INTERLINEAR Greek-English NEW TESTAMENT

JAY P. GREEN

MAC DONALD PUBLISHING COMPANY
P.O. Box 6006 Mac Dill AFB, Florida 33608

Fourth Edition

PREFACF

After nearly twenty centuries of desperate failure, has Satan, aided and cheerfully abetted by deceitful and desperately wicked men (Jer. 17:9), finally succeeded in destroying the Bible as a single-voiced witness to his great arch-enemy, Jesus Christ? Has the old devil, like a sleight-of-hand shell-game artist, finally brought us to the point where we are searching desperately for the true Word of God? Are we to believe that it cannot now be intact after all this time, having been run through the shredder of unholy hands and heads? God would not so easily permit Satan to touch His servant Job without His permission (Job 1:10), but now are we to believe that God had permitted the great adversary to hide the God-breathed Word so that we must search for the bread of life among the garbage pails of modern paraphrases and critically distorted 'versions'?

The answer to the above questions must be a resounding, crashing NO! And our basis for certainty in that answer is that same Word which modern textual critics, and their lazy dupes, claim to be blown to bits and pieces by the winds of time and the depravity of men. Our God and Savior, Jesus Christ, minces no words and leaves no pinhole for God-dishonoring textual theories to ooze through, saying,: *"Until the sky and the earth pass away, not one jot nor one tittle shall pass away from the Law until all has been fulfilled"* (Matt. 5:18). Who will you believe? Let God, our Lord Jesus, be true, and every man a liar. For no matter how scholarly the voice or how slick the hypothetical connivance, no 'logic' or 'scientific' investigation will ever prove anything untrue which passed from His lips — HE, God, assures us that not one jot, much less a word, of the Bible will be lost. It has not been lost, it is not lost, and it shall not be lost! Just as surely as Christ, the Word that is God, is with us today, so surely is His written Word with us today. If you love Him, because He first loved you, must you not then fall prostrate at His feet and cry out with joy and hope, *"Lord, I believe! Help my unbelief!"*?

WHY AN INTERLINEAR GREEK-ENGLISH NEW TESTAMENT IS NEEDED NOW MORE THAN EVER BEFORE

History is repeating itself again. During the first three centuries after Christ's atoning sacrifice for His own, there was an explosion of 'versions' claiming to exactly represent the originals as they left the hands of the New Testament writers. Besides the translations, however, they had a problem you and I do not have: the proliferation of actual Greek manuscripts purporting to be exact copies of the originals. Just as surely and, for a while at least, just as successfully as the magicians of Pharaoh were permitted to simulate the miracles of Moses and Aaron, so Marcion, Tatian, Valentinus, Justin Martyr, Clement of Alexandria, Origen, etc., were permitted to doctor Greek manuscripts and pass them off as exact copies of the original Greek manuscripts which were God-breathed through the apostles. Gnosticism reared its ugly head before John died in 100 A.D. The philosophers seized upon Christianity and mixed up a witches' brew which was as seductive to the intelligentsia as are today's mixtures of philosophy and Christianity. Man has always wanted to be as God, a god to himself, and he is easily misled into mystical societies and sects which assure him that he can study himself and work himself into godhood. Standing against this self-deceit is the Word of God. Through His written Word, by the power of the Holy Spirit of God, its Author, our God has breathed out for our benefit an all-encompassing answer to every conceit and evil imagination of any and all who oppose His truth with their error. The pure Word of God smashes, crushes, saps, overflows, etc., the entire output of error from all the demons and all the men who now live, who ever lived, and who ever shall live. Therefore, those who set themselves up as gods in this world have from the very beginning made it their primary effort to distort and dilute the Word of God written.

Today, nineteen centuries later, after enjoying a relatively quiet period in history, a time when one English version, at least, has been the Bible of the people, once more God has let loose the lust of the flesh, the lust of the eye, and the pride of life, that they may become the downfall of a world full of people who despise both God and His Word. Once more, there is a flood of 'versions' and false manuscripts bearing down upon us. There are few of you who have not been assaulted with the gleeful voices of the Bible-tinkerers who are much impressed with the Chester Beatty Papyri, the Bodmer Papyri, and the Dead Sea Scrolls. In mock-scholarship, they pretend to find in each new 'find' some corroboration of their pet hypotheses (and they have a million of them). The miserable, un-Biblical content of those same 'finds' are kept well out of sight. Why, the Dead Sea Scrolls no more represent any written word of God than do the false 'sacred' books of the Mormons, the Christian Scientists, and the Moslems. And they have the tell-tale signs of human engineering splattered all over every page. There is no hope in them. The other, the Papyri, we will discuss later. The singular fact we want you to see is this, that he who takes men captive through their fleshly lusts for a Bible after their own image is at work turning up false Bibles for them. There are unholy versions, and there are unholy manuscripts to seemingly give them some color of acceptability. Some of Satan's efforts are crude. Some of them are exceedingly subtle. Surprisingly, the crude, impostor 'Bible' seems to be as freely clasped to the breast of modern English readers as the subtle ones.

There you see the need for an interlinear Greek-English New Testament in every home that claims to be occupied by a true follower of Christ. So many magicians are practicing their deceptive arts with the Word of God, and so many are dancing to their mesmerizing music, that even the elect of God are sometimes for a while caught up in their webs of lying misrepresentations of God's holy legacy to His children, the Bible. You need this book to sit down and quietly ferret out the false from the true. Once you try it, you'll be eternally grateful that you have the means at hand to discover when you are being fooled. No one, no, not even a so-called Greek scholar, is able to read an English version purporting to be the Bible and tell for certain in each verse which is and which is not in the original. Even if you had the entire Greek New Testament memorized, you would still have to use some kind of comparative tools in order to keep from being deceived on some subtle changes which are being slipped in. Let no man think that he, in the power of his own intellect and learning, is a match for that old counterfeiter of God's word: for Satan has thousands of years of experience and an intellect which is superior to even our proudest claimant to intellectual championship.

Then take this book and start checking out those versions which you believe to be good representations of what God has said to you for the salvation of your soul and the good employment of your life. Yes, even check out the King James Version, that venerable old masterpiece which is the very matrix from which has come our high level of modern civilization.

THE QUESTION: WHO IS GOING TO BE YOUR MEDIATOR?

There is a simple explanation to the accelerating retrogression of our age back toward the dark ages, when the Word of God was counted as worthless, fit only for fanatic fools who hid themselves in monasteries on mountain tops. This explanation is not acceptable to the natural mind, however, for it must be spiritually discerned (I Cor. 2:15-17). The fact is, men prefer to have other men as their mediators, rather than the sinless God-Man, the Mediator appointed by God to purge the sins of men by the shedding of His blood, by the living of a perfect life which could be imputed to even the chief of sinners. Look back through the sin-blackened sands of time. You will see that mankind has in every age chosen for himself a priest, a necromantic wizard, a Balaam (one inferior in obedience to his donkey), a voodoo doctor, etc., to act as his instrument to ward off the righteous demands of God upon them. And these false 'mediators' are not, as is too often supposed, the superior intellects of their generation. Instead, as in the usual African witchdoctor, they are slick, deceitful tricksters who are able to devilishly deviate the mind of a man, appealing to him through their strong, perverted hatred of God's truth. Since men prefer a lie that makes them comfortable, they choose mediators who, right before their very eyes, change the truth of God into a lie (Rom. 1:25). In our day, there are two major strains of uncertain guides who do not hesitate to put on the robes of mediatorship in what we like to call 'civilized' countries: they are the 'scholar' and the 'scientist.' These Magi of our day may be read and heard daily throughout our corrupt world contradicting themselves, as well as categorically denying the precious and mightily preserved Word of God. And men hear them gladly. They are willing slaves, being taken captive at Satan's will because they are in truth, for the most part, children of that father of lies – they and their self-worshipping mediators. One of the hardiest of the scholar-mediator types is the exalted high-priest of the religious world, the textual critic.

THE TEXTUAL CRITIC AS MEDIATOR

The textual critic sets himself up as the subjective arbiter who deserves your fullest trust in determining which are and which are not the words of God. As you will see a few lines down, they may be Jews, Unitarians, mariolators, deniers of the substitutionary atonement of Christ, biased enemies of the true text, yet they may still be set up on a throne and trusted to provide the believer with the words he is supposed to believe and obey. How can an unbelieving man, scholar or not, be the judge of the trueness of a believing man's lifeblood, the written Word of God? Yet these enemies of the truth, these crooked guides become judges, are receiving deference which at times approaches worship.

The textual critics of the first centuries were of the same stripe as the present-day variety – each wanted to alter the written Word to make it more compatible to his own comfort and beliefs. Running into the two-edged sword of the Lord, able to slash through his most cunning deceits, discovering the Word hammering to pieces his self-centered world, he seizes upon the only remedy which appears to offer him any relief: if he cannot live with the Word as it is written, then he must rewrite the Word so he can live with it. Once he sets about his task, he follows the path of the old serpent who was so successful as the first textual critic. For did the serpent in the Garden not start this game of wits by which man determines what it is that God has said? Was it not the wily one who first suggested that what God has said is not necessarily what He means? Did he not whisper into Eve's itching ear, *"You shall not surely die . . . you shall be as God . . . " (Gen. 3:1-5)*? And do not our textual critics do the very same? What places in the Scriptures do they most question? Are they not the places that bring man face to face with his Maker, causing him to realize how impassable is the gulf between his performance and the duty God has laid on him? Is it not the deity and purity of Christ they impugn at every opportunity? Is it not His absolute power and worth which they subtly hide, or dilute, or simply deny by exalting man's will over the will of God? And how is it that they narrow this deep and wide canyon which separates God's commands from man's sinful disobedience? They first, as the old serpent, attempt to convince their hearers that God's Word does not mean what it says. This failing, they then set about distorting the true Word. By defining words against their natural meaning, by adding words to change the import of the verse, by subtracting words to leave the message of God short of its mark, by diluting the words of God, by substituting seemingly equal words, they ply their trade of deception. Then it becomes a nose of wax, designed so that they can twist it this way for one person, that way for another person, thus meeting the objections of those who seek to cling to God's word as a way of life. Throughout this entire distorting process is one abiding element, the appeal to the logic and natural reasoning power of a mind that has been born at enmity with God (*"Because the mind of the flesh is enmity towards God, for it is not subject to the law of God, for neither can it be,"* – Romans 8:7).

But you may say, How can the textual critic be blamed for merely reporting what he discovers? After all, if the manuscripts, and all the other evidence, appear to be hopelessly at variance, do we not need an 'expert' to make order out of all that chaos? For a fuller explanation, read *The Secret Spanking of Westcott and Hort*, J. W. Burgon (Grand Rapids: Associated Publishers & Authors). For now, we beg you not to accept at face value their claim that they are merely reporting what they have discovered. Not by any stretch of the truth can they say that what they are handing out to you as the carefully sorted out Word of God is anything more than a poisonous pot full of carnal conjectures, hypotheses, self-serving theories, and painted-over lies which have come down through centuries of similarity crooked minds with experience at distorting the truth. It is true there may sometimes be some ingenious hypothesis which seems to be a new wrinkle never before thrown upon the pile of man's wickedness, but be assured it is only a new face on an old heresy, and 999 times out of 1000 it can be found among the heresies of the first three centuries.

CHRIST IS THE ONE AND ONLY MEDIATOR.

God in His wisdom contrived the best means to accomplish the salvation of fallen, sinful men, and He appointed the One who was to be the Mediator between men and God, Christ Jesus, our Lord. Since He as the Second Adam has identified Himself with those who are His, and since He ever lives to make intercession for them, and since He as God was with the other Persons of the Godhead the Author of the God-breathed words by which we must live, who can be so idiotic as to prefer another mediator to identify which are and which are not the true written words of God?

But you may say, How can I look at a falsified record and see what is true and what is false? I have no man to guide me. *"If anyone desires to practice His will, he SHALL know of the teaching, whether it is from God . . . "* (John 7:17). *"But when He has come, the Spirit of Truth, He will guide you into all the truth. . . . He will glorify Me, for He will take that which is Mine and will tell it to you"* (John 16:13, 14). It is your faith that shall overcome the subtleties of the deceivers who in these last times are trying to trap you into basing your life on a Bible full of the miry clay of men's minds. Certainly, you may say in truth that they have more knowledge of Greek and other forms of higher learning than you. They may have the tools of deception which are beyond any defense you personally can put up against them. But you simply roll yourself over on Christ Jesus, your Mediator, and pray that He will protect you from following the wrong precepts. If you are a moron, uneducated, without clear discernment, having no sharpness of perception, yet you have faith – you shall be the victor. But God will demand of you the utmost of all the skills and talents and intellectual ability that He has given to you. If you are of normal intellect, if you can compare one thing with another, if you can learn the Greek alphabet and can read English in a passable way, then you are going to be held responsible to use those God-given abilities to arm yourself against error.

This Interlinear Greek-English New Testament is a tool which any ordinary intellect (and who admits to one that is only ordinary, except when he wants to doge a duty?) may use to try the spirits, to see if they are of God. With Christ as your Mediator, and with the use of your merciful provisions from God, you will have no excuse for being deceived by today's not-really-very-subtle perversions of God's Word.

WHAT MAKES THIS INTERLINEAR DIFFERENT?

The difference is really quite easy to state, since there are only two other interlinear New Testaments: There is the Englishman's Greek New Testament (which was photographed and has appeared in America as 'Berry's' Interlinear, though Berry supplied nothing but some notes and a short lexicon in the back of it); and there is the interlinear known as the Marshall-Nestle Interlinear Greek-English New Testament. We have taken the Englishman's Greek New Testament and have altered it in the following ways: (1) We have lengthened the pages, thus making a book with fewer pages, yet with larger print; (2) this was possible by eliminating the comments of certain early 'editors' which formerly appeared at the bottom of each page – we believe almost no one uses these any more; (3) we have placed on the side of the page the King James Version, Twentieth Century Edition, so that the modern reader may have a modern-language version of the Greek text appearing in this book. By doing this, it is hoped that you will see that it is quite possible to have a word-by-word translation, one which is really quite literal when compared to other productions of this century, and yet a translation which transmits in English a very great deal of the pregnant meanings of the Greek words which God chose as His instruments of expression.

Why did we eliminate the critical remarks of the 'editors'? No more explanation than a revealing of the character, drive, and work of these men should be necessary. Their remarks we consider to be of doubtful value because, except for Elzivir and Bishop Wordsworth, they were made by doubting men. In removing these particular editorial comments, however, we are not indicating that there is no work for textual critics to do. It appears that Erasmus (whose fourth or fifth edition of the Greek New Testament is represented in the third edition of Robert Stephens, 1550, the Greek text found in this book) simply translated from Latin manuscripts back into Greek and included them into this text. It is in matters like this that the true textual critic can be of value. He can discover, collate, evaluate, and publish manuscripts. This adds to the ever-growing mass of evidence which we have on the New Tesatment. There are now over 5000 manuscripts, or fragments of them, and the list is ever growing. But if the textual scholar is not honest with us, reporting only what appears to uphold some hypotheses which he had formerly put forth or some text to which he had attached himself, then he is a 'doctor of no value.' Particularly, when this man with extraordinary qualifications comes to us with a biased mind, determined to destroy our esteem for that text which has been most widely received and used through the history of Christianity, having that as a driving force in his life, we would do well to carefully sift whatever he offers us. This is not to say that even a crass unbeliever can be of no service to the Christian community. Many such have added to our knowledge, and they at times with great astuteness serve to knock down the false theories of other unbelieving critics.

May it be said here that there is nothing worthy of the name of 'science' in the textual field. You will discover this as you wade through the subjective opinions of the men engaged in textual criticism. They are far more apt to argue from the deep recesses of their egos than they are to argue from facts carefully collected, collated, and presented for the unbiased mind to consider.

These then are the men who formerly graced the pages of the Englishman's Greek New Testament as 'editors', who had thousands of suggested changes in the text of the New Testament, by far the most of them simply touting some favourite theory of theirs, or diluting the text in a way pleasing to them.

JOHANN GRIESBACH (1745-1812) has the name as the first of the modern-day textual critics, and is credited with being the first to classify all known 'variant readings' into three groups (which he called, Constantinopolitan, those you see in the Greek of this book; Alexandrian, those of the Clement-Origenic school, and Western, those of the Roman tradition). The father of the school of destructive textual criticism, to which Griesbach belongs, though he would have denied it, is none other than the French priest, Richard Simon (1638-1712), a Roman Catholic. Another Roman Catholic, Jean Astruc, began the now discredited J E D P theory which Wellhausen used to make a wasteland out of a century full of theological scholarship; and further developed by another priest, Alexander Geddes (1737-1802). All these putrefying sores developed quickly in Germany, Griesbach's home. Doubt was the order of the day. The determination of the Roman Catholics to destroy the true text was well-handled, to the point that they invariably found Protestants to do their dirty work. While Griesbach was adding and subtracting from the Received Text, another Roman Catholic named Mohler (1796-1838) began vigorous argumentation which produced as much agitation and excitement in the camp of the Protestants as the old serpent desired. Griesbach was a tame critic, compared to some since, and he was willing for the Received Text to keep its essential shape. But he preferred to alter it often by following the Alexandrian manuscripts before loved by Origen.

Before we consider the elimination of Lachmann, let it be noted that the thought of Mohler and the rules formulated by other Roman Catholic theologians were incorporated into a Greek grammar by Winer (1789-1858). For the first time since the great Reformation, when Christian thought expelled pagan thought, a Greek grammar wholeheartedly took its form and content from much earlier pagan Greek scholarship. The Reformers saw that the New Testament was its own witness to how its Greek words were to be understood, often having its Greek words cast in Hebrew forms of thought, and translated freely. Thus much was taken from the Greek translation of the Old Testament, the Septuagint. Winer's bold efforts to cause New Testament scholars to take their meanings from the Greek philosophers, etc., were gleefully received by those who sought to tear down the Received Text. For instance, in Matthew 5:22 we have the Hebraism, *hell fire;* which Winer states should be *hell of fire.* Of this, Vance Smith, a Unitarian, stated that the rendering *hell of fire* opened the way for the other hells of pagan mythology. Such, you see, was the subtlety of these early destroyers.

C. LACHMANN (1793-1851) published "a text constructed according to the principles of his own devising" (London: *Our Bible and the Ancient Manuscripts,* Frederic Kenyon, 1897). Lachmann simply did not believe it was possible for us to have the Bible in any large degree of purity. His best hope was that he might recover "the text of the N.T. as it was current in the fourth century. . . " (*ibid.,* p. 188). Three centuries of biased, corrupt, and careless men having intervened before the fourth century, Lachmann's unbelieving start could only have an unbelieving end – a man-oriented, corrupt text. Lachmann used only 4 manuscripts. Erasmus was severely criticized for using only a handful. Actually Lachmann had the fourth century text righte before his eyes, if he had only had his eyes opened by the Spirit to realize it.

A.F.C. TISCHENDORF (1815-1874) has the name of one of the mighty men, and no doubt he was a scholar in the fullest sense of the word, as to his talents and equipment. Unlike Westcott and Hort, who pontificated but never collated manuscripts nor dug deep into the original evidence, Tischendorf did both. In all, he published eight Greek texts, each one differing much from the previous one. Finally, his whole life was revolutionized by his discovery of the famous manuscript, *Aleph,* known as the Codex Sinaiticus. This he found literally in a wastebasket. So extremely corrupt and carelessly executed is it that it may as well have been left there. But Tischendorf was so elated over his discovery, he became like a Midas who fingered his treasure day and night until it was all the world to him. Yet we have it on the authority of the scholars at the British Museum that this manuscript was written by three different scribes: one who could spell, one who spelled poorly, and one "whose illiteracy is so startling that it is indeed a puzzle to understand how he can ever have been chosen to work on a manuscript of this class" (Oxford: *The Codex Sinaiticus and The Codex Alexandrinus,* British Museum, 1955). Since the careful scribe did most of his work on the Old Testament, and since we are here concerned only with the New Testament, the sober judgment of the British Museum should be believed, that the Sinaiticus was executed mainly by two men, one mediocre, and one so ignorant and so careless that it astounds even its advocates. Not only are there sleepy omissions where the scribe dropped down two or three lines and picked up the same word and went on, but there are silly errors of a variety that an elementary school child could have avoided. But discoverers tend to be excessively proud of their discoveries, and Tischendorf shattered his image as a respected scholar by introducing some 3572 changes in the New Testament in his eighth edition. Poor man, he had become unhinged by his bias, and the many-colored fibers which he and his contemporary critics thought should be woven together in order to recover the 'true Word of God' were for him the chaff from a very poor witness indeed. Tischendorf was an uncertain guide to begin with, being known to cite, for instance, Codex C as against a certain Received Text reading, when he knew all the while that Codex C did not even have that page. Such intellectual dishonesty would be enough to cause us to cease to pay attention to his opinions, then add his bias toward the Sinaiticus, and you have to find a better mediator.

S.P. TREGELLES (1813-1875), according to a friendly Kenyon, was liable to depend on personal preference in choosing out what he would allow to be called the Word of God. He also did not believe that there had been any special providential care over the text, having the usual idea of that day among scholars of his circle that the Bible was irrecoverable. He thought the Bible manuscripts more unreliable than those of Plato's works. He was also just trying to scrabble together as best he could the fourth century text.

ALFORD claimed to have constructed his text by taking the evidence of the most ancient authorities, allowing later evidence only when the oldest manuscripts disagreed (which, check it for yourself, is practically everywhere, when there is a point of important doctrine being done away with). He tried to account for variations, and given his critical viewpoint, claimed to be seeking the original text. As with the others, however, he started with a presupposition that the Received Text could not be, not by any stretch of the imagination, the true text, nor even virtually so.

WORDSWORTH was a good bishop of the Angelican church, one who never made up a Greek text of his own. But he did not try to disguise his belief that a superintending Providence was always watching over the text of the New Testament, guiding the Church of Christ, which He used as the guardian and keeper of Holy Writ. As such a believer, he accepted the Received Text as virtually the true text, and usually his desires to make a change are based on a true desire to have the words originally written. We do not believe his efforts were essentially destructive, as was the case with the others.

ELZEVIR reprinted the original Stephens text, his last edition being issued in 1633. Since his changes were very minor, the Elzevir text is also known as the Received Text. There are many editions of the Elzevir text as the Received Text, but the one we have printed here is the Stephens of 1550.

So there you have the 'editors' we have eliminated. Their notes at the bottom of the page have upset and distressed generations of believers. No one really needs their doubtful contributions, unless he is really going to take up the career of a textual critic – then he may be able to see some potholes to avoid.

If you believe that God did not allow His Word to disintegrate into bits and pieces to the point where men must scrape them out of wastebaskets and Egyptian sand, then you are a great deal more qualified to make judgments on the evidence than were most of these men. Just as the Israelites could not enter into Canaan because of unbelief (Heb. 3:19), so the average textual critic cannot enter into the promised land of a God-breathed text because of his everywhere-evident unbelief.

Because it was too costly to obliterate the marks indicating editors' changes within the Greek text, we have left them. If you need to examine the critical notes of the editors, then we suggest you buy the Englishman's Greek New Testament. We do not think they are worth your trouble, but we have not after all burned all other interlinears in order to force you to use this one.

A BRIEF WORD AS TO THE RELIABILITY OF THE RECEIVED TEXT

God has made it plain that *"Man shall not live by bread alone, but by every word that proceeds out of the mouth of God"* (Matt. 4:4). Therefore it is most important that you know which words you are to live by. Not only must you live by them, but you will be judged by them: *"the word which I spoke is that which will judge him in the last day"* (John 12:48). All judgment shall be simply this: did you believe the written Word of God, and did you therefore obey it? Nothing outside the Word shall be brought against you, because the Word of God is the sole and sufficient rule for faith and practice of every man.

It is then very important what we think about this Received Text that you will find in the following pages. It is usual in altogether too many Greek classes for the instructor to scoff openly at the text most commonly received and believed for the past 400 years in the English world, and for the past 1600 years in many other regions of the world. The most often-repeated deceit is this, that the Received Text was formed by Erasmus, a Roman Catholic, from very late manuscripts. Therefore, they say, any intelligent person should be able to see it can only be the worst of texts It is true that Erasmus chose only a handful of Greek texts to work from, and that there are a few places where he emended the text with poor evidence at hand, even translating from the Latin to the Greek in a place or two. But it is certainly a lie of the first order to imply that because of this there is no reason to believe that the Received Text is reliable. The few manuscripts used by Erasmus were excellent exemplars of the extant text, and these can be seen to be virtually the same as all the Byzantine Greek manuscripts which had been used as THE text since the fourth century. Furthermore, Erasmus was in correspondence with others getting manuscript readings from them. In fact, he had a correspondent at Rome who could give him readings from the now idolized Vaticanus Codex, but he counted it so unreliable that he would not use anything from it. The fact is, those same professors who are misleading their students into thinking that the Received Text is the worst text by using the argument that poor Erasmus just grabbed up a handful of texts and put forth what was essentially a fourteenth-century text, I say those professors simply have not made a thorough study of textual matters, carefully applying themselves to acquire a knowledge of all sides of the subject they are teaching. Because they are willing to pass on misinformation, because they have not studied what they are teaching at first hand, they are guilty of passing on deceptive academic tradition.

This has resulted in an ever-widening circle of false information being passed on not only in the schoolroom, but from the pulpit. The waves of error radiating from the pulpit have done incalculable harm already. Only a realization of the harm done can now cause the people to demand a complete restudy of the textual content of their Bibles, redress the wrong done, and set forth again a pure stream of truth for the benefit of all. Hort, who described the Received Text with hatred, said, "Think of that vile Textus Receptus," and, "I had no idea till the last few weeks of the importance of the texts, having read so little Greek Testament, and dragged on with the VILLAINOUS Textus Receptus" (London: *The Life of Fenton J.A. Hort,* Hort, Vol. i, p. 211, 1896); even that Hort admitted that the Received Text was the text used by the great men of Christianity from the mid-fourth century until the fifteenth. Why all this pretense? Must a poor text be proven so by lies about its lateness of origin?

There are other evidences of dishonesty and deceit being practiced under the name of the science of textual criticism. It has been popular to condemn the Received Text readings as late readings, or else it has been said they were borrowed from the other texts and 'conflated'; or else it is said there was a revision made by the church authorities (of which history tells us not a single word); or some other excuse. At any rate, thousands of the words you will find in this book have at one time or another been pronounced as 'late' and as 'unworthy to be called God's words.' Professors have a pecular relationship with their students, one which at times borders on adoration. They do not like to tell their students, nor have it get back to former students, that what they told them in the classroom was blatantly untrue, was prematurely adjudged valueless, etc. Therefore it should be no surprise to you to hear that when the Chester Beatty Papyri, and then the Bodmer Papyri, were found in the dry regions of N. Africa, the 'scholars' chortled with glee when they found that these fragments contained many of the readings of that which was formerly called the 'neutral' text. This text is just a shift dreamed up by Hort to try to establish the Alexandrian text as authoritative, by splitting the manuscripts into two groups and letting one-half take all the criticism, while the other half was proclaimed the purest manifestation of the Word of God. It should be noted that manuscripts are still being found in Egypt and other parts of the world where the lack of moisture has preserved them. In lands where rainfall is greater, the manuscripts have mouldered away, or else have been used so heavily as to come to pieces. At any rate, in those same Papyri which were so widely circulated as having corroborated the opinions of the textual critics, there were some very embarrassing discoveries. Some Papyri had large portions of those verses formerly described as 'late,' one even having the entire chapter of Matthew virtually the same as the Received Text found in this book, and it was dated as a third century manuscript. The so-much-revered Vaticanus, a fourth-century manuscript, was found to agree with some of the Papyri in no greater percentage than the Received Text. So also was there embarrassment with the first 14 chapters of John's Gospel in the oldest known fragment, the Bodmer Papyrus II. 13% of those readings which had been scornfully ejected from the Bible by know-it-all critics were found to be in this manuscript. Yet, was a single word about these distinctively Byzantine (Received Text) readings advertised in the news columns? Not a single word was breathed. So it was in virtually all classrooms. Why? The professors must not lose their adoration by letting it become known that they were fallible. To this day, they are still largely propagating the false statements that the Byzantine Text is a late text without the authority of the ancient manuscripts.

If they will not put back into the text those readings which now have the weight of that ancient authority, which they have claimed as being so important, then what hope is there that they are ever going to give you a better text? The fact is, the Byzantine (Received) Text alone can stand the test of time. It alone has net been splintered. Kirsopp Lake, a well-respected textual critic testifies that there is not one case of the transmission of an error to another Byzantine manuscript. Yet 95% of the extant manuscripts are of the same Byzantine variety. If, as some schoolroom experts assure us, we have a corrupted Received Text because copyists made errors, then transmitted them to the next manuscript, and added some more, etc., then why is it Kirsopp Lake could not find a single such instance, even though he desperately wanted to find such a case, for he believed that theory thoroughly. In Lake's words, "Speaking generally, the evidence in our collations for the grouping of the codices which contain this text is singularly negative. There is extraordinarily little evidence of close family relationship between the manuscripts even in the same library. They have essentially the same text with a large amount of spordiac variation." (Paris: *The Byzantine Text of the Gospels,* K. & S. Lake., 1940, p. 256).

The Byzantine text, essentially the Received Text, triumphed because it was the Bible of the people. The intelligentsia, the philosophers like Justin Martyr, and the scholars like Clement of Alexandria, and the heretics like Lucian, Marcion and Valentinus, all had one thing in common: their faith in God was not sufficiently strong to keep them from monkeying with the Word of God. They were led by their intellectual pride and theological presuppositions to make the Bible text say what they thought it should say. Origen was an example of one who thought it legitimate to use his intellect to emend the text, rather than submitting his mind to the Word of God. The preservation of God's Word was not uppermost in his mind, but rather a desire for fame distorted his actions, as he sought to accommodate the Christian faith to the thought of the pagan philosophers. In this way, he was the forerunner of Roman Catholic evangelistic thinking. But the common people, poor, ignorant souls, did not dare tamper with God's word. They actually believed that the dire threats in Revelation 22 would be executed against them if they changed God's Word by so much as an iota. So they carried their scrolls wherever they went, copying them if they were that talented, otherwise having another scribe copy them when they were wearing out. And these people went as missionaries to every part of the world. The Received Text appears among the Goths, in England, in Scotland, in Spain, in S. France, and it was the text used to evangelize the world in those days. These other sedate, ornate, doctored texts were used in scholarly circles, for they appealed to their pride. But never, not even exclusively in Caesarea or in Alexandria, did these texts become the Bible of the people. In this way God providentially protected His true words from being corrupted. Do you really believe that men who cannot even pass along a message from one to another in a circle are capable of keeping the Bible pure? Surely, only God could keep His word in a form which would be sufficiently pure to be the basis for His great Judgment Day. Only the Received Text is attested in any near-totality by the preponderant testimony of manuscripts, fathers, and versions. So many are the manuscripts that uphold it, that Westcott and Hort, and other clever fellows, had to invent the slogan, "Don't count the evidence, weigh it." But how did they weigh it? They weighed it like the crooked butcher who weighs his thumb in with the meat. They first assigned the weights to their favourite manuscripts, then they weighed them against the others. If Codex B and Codex *Aleph* were weighted at 10,000 each, and all other of the 5000 manuscripts weighted at one pound each, you can see that those two manuscripts need only to agree and the game is over. But who ever agreed to such a silly changing of the rules of evidence? Only those who sorely wanted to get rid of the stringent, holy, demanding, God-honoring Received Text!

THE TRANSLATION IN THE MARGINS

The level of Bible knowledge in the individual hearts of Christians everywhere determines the course of the generation in which they live. Not only are individual Christians the salt that preserves the world from total corruption (Matt. 5:13), but in those centuries when the Christian community has led the world in its quest for true knowledge, have proven that knowledge of the Bible is the first requisite for any scholarship worthy of the name. And this knowledge of the Bible must consist in more than a mere intellectual grasp of the propositions stated in the Bible, or of the now-overflowing pools of knowledge peripheral to the Bible, but an actual experimental knowledge, through faith, of the heart.

It will surprise some to read that Dr. Phelps, late professor of English literature at Yale, recognized the value of Bible knowledge: "Everyone who has a thorough knowledge of the Bible may truly be called educated; and no other learning or culture, no matter how extensive or elegant, can, among Europeans and Americans, form a proper substitute. Western civilization is founded upon the Bible. . . . I thoroughly believe in a university education for both men and women; but I BELIEVE A KNOWLEDGE OF THE BIBLE WITHOUT A COLLEGE COURSE IS MORE VALUABLE THAN A COLLEGE COURSE WITHOUT THE BIBLE. . . . " (New York: *Ladies Home Journal,* Nov., 1921).

Because of the importance of Biblical knowledge in your life and in the life of all men, a new translation of the Received Text has been made and placed in the margin of this book. This in no way is intended to take away the glory of the King James Version, which served the world admirably for nearly 400 years. It is merely an attempt to provide what is obviously needed, a Bible in the language of the people. The same motive that drove Tyndale and Coverdale to provide the Bible in English in the beginning is the motive driving those producing this *Twentieth Century Edition* of the *King James Version.* We want both the learned and the unlearned, and those in the process of learning, to be able to read the Bible in their own current English, so as to grasp immediately the meaning God has placed there for each individual. For surely it should be clear once it is called to a person's attention, that reading Elizabethan English requires a constant translation going on within the mind of the reader. When you read *"wot not"*, you say in your head, that means *"does not know."* Anyone with much intelligence can with strong motivation learn Elizabethan English. Yet it should be admitted that there are few indeed who today read the King James Version and at the same time truly know what they are reading at all points. Taking the statement of the apostle Paul in II Corinthians 8:1. I have tested hundreds of people, asking them the meaning of this statement: *"we do you to wit of the grace of God".* Not one person in fifty can translate this simple group of words into their own native, everyday English, which is, *"we make known to you the grace of God."* How then do they fare with such words as champlain, besom, neesing, bruit, etc.?

The question enters the minds of children, at least, as to why they should learn Elizabethan English at all. They find it even less comprehensible that the Bible must be read in Elizabethan English if it is to be read in its best English version. The answer of most who still cling to the King James Version is this, that it is the only version they can trust. It is for this reason that we have produced a modern-day version from the Received Text, one that can be trusted, and we are willing to lay it alongside of the Greek original so that you yourself may determine if the translation work is true and trustworthy.

THE METHOD OF TRANSLATION

The basic translation was made by one person, then submitted for correction to a Greek scholar for suggested corrections. From this point it was submitted to the faculty of a seminary for thorough inspection of individual books of the New Testament.

Next it was issued in a small edition and submitted to the public with an appeal for the scholarship and good-hearted inspection of Christians in general. For true knowledge and helpful propensities do not reside only in the breasts of so-called elite scholars. Thousands of changes were made, coming from all streams of English-reading Christians, those who were disciplined scholars, and those who merely questioned whether certain verses could not be more closely rendered so as to meet the original. Many of these last were using an interlinear to determine the need for improvement in the translation.

The process of improvement of the New Testament included in this book has continued, it now being in its eighth revision. Again thousands of improvements have been suggested by hundreds of persons who have taken the work to heart. It is of course evident that we believe that *this* is the way to bring forth a version which will best serve the general body of Christians. With Spurgeon, we believe that God works through individuals in doing lasting work, and that no truly lasting work is likely to come from a committee. As Spurgeon noted, what comes from the usual committee is a compromised version of what they all believe, the lowest denominator of their collective knowledge. And what they cannot persuade their fellow-translators to put into the text, modern translation committees have persuaded them to put into the marginal notes. In this way, they hope, the next generation will move their favorite readings into the text.

WHAT IS DIFFERENT ABOUT THIS TRANSLATION?

1. It was done with fear and trembling, with full realization that the translator was in the sight and presence of God, the Author of the words being translated. Since the fear of God is the beginning of wisdom, there was much consideration given to the translation work, that it be as nearly literal in meaning, as nearly word-for-word translation, as would prove to be readable. To the surprise of most, such a translation did not prove to be difficult to read, but rather achieved its purpose of being not only readable but more readily assimilated into the minds and hearts of the reader. Groups of readers, down to the second-grade level, were employed from time to time to mark those places considered to be difficult to understand. These then, if they could with fidelity to the original be changed, were carefully reconsidered. When adding words for sense, those words of God which forbid the adding or subtracting of words from His Word rang in our ears. Therefore these words were placed in italics, that the reader might tell the true from the supplied words. An exception was made when it was felt that certain supplied words were implied in the original.

2. It was done with the general Christian community in mind. No attempt to reduce the irreducible words of Scripture, words such as sanctification, justification, adoption, etc., was made. We believe every area of knowledge requires the learning of certain terms and their meanings, and theology is no different. But on the other hand, not having as a primary design the making of a translation which would be to the praise and glory of the translators, it was possible to keep in mind the glory of God and the good of His people.

3. This translation was done without mental reservations. Clement of Alexandria appears to have been one of those who performed his work of textual emendation with admitted mental reservations. He knew he was wrong to change the text so drastically, but he excused himself by various internal assurances that it was all for the good of the poor, ignorant public. Much later, the Jesuits knitted together this doctrine, openly commending murder in the name of Christ, writing it in their manuals that a Jesuit could do anything, however foul it may seem to be in the eyes of the people, so long as it was done for the good of the mother Church at Rome. This was Newman's salve for his

conscience as he strove to bring the Anglican church back into the church of Rome. It has marked the work of many of the enemies of truth such as the Puseyites, who in one generation poisoned the streams of Christian thought through the Oxford Movement, at least among English intelligentsia. And it most certainly has marked the work of recent translation committees. How can a Jew truly translate the Messianic prophecies when he does not believe Messiah has come? The question may not be how he can do it, but will he do it? For your answer, read the Jewish Publication Society translation of those passages. How can a Unitarian truly translate those passages which unquestionably express equality in the Godhead for the Son and for the Spirit of God? How can a Westcott and a Hort, who sat on the revision committee of 1881, truly translate passages having to do with the substitutionary atonement, when neither of them believe in a substitutionary atonement? How can the Revised Standard Version be true to the original languages which express the virgin birth, when one of them, Professor Grant, stood before an audience and admitted that not one of the translators of that version believed in the virgin birth? The fact is, there was much mental reservation evident in the work of various recent 'translations.' Most obvious of all has been the attempt to establish among Protestants translations which are acceptable to Roman Catholics. Roman Catholic publications have rejoiced at each new translation, making statements that at last the Protestants are coming back to the readings of their own Roman Catholic Bible, the Vulgate. They have been gleeful to see certain evidences that the newer translators do not believe in an inerrant and infallible Bible, one that was God-breathed, once and for all, not to be emended by tradition.

4. This translation attempts to render the tenses faithfully, though this is largely impossible when modern English idiom is also in view. In those places where it was of so much importance, however, this has been done irregardless of the smoothness of the reading. A case in point is Matthew 16, where the words *"having been bound in Heaven"* are so important to the understanding of the text. The same is true in I John 3:9; 4:7; and 5:1, where it is of the utmost importance to know that one must have been born of God before he will leave the practice of sin, before he will love truly, and before he can believe truly.

5. This translation attempts to keep interpretation to a minimum. It is admitted that the capitalization of Deity is an interpretation, but we deemed it of such help to the reader that it has been attempted. We warn the reader, however, that they themselves are responsible to read the context, backward and forward, and to decide for themselves if God is in view. We also warn the reader that the punctuation is of men, for there was no punctuation, chapters, verses, or any other of the helps of this kind to the reader in the original Greek. For that matter, there were only capital letters, so all capitalization is interpretive.

6. The translator admits to certain presuppositions (some call them biases). He believes that God not only produced a perfect Word, one by which He will judge all men, but that He has preserved that Word through the centuries. He believes that God's will is done on earth, that men cannot through sinful error alter the plan of God. He believes that God has loved His own from everlasting (Jer. 31:3) and that He is the Author and Finisher of his faith, using His Word both to give him life and to strengthen his life, both here and throughout all eternity.

The translator has attempted to avoid sectarianism, yet has been compelled to follow doctrinal fidelity to the point that many may object to certain renderings. Thus there is the presupposition that God's Word must be rendered for the widest possible use at the same time it is rendered faithfully and without personal interpretation. We have tried to allow the Word of God to be its own interpreter (II Peter 1:20), as God gave us grace.

7. This translation has varied from the Received Text at times when we deemed the evidence to be strongly variant to it, it being different from the traditional text which appears in the majority of the manuscripts, fathers and versions, in a few places. Yet in most cases, where there was Greek evidence, we have translated the Received Text, not

putting into italics those verses.

IT TAKES A GOOD HEART TO TRANSLATE THE SCRIPTURES.

With the firm belief that only a Christian with the love of God shed abroad in his heart is capable of giving an honest rendering of the Scriptures, we have proceeded step by step, in prayer, in study, in meditation on the Word, careful to consider not only the immediate context, but the entire book of the Bible, and finally the entire Bible as a context to each rendering. This is admittedly laborious, but it is the only cure for the deceitfulness of our minds, which is bent upon inserting in God's Word what we want it to say. On the other hand, one will not find any translation here which varies from what we have believed and published elsewhere. We believe that Genesis 1–3 is true history. Many recent translations have been executed by men who thought it was a myth, yet translated it as if it were a history. The same is true with John's Gospel, which most of the RSV translators believed to be more folklore than Scripture. As believer, we welcomed the thought that the Scriptures contain no errors, much less myths and folklore. As believers, we call upon all other believers to become involved in this effort to have the best possible translation into current English. All of those capable of making a contribution to the translation of the Scriptures are not necessarily in the schools, nor, for that matter, in the pulpits. There is no excuse, in our opinion, for failing to use the Biblical knowledge and sharp discernment of every competent Christian who is willing to contribute to the improvement of an English translation of the Bible. This translation has already been enriched by contributions of this sort, and this interlinear is intended as a tool which may be used in such a contribution. But this interlinear will serve in a much wider sense by placing the current translation not only closely attached but closely related to the ageless words of the Greek text of the Bible. If John Bunyan, who had only a third-grade education, could study and acquire a grasp of the Bible which has made him one of the most noted authors of all time, then certainly any Christian in our day should be able to take a tool like this interlinear and learn in order to go on to a higher place of Christian service. It is through the general use of the tools that God has provided, tools such as this interlinear, that God's Word shall be triumphant in every generation.

May God bless all of you who are determined to learn the utmost of Him, all that a sinful human being blessed by grace can learn.

By His Mercy,

JAY GREEN

Distinctively Byzantine Readings in Papyrus Bodmer II.

John 1:32	*ōsei* with K M P U X Delta Pi many others fam 1 fam 13 700 W.
John 3:24	*o* ante *iō.* with A L Delta Pi others very many fam 1 fam 13 700 W Theta Origen.
John 4:14	*dipsēsē* with Lambda Pi many others 118 209 700 W Origen.
John 4:51	*kai apēggeilan* with A C Gamma Delta Lambda others very many fam 13 700 W Theta.
John 5:8	*egeirai* with U V Gamma Delta many others 118 209 700.
John 6:10	*ōsei* with A Gamma Delta Lambda many others fam 1 fam 13 700 Theta.
John 6:57	*zēsetai* with Gamma Delta Lambda others very many fam 1 700 W.
John 7:3	*theorēsōsi* with X Gamma Lambda Pi others very many fam 1 fam 13 700 Theta.
John 7:39	*agion* post *pneuma* with L N X Gamma Delta Lambda fam 1 fam 13 W 700 Origen int.
	oudepō with L T X Gamma Delta Lambda Pi others very many fam 1 fam 13 700 W Origen.
John 8:41	*ou gegenēmetha* with C X Gamma Delta Lambda Pi many others fam 1 fam 13 700 W Theta Origen.
John 8:48	*eipon* with L X Gamma Delta Lambda Pi fam 1 fam 13 700.
John 8:55	*kai ean* with A C L X Gamma Delta Pi many others fam 1 fam 13 700 Theta.
John 9:23	*eipon* with A L X many others fam 1 fam 13 700 W Theta.
John 10:38	*pisteusate* with A E G H M S X Gamma Lambda others very many Pap. 45 118 209 fam 13 700.
John 12:36	*eōs* with X Gamma Delta Lambda Pi others very many fam 1 fam 13 700.
John 12:44	*all'* with A X Gamma Lambda Pi others very many fam 1 fam 13 700 Theta.
John 14:17	*auto* post *ginōskei* with A X many others fam 1 fam 13 700 Theta.

In the preparation of this table the following sources were consulted:

Tischendorf	N. T. Graece, Editio Octava.
von Soden	Die Schriften des N. T., Text und Apparat.
H. A. Sanders	The Washington MS of the Four Gospels.
G. Beermann und C. R. Gregory	Die Koridethi Evangelien.
K. Lake	Codex 1 of the Gospel and Its Allies.
W. H. Ferrar and T. K. Abbott	A Collation of Four Important MSS of the Gospels.
H. C. Hoskier	Collation of the Greek Cursive Codex Evangelium 604 (700).

FROM THE INTRODUCTION TO THE ENGLISHMAN'S GREEK NEW TESTAMENT

I.—The Greek Text.

We have taken the Greek Text of Stephens 1550, which is the common text in this country; but as the edition of Elzevir 1624 is the one often called the Received Text, or Textus Receptus, because of the words, "Textum. . . . . ab omnibus receptum," occurring in the preface (though this edition, as is manifest by its date, was *not* used for our English translation of 1611), we give the readings of this Elzevir edition in the notes, and mark them E. It is the text commonly reprinted on the Continent. In the main they are one and the same, and either of them may be referred to as the Textus Receptus.

There are a number of minute variations between the editors with which we have not thought it well to trouble the reader in such a work as the present; indeed some of the editors have not kept strictly to one form of accentuation, &c., for the same word in every instance. Thus we have not noticed the variation of θλίψις with θλῖψις; στῦλος with στύλος; κριμα and κρῖμα; ζῶον and ζῷον; Μωυσῆς and Μωϋσῆς; Ἡσαῦ and Ἡυαῦ, &c. So again in the division of words. We have not recorded such variations as οὐκέτι and οὐκ ἔτι; εἴ τις and εἴτις; εἴγε and εἴ γε; μήποτε and μή ποτε, &c. In all these cases we have followed the majority of modern editors.

With them we have also added the final ν to the third person singular and plural in σι; third singular in ε; in datives plural in σι, &c. For οὕτω we have given οὕτως, and αὐτοῦ where some have αὑτοῦ.

As to the *form* of the Greek text a few words are needed.

1. Paragraphs.—We were disappointed in finding nothing like *authority* for where a paragraph ought to be. Ancient manuscripts were no help: they have few or no paragraphs. The editors all differed, each making paragraphs according to his own judgment. We were therefore obliged, after referring to the best examples, to form paragraphs for ourselves. We are anxious that our readers should remember that the paragraphs have *no authority*, which they might have had if the ancient manuscripts had agreed in the placing of them.

2. Parentheses.—Most of the editors have placed here and there parentheses in their Greek texts. These we have disregarded, seeing that there are no such things in the early Greek copies. We have placed them in the English where we deemed them necessary to preserve the sense, but not being in the Greek they also have no authority.

3. Inverted Commas.—Some editors mark with inverted commas the words that are spoken, and others in a similar way mark the quotations from the Old Testament. But in some places it is doubtful where these quotations close, and it was thought best to omit them. These also, being absent from the ancient Greek copies, have no authority.

4. Points.—There is no authority anywhere for the punctuation. There are few or no points in the ancient copies, and editors naturally differ in their system of pointing. We have been obliged to punctuate for ourselves as we judged best. We have not attempted to note the difference in the punctuation of the various editors, except in places where it materially alters the sense.

5. Capitals.—The only remark needed here is in reference to the names of God, of Christ, and of the Holy Spirit. The greatest difficulty is touching the word 'Spirit.' In some places it is very difficult to say whether the Holy Spirit as a person or the spirit of the Christian is referred to (see Rom. viii. 9); and if sometimes a small letter and sometimes a capital had been placed to the word *πνεῦμα*, in the Greek, persons would naturally have concluded that the question was thus indisputably settled. It was therefore judged best to put a small *π* everywhere. In the English we have been obliged to put a capital S when the Holy Spirit was referred to and so have retained it wherever we thought this was the case; but in some places it is really doubtful, and becomes a question for the spiritual judgment of the reader. The Greek will not help in the difficulty, because in the earliest copies every letter was a capital. In the other names we have followed the usage of modern editors; putting in the Greek a capital to Jesus but a small letter for Christ, and a small letter for Lord and for God.

6. Verses.—In a few places it is doubtful where the verses should commence. In these cases we have followed Bruder's "Greek Concordance," though that work does not in all cases agree with itself.

II.—The Interlinear Translation.

Very few words will suffice for this. No *new* translation has been aimed at, but rather a selection from the best translations already existing.

1. The plan adopted can soon be explained. The Greek words have always been kept in their right order, and where the interlinear English would not make sense in the same order, the words have been numbered to shew how they must be read. Thus, "And [7]related [8]to [9]them [2]also [1]those [3]who [4]had [5]seen [[6]it] (Luke viii. 36) are numbered so as to read "And those also who had seen [it] related to them."

To prevent this numbering, and transposition in reading, being increased unnecessarily, a few words are often made into a phrase. This has been done at the commencement of each sentence, where needed, two or more words being joined with a *low* hyphen. Thus, instead of

Ἐγένετο δὲ	we have printed	Ἐγένετο.δὲ.
[2]It [3]came [4]to [5]pass [1]and		And it came to pass.

The words in brackets [ ] are what have been added in the English to complete the sense where there is no word in the Greek to correspond to the words added.

Where a Greek word occurs which the English idiom requires should *not* be translated, the word stands alone with no English word under it: as ὅτι, 'that,' in Mark xii. 7; and οὐ in verse 14, where there are *two* negatives, which, if both were translated, would in English destroy one another; and so of μή, where it simply marks the sentence as a question.

In a few places we have been obliged to put a double translation, mostly because of the double negatives used in the Greek, where they do not immediately follow one another, and so could not be translated by such strengthened expressions as 'not at all,' 'in no wise,' &c. In such cases we have placed a *literal* translation below the one required in English. Thus—

οὐδέν.
anything.
(*lit.* nothing.)

2. As to points of grammar we shall trouble the reader with but few remarks.

The Aorist. This tense of the Greek verb has been at all times the most difficult to deal with, being translated, in the Authorised Version (and by others), sometimes by the *present*, sometimes by the *past*, sometimes by the *future*, and sometimes by the *perfect*. Grammarians say that, in the main, it is the *indefinite past*, and we have endeavoured, as far as may be, to keep it to this, avoiding, except in a few places, the translation of it as a perfect. We all know what stress is often laid—and rightly so—upon the word 'have.' If I say, 'he *has* cleansed me,' it is more than saying 'he cleansed me.' The former expression indicates the *perfect*, and implies a continuance of the act, or its effects, to the present time; whereas the latter speaks of an act at some time in the past, without anything being implied as to its continuance.

For this reason it appeared unadvisable to translate the aorist as the perfect, except in a few places where the true sense would otherwise have been destroyed. It is true that the English idiom requires it elsewhere, but it was thought best to sacrifice the English for the sake of preserving the above distinction. An extreme case will illustrate this point. In 1 Corinthians v. 9 occurs the word ἔγραψα, 'I wrote;' and in verse 11 the same word precisely—'I wrote;' but the Authorised Version (and others) put for the latter 'I have written.' It is there accompanied with the word 'now'—'now I have written.' This is needed for good English; but we have sacrificed the English and put 'I wrote' in both places, but have put a comma after the word 'now' to make it read not quite so harshly. We were encouraged to preserve this uniformity by the fact of the Authorised

Version being in proximity, which will make all plain in the instances where this uncouthness occurs.

In a few places we have translated the aorist as a *present* where the sense demanded it. As, for instance, ἔγνω, in 2 Timothy ii. 19: "The Lord *knows* those that are his," instead of "the Lord knew," &c.

The Imperfect. This is mostly translated as 'I was writing,' or 'I wrote.' But there are a few places where this tense is said to have a different meaning. This will be best illustrated by the much-disputed passage in Romans ix. 3: "For *I could wish* that myself were accursed from Christ for my brethren." Here the word for 'I could wish' is in the imperfect. If the learned were agreed as to a translation we should have kept to the same, but while some translate 'I could wish,' as a *conditional present*, others give 'I could have wished' as a *conditional past.* We have thought it best to keep the sense of the simple imperfect as referred by Winer to this passage. "*I felt a wish,* and should do so still, could it be gratified . . . . . (a conditional clause being understood)." We have put "I was wishing."

The Perfect. This we have kept as uniform as we could, implying an act perfected, but continuing to the present in itself or its consequences. In a few places we have translated it as a *present*: as in Matthew xii. 47, in the sense of 'they have stood and still *are standing.*'

The Subjunctive. In this tense perhaps we have deviated further from ordinary practice than in any other, but we have endeavoured, as far as practicable, to keep it distinct from both the English *imperative* and the Greek *future.* Thus in Romans xiii. 9 for οὐ φονεύσεις (future indicative) we have, 'thou shalt not commit murder;' but in James ii. 11, for μὴ φονεύσῃς (aorist subjunctive) 'thou mayest not commit murder.'

The Pronouns. At times it is important to know whether the pronouns are emphatic or not. ἐγὼ γράφω and γράφω are both 'I write;' but where the ἐγώ is put in the Greek, it makes the pronoun emphatic. This however is somewhat due to the writer's style, and in John's Gospel and Epistles, it has been judged that, from his peculiar style of composition, he puts in the pronouns where emphasis is not always intended. John ix. 27 gives a good example of the same verb with and without the pronoun in the Greek: "Why again do ye wish to hear? do *ye* also wish to become his disciples?"

Compound Words. It was found impracticable to translate these uniformly throughout. For instance, if γνῶσις be translated 'knowledge,' it might be thought that ἐπίγνωσις should be 'full knowledge,' &c.; but on referring to a Concordance it will be seen that the latter word cannot be intensified in all places, and then to translate it by 'knowledge' in some places, and 'full knowledge' in others looks too much like interpretation. We have therefore translated both words by 'knowledge.' In the few places however where one of each of such words occurs in the same sentence, some distinction was imperative.

THE GREEK ALPHABET

The Greek alphabet has twenty-four letters : —

Form.		Equivalent.	Name.	
Α	α	a	ἄλφα	*Alpha*
Β	β	b	βῆτα	*Beta*
Γ	γ	g	γάμμα	*Gamma*
Δ	δ	d	δέλτα	*Delta*
Ε	ε	e (*short*)	εἶ, ἒ ψῑλόν	*Epsīlon*
Ζ	ζ	z	ζῆτα	*Zeta*
Η	η	e (*long*)	ἦτα	*Eta*
Θ	θ ϑ	th	θῆτα	*Theta*
Ι	ι	i	ἰῶτα	*Iota*
Κ	κ	k *or hard* c	κάππα	*Kappa*
Λ	λ	l	λά(μ)βδα	*Lambda*
Μ	μ	m	μῦ	*Mu*
Ν	ν	n	νῦ	*Nu*
Ξ	ξ	x	ξεῖ, ξῖ	*Xi*
Ο	ο	o (*short*)	οὖ, ὂ μῑκρόν	*Omīcron*
Π	π	p	πεῖ, πῖ	*Pi*
Ρ	ρ	r	ῥῶ	*Rho*
Σ	σ ς	s	σίγμα	*Sigma*
Τ	τ	t	ταῦ	*Tau*
Υ	υ	(u) y	ὖ, ὒ ψῑλόν	*Upsīlon*
Φ	φ	ph	φεῖ, φῖ	*Phi*
Χ	χ	kh	χεῖ, χῖ	*Chi*
Ψ	ψ	ps	ψεῖ, ψῖ	*Psi*
Ω	ω	o (*long*)	ὦ, ὦ μέγα	*Omĕga*

N. At the end of a word the form ς is used, elsewhere the form σ; thus, σύστασις.

ΒΙΒΛΟΣ γενέσεως Ἰησοῦ χριστοῦ, υἱοῦ [b]Δαβίδ,‖ υἱοῦ
BOOK of [the] generation of Jesus Christ, son of David, son
Ἀβραάμ.
of Abraham.

2 Ἀβραὰμ ἐγέννησεν τὸν Ἰσαάκ· Ἰσαὰκ.δὲ ἐγέννησεν τὸν
Abraham begat Isaac; and Isaac begat
Ἰακώβ· Ἰακὼβ.δὲ ἐγέννησεν τὸν Ἰούδαν καὶ τοὺς ἀδελφοὺς
Jacob; and Jacob begat Judas and [2]brethren
αὐτοῦ· 3 Ἰούδας.δὲ ἐγέννησεν τὸν Φαρὲς καὶ τὸν Ζαρὰ ἐκ
[1]his; and Judas begat Phares and Zara of
τῆς Θαμάρ· Φαρὲς.δὲ ἐγέννησεν τὸν Ἐσρώμ· Ἐσρὼμ.δὲ
Thamar; and Phares begat Esrom; and Esrom
ἐγέννησεν τὸν Ἀράμ· 4 Ἀρὰμ.δὲ ἐγέννησεν τὸν [c]Ἀμιναδάβ·‖
begat Aram; and Aram begat Aminadab;
[c]Ἀμιναδὰβ‖.δὲ ἐγέννησεν τὸν Ναασσών· Ναασσὼν.δὲ ἐγέννη-
and Aminadab begat Naasson; and Naasson be-
σεν τὸν Σαλμών· 5 Σαλμὼν.δὲ ἐγέννησεν τὸν [d]Βοὸζ‖ ἐκ τῆς
gat Salmon; and Salmon begat Booz of
Ῥαχάβ· [d]Βοὸζ‖.δὲ ἐγέννησεν τὸν [e]Ὠβὴδ‖ ἐκ τῆς Ῥούθ· [e]Ὠβὴδ‖
Rachab; and Booz begat Obed of Ruth; [2]Obed
δὲ ἐγέννησεν τὸν Ἰεσσαί· 6 Ἰεσσαὶ.δὲ ἐγέννησεν τὸν [b]Δαβὶδ‖
[1]and begat Jesse; and Jesse begat David
τὸν βασιλέα. [b]Δαβὶδ‖.δὲ [f]ὁ βασιλεὺς‖ ἐγέννησεν τὸν [g]Σολο-
the king. And David the king begat Solo-
μῶντα‖ ἐκ τῆς τοῦ Οὐρίου· 7 Σολομὼν.δὲ ἐγέν-
mon of the [one who had been wife] of Urias; and Solomon be-
νησεν τὸν Ῥοβοάμ· Ῥοβοὰμ.δὲ ἐγέννησεν τὸν Ἀβιά· Ἀβιὰ
gat Roboam; and Roboam begat Abia; [2]Abia
δὲ ἐγέννησεν τὸν [h]Ἀσά·‖ 8 [h]Ἀσὰ‖.δὲ ἐγέννησεν τὸν Ἰωσαφάτ·
[1]and begat Asa; and Asa begat Josaphat;
Ἰωσαφὰτ.δὲ ἐγέννησεν τὸν Ἰωράμ· Ἰωρὰμ δὲ ἐγέννησεν τὸν
and Josaphat begat Joram; and Joram begat
[i]Ὀζίαν· 9 [i]Ὀζίας‖.δὲ ἐγέννησεν τὸν Ἰωάθαμ· Ἰωάθαμ.δὲ
Ozias; and Ozias begat Joatham; and Joatham
ἐγέννησεν τὸν Ἄχαζ· Ἄχαζ.δὲ ἐγέννησεν τὸν [k]Ἐζεκίαν·‖
begat Achaz; and Achaz begat Ezekias;
10 [l]Ἐζεκίας‖.δὲ ἐγέννησεν τὸν Μανασσῆ· Μανασσῆς.δὲ ἐγέν-
and Ezekias begat Manasses; and Manasses be-
νησεν τὸν [m]Ἀμών‖· [m]Ἀμὼν‖.δὲ ἐγέννησεν τὸν [n]Ἰωσίαν·‖
gat Amon; and Amon begat Josias;
11 [o]Ἰωσίας‖.δὲ ἐγέννησεν τὸν Ἰεχονίαν καὶ τοὺς ἀδελφοὺς
and Josias begat Jechonias and [2]brethren
αὐτοῦ, ἐπὶ τῆς μετοικεσίας Βαβυλῶνος. 12 Μετὰ.δὲ
[1]his, at [the time] of the carrying away of Babylon. And after
τὴν μετοικεσίαν Βαβυλῶνος, Ἰεχονίας [q]ἐγέννησεν‖ τὸν Σαλα-
the carrying away of Babylon, Jechonias begat Sala-
θιήλ· Σαλαθιὴλ.δὲ [q]ἐγέννησεν‖ τὸν Ζοροβάβελ· 13 Ζοροβά-
thiel; and Salathiel begat Zorobabel; [2]Zoroba-
βελ.δὲ [q]ἐγέννησεν‖ τὸν Ἀβιούδ· Ἀβιοὺδ.δὲ ἐγέννησεν τὸν
bel [1]and begat Abiud; and Abiud begat
Ἐλιακείμ· Ἐλιακεὶμ.δὲ ἐγέννησεν τὸν Ἀζώρ· 14 Ἀζὼρ.δὲ
Eliakim; and Eliakim begat Azor; and Azor
ἐγέννησεν τὸν Σαδώκ· Σαδὼκ.δὲ ἐγέννησεν τὸν Ἀχείμ· Ἀχεὶμ
begat Sadoc; and Sadoc begat Achim; [2]Achim
δὲ ἐγέννησεν τὸν Ἐλιούδ· 15 Ἐλιοὺδ.δὲ ἐγέννησεν τὸν Ἐλεά-
[1]and begat Eliud; and Eliud begat Elea-
ζαρ· Ἐλεάζαρ.δὲ ἐγέννησεν τὸν [r]Ματθάν·‖ [r]Ματθὰν‖.δὲ ἐγέν-
zar; and Eleazar begat Matthan; and Matthan be-
νησεν τὸν Ἰακώβ· 16 Ἰακὼβ.δὲ ἐγέννησεν τὸν Ἰωσὴφ τὸν
gat Jacob; and Jacob begat Joseph the
ἄνδρα Μαρίας, ἐξ ἧς ἐγεννήθη Ἰησοῦς ὁ λεγόμενος χριστός.
husband of Mary, of whom was born Jesus, who is called Christ.

17 Πᾶσαι.οὖν αἱ γενεαὶ ἀπὸ Ἀβραὰμ ἕως [s]Δαβὶδ‖
So all the generations from Abraham to David [were]
γενεαὶ δεκατέσσαρες· καὶ ἀπὸ [s]Δαβὶδ‖ ἕως τῆς μετοικεσίας
[2]generations [1]fourteen; and from David until the carrying away
Βαβυλῶνος, γενεαὶ δεκατέσσαρες· καὶ ἀπὸ τῆς μετοικεσίας
of Babylon, [2]generations [1]fourteen; and from the carrying away
Βαβυλῶνος ἕως τοῦ χριστοῦ, γενεαὶ δεκατέσσαρες.
of Babylon to the Christ, [2]generations [1]fourteen.

18 Τοῦ.δὲ.[t]Ἰησοῦ‖ χριστοῦ ἡ [v]γέννησις‖ οὕτως ἦν. Μνη-
Now of Jesus Christ the birth thus was. [6]Having
στευθείσης [w]γὰρ‖ τῆς.μητρὸς.αὐτοῦ Μαρίας τῷ Ἰωσήφ, πρὶν.ἢ
[6]been [7]betrothed [1]for [3]his [4]mother [2]Mary to Joseph, before
συνελθεῖν αὐτοὺς εὑρέθη ἐν.γαστρὶ.ἔχουσα ἐκ πνεύματος
[2]came [3]together [1]they she was found to be with child of [the] [2]Spirit
ἁγίου. 19 Ἰωσὴφ.δὲ ὁ.ἀνὴρ.αὐτῆς, δίκαιος ὤν, καὶ μὴ θέλων
[1]Holy. But Joseph her husband, [2]righteous [1]being, and not willing
αὐτὴν [x]παραδειγματίσαι,‖ ἐβουλήθη [y]λάθρα‖ ἀπολῦσαι αὐτήν.
her to expose publicly, purposed secretly to put [2]away [1]her.

CHAPTER 1

1 The book of the generations of Jesus
Christ, the son of David, the son of
Abraham.
2 Abraham fathered Isaac, and Isaac fathered Jacob, and Jacob fathered Judah and his
brothers.
3 And Judah fathered Phar-ez and Zarah of
Tamar. And Phar-ez fathered Hez-ron, and
Hez-ron fathered Ram,
4 and Ram fathered Am-min-a-dab, and
Am-min-a-dab fathered Nah-shon, and Nah-
shon fathered Salmon.
5 And Salmon fathered Boaz of Rahab, and
Boaz fathered Obed of Ruth, and Obed
fathered Jesse, and Jesse fathered David the
king.
6 And David the king fathered Solomon of
her *who had been the wife* of Uriah,
Bathsheba.
7 And Solomon fathered Re-ho-bo-am, and
Re-ho-bo-am fathered A-bi-jah, and A-bi-jah
fathered Asa.
8 And Asa fathered Je-hosh-a-phat, and Je-
hosh-a-phat fathered Je-hor-am, and
Je-hor-am fathered Uzziah.
9 And Uzziah fathered Jotham, and Jotham
fathered Ahaz, and Ahaz fathered Hezekiah.
10 And Hezekiah fathered Ma-nas-seh, and
Ma-nas-seh fathered A-mon, and A-mon
fathered Jo-si-ah.
11 And Jo-si-ah fathered Je-hoi-a-chin and
his brothers, at the *time the Israelites were*
carried away to Bab-y-lon.
12 And after they were carried away to
Bab-y-lon, Je-hoi-a-chin fathered She-al-tiel,
and She-al-tiel fathered Ze-rub-ba-bel.
13 And Ze-rub-ba-bel fathered A-bi-ud, and
A-bi-ud fathered E-li-a-kim, and E-li-a-kim
fathered A-zor.
14 And A-zor fathered Sa-doc, and Sa-doc
fathered Achim, and Achim fathered E-li-ud,
15 and E-li-ud fathered El-e-a-zar, and El-
e-a-zar fathered Mat-than, and Mat-than
fathered Jacob.
16 And Jacob fathered Joseph, the husband
of Mary, *that Mary* of whom Jesus was born,
who is called Christ.
17 So all the generations from Abraham to
David are fourteen generations. And from
David to the carrying away into Babylon are
fourteen generations. And from the carrying
away into Babylon until Christ are fourteen
generations.
18 Now the birth of Jesus Christ happened
this way (for His mother Mary was engaged
to Joseph): Before they came together she
was discovered to be with child of the Holy
Spirit.
19 But Joseph, her *betrothed* husband, was
righteous and was not willing to make her a
public example. *So he* intended to put her
away secretly.

20 ταῦτα.δὲ αὐτοῦ.ἐνθυμηθέντος, ἰδού, ἄγγελος κυρίου
And [5]these [6]things [1]when [2]he [3]had [4]pondered, behold, an angel of [the] Lord
κατ' ὄναρ ἐφάνη αὐτῷ, λέγων, Ἰωσήφ, υἱὸς [a]Δαβίδ,[ǁ] μὴ
in a dream appeared to him, saying, Joseph, son of David, [2]not
φοβηθῇς παραλαβεῖν Μαριὰμ τὴν.γυναῖκά.σου· τὸ.γὰρ ἐν
[1]fear to take to [thee] Mary thy wife, for that which in
αὐτῇ γεννηθὲν ἐκ πνεύματός ἐστιν ἁγίου. 21 τέξεται.δὲ υἱόν,
her is begotten [2]of [[3]the] [5]Spirit [1]is [4]Holy. And she shall bring forth a son,
καὶ καλέσεις τὸ.ὄνομα.αὐτοῦ Ἰησοῦν· αὐτὸς.γὰρ σώσει τὸν
and thou shalt call his name Jesus; for he shall save
λαὸν αὐτοῦ ἀπὸ τῶν.ἁμαρτιῶν.αὐτῶν. 22 Τοῦτο.δὲ ὅλον
[2]people [1]his from their sins. Now this all
γέγονεν, ἵνα πληρωθῇ τὸ ῥηθὲν ὑπὸ [z]τοῦ[ǁ] κυρίου
came to pass, that might be fulfilled that which was spoken by the Lord
διὰ τοῦ προφήτου, λέγοντος, 23 Ἰδοὺ ἡ παρθένος ἐν
through the prophet, saying, Behold, the virgin [3]with
γαστρὶ.ἕξει καὶ τέξεται υἱόν, καὶ καλέσουσιν τὸ ὄνομα
[4]child [1]shall [2]be, and shall bring forth a son, and they shall call [2]name
αὐτοῦ Ἐμμανουήλ, ὅ ἐστιν μεθερμηνευόμενον, Μεθ' ἡμῶν
[1]his Emmanuel, which is, being interpreted, [2]With [3]us
[a]ὁ[ǁ] θεός. 24 [b]Διεγερθεὶς[ǁ].δὲ [c]ὁ[ǁ] Ἰωσὴφ ἀπὸ τοῦ ὕπνου, ἐποί-
[1]God. And [2]having [3]been [4]aroused [1]Joseph from the sleep, did
ησεν ὡς προσέταξεν αὐτῷ ὁ ἄγγελος κυρίου· καὶ παρέλαβεν
as had ordered him the angel of [the] Lord, and took to [him]
τὴν.γυναῖκα.αὐτοῦ, 25 καὶ οὐκ.ἐγίνωσκεν αὐτὴν ἕως οὗ
his wife, and knew not her until
ἔτεκεν [d]τὸν[ǁ] υἱὸν [e]αὐτῆς τὸν πρωτότοκον·[ǁ] καὶ ἐκάλεσεν
she brought forth [3]son [1]her [2]the firstborn; and he called
τὸ.ὄνομα.αὐτοῦ Ἰησοῦν.
his name Jesus.

2 Τοῦ.δὲ.Ἰησοῦ γεννηθέντος ἐν Βηθλεὲμ τῆς Ἰουδαίας,
Now Jesus having been born in Bethlehem of Judæa,
ἐν ἡμέραις Ἡρῴδου τοῦ βασιλέως, ἰδού, μάγοι ἀπὸ ἀνατολῶν
in [the] days of Herod the king, behold, magi from [the] east
παρεγένοντο εἰς Ἱεροσόλυμα, 2 λέγοντες, Ποῦ ἐστιν ὁ τεχ-
arrived at Jerusalem, saying, Where is he who has
θεὶς βασιλεὺς τῶν Ἰουδαίων; εἴδομεν γὰρ αὐτοῦ τὸν ἀστέρα
been born King of the Jews? for we saw his star
ἐν τῇ ἀνατολῇ, καὶ ἤλθομεν προσκυνῆσαι αὐτῷ. 3 Ἀκούσας
in the east, and are come to do homage to him. [3]Having [4]heard
δὲ [f]Ἡρώδης ὁ βασιλεὺς[ǁ] ἐταράχθη, καὶ πᾶσα Ἱεροσόλυμα
[1]but [2]Herod [3]the [4]king he was troubled, and all Jerusalem
μετ' αὐτοῦ· 4 καὶ συναγαγὼν πάντας τοὺς ἀρχιερεῖς καὶ
with him. And having gathered together all the chief priests and
γραμματεῖς τοῦ λαοῦ, ἐπυνθάνετο παρ' αὐτῶν, ποῦ ὁ χριστὸς
scribes of the people, he inquired of them where the Christ
γεννᾶται. 5 Οἱ.δὲ [g]εἶπον[ǁ] αὐτῷ, Ἐν Βηθλεὲμ τῆς Ἰουδαίας.
should be born. And they said to him, In Bethlehem of Judæa:
οὕτως.γὰρ γέγραπται διὰ τοῦ προφήτου, 6 Καὶ σὺ Βηθλεέμ,
for thus it has been written by the prophet, And thou, Bethlehem,
γῆ Ἰούδα, οὐδαμῶς ἐλαχίστη εἶ ἐν τοῖς ἡγεμόσιν Ἰούδα· ἐκ
land of Juda, in no wise least art among the governors of Juda, [2]out
σοῦ γὰρ ἐξελεύσεται ἡγούμενος, ὅστις ποιμανεῖ τὸν.λαόν.μου
[3]of [4]thee [1]for shall go forth a leader, who shall shepherd my people
τὸν Ἰσραήλ. 7 Τότε Ἡρώδης [h]λάθρα[ǁ] καλέσας τοὺς μάγους,
Israel. Then Herod, [2]secretly [1]having called the magi,
ἠκρίβωσεν παρ' αὐτῶν τὸν χρόνον τοῦ φαινομένου ἀστέρος·
inquired accurately of them the time of the [2]appearing [1]star.
8 καὶ πέμψας αὐτοὺς εἰς Βηθλεὲμ εἶπεν, Πορευθέντες [i]ἀκρι-
And having sent them to Bethlehem, he said, Having gone, accu-
βῶς ἐξετάσατε[ǁ] περὶ τοῦ παιδίου· ἐπὰν.δὲ εὕρητε,
rately inquire for the little child; and when ye shall have found [him]
ἀπαγγείλατέ μοι, ὅπως κἀγὼ ἐλθὼν προσκυνήσω αὐτῷ.
bring word back to me, that I also having come may do homage to him.
9 Οἱ.δὲ ἀκούσαντες τοῦ βασιλέως ἐπορεύθησαν· καὶ ἰδού, ὁ
And they having heard the king, went away; and behold, the
ἀστὴρ, ὃν εἶδον ἐν τῇ ἀνατολῇ, προῆγεν αὐτοὺς ἕως ἐλθὼν
star, which they saw in the east, went before them, until having come
[k]ἔστη[ǁ] ἐπάνω οὗ ἦν τὸ παιδίον. 10 ἰδόντες.δὲ τὸν ἀστέρα,
it stood over where was the little child. And having seen the star,
ἐχάρησαν χαρὰν μεγάλην σφόδρα· 11 καὶ ἐλθόντες εἰς
they rejoiced [with] joy [2]great [1]exceedingly. And having come into
τὴν οἰκίαν, [l]εὗρον[ǁ] τὸ παιδίον μετὰ Μαρίας τῆς.μητρὸς.αὐτοῦ,
the house, they found the little child with Mary his mother,
καὶ πεσόντες προσεκύνησαν αὐτῷ καὶ ἀνοίξαντες τοὺς
and having fallen down did homage to him: and having opened
θησαυροὺς αὐτῶν προσήνεγκαν αὐτῷ δῶρα, χρυσὸν καὶ
[2]treasures [1]their they offered to him gifts; gold and
λίβανον καὶ σμύρναν. 12 καὶ χρηματισθέντες κατ'
frankincense and myrrh. And having been divinely instructed in
ὄναρ μὴ ἀνακάμψαι πρὸς Ἡρῴδην, δι' ἄλλης ὁδοῦ
a dream not to return to Herod, by another way

20 And as he thought about these things,
behold, an angel of the Lord appeared to
him in a dream! And *he* said, Joseph, son of
David, do not be afraid to take Mary as your
wife. For that which is in her is born of the
Holy Spirit.
21 And she shall give birth to a son. And
you shall call His name Jesus – for He shall
save His people from their sins.
22 Now all this happened so that it might
be fulfilled which was spoken by the Lord
through the prophet, saying,
23 "Behold! The virgin shall be with child
and shall give birth to a son, and they shall
call His name Im-man-u-el" (which translated means, "God with us").
24 And having been aroused from sleep,
Joseph did as the angel of the Lord
commanded him, taking *Mary* as his wife.
25 And he did not know her until she had
brought forth her first-born son. And he
called His name Jesus.

CHAPTER 2

1 Now when Jesus had been born in
Beth-le-hem of Ju-de-a in the days of Herod
the king, behold, wise men came from the
east to Jerusalem.
2 And they said, Where is He who has been
born king of the Jews? For we have seen His
star in the east and have come to worship
Him.
3 But when Herod the king heard this, he
was troubled, and all Jerusalem with him.
4 And when he had gathered all the chief
priests and scribes of the people together, he
asked them where the Christ was to be born.
5 And they said to him, in Beth-le-hem of
Ju-d-ea, for the prophet has written it so:
6 "And you, Beth-le-hem *in the* land of
Judah, are not the least among the princes of
Judah, for out of you shall come a Governor
who shall shepherd My people Israel."
7 Then Herod secretly called the wise men
aside and asked them the exact time the star
appeared.
8 And sending them on to Bethlehem, he
said, Go and search carefully for the little
child. And when you have found him, bring
me word again so that I may come and
worship him also.
9 And they went away, after hearing the
king. And, behold! The star which they had
seen in the east went before them until it
had come *to where it* stood right over the
little child.
10 And seeing the star, they rejoiced with
great, overwhelming joy.
11 And when they had come into the
house, they found the little child with His
mother, Mary. And they fell down and
worshiped Him. And they opened their
treasures and presented gifts to Him: gold
and frankincense and myrrh.
12 Then being warned of God in a dream
not to return to Herod, they went away into

ἀνεχώρησαν εἰς τὴν.χώραν.αὐτῶν.
they withdrew into their own country.
13 Ἀναχωρησάντων.δὲ αὐτῶν, ἰδού, ἄγγελος κυρίου
Now [2]having [3]withdrawn [1]they, behold, an angel of [the] Lord
[m]φαίνεται κατ' ὄναρ" τῷ Ἰωσήφ, λέγων, Ἐγερθεὶς παράλαβε
appears in a dream to Joseph, saying, Having risen take with [thee]
τὸ παιδίον καὶ τὴν.μητέρα.αὐτοῦ, καὶ φεῦγε εἰς Αἴγυπτον,
the little child and his mother, and flee into Egypt,
καὶ ἴσθι ἐκεῖ ἕως ἂν εἴπω σοί· μέλλει γὰρ Ἡρώδης ζητεῖν τὸ
and be there until I shall tell thee; [3]is [4]about [1]for [2]Herod to seek the
παιδίον, τοῦ ἀπολέσαι αὐτό. 14 Ὁ.δὲ ἐγερθεὶς παρέλαβεν
little child, to destroy him. And he having risen took with [him]
τὸ παιδίον καὶ τὴν.μητέρα.αὐτοῦ νυκτός, καὶ ἀνεχώρησεν εἰς
the little child and his mother by night, and withdrew into
Αἴγυπτον, 15 καὶ ἦν ἐκεῖ ἕως τῆς τελευτῆς Ἡρώδου· ἵνα
Egypt, and was there until the death of Herod: that
πληρωθῇ τὸ ῥηθὲν ὑπὸ [n]τοῦ" κυρίου διὰ τοῦ
might be fulfilled that which was spoken by the Lord through the
προφήτου, λέγοντος, Ἐξ Αἰγύπτου ἐκάλεσα τὸν.υἱόν.μου.
prophet, saying, Out of Egypt have I called my son.
16 Τότε Ἡρώδης, ἰδὼν ὅτι ἐνεπαίχθη ὑπὸ τῶν μάγων,
Then Herod, having seen that he was mocked by the magi,
ἐθυμώθη λίαν, καὶ ἀποστείλας ἀνεῖλεν πάντας τοὺς
was enraged greatly, and having sent he put to death all the
παῖδας τοὺς ἐν Βηθλεὲμ καὶ ἐν πᾶσιν τοῖς.ὁρίοις.αὐτῆς, ἀπὸ
boys that [were] in Bethlehem and in all its borders, from
διετοῦς καὶ κατωτέρω, κατὰ τὸν χρόνον ὃν ἠκρίβω-
two years old and under, according to the time which he had accurately
σεν παρὰ τῶν μάγων. 17 Τότε ἐπληρώθη τὸ ῥηθὲν
inquired from the magi. Then was fulfilled that which was spoken
[o]ὑπὸ" Ἱερεμίου τοῦ προφήτου, λέγοντος, 18 Φωνὴ ἐν Ῥαμᾶ
by Jeremias the prophet, saying, A voice in Rama
ἠκούσθη, [p]θρῆνος καὶ" κλαυθμὸς καὶ ὀδυρμὸς πολύς, Ῥαχὴλ
was heard, lamentation and weeping and [2]mourning [1]great, Rachel
κλαίουσα τὰ.τέκνα.αὐτῆς, καὶ οὐκ [q]ἤθελεν" παρακληθῆναι,
weeping [for] her children. and [2]not [1]would be comforted,
ὅτι οὐκ.εἰσίν.
because they are not.
19 Τελευτήσαντος.δὲ τοῦ Ἡρώδου, ἰδού, ἄγγελος κυρίου
But [2]having [3]died [1]Herod, behold, an angel of [the] Lord
[r]κατ' ὄναρ φαίνεται" τῷ Ἰωσὴφ ἐν Αἰγύπτῳ, 20 λέγων, Ἐγερ-
in a dream appears to Joseph in Egypt, saying, Having
θεὶς παράλαβε τὸ παιδίον καὶ τὴν.μητέρα.αὐτοῦ, καὶ πορεύου
risen take with [thee] the little child and his mother, and go
εἰς γῆν Ἰσραήλ· τεθνήκασιν.γὰρ οἱ ζητοῦντες τὴν ψυχὴν
into [the] land of Israel: for they have died who were seeking the life
τοῦ παιδίου. 21 Ὁ.δὲ ἐγερθεὶς παρέλαβεν τὸ παιδίον καὶ
of the little child. And he having risen took with [him] the little child and
τὴν.μητέρα.αὐτοῦ, καὶ [s]ἦλθεν" εἰς γῆν Ἰσραήλ. 22 ἀκούσας
his mother, and came into [the] land of Israel. [2]Having [3]heard
δὲ ὅτι Ἀρχέλαος βασιλεύει [t]ἐπὶ" τῆς Ἰουδαίας ἀντὶ [v]Ἡρώδου
[1]but that Archelaus reigns over Judæa instead of Herod
τοῦ.πατρὸς.αὐτοῦ," ἐφοβήθη ἐκεῖ ἀπελθεῖν· χρηματισ-
his father, he was afraid there to go; [2]having [3]been [4]divinely
θεὶς δὲ κατ' ὄναρ, ἀνεχώρησεν εἰς τὰ μέρη τῆς Γαλιλαίας,
[5]instructed [1]and in a dream, he withdrew into the parts of Galilee:
23 καὶ ἐλθὼν κατῴκησεν εἰς πόλιν λεγομένην [w]Ναζαρέτ·"
and having come he dwelt in a city called Nazareth;
ὅπως πληρωθῇ τὸ ῥηθὲν διὰ τῶν προφητῶν, ὅτι
so that should be fulfilled that which was spoken by the prophets, that
Ναζωραῖος κληθήσεται.
a Nazaræan shall he be called.
3 Ἐν.δὲ ταῖς.ἡμέραις.ἐκείναις παραγίνεται Ἰωάννης ὁ
Now in those days comes John the
βαπτιστής, κηρύσσων ἐν τῇ ἐρήμῳ τῆς Ἰουδαίας, 2 [x]καὶ" λέγων,
Baptist, proclaiming in the wilderness of Judæa, and saying,
Μετανοεῖτε· ἤγγικεν.γὰρ ἡ βασιλεία τῶν οὐρανῶν. 3 Οὗτος.γάρ
Repent, for has drawn near the kingdom of the heavens. For this
ἐστιν ὁ ῥηθεὶς [y]ὑπὸ" Ἡσαΐου τοῦ προφήτου, λέγοντος,
is he who was spoken of by Esaias the prophet, saying,
Φωνὴ βοῶντος ἐν τῇ ἐρήμῳ, Ἑτοιμάσατε τὴν ὁδὸν κυ-
[The] voice of one crying in the wilderness, Prepare the way of [the]
ρίου· εὐθείας ποιεῖτε τὰς.τρίβους.αὐτοῦ. 4 Αὐτὸς.δὲ ὁ Ἰωάννης
Lord, straight make his paths. And [2]himself [1]John
εἶχεν τὸ.ἔνδυμα.αὐτοῦ ἀπὸ τριχῶν καμήλου, καὶ ζώνην δερ-
had his raiment of hair of a camel, and a girdle of
ματίνην περὶ τὴν.ὀσφὺν.αὐτοῦ· ἡ.δὲ τροφὴ [z]αὐτοῦ ἦν" ἀκρίδες
leather about his loins, and the food of him was locusts
καὶ μέλι ἄγριον.
and [2]honey [1]wild.
5 Τότε ἐξεπορεύετο πρὸς αὐτὸν Ἱεροσόλυμα καὶ πᾶσα ἡ
Then went out to him Jerusalem, and all

their own country another way.
13 And when they had departed, lo, an
angel appeared to Joseph in a dream, saying,
Get up! Take the little child and His mother
with you and escape into Egypt. And stay
there until I call you. For Herod is about to
look for the little child in order to kill Him.
14 And he arose and took the little child
and His mother with him. And he went by
night into Egypt.
15 And he remained there until the death of
Herod, so that it might be fulfilled which
was spoken by the Lord through the prophet, saying, "Out of Egypt I have called My
Son."
16 Then seeing that he was fooled by the
wise men, Herod was very angry. And he
sent men and killed all the boys that were in
Bethlehem, and in all of its borders, from
two years old and under – according to the
time which he had accurately inquired of the
wise men.
17 Then that which was spoken by
Jeremiah the prophet was fulfilled, when he
said,
18 "A voice was heard in Ramah, wailing
and bitter weeping and great mourning,
Rachel weeping for her children. And she
would not be comforted, because they are
gone."
19 But when Herod had died, behold, an
angel of the Lord appeared to Joseph in
Egypt, in a dream,
20 saying, Get up! Take the little child and
His mother and go into the land of Israel.
For those who were seeking the little child's
life have died.
21 And he arose and took the little child
and His mother with him and came into the
land of Israel.
22 But when he heard that Arch-e-la-us
ruled over Ju-de-a in the place of his father
Herod, *Joseph* was afraid to go there. And
being warned of God in a dream, he went
into a part of Galilee.
23 And he came and lived in a city called
Naz-a-reth – so that what the prophets had
spoken would be fulfilled, "He shall be
called a Naz-a-rene."

CHAPTER 3

1 Now in those days John the Baptist came
preaching in the wilderness of Ju-de-a.
2 And he was saying, Repent! For the kingdom of Heaven *is* coming *soon*.
3 (For this is he who was spoken of by
Isaiah the prophet, saying, "The voice of one
crying in the wilderness! Prepare the way of
the Lord! Make His paths straight!")
4 And John's clothing was of camel's hair,
and *he wore* a girdle of leather about his
loins. And his food was locusts and wild
honey.
5 Then Jerusalem and all Ju-de-a went out

Ἰουδαία καὶ πᾶσα ἡ περίχωρος τοῦ Ἰορδάνου· 6 καὶ ἐβαπτί-
Judæa, and all the country around the Jordan, and were bap-
ζοντο[a] ἐν τῷ Ἰορδάνῃ[b] ὑπ' αὐτοῦ, ἐξομολογούμενοι τὰς ἁμαρ-
tized in the Jordan by him, confessing [2]sins
τίας αὐτῶν. 7 Ἰδὼν.δὲ πολλοὺς τῶν Φαρισαίων καὶ Σαδδου-
[1]their But having seen many of the Pharisees and Saddu-
καίων ἐρχομένους ἐπὶ τὸ.βάπτισμα.[c]αὐτοῦ,‖ εἶπεν αὐτοῖς,
cees coming to his baptism, he said to them,
Γεννήματα ἐχιδνῶν, τίς ὑπέδειξεν ὑμῖν φυγεῖν ἀπὸ τῆς μελ-
Offspring of vipers, who forewarned you to flee from the com-
λούσης ὀργῆς; 8 ποιήσατε οὖν [d]καρποὺς ἀξίους‖ τῆς μετα-
ing wrath? Produce therefore fruits worthy of repent-
νοίας· 9 καὶ μὴ.δόξητε λέγειν ἐν ἑαυτοῖς, Πατέρα ἔχομεν
ance: and think not to say within yourselves [4For] [3]father [1]we [2]have
τὸν Ἀβραάμ· λέγω.γὰρ ὑμῖν, ὅτι δύναται ὁ θεὸς ἐκ τῶν λίθων
Abraham: for I say to you, that able is God from [2]stones
τούτων ἐγεῖραι τέκνα τῷ Ἀβραάμ. 10 ἤδη.δὲ [e]καὶ‖ ἡ ἀξίνη
[1]these to raise up children to Abraham. But already also the axe
πρὸς τὴν ῥίζαν τῶν δένδρων κεῖται· πᾶν οὖν δένδρον μὴ
to the root of the trees is applied: [2]every [1]therefore tree not
ποιοῦν καρπὸν καλὸν ἐκκόπτεται καὶ εἰς πῦρ βάλλεται.
producing [2]fruit [1]good is cut down and into [the] fire is cast.
11 Ἐγὼ μὲν [f]βαπτίζω ὑμᾶς‖ ἐν ὕδατι εἰς μετάνοιαν· ὁ.δὲ
I indeed baptize you with water to repentance; but he who
ὀπίσω μου ἐρχόμενος ἰσχυρότερός μου ἐστίν, οὗ οὐκ.εἰμὶ
after me [is] coming mightier than I is, of whom I am not
ἱκανὸς τὰ ὑποδήματα βαστάσαι· αὐτὸς ὑμᾶς βαπτίσει ἐν
fit the sandals to bear: he [2]you [1]will [3]baptize with [the]
πνεύματι ἁγίῳ καὶ πυρί. 12 οὗ τὸ πτύον ἐν τῇ χειρὶ
[2]Spirit [1]Holy and with fire. Of whom the winnowing fan [is] in [2]hand
αὐτοῦ, καὶ διακαθαριεῖ τὴν.ἅλωνα.αὐτοῦ, καὶ συνάξει
[1]his, and he will thoroughly purge his floor, and will gather
τὸν.σῖτον.αὐτοῦ εἰς τὴν ἀποθήκην,[g] τὸ.δὲ ἄχυρον κατακαύσει
his wheat into the granary, but the chaff he will burn up
πυρὶ ἀσβέστῳ.
with fire unquenchable.
13 Τότε παραγίνεται ὁ Ἰησοῦς ἀπὸ τῆς Γαλιλαίας ἐπὶ τὸν
Then comes Jesus from Galilee to the
Ἰορδάνην πρὸς τὸν Ἰωάννην, τοῦ βαπτισθῆναι ὑπ' αὐτοῦ.
Jordan to John, to be baptized by him.
14 ὁ.δὲ.[h]Ἰωάννης‖ διεκώλυεν αὐτόν, λέγων, Ἐγὼ χρείαν ἔχω
But John was hindering him, saying, I [2]need [1]have
ὑπὸ σοῦ βαπτισθῆναι, καὶ σὺ ἔρχῃ πρός με; 15 Ἀποκριθεὶς
by thee to be baptized, and [2]thou [1]comest to me? [2]Answering
δὲ ὁ Ἰησοῦς εἶπεν [i]πρὸς αὐτόν,‖ Ἄφες ἄρτι· οὕτως.γὰρ
[1]but [3]Jesus said to him, Suffer [it] now; for thus
πρέπον ἐστὶν ἡμῖν πληρῶσαι πᾶσαν δικαιοσύνην. Τότε
becoming it is to us to fulfil all righteousness. Then
ἀφίησιν αὐτόν. 16 [j]Καὶ βαπτισθεὶς‖ ὁ Ἰησοῦς [k]ἀνέβη
he suffers him. And having been baptized Jesus went up
εὐθὺς‖ ἀπὸ τοῦ ὕδατος, καὶ ἰδού, [l]ἀνεῴχθησαν‖ [m]αὐτῷ‖ οἱ
immediately from the water: and behold, were opened to him the
οὐρανοί, καὶ εἶδεν [n]τὸ‖ πνεῦμα [o]τοῦ‖ θεοῦ καταβαῖνον ὡσεὶ
heavens, and he saw the Spirit of God descending as
περιστεράν, [p]καὶ‖ ἐρχόμενον ἐπ' αὐτόν. 17 καὶ ἰδού, φωνὴ
a dove, and coming upon him: and lo, a voice
ἐκ τῶν οὐρανῶν, λέγουσα, Οὗτός ἐστιν ὁ.υἱός.μου ὁ ἀγα-
out of the heavens, saying, This is my Son the be-
πητός, ἐν ᾧ [q]εὐδόκησα‖.
loved, in whom I have found delight.
4 Τότε [r]ὁ‖ Ἰησοῦς ἀνήχθη εἰς τὴν ἔρημον ὑπὸ τοῦ πνεύ-
Then Jesus was led up into the wilderness by the Spi-
ματος, πειρασθῆναι ὑπὸ τοῦ διαβόλου. 2 καὶ νηστεύσας
rit to be tempted by the devil. And having fasted
ἡμέρας [s]τεσσαράκοντα‖ καὶ [t]νύκτας τεσσαράκοντα,‖ ὕστερον
[2]days [1]forty and [2]nights [1]forty, afterwards
ἐπείνασεν. 3 καὶ προσελθὼν [v]αὐτῷ‖ ὁ πειράζων εἶπεν[w], Εἰ
he hungered. And having come to him the tempter said, If
υἱὸς εἶ τοῦ θεοῦ, εἰπὲ ἵνα οἱ.λίθοι.οὗτοι ἄρτοι γένωνται.
[3]Son [1]thou [2]art of God, speak that these stones [3]loaves [1]may [2]become.
4 Ὁ δὲ ἀποκριθεὶς εἶπεν, Γέγραπται, Οὐκ ἐπ' ἄρτῳ μόνῳ
But he answering said, It has been written, Not by bread alone
ζήσεται [x]ἄνθρωπος, ἀλλ' [y]ἐπὶ‖ παντὶ ῥήματι ἐκπορευομένῳ διὰ
shall [2]live [1]man, but by every word going out through
στόματος θεοῦ. 5 Τότε παραλαμβάνει αὐτὸν ὁ διάβολος εἰς
[the] mouth of God. Then [2]takes [4]him [1]the [2]devil to
τὴν ἁγίαν πόλιν, καὶ [z]ἵστησιν‖ αὐτὸν ἐπὶ τὸ πτερύγιον τοῦ
the holy city, and sets him upon the edge of the
ἱεροῦ, 6 καὶ [a]λέγει‖ αὐτῷ, Εἰ υἱὸς εἶ τοῦ θεοῦ, βάλε σεαυ-
temple, and says to him, If [3]Son [1]thou [2]art of God, cast thy-
τὸν κάτω· γέγραπται.γάρ, Ὅτι τοῖς.ἀγγέλοις.αὐτοῦ ἐν-
self down: for it has been written, To his angels he

to him, and all those of the country around
the Jordan.
6 And they were baptized by him in the
Jordan, confessing their sins.
7 But when he saw many of the Phar-i-sees
and Sad-du-cees coming to his baptism, he
said to them, Children of vipers! Who
warned you to flee from the wrath to come?
8 Then bring forth fruits worthy of repentance!
9 And do not think *you* can say within
yourselves, We have Abraham *as our* father.
For I say to you that God is able to raise up
children to Abraham from these stones.
10 And even now the axe is laying at the
root of the trees – therefore every tree that
is not bearing good fruit is to be cut down
and thrown into the fire.
11 I indeed baptize you in water to repentance. But He who is coming after me is
mightier than I, whose sandals I am not fit
to carry. He shall baptize you in the Holy
Spirit and in fire.
12 His fan is in His hand and He will
completely clear His floor. And He will
gather His wheat into the storehouse. But He
will burn up the chaff, with fire that cannot
be put out.
13 Then Jesus came from Galilee to the
Jordan river to be baptized by John.
14 But John was restraining Him, saying, I
need to be baptized by You, and do You
come to me?
15 But answering, Jesus said to him, Allow
it now, for in this way it is becoming to us
to fulfill all righteousness. Then he gave way
to Him.
16 And Jesus went up immediately out of
the water after He was baptized. And,
behold! The heavens were opened to Him.
And He saw the Spirit of God coming down
like a dove. And He came upon Him.
17 And, behold! A voice *came* out of the
heavens, saying, This is My beloved Son, in
whom I am well-pleased.

CHAPTER 4

1 Then Jesus was led up into the wilderness
by the Spirit to be tempted by the devil.
2 And since He had not eaten for forty days
and forty nights, He afterwards was hungry.
3 And the Tempter came to Him and said,
If You are the Son of God, command that
these stones may become bread.
4 But He answered and said, It is written,
"Man shall not live by bread alone, but by
every word coming out of the mouth of
God."
5 Then the devil took Him to the holy city
and set Him on the edge of the Temple.
6 And he said to Him, If You are the Son of
God, throw Yourself down, for it is written,
"He shall give His angels charge of You, and

τελεῖται περὶ σοῦ, καὶ ἐπὶ χειρῶν ἀροῦσίν σε,
will give charge concerning thee, and in [their] hands shall they bear thee,
μήποτε προσκόψῃς πρὸς λίθον τὸν.πόδα.σου. 7 ᵃἜφη αὐτῷ
lest thou strike against a stone thy foot. ²Said ³to ⁴him
ὁ Ἰησοῦς, Πάλιν γέγραπται, Οὐκ.ἐκπειράσεις κύριον τὸν
¹Jesus, Again it has been written, Thou shalt not tempt [the] Lord
θεόν σου. 8 Πάλιν παραλαμβάνει αὐτὸν ὁ διάβολος εἰς
²God ¹thy. Again ²takes him ¹the ²devil to
ὄρος ὑψηλὸν λίαν, καὶ δείκνυσιν αὐτῷ πάσας τὰς βασι-
a mountain ²high ¹exceedingly, and shews to him all the king-
λείας τοῦ κόσμου καὶ τὴν.δόξαν.αὐτῶν, 9 καὶ ᵇλέγει‖ αὐτῷ,
doms of the world and their glory, and says to him,
ᶜΤαῦτα πάντα σοι‖ δώσω, ἐὰν πεσὼν προσκυνήσῃς
³These ²things ¹all to thee will I give if falling down thou wilt worship
μοι. 10 Τότε λέγει αὐτῷ ὁ Ἰησοῦς, Ὕπαγεᵈ, σατανᾶ·
me. Then ²says ³to ⁴him ¹Jesus, Get thee away, Satan;
γέγραπται.γάρ, Κύριον τὸν.θεόν.σου προσκυνήσεις, καὶ
for it has been written, [The] Lord thy God shalt thou worship, and
αὐτῷ μόνῳ λατρεύσεις. 11 Τότε ἀφίησιν αὐτὸν ὁ διάβολος·
him alone shalt thou serve. Then ³leaves ⁴him ¹the ²devil,
καὶ ἰδού, ἄγγελοι προσῆλθον καὶ διηκόνουν αὐτῷ.
and behold, angels came and ministered to him.
12 Ἀκούσας.δὲ ᵉὁ Ἰησοῦς‖ ὅτι Ἰωάννης παρεδόθη, ἀν-
But ⁴having ³heard ¹Jesus that John was delivered up, he
εχώρησεν εἰς τὴν Γαλιλαίαν. 13 καὶ καταλιπὼν τὴν ᶠΝαζαρέτ,‖
withdrew into Galilee: and having left Nazareth,
ἐλθὼν κατῴκησεν εἰς ᵍΚαπερναοὺμ‖ τὴν παραθαλασσίαν,
having come he dwelt at Capernaum, which [is] on the sea-side,
ἐν ὁρίοις Ζαβουλὼν καὶ Νεφθαλείμ, 14 ἵνα πληρωθῇ
in [the] borders of Zabulon and Nephthalim, that might be fulfilled
τὸ ῥηθὲν διὰ Ἡσαΐου τοῦ προφήτου, λέγοντος, 15 Γῆ
that which was spoken by Esaias the prophet, saying, Land
Ζαβουλὼν καὶ γῆ Νεφθαλείμ, ὁδὸν θαλάσσης πέραν τοῦ
of Zabulon, and land of Nephthalim, way of [the] sea, beyond the
Ἰορδάνου, Γαλιλαία τῶν ἐθνῶν, 16 ὁ λαὸς ὁ καθήμενος
Jordan, Galilee of the nations, the people which was sitting
ἐν ʰσκότει εἶδε φῶς‖ μέγα, καὶ τοῖς καθημένοις ἐν
in darkness has seen a ²light ¹great, and to those which were sitting in [the]
χώρᾳ καὶ σκιᾷ θανάτου, φῶς ἀνέτειλεν αὐτοῖς. 17 Ἀπὸ
country and shadow of death, light has sprung up to them. From
τότε ἤρξατο ὁ Ἰησοῦς κηρύσσειν καὶ λέγειν, Μετανοεῖτε·
that time began Jesus to proclaim and to say, Repent;
ἤγγικεν.γὰρ ἡ βασιλεία τῶν οὐρανῶν.
for has drawn near the kingdom of the heavens.
18 Περιπατῶν.δὲ ⁱὁ Ἰησοῦς‖ παρὰ τὴν θάλασσαν τῆς Γαλι-
And ²walking ¹Jesus by the sea of Gali-
λαίας εἶδεν δύο ἀδελφούς, Σίμωνα τὸν λεγόμενον Πέτρον, καὶ
lee he saw two brothers, Simon who is called Peter, and
Ἀνδρέαν τὸν.ἀδελφὸν.αὐτοῦ, βάλλοντας ἀμφίβληστρον εἰς
Andrew his brother, casting a large net into
τὴν θάλασσαν· ἦσαν.γὰρ ἁλιεῖς. 19 καὶ λέγει αὐτοῖς,ᵏ Δεῦτε
the sea, for they were fishers: and he says to them, Come
ὀπίσω μου, καὶ ποιήσω ὑμᾶς ἁλιεῖς ἀνθρώπων. 20 Οἱ.δὲ
after me, and I will make you fishers of men. And they
εὐθέως ἀφέντες τὰ δίκτυα ἠκολούθησαν αὐτῷ. 21 Καὶ
immediately having left the nets, followed him. And
προβὰς ἐκεῖθεν, εἶδεν ἄλλους δύο ἀδελφούς, Ἰάκωβον τὸν
having gone on thence, he saw other two brothers, James the [son]
τοῦ Ζεβεδαίου καὶ Ἰωάννην τὸν.ἀδελφὸν.αὐτοῦ, ἐν τῷ πλοίῳ
of Zebedee, and John his brother, in the ship
μετὰ Ζεβεδαίου τοῦ.πατρὸς.αὐτῶν, καταρτίζοντας τὰ δίκτυα
with Zebedee their father, mending ²nets
αὐτῶν· καὶ ἐκάλεσεν αὐτούς. 22 οἱ.δὲ εὐθέως ἀφέντες τὸ
¹their, and he called them; and they immediately having left the
πλοῖον καὶ τὸν.πατέρα.αὐτῶν ἠκολούθησαν αὐτῷ.
ship and their father followed him.
23 Καὶ περιῆγεν ˡὅλην τὴν Γαλιλαίαν ὁ Ἰησοῦς,‖ διδάσκων
And ²went ³about ⁴all ⁵Galilee ¹Jesus, teaching
ἐν ταῖς.συναγωγαῖς.αὐτῶν, καὶ κηρύσσων τὸ εὐαγγέλιον τῆς
in their synagogues, and proclaiming the glad tidings of the
βασιλείας, καὶ θεραπεύων πᾶσαν νόσον καὶ πᾶσαν μαλακίαν
kingdom, and healing every disease and every bodily weakness
ἐν τῷ λαῷ. 24 καὶ ἀπῆλθεν ἡ ἀκοὴ αὐτοῦ εἰς ὅλην τὴν Συ-
among the people. And went out the fame of him into all Sy-
ρίαν· καὶ προσήνεγκαν αὐτῷ πάντας τοὺς.κακῶς.ἔχοντας,
ria. And they brought to him all who were ill,
ποικίλαις νόσοις καὶ βασάνοις συνεχομένους, ᵐκαὶ‖ δαιμονιζο-
by various diseases and torments oppressed, and possessed by
μένους, καὶ σεληνιαζομένους, καὶ παραλυτικούς· καὶ ἐθερά-
demons, and lunatics, and paralytics; and he
πευσεν αὐτούς. 25 καὶ ἠκολούθησαν αὐτῷ ὄχλοι πολλοὶ ἀπὸ
healed them. And ³followed ⁴him ²crowds ¹great from

in their hands they shall hold You lest You
strike Your foot against a stone."
7 Jesus said to him, Again it is written,
"You shall not tempt the Lord your God."
8 Again, the devil took Him up to a very
high mountain and showed Him all the
kingdoms of the world and their glory.
9 And he said to Him, I will give You all
these things if You will fall down and
worship me.
10 Then Jesus said to him, Get away, Satan!
For it is written, "You shall worship the
Lord your God, and Him alone you shall
serve."
11 Then the devil left Him. And, behold!
Angels came and waited upon Him.
12 But when Jesus heard that John had
been betrayed, He drew back into Galilee.
13 And He *then* left Naz-a-reth and came to
stay in Ca-per-na-um, which is on the sea-
side, in the borders of Ze-bu-lun and
Naph-ta-li –
14 so that it might be fulfilled which was
spoken by Isaiah the prophet, saying,
15 "Land of Ze-bu-lun and land of
Naph-ta-li by the seaside, beyond the
Jordan, Galilee of the nations,
16 the people sitting in darkness have seen a
great Light! And Light has sprung up to
those sitting in the region and shadow of
death" [see Isaiah 9:1].
17 From that time Jesus began to preach
and to cry, Repent! For the kingdom of
Heaven has come near.

18 And as Jesus walked by the sea of
Galilee, He saw two brothers – Simon, who
is called Peter, and Andrew his brother –
throwing a net into the sea. For they were
fishermen.
19 And He said to them, Follow Me and I
will make you fishers of men.
20 And they immediately left their nets and
followed Him.
21 And going on from there He saw two
other brothers – James the son of Zeb-e-dee,
and his brother John – in the ship with their
father, Zeb-e-dee, mending their nets. And
he called them.
22 And they immediately left the ship and
their father and followed Him.
23 And Jesus went around all Galilee, teaching in their synagogues and preaching the
gospel of the kingdom. And He was healing
every *kind of* disease and ailment among the
people.
24 His fame went into all Syria. And they
brought to Him all who were sick, pressed
down by different diseases and torments,
and *the* demon-possessed and *the* lunatics
and *the* paralytics. And He healed them.
25 And great crowds followed Him from
Galilee and De-cap-o-lis and Jerusalem and

τῆς Γαλιλαίας καὶ Δεκαπόλεως καὶ Ἱεροσολύμων καὶ Ἰουδαίας
Galilee and Decapolis and Jerusalem and Judea
καὶ πέραν τοῦ Ἰορδάνου.
and beyond the Jordan.
5 Ἰδὼν.δὲ τοὺς ὄχλους, ἀνέβη εἰς τὸ ὄρος· καὶ καθίσαν-
But seeing the crowds, he went up into the mountain; and [2]having [3]sat
τος αὐτοῦ, "προσῆλθον" °αὐτῷ' οἱ.μαθηταὶ.αὐτοῦ. 2 καὶ ἀνοί-
[4]down [1]he, came to him his disciples. And having
ξας τὸ.στόμα.αὐτοῦ ἐδίδασκεν αὐτούς, λέγων, 3 Μακάριοι οἱ
opened his mouth he taught them, saying, Blessed [are] the
πτωχοὶ τῷ πνεύματι· ὅτι αὐτῶν ἐστιν ἡ βασιλεία τῶν οὐρανῶν.
poor in spirit; for theirs is the kingdom of the heavens.
4 ᴾμακάριοι οἱ πενθοῦντες· ὅτι αὐτοὶ παρακληθήσονται.
Blessed they who mourn; for they shall be comforted.
5 μακάριοι οἱ πραεῖς· ὅτι αὐτοὶ κληρονομήσουσιν τὴν γῆν."
Blessed the meek; for they shall inherit the earth.
6 μακάριοι οἱ πεινῶντες καὶ διψῶντες τὴν δικαιοσύνην· ὅτι
Blessed they who hunger and thirst after righteousness; for
αὐτοὶ χορτασθήσονται. 7 μακάριοι οἱ ἐλεήμονες· ὅτι αὐτοὶ
they shall be filled. Blessed the merciful; for they
ἐλεηθήσονται. 8 μακάριοι οἱ καθαροὶ τῇ καρδίᾳ· ὅτι αὐτοὶ τὸν
shall find mercy. Blessed the pure in heart; for they
θεὸν ὄψονται. 9 μακάριοι οἱ εἰρηνοποιοί· ὅτι ᵠαὐτοὶ" υἱοὶ θεοῦ
[3]God [1]shall [2]see. Blessed the peacemakers; for they sons of God
κληθήσονται. 10 μακάριοι οἱ δεδιωγμένοι ἕνεκεν δικαιο-
shall be called. Blessed they who have been persecuted on account of right-
σύνης· ὅτι αὐτῶν ἐστιν ἡ βασιλεία τῶν οὐρανῶν. 11 μακάριοί
eousness; for theirs is the kingdom of the heavens. Blessed
ἐστε, ὅταν ὀνειδίσωσιν ὑμᾶς καὶ διώξωσιν, καὶ εἴπωσιν πᾶν
are ye when they shall reproach you, and shall persecute, and shall say every
πονηρὸν ʳῥῆμα" καθ' ὑμῶν ˢψευδόμενοι," ἕνεκεν ἐμοῦ. 12 χαί-
wicked word against you, lying, on account of me. Re-
ρετε καὶ ἀγαλλιᾶσθε, ὅτι ὁ.μισθὸς.ὑμῶν πολὺς ἐν τοῖς οὐρανοῖς·
joice and exult, for your reward [is] great in the heavens;
οὕτως.γὰρ ἐδίωξαν τοὺς προφήτας τοὺς πρὸ ὑμῶν.
for thus they persecuted the prophets who [were] before you.
13 Ὑμεῖς ἐστε τὸ ἅλας τῆς γῆς· ἐὰν.δὲ τὸ ἅλας μωρανθῇ,
Ye are the salt of the earth: but if the salt become tasteless,
ἐν τίνι ἁλισθήσεται; εἰς οὐδὲν ἰσχύει ἔτι, εἰ.μὴ ᵗβλη-
with what shall it be salted? for nothing has it strength any longer, but to be
θῆναι" ἔξω, ᵛκαὶ" καταπατεῖσθαι ὑπὸ τῶν ἀνθρώπων. 14 Ὑμεῖς
cast out, and to be trampled upon by men. Ye
ἐστε τὸ φῶς τοῦ κόσμου· οὐ.δύναται πόλις κρυβῆναι ἐπάνω
are the light of the world, [3]cannot [1]a [2]city be hid on
ὄρους κειμένη· 15 οὐδὲ καίουσιν λύχνον καὶ τιθέασιν αὐτὸν
a mountain situated. Nor do they light a lamp and put it
ὑπὸ τὸν μόδιον, ἀλλ' ἐπὶ τὴν λυχνίαν, καὶ λάμπει πᾶσιν τοῖς
under the corn measure, but upon the lampstand; and it shines for all who
ἐν τῇ οἰκίᾳ. 16 οὕτως λαμψάτω τὸ.φῶς.ὑμῶν ἔμπροσθεν
[are] in the house. Thus let shine your light before
τῶν ἀνθρώπων, ὅπως ἴδωσιν ὑμῶν τὰ καλὰ ἔργα, καὶ δοξά-
men, so that they may see your good works, and may
σωσιν τὸν.πατέρα.ὑμῶν τὸν ἐν τοῖς οὐρανοῖς.
glorify your Father who [is] in the heavens.
17 Μὴ.νομίσητε ὅτι ἦλθον καταλῦσαι τὸν νόμον ἢ τοὺς προ-
Think not that I came to abolish the law or the pro-
φήτας· οὐκ.ἦλθον καταλῦσαι, ἀλλὰ πληρῶσαι. 18 ἀμὴν.γὰρ
phets: I came not to abolish, but to fulfil. For verily
λέγω ὑμῖν, ἕως.ἂν παρέλθῃ ὁ οὐρανὸς καὶ ἡ γῆ, ἰῶτα ἓν ἢ
I say to you, Until shall pass away the heaven and the earth, [2]iota [1]one or
μία κεραία οὐ.μὴ παρέλθῃ ἀπὸ τοῦ νόμου, ἕως.ἂν πάντα
one tittle in no wise shall pass away from the law until all
γένηται. 19 ὃς.ἐὰν οὖν λύσῃ μίαν τῶν.ἐντολῶν.τούτων τῶν
come to pass. Whoever then shall break one of these commandments the
ἐλαχίστων, καὶ διδάξῃ οὕτως τοὺς ἀνθρώπους, ἐλάχιστος κλη-
least, and shall teach [2]so [1]men, least shall
θήσεται ἐν τῇ βασιλείᾳ τῶν οὐρανῶν· ὃς.δ'.ἂν ποιήσῃ καὶ
be called in the kingdom of the heavens; but whoever shall practise and
διδάξῃ, οὗτος μέγας κληθήσεται ἐν τῇ βασιλείᾳ τῶν
shall teach [them], this [one] great shall be called in the kingdom of the
οὐρανῶν. 20 λέγω.γὰρ ὑμῖν, ὅτι ἐὰν.μὴ περισσεύσῃ ʷἡ δικαιο-
heavens. For I say to you, That unless shall abound [2]right-
σύνη ὑμῶν" πλεῖον τῶν γραμματέων καὶ Φαρισαίων, οὐ.μὴ
eousness [1]your above [that] of the scribes and Pharisees, in no wise
εἰσέλθητε εἰς τὴν βασιλείαν τῶν οὐρανῶν.
shall ye enter into the kingdom of the heavens.

21 Ἠκούσατε ὅτι ˣἐῤῥέθη" τοῖς ἀρχαίοις, Οὐ.φονεύσεις·
Ye have heard that it was said to the ancients, Thou shalt not commit murder;
ὃς.δ'.ἂν φονεύσῃ, ἔνοχος ἔσται τῇ κρίσει. 22 ἐγὼ.δὲ
but whoever shall commit murder, liable shall be to the judgment. But I
λέγω ὑμῖν, ὅτι πᾶς ὁ ὀργιζόμενος τῷ.ἀδελφῷ.αὐτοῦ ʸεἰκῇ"
say to you, That every one who is angry with his brother lightly,

Judea and beyond the Jordan.

5 [1]But seeing the multitudes, He went up
into the mountain. And when He had sat
down, His disciples came to Him.
[2]And He opened His mouth and taught
them, saying,
[3]Blessed *are* the poor in spirit! For theirs is
the kingdom of Heaven.
[4]Blessed *are* those who mourn! For they
shall be comforted.
[5]Blessed *are* the meek! For they shall
inherit the earth.
[6]Blessed *are* those who hunger and thirst
after righteousness! For they shall be filled.
[7]Blessed *are* the merciful! For they shall
obtain mercy.
[8]Blessed *are* the pure in heart! For they
shall see God.
[9]Blessed *are* the peacemakers! For they
shall be called the sons of God.
[10]Blessed *are* those who have been persecuted for righteousness' sake! For theirs is
the kingdom of Heaven.
[11]Blessed are you when they shall call you
names and shall persecute you, and when
they shall lie, saying every evil word against
you for My sake.
[12]Rejoice and leap for joy! For great is
your reward in Heaven. For so they persecuted the prophets who were before you.
[13]You are the salt of the earth. But if the
salt loses its taste, with what shall it be
salted? For it no longer has its strength, but
is to be thrown out and trampled upon by
men.
[14]You are the light of the world. A city
that is situated on a hill cannot be hidden.
[15]Nor do they light a lamp and put it
under a bushel, but *they put it* on the
lampstand. And it shines for all who are in
the house.
[16]Even so let your light so shine before
men that they may see your good works and
glorify your Father who is in Heaven.
[17]Do not think that I came to do away
with the Law or the Prophets. I did not
come to do away, but to fulfill.
[18]For truly I say to you, Until the sky and
the earth pass away, not one jot or one tittle
shall pass away from the Law until all has
been fulfilled.
[19]Whoever then shall break one of these
commandments, *even* the least, and shall
teach men so, *that one* shall be called the
least in the kingdom of Heaven. But whoever
shall practice and teach them, that one shall
be called great in the kingdom of Heaven.
[20]For I say to you that unless your righteousness shall be over and above *that* of the
scribes and Pharisees, you shall in no way
enter into the kingdom of Heaven.
[21]You have heard that it was said to the
ancient ones, "You shall not murder" —
also, "Whoever shall murder shall be in
danger of the Judgment."
[22]But I say to you that everyone who is

ἔνοχος ἔσται τῇ κρίσει· ὃς.δ'.ἂν εἴπῃ τῷ.ἀδελφῷ.αὐτοῦ,
liable shall be to the judgment: but whoever shall say to his brother,
[z]Ῥακά,‖ ἔνοχος ἔσται τῷ συνεδρίῳ· ὃς.δ'.ἂν εἴπῃ, Μωρέ,
Raca, liable shall be to the Sanhedrim: but whoever shall say, Fool,
ἔνοχος ἔσται εἰς τὴν γέενναν τοῦ πυρός.
liable shall be to the Gehenna of fire.
23 Ἐὰν οὖν προσ-
If therefore thou
φέρῃς τὸ.δῶρόν.σου ἐπὶ τὸ θυσιαστήριον, κἀκεῖ μνησθῇς
shalt offer thy gift at the altar, and there shalt remember
ὅτι ὁ.ἀδελφός.σου ἔχει τὶ κατὰ σοῦ,
that thy brother has something against thee,
24 ἄφες ἐκεῖ τὸ δῶρόν
leave there [2]gift
σου ἔμπροσθεν τοῦ θυσιαστηρίου, καὶ ὕπαγε, πρῶτον διαλ-
[1]thy before the altar, and go away, first be
λάγηθι τῷ.ἀδελφῷ.σου, καὶ τότε ἐλθὼν πρόσφερε τὸ δῶρόν
reconciled to thy brother, and then having come offer [2]gift
σου.
[1]thy.
25 Ἴσθι εὐνοῶν τῷ.ἀντιδίκῳ.σου ταχύ, ἕως.ὅτου εἶ
Be agreeing with thine adverse party quickly, whilst thou art
[a]ἐν τῇ ὁδῷ μετ' αὐτοῦ,‖ μήποτέ σε παραδῷ ὁ ἀντίδικος τῷ
in the way with him, lest [5]thee [4]deliver [1]the [2]adverse [3]party to the
κριτῇ, καὶ ὁ κριτὴς [b]σε παραδῷ‖ τῷ ὑπηρέτῃ, καὶ εἰς φυλακὴν
judge, and the judge thee deliver to the officer, and into prison
βληθήσῃ.
thou be cast.
26 ἀμὴν λέγω σοι, οὐ.μὴ ἐξέλθῃς ἐκεῖθεν,
Verily I say to thee, In no wise shalt thou come out thence,
ἕως.ἂν ἀποδῷς τὸν ἔσχατον κοδράντην.
until thou pay the last kodrantes.

27 Ἠκούσατε ὅτι [x]ἐῤῥέθη‖ [c]τοῖς ἀρχαίοις.‖ Οὐ.μοιχεύ-
Ye have heard that it was said to the ancients, Thou shalt not commit
σεις·
adultery:
28 ἐγὼ.δὲ λέγω ὑμῖν, ὅτι πᾶς ὁ βλέπων γυναῖκα πρὸς
but I say to you, that every one that looks upon a woman to
τὸ ἐπιθυμῆσαι [d]αὐτῆς,‖ ἤδη ἐμοίχευσεν αὐτὴν ἐν τῇ
lust after her, already has committed adultery with her in
καρδίᾳ [e]αὐτοῦ.‖
[2]heart [1]his.
29 εἰ.δὲ ὁ.ὀφθαλμός.σου ὁ δεξιὸς σκανδαλίζει
But if thine eye, the right, cause [2]to [3]offend
σε, ἔξελε αὐτὸν καὶ βάλε ἀπὸ σοῦ· συμφέρει.γάρ σοι ἵνα
[1]thee, pluck out it and cast [it] from thee: for it is profitable for thee that
ἀπόληται ἓν τῶν.μελῶν.σου, καὶ μὴ ὅλον τὸ.σῶμά.σου βληθῇ
should perish one of thy members, and not [2]whole [1]thy [3]body be cast
εἰς γέενναν.
into Gehenna.
30 καὶ εἰ ἡ.δεξιά.σου χεὶρ σκανδαλίζει σε, ἔκκοψον
And if thy right hand cause [2]to [3]offend [1]thee, cut off
αὐτὴν καὶ βάλε ἀπὸ σοῦ· συμφέρει.γάρ σοι ἵνα ἀπόληται
it and cast [it] from thee: for it is profitable for thee that should perish
ἓν τῶν.μελῶν.σου, καὶ μὴ ὅλον τὸ.σῶμά.σου [f]βληθῇ εἰς γέενναν.‖
one of thy members, and not [2]whole [1]thy [3]body be cast into Gehenna.
31 [g]Ἐῤῥέθη‖ δέ, [h]ὅτι‖ ὃς.ἂν ἀπολύσῃ τὴν.γυναῖκα.αὐτοῦ,
It was said also that whoever shall put away his wife,
δότω αὐτῇ ἀποστάσιον.
let him give to her a letter of divorce:
32 ἐγὼ.δὲ λέγω ὑμῖν, ὅτι [i]ὃς.ἂν
but I say to you, that whoever
ἀπολύσῃ‖ τὴν.γυναῖκα.αὐτοῦ, παρεκτὸς λόγου πορνείας, ποιεῖ
shall put away his wife, except on account of fornication, causes
αὐτὴν [k]μοιχᾶσθαι‖ καὶ [l]ὃς.ἐὰν‖ ἀπολελυμένην [m]γαμήσῃ,‖
her to commit adultery; and whoever her who has been put away shall marry,
μοιχᾶται.
commits adultery.

33 Πάλιν ἠκούσατε, ὅτι [g]ἐῤῥέθη‖ τοῖς ἀρχαίοις, Οὐκ.ἐπιορ-
Again, ye have heard that it was said to the ancients, Thou shalt not
κήσεις, ἀποδώσεις.δὲ τῷ κυρίῳ τοὺς.ὅρκους.σου·
forswear thyself, but thou shalt render to the Lord thine oaths.
34 ἐγὼ
[2]I
δὲ λέγω ὑμῖν μὴ ὀμόσαι ὅλως, μήτε ἐν τῷ οὐρανῷ, ὅτι θρόνος
[1]but say to you not to swear at all, neither by the heaven, because [the] throne
ἐστὶν τοῦ θεοῦ·
it is of God;
35 μήτε ἐν τῇ γῇ, ὅτι ὑποπόδιόν ἐστιν τῶν
nor by the earth, because [the] footstool it is
ποδῶν.αὐτοῦ· μήτε εἰς Ἱεροσόλυμα, ὅτι πόλις ἐστὶν τοῦ
of his feet: nor by Jerusalem, because [the] city it is of the
μεγάλου βασιλέως·
great King.
36 μήτε ἐν τῇ.κεφαλῇ.σου ὀμόσῃς, ὅτι
Neither by thy head shalt thou swear, because
οὐ.δύνασαι μίαν τρίχα λευκὴν [n]ἢ μέλαιναν ποιῆσαι.‖
thou art not able one hair white or black to make.
37 [o]ἔστω‖
[2]Let [5]be
δὲ ὁ.λόγος.ὑμῶν, ναὶ ναί, οὒ οὔ· τὸ.δὲ περισσὸν τούτων ἐκ
[1]but [3]your [4]word, Yea, yea; Nay, nay: but what [is] more than these from
τοῦ πονηροῦ ἐστιν.
evil is.

38 Ἠκούσατε ὅτι [g]ἐῤῥέθη,‖ Ὀφθαλμὸν ἀντὶ ὀφθαλμοῦ, καὶ
Ye have heard that it was said, Eye for eye, and
ὀδόντα ἀντὶ ὀδόντος·
tooth for tooth;
39 ἐγὼ.δὲ λέγω ὑμῖν μὴ ἀντιστῆναι τῷ
but I say to you not to resist
πονηρῷ· ἀλλ' ὅστις σε [p]ῥαπίσει ἐπὶ‖ τὴν.δεξιάν.[q]σου σιαγόνα,‖
evil; but whosoever thee shall strike on thy right cheek,
στρέψον αὐτῷ καὶ τὴν ἄλλην·
turn to him also the other;
40 καὶ τῷ θέλοντί σοι κρι-
and to him who would with thee go
θῆναι καὶ τὸν.χιτῶνά.σου λαβεῖν, ἄφες αὐτῷ καὶ τὸ ἱμάτιον·
to law and thy tunic take, yield to him also [thy] cloak;
41 καὶ ὅστις σε ἀγγαρεύσει μίλιον ἕν, ὕπαγε μετ' αὐτοῦ δύο.
and whosoever thee will compel to go [2]mile [1]one, go with him two.

angry with his brother, without cause, shall
be liable to the Judgment. But whoever shall
say to his brother, Raca, shall be liable to
the San-he-drin. But whoever shall say, Fool,
shall be in danger of the fire of hell.
23 If, then, you are offering your gift at the
altar and shall remember there that your
brother has something against you,
24 leave your gift there before the altar and
go. First be reconciled to your brother and
then return and offer your gift.
25 Agree quickly with him who has a cause
against you, while you are *still* in the highway with him, so that this adversary may
not deliver you up to the judge, and the
judge deliver you up to the officer, and you
may be thrown into prison.
26 Truly I say to you, You shall in no way
come out of there until you pay the last bit.
27 You have heard it was said to the men of
old, "You shall not commit adultery."
28 But I say to you that everyone who
looks on a woman to lust after her has already committed adultery with her in his
heart.
29 But if your right eye causes you to sin,
pluck it out and throw it from you. For it is
more profitable for you that one of your
members should be lost, and not that your
whole body should be thrown into hell.
30 And if your right hand causes you to sin,
cut it off and throw it from you. For it is
more profitable for you that one of your
members should be lost, and not that your
whole body be thrown into hell.
31 It was also said, "Whoever puts away his
wife, let him give her a letter of divorce."
32 But I say to you that whoever puts away
his wife, except on account of fornication,
causes her to commit adultery. And whoever
marries the divorced one commits adultery.
33 Again, you have heard it was said to the
ancient men, "You shall not swear falsely, but
you shall perform your oaths to the Lord."
34 But I say to you, Do not swear at all – not
by Heaven, because it is God's throne –
35 nor by the earth, because it is His footstool – not by Jerusalem, because it is the
city of the great King.
36 You shall not swear by your head, because you are not able to make one hair
white or black.
37 But let your word be, Yes, yes, No, no!
For whatever is more than these is from evil.
38 You have heard that it was said, "Eye
for eye and tooth for tooth."
39 But I say to you, Do not resist evil. But
whoever shall strike you on your right
cheek, turn the other to him also.
40 And to him who would sue you and take
your tunic, give him your coat also.
41 And whoever compels you to go one
mile, go two with him.

42 τῷ αἰτοῦντί σε [r]δίδου·ǁ καὶ τὸν.θέλοντα ἀπὸ σοῦ [s]δανεί-
To him who asks of thee give; and him that wishes from thee to bor-
σασθαιǁ μὴ.ἀποστραφῇς.
row thou shalt not turn away from.
43 Ἠκούσατε ὅτι [t]ἐῤῥέθη,ǁ Ἀγαπήσεις τὸν.πλησίον.σου καὶ
Ye have heard that it was said, Thou shalt love thy neighbour and
μισήσεις τὸν.ἐχθρόν.σου· 44 ἐγὼ.δὲ λέγω ὑμῖν, Ἀγαπᾶτε τοὺς
hate thine enemy. But I say to you, Love
ἐχθροὺς ὑμῶν, [v]εὐλογεῖτε τοὺς καταρωμένους ὑμᾶς, καλῶς
[2]enemies [1]your, bless those who curse you, [2]well
ποιεῖτε [w]τοὺς μισοῦντας ὑμᾶς,ǁ καὶ προσεύχεσθε ὑπὲρ τῶν
[1]do to those who hate you, and pray for those who
[x]ἐπηρεαζόντων ὑμᾶς καὶǁ διωκόντων ὑμᾶς· 45 ὅπως γένησθε
despitefully use you and persecute you; so that ye may be
υἱοὶ τοῦ.πατρὸς.ὑμῶν τοῦ ἐν οὐρανοῖς· ὅτι τὸν.ἥλιον.αὐτοῦ
sons of your Father who [is] in [the] heavens: for his sun
ἀνατέλλει ἐπὶ πονηροὺς καὶ ἀγαθούς, καὶ βρέχει ἐπὶ δικαίους
he causes to rise on evil and good, and sends rain on just
καὶ ἀδίκους. 46 ἐὰν.γὰρ ἀγαπήσητε τοὺς ἀγαπῶντας ὑμᾶς,
and unjust. For if ye love those who love you,
τίνα μισθὸν ἔχετε; οὐχὶ καὶ οἱ τελῶναι [y]τὸ αὐτὸǁ ποιοῦσιν;
what reward have ye? [2]not [3]also [4]the [5]tax [6]gatherers [7]the [8]same [1]do?
47 καὶ ἐὰν ἀσπάσησθε τοὺς.ἀδελφοὺς.ὑμῶν μόνον, τί περισ-
and if ye salute your brethren only, what extraordi-
σὸν ποιεῖτε; οὐχὶ καὶ οἱ [z]τελῶναιǁ [a]οὕτωςǁ ποιοῦσιν; 48 ἔσεσθε
nary do ye? [2]Not [3]also [4]the [5]tax [6]gatherers [7]so [1]do? [3]shall [4]be
οὖν ὑμεῖς τέλειοι, [b]ὥσπερǁ ὁ.πατὴρ.ὑμῶν [c]ὁ ἐν τοῖς οὐρανοῖςǁ
[2]therefore [1]ye perfect, even as your Father who [is] in the heavens
τέλειός ἐστιν.
perfect is.

42 Give to him who asks of you, and you shall not turn away from him that wishes to borrow from you.
43 You have heard it was said, "You shall love your neighbor and hate your enemy."
44 But I say to you, Love your enemies. Bless those who curse you. Do good to those who hate you. And pray for those who insult you and persecute you:
45 so that you may be sons of your Father who is in Heaven. For He makes His sun to rise on evil and good. And He sends rain on the just and unjust.
46 For if you love those who love you, what reward do you have? Do not the tax-collectors do the same?
47 And if you only greet your brothers, what do you do more *than others?* Do not the tax-collectors also do so?
48 Therefore, you shall be perfect, even as your Father who is in Heaven is perfect.

6 Προσέχετε[d] τὴν.[e]ἐλεημοσύνηνǁ.ὑμῶν μὴ ποιεῖν ἔμπροσθεν
Beware your alms not to do before
τῶν ἀνθρώπων, πρὸς.τὸ.θεαθῆναι αὐτοῖς· εἰ.δὲ.μήγε, μισθὸν
men, in order to be seen by them: otherwise reward
οὐκ.ἔχετε παρὰ τῷ.πατρὶ.ὑμῶν τῷ ἐν [f]τοῖςǁ οὐρανοῖς. 2 ὅταν
ye have not with your Father who [is] in the heavens. When
οὖν ποιῇς ἐλεημοσύνην, μὴ.σαλπίσῃς ἔμπροσθέν σου,
therefore thou doest alms, do not sound a trumpet before thee,
ὥσπερ οἱ ὑποκριταὶ ποιοῦσιν ἐν ταῖς συναγωγαῖς καὶ ἐν ταῖς
as the hypocrites do in the synagogues and in the
ῥύμαις, ὅπως δοξασθῶσιν ὑπὸ τῶν ἀνθρώπων· ἀμὴν λέγω
streets, that they may have glory from men. Verily I say
ὑμῖν, ἀπέχουσιν τὸν.μισθὸν.αὐτῶν. 3 σοῦ.δὲ ποιοῦντος ἐλεη-
to you, they have their reward. But thou doing
μοσύνην, μὴ.γνώτω ἡ.ἀριστερά.σου τί ποιεῖ ἡ.δεξιά.σου,
alms, let not [4]know [1]thy [2]left [3]hand what does thy right hand,
4 ὅπως [g]ᾖ σου ἡ.ἐλεημοσύνηǁ ἐν τῷ κρυπτῷ· καὶ ὁ.πατήρ.σου
so that [3]may [4]be [1]thine [2]alms in secret: and thy Father
ὁ βλέπων ἐν τῷ κρυπτῷ [h]αὐτὸςǁ ἀποδώσει σοι [i]ἐν.τῷ.φανερῷ.ǁ
who sees in secret himself shall render to thee openly.
5 Καὶ ὅταν [k]προσεύχῃ, οὐκ.ἔσῃ ὥσπερǁ οἱ ὑποκριταί,
And when thou prayest, thou shalt not be as the hypocrites,
ὅτι φιλοῦσιν ἐν ταῖς συναγωγαῖς καὶ ἐν ταῖς γωνίαις τῶν
for they love in the synagogues and in the corners of the
πλατειῶν ἑστῶτες προσεύχεσθαι, ὅπως [l]ἂνǁ.φανῶσιν τοῖς
streets standing to pray, so that they may appear
ἀνθρώποις· ἀμὴν λέγω ὑμῖν, [m]ὅτιǁ ἀπέχουσιν τὸν μισθὸν
to men. Verily I say to you, that they have [2]reward
αὐτῶν. 6 σὺ.δέ, ὅταν προσεύχῃ, εἴσελθε εἰς τὸ.[n]ταμιεῖόνǁ.σου,
[1]their. But thou, when thou prayest, enter into thy chamber,
καὶ κλείσας τὴν.θύραν.σου, πρόσευξαι τῷ.πατρί.σου τῷ ἐν
and having shut thy door, pray to thy Father who [is] in
τῷ κρυπτῷ· καὶ ὁ.πατήρ.σου ὁ βλέπων ἐν τῷ κρυπτῷ ἀπο-
secret; and thy Father who sees in secret will
δώσει σοι [o]ἐν.τῷ.φανερῷǁ. 7 Προσευχόμενοι.δὲ μὴ.[p]βαττολο-
render to thee openly. But when ye pray do not use vain
γήσητε,ǁ ὥσπερ οἱ ἐθνικοί· δοκοῦσιν.γὰρ ὅτι ἐν τῇ πολυλογίᾳ
repetitions, as the heathens: for they think that in [2]much [3]speaking
αὐτῶν εἰσακουσθήσονται. 8 μὴ οὖν ὁμοιωθῆτε αὐτοῖς·
[1]their they shall be heard. [2]Not [3]therefore [1]be like to them:
οἶδεν.γὰρ ὁ.πατὴρ.ὑμῶν ὧν χρείαν ἔχετε πρὸ τοῦ ὑμᾶς
for [3]knows [1]your [2]Father of what things [3]need [1]ye [2]have before ye
αἰτῆσαι αὐτόν. 9 οὕτως οὖν προσεύχεσθε ὑμεῖς· Πάτερ.ἡμῶν
ask him. Thus therefore pray ye: Our Father
ὁ ἐν τοῖς οὐρανοῖς, ἁγιασθήτω τὸ.ὄνομά.σου· 10 [q]ἐλθέτωǁ
who [art] in the heavens, sanctified be thy name; let come
ἡ.βασιλεία.σου· γενηθήτω τὸ.θέλημά.σου, ὡς ἐν οὐρανῷ, καὶ
thy kingdom; let be done thy will as in heaven, [so] also
ἐπὶ [r]τῆςǁ γῆς· 11 τὸν.ἄρτον.ἡμῶν τὸν ἐπιούσιον δὸς ἡμῖν σή-
upon the earth; our bread the needed give us to-
μερον· 12 καὶ ἄφες ἡμῖν τὰ.ὀφειλήματα.ἡμῶν, ὡς καὶ ἡμεῖς
day; and forgive us our debts, as also we

CHAPTER 6

1 Be careful that you do not do your good deeds before men in order to be seen by them. Otherwise you do not have any reward with your Father who is in Heaven.
2 Therefore, when you do good deeds, do not sound a trumpet before you, like the hypocrites do in the Synagogues and in the streets (so that they may have glory from men). Truly I say to you, they have their reward.
3 But when you are doing good deeds, do not let your left hand know what your right hand is doing
4 so that your good deeds may be in secret. And your Father, who is watching in secret, will Himself reward you openly.

5 And when you pray, you shall not be like the hypocrites, for they love to pray standing in the synagogues and in the corners of the streets (so that they may be seen by men). Truly, I say to you that they have their reward.
6 But when you pray, go into your inner room, shut your door, and pray to your Father who is in secret. And your Father, who sees in secret, shall reward you openly.
7 But when you pray, do not vainly babble words, as the heathen do. For they think that they shall be heard *because of* their many words.
8 Then do not be like them, for your Father knows what things you need before you ask Him.
9 Therefore, pray in this way: Our Father, who is in Heaven, Hallowed be Your name.
10 Let Your kingdom come, and let Your will be done, on earth as it is in Heaven.
11 Give us today our daily bread,
12 and forgive us our debts as we also for-

[s]ἀφίεμεν‖ τοῖς.ὀφειλέταις.ἡμῶν· 13 καὶ μὴ.εἰσενέγκῃς ἡμᾶς εἰς
forgive our debtors; And lead not us into
πειρασμόν, ἀλλὰ ῥῦσαι ἡμᾶς ἀπὸ τοῦ πονηροῦ. [t]ὅτι σοῦ ἐστιν
temptation, but deliver us from evil. For thine is
ἡ βασιλεία καὶ ἡ δύναμις καὶ ἡ δόξα εἰς τοὺς αἰῶνας. ἀμήν.‖
the kingdom and the power and the glory to the ages. Amen.
14 Ἐὰν.γὰρ ἀφῆτε τοῖς ἀνθρώποις τὰ.παραπτώματα.αὐτῶν,
For if ye forgive men their offences,
ἀφήσει καὶ ὑμῖν ὁ.πατὴρ.ὑμῶν ὁ οὐράνιος· 15 ἐὰν.δὲ μὴ
5will 6forgive 8also 7you 1your 2Father 3the 4heavenly. but if 3not
ἀφῆτε τοῖς ἀνθρώποις [u]τὰ.παραπτώματα.αὐτῶν,‖ οὐδὲ ὁ
1ye 2forgive men their offences, neither
πατὴρ.ὑμῶν ἀφήσει τὰ.παραπτώματα.ὑμῶν.
3Father 2your 1will forgive your offences.
16 Ὅταν.δὲ νηστεύητε, μὴ.γίνεσθε [v]ὥσπερ‖ οἱ ὑποκριταὶ
And when ye fast, be not as the hypocrites,
σκυθρωποί· ἀφανίζουσιν.γὰρ τὰ.πρόσωπα.[w]αὐτῶν,‖
downcast in countenance; for they disfigure their faces,
ὅπως φανῶσιν τοῖς ἀνθρώποις νηστεύοντες· ἀμὴν λέγω
so that they may appear to men fasting. Verily I say
ὑμῖν, [x]ὅτι‖ ἀπέχουσιν τὸν.μισθὸν.αὐτῶν. 17 σὺ.δὲ νηστεύων
to you, that they have their reward. But thou, fasting,
ἄλειψαί σου τὴν κεφαλήν, καὶ τὸ.πρόσωπόν.σου νίψαι· 18 ὅπως
anoint thy head, and 2thy 3face 1wash, so that
μὴ.φανῇς [y]τοῖς ἀνθρώποις νηστεύων,‖ ἀλλὰ τῷ πατρί
thou mayest not appear to men fasting, but to 2Father
σου τῷ ἐν τῷ [z]κρυπτῷ·‖ καὶ ὁ.πατήρ.σου ὁ βλέπων ἐν τῷ
1thy who [is] in secret; and thy Father who sees in
[z]κρυπτῷ‖ ἀποδώσει σοι [a]ἐν.τῷ.φανερῷ.‖
secret will render to thee openly.
19 Μὴ.θησαυρίζετε ὑμῖν θησαυροὺς ἐπὶ τῆς γῆς, ὅπου
Treasure not up for yourselves treasures upon the earth, where
σὴς καὶ βρῶσις ἀφανίζει, καὶ ὅπου κλέπται διορύσσουσιν καὶ
moth and rust spoil, and where thieves dig through and
κλέπτουσιν· 20 θησαυρίζετε.δὲ ὑμῖν θησαυροὺς ἐν οὐρανῷ,
steal: but treasure up for yourselves treasures in heaven,
ὅπου οὔτε σὴς οὔτε βρῶσις ἀφανίζει, καὶ ὅπου κλέπται οὐ.δι-
where neither moth nor rust spoils and where thieves do not
ορύσσουσιν οὐδὲ κλέπτουσιν. 21 ὅπου.γάρ ἐστιν ὁ θησαυρὸς
dig through nor steal: for where 3is 2treasure
[b]ὑμῶν,‖ ἐκεῖ ἔσται [c]καὶ‖ ἡ καρδία [b]ὑμῶν.‖ 22 Ὁ λύχνος τοῦ
1your, there will be also 2heart 1your. The lamp of the
σώματός ἐστιν ὁ ὀφθαλμός[d]· ἐὰν [e]οὖν‖ [f]ὁ.ὀφθαλμός.σου
body is the eye; if therefore thine eye
ἁπλοῦς ᾖ,‖ ὅλον τὸ.σῶμά.σου φωτεινὸν ἔσται· 23 ἐὰν.δὲ ὁ
single be, 2whole 1thy body light will be. But if
ὀφθαλμός.σου πονηρὸς ᾖ, ὅλον τὸ.σῶμά.σου σκοτεινὸν ἔσται.
thine eye evil be, 2whole 1thy body dark will be.
εἰ οὖν τὸ φῶς τὸ ἐν σοὶ σκότος ἐστίν, τὸ σκότος πόσον;
If therefore the light that [is] in thee darkness is, the darkness how great
24 Οὐδεὶς δύναται δυσὶ κυρίοις δουλεύειν· ἢ.γὰρ τὸν ἕνα
No one is able two lords to serve; for either the one
μισήσει, καὶ τὸν ἕτερον ἀγαπήσει· ἢ ἑνὸς ἀνθέξεται, καὶ
he will hate, and the other he will love; or [the] one he will hold to, and
τοῦ ἑτέρου καταφρονήσει. οὐ.δύνασθε θεῷ δουλεύειν καὶ [g]μαμ-
the other he will despise. Ye are not able 3God 1to 2serve and mam-
μωνᾷ.‖ 25 διὰ τοῦτο λέγω ὑμῖν, μὴ.μεριμνᾶτε τῇ.ψυχῇ.ὑμῶν,
mon. Because of this I say to you, be not careful as to your life,
τί φάγητε [h]καὶ‖ [i]τί πίητε·‖ μηδὲ τῷ.σώματι.ὑμῶν,
what ye should eat and what ye should drink; nor as to your body
τί ἐνδύσησθε. οὐχὶ ἡ ψυχὴ πλεῖόν ἐστιν τῆς τροφῆς καὶ
what ye should put on. 2Not 3the 4life 5more 1is than the food and
τὸ σῶμα τοῦ ἐνδύματος; 26 ἐμβλέψατε εἰς τὰ πετεινὰ τοῦ
the body than the raiment? Look at the birds of the
οὐρανοῦ, ὅτι οὐ.σπείρουσιν, οὐδὲ θερίζουσιν, οὐδὲ συνάγουσιν
heaven, that they sow not, nor do they reap, nor do they gather
εἰς ἀποθήκας, καὶ ὁ.πατὴρ.ὑμῶν ὁ οὐράνιος τρέφει αὐτά· οὐχ
into granaries, and your Father the heavenly feeds them: 2not
ὑμεῖς μᾶλλον διαφέρετε αὐτῶν; 27 τίς.δὲ ἐξ ὑμῶν μερι-
3ye 4much 1are better than they? But which out of you by being
μνῶν δύναται προσθεῖναι ἐπὶ τὴν.ἡλικίαν.αὐτοῦ πῆχυν ἕνα;
careful is able to add to his stature 2cubit 1one?
28 καὶ περὶ ἐνδύματος τί μεριμνᾶτε; καταμάθετε τὰ κρίνα
and about raiment why are ye careful? observe the lilies
τοῦ ἀγροῦ, πῶς [k]αὐξάνει·‖ οὐ.[l]κοπιᾷ‖ οὐδὲ [m]νήθει·‖ 29 λέ-
of the field, how they grow: they labour not nor do they spin: 2I
γω δὲ ὑμῖν, ὅτι οὐδὲ Σολομὼν ἐν πάσῃ τῇ.δόξῃ.αὐτοῦ περιε-
say 1but to you that not even Solomon in all his glory was
βάλετο ὡς ἓν τούτων. 30 εἰ.δὲ τὸν χόρτον τοῦ ἀγροῦ, σήμερον
clothed as one of these. But if the grass of the field, to-day
ὄντα, καὶ αὔριον εἰς κλίβανον βαλλόμενον, ὁ θεὸς οὕτως
4which is and to-morrow into an oven is cast, God thus

give our debtors.
13 And do not lead us into temptation, but deliver us from evil. For Yours is the kingdom and the power and the glory, forever. Amen.
14 For if you forgive men their offences, your heavenly Father will forgive you too.
15 But if you do not forgive men their offences, neither will your Father forgive your offences.

16 And when you fast, do not be sad like the hypocrites, for they disfigure their faces so as to appear to men to be fasting. Truly I say to you that they have their reward.
17 But you, when you fast, oil your head and wash your face,
18 so that you may not appear to men to be fasting. But *you fast* to your Father who is in secret. And your Father who sees in secret will reward you openly.

19 Do not store up for yourselves treasures on earth, where moth and rust spoil, and where thieves break through and steal.
20 But store up treasures for yourselves in Heaven, where neither moth nor rust spoil, and where thieves do not break through or steal.
21 For where your treasure is, your heart will be there also.
22 The lamp of the body is the eye. So if your eye is sound, your whole body will be illuminated.
23 But if your eye is evil, your whole body will be dark. Therefore, if the light that is in you is darkness, how great is the darkness!

24 No one is able to serve two lords. For either he will hate the one and he will love the other; or, he will hold to one and he will despise the other. You are not able to serve God and mammon.
25 Because of this I say to you, Do not be anxious as to your life – what you should eat and what you should drink – nor for your body, what you should put on. Is not the life more than the food, and the body more than the clothing?

26 Look at the birds of the sky. *You will see* that they do not sow, nor do they reap, nor do they gather into barns. Yet your heavenly Father feeds them. Are you not much better than they?
27 But which of you by being anxious is able to add one cubit to his height?
28 And why are you worried about clothing? Look at the lilies of the field, how they grow. They do not work and they do not spin.
29 But I say to you that not even Solomon in all his glory was clothed like one of these!
30 But if God so clothe the grass of the field (which is here today and is thrown into the oven tomorrow,), *will He* not much rath-

ἀμφιέννυσιν, οὐ πολλῷ μᾶλλον ὑμᾶς, ὀλιγόπιστοι; 31 μὴ
arrays, [will he] not much rather you, O [ye] of little faith? [2]not
οὖν μεριμνήσητε, λέγοντες, Τί φάγωμεν, ἢ τί πίωμεν,
[3]therefore [1]be careful, saying, What shall we eat? or what shall we drink?
ἢ τί περιβαλώμεθα; 32 πάντα.γὰρ ταῦτα τὰ ἔθνη [u]ἐπι-
or with what shall we be clothed? For all these things the nations seek
ζητεῖ· οἶδεν.γὰρ ὁ.πατὴρ.ὑμῶν ὁ οὐράνιος ὅτι χρῄζετε
after. For knows your Father the heavenly that ye have need
τούτων ἁπάντων· 33 ζητεῖτε.δὲ πρῶτον [o]τὴν βασιλείαν τοῦ
of [2]these [3]things [1]all. But seek ye first the kingdom
θεοῦ καὶ τὴν.δικαιοσύνην.αὐτοῦ, καὶ ταῦτα πάντα προσ-
of God and his righteousness, and [2]these [3]things [1]all shall
τεθήσεται ὑμῖν. 34 μὴ οὖν [p]μεριμνήσητε εἰς τὴν αὔριον·
be added to you. [2]Not [3]therefore [1]be careful for the morrow:
ἡ.γὰρ αὔριον μεριμνήσει [q]τὰ [r]ἑαυτῆς. ἀρκετὸν τῇ
for the morrow shall be careful about the [things] of itself. Sufficient to the
ἡμέρᾳ ἡ κακία αὐτῆς.
day [is] the evil of it.

7 Μὴ.κρίνετε, ἵνα μὴ.κριθῆτε· 2 ἐν ᾧ γὰρ.κρίματι κρίνετε,
Judge not, that ye be not judged: [2]with [3]what [1]for judgment ye judge,
κριθήσεσθε· καὶ ἐν ᾧ μέτρῳ μετρεῖτε, [s]ἀντιμετρηθήσεται
ye shall be judged; and with what measure ye mete, it shall be measured again
ὑμῖν. 3 Τί.δὲ βλέπεις τὸ κάρφος τὸ ἐν τῷ ὀφθαλμῷ τοῦ
to you. But why lookest thou on the mote that [is] in the eye
ἀδελφοῦ.σου, τὴν.δὲ ἐν τῷ.σῷ ὀφθαλμῷ δοκὸν οὐ.κατανοεῖς;
of thy brother, but the [2]in [3]thine [[4]own] [5]eye [1]beam perceivest not?
4 ἢ πῶς ἐρεῖς τῷ.ἀδελφῷ.σου, Ἄφες ἐκβάλω τὸ
Or how wilt thou say to thy brother, Suffer [that] I may cast out the
κάρφος [t]ἀπὸ τοῦ.ὀφθαλμοῦ.σου· καὶ ἰδού, ἡ δοκὸς ἐν τῷ
mote from thine eye: and behold, the beam [is] in
ὀφθαλμῷ.σου; 5 ὑποκριτά, ἔκβαλε πρῶτον [v]τὴν δοκὸν ἐκ
thine [own] eye! hypocrite, cast out first the beam out of
τοῦ.ὀφθαλμοῦ.σου, καὶ τότε διαβλέψεις ἐκβαλεῖν τὸ κάρφος
thine [own] eye, and then thou wilt see clearly to cast out the mote
ἐκ τοῦ ὀφθαλμοῦ τοῦ.ἀδελφοῦ.σου.
out of the eye of thy brother.

6 Μὴ.δῶτε τὸ ἅγιον τοῖς κυσίν· μηδὲ βάλητε τοὺς
Give not that which [is] holy to the dogs, nor cast
μαργαρίτας ὑμῶν ἔμπροσθεν τῶν χοίρων, μήποτε [w]κατα-
[2]pearls [1]your before the swine, lest they should
πατήσωσιν αὐτοὺς ἐν τοῖς.ποσὶν.αὐτῶν, καὶ στραφέντες
trample upon them with their feet, and having turned
ῥήξωσιν ὑμᾶς.
they rend you.

7 Αἰτεῖτε, καὶ δοθήσεται ὑμῖν· ζητεῖτε, καὶ εὑρήσετε·
Ask, and it shall be given to you: seek, and ye shall find:
κρούετε, καὶ ἀνοιγήσεται ὑμῖν. 8 πᾶς.γὰρ ὁ αἰτῶν λαμβάνει,
knock, and it shall be opened to you. For everyone that asks receives,
καὶ ὁ ζητῶν εὑρίσκει, καὶ τῷ κρούοντι [x]ἀνοιγήσεται.
and he that seeks finds, and to him that knocks it shall be opened.
9 ἢ τίς [y]ἐστιν ἐξ ὑμῶν ἄνθρωπος, ὃν [z]ἐὰν [a]αἰτήσῃ ὁ υἱὸς
Or what [2]is [3]there [4]of [5]you [1]man who if [3]should [4]ask [2]son
αὐτοῦ ἄρτον, μὴ λίθον ἐπιδώσει αὐτῷ; 10 [b]καὶ ἐὰν ἰχθὺν
[1]his bread, a stone will he give him? and if a fish
αἰτήσῃ, μὴ ὄφιν ἐπιδώσει αὐτῷ; 11 εἰ οὖν ὑμεῖς πονηροὶ
he should ask, a serpent will he give him? If therefore ye, [2]evil
ὄντες οἴδατε δόματα ἀγαθὰ διδόναι τοῖς.τέκνοις.ὑμῶν, πόσῳ
[1]being, know [how] [2]gifts [1]good to give to your children, how much
μᾶλλον ὁ.πατὴρ.ὑμῶν ὁ ἐν τοῖς οὐρανοῖς δώσει ἀγαθὰ
more your Father who [is] in the heavens will give good things
τοῖς αἰτοῦσιν αὐτόν;
to them that ask him?

12 Πάντα οὖν ὅσα.[c]ἂν θέλητε ἵνα ποιῶσιν ὑμῖν οἱ
All things therefore whatever ye desire that [2]should [3]do [4]to [5]you
ἄνθρωποι, οὕτως καὶ ὑμεῖς ποιεῖτε αὐτοῖς· οὗτος.γάρ ἐστιν ὁ
[1]men, so also [2]ye [1]do to them: for this is the
νόμος καὶ οἱ προφῆται.
law and the prophets.

13 [d]Εἰσέλθετε διὰ τῆς στενῆς πύλης· ὅτι πλατεῖα [e]ἡ πύλη
Enter in through the narrow gate; for wide the gate
καὶ εὐρύχωρος ἡ ὁδὸς ἡ ἀπάγουσα εἰς τὴν ἀπώλειαν, καὶ
and broad the way that leads to destruction, and
πολλοί εἰσιν οἱ εἰσερχόμενοι δι' αὐτῆς· 14 [f]ὅτι στενὴ [g]ἡ
many are they who enter through it: for narrow the
πύλη καὶ τεθλιμμένη ἡ ὁδὸς ἡ ἀπάγουσα εἰς τὴν ζωήν, καὶ
gate and straitened the way that leads to life, and
ὀλίγοι εἰσὶν οἱ εὑρίσκοντες αὐτήν.
few are they who find it.

15 Προσέχετε.[h]δὲ ἀπὸ τῶν ψευδοπροφητῶν, οἵτινες ἔρχονται
But beware of the false prophets, who come
πρὸς ὑμᾶς ἐν ἐνδύμασιν προβάτων, ἔσωθεν.δέ εἰσιν λύκοι ἅρ-
you in raiment of sheep, but within are [2]wolves [1]ra-

er *provide for* you? O *you* of little faith!
31 Therefore, do not be anxious, saying, What shall we eat; or, what shall we drink; or, With what shall we be clothed?
32 For the heathen seek all these things. But your heavenly Father knows that you have need of all these things.
33 But seek first the kingdom of God and His righteousness, and all these things shall be added to you.
34 Then, do not be anxious for tomorrow. For tomorrow will be anxious for its own *things. Each* day has enough evil of itself.

CHAPTER 7

1 Do not judge, so that you may not be judged.
2 For with whatever judgment you judge, you shall be judged. And with whatever measure you measure out, it shall be measured to you again.
3 But why do you look upon the twig in your brother's eye, but *you* do not see the log that is in your own eye?
4 Or how can you say to your brother, Let me pull the twig out of your eye, *when* behold, the log *is* in your eye?
5 Hypocrite! First pull the log out of your own eye, and then you will see clearly to pull the twig out of your brother's eye.

6 Do not give that which is holy to the dogs nor throw your pearls before the pigs, so that they may not trample on them with their feet, then turn and tear you.

7 Ask and it shall be given to you. Seek and you shall find. Knock and it shall be opened to you.
8 For everyone that asks does receive. And he that seeks does find. And to him that knocks, it shall be opened.

9 Or what one of you is there who will give his son a stone when he asks for bread?
10 Or if he should ask for a fish, will he give him a snake?
11 Then, if you, being evil, know how to give good gifts to your children, how much more your Father who is in Heaven will give good things to those who ask Him!

12 Therefore, all things that you desire that men should do for you, so you also should do for them; for this is the Law and the Prophets.
13 Go in through the narrow gate. For wide is the gate and broad is the way that leads to death, and they who go through it are many.
14 Because narrow is the gate and narrow is the way that leads to life, and they are few who find it.
15 But beware of the false prophets who come to you in sheep's clothing (but inside they are plundering wolves).

παγες. 16 ἀπὸ τῶν.καρπῶν.αὐτῶν ἐπιγνώσεσθε αὐτούς· μήτι
pacious. By their fruits ye shall know them.
συλλέγουσιν ἀπὸ ἀκανθῶν ⁱσταφυλὴν ‖ ἢ ἀπὸ τριβόλων σῦκα;
Do they gather from thorns a bunch of grapes, or from thistles figs?
17 οὕτως πᾶν δένδρον ἀγαθὸν καρποὺς καλοὺς ποιεῖ· τὸ.δὲ
So every ²tree ¹good ⁴fruits ³good produces, but the
σαπρὸν δένδρον καρποὺς πονηροὺς ποιεῖ. 18 οὐ.δύναται
corrupt tree ²fruits ¹bad produces. ⁴Cannot
δένδρον ἀγαθὸν καρποὺς πονηροὺς ʲποιεῖν,‖ οὐδὲ δένδρον σα-
¹a ³tree ²good ⁶fruits ⁵evil produce, nor a ²tree ¹cor-
πρὸν καρποὺς καλοὺς ʲποιεῖν.‖ 19 πᾶν^k δένδρον μὴ ποιοῦν
rupt ³fruits ⁴good ⁵produce. Every tree not producing
καρπὸν καλὸν ἐκκόπτεται καὶ εἰς πῦρ βάλλεται. 20 ˡἄραγε‖
²fruit ¹good is cut down and into fire is cast. Then surely
ᵐἀπὸ‖ τῶν.καρπῶν.αὐτῶν ἐπιγνώσεσθε αὐτούς.
by their fruits ye shall know them.

21 Οὐ πᾶς ὁ λέγων μοι, Κύριε, κύριε, εἰσελεύσεται εἰς
Not every one who says to me, Lord, Lord, shall enter into
τὴν βασιλείαν τῶν οὐρανῶν· ἀλλ' ὁ ποιῶν τὸ θέλημα τοῦ
the kingdom of the heavens, but he who does the will
πατρός.μου τοῦ ἐν ⁿ οὐρανοῖς. 22 πολλοὶ ἐροῦσίν μοι ἐν
of my Father who [is] in [the] heavens. Many will say to me in
ἐκείνῃ τῇ ἡμέρᾳ, Κύριε, κύριε, οὐ τῷ.σῷ ὀνόματι ᵒπροεφη-
that day, Lord, Lord, ³not ⁵through ⁶thy ⁷name ¹did ²we
τεύσαμεν,‖ καὶ τῷ.σῷ ὀνόματι δαιμόνια ἐξεβάλομεν, καὶ
⁴prophesy, and through thy name demons cast out, and
τῷ.σῷ ὀνόματι δυνάμεις πολλὰς ἐποιήσαμεν; 23 καὶ
through thy name ²works ³of ⁴power ¹many perform? And
τότε ὁμολογήσω αὐτοῖς, ὅτι οὐδέποτε ἔγνων ὑμᾶς· ἀποχωρεῖτε
then will I confess to them, Never knew I you: depart ye
ἀπ' ἐμοῦ, οἱ ἐργαζόμενοι τὴν ἀνομίαν.
from me, who work lawlessness.

24 Πᾶς οὖν ὅστις ἀκούει μου τοὺς λόγους ᵖτούτους,‖
Every one therefore whosoever hears ²my ³words ¹these,
καὶ ποιεῖ αὐτούς, ᵠὁμοιώσω αὐτὸν‖ ἀνδρὶ φρονίμῳ, ὅστις ᾠκοδό-
and does them, I will liken him to a ²man ¹prudent, who built
μησεν ʳτὴν.οἰκίαν.αὐτοῦ‖ ἐπὶ τὴν πέτραν· 25 καὶ κατέβη ἡ
his house upon the rock: and came down the
βροχὴ καὶ ˢἦλθον‖ οἱ ποταμοὶ καὶ ἔπνευσαν οἱ ἄνεμοι, καὶ
rain, and came the streams, and blew the winds, and
ᵗπροσέπεσον‖ τῇ.οἰκίᾳ.ἐκείνῃ, καὶ οὐκ.ἔπεσεν· τεθεμελίωτο.γὰρ
fell upon that house, and it fell not; for it had been founded
ἐπὶ τὴν πέτραν. 26 καὶ πᾶς ὁ ἀκούων μου τοὺς λόγους
upon the rock. and everyone who hears ²my ³words
τούτους καὶ μὴ.ποιῶν αὐτούς, ὁμοιωθήσεται ἀνδρὶ μωρῷ,
¹these and does not do them, he shall be likened to a ²man ¹foolish,
ὅστις ᾠκοδόμησεν ᵛτὴν.οἰκίαν.αὐτοῦ‖ ἐπὶ τὴν ἄμμον· 27 καὶ
who built his house upon the sand: and
κατέβη ἡ βροχὴ καὶ ἦλθον οἱ ποταμοὶ καὶ ἔπνευσαν οἱ
came down the rain, and came the streams, and blew the
ἄνεμοι, καὶ προσέκοψαν τῇ.οἰκίᾳ.ἐκείνῃ, καὶ ἔπεσεν, καὶ ἦν
winds, and beat upon that house, and it fell, and ⁵was
ἡ πτῶσις αὐτῆς μεγάλη.
¹the ²fall ³of ⁴it great.

28 Καὶ ἐγένετο ὅτε ʷσυνετέλεσεν‖ ὁ Ἰησοῦς τοὺς λόγους
And it came to pass when ²had ³finished ¹Jesus ⁵words
τούτους ἐξεπλήσσοντο οἱ ὄχλοι ἐπὶ τῇ.διδαχῇ.αὐτοῦ· 29 ἦν
⁴these astonished were the crowds at his teaching: ²he ³was
γὰρ διδάσκων αὐτοὺς ὡς ἐξουσίαν ἔχων, καὶ οὐχ ὡς οἱ
¹for teaching them as ²authority ¹having, and not as the
γραμματεῖς^x.
scribes.

8 ʸΚαταβάντι.δὲ αὐτῷ‖ ἀπὸ τοῦ ὄρους, ἠκολούθησαν αὐτῷ
And when ²had ³come ⁴down ¹he from the mountain, ³followed ⁴him
ὄχλοι πολλοί· 2 καὶ ἰδού, λεπρὸς ᶻἐλθὼν‖ προσεκύνει αὐτῷ,
²crowds ¹great. And behold, a leper having come did homage to him,
λέγων, Κύριε, ἐὰν θέλῃς, δύνασαί με καθαρίσαι. 3 Καὶ
saying, Lord, if thou wilt thou art able me to cleanse. And
ἐκτείνας τὴν.χεῖρα ἥψατο αὐτοῦ ᵃὁ Ἰησοῦς,‖ λέγων,
having stretched out [his] hand ²touched ³him ¹Jesus, saying,
Θέλω, καθαρίσθητι. Καὶ εὐθέως ᵇἐκαθαρίσθη‖ αὐτοῦ ἡ λέπρα.
I will, be thou cleansed. And immediately was cleansed his leprosy.
4 Καὶ λέγει αὐτῷ ὁ Ἰησοῦς, Ὅρα μηδενὶ εἴπῃς· ᶜἀλλ'‖ ὕπαγε,
And ²says ³to ⁴him ¹Jesus, See no one thou tell; but go
σεαυτὸν δεῖξον τῷ ἱερεῖ, καὶ ᵈπροσένεγκε‖ τὸ δῶρον ὃ προσ-
thyself shew to the priest, and offer the gift which ²or-
έταξεν ᵉΜωσῆς,‖ εἰς μαρτύριον αὐτοῖς.
dered ¹Moses for a testimony to them.

5 ᶠΕἰσελθόντι‖.δὲ ᵍτῷ Ἰησοῦ‖ εἰς ʰΚαπερναούμ,‖ προσῆλθεν
And ²having ³entered ¹Jesus into Capernaum, ³came
αὐτῷ ⁱἑκατόνταρχος‖ παρακαλῶν αὐτὸν 6 καὶ λέγων, Κύριε,
⁴to ⁵him ¹a ²centurion, beseeching him and saying, Lord,

16 By their fruits you shall know them. Do
men gather grapes from thorns, or figs from
thistles?
17 So every good tree produces good fruits.
But the corrupt tree produces evil fruits.
18 A good tree cannot produce evil fruit,
nor can a corrupt true produce good fruits.
19 Every tree not bringing forth good fruit
is cut down and is thrown into the fire.
20 Then surely, by their fruits you shall
know them.
21 Not everyone who says to Me, Lord!
Lord! shall enter into the kingdom of
Heaven. But he who does the will of My
Father who is in Heaven *shall enter in.*
22 Many will say to Me in that day, Lord!
Lord! Did we not prophesy through Your
name and through Your name throw out
demons? And *did we not* through Your
name do mighty works?
23 And then I will say to them, I never
knew you! Depart from Me, you who work
lawlessness!
24 Therefore, everyone who hears these
words of Mine, and does them, I will compare him to a wise man who built his house
on a rock.
25 And the rain came down, and the floods
came, and the winds blew and fell upon that
house. But it did not fall, for it had been
founded on a rock.
26 And everyone who hears these words of
Mine and does not do them, he shall be
compared to a foolish man who built his
house on the sand.
27 And the rain came down, and the floods
came, and the winds blew and beat upon
that house. And it fell, and great was the fall
of it.
28 And when Jesus had finished these
words, the people were astonished at His
teaching.
29 For He was teaching them as One who
had authority, and not like the scribes.

CHAPTER 8

1 And when He had come down from the
mountain, great crowds followed Him.
2 And behold, a leper came and worshiped
Him, saying, Lord, if You so desire, You are
able to make me clean.
3 And stretching out His hand, Jesus
touched him, saying, I desire it! Be clean!
And instantly his leprosy was gone.
4 And Jesus said to him, See that you do
not tell anyone. But go show yourself to the
priest and offer the gifts which Moses commanded for a witness to them.
5 And when Jesus had entered Ca-per-na-
um, a centurion came to Him, begging Him.
6 And he said, Lord, my servant has been

ὁ.παῖς.μου βέβληται ἐν τῇ οἰκίᾳ παραλυτικός, δεινῶς βασα-
my servant is laid in the house paralytic, grievously tor-
νιζόμενος. 7 [k]Καὶ‖ λέγει αὐτῷ [l]ὁ Ἰησοῦς,‖ Ἐγὼ ἐλθὼν θερα-
mented. And [2]says [3]to [4]him [1]Jesus, I having come will
πεύσω αὐτόν. 8 [m]Καὶ ἀποκριθεὶς‖ ὁ [l]ἑκατόνταρχος‖ ἔφη, Κύριε,
heal him. And [3]answering [1]the [2]centurion said, Lord,
οὐκ.εἰμὶ ἱκανὸς ἵνα μου ὑπὸ τὴν στέγην εἰσέλθῃς· ἀλλὰ μόνον
I am not worthy that [2]my [1]under roof thou shouldest come, but only
εἰπὲ [n]λόγον,‖ καὶ ἰαθήσεται ὁ.παῖς.μου. 9 καὶ.γὰρ ἐγὼ ἄν-
speak a word, and shall be healed my servant. For also I a
θρωπός εἰμι ὑπὸ ἐξουσίαν[o], ἔχων ὑπ' ἐμαυτὸν στρατιώτας·
man am under authority, having under myself soldiers;
καὶ λέγω τούτῳ, Πορεύθητι, καὶ πορεύεται· καὶ ἄλλῳ, Ἔρχου,
and I say to this [one], Go, and he goes; and to another, Come,
καὶ ἔρχεται· καὶ τῷ.δούλῳ.μου, Ποίησον τοῦτο, καὶ ποιεῖ.
and he comes; and to my bondman, Do this, and he does [it].
10 Ἀκούσας.δὲ ὁ Ἰησοῦς ἐθαύμασεν, καὶ εἶπεν τοῖς ἀκολου-
And [2]having [3]heard [1]Jesus wondered, and said to those follow-
θοῦσιν[p], Ἀμὴν λέγω ὑμῖν, [q]οὐδὲ ἐν τῷ Ἰσραὴλ τοσαύτην
ing, Verily I say to you, Not even in Israel so great
πίστιν‖ εὗρον. 11 λέγω.δὲ ὑμῖν, ὅτι πολλοὶ ἀπὸ ἀνατολῶν
faith have I found. But I say to you, that many from east
καὶ δυσμῶν ἥξουσιν, καὶ ἀνακλιθήσονται μετὰ Ἀβραὰμ καὶ
and west shall come, and shall recline [at table] with Abraham and
Ἰσαὰκ καὶ Ἰακὼβ ἐν τῇ βασιλείᾳ τῶν οὐρανῶν· 12 οἱ.δὲ υἱοὶ
Isaac and Jacob in the kingdom of the heavens; but the sons
τῆς βασιλείας [r]ἐκβληθήσονται‖ εἰς τὸ σκότος τὸ ἐξώτερον· ἐκεῖ
of the kingdom shall be cast out into the darkness the outer: there
ἔσται ὁ κλαυθμὸς καὶ ὁ βρυγμὸς τῶν ὀδόντων. 13 Καὶ εἶπεν
shall be the weeping and the gnashing of the teeth. And [2]said
ὁ Ἰησοῦς τῷ [s]ἑκατοντάρχῳ,‖ Ὕπαγε, [t]καὶ‖ ὡς ἐπίστευσας
[1]Jesus to the centurion, Go, and as thou hast believed
γενηθήτω σοι. Καὶ ἰάθη ὁ.παῖς.[v]αὐτοῦ‖ [w]ἐν τῇ ὥρᾳ
be it to thee. And was healed his servant in [2]hour
ἐκείνῃ.‖
[1]that.

14 Καὶ ἐλθὼν ὁ Ἰησοῦς εἰς τὴν οἰκίαν Πέτρου, εἶδεν
And [2]having [3]come [1]Jesus to the house of Peter, saw
τὴν.πενθερὰν.αὐτοῦ βεβλημένην καὶ πυρέσσουσαν, 15 καὶ
his wife's mother laid and in a fever; and
ἥψατο τῆς χειρὸς.αὐτῆς, καὶ ἀφῆκεν αὐτὴν ὁ πυρετός· καὶ
he touched her hand, and [3]left [4]her [1]the [2]fever; and
ἠγέρθη καὶ διηκόνει [x]αὐτοῖς.‖
she arose and ministered to them.

16 Ὀψίας.δὲ γενομένης προσήνεγκαν αὐτῷ δαιμονιζομένους
And evening being come, they brought to him [2]possessed [3]with [4]demons
πολλούς· καὶ ἐξέβαλεν τὰ πνεύματα λόγῳ καὶ πάντας τοὺς
[1]many, and he cast out the spirits by a word, and all who
κακῶς ἔχοντας ἐθεράπευσεν· 17 ὅπως πληρωθῇ τὸ
[2]ill [1]were he healed: So that might be fulfilled that which
ῥηθὲν διὰ Ἡσαΐου τοῦ προφήτου, λέγοντος, Αὐτὸς τὰς
was spoken by Esaias the prophet, saying, Himself the
ἀσθενείας ἡμῶν ἔλαβεν, καὶ τὰς νόσους ἐβάστασεν.
infirmities of us took, and the diseases bore.

18 Ἰδὼν.δὲ ὁ Ἰησοῦς [y]πολλοὺς ὄχλους‖ περὶ αὐτόν, ἐκέ-
And [2]seeing [1]Jesus great crowds around him, he com-
λευσεν ἀπελθεῖν εἰς τὸ πέραν. 19 καὶ προσελθὼν εἷς
manded to depart to the other side. And having come to [him] one
γραμματεὺς εἶπεν αὐτῷ, Διδάσκαλε, ἀκολουθήσω σοι ὅπου.ἐὰν
a scribe said to him, Teacher, I will follow thee whithersoever
ἀπέρχῃ. 20 Καὶ λέγει αὐτῷ ὁ Ἰησοῦς, Αἱ ἀλώπεκες φωλεοὺς
thou mayest go. And [2]says [3]to [4]him [1]Jesus, The foxes [2]holes
ἔχουσιν καὶ τὰ πετεινὰ τοῦ οὐρανοῦ κατασκηνώσεις, ὁ.δὲ υἱὸς
[1]have, and the birds of the heaven nests, but the Son
τοῦ ἀνθρώπου οὐκ.ἔχει ποῦ τὴν κεφαλὴν κλίνῃ. 21 Ἕτερος
of man has not where the head he may lay. [2]Another
δὲ τῶν.μαθητῶν.[z]αὐτοῦ‖ εἶπεν αὐτῷ, Κύριε, ἐπίτρεψόν μοι
[1]and of his disciples said to him, Lord, allow me
πρῶτον ἀπελθεῖν καὶ θάψαι τὸν.πατέρα.μου. 22 Ὁ.δὲ.[a]Ἰησοῦς‖
first to go and bury my father. But Jesus
[b]εἶπεν‖ αὐτῷ, Ἀκολούθει μοι, καὶ ἄφες τοὺς νεκροὺς θάψαι
said to him, Follow me, and leave the dead to bury
τοὺς.ἑαυτῶν νεκρούς.
their own dead.

23 Καὶ ἐμβάντι αὐτῷ εἰς [c]τὸ‖ πλοῖον, ἠκολούθησαν αὐτῷ
And [2]having [3]entered [1]he into the ship, [3]followed [4]him
οἱ.μαθηταὶ αὐτοῦ. 24 καὶ ἰδού, σεισμὸς μέγας ἐγένετο ἐν τῇ
[1]his [2]disciples. And lo, a [2]tempest [1]great arose in the
θαλάσσῃ, ὥστε τὸ πλοῖον καλύπτεσθαι ὑπὸ τῶν κυμάτων·
sea, so that the ship was covered by the waves;
αὐτὸς.δὲ ἐκάθευδεν. 25 καὶ προσελθόντες [d]οἱ μαθηταὶ‖ [e]αὐτοῦ‖
but he was sleeping. And having come to [him] the disciples of him

laid out in the house, a paralytic, fearfully tormented.
7 And Jesus said to him, I will come and heal him.
8 The centurion answered and said, Lord, I am not worthy that You should come under my roof. But only speak a word and my servant will be healed.
9 For I also am a man under authority, having soldiers under me. And I say to this one, Go! And he goes. And to another, Come! And he comes; and to my slave, Do this! and he does.
10 And having heard this, Jesus marveled. And He said to those following, Truly I say to you, Not even in Israel have I found such great faith.
11 But I say to you that many shall come from the east and west and shall sit down with Abraham and Isaac and Jacob in the kingdom of Heaven.
12 But the children of the kingdom shall be thrown into outer darkness. There shall be weeping and gnashing of teeth.
13 And Jesus said to the centurion, Go! And as you have believed, let it be done to you. And his servant was healed in that hour.

14 And when Jesus had come to Peter's house, He saw his wife's mother laid out *in bed* and sick of a fever.

15 And He touched her hand. And the fever left her. And she arose and served them.

16 And as evening was coming on, they brought to Him many that were demon-possessed. And He threw out the spirits by a word. And He healed all who were sick,
17 so that that which was spoken through Isaiah the prophet might be fulfilled, saying, "He took upon Himself our weaknesses and bore *our* sicknesses."

18 And seeing great crowds around Him, Jesus gave orders to go over to the other side.
19 And a certain scribe came and said to Him, Master, I will follow You wherever You go.
20 And Jesus said to him, The foxes have holes, and the birds of the sky nests, but the Son of man has nowhere to lay His head.
21 And another of His disciples said to Him, Lord, allow me first to go and bury my father.
22 But Jesus said to him, Follow Me and leave the dead to bury their own dead.

23 And when He had gone into the ship, His disciples followed Him.
24 And behold! A great tempest occurred in the sea, so that the ship was covered by the waves! But He was asleep.
25 And His disciples came and awoke Him,

ἤγειραν αὐτόν, λέγοντες, Κύριε, σῶσον [f]ἡμᾶς,ǁ ἀπολλύμεθα.
awoke him, saying, Lord, save us; we perish.
26 Καὶ λέγει αὐτοῖς, Τί δειλοί ἐστε, ὀλιγόπιστοι; Τότε
And he says to them, Why fearful are ye, O [ye] of little faith? Then,
ἐγερθεὶς ἐπετίμησεν τοῖς ἀνέμοις καὶ τῇ θαλάσσῃ, καὶ ἐγένετο
having arisen he rebuked the winds and the sea, and there was
γαλήνη μεγάλη. 27 οἱ.δὲ ἄνθρωποι ἐθαύμασαν, λέγοντες,
a [2]calm [1]great. And the men wondered, saying,
Ποταπός ἐστιν οὗτος, ὅτι [g]καὶǁ οἱ ἄνεμοι καὶ ἡ θάλασσα
What kind [of man] is this, that even the winds and the sea
[h]ὑπακούουσιν αὐτῷ;ǁ
obey him?
28 Καὶ [i]ἐλθόντι αὐτῷǁ εἰς τὸ πέραν εἰς τὴν χώραν τῶν
And when [2]had [3]come [1]he to the other side to the country of the
[k]Γεργεσηνῶνǁ ὑπήντησαν.αὐτῷ δύο δαιμονιζόμενοι ἐκ τῶν
Gergesenes, [5]met [6]him [1]two [2]possessed [3]by [4]demons out of the
μνημείων ἐξερχόμενοι, χαλεποὶ λίαν, ὥστε μὴ ἰσχύειν τινὰ
tombs coming, [2]violent [1]very, so that not [3]was [4]able [1]any [2]one
παρελθεῖν διὰ τῆς.ὁδοῦ.ἐκείνης· 29 καὶ ἰδού, ἔκραξαν λέγοντες,
to pass by that way. And lo, they cried out, saying,
Τί ἡμῖν καὶ σοί, [l]Ἰησοῦ,ǁ υἱὲ τοῦ θεοῦ; ἦλθες ὧδε πρὸ
What to us and to thee, Jesus, Son of God? art thou come here before [the]
καιροῦ βασανίσαι ἡμᾶς; 30 Ἦν.δὲ μακρὰν ἀπ' αὐτῶν ἀγέλη
time to torment us? Now there was far off from them a herd
χοίρων πολλῶν βοσκομένη. 31 οἱ.δὲ δαίμονες παρεκάλουν
of [2]swine [1]many feeding; And the demons besought
αὐτόν, λέγοντες, Εἰ ἐκβάλλεις ἡμᾶς, [m]ἐπίτρεψον ἡμῖν ἀπελθεῖνǁ
him, saying, If thou cast out us, allow us to go away
εἰς τὴν ἀγέλην τῶν χοίρων. 32 Καὶ εἶπεν αὐτοῖς[n], Ὑπάγετε.
into the herd of the swine. And he said to them, Go.
Οἱ.δὲ ἐξελθόντες [o]ἀπῆλθονǁ εἰς [p]τὴν ἀγέλην τῶν χοίρων·ǁ
And they having gone out went away into the herd of the swine:
καὶ ἰδού, ὥρμησεν πᾶσα ἡ ἀγέλη [q]τῶν χοίρωνǁ κατὰ τοῦ
and behold, [7]rushed [1]all [2]the [3]herd [4]of [5]the [6]swine down the
κρημνοῦ εἰς τὴν θάλασσαν, καὶ ἀπέθανον ἐν τοῖς ὕδασιν.
steep into the sea, and died in the waters.
33 οἱ.δὲ βόσκοντες ἔφυγον, καὶ ἀπελθόντες εἰς τὴν πόλιν
But those who fed [them] fled, and having gone away into the city
ἀπήγγειλαν πάντα, καὶ τὰ τῶν.δαιμονιζομένων.
related everything, and the [events] concerning those possessed by demons.
34 καὶ ἰδού, πᾶσα ἡ πόλις ἐξῆλθεν εἰς [r]συνάντησινǁ [s]τῷǁ Ἰησοῦ·
And behold, all the city went out to meet Jesus;
καὶ ἰδόντες αὐτόν, παρεκάλεσαν [t]ὅπωςǁ μεταβῇ ἀπὸ
and seeing him, they besought [him] that he would depart from
τῶν.ὁρίων.αὐτῶν.
their borders.
9 Καὶ ἐμβὰς εἰς [v]τὸǁ πλοῖον διεπέρασεν καὶ ἦλθεν εἰς
And having entered into the ship he passed over and came to
τὴν.ἰδίαν πόλιν. 2 καὶ ἰδού, [w]προσέφερονǁ αὐτῷ παραλυτικὸν
his own city. And behold, they brought to him a paralytic
ἐπὶ κλίνης βεβλημένον· καὶ ἰδὼν ὁ Ἰησοῦς τὴν.πίστιν.αὐτῶν
on a bed lying; and [2]seeing [1]Jesus their faith
εἶπεν τῷ παραλυτικῷ, Θάρσει, τέκνον, [x]ἀφέωνταίǁ
said to the paralytic, Be of good courage, child; [3]have [4]been [5]forgiven
[y]σοι αἱ.ἁμαρτίαι σου.ǁ 3 Καὶ ἰδού, τινὲς τῶν γραμματέων [z]εἶπονǁ
[6]thee [1]thy [2]sins. And lo, some of the scribes said
ἐν ἑαυτοῖς, Οὗτος βλασφημεῖ. 4 Καὶ [a]ἰδὼνǁ ὁ Ἰησοῦς τὰς
in themselves, This [man] blasphemes. And [2]perceiving [1]Jesus
ἐνθυμήσεις.αὐτῶν, εἶπεν, [b]Ἱνα.τίǁ [c]ὑμεῖςǁ ἐνθυμεῖσθε πονηρὰ
their thoughts, said, Why [2]ye [1]think evil
ἐν ταῖς.καρδίαις.ὑμῶν; 5 τί.γάρ ἐστιν εὐκοπώτερον, εἰπεῖν,
in your hearts? For which is easier, to say,
[d]Ἀφέωνταίǁ [e]σοιǁ αἱ ἁμαρτίαι· ἢ εἰπεῖν, [f]Ἔγειραιǁ καὶ
[3]Have [4]been [5]forgiven [6]thee [[1]thy] [2]sins, or to say, Arise and
περιπάτει; 6 ἵνα.δὲ εἰδῆτε ὅτι ἐξουσίαν ἔχει ὁ υἱὸς τοῦ ἀν-
walk? But that ye may know that authority has the Son of
θρώπου ἐπὶ τῆς γῆς ἀφιέναι ἁμαρτίας· τότε λέγει τῷ παρα-
man on the earth to forgive sins: then he says to the para-
λυτικῷ, [g]Ἐγερθεὶςǁ ἆρόν σου τὴν κλίνην, καὶ ὕπαγε εἰς τὸν
lytic, Having arisen, take up thy bed, and go to
οἶκόν σου 7 Καὶ ἐγερθεὶς ἀπῆλθεν εἰς τὸν.οἶκον.αὐτοῦ.
[2]house [1]thy. And having arisen he went away to his house.
8 ἰδόντες.δὲ οἱ ὄχλοι [h]ἐθαύμασαν,ǁ καὶ ἐδόξασαν τὸν θεόν,
And [3]having [4]seen [1]the [2]crowds wondered, and glorified God,
τὸν δόντα ἐξουσίαν τοιαύτην τοῖς ἀνθρώποις.
who gave [2]authority [1]such to men.
9 Καὶ παράγων ὁ Ἰησοῦς ἐκεῖθεν εἶδεν ἄνθρωπον καθήμενον
And [2]passing [1]Jesus thence saw a man sitting
ἐπὶ τὸ τελώνιον, [i]Ματθαῖονǁ λεγόμενον, καὶ λέγει αὐτῷ, Ἀκο-
at the tax-office, [2]Matthew [1]called, and says to him, Fol-
λούθει μοι. Καὶ ἀναστὰς [k]ἠκολούθησενǁ αὐτῷ. 10 Καὶ ἐγένετο
low me. And having arisen he followed him. And it came to pass

saying, Lord, save us! We are perishing!
26 And He said to them, Why are you afraid, O you of little faith? Then rising up, He rebuked the winds and the sea, and there was a great calm.
27 And the men marveled, saying, What kind of man is this, that even the winds and the sea obey Him?

28 And when He had come to the other side into the country of the Ger-ge-senes, two demon-possessed men met Him, coming out of the tombs – *men* so violent that no one was able to pass by that way.
29 And behold! They cried out, saying, What have we to do with You, Jesus, O Son of God? Have You come here before the time to torment us?
30 Now a herd of hogs was feeding at a distance from them.
31 And the demons begged Him, saying, If You are going to throw us out, allow us to go into the herd of hogs.
32 And He said to them, Go! And they came out and entered the herd of hogs. And, behold! The whole herd of hogs rushed down the cliff into the sea and died in the waters!
33 And those who fed them ran away. And going into the city, *they* told them everything, even about the demon-possessed ones.
34 And behold! The whole city went out to meet Jesus. And when they saw Him, they begged Him to go away from their borders.

CHAPTER 9

1 And entering into the ship, He crossed and came to His own city.
2 And, behold! They brought to Him a paralytic lying on a bed. And seeing their faith, Jesus said to the paralytic, Be comforted, child! Your sins have been forgiven you.
3 And behold! Some of the scribes said within themselves, This one blasphemes.
4 And knowing their thoughts, Jesus said, Why do you think evil in your hearts?
5 For which is easier, to say, *Your* sins are forgiven you; or to say, Arise and walk?
6 But so that you may know that the Son of Man has authority on earth to forgive sins, He then said to the paralytic, Arise! Take up your bed and go to your house.
7 And rising up, he went away to his house.
8 And seeing this, the multitudes marveled and glorified God, who had given such authority to men.

9 And as He went on, Jesus saw there a man named Matthew sitting at the tax-office. And He said to him, Follow Me! And he rose up and followed Him.
10 And as He was dining in the house,

[l]αὐτοῦ ἀνακειμένου" ἐν τῇ οἰκίᾳ, [m]καὶ" ἰδού, πολλοὶ τελῶναι
at his reclining [at table] in the house, that behold, many tax-gatherers
καὶ ἁμαρτωλοὶ ἐλθόντες συνανέκειντο τῷ Ἰησοῦ καὶ
and sinners having come were reclining [at table] with Jesus and
τοῖς.μαθηταῖς.αὐτοῦ. 11 καὶ ἰδόντες οἱ Φαρισαῖοι [n]εἶπον"
his disciples. And having seen [it] the Pharisees said
τοῖς.μαθηταῖς.αὐτοῦ, [o]Διατί" μετὰ τῶν τελωνῶν καὶ ἁμαρ-
to his disciples, Why with the tax-gatherers and sin-
τωλῶν ἐσθίει ὁ.διδάσκαλος.ὑμῶν; 12 Ὁ.δὲ.[p]Ἰησοῦς" ἀκούσας
ners eats your teacher? But Jesus having heard
εἶπεν [q]αὐτοῖς," Οὐ χρείαν ἔχουσιν οἱ ἰσχύοντες ἰατροῦ,
he said to them, [6]Not [5]need [4]have [1]they [2]who [3]are [4]strong of a physician,
[r]ἀλλ'" οἱ κακῶς ἔχοντες. 13 πορευθέντες δὲ μάθετε τί ἐστιν,
but they who ill are. But having gone learn what is,
[s]"Ἔλεον" θέλω, καὶ οὐ θυσίαν· οὐ γὰρ ἦλθον καλέσαι δικαίους,
Mercy I desire, and not sacrifice: [4]not [3]for [1]I [2]came to call righteous
[t]ἀλλ'" ἁμαρτωλοὺς [v]εἰς μετάνοιαν."
[ones], but sinners to repentance.

14 Τότε προσέρχονται αὐτῷ οἱ μαθηταὶ Ἰωάννου, λέγοντες,
Then come near to him the disciples of John, saying,
[w]Διατί" ἡμεῖς καὶ οἱ Φαρισαῖοι νηστεύομεν [x]πολλά," οἱ.δὲ.μαθη-
Why [2]we [3]and [4]the [5]Pharisees [1]do fast much, but [2]disci-
ταί.σου οὐ.νηστεύουσιν; 15 Καὶ εἶπεν αὐτοῖς ὁ Ἰησοῦς, Μὴ
ples [1]thy fast not? And [2]said [3]to [4]them [1]Jesus,
δύνανται οἱ υἱοὶ τοῦ νυμφῶνος πενθεῖν ἐφ'.ὅσον μετ' αὐτῶν
Can the sons of the bridechamber mourn while with them
ἐστιν ὁ νυμφίος; ἐλεύσονται δὲ ἡμέραι ὅταν ἀπαρθῇ
is the bridegroom? [3]will [4]come [1]but [2]days when will have been taken away
ἀπ' αὐτῶν ὁ νυμφίος, καὶ τότε νηστεύσουσιν. 16 οὐδεὶς.δὲ
from them the bridegroom, and then they will fast. But no one
ἐπιβάλλει ἐπίβλημα ῥάκους ἀγνάφου ἐπὶ ἱματίῳ.παλαιῷ·
puts a piece of [2]cloth [1]unfulled on an old garment:
αἴρει γὰρ τὸ.πλήρωμα.αὐτοῦ ἀπὸ τοῦ ἱματίου, καὶ χεῖρον
[3]takes [4]away [1]for [2]its filling up from the garment, and a worse
σχίσμα γίνεται. 17 οὐδὲ βάλλουσιν οἶνον νέον εἰς ἀσκοὺς
rent takes place. Nor put they [2]wine [1]new into [2]skins
παλαιούς· εἰ.δὲ.μήγε ῥήγνυνται οἱ ἀσκοί, καὶ ὁ οἶνος ἐκχεῖται,
[1]old, otherwise [3]are [4]burst [1]the [2]skins, and the wine is poured out,
καὶ οἱ ἀσκοὶ [y]ἀπολοῦνται·" ἀλλὰ [z]βάλλουσιν οἶνον νέον εἰς
and the skins will be destroyed; but they put [2]wine [1]new into
ἀσκοὺς" καινούς, καὶ [a]ἀμφότερα" συντηροῦνται.
[2]skins [1]new, and both are preserved together.

18 Ταῦτα αὐτοῦ.λαλοῦντος αὐτοῖς, ἰδού, ἄρχων[b] [c]ἐλθὼν"
[5]These [6]things [1]as [2]he [3]is [4]speaking to them, behold, a ruler having come
προσεκύνει αὐτῷ, λέγων, [d]"Ὅτι" ἡ.θυγάτηρ.μου ἄρτι ἐτελεύ-
did homage to him, saying, My daughter just now has
τησεν· ἀλλὰ ἐλθὼν ἐπίθες τὴν.χεῖρά.σου ἐπ' αὐτήν, καὶ
died; but having come lay thy hand upon her, and
ζήσεται. 19 καὶ ἐγερθεὶς ὁ Ἰησοῦς [e]ἠκολούθησεν" αὐτῷ
she shall live. And having arisen Jesus followed him,
καὶ οἱ.μαθηταὶ.αὐτοῦ.
and his disciples.

20 Καὶ ἰδού, γυνὴ αἱμοῤῥοοῦσα δώδεκα ἔτη, προσελ-
And behold, a woman having had a flux of blood twelve years, having
θοῦσα ὄπισθεν ἥψατο τοῦ κρασπέδου τοῦ.ἱματίου.αὐτοῦ.
come behind touched the border of his garment.
21 ἔλεγεν.γὰρ ἐν ἑαυτῇ, Ἐὰν μόνον ἅψωμαι τοῦ ἱματίου
For she said within herself, If only I shall touch [2]garment
αὐτοῦ σωθήσομαι. 22 Ὁ.δὲ.[f]Ἰησοῦς" [g]ἐπιστραφεὶς" καὶ ἰδὼν
[1]his I shall be cured. But Jesus having turned and having seen
αὐτὴν εἶπεν, Θάρσει, θύγατερ· ἡ.πίστις.σου σέσωκέν σε.
her he said, Be of good courage, daughter; thy faith hath cured thee.
καὶ ἐσώθη ἡ γυνὴ ἀπὸ τῆς.ὥρας.ἐκείνης.
And [3]was [4]cured [1]the [2]woman from that hour.
23 Καὶ ἐλθὼν ὁ Ἰησοῦς εἰς τὴν οἰκίαν τοῦ ἄρχοντος,
And [2]having [3]come [1]Jesus into the house of the ruler,
καὶ ἰδὼν τοὺς αὐλητὰς καὶ τὸν ὄχλον θορυβούμενον,
and having seen the flute-players and the crowd making a tumult,
24 [h]λέγει αὐτοῖς," Ἀναχωρεῖτε οὐ γὰρ ἀπέθανεν τὸ κοράσιον,
says to them, Withdraw, [4]not [3]for [3]is [4]dead [1]the [2]damsel,
ἀλλὰ καθεύδει. καὶ κατεγέλων αὐτοῦ. 25 ὅτε.δὲ ἐξεβλήθη
but sleeps. And they laughed at him. But when [3]had [4]been [5]put [6]out
ὁ ὄχλος, εἰσελθὼν ἐκράτησεν τῆς.χειρὸς.αὐτῆς, καὶ ἠγέρθη
[1]the [2]crowd, having entered he took hold of her hand, and [3]arose
τὸ κοράσιον. 26 καὶ ἐξῆλθεν ἡ.φήμη.αὕτη εἰς ὅλην τὴν
[1]the [2]damsel. And [3]went [4]out [1]this [2]report into all
γῆν ἐκείνην.
[2]land [1]that.

27 Καὶ παράγοντι ἐκεῖθεν τῷ Ἰησοῦ, ἠκολούθησαν [i]αὐτῷ"
And [2]passing [3]on [4]thence [1]Jesus, [5]followed [6]him
δύο τυφλοί, κράζοντες καὶ λέγοντες, Ἐλέησον ἡμᾶς, [k]υἱὲ
[3]two [4]blind [men], crying and saying, Have pity on us, Son

behold, many tax-collectors and sinners
came and dined with Jesus and His disciples.
[11]And the Pharisees saw it and said to His
disciples, Why does your master eat with
tax-collectors and sinners?
[12]But Jesus heard them and said to them,
They who are strong have no need of a
physician, but they who are sick.
[13]But go and learn what this is, "I desire
mercy and not sacrifice." For I did not come
to call the righteous to repentance, but *I
came to call* sinners.

[14]Then the disciples of John came near to
Him saying, Why do we and the Pharisees
fast often, but Your disciples do not fast at
all?
[15]And Jesus said to them, Can the sons of
the bridechamber mourn as long as the
bridegroom is with them? But the days will
come when the bridegroom will have been
taken away from them. And then they will
fast.
[16]But no one puts a piece of new cloth onto
an old piece of clothing. For filling it up
with new cloth takes away the clothing and
the tear is made worse,
[17]Nor do men put new wine into old wineskins, for if *they* do the wineskins burst and
the wine runs out, and the wineskins will be
ruined. But they put new wine into new
wineskins. And both are preserved together.

[18]While He was speaking these things to
them, behold, a ruler came and worshiped
Him, saying, My daughter has just died. But
come and lay Your hand on her and she shall
live.
[19]And Jesus and His disciples arose and
followed him.

[20]Lo and behold! A woman who had a
flow of blood for twelve years came up
behind and touched the hem of His robe.
[21]For she said within herself, If only I shall
touch the robe, I shall be cured.
[22]But turning and seeing her, Jesus said, Be
comforted, daughter, your faith has cured
you – and the woman was cured from that
hour.
[23]And when Jesus came to the house of the
ruler and saw the flute-players and the crowd
making a great noise,
[24]He said to them, Go back, for the little
girl is not dead but is asleep. And they
scornfully laughed at Him.
[25]But when the crowd had been put out,
He went in and took hold of her hand. And
the little girl rose up.
[26]And this story went into all that land.

[27]And as Jesus was leaving there, two blind
ones followed Him, crying out and saying,
Have mercy on us, Son of David!

Δαβίδ." 28 ἐλθόντι.δὲ εἰς τὴν οἰκίαν, [l]προσῆλθον" αὐτῷ οἱ
of David. And having come into the house, came to him the
τυφλοί, καὶ λέγει αὐτοῖς ὁ Ἰησοῦς, Πιστεύετε ὅτι δύναμαι
blind [men], and [2]says [3]to [4]them [1]Jesus, Believe ye that I am able
[m]τοῦτο ποιῆσαι;" Λέγουσιν αὐτῷ, Ναί, κύριε. 29 Τότε ἥψατο
this to do? They say to him, Yea, Lord. Then he touched
τῶν.ὀφθαλμῶν.αὐτῶν, λέγων, Κατὰ τὴν.πίστιν.ὑμῶν γενη-
their eyes, saying, According to your faith be
θήτω ὑμῖν. 30 Καὶ [n]ἀνεῴχθησαν" αὐτῶν οἱ ὀφθαλμοί· καὶ
it to you. And were opened their eyes; and
[o]ἐνεβριμήσατο" αὐτοῖς ὁ Ἰησοῦς, λέγων, Ὁρᾶτε μηδεὶς γινω-
[2]strictly [3]charged [4]them [1]Jesus, saying, See [2]no [3]one [1]let
σκέτω. 31 Οἱ.δὲ ἐξελθόντες διεφήμισαν αὐτὸν ἐν ὅλῃ τῇ
know [it]. But they having gone out made [2]known [1]him in all
γῇ ἐκείνῃ.
[3]land [2]that.

32 Αὐτῶν.δὲ ἐξερχομένων, ἰδού, προσήνεγκαν αὐτῷ [p]ἄν-
And as they were going out, behold, they brought to him a
θρωπον" κωφὸν δαιμονιζόμενον. 33 καὶ ἐκβληθέντος
man dumb, possessed by a demon. And [3]having [4]been [5]cast [6]out
τοῦ δαιμονίου, ἐλάλησεν ὁ κωφός· καὶ ἐθαύμασαν οἱ ὄχλοι,
[1]the [2]demon, [3]spake [1]the [2]dumb. And [3]wondered [1]the [2]crowds,
λέγοντες, [q]"Ὅτι" οὐδέποτε ἐφάνη οὕτως ἐν τῷ Ἰσραήλ. 34 Οἱ.δὲ
saying, Never was it seen thus in Israel. But the
Φαρισαῖοι ἔλεγον, Ἐν τῷ ἄρχοντι τῶν δαιμονίων ἐκβάλλει
Pharisees said, By the prince of the demons he casts out
τὰ δαιμόνια.
the demons.

35 Καὶ περιῆγεν ὁ Ἰησοῦς τὰς πόλεις πάσας καὶ τὰς κώμας,
And [2]went [3]about [1]Jesus [5]the [6]cities [4]all and the villages,
διδάσκων ἐν ταῖς.συναγωγαῖς.αὐτῶν, καὶ κηρύσσων τὸ εὐαγ-
teaching in their synagogues, and proclaiming the glad
γέλιον τῆς βασιλείας, καὶ θεραπεύων πᾶσαν νόσον καὶ πᾶσαν
tidings of the kingdom, and healing every disease and every
μαλακίαν [r]ἐν τῷ λαῷ." 36 ἰδὼν.δὲ τοὺς ὄχλους, ἐ-
bodily weakness among the people. And having seen the crowds he was
σπλαγχνίσθη περὶ αὐτῶν, ὅτι ἦσαν [s]ἐκλελυμένοι" καὶ
moved with compassion for them, because they were wearied and
[t]ἐρριμμένοι" [v]ὡσεὶ" πρόβατα μὴ ἔχοντα ποιμένα. 37 τότε λέγει
cast away as sheep not having a shepherd. Then he says
τοῖς.μαθηταῖς.αὐτοῦ, Ὁ μὲν θερισμὸς πολύς, οἱ.δὲ ἐργάται
to his disciples, The [2]indeed [1]harvest [is] great, but the workmen
ὀλίγοι· 38 δεήθητε οὖν τοῦ κυρίου τοῦ θερισμοῦ, ὅπως
[are] few; supplicate therefore the Lord of the harvest, that
ἐκβάλῃ ἐργάτας εἰς τὸν.θερισμὸν.αὐτοῦ.
he may send out workmen into his harvest.

10 Καὶ προσκαλεσάμενος τοὺς δώδεκα μαθητὰς αὐτοῦ,
And having called to [him] [2]twelve [3]disciples [1]his
ἔδωκεν αὐτοῖς ἐξουσίαν πνευμάτων ἀκαθάρτων, ὥστε
he gave to them authority over [2]spirits [1]unclean, so as
ἐκβάλλειν αὐτά, καὶ θεραπεύειν πᾶσαν νόσον καὶ πᾶσαν
to cast out them, and to heal every disease and every
[u]μαλακίαν.
bodily weakness.

2 Τῶν.δὲ δώδεκα ἀποστόλων τὰ ὀνόματά ἐστιν ταῦτα·
Now of the twelve apostles the names are these:
πρῶτος Σίμων ὁ λεγόμενος Πέτρος, καὶ Ἀνδρέας ὁ ἀδελφὸς
first Simon who is called Peter, and Andrew [2]brother
αὐτοῦ· [w]Ἰάκωβος ὁ τοῦ Ζεβεδαίου, καὶ Ἰωάννης ὁ ἀδελφὸς
[1]his; James the [son] of Zebedee, and John [2]brother
αὐτοῦ· 3 Φίλιππος, καὶ Βαρθολομαῖος· Θωμᾶς, καὶ [x]Ματθαῖος"
[1]his; Philip, and Bartholomew; Thomas, and Matthew
ὁ τελώνης· Ἰάκωβος ὁ τοῦ Ἀλφαίου, καὶ [y]Λεββαῖος ὁ
the tax-gatherer; James the [son] of Alphæus, and Lebbæus who
ἐπικληθεὶς Θαδδαῖος·" 4 Σίμων ὁ [z]Κανανίτης," καὶ Ἰούδας
was surnamed Thaddæus; Simon the Canaanite, and Judas
[a][b]Ἰσκαριώτης," ὁ καὶ παραδοὺς αὐτόν.
Iscariote, who also delivered up him.

5 Τούτους τοὺς δώδεκα ἀπέστειλεν ὁ Ἰησοῦς, παραγγείλας
These twelve [2]sent [3]forth [1]Jesus, having charged
αὐτοῖς, λέγων, Εἰς ὁδὸν ἐθνῶν μὴ.ἀπέλθητε, καὶ εἰς
them, saying, Into [the] way of the Gentiles go not off, and into
πόλιν [c]Σαμαρειτῶν" μὴ.εἰσέλθητε· 6 πορεύεσθε.δὲ μᾶλλον
a city of [the] Samaritans enter not; but go rather
πρὸς τὰ πρόβατα τὰ ἀπολωλότα οἴκου Ἰσραήλ. 7 πο-
to the sheep the lost of [the] house of Israel. [2]Go-
ρευόμενοι.δὲ κηρύσσετε, λέγοντες, Ὅτι ἤγγικεν ἡ βασιλεία
ing [1]and proclaim, saying, Has drawn near the kingdom
τῶν οὐρανῶν. 8 ἀσθενοῦντας θεραπεύετε, [d]λεπροὺς καθαρί-
of the heavens. Sick heal, lepers cleanse,
ζετε, νεκροὺς ἐγείρετε," δαιμόνια ἐκβάλλετε. δωρεὰν ἐλάβετε,
dead raise, demons cast out: gratuitously ye received,

28 And coming into the house, the blind
ones came to Him. And Jesus said to them,
Do you believe that I am able to do this?
They said to Him, Yes, Lord.
29 Then He touched their eyes, saying, Let
it be done to you according to your faith.
30 And their eyes were opened. And Jesus
strictly commanded them, saying, See that
you let no one know it.
31 But after they left, they made Him
known in all that land.

32 And as they were going out, behold! They
brought Him a man dumb, demon-possessed.
33 And when the demon had been thrown
out, the dumb one spoke. And the multitudes marveled, saying, Never was it seen
like this in Israel.
34 But the Pharisees said, He throws out
demons by the prince of demons.

35 And Jesus went about all the cities and
villages, teaching in their synagogues and
preaching the gospel of the kingdom. And
He was healing every sickness and weakness
of body among the people.
36 And seeing the crowds, He was moved
with compassion for them because they were
tired and scattered as sheep having no
shepherd.
37 Then He said to His disciples, The harvest truly is great, but the workers few.
38 Pray then that the Lord of the harvest
may send out workers into His harvest.

CHAPTER 10

1 And calling His twelve disciples, He gave
to them authority over unclean spirits so as
to throw them out, also *power* to heal every
disease and every weakness of body.

2 Now the names of the twelve disciples are
these: The first, Simon, who is called Peter;
and Andrew his brother – James the son of
Zeb-e-dee, and his brother John –
3 Philip and Bar-thol-o-mew – Thomas and
Matthew the tax-collector – James the son
of Al-phe-us, and Leb-be-us whose last name
was Thad-de-us –
4 Simon the Canaanite and Judas Is-car-i-ot
who also betrayed Him.

5 Jesus sent out these twelve, commanding
them, saying, Do not go into the way of the
Gentiles. And do not enter into a city of the
Sa-mar-i-tans.
6 But go rather to the lost sheep of the
house of Israel.
7 And as you go, preach, saying, The
kingdom of Heaven has drawn near.
8 Heal the sick, cleanse the lepers, raise the
dead, throw out demons. You have freely

δωρεὰν δότε. 9 Μὴ-κτήσησθε χρυσόν, μηδὲ ἄργυρον, μηδὲ
gratuitously impart. Provide not gold, nor silver, nor

χαλκὸν εἰς τὰς.ζώνας.ὑμῶν, 10 μὴ πήραν εἰς ὁδόν, μηδὲ
money in your belts, nor provision-bag for [the] way, nor

δύο χιτῶνας, μηδὲ ὑποδήματα, μηδὲ [e]ῥάβδον·ǁ ἄξιος.γὰρ ὁ
two tunics, nor sandals, nor a staff: for worthy the

ἐργάτης τῆς.τροφῆς.αὐτοῦ [f]ἐστιν.ǁ 11 Εἰς.ἣν.δ'.ἂν πόλιν ἢ
workman of his food is. And into whatever city or

κώμην εἰσέλθητε, ἐξετάσατε τίς ἐν αὐτῇ ἄξιός ἐστιν· κἀκεῖ
village ye enter, inquire who in it worthy is, and there

μείνατε, ἕως.ἂν ἐξέλθητε. 12 εἰσερχόμενοι.δὲ εἰς τὴν οἰκίαν,
remain until ye go forth. But entering into the house,

ἀσπάσασθε αὐτήν. 13 καὶ ἐὰν μὲν ᾖ ἡ οἰκία ἀξία, [g]ἐλθέτωǁ
salute it: and if indeed [3]be [1]the [2]house worthy, let come

ἡ.εἰρήνη.ὑμῶν ἐπ' αὐτήν· ἐὰν.δὲ μὴ.ᾖ ἀξία, ἡ.εἰρήνη.ὑμῶν
your peace upon it; but if it be not worthy, [1]your [2]peace

πρὸς ὑμᾶς ἐπιστραφήτω. 14 καὶ ὃς.[h]ἐὰνǁ μὴ.δέξηται ὑμᾶς,
[5]to [6]you [3]let [4]return. And whoever will not receive you,

μηδὲ ἀκούσῃ τοὺς.λόγους.ὑμῶν, ἐξερχόμενοι [i]τῆς οἰκίας ἢ τῆς
nor will hear your words, going forth of [that] house or

πόλεως ἐκείνης, ἐκτινάξατε τὸν κονιορτὸν [k]τῶν.ποδῶν.ὑμῶν.
[2]city [1]that, shake off the dust of your feet.

15 ἀμὴν λέγω ὑμῖν, ἀνεκτότερον ἔσται γῇ Σοδόμων
Verily I say to you, More tolerable it shall be for [the] land of Sodom

καὶ [l]Γομόῤῥωνǁ ἐν ἡμέρᾳ κρίσεως, ἢ τῇ.πόλει.ἐκείνῃ. 16 Ἰδού,
and of Gomorrha in day of judgment, than for that city. Lo,

ἐγὼ ἀποστέλλω ὑμᾶς ὡς πρόβατα ἐν μέσῳ λύκων· γίνεσθε
I send forth you as sheep in [the] midst of wolves: be ye

οὖν φρόνιμοι ὡς οἱ ὄφεις, καὶ ἀκέραιοι ὡς αἱ περιστεραί.
therefore prudent as the serpents, and harmless as the doves.

17 προσέχετε.δὲ ἀπὸ τῶν ἀνθρώπων· παραδώσουσιν.γὰρ ὑμᾶς
But beware of men; for they will deliver you

εἰς συνέδρια, καὶ ἐν ταῖς.συναγωγαῖς.αὐτῶν μαστιγώσουσιν
to sanhedrims, and in their synagogues they will scourge

ὑμᾶς· 18 καὶ ἐπὶ ἡγεμόνας δὲ καὶ βασιλεῖς ἀχθήσεσθε
you: and before governors also and kings ye shall be brought

ἕνεκεν ἐμοῦ, εἰς μαρτύριον αὐτοῖς καὶ τοῖς ἔθνεσιν.
on account of me, for a testimony to them and to the nations.

19 ὅταν.δὲ [l]παραδιδῶσινǁ ὑμᾶς, μὴ.μεριμνήσητε πῶς ἢ τί
But when they deliver up you, be not careful how or what

λαλήσητε· [m]δοθήσεται.γὰρ ὑμῖν ἐν ἐκείνῃ τῇ ὥρᾳ τί [n]λαλή-
ye should speak: for it shall be given you in that hour what ye shall

σετε·ǁ 20 οὐ.γὰρ ὑμεῖς ἐστε οἱ λαλοῦντες, ἀλλὰ τὸ πνεῦμα
speak: for [3]not [1]ye [2]are they who speak, but the Spirit

τοῦ.πατρὸς.ὑμῶν τὸ λαλοῦν ἐν ὑμῖν. 21 Παραδώσει.δὲ
of your Father which speaks in you. But [2]will [3]deliver [4]up

ἀδελφὸς ἀδελφὸν εἰς θάνατον, καὶ πατὴρ τέκνον· καὶ ἐπανα-
[1]brother brother to death; and father child: and [2]will

στήσονται τέκνα ἐπὶ γονεῖς, καὶ θανατώσουσιν αὐτούς.
[3]rise [4]up [1]children against parents, and will put to death them.

22 καὶ ἔσεσθε μισούμενοι ὑπὸ πάντων διὰ τὸ.ὄνομά.μου·
And ye will be hated by all on account of my name;

ὁ.δὲ ὑπομείνας εἰς τέλος, οὗτος σωθήσεται. 23 ὅταν.δὲ
but he that endures to [the] end, he shall be saved. But when

διώκωσιν ὑμᾶς ἐν τῇ.πόλει.ταύτῃ, φεύγετε εἰς [o]τὴν.ἄλλην·ǁ [p]
they persecute you in this city, flee to another:

ἀμὴν.γὰρ λέγω ὑμῖν, οὐ.μὴ τελέσητε τὰς πόλεις
for verily I say to you, In no wise will ye have completed the cities

[q]τοῦǁ Ἰσραὴλ ἕως.[r]ἂνǁ ἔλθῃ ὁ υἱὸς τοῦ ἀνθρώπου. 24 Οὐκ
of Israel until be come the Son of man. [4]Not

ἔστιν μαθητὴς ὑπὲρ τὸν διδάσκαλον, οὐδὲ δοῦλος ὑπὲρ
[3]is [1]a [2]disciple above the teacher, nor a bondman above

τὸν.κύριον.αὐτοῦ. 25 ἀρκετὸν τῷ μαθητῇ ἵνα γένηται ὡς
his lord. Sufficient for the disciple that he become as

ὁ.διδάσκαλος.αὐτοῦ, καὶ ὁ δοῦλος ὡς ὁ.κύριος.αὐτοῦ. εἰ [s]τὸν
his teacher, and the bondman as his lord. If [3]the

οἰκοδεσπότηνǁ Βεελζεβοὺλ [t]ἐκάλεσαν,ǁ πόσῳ μᾶλλον
[4]master [5]of [6]the [7]house [8]Beelzebul [1]they [2]called, how much more

[v]τοὺς οἰκιακοὺςǁ.αὐτοῦ; 26 Μὴ οὖν φοβηθῆτε αὐτούς
those of his household? [3]Not [4]therefore [1]ye [2]should fear them;

οὐδὲν.γάρ ἐστιν κεκαλυμμένον ὃ οὐκ.ἀποκαλυφθήσεται·
for nothing is covered which shall not be uncovered,

καὶ κρυπτὸν ὃ οὐ.γνωσθήσεται. 27 ὃ λέγω ὑμῖν ἐν τῇ
and hidden which shall not be known. What I tell you in the

σκοτίᾳ εἴπατε ἐν τῷ φωτί· καὶ ὃ εἰς τὸ οὖς ἀκούετε κη-
darkness speak in the light; and what in the ear ye hear pro-

ρύξατε ἐπὶ τῶν δωμάτων. 28 καὶ [w]μὴ.φοβηθῆτεǁ ἀπὸ
claim upon the housetops. And ye should not fear because of

τῶν [x]ἀποκτεινόντωνǁ τὸ σῶμα, τὴν.δὲ ψυχὴν μὴ.δυναμένων
those who kill the body, but the soul are not able

ἀποκτεῖναι· [y]φοβήθητε.ǁδὲ μᾶλλον τὸν δυνάμενον [z]καὶǁ
to kill; but ye should fear rather him who is able both

received, freely give.

9 Do not take either gold or silver or money in your purses –

10 nor a bag for the road, nor two coats, nor shoes, nor a staff. For the worker is worthy of his food.

11 And into whatever city or village you enter, ask who in it is worthy. And stay there until you leave.

12 And when you come into the house, greet it.

13 And if the house is truly worthy, let your peace come on it. But if it is not worthy, let your peace return to you.

14 And whoever will not receive you or hear your words, when *you* come out of that house or city, shake off the dust from your feet.

15 Truly I say to you that it shall be more bearable for the land of Sodom and Go-mor-rah in the day of judgment than for that city.

16 Behold! I send you out as sheep in the midst of wolves. Therefore be wise as serpents and harmless as doves.

17 But beware of men. For they will deliver you to the sanhedrins, and they will beat you in their synagogues.

18 And also you shall be brought before governors and kings for My sake, as a witness to them and to the Gentiles.

19 But when they deliver you up, do not be anxious how or what you should speak. For it shall be given you in that hour what you shall say.

20 For it is not you that speak, but the Spirit of your Father who speaks in you.

21 And brother will deliver up brother to death, and the father his child. And children will rise up against parents and will put them to death.

22 And you shall be hated by all on account of My name. But he that endures to the end is the one who shall be saved.

23 But when they persecute you in this city, flee into another. For truly I say to you, you will not have finished the cities of Israel until the Son of man has come.

24 The disciple is not above the teacher, nor a slave above his lord.

25 It is enough that the disciple become like his teacher and the slave like his lord. If they have called the Master of the house Be-el-ze-bub, how much more those of His household!

26 You should not fear them, then. For nothing is covered that shall not be uncovered, nor hidden which shall not become known.

27 What I tell you in the darkness, speak in the light. And what you hear in the ear, proclaim it on the housetops.

28 And you should not be afraid of those who kill the body but who are not able to kill the soul. But rather you should fear Him who is able to destroy both soul and body in

ψυχὴν καὶ σῶμα ἀπολέσαι ἐν γεέννῃ. 29 οὐχὶ δύο στρουθία
soul and body to destroy in Gehenna. [2]Not [3]two [4]sparrows
ἀσσαρίου πωλεῖται; καὶ ἓν ἐξ αὐτῶν οὐ.πεσεῖται ἐπὶ τὴν
[6]for [7]an [8]assarion [1]are [5]sold? and one of them shall not fall to the
γῆν ἄνευ τοῦ.πατρὸς.ὑμῶν· 30 ὑμῶν.δὲ καὶ αἱ τρίχες τῆς
ground without your Father. But of you even the hairs of the
κεφαλῆς πᾶσαι ἠριθμημέναι εἰσίν. 31 μὴ οὖν [a]φοβηθῆτε·[ll]
head all numbered are. [3]Not [2]therefore [1]ye [4]should [5]fear;
πολλῶν στρουθίων διαφέρετε ὑμεῖς. 32 Πᾶς οὖν ὅσ-
than many sparrows better are ye. Every one therefore whoso-
τις ὁμολογήσει ἐν ἐμοὶ ἔμπροσθεν τῶν ἀνθρώπων, ὁμολογήσω
ever shall confess me before men, [3]will [4]confess
κἀγὼ ἐν αὐτῷ ἔμπροσθεν τοῦ.πατρός.μου τοῦ ἐν [b] οὐρανοῖς
[2]also [1]I him before my Father who [is] in [the] heavens.
33 ὅστις.[c]δ' ἂν[ll] ἀρνήσηταί με ἔμπροσθεν τῶν ἀνθρώπων,
But whosoever shall deny me before men,
ἀρνήσομαι [d]αὐτὸν κἀγὼ[ll] ἔμπροσθεν τοῦ.πατρός.μου τοῦ ἐν
[3]will [4]deny [5]him [2]also [1]I before my Father who [is] in
[e] οὐρανοῖς. 34 Μὴ.νομίσητε ὅτι ἦλθον βαλεῖν εἰρήνην ἐπὶ
[the] heavens. Think not that I came to place peace on
τὴν γῆν· οὐκ.ἦλθον βαλεῖν εἰρήνην, ἀλλὰ μάχαιραν. 35 ἦλθον
the earth: I came not to place peace, but a sword. [2]I [3]came
γὰρ διχάσαι ἄνθρωπον κατὰ τοῦ.πατρὸς.αὐτοῦ, καὶ θυγα-
[1]for to set at variance a man against his father, and a daugh-
τέρα κατὰ τῆς.μητρὸς.αὐτῆς, καὶ νύμφην κατὰ τῆς πεν-
ter against her mother, and a daughter-in-law against [2]mother-
θερᾶς αὐτῆς· 36 καὶ ἐχθροὶ τοῦ.ἀνθρώπου οἱ οἰκιακοὶ
in-law [1]her. And enemies of the man [shall be] [2]household
αὐτοῦ. 37 Ὁ φιλῶν πατέρα ἢ μητέρα ὑπὲρ ἐμὲ οὐκ.ἔστιν
[1]his. He that loves father or mother above me is not
μου ἄξιος· καὶ ὁ φιλῶν υἱὸν ἢ θυγατέρα ὑπὲρ ἐμὲ οὐκ
of me worthy; and he that loves son or daughter above me [2]not
ἔστιν μου ἄξιος· 38 καὶ ὃς οὐ.λαμβάνει τὸν.σταυρὸν.αὐτοῦ
[1]is of me worthy. And he that takes not his cross
καὶ ἀκολουθεῖ ὀπίσω μου οὐκ ἔστιν μου ἄξιος. 39 ὁ εὑρὼν
and follows after me [2]not [1]is of me worthy. He that has found
τὴν.ψυχὴν.αὐτοῦ ἀπολέσει αὐτήν· καὶ ὁ ἀπολέσας τὴν
his life shall lose it; and he that has lost
ψυχὴν αὐτοῦ ἕνεκεν ἐμοῦ εὑρήσει αὐτήν. 40 Ὁ δεχόμενος
[2]life [1]his on account of me shall find it. He that receives
ὑμᾶς ἐμὲ δέχεται· καὶ ὁ ἐμὲ δεχόμενος δέχεται τὸν ἀπο-
you me receives; and he that me receives receives him who sent
στείλαντά με. 41 ὁ δεχόμενος προφήτην εἰς ὄνομα προ-
me. He that receives a prophet in [the] name of a
φήτου μισθὸν προφήτου [f]λήψεται·[ll] καὶ ὁ δεχόμενος
prophet [the] reward of a prophet shall receive; and he that receives
δίκαιον εἰς ὄνομα δικαίου μισθὸν δικαίου
a righteous [man] in [the] name of a righteous [man] the reward of a righteous
[f]λήψεται.[ll] 42 καὶ ὃς.[g]ἐὰν[ll] ποτίσῃ ἕνα τῶν μικρῶν
[man] shall receive. And whoever shall give to drink to one [2]little [1]ones
τούτων ποτήριον ψυχροῦ μόνον εἰς ὄνομα μαθητοῦ,
[3]of [4]these a cup of cold [water] only in [the] name of a disciple,
ἀμὴν λέγω ὑμῖν, οὐ.μὴ ἀπολέσῃ τὸν.μισθὸν.αὐτοῦ.
verily I say to you, in nowise shall he lose his reward.

11 Καὶ ἐγένετο ὅτε ἐτέλεσεν ὁ Ἰησοῦς διατάσσων τοῖς
And it came to pass when [2]had [3]finished [1]Jesus commanding
δώδεκα μαθηταῖς αὐτοῦ, μετέβη ἐκεῖθεν τοῦ διδάσκειν καὶ
[2]twelve [3]disciples [1]his, he departed thence to teach and
κηρύσσειν ἐν ταῖς.πόλεσιν.αὐτῶν.
to preach in their cities.

2 Ὁ.δὲ.Ἰωάννης ἀκούσας ἐν τῷ δεσμωτηρίῳ τὰ ἔργα τοῦ
Now John having heard in the prison the works of the
χριστοῦ, πέμψας [h]δύο[ll] τῶν.μαθητῶν.αὐτοῦ, 3 εἶπεν αὐτῷ,
Christ, having sent two of his disciples, said to him,
Σὺ.εἶ ὁ ἐρχόμενος, ἢ ἕτερον προσδοκῶμεν; 4 Καὶ ἀποκρι-
Art thou the coming [one], or another are we to look for? And [2]answer-
θεὶς ὁ Ἰησοῦς εἶπεν αὐτοῖς, Πορευθέντες ἀπαγγείλατε Ἰωάννῃ
ing [1]Jesus said to them, Having gone relate to John
ἃ ἀκούετε καὶ βλέπετε· 5 τυφλοὶ ἀναβλέπουσιν, [i]καὶ[ll]
what ye hear and see: blind receive sight, and
χωλοὶ περιπατοῦσιν· λεπροὶ καθαρίζονται, [k]καὶ[ll] κωφοὶ
lame walk; lepers are cleansed, and deaf
ἀκούουσιν· [l]νεκροὶ ἐγείρονται, [k]καὶ[ll] πτωχοὶ εὐαγγελίζονται·
hear; dead are raised, and poor are evangelized.
6 καὶ μακάριός ἐστιν, ὃς.[m]ἐὰν[ll] μὴ.σκανδαλισθῇ ἐν ἐμοί.
And blessed is, whoever shall not be offended in me.

7 Τούτων.δὲ πορευομένων ἤρξατο ὁ Ἰησοῦς λέγειν τοῖς
But as these were going [2]began [1]Jesus to say to the
ὄχλοις περὶ Ἰωάννου, Τί [n]ἐξήλθετε[ll] εἰς τὴν ἔρημον
crowds concerning John, What went ye out into the wilderness
θεάσασθαι; κάλαμον ὑπὸ ἀνέμου σαλευόμενον; 8 ἀλλὰ
to look at? a reed by [the] wind shaken? But

hell.
29 Are not two sparrows sold for a penny.
Yet not one of them shall fall to the ground
except the Father wills *it*.
30 Even the very hairs of your head are all
number.
31 You should not fear, then, for you are of
more value than many sparrows.
32 Therefore, everyone who shall confess
Me before men, I will also confess him
before My Father who is in Heaven.
33 But whoever shall deny Me before men, I
will also deny him before My Father who is
in Heaven.
34 Do not think that I have come to bring
peace on earth. I did not come to bring
peace, but a sword.
35 For I came to set a man against his
father – and a daughter against her mother
– and the daughter-in-law against her
mother-in-law.
36 And a man's enemies *shall be from* his
own household.
37 He that loves father or mother more
than Me is not worthy of Me! And he that
loves son or daughter more than Me is not
worthy of Me!
38 And he that does not take his cross and
follow after Me is not worthy of Me!
39 He that has found his life shall lose it.
And he that has lost his life on account of
Me shall find it.
40 He that receives you receives Me. And he
that receives Me receives Him who sent Me.
41 He that receives a prophet in the name
of a prophet shall receive a prophet's reward
– and he that receives a righteous man in the
name of a righteous man shall receive a
righteous man's reward.
42 And whoever shall give to one of these
little ones only a cup of cold *water* to drink
in the name of a disciple, truly I say to you
that he shall in no way lose his reward!

CHAPTER 11

1 And when Jesus had finished commanding
His twelve disciples, He left there in order to
teach and to preach in their cities.
2 Now hearing in the prison of the works of
the Christ, John sent two of his disciples.
3 They said to Him, Are You the One who
is to come? Or are we to look for another?
4 And Jesus answered, saying to them, Go!
Tell John what you hear and see:
5 The blind receive sight and the lame walk.
Lepers are cleansed and the deaf hear. *The*
dead are raised and the poor have the gospel
preached to them.
6 And blessed is he who shall not be offended in Me.
7 And as these were going away, Jesus
began to say to the multitude concerning
John – What did you go out into the wilderness to see, a reed shaken with the wind?
8 But what did you go out to see, a man

τί [n]ἐξήλθετε‖ ἰδεῖν; ἄνθρωπον ἐν μαλακοῖς [o]ἱματίοις‖ ἠμφιεσ-
what went ye out to see? a man in soft garments ar-
μένον; ἰδού, οἱ τὰ μαλακὰ φοροῦντες ἐν τοῖς οἴκοις
rayed? Behold, those who the soft [garments] wear in the houses
τῶν βασιλέων [p]εἰσίν.‖ 9 ἀλλὰ τί [q]ἐξήλθετε‖ [q]ἰδεῖν; προ-
of kings are. But what went ye out to see? a pro-
φήτην;‖ ναί, λέγω ὑμῖν, καὶ περισσότερον προφήτου.
phet? Yea, I say to you, and [one] more excellent than a prophet.
10 οὗτος [r]γάρ‖ ἐστιν περὶ οὗ γέγραπται, Ἰδού, [s]ἐγὼ‖
For this is [he] concerning whom it has been written, Behold, I
ἀποστέλλω τὸν ἄγγελόν μου πρὸ προσώπου σου, [t]ὃς‖ κατα-
send my messenger before thy face, who shall
σκευάσει τὴν ὁδόν σου ἔμπροσθέν σου. 11 Ἀμὴν λέγω ὑμῖν,
prepare thy way before thee. Verily I say to you,
οὐκ ἐγήγερται ἐν γεννητοῖς γυναικῶν μείζων Ἰωάννου
there has not risen among [those] born of women a greater than John
τοῦ βαπτιστοῦ· ὁ δὲ μικρότερος ἐν τῇ βασιλείᾳ τῶν
the Baptist. But he that [is] less in the kingdom of the
οὐρανῶν μείζων [v]αὐτοῦ ἐστιν.‖ 12 ἀπὸ δὲ τῶν ἡμερῶν Ἰωάννου
heavens greater than he is. But from the days of John
τοῦ βαπτιστοῦ ἕως ἄρτι, ἡ βασιλεία τῶν οὐρανῶν βιά-
the Baptist until now, the kingdom of the heavens is taken by
ζεται, καὶ βιασταὶ ἁρπάζουσιν αὐτήν. 13 πάντες γὰρ οἱ
violence, and [the] violent seize it. For all the
προφῆται καὶ ὁ νόμος ἕως Ἰωάννου [w]προεφήτευσαν.‖ 14 καὶ
prophets and the law [2]until [3]John [1]prophesied. And
εἰ θέλετε δέξασθαι, αὐτός ἐστιν [x]Ἠλίας‖ ὁ μέλλων ἔρχεσθαι.
if ye are willing to receive [it], he is Elias who is about to come.
15 ὁ ἔχων ὦτα [y]ἀκούειν,‖ ἀκουέτω. 16 Τίνι δὲ ὁμοιώσω
He that has ears to hear, let him hear. But to what shall I liken
τὴν γενεὰν ταύτην; ὁμοία ἐστὶν [z]παιδαρίοις‖ [a]ἐν ἀγοραῖς
this generation? [3]like [1]it [2]is to little children in [the] markets
καθημένοις,‖ [b]καὶ προσφωνοῦσιν τοῖς ἑταίροις αὐτῶν, 17 καὶ
sitting, and calling to their companions, and
λέγουσιν,‖ Ηὐλήσαμεν ὑμῖν, καὶ οὐκ ὠρχήσασθε· ἐθρηνήσαμεν
saying, We piped to you, and ye did not dance; we mourned
[c]ὑμῖν,‖ καὶ οὐκ ἐκόψασθε. 18 [d]Ἦλθεν γὰρ Ἰωάννης μήτε ἐσθίων
to you, and ye did not wail. For [2]came [1]John neither eating
μήτε πίνων, καὶ λέγουσιν, Δαιμόνιον ἔχει. 19 ἦλθεν ὁ υἱὸς
nor drinking, and they say, A demon he has. [5]Came [1]the [2]Son
τοῦ ἀνθρώπου ἐσθίων καὶ πίνων, καὶ λέγουσιν, Ἰδού,
[3]of [4]man eating and drinking, and they say, Behold,
ἄνθρωπος φάγος καὶ οἰνοπότης, τελωνῶν φίλος καὶ
a man a glutton and a wine bibber, of tax-gatherers a friend and
ἁμαρτωλῶν. καὶ ἐδικαιώθη ἡ σοφία ἀπὸ τῶν [d]τέκνων‖ αὐτῆς.
of sinners. And [2]was [3]justified [1]wisdom by [2]children [1]her.
20 Τότε ἤρξατο ὀνειδίζειν τὰς πόλεις ἐν αἷς ἐγένοντο
Then he began to reproach the cities in which had taken place
αἱ πλεῖσται δυνάμεις αὐτοῦ, ὅτι οὐ μετενόησαν. 21 Οὐαί
the most of his works of power, because they repented not. Woe
σοι, [e]Χοραζίν·‖ οὐαί σοι, [f]Βηθσαϊδάν·‖ ὅτι εἰ ἐν Τύρῳ καὶ
to thee, Chorazin! woe to thee, Bethsaida! for if in Tyre and
Σιδῶνι ἐγένοντο αἱ δυνάμεις αἱ γενόμεναι ἐν ὑμῖν,
Sidon had taken place the works of power which have taken place in you,
πάλαι ἂν ἐν σάκκῳ καὶ σποδῷ μετενόησαν. 22 πλὴν λέγω
long ago in sackcloth and ashes they had repented. But I say
ὑμῖν, Τύρῳ καὶ Σιδῶνι ἀνεκτότερον ἔσται ἐν ἡμέρᾳ κρίσεως
to you, For Tyre and Sidon more tolerable shall it be in day of judgment
ἢ ὑμῖν. 23 Καὶ σύ, [g]Καπερναούμ,‖ [h]ἡ‖ ἕως [i]τοῦ‖ οὐρανοῦ
than for you. And thou, Capernaum, who to the heaven
[k]ὑψωθεῖσα,‖ ἕως ᾅδου [l]καταβιβασθήσῃ·‖ ὅτι εἰ ἐν Σοδό-
hast been lifted up, to hades shalt be brought down: for if in Sod-
μοις [m]ἐγένοντο‖ αἱ δυνάμεις αἱ [n]γενόμεναι ἐν σοί,‖
om had taken place the works of power which have taken place in thee,
[o]ἔμειναν‖ ἂν μέχρι τῆς σήμερον. 24 πλὴν λέγω ὑμῖν, ὅτι
it had remained until to-day. But I say to you, that
γῇ Σοδόμων ἀνεκτότερον ἔσται ἐν ἡμέρᾳ κρίσεως
for [the] land of Sodom more tolerable shall it be in day of judgment
ἢ σοί.
than for thee.
25 Ἐν ἐκείνῳ τῷ καιρῷ ἀποκριθεὶς ὁ Ἰησοῦς εἶπεν, Ἐξομο-
At that time answering Jesus said, I
λογοῦμαί σοι, πάτερ, κύριε τοῦ οὐρανοῦ καὶ τῆς γῆς, ὅτι
praise thee, O Father, Lord of the heaven and the earth, that
[p]ἀπέκρυψας‖ ταῦτα ἀπὸ σοφῶν καὶ συνετῶν, καὶ ἀπεκάλυψας
thou didst hide these things from wise and prudent, and didst reveal
αὐτὰ νηπίοις. 26 ναί, ὁ πατήρ, ὅτι οὕτως [q]ἐγένετο εὐδοκία‖
them to babes. Yea, Father, for thus it was well-pleasing
ἔμπροσθέν σου. 27 Πάντα μοι παρεδόθη ὑπὸ τοῦ πατρός μου·
before thee. All things to me were delivered by my Father.
καὶ οὐδεὶς ἐπιγινώσκει τὸν υἱὸν εἰ μὴ ὁ πατήρ· οὐδὲ τὸν
And no one knows the Son except the Father; nor the

clothed in soft clothing? Behold! They that
wear soft things are in the houses of kings.
9 But what did you go out to see, a
prophet? Yes, I say to you, and one more
excellent than a prophet.
10 For this is *he* of whom it has been
written, "Behold! I send My messenger
before Your face, who shall prepare Your
way before You."
11 Truly I say to you, There has not ever
risen among those born of women any
greater than John the Baptist. But he that is
least in the kingdom of Heaven is greater than
he.
12 And from the days of John the Baptist
until now, the kingdom of Heaven is taken by
violence, and the violent take it by force.
13 For all the Prophets and the Law
prophesied until John.
14 And if you are willing to receive it, he is
Elijah who is to come.
15 He that has ears to hear, let him hear.
16 But to what shall I compare this generation? It is like little children sitting in the
markets and calling to their playmates,
17 saying, We played the flute to you, and
you did not dance! We mourned to you, but
you did not wail!
18 For John came neither eating nor
drinking and they say, He has a demon.
19 The Son of man came eating and
drinking and they say, Look! A gluttonous
man and a wine-drinker, a friend of tax-
collectors and sinners. But wisdom was
justified by her children.
20 Then He began to shame the cities in
which most of His mighty works had taken
place, because they did not repent.
21 Woe to you, Cho-ra-zin! Woe to you,
Beth-sa-i-da! For if the mighty works which
have taken place in you had happened in
Tyre and Sidon, they would have repented
long ago in sackcloth and ashes.
22 But I say to you, It shall be more
bearable for Tyre and Sidon in the day of
judgment than for you.
23 And you, Capernaum, who have been
lifted up to Heaven, shall be brought down
into hell. For if the mighty works which
have taken place in you had happened in
Sodom, it would have remained until this
day.
24 But I say to you that it shall be more
bearable for the land of Sodom in the day of
judgment than for you.
25 Answering at that time, Jesus said,
Thank You, O Father, Lord of Heaven and
earth, because You have hidden these things
from the sophisticated and cunning and have
revealed them to babes.
26 Even so, Father, for so it seemed good in
Your sight.
27 All things were delivered to Me by My
Father. And no one knows the Son except the
Father – nor does anyone know the Father

πατέρα τις ἐπιγινώσκει εἰ.μὴ ὁ υἱός, καὶ ᾧ.ἐὰν
Father 3any 2one 1does know except the Son, and he to whomsoever
βούληται ὁ υἱὸς ἀποκαλύψαι. 28 Δεῦτε πρός με, πάντες
3may 4will 1the 2Son to reveal [him]. Come to me, all
οἱ κοπιῶντες καὶ πεφορτισμένοι, κἀγὼ ἀναπαύσω ὑμᾶς.
ye that labour and are burdened, and I will give 2rest 1you.
29 ἄρατε τὸν.ζυγόν.μου ἐφ' ὑμᾶς, καὶ μάθετε ἀπ' ἐμοῦ, ὅτι
Take my yoke upon you, and learn from me, for
rπρᾷός" εἰμι καὶ ταπεινὸς τῇ.καρδίᾳ· καὶ εὑρήσετε ἀνάπαυσιν
meek I am and lowly in heart; and ye shall find rest
ταῖς.ψυχαῖς.ὑμῶν. 30 ὁ.γὰρ.ζυγός.μου χρηστὸς καὶ τὸ φορτίον
to your souls. For my yoke easy and 2burden
μου ἐλαφρόν ἐστιν.
1my light is.

12 Ἐν ἐκείνῳ τῷ καιρῷ ἐπορεύθη ὁ Ἰησοῦς τοῖς sσάββασιν"
At that time went Jesus on the Sabbath
διὰ τῶν σποριμων· οἱ.δὲ.μαθηταὶ.αὐτοῦ ἐπείνασαν, καὶ
through the corn-fields; and his disciples were hungry, and
ἤρξαντο τίλλειν στάχυας καὶ ἐσθίειν. 2 οἱ.δὲ Φαρισαῖοι
began to pluck [the] ears and to eat. But the Pharisees
ἰδόντες tεἶπον" αὐτῷ, Ἰδού, οἱ.μαθηταί.σου ποιοῦσιν ὃ
having seen said to him, Behold, thy disciples are doing what
οὐκ.ἔξεστιν ποιεῖν ἐν σαββάτῳ. 3 Ὁ.δὲ εἶπεν αὐτοῖς, Οὐκ
it is not lawful to do on sabbath. But he said to them, 2Not
ἀνέγνωτε τί ἐποίησεν vΔαβίδ," ὅτε ἐπείνασεν wαὐτὸς" καὶ
3ye 1have read what 2did 1David, when he hungered himself and
οἱ μετ' αὐτοῦ; 4 πῶς εἰσῆλθεν εἰς τὸν οἶκον τοῦ θεοῦ, καὶ
those with him? How he entered into the house of God, and
τοὺς ἄρτους τῆς προθέσεως xἔφαγεν," yοὓς" οὐκ ἐξὸν ἦν
the loaves of the presentation he ate, which 3not 4lawful 1it 2was
αὐτῷ φαγεῖν, οὐδὲ τοῖς μετ' αὐτοῦ, εἰ.μὴ τοῖς ἱερεῦσιν μόνοις;
for him to eat, nor for those with him, but for the priests only?
5 Ἢ οὐκ.ἀνέγνωτε ἐν τῷ νόμῳ, ὅτι τοῖς σάββασιν οἱ ἱερεῖς
Or have ye not read in the law, that on the sabbaths the priests
ἐν τῷ ἱερῷ τὸ σάββατον βεβηλοῦσιν, καὶ ἀναίτιοί εἰσιν;
in the temple the sabbath profane, and guiltless are?
6 λέγω.δὲ ὑμῖν, ὅτι τοῦ.ἱεροῦ zμείζων" ἐστὶν ὧδε. 7 εἰ.δὲ
But I say to you, that 3than 4the 5temple 1a 2greater is here. But if
ἐγνώκειτε τί ἐστιν, aἜλεον" θέλω καὶ οὐ θυσίαν, οὐκ ἂν
ye had known what is, Mercy I desire and not sacrifice, 3not
κατεδικάσατε τοὺς ἀναιτίους· 8 κύριος.γάρ ἐστιν bκαὶ" τοῦ
1ye 2had condemned the guiltless. For Lord 5is 1also 2of 3the
σαββάτου ὁ υἱὸς τοῦ.ἀνθρώπου.
4sabbath the son of man.
9 Καὶ μεταβὰς ἐκεῖθεν, ἦλθεν εἰς τὴν.συναγωγὴν.αὐτῶν.
And having departed thence, he went into their synagogue.
10 καὶ ἰδού, ἄνθρωπος cἦν τὴν" χεῖρα ἔχων ξηράν· καὶ
And behold, a man there was 2the 3hand 1having withered. And
ἐπηρώτησαν αὐτόν, λέγοντες, Εἰ.ἔξεστιν τοῖς σάββασιν
they asked him, saying, Is it lawful on the sabbaths
dθεραπεύειν;" ἵνα κατηγορήσωσιν αὐτοῦ. 11 Ὁ.δὲ εἶπεν αὐτοῖς,
to heal? that they might accuse him. But he said to them,
Τίς eἔσται" ἐξ ὑμῶν ἄνθρωπος, ὃς ἕξει πρόβατον ἕν,
What 2shall 3there 4be 5of 6you 1man, who shall have 2sheep 1one,
καὶ ἐὰν ἐμπέσῃ τοῦτο τοῖς σάββασιν εἰς βόθυνον, οὐχὶ
and if 2fall 1this on the sabbaths into a pit, will not
κρατήσει αὐτὸ καὶ fἐγερεῖ;" 12 πόσῳ οὖν διαφέρει ἄν-
lay hold of it and will raise [it] up? How much then is 3better 1a
θρωπος προβάτου; ὥστε ἔξεστιν τοῖς.gσάββασιν" καλῶς
2man than a sheep? So that it is lawful on the sabbaths 3well
ποιεῖν. 13 Τότε λέγει τῷ.ἀνθρώπῳ, Ἔκτεινον hτὴν χεῖρά
1to 2do. Then he says to the man, Stretch out 2hand
σου." Καὶ ἐξέτεινεν, καὶ iἀποκατεστάθη" ὑγιὴς ὡς ἡ
1thy. And he stretched [it] out, and it was restored sound as the
ἄλλη.
other.
14 kΟἱ.δὲ Φαρισαῖοι συμβούλιον ἔλαβον κατ' αὐτοῦ ἐξελ-
But the Pharisees 5a 6council 4held 7against 8him 1having
θόντες," ὅπως αὐτὸν ἀπολέσωσιν. 15 Ὁ.δὲ.Ἰησοῦς γνοὺς
2gone 3out how him they might destroy. But Jesus having known
ἀνεχώρησεν ἐκεῖθεν· καὶ ἠκολούθησαν αὐτῷ lὄχλοι" πολλοί,
withdrew thence, and followed him 2crowds 1great,
καὶ ἐθεράπευσεν αὐτοὺς πάντας· 16 καὶ ἐπετίμησεν αὐτοῖς
and he healed them all, and strictly charged them
ἵνα μὴ φανερὸν αὐτὸν ποιήσωσιν· 17 mὅπως" πλη-
that 3not 6publicly 7known 5him 1they 2should 4make. So that might
ρωθῇ τὸ ῥηθὲν διὰ Ἡσαΐου τοῦ προφήτου, λέγοντος,
be fulfilled that which was spoken by Esaias the prophet, saying,
18 Ἰδοὺ ὁ.παῖς.μου ὃν nᾑρέτισα," ὁ.ἀγαπητός.μου oεἰς
Behold my servant whom I have chosen, my beloved in
ὃν" pεὐδόκησεν" ἡ.ψυχή.μου· θήσω τὸ.πνεῦμά.μου ἐπ'
whom 3has 4found 5delight 1my 2soul. I will put my Spirit upon

except the Son, and he to whom the Son may
decide to reveal *Him*.
28 Come to Me, all you that labor and are
heavy laden, and I will give you rest.
29 Take My yoke upon you and learn of Me
– for I am meek and lowly in heart, and you
shall find rest to your souls.
30 For My yoke is easy and My burden is
light.

CHAPTER 12

1 At that time Jesus went through the field of
grain on the Sabbath day. And His disciples
were hungry. And they began to pluck the
ears of grain and to eat.
2 But seeing this, the Pharisees said to Him,
Look! Your disciples are doing what it is not
lawful to do on the Sabbath day.
3 But He said to them, Have you never read
what David did when he himself and those
with him were hungry?
4 *Remember* how he went into the house of
God and ate the showbread, which it was not
lawful for him to eat, nor for those with him –
but *it was* only for the priests?
5 Or have you never read in the Law that the
priests in the Temple profane the Sabbath on
the sabbaths, and yet are not guilty?
6 But I say to you that One greater than the
Temple is here.
7 But if you had know what *this means*, "I
desire mercy and not sacrifice," you would
not have condemned those who are not guilty.
8 For the Son of man is Lord even of the
Sabbath.
9 And He left there and went into their
synagogue.
10 And behold! There was a man with a
withered hand! And they asked Him, saying,
Is it lawful to heal on the sabbaths? – so that
they might accuse Him.
11 But He said to them, What, shall there be a
man of you who shall have one sheep, and if it
falls into a pit on the sabbaths, will he not take
hold of it and lift it out?
12 How much better, then, is a man than a
sheep? So it is lawful to do well on the
sabbaths.
13 Then He said to the man, Stretch out
your hand! And he stretched it out. And it
was made whole again, just like the other.
14 But when they had gone out, the
Pharisees held a meeting against Him, as to
how they might destroy Him.
15 And knowing it, Jesus left there. And
great crowds followed Him. And He healed
them all.
16 And He strictly commanded them that
they should not publicize Him
17 so that it might be fulfilled which was
spoken through Isaiah the prophet, saying,
18 "Behold My Servant, whom I have
chosen, My Beloved in whom My soul has
found delight! I will put My Spirit on Him,
and He shall declare judgment to the Gen-

αὐτόν, καὶ κρίσιν τοῖς ἔθνεσιν ἀπαγγελεῖ· 19 οὐκ.ἐρίσει
him, and judgment to the nations he shall declare. He shall not strive
οὐδὲ κραυγάσει, οὐδὲ ἀκούσει τις ἐν ταῖς πλατείαις τὴν
nor cry out, nor shall [3]hear [1]any [2]one in the streets
φωνὴν.αὐτοῦ. 20 κάλαμον συντετριμμένον οὐ.κατεάξει, καὶ
his voice. A [2]reed [1]bruised he shall not break, and
λίνον τυφόμενον οὐ.σβέσει, ἕως.ἂν ἐκβάλῃ εἰς νῖκος τὴν
[2]flax [1]smoking he shall not quench, until he bring forth [3]unto [4]victory [1]the
κρίσιν. 21 καὶ [q]ἐν‖ τῷ.ὀνόματι.αὐτοῦ ἔθνη ἐλπιοῦσιν.
[2]judgment. And in his name [the] nations shall hope.
22 Τότε [r]προσηνέχθη‖ αὐτῷ [s]δαιμονιζόμενος, τυφλὸς
Then was brought to him one possessed by a demon, blind
καὶ κωφός·‖ καὶ ἐθεράπευσεν αὐτόν, ὥστε τὸν [t]τυφλὸν καὶ‖
and dumb, and he healed him, so that the blind and
κωφὸν [v]καὶ‖ λαλεῖν καὶ βλέπειν. 23 καὶ ἐξίσταντο πάντες
dumb both spake and saw. And [4]were [5]amazed [1]all
οἱ ὄχλοι καὶ ἔλεγον, Μήτι οὗτός ἐστιν ὁ υἱὸς [w]Δαβίδ;‖
[2]the [3]crowds and said, [2]This [1]is the son of David?
24 Οἱ.δὲ Φαρισαῖοι ἀκούσαντες εἶπον, Οὗτος οὐκ.ἐκβάλλει
But the Pharisees having heard said, This [man] casts not out
τὰ δαιμόνια εἰ.μὴ ἐν τῷ Βεελζεβοὺλ ἄρχοντι τῶν δαιμονίων.
the demons except by Beelzebul prince of the demons.
25 Εἰδὼς.δὲ [x]ὁ Ἰησοῦς‖ τὰς.ἐνθυμήσεις.αὐτῶν εἶπεν αὐτοῖς,
But [2]knowing [1]Jesus their thoughts he said to them,
Πᾶσα βασιλεία μερισθεῖσα καθ' ἑαυτῆς ἐρημοῦται· καὶ
Every kingdom divided against itself is brought to desolation, and
πᾶσα πόλις ἢ.οἰκία μερισθεῖσα καθ' ἑαυτῆς οὐ.σταθήσεται.
every city or house divided against itself will not stand.
26 καὶ εἰ ὁ σατανᾶς τὸν σατανᾶν ἐκβάλλει, ἐφ' ἑαυτὸν ἐμε-
And if Satan [3]Satan [1]casts [2]out, against himself he was
ρίσθη· πῶς οὖν σταθήσεται ἡ.βασιλεία.αὐτοῦ; 27 καὶ εἰ ἐγὼ
divided. How then will stand his kingdom? And if I
ἐν Βεελζεβοὺλ ἐκβάλλω τὰ δαιμόνια οἱ.υἱοὶ.ὑμῶν ἐν τίνι
by Beelzebul cast out the demons, your sons by whom
ἐκβάλλουσιν; διὰ τοῦτο αὐτοὶ [y]ὑμῶν ἔσονται κριταί.‖
do they cast out? on account of this they of you shall be judges.
28 εἰ.δὲ [z]ἐγὼ ἐν πνεύματι θεοῦ‖ ἐκβάλλω τὰ δαιμόνια, ἄρα
But if I by [the] Spirit of God cast out the demons, then
ἔφθασεν ἐφ' ὑμᾶς ἡ βασιλεία τοῦ θεοῦ. 29 ἢ πῶς δύναταί
has come upon you the kingdom of God. Or how is able
τις εἰσελθεῖν εἰς τὴν οἰκίαν τοῦ ἰσχυροῦ καὶ τὰ σκεύη
anyone to enter into the house of the strong [man] and [2]goods
αὐτοῦ [a]διαρπάσαι,‖ ἐὰν.μὴ πρῶτον δήσῃ τὸν ἰσχυρόν;
[1]his to plunder, unless first he bind the strong [man]?
καὶ τότε τὴν.οἰκίαν.αὐτοῦ [b]διαρπάσει.‖ 30 ὁ μὴ.ὢν μετ' ἐμοῦ
and then his house he will plunder. He who is not with me
κατ' ἐμοῦ ἐστιν· καὶ ὁ μὴ.συνάγων μετ' ἐμοῦ σκορπίζει.
against me is; and he who gathers not with me scatters.
31 Διὰ τοῦτο λέγω ὑμῖν, Πᾶσα ἁμαρτία καὶ βλασφημία
Because of this I say to you, Every sin and blasphemy
ἀφεθήσεται [c]τοῖς ἀνθρώποις· ἡ.δὲ τοῦ.πνεύματος βλασ-
shall be forgiven to men; but the [2]concerning [3]the [4]Spirit [1]blas-
φημία οὐκ.ἀφεθήσεται [d]τοῖς ἀνθρώποις.‖ 32 καὶ ὃς.[e]ἂν‖ εἴπῃ
phemy shall not be forgiven to men. And whoever speaks
λόγον κατὰ τοῦ υἱοῦ τοῦ ἀνθρώπου, ἀφεθήσεται αὐτῷ·
a word against the Son of man, it shall be forgiven him;
ὃς.δ'.ἂν εἴπῃ κατὰ τοῦ πνεύματος τοῦ ἁγίου, [f]οὐκ.ἀφε-
but whoever speaks against the Spirit the Holy, it shall not
θήσεται‖ αὐτῷ, οὔτε ἐν τούτῳ τῷ αἰῶνι οὔτε ἐν τῷ μέλλον-
be forgiven him, neither in this age nor in the coming
τι. 33 Ἢ ποιήσατε τὸ δένδρον καλὸν καὶ τὸν καρπὸν
[one]. Either make the tree good and [2]fruit
αὐτοῦ καλόν, ἢ ποιήσατε τὸ δένδρον σαπρὸν καὶ τὸν καρπὸν
[1]its good, or make the tree corrupt and [2]fruit
αὐτοῦ σαπρόν· ἐκ.γὰρ τοῦ καρποῦ τὸ δένδρον γινώσκεται.
[1]its corrupt: for from the fruit the tree is known.
34 Γεννήματα ἐχιδνῶν, πῶς δύνασθε ἀγαθὰ λαλεῖν, πονηροὶ
Offspring of vipers, how are ye able good things to speak, [2]wicked
ὄντες; ἐκ.γὰρ τοῦ περισσεύματος τῆς καρδίας τὸ στόμα
[1]being? for out of the abundance of the heart the mouth
λαλεῖ. 35 ὁ ἀγαθὸς ἄνθρωπος ἐκ τοῦ ἀγαθοῦ θησαυροῦ
speaks. The good man out of the good treasure
[g]τῆς καρδίας‖ ἐκβάλλει [h]τὰ‖ ἀγαθά· καὶ ὁ πονηρὸς ἄνθρω-
of the heart puts forth the good things; and the wicked man
πος ἐκ τοῦ πονηροῦ θησαυροῦ ἐκβάλλει πονηρά. 36 λέγω.δὲ
out of the wicked treasure puts forth wicked things. But I say
ὑμῖν, ὅτι πᾶν ῥῆμα ἀργὸν ὃ.[i]ἐὰν‖ [k]λαλήσωσιν‖ οἱ ἄνθρωποι,
to you, that every [2]word [1]idle whatsoever [2]may [3]speak [1]men,
ἀποδώσουσιν περὶ αὐτοῦ λόγον ἐν ἡμέρᾳ κρίσεως. 37 ἐκ
they shall render of it an account in day of judgment. [2]By
γὰρ τῶν.λόγων.σου δικαιωθήσῃ, καὶ ἐκ τῶν.λόγων.σου
[1]for thy words thou shalt be justified, and by thy words

tiles.

19 He shall not strive nor cry out, nor shall anyone hear His voice in the streets.

20 A bruised reed He will not break, and a smoking wick He shall not quench, until He brings forth judgment to victory.

21 And the Gentiles shall hope in His name."

22 Then a demon-possessed man was led to Him, a blind and dumb one. And He healed him, so that the blind and dumb one both spoke and saw.

23 And all the people were amazed, saying, This is the son of David!

24 But hearing this the Pharisees said, This one does not throw out demons except by Be-el-ze-bub the prince of the demons.

25 But Jesus knew their thoughts and said to them, Every kingdom divided against itself is made helpless. And every city or house divided against itself will not stand.

26 And if Satan does throw out Satan, he has been divided against himself. How then will his kingdom stand?

27 And if I throw out demons by Be-el-ze-bub, by whom do your sons throw them out? Because of this they shall be your judges.

28 But if I throw out demons by the Spirit of God, then the kingdom of God has come upon you.

29 Or else how is anyone able to enter into the house of the strong one and take his goods, unless he first ties up the strong one? And then he will plunder his house.

30 He that is not with Me is against Me! And he who does not gather with Me scatters!

31 Because of this I say to you, Every *kind of* sin and blasphemy shall be forgiven to men, but blasphemy concerning the Spirit shall not be forgiven to men.

32 And whoever speaks a word against the Son of man, it shall be forgiven him. But whoever speaks against the Holy Spirit, it shall not be forgiven him – neither in this age, nor in that to come.

33 Either make the tree good and its fruit good, or else make the tree evil and its fruit evil – for the tree is known from the fruit.

34 Sons of vipers! How can you, being evil, speak good things? For the mouth speaks out of the overflowing of the heart.

35 The good man brings forth good things out of the good treasure of the heart. And the evil man brings forth evil things out of the evil treasure.

36 But I say to you that every idle word that men shall speak, they shall give an account of it in the day of judgment.

37 For by your words you shall be justified, and by your words you shall be condemned.

καταδικασθήσῃ.
thou shalt be condemned.
38 Τότε ἀπεκρίθησάν[l] τινες τῶν γραμματέων [m]καὶ Φαρι-
Then answered, some of the scribes and Phari-
σαίων,[ll] λέγοντες, Διδάσκαλε, θέλομεν ἀπὸ σοῦ σημεῖον ἰδεῖν.
sees, saying, Teacher, we wish from thee a sign to see.
39 Ὁ.δὲ ἀποκριθεὶς εἶπεν αὐτοῖς, Γενεὰ πονηρὰ καὶ μοι-
But he answering said to them, A generation wicked and adul-
χαλὶς σημεῖον ἐπιζητεῖ· καὶ σημεῖον οὐ.δοθήσεται αὐτῇ,
terous a sign seeks for, and a sign shall not be given to it,
εἰ.μὴ τὸ σημεῖον Ἰωνᾶ τοῦ προφήτου. 40 ὥσπερ.γὰρ ἦν Ἰωνᾶς
except the sign of Jonas the prophet. For even as was Jonas
ἐν τῇ κοιλίᾳ τοῦ κήτους τρεῖς ἡμέρας καὶ τρεῖς νύκτας, οὕτως
in the belly of the great fish three days and three nights, thus
ἔσται ὁ υἱὸς τοῦ ἀνθρώπου ἐν τῇ καρδίᾳ τῆς γῆς τρεῖς
shall be the Son of man in the heart of the earth three
ἡμέρας καὶ τρεῖς νύκτας. 41 Ἄνδρες [n]Νινευῖται[ll] ἀναστήσονται
days and three nights. Men Ninevites shall stand up
ἐν τῇ κρίσει μετὰ τῆς.γενεᾶς.ταύτης, καὶ κατακρινοῦσιν αὐτήν·
in the judgment with this generation, and shall condemn it;
ὅτι μετενόησαν εἰς τὸ κήρυγμα Ἰωνᾶ· καὶ ἰδού, πλεῖον
for they repented at the proclamation of Jonas; and behold, more
Ἰωνᾶ ὧδε. 42 βασίλισσα νότου ἐγερθήσεται ἐν τῇ κρίσει
than Jonas here. A queen of [the] south shall rise up in the judgment
μετὰ τῆς.γενεᾶς.ταύτης, καὶ κατακρινεῖ αὐτήν· ὅτι ἦλθεν
with this generation, and shall condemn it; for she came
ἐκ τῶν περάτων τῆς γῆς ἀκοῦσαι τὴν σοφίαν [o]Σολομῶντος·[ll]
from the ends of the earth to hear the wisdom of Solomon;
καὶ ἰδού, πλεῖον [o]Σολομῶντος[ll] ὧδε. 43 Ὅταν.δὲ τὸ ἀκάθαρτον
and behold, more than Solomon here. But when the unclean
πνεῦμα ἐξέλθῃ ἀπὸ τοῦ ἀνθρώπου, διέρχεται δι' ἀνύδρων
spirit is gone out from the man, he goes through waterless
τόπων, ζητοῦν ἀνάπαυσιν, καὶ οὐχ.εὑρίσκει. 44 τότε λέγει,
places, seeking rest, and finds not [it]. Then he says,
[q]Ἐπιστρέψω εἰς τὸν.οἶκόν.μου,[ll] ὅθεν ἐξῆλθον· καὶ ἐλθὸν
I will return to my house, whence I came out. And having come
εὑρίσκει σχολάζοντα, [r]σεσαρωμένον καὶ κεκοσμημένον. 45 τότε
he finds [it] unoccupied, swept and adorned. Then
πορεύεται καὶ παραλαμβάνει μεθ' ἑαυτοῦ ἑπτὰ ἕτερα πνεύματα
he goes and takes with himself seven other spirits
πονηρότερα ἑαυτοῦ, καὶ εἰσελθόντα κατοικεῖ ἐκεῖ· καὶ γίνεται
more wicked than himself and entering in they dwell there; and [6]becomes
τὰ ἔσχατα τοῦ.ἀνθρώπου.ἐκείνου χείρονα τῶν πρώτων. οὕτως
[1]the [2]last [3]of [4]that [5]man worse than the first. Thus
ἔσται καὶ τῇ.γενεᾷ.ταύτῃ τῇ πονηρᾷ.
it shall be also to this generation the wicked.
46 [s]Ἔτι.[s]δὲ[ll] αὐτοῦ λαλοῦντος τοῖς ὄχλοις, ἰδού, ἡ μήτηρ
But while yet he was speaking to the crowds, behold, [his] mother
καὶ οἱ.ἀδελφοὶ.[t]αὐτοῦ[ll] εἱστήκεισαν ἔξω, ζητοῦντες αὐτῷ λα-
and his brethren were standing without, seeking [3]to [4]him [1]to
λῆσαι. [v]47 εἶπεν.δέ τις αὐτῷ, Ἰδού, ἡ.μήτηρ.σου καὶ οἱ ἀδελφοί
[2]speak. Then said one to him, Behold, thy mother and [2]brethren
σου ἔξω ἑστήκασιν, ζητοῦντές σοι.λαλῆσαι.[ll] 48 Ὁ.δὲ ἀπο-
[1]thy without are standing, seeking [3]to [4]thee [1]to [2]speak. But he an-
κριθεὶς εἶπεν τῷ [w]εἰπόντι[ll] αὐτῷ, Τίς ἐστιν ἡ.μήτηρ.μου;
swering said to him who spoke to him, Who is my mother?
καὶ τίνες εἰσὶν οἱ.ἀδελφοί.μου; 49 Καὶ ἐκτείνας τὴν χεῖρα
and who are my brethren? And stretching out [2]hand
[x]αὐτοῦ[ll] ἐπὶ τοὺς.μαθητὰς.αὐτοῦ εἶπεν, Ἰδού, ἡ.μήτηρ.μου καὶ
[1]his to his disciples he said, Behold, my mother and
οἱ.ἀδελφοί.μου. 50 ὅστις.γὰρ ἂν [y]ποιήσῃ[ll] τὸ θέλημα τοῦ
my brethren. For whosoever shall do the will
πατρός.μου τοῦ ἐν οὐρανοῖς, αὐτός μου ἀδελφὸς καὶ
of my Father who [is] in [the] heavens, he my brother and
ἀδελφὴ καὶ μήτηρ ἐστίν.
sister and mother is.
13 Ἐν.[z]δὲ[ll] τῇ.ἡμέρᾳ.ἐκείνῃ ἐξελθὼν ὁ Ἰησοῦς [a]ἀπὸ[ll]
And in that day [2]having [3]gone [4]forth [1]Jesus from
τῆς οἰκίας ἐκάθητο παρὰ τὴν θάλασσαν· 2 καὶ συνήχθησαν
the house sat down by the sea. And were gathered together
πρὸς αὐτὸν ὄχλοι πολλοί, ὥστε αὐτὸν εἰς [b]τὸ[ll] πλοῖον ἐμ-
to him [2]crowds [1]great, so that he into the ship having
βάντα καθῆσθαι, καὶ πᾶς ὁ ὄχλος ἐπὶ τὸν αἰγιαλὸν εἱστήκει.
entered sat down, and all the crowd on the shore stood.
3 καὶ ἐλάλησεν αὐτοῖς πολλὰ ἐν παραβολαῖς, λέγων, Ἰδού,
And he spoke to them many things in parables, saying, Behold,
ἐξῆλθεν ὁ σπείρων τοῦ σπείρειν. 4 καὶ ἐν.τῷ.σπείρειν.αὐτὸν
[3]went [4]out [1]the [2]sower to sow. And as he sowed
ἃ.μὲν ἔπεσεν παρὰ τὴν ὁδόν, καὶ [c]ἦλθεν[ll] τὰ πετεινὰ [d]καὶ[ll]
some fell by the way, and [3]came [1]the [2]birds and
κατέφαγεν αὐτά. 5 ἄλλα.δὲ ἔπεσεν ἐπὶ τὰ πετρώδη, ὅπου
devoured them. And some fell upon the rocky places, where

38 Then some of the scribes and Pharisees answered, saying, Teacher, we want to see a sign from you.

39 But He answered, saying to them. A generation *full of* evil and adultery seeks for a sign. And a sign shall not be given to it, except the sign of Jonah the prophet.

40 For even as Jonah was three days and three nights in the belly of the great fish, so shall the Son of man be three days and three nights in the heart of the earth.

41 *The* men of Nin-e-veh shall stand up in the Judgment with this generation and shall condemn it. For they repented at the preaching of Jonah. And behold! One greater than Jonah is here.

42 The queen of the south shall rise up in the Judgment with this generation and shall condemn it. For she came from the other side of the earth to hear the wisdom of Solomon. And behold! One greater than Solomon is here.

43 But when the unclean spirit has gone out of a man, he walks through dry places looking for rest and does not find it.

44 Then he says, I will go back into my house from which I came. And coming back, he finds it empty, swept and decorated.

45 Then he goes and takes with himself seven other spirits more wicked than himself. And they go in and live there. And the last *condition* of that man becomes worse than the first. So also shall it be to this wicked generation.

46 While He was still speaking to the people – lo, His mother and brothers were standing outside wanting to speak to Him!

47 Then someone said to Him, Lo, Your mother and Your brothers are standing outside wanting to speak to You.

48 But He answered and said to the one who spoke to Him, Who is My mother? And who are My brothers?

49 And stretching out His hand toward His disciples He said, Look, My mother and My brothers!

50 For whoever shall do the will of My Father who is in Heaven, he is My brother and sister and mother.

CHAPTER 13

1 And going out from the house that day, Jesus sat down by the sea.

2 And great multitudes were gathered to Him, so that He entered into a boat and sat down. And all the crowd stood on the shore.

3 And He spoke to them many things in parables, saying, behold! A sower went out to sow.

4 And as He sowed, some *seeds* fell by the roadside. And the birds came and ate them.

5 And others fell upon the stony places,

οὐκ.εἶχεν γῆν πολλήν, καὶ εὐθέως ἐξανέτειλεν διὰ τὸ μὴ
they had not ²earth ¹much, and immediately sprang up because of not
ἔχειν βάθος ᵉ γῆς· 6 ἡλίου.δὲ ἀνατείλαντος ἐκαυματίσθη,
having depth of earth; and [the] sun having risen they were scorched,
καὶ διὰ τὸ.μὴ.ἔχειν ῥίζαν ἐξηράνθη. 7 ἄλλα.δὲ ἔπεσεν ἐπὶ
and because of not having root were dried up. And some fell upon
τὰς ἀκάνθας, καὶ ἀνέβησαν αἱ ἄκανθαι καὶ ᶠἀπέπνιξαν‖ αὐτά.
the thorns, and ³grew ⁴up ¹the ²thorns and choked them.
8 ἄλλα.δὲ ἔπεσεν ἐπὶ τὴν γῆν τὴν καλήν, καὶ ἐδίδου καρπόν,
And some fell upon the ground the good, and yielded fruit,
ὃ.μὲν ἑκατόν, ὃ.δὲ ἑξήκοντα, ὃ.δὲ τριάκοντα. 9 ὁ ἔχων
one a hundred, another sixty, another thirty. He that has
ὦτα ᵍἀκούειν‖ ἀκουέτω.
ears to hear let him hear.

10 Καὶ προσελθόντες οἱ μαθηταὶʰ ⁱεἶπον‖ αὐτῷ, ᵏΔιατί‖
And ³having ⁴come ⁵to [⁶him] ¹the ²disciples said to him, Why
ἐν παραβολαῖς λαλεῖς αὐτοῖς; 11 Ὁ.δὲ ἀποκριθεὶς εἶπεν
in parables speakest thou to them? And he, answering said
ˡαὐτοῖς,‖ Ὅτι ὑμῖν δέδοται γνῶναι τὰ μυστήρια τῆς
to them, Because to you it has been given to know the mysteries of the
βασιλείας τῶν.οὐρανῶν, ἐκείνοις.δὲ οὐ.δέδοται. 12 ὅστις
kingdom of the heavens, but to them it has not been given. ²Whosoever
γὰρ ἔχει, δοθήσεται αὐτῷ, καὶ περισσευθήσεται· ὅστις.δὲ
¹for has, ³shall ⁴be ⁵given ¹to ²him, and he shall be in abundance; but whosoever
οὐκ.ἔχει, καὶ ὃ ἔχει ἀρθήσεται ἀπ' αὐτοῦ. 13 διὰ τοῦτο
has not, even what he has shall be taken away from him. Because of this
ἐν παραβολαῖς αὐτοῖς λαλῶ, ὅτι βλέποντες οὐ.βλέπουσιν,
in parables to them I speak, because seeing they see not,
καὶ ἀκούοντες οὐκ.ἀκούουσιν, οὐδὲ συνιοῦσιν. 14 καὶ ἀνα-
and hearing they hear not, nor do they understand. And ³is
πληροῦται ᵐἐπ'‖ αὐτοῖς ἡ προφητεία Ἡσαΐου, ἡ λέγουσα,
⁴filled ⁵up ¹in ²them the prophecy of Esaias, which says,
Ἀκοῇ ἀκούσετε, καὶ οὐ.μὴ.συνῆτε· καὶ βλέποντες βλέ-
In hearing ye shall hear, and in no wise understand; and seeing ye shall
ψετε, καὶ οὐ.μὴ.ἴδητε. 15 ἐπαχύνθη.γὰρ ἡ καρδία τοῦ
see, and in no wise perceive: for ⁶has ⁷grown ⁸fat the ²heart
λαοῦ.τούτου, καὶ τοῖς ὠσὶνⁿ βαρέως ἤκουσαν, καὶ τοὺς
³of ⁴this ⁵people, and with the ears heavily they have heard, and
ὀφθαλμοὺς.αὐτῶν ἐκάμμυσαν· μήποτε ἴδωσιν τοῖς ὀφ-
their eyes they have closed; lest they should see with the
θαλμοῖς, καὶ τοῖς ὠσὶν ἀκούσωσιν, καὶ τῇ καρδίᾳ συν-
eyes, and with the ears they should hear, and with the heart they should
ῶσιν, καὶ ἐπιστρέψωσιν καὶ ᵒἰάσωμαι‖ αὐτούς. 16 Ὑμῶν.δὲ
understand, and should be converted and I should heal them. But of you
μακάριοι οἱ ὀφθαλμοί, ὅτι βλέπουσιν· καὶ τὰ ὦτα ᵖὑμῶν,‖
blessed [are] the eyes, because they see; and the ears of you,
ὅτι ᵠἀκούει.‖ 17 ἀμὴν.ʳγὰρ‖ λέγω ὑμῖν, ὅτι πολλοὶ προφῆται
because they hear. For verily I say to you, that many prophets
καὶ δίκαιοι ἐπεθύμησαν ἰδεῖν ἃ βλέπετε, καὶ οὐκ ˢεἶδον·‖
and righteous [men] desired to see what ye see, and ²not ¹saw;
καὶ ἀκοῦσαι ἃ ἀκούετε, καὶ οὐκ.ἤκουσαν.
and to hear what ye hear, and heard not.

18 Ὑμεῖς οὖν ἀκούσατε τὴν παραβολὴν τοῦ ᵗσπείροντος·‖
²Ye ³therefore ¹hear the parable of the sower.
19 Παντὸς.ἀκούοντος τὸν λόγον τῆς βασιλείας καὶ μὴ
When any one hears the word of the kingdom and not [it]
συνιέντος, ἔρχεται ὁ πονηρὸς καὶ ἁρπάζει τὸ ἐσπαρμένον
understands, ³comes ¹the ²wicked ⁴one and catches away that which was sown
ἐν τῇ.καρδίᾳ.αὐτοῦ· οὗτός ἐστιν ὁ παρὰ τὴν ὁδὸν σπαρείς.
in his heart. This is he who by the way was sown.
20 Ὁ.δὲ ἐπὶ τὰ πετρώδη σπαρείς, οὗτός ἐστιν ὁ τὸν λόγον
And he who upon the rocky places was sown, this is he who the word
ἀκούων καὶ εὐθὺς μετὰ χαρᾶς λαμβάνων αὐτόν· 21 οὐκ
hears and immediately with joy receives it; ³no
ἔχει δὲ ῥίζαν ἐν ἑαυτῷ, ἀλλὰ πρόσκαιρός ἐστιν· γενομένης.δὲ
²has ¹but root in himself, but temporary is; but ⁴having ⁵risen
θλίψεως ἢ διωγμοῦ διὰ τὸν λόγον, εὐθὺς σκαν-
¹tribulation ²or ³persecution on account of the word, immediately he is
δαλίζεται. 22 Ὁ.δὲ εἰς τὰς ἀκάνθας σπαρείς, οὗτός ἐστιν
offended. And he who among the thorns was sown, this is
ὁ τὸν λόγον ἀκούων, καὶ ἡ μέριμνα τοῦ.αἰῶνος.ᵛτούτου‖
he who the word hears, and the care of this life
καὶ ἡ ἀπάτη τοῦ πλούτου ʷσυμπνίγει‖ τὸν λόγον, καὶ ἄκαρπος
and the deceit of riches choke the word, and unfruitful
γίνεται. 23 Ὁ.δὲ ἐπὶ τὴν ˣγῆν τὴν καλὴν‖ σπαρείς, οὗτός
it becomes. But he who on the ground the good was sown, this
ἐστιν ὁ τὸν λόγον ἀκούων καὶ ʸσυνιών·‖ ὃς δὴ καρ-
is he who the word hears and understands; who indeed brings
ποφορεῖ, καὶ ποιεῖ ᶻὃ‖.μὲν ἑκατόν, ᶻὃ‖.δὲ ἑξήκοντα, ᶻὃ‖.δὲ
forth fruit, and produces one a hundred, another sixty, another
τριάκοντα.
thirty.

where they did not have much earth. And they sprang up immediately because they had no deepness of earth.

6 And when the sun came up they were scorched. And because they did not have any root, they dried up.

7 And some fell on the thorns. And the thorns sprang up and choked them.

8 And some fell on the good ground and yielded fruit – some a hundred times, another sixty, and another thirty.

9 He that has ears to hear, let him hear.

10 And coming to *Him*, the disciples said to Him, Why do you speak to them in parables?

11 He answered them, saying, Because it has been given to you to know the mysteries of the kingdom of Heaven, but it is not given to them.

12 For whoever has, *more* shall be given to him, and he shall have plenty. But whoever does not have, even what he has shall be taken away from him.

13 Because of this I speak to them in parables – because seeing, they do not see; and hearing, they do not hear, nor do they understand.

14 And the prophecy of Isaiah is fulfilled in them, which says, "In hearing you shall hear and in no way understand; and seeing, you shall see, yet in no way know.

15 For the heart of this people has grown fat and they have heard sluggishly with their ears. And they have closed their eyes so that they might not see with their eyes and hear with their ears, and so that they might not understand with their heart and be converted, and that I should heal them."

16 But your eyes *are* blessed because they see and your ears because they hear.

17 For truly I say to you that many prophets and righteous ones desired to see what you see, yet did not see; and to hear what you hear, yet did not hear.

18 Hear then the parable of the sower.

19 When anyone hears the word of the kingdom and does not understand it, the wicked one comes and catches away that which was sown in his heart. This is he who received seed by the roadside.

20 And he who received seed on the stony places is he who hears the word and immediately receives it with joy.

21 But he has no root in himself and is temporary. And when trouble or persecution rises on account of the word, he immediately sins.

22 And he who received seed among the thorns is he who hears the word, but the care of this life and the deceitfulness of riches choke the word, and it becomes unfruitful.

23 But he who received seed on the good ground is he who hears the word and understands. He indeed brings forth fruit and produces, one a hundred times, another sixty, another thirty.

24 [r]Ἄλλην παραβολὴν παρέθηκεν αὐτοῖς, λέγων, [s]Ὡμοιώ-
Another parable put he before them, saying, [6]has [7]become
θη ἡ βασιλεία τῶν οὐρανῶν ἀνθρώπῳ [a]σπείροντι‖ καλὸν
[8]like [1]the [2]kingdom [3]of [4]the [5]heavens to a man sowing good
σπέρμα ἐν τῷ.ἀγρῷ.αὐτοῦ· 25 ἐν.δὲ.τῷ.καθεύδειν τοὺς ἀνθρώ-
seed in his field; but while [3]slept [1]the [2]men
πους ἦλθεν αὐτοῦ ὁ ἐχθρὸς καὶ [b]ἔσπειρεν‖ ζιζάνια ἀνὰ μέσον
came his enemy and sowed darnel in [the] midst
τοῦ σίτου, καὶ ἀπῆλθεν. 26 ὅτε.δὲ ἐβλάστησεν ὁ χόρτος,
of the wheat, and went away. And when [3]sprouted [1]the [2]blade,
καὶ καρπὸν ἐποίησεν, τότε ἐφάνη καὶ τὰ ζιζάνια. 27 προσελ-
and fruit produced, then appeared also the darnel. [2]Having [3]come
θόντες δὲ οἱ δοῦλοι τοῦ οἰκοδεσπότου εἶπον αὐτῷ, Κύριε,
[4]to [5]him] [1]and the bondmen of the master of the house said to him, Sir,
οὐχὶ καλὸν σπέρμα [c]ἔσπειρας‖ ἐν τῷ σῷ ἀγρῷ; πόθεν οὖν
[3]not [5]good [6]seed [1]didst [2]thou [4]sow in thy field? whence then
ἔχει [d]τὰ‖ ζιζάνια; 28 Ὁ.δὲ ἔφη αὐτοῖς, Ἐχθρὸς ἄνθρωπος
has it the darnel? And he said to them, [3]an [4]enemy [1]a [2]man
τοῦτο ἐποίησεν. οἱ.δὲ [e]δοῦλοι‖ [f]εἶπον αὐτῷ,‖ Θέλεις οὖν
[6]this [5]did. And the bondmen said to him, Wilt thou then
ἀπελθόντες συλλέξωμεν αὐτά; 29 Ὁ.δὲ [g]ἔφη,‖ Οὔ·
[that] having gone forth we should gather them? But he said, No;
μήποτε συλλέγοντες τὰ ζιζάνια, ἐκριζώσητε ἅμα αὐτοῖς τὸν
lest gathering the darnel, ye should uproot with them the
σῖτον. 30 ἄφετε συναυξάνεσθαι ἀμφότερα [h]μέχρι‖ τοῦ θερισμοῦ·
wheat. Suffer to grow together both until the harvest;
καὶ ἐν [i]τῷ‖ καιρῷ τοῦ θερισμοῦ ἐρῶ τοῖς θερισταῖς, Συλ-
and in the time of the harvest I will say to the harvest men, Ga-
λέξατε πρῶτον τὰ ζιζάνια, καὶ δήσατε αὐτὰ [j]εἰς‖ δέσμας
ther first the darnel, and bind them into bundles
πρὸς.τὸ.κατακαῦσαι αὐτά· τὸν.δὲ σῖτον [k]συναγάγετε‖ εἰς τὴν
to burn them; but the wheat bring together into
ἀποθήκην.μου.
my granary.

[24]He presented another parable to them, saying, The kingdom of Heaven has become like a man sowing good seed in his field.
[25]But while men slept, his enemy came and sowed tares among the wheat and left.
[26]And when the blade sprouted and fruit came forth, then the tares appeared also.
[27]And the servants of the master of the house came and said to him, Sir, did you not sow good seed in your field? Then where have the tares come from?
[28]And he said to them, A man, an enemy, has done this. And the servants said to him, Then do you want us to go and gather them?
[29]But he said, No, lest in gathering the tares you should root up the wheat with them.
[30]Let both grow together until the harvest. And at harvest time I will say to the reapers, First, gather the tares and bundle them to burn them. But gather the wheat into my barn.

31 [r]Ἄλλην παραβολὴν παρέθηκεν αὐτοῖς, λέγων, Ὁμοία
Another parable put he before them, saying, Like
ἐστὶν ἡ βασιλεία τῶν οὐρανῶν κόκκῳ σινάπεως, ὃν λα-
is the kingdom of the heavens to a grain of mustard, which having
βὼν ἄνθρωπος ἔσπειρεν ἐν τῷ.ἀγρῷ.αὐτοῦ· 32 ὃ μικρότερον
taken, a man sowed in his field; which less
μέν ἐστιν πάντων τῶν σπερμάτων, ὅταν.δὲ αὐξηθῇ
indeed is than all the seeds, but when it be grown,
μεῖζον τῶν λαχάνων ἐστίν, καὶ γίνεται δένδρον, ὥστε
greater than the herbs is, and becomes a tree, so that
ἐλθεῖν τὰ πετεινὰ τοῦ οὐρανοῦ καὶ [l]κατασκηνοῦν‖ ἐν τοῖς
come the birds of the heaven and roost in the
κλάδοις αὐτοῦ.
branches of it.

[31]He put another parable before them, saying, The kingdom of Heaven is like a grain of mustard seed which a man has taken and sowed in his field.
[32]It is indeed less than all the seeds, but when it is grown it is greater than the *other* plants and becomes a tree, so that the birds of the air come and roost in the limbs of it.

33 [r]Ἄλλην παραβολὴν ἐλάλησεν αὐτοῖς, Ὁμοία ἐστὶν ἡ
Another parable spoke he to them, Like is the
βασιλεία τῶν οὐρανῶν ζύμῃ, ἣν λαβοῦσα γυνὴ ἐνέκρυψεν
kingdom of the heavens to leaven, which having taken, a woman hid
εἰς ἀλεύρου σάτα τρία, ἕως.οὗ ἐζυμώθη ὅλον.
in [3]of [4]meal [2]seahs [1]three, until [2]was [3]leavened [1]all.

[33]He spoke another parable to them: The kingdom of Heaven is like leaven, which a woman takes and hides in three measures of meal until the whole is leavened.

34 Ταῦτα πάντα ἐλάλησεν ὁ Ἰησοῦς ἐν παραβολαῖς τοῖς
[2]These [3]things [1]all spoke Jesus in parables to the
ὄχλοις, καὶ χωρὶς παραβολῆς [m]οὐκ‖ ἐλάλει αὐτοῖς· 35 ὅπως
crowds, and without a parable [3]not [1]he [2]spoke to them; so that
πληρωθῇ τὸ ῥηθὲν διὰ τοῦ προφήτου[n], λέγοντος,
might be fulfilled that which was spoken by the prophet, saying,
Ἀνοίξω ἐν παραβολαῖς τὸ.στόμα.μου· ἐρεύξομαι κεκρυμμένα
I will open in parables my mouth: I will utter things hidden
ἀπὸ καταβολῆς [o]κόσμου.‖
from [the] foundation of [the] world.

[34]Jesus spoke all these things to the multitudes in parables. And He spoke nothing to them without making use of a parable,
[35]so that which was spoken by the prophet might be fulfilled, saying, "I will open My mouth in parables. I will say things hidden from the foundation of the world."

36 Τότε ἀφεὶς τοὺς ὄχλους, ἦλθεν εἰς τὴν οἰκίαν
Then having dismissed the crowds, [2]went [3]into [4]the [5]house
[p]ὁ Ἰησοῦς·‖ καὶ [q]προσῆλθον‖ αὐτῷ οἱ.μαθηταὶ.αὐτοῦ, λέγοντες,
[1]Jesus; and came to him his disciples, saying,
[r]Φράσον‖ ἡμῖν τὴν παραβολὴν τῶν ζιζανίων τοῦ ἀγροῦ.
Expound to us the parable of the darnel of the field.
37 Ὁ.δὲ ἀποκριθεὶς εἶπεν [s]αὐτοῖς,‖ Ὁ σπείρων τὸ καλὸν
And he answering said to them, He who sows the good
σπέρμα ἐστὶν ὁ υἱὸς τοῦ ἀνθρώπου· 38 ὁ.δὲ ἀγρός ἐστιν ὁ
seed is the Son of man; and the field is the
κόσμος· τὸ.δὲ καλὸν σπέρμα, οὗτοί εἰσιν οἱ υἱοὶ τῆς βασιλείας·
world; and the good seed, these are the sons of the kingdom;
τὰ.δὲ ζιζάνιά εἰσιν οἱ υἱοὶ τοῦ πονηροῦ· 39 ὁ.δὲ ἐχθρὸς
but the darnel are the sons of the evil [one]; and the enemy
[t]ὁ σπείρας αὐτά ἐστιν‖ ὁ διάβολος· ὁ.δὲ θερισμὸς συν-
who sowed them is the devil; and the harvest [the] com-
τέλεια [v]τοῦ‖ αἰῶνός ἐστιν· οἱ.δὲ θερισταὶ ἄγγελοί εἰσιν.
pletion of the age is, and the harvest men angels are.

[36]Then Jesus sent the crowds away and went into the house. And His disciples came to Him and said, Explain to us the parable of the tares of the field.
[37]And answering He said to them, He who sows the good seed is the Son of man.
[38]And the field is the world. And the good seed are the sons of the kingdom. But the tares are the sons of the evil one.
[39]And the enemy who sowed them is the devil. And the harvest is the end of the world. And the reapers are the angels.

40 ὥσπερ οὖν συλλέγεται τὰ ζιζάνια, καὶ πυρὶ [w]κατα-
As therefore is gathered the darnel, and in fire is con-
καίεται,‖ οὕτως ἔσται ἐν τῇ συντελείᾳ τοῦ.αἰῶνος.[x]τούτου.‖
sumed, thus it shall be in the completion of this age.
41 ἀποστελεῖ ὁ υἱὸς τοῦ ἀνθρώπου τοὺς ἀγγέλους.αὐτοῦ,
[5]shall [6]send [7]forth [1]the [2]Son [3]of [4]man his angels,
καὶ συλλέξουσιν ἐκ τῆς.βασιλείας.αὐτοῦ πάντα τὰ σκάνδαλα
and they shall gather out of his kingdom all the offences
καὶ τοὺς ποιοῦντας τὴν ἀνομίαν, 42 καὶ βαλοῦσιν αὐτοὺς
and those who practise lawlessness, and they shall cast them
εἰς τὴν κάμινον τοῦ πυρός· ἐκεῖ ἔσται ὁ κλαυθμὸς καὶ ὁ
into the furnace of the fire: there shall be the weeping and the
βρυγμὸς τῶν ὀδόντων. 43 τότε οἱ δίκαιοι ἐκλάμψουσιν ὡς
gnashing of the teeth. Then the righteous shall shine forth as
ὁ ἥλιος ἐν τῇ βασιλείᾳ τοῦ.πατρὸς.αὐτῶν. Ὁ ἔχων ὦτα
the sun in the kingdom of their Father. He that has ears
[y]ἀκούειν‖ ἀκουέτω.
to hear let him hear.
44 [z]Πάλιν‖ ὁμοία ἐστὶν ἡ βασιλεία τῶν οὐρανῶν θησαυρῷ
Again like is the kingdom of the heavens to treasure
κεκρυμμένῳ ἐν τῷ ἀγρῷ, ὃν εὑρὼν ἄνθρωπος ἔκρυψεν,
hid in the field, which [3]having [4]found [1]a [2]man hid,
καὶ ἀπὸ τῆς χαρᾶς αὐτοῦ ὑπάγει καὶ [a]πάντα ὅσα ἔχει
and for the joy of it goes and all things as many as he has
πωλεῖ,‖ καὶ ἀγοράζει τὸν.ἀγρὸν.ἐκεῖνον.
he sells, and buys that field.
45 Πάλιν ὁμοία ἐστὶν ἡ βασιλεία τῶν οὐρανῶν ἀνθρώπῳ
Again like is the kingdom of the heavens to a man
ἐμπόρῳ, ζητοῦντι καλοὺς μαργαρίτας· 46 [b]ὃς εὑρὼν‖ ἕνα
a merchant, seeking beautiful pearls; who having found one
πολύτιμον μαργαρίτην, ἀπελθὼν πέπρακεν πάντα ὅσα
very precious pearl, having gone away has sold all things as many as
εἶχεν, καὶ ἠγόρασεν αὐτόν.
he had, and bought it.
47 Πάλιν ὁμοία ἐστὶν ἡ βασιλεία τῶν οὐρανῶν σαγήνῃ
Again like is the kingdom of the heavens to a drag net
βληθείσῃ εἰς τὴν θάλασσαν, καὶ ἐκ παντὸς γένους συναγα-
cast into the sea, and of every kind gathering
γούσῃ· 48 ἣν ὅτε ἐπληρώθη ἀναβιβάσαντες[c] [d]ἐπὶ τὸν
together; which when it was filled having drawn up on the
αἰγιαλόν, καὶ‖ καθίσαντες συνέλεξαν τὰ καλὰ εἰς [e]ἀγγεῖα,‖
shore, and having sat down they collected the good into vessels,
τὰ.δὲ σαπρὰ ἔξω ἔβαλον. 49 οὕτως ἔσται ἐν τῇ συντελείᾳ
and the corrupt [3]out [1]they [2]cast. Thus shall it be in the completion
τοῦ αἰῶνος· ἐξελεύσονται οἱ ἄγγελοι, καὶ ἀφοριοῦσιν τοὺς
of the age: [3]shall [4]go [5]out [1]the [2]angels, and shall separate the
πονηροὺς ἐκ μέσου τῶν δικαίων, 50 καὶ βαλοῦσιν αὐτοὺς
wicked from [the] midst of the righteous, and shall cast them
εἰς τὴν κάμινον τοῦ πυρός· ἐκεῖ ἔσται ὁ κλαυθμὸς καὶ ὁ
into the furnace of the fire: there shall be the wailing and the
βρυγμὸς τῶν ὀδόντων.
gnashing of the teeth.
51 [g]Λέγει αὐτοῖς ὁ Ἰησοῦς,‖ Συνήκατε ταῦτα πάντα;
[2]Says [3]to [4]them [1]Jesus, Have ye understood [2]these [3]things [1]all?
Λέγουσιν αὐτῷ, Ναί, [h]κύριε.‖ 52 Ὁ.δὲ [i]εἶπεν‖ αὐτοῖς, Διὰ
They say to him, Yea, Lord. And he said to them, Because of
τοῦτο πᾶς γραμματεὺς μαθητευθεὶς [k]εἰς τὴν βασιλείαν‖ τῶν
this every scribe discipled into the kingdom of the
οὐρανῶν ὅμοιός ἐστιν ἀνθρώπῳ οἰκοδεσπότῃ, ὅστις ἐκβάλλει
heavens [2]like [1]is to a man a master of a house, who puts forth
ἐκ τοῦ.θησαυροῦ.αὐτοῦ καινὰ καὶ παλαιά.
out of his treasure [things] new and old.
53 Καὶ ἐγένετο ὅτε ἐτέλεσεν ὁ Ἰησοῦς τὰς παραβολὰς
And it came to pass when [2]had [3]finished [1]Jesus [2]parables
ταύτας, μετῆρεν ἐκεῖθεν· 54 καὶ ἐλθὼν εἰς τὴν πατρίδα
[1]these, he withdrew thence; and having come into [3]country
αὐτοῦ, ἐδίδασκεν αὐτοὺς ἐν τῇ.συναγωγῇ.αὐτῶν, ὥστε [l]ἐκπλήτ-
[1]his [2]own], he taught them in their synagogue, so that [2]were
τεσθαι‖ αὐτοὺς καὶ λέγειν, Πόθεν τούτῳ ἡ.σοφία.αὕτη καὶ
[3]astonished [1]they and said, Whence to this [man] this wisdom and
αἱ δυνάμεις; 55 οὐχ οὗτός ἐστιν ὁ τοῦ τέκτονος υἱός;
the works of power? [2]not [3]this [1]is [4]the [6]of [7]the [8]carpenter [5]son? [Is]
[m]οὐχὶ‖ ἡ.μήτηρ.αὐτοῦ λέγεται Μαριάμ, καὶ οἱ.ἀδελφοὶ.αὐτοῦ
not his mother called Mary, and his brethren
Ἰάκωβος καὶ [n]Ἰωσῆς‖ καὶ Σίμων καὶ Ἰούδας; 56 καὶ αἱ
James and Joses and Simon and Judas? and
ἀδελφαὶ.αὐτοῦ οὐχὶ πᾶσαι πρὸς ἡμᾶς εἰσιν; πόθεν οὖν τούτῳ
[3]his [4]sisters [2]not [5]all [6]with [7]us [1]are? whence then to this
ταῦτα πάντα; 57 Καὶ ἐσκανδαλίζοντο ἐν αὐτῷ. Ὁ δὲ
[man] [2]these [3]things [1]all? And they were offended in him. But
Ἰησοῦς εἶπεν αὐτοῖς, Οὐκ ἔστιν προφήτης ἄτιμος εἰ.μὴ
Jesus said to them, [4]not [3]is [1]a [2]prophet without honour except

40 Therefore, just as the tares are gathered and burned in the fire, so it shall be at the end of the world.

41 The Son of man shall send forth His angels. And they shall gather out of His kingdom all things that offend, and those who practice lawlessness.

42 And they shall throw them into a furnace of fire. There shall be wailing and gnashing of teeth.

43 Then the righteous shall shine like the sun in the kingdom of their Father. He that has ears to hear, let him hear.

44 Again, the kingdom of Heaven is like treasure hidden in a field, which a man found and hid. And from the joy of it, he goes and sells all things, all that he has, and buys that field.

45 Again, the kingdom of Heaven is like a man, *who is* a merchant, looking for beautiful pearls.

46 *And* having found one very precious pearl, he goes away and sells all, as many things as he had, and buys it.

47 Again, the kingdom of Heaven is like a drag net that is thrown into the sea. And it gathers together some of every kind,

48 which, when it was filled, drawing it up on the shore and sitting down, they gathered the good into containers, and they threw out the bad.

49 So it shall be at the end of the world. The angels will go out and will separate the wicked from among the righteous.

50 And *they* shall throw them into the furnace of fire. There shall be wailing and gnashing of teeth.

51 Jesus said to them, Have you understood all these things? They said to Him, Yes, Lord.

52 And He said to them, Because of this every scribe schooled to the kingdom of Heaven is like a man *who is* a master of a house, who puts forth out of his treasure new and old things.

53 And when Jesus had finished these parables, He went away from there.

54 And He came to His own country and taught them in their synagogue, so that they were astonished. And *they* said, From where does this one get this wisdom and these mighty works?

55 Is this not the son of the carpenter? *Is* his mother not called Mary, and his brothers James and Joses and Simon and Judas?

56 And his sisters, are they not all with us? From where then does this one get all these things?

57 And they were offended in Him. But Jesus said to them, A prophet is never without honor except in his own country and in his

ἐν τῇ[o].πατρίδι.[p]αὐτοῦ" καὶ ἐν τῇ.οἰκίᾳ.αὐτοῦ. 58 Καὶ οὐκ
in his [own] country and in his [own] house. And [3]not
ἐποίησεν ἐκεῖ δυνάμεις πολλὰς διὰ τὴν.ἀπιστίαν.αὐτῶν.
[1]he-[2]did there [2]works [3]of [4]power [1]many because of their unbelief.
14 Ἐν ἐκείνῳ τῷ καιρῷ ἤκουσεν Ἡρώδης ὁ [q]τετράρχης"
At that time heard Herod the tetrarch
τὴν ἀκοὴν Ἰησοῦ, 2 καὶ εἶπεν τοῖς.παισὶν.αὐτοῦ, Οὗτός ἐστιν
the fame of Jesus, and said to his servants, This is
Ἰωάννης ὁ βαπτιστής· αὐτὸς ἠγέρθη ἀπὸ τῶν νεκρῶν, καὶ
John the Baptist: he is risen from the dead, and
διὰ τοῦτο αἱ δυνάμεις ἐνεργοῦσιν ἐν αὐτῷ. 3 Ὁ γὰρ
because of this the works of power operate in him. For
Ἡρώδης κρατήσας τὸν Ἰωάννην ἔδησεν [r]αὐτὸν" καὶ [s]ἔθετο
Herod having seized John bound him and put
ἐν φυλακῇ," διὰ Ἡρωδιάδα τὴν γυναῖκα [t]Φιλίππου"
[him] in prison, on account of Herodias the wife [4]Philip
τοῦ.ἀδελφοῦ.αὐτοῦ. 4 ἔλεγεν.γὰρ [v]αὐτῷ ὁ Ἰωάννης," Οὐκ
[1]of [2]his [3]brother. For [2]said [3]to [4]him [1]John, [7]Not
ἔξεστίν σοι ἔχειν αὐτήν. 5 Καὶ θέλων αὐτὸν ἀποκτεῖναι,
[5]it [6]is lawful for thee to have her. And wishing [3]him [1]to [2]kill,
ἐφοβήθη τὸν ὄχλον, ὅτι ὡς προφήτην αὐτὸν εἶχον.
he feared the multitude, because as a prophet him they held.
6 [w]γενεσίων.δὲ ἀγομένων" τοῦ Ἡρώδου, ὠρχήσατο ἡ θυγάτηρ
But a birthday being celebrated of Herod, [5]danced [1]the [2]daughter
τῆς Ἡρωδιάδος ἐν τῷ μέσῳ, καὶ ἤρεσεν τῷ Ἡρώδῃ· 7 ὅθεν
[3]of [4]Herodias in the midst, and pleased Herod; Whereupon
μεθ' ὅρκου ὡμολόγησεν αὐτῇ δοῦναι ὃ.[x]ἐὰν" αἰτήσηται. 8 Ἡ.δὲ
with oath he promised to her to give whatever she should ask. But she
προβιβασθεῖσα ὑπὸ τῆς.μητρὸς.αὐτῆς, Δός μοι, φησίν, ὧδε
being urged on by her mother, Give me, she says, here
ἐπὶ πίνακι τὴν κεφαλὴν Ἰωάννου τοῦ βαπτιστοῦ. 9 Καὶ
upon a dish the head of John the Baptist. And
[y]ἐλυπήθη" ὁ βασιλεύς· διὰ.[z]δὲ" τοὺς ὅρκους καὶ τοὺς
[3]was [4]grieved [1]the [2]king; but on account of the oaths and those who
συνανακειμένους ἐκέλευσεν δοθῆναι· 10 καὶ πέμψας
reclined with [him at table] he commanded [it] to be given. And having sent
ἀπεκεφάλισεν [a]τὸν" Ἰωάννην ἐν τῇ φυλακῇ. 11 καὶ ἠνέχθη
he beheaded John in the prison. And [3]was [4]brought
ἡ.κεφαλὴ.αὐτοῦ ἐπὶ πίνακι, καὶ ἐδόθη τῷ κορασίῳ· καὶ ἤν-
[1]his [2]head on a dish, and was given to the damsel, and she
εγκεν τῇ.μητρὶ.αὐτῆς. 12 καὶ προσελθόντες οἱ.μαθηταὶ.αὐτοῦ
brought [it] to her mother. And having come his disciples
ἦραν τὸ [b]σῶμα," καὶ ἔθαψαν [c]αὐτό·" καὶ ἐλθόντες ἀπήγγειλαν
took the body, and buried it; and having come told
τῷ Ἰησοῦ. 13 [d]καὶ ἀκούσας" ὁ Ἰησοῦς ἀνεχώρησεν ἐκεῖθεν
[it] to Jesus. And [2]having [3]heard [1]Jesus withdrew thence
ἐν πλοίῳ εἰς ἔρημον τόπον κατ'.ἰδίαν.
by ship to a desert place apart.
Καὶ ἀκούσαντες οἱ ὄχλοι ἠκολούθησαν αὐτῷ [e]πεζῇ"
And having heard [of it] the crowds followed him on foot
ἀπὸ τῶν πόλεων. 14 Καὶ ἐξελθὼν [f]ὁ Ἰησοῦς" εἶδεν πολὺν
from the cities. And having gone out Jesus saw [2]great
ὄχλον, καὶ ἐσπλαγχνίσθη ἐπ' [g]αὐτούς," καὶ ἐθεράπευσεν
[1]a crowd, and was moved with compassion towards them, and healed
τοὺς.ἀῤῥώστους.αὐτῶν. 15 Ὀψίας.δὲ γενομένης [h]προσῆλθον"
their infirm. And evening having come came
αὐτῷ οἱ.μαθηταὶ.[i]αὐτοῦ," λέγοντες, Ἔρημός ἐστιν ὁ τόπος,
to him his disciples, saying, Desert is the place,
καὶ ἡ ὥρα [k]ἤδη παρῆλθεν·" ἀπόλυσον [l]τοὺς ὄχλους, ἵνα
and the time already is gone by: dismiss the crowds, that
ἀπελθόντες εἰς τὰς κώμας ἀγοράσωσιν ἑαυτοῖς βρώματα.
having gone into the villages they may buy for themselves meat.
16 Ὁ.δὲ.[m]Ἰησοῦς" εἶπεν αὐτοῖς, Οὐ χρείαν ἔχουσιν ἀπελθεῖν·
But Jesus said to them, [3]No [4]need [1]they [2]have to go away:
δότε αὐτοῖς ὑμεῖς φαγεῖν. 17 Οἱ.δὲ λέγουσιν αὐτῷ, Οὐκ.ἔχομεν
give [2]to [3]them [1]ye to eat. But they say to him, We have not
ὧδε εἰ.μὴ πέντε ἄρτους καὶ δύο ἰχθύας. 18 Ὁ.δὲ εἶπεν, Φέρετέ
here except five loaves and two fishes. And he said, Bring
μοι [n]αὐτοὺς ὧδε." 19 Καὶ κελεύσας τοὺς ὄχλους ἀνα-
[2]to [3]me [1]them here. And having commanded the crowds to re-
κλιθῆναι ἐπὶ [o]τοὺς χόρτους," [p]καὶ" λαβὼν τοὺς πέντε ἄρτους
cline on the grass, and having taken the five loaves
καὶ τοὺς δύο ἰχθύας, ἀναβλέψας εἰς τὸν οὐρανὸν [q]εὐλόγησεν·"
and the two fishes, having looked up to the heaven he blessed;
καὶ κλάσας ἔδωκεν τοῖς μαθηταῖς τοὺς ἄρτους, οἱ.δὲ μα-
and having broken he gave to the disciples the loaves, and the dis-
θηταὶ τοῖς ὄχλοις. 20 καὶ ἔφαγον πάντες καὶ ἐχορτάσθησαν·
ciples to the crowds. And [2]ate [1]all and were satisfied;
καὶ ἦραν τὸ περισσεῦον τῶν κλασμάτων, δώδεκα
and they took up that which was over and above of the fragments, twelve
κοφίνους πλήρεις. 21 οἱ.δὲ ἐσθίοντες ἦσαν ἄνδρες ὡσεὶ
hand-baskets full. And those who ate were men about

own house.
58 And He did not do many mighty works
there because of their unbelief.

CHAPTER 14

1 At that time Herod the tetrarch heard the
fame of Jesus.
2 And *he* said to his servants, This is John
the Baptist! He has risen from the dead. And
because of this mighty works show themselves in him.
3 For after Herod had captured John, he
bound him and put him in prison (because
of He-ro-di-as the wife of his brother Philip).
4 For John said to him, It is not lawful for
you to have her.
5 And *when he* desired to kill him, he
feared the people, because they believed him
to be a prophet.
6 But when the birthday of Herod was
being celebrated, the daughter of He-ro-di-as
danced in their midst and pleased Herod.
7 So he promised with an oath to give her
whatever she should ask.
8 And (being urged on by her mother beforehand) she said, Give me here the head of
John the Baptist on a platter.
9 And the king was sad. But on account of
the oaths (and those who were at the table
with him,) he commanded it to be given.
10 And he sent and had John beheaded in
the prison.
11 And his head was brought on a platter
and was given to the girl. And she brought it
to her mother.
12 And his disciples came and took the body
and buried it. And they came and told Jesus.
13 And having heard, Jesus left there by ship
to *go* apart *to* a deserted place. And hearing of
it, the crowds followed Him on foot from the
cities.
14 And going out, Jesus saw a multitude and
was moved with compassion toward them.
And He healed their sick.
15 And since evening had come, His disciples
came to Him, saying, The place is deserted and
the time has already gone by. Send away the
multitude so that they may go into the villages
and buy food for themselves.
16 But Jesus said to them, They have no need
to go away. You give them *food* to eat.
17 But they said to Him, We have nothing
here but five loaves and two fish.
18 And He said, Bring them here to Me.
19 And after commanding the multitude to
rest on the grass, and after He had taken the
five loaves and the two fish, and after He
had looked up to Heaven, He blessed *them*.
And He broke and gave the loaves to the
disciples. And the disciples *gave them* to the
multitude.
20 And all ate and were satisfied. And they
took up twelve baskets full of the pieces that
were left over.
21 And those men who ate were about five

πεντακισχίλιοι, χωρὶς [r]γυναικῶν καὶ παιδίων.‖
five thousand, besides women and children.
22 Καὶ [s]εὐθέως‖ ἠνάγκασεν [t]ὁ Ἰησοῦς‖ τοὺς.μαθητὰς.[v]αὐτοῦ‖
And immediately [2]compelled [1]Jesus his disciples
ἐμβῆναι εἰς [w]τὸ‖ πλοῖον καὶ προάγειν αὐτὸν εἰς τὸ πέραν,
to enter into the ship and to go before him to the other side,
ἕως.οὗ ἀπολύσῃ τοὺς ὄχλους. 23 καὶ ἀπολύσας τοὺς
until he should have dismissed the crowds. And having dismissed the
ὄχλους ἀνέβη εἰς τὸ ὄρος κατ'.ἰδίαν προσεύξασθαι. Ὀψί-
crowds he went up into the mountain apart to pray. [2]Even-
ας δὲ γενομένης μόνος ἦν ἐκεῖ. 24 τὸ.δὲ πλοῖον ἤδη [x]μέσον
ing [1]and being come alone he was there. But the ship now in [the] midst
τῆς θαλάσσης ἦν,‖ βασανιζόμενον ὑπὸ τῶν κυμάτων· ἦν γὰρ
of the sea was, tossed by the waves, [4]was [1]for
ἐναντίος ὁ ἄνεμος. 25 Τετάρτῃ.δὲ φυλακῇ τῆς νυκτὸς
[5]contrary [2]the [3]wind. But in [the] fourth watch of the night
[y]ἀπῆλθεν‖ πρὸς αὐτοὺς [z]ὁ Ἰησοῦς,‖ περιπατῶν ἐπὶ [a]τῆς θαλάσ-
[2]went [3]to [4]them [1]Jesus, walking on the sea.
σης.‖ 26 [b]καὶ ἰδόντες αὐτὸν οἱ μαθηταὶ‖ ἐπὶ [c]τὴν θάλασσαν‖
And [3]seeing [4]him [1]the [2]disciples on the sea
περιπατοῦντα ἐταράχθησαν, λέγοντες, Ὅτι φάντασμά ἐστιν·
walking were troubled, saying, An apparition it is:
καὶ ἀπὸ τοῦ φόβου ἔκραξαν. 27 [d]εὐθέως‖.δὲ ἐλάλησεν [e]αὐ-
and through fear they cried out. But immediately [2]spoke [3]to
τοῖς ὁ Ἰησοῦς,‖ λέγων, Θαρσεῖτε, ἐγώ.εἰμι, μὴ.φοβεῖσθε.
[4]them [1]Jesus, saying, Be of good courage, I am [he], fear not.
28 Ἀποκριθεὶς δὲ [f]αὐτῷ ὁ Πέτρος εἶπεν,‖ Κύριε, εἰ σὺ.εἶ,
And answering him Peter said, Lord, if it be thou,
κέλευσόν με [g]πρός σε ἐλθεῖν‖ ἐπὶ τὰ ὕδατα. 29 Ὁ.δὲ εἶπεν,
bid me [3]to [4]thee [1]to [2]come upon the waters. And he said,
Ἐλθέ. Καὶ καταβὰς ἀπὸ τοῦ πλοίου [h]ὁ‖ Πέτρος περιεπά-
Come. And having descended from the ship Peter walk-
τησεν ἐπὶ τὰ ὕδατα, [i]ἐλθεῖν‖ πρὸς τὸν Ἰησοῦν. 30 βλέπων.δὲ
ed upon the waters, to go to Jesus. But seeing
τὸν ἄνεμον [k]ἰσχυρὸν‖ ἐφοβήθη, καὶ ἀρξάμενος καταπον-
the wind strong he was affrighted, and beginning to
τίζεσθαι ἔκραξεν, λέγων, Κύριε, σῶσόν με. 31 Εὐθέως.δὲ
sink he cried out, saying, Lord, save me. And immediately
ὁ Ἰησοῦς ἐκτείνας τὴν χεῖρα ἐπελάβετο αὐτοῦ, καὶ λέγει
Jesus having stretched out the hand took hold of him, and says
αὐτῷ, Ὀλιγόπιστε, εἰς.τί ἐδίστασας; 32 Καὶ [l]ἐμβάντων‖
to him, O [thou] of little faith, why didst thou doubt? And [2]having [3]entered
αὐτῶν εἰς τὸ πλοῖον ἐκόπασεν ὁ ἄνεμος· 33 οἱ.δὲ ἐν τῷ
[1]they into the ship [3]ceased [1]the [2]wind. And those in the
πλοίῳ [m]ἐλθόντες‖ προσεκύνησαν αὐτῷ, λέγοντες, Ἀληθῶς
ship having come worshipped him, saying, Truly
θεοῦ υἱὸς εἶ.
[3]of [2]God [1]Son thou art!
34 Καὶ διαπεράσαντες ἦλθον [n]εἰς‖ τὴν γῆν[o] [p]Γεννησαρέτ.‖
And having passed over they came to the land of Gennesaret.
35 καὶ ἐπιγνόντες αὐτὸν οἱ ἄνδρες τοῦ.τόπου.ἐκείνου ἀπέ-
And having recognized him the men of that place sent
στειλαν εἰς ὅλην τὴν.περίχωρον.ἐκείνην, καὶ προσήνεγκαν αὐτῷ
to all that country round, and brought to him
πάντας τοὺς κακῶς.ἔχοντας· 36 καὶ παρεκάλουν αὐτὸν ἵνα
all those who were ill; and besought him that
μόνον ἅψωνται τοῦ κρασπέδου τοῦ.ἱματίου.αὐτοῦ· καὶ
only they might touch the border of his garment; and
ὅσοι ἥψαντο διεσώθησαν.
as many as touched were cured.
15 Τότε προσέρχονται τῷ Ἰησοῦ [q]οἱ‖ ἀπὸ Ἱεροσολύμων
Then come to Jesus the [4]from [5]Jerusalem
[r]γραμματεῖς καὶ Φαρισαῖοι,‖ λέγοντες, 2 [s]Διατί‖ οἱ μαθηταί
[1]scribes [2]and [3]Pharisees, saying, Why [3]disciples
σου παραβαίνουσιν.τὴν παράδοσιν τῶν πρεσβυτέρων; οὐ
[2]thy [1]transgress the tradition of the elders? [4]not
γὰρ νίπτονται τὰς.χεῖρας.[t]αὐτῶν‖ ὅταν ἄρτον ἐσθίωσιν. 3 Ὁ.δὲ
[1]for [2]they [3]wash their hands when bread they eat. But he
ἀποκριθεὶς εἶπεν αὐτοῖς, [s]Διατί‖ καὶ ὑμεῖς παραβαίνετε τὴν
answering said to them, Why [2]also [1]ye [3]transgress the
ἐντολὴν τοῦ θεοῦ διὰ τὴν.παράδοσιν.ὑμῶν; 4 Ὁ γὰρ
commandment of God on account of your tradition? For
θεὸς [v]ἐνετείλατο, λέγων,‖ Τίμα τὸν.πατέρα.[w]σου‖ καὶ τὴν
God commanded, saying, Honour thy father and
μητέρα· καὶ Ὁ κακολογῶν πατέρα ἢ μητέρα, θανάτῳ τε-
mother; and, He who speaks evil of father or mother, by death let
λευτάτω. 5 ὑμεῖς.δὲ λέγετε, Ὃς.ἂν εἴπῃ τῷ πατρὶ ἢ τῇ
him die. But ye say, Whoever shall say to father or
μητρί, Δῶρον, ὃ.ἐὰν ἐξ ἐμοῦ ὠφεληθῇς, [x]καὶ‖
mother, [It is] a gift whatever by me thou mightest be profited—: and
οὐ.μὴ [y]τιμήσῃ‖ τὸν.πατέρα.αὐτοῦ [z]ἢ τὴν.μητέρα.αὐτοῦ·‖
in no wise honour his father or his mother:

thousand, besides women and children.
22 And immediately Jesus made His
disciples get into a ship and to go before
Him to the other side, until He had sent the
multitudes away.
23 And when He had sent the multitudes
away, He went up alone into a mountain to
pray. And when evening had come, He was
there alone.
24 But the ship now was in the middle of
the sea being tossed by the waves, for the
wind was contrary.
25 But in the fourth watch of the night,
Jesus went out to them, walking on the sea.
26 And seeing Him walking on the sea, the
disciples were troubled, saying, It is a ghost!
And they cried out from fear.
27 But immediately Jesus spoke to them,
saying, Be comforted, I AM *He*! Do not fear.
28 And Peter answered Him and said, Lord, if
it is You, tell me to come to You on the
waters.
29 And He said, Come! And Peter came
down out of the ship and walked on the
waters to go to Jesus.
30 But when he saw the wind was violent,
he was afraid. And beginning to sink, he
cried out, saying, Lord, save me!
31 And Jesus immediately stretched out His
hand and took hold of him. And He said to
him, *O you* of little faith, why did you doubt?
32 And after *they* had come into the ship, the
wind stopped.
33 And those in the ship came and worshiped Him, saying, Truly You are the Son
of God.
34 And after they had crossed over, they
came to the land of Gen-nes-a-ret.
35 And when the men of that place recognized Him, they sent out to all the surrounding country and brought to Him all that were
diseased.
36 And they begged Him that they might
only touch the hem of His coat. And as
many as touched were made perfectly well.

CHAPTER 15

1 Then scribes and Pharisees from Jerusalem
came to Jesus, saying,
2 Why do your disciples violate the tradition of the elders? For they do not wash
their hands when they eat bread.
3 And He answered them, saying, Why do
you also violate the commandment of God
on account of your tradition?
4 For God commanded saying, "Honor
your father and mother;" and, "He who
speaks evil of father or mother, by death let
him die."
5 But you say, Whoever shall say to father
or mother, Whatever you might have gained
from me *is* a gift *to God* – and in no way *do
you require him* to honor his father or his
mother.

6 καὶ ἠκυρώσατε [a]τὴν ἐντολὴν" τοῦ θεοῦ διὰ τὴν παρά-
and ye made void the commandment of God on account of [2]tra-
δοσιν ὑμῶν. 7 Ὑποκριταί, καλῶς [b]προεφήτευσεν" περὶ ὑμῶν
dition [1]your. Hypocrites! well prophesied concerning you
Ἡσαΐας, λέγων, 8 [c]Ἐγγίζει μοι" ὁ.λαὸς.οὗτος [d]τῷ στόματι
Esaias, saying, Draws near to me this people with [2]mouth
αὐτῶν, καὶ" τοῖς.χείλεσίν με τιμᾷ· ἡ.δὲ.καρδία.αὐτῶν πόῤῥω
their, and with the lips [3]me [1]it [2]honours; but their heart far
ἀπέχει ἀπ' ἐμοῦ. 9 μάτην.δὲ σέβονταί με, διδάσκοντες
is away from me: But in vain they worship me, teaching [as]
διδασκαλίας ἐντάλματα ἀνθρώπων. 10 Καὶ προσκαλεσάμενος
teachings injunctions of men. And having called to [him]
τὸν ὄχλον εἶπεν αὐτοῖς, Ἀκούετε καὶ συνίετε. 11 οὐ
the crowd he said to them, Hear and understand! not
τὸ εἰσερχόμενον εἰς τὸ στόμα κοινοῖ τὸν ἄνθρωπον·
that which enters into the mouth defiles the man;
ἀλλὰ τὸ ἐκπορευόμενον ἐκ τοῦ στόματος, τοῦτο κοινοῖ
but that which goes forth out of the mouth, this defiles
τὸν ἄνθρωπον.
the man.
12 Τότε προσελθόντες οἱ.μαθηταὶ.[e]αὐτοῦ" [f]εἶπον" αὐτῷ,
Then having come to [him] his disciples said to him,
Οἶδας ὅτι οἱ Φαρισαῖοι ἀκούσαντες τὸν λόγον ἐσκανδαλί-
Knowest thou that the Pharisees having heard the saying were of-
σθησαν; 13 ὁ.δὲ ἀποκριθεὶς εἶπεν, Πᾶσα φυτεία ἣν οὐκ
fended? But he answering said, Every plant which [6]not
ἐφύτευσεν ὁ.πατήρ.μου ὁ.οὐράνιος, ἐκριζωθήσεται. 14 ἄφετε
[5]has [7]planted [1]my [2]Father [3]the [4]heavenly, shall be rooted up. Leave
αὐτούς· [g]ὁδηγοί εἰσιν τυφλοὶ" τυφλῶν· τυφλὸς ·δὲ τυφλὸν
them; [4]leaders [1]they [2]are [3]blind of blind; [3]blind [1]and [5]blind
ἐὰν ὁδηγῇ, ἀμφότεροι εἰς βόθυνον πεσοῦνται. 15 Ἀποκριθεὶς.δὲ
[2]if [4]lead, both into a pit will fall. And answering
ὁ Πέτρος εἶπεν αὐτῷ, Φράσον ἡμῖν τὴν.παραβολὴν.[h]ταύτην."
Peter said to him, Expound to us this parable.
16 Ὁ.δὲ.[i]Ἰησοῦς" εἶπεν, Ἀκμὴν καὶ ὑμεῖς ἀσύνετοί ἐστε;
But Jesus said, [4]Still [3]also [2]ye [5]without [6]understanding [1]are?
17 [k]οὔπω" νοεῖτε ὅτι πᾶν τὸ εἰσπορευόμενον εἰς τὸ
[3]not [4]yet [1]perceive [2]ye that everything which enters into the
στόμα εἰς τὴν κοιλίαν χωρεῖ, καὶ εἰς ἀφεδρῶνα ἐκβάλλεται;
mouth into the belly goes, and into [the] draught is cast forth?
18 τὰ.δὲ ἐκπορευόμενα ἐκ τοῦ στόματος ἐκ τῆς
But the things which, go forth out of the mouth out of the
καρδίας ἐξέρχεται, κἀκεῖνα κοινοῖ τὸν ἄνθρωπον. 19 ἐκ.γὰρ
heart come forth, and these defile the man. For out of
τῆς καρδίας ἐξέρχονται διαλογισμοὶ πονηροί, φόνοι, μοιχεῖαι,
the heart come forth [2]reasonings [1]evil, murders, adulteries,
πορνεῖαι, κλοπαί, ψευδομαρτυρίαι, βλασφημίαι. 20 ταῦτά
fornications, thefts, false-witnessings, blasphemies. These things
ἐστιν τὰ κοινοῦντα τὸν ἄνθρωπον· τὸ.δὲ ἀνίπτοις
are they which defile the man; but the [2]with [3]unwashed
χερσὶν φαγεῖν οὐ.κοινοῖ τὸν ἄνθρωπον.
[4]hands [1]eating defiles not the man.
21 Καὶ ἐξελθὼν ἐκεῖθεν ὁ Ἰησοῦς ἀνεχώρησεν εἰς τὰ μέρη
And going forth thence Jesus withdrew to the parts
Τύρου καὶ Σιδῶνος. 22 καὶ ἰδού, γυνὴ Χαναναία ἀπὸ
of Tyre and Sidon; and behold, a [2]woman [1]Cananæan from
τῶν.ὁρίων.ἐκείνων ἐξελθοῦσα [l]ἐκραύγασεν" [m]αὐτῷ," λέγουσα,
those borders having come out cried to him, saying,
Ἐλέησόν με, κύριε, [n]υἱὲ Δαβίδ·" ἡ.θυγάτηρ.μου κακῶς δαι-
Have pity on me, Lord, Son of David; my daughter miserably is pos-
μονίζεται. 23 Ὁ.δὲ οὐκ.ἀπεκρίθη αὐτῇ λόγον. καὶ προσ-
sessed by a demon. But he answered [2]not [1]her a word. And having
ελθόντες οἱ.μαθηταὶ.αὐτοῦ [o]ἠρώτων" αὐτόν, λέγοντες,
come to [him] his disciples asked him, saying,
Ἀπόλυσον αὐτήν, ὅτι κράζει ὄπισθεν ἡμῶν· 24 Ὁ.δὲ ἀποκρι-
Dismiss her, for she cries after us. But he answer-
θεὶς εἶπεν, Οὐκ.ἀπεστάλην εἰ.μὴ εἰς τὰ πρόβατα τὰ ἀπολωλότα
ing said, I was not sent except to the sheep the lost
οἴκου Ἰσραήλ. 25 Ἡ.δὲ ἐλθοῦσα προσεκύνει αὐτῷ,
of [the] house of Israel. But she having come did homage to him,
λέγουσα, Κύριε, βοήθει μοι. 26 Ὁ.δὲ ἀποκριθεὶς εἶπεν, Οὐκ
saying, Lord, help me! But he answering said, [3]Not
[p]ἔστιν καλὸν" λαβεῖν τὸν ἄρτον τῶν τέκνων, καὶ βαλεῖν
[1]it [2]is good to take the bread of the children, and to cast [it]
τοῖς κυναρίοις. 27 Ἡ.δὲ εἶπεν, Ναί, κύριε· καὶ.γὰρ τὰ κυνάρια
to the little dogs. But she said, Yea, Lord: for even the little dogs
ἐσθίει ἀπὸ τῶν ψιχίων τῶν πιπτόντων ἀπὸ τῆς τραπέζης
eat of the crumbs which fall from the table
τῶν.κυρίων.αὐτῶν. 28 Τότε ἀποκριθεὶς ὁ Ἰησοῦς εἶπεν αὐτῇ,
of their masters. Then answering Jesus said to her,
Ὦ γύναι, μεγάλη σου ἡ πίστις· γενηθήτω σοι ὡς θέλεις.
O woman, great [is] thy faith: be it to thee as thou desirest.

6 And you have voided the commandment of God on account of your tradition.
7 Hypocrites! Well did Isaiah prophesy about you, saying,
8 "This people draws near to Me with their mouth, and with their lips honor Me, but their heart is far from Me:
9 but in vain they worship Me, teaching for doctrines the commandments of men."
10 And He called the multitude and said to them, Hear and understand!
11 Not that which enters into the mouth defiles a man, but that which goes forth out of the mouth, this defiles a man.
12 Then coming up to *Him*, His disciples said to Him, Do You know that the Pharisees were offended as they heard what You said?
13 But Jesus answered and said, Every plant which My heavenly Father has not planted shall be rooted up.
14 Leave them *alone*. They are blind leaders of the blind. And if the blind lead the blind, both will fall into the ditch.
15 Then Peter answered and said to Him, Explain this parable to us.
16 But Jesus said, Are you also still without understanding?
17 Do you not yet understand that everything which enters into the mouth goes into the belly and is thrown out into the wastebowl?
18 But the things which go forth out of the mouth come from the heart – and they defile a man.
19 For out of the heart comes forth evil thoughts, murders, adulteries, fornications, thefts, lies and blasphemies.
20 These are the things which defile a man, but eating with unwashed hands does not make a man unclean.
21 And leaving there, Jesus withdrew into the parts of Tyre and Sidon.
22 And, behold! A woman of Canaan came out of those borders and cried to Him, saying, Have mercy on me, O Lord, Son of David! My daughter is miserably possessed by a demon.
23 But He did not answer her a word. And His disciples came and asked Him, saying, Send her away, for she cries after us.
24 But He answered and said, I was not sent to any but the lost sheep of the house of Israel.
25 But she came up and bowed before Him, saying, Lord, help me!
26 But He answered and said, It is not good to take the children's bread and to throw it to the little dogs.
27 But she said, True, O Lord. But even the little dogs eat of the crumbs which fall from the table of their masters.
28 Then Jesus answered and said to her, O woman, great is your faith! So let it be to you, even as you wish. And her daughter was

Καὶ ἰάθη ἡ.θυγάτηρ.αὐτῆς ἀπὸ τῆς.ὥρας.ἐκείνης.
And was healed her daughter from that hour.
29 Καὶ μεταβὰς ἐκεῖθεν ὁ Ἰησοῦς ἦλθεν παρὰ τὴν θάλασ-
And having departed thence Jesus came towards the sea
σαν τῆς Γαλιλαίας· καὶ ἀναβὰς εἰς τὸ ὄρος ἐκάθητο
of Galilee; and having gone up into the mountain he was sitting
ἐκεῖ. 30 καὶ προσῆλθον αὐτῷ ὄχλοι πολλοί, ἔχοντες μεθ'
there. And came to him [2]crowds [1]great, having with
ἑαυτῶν χωλούς, τυφλούς, κωφούς, κυλλούς, καὶ ἑτέρους πολ-
them lame, blind, dumb, maimed, and [2]others [1]many,
λούς, καὶ [q]ἔρριψαν‖ αὐτοὺς παρὰ τοὺς πόδας [r]τοῦ Ἰησοῦ·‖
and they cast down them at the feet of Jesus,
καὶ ἐθεράπευσεν αὐτούς· 31 ὥστε [s]τοὺς ὄχλους‖ θαυμάσαι,
and he healed them; so that the crowds wondered,
βλέποντας κωφοὺς λαλοῦντας, κυλλοὺς ὑγιεῖς, [t] χωλοὺς περι-
seeing dumb speaking, maimed sound, lame walk-
πατοῦντας, καὶ τυφλοὺς βλέποντας· καὶ [v]ἐδόξασαν‖ τὸν θεὸν
ing, and blind seeing; and they glorified the God
Ἰσραήλ. 32 Ὁ.δὲ.Ἰησοῦς προσκαλεσάμενος τοὺς μαθητὰς
of Israel. But Jesus having called to [him] [2]disciples
αὐτοῦ εἶπεν, Σπλαγχνίζομαι ἐπὶ τὸν ὄχλον, ὅτι ἤδη
[1]his said, I am moved with compassion towards the crowd, because already
[w]ἡμέρας‖ τρεῖς προσμένουσίν μοι, καὶ οὐκ.ἔχουσιν τί φάγω-
[2]days [1]three they continue with me, and have not what they may
σιν· καὶ ἀπολῦσαι αὐτοὺς νήστεις οὐ.θέλω, μήποτε ἐκλυθῶσιν
eat; and to send away them fasting I am not willing, lest they faint
ἐν τῇ ὁδῷ. 33 Καὶ λέγουσιν αὐτῷ οἱ.μαθηταὶ.[x]αὐτοῦ,‖ Πόθεν
in the way. And [3]say [4]to [5]him [1]his [2]disciples, Whence
ἡμῖν ἐν ἐρημίᾳ ἄρτοι τοσοῦτοι ὥστε χορτάσαι ὄχλον τοσοῦτον;
to us in a desert loaves so many as to satisfy a crowd so great?
34 Καὶ λέγει αὐτοῖς ὁ Ἰησοῦς, Πόσους ἄρτους ἔχετε; Οἱ.δὲ
And [2]says [3]to [4]them [1]Jesus, How many loaves have ye? And they
εἶπον, Ἑπτά, καὶ ὀλίγα ἰχθύδια. 35 Καὶ [y]ἐκέλευσεν τοῖς
said, Seven, and a few small fishes. And he commanded the
ὄχλοις‖ ἀναπεσεῖν ἐπὶ τὴν γῆν· 36 [z]καὶ λαβὼν‖ τοὺς ἑπτὰ
crowds to recline on the ground; and having taken the seven
ἄρτους καὶ τοὺς ἰχθύας,[a] εὐχαριστήσας ἔκλασεν καὶ [b]ἔδωκεν‖
loaves and the fishes, having given thanks he broke and gave
τοῖς.μαθηταῖς.[c]αὐτοῦ,‖ οἱ.δὲ μαθηταὶ [d]τῷ ὄχλῳ.‖ 37 Καὶ
to his disciples, and the disciples to the crowd. And
ἔφαγον πάντες, καὶ ἐχορτάσθησαν καὶ [e]ἦραν τὸ περισ-
[2]ate [1]all, and were satisfied; and they took up that which was over
σεῦον τῶν κλασμάτων‖ ἑπτὰ σπυρίδας πλήρεις. 38 οἱ.δὲ
and above of the fragments seven baskets full; and they who
ἐσθίοντες ἦσαν τετρακισχίλιοι ἄνδρες, χωρὶς [f]γυναικῶν καὶ
ate were four thousand men, besides women and
παιδίων.‖ 39 Καὶ ἀπολύσας τοὺς ὄχλους [g]ἐνέβη‖ εἰς τὸ
children. And having dismissed the crowds he entered into the
πλοῖον, καὶ ἦλθεν εἰς τὰ ὅρια [h]Μαγδαλά.‖
ship, and came to the borders of Magdala.

16 Καὶ προσελθόντες οἱ Φαρισαῖοι καὶ Σαδδουκαῖοι
And having come to [him] the Pharisees and Sadducees
πειράζοντες [i]ἐπηρώτησαν‖ αὐτὸν σημεῖον ἐκ τοῦ οὐρανοῦ
tempting [him] asked him a sign out of the heaven
ἐπιδεῖξαι αὐτοῖς 2 ὁ.δὲ ἀποκριθεὶς εἶπεν αὐτοῖς, [k]Ὀψίας
to shew them. But he answering said to them, Evening
γενομένης λέγετε, Εὐδία· πυῤῥάζει.γὰρ ὁ οὐρανός. 3 καὶ
having come ye say, Fine weather; for [3]is [4]red [1]the [2]heaven. And
πρωΐ, Σήμερον χειμών· πυῤῥάζει.γὰρ στυγνάζων ὁ οὐρανός.
at morning, To-day a storm; for [3]is [4]red [5]lowering [1]the [2]heaven.
[l]ὑποκριταί,‖ τὸ μὲν πρόσωπον τοῦ οὐρανοῦ γινώσκετε
Hypocrites! the [5]indeed [1]face [2]of [3]the [4]heaven ye know [how]
διακρίνειν, τὰ.δὲ σημεῖα τῶν καιρῶν οὐ.δύνασθε;‖ 4 γενεὰ
to discern, but the signs of the times ye cannot! A generation
πονηρὰ καὶ μοιχαλὶς σημεῖον ἐπιζητεῖ· καὶ σημεῖον οὐ.δοθή-
wicked and adulterous a sign seeks, and a sign shall not be
σεται αὐτῇ, εἰ.μὴ τὸ σημεῖον Ἰωνᾶ [m]τοῦ προφήτου.‖ Καὶ
given to it, except the sign of Jonas the prophet. And
καταλιπὼν αὐτοὺς ἀπῆλθεν.
leaving them he went away.
5 Καὶ ἐλθόντες οἱ.μαθηταὶ.[n]αὐτοῦ‖ εἰς τὸ πέραν ἐπελάθοντο
And [3]having [4]come [1]his [2]disciples to the other side they forgot
ἄρτους λαβεῖν. 6 ὁ.δὲ.Ἰησοῦς εἶπεν αὐτοῖς, Ὁρᾶτε.καὶ προσ-
[2]loaves [1]to [2]take. And Jesus said to them, See and be-
έχετε ἀπὸ τῆς ζύμης τῶν Φαρισαίων καὶ Σαδδουκαίων. 7 Οἱ.δὲ
ware of the leaven of the Pharisees and Sadducees. And they
διελογίζοντο ἐν ἑαυτοῖς, λέγοντες, Ὅτι ἄρτους οὐκ ἐλά-
reasoned among themselves, saying, Because loaves [3]not [1]we
βομεν. 8 Γνοὺς.δὲ ὁ Ἰησοῦς εἶπεν [o]αὐτοῖς,‖ Τί δια-
[2]took. And having known [this] Jesus said to them, Why rea-
λογίζεσθε ἐν ἑαυτοῖς, ὀλιγόπιστοι, ὅτι ἄρτους οὐκ
son ye among yourselves, O [ye] of little faith, because loaves [3]not

made whole from that very hour.
29 And leaving there, Jesus came towards
the sea of Galilee. And He went up into a
mountain and sat down there.
30 And a great multitude came to Him,
having with them those who were lame,
blind, dumb, maimed and many others. And
they flung them down at Jesus' feet. And He
healed them,
31 so that the multitude wondered, seeing
the dumb speaking, the maimed sound, the
lame walking and the blind seeing. And they
glorified the God of Israel.
32 But Jesus called His disciples and said, I
am moved with compassion for the multitude, because they have been with Me three
days and have had nothing to eat. And I am
not willing to send them away fasting, for
fear that they will faint in the way.
33 And His disciples said to Him, Where
could we get so many loaves in a wilderness
so as to satisfy so great a crowd?
34 And Jesus said to them, How many
loaves do you have? And they said, Seven,
and a few little fish.
35 And He commanded the crowds to rest
on the ground.
36 And taking the seven loaves and the fish,
He gave thanks and broke *them*, giving *them*
to His disciples. And the disciples *gave them*
to the crowd.
37 And they all ate and were satisfied. And
they took up seven baskets full of the
broken pieces that were left.
38 And those who ate were four thousand
men, besides women and children.
39 And when He had sent away the crowd,
He entered into the ship and came to the
borders of Mag-da-la.

CHAPTER 16

1 And the Pharisees and Sad-du-cees came
to tempt *Him*, asking Him to show them a
sign from Heaven. But He answered and said
to them,
2 When evening has come, you say, Fair
weather; because the sky is red.
3 And in the morning, A storm today; for
the sky is red and gloomy. Hypocrites! You
indeed know how to tell the face of the sky,
but you cannot *tell* the signs of the times!
4 A wicked and adulterous generation seeks
a sign, but no sign shall be given to it except
the sign of Jonah the prophet. And leaving
them, he departed.
5 And when His disciples came to the other
side, they forgot to take loaves.
6 And Jesus said to them, Watch! Beware of
the leaven of the Pharisees and Sadducees!
7 And they reasoned among themselves,
saying, *It is* because we brought no bread.
8 And knowing this, Jesus said to them, *O
you* of little faith! Why do you reason
among yourselves because you have brought

[p]ἐλάβετε;" 9 οὔπω.νοεῖτε, οὐδὲ μνημονεύετε τοὺς πέντε
[1]ye [2]took? Do ye not yet perceive, nor remember the five
ἄρτους τῶν πεντακισχιλίων, καὶ πόσους κοφίνους ἐλάβετε,
loaves of the five thousand, and how many hand-baskets ye took [up]?
10 οὐδὲ τοὺς ἑπτὰ ἄρτους τῶν τετρακισχιλίων, καὶ πόσας
nor the seven loaves of the four thousand, and how many
[q]σπυρίδας" ἐλάβετε; 11 πῶς οὐ.νοεῖτε ὅτι οὐ περὶ
baskets ye took [up]? How perceive ye not that not concerning
[r]ἄρτου" εἶπον ὑμῖν [s]προσέχειν" ἀπὸ τῆς ζύμης τῶν Φαρισαίων
bread I spoke to you to beware of the leaven of the Pharisees
καὶ Σαδδουκαίων; 12 Τότε συνῆκαν ὅτι οὐκ.εἶπεν προσέχειν
and Sadducees? Then they understood that he said not to beware
ἀπὸ τῆς ζύμης [t]τοῦ ἄρτου," [v]ἀλλ'" ἀπὸ τῆς διδαχῆς τῶν
of the leaven of bread, but of the teaching of the
Φαρισαίων καὶ Σαδδουκαίων.
Pharisees and Sadducees.

13 Ἐλθὼν.δὲ ὁ Ἰησοῦς εἰς τὰ μέρη Καισαρείας τῆς
And [2]having [3]come [1]Jesus into the parts of Cæsarea
Φιλίππου ἠρώτα τοὺς.μαθητὰς.αὐτοῦ, λέγων, Τίνα [w]με"
Philippi he questioned his disciples, saying, Whom [4]me
λέγουσιν οἱ.ἄνθρωποι εἶναι τὸν υἱὸν τοῦ ἀνθρώπου; 14 Οἱ.δὲ
[1]do [3]pronounce [2]men [9]to [10]be [5]the [6]Son [7]of [8]man? And they
[x]εἶπον," Οἱ.μὲν Ἰωάννην τὸν βαπτιστήν· [y]ἄλλοι".δὲ [z]Ἠλίαν"
said, Some John the Baptist; and others Elias;
ἕτεροι.δὲ Ἱερεμίαν, ἢ ἕνα τῶν προφητῶν. 15 Λέγει αὐτοῖς,[a]
and others Jeremias, or one of the prophets. He says to them,
Ὑμεῖς.δὲ τίνα με λέγετε εἶναι; 16 [b]Ἀποκριθεὶς.δὲ" Σί-
But ye whom [4]me [1]do [2]ye [3]pronounce to be? And answering Si-
μων Πέτρος εἶπεν, Σὺ εἶ ὁ χριστός, ὁ υἱὸς τοῦ θεοῦ τοῦ
mon Peter said, Thou art the Christ, the Son of God the
ζῶντος. 17 [c]Καὶ ἀποκριθεὶς" ὁ Ἰησοῦς εἶπεν αὐτῷ, Μακάριος
living. And answering Jesus said to him, Blessed
εἶ, Σίμων [d]Βὰρ Ἰωνᾶ," ὅτι σὰρξ καὶ αἷμα οὐκ.ἀπεκάλυψέν
art thou, Simon Bar-Jonas, for flesh and blood revealed [it] not
σοι, ἀλλ' ὁ.πατήρ.μου ὁ ἐν [e]τοῖς" οὐρανοῖς. 18 Κἀγὼ.δὲ
to thee, but my Father who [is] in the heavens. And I also
σοι λέγω, ὅτι σὺ εἶ Πέτρος, καὶ ἐπὶ ταύτῃ τῇ πέτρᾳ οἰκοδο-
to thee say, That thou art Peter, and on this rock I will
μήσω μου τὴν ἐκκλησίαν, καὶ πύλαι ᾅδου οὐ.κατισχύσουσιν
build my assembly, and gates of hades shall not prevail against
αὐτῆς. 19 [f]καὶ" δώσω σοὶ τὰς [g]κλεῖς" τῆς βασιλείας τῶν
it. And I will give to thee the keys of the kingdom of the
οὐρανῶν· καὶ ὃ.[h]ἐὰν" δήσῃς ἐπὶ τῆς γῆς, ἔσται δεδεμένον
heavens: and whatever thou mayest bind on the earth, shall be bound
ἐν τοῖς οὐρανοῖς· καὶ ὃ.[i]ἐὰν" λύσῃς ἐπὶ τῆς γῆς, ἔσται
in the heavens; and whatever thou mayest loose on the earth, shall be
λελυμένον ἐν τοῖς οὐρανοῖς. 20 Τότε [k]διεστείλατο" τοῖς μαθη-
loosed in the heavens. Then charged he [2]dis-
ταῖς [l]αὐτοῦ" ἵνα μηδενὶ εἴπωσιν ὅτι αὐτός ἐστιν [m]Ἰησοῦς"
ciples [1]his that to no one they should say that he is Jesus
ὁ χριστός.
the Christ.

21 Ἀπὸ τότε ἤρξατο [n]ὁ" Ἰησοῦς δεικνύειν τοῖς μαθηταῖς
From that time began Jesus to show to [2]disciples
αὐτοῦ, ὅτι δεῖ αὐτὸν [o]ἀπελθεῖν εἰς Ἱεροσόλυμα," καὶ
[1]his that it is necessary for him to go away to Jerusalem, and
πολλὰ παθεῖν ἀπὸ τῶν πρεσβυτέρων καὶ ἀρχιερέων καὶ
many things to suffer from the elders and chief priests and
γραμματέων, καὶ ἀποκτανθῆναι, καὶ τῇ τρίτῃ ἡμέρᾳ ἐγερθῆναι.
scribes, and to be killed, and the third day to be raised.
22 καὶ προσλαβόμενος αὐτὸν ὁ Πέτρος [p]ἤρξατο" [q]ἐπιτιμᾶν
And [2]having [3]taken [5]to [[6]him] [4]him [1]Peter began to rebuke
αὐτῷ, λέγων," Ἵλεώς σοι, κύριε· οὐ.μὴ ἔσται σοι
him, saying, [God be] favourable to thee, Lord: in no wise shall be to thee
τοῦτο. 23 Ὁ.δὲ στραφεὶς εἶπεν τῷ Πέτρῳ, Ὕπαγε ὀπίσω μου,
this. But he having turned said to Peter, Get behind me,
σατανᾶ, σκάνδαλόν [r]μου εἶ·" ὅτι οὐ.φρονεῖς τὰ
Satan: an offence to me thou art, for thy thoughts are not of the things
τοῦ θεοῦ, ἀλλὰ τὰ τῶν ἀνθρώπων. 24 Τότε ὁ Ἰησοῦς εἶπεν
of God, but the things of men. Then Jesus said
τοῖς.μαθηταῖς.αὐτοῦ, Εἴ τις θέλει ὀπίσω μου ἐλθεῖν, ἀπαρ-
to his disciples, If any one desires after me to come, let
νησάσθω ἑαυτόν, καὶ ἀράτω τὸν.σταυρὸν.αὐτοῦ, καὶ ἀκο-
him deny himself, and let him take up his cross, and let
λουθείτω μοι. 25 ὃς.γὰρ.[s]ἂν" θέλῃ τὴν.ψυχὴν.αὐτοῦ σῶσαι,
him follow me. For whoever may desire his life to save,
ἀπολέσει αὐτήν· ὃς.δ'.ἂν ἀπολέσῃ τὴν.ψυχὴν.αὐτοῦ ἕνεκεν
shall lose it; but whoever may lose his life on account of
ἐμοῦ, εὑρήσει αὐτήν· 26 τί.γὰρ [t]ὠφελεῖται" ἄνθρωπος, ἐὰν
me, shall find it. For what is [3]profited [1]a [2]man, if
τὸν κόσμον ὅλον κερδήσῃ, τὴν.δὲ.ψυχὴν.αὐτοῦ ζημιωθῇ; ἢ
the [2]world [1]whole he gain, and his soul lose? or

no bread?

9 Do you not yet understand, nor remember the five loaves and the five thousand and how many baskets you took up?

10 – nor the seven loaves of the four thousand and how many baskets you took up?

11 How is it that you do not understand that I did not speak to you about bread, but to beware of the leaven of the Pharisees and Sadducees?

12 Then they understood that He was not saying to beware of the leaven of bread, but of the teaching of the Pharisees and Sadducees.

13 And when Jesus came into the environs of Caes-a-rea Phil-ip-pi, He questioned His disciples, saying, Who do men say that I the Son of man am?

14 And they said, Some say John the Baptist and others say Elijah, and others say Jeremiah or one of the prophets.

15 He said to them, But you, who do you say that I am?

16 And Simon Peter answered, saying, You are the Christ, the Son of the living God!

17 And answering Jesus said to him, Blessed are you, Simon, son of Jonah, for flesh and blood has not revealed it to you, but My Father who is in Heaven.

18 And I also say to you that you are Peter, and on this rock I will build My church. And the gates of hades shall not prevail against it.

19 And I will give to you the keys of the kingdom of Heaven. And whatever you may bind on earth shall occur, having been already bound in Heaven. And whatever you may loose on earth shall occur, having been already loosed in Heaven.

20 Then He charged His disciples that they should not say to anyone that He is Jesus the Christ.

21 From that time Jesus began to show to His disciples that it was necessary for Him to go away to Jerusalem and to suffer many things from the elders and chief priests and scribes – and to be killed, and to be raised the third day.

22 But taking Him aside, Peter began to rebuke Him, saying, *God be* gracious to You, Lord, this shall never be done to You.

23 But Jesus turned around and said to Peter, Get behind Me, Satan! You are a scandal to Me, for you do not think of the things of God, but of the things of men.

24 Then Jesus said to His disciples, If anyone desires to come after Me, let him deny himself and take up his cross and follow Me.

25 For whoever desires to save his life shall lose it, but whoever may lose his life for My sake shall find it.

26 For what profit is it to a man if he gain the whole world and lose his own soul? Or what will a man give in exchange for his soul?

τί δώσει ἄνθρωπος ἀντάλλαγμα τῆς.ψυχῆς.αὐτοῦ; 27 μέλ-
what will ³give ¹a ²man [as] an exchange for his soul? For ⁵is
λει.γὰρ ὁ υἱὸς τοῦ.ἀνθρώπου ἔρχεσθαι ἐν τῇ δόξῃ τοῦ πατρὸς
⁶about ¹the ²Son ³of ⁴man to come in the glory ³Father
αὐτοῦ μετὰ τῶν.ἀγγέλων.αὐτοῦ· καὶ τότε ἀποδώσει ἑκάστῳ
¹of ²his with his angels; and then he will render to each
κατὰ τὴν.πρᾶξιν.αὐτοῦ. 28 Ἀμὴν λέγω ὑμῖν, ᵛ εἰσίν
according to his doing. Verily I say to you, There are
τινες ʷτῶν ὧδε ἑστηκότων,‖ οἵτινες οὐ.μὴ γεύσωνται θανάτου
some of those here standing who in no wise shall taste of death
ἕως ἂν ἴδωσιν τὸν υἱὸν τοῦ ἀνθρώπου ἐρχόμενον ἐν τῇ
until they have seen the Son of man coming in
βασιλείᾳ.αὐτοῦ.
his kingdom.

17 Καὶ μεθ' ἡμέρας ἓξ παραλαμβάνει ὁ Ἰησοῦς τὸν Πέτρον
And after ²days ¹six ⁴takes ⁵with [⁶him] ³Jesus Peter
καὶ Ἰάκωβον καὶ Ἰωάννην τὸν.ἀδελφὸν.αὐτοῦ, καὶ ἀναφέρει
and James and John his brother, and brings up
αὐτοὺς εἰς ὄρος ὑψηλὸν κατ'.ἰδίαν. 2 καὶ μετεμορφώθη
them into a ²mountain ¹high apart. And he was transfigured
ἔμπροσθεν αὐτῶν, καὶ ἔλαμψεν τὸ.πρόσωπον.αὐτοῦ ὡς ὁ ἥλιος,
before them, and ³shone ¹his ²face as the sun,
τὰ.δὲ.ἱμάτια.αὐτοῦ ἐγένετο λευκὰ ὡς τὸ φῶς. 3 καὶ ἰδού, ˣὤφ-
and his garments became white as the light; and behold, ⁴ap-
θησαν‖ αὐτοῖς ʸΜωσῆς‖ καὶ ᶻἨλίας,| ᵃμετ' αὐτοῦ συλλαλοῦντες.‖
peared ⁵to ⁶them ¹Moses ²and ³Elias ⁸with ⁹him ⁷talking.
4 ἀποκριθεὶς.δὲ ὁ Πέτρος εἶπεν τῷ Ἰησοῦ, Κύριε, καλόν ἐστιν
And answering Peter said to Jesus, Lord, good it is
ἡμᾶς ὧδε εἶναι· εἰ θέλεις, ᵇποιήσωμεν‖ ὧδε τρεῖς σκηνάς,
for us here to be. If thou wilt, let us make here three tabernacles:
σοὶ μίαν, καὶ ᶜΜωσῇ‖ μίαν, καὶ ᵈμίαν Ἡλίᾳ.‖ 5 Ἔτι αὐτοῦ
for thee one, and for Moses one, and one for Elias. While yet he
λαλοῦντος, ἰδού, νεφέλη ᵉφωτεινὴ‖ ἐπεσκίασεν αὐτούς· καὶ
was speaking, behold, a ²cloud ¹bright overshadowed them. and
ἰδού, φωνὴ ἐκ τῆς νεφέλης, λέγουσα, Οὗτός ἐστιν ὁ.υἱός.μου
lo, a voice out of the cloud, saying, This is my Son
ὁ ἀγαπητός, ἐν ᾧ ᶠεὐδόκησα·‖ ᵍαὐτοῦ ἀκούετε.‖ 6 Καὶ
the beloved, in whom I have found delight: ³him ¹hear ²ye. And
ἀκούσαντες οἱ μαθηταὶ ʰἔπεσον‖ ἐπὶ πρόσωπον.αὐτῶν, καὶ
hearing [it] the ¹disciples fell upon their face, and
ἐφοβήθησαν σφόδρα. 7 καὶ ⁱπροσελθὼν‖ ὁ Ἰησοῦς ᵏἥψατο‖
were terrified greatly. And having come to [them] Jesus touched
αὐτῶν, ˡκαὶ‖ εἶπεν, Ἐγέρθητε, καὶ μὴ.φοβεῖσθε. 8 Ἐπάραντες
them, and said, Rise up, and be not terrified. ²Having ³lifted ⁴up
δὲ τοὺς.ὀφθαλμοὺς.αὐτῶν οὐδένα εἶδον εἰ.μὴ τὸν Ἰησοῦν
¹and their eyes ³no ⁴one ¹they ²saw except Jesus
μόνον.
alone.

9 Καὶ καταβαινόντων αὐτῶν ᵐἀπὸ‖ τοῦ ὄρους ἐνετείλατο
And as ²were ³descending ¹they from the mountain ²charged
αὐτοῖς ὁ Ἰησοῦς, λέγων, Μηδενὶ εἴπητε τὸ ὅραμα, ἕως.οὗ ὁ
³them ¹Jesus, saying, To no one tell the vision, until the
υἱὸς τοῦ ἀνθρώπου ἐκ νεκρῶν ⁿἀναστῇ.‖ 10 Καὶ ἐπη-
Son of man from among [the] dead be risen. And ³ask-
ρώτησαν αὐτὸν οἱ.μαθηταὶ.ᵒαὐτοῦ,‖ λέγοντες, Τί οὖν οἱ γραμ-
ed ⁴him ¹his ²disciples, saying, Why then ²the ³scribes
ματεῖς λέγουσιν ὅτι ᵖἨλίαν‖ δεῖ ἐλθεῖν πρῶτον; 11 Ὁ δὲ
¹say that Elias must come first? And
ᵍἸησοῦς‖ ἀποκριθεὶς εἶπεν ʳαὐτοῖς,‖ ˢἨλίας‖ μὲν ἔρχεται
Jesus answering said to them, Elias indeed comes
ᵗπρῶτον‖ καὶ ἀποκαταστήσει πάντα· 12 λέγω δὲ ὑμῖν ὅτι
first and shall restore all things. But I say to you that
ᵘἨλίας‖ ἤδη ἦλθεν, καὶ οὐκ.ἐπέγνωσαν αὐτόν, ᵛἀλλ'‖ ἐποίη-
Elias already is come, and they knew not him, but did
σαν ἐν αὐτῷ ὅσα ἠθέλησαν· οὕτως καὶ ὁ υἱὸς τοῦ ἀνθρώπου
to him whatever they desired. Thus also the Son of man
μέλλει πάσχειν ὑπ' αὐτῶν. 13 Τότε συνῆκαν οἱ μαθηταὶ ὅτι
is about to suffer from them. Then understood the disciples that
περὶ Ἰωάννου τοῦ βαπτιστοῦ εἶπεν αὐτοῖς.
concerning John the Baptist he spoke to them.

14 Καὶ ἐλθόντων ʷαὐτῶν‖ πρὸς τὸν ὄχλον προσῆλθεν
And ²having ³come ¹they to the crowd ³came
αὐτῷ ἄνθρωπος γονυπετῶν ˣαὐτῷ,‖ 15 καὶ λέγων, Κύριε,
⁴to ⁵him ¹a ²man kneeling down to him, and saying, Lord,
ἐλέησόν μου τὸν υἱόν, ὅτι σεληνιάζεται καὶ ʸκακῶς πάσχει·‖
have pity on my son, for he is lunatic and miserably suffers:
πολλάκις.γὰρ πίπτει εἰς τὸ πῦρ, καὶ πολλάκις εἰς τὸ ὕδωρ.
for often he falls into the fire, and often into the water.
16 καὶ προσήνεγκα αὐτὸν τοῖς.μαθηταῖς.σου, καὶ οὐκ.ἠδυνή-
And I brought him to thy disciples, and they were not
θησαν αὐτὸν θεραπεῦσαι. 17 Ἀποκριθεὶς.δὲ ὁ Ἰησοῦς εἶπεν,
able him to heal. And answering Jesus said,

27 For the Son of man is going to come in the
glory of His Father, with His angels. And then
He will give to each one according to his
works.
28 Truly I say to you, There are some of
those standing here who in no way shall
taste of death until they have seen the Son
of man coming in His kingdom.

CHAPTER 17

1 And after six days Jesus took Peter and
James and John, his brother. And He led
them into an isolated, high mountain.
2 And He was gloriously changed before
them. And His face shone as the sun! And
His clothes became white as the light!
3 And behold! Moses and Elijah appeared to
them, talking with Him.
4 And answering, Peter said to Jesus, Lord,
it is good for us to be here. If it pleases You,
let us make three tabernacles here: one for
You, and one for Moses, and one for Elijah.
5 While he was still speaking, lo and behold!
a bright cloud overshadowed them, and
behold, a voice out of the cloud said, This is
My beloved Son in whom I am well-pleased.
Listen to Him!
6 And hearing it, the disciples fell on their
face and were greatly terrified.
7 And Jesus came and touched them and
said, Rise up, and do not be afraid.
8 And lifting up their eyes, they saw no one
except Jesus, alone.

9 And as they were coming down from the
mountains, Jesus commanded them saying,
Tell the vision to no one until the Son of
man has arisen from the dead.
10 And His discipled asked Him, saying,
Why then do the scribes say that Elijah must
come first?
11 And answering, Jesus said to them,
Elijah indeed comes first and shall restore all
things.
12 But I say to you that Elijah already has
come, and they did not know him, but did
to him whatever they desired. In the same
way also the Son of man is going to suffer
from them.
13 Then the disciples understood that He
spoke to them of John the Baptist.
14 And when they came to the multitude,
there came to Him a man bowing to Him
and saying,
15 Lord, have mercy on my son! For he is a
lunatic and suffers miserably. For many
times he falls into the fire, and often into
the water.
16 And I brought him to Your disciples,
and they were not able to heal him.
17 And answering, Jesus said, O faithless

Ὦ γενεὰ ἄπιστος καὶ διεστραμμένη, ἕως πότε [z]ἔσομαι
O generation unbelieving and perverted, until when shall I be
μεθ' ὑμῶν;ǁ ἕως πότε ἀνέξομαι ὑμῶν; φέρετέ μοι αὐτὸν ὧδε.
with you? until when shall I bear with you? Bring to me him here.
18 Καὶ ἐπετίμησεν αὐτῷ ὁ Ἰησοῦς, καὶ ἐξῆλθεν ἀπ' αὐτοῦ τὸ
And [2]rebuked [3]him [1]Jesus, and went out from him the
δαιμόνιον, καὶ ἐθεραπεύθη ὁ παῖς ἀπὸ τῆς.ὥρας.ἐκείνης.
demon, and was healed the boy from that hour.
19 Τότε προσελθόντες οἱ μαθηταὶ τῷ Ἰησοῦ κατ'.ἰδίαν εἶπον,
Then [3]having [4]come [1]the [2]disciples to Jesus apart said,
[a]Διατίǁ ἡμεῖς οὐκ.ἠδυνήθημεν ἐκβαλεῖν αὐτό; 20 Ὁ.δὲ.[b]Ἰησοῦςǁ
Why [3]we [1]were [2]not able to cast out him? And Jesus
[c]εἶπενǁ αὐτοῖς, Διὰ τὴν [d]ἀπιστίανǁ ὑμῶν. ἀμὴν.γὰρ λέγω
said to them, Because of [2]unbelief [1]your. For verily I say
ὑμῖν, ἐὰν ἔχητε πίστιν ὡς κόκκον σινάπεως, ἐρεῖτε τῷ ὄρει
to you, If ye have faith as a grain of mustard, ye shall say [3]mountain
τούτῳ, [e]Μετάβηθι ἐντεῦθενǁ ἐκεῖ, καὶ μεταβήσεται· καὶ οὐδὲν
[1]to [2]this, Remove hence thither, and it shall remove; and nothing
ἀδυνατήσει ὑμῖν. 21 [f]τοῦτο.δὲ.τὸ.γένος οὐκ.ἐκπορεύεται
shall be impossible to you. But this kind goes not out
εἰ.μὴ ἐν προσευχῇ καὶ νηστείᾳ.ǁ
except by prayer and fasting.
22 [g]Ἀναστρεφομένωνǁ.δὲ αὐτῶν ἐν τῇ Γαλιλαίᾳ, εἶπεν αὐτοῖς
And while [2]were [3]abiding [1]they in Galilee, [2]said [3]to [4]them
ὁ Ἰησοῦς, Μέλλει ὁ υἱὸς τοῦ ἀνθρώπου παραδίδοσθαι εἰς
[1]Jesus, [9]is [10]about [5]the [6]Son [7]of [8]man to be delivered up into
χεῖρας ἀνθρώπων, 23 καὶ ἀποκτενοῦσιν αὐτόν, καὶ τῇ τρίτῃ
[the] hands of men, and they will kill him; and the third
ἡμέρᾳ [h]ἐγερθήσεται.ǁ Καὶ ἐλυπήθησαν σφόδρα.
day he shall be raised up. And they were grieved greatly.
24 Ἐλθόντων.δὲ αὐτῶν εἰς [i]Καπερναούμǁ προσῆλθον οἱ
And [2]having [3]come [1]they to Capernaum [6]came [1]those [2]who
τὰ δίδραχμα λαμβάνοντες τῷ Πέτρῳ καὶ [k]εἶπον,ǁ Ὁ διδάσ-
[4]the [5]didrachmas [3]received to Peter and said, [2]Teach-
καλος ὑμῶν οὐ.τελεῖ [l]τὰǁ δίδραχμα; 25 Λέγει, Ναί. Καὶ
er [1]your does he not pay the didrachmas? He says, Yes. And
[m]ὅτε εἰσῆλθενǁ εἰς τὴν οἰκίαν προέφθασεν αὐτὸν ὁ Ἰησοῦς,
when he entered into the house [2]anticipated [3]him [1]Jesus,
λέγων, Τί σοι.δοκεῖ, Σίμων; οἱ βασιλεῖς τῆς γῆς ἀπὸ τίνων
saying, What thinkest thou, Simon? The kings of the earth from whom
λαμβάνουσιν τέλη ἢ κῆνσον; ἀπὸ τῶν.υἱῶν.αὐτῶν, ἢ ἀπὸ
do they receive custom or tribute? from their sons, or from
τῶν ἀλλοτρίων; 26 [n]Λέγει αὐτῷǁ ὁ Πέτρος,ǁ Ἀπὸ τῶν ἀλ-
the strangers? [2]says [3]to [4]him [1]Peter, From the stran-
λοτρίων. [o]Ἔφη αὐτῷ ὁ Ἰησοῦς, [p]Ἄραγεǁ ἐλεύθεροί εἰσιν οἱ
gers. [2]said [3]to [4]him [1]Jesus, Then indeed free are the
υἱοί. 27 ἵνα.δὲ μὴ.[q]σκανδαλίσωμενǁ αὐτούς, πορευθεὶς εἰς
sons. But that we may not offend them, having gone to
[r]τὴνǁ θάλασσαν βάλε ἄγκιστρον, καὶ τὸν ἀναβάντα πρῶτον
the sea cast a hook, and the [3]coming [4]up [2]first
ἰχθὺν ἆρον· καὶ ἀνοίξας τὸ.στόμα.αὐτοῦ εὑρήσεις στα-
[1]fish take, and having opened its mouth thou shalt find a sta-
τῆρα· ἐκεῖνον λαβὼν δὸς αὐτοῖς ἀντὶ ἐμοῦ καὶ σοῦ.
ter; that having taken give to them for me and thee.

18 Ἐν ἐκείνῃ τῇ [s]ὥρᾳǁ προσῆλθον οἱ μαθηταὶ τῷ Ἰησοῦ,
In that hour came the disciples to Jesus,
λέγοντες, Τίς ἄρα μείζων ἐστὶν ἐν τῇ βασιλείᾳ τῶν οὐ-
saying, Who then [2the] [3]greater [1]is in the kingdom of the hea-
ρανῶν; 2 Καὶ προσκαλεσάμενος [t]ὁ Ἰησοῦςǁ παιδίον, ἔστησεν
vens? And [2]having [3]called [4]to [5him] [1]Jesus a little child, he set
αὐτὸ ἐν μέσῳ.αὐτῶν, 3 καὶ εἶπεν, Ἀμὴν λέγω ὑμῖν, ἐὰν.μὴ
it in their midst, and said, Verily I say to you, Unless
στραφῆτε καὶ γένησθε ὡς τὰ παιδία, οὐ.μὴ εἰσέλθητε εἰς
ye are converted and become as the little children, in no wise shall ye enter into
τὴν βασιλείαν τῶν οὐρανῶν. 4 ὅστις οὖν [v]ταπεινώσῃǁ
the kingdom of the heavens. Whosoever therefore will humble
ἑαυτὸν ὡς τὸ.παιδίον.τοῦτο, οὗτός ἐστιν ὁ μείζων ἐν τῇ βασι-
himself as this little child, he is the greater in the king-
λείᾳ τῶν οὐρανῶν. 5 καὶ ὃς.[w]ἐὰνǁ δέξηται [x]παιδίον τοιοῦτον
dom of the heavens; and whoever will receive [3]little [4]child [2]such
ἓνǁ ἐπὶ τῷ.ὀνόματί.μου, ἐμὲ δέχεται· 6 ὃς.δ'.ἂν σκανδαλίσῃ
[1]one in my name, [2]me [1]receives. But whoever shall cause [6]to [7]offend
ἕνα τῶν.μικρῶν.τούτων τῶν πιστευόντων. εἰς ἐμέ, συμφέρει
[1]one [2]of [3]these [4]little [5]ones who believe in me, it is profitable
αὐτῷ ἵνα κρεμασθῇ μύλος ὀνικὸς [y]ἐπὶǁ τὸν
for him that should be hung [4]a [5]millstone [6]turned [7]by [8]an [9]ass [1]upon
τράχηλον.αὐτοῦ, καὶ καταποντισθῇ ἐν τῷ πελάγει τῆς θαλάσ-
[2]his [3]neck, and he be sunk in the depth of the sea.
σης. 7 Οὐαὶ τῷ κόσμῳ ἀπὸ τῶν σκανδάλων· ἀνάγκη.γάρ
Woe to the world because of the offences! For necessary
[z]ἐστινǁ ἐλθεῖν τὰ σκάνδαλα, πλὴν οὐαὶ τῷ.ἀνθρώπῳ.[a]ἐκείνῳǁ
it is [3]to [4]come [1]the [2]offences, yet woe to that man

and perverted generation! How long shall I be with you? How long will I bear with you? Bring him here to Me.

18 And Jesus rebuked him, and the demon left him, and the boy was healed from that very hour.

19 Then coming aside to Jesus, the disciples said, Why were we not able to throw him out?

20 And Jesus said to them, Because of your unbelief. For truly I say to you, If you have faith as a grain of mustard seed, you shall say to this mountain, Move from here to there! And it will move. And nothing shall be impossible to you.

21 But this kind does not go out except by prayer and fasting.

22 And while they were staying in Galilee, Jesus said to them, The Son of man is about to be betrayed into the hands of men.

23 And they shall kill Him. And the third day He shall be raised up. And they were made very sad.

24 And after they had come to Ca-per-na-um, those who collected the tax-money came to Peter and said, Does your master not pay the tax money?

25 He said, Yes. And when he went into the house, Jesus spoke before him, saying, What do you think, Simon? From whom do the kings of the earth receive custom and tribute – from their sons or from strangers?

26 Peter answered Him, From strangers. Jesus said to him, Then truly the sons are free.

27 But that we may not offend them, when you go down to the sea, throw out a hook and take the first fish that comes up. And when you have opened its mouth, you will find a piece of money. Take that and give it to them for you and Me.

CHAPTER 18

1 In that hour the disciples came to Jesus, saying, Who then is greatest in the kingdom of Heaven?

2 And after Jesus had called a little child, He set him in the middle of them.

3 And He said, Truly I say to you that unless you are converted and become as the little children, you shall never enter into the kingdom of Heaven.

4 Therefore, whoever will humble himself as this little child, he is the greatest in the kingdom of Heaven.

5 And whoever shall receive one such little child in My name receives Me.

6 But whoever shall cause one of these little ones who believe in Me to stumble, it is better for him that a millstone should be hung on his neck and that he be sunk in the depth of the sea.

7 Woe to the world because of offenses! For it is necessary for the offenses to come, but

δι' οὗ τὸ σκάνδαλον ἔρχεται. 8 Εἰ.δὲ ἡ.χείρ.σου ἢ ὁ.πούς.σου
by whom the offence comes! And if thy hand or thy foot
σκανδαλίζει σε, ἔκκοψον [b]αὐτὰ‖ καὶ βάλε ἀπὸ σοῦ· καλόν
cause [2]to [3]offend [1]thee, cut off them and cast [them] from thee; good
σοι ἐστὶν εἰσελθεῖν εἰς τὴν ζωὴν [c]χωλὸν ἢ κυλλόν,‖ ἢ
for thee it is to enter into life lame or maimed, [rather] than
δύο χεῖρας ἢ δύο πόδας ἔχοντα βληθῆναι εἰς τὸ πῦρ τὸ αἰώνιον.
two hands or two feet having to be cast into the fire the eternal.
9 καὶ εἰ ὁ.ὀφθαλμός.σου σκανδαλίζει σε, ἔξελε αὐτὸν καὶ βάλε
And if thine eye cause [2]to [3]offend [1]thee, pluck out it and cast
ἀπὸ σοῦ· καλόν σοι ἐστὶν μονόφθαλμον εἰς τὴν ζωὴν
[it] from thee; good for thee it is one-eyed into life
εἰσελθεῖν, ἢ δύο ὀφθαλμοὺς ἔχοντα βληθῆναι εἰς τὴν
to enter, [rather] than two eyes having to be cast into the
γέενναν τοῦ πυρός. 10 Ὁρᾶτε μὴ.καταφρονήσητε ἑνὸς τῶν
Gehenna of the fire. See ye despise not one
μικρῶν.τούτων· λέγω.γὰρ ὑμῖν, ὅτι οἱ.ἄγγελοι.αὐτῶν [d]ἐν
of these little ones, for I say to you, that their angels in [the]
οὐρανοῖς‖ διὰ.παντὸς βλέπουσιν τὸ πρόσωπον τοῦ.πατρός.μου
heavens continually behold the face of my Father
τοῦ ἐν οὐρανοῖς. 11 [e]ἦλθεν.γὰρ ὁ υἱὸς τοῦ ἀνθρώπου
who [is] in [the] heavens. For is come the Son of man
σῶσαι τὸ ἀπολωλός.‖ 12 Τί ὑμῖν.δοκεῖ; ἐὰν γένηταί
to save that which has been lost. What think ye? If there should be
τινι ἀνθρώπῳ ἑκατὸν πρόβατα, καὶ πλανηθῇ ἓν ἐξ αὐτῶν,
to any man a hundred sheep, and be gone astray one of them,
οὐχὶ [f]ἀφεὶς‖ τὰ [g]ἐννενηκονταεννέα‖ ἐπὶ τὰ ὄρη
[does he] not, having left the ninety-nine on the mountains,
[h]πορευθεὶς ζητεῖ τὸ πλανώμενον; 13 καὶ ἐὰν γένηται
having gone seek that which is gone astray? and if it should be
εὑρεῖν αὐτό, ἀμὴν λέγω ὑμῖν, ὅτι χαίρει ἐπ' αὐτῷ μᾶλλον
that he find it, verily I say to you, that he rejoices over it more
ἢ ἐπὶ τοῖς [g]ἐννενηκονταεννέα‖ τοῖς μὴ.πεπλανημένοις. 14 οὕ-
than over the ninety-nine which have not gone astray. So
τως οὐκ.ἔστιν θέλημα ἔμπροσθεν τοῦ πατρὸς [i]ὑμῶν‖ τοῦ
it is not [the] will before [2]Father [1]your who [is]
ἐν οὐρανοῖς, ἵνα ἀπόληται [k]εἷς‖ τῶν.μικρῶν.τούτων.
in [the] heavens, that should perish one of these little ones.
15 Ἐὰν.δὲ ἁμαρτήσῃ [l]εἰς σὲ‖ ὁ.ἀδελφός.σου, ὕπαγε [m]καὶ‖
But if [3]sin [4]against [5]thee [1]thy [2]brother, go and
ἔλεγξον αὐτὸν μεταξὺ σοῦ καὶ αὐτοῦ μόνου. ἐάν σου ἀκούσῃ,
reprove him between thee and him alone. If thee he will hear,
ἐκέρδησας τὸν.ἀδελφόν.σου. 16 ἐὰν.δὲ μὴ.ἀκούσῃ, παράλαβε
thou hast gained thy brother. But if he will not hear, take
[n]μετὰ σοῦ‖ ἔτι ἕνα ἢ δύο[o], ἵνα ἐπὶ στόματος δύο μαρτύρων
with thee besides one or two, that upon [the] mouth of two witnesses
ἢ τριῶν σταθῇ πᾶν ῥῆμα. 17 ἐὰν.δὲ παρακούσῃ αὐτῶν,
or of three may stand every word. But if he fail to listen to them,
[p]εἰπὲ‖ τῇ ἐκκλησίᾳ· ἐὰν.δὲ καὶ τῆς ἐκκλησίας παρακούσῃ,
tell [it] to the assembly. And if also the assembly he fail to listen to,
ἔστω σοι ὥσπερ ὁ ἐθνικὸς καὶ ὁ τελώνης. 18 Ἀμὴν λέγω
let him be to thee as the heathen and the tax-gatherer. Verily I say
ὑμῖν, ὅσα.[q]ἐὰν‖ δήσητε ἐπὶ τῆς γῆς, ἔσται δεδεμένα ἐν [r]τῷ‖
to you, Whatsoever ye shall bind on the earth, shall be bound in the
οὐρανῷ· καὶ ὅσα.ἐὰν λύσητε ἐπὶ τῆς γῆς, ἔσται λελυμένα
heaven; and whatsoever ye shall loose on the earth, shall be loosed
ἐν [r]τῷ‖ οὐρανῷ. 19 [s]Πάλιν‖ λέγω ὑμῖν, ὅτι ἐὰν δύο [t]ὑμῶν
in the heaven. Again I say to you, that if two of you
συμφωνήσωσιν‖ ἐπὶ τῆς γῆς περὶ παντὸς πράγματος οὗ.ἐὰν
may agree on the earth concerning any matter whatever
αἰτήσωνται, γενήσεται αὐτοῖς παρὰ τοῦ.πατρός.μου τοῦ
they shall ask, it shall be done to them from my Father who [is]
ἐν οὐρανοῖς. 20 οὗ.γάρ εἰσιν δύο ἢ τρεῖς συνηγμένοι εἰς
in [the] heavens. For where are two or three gathered together unto
τὸ ἐμὸν ὄνομα, ἐκεῖ εἰμι ἐν μέσῳ αὐτῶν.
my name there am I in [the] midst of them.

21 Τότε προσελθὼν [u]αὐτῷ ὁ Πέτρος εἶπεν,‖ Κύριε, ποσάκις
Then having come to him Peter said, Lord, how often
ἁμαρτήσει εἰς ἐμὲ ὁ.ἀδελφός.μου καὶ ἀφήσω αὐτῷ; ἕως
shall [3]sin [4]against [5]me [1]my [2]brother and I forgive him? until
ἑπτάκις; 22 Λέγει αὐτῷ ὁ Ἰησοῦς, Οὐ.λέγω σοι ἕως ἑπτάκις,
seven times? [2]Says [3]to [4]him [1]Jesus, I say not to thee until seven times,
[v]ἀλλ'‖ ἕως ἑβδομηκοντάκις ἑπτά. 23 Διὰ.τοῦτο ὡμοιώθη
but until seventy times seven. Because of this [6]has [7]become [8]like
ἡ βασιλεία τῶν οὐρανῶν ἀνθρώπῳ βασιλεῖ, ὃς ἠθέλησεν
[1]the [2]kingdom [3]of [4]the [5]heavens to a man a king, who would
συνᾶραι.λόγον μετὰ τῶν.δούλων.αὐτοῦ. 24 ἀρξαμένου.δὲ αὐτοῦ
take account with his bondmen. And [2]having [3]begun [1]he
συναίρειν, [w]προσηνέχθη‖ [x]αὐτῷ εἷς‖ ὀφειλέτης μυρίων
to reckon, there was brought to him one debtor of ten thousand
ταλάντων. 25 μὴ.ἔχοντος.δὲ αὐτοῦ ἀποδοῦναι, ἐ-
talents. But [2]not [3]having [1]he [wherewith] to pay, [3]com-

woe to that man by whom the offense comes.

8 And if your hand or your foot causes you to sin, cut them off and throw *them* from you. It is better for you to enter into life lame or maimed than to have two hands or two feet to be thrown into everlasting fire.

9 And if your eye causes you to sin, pluck it out and throw it from you. It is better for you to enter into life one-eyed than to have two eyes to be thrown into hell-fire.

10 Take care that you do not despise one of these little ones, for I say to you that their angels in Heaven continually look upon the face of My Father who is in Heaven.

11 For the Son of man has come to save that which has been lost.

12 What do you think? If a man should have a hundred sheep, and one of them has gone astray, does he not leave the ninety-nine and go on the mountains to seek that which has gone astray?

13 And if it comes about that he finds it, truly I say to you that he rejoices more over it than over the ninety-nine which have not gone astray.

14 Even so it is not the will of your Father who is in Heaven that one of these little ones should perish.

15 And if your brother sin against you, go and show him his fault between you and him alone. If he will hear you, you have gained your brother.

16 But if he will not hear, take one or two more with you, so that in the mouth of two or three witnesses every word may stand.

17 But if he fails to listen to them, tell it to the church. And if he also fails to listen to the church, let him be to you as the heathen and the tax-collector.

18 Truly I say to you, Whatever you shall bind on earth shall occur, having been already bound in Heaven. And whatever you shall loose on earth shall occur, having been already loosed in Heaven.

19 Again I say to you, that if two of you agree on earth about anything, whatever they shall ask shall be done for them by My Father who is in Heaven.

20 For where two or three are gathered together in My name, I am there among them.

21 Then Peter came to Him and said, Lord, how often shall my brother sin against me and I forgive him, until seven times?

22 Jesus said to him, I do not say to you, Until seven times, but, until seventy times seven.

23 Because of this the kingdom of Heaven has been compared to a man, a king who decided on an accounting with his servants.

24 And when he had begun to count, one debtor was brought to him *who owed him* ten thousand talents.

25 But as he had nothing to pay, his lord

κέλευσεν αὐτὸν ὁ.κύριος.[j]αὐτοῦ‖ πραθῆναι, καὶ τὴν γυναῖκα
manded [4]him [1]his [2]lord to be sold, and [2]wife
[k]αὐτοῦ‖ καὶ τὰ τέκνα, καὶ πάντα ὅσα [a]εἶχεν,‖ καὶ ἀποδο-
[1]his and the children, and all as much as he had, and payment to
θῆναι. 26 πεσὼν οὖν ὁ δοῦλος[b] προσεκύνει αὐτῷ,
be made. Having fallen down therefore the bondman did homage to him,
λέγων, [c]Κύριε,‖ μακροθύμησον ἐπ' [d]ἐμοί,‖ καὶ πάντα [e]σοι
saying, Lord, have patience with me, and [6]all [4]to [5]thee
ἀποδώσω.‖ 27 σπλαγχνισθεὶς.δὲ ὁ κύριος τοῦ δούλου
[1]I [2]will [3]pay. And having been moved with compassion the lord [3]bondman
[f]ἐκείνου‖ ἀπέλυσεν αὐτόν, καὶ τὸ δάνειον ἀφῆκεν αὐτῷ.
[1]of [2]that released him, and [3]the [4]loan [1]forgave [2]him.
28 Ἐξελθὼν.δὲ ὁ.δοῦλος.[g]ἐκεῖνος‖ εὗρεν ἕνα τῶν συνδούλων
But having gone out that bondman found one [3]fellow [4]bondmen
αὐτοῦ, ὃς ὤφειλεν αὐτῷ ἑκατὸν δηνάρια, καὶ κρατήσας αὐτὸν
[1]of [2]his, who owed him a hundred denarii, and having seized him
ἔπνιγεν, λέγων, Ἀπόδος [h]μοι‖ [i]ὅ τι‖ ὀφείλεις. 29 πε-
he throttled [him], saying, Pay me what thou owest. [5]Having [6]fallen
σὼν οὖν ὁ.σύνδουλος.αὐτοῦ [k]εἰς τοὺς.πόδας.αὐτοῦ‖ παρε-
[7]down [4]therefore [1]his [2]fellow [3]bondman at his feet be-
κάλει αὐτόν, λέγων, Μακροθύμησον ἐπ' [l]ἐμοί,‖ καὶ [m]πάντα‖
sought him, saying, Have patience with me, and all
ἀποδώσω σοι. 30 Ὁ.δὲ οὐκ.ἤθελεν, [n]ἀλλὰ‖ ἀπελθὼν ἔβαλεν
I will pay thee. But he would not, but having gone he cast
αὐτὸν εἰς φυλακήν, ἕως.[o]οὗ‖ ἀποδῷ τὸ ὀφειλόμενον.
him into prison, until he should pay that which was owing.
31 ἰδόντες [p]δὲ οἱ.σύνδουλοι.αὐτοῦ‖ τὰ [q]γενόμενα‖
[5]Having [6]seen [1]but [2]his [3]fellow [4]bondmen what things had taken place,
ἐλυπήθησαν σφόδρα· καὶ ἐλθόντες διεσάφησαν τῷ.κυρίῳ.[r]αὐτῶν‖
were grieved greatly, and having gone narrated to their lord
πάντα τὰ γενόμενα. 32 Τότε προσκαλεσάμενος αὐτὸν ὁ
all that had taken place. Then [3]having [4]called [6]to [7]him] [5]him
κύριος.αὐτοῦ λέγει αὐτῷ, Δοῦλε πονηρέ, πᾶσαν τὴν ὀφειλὴν
[1]his [2]lord says to him, [2]Bondman [1]wicked, all [2]debt
ἐκείνην ἀφῆκά σοι, ἐπεὶ παρεκάλεσάς με· 33 οὐκ.ἔδει καὶ
[1]that I forgave thee, since thou besoughtest me; did it not behove [2]also
σὲ ἐλεῆσαι τὸν.σύνδουλόν.σου, ὡς [s]καὶ ἐγώ‖ σε ἠλέησα;
[1]thee to have pitied thy fellow bondman, as also I thee had pitied?
34 καὶ ὀργισθεὶς ὁ.κύριος.αὐτοῦ παρέδωκεν αὐτὸν τοῖς βασανι-
And being angry his lord delivered up him to the tormen-
σταῖς, ἕως.[t]οὗ‖ ἀποδῷ πᾶν τὸ ὀφειλόμενον [v]αὐτῷ‖ 35 Οὕτως
tors, until he should pay all that was owing to him. Thus
καὶ ὁ.πατήρ.μου ὁ [w]ἐπουράνιος‖ ποιήσει ὑμῖν ἐὰν.μὴ ἀφῆτε
also my Father the heavenly will do to you unless ye forgive
ἕκαστος τῷ.ἀδελφῷ.αὐτοῦ ἀπὸ τῶν.καρδιῶν.ὑμῶν [x]τὰ παρα-
each his brother from your hearts [2]of-
πτώματα αὐτῶν.‖
fences [1]their.

19 Καὶ ἐγένετο ὅτε ἐτέλεσεν ὁ Ἰησοῦς τοὺς λόγους
And it came to pass when [2]had [3]finished [1]Jesus [5]words
τούτους, μετῆρεν ἀπὸ [y]τῆς‖ Γαλιλαίας, καὶ ἦλθεν εἰς τὰ ὅρια
[4]these, he withdrew from Galilee, and came to the borders
τῆς Ἰουδαίας πέραν τοῦ Ἰορδάνου. 2 καὶ ἠκολούθησαν αὐτῷ
of Judæa beyond the Jordan: and [3]followed [4]him
ὄχλοι πολλοί, καὶ ἐθεράπευσεν αὐτοὺς ἐκεῖ.
[2]crowds [1]great, and he healed them there.
3 Καὶ προσῆλθον αὐτῷ [z]οἱ‖ Φαρισαῖοι πειράζοντες αὐτόν,
And [3]came [4]to [5]him [1]the [2]Pharisees tempting him,
καὶ λέγοντες [a]αὐτῷ,‖ Εἰ ἔξεστιν [b]ἀνθρώπῳ‖ ἀπολῦσαι τὴν
and saying to him, Is it lawful for a man to put away
γυναῖκα.αὐτοῦ κατὰ πᾶσαν αἰτίαν; 4 Ὁ.δὲ ἀποκριθεὶς εἶπεν
his wife for every cause? But he answering said
[c]αὐτοῖς,‖ Οὐκ.ἀνέγνωτε ὅτι ὁ [d]ποιήσας‖ ἀπ' ἀρ-
to them, Have ye not read that he who made [them] from [the] begin-
χῆς ἄρσεν καὶ θῆλυ ἐποίησεν αὐτούς, 5 καὶ εἶπεν, [e]Ἕνεκεν‖
ning male and female made them, and said, On account of
τούτου καταλείψει ἄνθρωπος τὸν πατέρα καὶ τὴν μητέρα, καὶ
this [3]shall [4]leave [1]a [2]man father and mother, and
[f]προσκολληθήσεται‖ τῇ.γυναικὶ.αὐτοῦ, καὶ ἔσονται οἱ δύο εἰς
shall be joined to his wife, and [3]shall [4]be [1]the [2]two [5]for
σάρκα μίαν; 6 ὥστε οὐκέτι εἰσὶν δύο, ἀλλὰ σὰρξ μία· ὃ
[7]flesh [6]one? So that no longer are they two, but [2]flesh [1]one. What
οὖν ὁ θεὸς συνέζευξεν, ἄνθρωπος μὴ.χωριζέτω. 7 Λέγουσιν
therefore God united together, [2]man [1]let [3]not separate. They say
αὐτῷ, Τί οὖν [g]Μωσῆς‖ ἐνετείλατο δοῦναι βιβλίον ἀπο-
to him, Why then [2]Moses [1]did command to give a bill of di-
στασίου, καὶ ἀπολῦσαι [h]αὐτήν;‖ 8 Λέγει αὐτοῖς, Ὅτι [g]Μωσῆς‖
vorce, and to put away her? He says to them, Moses
πρὸς τὴν.σκληροκαρδίαν.ὑμῶν ἐπέτρεψεν ὑμῖν ἀπολῦσαι
in view of your hard-heartedness allowed you to put away
τὰς.γυναῖκας.ὑμῶν· ἀπ' ἀρχῆς δὲ οὐ.γέγονεν οὕτως.
your wives; from [the] beginning however it was not thus.

commanded him to be sold, also his wife and children, and all that he had, and payment to be made.
26 The servant then fell down before him, saying, Lord, have patience with me and I will pay you all.
27 And being moved with pity, the lord of that servant released him and forgave him the debt.
28 But going out, the same servant found one of his fellow-servants who owed him a hundred coins. And he seized him and choked *him*, saying, Pay me what you owe.
29 His fellow-servant then fell down and begged him, saying, Have patience with me and I will pay you all.
30 But he would not, but he went out and threw him into prison until he should pay that which was owing.
31 But when his fellow-servants saw what things had taken place, they were very sorry and told their lord all that had happened.
32 Then his lord called him and said to him, Wicked servant! I forgave you all that debt because you begged me.
33 Should you not also have pitied your fellow-servant, even as I had pitied you?
34 And being angry, his lord delivered him up to the tormentors until he should pay all that was owing to him.
35 Even so shall My heavenly Father do to you unless every one of you from your heart forgives his brother his offences.

CHAPTER 19

1 And when Jesus had finished these words, He departed from Galilee and came into the borders of Judea beyond Jordan.
2 And great multitudes followed Him. And He healed them there.
3 And the Pharisees came to Him to tempt Him, saying to Him, is it lawful for a man to put away his wife for every reason?
4 But He answered them and said to them, Have you never read that He who created from the beginning made them male and female.
5 And *He* said, "For this reason a man shall leave father and mother and shall cleave to his wife, and the two shall become one flesh"?
6 So that they no longer are two, but one flesh. Then, what God has joined together, let not man separate.
7 They said to Him, Why then did Moses command to give a bill of divorce and to put her away?
8 He answered, because of the hardness of your heart Moses allowed you to put away your wives, but from the beginning it was not so.

9 λέγω.δὲ ὑμῖν, [l]ὅτι[ll] ὃς.ἂν ἀπολύσῃ τὴν.γυναῖκα.αὐτοῦ
And I say to you, that whoever shall put away his wife
[k]εἰ[ll] [l]μὴ ἐπὶ πορνείᾳ,[ll] καὶ γαμήσῃ ἄλλην, μοιχᾶται· [m]καὶ
if not for fornication, and shall marry another, commits adultery; and
ὁ ἀπολελυμένην γαμήσας μοιχᾶται.[ll] 10 Λέγουσιν
he who [2]her [4that [5]is] [6]put [6]away [1]marries commits adultery. [3]Say
αὐτῷ οἱ.μαθηταὶ.[n]αὐτοῦ,[ll] Εἰ οὕτως ἐστὶν ἡ αἰτία τοῦ ἀνθρώ-
[4]to [5]him [1]his [2]disciples, If thus is the case of the man
που μετὰ τῆς γυναικός, οὐ.συμφέρει γαμῆσαι. 11 Ὁ.δὲ εἶπεν
with the wife, it is not profitable to marry. But he said
αὐτοῖς, Οὐ πάντες χωροῦσιν τὸν.λόγον.[o]τοῦτον,[ll] ἀλλ'
to them, Not all receive this word, but [those]
οἷς δέδοται. 12 εἰσὶν.γὰρ εὐνοῦχοι οἵτινες ἐκ κοιλίας
to whom it has been given; for there are eunuchs who from [the] womb
μητρὸς ἐγεννήθησαν οὕτως, καί εἰσιν εὐνοῦχοι οἵτινες
of [their] mother were born thus, and there are eunuchs who
εὐνουχίσθησαν ὑπὸ τῶν ἀνθρώπων, καί εἰσιν εὐνοῦχοι οἵτινες
were made eunuchs by men, and there are eunuchs who
εὐνούχισαν ἑαυτοὺς διὰ τὴν βασιλείαν τῶν οὐρανῶν.
made eunuchs of themselves for the sake of the kingdom of the heavens.
ὁ δυνάμενος χωρεῖν χωρείτω.
He who is able to receive [it] let him receive [it].

13 Τότε [p]προσηνέχθη[ll] αὐτῷ παιδία, ἵνα τὰς χεῖρας
Then were brought to him little children, that [his] hands
ἐπιθῇ αὐτοῖς, καὶ προσεύξηται· οἱ.δὲ μαθηταὶ ἐπετίμησαν
he might lay on them, and might pray; but the disciples rebuked
αὐτοῖς· 14 ὁ.δὲ.Ἰησοῦς εἶπεν[q], [r]Ἄφετε τὰ παιδία, καὶ μὴ
them. But Jesus said, Suffer the little children, and [2]not
κωλύετε αὐτὰ ἐλθεῖν πρός [r]με·[ll] τῶν.γὰρ.τοιούτων ἐστὶν ἡ
[1]do forbid them to come to me; for of such is the
βασιλεία τῶν οὐρανῶν. 15 Καὶ ἐπιθεὶς [s]αὐτοῖς τὰς χεῖρας[ll]
kingdom of the heavens. And having laid upon them [his] hands
ἐπορεύθη ἐκεῖθεν.
he departed thence.

16 Καὶ ἰδού, εἷς προσελθὼν [t]εἶπεν αὐτῷ,[ll] Διδάσκαλε
And behold, one having come to [him] said to him, [2]Teacher
[u]ἀγαθέ,[ll] τί ἀγαθὸν ποιήσω ἵνα [w]ἔχω[ll] ζωὴν αἰώνιον;
[1]good, what good [thing] shall I do that I may have life eternal?
17 Ὁ.δὲ εἶπεν.αὐτῷ, [x]Τί με λέγεις ἀγαθόν; οὐδεὶς ἀγαθὸς
And he said to him, Why me callest thou good? no one [is] good
εἰ.μὴ εἷς, ὁ θεός.[ll] εἰ.δὲ θέλεις [y]εἰσελθεῖν εἰς τὴν ζωήν,[ll]
except one, God. But if thou desirest to enter into life,
[z]τήρησον[ll] τὰς ἐντολάς. 18 [a]Λέγει αὐτῷ,[ll] Ποίας; [b]Ὁ.δὲ.Ἰη-
keep the commandments. He says to him, Which? And Je-
σοῦς εἶπεν, Τό, οὐ.φονεύσεις· οὐ.μοιχεύσεις·
sus said, Thou shalt not commit murder; Thou shalt not commit adultery;
οὐ.κλέψεις· οὐ.ψευδομαρτυρήσεις· 19 τίμα τὸν πατέρα
Thou shalt not steal; Thou shalt not bear false witness; Honour [2]father
[c]σου[ll] καὶ τὴν μητέρα· καὶ ἀγαπήσεις τὸν.πλησίον.σου ὡς
[1]thy and mother; and Thou shalt love thy neighbour as
σεαυτόν. 20 Λέγει αὐτῷ ὁ νεανίσκος, [d]Πάντα ταῦτα[ll]
thyself. [4]Says [5]to [6]him [1]the [2]young [3]man, All these
[e]ἐφυλαξάμην[ll] [f]ἐκ νεότητός.μου·[l] τί ἔτι ὑστερῶ; 21 [g]Ἔφη[ll] αὐτῷ
have I kept from my youth, what yet lack I? [2]Said [3]to [4]him
ὁ Ἰησοῦς, Εἰ θέλεις τέλειος εἶναι, ὕπαγε πώλησόν σου τὰ
[1]Jesus, If thou desirest perfect to be, go sell thy
ὑπάρχοντα καὶ δὸς [h] πτωχοῖς, καὶ ἕξεις θησαυρὸν ἐν
property and give to [the] poor, and thou shalt have treasure in
[i]οὐρανῷ·[ll] καὶ δεῦρο ἀκολούθει μοι. 22 Ἀκούσας.δὲ ὁ νεανίσκος
heaven; and come follow me. But [4]having [5]heard [1]the [2]young [3]man
[k]τὸν λόγον[ll] [l] ἀπῆλθεν λυπούμενος, ἦν.γὰρ.ἔχων κτήματα
the word went away grieved, for he had [2]possessions
πολλά.
[1]many.

23 Ὁ.δὲ Ἰησοῦς εἶπεν τοῖς.μαθηταῖς.αὐτοῦ, Ἀμὴν λέγω
And Jesus said to his disciples, Verily I say
ὑμῖν, ὅτι [m]δυσκόλως [l]πλούσιος[ll] εἰσελεύσεται εἰς τὴν βασι-
to you, that with difficulty a rich man shall enter into the king-
λείαν τῶν οὐρανῶν. 24 πάλιν.δὲ λέγω ὑμῖν, [n] εὐκοπώτερόν ἐστιν
dom of the heavens. And again I say to you, easier is it
κάμηλον διὰ τρυπήματος ῥαφίδος [o]διελθεῖν,[ll] ἢ πλού-
a camel through [the] eye of a needle to pass, than a rich
σιον [p] εἰς τὴν βασιλείαν [q]τοῦ θεοῦ[ll] [r]εἰσελθεῖν.[ll] 25 Ἀκούσαντες
man into the kingdom of God to enter. [2]Having [3]heard
δὲ οἱ.μαθηταὶ.[s]αὐτοῦ[ll] ἐξεπλήσσοντο σφόδρα, λέγοντες,
[1]and [this] his disciples were astonished exceedingly, saying,
Τίς ἄρα δύναται σωθῆναι; 26 Ἐμβλέψας.δὲ ὁ Ἰησοῦς
Who then is able to be saved? But looking on [them] Jesus
εἶπεν αὐτοῖς, Παρὰ ἀνθρώποις τοῦτο ἀδύνατόν ἐστιν, παρὰ.δὲ
said to them, With men this impossible is, but with
θεῷ [t]πάντα δυνατά[ll] [v]ἐστιν.[ll]
God all things possible are.

9 And I say to you, Whoever shall put away his wife, if not for fornication, and shall marry another, commits adultery. And he who marries the one put away commits adultery.
10 His disciples asked Him, If this is the case of the man with a wife, it is not helpful to marry.
11 But He said to them, Not all receive this word, only the ones to whom it is given.
12 For there are eunuchs who from the mother's womb were born that way, and there are eunuchs who were made eunuchs by men. And there are eunuchs who have made themselves eunuchs for the sake of the kingdom of Heaven. He who is able to receive *it*, let him receive *it*.

13 Then little children were brought to Him so that He might lay hands on them and might pray. But the disciples rebuked them.
14 But Jesus said, Allow the little children and do not forbid them to come to Me, for of such is the kingdom of Heaven.
15 And laying hands upon them, He went away from there.

16 And behold! One came up to Him and said, Good Teacher, what good thing shall I do that I may have eternal life?
17 And He said to him, Why do you call Me good? No one is good, except One – God! But if you desire to enter into life, keep the commandments.
18 He asked Him, Which? Jesus said, You shall not murder; you shall not commit adultery; you shall not steal; you shall not bear false witness;
19 honor your father and mother; and you shall love your neighbor as yourself. The young man said to Him,
20 I have kept all these from my youth. What do I lack yet?
21 Jesus said to him, If you desire to be perfect, Go sell what you have and give to the poor, and you shall have treasure in Heaven. And come follow Me.
22 But when he heard that saying, the young man went away sorrowful, for he had a great many possessions.

23 And Jesus said to His disciples, Truly I say to you that a rich man shall with great difficulty enter into the kingdom of Heaven.
24 And again I say to you, It is easier for a camel to go through the eye of a needle than for a rich man to enter into the kingdom of God.
25 And His disciples were amazed when they heard this, saying, Who then can be saved?
26 But Jesus looked at them and said, With men this is impossible, but with God all things are possible.

27 Τότε ἀποκριθεὶς ὁ Πέτρος εἶπεν αὐτῷ, Ἰδού, ἡμεῖς ἀφή-
Then answering Peter said to him, Lo, we left
καμεν πάντα καὶ ἠκολουθήσαμέν σοι· τί ἄρα ἔσται ἡμῖν;
all things and followed thee; what then shall be to us?
28 Ὁ.δὲ.Ἰησοῦς εἶπεν αὐτοῖς, Ἀμὴν λέγω ὑμῖν, ὅτι ὑμεῖς οἱ
And Jesus said to them, Verily I say to you, that ye who
ἀκολουθήσαντές μοι, ἐν τῇ [w]παλιγγενεσίᾳ,ǁ ὅταν καθίσῃ
have followed me, in the regeneration, when shall sit down
ὁ υἱὸς τοῦ ἀνθρώπου ἐπὶ θρόνου δόξης.αὐτοῦ, καθίσεσθε
the Son of man upon [the] throne of his glory, [3]shall [4]sit
καὶ [x]ὑμεῖςǁ ἐπὶ δώδεκα θρόνους, κρίνοντες τὰς δώδεκα φυλὰς
[2]also [1]ye on twelve thrones, judging the twelve tribes
τοῦ Ἰσραήλ. 29 καὶ πᾶς [y]ὃςǁ ἀφῆκεν [z]οἰκίας, ἢǁ ἀδελφούς,
of Israel. And every one who has left houses, or brothers,
ἢ ἀδελφάς, ἢ πατέρα, ἢ μητέρα, [a]ἢ γυναῖκα,ǁ ἢ τέκνα, ἢ
or sisters, or father, or mother, or wife, or children, or
ἀγρούς,[b] [c]ἕνεκενǁ τοῦ.[da]ὀνόματός.μου,ǁ [ea]ἑκατονταπλασίονα
lands, for the sake of my name, a hundredfold
λήψεται,ǁ καὶ ζωὴν αἰώνιον κληρονομήσει. 30 πολλοὶ.δὲ
shall receive, and life eternal shall inherit; but many
ἔσονται πρῶτοι ἔσχατοι, καὶ ἔσχατοι πρῶτοι. 20 Ὁμοία.γάρ
[2]shall [3]be [1]first last, and last first. For [7]like
ἐστιν ἡ βασιλεία τῶν οὐρανῶν ἀνθρώπῳ οἰκοδεσπότῃ, ὅστις
[6]is [1]the [2]kingdom [3]of [4]the [5]heavens to a man a master of a house, who
ἐξῆλθεν ἅμα πρωῒ μισθώσασθαι ἐργάτας εἰς τὸν ἀμπελῶνα
went out with [the] morning to hire workmen for [2]vineyard
αὐτοῦ. 2 συμφωνήσας.δὲ μετὰ τῶν ἐργατῶν ἐκ δηναρίου τὴν
[1]his. And having agreed with the workmen for a denarius the
ἡμέραν, ἀπέστειλεν αὐτοὺς εἰς τὸν.ἀμπελῶνα.αὐτοῦ. 3 Καὶ
day, he sent them into his vineyard. And
ἐξελθὼν περὶ [f]τὴνǁ τρίτην ὥραν, εἶδεν ἄλλους ἑστῶτας
having gone out about the third hour, he saw others standing
ἐν τῇ ἀγορᾷ ἀργούς· 4 [g]κἀκείνοιςǁ εἶπεν, Ὑπάγετε καὶ
in the marketplace idle; and to them he said, Go also
ὑμεῖς εἰς τὸν ἀμπελῶνα, καὶ ὃ.ἐὰν ᾖ δίκαιον δώσω ὑμῖν.
ye into the vineyard, and whatever may be just I will give you.
5 οἱ.δὲ ἀπῆλθον. Πάλιν[h] ἐξελθὼν περὶ ἕκτην καὶ
And they went. Again having gone out about [the] sixth and
[i]ἐννάτηνǁ ὥραν, ἐποίησεν ὡσαύτως. 6 Περὶ.δὲ τὴν ἑνδεκάτην
ninth hour, he did likewise. And about the eleventh
[k]ὥρανǁ ἐξελθὼν εὗρεν ἄλλους ἑστῶτας [l]ἀργούς,ǁ καὶ λέγει
hour having gone out he found others standing idle, and says
αὐτοῖς, Τί ὧδε ἑστήκατε ὅλην τὴν ἡμέραν ἀργοί; 7 λέγουσιν
to them, Why here stand ye all the day idle? They say
αὐτῷ, Ὅτι οὐδεὶς ἡμᾶς ἐμισθώσατο. λέγει αὐτοῖς, Ὑπάγετε
to him, Because no one [3]us [1]has [2]hired. He says to them, Go
καὶ ὑμεῖς εἰς τὸν ἀμπελῶνα,[m] [n]καὶ ὃ.ἐὰν ᾖ δίκαιον λή-
also ye into the vineyard, and whatever may be just ye shall
ψεσθε.ǁ 8 Ὀψίας.δὲ γενομένης λέγει ὁ κύριος τοῦ ἀμπελῶνος
receive. But evening being come [6]says [1]the [2]lord [3]of [4]the [5]vineyard
τῷ.ἐπιτρόπῳ.αὐτοῦ, Κάλεσον τοὺς ἐργάτας, καὶ ἀπόδος [o]αὐ-
to his steward, Call the workmen, and pay them
τοῖςǁ τὸν μισθόν, ἀρξάμενος ἀπὸ τῶν ἐσχάτων ἕως τῶν
[their] hire, beginning from the last unto the
πρώτων. 9 [p]καὶ ἐλθόντεςǁ οἱ περὶ τὴν ἑνδεκάτην
first. And [7]having [8]come [1]those [[2]hired] [3]about [4]the [5]eleventh
ὥραν ἔλαβον ἀνὰ δηνάριον. 10 [q]ἐλθόντες.δὲǁ οἱ πρῶτοι
[6]hour they received each a denarius. And [3]having [4]come [1]the [2]first
ἐνόμισαν ὅτι [r]πλείονα λήψονται·ǁ καὶ ἔλαβον [s]καὶ αὐτοὶ
they thought that more they would receive, and they received also themselves
ἀνὰ δηνάριον.ǁ 11 λαβόντες.δὲ ἐγόγγυζον κατὰ τοῦ
each a denarius. And having received [it] they murmured against the
οἰκοδεσπότου, 12 λέγοντες, [t]Ὅτιǁ οὗτοι οἱ ἔσχατοι μίαν
master of the house, saying, These last one
ὥραν ἐποίησαν, καὶ ἴσους [v]ἡμῖν αὐτοὺςǁ ἐποίησας, τοῖς
hour have worked, and [5]equal [6]to [7]us [4]them [1]thou [2]hast [3]made, who
βαστάσασιν τὸ βάρος τῆς ἡμέρας καὶ τὸν καύσωνα.[w] 13 ὁ.δὲ
have borne the burden of the day and the heat. But he
ἀποκριθεὶς [x]εἶπεν ἑνὶ αὐτῶν,ǁ Ἑταῖρε, οὐκ.ἀδικῶ σε· οὐχὶ
answering said to one of them, Friend, I do not wrong thee. [3]Not
δηναρίου συνεφώνησάς μοι; 14 ἆρον τὸ.σὸν καὶ
[7]for [8]a [9]denarius [1]didst [2]thou [4]agree [5]with [6]me? Take thine own and
ὕπαγε. θέλω.[y]δὲǁ τούτῳ τῷ ἐσχάτῳ δοῦναι ὡς καὶ σοί· 15 [z]ἢǁ
go. But I will to this last give as also to thee: or
οὐκ.ἔξεστίν μοι [a]ποιῆσαι ὃ θέλωǁ ἐν τοῖς ἐμοῖς; [b]εἰǁ
is it not lawful for me to do what I will in that which [is] mine?
ὁ.ὀφθαλμός.σου πονηρός ἐστιν ὅτι ἐγὼ ἀγαθός εἰμι; 16 οὕτως
[2]thine [3]eye [4]evil [1]is because I good am? Thus
ἔσονται οἱ ἔσχατοι πρῶτοι, καὶ οἱ πρῶτοι ἔσχατοι· [c]πολλοὶ.γάρ
shall be the last first, and the first last: for many
εἰσιν κλητοί, ὀλίγοι.δὲ ἐκλεκτοί.ǁ
are called, but few chosen.

27 Then Peter answered Him and said,
Behold! We left all things and followed You.
What then will happen to us?
28 And Jesus said to them, Truly I say to
you who have followed Me: in the regeneration, when the Son of man shall sit on the
throne of His glory, you shall also sit on
twelve thrones, judging the twelve tribes of
Israel.
29 And everyone who has left houses or
brothers or sisters or father or mother or
wife or children or lands for My name's sake
shall receive a hundredfold and shall inherit
everlasting life.
30 But many *who are now* first shall be last,
and *the* last *shall be* first.

CHAPTER 20

1 For the kingdom of Heaven is like a man,
a master of a house, who went out in the
morning to hire workers for his vineyard.
2 And after agreeing with the workers for a
certain coin *for* the day, he sent them into
his vineyard.
3 And going out again the third hour, he
saw others standing idle in the marketplace.
4 And he said to them, You go also into the
vineyard, and whatever is right I will give
you And they went.
5 Going out again about the sixth and ninth
hour, he did likewise.
6 And going out about the eleventh hour,
he found others standing idle and said to
them, Why do you stand here all the day
idle?
7 They answered him, Because no one has
hired us. He said to them, You go also into
the vineyard. And whatever may be right,
you will receive.
8 And when evening came, the lord of the
vineyard said to his steward, Call the
workers and pay them *their* wages, beginning
from the last to the first.
9 And when those *hired* about the eleventh
hour came, they each received a certain coin.
10 And when the first ones had come, they
thought they would receive more. But they
also each one received a certain coin.
11 And when they received it, they grumbled against the master of the house,
12 saying, These last have worked one hour,
and you have made them equal to us who
have borne the burden and the heat of the
day.
13 But answering, he said to one of them,
Friend, I do no wrong to you. Did you not
agree with me for a certain coin?
14 Take your own and go. But I intend to
give to this last *one the same* as I also give to
you.
15 Is it not lawful for me to do what I wish
with that which is mine? Is your eye evil
because I am good?
16 So the last shall be first, and the first
last. For many are called, but few chosen.

17 Καὶ ἀναβαίνων ὁ Ἰησοῦς εἰς Ἱεροσόλυμα παρέλαβεν
And [2]going [3]up [1]Jesus to Jerusalem took
τοὺς δώδεκα [d]μαθητὰς‖ κατ' ἰδίαν [e]ἐν τῇ ὁδῷ, καὶ‖ εἶπεν αὐτοῖς,
the twelve disciples apart in the way, and said to them,
18 Ἰδού, ἀναβαίνομεν εἰς Ἱεροσόλυμα, καὶ ὁ υἱὸς τοῦ ἀνθρώ-
Behold, we go up to Jerusalem, and the Son of man
που παραδοθήσεται τοῖς ἀρχιερεῦσιν καὶ γραμματεῦσιν, καὶ
will be delivered up to the chief priests and scribes, and
κατακρινοῦσιν αὐτὸν [f]θανάτῳ,‖ 19 καὶ παραδώσουσιν αὐτὸν
they will condemn him to death, and they will deliver up him
τοῖς ἔθνεσιν εἰς τὸ ἐμπαῖξαι καὶ μαστιγῶσαι καὶ σταυρῶσαι·
to the Gentiles to mock and to scourge and to crucify;
καὶ τῇ τρίτῃ ἡμέρᾳ [g]ἀναστήσεται.‖
and the third day he will rise again.
20 Τότε προσῆλθεν αὐτῷ ἡ μήτηρ τῶν υἱῶν Ζεβεδαίου μετὰ
Then came to him the mother of the sons of Zebedee with
τῶν υἱῶν αὐτῆς, προσκυνοῦσα καὶ αἰτοῦσά τι [h]παρ'‖ αὐτοῦ.
her sons, doing homage and asking something from him.
21 ὁ δὲ εἶπεν αὐτῇ, Τί θέλεις; Λέγει αὐτῷ, Εἰπὲ ἵνα
And he said to her, What dost thou desire? She says to him, Say that
καθίσωσιν [i]οὗτοι‖ οἱ δύο υἱοί μου εἷς ἐκ δεξιῶν [k]σου‖ καὶ εἷς
[5]may [6]sit [1]these [3]two [4]sons [2]my one on thy right hand and one
ἐξ εὐωνύμων[l] ἐν τῇ βασιλείᾳ σου. 22 Ἀποκριθεὶς δὲ ὁ
on [thy] left in thy kingdom. But answering
Ἰησοῦς εἶπεν, Οὐκ οἴδατε τί αἰτεῖσθε. δύνασθε πιεῖν τὸ
Jesus said, Ye know not what ye ask for. Are ye able to drink the
ποτήριον ὃ ἐγὼ μέλλω πίνειν, [m]καὶ τὸ βάπτισμα ὃ ἐγὼ
cup which I am about to drink, and [5]the [6]baptism [7]which [8]I
βαπτίζομαι βαπτισθῆναι;‖ Λέγουσιν αὐτῷ, Δυνά-
[9]am [10]baptized [[11]with] [1]to [2]be [3]baptized [[4]with]? They say to him, We are
μεθα. 23 [n]Καὶ‖ λέγει αὐτοῖς, Τὸ μὲν ποτήριόν μου πίεσθε,
able. And he says to them, [3]Indeed [2]cup [1]my ye shall drink,
[o]καὶ τὸ βάπτισμα ὃ ἐγὼ βαπτίζομαι βαπτισθήσεσθε·‖
and the baptism which I am baptized [with] ye shall be baptized
τὸ δὲ καθίσαι ἐκ δεξιῶν μου καὶ ἐξ εὐωνύμων [p]μου‖ οὐκ
[with]; but to sit on my right hand and on my left [2]not
ἔστιν ἐμὸν[q] δοῦναι, ἀλλ' οἷς ἡτοίμασται ὑπὸ τοῦ
[1]is mine to give, but [to those] for whom it has been prepared by
πατρός μου. 24 [r]Καὶ ἀκούσαντες‖ οἱ δέκα ἠγανάκτησαν
my Father. And having heard [this] the ten were indignant
περὶ τῶν δύο ἀδελφῶν. 25 ὁ δὲ Ἰησοῦς προσκαλεσάμενος
about the two brothers. But Jesus having called [2]to [[3]him]
αὐτοὺς εἶπεν, Οἴδατε ὅτι οἱ ἄρχοντες τῶν ἐθνῶν κατακυριεύου-
[1]them said, Ye know that the rulers of the nations exercise lordship
σιν αὐτῶν, καὶ οἱ μεγάλοι κατεξουσιάζουσιν αὐτῶν. 26 οὐχ
over them, and the great ones exercise authority over them. Not
οὕτως [s]δὲ‖ [t]ἔσται‖ ἐν ὑμῖν· ἀλλ' ὃς [v]ἐὰν‖ θέλῃ [w]ἐν
thus however shall it be among you; but whoever would among
ὑμῖν‖ μέγας γενέσθαι, [x]ἔστω‖ ὑμῶν διάκονος· 27 καὶ ὃς [y]ἐὰν‖
you great become, let him be your servant; and whoever
θέλῃ ἐν ὑμῖν εἶναι πρῶτος, [z]ἔστω‖ ὑμῶν δοῦλος· 28 ὥσπερ
would among you be first, let him be your bondman; even as
ὁ υἱὸς τοῦ ἀνθρώπου οὐκ ἦλθεν διακονηθῆναι, ἀλλὰ διακονῆ-
the Son of man came not to be served, but to serve,
σαι καὶ δοῦναι τὴν ψυχὴν αὐτοῦ λύτρον ἀντὶ πολλῶν.
and to give his life a ransom for many.
29 Καὶ ἐκπορευομένων αὐτῶν ἀπὸ [a]Ἱεριχὼ‖ ἠκολούθησεν
And as [2]were [3]going [4]out [1]they from Jericho [4]followed
αὐτῷ ὄχλος πολύς. 30 καὶ ἰδού, δύο τυφλοὶ καθήμενοι
[5]him [1]a [3]crowd [2]great. And behold, two blind [men] sitting
παρὰ τὴν ὁδόν, ἀκούσαντες ὅτι Ἰησοῦς παράγει ἔκραξαν,
beside the way, having heard that Jesus is passing by cried out,
λέγοντες, [b]Ἐλέησον ἡμᾶς, κύριε,‖ [c]υἱὸς‖ [d]Δαβίδ.‖ 31 Ὁ δὲ ὄχλος
saying, Have pity on us, Lord, Son of David. But the crowd
ἐπετίμησεν αὐτοῖς ἵνα σιωπήσωσιν. οἱ δὲ μεῖζον [e]ἔκρα-
rebuked them that they should be silent. But they the more cried
ζον,‖ λέγοντες, [f]Ἐλέησον ἡμᾶς, κύριε,‖ [c]υἱὸς‖ [d]Δαβίδ‖. 32 Καὶ
out, saying, Have pity on us, Lord, Son of David. And
στὰς ὁ Ἰησοῦς ἐφώνησεν αὐτούς, καὶ εἶπεν, Τί θέλετε
having stopped, Jesus called them, and said, What do ye desire
[g]ποιήσω ὑμῖν; 33 Λέγουσιν αὐτῷ, Κύριε, ἵνα [h]ἀνοιχθῶσιν‖
I should do to you? They say to him, Lord, that [3]may [4]be [5]opened
[i]ἡμῶν οἱ ὀφθαλμοί.‖ 34 Σπλαγχνισθεὶς δὲ ὁ Ἰησοῦς ἥψατο
[1]our [2]eyes. And moved with compassion Jesus touched
τῶν [k]ὀφθαλμῶν‖ αὐτῶν· καὶ εὐθέως ἀνέβλεψαν [l]αὐτῶν οἱ
their eyes; and immediately [3]received [4]sight [1]their
ὀφθαλμοί,‖ καὶ ἠκολούθησαν αὐτῷ.
[2]eyes, and they followed him.
21 Καὶ ὅτε ἤγγισαν εἰς Ἱεροσόλυμα καὶ ἦλθον εἰς Βηθ-
And when they drew near to Jerusalem and came to Beth-
φαγῆ [m]πρὸς‖ τὸ ὄρος τῶν ἐλαιῶν, τότε [n]ὁ‖ Ἰησοῦς ἀπέστειλεν
phage towards the mount of Olives, then Jesus sent

17 And going up toward Jerusalem, Jesus took his disciples aside in the highway and said to them,
18 Behold! We are going up to Jerusalem and the Son of man will be betrayed to the chief priests and scribes. And they will condemn Him to death.
19 And they will deliver Him to the Gentiles to mock and to scourge and to crucify. And the third day He will rise again.
20 Then the mother of the sons of Zeb-e-dee came to Him with her sons, bowing down and asking something from Him.
21 And He said to her, What do you desire? She said to Him, Say that these my two sons may sit one on Your right hand and one on Your left in Your kingdom.
22 But Jesus answered and said, You do not know what you ask. Are you able to drink the cup which I am about to drink, and to be baptized with the baptism with which I am to be baptized? They said to Him, We are able.
23 And He said to them, Indeed you shall drink My cup and you will be baptized with the baptism with which I am baptized, but to sit on My right hand and on My left is not Mine to give, but *to those* for whom it has been prepared by My Father.
24 And when the ten heard this, they were indignant about the two brothers.
25 But Jesus called them to Him and said, You know that the rulers of the Gentiles lord it over them. And the great ones exercise authority over them.
26 However, it shall not be so among you. But whoever desires to become great among you, let him be your servant.
27 And whoever wants to be first among you, let him be your slave,
28 even as the Son of man did not come to be served, but to serve, and to give His life a ransom for many.
29 And as they were going out from Jer-i-cho, a great crowd followed Him.
30 And behold! Two blind ones sitting by the roadside heard that Jesus was passing by and cried out, saying, Have mercy on us, O Lord, Son of David!
31 But the crowd commanded them to be quiet. But they cried out the more, saying, Have mercy on us, O Lord, Son of David!
32 And Jesus stopped and called them, saying, What do you desire that I should do for you?
33 They said to Him, Lord, that our eyes may be opened.
34 And, moved with compassion, Jesus touched their eyes. And immediately their eyes received sight. And they followed Him.

CHAPTER 21

1 And when they drew near to Jerusalem and came to Beth-pha-ge towards the Mount

δύο μαθητάς, 2 λέγων αὐτοῖς, [o]Πορεύθητε‖ εἰς τὴν κώμην τὴν
two disciples, saying to them, Go into the village, that
[p]ἀπέναντι‖ ὑμῶν, καὶ [q]εὐθέως‖ εὑρήσετε ὄνον δεδεμένην, καὶ
opposite you, and immediately ye will find an ass tied, and
πῶλον μετ' αὐτῆς· λύσαντες [r]ἀγάγετέ‖ μοι. 3 καὶ ἐάν
a colt with her; having loosed [them] bring [them] to me. And if
τις ὑμῖν εἴπῃ τι, ἐρεῖτε, "Ὅτι ὁ κύριος αὐτῶν χρείαν
any one to you say anything, ye shall say, The Lord [3]of [4]them [2]need
ἔχει· [s]εὐθέως‖.δὲ [t]ἀποστελεῖ‖ αὐτούς. 4 Τοῦτο.δὲ [u]ὅλον‖ γέ-
[1]has. And immediately he will send them. But this all came
γονεν ἵνα πληρωθῇ τὸ ῥηθὲν διὰ τοῦ προφήτου,
to pass that might be fulfilled that which was spoken by the prophet,
λέγοντος, 5 Εἴπατε τῇ θυγατρὶ Σιών, Ἰδού, ὁ.βασιλεύς.σου
saying, Say to the daughter of Sion, Behold, thy king
ἔρχεταί σοι, πραῢς [v]καὶ‖ ἐπιβεβηκὼς ἐπὶ ὄνον καὶ [w] πῶλον
comes to thee, meek and mounted on an ass and a colt [the]
υἱὸν ὑποζυγίου. 6 Πορευθέντες.δὲ οἱ μαθηταί, καὶ ποιήσαν-
foal of a beast of burden. And [3]having [4]gone [1]the [2]disciples, and having
τες καθὼς [x]προσέταξεν‖ αὐτοῖς ὁ Ἰησοῦς, 7 ἤγαγον τὴν
done as [2]ordered [3]them [1]Jesus, they brought the
ὄνον καὶ τὸν πῶλον, καὶ ἐπέθηκαν [y]ἐπάνω‖ αὐτῶν τὰ ἱμάτια
ass and the colt, and put upon them [2]garments
[z]αὐτῶν,‖ καὶ [a]ἐπεκάθισεν‖ ἐπάνω αὐτῶν. 8 ὁ.δὲ πλεῖστος
[1]their, and he sat on them. And the greater part [of the]
ὄχλος ἔστρωσαν ἑαυτῶν τὰ ἱμάτια ἐν τῇ ὁδῷ, ἄλλοι.δὲ ἔκοπ-
crowd strewed their garments on the way, and others were cutting
τον κλάδους ἀπὸ τῶν δένδρων καὶ [b]ἐστρώννυον‖ ἐν τῇ
down branches from the trees and were strewing [them] on the
ὁδῷ. 9 οἱ.δὲ ὄχλοι οἱ προάγοντες[c] καὶ οἱ ἀκολουθοῦντες
way. And the crowds those going before and those following
ἔκραζον, λέγοντες, Ὡσαννὰ τῷ υἱῷ [d]Δαβίδ·‖ εὐλογημένος
were crying out, saying, Hosanna to the Son of David; blessed
ὁ ἐρχόμενος ἐν ὀνόματι κυρίου· Ὡσαννὰ ἐν τοῖς
[be] he who comes in [the] name of [the] Lord. Hosanna in the
ὑψίστοις. 10 Καὶ εἰσελθόντος.αὐτοῦ εἰς Ἱεροσόλυμα ἐσείσθη
highest. And as he entered into Jerusalem [4]was [5]moved
πᾶσα ἡ πόλις, λέγουσα, Τίς ἐστιν οὗτος; 11 Οἱ.δὲ ὄχλοι
[1]all [2]the [3]city, saying, Who is this? And the crowds
ἔλεγον, Οὗτός ἐστιν [e]Ἰησοῦς ὁ προφήτης,‖ ὁ ἀπὸ [f]Να-
said, This is Jesus the prophet, he who [is] from Na-
ζαρὲτ‖ τῆς Γαλιλαίας.
zareth of Galilee.

12 Καὶ εἰσῆλθεν [g]ὁ‖ Ἰησοῦς εἰς τὸ ἱερὸν [h]τοῦ θεοῦ,‖ καὶ
And [2]entered [1]Jesus into the temple of God, and
ἐξέβαλεν πάντας τοὺς πωλοῦντας καὶ ἀγοράζοντας ἐν τῷ
cast out all those selling and buying in the
ἱερῷ, καὶ τὰς τραπέζας τῶν κολλυβιστῶν κατέστρεψεν, καὶ
temple, and the tables of the money changers he overthrew, and
τὰς καθέδρας τῶν πωλούντων τὰς περιστεράς. 13 καὶ λέγει
the seats of those selling the doves. And he says
αὐτοῖς, Γέγραπται, Ὁ.οἶκός.μου οἶκος προσευχῆς κληθή-
to them, It has been written, My house, a house of prayer shall be
σεται· ὑμεῖς.δὲ αὐτὸν [i]ἐποιήσατε‖ σπήλαιον λῃστῶν. 14 Καὶ
called; but ye it have made a den of robbers. And
προσῆλθον αὐτῷ τυφλοὶ καὶ χωλοὶ ἐν τῷ ἱερῷ, καὶ ἐθεράπευ-
[4]came [5]to [6]him [1]blind [2]and [3]lame in the temple, and he healed
σεν αὐτούς. 15 Ἰδόντες.δὲ οἱ ἀρχιερεῖς καὶ οἱ γραμματεῖς
them. But [7]seeing [1]the [2]chief [3]priests [4]and [5]the [6]scribes
τὰ θαυμάσια ἃ ἐποίησεν, καὶ τοὺς παῖδας [k]κράζοντας ἐν τῷ
the wonders which he wrought, and the children crying in the
ἱερῷ, καὶ λέγοντας, Ὡσαννὰ τῷ υἱῷ [l]Δαβίδ,‖ ἠγανάκτησαν,
temple, and saying, Hosanna to the Son of David, they were indignant,
16 καὶ [m]εἶπον‖ αὐτῷ, Ἀκούεις τί οὗτοι λέγουσιν; Ὁ.δὲ.Ἰη-
and said to him, Hearest thou what these say? And Je-
σοῦς λέγει αὐτοῖς, Ναί· οὐδέποτε ἀνέγνωτε, "Ὅτι ἐκ στόμα-
sus says to them, Yea; [3]never [1]did [2]ye read, Out of [the] mouth
τος νηπίων καὶ θηλαζόντων κατηρτίσω αἶνον; 17 Καὶ
of babes and sucklings thou hast perfected praise? And
καταλιπὼν αὐτοὺς ἐξῆλθεν ἔξω τῆς πόλεως εἰς Βηθανίαν, καὶ
having left them he went out of the city to Bethany, and
ηὐλίσθη ἐκεῖ.
passed the night there.

18 [n]Πρωΐας‖.δὲ [o]ἐπανάγων‖ εἰς τὴν πόλιν ἐπείνασεν,
Now early in the morning coming back into the city he hungered,
19 καὶ ἰδὼν συκῆν μίαν ἐπὶ τῆς ὁδοῦ, ἦλθεν ἐπ' αὐτήν, καὶ
and seeing [2]fig-tree [1]one by the way, he came to it, and
οὐδὲν εὗρεν ἐν αὐτῇ εἰ.μὴ φύλλα μόνον· καὶ λέγει αὐτῇ,
nothing found on it except leaves only. And he says to it,
[p] Μηκέτι ἐκ σοῦ καρπὸς γένηται εἰς τὸν.αἰῶνα. Καὶ ἐξηράνθη
Never more of thee fruit let there be for ever. And [4]dried [5]up
παραχρῆμα ἡ συκῆ. 20 Καὶ ἰδόντες οἱ μαθηταὶ ἐθαύμασαν,
[1]immediately [2]the [3]fig-tree. And seeing [it] the disciples wondered,

of Olives, then Jesus sent two disciples,
2 saying to them, Go into the village across
from you. And you will immediately find an
ass tied, and a colt with her. Untie and bring
them to Me.
3 And if anyone says anything to you, you
shall say, The Lord has need of them. And
he will quickly send them.
4 But all this was so that which was spoken
by the prophet might be fulfilled, saying,
5 "Tell the daughter of Zion, Behold! Your
King comes to you, meek and mounted on
an ass, even a colt, the foal of a beast of
burden."
6 And the disciples left. And they did as
Jesus commanded them.
7 They brought the ass and the colt, and
they put their coats on them. And He sat on
the coats.
8 And most of the crowd spread their coats
on the road.
9 And others were cutting down branches
from the trees and were spreading *them* on
the road. And the multitudes, those going
before and those following, were crying out,
saying, Hosanna to the son of David! Blessed
is He who comes in the name of the Lord –
Hosanna in the highest!
10 And as He entered into Jerusalem, all the
city was moved, saying, Who is this?
11 And the multitudes said, This is Jesus
the Prophet, He who is from Nazareth of
Galilee.
12 And Jesus entered into the Temple of
God and threw out all those selling and
buying in the Temple. And He overthrew the
tables of the money-changers, and the seats
of those selling the doves.
13 And He said to them, It is written, "My
house shall be called a house of prayer," but
you have made it a den of thieves.
14 And the blind and the lame came to Him
in the Temple. And He healed them.
15 But when the chief priests and the
scribes saw the wonders which He did, and
the children crying in the Temple and
saying, Hosanna to the son of David, they
were angry.
16 And *they* said to Him, Do you hear what
these say? And Jesus said to them, Yes, have
you never read, "Out of the mouth of babes
and sucklings You have perfected praise"?
17 And He left them and went out of the
city to Bethany, and He spent the night
there.
18 Now early in the morning, coming back
into the city, He was hungry.
19 And seeing a fig-tree by the roadside, He
came to it and found nothing on it, only the
leaves. And He said to it, Let there be no
more fruit from you forever. And the fig-
tree immediately dried up.
20 And seeing it the disciples wondered
saying, How soon the fig-tree withered

λέγοντες, Πῶς παραχρῆμα ἐξηράνθη ἡ συκῆ; 21 Ἀποκριθεὶς
saying, How immediately is dried up the fig-tree! [2]Answering
δὲ ὁ Ἰησοῦς εἶπεν αὐτοῖς, Ἀμὴν λέγω ὑμῖν, ἐὰν ἔχητε πίστιν,
[1]and Jesus said to them, Verily, I say to you, If ye have faith,
καὶ μὴ.διακριθῆτε, οὐ μόνον τὸ τῆς συκῆς ποιήσετε,
and do not doubt, not only the [miracle] of the fig-tree shall ye do,
ἀλλὰ κἂν τῷ.ὄρει.τούτῳ εἴπητε, Ἄρθητι καὶ βλήθητι
but even if to this mountain ye should say, Be thou taken away and be thou cast
εἰς τὴν θάλασσαν, γενήσεται· 22 καὶ πάντα ὅσα.[q]ἂν‖
into the sea, it shall come to pass. And all things whatsoever
αἰτήσητε ἐν τῇ προσευχῇ, πιστεύοντες, [r]λήψεσθε.‖
ye may ask in prayer, believing, ye shall receive.

23 Καὶ [s]ἐλθόντι.αὐτῷ‖ εἰς τὸ ἱερὸν προσῆλθον αὐτῷ
And on his coming into the temple there came up to him, [when]
διδάσκοντι οἱ ἀρχιερεῖς καὶ οἱ πρεσβύτεροι τοῦ λαοῦ, λέγον-
teaching, the chief priests and the elders of the people, say-
τες, Ἐν ποίᾳ ἐξουσίᾳ ταῦτα ποιεῖς; καὶ τίς σοι ἔδωκεν τὴν
ing, By what authority these things doest thou? and who to thee gave
ἐξουσίαν.ταύτην; 24 Ἀποκριθεὶς.[t]δὲ‖ ὁ Ἰησοῦς εἶπεν αὐτοῖς,
this authority? And answering Jesus said to them,
Ἐρωτήσω ὑμᾶς κἀγὼ λόγον ἕνα, ὃν ἐὰν εἴπητέ μοι, κἀγὼ
[3]Will [4]ask [5]you [1]I [2]also [7]thing [6]one, which if ye tell me, I also
ὑμῖν ἐρῶ ἐν ποίᾳ ἐξουσίᾳ ταῦτα ποιῶ. 25 τὸ βάπτισμα
to you will say by what authority these things I do. The baptism
[v] Ἰωάννου πόθεν ἦν; ἐξ οὐρανοῦ, ἢ ἐξ ἀνθρώπων;
of John, whence was it? from heaven, or from men?
Οἱ.δὲ διελογίζοντο [w]παρ'‖ ἑαυτοῖς, λέγοντες, Ἐὰν εἴπω-
And they reasoned with themselves, saying, If we should
μεν, Ἐξ οὐρανοῦ, ἐρεῖ ἡμῖν, [x]Διατί‖ οὖν οὐκ.ἐπιστεύσατε
say, From heaven, he will say to us, Why then did ye not believe
αὐτῷ; 26 ἐὰν.δὲ εἴπωμεν, Ἐξ ἀνθρώπων, φοβούμεθα τὸν
him? but if we should say, From men, we fear the
ὄχλον· πάντες.γὰρ [y]ἔχουσιν τὸν Ἰωάννην ὡς προφήτην.‖
multitude; for all hold John as a prophet.
27 Καὶ ἀποκριθέντες τῷ Ἰησοῦ [z]εἶπον,‖ Οὐκ οἴδαμεν. Ἔφη
And answering Jesus they said, We know not. [3]Said
αὐτοῖς καὶ αὐτός, Οὐδὲ ἐγὼ λέγω ὑμῖν ἐν ποίᾳ ἐξουσίᾳ
[4]to [5]them [2]also [1]he, Neither [2]I [1]tell you by what authority
ταῦτα ποιῶ. 28 Τί.δὲ ὑμῖν.δοκεῖ; ἄνθρωπος[a] εἶχεν [b]τέκνα
these things I do. But what think ye? a man had [2]children
δύο,‖ [c]καὶ‖ προσελθὼν τῷ πρώτῳ εἶπεν, Τέκνον, ὕπαγε
[1]two, and having come to the first he said, Child, go
σήμερον ἐργάζου ἐν τῷ.ἀμπελῶνί.[d]μου.‖ 29 Ὁ.δὲ ἀποκριθεὶς
to-day work in my vineyard. And he answering
εἶπεν, Οὐ.θέλω· ὕστερον.[e]δὲ‖ μεταμεληθεὶς ἀπῆλθεν. 30 [f]Καὶ
said, I will not; but afterwards having repented he went. And
προσελθὼν‖ τῷ [g]δευτέρῳ‖ εἶπεν ὡσαύτως. ὁ.δὲ ἀποκριθεὶς
having come to the second he said likewise. And he answering
εἶπεν, Ἐγώ, κύριε· καὶ οὐκ.ἀπῆλθεν. 31 Τίς ἐκ τῶν δύο ἐποίη-
said, I [go], sir, and went not. Which of the two did
σεν τὸ θέλημα τοῦ πατρός; Λέγουσιν [h]αὐτῷ,‖ [i]Ὁ πρῶτος.‖
the will of the father? They say to him, The first.
Λέγει αὐτοῖς ὁ Ἰησοῦς, Ἀμὴν λέγω ὑμῖν, ὅτι οἱ τελῶναι καὶ
[2]Says [3]to [4]them [1]Jesus, Verily I say to you, that the tax-gatherers and
αἱ πόρναι προάγουσιν ὑμᾶς εἰς τὴν βασιλείαν τοῦ θεοῦ.
the harlots go before you into the kingdom of God.
32 ἦλθεν.γὰρ [k]πρὸς ὑμᾶς Ἰωάννης‖ ἐν ὁδῷ δικαιοσύνης,
For [2]came [3]to [4]you [1]John in [the] way of righteousness,
καὶ οὐκ.ἐπιστεύσατε αὐτῷ, οἱ.δὲ τελῶναι καὶ αἱ πόρναι
and ye did not believe him, but the tax-gatherers and the harlots
ἐπίστευσαν αὐτῷ· ὑμεῖς.δὲ ἰδόντες [l]οὐ‖.μετεμελήθητε ὕστερον
believed him; but ye having seen did not repent afterwards
τοῦ πιστεῦσαι αὐτῷ.
to believe him.

33 Ἄλλην παραβολὴν ἀκούσατε. Ἄνθρωπός [m]τις‖ ἦν
Another parable hear. A [2]man [1]certain there was
οἰκοδεσπότης, ὅστις ἐφύτευσεν ἀμπελῶνα, καὶ φραγμὸν αὐτῷ
a master of a house, who planted a vineyard, and [4]a [5]fence [3]it
περιέθηκεν, καὶ ὤρυξεν ἐν αὐτῷ ληνόν, καὶ ᾠκοδόμησεν
[1]placed [2]about, and dug in it a winepress, and built
πύργον, καὶ [n]ἐξέδοτο‖ αὐτὸν γεωργοῖς, καὶ ἀπεδήμησεν.
a tower, and let out it to husbandmen, and left the country.
34 ὅτε.δὲ ἤγγισεν ὁ καιρὸς τῶν καρπῶν, ἀπέστειλεν τοὺς
And when drew near the season of the fruits, he sent
δούλους.αὐτοῦ πρὸς τοὺς γεωργοὺς λαβεῖν τοὺς.καρποὺς.αὐτοῦ.
his bondmen to the husbandmen to receive his fruits.
35 καὶ λαβόντες οἱ γεωργοὶ τοὺς.δούλους.αὐτοῦ, ὃν.μὲν
And [3]having [4]taken [1]the [2]husbandmen his bondmen, one
ἔδειραν, ὃν.δὲ ἀπέκτειναν, ὃν.δὲ ἐλιθοβόλησαν. 36 πάλιν
they beat, and another they killed, and another they stoned. Again
ἀπέστειλεν ἄλλους δούλους πλείονας τῶν πρώτων, καὶ ἐποίη-
he sent other bondmen more than the first, and they

away!
21 Answering, Jesus said to them, Truly I say to you, If you have faith and do not doubt, not only the *miracle* of the fig-tree you shall do, but even if you should say to the mountain, Be moved! And, Be tossed into the sea! It shall happen.
22 And all things, whatever you may ask in prayer, believing, you shall receive.

23 And as He came into the Temple to teach, the chief priests and the elders of the people came up to Him and said, By what authority do You do these things? And, Who gave You this authority?
24 And Jesus answered and said to them, I will ask you one thing also, which if you tell Me I also will tell you by what authority I do these things.
25 The baptism of John, where was it from – from Heaven, or from men?
26 And they reasoned with themselves, saying, If we should say, From Heaven, He will say to us, Then why did you not believe him? But if we should say, From men, we fear the people. For all hold John to be a prophet.
27 And they answered Jesus, saying, We do not know. He also said to them, Neither do I tell you by what authority I do these things.
28 But what do you think? A man had two children. And he came to the first and said, Child, go work today in my vineyard.
29 And he answered, saying, I will not. But repenting afterwards, he went.
30 And coming to the second, he said the same. And he answered, saying, I *go*, sir – but he did not go.
31 Which of the two did the will of the father? They said to him, The first. Jesus said to them, Truly I say to you that the tax-collectors and the harlots go into the kingdom of God before you.
32 For John came to you in the way of righteousness, and you did not believe him – but the tax-collectors and harlots believed him. And when you had seen it, you did not repent afterwards so that you might believe him.

33 Hear another parable: There was a certain man, a master of a house, who planted a vineyard and placed a hedge around it. And *he* dug a winepress in it and built a tower. And he let it out to vinedressers and left the country.
34 And when the fruit season came, he sent his servants to the vinedressers to receive his fruits.
35 And after the vinedressers took his servants, they beat one, and another they killed, and another they stoned.
36 Again he sent other servants, more than the first. And they did to them the same.

σαν αὐτοῖς ὡσαύτως. 37 ὕστερον.δὲ ἀπέστειλεν πρὸς αὐτοὺς
did to them in like manner. And at last he sent to them

τὸν.υἱὸν.αὐτοῦ, λέγων, Ἐντραπήσονται τὸν.υἱόν.μου.
his son, saying, They will have respect for my son.

38 Οἱ.δὲ γεωργοὶ ἰδόντες τὸν υἱὸν εἶπον ἐν ἑαυτοῖς, Οὗτός
But the husbandmen seeing the son said among themselves, This

ἐστιν ὁ κληρονόμος· δεῦτε, ἀποκτείνωμεν αὐτόν, καὶ [o]κατά-
is the heir; come, let us kill him, and gain pos-

σχωμεν‖ τὴν.κληρονομίαν.αὐτοῦ. 39 καὶ λαβόντες αὐτὸν
session of his inheritance. And having taken him

ἐξέβαλον ἔξω τοῦ ἀμπελῶνος καὶ ἀπέκτειναν. 40 ὅταν οὖν
they cast [him] out of the vineyard and killed [him]. When therefore

ἔλθῃ ὁ κύριος τοῦ ἀμπελῶνος, τί ποιήσει τοῖς γεωργοῖς
shall come the lord of the vineyard, what will he do [3]husbandmen

ἐκείνοις; 41 Λέγουσιν αὐτῷ, Κακοὺς κακῶς ἀπολέσει
[1]to [2]those? They say to him, Evil [men]! miserably he will destroy

αὐτούς, καὶ τὸν ἀμπελῶνα [p]ἐκδόσεται‖ ἄλλοις γεωργοῖς,
them, and the vineyard he will let out to other husbandmen,

οἵτινες ἀποδώσουσιν αὐτῷ τοὺς καρποὺς ἐν τοῖς.καιροῖς.αὐτῶν.
who will render to him the fruits in their seasons.

42 Λέγει αὐτοῖς ὁ Ἰησοῦς, Οὐδέποτε.ἀνέγνωτε ἐν ταῖς γρα-
[2]Says [3]to [4]them [1]Jesus, Did ye never read in the scrip-

φαῖς, Λίθον ὃν ἀπεδοκίμασαν οἱ οἰκοδομοῦντες, οὗτος
tures, [The] stone which [4]rejected [1]those [2]who [3]build, this

ἐγενήθη εἰς κεφαλὴν γωνίας· παρὰ κυρίου ἐγένετο αὕτη,
is become head of [the] corner: from [the] Lord was this,

καὶ ἔστιν θαυμαστὴ ἐν ὀφθαλμοῖς.ἡμῶν; 43 Διὰ τοῦτο λέγω
and it is wonderful in our eyes? Because of this I say

ὑμῖν, ὅτι ἀρθήσεται ἀφ' ὑμῶν ἡ βασιλεία τοῦ θεοῦ, καὶ
to you, that [3]shall [4]be [5]taken [1]from [2]you the kingdom of God, and

δοθήσεται ἔθνει ποιοῦντι τοὺς καρποὺς αὐτῆς. 44 [q]καὶ
it shall be given to a nation producing the fruits of it. And

ὁ πεσὼν ἐπὶ τὸν.λίθον.τοῦτον συνθλασθήσεται· ἐφ'.ὃν.δ'.ἂν
he who falls on this stone shall be broken; but on whomsoever

πέσῃ, λικμήσει αὐτόν.‖ 45 [r]Καὶ ἀκούσαντες‖ οἱ
it shall fall it will grind to powder him. And [7]hearing [1]the

ἀρχιερεῖς καὶ οἱ Φαρισαῖοι τὰς.παραβολὰς.αὐτοῦ ἔγνωσαν
[2]chief [3]priests [4]and [5]the [6]Pharisees his parables knew

ὅτι περὶ αὐτῶν λέγει. 46 καὶ ζητοῦντες αὐτὸν κρατῆσαι,
that about them he speaks. And seeking him to lay hold of,

ἐφοβήθησαν τοὺς ὄχλους, [s]ἐπειδὴ‖ [t]ὡς‖ προφήτην αὐτὸν εἶχον.
they feared the crowds, because as a prophet him they held.

22 Καὶ ἀποκριθεὶς ὁ Ἰησοῦς πάλιν εἶπεν [v]αὐτοῖς ἐν παρα-
And answering Jesus again spoke to them in para-

βολαῖς,‖ λέγων, 2 Ὡμοιώθη ἡ βασιλεία τῶν οὐρανῶν
bles, saying, [6]Has [7]become [8]like [1]the [2]kingdom [3]of [4]the [5]heavens

ἀνθρώπῳ βασιλεῖ, ὅστις ἐποίησεν γάμους τῷ.υἱῷ.αὐτοῦ·
to a man a king, who made a wedding feast for his son:

3 καὶ ἀπέστειλεν τοὺς.δούλους.αὐτοῦ καλέσαι τοὺς κεκλη-
and sent his bondmen to call those who had been

μένους εἰς τοὺς γάμους, καὶ οὐκ.ἤθελον ἐλθεῖν. 4 Πάλιν
invited to the wedding feast, and they would not come. Again

ἀπέστειλεν ἄλλους δούλους, λέγων, Εἴπατε τοῖς κεκλη-
he sent other bondmen, saying, Say to those who had been

μένοις, Ἰδού, τὸ.ἄριστόν.μου [w]ἡτοίμασα,‖ οἱ.ταῦροί.μου καὶ
invited, Behold, my dinner I prepared, my oxen and

τὰ σιτιστὰ τεθυμένα, καὶ πάντα ἕτοιμα· δεῦτε εἰς τοὺς
the fatted beasts are killed, and all things [are] ready; come to the

γάμους. 5 Οἱ.δὲ ἀμελήσαντες ἀπῆλθον, [x]ὁ‖.μὲν εἰς τὸν
wedding feast. But they being negligent of [it] went away, one to

ἴδιον ἀγρόν, [y]ὁ‖.δὲ [z]εἰς‖ τὴν.ἐμπορίαν.αὐτοῦ. 6 οἱ.δὲ λοιποὶ
his own field, and another to his commerce. And the rest,

κρατήσαντες τοὺς.δούλους.αὐτοῦ ὕβρισαν καὶ ἀπέκτειναν.
having laid hold of his bondmen, insulted and killed [them].

7 [a]Ἀκούσας.δὲ ὁ βασιλεὺς ὠργίσθη, καὶ πέμψας τὰ
And having heard [it] the king was wroth, and having sent

στρατεύματα.αὐτοῦ ἀπώλεσεν τοὺς.φονεῖς.ἐκείνους, καὶ τὴν
his forces he destroyed those murderers, and

πόλιν.αὐτῶν ἐνέπρησεν. 8 Τότε λέγει τοῖς δούλοις.αὐτοῦ, Ὁ
their city he burnt. Then he says to his bondmen, The

μὲν γάμος ἕτοιμός ἐστιν, οἱ.δὲ κεκλημένοι οὐκ.ἦσαν
[3]indeed [1]wedding [2]feast [5]ready [4]is, but those who had been invited were not

ἄξιοι· 9 πορεύεσθε οὖν ἐπὶ τὰς διεξόδους τῶν ὁδῶν, καὶ
worthy; Go therefore into the thoroughfares of the highways, and

ὅσους [b]ἂν‖.εὕρητε, καλέσατε εἰς τοὺς γάμους. 10 Καὶ
as many as ye shall find, invite to the wedding feast. And

ἐξελθόντες οἱ.δοῦλοι.ἐκεῖνοι εἰς τὰς ὁδοὺς συνήγαγον πάντας
[3]having [4]gone [5]out [1]those [2]bondmen into the highways brought together all

ὅσους εὗρον, πονηρούς τε καὶ ἀγαθούς· καὶ ἐπλήσθη ὁ
as many as they found, [2]evil [1]both and good; and [4]became [5]full [1]the

[c]γάμος‖ ἀνακειμένων. 11 εἰσελθὼν.δὲ ὁ βασιλεὺς θεάσα-
[2]wedding [3]feast of guests. And [3]coming [4]in [1]the [2]king to see

[37]And at last he sent to them his son, saying, They will have respect for my son.

[38]But seeing the son, the vinedressers said among themselves, This is the heir! Come, let us kill him and get hold of his inheritance.

[39]And taking him, they threw *him* out of the vineyard and killed *him.*

[40]Therefore, when the lord of the vineyard shall come, what will he do to those vinedressers?

[41]They said to Him, Evil ones! He will miserably destroy them and he will let out the vineyard to other vinedressers who will give him the fruits in their seasons.

[42]Jesus said to them, Have you never read in the Scriptures, "*The* Stone which the builders rejected is the one that has become the head of the corner: this was from *the* Lord and it is wonderful in our eyes"?

[43]Because of this I say to you, The kingdom of God shall be taken from you, and it shall be given to a nation bringing forth the fruits of it.

[44]And he who falls on this Stone shall be broken, and on whomever it shall fall, it will grind him to powder.

[45]And the chief priests and the Pharisees hearing His parables knew that He spoke about them.

[46]And they sought to lay hold of Him, but they feared the multitude, because they held Him as a prophet.

22 [1]And answering, Jesus again spoke to them in parables, saying,

[2]The kingdom of Heaven has been compared to a man, a king, who made a wedding feast for his son.

[3]And *he* sent his servants to call those who had been invited to the wedding feast, and they would not come.

[4]Again he sent other servants, saying, Tell those who have been invited, Behold, I have prepared my dinner, my oxen and the fatlings are killed, and all things are ready. Come to the wedding feast.

[5]But paying no attention at all, they went away, one to his own field, and another to his business.

[6]And the rest, catching hold of his servants insulted and killed *them.*

[7]And hearing it, the king was angry. And he sent forth his armies to destroy those murderers, and he burned their city.

[8]Then he said to his servants, The wedding feast indeed is ready, but those who had been invited were not worthy.

[9]Therefore go into the highways and invite as many as you shall find to the wedding feast.

[10]And going out into the highways, those servants brought together as many as they found, both evil and good. And the wedding feast was full of guests.

[11]And coming in to see the guests, the king

σθαι τοὺς ἀνακειμένους εἶδεν ἐκεῖ ἄνθρωπον οὐκ ἐνδεδυμένον
the guests beheld there a man not clothed
ἔνδυμα γάμου. 12 καὶ λέγει αὐτῷ, Ἑταῖρε, πῶς
with a garment of [the] wedding feast; and he says to him, Friend, how
εἰσῆλθες ὧδε μὴ ἔχων ἔνδυμα γάμου; Ὁ.δὲ
didst thou enter here not having a garment of [the] wedding feast? But he
ἐφιμώθη. 13 τότε [d]εἶπεν ὁ βασιλεὺς‖ τοῖς διακόνοις, Δήσαν-
was speechless. Then said the king to the servants, Having
τες αὐτοῦ πόδας καὶ χεῖρας [e]ἄρατε αὐτὸν καὶ‖ ἐκβάλετε [f]
bound his feet and hands take away him and cast out [him]
εἰς τὸ σκότος τὸ ἐξώτερον· ἐκεῖ ἔσται ὁ κλαυθμὸς καὶ ὁ
into the darkness the outer: there shall be the weeping and the
βρυγμὸς τῶν ὀδόντων. 14 πολλοὶ.γάρ εἰσιν κλητοί, ὀλίγοι.δὲ
gnashing of the teeth. For many are called, but few
ἐκλεκτοί.
chosen.

15 Τότε πορευθέντες οἱ Φαρισαῖοι συμβούλιον ἔλαβον ὅπως
Then having gone the Pharisees [2]counsel [1]took how
αὐτὸν παγιδεύσωσιν ἐν λόγῳ. 16 καὶ ἀποστέλλουσιν αὐτῷ
him they might ensnare in discourse. And they send to him
τοὺς.μαθητὰς.αὐτῶν μετὰ τῶν Ἡρωδιανῶν, [g]λέγοντες,‖ Διδά-
their disciples with the Herodians, saying, Teacher,
σκαλε, οἴδαμεν ὅτι ἀληθὴς εἶ, καὶ τὴν ὁδὸν τοῦ θεοῦ ἐν ἀληθείᾳ
we know that true thou art, and the way of God in truth
διδάσκεις, καὶ οὐ μέλει σοι περὶ οὐδενός, οὐ.γὰρ βλέπεις
teachest, and there is care to thee about no one, for [3]not [1]thou [2]lookest
εἰς πρόσωπον ἀνθρώπων· 17 [h]εἰπὲ‖ οὖν ἡμῖν, τί [2]σοι
on [the] appearance of men; tell therefore us, what [2]thou
δοκεῖ; ἔξεστιν δοῦναι κῆνσον Καίσαρι ἢ οὔ; 18 Γνοὺς.δὲ
[1]thinkest? Is it lawful to give tribute to Cæsar or not? But [2]knowing
ὁ Ἰησοῦς τὴν.πονηρίαν.αὐτῶν εἶπεν, Τί με πειράζετε, ὑπο-
[1]Jesus their wickedness said, Why me do ye tempt, hypo-
κριταί; 19 ἐπιδείξατέ μοι τὸ νόμισμα τοῦ κήνσου. Οἱ.δὲ
crites? Shew me the coin of the tribute. And they
προσήνεγκαν αὐτῷ δηνάριον. 20 καὶ λέγει αὐτοῖς[i], Τίνος
presented to him a denarius. And he says to them, Whose [is]
ἡ.εἰκὼν.αὕτη καὶ ἡ ἐπιγραφή; 21 Λέγουσιν [k]αὐτῷ,‖ Καίσαρος.
this image and the inscription? They say to him, Cæsar's.
Τότε λέγει αὐτοῖς, Ἀπόδοτε οὖν τὰ Καίσαρος Καίσαρι,
Then he says to them, Render then the things of Cæsar to Cæsar,
καὶ τὰ τοῦ θεοῦ τῷ θεῷ. 22 Καὶ ἀκούσαντες ἐθαύμασαν·
and the things of God to God. And having heard they wondered;
καὶ ἀφέντες αὐτὸν [l]ἀπῆλθον.‖
and leaving him went away.

23 Ἐν ἐκείνῃ τῇ ἡμέρᾳ προσῆλθον αὐτῷ Σαδδουκαῖοι, [m]οἱ‖
On that day came to him Sadducees, who
λέγοντες μὴ.εἶναι ἀνάστασιν, καὶ ἐπηρώτησαν αὐτόν, 24 λέ-
say there is not a resurrection, and they questioned him, say-
γοντες, Διδάσκαλε, [n]Μωσῆς‖ εἶπεν, Ἐάν τις ἀποθάνῃ μὴ
ing, Teacher, Moses said, If any one should die not
ἔχων τέκνα, [o]ἐπιγαμβρεύσει ὁ.ἀδελφὸς.αὐτοῦ τὴν γυναῖκα
having children, [3]shall [4]marry [1]his [2]brother [5]wife
αὐτοῦ, καὶ ἀναστήσει σπέρμα τῷ.ἀδελφῷ.αὐτοῦ. 25 Ἦσαν.δὲ
[6]his, and shall raise up seed to his brother. Now there were
παρ' ἡμῖν ἑπτὰ ἀδελφοί· καὶ ὁ πρῶτος [p]γαμήσας‖ ἐτελεύτη-
with us seven brothers; and the first having married died,
σεν, καὶ μὴ ἔχων σπέρμα ἀφῆκεν τὴν.γυναῖκα.αὐτοῦ τῷ
and not having seed left his wife
ἀδελφῷ.αὐτοῦ. 26 ὁμοίως καὶ ὁ δεύτερος, καὶ ὁ τρίτος,
to his brother. In like manner also the second, and the third,
ἕως τῶν ἑπτά. 27 ὕστερον.δὲ πάντων ἀπέθανεν [q]καὶ‖ ἡ γυνή.
unto the seven. And last of all died also the woman.
28 ἐν τῇ [r]οὖν ἀναστάσει‖ τίνος τῶν ἑπτὰ ἔσται γυνή;
[2]In [3]the [1]therefore resurrection of which of the seven shall she be wife?
πάντες.γὰρ ἔσχον αὐτήν. 29 Ἀποκριθεὶς.δὲ ὁ Ἰησοῦς εἶπεν
for all had her. And answering Jesus said
αὐτοῖς, Πλανᾶσθε, μὴ εἰδότες τὰς γραφάς, μηδὲ τὴν δύναμιν
to them, Ye err, not knowing the scriptures, nor the power
τοῦ θεοῦ. 30 ἐν.γὰρ τῇ ἀναστάσει οὔτε γαμοῦσιν οὔτε
of God. For in the resurrection neither do they marry nor
[s]ἐκγαμίζονται,‖ ἀλλ' ὡς ἄγγελοι [t]τοῦ‖ [v]θεοῦ‖ ἐν [w] οὐρανῷ
are given in marriage, but as angels of God in heaven
εἰσιν. 31 περὶ.δὲ τῆς ἀναστάσεως τῶν νεκρῶν, οὐκ.ἀνέγνωτε
they are. But concerning the resurrection of the dead, have ye not read
τὸ ῥηθὲν ὑμῖν ὑπὸ τοῦ θεοῦ, λέγοντος, 32 Ἐγώ εἰμι
that which was spoken to you by God, saying, I am
ὁ θεὸς Ἀβραὰμ καὶ ὁ θεὸς Ἰσαὰκ καὶ ὁ θεὸς Ἰακώβ; οὐκ
the God of Abraham and the God of Isaac and the God of Jacob? [3]Not
ἔστιν [x]ὁ θεὸς‖ [y]θεὸς‖ νεκρῶν, ἀλλὰ ζώντων. 33 Καὶ ἀκού-
[2]is [1]God God of [the] dead, but of [the] living. And having
σαντες οἱ ὄχλοι ἐξεπλήσσοντο ἐπὶ τῇ.διδαχῇ.αὐτοῦ.
heard, the crowds were astonished at his teaching.

saw there a man not clothed with a wedding
garment.
12 And he said to him, Friend, how did you
come in here without a wedding garment?
But he was speechless.
13 Then the king said to the servants, After
binding his feet and hands, take him away
and throw him out into the outer darkness.
There shall be weeping and gnashing of teeth
14 – for many are called, but few chosen.

15 Then after they had left, the Pharisees
planned how they might trap *Him* in words.
16 And they sent their disciples to Him,
with the Herodians, saying, Teacher, we
know that you are true and teach the way of
God in truth, nor do you care for anyone,
for you do not look on the face of men.
17 Then tell us, what do you think? Is it
lawful to give tribute to Caesar or not?
18 But knowing their wickedness Jesus said,
Why do you tempt Me, hypocrites?
19 Show Me the tribute money. And they
brought a coin to Him.
20 And He said to them, Whose image and
writing is this?
21 They said to Him, Caesar's. Then He said
to them, Then give to Caesar the things of
Caesar, and to God the things of God.
22 And hearing this, they marveled. And
they left Him and went away.

23 On that day Sadducees (who say there is
no resurrection) came to Him. And they
questioned Him,
24 saying, Teacher, Moses said, If anyone
should die not having children, his brother
shall marry his wife and raise up seed to his
brother.
25 Now there were with us seven brothers.
And after he had married, the first one died,
and having no seed he left his wife to his
brother.
26 In the same way the second also died,
and the third, to the seventh.
27 And last of all the woman also died.
28 Then in the resurrection, of the seven,
whose wife shall she be? For they all had
her.
29 And answering, Jesus said to them, You
err, not knowing the Scriptures nor the
power of God.
30 For in the resurrection they neither
marry nor are given in marriage, but are as
the angels of God in Heaven.
31 But concerning the resurrection of the
dead, have you not read that which was
spoken to you by God, saying,
32 "I am the God of Abraham and the God
of Isaac and the God of Jacob"? God is not
God of the dead, but of the living.
33 And hearing this, the multitudes were
astonished at His teaching.

34 Οἱ.δὲ Φαρισαῖοι ἀκούσαντες ὅτι ἐφίμωσεν τοὺς Σαδ-
But the Pharisees, having heard that he had silenced the Sad-
δουκαίους, συνήχθησαν ἐπὶ.τὸ.αὐτό, 35 καὶ ἐπηρώτησεν
ducees, were gathered together, and [9]questioned [[10]him]
εἷς ἐξ αὐτῶν νομικός, πειράζων αὐτόν, [z]καὶ λέγων,"
[1]one [2]of [3]them [4]a [5]doctor [6]of [7]the [8]law, tempting him, and saying,
36 Διδάσκαλε, ποία ἐντολὴ μεγάλη ἐν τῷ νόμῳ;
Teacher, which [4]commandment [[1]is [2]the] [3]great in the law?
37 [a]Ὁ.δὲ.Ἰησοῦς εἶπεν αὐτῷ," Ἀγαπήσεις κύριον τὸν θεόν
And Jesus said to him, Thou shalt love [the] Lord [2]God
σου ἐν ὅλῃ [b]τῇ".καρδίᾳ σου, καὶ ἐν ὅλῃ τῇ.ψυχῇ.σου, καὶ ἐν
[1]thy with all thy heart, and with all thy soul, and with
ὅλῃ τῇ.διανοίᾳ.σου. 38 αὕτη ἐστὶν [c]πρώτη καὶ μεγάλη"
all thy mind. This is [the] first and great
ἐντολή. 39 δευτέρα.[d]δὲ" ὁμοία αὐτῇ, Ἀγαπήσεις τὸν
commandment. And [the] second [is] like it, Thou shalt love
πλησίον.σου ὡς σεαυτόν. 40 ἐν ταύταις ταῖς δυσὶν ἐντολαῖς
thy neighbour as thyself. On these two commandments
ὅλος ὁ νόμος [e]καὶ οἱ προφῆται κρέμανται."
all the law and the prophets hang.

41 Συνηγμένων.δὲ τῶν Φαρισαίων ἐπηρώτησεν
But [3]having [4]been [5]assembled [6]together, [1]the [2]Pharisees [8]questioned
αὐτοὺς ὁ Ἰησοῦς, 42 λέγων, Τί ὑμῖν δοκεῖ περὶ τοῦ χριστοῦ;
[9]them [7]Jesus, saying, What [2]ye [1]think concerning the Christ?
τίνος υἱός ἐστιν; Λέγουσιν αὐτῷ, Τοῦ.[f]Δαβίδ." 43 Λέγει
of whom [3]son [1]is [2]he? They say to him, Of David. He says
αὐτοῖς, Πῶς οὖν [f]Δαβὶδ" ἐν πνεύματι [g]κύριον αὐτὸν καλεῖ;"
to them, How then [2]David [3]in [4]spirit [7]Lord [6]him [1]does [5]call?
λέγων, 44 Εἶπεν [h]ὁ" κύριος τῷ.κυρίῳ.μου, Κάθου ἐκ δεξιῶν.μου
saying, [3]Said [1]the [2]Lord to my Lord, Sit on my right hand
ἕως.ἂν θῶ τοὺς.ἐχθρούς.σου [i]ὑποπόδιον" τῶν.ποδῶν.σου.
until I place thine enemies [as] a footstool for thy feet.
45 Εἰ οὖν [f]Δαβὶδ" καλεῖ αὐτὸν κύριον, πῶς υἱὸς.αὐτοῦ
If therefore David calls him Lord, how his son
ἐστιν; 46 Καὶ οὐδεὶς ἐδύνατο [k]αὐτῷ ἀποκριθῆναι" λόγον,
is he? And no one was able him to answer a word
οὐδὲ ἐτόλμησέν τις ἀπ' ἐκείνης τῆς ἡμέρας ἐπερωτῆσαι αὐτὸν
nor dared anyone from that day to question him
οὐκέτι.
any more (*lit.* no more).

23 Τότε ὁ Ἰησοῦς ἐλάλησεν τοῖς ὄχλοις καὶ τοῖς.μαθηταῖς
Then Jesus spoke to the crowds and to [2]disciples
αὐτοῦ, 2 λέγων, Ἐπὶ τῆς [l]Μωσέως" καθέδρας ἐκάθισαν οἱ
[1]his, saying, On the [2]of [3]Moses [1]seat have sat down the
γραμματεῖς καὶ οἱ Φαρισαῖοι· 3 πάντα οὖν ὅσα.[m]ἂν" εἴπω-
scribes and the Pharisees; all things therefore whatever they may
σιν ὑμῖν [n]τηρεῖν," [o]τηρεῖτε καὶ ποιεῖτε·" κατὰ.δὲ τὰ.ἔργα.αὐτῶν
tell you to keep, keep and do. But after their works
μὴ.ποιεῖτε λέγουσιν.γὰρ καὶ οὐ.ποιοῦσιν. 4 δεσμεύουσιν [p]γὰρ"
do not; for they say and do not. [2]They [3]bind [1]for
φορτία βαρέα [q]καὶ δυσβάστακτα," καὶ ἐπιτιθέασιν ἐπὶ τοὺς
burdens heavy and hard to bear, and lay [them] on the
ὤμους τῶν ἀνθρώπων· [r]τῷ δὲ.δακτύλῳ.αὐτῶν" οὐ.θέλουσιν
shoulders of men, but with their own finger they will not
κινῆσαι αὐτά. 5 πάντα.δὲ τὰ.ἔργα.αὐτῶν ποιοῦσιν πρὸς τὸ
move them. And all their works they do to
θεαθῆναι τοῖς ἀνθρώποις. πλατύνουσιν [s]δὲ" τὰ φυλακτήρια
be seen by men. [2]They [3]make [4]broad [1]and [5]phylacteries
αὐτῶν, καὶ μεγαλύνουσιν τὰ κράσπεδα [t]τῶν.ἱματίων.αὐτῶν·"
[6]their, and enlarge the borders of their garments,
6 φιλοῦσίν [v]τε" τὴν πρωτοκλισίαν ἐν τοῖς δείπνοις, καὶ τὰς
[2]love [1]and the first place in the suppers, and the
πρωτοκαθεδρίας ἐν ταῖς συναγωγαῖς, 7 καὶ τοὺς ἀσπασμοὺς ἐν
first seats in the synagogues, and the salutations in
ταῖς ἀγοραῖς, καὶ καλεῖσθαι ὑπὸ τῶν ἀνθρώπων [w]ῥαββί, ῥαββί·"
the market-places, and to be called by men Rabbi, Rabbi.
8 ὑμεῖς.δὲ μὴ.κληθῆτε [x]ῥαββί·" εἷς.γάρ ἐστιν ὑμῶν ὁ [y]καθηγητής,"
But [2]ye [1]be [3]not called Rabbi; for one is your leader,
[z]ὁ χριστός·" πάντες.δὲ ὑμεῖς ἀδελφοί ἐστε. 9 καὶ πατέρα μὴ
the Christ, and all ye brethren are. And [6]father [2]not
καλέσητε ὑμῶν ἐπὶ τῆς γῆς· εἷς.γάρ ἐστιν [a]ὁ.πατὴρ.ὑμῶν,"
[1]call [5]your [[3]any [4]one] on the earth; for one is your father,
[b]ὁ ἐν τοῖς οὐρανοῖς." 10 μηδὲ κληθῆτε καθηγηταί· [c]εἷς.γὰρ
who [is] in the heavens. Neither be called leaders; for one
ὑμῶν ἐστιν ὁ καθηγητής," ὁ χριστός. 11 ὁ.δὲ μείζων ὑμῶν
[2]your [1]is leader, the Christ. But the greater of you
ἔσται ὑμῶν διάκονος. 12 ὅστις.δὲ ὑψώσει ἑαυτὸν ταπεινωθή-
shall be your servant. And whosoever will exalt himself shall be
σεται· καὶ ὅστις ταπεινώσει ἑαυτὸν ὑψωθήσεται.
humbled; and whosoever will humble himself shall be exalted.
13 (14) [d]Οὐαὶ.[e]δὲ" ὑμῖν, γραμματεῖς καὶ Φαρισαῖοι, ὑποκριταί,
But woe to you, scribes and Pharisees, hypocrites,

34 But the Pharisees, hearing that He had
silenced the Sadducees, were gathered together.
35 And one of them, a doctor of the Law,
questioned *Him*, tempting Him and saying,
36 Teacher, which is the great commandment in the Law?
37 And Jesus said to him, You shall love the
Lord your God with all your heart and with
all your soul and with all your mind.
38 This is the first and great commandment.
39 And the second is like it. You shall love
your neighbor as yourself.
40 On these two commandments hang all
the Law and the Prophets.
41 But the Pharisees being gathered together, Jesus asked them,
42 saying, What do you think about the
Christ? Whose son is He? They said to Him,
the son of David.
43 He said to them, How then does David in
Spirit call Him Lord, saying,
44 "The Lord said to my Lord, Sit on My
right hand until I place Your enemies as a
footstool for Your feet"?
45 Then if David calls Him Lord, how is He
his son?
46 And no one was able to answer Him a
word, nor did anyone dare from that day to
question Him any more.

CHAPTER 23

1 Then Jesus spoke to the multitudes and to
His disciples, saying,
2 The scribes and the Pharisees have sat
down on Moses' seat.
3 All things, whatever they may tell you to
keep, keep and do. But do not as they do –
for they say and do not.
4 For they tie together heavy loads, and
hard ones to bear, and lay them on men's
shoulders. But they will not move them with
their own finger.
5 And all their works they do to be seen by
men. And they make their prayer-bands
broad and enlarge the borders of their robes.
6 And *they* love the chief place at feasts and
the chief seats in the synagogues,
7 and the greetings in the market-places,
and to be called by men, Rabbi, Rabbi.
8 But you must not be called Rabbi, for one
is your Teacher, the Christ, and you are all
brothers.
9 And do not call *anyone* father on earth,
for one is your Father, who is in Heaven.
10 And you may not be called leaders, for
one is your Leader, the Christ.
11 And the greater one among you shall be
your servant.
12 And whoever desires to exalt himself
shall be brought low. And whoever shall
humble himself shall be exalted.
13 But woe to you, scribes and Pharisees,
hypocrites! Because you shut up the king-

ὅτι κατεσθίετε τὰς οἰκίας τῶν χηρῶν, καὶ προφάσει μακρὰ
for ye devour the houses of widows, and as a pretext [2]at [3]great [4]length
προσευχόμενοι· διὰ τοῦτο λήψεσθε περισσότερον κρίμα.‖
[1]praying. Because of this ye shall receive more abundant judgment.
14 (13) Οὐαὶ [f] ὑμῖν, γραμματεῖς καὶ Φαρισαῖοι, ὑποκριταί, ὅτι
Woe to you, scribes and Pharisees, hypocrites, for
κλείετε τὴν βασιλείαν τῶν οὐρανῶν ἔμπροσθεν τῶν ἀνθρώπων·
ye shut up the kingdom of the heavens before men;
ὑμεῖς.γὰρ οὐκ.εἰσέρχεσθε, οὐδὲ τοὺς εἰσερχομένους ἀφίετε
for ye do not enter, nor even those who are entering do ye suffer
εἰσελθεῖν. 15 Οὐαὶ ὑμῖν, γραμματεῖς καὶ Φαρισαῖοι, ὑποκριταί,
to enter. Woe to you, scribes and Pharisees, hypocrites,
ὅτι περιάγετε τὴν θάλασσαν καὶ τὴν ξηρὰν ποιῆσαι ἕνα
for ye go about the sea and the dry [land] to make one
προσήλυτον, καὶ ὅταν γένηται, ποιεῖτε αὐτὸν υἱὸν γε-
proselyte, and when he has become [so], ye make him a son of Ge-
έννης διπλότερον ὑμῶν. 16 Οὐαὶ ὑμῖν, ὁδηγοὶ τυφλοί, οἱ
henna twofold more than yourselves. Woe to you, [2]guides [1]blind, who
λέγοντες, Ὃς.ἂν ὀμόσῃ ἐν τῷ ναῷ, οὐδέν ἐστιν· ὃς.δ᾽.ἂν
say, Whoever shall swear by the temple, nothing it is; but whoever
ὀμόσῃ ἐν τῷ χρυσῷ τοῦ ναοῦ, ὀφείλει. 17 μωροὶ καὶ τυφλοί·
shall swear by the gold of the temple, is a debtor. Fools and blind,
[g]τίς‖.γὰρ [h]μείζων‖ ἐστίν, ὁ χρυσός, ἢ ὁ ναὸς ὁ [i]ἁγιάζων‖
for which [2]greater [1]is, the gold, or the temple which sanctifies
τὸν χρυσόν; 18 καί, Ὃς.[k]ἐὰν‖ ὀμόσῃ ἐν τῷ θυσιαστηρίῳ,
the gold? And, Whoever shall swear by the altar,
οὐδέν ἐστιν· ὃς.δ᾽.ἂν ὀμόσῃ ἐν τῷ δώρῳ τῷ ἐπάνω αὐτοῦ,
nothing it is; but whoever shall swear by the gift that [is] upon it,
ὀφείλει. 19 [l]μωροὶ καὶ‖ τυφλοί, τί γὰρ μεῖζον, τὸ δῶρον,
is a debtor. Fools and blind, for which [is] greater, the gift,
ἢ τὸ θυσιαστήριον τὸ ἁγιάζον τὸ δῶρον; 20 ὁ οὖν ὀμόσας
or the altar which sanctifies the gift? He [2]that [1]therefore swears
ἐν τῷ θυσιαστηρίῳ ὀμνύει ἐν αὐτῷ καὶ ἐν πᾶσιν τοῖς ἐπάνω
by the altar swears by it and by all things that [are] upon
αὐτοῦ· 21 καὶ ὁ ὀμόσας ἐν τῷ ναῷ ὀμνύει ἐν αὐτῷ καὶ ἐν
it. And he that swears by the temple swears by it and by
τῷ [m]κατοικοῦντι‖ αὐτόν· 22 καὶ ὁ ὀμόσας ἐν τῷ οὐρανῷ
him who dwells in it. And he that swears by the heaven
ὀμνύει ἐν τῷ θρόνῳ τοῦ θεοῦ καὶ ἐν τῷ καθημένῳ ἐπάνω
swears by the throne of God and by him who sits upon
αὐτοῦ. 23 Οὐαὶ ὑμῖν, γραμματεῖς καὶ Φαρισαῖοι, ὑποκριταί, ὅτι
it. Woe to you, scribes and Pharisees, hypocrites, for
ἀποδεκατοῦτε τὸ ἡδύοσμον καὶ τὸ ἄνηθον καὶ τὸ κύμινον, καὶ
ye pay tithes of the mint and the anise and the cummin, and
ἀφήκατε τὰ βαρύτερα τοῦ νόμου, τὴν κρίσιν καὶ [n]τὸν
ye have left aside the weightier [matters] of the law, judgment, and
ἔλεον‖ καὶ τὴν πίστιν· ταῦτα[o] ἔδει ποιῆσαι, κἀκεῖνα μὴ
mercy and faith: these it behoved [you] to do, and those not
[p]ἀφιέναι.‖ 24 ὁδηγοὶ τυφλοί, [q]οἱ‖ διϋλίζοντες τὸν κώνωπα,
to be leaving aside. [2]Guides [1]blind, who filter out the gnat,
τὴν.δὲ κάμηλον καταπίνοντες. 25 Οὐαὶ ὑμῖν, γραμματεῖς καὶ
but the camel swallow. Woe to you, scribes and
Φαρισαῖοι, ὑποκριταί, ὅτι καθαρίζετε τὸ ἔξωθεν τοῦ ποτηρίου
Pharisees, hypocrites, for ye cleanse the outside of the cup
καὶ τῆς παροψίδος, ἔσωθεν.δὲ γέμουσιν [r]ἐξ‖ ἁρπαγῆς καὶ
and of the dish, but within they are full of plunder and
[s]ἀκρασίας.‖ 26 Φαρισαῖε τυφλέ, καθάρισον πρῶτον τὸ ἐντὸς
incontinence. [2]Pharisee [1]blind, cleanse first the inside
τοῦ ποτηρίου [t]καὶ τῆς παροψίδος,‖ ἵνα γένηται καὶ τὸ ἐκτὸς
of the cup and of the dish, that [6]may [7]become [5]also [1]the [2]outside
[v]αὐτῶν‖ καθαρόν. 27 Οὐαὶ ὑμῖν, γραμματεῖς καὶ Φαρισαῖοι,
[3]of [4]them clean. Woe to you, scribes and Pharisees,
ὑποκριταί, ὅτι [w]παρομοιάζετε‖ τάφοις κεκονιαμένοις, οἵτινες
hypocrites, for ye are like [2]sepulchres [1]whited, which
ἔξωθεν μὲν φαίνονται ὡραῖοι, ἔσωθεν.δὲ γέμουσιν ὀστέων
outwardly indeed appear beautiful, but within are full of bones
νεκρῶν καὶ πάσης ἀκαθαρσίας. 28 οὕτως καὶ ὑμεῖς ἔξωθεν
of [the] dead and of all uncleanness. Thus also ye outwardly
μὲν φαίνεσθε τοῖς ἀνθρώποις δίκαιοι, ἔσωθεν.δὲ [x]μεστοί ἐστε‖
indeed appear to men righteous, but within [2]full [1]are
ὑποκρίσεως καὶ ἀνομίας. 29 Οὐαὶ ὑμῖν, γραμματεῖς καὶ Φα-
of hypocrisy and lawlessness. Woe to you, scribes and Pha-
ρισαῖοι, ὑποκριταί, ὅτι οἰκοδομεῖτε τοὺς τάφους τῶν προφητῶν,
risees, hypocrites, for ye build the sepulchres of the prophets,
καὶ κοσμεῖτε τὰ μνημεῖα τῶν δικαίων, 30 καὶ λέγετε, Εἰ [y]ἤμεν‖
and adorn the tombs of the righteous, and ye say, If we had been
ἐν ταῖς ἡμέραις τῶν.πατέρων.ἡμῶν, οὐκ.ἂν.[y]ἤμεν‖ [z]κοινωνοὶ
in the days of our fathers we would not have been partakers
αὐτῶν‖ ἐν τῷ αἵματι τῶν προφητῶν. 31 ὥστε μαρτυρεῖτε
with them in the blood of the prophets. So that ye bear witness
ἑαυτοῖς, ὅτι υἱοί ἐστε τῶν φονευσάντων τοὺς προφήτας·
to yourselves, that sons ye are of those who murdered the prophets;

dom of Heaven in front of men. For you do
not enter, nor do you allow even those who
are going in to enter.
14 Woe to you, scribes and Pharisees,
hypocrites! For you devour the houses of
widows and for a pretense make long
prayers. Because of this you shall receive a
heavier sentence.
15 Woe to you, scribes and Pharisees, hypocrites! Because you go about the sea and the
dry *land* to make one convert. And when he
becomes one, you make him twofold more a
child of hell than yourselves.
16 Woe to you, blind guides, who say,
Whoever shall swear by the Temple, it is
nothing – but whoever shall swear by the
gold of the Temple is duty bound.
17 Fools and blind ones! For which is
greater, the gold, or the Temple which
sanctifies the gold?
18 And, whoever shall swear by the altar, it
is nothing – but whoever shall swear by the
gift that is upon it is duty bound.
19 Fools and blind ones! For which is
greater, the gift, or the altar which sanctifies
the gift?
20 He therefore that swears by the altar
swears by it and by all things on it.
21 And he that swears by the Temple
swears by it and by Him who dwells in it.
22 And he that swears by Heaven swears by
the throne of God and by Him who sits on it.
23 Woe to you, scribes and Pharisees, hypocrites! Because you pay tithes of mint and
dill and cummin, and you have left undone
the weightier *matters* of the Law – judgment and mercy and faith. *You* should have
done these and not left those undone.
24 Blind guides! *You* strain out the gnat,
but swallow the camel.
25 Woe to you, scribes and Pharisees, hypocrites! Because you cleanse the outside of
the cup and the plate, but within they are
full of robbery and excess.
26 Blind Pharisee! First clean the inside of
the cup and of the plate so that the outside
of them also may become clean.
27 Woe to you, scribes and Pharisees, hypocrites! For you are like whitewashed tombs,
which indeed appear beautiful outside, but
inside they are full of bones of *the* dead and
of all uncleanness.
28 Even so you also appear to men to be
righteous on the outside, but inside you are
full of hypocrisy and lawlessness.
29 Woe to you, scribes and Pharisees, hypocrites! Because you build the tombs of the
prophets and adorn the tombs of the righteous,
30 and you say, If we had been there in the
days of our fathers, we would not have been
partakers with them in the blood of the
prophets.
31 So you bear witness to yourselves, that
you are the sons of those who murdered the

32 καὶ ὑμεῖς πληρώσατε τὸ μέτρον τῶν.πατέρων.ὑμῶν. 33 ὄφεις,
and ye, fill ye up the measure of your fathers. Serpents,
γεννήματα ἐχιδνῶν, πῶς φύγητε ἀπὸ τῆς κρίσεως τῆς γε-
offspring of vipers, how shall ye escape from the judgment of Ge-
έννης; 34 Διὰ τοῦτο, ἰδού, ἐγὼ ἀποστέλλω πρὸς ὑμᾶς προ-
henna? Because of this, behold, I send to you pro-
φήτας καὶ σοφοὺς καὶ γραμματεῖς· [a]καὶ‖ ἐξ αὐτῶν ἀπο-
phets and wise [men] and scribes; and [some] of them ye will
κτενεῖτε καὶ σταυρώσετε, καὶ ἐξ αὐτῶν μαστιγώσετε ἐν ταῖς
kill and crucify, and [some] of them ye will scourge in
συναγωγαῖς.ὑμῶν, καὶ διώξετε ἀπὸ πόλεως εἰς πόλιν·
your synagogues, and will persecute from city to city;
35 ὅπως ἔλθῃ ἐφ' ὑμᾶς πᾶν αἷμα δίκαιον [b]ἐκχυνόμενον‖
so that should come upon you all [the] [2]blood [1]righteous poured out
ἐπὶ τῆς γῆς, ἀπὸ [c]τοῦ‖ αἵματος Ἄβελ τοῦ δικαίου, ἕως τοῦ
upon the earth from the blood of Abel the righteous, to the
αἵματος Ζαχαρίου υἱοῦ Βαραχίου, ὃν ἐφονεύσατε μεταξὺ τοῦ
blood of Zacharias son of Barachias, whom ye murdered between the
ναοῦ καὶ τοῦ θυσιαστηρίου. 36 ἀμὴν λέγω ὑμῖν, [d]ἥξει
temple and the altar. Verily I say to you, [4]shall [5]come
[e]ταῦτα πάντα‖ ἐπὶ τὴν.γενεὰν.ταύτην. 37 Ἱερουσαλήμ,
[2]these [3]things [1]all upon this generation. Jerusalem,
Ἱερουσαλήμ, ἡ ἀποκτείνουσα τοὺς προφήτας καὶ λιθοβολοῦσα
Jerusalem, who killest the prophets and stonest
τοὺς ἀπεσταλμένους πρὸς αὐτήν, ποσάκις ἠθέλησα ἐπισυν-
those who have been sent to her, how often would I have gath-
αγαγεῖν τὰ.τέκνα.σου, ὃν.τρόπον [f]ἐπισυνάγει, ὄρνις‖ τὰ
ered together thy children, in the way [3]gathers [4]together [1]a [2]hen
νοσσία.[g]ἑαυτῆς‖ ὑπὸ τὰς πτέρυγας[h], καὶ οὐκ.ἠθελήσατε;
her brood under [her] wings, and ye would not!
38 ἰδού, ἀφίεται ὑμῖν ὁ.οἶκος.ὑμῶν [i]ἔρημος.‖ 39 λέγω.γὰρ
Behold, is left to you your house desolate; for I say
ὑμῖν, Οὐ.μή με ἴδητε ἀπ'.ἄρτι ἕως.ἂν εἴπητε, Εὐλογη-
to you, In no wise me shall ye see henceforth until ye say, Bless-
μένος ὁ ἐρχόμενος ἐν ὀνόματι κυρίου.
ed [is] he who comes in [the] name of [the] Lord.

24 Καὶ ἐξελθὼν ὁ Ἰησοῦς [k]ἐπορεύετο ἀπὸ τοῦ ἱεροῦ,‖ καὶ
And going forth Jesus went away from the temple, and
προσῆλθον οἱ.μαθηταὶ.αὐτοῦ ἐπιδεῖξαι αὐτῷ τὰς οἰκοδομὰς
[3]came [4]to [5]him] [1]his [2]disciples to point out to him the buildings
τοῦ ἱεροῦ. 2 ὁ.δὲ.[l]Ἰησοῦς‖ εἶπεν αὐτοῖς, Οὐ.βλέπετε [m]πάντα
of the temple. But Jesus said to them, See ye not all
ταῦτα;‖ ἀμὴν λέγω ὑμῖν, οὐ.μὴ ἀφεθῇ ὧδε λίθος ἐπὶ λίθον
these things? Verily I say to you, not at all shall be left here stone upon stone
ὃς οὐ.[n]μὴ‖.καταλυθήσεται. 3 Καθημένου.δὲ αὐτοῦ ἐπὶ τοῦ
which shall not be thrown down. And as [2]was [3]sitting [1]he upon the
ὄρους τῶν ἐλαιῶν προσῆλθον αὐτῷ οἱ μαθηταὶ[o] κατ'.ἰδίαν, λέ-
mount of Olives [3]came [4]to [5]him [1]the [2]disciples apart, say-
γοντες, Εἰπὲ ἡμῖν, πότε ταῦτα ἔσται; καὶ τί τὸ σημεῖον
ing, Tell us, when [2]these [3]things [1]shall be? and what [is] the sign
τῆς.σῆς παρουσίας καὶ [p]τῆς‖ συντελείας τοῦ αἰῶνος; 4 Καὶ
of thy coming and of the completion of the age? And
ἀποκριθεὶς ὁ Ἰησοῦς εἶπεν αὐτοῖς, Βλέπετε, μή τις ὑμᾶς
answering Jesus said to them, Take heed, lest any one [2]you
πλανήσῃ. 5 πολλοὶ.γὰρ ἐλεύσονται ἐπὶ τῷ.ὀνόματί.μου, λέ-
[1]mislead. For many will come in my name,
γοντες, Ἐγώ εἰμι ὁ χριστός· καὶ πολλοὺς πλανήσουσιν.
saying, I am the Christ; and many they will mislead.
6 Μελλήσετε.δὲ ἀκούειν πολέμους καὶ ἀκοὰς πολέμων. ὁρᾶτε,
But ye shall be about to hear of wars and rumours of wars. See,
μὴ.θροεῖσθε· δεῖ.γὰρ [q]πάντα‖ γενέσθαι· ἀλλ' οὔπω
be not disturbed; for it is necessary all [these] things to take place, but not yet
ἐστὶν τὸ τέλος. 7 Ἐγερθήσεται.γὰρ ἔθνος [r]ἐπὶ‖ ἔθνος, καὶ
is the end. For [2]shall [3]rise [4]up [1]nation against nation, and
βασιλεία ἐπὶ βασιλείαν· καὶ ἔσονται λιμοὶ [s]καὶ λοιμοὶ‖
kingdom against kingdom; and there shall be famines and pestilences
καὶ σεισμοὶ κατὰ τόπους. 8 πάντα.δὲ ταῦτα ἀρχὴ ὠδί-
and earthquakes in [different] places. But all these [are] a beginning of
νων. 9 Τότε παραδώσουσιν ὑμᾶς εἰς θλίψιν, καὶ ἀποκτενοῦσιν
throes. Then will they deliver up you to tribulation, and will kill
ὑμᾶς· καὶ ἔσεσθε μισούμενοι ὑπὸ πάντων [t]τῶν‖ ἐθνῶν διὰ
you; and ye will be hated by all the nations on account of
τὸ.ὄνομά.μου. 10 καὶ τότε σκανδαλισθήσονται πολλοί, καὶ
my name. And then will be offended many, and
ἀλλήλους παραδώσουσιν καὶ μισήσουσιν ἀλλήλους· 11 καὶ
one another they will deliver up and will hate one another; and
πολλοὶ ψευδοπροφῆται ἐγερθήσονται, καὶ πλανήσουσιν πολ-
many false prophets will arise, and will mislead
λούς· 12 καὶ διὰ τὸ.πληθυνθῆναι τὴν ἀνομίαν, ψυγήσεται
many; and because shall have been multiplied lawlessness, [6]will [7]grow [8]cold
ἡ ἀγάπη τῶν πολλῶν· 13 ὁ.δὲ ὑπομείνας εἰς τέλος,
[1]the [2]love [3]of [4]the [5]many; but he who endures to [the] end

prophets,

32 and you fill up the measure of your fathers.

33 Serpents! Offspring of vipers! How shall you escape the judgment of hell?

34 Because of this, behold! I send to you prophets and wise men and scribes. And *some* of them you will kill and crucify, and *some* of them you will flog in your synagogues. And *you* will persecute *them* from city to city,

35 so that all *the* righteous blood poured out on the earth should come upon you, from the blood of righteous Abel to the blood of Zech-a-ri-ah the son of Ber-e-chi-ah, whom you murdered between the Temple and the altar.

36 Truly I say to you, All these things shall come upon this generation.

37 O Jerusalem, Jerusalem, who kill the prophets and stone those who have been sent to her. How often I would have gathered your children together, like a hen gathers her chicks under her wings, but you did not desire it.

38 Behold! Your house is left to you desolate.

39 For I say to you, In no way shall you see Me from now on until you say, "Blessed is He who comes in the name of the Lord."

24:1 And going out, Jesus left the Temple. And His disciples came to Him to point out to Him the buildings of the Temple.

2 But Jesus said to them, Do you not see all these things? Truly I say to you, There shall not be left here one stone upon another that shall not be thrown down.

3 And as He was sitting on the Mount of Olives, the disciples came to Him privately, saying, Tell us when these things shall happen – and, What is the sign of Your coming and of the end of the world?

4 And answering Jesus said to them, Be careful that no one fools you.

5 For many will come in My name, saying, I am the Christ. And they will fool many.

6 And you will begin to hear of wars and rumors of wars. See, do not be troubled, for all must take place. But the end is not yet.

7 For nation shall rise against nation and kingdom against kingdom. And there shall be famines and plagues and earthquakes in different places.

8 But all these are the beginning of sorrows.

9 Then they will deliver you up to trouble and will kill you. And you will be hated by all the nations for My name's sake.

10 And then many will be offended and will deliver up one another and will hate one another.

11 And many false prophets will rise up and will fool many.

12 And because lawlessness will abound, the love of many will grow cold.

13 But he who endures to the end shall be

οὗτος σωθήσεται. 14 καὶ κηρυχθήσεται τοῦτο.τὸ.εὐαγγέλιον
he shall be saved. And there shall be proclaimed these glad tidings
τῆς βασιλείας ἐν ὅλῃ τῇ οἰκουμένῃ, εἰς μαρτύριον πᾶσιν τοῖς
of the kingdom in all the habitable earth, for a testimony to all the
ἔθνεσιν· καὶ τότε ἥξει τὸ τέλος. 15 Ὅταν οὖν ἴδητε τὸ
nations; and then shall come the end. When therefore ye shall see the
βδέλυγμα τῆς ἐρημώσεως, τὸ ῥηθὲν διὰ Δανιὴλ τοῦ προ-
abomination of desolation, which was spoken of by Daniel the pro-
φήτου, [v]ἑστὸς" ἐν τόπῳ ἁγίῳ· ὁ ἀναγινώσκων [w]νοεί-
phet, standing in [the] [2]place [1]holy (he who reads let him un-
τω·" 16 τότε οἱ ἐν τῇ Ἰουδαίᾳ φευγέτωσαν [x]ἐπὶ" τὰ
derstand), then those in Judea let them flee to the
ὄρη· 17 ὁ ἐπὶ τοῦ δώματος μὴ.[y]καταβαινέτω" ἆραί [z]τι"
mountains; he on the housetop let him not come down to take anything
ἐκ τῆς.οἰκίας.αὐτοῦ· 18 καὶ ὁ ἐν τῷ ἀγρῷ μὴ.ἐπιστρεψάτω
out of his house; and he in the field let him not return
ὀπίσω ἆραι [a]τὰ ἱμάτια" αὐτοῦ. 19 οὐαὶ.δὲ ταῖς ἐν.γαστρὶ.ἐ-
back to take [2]garments [1]his. But woe to those that are with
χούσαις καὶ ταῖς θηλαζούσαις ἐν ἐκείναις ταῖς ἡμέραις.
child and to those that give suck in those days.
20 προσεύχεσθε.δὲ ἵνα μὴ.γένηται ἡ.φυγὴ.ὑμῶν χειμῶνος, μηδὲ
And pray that [3]may [4]not [5]be [1]your [2]flight in winter, nor
[b]ἐν" σαββάτῳ. 21 Ἔσται.γὰρ τότε θλίψις μεγάλη, οἵα [c]οὐ
on sabbath: for there shall be then [2]tribulation [1]great such as [2]not
γέγονεν" ἀπ' ἀρχῆς κόσμου ἕως τοῦ νῦν, οὐδ'.οὐ.μὴ
[1]has been from [the] beginning of [the] world until now, no, nor ever
γένηται. 22 καὶ εἰ.μὴ ἐκολοβώθησαν αἱ.ἡμέραι.ἐκεῖναι, οὐκ
shall be; and unless [3]had [4]been [5]shortened [1]those [2]days, [6]not
ἂν.ἐσώθη πᾶσα σάρξ· διὰ.δὲ τοὺς ἐκλεκτοὺς
[8]there [7]would have been saved any flesh, but on account of the elect
κολοβωθήσονται αἱ.ἡμέραι.ἐκεῖναι. 23 Τότε ἐάν τις ὑμῖν
[3]shall [4]be [5]shortened [1]those [2]days. Then if anyone to you
εἴπῃ, Ἰδού, ὧδε ὁ χριστός, ἤ ὧδε, μὴ.[d]πιστεύσητε." 24 Ἐγερ-
say, Behold, here [is] the Christ, or here, believe [it] not. [2]There [3]will
θήσονται γὰρ ψευδόχριστοι καὶ ψευδοπροφῆται, καὶ δώσουσιν
[4]arise [1]for false Christs and false prophets, and will give
σημεῖα μεγάλα καὶ τέρατα, ὥστε [e]πλανῆσαι", εἰ δυνατόν, καὶ
[2]signs [1]great and wonders, so as to mislead, if possible, even
τοὺς ἐκλεκτούς. 25 Ἰδού, προείρηκα ὑμῖν. 26 ἐὰν οὖν εἴπωσιν
the elect. Lo, I have foretold [it] to you. If therefore they say
ὑμῖν, Ἰδού, ἐν τῇ ἐρήμῳ ἐστίν, μὴ.ἐξέλθητε· Ἰδού, ἐν
to you, Behold, in the wilderness he is, go not forth: Behold, [he is] in
τοῖς ταμείοις, μὴ.πιστεύσητε. 27 ὥσπερ.γὰρ ἡ ἀστραπὴ ἐξέρ-
the chambers, believe [it] not. For as the lightning comes
χεται ἀπὸ ἀνατολῶν καὶ φαίνεται ἕως δυσμῶν, οὕτως
forth from [the] east and appears as far as [the] west, so
ἔσται [f]καὶ" ἡ παρουσία τοῦ υἱοῦ τοῦ ἀνθρώπου. 28 ὅπου.[g]γὰρ"
shall be also the coming of the Son of man. For wherever
ἐὰν ᾖ τὸ πτῶμα, ἐκεῖ συναχθήσονται οἱ ἀετοί. 29 Εὐ-
may be the carcase, there will be gathered together the eagles. [2]Immedi-
θέως δὲ μετὰ τὴν θλίψιν τῶν.ἡμερῶν.ἐκείνων ὁ ἥλιος σκοτι-
ately [1]but after the tribulation of those days the sun shall be
σθήσεται, καὶ ἡ σελήνη οὐ.δώσει τὸ.φέγγος.αὐτῆς, καὶ οἱ
darkened, and the moon shall not give her light, and the
ἀστέρες πεσοῦνται [h]ἀπὸ" τοῦ οὐρανοῦ, καὶ αἱ δυνάμεις τῶν
stars shall fall from the heaven, and the powers of the
οὐρανῶν σαλευθήσονται. 30 καὶ τότε φανήσεται τὸ σημεῖον
heavens shall be shaken. And then shall appear the sign
τοῦ υἱοῦ τοῦ ἀνθρώπου ἐν [i]τῷ" οὐρανῷ· καὶ [k]τότε" κό-
of the Son of man in the heaven; and then shall
ψονται πᾶσαι αἱ φυλαὶ τῆς γῆς. καὶ ὄψονται τὸν υἱὸν τοῦ
wail all the tribes of the land, and they shall see the Son
ἀνθρώπου, ἐρχόμενον ἐπὶ τῶν νεφελῶν τοῦ οὐρανοῦ μετὰ δυ-
of man, coming on the clouds of heaven with
νάμεως καὶ δόξης πολλῆς. 31 καὶ ἀποστελεῖ τοὺς ἀγγέλους
power and [2]glory [1]great. And he shall send [2]angels
αὐτοῦ μετὰ σάλπιγγος [l]φωνῆς" μεγάλης, καὶ ἐπισυνάξουσιν
[1]his with [3]of [4]a [5]trumpet [2]sound [1]great, and they shall gather together
τοὺς.ἐκλεκτοὺς.αὐτοῦ ἐκ τῶν τεσσάρων ἀνέμων, ἀπ' ἄκρων
his elect from the four winds, from [the] extremities
οὐρανῶν ἕως [m] ἄκρων αὐτῶν. 32 Ἀπὸ.δὲ τῆς συκῆς
of [the] heavens to [the] extremities of them. But from the fig-tree
μάθετε τὴν παραβολήν· ὅταν ἤδη ὁ.κλάδος.αὐτῆς γένηται
learn the parable: When already its branch is become
ἁπαλός, καὶ τὰ φύλλα [n]ἐκφύῃ," γινώσκετε ὅτι ἐγγὺς τὸ
tender, and the leaves it puts forth, ye know that near [is] the
θέρος· 33 οὕτως καὶ ὑμεῖς, ὅταν ἴδητε [o]πάντα ταῦτα,"
summer. Thus also ye, when ye see all these things,
γινώσκετε ὅτι ἐγγύς ἐστιν ἐπὶ θύραις. 34 ἀμὴν λέγω ὑμῖν,
know that near it is, at [the] doors. Verily I say to you,
οὐ.μὴ παρέλθῃ ἡ.γενεὰ.αὕτη ἕως.ἂν πάντα ταῦτα
In no wise will have passed away this generation until all these things

saved.
14 And this gospel of the kingdom shall be
preached in all the world for a witness to all
the nations. And then the end shall come.
15 Therefore, when you shall see the abomination of desolation (which was spoken of
by Daniel the prophet) standing in the holy
place (he who reads let him understand),
16 then let those in Judea flee into the
mountains?
17 he on the housetop, let him not come
down to take anything out of his house.
18 And he *that is* in the field, let him not go
back to take his clothes.
19 And woe to those that are with child,
and to those who give suck in those days!
20 And pray that your flight is not in
winter, or on a sabbath.
21 For there shall then be great trouble,
such as has not been from the beginning of
the world until now – no, nor ever shall be.
22 And unless those days had been
shortened, there would have been no flesh
saved. But because of the elect, those days
will be shortened.
23 Then if anyone says to you, Behold!
Here is the Christ! Or, Here! Do not believe
it.
24 For there will arise false christs and false
prophets. And they will give great miracles
and wonders, so as to mislead, if possible,
even the elect.
25 Behold! I have told you beforehand.
26 Then if they shall say to you, Look, He
is in the wilderness! Do not go. Look, *He is*
in the inner rooms. Do not believe it.
27 For as the lightning comes from the east
and appears as far as the west, so shall be
also the coming of the Son of man.
28 For wherever the dead body may be,
there the eagles will be gathered together.
29 And immediately after the trouble of
those days the sun shall be darkened, and
the moon shall not give its light. And the
stars shall fall from the sky, and the powers
of the heavens shall be shaken.
30 And then the sign of the Son of man
shall appear in the sky: and then all the
tribes of the earth shall mourn. And they
shall see the Son of man coming on the
clouds of the sky with power and great glory
31 – and He shall send His angels with a
great sound of a trumpet, and they shall
gather together His elect from the four
winds, from one end of the sky to the other.
32 Now from the fig-tree learn a parable.
When its branch has already become tender
and it leafs out, you know that summer is
near.
33 So also when you see all these things, you
know that it is near, at the very doors.
34 Truly I say to you, in no way will this
generation have passed away until all these
things have happened.

γένηται. 35 Ὁ οὐρανὸς καὶ ἡ γῆ [q]παρελεύσονται,‖
shall have taken place. The heaven and the earth shall pass away,
οἱ.δὲ.λόγοι.μου οὐ.μὴ παρέλθωσιν. 36 Περὶ.δὲ τῆς ἡμέρας
but my words in no wise shall pass away. But concerning [2]day
ἐκείνης καὶ [r]τῆς‖ ὥρας οὐδεὶς οἶδεν, οὐδὲ οἱ ἄγγελοι τῶν
[1]that and the hour no one knows, not even the angels of the
οὐρανῶν, [s]εἰ.μὴ ὁ.πατήρ.[t]μου‖ μόνος. 37 [u]Ὥσπερ.[v]δὲ‖ αἱ ἡμέραι
heavens, but my Father only. But as the days
τοῦ.Νῶε, οὕτως ἔσται [w]καὶ‖ ἡ παρουσία τοῦ υἱοῦ τοῦ ἀνθρώ-
of Noe, so shall be also the coming of the Son of
που. 38 [x]ὥσπερ‖ γὰρ ἦσαν ἐν ταῖς ἡμέραις[y] [z]ταῖς πρὸ‖
man. [2]As [1]for they were in the days which [were] before
τοῦ κατακλυσμοῦ, τρώγοντες καὶ πίνοντες, γαμοῦντες καὶ
the flood, eating and drinking, marrying and
[a]ἐκγαμίζοντες,‖ ἄχρι ἧς.ἡμέρας εἰσῆλθεν Νῶε εἰς τὴν κιβωτόν,
giving in marriage, until the day when [2]entered [1]Noe into the ark,
39 καὶ οὐκ.ἔγνωσαν, ἕως ἦλθεν ὁ κατακλυσμὸς καὶ ἦρεν
and they knew not till [3]came [1]the [2]flood and took away
ἅπαντας, οὕτως ἔσται [b]καὶ‖ ἡ παρουσία τοῦ υἱοῦ τοῦ ἀνθρώπου.
all; thus shall be also the coming of the Son of man.
40 Τότε [c]δύο ἔσονται‖ ἐν τῷ ἀγρῷ· [d]ὁ‖ εἷς παραλαμβάνεται,
Then two will be in the field, the one is taken,
καὶ [d]ὁ‖ εἷς ἀφίεται. 41 δύο ἀλήθουσαι ἐν τῷ [e]μύλωνι·‖ μία
and the one is left; two[women] grinding at the mill, one
παραλαμβάνεται, καὶ μία ἀφίεται. 42 Γρηγορεῖτε οὖν, ὅτι
is taken, and one is left. Watch therefore, for
οὐκ.οἴδατε ποίᾳ [f]ὥρᾳ‖ ὁ.κύριος.ὑμῶν ἔρχεται. 43 ἐκεῖνο.δὲ
ye know not in what hour your Lord comes. But this
γινώσκετε, ὅτι εἰ ᾔδει ὁ οἰκοδεσπότης ποίᾳ φυλακῇ
know, that if [6]had [7]known [1]the [2]master [3]of [4]the [5]house in what watch
ὁ κλέπτης ἔρχεται, ἐγρηγόρησεν.ἄν, καὶ οὐκ ἂν.εἴασεν [g]διο-
the thief comes, he would have watched, and not have suffered [3]to [4]be
ρυγῆναι‖ τὴν.οἰκίαν.αὐτοῦ. 44 διὰ.τοῦτο καὶ ὑμεῖς γίνεσθε
[5]dug [6]through [1]his [2]house. Wherefore also [2]ye [1]be
ἕτοιμοι· ὅτι ᾗ.[h]ὥρᾳ οὐ.δοκεῖτε‖ ὁ υἱὸς τοῦ ἀνθρώπου ἔρχεται.
ready, for in what hour ye think not the Son of man comes.
45 Τίς ἄρα ἐστὶν ὁ πιστὸς δοῦλος καὶ φρόνιμος, ὃν κατέ-
Who then is the faithful bondman and prudent, whom [3]has
στησεν ὁ.κύριος.[i]αὐτοῦ‖ ἐπὶ τῆς.[k]θεραπείας‖.αὐτοῦ, τοῦ [l]διδόναι‖
[4]set [1]his [2]lord over his household, to give
αὐτοῖς τὴν τροφὴν ἐν καιρῷ; 46 μακάριος ὁ.δοῦλος.ἐκεῖνος, ὃν,
to them the food in season? Blessed that bondman, whom
ἐλθὼν ὁ.κύριος.αὐτοῦ εὑρήσει [m]ποιοῦντα οὕτως.‖ 47 Ἀμὴν
[3]having [4]come [1]his [2]lord will find doing thus. Verily
λέγω ὑμῖν, ὅτι ἐπὶ πᾶσιν τοῖς.ὑπάρχουσιν.αὐτοῦ καταστήσει
I say to you, that over all his property he will set
αὐτόν. 48 Ἐὰν.δὲ εἴπῃ ὁ κακὸς δοῦλος [n]ἐκεῖνος‖ ἐν τῇ
him. But if [4]should [5]say [2]evil [3]bondman [1]that in
καρδίᾳ αὐτοῦ, Χρονίζει [o]ὁ.κύριός.μου‖ [p]ἐλθεῖν,‖ 49 καὶ ἄρξηται
his heart, [3]Delays [1]my [2]lord to come, and should begin
τύπτειν τοὺς συνδούλους[q], [r]ἐσθίειν‖.δὲ καὶ [s]πίνειν‖ μετὰ τῶν
to beat [his] fellow-bondmen, and to eat and to drink with the
μεθυόντων, 50 ἥξει ὁ κύριος τοῦ.δούλου ἐκείνου ἐν ἡμέρᾳ
drunken, [6]will [7]come [1]the [2]lord [3]of [4]that [5]bondman in a day
ᾗ οὐ.προσδοκᾷ, καὶ ἐν ὥρᾳ ᾗ οὐ.γινώσκει, 51 καὶ
in which he does not expect, and in an hour which he knows not, and
διχοτομήσει αὐτόν, καὶ τὸ.μέρος.αὐτοῦ μετὰ τῶν ὑποκριτῶν
will cut [2]in [3]two [1]him, and his portion with the hypocrites
θήσει· ἐκεῖ ἔσται ὁ κλαυθμὸς καὶ ὁ βρυγμὸς τῶν ὀδόντων.
will appoint: there will be the weeping and the gnashing of the teeth.
25 Τότε ὁμοιωθήσεται ἡ βασιλεία τῶν οὐρανῶν δέκα
Then [6]will [7]be [8]made [9]like [1]the [2]kingdom [3]of [4]the [5]heavens [to] ten
παρθένοις, αἵτινες λαβοῦσαι τὰς.λαμπάδας.[t]αὐτῶν‖ ἐξῆλθον
virgins, who having taken their lamps went forth
εἰς.[v]ἀπάντησιν‖ τοῦ νυμφίου. 2 πέντε.δὲ [w]ἦσαν ἐξ αὐτῶν‖
to meet the bridegroom. And five [3]were [1]of [2]them
[x]φρόνιμοι,‖ καὶ [y]αἱ‖ πέντε [z]μωραί.‖ 3 [a]αἵτινες‖ μωραί, λα-
prudent, and five foolish. They who [were] foolish, hav-
βοῦσαι τὰς.λαμπάδας.[b]ἑαυτῶν,‖ οὐκ.ἔλαβον μεθ' ἑαυτῶν
ing taken their lamps, did not take with themselves
ἔλαιον· 4 αἱ.δὲ φρόνιμοι ἔλαβον ἔλαιον ἐν τοῖς ἀγγείοις
oil; but the prudent took oil in [2]vessels
[c]αὐτῶν‖ μετὰ τῶν.λαμπάδων.[d]αὐτῶν.‖ 5 χρονίζοντος.δὲ τοῦ
[1]their with their lamps. But [3]tarrying [1]the
νυμφίου, ἐνύσταξαν πᾶσαι καὶ ἐκάθευδον. 6 μέσης.δὲ
[2]bridegroom, they [2]became [3]drowsy [1]all and slept. But in [the] middle
νυκτὸς κραυγὴ γέγονεν, Ἰδού, ὁ νυμφίος [e]ἔρχεται,‖ ἐξέρ-
of [the] night [3]a [4]cry [1]there [2]was, Behold, the bridegroom comes, go
χεσθε εἰς.ἀπάντησιν [f]αὐτοῦ.‖ 7 Τότε ἠγέρθησαν πᾶσαι αἱ
forth to meet him. Then arose all
παρθένοι.ἐκεῖναι, καὶ ἐκόσμησαν τὰς.λαμπάδας.[g]αὐτῶν.‖ 8 αἱ.δὲ
those virgins, and trimmed their lamps. And the

35 The sky and the earth will pass away,
but My words shall never in any way
disappear.
36 But as to that day and the hour, no one
knows, not even the angels of Heaven, but
only My Father.
37 But as the days of Noah, so shall be also
the coming of the Son of man.
38 For as they were in the days which were
before the flood – eating and drinking,
marrying and giving in marriage, until the
day that Noah entered into the ark,
39 (and they did not know until the flood
came and took all away), so shall be also the
coming of the Son of man.
40 Then two will be in the field, the one is
taken and the other left.
41 Two *shall* be grinding at the mill, one is
taken and the other left.
42 Watch, then, for you do not know in
what hour your Lord comes.
43 But know this, that if the master of the
house had known in what watch the thief
was coming, he would have watched and not
have allowed his house to be broken into.
44 So also, you be ready, for in an hour
that you do not think, the Son of man is
coming.
45 Who then is the faithful and wise servant
whom his lord has set over his household, to
give to them food at the right time?
46 That servant whom his lord shall find so
doing when he comes will be happy.
47 Truly I say to you that he will set him
over all he owns.
48 But if that evil servant should say in his
heart, My lord is delaying his coming,
49 and should begin to beat his fellow-
servants, and to eat and drink with those
who are drunkards,
50 the lord of that servant will come in a
day when he does not expect him, and in an
hour that he does not know.
51 And *he* will cut him in two and will appoint him his portion with the hypocrites –
there shall be weeping and gnashing of teeth.

CHAPTER 25

1 Then the kingdom of Heaven shall be
compared to ten virgins, who took their
lamps and went out to meet the bridegroom.
2 And five of them were wise, and five were
foolish.
3 When they took their lamps, the foolish
ones did not take oil with them.
4 But the wise took oil in their bottles with
their lamps.
5 And as the bridegroom delayed, they all
nodded and went to sleep.
6 And in the middle of the night there was a
cry, Look, the bridegroom is coming! Go
out to meet him.
7 Then all those virgins rose up and
trimmed their lamps.
8 And the foolish ones said to the wise,

μωραὶ ταῖς φρονίμοις [h]εἶπον,ǁ Δότε ἡμῖν ἐκ τοῦ.ἐλαίου.ὑμῶν,
foolish to the prudent said, Give us of your oil,
ὅτι αἱ.λαμπάδες.ἡμῶν σβέννυνται. 9 Ἀπεκρίθησαν.δὲ αἱ
for our lamps are going out. But [3]answered [1]the
φρόνιμοι, λέγουσαι, Μήποτε [i]οὐκǁ ἀρκέσῃ ἡμῖν καὶ ὑμῖν·
[2]prudent, saying, [No,] lest [3]not [1]it [2]may suffice for us and you:
πορεύεσθε.[k]δὲǁ μᾶλλον πρὸς τοὺς πωλοῦντας, καὶ ἀγοράσατε
but go rather to those who sell, and buy
ἑαυταῖς. 10 ἀπερχομένων.δὲ αὐτῶν ἀγοράσαι, ἦλθεν ὁ
for yourselves. But as [2]went [3]away [1]they to buy, [3]came [1]the
νυμφίος· καὶ αἱ ἕτοιμοι εἰσῆλθον μετ' αὐτοῦ εἰς τοὺς γά-
[2]bridegroom, and those ready went in with him to the wedding
μους, καὶ ἐκλείσθη ἡ θύρα. 11 ὕστερον.δὲ ἔρχονται [l]καὶǁ αἱ
feast, and [3]was [4]shut [1]the [2]door. And afterwards come also the
λοιπαὶ παρθένοι, λέγουσαι, Κύριε, κύριε, ἄνοιξον ἡμῖν. 12 Ὁ.δὲ
other virgins, saying, Lord, Lord, open to us. But he
ἀποκριθεὶς εἶπεν, Ἀμὴν λέγω ὑμῖν, οὐκ.οἶδα ὑμᾶς. 13 Γρη-
answering said, Verily I say to you, I do not know you. Watch
γορεῖτε οὖν, ὅτι οὐκ.οἴδατε τὴν ἡμέραν οὐδὲ τὴν ὥραν [m]ἐν
therefore, for ye do not know the day nor the hour in
ᾗ ὁ υἱὸς τοῦ ἀνθρώπου ἔρχεται.ǁ
which the Son of man comes.
14 Ὥσπερ.γὰρ ἄνθρωπος ἀποδημῶν ἐκάλεσεν τοὺς.ἰδίους
For [it is] as [if] a man leaving the country called his own
δούλους, καὶ παρέδωκεν αὐτοῖς τὰ.ὑπάρχοντα.αὐτοῦ. 15 καὶ
bondmen, and delivered to them his property. And
ᾧ.μὲν ἔδωκεν πέντε τάλαντα, ᾧ.δὲ δύο, ᾧ.δὲ ἕν,
to one he gave five talents, and to another two, and to another one,
ἑκάστῳ κατὰ τὴν.ἰδίαν δύναμιν καὶ [n]ἀπεδήμησεν εὐθέως.
to each according to his respective ability; and left the country immediately.
16 πορευθεὶςǁ.[o]δὲǁ ὁ τὰ πέντε τάλαντα λαβὼν [p]εἰργάσατοǁ
And [2]having [3]gone [1]he who the five talents received trafficked
ἐν αὐτοῖς, καὶ [q]ἐποίησενǁ ἄλλα πέντε [r]τάλαντα.ǁ 17 ὡσαύτως
with them, and made other five talents. In like manner
[s]καὶǁ ὁ τὰ δύο ἐκέρδησεν [t]καὶ αὐτὸςǁ ἄλλα δύο.
also he who [received] the two [3]gained [2]also [1]he other two.
18 ὁ.δὲ τὸ ἓν[v] λαβὼν ἀπελθὼν ὤρυξεν [w]ἐν τῇ γῇ,ǁ καὶ
But he who the one received having gone away dug in the earth, and
[x]ἀπέκρυψενǁ τὸ ἀργύριον τοῦ.κυρίου.αὐτοῦ. 19 Μετὰ.δὲ [y]χρόνον
hid the money of his lord. And after a [2]time
πολὺνǁ ἔρχεται ὁ κύριος τῶν.δούλων.ἐκείνων, καὶ συναίρει
[1]long comes the lord of those bondmen, and takes
[z]μετ' αὐτῶν λόγον.ǁ 20 καὶ προσελθὼν ὁ τὰ πέντε τά-
[2]with [3]them. [1]account. And [2]having [3]come [1]he who the five ta-
λαντα λαβὼν, προσήνεγκεν ἄλλα πέντε τάλαντα, λέγων,
lents received, brought to [him] other five talents, saying,
Κύριε, πέντε τάλαντά μοι παρέδωκας· ἴδε, ἄλλα πέντε
Lord, five talents to me thou didst deliver: behold, other five
[a]τάλανταǁ ἐκέρδησα [b]ἐπ' αὐτοῖς.ǁ 21 Ἔφη.[c]δὲǁ αὐτῷ ὁ κύριος
talents have I gained besides them. And [3]said [4]to [5]him [2]lord
αὐτοῦ, Εὖ, δοῦλε ἀγαθὲ καὶ πιστέ, ἐπὶ ὀλίγα ἦς
[1]his, Well! bondman good and faithful, over a few things thou wast
πιστός, ἐπὶ πολλῶν σε καταστήσω· εἴσελθε εἰς τὴν χαρὰν
faithful, over many things thee will I set: enter into the joy
τοῦ.κυρίου.σου. 22 Προσελθὼν.[d]δὲǁ καὶ ὁ τὰ δύο τά-
of thy lord. And having come to [him] [2]also [1]he who the two ta-
λαντα [e]λαβὼνǁ εἶπεν, Κύριε, δύο τάλαντά μοι παρέδωκας·
lents received said, Lord, two talents to me thou didst deliver;
ἴδε, ἄλλα δύο τάλαντα ἐκέρδησα [b]ἐπ' αὐτοῖς.ǁ 23 Ἔφη
behold, other two talents have I gained besides them. [3]Said
αὐτῷ ὁ.κύριος.αὐτοῦ, Εὖ, δοῦλε ἀγαθὲ καὶ πιστέ, ἐπὶ
[4]to [5]him [1]his [2]Lord, Well! bondman good and faithful, over
ὀλίγα ἦς πιστός, ἐπὶ πολλῶν σε καταστήσω· εἴσελθε
a few things thou wast faithful, over many things thee will I set: enter
εἰς τὴν χαρὰν τοῦ.κυρίου.σου. 24 Προσελθὼν.δὲ καὶ ὁ
into the joy of thy Lord. And having come to [him] [2]also [1]he who
τὸ ἓν τάλαντον εἰληφὼς εἶπεν, Κύριε, ἔγνων σε ὅτι σκληρὸς
the one talent had received said, Lord, I knew thee that [4]hard
εἶ ἄνθρωπος, θερίζων ὅπου οὐκ.ἔσπειρας, καὶ συνάγων
[1]thou [2]art [3]a [5]man, reaping where thou didst not sow, and gathering
ὅθεν οὐ.διεσκόρπισας· 25 καὶ φοβηθεὶς, ἀπελθὼν ἔκρυψα
whence thou didst not scatter, and being afraid, having gone away I hid
τὸ.τάλαντόν.σου ἐν τῇ γῇ· ἴδε, ἔχεις τὸ.σόν. 26 Ἀπο-
thy talent in the earth; behold, thou hast thine own. [4]An-
κριθεὶς δὲ ὁ.κύριος.αὐτοῦ εἶπεν αὐτῷ, [f]Πονηρὲ δοῦλεǁ καὶ
swering [1]and [2]his [3]Lord said to him, Wicked [3]bondman [1]and
ὀκνηρέ, ᾔδεις ὅτι θερίζω ὅπου οὐκ.ἔσπειρα, καὶ συνάγω ὅθεν
[2]slothful, thou knewest that I reap where I sowed not, and gather whence
οὐ.διεσκόρπισα; 27 ἔδει [g]οὖνǁ σεǁ βαλεῖν [h]τὸ.ἀργύριόν[i].μου
I scattered not; it behoved [2]therefore [1]thee to put my money
τοῖς [l]τραπεζίταις·ǁ καὶ ἐλθὼν ἐγὼ ἐκομισάμην.ἂν τὸ.ἐμὸν σὺν
to the money changers, and coming I should have received mine own with

Share your oil with us, for our lamps are
going out.
9 But the wise answered and said, *No*, lest
there should not be enough for us and for
you. But rather go to those who sell, and
buy *oil* for yourselves.
10 But as they went away to buy, the bridegroom came. And those who were ready
went in with him to the wedding feast. And
the door was shut.
11 And afterwards the other virgins also
came, saying, Lord, Lord, open to us!
12 But he answered and said, Truly I say to
you, I do not know you.
13 Then watch, for you do not know the
day or the hour in which the Son of man is
coming.
14 For *it is* as *if* a man leaving the country
called his own servants and gave them his
possessions.
15 And to one he gave five talents, to
another one, to each according to his own
ability. And he left the place immediately.
16 And he who received the five talents
went out and traded with them and made
another five talents.
17 In the same way also he who *received*
the two – he also gained another two.
18 But he who received the one went out
and dug in the ground and buried his lord's
money.
19 And after a long time the lord of those
servants came and took account with them.
20 And he who received the five talents
came up and brought another five talents,
saying, Lord, you gave me five talents. See, I
have gained another five talents above them.
21 And his lord said to him, Well done,
good and faithful servant. You were faithful
over a few things, I will set you over many
things. Enter into the joy of your lord.
22 And also he who received the two talents
came and said, Lord, you gave me two
talents. See, I have gained another two
talents above them.
23 His lord said to him, Well done, good
and faithful servant. You were faithful over
a few things, I will set you over many things.
Enter into the joy of your lord.
24 And also he who had received the one
talent came and said, Lord, I knew that you
were a hard man, reaping where you did not
sow, and gathering where you did not
scatter.
25 And being afraid, I went away and
buried your talent in the earth. See, you
have your own back.
26 But his lord answered and said to him,
Wicked and slothful servant! You knew that
I reaped where I did not sow and gathered
where I did not scatter.
27 Then you ought to have taken my
money to the money-lenders, and at my
coming I would have received my own back

τόκῳ. 28 ἄρατε οὖν ἀπ' αὐτοῦ τὸ τάλαντον, καὶ δότε ·τῷ
interest. Take therefore from him the talent, and give [it] to him who
ἔχοντι τὰ δέκα τάλαντα. 29 Τῷ.γὰρ ἔχοντι παντὶ δοθή-
has the ten talents. For [4]who [5]has [1]to [2]every [3]one shall
σεται, καὶ περισσευθήσεται· [k]ἀπὸ δὲ τοῦ" μὴ.ἔχοντος, καὶ
be given, and [he] shall be in abundance; [2]from [1]but him who has not, even
ὃ ἔχει ἀρθήσεται ἀπ' αὐτοῦ. 30 Καὶ τὸν ἀχρεῖον δοῦλον
that which he has shall be taken from him. And the useless bondman
[l]ἐκβάλλετε" εἰς τὸ σκότος τὸ ἐξώτερον· ἐκεῖ ἔσται ὁ κλαυθμὸς
cast ye out into the darkness the outer: there shall be the weeping
καὶ ὁ βρυγμὸς τῶν ὀδόντων.
and the gnashing of the teeth.

31 Ὅταν.δὲ ἔλθῃ ὁ υἱὸς τοῦ ἀνθρώπου ἐν τῇ.δόξῃ.αὐτοῦ,
But when [5]comes [1]the [2]Son [3]of [4]man in his glory,
καὶ πάντες οἱ [m]ἅγιοι" ἄγγελοι μετ' αὐτοῦ, τότε καθίσει ἐπὶ
and all the holy angels with him, then will he sit upon [the]
θρόνου δόξης.αὐτοῦ, 32 καὶ [n]συναχθήσεται" ἔμπροσθεν αὐτοῦ
throne of his glory, and shall be gathered before him
πάντα τὰ ἔθνη, καὶ [o]ἀφοριεῖ" αὐτοὺς ἀπ' ἀλλήλων, ὥσπερ ὁ
all the nations, and he will separate them from one another, as the
ποιμὴν ἀφορίζει τὰ πρόβατα ἀπὸ τῶν ἐρίφων, 33 καὶ στήσει
shepherd separates the sheep from the goats; and he will set
τὰ μὲν πρόβατα ἐκ δεξιῶν αὐτοῦ, τὰ.δὲ ἐρίφια ἐξ εὐωνύμων.
the sheep on [2]right [3]hand [1]his, but the goats on [his] left.
34 Τότε ἐρεῖ ὁ βασιλεὺς τοῖς ἐκ δεξιῶν αὐτοῦ, Δεῦτε, οἱ
Then [3]will [4]say [1]the [2]king to those on [2]right [3]hand [1]his, Come, the
εὐλογημένοι τοῦ.πατρός.μου, κληρονομήσατε τὴν ἡτοιμασμένην
blessed of my Father, inherit the [2]prepared
ὑμῖν βασιλείαν ἀπὸ καταβολῆς κόσμου. 35 ἐπείνασα.γάρ,
[3]for [4]you [1]kingdom from [the] foundation of [the] world. For I hungered,
καὶ ἐδώκατέ μοι φαγεῖν· ἐδίψησα, καὶ ἐποτίσατέ με· ξένος
and ye gave me to eat; I thirsted, and ye gave [2]to [3]drink [1]me; a stranger
ἤμην, καὶ συνηγάγετέ με· 36 γυμνός, καὶ περιεβάλετέ με· ἠσθέ-
I was, and ye took [2]in [1]me; naked, and ye clothed me; I was
νησα, καὶ ἐπεσκέψασθέ με· ἐν φυλακῇ ἤμην, καὶ [p]ἤλθετε" πρός
sick, and ye visited me; in prison I was, and ye came to
με. 37 Τότε ἀποκριθήσονται αὐτῷ οἱ δίκαιοι, λέγοντες, Κύριε,
me. Then will answer him the righteous, saying, Lord,
πότε σὲ [q]εἴδομεν" πεινῶντα, καὶ ἐθρέψαμεν; ἢ διψῶντα, καὶ
when [3]thee [1]saw [2]we hungering, and fed [thee]? or thirsting, and
ἐποτίσαμεν; 38 πότε.δέ σε εἴδομεν ξένον, καὶ συνηγάγομεν;
gave [thee] to drink? and when [3]thee [1]saw [2]we a stranger, and took [thee] in?
ἢ γυμνόν, καὶ περιεβάλομεν; 39 πότε.δέ σε εἴδομεν [r]ἀσθενῆ,"
or naked, and clothed [thee]? And when [3]thee [1]saw [2]we sick,
ἢ ἐν φυλακῇ, καὶ ἤλθομεν πρός σε; 40 Καὶ ἀποκριθεὶς ὁ
or in prison, and came to thee? And answering the
βασιλεὺς ἐρεῖ αὐτοῖς, Ἀμὴν λέγω ὑμῖν, ἐφ'.ὅσον ἐποιήσατε
king will say to them, Verily I say to you, Inasmuch as ye did [it]
ἑνὶ τούτων [s]τῶν.ἀδελφῶν.μου" τῶν ἐλαχίστων, ἐμοὶ ἐποιή-
to one of these my brethren the least, to me ye
σατε. 41 Τότε ἐρεῖ καὶ τοῖς ἐξ εὐωνύμων, Πορεύεσθε ἀπ'
did [it]. Then will he say also to those on [the] left, Go from
ἐμοῦ, [t]οἱ" κατηραμένοι, εἰς τὸ πῦρ τὸ αἰώνιον, τὸ ἡτοιμα-
me, the cursed, into the fire the eternal, which has been
σμένον τῷ διαβόλῳ καὶ τοῖς.ἀγγέλοις.αὐτοῦ. 42 ἐπείνασα.γάρ,
prepared for the devil and his angels. For I hungered,
καὶ οὐκ.ἐδώκατέ μοι φαγεῖν· ἐδίψησα, καὶ οὐκ.ἐποτίσατέ με·
and ye gave not to me to eat; I thirsted, and ye gave [2]not [3]to [4]drink [1]me;
43 ξένος ἤμην, καὶ οὐ.συνηγάγετέ με· γυμνός, καὶ οὐ.περιεβά-
a stranger I was, and ye took [2]not [3]in [1]me; naked, and ye did not
λετέ με· ἀσθενής, καὶ ἐν φυλακῇ, καὶ οὐκ.ἐπεσκέψασθέ με.
clothe me; sick, and in prison, and ye did not visit me.
44 Τότε ἀποκριθήσονται [v]αὐτῷ" καὶ αὐτοί, λέγοντες, Κύριε,
Then [3]will [4]answer [5]him [2]also [1]they, saying, Lord,
πότε σὲ εἴδομεν πεινῶντα, ἢ διψῶντα, ἢ ξένον, ἢ γυμνόν, ἢ
when [3]thee [1]saw [2]we hungering, or thirsting, or a stranger, or naked, or
ἀσθενῆ, ἢ ἐν φυλακῇ, καὶ οὐ.διηκονήσαμέν σοι; 45 Τότε ἀπο-
sick, or in prison, and did not minister to thee? Then will
κριθήσεται αὐτοῖς, λέγων, Ἀμὴν λέγω ὑμῖν, ἐφ'.ὅσον οὐκ.ἐποι-
he answer them, saying, Verily I say to you, Inasmuch as ye did not
ήσατε ἑνὶ τούτων τῶν ἐλαχίστων, οὐδὲ ἐμοὶ ἐποιήσατε. 46 Καὶ
[it] to one of these the least, neither to me did ye [it]. And
ἀπελεύσονται οὗτοι εἰς κόλασιν αἰώνιον· οἱ.δὲ δίκαιοι εἰς ζωὴν
[3]shall [2]go [4]away [1]these into punishment eternal, but the righteous into life
αἰώνιον.
eternal.

26 Καὶ ἐγένετο ὅτε ἐτέλεσεν ὁ Ἰησοῦς πάντας τοὺς
And it came to pass when [2]had [3]finished [1]Jesus all
λόγους.τούτους, εἶπεν τοῖς.μαθηταῖς.αὐτοῦ, 2 Οἴδατε ὅτι μετὰ
these sayings he said to his disciples, Ye know that after
δύο ἡμέρας τὸ πάσχα γίνεται, καὶ ὁ υἱὸς τοῦ ἀνθρώπου
two days the passover takes place, and the Son of man

with interest.
28 Therefore take the talent from him and
give it to him who has the ten talents.
29 For to everyone who has, *more* shall be
given, and he shall have plenty. But from
him who has not, even that which he has
shall be taken from him.
30 And throw this worthless servant into
the outer darkness – there shall be weeping
and gnashing of teeth.
31 But when the Son of man comes in His
glory, and all the holy angels with Him, then
He will sit upon the throne of His glory.
32 And before Him all the nations shall be
gathered. And He shall separate them from
one another, as a shepherd separates the
sheep from the goats.
33 And He will set the sheep on His right
hand; but the goats on the left.
34 Then the King will say to those on His
right hand, Come, the blessed of My Father.
Inherit the kingdom prepared for you from
the foundation of the world.
35 For I was hungry, and you gave Me food
– I was thirsty and you gave Me drink. I was
a stranger and you took Me in.
36 *I was* naked and you clothed Me. I was
sick and you visited Me. I was in prison and
you came to Me.
37 *Then* the righteous will answer Him, saying, Lord, when did we see You hungry and
fed You? – or thirsty and gave You drink?
38 And when did we see You a stranger and
took You in? – or naked and clothed You?
39 And when did we see You sick, or in
prison, and came to You?
40 And answering, the King will say to
them, Truly I say to you, Since you did it to
one of these, the least of My brothers, you
did it to Me.
41 Then He will say also to those on the
left, Go away from Me, you cursed ones,
into the everlasting fire which has been prepared for the devil and his angels.
42 For I was hungry and you gave Me
nothing to eat. I was thirsty and you gave
Me nothing to drink.
43 I was a stranger and you did not take Me
in – naked and you did not clothe Me – sick
and in prison, and you did not visit Me.
44 Then they will also answer Him, saying,
Lord, when did we see You hungry, or
thirsty, or a stranger, or naked, or sick, or in
prison, and did not serve You?
45 Then He will answer them, saying, Truly
I say to you, Since you did not do it to one
of the least of these, you did not do it to
Me.
46 And these shall go away into everlasting
punishment. But the righteous *shall go* into
everlasting life.
26 1 And when Jesus had finished all these
sayings, He said to His disciples,
2 You know that after two days the Passover takes place, and the Son of man is to be

παραδίδοται εἰς.τὸ.σταυρωθῆναι. 3 Τότε συνήχθησαν οἱ
is delivered up to be crucified. Then were gathered together the
ἀρχιερεῖς [w]καὶ οἱ γραμματεῖς" καὶ οἱ πρεσβύτεροι τοῦ λαοῦ
chief priests and the scribes and the elders of the people
εἰς τὴν αὐλὴν τοῦ ἀρχιερέως τοῦ λεγομένου Καϊάφα, 4 καὶ
to the court of the high priest who was called Caiaphas, and
συνεβουλεύσαντο ἵνα τὸν Ἰησοῦν [x]κρατήσωσιν δόλῳ."
took counsel together in order that Jesus they might seize by guile,
καὶ ἀποκτείνωσιν. 5 ἔλεγον.δέ, Μὴ ἐν τῇ ἑορτῇ, ἵνα μὴ
and kill [him]; but they said, Not during the feast, that [3]not
θόρυβος γένηται ἐν τῷ λαῷ.
[4]a [5]tumult [1]there [2]be among the people.

6 Τοῦ.δὲ.Ἰησοῦ γενομένου ἐν Βηθανίᾳ ἐν οἰκίᾳ Σίμωνος
Now Jesus being in Bethany in [the] house of Simon
τοῦ λεπροῦ, 7 προσῆλθεν αὐτῷ γυνὴ [y]ἀλάβαστρον μύρου
the leper, [3]came [4]to [5]him [1]a [2]woman, an alabaster flask of ointment
ἔχουσα" [z]βαρυτίμου," καὶ κατέχεεν ἐπὶ [a]τὴν.κεφαλὴν." αὐτοῦ
having, very precious, and poured [it] on his head
ἀνακειμένου. 8 ἰδόντες.δὲ οἱ.μαθηταὶ.[b]αὐτοῦ" ἠγανάκ-
as he reclined [at table]. But seeing [it] his disciples became
τησαν, λέγοντες, Εἰς τί ἡ.ἀπώλεια.αὕτη; 9 [c]ἠδύνατο".γὰρ τοῦτο
indignant, saying, For what this waste? for [3]could [1]this
[d]τὸ.μύρον" πραθῆναι πολλοῦ, καὶ δοθῆναι [e] πτωχοῖς.
[2]ointment have been sold for much, and have been given to [the] poor.
10 Γνοὺς.δὲ ὁ Ἰησοῦς εἶπεν αὐτοῖς, Τί κόπους παρέχετε
But knowing [this] Jesus said to them, Why trouble do ye cause
τῇ γυναικί; ἔργον.γὰρ καλὸν [f]εἰργάσατο" εἰς ἐμέ. 11 πάν-
to the woman? for a [2]work [1]good she wrought towards me. [2]Al-
τοτε γὰρ τοὺς πτωχοὺς ἔχετε μεθ' ἑαυτῶν, ἐμὲ.δὲ οὐ πάντοτε
ways [1]for the poor ye have with you, but me not always
ἔχετε. 12 βαλοῦσα.γὰρ αὕτη τὸ.μύρον.τοῦτο ἐπὶ τοῦ
ye have. For [3]in [4]pouring [1]this [[2]woman] this ointment on
σώματός.μου πρὸς τὸ.ἐνταφιάσαι.με ἐποίησεν. 13 ἀμὴν λέγω
my body for my burying she did [it]. Verily I say
ὑμῖν, ὅπου.ἐὰν κηρυχθῇ τὸ.εὐαγγέλιον.τοῦτο ἐν ὅλῳ
to you, Wheresoever shall be proclaimed these glad tidings in all
τῷ κόσμῳ, λαληθήσεται καὶ ὃ ἐποίησεν αὕτη, εἰς
the world, shall be spoken of also that which [3]did [1]this [[2]woman], for
μνημόσυνον αὐτῆς.
a memorial of her.

14 Τότε πορευθεὶς εἷς τῶν δώδεκα, ὁ λεγόμενος Ἰούδας
Then [10]having [11]gone [1]one [2]of [3]the [4]twelve, [5]who [6]was [7]called [8]Judas
Ἰσκαριώτης, πρὸς τοὺς ἀρχιερεῖς, 15 εἶπεν, Τί θέλετέ μοι
[9]Iscariote, to the chief priests, said, What are ye willing [3]me
δοῦναι, [g]κἀγὼ" ὑμῖν παραδώσω αὐτόν; Οἱ.δὲ ἔστησαν αὐτῷ
[1]to [2]give, and I to you will deliver up him? And they appointed to him
τριάκοντα ἀργύρια. 16 καὶ ἀπὸ τότε ἐζήτει εὐκαιρίαν
thirty pieces of silver. And from that time he sought an opportunity
ἵνα αὐτὸν παραδῷ.
that him he might deliver up.

17 Τῇ.δὲ πρώτῃ τῶν.ἀζύμων προσῆλθον οἱ μαθη-
Now on the first [day] of unleavened [bread] came the disci-
ταὶ τῷ Ἰησοῦ, λέγοντες [h]αὐτῷ," Ποῦ θέλεις ἑτοιμάσωμέν
ples to Jesus, saying to him, Where wilt thou [that] we should prepare
σοι φαγεῖν τὸ πάσχα; 18 Ὁ.δὲ εἶπεν, Ὑπάγετε εἰς τὴν
for thee to eat the passover? And he said, Go into the
πόλιν πρὸς τὸν.δεῖνα, καὶ εἴπατε αὐτῷ, Ὁ διδάσκαλος λέγει,
city unto such a one, and say to him, The teacher says,
Ὁ.καιρός.μου ἐγγύς ἐστιν· πρὸς σὲ ποιῶ τὸ πάσχα μετὰ
My time [2]near [1]is; with thee I will keep the passover with
τῶν.μαθητῶν.μου. 19 Καὶ ἐποίησαν οἱ μαθηταὶ ὡς συνέταξεν
my disciples. And [3]did [1]the [2]disciples [4]as [6]directed
αὐτοῖς ὁ Ἰησοῦς, καὶ ἡτοίμασαν τὸ πάσχα.
[7]them [5]Jesus, and prepared the passover.

20 Ὀψίας.δὲ γενομένης ἀνέκειτο μετὰ τῶν δώδεκα[i].
And evening being come he reclined [at table] with the twelve.
21 καὶ ἐσθιόντων.αὐτῶν εἶπεν, Ἀμὴν λέγω ὑμῖν, ὅτι εἷς ἐξ
And as they were eating he said, Verily I say to you, that one of
ὑμῶν παραδώσει με. 22 Καὶ λυπούμενοι σφόδρα ἤρξαντο
you will deliver up me. And being grieved exceedingly they began
λέγειν αὐτῷ [k]ἕκαστος αὐτῶν," Μήτι ἐγώ εἰμι, κύριε; 23 Ὁ.δὲ
to say to him, each of them, [2]I [1]am [he], Lord? But he
ἀποκριθεὶς εἶπεν, Ὁ ἐμβάψας μετ' ἐμοῦ [l]ἐν τῷ τρυβλίῳ
answering said, He who dipped with me in the dish
τὴν χεῖρα," οὗτός με παραδώσει. 24 ὁ μὲν υἱὸς τοῦ ἀνθρώ-
[his] hand, he me will deliver up. The [4]indeed [1]Son [2]of [3]man
που ὑπάγει, καθὼς γέγραπται περὶ αὐτοῦ, οὐαὶ.δὲ τῷ
goes, as it has been written concerning him, but woe
ἀνθρώπῳ.ἐκείνῳ δι' οὗ ὁ υἱὸς τοῦ ἀνθρώπου παραδίδοται·
to that man by whom the Son of man is delivered up;
καλὸν ἦν αὐτῷ εἰ οὐκ.ἐγεννήθη ὁ.ἄνθρωπος.ἐκεῖνος.
good were it for him if [3]had [4]not [5]been [6]born that [2]man.

handed over to be crucified.

3 Then the chief priests and the scribes and the elders of the people were gathered together into the court of the high priest, who was called Cai-a-phas.

4 And they plotted together in order that they might take Jesus by trickery and kill Him.

5 But they said, Not during the feast, so that there will not be an uproar among the people.

6 Now Jesus was in Bethany in the house of Simon the leper.

7 A woman came to Him with an alabaster cask of very precious ointment, and *she* poured it on His head as He sat at the table.

8 But seeing it, His disciples became very indignant, saying, For what purpose is this waste?

9 For the ointment could have been sold for much and given to the poor.

10 But knowing this, Jesus said to them, Why do you cause trouble to the woman? For she has done a good work towards Me.

11 For you always have the poor with you, but you do not always have Me.

12 For in pouring this ointment upon My body, she did it for My burying.

13 Truly I say to you, Wherever this gospel shall be preached to the whole world, that which this one did shall be spoken of also for a remembering of her.

14 Then one of the twelve, called Judas Is-car-i-ot, went to the chief priests.

15 And he said, What are you willing to give me, and I will betray Him to you? And they appointed to him thirty pieces of silver.

16 And from that time he looked for an opportunity, that he might betray Him.

17 Now on the first *day* of the unleavened bread the disciples came to Jesus, saying to Him, Where do You desire for us to prepare for You to eat the passover?

18 And He said, Go into the city to a certain one and say to him, The Master says, My time is near. I will keep the Passover at your house with My disciples.

19 And the disciples did as Jesus commanded them and prepared the passover.

20 And when evening had come, He was reclining at table with the twelve.

21 And as they were eating He said, Truly I say to you that one of you will betray Me.

22 And being very sorrowful, they began each of them to say to Him, Lord, is it I? But answering,

23 He said, He who dipped his hand with Me in the dish will betray Me.

24 Truly the Son of man does go, as it has been written concerning Him, but woe to that man through whom the Son of man is betrayed! It would have been good for that man if he had not been born.

25 'Αποκριθεὶς.δὲ 'Ιούδας ὁ παραδιδοὺς αὐτὸν εἶπεν, Μήτι
And answering Judas, who was delivering up him, said,
ἐγώ εἰμι, [m]ῥαββί;" Λέγει αὐτῷ, Σὺ εἶπας.
[2]I [1]am [he], Rabbi? He says to him, Thou hast said.
26 'Εσθιόντων.δὲ.αὐτῶν, λαβὼν ὁ 'Ιησοῦς [n]τὸν" ἄρτον,
And as they were eating, [2]having [3]taken [1]Jesus the bread,
καὶ εὐλογήσας, ἔκλασεν καὶ [o]ἐδίδου" τοῖς μαθηταῖς, [p]καὶ"
and having blessed, broke and gave to the disciples, and
εἶπεν, Λάβετε, φάγετε· τοῦτό ἐστιν τὸ.σῶμά.μου. 27 Καὶ
said, Take, eat; this is my body. And
λαβὼν [q]τὸ" ποτήριον, [r]καὶ" εὐχαριστήσας, ἔδωκεν αὐτοῖς,
having taken the cup, and having given thanks, he gave [it] to them,
λέγων, Πίετε ἐξ αὐτοῦ πάντες· 28 τοῦτο.γάρ ἐστιν τὸ.αἷμά.μου,
saying, [2]Drink [3]of [4]it [1]all. For this is my blood,
[t]τὸ" τῆς [v]καινῆς" διαθήκης, τὸ περὶ πολλῶν [w]ἐκχυνόμενον" εἰς
that of the new covenant, which for many is poured out for
ἄφεσιν ἁμαρτιῶν. 29 λέγω.δὲ ὑμῖν, [x]ὅτι" οὐ.μὴ πίω ἀπ'
remission of sins. But I say to you, that not at all will I drink hence-
ἄρτι ἐκ τούτου τοῦ [y]γεννήματος" τῆς ἀμπέλου, ἕως τῆς ἡμέρας
forth of this fruit of the vine, until [2]day
ἐκείνης ὅταν αὐτὸ πίνω μεθ' ὑμῶν καινὸν ἐν τῇ βασιλείᾳ τοῦ
[1]that when it I drink with you new in the kingdom
πατρός.μου. 30 Καὶ ὑμνήσαντες ἐξῆλθον εἰς τὸ ὄρος τῶν
of my father. And having sung a hymn they went out to the mount
ἐλαιῶν. 31 τότε λέγει αὐτοῖς ὁ 'Ιησοῦς, Πάντες ὑμεῖς σκανδα-
of Olives. Then [2]says [3]to [4]them [1]Jesus, All ye will be
λισθήσεσθε ἐν ἐμοὶ ἐν τῇ.νυκτὶ.ταύτῃ. γέγραπται.γάρ,
offended in me during this night. For it has been written,
Πατάξω τὸν ποιμένα, καὶ [z]διασκορπισθήσεται" τὰ πρόβατα
I will smite the shepherd, and will be scattered abroad the sheep
τῆς ποίμνης. 32 μετὰ.δὲ τὸ.ἐγερθῆναί.με προάξω ὑμᾶς
of the flock; but after my being raised I will go before you
εἰς τὴν Γαλιλαίαν. 33 'Αποκριθεὶς.δὲ. ὁ Πέτρος εἶπεν αὐτῷ,
into Galilee. And answering Peter said to him,
Εἰ [a]καὶ" πάντες σκανδαλισθήσονται ἐν σοί, ἐγὼ οὐδέποτε
If even all will be offended in thee, I never
σκανδαλισθήσομαι. 34 "Εφη αὐτῷ ὁ 'Ιησοῦς, 'Αμὴν λέγω σοι,
will be offended. [2]Said [3]to [4]him [1]Jesus, Verily I say to thee,
ὅτι ἐν ταύτῃ τῇ νυκτί, πρὶν ἀλέκτορα φωνῆσαι, τρὶς
that during this night, before [the] cock crows, thrice
ἀπαρνήσῃ με. 35 Λέγει αὐτῷ ὁ Πέτρος, Κἂν δέῃ με
thou wilt deny me. [2]Says [3]to [4]him [1]Peter, Even if it were needful for me
σὺν σοὶ ἀποθανεῖν, οὐ.μή σε ἀπαρνήσομαι. 'Ομοίως [b] καὶ
with thee to die, in no wise thee will I deny. Likewise also
πάντες οἱ μαθηταὶ εἶπον.
all the disciples said.

36 Τότε ἔρχεται μετ' αὐτῶν ὁ 'Ιησοῦς εἰς χωρίον λεγόμενον
Then comes with them Jesus to a place called
[c]Γεθσημανῆ," καὶ λέγει τοῖς μαθηταῖς[d], Καθίσατε αὐτοῦ, ἕως.οὗ
Gethsemane, and he says to the disciples, Sit here, until
ἀπελθὼν [f]προσεύξωμαι ἐκεῖ." 37 Καὶ παραλαβὼν τὸν
having gone away I shall pray yonder. And having taken with [him]
Πέτρον καὶ τοὺς δύο υἱοὺς Ζεβεδαίου, ἤρξατο λυπεῖσθαι καὶ
Peter and the two sons of Zebedee, he began to be sorrowful and
ἀδημονεῖν. 38 τότε λέγει αὐτοῖς[g], Περίλυπός ἐστιν ἡ.ψυχή.μου
deeply depressed. Then he says to them, Very sorrowful is my soul
ἕως θανάτου· μείνατε ὧδε καὶ γρηγορεῖτε μετ' ἐμοῦ. 39 Καὶ
even to death; remain here and watch with me. And
[h]προελθὼν" μικρὸν ἔπεσεν ἐπὶ πρόσωπον.αὐτοῦ προσευχό-
having gone forward a little he fell upon his face pray-
μενος, καὶ λέγων, Πάτερ.[i]μου," εἰ δυνατόν ἐστιν [k]παρελθέτω"
ing, and saying, my Father, if possible it is let pass
ἀπ' ἐμοῦ τὸ.ποτήριον.τοῦτο· πλὴν οὐχ ὡς ἐγὼ θέλω, ἀλλ' ὡς
from me this cup; nevertheless not as I will, but as
σύ. 40 Καὶ ἔρχεται πρὸς τοὺς μαθητὰς καὶ εὑρίσκει αὐτοὺς
thou. And he comes to the disciples and finds them
καθεύδοντας, καὶ λέγει τῷ Πέτρῳ, Οὕτως οὐκ.ἰσχύσατε μίαν
sleeping, and says to Peter, Thus were ye not able one
ὥραν γρηγορῆσαι μετ' ἐμοῦ; 41 γρηγορεῖτε καὶ προσεύχεσθε,
hour to watch with me? Watch and pray,
ἵνα μὴ.εἰσέλθητε εἰς πειρασμόν. τὸ μὲν πνεῦμα πρόθυμον,
that ye enter not into temptation: the [2]indeed [1]spirit [is] ready,
ἡ.δὲ. σὰρξ ἀσθενής. 42 Πάλιν ἐκ.δευτέρου ἀπελθὼν προσ-
but the flesh weak. Again a second time having gone away he
ηύξατο, λέγων, Πάτερ.μου, εἰ οὐ.δύναται τοῦτο [l]τὸ ποτήριον"
prayed, saying, my Father, if [3]cannot [1]this [2]cup
παρελθεῖν [m]ἀπ' ἐμοῦ ἐὰν.μὴ αὐτὸ πίω, γενηθήτω τὸ θέλημά
pass from me unless [3]it [1]I [2]drink, [5]be [7]done [6]will
σου. 43 Καὶ ἐλθὼν [n]εὑρίσκει αὐτοὺς πάλιν καθεύδοντας,
[4]thy. And having come he finds them again sleeping,

25 And Judas, who was betraying Him, answered and said, Master, am I the one? He said to him, You have said it.

26 And as they were eating, Jesus, taking the bread and blessing it, broke it and gave to the disciples. And *He* said, Take, eat. This is My body.

27 And taking the cup, and giving thanks, He gave to them, saying, All of you drink of it.

28 For this is My blood of the new covenant which is being poured out for many, to remission of sins.

29 But I say to you that I will not at all drink of this fruit of the vine after this, until that day when I drink it new with you in the kingdom of My Father.

30 And having sung a hymn, they went out to the Mount of Olives.

31 Then Jesus said to them, All of you will be offended in Me during this night. For it has been written, "I will smite the shepherd and the sheep of the flock will be scattered abroad."

32 But after My resurrection, I will go before you into Galilee.

33 And Peter answered and said to Him, Even if all will be offended in You, I will never be offended.

34 Jesus said to him, Truly I say to you that during this night you will deny Me three times, before the cock crows.

35 Peter said to Him, Even if it were necessary for me to die with You, I will never deny You. All the disciples said the same.

36 Then Jesus came with them to a place called Geth-sem-a-ne. And He said to the disciples, sit here while I go away. I shall pray over there.

37 And taking Peter and the two sons of Zeb-e-dee, He began to be sorrowful and deeply troubled.

38 Then He said to them, My soul is very sorrowful, even to death. Stay here and watch with Me.

39 And going forward a little He fell upon His face praying. And He said, O My Father, if it is possible let this cup pass from Me. Nevertheless, *let it* not *be* as I desire, but as You *desire.*

40 And He came to the disciples and found them sleeping. And He said to Peter, So! Were you not able to watch one hour with Me?

41 Watch and pray that you do not enter into temptation. The spirit is indeed willing, but the flesh is weak.

42 Again, going away a second time, He prayed, saying, O My Father, if this cup cannot pass away from Me without My drinking it, let Your will be done.

43 And coming back He found them sleeping again, for their eyes were heavy.

ἦσαν.γὰρ αὐτῶν.οἱ.ὀφθαλμοὶ βεβαρημένοι. 44 Καὶ ἀφεὶς
for were their eyes heavy. And leaving
αὐτούς, ἀπελθὼν πάλιν προσηύξατο ἐκ.τρίτου, τὸν αὐτὸν
them, having gone away again he prayed a third time, the same
λόγον εἰπών. 45 τότε ἔρχεται πρὸς τοὺς.μαθητὰς.αὐτοῦ,
thing saying. Then he comes to his disciples
καὶ λέγει αὐτοῖς, Καθεύδετε τὸ.λοιπὸν καὶ ἀναπαύεσθε·
and says to them, Sleep on now and take your rest;
ἰδού, ἤγγικεν ἡ ὥρα, καὶ ὁ υἱὸς τοῦ ἀνθρώπου παραδίδο-
lo, has drawn near the hour, and the Son of man is delivered
ται εἰς χεῖρας ἁμαρτωλῶν. 46 ἐγείρεσθε, ἄγωμεν· ἰδού,
up into [the] hands of sinners. Rise up, let us go; behold,
ἤγγικεν ὁ παραδιδούς με.
has drawn near he who is delivering up me.
47 Καὶ ἔτι αὐτοῦ.λαλοῦντος, ἰδού, Ἰούδας εἷς τῶν δώδεκα
And yet as he is speaking behold, Judas, one of the twelve,
ἦλθεν, καὶ μετ' αὐτοῦ ὄχλος πολὺς μετὰ μαχαιρῶν καὶ ξύλων,
came, and with him a crowd great with swords and staves,
ἀπὸ τῶν ἀρχιερέων καὶ πρεσβυτέρων τοῦ λαοῦ. 48 ὁ.δὲ
from the chief priests and elders of the people. And he who
παραδιδοὺς αὐτὸν ἔδωκεν αὐτοῖς σημεῖον, λέγων, Ὃν.ἂν
was delivering up him gave them a sign, saying, Whomsoever
φιλήσω, αὐτός ἐστιν· κρατήσατε αὐτόν. 49 Καὶ εὐθέως
I shall kiss, he it is: seize him. And immediately
προσελθὼν τῷ Ἰησοῦ εἶπεν, Χαῖρε, ῥαββί, καὶ κατεφίλησεν
having come up to Jesus he said, Hail, Rabbi, and ardently kissed
αὐτόν. 50 ὁ.δὲ.Ἰησοῦς εἶπεν αὐτῷ, Ἑταῖρε, ἐφ' ᾧ
him. But Jesus said to him, Friend, for what [purpose]
πάρει; Τότε προσελθόντες ἐπέβαλον τὰς χεῖρας ἐπὶ
art thou come? Then having come to [him] they laid hands on
τὸν Ἰησοῦν, καὶ ἐκράτησαν αὐτόν. 51 Καὶ ἰδού, εἷς τῶν
Jesus, and seized him. And behold, one of those
μετὰ Ἰησοῦ, ἐκτείνας τὴν χεῖρα ἀπέσπασεν τὴν μάχαι-
with Jesus, having stretched out [his] hand drew sword
ραν αὐτοῦ, καὶ πατάξας τὸν δοῦλον τοῦ ἀρχιερέως ἀφεῖλεν
his, and smiting the bondman of the high priest took off
αὐτοῦ τὸ ὠτίον. 52 τότε λέγει αὐτῷ ὁ Ἰησοῦς, Ἀπόστρεψόν
his ear. Then says to him Jesus, Return
σου τὴν μάχαιραν εἰς τὸν.τόπον.αὐτῆς· πάντες.γὰρ οἱ λα-
thy sword to its place; for all who
βόντες μάχαιραν ἐν μαχαίρᾳ ἀπολοῦνται. 53 ἢ δο-
take [the] sword by [the] sword shall perish. Or think-
κεῖς ὅτι οὐ.δύναμαι ἄρτι παρακαλέσαι τὸν.πατέρα.μου,
est thou that I am not able now to call upon my Father,
καὶ παραστήσει μοι πλείους ἢ δώδεκα λεγεῶνας ἀγ-
and he will furnish to me more than twelve legions of
γέλων; 54 πῶς οὖν πληρωθῶσιν αἱ γραφαὶ ὅτι οὕτως
angels? How then should be fulfilled the scriptures that thus
δεῖ γενέσθαι;
it must be?
55 Ἐν ἐκείνῃ τῇ ὥρᾳ εἶπεν ὁ Ἰησοῦς τοῖς ὄχλοις, Ὡς ἐπὶ
In that hour said Jesus to the crowds, As against
λῃστὴν ἐξήλθετε μετὰ μαχαιρῶν καὶ ξύλων συλλαβεῖν με;
a robber are ye come out with swords and staves to take me?
καθ'.ἡμέραν πρὸς ὑμᾶς ἐκαθεζόμην διδάσκων ἐν τῷ ἱερῷ,
Daily with you I sat teaching in the temple,
καὶ οὐκ.ἐκρατήσατέ με. 56 τοῦτο.δὲ ὅλον γέγονεν ἵνα πλη-
and ye did not seize me. But this all is come to pass that may
ρωθῶσιν αἱ γραφαὶ τῶν προφητῶν. Τότε οἱ μαθηταὶ πάντες
be fulfilled the scriptures of the prophets. Then the disciples all
ἀφέντες αὐτὸν ἔφυγον.
forsaking him fled.
57 Οἱ.δὲ κρατήσαντες τὸν Ἰησοῦν ἀπήγαγον πρὸς Καϊ-
But they who had seized Jesus led [him] away to Cai-
άφαν τὸν ἀρχιερέα, ὅπου οἱ γραμματεῖς καὶ οἱ πρεσβύτεροι
aphas the high priest, where the scribes and the elders
συνήχθησαν 58 Ὁ.δὲ.Πέτρος ἠκολούθει αὐτῷ ἀπὸ μακρό-
were gathered together. And Peter followed him from afar
θεν, ἕως τῆς αὐλῆς τοῦ ἀρχιερέως· καὶ εἰσελθὼν ἔσω ἐκάθητο
even to the court of the high priest; and having entered within he sat
μετὰ τῶν ὑπηρετῶν ἰδεῖν τὸ τέλος. 59 Οἱ.δὲ ἀρχιερεῖς καὶ οἱ
with the officers to see the end. And the chief priests and the
πρεσβύτεροι καὶ τὸ συνέδριον ὅλον ἐζήτουν ψευδομαρτυρίαν
elders and the sanhedrim whole sought false evidence
κατὰ τοῦ Ἰησοῦ, ὅπως αὐτὸν θανατώσωσιν, 60 καὶ οὐχ
against Jesus, so that him they might put to death, and not
εὗρον· καὶ πολλῶν ψευδομαρτύρων προσελθόντων οὐχ
found [any]: even many false witnesses having come forward not
εὗρον. 61 ὕστερον.δὲ προσελθόντες δύο ψευδομάρτυρες
they found [any]. But at last having come forward two false witnesses
εἶπον, Οὗτος ἔφη, Δύναμαι καταλῦσαι τὸν ναὸν τοῦ θεοῦ,
said, This [man] said, I am able to destroy the temple of God,

44 And leaving them, He went away again and prayed the third time, saying the same words.
45 Then He came to His disciples and said to them, Sleep on now and take your rest. Behold! The hour has come near and the Son of man is betrayed into the hands of sinners.
46 Rise, let us go. Lo! He who is betraying Me has come.
47 And while He was still speaking, Behold, Judas came, one of the twelve! And a great multitude with swords and staves *came* with him, *being sent* from the chief priests and elders of the people.
48 And he who was betraying Him gave them a sign saying, Whomever I shall kiss, it is He. Seize Him.
49 And he came up to Jesus immediately and said, Greetings, Master! And *he* kissed Him.
50 But Jesus said to him, Friend, why have you come? Then they came up and laid hands on Jesus and held Him.
51 And behold! One of those with Jesus stretched out his hand and drew his sword. And striking a servant of the high priest, *he* took off his ear.
52 Then Jesus said to him, Put your sword back into its place, for all who take the sword shall perish by the sword.
53 Or do you think that I am not able now to call upon My Father, and He will place beside Me more than twelve legions of angels?
54 How then would the Scriptures be fulfilled? *For they say,* it must happen like this.
55 In that hour Jesus said to the multitudes, You have come out with swords and staves to take Me, as against a thief. I sat daily with you, teaching in the Temple, and you did not lay hands on Me.
56 But this has all happened so that the Scriptures of the prophets may be fulfilled. Then all His disciples ran away, forsaking Him.
57 And those who had seized Jesus led *Him* away to Cai-a-phas, the high priest, where the scribes and the elders were gathered together.
58 And Peter followed Him from a distance – even to the court of the high priest. And he went inside and sat with the officers to see the end.
59 And the chief priests and the elders and the whole San-he-drin looked for false evidence against Jesus, so that they might put Him to death.
60 But none was found; even though many false witnesses came forward, they did not find any. But at last two false witnesses came up,
61 saying, This one said, I am able to destroy the Temple of God and in three days

καὶ διὰ τριῶν ἡμερῶν [q]οἰκοδομῆσαι αὐτόν." 62 Καὶ ἀναστὰς
and in three days to build it. And having stood up
ὁ ἀρχιερεὺς εἶπεν αὐτῷ, Οὐδὲν ἀποκρίνῃ; τί οὗτοί σου
the high priest said to him, Nothing answerest thou? What [2]these [5]thee
καταμαρτυροῦσιν; 63 Ὁ.δὲ.Ἰησοῦς ἐσιώπα. καὶ [r]ἀποκριθεὶς" ὁ
[1]do [3]witness [4]against? But Jesus was silent. And answering the
ἀρχιερεὺς εἶπεν αὐτῷ, Ἐξορκίζω σὲ κατὰ τοῦ θεοῦ τοῦ ζῶντος,
high priest said to him, I adjure thee by [3]God [1]the [2]living,
ἵνα ἡμῖν εἴπῃς. εἰ σὺ εἶ ὁ χριστός, ὁ υἱὸς τοῦ θεοῦ. 64 Λέγει
that us thou tell if thou art the Christ, the Son of God. [2]Says
αὐτῷ ὁ Ἰησοῦς, Σὺ εἶπας. πλὴν λέγω ὑμῖν, ἀπ'.ἄρτι ὄψεσθε
[3]to [4]him [1]Jesus, Thou hast said. Moreover I say to you, Henceforth ye shall see
τὸν υἱὸν τοῦ ἀνθρώπου καθήμενον ἐκ δεξιῶν τῆς δυνάμεως καὶ
the Son of man sitting at [the] right hand of power, and
ἐρχόμενον ἐπὶ τῶν νεφελῶν τοῦ οὐρανοῦ. 65 Τότε ὁ ἀρχιερεὺς
coming on the clouds of heaven. Then the high priest
διέρρηξεν τὰ.ἱμάτια.αὐτοῦ, λέγων, [t]"Ὅτι" ἐβλασφήμησεν· τί
rent his garments, saying, He has blasphemed; why
ἔτι χρείαν ἔχομεν μαρτύρων; ἴδε, νῦν ἠκούσατε τὴν βλασ-
any more [3]need [1]have [2]we of witnesses? lo, now ye have heard the blas-
φημίαν [v]αὐτοῦ." 66 τί ὑμῖν.δοκεῖ; Οἱ.δὲ ἀποκριθέντες εἶπον,
phemy of him. What do ye think? And they answering said,
Ἔνοχος θανάτου ἐστίν. 67 Τότε ἐνέπτυσαν εἰς τὸ πρόσωπον
Deserving of death he is. Then they spat in [2]face
αὐτοῦ, καὶ ἐκολάφισαν αὐτόν, οἱ.δὲ [w]ἐῤῥάπισαν,"
[1]his, and buffeted him, and some struck [him] with the palm of the
68 λέγοντες, Προφήτευσον ἡμῖν, χριστέ, τίς ἐστιν ὁ
hand, saying, Prophesy to us, Christ, Who is he that
παίσας σε;
struck thee?

69 Ὁ.δὲ.Πέτρος [x]ἔξω ἐκάθητο" ἐν τῇ αὐλῇ, καὶ προσῆλθεν
But Peter [3]without [1]was [2]sitting in the court, and [5]came
αὐτῷ μία.παιδίσκη, λέγουσα, Καὶ σὺ ἦσθα μετὰ Ἰησοῦ τοῦ
[4]to [5]him [1]a [2]maid, saying, And thou wast with Jesus the
Γαλιλαίου. 70 Ὁ.δὲ ἠρνήσατο ἔμπροσθεν [y]πάντων, λέγων, Οὐκ
Galilæan. But he denied before all, saying, [3]Not
οἶδα τί λέγεις. 71 Ἐξελθόντα.δὲ [z]αὐτὸν" εἰς τὸν πυλῶνα
[1]I [2]know what thou sayest. And [2]having [3]gone [4]out [1]he into the porch
εἶδεν αὐτὸν ἄλλη, καὶ λέγει [a]τοῖς" ἐκεῖ, [b]Καὶ" οὗτος
[3]saw [4]him [1]another [[2]maid], and says to those there, And this [man]
ἦν μετὰ Ἰησοῦ τοῦ Ναζωραίου. 72 Καὶ πάλιν ἠρνήσατο
was with Jesus the Nazaræan. And again he denied
[c]μεθ'" ὅρκου, "Ὅτι οὐκ.οἶδα τὸν ἄνθρωπον. 73 Μετὰ μικρὸν.δὲ
with an oath, I know not the man. After a little also
προσελθόντες οἱ ἑστῶτες εἶπον τῷ Πέτρῳ, Ἀληθῶς
[5]having [6]come [7]to [[8]him] [1]those [2]who [3]stood [4]by said to Peter, Truly
καὶ σὺ ἐξ αὐτῶν εἶ· καὶ.γὰρ ἡ.λαλιά.σου δῆλόν σε ποιεῖ.
also thou of them art, for even thy speech [3]manifest [2]thee [1]makes.
74 Τότε ἤρξατο [d]καταναθεματίζειν" καὶ ὀμνύειν, "Ὅτι οὐκ.οἶδα
Then he began to curse and to swear, I know not
τὸν ἄνθρωπον. Καὶ [e]εὐθέως" ἀλέκτωρ ἐφώνησεν. 75 καὶ
the man. And immediately a cock crew. And
ἐμνήσθη ὁ Πέτρος τοῦ ῥήματος [f]τοῦ" Ἰησοῦ εἰρηκότος [g]αὐτῷ",
[2]remembered [1]Peter the word of Jesus, who had said to him,
Ὅτι πρὶν ἀλέκτορα φωνῆσαι, τρὶς ἀπαρνήσῃ με· καὶ
Before [the] cock crow, thrice thou wilt deny me. And
ἐξελθὼν ἔξω ἔκλαυσεν πικρῶς.
having gone out he wept bitterly.

27 Πρωΐας.δὲ γενομένης, συμβούλιον ἔλαβον πάντες οἱ
And morning being come, [12]counsel [11]took [1]all [2]the
ἀρχιερεῖς καὶ οἱ πρεσβύτεροι τοῦ λαοῦ κατὰ τοῦ Ἰησοῦ,
[3]chief [4]priests [5]and [6]the [7]elders [8]of [9]the [10]people against Jesus,
ὥστε θανατῶσαι αὐτόν· 2 καὶ δήσαντες αὐτὸν ἀπήγα-
so that they might put to death him; and having bound him they led
γον καὶ παρέδωκαν [i]αὐτὸν" [k]Ποντίῳ" [l]Πιλάτῳ" τῷ
away [him] and delivered up him to Pontius Pilate the
ἡγεμόνι.
governor.

3 Τότε ἰδὼν Ἰούδας ὁ [m]παραδιδοὺς" αὐτὸν ὅτι κατ-
Then [6]having [7]seen [1]Judas [2]who [3]delivered [5]up [4]him that he was
εκρίθη, μεταμεληθεὶς [n]ἀπέστρεψεν" τὰ τριάκοντα ἀργύ-
condemned, having regretted [it] returned the thirty pieces of
ρια τοῖς ἀρχιερεῦσιν καὶ [o]τοῖς" πρεσβυτέροις, 4 λέγων,
silver to the chief priests and the elders, saying,
Ἥμαρτον παραδοὺς αἷμα [p]ἀθῷον". Οἱ.δὲ εἶπον, Τί
I sinned delivering up [2]blood [1]guiltless. But they said, What [is that]
πρὸς ἡμᾶς; σὺ [q]ὄψει." 5 Καὶ ῥίψας τὰ ἀργύρια
to us? thou wilt see [to it]. And having cast down the pieces of silver
[r]ἐν τῷ ναῷ" ἀνεχώρησεν, καὶ ἀπελθὼν ἀπήγξατο. 6 Οἱ.δὲ
in the temple he withdrew, and having gone away hanged himself. And the
ἀρχιερεῖς λαβόντες τὰ ἀργύρια [s]εἶπον," Οὐκ.ἔξεστιν βαλεῖν
chief priests having taken the pieces of silver said, It is not lawful to put

to build it.
62 And the high priest stood up, saying to
Him, Do you answer nothing? What do these
say against you?
63 But Jesus was silent. And the high priest
said to Him, I command you by the living
God that you tell us whether you are the
Christ, the Son of God.
64 Jesus said to him, You have said it! More
than that I say to you, From this time you
shall see the Son of man sitting on the right
hand of power and coming on the clouds of
heaven.
65 Then the high priest tore his clothes,
saying, He has blasphemed! Why do we have
any more need to hear witnesses? Behold!
Now you have heard his blasphemy.
66 What do you think? And answering, they
said, He is worthy of death.
67 Then they spat in His face and beat Him.
And some slapped *Him*,
68 saying, Prophesy to us, O Christ, Who is
he that slapped you?

69 And Peter was sitting outside in the
court. And a certain girl came to him, saying,
And you were with Jesus the Galilean.
70 But he denied it before all, saying, I do
not know what you say.
71 And after he had gone out into the
porch, another saw him and said to those
there, This one also was with Jesus the
Nazarean.
72 And again he denied with an oath, I do
not know the man.
73 And after a little while those standing
near came up and said to Peter, Indeed, you
are also one of them, for even your speech
betrays you.

74 Then he began to curse and to swear, I
do not know the man. And immediately the
cock crowed.
75 And Peter remembered the word of
Jesus, who had said to him, Before the cock
crow, you will deny Me three times. And he
went out and cried bitterly.
27 1 And when morning came, all the chief
priests and elders of the people plotted
against Jesus, so that they might put Him to
death.
2 And they tied Him up and led *Him* away
and handed Him over to Pontius Pilate, the
governor.
3 Then Judas, who had betrayed Him,
seeing that He was condemned, being sorry,
brought back the thirty pieces of silver to
the chief priests and elders,
4 saying, I have sinned. *I* have betrayed
innocent blood. But they said, What *is that*
to us? You will *have* to see *to that!*
5 And throwing down the pieces of silver in
the Temple, he left and went away and
hanged himself.
6 And the chief priests took the silver and

αὐτὰ εἰς τὸν κορβανᾶν, ἐπεὶ τιμὴ αἵματός ἐστιν. 7 Συμ-
them into the treasury, since [the] price of blood it is. [4]Coun-
βούλιον δὲ λαβόντες, ἠγόρασαν ἐξ αὐτῶν τὸν ἀγρὸν τοῦ
sel [1]and [2]having [3]taken, they bought with them the field of the
κεραμέως, εἰς ταφὴν τοῖς ξένοις. 8 διὸ ἐκλήθη ὁ
potter, for a burying ground for strangers. Wherefore [3]was [4]called
ἀγρὸς.ἐκεῖνος ἀγρὸς αἵματος ἕως τῆς.σήμερον. 9 τότε
[1]that [2]field Field of blood to this day. Then
ἐπληρώθη τὸ ῥηθὲν διὰ Ἱερεμίου τοῦ προφήτου, λέγον-
was fulfilled that which was spoken by Jeremias the prophet, say-
τος, Καὶ ἔλαβον τὰ τριάκοντα ἀργύρια, τὴν τιμὴν τοῦ
ing, And I took the thirty pieces of silver, the price of him who
τετιμημένου, ὃν ἐτιμήσαντο ἀπὸ υἱῶν Ἰσραήλ, 10 καὶ
was set a price on, whom they [6]set [7]a [8]price [9]on [1]of [[2]the] [3]sons [4]of [5]Israel, and
ἔδωκαν αὐτὰ εἰς τὸν ἀγρὸν τοῦ κεραμέως, καθὰ συνέταξέν
gave them for the field of the potter, according as [3]directed
μοι κύριος.
[4]me [[1]the] [2]Lord.

11 Ὁ.δὲ.Ἰησοῦς [t]ἔστη" ἔμπροσθεν τοῦ ἡγεμόνος· καὶ ἐπηρώ-
But Jesus stood before the governor; and [3]ques-
τησεν αὐτὸν ὁ ἡγεμών, λέγων, Σὺ εἶ ὁ βασιλεὺς τῶν
tioned [4]him [1]the [2]governor, saying, [2]Thou [1]art the king of the
Ἰουδαίων; Ὁ.δὲ.Ἰησοῦς ἔφη [v]αὐτῷ," Σὺ λέγεις. 12 Καὶ
Jews? And Jesus said to him, Thou sayest. And
ἐν.τῷ.κατηγορεῖσθαι αὐτὸν ὑπὸ τῶν ἀρχιερέων καὶ [w]τῶν" πρεσ-
when [2]was [3]accused [1]he by the chief priests and the el-
βυτέρων, οὐδὲν ἀπεκρίνατο. 13 τότε λέγει αὐτῷ ὁ [x]Πιλάτος,"
ders, nothing he answered. Then [2]says [3]to [4]him [1]Pilate,
Οὐκ.ἀκούεις πόσα σοῦ καταμαρτυροῦσιν; 14 Καὶ
Hearest thou not how many things [4]thee [1]they [2]witness [3]against? And
οὐκ.ἀπεκρίθη αὐτῷ πρὸς οὐδὲ ἓν ῥῆμα, ὥστε θαυμάζειν τὸν
he did not answer him to even one word, so that [3]wondered [1]the
ἡγεμόνα λίαν.
[2]governor exceedingly.

15 Κατὰ.δὲ ἑορτὴν εἰώθει ὁ ἡγεμὼν ἀπολύειν ἕνα
Now at [the] feast [3]was [4]accustomed [1]the [2]governor to release one
τῷ ὄχλῳ δέσμιον, ὃν ἤθελον. 16 εἶχον.δὲ τότε δέσ-
[2]to [3]the [4]multitude [1]prisoner, whom they wished. And they had then a [2]pri-
μιον ἐπίσημον, λεγόμενον Βαραββᾶν. 17 συνηγμένων
soner [1]notable, called Barabbas. [3]Being [4]gathered [5]together
οὖν αὐτῶν εἶπεν αὐτοῖς ὁ [y]Πιλάτος," Τίνα θέλετε ἀπο-
[2]therefore [1]they [7]said [8]to [9]them [6]Pilate, Whom will ye [that] I
λύσω ὑμῖν; Βαραββᾶν, ἢ Ἰησοῦν τὸν λεγόμενον χριστόν;
release to you? Barabbas, or Jesus who is called Christ?
18 ᾔδει.γὰρ ὅτι διὰ φθόνον παρέδωκαν αὐτόν. 19 Καθη-
For he knew that through envy they delivered up him. [2]As [4]was
μένου δὲ αὐτοῦ ἐπὶ τοῦ βήματος ἀπέστειλεν πρὸς αὐτὸν ἡ
[5]sitting [1]but [3]he on the judgment seat [3]sent [4]to [5]him
γυνὴ.αὐτοῦ, λέγουσα, Μηδέν σοι καὶ τῷ δικαίῳ
[1]his [2]wife, saying, [Let there be] nothing between thee and [2]righteous
ἐκείνῳ· πολλὰ.γὰρ ἔπαθον σήμερον κατ' ὄναρ δι'
[1]that [man]; for many things I suffered to-day in a dream because of
αὐτόν. 20 Οἱ.δὲ ἀρχιερεῖς καὶ οἱ πρεσβύτεροι ἔπεισαν τοὺς
him. But the chief priests and the elders persuaded the
ὄχλους ἵνα αἰτήσωνται τὸν Βαραββᾶν, τὸν.δὲ.Ἰησοῦν ἀπολ-
crowds that they should beg for Barabbas, and [3]Jesus [1]should
έσωσιν. 21 ἀποκριθεὶς.δὲ ὁ ἡγεμὼν εἶπεν αὐτοῖς, Τίνα θέλετε
[2]destroy. And [3]answering [1]the [2]governor said to them, Which will ye
ἀπὸ τῶν δύο ἀπολύσω ὑμῖν; Οἱ.δὲ [z]εἶπον", [a]Βαραββᾶν.
of the two [that] I release to you? And they said, Barabbas.
22 Λέγει αὐτοῖς ὁ [y]Πιλάτος," Τί οὖν ποιήσω Ἰησοῦν, τὸν
[2]Says [3]to [4]them [1]Pilate, What then shall I do with Jesus, who
λεγόμενον χριστόν; Λέγουσιν [b]αὐτῷ" πάντες, Σταυρωθήτω.
is called Christ? They [2]say [3]to [4]him [1]all, Let [him] be crucified.
23 Ὁ.δὲ [c]ἡγεμὼν" ἔφη, Τί γὰρ κακὸν ἐποίησεν; Οἱ.δὲ
And the governor said, What [2]then [1]evil did he commit? But they
περισσῶς ἔκραζον, λέγοντες, Σταυρωθήτω. 24 Ἰδὼν.δὲ ὁ
the more cried out, saying, Let [him] be crucified. And [2]seeing
[y]Πιλάτος" ὅτι οὐδὲν ὠφελεῖ, ἀλλὰ μᾶλλον θόρυβος γίνεται,
[1]Pilate that nothing it availed, but rather a tumult is arising,
λαβὼν ὕδωρ ἀπενίψατο τὰς χεῖρας [d]ἀπέναντι" τοῦ ὄχλου,
having taken water he washed [his] hands before the crowd,
λέγων, [e]Ἀθῷός" εἰμι ἀπὸ τοῦ αἵματος [f]τοῦ.δικαίου.τούτου·"
saying, Guiltless I am of the blood of this righteous [man];
ὑμεῖς ὄψεσθε. 25 Καὶ ἀποκριθεὶς πᾶς ὁ λαὸς εἶπεν, Τὸ
ye will see [to it]. And [4]answering [1]all [2]the [3]people said,
αἷμα.αὐτοῦ ἐφ' ἡμᾶς καὶ ἐπὶ τὰ.τέκνα.ἡμῶν. 26 Τότε ἀπέλυ-
His blood [be] on us and on our children. Then he re-
σεν αὐτοῖς τὸν Βαραββᾶν· τὸν.δὲ.Ἰησοῦν φραγελλώσας
leased to them Barabbas; but [3]Jesus [1]having [2]scourged
παρέδωκεν ἵνα σταυρωθῇ.
he delivered up [him] that he might be crucified.
27 Τότε οἱ στρατιῶται τοῦ ἡγεμόνος, παραλαβόντες
Then the soldiers of the governor, having taken with [them]

said, It is not lawful to put them into the
treasury, for it is the price of blood.
7 And after talking it over, they bought the
potter's field with them, for the burial of
strangers.
8 So that field was called Field of Blood
until this day.
9 Then that which was spoken by Jeremiah
the prophet was fulfilled, saying, "And I
took the thirty pieces of silver, the price of
Him who was priced, on whom they of the
sons of Israel set a price,
10 and gave them for the potter's field, as
the Lord commanded me."
11 And Jesus stood before the governor.
And the governor questioned Him, saying,
Are you the king of the Jews? And Jesus
said to him, You say it.
12 And when He was accused by the chief
priests and the elders, He answered nothing.
13 Then Pilate said to Him, Do you not
hear how many things they say against you?
14 And He did not answer him even to one
word, so that the governor greatly marveled.
15 Now at *this* feast-time the governor was
accustomed to release to the people a
prisoner, *anyone* whom they desired.
16 And they had then a noted prisoner,
called Bar-ab-bas.
17 Then, when they were gathered together,
Pilate said to them, Whom do you desire
that I release to you, Bar-ab-bas or Jesus
who is called Christ?
18 For he knew that they handed him over
through envy.
19 But as he was sitting on the judgment
seat, his wife sent to him, saying, *Let there
be* nothing between you and that righteous
one, for I have suffered many things today
in a dream because of him.
20 But the chief priests and elders persuaded the crowd that they should beg for
Bar-ab-bas and should destroy Jesus.
21 And the governor answered and said to
them, Which of the two do you desire that I
release to you? And they said, Bar-ab-bas.
22 Pilate said to them, What then shall I do
with Jesus who is called Christ?
23 They all said to him, Let him be
crucified! And the governor said, Why? What
evil has he done? But they cried out the
more, saying, Let him be crucified!
24 And when Pilate saw that it gained
nothing, but rather that an uproar was
arising, he took water and washed his hands
before the crowd, saying, I am innocent of
the blood of this just one – you will see.
25 And all the people answered and said,
Let his blood be on us and on our children.
26 Then he released Bar-ab-bas to them. But
he had Jesus whipped and handed *Him* over
that He might be crucified.

27 Then the soldiers of the governor, taking
Jesus with them into the palace, gathered all

τὸν Ἰησοῦν εἰς τὸ πραιτώριον, συνήγαγον ἐπ' αὐτὸν ὅλην
Jesus to the prætorium, gathered against him all
τὴν σπεῖραν· 28 καὶ [g]ἐκδύσαντες‖ αὐτὸν [h]περιέθηκαν αὐτῷ
the band; and having stripped him they put round him
χλαμύδα κοκκίνην·‖ 29 καὶ πλέξαντες στέφανον ἐξ ἀκανθῶν
a [2]cloak [1]scarlet; And having platted a crown of thorns
ἐπέθηκαν ἐπὶ [i]τὴν.κεφαλὴν‖.αὐτοῦ, καὶ κάλαμον [k]ἐπὶ τὴν
they put [it] on his head, and a reed in
δεξιὰν‖ αὐτοῦ· καὶ γονυπετήσαντες ἔμπροσθεν αὐτοῦ [l]ἐνέ-
[2]right [3]hand [1]his; and bowing the knees before him they
παιζον‖ αὐτῷ, λέγοντες, Χαῖρε, [m]ὁ βασιλεὺς‖ τῶν Ἰουδαίων·
mocked him, saying, Hail, king of the Jews!
30 καὶ ἐμπτύσαντες εἰς αὐτὸν ἔλαβον τὸν κάλαμον καὶ ἔτυπ-
And having spit upon him they took the reed and struck
τον εἰς τὴν.κεφαλὴν.αὐτοῦ. 31 Καὶ ὅτε ἐνέπαιξαν αὐτῷ
[him] on his head. And when they had mocked him
[n]ἐξέδυσαν‖ αὐτὸν τὴν χλαμύδα, [o]καὶ‖ ἐνέδυσαν αὐτὸν τὰ
they took off him the cloak, and they put on him
ἱμάτια.αὐτοῦ· καὶ ἀπήγαγον αὐτὸν εἰς τὸ.σταυρῶσαι.
his own garments; and led [2]away [1]him to crucify.
32 Ἐξερχόμενοι.δὲ εὗρον ἄνθρωπον Κυρηναῖον, ὀνόματι
And going forth they found a man a Cyrenæan, by name
Σίμωνα· τοῦτον ἠγγάρευσαν ἵνα ἄρῃ τὸν.σταυρὸν.αὐτοῦ.
Simon; him they compelled that he might carry his cross.
33 Καὶ ἐλθόντες εἰς τόπον λεγόμενον [p]Γολγοθᾶ,‖ [q]ὅς‖ ἐστιν
And having come to a place called Golgotha, which is
[r]λεγόμενος κρανίου τόπος,‖ 34 ἔδωκαν αὐτῷ [s]πιεῖν‖ [t]ὄξος‖
called [2]of [3]a [4]skull [1]place, they gave him to drink vinegar
μετὰ χολῆς μεμιγμένον· καὶ γευσάμενος οὐκ.[v]ἤθελεν‖ [s]πιεῖν.‖
with gall mingled; and having tasted he would not drink.
35 Σταυρώσαντες.δὲ αὐτὸν διεμερίσαντο τὰ.ἱμάτια.αὐτοῦ,
And having crucified him they divided his garments,
[w]βάλλοντες‖ κλῆρον· [x]ἵνα πληρωθῇ τὸ ῥηθὲν ὑπὸ
casting a lot; that might be fulfilled that which was spoken by
τοῦ προφήτου, Διεμερίσαντο τὰ.ἱμάτιά.μου ἑαυτοῖς, καὶ
the prophet, They divided my garments among themselves, and
ἐπὶ τὸν.ἱματισμόν.μου ἔβαλον κλῆρον.‖ 36 Καὶ καθήμενοι
for my vesture they cast a lot. And sitting down
ἐτήρουν αὐτὸν ἐκεῖ. 37 Καὶ ἐπέθηκαν ἐπάνω τῆς
they kept guard over him there. And they put up over
κεφαλῆς.αὐτοῦ τὴν.αἰτίαν.αὐτοῦ γεγραμμένην, Οὗτός ἐστιν
his head his accusation written: This is
Ἰησοῦς ὁ βασιλεὺς τῶν Ἰουδαίων. 38 Τότε σταυροῦνται σὺν
Jesus the king of the Jews. Then are crucified with
αὐτῷ δύο λῃσταί, εἷς ἐκ δεξιῶν καὶ εἷς ἐξ εὐωνύμων.
him two robbers, one at [the] right hand and one at [the] left.
39 Οἱ.δὲ παραπορευόμενοι ἐβλασφήμουν αὐτόν, κινοῦντες
But those passing by railed at him, shaking
τὰς.κεφαλὰς.αὐτῶν, 40 καὶ λέγοντες, Ὁ καταλύων τὸν ναὸν
their heads, and saying, Thou who destroyest the temple
καὶ ἐν τρισὶν ἡμέραις οἰκοδομῶν, σῶσον σεαυτόν.[y]εἰ υἱὸς
and in three days buildest [it], save thyself. If son
[y]εἶ τοῦ θεοῦ,‖ [z]κατάβηθι ἀπὸ τοῦ σταυροῦ. 41 Ὁμοίως
thou art of God, descend from the cross. [2]In [3]like [4]manner
[a]δὲ καὶ‖ οἱ ἀρχιερεῖς ἐμπαίζοντες μετὰ τῶν γραμματέων καὶ
[1]and also the chief priests, mocking, with the scribes and
πρεσβυτέρων ἔλεγον, 42 Ἄλλους ἔσωσεν, ἑαυτὸν οὐ.δύναται
elders, said, Others he saved, himself he is not able
σῶσαι. [b]εἰ‖ βασιλεὺς Ἰσραήλ ἐστιν, καταβάτω νῦν ἀπὸ τοῦ
to save. If king of Israel he is, let him descend now from the
σταυροῦ, καὶ [c]πιστεύσομεν‖ [d]αὐτῷ.‖ 43 πέποιθεν ἐπὶ [e]τὸν θεόν·‖
cross, and we will believe him. He trusted on God:
ῥυσάσθω νῦν [f]αὐτόν,‖ εἰ θέλει αὐτόν. εἶπεν.γάρ, Ὅτι θεοῦ
let him deliver [2]now [1]him, if he will [have] him. For he said, [4]Of [5]God
εἰμι υἱός. 44 Τὸ.δ'.αὐτὸ καὶ οἱ λῃσταὶ οἱ [g]συσταυρωθέν-
[1]I [2]am [3]Son. And [with] the same thing also the robbers who were crucified to-
τες‖ [h]αὐτῷ ὠνείδιζον [i]αὐτῷ.‖
gether with him reproached him.
45 Ἀπὸ.δὲ ἕκτης ὥρας σκότος ἐγένετο ἐπὶ πᾶσαν τὴν
Now from [2]sixth [[1]the] hour darkness was over all the
γῆν ἕως ὥρας [k]ἐννάτης‖ 46 περὶ.δὲ τὴν [l]ἐννάτην‖ ὥραν
land until [the] [2]hour [1]ninth; and about the ninth hour
[m]ἀνεβόησεν‖ ὁ Ἰησοῦς φωνῇ μεγάλῃ, λέγων, [n]Ἠλί, Ἠλί,‖
[2]cried [3]out [1]Jesus [4]with [5]a [7]voice [6]loud, saying, Eli, Eli,
[o]λαμὰ‖ [p]σαβαχθανί;‖ τοῦτ' ἔστιν, Θεέ.μου, θεέ.μου, [q]ἱνατί‖ με
lama sabachthani? that is, My God, my God, why me
ἐγκατέλιπες; 47 Τινὲς.δὲ τῶν ἐκεῖ [r]ἑστώτων‖ ἀκού-
hast thou forsaken? And some of those who there were standing having
σαντες, ἔλεγον, Ὅτι [s]Ἠλίαν‖ φωνεῖ οὗτος. 48 Καὶ εὐθέως
heard, said, [4]Elias [3]calls [1]this [[2]man]. And immediately
δραμὼν εἷς ἐξ αὐτῶν καὶ λαβὼν σπόγγον, πλήσας.τε
[4]having [5]run [1]one [2]of [3]them and taken a sponge, and filled [it]

the band against Him.
28 And stripping Him, they put a scarlet
robe around Him.
29 And they plaited a crown of thorns and
put it on His head. And *they put* a reed in His
right hand. And bowing before Him, they
mocked Him, saying, Hail, king of the Jews!
30 And after they spit upon Him, they took
the reed and struck Him on His head.
31 And when they had mocked Him, they
took the robe off of Him. And they put His
own clothes on Him and led Him away to
crucify *Him.*

32 And going out they found a man, a
Cy-ren-e-an named Simon. They forced him
to carry His cross.
33 And coming to a place called Gol-goth-a
(which is called 'Place of a Skull'),
34 they gave Him vinegar to drink, mixed
with gall. But He tasted it and would not
drink.
35 And when they had crucified Him, they
divided His garments, casting a lot (so that
that which was spoken by the prophet might
be fulfilled, "They divided My garments
among themselves, and for My clothing they
cast a lot").
36 And they sat down and watched Him
there.
37 And they put up over His head His
accusation, written, THIS IS JESUS THE
KING OF THE JEWS.
38 Then two thieves were crucified with
Him, one at His right hand and one at His left.
39 But those passing by blasphemed Him,
shaking their heads,
40 and saying, You who will destroy the
Temple and build it in three days, save Yourself. If You are the Son of God, come down
from the cross.
41 And in the same way also, the chief
priests and the elders mocked, saying,
42 He saved others. He is not able to save
himself. If he is the king of Israel, let him
now come down from the cross, and we will
believe him.
43 He has trusted on God, let Him deliver
him now, if He will *have* him. (For He said, I
am the Son of God.)
44 And in the same way the thieves who
were together with Him also reviled Him.

45 Now from the sixth hour there was darkness over all the land until the ninth hour.
46 And about the ninth hour Jesus cried
with a loud voice, saying, E-li, E-li, la-ma
sa-bach-tha-ni, that is to say, My God, My
God, why have You forsaken Me?
47 And some of those who were standing
there heard and said, He is calling Elijah.
48 And immediately one of them ran and
took a sponge. He filled it with vinegar and

ὄξους καὶ περιθεὶς καλάμῳ, ἐπότιζεν αὐτόν· 49 οἱ.δὲ
with vinegar and put [it] on a reed, gave [2]to [3]drink [1]him. But the
λοιποὶ [t]ἔλεγον,[ll] [u]Ἄφες, ἴδωμεν εἰ ἔρχεται [v]Ἠλίας[ll] σώσων
rest said, Let be; let us see [2]comes [1]Elias to save
αὐτόν.
him.

50 Ὁ.δὲ.Ἰησοῦς πάλιν κράξας φωνῇ μεγάλῃ ἀφῆκεν
And Jesus again having cried with a [2]voice [1]loud yielded up
τὸ πνεῦμα. 51 Καὶ ἰδού, τὸ καταπέτασμα τοῦ ναοῦ ἐσχίσθη
[his] spirit. And behold, the veil of the temple was rent
[w]εἰς δύο[ll] [x]ἀπὸ[ll] ἄνωθεν ἕως κάτω[w]· καὶ ἡ γῆ ἐσείσθη, καὶ
into two from top to bottom; and the earth was shaken, and
αἱ πέτραι ἐσχίσθησαν, 52 καὶ τὰ μνημεῖα ἀνεῴχθησαν, καὶ
the rocks were rent, and the tombs were opened, and
πολλὰ σώματα τῶν κεκοιμημένων ἁγίων [ya]ἠγέρθη,[ll] 53 καὶ
many bodies of the [2]fallen [3]asleep [1]saints arose, and
ἐξελθόντες ἐκ τῶν μνημείων μετὰ τὴν.ἔγερσιν.αὐτοῦ, εἰσῆλ-
having gone forth out of the tombs after his arising, entered
θον εἰς τὴν ἁγίαν πόλιν καὶ ἐνεφανίσθησαν πολλοῖς.
into the holy city and appeared to many.

54 Ὁ.δὲ [z]ἑκατόνταρχος[ll] καὶ οἱ μετ' αὐτοῦ τηροῦντες
But the centurion and they who with him kept guard over
τὸν Ἰησοῦν, ἰδόντες τὸν σεισμὸν καὶ τὰ [a]γενόμενα,[ll]
Jesus, having seen the earthquake and the things that took place,
ἐφοβήθησαν σφόδρα, λέγοντες, Ἀληθῶς [b]θεοῦ υἱὸς[ll] ἦν οὗτος.
feared greatly, saying, Truly [3]God's [4]Son [2]was [1]this.

55 Ἦσαν.δὲ ἐκεῖ γυναῖκες πολλαὶ ἀπὸ μακρόθεν θεωροῦ-
And there were there [2]women [1]many from afar off looking
σαι, αἵτινες ἠκολούθησαν τῷ Ἰησοῦ ἀπὸ τῆς Γαλιλαίας δια-
on, who followed Jesus from Galilee min-
κονοῦσαι αὐτῷ, 56 ἐν αἷς ἦν Μαρία ἡ Μαγδαληνή, καὶ
istering to him, among whom was Mary the Magdalene, and
Μαρία ἡ τοῦ Ἰακώβου καὶ [c]Ἰωσῆ[ll] μήτηρ, καὶ ἡ μήτηρ τῶν
Mary the [2]of [3]James [4]and [5]Joses [1]mother; and the mother of the
υἱῶν Ζεβεδαίου.
sons of Zebedee.

57 Ὀψίας.δὲ γενομένης ἦλθεν ἄνθρωπος πλούσιος ἀπὸ
And evening being come [4]came [1]a [3]man [2]rich from
[d]Ἀριμαθαίας,[ll] τοὔνομα Ἰωσήφ, ὃς καὶ αὐτὸς [e]ἐμαθήτευσεν[ll]
Arimathea, by name Joseph, who also himself was discipled
τῷ Ἰησοῦ· 58 οὗτος προσελθὼν τῷ [f]Πιλάτῳ[ll] ᾐτήσατο τὸ σῶμα
to Jesus. He having gone to Pilate begged the body
τοῦ Ἰησοῦ. τότε ὁ [g]Πιλάτος[ll] ἐκέλευσεν ἀποδοθῆναι [h]τὸ σῶμα.[ll]
of Jesus. Then Pilate commanded to be given up the body.
59 καὶ λαβὼν τὸ σῶμα ὁ Ἰωσὴφ ἐνετύλιξεν αὐτὸ [i] σινδόνι
And having taken the body Joseph wrapped it in a [2]linen [3]cloth
καθαρᾷ, 60 καὶ ἔθηκεν αὐτὸ ἐν τῷ.καινῷ.αὐτοῦ μνημείῳ ὃ
[1]clean, and placed it in his new tomb which
ἐλατόμησεν ἐν τῇ πέτρᾳ καὶ προσκυλίσας λίθον μέγαν
he had hewn in the rock; and having rolled a [2]stone [1]great
[k]τῇ θύρᾳ τοῦ μνημείου ἀπῆλθεν. 61 ἦν.δὲ ἐκεῖ [l]Μαρία[ll]
to the door of the tomb went away. And there was there Mary
ἡ Μαγδαληνὴ καὶ ἡ ἄλλη Μαρία, καθήμεναι ἀπέναντι τοῦ
the Magdalene and the other Mary, sitting opposite the
τάφου.
sepulchre.

62 Τῇ.δὲ ἐπαύριον, ἥτις ἐστὶν μετὰ τὴν παρασκευήν,
Now on the morrow, which is after the preparation,
συνήχθησαν οἱ ἀρχιερεῖς καὶ οἱ Φαρισαῖοι πρὸς [m]Πι-
were gathered together the chief priests and the Pharisees to Pi-
λάτον,[ll] 63 λέγοντες, Κύριε, ἐμνήσθημεν ὅτι ἐκεῖνος
late, saying, Sir, we have called to mind that that
ὁ πλάνος εἶπεν ἔτι ζῶν, Μετὰ τρεῖς ἡμέρας ἐγείρομαι. 64 κέ-
deceiver said whilst living, After three days I arise. Com-
λευσον οὖν ἀσφαλισθῆναι τὸν τάφον ἕως τῆς τρίτης ἡμέρας·
mand therefore to be secured the sepulchre until the third day,
μήποτε ἐλθόντες οἱ.μαθηταὶ.[n]αὐτοῦ[ll] [o]νυκτὸς[ll] κλέψωσιν αὐτόν,
lest [3]coming [1]his [2]disciples by night steal [4]away [1]him,
καὶ εἴπωσιν τῷ λαῷ, Ἠγέρθη ἀπὸ τῶν νεκρῶν· καὶ ἔσται
and say to the people, He is risen from the dead; and [4]shall [5]be
ἡ ἐσχάτη πλάνη χείρων τῆς πρώτης. 65 [p]Ἔφη.[p]δὲ[ll] αὐτοῖς
[1]the [2]last [3]deception worse than the first. And [2]said [3]to [4]them
ὁ [q]Πιλάτος,[ll] [r]Ἔχετε κουστωδίαν· ὑπάγετε ἀσφαλίσασθε ὡς
[1]Pilate, Ye have a guard: Go make [it as] secure as
οἴδατε. 66 Οἱ.δὲ πορευθέντες ἠσφαλίσαντο τὸν τάφον
ye know [how]. And they having gone made [3]secure [1]the [2]sepulchre
σφραγίσαντες τὸν λίθον, μετὰ τῆς κουστωδίας.
[7]sealing [8]the [9]stone, [4]with [5]the [6]guard.

28 Ὀψὲ.δὲ σαββάτων, τῇ.ἐπιφωσκούσῃ εἰς μίαν
Now late on Sabbath, as it was getting dusk toward [the] first [day]
σαββάτων, ἦλθεν [r]Μαρία[ll] ἡ Μαγδαληνὴ καὶ ἡ ἄλλη Μαρία
of [the] week, came Mary the Magdalene and the other Mary

put it on a reed, giving it to Him to drink.
49 But the rest said, Let *Him* alone! Let us see if Elijah will come to save him.
50 And Jesus cried again with a loud voice, giving up *His* spirit.
51 And, behold, the veil of the Temple was torn into two from top to bottom! And the earth quaked, and the rocks were sheared!
52 And the tombs were opened, and many bodies of the saints who had fallen asleep arose,
53 and coming forth out of the tombs after His resurrection, they went into the holy city and appeared to many.
54 And the centurion, and they who watched with him over Jesus, seeing the earthquake and the things that took place, feared greatly, saying, Truly this was the Son of God!
55 And there were many women there watching from afar off, who followed Jesus from Galilee, ministering to Him,
56 among whom was Mary Mag-da-lene, and Mary the mother of James and Joses, and the mother of the sons of Zeb-e-dee.
57 And when evening had come, a rich man from Ar-i-ma-the-a, named Joseph, came (who also himself was Jesus' disciple).
58 Going to Pilate, he begged the body of Jesus. Then Pilate commanded the body to be delivered.
59 And taking the body, Joseph wrapped it in a clean linen cloth
60 and laid it in his own new tomb which he had cut out in the rock. And when he had rolled a great stone to the door of the tomb, he departed.
61 And there was Mary Mag-da-lene and the other Mary, sitting across from the grave.
62 Now on the next day, which is after the preparation, the chief priests and the Pharisees were gathered together to Pilate,
63 saying, Sir, we have remembered what that deceiver said, while he was living, After three days I will arise.
64 Therefore command that the grave be made secure until the third day, for fear that his disciples may come by night and steal him away and say to the people, He has risen from the dead. And the last error will be worse than the first.
65 And Pilate said to them, You have a guard. Go away. Make it as secure as you know *how*.
66 And they went away and made the grave secure, sealing the stone, together with the guard.

CHAPTER 28

1 And at the end of the Sabbath, as it was dawning toward the first day of the week, Mary Mag-da-lene and the other Mary came

θεωρῆσαι τὸν τάφον.
to see the sepulchre.
2 Καὶ ἰδού, σεισμὸς ἐγένετο μέγας· ἄγγελος.γὰρ κυρίου
And behold, [3]a [5]earthquake [1]there [2]was [4]great; for an angel of [the] Lord
καταβὰς ἐξ οὐρανοῦ, [s] προσελθὼν ἀπεκύλισεν τὸν λίθον
having descended out of heaven, having come rolled away the stone
[t]ἀπὸ τῆς θύρας,‖ καὶ ἐκάθητο ἐπάνω αὐτοῦ. 3 ἦν.δὲ ἡ [v]ἰδέα‖
from the door, and was sitting upon it. And [3]was [2]look
αὐτοῦ ὡς ἀστραπή, καὶ τὸ.ἔνδυμα.αὐτοῦ λευκὸν [w]ὡσεὶ‖ χιών.
[1]his as lightning, and his raiment white as snow.
4 ἀπὸ.δὲ τοῦ φόβου αὐτοῦ ἐσείσθησαν οἱ τηροῦντες, καὶ [x]ἐγέ-
And from the fear of him [4]trembled [1]those [2]keeping [3]guard, and be-
νοντο ὡσεὶ‖ νεκροί. 5 Ἀποκριθεὶς.δὲ ὁ ἄγγελος εἶπεν ταῖς
came as dead [men]. But [3]answering [1]the [2]angel said to the
γυναιξίν, Μὴ.φοβεῖσθε ὑμεῖς· οἶδα.γὰρ ὅτι Ἰησοῦν τὸν ἐσταυ-
women, Fear not ye; for I know that Jesus who has been
ρωμένον ζητεῖτε. 6 οὐκ.ἔστιν ὧδε· ἠγέρθη.γάρ, καθὼς εἶπεν.
crucified ye seek. He is not here, for he is risen, as he said.
δεῦτε ἴδετε τὸν τόπον ὅπου ἔκειτο [y]ὁ κύριος.‖ 7 καὶ ταχὺ
Come see the place where [3]was [4]lying [1]the [2]Lord. And [2]quickly
πορευθεῖσαι εἴπατε τοῖς.μαθηταῖς.αὐτοῦ, ὅτι ἠγέρθη ἀπὸ τῶν
[1]going say to his disciples, that he is risen from the
νεκρῶν· καὶ ἰδού, προάγει ὑμᾶς εἰς τὴν Γαλιλαίαν· ἐκεῖ
dead; and behold, he goes before you into Galilee; there
αὐτὸν ὄψεσθε. ἰδού, εἶπον ὑμῖν. 8 Καὶ [z]ἐξελθοῦσαι‖ ταχὺ
him ye shall see. Lo, I have told you. And having gone out quickly
ἀπὸ τοῦ μνημείου μετὰ φόβου καὶ χαρᾶς μεγάλης, ἔδραμον
from the tomb with fear and [2]joy [1]great, they ran
ἀπαγγεῖλαι τοῖς.μαθηταῖς.αὐτοῦ. 9 [a]ὡς.δὲ ἐπορεύοντο
to tell [it] to his disciples. But as they were going
ἀπαγγεῖλαι τοῖς.μαθηταῖς.αὐτοῦ,‖ καὶ ἰδού, [b]ὁ‖ Ἰησοῦς [c]ἀπήν-
to tell [it] to his disciples, [2]also [1]behold, Jesus met
τησεν‖ αὐταῖς, λέγων, Χαίρετε. Αἱ.δὲ προσελθοῦσαι ἐκρά-
them, saying, Hail! And they having come to [him] seized
τησαν αὐτοῦ τοὺς πόδας, καὶ προσεκύνησαν αὐτῷ. 10 τότε
hold of his feet, and worshipped him. Then
λέγει αὐταῖς ὁ Ἰησοῦς, Μὴ.φοβεῖσθε· ὑπάγετε, ἀπαγγείλατε
[2]says [3]to [4]them [1]Jesus, Fear not: Go, tell
τοῖς.ἀδελφοῖς.μου ἵνα ἀπέλθωσιν εἰς τὴν Γαλιλαίαν, [d]κἀκεῖ‖ με
my brethren that they go into Galilee, and there me
ὄψονται.
shall they see.

11 Πορευομένων.δὲ αὐτῶν, ἰδού, τινὲς τῆς κουστωδίας ἐλ-
And as [2]were [3]going [1]they, lo, some of the guard hav-
θόντες εἰς τὴν πόλιν [e]ἀπήγγειλαν‖ τοῖς ἀρχιερεῦσιν ἅπαντα
ing gone into the city reported to the chief priests all things
τὰ γενόμενα. 12 καὶ συναχθέντες μετὰ τῶν πρεσ-
that were done. And having been gathered together with the el-
βυτέρων, συμβούλιόν.τε λαβόντες, ἀργύρια ἱκανὰ ἔδωκαν
ders, and counsel having taken, [2]money [1]much they gave
τοῖς στρατιώταις, 13 λέγοντες, Εἴπατε ὅτι οἱ.μαθηταὶ.αὐτοῦ
to the soldiers, saying, Say that his disciples
νυκτὸς ἐλθόντες ἔκλεψαν αὐτὸν ἡμῶν κοιμωμένων· 14 καὶ
by night having come stole him, we being asleep. And
ἐὰν ἀκουσθῇ τοῦτο [f]ἐπὶ‖ τοῦ ἡγεμόνος, ἡμεῖς πείσομεν [g]αὐτὸν‖
if [2]be [3]heard [1]this by the governor, we will persuade him
καὶ ὑμᾶς ἀμερίμνους ποιήσομεν. 15 Οἱ.δὲ λαβόντες τὰ
and [3]you [4]free [5]from [6]care [1]will [2]make. And they having taken the
ἀργύρια ἐποίησαν ὡς ἐδιδάχθησαν. καὶ [h]διεφημίσθη‖ ὁ λόγος
money did as they were taught. And [3]is [4]spread [5]abroad [2]report
οὗτος παρὰ Ἰουδαίοις μέχρι τῆς σήμερον[i].
[1]this among [the] Jews until the present.
16 Οἱ.δὲ ἕνδεκα μαθηταὶ ἐπορεύθησαν εἰς τὴν Γαλιλαίαν,
But the eleven disciples went into Galilee,
εἰς τὸ ὄρος οὗ ἐτάξατο αὐτοῖς ὁ Ἰησοῦς. 17 καὶ ἰδόντες
to the mountain whither [2]appointed [3]them [1]Jesus. And seeing
αὐτὸν προσεκύνησαν [k]αὐτῷ·‖ οἱ.δὲ ἐδίστασαν. 18 καὶ προσ-
him they worshipped him: but some doubted. And having
ελθὼν ὁ Ἰησοῦς ἐλάλησεν αὐτοῖς, λέγων, Ἐδόθη μοι
come to [them] Jesus spoke to them, saying, [3]Has [4]been [5]given [6]to [7]me
πᾶσα ἐξουσία ἐν οὐρανῷ καὶ ἐπὶ [l] γῆς. 19 πορευθέντες [m]οὖν‖
[1]all [2]authority in heaven and on earth. Going therefore
μαθητεύσατε πάντα τὰ ἔθνη, [n]βαπτίζοντες‖ αὐτοὺς εἰς τὸ
disciple all the nations, baptizing them to the
ὄνομα τοῦ πατρὸς καὶ τοῦ υἱοῦ καὶ τοῦ ἁγίου πνεύματος,
name of the Father and of the Son and of the Holy Spirit;
20 διδάσκοντες αὐτοὺς τηρεῖν πάντα ὅσα ἐνετειλάμην
teaching them to observe all things whatsoever I commanded
ὑμῖν· καὶ ἰδού, ἐγὼ μεθ' ὑμῶν εἰμι πάσας τὰς ἡμέρας ἕως τῆς
you. And lo, I with you am all the days until the
συντελείας τοῦ αἰῶνος. [o]Ἀμήν.‖ [p]
completion of the age. Amen.

to see the grave.
[2]And behold, there had been a great earthquake! For an angel of the Lord came down
out of Heaven and had rolled away the stone
from the door and was sitting upon it.
[3]And his face was as lightning, and his
clothing white as snow.
[4]And those keeping guard trembled from
fear of him, becoming like dead men.
[5]But answering, the angel said to the
women, You must not fear, for I know that
you seek Jesus who has been crucified.
[6]He is not here, for He is risen, as He said.
Come, see the place where the Lord was
lying.
[7]And go quickly, saying to His disciples
that He has risen from the dead. And, lo, He
goes before you into Galilee. There you shall
see Him. See, I have told you.
[8]And going out quickly from the tomb,
with great joy and fear, they ran to tell His
disciples.
[9]But as they were going to tell His disciples
– lo and behold! Jesus met them, saying,
Greetings. And coming up to *Him*, they laid
hold of His feet and worshiped Him.
[10]Then Jesus said to them, Fear not, Go
and tell My brothers that they should go
into Galilee. And there they shall see Me.

[11]And as they were going, behold, some of
the guard went into the city and reported to
the chief priest all things that were done.
[12]And gathering together with the elders,
and talking it over, they gave large *sums of*
money to the soldiers,
[13]saying, Say that his disciples came
by night and stole him, we being
asleep.
[14]And if this is heard by the governor, we
will persuade him and will make you free
from care.
[15]And taking the money, they did as they
were taught. And this saying is spread among
the Jews until the present day.

[16]And the eleven disciples went into
Galilee, to the mountain where Jesus
commanded them.
[17]And seeing Him, they worshiped Him.
But some doubted.
[18] And coming up to them, Jesus spoke to
them, saying, All authority has been given to
Me in Heaven and on earth.
[19]As you go therefore, teach all nations,
baptizing them into the name of the Father
and of the Son and of the Holy Spirit,
[20]teaching them to observe all things,
whatever I commanded you. And lo, I am
with you all the days until the end of the
world. Amen.

'ΑΡΧΗ τοῦ εὐαγγελίου 'Ιησοῦ χριστοῦ, [b]υἱοῦ τοῦ θεοῦ·
BEGINNING of the glad tidings of Jesus Christ, Son of God;
2 [c]ὡς γέγραπται ἐν [d]τοῖς.προφήταις, 'Ιδού, [e]ἐγὼ ἀποστέλλω
as it has been written in the prophets, Behold, I send
τὸν.ἄγγελόν.μου πρὸ προσώπου.σου, ὃς κατασκευάσει τὴν
my messenger before thy face, who shall prepare
ὁδόν.σου [f]ἔμπροσθέν σου. 3 Φωνὴ βοῶντος ἐν τῇ ἐρήμῳ,
thy way before thee. [The] voice of one crying in the wilderness,
Ἑτοιμάσατε τὴν ὁδὸν κυρίου, εὐθείας ποιεῖτε τὰς τρίβους
Prepare the way of [the] Lord, straight make [2]paths
αὐτοῦ.
[1]his.

4 Ἐγένετο Ἰωάννης [g] βαπτίζων ἐν τῇ ἐρήμῳ, [h]καὶ κηρύσ-
[2]Came [1]John baptizing in the wilderness, and proclaim-
σων βάπτισμα μετανοίας εἰς ἄφεσιν ἁμαρτιῶν. 5 καὶ
ing [the] baptism of repentance for remission of sins. And
ἐξεπορεύετο πρὸς αὐτὸν πᾶσα ἡ Ἰουδαία χώρα, καὶ οἱ [i]Ἱερο-
went out to him all the [2]of [3]Judæa [1]country, and they of Je-
σολυμῖται, [k]καὶ ἐβαπτίζοντο πάντες [l]ἐν τῷ Ἰορδάνῃ ποταμῷ
rusalem, and were [2]baptized [1]all in the [2]Jordan [1]river
ὑπ' αὐτοῦ, ἐξομολογούμενοι τὰς.ἁμαρτίας.αὐτῶν. 6 [m]ἦν.δὲ
by him, confessing their sins. And [2]was
[n]Ἰωάννης ἐνδεδυμένος τρίχας καμήλου, καὶ ζώνην δερματίνην
[1]John clothed in hair of a camel, and a girdle of leather
περὶ τὴν.ὀσφὺν.αὐτοῦ, καὶ [o]ἐσθίων ἀκρίδας καὶ μέλι ἄγριον.
about his loins, and eating locusts and [2]honey [1]wild.
7 Καὶ ἐκήρυσσεν, λέγων, Ἔρχεται ὁ ἰσχυρότερός μου ὀπίσω
And he proclaimed, saying, He comes who [is] mightier than I after
μου, οὗ οὐκ.εἰμὶ ἱκανὸς κύψας λῦσαι τὸν ἱμάντα
me, of whom I am not fit having stooped down to loose the thong
τῶν.ὑποδημάτων.αὐτοῦ. 8 ἐγὼ [p]μὲν ἐβάπτισα ὑμᾶς [q]ἐν ὕδατι,
of his sandals. I indeed baptized you with water,
αὐτὸς.δὲ βαπτίσει ὑμᾶς [r]ἐν πνεύματι ἁγίῳ.
but he will baptize you with [the] [2]Spirit [1]Holy.

9 [s]Καὶ ἐγένετο ἐν ἐκείναις ταῖς ἡμέραις ἦλθεν Ἰησοῦς
And it came to pass in those days [that] [2]came [1]Jesus
ἀπὸ [t]Ναζαρὲτ τῆς Γαλιλαίας, καὶ ἐβαπτίσθη [v]ὑπὸ Ἰωάν-
from Nazareth of Galilee, and was baptized by John
νου εἰς τὸν Ἰορδάνην. 10 καὶ [w]εὐθέως ἀναβαίνων [x]ἀπὸ τοῦ
in the Jordan. And immediately going up from the
ὕδατος, εἶδεν σχιζομένους τοὺς οὐρανούς, καὶ τὸ πνεῦμα
water, he saw parting asunder the heavens, and the Spirit
[y]ὡσεὶ περιστερὰν καταβαῖνον [z]ἐπ' αὐτόν· 11 καὶ φωνὴ [aa]ἐγένε-
as a dove descending upon him. And a voice came
το ἐκ τῶν οὐρανῶν, Σὺ εἶ ὁ.υἱός.μου ὁ ἀγαπητός, ἐν [b]ᾧ
out of the heavens, Thou art my Son the beloved, in whom
εὐδόκησα.
I have found delight.

12 Καὶ [c]εὐθὺς τὸ πνεῦμα αὐτὸν ἐκβάλλει εἰς τὴν ἔρη-
And immediately the Spirit [2]him [1]drives out into the wilder-
μον. 13 καὶ ἦν [d]ἐκεῖ ἐν τῇ ἐρήμῳ [e]ἡμέρας τεσσαράκοντα,
ness. And he was there in the wilderness [2]days [1]forty,
πειραζόμενος ὑπὸ τοῦ σατανᾶ, καὶ ἦν μετὰ τῶν θηρίων· καὶ
tempted by Satan, and was with the beasts; and
οἱ ἄγγελοι διηκόνουν αὐτῷ.
the angels ministered to him.

14 [f]Μετὰ.δὲ τὸ.παραδοθῆναι τὸν Ἰωάννην ἦλθεν ὁ Ἰησοῦς
And after [2]was [3]delivered [4]up [1]John came Jesus
εἰς τὴν Γαλιλαίαν, κηρύσσων τὸ εὐαγγέλιον [g]τῆς βασιλείας
into Galilee, proclaiming the glad tidings of the kingdom
τοῦ θεοῦ, 15 [h]καὶ λέγων, Ὅτι πεπλήρωται ὁ καιρός, καὶ ἤγ-
of God, and saying, [3]Has [4]been [5]fulfilled [1]the [2]time, and has
γικεν ἡ βασιλεία τοῦ θεοῦ· μετανοεῖτε, καὶ πιστεύετε ἐν τῷ
drawn near the kingdom of God; repent, and believe in the
εὐαγγελίῳ. 16 [i]Περιπατῶν.δὲ παρὰ τὴν θάλασσαν τῆς Γαλι-
glad tidings. And walking by the sea of Ga-
λαίας εἶδεν Σίμωνα καὶ Ἀνδρέαν τὸν ἀδελφὸν [k]αὐτοῦ [l]βάλ-
lilee he saw Simon and Andrew the brother of him cast-
λοντας [m]ἀμφίβληστρον ἐν τῇ θαλάσσῃ· ἦσαν.γὰρ [n]ἁλιεῖς.
ing a large net in the sea; for they were fishers.
17 καὶ εἶπεν αὐτοῖς ὁ Ἰησοῦς, Δεῦτε ὀπίσω μου, καὶ ποιήσω
And [2]said [3]to [4]them [1]Jesus, Come after me, and I will make
ὑμᾶς γενέσθαι [n]ἁλιεῖς ἀνθρώπων. 18 Καὶ [o]εὐθέως ἀφέντες
you to become fishers of men. And immediately having left
τὰ.δίκτυα.[p]αὐτῶν ἠκολούθησαν αὐτῷ. 19 Καὶ προβὰς
their nets they followed him. And having gone on
[q]ἐκεῖθεν ὀλίγον εἶδεν Ἰάκωβον τὸν τοῦ Ζεβεδαίου, καὶ
thence a little he saw James the [son] of Zebedee, and
Ἰωάννην τὸν.ἀδελφὸν.αὐτοῦ, καὶ αὐτοὺς ἐν τῷ πλοίῳ
John his brother, and these [were] in the ship
καταρτίζοντας τὰ δίκτυα. 20 καὶ [r]εὐθέως ἐκάλεσεν αὐτούς·
mending the nets. And immediately he called them;

CHAPTER 1

1 The beginning of the gospel of Jesus
Christ, the Son of God,
2 as it has been written in the prophets,
"Behold! I send My messenger before Your
face, who shall prepare Your way before
You,
3 *the* voice of one crying in the wilderness,
Prepare the way of the Lord. Make His paths
straight."
4 John came baptizing in the wilderness,
and preaching the baptism of repentance for
remission of sins.
5 And all the country of Judea and of
Jerusalem went out to him. And all were
baptized by him in the Jordan River,
confessing their sins.
6 And John was clothed in camel's hair and
a girdle of leather about his loins. And *he
was* eating locusts and wild honey.
7 And he preached, saying, He who comes
after me is mightier than I, of whom I am
not fit to stoop down to untie the latchet of
His sandals.
8 I indeed baptize you with water, but He
will baptize you with the Holy Spirit.
9 And in those days Jesus came from
Naz-a-reth of Galilee and was baptized by
John in the Jordan.
10 And immediately as He came up from
the water He saw the heavens opened and
the Spirit as a dove coming down upon Him.
11 And a voice came out of Heaven, You
are My Son, the Beloved, in whom I am
well-pleased.

12 And immediately the Spirit drove Him
out into the wilderness.
13 And He was there in the wilderness forty
days, tempted by Satan. And *He* was with
the wild animals. And the angels waited
upon Him.

14 And after John was delivered up, Jesus
came into Galilee, preaching the gospel of
the kingdom of God.
15 And *He was* saying, The time has been
fulfilled, and the kingdom of God has come
near. Repent and believe in the gospel.
16 And walking by the sea of Galilee, He
saw Simon and his brother Andrew casting a
net into the sea, for they were fishers.
17 And Jesus said to them, Come after Me
and I will make you fishers of men.
18 And immediately they left their nets and
followed Him.
19 And going on a little further, He saw
James the son of Zeb-e-dee, and his brother
John. And they were in the ship mending
their nets.
20 And immediately He called them. And

καὶ ἀφέντες τὸν πατέρα.αὐτῶν Ζεβεδαῖον ἐν τῷ πλοίῳ μετὰ
and having left their father Zebedee in the ship with
τῶν μισθωτῶν, ἀπῆλθον ὀπίσω αὐτοῦ.
the hired servants, they went away after him.

21 Καὶ εἰσπορεύονται εἰς [s]Καπερναούμ·‖ καὶ [t]εὐθέως‖ τοῖς
And they go into Capernaum; and immediately on the
σάββασιν [v]εἰσελθὼν‖ [w]εἰς τὴν συναγωγὴν ἐδίδασκεν.‖ 22 καὶ
sabbaths having entered into the synagogue he taught. And
ἐξεπλήσσοντο ἐπὶ τῇ.διδαχῇ.αὐτοῦ· ἦν.γὰρ διδάσκων αὐτοὺς
they were astonished at his teaching: for he was teaching them
ὡς ἐξουσίαν ἔχων, καὶ οὐχ ὡς οἱ γραμματεῖς[x]. 23 Καὶ [y] ἦν
as [2]authority [1]having, and not as the scribes. And there was
ἐν τῇ.συναγωγῇ.αὐτῶν ἄνθρωπος ἐν πνεύματι.ἀκαθάρτῳ, καὶ
in their synagogue a man with an unclean spirit, and
ἀνέκραξεν, 24 λέγων, [z]Ἔα,‖ τί ἡμῖν καὶ σοί, Ἰησοῦ Ναζαρηνέ;
he cried out, saying, Ah! what to us and to thee, Jesus, Nazarene?
ἦλθες ἀπολέσαι ἡμᾶς; [a]οἶδά‖ σε τίς εἶ, ὁ ἅγιος
art thou come to destroy us? I know thee who thou art, the Holy [One]
τοῦ θεοῦ. 25 Καὶ ἐπετίμησεν αὐτῷ ὁ Ἰησοῦς, [b]λέγων,‖ Φιμώ-
of God. And [2]rebuked [3]him [1]Jesus, saying, Be
θητι, καὶ ἔξελθε ἐξ αὐτοῦ. 26 Καὶ σπαράξαν
silent, and come forth out of him. And [5]having [6]thrown [8]into [9]convulsions
αὐτὸν τὸ πνεῦμα τὸ ἀκάθαρτον, καὶ [c]κράξαν‖ φωνῇ μεγάλῃ,
[7]him [1]the [4]spirit [2]the [3]unclean, and having cried with a [2]voice [1]loud,
ἐξῆλθεν [d]ἐξ‖ αὐτοῦ. 27 καὶ ἐθαμβήθησαν [e]πάντες,‖ ὥστε
came forth out of him. And [2]were [3]astonished [1]all, so that
[f]συζητεῖν‖ [g]πρὸς‖ [h]αὐτούς,‖ λέγοντας, Τί ἐστιν τοῦτο;
they questioned together among themselves, saying, What is this?
[i]τίς ἡ διδαχὴ ἡ καινὴ αὕτη, ὅτι‖ κατ' ἐξουσίαν καὶ τοῖς πνεύ-
what [3]teaching [2]new [1]this, that with authority even the spirits
μασιν τοῖς ἀκαθάρτοις ἐπιτάσσει, καὶ ὑπακούουσιν αὐτῷ;
the unclean he commands, and they obey him!
28 [k]Ἐξῆλθεν.δὲ‖ ἡ ἀκοὴ αὐτοῦ [l]εὐθὺς‖ [m]εἰς ὅλην τὴν περί-
And went out the fame of him immediately in all the [2]around
χωρον τῆς Γαλιλαίας.
[1]country Galilee.

29 Καὶ [n]εὐθέως‖ ἐκ τῆς συναγωγῆς [o]ἐξελθόντες ἦλθον[‖]
And immediately out of the synagogue having gone forth they came
εἰς τὴν οἰκίαν Σίμωνος καὶ Ἀνδρέου, μετὰ Ἰακώβου καὶ Ἰωάν-
into the house of Simon and Andrew, with James and John.
νου. 30 ἡ.δὲ πενθερὰ Σίμωνος κατέκειτο πυρέσσουσα· καὶ
And the mother-in-law of Simon was lying in a fever. And
[p]εὐθέως‖ λέγουσιν αὐτῷ περὶ αὐτῆς. 31 καὶ προσελθὼν
immediately they speak to him about her. And having come to [her]
ἤγειρεν αὐτήν, κρατήσας τῆς.χειρὸς.[q]αὐτῆς·‖ καὶ ἀφῆκεν
he raised up her, having taken her hand. And [3]left
αὐτὴν ὁ πυρετὸς [r]εὐθέως,‖ καὶ διηκόνει αὐτοῖς. 32 Ὀψίας
[4]her [1]the [2]fever immediately, and she ministered to them. [2]Evening
δὲ γενομένης, ὅτε [s]ἔδυ‖ ὁ ἥλιος, ἔφερον πρὸς αὐτὸν
[1]and being come, when went down the sun, they brought to him
πάντας τοὺς κακῶς ἔχοντας καὶ τοὺς δαιμονιζομένους· 33 καὶ
all who [2]ill [1]were and those possessed by demons; and
[t]ἡ πόλις ὅλη ἐπισυνηγμένη ἦν‖ πρὸς τὴν θύραν. 34 καὶ
the [2]city [1]whole [4]gathered [5]together [3]was at the door. And
ἐθεράπευσεν πολλοὺς κακῶς.ἔχοντας ποικίλαις νόσοις, καὶ
he healed many that were ill of various diseases, and
δαιμόνια πολλὰ ἐξέβαλεν, καὶ οὐκ.ἤφιεν λαλεῖν τὰ δαιμόνια,
[2]demons [1]many he cast out, and suffered not [3]to [4]speak [1]the [2]demons,
ὅτι ᾔδεισαν αὐτόν.
because they knew him.

35 Καὶ πρωῒ [v]ἔννυχον‖.λίαν ἀναστὰς ἐξῆλθεν καὶ
And very early while yet night having risen up he went out and
ἀπῆλθεν εἰς ἔρημον τόπον, [w]κἀκεῖ‖ προσηύχετο. 36 καὶ
departed into [2]desert [1]a place, and there was praying. And
[x]κατεδίωξαν‖ αὐτὸν [y]ὁ‖ Σίμων καὶ οἱ μετ' αὐτοῦ· 37 καὶ
[6]went [7]after [8]him [1]Simon [2]and [3]those [4]with [5]him; and
[z]εὑρόντες αὐτὸν‖ λέγουσιν αὐτῷ, Ὅτι πάντες [a]ζητοῦσίν σε.‖
having found him they say to him, All seek thee.
38 Καὶ λέγει αὐτοῖς, [*]Ἄγωμεν[b] εἰς τὰς ἐχομένας κωμοπόλεις,
And he says to them, Let us go into the neighbouring country towns,
ἵνα [c]κἀκεῖ‖ κηρύξω· εἰς τοῦτο γὰρ [d]ἐξελήλυθα.‖ 39 Καὶ
that there also I may preach; [2]for [3]this [1]because have I come forth. And
[e]ἦν‖ κηρύσσων [f]ἐν ταῖς.συναγωγαῖς‖.αὐτῶν εἰς ὅλην τὴν Γαλι-
he was preaching in their synagogues in all Ga-
λαίαν, καὶ τὰ δαιμόνια ἐκβάλλων.
lilee, and the demons casting out.

40 Καὶ ἔρχεται πρὸς αὐτὸν λεπρός, παρακαλῶν αὐτὸν [g]καὶ
And [2]comes [3]to [5]him [1]a [2]leper, beseeching him and
γονυπετῶν αὐτόν,‖ [h]καὶ‖ λέγων αὐτῷ, Ὅτι ἐὰν θέλῃς δύνασαί
kneeling down to him, and saying to him, If thou wilt thou art able
με καθαρίσαι. 41 [i]Ὁ.δὲ.Ἰησοῦς‖ σπλαγχνισθείς, ἐκ-
me to cleanse. And Jesus being moved with compassion, having

leaving their father Zeb-e-dee in the ship with the hired servants, they went away after Him.

21 And they went into Ca-per-na-um. And He immediately entered into the synagogue and taught on the sabbaths.

22 And they were astonished at His teaching. For He was teaching them as One who had authority, and not as the scribes.

23 And there was a man in their synagogue with an unclean spirit. And he cried out,

24 saying, Ha! What have we to do with You, Jesus, Naz-a-rene? Have You come to destroy us? I know You. You are the Holy One of God!

25 And Jesus rebuked him, saying, Be quiet and come out of him!

26 And after the unclean spirit had thrown him into fits and had cried with a loud voice, he came out of him.

27 And all were astonished, so that they questioned together among themselves, saying, What is this? What new teaching is this? For with authority He commands even the unclean spirits, and they obey Him.

28 And immediately His fame spread all through the country around Galilee.

29 And after coming out of the synagogue, they went at once into the house of Simon and Andrew, with James and John.

30 And the mother-in-law of Simon was lying in a fever. And at once they spoke to Him about her.

31 And He came to her and raised her up, taking her hand. And instantly the fever left her. And she served them.

32 And when evening had come, when the sun went down, they brought to Him all that were diseased, and those who were demon-possessed.

33 And the whole city was gathered together at the door.

34 And He healed many who were sick of various diseases. And He cast out many demons and did not allow the demons to speak, because they knew Him.

35 And very early, while *it was* still night, He rose up and went out and departed into a desert place. And He was there praying.

36 And Simon and those with him went after Him.

37 And finding Him, they said to Him, All are looking for You.

38 And He said to them, Let us go into the next towns so that I may preach there also, because for this I have come.

39 And He was preaching in their synagogues in all Galilee. And *He was* casting out the demons.

40 And a leper came to Him, begging Him. And he kneeled down to Him, saying to Him, If you desire You are able to make me clean.

41 And Jesus, being moved with compassion, put forth His hand and touched

τείνας τὴν χεῖρα ᵏἥψατο αὐτοῦ,ˡˡ καὶ λέγει ˡαὐτῷ,ˡˡ
stretched out [his] hand he touched him, and says to him,
Θέλω, καθαρίσθητι. 42 Καὶ ᵐεἰπόντος.αὐτοῦ,ˡˡ ⁿεὐθέως ˡˡ ἀπῆλ-
I will, be thou cleansed. And he having spoken, immediately depart-
θεν ἀπ' αὐτοῦ ἡ λέπρα, καὶ ᵒἐκαθαρίσθη.ˡˡ 43 Καὶ ἐμβριμησά-
ed from him the leprosy, and he was cleansed. And having strictly
μενος αὐτῷ, ᵖεὐθέωςˡˡ ἐξέβαλεν αὐτόν, 44 καὶ λέγει αὐτῷ,
charged him, immediately he sent away him, And says to him,
Ὅρα μηδενὶ ᵠμηδὲνˡˡ εἴπῃς· ʳἀλλ'ˡˡ ὕπαγε, σεαυτὸν δεῖξον
See to no one anything thou speak; but go, thyself shew
(lit. nothing)
τῷ ἱερεῖ, καὶ προσένεγκε περὶ τοῦ.καθαρισμοῦ.σου ἃ προσ-
to the priest, and offer for thy cleansing what ²or-
έταξεν ˢΜωσῆς,ˡˡ εἰς μαρτύριον αὐτοῖς. 45 Ὁ.δὲ ἐξελθὼν
dered ¹Moses, for a testimony to them. But he having gone out
ἤρξατο κηρύσσειν πολλὰ καὶ διαφημίζειν τὸν λόγον, ὥστε
began to proclaim [it] much and to spread abroad the matter, so that
μηκέτι αὐτὸν δύνασθαι ᵗφανερῶς εἰς πόλινˡˡ εἰσελθεῖν·
no longer he was able openly into [the] city to enter;
ᵛἀλλ'ˡˡ ἔξω ʷἐνˡˡ ἐρήμοις τόποις ˣἦν,ˡˡ καὶ ἤρχοντο πρὸς αὐτὸν
but without in desert places was, and they came to him
ʸπανταχόθεν.ˡˡ
from every quarter.

2 Καὶ ᶻπάλιν εἰσῆλθενˡˡ εἰς ᵃᵃΚαπερναοὺμˡˡ δι' ἡμερῶν,
And again he entered into Capernaum after [some] days,
ᵇᵇκαὶˡˡ ἠκούσθη ὅτι ᶜᶜεἰς οἶκόνˡˡ ἐστιν· 2 καὶ ᵈᵈεὐθέωςˡˡ συνη-
and it was heard that in [the] house he is; and immediately were
χθησαν πολλοί, ὥστε μηκέτι.χωρεῖν μηδὲ τὰ
gathered together many, so that there was no longer any room not even
πρὸς τὴν θύραν· καὶ ἐλάλει αὐτοῖς τὸν λόγον. 3 Καὶ ἔρχονται
at the door; and he spoke to them the word. And they come
ᵉπρὸς αὐτόν, παραλυτικὸν φέροντες,ˡˡ αἰρόμενον ὑπὸ τεσσάρων.
to him, ²a ³paralytic ¹bringing, borne by four.
4 καὶ μὴ δυνάμενοι ᶠπροσεγγίσαιˡˡ αὐτῷ διὰ τὸν ὄχλον,
And not being able to come near to him on account of the crowd,
ἀπεστέγασαν τὴν στέγην ὅπου ἦν, καὶ ἐξορύξαντες χα-
they uncovered the roof where he was, and having broken up [it] they
λῶσιν τὸν ᵍκράββατονˡˡ ʰἐφ' ᾧˡˡ ὁ παραλυτικὸς κατέκειτο.
let down the couch on which the paralytic was lying.
5 ⁱἰδὼν.δὲˡˡ ὁ Ἰησοῦς τὴν.πίστιν.αὐτῶν λέγει τῷ παραλυτικῷ,
And ²seeing ¹Jesus their faith says to the paralytic,
Τέκνον, ᵏἀφέωνταιˡˡ ˡσοι αἱ.ἁμαρτίαι.σου.ˡˡ 6 Ἦσαν.δέ τινες
Child, ³have ⁴been ⁵forgiven ⁶thee ¹thy ²sins. But there were some
τῶν γραμματέων ἐκεῖ καθήμενοι, καὶ διαλογιζόμενοι ἐν ταῖς
of the scribes ²there ¹sitting, and reasoning in
καρδίαις.αὐτῶν, 7 Τί οὗτος οὕτως λαλεῖ ᵐβλασφημίας;ˡˡ
their hearts, Why ²this [³man] ⁴thus ¹does ⁵speak blasphemies?
τίς δύναται ἀφιέναι ἁμαρτίας, εἰ.μὴ εἷς, ὁ θεός; 8 Καὶ
who is able to forgive sins, except one, [that is] God? And
ⁿεὐθέωςˡˡ ἐπιγνοὺς ὁ Ἰησοῦς τῷ.πνεύματι.αὐτοῦ ὅτι ᵒοὕτωςˡˡ ᵖ
immediately ²knowing ¹Jesus in his spirit that thus
διαλογίζονται ἐν ἑαυτοῖς, ᵠεἶπενˡˡ αὐτοῖς, Τί ταῦτα δια-
they are reasoning within themselves, said to them, Why these things rea-
λογίζεσθε ἐν ταῖς.καρδίαις.ὑμῶν; 9 τί ἐστιν εὐκοπώτερον,
son ye in your hearts? which is easier,
εἰπεῖν τῷ παραλυτικῷ, ʳἈφέωνταιˡˡ ˢσοιˡˡ αἱ ἁμαρτίαι,
to say to the paralytic, ³Have ⁴been ⁵forgiven ⁶thee [¹thy] ²sins,
ἢ εἰπεῖν, ᵗἜγειραι,ˡˡ ᵛκαὶˡˡ ἆρόν ʷσου τὸν κράββατονˡˡ καὶ
or to say, Arise, and take up thy couch and
ˣπεριπάτει;ˡˡ 10 ἵνα.δὲ εἰδῆτε ὅτι ἐξουσίαν ἔχει ὁ υἱὸς τοῦ
walk? but that ye may know that ⁶authority ⁵has ¹the ²Son
ἀνθρώπου ʸἀφιέναι ἐπὶ τῆς γῆςˡˡ ἁμαρτίας, λέγει τῷ παρα-
³of ⁴man to forgive on the earth sins,— he says to the para-
λυτικῷ, 11 Σοὶ λέγω, ᶻἔγειραι,ˡˡ ᵃκαὶˡˡ ἆρον τὸν ᵍκράββατόνˡˡ
lytic, To thee I say, arise, and take up ²couch
σου καὶ ὕπαγε εἰς τὸν.οἶκόν.σου. 12 Καὶ ἠγέρθη ᵇεὐθέως, καὶˡˡ
¹thy and go to thy house. And he arose immediately, and
ἄρας τὸν ᵍκράββατονˡˡ ἐξῆλθεν ᶜἐναντίονˡˡ πάντων,
having taken up the couch went forth before all,
ὥστε ἐξίστασθαι πάντας, καὶ δοξάζειν τὸν θεόν, ᵈλέγοντας,ˡˡ
so that ²were ³amazed ¹all, and glorified God, saying,
Ὅτι ᵉᵃοὐδέποτε οὕτωςˡˡ ᶠᵃεἴδομεν.ˡˡ
Never thus did we see [it].

13 Καὶ ἐξῆλθεν πάλιν ᵍᵃπαρὰˡˡ τὴν θάλασσαν, καὶ πᾶς ὁ
And he went forth again by the sea, and all the
ὄχλος ἤρχετο πρὸς αὐτόν, καὶ ἐδίδασκεν αὐτούς. 14 Καὶ
crowd came to him, and he taught them. And
παράγων εἶδεν ʰΛευῒνˡˡ τὸν τοῦ Ἀλφαίου καθήμενον ἐπὶ τὸ
passing on he saw Levi the [son] of Alphæus sitting at the
τελώνιον, καὶ λέγει αὐτῷ, Ἀκολούθει μοι. Καὶ ἀναστὰς
tax office, and says to him, Follow me. And having arisen
ἠκολούθησεν αὐτῷ. 15 Καὶ ⁱἐγένετοˡˡ ᵏἐν.τῷˡˡ.κατακεῖσθαι.αὐ-
he followed him. And it came to pass as he reclined

him. And *He* said to him, I desire it! Be clean!

42 And when He had spoken, the leprosy instantly left him, and he was made clean.

43 And strictly commanding him, He at once sent him away.

44 And He said to him, See that you say nothing to anyone. But go show yourself to the priest and offer for your cleansing those things which Moses commanded, for a witness to them.

45 But after he had left, he began to speak of it and very much to publicize it – so that *Jesus* was no longer able to enter into the city openly, but was outside in deserted places. And they came to Him from every quarter.

CHAPTER 2

1 And again He entered Ca-per-na-um after *some* days. And it was heard that He was in the house.

2 And immediately many were gathered together, so that there was no longer any room (not even at the door). And He spoke the word to them.

3 And they came to Him, bringing a paralytic, carried by four *men*.

4 And not being able to come near Him on account of the crowd, they uncovered the roof where He was. And breaking through, they let down the bed on which the paralytic was lying.

5 And Jesus, seeing their faith, said to the paralytic, Son, your sins have been forgiven you.

6 But there were some of the scribes sitting there. And *they were* questioning in their hearts,

7 Why does this one speak blasphemies this way? Who is able to forgive sins, except One, *that is,* God?

8 And instantly, knowing in His spirit that they were thinking this way inside themselves, Jesus said to them, Why do you question these things in your hearts?

9 Which is easier, to say to the paralytic, Your sins have been forgiven you! or to say, Arise, take up your bed and walk?

10 But that you may know that the Son of man has authority on earth to forgive sins, He said to the paralytic

11 I say to you, Arise and take up your bed and go to your house.

12 And he immediately rose up and took up the bed and went forth before them all, so that they were all amazed. And *they* glorified God, saying, Never did we see it so.

13 And He went forth again by the seaside. And all the multitude came to Him. And He taught them.

14 And as He went on He saw Levi, the son of Al-phe-us, sitting at the tax-office. And He said to him, Follow Me! And rising up, he followed Him.

15 And as He sat in *Levi's* house, many tax-

τὸν ἐν τῇ.οἰκίᾳ.αὐτοῦ, καὶ πολλοὶ τελῶναι καὶ ἁμαρτω-
[at table] in his house, that many tax-gatherers and sin-
λοὶ συνανέκειντο τῷ Ἰησοῦ καὶ τοῖς.μαθηταῖς.αὐτοῦ·
ners were reclining [at table] with Jesus and his disciples;
ἦσαν.γὰρ πολλοί, καὶ [l]ἠκολούθησαν‖ αὐτῷ. 16 καὶ [m]οἱ‖ γραμ-
for they were many, and they followed him. And the scribes
ματεῖς [n]καὶ οἱ Φαρισαῖοι,‖ [o]ἰδόντες [p]αὐτὸν ἐσθίοντα‖ μετὰ
and the Pharisees, having seen him eating with
τῶν [q]τελωνῶν καὶ ἁμαρτωλῶν,‖ ἔλεγον τοῖς.μαθηταῖς.αὐτοῦ,
the tax-gatherers and sinners, said to his disciples,
[r]Τί‖ ὅτι μετὰ τῶν [s]τελωνῶν καὶ ἁμαρτωλῶν‖ ἐσθίει [t]καὶ
Why [is it] that with the tax-gatherers and sinners he eats and
πίνει;‖ 17 Καὶ ἀκούσας ὁ Ἰησοῦς λέγει αὐτοῖς, Οὐ χρείαν
drinks? And [2]having [3]heard [1]Jesus says to them, [6]Not [7]need
ἔχουσιν οἱ ἰσχύοντες ἰατροῦ, ἀλλ' οἱ κακῶς ἔχον-
[5]have [1]they [2]who [3]are [4]strong of a physician, but they who ill are.
τες. οὐκ.ἦλθον καλέσαι δικαίους, ἀλλὰ ἁμαρτωλοὺς [v]εἰς
I came not to call righteous [ones], but sinners to
μετάνοιαν.‖
repentance.

18 Καὶ ἦσαν οἱ μαθηταὶ Ἰωάννου καὶ [w]οἱ τῶν Φαρισαίων‖
And [10]were [1]the [2]disciples [3]of [4]John [5]and [6]those [7]of [8]the [9]Pharisees
νηστεύοντες· καὶ ἔρχονται καὶ λέγουσιν αὐτῷ, [x]Διατί‖ οἱ μαθη-
fasting; and they come and say to him, Why [2]the [3]disci-
ταὶ Ἰωάννου καὶ οἱ [y] τῶν Φαρισαίων νηστεύουσιν, οἱ δὲ σοὶ
ples [4]of [5]John [6]and [7]those [8]of [9]the [10]Pharisees [1]fast, but thy
μαθηταὶ οὐ.νηστεύουσιν; 19 Καὶ εἶπεν αὐτοῖς ὁ Ἰησοῦς, Μὴ
disciples fast not? And [2]said [3]to [4]them [1]Jesus,
δύνανται οἱ υἱοὶ τοῦ νυμφῶνος, ἐν.ᾧ ὁ νυμφίος μετ' αὐτῶν
Can the sons of the bridechamber, while the bridegroom with them
ἐστιν, νηστεύειν; ὅσον.χρόνον [z]μεθ' ἑαυτῶν ἔχουσιν τὸν νυμ-
is, fast? as long as with them they have the bride-
φίον,‖ οὐ.δύνανται νηστεύειν· 20 ἐλεύσονται.δὲ ἡμέραι ὅταν
groom, they are not able to fast. But will come days when
ἀπαρθῇ ἀπ' αὐτῶν ὁ νυμφίος, καὶ τότε νη-
will have been taken away from them the bridegroom, and then they
στεύσουσιν ἐν [a]ἐκείναις ταῖς ἡμέραις.‖ 21 [b]καὶ‖ οὐδεὶς ἐπίβλημα
will fast in those days. And no one a piece
[c]ῥάκους‖ ἀγνάφου [d]ἐπιῤῥάπτει‖ ἐπὶ [e]ἱματίῳ.παλαιῷ‖· εἰ.δὲ.μή,
of [2]cloth [1]unfulled sews on an old garment; otherwise,
αἴρει [f] τὸ πλήρωμα[g] [ha]αὐτοῦ‖ τὸ καινὸν τοῦ παλαιοῦ, καὶ
[7]takes [8]away [1]the [2]filling [4]up [5]of [6]it [3]new from the old, and
χεῖρον σχίσμα γίνεται. 22 καὶ οὐδεὶς βάλλει οἶνον νέον εἰς
[2]worse [1]a rent takes place. And no one puts [2]wine [1]new into
ἀσκοὺς παλαιούς· εἰ.δὲ.μή, [i]ῥήσσει‖ ὁ οἶνος [k]ὁ νέος‖ τοὺς ἀσ-
[2]skins [1]old; otherwise, [4]bursts [1]the [3]wine [2]new the skins,
κούς, καὶ ὁ οἶνος [l]ἐκχεῖται καὶ οἱ ἀσκοὶ ἀπολοῦνται·‖ [m]ἀλλὰ
and the wine is poured out, and the skins will be destroyed; but
οἶνον νέον εἰς ἀσκοὺς καινοὺς βλητέον.‖
[2]wine [1]new [3]into [5]skins [4]new is to be put.

23 Καὶ ἐγένετο [n]παραπορεύεσθαι.αὐτὸν ἐν τοῖς σάββασιν‖
And it came to pass that he went on the sabbath
διὰ τῶν σπορίμων, καὶ [o]ἤρξαντο οἱ.μαθηταὶ αὐτοῦ‖ [p]ὁδὸν
through the corn-fields, and [3]began [1]his [2]disciples [their] way
ποιεῖν‖ τίλλοντες τοὺς στάχυας. 24 καὶ οἱ Φαρισαῖοι ἔλεγον
to make, plucking the ears. And the Pharisees said
αὐτῷ, Ἴδε, τί ποιοῦσιν [q]ἐν‖ τοῖς σάββασιν ὃ οὐκ.ἔξεστιν;
to him, Behold, why do they on the sabbath that which is not lawful?
25 Καὶ [r]αὐτὸς‖ [s]ἔλεγεν‖ αὐτοῖς, Οὐδέποτε ἀνέγνωτε τί ἐποίη-
And he said to them, [3]Never [1]did [2]ye read what [2]did
σεν [t]Δαβίδ,‖ ὅτε χρείαν ἔσχεν καὶ ἐπείνασεν, αὐτὸς καὶ οἱ
[1]David, when need he had and hungered, he and those
μετ' αὐτοῦ; 26 [v]πῶς‖ εἰσῆλθεν εἰς τὸν οἶκον τοῦ θεοῦ ἐπὶ
with him? how he entered into the house of God in
Ἀβιάθαρ [w]τοῦ‖ ἀρχιερέως, καὶ τοὺς ἄρτους τῆς
[the days of] Abiathar the high priest, and the loaves of the
προθέσεως ἔφαγεν, οὓς οὐκ.ἔξεστιν φαγεῖν εἰ.μὴ [x]τοῖς ἱερεῦ-
presentation ate, which it is not lawful to eat except for the priests,
σιν,‖ καὶ ἔδωκεν καὶ τοῖς σὺν αὐτῷ οὖσιν; 27 Καὶ ἔλεγεν
and gave even to those who with him were? And he said
αὐτοῖς, Τὸ σάββατον διὰ τὸν ἄνθρωπον ἐγένετο, [y]οὐχ ὁ
to them, The sabbath on account of man was made, not
ἄνθρωπος διὰ τὸ σάββατον. 28 ὥστε κύριός ἐστιν ὁ
man on account of the sabbath: so then Lord is the
υἱὸς τοῦ ἀνθρώπου καὶ τοῦ σαββάτου.
Son of man also of the sabbath.

3 Καὶ εἰσῆλθεν πάλιν εἰς [z]τὴν‖ συναγωγήν, καὶ [a]ἦν‖ ἐκεῖ
And he entered again into the synagogue, and there was there
ἄνθρωπος ἐξηραμμένην ἔχων τὴν χεῖρα, 2 καὶ [b]παρ-
a man [4]withered [1]having [[2]his] [3]hand, and they
ετήρουν‖ αὐτὸν εἰ [c] τοῖς σάββασιν [d]θεραπεύσει‖ αὐτόν,
were watching him whether on the sabbath he will heal him,

collectors and sinners also sat with Jesus and His disciples. For there were many, and they followed Him.

16 And the scribes and Pharisees, seeing Him eating with tax-collectors and sinners, said to His disciples, Why does He eat and drink with the tax-collectors and sinners?

17 And hearing this, Jesus said, They who are strong have no need of a physician, but they who are sick. I did not come to call the righteous to repentance, but *to call* sinners.

18 And the disciples of John and those of the Pharisees were fasting. And they came and said to Him, Why do the disciples of John and those of the Pharisees fast, but Your disciples do not fast?

19 And Jesus said to them, Can the children of the bridechamber fast while the bridegroom is with them? As long as they have the bridegroom with them they are not able to fast.

20 But the days will come when the bridegroom will have been taken away from them. And they they will fast in those days.

21 And no one sews a piece of new cloth on an old garment. Else the new piece inserted takes away from the old, and the tear becomes worse.

22 And no one puts new wine into old wineskins. Otherwise the new wine bursts the wineskins and the wine is poured out – and the wineskins will be ruined. But the new wine is to be put into new wineskins.

23 And He went through the grain fields on the Sabbath. And His disciples began to make a way, plucking the ears.

24 And the Pharisees said to Him, Behold, why do they do that which is not lawful on the Sabbath day?

25 And He said to them, Have you never read what David did when he had need and was hungry, he and those with him?

26 How he entered into the house of God in *the days of* A-bi-a-thar the high priest and ate the showbread, which it is not lawful to eat, except for the priests? And *he* even gave to those who were with him.

27 And He said to them, The sabbath was made for man, and not man for the sabbath.

28 So, then, the Son of man is Lord also of the sabbath.

CHAPTER 3

1 And He entered again into the synagogue. And there was a man there who had a withered hand.

2 And they were watching Him *to see* if He would heal him on the Sabbath (so that they

ἵνα [e]κατηγορήσωσιν‖ αὐτοῦ. 3 καὶ λέγει τῷ ἀνθρώπῳ
in order that they might accuse him. And he says to the man
τῷ [f]ἐξηραμμένην ἔχοντι τὴν χεῖρα,‖ [g]"Εγειραι‖ εἰς τὸ
who [3]withered [1]had [2]the hand, Arise [and come] into the
μέσον. 4 Καὶ λέγει αὐτοῖς, "Εξεστιν τοῖς σάββασιν [h]ἀγαθο-
midst. And he says to them, Is it lawful on the sabbaths to do
ποιῆσαι,‖ ἢ κακοποιῆσαι; ψυχὴν σῶσαι, ἢ ἀποκτεῖναι; Οἱ.δὲ
good, or to do evil? [3]life [1]to [2]save, or to kill? But they
ἐσιώπων. 5 καὶ περιβλεψάμενος αὐτοὺς μετ' ὀργῆς, [i]συλ-
were silent. And having looked around on them with anger, being
λυπούμενος‖ ἐπὶ τῇ πωρώσει τῆς.καρδίας.αὐτῶν, λέγει τῷ
grieved at the hardness of their heart, he says to the
ἀνθρώπῳ, "Εκτεινον τὴν.χεῖρά.[k]σου.‖ Καὶ ἐξέτεινεν, καὶ
man, Stretch out thy hand. And he stretched out [it], and
[l]ἀποκατεστάθη‖ ἡ.χεὶρ.αὐτοῦ [m]ὑγιὴς ὡς ἡ ἄλλη.‖ 6 καὶ ἐξελ-
[3]was restored [1]his [2]hand sound as the other. And having
θόντες οἱ Φαρισαῖοι [n]εὐθέως‖ μετὰ τῶν Ἡρωδιανῶν συμβούλιον
gone out the Pharisees immediately with the Herodians [2]counsel
[o]ἐποίουν‖ κατ' αὐτοῦ, ὅπως αὐτὸν ἀπολέσωσιν.
[1]took against him, how him they might destroy.

7 Καὶ ὁ Ἰησοῦς [p]ἀνεχώρησεν μετὰ τῶν.μαθητῶν.αὐτοῦ‖ [q]πρὸς‖
And Jesus withdrew with his disciples to
τὴν θάλασσαν· καὶ πολὺ πλῆθος ἀπὸ τῆς Γαλιλαίας
the sea; and [2]great [1]a multitude from Galilee
[r]ἠκολούθησαν‖ [s]αὐτῷ,‖ καὶ ἀπὸ τῆς Ἰουδαίας, 8 καὶ ἀπὸ Ἰε-
followed him, and from Judea, and from Je-
ροσολύμων, καὶ ἀπὸ τῆς Ἰδουμαίας, καὶ πέραν τοῦ Ἰορδάνου·
rusalem, and from Idumea, and beyond the Jordan;
καὶ [t]οἱ‖ περὶ Τύρον καὶ Σιδῶνα, πλῆθος πολύ, [v]ἀκούσαντες‖
and they around Tyre and Sidon, a [2]multitude [1]great, having heard
ὅσα [w]ἐποίει‖. ἦλθον πρὸς αὐτόν. 9 καὶ εἶπεν τοῖς.μαθη-
how much he was doing came to him. And he spoke to his dis-
ταῖς.αὐτοῦ, ἵνα πλοιάριον προσκαρτερῇ αὐτῷ διὰ τὸν
ciples, that a small ship might wait upon him, on account of the
ὄχλον, ἵνα μὴ.θλίβωσιν αὐτόν. 10 πολλοὺς.γὰρ ἐθερά-
crowd, that they might not press upon him. For many he
πευσεν, ὥστε ἐπιπίπτειν αὐτῷ, ἵνα αὐτοῦ ἅψωνται, ὅσοι
healed, so that they beset him, that him they might touch, as many as
εἶχον μάστιγας· 11 καὶ τὰ πνεύματα τὰ ἀκάθαρτα, ὅταν αὐτὸν
had scourges; and the spirits the unclean, when him
[x]ἐθεώρει, προσέπιπτεν‖ αὐτῷ, καὶ [y]ἔκραζεν‖, [z]λέγοντα,‖ "Ὅτι σὺ
they beheld, fell down before him, and cried, saying, Thou
εἶ ὁ υἱὸς τοῦ θεοῦ. 12 Καὶ πολλὰ ἐπετίμα αὐτοῖς, ἵνα μὴ
art the Son of God. And much he rebuked them, so that [3]not
[a]αὐτὸν φανερὸν‖ [b]ποιήσωσιν‖ [c].
[5]him [6]manifest [1]they [2]should [4]make.

13 Καὶ ἀναβαίνει εἰς τὸ ὄρος, καὶ προσκαλεῖται οὓς
And he goes up into the mountain, and calls to [him] whom
ἤθελεν αὐτός· καὶ ἀπῆλθον πρὸς αὐτόν. 14 καὶ ἐποίησεν
[2]would [1]he; and they went to him. And he appointed
δώδεκα ἵνα ὦσιν μετ' αὐτοῦ, καὶ ἵνα ἀποστέλλῃ αὐτοὺς
twelve that they might be with him, and that he might send them
κηρύσσειν, 15 καὶ ἔχειν ἐξουσίαν [d]θεραπεύειν τὰς νόσους καὶ‖
to preach, and to have authority to heal diseases and
ἐκβάλλειν τὰ δαιμόνια. 16 [e]καὶ ἐπέθηκεν [f]τῷ Σίμωνι ὄνομα‖
to cast out demons. And he added to Simon [the] name
Πέτρον· 17 καὶ Ἰάκωβον τὸν τοῦ Ζεβεδαίου, καὶ Ἰωάννην
Peter; and James the [son] of Zebedee, and John
τὸν ἀδελφὸν τοῦ Ἰακώβου· καὶ ἐπέθηκεν αὐτοῖς ὀνόματα
the brother of James; and he added to them [the] names
[g]Βοανεργές,‖ ὅ ἐστιν υἱοὶ βροντῆς· 18 καὶ Ἀνδρέαν, καὶ
Boanerges, which is Sons of thunder; and Andrew, and
Φίλιππον, καὶ Βαρθολομαῖον, καὶ [h]Ματθαῖον,‖ καὶ Θωμᾶν,
Philip, and Bartholomew, and Matthew, and Thomas,
καὶ Ἰάκωβον τὸν τοῦ Ἀλφαίου, καὶ Θαδδαῖον, καὶ Σίμωνα
and James the [son] of Alphæus, and Thaddæus, and Simon
τὸν [i]Κανανίτην,‖ 19 καὶ Ἰούδαν [k]Ἰσκαριώτην,‖ ὃς καὶ παρέ-
the Canaanite, and Judas Iscariote, who also deliver-
δωκεν αὐτόν.
ed up him.

Καὶ [l]ἔρχονται‖ εἰς οἶκον· 20 καὶ συνέρχεται πάλιν [m]ὄχλος,
And they come to a house: and [3]comes [4]together [5]again [1]a [2]crowd,
ὥστε μὴ.δύνασθαι.αὐτοὺς.[n]μήτε‖ ἄρτον φαγεῖν. 21 καὶ ἀκού-
so that they are not able so much as [3]bread [1]to [2]eat. And having
σαντες οἱ παρ' αὐτοῦ ἐξῆλθον κρατῆσαι αὐτόν·
heard [of it]. those belonging to him went out to lay hold of him;
ἔλεγον.γάρ, "Ὅτι ἐξέστη. 22 Καὶ οἱ γραμματεῖς οἱ ἀπὸ
for they said, He is beside himself. And the scribes who from
Ἱεροσολύμων καταβάντες ἔλεγον, "Ὅτι Βεελζεβοὺλ ἔχει· καὶ
Jerusalem came down said, Beelzebul he has; and
"Ὅτι ἐν τῷ ἄρχοντι τῶν δαιμονίων ἐκβάλλει τὰ δαιμόνια.
By the prince of the demons he casts out the demons.

might accuse Him).
3 And He said to the man who had the
withered hand, Get up and come into the
middle.
4 And He said to them, Is it lawful to do
good on the sabbath days, or to do evil, to
save life or to kill? But they were silent.
5 And looking around on them with anger,
being saddened at the hardness of their
heart, He commanded the man, Stretch out
your hand! And he stretched it out. And his
hand was restored whole like the other.
6 And the Pharisees left, immediately plot-
ting with the Herodians against Him, *as to*
how they might destroy Him.

7 And Jesus retired to the sea with His
disciples. And a great crowd from Galilee
and from Judea followed Him.
8 And *also they were* from Jerusalem and
from I-du-me-a and beyond the Jordan. And
when those around Tyre and Sidon heard
what great things He was doing, a great
crowd came to Him.
9 And He spoke to His disciples, that they
might have a boat ready for Him (on
account of the crowd, that they might not
press upon Him).
10 For He healed many, so that they threw
themselves upon Him, that they might touch
Him, all that had torments.
11 And when the unclean spirits saw Him,
they fell down before Him and cried out,
saying, You are the Son of God!
12 And He warned them many times, so
that they would not make Him known.
13 And He went up into the mountain and
called those He wanted. And they went to
Him.
14 And He appointed twelve to be with
Him, and that He might send them forth to
preach,
15 and that they might have authority to
heal diseases and to evict demons.
16 And He added to Simon the name Peter.
17 And there was James the son of
Zeb-e-dee, and John the brother of James
(and He added to their names Bo-an-er-ges,
which is, Sons of Thunder).
18 And *there was* Andrew and Philip and
Bar-thol-o-mew and Matthew and Thomas
and James the son of Al-phe-us, and Thad-
de-us and Simon the Ca-naan-ite,
19 and also Judas Is-car-i-ot, who betrayed
Him. And they came into a house.
20 And a multitude came together again, so
that they were not able even to eat bread.
21 And those belonging to Him heard and
went out to restrain Him. For they said, He
is beside Himself.
22 And the scribes who came down from
Jerusalem said, He has Be-el-ze-bub – and,
He throws out demons by the prince of the
demons.

23 Καὶ προσκαλεσάμενος αὐτοὺς ἐν παραβολαῖς ἔλεγεν
And having called to [him] them in parables he said
αὐτοῖς, Πῶς δύναται σατανᾶς σατανᾶν ἐκβάλλειν; 24 καὶ
to them, How can [3]Satan [1]cast [2]out? and
ἐὰν βασιλεία ἐφ' ἑαυτὴν μερισθῇ, οὐ.δύναται σταθῆναι ἡ
if a kingdom against itself be divided, [3]is [4]not [5]able [6]to [7]stand
βασιλεία.ἐκείνη· 25 καὶ ἐὰν οἰκία ἐφ' ἑαυτὴν μερισθῇ, [o]οὐ
[1]that [2]kingdom: and if a house against itself be divided, [4]not
δύναται‖ [p]σταθῆναι ἡ.οἰκία.ἐκείνη·‖ 26 καὶ εἰ ὁ σατανᾶς ἀνέστη
[3]is [5]able [6]to [7]stand [1]that [2]house: and if Satan has risen up
ἐφ' ἑαυτὸν [q]καὶ μεμέρισται,‖ οὐ.δύναται [r]σταθῆναι,‖ ἀλλὰ
against himself and has been divided, he is not able to stand, but
τέλος ἔχει. 27 [s t]οὐ.δύναται.οὐδεὶς‖ [v]τὰ σκεύη τοῦ ἰσχυροῦ,
an end has. No one in any wise is able the goods of the strong man,
εἰσελθὼν εἰς τὴν.οἰκίαν‖.αὐτοῦ, διαρπάσαι, ἐὰν.μὴ πρῶτον
having entered into his house, to plunder, unless first
τὸν ἰσχυρὸν δήσῃ, καὶ τότε τὴν.οἰκίαν.αὐτοῦ διαρπάσει. 28 ἀ-
the strong man he bind, and then his house he will plunder. Ve-
μὴν λέγω ὑμῖν, ὅτι πάντα ἀφεθήσεται [w]τὰ ἁμαρτήματα τοῖς
rily I say to you, that all [3]shall [4]be [5]forgiven [1]the [2]sins to the
υἱοῖς τῶν ἀνθρώπων,‖ καὶ [x] βλασφημίαι [y]ὅσας‖.[z]ἂν‖ βλασ-
sons of men, and blasphemies whatsoever they shall
φημήσωσιν· 29 ὃς.δ'.ἂν βλασφημήσῃ εἰς τὸ πνεῦμα τὸ
have blasphemed; but whosoever shall blaspheme against the Spirit the
ἅγιον, οὐκ.ἔχει ἄφεσιν εἰς τὸν αἰῶνα, [a]ἀλλ'‖ ἔνοχός [b]ἐστιν‖
Holy, has not forgiveness to eternity, but [2]liable [3]to [1]is
αἰωνίου [c]κρίσεως·‖ 30 ὅτι ἔλεγον, Πνεῦμα.ἀκάθαρτον ἔχει.
eternal judgment; because they said, An unclean spirit he has.
31 [d]Ἔρχονται.οὖν‖ [e]οἱ ἀδελφοὶ καὶ ἡ.μήτηρ.αὐτοῦ,‖ καὶ
Then come [his] brethren and his mother, and
ἔξω [f]ἑστῶτες‖ ἀπέστειλαν πρὸς αὐτόν, [g]φωνοῦντες‖ αὐτόν.
[2]without [1]standing sent to him, calling him.
32 καὶ ἐκάθητο [h]ὄχλος περὶ αὐτόν·‖ [i]εἶπον.δὲ‖ αὐτῷ, Ἰδού,
And [3]sat [1]a [2]crowd around him: and they said to him, Behold,
ἡ.μήτηρ.σου καὶ οἱ.ἀδελφοί.σου [k] ἔξω ζητοῦσίν σε. 33 Καὶ
thy mother and thy brethren without seek thee. And
[l]ἀπεκρίθη αὐτοῖς, λέγων,‖ Τίς ἐστιν ἡ.μήτηρ.μου [m]ἢ‖ οἱ ἀδελ-
he answered them, saying, Who is my mother or [2]breth-
φοί [n]μου‖; 34 Καὶ περιβλεψάμενος [o]κύκλῳ τοὺς περὶ
ren [1]my? And having looked around on [3]in [4]a [5]circuit [1]those [2]who around
αὐτὸν‖ καθημένους, λέγει, [p]Ἴδε,‖ ἡ.μήτηρ.μου καὶ οἱ ἀδελφοί
him were sitting, he says, Behold, my mother and [2]brethren
μου· 35 ὃς.[q]γὰρ‖.ἂν ποιήσῃ [r]τὸ θέλημα‖ τοῦ θεοῦ, οὗτος ἀδελ-
[1]my: for whoever shall do the will of God, he [2]bro-
φός μου καὶ ἀδελφή.[s]μου‖ καὶ μήτηρ ἐστίν.
ther [1]my and my sister and mother is.
4 Καὶ πάλιν ἤρξατο διδάσκειν παρὰ τὴν θάλασσαν· καὶ
And again he began to teach by the sea. And
[t]συνήχθη‖ πρὸς αὐτὸν ὄχλος [v]πολύς,‖ ὥστε αὐτὸν [w]ἐμ-
was gathered together to him a [2]crowd [1]great, so that he having
βάντα εἰς τὸ πλοῖον‖ καθῆσθαι ἐν τῇ θαλάσσῃ, καὶ πᾶς ὁ
entered into the ship sat in the sea, and all the
ὄχλος πρὸς τὴν θάλασσαν ἐπὶ τῆς γῆς [x]ἦν.‖ 2 καὶ ἐδίδασκεν
crowd close to the sea on the land was. And he taught
αὐτοὺς ἐν παραβολαῖς πολλά, καὶ ἔλεγεν αὐτοῖς ἐν τῇ δι-
them in parables many things, and said to them in [2]teach-
δαχῇ.αὐτοῦ, 3 Ἀκούετε· ἰδού, ἐξῆλθεν ὁ σπείρων [y]τοῦ‖ σπεῖραι
ing [1]his, Hearken: behold, went out the sower to sow.
4 καὶ ἐγένετο ἐν.τῷ.σπείρειν, ὃ.μὲν ἔπεσεν παρὰ τὴν ὁδόν,
And it came to pass as he sowed, one fell by the way,
καὶ ἦλθεν τὰ πετεινὰ [z]τοῦ. οὐρανοῦ‖ καὶ κατέφαγεν αὐτό.
and came the birds of the heaven and devoured it.
5 [a]ἄλλο.δὲ‖ ἔπεσεν ἐπὶ τὸ πετρῶδες, [b]ὅπου οὐκ.εἶχεν γῆν
And another fell upon the rocky place, where it had not [2]earth
πολλήν· καὶ [c]εὐθέως‖ ἐξανέτειλεν, διὰ τὸ.μὴ.ἔχειν βάθος[da]
[1]much, and immediately it sprang up, because of not having depth
γῆς· 6 [ea]ἡλίου.δὲ ἀνατείλαντος‖ [fa]ἐκαυματίσθη,‖ καὶ διὰ
of earth; and [the] sun having arisen it was scorched, and because of
τὸ.μὴ.ἔχειν ῥίζαν ἐξηράνθη. 7 καὶ ἄλλο ἔπεσεν εἰς [ga]τὰς‖
not having root it withered away. And another fell among the
ἀκάνθας· καὶ ἀνέβησαν αἱ ἄκανθαι, καὶ συνέπνιξαν αὐτό, καὶ
thorns, and [3]grew [4]up [1]the [2]thorns, and choked it, and
καρπὸν οὐκ.ἔδωκεν. 8 καὶ [ha]ἄλλο‖ ἔπεσεν εἰς τὴν γῆν τὴν
fruit it yielded not. And another fell into the ground the
καλήν· καὶ ἐδίδου καρπὸν ἀναβαίνοντα καὶ [i]αὐξάνοντα,‖ καὶ
good, and yielded fruit, growing up and increasing, and
ἔφερεν [k]ἓν‖ τριάκοντα, καὶ [k]ἓν‖ ἑξήκοντα, καὶ [k]ἓν‖ ἑκατόν.
bore one thirty, and one sixty, and one a hundred.
9 Καὶ ἔλεγεν [l]αὐτοῖς,‖ [m]Ὁ ἔχων‖ ὦτα ἀκούειν ἀκουέτω.
And he said to them, He that has ears to hear let him hear.
10 [n]Ὅτε.δὲ‖ ἐγένετο [o]καταμόνας,‖ [p]ἠρώτησαν‖ αὐτὸν οἱ περὶ
And when he was alone, [7]asked [8]him [1]those [2]about

23 And calling them, He said to them in parables, How can Satan evict Satan?
24 And if a kingdom is divided against itself that kingdom is not able to stand.
25 And if a house is divided against itself that house is not able to stand.
26 And if Satan has risen up against himself and has been divided, he is not able to stand, but has an end.
27 No one going into the house of the strong man is able to plunder his goods unless he first ties up the strong man. And then he will strip his house of goods.
28 Truly I say to you that all sins shall be forgiven to the sons of men (and whatever blasphemies they have blasphemed),
29 but whoever shall blaspheme against the Holy Spirit never has forgiveness to eternity, but is in danger of everlasting judgment,
30 because they said, He has an unclean spirit.
31 Then His brothers and His mother came. And standing outside, *they* sent to Him, calling Him.
32 And a crowd sat around Him, and they said to Him, Behold, Your mother and Your brothers are asking for You outside.
33 And He answered them, Who is My mother and My brothers?
34 And looking around in a circle on those who were sitting about Him, He said, See, My mother and My brothers –
35 for whoever shall do the will of God, he is My brother and My sister and My mother.

CHAPTER 4

1 And again He began to teach by the sea. And a great crowd gathered to Him, so that He entered into the ship in the sea and sat. And all the crowd was on the land close to the sea.
2 And He taught them many things in parables, saying to them in His teaching,
3 Listen! Behold! The sower went out to sow.
4 And as he sowed some fell by the roadside. And the birds of the air came and ate it.
5 And some fell on stony ground, where it did not have much earth; and it immediately sprang up, not having deepness of earth.
6 But after the sun had risen, it was scorched. And because it had no root, it withered away.
7 And some fell among thorns. And the thorns grew up and choked it. And it bore no fruit.
8 And another fell into the good ground, growing up and increasing, bearing fruit. And one bore thirty, and one sixty and one a hundred times.
9 And He said to them, He that has ears to hear let him hear.
10 And when He was alone the twelve and those around Him asked Him about the

αὐτὸν σὺν τοῖς δώδεκα [q]τὴν παραβολήν.ǁ 11 καὶ ἔλεγεν
[3]him [4]with [5]the [6]twelve [as to] the parable. And he said

αὐτοῖς, Ὑμῖν [r]δέδοται γνῶναι τὸ μυστήριονǁ τῆς βασιλείας
to them, To you has been given to know the mystery of the kingdom

τοῦ θεοῦ· ἐκείνοις.δὲ τοῖς ἔξω, ἐν παραβολαῖς [s]τὰǁ.πάντα
of God: but to those who are without, in parables all things

γίνεται· 12 ἵνα βλέποντες βλέπωσιν, καὶ μὴ ἴδωσιν· καὶ
are done, that seeing they may see, and not perceive; and

ἀκούοντες ἀκούωσιν, καὶ μὴ συνιῶσιν· μήποτε ἐπιστρέψω-
hearing they may hear, and not understand, lest they should be con-

σιν, καὶ ἀφεθῇ αὐτοῖς [t]τὰ ἁμαρτήματα.ǁ 13 Καὶ
verted, and [3]should [4]be [5]forgiven [6]them [[1]their] [2]sins. And

λέγει αὐτοῖς, Οὐκ.οἴδατε τὴν.παραβολὴν.ταύτην; καὶ πῶς
he says to them, Perceive ye not this parable? and how

πάσας τὰς παραβολὰς γνώσεσθε; 14 ὁ σπείρων τὸν λόγον
all the parables will ye know? The sower the word

σπείρει. 15 οὗτοι.δέ εἰσιν οἱ παρὰ τὴν ὁδόν, ὅπου σπείρεται
sows. And these are they by the way, where is sown

ὁ λόγος, καὶ ὅταν ἀκούσωσιν, [v]εὐθέωςǁ ἔρχεται ὁ σατανᾶς
the word, and when they hear, immediately comes Satan

καὶ αἴρει τὸν λόγον τὸν ἐσπαρμένον [w]ἐν ταῖς.καρδίαις.αὐ-
and takes away the word that has been sown in their hearts.

τῶν.ǁ 16 καὶ οὗτοί [x]εἰσιν ὁμοίωςǁ οἱ ἐπὶ τὰ πετρώδη
And these are in like manner they who upon the rocky places

σπειρόμενοι, οἵ, ὅταν ἀκούσωσιν τὸν λόγον, [y]εὐθέωςǁ μετὰ
are sown, who, when they hear the word, immediately with

χαρᾶς λαμβάνουσιν αὐτόν, 17 καὶ οὐκ.ἔχουσιν ῥίζαν ἐν ἑαυ-
joy receive it, and have not root in them-

τοῖς, ἀλλὰ πρόσκαιροί εἰσιν· εἶτα γενομένης θλίψεως ἢ
selves, but temporary are; then having arisen tribulation or

διωγμοῦ διὰ τὸν λόγον, [v]εὐθέωςǁ σκανδαλίζονται. 18 καὶ
persecution on account of the word, immediately they are offended. And

[z]οὗτοίǁ εἰσιν οἱ [a]εἰςǁ τὰς ἀκάνθας σπειρόμενοι, οὗτοί
these are they who among the thorns are sown, these

εἰσιν οἱ τὸν λόγον [b]ἀκούοντες,ǁ 19 καὶ αἱ μέριμναι τοῦ
are they who the word hear, and the cares

αἰῶνος.[c]τούτουǁ καὶ ἡ ἀπάτη τοῦ πλούτου καὶ αἱ περὶ
of this life and the deceit of riches and the [2]of

τὰ.λοιπὰ ἐπιθυμίαι εἰσπορευόμεναι [d]συμπνίγουσινǁ τὸν λόγον,
[3]other [4]things [1]desires entering in choke the word,

καὶ ἄκαρπος γίνεται. 20 καὶ [e]οὗτοίǁ εἰσιν οἱ ἐπὶ τὴν γῆν
and unfruitful it becomes. And these are they who upon the ground

τὴν καλὴν σπαρέντες, οἵτινες ἀκούουσιν τὸν λόγον καὶ
the good have been sown, such as hear the word and

παραδέχονται, καὶ καρποφοροῦσιν, [f]ἓνǁ τριάκοντα, καὶ [f]ἓνǁ
receive [it], and bring forth fruit, one thirty, and one

ἑξήκοντα, καὶ [f]ἓνǁ ἑκατόν. 21 Καὶ ἔλεγεν αὐτοῖς, [g]Μήτι [h]ὁ
sixty, and one a hundred. And he said to them, [2]The

λύχνος ἔρχεταιǁ ἵνα ὑπὸ τὸν μόδιον τεθῇ ἢ ὑπὸ τὴν
[3]lamp [1]comes that under the corn measure it may be put or under the

κλίνην; οὐχ ἵνα ἐπὶ τὴν λυχνίαν [i]ἐπιτεθῇǁ; 22 οὐ.γάρ
couch? [Is it] not that upon the lampstand it may be put? for not

ἐστίν [k]τιǁ κρυπτόν, [l]ὃǁ ἐὰν.μὴ [m] φανερωθῇ· οὐδὲ
[2]is [1]anything hidden, unless it should be made manifest, nor

ἐγένετο ἀπόκρυφον, ἀλλ' ἵνα [n]εἰς φανερὸν ἔλθῃ.ǁ
has [4]taken [5]place [1]a [2]secret [3]thing, but that to light it should come.

23 εἴ τις ἔχει ὦτα ἀκούειν, ἀκουέτω. 24 Καὶ ἔλεγεν αὐτοῖς,
If anyone has ears to hear, let him hear. And he said to them,

Βλέπετε τί ἀκούετε. ἐν ᾧ μέτρῳ μετρεῖτε μετρηθήσεται
Take heed what ye hear: with what measure ye mete it shall be measured

ὑμῖν, [o]καὶ προστεθήσεται ὑμῖνǁ [p]τοῖς ἀκούουσιν.ǁ 25 ὃς.γὰρ [q]ἂν
to you, and [5]shall [6]be [7]added [1]to [2]you [3]who [4]hear; for whoever

ἔχῃ,ǁ δοθήσεται αὐτῷ· καὶ ὃς οὐκ.ἔχει, καὶ ὃ ἔχει
may have, [3]shall [4]be [5]given [1]to [2]him; and he who has not, even that which he has

ἀρθήσεται ἀπ' αὐτοῦ.
shall be taken from him.

26 Καὶ ἔλεγεν, Οὕτως ἐστὶν ἡ βασιλεία τοῦ θεοῦ, ὡς [r]ἐὰνǁ
And he said, Thus is the kingdom of God, as if

ἄνθρωπος βάλῃ τὸν σπόρον ἐπὶ τῆς γῆς, 27 καὶ καθεύδῃ
a man should cast the seed upon the earth, and should sleep

καὶ ἐγείρηται νύκτα καὶ ἡμέραν, καὶ ὁ σπόρος [s]βλαστάνῃǁ
and rise night and day, and the seed should sprout

καὶ μηκύνηται ὡς οὐκ.οἶδεν αὐτός· 28 αὐτομάτη [t]γὰρǁ ἡ γῆ
and be lengthened how [2]knows [3]not [1]he; [2]of [3]itself [1]for the earth

καρποφορεῖ, πρῶτον χόρτον, [v]εἶταǁ στάχυν, [v]εἶταǁ [w]πλήρη
brings forth fruit, first a blade, then an ear, then full

σῖτονǁ ἐν τῷ στάχυϊ. 29 ὅταν.δὲ [x]παραδῷǁ ὁ καρπός,
corn in the ear. And when [3]offers [4]itself [1]the [2]fruit,

[y]εὐθέωςǁ ἀποστέλλει τὸ δρέπανον, ὅτι παρέστηκεν ὁ θερισμός.
immediately he sends the sickle, for has come the harvest.

30 Καὶ ἔλεγεν, [z]Τίνιǁ ὁμοιώσωμεν τὴν βασιλείαν τοῦ θεοῦ;
And he said, To what shall we liken the kingdom of God?

parable.
11 And He said to them, To you it has been
given to know the mystery of the kingdom
of God. But to those who are on the outside,
all things are done in parables,
12 "that seeing they may see and not perceive; and hearing they may hear and not
understand; lest they should be converted
and *their* sins should be forgiven them."
13 And He said to them, Do you not know
this parable? Then how will you know all
the parables?
14 The sower sows the word.
15 And these are the ones by the roadside
where the word is sown – and when they
hear, Satan comes immediately and takes
away the word that has been sown in their
hearts.
16 And in the same way, these are the ones
who are sown on the stony ground – who
when they hear the word receive it immediately with joy.
17 But having no root in themselves, *these*
last only a little while. Then when trouble or
torment has arisen on account of the word,
they are immediately scandalized.
18 And these are the ones who are sown
among the thorns – these are the ones who
hear the word,
19 but the cares of this world and the false
promises of riches and the lusts of other
things enter in and choke the word. And it
becomes unfruitful.
20 And these are the ones who are sown on
good ground – they who hear the word and
receive it and bring forth fruit, one thirty,
one sixty and one a hundred times.
21 And He said to them, Do they come
with the lamp in order to put it under a
basket, or under the bed? *Or, is it* not that it
may be put on the lampstand?
22 For nothing is hidden which shall not be
made clear. Nor has any secret thing taken
place except that it should come to light.
23 If anyone has ears to hear, let him hear.
24 And He said to them, Be careful what
you hear. With whatever measure you
measure, the same shall be measured to you.
And to you who hear, more shall be added.
25 For whoever has, to him shall be given.
And he who has not, even that which he has
shall be taken away from him.
26 And He said, This is the way the kingdom of God is – as if a man should throw
the seed on the ground,
27 then should sleep, but rising night and
day; and the seed should spring up and grow,
in a way he does not know,
28 for of itself the earth brings forth fruit –
first a blade, then an ear, then full grain in
the ear.
29 And when the fruit yields itself, immediately he sends out the sickle, because the
harvest has come.
30 And He said, To what shall we compare

ἢ ἐν [a]ποίᾳ παραβολῇ παραβάλωμεν αὐτήν;‖ 31 ὡς [b]κόκκῳ‖
or with what parable shall we compare it? As to a grain
σινάπεως, ὅς, ὅταν σπαρῇ ἐπὶ τῆς γῆς, [c]μικρότερος‖
of mustard, which, when it has been sown upon the earth, less
πάντων τῶν σπερμάτων [d]ἐστὶν‖ [e]τῶν ἐπὶ τῆς γῆς·‖ 32 καὶ
than all the seeds is which [are] upon the earth, and
ὅταν σπαρῇ, ἀναβαίνει, καὶ γίνεται [f]πάντων τῶν λαχάνων
when it has been sown, it grows up, and becomes [2]than [3]all [4]the [5]herbs
μείζων,‖ καὶ ποιεῖ κλάδους μεγάλους, ὥστε δύνασθαι ὑπὸ
[1]greater, and produces [2]branches [1]great, so that [6]are [7]able [1]under
τὴν σκιὰν αὐτοῦ τὰ πετεινὰ τοῦ οὐρανοῦ κατασκηνοῦν.
[2]the [3]shadow [4]of [5]it the birds of the heaven to roost.
33 Καὶ τοιαύταις παραβολαῖς πολλαῖς ἐλάλει αὐτοῖς τὸν
And with [2]such [3]parables [1]many he spoke to them the
λόγον, καθὼς [g]ἠδύναντο‖ ἀκούειν, 34 χωρὶς.δὲ παραβολῆς
word, as they were able to hear, but without a parable
οὐκ.ἐλάλει αὐτοῖς· κατ᾽.ἰδίαν.δὲ [h]τοῖς.μαθηταῖς.αὐτοῦ‖ ἐπέλυεν
spoke he not to them; and apart to his disciples he explained
πάντα.
all things.

35 Καὶ λέγει αὐτοῖς ἐν ἐκείνῃ τῇ ἡμέρᾳ, ὀψίας γενομένης,
And he says to them on that day, evening being come,
Διέλθωμεν εἰς τὸ πέραν. 36 Καὶ ἀφέντες τὸν ὄχλον,
Let us pass over to the other side. And having dismissed the crowd,
παραλαμβάνουσιν αὐτὸν ὡς ἦν ἐν τῷ πλοίῳ· καὶ ἄλλα
they take with [them] him as he was in the ship; [2]also [3]other
[i]δὲ‖ [k]πλοιάρια‖ [l]ἦν‖ μετ᾽ αὐτοῦ. 37 καὶ γίνεται λαῖλαψ
[1]but small ships were with him. And comes a [2]storm
[m]ἀνέμου μεγάλη,‖ [n]τὰ.δὲ‖ κύματα ἐπέβαλλεν εἰς τὸ πλοῖον,
[3]of [4]wind [1]violent, and the waves beat into the ship,
ὥστε [o]αὐτὸ ἤδη γεμίζεσθαι.‖ 38 καὶ ἦν αὐτὸς [p]ἐπὶ‖ τῇ πρύ-
so that it already was filled. And [2]was [1]he on the stern
μνῃ ἐπὶ τὸ προσκεφάλαιον καθεύδων· καὶ [q]διεγείρουσιν‖
on the cushion sleeping. And they arouse
αὐτόν, καὶ λέγουσιν αὐτῷ, Διδάσκαλε, οὐ.μέλει σοι ὅτι
him, and say to him, Teacher, is it no concern to thee that
ἀπολλύμεθα; 39 Καὶ διεγερθεὶς ἐπετίμησεν τῷ ἀνέμῳ,
we perish? And having been aroused he rebuked the wind,
καὶ εἶπεν τῇ θαλάσσῃ, Σιώπα, πεφίμωσο. Καὶ ἐκόπασεν ὁ
and said to the sea, Silence, be quiet. And [2]fell [1]the
ἄνεμος, καὶ ἐγένετο γαλήνη μεγάλη. 40 καὶ εἶπεν αὐτοῖς,
[3]wind, and there was a [2]calm [1]great. And he said to them,
Τί δειλοί ἐστε [r]οὕτως; πῶς οὐκ‖ ἔχετε πίστιν; 41 Καὶ ἐφο-
Why fearful are ye thus? How [3]not [1]have [2]ye faith? And they
βήθησαν φόβον μέγαν, καὶ ἔλεγον πρὸς.ἀλλήλους, Τίς
feared [with] [2]fear [1]great, and said one to another, Who
ἄρα οὗτός ἐστιν, ὅτι καὶ ὁ ἄνεμος καὶ ἡ θάλασσα [s]ὑπακούου-
then [2]this [1]is, that even the wind and the sea obey
σιν αὐτῷ‖;
him?

5 Καὶ ἦλθον εἰς τὸ πέραν τῆς θαλάσσης, εἰς τὴν χώραν
And they came to the other side of the sea, to the country
τῶν [t]Γαδαρηνῶν.‖ 2 καὶ [u]ἐξελθόντι.αὐτῷ‖ ἐκ τοῦ πλοίου,
of the Gadarenes. And on his having gone forth out of the ship,
[v]εὐθέως‖ [w]ἀπήντησεν‖ αὐτῷ ἐκ τῶν μνημείων ἄνθρωπος
immediately met him out of the tombs a man
ἐν πνεύματι.ἀκαθάρτῳ, 3 ὃς τὴν κατοίκησιν εἶχεν ἐν τοῖς
with an unclean spirit, who [his] dwelling had in the
[x]μνημείοις·‖ καὶ [y]οὔτε‖ [z]ἁλύσεσιν‖ [a]οὐδεὶς [b]ἠδύνατο‖ αὐτὸν
tombs; and not even with chains anyone was able him
(lit. no one)
δῆσαι, 4 διὰ τὸ αὐτὸν πολλάκις πέδαις καὶ ἁλύσεσιν δε-
to bind, because that he often with fetters and chains had
δέσθαι, καὶ διεσπᾶσθαι ὑπ᾽ αὐτοῦ τὰς ἁλύσεις, καὶ
been bound, and [3]had [4]been [5]torn [6]asunder [7]by [8]him [1]the [2]chains, and
τὰς πέδας συντετρίφθαι, καὶ οὐδεὶς [c]αὐτὸν ἴσχυεν‖ δαμάσαι·
the fetters had been shattered, and no one him was able to subdue.
5 καὶ [d]διαπαντὸς‖ νυκτὸς καὶ ἡμέρας ἐν τοῖς [e]ὄρεσιν καὶ ἐν
And continually night and day in the mountains and in
τοῖς μνήμασιν‖ ἦν κράζων καὶ κατακόπτων ἑαυτὸν λίθοις.
the tombs he was crying and cutting himself with stones.
6 [f]Ἰδὼν.δὲ‖ τὸν Ἰησοῦν ἀπὸ μακρόθεν, ἔδραμεν καὶ προσ-
And having seen Jesus from afar, he ran and did
εκύνησεν [g]αὐτῷ,‖ 7 καὶ κράξας φωνῇ μεγάλῃ [h]εἶπεν,‖ Τί ἐμοὶ
homage to him, and crying with a [2]voice [1]loud he said, What to me
καὶ σοί, Ἰησοῦ, υἱὲ τοῦ θεοῦ τοῦ ὑψίστου; ὁρκίζω σε τὸν
and to thee, Jesus, Son of God the Most High? I adjure thee
θεόν, μή με βασανίσῃς. 8 ἔλεγεν.γὰρ αὐτῷ, Ἔξελθε, τὸ
by God, [3]not [2]me [1]torment. For he was saying to him, Come forth, the
πνεῦμα τὸ ἀκάθαρτον, ἐκ τοῦ ἀνθρώπου. 9 Καὶ ἐπηρώτα
spirit the unclean, out of the man. And he asked
αὐτόν, Τί [i]σοι.ὄνομα‖; Καὶ [k]ἀπεκρίθη, λέγων,‖ [l]Λεγεὼν‖
him, What [is] thy name? And he answered, saying, Legion

the kingdom of God? Or with what parable shall we compare it?

31 *It is* like a grain of mustard. For when it has been sown on the earth, *it is* less than all the seeds which are on the earth.

32 But when it has been sown, it grows up and becomes larger than all the plants. And it produces great branches, so that the birds of the air are able to rest under its shadow.

33 And with many such parables He spoke to them the word, as much as they were able to hear.

34 But He did not speak to them except in a parable. And He explained all things to His disciples alone.

35 And when evening had come on that day, He said to them, Let us cross to the other side.

36 And as He was in the ship, they dismissed the crowd and took Him with them. And other small ships were also with Him.

37 Then there came a great storm of violent wind. And the waves beat into the ship, so that it was already filled.

38 And He was on the stern, sleeping on a pillow. And they awakened Him and said to Him, Master! Do You not care that we are about to die?

39 And being awake, He commanded the wind and said to the sea, Peace! Be still! And the wind ceased, and there was a great calm.

40 And He said to them, Why are you so afraid? How does it happen that you have no faith?

41 And they feared with very great fear, saying to one another, Who then is this, that even the wind and sea obey Him?

CHAPTER 5

1 And they came to the other side of the sea, to the country of the Gad-a-renes.

2 And when He came out of the ship, a man with an unclean spirit immediately met Him, coming out of the tombs,

3 *for he* had *his* home in the tombs. And no one was able to tie him up, not even with chains.

4 Because he had often been bound with shackles and chains. And he had torn the chains apart, and the shackles had been broken in pieces. And no one was able to tame him.

5 And night and day in the mountains and in the tombs, he was always crying and cutting himself with stones.

6 And seeing Jesus from a distance, he ran and bowed down to Him.

7 And with a loud voice he cried and said, What do I have to do with You, Jesus, Son of the most high God? I implore You by God not to torment me.

8 For He said to him, Unclean spirit, come out of the man!

9 And He asked him, What is your name? And he answered, saying, My name is Legion

ὄνομά.μοι,[m] ὅτι πολλοί ἐσμεν. 10 Καὶ παρεκάλει αὐτὸν
my name [is], because many we are. And he besought him
πολλά, ἵνα μὴ [n]αὐτοὺς‖ ἀποστείλῃ ἔξω τῆς χώρας. 11 ἦν.δὲ
much, that not them he would send out of the country. Now there was
ἐκεῖ πρὸς [o]τὰ ὄρη‖ ἀγέλη χοίρων μεγάλη βοσκομένη· 12 καὶ
there just at the mountains a [2]herd [3]of [4]swine [1]great feeding; and
παρεκάλεσαν αὐτὸν [p]πάντες οἱ δαίμονες,‖ λέγοντες, Πέμψον
[4]besought [5]him [1]all [2]the [3]demons, saying, Send
ἡμᾶς εἰς τοὺς χοίρους, ἵνα εἰς αὐτοὺς εἰσέλθωμεν. 13 Καὶ
us into the swine, that into them we may enter. And
ἐπέτρεψεν αὐτοῖς [q]εὐθέως ὁ Ἰησοῦς.‖ καὶ ἐξελθόντα τὰ
[2]allowed [3]them [4]immediately [1]Jesus. And having gone out the
πνεύματα τὰ ἀκάθαρτα εἰσῆλθον εἰς τοὺς χοίρους· καὶ ὥρμησεν
spirits the unclean entered into the swine, and [3]rushed
ἡ ἀγέλη κατὰ τοῦ κρημνοῦ εἰς τὴν θάλασσαν· [r]ἦσαν δὲ‖
[1]the [2]herd down the steep into the sea, (now they were
ὡς δισχίλιοι· καὶ ἐπνίγοντο ἐν τῇ θαλάσσῃ. 14 [s]Οἱ.δὲ‖
about two thousand), and they were choked in the sea. And those who
βόσκοντες [t]τοὺς χοίρους‖ ἔφυγον, καὶ [v]ἀνήγγειλαν‖ εἰς τὴν
fed the swine fled, and announced [it] to the
πόλιν καὶ εἰς τοὺς ἀγρούς. καὶ [w]ἐξῆλθον‖ ἰδεῖν τί ἐστιν τὸ
city and to the country. And they went out to see what it is that
γεγονός· 15 καὶ ἔρχονται πρὸς τὸν Ἰησοῦν, καὶ θεωροῦσιν
has been done. And they come to Jesus, and see
τὸν δαιμονιζόμενον καθήμενον [x]καὶ‖ ἱματισμένον καὶ σωφρο-
the possessed by demons sitting and clothed and of sound
νοῦντα, τὸν.ἐσχηκότα τὸν [y]λεγεῶνα·‖ καὶ ἐφοβήθησαν. 16 καὶ
mind, him who had the legion: and they were afraid. And
διηγήσαντο αὐτοῖς οἱ ἰδόντες, πῶς ἐγένετο τῷ δαι-
[6]related [7]to [8]them [1]those [2]who [3]had [4]seen [[5]it] how it happened to him pos-
μονιζομένῳ, καὶ περὶ τῶν χοίρων. 17 καὶ ἤρξαντο παρα-
sessed by demons, and concerning the swine. And they began to be-
καλεῖν αὐτὸν ἀπελθεῖν ἀπὸ τῶν.ὁρίων.αὐτῶν. 18 Καὶ
seech him to depart from their borders. And
[z]ἐμβάντος‖ αὐτοῦ εἰς τὸ πλοῖον, παρεκάλει αὐτὸν ὁ
[2]having [3]entered [1]he into the ship, [8]besought [9]him [1]he [2]who
δαιμονισθείς, ἵνα [a]ᾖ μετ' αὐτοῦ.‖ 19 [b]ὁ δὲ‖
[3]had [4]been [5]possessed [6]by [7]demons that he might be with him. But
[c]Ἰησοῦς‖ οὐκ.ἀφῆκεν αὐτόν, ἀλλὰ λέγει αὐτῷ, Ὕπαγε εἰς τὸν
Jesus did not suffer him, but says to him, Go to
οἶκόν.σου πρὸς τοὺς.σούς, καὶ [d]ἀνάγγειλον‖ αὐτοῖς ὅσα [e]σοι
thy house to thine own, and announce to them how much for thee
ὁ κύριος‖ [f]ἐποίησεν,‖ καὶ ἠλέησέν σε. 20 Καὶ ἀπῆλθεν καὶ
the Lord did, and pitied thee. And he departed and
ἤρξατο κηρύσσειν ἐν τῇ Δεκαπόλει, ὅσα ἐποίησεν αὐτῷ ὁ
began to proclaim in Decapolis, how much [2]had [3]done [4]for [5]him
Ἰησοῦς· καὶ πάντες ἐθαύμαζον.
[1]Jesus; and all wondered.
21 Καὶ διαπεράσαντος τοῦ Ἰησοῦ ἐν τῷ πλοίῳ [g]πάλιν εἰς
And [2]having [3]passed [4]over [1]Jesus in the ship again to
τὸ πέραν,‖ συνήχθη ὄχλος πολὺς ἐπ' αὐτόν, καὶ ἦν
the other side, [4]was [5]gathered [1]a [3]crowd [2]great to him, and he was
παρὰ τὴν θάλασσαν. 22 Καὶ [h]ἰδού,‖ ἔρχεται εἷς.τῶν ἀρχι-
by the sea. And behold, comes one of the rulers of
συναγώγων, ὀνόματι Ἰάειρος, καὶ ἰδὼν αὐτόν, πίπτει πρὸς
the synagogue. by name Jairus, and seeing him, falls at
τοὺς.πόδας.αὐτοῦ· 23 καὶ [i]παρεκάλει‖ αὐτὸν πολλά, λέγων,
his feet; and he besought him much, saying
Ὅτι τὸ.θυγάτριόν.μου ἐσχάτως.ἔχει· ἵνα ἐλθὼν
My little daughter is at the last extremity, [I pray] that having come
ἐπιθῇς [k]αὐτῇ τὰς χεῖρας,‖ [l]ὅπως‖ σωθῇ καὶ
thou wouldest lay on her [thy] hands, so that she may be cured, and
[m]ζήσεται.‖ 24 Καὶ ἀπῆλθεν μετ' αὐτοῦ, καὶ ἠκολούθει αὐτῷ
she shall live. And he departed with him, and [4]followed [5]him
ὄχλος πολύς, καὶ συνέθλιβον αὐτόν. 25 Καὶ γυνή [n]τις‖
[1]a [3]crowd [2]great, and pressed on him. And a [2]woman [1]certain
οὖσα ἐν ῥύσει αἵματος [o]ἔτη δώδεκα,‖ 26 καὶ πολλὰ παθοῦσα
being with a flux of blood [2]years [1]twelve, and much having suffered
ὑπὸ πολλῶν ἰατρῶν, καὶ δαπανήσασα τὰ.παρ'.[p]ἑαυτῆς‖
under many physicians, and having spent [2]her [3]means
πάντα, καὶ μηδὲν ὠφεληθεῖσα ἀλλὰ μᾶλλον εἰς τὸ.χεῖρον
[1]all, and in no way having benefited but rather [3]to [4]worse
ἐλθοῦσα, 27 ἀκούσασα [q] περὶ τοῦ Ἰησοῦ, ἐλθοῦσα ἐν
[1]having [2]come, having heard concerning Jesus, having come in
τῷ ὄχλῳ ὄπισθεν, ἥψατο τοῦ.ἱματίου.αὐτοῦ· 28 ἔλεγεν.γάρ,
the crowd behind, touched his garment; for she said,
Ὅτι [r]κἂν τῶν.ἱματίων.αὐτοῦ ἅψωμαι,‖ σωθήσομαι. 29 Καὶ
If but his garments I shall touch, I shall be cured. And
[s]εὐθέως‖ ἐξηράνθη ἡ πηγὴ τοῦ.αἵματος.αὐτῆς, καὶ ἔγνω
immediately was dried up the fountain of her blood, and she knew
τῷ σώματι ὅτι ἴαται ἀπὸ τῆς μάστιγος. 30 καὶ [s]εὐθέως‖
in [her] body that she was healed from the scourge. And immediately

for we are many.
10 And he begged Him very much that He
would not send them out of the country.
11 Now there was a great herd of pigs
feeding near the mountains.
12 And all the demons begged Him, saying,
Send us into the pigs, that we may enter into
them.
13 And Jesus immediately gave them
permission. And the unclean spirits left and
entered into the pigs. And the herd rushed
down a steep place into the sea. And they
were about two thousand. And they were
choked in the sea.
14 And those who fed the pigs ran and told
it to the city and to the countryside. And
they went out to see what had been done.
15 And they came to Jesus. And they saw
the one who had been demon-possessed, sitting and clothed and of sound mind – the
one who had the legion. And they were
afraid.
16 And those who had seen it told them
how it happened to the one who had been
demon-possessed, and *also* about the pigs.
17 And they began to beg Him to go away
from their borders.
18 And as He was entering into the ship, he
who had been demon-possessed begged Him,
that he might be with Him.
19 But Jesus did not allow him to go, but
said to him, Go away to your house, to your
own, and tell them how much the Lord
pitied you and worked for you.
20 And he went away and began to preach
in De-cap-o-lis how much Jesus had done for
him. And all greatly wondered.
21 And when Jesus had gone over to the
other side again in the ship, a great crowd
was gathered to Him, and He was by the sea.
22 And behold, one of the rulers of the
synagogue, named Ja-i-rus, came up. And
when he saw Him, he fell at His feet.
23 And he begged Him fervently, saying,
My little daughter is at the very end. *O* that
You would come and lay Your hands on her
so that she may be cured, then she shall live.
24 And He went with him. And a great
crowd followed Him and thronged Him.
25 And a certain woman *came, who* had
been *sick* with a flow of blood for twelve
years.
26 And *she* had suffered much under many
physicians. And *she* had spent all her means,
yet had gained in no way. But instead she
had become worse.
27 She had heard about Jesus and came in
the crowd behind *Him* and touched His
clothes.
28 For she said, If I shall but touch His
clothes I shall be cured.
29 And instantly the fountain of her blood
was dried up, and she knew in her body that
she was healed from the torment.
30 But Jesus, immediately knowing within

ὁ Ἰησοῦς, ἐπιγνοὺς ἐν ἑαυτῷ τὴν ἐξ αὐτοῦ δύναμιν
Jesus, knowing in himself [that] the [2]out [3]of [4]him [1]power
ἐξελθοῦσαν, ἐπιστραφεὶς ἐν τῷ ὄχλῳ, ἔλεγεν, Τίς μου ἥψατο
had gone forth, having turned in the crowd, said, Who of me touched
τῶν ἱματίων; 31 Καὶ ἔλεγον αὐτῷ οἱ.μαθηταὶ.αὐτοῦ, Βλέπεις
the garments? And [3]said [4]to [5]him [1]his [2]disciples, Thou seest
τὸν ὄχλον συνθλίβοντά σε, καὶ λέγεις, Τίς μου ἥψατο;
the crowd pressing on thee, and sayest thou, Who me touched?
32 Καὶ περιεβλέπετο ἰδεῖν τὴν τοῦτο ποιήσασαν. 33 ἡ.δὲ
And he looked round to see her who this had done. But the
γυνὴ φοβηθεῖσα καὶ τρέμουσα, εἰδυῖα ὃ γέγονεν [t]ἐπ'ǁ
woman being frightened and trembling, knowing what had been done upon
αὐτῇ, ἦλθεν καὶ προσέπεσεν αὐτῷ, καὶ εἶπεν αὐτῷ πᾶσαν
her, came and fell down before him, and told him all
τὴν ἀλήθειαν. 34 ὁ.δὲ [v] εἶπεν αὐτῇ, [w]Θύγατερ,ǁ ἡ.πίστις.σου
the truth. And he said to her, Daughter, thy faith
σέσωκέν σε· ὕπαγε εἰς εἰρήνην, καὶ ἴσθι ὑγιὴς ἀπὸ τῆς μάστι-
has cured thee; go in peace, and be sound from [2]scourge
γός σου. 35 Ἔτι αὐτοῦ.λαλοῦντος, ἔρχονται ἀπὸ τοῦ ἀρχι-
[1]thy. [While] yet he is speaking, they come from the ruler of
συναγώγου, λέγοντες, Ὅτι ἡ.θυγάτηρ.σου ἀπέθανεν· τί ἔτι
the synagogue's [house], saying, Thy daughter is dead; why still
σκύλλεις τὸν διδάσκαλον; 36 Ὁ.δὲ.Ἰησοῦς [x]εὐθέωςǁ [y]ἀκού-
troublest thou the teacher? But Jesus immediately, having
σαςǁ τὸν λόγον λαλούμενον λέγει τῷ ἀρχισυναγώγῳ, Μὴ
heard the word spoken, says to the ruler of the synagogue, [2]Not
φοβοῦ· μόνον πίστευε. 37 Καὶ οὐκ.ἀφῆκεν οὐδένα [z]αὐτῷǁ
[1]fear; only believe. And he suffered no one him
[a]συνακολουθῆσαι,ǁ εἰ.μὴ [b] Πέτρον καὶ Ἰάκωβον καὶ Ἰωάννην
to accompany, except Peter and James and John
τὸν ἀδελφὸν Ἰακώβου. 38 καὶ [c]ἔρχεταιǁ εἰς τὸν οἶκον τοῦ
the brother of James. And he comes to the house of the
ἀρχισυναγώγου, καὶ θεωρεῖ θόρυβον, [d] κλαίοντας καὶ
ruler of the synagogue, and he beholds a tumult, [people] weeping and
ἀλαλάζοντας πολλά. 39 καὶ εἰσελθὼν λέγει αὐτοῖς, Τί
wailing greatly. And having entered he says to them, Why
θορυβεῖσθε καὶ κλαίετε; τὸ παιδίον οὐκ.ἀπέθανεν, ἀλλὰ
make ye a tumult and weep? the child is not dead, but
καθεύδει. 40 Καὶ κατεγέλων αὐτοῦ. [e]ὁǁ.δὲ ἐκβαλὼν [f]ἅπαν-
sleeps. And they laughed at him. But he having put out all,
τας,ǁ παραλαμβάνει τὸν πατέρα τοῦ παιδίου καὶ τὴν
takes with [him] the father of the child and the
μητέρα καὶ τοὺς μετ' αὐτοῦ, καὶ εἰσπορεύεται ὅπου ἦν τὸ
mother and those with him, and enters in where [3]was [1]the
παιδίον [g]ἀνακείμενον.ǁ 41 καὶ κρατήσας τῆς χειρὸς τοῦ
[2]child lying. And having taken the hand of the
παιδίου, λέγει αὐτῇ, Ταλιθά, [h]κοῦμι·ǁ ὅ ἐστιν μεθερμηνευό-
child, he says to her, Talitha, koumi; which is, being inter-
μενον, Τὸ κοράσιον, σοὶ λέγω, [i]ἔγειραι.ǁ 42 Καὶ [k]εὐθέωςǁ
preted, Damsel, to thee I say, arise. And immediately
ἀνέστη τὸ κοράσιον καὶ περιεπάτει, ἦν γὰρ ἐτῶν δώδεκα.
arose the damsel and walked, for she was [2]years [1]twelve [old].
καὶ ἐξέστησαν [l] ἐκστάσει μεγάλῃ. 43 καὶ διεστείλατο
And they were amazed with [2]amazement [1]great. And he charged
αὐτοῖς πολλὰ ἵνα μηδεὶς [m]γνῷǁ τοῦτο· καὶ εἶπεν
them much that no one should know this; and he said [that some-
δοθῆναι αὐτῇ φαγεῖν.
thing] should be given to her to eat.

6 Καὶ ἐξῆλθεν ἐκεῖθεν, καὶ [n]ἦλθενǁ εἰς τὴν.πατρίδα.αὐτοῦ·
And he went out thence, and came into his [own] country;
καὶ ἀκολουθοῦσιν αὐτῷ οἱ.μαθηταὶ.αὐτοῦ· 2 καὶ γενομένου
and [3]follow [4]him [1]his [2]disciples. And [2]being [3]come
σαββάτου ἤρξατο [o]ἐν τῇ συναγωγῇ διδάσκειν·ǁ καὶ [p] πολλοὶ
[1]sabbath he began in the synagogue to teach; and many
ἀκούοντες ἐξεπλήσσοντο, λέγοντες, Πόθεν τούτῳ ταῦτα;
hearing were astonished, saying, Whence to this [man] these things?
καὶ τίς ἡ σοφία ἡ δοθεῖσα [q]αὐτῷ,ǁ [r]ὅτιǁ καὶ δυνάμεις
and what the wisdom that has been given to him, that even [2]works [3]of [4]power
τοιαῦται διὰ τῶν.χειρῶν.αὐτοῦ [s]γίνονται;ǁ 3 οὐχ οὗτός ἐστιν
[1]such by his hands are done? [2]not [3]this [1]is
ὁ τέκτων, ὁ υἱὸς [t]Μαρίας, [v]ἀδελφὸς.δὲǁ Ἰακώβου καὶ [w]Ἰωσῆǁ
the carpenter, the son of Mary, and brother of James and Joses
καὶ Ἰούδα καὶ Σίμωνος; καὶ οὐκ.εἰσὶν αἱ.ἀδελφαὶ.αὐτοῦ ὧδε
and Judas and Simon? and are not his sisters here
πρὸς ἡμᾶς; Καὶ ἐσκανδαλίζοντο ἐν αὐτῷ. 4 [x]ἔλεγεν.δὲǁ αὐτοῖς
with us? And they were offended in him. But [2]said [3]to [4]them
ὁ Ἰησοῦς, Ὅτι οὐκ ἔστιν προφήτης ἄτιμος, εἰ.μὴ ἐν τῇ
[1]Jesus, [6]Not [7]is [5]a [8]prophet without honour, except in
πατρίδι.[y]αὐτοῦǁ καὶ ἐν τοῖς [z]συγγενέσινǁ [a] καὶ ἐν τῇ
his [own] country and among [his] kinsmen and in
οἰκίᾳ.[b]αὐτοῦǁ. 5 Καὶ οὐκ [c]ἠδύνατοǁ ἐκεῖ [d]οὐδεμίαν δύναμιν
his [own] house. And he was [2]able [3]there [1]not any work of power

Himself that the power had gone forth out of Him, turning in the crowd, said, Who touched My clothes?

31 And His disciples said to Him, You see the multitude thronging You. And do You say, Who touched Me?

32 And He looked around to see who had done this thing.

33 But knowing what had been done to her, being afraid and trembling, the woman came and fell down before Him and told Him all the truth.

34 And He said to her, Daughter, your faith has cured you. Go in peace and be well from your torment.

35 As He yet was speaking, they came from the synagogue ruler's *house* saying, Your daughter is dead. Why do you still trouble the Teacher?

36 But Jesus heard what was said and immediately said to the ruler of the synagogue, Do not be afraid, only believe.

37 And He did not allow anyone to go with Him except Peter and James and John, the brother of James.

38 And He came to the house of the ruler of the synagogue.. And He saw a tumult, much weeping and wailing.

39 And going in, He said to them, Why do you make a noise and weep? The child is not dead, but sleeps.

40 And they laughed at Him. But putting them all out, He took the father and mother of the child, and those with Him, and He went in where the child was lying.

41 And taking the hand of the child, He said to her, Tal-ith-a kou-mi (which translated means, Little girl, I say to you, Get up!).

42 And immediately the little girl got up and walked, for she was twelve years old. And they were amazed with a great amazement.

43 And very distinctly He commanded that no one should know this: And He asked that *something* be given her to eat.

6 1 And He went out from there and came into His own country. And His disciples followed Him.

2 And Sabbath coming on, He began to teach in the synagogue. And hearing, many were astonished, saying, From where do these things come to this one? And, What is the wisdom that has been given to Him, that even such mighty works are done by His hands?

3 Is this not the carpenter, the son of Mary, and the brother of James and Joses and Judas and Simon? And are not his sisters here with us? And they were scandalized by Him.

4 But Jesus said to them, A prophet is not without honor, except in his own country and among his own kin and in his own house.

5 And He was not able to do any work of

ποιῆσαι,‖ εἰ.μὴ ὀλίγοις ἀῤῥώστοις ἐπιθεὶς τὰς χεῖρας
to do, except on a few infirm having laid [his] hands
ἐθεράπευσεν. 6 καὶ [e]ἐθαύμαζεν‖ διὰ τὴν.ἀπιστίαν.αὐ-
he healed [them]. And he wondered because of their unbelief.
τῶν· καὶ περιῆγεν τὰς κώμας κύκλῳ διδάσκων.
And he went about the villages in a circuit teaching.
7 Καὶ προσκαλεῖται τοὺς δώδεκα, καὶ ἤρξατο αὐτοὺς
And he calls to [him] the twelve, and began them
ἀποστέλλειν δύο.δύο, καὶ ἐδίδου αὐτοῖς ἐξουσίαν τῶν πνευμά-
to send forth two and two, and gave to them authority over the spirits
των τῶν ἀκαθάρτων· 8 καὶ παρήγγειλεν αὐτοῖς ἵνα μηδὲν
the unclean; and he charged them that nothing
αἴρωσιν εἰς ὁδόν, εἰ.μὴ ῥάβδον μόνον· μὴ [f]πήραν,
they should take for [the] way, except a staff only; no provision bag,
μὴ ἄρτον,‖ μὴ εἰς τὴν ζώνην χαλκόν· 9 [g]ἀλλ'‖ ὑποδεδεμένους
nor bread, nor in the belt money; but be shod
σανδάλια· καὶ μὴ.[h]ἐνδύσησθε‖ δύο χιτῶνας. 10 Καὶ ἔλεγεν
with sandals; and put not on two tunics. And he said
αὐτοῖς, Ὅπου.[i]ἐὰν‖ εἰσέλθητε εἰς οἰκίαν, ἐκεῖ μένετε ἕως ἂν
to them, Wherever ye enter into a house, there remain until
ἐξέλθητε ἐκεῖθεν. 11 καὶ [k]ὅσοι.ἂν μὴ.δέξωνται‖ ὑμᾶς, μηδὲ
ye go out thence. And as many as will not receive you, nor
ἀκούσωσιν ὑμῶν, ἐκπορευόμενοι ἐκεῖθεν, ἐκτινάξατε τὸν χοῦν
hear you, departing thence, shake off the dust
τὸν ὑποκάτω τῶν.ποδῶν.ὑμῶν, εἰς μαρτύριον αὐτοῖς. [l]ἀμὴν
which [is] under your feet, for a testimony to them. Verily
λέγω ὑμῖν, ἀνεκτότερον ἔσται Σοδόμοις ἢ Γομόῤῥοις ἐν ἡμέρᾳ
I say to you, more tolerable it shall be for Sodom or Gomorrha in day
κρίσεως, ἢ τῇ.πόλει.ἐκείνῃ.‖ 12 Καὶ ἐξελθόντες [m]ἐκήρυσ-
of judgment than for that city. And having gone out they pro-
σον‖ ἵνα [n]μετανοήσωσιν.‖ 13 καὶ δαιμόνια πολλὰ ἐξέβαλλον,
claimed that [men] should repent. And [2]demons [1]many they cast out,
καὶ ἤλειφον ἐλαίῳ πολλοὺς ἀῤῥώστους καὶ ἐθεράπευον.
and anointed with oil many infirm and healed [them].
14 Καὶ ἤκουσεν ὁ βασιλεὺς Ἡρώδης, φανερὸν.γὰρ
And [4]heard [2]the [3]king [1]Herod [of him], for public
ἐγένετο τὸ.ὄνομα.αὐτοῦ, καὶ [o]ἔλεγεν,‖ Ὅτι Ἰωάννης ὁ βαπ-
became his name, and he said, John the Bap-
τίζων [p]ἐκ νεκρῶν ἠγέρθη,‖ καὶ διὰ τοῦτο ἐνεργοῦ-
tist from among [the] dead is risen, and because of this [5]ope-
σιν αἱ δυνάμεις ἐν αὐτῷ. 15 [q]Ἄλλοι‖ ἔλεγον, Ὅτι [r]Ἠλίας‖
rate [1]the [2]works [3]of [4]power in him. Others said, Elias
ἐστίν· ἄλλοι.δὲ ἔλεγον, Ὅτι προφήτης [s]ἐστίν,‖ [t]ἢ‖ ὡς εἷς τῶν
it is; and others said, A prophet it is, or as one of the
προφητῶν. 16 Ἀκούσας.δὲ ὁ Ἡρώδης [v]εἶπεν,‖ [w]Ὅτι‖ ὃν
prophets. But having heard Herod said, [2]Whom
ἐγὼ ἀπεκεφάλισα Ἰωάννην, οὗτός [x]ἐστιν· αὐτὸς‖ ἠγέρθη
[3]I [4]beheaded [1]John, he it is. He is risen
[y]ἐκ νεκρῶν.‖ 17 Αὐτὸς.γὰρ ὁ Ἡρώδης ἀποστείλας
from among [the] dead. For [2]himself [1]Herod having sent
ἐκράτησεν τὸν Ἰωάννην, καὶ ἔδησεν αὐτὸν ἐν [z]τῇ‖ φυλακῇ,
seized John, and bound him in the prison,
διὰ Ἡρωδιάδα τὴν γυναῖκα Φιλίππου τοῦ.ἀδελφοῦ.αὐτοῦ,
on account of Herodias the wife of Philip his brother,
ὅτι αὐτὴν ἐγάμησεν. 18 ἔλεγεν.γὰρ ὁ Ἰωάννης τῷ Ἡρώδῃ,
because her he had married. For [2]said [1]John to Herod,
Ὅτι οὐκ.ἔξεστίν σοι ἔχειν τὴν γυναῖκα τοῦ.ἀδελφοῦ.σου.
It is not lawful for thee to have the wife of thy brother.
19 Ἡ.δὲ.Ἡρωδιὰς ἐνεῖχεν αὐτῷ, καὶ [a]ἤθελεν‖ αὐτὸν ἀπο-
But Herodias held it against him, and wished [3]him [1]to
κτεῖναι· καὶ οὐκ.ἠδύνατο. 20 ὁ.γὰρ.Ἡρώδης ἐφοβεῖτο τὸν
[2]kill, and was not able: for Herod feared
Ἰωάννην, εἰδὼς αὐτὸν ἄνδρα δίκαιον καὶ ἅγιον, καὶ
John, knowing him [to be] a man just and holy, and
συνετήρει αὐτόν· καὶ ἀκούσας αὐτοῦ, πολλὰ [b]ἐποίει,‖ καὶ
kept [2]safe [1]him; and having heard him, many things did, and
ἡδέως αὐτοῦ ἤκουεν. 21 καὶ γενομένης ἡμέρας.εὐκαίρου, [c]ὅτε‖
gladly him heard. And [4]being [5]come [1]an [2]opportune [3]day, when
Ἡρώδης τοῖς.γενεσίοις.αὐτοῦ δεῖπνον [d]ἐποίει‖ τοῖς μεγιστᾶσιν
Herod on his birthday a supper made to [2]great [3]men
αὐτοῦ καὶ τοῖς χιλιάρχοις καὶ τοῖς πρώτοις τῆς Γαλιλαίας,
[1]his and to the chief captains and to the first [men] of Galilee;
22 καὶ εἰσελθούσης τῆς θυγατρὸς αὐτῆς τῆς Ἡρωδιάδος, καὶ
and [6]having [7]come [8]in [1]the [2]daughter [3]of [5]herself [4]Herodias, and
ὀρχησαμένης, [e]καὶ ἀρεσάσης‖ τῷ Ἡρώδῃ καὶ τοῖς συνανα-
having danced, and pleased Herod and those reclining
κειμένοις, [f]εἶπεν ὁ βασιλεὺς‖ τῷ κορασίῳ, Αἴτησόν με
[at table] with [him], [3]said [1]the [2]king to the damsel, Ask me
ὃ.ἐὰν θέλῃς, καὶ δώσω σοί· 23 καὶ ὤμοσεν αὐτῇ, Ὅτι
whatever thou wilt, and I will give to thee. And he swore to her,
ὃ.ἐὰν με αἰτήσῃς, δώσω σοί, ἕως ἡμίσους τῆς βασιλείας
Whatever me thou mayest ask, I will give thee, to half of [2]kingdom

power there, except He laid hands on a few
sick people and healed *them.*
6 And He marveled because of their unbelief. And He went around the villages in a
circle teaching.
7 And He called the twelve to Him and began to send them out two by two. And He
gave them authority over the unclean spirits.
8 And He commanded them not to take
anything for their trip except a staff – no
bag, no bread, no money in the belt,
9 but to be shod with sandals, and not to
put on two coats.
10 And He said to them, Wherever you
enter a house, stay there until you leave that
place.
11 And as many as will not receive you or
hear you, as you go out from there shake off
the dust which is under your feet for a
witness to them. Truly I say to you, It shall
be more bearable for Sodom or Go-mor-rah
in the day of judgment than for that city.
12 And they went out and preached that
men should repent.
13 And they threw out many demons and
anointed many of the sick with oil and
healed them.

14 And king Herod heard, for His name was
spread abroad. And he said, John the Baptist
has risen from among the dead – and
because of this the mighty powers are
working in him.
15 Others said, It is Elijah. And others said,
It is a prophet, or like one of the prophets.
16 But Herod hearing it said, It is he whom
I beheaded, John. He has risen from the
dead.
17 For Herod himself had sent out and laid
hands on John. And he had put him in
prison, on account of He-ro-di-as, the wife of
his brother Philip (because he had married
her).
18 For John said to Herod, It is not lawful
for you to have the wife of your brother.
19 And He-ro-di-as set herself against him
and wanted to kill him. But she was not able
to do so.
20 For Herod feared John, knowing that he
was a just and holy man. And he kept him
safe. And when he heard him he did many
things. And he heard him gladly.
21 And a day of opportunity came, when
Herod made a feast to great men on his
birthday (also to the chief captains and to
the leaders of Galilee).
22 And the daughter of He-ro-di-as herself
came in and danced. And she pleased Herod
and those at table with *him.* The king said to
the girl, Ask me whatever you desire, and I
will give it to you,
23 And he swore to her, Whatever you may
ask me, I will give it to you, to half of my

μου. 24 [g]Ἡ.δὲ" ἐξελθοῦσα εἶπεν τῇ.μητρὶ.αὐτῆς, Τί [h]αἰτή-
[1]my. And she having gone out said to her mother, What shall I
σομαι;" Ἡ.δὲ εἶπεν, Τὴν [i]κεφαλὴν Ἰωάννου τοῦ [j]βαπτιστοῦ."
ask? And she said, The head of John the Baptist.
25 Καὶ εἰσελθοῦσα [k]εὐθέως" μετὰ σπουδῆς πρὸς τὸν βασιλέα,
And having entered immediately with haste to the king,
ᾐτήσατο, λέγουσα, Θέλω ἵνα [l]μοι δῷς ἐξ.αὐτῆς" ἐπὶ πίνακι
she asked, saying, I desire that to me thou give at once upon a dish
τὴν κεφαλὴν Ἰωάννου τοῦ βαπτιστοῦ. 26 Καὶ περίλυπος
the head of John the Baptist. And [5]very [6]sorrowful
γενόμενος ὁ βασιλεύς, διὰ τοὺς ὅρκους καὶ τοὺς
[[3]while] [4]made [1]the [2]king, on account of the oaths and those who
[m]συνανακειμένους" οὐκ.ἠθέλησεν [n]αὐτὴν ἀθετῆσαι." 27 καὶ
reclined [at table] with [him], would not [2]her [1]reject. And
[o]εὐθέως" ἀποστείλας ὁ βασιλεὺς [p]σπεκουλάτωρα" ἐπέταξεν
immediately [3]having [4]sent [1]the [2]king a guardsman ordered
[q]ἐνεχθῆναι" τὴν.κεφαλὴν.αὐτοῦ[r]. 28 [s]ὁ.δὲ" ἀπελθὼν ἀπεκε-
to be brought his head. And he having gone be-
φάλισεν αὐτὸν ἐν τῇ φυλακῇ, καὶ ἤνεγκεν τὴν.κεφαλὴν.αὐτοῦ
headed him in the prison, and brought his head
ἐπὶ πίνακι, καὶ ἔδωκεν αὐτὴν τῷ κορασίῳ· καὶ τὸ κοράσιον
upon a dish, and gave it to the damsel, and the damsel
ἔδωκεν αὐτὴν τῇ.μητρὶ.αὐτῆς. 29 Καὶ ἀκούσαντες οἱ μαθηταὶ
gave it to her mother. And having heard [it] [2]disciples
αὐτοῦ [t]ἦλθον," καὶ ἦραν τὸ.πτῶμα.αὐτοῦ, καὶ ἔθηκαν [u]αὐτὸ"
[1]his came, and took up his corpse, and laid it
ἐν [v]τῷ" μνημείῳ.
in the tomb.

30 Καὶ συνάγονται οἱ ἀπόστολοι πρὸς τὸν Ἰησοῦν, καὶ
And [3]are [4]gathered [5]together [1]the [2]apostles to Jesus, and
ἀπήγγειλαν αὐτῷ πάντα, [w]καὶ" ὅσα ἐποίησαν καὶ [x]ὅσα"
they related to him all things, both what they had done and what
ἐδίδαξαν. 31 καὶ [y]εἶπεν" αὐτοῖς, Δεῦτε ὑμεῖς αὐτοὶ
they had taught. And he said to them, Come ye yourselves
κατ'.ἰδίαν εἰς ἔρημον τόπον, καὶ [z]ἀναπαύεσθε" ὀλίγον. Ἦσαν
apart into [2]desert [1]a place, and rest a little. [7]Were
γὰρ οἱ ἐρχόμενοι καὶ οἱ ὑπάγοντες πολλοί, καὶ οὐδὲ φαγεῖν
[1]for [2]those [3]coming [4]and [5]those [6]going many, and not even to eat
[a]ηὐκαίρουν." 32 καὶ ἀπῆλθον [b]εἰς ἔρημον τόπον τῷ
had they opportunity. And they went away into [2]desert [1]a place by the
πλοίῳ" κατ'.ἰδίαν. 33 Καὶ εἶδον αὐτοὺς ὑπάγοντας [c]οἱ ὄχλοι,"
ship apart. And [3]saw [4]them [5]going [1]the [2]crowds,
καὶ [d]ἐπέγνωσαν" [e]αὐτὸν" πολλοί, καὶ πεζῇ ἀπὸ πασῶν τῶν
[6]and [8]recognized [9]him [7]many, and on foot from all the
πόλεων συνέδραμον ἐκεῖ, [f]καὶ προῆλθον αὐτούς," [g]καὶ συνῆλ-
cities ran together there, and went before them, and came to-
θον πρὸς αὐτόν." 34 καὶ ἐξελθὼν [h]εἶδεν ὁ Ἰησοῦς" πολὺν
gether to him. And having gone out [2]saw [1]Jesus [3]great
ὄχλον, καὶ [i]ἐσπλαγχνίσθη ἐπ' [j]αὐτοῖς," ὅτι ἦσαν
[4]a crowd, and was moved with compassion towards them, because they were
ὡς πρόβατα μὴ ἔχοντα ποιμένα· καὶ ἤρξατο διδάσκειν αὐτοὺς
as sheep not having a shepherd. And he began to teach them
πολλά. 35 Καὶ ἤδη ὥρας.πολλῆς [k]γενομένης," προσελ-
many things. And already a late hour [it] being, com-
θόντες [l]αὐτῷ" οἱ.μαθηταὶ.[m]αὐτοῦ" [n]λέγουσιν," Ὅτι ἔρημός ἐστιν
ing to him his disciples say, Desert is
ὁ τόπος, καὶ ἤδη ὥρα.πολλή· 36 ἀπόλυσον αὐτούς, ἵνα
the place, and already [it is] a late hour; dismiss them, that
ἀπελθόντες εἰς τοὺς κύκλῳ ἀγροὺς καὶ κώμας, ἀγοράσωσιν
having gone [4]to [5]the [1]in [2]a [3]circuit country and villages, they may buy
ἑαυτοῖς [o]ἄρτους·" τί [p]γὰρ" φάγωσιν [q]οὐκ.ἔχουσιν."
for themselves bread; [2]something [1]for to eat they have not.
37 Ὁ.δὲ ἀποκριθεὶς εἶπεν αὐτοῖς, Δότε αὐτοῖς ὑμεῖς φαγεῖν.
But he answering said to them, Give [2]to [3]them [1]ye to eat.
Καὶ λέγουσιν αὐτῷ, Ἀπελθόντες ἀγοράσωμεν [r]διακοσίων
And they say to him, Having gone shall we buy two hundred
δηναρίων" ἄρτους, καὶ [s]δῶμεν" αὐτοῖς φαγεῖν; 38 Ὁ.δὲ λέγει
denarii of bread, and give them to eat? And he says
αὐτοῖς, Πόσους ἄρτους ἔχετε; ὑπάγετε [t]καὶ" ἴδετε. Καὶ γνόν-
to them, How many loaves have ye? go and see. And having
τες λέγουσιν[v], Πέντε, καὶ δύο ἰχθύας. 39 Καὶ ἐπέταξεν αὐτοῖς
known they say, Five, and two fishes. And he ordered them
[w]ἀνακλῖναι" πάντας συμπόσια.συμπόσια ἐπὶ τῷ χλωρῷ χόρτῳ.
to make [2]recline [1]all by companies on the green grass.
40 καὶ [x]ἀνέπεσον" πρασιαὶ.πρασιαί, [y]ἀνὰ" ἑκατὸν καὶ [y]ἀνὰ"
And they sat down in ranks, by hundreds and by
πεντήκοντα. 41 καὶ λαβὼν τοὺς πέντε ἄρτους καὶ τοὺς δύο
fifties. And having taken the five loaves and the two
ἰχθύας, ἀναβλέψας εἰς τὸν οὐρανὸν εὐλόγησεν καὶ κατέκλα-
fishes, having looked up to the heaven he blessed and broke
σεν τοὺς ἄρτους, καὶ ἐδίδου τοῖς.μαθηταῖς.[z]αὐτοῦ" ἵνα [aa]παρα-
the loaves, and gave to his disciples that they might

kingdom.
24 And she went out and said to her
mother, What shall I ask? And she said, The
head of John the Baptist.
25 And immediately hurrying in to the king
she asked, saying, I want you to give to me
at once the head of John the Baptist on a
platter.
26 And the king was full of sorrow. *But* because of the oaths and those who were at
table with *him*, he would not refuse her.
27 And immediately the king sent a guard
and commanded his head to be brought.
And he went out and beheaded *John* in the
prison.
28 And he brought his head on a platter and
gave it to the girl. And the girl gave it to her
mother.
29 And when his disciples heard, they came
and took up his body and laid it in the grave.
30 And the apostles had met Jesus. And
they told Him all the things they had done,
and what they had taught.
31 And He said to them, You yourselves
come aside into a deserted place and rest a
little. For those coming and going were very
many. And they did not even have time to
eat.
32 And they went away by ship into a
deserted place, alone.
33 And the people saw them going away,
and many recognized Him. And they ran
together on foot from all the cities and went
before them. And they met Him.
34 And Jesus went out and saw a great
crowd. And He was moved with pity toward
them, because they were as sheep having no
shepherd. And He began to teach them
many things.
35 And it having become late already, His
disciples came to Him and said, The place is
deserted, and now the hour is late.
36 Send them away so that they may buy
bread for themselves *by* going to the
surrounding farms and villages. For they
have nothing to eat.
37 And answering He said to them, You
give them *something* to eat. And they said to
Him, Shall we go and buy two hundred silver
pieces' worth of bread and give them
something to eat.
38 And He said to them, How many loaves
do you have? Go and see. And when they
knew, they said, Five, and two fish.
39 And He commanded them to make
everyone sit down in companies on the green
grass.
40 And they sat down by rows, by
hundreds and by fifties.
41 And taking the five loaves and the two
fish, looking up to Heaven, He blessed. And
He broke the loaves and gave to His disciples
so that they might serve them. And the two
fish He divided among all.

θῶσιν" αὐτοῖς· καὶ τοὺς δύο ἰχθύας ἐμέρισεν πᾶσιν· 42 καὶ
set before them. And the two fishes he divided among all. And
ἔφαγον πάντες, καὶ ἐχορτάσθησαν· 43 καὶ ἦραν [b]κλασμά-
[2]ate [1]all, and were satisfied. And they took up of frag-
των" δώδεκα [c]κοφίνους" [d]πλήρεις," καὶ ἀπὸ τῶν ἰχθύων. 44 καὶ
ments twelve hand-baskets full, and of the fishes. And
ἦσαν οἱ φαγόντες τοὺς ἄρτους [e]ὡσεὶ" πεντακισχίλιοι
[7]were [1]those [2]that [3]ate [4]of [5]the [6]loaves about five thousand
ἄνδρες. 45 Καὶ [f]εὐθέως" ἠνάγκασεν τοὺς.μαθητὰς.αὐτοῦ
men. And immediately he compelled his disciples
ἐμβῆναι εἰς τὸ πλοῖον, καὶ προάγειν εἰς τὸ πέραν πρὸς Βηθ-
to enter into the ship, and to go before to the other side to Beth-
σαϊδάν, ἕως αὐτὸς [g]ἀπολύσῃ" τὸν ὄχλον. 46 καὶ ἀποταξάμενος
saida, until he should dismiss the crowd. And having taken leave of
αὐτοῖς, ἀπῆλθεν εἰς τὸ ὄρος προσεύξασθαι. 47 Καὶ ὀψίας
them, he departed into the mountain to pray. And evening
γενομένης, ἦν τὸ πλοῖον ἐν μέσῳ τῆς θαλάσσης, καὶ αὐτὸς
being come, [3]was [1]the [2]ship in the midst of the sea, and he
μόνος ἐπὶ τῆς γῆς. 48 Καὶ [h]εἶδεν" αὐτοὺς βασανιζομένους
alone upon the land. And he saw them labouring
ἐν τῷ ἐλαύνειν, ἦν.γὰρ ὁ ἄνεμος ἐναντίος αὐτοῖς· [i]καὶ[i] περὶ
in the rowing, for [3]was [1]the [2]wind contrary to them; and about
τετάρτην φυλακὴν τῆς νυκτὸς ἔρχεται πρὸς αὐτούς, περιπα-
[the] fourth watch of the night he comes to them, walk-
τῶν ἐπὶ τῆς θαλάσσης, καὶ ἤθελεν παρελθεῖν αὐτούς. 49 οἱ.δὲ
ing on the sea, and would have passed by them. But they,
ἰδόντες αὐτὸν [k]περιπατοῦντα ἐπὶ τῆς θαλάσσης," ἔδοξαν [l]
seeing him walking on the sea, thought [it]
φάντασμα [m]εἶναι," καὶ ἀνέκραξαν. 50 πάντες.γὰρ αὐτὸν
[3]an [4]apparition [1]to [2]be, and cried out: for all [2]him
[n]εἶδον," καὶ ἐταράχθησαν. [o]καὶ εὐθέως" ἐλάλησεν μετ' αὐτῶν,
[1]saw, and were troubled. And immediately he spoke with them,
καὶ λέγει αὐτοῖς, Θαρσεῖτε· ἐγώ εἰμι, μὴ.φοβεῖσθε.
and says to them, Be of good courage: I am [he]; fear not.
51 Καὶ ἀνέβη πρὸς αὐτοὺς εἰς τὸ πλοῖον, καὶ ἐκόπασεν ὁ
And he went up to them into the ship, and [3]fell [1]the
ἄνεμος· καὶ λίαν [p]ἐκ.περισσοῦ" ἐν ἑαυτοῖς ἐξίσταντο,
[2]wind. And exceedingly beyond measure in themselves they were amazed,
[q]καὶ ἐθαύμαζον·" 52 οὐ.γὰρ.συνῆκαν ἐπὶ τοῖς ἄρτοις· [r]ἦν.γὰρ"
and wondered; for they understood not by the loaves, for [3]was
[s]ἡ.καρδία.αὐτῶν" πεπωρωμένη.
[1]their [2]heart hardened.

53 Καὶ διαπεράσαντες [t]ἦλθον ἐπὶ τὴν γῆν" [v]Γεννησαρέτ,"
And having passed over they came to the land of Gennesaret,
καὶ προσωρμίσθησαν. 54 καὶ ἐξελθόντων.αὐτῶν ἐκ τοῦ
and drew to shore. And on their coming out of the
πλοίου, [f]εὐθέως" ἐπιγνόντες αὐτόν[w], 55 [x]περιδραμόντες"
ship, immediately having recognized him, running through
ὅλην τὴν.[y]περίχωρον".ἐκείνην [z]ἤρξαντο ἐπὶ τοῖς [a]κραββάτοις"
all that country around they began on couches
τοὺς κακῶς.ἔχοντας περιφέρειν, ὅπου ἤκουον ὅτι
those that were ill to carry about, where they were hearing that
[c]ἐκεῖ" ἐστιν. 56 καὶ ὅπου [d]ἂν" εἰσεπορεύετο εἰς κώμας ἢ [e]
there he was. (lit. he is.) And wherever he entered into villages or
πόλεις ἢ [e] ἀγρούς, ἐν ταῖς ἀγοραῖς [f]ἐτίθουν" τοὺς ἀσθενοῦν-
cities or fields, in the marketplaces they laid those who were sick,
τας, καὶ παρεκάλουν αὐτὸν ἵνα κἂν τοῦ κρασπέδου τοῦ
and besought him that if only the border
ἱματίου.αὐτοῦ ἅψωνται· καὶ ὅσοι ἂν [g]ἥπτοντο" αὐτοῦ
of his garment they might touch; and as many as touched him
ἐσώζοντο.
were healed.

7 Καὶ συνάγονται πρὸς αὐτὸν οἱ Φαρισαῖοι καί τινες
And are gathered together to him the Pharisees and some
τῶν γραμματέων, ἐλθόντες ἀπὸ Ἱεροσολύμων· 2 καὶ ἰδόντες
of the scribes, having come from Jerusalem; and having seen
τινὰς τῶν.μαθητῶν.αὐτοῦ [h] κοιναῖς χερσίν, [i]τοῦτ' ἔστιν"
some of his disciples with defiled hands, that is
ἀνίπτοις, [k]ἐσθίοντας" [l]ἄρτους, [m]ἐμέμψαντο·" 3 οἱ.γὰρ Φαρι-
unwashed, eating bread, they found fault; for the Phari-
σαῖοι καὶ πάντες οἱ Ἰουδαῖοι, ἐὰν.μὴ [n]πυγμῇ" νίψωνται τὰς
sees and all the Jews, unless with the fist they wash the
χεῖρας, οὐκ.ἐσθίουσιν, κρατοῦντες τὴν παράδοσιν τῶν πρεσ-
hands, eat not, holding the tradition of the el-
βυτέρων· 4 καὶ [o]ἀπὸ" ἀγορᾶς, ἐὰν.μὴ βαπτίσωνται
ders; and [on coming] from the market, unless they wash themselves
οὐκ.ἐσθίουσιν· καὶ ἄλλα πολλά ἐστιν ἃ παρέλαβον
they eat not; and [2]other [3]things [1]many there are which they received
κρατεῖν, βαπτισμοὺς ποτηρίων καὶ ξεστῶν καὶ χαλκίων [p]καὶ
to hold, washings of cups and vessels and brazen utensils and
κλινῶν·" 5 [q]ἔπειτα" ἐπερωτῶσιν αὐτὸν οἱ Φαρισαῖοι καὶ οἱ
couches: then question him the Pharisees and the

42 And they all ate and were filled.
43 And they took up twelve baskets full of
the pieces, and of the fish.
44 And those that ate of the loaves were
about five thousand men.
45 And immediately He made His disciples
enter into the ship and to go to the other
side, to Beth-sa-i-da, until He should send
away the people.
46 And leaving them, He went away into a
mountain to pray.
47 And when evening had come, the ship
was in the middle of the sea. And He was
alone on the land.
48 And He saw them laboring in rowing, for
the wind was contrary to them. And about
the fourth watch of the night He came to
them, walking on the sea. And He would
have gone by them.
49 But when they saw Him walking on the
sea, they thought it was a ghost. And they
cried out.
50 For they all saw Him and were afraid.
And He immediately spoke to them and said
to them, Be comforted! I AM *He!* Do not be
afraid.
51 And He went up into the ship to them.
And the wind stopped. And they were
greatly amazed within themselves, beyond
measure. And they wondered.
52 For they did not understand about the
loaves, because their hearts were hardened.
53 And when they had crossed over, they
came to the land of Gen-nes-a-ret and drew
near to the shore.
54 And when they came out of the ship,
immediately He was recognized.
55 And running all around through that
country, they began to carry those that were
ill on beds, wherever they heard that He was.
56 And wherever He entered into villages or
cities or countryside, they laid those who
were sick in the market-places. And they
begged Him, that they might touch only the
hem of His robe. And as many as touched
Him were healed.

CHAPTER 7

1 And having come from Jerusalem the
Pharisees and some of the scribes came to
Him.
2 And they found fault as they saw some of
His disciples eating bread with defiled, that
is, unwashed hands.
3 For the Pharisees and all the Jews do not
eat unless they wash the hands with the fist,
holding the tradition of the elders.
4 And *as they come* from market, they do
not eat unless they wash themselves. And
many other things there are which they have
agreed to keep: washings of cups and pots
and brass vessels and beds.
5 Then the Pharisees and the scribes asked

γραμματεῖς, [r]Διατί[‖] [s]οἱ.μαθηταί.σου οὐ.περιπατοῦσιν[‖] κατὰ
scribes, Why [3]thy [4]disciples [1]walk [2]not according to
τὴν παράδοσιν τῶν πρεσβυτέρων, ἀλλὰ [t]ἀνίπτοις[‖] χερσὶν
the tradition of the elders, but with unwashed hands
ἐσθίουσιν τὸν ἄρτον; 6 Ὁ.δὲ [v]ἀποκριθεὶς[‖] εἶπεν αὐτοῖς, [w]"Ὅτι[‖]
eat bread? But he answering said to them,
καλῶς [x]προεφήτευσεν[‖] Ἡσαΐας περὶ ὑμῶν τῶν ὑποκριτῶν,
Well prophesied Esaias concerning you, hypocrites,
ὡς γέγραπται, [y] [z]Οὗτος ὁ λαὸς[‖] τοῖς χείλεσίν με τιμᾷ,
as it has been written, This people with the lips me honour,
ἡ.δὲ.καρδία.αὐτῶν πόῤῥω ἀπέχει ἀπ' ἐμοῦ. 7 μάτην.δὲ σέβον-
but their heart far is away from me. But in vain they wor-
ταί με, διδάσκοντες διδασκαλίας ἐντάλματα ἀνθρώπων.
ship me, teaching [as] teachings injunctions of men.
8 Ἀφέντες.[a]γὰρ[‖] τὴν ἐντολὴν τοῦ θεοῦ, κρατεῖτε τὴν παρά-
For, leaving the commandment of God, ye hold the tra-
δοσιν τῶν ἀνθρώπων, [b]βαπτισμοὺς ξεστῶν καὶ ποτηρίων, καὶ
dition of men, washings of vessels and cups, and
ἄλλα παρόμοια τοιαῦτα πολλὰ ποιεῖτε.[‖] 9 Καὶ ἔλεγεν
[5]other [4]like [[6]things] [3]such [1]many ye do. And he said
αὐτοῖς, Καλῶς ἀθετεῖτε τὴν ἐντολὴν τοῦ θεοῦ, ἵνα τὴν
to them, Well do ye set aside the commandment of God, that
παράδοσιν.ὑμῶν τηρήσητε. 10 [c]Μωσῆς[‖].γὰρ εἶπεν, Τίμα
your tradition ye may observe. For Moses said, Honour
τὸν.πατέρα.σου καὶ τὴν.μητέρα.σου· καί, Ὁ κακολογῶν πατέρα
thy father and thy mother; and, He who speaks evil of father
ἢ μητέρα θανάτῳ τελευτάτω. 11 Ὑμεῖς.δὲ λέγετε, Ἐὰν εἴπῃ
or mother by death let him die. But ye say, If [3]say
ἄνθρωπος τῷ πατρὶ ἢ τῇ μητρί, Κορβᾶν ὅ ἐστιν, δῶρον,
[1]a [2]man to father or mother, [It is] a corban, (that is, a gift,)
ὃ.ἐὰν ἐξ ἐμοῦ ὠφεληθῇς· 12 [d]καὶ[‖] οὐκέτι ἀφίετε
whatever from me thou mightest be profited by:— and no longer ye suffer
αὐτὸν οὐδὲν ποιῆσαι τῷ.πατρὶ.[e]αὐτοῦ[‖] ἢ τῇ.μητρὶ.[e]αὐτοῦ,[‖]
him anything to do for his father or his mother,
(lit. nothing)
13 ἀκυροῦντες τὸν λόγον τοῦ θεοῦ τῇ.παραδόσει.ὑμῶν ᾗ
making void the word of God by your tradition which
παρεδώκατε· καὶ παρόμοια τοιαῦτα πολλὰ ποιεῖτε.
ye have delivered; and [3]like [[4]things] [2]such [1]many ye do.
14 Καὶ προσκαλεσάμενος [f]πάντα[‖] τὸν ὄχλον, ἔλεγεν αὐτοῖς,
And having called to [him] all the crowd, he said to them,
[g]Ἀκούετέ[‖] μου πάντες, καὶ [h]συνίετε.[‖] 15 οὐδέν ἐστιν ἔξω-
Hear ye me, all, and understand: Nothing there is from with-
θεν τοῦ ἀνθρώπου εἰσπορευόμενον εἰς αὐτόν, ὃ δύναται
out the man entering into him, which is able
[i]αὐτὸν κοινῶσαι·[‖] ἀλλὰ τὰ [k]ἐκπορευόμενα ἀπ' αὐτοῦ,[‖]
him to defile; but the things which go out from him,
[l]ἐκεῖνά[‖] ἐστιν τὰ κοινοῦντα τὸν ἄνθρωπον. 16 [m]εἴ τις
those are the things which defile the man. If anyone
ἔχει ὦτα ἀκούειν, ἀκουέτω.[‖] 17 Καὶ ὅτε εἰσῆλθεν εἰς [n] οἶκον
have ears to hear, let him hear. And when he went into a house
ἀπὸ τοῦ ὄχλου, ἐπηρώτων αὐτὸν οἱ.μαθηταὶ.αὐτοῦ [o]περὶ τῆς
from the crowd, [3]asked [4]him [1]his [2]disciples concerning the
παραβολῆς.[‖] 18 καὶ λέγει αὐτοῖς, Οὕτως καὶ ὑμεῖς ἀσύνε-
parable. And he says to them, [4]Thus [3]also [1]ye [5]without [6]un-
τοί ἐστε; οὐ.νοεῖτε ὅτι πᾶν τὸ ἔξωθεν εἰσπο-
derstanding [2]are? Perceive ye not that everything which from without en-
ρευόμενον εἰς τὸν ἄνθρωπον οὐ.δύναται αὐτὸν κοινῶσαι;
ters into the man is not able him to defile?
19 ὅτι οὐκ.εἰσπορεύεται αὐτοῦ εἰς τὴν καρδίαν, ἀλλ' εἰς τὴν
because it enters not [4]of [5]him [1]into [2]the [3]heart, but into the
κοιλίαν· καὶ εἰς τὸν ἀφεδρῶνα ἐκπορεύεται, [p]καθαρίζον[‖] πάντα
belly, and into the draught goes out, purifying all
τα βρώματα. 20 [q]Ἔλεγεν.δέ, "Ὅτι τὸ ἐκ τοῦ ἀνθρώπου
the food. And he said, That which out of the man
ἐκπορευόμενον, ἐκεῖνο κοινοῖ τὸν ἄνθρωπον. 21 ἔσωθεν.γὰρ
goes forth, that defiles the man. For from within
ἐκ τῆς καρδίας τῶν ἀνθρώπων οἱ διαλογισμοὶ οἱ κακοὶ ἐκ-
out of the heart of men [2]reasonings [1]evil go
πορεύονται, [q]μοιχεῖαι, πορνεῖαι, φόνοι, 22 κλοπαί,[‖] πλεον-
forth, adulteries, fornications, murders, thefts, covetous
εξίαι, πονηρίαι, δόλος, ἀσέλγεια, ὀφθαλμὸς πονηρός,
desires, wickednesses, guile, licentiousness, an eye wicked,
βλασφημία, ὑπερηφανία, ἀφροσύνη· 23 πάντα ταῦτα τὰ
blasphemy, haughtiness, folly: all these
πονηρὰ ἔσωθεν ἐκπορεύεται, καὶ κοινοῖ τὸν ἄνθρωπον.
evils from within go forth, and defile the man.
24 [r]Καὶ ἐκεῖθεν[‖] ἀναστὰς ἀπῆλθεν εἰς τὰ [s]μεθόρια[‖]
And thence having risen up he went away into the borders
Τύρου [t]καὶ Σιδῶνος[‖]. καὶ εἰσελθὼν εἰς [v]τὴν[‖] οἰκίαν, οὐδένα
of Tyre and Sidon; and having entered into the house, no one
[w]ἤθελεν[‖] γνῶναι, καὶ οὐκ.[x]ἠδυνήθη[‖] λαθεῖν. 25 [y]ἀκούσασα
he wished to know [it], and he could not be hid. [4]Having [5]heard

Him, Why is it that your disciples do not
walk according to the tradition of the elders,
but eat bread with unwashed hands?
6 But answering He said to them, Well did
Isaiah prophesy about you hypocrites, as it
has been written, "This people honor Me
with the lips, but their heart is far from Me.
7 But in vain they worship Me, teaching as
doctrines the commandments of men."
8 For laying aside the commandments of
God, you hold the tradition of men: washing
of pots and cups. And you do many other
such things.
9 And He said to them, Truly you reject the
commandment of God, so that you may
keep your own tradition.
10 For Moses said, "Honor your father and
your mother," and, "He who speaks evil of
father or mother, let him die the death."
11 But you say, If a man shall say to father
or mother, "Whatever you may gain by me,
Corban! (that is, A gift *to God*!)."
12 And you no longer allow him to do
anything for his father or his mother,
13 setting aside the word of God by your
tradition which you have delivered. And
many such things you do.
14 And calling all the crowd to Him, He
said to them, Everyone listen to me and
understand.
15 There is nothing from outside a man
which can enter into a man and defile him.
But the things that go out from him are the
things which defile the man.
16 If anyone has ears to hear, let him hear.
17 And when He went into a house away
from the people, His disciples asked Him
about the parable.
18 And He said to them, So you also are
without understanding? Do you not see that
everything which enters from outside into a
man is not able to defile him?
19 *It is* because it does not enter into his
heart but into the belly. And *then it* goes
out into the waste-bown, purifying all the
food.
20 And He said, That which comes out of
the man is that which defiles the man.
21 For from within, out of the heart of
men, come forth evil thoughts, adulteries,
fornications, murders,
22 thefts, greedy desires, wickednesses, deceit, lustful desires, a wicked eye,
blasphemy, pride, foolishness –
23 all these evil things come from within
and defile the man.

24 And He rose up from there and went
away into the borders of Tyre and Sidon.
And entering into the house, He wanted no
one to know. But He could not be hidden.
25 For hearing about Him, a certain woman
whose little daughter had a vicious spirit

γὰρ γυνὴ περὶ αὐτοῦ, ἧς εἶχεν τὸ.θυγάτριον.αὐτῆς πνεῦμα
for a woman about him, of whom had her little daughter a spirit
ἀκάθαρτον, [z]ἐλθοῦσα προσέπεσεν πρὸς τοὺς.πόδας.αὐτοῦ·
unclean, having come fell at his feet,
26 [a]ἦν.δὲ ἡ γυνὴ Ἑλληνίς, [b]Συροφοίνισσα τῷ γένει· καὶ
(now was the woman a Greek, Syrophenician by race), and
ἠρώτα αὐτὸν ἵνα τὸ δαιμόνιον [c]ἐκβάλλῃ ἐκ τῆς θυγατρὸς
asked him that the demon he should cast forth out of daughter
αὐτῆς. 27 [d]ὁ.δὲ.Ἰησοῦς εἶπεν αὐτῇ, Ἄφες πρῶτον χορτασ-
her. But Jesus said to her, Suffer first to be satis-
θῆναι τὰ τέκνα· οὐ.γὰρ [e]καλόν ἐστιν λαβεῖν τὸν ἄρτον τῶν
fied the children; for not good is it to take the bread of the
τέκνων, καὶ [f]βαλεῖν τοῖς κυναρίοις. 28 Ἡ.δὲ ἀπεκρίθη καὶ
children, and cast [it] to the dogs. But she answered and
λέγει αὐτῷ, Ναί, κύριε· καὶ.[g]γὰρ τὰ κυνάρια ὑποκάτω τῆς
says to him, Yea, Lord; for even the little dogs under the
τραπέζης [h]ἐσθίει ἀπὸ τῶν ψιχίων τῶν παιδίων. 29 Καὶ εἶπεν
table eat of the crumbs of the children. And he said
αὐτῇ, Διὰ τοῦτον τὸν λόγον ὕπαγε· ἐξελήλυθεν [i]τὸ δαι-
to her, Because of this word go; has gone forth the de-
μόνιον ἐκ τῆς.θυγατρός.σου. 30 Καὶ ἀπελθοῦσα εἰς τὸν
mon out of thy daughter. And having gone away to
οἶκον.αὐτῆς, εὗρεν [k]τὸ δαιμόνιον ἐξεληλυθός, καὶ τὴν θυγα-
her house, she found the demon had gone forth, and the daugh-
τέρα βεβλημένην ἐπὶ τῆς κλίνης.
ter laid on the bed.

31 Καὶ πάλιν ἐξελθὼν ἐκ τῶν ὁρίων Τύρου [l]καὶ Σιδῶνος,
And again having departed from the borders of Tyre and Sidon,
ἦλθεν [m]πρὸς τὴν θάλασσαν τῆς Γαλιλαίας, ἀνὰ μέσον
he came to the sea of Galilee, through [the] midst
τῶν ὁρίων Δεκαπόλεως. 32 καὶ φέρουσιν αὐτῷ κωφὸν [n]
of the borders of Decapolis. And they bring to him a deaf man
[o]μογιλάλον, καὶ παρακαλοῦσιν αὐτὸν ἵνα ἐπιθῇ
who spoke with difficulty, and they beseech him that he might lay
αὐτῷ τὴν χεῖρα. 33 καὶ ἀπολαβόμενος αὐτὸν ἀπὸ τοῦ
on him [his] hand. And having taken away him from the
ὄχλου κατ'.ἰδίαν, ἔβαλεν τοὺς.δακτύλους.[p]αὐτοῦ εἰς τὰ ὦτα
crowd apart, he put his fingers to ears
αὐτοῦ, καὶ πτύσας ἥψατο τῆς.γλώσσης.αὐτοῦ, 34 καὶ ἀνα-
his, and having spit he touched his tongue, and having
βλέψας εἰς τὸν οὐρανὸν ἐστέναξεν, καὶ λέγει αὐτῷ, Ἐφφαθά,
looked up to the heaven he groaned, and says to him, Ephphatha,
ὅ.ἐστιν, Διανοίχθητι. 35 Καὶ [q]εὐθέως [r]διηνοίχθησαν αὐτοῦ
that is, Be opened. And immediately were opened his
αἱ ἀκοαί, καὶ [s] ἐλύθη ὁ δεσμὸς τῆς.γλώσσης.αὐτοῦ, καὶ ἐλάλει
ears, and was loosed the band of his tongue, and he spoke
ὀρθῶς. 36 καὶ διεστείλατο αὐτοῖς ἵνα μηδενὶ [t]εἴπωσιν·
rightly. And he charged them that no one they should tell.
ὅσον.δὲ [v]αὐτὸς αὐτοῖς διεστέλλετο, [w]μᾶλλον περισσότερον
But as much as he them charged, exceeding more abundantly
ἐκήρυσσον. 37 καὶ ὑπερπερισσῶς ἐξεπλήσσοντο, λέγοντες,
they proclaimed [it]: and above measure they were astonished, saying,
Καλῶς πάντα πεποίηκεν· καὶ τοὺς κωφοὺς ποιεῖ ἀκούειν,
Well all things he has done: both the deaf he makes to hear,
καὶ [x]τοὺς ἀλάλους λαλεῖν.
and the dumb to speak.

8 Ἐν ἐκείναις.ταῖς.ἡμέραις [y]παμπόλλου ὄχλου ὄντος,
In those days very great [the] crowd being,
καὶ μὴ ἐχόντων τί φάγωσιν, προσκαλεσάμενος [z]ὁ Ἰη-
and not having what they may eat, having called to [him] Je-
σοῦς τοὺς.μαθητὰς.[a]αὐτοῦ λέγει αὐτοῖς, 2 Σπλαγχνίζομαι
sus his disciples he says to them, I am moved with compassion
ἐπὶ τὸν ὄχλον· ὅτι ἤδη [b]ἡμέρας τρεῖς προσμένουσίν [c]μοι,
on the crowd, because already days three they continue with me
καὶ οὐκ.ἔχουσιν τί φάγωσιν· 3 καὶ ἐὰν ἀπολύσω αὐτοὺς
and have not what they may eat; and if I shall send away them
[d]νήστεις εἰς οἶκον.αὐτῶν, ἐκλυθήσονται ἐν τῇ ὁδῷ· [e]τινὲς.γὰρ
fasting to their home, they will faint in the way; for some
αὐτῶν [f] μακρόθεν [g]ἥκασιν. 4 Καὶ ἀπεκρίθησαν αὐτῷ οἱ μαθη-
of them from afar are come. And answered him disci-
ταὶ αὐτοῦ, [h]Πόθεν τούτους δυνήσεταί τις ὧδε χορτάσαι
ples his, Whence these shall be able anyone here to satisfy
ἄρτων ἐπ'.ἐρημίας; 5 Καὶ [i]ἐπηρώτα αὐτούς, Πόσους ἔχετε
with bread in a desert? And he asked them, How many have ye
ἄρτους; Οἱ.δὲ [k]εἶπον, Ἑπτά. 6 Καὶ [l]παρήγγειλεν τῷ ὄχλῳ
loaves? And they said, Seven. And he ordered the crowd
ἀναπεσεῖν ἐπὶ τῆς γῆς· καὶ λαβὼν τοὺς ἑπτὰ ἄρτους,
to recline on the ground. And having taken the seven loaves,
[m]εὐχαριστήσας ἔκλασεν καὶ ἐδίδου τοῖς.μαθηταῖς.αὐτοῦ, ἵνα
having given thanks he broke and gave to his disciples, that
[n]παραθῶσιν· καὶ παρέθηκαν τῷ ὄχλῳ. 7 καὶ
they might set before [them]. And they set [it] before the crowd. And

came and fell down at His feet.
26 Now the woman was a Greek, a Syro-
phe-nic-i-an by race. And she begged Him
that He should throw the demon out of her
daughter.
27 But Jesus said to her, Let the children
first be filled, for it is not good to take the
children's bread and throw it to the dogs.
28 But she answered and said to Him, Yes,
Lord, for even the little dogs under the table
eat of the children's crumbs.
29 And He said to her, Because of these
words, Go! The demon has left your daughter.
30 And going away to her house, she found
the demon had left. And her daughter lay
upon the bed.
31 And again, He left the borders of Tyre
and Sidon and came to the sea of Galilee,
through the middle of the borders of
De-cap-o-lis.
32 And they brought a deaf man to Him,
one who spoke with difficulty. And they
asked Him to lay His hand on him.
33 And taking him away from the crowd,
He put His fingers to his ears. And He spit
and touched his tongue.
34 And looking up to Heaven, He groaned,
saying to him, Eph-pha-tha! (meaning, Be
opened!).
35 And immediately his ears were opened,
and the band on his tongue was removed.
And he spoke plainly.
36 And He commanded them that they
should tell no one. But as much as He
commanded them, *that* much more they
publicized it.
37 And they were astonished beyond com-
parison, saying, He has done all things well.
He makes both the deaf to hear and the
dumb to speak.

CHAPTER 8

1 In those days the crowd was very great.
And *they* had nothing to eat. Calling His
disciples to Him, Jesus said to them,
2 I am full of pity for the crowd because
they now have been with Me three days and
have nothing to eat.
3 And if I send them away to their homes
without any food, they will faint in the way
– for some of them come from far away.
4 And His disciples answered Him, From
where can anyone satisfy these with bread
here in the wilderness?
5 And He asked them, How many loaves do
you have? And they said, Seven.
6 And He commanded the people to rest on
the ground. And He took the seven loaves
and blessed *them, then* He broke and gave to
His disciples so that they might serve *them.*
And they set it before the people.
7 And they had a few small fish. And bless-

[o]εἶχον‖ ἰχθύδια ὀλίγα· καὶ [pa]εὐλογήσας [qa]εἶπεν παρα-
they had small fishes a few; and having blessed he desired [3]to [4]be [5]set
θεῖναι καὶ αὐτά.‖ 8 [r]ἔφαγον.δὲ‖ καὶ ἐχορτάσθησαν. καὶ
[6]before [[7]them] [2]also [1]these. And they ate and were satisfied. And
ἦραν περισσεύματα κλασμάτων ἑπτὰ [s]σπυρίδας.‖ 9 ἦσαν.δὲ
they took up [1]over [4]and [5]above [1]of [2]fragments seven baskets. And [5]were
[t]οἱ φαγόντες‖ ὡς τετρακισχίλιοι· καὶ ἀπέλυσεν αὐτούς.
[1]those [2]who [3]had [4]eaten about four thousand; and he sent [2]away [1]them.
10 Καὶ [v]εὐθέως‖ ἐμβὰς[w] εἰς τὸ πλοῖον μετὰ τῶν μαθητῶν
And immediately having entered into the ship with [2]disciples
αὐτοῦ, ἦλθεν εἰς τὰ μέρη Δαλμανουθά. 11 καὶ ἐξῆλθον οἱ
[1]his, he came into the parts of Dalmanutha. And [3]went [4]out [1]the
Φαρισαῖοι καὶ ἤρξαντο [x]συζητεῖν‖ αὐτῷ, ζητοῦντες παρ'
[2]Pharisees and began to dispute with him, seeking from
αὐτοῦ σημεῖον ἀπὸ τοῦ οὐρανοῦ, πειράζοντες αὐτόν. 12 καὶ
him a sign from the heaven, tempting him. And
ἀναστενάξας τῷ.πνεύματι.αὐτοῦ λέγει, Τί ἡ.γενεὰ.αὕτη
having groaned in his spirit he says, Why [2]this [3]generation
[y]σημεῖον ἐπιζητεῖ;‖ ἀμὴν λέγω [z]ὑμῖν,‖ εἰ.δοθήσεται τῇ
[4]a [5]sign [1]seeks? Verily I say to you, If there shall be given
γενεᾷ.ταύτῃ σημεῖον. 13 Καὶ ἀφεὶς αὐτούς, [a]ἐμβὰς
to this generation a sign. And having left them, having entered
πάλιν‖ [b]εἰς τὸ πλοῖον‖ ἀπῆλθεν εἰς τὸ πέραν.
again into the ship he went away to the other side.

14 Καὶ ἐπελάθοντο λαβεῖν ἄρτους, καὶ εἰ.μὴ ἕνα ἄρτον
And they forgot to take loaves, and except one loaf
οὐκ.εἶχον μεθ' ἑαυτῶν ἐν τῷ πλοίῳ. 15 καὶ διεστέλλετο
they had not [any] with them in the ship. And he charged
αὐτοῖς, λέγων, Ὁρᾶτε, [c]βλέπετε ἀπὸ τῆς ζύμης τῶν Φαρισαίων
them, saying, See, take heed of the leaven of the Pharisees
καὶ τῆς ζύμης Ἡρῴδου. 16 Καὶ διελογίζοντο πρὸς ἀλλήλους,
and of the leaven of Herod. And they reasoned with one another,
[d]λέγοντες,‖ Ὅτι ἄρτους οὐκ [e]ἔχομεν.‖ 17 Καὶ γνοὺς
saying, Because loaves [3]not [1]we [2]have. And knowing [it]
[f]ὁ Ἰησοῦς‖ λέγει αὐτοῖς, Τί διαλογίζεσθε ὅτι ἄρτους οὐκ
Jesus says to them, Why reason ye because loaves [3]not
ἔχετε; οὔπω.νοεῖτε οὐδὲ.συνίετε; [g]ἔτι‖ πεπωρωμένην
[1]ye [2]have? Do ye not yet perceive nor understand? Yet hardened
ἔχετε τὴν.καρδίαν.ὑμῶν; 18 ὀφθαλμοὺς ἔχοντες οὐ.βλέπετε;
have ye your heart? Eyes having, do ye not see?
καὶ ὦτα ἔχοντες οὐκ.ἀκούετε; καὶ οὐ.μνημονεύετε; 19 ὅτε
and ears having, do ye not hear? and do ye not remember? When
τοὺς πέντε ἄρτους ἔκλασα εἰς τοὺς πεντακισχιλίους, [h]πόσους
the five loaves I broke to the five thousand, how many
κοφίνους [i]πλήρεις κλασμάτων‖ ἤρατε; Λέγουσιν αὐτῷ,
hand-baskets full of fragments took ye up? They say to him,
Δώδεκα. 20 [j]Ὅτε.[k]δὲ‖ τοὺς ἑπτὰ [l]εἰς τοὺς τετρακισχιλίους,
Twelve. And when the seven to the four thousand,
πόσων σπυρίδων πληρώματα κλασμάτων ἤρατε; [m]Οἱ.δὲ
of how many baskets [the] fillings of fragments took ye up? And they
εἶπον,‖ Ἑπτά. 21 Καὶ ἔλεγεν αὐτοῖς, [n]Πῶς‖ [o]οὐ‖ συνίετε;
said, Seven. And he said to them, How [3]not [1]do [2]ye understand?
22 Καὶ [p]ἔρχεται‖ εἰς Βηθσαϊδάν· καὶ φέρουσιν αὐτῷ τυφλόν,
And he comes to Bethsaida; and they bring to him a blind
καὶ παρακαλοῦσιν αὐτὸν ἵνα αὐτοῦ ἅψηται. 23 καὶ
[man], and beseech him that him he might touch. And
ἐπιλαβόμενος τῆς χειρὸς τοῦ τυφλοῦ [q]ἐξήγαγεν‖ αὐτὸν
taking hold of the hand of the blind [man] he led forth him
ἔξω τῆς κώμης, καὶ πτύσας εἰς τὰ.ὄμματα.αὐτοῦ, ἐπιθεὶς
out of the village, and having spit upon his eyes, having laid
τὰς χεῖρας αὐτῷ ἐπηρώτα αὐτὸν εἴ τι [r]βλέπει.‖ 24 καὶ
[his] hands upon him he asked him if anything he beholds. And
ἀναβλέψας ἔλεγεν, Βλέπω τοὺς ἀνθρώπους, [s]ὅτι ὡς δένδρα
having looked up he said, I behold the men, for as trees
ὁρῶ‖ περιπατοῦντας. 25 Εἶτα πάλιν [t]ἐπέθηκεν‖ τὰς
I see [them] walking. Then again he laid [his]
χεῖρας ἐπὶ τοὺς.ὀφθαλμοὺς.αὐτοῦ, καὶ [v]ἐποίησεν αὐτὸν ἀνα-
hands upon his eyes, and made him look
βλέψαι.‖ καὶ [w]ἀποκατεστάθη,‖ καὶ [x]ἐνέβλεψεν‖ [y]τηλαυγῶς‖
up. And he was restored, and looked [2]on [1]clearly
[z]ἅπαντας.‖ 26 καὶ ἀπέστειλεν αὐτὸν εἰς [a]τὸν.‖οἶκον.αὐτοῦ,
all [men]. And he sent him to his house,
λέγων, [b]Μηδὲ‖ εἰς τὴν κώμην εἰσέλθῃς. [c]μηδὲ εἴπῃς
saying, Neither into the village mayest thou enter, nor mayest tell [it]
τινὶ ἐν τῇ κώμῃ.‖
to any one in the village.
27 Καὶ ἐξῆλθεν ὁ Ἰησοῦς καὶ οἱ.μαθηταὶ.αὐτοῦ εἰς τὰς κώ-
And [2]went [3]forth [1]Jesus and his disciples into the vil-
μας Καισαρείας τῆς Φιλίππου· καὶ ἐν τῇ ὁδῷ ἐπηρώτα
lages of Cæsarea Philippi. And by the way he was questioning
τοὺς.μαθητὰς.αὐτοῦ, λέγων [d]αὐτοῖς,‖ Τίνα με λέγουσιν οἱ
his disciples, saying to them, Whom [2]me [1]do [3]pronounce

ing, He also ordered these set before *them.*
8 And they ate and were satisfied. And they took up that which was left over of broken pieces, seven baskets full.
9 And those who had eaten were about four thousand. And He sent them away.
10 And immediately entering into the ship with His disciples, He came into the parts of Dal-ma-nu-tha.
11 And the Pharisees went out and began to argue with Him, looking for a sign from Heaven from Him, tempting Him.
12 And groaning in His spirit, He said, Why does this generation look for a sign? Truly I say to you, No sign shall be given this generation.
13 And leaving them there, He went into the ship again and went away to the other side.

14 And they forgot to take bread. And except for one loaf, they did not have any with them in the ship.
15 And He ordered them, saying, Be careful! Beware of the leaven of the Pharisees and of the leaven of Herod.
16 And they reasoned with one another, saying, *It is* because we have no bread.
17 And He knew and said to them, Why do you reason because you have no bread? Do you not yet see nor understand? Have you hardened your heart?
18 Do you have ears and do not see? And do you have ears and do not hear? And do you not remember?
19 When I broke the five loaves to the five thousand, how many baskets full of pieces did you take up? They said, Twelve.
20 And when *I broke* the seven *loaves* to the four thousand, how many baskets full of pieces did you take up? And they said, Seven.
21 And He said to them, How can it be that you do not understand?
22 And He came to Beth-sa-i-da. And they brought to Him a blind one and begged Him to touch him.
23 And taking hold of the blind one, He led him out of the town. And when He had spit on his eyes and had laid hands on him, He asked him if he saw anything.
24 And looking up he said, I see men. For as trees I see *them* walking.
25 Then again He laid His hands on his eyes and made him look up. And he was cured and saw everything clearly.
26 And He sent him away to his house, saying, But you may not go into the town and tell it to anyone in the town.
27 And Jesus and His disciples went out into the towns of Cae-sa-re-a Phil-ip-pi. And in the highway He asked His disciples, saying to them, Who do men say that I am?

ἄνθρωποι εἶναι; 28 Οἱ.δὲ [e]ἀπεκρίθησαν,[f] [g]Ἰωάννην τον βαπ-
²men to be? And they answered, John the Bap-
τιστήν· καὶ ἄλλοι [h]Ἡλίαν· ἄλλοι.δὲ [i]ἕνα τῶν.προφητῶν.
tist; and others, Elias; but others, one of the prophets.
29 Καὶ αὐτὸς [k]λέγει αὐτοῖς, Ὑμεῖς.δὲ τίνα με λέγετε
And he says to them, But ye, whom ⁴me ¹do ²ye ³pronounce
εἶναι; [l]Ἀποκριθεὶς [m]δὲ ὁ Πέτρος λέγει αὐτῷ, Σὺ.εἶ ὁ χριστός.
to be? ²Answering ¹and Peter says to him, Thou art the Christ.
30 Καὶ ἐπετίμησεν αὐτοῖς ἵνα μηδενὶ [n]λέγωσιν περὶ
And he strictly charged them that no one they should tell concerning
αὐτοῦ. 31 Καὶ ἤρξατο διδάσκειν αὐτοὺς ὅτι δεῖ τὸν
him. And he began to teach them that it is necessary for the
υἱὸν τοῦ ἀνθρώπου πολλὰ παθεῖν, καὶ ἀποδοκιμασθῆναι
Son of man many things to suffer, and to be rejected
[o]ἀπὸ τῶν πρεσβυτέρων καὶ [pa]ἀρχιερέων καὶ [pa]γραμματέων, και
of the elders and chief priests and scribes, and
ἀποκτανθῆναι, καὶ μετὰ τρεῖς ἡμέρας ἀναστῆναι· 32 καὶ
to be killed, and after three days to rise [again]. And
παῤῥησίᾳ τὸν λόγον ἐλάλει. Καὶ προσλαβόμενος [qa]αὐτὸν
openly the word he spoke. And ²having ³taken ⁵to [⁶him] ⁴him
ὁ Πέτρος ἤρξατο ἐπιτιμᾷν αὐτῷ. 33 ὁ.δὲ ἐπιστραφεὶς καὶ
¹Peter began to rebuke him. But he, turning and
ἰδὼν τοὺς.μαθητὰς.αὐτοῦ, ἐπετίμησεν [r]τῷ Πέτρῳ, [s]λέγων,
seeing his disciples, rebuked Peter, saying,
Ὕπαγε ὀπίσω μου, σατανᾶ· ὅτι οὐ.φρονεῖς τὰ
Get behind me, Satan, for thy thoughts are not of the things
τοῦ θεοῦ, ἀλλὰ τὰ τῶν ἀνθρώπων.
of God, but the things of men.
34 Καὶ προσκαλεσάμενος τὸν ὄχλον σὺν τοῖς μαθηταῖς
And having called to [him] the crowd with ²disciples
αὐτοῦ εἶπεν αὐτοῖς, [t]Ὅστις θέλει ὀπίσω μου [v]ἐλθεῖν, ἀπαρ-
¹his he said to them, Whosoever desires after me to come, let
νησάσθω ἑαυτόν, καὶ ἀράτω τὸν.σταυρὸν.αὐτοῦ, καὶ
him deny himself, and let him take up his cross, and
ἀκολουθείτω μοι. 35 ὃς.γὰρ.[w]ἂν θέλῃ τὴν.ψυχὴν.αὐτοῦ
let him follow me. For whoever may desire his life
σῶσαι, ἀπολέσει αὐτήν· ὃς.δ'.ἂν [x]ἀπολέσῃ τὴν.[y]ψυχὴν.αὐτοῦ
to save, shall lose it, but whoever may lose his life
ἕνεκεν ἐμοῦ καὶ τοῦ εὐαγγελίου, [z]οὗτος σώσει αὐτήν.
on account of me and of the glad tidings, he shall save it.
36 τί.γὰρ [a]ὠφελήσει [b]ἄνθρωπον [c]ἐὰν κερδήσῃ τὸν κόσμον
For what shall it profit a man if he gain the ²world
ὅλον καὶ [d]ζημιωθῇ τὴν.ψυχὴν.αὐτοῦ; 37 [e]ἢ τί δώσει
¹whole and lose his soul? or what shall ³give
ἄνθρωπος ἀντάλλαγμα τῆς.ψυχῆς.αὐτοῦ; 38 ὃς.γὰρ.[f]ἂν
¹a ²man [as] an exchange for his soul? For whoever
ἐπαισχυνθῇ με καὶ τοὺς ἐμοὺς λόγους ἐν τῇ.γενεᾷ.ταύτῃ
may have been ashamed of me and my words in this generation
τῇ μοιχαλίδι καὶ ἁμαρτωλῷ, καὶ ὁ υἱὸς τοῦ ἀνθρώπου ἐπαισ-
the adulterous and sinful, also the Son of man will be
χυνθήσεται αὐτόν, ὅταν ἔλθῃ ἐν τῇ δόξῃ τοῦ.πατρὸς.αὐτοῦ
ashamed of him when he shall come in the glory of his Father
μετὰ τῶν ἀγγέλων τῶν ἁγίων. 9 Καὶ ἔλεγεν αὐτοῖς, Ἀμὴν
with the angels the holy. And he said to them, Verily
λέγω ὑμῖν, ὅτι εἰσίν τινες [g]τῶν ὧδε ἑστηκότων, οἵτινες
I say to you, That there are some of those here standing, who
οὐ.μὴ γεύσωνται θανάτου ἕως.ἂν ἴδωσιν τὴν βασιλείαν τοῦ
in no wise shall taste of death until they see the kingdom
θεοῦ ἐληλυθυῖαν ἐν δυνάμει.
of God having come in power.
2 Καὶ [h]μεθ' ἡμέρας ἓξ παραλαμβάνει ὁ Ἰησοῦς τὸν
And after ²days ¹six ²takes ³with [⁶him] ¹Jesus
Πέτρον καὶ [i]τὸν Ἰάκωβον καὶ [k]τὸν Ἰωάννην, καὶ ἀναφέρει
Peter and James and John, and brings up
αὐτοὺς εἰς ὄρος ὑψηλὸν κατ'.ἰδίαν μόνους· καὶ μετεμορ-
them into a ²mountain ¹high apart alone. And he was trans-
φώθη ἔμπροσθεν αὐτῶν, 3 καὶ τὰ.ἱμάτια.αὐτοῦ [l]ἐγένετο
figured before them; and his garments became
στίλβοντα, λευκὰ λίαν [m]ὡς χιών, οἷα γναφεὺς ἐπὶ τῆς
shining, white exceedingly as snow, such as a fuller on the
γῆς οὐ.δύναται [n] λευκᾶναι. 4 καὶ ὤφθη αὐτοῖς [o]Ἠλίας σὺν
earth is not able to whiten. And ⁴appeared ⁵to ⁶them ¹Elias ²with
[p]Μωσεῖ, καὶ ἦσαν [q]συλλαλοῦντες τῷ Ἰησοῦ. 5 καὶ ἀποκριθεὶς
³Moses, and they were talking with Jesus. And ²answering
ὁ.Πέτρος λέγει τῷ Ἰησοῦ, [r]Ῥαββί, καλόν ἐστιν ἡμᾶς ὧδε
¹Peter says to Jesus, Rabbi, good it is for us here
εἶναι· καὶ ποιήσωμεν [s]σκηνὰς τρεῖς, σοὶ μίαν, καὶ [p]Μω-
to be; and let us make ²tabernacles ¹three, for thee one, and for Mo-
σεῖ μίαν, καὶ [t]Ἠλίᾳ μίαν. 6 οὐ.γὰρ.ᾔδει τί [v]λαλήσῃ·
ses one, and for Elias one. For he knew not what he should say,
[w]ἦσαν.γὰρ ἔκφοβοι. 7 καὶ ἐγένετο νεφέλη ἐπισκιάζουσα
for they were greatly afraid. And there came a cloud overshadowing

28 And they answered, John the Baptist. And others say, Elijah, but others, One of the prophets.
29 And He said to them, But who do you say that I am? And Peter answered and said to Him, You are the Christ!
30 And He strictly commanded them that they should not tell anyone about Him.
31 And He began to teach them that the Son of man must suffer many things and be rejected by the elders and by the chief priests and scribes – and be killed, and after three days rise again.
32 And He spoke the word openly. And taking im *aside* Peter began to rebuke Him.
33 But turning and looking on His disciples, He rebuked Peter, saying, Get behind Me, Satan! For your thoughts are not of the things of God, but of the things of men.
34 And calling the crowd together with His disciples, He said to them, Whoever desires to come after Me, let him deny himself and take up his cross and follow Me.
35 For whoever wants to save his life shall lose it, but whoever shall lose his life for My sake and for the gospel shall save it.
36 For what shall it profit a man if he gain the whole world and lose his own soul?
37 Or what shall a man give in exchange for his soul?
38 Whoever, then, shall be ashamed of Me and of My words in this adulterous and sinful generation, the Son of man shall also be ashamed of him when He comes with the holy angels in the glory of His Father.

CHAPTER 9

1 And He said to them, Truly I say to you that there are some of those standing here who shall in no way taste of death until they see the kingdom of God coming in power.
2 And after six days Jesus took Peter and James and John with Him. And He brought them up into a high mountain, alone, by themselves. And He was gloriously changed before them.
3 And His clothes became bright, exceedingly white as snow, in a way that no bleacher on earth could whiten them.
4 And Elijah appeared to them with Moses, and they were talking with Jesus.
5 And Peter answered and said to Jesus, Master, it is good for us to be here. Let us make three tabernacles, one for You and one for Moses and one for Elijah.
6 For he did not know what he should say, for they were greatly afraid.
7 And there came a cloud overshadowing them. And there came a voice out of the

αὐτοῖς· καὶ [x]ἦλθεν‖ φωνὴ ἐκ τῆς νεφέλης, [y]λέγουσα,‖ Οὗτός
them; and there came a voice out of the cloud, saying, This
ἐστιν ὁ.υἱός.μου ὁ ἀγαπητός· [z]αὐτοῦ ἀκούετε‖ 8 Καὶ ἐξάπινα
is my Son the beloved: [3]him [1]hear [2]ye. And suddenly
περιβλεψάμενοι οὐκέτι.οὐδένα εἶδον, [a]ἀλλὰ‖ τὸν Ἰησοῦν
having looked around no longer any one they saw, but Jesus
μόνον μεθ' ἑαυτῶν. 9 [b]Καταβαινόντων.δὲ‖ αὐτῶν [c]ἀπὸ‖ τοῦ
alone with themselves. And as [2]were [3]descending [1]they from the
ὄρους διεστείλατο αὐτοῖς ἵνα μηδενὶ [d]διηγήσωνται ἃ εἶ-
mountain he charged them that to no one they should relate what they
δον,‖ εἰ.μὴ ὅταν ὁ υἱὸς τοῦ ἀνθρώπου ἐκ νεκρῶν
had seen except when the Son of man from among [the] dead
ἀναστῇ. 10 καὶ τὸν λόγον ἐκράτησαν πρὸς ἑαυτούς, [e]συζη-
be risen. And that saying they kept among themselves, ques-
τοῦντες‖ τί ἐστιν τὸ ἐκ νεκρῶν ἀναστῆναι.
tioning what is the [2]from [3]among [[4]the] [5]dead [1]rising.
11 Καὶ ἐπηρώτων αὐτόν, λέγοντες, [f]Ὅτι‖ λέγουσιν [g] οἱ γραμ-
And they asked him, saying, That [3]say [1]the [2]scribes
ματεῖς ὅτι [h]Ἠλίαν‖ δεῖ ἐλθεῖν πρῶτον; 12 Ὁ.δὲ [i]ἀποκριθεὶς
that Elias must come first? And he answering
εἶπεν‖ αὐτοῖς, [k]Ἠλίας‖ [l]μὲν‖ ἐλθὼν πρῶτον, [m]ἀποκαθιστᾷ‖
said to them, Elias indeed having come first, restores
πάντα· καὶ πῶς γέγραπται ἐπὶ τὸν υἱὸν τοῦ ἀνθρώπου[na]
all things; and how it has been written of the Son of man
ἵνα πολλὰ πάθῃ καὶ [oa]ἐξουδενωθῇ.‖ 13 ἀλλὰ λέγω
that many things he should suffer and be set at nought: but I say
ὑμῖν, ὅτι καὶ [k]Ἠλίας‖ ἐλήλυθεν, καὶ ἐποίησαν αὐτῷ ὅσα
to you, that also Elias has come, and they did to him whatever
[pa]ἠθέλησαν,‖ καθὼς γέγραπται ἐπ' αὐτόν.
they desired, as it has been written of him.
14 Καὶ [qa]ἐλθὼν‖ πρὸς τοὺς μαθητὰς [ra]εἶδεν‖ ὄχλον πολὺν
And having come to the disciples he saw a [2]crowd [1]great
περὶ αὐτούς, καὶ γραμματεῖς [sa]συζητοῦντας [ta]αὐτοῖς.‖ 15 καὶ
around them, and scribes discussing with them. And
[va]εὐθέως‖ πᾶς ὁ ὄχλος [wa]ἰδὼν‖ αὐτὸν [xa]ἐξεθαμβήθη,‖ καὶ
immediately all the crowd seeing him were greatly amazed, and
προστρέχοντες ἠσπάζοντο αὐτόν. 16 καὶ ἐπηρώτησεν [y]τοὺς
running to [him] saluted him. And he asked the
γραμματεῖς,‖ Τί [z]συζητεῖτε‖ πρὸς [a]αὐτούς;‖ 17 Καὶ [b]ἀπο-
scribes, What discuss ye with them? And an-
κριθεὶς‖ εἷς ἐκ τοῦ ὄχλου [c]εἶπεν,‖ Διδάσκαλε, ἤνεγκα τὸν υἱόν
swering one out of the crowd said, Teacher, I brought [2]son
μου πρός σε, ἔχοντα πνεῦμα ἄλαλον. 18 καὶ ὅπου.[d]ἂν‖ αὐτὸν
[1]my to thee, having a [2]spirit [1]dumb; and wheresoever him
καταλάβῃ ῥήσσει [e]αὐτόν·‖ καὶ ἀφρίζει, καὶ τρίζει τοὺς
it seizes it dashes [2]down [1]him; and he foams, and gnashes
ὀδόντας.[f]αὐτοῦ,‖ καὶ ξηραίνεται· καὶ [g]εἶπον‖ τοῖς μαθηταῖς
his teeth, and is withering away. And I spoke to [2]disciples
σου ἵνα αὐτὸ ἐκβάλωσιν, καὶ οὐκ.ἴσχυσαν. 19 Ὁ.δὲ ἀπο-
[1]thy that it they might cast out, and they had not power. But he an-
κριθεὶς [h]αὐτῷ‖ λέγει, [i]Ὦ γενεὰ ἄπιστος, ἕως πότε πρὸς ὑμᾶς
swering him says, O [2]generation [1]unbelieving! until when with you
ἔσομαι; ἕως πότε ἀνέξομαι ὑμῶν; φέρετε αὐτὸν πρός με.
shall I be? until when shall I bear with you? Bring him to me.
20 Καὶ ἤνεγκαν αὐτὸν πρὸς αὐτόν· καὶ ἰδὼν αὐτὸν [i]εὐθέως
And they brought him to him. And seeing him immediately
τὸ πνεῦμα‖ [k]ἐσπάραξεν‖ αὐτόν, καὶ πεσὼν ἐπὶ τῆς
the spirit threw [2]into [3]convulsions [1]him, and having fallen upon the
γῆς ἐκυλίετο ἀφρίζων. 21 Καὶ ἐπηρώτησεν τὸν.πατέρα.αὐτοῦ,
earth he rolled foaming. And he asked his father,
Πόσος χρόνος ἐστὶν ὡς τοῦτο γέγονεν αὐτῷ; Ὁ.δὲ εἶπεν,
How long a time is it that this has been with him? And he said,
[l]Παιδιόθεν. 22 καὶ πολλάκις [m]αὐτὸν καὶ εἰς πῦρ‖ ἔβαλεν καὶ
From childhood. And often him both into fire it cast and
εἰς ὕδατα, ἵνα ἀπολέσῃ αὐτόν· [n]ἀλλ'‖ εἴ τι [o]δύνασαι,‖
into waters, that it might destroy him: but if anything thou art able
βοήθησον ἡμῖν, σπλαγχνισθεὶς ἐφ' ἡμᾶς. 23 Ὁ.δὲ.Ἰη-
[to do], help us, being moved with pity on us. And Je-
σοῦς εἶπεν αὐτῷ, Τὸ εἰ [o]δύνασαι‖ [p]πιστεῦσαι,‖ πάντα δυνατὰ
sus said to him, If thou art able to believe, all things are possible
τῷ πιστεύοντι. 24 [q]Καὶ‖ [r]εὐθέως‖ κράξας ὁ πατὴρ τοῦ
to him that believes. And immediately crying out the father of the
παιδίου [s]μετὰ δακρύων‖ ἔλεγεν, Πιστεύω, [t]Κύριε,‖ βοήθει
little child with tears said, I believe, Lord, help
μου.τῇ.ἀπιστίᾳ. 25 Ἰδὼν.δὲ ὁ Ἰησοῦς ὅτι ἐπισυντρέχει [v]
mine unbelief. But [2]seeing [1]Jesus that [3]was [4]running [5]together
ὄχλος, ἐπετίμησεν τῷ πνεύματι τῷ ἀκαθάρτῳ, λέγων αὐτῷ,
[1]a [2]crowd, rebuked the spirit the unclean, saying to it,
Τὸ [w]πνεῦμα τὸ ἄλαλον καὶ κωφόν,‖ ἐγὼ [x]σοι ἐπιτάσσω,‖ ἔξελθε
Spirit dumb and deaf, I thee command, come
[ya]ἐξ‖ αὐτοῦ, καὶ μηκέτι εἰσέλθῃς εἰς αὐτόν. 26 Καὶ [za]κρά-
out of him, and no more mayest thou enter into him. And having

cloud, saying, This is My beloved Son! Listen to Him!

8 And suddenly they looked around and no longer saw anyone with them, only Jesus.

9 And as they were coming down from the mountain, He commanded them not to tell anyone what they had seen, except when the Son of man should rise from the dead.

10 And they kept that saying among themselves, questioning with one another what the rising from the dead might be.

11 And they asked Him, saying, The scribes say that Elijah must come first?

12 And answering He said to them, Indeed Elijah does come first and restore all things. And has it not been written that the Son of man must suffer many things and be despised?

13 But I say to you that Elijah also has come. And they did to him all that they desired to do, as it is written of him.

14 And coming to the disciples, He saw a great crowd around them. And scribes *were* questioning with them.

15 And immediately all the crowd was much astonished to see Him. And they ran up to Him and greeted Him.

16 And He asked the scribes, What are you asking them?

17 And one answered out of the crowd and said, Teacher, I brought my son to You. For he has a spirit that will not let him speak.

18 And wherever it seizes him, it tears him. And he foams and gnashes his teeth and is wasting away. And I spoke to Your disciples to throw it out. But they could not.

19 But He answered him, saying, O unbelieving generation! How long shall I be with you? How long shall I bear with you? Bring him to Me.

20 And they brought him to Him. And when the spirit saw Him, *he* immediately threw him into fits. And he fell on the ground and was wallowing and foaming.

21 And He asked his father, How long is it that this has been happening to him? And he said, From childhood.

22 And it often throws him both into fire and into waters in order to destroy him. But if You are able to do anything, help us. Have pity on us.

23 And Jesus said to him, If you are able to believe, all things are possible to him that believes.

24 And crying out with tears in his eyes, the father of the child immediately said, I believe, Lord! Help my unbelief!

25 But Jesus saw that the people were running together. And *He* rebuked the impure spirit, saying to it, Deaf and dumb spirit, I command you, Come out of him! And you may never enter into him again.

26 And crying out, and tearing him, it came

ξαν,ǁ καὶ πολλὰ [aa]σπαράξανǁ [ba]αὐτόν,ǁ ἐξῆλθεν· καὶ
cried out, and [3]much [1]thrown [4]into [5]convulsions [2]him, it came out, and
ἐγένετο ὡσεὶ νεκρός, ὥστε [ca]πολλοὺς λέγειν ὅτι ἀπέθανεν.
he became as if dead, so that many said that he was dead.
27 ὁ.δὲ.Ἰησοῦς κρατήσας [d]αὐτὸν τῆς χειρόςǁ ἤγειρεν αὐτόν,
But Jesus, having taken him by the hand, raised [2]up [1]him,
καὶ ἀνέστη.
and he arose.

28 Καὶ [e]εἰσελθόντα.αὐτὸνǁ εἰς οἶκον οἱ.μαθηταὶ.αὐτοῦ
And when he was entered into a house his disciples
[f]ἐπηρώτων αὐτὸν κατ'.ἰδίαν,ǁ [g]"Ὅτιǁ ἡμεῖς οὐκ.ἠδυνή-
asked him apart, Because [of what] [2]we [1]were not
θημεν ἐκβαλεῖν αὐτό; 29 Καὶ εἶπεν αὐτοῖς, Τοῦτο τὸ γένος
able to cast out it? And he said to them, This kind
ἐν οὐδενὶ δύναται ἐξελθεῖν εἰ.μὴ ἐν προσευχῇ [h]καὶ νηστείᾳ.ǁ
by nothing can go out except by prayer and fasting.

30 [i]Καὶ ἐκεῖθενǁ ἐξελθόντες [k]παρεπορεύοντοǁ διὰ τῆς
And from thence having gone forth they went through
Γαλιλαίας· καὶ οὐκ.ἤθελεν ἵνα τις [l]γνῷ·ǁ 31 ἐδίδασ-
Galilee; and he would not that anyone should know [it]; [2]he [3]was [4]teach-
κεν γὰρ τοὺς.μαθητὰς.αὐτοῦ, καὶ ἔλεγεν αὐτοῖς, "Ὅτι ὁ υἱὸς
ing [1]for his disciples, and said to them, The Son
τοῦ ἀνθρώπου παραδίδοται εἰς χεῖρας ἀνθρώπων, καὶ
of man is delivered into [the] hands of men, and
ἀποκτενοῦσιν αὐτόν· καὶ ἀποκτανθείς, [m]τῇ τρίτῃ ἡμέρᾳǁ
they will kill him; and having been killed, on the third day
ἀναστήσεται. 32 Οἱ.δὲ ἠγνόουν τὸ ῥῆμα, καὶ ἐφοβοῦντο
he will arise. But they understood not the saying, and were afraid
αὐτὸν ἐπερωτῆσαι.
[3]him [1]to [2]ask.

33 Καὶ [n]ἦλθενǁ εἰς [o]Καπερναούμ·ǁ καὶ ἐν τῇ οἰκίᾳ γενόμενος
And he came to Capernaum; and [2]in [3]the [4]house [1]being
ἐπηρώτα αὐτούς, Τί ἐν τῇ ὁδῷ [p]πρὸς ἑαυτοὺςǁ διελογίζεσθε;
he asked them, What in the way among yourselves were ye discussing?
34 Οἱ.δὲ ἐσιώπων· πρὸς ἀλλήλους γὰρ διελέχθησαν [q]ἐν
But they were silent; [2]with [3]one [4]another [1]for they had been discussing by
τῇ ὁδῷ,ǁ τίς μείζων. 35 καὶ καθίσας ἐφώνησεν τοὺς
the way, who [was] greater. And sitting down he called the
δώδεκα, καὶ λέγει αὐτοῖς, Εἴ τις θέλει πρῶτος εἶναι, ἔσται
twelve, and he says to them, If anyone desires [3]first [1]to [2]be, he shall be
πάντων ἔσχατος καὶ πάντων διάκονος. 36 Καὶ λαβὼν
[2]of [3]all [1]last and [2]of [3]all [1]servant. And having taken
παιδίον ἔστησεν αὐτὸ ἐν μέσῳ.αὐτῶν· καὶ ἐναγκαλισάμενος
a little child he set it in their midst; and having taken [2]in [3]his] [4]arms
αὐτὸ εἶπεν αὐτοῖς, 37 "Ὃς.ἐὰνǁ ἓν τῶν [s]τοιούτων παιδίωνǁ
[1]it he said to them, Whoever one of such little children
δέξηται ἐπὶ τῷ.ὀνόματί.μου, ἐμὲ δέχεται· καὶ ὃς.[r]ἐὰνǁ ἐμὲ
shall receive in my name, me receives; and whoever me
[t]δέξηται,ǁ οὐκ ἐμὲ δέχεται, ἀλλὰ τὸν ἀποστείλαντά με.
shall receive, not me receives, but him who sent me.
38 [u]'Απεκρίθη.δὲǁ αὐτῷ [v]ὁǁ Ἰωάννης [w]λέγων,ǁ Διδάσκαλε, εἴδομέν
And [2]answered [3]him [1]John saying, Teacher, we saw
τινα [x]τῷ.ὀνόματί.σου ἐκβάλλοντα δαιμόνια, [y]ὃς οὐκ.ἀκολουθεῖ
some one in thy name casting out demons, who follows not
ἡμῖν·ǁ καὶ [z]ἐκωλύσαμενǁ αὐτόν, [a]ὅτι οὐκ.ἀκολουθεῖ ἡμῖν.ǁ
us, and we forbade him, because he follows not us.
39 'Ο.δὲ.Ἰησοῦς εἶπεν, Μὴ.κωλύετε αὐτόν· οὐδεὶς.γάρ ἐστιν
But Jesus said, Forbid not him; for no one there is
ὃς ποιήσει δύναμιν ἐπὶ τῷ.ὀνόματί.μου, καὶ δυνήσεται
who shall do a work of power in my name, and be able
ταχὺ κακολογῆσαί με. 40 ὃς.γὰρ οὐκ.ἔστιν καθ' [b]ὑμῶν,ǁ ὑπὲρ
readily to speak evil of me; for he who is not against you, for
[b]ὑμῶνǁ ἐστιν. 41 ὃς.γὰρ.ἂν ποτίσῃ ὑμᾶς ποτήριον
you is. For whoever may give [2]to [3]drink [1]you a cup
ὕδατος ἐν [c]τῷǁ.ὀνόματί.[d]μου,ǁ ὅτι χριστοῦ ἐστε, ἀμὴν λέγω
of water in my name, because [3]Christ's [1]ye [2]are, verily I say
ὑμῖν, [e]οὐ.μὴ [f]ἀπολέσῃǁ τὸν.μισθὸν.αὐτοῦ. 42 Καὶ ὃς.ἂν
to you, in no wise should he lose his reward. And whoever
σκανδαλίσῃ ἕνα τῶν μικρῶν [g]τῶν [h]πιστευόντων εἰς
may cause [5]to [6]offend [1]one [2]of [3]the [4]little ones who believe in
ἐμέ,ǁ καλόν ἐστιν αὐτῷ μᾶλλον εἰ περίκειται [i]λίθος.μυλικὸςǁ
me, good it is for him rather if is put a millstone
περὶ τὸν.τράχηλον.αὐτοῦ, καὶ βέβληται εἰς τὴν θάλασσαν.
about his neck, and he has been cast into the sea.

43 Καὶ ἐὰν [k]σκανδαλίζῃǁ σε ἡ.χείρ.σου, ἀπόκοψον αὐτήν·
And if [3]should [4]cause [5]to [6]offend [2]thee [1]thy [2]hand, cut off it:
καλόν [l]σοι ἐστὶνǁ κυλλὸν [m]εἰς τὴν ζωὴν εἰσελθεῖν,ǁ
good for thee it is maimed into life to enter, [rather]
ἢ τὰς δύο χεῖρας ἔχοντα ἀπελθεῖν εἰς τὴν γέενναν, εἰς τὸ
than the two hands having to go away into the Gehenna, into the
πῦρ τὸ ἄσβεστον, 44 [n]ὅπου ὁ.σκώληξ.αὐτῶν οὐ.τελευτᾷ, καὶ
fire the unquenchable, where their worm dies not, and

out. And he became as dead, so that many
said that he was dead.
27 But Jesus took him by the hand and
raised him up. And he got up.

28 And when He had gone into a house, His
disciples asked Him privately, Why were we
not able to throw it out?
29 And He said to them, This kind can go
out by nothing except by prayer and fasting.

30 And they left there and went through
Galilee. And He did not desire that anyone
should know.
31 For He was teaching His disciples. And
He said to them, The Son of man is now
delivered into the hands of men. And they
will kill Him. And after being killed, on the
third day He will arise.
32 But they did not understand the words
and were afraid to ask Him.

33 And He came to Ca-per-na-um. And in
the house He asked them, What were you
arguing among yourselves in the highway?
34 But they were silent. For they had been
arguing with one another in the highway as
to who was greater *among* them.
35 And He sat down and called the twelve.
And He said to them, If anyone desires to be
first, He shall be last of all and servant of all.
36 And taking a little child, He set him in
their midst. And taking him in His arms, He
said to them,
37 Whoever shall receive one of the little
children like this one, in My name receives
Me. And whoever shall receive Me, he
receives not Me but Him who sent Me.
38 And John answered Him, saying,
Teacher, we saw one who does not follow us
throwing out demons in Your name. And we
told him not to do it because he does not
follow us.
39 But Jesus said, Do not stop him. For
there is no one who shall do a work of
power in My name and be able to easily
speak evil of Me.
40 For he who is not against us is for us.
41 For whoever may give you a cup of
water to drink in My name, because you belong to Christ, truly I say to you that he
shall in no way lose his reward.
42 And whoever may cause one of the little
ones who believe in Me to sin, it would be
better for him if a millstone had been hung
around his neck and he had been thrown in
the sea.
43 And if your hand causes you to scandal-
ously sin, cut it off. It is better for you to
enter into life maimed than to have two
hands to go away into hell, into the fire that
cannot be put out –
44 where their worm does not die, and the
fire is never put out.

τὸ πῦρ οὐ.σβέννυται." 45 καὶ ἐὰν ὁ.πούς.σου σκανδαλίζῃ
the fire is not quenched. And if thy foot should cause [2]to [3]offend
σε, ἀπόκοψον αὐτόν· καλόν [o][p]ἐστίν σοι" εἰσελθεῖν εἰς τὴν
[1]thee, cut off it: good it is for thee to enter into
ζωὴν χωλόν, ἢ τοὺς δύο πόδας ἔχοντα βληθῆναι εἰς
life lame, [rather] than the two feet having to be cast into
τὴν γέενναν, [q]εἰς τὸ πῦρ τὸ ἄσβεστον," 46 [r]ὅπου ὁ σκώληξ
the Gehenna, into the fire the unquenchable, where [2]worm
αὐτῶν οὐ.τελευτᾷ, καὶ τὸ πῦρ οὐ.σβέννυται." 47 καὶ ἐὰν ὁ
[1]their dies not, and the fire is not quenched. And if
ὀφθαλμός.σου σκανδαλίζῃ σε, ἔκβαλε αὐτόν· καλόν
thine eye should cause [2]to [3]offend [1]thee, cast out it: good
[s]σοι ἐστίν" μονόφθαλμον εἰσελθεῖν εἰς τὴν βασιλείαν τοῦ
for thee it is with one eye to enter into the kingdom
θεοῦ, ἢ δύο ὀφθαλμοὺς ἔχοντα βληθῆναι εἰς τὴν γέεν-
of God, [rather] than two eyes having to be cast into the Gehen-
ναν [t]τοῦ πυρός," 48 ὅπου ὁ.σκώληξ.αὐτῶν οὐ.τελευτᾷ, καὶ τὸ
na of fire, where their worm dies not, and the
πῦρ οὐ.σβέννυται. 49 Πᾶς.γὰρ πυρὶ ἁλισθήσεται, [u]καὶ
fire is not quenched. For everyone with fire shall be salted, and
πᾶσα θυσία ἁλὶ ἁλισθήσεται." 50 καλὸν τὸ [v]ἅλας,"
every sacrifice with salt shall be salted. Good [is] the salt,
ἐὰν.δὲ τὸ [w]ἅλας" ἄναλον γένηται, ἐν τίνι αὐτὸ ἀρτύσετε;
but if the salt saltless is become, with what it will ye season?
ἔχετε ἐν ἑαυτοῖς [x]ἅλας," καὶ εἰρηνεύετε ἐν ἀλλήλοις.
Have in yourselves salt, and be at peace with one another.

10 [y]Κἀκεῖθεν" ἀναστὰς ἔρχεται εἰς τὰ ὅρια τῆς Ἰουδαίας,
And thence rising up he comes into the borders of Judæa,
[z]διὰ τοῦ" πέραν τοῦ Ἰορδάνου· καὶ [a]συμπορεύονται" πάλιν
by the other side of the Jordan. And come together again
ὄχλοι πρὸς αὐτόν, καὶ ὡς εἰώθει πάλιν ἐδίδασκεν
crowds to him, and as he had been accustomed again he taught
αὐτούς. 2 Καὶ προσελθόντες [b]οἱ" Φαρισαῖοι [c]ἐπηρώτησαν"
them. And coming to [him] the Pharisees asked
αὐτὸν εἰ ἔξεστιν ἀνδρὶ γυναῖκα ἀπολῦσαι, πειράζοντες
him if it is lawful for a husband a wife to put away, tempting
αὐτόν. 3 ὁ.δὲ ἀποκριθεὶς εἶπεν αὐτοῖς, Τί ὑμῖν ἐνετείλατο
him. But he answering said to them, What [4]you [1]did [3]command
[d]Μωσῆς;" 4 Οἱ.δὲ [e]εἶπον," [f]Μωσῆς ἐπέτρεψεν" βιβλίον ἀπο-
[2]Moses? And they said, Moses allowed a bill of di-
στασίου γράψαι, καὶ ἀπολῦσαι. 5 [g]Καὶ ἀποκριθεὶς ὁ" Ἰησοῦς
vorce to write, and to put away. And answering Jesus
εἶπεν αὐτοῖς, Πρὸς τὴν.σκληροκαρδίαν.ὑμῶν ἔγραψεν ὑμῖν
said to them, In view of your hardheartedness he wrote for you
τὴν.ἐντολὴν.ταύτην· 6 ἀπὸ.δὲ ἀρχῆς κτίσεως ἄρσεν καὶ
this commandment; but from [the] beginning of creation male and
θῆλυ ἐποίησεν αὐτοὺς [h]ὁ θεός." 7 ἕνεκεν τούτου καταλείψει
female, [2]made [3]them [1]God. On account of this shall [3]leave
ἄνθρωπος τὸν.πατέρα.αὐτοῦ καὶ τὴν μητέρα, [i]καὶ προσκολ-
[1]a [2]man his father and mother, and shall be
ληθήσεται" [k]πρὸς τὴν.γυναῖκα".αὐτοῦ, 8 καὶ ἔσονται οἱ δύο
joined to his wife, and [3]shall [4]be [1]the [2]two
εἰς σάρκα μίαν· ὥστε οὐκέτι εἰσὶν δύο, ἀλλὰ μία σάρξ. 9 ὃ
[5]for [7]flesh [6]one; so that no longer are they two, but one flesh. What
οὖν ὁ θεὸς συνέζευξεν, ἄνθρωπος μὴ.χωριζέτω. 10 Καὶ [l]ἐν
therefore God united together, [3]man [1]let [2]not separate. And in
τῇ οἰκίᾳ" πάλιν οἱ.μαθηταὶ.[m]αὐτοῦ" περὶ [n]τοῦ.αὐτοῦ" [o]ἐπη-
the house again his disciples concerning the same thing
ρώτησαν" αὐτόν. 11 καὶ λέγει αὐτοῖς, [p]Ὃς.[p]ἐὰν" ἀπολύσῃ
asked him. And he says to them, Whoever should put away
τὴν.γυναῖκα.αὐτοῦ καὶ γαμήσῃ ἄλλην, μοιχᾶται ἐπ'
his wife and should marry another, commits adultery against
αὐτήν. 12 καὶ ἐὰν [q]γυνὴ ἀπολύσῃ" τὸν.ἄνδρα.αὐτῆς [r]καὶ"
her. And if a woman should put away her husband and
[s]γαμηθῇ ἄλλῳ," μοιχᾶται.
be married to another, she commits adultery.

13 Καὶ προσέφερον αὐτῷ παιδία, ἵνα ἅψηται αὐτῶν·
And they brought to him little children, that he might touch them.
οἱ.δὲ μαθηταὶ ἐπετίμων τοῖς προσφέρουσιν. 14 ἰδὼν.δὲ
But the disciples rebuked those who brought them. But having seen [it]
ὁ Ἰησοῦς ἠγανάκτησεν, καὶ εἶπεν αὐτοῖς, Ἄφετε τὰ παιδία
Jesus was indignant, and said to them, Suffer the little children
ἔρχεσθαι πρός με, [t]καὶ" μὴ.κωλύετε αὐτά· τῶν.γὰρ.τοιούτων
to come to me, and do not hinder them; for of such
ἐστὶν ἡ βασιλεία τοῦ θεοῦ. 15 ἀμὴν λέγω ὑμῖν, ὃς.[v]ἐὰν"
is the kingdom of God. Verily I say to you, Whoever
μὴ.δέξηται τὴν βασιλείαν τοῦ θεοῦ ὡς παιδίον, οὐ.μὴ
shall not receive the kingdom of God as a little child, in no wise
εἰσέλθῃ εἰς αὐτήν. 16 Καὶ ἐναγκαλισάμενος αὐτά, [w]
shall enter into it. And having taken [2]in [[3]his] [4]arms [1]them,
τιθεὶς τὰς χεῖρας ἐπ' αὐτὰ [x]ηὐλόγει αὐτά."
having laid [his] hands on them he blessed them.

45 And if your foot causes you to scandal-
ously sin, cut it off. It is better for you to
enter into life lame than to have two feet to
be thrown into hell, into the fire that cannot
be put out –
46 where their worm does not die, and the
fire is never put out.
47 And if your eye causes you to scandal-
ously sin, pluck it out. It is better for you to
enter into the kingdom of God with one eye
than to have two eyes to be thrown into
hell-fire –
48 where their worm does not die, and the
fire is never put out.
49 For everyone shall be salted with fire.
And every sacrifice shall be salted with salt.
50 Salt is good, but if the salt become saltless, with what will you season? Have salt in
yourselves and be at peace with one another.

CHAPTER 10

1 And He got up and went into the borders
of Judea, by the other side of Jordan. And
the people gathered again to Him. And as He
had always done, He again taught them.
2 And the Pharisees came to Him and asked
Him if it is lawful for a man to put away a
wife, tempting Him.
3 But answering He said to them, What did
Moses command you?
4 And they said, Moses allowed the writing
of a bill of divorce and to put *her* away.
5 And answering Jesus said to them, Because of the hardness of your heart he wrote
you this commandment.
6 But from the beginning of creation, God
made them male and female.
7 Because of this a man shall leave his father
and mother and shall be joined to his wife
8 and the two shall be one flesh – so that
they are no longer two, but one flesh.
9 Therefore what God joined together, let
not man separate.
10 And in the house His disciples asked Him
again about the same thing.
11 And He said to them that whoever
should put away his wife and marry another
would commit adultery against her.
12 And if a woman should put away her
husband and be married to another, she
commits adultery.
13 And they brought little children to Him
for Him to touch. But the disciples rebuked
those who brought them.
14 But when Jesus observed *this,* He was
very displeased. And *He* said to them, Allow
the little children to come to Me and do not
stop them. For of such is the kingdom of
God.
15 Truly I say to you, Whoever shall not
receive the kingdom of God like a little child
shall in no way enter into it.
16 And taking them in His arms, laying His
hands on them, He blessed them.

17 Καὶ ἐκπορευομένου.αὐτοῦ εἰς ὁδόν, προσδραμὼν εἷς καὶ
And as he went forth into [the] way, [2]running [3]up [1]one and
γονυπετήσας αὐτὸν ἐπηρώτα αὐτόν, Διδάσκαλε ἀγαθέ, τί
kneeling down to him asked him, [2]Teacher [1]good, what
ποιήσω ἵνα ζωὴν αἰώνιον κληρονομήσω; 18 Ὁ.δὲ.Ἰησοῦς
shall I do that life eternal I may inherit? But Jesus
εἶπεν αὐτῷ, Τί με λέγεις ἀγαθόν; οὐδεὶς ἀγαθὸς εἰ.μὴ
said to him, Why me callest thou good? No one [is] good except
εἷς, ὁ θεός. 19 τὰς ἐντολὰς οἶδας, [y]Μὴ.μοιχεύσῃς·
one, God. The commandments thou knowest: Thou shouldest not commit
μὴ.φονεύσῃς·" · μὴ.κλέψῃς·
adultery; thou shouldest not commit murder; thou shouldest not steal; thou
μὴ.ψευδομαρτυρήσῃς· μὴ.ἀποστερήσῃς· τίμα τὸν
shouldest not bear false witness; thou shouldest not defraud; honour
πατέρα.σου καὶ τὴν μητέρα[z]. 20 Ὁ.δὲ [a]ἀποκριθεὶς" [b]εἶπεν"
thy father and mother. And he answering said
αὐτῷ, Διδάσκαλε, [c]ταῦτα πάντα" [d]ἐφυλαξάμην" ἐκ νεότητός
to him, Teacher, [2]these [1]all have I kept from [2]youth
μου. 21 Ὁ.δὲ.Ἰησοῦς ἐμβλέψας αὐτῷ ἠγάπησεν αὐτόν, καὶ
[1]my. And Jesus looking upon him loved him, and
εἶπεν αὐτῷ, Ἕν [e]σοι" ὑστερεῖ· ὕπαγε, ὅσα ἔχεις πώλη-
said to him, One thing to thee is lacking: go, as much as thou hast sell
σον καὶ δὸς [f]τοῖς" πτωχοῖς, καὶ ἕξεις θησαυρὸν ἐν
and give to the poor, and thou shalt have treasure in
οὐρανῷ· καὶ δεῦρο, ἀκολούθει μοι, [g]ἄρας τὸν σταυρόν." 22 Ὁ.δὲ
heaven; and come, follow me, taking up the cross. But he,
στυγνάσας ἐπὶ τῷ λόγῳ ἀπῆλθεν λυπούμενος· ἦν.γὰρ.ἔχων
being sad at the word, went away grieved, for he had
κτήματα πολλά. 23 Καὶ περιβλεψάμενος ὁ Ἰησοῦς λέγει τοῖς
[2]possessions [1]many. And looking around Jesus says
μαθηταῖς.αὐτοῦ, Πῶς δυσκόλως οἱ τὰ χρήματα ἔχοντες εἰς
to his disciples, How difficultly those [2]riches [1]having into
τὴν βασιλείαν τοῦ θεοῦ εἰσελεύσονται. 24 Οἱ.δὲ μαθηταὶ ἐθαμ-
the kingdom of God shall enter! And the disciples were as-
βοῦντο ἐπὶ τοῖς.λόγοις.αὐτοῦ. Ὁ.δὲ.Ἰησοῦς πάλιν ἀποκριθεὶς
tonished at his words. And Jesus again answering
λέγει αὐτοῖς, [h]Τέκνα," πῶς δύσκολόν ἐστιν [i]τοὺς πεποιθότας
says to them, Children, how difficult it is [for] those who trust
ἐπὶ [k]τοῖς' χρήμασιν" εἰς τὴν βασιλείαν τοῦ θεοῦ εἰσελθεῖν.
in riches into the kingdom of God to enter!
25 εὐκοπώτερόν ἐστιν κάμηλον διὰ [l]τῆς' τρυμαλιᾶς [l]τῆς"
Easier it is [for] a camel through the eye of the
ῥαφίδος [m]εἰσελθεῖν," ἢ πλούσιον εἰς τὴν βασιλείαν τοῦ θεοῦ
needle to pass, than [for] a rich man into the kingdom of God
εἰσελθεῖν. 26 Οἱ.δὲ περισσῶς ἐξεπλήσσοντο, λέγοντες πρὸς
to enter. And they exceedingly were astonished, saying among
ἑαυτούς, Καὶ τίς δύναται σωθῆναι; 27 Ἐμβλέψας.[n]δὲ" αὐτοῖς
themselves, And who is able to be saved? But looking on them
ὁ Ἰησοῦς λέγει, Παρὰ ἀνθρώποις [o] ἀδύνατον, ἀλλ' οὐ παρὰ
Jesus says, With men [it is] impossible, but not with
[p]τῷ" θεῷ· πάντα.γὰρ δυνατά [q]ἐστιν" παρὰ τῷ θεῷ. ⌐28 [r]Καὶ"
God; for all things [2]possible [1]are with God. And
ἤρξατο [s]ὁ Πέτρος λέγειν' αὐτῷ, Ἰδού, ἡμεῖς ἀφήκαμεν πάντα,
[2]began [1]Peter to say to him, Lo, we left all,
καὶ [t]ἠκολουθήσαμέν" σοι. 29 [v]Ἀποκριθεὶς.δὲ ὁ Ἰησοῦς εἶπεν,"
and followed thee. But answering Jesus said,
Ἀμὴν λέγω ὑμῖν, οὐδείς ἐστιν ὃς ἀφῆκεν οἰκίαν, ἢ ἀδελφούς,
Verily I say to you, No one there is who has left house, or brothers,
ἢ ἀδελφάς, [w]ἢ πατέρα, ἢ μητέρα," [x]ἢ γυναῖκα," ἢ τέκνα, ἢ
or sisters, or father, or mother, or wife, or children, or
ἀγρούς, ἕνεκεν ἐμοῦ καὶ [y] τοῦ εὐαγγελίου, 30 ἐὰν.μὴ.λάβῃ
lands, for the sake of me and of the glad tidings, that shall not receive
ἑκατονταπλασίονα νῦν ἐν τῷ.καιρῷ.τούτῳ, οἰκίας καὶ ἀδελ-
a hundredfold now in this time: houses and bro-
φοὺς καὶ ἀδελφὰς καὶ [z]μητέρας' καὶ τέκνα καὶ ἀγρούς, μετὰ
thers and sisters and mothers and children and lands, with
διωγμῶν, καὶ ἐν τῷ αἰῶνι τῷ.ἐρχομένῳ ζωὴν αἰώνιον. 31 πολ-
persecutions, and in the age that is coming life eternal. [2]Many
λοὶ δὲ ἔσονται πρῶτοι ἔσχατοι, καὶ [a]οἱ" ἔσχατοι πρῶτοι.
[1]but [4]shall [5]be [3]first last, and the last first.
32 Ἦσαν.δὲ ἐν τῇ ὁδῷ ἀναβαίνοντες εἰς Ἱεροσόλυμα· καὶ
And they were in the way going up to Jerusalem, and
ἦν προάγων αὐτοὺς ὁ Ἰησοῦς, καὶ ἐθαμβοῦντο, [b]καὶ"
[2]was [3]going [4]on [5]before [6]them [1]Jesus, and they were astonished, and
ἀκολουθοῦντες ἐφοβοῦντο. καὶ παραλαβὼν πάλιν τοὺς
following were afraid. And having taken to [him] again the
δώδεκα, ἤρξατο αὐτοῖς λέγειν τὰ μέλλοντα αὐτῷ
twelve, he began them to tell the things which were about [3]to [4]him
συμβαίνειν· 33 Ὅτι, ἰδού, ἀναβαίνομεν εἰς Ἱεροσόλυμα, καὶ
[1]to [2]happen: Behold, we go up to Jerusalem, and
ὁ υἱὸς τοῦ ἀνθρώπου παραδοθήσεται τοῖς ἀρχιερεῦσιν καὶ
the Son of man will be delivered up to the chief priests and

17 And as He went out into the highway, one came running up. And kneeling down to Him he asked Him, Good master, what shall I do that I may inherit eternal life?

18 And Jesus said to him, Why do you call Me good? No one is good except One, *that is,* God.

19 You know the commandments: Do not commit adultery, do not commit murder; do not steal; do not bear false witness; do not cheat; honor your father and your mother.

20 And answering he said to Him, Master, I have kept all these from my youth.

21 And looking upon him Jesus loved him. And He said to him, You lack one thing. Go sell all that you have and give to the poor, and you shall have treasure in Heaven. And come, follow Me, taking up the cross.

22 But being saddened at that saying, he went away sorrowful – for he had many possessions.

23 And looking around Jesus said to His disciples, How difficult it is for those who have riches to enter into the kingdom of God!

24 And the disciples were astonished at His words. And Jesus answered again, saying to them, Children, how difficult it is for those who trust in riches to enter into the kingdom of God!

25 It is easier for a camel to go through the eye of a needle than for a rich man to enter into the kingdom of God.

26 And they were very much astonished, saying among themselves, Who then can be saved?

27 But Jesus looked on them and said, With men *it is* impossible, but not with God – for with God all things are possible.

28 And Peter began to say to Him, Lo, we have left all and followed You!

29 But answering Jesus said, Truly I say to you, There is no one who has left house or brothers or sisters or father or mother or wife or children or lands for My sake, and for the gospel,

30 that shall not receive a hundred times now in this time: houses and brothers and sisters and mothers and children and lands, with persecutions – and in the world that is coming, everlasting life.

31 But many *who are* first shall be last, and the last *shall be* first.

32 And they were in the highway going up to Jerusalem. And Jesus was going on ahead of them. And they were filled with holy fear and were afraid as they followed. And taking the twelve to Him again, He began to tell them the things that were about to happen to Him.

33 Behold, we go up to Jerusalem! And the Son of man will be delivered up to the chief priests and to the scribes. And they will condemn Him to death and will deliver Him

[c]τοῖς' γραμματεῦσιν, καὶ κατακρινοῦσιν αὐτὸν θανάτῳ, καὶ
to the scribes, and they will condemn him to death, and
παραδώσουσιν αὐτὸν τοῖς ἔθνεσιν, 34 καὶ ἐμπαίξουσιν αὐτῷ,
will deliver up him to the Gentiles. And they will mock him,
[d]καὶ μαστιγώσουσιν αὐτόν, καὶ ἐμπτύσουσιν αὐτῷ,' καὶ ἀπο-
and will scourge him, and will spit upon him, and will
κτενοῦσιν [e]αὐτόν" καὶ [f]τῇ τρίτῃ ἡμέρᾳ' ἀναστήσεται.
kill him; and on the third day he will rise again.
35 Καὶ προσπορεύονται αὐτῷ Ἰάκωβος καὶ Ἰωάννης [g]οἱ"
And come up to him James and John, the
υἱοὶ Ζεβεδαίου, λέγοντες[h], Διδάσκαλε, θέλομεν ἵνα ὃ.ἐὰν
sons of Zebedee, saying, Teacher, we de re that whatever
αἰτήσωμεν [i] ποιήσῃς ἡμῖν. 36 Ὁ.δὲ εἶπεν αὐτοῖς, Τί θέλετε
we may ask thou wouldest do for us. And he said to them, What do ye desire
[k]ποιῆσαί με" ὑμῖν; 37 Οἱ.δὲ [l]εἶπον" αὐτῷ, Δὸς ἡμῖν, ἵνα εἷς
to do for you? And they said to him, Give to us, that one
[m]ἐκ δεξιῶν.σου" καὶ εἷς [n] ἐξ [o]εὐωνύμων"[p]σου" καθίσωμεν ἐν
at thy right hand and one at thy left hand we may sit in
τῇ.δόξῃ.σου. 38 Ὁ.δὲ.Ἰησοῦς εἶπεν αὐτοῖς, Οὐκ.οἴδατε τί
thy glory. But Jesus said to them, Ye know not what
αἰτεῖσθε. δύνασθε πιεῖν τὸ ποτήριον· ὃ ἐγὼ πίνω, [q]καὶ" τὸ
ye ask. Are ye able to drink the cup which I drink, and the
βάπτισμα ὃ ἐγὼ βαπτίζομαι, βαπτισθῆναι;
baptism which I am baptized [with], to be baptized [with]?
39 Οἱ.δὲ [r]εἶπον" αὐτῷ, Δυνάμεθα. Ὁ.δὲ.Ἰησοῦς εἶπεν αὐτοῖς,
And they said to him, We are able. But Jesus said to them,
Τὸ [s]μὲν" ποτήριον ὃ ἐγὼ πίνω, πίεσθε· καὶ τὸ βάπτισμα
The indeed cup which I drink, ye shall drink; and the baptism
ὃ ἐγὼ βαπτίζομαι, βαπτισθήσεσθε· 40 τὸ.δὲ.καθί-
which I am baptized [with], ye shall be baptized [with]; but to sit
σαι ἐκ δεξιῶν.μου [q]καὶ" ἐξ εὐωνύμων.[t]μου" οὐκ.ἔστιν ἐμὸν
at my right hand and at my left hand is not mine
δοῦναι, ἀλλ' οἷς ἡτοίμασται. 41 Καὶ ἀκούσαν-
to give, but [to those] for whom it has been prepared. And having
τες οἱ δέκα ἤρξαντο ἀγανακτεῖν περὶ Ἰακώβου καὶ
heard [this] the ten began to be indignant about James and
Ἰωάννου 42 [v]ὁ.δὲ.Ἰησοῦς προσκαλεσάμενος αὐτοὺς" λέγει
John. But Jesus having called to [him] them says
αὐτοῖς, Οἴδατε ὅτι οἱ δοκοῦντες ἄρχειν τῶν ἐθνῶν
to them, Ye know that those who are accounted to rule over the nations
κατακυριεύουσιν αὐτῶν· καὶ οἱ.μεγάλοι.αὐτῶν κατεξουσιάζου-
exercise lordship over them; and their great ones exercise authority
σιν αὐτῶν. 43 οὐχ οὕτως δὲ [w]ἔσται" ἐν ὑμῖν· ἀλλ'
over them; not thus however shall it be among you; but
ὃς.[x]ἐὰν" θέλῃ [y]γενέσθαι μέγας" ἐν ὑμῖν, ἔσται [z]διάκονος
whoever desires to become great among you, shall be servant
ὑμῶν." 44 καὶ ὃς.[a]ἂν" θέλῃ [b]ὑμῶν" [c]γενέσθαι" πρῶτος, ἔσται
your; and whoever desires of you to become first, shall be
πάντων δοῦλος· 45 καὶ.γὰρ ὁ υἱὸς τοῦ ἀνθρώπου οὐκ.ἦλθεν
of all bondman. For even the Son of man came not
διακονηθῆναι, ἀλλὰ διακονῆσαι, καὶ δοῦναι τὴν.ψυχὴν.αὐτοῦ
to be served, but to serve, and to give his life
λύτρον ἀντὶ πολλῶν.
a ransom for many.

46 Καὶ [d]ἔρχονται" εἰς [e]Ἱεριχώ·" καὶ ἐκπορευομένου.αὐτοῦ
And they come to Jericho; and as he was going out
ἀπὸ [e]Ἱεριχώ," καὶ τῶν.μαθητῶν.αὐτοῦ, καὶ ὄχλου ἱκανοῦ,
from Jericho, and his disciples, and a crowd large,
[f]υἱὸς Τιμαίου Βαρτίμαιος [g]ὁ" τυφλὸς [ha] ἐκάθητο παρὰ τὴν
a son of Timæus, Bartimæus the blind [man], was sitting beside the
ὁδὸν [i]προσαιτῶν." 47 καὶ ἀκούσας ὅτι Ἰησοῦς ὁ [k]Ναζωραῖός"
way, begging. And having heard that Jesus the Nazaræan
ἐστιν, ἤρξατο κράζειν καὶ λέγειν, [l]Ὁ υἱὸς" [m]Δαβίδ," Ἰησοῦ,
it was, he began to cry out and to say, Son of David, Jesus,
(lit. it is)
ἐλέησόν με. 48 Καὶ ἐπετίμων αὐτῷ πολλοὶ ἵνα σιωπήσῃ·
have pity on me. And rebuked him many that he should be silent;
ὁ.δὲ πολλῷ μᾶλλον ἔκραζεν, Υἱὲ [m]Δαβίδ," ἐλέησόν με.
but he much more cried out, Son of David, have pity on me.
49 Καὶ στὰς ὁ Ἰησοῦς [n]εἶπεν αὐτὸν φωνηθῆναι·" καὶ
And having stopped Jesus asked for him to be called. And
φωνοῦσιν τὸν τυφλόν, λέγοντες αὐτῷ, Θάρσει·
they call the blind [man], saying to him, Be of good courage;
[o]ἔγειραι," φωνεῖ σε. 50 Ὁ.δὲ ἀποβαλὼν τὸ.ἱμάτιον.αὐτοῦ,
rise up, he calls thee. And he casting away his garment,
[p]ἀναστὰς" ἦλθεν πρὸς τὸν Ἰησοῦν· 51 καὶ ἀποκριθεὶς [q]λέγει
having risen up he came to Jesus. And answering says
αὐτῷ ὁ Ἰησοῦς," Τί [r]θέλεις ποιήσω σοί;" Ὁ.δὲ τυφλὸς
to him Jesus, What dost thou desire I should do to thee? And the blind
εἶπεν αὐτῷ, [s]Ῥαββονί," ἵνα ἀναβλέψω. 52 Ὁ.δὲ.Ἰη-
[man] said to him, Rabboni, that I may receive sight. And Je-

up to the Gentiles.
34 And they will ridicule Him. And *they* will
whip Him and spit on Him and will kill Him –
and on the third day He will rise again.

35 And James and John, the sons of Zeb-e-
dee, came to Him, saying, Teacher, we ask
that you do for us whatever we may ask.
36 And He said to them, What do you want
Me to do for you?
37 And they said to Him, allow us to sit in
Your glory, one on Your right hand and one
on Your left.
38 But Jesus said to them, You do not
know what you ask. Are you able to drink
the cup which I drink, and to be baptized
with the baptism which I am baptized with?
39 And they said to Him, We are able. But
Jesus said to them, You shall indeed drink of
the cup which I drink. And you shall be
baptized with the baptism that I am
baptized with.
40 But to sit on My right hand and at My
left hand is not Mine to give – but to those
for whom it has been prepared.
41 And when the ten heard this *they* began to
be indignant about James and John.
42 But calling them to Him, Jesus said to
them, You know that those who are counted
rulers over the nations exercise lordship over
them. And their great ones exercise
authority over them.
43 But it shall not be so among you, but
whoever desires to be great among you shall
be your servant.
44 And whoever of you desires to be first,
he shall be servant of all.
45 For even the Son of man did not come
to be served, but to serve, and to give His life
a ransom for many.

46 And they came to Jericho. And as He
and His disciples and a great number of
people were going out of Jericho. Blind
Bar-ti-me-us the son of Ti-me-us was sitting
beside the highway begging.
47 And hearing that it was Jesus the Naz-a-
rene, he began to cry out and to say, Jesus,
Son of David! Have pity on me!
48 And many warned him that he should be
still. But he cried out much more, Son of
David! Have pity on me!
49 And Jesus stopped and asked for him to
be called. And they called the blind one,
saying to him, Be comforted. Get up! He is
calling you.
50 And throwing aside his coat, he got up
and went to Jesus.
51 And answering Jesus said to him, What
do you want Me to do to you? And the
blind one said to Him, Master, that I may be
given sight.
52 And Jesus said to him, Go! Your faith
has healed you. And instantly he received his

σοῦς εἶπεν αὐτῷ, "Ὕπαγε· ἡ.πίστις.σου σέσωκέν σε Καὶ
sus said to him, Go, thy faith has healed thee. And
[t]εὐθέως" ἀνέβλεψεν, καὶ ἠκολούθει [v]τῷ Ἰησοῦ' ἐν τῇ ὁδῷ.
immediately he received sight, and followed Jesus in the way.
11 Καὶ ὅτε ἐγγίζουσιν εἰς [w]Ἱερουσαλήμ," [x]εἰς Βηθφαγὴ
And when they drew near to Jerusalem, to Bethphage
καὶ Βηθανίαν," πρὸς τὸ ὄρος τῶν Ἐλαιῶν, [y]ἀποστέλλει" δύο
and Bethany, towards the mount of Olives, he sends two
τῶν.μαθητῶν.αὐτοῦ, 2 καὶ λέγει αὐτοῖς, Ὑπάγετε εἰς τὴν
of his disciples, and says to them, Go into the
κώμην τὴν.κατέναντι ὑμῶν· καὶ [z]εὐθέως" εἰσπορευόμενοι εἰς
village, that opposite you, and immediately entering into
αὐτὴν εὑρήσετε πῶλον δεδεμένον, ἐφ' ὃν οὐδεὶς[a] ἀνθρώπων[b]
it ye will find a colt tied, upon which no one of men
κεκάθικεν· [c]λύσαντες αὐτὸν [d]ἀγάγετε." 3 καὶ ἐάν τις ὑμῖν
has sat: having loosed it lead [it]. And if anyone to you
εἴπῃ, Τί ποιεῖτε τοῦτο; εἴπατε, [e]"Οτι" ὁ κύριος αὐτοῦ χρείαν
say, Why do ye this? say, The Lord [3]of [4]it [2]need
ἔχει· καὶ [f]εὐθέως" αὐτὸν [g]ἀποστελεῖ' [h] ὧδε. 4 [ia]Ἀπῆλθον.δέ,"
[1]has, and immediately it he will send hither. And they departed,
καὶ εὗρον [ka]τὸν" πῶλον δεδεμένον πρὸς [la]τὴν" θύραν ἔξω ἐπὶ
and found the colt tied at the door without, by
τοῦ ἀμφόδου, καὶ λύουσιν αὐτόν. 5 καί τινες τῶν ἐκεῖ ἑστη-
the cross way, and they loose it. And some of those there stand-
κότων ἔλεγον αὐτοῖς, Τί ποιεῖτε λύοντες τὸν πῶλον; 6 Οἱ.δὲ
ing said to them, What are ye doing loosing the colt? And they
[ma]εἶπον" αὐτοῖς καθὼς [na]ἐνετείλατο' ὁ Ἰησοῦς· καὶ ἀφῆκαν
said to them as [2]commanded [1]Jesus. And they allowed
αὐτούς. 7 καὶ [o]ἤγαγον" τὸν πῶλον πρὸς τὸν Ἰησοῦν· καὶ
them. And they led the colt to Jesus. And
[p]ἐπέβαλον" αὐτῷ τὰ.ἱμάτια.αὐτῶν, καὶ ἐκάθισεν ἐπ' [q]αὐτῷ."
they cast upon it their garments, and he sat on it;
8 [r]πολλοὶ.δὲ" τὰ.ἱμάτια.αὐτῶν ἔστρωσαν εἰς τὴν ὁδόν· ἄλλοι.δὲ
and many their garments strewed on the way, and others
[s]στοιβάδας" [t]ἔκοπτον" ἐκ τῶν [v]δένδρων," [w]καὶ ἐστρώννυον
branches were cutting down from the trees, and were strewing
εἰς τὴν ὁδόν." 9 καὶ οἱ προάγοντες καὶ οἱ ἀκολουθοῦν-
[them] on the way. And those going before and those follow-
τες ἔκραζον, [x]λέγοντες," Ὡσαννά· εὐλογημένος ὁ
ing were crying out, saying, Hosanna! blessed [be] he who
ἐρχόμενος ἐν ὀνόματι κυρίου. 10 εὐλογημένη ἡ ἐρχο-
comes in [the] name of [the] Lord. Blessed [be] the com-
μένη βασιλεία [y]ἐν ὀνόματι κυρίου" τοῦ.πατρὸς.ἡμῶν
ing kingdom [5]in [[6]the] [7]name [8]of [[9]the] [10]Lord [1]of [2]our [3]father
[z]Δαβίδ·" ' Ὡσαννὰ ἐν τοῖς ὑψίστοις. 11 Καὶ εἰσῆλθεν εἰς
[4]David. Hosanna in the highest! And [2]entered [3]into
Ἱεροσόλυμα [a]ὁ Ἰησοῦς καὶ" εἰς τὸ ἱερόν· καὶ περιβλεψάμενος
[4]Jerusalem [1]Jesus and into the temple; and having looked round on
πάντα, [b]ὀψίας" ἤδη οὔσης τῆς ὥρας, ἐξῆλθεν εἰς Βηθανίαν
all things, late already being the hour, he went out to Bethany
μετὰ τῶν δώδεκα.
with the twelve.
12 Καὶ τῇ ἐπαύριον ἐξελθόντων αὐτῶν ἀπὸ Βηθανίας,
And on the morrow [2]having [3]gone [4]out [1]they from Bethany,
ἐπείνασεν· 13 καὶ ἰδὼν συκῆν [c] μακρόθεν ἔχουσαν φύλλα,
he hungered. And seeing a fig-tree afar off having leaves,
ἦλθεν εἰ ἄρα [d]εὑρήσει τι" ἐν αὐτῇ· καὶ ἐλθὼν ἐπ'
he went if perhaps he will find anything on it. And having come to
αὐτήν, οὐδὲν εὗρεν εἰ.μὴ φύλλα·[e] [f]οὐ.γὰρ.ἦν καιρὸς" σύκων.
it, nothing he found except leaves, for it was not [the] season of figs.
14 καὶ ἀποκριθεὶς [g]ὁ Ἰησοῦς" εἶπεν αὐτῇ, Μηκέτι [h]ἐκ σοῦ εἰς
And [2]answering [1]Jesus said to it, No more of thee for
τὸν αἰῶνα" [i]μηδεὶς" καρπὸν φάγοι. Καὶ ἤκουον οἱ μαθηταὶ
ever [2]any [3]one [5]fruit [1]let [4]eat. And [3]heard [2]disciples
(*lit.* no one)
αὐτοῦ. 15 Καὶ ἔρχονται εἰς Ἱεροσόλυμα· καὶ εἰσελθὼν
[1]his. And they come to Jerusalem; and [2]having [3]entered
[k]ὁ Ἰησοῦς" εἰς τὸ ἱερὸν ἤρξατο ἐκβάλλειν τοὺς πωλοῦντας
[1]Jesus into the temple he began to cast out those selling
καὶ [l] ἀγοράζοντας ἐν τῷ ἱερῷ· καὶ τὰς τραπέζας τῶν κολλυ-
and buying in the temple, and the tables of the money
βιστῶν καὶ τὰς καθέδρας τῶν πωλούντων τὰς περιστερὰς
changers and the seats of those selling the doves
κατέστρεψεν· 16 καὶ οὐκ.ἤφιεν ἵνα τις διενέγκῃ σκεῦος
he overthrew, and suffered not that anyone should carry a vessel
διὰ τοῦ ἱεροῦ. 17 καὶ ἐδίδασκεν, [m]λέγων" [n]αὐτοῖς," Οὐ
through the temple. And he taught, saying to them, [3]Not
γέγραπται, [o]"Οτι" ὁ.οἶκός.μου οἶκος προσευχῆς κληθήσεται
[1]has [2]it been written, My house a house of prayer shall be called
πᾶσιν τοῖς ἔθνεσιν; ὑμεῖς.δὲ [p]ἐποιήσατε" αὐτὸν σπήλαιον
for all the nations? but ye made it a den
λῃστῶν. 18 Καὶ ἤκουσαν οἱ [q]γραμματεῖς καὶ οἱ ἀρχιερεῖς,"
of robbers. And [7]heard [[8]it] [1]the [2]scribes [3]and [4]the [5]chief [6]priests,

sight and followed Jesus in the highway.

CHAPTER 11

1 And when they came close to Jerusalem, to Beth-pha-ge and Beth-a-ny, to the Mount of Olives, He sent two of His disciples out.

2 And *He* said to them, Go into the village that is across from you. And immediately when you enter it you will find a colt tied, on which no one has sat. Untie it and bring it.

3 And if anyone says to you, Why do you do this? Say, The Lord needs it. And he will send it here at once.

4 And they left and found the colt tied outside the door, by the crossing of two ways. And they untied it.

5 And some of those standing there said to them, What are you doing untying the colt?

6 And they told them what Jesus had commanded. And they allowed them *to go.*

7 And they led the colt to Jesus. And they threw their robes on it. And He sat on it.

8 And many spread their robes in the highway. And others were cutting down branches from the trees and were scattering them in the highway.

9 And those that went before and those that followed were crying out, saying, "Hosanna! Blessed is He who comes in the name of the Lord!"

10 Blessed is the kingdom of our father David, coming in the name of the Lord. Hosanna in the highest!

11 And Jesus entered into Jerusalem and into the Temple. And looking around on all things, the hour already being late, He went out to Bethany with the twelve.

12 And on the next day, after they had left Bethany, He was hungry.

13 And seeing a fig-tree with leaves ahead, He came to see if He might find anything on it. And coming to it, He found nothing but leaves, for it was not the season for figs.

14 And answering Jesus said to it, Let no one ever eat any more fruit of you forever. And His disciples heard *it.*

15 And they came to Jerusalem. And after He entered into the Temple, Jesus began to throw out those selling and buying in the Temple. And He overthrew the tables of the money-changers and the seats of those selling doves.

16 And He would not permit anyone to carry a vessel through the Temple.

17 And He taught, saying to them, Has it not been written, "My house shall be called a house of prayer for all the nations"? But you made it a den of thieves

18 And the scribes and the chief priests heard. And they began seeking how they might destroy Him. For they feared Him because all the people were astonished at His teaching.

καὶ ἐζήτουν πῶς αὐτὸν [r]ἀπολέσουσιν·‖ ἐφοβοῦντο.γὰρ [s]αὐτόν,‖
and they sought how him they shall destroy; for they feared him,
[t]ὅτι πᾶς‖ ὁ ὄχλος [v]ἐξεπλήσσετο‖ ἐπὶ τῇ.διδαχῇ.αὐτοῦ.
because all the crowd were astonished at his teaching.
19 Καὶ [w]ὅτε‖ ὀψὲ ἐγένετο [x]ἐξεπορεύετο‖ ἔξω τῆς πόλεως.
And when evening came he went forth out of the city.
20 Καὶ [y]πρωῒ παραπορευόμενοι‖ εἶδον τὴν συκῆν
And in the morning passing by they saw the fig-tree
ἐξηραμμένην ἐκ ῥιζῶν. 21 καὶ ἀναμνησθεὶς ὁ Πέτρος
dried up from [the] roots. And having remembered Peter
λέγει αὐτῷ, [z]Ῥαββί,‖ ἴδε, ἡ συκῆ ἣν κατηράσω ἐξήρανται.
says to him Rabbi, see, the fig-tree which thou cursedst is dried up.
22 Καὶ ἀποκριθεὶς [a]Ἰησοῦς λέγει αὐτοῖς, Ἔχετε πίστιν θεοῦ.
And answering Jesus says to them, Have faith in God.
23 ἀμὴν.[b]γὰρ‖ λέγω ὑμῖν, ὅτι ὃς.ἂν εἴπῃ τῷ.ὄρει.τούτῳ,
For verily I say to you, that whoever shall say to this mountain,
Ἄρθητι καὶ βλήθητι εἰς τὴν θάλασσαν, καὶ μὴ.δια-
Be thou taken away and be thou cast into the sea, and shall not
κριθῇ ἐν τῇ.καρδίᾳ.αὐτοῦ, ἀλλὰ [c]πιστεύσῃ‖ ὅτι [d]ἃ‖ [e]λέγει‖
doubt in his heart, but shall believe that what he says
γίνεται· ἔσται αὐτῷ [f]ὃ.ἐὰν εἴπῃ.‖ 24 διὰ.τοῦτο λέγω
takes place, there shall be to him whatever he shall say. For this reason I say
ὑμῖν, Πάντα ὅσα.[g]ἂν‖ [h]προσευχόμενοι‖, αἰτεῖσθε, πιστεύετε
to you, All things whatsoever praying ye ask, believe
ὅτι [i]λαμβάνετε,‖ καὶ ἔσται ὑμῖν. 25 Καὶ ὅταν [k]στήκητε‖
that ye receive, and [they] shall be to you. And when ye may stand
προσευχόμενοι, ἀφίετε εἴ τι ἔχετε κατά τινος· ἵνα καὶ
praying, forgive if anything ye have against anyone, that also
ὁ.πατὴρ.ὑμῶν ὁ ἐν τοῖς οὐρανοῖς ἀφῇ ὑμῖν τὰ παρα-
your Father who [is] in the heavens may forgive you of-
πτώματα ὑμῶν. 26 [l]εἰ.δὲ ὑμεῖς οὐκ.ἀφίετε, οὐδὲ ὁ.πατὴρ.ὑμῶν
fences your. But if ye forgive not, neither your Father
ὁ ἐν [m]τοῖς‖ οὐρανοῖς ἀφήσει τὰ.παραπτώματα.ὑμῶν.‖
who [is] in the heavens will forgive your offences.
27 Καὶ ἔρχονται πάλιν εἰς Ἱεροσόλυμα· καὶ ἐν τῷ ἱερῷ
And they come again to Jerusalem. And in the temple
περιπατοῦντος.αὐτοῦ ἔρχονται πρὸς αὐτὸν οἱ ἀρχιερεῖς καὶ
as he is walking come to him the chief priests and
οἱ γραμματεῖς καὶ οἱ πρεσβύτεροι, 28 καὶ [n]λέγουσιν‖ αὐτῷ,
the scribes and the elders, and they say to him,
Ἐν ποίᾳ ἐξουσίᾳ ταῦτα ποιεῖς; [o]καὶ‖ τίς σοι [p]τὴν ἐξουσίαν
By what authority these things doest thou? and who thee authority
ταύτην ἔδωκεν,‖ ἵνα ταῦτα ποιῇς; 29 Ὁ.δὲ.Ἰησοῦς
this gave, that these things thou shouldst do? And Jesus
[r]ἀποκριθεὶς‖ εἶπεν αὐτοῖς, Ἐπερωτήσω [s]ὑμᾶς κἀγὼ‖ ἕνα λόγον,
answering said to them Will ask you I also one thing,
καὶ ἀποκρίθητέ μοι, καὶ ἐρῶ ὑμῖν ἐν ποίᾳ ἐξουσίᾳ ταῦτα
and answer me, and I will tell you by what authority these things
ποιῶ. 30 Τὸ βάπτισμα [t]Ἰωάννου ἐξ οὐρανοῦ ἦν ἢ ἐξ
I do: The baptism of John from heaven was it or from
ἀνθρώπων; ἀποκρίθητέ μοι. 31 Καὶ [v]ἐλογίζοντο‖ πρὸς ἑαυ-
men? answer me. And they reasoned with them
τούς, λέγοντες, Ἐὰν εἴπωμεν, Ἐξ οὐρανοῦ, ἐρεῖ, [w]Διατί‖
selves, saying, If we should say, From heaven, he will say, Why
[x]οὖν‖ οὐκ.ἐπιστεύσατε αὐτῷ; 32 [y]ἀλλ' ἐὰν‖ εἴπωμεν, Ἐξ
then did ye not believe him? but if we should say, From
ἀνθρώπων, ἐφοβοῦντο τὸν λαόν· [z]ἅπαντες‖.γὰρ εἶχον τὸν
men,— they feared the people; for all held
Ἰωάννην [a]ὅτι ὄντως‖ προφήτης ἦν. 33 καὶ ἀποκριθέντες [b]λέ-
John that indeed a prophet he was. And answering they
γουσιν τῷ Ἰησοῦ,‖ Οὐκ.οἴδαμεν. Καὶ [c]ὁ Ἰησοῦς ἀποκριθεὶς‖ λέγει
say to Jesus, We know not. And Jesus answering says
αὐτοῖς, Οὐδὲ ἐγὼ λέγω ὑμῖν ἐν ποίᾳ ἐξουσίᾳ ταῦτα ποιῶ.
to them, Neither I tell you by what authority these things I do.
12 Καὶ ἤρξατο αὐτοῖς ἐν παραβολαῖς [d]λέγειν.‖ Ἀμπελῶνα
And he began to them in parables to say, A vineyard
[e]ἐφύτευσεν ἄνθρωπος,‖ καὶ περιέθηκεν φραγμόν, καὶ ὤρυξεν
planted a man, and placed about [it] a fence, and dug
ὑπολήνιον, καὶ ᾠκοδόμησεν πύργον, καὶ [f]ἐξέδοτο‖ αὐτὸν
a wine-vat, and built a tower, and let out it
γεωργοῖς, καὶ ἀπεδήμησεν. 2 καὶ ἀπέστειλεν πρὸς τοὺς
to husbandmen, and left the country. And he sent to the
γεωργοὺς τῷ καιρῷ δοῦλον, ἵνα παρὰ τῶν γεωργῶν
husbandmen at the season a bondman, that from the husbandmen
λάβῃ ἀπὸ [g]τοῦ καρποῦ‖ τοῦ ἀμπελῶνος 3 [h]οἱ.δὲ‖ λα-
he might receive from the fruit of the vineyard. But they having
βόντες αὐτὸν ἔδειραν, καὶ ἀπέστειλαν κενόν. 4 καὶ πάλιν
taken him beat, and sent [him] away empty. And again
ἀπέστειλεν πρὸς αὐτοὺς ἄλλον δοῦλον· κἀκεῖνον [i]λιθοβολή-
he sent to them another bondman, and him having
σαντες‖ [j]ἐκεφαλαίωσαν,‖ καὶ [k]ἀπέστειλαν ἠτιμωμένον.‖
stoned they struck on the head, and sent [him] away having insulted [him].

19 And when evening came, He went out of
the city.
20 And in the morning, as they passed by,
they saw the fig-tree dried up from the
roots.
21 And remembering, Peter said to Him,
Master, Look! The fig-tree which You cursed
is dried up.
22 And answering Jesus said to them, Have
faith in God.
23 For truly I say to you that whoever shall
say to this mountain, Move and be thrown
into the sea! and shall not doubt in his heart
but shall believe that what he says will
happen, it shall happen to him, whatever he
shall say.
24 For this reason I say to you, All things,
whatever you ask, praying, believe that you
shall get it and it shall happen to you.
25 And whenever you stand praying, if you
have anything against anyone, forgive so that
your Father who is in Heaven may also forgive you your sins.
26 But if you do not forgive, neither will
your Father who is in Heaven forgive your
sins.
27 And they came again to Jerusalem. And
as He was walking in the Temple, the chief
priests and the scribes and the elders came to
Him
28 and said to Him, By what authority do
You do these things? And, Who gave You
this authority that you should do these
things?
29 And answering Jesus said to them, I will
also ask you one question. Now answer Me
and I will tell you by what authority I do
these things:
30 The baptism of John, was it from
Heaven or from men? Answer Me!
31 And they reasoned among themselves,
saying, If we should say, From Heaven, He
will say, Why then did you not believe him?
32 But if we should say, From men – they
feared the people, for all men held that John
truly was a prophet.
33 And they answered and said to Jesus, we
do not know. And Jesus answered, saying to
them, Neither do I tell you by what
authority I do these things.

CHAPTER 12

1 And He began to speak to them in parables, A man planted a vineyard and set a
hedge around it. And he dug a wine-vat and
built a tower. And he let it out to vinedressers and left the country.
2 And in due season he sent a servant to the
vinedressers in order that he might receive
the fruit of the vineyard from the vinedressers.
3 But they caught and beat him and sent
him away empty.
4 And again he sent another servant to

5 καὶ [l]πάλιν‖ ἄλλον ἀπέστειλεν· κἀκεῖνον ἀπέκτειναν· καὶ
And again another he sent, and him they killed; also
πολλοὺς ἄλλους, [m]τοὺς‖ μὲν δέροντες, [m]τοὺς‖.δὲ [n]ἀποκτείνον-
many others, [2]some [1]beating, and [2]others [1]killing.
τες.‖ 6 ἔτι [o]οὖν‖ ἕνα [p]υἱὸν ἔχων‖ ἀγαπητὸν [q]αὐτοῦ,‖
Yet therefore [2]one [3]son [1]having [6]beloved [4]his [5]own,
ἀπέστειλεν [r]καὶ‖ αὐτὸν [s]πρὸς αὐτοὺς ἔσχατον,‖ λέγων, Ὅτι
he sent also him to them last, saying,
ἐντραπήσονται τὸν.υἱόν.μου. 7 ἐκεῖνοι.δὲ οἱ γεωργοὶ [t]εἶπον
They will have respect for my son. But those husbandmen said
πρὸς ἑαυτούς,‖ Ὅτι οὗτός ἐστιν ὁ κληρονόμος· δεῦτε, ἀπο-
among themselves, This is the heir: come, let us
κτείνωμεν αὐτόν, καὶ ἡμῶν ἔσται ἡ κληρονομία. 8 καὶ λαβόντες
kill him, and ours will be the inheritance. And having taken
[v]αὐτὸν ἀπέκτειναν,‖ καὶ ἐξέβαλον [w] ἔξω τοῦ ἀμπελῶνος.
him they killed [him], and cast forth [him] outside the vineyard.
9 τί [x]οὖν‖ ποιήσει ὁ κύριος τοῦ ἀμπελῶνος; ἐλεύσεται καὶ
What therefore will do the lord of the vineyard? He will come and
ἀπολέσει τοὺς γεωργούς, καὶ δώσει τὸν ἀμπελῶνα ἄλλοις.
will destroy the husbandmen, and will give the vineyard to others.
10 Οὐδὲ τὴν.γραφὴν.ταύτην ἀνέγνωτε; Λίθον ὃν
[3]Not [4]even [6]this [5]scripture [1]did [2]ye [5]read? [The] stone which
ἀπεδοκίμασαν οἱ οἰκοδομοῦντες, οὗτος ἐγενήθη εἰς κεφαλὴν
[4]rejected [1]those [2]who [3]build, this is become head
γωνίας. 11 παρὰ κυρίου ἐγένετο αὕτη, καὶ ἔστιν θαυ-
of [the] corner: from [the] Lord was this, and it is won-
μαστὴ ἐν ὀφθαλμοῖς.ἡμῶν. 12 Καὶ ἐζήτουν αὐτὸν κρατῆσαι,
derful in our eyes. And they sought him to lay hold of,
καὶ ἐφοβήθησαν τὸν ὄχλον· ἔγνωσαν.γὰρ ὅτι πρὸς αὐτοὺς
and they feared the crowd; for they knew that against them
τὴν παραβολὴν εἶπεν· καὶ ἀφέντες αὐτὸν ἀπῆλθον.
the parable he speaks. And leaving him they went away.
13 Καὶ ἀποστέλλουσιν πρὸς αὐτόν τινας τῶν Φαρισαίων
And they send to him some of the Pharisees
καὶ τῶν Ἡρωδιανῶν, ἵνα αὐτὸν ἀγρεύσωσιν λόγῳ. 14 [y]οἱ.δὲ‖
and of the Herodians, that him they might catch in discourse. And they
ἐλθόντες λέγουσιν αὐτῷ, Διδάσκαλε, οἴδαμεν ὅτι ἀληθὴς εἶ,
having come say to him, Teacher, we know that true thou art,
καὶ οὐ μέλει σοι περὶ οὐδενός· οὐ.γὰρ βλέπεις εἰς
and there is care to thee about no one; for [3]not [1]thou [2]lookest on [the]
πρόσωπον ἀνθρώπων, ἀλλ' ἐπ' ἀληθείας τὴν ὁδὸν τοῦ θεοῦ
appearance of men, but with truth the way of God
διδάσκεις. [z]ἔξεστιν [a]κῆνσον Καίσαρι δοῦναι‖ ἢ οὔ; 15 δῶμεν
teachest: Is it lawful tribute to Cæsar to give or not? Should we give
ἢ μὴ.δῶμεν; Ὁ.δὲ [b]εἰδὼς‖ αὐτῶν.τὴν.ὑπόκρισιν εἶπεν
or should we not give? But he knowing their hypocrisy said
αὐτοῖς, Τί με πειράζετε; φέρετέ μοι δηνάριον ἵνα ἴδω.
to them, Why me do ye tempt? Bring me a denarius that I may see [it].
16 Οἱ.δὲ ἤνεγκαν. Καὶ λέγει αὐτοῖς, Τίνος ἡ.εἰκὼν.αὕτη καὶ
And they brought [it]. And he says to them, Whose [is] this image and
ἡ ἐπιγραφή; [c]Οἱ.δὲ‖ [d]εἶπον‖ αὐτῷ, Καίσαρος. 17 [e]Καὶ
the inscription? And they said to him, Cæsar's. And
ἀποκριθεὶς ὁ‖ Ἰησοῦς εἶπεν [f]αὐτοῖς,‖ [g]Ἀπόδοτε τὰ Καί-
[2]answering [1]Jesus said to them, Render the things of Cæ-
σαρος‖ Καίσαρι, καὶ τὰ τοῦ θεοῦ τῷ θεῷ. Καὶ [h]ἐθαύμασαν‖
sar to Cæsar, and the things of God to God. And they wondered
ἐπ' αὐτῷ,
at him.

18 Καὶ ἔρχονται Σαδδουκαῖοι πρὸς αὐτόν, οἵτινες λέγουσιν
And [2]come [1]Sadducees to him, who say
ἀνάστασιν μὴ.εἶναι· καὶ [i]ἐπηρώτησαν‖ αὐτόν, λέγοντες,
a resurrection there is not. And they questioned him, saying,
19 Διδάσκαλε, [k]Μωσῆς‖ ἔγραψεν ἡμῖν, ὅτι ἐάν τινος ἀδελ-
Teacher, Moses wrote for us, that if of anyone a bro-
φὸς ἀποθάνῃ καὶ καταλίπῃ γυναῖκα καὶ [l]τέκνα μὴ.ἀφῇ,‖
ther should die and leave behind a wife and children leave not,
ἵνα λάβῃ ὁ.ἀδελφὸς.αὐτοῦ τὴν γυναῖκα [m]αὐτοῦ‖ καὶ
that [3]should [4]take [1]his [2]brother the wife of him and
ἐξαναστήσῃ σπέρμα τῷ.ἀδελφῷ.αὐτοῦ. 20 ἑπτὰ [n] ἀδελφοὶ
raise up seed to his brother. Seven brethren
ἦσαν· καὶ ὁ πρῶτος ἔλαβεν γυναῖκα, καὶ ἀποθνήσκων
there were; and the first took a wife, and dying
οὐκ.ἀφῆκεν σπέρμα· 21 καὶ ὁ δεύτερος ἔλαβεν αὐτήν, καὶ
left no seed; and the second took her, and
ἀπέθανεν, [o]καὶ οὐδὲ αὐτὸς ἀφῆκεν‖ σπέρμα· καὶ ὁ τρίτος
died, and neither he left seed; and the third
ὡσαύτως· 22 καὶ [p]ἔλαβον αὐτὴν‖ οἱ ἑπτά, [q]καὶ‖ οὐκ.ἀφῆκαν
likewise. And [3]took [4]her [1]the [2]seven, and left no
σπέρμα. [r]ἐσχάτη‖ πάντων [s]ἀπέθανεν καὶ ἡ γυνή.‖ 23 ἐν.τῇ
seed. Last of all died also the woman. In the
[t]οὖν‖ ἀναστάσει, [v]ὅταν ἀναστῶσιν,‖ τίνος αὐτῶν ἔσται
[2]therefore [1]resurrection, when they shall arise, of which of them shall she be

them. And *they* stoned him and wounded
him in the head and sent him away, treating
him shamefully.
5 And again he sent another. And they
killed him – and many others, beating some
and killing others.
6 Yet, then, having one son, his own
beloved, he also sent him to them at last,
saying, They will respect my son.
7 But those men said among themselves,
This is the heir. Come, let us kill him and the
inheritance will be ours.
8 And they took him and killed him and
threw him out of the vineyard.
9 What, then, will the lord of the vineyard
do? He will come and will destroy the vinedressers. And he will give the vineyard to
others.
10 Have you never even read this Scripture,
"The Stone which the builders rejected has
become the head of the corner.
11 This was from the Lord, and it is
marvelous in our eyes"?
12 And they wanted to seize Him, but they
feared the people. For they knew that He
had spoken the parable against them. And
they left Him and went away.
13 And they sent to Him some of the
Pharisees and some of the He-ro-di-ans in
order to catch Him in conversation.
14 And they came and said to Him,
Teacher, we know that you are true and that
you care about no one, for you do not look
on the outward appearance of men. But *you*
teach with truth the way of God. Is it right
to give taxes to Caesar, or not?
15 Should we give, or should we not give?
But knowing their hypocrisy, He said to
them, Why do you tempt Me? Bring Me a
coin so that I may see.
16 And they brought it. And He said to
them, Whose likeness and engraving is this?
And they said to Him, Caesar's.
17 And answering Jesus said to them, Give
to Caesar the things that are Caesar's and to
God the things that are God's. And they
marveled at Him.
18 And the Sad-du-cees came to Him (who
say there is no resurrection). And they asked
Him, saying,
19 Teacher, Moses wrote to us that if
anyone's brother should die and leave
behind a wife, having no children, that his
brother should take his wife and raise up
seed to his brother.
20 There were seven brothers. And the first
took a wife. And he died and left no seed.
21 And the second took her and died, and
neither did he leave any seed; and the third
likewise.
22 And the seven took her and left no seed.
Last of all the woman died also.
23 In the resurrection, then, when they
shall arise, which of these shall have her as a

γυνή; οἱ.γὰρ ἑπτὰ ἔσχον αὐτὴν γυναῖκα. 24 [w]Καὶ ἀποκριθεὶς
wife? for the seven had her as wife. And [2]answering
ὁ Ἰησοῦς εἶπεν αὐτοῖς," Οὐ διὰ.τοῦτο πλανᾶσθε, μὴ εἰδότες
[1]Jesus said to them, [3]Not [4]therefore [1]do [2]ye err, not knowing
τὰς γραφὰς μηδὲ τὴν δύναμιν τοῦ θεοῦ; 25 ὅταν.γὰρ ἐκ
the scriptures nor the power of God? For when from among
νεκρῶν ἀναστῶσιν, οὔτε γαμοῦσιν οὔτε [x]γαμίσκονται,"
[the] dead they rise, neither do they marry nor are given in marriage,
ἀλλ' εἰσὶν ὡς ἄγγελοι [y]οἱ" ἐν τοῖς οὐρανοῖς. 26 περὶ.δὲ
but [1]are as angels who [are] in the heavens. But concerning
τῶν νεκρῶν, ὅτι ἐγείρονται, οὐκ.ἀνέγνωτε ἐν τῇ βίβλῳ
the dead, that they rise, have ye not read in the book
[z]Μωσέως," ἐπὶ [a]τῆς" βάτου, [b]ὡς" εἶπεν αὐτῷ ὁ θεός,
of Moses, [in the part] on the bush, how [2]spoke [3]to [4]him [1]God,
λέγων, Ἐγὼ ὁ θεὸς Ἀβραὰμ καὶ [c]ὁ" θεὸς Ἰσαὰκ καὶ [c]ὁ"
saying, I [am] the God of Abraham and the God of Isaac and the
θεὸς Ἰακώβ; 27 Οὐκ.ἔστιν [c]ὁ" θεὸς νεκρῶν, ἀλλὰ [d]θεὸς"
God of Jacob? He is not the God of [the] dead, but God
ζώντων· [e]ὑμεῖς οὖν" πολὺ πλανᾶσθε. 28 Καὶ προσελθὼν
of [the] living. Ye therefore greatly err. And [5]having [6]come [7]up
εἷς τῶν γραμματέων, ἀκούσας αὐτῶν [f]συζητούντων," [g]εἰδὼς"
[1]one [2]of [3]the [4]scribes, having heard them reasoning together, perceiving
ὅτι καλῶς [h]αὐτοῖς ἀπεκρίθη," ἐπηρώτησεν αὐτόν, Ποία ἐστὶν
that well them he answered, questioned him, Which is
[i]πρώτη πασῶν ἐντολή"; 29 [k]Ὁ.δὲ.Ἰησοῦς ἀπεκρίθη"
[the] first [2]of [3]all [1]commandment? And Jesus answered
[l]αὐτῷ," Ὅτι πρώτη [m]πασῶν τῶν ἐντολῶν," Ἄκουε,
him, [The] first of all the commandments [is], Hear,
Ἰσραήλ· κύριος ὁ.θεὸς.ἡμῶν κύριος εἷς ἐστίν. 30 καὶ
Israel: [the] Lord our God [3]Lord [2]one [1]is. And
ἀγαπήσεις κύριον τὸν.θεόν.σου ἐξ ὅλης τῆς.καρδίας.σου
thou shalt love [the] Lord thy God with all thy heart
καὶ ἐξ ὅλης τῆς.ψυχῆς.σου καὶ ἐξ ὅλης τῆς.διανοίας.σου
and with all thy soul and with all thy mind
καὶ ἐξ ὅλης τῆς.ἰσχύος.σου. [n]αὕτη πρώτη ἐντολή."
and with all thy strength. This [is the] first commandment.
31 [o]καὶ" δευτέρα [p]ὁμοία" [q]αὕτη," Ἀγαπήσεις τὸν πλη-
And [the] second like [it is] this: Thou shalt love [2]neigh-
σίον σου ὡς σεαυτόν. Μείζων τούτων ἄλλη ἐντολὴ
bour [1]thy as thyself. Greater than these another commandment
οὐκ.ἔστιν. 32 Καὶ εἶπεν αὐτῷ ὁ γραμματεύς, Καλῶς, διδάσ-
there is not. And [3]said [4]to [5]him [1]the [2]scribe, Right, teach-
καλε, ἐπ' ἀληθείας [r]εἶπας" ὅτι εἷς ἐστιν [s]θεός," καὶ
er, according to truth thou hast said that [3]one [2]is [1]God, and
οὐκ.ἔστιν ἄλλος πλὴν αὐτοῦ. 33 καὶ τὸ ἀγαπᾷν αὐτὸν ἐξ
there is not another besides him: and to love him with
ὅλης τῆς καρδίας καὶ ἐξ ὅλης τῆς συνέσεως [t]καὶ ἐξ ὅλης
all the heart and with all the understanding and with all
τῆς ψυχῆς" καὶ ἐξ ὅλης τῆς ἰσχύος, καὶ τὸ ἀγαπᾷν
the soul and with all the strength, and to love [one's]
τὸν πλησίον ὡς ἑαυτόν, [v]πλεῖόν" ἐστιν πάντων τῶν ὁλοκαυ-
neighbour as oneself, [2]more [1]is than all the burnt
τωμάτων καὶ [w]τῶν" θυσιῶν. 34 Καὶ ὁ Ἰησοῦς ἰδὼν [x]αὐτὸν"
offerings and the sacrifices. And Jesus seeing him
ὅτι νουνεχῶς ἀπεκρίθη, εἶπεν αὐτῷ, Οὐ μακρὰν εἶ
that intelligently he answered, said to him, Not far art thou
ἀπὸ τῆς βασιλείας τοῦ θεοῦ. Καὶ οὐδεὶς.οὐκέτι ἐτόλμα αὐτὸν
from the kingdom of God. And no one any more dared [3]him
ἐπερωτῆσαι.
[1]to [2]question.

35 Καὶ ἀποκριθεὶς ὁ Ἰησοῦς ἔλεγεν, διδάσκων ἐν τῷ ἱερῷ,
And [2]answering [1]Jesus said, teaching in the temple,
Πῶς λέγουσιν οἱ γραμματεῖς ὅτι ὁ χριστὸς υἱός [y]ἐστιν Δαβίδ";
How say the scribes that the Christ [2]son [1]is of David?
36 αὐτὸς [z]γὰρ" [a]Δαβὶδ" [b]εἶπεν" ἐν [c]τῷ" πνεύματι [c]τῷ" ἁγίῳ,
[3]himself [1]for [2]David said by the Spirit the Holy,
[d]Εἶπεν" [e]ὁ" κύριος τῷ.κυρίῳ.μου, [f]Κάθου" ἐκ δεξιῶν.μου ἕως.ἂν
[3]Said [1]the [2]Lord to my Lord, Sit at my right hand until
θῶ τοὺς.ἐχθρούς.σου [g]ὑποπόδιον" τῶν ποδῶν.σου. 37 Αὐτὸς
I place thine enemies [as] a footstool for thy feet. [2]Himself
[h]οὖν" [a]Δαβὶδ" λέγει αὐτὸν κύριον· καὶ πόθεν [i]υἱὸς.αὐτοῦ
[3]therefore [1]David calls him Lord, and whence his son
ἐστιν;" Καὶ ὁ πολὺς ὄχλος ἤκουεν αὐτοῦ ἡδέως.
is he? And the great crowd heard him gladly.

38 Καὶ [k]ἔλεγεν αὐτοῖς ἐν τῇ.διδαχῇ.αὐτοῦ," Βλέπετε ἀπὸ
And he said to them in his teaching, Take heed of
τῶν γραμματέων, τῶν θελόντων ἐν στολαῖς περιπατεῖν, καὶ
the scribes, who like in robes to walk about, and
ἀσπασμοὺς ἐν ταῖς ἀγοραῖς 39 καὶ πρωτοκαθεδρίας ἐν ταῖς
salutations in the market-places and first seats in the
συναγωγαῖς καὶ πρωτοκλισίας ἐν τοῖς δείπνοις· 40 οἱ [l]κατεσ-
synagogues and first places at the suppers; who de-

wife? For the seven had her as a wife.
24 And answering Jesus said to them, Do
you not err because of this, not knowing
either the Scriptures or the power of God?
25 For when they rise from among the
dead, they neither marry nor are given in
marriage. But they are as the angels who are
in Heaven.
26 But as to the dead, that they do rise,
have you never read in the book of Moses
how God spoke to him at the bush, saying, I
am the God of Abraham and the God of
Isaac and the God of Jacob?
27 He is not the God of the dead, but God
of the living! You therefore greatly err.
28 And one of the scribes came and heard
them reasoning together. Observing that He
answered them well, he asked Him, Which is
the first commandment of all?
29 And Jesus answered him, The first of all
the commandments is, "Hear, O Israel! The
Lord our God is one Lord.
30 And you shall love the Lord your God
with all your heart and with all your soul
and with all your mind and with all your
strength." This is the first commandment.
31 And the second is like this, "You shall
love your neighbor as yourself." There is no
other commandment greater than these.
32 And the scribe said to Him, Teacher, *you
are* right. You have truly said that God is
one and there is none other besides Him;
33 and to love Him with all the heart and
with all the understanding and with all the
soul and with all the strength, and to love
one's neighbor as oneself, is more than all
the whole burnt offerings and the sacrifices.
34 And when Jesus saw that he answered
with understanding, He said to him, You are
not far from the kingdom of God. And no
one after that dared to question Him.

35 And teaching in the Temple, Jesus
answered, saying, How can the scribes say
that Christ is the son of David?
36 For David himself said by the Holy
Spirit, "The Lord said to my Lord, Sit at My
right hand until I place Your enemies as a
footstool for Your feet."
37 Therefore David himself calls Him Lord.
But how then is He his son? And the great
crowd heard Him gladly.

38 And He said to them in His teaching, Be
careful of the scribes who like to walk about
in long robes and love greetings in the
market-places,
39 and the chief seats in the synagogues,
and the highest places at the feasts,
40 who devour widows' houses, and as a
pretense make long prayers. These shall

θιοντες" τὰς οἰκίας τῶν χηρῶν, καὶ προφάσει μακρὰ
your the houses of widows, and as a pretext [2]at [3]great [4]length
προσευχόμενοι· οὗτοι [m]λήψονται" περισσότερον κρίμα.
[1]pray. These shall receive more abundant judgment.
41 Καὶ καθίσας [n]ὁ Ἰησοῦς" [o]κατέναντι" τοῦ γαζοφυλα-
And [2]having [3]sat [4]down [1]Jesus opposite the treasury,
κίου ἐθεώρει πῶς ὁ ὄχλος βάλλει χαλκὸν εἰς τὸ γαζοφυλά-
he saw how the crowd cast money into the treasury;
κιον· καὶ πολλοὶ πλούσιοι ἔβαλλον πολλά. 42 καὶ ἐλθοῦσα
and many rich were casting [in] much. And [4]having [5]come
μία χήρα πτωχὴ ἔβαλεν λεπτὰ δύο, ὅ ἐστιν κοδράντης.
[1]one [3]widow [2]poor cast [in] [2]lepta [1]two, which is a kodrantes.
43 καὶ προσκαλεσάμενος τοὺς.μαθητὰς.αὐτοῦ [p]λέγει" αὐτοῖς,
And having called to [him] his disciples he says to them,
Ἀμὴν λέγω ὑμῖν, ὅτι ἡ.χήρα.αὕτη ἡ πτωχὴ πλεῖον πάντων
Verily I say to you, that this [2]widow [1]poor more than all
[q]βέβληκεν" τῶν [r]βαλόντων" εἰς τὸ γαζοφυλάκιον. 44 πάν-
has cast [in] of those casting into the treasury. [2]All
τες γὰρ ἐκ τοῦ περισσεύοντος αὐτοῖς ἔβαλον· αὕτη.δὲ
[1]for out of that which was abounding to them cast [in], but she
ἐκ τῆς.ὑστερήσεως.αὐτῆς πάντα ὅσα εἶχεν ἔβαλεν,
out of her destitution [3]all [4]as [5]much [6]as [7]she [8]had [1]cast [[2]in],
ὅλον τὸν.βίον.αὐτῆς.
[10]whole [9]her [11]livelihood.

13 Καὶ ἐκπορευομένου.αὐτοῦ ἐκ τοῦ ἱεροῦ λέγει αὐτῷ
And as he was going forth out of the temple [5]says [6]to [7]him
εἷς [s] τῶν.μαθητῶν.αὐτοῦ, Διδάσκαλε, ἴδε, ποταποὶ λίθοι καὶ
[1]one [2]of [3]his [4]disciples, Teacher, see, what stones and
ποταπαὶ οἰκοδομαί. 2 Καὶ [t]ὁ Ἰησοῦς ἀποκριθεὶς" εἶπεν αὐτῷ,
what buildings! And Jesus answering said to him,
Βλέπεις ταύτας τὰς μεγάλας οἰκοδομάς; οὐ.μὴ ἀφεθῇ [u]
Seest thou these great buildings? not at all shall be left
λίθος ἐπὶ [v]λίθῳ" ὃς οὐ.μὴ.καταλυθῇ. 3 Καὶ καθημένου
stone upon stone which shall not be thrown down. And as [2]was [3]sitting
αὐτοῦ εἰς τὸ ὄρος τῶν Ἐλαιῶν κατέναντι τοῦ ἱεροῦ, [w]ἐπηρώ-
[1]he upon the mount of Olives opposite the temple, [8]ask-
των" αὐτὸν κατ᾽.ἰδίαν [x]Πέτρος καὶ Ἰάκωβος καὶ Ἰωάννης καὶ
ed [9]him [10]apart [1]Peter [2]and [3]James [4]and [5]John [6]and
Ἀνδρέας, 4 [y]Εἰπὲ" ἡμῖν πότε ταῦτα ἔσται; καὶ τί τὸ
[7]Andrew, Tell us when [2]these [3]things [1]shall be? and what the
σημεῖον ὅταν μέλλῃ [z]πάντα ταῦτα συντελεῖσθαι" ;
sign when [4]should [5]be [6]about [1]all [2]these [3]things to be accomplished?
5 Ὁ.δὲ.Ἰησοῦς [a]ἀποκριθεὶς" [b]αὐτοῖς ἤρξατο λέγειν," Βλέπετε
And Jesus answering to them began to say, Take heed
μή τις ὑμᾶς πλανήσῃ. 6 πολλοὶ.[c]γὰρ" ἐλεύσονται ἐπὶ τῷ
lest anyone [2]you [1]mislead. For many will come in
ὀνόματί.μου, λέγοντες, Ὅτι ἐγώ εἰμι· καὶ πολλοὺς πλανή-
my name, saying, I am [he], and many they will
σουσιν. 7 ὅταν.δὲ [d]ἀκούσητε" πολέμους καὶ ἀκοὰς πολέμων,
mislead. But when ye shall hear of wars and rumours of wars,
μὴ.θροεῖσθε· δεῖ [e]γὰρ" γενέσθαι· ἀλλ᾽ οὔπω τὸ
be not disturbed; [2]it [3]must [4]needs [1]for come to pass, but [4]not [5]yet [[3]is] [1]the
τέλος. 8 Ἐγερθήσεται.γὰρ ἔθνος [f]ἐπὶ" ἔθνος καὶ βασιλεία
[2]end. For [2]shall [3]rise [4]up [1]nation against nation and kingdom
ἐπὶ βασιλείαν· [g]καὶ" ἔσονται σεισμοὶ κατὰ.τόπους, [h]καὶ"
against kingdom; and there shall be earthquakes in different places, and
ἔσονται λιμοὶ [i]καὶ ταραχαί." [k]ἀρχαὶ" ὠδίνων ταῦτα.
there shall be famines and troubles. Beginnings of throes [are] these.
9 Βλέπετε.δὲ ὑμεῖς ἑαυτούς. παραδώσουσιν.[l]γὰρ" ὑμᾶς εἰς
But take heed ye to yourselves; for they will deliver up you to
συνέδρια καὶ εἰς συναγωγὰς· δαρήσεσθε, καὶ ἐπὶ ἡγεμόνων
sanhedrims and to synagogues: ye will be beaten, and before governors
καὶ βασιλέων σταθήσεσθε ἕνεκεν.ἐμοῦ, εἰς μαρτύριον αὐτοῖς·
and kings ye will be brought for my sake, for a testimony to them;
10 καὶ εἰς πάντα τὰ ἔθνη [m]δεῖ πρῶτον" κηρυχθῆναι τὸ
and to all the nations must first be proclaimed the
εὐαγγέλιον. 11 [n]ὅταν.δὲ" [o]ἀγάγωσιν" ὑμᾶς παραδιδόντες,
glad tidings. But whenever they may lead away you delivering [you] up,
μὴ.προμεριμνᾶτε τί λαλήσητε, [p]μηδὲ μελετᾶτε·"
be not careful beforehand what ye should say, nor meditate [your reply];
ἀλλ᾽ ὃ.[q]ἐὰν" δοθῇ ὑμῖν ἐν ἐκείνῃ.τῇ.ὥρᾳ, τοῦτο λαλεῖτε·
but whatever may be given to you in that hour, that speak;
οὐ.γάρ ἐστε ὑμεῖς οἱ λαλοῦντες, ἀλλὰ τὸ πνεῦμα τὸ ἅγιον.
for [3]not [2]are [1]ye they who speak, but the Spirit the Holy.
12 [r]παραδώσει.δὲ" ἀδελφὸς ἀδελφὸν εἰς θάνατον, καὶ πατὴρ
And [2]will [3]deliver [4]up [1]brother brother to death, and father
τέκνον· καὶ ἐπαναστήσονται τέκνα ἐπὶ γονεῖς, καὶ θανατώ-
child; and [2]will [3]rise [4]up [1]children against parents, and will put to
σουσιν αὐτούς· 13 καὶ ἔσεσθε μισούμενοι ὑπὸ πάντων διὰ
death them. And ye will be hated by all on account of
τὸ.ὄνομά.μου· ὁ.δὲ ὑπομείνας εἰς τέλος, οὗτος σωθήσε-
my name; but he who endures to [the] end, he shall be

receive more abundant judgment.
41 And sitting down across from the treasury, Jesus watched the crowd put money into the treasury. And many of the rich were putting in much.
42 And one poor widow came and put in two bits of money (which makes a kodran-tes).
43 And calling His disciples to Him, He said to them, Truly I say to you that this poor widow has put in more than all of those donating to the treasury.
44 For all *others* donated out of their abundance, but she out of her poverty put in all that she had – her whole living!

CHAPTER 13

1 And as He was going out of the Temple, one of His disciples said to Him, Teacher, Look! What stones and what buildings!
2 And answering Jesus said to him, Do you see these great buildings? There shall not be left a stone on top of a stone which shall not be thrown down.
3 And as He was sitting on the Mount of Olives across from the Temple, Peter and James and John and Andrew asked Him privately,
4 Tell us, when shall these things happen? And what *shall be* the sign when all these things are fulfilled?
5 And answering them Jesus began to say, Watch out! For someone may lead you astray.
6 For many will come in My name, saying, I AM *He*. And they will lead many into error.
7 But when you shall hear of wars and rumors of wars, do not be troubled. For this must happen. But the end is not yet.
8 For nation shall rise up against nation, and kingdom against kingdom. And there shall be earthquakes in different places. And there shall be famines and troubles. These are the beginnings of anguish.
9 But watch out for yourselves, for they will deliver you to sanhedrins and synagogues. You will be beaten. And you will be brought before governors and kings for My sake, as a witness to them.
10 But the gospel must first be preached to all nations.
11 But whenever they lead you away and deliver you, do not be anxious beforehand as to what you should say or think. But speak whatever is given to you in that hour – for you are not the ones who speak, but the Holy Spirit *speaks*.
12 And brother will betray brother to death and a father *his* child. And children will rise up against parents and will put them to death.
13 And you will be hated by all because of My name. But he that endures to the end, he shall be saved.

ται. 14 "Οταν.δὲ ἴδητε τὸ βδέλυγμα ˙τῆς ἐρημώσεως [s]τὸ
saved. But when ye see the abomination of the desolation which
ῥηθὲν ὑπὸ Δανιὴλ τοῦ προφήτου,ǁ [t]ἑστὸςǁ ὅπου οὐ.δεῖ·
was spoken of by Daniel the prophet, standing where it should not
ὁ ἀναγινώσκων νοείτω· τότε οἱ ἐν τῇ Ἰουδαίᾳ φευ-
(he who reads let him understand), then those in Judæa let
γέτωσαν εἰς.τὰ ὄρη· 15 ὁ [v]δὲǁ ἐπὶ τοῦ δώματος μὴ κατα-
them flee to the mountains, [2]he [1]and upon the housetop [3]not [4]let [5]him
βάτω [w]εἰς τὴν οἰκίαν,ǁ μηδὲ [x]εἰσελθέτωǁ [y]ἆραί τιǁ ἐκ
come down into the house, nor go in to take any thing out of
τῆς.οἰκίας.αὐτοῦ· 16 καὶ ὁ εἰς τὸν ἀγρὸν [z]ὢνǁ μὴ.ἐπιστρεψάτω
his house; and he that in the field is let him not return
εἰς τὰ ὀπίσω ἆραι τὸ.ἱμάτιον.αὐτοῦ. 17 οὐαὶ.δὲ ταῖς
to the things behind to take his garment. But woe to those that
ἐν.γαστρὶ.ἐχούσαις καὶ ταῖς θηλαζούσαις ἐν ἐκείναις ταῖς
are with child and to those that give suck in those
ἡμέραις. 18 προσεύχεσθε.δὲ ἵνα μὴ.γένηται [a]ἡ.φυγὴ.ὑμῶνǁ
days! And pray that [3]may [4]not [5]be [1]your [2]flight
χειμῶνος. 19 ἔσονται.γὰρ αἱ.ἡμέραι.ἐκεῖναι θλίψις, οἵα
in winter; for [4]shall [5]be [[1]in] [2]those [3]days tribulation, such as
οὐ.γέγονεν τοιαύτη ἀπ' ἀρχῆς κτίσεως [b]ἧςǁ ἔκτισεν ὁ
has not been the like from [the] beginning of creation which [2]created
θεὸς ἕως τοῦ νῦν, καὶ οὐ.μὴ γένηται. 20 καὶ εἰ.μὴ [c]κύριος
[1]God until now, and not at all shall be; and unless [the] Lord
ἐκολόβωσενǁ τὰς ἡμέρας, οὐκ.ἂν.ἐσώθη πᾶσα σάρξ·
had shortened the days, there would not have been saved any flesh;
ἀλλὰ διὰ τοὺς ἐκλεκτοὺς οὓς ἐξελέξατο, ἐκολόβωσεν τὰς
but on account of the elect whom he chose, he has shortened the
ἡμέρας. 21 Καὶ τότε ἐάν τις ὑμῖν εἴπῃ, [d]Ἰδού,ǁ ὧδε ὁ
days. And then if anyone to you say, Behold, here [is] the
χριστός, [e]ἢǁ [f]ἰδού,ǁ ἐκεῖ, [g]μὴ.πιστεύσητε.ǁ 22 ἐγερθήσονται
Christ, or Behold, there, ye shall not believe [it] [2]There [3]will [4]arise
[h]γὰρǁ [i]ψευδόχριστοι καὶǁ ψευδοπροφῆται, καὶ [j]δώσουσινǁ σημεῖα
[1]for false Christs and false prophets, and will give signs
καὶ τέρατα, πρὸς τὸ ἀποπλανᾶν εἰ δυνατὸν [k]καὶǁ τοὺς ἐκλεκ-
and wonders, to deceive if possible even the elect.
τούς. 23 ὑμεῖς.δὲ βλέπετε· [l]ἰδού,ǁ προείρηκα ὑμῖν πάντα.
But [2]ye [1]take heed: lo, I have foretold to you all things.
24 [m]Ἀλλ'ǁ ἐν ἐκείναις ταῖς ἡμέραις, μετὰ τὴν.θλῖψιν.ἐκείνην,
But in those days, after that tribulation,
ὁ ἥλιος σκοτισθήσεται, καὶ ἡ σελήνη οὐ.δώσει τὸ φέγγος
the sun shall be darkened, and the moon shall not give [2]light
αὐτῆς, 25 καὶ οἱ ἀστέρες [n]τοῦ οὐρανοῦ ἔσονται ἐκπίπτοντες,ǁ
[1]her; and the stars of the heaven shall be falling out,
καὶ αἱ δυνάμεις αἱ ἐν τοῖς οὐρανοῖς σαλευθήσονται.
and the powers which [are] in the heavens shall be shaken;
26 καὶ τότε ὄψονται τὸν υἱὸν τοῦ ἀνθρώπου ἐρχόμενον ἐν
and then shall they see the Son of man coming in
νεφέλαις μετὰ δυνάμεως [o]πολλῆς καὶ δόξης.ǁ 27 καὶ τότε
clouds with [2]power [1]great and glory, and then
ἀποστελεῖ τοὺς.ἀγγέλους.[p]αὐτοῦ,ǁ καὶ ἐπισυνάξει τοὺς
he will send his angels, and will gather together
ἐκλεκτοὺς.[q]αὐτοῦǁ ἐκ τῶν τεσσάρων ἀνέμων, ἀπ' ἄκρου
his elect from the four winds, from [the] extremity
γῆς ἕως ἄκρου οὐρανοῦ. 28 Ἀπὸ.δὲ τῆς συκῆς μάθετε
of earth to [the] extremity of heaven. But from the fig-tree learn
τὴν παραβολήν· ὅταν [r]αὐτῆς ἤδη ὁ κλάδοςǁ ἁπαλὸς γένη-
the parable: when of it already the branch tender is be-
ται, καὶ [s]ἐκφυῇǁ τὰ φύλλα, [t]γινώσκετεǁ ὅτι ἐγγὺς τὸ θέρος
come, and it puts forth the leaves, ye know that near the summer
ἐστίν· 29 οὕτως καὶ ὑμεῖς, ὅταν [u]ταῦτα ἴδητεǁ γινόμενα,
is. So also ye, when these things ye see coming to pass,
γινώσκετε ὅτι ἐγγύς ἐστιν ἐπὶ θύραις. 30 Ἀμὴν λέγω ὑμῖν,
know that near it is, at [the] doors. Verily I say to you,
ὅτι οὐ.μὴ παρέλθῃ ἡ.γενεὰ.αὕτη, μέχρις οὗ [v]πάντα
that in no wise will have passed away this generation, until all
ταῦταǁ γένηται. 31 ὁ οὐρανὸς καὶ ἡ γῆ [w]παρε-
these things shall have taken place. The heaven and the earth shall
λεύσονται·ǁ οἱ.δὲ.λόγοι.μου οὐ.[x]μὴǁ [y]παρέλθωσιν.ǁ 32 Περὶ.δὲ
pass away, but my words in no wise shall pass away. But concerning
τῆς.ἡμέρας.ἐκείνης [z]καὶǁ τῆς ὥρας, οὐδεὶς οἶδεν, οὐδὲ [a]οἱ ἄγ-
that day and the hour, no one knows, not even the an-
γελοιǁ [b]οἱǁ ἐν οὐρανῷ, οὐδὲ ὁ υἱός, εἰ.μὴ ὁ πατήρ. 33 Βλέπετε,
gels those in heaven, nor the Son, but the Father. Take heed,
ἀγρυπνεῖτε [c]καὶ προσεύχεσθε·ǁ οὐκ.οἴδατε.γὰρ πότε ὁ καιρός
watch and pray; for ye know not when the time
ἐστιν 34 ὡς ἄνθρωπος ἀπόδημος ἀφεὶς τὴν οἰκίαν
is; as a man going out of the country, leaving [2]house
αὐτοῦ, καὶ δοὺς τοῖς.δούλοις.αὐτοῦ τὴν ἐξουσίαν, [d]καὶǁ ἑκάστῳ
[1]his, and giving to his bondmen the authority, and to each one
τὸ.ἔργον.αὐτοῦ, καὶ τῷ θυρωρῷ ἐνετείλατο ἵνα γρηγορῇ.
his work, and [2]the [3]door-keeper [1]commanded that he should watch.

14 But when you see the abomination of desolation spoken of by Daniel the prophet, standing where it ought not, then let the ones who are in Judea flee to the mountains (let him who reads understand).
15 And he on the housetop, let him not come down into the house nor go in to take anything out of his house.
16 And he who is in the field, let him not return to the things behind in order to take his clothing.
17 But woe to those who are with child, and to those who are breast-feeding in those days!
18 And pray that your flight may not be in winter.
19 For in those days there shall be trouble such as has not occurred from the beginning of the creation which God created until now – and never shall be.
20 And if the Lord had not shortened the days, there would not have been any flesh saved. But because of the elect, those whom He chose, He has shortened the days.
21 And then if anyone shall say to you, Look! Here is the Christ! Or, Look there! You are not to believe.
22 For there will arise false christs and false prophets. And they will give signs and miracles in order to deceive, if possible, even the elect.
23 But be careful. See, I have told you all things beforehand.
24 But in those days, after that great trouble, the sun will be darkened and the moon will not give her light.
25 And the stars of the sky will be falling. And the powers that are in the heavens will be shaken.
26 And then they will see the Son of man coming in the clouds with great power and glory.
27 And then He will send His angels and will gather together His elect from the four winds, from the furthest part of the earth to the furthest part of Heaven.
28 But learn a parable from the fig-tree: when its branch has already become tender and put out leaves, you know that the summer is near.
29 So also when you see these things happening, *you will* know that it is near, at the very doors.
30 Truly I say to you that this generation will not have passed away until all these things have taken place.
31 The sky and the earth shall perish, but My words shall never perish.
32 But concerning that day and the hour no one knows, no, not even the angels who are in Heaven, nor the Son – but *only* the Father.
33 Be careful! Watch and pray! For you do not know when the time is.
34 As *When* a man leaves his house, going

35 γρηγορεῖτε οὖν· οὐκ.οἴδατε.γὰρ πότε ὁ.κύριος τῆς οἰκίας
Watch therefore, for ye know not when the master of the house
ἔρχεται. [e]ὀψέ, ἢ [f]μεσονυκτίου," ἢ ἀλεκτοροφωνίας, ἢ πρωΐ·
comes: at evening, or at midnight, or at cock-crowing, or morning;
36 μὴ ἐλθὼν ἐξαίφνης εὕρῃ ὑμᾶς καθεύδοντας. 37 [g]ἃ".δὲ
lest coming suddenly he should find you sleeping. And what
ὑμῖν λέγω, πᾶσιν λέγω, Γρηγορεῖτε.
to you I say, to all I say, Watch.

14 Ἦν.δὲ τὸ πάσχα καὶ τὰ ἄζυμα μετὰ δύο
Now it was the passover and the [feast of] unleavened bread after two
ἡμέρας· καὶ ἐζήτουν οἱ ἀρχιερεῖς καὶ οἱ γραμματεῖς πῶς
days. And [7]were [8]seeking [1]the [2]chief [3]priests [4]and [5]the [6]scribes how
αὐτὸν ἐν δόλῳ κρατήσαντες ἀποκτείνωσιν· 2 ἔλεγον [h]δέ,"
him by guile getting hold of they might kill [him]. [2]They [3]said [1]but,
Μὴ ἐν τῇ ἑορτῇ, μήποτε [i]θόρυβος ἔσται" τοῦ λαοῦ.
Not in the feast, lest a tumult there shall be of the people.

3 Καὶ ὄντος αὐτοῦ ἐν Βηθανίᾳ, ἐν τῇ οἰκίᾳ Σίμωνος τοῦ
And [2]being [1]he in Bethany, in the house of Simon the
λεπροῦ, κατακειμένου.αὐτοῦ, ἦλθεν γυνὴ ἔχουσα ἀλά-
leper, as he reclined [at table], [3]came [1]a [2]woman having an ala-
βαστρον μύρου νάρδου πιστικῆς πολυτελοῦς· [k]καὶ" συν-
baster flask of ointment of [2]nard [1]pure of great price; and having
τρίψασα [l]τὸ" ἀλάβαστρον, κατέχεεν αὐτοῦ [m]κατὰ" τῆς
broken the alabaster flask, she poured [it] [2]his [1]on
κεφαλῆς. 4 ἦσαν.δέ τινες ἀγανακτοῦντες πρὸς.ἑαυτούς, [n]καὶ
head. And [2]were [1]some indignant within themselves, and
λέγοντες," Εἰς τί ἡ.ἀπώλεια.αὕτη τοῦ μύρου γέγονεν;
saying, For what [2]this [3]waste [4]of [5]the [6]ointment [1]has been made?
5 ἠδύνατο.γὰρ τοῦτο [o] πραθῆναι ἐπάνω [p]τριακοσίων
for it was possible [for] this to have been sold for above three hundred
δηναρίων," καὶ δοθῆναι τοῖς πτωχοῖς· καὶ [q]ἐνεβριμῶντο"
denarii, and to have been given to the poor. And they murmured
αὐτῇ. 6 Ὁ.δὲ.Ἰησοῦς εἶπεν, Ἄφετε αὐτήν· τί αὐτῇ κόπους
at her. But Jesus said, Let [2]alone [1]her; why to her trouble
παρέχετε; καλὸν ἔργον [r]εἰργάσατο" [s]εἰς ἐμέ." 7 πάντοτε.γὰρ
do ye cause? a good work she wrought towards me. For always
τοὺς πτωχοὺς ἔχετε μεθ' ἑαυτῶν, καὶ ὅταν θέλητε δύνασθε
the poor ye have with you, and whenever ye desire ye are able
[t]αὐτοὺς" εὖ.ποιῆσαι· ἐμὲ.δὲ οὐ πάντοτε ἔχετε. 8 ὃ [v]εἶχεν"
[3]them [1]to [2]do good; but me not always ye have. What [2]could
[w]αὕτη," ἐποίησεν· προέλαβεν μυρίσαι [x]μου.τὸ.σῶμα" εἰς
[1]she, she did. She came beforehand to anoint my body for
τὸν ἐνταφιασμόν. 9 ἀμὴν [y] λέγω ὑμῖν, ὅπου.[z]ἂν" κηρυχθῇ
the burial. Verily I say to you, Wheresoever shall be proclaimed
τὸ.εὐαγγέλιον.[a]τοῦτο" εἰς ὅλον τὸν κόσμον, καὶ ὃ ἐποίησεν
this glad tidings in [2]whole [1]the world, also what [3]has [4]done
αὕτη λαληθήσεται εἰς μνημόσυνον αὐτῆς.
[1]this [[2]woman] shall be spoken of for a memorial of her.

10 Καὶ [b]ὁ" Ἰούδας [b]ὁ" [c]Ἰσκαριώτης," [d] εἷς τῶν δώδεκα,
And Judas the Iscariote, one of the twelve,
ἀπῆλθεν πρὸς τοὺς ἀρχιερεῖς, ἵνα [e]παραδῷ αὐτὸν"
went away to the chief priests, that he might deliver up him
αὐτοῖς. 11 Οἱ.δὲ ἀκούσαντες ἐχάρησαν, καὶ ἐπηγγείλαντο
to them. And they having heard rejoiced, and promised
αὐτῷ ἀργύριον δοῦναι· καὶ ἐζήτει πῶς [f]εὐκαίρως αὐτὸν
[3]him [4]money [1]to [2]give. And he sought how [3]conveniently [5]him
παραδῷ."
[1]he [2]might [4]deliver [6]up.

12 Καὶ τῇ πρώτῃ ἡμέρᾳ τῶν ἀζύμων, ὅτε τὸ πάσχα
And on the first day of unleavened [bread], when the passover
ἔθυον, λέγουσιν αὐτῷ οἱ.μαθηταὶ.αὐτοῦ, Ποῦ θέλεις
they killed, [3]say [4]to [5]him [1]his [2]disciples, Where desirest thou [that]
ἀπελθόντες ἑτοιμάσωμεν ἵνα φάγῃς τὸ πάσχα; 13 Καὶ
going we should prepare that thou mayest eat the passover? And
ἀποστέλλει δύο τῶν.μαθητῶν.αὐτοῦ, καὶ λέγει αὐτοῖς, Ὑπάγετε
he sends forth two of his disciples, and says to them, Go
εἰς τὴν πόλιν· καὶ ἀπαντήσει ὑμῖν ἄνθρωπος κεράμιον ὕδατος
into the city, and [3]will [4]meet [5]you [1]a [2]man a pitcher of water
βαστάζων· ἀκολουθήσατε αὐτῷ, 14 καὶ ὅπου.[g]ἐὰν" εἰσέλθῃ,
carrying; follow him; and wherever he may enter,
εἴπατε τῷ οἰκοδεσπότῃ, Ὅτι ὁ διδάσκαλος λέγει, Ποῦ
say to the master of the house, The teacher says, Where
ἐστιν τὸ κατάλυμα [h] ὅπου τὸ πάσχα μετὰ τῶν.μαθητῶν.μου
is the guest-chamber where the passover with my disciples
φάγω; 15 καὶ αὐτὸς ὑμῖν δείξει [i]ἀνώγεον" μέγα ἐστρω-
I may eat? and he [3]you [1]will [2]shew an upper room large, fur-
μένον [k]ἕτοιμον." [l]ἐκεῖ" ἑτοιμάσατε ἡμῖν. 16 Καὶ ἐξῆλθον οἱ
nished ready. There prepare for us. And went away
μαθηταὶ.[m]αὐτοῦ," καὶ ἦλθον εἰς τὴν πόλιν, καὶ εὗρον καθὼς
his disciples, and came into the city, and found as
εἶπεν αὐτοῖς, καὶ ἡτοίμασαν τὸ πάσχα. 17 Καὶ ὀψίας
he had said to them, and they prepared the passover. And evening

to a foreign country, giving authority to his
servants and to each one his work, and commanding the doorkeeper to watch
35 watch, then, for you do not know
when the Master of the house comes – at
evening or at midnight or at the time the
cock crows or morning –
36 so that he should not come suddenly and
find you sleeping.
37 And what I say to you, I say to all.
Watch!
14 1 Now after two days it was the Passover
and the feast of unleavened bread. And the
chief priests and the scribes were looking for
a way to seize Him by trickery and kill
Him.
2 But they said, Not during the feast, for
fear that there may be a riot among the
people.
3 And when He was in the house of Simon
the leper in Bethany, as He rested, a woman
came with a very precious alabaster bottle of
ointment of spikenard. And breaking the
alabaster bottle, she poured it on His head.
4 And some were angry within themselves.
And *they* said, Why has this waste occurred?
5 For this could have been sold for more
than three hundred coins and given to the
poor. And they grumbled at her.
6 But Jesus said, Let her alone. Why do you
trouble her? She has done a good work
towards Me.
7 For you always have the poor with you.
And you can do them good whenever you
wish. But you do not always have Me.
8 She has done what she could. She came
beforehand to anoint My body for burial.
9 Truly I say to you that wherever this
gospel shall be preached throughout the
whole world, also what this one has done
shall be spoken of for a memorial of her.
10 And Judas Is-car-i-ot, one of the twelve,
went to the chief priests in order to betray
Him to them.
11 And hearing *this* they rejoiced and promised to give him money. And he was looking
for a way to conveniently betray Him.
12 And on the first day of unleavened
bread, when they killed the passover lamb,
His disciples said to Him, Where do you
desire for us to go to prepare so that You
may eat the passover?
13 And He sent out two of His disciples,
saying to them, Go into the city. And a man
carrying a pitcher of water will meet you –
follow him.
14 And wherever he goes in, say to the
master of the house, The Teacher says,
Where is the guest-room where I may eat the
passover with My disciples?
15 And he will show you a large upper
room, furnished and ready. Make ready for
us there.
16 And His disciples went out and came
into the city. And they found it as He had
said to them. And they prepared the

γινομένης ἔρχεται μετὰ τῶν δώδεκα· 18 καὶ ἀνακειμένων
being come he comes with the twelve. And as ²were ³reclining
αὐτῶν καὶ ἐσθιόντων [n]εἶπεν ὁ Ἰησοῦς,[ǁ] Ἀμὴν λέγω
[⁴at ⁵table] ¹they and were eating ²said ¹Jesus, Verily I say
ὑμῖν, ὅτι εἷς ἐξ ὑμῶν παραδώσει με, ὁ ἐσθίων μετ' ἐμοῦ.
to you, that one of you will deliver up me, who is eating with me.
19 [o]Οἱ.δὲ[ǀ] ἤρξαντο λυπεῖσθαι, καὶ λέγειν αὐτῷ, εἷς [p]καθ'[ǁ] εἷς,
And they began to be grieved, and to say to him, one by one,
Μήτι ἐγώ; [q]Καὶ ἄλλος, Μήτι ἐγώ;[ǁ] 20 Ὁ.δὲ [r]ἀπο-
[Is it] I? And another, [Is it] I? But he an-
κριθεὶς[ǁ] εἶπεν αὐτοῖς, Εἷς [s]ἐκ[ǀ] τῶν δώδεκα, ὁ ἐμβαπτό-
swering said to them, [It is] one of the twelve, who is dip-
μενος μετ' ἐμοῦ [t]εἰς τὸ τρυβλίον. 21 [v]ὁ μὲν υἱὸς τοῦ ἀνθρώπου
ping with me in the dish. The ⁵indeed ¹Son ²of ³man
ὑπάγει, καθὼς γέγραπται περὶ αὐτοῦ· οὐαὶ.δὲ τῷ
⁴goes, as it has been written concerning him; but woe
ἀνθρώπῳ.ἐκείνῳ δι' οὗ ὁ υἱὸς τοῦ ἀνθρώπου παραδίδοται·
to that man by whom the Son of man is delivered up;
καλὸν [w]ἦν[ǁ] αὐτῷ εἰ οὐκ.ἐγεννήθη ὁ.ἄνθρωπος.ἐκεῖνος.
good were it for him if ³had ⁴not ⁵been ⁶born ¹that ²man.
22 Καὶ ἐσθιόντων.αὐτῶν, λαβὼν [x]ὁ Ἰησοῦς[ǁ] ἄρτον,
And as they were eating, ²having ³taken ¹Jesus a loaf,
εὐλογήσας ἔκλασεν, καὶ ἔδωκεν αὐτοῖς, καὶ εἶπεν, Λάβετε,
having blessed he brake, and gave to them, and said, Take,
[y]φάγετε·[ǁ] τοῦτό ἐστιν τὸ.σῶμά.μου. 23 Καὶ λαβὼν [z]τὸ[ǁ]
eat; this is my body. And having taken the
ποτήριον, εὐχαριστήσας ἔδωκεν αὐτοῖς· καὶ ἔπιον ἐξ αὐτοῦ
cup, having given thanks he gave to them, and they ²drank ³of ⁴it
πάντες· 24 καὶ εἶπεν αὐτοῖς, Τοῦτό ἐστιν τὸ.αἷμά.μου [a]τὸ[ǁ]
¹all And he said to them, This is my blood that
τῆς [b]καινῆς[ǁ] διαθήκης, τὸ [c]περὶ πολλῶν ἐκχυνόμενον.[ǁ]
of the new covenant, which for many is poured out.
25 ἀμὴν λέγω ὑμῖν, ὅτι οὐκέτι.οὐ.μὴ πίω ἐκ τοῦ
Verily I say to you, that not any more in any wise will I drink of the
[d]γεννήματος[ǁ] τῆς ἀμπέλου, ἕως τῆς.ἡμέρας.ἐκείνης ὅταν αὐτὸ
fruit of the vine, until that day when it
πίνω καινὸν ἐν τῇ βασιλείᾳ τοῦ θεοῦ.
I drink new in the kingdom of God.
26 Καὶ ὑμνήσαντες ἐξῆλθον εἰς τὸ ὄρος τῶν Ἐλαιῶν.
And having sung a hymn they went out to the mount of Olives.
27 καὶ λέγει αὐτοῖς ὁ Ἰησοῦς, Ὅτι πάντες σκανδαλισθήσεσθε
And ²says ³to ⁴them ¹Jesus, All ye will be offended
[e]ἐν ἐμοὶ[ǀ] [f]ἐν τῇ.νυκτὶ.ταύτῃ·[ǁ] ὅτι γέγραπται, Πατάξω τὸν
in me in this night; for it has been written, I will smite the
ποιμένα, καὶ [g]διασκορπισθήσεται τὰ πρόβατα.[ǁ] 28 Ἀλλὰ
shepherd, and will be scattered abroad the sheep. But
μετὰ τὸ.ἐγερθῆναί.με, προάξω ὑμᾶς εἰς τὴν Γαλιλαίαν.
after my arising, I will go before you into Galilee.
29 Ὁ.δὲ.Πέτρος ἔφη αὐτῷ, [h]Καὶ εἰ[ǀ] πάντες σκανδαλισθήσονται,
But Peter said to him, Even if all shall be offended,
ἀλλ' οὐκ ἐγώ. 30 Καὶ λέγει αὐτῷ ὁ Ἰησοῦς, Ἀμὴν λέγω σοι,
yet not I. And ²says ³to ⁴him ¹Jesus, Verily I say to thee,
ὅτι [i]σήμερον [j]ἐν τῇ.νυκτὶ.ταύτῃ,[ǁ] πρὶν ἢ δὶς ἀλέκτορα
that to-day in this night, before that twice [the] cock
φωνῆσαι, τρίς [k]ἀπαρνήσῃ με.[ǁ] 31 Ὁ.δὲ [l]ἐκ.περισσοῦ ἔλεγεν
crow, thrice thou wilt deny me. But he ²vehemently ⁴said
μᾶλλον,[ǁ] Ἐάν [m]με.δέῃ[ǁ] συναποθανεῖν σοι, οὐ.μή σε
¹the ³more, If it were needful for me to die with thee, in no wise thee
[n]ἀπαρνήσομαι.[ǁ] Ὡσαύτως.δὲ καὶ πάντες ἔλεγον.
will I deny. And in like manner also ³all ²they ¹spake.
32 Καὶ ἔρχονται εἰς χωρίον [o]οὗ τὸ[ǁ] ὄνομα [p]Γεθσημανῆ·[ǁ]
And they come to a place of which the name [is] Gethsemane;
καὶ λέγει τοῖς.μαθηταῖς.αὐτοῦ, Καθίσατε ὧδε, ἕως προσεύξω-
and he says to his disciples, Sit here, while I shall
μαι. 33 Καὶ παραλαμβάνει τὸν Πέτρον καὶ [q]τὸν[ǁ] Ἰάκωβον
pray. And he takes Peter and James
καὶ Ἰωάννην [r]μεθ' ἑαυτοῦ.[ǁ] Καὶ ἤρξατο ἐκθαμβεῖσθαι καὶ
and John with him; and he began to be greatly amazed and
ἀδημονεῖν. 34 καὶ λέγει αὐτοῖς, Περίλυπός ἐστιν ἡ.ψυχή.μου
deeply depressed. And he says to them, Very sorrowful is my soul
ἕως θανάτου· μείνατε ὧδε καὶ γρηγορεῖτε. 35 Καὶ [s]προελ-
even to death; remain here and watch. And having gone
θὼν[ǁ] μικρὸν [t]ἔπεσεν[ǁ] ἐπὶ τῆς γῆς, καὶ προσηύχετο ἵνα, εἰ
forward a little he fell upon the earth, and prayed that, if
δυνατόν ἐστιν, παρέλθῃ ἀπ' αὐτοῦ ἡ ὥρα. 36 καὶ ἔλεγεν,
possible it is, might pass from him the hour. And he said,
Ἀββᾶ, ὁ πατήρ, πάντα δυνατά σοι· παρένεγκε τὸ ποτή-
Abba, Father, all things [are] possible to thee; take away ²cup
ριον [v]ἀπ' ἐμοῦ τοῦτο·[ǁ] ἀλλ' οὐ τί ἐγὼ θέλω, ἀλλὰ τί σύ.
³from ⁴me ¹this; but not what I will, but what thou.
37 Καὶ ἔρχεται καὶ εὑρίσκει αὐτοὺς καθεύδοντας· καὶ λέγει τῷ
And he comes and finds them sleeping. And he says

passover.

17 And when evening had come, He came with the Twelve.

18 And as they sat at table and were eating, Jesus said to them, Truly I say to you that one of you who is eating with Me will betray Me.

19 And they began to be sorrowful and to say to Him one by one, Is it I? And another, Is it I?

20 But answering He said to them, It is one of the Twelve, the one who is dipping with Me in the dish.

21 Indeed the Son of man goes, as it has been written about Him. But woe to that man by whom the Son of man is betrayed! It would be good for that man if he had never been born.

22 And as they were eating, Jesus took a loaf. *And He* blessed it, broke, and gave to them. And *He* said, Take, eat! This is My body.

23 And taking the cup and giving thanks, He gave to them. And they all drank of it.

24 And He said to them, This is My blood of the new covenant, which is poured out for many.

25 Truly I say to you that I will not drink of the fruit of the vine any more until that day when I will drink it new in the kingdom of God.

26 And singing a hymn, they went out to the Mount of Olives.

27 And Jesus said to them, All of you will be ashamed of Me tonight. For it is written, "I will strike the Shepherd and the sheep shall be scattered."

28 But after I have risen, I will go before you into Galilee.

29 But Peter said to Him, Even if all shall be offended, yet I will not.

30 And Jesus said to him, Truly I say to you that today, in this *very* night, you will deny Me three times before the cock crows twice.

31 But he spoke more strongly, If it were necessary for me to die with You, I will never deny You. And they all also spoke in the same way.

32 And they came to a place named Geth-sem-a-ne. And He said to His disciples, Sit here while I pray.

33 And He took Peter and James and John with Him. And He began to be greatly amazed and heavy-hearted.

34 And He said to them, My soul is sorrowful beyond words, even to death. Stay here and watch.

35 And going forward a little, He fell on the ground and prayed that, if it were possible, the hour might pass from Him.

36 And He said, Abba! Father, all things are possible to You. Take away this cup from Me, but not as I desire, but as You will.

37 And He came and found them sleeping.

Πέτρῳ, Σίμων, καθεύδεις; οὐκ.ἴσχυσας μίαν ὥραν γρη-
to Peter, Simon, sleepest thou? wast thou not able one hour to
γορῆσαι; 38 γρηγορεῖτε καὶ προσεύχεσθε, ἵνα μὴ.[w]εἰσέλθητε‖
watch? Watch and pray, that ye enter not
εἰς πειρασμόν. τὸ μὲν πνεῦμα πρόθυμον, ἡ.δὲ σὰρξ
into temptation. The [2]indeed [1]spirit [is] ready, but the flesh
ἀσθενής. 39 Καὶ πάλιν ἀπελθὼν προσηύξατο, τὸν αὐτὸν
weak. And again having gone away he prayed, [2]the [3]same
λόγον εἰπών. 40 καὶ [x]ὑποστρέψας‖ εὗρεν αὐτοὺς [y]πάλιν‖
[4]thing [1]saying. And having returned he found them again
καθεύδοντας· ἦσαν.γὰρ [z]οἱ.ὀφθαλμοὶ.αὐτῶν‖ [a]βεβαρημένοι.‖
sleeping, for [3]were [1]their [2]eyes heavy;
καὶ οὐκ.ᾔδεισαν τί [b]αὐτῷ ἀποκριθῶσιν.‖ 41 Καὶ ἔρχεται
and they knew not what [4]him [1]they [2]should [3]answer. And he comes
τὸ τρίτον, καὶ λέγει αὐτοῖς, Καθεύδετε [c]τὸ‖ λοιπὸν καὶ
the third time, and says to them, Sleep on now and
ἀναπαύεσθε. ἀπέχει· ἦλθεν ἡ ὥρα· ἰδού, παραδίδοται
take your rest. It is enough; has come the hour; lo, [5]is [6]delivered [7]up
ὁ υἱὸς τοῦ ἀνθρώπου εἰς τὰς χεῖρας τῶν ἁμαρτωλῶν. 42 ἐγεί-
[1]the [2]Son [3]of [4]man into the hands of sinners. Rise,
ρεσθε, ἄγωμεν· ἰδού, ὁ παραδιδούς με [d]ἤγγικεν.‖
let us go; behold, he who is delivering up me has drawn near.

43 Καὶ [e]εὐθέως‖ ἔτι αὐτοῦ.λαλοῦντος παραγίνεται [f]Ἰού-
And immediately [4]yet [1]as [2]he [3]is speaking, comes up Ju
δας[g], εἷς [h]ὢν‖ τῶν δώδεκα, καὶ μετ' αὐτοῦ ὄχλος [i]πολὺς‖
das, [2]one [1]being of the twelve, and with him a [2]crowd [1]great,
μετὰ μαχαιρῶν καὶ ξύλων, παρὰ τῶν ἀρχιερέων καὶ τῶν
with swords and staves, from the chief priests and the
γραμματέων καὶ [k]τῶν‖ πρεσβυτέρων. 44 δεδώκει.δὲ ὁ
scribes and the elders. Now [7]had [8]given [1]he [2]who
παραδιδοὺς αὐτὸν [l]σύσσημον‖ αὐτοῖς, λέγων, Ὃν.ἂν
[3]was [4]delivering [6]up [5]him a sign to them, saying, Whomsoever
φιλήσω αὐτός ἐστιν· κρατήσατε αὐτόν, καὶ [m]ἀπαγάγετε‖
I shall kiss [2]he [1]is; seize him, and lead [him] away
ἀσφαλῶς. 45 Καὶ ἐλθών, [e]εὐθέως‖ προσελθὼν αὐτῷ λέγει,
safely. And being come, immediately coming up to him he says,
[n]Ῥαββί, ῥαββί‖ καὶ κατεφίλησεν αὐτόν. 46 Οἱ.δὲ [o]ἐπέβαλον‖
Rabbi, Rabbi; and ardently kissed him. And they laid
[p]ἐπ' αὐτὸν τὰς χεῖρας αὐτῶν,‖ καὶ ἐκράτησαν αὐτόν. 47 Εἷς.δέ
upon him [2]hands [1]their, and seized him. But [3]one
[q]τις‖ τῶν παρεστηκότων σπασάμενος τὴν μάχαιραν
[1]a [2]certain of those standing by, having drawn the sword
ἔπαισεν τὸν δοῦλον τοῦ ἀρχιερέως καὶ ἀφεῖλεν αὐτοῦ τὸ
struck the bondman of the high priest and took off his
[r]ὠτίον.‖ 48 Καὶ ἀποκριθεὶς ὁ Ἰησοῦς εἶπεν αὐτοῖς, Ὡς ἐπὶ
ear. And [2]answering [1]Jesus said to them, As against
λῃστὴν [s]ἐξήλθετε‖ μετὰ μαχαιρῶν καὶ ξύλων συλλαβεῖν με;
a robber are ye come out with swords and staves to take me?
49 καθ'.ἡμέραν ἤμην πρὸς ὑμᾶς ἐν τῷ ἱερῷ διδάσκων, καὶ
Daily I was with you in the temple teaching, and
οὐκ ἐκρατήσατέ με· ἀλλ' ἵνα πληρωθῶσιν αἱ γραφαί.
ye did not seize me: but [it is] that [3]may [4]be [5]fulfilled [1]the [2]scriptures.
50 Καὶ ἀφέντες αὐτὸν [t]πάντες ἔφυγον.‖ 51 Καὶ [u]εἷς τις
And leaving him all fled. And one a certain
νεανίσκος‖ [v]ἠκολούθει‖ αὐτῷ, περιβεβλημένος σινδόνα ἐπὶ
young man was following him, having cast a linen cloth about
γυμνοῦ· καὶ κρατοῦσιν αὐτὸν [w]οἱ νεανίσκοι·‖ 52 ὁ δὲ
[his] naked [body]; and [4]seize [5]him [1]the [2]young [3]men, but he,
καταλιπὼν τὴν σινδόνα γυμνὸς ἔφυγεν [x]ἀπ' αὐτῶν.‖
leaving behind the linen cloth, [2]naked [1]fled from them.

53 Καὶ ἀπήγαγον τὸν Ἰησοῦν πρὸς τὸν ἀρχιερέα· καὶ
And they led away Jesus to the high priest. And
συνέρχονται [y]αὐτῷ πάντες οἱ ἀρχιερεῖς καὶ οἱ [z]πρεσβύτεροι
there come together to him all the chief priests and the elders
καὶ οἱ γραμματεῖς.‖ 54 Καὶ ὁ Πέτρος ἀπὸ μακρόθεν ἠκολού-
and the scribes. And Peter from afar off fol-
θησεν αὐτῷ ἕως ἔσω εἰς τὴν αὐλὴν τοῦ ἀρχιερέως· καὶ ἦν
lowed him as far as within to the court of the high priest; and he was
[a]συγκαθήμενος‖ μετὰ.τῶν ὑπηρετῶν, καὶ θερμαινόμενος πρὸς
sitting with the officers, and warming himself at
[b]τὸ‖ φῶς. 55 Οἱ.δὲ ἀρχιερεῖς καὶ ὅλον τὸ συνέδριον ἐζήτουν
the fire (lit. light). And the chief priests and [2]whole [1]the sanhedrim sought
κατὰ τοῦ Ἰησοῦ μαρτυρίαν, εἰς τὸ θανατῶσαι αὐτόν· καὶ οὐχ
against Jesus testimony, to put to death him, and [2]not
[c]εὕρισκον.‖ 56 πολλοὶ.γὰρ ἐψευδομαρτύρουν κατ' αὐτοῦ,
[1]did find [any]. For many bore false testimony against him,
καὶ ἴσαι αἱ μαρτυρίαι οὐκ.ἦσαν. 57 καί τινες ἀναστάντες
and alike their testimonies were not. And some having risen up
ἐψευδομαρτύρουν κατ' αὐτοῦ, λέγοντες, 58 Ὅτι ἡμεῖς ἠκούσα-
bore false testimony against him, saying, We heard

And He said to Peter, Simon, do you sleep?
Could you not watch one hour?
38 Watch and pray that you do not enter
into temptation. The spirit truly is willing,
but the flesh is weak.
39 And going away again, He prayed and
spoke the same words.
40 And returning He found them asleep
again, for their eyes were heavy. And they
did not know what they should answer Him.
41 And He came the third time and said to
them, Sleep on now and take your rest. It is
enough. The hour has come. Behold, the Son
of man has been betrayed into the hands of
sinners!
42 Get up. Let us go. See, he who is
betraying Me has come.
43 And immediately while He was still
speaking, Judas, who was one of the twelve,
came up And a great crowd with swords and
sticks was with him, sent from the chief
priests and the scribes and the elders.
44 Now he who was betraying Him had
given them a signal, saying, Whomever I shall
kiss is the one. Catch hold of him and lead
him safely away.
45 And having arrived, he immediately
came up to Him and said, Master! Master!
And he kissed Him.
46 And they laid their hands on Him and
took hold of Him.
47 But one of those standing by drew a
sword and struck a servant of the high priest,
taking off his ear.
48 And answering, Jesus said to them, Have
you come out as against a thief, to take Me
with swords and sticks?
49 I was with you in the Temple teaching
daily and you did not lay hold on Me. But *it
must be* so that the Scriptures may be
fulfilled.
50 And forsaking Him, they all ran away.
51 And a certain young man was following
Him, wearing a linen cloth about his naked
body. And the young men seized him.
52 But leaving behind the linen cloth, he
fled from them naked.

53 And they led Jesus away to the high
priest. And all the chief priests and the
elders and the scribes gathered with him.
54 And Peter followed Him at a distance; as
far as the inside of the high priest's hall. And
he was sitting with the officers and was
warming himself near the fire.
55 And the chief priests and the whole
sanhedrin sought testimony against Jesus, in
order to put Him to death. But none was
found.
56 For many bore false witness against Him,
but their stories were not alike.
57 And some rose up to bear false witness
against Him, saying,
58 We heard him saying, I will destroy this

μεν αὐτοῦ λέγοντος, "Οτι ἐγὼ καταλύσω τὸν.ναὸν.τοῦτον τὸν
him saying, I will destroy this temple the
χειροποίητον, καὶ διὰ τριῶν ἡμερῶν ἄλλον ἀχειροποίητον
[one] made with hands, and in three days another not made with hands
οἰκοδομήσω. 59 Καὶ οὐδὲ οὕτως ἴση ἦν ἡ.μαρτυρία.αὐτῶν.
I will build. And neither thus alike was their testimony.
60 Καὶ ἀναστὰς ὁ ἀρχιερεὺς εἰς [e]τὸ" μέσον ἐπηρώτησεν
And [4]having [5]stood [6]up [1]the [2]high [3]priest in the midst questioned
τὸν Ἰησοῦν, λέγων, Οὐκ ἀποκρίνῃ οὐδέν; τί οὗτοί σου
Jesus, saying, Answerest thou nothing? What [2]these [4]thee
καταμαρτυροῦσιν; 61 Ὁ.δὲ ἐσιώπα, καὶ [f]οὐδὲν ἀπεκρίνατο."
[1]testify [3]against? But he was silent, and nothing answered.
Πάλιν ὁ ἀρχιερεὺς ἐπηρώτα αὐτόν, καὶ λέγει αὐτῷ, Σὺ
Again the high priest was questioning him, and says to him, [2]Thou
εἶ ὁ χριστός, ὁ υἱὸς τοῦ εὐλογητοῦ; 62 Ὁ.δὲ.Ἰησοῦς εἶπεν,
[1]art the Christ, the Son of the blessed? And Jesus said,
Ἐγώ εἰμι. καὶ ὄψεσθε τὸν υἱὸν τοῦ ἀνθρώπου [g]καθήμενον
I am. And ye shall see the Son of man sitting
ἐκ δεξιῶν" τῆς δυνάμεως, καὶ ἐρχόμενον μετὰ τῶν νεφελῶν
at [the] right hand of power, and coming with the clouds
τοῦ οὐρανοῦ. 63 Ὁ.δὲ ἀρχιερεὺς διαῤῥήξας τοὺς.χιτῶνας.αὐτοῦ
of the heaven. And the high priest having rent his garments
λέγει, Τί ἔτι χρείαν ἔχομεν μαρτύρων; 64 ἠκούσατε [h]τῆς
says, What any more need have we of witnesses? Ye heard the
βλασφημίας." τί ὑμῖν φαίνεται; Οἱ.δὲ πάντες κατέκριναν
blasphemy: what [2]to [3]you [1]appears? And they all condemned
αὐτὸν [i]εἶναι ἔνοχον[i] θανάτου. 65 Καὶ ἤρξαντό τινες ἐμπτύειν
him to be deserving of death. And [2]began [1]some to spit upon
αὐτῷ, καὶ περικαλύπτειν [k]τὸ.πρόσωπον.αὐτοῦ," καὶ κολα-
him, and to cover up his face, and to buf-
φίζειν αὐτόν, καὶ λέγειν αὐτῷ, Προφήτευσον· καὶ οἱ ὑπηρέται
fet him, and to say to him, Prophesy; and the officers
ῥαπίσμασιν αὐτὸν [m]ἔβαλλον."
with the palm of the hand [2]him [1]struck.
66 Καὶ ὄντος τοῦ Πέτρου [n]ἐν τῇ αὐλῇ κάτω," ἔρχεται μία
And [2]being [1]Peter in the court below, comes one
τῶν παιδισκῶν τοῦ ἀρχιερέως, 67 καὶ ἰδοῦσα τὸν Πέτρον
of the maids of the high priest, and seeing Peter
θερμαινόμενον, ἐμβλέψασα αὐτῷ λέγει, Καὶ σὺ μετὰ τοῦ
warming himself, having looked at him says, And thou [2]with [3]the
Ναζαρηνοῦ [o]Ἰησοῦ ἦσθα." 68 Ὁ.δὲ ἠρνήσατο, λέγων, [p]Οὐκ
[4]Nazarene [5]Jesus [1]wast. But he denied, saying, [3]Not
οἶδα [q]οὐδὲ" ἐπίσταμαι [r]τί σὺ" λέγεις. Καὶ ἐξῆλθεν ἔξω
[1]I [2]know nor even understand what thou sayest. And he went forth out
εἰς τὸ προαύλιον· [s]καὶ ἀλέκτωρ ἐφώνησεν." 69 Καὶ ἡ παιδίσκη
into the porch, and a cock crew. And the maid
ἰδοῦσα αὐτὸν [t]πάλιν ἤρξατο" λέγειν τοῖς [v]παρεστηκόσιν," "Οτι
seeing him again began to say to those standing by,
οὗτος ἐξ αὐτῶν ἐστιν. 70 Ὁ.δὲ πάλιν ἠρνεῖτο. Καὶ μετὰ
This [[2]one] [3]of [4]them [1]is. And he again denied. And after
μικρὸν πάλιν οἱ παρεστῶτες ἔλεγον τῷ Πέτρῳ, Ἀληθῶς
a little again those standing by said to Peter, Truly
ἐξ αὐτῶν εἶ· καὶ.γὰρ Γαλιλαῖος εἶ, [w]καὶ ἡ λαλιά
from among them thou art, for both a Galilean thou art, and [2]speech
σου ὁμοιάζει." 71 Ὁ.δὲ ἤρξατο ἀναθεματίζειν καὶ [x]ὀμνύειν,"
[1]thy agrees. But he began to curse and to swear,
"Οτι οὐκ.οἶδα τὸν.ἄνθρωπον.τοῦτον ὃν λέγετε. 72 Καὶ [y]
I know not this man whom ye speak of. And
ἐκ.δευτέρου ἀλέκτωρ ἐφώνησεν. Καὶ ἀνεμνήσθη ὁ Πέτρος [z]τοῦ
the second time a cock crew. And [2]remembered [1]Peter the
ῥήματος οὗ" εἶπεν αὐτῷ ὁ Ἰησοῦς, "Οτι πρὶν ἀλέκτορα
word that [2]said [3]to [4]him [1]Jesus, Before [the] cock
[a]φωνῆσαι δὶς" [b]ἀπαρνήσῃ με τρίς·" καὶ ἐπιβαλὼν
crow twice thou wilt deny me thrice; and having thought thereon
ἔκλαιεν.
he wept.

15 Καὶ [c]εὐθέως" [d]ἐπὶ τὸ" πρωῒ συμβούλιον [e]ποιήσαντες"
And immediately in the morning [6]a [7]counsel [4]having [5]formed
οἱ ἀρχιερεῖς μετὰ τῶν πρεσβυτέρων καὶ [f]γραμματέων καὶ
[1]the [2]chief [3]priests with the elders and scribes and
ὅλον τὸ συνέδριον, δήσαντες τὸν Ἰησοῦν ἀπήνεγκαν καὶ
[2]whole [1]the sanhedrim, having bound Jesus carried [him] away and
παρέδωκαν [g]τῷ" [h]Πιλάτῳ." 2 καὶ ἐπηρώτησεν αὐτὸν ὁ
delivered up [him] to Pilate. And [2]questioned [3]him
[i]Πιλάτος," Σὺ εἶ ὁ βασιλεὺς τῶν Ἰουδαίων; Ὁ.δὲ ἀπο-
[1]Pilate, [5]Thou [4]art the King of the Jews? And he an-
κριθεὶς [j]εἶπεν αὐτῷ," Σὺ λέγεις. 3 Καὶ κατηγόρουν αὐτοῦ οἱ
swering said to him, Thou sayest. And [4]were [5]accusing [6]him [1]the
ἀρχιερεῖς πολλά· 4 ὁ.δὲ.[i]Πιλάτος" πάλιν [k]ἐπηρώτησεν" αὐτόν,
[2]chief [3]priests urgently. And Pilate again questioned him,
[l]λέγων," Οὐκ ἀποκρίνῃ οὐδέν; ἴδε, πόσα σου
saying, Answerest thou nothing? See, of how many things [4]thee

Temple that is made with hands, and in
three days I will build another which is not
made with hands.
59 And neither was their testimony alike in
this.
60 And standing up in the middle, the high
priest questioned Jesus, saying, Do you
answer nothing? What do these witness
against you?
61 But He was silent and answered nothing.
Again the high priest asked Him, saying to
Him, Are you the Christ, the Son of the
Blessed?
62 And Jesus said, I AM! And you will see
the Son of man sitting at the right hand of
power and coming with the clouds of the
heavens.
63 And tearing his clothes, the high priest
said, What need do we have of any more
witnesses?
64 You have heard the blasphemy. How
does it look to you? And they all condemned Him to be worthy of death.
65 And some began to spit on Him and to
cover His face and to beat Him with their
fists, saying to Him, Prophesy! And the
officers hit Him with the palms of their
hands.
66 Peter was in the court below. And one of
the maids of the high priest came up.
67 And seeing Peter warming himself,
staring at him, she said, You also were with
Jesus the Naz-a-re-an.
68 But he denied it, saying, I do not know
nor even understand what you say. And he
went out into the porch. And the cock crew.
69 And seeing him again, the maid began to
say to those standing there, This is one of
them.
70 And he again denied it. And after a little,
those standing by again said to Peter, You
really are one of them, for you are both a
Gal-i-le-an and you speak like them.
71 But he began to curse and to swear, I do
not know this man of whom you speak.
72 And the cock crowed the second time.
And Peter remembered the word that Jesus
said to him, Before the cock crows two
times, you will deny Me three times. And
thinking of this, he broke out into tears.
15 1 And immediately in the morning, having
consulted with the elders and scribes and the
whole sanhedrin, the chief priests tied Jesus
up and carried Him away and delivered Him
up to Pilate.
2 And Pilate questioned Him, Are you the
king of the Jews? And answering He said to
him, You say it.
3 And the chief priests were accusing Him
of many things.
4 And again Pilate questioned Him, saying,
Do you answer nothing? See how many
things they witness against you?
5 But Jesus did not answer anything any
more, so that Pilate wondered.

ᵐκαταμαρτυροῦσιν.ᐥ 5 Ὁ.δὲ.Ἰησοῦς οὐκέτι.οὐδὲν ἀπεκρίθη,
¹they ²witness ³against. But Jesus not any more any thing answered,
ὥστε θαυμάζειν τὸν ⁿΠιλάτον.ᐥ 6 Κατὰ.δὲ ἑορτὴν ἀπέλυεν
so that ²wondered ¹Pilate. Now at [the] feast he released
αὐτοῖς ἕνα δέσμιον, ᵒὅνπερ ᾐτοῦντο.ᐥ 7 ἦν.δὲ ὁ λεγό-
to them one prisoner, whomsoever they asked. And there was the [one] call-
μενος Βαραββᾶς μετὰ τῶν ᵖσυστασιαστῶνᐥ δεδεμένος,
ed Barabbas with the associates in insurrection bound,
οἵτινες ἐν τῇ στάσει φόνον πεποιήκεισαν. 8 καὶ ᵠἀναβοήσαςᐥ
who in the insurrection murder had committed. And crying out
ὁ ὄχλος ἤρξατο αἰτεῖσθαι καθὼς ʳἀεὶᐥ ἐποίει αὐτοῖς
the crowd began to beg [him to do] as always he did to them.
9 ὁ.δὲ.ˢΠιλάτοςᐥ ἀπεκρίθη αὐτοῖς, λέγων, Θέλετε ἀπολύσω
But Pilate answered them, saying, Will ye I should release
ὑμῖν τὸν βασιλέα τῶν Ἰουδαίων; 10 Ἐγίνωσκεν.γὰρ ὅτι διὰ
to you the King of the Jews? for he knew that through
φθόνον παραδεδώκεισαν αὐτὸν οἱ ἀρχιερεῖς. 11 οἱ.δὲ ἀρχ-
envy ⁴had ⁵delivered ⁷up ⁶him ¹the ²chief ³priests. But the chief
ιερεῖς ἀνέσεισαν τὸν ὄχλον ἵνα μᾶλλον τὸν Βαραββᾶν
priests stirred up the crowd that rather Barabbas
ἀπολύσῃ αὐτοῖς. 12 ὁ.δὲ.ˢΠιλάτοςᐥ ᵗἀποκριθεὶς πάλινᐥ
he might release to them. And Pilate answering again
ᵛεἶπενᐥ αὐτοῖς, Τί οὖν ʷθέλετεᐥ ποιήσω ˣὃν λέγετεᐥ
said to them, What then will ye I should do [to him] whom ye call
ʸβασιλέα τῶν Ἰουδαίων; 13 Οἱ.δὲ πάλιν ἔκραξαν,ᶻ Σταύρω-
King of the Jews? But they again cried out Cruci-
σον αὐτόν. 14 Ὁ.δὲ.ˢΠιλάτοςᐥ ἔλεγεν αὐτοῖς, Τί γὰρ ᵃκακὸν
fy him. And Pilate said to them, What ²then ¹evil
ἐποίησενᐥ; Οἱ.δὲ ᵇπερισσοτέρωςᐥ ᶜἔκραξαν,ᐥ Σταύρωσον αὐ-
did he commit? But they much more cried out, Crucify him.
τόν. 15 Ὁ.δὲ.ˢΠιλάτοςᐥ βουλόμενος ᵈτῷ ὄχλῳ τὸ
And Pilate, desiring ⁷to ⁸the ⁹crowd ³that ⁴which [⁵was]
ἱκανὸν ποιῆσαι,ᐥ ἀπέλυσεν αὐτοῖς τὸν Βαραββᾶν· καὶ παρέ-
⁶satisfactory ¹to ²do, released to them Barabbas, and de-
δωκεν τὸν Ἰησοῦν, φραγελλώσας, ἵνα σταυρωθῇ.
livered up Jesus, having scourged [him], that he might be crucified.

16 Οἱ.δὲ στρατιῶται ἀπήγαγον αὐτὸν ἔσω τῆς αὐλῆς, ὅ
And the soldiers led away him within the court, which
ἐστιν πραιτώριον, καὶ ᵉσυγκαλοῦσινᐥ ὅλην τὴν σπεῖραν·
is [the] prætorium, and they call together ²whole ¹the band.
17 καὶ ᶠἐνδύουσινᐥ αὐτὸν πορφύραν, καὶ περιτιθέασιν αὐτῷ
And they put on him purple, and placed on him
πλέξαντες ἀκάνθινον στέφανον, 18 καὶ ἤρξαντο ἀσπάζε-
having platted [it] ²thorny ¹a crown, and they began to sa-
σθαι αὐτόν, Χαῖρε, ᵍβασιλεῦᐥ τῶν Ἰουδαίων· 19 καὶ ἔτυπτον
lute him, Hail, King of the Jews! And they struck
αὐτοῦ τὴν κεφαλὴν καλάμῳ, καὶ ἐνέπτυον αὐτῷ, καὶ τιθέντες
his head with a reed, and spat on him, and bending
τὰ γόνατα προσεκύνουν αὐτῷ. 20 Καὶ ὅτε ἐνέπαιξαν αὐτῷ,
the knees did homage to him. And when they had mocked him,
ἐξέδυσαν αὐτὸν τὴν πορφύραν, καὶ ἐνέδυσαν αὐτὸν τὰ
they took off him the purple, and put on him
ʰἱμάτια.τὰ.ἴδια·ᐥ καὶ ⁱἐξάγουσινᐥ αὐτὸν ἵνα ᵏσταυρώσωσινᐥ
his own garments; and they lead ²out ¹him that they may crucify
ˡαὐτόν.ᐥ 21 καὶ ἀγγαρεύουσιν παράγοντά τινα Σίμωνα Κυ-
him. And they compel ²passing ³by ¹one, Simon a Cy-
ρηναῖον, ἐρχόμενον ᵐἀπ'ᐥ ἀγροῦ, τὸν πατέρα Ἀλεξάνδρου καὶ
renian, coming from a field, the father of Alexander and
Ῥούφου, ἵνα ἄρῃ τὸν.σταυρὸν.αὐτοῦ.
Rufus, that he might carry his cross.

22 Καὶ φέρουσιν αὐτὸν ἐπὶ ⁿΓολγοθᾶᐥ τόπον, ὅ ἐστιν
And they bring him to ³Golgotha ¹a ²place, which is
μεθερμηνευόμενον, κρανίου τόπος. 23 Καὶ ἐδίδουν αὐτῷ
being interpreted, ²of ³a ⁴skull ¹place. And they gave him
ᵒπιεῖνᐥ ἐσμυρνισμένον οἶνον· ᵖὁ.δὲᐥ οὐκ.ἔλαβεν. 24 Καὶ
to drink ²medicated ³with ⁴myrrh ¹wine; but he did not take [it] And
ᵠσταυρώσαντες αὐτὸνᐥ ʳδιεμέριζονᐥ τὰ.ἱμάτια.αὐτοῦ, βάλλον-
having crucified him they divided his garments, cast-
τες κλῆρον ἐπ' αὐτά, τίς τί ἄρῃ. 25 ἦν.δὲ
ing a lot on them, who [and] what [each] should take. And it was [the]
ὥρα τρίτη, καὶ ἐσταύρωσαν αὐτόν. 26 Καὶ ἦν ἡ ἐπιγραφὴ
²hour ¹third, and they crucified him. And ⁴was ¹the ²inscription
τῆς.αἰτίας.αὐτοῦ ἐπιγεγραμμένη, Ὁ βασιλεὺς τῶν Ἰουδαίων.
³of ⁴his ⁵accusation written up, The King of the Jews.
27 Καὶ σὺν αὐτῷ σταυροῦσιν δύο λῃστάς, ἕνα ἐκ δεξιῶν
And with him they crucify two robbers, one at [the] right hand
καὶ ἕνα ἐξ εὐωνύμων αὐτοῦ. 28 ˢκαὶ ἐπληρώθη ἡ γραφὴ
and one at [the] left of him. And was fulfilled the scripture
ἡ λέγουσα, Καὶ μετὰ ἀνόμων ἐλογίσθη.ᐥ 29 Καὶ οἱ
which says, And with [the] lawless he was reckoned. And those
παραπορευόμενοι ἐβλασφήμουν αὐτόν, κινοῦντες τὰς κεφαλὰς
passing by railed at him, shaking ²heads

6 Now at the feast he released to them one
prisoner, whoever they desired.
7 And there was one called Bar-ab-bas
locked up with those who rioted with him,
who had committed murder in the riot.
8 And the crowd began to cry out and beg
him to do as he always did to them.
9 But Pilate answered them, saying, Do you
want me to release to you the king of the
Jews?
10 For he knew that the chief priests
delivered Him up through envy.
11 But the chief priests stirred the people
up in order that he might rather release
Bar-ab-bas to them.
12 And answering again Pilate said to them,
What then do you want me to do with the
one whom you call king of the Jews?
13 And they cried out again, Crucify him!
14 And Pilate said to them, Why? What evil
did he do? But they cried out much more
vehemently, Crucify him!
15 And wanting to do what was pleasing to
the people, Pilate released Bar-ab-bas to
them. And after he had *Him* whipped, he
delivered Him so that He could be crucified.
16 And the soldiers led Him away into that
hall which is the governor's palace. And they
called together the whole band.
17 And they put purple on Him. And they
plaited and placed a crown of thorns on
Him.
18 And they began to salute Him, *saying,*
Hail, King of the Jews!
19 And they struck Him on the head with a
reed and spat on Him. And bending their
knees, they bowed down to Him.
20 And when they had made fun of Him,
they took the purple off of Him and put His
own clothes on Him. And they led Him out
so that they might crucify Him.
21 And they forced a certain one passing by
(Simon, a Cy-ren-i-an, the father of
Alexander and Rufus, *who was* coming from
the field,) in order that he might carry His
cross.
22 And they brought Him to a place *called*
Gol-goth-a (which means, The place of a
skull).
23 And they gave Him wine mixed with
myrrh to drink. But He did not take it.
24 And after they had crucified Him, they
divided His clothes, throwing a lot upon
them *to see* what *each* should take.
25 And it was the third hour. And they
crucified Him.
26 And the title of His accusation was written above: THE KING OF THE JEWS.
27 And they crucified two thieves with Him
– one at the right hand and one at the left
of Him.
28 And the Scripture which says "And He
was numbered with *the* lawless" was fulfilled.
29 And those passing by blasphemed Him,

αὐτῶν, καὶ λέγοντες, Οὐά, ὁ.καταλύων τὸν ναὸν καὶ ἐν
their, and saying, Aha, thou who destroyest the temple and in
τρισὶν ἡμέραις οἰκοδομῶν, 30 σῶσον σεαυτόν, καὶ κατάβα
three days buildest [it], save thyself, and descend
ἀπὸ τοῦ σταυροῦ. 31 Ὁμοίως.δὲ καὶ οἱ ἀρχιερεῖς, ἐμπαί-
from the cross. And in like manner also the chief priests, mock-
ζοντες πρὸς ἀλλήλους μετὰ τῶν γραμματέων, ἔλεγον, Ἄλλους
ing among one another with the scribes, said, Others
ἔσωσεν, ἑαυτὸν οὐ.δύναται σῶσαι. 32 ὁ χριστὸς ὁ βασιλεὺς
he saved, himself he is not able to save. The Christ the King
τοῦ Ἰσραὴλ καταβάτω νῦν ἀπὸ τοῦ σταυροῦ, ἵνα ἴδωμεν
of Israel! let him descend now from the cross, that we may see
καὶ πιστεύσωμεν. Καὶ οἱ συνεσταυρωμένοι αὐτῷ ὠνείδιζον
and believe. And they who were crucified with him reproached
αὐτόν. 33 Γενομένης.δὲ ὥρας ἕκτης, σκότος ἐγένετο ἐφ'
him. And being come [the] hour sixth, darkness came over
ὅλην τὴν γῆν, ἕως ὥρας ἐννάτης· 34 καὶ τῇ ὥρᾳ τῇ
all the land, until [the] hour ninth; and at the hour the
ἐννάτῃ ἐβόησεν ὁ Ἰησοῦς φωνῇ μεγάλῃ, λέγων, Ἐλωΐ,
ninth cried Jesus with a voice loud, saying, Eloi,
Ἐλωΐ, λαμμᾶ σαβαχθανί; ὅ ἐστιν μεθερμηνευόμενον,
Eloi, lama sabachthani? which is being interpreted,
Ὁ.θεός.μου, ὁ.θεός.μου, εἰς.τί με ἐγκατέλιπες; 35 Καί τινες
My God, My God, why me hast thou forsaken? And some
τῶν παρεστηκότων ἀκούσαντες ἔλεγον, Ἰδού, Ἠλίαν
of those standing by having heard said, Lo, Elias
φωνεῖ. 36 Δραμὼν.δὲ εἷς καὶ γεμίσας σπόγγον ὄξους,
he calls. And having run one and filled a sponge with vinegar,
περιθείς τε καλάμῳ ἐπότιζεν αὐτόν, λέγων, Ἄφετε,
having put [it] on and a reed gave to drink him, saying, Let be,
ἴδωμεν εἰ ἔρχεται Ἠλίας καθελεῖν αὐτόν.
let us see if comes Elias to take down him.
37 Ὁ.δὲ.Ἰησοῦς ἀφεὶς φωνὴν μεγάλην ἐξέπνευσεν.
And Jesus having uttered a cry loud expired.
38 καὶ τὸ καταπέτασμα τοῦ ναοῦ ἐσχίσθη εἰς δύο, ἀπὸ ἄνω-
And the veil of the temple was rent into two, from top
θεν ἕως κάτω. 39 Ἰδὼν.δὲ ὁ κεντυρίων ὁ παρεστηκὼς
to bottom. And having seen the centurion who stood by
ἐξ.ἐναντίας αὐτοῦ ὅτι οὕτως κράξας ἐξέπνευσεν, εἶπεν,
opposite him that thus having cried out he expired, said,
Ἀληθῶς ὁ.ἄνθρωπος.οὗτος υἱὸς ἦν θεοῦ. 40 Ἦσαν.δὲ καὶ
Truly this man Son was of God. And there were also
γυναῖκες ἀπὸ μακρόθεν θεωροῦσαι, ἐν αἷς ἦν καὶ Μαρία
women from afar off looking on, among whom was also Mary
ἡ Μαγδαληνή, καὶ Μαρία ἡ τοῦ Ἰακώβου τοῦ μικροῦ καὶ
the Magdalene, and Mary the of James the less and
Ἰωσῆ μήτηρ, καὶ Σαλώμη, 41 αἳ καὶ ὅτε ἦν ἐν τῇ Γαλι-
of Joses mother, and Salome; who also when he was in Gali-
λαίᾳ ἠκολούθουν αὐτῷ καὶ διηκόνουν αὐτῷ, καὶ ἄλλαι πολλαὶ
lee followed him and ministered to him, and others many
αἱ συναναβᾶσαι αὐτῷ εἰς Ἱεροσόλυμα.
who came up with him to Jerusalem.
42 Καὶ ἤδη ὀψίας γενομένης, ἐπεὶ ἦν παρασκευή,
And already evening being come, since it was [the] preparation,
ὅ ἐστιν προσάββατον, 43 ἦλθεν Ἰωσὴφ ὁ ἀπὸ
that is [the day] before sabbath, came Joseph who [was] from
Ἀριμαθαίας, εὐσχήμων βουλευτής, ὃς καὶ αὐτὸς ἦν προσ-
Arimathæa, [an] honourable counsellor, who also himself was wait-
δεχόμενος τὴν βασιλείαν τοῦ θεοῦ· τολμήσας εἰσῆλθεν πρὸς
ing for the kingdom of God, having boldness he went in to
Πιλάτον καὶ ᾐτήσατο τὸ σῶμα τοῦ Ἰησοῦ. 44 ὁ.δὲ.Πιλάτος
Pilate and begged the body of Jesus. And Pilate
ἐθαύμασεν εἰ ἤδη τέθνηκεν· καὶ προσκαλεσάμενος τὸν
wondered if already he were dead; and having called to [him] the
κεντυρίωνα ἐπηρώτησεν αὐτὸν εἰ πάλαι ἀπέθανεν· 45 καὶ
centurion he questioned him if long he had died. And
γνοὺς ἀπὸ τοῦ κεντυρίωνος ἐδωρήσατο τὸ σῶμα τῷ
having known [it] from the centurion he granted the body
Ἰωσήφ. 46 καὶ ἀγοράσας σινδόνα, καὶ καθελὼν
to Joseph. And having bought a linen cloth, and having taken down
αὐτὸν ἐνείλησεν τῇ σινδόνι, καὶ κατέθηκεν αὐτὸν ἐν
him he wrapped [him] in the linen cloth, and laid him in
μνημείῳ, ὃ ἦν λελατομημένον ἐκ πέτρας· καὶ προσ-
a tomb, which was cut out of a rock. and roll-
εκύλισεν λίθον ἐπὶ τὴν θύραν τοῦ μνημείου. 47 ἡ.δὲ.Μαρία ἡ
ed a stone to the door of the tomb. And Mary the
Μαγδαληνὴ καὶ.Μαρία Ἰωσῆ ἐθεώρουν ποῦ τίθεται.
Magdalene and Mary [mother] of Joses saw where he is laid.
16 Καὶ διαγενομένου τοῦ σαββάτου, Μαρία ἡ Μαγδαληνὴ
And being past the sabbath, Mary the Magdalene
καὶ Μαρία ἡ τοῦ Ἰακώβου καὶ Σαλώμη ἠγόρασαν
and Mary the [mother] of James and Salome bought

shaking their heads and saying, Aha, you
who will destroy the Temple and build it in
three days!
30 Save yourself and come down from the
cross.
31 And in the same way, the chief priests
mocking with the scribes and one another
said, He saved others. He is not able to save
himself.
32 The Christ? The King of Israel? Let him
come down now from the cross so that we
may see and believe. And they who were
crucified with Him insulted Him.
33 And as the sixth hour arrived, darkness
came over all the land until the ninth hour.
34 And at the ninth hour Jesus cried with a
loud voice saying, E-lo-i, E-lo-i, la-ma, sa-
bach-tha-ni (which means, My God! My
God! Why have You forsaken Me?)
35 And hearing *this* some of those standing
by said, Look! He is calling Elijah.
36 And one ran and filled a sponge with
vinegar. And putting it on a reed, *he* gave *it*
to Him to drink, saying, Let alone! Let us
see if Elijah comes to take him down.
37 And uttering a loud cry Jesus breathed
forth his spirit.
38 And the veil of the Temple was torn in
two, from top to bottom.
39 And the centurion who stood by across
from Him, seeing that He cried out so and
gave up the spirit, said, This man was truly
the Son of God.
40 And there were also women looking on
from a distance, among whom was Mary
Mag-da-lene and Mary the mother of James
the less, and Joses and Salome,
41 (who also followed Him and ministered
to Him when He was in Galilee,) and many
others who came up with Him to Jerusalem.
42 And now when evening had come –
since it was the preparation, that is *the day*
before sabbath –
43 Joseph of Ar-i-ma-the-a, an honorable
councillor who himself was also waiting for
the kingdom of God, came and begged the
body of Jesus (having great courage in going
in to Pilate).
44 And Pilate wondered if He were already
dead. And calling the centurion to him, he
asked him if He had been dead long.
45 And having known it from the centurion, he granted the body to Joseph.
46 And he bought fine linen. And taking
Him down, he wrapped Him in the fine linen
and laid Him in a tomb which was cut out of
a rock. And he rolled a stone to the door of
the tomb.
47 And Mary Mag-da-lene and Mary *the*
mother of Joses saw where He was laid.

CHAPTER 16

1 And the sabbath being past, Mary Mag-

ἀρώματα, ἵνα ἐλθοῦσαι ἀλείψωσιν αὐτόν. 2 καὶ λίαν πρωῒ
aromatics, that having come they might anoint him. And very early
[o]τῆς μιᾶς" σαββάτων ἔρχονται ἐπὶ τὸ [p]μνημεῖον," ἀνατεί-
on the first [day] of the week they come to the tomb, [3]having
λαντος τοῦ ἡλίου. 3 καὶ ἔλεγον πρὸς ἑαυτάς, Τίς ἀποκυλίσει
[4]risen [1]the [2]sun. And they said among themselves, Who will roll away
ἡμῖν τὸν λίθον [q]ἐκ" τῆς θύρας τοῦ μνημείου; 4 Καὶ ἀνα-
for us the stone out of the door of the tomb? And having
βλέψασαι θεωροῦσιν ὅτι [r]ἀποκεκύλισται" ὁ λίθος· ἦν.γὰρ
looked up they see that has been rolled away the stone: for it was
μέγας σφόδρα. 5 καὶ [s]εἰσελθοῦσαι" εἰς τὸ μνημεῖον, εἶδον
[2]great [1]very. And having entered into the tomb, they saw
νεανίσκον καθήμενον ἐν τοῖς δεξιοῖς, περιβεβλημένον στολὴν
a young man sitting on the right, clothed with a [2]robe
λευκήν· καὶ ἐξεθαμβήθησαν. 6 ὁ.δὲ λέγει αὐταῖς, Μὴ
[1]white, and they were greatly amazed. But he says to them, [2]Not
ἐκθαμβεῖσθε. Ἰησοῦν ζητεῖτε τὸν Ναζαρηνὸν τὸν ἐσταυ-
[1]be amazed. [3]Jesus [1]ye [2]seek the Nazarene, who has been
ρωμένον· ἠγέρθη, οὐκ.ἔστιν ὧδε· ἴδε ὁ τόπος ὅπου ἔθηκαν
crucified. He is risen, he is not here; behold the place where they laid
αὐτόν· 7 [t]ἀλλ'" ὑπάγετε, εἴπατε τοῖς.μαθηταῖς.αὐτοῦ καὶ τῷ
him. But go, say to his disciples and
Πέτρῳ, ὅτι προάγει ὑμᾶς εἰς τὴν Γαλιλαίαν· ἐκεῖ αὐτὸν
to Peter, that he goes before you into Galilee; there him
ὄψεσθε, καθὼς εἶπεν ὑμῖν. 8 Καὶ ἐξελθοῦσαι [v]ταχὺ"
shall ye see, as he said to you. And having gone out quickly
ἔφυγον ἀπὸ τοῦ μνημείου· εἶχεν.[w]δὲ" αὐτὰς τρόμος καὶ
they fled from the tomb. And [4]possessed [5]them [1]trembling [2]and
ἔκστασις· καὶ οὐδενὶ [x]οὐδὲν" εἶπον, ἐφοβοῦντο.γάρ.[y]
[3]amazement, and to no one anything they spoke, for they were afraid.
(*lit.* nothing)
9 [z]Ἀναστὰς.δὲ πρωῒ πρώτῃ σαββάτου ἐφάνη πρῶ-
Now having risen early [the] first [day] of the week he appeared first
τον Μαρίᾳ τῇ Μαγδαληνῇ, [a]ἀφ'" ἧς ἐκβεβλήκει ἑπτὰ δαιμό-
to Mary the Magdalene, from whom he had cast out seven demons.
νια. 10 ἐκείνη[b] πορευθεῖσα ἀπήγγειλεν τοῖς μετ' αὐτοῦ γε-
She having gone told [it] to those who with him had
νομένοις, πενθοῦσιν καὶ κλαίουσιν. 11 κἀκεῖνοι ἀκούσαντες
been, [who were] grieving and weeping. And they having heard
ὅτι ζῇ καὶ ἐθεάθη ὑπ' αὐτῆς ἠπίστησαν. 12 Μετὰ.δὲ
that he is alive and has been seen by her disbelieved [it]. And after
ταῦτα δυσὶν ἐξ αὐτῶν περιπατοῦσιν ἐφανερώθη ἐν ἑτέρᾳ
these things to two of them as they walked he was manifested in another
μορφῇ, πορευομένοις εἰς ἀγρόν. 13 κἀκεῖνοι ἀπελθόντες ἀπ-
form, going into [the] country; and they having gone
ήγγειλαν τοῖς λοιποῖς· οὐδὲ ἐκείνοις ἐπίστευσαν. 14 "Ὕστερον[c]
told [it] to the rest; neither them did they believe. Afterwards
ἀνακειμένοις αὐτοῖς τοῖς ἕνδεκα ἐφανερώθη, καὶ ὠνεί-
as [2]reclined [[3]at [4]table] [1]they to the eleven he was manifested, and re-
δισεν τὴν.ἀπιστίαν.αὐτῶν καὶ σκληροκαρδίαν, ὅτι τοῖς
proached their unbelief and hardness of heart, because [4]those [5]who
θεασαμένοις αὐτὸν ἐγηγερμένον[d] οὐκ.ἐπίστευσαν. 15 Καὶ εἶπεν
[6]had [7]seen [8]him [9]arisen [1]they [2]believed [3]not. And he said
αὐτοῖς, Πορευθέντες εἰς τὸν κόσμον ἅπαντα κηρύξατε τὸ εὐαγ-
to them, Having gone into [2]the [3]world [1]all proclaim the glad
γέλιον πάσῃ τῇ κτίσει. 16 ὁ πιστεύσας καὶ βαπτισθεὶς σωθήσε-
tidings to all the creation. He that believes and is baptized shall be
ται· ὁ.δὲ ἀπιστήσας κατακριθήσεται. 17 σημεῖα.δὲ τοῖς
saved, and he that disbelieves shall be condemned. And [2]signs [5]those [6]that
πιστεύσασιν [e]ταῦτα παρακολουθήσει". ἐν τῷ.ὀνόματί.μου δαι-
[7]believe [1]these [3]shall [4]follow: in my name de-
μόνια ἐκβαλοῦσιν· γλώσσαις λαλήσουσιν [f]καιναῖς·"
mons they shall cast out; with [2]tongues [3]they [4]shall [5]speak [1]new;
18 [g]ὄφεις ἀροῦσιν· κἂν θανάσιμόν τι πίωσιν οὐ.μὴ
serpents they shall take up; and if [2]deadly [1]anything they drink in no wise
αὐτοὺς [h]βλάψει·" ἐπὶ ἀρρώστους χεῖρας ἐπιθήσουσιν, καὶ
them shall it injure; upon [the] infirm [4]hands [1]they [2]shall [3]lay, and
καλῶς ἕξουσιν.
[4]well [1]they [2]shall [3]be.
19 Ὁ μὲν οὖν κύριος[i] μετὰ τὸ λαλῆσαι αὐτοῖς [k]ἀνελή-
The [2]indeed [3]therefore [1]Lord after speaking to them was taken
φθη" εἰς τὸν οὐρανόν, καὶ ἐκάθισεν ἐκ δεξιῶν τοῦ θεοῦ·
up into the heaven, and sat at [the] right hand of God.
20 ἐκεῖνοι.δὲ ἐξελθόντες ἐκήρυξαν πανταχοῦ, τοῦ κυρίου συνερ-
And they having gone forth preached everywhere, the Lord working
γοῦντος, καὶ τὸν λόγον βεβαιοῦντος διὰ τῶν ἐπακολουθούν-
with [them], and the word confirming by the [2]following [3]upon
των σημείων. [l]Ἀμήν."
[[4]it] [1]signs. Amen.

[m]Τὸ κατὰ Μάρκον εὐαγγέλιον."
The [3]according [4]to [5]Mark [1]glad [2]tidings.

da-lene and Mary *the mother* of James and Salome brought sweet spices that they might come and anoint Him.

2 And very early on the first *day* of the week, they came to the tomb as the sun rose.

3 And they said among themselves, Who will roll away the stone from the door of the tomb?

4 And looking up they saw that the stone had been rolled away. For it was very large.

5 And going into the tomb they saw a young man sitting on the right, clothed with a white robe. And they were astonished.

6 But he said to them, Do not be distressed. You look for Jesus the Naz-a-rene who has been crucified. He has risen. He is not here. See the place where they laid Him?

7 But go say to His disciples and to Peter that He has gone before you into Galilee. You shall see Him there, as He said to you.

8 And going out quickly, they fled from the tomb. And trembling and ecstasy took hold of them. And neither did they say anything to anyone, for they were afraid.

9 Now rising early *the* first *day* of the week, He first appeared to Mary Mag-da-lene, from whom He had thrown out seven demons.

10 She went and told it to those who had been with Him, *those* grieving and weeping.

11 And hearing that He was alive and had been seen by her, they did not believe it.

12 And after these things, He was revealed in another form to two of them as they walked, going into the country.

13 And they went away and told it to the rest of them. Neither did they believe them.

14 Afterwards, as they sat at table, He was revealed to the Eleven. And He censured their unbelief and hardness of heart, because they did not believe those who had seen Him risen.

15 And He said to them, Go into all the world and preach the gospel to every creature.

16 He that believes and is baptized shall be saved. And he that does not believe shall be condemned.

17 And these signs shall follow those that believe: In My name they shall throw out demons; they shall speak with new tongues;

18 they shall take up serpents; and if they drink any deadly thing, it shall not hurt them; they shall lay hands on the sick and they shall recover.

19 Then, after speaking to them, the Lord was received up into Heaven and sat at the right hand of God.

20 And they went out and preached everywhere, the Lord working with them and confirming the word by the miracles following. Amen.

The Gospel According to LUKE

᾿ΕΠΕΙΔΗΠΕΡ πολλοὶ ἐπεχείρησαν ἀνατάξασθαι διήγησιν
FORASMUCH AS many took in hand to draw up a narration
περὶ τῶν πεπληροφορημένων ἐν ἡμῖν πραγμά-
concerning the [2]which [3]have [4]been [5]fully [6]believed [7]among [8]us [1]mat-
των, 2 καθὼς παρέδοσαν ἡμῖν οἱ ἀπ' ἀρχῆς
ters, as they delivered [them] to us, they [3]from [4the] [5]beginning
αὐτόπται καὶ ὑπηρέται γενόμενοι τοῦ λόγου, 3 ἔδοξεν
[6]eye-witnesses [7]and [8]attendants [1]having [2]been of the Word, it seemed good
κἀμοί, παρηκολουθηκότι ἄνωθεν πᾶσιν ἀκριβῶς, κα-
also to me, having been acquainted from the first with all things accurately, with
θεξῆς σοι γράψαι, κράτιστε Θεόφιλε, 4 ἵνα ἐπιγνῷς
method to thee to write, most excellent Theophilus, that thou mightest know
περὶ ὧν κατηχήθης λόγων τὴν ἀσφάλειαν.
[6]concerning [7]which [8]thou [9]wast [10]instructed [3]of [4the] [5]things [1]the [2]certainty.
5 Ἐγένετο ἐν ταῖς ἡμέραις Ἡρώδου [b]τοῦ βασιλέως τῆς
There was in the days of Herod the king
Ἰουδαίας ἱερεύς τις ὀνόματι Ζαχαρίας, ἐξ ἐφημερίας
of Judæa a [2]priest [1]certain, by name Zacharias, of [the] course
Ἀβιά· καὶ [c]ἡ γυνὴ αὐτοῦ ἐκ τῶν θυγατέρων Ἀαρών, καὶ τὸ
of Abia, and his wife of the daughters of Aaron, and
ὄνομα αὐτῆς Ἐλισάβετ. 6 ἦσαν δὲ δίκαιοι ἀμφότεροι [d]ἐνώ-
her name Elizabeth. And they were [2]just [1]both be-
πιον τοῦ θεοῦ, πορευόμενοι ἐν πάσαις ταῖς ἐντολαῖς καὶ
fore God, walking in all the commandments and
δικαιώμασιν τοῦ κυρίου ἄμεμπτοι. 7 καὶ οὐκ ἦν αὐτοῖς
ordinances of the Lord blameless. And there was not to them
τέκνον, καθότι [e]ἡ Ἐλισάβετ ἦν στεῖρα, καὶ ἀμφότεροι προ-
a child, inasmuch as Elizabeth was barren, and both ad-
βεβηκότες ἐν ταῖς ἡμέραις αὐτῶν ἦσαν. 8 Ἐγένετο δὲ ἐν
vanced in their days were. And it came to pass in
τῷ ἱερατεύειν αὐτὸν ἐν τῇ τάξει τῆς ἐφημερίας αὐτοῦ ἔναντι
fulfilling his priestly service in the order of his course before
τοῦ θεοῦ, 9 κατὰ τὸ ἔθος τῆς ἱερατείας, ἔλαχεν
God, according to the custom of the priestly service, it fell to him by lot
τοῦ θυμιᾶσαι εἰσελθὼν εἰς τὸν ναὸν τοῦ κυρίου· 10 καὶ
to burn incense, having entered into the temple of the Lord. And
πᾶν τὸ πλῆθος [f]τοῦ λαοῦ ἦν προσευχόμενον ἔξω τῇ ὥρᾳ
all the multitude of the people were praying without at the hour
τοῦ θυμιάματος. 11 ὤφθη δὲ αὐτῷ ἄγγελος κυρίου, ἑ-
of incense. And [6]appeared [7]to [8]him [1]an [2]angel [3]of [4the] [5]Lord, stand-
στὼς ἐκ δεξιῶν τοῦ θυσιαστηρίου τοῦ θυμιάματος· 12 καὶ
ing at [the] right of the altar of incense. and
ἐταράχθη Ζαχαρίας ἰδών, καὶ φόβος ἐπέπεσεν ἐπ' αὐτόν.
[4]was [5]troubled [1]Zacharias [2]seeing [3him], and fear fell upon him.
13 Εἶπεν δὲ πρὸς αὐτὸν ὁ ἄγγελος, Μὴ φοβοῦ, Ζαχαρία·
But [3]said [4]to [5]him [1]the [2]angel, Fear not, Zacharias,
διότι εἰσηκούσθη ἡ δέησίς σου, καὶ ἡ γυνή σου Ἐλισάβετ γεν-
because has been heard thy supplication, and thy wife Elizabeth shall
νήσει υἱόν σοι, καὶ καλέσεις τὸ ὄνομα αὐτοῦ [g]Ἰωάννην.
bear a son to thee, and thou shalt call his name John.
14 καὶ ἔσται χαρά σοι καὶ ἀγαλλίασις, καὶ πολλοὶ ἐπὶ τῇ
And he shall be joy to thee and exultation, and many at
[h]γεννήσει αὐτοῦ χαρήσονται. 15 ἔσται γὰρ μέγας ἐνώπιον
his birth shall rejoice. For he shall be great before
[i]τοῦ κυρίου· καὶ οἶνον καὶ σίκερα οὐ μὴ πίῃ, καὶ
the Lord; and wine and strong drink in no wise shall he drink, and
πνεύματος ἁγίου πλησθήσεται ἔτι ἐκ κοιλίας μητρὸς
with [the] [2]Spirit [1]Holy he shall be filled even from [the] womb [3]mother
αὐτοῦ. 16 καὶ πολλοὺς τῶν υἱῶν Ἰσραὴλ ἐπιστρέψει ἐπὶ
[1]of [2]his. And many of the sons of Israel shall he turn to [the]
κύριον τὸν θεὸν αὐτῶν. 17 καὶ αὐτὸς προελεύσεται ἐνώπιον
Lord their God. And he shall go forth before
αὐτοῦ ἐν πνεύματι καὶ δυνάμει [k]Ἠλίου, ἐπιστρέψαι καρδίας
him in [the] spirit and power of Elias, to turn hearts
πατέρων ἐπὶ τέκνα, καὶ ἀπειθεῖς ἐν φρονήσει δι-
of fathers to children, and [the] disobedient to [the] wisdom of [the]
καίων, ἑτοιμάσαι κυρίῳ λαὸν κατεσκευασμένον. 18 Καὶ
righteous, to make ready for [the] Lord a people prepared. And
εἶπεν Ζαχαρίας πρὸς τὸν ἄγγελον, Κατὰ τί γνώσομαι τοῦτο;
[2]said [1]Zacharias to the angel, By what shall I know this?
ἐγὼ γάρ εἰμι πρεσβύτης, καὶ ἡ γυνή μου προβεβηκυῖα ἐν ταῖς
for I am an old man, and my wife advanced in
ἡμέραις αὐτῆς. 19 Καὶ ἀποκριθεὶς ὁ ἄγγελος εἶπεν αὐτῷ,
her days. And [3]answering [1]the [2]angel said to him,
Ἐγώ εἰμι Γαβριὴλ ὁ παρεστηκὼς ἐνώπιον τοῦ θεοῦ· καὶ
I am Gabriel, who stand before God, and
ἀπεστάλην λαλῆσαι πρός σε, καὶ εὐαγγελίσασθαί σοι
I was sent to speak to thee, and to announce [2]glad [3]tidings [4]to [5]thee
ταῦτα. 20 καὶ ἰδού, ἔσῃ σιωπῶν καὶ μὴ δυνάμενος λαλῆσαι
[1]these; and lo, thou shalt be silent and not able to speak
ἄχρι ἧς ἡμέρας γένηται ταῦτα· ἀνθ' ὧν οὐκ ἐπίστευσας
till the day in which shall take place these things, because thou didst not believe

CHAPTER 1

1 Since many others have taken in hand to draw up an account of those things which have been fully believed among us,
2 even as they who were eye-witnesses and ministers of the word from the beginning delivered them to us,
3 it seemed good to me also, having carefully traced out these things from the first, to write to you in order, most excellent The-oph-i-lus,
4 so that you may know the certainty of those things in which you were taught.
5 In the days of Herod, king of Judea, there was a certain priest named Zach-a-ri-as, of Abi-jah's course. And his wife was of Aaron's daughters, and her name was Elizabeth.
6 And they were both righteous before God, walking blameless in the commandments and ordinances of the Lord.
7 And they were childless, because Elizabeth was barren. And both were advanced in years.
8 And as *Zach-a-ri-as* was doing his priestly service in the order of his course before God,
9 according to the custom of the priestly office, it was his duty to enter the Temple of the Lord to burn incense.
10 And all the multitude of the people were praying outside at the hour of incense.
11 And an angel of the Lord appeared to him, standing at the right of the altar of incense.
12 And seeing him Zach-a-ri-as was troubled and fear fell on him.
13 But the angel said to him, Do not fear, Zach-a-ri-as, because your prayer has been heard. And your wife Elizabeth shall bear a son to you. And you shall call his name John.
14 And he shall be joy and gladness to you. And many shall rejoice at his birth.
15 For he shall be great before the Lord and shall never drink wine or strong drink. And he shall be filled with the Holy Spirit, even from his mother's womb.
16 And he shall turn many of the children of Israel to the Lord their God.
17 And he shall go before Him, in the spirit and power of Elijah, to turn hearts of fathers to children, and the ones who disobey to the wisdom of the righteous, to make ready a people prepared for the Lord.
18 And Zach-a-ri-as said to the angel, By what shall I know this? For I am an old man and my wife is advanced in years.
19 And answering the angel said to him, I am Ga-bri-el, who stands before God. And I was sent to speak to you and to bring you the good news of these things.
20 And behold, you shall be dumb and unable to speak until the day in which these things take place; because you did not be-

τοῖς.λόγοις.μου, οἵτινες πληρωθήσονται εἰς τὸν.καιρὸν.αὐτῶν.
my words, which shall be fulfilled in their season.
21 Καὶ ἦν ὁ λαὸς προσδοκῶν τὸν Ζαχαρίαν· καὶ ἐθαύμαζον ἐν
And [3]were [1]the [2]people expecting Zacharias, and they wondered at
τῷ.χρονίζειν.αὐτὸν ἐν τῷ ναῷ. 22 ἐξελθὼν.δὲ [l]οὐκ.ἠδύνατο‖
his delaying in the temple. But having come out he was not able
λαλῆσαι αὐτοῖς· καὶ ἐπέγνωσαν ὅτι ὀπτασίαν ἑώρακεν ἐν
to speak to them, and they recognized that a vision he has seen in
τῷ ναῷ· καὶ αὐτὸς ἦν διανεύων αὐτοῖς, καὶ διέμενεν κωφός.
the temple. And he was making signs to them, and continued dumb.
23 καὶ ἐγένετο ὡς ἐπλήσθησαν αἱ ἡμέραι τῆς λειτουργίας
And it came to pass, when were fulfilled the days [3]service
αὐτοῦ ἀπῆλθεν εἰς τὸν.οἶκον.αὐτοῦ.
[1]of [2]his he departed to his house.
24 Μετὰ.δὲ ταύτας τὰς ἡμέρας συνέλαβεν Ἐλισάβετ ἡ
Now after these days [4]conceived [1]Elizabeth
γυνὴ.αὐτοῦ, καὶ περιέκρυβεν ἑαυτὴν μῆνας πέντε, λέγουσα,
[2]his [3]wife, and hid herself [2]months [1]five, saying,
25 Ὅτι.οὕτως μοι πεποίηκεν [m]ὁ‖ κύριος ἐν ἡμέραις αἷς
Thus to me has done the Lord in [the] days in which
ἐπεῖδεν ἀφελεῖν [n]τὸ‖.ὄνειδός.μου ἐν ἀνθρώποις.
he looked upon [me] to take away my reproach among men.
26 Ἐν.δὲ τῷ μηνὶ τῷ ἕκτῳ ἀπεστάλη ὁ ἄγγελος Γαβριὴλ
And in the month the sixth was sent the angel Gabriel
[o]ὑπὸ‖ τοῦ θεοῦ εἰς πόλιν τῆς Γαλιλαίας, ᾗ ὄνομα [p]Να-
by God to a city of Galilee, whose name [was] Na-
ζαρέτ,‖ 27 πρὸς παρθένον [q]μεμνηστευμένην‖ ἀνδρὶ ᾧ ὄνομα
zareth, to a virgin betrothed to a man whose name
Ἰωσήφ, ἐξ οἴκου [r]Δαβίδ·‖ καὶ τὸ ὄνομα τῆς παρθένου
[was] Joseph, of [the] house of David, and the name of the virgin
Μαριάμ. 28 καὶ εἰσελθὼν [s]ὁ ἄγγελος‖ πρὸς αὐτὴν [t] εἶπεν,
[was] Mary. And [3]coming [1]the [2]angel to her said,
Χαῖρε, κεχαριτωμένη· ὁ κύριος μετὰ σοῦ, [v]εὐλογημένη
Hail, [thou] favoured one! the Lord [is] with thee, blessed [art]
σὺ ἐν γυναιξίν.‖ 29 Ἡ.δὲ [w]ἰδοῦσα‖ [x]διεταράχθη ἐπὶ
thou amongst women. But she seeing [him] was troubled at
τῷ.λόγῳ.αὐτοῦ,‖ καὶ διελογίζετο ποταπὸς εἴη ὁ ἀσπασμὸς
his word, and was reasoning of what kind might be [2]salutation
οὗτος. 30 Καὶ εἶπεν ὁ ἄγγελος αὐτῇ, Μὴ.φοβοῦ, Μαριάμ·
[1]this. And [3]said [1]the [2]angel to her, Fear not, Mary,
εὗρες.γὰρ χάριν παρὰ τῷ θεῷ· 31 καὶ ἰδού, [y]συλλήψῃ‖
for thou hast found favour with God; and lo, thou shalt conceive
ἐν γαστρὶ καὶ τέξῃ υἱόν, καὶ καλέσεις τὸ.ὄνομα.αὐτοῦ
in [thy] womb and bring forth a son, and thou shalt call his name
Ἰησοῦν. 32 οὗτος ἔσται μέγας, καὶ υἱὸς ὑψίστου κληθήσε-
Jesus. He shall be great, and Son of [the] Highest shall be
ται· καὶ δώσει αὐτῷ κύριος ὁ θεὸς τὸν θρόνον [z]Δαβὶδ‖
called; and [4]shall [5]give [6]him [[1]the] [2]Lord [3]God the throne of David
τοῦ.πατρὸς.αὐτοῦ, 33 καὶ βασιλεύσει ἐπὶ τὸν οἶκον Ἰακὼβ εἰς
his father; and he shall reign over the house of Jacob to
τοὺς αἰῶνας, καὶ τῆς.βασιλείας.αὐτοῦ οὐκ.ἔσται τέλος.
the ages, and of his kingdom there shall not be an end.
34 Εἶπεν.δὲ Μαριὰμ πρὸς τὸν ἄγγελον, Πῶς ἔσται τοῦτο ἐπεὶ
But [2]said [1]Mary to the angel, How shall [2]be [1]this since
ἄνδρα οὐ.γινώσκω; 35 Καὶ ἀποκριθεὶς ὁ ἄγγελος εἶπεν αὐτῇ,
a man I know not? And answering the angel said to her,
Πνεῦμα ἅγιον ἐπελεύσεται ἐπὶ σέ, καὶ δύναμις ὑψίστου
[The] [2]Spirit [1]Holy shall come upon thee, and power of [the] Highest
ἐπισκιάσει σοι· διὸ καὶ τὸ γεννώμενον[a] ἅγιον κληθή-
shall overshadow thee; wherefore also the [3]born [1]holy [2]thing shall be
σεται υἱὸς θεοῦ. 36 καὶ ἰδού, Ἐλισάβετ ἡ.[b]συγγενής‖.σου καὶ
called Son of God. And lo, Elizabeth thy kinswoman [2]also
αὐτὴ [c]συνειληφυῖα‖ υἱὸν ἐν [d]γήρᾳ‖.αὐτῆς· καὶ οὗτος μὴν
[1]she has conceived a son in her old age, and this [the] [2]month
ἕκτος ἐστὶν αὐτῇ τῇ καλουμένῃ στείρᾳ· 37 ὅτι οὐκ ἀδυνα-
[1]sixth is to her who [was] called barren; for not [3]shall [4]be
τήσει παρὰ [e]τῷ θεῷ‖ πᾶν ῥῆμα. 38 Εἶπεν.δὲ Μαριάμ,
[5]impossible [6]with [7]God [1]any [2]thing. And [2]said [1]Mary,
(lit. every)
Ἰδού, ἡ δούλη κυρίου· γένοιτό μοι κατὰ τὸ.ῥῆμά.σου.
Behold, the bondmaid of [the] Lord; be it to me according to thy word.
Καὶ ἀπῆλθεν ἀπ' αὐτῆς ὁ ἄγγελος.
And departed from her the angel.
39 Ἀναστᾶσα.δὲ Μαριὰμ ἐν ταῖς.ἡμέραις.ταύταις ἐπορεύθη
And [2]rising [3]up [1]Mary in those days went
εἰς τὴν ὀρεινὴν μετὰ σπουδῆς, εἰς πόλιν Ἰούδα, 40 καὶ
into the hill-country with haste, to a city of Judah, and
εἰσῆλθεν εἰς τὸν οἶκον Ζαχαρίου καὶ ἠσπάσατο τὴν Ἐλισάβετ.
entered into the house of Zacharias and saluted Elizabeth.
41 καὶ ἐγένετο ὡς ἤκουσεν [f]ἡ Ἐλισάβετ τὸν ἀσπασμὸν τῆς
And it came to pass as [2]heard [1]Elizabeth the salutation
Μαρίας,‖ ἐσκίρτησεν τὸ βρέφος ἐν τῇ.κοιλίᾳ.αὐτῆς· καὶ ἐπλήσθη
of Mary, [3]leaped [1]the [2]babe in her womb; and [2]was [3]filled

lieve my words, which shall be fulfilled in their time.
21 And the people were expecting Zach-a-ri-as. And they wondered at his staying in the Temple.
22 But when he came out he was not able to speak to them. And they saw that he had seen a vision in the Temple. And he was making signs to them, and remained dumb.
23 And when the days of his service were finished, he went to his house.
24 Now afterwards his wife Elizabeth conceived – then hid herself five months, saying,
25 So has the Lord done to me in the days in which He looked on me to take away my reproach among men.
26 And in the sixth month the angel Ga-bri-el was sent from God to a city of Galilee named Naz-a-reth,
27 to a virgin betrothed to a man whose name was Joseph, of the house of David. And the name of the virgin was Mary.
28 And coming to her the angel said, Greetings, O favored one! The Lord is with you. Blessed are you among women.
29 But seeing *him* she was troubled at his words and was considering what kind of greeting this might be.
30 And the angel said to her, Do not fear, Mary, for you have found favor with God.
31 And behold, you shall conceive in your womb and bring forth a son! And you shall call His name Jesus.
32 He shall be great. And He shall be called the Son of the Highest. And the Lord God shall give Him the throne of David His father
33 and He shall reign over the house of Jacob forever. And of His kingdom there shall never be an end.
34 But Mary said to the angel, How shall this be since I know not a man?
35 And answering the angel said to her, The Holy Spirit shall come upon you, and the power of the Highest shall overshadow you – for this reason also the holy thing born of you shall be called Son of God.
36 And behold, Elizabeth of your family has also conceived a son in her old age! And this is the sixth month with her who *had been* called barren.
37 For nothing shall be impossible with God.
38 And Mary said, See, *I am* the servant of the Lord. Let it be done to me according to your word. And the angel left her.
39 And in those days Mary got up and went into the hill-country with haste, to a city of Judah.
40 And she entered the house of Zach-a-ri-as and embraced Elizabeth.
41 And as Elizabeth heard Mary's report, the babe leaped in her womb. And Elizabeth was

πνεύματος ἁγίου ἡ Ἐλισάβετ, 42 καὶ ἀνεφώνησεν [k]φωνῇ[ll]
[4]with [[5]the] [7]Spirit [6]Holy [1]Elizabeth, and cried out with a [2]voice
μεγάλῃ καὶ εἶπεν, Εὐλογημένη σὺ ἐν γυναιξίν, καὶ εὐλο-
[1]loud and said, Blessed [art] thou among women, and bless-
γημένος ὁ καρπὸς τῆς.κοιλίας.σου. 43 καὶ πόθεν μοι τοῦτο,
ed the fruit of thy womb. And whence to me this,
ἵνα ἔλθῃ ἡ μήτηρ τοῦ.κυρίου.μου πρός [h]με[i]; 44 ἰδοὺ.γάρ,
that should come the mother of my Lord to me? For lo,
ὡς ἐγένετο ἡ φωνὴ τοῦ.ἀσπασμοῦ.σου εἰς τὰ.ὦτά.μου ἐσκίρ-
as came the voice of thy salutation into mine ears, leap-
τησεν [i]ἐν ἀγαλλιάσει τὸ βρέφος[ll] ἐν τῇ.κοιλίᾳ.μου. 45 καὶ
ed in exultation the babe in my womb; and
μακαρία ἡ πιστεύσασα, ὅτι ἔσται τελείωσις τοῖς
blessed [is] she who believed, for there shall be a fulfilment to the things
λελαλημένοις αὐτῇ παρὰ κυρίου
spoken to her from [the] Lord.

46 Καὶ εἶπεν Μαριάμ, Μεγαλύνει ἡ.ψυχή.μου τὸν κύριον,
And said Mary, [3]Magnifies [1]my [2]soul the Lord,
47 καὶ ἠγαλλίασεν τὸ.πνεῦμά.μου ἐπὶ τῷ θεῷ τῷ.σωτῆρί.μου·
and [3]exulted [1]my [2]spirit in God my Saviour.
48 ὅτι ἐπέβλεψεν ἐπὶ τὴν ταπείνωσιν τῆς.δούλης.αὐτοῦ· ἰδοὺ
For he looked upon the humiliation of his bondmaid; [2]lo
γάρ, ἀπὸ τοῦ.νῦν μακαριοῦσίν.με πᾶσαι αἱ γενεαί. 49 ὅτι
[1]for, from henceforth [3]will [4]count [5]me [6]blessed [1]all [2]generations. For
ἐποίησέν μοι [k]μεγαλεῖα[ll] ὁ δυνατός, καὶ ἅγιον τὸ ὄνομα
[4]has [5]done [6]to [7]me [8]great [9]things [1]the [2]mighty [3]one, and holy [is] [2]name
αὐτοῦ· 50 καὶ τὸ.ἔλεος.αὐτοῦ εἰς γενεὰς [l]γενεῶν[ll] τοῖς
[1]his; and his mercy [is] to generations of generations to those
φοβουμένοις αὐτόν. 51 ἐποίησεν κράτος ἐν βραχίονι.αὐτοῦ·
fearing him. He wrought strength with his arm,
διεσκόρπισεν ὑπερηφάνους διανοίᾳ καρδίας.αὐτῶν.
he scattered [the] haughty in [the] thought of their heart.
52 καθεῖλεν δυνάστας ἀπὸ θρόνων, καὶ ὕψωσεν ταπεινούς.
He put down rulers from thrones, and exalted [the] lowly:
53 πεινῶντας ἐνέπλησεν ἀγαθῶν, καὶ πλουτοῦντας
[the] hungry he filled with good things, and [the] rich
ἐξαπέστειλεν κενούς. 54 ἀντελάβετο Ἰσραὴλ παιδὸς αὐτοῦ,
he sent away empty. He helped Israel [2]servant [1]his,
μνησθῆναι ἐλέους, 55 καθὼς ἐλάλησεν πρὸς τοὺς
[in order] to remember mercy, according as he spoke to
πατέρας.ἡμῶν, τῷ Ἀβραὰμ καὶ τῷ.σπέρματι.αὐτοῦ [m]εἰς τὸν
our fathers, to Abraham and to his seed for
αἰῶνα.[ll] 56 Ἔμεινεν.δὲ Μαριὰμ σὺν αὐτῇ [n]ὡσεὶ[ll] μῆνας τρεῖς,
ever. And [2]abode [1]Mary with her about [2]months [1]three,
καὶ ὑπέστρεψεν εἰς τὸν.οἶκον.αὐτῆς.
and returned to her house.

57 Τῇ.δὲ.Ἐλισάβετ ἐπλήσθη ὁ χρόνος τοῦ.τεκεῖν.αὐτήν,
Now to Elizabeth was fulfilled the time that she should bring forth,
καὶ ἐγέννησεν υἱόν· 58 καὶ ἤκουσαν οἱ περίοικοι καὶ οἱ συγ-
and she bore a son. And [3]heard [1]the [2]neighbours and [2]kins-
γενεῖς αὐτῆς ὅτι ἐμεγάλυνεν κύριος τὸ.ἔλεος.αὐτοῦ μετ'
folk [1]her that [3]was [4]magnifying [[1]the] [2]Lord his mercy with
αὐτῆς, καὶ συνέχαιρον αὐτῇ. 59 Καὶ ἐγένετο ἐν τῇ [o]ὀγδόῃ
her, and they rejoiced with her. And it came to pass on the eighth
ἡμέρᾳ[ll] ἦλθον περιτεμεῖν τὸ παιδίον· καὶ ἐκάλουν αὐτὸ
day they came to circumcise the little child, and were calling it
ἐπὶ τῷ ὀνόματι τοῦ.πατρὸς.αὐτοῦ Ζαχαρίαν. 60 καὶ ἀπο-
after the name of his father Zacharias. And [3]an-
κριθεῖσα ἡ.μήτηρ.αὐτοῦ εἶπεν, Οὐχί, ἀλλὰ κληθήσεται [p]Ἰωάν-
swering [1]his [2]mother said, No; but he shall be called John.
νης.[ll] 61 Καὶ [q]εἶπον[ll] πρὸς αὐτήν, Ὅτι οὐδείς ἐστιν [r]ἐν τῇ
And they said to her, No one is among the
συγγενείᾳ[ll] σου ὃς καλεῖται τῷ.ὀνόματι.τούτῳ. 62 Ἐνένευον
kinsfolk of thee who is called by this name. [2]They [3]made [4]signs
δὲ τῷ.πατρὶ.αὐτοῦ τὸ.τί ἂν.θέλοι καλεῖσθαι [s]αὐτόν.[ll]
[1]and to his father [as to] what he might wish [2]to [3]be [4]called [1]him.
63 καὶ αἰτήσας πινακίδιον ἔγραψεν, λέγων, [p]Ἰωάννης[ll]
And having asked for a writing tablet he wrote, saying, John
ἐστὶν [t]τὸ[ll] ὄνομα.αὐτοῦ· καὶ ἐθαύμασαν πάντες. 64 Ἀνεῴχθη.δὲ
is his name. And they [2]wondered [1]all. And was opened
τὸ.στόμα.αὐτοῦ παραχρῆμα καὶ ἡ.γλῶσσα.αὐτοῦ, καὶ
his mouth immediately and his tongue [loosed], and
ἐλάλει εὐλογῶν τὸν θεόν. 65 Καὶ ἐγένετο ἐπὶ πάντας φόβος
he spoke, blessing God. And [2]came [3]upon [4]all [1]fear
τοὺς περιοικοῦντας αὐτούς· καὶ ἐν ὅλῃ τῇ ὀρεινῇ τῆς
those who dwelt around them; and in [2]whole [1]the hill-country
Ἰουδαίας διελαλεῖτο πάντα τὰ.ῥήματα.ταῦτα· 66 καὶ
of Judæa [4]were [5]being [6]talked [7]of [1]all [2]these [3]things. And
ἔθεντο πάντες οἱ ἀκούσαντες ἐν τῇ.καρδίᾳ.αὐτῶν, λέ-
[4]laid [[5]them] [6]up [1]all [2]who [3]heard in their heart, say-
γοντες, Τί ἄρα τὸ.παιδίον.τοῦτο ἔσται; Καὶ [w] χεὶρ
ing, What then [3]this [4]little [5]child [1]will [2]be? And [the] hand

filled with the Holy Spirit.

42 And she cried out with a loud voice and said, Blessed are you among women, and blessed is the fruit of your womb.

43 And why is this, that the mother of my Lord should come to me?

44 For, lo, as the voice of your greeting came into my ears, the babe leaped for joy in my womb.

45 And blessed is she who believed, for there shall be a fulfillment to the things spoken to her from the Lord.

46 And Mary said, My soul glorifies the Lord,

47 and my spirit has rejoiced in God my Savior.

48 For He looked down on the lowliness of His servant. For behold, from now on all generations will call me blessed.

49 For the Mighty One has done great things to me, and holy is His name.

50 And His mercy is to generations of generations to those who fear Him.

51 He worked powerfully with His arm, He scattered the proud in the imagination of their hearts.

52 He put down rulers from thrones and raised up the lowly.

53 He filled the hungry with good things, and the rich He sent away empty.

54 He helped His servant Israel in order to remember mercy,

55 even as He spoke to our fathers, to Abraham and to his seed forever.

56 And Mary stayed with her about three months, then returned to her own house.

57 Now the time was fulfilled to Elizabeth that she should give birth. And she gave birth to a son.

58 And the neighbors and relatives heard that the Lord was magnifying His mercy with her and they greatly rejoiced with her.

59 And on the eighth day they came to circumcise the little child. And they were calling him after the name of his father, Zach-a-ri-as.

60 But answering, his mother said, No, but he shall be called John.

61 And they said to her, There is not one of your relatives who is called by this name.

62 And they signaled to his father as to what he wanted him to be called.

63 And asking for a writing tablet he wrote, saying, John is his name; and they all marveled.

64 And immediately his mouth opened and his tongue *was untied.* And he spoke, blessing God.

65 And fear came on all those who lived around them. And in the whole hill-country of Judea these things were told.

66 And all who heard laid them up in their hearts, saying, What then will this child be? And the hand of the Lord was with him.

κυρίου ἦν μετ' αὐτοῦ.
of [the] Lord was with him.

67 Καὶ Ζαχαρίας ὁ.πατὴρ.αὐτοῦ ἐπλήσθη πνεύματος
And Zacharias his father was filled with [the] [2]Spirit
ἁγίου, καὶ [x]προεφήτευσεν,[ll] λέγων, 68 Εὐλογητὸς κύριος ὁ
[1]Holy, and prophesied, saying, Blessed be [the] Lord the
θεὸς τοῦ Ἰσραήλ, ὅτι ἐπεσκέψατο καὶ ἐποίησεν λύτρωσιν
God of Israel, because he looked upon and wrought redemption
τῷ.λαῷ.αὐτοῦ· 69 καὶ ἤγειρεν κέρας σωτηρίας ἡμῖν ἐν [y]τῷ[l]
for his people, and raised up a horn of salvation for us in the
οἴκῳ [z]Δαβὶδ[ll] [a]τοῦ[l].παιδὸς.αὐτοῦ· 70 καθὼς ἐλάλησεν διὰ
house of David his servant; according as he spoke by [the]
στόματος τῶν ἁγίων [b]τῶν[l].ἀπ'.αἰῶνος προφητῶν αὐτοῦ·
mouth [3]holy [5]since [6]time [7]began [4]prophets [1]of [2]his;
71 σωτηρίαν ἐξ ἐχθρῶν.ἡμῶν καὶ ἐκ χειρὸς πάντων
salvation from our enemies and from [the] hand of all
τῶν μισούντων ἡμᾶς· 72 ποιῆσαι ἔλεος μετὰ τῶν πατέρων
those who hate us; to fulfil mercy with [2]fathers
ἡμῶν, καὶ μνησθῆναι διαθήκης ἁγίας αὐτοῦ, 73 ὅρκον ὃν
[1]our, and to remember [3]covenant [2]holy [1]his, [the] oath which
ὤμοσεν πρὸς Ἀβραὰμ τὸν.πατέρα.ἡμῶν, τοῦ δοῦναι ἡμῖν
he swore to Abraham our father, to give us [that]
74 ἀφόβως ἐκ χειρὸς [c]τῶν[ll].ἐχθρῶν.[d]ἡμῶν[l] ῥυσθέντας,
without fear out of [the] hand of our enemies being saved,
λατρεύειν αὐτῷ 75 ἐν ὁσιότητι καὶ δικαιοσύνῃ ἐνώπιον αὐτοῦ
we should serve him in holiness and righteousness before him,
πάσας τὰς ἡμέρας [e]τῆς.ζωῆς[l].ἡμῶν. 76 Καὶ σύ[f], παιδίον,
all the days of our life. And thou, little child,
προφήτης ὑψίστου κληθήσῃ· προπορεύσῃ.γὰρ πρὸ
prophet of [the] Highest shalt be called; for thou shalt go before [the]
προσώπου κυρίου ἑτοιμάσαι ὁδοὺς.αὐτοῦ· 77 τοῦ δοῦναι
face of [the] Lord to prepare his ways; to give
γνῶσιν σωτηρίας τῷ.λαῷ.αὐτοῦ ἐν ἀφέσει ἁμαρτιῶν.αὐτῶν,
knowledge of salvation to his people in remission of their sins,
78 διὰ σπλάγχνα ἐλέους θεοῦ.ἡμῶν, ἐν οἷς ἐπεσκέψατο
through [the] bowels of compassion of our God, in which has visited
ἡμᾶς ἀνατολὴ ἐξ ὕψους, 79 ἐπιφᾶναι τοῖς ἐν σκότει
us [the] day-spring from on high, to shine upon those [2]in [3]darkness
καὶ σκιᾷ θανάτου καθημένοις· τοῦ κατευθῦναι τοὺς
[4]and [5]in [6]the [7]shadow [8]of [9]death [1]sitting; to direct
πόδας.ἡμῶν εἰς ὁδὸν εἰρήνης. 80 Τὸ.δὲ παιδίον ηὔξανεν
our feet into [the] way of peace. And the little child grew
καὶ ἐκραταιοῦτο πνεύματι· καὶ ἦν ἐν ταῖς ἐρήμοις ἕως
and was strengthened in spirit; and he was in the deserts until [the]
ἡμέρας ἀναδείξεως.αὐτοῦ πρὸς τὸν Ἰσραήλ.
day of his shewing to Israel.

2 Ἐγένετο.δὲ ἐν ταῖς.ἡμέραις.ἐκείναις ἐξῆλθεν δόγμα
And it came to pass in those days [3]went [4]out [1]a [2]decree
παρὰ Καίσαρος Αὐγούστου, ἀπογράφεσθαι πᾶσαν τὴν
from Caesar Augustus, that should be registered all the
οἰκουμένην· 2 αὕτη.[g]ἡ ἀπογραφὴ [h]πρώτη ἐγένετο[ll] ἡγε-
habitable world; this registration first took place when
μονεύοντος τῆς Συρίας [i]Κυρηνίου.[ll] 3 καὶ ἐπορεύοντο πάντες
[2]was [3]governor [4]of [5]Syria [1]Cyrenius. And [2]went [1]all
ἀπογράφεσθαι, ἕκαστος εἰς τὴν.[k]ἰδίαν[l].πόλιν. 4 Ἀνέβη.δὲ καὶ
to be registered, each to his own city: and [3]went [4]up [2]also
Ἰωσὴφ ἀπὸ τῆς Γαλιλαίας ἐκ πόλεως [l]Ναζαρέτ[l] εἰς τὴν
[1]Joseph from Galilee out of [the] city Nazareth to
Ἰουδαίαν, εἰς πόλιν [m]Δαβὶδ[l] ἥτις καλεῖται Βηθλεέμ, διὰ
Judæa, to a city of David which is called Bethlehem, because
τὸ.εἶναι.αὐτὸν ἐξ οἴκου καὶ πατριᾶς [m]Δαβίδ,[l] 5 [n]ἀπο-
of his being of [the] house and family of David, to re-
γράψασθαι[ll] σὺν Μαριὰμ τῇ [o]μεμνηστευμένῃ[ll] αὐτῷ [p]γυναικί,[ll]
gister himself with Mary who was betrothed to him as wife,
οὔσῃ ἐγκύῳ. 6 Ἐγένετο.δὲ ἐν τῷ εἶναι.αὐτοὺς
she being great with child. And it came to pass in the [time] they were
ἐκεῖ ἐπλήσθησαν αἱ ἡμέραι τοῦ.τεκεῖν.αὐτήν· 7 καὶ ἔτε-
there [3]were [4]fulfilled [1]the [2]days for her bringing forth, and she brought
κεν τὸν.υἱὸν.αὐτῆς τὸν πρωτότοκον, καὶ ἐσπαργάνωσεν
forth her son the first-born, and wrapped [2]in [3]swaddling [4]clothes
αὐτόν, καὶ ἀνέκλινεν αὐτὸν ἐν [q]τῇ[l] φάτνῃ, διότι οὐκ.ἦν
[1]him, and laid him in the manger, because there was not
αὐτοῖς τόπος ἐν τῷ καταλύματι.
for them a place in the inn.

8 Καὶ ποιμένες ἦσαν ἐν τῇ χώρᾳ τῇ αὐτῇ, ἀγραυλοῦντες
And shepherds were in the [2]country [1]same, lodging in the fields
καὶ φυλάσσοντες φυλακὰς τῆς νυκτὸς ἐπὶ τὴν.ποίμνην.αὐτῶν.
and keeping watch by night over their flock;
9 καὶ [r]ἰδού,[ll] ἄγγελος κυρίου ἐπέστη αὐτοῖς, καὶ δόξα
and behold, an angel of [the] Lord stood by them, and [the] glory
κυρίου περιέλαμψεν αὐτούς· καὶ ἐφοβήθησαν φόβον
of [the] Lord shone around them, and they feared [with] [2]fear

67 And his father Zach-a-ri-as was filled with the Holy Spirit and prophesied, saying,

68 Blessed be the Lord, the God of Israel, because He looked on His people and worked out redemption for them.

69 And He raised up a Horn of salvation for us in the house of his servant David

70 even as He spoke by the mouth of His holy prophets (*all who* have been since the world began) –

71 salvation from our enemies and from the hand of those who hate us –

72 to fulfil mercy with our fathers and to remember His holy covenant,

73 the oath which He swore to Abraham our father,

74 to grant to us that we, being delivered out of the hand of our enemies, should serve Him without fear,

75 in holiness and righteousness before Him all the days of our lives.

76 And you, child, shall be called the prophet of the Highest. For you shall go before the face of the Lord to prepare His way,

77 to give knowledge of salvation to His people in remission of their sins,

78 through the tender mercies of our God, in which the Dayspring from on high has visited us,

79 to shine on those sitting in darkness and in the shadow of death, to guide our feet into the way of peace.

80 And the little child grew and was made stronger in spirit. And he was in the deserts until the day of his showing to Israel.

CHAPTER 2

1 And a decree went out from Caesar Augustus that all the world should be registered.

2 This census first began when Cy-ren-i-us was governor of Syria.

3 And all went to be registered, each to his own city.

4 And Joseph also went up from Galilee, out of the city Naz-a-reth, to Judea, to the city of David which is called Beth-le-hem, because he was of the house and family of David,

5 in order to register himself with Mary (who was betrothed to him as wife,) she being great with child.

6 And while they were there, the days were fulfilled for her to give birth.

7 And she bore her first-born son and wrapped him in a navel-band and laid Him in the manger because there was no room for them in the inn.

8 And there were shepherds in the same country, living in the fields and keeping watch by night over their flock.

9 And, behold! The angel of the Lord stood by them and the Lord's glory shone around them. And they feared with great fear.

μέγαν. 10 καὶ εἶπεν αὐτοῖς ὁ ἄγγελος, Μὴ.φοβεῖσθε· ἰδοὺ
[1]great. And [3]said [4]to [5]them [1]the [2]angel, Fear not; [2]behold
γάρ, εὐαγγελίζομαι ὑμῖν χαρὰν μεγάλην, ἥτις ἔσται
[1]for, I announce glad tidings to you [of] [2]joy [1]great, which shall be
παντὶ τῷ λαῷ· 11 ὅτι ἐτέχθη ὑμῖν σήμερον σωτήρ, ὅς ἐστιν
to all the people; for was born to you to-day a Saviour, who is
χριστὸς κύριος, ἐν πόλει [s]Δαβίδ.‖ 12 καὶ τοῦτο ὑμῖν
Christ [the] Lord, in [the] city of David. And this [is] to you
τὸ σημεῖον· εὑρήσετε βρέφος ἐσπαργανωμένον, [t][v]κεί-
the sign: ye shall find a babe wrapped in swaddling clothes, ly-
μενον‖ ἐν [w]τῇ‖ φάτνῃ. 13 Καὶ ἐξαίφνης ἐγένετο σὺν τῷ
ing in the manger. And suddenly there was with the
ἀγγέλῳ πλῆθος στρατιᾶς [x]οὐρανίου,‖ αἰνούντων τὸν θεόν,
angel a multitude of [the] [2]host [1]heavenly, praising God,
καὶ λεγόντων, 14 Δόξα ἐν ὑψίστοις θεῷ, καὶ ἐπὶ γῆς
and saying, Glory in [the] highest to God, and on earth
εἰρήνη, ἐν ἀνθρώποις [y]εὐδοκία.‖ 15 Καὶ ἐγένετο, ὡς ἀπῆλ-
peace, in men good pleasure. And it came to pass, as [3]depart-
θον ἀπ' αὐτῶν εἰς τὸν οὐρανὸν οἱ ἄγγελοι, [z]καὶ οἱ ἄνθρωποι‖
ed [4]from [5]them [6]into [7]the [8]heaven [1]the [2]angels, that the men
οἱ ποιμένες [a]εἶπον‖ πρὸς ἀλλήλους, Διέλθωμεν δὴ ἕως
the shepherds said to one another, Let us go through indeed as far as
Βηθλεέμ, καὶ ἴδωμεν τὸ.ῥῆμα.τοῦτο τὸ γεγονὸς ὃ ὁ
Bethlehem, and let us see this thing that has come to pass which the
κύριος ἐγνώρισεν ἡμῖν. 16 Καὶ [b]ἦλθον‖ σπεύσαντες καὶ
Lord made known to us. And they came having hasted and
[c]ἀνεῦρον‖ τήν.τε.Μαριὰμ καὶ τὸν Ἰωσήφ, καὶ τὸ βρέφος κεί-
found both Mary and Joseph, and the babe ly-
μενον ἐν τῇ φάτνῃ. 17 ἰδόντες.δὲ [d]διεγνώρισαν‖
ing in the manger. And having seen, they made known abroad
περὶ τοῦ ῥήματος τοῦ λαληθέντος αὐτοῖς περὶ τοῦ
concerning the saying which had been told them concerning
παιδίου.τούτου. 18 καὶ πάντες οἱ ἀκούσαντες ἐθαύμασαν
this little child. And all who heard wondered
περὶ τῶν λαληθέντων ὑπὸ τῶν ποιμένων πρὸς
concerning the things which had been spoken by the shepherds to
αὐτούς. 19 ἡ.δὲ.[e]Μαριὰμ‖ πάντα συνετήρει τὰ.ῥήματα.ταῦτα,
them. But Mary [2]all [1]kept these sayings,
[f]συμβάλλουσα‖ ἐν τῇ.καρδίᾳ.αὐτῆς. 20 καὶ [g]ἐπέστρεψαν‖
pondering [them] in her heart. And [3]returned
οἱ ποιμένες, δοξάζοντες καὶ αἰνοῦντες τὸν θεὸν ἐπὶ πᾶσιν
[1]the [2]shepherds, glorifying and praising God for all things
οἷς ἤκουσαν καὶ [h]εἶδον,‖ καθὼς ἐλαλήθη πρὸς αὐτούς.
which they had heard and seen, as it was said to them.
21 Καὶ ὅτε ἐπλήσθησαν ἡμέραι ὀκτὼ τοῦ περιτεμεῖν [i]τὸ
And when were fulfilled [2]days [1]eight for the circumcising the
παιδίον,‖ καὶ ἐκλήθη τὸ.ὄνομα.αὐτοῦ Ἰησοῦς, τὸ κλη-
little child, [3]was [4]called [1]his [2]name Jesus, which [he] was
θὲν ὑπὸ τοῦ ἀγγέλου πρὸ τοῦ [k]συλληφθῆναι‖ αὐτὸν ἐν τῇ
called by the angel before [2]was [3]conceived [1]he in the
κοιλίᾳ.
womb.
22 Καὶ ὅτε ἐπλήσθησαν αἱ ἡμέραι τοῦ.καθαρισμοῦ.[l]αὐτῶν‖
And when were fulfilled the days for their purification
κατὰ τὸν νόμον [m]Μωσέως,‖ ἀνήγαγον αὐτὸν εἰς Ἱεροσό-
according to the law of Moses, they brought him to Jerusa-
λυμα παραστῆσαι τῷ κυρίῳ, 23 καθὼς γέγραπται ἐν [n]
lem to present to the Lord, as it has been written in [the]
νόμῳ κυρίου, Ὅτι πᾶν ἄρσεν διανοῖγον μήτραν ἅγιον
law of [the] Lord, That every male opening a womb [4]holy
τῷ κυρίῳ κληθήσεται· 24 καὶ τοῦ δοῦναι θυσίαν κατὰ
[5]to [6]the [7]Lord [1]shall [2]be [3]called; and to offer a sacrifice according to
τὸ εἰρημένον ἐν [o] νόμῳ κυρίου, Ζεῦγος τρυγόνων
that which has been said in [the] law of [the] Lord, A pair of turtle doves
ἢ δύο [p]νεοσσοὺς‖ περιστερῶν.
or two young of pigeons.
25 Καὶ ἰδού, [q]ἦν ἄνθρωπος‖ ἐν Ἱερουσαλὴμ ᾧ ὄνομα
And behold, there was a man in Jerusalem whose name
Συμεών, καὶ ὁ.ἄνθρωπος.οὗτος δίκαιος καὶ εὐλαβής,
[was] Simeon; and this man [was] just and pious,
προσδεχόμενος παράκλησιν τοῦ Ἰσραήλ, καὶ πνεῦμα
waiting for [the] consolation of Israel, and [the] [2]Spirit
[r]ἅγιον ἦν‖ ἐπ' αὐτόν· 26 καὶ ἦν αὐτῷ κεχρηματισμένον ὑπὸ
[1]Holy was upon him. And it was to him divinely communicated by
τοῦ πνεύματος τοῦ ἁγίου μὴ.ἰδεῖν θάνατον πρὶν [s]ἢ [t]
the Spirit the Holy that he should not see death before
ἴδῃ τὸν χριστὸν κυρίου. 27 καὶ ἦλθεν ἐν τῷ πνεύματι
he should see the Christ of [the] Lord. And he came in the Spirit
εἰς τὸ ἱερόν· καὶ ἐν.τῷ.εἰσαγαγεῖν τοὺς γονεῖς τὸ παιδίον Ἰη-
into the temple; and when [3]brought [4]in [1]the [2]parents the little child Je-
σοῦν, τοῦ.ποιῆσαι.αὐτοὺς κατὰ τὸ.εἰθισμένον
sus, that they might do [3]according [4]to [5]what [6]had [7]become [8]customary

10 And the angel said to them, Do not fear. Lo, I bring you good news of great joy, which shall be to all people.

11 For a Savior was born to you today, who is Christ the Lord, in the city of David.

12 And this is the sign to you, You shall find a babe wrapped in a navel-band, lying in a manger.

13 And suddenly there was with the angel a multitude of the heavenly host, praising God and saying,

14 Glory to God in the highest, and peace on earth, good will toward men.

15 And as the angels were going away from them into Heaven, the shepherd men said to one another, Indeed, let us go over to Beth-le-hem, and let us see this thing which has happened, which the Lord made known to us.

16 And hurrying, they came and found both Mary and Joseph, and the babe lying in the manger.

17 And seeing, they spoke out about the story which they had been told regarding the child.

18 And all who heard wondered about these things which the shepherds had told them.

19 But Mary treasured all these words, keeping them afresh in her heart.

20 And the shepherds returned, glorifying and praising God for all those things which they had heard and seen, as it was told them.

21 And when eight days were fulfilled for the circumcising of the child, His name was called Jesus (which *He* was called by the angel before He was conceived in the womb).

22 And when the days for their purification were fulfilled according to the Law of Moses, they brought Him to Jerusalem to present Him to the Lord –

23 even as it has been written in the Law of the Lord, "Every male opening a womb shall be called holy to the Lord,"

24 and to offer a sacrifice according to that which had been written in the Law of the Lord – a pair of turtledoves, or two young pigeons.

25 And lo, there was a man in Jerusalem whose name was Simeon. And this man was righteous and godly, waiting for the Comfort of Israel. And the Holy Spirit was on him.

26 And it was divinely revealed to him by the Holy Spirit that he should not see death before he should see the Christ of the Lord.

27 And he came in the Spirit into the Temple. And when the parents brought in the child Jesus, that they might do according to the custom of the Law for Him,

τοῦ νόμου περὶ αὐτοῦ, 28 καὶ.αὐτὸς ἐδέξατο αὐτὸ εἰς τὰς ἀγκά-
9by 10the 11law 1for 2him, he also received him into 2arms,
λας αὐτοῦ, καὶ εὐλόγησεν τὸν θεόν, καὶ εἶπεν, 29 Νῦν ἀπολύεις
1his, and blessed God, and said, Now thou lettest go
τὸν.δοῦλόν.σου, δέσποτα, κατὰ τὸ.ῥῆμά.σου, ἐν εἰρήνῃ·
thy bondman, O Master, according to thy word, in peace;
30 ὅτι εἶδον οἱ.ὀφθαλμοί.μου τὸ.σωτήριόν.σου, 31 ὃ
for 3have 4seen 1mine 2eyes thy salvation, which
ἡτοίμασας κατὰ πρόσωπον πάντων τῶν λαῶν· 32 φῶς
thou hast prepared before [the] face of all the peoples; a light
εἰς ἀποκάλυψιν ἐθνῶν καὶ δόξαν λαοῦ.σου Ἰσραήλ.
for revelation of [the] Gentiles and glory of thy people Israel.
33 Καὶ ἦν Ἰωσὴφ καὶ ἡ.μήτηρ.αὐτοῦ θαυμάζοντες ἐπὶ
And 5were 1Joseph 2and 3his 4mother wondering at
τοῖς λαλουμένοις περὶ αὐτοῦ. 34 καὶ εὐλόγησεν
the things which were spoken concerning him. And 2blessed
αὐτοὺς Συμεών, καὶ εἶπεν πρὸς Μαριὰμ τὴν.μητέρα αὐτοῦ,
3them 1Simeon, and said to Mary his mother,
Ἰδού, οὗτος κεῖται εἰς πτῶσιν καὶ ἀνάστασιν πολλῶν
Lo, this [child] is set for [the] fall and rising up of many
ἐν τῷ Ἰσραήλ, καὶ εἰς σημεῖον ἀντιλεγόμενον· 35 καὶ σοῦ δὲ
in Israel, and for a sign spoken against; (and of thee also
αὐτῆς τὴν ψυχὴν διελεύσεται ῥομφαία· ὅπως ἂν.ἀποκαλυ-
6thy 7soul 3shall 4go 5through 1a 2sword;) so that may be re-
φθῶσιν ἐκ πολλῶν καρδιῶν διαλογισμοί.
vealed of many hearts [the] reasonings.
36 Καὶ ἦν Ἄννα προφῆτις, θυγάτηρ Φανουήλ, ἐκ
And there was Anna a prophetess, daughter of Phanuel, of [the]
φυλῆς Ἀσήρ· αὕτη προβεβηκυῖα ἐν ἡμέραις πολλαῖς, ζήσασα
tribe of Asher, she was advanced in 2days 1many, having lived
ἔτη μετὰ ἀνδρὸς ἑπτὰ ἀπὸ τῆς.παρθενίας.αὐτῆς, 37 καὶ
6years 3with 4a 5husband 1seven from her virginity, and
αὕτη χήρα ὡς ἐτῶν ὀγδοηκοντατεσσάρων, ἣ οὐκ
she [was] a widow 2about 4years 1of 3eighty-four, 5who 7not
ἀφίστατο ἀπὸ τοῦ ἱεροῦ, νηστείαις καὶ δεήσεσιν λατρεύουσα
8departed from the temple, with fastings and supplications serving
νύκτα καὶ ἡμέραν· 38 καὶ αὕτη αὐτῇ.τῇ ὥρᾳ ἐπιστᾶσα
night and day: and she at the same hour coming up
ἀνθωμολογεῖτο τῷ κυρίῳ, καὶ ἐλάλει περὶ αὐτοῦ πᾶσιν
gave praise to the Lord, and spoke concerning him to all
τοῖς προσδεχομένοις λύτρωσιν ἐν Ἱερουσαλήμ.
those waiting for redemption in Jerusalem.
39 Καὶ ὡς ἐτέλεσαν ἅπαντα.τὰ κατὰ τὸν νόμον
And when they had completed all things according to the law
κυρίου, ὑπέστρεψαν εἰς τὴν Γαλιλαίαν, εἰς τὴν πόλιν
of [the] Lord they returned to Galilee, to 3city
αὐτῶν Ναζαρέτ. 40 Τὸ.δὲ παιδίον ηὔξανεν καὶ ἐκρα-
1their [2own], Nazareth. And the little child grew, and became
ταιοῦτο πνεύματι, πληρούμενον σοφίας, καὶ χάρις
strong in spirit, being filled with wisdom, and [the] grace
θεοῦ ἦν ἐπ' αὐτό.
of God was upon him.
41 Καὶ ἐπορεύοντο οἱ.γονεῖς.αὐτοῦ κατ'.ἔτος εἰς Ἱερουσαλὴμ
And 3went 1his 2parents yearly to Jerusalem
τῇ ἑορτῇ τοῦ πάσχα. 42 καὶ ὅτε ἐγένετο ἐτῶν δώδεκα,
at the feast of the passover. And when he was 2years [3old] 1twelve,
ἀναβάντων αὐτῶν εἰς Ἱεροσόλυμα κατὰ τὸ ἔθος τῆς
5having 6gone 7up 4they to Jerusalem according to the custom of the
ἑορτῆς, 43 καὶ τελειωσάντων τὰς ἡμέρας, ἐν.τῷ.ὑποστρέφειν
feast, and having completed the days, as 2returned
αὐτοὺς ὑπέμεινεν Ἰησοῦς ὁ παῖς ἐν Ἱερουσαλήμ, καὶ
1they 6remained 7behind 5Jesus 3the 4child in Jerusalem, and
οὐκ.ἔγνω Ἰωσὴφ καὶ ἡ.μήτηρ.αὐτοῦ· 44 νομίσαντες.δὲ αὐτὸν
5knew [6it] 7not 1Joseph 2and 3his 4mother; but supposing him
ἐν τῇ συνοδίᾳ εἶναι ἦλθον ἡμέρας ὁδόν, καὶ ἀνεζήτουν
in the company to be they went a day's journey, and sought
αὐτὸν ἐν τοῖς συγγενέσιν καὶ ἐν τοῖς γνωστοῖς· 45 καὶ
him among the relations and among the acquaintances: and
μὴ εὑρόντες αὐτὸν ὑπέστρεψαν εἰς Ἱερουσαλήμ, ζητοῦντες
not having found him they returned to Jerusalem, seeking
αὐτόν. 46 Καὶ ἐγένετο μεθ' ἡμέρας τρεῖς εὗρον αὐτὸν ἐν
him. And it came to pass after 2days 1three they found him in
τῷ ἱερῷ, καθεζόμενον ἐν μέσῳ τῶν διδασκάλων, καὶ ἀκού-
the temple, sitting in [the] midst of the teachers, both hear-
οντα αὐτῶν καὶ ἐπερωτῶντα αὐτούς. 47 ἐξίσταντο.δὲ πάντες
ing them and questioning them. And 5were 6amazed 1all
οἱ ἀκούοντες αὐτοῦ ἐπὶ τῇ συνέσει καὶ ταῖς ἀποκρίσεσιν
2those 3hearing 4him at [his] understanding and 2answers
αὐτοῦ. 48 Καὶ ἰδόντες αὐτὸν ἐξεπλάγησαν· καὶ πρὸς αὐτὸν
1his. And seeing him they were astonished: and to him
ἡ.μήτηρ.αὐτοῦ εἶπεν, Τέκνον, τί ἐποίησας ἡμῖν οὕτως;
his mother said, Child, why hast thou done to us thus?

28 he also received Him into his arms. And he blessed God and said,
29 Now You will let Your servant go in peace, Lord, according to Your word.
30 For my eyes have seen Your salvation,
31 which You have prepared before the face of all the nations,
32 a light for enlightening the Gentiles, and the glory of Your people Israel.
33 And Joseph and His mother were wondering at the things which were spoken of Him.
34 And Simeon blessed them and said to Mary His mother, Behold! This One is set for the fall and rising up of many in Israel, and for a sign spoken against –
35 yea, a sword shall pierce your own soul also – so that the thoughts of many hearts may be revealed.

36 And there was Anna, a prophetess, Phanuel's daughter, of the tribe of Asher. She was much advanced in days, having lived seven years with a husband from her virginity,
37 and she was a widow of about eighty-four years. *And she* never left the Temple, serving with fastings and prayers night and day.
38 And coming up at the same time she gave praise to the Lord and spoke about Him to all those waiting for redemption at Jerusalem.

39 And when they had done all things according to the Law of the Lord, they returned to Galilee, to their own city of Naz-a-reth.
40 And the child grew and became strong in spirit, being filled with wisdom. And God's grace was upon Him.

41 And His parents went to Jerusalem every year at the Feast of the Passover.
42 And when He was twelve years old they went up to Jerusalem, according to the custom of the Feast.
43 And when they had completed the days, as they returned, the child Jesus stayed behind in Jerusalem. But Joseph and His mother did not know.
44 And supposing Him to be in the group, they went a day's journey. And *then they* looked for Him among the relatives and among the friends.
45 And when they did not find Him, they returned to Jerusalem looking for Him.
46 And after three days they found Him in the Temple, sitting in the midst of the ones who taught, both hearing them and asking questions.
47 And all those hearing Him were amazed at His understanding and answers.
48 And they were astonished when they saw Him. And His mother said to Him, Son, why have You done this to us? See, Your

ἰδού, ὁ.πατήρ.σου κἀγὼ ὀδυνώμενοι ἐζητοῦμέν σε. 49 Καὶ
behold, thy father and I distressed were seeking thee. And

εἶπεν πρὸς αὐτούς, Τί ὅτι ἐζητεῖτέ με; οὐκ.ᾔδειτε ὅτι
he said to them, Why [is it] that ye were seeking me? knew ye not that

ἐν τοῖς τοῦ.πατρός.μου δεῖ εἶναί με; 50 Καὶ αὐτοὶ
in the [affairs] of my Father it behoves [2]to [3]be [1]me? And they

οὐ.συνῆκαν τὸ ῥῆμα ὃ ἐλάλησεν αὐτοῖς. 51 Καὶ κατέβη
understood not the word which he spoke to them. And he went down

μετ' αὐτῶν καὶ ἦλθεν εἰς [b]Ναζαρέτ·‖ καὶ ἦν ὑποτασσόμενος
with them and came to Nazareth, and he was subject

αὐτοῖς. καὶ ἡ.μήτηρ.αὐτοῦ διετήρει [c]πάντα τὰ.ῥήματα [d]ταῦτα‖
to them. And his mother kept all these things

ἐν τῇ.καρδίᾳ.αὐτῆς. 52 καὶ Ἰησοῦς προέκοπτεν [e] [f]σοφίᾳ καὶ
in her heart. And Jesus advanced in wisdom and

ἡλικίᾳ,‖ καὶ χάριτι παρὰ θεῷ καὶ ἀνθρώποις.
stature, and in favour with God and men.

3 Ἐν ἔτει δὲ πεντεκαιδεκάτῳ τῆς ἡγεμονίας Τιβερίου
[2]In [5]year [1]now [[3]the] [4]fifteenth of the government of Tiberius

Καίσαρος, ἡγεμονεύοντος Ποντίου [g]Πιλάτου‖ τῆς Ἰουδαίας,
Cæsar, [3]being [4]governor [1]Pontius [2]Pilate of Judæa,

καὶ [h]τετραρχοῦντος‖ τῆς Γαλιλαίας Ἡρῴδου, Φιλίππου.δὲ τοῦ
and [2]being [3]tetrarch [4]of [5]Galilee [1]Herod, and Philip

ἀδελφοῦ.αὐτοῦ [h]τετραρχοῦντος‖ τῆς Ἰτουραίας καὶ Τραχωνί-
his brother being tetrarch of Ituræa and [3]of [4]Tracho-

τιδος χώρας, καὶ Λυσανίου τῆς Ἀβιληνῆς [h]τετραρχοῦντος,‖
nitis [the] [2]region, and Lysanias [3]of [4]Abilene [1]being [2]tetrarch,

2 [i]ἐπ' ἀρχιερέων‖ Ἄννα καὶ [k]Καϊάφα,‖ ἐγένετο ῥῆμα
in [the] high-priesthood of Annas and Caiaphas, came [the] word

θεοῦ ἐπὶ [l]Ἰωάννην‖ τὸν [m]τοῦ‖ Ζαχαρίου υἱὸν ἐν τῇ ἐρήμῳ·
of God upon John the [2]of [3]Zacharias [1]son in the wilderness.

3 καὶ ἦλθεν εἰς πᾶσαν [n]τὴν‖ περίχωρον τοῦ Ἰορδάνου,
And he went into all the country around the Jordan,

κηρύσσων βάπτισμα μετανοίας εἰς ἄφεσιν ἁμαρτιῶν·
proclaiming [the] baptism of repentance for remission of sins;

4 ὡς γέγραπται ἐν βίβλῳ λόγων Ἡσαΐου τοῦ
as it has been written in [the] book of [the] words of Esaias the

προφήτου, [o]λέγοντος,‖ Φωνὴ βοῶντος ἐν τῇ ἐρήμῳ,
prophet, saying, [The] voice of one crying in the wilderness,

Ἑτοιμάσατε τὴν ὁδὸν κυρίου· εὐθείας ποιεῖτε τὰς τρίβους
Prepare the way of [the] Lord; [2]straight [1]make [4]paths

αὐτοῦ. 5 πᾶσα φάραγξ πληρωθήσεται, καὶ πᾶν ὄρος καὶ
[3]his. Every ravine shall be filled up, and every mountain and

βουνὸς ταπεινωθήσεται· καὶ ἔσται τὰ σκολιὰ εἰς
hill shall be made low; and [4]shall [5]become [1]the [2]crooked [[3]places] into

[p]εὐθεῖαν,‖ καὶ αἱ τραχεῖαι εἰς ὁδοὺς λείας· 6 καὶ ὄψεται
a straight [path], and the rough into [2]ways [1]smooth; and [3]shall [4]see

πᾶσα σὰρξ τὸ σωτήριον τοῦ θεοῦ. 7 Ἔλεγεν οὖν τοῖς
[1]all [2]flesh the salvation of God. He said therefore to the

ἐκπορευομένοις ὄχλοις βαπτισθῆναι ὑπ' αὐτοῦ, Γεννήματα
[2]coming [3]out [1]crowds to be baptized by him, Offspring

ἐχιδνῶν, τίς ὑπέδειξεν ὑμῖν φυγεῖν ἀπὸ τῆς μελλούσης ὀργῆς;
of vipers, who forewarned you to flee from the coming wrath?

8 ποιήσατε οὖν καρποὺς ἀξίους τῆς μετανοίας· καὶ μὴ
Produce therefore fruits worthy of repentance; and [2]not

ἄρξησθε λέγειν ἐν ἑαυτοῖς, Πατέρα ἔχομεν τὸν Ἀβραάμ·
[1]begin to say in yourselves, [[4]For] [5]father [1]we [2]have [3]Abraham,

λέγω.γὰρ ὑμῖν, ὅτι δύναται ὁ θεὸς ἐκ τῶν.λίθων.τούτων
for I say to you, that [2]is [3]able [1]God from these stones

ἐγεῖραι τέκνα τῷ Ἀβραάμ. 9 ἤδη.δὲ καὶ ἡ ἀξίνη πρὸς τὴν
to raise up children to Abraham. But already also the axe to the

ῥίζαν τῶν δένδρων κεῖται· πᾶν οὖν δένδρον μὴ ποιοῦν
root of the trees is applied: [2]every [1]therefore tree not producing

καρπὸν [r]καλὸν‖ ἐκκόπτεται καὶ εἰς πῦρ βάλλεται. 10 Καὶ
[2]fruit [1]good is cut down and into [the] fire is cast. And

ἐπηρώτων αὐτὸν οἱ ὄχλοι, λέγοντες, Τί οὖν [s]ποιήσομεν‖;
[3]asked [4]him [1]the [2]crowds, saying, What then shall we do?

11 Ἀποκριθεὶς.δὲ [t]λέγει‖ αὐτοῖς, Ὁ ἔχων δύο χιτῶνας μετα-
And answering he says to them, He that has two tunics let him

δότω τῷ μὴ.ἔχοντι· καὶ ὁ ἔχων βρώματα ὁμοίως
impart to him that has not; and he that has victuals [4]likewise

ποιείτω. 12 Ἦλθον.δὲ καὶ τελῶναι βαπτισθῆναι, καὶ
[1]let [2]him [3]do. And [3]came [2]also [1]tax-gatherers to be baptized, and

[v]εἶπον‖ πρὸς αὐτόν, Διδάσκαλε, τί [s]ποιήσομεν‖; 13 Ὁ.δὲ εἶπεν
they said to him, Teacher, what shall we do? And he said

πρὸς αὐτούς, Μηδὲν πλέον παρὰ τὸ διατεταγμένον
to them, [2]Nothing [3]more [4]beyond [5]that [6]which [7]is [8]appointed

ὑμῖν πράσσετε. 14 Ἐπηρώτων.δὲ αὐτὸν καὶ στρατευόμενοι,
[9]to [10]you [1]exact. And asked him also those who were soldiers,

λέγοντες, [w]Καὶ ἡμεῖς τί ποιήσομεν‖; Καὶ εἶπεν [x]πρὸς αὐτούς,‖
saying, And we what shall we do? And he said to them,

Μηδένα διασείσητε [y]μηδὲ‖ συκοφαντήσητε, καὶ ἀρκεῖσθε τοῖς
[2]No [3]one [1]oppress nor accuse falsely, and be satisfied

father and I were looking for You, full of sorrow.

49 And He said to them, Why were you looking for Me? Do you not know that I must be about My Father's business?

50 And they did not understand what He was saying to them.

51 And He went down with them and came to Nazareth. And He was obedient to them. And His mother kept all these things in her heart.

52 And Jesus advanced in wisdom and size, and in favor with God and men.

CHAPTER 3

1 Now in the fifteenth year of the reign of Ti-ber-i-as Caesar, Pontius Pilate was governor of Judea and Herod was tetrarch of Galilee. And his brother Philip was tetrarch of I-tu-re-a and of the region of Trach-o-ni-tis. And Ly-sa-ni-as was the tetrarch of Ab-i-le-ne.

2 During the high-priesthood of Annas and Cai-a-phas, the word of God came on John the son of Zach-a-ri-as in the wilderness.

3 And he went into all the country around the Jordan, preaching the baptism of repentance for remission of sins –

4 as it has been written in the book of the words of Isaiah the prophet, saying, "The voice of one crying in the wilderness. Prepare the way of the Lord. Make His paths straight

5 – every valley shall be filled and every mountain and hill shall be brought low. And the crooked places shall become a straight *path,* and the rough roads shall become smooth,

6 and all flesh shall see the salvation of God."

7 Then he said to the crowd coming out to be baptized by him, Children of vipers! Who has warned you to flee from the wrath to come?

8 Then bring forth fruits worthy of repentance. And do not begin to say within yourselves, We have Abraham for *our* father. For I say to you that God is able to raise up children to Abraham from these stones.

9 And also the axe is already laid to the root of the trees: therefore every tree which does not bear good fruit is cut down and is thrown into the fire.

10 And the people asked him, saying, What then shall we do?

11 And answering he said to them, He that has two coats, let him give to him that has none. And he that has food, let him do likewise.

12 And tax-collectors also came to be baptized. And they said to him, Teacher, what shall we do?

13 And he said to them, Exact no more than that which is appointed to you.

14 And those who were soldiers also asked him, saying, And what shall we do? And he said to them, Treat no one cruelly, nor accuse falsely, and be satisfied with your pay.

ὀψωνίοις.ὑμῶν.
with your wages.
15 Προσδοκῶντος.δὲ τοῦ λαοῦ, καὶ διαλογιζομένων πάν-
But as [3]were [4]in [5]expectation [1]the [2]people, and [2]were [3]reasoning [1]all
των ἐν ταῖς.καρδίαις.αὐτῶν περὶ τοῦ [z]Ἰωάννου,‖ μήποτε
in their hearts concerning John, whether or not
αὐτὸς εἴη ὁ χριστός, 16 ἀπεκρίνατο [a]ὁ Ἰωάννης ἅπασιν,
he might be the Christ, [2]answered [1]John all,
λέγων,‖ Ἐγὼ μὲν ὕδατι βαπτίζω ὑμᾶς[b]· ἔρχεται.δὲ ὁ
saying, I indeed with water baptize you, but he comes who [is]
ἰσχυρότερός μου, οὗ οὐκ.εἰμὶ ἱκανὸς λῦσαι τὸν ἱμάντα τῶν
mightier than I, of whom I am not fit to loose the thong
ὑποδημάτων.αὐτοῦ· αὐτὸς ὑμᾶς βαπτίσει ἐν πνεύματι
of his sandals; he [3]you [1]will [2]baptize with [the] [2]Spirit
ἁγίῳ καὶ πυρί· 17 οὗ τὸ πτύον ἐν τῇ.χειρὶ.αὐτοῦ,
[1]Holy and with fire; of whom the winnowing fan [is] in his hand,
[c]καὶ διακαθαριεῖ‖ τὴν.ἅλωνα.αὐτοῦ, καὶ [d]συνάξει‖ τὸν
and he will thoroughly purge his floor, and will gather the
σῖτον εἰς τὴν.ἀποθήκην.αὐτοῦ, τὸ.δὲ ἄχυρον κατακαύσει
wheat into his granary, but the chaff he will burn
πυρὶ ἀσβέστῳ. 18 Πολλὰ μὲν.οὖν καὶ ἕτερα παρακαλῶν
with fire unquenchable. [3]Many [2]therefore [1]and other things exhorting
εὐηγγελίζετο τὸν λαόν. 19 Ὁ.δὲ.Ἡρώδης ὁ [e]τε-
he announced the glad tidings to the people. But Herod the te-
τράρχης‖ ἐλεγχόμενος ὑπ' αὐτοῦ περὶ Ἡρωδιάδος τῆς
trarch being reproved by him concerning Herodias the
γυναικὸς [f]Φιλίππου‖ τοῦ.ἀδελφοῦ.αὐτοῦ, καὶ περὶ πάντων
wife of Philip his brother, and concerning all
ὧν ἐποίησεν πονηρῶν ὁ Ἡρώδης, 20 προσέθηκεν [g]καὶ‖
[3]which [5]had [6]done [[1]the] [2]evils [4]Herod, added also
τοῦτο ἐπὶ πᾶσιν [h]καὶ‖ κατέκλεισεν τὸν [i]Ἰωάννην‖ ἐν [k]τῇ‖
this to all that he shut up John in the
φυλακῇ.
prison.
21 Ἐγένετο.δὲ ἐν.τῷ.βαπτισθῆναι ἅπαντα τὸν λαόν, καὶ
Now it came to pass [4]having [5]been [6]baptized [1]all [2]the [3]people, and
Ἰησοῦ βαπτισθέντος καὶ προσευχομένου, ἀνεῳχθῆναι τὸν
Jesus having been baptized and praying, [3]was [4]opened [1]the
οὐρανόν, 22 καὶ καταβῆναι τὸ πνεῦμα τὸ ἅγιον σωματικῷ
[2]heaven, and descended the Spirit the Holy in a bodily
εἴδει [l]ὡσεὶ‖ περιστερὰν ἐπ' αὐτόν, καὶ φωνὴν ἐξ οὐρανοῦ
form as a dove upon him, and a voice out of heaven
γενέσθαι, [m]λέγουσαν,‖ Σὺ εἶ ὁ.υἱός.μου ὁ ἀγαπητός, ἐν σοὶ
came, saying, Thou art my Son the beloved, in thee
[n]ηὐδόκησα.‖
I have found delight.
23 Καὶ αὐτὸς ἦν [o]ὁ‖ Ἰησοῦς [p]ὡσεὶ ἐτῶν τριάκοντα
And [2]himself [3]was [1]Jesus [7]about [9]years [[10]old] [8]thirty
ἀρχόμενος,‖ [q]ὤν, ὡς ἐνομίζετο, υἱὸς‖ Ἰωσήφ, τοῦ [r]Ἡλί,‖
[4]beginning [[5]to [6]be], being, as was supposed, son of Joseph, of Eli,
24 τοῦ [s]Ματθάτ,‖ τοῦ [t]Λευΐ,‖ τοῦ [v]Μελχί,‖ τοῦ [w]Ἰαννά,‖ τοῦ
of Matthat, of Levi, of Melchi, of Janna,
Ἰωσήφ, 25 τοῦ [x]Ματταθίου,‖ τοῦ Ἀμώς, τοῦ Ναούμ, τοῦ [y]Ἐσλί,‖
of Joseph, of Mattathias, of Amos, of Naoum, of Esli,
τοῦ Ναγγαί, 26 τοῦ Μαάθ, τοῦ Ματταθίου, τοῦ [z]Σεμεΐ,‖ τοῦ
of Naggai, of Maath, of Mattathias, of Semei,
[a']Ἰωσήφ,‖ τοῦ [b']Ἰούδα,‖ 27 τοῦ [c']Ἰωαννᾶ,‖ τοῦ Ῥησά, τοῦ Ζορο-
of Joseph, of Juda, of Joannes, of Rhesa, of Zoro-
βάβελ, τοῦ Σαλαθιήλ, τοῦ [d]Νηρί,‖ 28 τοῦ [v]Μελχί,‖ τοῦ [ea]Ἀδδί,‖
babel, of Salathiel, of Neri, of Melchi, of Addi,
τοῦ Κωσάμ, τοῦ [fa]Ἐλμωδάμ,‖ τοῦ Ἤρ, 29 τοῦ [ga]Ἰωσή,‖ τοῦ Ἐλι-
of Cosam, of Elmodam, of Er, of Joses, of Eli-
έζερ, τοῦ Ἰωρείμ, τοῦ [ha]Ματθάτ,‖ τοῦ [ia]Λευΐ,‖ 30 τοῦ Συμεών,
ezer, of Joreim, of Matthat, of Levi, of Simeon,
τοῦ Ἰούδα, τοῦ Ἰωσήφ, τοῦ [ka]Ἰωνάν,‖ τοῦ Ἐλιακείμ, 31 τοῦ [la]Με-
of Juda, of Joseph, of Jonan, of Eliakim, of Me-
λεᾶ,‖ [ma]τοῦ Μαϊνάν,‖ τοῦ Ματταθά, τοῦ [na]Ναθάν,‖ τοῦ [oa]Δα-
leas, of Menna, of Mattatha, of Nathan, of Da-
βίδ,‖ 32 τοῦ Ἰεσσαί, τοῦ [pa]Ὠβήδ,‖ τοῦ [qa]Βοόζ,‖ τοῦ [ra]Σαλμών,‖
vid, of Jesse, of Obed, of Booz, of Salmon,
τοῦ Ναασσών, 33 τοῦ [s]Ἀμιναδάβ,‖ τοῦ [t]Ἀράμ,‖ τοῦ [v]Ἐσρώμ,‖
of Naasson, of Aminadab, of Aram, of Esrom,
τοῦ Φαρές, τοῦ Ἰούδα, 34 τοῦ Ἰακώβ, τοῦ Ἰσαάκ, τοῦ Ἀβραάμ,
of Phares, of Juda, of Jacob, of Isaac, of Abraham,
τοῦ Θάρα, τοῦ Ναχώρ, 35 τοῦ [w]Σαρούχ,‖ τοῦ Ῥαγαῦ, τοῦ Φαλέκ,
of Terah, of Nachor, of Saruch, of Ragau, of Phalek,
τοῦ [x]Ἔβερ,‖ τοῦ Σαλά, 36 τοῦ [y]Καϊνάν,‖ τοῦ Ἀρφαξάδ, τοῦ
of Eber, of Sala, of Cainan, of Arphaxad,
Σήμ, τοῦ Νῶε, τοῦ Λάμεχ, 37 τοῦ Μαθουσάλα, τοῦ Ἐνώχ,
of Sem, of Noe, of Lamech, of Mathusala, of Enoch,
τοῦ [z]Ἰαρέδ,‖ τοῦ [a]Μαλελεήλ,‖ τοῦ [b]Καϊνάν,‖ 38 τοῦ Ἐνώς,
of Jared, of Maleleel, of Cainan, of Enos,

15 But as the people were in suspense and
were reasoning in their hearts about John,
whether or not he might be the Christ,
16 John answered, saying to all, I indeed
baptize you with water, but He comes who is
mightier than I, of whom I am not worthy to
untie the thong of His sandals. He will baptize
you with the Holy Spirit and with fire.
17 *His* sifting fan is in His hand and He will
thoroughly purge His floor. And He will gather the wheat into His storehouse. But He will
burn the chaff with fire that cannot be put
out.
18 And then imploring them with many
other things, he truly preached the gospel to
the people.
19 But Herod the tetrarch had been shamed
by John as to He-ro-di-as the wife of his
brother Philip, and as to all the evils which
Herod had done.
20 He also added this to all the *evils*, that he
locked John up in the prison.
21 Now when all the people had been baptized, and Jesus had been baptized and was
praying, the heavens were opened
22 and the Holy Spirit came down upon
Him in a bodily form as a dove. And a voice
out of Heaven came, saying, You are My
beloved Son! In You I have found delight!
23 And Jesus Himself was beginning to be
about thirty years old, being, as was supposed, the son of Joseph, the *son* of Heli,
24 the *son* of Mat-that, the *son* of Levi, the
son of Mel-chi, the *son* of Janna, the *son* of
Joseph,
25 the *son* of Mat-ta-thi-as, the *son* of
Amos, the *son* of Nahum, the *son* of Esli,
the *son* of Nag-ga-i,
26 the *son* of Ma-ath, the *son* of Mat-ta-
thi-as, the *son* of Sem-e-i, the *son* of Joseph,
the *son* of Juda,
27 the *son* of Jo-ann-es, the *son* of Rhesa,
the *son* of Ze-rub-ba-bel, the *son* of She-al-
ti-el, the *son* of Neri,
28 the *son* of Mel-chi, the *son* of Addi, the
son of Co-sam, the *son* of El-mo-dam, the
son of Er,
29 the *son* of Joses, the *son* of El-i-e-zer, the
son of Jorim, the *son* of Mat-that, the *son* of
Levi,
30 the *son* of Sim-e-on, the *son* of Juda, the
son of Joseph, the *son* of Jonan, the *son* of
E-li-a-kim,
31 the *son* of Mel-e-a, the *son* of Menna, the
son of Mat-ta-tha, the *son* of Nathan, the *son*
of David,
32 the *son* of Jesse, the *son* of Obed, the
son of Boaz, the *son* of Salmon, the *son* of
Nah-shon,
33 the *son* of Am-min-a-dab, the *son* of
Aram, the *son* of Hez-ron, the *son* of Phar-
ez, the *son* of Judah,
34 the *son* of Jacob, the *son* of Isaac, the
son of Abraham, the *son* of Terah, the *son*
of Na-hor,
35 the *son* of Se-rug, the *son* of Reu, the
son of Peleg, the *son* of Eber, the *son* of
Salah,
36 the *son* of Ca-i-nan, the *son* or Ar-phax-
ad, the *son* of Shem, the *son* of Noah, the
son of La-mech,
37 the *son* of Me-thu-se-lah, the *son* of
E-noch, the *son* of Jar-ed, the *son* of
Ma-hal-a-leel, the *son* of Ca-i-nan,

τοῦ Σήθ, τοῦ Ἀδάμ, τοῦ θεοῦ.
of Seth, of Adam, of God.

4 Ἰησοῦς.δὲ [c]πνεύματος ἁγίου πλήρης' ὑπέστρεψεν ἀπὸ
And Jesus, [2]of [3]the [5]Spirit [4]Holy [1]full, returned from
τοῦ Ἰορδάνου καὶ ἤγετο ἐν τῷ πνεύματι [d]εἰς τὴν ἔρημον[d]
the Jordan, and was led by the Spirit into the wilderness
2 ἡμέρας [e]τεσσαράκοντα,' πειραζόμενος ὑπὸ τοῦ διαβόλου·
[2]days [1]forty, being tempted by the devil;
καὶ οὐκ ἔφαγεν οὐδὲν ἐν ταῖς.ἡμέραις.ἐκείναις, καὶ συντελεσ-
and he ate nothing in those days, and [2]being
θεισῶν αὐτῶν [f]ὕστερον' ἐπείνασεν. 3 [g]καὶ εἶπεν[g] αὐτῷ ὁ
[3]ended [1]they afterwards he hungered. And [2]said [4]to [5]him [1]the
διάβολος, Εἰ υἱὸς εἶ τοῦ θεοῦ, εἰπὲ τῷ.λίθῳ τούτῳ ἵνα
[2]devil, If Son thou art of God, speak to this stone that
γένηται ἄρτος. 4 Καὶ ἀπεκρίθη [h] Ἰησοῦς πρὸς αὐτόν,' Λέγων,[i]
it become bread. And [2]answered [1]Jesus to him, saying,
Γέγραπται, Ὅτι οὐκ ἐπ' ἄρτῳ μόνῳ ζήσεται ὁ ἄνθρωπος,
It has been written, That not on bread alone shall [2]live [1]man,
[k]ἀλλ' ἐπὶ παντὶ ῥήματι θεοῦ.' 5 Καὶ ἀναγαγὼν αὐτὸν [l]ὁ
but on every word of God. And [3]leading [5]up [4]him [1]the
διάβολος[l] [m]εἰς ὄρος ὑψηλὸν' ἔδειξεν αὐτῷ πάσας τὰς βασι-
[2]devil into a [2]mountain [1]high shewed him all the king-
λείας τῆς οἰκουμένης ἐν στιγμῇ χρόνου· 6 καὶ εἶπεν αὐτῷ
doms of the habitable world in a moment of time. And [3]said [4]to [5]him
ὁ διάβολος, Σοὶ δώσω τὴν.ἐξουσίαν.ταύτην ἅπασαν καὶ
[1]the [2]devil, To thee will I give [2]this [3]authority [1]all and
τὴν.δόξαν.αὐτῶν· ὅτι ἐμοὶ παραδέδοται, καὶ ᾧ.[n]ἐὰν[n] θέλω
their glory; for to me it has been delivered, and to whomsoever I wish
δίδωμι αὐτήν· 7 σὺ οὖν ἐὰν προσκυνήσῃς ἐνώπιόν [o]μου,[o]
I give it. Thou therefore if thou wilt worship before me,
ἔσται σου [p]πάντα.' 8 Καὶ ἀποκριθεὶς [q]αὐτῷ εἶπεν ὁ Ἰησοῦς,[q]
[3]shall [4]be [5]thine [1]all [2]things. And answering him [2]said [1]Jesus,
[r]Ὕπαγε ὀπίσω μου, σατανᾶ·[r] γέγραπται.[sa]γάρ,' [ta]Προσκυνή-
Get thee behind me, Satan; for it has been written, Thou shalt wor-
σεις κύριον τὸν.θεόν.σου,' καὶ αὐτῷ μόνῳ λατρεύσεις.
ship [the] Lord thy God, and him only shalt thou serve.
9 [va]Καὶ ἤγαγεν' αὐτὸν εἰς Ἱερουσαλήμ, καὶ ἔστησεν [wa]αὐτὸν[w]
And he led him to Jerusalem, and set him
ἐπὶ τὸ πτερύγιον τοῦ ἱεροῦ, καὶ εἶπεν αὐτῷ, Εἰ [x]ὁ[x] υἱὸς εἶ
upon the edge of the temple, and said to him, If the Son thou art
τοῦ θεοῦ, βάλε σεαυτὸν ἐντεῦθεν κάτω. 10 γέγραπται.γάρ,
of God, cast thyself [2]hence [1]down; for it has been written,
Ὅτι τοῖς.ἀγγέλοις.αὐτοῦ ἐντελεῖται περὶ σοῦ, τοῦ δια-
That to his angels he will give charge concerning thee, to
φυλάξαι σε· 11 καὶ ὅτι ἐπὶ χειρῶν ἀροῦσίν σε, μήποτε
keep thee; and that in [their] hands shall they bear thee, lest
προσκόψῃς πρὸς λίθον τὸν.πόδα.σου. 12 Καὶ ἀποκριθεὶς εἶπεν
thou strike against a stone thy foot. And answering [2]said
αὐτῷ ὁ Ἰησοῦς, Ὅτι Εἴρηται, Οὐκ.ἐκπειράσεις κύριον
[3]to [4]him [1]Jesus, It has been said, Thou shalt not tempt [the] Lord
τὸν.θεόν.σου. 13 Καὶ συντελέσας πάντα πειρασμὸν ὁ διά-
thy God. And having finished every temptation the de-
βολος ἀπέστη ἀπ' αὐτοῦ ἄχρι.καιροῦ.
vil departed from him for a time.

14 Καὶ ὑπέστρεψεν ὁ Ἰησοῦς ἐν τῇ δυνάμει τοῦ πνεύματος
And [2]returned [1]Jesus in the power of the Spirit
εἰς τὴν Γαλιλαίαν· καὶ φήμη ἐξῆλθεν καθ' ὅλης τῆς περι-
to Galilee; and a rumour went out into [2]whole [1]the country
χώρου περὶ αὐτοῦ. 15 καὶ αὐτὸς ἐδίδασκεν ἐν ταῖς συν-
around concerning him. and he taught in [2]syn-
αγωγαῖς αὐτῶν, δοξαζόμενος ὑπὸ πάντων. 16 καὶ ἦλθεν εἰς
agogues [1]their, being glorified by all. And he came to
[y]τὴν[y].[z]Ναζαρέτ,[z] οὗ ἦν [a]τεθραμμένος·[a] καὶ εἰσῆλθεν κατὰ
Nazareth, where he was brought up; and he entered according to
τὸ.εἰωθὸς.αὐτῷ ἐν τῇ ἡμέρᾳ τῶν σαββάτων εἰς τὴν συναγωγήν,
his custom on the day of the sabbaths into the synagogue,
καὶ ἀνέστη ἀναγνῶναι. 17 καὶ ἐπεδόθη αὐτῷ βιβλίον
and stood up to read. And there was given to him [the] book
[b]Ἡσαΐου τοῦ προφήτου,[b] καὶ [c]ἀναπτύξας[c] τὸ βιβλίον εὗρεν
of Esaias the prophet, and having unrolled the book he found
[d]τὸν[d] τόπον οὗ ἦν γεγραμμένον, 18 Πνεῦμα κυρίου
the place where it was written, [The] Spirit of [the] Lord [is]
ἐπ' ἐμέ, οὗ.[e]εἵνεκεν[e] ἔχρισέν με. [f]εὐαγγελίζεσθαι[f]
upon me, on account of which he anointed me to announce the glad tidings
πτωχοῖς, ἀπέσταλκέν με [g]ἰάσασθαι τοὺς συντετριμμένους
to [the] poor, he has sent me to heal the broken
τὴν καρδίαν,[g] κηρύξαι αἰχμαλώτοις ἄφεσιν καὶ τυφλοῖς
in heart, to proclaim to captives deliverance and to [the] blind
ἀνάβλεψιν, ἀποστεῖλαι τεθραυσμένους ἐν ἀφέσει· 19 κηρύ-
recovery of sight, to send forth [the] crushed in deliverance, to pro-
ξαι ἐνιαυτὸν κυρίου δεκτόν. 20 Καὶ πτύξας τὸ
claim [the] [2]year [3]of [4the] [5]Lord [1]acceptable. And having rolled up the

38 the *son* of Enos, the *son* of Seth, the *son* of Adam, the *son* of God.

CHAPTER 4

1 And Jesus, full of the Holy Spirit, returned from the Jordan and was led by the Spirit into the wilderness

2 forty days, being tempted by the devil. And He ate nothing in those days. And when they were ended, He afterwards was hungry.

3 And the devil said to Him, If you are the Son of God, speak to this stone that it might become bread.

4 And Jesus answered him saying, It has been written, "Man shall not live by bread alone, but by every word of God."

5 And the devil took Him up into a high mountain and showed Him all the kingdoms of the world in a moment of time.

6 And the devil said to Him, I will give you all this authority and all their glory, for it has been given to me. And I give it to whomever I wish.

7 Therefore, if you will worship before me, all things shall be yours.

8 And answering him, Jesus said, Get behind Me, Satan! For it has been written, "You shall worship the Lord your God, and Him only shall you serve."

9 And he led Him to Jerusalem and set Him on the pinnacle of the Temple. And he said to Him, If you are the Son of God, throw yourself down from here,

10 for it has been written, "He will give His angels command about you, to keep you,

11 and that they shall bear you up in *their* hands, for fear that you may strike your foot against a stone."

12 And answering, Jesus said to him, It has been said, "You shall not tempt the Lord your God."

13 And when the devil had finished every temptation, he left Him for a while.

14 And Jesus returned in the power of the Spirit into Galilee. And a report about Him went out through all the countryside.

15 And He taught in their synagogues, being glorified by all.

16 And He came to Nazareth, where He had been brought up. And according to His custom, He went into the synagogue on the Sabbath day and stood up to read.

17 And the book of Isaiah the prophet was given to Him. And unrolling the book He found the place where it was written,

18 "The Spirit of the Lord is upon Me, because He has anointed Me to preach the gospel to the poor, He has sent Me to heal the brokenhearted, to announce deliverance to the captives and recovery of sight to the blind, to send forth the bruised with deliverance,

19 to proclaim the acceptable year of the Lord."

20 And rolling up the book, He gave it to

βιβλίον, ἀποδοὺς τῷ ὑπηρέτῃ ἐκάθισεν, καὶ πάντων
book, having delivered [it] to the attendant he sat down, and of all
ἐν τῇ συναγωγῇ οἱ ὀφθαλμοὶ ἦσαν ἀτενίζοντες αὐτῷ.
in the synagogue the eyes were fixed upon him.
21 Ἤρξατο.δὲ λέγειν πρὸς αὐτούς, Ὅτι σήμερον πεπλήρωται
And he began to say to them, To-day is fulfilled
ἡ.γραφὴ.αὕτη ἐν τοῖς.ὠσὶν.ὑμῶν. 22 Καὶ πάντες ἐμαρτύρουν
this scripture in your ears. And all bore witness
αὐτῷ, καὶ ἐθαύμαζον ἐπὶ τοῖς λόγοις τῆς χάριτος τοῖς ἐκπορευο-
to him, and wondered at the words of grace which pro-
μένοις ἐκ τοῦ.στόματος.αὐτοῦ, καὶ ἔλεγον, Οὐχ οὗτός ἐστιν
ceeded out of his mouth; and they said, Not this is
ὁ υἱὸς Ἰωσήφ; 23 Καὶ εἶπεν πρὸς αὐτούς, Πάντως ἐρεῖτέ
the son of Joseph? And he said to them, Surely ye will say
μοι τὴν.παραβολὴν.ταύτην, Ἰατρέ, θεράπευσον σεαυτόν·
to me this parable, Physician, heal thyself;
ὅσα ἠκούσαμεν γενόμενα ἐν τῇ Καπερναούμ, ποίησον
whatsoever we have heard being done in Capernaum, do
καὶ ὧδε ἐν τῇ.πατρίδι.σου. 24 Εἶπεν.δέ, Ἀμὴν λέγω ὑμῖν, ὅτι
also here in thine [own] country. But he said, Verily I say to you, that
οὐδεὶς προφήτης δεκτός ἐστιν ἐν τῇ.πατρίδι.αὐτοῦ. 25 ἐπ'
no prophet acceptable is in his [own] country. In
ἀληθείας.δὲ λέγω ὑμῖν, πολλαὶ χῆραι ἦσαν ἐν ταῖς ἡμέραις
but truth I say to you, many widows were in the days
Ἡλίου ἐν τῷ Ἰσραήλ, ὅτε ἐκλείσθη ὁ οὐρανὸς ἐπὶ ἔτη
of Elias in Israel, when was shut up the heaven for years
τρία καὶ μῆνας ἕξ, ὡς ἐγένετο λιμὸς μέγας ἐπὶ πᾶσαν τὴν
three and months six, when there was a famine great upon all the
γῆν, 26 καὶ πρὸς οὐδεμίαν αὐτῶν ἐπέμφθη Ἠλίας εἰ.μὴ εἰς
land, and to none of them was sent Elias except to
Σάρεπτα τῆς Σιδῶνος, πρὸς γυναῖκα χήραν. 27 καὶ πολλοὶ
Sarepta of Sidonia, to a woman widow. And many
λεπροὶ ἦσαν ἐπὶ Ἐλισσαίου τοῦ προφήτου ἐν τῷ Ἰσραήλ,
lepers were in the time of Elisha the prophet in Israel,
καὶ οὐδεὶς αὐτῶν ἐκαθαρίσθη εἰ.μὴ Νεεμὰν ὁ Σύρος. 28 Καὶ
and none of them was cleansed except Naaman the Syrian. And
ἐπλήσθησαν πάντες θυμοῦ ἐν τῇ συναγωγῇ, ἀκούοντες
were filled all with indignation in the synagogue, hearing
ταῦτα. 29 καὶ ἀναστάντες ἐξέβαλον αὐτὸν ἔξω τῆς
these things; and having risen up they cast him out of [the]
πόλεως, καὶ ἤγαγον αὐτὸν ἕως τῆς ὀφρύος τοῦ ὄρους ἐφ'
city, and led him unto the brow of the mountain upon
οὗ ἡ.πόλις.αὐτῶν ᾠκοδόμητο, εἰς τὸ κατακρημνίσαι
which their city had been built, for to throw down headlong
αὐτόν· 30 αὐτὸς.δὲ διελθὼν διὰ μέσου αὐτῶν ἐπορεύετο
him; but he passing through [the] midst of them went away.
31 Καὶ κατῆλθεν εἰς Καπερναοὺμ πόλιν τῆς Γαλιλαίας·
And he went down to Capernaum a city of Galilee,
καὶ ἦν διδάσκων αὐτοὺς ἐν τοῖς σάββασιν. 32 καὶ ἐξεπλήσ-
and was teaching them on the sabbaths. And they were as-
σοντο ἐπὶ τῇ.διδαχῇ.αὐτοῦ, ὅτι ἐν ἐξουσίᾳ ἦν ὁ.λόγος.αὐτοῦ.
tonished at his teaching, for with authority was his word.
33 Καὶ ἐν τῇ συναγωγῇ ἦν ἄνθρωπος ἔχων πνεῦμα δαιμονίου
And in the synagogue was a man having a spirit of a demon
ἀκαθάρτου, καὶ ἀνέκραξεν φωνῇ μεγάλῃ, 34 λέγων, Ἔα,
unclean; and he cried out with a voice loud, saying, Ah!
τί ἡμῖν καὶ σοί, Ἰησοῦ Ναζαρηνέ; ἦλθες ἀπολέσαι ἡμᾶς;
what to us and to thee, Jesus, Nazarene? Art thou come to destroy us?
οἶδά σε τίς εἶ, ὁ ἅγιος τοῦ θεοῦ. 35 Καὶ ἐπετίμησεν
I know thee who thou art, the Holy [One] of God. And rebuked
αὐτῷ ὁ Ἰησοῦς, λέγων, Φιμώθητι, καὶ ἔξελθε ἐξ αὐτοῦ.
him Jesus, saying, Hold thy peace, and come forth out of him.
Καὶ ῥίψαν αὐτὸν τὸ δαιμόνιον εἰς τὸ μέσον ἐξῆλθεν
And having thrown him the demon into the midst came out
ἀπ' αὐτοῦ, μηδὲν βλάψαν αὐτόν. 36 καὶ ἐγένετο θάμβος
from him, in nothing having hurt him. And came astonishment
ἐπὶ πάντας, καὶ συνελάλουν πρὸς ἀλλήλους, λέγοντες, Τίς
upon all, and they spoke to one another, saying, What
ὁ λόγος οὗτος, ὅτι ἐν ἐξουσίᾳ καὶ δυνάμει ἐπιτάσσει τοῖς
word [is] this, that with authority and power he commands the
ἀκαθάρτοις πνεύμασιν, καὶ ἐξέρχονται; 37 Καὶ ἐξεπορεύετο
unclean spirits, and they come out? And went out
ἦχος περὶ αὐτοῦ εἰς πάντα τόπον τῆς περιχώρου.
a rumour concerning him into every place of the country around.
38 Ἀναστὰς.δὲ ἐκ τῆς συναγωγῆς εἰσῆλθεν εἰς τὴν οἰκίαν
And rising up out of the synagogue he entered into the house
Σίμωνος· ἡ πενθερὰ δὲ τοῦ Σίμωνος ἦν συνεχομένη
of Simon. The mother-in-law and of Simon was oppressed with
πυρετῷ μεγάλῳ· καὶ ἠρώτησαν αὐτὸν περὶ αὐτῆς. 39 καὶ
a fever great; and they asked him for her. And
ἐπιστὰς ἐπάνω αὐτῆς ἐπετίμησεν τῷ πυρετῷ, καὶ ἀφῆκεν αὐτήν·
standing over her he rebuked the fever, and it left her;

the officers and sat down. And the eyes of
all in the synagogue were fastened on Him.
21 And He began to say to them, Today
this Scripture is fulfilled in your ears.
22 And all bore witness to Him and wondered at the gracious words which came out
of His mouth. And they said, Is this not the
son of Joseph?
23 And He said to them, Surely you will say
to Me this proverb, Physician, heal yourself.
Whatever *things* we have heard were being
done in Ca-per-na-um, do also here in your
own country.
24 But He said, Truly I say to you that no
prophet is accepted in his own country.
25 But truly I say to you, there were many
widows in Israel in the days of Elijah, when
the sky was shut up for three years and six
months, when there was a great famine on
all the land.
26 And to none of them was Elijah sent
except to Zar-e-phath of Sidon, to a woman,
a widow.
27 And many lepers were in Israel in the
time of Elisha the prophet, and none of
them were cleansed except Na-a-man the
Syrian.
28 And hearing these things, all those in the
synagogue were filled with anger.
29 And they rose up and threw Him out of
the city. And they led Him to the brow of the
hill on which their city had been built, in
order to throw Him headlong down it.
30 But passing through the midst of them, He
went away.

31 And He went down to Ca-per-na-um, a
city of Galilee, and was teaching them on the
sabbaths.
32 And they were astonished at His teaching
for His word was with authority.
33 And in the synagogue was a man who had
a spirit of an unclean demon. And he cried out
with a loud voice,
34 saying, Ha! What do we have to do with
You, Jesus, Naz-a-rene? Have you come to
destroy us? I know You. You are the Holy
One of God.
35 And Jesus warned him, saying, Be quiet
and come out of him! And after the demon
had thrown him into the middle, he came out
from him, not having hurt him.
36 And amazement came on all. And they
spoke to one another, saying, What is this
word, that with authority and power he commands the unclean spirits and they come out?
37 And a report about Him went out into
every place of the country around there.

38 And leaving the synagogue, He went into
the house of Simon. And Simon's mother-
in-law was pressed with a great fever. And
they asked Him about her.
39 And standing over her, He solemnly
spoke to the fever and it left her. And

παραχρῆμα.δὲ ἀναστᾶσα διηκόνει αὐτοῖς.
and immediately arising she served them.

40 Δύνοντος.δὲ τοῦ ἡλίου πάντες ὅσοι εἶχον
And at the going down of the sun all as many as had [persons]
ἀσθενοῦντας νόσοις ποικίλαις ἤγαγον αὐτοὺς πρὸς αὐτόν·
sick with ²diseases ¹various brought them to him,
ὁ.δὲ ἑνὶ ἑκάστῳ αὐτῶν τὰς χεῖρας ʰἐπιθεὶς ⁱἐθεράπευ-
and he ⁴on ⁵one ⁶each ⁷of ⁸them ³hands ¹having ²laid healed
σεν αὐτούς· 41 ᵏἐξήρχετο.δὲ καὶ δαιμόνια ἀπὸ πολλῶν,
them; and ²went ³out ⁴also ¹demons from many,
ˡκράζοντα καὶ λέγοντα, Ὅτι σὺ εἶ ᵐὁ χριστὸς ὁ υἱὸς τοῦ
crying out and saying, Thou art the Christ the Son
θεοῦ. Καὶ ἐπιτιμῶν οὐκ.εἴα αὐτὰ λαλεῖν ὅτι ᾔδεισαν
of God. And rebuking he suffered not them to speak because they knew
τὸν χριστὸν αὐτὸν εἶναι.
⁴the ⁵Christ ¹him ²to ³be.

42 Γενομένης.δὲ ἡμέρας ἐξελθὼν ἐπορεύθη εἰς ἔρημον
And ²being come ¹day having gone out he went into a desert
τόπον, καὶ οἱ ὄχλοι ⁿἐζήτουν αὐτόν, καὶ ἦλθον ἕως αὐτοῦ
place, and the crowds sought him, and came up to him
καὶ κατεῖχον αὐτὸν τοῦ.μὴ.πορεύεσθαι ἀπ' αὐτῶν. 43 ὁ.δὲ
and were detaining him that he might not go from them. But he
εἶπεν πρὸς αὐτούς, Ὅτι καὶ ταῖς ἑτέραις πόλεσιν εὐαγ-
said to them, Also to the other cities ⁴to ⁵announce
γελίσασθαί ᵒμε.δεῖ τὴν βασιλείαν τοῦ θεοῦ· ὅτι
⁶the ⁷glad ⁸tidings ¹it ²behoves ³me, the kingdom of God; because
ᵖεἰς τοῦτο ᑫἀπέσταλμαι. 44 Καὶ ἦν κηρύσσων ʳἐν ταῖς
for this have I been sent forth. And he was preaching in the
συναγωγαῖς τῆς ˢΓαλιλαίας.
synagogues of Galilee.

immediately she got up and served them.
40 And at the setting of the sun, all those
who had sick ones with various disease
brought them to Him. And He laid His hands
on each one of them and healed them.
41 And also many demons went out from
many, crying out and saying, You are the
Christ, the Son of God! And He warned
them, not allowing them to speak because
they knew that He was the Christ.
42 And when it was day, He came out and
went into a deserted place. And the people
were seeking Him and came up to Him. And
they were holding Him so that He might not
go away from them.
43 But He said to them, It is necessary for
Me to preach the gospel of the kingdom of
God in the other cities also, because it was
for this that I have been sent.
44 And He was preaching in the synagogues
of Galilee.

5 Ἐγένετο.δὲ ἐν τῷ τὸν ὄχλον ἐπικεῖσθαι αὐτῷ
And it came to pass during the [time] the crowd pressed on him
ᵗτοῦ ἀκούειν τὸν λόγον τοῦ θεοῦ, καὶ αὐτὸς ἦν ἑστὼς παρὰ
to hear the word of God, that he was standing by
τὴν λίμνην Γεννησαρέτ· 2 καὶ ᵛεἶδεν δύο ʷπλοῖα ἑστῶτα
the lake of Gennesaret: and he saw two ships standing
παρὰ τὴν λίμνην· οἱ.δὲ ˣἁλιεῖς ʸἀποβάντες ἀπ' αὐτῶν
by the lake, but the fishermen having gone out from them
ᶻἀπέπλυναν τὰ δίκτυα. 3 ἐμβὰς.δὲ εἰς ἓν τῶν πλοίων
washed the nets. And having entered into one of the ships
ὃ ἦν ᵃτοῦ Σίμωνος, ἠρώτησεν αὐτὸν ἀπὸ τῆς γῆς ἐπαναγα-
which was Simon's, he asked him from the land to put
γεῖν ὀλίγον· ᵇκαὶ καθίσας ᶜἐδίδασκεν ἐκ τοῦ πλοίου τοὺς
off a little; and having sat down he taught from the ship the
ὄχλους. 4 Ὡς.δὲ ἐπαύσατο λαλῶν εἶπεν πρὸς τὸν Σίμωνα,
crowds. And when he ceased speaking he said to Simon,
Ἐπανάγαγε εἰς τὸ βάθος καὶ χαλάσατε τὰ.δίκτυα.ὑμῶν εἰς
Put off into the deep and let down your nets for
ἄγραν. 5 Καὶ ἀποκριθεὶς ᵈὁ Σίμων εἶπεν ᵉαὐτῷ, Ἐπιστάτα,
a haul. And answering Simon said to him, Master,
δι' ὅλης ᶠτῆς νυκτὸς κοπιάσαντες οὐδὲν ἐλάβομεν·
through ²whole ¹the night having laboured, nothing have we taken,
ἐπὶ.δὲ τῷ.ῥήματί.σου χαλάσω ᵍτὸ δίκτυον. 6 Καὶ τοῦτο
but at thy word I will let down the net. And this
ποιήσαντες συνέκλεισαν ʰἰχθύων πλῆθος πολύ· ⁱδιερρήγνυτο
having done they enclosed of fishes a ²shoal ¹great; ⁴was ⁵breaking
δὲ ʲτὸ δίκτυον αὐτῶν. 7 καὶ κατένευσαν τοῖς μετόχοις
¹and ²net ³their. And they beckoned to the partners
ᵏτοῖς ἐν τῷ ἑτέρῳ πλοίῳ, τοῦ.ἐλθόντας συλλαβέσθαι αὐτοῖς·
those in the other ship, that coming they should help them;
καὶ ˡἦλθον, καὶ ἔπλησαν ἀμφότερα τὰ πλοῖα, ὥστε βυθίζε-
and they came, and filled both the ships, so that ²were ³sink-
σθαι αὐτά. 8 ἰδὼν.δὲ Σίμων Πέτρος προσέπεσεν τοῖς γόνασιν
ing ¹they. And ³having ⁴seen ¹Simon ²Peter fell at the knees
ᵐτοῦ Ἰησοῦ, λέγων, Ἔξελθε ἀπ' ἐμοῦ, ὅτι ἀνὴρ ἁμαρτωλός
of Jesus, saying, Depart from me, for a man a sinner
εἰμι, κύριε. 9 Θάμβος.γὰρ περιέσχεν αὐτὸν καὶ πάντας τοὺς
am I, Lord. For astonishment laid hold on him and all those
σὺν αὐτῷ, ἐπὶ τῇ ἄγρᾳ τῶν ἰχθύων ⁿᾗ συνέλαβον·
with him, at the haul of the fishes which they had taken;
10 ὁμοίως.δὲ καὶ Ἰάκωβον καὶ ᵒἸωάννην, υἱοὺς Ζεβεδαίου,
and in like manner also James and John, sons of Zebedee,
οἳ ἦσαν κοινωνοὶ τῷ Σίμωνι. Καὶ εἶπεν πρὸς τὸν Σίμωνα
who were partners with Simon. And ²said ³to ⁴Simon
ᵖὁ Ἰησοῦς, Μὴ.φοβοῦ· ἀπὸ τοῦ.νῦν ἀνθρώπους ἔσῃ
¹Jesus, Fear not; from henceforth men thou shalt be
ζωγρῶν. 11 Καὶ καταγαγόντες τὰ πλοῖα ἐπὶ τὴν γῆν, ἀφέντες
capturing. And having brought the ships to land, leaving
ᑫἅπαντα ἠκολούθησαν αὐτῷ.
all they followed him.

12 Καὶ ἐγένετο ἐν.τῷ.εἶναι αὐτὸν ἐν μιᾷ τῶν πόλεων,
And it came to pass as ²was ¹he in one of the cities,

CHAPTER 5

1 And as the people pressed upon Him to
hear the word of God, He was standing by
the lake of Gen-nes-a-ret.
2 And He saw two ships standing by the
lake, but the fishermen had left them and
were washing their nets.
3 And going onto one of the ships, which
was Simon's, He asked him to put back a
little from the land. And sitting down, He
taught the people from the ship.
4 And when He quit speaking, He said to
Simon, Move out into the deep and let down
your nets for a haul.
5 And answering, Simon said to Him,
Master, we have worked through the whole
night and have taken nothing. But at Your
word I will let down the net.
6 And doing this, they took in a big multitude of fish. And their net was breaking.
7 And they signaled to the partners, those
in the other ship, that they should come to
help them. And they came and filled both
the ships, so that they were sinking.
8 And having seen this, Simon Peter fell
down at the knees of Jesus, saying, Depart
from me, Lord, for I am a man, a sinner.
9 For amazement seized him and all with
him, at the haul of fish which they had taken.
10 And so also were James and John, sons of
Zeb-e-dee, who were partners with Simon.
And Jesus said to Simon, Do not fear. From
now on you shall be catching men.
11 And bringing the ships to the land, they
left all and followed Him.

12 And as He was in one of the cities, there

καὶ ἰδού, ἀνὴρ πλήρης λέπρας· [r]καὶ ἰδὼνǁ τὸν Ἰησοῦν, πεσὼν
that behold, a man full of leprosy, and seeing Jesus, falling
ἐπὶ πρόσωπον ἐδεήθη αὐτοῦ, λέγων, Κύριε, ἐὰν θέλῃς
upon [his] face he besought him, saying, Lord, if thou wilt
δύνασαί με καθαρίσαι. 13 Καὶ ἐκτείνας τὴν χεῖρα
thou art able me to cleanse. And having stretched out [his] hand
ἥψατο αὐτοῦ, [s]εἰπών,ǁ Θέλω, καθαρίσθητι. Καὶ εὐθέως ἡ
he touched him, saying, I will; be thou cleansed. And immediately the
λέπρα ἀπῆλθεν ἀπ' αὐτοῦ. 14 καὶ αὐτὸς παρήγγειλεν αὐτῷ
leprosy departed from him. And he charged him
μηδενὶ εἰπεῖν· ἀλλὰ ἀπελθὼν δεῖξον σεαυτὸν τῷ ἱερεῖ, καὶ
no one to tell; but having gone show thyself to the priest, and
προσένεγκε περὶ τοῦ.καθαρισμοῦ.σου, καθὼς προσέταξεν [t]Μω-
offer for thy cleansing, as [2]ordered [1]Mo-
σῆς,ǁ εἰς μαρτύριον αὐτοῖς. 15 Διήρχετο.δὲ μᾶλλον ὁ
ses, for a testimony to them. But was spread abroad still more the
λόγος περὶ αὐτοῦ· καὶ συνήρχοντο ὄχλοι πολλοὶ ἀκούειν,
report concerning him; and [3]were [4]coming [2]crowds [1]great to hear,
καὶ θεραπεύεσθαι [v]ὑπ' αὐτοῦǁ ἀπὸ τῶν.ἀσθενειῶν.αὐτῶν·
and to be healed by him from their infirmities.
16 αὐτὸς.δὲ ἦν ὑποχωρῶν ἐν ταῖς ἐρήμοις καὶ προσευχό-
But he was retiring in the deserts and pray-
μενος.
ing.

17 Καὶ ἐγένετο ἐν μιᾷ τῶν ἡμερῶν καὶ αὐτὸς ἦν διδάσ-
And it came to pass on one of the days that he was teach-
κων, καὶ ἦσαν καθήμενοι [w]Φαρισαῖοι καὶ νομοδιδάσκαλοι,
ing, and there were sitting by Pharisees and teachers of the law,
οἳ ἦσαν [x]ἐληλυθότεςǁ ἐκ πάσης κώμης τῆς Γαλιλαίας καὶ
who were come out of every village of Galilee and
Ἰουδαίας καὶ Ἱερουσαλήμ· καὶ δύναμις κυρίου ἦν εἰς
of Judæa and of Jerusalem: and power of [the] Lord was [there] for
τὸ ἰᾶσθαι [y]αὐτούς.ǁ 18 καὶ ἰδού, ἄνδρες φέροντες ἐπὶ κλίνης
to heal them. And behold, men carrying upon a couch
ἄνθρωπον ὃς ἦν παραλελυμένος, καὶ ἐζήτουν αὐτὸν εἰσενεγ-
a man who was paralysed, and they sought [3]him [1]to [2]bring
κεῖν καὶ θεῖναι [z] ἐνώπιον αὐτοῦ· 19 καὶ μὴ εὑρόντες [a]διὰǁ
in and to place [him] before him. And not having found by
ποίας εἰσενέγκωσιν αὐτὸν διὰ τὸν ὄχλον, ἀναβάντες
what way they should bring in him on account of the crowd, going up
ἐπὶ τὸ δῶμα, διὰ τῶν κεράμων καθῆκαν αὐτὸν σὺν τῷ
on the housetop, through the tiles they let down him with the
κλινιδίῳ εἰς τὸ μέσον ἔμπροσθεν τοῦ Ἰησοῦ. 20 καὶ ἰδὼν τὴν
little couch into the midst before Jesus. And seeing
πίστιν.αὐτῶν εἶπεν [b]αὐτῷ,ǁ Ἄνθρωπε, ἀφέωνταί σοι
their faith he said to him, Man, [3]have [4]been [5]forgiven [6]thee
αἱ.ἁμαρτίαι.σου. 21 Καὶ ἤρξαντο διαλογίζεσθαι οἱ γραμματεῖς
[1]thy [2]sins. And began to reason the scribes
καὶ οἱ Φαρισαῖοι, λέγοντες, Τίς ἐστιν οὗτος ὃς λαλεῖ βλασ-
and the Pharisees, saying, Who is this who speaks blas-
φημίας; τίς δύναται [c]ἀφιέναι ἁμαρτίας,ǁ εἰ.μὴ μόνος ὁ θεός;
phemies? who is able to forgive sins, except [2]alone [1]God?
22 Ἐπιγνοὺς.δὲ ὁ Ἰησοῦς τοὺς.διαλογισμοὺς.αὐτῶν [d]ἀπο-
But [2]knowing [1]Jesus their reasonings an-
κριθεὶςǁ εἶπεν πρὸς αὐτούς, Τί διαλογίζεσθε ἐν ταῖς καρδίαις
swering said to them, Why reason ye in [2]hearts
ὑμῶν; 23 τί ἐστιν εὐκοπώτερον, εἰπεῖν, Ἀφέωνταί σοι
[1]your? which is easier, to say, Have been forgiven thee
αἱ.ἁμαρτίαι.σου, ἢ εἰπεῖν, [e]Ἔγειραιǁ καὶ περιπάτει; 24 ἵνα.δὲ
thy sins, or to say, Arise and walk? But that
εἰδῆτε ὅτι [f]ἐξουσίαν ἔχει ὁ υἱὸς τοῦ ἀνθρώπουǁ ἐπὶ τῆς
ye may know that authority has the Son of man on the
γῆς ἀφιέναι ἁμαρτίας, εἶπεν τῷ [g]παραλελυμένῳ,ǁ Σοὶ λέγω,
earth to forgive sins, he said to the paralysed, To thee I say,
[h]ἔγειραι,ǁ καὶ ἄρας τὸ.κλινίδιόν.σου πορεύου εἰς τὸν οἶκόν
Arise, and having taken up thy little couch go to [2]house
σου. 25 Καὶ παραχρῆμα ἀναστὰς ἐνώπιον αὐτῶν, ἄρας
[1]thy. And immediately having stood up before them, having taken up
ἐφ' [i]ᾧǁ κατέκειτο, ἀπῆλθεν εἰς τὸν.οἶκον.αὐτοῦ, δοξάζων
[that] on which he was lying, he departed to his house, glorifying
τὸν θεόν. 26 καὶ ἔκστασις ἔλαβεν ἅπαντας, καὶ ἐδόξαζον
God. And amazement seized all, and they glorified
τὸν θεόν, καὶ ἐπλήσθησαν φόβου, λέγοντες, Ὅτι εἴδομεν
God, and were filled with fear, saying, We have seen
παράδοξα σήμερον.
strange things to-day.

27 Καὶ μετὰ ταῦτα ἐξῆλθεν, καὶ ἐθεάσατο τελώνην,
And after these things he went forth, and saw a tax-gatherer,
ὀνόματι [j]Λευΐν,ǁ καθήμενον ἐπὶ τὸ τελώνιον, καὶ εἶπεν αὐτῷ,
by name Levi, sitting at the tax office, and said to him,
Ἀκολούθει μοι. 28 Καὶ καταλιπὼν [k]ἅπαντα,ǁ ἀναστὰς [l]ἠκο-
Follow me. And having left all, having arisen he fol-

was a man full of leprosy. And when he saw Jesus, he fell on his face and begged Him, saying, Lord, if you desire, you are able to make me clean.
13 And He stretched out His hand and touched him, saying, I desire it, Be clean! And instantly the leprosy left him.
14 And He commanded him to tell no one, *saying*, But go and show yourself to the priest and offer for your cleansing, as Moses commanded – for a witness to them.
15 But still more the report about Him was spread abroad. And great crowds were coming to hear and to be healed from their sicknesses by Him.
16 But He drew Himself back into the deserted places and was praying.

17 And on one of the days He was teaching, Pharisees and teachers of the Law were sitting there, who had come out of every town of Galilee and of Judea and of Jerusalem. And the power of the Lord was *there* to heal them.
18 And, behold! Men *appeared* carrying a man who was paralyzed on a bed. And they were trying to bring him in so as to place him before Him.
19 But because of the multitude, they did not find a way to bring him in. So, going up on the housetop, they let him down through the tiles, with the little bed into the midst, in front of Jesus.
20 And seeing their faith, He said to him, Man, your sins have been forgiven you!
21 And the scribes and the Pharisees began to question, saying, Who is this who speaks blasphemies? Who is able to forgive sins except God alone?
22 But knowing their thoughts, Jesus answered, saying to them, Why do you doubt in your hearts?
23 Which is easier, to say, Your sins have been forgiven you, or to say, Get up and walk?
24 But so that you may know that the Son of man has authority on earth to forgive sins, He said to the paralyzed one, I say to you, Get up! And take up your bed and go to your house.
25 And immediately he stood up before them and took up *the bed* on which he was lying and went away to his house, glorifying God.
26 And amazement took hold on all. And they glorified God and were filled with fear, saying, We have seen wonderful things today.

27 And after these things, He went out and saw a tax-collector named Levi sitting at the tax office. And He said to him, Follow Me!
28 And leaving all, he rose up and followed

λούθησεν" αὐτῷ. 29 Καὶ ἐποίησεν δοχὴν μεγάλην " ὁ"
lowed him. And ²made ⁵entertainment ³a ⁴great
ⁿΛευῒς' αὐτῷ ἐν τῇ.οἰκίᾳ.αὐτοῦ, καὶ ἦν ὄχλος ᵒτελω-
¹Levi for him in his house, and there was a ²multitude ³of ⁴tax-
νῶν πολύς' καὶ ἄλλων οἳ ἦσαν μετ' αὐτῶν κατακείμενοι.
gatherers ¹great and others who were with them reclining
30 καὶ ἐγόγγυζον οἱ.ᵖγραμματεῖς.αὐτῶν καὶ οἱ Φαρι-
[at table]. And murmured their scribes and the Phari-
σαῖοι' πρὸς τοὺς.μαθητὰς.αὐτοῦ, λέγοντες, ᵠΔιατί" μετὰ
sees at his disciples, saying, Why with
ʳτελωνῶν ˢκαὶ ἁμαρτωλῶν" ἐσθίετε καὶ πίνετε; 31 καὶ ἀπο-
tax-gatherers and sinners do ye eat and drink? And an-
κριθεὶς ὁ Ἰησοῦς εἶπεν πρὸς αὐτούς, Οὐ χρείαν ἔχουσιν οἱ
swering Jesus said to them, No need have they who
ὑγιαίνοντες ἰατροῦ, ᵗἀλλ'" οἱ κακῶς ἔχοντες. 32 οὐκ
are in health of a physician, but they who ill are. ³Not
ἐλήλυθα καλέσαι δικαίους, ἀλλὰ ἁμαρτωλοὺς εἰς μετά-
¹I ²have come to call righteous [ones], but sinners to repent-
νοιαν. 33 Οἱ.δὲ ᵛεἶπον" πρὸς αὐτόν, ʷΔιατί" οἱ μαθηταὶ
ance. And they said to him, Why ²the ³disciples
ˣἸωάννου" νηστεύουσιν πυκνὰ καὶ δεήσεις ποιοῦνται, ὁ-
⁴of ⁵John ¹fast often and supplications make, in like
μοίως καὶ οἱ τῶν Φαρισαίων, οἱ.δὲ σοὶ ἐσθίουσιν καὶ
manner also those of the Pharisees, but those of thee eat and
πίνουσιν; 34 Ὁ.δὲ ʸ εἶπεν πρὸς αὐτούς, Μὴ δύνασθε τοὺς
drink? And he said to them, Are ye able ³the
υἱοὺς τοῦ νυμφῶνος, ἐν.ᾧ ὁ νυμφίος μετ' αὐτῶν ἐστιν
⁴sons ⁵of ⁶the ⁷bridechamber ¹⁰while ¹¹the ¹²bridegroom ¹⁴with ¹⁵them ¹³is
ποιῆσαι ᶻνηστεύειν"; 35 ἐλεύσονται δὲ ἡμέραι ᵃκαὶ" ὅταν
¹to ²make ⁸to ⁹fast? But will come days ²also ¹when
ἀπαρθῇ ἀπ' αὐτῶν ὁ νυμφίος, τότε νηστεύσουσιν ἐν
shall be taken away from them the bridegroom, then they will fast in
ἐκείναις ταῖς ἡμέραις. 36 Ἔλεγεν.δὲ καὶ παραβολὴν πρὸς
these days. And he spoke also a parable to
αὐτούς, Ὅτι οὐδεὶς ἐπίβλημα ᵇ ἱματίου καινοῦ ᶜ ἐπιβάλλει ἐπὶ
them, No one a piece of a ²garment ¹new puts on
ἱμάτιον παλαιόν· εἰ.δὲ.μήγε καὶ τὸ καινὸν ᵈσχίζει," καὶ
²garment ¹an ²old, otherwise both the new he rends, and
τῷ παλαιῷ ᵉοὐ.συμφωνεῖ'. ᶠ ἐπίβλημα τὸ ἀπὸ τοῦ
with the old does not agree [the] piece which [is] from the
καινοῦ. 37 καὶ οὐδεὶς βάλλει οἶνον νέον εἰς ἀσκοὺς παλαιούς·
new. And no one puts ²wine ¹new into ²skins ¹old,
εἰ.δὲ.μήγε ῥήξει ᵍὁ νέος οἶνος" τοὺς ἀσκούς, καὶ αὐτὸς
otherwise ⁴will ⁵burst ¹the ²new ³wine the skins, and it
ἐκχυθήσεται, καὶ οἱ ἀσκοὶ ἀπολοῦνται· 38 ἀλλὰ οἶνον νέον
will be poured out, and the skins will be destroyed; but ²wine ¹new
εἰς ἀσκοὺς καινοὺς βλητέον, ʰκαὶ ἀμφότεροι συντηροῦνται."
into ²skins ¹new is to be put, and both are preserved together.
39 καὶ οὐδεὶς πιὼν παλαιὸν ⁱεὐθέως' θέλει νέον·
And no one having drunk old [wine] immediately desires new;
λέγει.γάρ, Ὁ παλαιὸς ᵏχρηστότερός" ἐστιν.
for he says, The old ²better ¹is.
6 Ἐγένετο.δὲ ἐν σαββάτῳ ˡδευτεροπρώτῳ" διαπο-
And it came to pass on ⁴sabbath [¹the] ²second ³first ⁶passed
ρεύεσθαι αὐτὸν διὰ ᵐτῶν" σπορίμων· καὶ ἔτιλλον οἱ
⁷along ⁵he through the corn fields; and ³were ⁴plucking
μαθηταὶ.αὐτοῦ ⁿτοὺς στάχυας, καὶ ἤσθιον,' ψώχοντες
¹his ²disciples the ears, and were eating, rubbing [them]
ταῖς χερσίνᵒ. 2 τινὲς.δὲ τῶν Φαρισαίων εἶπον ᵖαὐτοῖς," Τί
in the hands. But some of the Pharisees said to them, Why
ποιεῖτε ὃ οὐκ.ἔξεστιν ᵠποιεῖν ἐν" τοῖς σάββασιν; 3 Καὶ
do ye that which it is not lawful to do on the sabbaths? And
ἀποκριθεὶς ʳπρὸς αὐτοὺς εἶπεν ὁ Ἰησοῦς," Οὐδὲ τοῦτο ἀνέγνωτε,
answering to them ²said ¹Jesus, Not even this did ye read,
ὃ ἐποίησεν ˢΔαβίδ," ᵗὁπότε' ἐπείνασεν αὐτὸς καὶ οἱ
that which ²did ¹David, when he hungered, himself and those who
μετ' αὐτοῦ ᵛὄντες"; 4 ʷὡς" εἰσῆλθεν εἰς τὸν οἶκον τοῦ θεοῦ,
with him were? how he entered into the house of God,
καὶ τοὺς ἄρτους τῆς προθέσεως ˣᵃἔλαβεν, καὶ" ἔφαγεν, καὶ
and the loaves of the presentation took, and ate, and
ἔδωκεν ʸκαὶ" τοῖς μετ' αὐτοῦ, οὓς οὐκ.ἔξεστιν φαγεῖν εἰ.μὴ
gave also to those with him, which it is not lawful to eat except
μόνους τοὺς ἱερεῖς; 5 Καὶ ἔλεγεν αὐτοῖς, ᶻὍτι" κύριός ἐστιν
³only ¹the ²priests? And he said to them, ⁶Lord ⁵is
ὁ υἱὸς τοῦ ἀνθρώπου καὶ τοῦ σαββάτου.
¹the ²Son ³of ⁴man also of the sabbath.
6 Ἐγένετο.δὲ ᵃκαὶ" ἐν ἑτέρῳ σαββάτῳ εἰσελθεῖν αὐτὸν
And it came to pass also on another sabbath ²entered ¹he
εἰς τὴν συναγωγὴν καὶ διδάσκειν· καὶ ἦν ᵇἐκεῖ ἄνθρωπος,"
into the synagogue and taught; and there was there a man,
καὶ ἡ.χεὶρ.αὐτοῦ ἡ δεξιὰ ἦν ξηρά. 7 ᶜπαρετήρουν".δὲ ᵈαὐτὸν"
and his hand the right was withered. And ⁶were ⁷watching ⁸him

Him.
29 And Levi made a great feast in his own house. And there was a great company of tax-collectors and others who were with them at the table.
30 And their scribes and the Pharisees murmured at His disciples, saying, Why do you eat and drink with tax-collectors and sinners?
31 And answering Jesus said to them, They who are well do not need a physician, but they who are sick.
32 I did not come to call the righteous to repentance, but sinners.
33 And they said to Him, Why do the disciples of John fast often and make prayers, and also those of the Pharisees, but yours eat and drink?
34 And He said to them, Are you able to make the sons of the bride-chamber fast while the bridegroom is with them?
35 But the days will come also when the bridegroom shall be taken away from them. Then they will fast in those days.
36 And He spoke also a parable to them: No one puts a piece of new cloth on an old piece of cloth. Otherwise, he both tears the new and the old does not match the piece which is from the new.
37 And no one puts new wine into old wineskins. Else the new wine will burst the skins and it will be spilled, and the wineskins will be ruined.
38 But new wine is to be put into new wineskins, and both are preserved together.
39 And no one who has drunk old *wine* immediately desires new, for he says, The old is better.

CHAPTER 6

1 And on the second sabbath *after the* first, He passed along through the grain fields. And His disciples were plucking the ears and were eating, rubbing in their hands.
2 But some of the Pharisees said to them, Why do you do that which it is not lawful to do on the sabbaths?
3 And answering to them, Jesus said, Have you not even read this, that which David did when he was hungry, himself and those who were with him,
4 how he went into the house of God and took the showbread and ate (and he also gave to those with him) – which it is not lawful to eat, but only the priests?
5 And He said to them, The Son of man is Lord also of the sabbath.
6 And also on another sabbath He went into the synagogue and taught. And there was a man there, and his right hand was withered.
7 And the scribes and the Pharisees were watching Him, whether He would heal on

οἱ γραμματεῖς καὶ οἱ Φαρισαῖοι, εἰ ἐν τῷ σαββάτῳ [e]θερα-
[1]the [2]scribes [3]and [4]the [5]Pharisees, whether on the sabbath he will
πεύσει,‖ ἵνα εὕρωσιν [f]κατηγορίαν‖ αὐτοῦ. 8 αὐτὸς.δὲ
heal, that they might find an accusation against him. But he
ᾔδει τοὺς.διαλογισμοὺς.αὐτῶν, [g]καὶ εἶπεν‖ τῷ [h]ἀνθρώπῳ‖ τῷ
knew their reasonings, and said to the man who
ξηρὰν ἔχοντι τὴν χεῖρα, [i]Ἔγειραι,‖ καὶ στῆθι εἰς τὸ μέσον.
[3]withered [1]had [2]the hand, Arise, and stand in the midst.
[k]Ὁ.δὲ‖ ἀναστὰς ἔστη. 9 Εἶπεν [l]οὖν‖ ὁ Ἰησοῦς πρὸς αὐτούς,
And he having risen up stood. [3]Said [1]then [2]Jesus to them,
[m]Ἐπερωτήσω‖ ὑμᾶς, [n]τί‖ ἔξεστιν [o]τοῖς σάββασιν‖ ἀγαθο-
I will ask you, whether it is lawful on the sabbaths to do
ποιῆσαι ἢ κακοποιῆσαι; ψυχὴν σῶσαι ἢ [p]ἀπολέσαι‖; 10 Καὶ
good or to do evil? [3]life [1]to [2]save or to destroy? And
περιβλεψάμενος πάντας αὐτοὺς εἶπεν [q]τῷ ἀνθρώπῳ,‖
having looked around on all them he said to the man,
Ἔκτεινον τὴν.χεῖρά.σου. Ὁ.δὲ ἐποίησεν [r]οὕτως·‖ καὶ [s]ἀπο-
Stretch out thy hand. And he did so, and [2]was
κατεστάθη‖ ἡ.χεὶρ.αὐτοῦ [t]ὑγιὴς‖ [v]ὡς ἡ ἄλλη.‖ 11 αὐτοὶ.δὲ
[4]restored [1]his [2]hand sound as the other. But they
ἐπλήσθησαν ἀνοίας, καὶ διελάλουν πρὸς ἀλλήλους τί
were filled with madness, and consulted with one another [as to] what
ἂν [w]ποιήσειαν‖ τῷ Ἰησοῦ.
they should do to Jesus.

12 Ἐγένετο.δὲ ἐν ταῖς.ἡμέραις.ταύταις [x]ἐξῆλθεν‖ εἰς τὸ
And it came to pass in those days he went out into the
ὄρος προσεύξασθαι· καὶ ἦν διανυκτερεύων ἐν τῇ προσευχῇ
mountain to pray, and he was spending the night in prayer
τοῦ θεοῦ. 13 καὶ ὅτε ἐγένετο ἡμέρα προσεφώνησεν τοὺς
of God. And when it became day he called to [him]
μαθητὰς.αὐτοῦ· καὶ ἐκλεξάμενος ἀπ' αὐτῶν δώδεκα, οὓς καὶ
his disciples, and chose out from them twelve, whom also
ἀποστόλους ὠνόμασεν, 14 Σίμωνα ὃν καὶ ὠνόμασεν Πέτρον
[2]apostles [1]he [2]named: Simon whom also he named Peter
καὶ Ἀνδρέαν τὸν.ἀδελφὸν.αὐτοῦ, [ya]Ἰάκωβον καὶ [za]Ἰωάννην,‖
and Andrew his brother, James and John,
[ya]Φίλιππον καὶ Βαρθολομαῖον, 15 [ya aa]Ματθαῖον‖ καὶ Θωμᾶν,
Philip and Bartholomew, Matthew and Thomas,
[a]Ἰάκωβον [b]τὸν τοῦ‖ Ἀλφαίου καὶ Σίμωνα τὸν καλού-
James the [son] of Alphæus and Simon who [was] call-
μενον Ζηλωτήν, 16 [c] Ἰούδαν Ἰακώβου, καὶ Ἰούδαν
ed Zealot, Judas [brother] of James, and Judas
[d]Ἰσκαριώτην,‖ ὃς [e]καὶ‖ ἐγένετο προδότης· 17 καὶ καταβὰς
Iscariote, who also became [the] betrayer. And descending
μετ' αὐτῶν ἔστη ἐπὶ τόπου πεδινοῦ, καὶ ὄχλος [f] μαθητῶν
with them he stood on a [2]place [1]level, and a crowd of [2]disciples
αὐτοῦ καὶ πλῆθος πολὺ τοῦ λαοῦ ἀπὸ πάσης τῆς Ἰουδαίας
[1]his and a [2]multitude [1]great of the people from all Judæa
καὶ Ἰερουσαλὴμ καὶ τῆς παραλίου Τύρου καὶ Σιδῶνος, οἳ
and Jerusalem and the sea coast of Tyre and Sidon, who
ἦλθον ἀκοῦσαι αὐτοῦ, καὶ ἰαθῆναι ἀπὸ τῶν.νόσων.αὐτῶν,
came to hear him, and to be healed of their diseases,
18 καὶ οἱ [g]ὀχλούμενοι‖ [h]ὑπὸ‖ πνευμάτων ἀκαθάρτων, [i]καὶ‖
and those beset by [2]spirits [1]unclean, and
ἐθεραπεύοντο. 19 καὶ πᾶς ὁ ὄχλος [k]ἐζήτει‖ ἅπτεσθαι αὐτοῦ·
they were healed. And all the crowd sought to touch him;
ὅτι δύναμις παρ' αὐτοῦ ἐξήρχετο καὶ ἰᾶτο πάντας.
for power from him went out and healed all.
20 Καὶ αὐτὸς ἐπάρας τοὺς.ὀφθαλμοὺς.αὐτοῦ εἰς τοὺς μαθη-
And he lifting up his eyes upon [2]disci-
τὰς αὐτοῦ ἔλεγεν, Μακάριοι οἱ πτωχοί, ὅτι ὑμετέρα ἐστὶν
ples [1]his said, Blessed [are] the poor, for yours is
ἡ βασιλεία τοῦ θεοῦ. 21 μακάριοι οἱ πεινῶντες νῦν, ὅτι
the kingdom of God. Blessed [ye] who hunger now, for
χορτασθήσεσθε. μακάριοι οἱ κλαίοντες νῦν, ὅτι γελάσετε.
ye shall be filled. Blessed [ye] who weep now, for ye shall laugh.
22 μακάριοί ἐστε ὅταν μισήσωσιν ὑμᾶς οἱ ἄνθρωποι, καὶ ὅταν
Blessed are ye when [2]shall [3]hate [4]you [1]men, and when
ἀφορίσωσιν ὑμᾶς, καὶ ὀνειδίσωσιν, καὶ ἐκβάλωσιν τὸ
they shall cut [2]off [1]you, and shall reproach [you], and cast out
ὄνομα.ὑμῶν ὡς πονηρόν, [l]ἕνεκα‖ τοῦ υἱοῦ τοῦ ἀνθρώπου·
your name as wicked, on account of the Son of man:
23 [m]χαίρετε‖ ἐν ἐκείνῃ τῇ ἡμέρᾳ καὶ σκιρτήσατε· ἰδοὺ.γάρ, ὁ
rejoice in that day and leap for joy; for lo,
μισθὸς.ὑμῶν πολὺς ἐν τῷ οὐρανῷ· κατὰ [n]ταῦτα‖ γὰρ
your reward [is] great in the heaven, [2]according [3]to [4]these [5]things [1]for
ἐποίουν τοῖς προφήταις οἱ.πατέρες.αὐτῶν. 24 Πλὴν οὐαὶ
did [3]to [4]the [5]prophets [1]their [2]fathers. But woe
ὑμῖν τοῖς πλουσίοις, ὅτι ἀπέχετε τὴν.παράκλησιν.ὑμῶν.
to you the rich, for ye are receiving your consolation.
25 οὐαὶ ὑμῖν οἱ ἐμπεπλησμένοι[o], ὅτι πεινάσετε. οὐαὶ [p]ὑμῖν‖
Woe to you who have been filled, for ye shall hunger. Woe to you

the Sabbath, that they might find a charge against Him.

8 But He knew their thoughts and said to the man who had the withered hand, Get up and stand in the middle! And he got up and stood.

9 Then Jesus said to them, I will ask you one thing, Is it lawful to do good on the sabbath days, or to do evil – to save life, or to destroy?

10 And looking around on all of them, He said to the man, Stretch out your hand! And he did so. And his hand was restored as sound as the other.

11 But they were filled with fury and plotted with one another *as to* what they should do to Jesus.

12 And in those days Jesus went out into the mountain to pray. And He was spending the night in prayer to God.

13 And when daylight arrived, He called His disciples and chose out twelve from them, whom also He named apostles:

14 Simon (whom He also called Peter), and his brother Andrew – James and John – Philip and Bar-thol-o-mew –

15 Matthew and Thomas – James the *son* of Al-phe-us and Simon (who was called Ze-lo-tes) –

16 Judas *the brother* of James and Judas Is-car-i-ot (who also became the betrayer).

17 And going down with them, He stood on a level plain and *looked upon* a crowd of His disciples and a great multitude of people from all Judea, and from Jerusalem, and from the sea coast of Tyre and Sidon – who had come to hear Him and to be healed of their diseases.

18 And those troubled by unclean spirits *also came.* And they were all healed.

19 And the whole crowd was trying to touch Him, for power was going out from Him and healing all.

20 And lifting up His eyes on His disciples, He said, Blessed are the poor, for yours is the kingdom of God.

21 Blessed *are you* who hunger now, for you shall be filled. Blessed *are you* who weep now, for you shall laugh.

22 Blessed *are you* when men hate you, and when they shall cut you off and shall insult *you,* and throw out your name as evil because of the Son of man.

23 Rejoice in that day and leap for joy. For, behold! Your reward in Heaven is great, for so their fathers did to the prophets.

24 But woe to you that are rich, for you are receiving your comfort!

25 Woe to you who have been filled, for you shall hunger! Woe to you who laugh

οἱ γελῶντες νῦν, ὅτι πενθήσετε καὶ κλαύσετε. 26 οὐαὶ [q]ὑμῖν·
who laugh now, for ye shall mourn and weep. Woe to you
ὅταν καλῶς [r]ὑμᾶς εἴπωσιν‖ [s]πάντες‖ οἱ ἄνθρωποι· κατὰ
when well of you speak all men, [2]according [3]to
[n]ταῦτα‖ γὰρ ἐποίουν τοῖς ψευδοπροφήταις οἱ.πατέρες.αὐτῶν.
[4]these [5]things [1]for did [3]to [4]the [5]false [6]prophets [1]their [2]fathers.
27 [t]Ἀλλ'‖ ὑμῖν λέγω τοῖς ἀκούουσιν, Ἀγαπᾶτε τοὺς ἐχθροὺς
But to you I say who hear, Love [2]enemies
ὑμῶν, καλῶς ποιεῖτε τοῖς μισοῦσιν ὑμᾶς, 28 εὐλογεῖτε
[1]your, [4]well [3]do to those who hate you, bless
τοὺς καταρωμένους [v]ὑμῖν,‖ [w]καὶ‖ προσεύχεσθε [x]ὑπὲρ‖ τῶν
those who curse you, and pray for those who
ἐπηρεαζόντων ὑμᾶς. 29 τῷ τύπτοντί σε [y]ἐπὶ‖ τὴν σιαγόνα,
despitefully use you. To him who strikes thee on the cheek,
πάρεχε καὶ τὴν ἄλλην· καὶ ἀπὸ τοῦ αἴροντός σου τὸ
offer also the other; and from him who takes away thy
ἱμάτιον, καὶ τὸν χιτῶνα μὴ.κωλύσῃς. 30 παντὶ [z]δὲ τῷ‖
cloak, also the tunic do not forbid. [2]To [3]every [4]one [1]and who
αἰτοῦντί σε, δίδου· καὶ ἀπὸ τοῦ αἴροντος τὰ.σά,
asks thee, give; and from him who takes away what [is] thine,
μὴ.ἀπαίτει. 31 καὶ καθὼς θέλετε ἵνα ποιῶσιν ὑμῖν οἱ
ask [it] not back; and according as ye desire that [2]should [3]do [4]to [5]you
ἄνθρωποι, [a]καὶ ὑμεῖς‖ ποιεῖτε αὐτοῖς ὁμοίως. 32 καὶ εἰ
[1]men, also [2]ye [1]do to them in like manner. And if
ἀγαπᾶτε τοὺς ἀγαπῶντας ὑμᾶς, ποία ὑμῖν χάρις ἐστίν;
ye love those who love you, what [4]to [5]you [1]thank [2]is [3]it?
καὶ.γὰρ οἱ ἁμαρτωλοὶ τοὺς ἀγαπῶντας αὐτοὺς ἀγαπῶσιν.
for even sinners [2]those [3]who [4]love [5]them [1]love.
33 καὶ [b]ἐὰν ἀγαθοποιῆτε τοὺς ἀγαθοποιοῦντας ὑμᾶς,
And if ye do good to those who do good to you,
ποία ὑμῖν [c]χάρις ἐστίν‖; καὶ [d]γὰρ‖ οἱ ἁμαρτωλοὶ τὸ αὐτὸ
what [2]to [3]you [1]thank is it? [2]even [1]for sinners [2]the [3]same
ποιοῦσιν. 34 καὶ ἐὰν [e]δανείζητε‖ παρ' ὧν ἐλπίζετε
[1]do. And if ye lend [to those] from whom ye hope
[f]ἀπολαβεῖν,‖ ποία ὑμῖν χάρις ἐστίν; καὶ [g]γὰρ‖ [h]οἱ‖ ἁμαρτωλοὶ
to receive, what [2]to [3]you [1]thank is it? [2]even [1]for sinners
ἁμαρτωλοῖς [i]δανείζουσιν,‖ ἵνα ἀπολάβωσιν τὰ [k]ἴσα.‖ 35 πλὴν
[2]to [3]sinners [1]lend, that they may receive the like. But
ἀγαπᾶτε τοὺς.ἐχθροὺς.ὑμῶν, καὶ ἀγαθοποιεῖτε, καὶ [l]δανείζετε‖
love your enemies, and do good, and lend,
[m]μηδὲν‖ [n]ἀπελπίζοντες‖ καὶ ἔσται ὁ.μισθὸς.ὑμῶν πολὺς[o],
[3]nothing [1]hoping [2]for again; and [3]shall [4]be your [2]reward great,
καὶ ἔσεσθε υἱοὶ [p]τοῦ‖ ὑψίστου· ὅτι αὐτὸς χρηστός ἐστιν ἐπὶ
and ye shall be sons of the Highest; for he [2]good [1]is to
τοὺς ἀχαρίστους καὶ πονηρούς. 36 γίνεσθε [q]οὖν‖ οἰκτίρμονες,
the unthankful and wicked. Be ye therefore compassionate,
καθὼς [r]καὶ‖ ὁ.πατὴρ.ὑμῶν οἰκτίρμων ἐστίν. 37 καὶ μὴ.κρίνετε,
as also your father [2]compassionate [1]is. And judge not,
[s]καὶ οὐ‖.μὴ κριθῆτε· [t] μὴ.καταδικάζετε, καὶ οὐ.μὴ κατα-
that in no wise ye be judged; condemn not, that in no wise ye be
δικασθῆτε. ἀπολύετε, καὶ ἀπολυθήσεσθε· 38 δίδοτε, καὶ
condemned. Release, and ye shall be released. Give, and
δοθήσεται ὑμῖν. μέτρον καλόν πεπιεσμένον [va]καὶ‖ σεσαλευ-
it shall be given to you, [2]measure [1]good, pressed down and shaken to-
μένον [va]καὶ‖ [wa]ὑπερεκχυνόμενον‖ δώσουσιν εἰς τὸν κόλπον
gether and running over shall they give into [2]bosom
ὑμῶν· [xa]τῷ γὰρ αὐτῷ μέτρῳ ᾧ‖ μετρεῖτε, ἀντιμε-
[1]your: [4]with [5]the [1]for same measure with which ye mete, it shall be
τρηθήσεται ὑμῖν.‖ 39 Εἶπεν.δὲ [y] παραβολὴν αὐτοῖς, Μήτι
measured again to you. And he spoke a parable to them,
δύναται τυφλὸς τυφλὸν ὁδηγεῖν; οὐχὶ ἀμφότεροι εἰς
Is [4]able [1]a [2]blind [[3]man] a blind [man] to lead? [2]not [3]both [4]into
βόθυνον [z]πεσοῦνται‖; 40 οὐκ ἔστιν μαθητὴς ὑπὲρ τὸν διδάσκα-
[5]a [6]pit [1]will fall? [4]not [3]is [1]a [2]disciple above the teacher
λον [a]αὐτοῦ·‖ κατηρτισμένος.δὲ πᾶς ἔσται ὡς ὁ διδάσκαλος
of him; but [3]perfected [1]every [2]one shall be as [2]teacher
αὐτοῦ. 41 τί.δὲ βλέπεις τὸ κάρφος τὸ ἐν τῷ ὀφθαλμῷ
[1]his. But why lookest thou on the mote that [is] in the eye
τοῦ.ἀδελφοῦ.σου, τὴν.δὲ δοκὸν τὴν ἐν τῷ.ἰδίῳ ὀφθαλμῷ
of thy brother, but the beam that [is] in thine own eye
οὐ.κατανοεῖς; 42 [b]ἢ‖ πῶς δύνασαι λέγειν τῷ.ἀδελφῷ.σου,
perceivest not? or how art thou able to say to thy brother,
Ἀδελφέ, ἄφες ἐκβάλω τὸ κάρφος τὸ ἐν τῷ ὀφθαλμῷ
Brother, suffer [that] I may cast out the mote that [is] in [2]eye
σου, αὐτὸς τὴν ἐν τῷ.ὀφθαλμῷ.σου δοκὸν οὐ βλέπων; ὑπο-
[1]thine, thyself the [2]in [3]thine [[4]own] [5]eye [1]beam not seeing? Hypo-
κριτά, ἔκβαλε πρῶτον τὴν.δοκὸν ἐκ τοῦ.ὀφθαλμοῦ.σου, καὶ
crite, cast out first the beam out of thine [own] eye, and
τότε διαβλέψεις [c]ἐκβαλεῖν‖ τὸ κάρφος τὸ ἐν τῷ ὀφθαλμῷ
then thou wilt see clearly to cast out the mote that [is] in the eye
τοῦ.ἀδελφοῦ.σου[d]. 43 οὐ.γάρ ἐστιν δένδρον καλὸν ποιοῦν
of thy brother. For [3]not [1]there [2]is [4]a [6]tree [5]good producing

now, for you shall mourn and weep!
26 Woe to you when all men shall speak
well of you, for so their fathers did to the
false prophets!
27 But I say to you who hear, Love your
enemies. Do good to those who hate you.
28 Bless those who curse you, and pray for
those who spitefully use you.
29 And to him who strikes you on the *one*
cheek, offer also the other. And from him
who takes away your cloak, do not forbid
him to take your coat also.
30 And give to everyone who asks you. And
from him who takes away what is yours, do
not ask for it again.
31 And even as you desire that men should
do to you, you also do to them in the same
way.
32 And if you love those who love you, what
thanks is it to you? For even sinners love those
who love them.
33 And if you do good to those who do good
to you, what thanks is it to you? For even
sinners do the same.
34 And if you lend to those from whom
you hope to receive, what thanks is it to
you? For even sinners lend to sinners so that
they may receive as much again.
35 But love your enemies, and do good, and
lend, hoping for nothing again. And your
reward will be great. And you shall be the
children of the Highest, for He is good to the
unthankful and to the evil.
36 Therefore be merciful, as your Father is
also merciful.
37 And do not judge, so that in no way you
may be judged. Do not condemn, so that in
no way you may be condemned. Forgive and
you shall be forgiven.
38 Give, and it shall be given to you – good
measure, pressed down and shaken together
and running over, they shall give into your
bosom. For with the same measure with
which you measure, it shall be measured to
you again.
39 And He spoke a parable to them. Can the
blind lead the blind? Shall they not both fall
into a ditch?
40 The disciple is not above his teacher, but
everyone who is perfected shall be like his
teacher.
41 But why do you look on the twig that is
in the eye of your brother, but do not see
the log that is in your own eye?
42 Or how can you say to your brother,
Brother, let me pull out the twig that is in
your eye, *when you* yourself do not see the
log in your own eye? Hypocrite! First, pull
the log out of your own eye. And then you
will see clearly to pull out the twig that is in
your brother's eye.
43 For there is not any good tree that pro-

καρπὸν σαπρόν· οὐδὲ[e] δένδρον σαπρὸν ποιοῦν καρπὸν καλόν·
[2]fruit [1]corrupt; nor a [2]tree [1]corrupt producing [2]fruit [1]good;
44 ἕκαστον.γὰρ δένδρον ἐκ τοῦ.ἰδίου καρποῦ γινώσκεται· οὐ.γὰρ
for each tree by its own fruit is known, for not
ἐξ ἀκανθῶν συλλέγουσιν σῦκα, οὐδὲ ἐκ βάτου [f]τρυγῶσιν
from thorns do they gather figs, nor from a bramble gather they
σταφυλήν.‖ 45 ὁ ἀγαθὸς ἄνθρωπος ἐκ τοῦ ἀγαθοῦ θησαυροῦ
a bunch of grapes. The good man out of the good treasure
τῆς.καρδίας.[g]αὐτοῦ‖ προφέρει τὸ ἀγαθόν· καὶ ὁ πονη-
of his heart brings forth that which [is] good; and the wick-
ρὸς [h]ἄνθρωπος‖ ἐκ τοῦ πονηροῦ [i]θησαυροῦ τῆς καρδίας
ed man out of the wicked treasure of [2]heart
αὐτοῦ‖ προφέρει τὸ πονηρόν· ἐκ.γὰρ [k]τοῦ[l] περισσεύ-
[1]his brings forth that which [is] wicked; for out of the abun-
ματος [l]τῆς‖ καρδίας [m]λαλεῖ τὸ.στόμα.αὐτοῦ.‖ 46 Τί.δέ με
dance of the heart [3]speaks [1]his [2]mouth. And why me
καλεῖτε Κύριε, κύριε, καὶ οὐ.ποιεῖτε ἃ λέγω; 47 πᾶς ὁ ἐρ-
do ye call Lord, Lord, and do not what I say? Every one who
χόμενος πρός με καὶ ἀκούων μου.τῶν.λόγων καὶ ποιῶν αὐτούς,
is coming to me and hearing my words and doing them,
ὑποδείξω ὑμῖν τίνι ἐστὶν ὅμοιος. 48 ὅμοιός ἐστιν ἀνθρώπῳ
I will shew you to whom he is like. Like he is to a man
οἰκοδομοῦντι οἰκίαν, ὃς ἔσκαψεν καὶ ἐβάθυνεν, καὶ ἔθηκεν
building a house, who dug and deepened, and laid
θεμέλιον ἐπὶ τὴν πέτραν· [n]πλημμύρας[l].δὲ γενομένης [o]προσέρ-
a foundation on the rock; and a flood having come [3]burst
ρηξεν‖ ὁ ποταμὸς τῇ.οἰκίᾳ.ἐκείνῃ, καὶ οὐκ.ἴσχυσεν σαλεῦσαι
[4]upon [1]the [2]stream that house, and could not shake
αὐτήν· [p]τεθεμελίωτο.γὰρ ἐπὶ τὴν πέτραν.‖ 49 ὁ.δὲ ἀκούσας
it, for it had been founded upon the rock. But he who heard
καὶ μὴ.ποιήσας ὅμοιός ἐστιν ἀνθρώπῳ [q]οἰκοδομήσαντι‖ οἰκίαν
and did not [2]like [1]is to a man having built a house
ἐπὶ τὴν γῆν χωρὶς θεμελίου· ᾗ [r]προσέρρηξεν‖ ὁ ποτα-
on the earth without a foundation; on which [3]burst [1]the [2]stream,
μός, καὶ [s]εὐθέως ἔπεσεν,‖ καὶ ἐγένετο τὸ ῥῆγμα τῆς οἰκίας
and immediately it fell, and [6]was [1]the [2]ruin [3]of [5]house
ἐκείνης μέγα.
[4]that great.

7 [t]Ἐπεὶ.δὲ‖ ἐπλήρωσεν πάντα τὰ.ῥήματα.αὐτοῦ εἰς τὰς
And when he had completed all his words in the
ἀκοὰς τοῦ λαοῦ εἰσῆλθεν εἰς [u]Καπερναούμ.[l] 2 Ἑκατοντάρχου
ears of the people he entered into Capernaum. [4]Of [5]a [7]centurion
δέ τινος δοῦλος κακῶς ἔχων ἤμελλεν τελευτᾶν, ὃς ἦν
[1]and [6]certain [2]a [3]bondman [9]ill [8]being was about to die, who was
αὐτῷ ἔντιμος. 3 ἀκούσας.δὲ περὶ τοῦ Ἰησοῦ ἀπέστειλεν πρὸς
by him honoured. And having heard about Jesus he sent to
αὐτὸν πρεσβυτέρους τῶν Ἰουδαίων, ἐρωτῶν αὐτὸν ὅπως
him elders of the Jews, begging him that
ἐλθὼν διασώσῃ τὸν.δοῦλον.αὐτοῦ. 4 οἱ.δὲ παραγενόμενοι
having come he might cure his bondman. And they having come
πρὸς τὸν Ἰησοῦν [v]παρεκάλουν[l] αὐτὸν σπουδαίως, λέγοντες,
to Jesus besought him diligently, saying,
Ὅτι ἄξιός ἐστιν ᾧ [w]παρέξει‖ τοῦτο· 5 ἀγαπᾷ.γὰρ τὸ
that [3]worthy [1]he [2]is to whom he shall grant this, for he loves
ἔθνος.ἡμῶν καὶ τὴν συναγωγὴν αὐτὸς ᾠκοδόμησεν ἡμῖν.
our nation and the synagogue he built for us.
6 Ὁ.δὲ.Ἰησοῦς ἐπορεύετο σὺν αὐτοῖς· ἤδη.δὲ αὐτοῦ οὐ μακρὰν
And Jesus went with them; but already he [2]not [3]far
ἀπέχοντος [x]ἀπὸ‖ τῆς οἰκίας, ἔπεμψεν [y]πρὸς αὐτὸν[l] [z]ὁ ἑκατόν-
[1]being distant from the house, [3]sent [4]to [5]him [1]the [2]cen-
ταρχος φίλους,[l] λέγων [a]αὐτῷ,[l] Κύριε, μὴ.σκύλλου· οὐ
turion friends, saying to him, Lord, trouble not [thyself], [4]not
γάρ [b]εἰμι ἱκανὸς[l] ἵνα [c]ὑπὸ τὴν.στέγην.μου[l] εἰσέλθῃς·
[1]for [2]I [3]am worthy that under my roof thou shouldest come;
7 διὸ οὐδὲ ἐμαυτὸν ἠξίωσα πρός σε ἐλθεῖν· ἀλλὰ
wherefore neither myself counted I worthy [3]to [4]thee [1]to [2]come; but
εἰπὲ λόγῳ, καὶ [d]ἰαθήσεται[l] ὁ.παῖς.μου. 8 καὶ.γὰρ ἐγὼ ἄν-
say by a word, and shall be healed my servant. For also I a
θρωπός εἰμι ὑπὸ ἐξουσίαν τασσόμενος, ἔχων ὑπ' ἐμαυτὸν
man am under authority appointed, having under myself
στρατιώτας, καὶ λέγω τούτῳ Πορεύθητι, καὶ πορεύεται·
soldiers, and I say to this [one] Go, and he goes;
καὶ ἄλλῳ, Ἔρχου. καὶ ἔρχεται· καὶ τῷ.δούλῳ.μου, Ποίησον
and to another, Come, and he comes; and to my bondman, Do
τοῦτο, καὶ ποιεῖ. 9 Ἀκούσας.δὲ ταῦτα ὁ Ἰησοῦς ἐθαύ-
this, and he does [it]. And having heard these things Jesus won-
μασεν αὐτόν· καὶ στραφεὶς τῷ ἀκολουθοῦντι αὐτῷ ὄχλῳ
dered at him; and turning to the [2]following [3]him [1]crowd
εἶπεν, Λέγω ὑμῖν, οὐδὲ ἐν τῷ Ἰσραὴλ τοσαύτην πίστιν εὗρον.
said, I say to you, not even in Israel so great faith did I find.
10 Καὶ ὑποστρέψαντες [e]οἱ πεμφθέντες εἰς τὸν οἶκον‖ εὗρον
And [3]having [4]returned [1]those [2]sent to the house found

duces bad fruit, nor any bad tree that produces good fruit.
44 For every tree is known by its own fruit.
For they do not gather figs from thorns, nor
do they gather a bunch of grapes from a
bramble bush.
45 A good man out of the good treasure of
his heart brings out that which is good. And
an evil man out of the evil treasure of his
heart brings out that which is evil. For out
of the abundance of the heart his mouth
speaks.
46 And why do you call Me Lord, Lord,
and do not do the things which I say?
47 Whoever comes to Me and hears My
words, and does them, I will show you to
whom he is to be compared:
48 He is like a man building a house, who
dug and deepened and laid the foundation
on a rock. And a flood came up and the
stream burst upon that house, but could not
shake it, for it had been founded on a rock.
49 But he who hears and does not do is like
a man who had built a house on the earth
without a foundation, against which the
stream broke forth. And immediately it fell,
and the ruin of that house was great.

CHAPTER 7

1 Now when He had completed all His
sayings in the ears of the people, He went
into Ca-per-na-um.
2 And a certain centurion's servant, who
was dear to him, was sick and was about to
die.
3 And *he* had heard about Jesus and sent to
Him elders of the Jews begging Him that He
would come and heal his servant.
4 And when they had come to Jesus, they
begged Him earnestly, saying that the one to
whom He should grant this was worthy;
5 for he loves our nation, and he built a
synagogue for us.
6 And Jesus went with them. But when He
was already nearly to the house, the centurion sent friends to Him, saying to Him,
Lord, Do not go to any trouble, for I am not
worthy for You to come under my roof.
7 It was for this reason that I did not consider myself worthy to come to You. But
speak a word and my servant will be healed.
8 For I also am a man placed under
authority, having soldiers under myself. And
I say to this one, Go! And he goes. And to
another, *I say*, Come! And he comes. And to
my servant, Do this! And he does it.
9 And hearing these things, Jesus marveled
at him. And turning to the people following
Him, He said, I say to you that not even in
Israel have I found such great faith.
10 And returning to the house, those who
were sent found the ailing servant well.

τὸν [f]ἀσθενοῦντα" δοῦλον ὑγιαίνοντα.
the sick bondman in good health.
11 Καὶ ἐγένετο ἐν [g]τῇ' ἑξῆς [h]ἐπορεύετο" εἰς πόλιν
And it came to pass on the next [day] he went into a city
καλουμένην Ναΐν, καὶ συνεπορεύοντο αὐτῷ οἱ.μαθηταὶ.αὐτοῦ
called Nain, and went with him his [2]disciples
[i]ἱκανοὶ" καὶ ὄχλος πολύς. 12 ὡς.δὲ ἤγγισεν τῇ πύλῃ τῆς
[1]many and a [2]crowd [1]great. And as he drew near to the gate of the
πόλεως καὶ ἰδού, ἐξεκομίζετο [k]τεθνηκώς," [l]υἱὸς μονο-
city [2]also [1]behold, was being carried out [one] who had died, an [2]son [1]only
γενὴς" τῇ.μητρὶ.αὐτοῦ, καὶ [m]αὕτη ἦν" χήρα· καὶ ὄχλος τῆς
to his mother, and she was a widow, and a [2]crowd [3]of [4]the
πόλεως ἱκανὸς [n] σὺν αὐτῇ. 13 καὶ ἰδὼν αὐτὴν ὁ κύριος
[5]city [1]considerable [was] with her. And seeing her the Lord
ἐσπλαγχνίσθη ἐπ' [o]αὐτῇ" καὶ εἶπεν αὐτῇ, Μὴ.κλαῖε.
was moved with compassion on her and said to her, Weep not.
14 Καὶ προσελθὼν ἥψατο τῆς σοροῦ· οἱ.δὲ βαστάζοντες
And coming up he touched the bier, and those bearing [it]
ἔστησαν· καὶ εἶπεν, Νεανίσκε, σοὶ λέγω, ἐγέρθητι. 15 Καὶ
stopped. And he said, Young man, to thee I say, Arise. And
ἀνεκάθισεν ὁ νεκρὸς καὶ ἤρξατο λαλεῖν· καὶ ἔδωκεν αὐτὸν τῇ
[3]sat [4]up [1]the [2]dead and began to speak, and he gave him
μητρὶ.αὐτοῦ. 16 ἔλαβεν.δὲ φόβος [p]ἅπαντας," καὶ ἐδόξαζον
to his mother. And [2]seized [1]fear all, and they glorified
τὸν θεόν, λέγοντες, "Οτι προφήτης μέγας [q]ἐγήγερται" ἐν
God, saying, A [2]prophet [1]great has risen up amongst
ἡμῖν, καὶ "Οτι ἐπεσκέψατο ὁ θεὸς τὸν.λαὸν.αὐτοῦ. 17 Καὶ
us; and [2]Has [3]visited [1]God his people. And
ἐξῆλθεν ὁ.λόγος.οὗτος ἐν ὅλῃ τῇ Ἰουδαίᾳ περὶ αὐτοῦ, καὶ
went out this report in all Judæa concerning him, and
[r]ἐν" πάσῃ τῇ περιχώρῳ.
in all the country around.

18 Καὶ ἀπήγγειλαν [s]Ἰωάννῃ" οἱ.μαθηταὶ.αὐτοῦ περὶ
And [5]brought [6]word [1]to [2]John [3]his [4]disciples concerning
πάντων τούτων. 19 καὶ προσκαλεσάμενος δύο τινὰς τῶν
all these things. And having called to [him] [2]two [1]certain
μαθητῶν.αὐτοῦ ὁ [t]Ἰωάννης" ἔπεμψεν πρὸς [v]τὸν Ἰησοῦν,"
of his disciples John sent [them] to Jesus,
λέγων, Σὺ.εἶ ὁ ἐρχόμενος ἢ [w]ἄλλον" προσδοκῶμεν;
saying, Art thou the coming [one] or another are we to look for?
20 Παραγενόμενοι.δὲ πρὸς αὐτὸν οἱ ἄνδρες [x]εἶπον," [y]Ἰωάν-
And having come to him the men said, John
νης" ὁ βαπτιστὴς ἀπέσταλκεν ἡμᾶς πρός σε, λέγων, Σὺ.εἶ
the Baptist has sent us to thee, saying, Art thou
ὁ ἐρχόμενος ἢ ἄλλον προσδοκῶμεν; 21 Ἐν [z]αὐτῇ" [a]δὲ"
the coming [one] or another are we to look for? [4]In [5]the [6]same [1]and
τῇ ὥρᾳ ἐθεράπευσεν πολλοὺς ἀπὸ νόσων καὶ μαστίγων καὶ
hour he healed many of diseases and scourges and
πνευμάτων πονηρῶν, καὶ τυφλοῖς πολλοῖς ἐχαρίσατο [b]τὸ"
[2]spirits [1]evil, and to [2]blind [1]many he granted
βλέπειν. 22 καὶ ἀποκριθεὶς [c]ὁ Ἰησοῦς" εἶπεν αὐτοῖς, Πορευθέν-
to see. And [2]answering [1]Jesus said to them, Having
τες ἀπαγγείλατε [d]Ἰωάννῃ" ἃ εἴδετε καὶ ἠκούσατε· [e]ὅτι"
gone relate to John what ye have seen and heard; that
τυφλοὶ ἀναβλέπουσιν, χωλοὶ περιπατοῦσιν, λεπροὶ καθαρίζον-
blind receive sight, lame walk, lepers are cleansed,
ται, κωφοὶ ἀκούουσιν, νεκροὶ ἐγείρονται, πτωχοὶ εὐαγγελίζονται·
deaf hear, dead are raised, poor are evangelized;

23 καὶ μακάριός ἐστιν ὃς.ἐὰν μὴ.σκανδαλισθῇ ἐν ἐμοί.
and blessed is whoever shall not be offended in me.
24 Ἀπελθόντων.δὲ τῶν ἀγγέλων [f]Ἰωάννου" ἤρξατο λέγειν
And [5]having [6]departed [1]the [2]messengers [3]of [4]John he began to speak
πρὸς τοὺς ὄχλους περὶ [f]Ἰωάννου," Τί [g]ἐξεληλύθατε" εἰς
to the crowds concerning John: What have ye gone out into
τὴν ἔρημον θεάσασθαι; κάλαμον ὑπὸ ἀνέμου σαλευό-
the wilderness to look at? a reed by [the] wind shaken?
μενον; 25 ἀλλὰ τί [g]ἐξεληλύθατε" ἰδεῖν; ἄνθρωπον ἐν μαλα-
But what have ye gone out to see? a man in soft
κοῖς ἱματίοις ἠμφιεσμένον; ἰδού, οἱ ἐν ἱματισμῷ ἐνδόξῳ
clothing arrayed? Behold, they who in [2]clothing [1]splendid
καὶ τρυφῇ ὑπάρχοντες ἐν τοῖς βασιλείοις εἰσίν. 26 ἀλλὰ τί
and in luxury are living [2]in [3]the [4]palaces [1]are. But what
[g]ἐξεληλύθατε" ἰδεῖν; προφήτην; ναί, λέγω ὑμῖν, καὶ
have ye gone out to see? a prophet? Yea, I say to you, and [one]
περισσότερον προφήτου. 27 οὗτός ἐστιν περὶ οὗ γέ-
more excellent than a prophet. This is he concerning whom it has
γραπται, Ἰδού, [h]ἐγὼ" ἀποστέλλω τὸν.ἄγγελόν.μου πρὸ
been written, Behold, I send my messenger before
προσώπου.σου, ὃς κατασκευάσει τὴν.ὁδόν.σου ἔμπροσθέν σου.
thy face, who shall prepare thy way before thee.
28 Λέγω [i]γὰρ" ὑμῖν, μείζων ἐν γεννητοῖς γυναικῶν
[2]I [3]say [1]for to you, [6]a [7]greater [1]among [[2]those] [3]born [4]of [5]women

11 And on the next day, He went into a city called Nain. And many of His disciples and a great crowd went with Him.

12 And as He drew near to the gate of the city, behold, one who had died was being carried out, an only son to his mother. And she was a widow. And many people of the city were with her.

13 And seeing her, the Lord was moved with compassion on her. And He said to her, Do not weep.

14 And coming up, He touched the bier, and those bearing it stood still. And He said, Young man, I say to you, Arise!

15 And the dead one sat up and began to speak. And He gave him to his mother.

16 And fear clutched them all. And they glorified God, saying, A great prophet has appeared among us – and, God has visited His people.

17 And this report about Him went out into all Judea and into all the region around it.

18 And the disciples of John brought word of all these things.

19 And calling to him two particular ones of his disciples, John sent to Jesus, saying, Are You the One who is coming, or are we to look for another?

20 And coming to Him, the men said, John the Baptist has sent us to You, saying, Are You the One who is coming, or are we to look for another?

21 And in the same hour He healed many of sicknesses and plagues and evil spirits. And to many of the blind, He gave power to see.

22 And answering Jesus said to them, When you return, tell John what you have seen and heard – that the blind receive sight, the lame walk, the lepers are cleansed, the deaf hear, the dead are raised, the gospel is preached to the poor.

23 And blessed is he, whoever shall not be offended in Me.

24 And after the messengers of John had left, He began to speak to the people about John: What have you gone out into the wilderness to see, a reed shaken by the wind?

25 But what have you gone out to see, a man clothed in soft clothing? Behold, they who are in gorgeous clothes and who are in luxury are living in palaces.

26 But what have you gone out to see, a prophet? Yes, I say to you, and one more excellent than a prophet.

27 This is he about whom it has been written, "Behold! I send My messenger before Your face, who shall prepare Your way before You."

28 For I say to you, among those born of

[k]προφήτης‖ [r]Ἰωάννου‖ [l]τοῦ βαπτιστοῦ‖ οὐδείς ἐστιν· ὁ.δὲ
prophet than John the Baptist no one is; but he that [is]
μικρότερος ἐν τῇ βασιλείᾳ τοῦ θεοῦ μείζων αὐτοῦ ἐστιν. 29 Καὶ
less in the kingdom of God greater than he is. And
πᾶς ὁ λαὸς ἀκούσας καὶ οἱ τελῶναι ἐδικαίωσαν τὸν θεόν,
all the people having heard and the tax-gatherers justified God,
βαπτισθέντες τὸ βάπτισμα [r]Ἰωάννου·‖ 30 οἱ.δὲ Φα-
having been baptized [with] the baptism of John; but the Pha-
ρισαῖοι καὶ οἱ νομικοὶ τὴν βουλὴν τοῦ θεοῦ ἠθέτησαν
risees and the doctors of the law the counsel of God set aside
εἰς ἑαυτούς, μὴ βαπτισθέντες ὑπ' αὐτοῦ. 31 [m]εἶπεν.δὲ ὁ
as to themselves, not having been baptized by him. And [3]said [1]the
κύριος,‖ Τίνι οὖν ὁμοιώσω τοὺς ἀνθρώπους τῆς γενεᾶς
[2]Lord, To what therefore shall I liken the men of [2]generation
ταύτης; καὶ τίνι εἰσὶν ὅμοιοι; 32 ὅμοιοί εἰσιν παιδίοις
[1]this? and to what are they like? Like are they to little children
τοῖς ἐν ἀγορᾷ καθημένοις, καὶ προσφωνοῦσιν ἀλλήλοις
in a market-place sitting, and calling one to another
[n]καὶ λέγουσιν,‖ Ηὐλήσαμεν ὑμῖν, καὶ οὐκ.ὠρχήσασθε· ἐθρη-
and saying, We piped to you, and ye did not dance; we
νήσαμεν [o]ὑμῖν,‖ καὶ οὐκ.ἐκλαύσατε. 33 ἐλήλυθεν.γὰρ [p]Ἰωάννης‖
mourned to you, and ye did not weep. For [4]has [5]come [1]John
ὁ βαπτιστὴς [q]μήτε‖ [r]ἄρτον ἐσθίων‖ [s]μήτε‖ [t]οἶνον πίνων,‖
[2]the [3]Baptist neither [2]bread [1]eating nor [2]wine [1]drinking,
καὶ λέγετε, Δαιμόνιον ἔχει. 34 ἐλήλυθεν ὁ υἱὸς τοῦ ἀνθρώπου
and ye say, A demon he has. [5]Has [6]come [1]the [2]Son [3]of [4]man
ἐσθίων καὶ πίνων, καὶ λέγετε, Ἰδού, ἄνθρωπος φάγος καὶ
eating and drinking, and ye say, Behold, a man a glutton and
οἰνοπότης, [v]τελωνῶν φίλος‖ καὶ ἁμαρτωλῶν. 35 καὶ ἐδι-
a wine-bibber, of tax-gatherers a friend and of sinners; and [2]was
καιώθη ἡ σοφία ἀπὸ [w]τῶν.τέκνων.αὐτῆς πάντων.‖
[3]justified [1]wisdom by [2]her [3]children [1]all.

36 Ἠρώτα.δέ τις αὐτὸν τῶν Φαρισαίων ἵνα φάγῃ μετ'
And [5]asked [1]one [6]him [2]of [3]the [4]Pharisees that he should eat with
αὐτοῦ· καὶ εἰσελθὼν εἰς [x]τὴν οἰκίαν‖ τοῦ Φαρισαίου [y]ἀνε-
him And having entered into the house of the Pharisee he re-
κλίθη.‖ 37 Καὶ ἰδού, γυνὴ [z]ἐν τῇ πόλει ἥτις ἦν‖
clined [at table]; and behold, a woman in the city who was
ἁμαρτωλός, [a]ἐπιγνοῦσα ὅτι [b]ἀνάκειται‖ ἐν τῇ οἰκίᾳ
a sinner, having known that he had reclined [at table] in the house
τοῦ Φαρισαίου, κομίσασα ἀλάβαστρον μύρου, 38 καὶ στᾶσα
of the Pharisee, having taken an alabaster flask of ointment, and standing
[c]παρὰ τοὺς.πόδας.αὐτοῦ ὀπίσω‖ κλαίουσα, [d]ἤρξατο βρέχειν
at his feet behind weeping, began to bedew
τοὺς.πόδας.αὐτοῦ τοῖς.δάκρυσιν,‖ καὶ ταῖς θριξὶν τῆς κεφαλῆς
his feet with tears, and with the hairs of [2]head
αὐτῆς [e]ἐξέμασσεν,‖ καὶ κατεφίλει τοὺς.πόδας.αὐτοῦ,
[1]her she was wiping [them], and was ardently kissing his feet,
καὶ ἤλειφεν τῷ μύρῳ. 39 ἰδὼν.δὲ ὁ Φαρισαῖος
and was anointing [them] with the ointment. But having seen, the Pharisee
ὁ καλέσας αὐτὸν εἶπεν ἐν ἑαυτῷ, λέγων, Οὗτος εἰ
who invited him spoke within himself, saying, This [person] if
ἦν προφήτης, ἐγίνωσκεν.ἂν τίς καὶ ποταπὴ ἡ γυνὴ
he were a prophet, would have known who and what the woman [is]
ἥτις ἅπτεται αὐτοῦ, ὅτι ἁμαρτωλός ἐστιν. 40 Καὶ ἀποκριθεὶς
who touches him, for a sinner she is. And [2]answering
ὁ Ἰησοῦς εἶπεν πρὸς αὐτόν, Σίμων, ἔχω σοί τι εἰπεῖν.
[1]Jesus said to him, Simon, I have to thee something to say.
Ὁ.δὲ [f]φησιν, Διδάσκαλε, εἰπέ.‖ 41 Δύο [g]χρεωφειλέται‖ ἦσαν
And he says, Teacher, say [it]. Two debtors there were
[h]δανειστῇ‖ τινι· ὁ εἷς ὤφειλεν δηνάρια πεντακόσια, ὁ.δὲ
to a [2]creditor [1]certain; the one owed [3]denarii [1]five [2]hundred, and the
ἕτερος πεντήκοντα. 42 μὴ.ἐχόντων.[i]δὲ‖ αὐτῶν ἀπο-
other fifty. But [2]not [3]having [1]they [wherewith] to
δοῦναι ἀμφοτέροις ἐχαρίσατο· τίς οὖν αὐτῶν, [k]εἰπέ,‖ πλεῖον
pay, both he forgave: which therefore of them, say, [4]most
[l]αὐτὸν ἀγαπήσει‖; 43 Ἀποκριθεὶς.[j]δὲ‖ [m]ὁ‖ Σίμων εἶπεν, Ὑπο-
[3]him [1]will [2]love? And [2]answering [1]Simon said, I
λαμβάνω ὅτι ᾧ τὸ πλεῖον ἐχαρίσατο. Ὁ.δὲ εἶπεν αὐτῷ,
take it that [he] to whom the more he forgave. And he said to him,
Ὀρθῶς ἔκρινας. 44 Καὶ στραφεὶς πρὸς τὴν γυναῖκα, τῷ
Rightly thou hast judged And having turned to the woman,
Σίμωνι ἔφη, Βλέπεις ταύτην τὴν γυναῖκα; εἰσῆλθόν σου εἰς
to Simon he said, Seest thou this woman? I entered [2]thy [1]into
τὴν οἰκίαν, ὕδωρ [n]ἐπὶ τοὺς.πόδας.μου‖ οὐκ.ἔδωκας· αὕτη.δὲ
house, water for my feet thou gavest not, but she
τοῖς δάκρυσιν ἔβρεξέν μου τοὺς πόδας, καὶ ταῖς θριξὶν [o]τῆς
with tears bedewed my feet, and with the hairs
κεφαλῆς‖ αὐτῆς ἐξέμαξεν. 45 φίλημά μοι οὐκ.ἔδωκας·
[3]head [1]of [2]her wiped [them]. A kiss to me thou gavest not,
αὕτη.δὲ ἀφ' ἧς εἰσῆλθον οὐ.[p]διέλιπεν‖ καταφιλοῦσά
but she from which [time] I came in ceased not ardently kissing

women there is not a greater prophet than John the Baptist. But he that is least in the kingdom of God is greater than he.

29 And having heard, all the people and the tax-collectors who had been baptized with the baptism of John justified God.

30 But the Pharisees and the lawyers who had not been baptized by him rejected the purpose of God as to themselves.

31 And the Lord said, Then to what shall I compare the men of this generation; and, What are they like?

32 They are like little children sitting in the market place and calling to one another, and saying, We have piped to you and you did not dance – we mourned to you and you did not weep.

33 For John the Baptist has come neither eating bread nor drinking wine. And you say he has a demon.

34 The Son of man has come eating and drinking. And you say, See, a glutton and a drunkard, a friend of tax-collectors and sinners!

35 Yet wisdom was justified by all her children.

36 And one of the Pharisees begged Him that He would eat with him. And going into the house of the Pharisee, He sat at table.

37 And, behold, a woman in the city who was a sinner, knowing that He had sat down to eat in the Pharisee's house, brought an alabaster bottle of ointment!

38 And standing behind, weeping beside His feet, she began to wash His feet with tears. And she was wiping *them* with the hairs of her head. And *she* was lovingly kissing His feet and anointing *them* with ointment.

39 But seeing *this,* the Pharisee who invited Him spoke within himself, saying, This one, if he were a prophet, would have known who and what kind of woman this is who touches him. For she is a great sinner.

40 And Jesus said to him, Simon, I have something to say to you. And he said, Teacher, speak.

41 There were two men who owed a certain lender – the one owed five hundred pieces of silver, and the other fifty.

42 But as they had nothing to repay, he forgave both. Which of them, then, do you say will love him most?

43 And answering Simon said, I suppose that one to whom he forgave the most. And He said to him, you have judged rightly.

44 And turning to the woman, He said to Simon, Do you see this woman? I came into your house. You gave Me no water for My feet, but she has washed My feet with tears and wiped *them* with the hairs of her head.

45 You gave Me no kiss, but since I arrived this woman has not ceased to lovingly kiss My

[q]μου τοὺς πόδας.‖ 46 ἐλαίῳ τὴν.κεφαλήν.μου οὐκ.ἤλειψας·
my feet. With oil my head thou didst not anoint,
αὕτη.δὲ μύρῳ ἤλειψέν [r]μου τοὺς πόδας.‖ 47 οὗ.χάριν
but she with ointment anointed my feet. For which cause
λέγω σοι, ἀφέωνται [s]αἱ.ἁμαρτίαι.αὐτῆς‖ αἱ πολλαί, ὅτι
I say to thee, forgiven have been her [2]sins [1]many; for
ἠγάπησεν πολύ· ᾧ.δὲ ὀλίγον ἀφίεται ὀλίγον ἀγαπᾷ.
she loved much; but to whom little is forgiven little he loves.
48 Εἶπεν.δὲ αὐτῇ, Ἀφέωνταί σου αἱ ἁμαρτίαι. 49 Καὶ
And he said to her, Forgiven have been thy sins. And
ἤρξαντο οἱ συνανακείμενοι λέγειν ἐν ἑαυτοῖς, Τίς [t]οὗτός
began those reclining with [him] to say within themselves, Who [2]this
ἐστιν‖ ὃς καὶ ἁμαρτίας ἀφίησιν; 50 Εἶπεν.δὲ πρὸς τὴν γυ-
[1]is who even [2]sins [1]forgives? But he said to the wo-
ναῖκα, Ἡ.πίστις.σου σέσωκέν σε· πορεύου εἰς εἰρήνην.
man, Thy faith has saved thee; go in peace.

8 Καὶ ἐγένετο ἐν.τῷ.καθεξῆς καὶ αὐτὸς διώδευεν
And it came to pass afterwards that he journeyed through
κατὰ.πόλιν καὶ κώμην, κηρύσσων καὶ εὐαγγελιζό-
city by city and village by village, preaching and announcing the glad
μενος τὴν βασιλείαν τοῦ θεοῦ· καὶ οἱ δώδεκα σὺν αὐτῷ,
tidings, the kingdom of God, and the twelve [were] with him,
2 καὶ γυναῖκές τινες αἳ ἦσαν.τεθεραπευμέναι ἀπὸ πνευμάτων
and [2]women [1]certain who had been cured from [2]spirits
πονηρῶν καὶ ἀσθενειῶν, Μαρία ἡ καλουμένη Μαγδαληνή,
[1]wicked and infirmities, Mary who is called Magdalene,
ἀφ᾽ ἧς δαιμόνια ἑπτὰ ἐξεληλύθει, 3 καὶ [v]Ἰωάννα‖ γυνὴ
from whom [2]demons [1]seven had gone out; and Joanna wife
Χουζᾶ ἐπιτρόπου Ἡρώδου, καὶ Σουσάννα, καὶ ἕτεραι πολλαί,
of Chuza a steward of Herod; and Susanna, and [2]others [1]many,
αἵτινες διηκόνουν [w]αὐτῷ‖ [x]ἀπὸ‖ τῶν.ὑπαρχόντων.αὐταῖς.
who were ministering to him of their property.
4 Συνιόντος.δὲ ὄχλου πολλοῦ, καὶ τῶν κατὰ.πόλιν ἐπι-
And [4]assembling [1]a [3]crowd [2]great, and those who from each city were
πορευομένων πρὸς αὐτόν, εἶπεν διὰ παραβολῆς. 5 Ἐξῆλθεν
coming to him, he spoke by a parable. [3]Went [4]out
ὁ σπείρων τοῦ σπεῖραι τὸν.σπόρον.αὐτοῦ· καὶ ἐν.τῷ.σπείρειν
[1]the [2]sower to sow his seed; and as [2]sowed
αὐτὸν ὃ.μὲν ἔπεσεν παρὰ τὴν ὁδόν, καὶ κατεπατήθη, καὶ τὰ
[1]he some fell by the way, and it was trampled upon, and the
πετεινὰ τοῦ οὐρανοῦ κατέφαγεν αὐτό. 6 καὶ ἕτερον [y]ἔπεσεν‖
birds of the heaven devoured it. And other fell
ἐπὶ τὴν πέτραν, καὶ φυὲν ἐξηράνθη, διὰ τὸ μὴ.ἔχειν
upon the rock, and having sprung up it withered, because it had not
ἰκμάδα. 7 καὶ ἕτερον ἔπεσεν ἐν μέσῳ τῶν ἀκανθῶν, καὶ
moisture; and other fell in [the] midst of the thorns, and
[z]συμφυεῖσαι‖ αἱ ἄκανθαι ἀπέπνιξαν αὐτό. 8 καὶ ἕτερον
having sprung up together the thorns choked it; and other
ἔπεσεν [a]ἐπὶ‖ τὴν γῆν τὴν ἀγαθήν, καὶ φυὲν ἐποίησεν
fell upon the ground the good, and having sprung up produced
καρπὸν ἑκατονταπλασίονα. Ταῦτα λέγων ἐφώνει, Ὁ ἔχων
fruit a hundredfold. These things saying he cried, He that has
ὦτα ἀκούειν ἀκουέτω. 9 Ἐπηρώτων.δὲ αὐτὸν οἱ.μαθηταὶ.αὐτοῦ,
ears to hear let him hear. And [3]asked [4]him [1]his [2]disciples,
[b]λέγοντες,‖ Τίς [c]εἴη ἡ.παραβολὴ.αὕτη‖; 10 Ὁ.δὲ εἶπεν,
saying, What may be this parable? And he said,
Ὑμῖν δέδοται γνῶναι τὰ μυστήρια τῆς βασιλείας τοῦ
To you it has been given to know the mysteries of the kingdom
θεοῦ· τοῖς.δὲ λοιποῖς ἐν παραβολαῖς, ἵνα βλέποντες μὴ
of God, but to the rest in parables, that seeing [3]not
βλέπωσιν, καὶ ἀκούοντες μὴ.συνιῶσιν. 11 Ἔστιν.δὲ
[1]they [2]may see, and hearing they may not understand. Now [4]is
αὕτη ἡ παραβολή· ὁ σπόρος ἐστὶν ὁ λόγος τοῦ θεοῦ· 12 οἱ.δὲ
[3]this [1]the [2]parable: The seed is the word of God: and those
παρὰ τὴν ὁδὸν εἰσὶν οἱ [d]ἀκούοντες,‖ εἶτα ἔρχεται ὁ διά-
by the way are those who hear; then comes the de-
βολος καὶ αἴρει τὸν λόγον ἀπὸ τῆς.καρδίας.αὐτῶν, ἵνα.μὴ
vil and takes away the word from their heart, lest,
πιστεύσαντες σωθῶσιν. 13 οἱ.δὲ ἐπὶ [e]τῆς πέτρας,‖ οἳ
having believed they should be saved. And those upon the rock, those who
ὅταν ἀκούσωσιν, μετὰ χαρᾶς δέχονται τὸν λόγον, καὶ οὗτοι
when they hear, with joy receive the word, and these
ῥίζαν οὐκ.ἔχουσιν, οἳ πρὸς καιρὸν πιστεύουσιν, καὶ ἐν καιρῷ
a root have not, who for a time believe, and in time
πειρασμοῦ ἀφίστανται. 14 τὸ.δὲ εἰς τὰς ἀκάνθας πεσόν,
of trial fall away. And that which into the thorns fell,
οὗτοί εἰσιν οἱ ἀκούσαντες, καὶ ὑπὸ μεριμνῶν καὶ πλούτου
these are they who having heard, and under cares and riches
καὶ ἡδονῶν τοῦ βίου πορευόμενοι [f]συμπνίγονται,‖ καὶ οὐ
and pleasures of life moving along are choked, and [2]not
τελεσφοροῦσιν. 15 τὸ.δὲ ἐν τῇ καλῇ γῇ, οὗτοί εἰσιν
[1]do bring to perfection. And that in the good ground, these are

feet.
46 You did not anoint My head with oil, but
this woman has anointed My feet with
ointment.
47 Because of this I say to you, her many sins
have been forgiven, for she loved much. But to
whom little is forgiven, he loves little.
48 And He said to her, Your sins have been
forgiven.
49 And those at table began to say within
themselves, Who is this who even forgives
sins?
50 But He said to the woman, Your faith has
saved you. Go in peace.

CHAPTER 8

1 And afterwards He was going through every
city and village preaching and announcing the
gospel of the kingdom of God. And the twelve
were with Him.
2 And certain women who had been healed
of evil spirits and infirmities *also were with
Him* – Mary (who is called Mag-da-lene) from
whom seven demons had gone out,
3 and Joanna the wife of Chuza, a steward
of Herod, and Susanna, and many others
who ministered to Him from their property.
4 And a great crowd came together. And
those who were from each city came to Him.
And He spoke by a parable:
5 The sower went out to sow his seed. And as
he sowed, some fell by the roadside. And it
was trampled upon, and the birds ate it.
6 And other *seed* fell on a rock. And after it
had sprouted, it withered away because it had
no moisture.
7 And other *seed* fell in the middle of thorns,
and after springing up together, the thorns
choked it.
8 And other *seed* fell on the good ground,
and springing up bore fruit a hundred times.
Having said these things, He cried, He that has
ears to hear, let him hear!
9 And His disciples asked Him, saying, What
does this parable mean?
10 And He said, It has been given to you to
know the mysteries of the kingdom of God,
but to the rest *I speak* in parables – so that
seeing they may not see and hearing they may
not understand.
11 Now the parable is this: The seed is the
word of God.
12 And those by the roadside are those who
hear. Then the devil comes and takes away the
word from their heart for fear they may
believe and be saved.
13 And those on the rock are those who,
when they hear, receive the word with joy.
But these who believe for a time but in time of
temptation fall away have no root.
14 And that which fell into the thorns are the
ones who after they have heard and have gone
forth are choked with cares and riches and
pleasures of life – and bring nothing to
perfection.
15 And that in the good ground are the ones

οἵτινες ἐν καρδίᾳ καλῇ καὶ ἀγαθῇ ἀκούσαντες τὸν λόγον
they who in a heart right and good having heard the word
κατέχουσιν, καὶ καρποφοροῦσιν ἐν ὑπομονῇ. 16 Οὐδεὶς δὲ
keep [it], and bring forth fruit with endurance. And no one
λύχνον ἅψας καλύπτει αὐτὸν σκεύει, ἢ ὑποκάτω κλίνης
a lamp having lighted covers it with a vessel, or under a couch
τίθησιν· ἀλλ' ἐπὶ λυχνίας ἐπιτίθησιν, ἵνα οἱ
puts [it], but on a lamp-stand puts [it], that they who
εἰσπορευόμενοι βλέπωσιν τὸ φῶς. 17 οὐ.γάρ ἐστιν
enter in may see the light. For not [anything] is
κρυπτὸν ὃ οὐ φανερὸν γενήσεται· οὐδὲ ἀπόκρυφον ὃ
hidden which not manifest shall become; nor secret which
οὐ.γνωσθήσεται καὶ εἰς φανερὸν ἔλθῃ. 18 βλέπετε οὖν
shall not be known and to light come. Take heed therefore
πῶς ἀκούετε· ὃς.γὰρ.ἂν ἔχῃ, δοθήσεται αὐτῷ· καὶ
how ye hear; for whoever may have, shall be given to him; and
ὃς.ἂν μὴ.ἔχῃ, καὶ ὃ δοκεῖ ἔχειν ἀρθήσεται ἀπ' αὐτοῦ.
whoever may not have, even what he seems to have shall be taken from him.
19 Παρεγένοντο.δὲ πρὸς αὐτὸν ἡ μήτηρ καὶ οἱ ἀδελ-
And came to him [his] mother and brethren
φοὶ αὐτοῦ, καὶ οὐκ.ἠδύναντο συντυχεῖν αὐτῷ διὰ τὸν
his, and were not able to get to him because of the
ὄχλον. 20 καὶ ἀπηγγέλη αὐτῷ, λεγόντων, Ἡ.μήτηρ.σου
crowd. And it was told him, saying, Thy mother
καὶ οἱ.ἀδελφοί.σου ἑστήκασιν ἔξω, ἰδεῖν σε θέλοντες.
and thy brethren are standing without, to see thee wishing.
21 Ὁ.δὲ ἀποκριθεὶς εἶπεν πρὸς αὐτούς, Μήτηρ.μου καὶ
And he answering said to them, My mother and
ἀδελφοί.μου οὗτοί εἰσιν οἱ τὸν λόγον τοῦ θεοῦ ἀκούοντες καὶ
my brethren those are who the word of God are hearing and
ποιοῦντες αὐτόν.
doing it.

22 Καὶ ἐγένετο ἐν μιᾷ τῶν ἡμερῶν καὶ αὐτὸς ἐνέβη
And it came to pass on one of the days that he entered
εἰς πλοῖον καὶ οἱ.μαθηταὶ.αὐτοῦ, καὶ εἶπεν πρὸς αὐτούς,
into a ship, and his disciples, and he said to them,
Διέλθωμεν εἰς τὸ πέραν τῆς λίμνης· καὶ ἀνήχθησαν.
Let us pass over to the other side of the lake; and they put off.
23 πλεόντων.δὲ.αὐτῶν ἀφύπνωσεν· καὶ κατέβη λαῖλαψ
And as they sailed he fell asleep; and came down a storm
ἀνέμου εἰς τὴν λίμνην, καὶ συνεπληροῦντο, καὶ ἐκινδύνευον.
of wind on the lake, and they were being filled, and were in danger.
24 προσελθόντες.δὲ διήγειραν αὐτόν, λέγοντες, Ἐπιστάτα,
And having come to [him] they aroused him, saying, Master,
ἐπιστάτα, ἀπολλύμεθα. Ὁ.δὲ ἐγερθεὶς ἐπετίμησεν τῷ
Master, we are perishing. And he having arisen rebuked the
ἀνέμῳ καὶ τῷ κλύδωνι τοῦ ὕδατος· καὶ ἐπαύσαντο, καὶ ἐγένετο
wind and the raging of the water; and they ceased, and there was
γαλήνη. 25 εἶπεν.δὲ αὐτοῖς, Ποῦ ἐστιν ἡ.πίστις.ὑμῶν;
a calm. And he said to them, Where is your faith?
Φοβηθέντες.δὲ ἐθαύμασαν, λέγοντες πρὸς ἀλλήλους, Τίς ἄρα
And being afraid they wondered, saying to one another, Who then
οὗτός ἐστιν, ὅτι καὶ τοῖς ἀνέμοις ἐπιτάσσει καὶ τῷ ὕδατι,
this is, that even the winds he commands and the water,
καὶ ὑπακούουσιν αὐτῷ;
and they obey him?

26 Καὶ κατέπλευσαν εἰς τὴν χώραν τῶν Γαδαρηνῶν,
And they sailed down to the country of the Gadarenes,
ἥτις ἐστὶν ἀντιπέραν τῆς Γαλιλαίας. 27 ἐξελθόντι.δὲ.αὐτῷ
which is over against Galilee. And on his having gone forth
ἐπὶ τὴν γῆν ὑπήντησεν αὐτῷ ἀνήρ τις ἐκ τῆς πόλεως,
upon the land met him a man certain out of the city,
ὃς εἶχεν δαιμόνια ἐκ χρόνων.ἱκανῶν, καὶ ἱμάτιον οὐκ
who had demons for a long time, and a garment not
ἐνεδιδύσκετο, καὶ ἐν οἰκίᾳ οὐκ.ἔμενεν, ἀλλ' ἐν τοῖς μνήμασιν.
was wearing, and in a house did not abide, but in the tombs.
28 ἰδὼν.δὲ τὸν Ἰησοῦν καὶ ἀνακράξας προσέπεσεν αὐτῷ,
But having seen Jesus and having cried out he fell down before him,
καὶ φωνῇ μεγάλῃ εἶπεν, Τί ἐμοὶ καὶ σοί, Ἰησοῦ, υἱὲ τοῦ
and with a voice loud said, What to me and to thee, Jesus, Son
θεοῦ τοῦ ὑψίστου; δέομαί σου μή με βασανίσῃς.
of God the Most High? I beseech of thee not me thou mayest torment.
29 Παρήγγελλεν.γὰρ τῷ πνεύματι τῷ ἀκαθάρτῳ ἐξελθεῖν
For he was charging the spirit the unclean to come out
ἀπὸ τοῦ ἀνθρώπου· πολλοῖς.γὰρ χρόνοις συνηρπάκει αὐτόν,
from the man. For many times it had seized him;
καὶ ἐδεσμεῖτο, ἁλύσεσιν καὶ πέδαις φυλασσόμενος, καὶ διαρ-
and he was bound, with chains and fetters being kept, and break-
ρήσσων τὰ δεσμὰ ἠλαύνετο ὑπὸ τοῦ δαίμονος εἰς τὰς
ing the bonds he was driven by the demon into the
ἐρήμους. 30 ἐπηρώτησεν.δὲ αὐτὸν ὁ Ἰησοῦς, λέγων, Τί σοι
desert. And asked him Jesus, saying, What thy

who in an honest and good heart hear the
word and keep it - and bear fruit with
patience.
16 And no one who is lighting a lamp covers
it with a vessel or puts it under a bed. But he
puts it on a lampstand so that they who enter
may see the light.
17 For nothing is hidden which shall not be
uncovered, nor secret which shall not be
known and come to light.
18 Be careful then, how you hear. For
whoever may have, *more* shall be given to him.
And whoever may not have, even what he
seems to have shall be taken from him.
19 And His mother and His brothers came to
Him and were not able to get to Him because
of the crowd.
20 And He was told that His mother and His
brothers were standing outside, desiring to see
Him.
21 And answering He said to them, My
mother and My brothers are those who are
hearing the word of God and doing it.

22 And on a certain day He and His disciples
entered a ship. And He said to them, Let us go
over to the other side of the lake. And they
shoved off from shore.
23 And as they sailed, He fell asleep. And a
storm of wind came down on the lake. And
they were being flooded and were in danger.
24 And coming to Him, they awakened Him,
saying, Master! Master! We are sinking! And
He arose and stopped the wind and the raging
of the water. And they ceased, and there was a
calm.
25 And He said to them, Where is your faith?
And they wondered, being afraid, saying to
one another, Who then is this, that He
commands even the winds and the water and
they obey Him?

26 And they sailed down to the country of
the Gad-a-renes, which is across from Galilee
27 – and as He went out on the land, a
certain man out of the city met Him (one who
had demons for a long time, and who was
wearing no clothes, and who was not living in
a house, but in the tombs).
28 And seeing Jesus, and crying out, he fell
down before Him. And with a loud voice *he*
cried, What do I have to do with You, Jesus,
Son of the most high God? I beg You, do not
torment me.
29 For He was commanding the evil spirit
to come out of the man. For it had often
seized him. And he had been guarded, being
kept with chains and iron bands, but he broke
the bonds and was driven by the demon into
the deserted places.
30 And Jesus asked him, saying, What is your

kἐστὶν ὄνομα"; Ὁ.δὲ εἶπεν, lΛεγεών·" ὅτι mδαιμόνια πολλὰ
'is name? And he said, Legion, because demons many
εἰσῆλθεν" εἰς αὐτόν. 31 καὶ nπαρεκάλει" αὐτὸν ἵνα μὴ ἐπι-
had entered into him. And he besought him that ³not ¹he ²would
τάξῃ αὐτοῖς εἰς τὴν ἄβυσσον ἀπελθεῖν. 32 ἦν.δὲ ἐκεῖ
command them into the abyss to go away. Now there was there
ἀγέλη χοίρων ἱκανῶν oβοσκομένων' ἐν τῷ ὄρει· καὶ pπαρε-
a herd of ²swine ¹many feeding in the mountain, and they be-
κάλουν' αὐτὸν ἵνα ἐπιτρέψῃ αὐτοῖς εἰς ἐκείνους εἰσελθεῖν.
sought him that he would allow them into those to enter;
καὶ ἐπέτρεψεν αὐτοῖς. 33 ἐξελθόντα.δὲ τὰ δαιμόνια ἀπὸ τοῦ
and he allowed them. And having gone out the demons from the
ἀνθρώπου qεἰσῆλθεν" εἰς τοὺς χοίρους· καὶ ὥρμησεν ἡ ἀγέλη
man they entered into the swine, and ³rushed ¹the ²herd
κατὰ τοῦ κρημνοῦ εἰς τὴν λίμνην, καὶ ἀπεπνίγη 34 ἰδόντες.δὲ
down the steep into the lake, and were choked. And ⁵having ⁶seen
οἱ βόσκοντες τὸ rγεγενημένον" ἔφυγον, καὶ sἀπελ-
¹those ²who ³fed [⁴them] what had taken place fled, and having
θόντες" ἀπήγγειλαν εἰς τὴν πόλιν καὶ εἰς τοὺς ἀγρούς.
gone away related [it] to the city and to the country.
35 ἐξῆλθον.δὲ ἰδεῖν τὸ γεγονός· καὶ tἦλθον' πρὸς τὸν
And they went out to see what had taken place, and came to
Ἰησοῦν, καὶ vεὗρον' καθήμενον τὸν ἄνθρωπον ἀφ' οὗ τὰ
Jesus, and found seated the man from whom the
δαιμόνια wἐξεληλύθει," ἱματισμένον καὶ σωφρονοῦντα, παρὰ
demons had gone out, clothed and of sound mind, at
τοὺς πόδας τοῦ Ἰησοῦ. καὶ ἐφοβήθησαν. 36 ἀπήγγειλαν.δὲ
the feet of Jesus. And they were afraid. And ⁷related
αὐτοῖς xκαὶ" οἱ ἰδόντες πῶς ἐσώθη ὁ δαι-
⁸to ⁹them ²also ¹those ³who ⁴had ⁵seen [⁶it] how was healed he who had been pos-
μονισθείς. 37 καὶ yἠρώτησαν" αὐτὸν ἅπαν τὸ πλῆθος τῆς
sessed by demons. And asked him all the multitude of the
περιχώρου τῶν zΓαδαρηνῶν" ἀπελθεῖν ἀπ' αὐτῶν, ὅτι φόβῳ
country around of the Gadarenes to depart from them, for with ²fear
μεγάλῳ συνείχοντο· αὐτὸς.δὲ ἐμβὰς εἰς aτὸ" πλοῖον
¹great they were possessed. And he having entered into the ship
ὑπέστρεψεν. 38 bἐδέετο".δὲ αὐτοῦ ὁ ἀνὴρ ἀφ' οὗ ἐξελη-
returned. And ⁹was ¹⁰begging ¹¹him ¹the ²man ³from ⁴whom ⁵had
λύθει τὰ δαιμόνια εἶναι σὺν αὐτῷ. ἀπέλυσεν.δὲ αὐτὸν
⁶gone ⁷the ⁸demons to be [taken] with him. But ²sent ⁴away ³him
cὁ Ἰησοῦς," λέγων, 39 Ὑπόστρεφε εἰς τὸν.οἶκόν.σου καὶ διηγοῦ
¹Jesus, saying, Return to thy house and relate
ὅσα dἐποίησέν σοι" ὁ θεός. Καὶ ἀπῆλθεν, καθ' ὅλην τὴν
all that ²has ³done ⁴for ⁵thee ¹God. And he departed, through ²whole ¹the
πόλιν κηρύσσων ὅσα ἐποίησεν αὐτῷ ὁ Ἰησοῦς.
city proclaiming all that ²had ³done ⁴for ⁵him ¹Jesus.

40 eἘγένετο δὲ ἐν" τῷ fὑποστρέψαι" τὸν Ἰησοῦν ἀπ-
²It ³came ⁴to ⁵pass ¹and ⁶on ⁸returning ⁷Jesus, gladly
εδέξατο αὐτὸν ὁ ὄχλος· ἦσαν.γὰρ πάντες προσδοκῶντες
received him the crowd, for they were all looking for
αὐτόν. 41 Καὶ ἰδού, ἦλθεν ἀνὴρ ᾧ ὄνομα Ἰάειρος, καὶ
him. And behold, ³came ¹a ²man whose name [was] Jairus, and
gαὐτὸς" ἄρχων τῆς συναγωγῆς ὑπῆρχεν, καὶ πεσὼν παρὰ
he a ruler of the synagogue was, and having fallen at
τοὺς πόδας hτοῦ' Ἰησοῦ παρεκάλει αὐτὸν εἰσελθεῖν εἰς τὸν
the feet of Jesus he besought him to come to
οἶκον.αὐτοῦ· 42 ὅτι θυγάτηρ μονογενὴς ἦν αὐτῷ ὡς ἐτῶν
his house, because ³daughter ¹an ²only was to him, about ²years
δώδεκα, καὶ αὕτη ἀπέθνησκεν. iἘν.δὲ.τῷ.ὑπάγειν αὐτὸν"
[³old] ¹twelve, and she was dying. And as ²went ¹he
οἱ ὄχλοι συνέπνιγον αὐτόν. 43 Καὶ γυνὴ οὖσα ἐν ῥύσει
the crowds thronged him. And a woman being with a flux
αἵματος ἀπὸ ἐτῶν δώδεκα, ἥτις kεἰς ἰατροὺς" προσαναλώσασα
of blood since ²years ¹twelve, who on physicians having spent
ὅλον τὸν βίον l οὐκ ἴσχυσεν mὑπ'" οὐδενὸς θεραπευθῆναι,
²whole ³living [¹her] could by no one be cured,
44 προσελθοῦσα ὄπισθεν ἥψατο τοῦ κρασπέδου τοῦ ἱματίου
having come behind touched the border of ²garment
αὐτοῦ, καὶ παραχρῆμα ἔστη ἡ ῥύσις τοῦ.αἵματος.αὐτῆς.
¹his, and immediately stopped the flux of her blood.
45 καὶ εἶπεν ὁ Ἰησοῦς, Τίς ὁ ἁψάμενός μου; Ἀρνου-
And ²said ¹Jesus, Who [is it] that was touching me? ³Deny-
μένων δὲ πάντων, εἶπεν ὁ Πέτρος καὶ οἱ nμετ' αὐτοῦ," Ἐπι-
ing ¹and ²all, ⁵said ⁴Peter ⁶and ⁶those ⁷with ⁸him, Mas-
στάτα, οἱ ὄχλοι συνέχουσίν σε καὶ ἀποθλίβουσιν, oκαὶ λέγεις,
ter, the crowds throng thee and press, and sayest thou,
Τίς ὁ ἁψάμενός μου;" 46 Ὁ.δὲ.Ἰησοῦς εἶπεν, "Ἥψατό
Who [is it] that was touching me? And Jesus said, ³Touched
μου τίς· ἐγὼ.γὰρ ἔγνων δύναμιν pἐξελθοῦσαν" ἀπ'
⁴me ¹some ²one, for I knew [that] power went out from
μοῦ. 47 Ἰδοῦσα.δὲ ἡ γυνὴ ὅτι οὐκ.ἔλαθεν, τρέμουσα ἦλ-
me. And ³seeing ¹the ²woman that she was not hid, trembling she

name? And he said, Legion (because many demons had entered into him).

31 And they begged Him that He would not command them to go away into the bottomless pit.

32 Now there was there a herd of many pigs feeding in the mountains. And they begged Him that He would allow them to go into those. And He allowed them.

33 And having left the man, the demons entered into the pigs. And the herd ran violently down the steep bank into the lake and were drowned.

34 And seeing what had happened, those who fed them fled. And going to the city and to the countryside, they reported it.

35 And they went out to see what had happened and came to Jesus. And *they* found the man from whom the demons had gone out, sitting and clothed and of sound mind, at the feet of Jesus. And they were afraid.

36 And also those who had seen it told them how he who had been demon-possessed was healed.

37 And the whole multitude of the country of the Gad-a-renes all around begged Him to go away from them – for they were filled with great fear. And He entered into the ship and returned.

38 And the man from whom the demons had gone out was begging Him to be with Him. But Jesus sent him away, saying,

39 Return to your house and tell all that God has done for you. And he went his way, telling all that Jesus had done throughout the whole city.

40 And when Jesus had returned, it happened that the people gladly received Him – for they were all looking for Him.

41 And, behold! A man named Ja-i-rus came. And he was a ruler of the synagogue. And falling down at the feet of Jesus, he begged Him to come to his house,

42 because he had an only daughter about twelve years old, and she was dying. And as He went, the people thronged Him.

43 And a woman *came who* had been *sick* with a flow of blood *for* twelve years, *and* she had spent her whole living on physicians, *but* could be cured by none.

44 Coming up behind, she touched the border of His robe. And instantly her flow of blood was stopped!

45 And Jesus said, Who was that touching Me? And when all denied, Peter and those with Him said, Master, the crowds throng and press upon You, and do You say, Who was that touching Me?

46 And Jesus said, Someone has touched Me, for I realized that power went forth from Me.

47 And seeing that she was not hidden, the woman came up, trembling. And falling down

θεν, καὶ προσπεσοῦσα αὐτῷ,ˋ δι' ἣν αἰτίαν ἥψατο
came, and having fallen down before him, for what cause she touched
αὐτοῦ ἀπήγγειλεν ᵠαὐτῷˡ ἐνώπιον παντὸς τοῦ λαοῦ, καὶ ὡς
him she declared to him before all the people, and how
ἰάθη παραχρῆμα. 48 ὁ.δὲ εἶπεν αὐτῇ, ʳΘάρσει,ˡˡ
she was healed immediately. And he said to her, Be of good courage,
ˢθύγατερ,ˡˡ ἡ.πίστις.σου σέσωκέν σε· πορεύου εἰς εἰρήνην.
daughter, thy faith has cured thee: go in peace.
49 ᵗἜτι.αὐτοῦ.λαλοῦντος ἔρχεταί τις ᵘπαρὰˡˡ τοῦ ἀρχισυναγώ-
As yet he was speaking comes one from the ruler of the syna-
γου, λέγων ᵛαὐτῷ,ˡˡ ῞Οτι τέθνηκεν ἡ.θυγάτηρ.σου· ʷμὴˡ σκύλλε
gogue, saying to him, ³Has ⁴died ¹thy ²daughter; ⁶not ⁵trouble
τὸν διδάσκαλον. 50 Ὁ.δὲ.Ἰησοῦς ἀκούσας ἀπεκρίθη αὐτῷ,
the teacher. But Jesus having heard answered him,
ˣλέγων,ˡˡ Μὴ.φοβοῦ· μόνον ʸπίστευε.ˡˡ καὶ σωθήσεται.
saying, Fear not; only believe, and she shall be restored.
51 ᶻΕἰσελθὼνˡˡ.δὲ εἰς τὴν οἰκίαν οὐκ.ἀφῆκεν εἰσελθεῖν ᵃοὐδέναˡˡ
And having entered into the house he did not suffer ³to ⁴go ⁵in ¹any ²one (lit. no one)
εἰ.μὴ Πέτρον καὶ ᵇἸάκωβον καὶ Ἰωάννην,ˡˡ καὶ τὸν πατέρα
except Peter and James and John, and the father
τῆς παιδὸς καὶ τὴν μητέρα. 52 ἔκλαιον.δὲ πάντες καὶ
of the child and the mother. And they were ²weeping ¹all and
ἐκόπτοντο αὐτήν. ὁ.δὲ εἶπεν, Μὴ.κλαίετε· ᶜοὐκˡˡ.ἀπέθανεν,
bewailing her. But he said, Weep not; she is not dead,
ἀλλὰ καθεύδει. 53 Καὶ κατεγέλων αὐτοῦ, εἰδότες ὅτι ἀπέ-
but sleeps. And they laughed at him, knowing that she was
θανεν. 54 αὐτὸς.δὲ ᵈἐκβαλὼν ἔξω πάντας, καὶˡ κρατήσας
dead. But he having put out all, and having taken hold
τῆς.χειρὸς.αὐτῆς, ἐφώνησεν, λέγων, Ἡ παῖς, ᵉἐγείρου.ˡ 55 Καὶ
of her hand, cried, saying, Child, arise. And
ἐπέστρεψεν τὸ.πνεῦμα.αὐτῆς, καὶ ἀνέστη παραχρῆμα· καὶ
³returned ¹her ²spirit, and she arose immediately; and
διέταξεν αὐτῇˋ δοθῆναι φαγεῖν. 56 καὶ
he directed [that] ⁵to ⁶her [¹something] ²should ³be ⁴given to eat. And
ἐξέστησαν οἱ.γονεῖς.αὐτῆς· ὁ.δὲ παρήγγειλεν αὐτοῖς μηδενὶ
³were ⁴amazed ¹her ²parents; and he charged them to no one
εἰπεῖν τὸ γεγονός.
to tell what had happened.

9 ᶠΣυγκαλεσάμενοςˡˡ.δὲ τοὺς δώδεκα ᵍμαθητὰς αὐτοῦˡˡ ἔδωκεν
And having called together the twelve disciples of him he gave
αὐτοῖς δύναμιν καὶ ἐξουσίαν ἐπὶ πάντα τὰ δαιμόνια, καὶ
to them power and authority over all the demons, and
νόσους θεραπεύειν· 2 καὶ ἀπέστειλεν αὐτοὺς κηρύσσειν τὴν
diseases to heal, and sent them to proclaim the
βασιλείαν τοῦ θεοῦ, καὶ ἰᾶσθαι ʰτοὺς ἀσθενοῦντας.ˡˡ 3 καὶ
kingdom of God, and to heal those being sick. And
εἶπεν πρὸς αὐτούς, Μηδὲν αἴρετε εἰς τὴν ὁδόν· μήτε ⁱῥάβδους,ˡˡ
he said to them, Nothing take for the way; neither staves,
μήτε πήραν, μήτε ἄρτον, μήτε ἀργύριον, μήτε ᵏἀνὰˡˡ δύο
nor provision bag, nor bread, nor money, nor each two
χιτῶνας ἔχειν. 4 καὶ εἰς ἣν.ἂν οἰκίαν εἰσέλθητε, ἐκεῖ μένετε,
tunics to have. And into whatever house ye may enter, there remain,
καὶ ἐκεῖθεν ἐξέρχεσθε. 5 καὶ ὅσοι ἂν μὴ.ˡδέξωνταιˡˡ ὑμᾶς,
and thence go forth. And as many as may not receive you,
ἐξερχόμενοι ἀπὸ τῆς.πόλεως.ἐκείνης ᵐκαὶˡˡ τὸν κονιορτὸν ἀπὸ
going forth from that city even the dust from
τῶν.ποδῶν.ὑμῶν ⁿἀποτινάξατε,ˡˡ εἰς μαρτύριον ἐπ' αὐτούς.
your feet shake off, for a testimony against them.
6 Ἐξερχόμενοι.δὲ διήρχοντο κατὰ τὰς κώμας, εὐαγγελιζό-
And going forth they passed through the villages, announcing the
μενοι καὶ θεραπεύοντες πανταχοῦ.
glad tidings and healing everywhere.
7 Ἤκουσεν.δὲ Ἡρώδης ὁ ᵒτετράρχηςˡˡ τὰ γινόμενα
And ⁴heard ⁵of ¹Herod ²the ³tetrarch ⁷the ⁸things ⁹being ¹⁰done
ᵖὑπ' αὐτοῦˡˡ πάντα· καὶ διηπόρει, διὰ τὸ λέγεσθαι ὑπό
¹¹by ¹²him ⁶all, and was perplexed, because it was said by
τινων, ῞Οτι ᵠἸωάννηςˡˡ ʳἐγήγερταιˡˡ ἐκ νεκρῶν·
some, John has been raised from among [the] dead;
8 ὑπό τινων δέ, ῞Οτι ˢἩλίαςˡˡ ἐφάνη· ἄλλων δέ, ῞Οτι
by some also, that Elias had appeared; by others also, that
προφήτης ᵗεἷςˡˡ τῶν ἀρχαίων ἀνέστη. 9 ᵛΚαὶ εἶπενˡ ʷὁˡ
a prophet one of the ancients had arisen. And ²said
Ἡρώδης, ˣἸωάννηνˡ ἐγὼ ἀπεκεφάλισα· τίς.δέ ἐστιν οὗτος
¹Herod, John I beheaded, but who is this
περὶ οὗ ʸἐγὼˡ ἀκούω τοιαῦτα; Καὶ ἐζήτει ἰδεῖν αὐτόν.
concerning whom I hear such things? And he sought to see him.
10 Καὶ ὑποστρέψαντες οἱ ἀπόστολοι διηγήσαντο αὐτῷ
And ³having ⁴returned ¹the ²apostles related to him
ὅσα ἐποίησαν· καὶ παραλαβὼν αὐτοὺς ὑπεχώρησεν
whatsoever they had done. And having taken them he retired
κατ'.ἰδίαν εἰς ᶻτόπον ἔρημον πόλεως καλουμένηςˡˡ Βηθσαϊδά.
apart into a ²place ¹desert of a city called Bethsaida.

before Him, she told Him before all the people for what reason she had touched Him, and how she was healed instantly.

48 And He said to her, Daughter, be comforted, your faith has cured you. Go in peace.

49 While He was still speaking, one came from *the house of* the ruler of the synagogue and said to him, Your daughter has died. Do not trouble the Master.

50 But Jesus heard and answered him, saying, Do not fear, only believe and she shall be restored.

51 And going into the house, He allowed no one to go in except Peter and James and John, and the father and the mother of the child.

52 And they were all weeping and beating the breast for her. But He said, Do not weep, she is not dead, but is sleeping.

53 And they laughed scornfully at Him, knowing that she was dead.

54 But putting them all out, and taking her hand, He called, saying, Child, arise!

55 And her spirit came again. And she immediately got up. And He commanded that *something* should be given her to eat.

56 And her parents were amazed, but He commanded them that they should tell no one what had happened.

CHAPTER 9

1 And calling His disciples together, He gave to them power and authority over all the demons, and to heal diseases.

2 And *He* sent them to preach the kingdom of God, and to heal those who were sick.

3 And He said to them, Take nothing for the highway, no walking sticks, no bag, no bread, no money, and do not have two coats apiece.

4 And into whatever house you go, stay there, and depart from there.

5 And as many as may not receive you, *as you are* going forth from that city, even the dust of your feet shake off for a witness against them.

6 And they went out through the towns, preaching the gospel and healing everywhere.

7 And Herod the tetrarch heard of all the things being done by Him and was puzzled, because it was said by certain ones, John has been raised from the dead.

8 And certain ones *said* that Elijah had appeared, others also that a prophet, one of the ancients, had arisen.

9 And Herod said, I beheaded John, but who is this of whom I hear such things? And he desired to see Him.

10 And the apostles returned and told Him all that they had done. And taking them along, He drew them aside into a deserted place of a city called Beth-sa-i-da.

11 οἱ.δὲ ὄχλοι γνόντες ἠκολούθησαν αὐτῷ· καὶ [a]δεξά-
But the crowds having known [it] followed him; and having
μενος" αὐτοὺς ἐλάλει αὐτοῖς περὶ τῆς βασιλείας τοῦ θεοῦ,
received them he spoke to them concerning the kingdom of God,
καὶ τοὺς χρείαν ἔχοντας θεραπείας ἰᾶτο. 12 Ἡ.δὲ ἡμέρα
and those [2]need [1]having of healing he cured. But the day
ἤρξατο κλίνειν· προσελθόντες.δὲ οἱ δώδεκα εἶπον αὐτῷ, Ἀπό-
began to decline, and having come the twelve said to him, Dis-
λυσον τὸν ὄχλον, ἵνα [b]ἀπελθόντες" εἰς τὰς κύκλῳ κώμας καὶ
miss the crowd, that having gone into the [2]around [1]villages and
[c]τοὺς" ἀγροὺς καταλύσωσιν, καὶ εὕρωσιν ἐπισιτισμόν· ὅτι ὧδε
the country they may lodge, and may find provisions; for here
ἐν ἐρήμῳ τόπῳ ἐσμέν. 13 Εἶπεν.δὲ πρὸς αὐτούς, Δότε αὐτοῖς
in [2]desert [1]a place we are. But he said to them, Give [2]to [3]them
[d]ὑμεῖς φαγεῖν." Οἱ.δὲ [e]εἶπον," Οὐκ.εἰσὶν ἡμῖν πλεῖον ἢ
[1]ye to eat. But they said, There are not to us more than
[f]πέντε ἄρτοι" καὶ [g]δύο ἰχθύες," εἰ.[h]μήτι" πορευθέντες ἡμεῖς
five loaves and two fishes, unless indeed having gone we
ἀγοράσωμεν εἰς πάντα τὸν.λαὸν.τοῦτον βρώματα. 14 [i]Ἦσαν
should buy for all this people victuals; [2]they [3]were
γὰρ" ὡσεὶ ἄνδρες πεντακισχίλιοι. Εἶπεν.δὲ πρὸς τοὺς μαθητὰς
[1]for about [3]men [1]five [2]thousand. But he said to [2]disciples
αὐτοῦ, Κατακλίνατε αὐτοὺς κλισίας [k] ἀνὰ πεντήκοντα. 15 Καὶ
[1]his, Make [2]recline [1]them in companies by fifties. And
ἐποίησαν οὕτως, καὶ [l]ἀνέκλιναν" ἅπαντας. 16 Λαβὼν.δὲ
they did so, and made [2]recline [1]all. And having taken
τοὺς πέντε ἄρτους καὶ τοὺς δύο ἰχθύας, ἀναβλέψας εἰς τὸν
the five loaves and the two fishes, having looked up to the
οὐρανὸν εὐλόγησεν αὐτοὺς καὶ κατέκλασεν, καὶ ἐδίδου τοῖς
heaven he blessed them and broke, and gave to the
μαθηταῖς [m]παρατιθέναι" τῷ ὄχλῳ. 17 καὶ ἔφαγον καὶ ἐχορ-
disciples to set before the crowd. And they ate and were
τάσθησαν πάντες· καὶ ἤρθη τὸ περισσεῦσαν αὐτοῖς
[2]satisfied [1]all; and was taken up that which was over and above to them
κλασμάτων κόφινοι δώδεκα.
of fragments [2]hand-[3]baskets [1]twelve.

18 Καὶ ἐγένετο ἐν.τῷ.εἶναι αὐτὸν προσευχόμενον [n]κατα-
And it came to pass as [2]was [1]he praying a-
μόνας," συνῆσαν αὐτῷ οἱ μαθηταί· καὶ ἐπηρώτησεν αὐτούς,
lone, [3]were [4]with [5]him [1]the [2]disciples, and he questioned them,
λέγων, Τίνα με [o]λέγουσιν οἱ ὄχλοι" εἶναι; 19 Οἱ.δὲ ἀπο-
saying, Whom [5]me [1]do [4]pronounce [2]the [3]crowds to be? And they an-
κριθέντες [p]εἶπον," [q]Ἰωάννην" τὸν βαπτιστήν· ἄλλοι.δὲ
swering said, John the Baptist; and others,
[r]Ἠλίαν·" ἄλλοι.δέ, ὅτι προφήτης τις τῶν ἀρχαίων ἀνέστη.
Elias; and others, that [2]prophet [1]some of the ancients has arisen.
20 Εἶπεν.δὲ αὐτοῖς, Ὑμεῖς.δὲ τίνα με λέγετε εἶναι;
And he said to them, But ye whom [4]me [1]do [2]ye [3]pronounce to be?
[s]Ἀποκριθεὶς.δὲ ὁ Πέτρος" εἶπεν, Τὸν χριστὸν τοῦ θεοῦ. 21 Ὁ.δὲ
And answering Peter said, The Christ of God. And he
ἐπιτιμήσας αὐτοῖς παρήγγειλεν μηδενὶ [t]εἰπεῖν" τοῦτο,
strictly enjoining them charged [them] to no one to tell this,
22 εἰπών, Ὅτι δεῖ τὸν υἱὸν τοῦ ἀνθρώπου πολλὰ
saying, It is necessary for the Son of man many things
παθεῖν, καὶ ἀποδοκιμασθῆναι ἀπὸ τῶν πρεσβυτέρων καὶ ἀρχ-
to suffer, and to be rejected by the elders and chief
ιερέων καὶ γραμματέων, καὶ ἀποκτανθῆναι, καὶ τῇ τρίτῃ
priests and scribes, and to be killed, and the third
ἡμέρᾳ [u]ἐγερθῆναι." 23 [v]Ἔλεγεν.δὲ πρὸς πάντας, Εἴ τις θέλει
day to be raised. And he said to all, If any one desires
ὀπίσω μου [w]ἐλθεῖν, ἀπαρνησάσθω" ἑαυτόν, καὶ ἀράτω
after me to come, let him deny himself, and let him take up
τὸν.σταυρὸν.αὐτοῦ [x]καθ'.ἡμέραν," καὶ ἀκολουθείτω μοι.
his cross daily, and let him follow me;
24 ὃς.γὰρ.[y]ἂν" θέλῃ τὴν.ψυχὴν.αὐτοῦ σῶσαι, ἀπολέσει αὐ-
for whoever may desire his life to save, shall lose it,
τήν· ὃς.δ'.ἂν ἀπολέσῃ τὴν.ψυχὴν.αὐτοῦ ἕνεκεν ἐμοῦ, οὗτος
but whoever may lose his life on account of me, he
σώσει αὐτήν. 25 τί.γὰρ ὠφελεῖται ἄνθρωπος, κερδήσας
shall save it. For what is [3]profited [1]a [2]man, having gained
τὸν κόσμον ὅλον, ἑαυτὸν.δὲ ἀπολέσας ἢ ζημιωθείς;
the [2]world [1]whole, but himself having destroyed or suffered the loss of?
26 ὃς.γὰρ.ἂν ἐπαισχυνθῇ με καὶ τοὺς ἐμοὺς λόγους,
For whoever may have been ashamed of me and my words,
τοῦτον ὁ υἱὸς τοῦ ἀνθρώπου ἐπαισχυνθήσεται ὅταν ἔλθῃ
him the Son of man will be ashamed of when he shall come
ἐν τῇ δόξῃ αὐτοῦ καὶ τοῦ πατρὸς καὶ τῶν ἁγίων ἀγγέλων.
in the glory of himself and of the Father and of the holy angels.
27 Λέγω.δὲ ὑμῖν ἀληθῶς, εἰσίν τινες τῶν [z]ὧδε" [a]ἑστηκό-
But I say to you of a truth, there are some of those here stand-
των," οἳ οὐ.μὴ [b]γεύσονται" θανάτου ἕως.ἂν ἴδωσιν
ing who in no wise shall taste of death until they shall have seen

11 But knowing it, the people followed Him. And receiving them, He spoke to them about the kingdom of God. And those who needed healing He cured.

12 But the day began to wane. And the twelve came near and said to Him, Turn the crowd loose so that they may go into the towns and the country around here, so that they may lodge and find food. For here we are in a deserted place.

13 But He said to them, You provide them food. But they said, We have no more than five loaves and two fish, unless we should go to buy food for all this people.

14 For they were about five thousand men. But He said to His disciples, Make them rest in companies of fifties.

15 And they did so, making all to rest.

16 And taking the five loaves and the two fish, looking up into Heaven, He blessed them and broke and gave to the disciples to set before the crowd.

17 And they ate and were all satisfied. And that which was taken up of the pieces that were left over and above to them was twelve baskets *full.*

18 And as He was alone praying, the disciples were with Him. And He questioned them, saying, Who do the people say that I am?

19 And answering they said, John the Baptist, but others say, Elijah, and others that some prophet of the ancients has risen.

20 And He said to them, But who do you say that I am? And answering Peter said, The Christ of God.

21 And strictly warning them, He commanded *them* to tell no one of this,

22 saying, The Son of man must suffer many things and is to be rejected by the elders and chief priests and scribes. And *He is* to be killed and to be raised the third day.

23 And He said to all, If anyone desires to come after Me, let him deny himself, and let him take up his cross day by day. And let him follow Me.

24 For whoever desires to save his life shall lose it. But whoever may lose his life for My sake, he shall save it.

25 For what is man profited who has gained the whole world, but who has destroyed or lost himself?

26 For whoever may have been ashamed of Me and My words, the Son of man will be ashamed of him when He shall come in His own glory, and *in His* Father's *glory,* and of the holy angels.

27 But I say to you, there truly are some of those standing here who shall not taste of death until they have seen the kingdom of

τὴν βασιλείαν τοῦ θεοῦ.
the kingdom of God.

28 Ἐγένετο.δὲ μετὰ τοὺς.λόγους.τούτους ὡσεὶ ἡμέραι ὀκτὼ
And it came to pass after these words about [2]days [1]eight
[c]καὶ[1] παραλαβὼν [d]τὸν[1] Πέτρον καὶ [e]Ἰωάννην‖ καὶ Ἰάκωβον
that having taken Peter and John and James
ἀνέβη εἰς τὸ ὄρος προσεύξασθαι. 29 καὶ ἐγένετο
he went up into the mountain to pray. And it came to pass
ἐν.τῷ προσεύχεσθαι αὐτὸν τὸ εἶδος τοῦ.προσώπου.αὐτοῦ
as [2]prayed [1]he the appearance of his face
ἕτερον, καὶ ὁ.ἱματισμὸς.αὐτοῦ λευκὸς ἐξαστράπτων.
[became] altered, and his clothing white effulgent.
30 Καὶ ἰδού, ἄνδρες δύο συνελάλουν αὐτῷ, οἵτινες ἦσαν
And behold, [2]men [1]two talked with him, who were
[f]Μωσῆς[1] καὶ [g]Ἠλίας‖ 31 οἳ ὀφθέντες ἐν δόξῃ ἔλεγον[h] τὴν
Moses and Elias, who appearing in glory spoke of
ἔξοδον.αὐτοῦ ἣν [i]ἔμελλεν‖ πληροῦν ἐν Ἱερουσαλήμ.
his departure which he was about to accomplish in Jerusalem.
32 ὁ.δὲ.Πέτρος καὶ οἱ σὺν αὐτῷ ἦσαν βεβαρημένοι ὕπνῳ.
But Peter and those with him were oppressed with sleep.
διαγρηγορήσαντες.δὲ [k]εἶδον[1] τὴν.δόξαν.αὐτοῦ, καὶ τοὺς δύο
and having awoke fully they saw his glory, and the two
ἄνδρας τοὺς συνεστῶτας αὐτῷ. 33 καὶ ἐγένετο ἐν.τῷ.δια-
men who stood with him. And it came to pass as [2]de-
χωρίζεσθαι αὐτοὺς ἀπ' αὐτοῦ, εἶπεν ὁ Πέτρος πρὸς τὸν
parted [1]these from him, [2]said [1]Peter to
Ἰησοῦν, Ἐπιστάτα, καλόν ἐστιν ἡμᾶς ὧδε εἶναι· καὶ ποιήσωμεν
Jesus, Master, good it is for us here to be; and let us make
σκηνὰς τρεῖς, μίαν σοί, καὶ [l]Μωσεῖ μίαν,‖ καὶ μίαν
[2]tabernacles [1]three, one for thee, and for Moses one, and one
[m]Ἠλίᾳ,‖ μὴ εἰδὼς ὃ λέγει. 34 ταῦτα.δὲ αὐτοῦ.λέγοντος
for Elias, not knowing what he is saying. But these things as he was saying
ἐγένετο νεφέλη καὶ [n]ἐπεσκίασεν‖ αὐτούς· ἐφοβήθησαν.δὲ ἐν.τῷ
[3]came [1]a [2]cloud and overshadowed them, and they feared as
[o]ἐκείνους εἰσελθεῖν‖ εἰς τὴν νεφέλην. 35 καὶ φωνὴ ἐγένετο ἐκ
those entered into the cloud: and a voice came out of
τῆς νεφέλης, λέγουσα, Οὗτός ἐστιν ὁ.υἱός.μου ὁ [p]ἀγαπητός·‖
the cloud, saying, This is my Son the beloved;
αὐτοῦ ἀκούετε. 36 Καὶ ἐν.τῷ γενέσθαι τὴν φωνὴν εὑρέθη
[3]him [1]hear [2]ye. And as occurred the voice [2]was [3]found
[q]ὁ‖ Ἰησοῦς μόνος. Καὶ αὐτοὶ ἐσίγησαν, καὶ οὐδενὶ ἀπήγγειλαν
[1]Jesus alone: and they were silent, and to no one they told
ἐν ἐκείναις ταῖς ἡμέραις οὐδὲν ὧν [r]ἑωράκασιν.‖
in those days anything of what they had seen.

God.
[28]And about eight days after these words,
He took Peter and John and James and went
up into a mountain to pray.
[29]And as He prayed, the appearance of His
face changed, and His clothing was dazzling
white.
[30]And, behold! Two men talked with Him,
who were Moses and Elijah –
[31]who appearing in glory spoke of His
exodus, which He was about to complete in
Jerusalem.
[32]But Peter and those with him were heavy
with sleep. And when they were fully awake,
they saw His glory and the two men who
stood with Him.
[33]And as they were leaving Him, Peter said
to Jesus, Master, it is good for us to be here.
And, Let us make three tabernacles, one for
You and one for Moses and one for Elijah –
not knowing what he was saying.
[34]But as he was saying these things, a cloud
came and overshadowed them. And they were
afraid as these men entered the cloud.
[35]And a voice came out of the cloud, saying,
This is My beloved Son, hear Him!
[36]And when the voice had faded away, Jesus
was seen to be alone. And they were silent.
And they did not tell anyone in those days,
not any of the things which they had seen.

37 Ἐγένετο.δὲ [s]ἐν‖ τῇ ἑξῆς ἡμέρᾳ, κατελθόντων.αὐτῶν
And it came to pass on the next day, on their having come down
ἀπὸ τοῦ ὄρους, συνήντησεν αὐτῷ ὄχλος πολύς. 38 Καὶ
from the mountain, [4]met [5]him [1]a [3]crowd [2]great. And
ἰδού, ἀνὴρ ἀπὸ τοῦ ὄχλου [t]ἀνεβόησεν,‖ λέγων, Διδάσκαλε,
behold, a man from the crowd cried out, saying, Teacher,
δέομαί σου [v]ἐπίβλεψον‖ ἐπὶ τὸν.υἱόν.μου, ὅτι μονογενής
I beseech thee look upon my son, for an only child
[w]ἐστίν μοι·‖ 39 καὶ ἰδού, πνεῦμα λαμβάνει αὐτὸν καὶ ἐξ-
he is to me: and behold, a spirit takes him and sud-
αίφνης κράζει, καὶ σπαράσσει αὐτὸν μετὰ ἀφροῦ,
denly he cries out, and it throws [2]into [3]convulsions [1]him with foaming,
καὶ μόγις ἀποχωρεῖ ἀπ' αὐτοῦ, συντρῖβον αὐτόν. 40 καὶ
and with difficulty departs from him, bruising him. And
ἐδεήθην τῶν.μαθητῶν.σου ἵνα [x]ἐκβάλλωσιν‖ αὐτό, καὶ οὐκ
I besought thy disciples that they might cast out it, and [3]not
ἠδυνήθησαν. 41 Ἀποκριθεὶς.δὲ ὁ Ἰησοῦς εἶπεν, Ὦ γενεὰ
[1]they [2]were able. And [2]answering [1]Jesus said, O generation
ἄπιστος καὶ διεστραμμένη, ἕως πότε ἔσομαι πρὸς ὑμᾶς καὶ
unbelieving and perverted, until when shall I be with you and
ἀνέξομαι ὑμῶν; προσάγαγε [y]ὧδε τὸν.υἱόν.σου.‖ 42 Ἔτι.δὲ
bear with you? Bring hither thy son. But [4]yet
προσερχομένου.αὐτοῦ ἔρρηξεν αὐτὸν τὸ δαιμόνιον καὶ συν-
[5]as [2]he [3]was coming near [8]dashed [9]down [7]him [1]the [2]demon and threw
εσπάραξεν· ἐπετίμησεν.δὲ ὁ Ἰησοῦς τῷ πνεύματι τῷ
[him] into convulsions. And rebuked [1]Jesus the spirit the
ἀκαθάρτῳ, καὶ ἰάσατο τὸν παῖδα, καὶ ἀπέδωκεν αὐτὸν τῷ
unclean, and healed the child, and gave back him to
πατρὶ.αὐτοῦ. 43 ἐξεπλήσσοντο.δὲ πάντες ἐπὶ τῇ μεγαλειότητι
his father. And [2]were [3]astonished [1]all at the majesty
τοῦ θεοῦ.
of God.

[37]And on the next day, on coming down
from the mountain, a great crowd met Him.
[38]And, behold! A man cried out of the
crowd, saying, Teacher, I beg You to look
upon my son, for he is an only child to me.
[39]And, behold! A spirit takes him and he
suddenly cries out. And it throws him into
convulsions with foaming, then painfully
leaves him, bruising him.
[40]And I pleaded with Your disciples that
they might throw it out, but they could not.
[41]And answering Jesus said, O faithless and
crooked generation, how long shall I be with
you and bear with you? Bring your son here.
[42]But as he was coming up, the demon
dashed him down and threw him into convulsions. And Jesus rebuked the evil spirit.
And He healed the child and gave him back to
his father again.
[43]And all were amazed at the majesty of
God.

Πάντων.δὲ θαυμαζόντων ἐπὶ πᾶσιν οἷς [z]ἐποίησεν‖ [a]ὁ Ἰη-
And [as] all were wondering at all which [2]did [1]Je-
σοῦς,[1] εἶπεν πρὸς τοὺς.μαθητὰς.αὐτοῦ, 44 Θέσθε ὑμεῖς εἰς τὰ
sus, he said to his disciples, Lay [2]by [1]ye into
ὦτα.ὑμῶν τοὺς.λόγους.τούτους· ὁ.γὰρ.υἱὸς τοῦ ἀνθρώπου μέλ-
your ears these words: For the Son of man is a-

And as all were wondering at all things
which Jesus did, He said to His disciples,
[44]Let these words sink into your ears, for
the Son of man is about to be betrayed into

λει παραδίδοσθαι εἰς χεῖρας ἀνθρώπων. 45 Οἱ.δὲ ἠγνόουν
bout to be delivered up into [the] hands of men. But they understood not

τὸ.ῥῆμα.τοῦτο, καὶ ἦν παρακεκαλυμμένον ἀπ' αὐτῶν ἵνα
this saying, and it was veiled from them that

μὴ.αἴσθωνται αὐτό· καὶ ἐφοβοῦντο [b]ἐρωτῆσαι" αὐτὸν
they should not perceive it. And they feared to ask him

περὶ τοῦ ῥήματος τούτου. 46 Εἰσῆλθεν.δὲ διαλογισμὸς ἐν
concerning [2]saying [1]this. But [3]came [4]up [1]a [2]reasoning among

αὐτοῖς, τό, τίς ἂν εἴη μείζων αὐτῶν. 47 ὁ.δὲ.Ἰησοῦς [c]ἰδὼν"
them, this, who might be greatest of them. And Jesus having seen

τὸν διαλογισμὸν τῆς.καρδίας.αὐτῶν, ἐπιλαβόμενος [d]παιδίου"
the reasoning of their heart, having taken hold of a little child

ἔστησεν αὐτὸ παρ' ἑαυτῷ, 48 καὶ εἶπεν αὐτοῖς, "Ος.[e]ἐὰν"
he set it by him, and said to them, Whoever

δέξηται τοῦτο τὸ παιδίον ἐπὶ τῷ.ὀνόματί.μου, ἐμὲ δέχεται·
shall receive this little child in my name, me receives;

καὶ ὃς.[f]ἐὰν" ἐμὲ δέξηται, δέχεται τὸν ἀποστείλαντά με.
and whoever me shall receive, receives him who sent me.

ὁ.γὰρ μικρότερος ἐν πᾶσιν ὑμῖν ὑπάρχων οὗτος [g]ἔσται"
For he who [2]less [3]among [5]all [4]you [1]is he shall be

μέγας. 49 Ἀποκριθεὶς.δὲ [h]ὁ" [i]Ἰωάννης" εἶπεν, Ἐπιστάτα,
great. And answering John said, Master,

εἴδομέν τινα ἐπὶ τῷ.ὀνόματί σου ἐκβάλλοντα [k]τὰ" δαιμόνια·
we saw some one in thy name casting out the demons,

καὶ ἐκωλύσαμεν αὐτόν, ὅτι οὐκ.ἀκολουθεῖ μεθ' ἡμῶν· 50 [l]Καὶ
and we forbade him, because he follows not with us. And

εἶπεν" πρὸς αὐτὸν [m]ὁ" Ἰησοῦς, Μὴ.κωλύετε· ὃς.γὰρ οὐκ
[2]said [3]to [4]him [1]Jesus, Forbid not; for whosoever [2]not

ἔστιν καθ' [n]ἡμῶν," ὑπὲρ [n]ἡμῶν" ἐστιν.
[1]is against us, for us is.

51 Ἐγένετο.δὲ ἐν.τῷ.συμπληροῦσθαι τὰς ἡμέρας τῆς
And it came to pass when were being fulfilled the days of the

[o]ἀναλήψεως[l].αὐτοῦ, καὶ αὐτὸς τὸ.πρόσωπον.[p]αὐτοῦ" [q]ἐστή-
receiving him up, that he his face sted-

ριξεν" τοῦ πορεύεσθαι εἰς Ἱερουσαλήμ. 52 καὶ ἀπέστειλεν
fastly set to go to Jerusalem. And he sent

ἀγγέλους πρὸ προσώπου αὐτοῦ. καὶ πορευθέντες εἰσῆλθον
messengers before [2]face [1]his. And having gone they entered

εἰς [r]κώμην Σαμαρειτῶν," ὥστε ἑτοιμάσαι αὐτῷ. 53 καὶ οὐκ
into a village of Samaritans, so as to make ready for him. And [3]not

ἐδέξαντο αὐτόν, ὅτι τὸ.πρόσωπον.αὐτοῦ ἦν πορευό-
[1]they [2]did receive him, because his face was [as] go-

μενον εἰς Ἱερουσαλήμ. 54 ἰδόντες.δὲ οἱ.μαθηταὶ.[s]αὐτοῦ"
ing to Jerusalem. And seeing [it] his disciples

Ἰάκωβος καὶ [t]Ἰωάννης" [w]εἶπον," Κύριε, θέλεις εἴπω-
James and John said, Lord, wilt thou [that] we should

μεν πῦρ καταβῆναι [x]ἀπὸ" τοῦ οὐρανοῦ, καὶ ἀναλῶσαι αὐτούς,
call fire to come down from the heaven, and consume them,

[y]ὡς καὶ Ἠλίας ἐποίησεν"; 55 Στραφεὶς.δὲ ἐπετίμησεν αὐτοῖς,
as also Elias did? But turning he rebuked them,

[z]καὶ εἶπεν, Οὐκ.οἴδατε οἵου πνεύματός ἐστε ὑμεῖς· 56 [z]ὁ.γὰρ
and said, Ye know not of what spirit [2]are [1]ye. For the

υἱὸς τοῦ ἀνθρώπου οὐκ.ἦλθεν ψυχὰς ἀνθρώπων ἀπολέσαι,
Son of man did not come [the] lives of men to destroy,

ἀλλὰ σῶσαι." Καὶ ἐπορεύθησαν εἰς ἑτέραν κώμην.
but to save. And they went to another village.

57 [a]Ἐγένετο.δὲ" πορευομένων.αὐτῶν ἐν τῇ ὁδῷ εἶπέν τις
And it came to pass as they were going in the way [3]said [1]some [2]one

πρὸς αὐτόν, Ἀκολουθήσω σοι ὅπου [b]ἂν" ἀπέρχῃ, [c]κύριε."
to him, I will follow thee wherever thou mayest go, Lord.

58 Καὶ εἶπεν αὐτῷ ὁ Ἰησοῦς, Αἱ ἀλώπεκες φωλεοὺς ἔχουσιν,
And [2]said [3]to [4]him [1]Jesus, The foxes holes have,

καὶ τὰ πετεινὰ τοῦ οὐρανοῦ κατασκηνώσεις· ὁ.δὲ υἱὸς τοῦ
and the birds of the heaven nests; but the Son

ἀνθρώπου οὐκ.ἔχει ποῦ τὴν κεφαλὴν κλίνῃ. 59 Εἶπεν.δὲ
of man has not where the head he may lay. And he said

πρὸς ἕτερον, Ἀκολούθει μοι. Ὁ δὲ εἶπεν, [d]Κύριε," ἐπίτρεψόν
to another, Follow me. But he said, Lord, allow

μοι [e]ἀπελθόντι πρῶτον" θάψαι τὸν.πατέρα.μου. 60 Εἶπεν.δὲ
me going away first to bury my father. But [2]said

αὐτῷ [f]ὁ Ἰησοῦς," Ἄφες τοὺς νεκροὺς θάψαι τοὺς ἑαυτῶν
[3]to [4]him [1]Jesus, Leave the dead to bury their own

νεκρούς· σὺ.δὲ ἀπελθὼν διάγγελλε τὴν βασιλείαν τοῦ θεοῦ.
dead; but thou going forth declare the kingdom of God.

61 Εἶπεν.δὲ καὶ ἕτερος, Ἀκολουθήσω σοι, κύριε· πρῶτον.δὲ
And [2]said [3]also [1]another, I will follow thee, Lord, but first

ἐπίτρεψόν μοι ἀποτάξασθαι τοῖς εἰς τὸν.οἶκόν μου. 62 Εἶπεν.δὲ
allow me to take leave of those at my house. But [2]said

[g]πρὸς αὐτὸν ὁ Ἰησοῦς," Οὐδεὶς [h]ἐπιβαλὼν" τὴν.χεῖρα.[i]αὐτοῦ"
[3]to [4]him [1]Jesus, No one having laid his hand

ἐπ' ἄροτρον, καὶ βλέπων εἰς τὰ ὀπίσω, εὔθετός ἐστιν
upon [the] plough, and looking on the things behind, [2]fit [1]is

the hands of men.

45 But they did not understand this saying, and it was hidden from them so that they should not see it. And they were afraid to ask Him about that saying.

46 And an argument developed among them this, who might be the greatest of them.

47 And Jesus seeing the thought of their heart, taking a little child, He set it beside Him

48 and said to them, Whoever shall receive this little child in My name receives Me. And whoever shall receive Me receives Him who sent Me. For he who is least among you all is he who shall be great.

49 And answering John said, Master, we saw someone throwing out demons in Your name. And we ordered him to stop because he does not follow along with us.

50 And Jesus said to him, Do not stop him, for whoever is not against us is for us.

51 And when the days of His taking up were being fulfilled, He set His face to go to Jerusalem.

52 And He sent messengers before His face to go to Jerusalem. And going on they entered a village of the Sa-mar-i-tans, so as to make ready for Him.

53 And they did not receive Him because His face was set to go to Jerusalem.

54 And when His disciples saw it, James and John said, Lord, do You desire that we should call fire to come down from Heaven and burn them up, even as Elijah did?

55 But turning He warned them and said, You do not know of what spirit you are!

56 But the Son of man did not come to destroy men's lives, but to save. And they went into another village.

57 And it happened that as they were going in the highway, someone said to Him, Lord, wherever You go, I will follow You.

58 And Jesus said to him, The foxes have holes and the birds of the air have nests, but the Son of man has nowhere He may lay His head.

59 And He said to another, Follow Me! But he said, Lord, let me first go away to bury my father.

60 But Jesus said to him, Leave the dead to bury their own dead, but you go out and preach the kingdom of God.

61 And another also said, Lord, I will follow You, but first let me go say goodbye to those at my house.

62 But Jesus said to him, No one who has put his hand on the plow and *still* looks back at the things behind is fit for the kingdom of

kεἰς τὴν βασιλείαν" τοῦ θεοῦ.
for the kingdom of God.

10 Μετὰ.δὲ .ταῦτα ἀνέδειξεν ὁ κύριος lκαὶ" ἑτέρους ἑβδο-
Now after these things 3appointed 1the 2Lord 4also 5others 6seven-
μήκονταm, καὶ ἀπέστειλεν αὐτοὺς ἀνὰ.δύο πρὸ προσώπου
ty, and sent them two and two before 2face
αὐτοῦ, εἰς πᾶσαν πόλιν καὶ τόπον οὗ "ἔμελλεν" αὐτὸς
1his, into every city and place where he was about himself
ἔρχεσθαι. 2 "Ἔλεγεν οοὖν" πρὸς αὐτούς, Ὁ μὲν θερισμὸς
to come. He said therefore to them, The 2indeed 1harvest [is]
πολύς, οἱ.δὲ ἐργάται ὀλίγοι· δεήθητε οὖν τοῦ κυρίου
great, but the workmen [are] few. Supplicate therefore the Lord
τοῦ θερισμοῦ, ὅπως pἐκβάλλῃ ἐργάτας" εἰς τὸν θερισμὸν
of the harvest, that he may send out workmen into 2harvest
αὐτοῦ. 3 Ὑπάγετε· ἰδού, qἐγὼ" ἀποστέλλω ὑμᾶς ὡς ἄρνας ἐν
1his. Go; lo, I send forth you as lambs in
μέσῳ λύκων. 4 μὴ βαστάζετε rβαλάντιον" μὴ πήραν
[the] midst of wolves. Neither carry purse nor provision bag
sμηδὲ" ὑποδήματα· tκαὶ" μηδένα κατὰ τὴν ὁδὸν ἀσπάσησθε.
nor sandals, and no one on the way salute.
5 Εἰς.ἣν.δ'.ἂν vοἰκίαν εἰσέρχησθε," πρῶτον λέγετε, Εἰρήνη τῷ
And into whatever house ye may enter, first say, Peace
οἴκῳ.τούτῳ. 6 καὶ ἐὰν wμὲν" ᾖ ἐκεῖ xὁ υἱὸς εἰρήνης, yἐπανα-
to this house. And if indeed be there a son of peace, 3shall
παύσεται" ἐπ' αὐτὸν ἡ.εἰρήνη.ὑμῶν· εἰ.δὲ μήγε, ἐφ' ὑμᾶς
4rest 5upon 6it 1your 2peace; but if not so, to you
ἀνακάμψει. 7 ἐν αὐτῇ δὲ τῇ οἰκίᾳ μένετε, zἐσθίοντες" καὶ
it shall return. 2In 3the 4same 1and house abide, eating and
πίνοντες τὰ παρ' αὐτῶν· ἄξιος.γὰρ ὁ ἐργάτης
drinking the things [supplied] by them; for worthy 2the 3workman
τοῦ.μισθοῦ.αὐτοῦ aἐστιν." μὴ.μεταβαίνετε ἐξ οἰκίας εἰς οἰκίαν.
4of 5his 6hire 1is. Remove not from house to house.
8 καὶ εἰς ἣν.bδ'".ἂν πόλιν εἰσέρχησθε, καὶ δέχωνται ὑμᾶς,
And into whatever 2also 1city ye may enter, and they receive you,
ἐσθίετε τὰ παρατιθέμενα ὑμῖν, 9 καὶ θεραπεύετε τοὺς ἐν
eat the things set before you, and heal the 2in
αὐτῇ ἀσθενεῖς, καὶ λέγετε αὐτοῖς, Ἤγγικεν ἐφ' ὑμᾶς ἡ βασι-
3it 1sick, and say to them, Has drawn near to you the king-
λεία τοῦ θεοῦ. 10 εἰς.ἣν.δ'.ἂν πόλιν cεἰσέρχησθε," καὶ μὴ
dom of God. But into whatever city ye may enter, and 3not
δέχωνται ὑμᾶς, ἐξελθόντες εἰς τὰς.πλατείας.αὐτῆς, εἴπατε,
1they 2do receive you, having gone out into its streets, say,
11 Καὶ τὸν κονιορτὸν τὸν κολληθέντα ἡμῖν ἐκ τῆς πόλεως
Even the dust which clung to us out of 2city
ὑμῶν d ἀπομασσόμεθα ὑμῖν· πλὴν τοῦτο γινώσκετε, ὅτι
1your we wipe off against you; yet this know, that
ἤγγικεν eἐφ' ὑμᾶς" ἡ βασιλεία τοῦ θεοῦ. 12 λέγω.fδὲ" ὑμῖν,
has drawn near to you the kingdom of God. And I say to you,
ὅτι Σοδόμοις ἐν τῇ.ἡμέρᾳ.ἐκείνῃ ἀνεκτότερον ἔσται ἢ τῇ
that for Sodom in that day more tolerable it shall be than
πόλει.ἐκείνῃ. 13 Οὐαί σοι, gΧωραζίν," οὐαί σοι, Βηθσαϊδά·
for that city. Woe to thee, Chorazin! woe to thee, Bethsaida!
ὅτι εἰ ἐν Τύρῳ καὶ Σιδῶνι hἐγένοντο" αἱ δυνάμεις αἱ
for if in Tyre and Sidon had taken place the works of power which
γενόμεναι ἐν ὑμῖν, πάλαι ἂν ἐν σάκκῳ καὶ σποδῷ
have been taking place in you, long ago in sackcloth and ashes
iκαθήμεναι" μετενόησαν. 14 πλὴν Τύρῳ καὶ Σιδῶνι ἀνεκ-
sitting they had repented. But for Tyre and Sidon more
τότερον ἔσται ἐν τῇ κρίσει ἢ ὑμῖν. 15 καὶ σύ, kΚαπερ-
tolerable will it be in the judgment than for you. And thou, Caper-
ναούμ," lἡ" ἕως mτοῦ" οὐρανοῦ nὑψωθεῖσα," ἕως o ᾅδου
naum, who to the heaven hast been lifted up, to hades
καταβιβασθήσῃ. 16 Ὁ ἀκούων ὑμῶν ἐμοῦ ἀκούει· καὶ
thou shalt be brought down. He that hears you 2me 1hears, and
ὁ ἀθετῶν ὑμᾶς ἐμὲ ἀθετεῖ· ὁ.δὲ ἐμὲ ἀθετῶν ἀθετεῖ τὸν
he that rejects you 2me 1rejects, and he that 2me 1rejects rejects him
ἀποστείλαντά με.
who sent me.

17 Ὑπέστρεψαν.δὲ οἱ ἑβδομήκονταp μετὰ χαρᾶς, λέγοντες,
And 3returned 1the 2seventy with joy, saying,
Κύριε, καὶ τὰ δαιμόνια ὑποτάσσεται ἡμῖν ἐν τῷ ὀνόματί
Lord, even the demons are subject to us through 2name
σου. 18 Εἶπεν.δὲ αὐτοῖς, Ἐθεώρουν τὸν σατανᾶν ὡς ἀστραπὴν
1thy. And he said to them, I beheld Satan as lightning
ἐκ τοῦ οὐρανοῦ πεσόντα. 19 ἰδού, qδίδωμι" ὑμῖν τὴν ἐξουσίαν
out of the heaven falling. Lo, I give you the authority
τοῦ πατεῖν ἐπάνω ὄφεων καὶ σκορπίων, καὶ ἐπὶ πᾶσαν τὴν
to tread upon serpents and scorpions, and upon all the
δύναμιν τοῦ ἐχθροῦ· καὶ οὐδὲν ὑμᾶς οὐ.μὴ rἀδικήσῃ."
power of the enemy, and nothing you in anywise shall injure.
(lit. in no wise)
20 πλὴν ἐν τούτῳ μὴ.χαίρετε, ὅτι τὰ πνεύματα ὑμῖν ὑποτάσ-
Yet in this rejoice not, that the spirits to you are sub-

God.

CHAPTER 10

1Now after these things, the Lord also appointed seventy others and sent them two by two before Him into every city and place where He himself was about to come.

2Therefore He said to them, The harvest truly is great, but the laborers are few. Then pray to the Lord of the harvest that He may send laborers into His harvest.

3Go! Lo, I send you out as lambs in the midst of wolves.

4Do not carry purse or bag or shoes. And do not greet anyone on the highway.

5And into whatever house you may enter, first say, Peace to this house.

6And if indeed there is a son of peace there, your peace shall rest upon it. But if not, it shall return to you.

7And stay in that same house, eating and drinking the things *provided* by them – for the laborer is worthy of his hire. Do not go from house to house.

8And into whatever city you may go, and should they receive you, eat the things set before you.

9And heal the sick in it. And say to them, The kingdom of God has come near to you.

10But into whatever city you may go, and they do not receive you, go out into its streets and cry,

11Even the dust which has clung to us out of your city we wipe off against you. Yet know this, that the kingdom of God has come near to you.

12And I say to you it shall be more bearable in that Day for Sodom than for that city.

13Woe to you, Chor-a-zin! Woe to you, Beth-sa-i-da! For if the mighty works had been done in Tyre and Sidon which have been taking place in you, they long ago would have repented, sitting in sackcloth and ashes.

14But it shall be more bearable for Tyre and Sidon in the Judgment than for you.

15And you, Ca-per-na-um, who have been lifted up to Heaven, you shall be thrust down to hell.

16He that hears you hears Me. And he who despises you despises Me. And he that despises Me despises Him who sent Me.

17And the seventy returned again with joy, saying, Lord, even the demons are subject to us through Your name.

18And He said to them, I saw Satan falling out of Heaven, like lightning.

19Behold! I give you the authority to walk on serpents and scorpions, and on all the power of the enemy. And nothing in any way shall hurt you.

20Yet do not rejoice in this, that the spirits are subject to you. But rather rejoice that

σεται· χαίρετε.δὲ [s]μᾶλλον" ὅτι τὰ.ὀνόματα.ὑμῶν [t]ἐγράφη"
jected, but rejoice rather that your names are written
ἐν τοῖς οὐρανοῖς. 21 Ἐν αὐτῇ.τῇ ὥρᾳ ἠγαλλιάσατο [v] τῷ
in the heavens. In the same hour [2]rejoiced [3]in [4]the
πνεύματι[w] [x]ὁ Ἰησοῦς," καὶ εἶπεν, Ἐξομολογοῦμαί σοι, πάτερ,
[5]Spirit [1]Jesus, and said, I praise thee, O Father,
κύριε τοῦ οὐρανοῦ καὶ τῆς γῆς, ὅτι ἀπέκρυψας ταῦτα ἀπὸ
Lord of the heaven and of the earth, that thou didst hide these things from
σοφῶν καὶ συνετῶν, καὶ ἀπεκάλυψας αὐτὰ νηπίοις· ναί, ὁ πα-
wise and prudent, and didst reveal them to babes: yea, Fa-
τήρ, ὅτι οὕτως [y]ἐγένετο εὐδοκία" ἔμπροσθέν σου. 22 [z]Καὶ
ther, for thus was it well pleasing before thee. And
στραφεὶς πρὸς τοὺς μαθητὰς εἶπεν," Πάντα [a]παρεδόθη μοι"
having turned to the disciples he said, All things were delivered to me
ὑπὸ τοῦ.πατρός.μου· καὶ οὐδεὶς γινώσκει τίς ἐστιν ὁ υἱὸς εἰ.μὴ
by my Father, and no one knows who is the Son except
ὁ πατήρ, καὶ τίς ἐστιν ὁ πατήρ, εἰ.μὴ ὁ υἱός, καὶ ᾧ.[b]ἐὰν"
the Father, and who is the Father, except the Son, and he to whomsoever
βούληται ὁ υἱὸς ἀποκαλύψαι. 23 Καὶ στραφεὶς πρὸς
[3]may [4]will [1]the [2]Son to reveal [him]. And having turned to
τοὺς μαθητὰς κατ'.ἰδίαν εἶπεν, Μακάριοι οἱ ὀφθαλμοὶ
the disciples apart he said, Blessed [are] the eyes
οἱ βλέποντες ἃ βλέπετε. 24 λέγω.γὰρ ὑμῖν, ὅτι πολλοὶ
which see what ye see. For I say to you, that many
προφῆται καὶ βασιλεῖς ἠθέλησαν ἰδεῖν ἃ ὑμεῖς βλέπετε,
prophets and kings desired to see what ye see,
καὶ οὐκ [c]εἶδον·" καὶ ἀκοῦσαι ἃ ἀκούετε, καὶ οὐκ.ἤκουσαν.
and saw not; and to hear what ye hear, and heard not.
25 Καὶ ἰδού, νομικός τις ἀνέστη, ἐκπειράζων
And behold, a [2]doctor [3]of [4]the [5]law [1]certain stood up, tempting
αὐτόν, [d]καὶ" λέγων, Διδάσκαλε, τί ποιήσας ζωὴν αἰώνιον
him, and saying, Teacher, [3]what [1]having [2]done life eternal
κληρονομήσω; 26 Ὁ.δὲ εἶπεν πρὸς αὐτόν, Ἐν τῷ νόμῳ τί
shall I inherit? And he said to him, In the law what
γέγραπται; πῶς ἀναγινώσκεις; 27 Ὁ.δὲ ἀποκριθεὶς εἶπεν,
has been written? how readest thou? And he answering said,
Ἀγαπήσεις κύριον τὸν.θεόν.σου ἐξ ὅλης [e]τῆς" καρδίας
Thou shalt love [the] Lord thy God with all [2]heart
σου καὶ [f]ἐξ ὅλης τῆς.ψυχῆς.σου καὶ ἐξ ὅλης τῆς.ἰσχύος".σου
[1]thy and with all thy soul and with all thy strength
καὶ [g]ἐξ ὅλης τῆς.διανοίας".σου· καὶ τὸν.πλησίον.σου ὡς σεαυ-
and with all thy mind; and thy neighbour as thy-
τόν. 28 Εἶπεν.δὲ αὐτῷ, Ὀρθῶς ἀπεκρίθης· τοῦτο ποίει,
self. And he said to him, Rightly thou hast answered: this do,
καὶ ζήσῃ. 29 Ὁ.δὲ θέλων [h]δικαιοῦν" ἑαυτὸν εἶπεν πρὸς
and thou shalt live. But he desiring to justify himself said to
τὸν Ἰησοῦν, Καὶ τίς ἐστίν μου πλησίον; 30 Ὑπολαβὼν.[i]δὲ"
Jesus, And who is my neighbour? And taking [it] up
ὁ Ἰησοῦς εἶπεν, Ἄνθρωπός τις κατέβαινεν ἀπὸ Ἱερουσαλὴμ
Jesus said, A [2]man [1]certain was going down from Jerusalem
εἰς [k]Ἱεριχώ," καὶ λῃσταῖς περιέπεσεν, οἳ καὶ ἐκδύσαντες
to Jericho, and [3]robbers [1]fell [2]among, who both having stripped
αὐτὸν καὶ πληγὰς ἐπιθέντες ἀπῆλθον, ἀφέντες ἡμιθανῆ
him and wounds having inflicted went away, leaving [him], half dead
[l]τυγχάνοντα." 31 κατὰ συγκυρίαν δὲ ἱερεύς τις κατ-
being. [2]By [3]a [4]coincidence [1]now [5]a [7]priest [6]certain went
έβαινεν ἐν τῇ.ὁδῷ.ἐκείνῃ, καὶ ἰδὼν αὐτὸν ἀντιπαρῆλ-
down in that road, and having seen him he passed by on the op-
θεν· 32 ὁμοίως.δὲ καὶ [m]Λευΐτης," [n]γενόμενος" κατὰ τὸν
posite side; and in like manner also a Levite, being at the
τόπον, ἐλθὼν καὶ ἰδὼν [o] ἀντιπαρῆλθεν. 33 [p]Σα-
spot, having come and having seen passed by on the opposite side. [2]A [4]Sa-
μαρείτης" δέ τις ὁδεύων ἦλθεν κατ' αὐτόν, καὶ ἰδὼν
maritan [1]but [3]certain journeying came to him, and having seen
[q]αὐτὸν" ἐσπλαγχνίσθη· 34 καὶ προσελθὼν κατέδησεν τὰ
him was moved with compassion, and having approached bound up
τραύματα.αὐτοῦ, ἐπιχέων ἔλαιον καὶ οἶνον· [r]ἐπιβιβάσας.δὲ"
his wounds, pouring on oil and wine; and having put
αὐτὸν ἐπὶ τὸ.ἴδιον κτῆνος ἤγαγεν αὐτὸν εἰς [s]πανδοχεῖον,".καὶ
him on his own beast brought him to an inn, and
ἐπεμελήθη αὐτοῦ. 35 καὶ ἐπὶ τὴν αὔριον [t]ἐξελθών," ἐκβαλὼν
took care of him. And on the morrow going forth, taking out
δύο δηνάρια ἔδωκεν τῷ [v]πανδοχεῖ," καὶ εἶπεν [w]αὐτῷ,"
two denarii he gave [them] to the innkeeper, and said to him,
Ἐπιμελήθητι αὐτοῦ· καὶ ὅ.τι.ἂν προσδαπανήσῃς, ἐγὼ ἐν
Take care of him, and whatsoever thou mayest expend more, I on
τῷ.ἐπανέρχεσθαί.με ἀποδώσω σοι. 36 Τίς [x]οὖν" τούτων
my coming back will repay thee. Which therefore of these
τῶν τριῶν [y]δοκεῖ σοι πλησίον" γεγονέναι τοῦ ἐμπεσόντος
three seems to thee [4]neighbour [1]to [2]have [3]been of him who fell
εἰς τοὺς λῃστάς; 37 Ὁ.δὲ εἶπεν, Ὁ ποιήσας τὸ ἔλεος
among the robbers? And he said, He who shewed compassion

your names are written in Heaven.
21 In that same hour Jesus rejoiced in the Spirit and said, I thank You, O Father, Lord of Heaven and of earth, that You have hidden these things from the sophisticated and cunning and have revealed them to babes. Yes, Father, for so it was pleasing in Your sight.
22 And He turned to the disciples and said, All things are given to Me by My Father. And no one but the Father knows who the Son is, and who the Father is but the Son – and he to whom the Son will reveal *Him.*
23 And turning to the disciples, He said privately, Blessed are the eyes which see what you see.
24 For I say to you that many prophets and kings have desired to see what you see and did not see them – and to hear what you hear, and did not hear.

25 And, behold! A certain lawyer stood up, tempting Him, and saying, Teacher, what shall I do to inherit eternal life?
26 And He said to him, What is written in the Law? How do you read?
27 And answering he said, You shall love the Lord your God with all your heart and with all your soul and with all your strength and with all your mind – and your neighbor as yourself.
28 And He said to him, You have answered right. Do this and you shall live.
29 But desiring to justify himself, he said to Jesus, And who is my neighbor?
30 And taking it up Jesus said, A certain man was going down from Jerusalem to Jericho. And he fell among thieves who stripped and wounded him and left him half dead.
31 Now it so happened a certain priest went down that road. And seeing him, he passed by on the other side.
32 And in the same way also a Levite who was traveling there came up and saw *him. And he* went around on the other side.
33 But a certain Sa-mar-i-tan traveling *that way* came up to him. And seeing him, he was moved with pity.
34 And he came near and bandaged his wounds, pouring on oil and wine. And putting him on his own animal, he brought him to an inn and took care of him.
35 And on leaving the next day, he took out two coins and gave them to the innkeeper. And he said to him, Take care of him. And whatever you spend more than this, I will repay you when I return.
36 Who, then, of these three seems to you to have been a neighbor to him who fell among the thieves?
37 And he said, He who showed him pity.

μετ' αὐτοῦ. Εἶπεν [z]οὖν[ǁ] αὐτῷ ὁ Ἰησοῦς, Πορεύου, καὶ
towards him. [3]Said [2]therefore [4]to [5]him [1]Jesus, Go [2]and
σὺ ποίει ὁμοίως.
[1]thou do likewise.
38 [a]Ἐγένετο.δὲ.ἐν[ǁ] τῷ.πορεύεσθαι αὐτοὺς [b]καὶ[ǁ] αὐτὸς εἰσῆλ-
And it came to pass as [2]proceeded [1]they that he enter-
θεν εἰς κώμην τινά· γυνὴ.δέ τις ὀνόματι Μάρθα ὑπ-
ed into a [2]village [1]certain; and a [2]woman [1]certain by name Martha re-
εδέξατο αὐτὸν εἰς [c]τὸν.οἶκον[ǁ].[d]αὐτῆς.[ǁ] 39 καὶ τῇδε.ἦν ἀδελφὴ
ceived him into her house. And she had a sister
καλουμένη [e]Μαρία,[ǁ] ἣ καὶ [f]παρακαθίσασα[ǁ] [g]παρὰ[ǁ] τοὺς πόδας
called Mary, who also having sat down at the feet
[h]τοῦ Ἰησοῦ[ǁ] ἤκουεν τὸν.λόγον.αὐτοῦ. 40 ἡ.δὲ.Μάρθα
of Jesus was listening to his word. But Martha
περιεσπᾶτο περὶ πολλὴν διακονίαν· ἐπιστᾶσα.δὲ εἶπεν, Κύριε,
was distracted about much service; and coming up she said, Lord,
οὐ.μέλει σοι ὅτι ἡ.ἀδελφή.μου μόνην με [i]κατέλιπεν[ǁ] δια-
is it no concern to thee that my sister [3]alone [2]me [1]left to
κονεῖν; [k]εἰπὲ[ǁ] οὖν αὐτῇ ἵνα μοι συναντιλάβηται. 41 Ἀπο-
serve? Speak therefore to her that me she may help. [3]An-
κριθεὶς δὲ εἶπεν αὐτῇ [l]ὁ Ἰησοῦς,[ǁ] Μάρθα, Μάρθα, μεριμνᾷς
swering [1]but [4]said [5]to [6]her [2]Jesus, Martha, Martha, thou art careful
καὶ [m]τυρβάζῃ[ǁ] περὶ πολλά· 42 ἑνὸς.δέ ἐστιν χρεία· Μαρία
and troubled about many things; but of one there is need; [2]Mary
[n]δὲ[ǁ] τὴν ἀγαθὴν μερίδα ἐξελέξατο, ἥτις οὐκ.ἀφαιρεθήσεται
[1]and the good part chose, which shall not be taken
[o]ἀπ'[ǁ] αὐτῆς.
from her.

11 Καὶ ἐγένετο ἐν.τῷ.εἶναι αὐτὸν ἐν τόπῳ τινὶ προσ-
And it came to pass as [2]was [1]he in a [2]place [1]certain pray-
ευχόμενον, ὡς ἐπαύσατο, εἶπέν τις τῶν.μαθητῶν.αὐτοῦ πρὸς
ing, when he ceased, said one of his disciples to
αὐτόν, Κύριε, δίδαξον ἡμᾶς προσεύχεσθαι, καθὼς καὶ [p]Ἰωάν-
him, Lord, teach us to pray, as also John
νης[ǁ] ἐδίδαξεν τοὺς.μαθητὰς.αὐτοῦ. 2 Εἶπεν.δὲ αὐτοῖς, Ὅταν
taught his disciples. And he said to them, When
προσεύχησθε λέγετε, Πάτερ [q]ἡμῶν ὁ ἐν τοῖς οὐρανοῖς,[ǁ]
ye pray say, [2]Father [1]our, who [art] in the heavens,
ἁγιασθήτω τὸ.ὄνομά.σου· [r]ἐλθέτω[ǁ] [s]ἡ.βασιλεία.σου·[ǁ] [t]γενηθήτω
sanctified be thy name; let come thy kingdom; let be done
τὸ.θέλημά.σου,[ǁ] [v]ὡς ἐν οὐρανῷ, καὶ ἐπὶ τῆς γῆς.[ǁ] 3 τὸν
thy will, as in heaven, [so] also upon the earth.
ἄρτον.ἡμῶν τὸν ἐπιούσιον δίδου ἡμῖν τὸ.καθ'.ἡμέραν· 4 καὶ
Our bread the needed give us daily; and
ἄφες ἡμῖν τὰς.ἁμαρτίας.ἡμῶν, καὶ.γὰρ αὐτοὶ [w]ἀφίεμεν[ǁ]
forgive us our sins, for [3]also [2]ourselves [1]we forgive
παντὶ ὀφείλοντι ἡμῖν· καὶ μὴ.εἰσενέγκῃς ἡμᾶς εἰς πειρασμόν,
every one indebted to us; and lead not us into temptation,
[x]ἀλλὰ ῥῦσαι ἡμᾶς ἀπὸ τοῦ πονηροῦ.[ǁ] 5 Καὶ εἶπεν πρὸς
but deliver us from evil. And he said to
αὐτούς, Τίς ἐξ ὑμῶν ἕξει φίλον, καὶ πορεύσεται πρὸς
them, Who among you shall have a friend, and shall go to
αὐτὸν μεσονυκτίου, καὶ [y]εἴπῃ[ǁ] αὐτῷ, Φίλε, χρῆσόν μοι τρεῖς
him at midnight, and say to him, Friend, lend me three
ἄρτους, 6 ἐπειδὴ φίλος μου παρεγένετο ἐξ ὁδοῦ πρός με,
loaves, since a friend of mine is come off a journey to me,
καὶ οὐκ.ἔχω ὃ παραθήσω αὐτῷ· 7 κἀκεῖνος ἔσωθεν
and I have not what I shall set before him; and he from within
ἀποκριθεὶς εἴπῃ, Μή μοι κόπους πάρεχε· ἤδη ἡ θύρα
answering should say, [3]Not [2]me [4]trouble [1]cause; already the door
κέκλεισται, καὶ τὰ.παιδία.μου μετ' ἐμοῦ εἰς τὴν κοίτην εἰσίν·
has been shut, and my children with me in bed are;
οὐ.δύναμαι ἀναστὰς δοῦναί σοι. 8 Λέγω ὑμῖν, εἰ καὶ οὐ
I cannot rise up to give to thee. I say to you, if even [3]not
δώσει αὐτῷ ἀναστάς, διὰ τὸ.εἶναι [z]αὐτοῦ φίλον,[ǁ]
[1]he [2]will give to him, having risen up, because of [his] being his friend,
διά.γε τὴν.[a]ἀναίδειαν[ǁ].αὐτοῦ ἐγερθεὶς δώσει αὐτῷ
yet because of his importunity having risen he will give him
ὅσων χρῄζει. 9 Κἀγὼ ὑμῖν λέγω, Αἰτεῖτε, καὶ δοθήσεται
as many as he needs. And I to you say, Ask, and it shall be given
ὑμῖν· ζητεῖτε, καὶ εὑρήσετε· κρούετε, καὶ [b]ἀνοιγήσεται[ǁ] ὑμῖν.
to you; seek, and ye shall find; knock, and it shall be opened to you.
10 πᾶς.γὰρ ὁ αἰτῶν λαμβάνει· καὶ ὁ ζητῶν εὑρίσκει· καὶ
For every one that asks receives; and he that seeks finds; and
τῷ κρούοντι [c]ἀνοιγήσεται.[ǁ] 11 τίνα.δὲ [d] ὑμῶν τὸν
to him that knocks it will be opened. And which of you who [is]
πατέρα αἰτήσει ὁ υἱὸς ἄρτον, μὴ λίθον ἐπιδώσει αὐτῷ;
a father shall [3]ask [4]for [1]the [2]son bread, a stone will he give to him?
[e]εἰ[ǁ] καὶ ἰχθύν, μὴ ἀντὶ ἰχθύος ὄφιν [f]ἐπιδώσει αὐτῷ[ǁ]; 12 ἢ
if also a fish, instead of a fish a serpent will he give to him? or
καὶ [g]ἐὰν[ǁ] [h]αἰτήσῃ[ǁ] ᾠόν, μὴ ἐπιδώσει αὐτῷ σκορπίον; 13 εἰ
also if he should ask an egg, will he give to him a scorpion? If

Then Jesus said to him, You go do the same.

38 And as they went on He entered into a certain village. And a certain woman named Martha received Him into her house.

39 And she had a sister called Mary who was sitting at the feet of Jesus and listening to His word.

40 But Martha was troubled with so much serving. And standing by Him she said, Lord, Do You not care that my sister has left me alone to serve? Speak to her, then, that she should help me.

41 But in answer Jesus said to her, Martha! Martha! You are anxious and troubled about many things.

42 But only one thing is needful, and Mary has chosen the good part, which shall not be taken away from her.

CHAPTER 11

1 And as He was praying in a certain place, when He was finished, one of His disciples asked Him, Lord, teach us to pray, even as John taught his disciples.

2 And He said to them, When you pray. say, Our Father who is in Heaven, holy is Your name. *May* Your kingdom come and Your will be done, on earth as it is in Heaven.

3 Give us day by day our daily bread. And forgive us our sins, for we also forgive everyone who is indebted to us.

4 And lead us not into temptation, but deliver us from evil.

5 And He said to them, Who among you shall have a friend and shall go to him at midnight and say to him, Friend, Let me borrow three loaves.

6 For a friend of mine has come to me from a journey and I have nothing to serve him.

7 And *what if* he from the inside should answer, Do not bother me, for the door is already shut and my children are in bed with me. I cannot get up and give it to you.

8 I say to you that even if he will not get up and give to him because he is his friend, yet because of his shameless insisting he will get up and give as many as he needs.

9 And I say to you, Ask and it shall be given to you. Seek and you shall find. Knock and it shall be opened to you.

10 For everyone that asks receives. And he that seeks finds. And to him that knocks, it will be opened.

11 And which of you who is a father, if the son shall ask a loaf, will he give him a rock? And if he asks for a fish, will he give him a snake instead?

12 Or if he asks for an egg, will he give him a scorpion?

13 If, then, you who are evil know how to

οὖν ὑμεῖς πονηροὶ ὑπάρχοντες οἴδατε ἰἀγαθὰ δόματα‖
therefore ye, ²evil ¹being, know [how] good gifts
διδόναι τοῖς.τέκνοις.ὑμῶν, πόσῳ μᾶλλον ὁ πατὴρ[k] ὁ ἐξ
to give to your children, how much more the Father who[is] of
οὐρανοῦ δώσει πνεῦμα ἅγιον τοῖς αἰτοῦσιν αὐτόν;
heaven will give [the] ²Spirit ¹Holy to those that ask him?
14 Καὶ ἦν ἐκβάλλων δαιμόνιον, ˡκαὶ αὐτὸ ἦνˡ κωφόν·
And he was casting out a demon, and it was dumb;
ἐγένετο.δὲ τοῦ.δαιμονίου ᵐἐξελθόντος,ˡ ἐλάλησεν ὁ κωφός·
and it came to pass on the demon having gone out, ³spoke ¹the ²dumb.
καὶ ἐθαύμασαν οἱ ὄχλοι. 15 τινὲς.δὲ ἐξ αὐτῶν ⁿεἶπον,‖ Ἐν
And ³wondered ¹the ²crowds. But some of them said, By
Βεελζεβοὺλ ᵒ ἄρχοντι τῶν δαιμονίων ἐκβάλλει τὰ δαιμόνια.
Beelzebul prince of the demons he casts out the demons.
16 Ἕτεροι.δὲ πειράζοντες σημεῖον ᵖπαρ' αὐτοῦ ἐζήτουν ἐξ
And others, tempting, a sign from him were seeking from
οὐρανοῦ.‖ 17 Αὐτὸς.δὲ εἰδὼς ᵠαὐτῶν τὰ διανοήματαˡ εἶπεν
heaven. But he knowing their thoughts said
αὐτοῖς, Πᾶσα βασιλεία ʳἐφ' ἑαυτὴν διαμερισθεῖσα‖ ἐρη-
to them, Every kingdom ²against ³itself ¹divided is brought to
μοῦται· καὶ οἶκος ἐπὶ οἶκον πίπτει. 18 εἰ.δὲ καὶ ὁ σατανᾶς
desolation; and a house against a house falls. And if also Satan
ἐφ' ἑαυτὸν διεμερίσθη, πῶς σταθήσεται ἡ.βασιλεία.αὐτοῦ;
against himself be divided, how shall stand his kingdom?
ὅτι λέγετε, ἐν Βεελζεβοὺλ ἐκβάλλειν.με τὰ δαιμόνια. 19 εἰ.δὲ
because ye say, by Beelzebul I cast out the demons. And if
ἐγὼ ἐν Βεελζεβοὺλ ἐκβάλλω τὰ δαιμόνια, ˢοἱˡ.υἱοὶ.ὑμῶν ἐν
I by Beelzebul cast out the demons, your sons by
τίνι ἐκβάλλουσιν; διὰ τοῦτο ᵗκριταὶ ὑμῶν αὐτοὶ ἔσον-
whom do they cast out? on account of this judges of you they shall
ται.‖ 20 εἰ.δὲ ἐν δακτύλῳ θεοῦ ᵛἐκβάλλω τὰ δαιμόνια,
be. But if by [the] finger of God I cast out the demons,
ἄρα ἔφθασεν ἐφ' ὑμᾶς ἡ βασιλεία τοῦ θεοῦ. 21 ὅταν ὁ
then is come upon you the kingdom of God. When the
ἰσχυρὸς καθωπλισμένος φυλάσσῃ τὴν.ἑαυτοῦ.αὐλήν, ἐν
strong [man] being armed may keep his own dwelling, in
εἰρήνῃ ἐστὶν τὰ.ὑπάρχοντα.αὐτοῦ· 22 ἐπὰν.δὲ ʷὁ‖ ἰσχυρό-
peace are his goods; but as soon as the stronger
τερος αὐτοῦ ἐπελθὼν νικήσῃ αὐτόν, τὴν πανοπλίαν
than he coming upon [him] shall overcome him, ²panoply
αὐτοῦ αἴρει ἐφ' ᾗ ἐπεποίθει, καὶ τὰ.σκῦλα.αὐτοῦ δια-
¹his he takes away in which he had trusted, and his spoils he
δίδωσιν. 23 ὁ μὴ.ὢν μετ' ἐμοῦ κατ' ἐμοῦ ἐστιν· καὶ ὁ
divides. He that is not with me against me is, and he that
μὴ.συνάγων μετ' ἐμοῦ σκορπίζει. 24 Ὅταν τὸ ἀκάθαρτον
gathers not with me scatters. When the unclean
πνεῦμα ἐξέλθῃ ἀπὸ τοῦ ἀνθρώπου, διέρχεται δι' ἀνύδρων
spirit is gone out from the man, he goes through waterless
τόπων, ζητοῦν ἀνάπαυσιν· καὶ μὴ εὑρίσκον ˣλέγει, Ὑπο-
places, seeking rest; and not finding [any] he says, I will
στρέψω εἰς τὸν.οἶκόν.μου ὅθεν ἐξῆλθον· 25 καὶ ἐλθὸν
return to my house whence I came out. And having come
εὑρίσκει σεσαρωμένον καὶ κεκοσμημένον. 26 τότε πορεύεται
he finds [it] swept and adorned. Then he goes
καὶ παραλαμβάνει ʸἑπτὰ ἕτερα πνεύματα πονηρότερα ἑαυτοῦ,‖
and takes seven other spirits more wicked than himself,
καὶ εἰσελθόντα κατοικεῖ ἐκεῖ· καὶ γίνεται τὰ ἔσχατα τοῦ
and having entered they dwell there; and becomes the last
ἀνθρώπου ἐκείνου χείρονα τῶν πρώτων. 27 Ἐγένετο.δὲ
³man ¹of ²that worse than the first. And it came to pass
ἐν.τῷ.λέγειν αὐτὸν ταῦτα, ἐπάρασά τις ᶻγυνὴ φωνὴν‖
as ²spoke ¹he these things, ⁴lifting ⁵up ²certain ¹a ³woman [her] voice
ἐκ τοῦ ὄχλου εἶπεν αὐτῷ, Μακαρία ἡ κοιλία ἡ βαστάσασά
from the crowd said to him, Blessed the womb that bore
σε, καὶ μαστοὶ οὓς ἐθήλασας. 28 Αὐτὸς.δὲ εἶπεν, ᵃΜεν-
thee, and [the] breasts which thou didst suck. But he said, Yea
οῦνγεˡ μακάριοι οἱ ἀκούοντες τὸν λόγον τοῦ θεοῦ καὶ
rather blessed they who hear the word of God and
φυλάσσοντες ᵇαὐτόν.‖
keep it.

29 Τῶν.δὲ ὄχλων ἐπαθροιζομένων ἤρξατο λέγειν, Ἡ γενεὰ
But the crowds being thronged together he began to say, ²generation
αὕτη ᶜ πονηρά ἐστιν· σημεῖον ᵈἐπιζητεῖ,‖ καὶ σημεῖον οὐ
¹this ⁴wicked ³is; a sign it seeks after, and a sign ²not
δοθήσεται αὐτῇ, εἰ.μὴ τὸ σημεῖον Ἰωνᾶ ᵉτοῦ προφήτου.‖
¹shall be given to it except the sign of Jonas the prophet.
30 καθὼς.γὰρ ἐγένετο Ἰωνᾶς ᶠσημεῖον τοῖς Νινευΐταις,ˡ οὕτως
For as was Jonas a sign to the Ninevites, thus
ἔσται καὶ ὁ υἱὸς τοῦ ἀνθρώπου τῇ.γενεᾷ.ταύτῃ. 31 Βασίλισσα
shall be also the Son of man to this generation. A queen
νότου ἐγερθήσεται ἐν τῇ κρίσει μετὰ τῶν ἀνδρῶν τῆς
of [the] south shall rise up in the judgment with the men

give good gifts to your children, how much
more your Father in Heaven will give the Holy
Spirit to those who ask Him!

14 And He was throwing out a demon, and it
was dumb. And the demon having left, the
dumb one spoke. And the people wondered.
15 But some of them said, He throws out
demons by Be-el-ze-bub the chief of demons.
16 And others were tempting by asking for a
miracle from Heaven from Him.
17 But knowing their thoughts, He said to
them, Every kingdom divided against itself is
brought to ruin. And a house *divided* against a
house falls.
18 And if Satan also is divided against himself, how shall his kingdom stand? *I ask*
because you say that I throw out demons by
Be-el-ze-bub.
19 And if I cast out demons by Be-el-ze-bub,
by whom do your sons throw them out? Because of this, they shall be judges of you.
20 But if I throw them out by God's finger,
then the kingdom of God has come on you.
21 When the strong is able to keep his house
safe, his possessions are in peace.
22 But as soon as one stronger than he comes
upon him, he will overcome him and take
from him all the armor in which he had
trusted and will divide his riches.
23 He that is not with Me is against Me! And
he who does not gather with Me scatters!
24 When the evil spirit has left a man, he goes
through dry places looking for rest. And
finding none he says, I will return to my house
from which I came.
25 And returning, he finds it swept and
decorated.
26 Then he goes and takes seven other spirits
more wicked than himself. And they go in and
live there. And the last state of that man is
worse than the first.
27 And as He spoke these things, a certain
woman cried out from the crowd to Him,
Blessed is the womb that bore You and the
breasts which You sucked.
28 But He said, Yes, but rather, Blessed are
those who hear the word of God and keep it.

29 And as the people crowded together, He
began to say, This generation is evil. It looks
for a sign, but a sign shall not be given to it,
except the sign of Jonah the prophet.
30 For as Jonah was a sign to the Ninevites,
so shall the Son of man also be to this generation.
31 The queen of the south shall stand up in
the Judgment with the men of this generation

γενεᾶς.ταύτης, καὶ κατακρινεῖ αὐτούς· ὅτι ἦλθεν ἐκ τῶν
of this generation, and shall condemn them; for she came from the
περάτων τῆς γῆς ἀκοῦσαι τὴν σοφίαν [g]Σολομῶντος, καὶ ἰδού,
ends of the earth to hear the wisdom of Solomon, and behold,
πλεῖον [g]Σολομῶντος ὧδε. 32 ἄνδρες [h]Νινευῒ ἀναστήσονται
more than Solomon here. Men of Nineveh shall stand up
ἐν τῇ κρίσει μετὰ τῆς.γενεᾶς ταύτης, καὶ κατακρινοῦσιν αὐτήν·
in the judgment with this generation, and shall condemn it,
ὅτι μετενόησαν εἰς τὸ κήρυγμα Ἰωνᾶ. καὶ ἰδού, πλεῖον
because they repented at the proclamation of Jonas: and behold, more
Ἰωνᾶ ὧδε. 33 Οὐδεὶς.δὲ λύχνον ἅψας εἰς [k]κρυπτὸν
than Jonas here. But no one a lamp having [2]it [3]in [4]secret
τίθησιν, οὐδὲ ὑπὸ τὸν μόδιον, [l]ἀλλ' ἐπὶ τὴν λυχνίαν,
[1]sets [2]it, nor under the corn-measure, but upon the lampstand,
ἵνα οἱ εἰσπορευόμενοι τὸ [m]φέγγος βλέπωσιν. 34 ὁ λύχνος
that they who enter in the light may see. The lamp
τοῦ σώματός ἐστιν ὁ ὀφθαλμός[n]· ὅταν [o]οὖν ὁ.ὀφθαλμός.σου
of the body is the eye: when therefore thine eye
ἁπλοῦς ᾖ, [p]καὶ ὅλον τὸ.σῶμά.σου φωτεινόν ἐστιν· ἐπὰν.δὲ
[2]single [1]be, also [2]whole [1]thy body light is; but when
πονηρὸς ᾖ, καὶ τὸ.σῶμά.σου σκοτεινόν. 35 σκόπει οὖν
evil it be, also thy body [is] dark. See therefore
μὴ τὸ φῶς τὸ ἐν σοὶ σκότος ἐστίν. 36 εἰ οὖν τὸ σῶμά
lest the light that [is] in thee [2]darkness [1]is. If therefore [2]body
σου ὅλον φωτεινόν, μὴ ἔχον [q]τὶ μέρος σκοτεινόν, ἔσται
[1]thy [3]whole [is] light, not having any part dark, it shall be
φωτεινὸν ὅλον, ὡς ὅταν ὁ λύχνος τῇ.ἀστραπῇ φωτίζῃ σε.
[2]light [1]all, as when the lamp with [its] brightness may light thee.
37 Ἐν.δὲ.τῷ.λαλῆσαι [r] [s]ἠρώτα αὐτὸν Φαρισαῖός [t]τις
Now as [2]was [3]speaking [[1]he] asked him [1]a [3]Pharisee [2]certain
ὅπως ἀριστήσῃ παρ' αὐτῷ· εἰσελθὼν.δὲ ἀνέπεσεν.
that he would dine with him: and having entered he reclined himself.
38 ὁ.δὲ Φαρισαῖος ἰδὼν ἐθαύμασεν ὅτι οὐ πρῶτον ἐβαπτίσθη
But the Pharisee seeing [it] wondered that not first he washed
πρὸ τοῦ ἀρίστου. 39 εἶπεν.δὲ ὁ κύριος πρὸς αὐτόν, Νῦν ὑμεῖς
before the dinner. But said the Lord to him, Now ye
οἱ Φαρισαῖοι τὸ ἔξωθεν τοῦ ποτηρίου καὶ τοῦ πίνακος καθαρίζετε,
Pharisees the outside of the cup and of the dish ye cleanse,
τὸ.δὲ ἔσωθεν ὑμῶν γέμει ἁρπαγῆς καὶ πονηρίας. 40 ἄφρονες,
but the inside of you is full of plunder and wickedness. Fools,
οὐχ ὁ ποιήσας τὸ ἔξωθεν καὶ τὸ ἔσωθεν ἐποίησεν;
[did] not he who made the outside also the inside make?
41 πλὴν τὰ.ἐνόντα δότε ἐλεημοσύνην, καὶ ἰδού,
But [of] the things which are within give alms, and lo,
πάντα καθαρὰ ὑμῖν ἐστιν. 42 [v]ἀλλ' οὐαὶ ὑμῖν τοῖς Φαρισαίοις,
all things clean to you are. But woe to you Pharisees,
ὅτι ἀποδεκατοῦτε τὸ ἡδύοσμον καὶ τὸ πήγανον καὶ πᾶν
for ye pay tithes of the mint and the rue and every
λάχανον, καὶ παρέρχεσθε τὴν κρίσιν καὶ τὴν ἀγάπην τοῦ θεοῦ·
herb, and pass by the judgment and the love of God
ταῦτα[w] ἔδει ποιῆσαι, κἀκεῖνα μὴ [x]ἀφιέναι.
These things it behoved [you] to do, and those not to be leaving aside.
43 οὐαὶ ὑμῖν τοῖς Φαρισαίοις, ὅτι ἀγαπᾶτε τὴν πρωτοκαθεδρίαν
Woe to you Pharisees, for ye love the first seat
ἐν ταῖς συναγωγαῖς καὶ τοὺς ἀσπασμοὺς ἐν ταῖς ἀγοραῖς[y].
in the synagogues and the salutations in the market-places.
44 οὐαὶ ὑμῖν, [z]γραμματεῖς καὶ Φαρισαῖοι, ὑποκριταί, ὅτι ἐστὲ
Woe to you, scribes and Pharisees, hypocrites, for ye are
ὡς τὰ μνημεῖα τὰ ἄδηλα, καὶ οἱ ἄνθρωποι [a]οἱ περιπατοῦντες
as the [2]tombs [1]unseen, and the men who walk
ἐπάνω οὐκ.οἴδασιν. 45 Ἀποκριθεὶς δέ τις τῶν νομι-
over [them] do not know [it]. And answering one of the doctors of the
κῶν λέγει αὐτῷ, Διδάσκαλε, ταῦτα λέγων καὶ ἡμᾶς ὑβρίζεις.
law says to him, Teacher, these things saying [2]also [1]us thou insultest.
46 Ὁ.δὲ εἶπεν, Καὶ ὑμῖν τοῖς νομικοῖς οὐαί, ὅτι φορτίζετε
And he said, Also to you the doctors of the law woe, for ye burden
τοὺς ἀνθρώπους φορτία δυσβάστακτα, καὶ αὐτοὶ ἑνὶ
men [with] burdens heavy to bear, and yourselves with one
τῶν.δακτύλων.ὑμῶν οὐ.προσψαύετε τοῖς φορτίοις. 47 οὐαὶ
of your fingers do not touch the burdens. Woe
ὑμῖν, ὅτι οἰκοδομεῖτε τὰ μνημεῖα τῶν προφητῶν, [b]οἱ δὲ πα-
to you, for ye build the tombs of the prophets, and [2]fa-
τέρες ὑμῶν ἀπέκτειναν αὐτούς. 48 ἄρα [c]μαρτυρεῖτε καὶ
thers [1]your killed them. Hence ye bear witness and
συνευδοκεῖτε τοῖς ἔργοις τῶν.πατέρων.ὑμῶν· ὅτι αὐτοὶ μὲν
consent to the works of your fathers; for they indeed
ἀπέκτειναν αὐτούς, ὑμεῖς.δὲ οἰκοδομεῖτε [d]αὐτῶν τὰ μνημεῖα.
killed them, and ye build their tombs.
49 διὰ τοῦτο καὶ ἡ σοφία τοῦ θεοῦ εἶπεν, Ἀποστελῶ εἰς
Because of this also the wisdom of God said, I will send to
αὐτοὺς προφήτας καὶ ἀποστόλους, καὶ ἐξ αὐτῶν ἀποκτε-
them prophets and apostles, and [some] of them they will

and she shall condemn them. For she came from the ends of the earth to hear the wisdom of Solomon. And, behold! One greater than Solomon is here.

32 Men of Nineveh shall stand up in the Judgment with this generation and shall condemn it. For they repented at the preaching of Jonah. And, behold! One greater than Jonah is here.

33 But no one who has lighted a lamp puts it in a secret place, or under a basket, but on a lampstand – so that those who come in may see the light.

34 The lamp of the body is the eye. So when your eye is clear, your whole body is full of light. But when *your eye* is filled with evil, your *whole* body is also darkened.

35 Then be careful that the light that is in you is not darkness.

36 If, then, your whole body is made light, not having any part dark, the whole will be made light, as when the brightness of a lamp gives you light.

37 Now as He was speaking, a certain Pharisee asked Him to dine with him. And He went in and sat at table.

38 But the Pharisee was watching, being surprised that He had not first washed before the dinner.

39 But the Lord said to him, Now you Pharisees clean the outside of the cup and of the dish, but your inner man is full of robbery and wickedness.

40 Fools! Did not He who made the outside also make the inside?

41 But give alms of the things you have inside, and behold, all things are clean to you.

42 But woe to you, Pharisees! For you pay tithes of mint and rue and every kind of plant, but you omit judgment and the love of God. You ought to have done these things and not to have neglected those.

43 Woe to you, Pharisees! For you love the best seats in the synagogues and the greetings in the markets.

44 Woe to you, scribes and Pharisees! Hypocrites! For you are like unseen graves, and the men who walk over them do not know.

45 And answering, one of the lawyers said to Him, Teacher, you also insult us when you say these things.

46 And He said, Woe to you also, lawyers! For you load men down with burdens too heavy to bear, but you yourselves do not touch the burdens with one of your fingers.

47 Woe to you! For you build the tombs of the prophets, yet your fathers killed them.

48 You truly bear witness and consent to the deeds of your fathers. For they indeed killed them, and you build their tombs.

49 Also for this the wisdom of God said, I will send prophets and apostles to them and they will kill and persecute some of them,

νοῦσιν καὶ [c]ἐκδιώξουσιν·‖ 50 ἵνα ἐκζητηθῇ τὸ αἷμα πάντων
kill and drive out, that may be required the blood of all
τῶν προφητῶν [f]τὸ ἐκχυνόμενον‖ ἀπὸ καταβολῆς κόσμου
the prophets poured out from [the] foundation of [the] world,
ἀπὸ τῆς γενεᾶς.ταύτης, 51 ἀπὸ [g]τοῦ' αἵματος Ἄβελ ἕως [g]τοῦ'
of this generation, from the blood of Abel to the
αἵματος Ζαχαρίου τοῦ ἀπολομένου μεταξὺ τοῦ θυσιαστηρίου
blood of Zacharias, who perished between the altar
καὶ τοῦ οἴκου· ναί, λέγω ὑμῖν, ἐκζητηθήσεται ἀπὸ τῆς γενεᾶς
and the house; yea, I say to you, it shall be required of [2]generation
ταύτης. 52 Οὐαὶ ὑμῖν τοῖς νομικοῖς, ὅτι ἤρατε τὴν
[1]this. Woe to you the doctors of the law, for ye took away the
κλεῖδα τῆς γνώσεως· αὐτοὶ οὐκ.[h]εἰσήλθετε,' καὶ τοὺς εἰσερ-
key of knowledge; yourselves did not enter, and those who were
χομένους ἐκωλύσατε. 53 [i]Λέγοντος.δὲ αὐτοῦ ταῦτα πρὸς
entering ye hindered. And as [2]was [3]saying [1]he these things to
αὐτοὺς' ἤρξαντο οἱ γραμματεῖς καὶ οἱ Φαρισαῖοι δεινῶς ἐν-
them began the scribes and the Pharisees urgently to press
έχειν, καὶ ἀποστοματίζειν αὐτὸν περὶ πλειόνων, 54 ἐνε-
upon [him], and to make [2]speak [1]him about many things; watch-
δρεύοντες [k]αὐτὸν' [l]καὶ‖ [m]ζητοῦντες' θηρεῦσαί τι ἐκ τοῦ
ing him and seeking to catch something out of
στόματος.αὐτοῦ [n]ἵνα κατηγορήσωσιν αὐτοῦ.‖
his mouth that they might accuse him.
12 Ἐν οἷς ἐπισυναχθεισῶν τῶν μυριάδων τοῦ
During which [things] being gathered together the myriads of the
ὄχλου, ὥστε καταπατεῖν ἀλλήλους, ἤρξατο λέγειν πρὸς τοὺς
crowd, so as to trample upon one another, he began to say to
μαθητὰς.αὐτοῦ πρῶτον, Προσέχετε ἑαυτοῖς ἀπὸ τῆς ζύμης
his disciples first, Take heed to yourselves of the leaven
τῶν Φαρισαίων, ἥτις ἐστὶν ὑπόκρισις. 2 οὐδὲν.δὲ συγκεκαλυμ-
of the Pharisees, which is hypocrisy; but nothing [2]covered
μένον ἐστὶν ὃ οὐκ.ἀποκαλυφθήσεται, καὶ κρυπτὸν ὃ οὐ
[3]up [1]is which shall not be uncovered, nor hidden which [2]not
γνωσθήσεται. 3 ἀνθ'.ὧν ὅσα ἐν τῇ σκοτίᾳ εἴπατε, ἐν τῷ
[3]shall be known; wherefore whatever in the darkness ye said, in the
φωτὶ ἀκουσθήσεται· καὶ ὃ πρὸς τὸ οὖς ἐλαλήσατε ἐν τοῖς
light shall be heard; and what in the ear ye spoke in
ταμείοις, κηρυχθήσεται ἐπὶ τῶν δωμάτων. 4 Λέγω.δὲ ὑμῖν
chambers, shall be proclaimed upon the housetops. But I say to you,
τοῖς.φίλοις.μου, Μὴ.φοβηθῆτε ἀπὸ τῶν [p]ἀποκτεινόντων‖
my friends, Ye should not fear because of those who kill
τὸ σῶμα, καὶ μετὰ ταῦτα μὴ.ἐχόντων [q]περισσότερόν‖.τι
the body, and after these things are not able anything more
ποιῆσαι. 5 ὑποδείξω.δὲ ὑμῖν τίνα φοβηθῆτε· φοβήθητε
to do. But I will shew you whom ye should fear: Fear
τὸν μετὰ τὸ ἀποκτεῖναι [r]ἐξουσίαν ἔχοντα‖ ἐμβαλεῖν εἰς τὴν
him who after having killed, authority has to cast into the
γέενναν· ναί, λέγω ὑμῖν, τοῦτον φοβήθητε. 6 Οὐχὶ πέντε
gehenna; yea, I say to you, [2]him [1]fear. [2]Not [3]five
στρουθία [s]πωλεῖται‖ ἀσσαρίων δύο; καὶ ἓν ἐξ αὐτῶν οὐκ
[4]sparrows [1]are sold for [2]assaria [1]two? and one of them [2]not
ἔστιν ἐπιλελησμένον ἐνώπιον τοῦ θεοῦ· 7 ἀλλὰ.καὶ αἱ τρίχες
[1]is forgotten before God. But even the hairs
τῆς.κεφαλῆς.ὑμῶν πᾶσαι ἠρίθμηνται. μὴ [t]οὖν‖ φοβεῖσθε·
of your head [2]all [1]have been numbered. [2]Not [3]therefore [1]fear,
πολλῶν στρουθίων διαφέρετε. 8 Λέγω.δὲ ὑμῖν, Πᾶς ὃς.ἂν
than many sparrows ye are better. But I say to you, Every one whoever
ὁμολογήσῃ ἐν ἐμοὶ ἔμπροσθεν τῶν ἀνθρώπων, καὶ ὁ υἱὸς τοῦ
may confess me before men, also the Son
ἀνθρώπου ὁμολογήσει ἐν αὐτῷ ἔμπροσθεν τῶν ἀγγέλων τοῦ
of man will confess him before the angels
θεοῦ· 9 ὁ.δὲ ἀρνησάμενός με [v]ἐνώπιον' τῶν ἀνθρώπων
of God; but he that has denied me before men
ἀπαρνηθήσεται ἐνώπιον τῶν ἀγγέλων τοῦ θεοῦ. 10 καὶ πᾶς
will be denied before the angels of God; and every one
ὃς ἐρεῖ λόγον εἰς τὸν υἱὸν τοῦ ἀνθρώπου, ἀφεθήσεται
who shall say a word against the Son of man, it will be forgiven
αὐτῷ· τῷ.δὲ εἰς τὸ ἅγιον πνεῦμα βλασφημήσαντι
him; but to him who against the Holy Spirit has blasphemed
οὐκ.ἀφεθήσεται. 11 ὅταν.δὲ [w]προσφέρωσιν‖ ὑμᾶς ἐπὶ τὰς
it will not be forgiven. But when they bring you before the
συναγωγὰς καὶ τὰς ἀρχὰς καὶ τὰς ἐξουσίας, [x]μὴ.μεριμνᾶτε‖
synagogues and the rulers and the authorities, be not careful
πῶς [y]ἢ τί‖ ἀπολογήσησθε, ἢ τί εἴπητε· 12 τὸ.γὰρ
how or what ye shall reply in defence, or what ye should say; for the
ἅγιον πνεῦμα διδάξει ὑμᾶς ἐν αὐτῇ.τῇ ὥρᾳ ἃ δεῖ
Holy Spirit will teach you in that same hour what it behoves [you]
εἰπεῖν.
to say.
13 Εἶπεν.δέ τις [z]αὐτῷ ἐκ τοῦ ὄχλου,‖ Διδάσκαλε, εἰπὲ τῷ
And [2]said [1]one to him from the crowd, Teacher, speak

50 so that the blood of all the prophets poured out from the foundation of the world may be required of this generation

51 from the blood of Abel to the blood of Zech-a-ri-ah, who died between the altar and the House *of God.* Yes, I say to you, it will be charged to this generation.

52 Woe to you, lawyers! For you took away the key of knowledge. You did not enter yourselves, yet you stood in the way of those who were entering.

53 And as He was saying these things to them, the scribes and Pharisees began to press furiously and *tried* to force Him to speak of many things,

54 watching Him closely and trying to catch something out of His mouth that they might use to accuse Him.

CHAPTER 12

1 In the meantime myriads of people were gathering, so as to trample on one another. He began to say to His disciples first of all, Look out for the leaven of the Pharisees (which is hypocrisy).

2 But nothing is concealed which shall not be uncovered, nor hidden which shall not be revealed.

3 Therefore whatever you said in the darkness will be heard in the light. And what you spoke in the ear in secret rooms will be shouted from the housetops.

4 But I say to you, my friends, Do not be afraid of those who kill the body and after that are not able to do anything else.

5 But I will show you whom you should fear. Fear *the One* who after He has killed has the authority to throw *you* into hell. Yes, I say to you, Fear Him!

6 Are not five sparrows sold for two coins? Yet not one of them is forgotten by God.

7 But even the hairs of your head have all been numbered. So do not fear, you are of more value than many sparrows.

8 But I say to you, Everyone who confesses Me before men, the Son of man will also acknowledge him in the presence of the angels of God.

9 But he who has denied Me before men will be denied before the angels of God.

10 And everyone who shall say a word against the Son of man, it will be forgiven him. But it will not be forgiven to him who has blasphemed the Holy Spirit.

11 But when they bring you in front of the synagogues and the rulers and the authorities, do not be anxious as to how or what you shall reply, or what you shall say –

12 for the Holy Spirit will teach you in that same hour what you ought to say.

13 And one of the company said to Him, Teacher, command my brother to divide the

ἀδελφῷ.μου μερίσασθαι μετ' ἐμοῦ τὴν κληρονομίαν. 14 Ὁ.δὲ
to my brother to divide with me the inheritance. But he
εἶπεν αὐτῷ, Ἄνθρωπε, τίς με κατέστησεν [a]δικαστὴν[||] ἢ μερισ-
said to him, Man, who [2]me [1]appointed a judge or a di-
τὴν ἐφ' ὑμᾶς; 15 Εἶπεν.δὲ πρὸς αὐτούς, Ὁρᾶτε καὶ φυλάσ-
vider over you? And he said to them, See and keep your-
σεσθε ἀπὸ [b]τῆς[||] πλεονεξίας· ὅτι οὐκ ἐν τῷ περισσεύειν
selves from covetousness; for not in the abundance
τινὶ ἡ.ζωὴ.αὐτοῦ ἐστιν ἐκ τῶν ὑπαρχόντων.[c]αὐτοῦ.[||]
[7]to [8]anyone [9]his [10]life [3]is [4]of [5]that [6]which [8]he [5]possesses.
16 Εἶπεν.δὲ παραβολὴν πρὸς αὐτούς, λέγων, Ἀνθρώπου
And he spoke a parable to them, saying, [3]Of [4]a [7]man
τινὸς πλουσίου [d]εὐφόρησεν[||] ἡ χώρα· 17 καὶ
[5]certain [6]rich [8]brought [9]forth [10]abundantly [1]the [2]ground. And
διελογίζετο ἐν ἑαυτῷ, λέγων, Τί ποιήσω, ὅτι οὐκ.ἔχω
he was reasoning within himself, saying, What shall I do, for I have not
ποῦ συνάξω τοὺς.καρπούς.μου; 18 καὶ εἶπεν, Τοῦτο ποιήσω·
where I shall lay up my fruit? and he said, This will I do:
καθελῶ μου τὰς ἀποθήκας, καὶ μείζονας οἰκοδομήσω, καὶ
I will take away my granaries, and greater will build, and
συνάξω ἐκεῖ πάντα [e]τὰ.γενήματά[?].[f]μου[||] καὶ τὰ.ἀγαθά.μου,
will lay up there all my produce and my good things,
19 καὶ ἐρῶ τῇ.ψυχῇ.μου, Ψυχή, ἔχεις πολλὰ ἀγαθὰ
and I will say to my soul, Soul, thou hast many good things
κείμενα εἰς ἔτη πολλά· ἀναπαύου, φάγε, πίε, εὐφραίνου.
laid by for [2]years [1]many; take thy rest, eat, drink, be merry.
20 εἶπεν.δὲ αὐτῷ ὁ θεός, [g]Ἄφρων,[||] ταύτῃ τῇ νυκτὶ τὴν ψυχήν
But [2]said [3]to [4]him [1]God, Fool, this night [4]soul
σου [h]ἀπαιτοῦσιν[||] ἀπὸ σοῦ· ἃ.δὲ ἡτοίμασας τίνι
[1]thy they require of thee; and [5]what [6]thou [7]didst [8]prepare [1]to [2]whom
ἔσται; 21 οὕτως ὁ θησαυρίζων [i]ἑαυτῷ,[||] καὶ μὴ εἰς
[3]shall [4]be? Thus [is] he who treasures up for himself, and not toward
θεὸν πλουτῶν. 22 Εἶπεν.δὲ πρὸς τοὺς.μαθητὰς.[k]αὐτοῦ,[||] Διὰ
God is rich. And he said to his disciples, Because of
τοῦτο [l]ὑμῖν λέγω,[||] μὴ.μεριμνᾶτε τῇ.ψυχῇ.[m]ὑμῶν[||] τί φάγητε,
this to you I say, Be not careful as to your life what ye should eat,
μηδὲ τῷ σώματι[n] τί ἐνδύσησθε. 23 ἡ[o] ψυχὴ πλεῖόν ἐστιν
nor as to the body what ye should put on. The life more is
τῆς τροφῆς, καὶ τὸ σῶμα τοῦ ἐνδύματος. 24 Κατανοήσατε
than the food, and the body than the raiment. Consider
τοὺς κόρακας, ὅτι [p]οὐ[||] σπείρουσιν [q]οὐδὲ[||] θερίζουσιν, οἷς
the ravens, for [3]not [1]they [2]sow nor reap, to which
οὐκ.ἔστιν ταμεῖον οὐδὲ ἀποθήκη, καὶ ὁ θεὸς τρέφει αὐτούς·
there is not storehouse nor granary, and God feeds them.
πόσῳ μᾶλλον ὑμεῖς διαφέρετε τῶν πετεινῶν; 25 τίς.δὲ ἐξ
How much more [2]ye [1]are better than the birds? And who of
ὑμῶν [r]μεριμνῶν[||] δύναται [s]προσθεῖναι ἐπὶ τὴν.ἡλικίαν.αὐτοῦ[t]
you [by] being careful is able to add to his stature
πῆχυν [t]ἕνα[||]; 26 εἰ οὖν [v]οὔτε[||] ἐλάχιστον δύνασθε,
[2]cubit [1]one? If therefore not even [the] least ye are able [to do],
τί περὶ τῶν λοιπῶν μεριμνᾶτε; 27 Κατανοήσατε τὰ κρίνα,
why about the rest are ye careful? Consider the lilies,
πῶς [w]αὐξάνει· οὐ.κοπιᾷ, οὐδὲ νήθει·[||] λέγω.δὲ ὑμῖν,[x]
how they grow; they labour not, nor do they spin; but I say to you,
οὐδὲ Σολομὼν ἐν πάσῃ τῇ.δόξῃ.αὐτοῦ περιεβάλετο ὡς ἓν
Not even Solomon in all his glory was clothed as one
τούτων. 28 εἰ.δὲ [y]τὸν χόρτον ἐν τῷ ἀγρῷ σήμερον ὄντα,[||] καὶ
of these. But if the grass [3]in [4]the [5]field [6]to-day [1]which [2]is, and
αὔριον εἰς κλίβανον βαλλόμενον, ὁ θεὸς οὕτως [z]ἀμφιέννυσιν,[||]
to-morrow into an oven is cast, God thus arrays,
πόσῳ μᾶλλον ὑμᾶς, ὀλιγόπιστοι; 29 καὶ ὑμεῖς μὴ.ζητεῖτε
how much rather you, O [ye] of little faith? And ye seek ye not
τί φάγητε [a]ἢ[||] τί πίητε, καὶ μὴ.μετεωρίζεσθε. 30 ταῦτα
what ye may eat or what ye may drink, and be not in anxiety; [2]these [3]things
γὰρ πάντα τὰ ἔθνη τοῦ κόσμου [b]ἐπιζητεῖ·[||] ὑμῶν.δὲ ὁ πατὴρ
[1]for all the nations of the world seek after; and your Father
οἶδεν ὅτι χρῄζετε τούτων. 31 πλὴν ζητεῖτε τὴν βασιλείαν
knows that ye have need of these things. But seek ye the kingdom
[c]τοῦ θεοῦ,[||] καὶ ταῦτα [d]πάντα[||] προστεθήσεται ὑμῖν. 32 μὴ
of God, and [2]these [3]things [1]all shall be added to you. [2]Not
φοβοῦ, τὸ μικρὸν ποίμνιον· ὅτι εὐδόκησεν ὁ.πατὴρ.ὑμῶν
[1]fear, little flock, for [3]took [4]delight [1]your [2]Father
δοῦναι ὑμῖν τὴν βασιλείαν. 33 πωλήσατε τὰ.ὑπάρχοντα.ὑμῶν,
in giving you the kingdom. Sell your possessions,
καὶ δότε ἐλεημοσύνην· ποιήσατε ἑαυτοῖς [e]βαλάντια[||] μὴ
and give alms; make to yourselves purses not
παλαιούμενα, θησαυρὸν ἀνέκλειπτον ἐν τοῖς οὐρανοῖς, ὅπου
growing old, a treasure unfailing in the heavens, where
κλέπτης οὐκ.ἐγγίζει, οὐδὲ σὴς διαφθείρει· 34 ὅπου.γάρ ἐστιν
thief does not draw near, nor moth destroy. For where is
ὁ.θησαυρὸς.ὑμῶν, ἐκεῖ καὶ ἡ.καρδία.ὑμῶν ἔσται. 35 Ἔστωσαν
your treasure, there also your heart will be. Let be

inheritance with me.
14 But He said to him, Man, who made Me a
judge or a divider over you?
15 And He said to them, Watch! And keep
yourselves from lusting for more and more.
For a man's life is not in the fullness of the
things he owns.
16 And He told them a parable, saying, The
ground of a certain rich man produced
abundantly.
17 And he was thinking within himself,
saying, What shall I do, for I have no room to
store my fruits.
18 And he said, I will do this: I will remove
my barns and will build bigger ones. And I will
store all my crops and good things there.
19 And I will say to my soul, Soul, you have
many good things laid up for many years. Rest
yourself; eat, drink and be merry.
20 But God said to him, Fool! This is the
night your soul shall be demanded of you.
And that which you have gathered, to whom
will it be given?
21 So is he who lays up treasure for himself
and is not rich toward God.
22 And He said to His disciples, Because of
this I say to you, Do not be anxious as to your
life, what you should eat – nor as to the body,
what you should put on.
23 Life is more than food, and the body is
more than clothing.
24 Think of the ravens, for they do not sow
or reap. There is no barn or storehouse for
them, yet God feeds them. How much better
are you than the birds!
25 And who of you is able to add one cubit to
his height by being anxious?
26 Then if you cannot do even the least
thing, why are you anxious about the rest?
27 Think of the lilies, how they grow. They
do not work, nor do they spin. But I tell you
that not even Solomon in all his glory was
clothed like one of these.
28 But if God so dresses the grass – which is
here today but is thrown into the oven tomorrow – how much rather you! O you of little
faith.
29 And you, do not seek what you may eat,
or what you may drink, and do not live in
anxiety.
30 For the nations of the world seek after all
these things, and your Father knows that you
need these things.
31 But rather seek the kingdom of God and
all these things will be added to you.
32 Do not be afraid, little flock, for your
Father delighted to give you the kingdom.
33 Sell what you own and give charitably.
Make yourselves purses that will not grow old,
a treasure in Heaven that will not fail – where
the thief does not come nor the moth destroy.
34 For where your treasure is, there your
heart will be also.
35 Keep your robe tight around your waist

[f]ὑμῶν αἱ ὀσφύες‖ περιεζωσμέναι καὶ οἱ λύχνοι καιόμενοι· 36 καὶ
your loins ·girded about and lamps burning; and
ὑμεῖς ὅμοιοι ἀνθρώποις προσδεχομένοις τὸν.κύριον.ἑαυτῶν,
ye like to men waiting for their lord,
πότε [g]ἀναλύσει‖ · ἐκ τῶν γάμων, ἵνα ἐλθόντος καὶ κρού-
whenever he shall return from the wedding feasts, that having come and having
σαντος, εὐθέως ἀνοίξωσιν αὐτῷ. 37 μακάριοι οἱ δοῦλοι
knocked, immediately they may open to him. Blessed [2]bondmen
ἐκεῖνοι οὓς ἐλθὼν ὁ κύριος εὑρήσει γρηγοροῦντας. ἀμὴν
[1]those whom coming the Lord shall find watching. Verily
λέγω ὑμῖν, ὅτι περιζώσεται καὶ ἀνακλινεῖ αὐτούς, καὶ
I say to you, that he will gird himself and will make [2]recline [1]them, and
παρελθὼν διακονήσει αὐτοῖς. 38 [h]καὶ ἐὰν ἔλθῃ ἐν τῇ δευτέρᾳ
coming up will serve them. And if he come in the second
φυλακῇ, καὶ‖ ἐν τῇ τρίτῃ φυλακῇ ἔλθῃ, καὶ εὕρῃ οὕτως,
watch, and in the third watch he come, and find [them] thus,
μακάριοί εἰσιν [i]οἱ δοῦλοι ἐκεῖνοι.‖ 39 τοῦτο.δὲ γινώσκετε, ὅτι
blessed are [2]bondmen [1]those. But this know, that
εἰ ᾔδει ὁ οἰκοδεσπότης ·ποίᾳ ὥρᾳ ὁ κλέπτης ἔρχεται,
if [6]had [7]known [1]the [2]master [3]of [4]the [5]house in what hour the thief is coming,
[k]ἐγρηγόρησεν ἄν, καὶ‖ οὐκ.[l]ἂν‖.ἀφῆκεν [m]διορυγῆναι‖
he would have watched, and would not have suffered to be dug through
τὸν.οἶκον.αὐτοῦ. 40 καὶ ὑμεῖς [n]οὖν‖ γίνεσθε ἕτοιμοι· ὅτι
his house. And ye therefore be ye ready; for
ᾗ ὥρᾳ οὐ.δοκεῖτε, ὁ υἱὸς τοῦ ἀνθρώπου ἔρχεται. 41 Εἶπεν.δὲ
in the hour ye think not, the Son of man comes. And [2]said
[o]αὐτῷ‖ ὁ Πέτρος, Κύριε, πρὸς ἡμᾶς τὴν.παραβολὴν.ταύτην
[3]to [4]him [1]Peter, Lord, to us this parable
λέγεις, ἢ καὶ πρὸς πάντας; 42 [p]Εἶπεν.δὲ‖ ὁ κύριος, Τίς
speakest thou, or also to all? And said the Lord, Who
ἄρα ἐστὶν ὁ πιστὸς οἰκονόμος [q]καὶ‖ φρόνιμος, ὃν καταστήσει
then is the faithful steward and prudent, whom [3]will [4]set
ὁ κύριος ἐπὶ τῆς.θεραπείας.αὐτοῦ, [r]τοῦ‖ διδόναι ἐν καιρῷ [s]τὸ‖
[1]the [2]Lord over his household, to give in season the
σιτομέτριον; 43 μακάριος ὁ.δοῦλος.ἐκεῖνος ὃν ἐλθὼν
measure of corn? Blessed that bondman whom [3]having [4]come
ὁ.κύριος.αὐτοῦ εὑρήσει ποιοῦντα οὕτως. 44 ἀληθῶς λέγω ὑμῖν,
[1]his [2]Lord will find doing thus. Of a truth I say to you,
ὅτι ἐπὶ πᾶσιν τοῖς.ὑπάρχουσιν.αὐτοῦ καταστήσει αὐτόν.
that over all his possessions he will set him.
45 Ἐὰν.δὲ εἴπῃ ὁ.δοῦλος.ἐκεῖνος ἐν τῇ.καρδίᾳ.αὐτοῦ, Χρο-
But if [3]should [4]say [1]that [2]bondman in his heart, [3]De-
νίζει ὁ.κύριός.μου ἔρχεσθαι· καὶ ἄρξηται τύπτειν τοὺς
lays [1]my [2]Lord to come, and should begin to beat the
παῖδας καὶ τὰς παιδίσκας, ἐσθίειν.τε καὶ πίνειν καὶ με-
men-servants and the maid-servants, and to eat and to drink and to be
θύσκεσθαι· 46 ἥξει ὁ κύριος τοῦ.δούλου.ἐκείνου ἐν ἡμέρᾳ
drunken, [6]will [7]come [1]the [2]Lord [3]of [4]that [5]bondman in a day
ᾗ οὐ.προσδοκᾷ, καὶ ἐν ὥρᾳ ᾗ οὐ.γινώσκει, καὶ
in which he does not expect, and in an hour which he knows not, and
διχοτομήσει αὐτόν, καὶ τὸ.μέρος.αὐτοῦ μετὰ τῶν ἀπίστων
will cut [2]in [3]two [1]him, and his portion with the unbelievers
θήσει. 47 ἐκεῖνος.δὲ ὁ δοῦλος ὁ γνοὺς τὸ θέλημα τοῦ
will appoint. But that bondman who knew the will
κυρίου.[t]ἑαυτοῦ,‖ καὶ μὴ.ἑτοιμάσας [v]μηδὲ‖ ποιήσας πρὸς
of his Lord, and prepared not nor did according to
τὸ.θέλημα.αὐτοῦ, δαρήσεται πολλάς· 48 ὁ.δὲ μὴ
his will, shall be beaten with many [stripes]; but he who [2]not
γνούς, ποιήσας.δὲ ἄξια πληγῶν, δαρήσεται ὀλίγας.
[1]knew, and did [things] worthy of stripes, shall be beaten with few.
παντὶ.δὲ ᾧ ἐδόθη πολύ, πολὺ ζητηθήσεται παρ' αὐτοῦ·
And everyone to whom was given much, much will be required from him;
καὶ ᾧ παρέθεντο πολύ, περισσότερον αἰτήσουσιν αὐτόν.
and to whom was committed much, the more will they ask of him.
49 Πῦρ ἦλθον βαλεῖν [w]εἰς‖ τὴν γῆν, καὶ τί θέλω εἰ ἤδη
Fire I came to cast into the earth, and what will I if already
ἀνήφθη; 50 βάπτισμα.δὲ ἔχω βαπτισθῆναι, καὶ πῶς συν-
it be kindled? But a baptism I have to be baptized [with], and how am I
έχομαι ἕως.[x]οὗ‖ τελεσθῇ. 51 δοκεῖτε ὅτι εἰρήνην παρε-
straitened until it be accomplished! Think ye that peace I
γενόμην δοῦναι ἐν τῇ γῇ; οὐχί, λέγω ὑμῖν, ἀλλ' ἢ
came to give in the earth? No, I say to you, but rather
διαμερισμόν. 52 ἔσονται.γὰρ ἀπὸ τοῦ.νῦν πέντε ἐν [y]οἴκῳ
division; for there will be from henceforth five in [2]house
ἑνὶ‖ διαμεμερισμένοι, τρεῖς ἐπὶ δυσὶν καὶ δύο ἐπὶ [z]τρισίν.
[1]one divided, three against two and two against three.
53 διαμερισθήσεται‖ πατὴρ [a]ἐφ'‖ υἱῷ, καὶ υἱὸς ἐπὶ πατρί
[4]Will [5]be [6]divided [1]father against son, and son against father
μήτηρ ἐπὶ [b]θυγατρί,‖ καὶ θυγάτηρ ἐπὶ [c]μητρί·‖ πενθερὰ
mother against daughter, and daughter against mother; mother-in-law
ἐπὶ τὴν νύμφην [d]αὐτῆς,‖ καὶ νύμφη ἐπὶ τὴν
against [2]daughter-in-law [1]her, and daughter-in-law against

and your lights on.
36 And be like men waiting for their lord
whenever he returns from the wedding feasts,
so that when he comes and knocks they may
immediately open to him.
37 Blessed are those servants whom the lord
shall find waiting alertly when he comes. I tell
you truly that he will prepare himself and will
make them recline. And He will come near
and serve them.
38 And if he returns in the second watch *or* in
the third watch and finds *them* so, blessed are
those servants.

39 But know this, that if the master of the
house had known in what hour the thief was
coming, he would have watched and would
not have allowed his house to be robbed.
40 Then, you be ready. For at a time that you
do not expect, the Son of man comes.
41 And Peter said to Him, Lord, do You
speak this parable to us, or also to all?
42 And the Lord said, Who then is the
faithful and wise manager, whom *his* lord shall
set over his household as ruler, to give the
portion of grain in due time?
43 Blessed is that servant who will be found
doing so when his lord comes.
44 Indeed I tell you that he will make him
ruler over all that he has.
45 But if that servant should say in his heart,
my lord is delaying to come, and should begin
to beat men and women under him (and to eat
and drink and become drunk),
46 that servant's lord will come in a day when
he does not expect him, and in an hour he
does not know. And he will cut him in two
and will give him his portion with the
unbelievers.
47 But the servant who knew the will of his
lord and did not prepare, nor acted according
to his will, will be beaten with many *stripes*.
48 But he who did not know, yet did things
worthy of stripes, will be beaten with few.
And to whom much was given, much will be
demanded from him. And to whom much is
entrusted, the more they will ask of him.
49 I came to hurl fire into the earth, and what
if I desire it already to be kindled?
50 But I have a baptism I must be immersed
in. And O how I am pressed until it is done!
51 Do you think that I came to give peace on
earth? No, I say to you, but rather to divide.
52 For from now on there will be five divided
in one house, three against two, and two
against three.
53 Father will be divided against son and son
against father; mother against daughter and
daughter against mother – mother-in-law
against her daughter-in-law and daughter-in-
law against her mother-in-law.

πενθερὰν ᵉαὐτῆς."
²mother-in-law ¹her.

54 ᶠἜλεγεν.δὲ καὶ τοῖς ὄχλοις, "Ὅταν ἴδητε ᶠτὴν" νεφέλην
And he said also to the crowds, When ye see the cloud

ἀνατέλλουσαν ᵍἀπὸ" δυσμῶν, εὐθέως λέγετε, ʰ"Ὄμβρος
rising up from [the] west, immediately ye say, A shower

ἔρχεται· καὶ γίνεται οὕτως. 55 καὶ ὅταν νότον πνέοντα,
is coming; and it happens so. And when a south wind [is] blowing,

λέγετε, "Ὅτι καύσων ἔσται· καὶ γίνεται. 56 ὑποκριταί, τὸ
ye say, Heat there will be; and it happens. Hypocrites, the

πρόσωπον τῆς γῆς καὶ τοῦ οὐρανοῦ οἴδατε δοκιμάζειν·
appearance of the earth and of the heaven ye know [how] to discern,

τὸν.δὲ.καιρὸν.τοῦτον πῶς ⁱοὐ.δοκιμάζετε"; 57 τί.δὲ καὶ ἀφ'
but this time how do ye not discern? And why even of

ἑαυτῶν οὐ.κρίνετε τὸ δίκαιον; 58 ὡς.γὰρ ὑπάγεις μετὰ
yourselves judge ye not what [is] right? For as thou goest with

τοῦ.ἀντιδίκου.σου ἐπ' ἄρχοντα, ἐν τῇ ὁδῷ δὸς ἐργασίαν
thine adverse party before a magistrate, in the way give diligence

ἀπηλλάχθαι ἀπ' αὐτοῦ· μήποτε κατασύρῃ σε πρὸς
to be set free from him, lest he should drag away thee to

τὸν κριτήν, καὶ ὁ κριτής σε ᵏπαραδῷ" τῷ πράκτορι, καὶ
the judge, and the judge thee should deliver to the officer, and

ὁ πράκτωρ σε ˡβάλλῃ" εἰς φυλακήν. 59 λέγω σοι, οὐ.μὴ
the officer thee should cast into prison. I say to thee, In no wise

ἐξέλθῃς ἐκεῖθεν ἕως.ᵐοὗ" καὶ τὸ ἔσχατον λεπτὸν
shalt thou come out thence until even the last lepton

ἀποδῷς.
thou shalt have paid.

13 Παρῆσαν.δέ τινες ἐν αὐτῷ.τῷ καιρῷ ἀπαγγέλλοντες
And ²were ³present ¹some at the same time telling

αὐτῷ περὶ τῶν Γαλιλαίων, ὧν τὸ αἷμα ⁿΠιλάτος" ἔμιξεν
him about the Galileans, of whom the blood Pilate mingled

μετὰ τῶν.θυσιῶν.αὐτῶν. 2 καὶ ἀποκριθεὶς ᵒὁ Ἰησοῦς" εἶπεν
with their sacrifices. And answering Jesus said

αὐτοῖς, Δοκεῖτε ὅτι οἱ Γαλιλαῖοι.οὗτοι ἁμαρτωλοὶ παρὰ πάν-
to them, Think ye that these Galileans sinners beyond all

τας τοὺς Γαλιλαίους ἐγένοντο, ὅτι ᵖτοιαῦτα" πεπόνθασιν;
the Galileans were, because such things they have suffered?

3 οὐχί, λέγω ὑμῖν· ἀλλ' ἐὰν μὴ.ᵠμετανοῆτε," πάντες ʳὡσαύ-
No, I say to you; but if ye repent not, all ²in ³like

τως" ἀπολεῖσθε. 4 ἢ ἐκεῖνοι οἱ ˢδέκα.καὶ.ὀκτὼ" ἐφ' οὓς
⁴manner ¹ye shall perish. Or those eighteen on whom

ἔπεσεν ὁ πύργος ἐν τῷ Σιλωὰμ καὶ ἀπέκτεινεν αὐτούς, δοκεῖτε
fell the tower in Siloam and killed them, think ye

ὅτι ᵗοὗτοι" ὀφειλέται ἐγένοντο παρὰ πάντας ᵛ ἀνθρώπους
that these debtors were beyond all men

τοὺς κατοικοῦντας ʷἐν" Ἱερουσαλήμ; 5 οὐχί, λέγω ὑμῖν· ἀλλ'
who dwelt in Jerusalem? No, I say to you; but

ἐὰν μὴ.ˣμετανοῆτε," πάντες ʸὁμοίως" ἀπολεῖσθε.
if ye repent not, all ²in ³like ⁴manner ¹ye shall perish.

6 ᶻἜλεγεν.δὲ ταύτην τὴν παραβολήν· Συκῆν εἶχέν τις
And he spoke this parable: ⁵A ⁶fig-tree ⁴had ¹a ²certain

ᶻἐν τῷ.ἀμπελῶνι.αὐτοῦ πεφυτευμένην·" καὶ ἦλθεν ᵃκαρπὸν
[³man] in his vineyard planted; and he came fruit

ζητῶν" ἐν αὐτῇ καὶ οὐχ.εὗρεν. 7 εἶπεν.δὲ πρὸς τὸν ἀμ-
seeking on it and did not find [any]. And he said to the vine-

πελουργόν, Ἰδού, τρία ἔτηᵇ ἔρχομαι ζητῶν καρπὸν ἐν τῇ
dresser, Behold, three years I come seeking fruit on

συκῇ.ταύτῃ καὶ οὐχ.εὑρίσκω· ἔκκοψον ᶜ αὐτήν· ᵈἱνατί" καὶ
this fig-tree and do not find [any]: cut ²down ¹it, why even

τὴν γῆν καταργεῖ; 8 ὁ.δὲ ἀποκριθεὶς λέγει αὐτῷ,
the ground does it render useless? But he answering says to him,

Κύριε, ἄφες αὐτὴν καὶ τοῦτο τὸ ἔτος, ἕως.ὅτου σκάψω περὶ
Sir, let ²alone ¹it also this year, until I shall dig about

αὐτὴν καὶ βάλω ᵉκοπρίαν·" 9 κἂν μὲν ποιήσῃ ᶠκαρπόν·
it and put manure, and if indeed it should bear fruit—;

εἰ.δὲ μήγε, εἰς.τὸ μέλλον" ἐκκόψεις αὐτήν.
but if not, hereafter thou shalt cut ²down ¹it.

10 Ἦν.δὲ διδάσκων ἐν μιᾷ τῶν συναγωγῶν ἐν τοῖς σάβ-
And he was teaching in one of the synagogues on the sab-

βασιν· 11 καὶ ἰδού, γυνὴ ᵍἦν" πνεῦμα ἔχουσα ἀσθενείας
baths. And behold, a woman there was ²a ³spirit ¹having of infirmity

ἔτη ˢδέκα.καὶ.ὀκτώ," καὶ ἦν ʰσυγκύπτουσα' καὶ μὴ.δυναμένη
³years ¹eighteen, and she was bent together and ²unable

ἀνακύψαι εἰς.τὸ.παντελές. 12 ἰδὼν.δὲ αὐτὴν ὁ Ἰησοῦς
³to ⁴lift ⁵up ⁶herself ¹wholly. And seeing her Jesus

προσεφώνησεν καὶ εἶπεν αὐτῇ, Γύναι, ἀπολέλυσαι ⁱ
called to [her] and said to her, Woman, thou hast been loosed from

τῆς.ἀσθενείας.σοῦ. 13 Καὶ ἐπέθηκεν αὐτῇ τὰς χεῖρας·
thine infirmity. And he laid upon her [his] hands,

καὶ παραχρῆμα ᵏἀνωρθώθη," καὶ ἐδόξαζεν τὸν θεόν.
and immediately she was made straight, and glorified God.

54 And He also said to the people, When you
see a cloud coming from the west, you quickly
say, A shower is coming, and it is so.
55 And when a south wind blows, you say,
There will be heat – and it happens.
56 Hypocrites! You know how to judge the
face of the sky and of the earth, but how is it
you do not know this time?
57 Yes, and why do you not judge what is
right even of yourselves?
58 For as you go with your opponent to the
magistrates, try hard to be set free from him in
the way, for fear that he may drag you away
to the judge (and the judge may deliver you to
the officer, and the officer may throw you
into prison).
59 I tell you that in no way will you come out
of there until you have paid even the last piece
of *your* money.

CHAPTER 13

1 And some of those there at the same time
were telling Him about the Galileans whose
blood Pilate had mixed with their sacrifices.
2 And answering Jesus said to them, Do you
think that these Galileans were sinners above
all the Galileans because they have suffered
these things?
3 No, I tell you, but if you do not repent, you
will all be destroyed the same way.
4 Or those eighteen on whom the tower of
Siloam fell and killed them, do you think that
these were sinners beyond all men who lived
in Jerusalem?
5 No, I tell you, but if you do not repent, you
will all be destroyed the same way.

6 And He told this parable: A certain one had
a fig-tree planted in his vineyard. And he came
looking for fruit on it, but found none.
7 And he said to the vinedresser, See! For
three years I have come looking for fruit on
this fig-tree and have found none. Cut it
down! Why does it still waste this land?
8 And he answered him, Sir, let it alone this
year also, until I have dug around it and
fertilized it.
9 Perhaps it may really bear fruit. But if not,
then you may cut it down.
10 And He was teaching in one of the
synagogues on a sabbath.
11 And, behold! There was a woman who
had a spirit of unsoundness eighteen years.
And she was bowed together and in no way
able to lift herself up.
12 And seeing her, Jesus called and said to
her, Woman, you have been turned loose from
your deformity!
13 And He laid His hands on her. And instantly she was made straight. And she
glorified God.

14 Ἀποκριθεὶς.δὲ ὁ ἀρχισυνάγωγος, ἀγανακτῶν ὅτι
But 6answering 1the 2ruler 3of 4the 5synagogue indignant because
τῷ σαββάτῳ ἐθεράπευσεν ὁ Ἰησοῦς, ἔλεγεν τῷ ὄχλῳ,[l]
on the sabbath 2healed 1Jesus, said to the crowd,
[m]Ἓξ ἡμέραι εἰσίν, ἐν αἷς δεῖ ἐργάζεσθαι· ἐν [m]ταύ-
Six days there are, in which it behoves [men] to work; in these
ταις‖ οὖν ἐρχόμενοι θεραπεύεσθε, καὶ μὴ τῇ ἡμέρᾳ τοῦ
therefore coming be healed, and not on the 2day
σαββάτου. 15 Ἀπεκρίθη [o]οὖν‖ αὐτῷ ὁ κύριος, καὶ εἶπεν,
1sabbath. 4Answered 1therefore 5him 2the 3Lord, and said,
[p]Ὑποκριτά,‖ ἕκαστος ὑμῶν τῷ σαββάτῳ οὐ.λύει τὸν
Hypocrite, each one of you on the sabbath does he not loose
βοῦν.αὐτοῦ ἢ τὸν ὄνον ἀπὸ τῆς φάτνης, καὶ ἀπαγαγὼν
his ox or ass from the manger, and having led [it] away
ποτίζει; 16 ταύτην.δὲ θυγατέρα Ἀβραὰμ οὖσαν,
give [it] drink? And this [woman], 2a 3daughter 4of 5Abraham 1being,
ἣν ἔδησεν ὁ σατανᾶς, ἰδού, δέκα.καὶ.ὀκτὼ ἔτη, οὐκ.ἔδει
whom 2has 3bound 1Satan, lo, eighteen years, ought [she] not
λυθῆναι ἀπὸ τοῦ.δεσμοῦ.τούτου τῇ ἡμέρᾳ τοῦ σαββάτου;
to be loosed from this bond on the 2day 1sabbath?
17 Καὶ ταῦτα λέγοντος.αὐτοῦ κατῃσχύνοντο πάντες οἱ
And 4these 5things 1on 2his 3saying 7were 8ashamed 6all who
ἀντικείμενοι αὐτῷ· καὶ πᾶς ὁ ὄχλος ἔχαιρεν ἐπὶ πᾶσιν
were opposed to him; and all the crowd were rejoicing at all
τοῖς ἐνδόξοις τοῖς γινομένοις ὑπ' αὐτοῦ.
the glorious things which were being done by him.

18 Ἔλεγεν [q]δέ,‖ Τίνι ὁμοία ἐστὶν ἡ βασιλεία τοῦ θεοῦ;
3He 2said 1and, To what 2like 1is the kingdom of God?
καὶ τίνι ὁμοιώσω αὐτήν; 19 ὁμοία ἐστὶν κόκκῳ σινάπεως,
and to what shall I liken it? Like it is to a grain of mustard,
[r]ὃν‖ λαβὼν ἄνθρωπος ἔβαλεν εἰς κῆπον ἑαυτοῦ· καὶ
which 3having 4taken 1a 2man cast into 2garden 1his; and
ηὔξησεν καὶ ἐγένετο εἰς δένδρον [s]μέγα,‖ καὶ τὰ πετεινὰ τοῦ
it grew and came into a 2tree 1great, and the birds of the
οὐρανοῦ κατεσκήνωσεν ἐν τοῖς.κλάδοις.αὐτοῦ. 20 [t]Καὶ‖ πάλιν
heaven roosted in its branches. And again
εἶπεν, Τίνι ὁμοιώσω τὴν βασιλείαν τοῦ θεοῦ; 21 ὁμοία
he said, To what shall I liken the kingdom of God? Like
ἐστὶν ζύμῃ, ἣν λαβοῦσα γυνὴ [v]ἐνέκρυψεν‖ εἰς ἀλεύρου
it is to leaven, which 3having 4taken 1a 2woman hid in 3of 4meal
σάτα τρία, ἕως.οὗ ἐζυμώθη ὅλον.
2seahs 1three, until 2was 3leavened 1all.

22 Καὶ διεπορεύετο κατὰ πόλεις καὶ κώμας διδάσκων, καὶ
And he went through by cities and villages teaching, and
πορείαν ποιούμενος εἰς [w]Ἱερουσαλήμ.‖ 23 εἶπεν.δέ τις αὐτῷ,
2progress 1making towards Jerusalem. And said one to him,
Κύριε, εἰ ὀλίγοι οἱ σωζόμενοι; Ὁ.δὲ εἶπεν πρὸς αὐτούς,
Lord, [are] 4few 1those 2being 3saved? But he said to them,
24 Ἀγωνίζεσθε εἰσελθεῖν διὰ τῆς στενῆς [x]πύλης·‖ ὅτι
Strive with earnestness to enter in through the narrow gate; for
πολλοί, λέγω ὑμῖν, ζητήσουσιν εἰσελθεῖν, καὶ οὐκ.ἰσχύσουσιν.
many, I say to you, will seek to enter in, and will not be able.
25 ἀφ'.οὗ.ἂν ἐγερθῇ ὁ οἰκοδεσπότης, καὶ ἀπο-
From the time 6shall 7have 8risen 9up 1the 2master 3of 4the 5house, and shall
κλείσῃ τὴν θύραν, καὶ ἄρξησθε ἔξω ἑστάναι καὶ κρούειν τὴν
have shut the door, and ye begin without to stand and to knock at the
θύραν, λέγοντες, Κύριε, [y]κύριε,‖ ἄνοιξον ἡμῖν· καὶ ἀποκριθεὶς
door, saying, Lord, Lord, open to us; and he answering
ἐρεῖ ὑμῖν, Οὐκ οἶδα ὑμᾶς πόθεν ἐστέ. 26 τότε ἄρξεσθε
will say to you, I do not know you whence ye are. Then will ye begin
λέγειν, Ἐφάγομεν ἐνώπιόν.σου καὶ ἐπίομεν, καὶ ἐν ταῖς
to say, We ate in thy presence and drank, and in
πλατείαις ἡμῶν ἐδίδαξας. 27 καὶ ἐρεῖ, Λέγω ὑμῖν, οὐκ
our streets thou didst teach. And he will say, I tell you, 3Not
οἶδα [z]ὑμᾶς‖ πόθεν ἐστέ· ἀπόστητε ἀπ' ἐμοῦ πάντες
1I 2do know you whence ye are; depart from me, all [ye]
[a]οἱ‖ ἐργάται [b]τῆς‖ ἀδικίας. 28 ἐκεῖ ἔσται ὁ κλαυθμὸς καὶ
the workers of unrighteousness. There shall be the weeping and
ὁ βρυγμὸς τῶν ὀδόντων, ὅταν [c]ὄψησθε‖ Ἀβραὰμ καὶ Ἰσαὰκ
the gnashing of the teeth, when ye see Abraham and Isaac
καὶ Ἰακὼβ καὶ πάντας τοὺς προφήτας ἐν τῇ βασιλείᾳ τοῦ
and Jacob and all the prophets in the kingdom
θεοῦ, ὑμᾶς.δὲ ἐκβαλλομένους ἔξω. 29 καὶ ἥξουσιν ἀπὸ
of God, but yourselves being cast out. And they shall come from
ἀνατολῶν καὶ δυσμῶν, καὶ [d]ἀπὸ‖ βοῤῥᾶ καὶ νότου, καὶ ἀνα-
east and west, and from north and south, and shall
κλιθήσονται ἐν τῇ βασιλείᾳ τοῦ θεοῦ. 30 καὶ ἰδού, εἰσὶν
recline in the kingdom of God. And lo, there are
ἔσχατοι οἳ ἔσονται πρῶτοι, καὶ εἰσὶν πρῶτοι οἳ ἔσονται
last who shall be first, and there are first who shall be
ἔσχατοι.
last.

14 But the ruler of the synagogue answered, being angry because Jesus healed on the sabbath, saying to the people, There are six days in which men ought to work. Therefore, come to be healed in these, and not on the Sabbath day.
15 Then the Lord answered, saying to him, Hypocrite! Does not every one of you untie his ox or his ass from the manger and lead it away and give it water?
16 And this one is a daughter of Abraham whom Satan has held tight lo *these* eighteen years! Is it not right that she be turned loose from this bond on the Sabbath?
17 And when He said these things, all who were against Him were ashamed. And all the people were rejoicing at all the glorious things which were being done by Him.

18 And He said, What is the kingdom of God like? And to what shall I compare it?
19 It is like a grain of mustard which a man took and threw into his garden. And it grew and became a great tree, and the birds roosted in the branches of it.
20 And again He said, To what shall I compare the kingdom of God?
21 It is like leaven, which a woman took and hid in three measures of meal, until all of it was leavened.

22 And He was going through cities and villages teaching and making progress toward Jerusalem.
23 And one said to Him, Lord, are those being saved few? But He said to them,
24 Labor to enter in through the narrow gate. For I tell you that many will try to enter in and will not be able.
25 From the time the master of the house has risen up and has shut the door, then you may begin to stand outside and knock at the door, crying, Lord! Lord! Open to us. But He will answer you, I do not know you. Where are you from?
26 Then you will begin to say, We ate and drank in Your presence, and You have taught in our streets.
27 And He will say, I tell you, I do not know where you are from. Depart from Me, all you workers of unrighteousness!
28 There will be weeping and gnashing of teeth when you see Abraham and Isaac and Jacob and all the prophets in the kingdom of God and you yourselves being thrown out.
29 And they shall come from east and west, and from north and south, and shall lie down in the kingdom of God.
30 And, behold! There are those who are *now* last who shall *then* be first, and there are first ones who shall be last.

31 Ἐν.αὐτῇ τῇ [c]ἡμέρᾳ" [f]προσῆλθόν" τινες Φαρισαῖοι,
On the same day came to [him] certain Pharisees,
λέγοντες αὐτῷ, Ἔξελθε καὶ πορεύου ἐντεῦθεν, ὅτι Ἡρώδης
saying to him, Go out and proceed hence, for Herod
θέλει σε ἀποκτεῖναι. 32 Καὶ εἶπεν αὐτοῖς, Πορευθέντες
desires [3]thee [1]to [2]kill. And he said to them, Having gone
εἴπατε τῇ ἀλώπεκι ταύτῃ, Ἰδού, ἐκβάλλω δαιμόνια καὶ ἰάσεις
say to that fox, Lo, I cast out demons and cures
[g]ἐπιτελῶ" σήμερον καὶ αὔριον, καὶ τῇ τρίτῃ[h] τελειοῦμαι.
I complete to-day and to-morrow, and the third [day] I am perfected;
33 πλὴν δεῖ με σήμερον καὶ αὔριον καὶ τῇ ἐχομένῃ
but it behoves me [2]to-day and to-morrow and the [day] following
πορεύεσθαι· ὅτι οὐκ.ἐνδέχεται προφήτην ἀπολέσθαι ἔξω
to proceed; for it is not possible [for] a prophet to perish out of
Ἱερουσαλήμ. 34 Ἱερουσαλήμ, Ἱερουσαλήμ, ἡ ἀποκτείνουσα
Jerusalem. Jerusalem, Jerusalem, who killest
τοὺς προφήτας, καὶ λιθοβολοῦσα τοὺς ἀπεσταλμένους πρὸς
the prophets, and stonest those who have been sent to
αὐτήν, ποσάκις ἠθέλησα ἐπισυνάξαι τὰ τέκνα.σου, ὃν.τρόπον
her, how often would I have gathered thy children, in the way
[i]ὄρνις" [k]τὴν" ἑαυτῆς [l]νοσσιὰν" ὑπὸ τὰς πτέρυγας,
a hen [gathers] her brood under [her] wings,
καὶ οὐκ ἠθελήσατε. 35 ἰδού, ἀφίεται ὑμῖν ὁ.οἶκος.ὑμῶν [m]ἔρη-
and ye would not. Behold, is left to you your house de-
μος·" [n]ἀμὴν δὲ λέγω" ὑμῖν, [o]ὅτι" οὐ.μή [p]με ἴδητε" ἕως.[q]ἂν"
solate; [2]verily [1]and I say to you, that not at all me shall ye see until
[r]ἥξῃ," [s]ὅτε" εἴπητε, Εὐλογημένος ὁ ἐρχόμενος ἐν ὀνό-
it come when ye say, Blessed [is] he who comes in [the] name
ματι κυρίου.
of [the] Lord.

14 Καὶ ἐγένετο ἐν τῷ.ἐλθεῖν.αὐτὸν εἰς οἶκόν τινος τῶν
And it came to pass on his having gone into a house of one of the
ἀρχόντων [t]τῶν[t] Φαρισαίων σαββάτῳ φαγεῖν ἄρτον, καὶ αὐτοὶ
rulers of the Pharisees on a sabbath to eat bread, that they
ἦσαν παρατηρούμενοι αὐτόν. 2 καὶ ἰδού, ἄνθρωπός τις
were watching him. And behold, a [2]man [1]certain
ἦν ὑδρωπικὸς ἔμπροσθεν αὐτοῦ. 3 καὶ ἀποκριθεὶς ὁ Ἰησοῦς
there was dropsical before him. And answering Jesus
εἶπεν πρὸς τοὺς νομικοὺς καὶ Φαρισαίους, [v]λέγων," [w]Εἰ"
spoke to the doctors of the law and to [the] Pharisees, saying,
ἔξεστιν τῷ σαββάτῳ [x]θεραπεύειν" [y]; 4 Οἱ.δὲ ἡσύχασαν.
Is it lawful on the sabbath to heal? But they were silent.
καὶ ἐπιλαβόμενος ἰάσατο αὐτόν, καὶ ἀπέλυσεν. 5 καὶ
And taking hold [of him] he healed him, and let [him] go. And
[z]ἀποκριθεὶς" [a]πρὸς αὐτοὺς εἶπεν," Τίνος ὑμῶν [b]ὄνος" ἢ βοῦς
answering to them he said, Of which of you [2]an [3]ass [4]or [5]an [6]ox
εἰς φρέαρ [c]ἐμπεσεῖται," καὶ οὐκ εὐθέως ἀνασπάσει αὐτὸν
[8]into [9]a [10]pit [1]shall [7]fall, and [2]not [4]immediately [1]he [3]will pull up him
[d]ἐν" [e]τῇ" ἡμέρᾳ τοῦ σαββάτου; 6 Καὶ οὐκ.ἴσχυσαν ἀνταπο-
on the [2]day [1]sabbath? And they were not able to re-
κριθῆναι [f]αὐτῷ" πρὸς ταῦτα.
ply to him as to these things.

7 Ἔλεγεν.δὲ πρὸς τοὺς κεκλημένους παραβολήν, ἐπέχων
And he spoke to those who were invited a parable, remarking
πῶς τὰς πρωτοκλισίας ἐξελέγοντο, λέγων πρὸς αὐτούς,
how the first places they were choosing out, saying to them,
8 Ὅταν κληθῇς ὑπό τινος εἰς γάμους, μὴ.κατακλιθῇς
When thou art invited by anyone to wedding feasts, do not recline
εἰς τὴν πρωτοκλισίαν, μήποτε ἐντιμότερός σου ᾖ.κεκλη-
in the first place, lest a more honourable than thou may have
μένος ὑπ' αὐτοῦ, 9 καὶ ἐλθὼν ὁ σὲ καὶ αὐτὸν καλέσας
been invited by him, and having come he who thee and him invited
ἐρεῖ σοι, Δὸς τούτῳ τόπον· καὶ τότε ἄρξῃ [g]μετ'"
shall say to thee, Give [2]to [3]this [4]one [1]place, and then thou begin with
αἰσχύνης τὸν ἔσχατον τόπον κατέχειν. 10 ἀλλ' ὅταν κλη-
shame the last place to take. But when thou art
θῇς, πορευθεὶς [h]ἀνάπεσον" εἰς τὸν ἔσχατον τόπον· ἵνα
invited, having gone recline in the last place, that
ὅταν ἔλθῃ ὁ κεκληκώς σε, [i]εἴπῃ" σοι, Φίλε, προσ-
when he may come who has invited thee, he may say to thee, Friend, come
ανάβηθι ἀνώτερον· τότε ἔσται σοι δόξα ἐνώπιον [k] τῶν
up higher. Then shall be to thee glory before those who
συνανακειμένων σοί. 11 ὅτι πᾶς ὁ ὑψῶν ἑαυτὸν ταπεινω-
recline [at table] with thee; for everyone that exalts himself shall be
θήσεται· καὶ ὁ ταπεινῶν ἑαυτὸν ὑψωθήσεται.
humbled, and he that humbles himself shall be exalted.

12 Ἔλεγεν.δὲ καὶ τῷ κεκληκότι.αὐτόν, Ὅταν ποιῇς
And he said also to him who had invited him, When thou makest
ἄριστον ἢ δεῖπνον, μὴ.φώνει τοὺς.φίλους.σου μηδὲ τοὺς ἀδελ-
a dinner or a supper, call not thy friends nor [2]breth-
φούς σου μηδὲ τοὺς.συγγενεῖς.σου μηδὲ γείτονας πλουσίους·
ren [1]thy nor thy kinsfolk nor [4]neighbours [3]rich,

31 On the same day some of the Pharisees came to Him and said, Get out! And, Go away from here! For Herod wants to kill you.

32 And He said to them, When you go back, say to that fox, Behold, I throw out demons and I finish cures today and tomorrow, and on the third day I am perfected.

33 But it is necessary for Me to go on today and tomorrow and the day after, for it is not possible for a prophet to be destroyed outside of Jerusalem.

34 O Jerusalem! Jerusalem that kills the prophets and stones those who have been sent to her! How often I would have gathered your children, as a hen her brood under her wings, but you were not willing.

35 See! Your house is left to you in ruins. And truly I tell you, You shall not see Me until *the time* comes when you say, Blessed is He who comes in the name of the Lord.

CHAPTER 14

1 And as He went into the house of one of the chief Pharisees on a sabbath to eat bread, they were watching Him.

2 And, behold! There was a certain man in front of Him, one who had dropsy.

3 And answering Jesus spoke to the lawyers and Pharisees, saying, Is it lawful to heal on the Sabbath?

4 And they were silent. And taking hold, He healed him and let him go.

5 And answering them He said, Which of you shall have an ass or an ox fall into a pit and will not immediately pull him out on the Sabbath day?

6 And they were not able to answer Him as to these things.

7 And He spoke a parable to those who were invited, noticing how they were choosing out the chief places, saying,

8 When you are invited by anyone to wedding feasts, do not sit in the chief place, for fear that one more honorable than you may have been invited by him.

9 And he who invited both you and him may come up and say to you, Give place to this one. And then you *would* with shame start toward the last place.

10 But when you are invited, go in and sit in the last place, so that when he who has invited you comes he may say to you, Friend, come up higher. Then you shall be honored before those at table with you.

11 For everyone that exalts himself shall be humbled. And he that humbles himself shall be exalted.

12 And He said also to the one who had invited Him, When you prepare a dinner or a supper, do not call your friends or your brothers or your relatives or rich neighbors, for fear

μήποτε καὶ αὐτοί [l]σε ἀντικαλέσωσιν,[l] καὶ γένηταί [m]σοι
lest also they thee should invite in return, and [3]be [4]made [5]thee
ἀνταπόδομα.[ll] 13 ἀλλ' ὅταν ποιῇς δοχήν, κάλει πτωχούς,
[1]a [2]recompense; but when thou makest a feast, call poor,
[n]ἀναπήρους,[ll] χωλούς, τυφλούς· 14 καὶ μακάριος ἔσῃ·
crippled, lame, blind; and blessed thou shalt be;
ὅτι οὐκ.ἔχουσιν ἀνταποδοῦναί σοι· ἀνταποδοθήσεται
for they have not [wherewith] to recompense thee; [2]it [3]shall [4]be [5]recompensed
[o]γάρ[l] σοι ἐν τῇ ἀναστάσει τῶν δικαίων.
[1]for thee in the resurrection of the just.

15 Ἀκούσας.δέ τις τῶν συνανακειμένων ταῦ-
And [9]having [10]heard [1]one [2]of [3]those [4]reclining [[5]at [6]table] [7]with [[8]him] these
τα εἶπεν αὐτῷ, Μακάριος [p]ὃς[l] φάγεται ἄρτον ἐν τῇ
things said to him, Blessed [he] who shall eat bread in the
βασιλείᾳ τοῦ θεοῦ. 16 Ὁ.δὲ εἶπεν αὐτῷ, Ἄνθρωπός τις
kingdom of God. But he said to him, A [2]man [1]certain
[q]ἐποίησεν[l] δεῖπνον [r]μέγα,[l] καὶ.ἐκάλεσεν πολλούς· 17 καὶ ἀπέ-
made a [2]supper [1]great, and invited many. And he
στειλεν τὸν.δοῦλον.αὐτοῦ τῇ ὥρᾳ τοῦ δείπνου εἰπεῖν τοῖς
sent his bondman at the hour of the supper to say to those who
κεκλημένοις, Ἔρχεσθε, ὅτι ἤδη ἕτοιμά [s]ἐστιν[l] [t]πάντα.[ll] 18 Καὶ
had been invited, Come, for now [1]ready [2]is [1]all. And
ἤρξαντο ἀπὸ μιᾶς [v]παραιτεῖσθαι πάντες.[ll] [w] ὁ πρῶ-
[2]began [3]with [4]one [[5]consent] [6]to [7]excuse [8]themselves [1]all. The first
τος εἶπεν αὐτῷ, Ἀγρὸν ἠγόρασα, καὶ [x]ἔχω ἀνάγκην[l]
said to him, [4]A [5]field [1]I [2]have [3]bought, and I have need
[y]ἐξελθεῖν καὶ[l] ἰδεῖν αὐτόν· ἐρωτῶ σε ἔχε με παρῃτημένον.
to go out and to see it; I pray thee hold me excused.
19 καὶ ἕτερος εἶπεν, Ζεύγη βοῶν ἠγόρασα πέντε, καὶ
And another said, [5]Pairs [6]of [7]oxen [1]I [2]have [3]bought [4]five, and
πορεύομαι δοκιμάσαι αὐτά· ἐρωτῶ σε ἔχε με παρῃτημένον.
I go to prove them; I pray thee hold me excused.
20 καὶ ἕτερος εἶπεν, Γυναῖκα ἔγημα, καὶ διὰ τοῦτο
And another said, A wife I have married, and because of this
οὐ.δύναμαι ἐλθεῖν. 21 καὶ παραγενόμενος ὁ.δοῦλος.[z]ἐκεῖνος[ll]
I am unable to come. And having come that bondman
ἀπήγγειλεν τῷ.κυρίῳ.αὐτοῦ ταῦτα. Τότε ὀργισθεὶς ὁ οἰκο-
reported to his lord these things. Then being angry the master
δεσπότης εἶπεν τῷ.δούλῳ.αὐτοῦ, Ἔξελθε ταχέως εἰς τὰς
of the house said to his bondman, Go out quickly into the
πλατείας καὶ ῥύμας τῆς πόλεως, καὶ τοὺς πτωχοὺς καὶ [a]ἀνα-
streets and lanes of the city, and the poor and crip-
πήρους[l] καὶ [b]χωλοὺς καὶ τυφλοὺς[ll] εἰσάγαγε ὧδε. 22 Καὶ εἶπεν
pled and lame and blind bring in here. And said
ὁ δοῦλος, Κύριε, γέγονεν [c]ὡς[l] ἐπέταξας, καὶ ἔτι
the bondman, Sir, it has been done as thou didst command, and still
τόπος ἐστίν. 23 Καὶ εἶπεν ὁ κύριος πρὸς τὸν δοῦλον,
room there is. And said the lord to the bondman,
Ἔξελθε εἰς τὰς ὁδοὺς καὶ φραγμούς, καὶ ἀνάγκασον εἰσελθεῖν,
Go out into the ways and hedges, and compel to come in,
ἵνα γεμισθῇ [d]ὁ.οἶκός.μου.[ll] 24 λέγω.γὰρ ὑμῖν, ὅτι οὐδεὶς τῶν
that may be filled my house; for I say to you, that not one
ἀνδρῶν.ἐκείνων τῶν κεκλημένων γεύσεταί μου τοῦ δείπνου.
of those men who have been invited shall taste of my supper.

25 Συνεπορεύοντο.δὲ αὐτῷ ὄχλοι πολλοί· καὶ στραφεὶς
And [3]were [4]going [5]with [6]him [2]crowds [1]great; and having turned
εἶπεν πρὸς αὐτούς, 26 Εἴ τις ἔρχεται πρός με, καὶ οὐ.μισεῖ
he said to them, If any one comes to me, and hates not
τὸν.πατέρα.[f]ἑαυτοῦ[l] καὶ τὴν μητέρα καὶ τὴν γυναῖκα καὶ τὰ
his father and mother and wife and
τέκνα καὶ τοὺς ἀδελφοὺς καὶ τὰς ἀδελφάς, ἔτι.[g]δὲ[ll] καὶ τὴν
children and brothers and sisters, and besides also
ἑαυτοῦ.ψυχήν, οὐ.δύναταί [h]μου.μαθητὴς εἶναι·[h] 27 [i]καὶ[ll] ὅστις
his own life, he cannot my disciple be; and whosoever
οὐ.βαστάζει τὸν.σταυρὸν.[k]αὐτοῦ,[ll] καὶ ἔρχεται ὀπίσω μου,
carries not his cross, and comes after me,
οὐ.δύναταί [l]μου εἶναι[ll] μαθητής. 28 τίς.γὰρ ἐξ ὑμῶν θέλων
cannot [2]my [1]be disciple. For which of you desiring
πύργον οἰκοδομῆσαι, οὐχὶ πρῶτον καθίσας ψηφίζει τὴν
a tower to build, [5]not [6]first [1]having [2]sat [3]down [4]counts the
δαπάνην, εἰ ἔχει [m]τὰ[ll] [n]πρὸς[l] ἀπαρτισμόν; 29 ἵνα μήποτε
cost, if he has the [means] for [its] completion? that lest
θέντος αὐτοῦ θεμέλιον καὶ μὴ ἰσχύοντος ἐκτελέσαι, πάντες
having laid of it a foundation and not being able to finish, all
οἱ θεωροῦντες ἄρξωνται [o]ἐμπαίζειν αὐτῷ,[l] 30 λέγοντες, Ὅτι
who see [it] should begin to mock at him, saying,
οὗτος ὁ ἄνθρωπος ἤρξατο οἰκοδομεῖν, καὶ οὐκ.ἴσχυσεν ἐκτελέσαι.
This man began to build, and was not able to finish.
31 Ἢ τίς βασιλεὺς πορευόμενος [p]συμβαλεῖν ἑτέρῳ βασι-
Or what king proceeding to engage with another king
λεῖ[ll] εἰς πόλεμον οὐχὶ καθίσας πρῶτον [q]βουλεύεται[l]
in war [6]not [1]having [2]sat [3]down [4]first [5]takes [7]counsel

that they also should invite you in return and
repay you.
13 But when you make a feast, call the poor,
the maimed, the lame and the blind,
14 and you shall be blessed. For they have
nothing to repay you. For it shall be repaid to
you in the resurrection of the just.

15 And hearing these things, one of those
sitting with Him said to Him, Blessed is he
who shall eat bread in the kingdom of God.
16 But He said to him, A certain man made a
great supper and invited many.
17 And he sent his servant at supper time to
say to those invited, Come, for all is ready.
18 And they all with one *mind* began to make
excuse. The first said to him, I have bought a
piece of land and I have to go and see it. I beg
you, count me excused.
19 And another said, I have bought five yoke
of oxen and I am going to try them out. Please
have me excused.
20 And another said, I have married a wife
and for this reason I cannot come.
21 And returning that servant reported these
things to his master. Then the master of the
house was angry and said to his servant, Go
out quickly into the streets and lanes of the
city and bring in here the poor and maimed,
the lame and the blind.
22 And the servant said, Master, it is done as
you commanded, and there is yet room.
23 And the lord said to the servant, Go out
into the highways and hedges and compel
them to come, that my house may be filled.
24 For I say to you that not one of those men
who have been invited shall taste of my
supper.

25 And great multitudes were going with
Him. And He turned and said to them,
26 If anyone comes to Me and does not hate
his father and mother and wife and children
and brothers and sisters, and his own life too,
he cannot be My disciple.
27 And whoever does not bear his cross and
come after Me cannot be My disciple.
28 For which of you, desiring to build a
tower, does not first sit down and count the
cost – whether he has enough to finish –
29 so that all who watch may not begin to
make fun of him when he has laid a foundation and is not able to finish,
30 saying, This man began to build and was
not able to finish.
31 Or what king going out to make war with
another king does not sit down and first con-

εἰ δυνατός ἐστιν ἐν δέκα χιλιάσιν [r]ἀπαντῆσαι' τῷ μετὰ
whether able he is with ten thousand to meet him with
εἴκοσι χιλιάδων ἐρχομένῳ ἐπ' αὐτόν; 32 εἰ.δὲ μήγε, ἔτι
twenty thousand who comes against him? But if not, [2]still
[s]αὐτοῦ πόρρω' ὄντος, πρεσβείαν ἀποστείλας ἐρωτᾷ τὰ
[1]he [4]far [5]off [3]being, an embassy having sent he asks the [terms]
πρὸς εἰρήνην. 33 οὕτως οὖν πᾶς ἐξ ὑμῶν ὃς οὐκ ἀπο-
for peace. Thus therefore everyone of you who [2]not [1]does take
τάσσεται πᾶσιν τοῖς ἑαυτοῦ ὑπάρχουσιν, οὐ.δύναταί [t]μου
leave of all that he himself possesses, cannot [2]my
εἶναι' μαθητής. 34 καλὸν [v] τὸ [w]ἅλας·' ἐὰν.δὲ [x] τὸ [w]ἅλας'
[1]be disciple. Good [is] the salt, but if the salt
μωρανθῇ ἐν τίνι ἀρτυθήσεται; 35 οὔτε εἰς γῆν οὔτε
become tasteless with what shall it be seasoned? Neither for land nor
εἰς κοπρίαν εὔθετόν ἐστιν· ἔξω βάλλουσιν αὐτό. Ὁ ἔχων
for manure fit is it: [4]out [1]they [2]cast [3]it. He that has
ὦτα [y]ἀκούειν' ἀκουέτω.
ears to hear let him hear.

15 [z]Ἦσαν.δὲ [z]ἐγγίζοντες αὐτῷ' πάντες οἱ τελῶναι καὶ
And were drawing near to him all the tax-gatherers and
οἱ ἁμαρτωλοὶ ἀκούειν αὐτοῦ· 2 καὶ διεγόγγυζον οἱ [a] Φαρισαῖοι
the sinners to hear him; and murmured the Pharisees
καὶ οἱ γραμματεῖς, λέγοντες, Ὅτι οὗτος ἁμαρτωλοὺς
and the scribes, saying, This [man] sinners
προσδέχεται καὶ συνεσθίει αὐτοῖς. 3 Εἶπεν.δὲ πρὸς αὐτοὺς
receives and eats with them. And he spoke to them
τὴν.παραβολὴν.ταύτην, λέγων, 4 Τίς ἄνθρωπος ἐξ ὑμῶν
this parable, saying, What man of you
ἔχων ἑκατὸν πρόβατα, καὶ [b]ἀπολέσας' [c]ἓν ἐξ αὐτῶν,' οὐ
having a hundred sheep, and having lost one of them, [2]not
καταλείπει τὰ [d]ἐννενηκονταεννέα' ἐν τῇ ἐρήμῳ καὶ πορεύεται
[1]leaves the ninety nine in the wilderness and goes
ἐπὶ τὸ ἀπολωλός, ἕως εὕρῃ αὐτό; 5 καὶ εὑρὼν
after that which has been lost, until he find it? And having found [it]
ἐπιτίθησιν ἐπὶ τοὺς.ὤμους.[e]ἑαυτοῦ' χαίρων, 6 καὶ ἐλθὼν
he lays [it] on his shoulders rejoicing, and having come
εἰς τὸν οἶκον [f]συγκαλεῖ' τοὺς φίλους καὶ τοὺς γείτονας, λέ-
to the house he calls together friends and neighbours, say-
γων αὐτοῖς, [g]Συγχάρητέ' μοι, ὅτι εὗρον τὸ.πρόβατόν.μου
ing to them, Rejoice with me, for I have found my sheep
τὸ ἀπολωλός. 7 λέγω ὑμῖν, ὅτι οὕτως χαρὰ [h]ἔσται ἐν τῷ
that was lost. I say to you, that thus joy shall be in the
οὐρανῷ' ἐπὶ ἑνὶ ἁμαρτωλῷ μετανοοῦντι, ἢ ἐπὶ [d]ἐννενη-
heaven over one sinner repenting, [more] than over ninety
κονταεννέα' δικαίοις, οἵτινες οὐ χρείαν ἔχουσιν μετανοίας.
nine righteous ones, who [2]no [3]need [1]have of repentance.
8 Ἢ τίς γυνὴ δραχμὰς ἔχουσα δέκα, ἐὰν ἀπολέσῃ δραχμὴν
Or what woman [3]drachmas [1]having [2]ten, if she should lose [2]drachma
μίαν, οὐχὶ.ἅπτει λύχνον καὶ σαροῖ τὴν οἰκίαν καὶ ζητεῖ ἐπι-
[1]one, lights not a lamp and sweeps the house and seeks care-
μελῶς ἕως.[i]ὅτου' εὕρῃ; 9 καὶ εὑροῦσα [f]συγκαλεῖται'
fully until she find [it]? and having found [it] she calls together
τὰς φίλας καὶ [k]τὰς' γείτονας, λέγουσα, [g]Συγχάρητέ' μοι, ὅτι
friends and neighbours, saying, Rejoice with me, for
εὗρον τὴν δραχμὴν ἣν ἀπώλεσα. 10 οὕτως, λέγω ὑμῖν,
I have found the drachma which I lost. Thus, I say to you,
[l]χαρὰ γίνεται' ἐνώπιον τῶν ἀγγέλων τοῦ θεοῦ ἐπὶ ἑνὶ ἁμαρ-
joy there is before the angels of God over one sin-
τωλῷ μετανοοῦντι.
ner repenting.

11 Εἶπεν.δέ, Ἄνθρωπός τις εἶχεν δύο υἱούς· 12 καὶ εἶπεν
And he said, A [2]man [1]certain had two sons; and said
ὁ νεώτερος αὐτῶν τῷ.πατρί, Πάτερ, δός μοι τὸ ἐπιβάλ-
the younger of them to [his] father, Father, give to me that [4]fall-
λον μέρος τῆς οὐσίας. [m]καὶ' διεῖλεν αὐτοῖς τὸν βίον.
ing [[3]to [4]me] [1]portion of the property. And he divided to them the living.
13 καὶ μετ' οὐ πολλὰς ἡμέρας συναγαγὼν [n]ἅπαντα'
And after not many days having gathered together all
ὁ νεώτερος υἱὸς ἀπεδήμησεν εἰς χώραν μακράν, καὶ ἐκεῖ
the younger son went away into a [2]country [1]distant, and there
διεσκόρπισεν τὴν.οὐσίαν.αὐτοῦ, ζῶν ἀσώτως. 14 δαπανή-
wasted his property, living dissolutely. [3]Having
σαντος δὲ αὐτοῦ πάντα ἐγένετο λιμὸς [o]ἰσχυρὸς' κατὰ
[4]spent [1]but [2]he all there arose a [2]famine [1]violent throughout
τὴν.χώραν.ἐκείνην, καὶ αὐτὸς ἤρξατο ὑστερεῖσθαι. 15 καὶ
that country, and he began to be in want. And
πορευθεὶς ἐκολλήθη ἑνὶ τῶν πολιτῶν τῆς.χώρας.ἐκείνης·
having gone he joined himself to one of the citizens of that country,
καὶ ἔπεμψεν αὐτὸν εἰς τοὺς.ἀγροὺς.αὐτοῦ βόσκειν χοίρους.
and he sent him into his fields to feed swine.
16 καὶ ἐπεθύμει γεμίσαι τὴν.κοιλίαν.αὐτοῦ ἀπὸ τῶν κερατίων
And he was longing to fill his belly from the husks'

sider whether he is able with ten thousand to meet him who is coming against him with twenty thousand?

32 But if not, while he is still far off, sending a group of ambassadors, he asks the *terms* of peace.

33 So in the same way every one of you who does not abandon all that he himself owns cannot be My disciple.

34 Salt is good, but if the salt becomes tasteless, with what shall it be seasoned?

35 It is neither fit for land nor for fertilizer. They throw it out. He that has ears to hear, let him hear.

CHAPTER 15

1 And all the tax-collectors and sinners were coming to Him to hear Him.

2 And the Pharisees and the scribes complained, saying, This one receives sinners and eats with them.

3 And He told them this parable, saying,

4 What man of you who has a hundred sheep and has lost one of them does not leave the ninety-nine in the field and go on after the one that is lost until he finds it?

5 And finding it he lays it on his shoulders rejoicing.

6 And he comes to the house and calls together friends and neighbors, saying to them, Rejoice with me, for I have found my sheep that was lost.

7 And I tell you that in the same way joy shall be in Heaven over one sinner repenting, *more* than over ninety-nine righteous ones who have no need of repentance.

8 Or what woman who has ten pieces of silver, if she should lose one piece, does not light a lamp and sweep the house and look carefully until she finds it?

9 And finding it she calls together friends and neighbors and says, Rejoice with me, for I have found the piece which I lost.

10 In the same way I tell you that there is joy in the presence of the angels of God over one sinner repenting.

11 And He said, A certain man had two sons.

12 And the youngest said to his father, Father, give me my part of the property. And he divided to them all *his* resources.

13 And not many days after, the younger son gathered together all and went away into a far country. And there he wasted his property with riotous living.

14 But when he had spent all, a mighty famine came throughout the country. And he began to be in need.

15 And he went over and joined himself to one of the citizens of that country. And he sent him into his fields to feed pigs.

16 And he was longing to fill his belly from the husks which the pigs were eating. But no

ὧν ἤσθιον οἱ χοῖροι· καὶ οὐδεὶς ἐδίδου αὐτῷ. 17 Εἰς
which [3]were [4]eating [1]the [2]swine; and no one gave to him. [4]To
ἑαυτὸν δὲ ἐλθὼν [p]εἶπεν,[ll] Πόσοι μίσθιοι τοῦ πατρός
[5]himself [1]but [2]having [3]come he said, How many hired servants [3]father
μου [q]περισσεύουσιν[ll] ἄρτων, ἐγὼ.δὲ [r] λιμῷ [s] ἀπόλλυμαι;
[1]of my have abundance of bread, and I with famine am perishing?
18 ἀναστὰς πορεύσομαι πρὸς τὸν.πατέρα.μου, καὶ ἐρῶ
Having risen up I will go to my father, and I will say
αὐτῷ, Πάτερ, ἥμαρτον εἰς τὸν οὐρανὸν καὶ ἐνώπιόν σου·
to him, Father, I have sinned against heaven and before thee;
19 [t]καὶ[ll] οὐκέτι εἰμὶ ἄξιος κληθῆναι υἱός.σου· ποίησόν με ὡς
and no longer am I worthy to be called thy son: make me as
ἕνα τῶν.μισθίων.σου. 20 καὶ ἀναστὰς ἦλθεν πρὸς τὸν πα-
one of thy hired servants. And having risen up he went to [2]fa-
τέρα [v]ἑαυτοῦ.[ll] [w]Ἔτι δὲ αὐτοῦ μακρὰν ἀπέχοντος εἶδεν αὐτὸν
ther [1]his. But [2]yet [1]he [4]far [3]being distant [5]saw [6]him
ὁ πατὴρ αὐτοῦ καὶ ἐσπλαγχνίσθη, καὶ δραμὼν ἐπέπεσεν
[1]his [2]father and was moved with compassion, and running fell
ἐπὶ τὸν.τράχηλον.αὐτοῦ καὶ κατεφίλησεν αὐτόν. 21 εἶπεν.δὲ
upon his neck and ardently kissed him. And [4]said
[w]αὐτῷ ὁ υἱός,[ll] Πάτερ, ἥμαρτον εἰς τὸν οὐρανὸν καὶ ἐνώ-
[3]to [4]him [1]the [2]son, Father, I have sinned against heaven and be-
πιόν σου, [x]καὶ[ll] οὐκέτι εἰμὶ ἄξιος κληθῆναι υἱός.σου. 22 Εἶπεν
fore thee, and no longer am I worthy to be called thy son. [2]Said
δὲ ὁ πατὴρ πρὸς τοὺς.δούλους.αὐτοῦ, [y] Ἐξενέγκατε [z]τὴν[ll]
[1]but the father to his bondmen, Bring out the
στολὴν τὴν πρώτην καὶ ἐνδύσατε αὐτόν, καὶ δότε δακτύλιον
robe the best and clothe him, and give a ring
εἰς τὴν χεῖρα.αὐτοῦ καὶ ὑποδήματα εἰς τοὺς πόδας· 23 καὶ
for his hand and sandals for the feet; and
[a]ἐνέγκαντες[ll] τὸν μόσχον τὸν σιτευτὸν θύσατε, καὶ φαγόντες
having brought the [2]calf [1]fattened kill [it], and eating
εὐφρανθῶμεν 24 ὅτι οὗτος ὁ υἱός.μου νεκρὸς ἦν, καὶ ἀνέζη-
let us be merry: for this my son [2]dead [1]was, and is alive
σεν· [b]καὶ ἀπολωλὼς ἦν,[ll] καὶ εὑρέθη. Καὶ ἤρξαντο εὐ-
again; and [2]lost [1]was, and is found. And they began to
φραίνεσθαι. 25 Ἦν.δὲ ὁ.υἱὸς.αὐτοῦ ὁ πρεσβύτερος ἐν ἀγρῷ·
be merry. And [5]was [1]his [2]son [3]the [4]elder in a field;
καὶ ὡς ἐρχόμενος ἤγγισεν τῇ οἰκίᾳ ἤκουσεν συμφωνίας
and as coming [up] he drew near to the house he heard music
καὶ χορῶν· 26 καὶ προσκαλεσάμενος ἕνα τῶν.παίδων.[c]αὐτοῦ,[ll]
and dancing. And having called near one of his servants,
ἐπυνθάνετο τί [d] εἴη ταῦτα. 27 ὁ.δὲ εἶπεν αὐτῷ, [e]Ὅτι
he inquired what might be these things. And he said to him,
ὁ ἀδελφός σου ἥκει· καὶ ἔθυσεν ὁ.πατήρ σου τὸν μόσχον τὸν
Thy brother is come, and [3]killed [1]thy [2]father the [2]calf
σιτευτόν, ὅτι ὑγιαίνοντα αὐτὸν ἀπέλαβεν. 28 Ὠργίσθη
[1]fattened, because safe and well [3]him [1]he [2]received. [2]He [3]was [1]angry
δὲ καὶ οὐκ.ἤθελεν εἰσελθεῖν. ὁ [f]οὖν[ll] πατὴρ αὐτοῦ
[1]but and was not willing to go in. [2]The [1]therefore father of him
ἐξελθὼν παρεκάλει αὐτόν. 29 ὁ.δὲ ἀποκριθεὶς εἶπεν τῷ.πα-
having gone out besought him. But he answering said to [2]fa-
τρί,[f] Ἰδού, τοσαῦτα ἔτη δουλεύω σοι καὶ οὐδέποτε ἐντολήν
ther [1]his], Lo, so many years I serve thee and never [4]commandment
σου παρῆλθον, καὶ ἐμοὶ οὐδέποτε ἔδωκας ἔριφον ἵνα μετὰ
[3]thy [1]transgressed [2]I, and to me never didst thou give a kid that with
τῶν φίλων.μου εὐφρανθῶ· 30 ὅτε δὲ ὁ υἱός.σου οὗτος
my friends I might make merry; but when [2]thy [3]son [1]this
ὁ καταφαγών σου τὸν βίον μετὰ [g] πορνῶν ἦλθεν, ἔθυσας
who devoured thy living with harlots came, thou didst kill
αὐτῷ τὸν [h]μόσχον τὸν σιτευτόν.[ll] 31 ὁ.δὲ εἶπεν αὐτῷ, Τέκνον,
for him the [2]calf [1]fattened. But he said to him, Child,
σὺ πάντοτε μετ' ἐμοῦ εἶ, καὶ πάντα τὰ ἐμὰ σά ἐστιν.
thou always with me art, and all that [is] mine [2]thine [1]is.
32 εὐφρανθῆναι δὲ καὶ χαρῆναι ἔδει, ὅτι ὁ.ἀδελφός σου
But to make merry and rejoice was becoming, because [2]thy [3]brother
οὗτος νεκρὸς ἦν, καὶ [i]ἀνέζησεν·[ll] [k]καὶ[ll] ἀπολωλὼς [l]ἦν,[ll] καὶ
[1]this [3]dead [4]was, and is alive again; and [2]lost [1]was, and
εὑρέθη.
is found.

16 [l]Ἔλεγεν δὲ καὶ πρὸς τοὺς μαθητὰς.[m]αὐτοῦ,[ll] [n]Ἄνθρωπός
And he said also to his disciples, A [3]man
τις ἦν πλούσιος, ὃς εἶχεν οἰκονόμον· καὶ οὗτος διε-
[1]certain [4]there [5]was [2]rich who had a steward, and he was
βλήθη αὐτῷ ὡς διασκορπίζων τὰ.ὑπάρχοντα.αὐτοῦ. 2 καὶ
accused to him as wasting his goods. And
φωνήσας αὐτὸν εἶπεν αὐτῷ, Τί τοῦτο ἀκούω περὶ
having called him he said to him, What [is] this I hear concerning
σοῦ; ἀπόδος τὸν λόγον τῆς οἰκονομίας σου· οὐ.γὰρ.[n]δυνήσῃ[ll]
thee? render the account of thy stewardship; for thou canst not
ἔτι οἰκονομεῖν. 3 Εἶπεν.δὲ ἐν ἑαυτῷ ὁ οἰκονόμος,
any longer be steward. And [1]said [4]within [5]himself [1]the [2]steward,

one gave to him.
17 And coming to himself, he said, How
many of my father's hired servants have bread
in abundance, and I am dying with hunger.
18 I will get up and go to my father. And I
will say to him, Father, I have sinned against
Heaven and in your sight.
19 And I am no longer worthy to be called
your son. Make me as one of your hired men.
20 And he got up and went to his father.
But while he was still at a distance, his father
saw him and was moved with loving pity. And
he ran and fell on his neck and lovingly kissed
him.
21 And the son said to him, Father, I have
sinned against Heaven and in your sight, and I
am no longer worthy to be called your son.
22 But the father said to his servants, Bring
out the best robe and put it on him. And give a
ring for his hand and sandals for his feet.
23 And when you have brought the fattened
calf, kill it and let us eat and be happy.
24 For my son was dead and is alive again,
and was lost and is found. And they began to
be merry.
25 And his elder son was in the field. And as
he came back and drew near to the house, he
heard music and dancing.
26 And calling one of his servants, he asked
what these things meant.
27 And he said to him, Your brother has
come and your father killed the fattened calf
because he has received him safe and well.
28 He was angry and would not go in. So his
father went out and begged him.
29 But he answered and said to his father,
See! I have served you these many years and
never disobeyed your commandment. And
you never gave a kid to me that I might make
merry with my friends.
30 But when this son of yours came, who has
wasted your living with harlots, you killed the
fattened calf for him.
31 But he said to him, Son, you are always
with me, and all that is mine is yours.
32 But it was right to be happy and rejoice,
because your brother was dead, and is alive
again – and was lost, but is found.

CHAPTER 16

1 And He also said to His disciples, A certain
rich man had a manager. And he was accused
to him, that he wasted his goods.
2 And calling him, he said, What *is* this I hear
of you? Account *to me* for your management
for you no longer can be manager.
3 And the manager said within himself, What

Τί ποιήσω, ὅτι ὁ.κύριός.μου ἀφαιρεῖται τὴν οἰκονομίαν ἀπ'
What shall I do, for my lord is taking away the stewardship from
ἐμοῦ; σκάπτειν οὐκ.ἰσχύω, ἐπαιτεῖν αἰσχύνομαι. 4 ἔγνων
me? To dig I am unable; to beg I am ashamed. I know
τί ποιήσω, ἵνα, ὅταν μετασταθῶ °τῆς οἰκονο-
what I will do, that, when I shall have been removed [from] the steward-
μίας, δέξωνταί με εἰς τοὺς.οἴκους.[p]αὐτῶν.ǁ 5 Καὶ προσ-
ship, they may receive me into their houses. And call-
καλεσάμενος ἕνα ἕκαστον τῶν [q]χρεωφειλετῶνǁ τοῦ κυρίου
ing to [him] [2]one [1]each of the debtors [3]lord
ἑαυτοῦ ἔλεγεν τῷ πρώτῳ, Πόσον ὀφείλεις τῷ.κυρίῳ.μου;
[4]of [5]his he said to the first, How much owest thou to my lord?
6 Ὁ.δὲ εἶπεν, Ἑκατὸν βάτους ἐλαίου. [r]Καὶǁ εἶπεν αὐτῷ,
And he said, A hundred baths of oil. And he said to him,
Δέξαι σου [s]τὸ γράμμαǁ καὶ καθίσας ταχέως γράψον πεντή-
Take thy bill and sitting down quickly write fifty.
κοντα. 7 Ἔπειτα ἑτέρῳ εἶπεν, Σὺ.δὲ πόσον ὀφείλεις;
Then to another he said, And thou how much owest thou?
Ὁ.δὲ εἶπεν, Ἑκατὸν κόρους σίτου. [t]Καὶǁ λέγει αὐτῷ, Δέξαι
And he said, A hundred cors of wheat. And he says to him, Take
σου [u]τὸ γράμμαǁ καὶ γράψον ὀγδοήκοντα. 8 Καὶ ἐπῄνεσεν
thy bill and write eighty. And [4]praised
ὁ κύριος τὸν οἰκονόμον τῆς ἀδικίας ὅτι φρονίμως ἐποίη-
[1]the [2]lord the [3]steward [1]unrighteous because prudently he had
σεν· ὅτι οἱ υἱοὶ τοῦ.αἰῶνος.τούτου φρονιμώτεροι ὑπὲρ τοὺς
done. For the sons of this age [6]more [7]prudent [8]than [9]the
υἱοὺς τοῦ φωτὸς εἰς τὴν γενεὰν τὴν.ἑαυτῶν εἰσιν. 9 [v]Κἀγὼǁ
[10]sons [11]of [12]the [13]light [2]in [5]generation [3]their [4]own [1]are. And I
ὑμῖν λέγω, [w]Ποιήσατε ἑαυτοῖςǁ φίλους ἐκ τοῦ μαμωνᾶ τῆς
to you say, Make to yourselves friends by the mammon
ἀδικίας, ἵνα ὅταν [x]ἐκλίπητεǁ δέξωνται ὑμᾶς εἰς τὰς
of unrighteousness, that when ye fail they may receive you into the
αἰωνίους σκηνάς[y]. 10 Ὁ πιστὸς ἐν ἐλαχίστῳ καὶ
eternal dwellings. He that [is] faithful in [the] least also
ἐν πολλῷ πιστός ἐστιν· καὶ ὁ ἐν ἐλαχίστῳ ἄδικος
in much faithful is; and he that in [the] least [is] unrighteous
καὶ ἐν πολλῷ ἄδικός ἐστιν. 11 εἰ οὖν ἐν τῷ ἀδίκῳ
also in much unrighteous is. If therefore in the unrighteous
μαμωνᾷ πιστοὶ οὐκ.ἐγένεσθε, τὸ ἀληθινὸν τίς ὑμῖν πιστεύσει;
mammon faithful ye have not been, the true who to you will entrust?
12 καὶ εἰ ἐν τῷ ἀλλοτρίῳ πιστοὶ οὐκ.ἐγένεσθε, τὸ
And if in that which [is] another's faithful ye have not been,
ὑμέτερον τίς [z]ὑμῖν δώσει;ǁ 13 Οὐδεὶς οἰκέτης δύναται δυσὶ
your own who to you will give? No servant is able two
κυρίοις δουλεύειν· ἢ.γὰρ τὸν ἕνα μισήσει, καὶ τὸν ἕτερον
lords to serve, for either the one he will hate, and the other
ἀγαπήσει· ἢ ἑνὸς ἀνθέξεται, καὶ τοῦ ἑτέρου καταφρονήσει.
he will love; or one he will hold to, and the other he will despise.
οὐ.δύνασθε θεῷ δουλεύειν καὶ μαμωνᾷ.
Ye are unable [3]God [1]to [2]serve and mammon.
14 Ἤκουον.δὲ ταῦτα πάντα [a]καὶǁ οἱ Φαρισαῖοι, φιλάρ-
And [4]heard [2]these [3]things [1]all also the Pharisees, [2]covet-
γυροι ὑπάρχοντες, καὶ ἐξεμυκτήριζον αὐτόν. 15 καὶ εἶπεν
ous [1]being, and they derided him. And he said
αὐτοῖς, Ὑμεῖς ἐστε οἱ δικαιοῦντες ἑαυτοὺς ἐνώπιον τῶν
to them, Ye are they who justify themselves before
ἀνθρώπων, ὁ.δὲ.θεὸς γινώσκει τὰς.καρδίας.ὑμῶν· ὅτι τὸ ἐν
men, but God knows your hearts; for that [4]among
ἀνθρώποις ὑψηλὸν βδέλυγμα ἐνώπιον τοῦ θεοῦ [b]ἐστιν.ǁ
[5]men [1]highly [2]thought [3]of an abomination before God is.
16 Ὁ νόμος καὶ οἱ προφῆται [c]ἕωςǁ [d]Ἰωάννου·ǁ ἀπὸ
The law and the prophets [were] until John: from
τότε ἡ βασιλεία τοῦ θεοῦ εὐαγγελίζεται, καὶ πᾶς εἰς
that time the kingdom of God is announced, and everyone [2]into
αὐτὴν βιάζεται. 17 Εὐκοπώτερον.δέ ἐστιν τὸν οὐρανὸν καὶ
[3]it [1]forces. But easier it is [for] the heaven and
τὴν γῆν παρελθεῖν, ἢ τοῦ νόμου μίαν κεραίαν πεσεῖν.
the earth to pass away, than of the law one tittle to fail.
18 Πᾶς ὁ ἀπολύων τὴν.γυναῖκα.αὐτοῦ καὶ γαμῶν ἑτέραν
Everyone who puts away his wife and marries another
μοιχεύει· καὶ [e]πᾶςǁ ὁ ἀπολελυμένην ἀπὸ ἀνδρὸς
commits adultery, and everyone who [2]her [3]put [4]away [5]from [6]a [7]husband
γαμῶν μοιχεύει.
[1]marries commits adultery.
19 Ἄνθρωπος.δέ τις ἦν πλούσιος, καὶ ἐνεδιδύσκετο
Now [3]a [6]man [4]certain [1]there [2]was [5]rich, and he was clothed in
πορφύραν καὶ βύσσον, εὐφραινόμενος καθ'.ἡμέραν λαμπρῶς.
purple and fine linen, making good cheer daily in splendour.
20 πτωχὸς.δέ τις [f]ἦνǁ ὀνόματι Λάζαρος, [g]ὃςǁ ἐβέβλητο
And a [4]poor [3]man [1]certain there was, by name Lazarus, who was laid
πρὸς τὸν.πυλῶνα.αὐτοῦ [h]ἡλκωμένος,ǁ 21 καὶ ἐπιθυμῶν χορ-
at his porch being full of sores, and desiring to be

shall I do. For my master is taking away the
management from me. I am not able to dig,
and I am ashamed to beg.
4 I know what I will do, so that when I have
been removed from the management they will
receive me into their houses.
5 And calling each one of his master's debtors
to *him*, he said to the first, How much do you
owe my lord?
6 And he said, A hundred baths of oil. And he
said to him, Sit down, take your bill and
quickly write fifty.
7 Then to another he said, And how much do
you owe? And he said, A hundred homers of
wheat. And he said to him, Take your bill and
write eighty.
8 And the master praised the unjust manager
in that he had acted shrewdly. For the children of this world are in their generation more
mindful of their interests than the children of
the light in their own generation.
9 And I tell you, Make friends for yourselves
out of the riches of unrighteousness so that
when you fail they may receive you into the
everlasting dwellings.
10 He that is faithful in the least is faithful in
much. And he that is unrighteous in the least
is also unrighteous in much.
11 If, then, you have not been faithful in the
untrustworthy riches, who will entrust to you
the true riches?
12 And if you have not been faithful in that
which is another's, who will give you that
which is your own?
13 No servant is able to serve two masters.
For either he will hate the one and he will love
the other, or else he will cling to the one and
he will despise the other. You cannot serve
both God and worldly riches.

14 And the Pharisees, who were greedy,
also heard these things. And they scoffed
at Him.
15 And He said to them, You are they who
justify themselves before men. But God knows
your hearts, for that which is highly prized
among men is a hateful thing before God.
16 The Law and the Prophets were until John
– from that time the kingdom of God is
proclaimed, and everyone forces his way into
it.
17 But it is easier for the sky and the earth to
vanish than for one bit of the law to fail.
18 Everyone who puts away his wife and
marries another commits adultery. And
everyone who marries her who is divorced
from her husband commits adultery.

19 Now there was a certain rich man. And
he was clothed in purple and fine linen,
making merry every day in luxury.
20 And there was a certain beggar named
Lazarus, who was full of sores, and who was
laid at his gate.
21 And he wanted to be fed with the

χορτασθῆναι ἀπὸ τῶν ψιχίων τῶν" πιπτόντων ἀπὸ τῆς τραπέζης
satisfied from the crumbs which fell from the table
τοῦ πλουσίου· ἀλλὰ καὶ οἱ κύνες ἐρχόμενοι ^kἀπέλειχον" τὰ
of the rich man; but even the dogs coming licked
ἕλκη.αὐτοῦ. 22 ἐγένετο.δὲ ἀποθανεῖν τὸν πτωχόν, καὶ
his sores. And it came to pass ⁴died ¹the ²poor ³man, and
ἀπενεχθῆναι αὐτὸν ὑπὸ τῶν ἀγγέλων εἰς τὸν κόλπον ^lτοῦ"
²was ³carried ⁴away ¹he by the angels into the bosom
Ἀβραάμ· ἀπέθανεν.δὲ καὶ ὁ πλούσιος, καὶ ἐτάφη. 23 καὶ ἐν
of Abraham. And died also the rich man, and was buried. And in
τῷ ᾅδῃ ἐπάρας τοὺς ὀφθαλμοὺς.αὐτοῦ, ὑπάρχων ἐν βα-
the hades having lifted up his eyes, being in tor-
σάνοις, ὁρᾷ ^mτὸν" Ἀβραὰμ ἀπὸ.μακρόθεν, καὶ Λάζαρον ἐν
ments, he sees Abraham afar off, and Lazarus in
τοῖς.κόλποις.αὐτοῦ· 24 καὶ αὐτὸς φωνήσας εἶπεν, Πάτερ
his bosom. And he crying out said, Father
Ἀβραάμ, ἐλέησόν με, καὶ πέμψον Λάζαρον, ἵνα βάψῃ
Abraham, have compassion on me, and send Lazarus, that he may dip
τὸ ἄκρον τοῦ.δακτύλου.αὐτοῦ ὕδατος, καὶ καταψύξῃ τὴν γλῶσ-
the tip of his finger in water, and cool ²tongue
σάν μου· ὅτι ὀδυνῶμαι ἐν τῇ.φλογὶ.ταύτῃ. 25 Εἶπεν.δὲ
¹my; for I am suffering in this flame. But ²said
Ἀβραάμ, Τέκνον, μνήσθητι ὅτι ^nἀπέλαβες "σὺ" τὰ
¹Abraham, Child, recollect that ²didst ³fully ⁴receive ¹thou
ἀγαθά.σου ἐν τῇ.ζωῇ.σου, καὶ Λάζαρος ὁμοίως τὰ.κακά·
thy good things in thy lifetime, and Lazarus likewise evil things.
νῦν.δὲ ^oὅδε" παρακαλεῖται, σὺ.δὲ ὀδυνᾶσαι. 26 καὶ ^pἐπὶ"
But now he is comforted, and thou art suffering. And besides
πᾶσιν τούτοις, μεταξὺ ἡμῶν καὶ ὑμῶν χάσμα μέγα ἐστήρικ-
all these things, between us and you a ²chasm ¹great has been
ται, ὅπως οἱ θέλοντες διαβῆναι ^qἐντεῦθεν" πρὸς ὑμᾶς
fixed, so that they who desire to pass hence to you
μὴ.δύνωνται, μηδὲ ^rοἱ" ἐκεῖθεν πρὸς ἡμᾶς διαπερῶσιν.
are unable, nor ²they ⁴thence ⁵to ⁶us ¹can ³pass
27 Εἶπεν.δέ, Ἐρωτῶ ^sοὖν σε," πάτερ, ἵνα πέμψῃς
And he said, I beseech ²then ¹thee, father, that thou wouldest send
αὐτὸν εἰς τὸν οἶκον τοῦ.πατρός.μου, 28 ἔχω.γὰρ πέντε ἀδελ-
him to the house of my father, for I have five bro-
φούς· ὅπως διαμαρτύρηται αὐτοῖς, ἵνα μὴ καὶ αὐτοὶ
thers, so that he may earnestly testify to them, that ²not ³also ¹they
ἔλθωσιν εἰς τὸν.τόπον.τοῦτον τῆς βασάνου· 29 λέγει^t ^vαὐτῷ"
may come to this place of torment. ²Says ³to ⁴him
Ἀβραάμ, Ἔχουσιν ^wΜωσέα" καὶ τοὺς προφήτας· ἀκουσάτωσαν
¹Abraham, They have Moses and the prophets: let them hear
αὐτῶν. 30 Ὁ.δὲ εἶπεν, Οὐχί, πάτερ Ἀβραάμ· ἀλλ' ἐάν τις
them. But he said, No, father Abraham, but if one
ἀπὸ νεκρῶν πορευθῇ πρὸς αὐτούς, μετανοήσουσιν.
from [the] dead should go to them, they will repent.
31 Εἶπεν.δὲ αὐτῷ, Εἰ ^xΜωσέως" καὶ τῶν προφητῶν οὐκ
And he said to him, If Moses and the prophets ³not
ἀκούουσιν, ^yοὐδὲ". ἐάν τις ἐκ νεκρῶν ἀναστῇ πεισθή-
¹they ²hear, not even if one from [the] dead should rise will they
σονται.
be persuaded.

17 Εἶπεν.δὲ πρὸς τοὺς μαθητάς,^z Ἀνένδεκτόν ἐστιν ^aτοῦ"
And he said to the disciples, Impossible it is that
^bμὴ.ἐλθεῖν τὰ σκάνδαλα·" ^cοὐαὶ.δὲ" δι' οὗ ἔρχεται.
²should ³not ⁴come ¹offences, but woe [to him] by whom they come.
2 λυσιτελεῖ αὐτῷ εἰ ^dμύλος ὀνικὸς" περίκειται περὶ
It is profitable for him if a millstone turned by an ass is put about
τὸν.τράχηλον.αὐτοῦ, καὶ ἔρριπται εἰς τὴν θάλασσαν, ἢ ἵνα
his neck, and he is cast into the sea, than that
σκανδαλίσῃ ^eἕνα τῶν.μικρῶν.τούτων." 3 προσέχετε
he should cause ⁶to ⁷offend ¹one ²of ³these ⁴little ⁵ones. Take heed
ἑαυτοῖς. ἐὰν.^fδὲ" ἁμάρτῃ ^gεἰς σὲ" ὁ.ἀδελφός.σου, ἐπι-
to yourselves: and if ³should ⁴sin ⁵against ⁶thee ¹thy ²brother, re-
τίμησον αὐτῷ· καὶ ἐὰν μετανοήσῃ, ἄφες αὐτῷ. 4 καὶ ἐὰν
buke him; and if he should repent, forgive him. And if
ἑπτάκις τῆς ἡμέρας ^hἁμάρτῃ" εἰς σέ, καὶ ^iἑπτάκις ^kτῆς
seven times in the day he should sin against thee, and seven times in the
ἡμέρας" ἐπιστρέψῃ ^lἐπὶ σέ," λέγων, Μετανοῶ, ἀφήσεις
day should return to thee, saying, I repent, thou shalt forgive
αὐτῷ.
him.

5 Καὶ ^mεἶπον" οἱ ἀπόστολοι τῷ κυρίῳ, Πρόσθες ἡμῖν
And said the apostles to the Lord, Give more ²to ³us
πίστιν. 6 Εἶπεν.δὲ ὁ κύριος, Εἰ ^nεἴχετε" πίστιν, ὡς κόκκον
¹faith. But ³said ¹the ²Lord, If ye had faith, as a grain
σινάπεως, ἐλέγετε.ἂν τῇ.συκαμίνῳ.ταύτῃ, Ἐκριζώθητι, καὶ
of mustard, ye might say to this sycamine tree, Be thou rooted up, and
φυτεύθητι ἐν τῇ θαλάσσῃ· καὶ ὑπήκουσεν.ἂν ὑμῖν. 7 Τίς.δὲ
be thou planted in the sea, and it would obey you. But which

crumbs that fell from the table of the rich man. Yes, even the dogs came and licked his sores.
22 And the beggar died. And he was carried away by the angels into Abraham's bosom. And the rich man also died and was buried.
23 And being in torment in hell, lifting up his eyes he saw Abraham afar off, and Lazarus in his bosom.
24 And he cried out and said, Father Abraham, have mercy on me and send Lazarus so that he may dip the tip of his finger in water and cool my tongue. For I am tormented in this flame.
25 But Abraham said, Son, remember that you fully received your good things in your lifetime, and Lazarus evil things also. But now he is comforted and you are suffering.
26 And besides all these things, a great gulf has been fixed between you and us, so that those who want to go from here to you cannot do so. Nor can those there come to us.
27 And he said, Then I beg you, father, that you send him to the house of my father,
28 for I have five brothers, so that he may earnestly witness to them, so that they may not come to this place of torment also.
29 Abraham said to him, They have Moses and the Prophets, let them hear them.
30 But he said, No, father Abraham, but if one should go to them from the dead they will repent.
31 And he said to him, If they do not hear Moses and the Prophets, they will not believe even if one should rise from the dead.

CHAPTER 17

1 And He said to the disciples, It is impossible for the scandals not to come, but woe *to him* by whom they come.
2 It is better for him if a millstone were hung around his neck and he were thrown into the sea, than that he should cause one of these little ones to stumble.
3 Be careful of yourselves, and if your brother sins against you, warn him. And if he should repent, forgive him.
4 And if he should sin against you seven times a day, and seven times in a day should return to you saying, I repent – you shall forgive him.
5 And the apostles said to the Lord, Give us more faith.
6 But the Lord said, If you had faith, as much as a grain of mustard, you might say to this sycamine tree, Be rooted up! And, Be planted in the sea! And it would obey you.
7 But which of you who has a servant plow-

[o]ἐξ‖ ὑμῶν δοῦλον ἔχων ἀροτριῶντα ἢ ποιμαίνοντα, ὃς
of you [2]a [3]bondman [1]having ploughing or shepherding, who
εἰσελθόντι ἐκ τοῦ ἀγροῦ ἐρεῖ [p] [q]εὐθέως, Παρελθὼν‖
[to him] come in out of the field will say immediately, Having come
[r]ἀνάπεσαι‖; 8 ἀλλ' οὐχὶ.ἐρεῖ αὐτῷ, Ἑτοίμασον τί
recline [at table]? but will he not say to him, Prepare what
δειπνήσω, καὶ περιζωσάμενος διακόνει μοι, ἕως φάγω καὶ
I may sup on, and girding thyself about serve me, while I eat and
πίω· καὶ μετὰ ταῦτα φάγεσαι καὶ πίεσαι σύ; 9 Μὴ
drink; and after these things [2]shalt [3]eat [4]and [5]drink [1]thou?
[s]χάριν.ἔχει‖ τῷ.δούλῳ.[t]ἐκείνῳ‖ ὅτι ἐποίησεν τὰ διατα-
Is he thankful to that bondman because he did the things com-
χθέντα [v]αὐτῷ‖; [w]οὐ.δοκῶ.‖ 10 οὕτως καὶ ὑμεῖς, ὅταν
manded him? I judge not. Thus also ye, when
ποιήσητε πάντα.τὰ διαταχθέντα ὑμῖν, λέγετε, [x]Ὅτι‖ δοῦ-
ye may have done all things commanded you, say, [2]Bond-
λοι ἀχρεῖοί ἐσμεν· [y]ὅτι‖ ὃ ὠφείλομεν ποιῆσαι πεποιή-
men [1]unprofitable are we, for that which we were bound to do we have
καμεν.
done.

ing or feeding will say immediately when he
has come from the field, Go and eat?
8 But will he not say to him, Prepare so that
I may eat. And, Get ready and serve me
while I eat and drink. And after this you will
eat and drink?
9 Is he thankful to that servant because he
did the things commanded him? I think not.
10 So you also, when you have done all that
is commanded you, say, We are unprofitable
servants, for we have done that which it was
our duty to do.

11 Καὶ ἐγένετο ἐν τῷ.πορεύεσθαι.[z]αὐτὸν‖ εἰς Ἱερουσαλὴμ
And it came to pass in his going up to Jerusalem
καὶ αὐτὸς διήρχετο διὰ [a]μέσου‖ [b]Σαμαρείας‖ καὶ Γαλι-
that he passed through [the] midst of Samaria and Gali-
λαίας. 12 καὶ εἰσερχομένου.αὐτοῦ εἴς τινα κώμην [c]ἀπήντησαν‖
lee. And on his entering into a certain village [4]met
[d]αὐτῷ‖ δέκα λεπροὶ ἄνδρες, οἳ ἔστησαν πόρρωθεν· 13 καὶ
[5]him [1]ten [2]leprous [3]men, who stood afar off. And
αὐτοὶ ἦραν φωνὴν λέγοντες, Ἰησοῦ, ἐπιστάτα, ἐλέη-
they lifted up [their] voice saying, Jesus. Master, have compas-
σον ἡμᾶς. 14 Καὶ ἰδὼν εἶπεν αὐτοῖς, Πορευθέντες
sion on us. And seeing [them] he said to them, Having gone
ἐπιδείξατε ἑαυτοὺς τοῖς ἱερεῦσιν. Καὶ ἐγένετο ἐν τῷ ὑπά-
shew yourselves to the priests. And it came to pass in [2]go-
γειν αὐτοὺς ἐκαθαρίσθησαν. 15 εἷς.δὲ ἐξ αὐτῶν, ἰδὼν ὅτι
ing [1]their they were cleansed. And one of them, seeing that
ἰάθη, ὑπέστρεψεν, μετὰ φωνῆς μεγάλης δοξάζων τὸν
he was healed, turned back, with a [2]voice [1]loud glorifying
θεόν· 16 καὶ ἔπεσεν ἐπὶ πρόσωπον παρὰ τοὺς.πόδας.αὐτοῦ,
God, and fell on [his] face at his feet,
εὐχαριστῶν αὐτῷ· καὶ αὐτὸς ἦν [e]Σαμαρείτης.‖ 17 ἀποκριθεὶς
giving thanks to him: and he was a Samaritan. [2]Answering
δὲ ὁ Ἰησοῦς εἶπεν, [f]Οὐχὶ‖ οἱ δέκα ἐκαθαρίσθησαν; οἱ.[g]δὲ‖
[1]and Jesus said, [2]Not [3]the [4]ten [1]were cleansed? but [3]the
ἐννέα ποῦ; 18 οὐχ.εὑρέθησαν ὑποστρέψαντες δοῦναι
[4]nine [1]where [[2]are]? Were there not found [any] returning to give
δόξαν τῷ θεῷ εἰ.μὴ ὁ.ἀλλογενὴς.οὗτος; 19 Καὶ εἶπεν αὐτῷ,
glory to God except this stranger? And he said to him,
Ἀναστὰς πορεύου· ἡ.πίστις.σου σέσωκέν σε.
Having risen up go forth; thy faith has cured thee.

11 And as He went toward Jerusalem He
traveled through the middle of Sa-mar-i-a
and Galilee.
12 And as He entered into a certain village,
ten men who were lepers met Him, standing
at a distance.
13 And they lifted up their voice, saying,
Jesus! Master! Have mercy on us.
14 And He saw them and said, Go! Show
yourselves to the priests. And as they went
they were made clean.
15 And seeing that he was healed, one of
them turned back. And with a loud voice
praising God,
16 he fell on his face at His feet, giving
thanks to Him. And he was a Sa-mar-i-tan.
17 And answering Jesus said, Were not the
ten made clean? But where are the nine?
18 Was there no one found that returned to
give glory to God except this stranger?
19 And He said to him, Get up and go.
Your faith has cured you.

20 Ἐπερωτηθεὶς.δὲ ὑπὸ τῶν Φαρισαίων, πότε ἔρχεται ἡ
And having been asked by the Pharisees, when is coming the
βασιλεία τοῦ θεοῦ, ἀπεκρίθη αὐτοῖς καὶ εἶπεν, Οὐκ.ἔρχεται ἡ
kingdom of God, he answered them and said, [5]Comes [6]not [1]the
βασιλεία τοῦ θεοῦ μετὰ παρατηρήσεως· 21 οὐδὲ ἐροῦσιν,
[2]kingdom [3]of [4]God with observation; nor shall they say,
Ἰδοὺ ὧδε, ἤ [h]ἰδοὺ‖ ἐκεῖ· ἰδοὺ.γάρ, ἡ βασιλεία τοῦ θεοῦ ἐντὸς
Lo here, or Lo there; for lo, the kingdom of God in the midst
ὑμῶν ἐστίν. 22 Εἶπεν.δὲ πρὸς τοὺς μαθητάς, [i]Ἐλεύσονται
of you is. And he said to the disciples, [2]Will [3]come
ἡμέραι, ὅτε ἐπιθυμήσετε μίαν τῶν ἡμερῶν τοῦ υἱοῦ τοῦ ἀν-
[1]days, when ye will desire one of the days of the Son of
θρώπου ἰδεῖν, καὶ οὐκ.ὄψεσθε. 23 καὶ ἐροῦσιν ὑμῖν, Ἰδοὺ
man to see, and shall not see [it]. And they will say to you, Lo
[k]ὧδε, ἢ ἰδοὺ ἐκεῖ·‖ μὴ.ἀπέλθητε μηδὲ διώξητε. 24 ὥσπερ.γὰρ
here, or Lo there; go not forth nor follow. For as
ἡ ἀστραπὴ [l]ἡ‖ ἀστράπτουσα ἐκ τῆς [m]ὑπ'‖ οὐρανὸν
the lightning which lightens from the [one end] under heaven
εἰς τὴν ὑπ' οὐρανὸν λάμπει, οὕτως ἔσται [n]καὶ‖ ὁ
to the [other end] under heaven shines, thus will be also the
υἱὸς τοῦ ἀνθρώπου [o]ἐν τῇ.ἡμέρᾳ.αὐτοῦ.‖ 25 πρῶτον.δὲ δεῖ
Son of man in his day. But first it behoves
αὐτὸν πολλὰ παθεῖν, καὶ ἀποδοκιμασθῆναι ἀπὸ τῆς γενεᾶς
him many things to suffer, and to be rejected of [2]generation
ταύτης. 26 καὶ καθὼς ἐγένετο ἐν ταῖς ἡμέραις [p]τοῦ‖ Νῶε,
[1]this. And as it came to pass in the days of Noe,
οὕτως ἔσται καὶ ἐν ταῖς ἡμέραις [q]τοῦ‖ υἱοῦ τοῦ ἀνθρώπου.
thus shall it be also in the days of the Son of man.
27 ἤσθιον, ἔπινον, ἐγάμουν, [r]ἐξεγα-
They were eating, they were drinking, they were marrying, they were being
μίζοντο,‖ ἄχρι ἧς.ἡμέρας εἰσῆλθεν Νῶε εἰς τὴν κιβωτόν,
given in marriage, until the day [2]entered [1]Noe into the ark,

20 And being asked by the Pharisees when
the kingdom of God was coming, He answered them and said, The kingdom of God
does not come with careful surveilance.
21 Nor shall they say, Look, here! Or,
Look, there! For, behold! The kingdom of
God is among you.
22 And He said to the disciples, The days
will come when you will want to see one of
the days of the Son of man and will not see.
23 And they will say to you, Look, here!
Or, Look, there! Do not go out nor follow.
24 For as the lightning that flashes out of
the *one part* under heaven and shines to the
other part of heaven, so will the Son of man
be in His day.
25 But first it is necessary for Him to suffer
many things and to be rejected by this
generation.
26 And as it was in Noah's days, so shall it
be also in the days of the Son of man.
27 They were eating – they were drinking
– they were marrying – they were being
given in marriage, until the day Noah

καὶ ἦλθεν ὁ κατακλυσμὸς καὶ ἀπώλεσεν [s]ἅπαντας." 28 ὁμοίως
and came the flood and destroyed all. [2]In [3]like [4]manner
[t]καὶ ὡς" ἐγένετο ἐν ταῖς ἡμέραις Λώτ· ἤσθιον, ἔπι-
[1]and as it came to pass in the days of Lot; they were eating, they were
νον, ἠγόραζον, ἐπώλουν, ἐφύτευον, ᾠκοδό-
drinking, they were buying, they were selling, they were planting, they were
μουν· 29 ᾗ.δὲ ἡμέρᾳ ἐξῆλθεν Λὼτ ἀπὸ Σοδόμων ἔβρεξεν
building; but on the day [2]went [3]out [1]Lot from Sodom it rained
πῦρ καὶ θεῖον ἀπ' οὐρανοῦ καὶ ἀπώλεσεν [s]ἅπαντας·" 30 κα-
fire and sulphur from heaven and destroyed all. In
τὰ.[v]ταῦτα" ἔσται ᾗ.ἡμέρᾳ ὁ υἱὸς τοῦ ἀνθρώπου ἀποκαλύπ-
this way shall it be in the day the Son of man is revealed.
τεται. 31 ἐν ἐκείνῃ τῇ ἡμέρᾳ ὃς ἔσται ἐπὶ τοῦ δώματος, καὶ
In that day [he] who shall be on the housetop, and
τὰ.σκεύη.αὐτοῦ ἐν τῇ οἰκίᾳ, μὴ.καταβάτω ἆραι αὐτά·
his goods in the house, let him not come down to take away them;
καὶ ὁ ἐν [w]τῷ" ἀγρῷ ὁμοίως μὴ.ἐπιστρεψάτω εἰς τὰ ὀπίσω.
and he in the field likewise let him not return to the things behind.
32 μνημονεύετε τῆς γυναικὸς Λώτ. 33 ὃς.ἐὰν ζητήσῃ τὴν
Remember the wife of Lot. Whoever may seek
ψυχὴν.αὐτοῦ [x]σῶσαι," ἀπολέσει αὐτήν· καὶ ὃς.[y]ἐὰν" [z]ἀπολέσῃ"
his life to save, shall lose it; and whoever may lose
[a]αὐτήν," ζωογονήσει αὐτήν. 34 λέγω ὑμῖν, ταύτῃ.τῇ νυκτὶ
it, shall preserve it. I say to you, In that night
ἔσονται δύο ἐπὶ κλίνης [b]μιᾶς·" [c]ὁ" εἷς [d]παραληφθήσε-
there shall be two [men] upon [2]bed [1]one; the one shall be ta-
ται," καὶ ὁ ἕτερος ἀφεθήσεται. 35 [e]δύο ἔσονται" ἀλή-
ken, and the other shall be left. Two [women] shall be grind-
θουσαι ἐπὶ τὸ.αὐτό· [f]μία [g]παραληφθήσεται," [h]καὶ ἡ" ἑτέρα
ing together; one shall be taken, and the other
ἀφεθήσεται.[i] 37 Καὶ ἀποκριθέντες λέγουσιν αὐτῷ, Ποῦ,
shall be left. And answering they say to him, Where,
κύριε; Ὁ.δὲ εἶπεν αὐτοῖς, Ὅπου τὸ σῶμα ἐκεῖ [j]συναχθή-
Lord? And he said to them, Where the body [is] there will be gathered
σονται οἱ ἀετοί."
together the eagles.

18 [k]Ἔλεγεν.δὲ [k]καὶ" παραβολὴν αὐτοῖς πρὸς.τὸ δεῖν
And he spoke also a parable to them to the purport that it behoves
πάντοτε προσεύχεσθαι,[l] καὶ μὴ [m]ἐκκακεῖν," 2 λέγων,
[2]always [3]to [4]pray [[1]them] and not to faint, saying,
Κριτής τις ἦν ἔν τινι πόλει, τὸν θεὸν μὴ φοβούμενος
A [2]judge [1]certain there was in [2]certain [1]a city, God not fearing
καὶ ἄνθρωπον μὴ ἐντρεπόμενος. 3 χήρα.δὲ [n] ἦν ἐν τῇ
and man not respecting. And a widow there was in
πόλει.ἐκείνῃ, καὶ ἤρχετο πρὸς αὐτόν, λέγουσα, Ἐκδίκησόν
that city, and she was coming to him, saying, Avenge
με ἀπὸ τοῦ.ἀντιδίκου.μου. 4 Καὶ οὐκ.[o]ἠθέλησεν" ἐπὶ χρόνον·
me of mine adverse party. And he would not for a time;
μετὰ.[p]δὲ.ταῦτα" εἶπεν ἐν ἑαυτῷ, Εἰ καὶ τὸν θεὸν οὐ.φοβοῦμαι
but afterwards he said within himself, If even God I fear not
[q]καὶ" ἄνθρωπον οὐκ" ἐντρέπομαι· 5 διά.γε τὸ παρέχειν μοι
and man [2]not [1]respect, yet because [3]causes [4]me
κόπον τὴν.χήραν.ταύτην ἐκδικήσω αὐτήν, ἵνα.μὴ εἰς.τέλος
[5]trouble [1]this [2]widow I will avenge her, lest perpetually
ἐρχομένη ὑπωπιάζῃ με. 6 Εἶπεν.δὲ ὁ κύριος, Ἀκούσατε τί
coming she harass me. And said the Lord, Hear what
ὁ κριτὴς τῆς ἀδικίας λέγει· 7 ὁ.δὲ.θεὸς οὐ.μὴ [r]ποιήσει" τὴν
the [2]judge [1]unrighteous says. And [3]God [2]not [1]shall execute the
ἐκδίκησιν τῶν.ἐκλεκτῶν.αὐτοῦ τῶν βοώντων [s]πρὸς αὐτὸν"
avenging of his elect who cry to him
ἡμέρας καὶ νυκτός, καὶ [t]μακροθυμῶν" ἐπ' αὐτοῖς; 8 λέγω
day and night, and [is] being patient over them? I say
ὑμῖν, ὅτι ποιήσει τὴν ἐκδίκησιν αὐτῶν ἐν.τάχει. πλὴν
to you, that he will execute the avenging of them speedily. Nevertheless
ὁ υἱὸς τοῦ ἀνθρώπου ἐλθὼν ἆρα εὑρήσει τὴν πίστιν
the Son of man having come [3]indeed [1]will [2]he find faith
ἐπὶ τῆς γῆς;
on the earth?

9 Εἶπεν.δὲ [v]καὶ" πρός τινας τοὺς πεποιθότας ἐφ' ἑαυτοῖς
And he spoke also to some who trusted in themselves
ὅτι εἰσὶν δίκαιοι καὶ ἐξουθενοῦντας τοὺς λοιποὺς τὴν παρα-
that they are righteous and despised the rest [2]para-
βολὴν ταύτην. 10 [w]Ἄνθρωποι δύο ἀνέβησαν εἰς τὸ ἱερὸν
ble [1]this: [2]Men [1]two went up into the temple
προσεύξασθαι· [w]ὁ" εἷς Φαρισαῖος καὶ ὁ ἕτερος τελώνης 11 ὁ
to pray; the one a Pharisee and the other a tax-gatherer. The
Φαρισαῖος σταθεὶς [x]πρὸς ἑαυτὸν ταῦτα" προσηύχετο, Ὁ θεός,
Pharisee standing, with himself thus was praying, God,

entered into the ark. And the flood came and destroyed all of them.

28 And in the same way as it was in the days of Lot: they were eating – they were drinking – they were buying – they were selling – they were planting – they were building,

29 but on the day Lot went out from Sodom, fire and brimstone rained from Heaven and destroyed all of them.

30 Even so it shall be in the day the Son of man is revealed.

31 In that day he who is on the housetop and his goods in the house, let him not come to take them away. And likewise, he in the field, let him not return to the things behind.

32 Remember Lot's wife!

33 Whoever may try to save his life will lose it. And whoever may lose it will save it.

34 I say to you, In that night there will be two men on one bed – the one will be taken and the other will be left.

35 Two will be grinding together – one will be taken and the other left.

36 Two will be in the field – the one will be taken and the other left.

37 And they answered, saying to Him, Where, Lord? And He said to them, Wherever the body is, there the eagles will be gathered.

CHAPTER 18

1 And He also told them a parable to show that it is necessary to pray without ceasing and not to lose heart,

2 saying, There was a certain judge in a city who neither feared God nor respected man.

3 And there was a widow in that city. And she came to him, saying, Give me justice against my enemy.

4 And he would not for a while. But afterwards he said within himself, Even though I do not fear God and do not respect man,

5 yet because this widow troubles me I will give her justice so that she will not wear me out by coming again and again.

6 And the Lord said, Hear what the unrighteous judge says?

7 And shall not God avenge His elect who cry to Him day and night, also being patient with them?

8 I say to you that He will avenge them speedily. But when the Son of man comes, will He indeed find faith on the earth?

9 And He also spoke this parable to certain ones who trusted in themselves that they were righteous and who despised others.

10 Two men went up to the Temple to pray – the one a Pharisee and the other a tax-collector.

11 The Pharisee was standing and praying within himself in this way, God, I thank You

εὐχαριστῶ σοι ὅτι οὐκ.εἰμὶ ʸὥσπερ" οἱ λοιποὶ τῶν ἀνθρώπων,
I thank thee that I am not as the rest of men,
ἅρπαγες, ἄδικοι, μοιχοί, ἢ καὶ ὡς οὗτος ὁ τελώνης. 12 νη-
rapacious, unrighteous, adulterers, or even as this tax-gatherer. I
στεύω δὶς τοῦ σαββάτου, ᶻἀποδεκατῶ¹ πάντα ὅσα κτῶμαι.
fast twice in the week, I tithe all things as many as I gain.
13 ᵃΚαὶ ὁ" τελώνης μακρόθεν ἑστὼς οὐκ ἤθελεν οὐδὲ τοὺς
And the tax-gatherer afar off standing would not even the
ὀφθαλμοὺς ᵇεἰς τὸν οὐρανὸν ἐπᾶραι"· ἀλλ' ἔτυπτεν ᶜεἰς" τὸ
eyes to the heaven lift up, but was striking upon
στῆθος ᵈαὐτοῦ,¹ λέγων, Ὁ θεός, ἱλάσθητί μοι τῷ ἁμαρτωλῷ.
his breast, saying, God, be propitious to me the sinner.
14 Λέγω ὑμῖν, ᵉ κατέβη οὗτος δεδικαιωμένος εἰς τὸν οἶκον
I say to you, Went down this one justified to ²house
αὐτοῦ ᶠἢ ἐκεῖνος." ὅτι πᾶς ὁ ὑψῶν ἑαυτὸν ταπεινω-
¹his rather than that. For everyone that exalts himself shall be
θήσεται ᵍὁ.δὲ¹ ταπεινῶν ἑαυτὸν ὑψωθήσεται.
humbled; and he that humbles himself shall be exalted.

15 Προσέφερον.δὲ αὐτῷ καὶ τὰ βρέφη, ἵνα αὐτῶν ἅπτη-
And they brought to him also the babes, that them he might
ται· ἰδόντες.δὲ οἱ μαθηταὶ ʰἐπετίμησαν" αὐτοῖς. 16 ὁ δὲ
touch; but having seen [it] the disciples rebuked them. But
Ἰησοῦς ⁱπροσκαλεσάμενος αὐτὰ εἶπεν," Ἄφετε τὰ παιδία
Jesus having called ⁴to [³him] ¹them said, Suffer the little children
ἔρχεσθαι πρός με, καὶ μὴ.κωλύετε αὐτά· τῶν.γὰρ.τοιούτων
to come to me, and do not forbid them; for of such
ἐστὶν ἡ βασιλεία τοῦ θεοῦ. 17 ἀμὴν λέγω ὑμῖν, ὃς.ᵏἐὰν" μὴ
is the kingdom of God. Verily I say to you, Whoever ²not
δέξηται τὴν βασιλείαν τοῦ θεοῦ ὡς παιδίον οὐ.μὴ εἰσέλθῃ
¹shall receive the kingdom of God as a little child in no wise shall enter
εἰς αὐτήν.
into it.

18 Καὶ ἐπηρώτησέν τις αὐτὸν ἄρχων, λέγων, Διδάσκαλε
And ⁴asked ¹a ²certain ⁵him ³ruler, saying, ²Teacher
ἀγαθέ, τί ποιήσας ζωὴν αἰώνιον κληρονομήσω; 19 Εἶπεν
¹good, what having done life eternal shall I inherit? ³Said
δὲ αὐτῷ ὁ Ἰησοῦς, Τί με λέγεις ἀγαθόν; οὐδεὶς ἀγαθὸς
¹but ⁴to him ²Jesus, Why me callest thou good? No one [is] good
εἰ μὴ εἷς, ˡὁ" θεός. 20 τὰς ἐντολὰς οἶδας· Μὴ μοι-
except one, God. The commandments thou knowest: Thou shouldest not
χεύσῃς· μὴ φονεύσῃς· μὴ.κλέψῃς·
commit adultery; thou shouldest not commit murder; thou shouldest not steal;
μὴ ψευδομαρτυρήσῃς· τίμα τὸν.πατέρα.σου καὶ τὴν
thou shouldest not bear false witness; honour thy father and
μητέρα ᵐσου." 21 Ὁ δὲ εἶπεν, Ταῦτα πάντα ⁿἐφυλαξάμην" ἐκ
thy mother. And he said, ²These ¹all have I kept from
νεότητός ᵒμου." 22 Ἀκούσας.δὲ ᵖταῦτα" ὁ Ἰησοῦς εἶπεν
²youth ¹my. And having heard these things Jesus said
αὐτῷ, Ἔτι ἕν σοι λείπει· πάντα ὅσα ἔχεις πώλη-
to him, Yet one thing to thee is lacking; all as much as thou hast sell,
σον, καὶ ᵠδιάδος" πτωχοῖς, καὶ ἕξεις θησαυρὸν ἐν ʳοὐ-
and distribute to [the] poor, and thou shalt have treasure in hea-
ρανῷ" καὶ δεῦρο ἀκολούθει μοι. 23 Ὁ.δὲ ἀκούσας ταῦτα
ven, and come follow me. But he having heard these things
περίλυπος ˢἐγένετο·" ἦν γὰρ πλούσιος σφόδρα. 24 Ἰδὼν.δὲ
very sorrowful became, for he was ²rich ¹very. But ²seeing
αὐτὸν ὁ Ἰησοῦς ᵗπερίλυπον γενόμενον" εἶπεν, Πῶς δυσκό-
³him ¹Jesus ⁵very ⁷sorrowful ⁴having ⁶become said, How diffi-
λως οἱ τὰ χρήματα ἔχοντες ᵛεἰσελεύσονται εἰς τὴν βασιλείαν
cultly those ²riches ¹having shall enter into the kingdom
τοῦ θεοῦ." 25 Εὐκοπώτερον.γάρ ἐστιν κάμηλον διὰ ʷτρυμαλιᾶς
of God. For easier it is a camel through an eye
ῥαφίδος" ˣεἰσελθεῖν" ἢ πλούσιον εἰς τὴν βασιλείαν τοῦ θεοῦ
of a needle to enter than a rich man into the kingdom of God
εἰσελθεῖν. 26 ʸΕἶπον".δὲ οἱ ἀκούσαντες, Καὶ τίς δύναται
to enter. And said those who heard, ²Then ¹who is able
σωθῆναι; 27 Ὁ δὲ εἶπεν, Τὰ ἀδύνατα παρὰ ἀνθρώποις
to be saved? But he said, The things impossible with men
δυνατά ᶻἐστιν παρὰ τῷ θεῷ." 28 Εἶπεν δὲ ᵃὁ" Πέτρος, Ἰδού,
²possible ¹are with God. And ²said ¹Peter, Lo,
ἡμεῖς ᵇἀφήκαμεν πάντα καὶ" ἠκολουθήσαμέν σοι. 29 Ὁ.δὲ
we left all and followed thee. And he
εἶπεν αὐτοῖς, Ἀμὴν λέγω ὑμῖν, ᶜὅτι" οὐδείς ἐστιν ὃς ἀφῆκεν
said to them, Verily I say to you, That no one there is who has left
οἰκίαν ᵈἢ γονεῖς ἢ ἀδελφοὺς ἢ γυναῖκα" ἢ τέκνα ᵉἕνεκεν¹
house or parents or brethren or wife or children for the sake of
τῆς βασιλείας τοῦ θεοῦ, 30 ὃς ᶠοὐ" μὴ ᵍἀπολάβῃ" πολ-
the kingdom of God, who shall not receive mani-
λαπλασίονα ἐν τῷ.καιρῷ.τούτῳ, καὶ ἐν τῷ αἰῶνι τῷ ἐρχομένῳ
fold more in this time and in the age that is coming
ζωὴν αἰώνιον.
life eternal.

that I am not like other men – robbers, unrighteous ones, adulterers, or even like this
tax-collector.
12 I fast twice a week, I tithe all that I get.
13 And standing at a distance, the
tax-collector would not even lift up his eyes
to Heaven. But he beat on his breast, saying,
O God, be merciful to me, a sinner!
14 I tell you, this one went down to his
house justified, rather than the other. For
everyone that exalts himself shall be brought
low. And he that humbles himself shall be
exalted.

15 And they brought infants to Him too, so
that He might touch them. But seeing it, the
disciples scolded them.
16 But calling them, Jesus said, Allow the
little children to come to Me and do not
forbid them. For of such as these is the
kingdom of God.
17 I tell you truly, Whoever shall not
receive the kingdom of God like a little child
shall in no way enter into it.

18 And a certain ruler asked Him, saying,
Good Teacher, what shall I do to inherit
eternal life?
19 And Jesus said to him, Why do you call
Me good? No one is good except one God!
20 You know the commandments: Do not
commit adultery, do not commit murder, do
not steal, do not bear false witness, honor
your father and your mother.
21 And he said, I have kept all these from
my youth.
22 And hearing these things, Jesus said to
him, Still one thing is lacking to you: Sell all
you have and give to the poor, and you will
have treasure in Heaven; and come, follow
Me.
23 But hearing these things, he became very
sorrowful, for he was very rich.
24 And seeing him being filled with sorrow,
Jesus said, How difficult it is for those
having riches to enter into the kingdom of
God.
25 For it is easier for a camel to go through
the eye of a needle than for a rich man to
enter into the kingdom of God.
26 And those who heard said, Who then is
able to be saved?
27 But He said, The things which are impossible with men are possible with God.
28 And Peter said, See, we have left all and
have followed You.
29 And He said to them, I tell you truly
that there is no one who has left house or
parents or brothers or wife or children for
the sake of the kingdom of God,
30 who shall not receive many times more
in this present time, and life everlasting in
the world that is coming.

31 Παραλαβὼν.δὲ τοὺς δώδεκα εἶπεν πρὸς αὐτούς,
And having taken to [him] the twelve he said to them,

Ἰδού, ἀναβαίνομεν εἰς [h]Ἱεροσόλυμα,[‖] καὶ τελεσθήσεται
Behold, we go up to Jerusalem, and [3]shall [4]be [5]accomplished

πάντα τὰ γεγραμμένα διὰ τῶν προφητῶν τῷ υἱῷ τοῦ
[1]all [2]things which have been written by the prophets about the Son

ἀνθρώπου. 32 παραδοθήσεται.γὰρ τοῖς ἔθνεσιν, καὶ ἐμπαι-
of man; for he will be delivered up to the Gentiles, and will be

χθήσεται καὶ ὑβρισθήσεται καὶ ἐμπτυσθήσεται. 33 καὶ μα-
mocked and will be insulted and will be spit upon. And having

στιγώσαντες ἀποκτενοῦσιν αὐτόν· καὶ τῇ ἡμέρᾳ τῇ τρίτῃ
scourged they will kill him; and on the [2]day [1]third

ἀναστήσεται. 34 Καὶ αὐτοὶ οὐδὲν τούτων συνῆκαν, καὶ
he will rise again. And they nothing of these things understood, and

ἦν τὸ ῥῆμα τοῦτο κεκρυμμένον ἀπ᾽ αὐτῶν, καὶ οὐκ ἐγίνωσκον
[3]was [1]this [2]saying hid from them, and they knew not

τὰ λεγόμενα.
that which was said.

35 Ἐγένετο.δὲ ἐν.τῷ ἐγγίζειν αὐτὸν εἰς [i]Ἱεριχώ,[‖] τυφλός
And it came to pass as he drew near to Jericho, a [2]blind

τις ἐκάθητο παρὰ τὴν ὁδὸν [k]προσαιτῶν·[‖] 36 ἀκούσας
[3man] [1]certain sat beside the way begging. [2]Having heard

δὲ ὄχλου διαπορευομένου ἐπυνθάνετο τί [l] εἴη τοῦτο.
[1]and a crowd passing along he asked what [2]might [3]be [1]this.

37 ἀπήγγειλαν.δὲ αὐτῷ, Ὅτι Ἰησοῦς ὁ Ναζωραῖος παρέρχεται.
And they told him, Jesus the Nazaræan is passing by.

38 Καὶ ἐβόησεν λέγων, Ἰησοῦ, υἱὲ [m]Δαβίδ,[‖] ἐλέησόν με.
And he called out saying, Jesus, Son of David, have pity on me.

39 Καὶ οἱ προάγοντες ἐπετίμων αὐτῷ ἵνα [n]σιωπήσῃ·[‖]
And those going before rebuked him that he should be silent,

αὐτὸς.δὲ πολλῷ μᾶλλον ἔκραζεν, Υἱὲ [m]Δαβίδ,[‖] ἐλέησόν με.
but he much more cried out, Son of David, have pity on me.

40 Σταθεὶς.δὲ [o]ὁ Ἰησοῦς ἐκέλευσεν αὐτὸν ἀχθῆναι πρὸς
And [2]having [3]stopped [1]Jesus commanded him to be brought to

αὐτόν· ἐγγίσαντος.δὲ αὐτοῦ ἐπηρώτησεν αὐτόν, 41 [p]λέ-
him. And having drawn near he asked him, say-

γων,[‖] Τί σοι θέλεις ποιήσω; Ὁ.δὲ εἶπεν, Κύριε, ἵνα
ing, What [6]to [7]thee [1]desirest [2]thou [3]I [4]shall [5]do? And he said, Lord, that

ἀναβλέψω. 42 Καὶ ὁ Ἰησοῦς εἶπεν αὐτῷ, Ἀνάβλεψον·
I may receive sight. And Jesus said to him, Receive sight:

ἡ.πίστις.σου σέσωκέν σε. 43 Καὶ παραχρῆμα ἀνέβλεψεν,
thy faith hath healed thee. And immediately he received sight,

καὶ ἠκολούθει αὐτῷ, δοξάζων τὸν θεόν· καὶ πᾶς ὁ λαὸς
and followed him, glorifying God. And all the people

ἰδὼν ἔδωκεν αἶνον τῷ θεῷ.
having seen [it] gave praise to God.

19 Καὶ εἰσελθὼν διήρχετο τὴν [q]Ἱεριχώ·[‖] 2 καὶ ἰδού,
And having entered he passed through Jericho. And behold,

ἀνὴρ ὀνόματι καλούμενος Ζακχαῖος, καὶ αὐτὸς ἦν ἀρχι-
a man by name called Zacchæus, and he was a chief

τελώνης, καὶ [r]οὗτος ἦν[‖] πλούσιος· 3 καὶ ἐζήτει ἰδεῖν τὸν
tax-gatherer, and he was rich. And he was seeking to see

Ἰησοῦν τίς ἐστιν, καὶ οὐκ.ἠδύνατο ἀπὸ τοῦ ὄχλου, ὅτι τῇ
Jesus— who he is: and he was not able for the crowd, because

ἡλικίᾳ μικρὸς ἦν. 4 καὶ προδραμὼν [s]ἔμπροσθεν ἀνέβη
in stature small he was. And having run forward before, he went up

ἐπὶ [t]συκομωραίαν,[‖] ἵνα ἴδῃ αὐτόν· ὅτι [v]δι'[‖] ἐκείνης
into a sycomore, that he might see him, for by that [way]

ἤμελλεν διέρχεσθαι. 5 καὶ ὡς ἦλθεν ἐπὶ τὸν τόπον, ἀνα-
he was about to pass. And as he came to the place, look-

βλέψας ὁ Ἰησοῦς [w]εἶδεν αὐτόν, καὶ[‖] εἶπεν πρὸς αὐτόν,
ing up Jesus saw him, and said to him,

Ζακχαῖε, σπεύσας κατάβηθι· σήμερον.γὰρ ἐν τῷ.οἴκῳ.σου
Zacchæus, making haste come down, for to-day in thy house

δεῖ με μεῖναι. 6 Καὶ σπεύσας κατέβη καὶ ὑπεδέξατο
it behoveth me to remain. And making haste he came down and received

αὐτὸν χαίρων. 7 καὶ ἰδόντες [x]ἅπαντες[‖] διεγόγγυζον,
him rejoicing. And having seen [it] all murmured,

λέγοντες, Ὅτι παρὰ ἁμαρτωλῷ ἀνδρὶ εἰσῆλθεν καταλῦσαι.
saying, With a sinful man he has entered to lodge.

8 Σταθεὶς δὲ Ζακχαῖος εἶπεν πρὸς τὸν κύριον, Ἰδού, τὰ
But standing Zacchæus said to the Lord, Lo, the

[y]ἡμίση[‖] [z]τῶν.ὑπαρχόντων.μου,[‖] κύριε, [a]δίδωμι τοῖς πτωχοῖς·[‖]
half of my possessions, Lord, I give to the poor,

καὶ εἴ τινός τι ἐσυκοφάντησα, ἀποδίδωμι τετρα-
and if of anyone anything I took by false accusation, I return four-

πλοῦν. 9 Εἶπεν.δὲ πρὸς αὐτὸν ὁ Ἰησοῦς, Ὅτι σήμερον σωτηρία
fold. And [2]said [3]to [4]him [1]Jesus, To-day salvation

τῷ.οἴκῳ.τούτῳ ἐγένετο, καθότι καὶ αὐτὸς υἱὸς Ἀβραάμ
to this house is come, inasmuch as also he a son of Abraham

[b]ἐστιν·[‖] 10 ἦλθεν.γὰρ ὁ υἱὸς τοῦ ἀνθρώπου ζητῆσαι καὶ σῶσαι
is: for [5]came [1]the [2]Son [3]of [4]man to seek and to save

31 And taking the twelve to Him, He said to
them, Behold! We are going up to Jerusalem
and all things that are written by the prophets
about the Son of man shall be fulfilled.
32 For He will be delivered up to the Gentiles
and will be laughed at. And He will be insulted
and will be spit upon.
33 And after they beat Him, they will kill
Him. And on the third day He will arise again.
34 And they did not understand any of these
things. And this saying was hidden from them.
And they did not know that which was said.
35 And as He drew near to Jericho, a certain
blind one sat beside the road begging.
36 And hearing the crowd passing by, he
asked what this might mean.
37 And they told him, Jesus the Nazarene is
going by.
38 And he cried out, saying, Jesus, Son of
David, have mercy on me!
39 And those going before scolded him, that
he should be quiet. But he cried out the more,
Son of David, have mercy on me!
40 And Jesus stopped and commanded him
to be brought to Him. And when he came
near, He asked him,
41 saying, What do you want Me to do to
you? And he said, Lord, that I may receive
sight.
42 And Jesus said to him, Look up! Your
faith has healed you.
43 And instantly he regained his sight. And
he followed Him, praising God. And when the
people saw, they praised God.

CHAPTER 19

1 And entering Jericho, He passed through it.
2 And, behold! *There was* a man named
Zac-che-us. And he was a chief tax-collector.
And he was rich.
3 And he was trying to see Jesus – who He
was. But he was not able because of the
crowd, for he was small in height.
4 And having run ahead beforehand, he
climbed up into a sycamore tree so that he
might see Him (for He was about to pass).
5 And as He came to the place, Jesus looked
up and saw him. And He said to him, Zac-
che-us! Hurry and come down! For today I
must stay in your house.
6 And hurrying he came down and joyfully
received Him.
7 And seeing it, all murmured, saying, He
has gone in to stay with a sinful man.
8 And standing up, Zac-che-us said to the
Lord, See, Lord, I give half of what I own to
the poor! And if I have taken anything from
anyone by lying charges, I give him back
four times as much.
9 And Jesus said to him, Salvation has come
to this house today, because he also is a son
of Abraham.
10 For the Son of man has come to seek
and to save that which has been lost.

τὸ ἀπολωλός.
that which has been lost.
11 Ἀκουόντων.δὲ αὐτῶν ταῦτα, προσθεὶς εἶπεν παρα-
But as ²were ³hearing ¹they these things, adding he spoke a para-
βολήν, διὰ τὸ ἐγγὺς [c]αὐτὸν εἶναι Ἱερουσαλήμ,‖ καὶ δοκεῖν
ble, because ³near ¹he , ²was Jerusalem, and ²thought
αὐτοὺς ὅτι παραχρῆμα μέλλει ἡ βασιλεία τοῦ θεοῦ ἀνα-
¹they that immediately was about the kingdom of God to be
φαίνεσθαι· 12 εἶπεν οὖν, Ἄνθρωπός τις εὐγενὴς ἐπορεύθη
manifested. He said therefore, A ³man ¹certain high born proceeded
εἰς χώραν μακράν, λαβεῖν ἑαυτῷ βασιλείαν καὶ ὑποστρέψαι.
to a ²country ¹distant, to receive for himself a kingdom and to return.
13 καλέσας.δὲ δέκα δούλους.ἑαυτοῦ ἔδωκεν αὐτοῖς δέκα μνᾶς,
And having called ten of his bondmen he gave to them ten minas,
καὶ εἶπεν πρὸς αὐτούς, Πραγματεύσασθε [d]ἕως‖ ἔρχομαι.
and said to them, Trade until I come.
14 Οἱ.δὲ.πολῖται.αὐτοῦ ἐμίσουν αὐτόν, καὶ ἀπέστειλαν πρεσ-
But his citizens hated him and sent an em-
βείαν ὀπίσω αὐτοῦ, λέγοντες, Οὐ.θέλομεν τοῦτον
bassy after him, saying, We are unwilling [for] this [man]
βασιλεῦσαι ἐφ' ἡμᾶς. 15 Καὶ ἐγένετο ἐν τῷ ἐπανελθεῖν
to reign over us. And it came to pass on ²coming ³back ⁴again
αὐτὸν λαβόντα τὴν βασιλείαν, καὶ εἶπεν φωνηθῆναι αὐτῷ
¹his having received the kingdom, that he directed to be called to him
τοὺς.δούλους.τούτους οἷς [e]ἔδωκεν‖ τὸ ἀργύριον, ἵνα
these bondmen to whom he gave the money, in order that
[f]γνῷ‖ [g]τίς.τί διεπραγματεύσατο.‖ 16 παρεγένετο.δὲ ὁ
he might know what each had gained by trading. And came up the
πρῶτος, λέγων, Κύριε, ἡ.μνᾶ.σου [h]προσειργάσατο δέκα‖ μνᾶς.
first, saying, Lord, thy mina has produced ten minas.
17 Καὶ εἶπεν αὐτῷ, [i]Εὖ,‖ ἀγαθὲ δοῦλε· ὅτι ἐν ἐλαχίστῳ
And he said to him, Well! good bondman; because in a very little
πιστὸς ἐγένου, ἴσθι ἐξουσίαν ἔχων ἐπάνω δέκα πόλεων.
faithful thou wast, be thou ²authority ¹having over ten cities.
18 Καὶ ἦλθεν ὁ δεύτερος, λέγων, [k]Κύριε, ἡ.μνᾶ.σου‖ ἐποίησεν
And came the second, saying, Lord, thy mina has made
πέντε μνᾶς. 19 Εἶπεν.δὲ καὶ τούτῳ, Καὶ σὺ [l]γίνου ἐπάνω‖
five minas. And he said also to this one, And ²thou ¹be over
πέντε πόλεων. 20 Καὶ [m]ἕτερος ἦλθεν, λέγων, Κύριε, ἰδοὺ ἡ
five cities. And another came, saying, Lord, behold
μνᾶ.σου, ἣν εἶχον ἀποκειμένην ἐν σουδαρίῳ· 21 ἐφοβούμην
thy mina, which I kept laid up in a handkerchief. ²I ³feared
γάρ σε, ὅτι ἄνθρωπος αὐστηρὸς εἶ· αἴρεις ὃ
¹for thee, because a man harsh thou art; thou takest up what
οὐκ.ἔθηκας καὶ θερίζεις ὃ οὐκ.ἔσπειρας. 22 Λέγει
thou didst not lay down and thou reapest what thou didst not sow. ²He ³says
[n]δὲ‖ αὐτῷ, Ἐκ τοῦ.στόματός.σου κρινῶ σε, πονηρὲ δοῦ-
¹but to him, Out of thy mouth I will judge thee, wicked bond-
λε. ᾔδεις ὅτι ἐγὼ ἄνθρωπος αὐστηρός εἰμι, αἴρων ὃ
man: thou knewest that I ²a ⁴man ³harsh ¹am, taking up what
οὐκ.ἔθηκα καὶ θερίζων ὃ οὐκ.ἔσπειρα. 23 καὶ [o]διατί‖
I did not lay down and reaping what I did not sow! and why
οὐκ.ἔδωκας [p]τὸ.ἀργύριόν.μου‖ ἐπὶ [q]τὴν‖ τράπεζαν, [r]καὶ ἐγὼ‖
didst thou not give my money to the bank, that I
ἐλθὼν σὺν τόκῳ ἂν.[s]ἔπραξα αὐτό‖; 24 Καὶ τοῖς παρε-
coming with interest might have required it? And to those stand-
στῶσιν εἶπεν, Ἄρατε ἀπ' αὐτοῦ τὴν μνᾶν, καὶ δότε τῷ
ing by he said, Take from him the mina, and give [it] to him who
τὰς δέκα μνᾶς ἔχοντι. 25 Καὶ [t]εἶπον‖ αὐτῷ, Κύριε, ἔχει
the ten minas has. (And they said to him, Lord, he has
δέκα μνᾶς. 26 Λέγω.[v]γὰρ‖ ὑμῖν, ὅτι παντὶ τῷ ἔχοντι δο-
ten minas.) For I say to you, that to everyone who has shall be
θήσεται· ἀπὸ.δὲ τοῦ μὴ.ἔχοντος, καὶ ὃ ἔχει ἀρθήσεται
given; but from him who has not, even that which he has shall be taken
[w]ἀπ' αὐτοῦ.‖ 27 Πλὴν τοὺς.ἐχθρούς.μου [x]ἐκείνους‖ τοὺς
from him. Moreover ²mine ³enemies ¹those who
μὴ.θελήσαντάς με βασιλεῦσαι ἐπ' αὐτούς, ἀγάγετε ὧδε
were unwilling [for] me to reign over them, bring here
καὶ κατασφάξατε [y] ἔμπροσθέν μου.
and slay [them] before me.

28 Καὶ εἰπὼν ταῦτα ἐπορεύετο ἔμπροσθεν, ἀναβαίνων
And having said these things he went on before, going up
εἰς Ἱεροσόλυμα· 29 Καὶ ἐγένετο ὡς ἤγγισεν εἰς Βηθ-
to Jerusalem. And it came to pass as he drew near to Beth-
φαγὴ καὶ [z]Βηθανίαν,‖ πρὸς τὸ ὄρος τὸ καλούμενον ἐλαιῶν,
phage and Bethany, towards the mount called of Olives,
ἀπέστειλεν δύο τῶν.μαθητῶν.[a]αὐτοῦ,‖ 30 [b]εἰπών,‖ Ὑπάγετε εἰς
he sent two of his disciples, saying, Go into
τὴν κατέναντι κώμην· ἐν ᾗ εἰσπορευόμενοι εὑρήσετε
the ²opposite [³you] ¹village, in which entering ye will find
πῶλον δεδεμένον, ἐφ' ὃν οὐδεὶς πώποτε ἀνθρώπων ἐκάθισεν·
a colt tied, on which no one ³ever ⁴yet ¹of ²men sat:

11 And as they were hearing these things,
He spoke, adding a parable because He was
near Jerusalem (and because they thought
that the kingdom of God was going to be
immediately revealed).
12 Because of this He said, A certain high-
born one went into a distant country to
receive a kingdom for himself, and *planned*
to return.
13 And he called ten of his servants and
gave to them ten minas. And he said to them,
Buy and sell until I return.
14 But his citizens hated him and sent a
group of men after him, saying, We do not
want this man to rule over us.
15 And when he returned, after receiving
the kingdom, he commanded these servants
to be called to him, those to whom he gave
the money, so that he might know what
each had gained by trading.
16 And the first one came up, saying, Lord
your mina has gained ten minas.
17 And he said to him, Well done, good
servant! Since you have been faithful in a
very little, you have authority over ten
cities.
18 And the second one came, saying, Lord,
your mina has gained five minas.
19 And he said also to this one, And you be
over five cities.
20 And another one came, saying, Lord, See
your mina which I have kept in a
handkerchief.
21 For I feared you because you are a harsh
man. You take up what you did not lay
down and you reap what you did not sow.
22 And he said to him, I will judge you out
of your own mouth, wicked servant. You
knew I was a harsh man, taking up what I
did not lay down and reaping what I did not
sow.
23 But why did you not give my money to
the bank so that when I came I could have
exacted it with interest.
24 And he said to those standing by, Take
the mina away from him and give it to him
who has ten minas.
25 (And they said to him, Lord, he has ten
minas!)
26 For I say to you that to everyone who
has, *more* shall be given. But from him who
does not have, even that which he has shall
be taken from him.
27 Furthermore, bring here those who were
unwilling for me to rule over them and kill
them in front of me.
28 And saying these things He went on
before, going up to Jerusalem.
29 And as He drew near to Beth-pha-ge and
Bethany, toward that called the Mount of
Olives, He sent two of His disciples away,
30 saying, Go into the village over on the
other side, in which, going in, you will find a
colt tied up (on which no one has ever yet

ᶜλύσαντες αὐτὸν ἀγάγετε. 31 καὶ ἐάν τις ὑμᾶς ἐρωτᾷ,
having loosed it bring [it]. And if anyone ²you ¹ask,
ᵈΔιατί" λύετε; οὕτως ἐρεῖτε ᵉαὐτῷ," "Οτι ὁ κύριος
Why do ye loose [it]? thus shall ye say to him, Because the ·Lord
αὐτοῦ χρείαν ἔχει. 32 Ἀπελθόντες.δὲ οἱ ἀπεσταλμένοι
³of ⁴it ²need ¹has. And having departed those who had been sent
εὗρον καθὼς εἶπεν αὐτοῖς. 33 λυόντων.δὲ.αὐτῶν τὸν πῶλον
found as he had said to them. And on their loosing the colt
ᶠεἶπον" οἱ κύριοι αὐτοῦ πρὸς αὐτούς, Τί λύετε τὸν πῶλον;
⁵said ¹the ²masters ³of ⁴it to them, Why loose ye the colt?
34 Οἱ.δὲ ᶠεἶπον," ᵍὉ κύριος αὐτοῦ χρείαν ἔχει. 35 Καὶ ἤγαγον
And they said, The Lord ³of ⁴it ²need ¹has. And they led
αὐτὸν πρὸς τὸν Ἰησοῦν· καὶ ʰἐπιρρίψαντες" ⁱἑαυτῶν" τὰ ἱμά-
it to Jesus; and having cast their gar-
τια· ἐπὶ τὸν πῶλον, ἐπεβίβασαν τὸν Ἰησοῦν. 36 πορευο-
ments on the colt, they put ²on [³it] ¹Jesus.
μένου.δὲ.αὐτοῦ ὑπεστρώννυον τὰ.ἱμάτια.ᵏαὐτῶν" ἐν τῇ ὁδῷ.
And as he went they were strewing their garments in the way.
37 Ἐγγίζοντος.δὲ.αὐτοῦ ἤδη πρὸς τῇ καταβάσει τοῦ ὄρους
And as he drew near already at the descent of the mount
τῶν ἐλαιῶν ἤρξαντο ἅπαν τὸ πλῆθος τῶν μαθητῶν χαιρον-
of Olives began all the multitude of the disciples, rejoic-
τες αἰνεῖν τὸν θεὸν φωνῇ μεγάλῃ περὶ ˡπασῶν" ὧν
ing, to praise God with a ²voice ¹loud for all ⁸which
εἶδον δυνάμεων, 38 λέγοντες, Εὐλογημένος ὁ
⁶they ⁷had ⁸seen [¹the] ²works ³of ⁴power, saying, Blessed the
ᵐἐρχόμενος" βασιλεὺς ἐν ὀνόματι κυρίου· ⁿεἰρήνη ἐν
²coming ¹king in [the] name of [the] Lord. Peace in
οὐρανῷ" καὶ δόξα ἐν ὑψίστοις. 39 Καί τινες τῶν Φαρισαίων
heaven and glory in [the] highest. And some of the Pharisees
ἀπὸ τοῦ ὄχλου ᵒεἶπον" πρὸς αὐτόν, Διδάσκαλε, ἐπιτίμησον
from the crowd said to him, Teacher, rebuke
τοῖς.μαθηταῖς.σου. 40 Καὶ ἀποκριθεὶς εἶπεν ᵖαὐτοῖς," Λέγω
thy disciples. And answering he said to them, I say
ὑμῖν, ᵠὅτι" ἐὰν οὗτοι ʳσιωπήσωσιν" οἱ λίθοι ˢκεκράξονται."
to you, that if these should be silent the stones will cry out.
41 Καὶ ὡς ἤγγισεν, ἰδὼν τὴν πόλιν ἔκλαυσεν ἐπ' ᵗαὐτῇ,"
And as he drew near, seeing the city he wept over it,
42 λέγων, "Οτι εἰ ἔγνως καὶ σύ, ᵛκαί.γε" ἐν τῇ ἡμέρᾳ
saying, If thou hadst known, even thou, even at least in ³day
ʷσου" ταύτῃ, τὰ πρὸς εἰρήνην ˣσου·" νῦν.δὲ ἐκρύβη ἀπὸ
²thy ¹this, the things for ²peace ¹thy: but now they are hid from
ὀφθαλμῶν.σου· 43 ὅτι ἥξουσιν ἡμέραι ἐπὶ σὲ καὶ ʸπεριβα-
thine eyes; for ²shall ³come ¹days upon thee that ⁵shall ⁶cast
λοῦσιν" οἱ.ἐχθροί.σου χάρακά σοι, καὶ περικυκλώσουσίν σε
⁸about ¹thine ²enemies ⁷a ⁸rampart ⁹thee, and shall close around thee
καὶ συνέξουσίν σε πάντοθεν, 44 καὶ ἐδαφιοῦσίν
and keep in thee on every side, and shall level ²with ¹the ³ground
σε καὶ τὰ.τέκνα.σου ἐν σοί, καὶ οὐκ.ἀφήσουσιν ᶻἐν σοὶ λίθον
¹thee and thy children in thee, and shall not leave in thee a stone
ἐπὶ λίθῳ·" ἀνθ'.ὧν οὐκ.ἔγνως τὸν καιρὸν τῆς ἐπισκοπῆς
upon a stone, because thou knowest not the season of ²visitation
σου.
¹thy.

45 Καὶ εἰσελθὼν εἰς τὸ ἱερὸν ἤρξατο ἐκβάλλειν τοὺς
And having entered into the temple he began to cast out those
πωλοῦντας ᵃἐν αὐτῷ καὶ ἀγοράζοντας," 46 λέγων αὐτοῖς,
selling in it and buying, saying to them,
Γέγραπται, ᵇὉ.οἶκός.μου οἶκος προσευχῆς ᶜἐστίν·" ὑμεῖς.δὲ
It has been written, My house a house of prayer is; but ye
αὐτὸν ἐποιήσατε σπήλαιον λῃστῶν. 47 Καὶ ἦν διδάσκων
it have made a den of robbers. And he was teaching
τὸ.καθ'.ἡμέραν ἐν τῷ ἱερῷ· οἱ.δὲ ἀρχιερεῖς καὶ οἱ γραμματεῖς
day by day in the temple; and the chief priests and the scribes
ἐζήτουν αὐτὸν ἀπολέσαι, καὶ οἱ πρῶτοι τοῦ λαοῦ· 48 καὶ
⁷were ⁸seeking ¹¹him ⁹to ¹⁰destroy, ¹and ²the ³first ⁴of ⁵the ⁶people, and
οὐχ.ᵈεὕρισκον" τὸ τί ποιήσωσιν, ὁ.λαὸς γὰρ ἅπας ᵉἐξεκρέματο"
found not what they might do, for ²the ³people ¹all ⁴were ⁵hanging ⁷on
αὐτοῦ ἀκούων.
⁸him ⁶listening.

20 Καὶ ἐγένετο ἐν μιᾷ τῶν.ἡμερῶν.ᶠἐκείνων," διδάσκον-
And it came to pass on one of those days, as ²was ³teach-
τος αὐτοῦ τὸν λαὸν ἐν τῷ ἱερῷ καὶ εὐαγγελιζομένου,
ing ¹he the people in the temple and announcing the glad tidings,
ἐπέστησαν οἱ ᵍἀρχιερεῖς" καὶ οἱ γραμματεῖς σὺν τοῖς πρεσβυ-
came up the chief priests and the scribes with the elders
τέροις, 2 καὶ ʰεἶπον" ⁱπρὸς αὐτόν, λέγοντες," ᵏΕἰπὲ" ἡμῖν ἐν
and spoke to him, saying, Tell us by
ποίᾳ ἐξουσίᾳ ταῦτα ποιεῖς, ἢ τίς ἐστιν ὁ δούς σοι τὴν
what authority these things thou doest, or who it is who gave to thee
ἐξουσίαν.ταύτην; 3 Ἀποκριθεὶς.δὲ εἶπεν πρὸς αὐτούς, Ἐρω-
this authority? And answering he said to them, ³Will

sat). After untying it, bring it.
31 And if anyone asks you, Why do you
untie it? You shall say to him, Because the
Lord needs it.
32 And going away, the ones who had been
sent found it just as He had said to them.
33 And as they untied the colt, its owners
said to them, Why do you untie the colt?
34 And they said, The Lord needs him.
35 And they led it to Jesus. And throwing
their coats on the colt, they set Jesus on it.
36 And as He went, they were spreading
their coats in the road.
37 And as He was coming near, now at the
descent of the Mount of Olives, all the
multitude of the disciples began to praise
God, rejoicing with a loud voice for all the
mighty works they had seen,
38 saying, Blessed is the King coming in the
name of the Lord! Peace in Heaven and
glory in the highest!
39 And some of the Pharisees said to Him
out of the crowd, Teacher, censure your
disciples.
40 And answering He said to them, I tell
you that if these should be silent the stones
will cry out.
41 And as He drew near, seeing the city, He
wept over it,
42 saying, If you had known, even you,
even at least in this day of yours, the things
which are for your peace! But now they are
hidden from your eyes.
43 Because days will come upon you that
your enemies shall throw up a rampart around
you, and surround you, and hem you in on
every side.
44 And *they* shall level you to the ground,
you and your children in you. And they
shall not leave in you one stone on top of
another stone – because you did not know
the time of your visitation.

45 And going into the Temple, He began to
throw out those selling and buying inside it,
46 saying to them, It has been written, "My
house is a house of prayer" but you have
made it a den of thieves.
47 And He was teaching daily in the Temple
– but the chief priests and scribes were lusting to kill Him (also the chief of the people).
48 But they did not find what they could
do, for the people were all hanging onto
Him, listening.

CHAPTER 20

1 And on one of those days, as He was
teaching the people in the Temple and
preaching the gospel, the chief priests and
the scribes came up with the elders,
2 and spoke to Him, saying, Tell us, by
what authority do you do these things? Or
who is it who gave you this authority?
3 And answering He said to them, I will ask

τήσω ὑμᾶς κἀγὼ ἕνα" λόγον, καὶ εἴπατέ μοι· 4 Τὸ·βάπτισμα
4ask 5you 1I 2also one thing, and tell me, The baptism
Ἰωάννου" ἐξ οὐρανοῦ ἦν ἢ ἐξ ἀνθρώπων; 5 Οἱ.δὲ
of John from heaven was it or from men? And they
συνελογίσαντο" πρὸς ἑαυτούς, λέγοντες, Ὅτι ἐὰν εἴπωμεν
reasoned among themselves, saying, If we should say
Ἐξ οὐρανοῦ, ἐρεῖ Διατί" οὖν" οὐκ.ἐπιστεύσατε αὐτῷ;
From heaven, he will say Why then did ye not believe him?
6 ἐὰν.δὲ εἴπωμεν Ἐξ ἀνθρώπων, πᾶς ὁ λαὸς' καταλιθάσει
But if we should say From men, all the people will stone
ἡμᾶς· πεπεισμένος.γάρ.ἐστιν Ἰωάννην' προφήτην εἶναι.
us; for they are persuaded [that] John 2a 3prophet 1was.
7 Καὶ ἀπεκρίθησαν μὴ.εἰδέναι πόθεν. 8 καὶ ὁ Ἰησοῦς εἶπεν
And they answered they knew not whence. And Jesus said
αὐτοῖς, Οὐδὲ ἐγὼ λέγω ὑμῖν ἐν ποίᾳ ἐξουσίᾳ ταῦτα ποιῶ.
to them, Neither 2I 1tell you by what authority these things I do.

9 Ἤρξατο δὲ πρὸς τὸν λαὸν λέγειν" τὴν.παραβολὴν.ταύτην·
And he began to the people to speak this parable:
Ἄνθρωπός τις' ἐφύτευσεν ἀμπελῶνα," καὶ ἐξέδοτο" αὐτὸν
A 2man 1certain planted a vineyard, and let out it
γεωργοῖς, καὶ ἀπεδήμησεν χρόνους ἱκανούς. 10 καὶ ἐν"
to husbandmen, and left the country for a long time. And in [the]
καιρῷ ἀπέστειλεν πρὸς τοὺς γεωργοὺς δοῦλον, ἵνα ἀπὸ τοῦ
season he sent to the husbandmen a bondman, that from the
καρποῦ τοῦ ἀμπελῶνος δῶσιν" αὐτῷ· οἱ.δὲ γεωργοὶ
fruit of the vineyard they might give to him; but the husbandmen
δείραντες αὐτὸν ἐξαπέστειλαν' κενόν. 11 καὶ προσέθετο
having beat him sent [him] away empty. And he added
πέμψαι ἕτερον' δοῦλον· οἱ.δὲ κἀκεῖνον δείραντες καὶ ἀτι-
to send another bondman; but they 4also 3him 1having 2beat and dis-
μάσαντες ἐξαπέστειλαν κενόν. 12 καὶ προσέθετο πέμψαι
honoured [him] sent [him] away empty. And he added to send
τρίτον·" οἱ.δὲ καὶ τοῦτον" τραυματίσαντες ἐξέβαλον.
a third; and they 4also 3him 1having 2wounded cast [him] out.
13 εἶπεν.δὲ ὁ κύριος τοῦ ἀμπελῶνος, Τί ποιήσω; πέμψω
And said the lord of the vineyard, What shall I do? I will send
τὸν.υἱόν μου τὸν ἀγαπητόν· ἴσως τοῦτον ἰδόντες" ἐντρα-
my son the beloved; perhaps him having seen they will
πήσονται. 14 Ἰδόντες.δὲ αὐτὸν οἱ γεωργοὶ διελογίζοντο"
respect. But having seen him the husbandmen reasoned
πρὸς ἑαυτούς," λέγοντες, Οὗτός ἐστιν ὁ κληρονόμος· δεῦτε"
among themselves, saying, This is the heir; come
ἀποκτείνωμεν αὐτόν, ἵνα ἡμῶν γένηται ἡ κληρονομία.
let us kill him, that 5ours 3may 4become 1the 2inheritance.
15 Καὶ ἐκβαλόντες αὐτὸν ἔξω τοῦ ἀμπελῶνος ἀπέκτειναν.
And having cast forth him outside the vineyard they killed
Τί οὖν ποιήσει αὐτοῖς ὁ κύριος τοῦ ἀμπελῶνος;
[him]. What therefore will do to them the lord of the vineyard?
16 ἐλεύσεται καὶ ἀπολέσει τοὺς.γεωργοὺς.τούτους, καὶ δώσει
He will come and will destroy these husbandmen, and will give
τὸν ἀμπελῶνα ἄλλοις. Ἀκούσαντες.δὲ' εἶπον," Μὴ
the vineyard to others. And having heard [it] they said, 1Not
γένοιτο. 17 Ὁ.δὲ ἐμβλέψας αὐτοῖς εἶπεν, Τί οὖν ἐστιν τὸ
2may 3it be! But he looking at them said, What then is 2that
γεγραμμένον τοῦτο, Λίθον ὃν ἀπεδοκίμασαν οἱ
3has 4been 5written 1this, [The] stone which 4rejected 1they 2that
οἰκοδομοῦντες, οὗτος ἐγενήθη εἰς κεφαλὴν γωνίας; 18 Πᾶς
3build, this is become head of [the] corner? Everyone
ὁ πεσὼν ἐπ' ἐκεῖνον τὸν λίθον συνθλασθήσεται· ἐφ'.ὃν.δ'.ἂν
that falls on that stone will be broken, but on whomsoever
πέσῃ λικμήσει αὐτόν. 19 Καὶ ἐζήτησαν" οἱ
it may fall it will grind 2to 3powder 1him. And 7sought 1the
ἀρχιερεῖς καὶ οἱ γραμματεῖς" ἐπιβαλεῖν ἐπ' αὐτὸν τὰς χεῖρας
2chief 3priests 4and 5the 6scribes to lay 2on 3him 1hands
ἐν αὐτῇ τῇ.ὥρᾳ, καὶ ἐφοβήθησαν τὸν λαόν· ἔγνωσαν.γὰρ ὅτι
in that hour, and they feared the people; for they knew that
πρὸς αὐτοὺς τὴν.παραβολὴν.ταύτην εἶπεν."
against them this parable he speaks.

20 Καὶ παρατηρήσαντες ἀπέστειλαν ἐγκαθέτους," ὑπο-
And having watched [him] they sent secret agents, feign-
κρινομένους ἑαυτοὺς δικαίους εἶναι, ἵνα ἐπιλάβωνται
ing themselves 3righteous 1to 2be, that they might take hold
αὐτοῦ λόγου," εἰς τὸ" παραδοῦναι αὐτὸν τῇ ἀρχῇ καὶ
of him in discourse, to the [end] to deliver up him to the power and
τῇ ἐξουσίᾳ τοῦ ἡγεμόνος. 21 καὶ ἐπηρώτησαν αὐτόν, λέγον-
to the authority of the governor. And they questioned him, say-
τες, Διδάσκαλε, οἴδαμεν ὅτι ὀρθῶς λέγεις καὶ διδάσκεις, καὶ
ing, Teacher, we know that rightly thou sayest and teachest, and
οὐ.λαμβάνεις πρόσωπον, ἀλλ' ἐπ' ἀληθείας τὴν ὁδὸν
acceptest not [any man's] person, but with truth the way

you one thing also. Then tell me,
4 The baptism of John, was it from Heaven or from men?
5 And they talked it over among themselves, saying, If we should say, From Heaven, he will say, Why then did you not believe him?
6 But if we should say, From men, all the people will stone us, for they are persuaded that John was a prophet.
7 And they answered that they did not know where.
8 And Jesus said to them, Neither do I tell you by what authority I do these things.
9 And He began to tell this parable to the people: A certain man planted a vineyard and let it out to vinedressers. And he left the country for a long time.
10 And in time he sent a servant to the vinedressers so that they might give him his fruit from the vineyard. But the vinedressers beat him and sent him away empty.
11 And besides this, he sent another servant – but beating him also and shamefully treating him, they sent him away empty.
12 And besides this, he sent a third. And they wounded him also and threw him out.
13 And the vineyard owner said, What shall I do? I will send my beloved son. It may be that seeing him they will respect him.
14 But seeing him, the vinedressers talked it over among themselves, saying, This is the heir. Come, let us kill him so that the inheritance may be ours.
15 And throwing him out of the vineyard, they killed him. What then will the owner of the vineyard do to them?
16 He will come and destroy these vinedressers. And he will give the vineyard to others. And they heard and said, Let it not be!
17 And looking at them He said, What then is this that has been written, "The Stone which the builders despised, this has become the chief Cornerstone?"
18 Everyone that falls on that stone will be broken, but on whomever it may fall, it will grind him to powder.
19 And the chief priests and the scribes lusted to seize Him then, but they were afraid of the people. For they knew that He had spoken the parable against them.

20 And they sent out spies to watch, pretending themselves to be righteous men (so that they might seize upon a word of His, in order to betray Him to the power and to the authority of the governor).
21 And they questioned Him, saying, Teacher, we know that you say and teach rightly and accept no one's person, but

τοῦ θεοῦ διδάσκεις. 22 ἔξεστιν [s]ἡμῖν" Καίσαρι φόρον δοῦναι
of God teachest: is it lawful for us [4]to [5]Cæsar [3]tribute [1]to [2]give
ἢ οὔ; 23 Κατανοήσας.δὲ αὐτῶν τὴν πανουργίαν εἶπεν πρὸς
or not? But perceiving their craftiness he said to
αὐτούς, [t]Τί με πειράζετε"; 24 [v]ἐπιδείξατέ" μοι δηνάριον·[w]
them, Why me do ye tempt? Shew me a denarius:
τίνος ἔχει εἰκόνα καὶ ἐπιγραφήν; [x]Ἀποκριθέντες".δὲ [y]εἶπον,[z]
whose [4]has [5]it [1]image [2]and [3]inscription? And answering they said,
Καίσαρος. 25 Ὁ.δὲ εἶπεν [z]αὐτοῖς," [a]Ἀπόδοτε τοίνυν" τὰ
Cæsar's. And he said to them, Render therefore the things
Καίσαρος [b] Καίσαρι, καὶ τὰ τοῦ θεοῦ τῷ θεῷ. 26 Καὶ
of Cæsar to Cæsar, and the things of God to God. And
οὐκ.ἴσχυσαν ἐπιλαβέσθαι [c]αὐτοῦ".ῥήματος ἐναντίον τοῦ
they were not able to take hold of his speech before the
λαοῦ· καὶ θαυμάσαντες ἐπὶ τῇ.ἀποκρίσει.αὐτοῦ ἐσίγησαν.
people; and wondering at his answer they were silent.

27 Προσελθόντες.δέ τινες τῶν Σαδδουκαίων, οἱ [d]ἀντι-
And having come to [him] some of the Sadducees, who deny
λεγοντες" ἀνάστασιν μὴ εἶναι, ἐπηρώτησαν αὐτόν, 28 λέγον-
[3]a [4]resurrection [1]there [2]is, they questioned him, say-
τες, Διδάσκαλε, [e]Μωσῆς" ἔγραψεν ἡμῖν, ἐάν τινος ἀδελφὸς
ing, Teacher, Moses wrote to us, If anyone's brother
ἀποθάνῃ ἔχων γυναῖκα, καὶ οὗτος ἄτεκνος [f]ἀποθάνῃ," ἵνα
should die having a wife, and he childless should die, that
λάβῃ ὁ.ἀδελφὸς.αὐτοῦ τὴν γυναῖκα καὶ ἐξαναστήσῃ σπέρμα
[3]should [4]take [1]his [2]brother the wife and should raise up seed
τῷ.ἀδελφῷ.αὐτοῦ. 29 ἑπτὰ οὖν ἀδελφοὶ ἦσαν· καὶ ὁ πρῶτος
to his brother. [4]Seven [3]then [5]brethren [1]there [2]were; and the first
λαβὼν γυναῖκα ἀπέθανεν ἄτεκνος· 30 καὶ [g]ἔλαβεν" ὁ
having taken a wife died childless; and [3]took [1]the
δεύτερος [h]τὴν γυναῖκα, καὶ οὗτος ἀπέθανεν ἄτεκνος·" 31 καὶ
[2]second the woman, and he died childless; and
ὁ τρίτος ἔλαβεν αὐτήν[i]· ὡσαύτως.δὲ καὶ οἱ ἑπτὰ [k] οὐ.κατ-
the third took her; and likewise also the seven did not
έλιπον τέκνα, καὶ ἀπέθανον· 32 ὕστερον [l]δὲ πάντων" [m]ἀπέ-
leave children, and died; [2]last [1]and of all died
θανεν καὶ ἡ γυνή." 33 [n]ἐν.τῇ.οὖν" ἀναστάσει τίνος αὐτῶν
also the woman. Therefore in the resurrection of which of them
γίνεται γυνή; οἱ.γὰρ ἑπτὰ ἔσχον αὐτὴν γυναῖκα. 34 Καὶ
does she become wife? for the seven had her as wife. And
[o]ἀποκριθεὶς" εἶπεν αὐτοῖς ὁ Ἰησοῦς, Οἱ υἱοὶ τοῦ.αἰῶνος.τούτου
answering [2]said [3]to [4]them [1]Jesus, The sons of this age
γαμοῦσιν καὶ [p]ἐκγαμίσκονται·" 35 οἱ.δὲ καταξιωθέντες τοῦ
marry and are given in marriage; but those accounted worthy
αἰῶνος.ἐκείνου τυχεῖν καὶ τῆς ἀναστάσεως τῆς ἐκ
[3]that [4]age [1]to [2]obtain and the resurrection which [is] from among
νεκρῶν οὔτε γαμοῦσιν οὔτε [q]ἐκγαμίσκονται·" 36 [r]οὔτε"
[the] dead neither marry nor are given in marriage; [2]neither
γὰρ ἀποθανεῖν ἔτι δύνανται· ἰσάγγελοι.γάρ εἰσιν, καὶ
[1]for [5]die [6]any [7]more [4]they [3]can; for equal to angels they are, and
υἱοί εἰσιν [s]τοῦ" θεοῦ, τῆς ἀναστάσεως υἱοὶ ὄντες. 37 Ὅτι.δὲ
sons are of God, [3]of [4]the [5]resurrection [2]sons [1]being. But that
ἐγείρονται οἱ νεκροί, καὶ [e]Μωσῆς" ἐμήνυσεν ἐπὶ τῆς
are raised the dead, even Moses shewed [in the part] on the
βάτου, ὡς λέγει κύριον τὸν θεὸν Ἀβραὰμ καὶ [t]τὸν" θεὸν
bush, when he called [the] Lord the God of Abraham and the God
Ἰσαὰκ καὶ [t]τὸν" θεὸν Ἰακώβ· 38 θεὸς.δὲ οὐκ.ἔστιν νεκρῶν,
of Isaac and the God of Jacob; but God he is not of [the] dead,
ἀλλὰ ζώντων. πάντες.γὰρ αὐτῷ ζῶσιν. 39 Ἀποκριθέν-
but of [the] living; for all for him live. [2]Answering
τες δέ τινες τῶν γραμματέων [v]εἶπον," Διδάσκαλε, καλῶς
[1]and some of the scribes said, Teacher, well
εἶπας. 40 Οὐκέτι [x]δὲ" ἐτόλμων ἐπερωτᾷν αὐτὸν
thou hast spoken. [2]Not [3]any [4]more [1]and did they dare to ask him
οὐδέν.
anything.
(lit. nothing.)

41 Εἶπεν.δὲ πρὸς αὐτούς, Πῶς λέγουσιν τὸν χριστὸν [y]υἱὸν
And he said to them, How do they say the Christ [2]Son
[z]Δαβὶδ" εἶναι"; 42 [a]καὶ αὐτὸς" [z]Δαβὶδ" λέγει ἐν βίβλῳ
[3]of [4]David [1]is? and [2]himself [1]David says in [the] book
[b]ψαλμῶν, Εἶπεν [c]ὁ" κύριος τῷ.κυρίῳ.μου, Κάθου ἐκ δεξιῶν.μου,
of Psalms, [3]Said [1]the [2]Lord to my Lord, Sit on my right hand,
43 ἕως.ἂν θῶ τοὺς.ἐχθρούς.σου ὑποπόδιον τῶν.ποδῶν.σου.
until I place thine enemies [as] a footstool for thy feet.
44 [z]Δαβὶδ" οὖν [d]κύριον αὐτὸν" καλεῖ, καὶ πῶς [e]υἱὸς.αὐτοῦ"
David therefore [3]Lord [2]him [1]calls, and how his son
ἐστιν;
is he?
45 Ἀκούοντος.δὲ παντὸς τοῦ λαοῦ εἶπεν [f]τοῖς μαθηταῖς
And as were listening all the people he said to [2]disciples

really teach the way of God.
22 Is it right for us to give tribute to Caesar
or not?
23 But seeing through their slyness, He said
to them, Why do you tempt Me?
24 Show Me a coin. Whose likeness and
writing is this? And they said, Caesar's.
25 And He said to them, Then give Caesar's
things to Caesar and God's things to God.
26 And they were not able to seize upon
His words before the people. And wondering
at His answer, they were silent.

27 And some of the Sad-du-cees came up
(who deny there is a resurrection). They
asked Him,
28 saying, Teacher, Moses wrote to us, If
anyone's brother should have a wife and he
should die without children, then his brother
should take the wife and should raise up
seed to his brother.
29 Then there were seven brothers. And the
first one took a wife and died childless.
30 And the second one took the woman.
And he died without children.
31 And the third took her, and in the same
way the seven also died and left no children.
32 And last of all the woman also died.
33 Then, in the resurrection, of which one
of these does she become the wife? For *all*
the seven had her as wife.
34 And answering Jesus said to them, The
children of this world marry and are given in
marriage.
35 But those counted worthy to reach that
world, and the resurrection which is from
among the dead, neither marry nor are given
in marriage –
36 neither can they die any more – for they
are equal to angels and are the children of
God, being the children of the resurrection.
37 But that the dead are raised, even Moses
made plain at the Bush, when he called the
Lord the God of Abraham and the God of
Isaac and the God of Jacob.
38 But He is not God of the dead, but of
the living, for all live for His sake.
39 And then some of the scribes answered
and said, Teacher, you have spoken well.
40 And never again did they dare to ask
Him anything.

41 And He said to them, How do they say
that Christ is the son of David?
42 And David himself said in the book of
Psalms, "The Lord said to my Lord, Sit on
My right hand
43 until I place Your enemies as a footstool
for Your feet."
44 David, then, calls Him Lord. And how
then is He his son?

45 And as all the people were listening, He
said to His disciples,

αὐτοῦ," 46 Προσέχετε ἀπὸ τῶν γραμματέων τῶν θελόντων
his, Beware of the scribes who like
περιπατεῖν ἐν στολαῖς, καὶ φιλούντων ἀσπασμοὺς ἐν ταῖς
to walk in robes, and love salutations in the
ἀγοραῖς καὶ πρωτοκαθεδρίας ἐν ταῖς συναγωγαῖς καὶ πρω-
market-places and first seats in the synagogues and first
τοκλισίας ἐν τοῖς δείπνοις· 47 οἳ κατεσθίουσιν τὰς οἰκίας
places in the suppers, who devour the houses
τῶν χηρῶν, καὶ προφάσει μακρὰ προσεύχονται." οὗτοι
of widows, and as a pretext at great length pray. These
λήψονται" περισσότερον κρίμα.
shall receive more abundant judgment

21 Ἀναβλέψας.δὲ εἶδεν τοὺς βάλλοντας τὰ δῶρα αὐτῶν
And having looked up he saw the casting their gifts
εἰς τὸ γαζοφυλάκιον" πλουσίους· 2 εἶδεν δὲ καί τινα"
into the treasury rich, and he saw also a certain
χήραν πενιχρὰν βάλλουσαν ἐκεῖ δύο λεπτά·" 3 καὶ εἶπεν,
widow poor casting therein two lepta. And he said,
Ἀληθῶς λέγω ὑμῖν, ὅτι ἡ χήρα ἡ πτωχὴ αὕτη" πλεῖον"
Of a truth I say to you, that widow poor this more
πάντων ἔβαλεν· 4 ἅπαντες".γὰρ οὗτοι ἐκ τοῦ περισ-
than all cast in; for all these out of that which was
σεύοντος αὐτοῖς ἔβαλον εἰς τὰ δῶρα τοῦ θεοῦ," αὕτη.δὲ
abounding to them cast into the gifts of God; but she
ἐκ τοῦ.ὑστερήματος.αὐτῆς ἅπαντα" τὸν βίον ὃν εἶχεν
out of her poverty all the livelihood which she had
ἔβαλεν.
did cast.

5 Καί τινων λεγόντων περὶ τοῦ ἱεροῦ, ὅτι λίθοις καλοῖς
And as some were speaking about the temple, that with stones goodly
καὶ ἀναθήμασιν" κεκόσμηται, εἶπεν, 6 Ταῦτα ἃ θεω-
and consecrated gifts it was adorned, he said, [As to] these things which ye are
ρεῖτε, ἐλεύσονται ἡμέραι ἐν αἷς οὐκ.ἀφεθήσεται λίθος ἐπὶ
beholding, will come days in which shall not be left stone upon
λίθῳ ὃς οὐ.καταλυθήσεται. 7 Ἐπηρώτησαν δὲ αὐτόν, λέ-
stone which shall not be thrown down. And they asked him, say-
γοντες, Διδάσκαλε, πότε οὖν ταῦτα ἔσται; καὶ τί τὸ
ing, Teacher, when then these things will be? and what the
σημεῖον ὅταν μέλλῃ ταῦτα γίνεσθαι; 8 Ὁ.δὲ εἶπεν,
sign when are about these things to take place? And he said,
Βλέπετε μὴ πλανηθῆτε· πολλοὶ γὰρ ἐλεύσονται ἐπὶ τῷ
Take heed ye be not led astray; for many will come in
ὀνόματί.μου, λέγοντες, "Ὅτι" ἐγώ εἰμι· καί, Ὁ καιρὸς ἤγ-
my name, saying, I am [he]; and, The time is
γικεν. μὴ οὖν" πορευθῆτε ὀπίσω αὐτῶν. 9 ὅταν δὲ
drawn near. Not therefore go ye after them. And when
ἀκούσητε πολέμους καὶ ἀκαταστασίας, μὴ.πτοηθῆτε· δεῖ
ye shall hear of wars and commotions, be not terrified; must
γὰρ ταῦτα γενέσθαι" πρῶτον, ἀλλ' οὐκ εὐθέως τὸ
for these things take place first, but not immediately [is] the
τέλος. 10 Τότε ἔλεγεν αὐτοῖς, Ἐγερθήσεται ἔθνος ἐπὶ"
end. Then he was saying to them, Shall rise up nation against
ἔθνος, καὶ βασιλεία ἐπὶ βασιλείαν· 11 σεισμοί.τε μεγάλοι
nation, and kingdom against kingdom; also earthquakes great
κατὰ τόπους καὶ" λιμοὶ καὶ λοιμοὶ" ἔσονται, φόβη-
in different places and famines and pestilences shall there be, fearful
τρά" τε καὶ σημεῖα ἀπ' οὐρανοῦ" μεγάλα ἔσται. 12 Πρὸ
sights and and signs from heaven great shall there be. Before
δὲ τούτων ἁπάντων" ἐπιβαλοῦσιν ἐφ' ὑμᾶς τὰς χεῖρας
but these things all they will lay upon you hands
αὐτῶν, καὶ διώξουσιν, παραδιδόντες εἰς συναγωγὰς καὶ
their, and will persecute [you], delivering up to synagogues and
φυλακάς, ἀγομένους" ἐπὶ βασιλεῖς καὶ ἡγεμόνας, ἕνεκεν
prisons, bringing [you] before kings and governors, on account of
τοῦ.ὀνόματός.μου. 13 ἀποβήσεται.δὲ" ὑμῖν εἰς μαρτύριον·
my name; but it shall turn out to you for a testimony.
14 Θέσθε" οὖν εἰς τὰς καρδίας".ὑμῶν μὴ προμελετᾷν ἀπο-
Settle therefore in your hearts not to premeditate to make
λογηθῆναι· 15 ἐγὼ.γὰρ δώσω ὑμῖν στόμα καὶ σοφίαν, ἣ
a defence; for I will give you a mouth and wisdom, which
οὐ.δυνήσονται ἀντειπεῖν οὐδὲ' ἀντιστῆναι" πάντες" οἱ
shall not be able to reply to nor to resist all those
ἀντικείμενοι ὑμῖν. 16 παραδοθήσεσθε.δὲ καὶ ὑπὸ γονέων καὶ
opposing you. But ye will be delivered up even by parents and
ἀδελφῶν καὶ συγγενῶν καὶ φίλων, καὶ θανατώσουσιν
brethren and relations and friends, and they will put to death [some]
ἐξ ὑμῶν· 17 καὶ ἔσεσθε μισούμενοι ὑπὸ πάντων διὰ
from among you, and ye will be hated by all because of
τὸ.ὄνομά.μου. 18 καὶ θρὶξ ἐκ τῆς.κεφαλῆς.ὑμῶν οὐ.μὴ ἀπό-
my name. And a hair of your head in no wise may
ληται. 19 ἐν τῇ.ὑπομονῇ.ὑμῶν "κτήσασθε" τὰς.ψυχὰς.ὑμῶν.
perish. By your patient endurance gain your souls.

46 Look out for the scribes, who like to walk in long robes and love greetings in the market-places and the first seats in the synagogues and the first places in the feasts
47 who devour the houses of widows and as a pretense pray long prayers. These will receive a greater judgment.

CHAPTER 21

1 And looking up, He saw the rich men putting their gifts into the treasury.
2 And He also saw a certain poor widow putting two little coins in there.
3 And He said, I tell you truly that this poor widow has put in more than all.
4 For all these have put into the offerings of God out of their plenty, but she out of her poverty has put in all the livelihood she had
5 And as some were speaking about the Temple, that it was decorated with beautiful stones and gifts, He said,
6 As *to* these things which you are seeing, the days will come in which there shall not be left a stone on top of a stone which shall not be thrown down.
7 And they asked Him, saying, Teacher, but when will these things happen? And what *will be* the sign when these things are about to take place?
8 And He said, Be careful that you are not led astray. For many will come in My name, saying, I AM! And, The time has come! Do not follow them.
9 And when you shall hear of wars and disturbances, do not be terrified. For all things must take place first. But the end is not immediately.
10 Then He was saying to them, Nation will rise up against nation and kingdom against kingdom.
11 Also there will be great earthquakes in different places and famines and plagues. There shall be fearful sights and great signs from Heaven.
12 But before all these things, they will lay their hands on you and will persecute *you*, delivering you up to the synagogues and prisons, bringing you before kings and governors for My name's sake.
13 But it shall return to you for a testimony.
14 Then settle in your hearts not to be studying beforehand how to reply.
15 For I will give you a mouth and wisdom which all those who are against you will not be able to answer or resist.
16 But you will be betrayed even by parents and brothers and relatives and friends. And they will put *some* of you to death.
17 And you will be hated by all for My name's sake.
18 But in no way may a hair of your head be destroyed.
19 In your patience you shall gain the life of your souls.

20 "Ὅταν.δὲ ἴδητε κυκλουμένην ὑπὸ στρατοπέδων °τὴν" Ἱερου-
But when ye see [2]being [3]encircled [4]with [5]armies [1]Jeru-
σαλήμ, τότε γνῶτε ὅτι ἤγγικεν ἡ.ἐρήμωσις.αὐτῆς. 21 τότε
salem then know that has drawn near her desolation. Then
οἱ ἐν τῇ Ἰουδαίᾳ φευγέτωσαν εἰς τὰ ὄρη· καὶ οἱ ἐν
those in Judæa let them flee to the mountains; and those in
μέσῳ.αὐτῆς ἐκχωρείτωσαν· καὶ οἱ ἐν ταῖς χώραις μὴ εἰσερχέ-
her midst let them depart out, and those in the countries [3]not [1]let [2]them
σθωσαν εἰς αὐτήν. 22 ὅτι ἡμέραι ἐκδικήσεως αὗταί εἰσιν, τοῦ
enter into her; for days of avenging these are,
[p]πληρωθῆναι" πάντα τὰ γεγραμμένα. 23 οὐαὶ.[q]δὲ' ταῖς
that may be accomplished all things that have been written. But woe to those
ἐν.γαστρὶ.ἐχούσαις καὶ ταῖς θηλαζούσαις ἐν ἐκείναις ταῖς ἡμέ-
with child and to those giving suck in those days,
ραις· ἔσται.γὰρ ἀνάγκη μεγάλη ἐπὶ τῆς γῆς καὶ ὀργὴ [r]ἐν"
for there shall be [2]distress [1]great upon the land and wrath among
τῷ.λαῷ.τούτῳ. 24 καὶ πεσοῦνται στόματι [s]μαχαίρας," καὶ
this people. And they shall fall by [the] mouth of [the] sword, and
αἰχμαλωτισθήσονται εἰς [t]πάντα τὰ ἔθνη·" καὶ Ἱερουσαλὴμ
shall be led captive into all the nations; and Jerusalem
ἔσται πατουμένη ὑπὸ ἐθνῶν [v]ἄχρι" [w] πληρωθῶσιν
shall be trodden down by [the] nations until be fulfilled [the]
καιροὶ ἐθνῶν. 25 Καὶ [x]ἔσται" σημεῖα ἐν ἡλίῳ καὶ σελήνῃ
times of [the] nations. And there shall be signs in sun and moon
καὶ ἄστροις, καὶ ἐπὶ τῆς γῆς συνοχὴ ἐθνῶν ἐν ἀπορίᾳ,
and stars, and upon the earth distress of nations with perplexity,
[y]ἠχούσης" θαλάσσης καὶ σάλου, 26 ἀποψυχόντων ἀνθρώ-
roaring of [the] sea and rolling surge, [2]fainting [3]at [4]heart [1]men
πων ἀπὸ φόβου καὶ προσδοκίας τῶν ἐπερχομένων τῇ
from fear and expectation of that which is coming on the
οἰκουμένῃ· αἱ.γὰρ δυνάμεις τῶν οὐρανῶν σαλευθήσονται.
habitable earth; for the powers of the heavens shall be shaken.
27 καὶ τότε ὄψονται τὸν υἱὸν τοῦ ἀνθρώπου ἐρχόμενον ἐν
And then shall they see the Son of man coming in
νεφέλῃ μετὰ δυνάμεως καὶ δόξης πολλῆς. 28 Ἀρχομένων.δὲ
a cloud with power and [2]glory [1]great. But beginning
τούτων γίνεσθαι ἀνακύψατε καὶ ἐπάρατε τὰς κεφαλὰς
[1]these [2]things to come to pass look up and lift up [2]heads
ὑμῶν· διότι ἐγγίζει ἡ.ἀπολύτρωσις.ὑμῶν. 29 Καὶ εἶπεν
[1]your, because draws near your redemption. And he spoke
παραβολὴν αὐτοῖς, "Ἴδετε τὴν συκῆν καὶ πάντα τὰ δένδρα.
a parable to them: Behold the fig-tree and all the trees:
30 ὅταν προβάλωσιν ἤδη, βλέποντες ἀφ' ἑαυτῶν
when [2]they [3]sprout [1]already, looking [on them] of yourselves
γινώσκετε ὅτι ἤδη ἐγγὺς τὸ θέρος ἐστίν. 31 οὕτως καὶ ὑμεῖς,
ye know that already near the summer is. So also ye,
ὅταν ἴδητε ταῦτα γινόμενα γινώσκετε ὅτι ἐγγύς ἐστιν ἡ
when ye see these things coming to pass know that near is the
βασιλεία τοῦ θεοῦ. 32 ἀμὴν λέγω ὑμῖν, ὅτι οὐ.μὴ παρ-
kingdom of God. Verily I say to you, that in no wise will have
έλθῃ ἡ.γενεὰ.αὕτη ἕως.ἂν πάντα γένηται. 33 ὁ
passed away this generation until all shall have taken place. The
οὐρανὸς καὶ ἡ γῆ παρελεύσονται, οἱ.δὲ.λόγοι.μου οὐ.μὴ
heaven and the earth shall pass away, but my words in no wise
[z]παρέλθωσιν." 34 Προσέχετε.δὲ ἑαυτοῖς, μήποτε [a]βαρυνθῶ-
may pass away. But take heed to yourselves, lest be laden
σιν" [b]ὑμῶν αἱ καρδίαι" ἐν κραιπάλῃ καὶ μέθῃ καὶ μερίμναις
your hearts with surfeiting and drinking and cares
βιωτικαῖς, καὶ [c]αἰφνίδιος ἐφ' ὑμᾶς ἐπιστῇ" ἡ.ἡμέρα.ἐκείνη·
of life, and suddenly upon you should come that day;
35 ὡς.[d]παγὶς.γὰρ ἐπελεύσεται" ἐπὶ πάντας τοὺς καθημένους
for as a snare shall it come upon all those sitting
ἐπὶ πρόσωπον πάσης τῆς γῆς. 36 ἀγρυπνεῖτε [e]οὖν" ἐν
upon the face of all the earth. Watch therefore at
παντὶ καιρῷ δεόμενοι, ἵνα [f]καταξιωθῆτε" ἐκφυγεῖν ταῦ-
every season praying, that ye may be accounted worthy to escape [2]these
τα πάντα τὰ μέλλοντα γίνεσθαι, καὶ σταθῆναι ἔμπρο-
[3]things [1]all which are about to come to pass, and to stand before
σθεν τοῦ υἱοῦ τοῦ ἀνθρώπου.
the Son of man.
37 "Ἦν.δὲ τὰς.ἡμέρας [g]ἐν τῷ ἱερῷ διδάσκων·" τὰς.δὲ.νύκτας
And he was by day in the temple teaching, and by night
ἐξερχόμενος ηὐλίζετο εἰς τὸ ὄρος τὸ καλούμενον ἐλαιῶν·
going out he lodged on the mount called of Olives;
38 καὶ πᾶς ὁ λαὸς ὤρθριζεν πρὸς αὐτὸν ἐν τῷ
and all the people came early in the morning to him in the
ἱερῷ ἀκούειν αὐτοῦ.
temple to hear him.
22 "Ἤγγιζεν.δὲ ἡ ἑορτὴ τῶν.ἀζύμων ἡ λεγομένη
And drew near the feast of unleavened [bread] which [is] called
πάσχα· 2 καὶ ἐζήτουν οἱ ἀρχιερεῖς καὶ οἱ γραμματεῖς
passover; and [7]were [8]seeking [1]the [2]chief [3]priests [4]and [5]the [6]scribes

20 But when you see Jerusalem being encircled with armies, then you know that her
ruin has come.
21 Then those in Judea, let them flee into
the mountains. And those in the midst of
her, let them go out. And those in the
countries, let them not enter into her –
22 for these are the days of vengeance, so
that all things that have been written may be
accomplished.
23 But woe to those with child and those
giving suck in those days! For there shall be
a great misery on the land and anger against
this people.
24 And they shall fall by the edge of the
sword and shall be led captive into all
nations. And Jerusalem shall be trampled
upon by the Gentiles until the times of the
Gentiles are fulfilled.
25 And there shall be signs in the sun and
moon and stars. And *there shall be* a stran-
gling of nations on the earth, with bewilder-
ment, with the sea and the waves roaring,
26 men's hearts failing them from fear and
looking for that which is coming on earth –
for the powers of the heavens shall be
shaken.
27 And then they shall see the Son of man
coming in a cloud, with great power and
glory.
28 But when these things begin to happen,
look up, and lift up your heads, because
your redemption draws near.
29 And He told them a parable: Look at the
fig-tree and all the trees.
30 Now when they sprout, you know and
see for yourselves that summer is now near.
31 So, too, when you see these things begin,
you know that the kingdom of God is near.
32 I tell you truly that this generation will
not in any way have passed away until all
this has happened.
33 The sky and the earth may come to an
end, but My words in no way will disappear.
34 But be careful of yourselves for fear that
your hearts may be burdened with head-
aches and drunkenness and cares of this life,
and that day should suddenly come on you,
35 for it shall come as a snare on all those
sitting on the face of the whole earth.
36 Then watch, praying in every season that
you may be counted worthy to escape all
these things which are about to happen and
to stand before the Son of man.
37 And He was teaching in the Temple
during the day and going out by night. He
was staying on the Mount of Olives.
38 And all the people came early in the
morning to Him, to hear Him in the Temple.

CHAPTER 22

1 And the feast of the unleavened bread,
which is called Passover, drew near.
2 And the chief priests and the scribes were

τὸ.πῶς ἀνέλωσιν αὐτόν· ἐφοβοῦντο.γὰρ τὸν λαόν.
as to how they might put [2]to [3]death [1]him, for they feared the people.
3 Εἰσῆλθεν.δὲ [h]ὁ' σατανᾶς εἰς Ἰούδαν τὸν [i]ἐπικαλούμενον‖
And [2]entered [1]Satan into Judas who is surnamed
Ἰσκαριώτην, ὄντα ἐκ τοῦ ἀριθμοῦ τῶν δώδεκα· 4 καὶ ἀπελ-
Iscariote, being of the number of the twelve. And having gone
θὼν συνελάλησεν τοῖς ἀρχιερεῦσιν [k] καὶ [l]τοῖς‖ στρατηγοῖς
away he spoke with the chief priests and the captains
τὸ.πῶς [m]αὐτὸν παραδῷ αὐτοῖς.‖ 5 καὶ ἐχάρησαν, καὶ
as to how him he might deliver up to them. And they rejoiced, and
συνέθεντο αὐτῷ ἀργύριον δοῦναι· 6 [n]καὶ ἐξωμολόγησεν,‖ καὶ
agreed [3]him [4]money [1]to [2]give. And he promised, and
ἐζήτει εὐκαιρίαν τοῦ παραδοῦναι αὐτὸν [o]αὐτοῖς ἄτερ
sought opportunity to deliver up him to them away from [the]
ὄχλου.‖
crowd.
7 [p]Ἦλθεν.δὲ ἡ ἡμέρα τῶν.ἀζύμων [p]ἐν‖ ᾗ ἔδει
And came the day of unleavened [bread] in which was needful
θύεσθαι τὸ πάσχα. 8 καὶ ἀπέστειλεν Πέτρον καὶ [q]Ἰωάννην,‖
to be killed the passover. And he sent Peter and John,
εἰπών, Πορευθέντες ἑτοιμάσατε ἡμῖν τὸ πάσχα, ἵνα φάγω-
saying, Having gone prepare for us the passover, that we may
μεν. 9 Οἱ.δὲ [r]εἶπον‖ αὐτῷ, Ποῦ θέλεις ἑτοιμάσωμεν[s];
eat [it]. But they said to him, Where willest thou we should prepare?
10 Ὁ.δὲ εἶπεν αὐτοῖς, Ἰδού, εἰσελθόντων.ὑμῶν εἰς τὴν πόλιν
And he said to them, Lo, on your having entered into the city
συναντήσει ὑμῖν ἄνθρωπος κεράμιον ὕδατος βαστάζων· ἀκο-
[3]will [4]meet [5]you [1]a [2]man, a pitcher of water carrying; fol-
λουθήσατε αὐτῷ εἰς τὴν οἰκίαν [t]οὗ' εἰσπορεύεται· 11 καὶ
low him into the house where he enters; and
ἐρεῖτε τῷ οἰκοδεσπότῃ τῆς οἰκίας, Λέγει σοι ὁ διδάσ-
ye shall say to the master of the house, [3]Says [4]to [5]thee [1]the [2]teach-
καλος, Ποῦ ἐστιν τὸ κατάλυμα ὅπου τὸ πάσχα μετὰ τῶν
er, Where is the guest-chamber where the passover with
μαθητῶν.μου φάγω; 12 Κἀκεῖνος ὑμῖν δείξει [v]ἀνώγεον‖
my disciples I may eat? And he [3]you [1]will [2]shew [6]upper [7]room
μέγα ἐστρωμένον· ἐκεῖ ἑτοιμάσατε. 13 Ἀπελθόντες.δὲ εὗρον
[4]a [5]large furnished: there prepare. And having gone they found
καθὼς [w]εἴρηκεν‖ αὐτοῖς· καὶ ἡτοίμασαν τὸ πάσχα.
as he had said to them; and they prepared the passover.
14 Καὶ ὅτε ἐγένετο ἡ ὥρα ἀνέπεσεν, καὶ οἱ [x]δώδεκα‖
And when was come the hour he reclined [at table], and the twelve
ἀπόστολοι σὺν αὐτῷ. 15 καὶ εἶπεν πρὸς αὐτούς, Ἐπιθυμίᾳ
apostles with him. And he said to them, With desire
ἐπεθύμησα τοῦτο τὸ πάσχα φαγεῖν μεθ' ὑμῶν πρὸ τοῦ.με.πα-
I desired this passover to eat with you before I suf-
θεῖν· 16 λέγω.γὰρ ὑμῖν, ὅτι [y]οὐκέτι‖ οὐ.μὴ φάγω [z]ἐξ
fer. For I say to you, that [4]any [5]more [1]not [2]at [3]all will I eat of
(lit. no more)
αὐτοῦ‖ ἕως.ὅτου πληρωθῇ ἐν τῇ βασιλείᾳ τοῦ θεοῦ. 17 Καὶ
it until it be fulfilled in the kingdom of God. And
δεξάμενος [a] ποτήριον, εὐχαριστήσας εἶπεν, Λάβετε τοῦτο,
having received a cup having given thanks he said, Take this,
καὶ διαμερίσατε [b]ἑαυτοῖς·‖ 18 λέγω.γὰρ ὑμῖν, [c]ὅτι‖ οὐ.μὴ
and divide [it] among yourselves. For I say to you, that not at all
πίω [d] ἀπὸ τοῦ [e]γεννήματος‖ τῆς ἀμπέλου ἕως.[f]ὅτου‖ ἡ
will I drink of the fruit of the vine until the
βασιλεία τοῦ θεοῦ ἔλθῃ. 19 Καὶ λαβὼν ἄρτον, εὐχαριστή-
kingdom of God be come. And having taken a loaf, having given
σας ἔκλασεν, καὶ ἔδωκεν αὐτοῖς, λέγων, Τοῦτό ἐστιν τὸ σῶμά
thanks he broke, and gave to them, saying, This is [2]body
μου, τὸ ὑπὲρ ὑμῶν διδόμενον· τοῦτο ποιεῖτε [g]εἰς' τὴν ἐμὴν
[1]my, which for you is given: this do in the [2]of [3]me
ἀνάμνησιν. 20 [h]Ὡσαύτως καὶ τὸ ποτήριον‖ μετὰ τὸ.δειπνῆ-
[1]remembrance. In like manner also the cup after having supped,
σαι, λέγων, Τοῦτο τὸ ποτήριον ἡ καινὴ διαθήκη ἐν τῷ
saying, This cup [is] the new covenant in
αἵματί.μου, τὸ ὑπὲρ ὑμῶν [i]ἐκχυνόμενον.‖ 21 Πλὴν ἰδού,
my blood, which for you is poured out. Moreover, behold,
ἡ χεὶρ τοῦ παραδιδόντος με μετ' ἐμοῦ ἐπὶ τῆς τραπέζης.
the hand of him delivering up me [is] with me on the table;
22 [k]καὶ ὁ.μὲν.υἱὸς' τοῦ ἀνθρώπου [l]πορεύεται κατὰ τὸ
and indeed the Son of man goes according as
ὡρισμένον·‖ πλὴν οὐαὶ τῷ.ἀνθρώπῳ.ἐκείνῳ δι' οὗ παρα-
it has been determined, but woe to that man by whom he is de-
δίδοται. 23 Καὶ αὐτοὶ ἤρξαντο [m]συζητεῖν‖ πρὸς ἑαυτούς,
livered up. And they began to question together among themselves,
τό, τίς ἄρα εἴη ἐξ αὐτῶν ὁ τοῦτο μέλλων πράσσειν.
this, who then it might be of them who this was about to do.
24 Ἐγένετο.δὲ καὶ φιλονεικία ἐν αὐτοῖς, τό, τίς αὐτῶν
And there was also a strife among them, this, which of them
δοκεῖ εἶναι μείζων. 25 ὁ.δὲ εἶπεν αὐτοῖς, Οἱ βασιλεῖς
is thought to be [the] greater. And he said to them, The kings

looking for a way to put Him to death – for
they were afraid of the people.
3 And Satan entered into Judas (whose last
name was Is-car-i-ot,) being of the number of
the twelve.
4 And he went away and spoke with the
chief priests and the captains as to how he
might betray Him to them.
5 And they rejoiced and agreed to pay him.
6 And he promised, then looked for a good
time to betray Him to them, away from the
crowd.
7 And the day of unleavened bread came, in
which the passover must be sacrificed.
8 And He sent Peter and John, saying, Go
and prepare the passover for us so that we
may eat.
9 But they said to Him, Where do you
desire that we should make ready?
10 And He said to them, Behold, as you go
into the city you will meet a man carrying a
pitcher of water. Follow him to the house
where he goes.
11 And you shall say to the master of the
house, The Teacher says to you, Where is the
guest-room where My disciples and I may eat
the passover?
12 And he will show you a large furnished
upper room.
13 Make preparations there. And they went
and found it just as He had said to them.
And they made the passover ready.
14 And when the hour arrived, He and the
twelve apostles sat at table.
15 And He said to them, With great longing
I have desired to eat this Passover with you
before I suffer.
16 For I tell you that I will never eat with
you any more until it is fulfilled in the kingdom of God.
17 And taking a cup He gave thanks, saying,
Take this and divide it among yourselves.
18 For I say to you that I will never again
drink of the fruit of the vine until the kingdom of God has come.
19 And taking a loaf, giving thanks, He
broke and gave to them, saying, This is My
body which is given for you: this do in the
remembrance of Me.
20 And likewise the cup, after the taking of
supper, saying, This cup is the new covenant
in My blood which is poured out for you.
21 But, look! The hand of him who betrays
Me is with Me on the table.
22 And truly the Son of Man goes just as it
has been foredetermined, but woe to that
man by whom He is betrayed!
23 And they began to ask among themselves
then as to which of them it might be who
would do this thing.
24 And there was a dispute among them –
this, which of them is to be thought greater.
25 And He said to them, The kings of the

τῶν ἐθνῶν κυριεύουσιν αὐτῶν, καὶ οἱ ἐξουσιάζοντες
of the nations rule over them, and those exercising authority over
αὐτῶν εὐεργέται καλοῦνται. 26 ὑμεῖς.δὲ οὐχ οὕτως· ἀλλ'
them well-doers are called. But ye not thus [shall be]; but
ὁ μείζων ἐν ὑμῖν [n]γενέσθω‖ ὡς ὁ νεώτερος· καὶ ὁ
the greater among you let him be as the younger, and he that
ἡγούμενος ὡς ὁ διακονῶν. 27 τίς.γὰρ μείζων, ὁ
leads as he that serves. For which [is] greater, he that
ἀνακείμενος ἢ ὁ διακονῶν; οὐχὶ ὁ ἀνακείμε-
reclines [at table] or he that serves? [Is] not he that reclines
νος; ἐγὼ.δέ [o]εἰμι ἐν μέσῳ ὑμῶν‖ ὡς ὁ διακονῶν.
[at table]? But I am in [the] midst of you as he that serves.
28 Ὑμεῖς.δέ ἐστε οἱ διαμεμενηκότες μετ' ἐμοῦ ἐν τοῖς
But ye are they who have continued with me in
πειρασμοῖς μου· 29 κἀγὼ διατίθεμαι ὑμῖν, καθὼς διέθετό
my temptations. And I appoint to you, as [3]appointed
μοι ὁ.πατήρ μου, βασιλείαν, 30 ἵνα [p]ἐσθίητε‖ καὶ πίνητε
[4]to [5]me [1]my [2]father, a kingdom, that ye may eat and may drink
ἐπὶ τῆς.τραπέζης.μου ἐν τῇ.βασιλείᾳ.μου, καὶ [q]καθίσησθε‖ ἐπὶ
at my table in my kingdom, and may sit on
θρόνων, κρίνοντες τὰς δώδεκα φυλὰς τοῦ Ἰσραήλ.
thrones, judging the twelve tribes of Israel.
31 [r]Εἶπεν.δὲ ὁ κύριος,‖ Σίμων, Σίμων, ἰδού, ὁ σατανᾶς
And [3]said [1]the [2]Lord, Simon, Simon, lo, Satan
ἐξῃτήσατο ὑμᾶς, τοῦ σινιάσαι ὡς τὸν σῖτον· 32 ἐγὼ
demanded to have you, for the sifting [you] as wheat; [2]I
δὲ ἐδεήθην περὶ σοῦ, ἵνα μὴ.[s]ἐκλείπῃ‖ ἡ.πίστις.σου· καὶ σύ
[1]but besought for thee, that may not fail thy faith; and [2]thou
ποτε ἐπιστρέψας [t]στήριξον‖ τοὺς.ἀδελφούς.σου. 33 Ὁ.δὲ
[1]when hast turned back confirm thy brethren. And he
εἶπεν αὐτῷ, Κύριε, μετὰ σοῦ ἕτοιμός εἰμι καὶ εἰς φυλακὴν καὶ
said to him, Lord, with thee ready I am both to prison and
εἰς θάνατον πορεύεσθαι. 34 Ὁ.δὲ εἶπεν, Λέγω σοι, Πέτρε,
to death to go. And he said, I tell thee, Peter,
οὐ.[v]μὴ‖ φωνήσει σήμερον ἀλέκτωρ [w]πρὶν.ἢ‖ τρὶς [x]ἀπαρ-
in no wise shall crow to-day [the] cock before that thrice thou wilt
νήσῃ [y]μὴ‖ εἰδέναι με.‖
deny knowing me.

35 Καὶ εἶπεν αὐτοῖς, Ὅτε ἀπέστειλα ὑμᾶς ἄτερ [z]βαλαν-
And he said to them, When I sent you without purse
τίου‖ καὶ πήρας καὶ ὑποδημάτων, μή τινος ὑστερήσατε;
and provision bag and sandals, anything did ye lack?
Οἱ.δὲ [a]εἶπον,‖ [b]Οὐδενός.‖ 36 [c]Εἶπεν οὖν‖ αὐτοῖς, Ἀλλὰ
And they said, Nothing. He said therefore to them, [2]However
νῦν ὁ ἔχων [d]βαλάντιον‖ ἀράτω, ὁμοίως καὶ πήραν·
[1]now he who has a purse let him take [it] in like manner also provision bag;
καὶ ὁ μὴ.ἔχων πωλησάτω τὸ.ἱμάτιον.αὐτοῦ καὶ ἀγορασάτω
and he who has not [one] let him sell his garment and buy
μάχαιραν· 37 λέγω.γὰρ ὑμῖν, ὅτι [e]ἔτι τοῦτο τὸ γεγραμμένον
a sword; for I say to you, that yet this that has been written
δεῖ τελεσθῆναι ἐν ἐμοί, [f]τό‖ Καὶ μετὰ ἀνόμων ἐλογίσθη·
must be accomplished in me, And with [the] lawless he was reckoned:
καὶ.[g]γὰρ‖ [h]τὰ‖ περὶ ἐμοῦ τέλος ἔχει. 38 Οἱ.δὲ [a]εἶπον,‖
for also the things concerning me an end have. And they said,
Κύριε, ἰδού, μάχαιραι ὧδε δύο. Ὁ.δὲ εἶπεν αὐτοῖς,
Lord, behold, [4]swords [1]here [[2]are] [3]two. And he said to them,
Ἱκανόν ἐστιν.
[3]Enough [1]it [2]is.

39 Καὶ ἐξελθὼν ἐπορεύθη κατὰ τὸ ἔθος εἰς τὸ ὄρος
And going forth he went according to custom to the mount
τῶν ἐλαιῶν· ἠκολούθησαν.δὲ αὐτῷ καὶ οἱ.μαθηταὶ.[i]αὐτοῦ.‖
of Olives, and followed him also his disciples.
40 γενόμενος.δὲ ἐπὶ τοῦ τόπου εἶπεν αὐτοῖς, Προσεύχεσθε
And having arrived at the place he said to them, Pray
μὴ.εἰσελθεῖν εἰς πειρασμόν. 41 Καὶ αὐτὸς ἀπεσπάσθη ἀπ'
not to enter into temptation. And he was withdrawn from
αὐτῶν ὡσεὶ λίθου βολήν, καὶ θεὶς.τὰ.γόνατα προσηύχετο,
them about a stone's throw, and falling on [his] knees he prayed,
42 λέγων, Πάτερ, εἰ βούλει [k]παρενεγκεῖν‖ [l]τὸ ποτήριον
saying, Father, if thou art willing to take away [2]cup
τοῦτο‖ ἀπ' ἐμοῦ· πλὴν μὴ τὸ.θέλημά μου, ἀλλὰ τὸ.σὸν [m]γε-
[1]this from me—; but not my will, but thine be
νέσθω.‖ 43 [n]Ὤφθη.δὲ αὐτῷ ἄγγελος [o]ἀπ'‖ οὐρανοῦ ἐνισχύων
done. And appeared to him an angel from heaven strengthening
αὐτόν. 44 καὶ γενόμενος ἐν ἀγωνίᾳ ἐκτενέστερον προσηύχετο.
him. And being in conflict more intently he prayed.
[p]ἐγένετο.δὲ ὁ‖ ἱδρὼς.αὐτοῦ ὡσεὶ θρόμβοι αἵματος [q]κατα-
And became his sweat as great drops of blood falling
βαίνοντες‖ ἐπὶ τὴν γῆν.‖ 45 Καὶ ἀναστὰς ἀπὸ τῆς
down to the earth. And having risen up from
προσευχῆς, ἐλθὼν πρὸς τοὺς μαθητὰς [r] εὗρεν [s]αὐτοὺς κοιμω-
prayer, coming to the disciples he found them sleep-

Gentiles lord it over them. And those who exercise authority over them are called benefactors.

26 But not so with you, but he who is greater among you, let him be as the younger, and he who leads as he that serves.

27 For which is greater? He that sits at table or he that serves? *Is it* not he who sits? But I am among you as one who serves.

28 However, you are they who have continued with Me in My temptations.

29 And I appoint to you a kingdom, as My Father has appointed to Me,

30 so that you may eat and drink at My table in My kingdom, and that you may sit on thrones judging the twelve tribes of Israel.

31 And the Lord said, Simon, Simon, Behold! Satan has claimed you *for himself,* in order to sift you as wheat.

32 But I have prayed for you, that your faith may not fail. And when you have been restored, make your brothers strong.

33 And he said to Him, Lord, I am ready to go with You both into prison and into death.

34 And He said, I tell you, Peter, surely the cock will not crow today before you deny knowing Me three times.

35 And He said to them, When I sent you without purse and bag and shoes, did you lack anything? And they said, Nothing.

36 Then He said to them, But, now he who has a purse, let him take it. And in the same way also a bag. And he who does not have one, let him sell his coat and buy a sword.

37 For I tell you that this that has been written must still be fulfilled in Me, "And He was numbered with the transgressors" — for the things concerning Me have an end too.

38 And they said, Lord, See, here are two swords. And He said to them, It is enough.

39 And going out, according to custom, He went to the Mount of Olives. And His disciples also followed him.

40 And arriving there, He said to them, Pray that you do not enter into temptation.

41 And He was withdrawn from them about a stone's throw. And falling on His knees He prayed,

42 saying, Father, if You are willing, remove this cup from Me. Nevertheless, not My will be done, but Yours.

43 And an angel appeared to Him from Heaven, strengthening Him.

44 And being in an agony, He prayed more earnestly. And His sweat became as great drops of blood falling down to the ground.

45 And rising up from prayer, coming to His disciples, He found them sleeping from

μένους" ἀπὸ τῆς λύπης, 46 καὶ εἶπεν αὐτοῖς, Τί καθεύδετε;
ing from grief, and he said to them, Why sleep ye?
ἀναστάντες προσεύχεσθε, ἵνα μὴ.εἰσέλθητε εἰς πειρασμόν.
Having risen up pray, that ye may not enter into temptation.
47 [v]Ἔτι.[v]δὲ" αὐτοῦ.λαλοῦντος, ἰδοὺ ὄχλος, καὶ ὁ λεγό-
And [4]yet [1]as [2]he [3]was speaking, behold a crowd, and he who was
μενος Ἰούδας, εἷς τῶν δώδεκα, προήρχετο [w]αὐτῶν," καὶ
called Judas, one of the twelve, was going before them, and
ἤγγισεν τῷ Ἰησοῦ φιλῆσαι αὐτόν. 48 [x]ὁ.δὲ.Ἰησοῦς" εἶπεν
drew near to Jesus to kiss him. But Jesus said
αὐτῷ, Ἰούδα, φιλήματι τὸν υἱὸν τοῦ ἀνθρώπου παραδίδως;
to him, Judas, with a kiss the Son of man deliverest thou up?
49 Ἰδόντες.δὲ οἱ περὶ αὐτὸν τὸ ἐσόμενον [y]εἶπον"
And [4]seeing [1]those [2]around [3]him what was about to happen said
[z]αὐτῷ," Κύριε, εἰ πατάξομεν ἐν [a]μαχαίρᾳ"; 50 Καὶ ἐπά-
to him, Lord, shall we smite with [the] sword? And [6]smote
ταξεν εἷς τις ἐξ αὐτῶν [b]τὸν δοῦλον τοῦ ἀρχιερέως," καὶ
[3]one [1]a [2]certain [4]of [5]them the bondman of the high priest, and
ἀφεῖλεν [c]αὐτοῦ τὸ οὖς" τὸ δεξιόν. 51 ἀποκριθεὶς.δὲ ὁ Ἰησοῦς
took off his [2]ear [1]right. And answering Jesus
εἶπεν, Ἐᾶτε ἕως.τούτου. Καὶ ἁψάμενος τοῦ ὠτίου [d]αὐτοῦ"
said, Suffer thus far. And having touched the ear of him
ἰάσατο αὐτόν. 52 Εἶπεν.δὲ [e]ὁ" Ἰησοῦς πρὸς τοὺς παρα-
he healed him. And [2]said [1]Jesus to those who were
γενομένους [f]ἐπ'" αὐτὸν ἀρχιερεῖς καὶ στρατηγοὺς τοῦ ἱεροῦ
come against him, chief priests and captains of the temple
καὶ πρεσβυτέρους, Ὡς ἐπὶ λῃστὴν [g]ἐξεληλύθατε" μετὰ
and elders, As against a robber have ye come out with
μαχαιρῶν καὶ ξύλων; 53 καθ'.ἡμέραν ὄντος.μου μεθ' ὑμῶν
swords and staves? Daily when I was with you
ἐν τῷ ἱερῷ οὐκ.ἐξετείνατε τὰς χεῖρας ἐπ' ἐμέ. [h]ἀλλ'"
in the temple ye stretched not out [your] hands against me; but
αὕτη [i]ὑμῶν ἐστιν" ἡ ὥρα, καὶ ἡ ἐξουσία τοῦ σκότους.
this [2]your [1]is hour, and the power of darkness.

54 Συλλαβόντες.δὲ αὐτὸν ἤγαγον, καὶ εἰσήγαγον
And having seized him they led [him away], and led
[k]αὐτὸν" εἰς [l]τὸν οἶκον" τοῦ ἀρχιερέως· ὁ.δὲ.Πέτρος ἠκολούθει
him into the house of the high priest. And Peter was following
μακρόθεν. 55 [m]ἁψάντων".δὲ πῦρ ἐν μέσῳ τῆς αὐλῆς,
afar off. And having kindled a fire in [the] midst of the court,
καὶ [n]συγκαθισάντων" [o]αὐτῶν" ἐκάθητο ὁ Πέτρος [p]ἐν.μέσῳ"
and [2]having [3]sat [4]down [5]together [1]they [7]sat [6]Peter among
αὐτῶν. 56 ἰδοῦσα.δὲ αὐτὸν παιδίσκη τις καθήμενον πρὸς
them. And [4]having [5]seen [6]him [1]a [3]maid [2]certain sitting by
τὸ φῶς, καὶ ἀτενίσασα αὐτῷ, εἶπεν, Καὶ οὗτος σὺν
the light, and having looked intently on him, said, And this one with
αὐτῷ ἦν. 57 Ὁ.δὲ ἠρνήσατο [q]αὐτόν," λέγων, [r]Γύναι, οὐκ
him was. But he denied him, saying, Woman, [3]not
οἶδα αὐτόν." 58 Καὶ μετὰ βραχὺ ἕτερος ἰδὼν αὐτὸν ἔφη,
[1]I [2]do know him. And after a little another seeing him said,
Καὶ σὺ ἐξ αὐτῶν εἶ. Ὁ.δὲ.Πέτρος [s]εἶπεν," Ἄνθρωπε, οὐκ.εἰμί.
And thou of them art. But Peter said, Man, I am not.
59 Καὶ διαστάσης ὡσεὶ ὥρας μιᾶς, ἄλλος τις διϊσχυρίζετο,
And having elapsed about [2]hour [1]one, [5]other [3]a [4]certain strongly affirmed,
λέγων, Ἐπ' ἀληθείας καὶ οὗτος μετ' αὐτοῦ ἦν· καὶ.γὰρ Γαλι-
saying, In truth also this one with him was; for also a Gali-
λαῖός ἐστιν. 60 Εἶπεν.δὲ ὁ Πέτρος, Ἄνθρωπε, οὐκ.οἶδα ὃ
lean he is. And [2]said [1]Peter, Man, I know not what
λέγεις. Καὶ παραχρῆμα, ἔτι λαλοῦντος.αὐτοῦ, ἐφώνησεν
thou sayest. And immediately, [2]yet [1]as he was speaking, [3]crew
[t]ὁ" ἀλέκτωρ· 61 καὶ στραφεὶς ὁ κύριος ἐνέβλεψεν τῷ Πέτρῳ·
[1]the [2]cock. And having turned, the Lord looked at Peter;
καὶ ὑπεμνήσθη ὁ Πέτρος τοῦ λόγου τοῦ κυρίου, ὡς εἶπεν αὐτῷ,
and [2]remembered [1]Peter the word of the Lord, how he said to him,
Ὅτι πρὶν ἀλέκτορα φωνῆσαι [v] ἀπαρνήσῃ με τρίς. 62 Καὶ
Before [the] cock crow thou wilt deny me thrice. And
ἐξελθὼν ἔξω [w]ὁ Πέτρος" ἔκλαυσεν πικρῶς.
having gone forth outside Peter wept bitterly.

63 Καὶ οἱ ἄνδρες οἱ συνέχοντες [x]τὸν Ἰησοῦν" ἐνέπαιζον
And the men who were holding Jesus mocked
αὐτῷ, δέροντες· 64 καὶ περικαλύψαντες αὐτὸν [y]ἔτυπτον
him, beating [him]; and having covered up him they were striking
αὐτοῦ τὸ πρόσωπον, καὶ" ἐπηρώτων [z]αὐτόν," λέγοντες, Προ-
his face, and were asking him, saying, Pro-
φήτευσον, τίς ἐστιν ὁ παίσας σε; 65 Καὶ ἕτερα πολλὰ
phesy, who is it that struck thee? And [2]other [3]things [1]many
βλασφημοῦντες ἔλεγον εἰς αὐτόν.
blasphemously they said to him.

66 Καὶ ὡς [a]ἐγένετο ἡμέρα συνήχθη τὸ πρεσβυτέριον
And when it became day were gathered together the elderhood
τοῦ λαοῦ, ἀρχιερεῖς.τε καὶ γραμματεῖς, καὶ [a]ἀνήγαγον" αὐτὸν
of the people, both chief priests and scribes, and they led him

the sorrow.
46 And He said to them, Why do you sleep?
Get up and pray, so that you may not enter
into temptation.
47 And as He was still speaking, behold, a
multitude! And he who was called Judas,
one of the twelve, was coming in front of
them. And he came to Jesus to kiss Him.
48 But Jesus said to him, Judas, do you
betray the Son of man with a kiss?
49 And seeing what was about to happen,
those around Him said to Him, Lord, shall
we strike with the sword?
50 And a certain one of them struck the
high priest's servant and cut off his right ear.
51 And answering Jesus said, Allow it this
far. And He touched *the man's* ear, healing
him.
52 And Jesus said to those who had come
out against Him, the chief priests and captains and elders, Have you come out with
swords and sticks as if against a thief?
53 When I was with you daily in the Temple
you did not lift your hands against Me. But
this is your hour, and the power of darkness.

54 And they seized Him and led Him,
taking Him to the house of the high priest.
And Peter was following at a distance.
55 And they kindled a fire in the middle of
the court and sat down together, and Peter
sat among them.
56 And seeing him sitting by the light, and
looking closely at him, a certain girl said,
This one was with Him too!
57 But he denied Him, saying, Woman, I do
not know Him.
58 And after a little while, another looked
at him and said, You are one of them too.
But Peter said, Man, I am not!
59 And about an hour later, a certain one
said boldly, Really, this one was with Him
too, for he is a Galilean.
60 And Peter said, Man, I do not know
what you say. And immediately, while he
was yet speaking, the cock crowed.
61 And the Lord turned around and looked
at Peter. And Peter remembered the word of
the Lord, how He had said to him, Before
the cock crow, you will deny Me three
times.
62 And going out, Peter cried bitterly.

63 And the men who were holding Jesus
ridiculed Him, beating Him.
64 And blindfolding Him, they were
slapping His face and asking Him, saying,
Prophesy! Who is it that hit you?
65 And they said many other things to Him,
blaspheming Him.
66 And when day came, the elders of the
people, both the chief priests and scribes
gathered together. And they led Him in to

εἰς τὸ συνέδριον [b]ἑαυτῶν," λέγοντες, 67 Εἰ σὺ εἶ ὁ χριστός,
into [2]sanhedrim [1]their, saying, If thou art the Christ,
[c]εἰπὲ" ἡμῖν. Εἶπεν.δὲ αὐτοῖς, Ἐὰν ὑμῖν εἴπω, οὐ.μὴ
tell us. And he said to them, If you I should tell, not at all
πιστεύσητε· 68 ἐὰν.δὲ [d]καὶ" ἐρωτήσω, οὐ.μὴ ἀποκρι-
would ye believe; and if also I should ask [you], not at all would ye
θῆτέ [e]μοι, ἢ ἀπολύσητε." 69 ἀπὸ.τοῦ.νῦν [f]ἔσται ὁ υἱὸς τοῦ
answer me, nor let [me] go. Henceforth shall be the Son
ἀνθρώπου καθήμενος ἐκ δεξιῶν τῆς δυνάμεως τοῦ θεοῦ.
of man sitting at [the] right hand of the power of God.
70 [g]Εἶπον".δὲ πάντες, Σὺ οὖν εἶ ὁ υἱὸς τοῦ θεοῦ; Ὁ.δὲ
And they [2]said [1]all, Thou then art the Son of God? And he
πρὸς αὐτοὺς ἔφη, Ὑμεῖς λέγετε, ὅτι ἐγώ εἰμι. 71 Οἱ.δὲ [h]εἶπον,"
to them said, Ye say, that I am. And they said,
Τί ἔτι [i]χρείαν ἔχομεν μαρτυρίας"; αὐτοὶ.γὰρ ἠκούσαμεν
What any more need have we of witness? for ourselves have heard
ἀπὸ τοῦ.στόματος.αὐτοῦ.
from his [own] mouth.

23 Καὶ ἀναστὰν ἅπαν τὸ πλῆθος αὐτῶν [k]ἤγαγεν"
And having risen up all the multitude of them led
αὐτὸν ἐπὶ τὸν [l]Πιλᾶτον." 2 ἤρξαντο.δὲ κατηγορεῖν αὐτοῦ,
him to Pilate. And they began to accuse him,
λέγοντες, Τοῦτον [m]εὕρομεν" διαστρέφοντα τὸ ἔθνος[n], καὶ
saying, This [man] we found perverting the nation, and
κωλύοντα [o]Καίσαρι φόρους" διδόναι, [p]λέγοντα ἑαυτὸν χριστὸν
forbidding [4]to [5]Cæsar [3]tribute [1]to [2]give, saying himself [2]Christ
βασιλέα εἶναι. 3 Ὁ.δὲ.[q]Πιλᾶτος" [r]ἐπηρώτησεν" αὐτόν, λέγων,
[3]a [4]king [1]is. And Pilate questioned him, saying,
Σὺ εἶ ὁ βασιλεὺς τῶν Ἰουδαίων; Ὁ.δὲ ἀποκριθεὶς αὐτῷ
[2]Thou [1]art the king of the Jews? And he answering him
ἔφη, Σὺ λέγεις. 4 Ὁ.δὲ.[q]Πιλᾶτος" εἶπεν πρὸς τοὺς ἀρχιερεῖς
said, Thou sayest. And Pilate said to the chief priests
καὶ τοὺς ὄχλους, Οὐδὲν εὑρίσκω αἴτιον ἐν τῷ.ἀνθρώπῳ.τούτῳ.
and the crowds, Nothing find I blamable in this man.
5 Οἱ.δὲ ἐπίσχυον, λέγοντες, Ὅτι ἀνασείει τὸν λαόν, διδάσ-
But they were insisting, saying, He stirs up the people, teach-
κων καθ' ὅλης τῆς Ἰουδαίας, [s]ἀρξάμενος ἀπὸ τῆς Γαλι-
ing throughout [2]whole [1]the of Judæa, beginning from Gali-
λαίας ἕως ὧδε. 6 [q]Πιλᾶτος".δὲ ἀκούσας [t]Γαλιλαίαν"
lee even to here. But Pilate having heard Galilee [named]
ἐπηρώτησεν εἰ ὁ ἄνθρωπος Γαλιλαῖός ἐστιν· 7 καὶ ἐπι-
asked whether the man [2]a [3]Galilean [1]is; and having
γνοὺς ὅτι ἐκ τῆς ἐξουσίας Ἡρῴδου ἐστίν, ἀνέπεμψεν αὐτὸν
known that from the jurisdiction of Herod he is, he sent [2]up [1]him
πρὸς [v]Ἡρῴδην, ὄντα καὶ αὐτὸν ἐν Ἱεροσολύμοις ἐν ταύταις
to Herod, [3]being [2]also [1]he at Jerusalem in those
ταῖς ἡμέραις. 8 ὁ.δὲ.Ἡρῴδης ἰδὼν τὸν Ἰησοῦν ἐχάρη λίαν
days. And Herod seeing Jesus rejoiced greatly,
ἦν.γὰρ [w]θέλων ἐξ.ἱκανοῦ" ἰδεῖν αὐτόν, διὰ τὸ ἀκούειν
for he was wishing for long to see him, because of hearing
[x]πολλὰ" περὶ αὐτοῦ καὶ ἤλπιζέν τι σημεῖον ἰδεῖν ὑπ'
many things concerning him; and he was hoping some sign to see [4]by
αὐτοῦ γινόμενον. 9 ἐπηρώτα.δὲ αὐτὸν ἐν λόγοις ἱκανοῖς·
[5]him [3]done. And he questioned him in [2]words [1]many,
αὐτὸς.δὲ οὐδὲν ἀπεκρίνατο αὐτῷ. 10 εἱστήκεισαν.δὲ οἱ ἀρχ-
but he nothing answered him. And [7]had [8]stood [1]the [2]chief
ιερεῖς καὶ οἱ γραμματεῖς, εὐτόνως κατηγοροῦντες αὐτοῦ.
[3]priests [4]and [5]the [6]scribes, violently accusing him.
11 ἐξουθενήσας.δὲ αὐτὸν [y]ὁ Ἡρῴδης σὺν τοῖς στρατεύμασιν
And [2]having [3]set [5]at [6]nought [4]him [1]Herod with [2]troops
αὐτοῦ, καὶ ἐμπαίξας, περιβαλὼν [z]αὐτὸν" ἐσθῆτα λαμ-
[1]his, and having mocked [him], having put on him [2]apparel [1]splen-
πρὰν ἀνέπεμψεν αὐτὸν τῷ [a]Πιλάτῳ." 12 ἐγένοντο.δὲ φίλοι
did he sent [2]back [1]him to Pilate. And became friends
ὅ.τε.[b]Πιλᾶτος καὶ ὁ Ἡρῴδης" ἐν αὐτῇ.τῇ ἡμέρᾳ μετ' ἀλλήλων·
both Pilate and Herod on that same day with one another;
προϋπῆρχον.γὰρ ἐν ἔχθρᾳ ὄντες πρὸς [c]ἑαυτούς."
for before they were at enmity between themselves.
13 [q]Πιλᾶτος".δὲ [d]συγκαλεσάμενος" τοὺς ἀρχιερεῖς καὶ τοὺς
And Pilate having called together the chief priests and the
ἄρχοντας καὶ τὸν λαόν, 14 εἶπεν πρὸς αὐτούς, Προσηνέγκατέ
rulers and the people, said to them, Ye brought
μοι τὸν.ἄνθρωπον.τοῦτον, ὡς ἀποστρέφοντα τὸν λαόν· καὶ
to me this man, as turning away the people; and
ἰδού, ἐγὼ ἐνώπιον ὑμῶν ἀνακρίνας [e]οὐδὲν" εὗρον ἐν τῷ
behold, I before you having examined [him] [2]nothing [1]found in
ἀνθρώπῳ.τούτῳ αἴτιον ὧν κατηγορεῖτε
this man blamable [as to the things] of which ye bring accusation
κατ' αὐτοῦ· 15 ἀλλ'.οὐδὲ Ἡρῴδης· [f]ἀνέπεμψα.γὰρ ὑμᾶς πρὸς
against him; nor even Herod, for I sent [2]up [1]you to
αὐτόν," καὶ ἰδού, οὐδὲν ἄξιον θανάτου ἐστὶν πεπραγμένον
him, and lo, nothing worthy of death is done

their san-he-drin, saying,
67 If you are the Christ, tell us. And He said
to them, If I tell you, you will never believe.
68 And if I also ask, you will not at all
answer Me nor let Me go.
69 From now on the Son of man shall be
sitting at the right hand of the power of
God.
70 And they all said, Are you then the Son
of God? And He said to them, You say that
I am.
71 And they said, What need do we have of
any further testimony? For we ourselves
have heard from his *own* mouth.

CHAPTER 23

1 And rising the whole multitude of them
led Him to Pilate.
2 And they began to accuse Him, saying, We
found this man leading the nation astray and
forbidding to give tribute to Caesar, saying
that he is Christ, a king.
3 And Pilate questioned Him, saying, Are
you the king of the Jews? And answering
him He said, You say it.
4 And Pilate said to the chief priests and the
people, I do not find any fault in this man.
5 But they kept insisting, saying, He stirs up
the people, teaching all through Judea,
beginning from Galilee even to here.
6 But hearing Galilee, Pilate asked if the
man was a Galilean.
7 And learning that He was from Herod's
district, he sent Him to Herod (he also being
at Jerusalem in those days).
8 And seeing Jesus, Herod rejoiced greatly,
for he had been wishing to see Him for a
long time, for he had heard many things
about Him. And he was hoping to see some
miracles performed by Him.
9 And he questioned Him in many words,
but He answered him nothing.
10 And the chief priests and the scribes had
stood furiously making charges against Him.
11 And Herod humiliated and ridiculed Him
with his troops. And dressing Him in luxur-
ious clothing, he sent Him back to Pilate.
12 And that same day Pilate and Herod be
came friends with one another (for before
they were at odds between themselves).

13 And calling the chief priests and the
rulers and the people,
14 Pilate said to them, You brought this
man to me as one turning away the people.
But, behold, I have examined him in front of
you. I found no fault in this man as to the
things you charge against Him.
15 Neither did Herod, for I sent you up to
him, and, see, nothing worthy of death has
been done by Him.

αὐτῷ. 16 παιδεύσας οὖν αὐτὸν ἀπολύσω. 17 [g]Ἀνάγκην
by him. Having [2]chastised [1]therefore him I will release [him]. [4]Necessity

δὲ εἶχεν ἀπολύειν αὐτοῖς κατὰ ἑορτὴν ἕνα.‖ 18 [h]ἀνέ-
[1]now [2]he [3]had to release to them at [the] feast one. [2]they

κραξαν‖ δὲ [k]παμπληθεί,‖ λέγοντες, Αἶρε τοῦτον, ἀπόλυ-
[3]cried [4]out [1]but [5]in a mass, saying, Away with this [man], [2]re-

σον δὲ ἡμῖν τὸν Βαραββᾶν· 19 ὅστις ἦν διὰ στάσιν
lease [1]and to us Barabbas; who was on account of [3]insurrection

τινὰ γενομένην ἐν τῇ πόλει καὶ φόνον [l]βεβλημένος εἰς
[1]a [2]certain made in the city and murder cast into

φυλακήν.‖ 20 Πάλιν [m]οὖν‖ ὁ [n]Πιλάτος‖ προσεφώνησεν[o],
prison. Again therefore Pilate called to [them],

θέλων ἀπολῦσαι τὸν Ἰησοῦν. 21 οἱ.δὲ ἐπεφώνουν, λέγοντες,
wishing to release Jesus. But they were crying out, saying,

[p]Σταύρωσον, σταύρωσον‖ αὐτόν. 22 Ὁ.δὲ τρίτον εἶπεν
Crucify, crucify him. And he a third [time] said

πρὸς αὐτούς, Τί γὰρ κακὸν ἐποίησεν οὗτος; οὐδὲν
to them, What [2]then [1]evil did [3]commit [1]this [[2]man]? No

αἴτιον θανάτου εὗρον ἐν αὐτῷ· παιδεύσας οὖν αὐτὸν
cause of death found I in him. Having [2]chastised [1]therefore him

ἀπολύσω. 23 Οἱ.δὲ ἐπέκειντο φωναῖς μεγάλαις, αἰτού-
I will release [him]. But they were urgent with [2]voices [1]loud, asking

μενοι αὐτὸν σταυρωθῆναι· καὶ κατίσχυον αἱ φωναὶ αὐτῶν
for him to be crucified. And prevailed the voices of them

[q]καὶ τῶν ἀρχιερέων.‖ 24 [r]Ὁ.δὲ‖ [n]Πιλάτος‖ ἐπέκρινεν γενέσθαι
and of the chief priests. And Pilate adjudged [3]to [4]be [5]done

τὸ.αἴτημα.αὐτῶν. 25 ἀπέλυσεν.δὲ [s]αὐτοῖς‖ τὸν διὰ
[1]their [2]request. And he released to them him who on account of

στάσιν καὶ φόνον βεβλημένον εἰς [t]τὴν‖ φυλακήν, ὃν
insurrection and murder had been cast into the prison, whom

ᾐτοῦντο· τὸν.δὲ.Ἰησοῦν παρέδωκεν τῷ.θελήματι.αὐτῶν.
they asked for; but Jesus he delivered up to their will.

26 Καὶ ὡς ἀπήγαγον αὐτόν, ἐπιλαβόμενοι [v]Σίμωνός
And as they led [2]away [1]him, having laid hold on [3]Simon

τινος Κυρηναίου [w]τοῦ‖ ἐρχομένου‖ [x]ἀπ'‖ ἀγροῦ, ἐπέθηκαν
[1]a [2]certain a Cyrenian coming from a field, they put upon

αὐτῷ τὸν σταυρὸν φέρειν ὄπισθεν τοῦ Ἰησοῦ. 27 Ἠκολούθει
him the cross to bear [it] behind Jesus. [2]Were [3]following

δὲ αὐτῷ πολὺ πλῆθος τοῦ λαοῦ καὶ γυναικῶν, αἳ [y]καὶ‖
[1]and him a great multitude of the people and of women, who also

ἐκόπτοντο καὶ ἐθρήνουν αὐτόν. 28 στραφεὶς.δὲ πρὸς αὐτὰς
were bewailing and lamenting him. And turning to them

[z]ὁ‖ Ἰησοῦς εἶπεν, Θυγατέρες Ἱερουσαλήμ, μὴ.κλαίετε ἐπ' ἐμέ,
Jesus said, Daughters of Jerusalem, weep not for me,

πλὴν ἐφ' ἑαυτὰς κλαίετε καὶ ἐπὶ τὰ.τέκνα.ὑμῶν· 29 ὅτι ἰδού,
but [2]for [3]yourselves [1]weep and for your children: for lo,

ἔρχονται ἡμέραι ἐν αἷς ἐροῦσιν, Μακάριαι αἱ στεῖραι
are coming days in which they will say, Blessed [are] the barren

καὶ [a]κοιλίαι αἳ οὐκ.ἐγέννησαν καὶ μαστοὶ οἳ [b]οὐκ ἐθήλασαν.‖
and wombs which did not bear and breasts which gave not suck.

30 τότε ἄρξονται λέγειν τοῖς ὄρεσιν, [c]Πέσετε‖ ἐφ' ἡμᾶς
Then shall they begin to say to the mountains, Fall upon us;

καὶ τοῖς βουνοῖς, Καλύψατε ἡμᾶς. 31 ὅτι εἰ ἐν [d]τῷ‖ ὑγρῷ
and to the hills, Cover us: for if in the green

ξύλῳ ταῦτα ποιοῦσιν, ἐν τῷ ξηρῷ τί γένηται; 32 Ἤγοντο
tree these things they do, in the dry what may take place? [2]Were [3]led

δὲ καὶ ἕτεροι δύο κακοῦργοι σὺν αὐτῷ ἀναιρεθῆναι. 33 Καὶ
[1]and also [3]other [2]two malefactors with him to be put to death. And

ὅτε [e]ἀπῆλθον‖ ἐπὶ τὸν τόπον τὸν καλούμενον κρανίον ἐκεῖ
when they came to the place called a Skull there

ἐσταύρωσαν αὐτόν, καὶ τοὺς κακούργους, ὃν.μὲν ἐκ δεξιῶν
they crucified him, and the malefactors, the one on [the] right

ὃν.δὲ ἐξ ἀριστερῶν. 34 [f]ὁ.δὲ.Ἰησοῦς ἔλεγεν, Πάτερ, ἄφες
and one on [the] left. And Jesus said, Father, forgive

αὐτοῖς· οὐ.γὰρ.οἴδασιν τί ποιοῦσιν.‖ Διαμεριζόμενοι.δὲ τὰ
them, for they know not what they do. And dividing

ἱμάτια.αὐτοῦ ἔβαλον [g]κλῆρον.‖ 35 καὶ εἱστήκει ὁ λαὸς θεω-
his garments they cast a lot. And [3]stood [1]the [2]people behold-

ρῶν· ἐξεμυκτήριζον.δὲ [h]καὶ‖ οἱ ἄρχοντες [i]σὺν αὐτοῖς,‖ λέγον-
ing, and [4]were [5]deriding [3]also [1]the [2]rulers with them, say-

τες, Ἄλλους ἔσωσεν, σωσάτω ἑαυτόν εἰ οὗτός ἐστιν ὁ χριστὸς
ing, Others he saved, let him save himself if this is the Christ

[k]ὁ τοῦ θεοῦ‖ ἐκλεκτός. 36 [l]Ἐνέπαιζον‖.δὲ αὐτῷ καὶ οἱ στρα-
the [2]of [3]God [1]chosen. And mocked him also the sol-

τιῶται, προσερχόμενοι [m]καὶ‖ ὄξος προσφέροντες αὐτῷ, 37 καὶ
diers, coming near and [3]vinegar [1]offering [2]him, and

λέγοντες, [n]Εἰ‖ σὺ εἶ ὁ βασιλεὺς τῶν Ἰουδαίων, σῶσον σεαυ-
saying, If thou art the king of the Jews, save thy-

τόν. 38 Ἦν.δὲ καὶ ἐπιγραφὴ [o]γεγραμμένη‖ ἐπ' αὐτῷ
self. And there was also an inscription written over him

[p]γράμμασιν Ἑλληνικοῖς καὶ Ῥωμαϊκοῖς καὶ Ἑβραϊκοῖς,‖
in letters Greek and Latin and Hebrew:

16 So, after I beat Him, I will let Him go.

17 (For it was needful for him to release one to them at every feast.)

18 And they cried out all together, Away with this man! And, Release Barabbas to us

19 (who was thrown into prison because of a certain revolt and murder done in the city).

20 Again, then, Pilate called to them, wishing to let Jesus go.

21 But they were crying out, saying, Crucify! Crucify Him!

22 And he said to them a third time, Why, then, what evil did this one do? I have found no cause of death in him. So, after I beat him, I will let him go.

23 But they were violently pressing him with loud voices, asking for Him to be crucified. And their voices and those of the chief priests prevailed.

24 And Pilate gave judgment that their request should be granted.

25 And he released to them the one who had been thrown into prison for revolt and murder, whom they had requested. But he delivered up Jesus to their will.

26 And as they led Him away, laying hold on one Simon (a Cy-re-ni-an coming from the country) they put the cross on him, to carry it behind Jesus.

27 And a great crowd of the people were following Him, and of women who were beating their breasts and weeping over Him.

28 But turning to them, Jesus said, Daughters of Jerusalem, do not weep for Me, but weep for yourselves and for your children.

29 For, behold! The days are coming in which they will say, Happy are the barren and the wombs which did not bear, and the breasts which never gave suck.

30 Then they will begin to say to the mountains, Fall on us; and to the hills, Cover us!

31 For if they do these things in the green tree, what may happen in the dry?

32 And there were others with Him – two criminals – to be put to death.

33 And when they came to the place called The Skull, they crucified Him and the criminals, one on the right and the other on the left.

34 And Jesus said, Father, forgive them, for they do not know what they are doing. And dividing His clothes, they threw a lot.

35 And the people stood looking on. And the rulers also ridiculed Him, saying, He saved others, let him save Himself if this is the Christ, the chosen of God.

36 And the soldiers also ridiculed Him, coming near and offering Him vinegar,

37 and saying, If you are the king of the Jews, save yourself.

38 And there was also a sign written over Him in Greek and Latin and Hebrew letters:

[q]Οὗτός ἐστιν ὁ βασιλεὺς τῶν Ἰουδαίων."
This is the king of the Jews.
39 Εἷς.δὲ τῶν κρεμασθέντων κακούργων ἐβλασφήμει
Now one of the [2]who [3]had [4]been [5]hanged [1]malefactors railed at
αὐτόν, [r]λέγων," [s]Εἰ σὺ εἶ ὁ χριστός," σῶσον σεαυτὸν καὶ
him, saying, If thou art the Christ, save thyself and
ἡμᾶς. 40 Ἀποκριθεὶς.δὲ ὁ ἕτερος [t]ἐπετίμα αὐτῷ, λέγων,"
us. But answering the other rebuked him, saying,
Οὐδὲ φοβῇ σὺ τὸν θεόν, ὅτι ἐν τῷ αὐτῷ κρίματι εἶ;
[2]Not [3]even [1]dost [5]fear [4]thou God, [thou] that under the same judgment art?
41 καὶ ἡμεῖς μὲν δικαίως· ἄξια.γὰρ ὧν ἐπράξαμεν
And we indeed justly; for [3]a [4]due [5]recompense [6]of [7]what [8]we [9]did
ἀπολαμβάνομεν· οὗτος.δὲ οὐδὲν ἄτοπον ἔπραξεν. 42 Καὶ
[1]we [2]receive; but this [man] [2]nothing [3]amiss [1]did. And
ἔλεγεν [v]τῷ" Ἰησοῦ, Μνήσθητί μου, [w]κύριε," ὅταν ἔλθῃς ἐν
he said to Jesus, Remember me, Lord, when thou comest in
τῇ.βασιλείᾳ.σου. 43 Καὶ εἶπεν αὐτῷ [x]ὁ Ἰησοῦς," Ἀμὴν [y]λέγω
thy kingdom. And [2]said [3]to [4]him [1]Jesus, Verily I say
σοι," σήμερον μετ' ἐμοῦ ἔσῃ ἐν τῷ παραδείσῳ.
to thee, To-day with me thou shalt be in Paradise.
44 [z]Ἦν.δὲ" ὡσεὶ ὥρα ἕκτη, καὶ σκότος ἐγένετο ἐφ' ὅλην
And it was about [the] [2]hour [1]sixth, and darkness came over [2]whole
τὴν γῆν ἕως ὥρας [a]ἐννάτης·" 45 [b]καὶ ἐσκοτίσθη ὁ ἥλιος,"
[1]the land until [the] [2]hour [1]ninth; and [3]was [4]darkened [1]the [2]sun;
[c]καὶ ἐσχίσθη" τὸ καταπέτασμα τοῦ ναοῦ μέσον· 46 καὶ
and [6]was [7]rent [1]the [2]veil [3]of [4]the [5]temple in [the] midst. And
φωνήσας φωνῇ μεγάλῃ ὁ Ἰησοῦς εἶπεν, Πάτερ, εἰς χεῖράς
having cried with a [2]voice [1]loud Jesus said, Father, into [2]hands
σου [d]παραθήσομαι" τὸ.πνεῦμά μου. [e]Καὶ ταῦτα" εἰπὼν
[1]thy I will commit my spirit. And these things having said
ἐξέπνευσεν. 47 Ἰδὼν.δὲ ὁ [f]ἑκατόνταρχος" τὸ γενόμενον
he expired. Now [3]having [4]seen [1]the [2]centurion that which took place
[g]ἐδόξασεν" τὸν θεόν, λέγων, Ὄντως ὁ.ἄνθρωπος.οὗτος δίκαιος
glorified God, saying, Indeed this man [2]just
ἦν. 48 Καὶ πάντες οἱ [h]συμπαραγενόμενοι" ὄχλοι ἐπὶ τὴν
[1]was. And all the [2]who [3]were [4]come [5]together [1]crowds to
θεωρίαν.ταύτην, [i]θεωροῦντες" τὰ γενόμενα, τύπτοντες
this sight, seeing the things which took place, beating
[k]ἑαυτῶν" τὰ στήθη ὑπέστρεφον. 49 εἱστήκεισαν.δὲ πάντες
their breasts returned. And [6]stood [1]all
οἱ γνωστοὶ [l]αὐτοῦ" [m]μακρόθεν, καὶ γυναῖκες αἱ [n]συν-
[2]those [3]who [4]knew [5]him afar off, also women who fol-
ακολουθήσασαι" αὐτῷ ἀπὸ τῆς Γαλιλαίας, ὁρῶσαι ταῦτα.
lowed with him from Galilee, beholding these things.
50 Καὶ ἰδού, ἀνὴρ ὀνόματι Ἰωσήφ, βουλευτὴς ὑπάρχων,
And behold, a man by name Joseph, a counsellor being,
[o]ἀνὴρ ἀγαθὸς καὶ δίκαιος, 51 οὗτος οὐκ.ἦν.[p]συγκατατεθειμένος"
a man good and just, (he had not assented
τῇ βουλῇ καὶ τῇ πράξει αὐτῶν, ἀπὸ Ἀριμαθαίας πόλεως
to the counsel and the deed of them,) from Arimathæa a city
τῶν Ἰουδαίων, ὃς.[q]καὶ" προσεδέχετο [r]καὶ αὐτὸς" τὴν βασι-
of the Jews, and who [3]was [4]waiting [5]for [1]also [2]himself the king-
λείαν τοῦ θεοῦ, 52 οὗτος προσελθὼν τῷ [s]Πιλάτῳ" ᾐτήσατο τὸ
dom of God, he having gone to Pilate begged the
σῶμα τοῦ Ἰησοῦ. 53 καὶ καθελὼν [t]αὐτὸ" ἐνετύλιξεν αὐτὸ
body of Jesus. And having taken [2]down [1]it he wrapped it
σινδόνι καὶ ἔθηκεν [v]αὐτὸ" ἐν μνήματι λαξευτῷ, οὗ
in a linen cloth and placed it in a tomb hewn in a rock, in which
οὐκ ἦν [w]οὐδέπω.οὐδεὶς" κείμενος. 54 καὶ ἡμέρα ἦν [x]παρα-
[3]was [1]no [2]one ever yet laid. And [4]day [1]it [2]was [3]pre-
σκευή," καὶ σάββατον ἐπέφωσκεν.
paration, and Sabbath was coming on.
55 Κατακολουθήσασαι.δὲ [y]καὶ" [z]γυναῖκες, αἵτινες ἦσαν
And [3]having [4]followed [2]also [1]women, who were
συνεληλυθυῖαι [a]αὐτῷ" ἐκ τῆς Γαλιλαίας[b], ἐθεάσαντο τὸ
come with him out of Galilee, saw the
μνημεῖον, καὶ ὡς ἐτέθη τὸ.σῶμα.αὐτοῦ. 56 ὑποστρέψασαι.δὲ
tomb, and how was laid his body. And having returned
ἡτοίμασαν ἀρώματα καὶ μύρα. καὶ τὸ.μὲν.σάββατον ἡσύχα-
they prepared aromatics and ointments, and on the sabbath remained
σαν κατὰ τὴν ἐντολήν. 24 τῇ.δὲ μιᾷ τῶν σαβ-
quiet, according to the commandment. But on the first [day] of the week
βάτων ὄρθρου.[c]βαθέος" [d]ἦλθον ἐπὶ τὸ μνῆμα," φέρουσαι ἃ
at early dawn they came to the tomb, bringing [2]which
ἡτοίμασαν ἀρώματα, [e]καί τινες σὺν αὐταῖς." 2 Εὗ-
[3]they [4]had [5]prepared [1]aromatics, and some [others] with them. [2]They
ρον δὲ τὸν λίθον ἀποκεκυλισμένον ἀπὸ τοῦ μνημείου, 3 [f]καὶ
[3]found [1]and the stone rolled away from the tomb; and
εἰσελθοῦσαι" οὐχ.εὗρον τὸ σῶμα τοῦ κυρίου Ἰησοῦ. 4 καὶ
having entered they found not the body of the Lord Jesus. And
ἐγένετο ἐν.τῷ.[g]διαπορεῖσθαι" αὐτὰς περὶ τούτου, καὶ ἰδού,
it came to pass as [2]were [3]perplexed [1]they about this, that behold,

THIS IS THE KING OF THE JEWS.
39 Now one of the criminals who had been
hanged blasphemed Him, saying, If you are
the Christ, save yourself and us.
40 But the other answered and warned him,
saying, Do you not even fear God, you that
are under the same judgment?
41 And we indeed justly, for we are getting
what we deserve for what we did – but this
One did nothing wrong.
42 And he said to Jesus, Remember me,
Lord, when You come in Your kingdom.
43 And Jesus said to him, I tell you truly
that you shall be with Me in Paradise today.
44 And it was about the sixth hour. And
darkness came over the whole land until the
ninth hour.
45 And the sun was darkened. And the veil
of the Temple was torn in the middle.
46 And crying out with a loud voice, Jesus
said, Father, into Your hands I commit My
spirit! And saying these things, He breathed
forth the spirit.
47 Now the centurion, seeing that which
had taken place, praised God, saying, Surely
this Man was righteous.
48 And all the people who had come together to see this sight, seeing the things
which took place, returned beating their
breasts.
49 And all those who knew Him, and the
women who followed Him from Galilee,
stood at a distance watching these things.
50 And, behold, a man named Joseph! He
was a good and righteous man, a councillor
51 who had not agreed to their decision and
deed. *And he was* from Ar-i-ma-the-a, a city
of the Jews, one who himself was also
waiting for the kingdom of God.
52 Going to Pilate, he begged the body of
Jesus.
53 And taking it down, he wrapped it in a
linen cloth and laid it in a tomb cut in a
rock, in which no one ever had been laid.
54 And it was the day of preparation, and
sabbath was coming on.
55 And the women who had come with
Him out of Galilee also followed. And they
saw the tomb and how His body was laid.
56 And returning they prepared spices and
ointments. And on the sabbath *they* rested,
according to the commandment.

CHAPTER 24

1 But on the first day of the week at early
dawn they came to the tomb, bringing spices
which they had prepared. And certain ones
were with them.
2 And they found the stone rolled away
from the tomb.
3 And going in, they did not find the body
of the Lord Jesus.
4 And as they wondered about this, behold!

[h]δύο ἄνδρες" ἐπέστησαν αὐταῖς ἐν [1]ἐσθήσεσιν ἀστραπτούσαις.[1]
two men stood by them in [2]garments [1]shining
5 ἐμφόβων δὲ γενομένων αὐτῶν καὶ κλινουσῶν [k]τὸ πρόσωπον" εἰς τὴν γῆν, [1]εἶπον" πρὸς αὐτάς, Τί ζητεῖτε τὸν ζῶντα
And [3]filled [4]with [5]fear [2]becoming [1]they and bowing the face to the earth, they said to them, Why seek ye the living
μετὰ τῶν νεκρῶν; 6 οὐκ.ἔστιν ὧδε, [m]ἀλλ'" ἠγέρθη· μνήσθητε
with the dead? He is not here, but is risen: remember
ὡς ἐλάλησεν ὑμῖν, ἔτι ὢν ἐν τῇ Γαλιλαίᾳ, 7 λέγων, [n]"Ὅτι
how he spoke to you, yet being in Galilee, saying,
δεῖ τὸν υἱὸν τοῦ ἀνθρώπου" παραδοθῆναι εἰς χεῖρας
It behoveth the Son of man to be delivered up into hands
ἀνθρώπων ἁμαρτωλῶν, καὶ σταυρωθῆναι, καὶ τῇ τρίτῃ ἡμέρᾳ
of [2]men [1]sinful, and to be crucified, and the third day
ἀναστῆναι. 8 Καὶ ἐμνήσθησαν τῶν.ῥημάτων.αὐτοῦ· 9 καὶ
to arise. And they remembered his words; and
ὑποστρέψασαι ἀπὸ τοῦ μνημείου ἀπήγγειλαν [o]ταῦτα πάντα"
having returned from the tomb they related [2]these [3]things [1]all
τοῖς ἕνδεκα καὶ πᾶσιν τοῖς λοιποῖς. 10 [p]ἦσαν.δὲ" ἡ Μαγδαληνὴ
to the eleven and to all the rest. Now it was [2]Magdalene
Μαρία καὶ [q]Ἰωάννα" καὶ Μαρία [r] Ἰακώβου, καὶ αἱ λοιπαὶ σὺν
[1]Mary and Joanna and Mary of James, and the rest with
αὐταῖς, [s]αἳ" ἔλεγον.πρὸς τοὺς ἀποστόλους ταῦτα. 11 Καὶ
them, who told to the apostles these things. And
ἐφάνησαν ἐνώπιον αὐτῶν ὡσεὶ λῆρος τὰ.ῥήματα [t]αὐτῶν,"
[3]appeared [4]before [5]them [6]like [7]idle [8]talk [2]words [1]their,
καὶ ἠπίστουν αὐταῖς. 12 [v]ὁ.δὲ.Πέτρος ἀναστὰς ἔδραμεν
and they disbelieved them. But Peter having risen up ran
ἐπὶ τὸ μνημεῖον, καὶ παρακύψας βλέπει τὰ ὀθόνια
to the tomb, and having stooped down he sees the linen clothes
[w]κείμενα μόνα·" καὶ ἀπῆλθεν πρὸς [x]ἑαυτὸν" θαυμάζων τὸ
lying alone, and went away home wondering at that which
γεγονός."
had come to pass.
13 Καὶ ἰδού, δύο ἐξ αὐτῶν [y]ἦσαν πορευόμενοι ἐν αὐτῇ τῇ
And lo, two of them were going on [2]same [1]the
ἡμέρᾳ" εἰς κώμην ἀπέχουσαν σταδίους ἑξήκοντα ἀπὸ Ἱερου-
day to a village being distant [2]furlongs [1]sixty from Jeru-
σαλήμ, ᾗ ὄνομα Ἐμμαούς· 14 καὶ αὐτοὶ ὡμίλουν πρὸς
salem, whose name [is] Emmaus; and they were conversing with
ἀλλήλους περὶ πάντων τῶν συμβεβηκότων τούτων. 15 καὶ
one another about all [3]which [4]had [5]taken [6]place [1]these [2]things. And
ἐγένετο ἐν.τῷ.ὁμιλεῖν.αὐτοὺς καὶ [z]συζητεῖν," καὶ αὐτὸς [a]ὁ"
it came to pass as they conversed and reasoned, that [2]himself
Ἰησοῦς ἐγγίσας συνεπορεύετο αὐτοῖς· 16 οἱ δὲ ὀφθαλμοὶ
[1]Jesus having drawn near went with them; but the eyes
αὐτῶν ἐκρατοῦντο τοῦ μὴ ἐπιγνῶναι αὐτόν. 17 Εἶπεν.δὲ
of them were holden [so as] not to know him. And he said
πρὸς αὐτούς, Τίνες οἱ λόγοι οὗτοι οὓς ἀντιβάλλετε πρὸς
to them, What words [are] these which ye exchange with
ἀλλήλους περιπατοῦντες, [b]καί ἐστε σκυθρωποί;"
one another as ye walk, and are downcast in countenance?
18 Ἀποκριθεὶς.δὲ [c]ὁ" εἷς[d], [e]ᾧ ὄνομα" Κλεόπας, εἶπεν πρὸς
And answering the one, whose name [was] Cleopas, said to
αὐτόν, Σὺ μόνος παροικεῖς [f]ἐν" Ἱερουσαλήμ, καὶ οὐκ.ἔγνως
him, [2]Thou [3]alone [1]sojournest in Jerusalem, and hast not known
τὰ γενόμενα ἐν αὐτῇ ἐν ταῖς.ἡμέραις.ταύταις;
the things which are come to pass in it in these days?
19 Καὶ εἶπεν αὐτοῖς, Ποῖα; Οἱ.δὲ [g]εἶπον" αὐτῷ, Τὰ
And he said to them, What things? And they said to him, The things
περὶ Ἰησοῦ τοῦ [h]Ναζωραίου," ὃς ἐγένετο ἀνὴρ προφήτης,
concerning Jesus the Nazaræan, who was a man a prophet,
δυνατὸς ἐν ἔργῳ καὶ [1] λόγῳ ἐναντίον τοῦ θεοῦ καὶ παντὸς τοῦ
mighty in deed and word before God and all the
λαοῦ· 20 ὅπως.τε [k]παρέδωκαν αὐτὸν" οἱ ἀρχιερεῖς καὶ οἱ
people; and how [7]delivered [8]up [9]him [1]the [2]chief [3]priests [4]and
ἄρχοντες.ἡμῶν εἰς κρίμα θανάτου, καὶ ἐσταύρωσαν αὐτόν·
[5]our [6]rulers to judgment of death, and crucified him.
21 ἡμεῖς.δὲ ἠλπίζομεν ὅτι αὐτός ἐστιν ὁ μέλλων λυτροῦσθαι
But we were hoping he it is who is about to redeem
τὸν Ἰσραήλ. ἀλλά.γε [1] σὺν πᾶσιν τούτοις τρίτην ταύτην
Israel. But then with all these things [4]third [3]this
ἡμέραν ἄγει [m]σήμερον" ἀφ'.οὗ ταῦτα ἐγένετο. 22 ἀλλὰ.καὶ
[5]day [2]brings [1]to-day since these things came to pass. And withal
γυναῖκές τινες ἐξ ἡμῶν ἐξέστησαν ἡμᾶς, γενόμεναι
[2]women [1]certain from amongst us astonished us, having been
[n]ὄρθριαι" ἐπὶ τὸ μνημεῖον· 23 καὶ μὴ εὑροῦσαι τὸ.σῶμα.αὐτοῦ
early to the tomb, and not having found his body
ἦλθον, λέγουσαι καὶ ὀπτασίαν ἀγγέλων ἑωρακέναι, οἳ λέγουσιν
came, declaring also a vision of angels to have seen, who say
αὐτὸν ζῆν. 24 καὶ ἀπῆλθόν τινες τῶν σὺν ἡμῖν ἐπὶ τὸ
he is living. And [5]went [1]some [2]of [3]those [4]with [5]us to the

Two men stood beside them in brilliantly
white clothes.
5 And they began to be filled with fear and
bowed down their faces to the earth. They
said to them, Why do you look for the living
among the dead?
6 He is not here, but has risen. Remember
how He spoke to you while He was yet in
Galilee,
7 saying, It is necessary for the Son of man
to be delivered into the hands of sinful men
and to be crucified, and to rise again the
third day?
8 And they remembered His words.
9 And returning from the tomb, they told
all these things to the Eleven, and to all the
rest.
10 Now it was Mary Mag-da-lene and
Joanna and Mary, *mother* of James, and the
rest of them who told these things to the
apostles.
11 And their words seemed to them like
idle talk, and they did not believe them.
12 But Peter got up and ran to the tomb.
And stooping down, he saw the linen clothes
laying by themselves. And he went away
wondering at that which had happened.

13 And, behold! Two of them were going to
a village called Em-ma-us on that same day,
which was seven and a half miles from
Jerusalem.
14 And they were talking with one another
about all these things which had happened.
15 And as they talked and reasoned together, Jesus Himself came up and went with
them.
16 But their eyes were kept from knowing
Him.
17 And He said to them, What kind of
words are these which you debate with one
another as you walk in sadness?
18 And answering, the one named Cle-o-pas
said to Him, Are you only a stranger in
Jerusalem and have not known the things
which have happened there in these days?
19 And He said to them, What things? And
they said to Him, The things about Jesus the
Nazarene, who was a man, a prophet mighty
in deed and word before God and all the
people,
20 and how the chief priests and our rulers
gave Him to a death charge and crucified
Him?
21 But we were hoping that He was the One
who is going to redeem Israel. But also with
all these things this is the third day since
these things happened.
22 But also certain women from among us,
astounded us, having gone to the tomb early,
23 and not finding His body, they came
claiming to have seen also a vision of angels,
who say He is alive.
24 And some of those with us went to the

μνημεῖον καὶ εὗρον οὕτως καθὼς °καὶ¹ αἱ γυναῖκες εἶπον,
tomb and found [it] so as also the women said,
αὐτὸν.δὲ οὐκ.εἶδον. 25 Καὶ αὐτὸς εἶπεν πρὸς αὐτούς, Ὦ
but him they saw not. And he said to them, O
ἀνόητοι καὶ βραδεῖς τῇ καρδίᾳ τοῦ πιστεύειν ἐπὶ πᾶσιν οἷς
senseless and slow of heart to believe in all which
ἐλάλησαν οἱ προφῆται· 26 οὐχὶ ταῦτα ἔδει
spoke the prophets. ⁹Not ¹⁰these ¹¹things ¹was ²it ⁴needful ⁵for
παθεῖν τὸν χριστόν, καὶ εἰσελθεῖν εἰς τὴν.δόξαν.αὐτοῦ;
⁸to ⁸suffer ⁶the ⁷Christ, and to enter into his glory?
27 Καὶ ἀρξάμενος ἀπὸ ᵖΜωσέως¹ καὶ ἀπὸ πάντων τῶν προ-
And beginning from Moses and from all the pro-
φητῶν ᵠδιηρμήνευεν¹ αὐτοῖς ἐν πάσαις ταῖς γραφαῖς τὰ
phets he interpreted to them in all the scriptures the things
περὶ ʳἑαυτοῦ.¹ 28 Καὶ ἤγγισαν εἰς τὴν κώμην οὗ
concerning himself. And they drew near to the village where
ἐπορεύοντο, καὶ αὐτὸς ˢπροσεποιεῖτο¹ ᵗπορρωτέρω¹ πορεύεσθαι.
they were going, and he appeared ⁴farther ¹to ²be ³going.
29 καὶ παρεβιάσαντο αὐτόν, λέγοντες, Μεῖνον μεθ' ἡμῶν, ὅτι
And they constrained him, saying, Abide with us, for
πρὸς ἑσπέραν ἐστίν, καὶ κέκλικεν ᵛ ἡ ἡμέρα. Καὶ εἰσῆλθεν
towards evening it is, and has declined the day. And he entered in
τοῦ μεῖναι σὺν αὐτοῖς. 30 καὶ ἐγένετο ἐν.τῷ.κατακλιθῆναι
to abide with them. And it came to pass as ²reclined
αὐτὸν μετ' αὐτῶν, λαβὼν τὸν ἄρτον ʷεὐλόγησεν,¹
[³at ⁴table] ¹he with them, having taken the bread he blessed,
καὶ κλάσας ἐπεδίδου αὐτοῖς. 31 αὐτῶν.δὲ διηνοίχθησαν οἱ
and having broken he gave [it] to them. And their ²were ³opened
ὀφθαλμοὶ καὶ ἐπέγνωσαν αὐτόν· καὶ αὐτὸς ἄφαντος.ἐγένετο
¹eyes and they knew him. And he disappeared
ἀπ' αὐτῶν. 32 Καὶ ˣεἶπον¹ πρὸς ἀλλήλους, Οὐχὶ ἡ καρδία
from them. And they said to one another, ²Not ⁴heart
ἡμῶν καιομένη ἦν ʸἐν ἡμῖν¹ ὡς ἐλάλει ἡμῖν ἐν τῇ ὁδῷ,
³our ⁵burning ¹was in us as he was speaking to us in the way,
ᶻκαὶ¹ ὡς διήνοιγεν ἡμῖν τὰς γραφάς; 33 Καὶ ἀναστάντες
and as he was opening to us the scriptures? And rising up
αὐτῇ.τῇ ὥρᾳ ὑπέστρεψαν εἰς Ἱερουσαλήμ, καὶ εὗρον ᵃσυνη-
the same hour they returned to Jerusalem, and they found gathered
θροισμένους¹ τοὺς ἕνδεκα καὶ τοὺς σὺν αὐτοῖς, 34 λέγοντας,
together the eleven and those with them, saying,
Ὅτι ᵇἠγέρθη ὁ κύριος ὄντως,¹ καὶ ὤφθη Σίμωνι. 35 Καὶ
³Is ⁴risen ¹the ²Lord indeed, and appeared to Simon. And
αὐτοὶ ἐξηγοῦντο τὰ ἐν τῇ ὁδῷ, καὶ ὡς ἐγνώσθη αὐτοῖς
they related the things in the way, and how he was known to them
ἐν τῇ κλάσει τοῦ ἄρτου.
in the breaking of the bread.

36 Ταῦτα.δὲ αὐτῶν.λαλούντων, αὐτὸς ᶜὁ.Ἰησοῦς¹ ἔστη ἐν
And these things as they were telling, ²himself ¹Jesus stood in
μέσῳ αὐτῶν ᵈκαὶ λέγει αὐτοῖς, Εἰρήνη ὑμῖν.¹ ᵉ 37 Πτοηθέντες
³midst ¹their and says to them, Peace to you. ³Terrified
δὲ καὶ ἔμφοβοι γενόμενοι ἐδόκουν πνεῦμα θεωρεῖν.
¹but ⁴and ⁵filled ⁶with ⁷fear ²being they thought a spirit they beheld.
38 καὶ εἶπεν αὐτοῖς, Τί τεταραγμένοι ἐστέ; καὶ ᶠδιατί¹ δια-
And he said to them, Why troubled are ye? and wherefore ²rea-
λογισμοὶ ἀναβαίνουσιν ἐν ᵍταῖς καρδίαις¹ ὑμῶν; 39 ἴδετε
sonings ¹do come up in ²hearts ¹your? see
τὰς.χεῖράς.μου καὶ τοὺς.πόδας.μου, ὅτι ʰαὐτὸς ἐγώ εἰμι.¹
my hands and my feet, that ³he ¹I ²am.
ψηλαφήσατέ με καὶ ἴδετε· ὅτι πνεῦμα ⁱσάρκα¹ καὶ ὀστέα οὐκ
Handle me and see, for a spirit flesh and bones ²not
ἔχει, καθὼς ἐμὲ θεωρεῖτε ἔχοντα. 40 ᵏΚαὶ τοῦτο εἰπὼν
¹has, as ³me ¹ye ²see having. And this having said
ˡἐπέδειξεν¹ αὐτοῖς τὰς χεῖρας καὶ τοὺς πόδας.¹ 41 ἔτι.δὲ
he shewed to them [his] hands and feet. But yet
ἀπιστούντων.αὐτῶν ᵐἀπὸ τῆς χαρᾶς καὶ θαυμαζόντων,¹ εἶπεν
while they were disbelieving for joy and were wondering, he said
αὐτοῖς, Ἔχετέ τι βρώσιμον ἐνθάδε; 42 Οἱ.δὲ ἐπέδωκαν
to them, Have ye anything eatable here? And they gave
αὐτῷ ἰχθύος ὀπτοῦ μέρος ⁿκαὶ ἀπὸ μελισσίου.κηρίου.¹ 43 καὶ
to him ²of ³a ⁵fish ⁴broiled ¹part and of a honeycomb. And
λαβὼν ἐνώπιον αὐτῶν ἔφαγεν. 44 Εἶπεν.δὲ °αὐτοῖς,¹
having taken [it] ³before ⁴them ¹he ²ate. And he said to them,
Οὗτοι οἱ λόγοιᵖ οὓς ἐλάλησα πρὸς ὑμᾶς ἔτι ὢν σὺν ὑμῖν,
These [are] the words which I spoke to you yet being with you,
ὅτι δεῖ πληρωθῆναι πάντα τὰ γεγραμμένα ἐν τῷ νόμῳ
that must be fulfilled all things that have been written in the law
ᵠΜωσέως¹ καὶ ʳ προφήταις καὶ ψαλμοῖς περὶ ἐμοῦ. 45 Τότε
of Moses and prophets and psalms concerning me. Then
διήνοιξεν αὐτῶν τὸν νοῦν τοῦ συνιέναι τὰς γραφάς·
he opened their understanding to understand the scriptures,
46 καὶ εἶπεν αὐτοῖς, Ὅτι οὕτως γέγραπται, ˢκαὶ οὕτως
and said to them, Thus it has been written, and ¹hus

tomb and found it even as the women said,
but they did not see Him.
25 And He said to them, O fools and slow
of heart to believe all that the prophets
spoke!
26 Was it not necessary for Christ to have
suffered these things and to enter into His
glory?
27 And beginning from Moses, and from all
the prophets, He explained to them the
things about Himself in all the Scriptures.
28 And they came to the village where they
were going, and He appeared to be going on.
29 But they pressed Him, saying, Stay with
us, for it is towards evening and the day has
declined. And He went in to stay with them.
30 And as He sat at table with them, taking
the bread He blessed it. And breaking it, He
gave it to them.
31 And their eyes were opened and they
knew Him. And He vanished from them.
32 And they said to one another, Did not
our heart burn within us while He was
speaking to us in the way, and as He was
opening the Scriptures to us?
33 And rising up that same hour they returned to Jerusalem. And they found the Eleven
gathered together, and those with them.
34 *And they* said, The Lord has truly risen
and has appeared to Simon.
35 And they told what things *happened* in
the way, and how He was known to them in
the breaking of the bread.

36 And as they were telling these things,
Jesus Himself stood among them and said to
them, Peace to you!
37 But they were terrified and filled with
fear, thinking they saw a ghost.
38 And He said to them, Why are you
fearful? And why do doubts come into your
heart?
39 Look at My hands and My feet – that I am
He. Touch Me and see, for a ghost does not
have flesh and bones as you see Me have.
40 And saying this He showed them His feet
and hands.
41 And as they still did not believe and
were wondering, full of joy, He said to them,
Have you anything here to eat?
42 And they gave Him a piece of a broiled
fish and a piece of honeycomb.
43 And He took it and ate before them.
44 And He said to them, These are the
words which I spoke to you while I was still
with you, that all things must be fulfilled
which have been written in the Law of Moses
and Prophets and Psalms about Me.
45 Then He opened their understanding that
they might understand the Scriptures.
46 And He said to them, So it has been
written and so it was necessary that the

ἔδει" παθεῖν τὸν χριστὸν καὶ ἀναστῆναι ἐκ νεκρῶν
it behoved [3]to [4]suffer [1]the [2]Christ and to rise from among [the] dead
τῇ τρίτῃ ἡμέρᾳ, 47 καὶ κηρυχθῆναι ἐπὶ τῷ.ὀνόματι.αὐτοῦ
the third day; and should be proclaimed in his name
μετάνοιαν [t]καὶ" ἄφεσιν ἁμαρτιῶν εἰς πάντα τὰ ἔθνη, [u]ἀρξά-
repentance and remission of sins to all nations, begin-
μενον" ἀπὸ Ἱερουσαλήμ. 48 ὑμεῖς [v]δέ ἐστε" μάρτυρες τούτων.
ning at Jerusalem. [2]Ye [1]and are witnesses of these things.
49 [w]καὶ ἰδού, ἐγὼ" [x]ἀποστέλλω" τὴν ἐπαγγελίαν τοῦ πατρός
And lo, I send the promise of [2]Father
μου ἐφ' ὑμᾶς· ὑμεῖς.δὲ καθίσατε ἐν τῇ πόλει [y]Ἱερουσαλὴμ"
[1]my upon you; but [2]ye [1]remain in the city of Jerusalem
ἕως.οὗ ἐνδύσησθε [z]δύναμιν ἐξ ὕψους."
till ye be clothed with power from on high.

50 Ἐξήγαγεν.δὲ αὐτοὺς [a]ἔξω" ἕως [b]εἰς" Βηθανίαν, καὶ
And he led them out as far as to Bethany, and
ἐπάρας τὰς.χεῖρας.αὐτοῦ εὐλόγησεν αὐτούς. 51 καὶ
having lifted up his hands he blessed them. And
ἐγένετο ἐν.τῷ.εὐλογεῖν αὐτὸν αὐτοὺς διέστη ἀπ' αὐτῶν
it came to pass as [2]was [3]blessing [1]he them he was separated from them
[c]καὶ ἀνεφέρετο εἰς τὸν οὐρανόν." 52 καὶ αὐτοὶ [d]προσκυνή-
and was carried up into the heaven. And they having wor-
σαντες αὐτὸν" ὑπέστρεψαν εἰς Ἱερουσαλὴμ μετὰ χαρᾶς μεγά-
shipped him returned to Jerusalem with [2]joy [1]great,
λης· 53 καὶ ἦσαν [e]διαπαντὸς" ἐν τῷ ἱερῷ, [f]αἰνοῦντες καὶ
and were continually in the temple, praising and
εὐλογοῦντες" τὸν θεόν. [g]Ἀμήν."
blessing God. Amen.

[h]Τὸ κατὰ Λουκᾶν εὐαγγέλιον."
The [3]according [4]to [5]Luke [1]glad [2]tidings.

Christ should suffer and rise from among the dead the third day –
47 and that repentance and remission of sins should be preached in His name in all nations, beginning at Jerusalem.
48 And you are witnesses of these things.
49 And, behold! I send the promise of My Father upon you. But remain in the city of Jerusalem until you are clothed with power from on high.

50 And He led them out as far as Bethany. And lifting up His hands, He blessed them.
51 And as He was blessing them, He was taken from them and was carried up into Heaven.
52 And after they had worshiped Him, they returned to Jerusalem with great joy.
53 And they were continually in the Temple, praising and blessing God. Amen.

The Gospel According to JOHN

ἘΝ ἀρχῇ ἦν ὁ λόγος, καὶ ὁ λόγος ἦν πρὸς τὸν θεόν,
In [the] beginning was the Word, and the Word was with God,
καὶ θεὸς ἦν ὁ λόγος. 2 οὗτος ἦν ἐν ἀρχῇ πρὸς τὸν
and [4]God [3]was [1]the [2]Word. He was in [the] beginning with
θεόν. 3 Πάντα δι' αὐτοῦ ἐγένετο, καὶ χωρὶς αὐτοῦ
God. All things through him came into being, and without him
ἐγένετο οὐδὲ [k]ἕν ὃ γέγονεν. 4 ἐν" αὐτῷ ζωὴ
came into being not even one [thing] which has come into being. In him [2]life
[l]ἦν," καὶ ἡ ζωὴ ἦν τὸ φῶς τῶν ἀνθρώπων· 5 καὶ τὸ φῶς ἐν
[1]was, and the life was the light of men. And the light in
τῇ σκοτίᾳ φαίνει, καὶ ἡ σκοτία αὐτὸ οὐ.κατέλαβεν.
the darkness appears, and the darkness [2]it [1]apprehended not.
6 Ἐγένετο ἄνθρωπος ἀπεσταλμένος παρὰ θεοῦ, ὄνομα
There was a man sent from God, [2]name
αὐτῷ [m]Ἰωάννης." 7 οὗτος ἦλθεν εἰς μαρτυρίαν, ἵνα μαρτυ-
[1]his John. He came for a witness, that he might
ρήσῃ περὶ τοῦ φωτός, ἵνα πάντες πιστεύσωσιν δι' αὐτοῦ.
witness concerning the light, that all might believe through him.
8 οὐκ.ἦν ἐκεῖνος τὸ φῶς, ἀλλ' ἵνα μαρτυρήσῃ περὶ τοῦ
[3]Was [2]not [1]he the light, but that he might witness concerning the
φωτός. 9 ἦν τὸ φῶς τὸ ἀληθινόν ὃ φωτίζει πάντα
light. [4]Was [1]the [3]light [2]true that which lightens every
ἄνθρωπον ἐρχόμενον εἰς τὸν κόσμον. 10 ἐν τῷ κόσμῳ ἦν,
man coming into the world. In the world he was,
καὶ ὁ κόσμος δι' αὐτοῦ ἐγένετο, καὶ ὁ κόσμος αὐτὸν
and the world through him came into being, and the world him
οὐκ.ἔγνω. 11 εἰς τὰ.ἴδια ἦλθεν, καὶ οἱ.ἴδιοι αὐτὸν οὐ.παρέλα-
knew not. To his own he came, and his own him received not;
βον· 12 ὅσοι.δὲ [n]ἔλαβον" αὐτὸν ἔδωκεν αὐτοῖς ἐξουσίαν
but as many as received him he gave to them authority
τέκνα θεοῦ γενέσθαι, τοῖς πιστεύουσιν εἰς τὸ ὄνομα
children of God to be, to those that believe on [2]name
αὐτοῦ· 13 οἳ οὐκ ἐξ αἱμάτων οὐδὲ ἐκ θελήματος σαρκὸς οὐδὲ
[1]his; who not of bloods nor of will of flesh nor
ἐκ θελήματος ἀνδρὸς ἀλλ' ἐκ θεοῦ ἐγεννήθησαν.
of will of man but of God were born.
14 Καὶ ὁ λόγος σὰρξ ἐγένετο, καὶ ἐσκήνωσεν ἐν ἡμῖν,
And the Word flesh became, and tabernacled among us,
καὶ ἐθεασάμεθα τὴν.δόξαν.αὐτοῦ, δόξαν ὡς μονογενοῦς παρὰ
(and we discerned his glory, a glory as of an only-begotten with
πατρός, πλήρης χάριτος καὶ ἀληθείας. 15 [o]Ἰωάννης" μαρτυρεῖ
a father, full of grace and truth. John witnesses
περὶ αὐτοῦ, καὶ κέκραγεν, λέγων, Οὗτος ἦν ὃν εἶπον,
concerning him, and cried, saying, This was he of whom I said,

CHAPTER 1

1 In the beginning was the Word, and the Word was with God, and the Word was God.
2 He was in the beginning with God.
3 All things came into being through Him. And without Him not even one thing was made that has come into being.
4 In Him was life, and the life was the light of men.
5 And the light shines in the darkness, and the darkness does not overcome it.
6 There was a man sent from God, whose name was John.
7 He came for a witness that he might witness concerning the Light, so that all might believe through Him.
8 He was not the Light, but he *came* so that he might witness concerning the Light –
9 That was the true Light, that which enlightens every man coming into the world.
10 He was in the world, and the world was made through Him, but the world did not know Him.
11 He came to that which was His own, but His own did not receive Him.
12 But as many as did receive Him, He gave to them authority to become children of God – to those that believe in His name –
13 who were not born of blood, nor of the will of flesh, nor of the will of man, but were born of God.
14 And the Word became flesh and lived among us. And we saw His glory, the glory as of the only-begotten of the Father – full of grace and truth.
15 John bore witness about Him and cried out, saying, This was He of whom I said, He

Ὁ ὀπίσω μου ἐρχόμενος, ἔμπροσθέν μου γέγονεν· ὅτι
He who after me comes, [2]precedence [3]of [4]me [1]has, for
πρῶτός μου ἦν. 16 [p]Καὶ" ἐκ τοῦ-πληρώματος-αὐτοῦ ἡμεῖς
before me he was. And of his fulness we
πάντες ἐλάβομεν, καὶ χάριν ἀντὶ χάριτος· 17 ὅτι ὁ νόμος
all received, and grace upon grace. For the law
διὰ [q]Μωσέως' ἐδόθη. ἡ χάρις καὶ ἡ ἀλήθεια διὰ Ἰησοῦ
through Moses was given; the grace and the truth through Jesus
χριστοῦ ἐγένετο. 18 θεὸν οὐδεὶς ἑώρακεν πώποτε· [r]ὁ" μονο-
Christ came. [4]God [1]no [2]one [3]has [5]seen at any time; the only-
γενὴς [s]υἱός," ὁ ὢν εἰς τὸν κόλπον τοῦ πατρός, ἐκεῖνος ἐξη-
begotten Son, who is in the bosom of the Father, he de-
γήσατο. 19 Καὶ αὕτη ἐστὶν ἡ μαρτυρία τοῦ [t]Ἰωάννου,"
clared [him]. And this is the witness of John,
ὅτε ἀπέστειλαν [v] οἱ Ἰουδαῖοι ἐξ Ἱεροσολύμων ἱερεῖς καὶ
when [3]sent [1]the [2]Jews from Jerusalem priests and
[w]Λευΐτας,' ἵνα ἐρωτήσωσιν αὐτόν, Σὺ τίς εἶ; 20 Καὶ
Levites, that they might ask him, Thou who art thou? And
ὡμολόγησεν καὶ οὐκ.ἠρνήσατο, καὶ ὡμολόγησεν, "Ὅτι [x]οὐκ εἰμὶ
he confessed and denied not, and confessed, [3]Not [2]am
ἐγὼ' ὁ χριστός. 21 Καὶ ἠρώτησαν αὐτόν, [y]Τί οὖν; Ἠλίας
[1]I the Christ. And they asked him, What then? Elias
εἶ σύ; [z]Καὶ" λέγει, Οὐκ.εἰμί. Ὁ προφήτης εἶ σύ; Καὶ
art thou? And he says, I am not. The prophet art thou? And
ἀπεκρίθη, Οὔ. 22 [a]Εἶπον' [b]οὖν" αὐτῷ, Τίς εἶ; ἵνα ἀπό-
he answered, No. They said therefore to him, Who art thou? that an
κρισιν δῶμεν τοῖς πέμψασιν ἡμᾶς· τί λέγεις περὶ
answer we may give to those who sent us: what sayest thou about
σεαυτοῦ; 23 Ἔφη, Ἐγὼ φωνὴ βοῶντος ἐν τῇ ἐρήμῳ,
thyself? He said, I [am] a voice crying in the wilderness,
Εὐθύνατε τὴν ὁδὸν κυρίου· καθὼς εἶπεν Ἠσαΐας ὁ προ-
Make straight the way of [the] Lord, as said Esaias the pro-
φήτης. 24 Καὶ [c]οἱ" ἀπεσταλμένοι ἦσαν ἐκ τῶν Φαρι-
phet. And those who had been sent were from among the Phari-
σαίων. 25 καὶ ἠρώτησαν αὐτὸν καὶ [d]εἶπον" αὐτῷ, Τί οὖν
sees. And they asked him and said to him, Why then
βαπτίζεις, εἰ σὺ οὐκ.εἶ ὁ χριστός, [e]οὔτε" [f]Ἠλίας," [e]οὔτε"
baptizest thou, if thou art not the Christ, nor Elias, nor
ὁ προφήτης; 26 Ἀπεκρίθη αὐτοῖς ὁ [g]Ἰωάννης" λέγων, Ἐγὼ
the prophet? [2]Answered [3]them [1]John saying, I
βαπτίζω ἐν ὕδατι· μέσος.[h]δὲ" ὑμῶν [i]ἕστηκεν" ὃν ὑμεῖς
baptize with water; but in [the] midst of you stands [one] whom ye
οὐκ.οἴδατε 27 [k]αὐτός ἐστιν" [l]ὁ" ὀπίσω μου ἐρχόμενος, [m]ὃς
know not; he it is who after me comes, who
ἔμπροσθέν μου γέγονεν·" οὗ [n]ἐγὼ" οὐκ εἰμὶ [o] ἄξιος ἵνα
[2]precedence [3]of [4]me [1]has, of whom I [2]not [1]am worthy that
λύσω αὐτοῦ τὸν ἱμάντα τοῦ ὑποδήματος. 28 Ταῦτα ἐν
I should loose of him the thong of the sandal. These things in
[p]Βηθαβαρᾷ' ἐγένετο πέραν τοῦ Ἰορδάνου, ὅπου ἦν [q] [r]Ἰωάν-
Bethabara took place across the Jordan, where [2]was [1]John
νης" βαπτίζων.
baptizing.

29 Τῇ ἐπαύριον βλέπει [s]ὁ Ἰωάννης" τὸν Ἰησοῦν ἐρχόμενον
On the morrow [2]sees [1]John Jesus coming
πρὸς αὐτόν, καὶ λέγει, Ἴδε ὁ ἀμνὸς τοῦ θεοῦ, ὁ αἴρων
to him, and says, Behold the Lamb of God, who takes away
τὴν ἁμαρτίαν τοῦ κόσμου. 30 οὗτός ἐστιν [t]περὶ" οὗ ἐγὼ
the sin of the world. He it is concerning whom I
εἶπον, Ὀπίσω μου ἔρχεται ἀνήρ, ὃς ἔμπροσθέν μου γέγονεν,
said, After me comes a man, who [2]precedence [3]of [4]me [1]has,
ὅτι πρῶτός μου ἦν. 31 κἀγὼ οὐκ.ᾔδειν αὐτόν· ἀλλ' ἵνα
because before me he was. And I knew not him; but that
φανερωθῇ τῷ Ἰσραήλ, διὰ.τοῦτο ἦλθον ἐγὼ ἐν [v]τῷ"
he might be manifested to Israel, therefore came I with
ὕδατι βαπτίζων. 32 Καὶ ἐμαρτύρησεν [r]Ἰωάννης" λέγων, "Ὅτι
water baptizing. And [2]bore [3]witness [1]John saying,
τεθέαμαι τὸ πνεῦμα καταβαῖνον [w]ὡσεὶ" περιστερὰν ἐξ οὐ-
I have beheld the Spirit descending as a dove out of hea-
ρανοῦ, καὶ ἔμεινεν ἐπ' αὐτόν. 33 κἀγὼ οὐκ.ᾔδειν αὐτόν· ἀλλ'
ven, and it abode upon him. And I knew not him; but
ὁ πέμψας με βαπτίζειν ἐν ὕδατι, ἐκεῖνός μοι εἶπεν, Ἐφ'
he who sent me to baptize with water, he to me said, Upon
ὃν ἂν ἴδῃς τὸ πνεῦμα καταβαῖνον καὶ μένον ἐπ'
whom thou shalt see the Spirit descending and abiding on
αὐτόν, οὗτός ἐστιν ὁ βαπτίζων ἐν πνεύματι ἁγίῳ.
him, he it is who baptizes with [the] [2]Spirit [1]Holy.
34 κἀγὼ ἑώρακα, καὶ μεμαρτύρηκα ὅτι οὗτός ἐστιν ὁ υἱὸς
And I have seen, and have borne witness that this is the Son
τοῦ θεοῦ.
of God.
35 Τῇ ἐπαύριον πάλιν εἱστήκει [x]ὁ" [r]Ἰωάννης," καὶ ἐκ
On the morrow again [2]was [3]standing [1]John, and [2]of

who comes after me has the right to go
before me, for He was before me.
16 And we all received of His fullness and
grace on top of grace.
17 For the Law was given through Moses,
but grace and truth came into being through
Jesus Christ.
18 No one has seen God at any time, the
only-begotten Son who is in the bosom of
the Father, He has revealed *Him*.
19 And this is the witness of John, when
the Jews sent priests and Levites from
Jerusalem that they might ask him, Who are
you?
20 And he confessed and did not deny, but
said, I am not the Christ.
21 And they asked him, What then? Are
you Elijah? And he said, I am not. Are you
the Prophet? And he answered, No!
22 Then they said to him, Who are you, so
that we can tell those who sent us? What do
you say about yourself?
23 He said, "I am a voice crying in the
wilderness, Make straight the way of the
Lord," as Isaiah the prophet said.
24 And those who had been sent were from
among the Pharisees.
25 And they asked, saying to him, Why
then do you baptize if you are not the Christ
or Elijah or the Prophet?
26 John answered them saying, I baptize
with water, but *One* stands among you
whom you do not know.
27 It is He who is coming after me, who has
been before me, of whom I am not worthy
to untie the thong of His sandal.
28 These things happened in Beth-ab-a-ra
beyond the Jordan, where John was
baptizing.

29 The next day John saw Jesus coming
toward him and said, Look! The Lamb of
God who takes away the sin of the world!
30 This is He about whom I said, After me a
Man comes who has the right to go before
me, because He was before me.
31 And I did not know Him. But in order
that He might be shown to Israel, therefore I
came baptizing with water.
32 And John witnessed, saying, I have seen
the Spirit coming down like a dove out of
Heaven and remaining upon Him.
33 And I did not know Him, but He who
sent me to baptize in water said to me, He
on whom you shall see the Spirit coming
down and remaining on Him, this is He who
baptizes in the Holy Spirit.
34 And I have seen and have borne witness
that this is the Son of God.

35 Again the next day John and two of his
disciples were standing together.

τῶν.μαθητῶν.αὐτοῦ δύο. 36 καὶ ἐμβλέψας τῷ Ἰησοῦ περιπα-
his disciples two. And looking at Jesus walk-
τοῦντι, λέγει, Ἴδε ὁ ἀμνὸς τοῦ θεοῦ. 37 Καὶ ἤκουσαν
ing, he says, Behold the Lamb of God! And heard
αὐτοῦ οἱ δύο μαθηταὶ λαλοῦντος, καὶ ἠκολούθησαν τῷ
him the two disciples speaking, and followed
Ἰησοῦ. 38 στραφεὶς δὲ ὁ Ἰησοῦς, καὶ θεασάμενος αὐτοὺς
Jesus. Having turned but Jesus, and beheld them
ἀκολουθοῦντας, λέγει αὐτοῖς, 39 Τί ζητεῖτε; Οἱ.δὲ εἶπον
following, says to them, What seek ye? And they said
αὐτῷ, Ῥαββί, ὃ λέγεται ἑρμηνευόμενον διδάσκαλε, ποῦ
to him, Rabbi, which is to say being interpreted Teacher, where
μένεις; 40 Λέγει αὐτοῖς, Ἔρχεσθε καὶ ἴδετε. Ἦλθον
abidest thou? He says to them, Come and see. They went
καὶ εἶδον ποῦ μένει· καὶ παρ' αὐτῷ ἔμειναν τὴν ἡμέραν
and saw where he abides; and with him they abode day
ἐκείνην· ὥρα δὲ ἦν ὡς δεκάτη. 41 Ἦν Ἀνδρέας
that. [The] hour now was about [the] tenth. Was Andrew
ὁ ἀδελφὸς Σίμωνος Πέτρου εἷς ἐκ τῶν δύο τῶν ἀκουσάντων
the brother of Simon Peter one of the two who heard
παρὰ Ἰωάννου, καὶ ἀκολουθησάντων αὐτῷ. 42 εὑρίσκει
[this] from John, and followed him. Finds
οὗτος πρῶτος τὸν ἀδελφὸν τὸν.ἴδιον Σίμωνα, καὶ λέγει
he first brother his own Simon, and says
αὐτῷ, Εὑρήκαμεν τὸν μεσσίαν, ὅ ἐστιν μεθερμηνευόμενον
to him, We have found the Messias, which is being interpreted
ὁ χριστός· 43 καὶ ἤγαγεν αὐτὸν πρὸς τὸν Ἰησοῦν.
the Christ. And he led him to Jesus.
ἐμβλέψας.δὲ αὐτῷ ὁ Ἰησοῦς εἶπεν, Σὺ εἶ Σίμων ὁ υἱὸς
And looking at him Jesus said, Thou art Simon the son
Ἰωνᾶ· σὺ κληθήσῃ Κηφᾶς, ὃ ἑρμηνεύεται Πέτρος.
of Jonas; thou shalt be called Cephas, which is interpreted Stone.
44 Τῇ ἐπαύριον ἠθέλησεν ὁ Ἰησοῦς ἐξελθεῖν εἰς τὴν
On the morrow desired Jesus to go forth into
Γαλιλαίαν· καὶ εὑρίσκει Φίλιππον καὶ λέγει αὐτῷ, Ἀκολούθει
Galilee, and he finds Philip and says to him, Follow
μοι. 45 Ἦν.δὲ ὁ Φίλιππος ἀπὸ Βηθσαϊδά, ἐκ τῆς πόλεως
me. Now was Philip from Bethsaida, of the city
Ἀνδρέου καὶ Πέτρου. 46 Εὑρίσκει Φίλιππος τὸν Ναθαναὴλ
of Andrew and Peter. Finds Philip Nathanael
καὶ λέγει αὐτῷ, Ὃν ἔγραψεν Μωσῆς ἐν τῷ νόμῳ καὶ
and says to him, [Him] whom wrote of Moses in the law and
οἱ προφῆται, εὑρήκαμεν, Ἰησοῦν τὸν υἱὸν τοῦ Ἰωσὴφ τὸν
the prophets, we have found, Jesus the son of Joseph who
ἀπὸ Ναζαρέτ. 47 Καὶ εἶπεν αὐτῷ Ναθαναήλ, Ἐκ
[is] from Nazareth. And said to him Nathanael, Out of
Ναζαρὲτ δύναταί τι ἀγαθὸν εἶναι; Λέγει αὐτῷ Φίλιππος,
Nazareth can any good thing be? Says to him Philip,
Ἔρχου καὶ ἴδε. 48 Εἶδεν ὁ Ἰησοῦς τὸν Ναθαναὴλ ἐρχόμενον
Come and see. Saw Jesus Nathanael coming
πρὸς αὐτόν, καὶ λέγει περὶ αὐτοῦ, Ἴδε ἀληθῶς Ἰσραηλ-
to him, and says concerning him, Behold truly an Israel-
ίτης, ἐν ᾧ δόλος οὐκ.ἔστιν. 49 Λέγει αὐτῷ Ναθαναήλ,
ite, in whom guile is not. Says to him Nathanael,
Πόθεν με γινώσκεις; Ἀπεκρίθη ὁ Ἰησοῦς καὶ εἶπεν αὐτῷ,
Whence me knowest thou? Answered Jesus and said to him,
Πρὸ τοῦ σὲ Φίλιππον φωνῆσαι, ὄντα ὑπὸ τὴν συκῆν,
Before that thee Philip called, [thou] being under the fig-tree,
εἶδόν σε. 50 Ἀπεκρίθη Ναθαναὴλ καὶ λέγει αὐτῷ, Ῥαββί,
I saw thee. Answered Nathanael and says to him, Rabbi,
σὺ εἶ ὁ υἱὸς τοῦ θεοῦ, σὺ εἶ ὁ βασιλεὺς τοῦ Ἰσραήλ.
thou art the Son of God, thou art the King of Israel.
51 Ἀπεκρίθη Ἰησοῦς καὶ εἶπεν αὐτῷ, Ὅτι εἶπόν σοι, Εἶδόν
Answered Jesus and said to him, Because I said to thee, I saw
σε ὑποκάτω τῆς συκῆς, πιστεύεις; μείζω τούτων
thee under the fig-tree, believest thou? Greater things than these
ὄψει. 52 Καὶ λέγει αὐτῷ, Ἀμὴν ἀμὴν λέγω ὑμῖν,
thou shalt see. And he says to him, Verily verily I say to you,
ἀπ'.ἄρτι ὄψεσθε τὸν οὐρανὸν ἀνεῳγότα, καὶ τοὺς ἀγ-
Henceforth ye shall see the heaven opened, and the an-
γέλους τοῦ θεοῦ ἀναβαίνοντας καὶ καταβαίνοντας ἐπὶ τὸν
gels of God ascending and descending on the
υἱὸν τοῦ ἀνθρώπου.
Son of man.

2 Καὶ τῇ ἡμέρᾳ τῇ τρίτῃ γάμος ἐγένετο ἐν Κανᾷ
And on the day third a marriage took place in Cana
τῆς Γαλιλαίας· καὶ ἦν ἡ μήτηρ τοῦ Ἰησοῦ ἐκεῖ. 2 ἐκλήθη.δὲ
of Galilee, and was the mother of Jesus there. And was invited
καὶ ὁ Ἰησοῦς καὶ οἱ μαθηταὶ.αὐτοῦ εἰς τὸν γάμον. 3 καὶ
also Jesus and his disciples to the marriage. And
ὑστερήσαντος οἴνου λέγει ἡ μήτηρ τοῦ Ἰησοῦ πρὸς αὐτόν,
being deficient of wine says the mother of Jesus to him,

36 And looking at Jesus as He walked, he
said, Look! The Lamb of God!
37 And the two disciples heard him say it.
And they followed Jesus.
38 But Jesus turned and looked at them as
they followed. And He said, What are you
looking for? And they said to Him, Rabbi
(which translated means teacher), where are
you staying?
39 He said to them, Come and see. They
went and saw where He was staying. And
they stayed with Him that day. And it was
about the tenth hour.
40 Andrew, the brother of Simon Peter, was
one of the two who heard this from John
and followed Him.
41 He first found his own brother, Simon,
and said to him, We have found the Messiah
(which translated means, The Christ).
42 And he brought him to Jesus. And looking at him Jesus said, You are Simon the son
of Jonah, you shall be called Ce-phas (which
translated means, A stone).
43 On the next day Jesus wanted to go into
Galilee. And He found Philip and said to
him, Follow Me!
44 Now Philip was from Beth-sa-i-da, the
city of Andrew and Peter.
45 Philip found Na-than-a-el and said to
him, We have found *Him* of whom Moses
wrote in the Law and the Prophets – Jesus
the son of Joseph, who is from Naz-a-reth.
46 And Na-than-a-el said to him, Can any
good thing come out of Naz-a-reth? Philip
answered, Come and see.
47 Jesus saw Na-than-a-el coming to Him
and said of him, Look, an Israelite indeed, in
whom *there* is no guile!
48 Na-than-a-el said to Him, From where do
you know me? Jesus answered and said to
him, Before Philip called you I saw you,
when you were under the fig-tree.
49 Na-than-a-el said to Him, Rabbi, You are
the Son of God! You are the King of Israel!
50 Jesus answered and said to him, Do you
believe because I said that I saw you under
the fig-tree? You shall see greater things than
these.
51 And He said to him, Indeed, I tell you
truly that from now on you shall see Heaven
opened and the angels of God going up and
coming down on the Son of man.

CHAPTER 2

1 And the third day there was a marriage in
Cana of Galilee. And Jesus' mother was
there.
2 And Jesus was invited to the marriage,
and His disciples also.
3 And when the wine was gone, Jesus'
mother said to Him, they have no wine.

Οἶνον οὐκ.ἔχουσιν. 4 [b]Λέγει αὐτῇ ὁ Ἰησοῦς, Τί ἐμοὶ καὶ
Wine they have not. 2Says 3to 4her 1Jesus, What to me and
σοί, γύναι; οὔπω ἥκει ἡ ὥρα μου. 5 Λέγει ἡ.μήτηρ.αὐτοῦ
to thee, woman? not yet is come mine hour. 2Says 1his 2mother
τοῖς διακόνοις, Ὅ.τι ἂν λέγῃ ὑμῖν, ποιήσατε. 6 Ἦσαν
to the servants, Whatever he may say to you, do. 2There 3were
δὲ ἐκεῖ ὑδρίαι λιθιναι ἓξ κείμεναι κατὰ τὸν καθα-
1and there 7water-vessels 6of 5stone 4six standing according to the puri-
ρισμὸν τῶν Ἰουδαίων, χωροῦσαι ἀνὰ μετρητὰς δύο ἢ τρεῖς.
fication of the Jews, holding each metretæ two or three.
7 λέγει αὐτοῖς ὁ Ἰησοῦς, Γεμίσατε τὰς ὑδρίας ὕδατος.
2Says 3to 4them 1Jesus, Fill the water-vessels with water.
Καὶ ἐγέμισαν αὐτὰς ἕως ἄνω. 8 Καὶ λέγει αὐτοῖς, Ἀν-
And they filled them unto [the] brim. And he says to them, Draw
τλήσατε νῦν καὶ φέρετε τῷ ἀρχιτρικλίνῳ. [e]Καὶ ἤνεγκαν.
out now and carry to the master of the feast. And they carried [it].
9 ὡς.δὲ ἐγεύσατο ὁ ἀρχιτρίκλινος τὸ ὕδωρ οἶνον γεγενη-
But when 6had 7tasted 1the 2master 3of 4the 5feast the water 4wine 1that 2had
μένον, καὶ οὐκ ᾔδει πόθεν ἐστίν· οἱ.δὲ διάκονοι ᾔδεισαν οἱ
3become, and knew not whence it is, (but the servants knew who
ἠντληκότες τὸ ὕδωρ· φωνεῖ τὸν νυμφίον ὁ ἀρχιτρίκλινος
had drawn the water,) 6calls 7the 8bridegroom 1the 2master 3of 4the 5feast
10 καὶ λέγει αὐτῷ, Πᾶς ἄνθρωπος πρῶτον τὸν καλὸν οἶνον
and says to him, Every man first the good wine
τίθησιν, καὶ ὅταν μεθυσθῶσιν [f]τότε τὸν ἐλάσσω·
sets on, and when they may have drunk freely then the inferior;
σὺ τετήρηκας τὸν καλὸν οἶνον ἕως ἄρτι. 11 Ταύτην ἐποίησεν
thou hast kept the good wine until now. This 5did
[g]τὴν ἀρχὴν τῶν σημείων ὁ Ἰησοῦς ἐν [z]Κανᾷ τῆς Γαλιλαίας,
1beginning 2of 3the 4signs Jesus in Cana of Galilee,
καὶ ἐφανέρωσεν τὴν.δόξαν.αὐτοῦ· καὶ ἐπίστευσαν εἰς αὐτὸν
and manifested his glory; and 3believed 4on 5him
οἱ.μαθηταὶ.αὐτοῦ.
1his 2disciples.

12 Μετὰ τοῦτο κατέβη εἰς [a]Καπερναούμ, αὐτὸς καὶ ἡ
After this he went down to Capernaum, he and
μήτηρ.αὐτοῦ καὶ οἱ ἀδελφοὶ [b]αὐτοῦ καὶ οἱ.μαθηταὶ.αὐτοῦ, καὶ
his mother and 2brethren 1his and his disciples, and
ἐκεῖ ἔμειναν οὐ πολλὰς ἡμέρας. 13 Καὶ ἐγγὺς ἦν τὸ πάσχα
there they abode not many days. And near was the passover
τῶν Ἰουδαίων, καὶ ἀνέβη εἰς Ἱεροσόλυμα ὁ Ἰησοῦς. 14 καὶ
of the Jews, and 2went 3up 4to 5Jerusalem 1Jesus. And
εὗρεν ἐν τῷ ἱερῷ τοὺς πωλοῦντας βόας καὶ πρόβατα καὶ
he found in the temple those who sold oxen and sheep and
περιστεράς, καὶ τοὺς κερματιστὰς καθημένους· 15 καὶ ποιή-
doves, and the money-changers sitting; and having
σας φραγέλλιον ἐκ σχοινίων πάντας ἐξέβαλεν ἐκ τοῦ
made a scourge of cords 4all 1he 2drove 3out from the
ἱεροῦ, τά.τε πρόβατα καὶ τοὺς βόας. καὶ τῶν κολλυβιστῶν
temple, both the sheep and the oxen; and of the money-changers
ἐξέχεεν [c]τὸ κέρμα καὶ τὰς τραπέζας ἀνέστρεψεν. 16 καὶ
he poured out the coin and the tables overthrew. And
τοῖς τὰς περιστερὰς πωλοῦσιν εἶπεν, Ἄρατε ταῦτα
to those who 2the 3doves 1sold he said, Take these things
ἐντεῦθεν· [d]μὴ.ποιεῖτε τὸν οἶκον τοῦ.πατρός.μου οἶκον ἐμ-
hence; make not the house of my father a house of mer-
πορίου. 17 Ἐμνήσθησαν.[e]δὲ οἱ.μαθηταὶ.αὐτοῦ ὅτι γε-
chandise. And 3remembered 1his 2disciples that writ-
γραμμένον ἐστίν, Ὁ ζῆλος τοῦ.οἴκου.σου [f]κατέφαγέν με.
ten it is, The zeal of thine house has eaten 2up 1me.
18 Ἀπεκρίθησαν οὖν οἱ Ἰουδαῖοι καὶ [g]εἶπον αὐτῷ, Τί
4Answered 3therefore 1the 2Jews and said to him, What
σημεῖον δεικνύεις ἡμῖν ὅτι ταῦτα ποιεῖς; 19 Ἀπεκρίθη
sign shewest thou to us that these things thou doest? 2Answered
[h]ὁ Ἰησοῦς καὶ εἶπεν αὐτοῖς, Λύσατε τὸν.ναὸν.τοῦτον, καὶ [i]ἐν
1Jesus and said to them, Destroy this temple, and in
τρισὶν ἡμέραις ἐγερῶ αὐτόν. 20 [g]Εἶπον οὖν οἱ Ἰουδαῖοι,
three days I will raise up it. 4Said 3therefore 1the 2Jews,
[k]Τεσσαράκοντα καὶ ἓξ ἔτεσιν [l]ᾠκοδομήθη ὁ.ναὸς.οὗτος, καὶ
Forty and six years was building this temple, and
σὺ ἐν τρισὶν ἡμέραις ἐγερεῖς αὐτόν; 21 Ἐκεῖνος.δὲ ἔλεγεν
thou in three days wilt raise up it? But he spoke
περὶ τοῦ ναοῦ τοῦ.σώματος.αὐτοῦ. 22 ὅτε οὖν ἠγέρ-
concerning the temple of his body. When therefore he was
θη ἐκ νεκρῶν ἐμνήσθησαν οἱ.μαθηταὶ.αὐτοῦ ὅτι
raised up from among [the] dead 3remembered 1his 2disciples that
τοῦτο ἔλεγεν [m]αὐτοῖς, καὶ ἐπίστευσαν τῇ γραφῇ καὶ τῷ
this he had said to them, and believed the scripture and the
λόγῳ [n]ᾧ εἶπεν ὁ Ἰησοῦς.
word which 2had 3spoken 1Jesus.
23 Ὡς.δὲ ἦν ἐν [o]Ἱεροσολύμοις ἐν τῷ πάσχα, [p]ἐν τῇ
But when he was in Jerusalem at the passover, at the

4 Jesus answered her, What *is that* to Me and you, woman? My time has not yet come.

5 His mother said to the servants, Whatever He may say to you, do it.

6 And six stone waterpots were there, placed according to the cleansing *laws* of the Jews, each one holding two or three measures.

7 Jesus said to them, Fill the waterpots with water. And they filled them to the brim.

8 And He said to them, Draw out now and carry to the master of the feast. And they carried it.

9 But when the master of the feast had tasted the water that had become wine, he did not know its origin (but the servants who had drawn the water knew). The master of the feast called the bridegroom

10 and said to him, Every man first sets out the good wine. And when they have drunk freely, then that which is worse. But you have kept the good wine until now.

11 This, the beginning of the miracles, Jesus did in Cana of Galilee, revealing His glory. And His disciples believed on Him.

12 After this He went down to Ca-per-na-um, He and His mother and His brothers and His disciples. And they did not remain there many days.

13 And the Passover of the Jews was near. And Jesus went up to Jerusalem.

14 And He found in the Temple those who sold oxen and sheep and doves, and the money-changers sitting *there*.

15 And making a whip of small cords, He drove them all out of the Temple, and the sheep and the oxen. And He poured out the money of the money-changers and overthrew the tables.

16 And He said to those who sold the doves, Take these things away from here! Do not make My Father's house a house for gain.

17 And His disciples remembered that it was written, "The zeal of Your house has eaten Me up."

18 Then the Jews answered and said to Him, What sign do you show us that you do these things?

19 Jesus said to them, Destroy this Temple and I will raise it up in three days.

20 Then the Jews said, This Temple was forty-six years in building, and will you raise it up in three days?

21 But He spoke as to the temple of His body.

22 Therefore when He was raised from the dead, His disciples remembered that He had said this to them. And they believed the Scripture and the word which Jesus had said

23 But when He was in Jerusalem at the Passover, many believed in His name during

ἑορτῇ, πολλοὶ ἐπίστευσαν εἰς τὸ.ὄνομα.αὐτοῦ, θεωροῦντες αὐτοῦ
feast, many believed on his name, beholding his
τὰ σημεῖα ἃ ἐποίει. 24 αὐτὸς.δὲ ὁ Ἰησοῦς οὐκ.ἐπίστευεν
signs which he was doing. But himself Jesus did not trust
ἑαυτὸν αὐτοῖς, διὰ τὸ.αὐτὸν γινώσκειν πάντας, 25 καὶ
himself to them, because of his knowing all [men], and
ὅτι οὐ χρείαν εἶχεν ἵνα τις μαρτυρήσῃ περὶ τοῦ ἀνθρώ-
that no need he had that any should testify concerning man,
που· αὐτὸς.γὰρ ἐγίνωσκεν τί ἦν ἐν τῷ ἀνθρώπῳ.
for he knew what was in man.

3 Ἦν.δὲ ἄνθρωπος ἐκ τῶν Φαρισαίων, Νικόδημος ὄνομα
But there was a man of the Pharisees, Nicodemus name
αὐτῷ, ἄρχων τῶν Ἰουδαίων· 2 οὗτος ἦλθεν πρὸς τὸν Ἰησοῦν
his, a ruler of the Jews; he came to Jesus
νυκτός, καὶ εἶπεν αὐτῷ, Ῥαββί, οἴδαμεν ὅτι ἀπὸ θεοῦ ἐλή-
by night, and said to him, Rabbi, we know that from God thou
λυθας διδάσκαλος· οὐδεὶς γὰρ ταῦτα τὰ σημεῖα δύναται
hast come a teacher, for no one these signs is able
ποιεῖν ἃ σὺ ποιεῖς ἐὰν.μὴ ᾖ ὁ θεὸς μετ' αὐτοῦ. 3 Ἀπεκρίθη
to do which thou doest unless be God with him. Answered
ὁ Ἰησοῦς καὶ εἶπεν αὐτῷ, Ἀμὴν ἀμὴν λέγω σοι, ἐὰν.μή
Jesus and said to him, Verily verily I say to thee, Unless
τις γεννηθῇ ἄνωθεν, οὐ.δύναται ἰδεῖν τὴν βασιλείαν τοῦ
anyone be born anew, he cannot see the kingdom
θεοῦ. 4 Λέγει πρὸς αὐτὸν ὁ Νικόδημος, Πῶς δύναται ἄν-
of God. Says to him Nicodemus, How can a
θρωπος γεννηθῆναι γέρων ὤν; μὴ δύναται εἰς τὴν κοιλίαν
man be born old being? can he into the womb
τῆς.μητρὸς.αὐτοῦ δεύτερον εἰσελθεῖν καὶ γεννηθῆναι; 5 Ἀπε-
of his mother a second time enter and be born? An-
κρίθη ὁ Ἰησοῦς, Ἀμὴν ἀμὴν λέγω σοι, ἐὰν.μή τις γεννηθῇ
swered Jesus, Verily verily I say to thee, Unless anyone be born
ἐξ ὕδατος καὶ πνεύματος οὐ.δύναται εἰσελθεῖν εἰς τὴν βασιλείαν
of water and of Spirit he cannot enter into the kingdom
τοῦ θεοῦ. 6 τὸ γεγεννημένον ἐκ τῆς σαρκὸς σάρξ ἐστιν·
of God. That which has been born of the flesh flesh is;
καὶ τὸ γεγεννημένον ἐκ τοῦ πνεύματος πνεῦμά ἐστιν.
and that which has been born of the Spirit spirit is.
7 μὴ.θαυμάσῃς ὅτι εἶπόν σοι, Δεῖ ὑμᾶς γεννηθῆναι
Do not wonder that I said to thee, It is needful for you to be born
ἄνωθεν. 8 τὸ πνεῦμα ὅπου θέλει πνεῖ, καὶ τὴν.φωνὴν.αὐτοῦ
anew. The wind where it wills blows, and its sound
ἀκούεις, ἀλλ' οὐκ.οἶδας πόθεν ἔρχεται καὶ ποῦ ὑπάγει
thou hearest, but knowest not whence it comes and where it goes:
οὕτως ἐστὶν πᾶς ὁ γεγεννημένος ἐκ τοῦ πνεύματος. 9 Ἀπε-
thus is everyone that has been born of the Spirit. An-
κρίθη Νικόδημος καὶ εἶπεν αὐτῷ, Πῶς δύναται ταῦτα γενέ-
swered Nicodemus and said to him, How can these things be?
σθαι; 10 Ἀπεκρίθη ὁ Ἰησοῦς καὶ εἶπεν αὐτῷ, Σὺ εἶ ὁ
Answered Jesus and said to him, Thou art the
διδάσκαλος τοῦ Ἰσραήλ, καὶ ταῦτα οὐ.γινώσκεις; 11 ἀμὴν
teacher of Israel, and these things knowest not? Verily
ἀμὴν λέγω σοι, ὅτι ὃ οἴδαμεν λαλοῦμεν, καὶ ὃ ἑωρά-
verily I say to thee, That which we know we speak, and that which we
καμεν μαρτυροῦμεν· καὶ τὴν.μαρτυρίαν.ἡμῶν οὐ.λαμβάνετε.
have seen we bear witness of; and our witness ye receive not.
12 εἰ τὰ.ἐπίγεια εἶπον ὑμῖν, καὶ οὐ.πιστεύετε, πῶς ἐὰν εἴπω
If earthly things I said to you, and ye believe not, how if I say
ὑμῖν τὰ.ἐπουράνια πιστεύσετε; 13 καὶ οὐδεὶς ἀναβέβηκεν
to you heavenly things will ye believe? And no one has gone up
εἰς τὸν οὐρανὸν εἰ.μὴ ὁ ἐκ τοῦ οὐρανοῦ καταβάς, ὁ υἱὸς
into the heaven except he who out of the heaven came down, the Son
τοῦ ἀνθρώπου ὁ ὢν ἐν τῷ οὐρανῷ. 14 καὶ καθὼς Μωσῆς
of man who is in the heaven. And even as Moses
ὕψωσεν τὸν ὄφιν ἐν τῇ ἐρήμῳ, οὕτως ὑψωθῆναι δεῖ
lifted up the serpent in the wilderness, thus to be lifted up it behoves
τὸν υἱὸν τοῦ ἀνθρώπου· 15 ἵνα πᾶς ὁ πιστεύων εἰς αὐτὸν
the Son of man, that everyone that believes on him
μὴ.ἀπόληται, ἀλλ' ἔχῃ ζωὴν αἰώνιον. 16 οὕτως.γὰρ
may not perish, but may have life eternal. For so
ἠγάπησεν ὁ θεὸς τὸν κόσμον ὥστε τὸν.υἱὸν.αὐτοῦ τὸν μονο-
loved God the world that his Son the only be-
γενῆ ἔδωκεν, ἵνα πᾶς ὁ πιστεύων εἰς αὐτὸν μὴ.ἀπόληται,
gotten he gave, that everyone who believes on him may not perish,
ἀλλ' ἔχῃ ζωὴν αἰώνιον. 17 οὐ.γὰρ.ἀπέστειλεν ὁ θεὸς τὸν
but may have life eternal. For sent not God
υἱὸν.αὐτοῦ εἰς τὸν κόσμον ἵνα κρίνῃ τὸν κόσμον, ἀλλ'
his Son into the world that he might judge the world, but
ἵνα σωθῇ ὁ κόσμος δι' αὐτοῦ. 18 ὁ πιστεύων εἰς
that might be saved the world through him. He that believes on
αὐτὸν οὐ.κρίνεται· ὁ.δὲ μὴ.πιστεύων ἤδη κέκριται,
him is not judged; but he that believes not already has been judged,

the feast, seeing His miracles which He was doing.

24 But Jesus did not trust Himself to them, because of His knowing all,

25 and because He did not need for any to testify about man, for He knew what was in man.

CHAPTER 3

1 And there was a man of the Pharisees named Nic-o-de-mus, a ruler of the Jews.

2 He came to Jesus by night and said to Him, Rabbi, we know that You are a teacher come from God, for no one is able to do these miracles which You are doing unless God is with him.

3 Jesus answered and said to him, Indeed, I tell you truly that unless one is born again, he cannot see the kingdom of God.

4 Nic-o-de-mus said to Him, How can a man be born when he is old? Can he enter into his mother's womb and be born the second time?

5 Jesus answered, Indeed, I tell you truly that unless one is born of water and of *the* Spirit he cannot enter into the kingdom of God.

6 That which has been born of the flesh is flesh. And that which has been born of the Spirit is spirit.

7 Do not wonder that I said to you, You need to be born again.

8 The Spirit breathes where He desires, and you hear His voice, but you do not know from where He comes and where He goes – so is everyone who has been born of the Spirit.

9 Nic-o-de-mus answered and said to Him, How can these things be?

10 Jesus answered him, Are you the teacher of Israel and do not know these things?

11 Indeed, I tell you truly that we speak that which we know and bear witness to that which we have seen, yet you do not receive our witness.

12 If I told you earthly things and you do not believe, how will you believe if I tell you heavenly things?

13 And no one has gone up into Heaven except He who came down out of Heaven – the Son of man who is in Heaven.

14 And even as Moses lifted up the serpent in the wilderness, so must the Son of man be lifted up,

15 so that everyone who believes on Him may not perish, but have everlasting life.

16 For God so loved the world that He gave His only-begotten Son, that whoever believes on Him may not perish, but have everlasting life.

17 For God did not send His Son into the world that He might judge the world, but that the world might be saved through Him.

18 He that believes on Him is not condemned, but he that does not believe has already been condemned – because he has not

ὅτι μὴ.πεπίστευκεν εἰς τὸ ὄνομα τοῦ μονογενοῦς υἱοῦ τοῦ
because he has not believed on the name of the only begotten Son
θεοῦ. 19 αὕτη.δέ ἐστιν ἡ κρίσις, ὅτι τὸ φῶς ἐλήλυθεν εἰς
of God. And this is the judgment, that the light has come into
τὸν κόσμον, καὶ ἠγάπησαν οἱ.ἄνθρωποι μᾶλλον τὸ σκότος
the world, and [2]loved [1]men [5]rather [3]the [4]darkness
ἢ τὸ φῶς· ἦν.γὰρ [u]πονηρὰ αὐτῶν‖ τὰ ἔργα. 20 πᾶς.γὰρ
than the light; for [2]were [1]evil their works. For everyone
ὁ φαῦλα πράσσων μισεῖ τὸ φῶς, καὶ οὐκ.ἔρχεται πρὸς τὸ
that evil does hates the light, and comes not to the
φῶς, ἵνα μὴ.ἐλεγχθῇ τὰ.ἔργα.αὐτοῦ· 21 ὁ.δὲ ποιῶν τὴν
light, that may not be exposed his works; but he that practises the
ἀλήθειαν ἔρχεται πρὸς τὸ φῶς, ἵνα φανερωθῇ αὐτοῦ τὰ
truth comes to the light, that may be manifested his
ἔργα ὅτι ἐν θεῷ ἐστιν.εἰργασμένα.
works that in God they have been wrought.

22 Μετὰ ταῦτα ἦλθεν ὁ Ἰησοῦς καὶ οἱ.μαθηταὶ.αὐτοῦ εἰς
After these things came Jesus and his disciples into
τὴν Ἰουδαίαν.γῆν. καὶ ἐκεῖ διέτριβεν μετ' αὐτῶν καὶ ἐβάπ-
the land of Judæa; and there he stayed with them and was bap-
τιζεν. 23 ἦν.δὲ καὶ [o]Ἰωάννης‖ βαπτίζων ἐν Αἰνὼν ἐγγὺς
tizing. And [3]was [2]also [1]John baptizing in Ænon, near
τοῦ Σαλείμ, ὅτι ὕδατα.πολλὰ ἦν ἐκεῖ· καὶ παρεγίνοντο καὶ
Salim, because [2]waters [1]many were there; and they were coming and
ἐβαπτίζοντο. 24 οὔπω.γὰρ ἦν βεβλημένος εἰς τὴν φυλακὴν
being baptized. For not yet was [5]cast [6]into [7]the [8]prison
[p]ὁ‖ [o]Ἰωάννης.‖ 25 Ἐγένετο οὖν ζήτησις ἐκ τῶν μαθητῶν
[1]John. Arose then a question [on the part] of the disciples
[q]Ἰωάννου‖ μετὰ [r]Ἰουδαίων‖ περὶ καθαρισμοῦ· 26 καὶ [s]ἦλθον‖
of John with [some] Jews about purification. And they came
πρὸς τὸν [t]Ἰωάννην‖ καὶ [v]εἶπον‖ αὐτῷ, [w]Ῥαββί,‖ ὃς ἦν μετὰ
to John and said to him, Rabbi, he who was with
σοῦ πέραν τοῦ Ἰορδάνου, ᾧ σὺ μεμαρτύρηκας, ἴδε οὗτος
thee beyond the Jordan, to whom thou hast borne witness, behold he
βαπτίζει, καὶ πάντες ἔρχονται πρὸς αὐτόν. 27 Ἀπεκρίθη
baptizes, and all come to him. [2]Answered
[o]Ἰωάννης‖ καὶ εἶπεν, Οὐ δύναται ἄνθρωπος λαμβάνειν οὐδὲν
[1]John and said, [3]Is [4]able [1]a [2]man to receive nothing
ἐὰν.μὴ ᾖ δεδομένον αὐτῷ ἐκ τοῦ οὐρανοῦ. 28 αὐτοὶ.ὑμεῖς
unless it be given to him from the heaven. Ye yourselves
μοι μαρτυρεῖτε ὅτι εἶπον, [x]Οὐκ.εἰμὶ ἐγὼ‖ ὁ χριστός, ἀλλ' ὅτι
to me bear witness that I said, [2]Am [3]not [1]I the Christ, but that
ἀπεσταλμένος εἰμὶ ἔμπροσθεν ἐκείνου. 29 ὁ ἔχων τὴν νύμ-
[3]sent [1]I [2]am before him. He that has the bride
φην, νυμφίος ἐστίν· ὁ.δὲ φίλος τοῦ νυμφίου, ὁ ἑστηκὼς καὶ
[2]bridegroom [1]is; but the friend of the bridegroom, who stands and
ἀκούων αὐτοῦ, χαρᾷ χαίρει διὰ τὴν φωνὴν τοῦ νυμφίου·
hears him, with joy rejoices because of the voice of the bridegroom,
αὕτη οὖν ἡ χαρὰ ἡ ἐμὴ πεπλήρωται. 30 ἐκεῖνον δεῖ
this then [2]joy [1]my is fulfilled. [2]Him [1]It [3]behoves
αὐξάνειν, ἐμὲ.δὲ ἐλαττοῦσθαι. 31 ὁ ἄνωθεν ἐρχόμενος ἐπάνω
to increase, but me to decrease. He who from above comes, above
πάντων ἐστίν. ὁ ὢν ἐκ τῆς γῆς ἐκ τῆς γῆς ἐστιν, καὶ
all is. He who is from the earth from the earth is, and
ἐκ τῆς γῆς λαλεῖ· ὁ ἐκ τοῦ οὐρανοῦ ἐρχόμενος [y]ἐπάνω
from the earth speaks. He who from the heaven comes above
πάντων ἐστίν,‖ 32 [z]καὶ‖ ὃ ἑώρακεν καὶ ἤκουσεν [a]τοῦτο‖
all is, and what he has seen and heard this
μαρτυρεῖ· καὶ τὴν.μαρτυρίαν.αὐτοῦ οὐδεὶς λαμβάνει. 33 ὁ
he testifies; and his testimony no one receives. He that
λαβὼν αὐτοῦ τὴν μαρτυρίαν ἐσφράγισεν ὅτι ὁ θεὸς ἀληθής
has received his testimony has set to his seal that God [2]true
ἐστιν. 34 ὃν.γὰρ ἀπέστειλεν ὁ θεὸς τὰ ῥήματα τοῦ θεοῦ
[1]is; for he whom [2]sent [1]God the words of God
λαλεῖ· οὐ.γὰρ ἐκ μέτρου δίδωσιν [b]ὁ θεὸς‖ τὸ πνεῦμα. 35 ὁ
speaks; for not by measure [2]gives [1]God the Spirit. The
πατὴρ ἀγαπᾷ τὸν υἱόν, καὶ πάντα δέδωκεν ἐν τῇ.χειρὶ.αὐ-
Father loves the Son, and all things has given into his hand.
τοῦ. 36 ὁ πιστεύων εἰς τὸν υἱὸν ἔχει ζωὴν αἰώνιον· ὁ.[c]δὲ‖
He that believes on the Son has life eternal; and he that
ἀπειθῶν τῷ υἱῷ οὐκ.ὄψεται ζωήν, ἀλλ' ἡ ὀργὴ τοῦ θεοῦ
is not subject to the Son shall not see life, but the wrath of God
μένει ἐπ' αὐτόν.
abides on him.

4 Ὡς οὖν ἔγνω ὁ [d]κύριος‖ ὅτι ἤκουσαν οἱ Φαρισαῖοι,
When therefore [3]knew [1]the [2]Lord that [3]heard [1]the [2]Pharisees,
ὅτι Ἰησοῦς πλείονας μαθητὰς ποιεῖ καὶ βαπτίζει ἢ [e]Ἰωάν-
that Jesus more disciples makes and baptizes than John
νης‖ 2 καίτοιγε Ἰησοῦς αὐτὸς οὐκ.ἐβάπτιζεν, ἀλλ' οἱ
(although indeed Jesus himself was not baptizing but
μαθηταὶ.αὐτοῦ· 3 ἀφῆκεν τὴν Ἰουδαίαν, καὶ ἀπῆλθεν πάλιν
his disciples), he left Judæa, and went away again

believed on the name of the only-begotten
Son of God.
19 And this is the judgment, that the Light
has come into the world and men loved the
darkness rather than the Light – for their
works were evil.
20 For everyone that practices evil hates the
Light and does not come to the Light, so
that his works may not be discovered.
21 But he that practices the truth comes to
the Light, so that his works may be known,
that they have been worked in him by God.
22 After these things Jesus and His disciples
came into the land of Judea. And He stayed
there with them and was baptizing.
23 And John was also baptizing, in Enon,
near Salim, because there were many waters
there. And they were coming and were being
baptized –
24 for John was not yet thrown into prison.
25 Then there arose a question from the
disciples of John with Jews about cleansing.
26 And they came to John and said to him,
Rabbi, He who was with you beyond the
Jordan, to whom you have borne witness –
see, He is baptizing and all are coming to
Him.
27 John answered and said, A man is not
able to receive anything unless it is given to
him from Heaven.
28 You yourselves bear me witness that I
said, I am not the Christ, but that I am sent
before Him.
29 He that has the bride is the bridegroom.
But the friend of the bridegroom, who
stands and hears him, rejoices greatly because of the bridegroom's voice. So my joy
is full.
30 It is right for Him to increase, but me to
decrease.
31 He who comes from above is above all.
He who is from the earth is of the earth, and
he speaks of the earth. He who comes from
Heaven is above all,
32 and what He has seen and heard, this He
testifies, but no one receives His witness.
33 He who has received His witness has set
his seal, that God is true.
34 For He whom God has sent speaks the
words of God, for God does not give the
Spirit by measure.
35 The Father loves the Son and has given
all things into His hand.
36 He that believes on the Son has everlasting life. But he that refuses to obey the Son
shall not see life, but the wrath of God remains on him.

CHAPTER 4

1 Then when the Lord knew that the Pharisees had heard that Jesus was making and
baptizing more disciples than John
2 (although indeed Jesus Himself was not
baptizing, but His disciples,)
3 He left Judea and went away again into
Galilee.

εἰς τὴν Γαλιλαίαν. 4 ἔδει.δὲ αὐτὸν διέρχεσθαι διὰ τῆς
into Galilee. And it was necessary for him to pass through
[f]Σαμαρείας." 5 ἔρχεται οὖν εἰς πόλιν τῆς [f]Σαμαρείας" λεγο-
Samaria. He comes therefore to a city of Samaria call-
μένην [k]Συχάρ," πλησίον τοῦ χωρίου [h]ὃ" ἔδωκεν Ἰακὼβ
ed Sychar, near the land which [2]gave [1]Jacob
Ἰωσὴφ τῷ.υἱῷ.αὐτοῦ. 6 ἦν.δὲ ἐκεῖ πηγὴ τοῦ Ἰακώβ.
to Joseph his son. Now [3]was [4]there [2]fountain [1]Jacob's;
ὁ.οὖν.Ἰησοῦς κεκοπιακὼς ἐκ τῆς ὁδοιπορίας ἐκαθέζετο οὕτως
Jesus therefore, being wearied from the journey, sat thus
ἐπὶ τῇ πηγῇ. ὥρα ἦν [i]ὡσεὶ" ἕκτη. 7 Ἔρχεται γυνὴ
at the fountain. [The] hour was about [the] sixth. Comes a woman
ἐκ τῆς [f]Σαμαρείας" ἀντλῆσαι ὕδωρ. λέγει αὐτῇ ὁ Ἰησοῦς,
out of Samaria to draw water. [2]Says [3]to [4]her [1]Jesus,
Δός μοι [k]πιεῖν." 8 οἱ.γὰρ.μαθηταὶ.αὐτοῦ ἀπεληλύθεισαν εἰς
Give me to drink; for his disciples had gone away into
τὴν πόλιν, ἵνα τροφὰς ἀγοράσωσιν. 9 Λέγει [l]οὖν" αὐτῷ
the city, that provisions they might buy. [5]Says [4]therefore [6]to [7]him
ἡ γυνὴ ἡ [m]Σαμαρεῖτις," Πῶς σὺ Ἰουδαῖος ὢν παρ' ἐμοῦ
[1]the [3]woman [2]Samaritan, How [2]thou [4]a [5]Jew [3]being [9]from [10]me
[n]πιεῖν αἰτεῖς, [o]οὔσης γυναικὸς Σαμαρείτιδος"; [p]οὐ.γὰρ
[7]to [8]drink [1]dost [6]ask, being a [2]woman [1]Samaritan? For [3]no
συγχρῶνται Ἰουδαῖοι Σαμαρείταις." 10 Ἀπεκρίθη Ἰησοῦς
[2]have [4]intercourse [1]Jews with Samaritans. [2]Answered [1]Jesus
καὶ εἶπεν αὐτῇ, Εἰ ᾔδεις τὴν δωρεὰν τοῦ θεοῦ, καὶ τίς
and said to her, If thou hadst known the gift of God, and who
ἐστιν ὁ λέγων σοι, Δός μοι [k]πιεῖν," σὺ ἂν.ᾔτησας
it is that says to thee, Give me to drink, thou wouldest have asked
αὐτόν, καὶ ἔδωκεν.ἂν σοι ὕδωρ ζῶν. 11 Λέγει αὐτῷ [q]ἡ
him, and he would have given to thee [2]water [1]living. [3]Says [4]to [5]him [1]the
γυνή," Κύριε, οὔτε ἄντλημα ἔχεις, καὶ τὸ φρέαρ ἐστὶν
[2]woman, Sir, nothing to draw with thou hast, and the well is
βαθύ· πόθεν [l]οὖν" ἔχεις τὸ ὕδωρ τὸ ζῶν; 12 μὴ σὺ.μείζων.εἶ
deep; whence then hast thou the [2]water [1]living? Art thou greater
τοῦ.πατρὸς.ἡμῶν Ἰακώβ, ὃς ἔδωκεν ἡμῖν τὸ φρέαρ, καὶ αὐτὸς
than our father Jacob, who gave us the well, and himself
ἐξ αὐτοῦ ἔπιεν, καὶ οἱ.υἱοὶ.αὐτοῦ καὶ τὰ.θρέμματα.αὐτοῦ;
of it drank, and his sons and his cattle?
13 Ἀπεκρίθη [r]ὁ" Ἰησοῦς καὶ εἶπεν αὐτῇ, Πᾶς ὁ πίνων ἐκ
[2]Answered [1]Jesus and said to her, Everyone that drinks of
τοῦ.ὕδατος.τούτου διψήσει πάλιν· 14 ὃς.δ'.ἂν πίῃ ἐκ τοῦ
this water will thirst again; but whoever may drink of the
ὕδατος οὗ ἐγὼ δώσω αὐτῷ [v]οὐ.μὴ [w]διψήσῃ' εἰς τὸν.αἰῶνα·
water which I will give him in no wise shall thirst for ever,
ἀλλ' τὸ ὕδωρ ὃ [x] δώσω αὐτῷ" γενήσεται ἐν αὐτῷ πηγὴ
but the water which I will give to him shall become in him a fountain
ὕδατος ἁλλομένου εἰς ζωὴν αἰώνιον. 15 Λέγει πρὸς αὐτὸν
of water springing up into life eternal. [3]Says [4]to [5]him
ἡ γυνή, Κύριε, δός μοι τοῦτο τὸ ὕδωρ, ἵνα μὴ.διψῶ
[1]the [2]woman, Sir, give me this water, that I may not thirst
μηδὲ [y]ἔρχωμαι" ἐνθάδε ἀντλεῖν. 16 Λέγει αὐτῇ [z]ὁ" [a]Ἰησοῦς,"
nor come here to draw. [2]Says [3]to [4]her [1]Jesus,
Ὕπαγε, φώνησον [b]τὸν.ἄνδρα σου" καὶ ἐλθὲ ἐνθάδε. 17 Ἀπε-
Go, call thy husband and come here. [2]An-
κρίθη ἡ γυνὴ καὶ εἶπεν[c], [d]Οὐκ.ἔχω ἄνδρα." Λέγει αὐτῇ ὁ
swered [1]the [2]woman and said, I have not a husband. [2]Says [3]to [4]her
Ἰησοῦς, Καλῶς [e]εἶπας," Ὅτι ἄνδρα οὐκ.ἔχω· 18 πέντε
[1]Jesus, Well didst thou say, A husband I have not; [2]five
γὰρ ἄνδρας ἔσχες. καὶ νῦν ὃν ἔχεις οὐκ.ἔστιν σου
[1]for husbands thou hast had, and now he whom thou hast is not thy
ἀνήρ· τοῦτο ἀληθὲς εἴρηκας. 19 Λέγει αὐτῷ ἡ γυνή,
husband: this truly thou hast spoken. [3]Says [4]to [5]him [1]the [2]woman,
Κύριε, θεωρῶ ὅτι προφήτης εἶ σύ. 20 οἱ πατέρες.ἡμῶν ἐν
Sir, I perceive that a prophet [2]art [1]thou. Our fathers in
[f]τούτῳ τῷ ὄρει" προσεκύνησαν· καὶ ὑμεῖς λέγετε ὅτι ἐν Ἱε-
this mountain worshipped, and ye say that in Je-
ροσολύμοις ἐστὶν ὁ τόπος ὅπου [g]δεῖ προσκυνεῖν." 21 Λέγει
rusalem is the place where it is necessary to worship. [2]Says
αὐτῇ ὁ Ἰησοῦς, [h]Γύναι, πίστευσόν μοι," ὅτι ἔρχεται ὥρα ὅτε
[3]to [4]her [1]Jesus, Woman, believe me, that is coming an hour when
οὔτε ἐν τῷ.ὄρει.τούτῳ οὔτε ἐν Ἱεροσολύμοις προσκυνήσετε
neither in this mountain nor in Jerusalem shall ye worship
τῷ πατρί. 22 ὑμεῖς προσκυνεῖτε ὃ οὐκ.οἴδατε· ἡμεῖς προσ-
the Father. Ye worship what ye know not: we wor-
κυνοῦμεν ὃ οἴδαμεν· ὅτι ἡ σωτηρία ἐκ τῶν Ἰουδαίων ἐστίν.
ship what we know; for salvation of the Jews is.
23 [i]ἀλλ'" ἔρχεται ὥρα καὶ νῦν ἐστιν, ὅτε οἱ ἀληθινοὶ προσ-
But is coming an hour and now is, when the true wor-
κυνηταὶ προσκυνήσουσιν τῷ πατρὶ ἐν πνεύματι καὶ ἀληθείᾳ·
shippers will worship the Father in spirit and truth;
καὶ γὰρ ὁ πατὴρ τοιούτους ζητεῖ τοὺς προσκυνοῦντας αὐτόν.
for also the Father [2]such [1]seeks who worship him.

4 And it was necessary for Him to go through Sa-mar-i-a.

5 Then He came to a city of Sa-mar-i-a called Sy-char, near the piece of ground which Jacob gave to his son Joseph.

6 And Jacob's well was there. Jesus, then, being wearied from the journey, sat on the well in a certain way, about the sixth hour.

7 A woman came out of Sa-mar-i-a to draw water. Jesus said to her, Give Me a drink.

8 (For His disciples had gone into the city in order to buy food.)

9 The Sa-mar-i-tan woman said to Him, How is it that you, being a Jew, ask a drink of me, being a Sa-mar-i-tan woman? For Jews do not have any dealings with Sa-mar-i-tans.

10 Jesus answered and said to her, If you had known the gift of God and who it is that says to you, Give Me a drink, you would have asked Him and He would have given living water to you.

11 The woman said to Him, Sir, you have nothing to draw with, and the well is deep. Where then do you get the living water?

12 Are you greater than our father Jacob, who gave us this well and drank of it himself, also his sons and his cattle?

13 Jesus answered and said to her, Everyone that drinks of this water will thirst again.

14 But whoever may drink of the water which I will give him will never ever thirst – but the water which I will give to him shall become within him a well of water springing up into everlasting life.

15 The woman said to Him, Sir, give me this water so that I may not thirst nor come here to draw.

16 Jesus said to her, Go call your husband and come back here.

17 The woman answered and said, I have no husband. Jesus said to her, Well did you say, I have no husband.

18 For you have had five husbands, and he whom you now have is not your husband. You have truly spoken this.

19 The woman said to Him, Sir, I see that you are a prophet.

20 Our fathers worshiped in this mountain and you say that in Jerusalem is the place where it is right to worship.

21 Jesus said to her, Woman, believe Me that the time will be when you will neither worship the Father in this mountain nor in Jerusalem.

22 You worship what you do not know. We worship that we know. For salvation is of the Jews.

23 But the hour is coming, and now is, when the true worshipers will worship the Father in spirit and in truth. For the Father also desires to find those who worship Him.

24 Πνεῦμα ὁ θεός· καὶ τοὺς προσκυνοῦντας ᵏαὐτὸν‖ ἐν
A spirit God [is], and they that worship him, in
πνεύματι καὶ ἀληθείᾳ ˡδεῖ προσκυνεῖν.‖ 25 Λέγει αὐτῷ ἡ
spirit and truth must worship. ³Says ⁴to ⁵him ¹the
γυνή, Οἶδα ὅτι μεσσίας ἔρχεται, ὁ λεγόμενος χριστός· ὅταν
²woman, I know that Messias is coming, who is called Christ; when
ἔλθῃ ἐκεῖνος ἀναγγελεῖ ἡμῖν ᵐπάντα.‖ 26 Λέγει αὐτῇ ὁ Ἰη-
²comes ¹he he will tell us all things. ²Says ³to ⁴her ¹Je-
σοῦς, Ἐγώ εἰμι, ὁ λαλῶν σοι. 27 Καὶ ἐπὶ τούτῳ
sus, I ⁶am [⁷he],·¹who ²am ³speaking ⁴to ⁵thee. And upon this
ⁿἦλθον‖ οἱ.μαθηταὶ.αὐτοῦ, καὶ ᵒἐθαύμασαν‖ ὅτι μετὰ γυναικὸς
came his disciples, and wondered that with a woman
ἐλάλει· οὐδεὶς μέντοι εἶπεν, Τί ζητεῖς; ἤ Τί λα-
he was speaking; no one however said, What seekest thou? or Why speakest
λεῖς μετ' αὐτῆς;
thou with her?

28 Ἀφῆκεν οὖν τὴν.ὑδρίαν.αὐτῆς ἡ γυνὴ καὶ ἀπῆλθεν εἰς
⁴Left ³then ⁵her ⁶waterpot ¹the ²woman and went away into
τὴν πόλιν, καὶ λέγει τοῖς ἀνθρώποις, 29 Δεῦτε, ἴδετε ἄνθρω-
the city, and says to the men, Come, see a man
πον ὃς εἶπέν μοι πάντα ᵖὅσα‖ ἐποίησα· μήτι οὗτός ἐστιν
who told me all things whatsoever I did: ³perchance ²this ¹is
ὁ χριστός; 30 ᑫἘξῆλθον ʳοὖν‖ ἐκ τῆς πόλεως, καὶ ἤρ-
the Christ! They went forth therefore out of the city, and came
χοντο πρὸς αὐτόν.
unto him.

31 Ἐν.ˢδὲ‖ τῷ μεταξὺ ἠρώτων αὐτὸν οἱ μαθηταί, λέ-
But in the meantime ³were ⁴asking ⁵him ¹the ²disciples, say-
γοντες, ᵗῬαββί,‖ φάγε. 32 Ὁ.δὲ εἶπεν αὐτοῖς, Ἐγὼ βρῶσιν
ing, Rabbi, eat. But he said to them, I meat
ἔχω φαγεῖν ἣν ὑμεῖς οὐκ.οἴδατε. 33 Ἔλεγον ᵛοὖν‖ οἱ μαθη-
have to eat which ye know not. ⁴Said ³therefore ¹the ²disci-
ταὶ πρὸς ἀλλήλους, Μή τις ἤνεγκεν αὐτῷ φαγεῖν;
ples to one another, ²Anyone ¹did bring him [anything] to eat?
34 Λέγει αὐτοῖς ὁ Ἰησοῦς, Ἐμὸν βρῶμά ἐστιν ἵνα ˣποιῶ‖ τὸ
²Says ³to ⁴them ¹Jesus, My meat is that I should do the
θέλημα τοῦ πέμψαντός με, καὶ τελειώσω αὐτοῦ τὸ ἔργον.
will of him who sent me, and should finish his work.
35 οὐχ ὑμεῖς λέγετε, ὅτι ἔτι ʸτετράμηνόν‖ ἐστιν καὶ ὁ θερισμὸς
²Not ³ye ¹say, that yet four months it is and the harvest
ἔρχεται; ἰδού, λέγω ὑμῖν, Ἐπάρατε τοὺς.ὀφθαλμοὺς.ὑμῶν καὶ
comes? Behold, I say to you, Lift up your eyes and
θεάσασθε τὰς χώρας, ὅτι λευκαί εἰσιν πρὸς θερισμὸν ᶻἤδη.‖
see the fields, for white they are to harvest already.
36 ᵃκαὶ‖ ὁ θερίζων μισθὸν λαμβάνει, καὶ συνάγει καρπὸν
And he that reaps a reward receives, and gathers fruit
εἰς ζωὴν αἰώνιον· ἵνα ᵇκαὶ‖ ὁ σπείρων ὁμοῦ χαίρῃ
unto life eternal, that both he that sows ⁷together ⁵may ⁶rejoice
καὶ ὁ θερίζων. 37 ἐν.γὰρ τούτῳ ὁ λόγος ἐστὶν ᶜὁ‖ ἀλη-
¹and ²he ³that ⁴reaps. For in this the saying is true,
θινός, ὅτι ἄλλος ἐστὶν ὁ σπείρων, καὶ ἄλλος ὁ θερίζων.
That ³one ¹it ²is who sows, and another who reaps.
38 ἐγὼ ᵈἀπέστειλα‖ ὑμᾶς θερίζειν ὃ οὐχ ὑμεῖς κεκοπιάκατε·
I sent you to reap on which ³not ¹ye ²have laboured;
ἄλλοι κεκοπιάκασιν, καὶ ὑμεῖς εἰς τὸν.κόπον.αὐτῶν εἰσεληλύ-
others have laboured, and ye into their labour have en-
θατε.
tered.

39 Ἐκ.δὲ τῆς.πόλεως.ἐκείνης πολλοὶ ἐπίστευσαν εἰς αὐτὸν
But out of that city many believed on him
τῶν ᵉΣαμαρειτῶν,‖ διὰ τὸν λόγον τῆς γυναικὸς μαρ-
of the Samaritans, because of the word of the woman tes-
τυρούσης, Ὅτι εἶπέν μοι πάντα ᶠὅσα‖ ἐποίησα. 40 Ὡς
tifying, He told me all things whatsoever I did. When
οὖν ἦλθον πρὸς αὐτὸν οἱ ᵍΣαμαρεῖται,‖ ἠρώτων αὐτὸν
therefore came to him the Samaritans, they asked him
μεῖναι παρ' αὐτοῖς· καὶ ἔμεινεν ἐκεῖ δύο ἡμέρας. 41 καὶ
to abide with them, and he abode there two days. And
πολλῷ.πλείους ἐπίστευσαν διὰ τὸν.λόγον.αὐτοῦ· 42 τῇ.τε
many more believed because of his word; and to the
γυναικὶ ἔλεγον, ʰὍτι‖ οὐκέτι διὰ τὴν σὴν λαλιὰν πισ-
woman they said, No longer because of thy saying we
τεύομεν· αὐτοὶ.γὰρ ἀκηκόαμεν, καὶ οἴδαμεν ὅτι οὗτός ἐστιν
believe, for ourselves have heard, and we know that this is
ἀληθῶς ὁ σωτὴρ τοῦ κόσμου, ⁱὁ χριστός.‖
truly the Saviour of the world, the Christ.

43 Μετὰ.δὲ τὰς δύο ἡμέρας ἐξῆλθεν ἐκεῖθεν, ᵏκαὶ ἀπῆλ-
But after the two days he went forth thence, and went
θεν‖ εἰς τὴν Γαλιλαίαν. 44 αὐτὸς.γὰρ ˡὁ‖ Ἰησοῦς ἐμαρτύρη-
away into Galilee; for ²himself ¹Jesus testified,
σεν, ὅτι προφήτης ἐν τῇ.ἰδίᾳ πατρίδι τιμὴν οὐκ.ἔχει.
that a prophet in his own country honour has not.

24 God is a spirit, and they that worship Him must worship in spirit and truth.
25 The woman said to Him, I know that Messiah is coming, who is called Christ. When He comes He will tell us all things.
26 Jesus said to her, I AM *is the* one speaking to you.
27 And on this His disciples came and wondered that He talked with the woman. But no one said, What do You desire? Or, Why do You speak with her?

28 The woman then left her waterpot and went into the city and said to the men,
29 Come and see a Man who told me all the things I ever did. Is this not the Christ?
30 So they left the city and came to Him.

31 But in the meantime, His disciples were asking Him, saying, Master, eat.
32 But He said to them, I have food to eat which you do not know.
33 So the disciples said to one another, Did anyone bring Him *anything* to eat?
34 Jesus said to them, My food is to do the will of Him who sent Me and to finish His work.
35 Do not say that it is yet four months and the harvest comes. Behold! I say to you, Lift up your eyes and look at the fields, for they are white to harvest already.
36 And he that reaps receives a reward and gathers fruit to everlasting life, so that both he that is sowing and he that is reaping may rejoice together.
37 For in this the saying is true, that there is one who sows and another who reaps
38 I sent you to reap that on which you have not labored. Others have labored and you have entered into their labor.

39 And many of the Sa-mar-i-tans out of that city believed on Him, because of the woman's word, saying, He told me all things I ever did.
40 Then when the Sa-mar-i-tans came to Him, they asked Him to stay with them. And He stayed there two days.
41 And many more believed because of His word
42 and said to the woman, We no longer believe because of your saying, for we ourselves have heard. And we know that this is truly the Savior of the world, the Christ.

43 But after the two days, He left and went into Galilee.
44 For Jesus Himself witnessed that a prophet has no honor in his own country.

45 [m]"Ότε" οὖν ἦλθεν εἰς τὴν Γαλιλαίαν ἐδέξαντο αὐτὸν
When therefore he came into Galilee [3]received [4]him
οἱ Γαλιλαῖοι, πάντα ἑωρακότες [n]ἃ" ἐποίησεν ἐν Ἱε-
[1]the [2]Galileans, all things having seen which he did in Je-
ροσολύμοις ἐν τῇ ἑορτῇ· καὶ.αὐτοὶ.γὰρ ἦλθον εἰς τὴν
rusalem during the feast, for they also went to the
ἑορτήν.
feast.
46 Ἦλθεν οὖν [o]ὁ Ἰησοῦς" πάλιν [p]εἰς τὴν Κανᾶ τῆς
[2]Came [3]therefore [1]Jesus again to Cana
Γαλιλαίας, ὅπου ἐποίησεν τὸ ὕδωρ οἶνον. [q]καὶ ἦν" τις
of Galilee, where he made the water wine. And there was a certain
βασιλικός, οὗ ὁ υἱὸς ἠσθένει ἐν [r]Καπερναούμ." 47 οὗτος
courtier, whose son was sick in Capernaum. He
ἀκούσας ὅτι Ἰησοῦς ἥκει ἐκ τῆς Ἰουδαίας εἰς τὴν Γαλι-
having heard that Jesus had come out of Judæa into Gali-
λαίαν, ἀπῆλθεν πρὸς αὐτόν, καὶ ἠρώτα [s]αὐτὸν" ἵνα κατα-
lee, went to him, and asked him that he would
βῇ καὶ ἰάσηται αὐτοῦ τὸν υἱόν· ἤμελλεν.γὰρ ἀποθνήσκειν.
come down and heal his son; for he was about to die.
48 εἶπεν οὖν ὁ Ἰησοῦς πρὸς αὐτόν, Ἐὰν.μὴ σημεῖα καὶ
[3]Said [2]therefore [1]Jesus to him, Unless signs and
τέρατα ἴδητε οὐ.μὴ πιστεύσητε. 49 Λέγει πρὸς αὐτὸν ὁ
wonders ye see in no wise will ye believe. [3]Says [4]to [5]him [1]the
βασιλικός, Κύριε, κατάβηθι πρὶν ἀποθανεῖν τὸ.παιδίον.μου.
[2]courtier, Sir, come down before [4]dies [1]my [2]little [3]child.
50 Λέγει αὐτῷ ὁ Ἰησοῦς, Πορεύου· ὁ.υἱός.σου ζῇ. [t]Καὶ"
[2]Says [3]to [4]him [1]Jesus, Go, thy son lives. And
ἐπίστευσεν ὁ ἄνθρωπος τῷ λόγῳ [v]ᾧ" εἶπεν αὐτῷ [w]Ἰησοῦς,
[3]believed [1]the [2]man the word which [2]said [3]to [4]him [1]Jesus,
καὶ ἐπορεύετο. 51 ἤδη.δὲ αὐτοῦ.καταβαίνοντος οἱ.δοῦλοι.[x]αὐ-
and went away. But already as he was going down his bondmen
τοῦ" [y]ἀπήντησαν" αὐτῷ, [z]καὶ ἀπήγγειλαν" [a]λέγοντες," "Οτι
met him, and reported, saying,
ὁ.παῖς.[b]σου" ζῇ. 52 Ἐπύθετο οὖν [c]παρ' αὐτῶν τὴν ὥραν"
Thy child lives. He inquired therefore from them the hour
ἐν ᾗ κομψότερον ἔσχεν. [d]καὶ εἶπον" αὐτῷ, "Οτι [e]χθὲς"
in which [3]better [1]he [2]got. And they said to him, Yesterday
ὥραν ἑβδόμην ἀφῆκεν αὐτὸν ὁ πυρετός. 53 "Εγνω
[at the] [2]hour [1]seventh left him the fever. [3]Knew
οὖν ὁ πατὴρ ὅτι [f]ἐν" ἐκείνῃ τῇ ὥρᾳ ἐν ᾗ εἶπεν
[4]therefore [1]the [2]father that [it was] at that hour in which [2]said
αὐτῷ ὁ Ἰησοῦς, [g]"Οτι" ὁ.υἱός.σου ζῇ. Καὶ ἐπίστευσεν αὐτὸς
[3]to [4]him [1]Jesus, Thy son lives. And he [2]believed [1]himself
καὶ ἡ.οἰκία.αὐτοῦ ὅλη. 54 τοῦτο [h]πάλιν δεύτερον σημεῖον
and his [2]house [1]whole. This again a second sign
ἐποίησεν ὁ Ἰησοῦς, ἐλθὼν ἐκ τῆς Ἰουδαίας εἰς τὴν Γα-
did Jesus, having come out of Judæa into Ga-
λιλαίαν.
lilee.
5 Μετὰ ταῦτα ἦν [i]ἑορτὴ τῶν Ἰουδαίων, καὶ ἀνέβη [k]ὁ"
After these things was a feast of the Jews, and [2]went [3]up
Ἰησοῦς εἰς Ἱεροσόλυμα. 2 ἔστιν.δὲ ἐν τοῖς Ἱεροσολύμοις
[1]Jesus to Jerusalem. And there is in Jerusalem
ἐπὶ τῇ προβατικῇ κολυμβήθρα, [l]ἡ ἐπιλεγομένη" Ἑβραϊστὶ
at the sheepgate a pool, which [is] called in Hebrew
[m]Βηθεσδά," πέντε στοὰς ἔχουσα. 3 ἐν ταύταις κατέκειτο
Bethesda, five porches having. In these were lying
πλῆθος [n]πολὺ" τῶν ἀσθενούντων, τυφλῶν, χωλῶν,
a [2]multitude [1]great of those who were sick, blind, lame,
ξηρῶν, [o]ἐκδεχομένων τὴν τοῦ ὕδατος κίνησιν. 4 ἄγγελος
withered, awaiting the [2]of [3]the [4]water [1]moving. [2]An [1]angel
γὰρ [p] κατὰ.καιρὸν κατέβαινεν ἐν τῇ κολυμβήθρᾳ, καὶ ἐτά-
[1]for from time to time descended in the pool, and agi-
ρασσεν τὸ ὕδωρ· ὁ οὖν πρῶτος ἐμβὰς μετὰ τὴν ταραχὴν
tated the water. He who therefore first entered after the agitation
τοῦ ὕδατος, ὑγιὴς ἐγίνετο, [q]ᾧ.δήποτε" κατείχετο νοσήματι."
of the water, [2]well [1]became, whatever [2]he [3]was [4]held [5]by [1]disease.
5 Ἦν.δέ τις ἄνθρωπος ἐκεῖ [r]τριακονταοκτὼ" ἔτη ἔχων ἐν
But [4]was [1]a [2]certain [3]man there [2]thirty [3]eight [4]years [1]being in
τῇ ἀσθενείᾳ[s]. 6 τοῦτον ἰδὼν ὁ Ἰησοῦς κατακείμενον, καὶ
infirmity. [3]Him [2]seeing [1]Jesus lying, and
γνοὺς ὅτι πολὺν ἤδη χρόνον ἔχει, λέγει αὐτῷ, Θέλεις
knowing that a long [2]already [1]time he has been, says to him, Desirest thou
ὑγιὴς γενέσθαι; 7 ἀπεκρίθη αὐτῷ ὁ ἀσθενῶν, Κύριε, ἄν-
well to become? [4]Answered [5]him [1]the [2]infirm [[3]man], Sir, a
θρωπον οὐκ.ἔχω, ἵνα ὅταν ταραχθῇ τὸ ὕδωρ [t]βάλλῃ"
man I have not, that when [3]has [4]been [5]agitated [1]the [2]water he may put
με εἰς τὴν κολυμβήθραν· ἐν.ᾧ.δὲ ἔρχομαι ἐγὼ ἄλλος πρὸ
me into the pool; but while [2]am [3]coming [1]I another before
ἐμοῦ καταβαίνει. 8 Λέγει αὐτῷ ὁ Ἰησοῦς, [v]"Εγειραι," [w]ἆρον
me descends. [2]Says [3]to [4]him [1]Jesus, Arise, take up

45 Then when He came into Galilee, the Galileans received Him (having seen all the things He did in Jerusalem during the feast – for they also went to the feast).

46 Then Jesus came again into Cana of Galilee, where He made the water into wine. And there was a certain nobleman whose son was ill in Ca-per-na-um.

47 Hearing that Jesus had come out of Judea into Galilee, he went to Him and begged Him that He might come down and heal his son – for he was about to die.

48 Then Jesus said to him, Unless you see miracles and wonders, you will not believe.

49 The nobleman said to Him, Sir, come down before my little child dies.

50 Jesus said to him, Go! Your son lives! And the man believed the word which Jesus spoke to him and went away.

51 But even as he was going down, his servants met him and reported, saying, Your child is alive.

52 He then asked them the hour in which he got better. And they said to him, Yesterday at the seventh hour the fever left him.

53 So the father knew that *it was* at that hour in which Jesus said to him, Your son lives! And he himself believed, also his whole household.

54 This again is a second miracle that Jesus did, coming out of Judea into Galilee.

CHAPTER 5

1 After these things there was a feast of the Jews, and Jesus went up to Jerusalem.

2 Now there is a pool at the Sheepgate in Jerusalem, which is called in Hebrew, Beth-es-da, having five porches.

3 In these were lying a great crowd of those who were sick, blind, lame and withered – awaiting the moving of the water.

4 For at a certain time an angel came down into the pool and stirred the water. Then the first one who entered after the stirring of the water became well, whatever disease held him.

5 And a certain man was there, who had been ill thirty-eight years.

6 Seeing him lying there, and knowing that he had already been there a long time, Jesus said to him, Do you want to become well?

7 The ailing man answered Him, Sir, I have no man, that he may put me into the pool when the water has been stirred. But while I am coming, another goes down in front of me.

8 Jesus said to him, Get up! Take up your bed and walk!

τὸν.xκράββατόν‖.σου, καὶ περιπάτει. 9 Καὶ yεὐθέως‖ ἐγένετο
thy bed, and walk. And immediately 3became
ὑγιὴς ὁ ἄνθρωπος, καὶ ἦρεν τὸν.xκράββατον‖.αὐτοῦ, καὶ
4well 1the 2man, and took up his bed, and
περιεπάτει· ἦν.δὲ σάββατον ἐν ἐκείνῃ τῇ ἡμέρᾳ. 10 zἜλεγον
walked; and it was sabbath on that day. 3Said
οὖν οἱ Ἰουδαῖοι τῷ τεθεραπευμένῳ, Σάββατόν ἐστιν·
4therefore 1the 2Jews to him who had been healed, Sabbath it is,
zοὐκ.ἔξεστίν σοι ἆραι τὸν xκράββατον‖a. 11 b Ἀπεκρίθη
it is not lawful for thee to take up the bed. He answered
αὐτοῖς, Ὁ ποιήσας με ὑγιῆ, ἐκεῖνός μοι εἶπεν, Ἆρον τὸν
them, He who made me well, he to me said, Take up
xκράββατόν‖.σου καὶ περιπάτει. 12 Ἠρώτησαν cοὖν‖ αὐτόν,
thy bed and walk. They asked 2therefore 1him,
Τίς ἐστιν ὁ ἄνθρωπος ὁ εἰπών σοι, Ἆρον dτὸν eκράββατόν
Who is the man who said to thee, Take up 2bed
σου καὶ περιπάτει; 13 Ὁ.δὲ fἰαθεὶς‖ οὐκ.ᾔδει τίς ἐστιν·
1thy and walk? But he who had been healed knew not who it is,
ὁ.γὰρ.Ἰησοῦς ἐξένευσεν, ὄχλου ὄντος ἐν τῷ τόπῳ. 14 Μετὰ
for Jesus had moved away, a crowd being in the place. After
ταῦτα εὑρίσκει αὐτὸν ὁ Ἰησοῦς ἐν τῷ ἱερῷ, καὶ εἶπεν αὐτῷ,
these things 2finds 3him 1Jesus in the temple, and said to him,
Ἴδε ὑγιὴς γέγονας· μηκέτι ἁμάρτανε, ἵνα μὴ χεῖρόν
Behold, well thou hast become: 2no 3more 1sin, that 4not 4worse
gτί σοι‖ γένηται. 15 hἈπῆλθεν ὁ ἄνθρωπος καὶ iἀνήγγειλεν‖
something 5to 6thee 7happens. Went away the man and told
τοῖς Ἰουδαίοις ὅτι Ἰησοῦς ἐστιν ὁ ποιήσας αὐτὸν
the Jews that Jesus it is who made him
ὑγιῆ. 16 Καὶ διὰ τοῦτο ἐδίωκον kτὸν Ἰησοῦν οἱ Ἰουδαῖοι,‖
well. And because of this 3persecuted 4Jesus 1the 2Jews,
lκαὶ ἐζήτουν αὐτὸν ἀποκτεῖναι,‖ ὅτι ταῦτα ἐποίει ἐν σαββάτῳ.
and sought him to kill, because these things he did on a sabbath.
17 ὁ.δὲ.mἸησοῦς‖ ἀπεκρίνατο αὐτοῖς, Ὁ.πατήρ.μου
But Jesus answered them, My Father
ἕως ἄρτι ἐργάζεται, κἀγὼ ἐργάζομαι. 18 Διὰ τοῦτο nοὖν‖
until now works, and I work. Because of this therefore
μᾶλλον ἐζήτουν αὐτὸν οἱ Ἰουδαῖοι ἀποκτεῖναι, ὅτι οὐ μόνον
the more sought 5him 1the 2Jews 3to 4kill, because not only
ἔλυεν τὸ σάββατον, ἀλλὰ καὶ πατέρα ἴδιον ἔλεγεν τὸν
did he break the sabbath, but also 5Father 3his 4own 1called
θεόν, ἴσον ἑαυτὸν ποιῶν τῷ θεῷ. 19 Ἀπεκρίνατο οὖν ὁ
2God, equal 2himself 1making to God. 3Answered 2therefore
Ἰησοῦς καὶ oεἶπεν‖ αὐτοῖς, Ἀμὴν ἀμὴν λέγω ὑμῖν, οὐ δύναται
1Jesus and said to them, Verily verily I say to you, 3is 4able
ὁ υἱὸς ποιεῖν ἀφ' ἑαυτοῦ οὐδέν, pἐὰν‖.μή τι βλέπῃ
1the 2Son to do from himself nothing, unless anything he may see
τὸν πατέρα ποιοῦντα· ἃ.γὰρ.qἂν‖ ἐκεῖνος ποιῇ, ταῦτα καὶ
the Father doing: for whatever he does, these things also
ὁ υἱὸς rὁμοίως ποιεῖ.‖ 20 ὁ γὰρ πατὴρ φιλεῖ τὸν υἱόν, καὶ
the Son in like manner does. For the Father loves the Son, and
πάντα δείκνυσιν αὐτῷ ἃ αὐτὸς ποιεῖ· καὶ μείζονα τούτων
all things shews to him which 2himself 1he does; and greater 2than
δείξει αὐτῷ ἔργα, ἵνα ὑμεῖς sθαυμάζητε.‖ 21 ὥσπερ
3these 4he 5will 6shew 7him 1works, that ye may wonder. 2Even 3as
γὰρ ὁ πατὴρ ἐγείρει τοὺς νεκροὺς καὶ ζωοποιεῖ, οὕτως καὶ ὁ
1for the Father raises up the dead and quickens, thus also the
υἱὸς οὓς θέλει ζωοποιεῖ. 22 οὐδὲ γὰρ ὁ πατὴρ κρίνει οὐδένα,
Son whom he will quickens; for the Father judges no one,
ἀλλὰ τὴν κρίσιν πᾶσαν δέδωκεν τῷ υἱῷ, 23 ἵνα πάντες
but 2judgment 1all has given to the Son, that all
τιμῶσιν τὸν υἱὸν καθὼς τιμῶσιν τὸν πατέρα. ὁ μὴ.τιμῶν
may honour the Son even as they honour the Father. He that honours not
τὸν υἱὸν οὐ τιμᾷ τὸν πατέρα τὸν πέμψαντα αὐτόν. 24 Ἀμὴν
the Son honours not the Father who sent him. Verily
ἀμὴν λέγω ὑμῖν, ὅτι ὁ τὸν λόγον.μου ἀκούων, καὶ πιστεύων
verily I say to you that he that my word hears, and believes
τῷ πέμψαντί με, ἔχει ζωὴν αἰώνιον, καὶ εἰς κρίσιν οὐκ
him who sent me has life eternal, and into judgment 2not
ἔρχεται, ἀλλὰ μεταβέβηκεν ἐκ τοῦ θανάτου εἰς τὴν ζωήν.
1comes, but has passed out of death into life.
25 Ἀμὴν ἀμὴν λέγω ὑμῖν, ὅτι ἔρχεται ὥρα καὶ νῦν ἐστιν,
Verily verily I say to you, that is coming an hour and now is,
ὅτε οἱ νεκροὶ tἀκούσονται‖ τῆς φωνῆς τοῦ υἱοῦ τοῦ θεοῦ, καὶ
when the dead shall hear the voice of the Son of God, and
οἱ ἀκούσαντες vζήσονται.‖ 26 ὥσπερ.γὰρ ὁ πατὴρ ἔχει
those having heard shall live. For even as the Father has
ζωὴν ἐν ἑαυτῷ, οὕτως wἔδωκεν καὶ τῷ υἱῷ ζωὴν ἔχειν
life in himself, so he gave also to the Son life to have
ἐν ἑαυτῷ. 27 καὶ ἐξουσίαν ἔδωκεν αὐτῷ xκαὶ‖ κρίσιν
in himself, and authority gave to him also judgment
ποιεῖν, ὅτι υἱὸς ἀνθρώπου ἐστίν. 28 μὴ.θαυμάζετε τοῦτο·
to execute, because Son of man he is. Wonder not at this,

9 And instantly the man was cured and took up his bed. And he was walking – and that day was a sabbath.

10 So the Jews said to the one who had been healed, It is the Sabbath! It is not lawful for you to carry your bed.

11 He answered them, He who made me well, He said to me, Take up your bed and walk.

12 Then they asked him, Who is the man who said to you, Take up your bed and walk?

13 But he who had been healed did not know who He was. For Jesus had moved away, since a crowd was in that place.

14 Afterward Jesus found him in the Temple and said to him, See, you have become well! Do not sin any more, so that a worse thing does not happen to you.

15 The man went away and told the Jews that it was Jesus who made him well.

16 And because of this the Jews persecuted Jesus and wanted to kill Him, because He had done these things on the Sabbath.

17 But Jesus answered them, My Father works until now, and I work.

18 Because of this, then, the Jews wanted all the more to kill Him, because He not only broke the sabbath, but also called God His own Father, making Himself equal with God.

19 Then Jesus answered and said to them, Indeed, I tell you truly that the Son is not able to do anything of Himself, except what He may see the Father doing – for whatever He does, the Son does these things also in the same way.

20 For the Father loves the Son and shows all things to Him which He Himself does. And He will show Him greater works than these in order that you may marvel.

21 For even as the Father raises up the dead and gives life, so the Son also gives life to whomever He will.

22 For the Father judges no one, but has given all judgment to the Son,

23 so that all may honor the Son even as they honor the Father. He that does not honor the Son does not honor the Father who sent Him.

24 Indeed, I tell you truly that He that hears My word and believes on Him who sent Me has everlasting life and does not come into judgment, but has passed out of death into life.

25 Indeed, I tell you truly that the time is coming, and now is, when the dead shall hear the voice of the Son of God, and those that hear shall live.

26 For even as the Father has life in Himself, so also He gave to the Son to have life in Himself.

27 And He gave to Him also authority to execute judgment, because He is the Son of man.

28 Do not wonder at this, for the time is coming in which all those in the graves shall hear His voice

ὅτι ἔρχεται ὥρα ἐν ᾗ πάντες οἱ ἐν τοῖς μνημείοις [l]ἀκού-
for [3]is [4]coming [1]an [2]hour in which all those in the tombs shall
σονται‖ τῆς.φωνῆς.αὐτοῦ, 29 καὶ ἐκπορεύσονται, οἱ τὰ
hear his voice, and shall come forth, those that
ἀγαθὰ ποιήσαντες εἰς ἀνάστασιν ζωῆς, οἱ.[y]δὲ‖ τὰ φαῦλα
good practised to a resurrection of life, and those that evil
πράξαντες εἰς ἀνάστασιν κρίσεως. 30 οὐ δύναμαι ἐγὼ ποιεῖν
did to a resurrection of judgment. [2]Am [3]able [1]I to do
ἀπ' ἐμαυτοῦ οὐδέν· καθὼς ἀκούω κρίνω, καὶ ἡ κρίσις ἡ
from myself nothing; even as I hear I judge, and [2]judgment
ἐμὴ δικαία ἐστίν· ὅτι οὐ.ζητῶ τὸ θέλημα τὸ ἐμόν, ἀλλὰ τὸ
[1]my [4]just [3]is, because I seek not [2]will [1]my, but the
θέλημα τοῦ πέμψαντός με [z]πατρός.‖ 31 Ἐὰν ἐγὼ μαρτυρῶ
will of the [2]who [3]sent [4]me [1]Father. If I bear witness
περὶ ἐμαυτοῦ, ἡ.μαρτυρία.μου οὐκ.ἔστιν ἀληθής. 32 ἄλλος
concerning myself, my witness is not true. Another
ἐστὶν ὁ μαρτυρῶν περὶ ἐμοῦ, καὶ [a]οἶδα‖ ὅτι ἀληθής ἐστιν
it is who bears witness concerning me, and I know that true is
ἡ μαρτυρία ἣν μαρτυρεῖ περὶ ἐμοῦ. 33 Ὑμεῖς ἀπεστάλ-
the witness which he witnesses concerning me. Ye have
κατε πρὸς [b]Ἰωάννην‖ καὶ μεμαρτύρηκεν τῇ ἀληθείᾳ· 34 ἐγὼ
sent unto John and he has borne witness to the truth. [2]I
δὲ οὐ παρὰ ἀνθρώπου τὴν μαρτυρίαν λαμβάνω, ἀλλὰ ταῦ-
[1]but [4]not [6]from [7]man [5]witness [3]receive, but these
τα λέγω ἵνα ὑμεῖς σωθῆτε. 35 ἐκεῖνος ἦν ὁ λύχνος ὁ
things I say that ye may be saved. He was the [4]lamp
καιόμενος καὶ φαίνων, ὑμεῖς.δὲ ἠθελήσατε [c]ἀγαλλιασθῆναι‖
[1]burning [2]and [3]shining, and ye were willing to rejoice
πρὸς ὥραν ἐν τῷ.φωτὶ.αὐτοῦ. 36 ἐγὼ.δὲ ἔχω τὴν μαρτυρίαν
for an hour in his light. But I have the witness
[d]μείζω‖ τοῦ [e]Ἰωάννου·‖ τὰ.γὰρ ἔργα ἃ [f]ἔδωκέν‖ μοι ὁ
greater than John's for the works which [3]gave [4]me [1]the
πατὴρ ἵνα τελειώσω αὐτά, αὐτὰ.τὰ.ἔργα ἃ [g]ἐγὼ‖
[2]Father that I should complete them, the works themselves which I
ποιῶ, μαρτυρεῖ περὶ ἐμοῦ ὅτι ὁ πατήρ με ἀπέσταλκεν.
do, bear witness concerning me that the Father me has sent.
37 καὶ ὁ πέμψας με πατήρ, [h]αὐτὸς‖ μεμαρτύρηκεν περὶ
And the [2]who [3]sent [4]me [1]Father, himself has borne witness concerning
ἐμοῦ. οὔτε φωνὴν.αὐτοῦ [i]ἀκηκόατε πώποτε,‖ οὔτε εἶδος
me. Neither his voice have ye heard at any time, nor [2]form
αὐτοῦ ἑωράκατε. 38 καὶ τὸν.λόγον.αὐτοῦ οὐκ.ἔχετε [k]μένοντα
[1]his have ye seen. And his word ye have not abiding
ἐν ὑμῖν,‖ ὅτι ὃν ἀπέστειλεν ἐκεῖνος, τούτῳ ὑμεῖς οὐ.πιστεύετε.
in you, for whom [2]sent [1]he, him ye believe not.
39 [l]Ἐρευνᾶτε‖ τὰς γραφάς, ὅτι ὑμεῖς δοκεῖτε ἐν αὐταῖς ζωὴν
Ye search the scriptures, for ye think in them life
αἰώνιον ἔχειν, καὶ ἐκεῖναί εἰσιν αἱ μαρτυροῦσαι περὶ
eternal to have, and they are they which bear witness concerning
ἐμοῦ· 40 καὶ οὐ.θέλετε ἐλθεῖν πρός με, ἵνα ζωὴν ἔχητε.
me; and ye are unwilling to come to me, that life ye may have.
41 Δόξαν παρὰ ἀνθρώπων οὐ.λαμβάνω· 42 [m]ἀλλ'‖ ἔγνωκα
Glory from men I receive not; but I have known
ὑμᾶς ὅτι [n]τὴν ἀγάπην τοῦ θεοῦ οὐκ.ἔχετε‖ ἐν ἑαυτοῖς. 43 ἐγὼ
you that the love of God ye have not in yourselves. I
ἐλήλυθα ἐν τῷ ὀνόματι τοῦ.πατρός.μου, καὶ οὐ.λαμβάνετέ με·
have come in the name of my Father, and ye receive not me;
ἐὰν ἄλλος ἔλθῃ ἐν τῷ ὀνόματι τῷ.ἰδίῳ, ἐκεῖνον [o]λήψεσθε.‖
if another should come in [3]name [1]his [2]own, him ye will receive.
44 πῶς δύνασθε.ὑμεῖς πιστεῦσαι, δόξαν [p]παρὰ‖ ἀλλήλων
How are ye able to believe, [3]glory [4]from [5]one [6]another
λαμβάνοντες, καὶ τὴν δόξαν τὴν παρὰ τοῦ μόνου [q]θεοῦ‖
[1]who [2]receive, and the glory which [is] from the only God
οὐ.ζητεῖτε; 45 μὴ.δοκεῖτε ὅτι ἐγὼ κατηγορήσω ὑμῶν πρὸς τὸν
ye seek not? Think not that I will accuse you to the
πατέρα· ἔστιν ὁ κατηγορῶν ὑμῶν, [r]Μωσῆς,‖ εἰς ὃν
Father: there is [one] who accuses you, Moses, in whom
ὑμεῖς ἠλπίκατε. 46 εἰ.γὰρ ἐπιστεύετε [s]Μωσῇ,‖ ἐπιστεύετε.ἂν
ye have hoped. For if ye believed Moses, ye would have believed
ἐμοί· περὶ.γὰρ ἐμοῦ ἐκεῖνος ἔγραψεν. 47 εἰ.δὲ τοῖς ἐκείνου
me, for concerning me he wrote. But if his
γράμμασιν οὐ.πιστεύετε, πῶς τοῖς.ἐμοῖς.ῥήμασιν πιστεύ-
writings ye believe not, how my words shall ye
σετε;
believe?

6 Μετὰ ταῦτα ἀπῆλθεν ὁ Ἰησοῦς πέραν τῆς θαλάσσης
After these things [2]went [3]away [1]Jesus over the sea
τῆς Γαλιλαίας τῆς Τιβεριάδος· 2 [t]καὶ ἠκολούθει‖ αὐτῷ ὄχλος
of Galilee (of Tiberias), and [4]followed [5]him [1]a [3]crowd
πολύς, ὅτι [v]ἑώρων‖ [w]αὐτοῦ‖ τὰ σημεῖα ἃ ἐποίει ἐπὶ
[2]great, because they saw of him the signs which he wrought upon
τῶν ἀσθενούντων. 3 ἀνῆλθεν.δὲ εἰς τὸ ὄρος [x]ὁ‖ Ἰησοῦς,
those who were sick. And [2]went [3]up [4]into [5]the [6]mountain [1]Jesus,

29 and shall come forth – those who practiced good to the resurrection of life – and
those who practiced evil to the resurrection
of judgment.
30 I am not able to do anything of Myself.
Even as I hear, I judge. And My judgment is
right because I do not seek My own will but
the will of the Father who sent Me.
31 If I bear witness about Myself, My
witness is not true.
32 There is another who witnesses about
Me, and I know that the testimony which He
witnesses about Me is true.
33 You have sent to John, and he has witnessed to the truth.
34 But I do not receive witness from man,
but these things I say that you may be saved.
35 He was a burning and shining lamp, and
you were willing to rejoice for an hour in his
light.
36 But I have a witness greater than John's.
For the works which the Father gave Me, that
I should finish them, the works which I do
themselves witness about Me, that the Father
has sent Me.
37 And the Father who sent Me has Himself
witnessed about Me. Neither have you heard
His voice at any time, nor have you seen His
shape.
38 And you do not have His word living
within you, for you do not believe Him whom
He sent.
39 You search the Scriptures, for you think
that in them you have everlasting life. And
those *Scriptures* are they which are witnessing about Me –
40 and you are not willing to come to Me so
that you may have life.
41 I do not receive glory from men –
42 but I have known you, that you do not
have the love of God in yourselves.
43 I have come in the name of My Father,
and you do not receive Me. If another
should come in his own name, you will receive him.
44 How can you believe, you who receive
glory from one another, and the glory which
is from the only God you do not desire?
45 Do not think that I will accuse you to
the Father. There is *one* who accuses you,
Moses, in whom you have hoped.
46 For if you believed Moses, you would
have believed Me, for he wrote of Me.
47 But if you do not believe his writings,
how shall you believe My words?

CHAPTER 6

1 After these things Jesus went away over
the Sea of Galilee, the Ti-ber-i-an *Sea*,
2 and a great crowd followed Him, because
they saw His miracles which He worked on
those who were sick.

καὶ ἐκεῖ [y]ἐκάθητο" μετὰ τῶν.μαθητῶν.αὐτοῦ. 4 ἦν δὲ ἐγγὺς
and there sat with his disciples; and 3was 4near
τὸ πάσχα ἡ ἑορτὴ τῶν Ἰουδαίων. 5 ἐπάρας οὖν [z]ὁ Ἰη-
1the 2passover, the feast of the Jews. 3Having 4lifted 5up 2then 1Je-
σοῦς τοὺς ὀφθαλμούς," καὶ θεασάμενος ὅτι πολὺς ὄχλος
sus [his] eyes, and having seen that a great crowd
ἔρχεται πρὸς αὐτόν, λέγει πρὸς [a]τὸν" Φίλιππον, Πόθεν
is coming to him, he says to Philip, Whence
[b]ἀγοράσομεν" ἄρτους ἵνα φάγωσιν οὗτοι; 6 Τοῦτο.δὲ ἔλεγεν
shall we buy loaves that 2may 3eat 1these? But this he said
πειράζων αὐτόν· αὐτὸς.γὰρ ᾔδει τί ἔμελλεν ποιεῖν. 7 [c]ἀπε-
trying him, for he knew what he was about to do. An-
κρίθη" αὐτῷ [d] Φίλιππος, Διακοσίων δηναρίων ἄρτοι οὐκ
swered him Philip, 6For 3two 4hundred 5denarii 1loaves 7not
ἀρκοῦσιν αὐτοῖς ἵνα ἕκαστος [e]αὐτῶν" βραχύ.[f]τι" λάβῃ.
8are sufficient for them that each of them some little may receive.
8 Λέγει αὐτῷ εἷς ἐκ τῶν.μαθητῶν.αὐτοῦ, Ἀνδρέας ὁ ἀδελφὸς
Says to him one of his disciples, Andrew the brother
Σίμωνος Πέτρου, 9 "Ἔστιν παιδάριον [g]ἓν" ὧδε, [h]ὃ" ἔχει πέντε
of Simon Peter, 4Is 2little 3boy 1a here, who has five
ἄρτους κριθίνους καὶ δύο ὀψάρια· ἀλλὰ ταῦτα τί ἐστιν εἰς
2loaves 1barley and two small fishes; but 3these 1what 2are for
τοσούτους; 10 Εἶπεν.[i]δὲ" ὁ Ἰησοῦς, Ποιήσατε τοὺς ἀνθρώπους
so many? And 2said 1Jesus, Make the men
ἀναπεσεῖν. ἦν.δὲ χόρτος πολὺς ἐν τῷ τόπῳ. [k]ἀνέπεσον"
to recline. Now 3was 2grass 1much in the place: reclined
οὖν οἱ ἄνδρες τὸν ἀριθμὸν [l]ὡσεὶ" πεντακισχίλιοι. 11 ἔλαβεν
therefore the men, the number about five thousand. 3Took
[m]δὲ" τοὺς ἄρτους ὁ Ἰησοῦς, καὶ [n]εὐχαριστήσας διέδωκεν" [o]τοῖς
1and 4the 5loaves 2Jesus, and having given thanks distributed to the
μαθηταῖς, οἱ.δὲ μαθηταὶ" τοῖς ἀνακειμένοις· ὁμοίως.καὶ
disciples, and the disciples to those reclining; and in like manner
ἐκ τῶν ὀψαρίων ὅσον ἤθελον. 12 ὡς.δὲ ἐνεπλήσθησαν
of the small fishes as much as they wished. And when they were filled
λέγει τοῖς.μαθηταῖς.αὐτοῦ, Συναγάγετε τὰ περισσεύσαντα
he says to his disciples, Gather together the 2over 3and 4above
κλάσματα, ἵνα μή.τι ἀπόληται. 13 Συνήγαγον οὖν
1fragments, that nothing may be lost. They gathered together therefore
καὶ ἐγέμισαν δώδεκα κοφίνους κλασμάτων ἐκ τῶν πέντε
and filled twelve hand-baskets of fragments from the five
ἄρτων τῶν κριθίνων ἃ [p]ἐπερίσσευσεν" τοῖς βεβρω-
2loaves 1barley which were over and above to those who had
κόσιν. 14 οἱ.οὖν.ἄνθρωποι ἰδόντες ὃ ἐποίησεν σημεῖον
eaten. The men therefore having seen what 3had 4done 1sign
[q]ὁ Ἰησοῦς," ἔλεγον, Ὅτι οὗτός ἐστιν ἀληθῶς ὁ προφήτης ὁ
2Jesus, said, This is truly the prophet who
[r]ἐρχόμενος εἰς τὸν κόσμον." 15 Ἰησοῦς οὖν γνοὺς ὅτι μέλ-
is coming into the world. Jesus therefore knowing that they
λουσιν ἔρχεσθαι καὶ ἁρπάζειν αὐτόν, ἵνα ποιήσωσιν [s]αὐτὸν"
are about to come and seize him, that they may make him
βασιλέα, [t]ἀνεχώρησεν" πάλιν εἰς τὸ ὄρος αὐτὸς μόνος.
king, withdrew again to the mountain himself alone.
16 Ὡς.δὲ ὀψία ἐγένετο κατέβησαν οἱ.μαθηταὶ.αὐτοῦ ἐπὶ
And when evening it became 3went 4down 1his 2disciples to
τὴν θάλασσαν, 17 καὶ ἐμβάντες εἰς [v]τὸ" πλοῖον ἤρχοντο
the sea, and having entered into the ship they were going
πέραν τῆς θαλάσσης εἰς [w]Καπερναούμ." [x]καὶ σκοτία ἤδη
over the sea to Capernaum. And dark already
ἐγεγόνει," καὶ [y]οὐκ" ἐληλύθει [z]πρὸς αὐτοὺς ὁ Ἰησοῦς," 18 ἥ.τε
it had become, and 3not 2had 4come 5to 6them 1Jesus, and the
θάλασσα ἀνέμου μεγάλου πνέοντος [a]διηγείρετο." 19 ἐληλα-
sea by a 2wind 1strong blowing was agitated. Having
κότες οὖν [b]ὡς" [c]σταδίους" [d]εἰκοσιπέντε" ἢ τριάκοντα θεωροῦσιν
rowed then about 4furlongs 1twenty-five 2or 3thirty they see
τὸν Ἰησοῦν περιπατοῦντα ἐπὶ τῆς θαλάσσης, καὶ ἐγγὺς τοῦ
Jesus walking on the sea, and near the
πλοίου γινόμενον· καὶ ἐφοβήθησαν. 20 ὁ.δὲ λέγει αὐτοῖς,
ship coming, and they were frightened. But he says to them,
Ἐγώ εἰμι· μὴ.φοβεῖσθε. 21 "Ἤθελον οὖν λαβεῖν αὐτὸν
I am [he]; fear not. They were willing then to receive him
εἰς τὸ πλοῖον, καὶ εὐθέως [e]τὸ πλοῖον ἐγένετο" ἐπὶ [f]τῆς γῆς"
into the ship, and immediately the ship was at the land
εἰς ἣν ὑπῆγον.
to which they were going.
22 Τῇ ἐπαύριον ὁ ὄχλος ὁ ἑστηκὼς πέραν τῆς θα-
On the morrow the crowd which stood the other side of the
λάσσης, [g]ἰδὼν" ὅτι πλοιάριον ἄλλο οὐκ ἦν ἐκεῖ εἰ.μὴ ἓν
sea, having seen that 3small 4ship 2other 1no was there except one
[h]ἐκεῖνο εἰς ὃ ἐνέβησαν οἱ.μαθηταὶ.αὐτοῦ," καὶ ὅτι οὐ
that into which entered his disciples, and that 3not
συνεισῆλθεν τοῖς.μαθηταῖς.αὐτοῦ ὁ Ἰησοῦς εἰς τὸ [i]πλοιάριον,"
2went 4with 5his 6disciples 1Jesus into the small ship,

3 And Jesus went up into the mountain and
sat there with His disciples.
4 And the feast of the Jews, the Passover,
was near.
5 Then lifting His eyes and seeing that a
great crowd was coming to Him, Jesus said
to Philip, Where shall we buy loaves that
these may eat?
6 But He said this to test him, for He knew
what He was about to do.
7 Philip answered Him, Two hundred pieces
of silver worth of loaves are not enough for
them, so that each of them may have a little.
8 One of His disciples, Simon Peter's brother,
Andrew, said to Him,
9 Here is a little boy who has five barley
loaves and two small fish. But what are these
for so many?
10 And Jesus said, Make the men sit. Now
there was much grass in the place. So the
men sat about five thousand in number.
11 And Jesus took the loaves. And giving
thanks, He gave to the disciples. And the
disciples gave to those who were sitting.
12 And in the same way *He gave* as many of
the small fish as they wanted. And when
they were full, He said to His disciples,
Gather up the broken pieces which are left,
so that nothing may be lost.
13 Then they gathered up and filled twelve
hand-baskets with broken pieces from the
five barley loaves which were left over to
those who had eaten.
14 Then seeing the miracle which Jesus had
worked, the men said, This is truly the
Prophet who is coming into the world.
15 Then knowing that they were going to
come and take Him by force (so that they
might make Him king,) Jesus drew back
again into the mountain alone.
16 And when evening came, His disciples
went down to the sea.
17 And entering into the ship, they were
going over the sea to Ca-per-na-um. And it
had already become dark. And Jesus had not
come to them.
18 And the sea was turbulent because of a
strong wind blowing.
19 Then after they had pressed forward
about three or four miles, they saw Jesus
walking on the sea. And He was coming near
the ship. And they were afraid.
20 But He said to them, I AM! Do not be
afraid.
21 They were willing, then, to receive Him
into the ship. And instantly the ship was at
the land where they were going.
22 On the following day the people that
stood on the other side of the sea saw that
there was no other small ship there, except
one – the one which His disciples had taken.
And *they saw* that Jesus did not go with His
disciples into the small ship, but that His
disciples went away alone.

ἀλλὰ μόνοι οἱ.μαθηταὶ.αὐτοῦ ἀπῆλθον, 23 ἄλλα.[k]δὲ" [l]ἦλθεν"
but alone his disciples went away, (but other [2]came
[m]πλοιάρια" ἐκ Τιβεριάδος ἐγγὺς τοῦ τόπου ὅπου ἔφαγον τὸν
[1]small [2]ships from Tiberias near the place where they ate the
ἄρτον, εὐχαριστήσαντος τοῦ κυρίου· 24 ὅτε οὖν εἶδεν ὁ
bread, [3]having [4]given [5]thanks [1]the [2]Lord;) when therefore [3]saw [1]the
ὄχλος ὅτι Ἰησοῦς οὐκ ἔστιν ἐκεῖ οὐδὲ οἱ.μαθηταὶ.αὐτοῦ, ἐνέ-
[2]crowd that Jesus [2]not [1]is there nor his disciples, they
βησαν "καὶ" αὐτοὶ εἰς τὰ [o]πλοῖα" καὶ ἦλθον εἰς [p]Καπερ-
[3]entered [1]also [2]themselves into the ships and came to Caper-
ναούμ," ζητοῦντες τὸν Ἰησοῦν. 25 καὶ εὑρόντες αὐτὸν
naum, seeking Jesus. And having found him
πέραν τῆς θαλάσσης, εἶπον αὐτῷ, [q]Ῥαββί," πότε ὧδε
the other side of the sea, they said to him, Rabbi, when here
γέγονας; 26 Ἀπεκρίθη αὐτοῖς ὁ Ἰησοῦς καὶ εἶπεν, Ἀμὴν
hast thou come? [2]Answered [3]them [1]Jesus and said, Verily
ἀμὴν λέγω ὑμῖν, ζητεῖτέ με, οὐχ ὅτι εἴδετε σημεῖα, ἀλλ'
verily I say to you, Ye seek me, not because ye saw signs, but
ὅτι ἐφάγετε ἐκ τῶν ἄρτων καὶ ἐχορτάσθητε. 27 ἐργάζεσθε
because ye ate of the loaves and were satisfied. Work
μὴ τὴν βρῶσιν τὴν.ἀπολλυμένην, ἀλλὰ τὴν βρῶσιν
not [for] the food which perishes, but [for] the food
τὴν μένουσαν εἰς ζωὴν αἰώνιον, ἣν ὁ υἱὸς τοῦ ἀνθρώπου
which abides unto life eternal, which the Son of man
[r]ὑμῖν δώσει·" τοῦτον.γὰρ ὁ πατὴρ ἐσφράγισεν ὁ θεός.
to you will give; for him the Father sealed, [even] God.
28 Εἶπον οὖν πρὸς αὐτόν, Τί [s]ποιοῦμεν," ἵνα ἐργαζώμεθα
They said therefore to him, What do we, that we may work
τὰ ἔργα τοῦ θεοῦ; 29 Ἀπεκρίθη [t]ὁ" Ἰησοῦς καὶ εἶπεν αὐτοῖς,
the works of God? [2]Answered [1]Jesus and said to them,
Τοῦτό ἐστιν τὸ ἔργον τοῦ θεοῦ, ἵνα [v]πιστεύσητε" εἰς ὃν
This is the work of God, that ye should believe on him whom
ἀπέστειλεν ἐκεῖνος. 30 Εἶπον οὖν αὐτῷ, Τί οὖν ποιεῖς
[2]sent [1]he. They said therefore to him, What [2]then [3]doest
σὺ σημεῖον, ἵνα ἴδωμεν καὶ πιστεύσωμέν σοι; τί ἐργάζῃ;
[4]thou [1]sign, that we may see and may believe thee? what dost thou work?
31 οἱ.πατέρες.ἡμῶν τὸ μάννα ἔφαγον ἐν τῇ ἐρήμῳ, καθώς
Our fathers the manna ate in the wilderness, as
ἐστιν γεγραμμένον, Ἄρτον ἐκ τοῦ οὐρανοῦ ἔδωκεν αὐτοῖς
it is written, Bread out of the heaven he gave them
φαγεῖν. 32 Εἶπεν οὖν αὐτοῖς ὁ Ἰησοῦς, Ἀμὴν ἀμὴν λέγω
to eat. [2]Said [3]therefore [4]to [5]them [1]Jesus, Verily verily I say
ὑμῖν, Οὐ [w]Μωσῆς" [x]δέδωκεν" ὑμῖν τὸν ἄρτον ἐκ τοῦ οὐρα-
to you, [2]Not [1]Moses [3]has [4]given you the bread out of the hea-
νοῦ· ἀλλ' ὁ.πατήρ.μου δίδωσιν ὑμῖν τὸν ἄρτον ἐκ τοῦ οὐ-
ven; but my Father gives you the [2]bread [3]out [4]of [5]the [6]hea-
ρανοῦ τὸν ἀληθινόν. 33 ὁ.γὰρ ἄρτος [y] τοῦ θεοῦ ἐστιν ὁ
ven [1]true. For the bread of God is he who
καταβαίνων ἐκ τοῦ οὐρανοῦ, καὶ ζωὴν διδοὺς τῷ κόσμῳ.
comes down out of the heaven, and life gives to the world.
34 Εἶπον οὖν πρὸς αὐτόν, Κύριε, πάντοτε δὸς ἡμῖν τὸν
They said therefore to him, Lord, always give to us
ἄρτον.τοῦτον. 35 Εἶπεν [z]δὲ" αὐτοῖς ὁ Ἰησοῦς, Ἐγώ εἰμι ὁ
this bread. [2]Said [1]and [4]to [5]them [3]Jesus, I am the
ἄρτος τῆς ζωῆς· ὁ ἐρχόμενος πρός [a]με" οὐ.μὴ [b]πεινάσῃ·"
bread of life: he that comes to me in no wise may hunger,
καὶ ὁ πιστεύων εἰς ἐμὲ οὐ.μὴ [c]διψήσῃ" πώποτε. 36 ἀλλ'
and he that believes on me in no wise may thirst at any time. But
εἶπον ὑμῖν ὅτι καὶ ἑωράκατέ [d]με" καὶ οὐ.πιστεύετε. 37 πᾶν
I said to you that also ye have seen me and believe not. All
ὃ δίδωσίν μοι ὁ πατὴρ πρὸς ἐμὲ ἥξει· καὶ τὸν ἐρχό-
that [3]gives [4]me [1]the [2]Father to me shall come, and him that comes
μενον πρός [e]με" οὐ.μὴ ἐκβάλω ἔξω· 38 ὅτι καταβέβηκα
to me not at all will I cast out. For I have come down
[f]ἐκ" τοῦ οὐρανοῦ, οὐχ ἵνα [g]ποιῶ" τὸ θέλημα τὸ ἐμόν, ἀλλὰ
out of the heaven, not that I should do [2]will [1]my, but
τὸ θέλημα τοῦ πέμψαντός με. 39 τοῦτο.δέ ἐστιν τὸ
the will of him who sent me. And this is the
θέλημα τοῦ πέμψαντός με [h]πατρός," ἵνα πᾶν ὃ δέδωκέν
will of the [2]who [3]sent [4]me [1]Father, that [of] all that he has given
μοι, μὴ.ἀπολέσω ἐξ.αὐτοῦ, ἀλλὰ ἀναστήσω αὐτὸ [i]ἐν"
me, I should not lose [any] of it, but should raise up it in
τῇ ἐσχάτῃ ἡμέρᾳ. 40 τοῦτο.[k]δέ" ἐστιν τὸ θέλημα [l]τοῦ
the last day. And this is the will of him who
πέμψαντός με," ἵνα πᾶς ὁ θεωρῶν τὸν υἱὸν καὶ πιστεύων
sent me, that everyone who sees the Son and believes
εἰς αὐτόν, ἔχῃ ζωὴν αἰώνιον, καὶ ἀναστήσω αὐτὸν [m]ἐγὼ"
on him, should have life eternal; and [2]will [3]raise [4]up [5]him [1]I
[n]τῇ ἐσχάτῃ ἡμέρᾳ. 41 Ἐγόγγυζον οὖν οἱ Ἰουδαῖοι περὶ
at the last day. Were murmuring therefore the Jews about
αὐτοῦ, ὅτι εἶπεν, Ἐγώ εἰμι ὁ ἄρτος ὁ καταβὰς ἐκ τοῦ
him, because he said, I am the bread which came down out of the

23 (But other little ships came from Ti-ber-
i-as near the place where they ate the bread,
after the Lord had given thanks.)

24 Then when the people saw that neither
Jesus nor His disciples were there, they also
themselves entered ships. And they came to
Ca-per-na-um looking for Jesus.

25 And when they found Him on the other
side of the sea, they said to Him, Rabbi,
when did you come here?
26 Jesus answered them and said, Indeed, I
tell you truly that you do not seek Me because you saw signs, but because you ate of
the loaves and were satisfied.

27 Do not labor for the food which vanishes
away, but for the food which endures to everlasting life, which the Son of man will give to
you – for Him the Father sealed, *even* God.
28 Then they said to Him, What shall we do
that we may work the works of God?
29 Jesus answered and said to them, This is
the work of God, that you should believe on
Him whom He has sent.
30 Then they said to Him, What miracle will
you do so that we may see and believe you?
What work will you do?
31 Our fathers ate the manna in the wilderness, as it is written, "He gave them bread
out of Heaven to eat."
32 Then Jesus said to them, Indeed, I tell
you truly that Moses did not give you the
bread out of Heaven, but My Father gives
you the true bread out of Heaven.
33 For the bread of God is He who comes
down out of Heaven and gives life to the
world.

34 Then they said to Him, Lord, always give
us this bread.
35 But Jesus said to them, I am the Bread
of life! He that comes to Me shall never ever
hunger. And he that believes on Me shall
never thirst at any time.
36 But I said to you that you also have seen
Me and still do not believe.
37 All that the Father gives Me shall come
to Me, and him that comes to Me I will in no
ways cast out.
38 For I have come down out of Heaven,
not to do My own will, but the will of Him
who sent Me.
39 And this is the will of the Father who
sent Me, that of all that He has given Me I
should not lose *any* of it, but should raise it
up in the last day.
40 And this is the will of Him who sent Me,
that everyone who sees the Son and believes
on Him should have everlasting life – and I
will raise him up at the last day.
41 The Jews then were complaining about
Him, because He said, I am the bread which
came down out of Heaven.

οὐρανοῦ. 42 καὶ ἔλεγον, °Οὐχ"-οὗτός.ἐστιν Ἰησοῦς ὁ υἱὸς
heaven. And were saying, Is not this Jesus the Son

Ἰωσήφ, οὗ ἡμεῖς οἴδαμεν τὸν πατέρα καὶ τὴν μητέρα;
of Joseph, of whom we know the father and the mother?

πῶς [p]οὖν" λέγει [q]οὗτος," Ὅτι ἐκ τοῦ οὐρανοῦ καταβέβηκα;
how therefore says he, Out of the heaven I have come down?

43 Ἀπεκρίθη [r]οὖν" [s]ὁ" Ἰησοῦς καὶ εἶπεν αὐτοῖς, Μὴ.γογγύζετε
[3]Answered [2]therefore [1]Jesus and said to them, Murmur not

[t]μετ'" ἀλλήλων. 44 οὐδεὶς δύναται ἐλθεῖν πρός [v]με" ἐὰν.μὴ
with one another. No one is able to come to me unless

ὁ πατὴρ ὁ πέμψας με ἑλκύσῃ αὐτόν, [w]καὶ ἐγὼ" ἀναστήσω
the Father who sent me draw him, and I will raise up

αὐτὸν [x] τῇ ἐσχάτῃ ἡμέρᾳ. 45 ἔστιν γεγραμμένον ἐν τοῖς προ-
him at the last day. It is written in the pro-

φήταις, Καὶ ἔσονται πάντες διδακτοὶ [y]τοῦ" θεοῦ. Πᾶς
phets, And they shall be all taught of God. Everyone

[z]οὖν" ὁ ἀκούσας παρὰ τοῦ πατρὸς καὶ μαθών, ἔρχεται
therefore that has heard from the Father and has learnt, comes

πρός [a]με·" 46 οὐχ ὅτι τὸν πατέρα [b]τις ἑώρακεν," εἰ.μὴ ὁ
to me: not that [4]the [5]Father [1]anyone [2]has [3]seen, except he who

ὢν παρὰ τοῦ θεοῦ, οὗτος ἑώρακεν τὸν [c]πατέρα." 47 ἀμὴν
is from God, he has seen the Father. Verily

ἀμὴν λέγω ὑμῖν, ὁ πιστεύων [d]εἰς ἐμὲ" ἔχει ζωὴν αἰώνιον.
verily I say to you, He that believes on me has life eternal.

48 ἐγώ εἰμι ὁ ἄρτος τῆς ζωῆς. 49 οἱ.πατέρες.ὑμῶν ἔφαγον
I am the bread of life. Your Fathers ate

[e]τὸ μάννα ἐν τῇ ἐρήμῳ," καὶ ἀπέθανον· 50 οὗτός ἐστιν ὁ
the manna in the desert, and died. This is the

ἄρτος ὁ ἐκ τοῦ οὐρανοῦ καταβαίνων, ἵνα τις ἐξ αὐτοῦ
bread which out of heaven comes down, that anyone of it

φάγῃ καὶ μὴ ἀποθάνῃ. 51 ἐγώ εἰμι ὁ ἄρτος ὁ ζῶν, ὁ
may eat and not die. I am the [2]bread [1]living, which

ἐκ τοῦ οὐρανοῦ καταβάς· ἐάν τις φάγῃ [f]ἐκ τούτου
out of the heaven came down: if anyone shall have eaten of this

τοῦ ἄρτου ζήσεται" εἰς.τὸν.αἰῶνα. καὶ ὁ ἄρτος δὲ ὃν ἐγὼ
bread he shall live for ever; and the bread also which I

δώσω, [g]ἡ.σάρξ.μου ἐστίν, [h]ἣν ἐγὼ δώσω' ὑπὲρ τῆς τοῦ
will give, my flesh is, which I will give for the [2]of [3]the

κόσμου ζωῆς." 52 Ἐμάχοντο οὖν [i]πρὸς ἀλλήλους οἱ Ἰου-
[4]world [1]life. Were contending therefore with one another the Jews

δαῖοι," λέγοντες, Πῶς δύναται [k]οὗτος ἡμῖν" δοῦναι τὴν
saying, How is [2]able [1]he [5]us [3]to [4]give

σάρκα [l] φαγεῖν; 53 Εἶπεν οὖν αὐτοῖς ὁ Ἰησοῦς, Ἀμὴν
[7]flesh [[6]his] to eat? [2]Said [3]therefore [4]to [5]them [1]Jesus, Verily

ἀμὴν λέγω ὑμῖν, ἐὰν.μὴ φάγητε τὴν σάρκα τοῦ υἱοῦ
verily I say to you, Unless ye shall have eaten the flesh of the Son

τοῦ ἀνθρώπου καὶ πίητε αὐτοῦ τὸ αἷμα, οὐκ.ἔχετε ζωὴν
of man and shall have drunk his blood, ye have not life

ἐν ἑαυτοῖς. 54 ὁ τρώγων μου τὴν σάρκα, καὶ πίνων μου
in yourselves. He that eats my flesh, and drinks my

τὸ αἷμα, ἔχει ζωὴν αἰώνιον, [m]καὶ ἐγὼ" ἀναστήσω αὐτὸν [n] τῇ
blood, has life eternal, and I will raise up him in the

ἐσχάτῃ ἡμέρᾳ· 55 ἡ γὰρ.σάρξ μου °ἀληθῶς" ἐστιν βρῶσις, καὶ
last day; for my flesh truly is food, and

τὸ.αἷμά.μου °ἀληθῶς" ἐστιν πόσις. 56 ὁ τρώγων μου τὴν
my blood truly is drink. He that eats my

σάρκα καὶ πίνων μου τὸ αἷμα, ἐν ἐμοὶ μένει, κἀγὼ ἐν αὐτῷ.
flesh and drinks my blood, in me abides, and I in him.

57 καθὼς ἀπέστειλέν με ὁ ζῶν πατήρ, κἀγὼ ζῶ διὰ
As [4]sent [5]me [1]the [2]living [3]Father, and I live because of

τὸν πατέρα· καὶ ὁ τρώγων με, κἀκεῖνος [p]ζήσεται" δι'
the Father, also he that eats me, he also shall live because of

ἐμέ. 58 οὗτός ἐστιν ὁ ἄρτος ὁ [q]ἐκ τοῦ" οὐρανοῦ καταβάς·
me. This is the bread which out of the heaven came down.

οὐ καθὼς ἔφαγον οἱ πατέρες [r]ὑμῶν" [s]τὸ μάννα," καὶ ἀπέθα-
Not as [5]ate [1]the [2]fathers [3]of [4]you the manna, and died:

νον· ὁ τρώγων τοῦτον τὸν ἄρτον [t]ζήσεται" εἰς.τὸν.αἰῶνα.
he that eats this bread shall live for ever.

59 Ταῦτα εἶπεν ἐν συναγωγῇ διδάσκων ἐν [v]Καπερναούμ."
These things he said in [the] synagogue teaching in Capernaum.

60 Πολλοὶ οὖν ἀκούσαντες ἐκ τῶν.μαθητῶν αὐτοῦ εἶπον,
Many therefore [4]having [5]heard [1]of [2]his [3]disciples said,

Σκληρός ἐστιν [w]οὗτος ὁ λόγος·" τίς δύναται αὐτοῦ ἀκούειν;
Hard is this word; who is able it to hear?

61 Εἰδὼς δὲ ὁ Ἰησοῦς ἐν ἑαυτῷ ὅτι γογγύζουσιν περὶ
[3]Knowing [1]but [2]Jesus in himself that [5]murmur [6]concerning

τούτου οἱ.μαθηταὶ.αὐτοῦ εἶπεν αὐτοῖς, Τοῦτο ὑμᾶς σκανδα-
[7]this [3]his [4]disciples said to them, [2]This [5]you [1]does [3]of-

λίζει; 62 ἐὰν οὖν θεωρῆτε τὸν υἱὸν τοῦ ἀνθρώπου ἀνα-
fend? If then ye should see the Son of man ascend-

βαίνοντα ὅπου ἦν τὸ πρότερον; 63 τὸ πνεῦμά ἐστιν τὸ
ing up where he was before? The Spirit it is which

42 And they were saying, Is this not Jesus the son of Joseph, whose father and mother we know? Then how does he now say, I have come down out of Heaven?

43 Jesus then answered them and said, Do not murmur with one another.

44 No one can come to Me unless the Father who sent Me draw him, and I will raise him up at the last day.

45 It is written in the Prophets, "And they shall all be taught of God." So everyone that has heard and has learned from the Father comes to Me –

46 not that anyone has seen the Father – only He who is from God, He has seen the Father.

47 Indeed, I tell you truly that he who believes on Me has everlasting life.

48 I am the Bread of life.

49 Your fathers ate the manna in the desert and died.

50 This is the Bread which comes down out of Heaven, so that anyone may eat of it and not die.

51 I am the Living Bread which came down out of Heaven. If anyone eats of this Bread, he shall live forever. And the bread which I will give for the life of the world is My flesh.

52 So the Jews were arguing with one another, saying, How is he able to give his flesh to eat?

53 Then Jesus said to them, Indeed, I tell you truly that unless you have eaten the flesh of the Son of man and have drunk His blood, you do not have life in yourselves.

54 He that eats My flesh and drinks My blood has everlasting life, and I will raise him up in the last day.

55 For My flesh truly is food, and My blood truly is drink.

56 He that eats My flesh and drinks My blood is living in Me and I in him.

57 As the living Father sent Me, and I live by means of the Father, so he that eats Me also shall live because of Me.

58 This is the Bread which came down out of Heaven, not as your fathers ate the manna and died. He who feeds on this Bread shall live forever.

59 He said these things in the synagogue, teaching in Ca-per-na-um.

60 Then many of His disciples, having heard, said, This word is hard, who is able to hear it?

61 But knowing in Himself that His disciples murmured about this, Jesus said to them, Does this offend you?

62 Then what if you should see the son of man going up where He was before?

63 It is the Spirit who gives life, the flesh

ζωοποιοῦν, ἡ σὰρξ οὐκ ὠφελεῖ οὐδέν· τὰ ῥήματα ἃ ·ἐγὼ
quickens, the flesh profits nothing; the words which I
[x]λαλῶ" ὑμῖν, πνεῦμά ἐστιν καὶ ζωή ἐστιν. 64 [y]ἀλλ'" εἰσὶν
speak to you, spirit are and life are; but there are
ἐξ ὑμῶν τινες οἳ οὐ.πιστεύουσιν. ᾔδει.γὰρ ἐξ ἀρχῆς
of you some who believe not. For [2]knew [3]from [[4]the] [5]beginning
ὁ Ἰησοῦς τίνες εἰσὶν οἱ μὴ.πιστεύοντες, καὶ τίς ἐστιν ὁ
[1]Jesus who they are who believe not, and who is he who
παραδώσων αὐτόν. 65 καὶ ἔλεγεν, Διὰ.τοῦτο εἴρηκα ὑμῖν,
shall deliver up him. And he said, Therefore have I said to you,
ὅτι οὐδεὶς δύναται ἐλθεῖν πρός [z]με" ἐὰν.μὴ ᾖ δεδομένον
that no one is able to come to me unless it be given
αὐτῷ ἐκ τοῦ.πατρός.[a]μου." 66 Ἐκ τούτου [b] πολλοὶ [c]
to him from my Father. From that [time] many
[d]ἀπῆλθον τῶν.μαθητῶν.αὐτοῦ" εἰς.τὰ.ὀπίσω, καὶ οὐκέτι μετ'
[4]went [5]away [1]of [2]his [3]disciples back, and no more with
αὐτοῦ περιεπάτουν. 67 εἶπεν οὖν ὁ Ἰησοῦς τοῖς δώδεκα,
him walked. [2]Said [3]therefore [1]Jesus to the twelve,
Μὴ καὶ ὑμεῖς θέλετε ὑπάγειν; 68 Ἀπεκρίθη [e]οὖν" αὐτῷ
[3]Also [2]ye [1]are [4]wishing to go away? [4]Answered [5]therefore [6]him
Σίμων Πέτρος, Κύριε, πρὸς τίνα ἀπελευσόμεθα; ῥήματα ζωῆς
[1]Simon [2]Peter, Lord, to whom shall we go? words of life
αἰωνίου ἔχεις· 69 καὶ ἡμεῖς πεπιστεύκαμεν καὶ ἐγνώκαμεν
eternal thou hast; and we have believed and have known
ὅτι σὺ εἶ [f]ὁ χριστὸς ὁ υἱὸς" τοῦ θεοῦ [g]τοῦ ζῶντος." 70 Ἀπε-
that thou art the Christ the Son of [3]God [1]the [2]living. An-
κρίθη αὐτοῖς ὁ Ἰησοῦς, Οὐκ ἐγὼ ὑμᾶς τοὺς δώδεκα ἐξελεξάμην,
swered them Jesus, [3]Not [2]I [5]you [6]the [7]twelve [1]did [4]choose,
καὶ ἐξ ὑμῶν εἷς διάβολός ἐστιν; 71 Ἔλεγεν.δὲ τὸν Ἰούδαν
and of you one a devil is? But he spoke of Judas
Σίμωνος [h]Ἰσκαριώτην·" οὗτος.γὰρ [i]ἤμελλεν" [k]αὐτὸν παρα-
Simon's [son], Iscariote, for he was about him to de-
διδόναι," εἷς [l]ὤν" ἐκ τῶν δώδεκα.
liver up, [2]one [1]being of the twelve.

7 [m]Καὶ" [n]περιεπάτει ὁ Ἰησοῦς μετὰ ταῦτα" ἐν τῇ Γαλι-
And [2]was [3]walking [1]Jesus after these things in Gali-
λαίᾳ· οὐ γὰρ ἤθελεν ἐν τῇ Ἰουδαίᾳ περιπατεῖν, ὅτι
lee, [4]not [1]for [2]he [3]did desire in Judæa to walk, because
ἐζήτουν αὐτὸν οἱ Ἰουδαῖοι ἀποκτεῖναι. 2 Ἦν.δὲ ἐγγὺς ἡ
[3]were [4]seeking [5]him [1]the [2]Jews to kill. Now was near the
ἑορτὴ τῶν Ἰουδαίων ἡ σκηνοπηγία. 3 εἶπον οὖν πρὸς αὐτὸν
feast of the Jews, the tabernacles. [3]Said [4]therefore [5]to [6]him
οἱ.ἀδελφοὶ.αὐτοῦ, Μετάβηθι ἐντεῦθεν, καὶ ὕπαγε εἰς τὴν Ἰου-
[1]his [2]brethren, Remove hence, and go into Ju-
δαίαν, ἵνα καὶ οἱ.μαθηταί.σου [o]θεωρήσωσιν" [p]τὰ.ἔργα.σου" ἃ
dæa, that also thy disciples may see thy works which
ποιεῖς· 4 οὐδεὶς.γὰρ [q]ἐν κρυπτῷ τι" ποιεῖ, καὶ ζητεῖ
thou doest; for no one in secret anything does, and seeks
[r]αὐτὸς" ἐν παρρησίᾳ εἶναι. εἰ ταῦτα ποιεῖς, φανέρωσον
himself [3]in [4]public [1]to [2]be. If these things thou doest, manifest
σεαυτὸν τῷ κόσμῳ. 5 Οὐδὲ.γὰρ οἱ.ἀδελφοὶ.αὐτοῦ ἐπίστευον
thyself to the world. For neither [2]his [3]brethren [1]believed
εἰς αὐτόν. 6 Λέγει [s]οὖν" αὐτοῖς ὁ Ἰησοῦς, Ὁ καιρὸς ὁ ἐμὸς
on him. [2]Says [3]therefore [4]to [5]them [1]Jesus, [2]Time [1]my
οὔπω πάρεστιν· ὁ.δὲ καιρὸς ὁ ὑμέτερος πάντοτέ ἐστιν ἕτοιμος.
not yet is come, but [2]time [1]your always is ready.
7 οὐ.δύναται ὁ κόσμος μισεῖν ὑμᾶς· ἐμὲ.δὲ μισεῖ, ὅτι ἐγὼ
[3]Is [4]unable [1]the [2]world to hate you, but me it hates, because I
μαρτυρῶ περὶ αὐτοῦ, ὅτι τὰ ἔργα αὐτοῦ πονηρά ἐστιν.
bear witness concerning it, that the works of it evil are.
8 ὑμεῖς ἀνάβητε εἰς τὴν.ἑορτὴν.[t]ταύτην·" ἐγὼ [v]οὔπω" ἀνα-
Ye, go ye up to this feast. I not yet am
βαίνω εἰς τὴν.ἑορτὴν.ταύτην, ὅτι ὁ [w]καιρὸς ὁ ἐμὸς" οὔπω
going up to this feast, for [2]time [1]my not yet
πεπλήρωται. 9 Ταῦτα [x]δὲ" εἰπὼν [y]αὐτοῖς" ἔμεινεν ἐν τῇ
has been fulfilled. And these things having said to them he abode in
Γαλιλαίᾳ. 10 Ὡς.δὲ ἀνέβησαν οἱ ἀδελφοὶ.αὐτοῦ [z]τότε καὶ
Galilee. But when were gone up his brethren then also
αὐτὸς ἀνέβη εἰς τὴν ἑορτήν," οὐ φανερῶς, [a]ἀλλ'" [b]ὡς" ἐν
he went up to the feast, not openly, but as in
κρυπτῷ. 11 Οἱ οὖν Ἰουδαῖοι ἐζήτουν αὐτὸν ἐν τῇ ἑορτῇ,
secret. The [2]therefore [1]Jews were seeking him at the feast,
καὶ ἔλεγον, Ποῦ ἐστιν ἐκεῖνος; 12 Καὶ γογγυσμὸς [c]πολὺς
and said, Where is he? And [2]murmuring [1]much
περὶ αὐτοῦ ἦν" ἐν [d]τοῖς ὄχλοις." οἱ.μὲν ἔλεγον,
concerning him there was among the crowds. Some said,
Ὅτι ἀγαθός ἐστιν· ἄλλοι.[e]δὲ" ἔλεγον, Οὔ· ἀλλὰ πλανᾷ τὸν
[3]Good [1]he [2]is; but others said, No; but he deceives the
ὄχλον. 13 Οὐδεὶς μέντοι παρρησίᾳ ἐλάλει περὶ αὐτοῦ,
crowd. No one however publicly spoke concerning him,
διὰ τὸν φόβον τῶν Ἰουδαίων.
because of the fear of the Jews.

does not profit anything. The words which I speak to you are spirit and are life.
64 But there are some of you who do not believe. For Jesus had known from the beginning who they were who do not believe, and who he was who would betray Him.
65 And He said, Because of this I said to you that no one can come to Me unless it shall have been given to him from My Father.
66 From that *time* many of His disciples fell back and did not walk any more with Him.
67 Then Jesus said to the twelve, Are you also wishing to go away?
68 Then Simon Peter answered Him, Lord, to whom shall we go? You have the words of everlasting life.
69 And we have believed and have known that You are the Christ, the Son of the living God.
70 Jesus answered them, Did I not choose you as the Twelve, and one of you is a devil?
71 But He spoke of Judas Is-car-i-ot, Simon's son, for he was about to betray Him, being one of the Twelve.

CHAPTER 7

1 And after these things Jesus was walking in Galilee, for He did not wish to walk in Judea – because the Jews were trying to kill Him.
2 Now the Jewish Feast of the Tabernacles was near.
3 So His brothers said to Him, Move away from here and go to Judea so that your disciples may also see your works which you do
4 – for no one does anything in secret and he himself seeks to be *seen* in public. If you do these things, show yourself to the world.
5 For neither did His brothers believe in Him.
6 Then Jesus said to them, My time has not yet come, but your time is always ready.
7 The world cannot hate you, but it hates Me because I witness concerning it, that its works are evil.
8 You go up to this feast. I am not yet going to this feast, for My time has not yet been fulfilled.
9 And saying these things to them, He stayed in Galilee.
10 But when His brothers went up, then He also went up to the feast – not openly, but in secret.
11 Then the Jews were looking for Him at the feast, saying, Where is He?
12 And there was much talking about Him among the people. Some said, He is good. But others said, No, but he leads the people astray.
13 But no one spoke about Him publicly, because of the fear of the Jews.

14 Ἤδη.δὲ τῆς ἑορτῆς μεσούσης ἀνέβη [f]ὁ" Ἰησοῦς
But now [5]of [6]the [7]feast [[1]it] [2]being [3]the [4]middle went up Jesus
εἰς τὸ ἱερόν, καὶ ἐδίδασκεν. 15 [g]καὶ ἐθαύμαζον" οἱ Ἰουδαῖοι
into the temple, and was teaching: and [3]were [4]wondering [1]the [2]Jews
λέγοντες, Πῶς οὗτος γράμματα οἶδεν, μὴ μεμαθηκώς;
saying, How [2]this [3]one [4]letters [1]knows, not having learned?
16 Ἀπεκρίθη [h] αὐτοῖς [i]ὁ" Ἰησοῦς καὶ εἶπεν, Ἡ.ἐμὴ.διδαχὴ οὐκ
[2]Answered [3]them [1]Jesus and said, My teaching [2]not
ἔστιν ἐμή, ἀλλὰ τοῦ πέμψαντός με· 17 ἐάν τις θέλῃ τὸ
[1]is mine, but his who sent me. If anyone desire
θέλημα.αὐτοῦ ποιεῖν, γνώσεται περὶ τῆς διδαχῆς πότερον
his will to practise, he shall know concerning the teaching whether
ἐκ [k]τοῦ" θεοῦ ἐστιν, ἢ ἐγὼ ἀπ' ἐμαυτοῦ λαλῶ. 18 ὁ ἀφ'
from God it is, or I from myself speak. He that from
ἑαυτοῦ λαλῶν, τὴν.δόξαν.τὴν.ἰδίαν ζητεῖ· ὁ.δὲ ζητῶν τὴν
himself speaks, his own glory seeks; but he that seeks the
δόξαν τοῦ πέμψαντος αὐτόν, οὗτος ἀληθής ἐστιν, καὶ
glory of him that sent him, he true is, and
ἀδικία ἐν αὐτῷ οὐκ.ἔστιν. 19 οὐ [l]Μωσῆς" [m]δέδωκεν"
unrighteousness in him is not. [2]Not [3]Moses [1]has given
ὑμῖν τὸν νόμον, καὶ οὐδεὶς ἐξ ὑμῶν ποιεῖ τὸν νόμον; τί
you the law, and no one of you practises the law? Why
με ζητεῖτε ἀποκτεῖναι; 20 Ἀπεκρίθη ὁ ὄχλος [n]καὶ εἶπεν,"
me do ye seek to kill? [3]Answered [1]the [2]crowd and said,
Δαιμόνιον ἔχεις· τίς σε ζητεῖ ἀποκτεῖναι; 21 Ἀπεκρίθη
A demon thou hast; who thee seeks to kill? [2]Answered
[o]ὁ" Ἰησοῦς καὶ εἶπεν αὐτοῖς, Ἓν ἔργον ἐποίησα, καὶ πάντες
[1]Jesus and said to them, One work I did, and [2]all
[p]θαυμάζετε. 22 διὰ.τοῦτο" [q]Μωσῆς" δέδωκεν ὑμῖν τὴν περι-
[1]ye wonder. Therefore Moses has given you circum-
τομήν, οὐχ ὅτι ἐκ τοῦ [r]Μωσέως" ἐστίν, ἀλλ' ἐκ τῶν πατέρων·
cision, not that of Moses it is, but of the fathers,
καὶ [s]ἐν" σαββάτῳ περιτέμνετε ἄνθρωπον. 23 εἰ περιτομὴν
and on sabbath ye circumcise a man. If [4]circumcision
λαμβάνει ἄνθρωπος ἐν σαββάτῳ ἵνα μὴ.λυθῇ ὁ νόμος [t]
[3]receives [1]a [2]man on sabbath, that may not be broken the law
[r]Μωσέως," ἐμοὶ χολᾶτε ὅτι ὅλον ἄνθρωπον ὑγιῆ ἐποίησα
of Moses, with me are ye angry because entirely [2]a [3]man [1]sound I made
ἐν σαββάτῳ; 24 μὴ.κρίνετε κατ' ὄψιν, ἀλλὰ τὴν δικαίαν
on sabbath? Judge not according to sight, but righteous
κρίσιν [v]κρίνατε." 25 Ἔλεγον οὖν τινες ἐκ τῶν [w]Ἱεροσο-
judgment judge. [7]Said [6]therefore [1]some [2]of [3]those [4]of [5]Jeru-
λυμιτῶν," Οὐχ.οὗτός.ἐστιν ὃν ζητοῦσιν ἀποκτεῖναι; 26 καὶ
salem, Is not this he whom they seek to kill? and
ἴδε, παῤῥησίᾳ λαλεῖ, καὶ οὐδὲν αὐτῷ λέγουσιν. μήποτε
lo, publicly he speaks, and nothing to him they say.
ἀληθῶς ἔγνωσαν οἱ ἄρχοντες, ὅτι οὗτός ἐστιν
[5]Truly [1]have [6]recognized [2]those [3]who [4]rule, that this is
[x]ἀληθῶς" ὁ χριστός; 27 ἀλλὰ τοῦτον οἴδαμεν πόθεν ἐστίν·
truly the Christ? But this one we know whence he is.
ὁ.δὲ.χριστὸς ὅταν [y]ἔρχηται," οὐδεὶς γινώσκει πόθεν ἐστίν.
But the Christ, whenever he may come, no one knows whence he is.
28 Ἔκραξεν οὖν ἐν τῷ ἱερῷ διδάσκων ὁ Ἰησοῦς καὶ λέγων,
[3]Cried [2]therefore [4]in [5]the [6]temple [7]teaching [1]Jesus and saying,
Κἀμὲ οἴδατε, καὶ οἴδατε πόθεν εἰμί· καὶ ἀπ' ἐμαυτοῦ οὐκ
Both me ye know, and ye know whence I am; and of myself [3]not
ἐλήλυθα, ἀλλ' ἔστιν ἀληθινὸς ὁ πέμψας με, ὃν ὑμεῖς
[1]I [2]have come, but [5]is [6]true [1]he [2]who [3]sent [4]me, whom ye
οὐκ.οἴδατε· 29 ἐγὼ.[z]δὲ" οἶδα αὐτόν, ὅτι παρ' αὐτοῦ εἰμι,
know not. But I know him, because from him I am,
κἀκεῖνός με [a]ἀπέστειλεν." 30 Ἐζήτουν οὖν αὐτὸν πιά-
and he me sent. They were seeking therefore him to
σαι· καὶ οὐδεὶς ἐπέβαλεν ἐπ' αὐτὸν τὴν χεῖρα, ὅτι οὔπω
take, but no one laid upon him [his] hand, because not yet
ἐληλύθει ἡ.ὥρα.αὐτοῦ. 31 [b]Πολλοὶ.δὲ ἐκ τοῦ ὄχλου ἐπίστευ-
had come his hour. But many of the crowd believed
σαν" εἰς αὐτόν, καὶ ἔλεγον, [c]"Ὅτι" ὁ χριστὸς ὅταν ἔλθῃ
on him, and said, The Christ, when he comes,
[d]μήτι" πλείονα σημεῖα [e]τούτων" ποιήσει ὧν οὗτος
[4]more [5]signs [6]than [7]these [1]will [2]he [3]do which this [man]
[f]ἐποίησεν"; 32 Ἤκουσαν οἱ Φαρισαῖοι τοῦ ὄχλου γογγύζοντος
did? [3]Heard [1]the [2]Pharisees of the crowd murmuring
περὶ αὐτοῦ ταῦτα· καὶ ἀπέστειλαν [g]οἱ Φαρισαῖοι καὶ
[3]concerning [4]him [1]these [2]things, and [7]sent [1]the [2]Pharisees [3]and
οἱ ἀρχιερεῖς ὑπηρέτας," ἵνα πιάσωσιν αὐτόν. 33 εἶπεν
[4]the [5]chief [6]priests officers, that they might take him. [3]Said
οὖν [h]αὐτοῖς" ὁ Ἰησοῦς, Ἔτι [i]μικρὸν χρόνον" μεθ' ὑμῶν
[2]therefore [4]to [5]them [1]Jesus, Yet a little time with you
εἰμι, καὶ ὑπάγω πρὸς τὸν πέμψαντά με. 34 ζητήσετέ με καὶ
I am, and I go to him who sent me. Ye will seek me and
οὐχ.εὑρήσετε[k]· καὶ ὅπου εἰμὶ ἐγὼ ὑμεῖς οὐ.δύνασθε ἐλθεῖν.
shall not find [me], and where [2]am [1]I ye are unable to come.

14 But now in the middle of the feast, Jesus went up into the Temple and was teaching.

15 And the Jews were wondering, saying, How does this one know letters, having never learned?

16 Jesus answered them and said, My teaching is not Mine, but His who sent Me.

17 If anyone desires to practice His will, he shall know of the teaching, whether it is from God, or if I speak from Myself.

18 He who speaks from himself seeks his own glory. But He who is seeking the glory of Him who sent Him, He is true and no unrighteousness is in Him.

19 Has not Moses given you the Law? And not one of you practices the Law! Why do you want to kill Me?

20 The people answered and said, You have a demon! Who wants to kill you?

21 Jesus answered and said to them, I did one work and you all wonder.

22 For this reason Moses has given you circumcision (not that it is of Moses, but of the fathers), and you circumcise a man on the Sabbath.

23 If a man receives circumcision on the Sabbath in order that the Law of Moses may not be broken, are you angry with Me because I made a man perfectly whole on the Sabbath?

24 Do not judge according to sight, but judge righteous judgment.

25 Then some of those from Jerusalem said, Is this not he whom they are seeking to kill?

26 And, look, He speaks out publicly and they say nothing to him. Have the rulers indeed recognized that this is truly the Christ?

27 But we know where this one is from. But the Christ, whenever He comes, no one knows where He is from.

28 Then Jesus cried out in the Temple, teaching and saying, You both know Me and you know where I am from. And, I have not come from Myself, but He who sent Me is true, whom you do not know.

29 But I know Him because I am from Him, and He sent Me.

30 They were then wishing to seize Him, but no one laid a hand on Him because His time had not yet come.

31 And many out of the crowd believed on Him and said, The Christ, when He comes, will He do more miracles than these which this One has done?

32 The Pharisees heard the people murmuring these things about Him. And the Pharisees and the chief priests sent officers that they might seize Him.

33 So Jesus said to them, Yet a little while I am with you, and I go to Him who sent Me.

34 You will look for Me and will not find Me. And, Where I am, you cannot come.

35 Εἶπον οὖν οἱ Ἰουδαῖοι πρὸς ἑαυτούς, Ποῦ [l]οὗτος
[4]Said [3]therefore [1]the [2]Jews among themselves, Where [2]he
μέλλει‖ πορεύεσθαι ὅτι [m]ἡμεῖς‖ οὐχ.εὑρήσομεν αὐτόν; μὴ εἰς
[1]is about to go that we shall not find him? to
τὴν διασπορὰν τῶν Ἑλλήνων μέλλει πορεύεσθαι, καὶ
the dispersion among the Greeks is he about to go, and
διδάσκειν τοὺς Ἕλληνας; 36 τίς ἐστιν [n]οὗτος ὁ λόγος‖ ὃν
teach the Greeks? What is this word which
εἶπεν, Ζητήσετέ με, καὶ οὐχ.εὑρήσετε[k], καὶ "Ὅπου εἰμὶ ἐγὼ
he said, Ye will seek me, and shall not find [me]; and Where [2]am [1]I
ὑμεῖς οὐ.δύνασθε ἐλθεῖν;
ye are unable to come?
37 Ἐν.δὲ τῇ ἐσχάτῃ ἡμέρᾳ τῇ μεγάλῃ τῆς ἑορτῆς εἱστήκει
And in the last [3]day [1]the [2]great of the feast stood
ὁ Ἰησοῦς, καὶ [o]ἔκραξεν‖ λέγων, Ἐάν τις διψᾷ, ἐρχέσθω
Jesus, and cried, saying, If anyone thirst, let him come
[p]πρός με‖ καὶ πινέτω. 38 ὁ πιστεύων εἰς ἐμέ, καθὼς εἶπεν
to me and drink. He that believes on me, as said
ἡ γραφή, ποταμοὶ ἐκ τῆς.κοιλίας.αὐτοῦ ῥεύσουσιν ὕδατος
the scripture, rivers out of his belly shall flow of [2]water
ζῶντος. 39 Τοῦτο.δὲ εἶπεν περὶ τοῦ πνεύματος οὗ [q]ἔμελ-
[1]living. But this he said concerning the Spirit which [5]were
λον‖ λαμβάνειν οἱ [r]πιστεύοντες‖ εἰς αὐτόν· οὔπω.γὰρ ἦν
[6]about [7]to [8]receive [1]those [2]believing [3]on [4]him; for not yet was
πνεῦμα [s]ἅγιον‖ [t]; ὅτι [v]ὁ‖ Ἰησοῦς [w]οὐδέπω‖ ἐδοξάσθη.
[the] [2]Spirit [1]Holy, because Jesus not yet was glorified.
40 [x]πολλοὶ οὖν ἐκ τοῦ ὄχλου‖ ἀκούσαντες [y]τὸν λόγον‖
Many therefore out of the crowd having heard the word
ἔλεγον, [z] Οὗτός ἐστιν ἀληθῶς ὁ προφήτης. 41 "Ἄλλοι[a] ἔλεγον,
said, This is truly the prophet. Others said,
Οὗτός ἐστιν ὁ χριστός. [b]"Ἄλλοι‖ [c]δὲ‖ ἔλεγον, Μὴ γὰρ ἐκ
This is the Christ. [2]Others [1]and said, [4]Then [5]out [6]of
τῆς Γαλιλαίας ὁ χριστὸς ἔρχεται; 42 [d]οὐχὶ‖ ἡ γραφὴ εἶπεν,
[7]Galilee [2]the [3]Christ [1]comes? [9]Not [10]the [11]scripture [8]said,
ὅτι ἐκ τοῦ σπέρματος [e]Δαβίδ,‖ καὶ ἀπὸ Βηθλεὲμ τῆς κώμης
that out of the seed of David, and from Bethlehem the village
ὅπου ἦν [e]Δαβίδ,‖ [f a]ὁ χριστὸς ἔρχεται;‖ 43 Σχίσμα οὖν [g a]ἐν
where [2]was [1]David, the Christ comes? A division therefore in
τῷ ὄχλῳ ἐγένετο‖ δι' αὐτόν. 44 τινὲς.δὲ ἤθελον ἐξ αὐτῶν
the crowd occurred because of him. But some [3]desired [1]of [2]them
πιάσαι αὐτόν, ἀλλ' οὐδεὶς [h]ἐπέβαλεν‖ ἐπ' αὐτὸν τὰς χεῖρας.
to take him, but no one laid [2]on [3]him [1]hands.
45 ἦλθον οὖν οἱ ὑπηρέται πρὸς τοὺς ἀρχιερεῖς καὶ Φαρι-
Came therefore the officers to the chief priests and Phari-
σαίους· καὶ εἶπον αὐτοῖς ἐκεῖνοι, [i]Διατί‖ οὐκ.ἠγάγετε αὐτόν;
sees, and [2]said [3]to [4]them [1]they, Why did ye not bring him?
46 Ἀπεκρίθησαν οἱ ὑπηρέται, Οὐδέποτε [k]οὕτως ἐλάλησεν‖
[3]Answered [1]the [2]officers, Never thus spoke
ἄνθρωπος [l]ὡς οὗτος [m] ὁ ἄνθρωπος.‖ 47 Ἀπεκρίθησαν [n]οὖν‖
man as this man. [4]Answered [3]therefore
[o]αὐτοῖς‖ οἱ Φαρισαῖοι, Μὴ καὶ ὑμεῖς πεπλάνησθε; 48 μή
[5]them [1]the [2]Pharisees, [6]also [7]ye [8]have been deceived?
τις ἐκ τῶν ἀρχόντων ἐπίστευσεν εἰς αὐτόν, ἢ ἐκ τῶν
[2]Any [3]one [4]of [5]the [6]rulers [1]has believed on him, or of the
Φαρισαίων; 49 [p]ἀλλ'‖ ὁ.ὄχλος.οὗτος ὁ μὴ.γινώσκων τὸν
Pharisees? But this crowd, which knows not the
νόμον [q]ἐπικατάρατοί‖ εἰσιν. 50 Λέγει Νικόδημος πρὸς αὐτούς,
law, accursed are. [2]Says [1]Nicodemus to them,
[r]ὁ ἐλθὼν [s]νυκτὸς[t] πρὸς αὐτόν,‖ [t] εἷς ὢν ἐξ αὐτῶν, 51 Μὴ
(he who came by night to him, [2]one [1]being of themselves,)
ὁ.νόμος.ἡμῶν κρίνει τὸν ἄνθρωπον, ἐὰν.μὴ ἀκούσῃ [v]παρ'
[2]Our [3]law [1]does judge the man, unless it have heard from
αὐτοῦ πρότερον,‖ καὶ γνῷ τί ποιεῖ; 52 Ἀπεκρίθησαν καὶ
himself first, and known what he does? They answered and
[w]εἶπον‖ αὐτῷ, Μὴ καὶ σὺ ἐκ τῆς Γαλιλαίας εἶ; [x]ἐρεύνησον‖
said to him, [3]Also [2]thou [4]of [5]Galilee [1]art? Search
καὶ ἴδε, ὅτι [y]προφήτης ἐκ τῆς Γαλιλαίας‖ [z]οὐκ.ἐγήγερται.‖
and look, that a prophet out of Galilee has not arisen.
53 [a]Καὶ ἐπορεύθη ἕκαστος εἰς τὸν.οἶκον.αὐτοῦ.
And [2]went [1]each to his house.
8 Ἰησοῦς.δὲ ἐπορεύθη εἰς τὸ ὄρος τῶν ἐλαιῶν· 2 ὄρθρου.δὲ
But Jesus went to the mount of Olives. And at dawn
πάλιν παρεγένετο εἰς τὸ ἱερόν, καὶ πᾶς ὁ λαὸς ἤρχετο πρὸς
again he came into the temple, and all the people came to
αὐτόν· καὶ καθίσας ἐδίδασκεν αὐτούς. 3 ἄγουσιν δὲ οἱ
him; and having sat down he was teaching them. [7]Bring [1]and [2]the
γραμματεῖς καὶ οἱ Φαρισαῖοι πρὸς αὐτὸν γυναῖκα ἐν μοιχείᾳ
[3]scribes [4]and [5]the [6]Pharisees to him a woman in adultery
κατειλημμένην, καὶ στήσαντες αὐτὴν ἐν μέσῳ, 4 λέγουσιν
having been taken, and having set her in [the] midst, they say
αὐτῷ, Διδάσκαλε, αὕτη ἡ γυνὴ κατειλήφθη [b]ἐπαυτοφώρῳ‖
to him, Teacher, this woman was taken in the very act

[35]Then the Jews said among themselves, Where is he about to go that we shall not find him? Is he about to go to the Dispersion among the Greeks and to teach the Greeks?
[36]What is this word which he said, You will look for Me and will not find Me? And, Where I am you are not able to come.

[37]And in the last day, the great one of the feast, Jesus stood and cried, saying, If anyone thirst, let him come to Me and drink.
[38]He that believes on Me, as the Scripture said, "Out of his belly shall flow rivers of living water."
[39]But He said this concerning the Spirit which those believing on Him were about to receive (for the Holy Spirit was not yet *given* because Jesus was not yet glorified).
[40]Many out of the multitude, then, hearing the word, said, This truly is the Prophet.
[41]Others said, This is the Christ. And others said, Does the Christ then come out of Galilee?
[42]Did not the Scriptures say that the Christ comes from the seed of David and from Bethlehem, the city where David lived?
[43]So a division arose among the people because of Him.
[44]And some of them wanted to seize Him, but no one laid hands on Him.
[45]Then the officers came to the chief priests and Pharisees. And they said to them, Why did you not bring Him?
[46]The officers answered, Never did *any* man speak like this man.
[47]Then the Pharisees answered them, Have you also been led astray?
[48]Has anyone of the rulers believed on him, or of the Pharisees?
[49]But this crowd which does not know the Law is cursed.
[50]Nic-o-de-mus said to them (he who came by night to Him,) being one of themselves,
[51]Does our Law judge a man unless it has first heard from him and know what he does?
[52]They answered and said to him, Are you also of Galilee? Search and see that no prophet has arisen out of Galilee.
[53]And each one went on to his house.

CHAPTER 8

[1]But Jesus went on to the Mount of Olives.
[2]And at dawn He came again into the Temple. And all the people came to Him. And sitting down, He taught them.
[3]And the scribes and the Pharisees brought to Him a woman taken in adultery. And sitting her in the middle,
[4]they said to Him, Teacher, this woman was taken in the very act, committing adultery.

μοιχευομένη. 5 ἐν.δὲ τῷ νόμῳ ᶜΜωσῆς" ἡμῖν ἐνετείλατο
committing adultery. Now in the law Moses us commanded
τὰς τοιαύτας. ᵈλιθοβολεῖσθαι·" σὺ οὖν τί λέγεις ᵉ;
such to be stoned: thou therefore what sayest thou?
6 Τοῦτο.δὲ ἔλεγον πειράζοντες αὐτὸν ἵνα ἔχωσιν κατη-
But this they said tempting him that they might have to ac-
γορεῖν αὐτοῦ. ὁ δὲ Ἰησοῦς κάτω.κύψας, τῷ δακτύλῳ
cuse him. But Jesus having stooped down, with [his] finger
ἔγραφεν εἰς τὴν γῆν. 7 ὡς.δὲ ἐπέμενον ἐρωτῶντες αὐτόν,
wrote on the ground. But as they continued asking him,
ἀνακύψας εἶπεν πρὸς αὐτούς, Ὁ ἀναμάρτητος ὑ-
having lifted up himself he said to them, The sinless one among
μῶν πρῶτος τὸν λίθον ἐπ' αὐτῇ βαλέτω. 8 καὶ πάλιν
you [5]first [4]the [6]stone [7]at [8]her [1]let [2]him [3]cast. And again
κάτω.κύψας ἔγραφεν εἰς τὴν γῆν. 9 οἱ.δὲ ἀκούσαντες,
having stooped down he wrote on the ground. But they having heard,
καὶ ὑπὸ τῆς συνειδήσεως ἐλεγχόμενοι, ἐξήρχοντο εἷς καθ' εἷς,
and by the conscience being convicted, went out one by one,
ἀρξάμενοι ἀπὸ τῶν πρεσβυτέρων ἕως τῶν ἐσχάτων· καὶ
beginning from the elder ones until the last; and
κατελείφθη μόνος ὁ Ἰησοῦς, καὶ ἡ γυνὴ ἐν μέσῳ ᶠἑστῶσα."
was left alone Jesus, and the woman in [the] midst standing.
10 ἀνακύψας.δὲ ὁ Ἰησοῦς, καὶ μηδένα θεασάμενος
And [2]having [3]lifted [4]up [5]himself [1]Jesus, and [2]no [3]one [1]seeing
πλὴν τῆς γυναικός, εἶπεν αὐτῇ, ᵍἩ γυνή," ποῦ εἰσιν ἐκεῖνοι
but the woman, said to her, Woman, where are those
οἱ.κατήγοροί.σου, οὐδείς σε κατέκρινεν; 11 Ἡ.δὲ εἶπεν,
thine accusers, [2]no [3]one [5]thee [1]did [4]condemn? And she said,
Οὐδείς, κύριε. Εἶπεν.δὲ αὐτῇ ὁ Ἰησοῦς, Οὐδὲ ἐγώ σε κατα-
No one, Sir. And [2]said [3]to [4]her [1]Jesus, Neither [2]I [4]thee [1]do
κρίνω· πορεύου καὶ μηκέτι ἁμάρτανε."
[3]condemn: go, and no more sin.

12 Πάλιν οὖν ʰὁ Ἰησοῦς αὐτοῖς ἐλάλησεν," λέγων, Ἐγώ
Again therefore Jesus to them spoke, saying, I
εἰμι τὸ φῶς τοῦ κόσμου· ὁ ἀκολουθῶν ⁱἐμοὶ" οὐ.μὴ
am the light of the world; he that follows me in no wise
ᵏπεριπατήσει" ἐν τῇ σκοτίᾳ, ἀλλ' ἕξει τὸ φῶς τῆς ζωῆς.
shall walk in the darkness, but shall have the light of the life.
13 Εἶπον οὖν αὐτῷ οἱ Φαρισαῖοι, Σὺ περὶ σεαυτοῦ
[3]Said [4]therefore [5]to [6]him [1]the [2]Pharisees, Thou concerning thyself
μαρτυρεῖς· ἡ.μαρτυρία.σου οὐκ.ἔστιν ἀληθής. 14 Ἀπεκρίθη
bearest witness; thy witness is not true. [2]Answered
Ἰησοῦς καὶ εἶπεν αὐτοῖς, Κἂν ἐγὼ μαρτυρῶ περὶ ἐμαυτοῦ,
[1]Jesus and said to them, Even if I bear witness concerning myself,
ἀληθής ἐστιν ἡ.μαρτυρία.μου, ὅτι οἶδα πόθεν ἦλθον καὶ
true is my witness, because I know whence I came and
ποῦ ὑπάγω· ὑμεῖς.ˡδὲ" οὐκ.οἴδατε πόθεν ἔρχομαι ᵐκαὶ" ποῦ
whither I go: but ye know not whence I come and whither
ὑπάγω. 15 ὑμεῖς κατὰ τὴν σάρκα κρίνετε· ἐγὼ οὐ κρίνω
I go. Ye according to the flesh judge, I judge
οὐδένα. 16 καὶ ἐὰν κρίνω δὲ ἐγώ, ἡ κρίσις ἡ ἐμὴ ⁿἀληθής"
no one. And if [3]judge [2]also [1]I, [5]judgment [4]my true
ἐστιν· ὅτι μόνος οὐκ.εἰμί, ἀλλ' ἐγὼ καὶ ὁ πέμψας με ᵒπα-
is, because alone I am not, but I and the [2]who [3]sent [4]me [1]Fa-
τήρ." 17 καὶ ἐν τῷ νόμῳ δὲ τῷ ὑμετέρῳ ᵖγέγραπται," ὅτι
ther. And in [2]law [3]also [1]your it has been written, that
δύο ἀνθρώπων ἡ μαρτυρία ἀληθής ἐστιν. 18 ἐγώ εἰμι ὁ
of two men the witness true is. I am [one] who
μαρτυρῶν περὶ ἐμαυτοῦ, καὶ μαρτυρεῖ περὶ ἐμοῦ ὁ
bears witness concerning myself, and [6]bears [7]witness [8]concerning [9]me [1]the
πέμψας με πατήρ. 19 Ἔλεγον οὖν αὐτῷ, Ποῦ ἐστιν ὁ
[3]who [4]sent [5]me [2]Father. They said therefore to him, Where is
πατήρ.σου; Ἀπεκρίθη ᵠὁ" Ἰησοῦς, Οὔτε ἐμὲ οἴδατε οὔτε τὸν
thy Father? [2]Answered [1]Jesus, Neither me ye know nor
πατέρα.μου· εἰ ἐμὲ ᾔδειτε, καὶ τὸν.πατέρα.μου ʳᾔδειτε.ἄν."
my Father. If me ye had known, also my Father ye would have known.
20 Ταῦτα τὰ ῥήματα ἐλάλησεν ˢὁ Ἰησοῦς" ἐν τῷ γαζοφυλακίῳ,
These words spoke Jesus in the treasury,
διδάσκων ἐν τῷ ἱερῷ· καὶ οὐδεὶς ἐπίασεν αὐτόν, ὅτι οὔπω
teaching in the temple; and no one took him, for not yet
ἐληλύθει ἡ.ὥρα.αὐτοῦ.
had come his hour.

21 Εἶπεν οὖν πάλιν αὐτοῖς ᵗὁ Ἰησοῦς," Ἐγὼ ὑπάγω,
[2]Said [3]therefore [4]again [5]to [6]them [1]Jesus, I go away,
καὶ ζητήσετέ με, καὶ ἐν τῇ.ἁμαρτίᾳ.ὑμῶν ἀποθανεῖσθε· ὅπου
and ye will seek me, and in your sin ye will die; where
ἐγὼ ὑπάγω ὑμεῖς οὐ.δύνασθε ἐλθεῖν. 22 Ἔλεγον οὖν οἱ
I go ye are unable to come. [4]Said [3]therefore [1]the
Ἰουδαῖοι, Μήτι ἀποκτενεῖ ἑαυτόν, ὅτι λέγει, Ὅπου ἐγὼ ὑπάγω
[2]Jews, Will he kill himself, that he says, Where I go
ὑμεῖς οὐ.δύνασθε ἐλθεῖν; 23 Καὶ ᵛεἶπεν" αὐτοῖς, Ὑμεῖς ἐκ
ye are unable to come? And he said to them, Ye from

5 Now in the Law, Moses commanded us
that such ones were to be stoned. What then
do you say?
6 But they said this to tempt Him, so that
they might be able to accuse Him. But
stooping down, Jesus wrote with His finger
on the ground.
7 And as they continued asking Him, He
lifted Himself up and said to them, He
among you who is without sin, let him
throw the first stone at her.
8 And stooping down again, He wrote on
the ground.
9 And hearing, and being convicted by conscience, they left, one by one, beginning from
the elders, to the last one. And Jesus was left
alone *with* the woman standing in the middle.
10 And lifting Himself up and seeing no one
but the woman, Jesus said to her, Woman,
where are those *men*, your accusers? Did no
one give judgment against you?
11 And she said, No one, Lord. And Jesus
said to her, Neither do I judge you. Go! And
do not sin any more.

12 Then again Jesus spoke to them, saying,
I am the Light of the world! He who follows
Me shall in no way walk in the darkness, but
shall have the light of life.
13 Then the Pharisees said to Him, You witness of yourself. Your witness is not true.
14 Jesus answered and said to them, Even if
I witness of Myself, My witness is true, because I know where I came from and where I
go. But you do not know where I come from
and where I go.
15 You judge according to the flesh. I judge
no one.
16 And even if I judge, My judgment is true,
because I am not alone, but I and the Father
who sent Me.
17 And it has also been written in your Law
that the witness of two men is true.
18 I am *one* who witnesses about Myself,
and the Father who sent Me witnesses about
Me.
19 Then they said to Him, Where is your
Father? Jesus answered, You do not know
Me or My Father. If you had known Me you
would have known My Father also.
20 Jesus spoke these words in the treasury,
teaching in the Temple. And no one laid
hold on Him, for His hour had not yet come.

21 Then Jesus said to them, again, I go
away and you will look for Me. And you will
die in your sin, for where I go, you cannot
come.
22 Then the Jews said, Will he kill himself?
– because He said, Where I go you are not
able to come.
23 And He said to them, You are from be-

τῶν.κάτω ἐστέ, ἐγὼ ἐκ τῶν.ἄνω εἰμι· ὑμεῖς ἐκ ʷτοῦ κόσμου
beneath are, I from above am; Ye of ²world
τούτου" ἐστέ, ἐγὼ οὐκ.εἰμὶ ἐκ τοῦ.κόσμου τούτου. 24 εἶπον
¹this are, I am not of this world. I said
οὖν ὑμῖν ὅτι ἀποθανεῖσθε ἐν ταῖς.ἁμαρτίαις ὑμῶν· ἐὰν.γὰρ
therefore to you that ye will die in your sins; for if
μὴ.πιστεύσητε ὅτι ἐγώ εἰμι, ἀποθανεῖσθε ἐν ταῖς ἁμαρτίαις
ye believe not that I am [he], ye will die in ²sins
ὑμῶν. 25 ˣἜλεγον οὖν αὐτῷ, Σὺ τίς εἶ; ˣΚαὶ" εἶπεν
¹your. They said therefore to him, ³Thou ¹who ²art? And ²said
αὐτοῖς ʸὁ" Ἰησοῦς, Τὴν.ἀρχὴν ὅ.τι καὶ λαλῶ ὑμῖν.
³to ⁴them ¹Jesus, Altogether that which also I say to you.
26 πολλὰ ἔχω περὶ ὑμῶν λαλεῖν καὶ κρίνειν· ἀλλ' ὁ
Many things I have concerning you to say and to judge; but he who
πέμψας με ἀληθής ἐστιν, κἀγὼ ἃ ἤκουσα παρ' αὐτοῦ, ταῦτα
sent me true is, and I what I heard from him, these things
ᶻλέγω" εἰς τὸν κόσμον. 27 Οὐκ.ἔγνωσαν ὅτι τὸν πατέρα αὐτοῖς
I say to the world. They knew not that the Father to them
ἔλεγεν. 28 Εἶπεν οὖν ᵃαὐτοῖς" ὁ Ἰησοῦς, Ὅταν ὑψώ-
he spoke of. ³Said ²therefore ⁴to ⁵them ¹Jesus, When ye shall have
σητε τὸν υἱὸν τοῦ ἀνθρώπου, τότε γνώσεσθε ὅτι ἐγώ εἰμι·
lifted up the Son of man, then ye shall know that I am [he],
καὶ ἀπ' ἐμαυτοῦ ποιῶ οὐδέν, ἀλλὰ καθὼς ἐδίδαξέν με ὁ
and from myself I do nothing, but as ³taught ⁴me
πατήρ.ᵇμου," ταῦτα λαλῶ. 29 καὶ ὁ πέμψας με, μετ'
¹my ²Father, these things I speak. And he who sent me, with
ἐμοῦ ἐστιν· οὐκ.ἀφῆκέν με μόνον ᶜὁ πατήρ," ὅτι ἐγὼ τὰ
me is; ³left ³not ⁴me ⁶alone ¹the ²Father, because I the things
ἀρεστὰ αὐτῷ ποιῶ πάντοτε. 30 Ταῦτα αὐτοῦ.λαλοῦντος
pleasing to him do always. ⁴These ⁵things ¹as ²he ³spoke
πολλοὶ ἐπίστευσαν εἰς αὐτόν.
many believed on him.

31 Ἔλεγεν οὖν ὁ Ἰησοῦς πρὸς τοὺς πεπιστευκότας αὐτῷ
³Said ²therefore ¹Jesus to the ²who ³had ⁴believed ⁵on ⁶him
Ἰουδαίους, Ἐὰν ὑμεῖς μείνητε ἐν τῷ λόγῳ τῷ ἐμῷ, ἀληθῶς
¹Jews, If ye abide in ²word ¹my, truly
μαθηταί μου ἐστέ· 32 καὶ γνώσεσθε τὴν ἀλήθειαν, καὶ ἡ
²disciples ¹my ye are. And ye shall know the truth, and the
ἀλήθεια ἐλευθερώσει ὑμᾶς. 33 Ἀπεκρίθησαν ᵈαὐτῷ," Σπέρμα
truth shall set free you. They answered him, ²Seed
Ἀβραάμ ἐσμεν, καὶ οὐδενὶ δεδουλεύκαμεν πώποτε· πῶς
¹Abraham's we are, and to anyone have been under bondage never; how
(lit. to no one)
σὺ λέγεις, Ὅτι ἐλεύθεροι γενήσεσθε; 34 Ἀπεκρίθη αὐτοῖς
²thou ¹sayest, Free ye shall become? ²Answered ³them
ᵉὁ" Ἰησοῦς, Ἀμὴν ἀμὴν λέγω ὑμῖν, ὅτι πᾶς ὁ ποιῶν
¹Jesus, Verily verily I say to you, that everyone that practises
τὴν ἁμαρτίαν δοῦλός ἐστιν τῆς ἁμαρτίας. 35 ὁ.δὲ δοῦλος
sin a bondman is of sin. Now the bondman
οὐ.μένει ἐν τῇ οἰκίᾳ εἰς.τὸν.αἰῶνα· ὁ υἱὸς μένει εἰς.τὸν.αἰῶνα.
abides not in the house for ever; the Son abides for ever.
36 ἐὰν οὖν ὁ υἱὸς ὑμᾶς ἐλευθερώσῃ, ὄντως ἐλεύθεροι ἔσ-
If therefore the Son ³you ¹shall ²set free, really free ye
εσθε. 37 οἶδα ὅτι σπέρμα Ἀβραάμ ἐστε· ἀλλὰ ζητεῖτέ με
shall be. I know that ²seed ¹Abraham's ye are; but ye seek me
ἀποκτεῖναι, ὅτι ὁ λόγος ὁ ἐμὸς οὐ.χωρεῖ ἐν ὑμῖν. 38 ᶠἐγὼ
to kill, because ²word ¹my has no entrance in you. I
ᵍὃ" ἑώρακα παρὰ τῷ.πατρί.ᵍμου" λαλῶ· καὶ ὑμεῖς οὖν ʰὃ
what I have seen with my Father speak; and ye therefore what
ἑωράκατε" παρὰ ⁱτῷ.πατρὶ.ὑμῶν" ποιεῖτε. 39 Ἀπεκρίθησαν
ye have seen with your father do. They answered
καὶ ᵏεἶπον" αὐτῷ, Ὁ.πατὴρ.ἡμῶν Ἀβραάμ ἐστιν. Λέγει αὐτοῖς
and said to him, ³Our ⁴Father ¹Abraham ²is. ⁶Says ⁷to ⁸them
ˡὁ" Ἰησοῦς, Εἰ τέκνα τοῦ Ἀβραὰμ ᵐἦτε," τὰ ἔργα τοῦ Ἀβραὰμ
⁵Jesus, If children of Abraham ye were, the works of Abraham
ἐποιεῖτε."ἄν·" 40 νῦν.δὲ ζητεῖτέ με ἀποκτεῖναι, ἄνθρωπον ὃς
ye would do; but now ye seek me to kill, a man who
τὴν ἀλήθειαν ὑμῖν λελάληκα, ἣν ἤκουσα παρὰ τοῦ θεοῦ·
the truth to you has spoken, which I heard from God:
τοῦτο Ἀβραὰμ οὐκ.ἐποίησεν. 41 ὑμεῖς ποιεῖτε τὰ ἔργα τοῦ
this Abraham did not. Ye do the works
πατρὸς.ὑμῶν. ᵒΕἶπον" ᵖοὖν" αὐτῷ, Ἡμεῖς ἐκ πορνείας ᵠοὐ
of your father. They said therefore to him, We of fornication ²not
γεγεννήμεθα." ἕνα πατέρα ἔχομεν, τὸν θεόν. 42 Εἶπεν ʳοὖν"
¹have been born; one Father we have, God. ³Said ²therefore
αὐτοῖς ˢὁ" Ἰησοῦς, Εἰ ὁ θεὸς ᵗ πατὴρ ὑμῶν ἦν, ἠγαπᾶτε.ἂν
⁴to ⁵them ¹Jesus, If God Father of you were, ye would have loved
ἐμέ· ἐγὼ.γὰρ ἐκ τοῦ θεοῦ ἐξῆλθον καὶ ἥκω· οὐδὲ.γὰρ ἀπ'
me, for I from God came forth and am come; for neither of
ἐμαυτοῦ ἐλήλυθα, ἀλλ' ἐκεῖνός με ἀπέστειλεν. 43 ᵛδιατί" τὴν
myself have I come, but he ²me ¹sent. Why
λαλιὰν τὴν ἐμὴν οὐ.γινώσκετε; ὅτι οὐ.δύνασθε ἀκούειν τὸν
²speech ¹my do ye not know? Because ye are unable to hear

neath. I am from above. You are of this world. I am not of this world.
24 So I said to you that you shall die in your sins. For if you do not believe that I Am, you will die in your sins.
25 Then they said to Him, Who are you? And Jesus said to them, Even the same which I also say to you.
26 I have many things to say and to judge concerning you. But He who sent Me is true, and those things I heard from Him, these I say to the world.
27 They did not know that He spoke to them of the Father.
28 Then Jesus said to them, When you have lifted up the Son of man, then you shall know that I Am. And I do nothing of Myself, but I speak these things, just as the Father taught Me.
29 And He who sent Me is with Me. The Father did not leave Me alone, because I always do the things that are pleasing to Him.
30 As He spoke these things, many believed on Him.
31 Then Jesus said to the Jews who had believed on Him, If you continue in My word you are really My disciples.
32 And you shall know the truth, and the truth shall set you free.
33 They answered Him, We are Abraham's seed and we have never been under bondage to anyone. How can you say, You shall become free?
34 Jesus answered them, Indeed, I tell you truly that everyone that practices sin is the slave of sin.
35 Now the slave does not stay in the house forever the Son continues forever.
36 So if the Son shall set you free, you shall be free indeed.
37 I know that you are Abraham's seed, but you want to kill Me because My word has no place to enter into you.
38 I speak what I have seen with My Father, and so do you always do what you have seen with your father.
39 They answered and said to Him, Our father is Abraham. Jesus said to them, If you were the children of Abraham, you would always do the works of Abraham.
40 But now you want to kill Me, · man who has spoken the truth to you, which I heard from God. Abraham did not do this.
41 You are always doing the works of your father. They said to Him then, We are not born of fornication. We have one father – God!
42 Then Jesus said to them, If God were your Father you would love Me. For I came forth and am come from God. For I have not come of Myself, but He sent Me.
43 Why do you not understand My speech? Because you are not able to hear My word.

λόγον τὸν ἐμόν. 44 ὑμεῖς ἐκ[w] πατρὸς τοῦ διαβόλου ἐστέ,
[2]word [1]my. Ye of [the] father the devil are,
καὶ τὰς ἐπιθυμίας τοῦ.πατρὸς.ὑμῶν θέλετε ποιεῖν. ἐκεῖνος
and the lusts of your father ye desire to do. He
ἀνθρωποκτόνος ἦν ἀπ' ἀρχῆς, καὶ ἐν τῇ ἀληθείᾳ [x]οὐχ[ll]
a murderer was from [the] beginning, and in the truth [2]not
ἕστηκεν· ὅτι οὐκ.ἔστιν ἀλήθεια ἐν αὐτῷ. ὅταν λαλῇ
[1]has stood, because there is not truth in him. Whenever he may speak
τὸ ψεῦδος, ἐκ τῶν.ἰδίων λαλεῖ· ὅτι ψεύστης ἐστὶν καὶ ὁ
falsehood, from his own he speaks; for a liar he is and the
πατὴρ αὐτοῦ. 45 ἐγὼ δὲ ὅτι τὴν ἀλήθειαν λέγω[y], οὐ
father of it. [2]I [1]and [2]because the truth speak, [3]not
πιστεύετέ μοι. 46 τίς ἐξ ὑμῶν ἐλέγχει με περὶ ἁμαρτίας;
[1]ye [2]do believe me. Which of you convinces me concerning sin?
εἰ.[z]δὲ[ll] ἀλήθειαν λέγω, [a]διατί[ll] ὑμεῖς οὐ.πιστεύετέ μοι; 47 ὁ
But if truth I speak, why [2]ye [1]do [3]not believe me? He that
ὢν ἐκ τοῦ θεοῦ τὰ ῥήματα τοῦ θεοῦ ἀκούει· διὰ.τοῦτο ὑμεῖς
is of God the words of God hears: therefore ye
οὐκ.ἀκούετε, ὅτι ἐκ τοῦ θεοῦ οὐκ.ἐστέ. 48 Ἀπεκρίθησαν
hear not, because of God ye are not. Answered
[b]οὖν[ll] οἱ Ἰουδαῖοι καὶ [c]εἶπον[ll] αὐτῷ, Οὐ καλῶς λέγομεν ἡμεῖς
therefore the Jews and said to him, [3]Not [4]well [1]say [2]we
ὅτι [d]Σαμαρείτης[ll] εἶ σύ, καὶ δαιμόνιον ἔχεις; 49 Ἀπεκρίθη
that a Samaritan [2]art [1]thou, and a demon hast? [2]Answered
Ἰησοῦς, Ἐγὼ δαιμόνιον οὐκ.ἔχω, ἀλλὰ τιμῶ τὸν.πατέρα.μου,
[1]Jesus, I a demon have not; but I honour my Father,
καὶ ὑμεῖς ἀτιμάζετέ με. 50 ἐγὼ.δὲ οὐ.ζητῶ τὴν.δόξαν.μου·
and ye dishonour me. But I seek not my glory:
ἔστιν ὁ ζητῶν καὶ κρίνων. 51 ἀμὴν ἀμὴν λέγω ὑμῖν, ἐάν
there is he who seeks and judges. Verily verily I say to you, If
τις τὸν [e]λόγον τὸν ἐμὸν[ll] τηρήσῃ, θάνατον οὐ.μὴ θεωρήσῃ
anyone [2]word [3]my [1]keep, death in no wise shall he see
εἰς.τὸν.αἰῶνα. 52 [f]Εἶπον[ll] [g]οὖν[ll] αὐτῷ οἱ Ἰουδαῖοι, Νῦν
for ever. [4]Said [5]therefore [6]to [7]him [1]the [2]Jews, Now
ἐγνώκαμεν ὅτι δαιμόνιον ἔχεις. Ἀβραὰμ ἀπέθανεν καὶ οἱ
we know that a demon thou hast. Abraham died and the
προφῆται, καὶ σὺ λέγεις, Ἐάν τις τὸν.λόγον.μου τηρήσῃ,
prophets, and thou sayest, If anyone [2]my [3]word [1]keep,
οὐ.μὴ [h]γεύσεται[ll] θανάτου εἰς.τὸν.αἰῶνα. 53 μὴ σὺ μείζων
in no wise shall he taste of death for ever. [2]Thou [3]greater
εἶ τοῦ.πατρὸς.ἡμῶν Ἀβραάμ, ὅστις ἀπέθανεν; καὶ οἱ προ-
[1]art than our father Abraham, who died? and the pro-
φῆται ἀπέθανον· τίνα σεαυτὸν [i]σὺ[ll] ποιεῖς; 54 Ἀπεκρίθη
phets died! whom [3]thyself [2]thou [1]makest? [2]Answered
Ἰησοῦς, Ἐὰν ἐγὼ [k]δοξάζω[ll] ἐμαυτόν, ἡ.δόξα.μου οὐδέν ἐστιν·
[1]Jesus, If I glorify myself, my glory nothing is;
ἔστιν ὁ.πατήρ μου ὁ δοξάζων με, ὃν ὑμεῖς λέγετε, ὅτι
it is my Father who glorifies me, [of] whom ye say, that
θεὸς [l]ὑμῶν[ll] ἐστιν, 55 καὶ οὐκ.ἐγνώκατε αὐτόν, ἐγὼ.δὲ οἶδα
[2]God [1]your he is. And ye have not known him, but I know
αὐτόν· [m]καὶ ἐὰν[ll] εἴπω ὅτι οὐκ.οἶδα αὐτόν, ἔσομαι ὅμοιος
him; and if I say that I know not him, I shall be like
[n]ὑμῶν,[ll] ψεύστης· [o]ἀλλ'[ll] οἶδα αὐτόν, καὶ τὸν.λόγον.αὐτοῦ
you, a liar. But I know him, and his word
τηρῶ. 56 Ἀβραὰμ ὁ.πατὴρ.ὑμῶν ἠγαλλιάσατο ἵνα [p]ἴδῃ[ll]
I keep. Abraham your Father exulted in that he should see
τὴν ἡμέραν τὴν ἐμήν· καὶ εἶδεν καὶ ἐχάρη. 57 [q]Εἶπον[ll] οὖν
[2]day [1]my, and he saw and rejoiced. Said therefore
οἱ Ἰουδαῖοι πρὸς αὐτόν, Πεντήκοντα ἔτη οὔπω ἔχεις,
the Jews to him, Fifty years [old] not yet art thou,
καὶ Ἀβραὰμ ἑώρακας; 58 Εἶπεν αὐτοῖς [r]ὁ[ll] Ἰησοῦς, Ἀμὴν
and Abraham hast thou seen? [2]Said [3]to [4]them [1]Jesus, Verily
ἀμὴν λέγω ὑμῖν, πρὶν Ἀβραὰμ γενέσθαι ἐγώ εἰμι. 59 Ἦραν
verily I say to you, Before Abraham was I am. They took up
οὖν λίθους ἵνα βάλωσιν ἐπ' αὐτόν· Ἰησοῦς.δὲ ἐκρύβη,
therefore stones that they might cast at him; but Jesus hid himself,
καὶ ἐξῆλθεν ἐκ τοῦ ἱεροῦ, [s]διελθὼν διὰ μέσου αὐτῶν·
and went forth out of the temple, going through the midst of them,
καὶ παρῆγεν οὕτως.[ll]
and [2]passed [3]on [1]thus.

9 Καὶ παράγων εἶδεν ἄνθρωπον τυφλὸν ἐκ γενετῆς. 2 καὶ
And passing on he saw a man blind from birth. And
ἠρώτησαν αὐτὸν οἱ.μαθηταὶ.αὐτοῦ λέγοντες, [t]Ῥαββί,[ll] τίς
[3]asked [4]him [1]his [2]disciples saying, Rabbi, who
ἥμαρτεν, οὗτος ἢ οἱ.γονεῖς.αὐτοῦ, ἵνα τυφλὸς γεννηθῇ;
sinned, this [man] or his parents, that blind he should be born?
3 Ἀπεκρίθη [u]ὁ[ll] Ἰησοῦς, Οὔτε οὗτος ἥμαρτεν οὔτε οἱ.γονεῖς
[2]Answered [1]Jesus, Neither this [man] sinned nor [2]parents
αὐτοῦ· ἀλλ' ἵνα φανερωθῇ τὰ ἔργα τοῦ θεοῦ ἐν αὐτῷ.
[1]his; but that should be manifested the works of God in him.
4 [v]ἐμὲ[ll] δεῖ ἐργάζεσθαι τὰ ἔργα τοῦ πέμψαντος [w]με[ll]
[2]Me [1]it [2]behoves to work the works of him who sent me

44 You have a father – the devil! And you desire to do the lusts of your father – he was a murderer from the beginning and has not stood in the truth because there is no truth in him. When he speaks a lie, he speaks of his own – for he is a liar and the father of it.
45 And because I speak the truth, you do not believe Me.
46 Who of you convicts Me of sin? But if I speak truth, why do you not believe Me?
47 He who is of God hears the words of God. Therefore you do not hear them because you are not of God.
48 Then the Jews answered and said to Him, Do we not say rightly that you are a Samaritan and have a demon?
49 Jesus answered, I do not have a demon! But I honor My Father, and you dishonor Me.
50 But I do not desire My own glory – there is *One* who searches and judges.
51 Indeed, I tell you truly that if anyone keeps My word he shall never ever see death.
52 Then the Jews said to Him, Now we know that you have a demon. Abraham and the prophets died, yet you say, If anyone keeps my word, he shall in no way taste of death forever.
53 Are you greater than our father Abraham, who died? And the prophets died *also*. Whom do you make yourself?
54 Jesus answered, If I glorify Myself, My glory is nothing. It is My Father who glorifies Me, of whom you say He is your God.
55 And you have not known Him, but I know Him. And if I say I do not know Him, I shall be like you, a liar! But I know Him and I keep His word.
56 Your father Abraham greatly rejoiced that he might see My day, and he saw and was glad.
57 Then the Jews said to Him, You are not yet fifty years old and have you seen Abraham?
58 Jesus said to them, Indeed, I tell you truly that before Abraham began to be, I AM!
59 Then they took up stones to throw at Him, but Jesus hid Himself. And He left the Temple, going through their midst *as He* left.

CHAPTER 9

1 And as He went He saw a man blind from birth.
2 And His disciples asked Him, saying, Master, who sinned, this man or his parents, that he should be born blind?
3 Jesus answered, Neither this one nor his parents sinned, but that the works of God might be shown in him.
4 It is necessary for Me to work the works

ἕως ἡμέρα ἐστίν· ἔρχεται νύξ, ὅτε οὐδεὶς δύναται ἐργάζεσθαι.
while day it is; [2]comes [1]night, when no one is able to work.
5 ὅταν ἐν τῷ κόσμῳ ὦ, φῶς εἰμι τοῦ κόσμου. 6 Ταῦ-
While in the world I may be, [the] light I am of the world. These
τα εἰπών, ἔπτυσεν χαμαί, καὶ ἐποίησεν πηλὸν ἐκ
things having said, he spat on [the] ground, and made clay of
τοῦ πτύσματος, καὶ ἐπέχρισεν [x] τὸν πηλὸν ἐπὶ τοὺς ὀφθαλμοὺς
the spittle, and applied the clay to the eyes
[y]τοῦ τυφλοῦ·‖ 7 καὶ εἶπεν αὐτῷ, Ὕπαγε, [z]νίψαι‖ εἰς τὴν
of the blind [man]. And he said to him, Go, wash in the
κολυμβήθραν τοῦ Σιλωάμ, ὃ ἑρμηνεύεται, ἀπεσταλμένος.
pool of Siloam, which is interpreted, Sent.
ἀπῆλθεν οὖν καὶ ἐνίψατο, καὶ ἦλθεν βλέπων. 8 Οἱ οὖν
He went therefore and washed, and came seeing. The [2]therefore
γείτονες καὶ οἱ θεωροῦντες αὐτὸν τὸ πρότερον ὅτι [a]τυφλὸς‖
[1]neighbours and those who saw him before that blind
ἦν, ἔλεγον, Οὐχ οὗτός ἐστιν ὁ καθήμενος καὶ προσαιτῶν;
he was, said, [2]Not [3]this [1]is he who was sitting and begging?
9 Ἄλλοι ἔλεγον, Ὅτι οὗτός ἐστιν· ἄλλοι.[b]δέ,‖ [c]Ὅτι ὅμοιος
Some said, [3]He [1]it [2]is, but others, [3]Like
αὐτῷ ἐστιν. Ἐκεῖνος[d] ἔλεγεν, Ὅτι ἐγώ εἰμι. 10 Ἔλεγον
[4]him [1]he [2]is. He said, I am [he]. They said
οὖν αὐτῷ, Πῶς[e] [f]ἀνεῴχθησάν‖ [g]σου‖ οἱ ὀφθαλμοί; 11 Ἀπ-
therefore to him, How were opened thine eyes? [2]An-
εκρίθη ἐκεῖνος [h]καὶ εἶπεν,‖ [i]Ἄνθρωπος [i] λεγόμενος Ἰησοῦς
swered [1]he and said, A man called Jesus
πηλὸν ἐποίησεν καὶ ἐπέχρισέν μου τοὺς ὀφθαλμούς, καὶ εἶπέν
clay made and applied to mine eyes, and said
μοι,[k] Ὕπαγε εἰς [l]τὴν κολυμβήθραν τοῦ‖ Σιλωὰμ καὶ νίψαι.
to me, Go to the pool of Siloam and wash:
ἀπελθὼν [m]δὲ‖ καὶ νιψάμενος ἀνέβλεψα. 12 [n]Εἶπον‖ [p]οὖν‖
[2]having [3]gone [1]and and washed I received sight. They said therefore
αὐτῷ, Ποῦ ἐστιν ἐκεῖνος; Λέγει, Οὐκ.οἶδα.
to him, Where is he? He says, I know not.

13 Ἄγουσιν αὐτὸν πρὸς τοὺς Φαρισαίους, τόν ποτε
They bring [4]him [1]to [2]the [3]Pharisees, who once [was]
τυφλόν. 14 ἦν.δὲ σάββατον [q]ὅτε‖ τὸν πηλὸν ἐποίησεν ὁ
blind. Now it was sabbath when [3]the [4]clay [2]made
Ἰησοῦς καὶ ἀνέῳξεν αὐτοῦ τοὺς ὀφθαλμούς. 15 πάλιν οὖν
[1]Jesus and opened his eyes. Again therefore
ἠρώτων αὐτὸν καὶ οἱ Φαρισαῖοι πῶς ἀνέβλεψεν. ὁ.δὲ εἶπεν
asked him also the Pharisees how he received sight. And he said
αὐτοῖς, Πηλὸν ἐπέθηκεν [r]ἐπὶ τοὺς.ὀφθαλμούς.μου,‖ καὶ ἐνι-
to them, Clay he put on mine eyes, and I
ψάμην, καὶ βλέπω. 16 Ἔλεγον οὖν ἐκ τῶν Φαρισαίων τινές,
washed, and I see. Said therefore [2]of [3]the [4]Pharisees [1]some,
[s]Οὗτος ὁ ἄνθρωπος οὐκ.ἔστιν παρὰ τοῦ θεοῦ,‖ ὅτι τὸ σάββατον
This man is not from God, for the sabbath
οὐ.τηρεῖ. Ἄλλοι ἔλεγον, Πῶς δύναται ἄνθρωπος ἁμαρτωλὸς
he does not keep. Others said, How can a man a sinner
τοιαῦτα σημεῖα ποιεῖν; Καὶ σχίσμα ἦν ἐν αὐτοῖς. 17 Λέγ-
such signs do? And a division was among them. They
ουσιν[t] τῷ τυφλῷ πάλιν, [v]Σὺ τί‖ λέγεις περὶ αὐτοῦ,
say to the blind [man] again, [3]Thou [1]what [2]sayest concerning him,
ὅτι [w]ἤνοιξέν‖ σου τοὺς ὀφθαλμούς; Ὁ.δὲ εἶπεν, Ὅτι προ-
for he opened thine eyes? And he said, A pro-
φήτης ἐστίν. 18 Οὐκ.ἐπίστευσαν οὖν οἱ Ἰουδαῖοι περὶ
phet he is. [4]Did [5]not [6]believe [3]therefore [1]the [2]Jews concerning
αὐτοῦ, ὅτι [x]τυφλὸς ἦν‖ καὶ ἀνέβλεψεν, ἕως.ὅτου ἐφώνησαν
him, that [3]blind [1]he [2]was and received sight, until they called
τοὺς γονεῖς αὐτοῦ τοῦ ἀναβλέψαντος· 19 καὶ ἠρώτησαν
the parents of him who had received sight. And they asked
αὐτοὺς λέγοντες, Οὗτός ἐστιν ὁ.υἱὸς.ὑμῶν ὃν ὑμεῖς λέγετε
them saying, [2]This [1]is your son, of whom ye say
ὅτι τυφλὸς.ἐγεννήθη; πῶς οὖν [y]ἄρτι βλέπει‖; 20 Ἀπεκρίθη-
that blind he was born? how then now does he see? [3]Answered
σαν[z] [a]αὐτοῖς‖ οἱ.γονεῖς.αὐτοῦ καὶ [b]εἶπον,‖ Οἴδαμεν ὅτι οὗτός
[4]them [1]his [2]parents and said, We know that this
ἐστιν ὁ.υἱὸς.ἡμῶν, καὶ ὅτι τυφλὸς ἐγεννήθη· 21 πῶς.δὲ νῦν
is our son, and that blind he was born; but how now
βλέπει οὐκ.οἴδαμεν, ἢ τίς ἤνοιξεν αὐτοῦ τοὺς ὀφθαλμοὺς
he sees we know not, or who opened his eyes
ἡμεῖς οὐκ.οἴδαμεν· [d]αὐτὸς ἡλικίαν.ἔχει, αὐτὸν ἐρωτήσατε,‖
we know not; he is of age, [2]him [1]ask,
αὐτὸς περὶ [e]αὐτοῦ‖ λαλήσει. 22 Ταῦτα εἶπον οἱ γονεῖς
he concerning himself shall speak. These things said [2]parents
αὐτοῦ, ὅτι ἐφοβοῦντο τοὺς Ἰουδαίους· ἤδη.γὰρ συνε-
[1]his, because they feared the Jews; for already had agreed
τέθειντο οἱ Ἰουδαῖοι, ἵνα ἐάν τις αὐτὸν ὁμολογήσῃ
together the Jews, that if anyone him should confess [to be the]
χριστόν, ἀποσυνάγωγος γένηται. 23 διὰ τοῦτο οἱ γονεῖς
Christ, put out of the synagogue he should be. Because of this [2]parents

of Him who sent Me while it is day. Night is coming when no one will be able to work.
5 As long as I am in the world, I am the Light of the world.
6 Saying these things, He spat on the ground and made clay of the spittle. And He spread the clay on the eyes of the blind one.
7 And He said to him, Go! Wash in the pool of Siloam (which means, Sent). He then went away and washed. And he came away seeing.
8 Then the neighbors and those who saw him before, that he was blind, said, Is this not he who was sitting and begging?
9 Some said, It is he. But others, He is like him. He said, I am the one.
10 Then they said to him, How were your eyes opened?
11 He answered and said, A man called Jesus made clay and spread it on my eyes and said to me, Go to the pool of Siloam and wash. And after I had gone and washed I received sight.
12 Then they said to him, Where is he? He said, I do not know.

13 So they brought him who once was blind to the Pharisees.
14 Now it was the Sabbath when Jesus made the clay and opened his eyes.
15 Again, then, the Pharisees also asked him how he received sight. And he said to them, He put clay on my eyes and I washed, and I see.
16 Then some of the Pharisees said, This man is not of God because he does not keep the Sabbath. Others said, How can a man, a sinner, do such miracles? And there was a division among them.
17 They said to the blind one again, What do you say about him, for he opened your eyes? And he said, He is a prophet.

18 The Jews, then, did not believe concerning him, that he was blind and received sight, until they called the parents of him who had received sight.
19 And they asked them, saying, Is this your son, who you say was born blind? How then does he see?
20 His parents answered and said, We know that this is our son and he was born blind.

21 But we do not know how he now sees, nor do we know who opened his eyes. Ask him. He is of age. He will tell about himself.
22 His parents said these things because they feared the Jews. For the Jews had already agreed together that if anyone should confess Him *to be the* Christ, he should be put out of the synagogue.
23 Because of this, his parents said, Ask him, he is of age.

αὐτοῦ [f]εἶπον," Ὅτι ἡλικίαν.ἔχει, αὐτὸν [g]ἐρωτήσατε." 24 Ἐφώ-
[1]his said, He is of age, [2]him [1]ask. They
νησαν οὖν [h]ἐκ.δευτέρου τὸν ἄνθρωπον" ὃς ἦν τυφλός, καὶ
called therefore a second time the man who was blind, and
[f]εἶπον' αὐτῷ, Δὸς δόξαν τῷ θεῷ· ἡμεῖς οἴδαμεν ὅτι [i]ὁ ἄνθρω-
said to him, Give glory to God; we know that [2]man
πος οὗτος" ἁμαρτωλός ἐστιν. 25 Ἀπεκρίθη οὖν ἐκεῖνος
[1]this a sinner is. [3]Answered [2]therefore [1]he
[k]καὶ εἶπεν," Εἰ ἁμαρτωλός ἐστιν οὐκ.οἶδα· ἓν οἶδα, ὅτι
and said, If a sinner he is I know not. One [thing] I know, that
τυφλὸς ὢν ἄρτι βλέπω. 26 Εἶπον.[l]δὲ" αὐτῷ [m]πάλιν," Τί
[2]blind [1]being now I see. And they said to him again, What
ἐποίησέν σοι; πῶς ἤνοιξέν σου τοὺς ὀφθαλμούς; 27 Ἀπε-
did he to thee? how opened he thine eyes? He an-
κρίθη αὐτοῖς, Εἶπον ὑμῖν ἤδη, καὶ οὐκ.ἠκούσατε· τί πάλιν
swered them, I told you already, and ye did not hear: why again
θέλετε ἀκούειν; μὴ καὶ ὑμεῖς.θέλετε αὐτοῦ μαθηταὶ γενέσθαι;
do ye wish to hear? [3]also [1]do [2]ye wish his disciples to become?
28 [n]Ἐλοιδόρησαν [o]οὖν" αὐτόν, καὶ [p]εἶπον," Σὺ [q]εἶ μαθητὴς"
They [2]railed [3]at [1]therefore him, and said, Thou art [2]disciple
ἐκείνου· ἡμεῖς.δὲ τοῦ [r]Μωσέως" ἐσμὲν μαθηταί. 29 ἡμεῖς οἴδα-
[1]his, but we of Moses are disciples. We know
μεν ὅτι [s]Μωσῇ" λελάληκεν ὁ θεός· τοῦτον.δὲ οὐκ.οἴδαμεν
that to Moses [2]has [3]spoken [1]God; but this [man] we know not
πόθεν ἐστίν. 30 Ἀπεκρίθη ὁ ἄνθρωπος καὶ εἶπεν αὐτοῖς, Ἐν
whence he is. [3]Answered [1]the [2]man and said to them, [2]In
[t]γὰρ τούτῳ" [v]θαυμαστόν ἐστιν, ὅτι ὑμεῖς οὐκ.οἴδατε πόθεν
[1]indeed this a wonderful thing is, that ye know not whence
ἐστίν, καὶ [w]ἀνέῳξέν" μου τοὺς ὀφθαλμούς. 31 οἴδαμεν.[x]δὲ" ὅτι
he is, and he opened mine eyes. But we know that
[y]ἁμαρτωλῶν ὁ θεὸς" οὐκ.ἀκούει· ἀλλ' ἐάν τις θεοσεβὴς ᾖ,
sinners God does not hear; but if anyone God-fearing be,
καὶ τὸ θέλημα αὐτοῦ ποιῇ, τούτου ἀκούει. 32 ἐκ.τοῦ.αἰῶνος
and the will of him do, him he hears. [4]Ever
οὐκ.ἠκούσθη, ὅτι [z]ἤνοιξέν" τις ὀφθαλμοὺς τυφλοῦ
[5]it [2]was [3]not heard that [2]opened [1]anyone [the] eyes of [one] [4]blind
γεγεννημένου. 33 εἰ μὴ ἦν οὗτος παρὰ θεοῦ οὐκ ἠ-
[5]having [2]been [3]born. If [4]not [3]were [1]this [[2]man] from God he
δύνατο ποιεῖν οὐδέν. 34 Ἀπεκρίθησαν καὶ [a]εἶπον" αὐτῷ, Ἐν
could do nothing. They answered and said to him, In
ἁμαρτίαις σὺ ἐγεννήθης ὅλος, καὶ σὺ διδάσκεις ἡμᾶς; Καὶ
sins thou wast born wholly, and [2]thou [1]teachest us? And
ἐξέβαλον αὐτὸν ἔξω. 35 Ἤκουσεν [b]ὁ" Ἰησοῦς ὅτι ἐξέβαλον
they cast him out. [2]Heard [1]Jesus that they cast
αὐτὸν ἔξω· καὶ εὑρὼν αὐτὸν εἶπεν [c]αὐτῷ," Σὺ πιστεύεις
him out, and having found him said to him, [2]Thou [1]believest
εἰς τὸν υἱὸν τοῦ [d]θεοῦ;" 36 Ἀπεκρίθη ἐκεῖνος [e]καὶ εἶπεν," [f]Τίς
on the Son of God? [2]Answered [1]he and said, Who
ἐστιν, κύριε, ἵνα πιστεύσω εἰς αὐτόν; 37 Εἶπεν [g]δὲ" αὐτῷ
is he, Lord, that I may believe on him? And [2]said [3]to [4]him
ὁ Ἰησοῦς, Καὶ ἑώρακας αὐτόν, καὶ ὁ λαλῶν μετὰ σοῦ
[1]Jesus, [7]Both [5]thou [6]hast seen him, and he who speaks with thee
ἐκεῖνός ἐστιν. 38 Ὁ.δὲ ἔφη, Πιστεύω, κύριε· καὶ προσεκύνη-
[2]he [1]is. And he said, I believe, Lord: and he worshipped
σεν αὐτῷ. 39 καὶ εἶπεν ὁ Ἰησοῦς, Εἰς κρίμα ἐγὼ εἰς τὸν
him. And [2]said [1]Jesus, For judgment I into
κόσμον.τοῦτον ἦλθον, ἵνα οἱ μὴ.βλέποντες βλέπωσιν, καὶ
this world came, that they that see not might see, and
οἱ βλέποντες τυφλοὶ γένωνται. 40 [h]Καὶ" ἤκουσαν ἐκ τῶν
they that see blind might become. And [9]heard [2]of [3]the
Φαρισαίων [i]ταῦτα" οἱ [k]ὄντες μετ' αὐτοῦ," καὶ [l]εἶ-
[4]Pharisees [10]these [11]things [1]those [5]who [6]were [7]with [8]him, and they
πον" αὐτῷ, Μὴ καὶ ἡμεῖς τυφλοί ἐσμεν; 41 Εἶπεν αὐτοῖς ὁ
said to him, [3]Also [2]we [4]blind [1]are? Said to them
Ἰησοῦς, Εἰ τυφλοὶ ἦτε, οὐκ.ἂν.εἴχετε ἁμαρτίαν· νῦν.δὲ λέ-
Jesus, If blind ye were, ye would not have sin; but now ye
γετε, Ὅτι βλέπομεν· ἡ [m]οὖν" ἁμαρτία ὑμῶν μένει.
say We see, the [2]therefore [1]sin of you remains.

10 Ἀμὴν ἀμὴν λέγω ὑμῖν, ὁ μὴ.εἰσερχόμενος διὰ τῆς
Verily verily I say to you, He that enters not in by the
θύρας εἰς τὴν αὐλὴν τῶν προβάτων, ἀλλὰ ἀναβαίνων ἀλ-
door to the fold of the sheep, but mounts up else-
λαχόθεν, ἐκεῖνος κλέπτης ἐστὶν καὶ λῃστής· 2 ὁ.δὲ εἰσερ-
where, he a thief is and a robber; but he that en-
χόμενος διὰ τῆς θύρας ποιμήν ἐστιν τῶν προβάτων. 3 τούτῳ
ters in by the door shepherd is of the sheep. To him
ὁ θυρωρὸς ἀνοίγει, καὶ τὰ πρόβατα τῆς.φωνῆς.αὐτοῦ ἀκούει,
the door-keeper opens, and the sheep his voice hear,
καὶ τὰ.ἴδια πρόβατα [n]καλεῖ" κατ' ὄνομα, καὶ ἐξάγει αὐτά.
and his own sheep he calls by name, and leads [2]out [1]them.
4 [o]καὶ" ὅταν τὰ.ἴδια [p]πρόβατα" ἐκβάλῃ ἔμπροσθεν αὐτῶν
And when his own sheep he puts forth before them

24 Then a second time they called the man
who was blind and said to him, Give glory to
God. We know that this man is a sinner.
25 Then he answered and said, I do not
know if he is a sinner. One thing I do know,
that I was blind *but* now I see.
26 They said to him again, What did he do
to you? How did he open your eyes?
27 He answered them, I told you before and
you did not listen. Why do you want to hear
again? Do you also want to become his disciples?
28 And they shouted at him and said, You
are his disciple, but we are Moses' disciples.
29 We know that God has spoken to Moses,
but we do not know where this one is from.
30 The man answered and said to them,
Why, this is a wonderful thing indeed, that
you do not know where he is from, and he
opened my eyes.
31 But we know that God does not hear
sinners. And if anyone is a worshiper of God
and does His will, He hears him.
32 Since the world began it was never heard
that anyone opened the eyes of one who was
born blind!
33 If this one were not from God, he could
do nothing.
34 They answered and said to him, You
were born totally in sins, and do you teach
us? And they threw him out.
35 Jesus heard that they threw him out.
And finding him He said to him, Do you
believe on the Son of God?
36 He answered and said, Who is He, Lord,
that I may believe on Him?
37 And Jesus said to him, You have both
seen Him and He who speaks with you is He.
38 And he said, I believe, Lord! And he
worshiped Him.
39 And Jesus said, I came into this world
for judgment, so that they who do not see
may see, and those who see may become
blind.
40 And those of the Pharisees who were
with Him heard these things. And they said,
Are we blind too?
41 Jesus said to them, If you were blind,
you would have no sin. But now you say, We
see! Therefore your sin remains.

CHAPTER 10

1 Indeed, I say to you, He that does not
enter in by the door of the sheepfold, but
climbs up some other place, that one is a
thief and a robber.
2 But he that goes in by the door is the
shepherd of the sheep.
3 The gatekeeper opens to him. And the
sheep hear his voice, and he calls his own
sheep by name and leads them out.
4 And when he takes out his own sheep, he
goes in front of them. And the sheep follow

πορεύεται· καὶ τὰ πρόβατα αὐτῷ ἀκολουθεῖ, ὅτι οἴδασιν
he goes; and the sheep him follow, because they know
τὴν.φωνὴν.αὐτοῦ. 5 ἀλλοτρίῳ.δὲ οὐ.μὴ [q]ἀκολουθήσωσιν,‖
his voice. But a stranger in no wise they should follow,
ἀλλὰ φεύξονται ἀπ' αὐτοῦ· ὅτι οὐκ.οἴδασιν τῶν ἀλλοτρίων
but will flee from him, because they know not of strangers
τὴν φωνήν. 6 Ταύτην τὴν παροιμίαν εἶπεν αὐτοῖς ὁ Ἰησοῦς,
the voice. This allegory 2spoke 3to 4them 1Jesus,
ἐκεῖνοι.δὲ οὐκ.ἔγνωσαν τίνα [r]ἦν‖ ἃ ἐλάλει αὐτοῖς.
but they knew not what it was which he spoke to them.
7 Εἶπεν οὖν [s]πάλιν αὐτοῖς‖ ὁ Ἰησοῦς, Ἀμὴν ἀμὴν λέγω
2Said 3therefore 4again 5to 6them 1Jesus, Verily verily I say
ὑμῖν, [t]ὅτι‖ ἐγώ εἰμι ἡ θύρα τῶν προβάτων. 8 πάντες ὅσοι
to you, that I am the door of the sheep. All whoever
[v]πρὸ ἐμοῦ ἦλθον‖ κλέπται εἰσὶν καὶ λῃσταί· ἀλλ' οὐκ.ἤκουσαν
before me came thieves are and robbers; but 3did 4not 5hear
αὐτῶν τὰ πρόβατα. 9 ἐγώ εἰμι ἡ θύρα· δι' ἐμοῦ ἐάν τις
6them 1the 2sheep. I am the door: by me if anyone
εἰσέλθῃ σωθήσεται, καὶ εἰσελεύσεται καὶ ἐξελεύσεται, καὶ
enter in he shall be saved, and shall go in and shall go out, and
νομὴν εὑρήσει. 10 ὁ κλέπτης οὐκ.ἔρχεται εἰ.μὴ ἵνα κλέψῃ
pasture shall find. The thief comes not except that he may steal
καὶ θύσῃ καὶ ἀπολέσῃ· ἐγὼ ἦλθον ἵνα ζωὴν ἔχωσιν,
and may kill and may destroy: I came that life they might have,
καὶ περισσὸν ἔχωσιν. 11 Ἐγώ εἰμι ὁ ποιμὴν ὁ καλός· ὁ
and abundantly might have [it]. I am the 2shepherd 1good. The
ποιμὴν ὁ καλὸς τὴν.ψυχὴν.αὐτοῦ τίθησιν ὑπὲρ τῶν προβά-
2shepherd 1good his life lays down for the sheep:
των. 12 ὁ.μισθωτὸς.[w]δέ,‖ καὶ οὐκ.ὢν ποιμήν, οὗ οὐκ
but the hired servant, and who is not [the] shepherd, whose 5not
[x]εἰσὶν‖ τὰ πρόβατα ἴδια, θεωρεῖ τὸν λύκον ἐρχόμενον, καὶ
4are 2the 3sheep 1own, sees the wolf coming, and
ἀφίησιν τὰ πρόβατα καὶ φεύγει· καὶ ὁ λύκος ἁρπάζει αὐτὰ
leaves the sheep, and flees; and the wolf seizes them
καὶ σκορπίζει [y]τὰ πρόβατα. 13 ὁ.δὲ μισθωτὸς φεύγει‖ ὅτι
and scatters the sheep. Now the hired servant flees because
μισθωτός ἐστιν, καὶ οὐ.μέλει.αὐτῷ περὶ τῶν προβάτων.
a hired servant he is, and is not himself concerned about the sheep.
14 ἐγώ εἰμι ὁ ποιμὴν ὁ καλός· καὶ γινώσκω τὰ ἐμά,
I am the 2shepherd 1good; and I know those that [are] mine,
καὶ [z]γινώσκομαι ὑπὸ τῶν ἐμῶν.‖ 15 καθὼς γινώσκει
and am known of those that [are] mine. As 3knows
με ὁ πατήρ, κἀγὼ γινώσκω τὸν πατέρα· καὶ τὴν.ψυχήν.μου
4me 1the 2Father, I also know the Father; and my life
τίθημι ὑπὲρ τῶν προβάτων. 16 καὶ ἄλλα πρόβατα ἔχω,
I lay down for the sheep. And other sheep I have,
ἃ οὐκ.ἔστιν ἐκ τῆς.αὐλῆς.ταύτης· κἀκεῖνά [a]με δεῖ‖
which are not of this fold; those also 3me 1it 2behoves
ἀγαγεῖν, καὶ τῆς.φωνῆς.μου ἀκούσουσιν· καὶ [b]γενήσεται‖ μία
to bring, and my voice they will hear; and there shall be one
ποίμνη, εἷς ποιμήν. 17 διὰ.τοῦτο [c]ὁ πατήρ με‖ ἀγαπᾷ,
flock, one shepherd. On this account the Father me loves,
ὅτι ἐγὼ τίθημι τὴν.ψυχήν.μου, ἵνα πάλιν λάβω αὐτήν.
because I lay down my life, that again I may take it.
18 οὐδεὶς αἴρει αὐτὴν ἀπ' ἐμοῦ, ἀλλ' ἐγὼ τίθημι αὐτὴν ἀπ'
No one takes it from me, but I lay down it of
ἐμαυτοῦ. ἐξουσίαν ἔχω θεῖναι αὐτήν, καὶ ἐξουσίαν ἔχω
myself. Authority I have to lay down it, and authority I have
πάλιν λαβεῖν αὐτήν· ταύτην τὴν ἐντολὴν ἔλαβον παρὰ
again to take it. This commandment I received from
τοῦ.πατρός.μου. 19 Σχίσμα [d]οὖν‖ πάλιν ἐγένετο ἐν τοῖς
my Father. A division therefore again there was among the
Ἰουδαίοις διὰ τοὺς.λόγους.τούτους. 20 ἔλεγον [e]δὲ‖
Jews on account of these words; 2said 1but
πολλοὶ ἐξ αὐτῶν, Δαιμόνιον ἔχει καὶ μαίνεται· τί αὐτοῦ
many of them, A demon he has and is mad; why him
ἀκούετε; 21 Ἄλλοι ἔλεγον, Ταῦτα τὰ ῥήματα οὐκ.ἔστιν
do ye hear? Others said, These sayings are not [those]
δαιμονιζομένου· μὴ δαιμόνιον δύναται τυφλῶν
of one possessed by a demon. 2A 3demon 1is able of [the] blind [the]
ὀφθαλμοὺς [f]ἀνοίγειν‖;
eyes to open?
22 Ἐγένετο.δὲ τὰ [g]ἐγκαίνια‖ ἐν [h]τοῖς‖ Ἱεροσολύμοις,
And took place the feast of dedication at Jerusalem,
[i]καὶ‖ χειμὼν ἦν· 23 καὶ περιεπάτει [k]ὁ‖ Ἰησοῦς ἐν τῷ ἱερῷ
and winter it was. And 2was 3walking 1Jesus in the temple
ἐν τῇ στοᾷ [l]τοῦ Σολομῶντος.‖ 24 ἐκύκλωσαν οὖν αὐτὸν
in the porch of Solomon. 4Encircled 3therefore 5him
οἱ Ἰουδαῖοι, καὶ ἔλεγον αὐτῷ, Ἕως πότε τὴν.ψυχὴν.ἡμῶν
1the 2Jews, and said to him, Until when our soul
αἴρεις; εἰ σὺ εἶ ὁ χριστός, [m]εἰπὲ‖ ἡμῖν παρ-
holdest thou in suspense? If thou art the Christ, tell us plain-

him because they know his voice.
5 But they will not follow a stranger, but
will flee from him because they do not know
the voice of strangers.
6 Jesus spoke this parable to them, but they
did not understand what it was which He
spoke to them.

7 Then Jesus said again to them, Indeed, I tell
you truly that I am the door of the sheep.
8 All those who came before Me are thieves
and robbers, but the sheep did not hear them.
9 I am the door. If anyone enter in through
Me he shall be saved and shall go in and shall
go out and shall find pasture.
10 The thief does not come except that he
may steal and kill and destroy. I have come
that they may have life and might have it
abundantly.
11 I am the Good Shepherd! The Good Shepherd lays down His life for the sheep.
12 But the hired servant, and he who is not
the shepherd, who does not own the sheep,
sees the wolf coming and leaves the sheep
and runs away. And the wolf catches them
and scatters the sheep.
13 Now the hired servant runs away because
he is a hired servant and does not care about
the sheep.

14 I am the Good Shepherd, and I know
those that are Mine. And I am known by
those who are Mine.
15 Even as the Father knows Me, I also
know the Father. And I lay down My life for
the sheep.
16 And I have other sheep which are not of
this fold. It is needful that I bring these also,
and they shall hear My voice, and there shall
be one flock, one Shepherd.
17 Because of this the Father loves Me, because I lay down My life, in order that I
might take it up again.

18 No one takes it from Me, but I lay it down
of Myself. I have authority to lay it down and
I have authority to take it up again. I received
this commandment from My Father.
19 Then again there was a division among the
Jews, because of these words.
20 And many of them said, He has a demon
and is insane. Why do you listen to him?
21 Others said, These are not the words of
one who is demon-possessed. Is a demon
able to open the eyes of the blind?

22 Now the Feast of Dedication took place
at Jerusalem, and it was winter.
23 And Jesus was walking in the Temple, in
the porch of Solomon.
24 Then the Jews came around Him and said
to Him, How long do you hold our soul in
suspense? If you are the Christ, tell us plainly.

ῥησίᾳ. 25 Ἀπεκρίθη [n]αὐτοῖς[‖] [k]ὁ[‖] Ἰησοῦς, Εἶπον ὑμῖν, καὶ
ly. [2]Answered [3]them [1]Jesus, I told you, and
οὐ.πιστεύετε. τὰ ἔργα ἃ ἐγὼ ποιῶ.ἐν τῷ ὀνόματι τοῦ πατρός
ye believe not. The works which I do in the name of [2]Father
μου, ταῦτα μαρτυρεῖ περὶ ἐμοῦ· 26 [o]ἀλλ'[‖] ὑμεῖς οὐ
[1]my, these bear witness concerning me: but ye [2]not
πιστεύετε· [p]οὐ.γάρ[‖].ἐστε ἐκ τῶν προβάτων τῶν ἐμῶν, [q]καθὼς
[1]believe, for ye are not of [2]sheep [1]my, as
εἶπον ὑμῖν.[‖] 27 τὰ πρόβατα τὰ ἐμὰ τῆς.φωνῆς.μου [r]ἀκούει,[r]
I said to you. [2]Sheep [1]my my voice hear,
κἀγὼ γινώσκω αὐτά· καὶ ἀκολουθοῦσίν μοι, 28 κἀγὼ [s]ζωὴν
and I know them, and they follow me; and I life
αἰώνιον δίδωμι αὐτοῖς·[‖] καὶ οὐ.μὴ ἀπόλωνται εἰς τὸν
eternal give them; and in no wise shall they perish for
αἰῶνα, καὶ οὐχ.ἁρπάσει τις αὐτὰ ἐκ τῆς.χειρός.μου. 29 ὁ
ever, and [3]shall [1]not [4]seize [2]anyone them out of my hand.
πατήρ.[t]μου[‖] [v]ὃς[‖] δέδωκέν μοι [w]μείζων πάντων[‖] ἐστίν· καὶ
My Father who has given [them] to me greater than all is, and
οὐδεὶς δύναται ἁρπάζειν ἐκ τῆς χειρὸς τοῦ.πατρός.[x]μου.[‖]
no one is able to seize out of the hand of my Father.
30 ἐγὼ καὶ ὁ πατὴρ ἕν ἐσμεν. 31 Ἐβάστασαν [y]οὖν[‖] πάλιν
I and the Father one are. [5]Took [6]up [3]therefore [4]again
λίθους οἱ Ἰουδαῖοι ἵνα λιθάσωσιν αὐτόν. 32 ἀπεκρίθη
[7]stones [1]the [2]Jews that they might stone him. [2]Answered
αὐτοῖς ὁ Ἰησοῦς, Πολλὰ [z]καλὰ ἔργα[‖] ἔδειξα ὑμῖν ἐκ τοῦ
[3]them [1]Jesus, Many good works I shewed you from
πατρός.[a]μου·[‖] διὰ ποῖον αὐτῶν ἔργον [b]λιθάζετέ με[‖];
my Father; because of which [2]of [3]them [1]work do ye stone me?
33 Ἀπεκρίθησαν αὐτῷ οἱ Ἰουδαῖοι [c]λέγοντες,[‖] Περὶ καλοῦ
[3]Answered [4]him [1]the [2]Jews, saying, For a good
ἔργου οὐ.λιθάζομέν σε, ἀλλὰ περὶ βλασφημίας, καὶ ὅτι
work we do not stone thee, but for blasphemy, and because
σὺ ἄνθρωπος ὢν ποιεῖς σεαυτὸν θεόν. 34 Ἀπεκρίθη αὐτοῖς
thou [2]a [3]man [1]being makest thyself God. [2]Answered [3]them
[d]ὁ[‖] Ἰησοῦς, Οὐκ.ἔστιν γεγραμμένον ἐν τῷ.νόμῳ.ὑμῶν, [e]Ἐγὼ
[1]Jesus, Is it not written in your law, I
[f]εἶπα,[‖] θεοί ἐστε; 35 Εἰ ἐκείνους εἶπεν θεούς, πρὸς οὓς ὁ
said, [3]gods [1]ye [2]are? If them he called gods, to whom the
λόγος [g]τοῦ θεοῦ ἐγένετο,[‖] καὶ οὐ.δύναται λυθῆναι ἡ γραφή·
word of God came, (and [3]cannot [4]be [5]broken [1]the [2]scripture,)
36 ὃν ὁ πατὴρ ἡγίασεν καὶ ἀπέστειλεν εἰς τὸν κόσμον,
[of him] whom the Father sanctified and sent into the world,
ὑμεῖς.λέγετε, Ὅτι βλασφημεῖς, ὅτι εἶπον, Υἱὸς [h]τοῦ[‖] θεοῦ
do ye say, Thou blasphemest, because I said, Son of God
εἰμι; 37 εἰ οὐ.ποιῶ τὰ ἔργα τοῦ.πατρός.μου, μὴ.πιστεύετέ
I am? If I do not the works of my Father, believe not
μοι· 38 εἰ.δὲ ποιῶ, κἂν ἐμοὶ μὴ.[i]πιστεύητε,[‖] τοῖς ἔργοις
me; but if I do, even if me ye believe not, the works
[k]πιστεύσατε,[‖] ἵνα γνῶτε καὶ [l]πιστεύσητε[‖] ὅτι ἐν ἐμοὶ
believe, that ye may perceive and may believe that in me [is]
ὁ πατήρ, κἀγὼ ἐν [m]αὐτῷ.[‖] 39 Ἐζήτουν [n]οὖν[‖] [o]πάλιν[‖]
the Father, and I in him. They sought therefore again
αὐτὸν πιάσαι· καὶ ἐξῆλθεν ἐκ τῆς.χειρὸς.αὐτῶν. 40 Καὶ
him to take, and he went forth out of their hand; and
ἀπῆλθεν πάλιν πέραν τοῦ Ἰορδάνου, εἰς τὸν τόπον ὅπου ἦν
departed again beyond the Jordan, to the place where was
[p]Ἰωάννης[‖] τὸ πρῶτον βαπτίζων· καὶ [q]ἔμεινεν[‖] ἐκεῖ. 41 καὶ
John first baptizing; and he abode there. And
πολλοὶ ἦλθον πρὸς αὐτόν, καὶ ἔλεγον, Ὅτι [p]Ἰωάννης[‖] μὲν
many came to him, and said, John indeed
σημεῖον ἐποίησεν οὐδέν· πάντα.δὲ ὅσα εἶπεν [p]Ἰωάννης[‖]
[3]sign [1]did [2]no; but all whatsoever [2]said [1]John
περὶ τούτου, ἀληθῆ ἦν. 42 Καὶ [r]ἐπίστευσαν πολλοὶ
concerning this [man], true were. And [2]believed [1]many
ἐκεῖ εἰς αὐτόν.[‖]
there on him.

11 Ἦν.δέ τις ἀσθενῶν Λάζαρος ἀπὸ Βηθανίας,
Now there was a certain [man] sick, Lazarus of Bethany,
ἐκ τῆς κώμης [s] Μαρίας καὶ Μάρθας τῆς.ἀδελφῆς.αὐτῆς. 2 ἦν
of the village of Mary and Martha her sister. [2]It [3]was
δὲ [t]Μαρία[‖] ἡ ἀλείψασα τὸν κύριον μύρῳ καὶ ἐκμάξασα
[1]and Mary who anointed the Lord with ointment and wiped
τοὺς.πόδας.αὐτοῦ ταῖς.θριξὶν.αὐτῆς, ἧς ὁ ἀδελφὸς Λάζαρος
his feet with her hair, whose brother Lazarus
ἠσθένει. 3 ἀπέστειλαν οὖν αἱ ἀδελφαὶ πρὸς αὐτὸν λέγου-
was sick. [4]Sent [3]therefore [1]the [2]sisters to him, say-
σαι, Κύριε, ἴδε ὃν φιλεῖς ἀσθενεῖ. 4 Ἀκούσας.δὲ ὁ Ἰησοῦς
ing, Lord, lo, he whom thou lovest is sick. But [2]having [3]heard [1]Jesus
εἶπεν, Αὕτη ἡ ἀσθένεια οὐκ.ἔστιν πρὸς θάνατον, ἀλλ' ὑπὲρ
said, This sickness is not unto death, but for

25 Jesus answered them, I told you and you
do not believe. The works which I do in the
name of My Father, these witness about Me.
26 But you do not believe because you are
not of My sheep. As I told you,
27 My sheep hear My voice and I know
them. And they follow Me.
28 And I give to them eternal life. And they
shall never perish, nor shall anyone pluck
them out of My hand.
29 My Father who has given *them* to Me is
greater than all, and no one is able to pluck
them out of My Father's hand.
30 The Father and I are one!
31 Then again the Jews took up stones that
they might stone Him.
32 Jesus answered them, I showed you
many good works from My Father. For
which work of these are you stoning Me?
33 The Jews answered Him, saying, We are
not stoning you for a good work, but for
blasphemy – and because you, being a man,
make yourself God.
34 Jesus answered them, Is it not written in
your Law, "I said, you are gods"?
35 If He called them gods to whom the
word of God came – and the Scriptures cannot be broken –
36 do you say *of Him* whom the Father set
apart and sent into the world, You blaspheme! – because I said, I am the Son of
God?
37 If I do not the works of My Father, do
not believe Me.
38 But if I do, even if you do not believe
Me, believe the works so that you may know
and believe that the Father is in Me and I in
Him.
39 Then they tried again to seize Him, but
He departed out of their hand.
40 And He went again beyond the Jordan
into the place where John was at first baptizing. And He stayed there.
41 And many came to Him and said, John
really did no miracle, but all things that
John said about this One were true.
42 And many believed on Him there.

CHAPTER 11

1 Now there was a certain sick one, Laz-a-
rus of Bethany, of the town of Mary and her
sister Martha.
2 And it was Mary who anointed the Lord
with ointment and wiped His feet with her
hair, whose brother Laz-a-rus was sick.
3 So the sisters sent to Him, saying, Behold,
Lord, the one You love is sick.
4 And Jesus listened and said, This illness is
not to death, but for the glory of God, so
that the Son of God may be glorified by it.

τῆς δόξης τοῦ θεοῦ, ἵνα δοξασθῇ ὁ υἱὸς τοῦ θεοῦ δι'
the glory of God, that may be glorified the Son of God by
αὐτῆς. 5 Ἠγάπα δὲ ὁ Ἰησοῦς τὴν Μάρθαν καὶ τὴν ἀδελφὴν
it. [3]Loved [1]now [2]Jesus Martha and [2]sister
αὐτῆς καὶ τὸν Λάζαρον. 6 ὡς οὖν ἤκουσεν ὅτι ἀσθενεῖ,
[1]her and Lazarus. When therefore he heard that he is sick,
τότε μὲν ἔμεινεν ἐν ᾧ ἦν τόπῳ δύο ἡμέρας. 7 [v]Ἔπειτα
then indeed he remained in which [2]he [3]was [1]place two days. Then
μετὰ τοῦτο λέγει τοῖς μαθηταῖς,[w] [x]Ἄγωμεν εἰς τὴν Ἰουδαίαν
after this he says to the disciples, Let us go into Judæa
πάλιν. 8 Λέγουσιν αὐτῷ οἱ μαθηταί, [x]Ῥαββί,ǁ νῦν ἐζή-
again. [3]Say [4]to [5]him [1]the [2]disciples, Rabbi, just now [3]were
τουν σε λιθάσαι οἱ Ἰουδαῖοι, καὶ πάλιν ὑπάγεις ἐκεῖ;
[4]seeking [7]thee [5]to [6]stone [1]the [2]Jews, and again goest thou thither?
9 Ἀπεκρίθη [y]ὁ Ἰησοῦς, Οὐχὶ δώδεκά [z]εἰσιν ὧραιǁ τῆς
[2]Answered [1]Jesus, [5]Not [6]twelve [3]are [4]there hours in the
ἡμέρας; ἐάν τις περιπατῇ ἐν τῇ ἡμέρᾳ, οὐ.προσκόπτει,
day? If anyone walk in the day, he stumbles not,
ὅτι τὸ φῶς τοῦ.κόσμου.τούτου βλέπει· 10 ἐὰν.δέ τις
because the light of this world he sees; but if anyone
περιπατῇ ἐν τῇ νυκτί, προσκόπτει, ὅτι τὸ φῶς οὐκ.ἔστιν ἐν
walk in the night, he stumbles, because the light is not in
αὐτῷ. 11 Ταῦτα εἶπεν, καὶ μετὰ τοῦτο λέγει αὐτοῖς, Λά-
him. These things he said; and after this he says to them, La-
ζαρος ὁ.φίλος.ἡμῶν κεκοίμηται· ἀλλὰ πορεύομαι ἵνα ἐξ-
zarus our friend has fallen asleep; but I go that I may
υπνίσω αὐτόν. 12 Εἶπον οὖν[a] [b]οἱ.μαθηταὶǁ.[c]αὐτοῦ,ǁ Κύριε,
awake him. [2]Said [1]therefore his disciples, Lord,
εἰ κεκοίμηται σωθήσεται. 13 Εἰρήκει.δὲ ὁ Ἰησοῦς περὶ
if he has fallen asleep he will get well. But [2]had [3]spoken [1]Jesus of
τοῦ.θανάτου.αὐτοῦ· ἐκεῖνοι.δὲ ἔδοξαν ὅτι περὶ τῆς κοιμήσεως
his death, but they thought that of the rest
τοῦ ὕπνου λέγει. 14 τότε [d]οὖνǁ εἶπεν αὐτοῖς ὁ Ἰησοῦς
of sleep he speaks. Then therefore [2]said [3]to [4]them [1]Jesus
παῤῥησίᾳ, Λάζαρος ἀπέθανεν· 15 καὶ χαίρω δι'.ὑμᾶς,
plainly, Lazarus died. And I rejoice on your account,
ἵνα πιστεύσητε, ὅτι οὐκ.ἤμην ἐκεῖ· [e]ἀλλ'ǁ ἄγωμεν πρὸς
in order that ye may believe, that I was not there. But let us go to
αὐτόν. 16 Εἶπεν οὖν Θωμᾶς, ὁ λεγόμενος Δίδυμος, τοῖς
him. [2]Said [1]therefore Thomas, called Didymus, to the
[f]συμμαθηταῖς,ǁ [x]Ἄγωμεν καὶ ἡμεῖς, ἵνα ἀποθάνωμεν μετ'
fellow-disciples, Let [3]go [2]also [1]us, that we may die with
αὐτοῦ.
him.

17 [g]Ἐλθὼνǁ οὖν ὁ Ἰησοῦς [h] εὗρεν αὐτὸν τέσσαρας
[3]Having [4]come [2]therefore [1]Jesus found him four
[i]ἡμέρας ἤδηǁ ἔχοντα ἐν τῷ μνημείῳ. 18 ἦν.δὲ [k]ἡǁ Βηθανία
days already having been in the tomb. Now [2]was [1]Bethany
ἐγγὺς τῶν Ἱεροσολύμων, ὡς ἀπὸ σταδίων δεκαπέντε 19 [l]καὶ
near to Jerusalem, about [3]off [2]furlongs [1]fifteen, and
πολλοὶǁ ἐκ τῶν Ἰουδαίων ἐληλύθεισαν πρὸς [m]τὰς περὶǁ
many of the Jews had come unto those around
Μάρθαν καὶ [n]Μαρίαν,ǁ ἵνα παραμυθήσωνται αὐτὰς περὶ
Martha and Mary, that they might console them concerning
τοῦ ἀδελφοῦ.[o]αὐτῶν.ǁ 20 ἡ.οὖν Μάρθα ὡς ἤκουσεν ὅτι [p]ὁǁ
their brother. Martha therefore when she heard that
Ἰησοῦς ἔρχεται, ὑπήντησεν αὐτῷ· Μαρία.δὲ ἐν τῷ οἴκῳ ἐκα-
Jesus is coming, met him; but Mary in the house was
θέζετο. 21 εἶπεν.οὖν [q]ἡ Μάρθα πρὸς [r]τὸνǁ Ἰησοῦν, Κύριε, εἰ
sitting. Then said Martha to Jesus, Lord, if
ἦς ὧδε, [s]ὁ.ἀδελφός μου οὐκ ἂν.ἐτεθνήκει.ǁ 22 [t]ἀλλὰǁ
thou hadst been here, my brother had not died; but
καὶ νῦν οἶδα ὅτι ὅσα ἂν.αἰτήσῃ τὸν θεόν, δώσει
even now I know that whatsoever thou mayest ask of God, [2]will [3]give
σοι ὁ θεός. 23 Λέγει αὐτῇ ὁ Ἰησοῦς, Ἀναστήσεται ὁ ἀδελφός
[4]thee [1]God. Says to her Jesus, [3]Will [4]rise [5]again [2]brother
σου. 24 Λέγει αὐτῷ [v] Μάρθα, Οἶδα ὅτι ἀναστήσεται ἐν τῇ
[1]thy. Says to him Martha, I know that he will rise again in the
ἀναστάσει ἐν τῇ ἐσχάτῃ ἡμέρᾳ. 25 Εἶπεν αὐτῇ ὁ Ἰησοῦς,
resurrection in the last day. [2]Said [3]to [4]her [1]Jesus,
Ἐγώ εἰμι ἡ ἀνάστασις καὶ ἡ ζωή. ὁ πιστεύων εἰς ἐμέ,
I am the resurrection and the life: he that believes on me,
κἂν ἀποθάνῃ ζήσεται· 26 καὶ πᾶς ὁ ζῶν καὶ πιστεύων
though he die he shall live; and everyone who lives and believes
εἰς ἐμέ, οὐ μὴ ἀποθάνῃ εἰς.τὸν αἰῶνα. πιστεύεις τοῦτο;
on me, in no wise shall die for ever. Believest thou this?
27 Λέγει αὐτῷ, Ναί, κύριε· ἐγὼ πεπίστευκα ὅτι σὺ εἶ ὁ
She says to him, Yea, Lord; I have believed that thou art the
χριστός, ὁ υἱὸς τοῦ θεοῦ, ὁ εἰς τὸν κόσμον ἐρχόμενος.
Christ, the Son of God, who into the world comes.

5 Now Jesus loved Martha and her sister and
Laz-a-rus.
6 So when He heard that he was sick, then
indeed He remained where He was two days.
7 Then after this He said to the disciples,
Let us go into Judea again.
8 The disciples said to Him, Master, the
Jews were just now trying to stone You and
are You now going back there again?
9 Jesus answered, Are there not twelve
hours in daytime? If anyone walks in the
daytime he does not stumble because he sees
the light of the world.
10 But if anyone walks in the nighttime, he
stumbles because the light is not in him.
11 He said these things. And afterward He
said to them, Our friend Laz-a-rus has fallen
asleep, but I am going that I may awaken him.
12 Then His disciples said, Lord, if he has
fallen asleep, he will get well.
13 But Jesus had spoken of his death, and
they thought that He had spoken of the rest of
sleep.
14 So then Jesus said to them plainly, Laz-a-
rus died.
15 And I rejoice for your sakes that I was not
there, so that you may believe. But let us go to
him.
16 Then Thomas, the one called Did-y-mus,
said to his fellow-disciples, Let us go too, so
that we may die with him.
17 So when Jesus came, He found him. He
had already been four days in the tomb.
18 Now Bethany was near Jerusalem, about
two miles away.
19 And many of the Jews had come to
those around Martha and Mary, so that they
might comfort them about their brother.
20 Then when she heard that Jesus was
coming, Martha met Him. But Mary was still
sitting in the house.
21 Then Martha said to Jesus, Lord, if You
had been here my brother would not have
died.
22 But I know even now that whatever You
ask of God, God will give it to You.
23 Jesus said to her, Your brother will rise
again.
24 Martha said to Him, I know that he will
rise again in the resurrection in the last day.
25 Jesus said to her, I am the Resurrection
and the Life. He that believes on Me, though
he die, he shall live.
26 And everyone who lives and believes on
Me shall never die. Do you believe this?
27 She said to Him, Yes, Lord, I have
believed that You are the Christ, the Son of
God who is coming into the world.

28 Καὶ [w]ταῦτα" εἰποῦσα ἀπῆλθεν, καὶ ἐφώνησεν [x]Μαρίαν"
And these things having said she went away, and called Mary
τὴν.ἀδελφὴν.αὐτῆς [y]λάθρα," [z]εἰποῦσα," Ὁ διδάσκαλος πάρ-
her sister secretly, saying, The teacher is
εστιν καὶ φωνεῖ σε. 29 Ἐκείνη [a] ὡς ἤκουσεν [b]ἐγείρεται" ταχὺ
come and calls thee. She when she heard rises up quickly
καὶ [c]ἔρχεται" πρὸς αὐτόν. 30 οὔπω.δὲ ἐληλύθει ὁ Ἰησοῦς
and comes to him. Now not yet had ²come ¹Jesus
εἰς τὴν κώμην, ἀλλ' ἦν [d] ἐν τῷ τόπῳ ὅπου ὑπήντησεν αὐτῷ
into the village, but was in the place where ²met ³him
ἡ Μάρθα. 31 οἱ.οὖν.Ἰουδαῖοι οἱ ὄντες μετ' αὐτῆς ἐν τῇ οἰκίᾳ
¹Martha. The Jews therefore who were with her in the house
καὶ παραμυθούμενοι αὐτήν, ἰδόντες τὴν [e]Μαρίαν' ὅτι ταχέως
and consoling her, having seen Mary that quickly
ἀνέστη καὶ ἐξῆλθεν, ἠκολούθησαν αὐτῇ, [f]λέγοντες,' Ὅτι
she rose up and went out, followed her, saying,
ὑπάγει εἰς τὸ μνημεῖον ἵνα κλαύσῃ ἐκεῖ. 32 Ἡ.οὖν.[g]Μαρία'
She is going to the tomb that she may weep there. Mary therefore
ὡς ἦλθεν ὅπου ἦν [h]ὁ" Ἰησοῦς, ἰδοῦσα αὐτὸν ἔπεσεν [i]εἰς
when she came where ²was ¹Jesus, seeing him, fell at
τοὺς.πόδας.αὐτοῦ," λέγουσα αὐτῷ, Κύριε, εἰ ἦς ὧδε
his feet, saying to him, Lord, if thou hadst been here
οὐκ.ἂν.[k]ἀπέθανέν μου" ὁ ἀδελφός. 33 Ἰησοῦς οὖν ὡς εἶδεν
³had ⁴not ⁵died ¹my ²brother. Jesus therefore when he saw
αὐτὴν κλαίουσαν, καὶ τοὺς συνελθόντας αὐτῇ Ἰουδαίους
her weeping, and the ²who ³came ⁴with ⁵her ¹Jews
κλαίοντας, ἐνεβριμήσατο τῷ πνεύματι, καὶ ἐτάραξεν ἑαυτόν,
weeping, he groaned in spirit, and troubled himself,
34 καὶ εἶπεν, Ποῦ τεθείκατε αὐτόν; Λέγουσιν αὐτῷ, Κύριε,
and said, Where have ye laid him? They say to him, Lord,
ἔρχου καὶ ἴδε. 35 Ἐδάκρυσεν ὁ Ἰησοῦς. 36 ἔλεγον οὖν οἱ
come and see. ²Wept ¹Jesus. ³Said ⁴therefore ¹the
Ἰουδαῖοι, Ἴδε πῶς ἐφίλει αὐτόν. 37 Τινὲς.δὲ ἐξ αὐτῶν
²Jews, Behold how he loved him! But some of them
εἶπον, Οὐκ.[l]ἠδύνατο" οὗτος ὁ ἀνοίξας τοὺς ὀφθαλμοὺς
said, Was not ²able ¹this [²man] who opened the eyes
τοῦ τυφλοῦ, ποιῆσαι ἵνα καὶ οὗτος μὴ.ἀποθάνῃ;
of the blind [man], to have caused that also this one should not have died?
38 Ἰησοῦς οὖν πάλιν [m]ἐμβριμώμενος" ἐν ἑαυτῷ ἔρχεται
Jesus therefore again groaning in himself comes
εἰς τὸ μνημεῖον. ἦν.δὲ σπήλαιον, καὶ λίθος ἐπέκειτο ἐπ'
to the tomb. Now it was a cave, and a stone was lying upon
αὐτῷ. 39 λέγει [n]ὁ" Ἰησοῦς, Ἄρατε τὸν λίθον. Λέγει αὐτῷ
it. ²Says ¹Jesus, Take away the stone. ³Says ¹to ²him
ἡ ἀδελφὴ τοῦ [o]τεθνηκότος" Μάρθα, Κύριε, ἤδη ὄζει·
⁵the ⁶sister ⁷of ⁸him ⁹who ¹⁰has ¹¹died, ⁴Martha, Lord, already he stinks,
τεταρταῖος γάρ ἐστιν. 40 Λέγει αὐτῇ ὁ Ἰησοῦς, Οὐκ.εἶπόν
⁴four ⁵days for ²it ³is. ²Says ³to ⁴her ¹Jesus, Said I not
σοι, ὅτι ἐὰν πιστεύσῃς, [p]ὄψει" τὴν δόξαν τοῦ θεοῦ;
to thee, that if thou shouldest believe, thou shalt see the glory of God?
41 Ἦραν οὖν τὸν λίθον [q]οὗ ἦν ὁ τεθνηκὼς κείμενος.[r]
They took away therefore the stone where ³was ¹the ²dead ⁴laid.
Ὁ.δὲ.Ἰησοῦς ἦρεν τοὺς ὀφθαλμοὺς ἄνω, καὶ εἶπεν, Πά-
And Jesus lifted [his] eyes upwards, and said, Fa-
τερ, εὐχαριστῶ σοι ὅτι ἤκουσάς μου. 42 ἐγὼ.δὲ ᾔδειν ὅτι
ther, I thank thee that thou heardest me; and I knew that
πάντοτέ μου ἀκούεις· ἀλλὰ διὰ τὸν ὄχλον τὸν περι-
always me thou hearest; but on account of the crowd who stand
εστῶτα εἶπον ἵνα πιστεύσωσιν ὅτι σύ με ἀπέστειλας.
around I said [it], that they might believe that thou me didst send.
43 Καὶ ταῦτα εἰπών, φωνῇ μεγάλῃ ἐκραύγασεν, Λά-
And these things having said, with a ²voice ¹loud he cried, La-
ζαρε, δεῦρο ἔξω. 44 [r]Καὶ" ἐξῆλθεν ὁ τεθνηκώς, δεδεμένος
zarus, come forth. And came forth he who had been dead, bound
τοὺς πόδας καὶ τὰς χεῖρας κειρίαις, καὶ ἡ.ὄψις.αὐτοῦ
feet and hands with grave clothes, and his face
σουδαρίῳ περιεδέδετο. λέγει αὐτοῖς ὁ Ἰησοῦς, Λύσατε
with a handkerchief bound about. ²Says ³to ⁴them ¹Jesus, Loose
αὐτὸν καὶ ἄφετε [s] ὑπάγειν.
him and let [him] go.

45 Πολλοὶ οὖν ἐκ τῶν Ἰουδαίων οἱ ἐλθόντες πρὸς τὴν
Many therefore of the Jews who came to
[t]Μαρίαν" καὶ θεασάμενοι [v]ἃ" ἐποίησεν [w]ὁ Ἰησοῦς," ἐπίστευσαν
Mary and saw what ²did ¹Jesus, believed
εἰς αὐτόν. 46 τινὲς.δὲ ἐξ αὐτῶν ἀπῆλθον πρὸς τοὺς Φαρι-
on him; but some of them went to the Phari-
σαίους καὶ [x]εἶπον" αὐτοῖς [y]ἃ" ἐποίησεν [z]ὁ" Ἰησοῦς. 47 συνήγα-
sees and told them what ²did ¹Jesus. Gathered
γον οὖν οἱ ἀρχιερεῖς καὶ οἱ Φαρισαῖοι συνέδριον, καὶ ἔλεγον,
therefore the chief priests and the Pharisees a council, and said,
Τί ποιοῦμεν; ὅτι οὗτος ὁ ἄνθρωπος πολλὰ [a]σημεῖα ποιεῖ."
What do we? for this man many signs does.

28 And saying these things she left. And she called[d] her sister Mary secretly, saying, The Master has come and is calling you.
29 When she heard, she rose up quickly and came to Him.
30 Now Jesus had not yet come into the town, but was in that place where Martha met Him.
31 Then the Jews who were with her in the house, who were there to comfort her, saw that Mary was quickly getting up to go out. They followed her, saying, She is going to the tomb that she may weep there.
32 Then when she came and saw where Jesus was, Mary fell down at His feet and said to Him, If you had been here, my brother would not have died.
33 Then when Jesus saw her weeping, and the Jews who came with her weeping, He groaned in spirit *and was* Himself troubled.
34 And He said, Where have you laid him? They said to Him, Lord, come and see.
35 Jesus wept.
36 Then the Jews said, See how He loved him!
37 But some of them said, Would not this One who opened the eyes of the blind have been able to prevent this one from dying?
38 Then again groaning within Himself, Jesus came to the tomb. Now it was a cave, and a stone was lying upon it.
39 Jesus said, Take away the stone. Martha the sister of him who had died said to Him, Lord, by now he stinks, for it is four days.
40 Jesus said to her, Did I not say to you that if you would believe you will see the glory of God?
41 Then they took away the stone where the dead was laid. And Jesus lifted His eyes and said, Father, I thank You that You have heard Me,
42 and I know that You always hear Me. But I said it on account of the people who are standing around, in order that they may believe that You have sent Me.
43 And saying these things, He cried out with a loud voice, Laz-a-rus! Come out!
44 And he who had been dead came out, bound hand and foot with graveclothes. And his face was tied up with a gravecloth. Jesus said to them, Untie him and let him go.

45 Then many of the Jews, who came to Mary and saw what Jesus did, believed on Him.
46 But some of them went to the Pharisees and told them what Jesus did.
47 Then the chief priests and the Pharisees gathered a council, saying, What can we do? For this man does many miracles.

48 ἐὰν ἀφῶμεν αὐτὸν οὕτως, πάντες πιστεύσουσιν εἰς αὐτόν·
If we let alone him thus, all will believe on him,
καὶ ἐλεύσονται οἱ Ῥωμαῖοι καὶ ἀροῦσιν ἡμῶν καὶ τὸν τόπον
and will come the Romans and will take away from us both the place
καὶ τὸ ἔθνος. 49 Εἷς.δέ.τις ἐξ αὐτῶν, Καϊάφας, ἀρχιερεὺς
and the nation. But a certain one of them, Caiaphas, high priest
ὢν τοῦ.ἐνιαυτοῦ.ἐκείνου, εἶπεν αὐτοῖς, Ὑμεῖς οὐκ οἴδατε
being of that year, said to them, Ye know
οὐδέν, 50 οὐδὲ [b]διαλογίζεσθε‖ ὅτι συμφέρει [c]ἡμῖν‖ ἵνα εἷς
nothing, nor consider that it is profitable for us that one
ἄνθρωπος ἀποθάνῃ ὑπὲρ τοῦ λαοῦ, καὶ μὴ ὅλον τὸ ἔθνος
man should die for the people, and not [2]whole [1]the nation
ἀπόληται. 51 Τοῦτο.δὲ ἀφ' ἑαυτοῦ οὐκ.εἶπεν, ἀλλὰ ἀρχ-
should perish. But this from himself he said not, but high
ιερεὺς ὢν τοῦ.ἐνιαυτοῦ.ἐκείνου, [d]προεφήτευσεν‖ ὅτι [e]ἔμελλεν‖
priest being of that year, prophesied that [2]was [3]about
[f]ὁ‖ Ἰησοῦς ἀποθνήσκειν ὑπὲρ τοῦ ἔθνους, 52 καὶ οὐχ ὑπὲρ
[1]Jesus to die for the nation; and not for
τοῦ ἔθνους μόνον, ἀλλ' ἵνα καὶ τὰ τέκνα τοῦ θεοῦ τὰ διεσκορ-
the nation only, but that also the children of God who have been
πισμένα συναγάγῃ εἰς ἕν. 53 ἀπ' ἐκείνης οὖν
scattered abroad he might gather together into one. From that [2]therefore
τῆς ἡμέρας [g]συνεβουλεύσαντο‖ ἵνα ἀποκτείνωσιν αὐτόν.
[1]day they took counsel together that they might kill him.
54 [h]Ἰησοῦς οὖν‖ [i]οὐκ ἔτι‖ παρρησίᾳ περιεπάτει ἐν τοῖς
Jesus therefore no longer publicly walked among the
Ἰουδαίοις, ἀλλὰ ἀπῆλθεν ἐκεῖθεν εἰς τὴν χώραν ἐγγὺς τῆς
Jews, but went away thence into the country near the
ἐρήμου, εἰς Ἐφραῒμ λεγομένην πόλιν, κἀκεῖ [k]διέτριβεν‖
desert, to [4]Ephraim [3]called [1]a [2]city, and there he stayed
μετὰ τῶν.μαθητῶν.[l]αὐτοῦ.‖
with his disciples.

55 Ἦν.δὲ ἐγγὺς τὸ πάσχα τῶν Ἰουδαίων, καὶ ἀνέβησαν
Now [6]was [7]near [1]the [2]passover [3]of [4]the [5]Jews, and went up
πολλοὶ εἰς Ἱεροσόλυμα ἐκ τῆς χώρας πρὸ τοῦ πάσχα, ἵνα
many to Jerusalem out of the country before the passover, that
ἁγνίσωσιν ἑαυτούς. 56 ἐζήτουν οὖν τὸν Ἰησοῦν, καὶ
they might purify themselves. They were seeking therefore Jesus, and
[m]ἔλεγον‖ μετ' ἀλλήλων ἐν τῷ ἱερῷ ἑστηκότες, Τί δοκεῖ
were saying among one another in the temple standing, What does it seem
ὑμῖν, ὅτι οὐ.μὴ ἔλθῃ εἰς τὴν ἑορτήν; 57 Δεδώκεισαν.δὲ
to you, that in no wise he will come to the feast? Now had given
[n]καὶ‖ οἱ ἀρχιερεῖς καὶ οἱ Φαρισαῖοι [o]ἐντολήν,‖ ἵνα ἐάν τις
both the chief priests and the Pharisees a command, that if anyone
γνῷ ποῦ ἐστιν μηνύσῃ, ὅπως πιάσωσιν αὐτόν.
should know where he is he should shew [it], that they might take him.

12 Ὁ.οὖν.Ἰησοῦς πρὸ ἓξ ἡμερῶν τοῦ πάσχα ἦλθεν εἰς
Jesus therefore [3]before [1]six [2]days the passover came to
Βηθανίαν, ὅπου ἦν Λάζαρος [p]ὁ τεθνηκώς,‖ ὃν ἤγειρεν
Bethany, where was Lazarus who had died, whom he raised
ἐκ νεκρῶν[q]. 2 ἐποίησαν οὖν αὐτῷ δεῖπνον ἐκεῖ,
from among [the] dead. They made therefore him a supper there,
καὶ ἡ Μάρθα διηκόνει· ὁ.δὲ.Λάζαρος εἷς ἦν [r]τῶν [s]συνανα-
and Martha served, but Lazarus one was of those re-
κειμένων‖ αὐτῷ. 3 Ἡ.οὖν.[t]Μαρία‖ λαβοῦσα λίτραν μύρου
clining with him. Mary therefore having taken a pound of ointment
νάρδου πιστικῆς πολυτίμου, ἤλειψεν τοὺς πόδας [v]τοῦ‖ Ἰησοῦ,
of [2]nard [1]pure of great price, anointed the feet of Jesus,
καὶ ἐξέμαξεν ταῖς.θριξὶν.αὐτῆς τοὺς.πόδας.αὐτοῦ· ἡ.δὲ οἰκία
and wiped with her hair his feet; and the house
ἐπληρώθη ἐκ τῆς ὀσμῆς τοῦ μύρου. 4 λέγει [w]οὖν‖ [x]εἷς ἐκ
was filled with the odour of the ointment. Says therefore one of
τῶν.μαθητῶν.αὐτοῦ, Ἰούδας, Σίμωνος Ἰσκαριώτης,‖ ὁ
his disciples, Judas, Simon's [son] Iscariote, who
μέλλων αὐτὸν παραδιδόναι, 5 [y]Διατί‖ τοῦτο τὸ μύρον οὐκ
was about him to deliver up, Why [3]this [4]ointment [2]not
ἐπράθη τριακοσίων δηναρίων, καὶ ἐδόθη πτωχοῖς; 6 Εἶπεν
[1]was sold for three hundred denarii, and given to [the] poor? [2]he [3]said
δὲ τοῦτο, οὐχ ὅτι περὶ τῶν πτωχῶν ἔμελεν.αὐτῷ, ἀλλ' ὅτι
[1]but this, not that for the poor he was caring, but because
κλέπτης ἦν, καὶ τὸ γλωσσόκομον [z]εἶχεν, καὶ‖ τὰ βαλλόμενα
a thief he was, and the bag had, and what was put into
ἐβάσταζεν. 7 εἶπεν οὖν ὁ Ἰησοῦς, Ἄφες αὐτήν· [a]εἰς
[it] carried. [3]Said [2]therefore [1]Jesus, Let [2]alone [1]her: for
τὴν ἡμέραν τοῦ.ἐνταφιασμοῦ.μου [b]τετήρηκεν‖ αὐτό. 8 τοὺς
the day of my burial has she kept it: [2]the
πτωχοὺς γὰρ πάντοτε ἔχετε μεθ' ἑαυτῶν, ἐμὲ.δὲ οὐ πάντοτε
[3]poor [1]for always ye have with you, but me not always
ἔχετε.
ye have.

9 Ἔγνω οὖν [c] ὄχλος πολὺς ἐκ τῶν Ἰουδαίων ὅτι ἐκεῖ
[7]Knew [8]therefore [1]a [3]crowd [2]great [4]of [5]the [6]Jews that there

48 If we let him alone this way, all will believe on him and the Romans will come and take away from us both our place and nation.

49 But a certain one of them, Cai-a-phas, being high priest of that year, said to them, You do not know anything,

50 nor consider that it is good for us that one man should die for the people, and not that the whole nation should be lost.

51 And he did not say this of himself, but being high priest of that year prophesied that Jesus was about to die for the nation –

52 and not for the nation only, but that also He might gather together into one the children of God, who have been scattered.

53 Then from that day on they consulted together that they might put Him to death.

54 So Jesus no longer walked openly among the Jews, but went away from there into the region near the desert, to a city called Ephraim – and He stayed there with His disciples.

55 Now the Passover of the Jews was near. And many went up to Jerusalem out of the country before the Passover, so that they might purify themselves.

56 Then they were looking for Jesus and were saying among one another as they stood in the Temple, What do you think? Will He come to the feast or not?

57 Now both the chief priests and the Pharisees had given a command that if anyone should come to know where He was, he was to make it known, so they could seize Him.

CHAPTER 12

1 Then six days before the Passover, Jesus came to Bethany, where Lazarus lived (who had died, whom He raised from the dead).

2 So they made a supper for Him there, and Martha served. And Lazarus was one of those at table with Him.

3 Then taking a pound of ointment of pure spikenard, of great value, Mary anointed the feet of Jesus and wiped His feet with her hair. And the house was filled with the odor of the ointment.

4 Then one of His disciples, Judas Is-car-i-ot, Simon's son, who was about to betray Him, said,

5 Why was this ointment not sold for three hundred silver pieces and given to the poor?

6 Now he did not say this because he cared for the poor, but because he was a thief and had the purse. And he carried away whatever was put in it.

7 Then Jesus said, Let her alone! She has kept it for the day of My burial.

8 For you always have the poor with you, but you do not always have Me.

9 Then a great crowd of the Jews learned that He was there. And they came, not only be-

ἐστιν, καὶ ἦλθον, οὐ διὰ τὸν Ἰησοῦν μόνον, ἀλλ' ἵνα
he is; and they came, not because of Jesus only, but that
καὶ τὸν Λάζαρον ἴδωσιν ὃν ἤγειρεν ἐκ νεκρῶν.
also Lazarus they might see whom he raised from among [the] dead.
10 ἐβουλεύσαντο.δὲ οἱ ἀρχιερεῖς ἵνα καὶ τὸν Λάζαρον ἀπο-
But [4]took [5]counsel [1]the [2]chief [3]priests that also Lazarus they
κτείνωσιν, 11 ὅτι πολλοὶ δι' αὐτὸν ὑπῆγον
might kill, because many [4]by [5]reason [6]of [7]him [8]were [9]going [10]away
τῶν Ἰουδαίων καὶ ἐπίστευον εἰς τὸν Ἰησοῦν.
[1]of [2]the [3]Jews and were believing on Jesus.
12 Τῇ.ἐπαύριον ὄχλος πολὺς ὁ ἐλθὼν εἰς τὴν ἑορτήν,
On the morrow a [2]crowd [1]great who came to the feast,
ἀκούσαντες ὅτι ἔρχεται [d]ὁ‖ Ἰησοῦς εἰς Ἱεροσόλυμα, 13 ἔλα-
having heard that [2]is [3]coming [1]Jesus into Jerusalem, took
βον τὰ βαΐα τῶν φοινίκων καὶ ἐξῆλθον εἰς ὑπάντησιν [e]αὐτῷ,‖
branches of the palms and went out to meet him,
καὶ [f]ἔκραζον,‖ [g]Ὡσαννά, εὐλογημένος ὁ ἐρχόμενος ἐν
and were crying, Hosanna, blessed [is] he who comes in [the]
ὀνόματι κυρίου, [h]ὁ βασιλεὺς τοῦ Ἰσραήλ. 14 Εὑρὼν δὲ
name of [the] Lord, the king of Israel. [3]Having [4]found [1]and
ὁ Ἰησοῦς ὀνάριον ἐκάθισεν ἐπ' αὐτό, καθώς ἐστιν γεγραμ-
[2]Jesus a young ass sat upon it, as it is writ-
μένον, 15 Μὴ.φοβοῦ, [i]θύγατερ‖ Σιών· ἰδού, ὁ.βασιλεύς.σου
ten, Fear not, daughter of Sion: behold, thy king
ἔρχεται, καθήμενος ἐπὶ πῶλον ὄνου 16 ταῦτα [k]δὲ‖ οὐκ
comes, sitting on a colt of an ass. [2]These [3]things [1]now [7]not
ἔγνωσαν [l]οἱ.μαθηταὶ.αὐτοῦ‖ τὸ.πρῶτον, ἀλλ' ὅτε ἐδοξάσθη
[8]knew [4]his [5]disciples at the first, but when was glorified
[m]ὁ‖ Ἰησοῦς τότε ἐμνήσθησαν ὅτι ταῦτα ἦν ἐπ' αὐτῷ
Jesus then they remembered that these things were of him
γεγραμμένα, καὶ ταῦτα ἐποίησαν αὐτῷ. 17 ἐμαρτύρει οὖν
written, and these things they did to him. Bore witness therefore
ὁ ὄχλος ὁ ὢν μετ' αὐτοῦ, [n]ὅτε‖ τὸν Λάζαρον ἐφώνησεν ἐκ
the crowd that was with him, when Lazarus he called out of
τοῦ μνημείου, καὶ ἤγειρεν αὐτὸν ἐκ νεκρῶν. 18 διὰ
the tomb, and raised him from among [the] dead. On account of
τοῦτο [o]καὶ‖ ὑπήντησεν αὐτῷ ὁ ὄχλος, ὅτι [p]ἤκουσεν‖ τοῦτο
this also met him the crowd, because it heard [5]this
αὐτὸν.πεποιηκέναι τὸ σημεῖον. 19 οἱ οὖν Φαρισαῖοι [q]εἶπον‖
[1]of [2]his [3]having [4]done sign. The [2]therefore [1]Pharisees said
πρὸς ἑαυτούς, Θεωρεῖτε ὅτι οὐκ ὠφελεῖτε οὐδέν; ἴδε, ὁ κόσμος
among themselves, Do ye see that ye gain nothing? lo, the world
ὀπίσω αὐτοῦ ἀπῆλθεν.
after him is gone.
20 Ἦσαν.δέ [r]τινες [s]Ἕλληνες‖ ἐκ τῶν ἀναβαινόντων ἵνα
And there were certain Greeks among those coming up that
[t]προσκυνήσωσιν‖ ἐν τῇ ἑορτῇ· 21 οὗτοι οὖν προσῆλθον
they might worship in the feast; these therefore came
Φιλίππῳ, τῷ ἀπὸ Βηθσαϊδὰ τῆς Γαλιλαίας, καὶ ἠρώτων
to Philip, who was from Bethsaida of Galilee, and they asked
αὐτὸν λέγοντες, Κύριε, θέλομεν τὸν Ἰησοῦν ἰδεῖν. 22 [u]Ἔρχε-
him saying, Sir, we desire [2]Jesus [1]to [3]see. [2]Comes
ται [t]Φίλιππος καὶ λέγει τῷ Ἀνδρέᾳ· [v]καὶ πάλιν‖ Ἀνδρέας
[1]Philip and tells Andrew, and again Andrew
καὶ Φίλιππος [w]λέγουσιν τῷ Ἰησοῦ. 23 ὁ.δὲ.Ἰησοῦς [x]ἀπε-
and Philip tell Jesus. But Jesus an-
κρίνατο‖ αὐτοῖς λέγων, Ἐλήλυθεν ἡ ὥρα ἵνα δοξασθῇ
swered them saying, [3]Has [4]come [1]the [2]hour that should be glorified
ὁ υἱὸς τοῦ ἀνθρώπου. 24 ἀμὴν ἀμὴν λέγω ὑμῖν, ἐὰν.μὴ ὁ
the Son of man. Verily verily I say to you, Unless the
κόκκος τοῦ σίτου πεσὼν εἰς τὴν γῆν ἀποθάνῃ, αὐτὸς μόνος
grain of wheat falling into the ground should die, it alone
μένει· ἐὰν.δὲ ἀποθάνῃ, πολὺν καρπὸν φέρει. 25 ὁ φιλῶν
abides; but if it should die, much fruit it bears. He that loves
τὴν.ψυχὴν.αὐτοῦ [y]ἀπολέσει‖ αὐτήν, καὶ ὁ μισῶν τὴν
his life shall lose it, and he that hates
ψυχὴν αὐτοῦ ἐν τῷ.κόσμῳ.τούτῳ εἰς ζωὴν αἰώνιον φυλάξει
[2]life [1]his in this world to life eternal shall keep
αὐτήν. 26 ἐὰν ἐμοί [z]διακονῇ τις,‖ ἐμοὶ ἀκολουθείτω· καὶ
it. If [2]me [3]serve [1]anyone, me let him follow; and
ὅπου εἰμὶ ἐγὼ ἐκεῖ καὶ ὁ διάκονος ὁ ἐμὸς ἔσται· [a]καὶ‖ ἐάν
where [2]am [1]I there also [2]servant [1]my shall be. And if
τις ἐμοὶ διακονῇ, τιμήσει αὐτὸν ὁ πατήρ.
anyone me serve, [2]will [5]honour [1]him [3]the [4]Father.
27 Νῦν ἡ.ψυχή.μου τετάρακται, καὶ τί εἴπω; Πάτερ,
Now my soul has been troubled, and what shall I say? Father,
σῶσόν με ἐκ τῆς.ὥρας.ταύτης.[b] ἀλλὰ διὰ τοῦτο ἦλθον
save me from this hour. But on account of this I came
εἰς τὴν.ὥραν.ταύτην. 28 Πάτερ, δόξασόν σου τὸ ὄνομα.
to this hour. Father, glorify thy name.
[c]Ἦλθεν.οὖν φωνὴ ἐκ τοῦ οὐρανοῦ, Καὶ ἐδόξασα καὶ πάλιν
Therefore came a voice out of heaven, [2]Both [1]I glorified and again

cause of Jesus, but that they might also see Lazarus, whom He raised from the dead.

10 But the chief priests plotted together so that they might also put Lazarus to death,

11 because many of the Jews were leaving and were believing on Jesus because of him.

12 On the next day a great crowd that had come to the feast, hearing that Jesus was coming into Jerusalem,

13 took branches of palm trees and went out to meet Him. And *they* were crying, Hosanna! "Blessed is He who comes in the name of the Lord, the King of Israel."

14 And finding a young ass colt, Jesus sat on it, as it is written,

15 "Do not fear, daughter of Zion. Behold! Your king comes sitting on the colt of an ass."

16 Now His disciples did not understand these things at first, but when Jesus was glorified, then they remembered that these things were written of Him, and that they did these things to Him.

17 Then the people were testifying (those who were with Him when He called Lazarus out of the grave and raised him from among the dead).

18 Also *it was* because they had heard that He had done this miracle that the people met Him.

19 Then the Pharisees said among themselves, Do you see that you gain nothing? Look! The world has gone after Him!

20 And there were certain Greeks among those who came up in order that they might worship in the feast.

21 Then these came to Philip, who was from Beth-sa-i-da of Galilee. And they asked him, saying, Sir, we want to see Jesus.

22 Philip came and told Andrew. And again, Andrew and Philip told Jesus.

23 But Jesus answered them, saying, The time has come for the Son of man to be glorified.

24 Indeed, I tell you truly that unless the grain of wheat falling into the ground should die, it remains alone. But if it dies, it bears much fruit.

25 He that loves his life shall lose it. And he that hates his life in this world shall keep it to life everlasting.

26 If anyone serves Me, let him follow Me. And where I am, My servant shall also be there. And if anyone serves Me, the Father will honor him.

27 Now My soul has been troubled. And what shall I say? Father, save Me from this hour. But it was for this reason that I came to this hour –

28 Father, glorify Your name. Then a voice came out of Heaven, *saying,* I both have glorified it and will glorify it again.

δοξάσω. 29 Ὁ.[c]οὖν‖.ὄχλος ὁ [d]ἑστὼς‖ [e]καὶ‖ ἀκούσας
will glorify [it]. Therefore the crowd which stood [there] and heard
ἔλεγεν βροντὴν.γεγονέναι. ἄλλοι ἔλεγον, [f]Ἄγγελος αὐτῷ
said, Thunder there has been: others said, An angel to him
λελάληκεν. 30 Ἀπεκρίθη [f]ὁ‖ Ἰησοῦς καὶ εἶπεν, Οὐ δι' ἐμὲ
has spoken. [2]Answered [1]Jesus and said, Not because of me
[g]αὕτη ἡ φωνὴ‖ γέγονεν, ἀλλὰ δι' ὑμᾶς. 31 νῦν κρίσις
this voice has come, but because of you. Now judgment
ἐστὶν τοῦ.κόσμου.τούτου· νῦν ὁ ἄρχων τοῦ.κόσμου.τούτου
is of this world; now the prince of this world
ἐκβληθήσεται ἔξω· 32 κἀγὼ ἐὰν ὑψωθῶ ἐκ τῆς γῆς, πάν-
shall be cast out: and I if I be lifted up from the earth, [3]all
τας ἑλκύσω πρὸς ἐμαυτόν. 33 Τοῦτο.δὲ ἔλεγεν, σημαίνων
[1]will [2]draw to myself. But this he said, signifying
ποίῳ θανάτῳ ἤμελλεν ἀποθνήσκειν. 34 ἀπεκρίθη [h] αὐτῷ
by what death he was about to die. [3]Answered [4]him
ὁ ὄχλος, Ἡμεῖς ἠκούσαμεν ἐκ τοῦ νόμου ὅτι ὁ χριστὸς
[1]the [2]crowd, We heard out of the law that the Christ
μένει εἰς.τὸν.αἰῶνα, καὶ πῶς [i]σὺ λέγεις,‖ Ὅτι δεῖ ὑψωθῆναι
abides for ever, and how [2]thou [1]sayest, that must be lifted up
τὸν υἱὸν τοῦ ἀνθρώπου; τίς ἐστιν οὗτος ὁ υἱὸς τοῦ ἀνθρώπου;
the Son of man? Who is this Son of man?
35 Εἶπεν οὖν αὐτοῖς ὁ Ἰησοῦς, Ἔτι μικρὸν χρόνον τὸ
[3]Said [2]therefore [4]to [5]them [1]Jesus, Yet a little while the
φῶς [k]μεθ' ὑμῶν‖ ἐστιν. περιπατεῖτε [l]ἕως‖ τὸ φῶς ἔχετε, ἵνα
light with you is. Walk while the light ye have, that
μὴ σκοτία ὑμᾶς καταλάβῃ· καὶ ὁ περιπατῶν ἐν τῇ
[3]not [1]darkness [5]you [2]may [4]overtake. And he who walks in the
σκοτίᾳ οὐκ.οἶδεν ποῦ ὑπάγει. 36 [l]ἕως‖ τὸ φῶς ἔχετε, πισ-
darkness knows not where he goes. While the light ye have, be-
τεύετε εἰς τὸ φῶς, ἵνα υἱοὶ φωτὸς γένησθε. Ταῦτα
lieve in the light, that sons of light ye may become. These things
ἐλάλησεν [m]ὁ‖ Ἰησοῦς, καὶ ἀπελθὼν ἐκρύβη ἀπ' αὐτῶν.
spoke Jesus, and going away was hid from them.
37 Τοσαῦτα.δὲ αὐτοῦ σημεῖα πεποιηκότος ἔμπροσθεν αὐτῶν
But [though] so many [2]he [1]signs had done before them
οὐκ.ἐπίστευον εἰς αὐτόν, 38 ἵνα ὁ λόγος Ἠσαΐου τοῦ προ-
they believed not on him, that the word of Esaias the pro-
φήτου πληρωθῇ, ὃν εἶπεν, Κύριε, τίς ἐπίστευσεν τῇ
phet might be fulfilled, which he said, Lord, who believed
ἀκοῇ.ἡμῶν; καὶ ὁ βραχίων κυρίου τίνι ἀπεκαλύφθη;
our report? and the arm of [the] Lord to whom was it revealed?
39 Διὰ.τοῦτο οὐκ.ἠδύναντο πιστεύειν, ὅτι πάλιν εἶπεν
On this account they could not believe, because again said
Ἡσαΐας, 40 Τετύφλωκεν αὐτῶν τοὺς ὀφθαλμοὺς καὶ [n]πε-
Esaias, He has blinded their eyes and has
πώρωκεν‖ αὐτῶν τὴν καρδίαν· ἵνα μὴ.ἴδωσιν τοῖς ὀφ-
hardened their heart, that they should not see with the
θαλμοῖς καὶ νοήσωσιν τῇ καρδίᾳ καὶ [o]ἐπιστραφῶσιν,‖ καὶ
eyes and understand with the heart and be converted, and
[p]ἰάσωμαι‖ αὐτούς. 41 Ταῦτα εἶπεν Ἠσαΐας, [q]ὅτε‖ εἶδεν
I should heal them. These things said Esaias, when he saw
τὴν.δόξαν.αὐτοῦ, καὶ ἐλάλησεν περὶ αὐτοῦ. 42 ὅμως μέντοι
his glory, and spoke concerning him. Although indeed
καὶ ἐκ τῶν ἀρχόντων πολλοὶ ἐπίστευσαν εἰς αὐτόν·
even from among the rulers many believed on him,
ἀλλὰ διὰ τοὺς Φαρισαίους οὐχ.ὡμολόγουν, ἵνα μὴ
but on account of the Pharisees they confessed not, that not
ἀποσυνάγωγοι γένωνται. 43 ἠγάπησαν.γὰρ τὴν δόξαν
put out of the synagogue they might be; for they loved the glory
τῶν ἀνθρώπων μᾶλλον ἤπερ τὴν δόξαν τοῦ θεοῦ. 44 Ἰησοῦς
of men more than the glory of God. [2]Jesus
δὲ ἔκραξεν καὶ εἶπεν, Ὁ πιστεύων εἰς ἐμέ, οὐ.πιστεύει εἰς
[1]but cried and said, He that believes on me, believes not on
ἐμέ, [r]ἀλλ'‖ εἰς τὸν πέμψαντά με· 45 καὶ ὁ θεωρῶν ἐμέ,
me, but on him who sent me; and he that beholds me,
θεωρεῖ τὸν πέμψαντά με. 46 ἐγὼ φῶς εἰς τὸν κόσμον
beholds him who sent me. I a light into the world
ἐλήλυθα, ἵνα πᾶς ὁ πιστεύων εἰς ἐμὲ ἐν τῇ σκοτίᾳ μὴ
have come, that everyone that believes on me in the darkness [2]not
μείνῃ. 47 καὶ ἐάν τις μου ἀκούσῃ τῶν ῥημάτων καὶ μὴ
[1]may abide. And if anyone [4]of [5]me [1]hear [2]the [3]words and [2]not
[s]πιστεύσῃ,‖ ἐγὼ οὐ.κρίνω αὐτόν· οὐ.γὰρ.ἦλθον ἵνα κρίνω
[1]believe, I do not judge him, for I came not that I might judge
τὸν κόσμον, ἀλλ' ἵνα σώσω τὸν κόσμον. 48 ὁ ἀθετῶν
the world, but that I might save the world. He that rejects
ἐμὲ καὶ μὴ.λαμβάνων τὰ.ῥήματα.μου, ἔχει τὸν κρίνοντα
me and does not receive my words, has him who judges
αὐτόν· ὁ λόγος ὃν ἐλάλησα, ἐκεῖνος κρινεῖ αὐτὸν ἐν τῇ
him: the word which I spoke, that shall judge him in the
ἐσχάτῃ ἡμέρᾳ. 49 ὅτι ἐγὼ ἐξ ἐμαυτοῦ οὐκ.ἐλάλησα· ἀλλ'
last day; for I from myself spoke not, but

29 Then the people who were standing
there and heard said, It has thundered.
Others said, An angel has spoken to Him.
30 Jesus answered and said, This voice has
not come because of Me, but for your sake.
31 Now there is a judging of this world!
Now the prince of this world will be throwr
out!
32 And I, if I shall be lifted up from the
earth, I will draw all to Myself.
33 But He said this showing by what kind
of death He was about to die.
34 The people answered Him, We heard out
of the Law that the Christ lives forever. And
how is it that You say that the Son of man
must be lifted up. Who is this Son of man?
35 Jesus then said to them, Yet a little
while the Light is with you. Walk while you
have the Light, so that darkness may not
overtake you. And he who walks in the darkness does not know where he goes.
36 While you have the Light, believe in the
Light, so that you may become sons of light.
Jesus spoke these things and went away, being hidden from them.
37 Although He had done so many miracles
before them, they did not believe on Him,
38 so that the word of Isaiah the prophet
might be fulfilled which he said, "Lord, who
believed our report – and the arm of the
Lord, to whom was it revealed?"
39 Because of this, then, they could not believe. And again, because Isaiah said,
40 "He has blinded their eyes and has hardened their heart so that they should not see
with their eyes and understand with their
heart and be converted, and I should heal
them."
41 Isaiah said these things when he saw His
glory and spoke about Him.
42 Still, even among the rulers, many did
believe on Him. But because of the Pharisees
they did not confess, so that they might not
be put out of the synagogue.
43 For they loved the glory of men more
than the glory of God.
44 And Jesus cried and said, He that believes on Me does not believe on Me but on
Him who sent Me.
45 And he who sees Me sees Him who sent
Me.
46 I have come as a Light into the world, so
that everyone who believes on Me may not
remain in the darkness.
47 And if anyone hears My words and does
not believe, I do not judge him – because I
did not come that I might judge the world,
but that I might save the world.
48 He that rejects Me and does not receive
My words has one that judges him: the word
which I spoke is that which will judge him in
the last day.
49 Because I did not speak from Myself, but
from the Father who sent Me, He Himself

ὁ πέμψας με πατήρ, αὐτός μοι ἐντολὴν [r]ἔδωκεν‖ τί
the [2]who [3]sent [4]me [1]Father, himself me commandment gave what
εἴπω καὶ τί λαλήσω· 50 καὶ οἶδα ὅτι ἡ.ἐντολὴ.αὐτοῦ
I should say and what I should speak; and I know that his commandment
ζωὴ αἰώνιός ἐστιν· ἃ οὖν [s]λαλῶ ἐγώ,‖ καθὼς εἴρηκέν μοι
life eternal is. What therefore [2]speak [1]I, as has said to me
ὁ πατήρ, οὕτως λαλῶ.
the Father, so I speak.
13 Πρὸ.δὲ τῆς ἑορτῆς του πάσχα; εἰδὼς ὁ Ἰησοῦς ὅτι
Now before the feast of the passover, [2]knowing [1]Jesus that
[w]ἐλήλυθεν‖ αὐτοῦ ἡ ὥρα ἵνα μεταβῇ ἐκ τοῦ.κόσμου.τού-
has come his hour that he should depart out of this world
του πρὸς τὸν πατέρα, ἀγαπήσας τοὺς.ἰδίους τοὺς ἐν τῷ
to the Father, having loved his own which [were] in the
κόσμῳ εἰς τέλος ἠγάπησεν αὐτούς. 2 καὶ δείπνου [x]γενο-
world to [the] end, he loved them. And supper taking
μένου,‖ τοῦ διαβόλου ἤδη βεβληκότος εἰς τὴν καρδίαν
place, the devil already having put into the heart
[y]Ἰούδα Σίμωνος Ἰσκαριώτου, ἵνα αὐτὸν παραδῷ,‖
of Judas, Simon's [son] Iscariote, that him he should deliver up,
3 εἰδὼς [z]ὁ Ἰησοῦς‖ ὅτι πάντα [a]δέδωκεν‖ αὐτῷ ὁ πατὴρ
[2]knowing [1]Jesus [3]that [9]all [10]things [6]has [7]given [8]him [4]the [5]Father
εἰς τὰς χεῖρας, καὶ ὅτι ἀπὸ θεοῦ ἐξῆλθεν καὶ πρὸς τὸν
into [his] hands, and that from God he came out and to
θεὸν ὑπάγει, 4 ἐγείρεται ἐκ τοῦ δείπνου καὶ τίθησιν τὰ
God goes, he rises from the supper and lays aside [his]
ἱμάτια, καὶ λαβὼν λέντιον διέζωσεν ἑαυτόν· 5 εἶτα βάλ-
garments and having taken a towel he girded himself: afterwards he
λει ὕδωρ εἰς τὸν νιπτῆρα, καὶ ἤρξατο νίπτειν τοὺς πόδας
pours water into the washing-basin, and began to wash the feet
τῶν μαθητῶν, καὶ ἐκμάσσειν τῷ λεντίῳ ᾧ ἦν
of the disciples, and to wipe [them] with the towel with which he was
διεζωσμένος. 6 ἔρχεται οὖν πρὸς Σίμωνα Πέτρον· [b]καὶ‖
girded. He comes therefore to Simon Peter, and
λέγει αὐτῷ [c]ἐκεῖνος,‖ Κύριε, σύ μου νίπτεις τοὺς πόδας;
[2]says [3]to [4]him [1]he, Lord, [2]thou [3]of [4]me [1]dost wash the feet?
7 Ἀπεκρίθη Ἰησοῦς καὶ εἶπεν αὐτῷ, Ὃ ἐγὼ ποιῶ σὺ οὐκ
[2]Answered [1]Jesus and said to him, What I do thou [2]not
οἶδας ἄρτι, γνώσῃ.δὲ μετὰ.ταῦτα. 8 Λέγει αὐτῷ Πέ-
[1]knowest now, but thou shalt know hereafter. [2]Says [3]to [4]him [1]Pe-
τρος, Οὐ.μὴ νίψῃς [d]τοὺς.πόδας.μου‖ εἰς.τὸν.αἰῶνα.
ter, In no wise mayest thou wash my feet for ever.
Ἀπεκρίθη [e]αὐτῷ ὁ Ἰησοῦς,‖ Ἐὰν.μὴ νίψω σε, οὐκ.ἔχεις
[2]Answered [3]him [1]Jesus, Unless I wash thee, thou hast not
μέρος μετ' ἐμοῦ. 9 Λέγει αὐτῷ Σίμων Πέτρος, Κύριε, μὴ
part with me. [3]Says [4]to [5]him [1]Simon [2]Peter, Lord, not
τοὺς.πόδας.μου μόνον, ἀλλὰ καὶ τὰς χεῖρας καὶ τὴν κεφαλήν.
my feet only, but also the hands and the head.
10 Λέγει αὐτῷ [f]ὁ‖ Ἰησοῦς, Ὁ λελουμένος [g]οὐ χρείαν
[2]Says [3]to [4]him [1]Jesus, He that has been laved [2]not [3]need
ἔχει‖ [h]ἢ‖ [i]τοὺς πόδας‖ νίψασθαι, ἀλλ' ἔστιν καθαρὸς
[1]has [other] than the feet to wash, but is clean
ὅλος· καὶ ὑμεῖς καθαροί ἐστε, ἀλλ' οὐχὶ πάντες. 11 ᾔδει.γὰρ
wholly; and ye clean are, but not all. For he knew
τὸν παραδιδόντα αὐτόν· διὰ τοῦτο εἶπεν, [k]Οὐχὶ πάν-
him who was delivering up him: on account of this he said, [3]Not [4]all
τες καθαροί ἐστε. 12 Ὅτε οὖν ἔνιψεν τοὺς.πόδας.αὐτῶν,
[5]clean [1]ye [2]are. When therefore he had washed, their feet,
[l]καὶ‖ ἔλαβεν τὰ.ἱμάτια.αὐτοῦ, [m] [n]ἀναπεσὼν‖ πάλιν, εἶπεν
and taken his garments, having reclined again, he said
αὐτοῖς, Γινώσκετε τί πεποίηκα ὑμῖν; 13 ὑμεῖς φωνεῖτέ με
to them, Do ye know what I have done to you? Ye call me
ὁ διδάσκαλος καὶ ὁ κύριος, καὶ καλῶς λέγετε, εἰμὶ γάρ.
the Teacher and the Lord, and well ye say, [2]I [3]am [[4]so] [1]for.
14 εἰ οὖν ἐγὼ ἔνιψα ὑμῶν τοὺς πόδας, ὁ κύριος καὶ ὁ
If therefore I washed your feet, the Lord and the
διδάσκαλος, καὶ ὑμεῖς ὀφείλετε ἀλλήλων νίπτειν τοὺς πόδας.
Teacher, also ye ought of one another to wash the feet;
15 ὑπόδειγμα.γὰρ [o]ἔδωκα‖ ὑμῖν, ἵνα καθὼς ἐγὼ ἐποίησα ὑμῖν,
for an example I gave you, that as I did to you,
καὶ ὑμεῖς ποιῆτε. 16 ἀμὴν ἀμὴν λέγω ὑμῖν, οὐκ.ἔστιν δοῦλος
also ye should do. Verily verily I say to you, [3]Is [4]not [1]a [2]bondman
μείζων τοῦ.κυρίου.αὐτοῦ, οὐδὲ ἀπόστολος μείζων τοῦ.πέμψαν-
greater than his lord, nor a messenger greater than he who sent
τος αὐτόν. 17 εἰ ταῦτα οἴδατε, μακάριοί ἐστε ἐὰν ποιῆτε
him. If these things ye know, blessed are ye if ye do
αὐτά. 18 οὐ περὶ πάντων ὑμῶν λέγω· ἐγὼ[p] οἶδα [q]οὓς‖
them. Not of [2]all [1]you I speak. I know whom
ἐξελεξάμην· ἀλλ' ἵνα ἡ γραφὴ πληρωθῇ, Ὁ τρώγων
I chose, but that the scripture might be fulfilled, He that eats
[r]μετ' ἐμοῦ‖ τὸν ἄρτον [s]ἐπῆρεν‖ ἐπ' ἐμὲ τὴν.πτέρναν.αὐτοῦ.
[2]with [3]me [1]bread lifted up against me his heel.

commanded Me what I should say and what
I should preach.
50 And I know that His commandment is
life everlasting. So what I speak, I speak just
as the Father has spoken to Me.

CHAPTER 13

1 Now before the feast of the Passover,
Jesus knew that His time had come, when
He would leave this world to go to the
Father. Having loved His own which were in
the world, He loved them to the end.
2 And as the supper was taking place, the
devil had already put it into the heart of
Judas Is-car-i-ot, Simon's son, that he should
betray Him.
3 And Jesus knew that the Father had given
all things into His hands, and that He came
out from God, and that He was going to God
4 – so He arose from the supper and laid
aside His robes. And He took a towel and
tied it around Himself.
5 Then He poured water into the washbowl
and began to wash the feet of the disciples
and to wipe them with the towel which He
had tied around Him.
6 He then came to Simon Peter. And Peter
said to Him, Lord, will You wash my feet?
7 Jesus answered and said to him, You do
not know what I am doing now, but You
shall know later.
8 Peter said to Him, You shall not in any
way wash my feet! Never! Jesus answered
him, Unless I wash you, you have no part
with Me.
9 Simon Peter said to Him, Lord, wash not
only my feet but also my hands and my
head.
10 Jesus said to him, He that has been
bathed has no need, except to wash his feet
yea, he is altogether clean. And you are
clean, but not all.
11 For He knew the one who was betraying
Him. Because of this He said, You are not all
clean.
12 Then when He had washed their feet and
had taken up His robes, He sat again and said
to them, Do you know what I have done to
you?
13 You call Me the Teacher, and the Lord.
And you are right to say it, for I am.
14 Then if I, the Lord and Teacher, have
washed your feet, you also ought to wash
each other's feet.
15 For I gave you an example, that as I did
to you, you should do also.
16 Indeed, I tell you truly that the slave is
not greater than his lord, nor an apostle
greater than He who sent him.
17 If you know these things, you are blessed if you do them.
18 I do not speak of all of you. I know the
ones I chose – but that the Scripture might
be fulfilled, "He that eats bread with Me lifted up his heel against Me."

19 [t]ἀπ'.ἄρτι" λέγω ὑμῖν πρὸ τοῦ.γενέσθαι, ἵνα [v]ὅταν γένη-
From this time I tell you, before it comes to pass, that when it come
ται, πιστεύσητε" ὅτι ἐγώ εἰμι. 20 ἀμὴν ἀμὴν λέγω ὑμῖν,
to pass, ye may believe that I am [he]. Verily verily I say to you,
Ὁ λαμβάνων [w]ἐάν".τινα πέμψω, ἐμὲ λαμβάνει· ὁ.δὲ
He that receives whomsoever I shall send, me receives; and he that
ἐμὲ λαμβάνων, λαμβάνει τὸν πέμψαντά με. 21 Ταῦτα
me receives, receives him who sent me. These things
εἰπὼν [x]ὁ" Ἰησοῦς ἐταράχθη τῷ πνεύματι, καὶ ἐμαρτύρησεν
saying Jesus was troubled in spirit, and testified
καὶ εἶπεν, Ἀμὴν ἀμὴν λέγω ὑμῖν, ὅτι εἷς ἐξ ὑμῶν παραδώσει
and said, Verily verily I say to you, that one of you will deliver up
με. 22 Ἔβλεπον [y]οὖν" εἰς ἀλλήλους οἱ μαθηταί, ἀπορού-
me. [4]Looked [3]therefore [5]upon [6]one [7]another [1]the [2]disciples, doubt-
μενοι περὶ τίνος λέγει. 23 ἦν.[z]δὲ" ἀνακείμενος εἷς [a] τῶν
ing of whom he speaks. But there was reclining one
μαθητῶν.αὐτοῦ ἐν τῷ κόλπῳ τοῦ.Ἰησοῦ, ὃν ἠγάπα ὁ Ἰησοῦς·
of his disciples in the bosom of Jesus, whom [2]loved [1]Jesus.
24 νεύει οὖν τούτῳ Σίμων Πέτρος [b]πυθέσθαι τίς
[6]Makes [7]a [8]sign [5]therefore [9]to [10]him [3]Simon [4]Peter to ask who
ἂν.εἴη" περὶ οὗ λέγει. 25 [c]ἐπιπεσὼν" [d]δὲ" ἐκεῖνος[e] ἐπὶ τὸ
it might be of whom he speaks. [3]Having [4]leaned [1]and [2]he on the
στῆθος τοῦ Ἰησοῦ, λέγει αὐτῷ, Κύριε, τίς ἐστιν; 26 Ἀπο-
breast of Jesus, says to him, Lord, who is it? [2]An-
κρίνεται[f] [g]ὁ" Ἰησοῦς, Ἐκεῖνός ἐστιν ᾧ ἐγὼ [h]βάψας" τὸ
swers [1]Jesus, He it is to whom I, having dipped the
ψωμίον [i]ἐπιδώσω." [k]Καὶ ἐμβάψας" τὸ ψωμίον [l] δίδωσιν
morsel, shall give [it]. And having dipped the morsel he gives [it]
Ἰούδᾳ Σίμωνος [m]Ἰσκαριώτῃ." 27 καὶ μετὰ τὸ ψωμίον,
to Judas, Simon's [son] Iscariote. And after the morsel,
τότε εἰσῆλθεν εἰς ἐκεῖνον ὁ σατανᾶς. λέγει οὖν αὐτῷ [n]ὁ"
then entered into him Satan. [3]Says [2]therefore [4]to [5]him
Ἰησοῦς, Ὃ ποιεῖς, ποίησον τάχιον. 28 Τοῦτο.δὲ οὐδεὶς
[1]Jesus, What thou doest, do quickly. But this no one
ἔγνω τῶν ἀνακειμένων πρὸς.τί εἶπεν αὐτῷ. 29 τινὲς.γὰρ
knew of those reclining wherefore he spoke to him; for some
ἐδόκουν, ἐπεὶ τὸ γλωσσόκομον εἶχεν [o]ὁ" Ἰούδας, ὅτι λέγει
thought, since [3]the [4]bag [2]had [1]Judas, that [2]is [3]saying
αὐτῷ [p]ὁ" Ἰησοῦς, Ἀγόρασον ὧν χρείαν ἔχομεν εἰς
[4]to [5]him [1]Jesus, Buy what things need [of] we have for
τὴν ἑορτήν· ἢ τοῖς πτωχοῖς ἵνα τι δῷ. 30 λα-
the feast; or to the poor that something he should give. Having
βὼν οὖν τὸ ψωμίον ἐκεῖνος [q]εὐθέως ἐξῆλθεν·" ἦν.δὲ
received therefore the morsel he immediately went out; and it was
νύξ.
night.

31 Ὅτε [r] ἐξῆλθεν λέγει [s]ὁ" Ἰησοῦς, Νῦν ἐδοξάσθη
When he was gone out [2]says [1]Jesus, Now has been glorified
ὁ υἱὸς τοῦ ἀνθρώπου, καὶ ὁ θεὸς ἐδοξάσθη ἐν αὐτῷ. 32 [t]εἰ
the Son of man, and God has been glorified in him. If
ὁ θεὸς ἐδοξάσθη ἐν αὐτῷ," καὶ ὁ θεὸς δοξάσει αὐτὸν ἐν
God has been glorified in him, also God shall glorify him in
[v]ἑαυτῷ," καὶ εὐθὺς δοξάσει αὐτόν. 33 Τεκνία, ἔτι
himself, and immediately shall glorify him. Little children, yet
μικρὸν μεθ' ὑμῶν εἰμι. ζητήσετέ με, καὶ καθὼς εἶπον τοῖς
a little while with you I am. Ye will seek me; and, as I said to the
Ἰουδαίοις, Ὅτι ὅπου [w]ὑπάγω ἐγώ," ὑμεῖς οὐ.δύνασθε ἐλθεῖν,
Jews, That where [2]go [1]I, ye are not able to come,
καὶ ὑμῖν λέγω ἄρτι. 34 ἐντολὴν καινὴν δίδωμι ὑμῖν, ἵνα
also to you I say now. A [2]commandment [1]new I give to you, that
ἀγαπᾶτε ἀλλήλους· καθὼς ἠγάπησα ὑμᾶς, ἵνα καὶ ὑμεῖς
ye should love one another; according as I loved you, that [2]also [1]ye
ἀγαπᾶτε ἀλλήλους. 35 ἐν τούτῳ γνώσονται πάντες ὅτι ἐμοὶ
should love one another. By this shall [2]know [1]all that to me
μαθηταί ἐστε, ἐὰν ἀγάπην ἔχητε ἐν ἀλλήλοις. 36 Λέγει
disciples ye are, if love ye have among one another. [3]Says
αὐτῷ Σίμων Πέτρος, Κύριε, ποῦ ὑπάγεις; ἀπεκρίθη [x]αὐτῷ
[4]to [5]him [1]Simon [2]Peter, Lord, where goest thou? [2]Answered [3]him
ὁ" Ἰησοῦς, Ὅπου[y] ὑπάγω οὐ.δύνασαί μοι νῦν ἀκολουθῆσαι·
[1]Jesus, Where I go thou art not able me now to follow,
[z]ὕστερον.δὲ ἀκολουθήσεις μοι." 37 Λέγει αὐτῷ [a]ὁ" Πέτρος,
but afterwards thou shalt follow me. [2]Says [3]to [4]him [1]Peter,
Κύριε, [b]διατί" οὐ.δύναμαί σοι [c]ἀκολουθῆσαι" ἄρτι; τὴν ψυχήν
Lord, why am I not able thee to follow now? [2]life
μου ὑπὲρ σοῦ θήσω. 38 [d]Ἀπεκρίθη αὐτῷ ὁ" Ἰησοῦς,
[1]my for thee I will lay down. [2]Answered [3]him [1]Jesus,
Τὴν.ψυχήν.σου ὑπὲρ ἐμοῦ θήσεις; ἀμὴν ἀμὴν λέγω
Thy life for me thou wilt lay down! Verily verily I say
σοι, οὐ.μὴ ἀλέκτωρ [e]φωνήσει" ἕως.οὗ [f]ἀπαρνήσῃ" με
to thee, in no wise [the] cock will crow until thou wilt deny me
τρίς.
thrice.

19 From this time I tell you, before it happens, so that when it happens you may believe that I am.

20 Indeed, I tell you truly that he who receives whoever I shall send receives Me. And he who receives Me receives Him who sent Me.

21 Saying these things, Jesus was troubled in spirit and witnessed and said, Indeed I tell you truly that one of you will betray Me.

22 Then the disciples looked toward one another, wondering whom He was talking about.

23 And there was one of His disciples lying on the breast of Jesus, whom Jesus loved.

24 So Simon Peter signaled *for him* to find out who it was of whom He spoke.

25 And leaning on the breast of Jesus, he said to Him, Lord, who is it?

26 Jesus answered, It is he to whom I shall give the piece of bread, after dipping it. And He dipped the piece of bread and gave it to Judas Is-car-i-ot, Simon's son.

27 And after the morsel, Satan then entered into him. Then Jesus said to him, What you are going to do, do quickly!

28 But no one of those at table knew why He said this to him.

29 For some thought, since Judas had the purse, that Jesus said to him, Buy those things we need for the feast. Or, that he should give something to the poor.

30 Then after receiving the piece of bread, he immediately left. And it was nighttime.

31 Then when he had left, Jesus said, Now the Son of man has been glorified, and God has been glorified in Him.

32 If God has been glorified in Him, God will also glorify Him in Himself. And He will glorify Him at once.

33 Little children, I am with you a little while longer. You will look for Me, and as I said to the Jews, Where I go, you are not able to come. This I now also say to you.

34 I give you a new commandment, that you should love one another. Even as I loved you, so you also should love one another.

35 By this all will know that you are My disciples, if you have love among one another.

36 Simon Peter said to Him, Lord, where are You going? Jesus answered him, Where I go you are not able to follow now, but you will follow Me afterwards.

37 Peter said to Him, Lord, why am I not able to follow You now? I will lay down my life for You.

38 Jesus answered him, Will you lay down your life for Me? Indeed, I tell you truly that the cock will not crow until you have denied Me three times.

14 Μὴ-ταρασσέσθω ὑμῶν ἡ καρδία· πιστεύετε εἰς τὸν θεόν,
Let not be troubled your heart; ye believe on God,

καὶ εἰς ἐμὲ πιστεύετε. 2 ἐν τῇ οἰκίᾳ τοῦ-πατρός-μου μοναὶ
also on me believe. In the house of my Father [2]abodes

πολλαί εἰσιν· εἰ.δὲ.μή, εἶπον.ἂν ὑμῖν· [g]πορεύομαι ἑτοι-
[1]many there are; otherwise I would have told you; I go to pre-

μάσαι τόπον ὑμῖν. 3 καὶ ἐὰν πορευθῶ [h]καὶ[h] ἑτοιμάσω [i]ὑμῖν
pare a place for you; and if I go and prepare for you

τόπον,[i] πάλιν ἔρχομαι καὶ [k]παραλήψομαι[k] ὑμᾶς πρὸς ἐμαυ-
a place, again I am coming and will receive you to my-

τόν· ἵνα ὅπου εἰμὶ ἐγώ, καὶ ὑμεῖς ἦτε. 4 καὶ ὅπου [l]ἐγὼ[l]
self, that where [2]am [1]I [4]also [3]ye may be. And where I

ὑπάγω οἴδατε [m]καὶ[m] τὴν ὁδὸν [n]οἴδατε.[n] 5 Λέγει αὐτῷ Θωμᾶς,
go ye know and the way ye know. [2]Says [3]to [4]him [1]Thomas,

Κύριε, οὐκ.οἴδαμεν ποῦ ὑπάγεις, [o]καὶ[o] πῶς [p]δυνάμεθα τὴν
Lord, we know not where thou goest, and how can we the

ὁδὸν εἰδέναι;[p] 6 Λέγει αὐτῷ [q]ὁ[q] Ἰησοῦς, Ἐγώ εἰμι ἡ ὁδὸς
way know? [2]Says [3]to [4]him [1]Jesus, I am the way

καὶ ἡ ἀλήθεια καὶ ἡ ζωή· οὐδεὶς ἔρχεται πρὸς τὸν πατέρα
and the truth and the life. No one comes to the Father

εἰ.μὴ δι' ἐμοῦ. 7 εἰ [r]ἐγνώκειτέ με,[r] καὶ τὸν.πατέρα.μου
but by me. If ye had known me, also my Father

[s]ἐγνώκειτε.ἄν·[s] [t]καὶ[t] [v]ἀπ'.ἄρτι[v] γινώσκετε αὐτόν, καὶ ἑωρά-
ye would have known; and henceforth ye know him, and have

κατε [w]αὐτόν.[w] 8 Λέγει αὐτῷ Φίλιππος, Κύριε, δεῖξον ἡμῖν
seen him. [2]Says [3]to [4]him [1]Philip, Lord, shew us

τὸν πατέρα, καὶ ἀρκεῖ ἡμῖν. 9 Λέγει αὐτῷ ὁ Ἰησοῦς,
the Father, and it suffices us. [2]Says [3]to [4]him [1]Jesus,

[x]Τοσοῦτον χρόνον[x] μεθ' ὑμῶν εἰμι, καὶ οὐκ.ἔγνωκάς με,
So long a time with you am I, and thou hast not known me,

Φίλιππε; ὁ ἑωρακὼς ἐμέ, ἑώρακεν τὸν πατέρα· [y]καὶ[y] πῶς
Philip? He that has seen me, has seen the Father; and how

σὺ λέγεις, Δεῖξον ἡμῖν τὸν πατέρα; 10 οὐ.πιστεύεις ὅτι
[2]thou [1]sayest, Shew us the Father? Believest thou not that

ἐγὼ ἐν τῷ πατρί, καὶ ὁ πατὴρ ἐν ἐμοί ἐστιν; τὰ ῥήματα
I [am] in the Father, and the Father [2]in [3]me [1]is? The words

ἃ ἐγὼ [z]λαλῶ[z] ὑμῖν, ἀπ' ἐμαυτοῦ οὐ.λαλῶ· ὁ.δὲ πατὴρ
which I speak to you, from myself I speak not; but the Father

[a]ὁ[a] ἐν ἐμοὶ μένων [b]αὐτὸς ποιεῖ τὰ ἔργα[b] [c]. 11 πιστεύετέ μοι
who in me abides he does the works. Believe me

ὅτι ἐγὼ ἐν τῷ πατρί, καὶ ὁ πατὴρ ἐν ἐμοί[d]· εἰ.δὲ μή,
that I [am] in the Father, and the Father in me; but if not,

διὰ τὰ ἔργα αὐτὰ πιστεύετέ [e]μοι.[e] 12 Ἀμὴν ἀμὴν λέγω
because of the works themselves believe me. Verily verily I say

ὑμῖν, ὁ πιστεύων εἰς ἐμέ, τὰ ἔργα ἃ ἐγὼ ποιῶ, κἀκεῖνος
to you, He that believes on me, the works which I do, also he

ποιήσει, καὶ μείζονα τούτων ποιήσει, ὅτι ἐγὼ πρὸς τὸν
shall do, and greater than these he shall do, because I to

πατέρα.[f]μου[f] πορεύομαι. 13 καὶ ὅ.τι.ἂν αἰτήσητε ἐν τῷ
my Father go. And whatsoever ye may ask in

ὀνόματί.μου, τοῦτο ποιήσω, ἵνα δοξασθῇ ὁ πατὴρ ἐν τῷ
my name, this will I do, that may be glorified the Father in the

υἱῷ. 14 ἐάν τι αἰτήσητε[g] ἐν τῷ.ὀνόματί.μου, ἐγὼ ποιήσω.
Son. If anything ye ask in my name, I will do [it].

15 ἐὰν ἀγαπᾶτέ με, τὰς ἐντολὰς τὰς ἐμὰς [h]τηρήσατε.[h]
If ye love me, [2]commandments [1]my keep.

16 [i]καὶ ἐγὼ[i] ἐρωτήσω τὸν πατέρα, καὶ ἄλλον παράκλητον
And I will ask the Father, and another Paraclete

δώσει ὑμῖν, ἵνα [k]μένῃ μεθ' ὑμῶν εἰς.τὸν.αἰῶνα,[k] 17 τὸ
he will give you, that he may remain with you for ever, the

πνεῦμα τῆς ἀληθείας, ὃ ὁ κόσμος οὐ.δύναται λαβεῖν, ὅτι
Spirit of truth, whom the world cannot receive, because

οὐ.θεωρεῖ αὐτό, οὐδὲ γινώσκει [l]αὐτό·[l] ὑμεῖς.[m]δὲ[m] γινώσκετε
it does not see him, nor know him; but ye know

αὐτό, ὅτι παρ' ὑμῖν μένει, καὶ ἐν ὑμῖν [n]ἔσται.[n] 18 οὐκ.ἀφήσω
him, for with you he abides, and in you shall be. I will not leave

ὑμᾶς ὀρφανούς· ἔρχομαι πρὸς ὑμᾶς. 19 ἔτι μικρὸν καὶ ὁ
you orphans, I am coming to you. Yet a little while and the

κόσμος με [o]οὐκ ἔτι[o] θεωρεῖ, ὑμεῖς.δὲ θεωρεῖτέ με· ὅτι ἐγὼ
world me no longer sees, but ye see me: because I

ζῶ, καὶ ὑμεῖς [p]ζήσεσθε.[p] 20 ἐν ἐκείνῃ τῇ ἡμέρᾳ [q]γνώσεσθε
live, [2]also [1]ye shall live. In that day shall [2]know

ὑμεῖς[q] ὅτι ἐγὼ ἐν τῷ.πατρί.μου, καὶ ὑμεῖς ἐν ἐμοί, κἀγὼ
[1]ye that I [am] in my Father, and ye in me, and I

ἐν ὑμῖν· 21 ὁ ἔχων τὰς.ἐντολάς.μου καὶ τηρῶν αὐτάς,
in you. He that has my commandments and keeps them,

ἐκεῖνός ἐστιν ὁ ἀγαπῶν με· ὁ.δὲ ἀγαπῶν με, ἀγαπηθήσε-
he it is that loves me; but he that loves me, shall be loved

ται ὑπὸ τοῦ.πατρός.μου· [r]καὶ ἐγὼ[r] ἀγαπήσω αὐτόν, καὶ
by my Father; and I will love him, and

ἐμφανίσω αὐτῷ ἐμαυτόν. 22 Λέγει αὐτῷ Ἰούδας, οὐχ
will manifest to him myself. [2]Says [3]to [4]him [1]Judas, (not

CHAPTER 14

1 Do not let your heart be troubled. You believe on God, believe also on Me.

2 In My Father's house are many places to live. If it were not so I would have told you. I am going to prepare a place for you.

3 And if I go and prepare a place for you, I am coming again and will take you to Myself, so that wherever I am you may be also.

4 And you know where I am going, and you know the way.

5 Thomas said to Him, Lord, we do not know where You are going, and how can we know the way?

6 Jesus said to him, I am the Way, the Truth, and the Life. No one comes to the Father in any other way than by Me.

7 If you had known Me, you would also have known My Father. And from now on you do know Him and have seen Him.

8 And Philip said to Him, Lord, show us the Father and it is enough for us.

9 Jesus said to him, Have I been with you for such a long time and you have not known Me, Philip? He who has seen Me has seen the Father. Then how is it that you say, Show us the Father?

10 Do you not believe that the Father is in Me and I in the Father? The words which I speak to you, I do not speak from Myself. But the Father who lives in Me, He does the works.

11 Believe Me that I am in the Father and the Father is in Me. But if not, believe Me because of the works themselves.

12 Indeed, I say to you truly that He who believes on Me will also do the works which I do. And he will do greater than these, because I am going to My Father.

13 And whatever you may ask in My name, I will do this, so that the Father may be glorified in the Son.

14 If you ask anything in My name, I will do it.

15 If you love Me, keep My commandments.

16 And I will ask the Father and He will give you another Comforter, that He may be with you forever –

17 the Spirit of Truth, whom the world cannot receive because it does not see Him or know Him. But you know Him, for He remains with you and shall be in you.

18 I will not leave you orphans. I am coming to you.

19 Yet a little while and the world will see Me no more. But you will see Me. Because I live, you will live also.

20 In that day you shall know that I am in the Father, and you in Me, and I in you.

21 He that has My commandments and keeps them is the one that loves Me. But he who loves Me shall be loved by My Father, and I will love him and will reveal Myself to him.

ὁ Ἰσκαριώτης, Κύριε, ˢτί γέγονεν ὅτι ἡμῖν μέλλεις
the Iscariote,) Lord, what has occurred that to us thou art about
ἐμφανίζειν σεαυτόν, καὶ οὐχὶ τῷ κόσμῳ; 23 Ἀπεκρίθη ˢὁ
to manifest thyself, and not to the world? ²Answered
Ἰησοῦς καὶ εἶπεν αὐτῷ, Ἐάν τις ἀγαπᾷ με, τὸν.λόγον.μου
¹Jesus and said to him, If anyone love me, my word
τηρήσει, καὶ ὁ.πατήρ.μου ἀγαπήσει αὐτόν, καὶ πρὸς αὐτὸν
he will keep, and my Father will love him, and to him
ἐλευσόμεθα, καὶ μονὴν παρ' αὐτῷ ᵛποιήσομεν.‖ 24 ὁ μὴ
we will come, and an abode with him will make. He that ²not
ἀγαπῶν με, τοὺς.λόγους.μου οὐ.τηρεῖ· καὶ ὁ λόγος ὃν
¹loves me, my words does not keep; and the word which
ἀκούετε οὐκ.ἔστιν ἐμός, ἀλλὰ τοῦ πέμψαντός με πατρός.
ye hear is not mine, but of the ²who ³sent ⁴me ¹Father.
25 Ταῦτα λελάληκα ὑμῖν παρ' ὑμῖν μένων· 26 ὁ.δὲ παρά-
These things I have said to you, with you abiding; but the Para-
κλητος, τὸ πνεῦμα τὸ ἅγιον, ὃ πέμψει ὁ πατὴρ ἐν τῷ
clete, the Spirit the Holy, whom ³will ⁴send ¹the ²Father in
ὀνόματί.μου, ἐκεῖνος ὑμᾶς διδάξει πάντα, καὶ ὑπο-
my name, he ⁴you ¹will ²teach all things, and will bring to ²re-
μνήσει ὑμᾶς πάντα ἃ εἶπον ὑμῖν. 27 εἰρήνην ἀφίημι
membrance ¹your all things which I said to you. Peace I leave
ὑμῖν, εἰρήνην τὴν ἐμὴν δίδωμι ὑμῖν· οὐ καθὼς ὁ κόσμος
with you; ²peace ¹my I give to you; not as the world
δίδωσιν, ἐγὼ δίδωμι ὑμῖν· μὴ.ταρασσέσθω ὑμῶν ἡ καρδία, μηδὲ
gives, ²I ¹give to you. Let not be troubled your heart, nor
δειλιάτω. 28 ἠκούσατε ὅτι ἐγὼ εἶπον ὑμῖν, Ὑπάγω καὶ
let it fear. Ye heard that I said to you, I am going away and
ἔρχομαι πρὸς ὑμᾶς. εἰ ἠγαπᾶτέ με, ἐχάρητε.ἂν ὅτι
I am coming to you. If ye loved me, ye would have rejoiced that
ʷεἶπον,‖ Πορεύομαι πρὸς τὸν πατέρα· ὅτι ὁ.πατήρ.ˣμου‖
I said, I am going to the Father, for my Father
μείζων μου ἐστίν. 29 καὶ νῦν εἴρηκα ὑμῖν πρὶν γενέ-
²greater ³than ⁴I ¹is. And now I have told you before it comes to
σθαι, ἵνα ὅταν γένηται πιστεύσητε. 30 ʸοὐκ ἔτι‖
pass, that when it shall have come to pass ye may believe. No longer
πολλὰ λαλήσω μεθ' ᶻὑμῶν·‖ ἔρχεται.γὰρ ὁ τοῦ κόσμου
much I will speak with you, for comes the ²of ⁴world
ᵃτούτου‖ ἄρχων, καὶ ἐν ἐμοὶ οὐκ ἔχει οὐδέν· 31 ἀλλ' ἵνα
³this ¹ruler, and in me he has nothing; but that
γνῷ ὁ κόσμος ὅτι ἀγαπῶ τὸν πατέρα, ᵇκαὶ‖ καθὼς
³may ⁴know ¹the ²world that I love the Father, and as
ᶜἐνετείλατό‖ μοι ὁ πατήρ, οὕτως ποιῶ· ἐγείρεσθε, ἄγωμεν
³commanded ⁴me ¹the ²Father, thus I do. Rise up, let us go
ἐντεῦθεν.
hence.

15 Ἐγώ εἰμι ἡ ἄμπελος ἡ ἀληθινή, καὶ ὁ.πατήρ.μου ὁ
I am the ²vine ¹true, and my Father the
γεωργός ἐστιν. 2 πᾶν κλῆμα ἐν ἐμοὶ μὴ φέρον καρπόν,
husbandman is. Every branch in me not bearing fruit,
αἴρει αὐτό· καὶ πᾶν τὸ καρπὸν φέρον, καθαίρει αὐτὸ
he takes away it; and everyone that fruit bears, he cleanses it
ἵνα ᵈπλείονα καρπὸν‖ φέρῃ. 3 ἤδη ὑμεῖς καθαροί ἐστε
that more fruit it may bear. Already ye clean are
διὰ τὸν λόγον ὃν λελάληκα ὑμῖν. 4 μείνατε ἐν ἐμοί,
by reason of the word which I have spoken to you. Abide in me,
κἀγὼ ἐν ὑμῖν. καθὼς τὸ κλῆμα οὐ.δύναται καρπὸν φέρειν ἀφ'
and I in you. As the branch is not able fruit to bear of
ἑαυτοῦ ἐὰν.μὴ ᵉμείνῃ‖ ἐν τῇ ἀμπέλῳ, οὕτως οὐδὲ ὑμεῖς
itself unless it abide in the vine, so neither [can] ye
ἐὰν.μὴ ἐν ἐμοὶ ᶠμείνητε.‖ 5 ἐγώ εἰμι ἡ ἄμπελος, ὑμεῖς τὰ
unless in me ye abide. I am the vine, ye [are] the
κλήματα. ὁ μένων ἐν ἐμοί, κἀγὼ ἐν αὐτῷ, οὗτος φέρει
branches. He that abides in me, and I in him, he bears
καρπὸν πολύν· ὅτι χωρὶς ἐμοῦ οὐ δύνασθε ποιεῖν οὐδέν.
²fruit ¹much; for apart from me ye are able to do nothing.
6 ἐὰν.μή τις ᵍμείνῃ‖ ἐν ἐμοί, ἐβλήθη ἔξω ὡς τὸ κλῆμα, καὶ
Unless anyone abide in me, he is cast out as the branch, and
ἐξηράνθη, καὶ συνάγουσιν ʰαὐτὰ‖ καὶ εἰς ⁱπῦρ βάλλουσιν, καὶ
is dried up, and they gather them and into a fire cast, and
καίεται. 7 ἐὰν μείνητε ἐν ἐμοί, καὶ τὰ.ῥήματά.μου ἐν ὑμῖν
it is burned. If ye abide in me, and my words in you
μείνῃ, ὃ.ᵏἐὰν‖ θέλητε ˡαἰτήσεσθε,‖ καὶ γενήσεται ὑμῖν.
abide, whatever ye will ye shall ask, and it shall come to pass to you.
8 ἐν τούτῳ ἐδοξάσθη ὁ.πατήρ.μου, ἵνα καρπὸν πολὺν φέρητε,
In this is glorified my Father, that ²fruit ¹much ye should bear,
καὶ ᵐγενήσεσθε‖ ἐμοὶ μαθηταί. 9 καθὼς ἠγάπησέν με ὁ
and ye shall become ²to ³me ¹disciples. As loved me the
πατήρ, κἀγὼ ⁿἠγάπησα ὑμᾶς·‖ μείνατε ἐν τῇ ἀγάπῃ τῇ ἐμῇ.
Father, I also loved you: abide in ²love ¹my.
10 ἐὰν τὰς.ἐντολάς.μου τηρήσητε, μενεῖτε ἐν τῇ.ἀγάπῃ.μου·
If my commandments ye keep, ye shall abide in my love,

22 Judas (not the Is-car-i-ot) said to Him,
Lord, what has happened that You are about
to reveal Yourself to us and not to the
world?
23 Jesus answered and said to him, If anyone loves Me he will keep My word. And My
Father will love him and We will come to
him and will make Our home with him.
24 He that does not love Me does not keep
My words. And the word which you hear is
not Mine, but of the Father who sent Me.
25 I have spoken these things to you while I
am still with you.
26 But the Comforter, the Holy Spirit
whom the Father will send in My name, He
will teach you all things. And He will bring
to your memory all the things which I told
you.
27 I leave peace with you. My peace I give
to you I do not give as the world gives to
you. Do not let your heart be troubled,
neither let it be afraid.
28 You heard Me say to you that I am going
away and I am coming to you. If you loved
Me, you would have been happy that I said,
I am going to the Father, for My Father is
greater than I.
29 And now I have told you before it
happens, so that when it has happened you
may believe.
30 I will not speak with you much longer,
for the prince of this world is coming and
has nothing in Me.
31 But that the world may know that I love
the Father, and as the Father commanded
Me, that I do. Arise, let us go away from
here.

CHAPTER 15

1 I am the True Vine and My Father is the
Vinedresser.
2 He takes away every branch in Me that
bears no fruit. And He prunes every one that
bears fruit, so that it may bear more fruit.
3 Now you are clean through the word
which I have spoken to you.
4 Remain in Me and I *will continue* in you.
As the branch is not able to bear fruit of
itself unless it remain in the vine, so neither
can you unless you continue in Me.
5 I am the Vine. You are the branches. He
that remains in Me and I in him will bear
much fruit. For apart from Me you are not
able to do anything.
6 If anyone does not remain in Me, he is
thrown out as a branch and is dried up. And
they gather and throw them into the fire.
And they are burned.
7 If you remain in Me and My words live in
you, you shall ask whatever you desire and it
shall be done to you.
8 In this My Father is glorified, that you
should bear much fruit, and you shall
become My disciples.
9 As the Father loved Me, I also loved you.
Continue in My love.
10 If you keep My commandments, you

καθὼς [o]ἐγὼ" [p]τὰς ἐντολὰς τοῦ.πατρός".[q]μου" τετήρηκα, καὶ
as I the commandments of my Father have kept, and
μένω αὐτοῦ ἐν τῇ ἀγάπῃ. 11 ταῦτα λελάληκα ὑμῖν, ἵνα
abide [2]his [1]in love. These things I have spoken to you, that
ἡ χαρὰ ἡ ἐμὴ ἐν ὑμῖν [r]μείνῃ," καὶ ἡ.χαρὰ.ὑμῶν πληρωθῇ.
[2]joy [1]my in you may abide, and your joy may be full.
12 αὕτη ἐστὶν ἡ ἐντολὴ ἡ ἐμή, ἵνα ἀγαπᾶτε ἀλλήλους,
This is [2]commandment [1]my, that ye love one another,
καθὼς ἠγάπησα ὑμᾶς. 13 μείζονα ταύτης ἀγάπην οὐδεὶς
as I loved you. Greater than this love no one
ἔχει, ἵνα [s]τις" τὴν.ψυχὴν.αὐτοῦ θῇ ὑπὲρ τῶν φίλων
has, that one his life should lay down for [2]friends
αὐτοῦ. 14 ὑμεῖς φίλοι μου ἐστὲ ἐὰν ποιῆτε [t]ὅσα" ἐγὼ
[1]his. Ye [2]friends [1]my are if ye practise whatsoever I
ἐντέλλομαι ὑμῖν. 15 οὐκέτι [v]ὑμᾶς λέγω" δούλους, ὅτι ὁ δοῦ-
command you. No longer you I call bondmen, for the bond-
λος οὐκ.οἶδεν τί ποιεῖ αὐτοῦ ὁ κύριος· ὑμᾶς.δὲ εἴρηκα
man knows not what [3]is [4]doing [1]his [2]master. But you I have called
φίλους, ὅτι πάντα ἃ ἤκουσα παρὰ τοῦ.πατρός.μου ἐγνώ-
friends, for all things which I heard of my Father I made
ρισα ὑμῖν. 16 οὐχ ὑμεῖς με ἐξελέξασθε, ἀλλ' ἐγὼ ἐξελεξάμην
known to you. [3]Not [1]ye [4]me [2]chose, but I chose
ὑμᾶς, καὶ ἔθηκα ὑμᾶς ἵνα ὑμεῖς ὑπάγητε καὶ καρπὸν φέ-
you, and appointed you that ye should go and fruit ye should
ρητε, καὶ ὁ.καρπὸς.ὑμῶν μένῃ· ἵνα ὅ.τι.ἂν αἰτήσητε τὸν
bear, and your fruit should abide; that whatsoever ye may ask the
πατέρα ἐν τῷ.ὀνόματί.μου δῷ ὑμῖν. 17 ταῦτα ἐντέλ-
Father in my name he may give you. These things I com-
λομαι ὑμῖν, ἵνα ἀγαπᾶτε ἀλλήλους. 18 Εἰ ὁ κόσμος ὑμᾶς
mand you, that ye love one another. If the world you
μισεῖ, γινώσκετε ὅτι ἐμὲ πρῶτον [w]ὑμῶν" μεμίσηκεν. 19 εἰ ἐκ
hates, ye know that me before you it has hated. If of
τοῦ κόσμου ἦτε, ὁ κόσμος ἂν.τὸ.ἴδιον.ἐφίλει· ὅτι.δὲ ἐκ τοῦ
the world ye were, the world would love its own; but because of the
κόσμου οὐκ.ἐστέ, ἀλλ' ἐγὼ ἐξελεξάμην ὑμᾶς ἐκ τοῦ κόσμου,
world ye are not, but I chose you out of the world,
διὰ τοῦτο μισεῖ ὑμᾶς ὁ κόσμος. 20 μνημονεύετε τοῦ
on account of this [3]hates [4]you [1]the [2]world. Remember the
λόγου οὗ ἐγὼ εἶπον ὑμῖν, Οὐκ.ἔστιν δοῦλος μείζων τοῦ
word which I said to you, [3]Is [4]not [1]a [2]bondman greater
κυρίου.αὐτοῦ. εἰ ἐμὲ ἐδίωξαν, καὶ ὑμᾶς διώξουσιν· εἰ
than his master. If me they persecuted, also you they will persecute; if
τὸν.λόγον.μου ἐτήρησαν, καὶ τὸν ὑμέτερον τηρήσουσιν. 21 ἀλλὰ
my word they kept, also yours they will keep. But
ταῦτα πάντα ποιήσουσιν [x]ὑμῖν" διὰ τὸ.ὄνομά.μου,
[3]these [4]things [1]all they will do to you on account of my name,
ὅτι οὐκ.οἴδασιν τὸν πέμψαντά με. 22 εἰ μὴ.ἦλθον καὶ
because they know not him who sent me. If I had not come and
ἐλάλησα αὐτοῖς, ἁμαρτίαν οὐκ.[y]εἶχον·" νῦν.δὲ πρόφασιν
spoken to them, sin they had not had; but now a pretext
οὐκ.ἔχουσιν περὶ τῆς.ἁμαρτίας.αὐτῶν. 23 ὁ ἐμὲ μισῶν, καὶ
they have not for their sin. He that [2]me [1]hates, [3]also
τὸν.πατέρα.μου μισεῖ. 24 εἰ τὰ ἔργα μὴ.ἐποίησα ἐν
[5]my [6]Father [4]hates. If [7]the [8]works [1]I [2]had [3]not [4]done [5]among
αὐτοῖς ἃ οὐδεὶς.ἄλλος [z]πεποίηκεν," ἁμαρτίαν οὐκ.[a]εἶχον·"
[6]them which no other one has done, sin they had not had,
νῦν.δὲ καὶ ἑωράκασιν καὶ μεμισήκασιν καὶ ἐμὲ καὶ τὸν πατέρα
but now both they have seen and have hated both me and [2]Father
μου· 25 ἀλλ' ἵνα πληρωθῇ ὁ λόγος ὁ [b]γεγραμμένος ἐν
[1]my. But that might be fulfilled the word that has been written in
τῷ.νόμῳ.αὐτῶν," Ὅτι ἐμίσησάν με δωρεάν. 26 Ὅταν.[c]δὲ"
their law, They hated me without cause. But when
ἔλθῃ ὁ παράκλητος, ὃν ἐγὼ πέμψω ὑμῖν παρὰ τοῦ πατρός,
is come the Paraclete, whom I will send to you from the Father,
τὸ πνεῦμα τῆς ἀληθείας, ὃ παρὰ τοῦ πατρὸς ἐκπορεύεται,
the Spirit of truth, who from the Father goes forth,
ἐκεῖνος μαρτυρήσει περὶ ἐμοῦ· 27 καὶ ὑμεῖς δὲ μαρ-
he will bear witness concerning me; [3]also [2]ye [1]and bear
τυρεῖτε, ὅτι ἀπ' ἀρχῆς μετ' ἐμοῦ ἐστε.
witness, because from [the] beginning with me ye are.
16 Ταῦτα λελάληκα ὑμῖν ἵνα μὴ.σκανδαλισθῆτε. 2 ἀπο-
These things I have spoken to you that ye may not be offended. Out of
συναγώγους ποιήσουσιν ὑμᾶς· ἀλλ' ἔρχεται ὥρα ἵνα πᾶς
the synagogues they will put you; but is coming an hour that everyone
ὁ ἀποκτείνας ὑμᾶς δόξῃ λατρείαν προσφέρειν τῷ θεῷ.
who kills you will think service to render to God;
3 καὶ ταῦτα ποιήσουσιν [d]ὑμῖν" ὅτι οὐκ.ἔγνωσαν τὸν πα-
and these things they will do to you because they know not the Fa-
τέρα οὐδὲ ἐμέ. 4 ἀλλὰ ταῦτα λελάληκα ὑμῖν, ἵνα ὅταν
ther nor me. But these things I have said to you, that when
ἔλθῃ ἡ ὥρα [e] μνημονεύητε [f]αὐτῶν" ὅτι ἐγὼ εἶπον
may have come the hour ye may remember them that I said [them]

shall continue in My love, even as I have
kept the commandments of My Father and
continue in His love.
11 I have spoken these things to you that
My joy may abide in you and your joy may
be full.
12 This is My commandment, that you love
one another, even as I loved you.
13 No one has greater love than this, that
one should lay down his life for his friends.
14 You are My friends, if you practice
whatever I command you.
15 I do not call you servants any more, for
the servant does not know what his lord is
doing. But I have called you friends, for all
things which I heard of My Father I have
made known to you.
16 You did not choose Me, but I chose you.
And I planted you in order that you should
go and bear fruit, and that your fruit should
last – so that whatever you may ask the
Father in My name, He may give to you.
17 I command you these things, that you
love one another.
18 If the world hates you, you know that it
has hated Me before it hated you.
19 If you were of the world, the world
would love its own. But because you are not
of the world, but I chose you out of the
world, the world hates you because of this.
20 Remember the word that I told you, The
slave is not greater than his lord. If they have
persecuted Me, they will also persecute you,
If they keep My word, they will keep yours
too.
21 But they will do all these things to you
on account of My name, because they do
not know Him who sent Me.
22 If I had not come and had not spoken to
them, they would not have had sin. But now
they have no excuse for their sin.
23 He that hates Me hates My Father also.
24 If I had not done among them the works
which no other one did, they would not
have had sin. But now they have both seen
and have hated both Me and My Father.
25 But *it is* in order that the word might be
fulfilled that has been written in their law,
"They hated Me without a cause."
26 But when the Comforter comes (whom I
will send to you from the Father, the Spirit
of Truth who comes from the Father) He
will bear witness about Me.
27 And you also bear witness because you
were with Me from the beginning.

CHAPTER 16

1 I have spoken these things to you so that
you may not stumble.
2 They will put you out of the synagogues.
And the time is coming when everyone who
kills you will think he is doing service to
God.
3 And they will do these things to you because they do not know the Father or Me.
4 But I have said these things to you, so

ὑμῖν· ταῦτα.δὲ ὑμῖν ἐξ ἀρχῆς οὐκ.εἶπον ὅτι
to you. But these things to you from [the] beginning I did not say, because
μεθ' ὑμῶν ἤμην. 5 νῦν.δὲ ὑπάγω πρὸς τὸν πέμψαντά με,
with you I was. But now I go to him who sent me,
καὶ οὐδεὶς ἐξ ὑμῶν ἐρωτᾷ με, Ποῦ ὑπάγεις; 6 ἀλλ' ὅτι
and none of you asks me, Where goest thou? But because
ταῦτα λελάληκα ὑμῖν ἡ λύπη πεπλήρωκεν ὑμῶν τὴν
these things I have said to you grief has filled your
καρδίαν. 7 ἀλλ' ἐγὼ τὴν ἀλήθειαν λέγω ὑμῖν, συμφέρει
heart. But I the truth say to you, It is profitable
ὑμῖν ἵνα ἐγὼ ἀπέλθω· ἐὰν.γὰρ [k]μὴ.ἀπέλθω ὁ παράκλη-
for you that I should go away; for if I go not away the Paraclete
τος [h]οὐκ.ἐλεύσεται" πρὸς ὑμᾶς· ἐὰν.δὲ πορευθῶ, πέμψω
will not come to you; but if I go, I will send
αὐτὸν πρὸς ὑμᾶς· 8 καὶ ἐλθὼν ἐκεῖνος ἐλέγξει τὸν κόσμον
him to you. And having come he will convict the world
περὶ ἁμαρτίας καὶ περὶ δικαιοσύνης καὶ περὶ κρίσεως.
concerning sin and concerning righteousness and concerning judgment.
9 περὶ ἁμαρτίας μέν, ὅτι οὐ.πιστεύουσιν εἰς ἐμέ· 10 περὶ
Concerning sin, because they believe not on me; concerning
δικαιοσύνης δέ, ὅτι πρὸς τὸν.πατέρα.[i]μου" ὑπάγω, καὶ [k]οὐκ
righteousness because to my Father I go away, and no
ἔτι" θεωρεῖτέ με· 11 περὶ.δὲ κρίσεως, ὅτι ὁ ἄρχων τοῦ
longer ye behold me; and concerning judgment, because the ruler
κόσμου.τούτου κέκριται. 12 'Ἔτι πολλὰ ἔχω [l]λέγειν
of this world has been judged. Yet many things I have to say
ὑμῖν," ἀλλ' οὐ.δύνασθε βαστάζειν ἄρτι· 13 ὅταν.δὲ ἔλθῃ
to you, but ye are not able to bear them now. But when [2]may [3]have [4]come
ἐκεῖνος, τὸ πνεῦμα τῆς ἀληθείας, ὁδηγήσει ὑμᾶς [m]εἰς πᾶσαν
[1]he, the Spirit of truth, he will guide you into all
τὴν ἀλήθειαν·" οὐ γὰρ λαλήσει ἀφ' ἑαυτοῦ, ἀλλ' ὅσα.[n]ἂν"
the truth; [4]not [1]for [2]he [3]will speak from himself, but whatsoever
[o]ἀκούσῃ" λαλήσει, καὶ τὰ ἐρχόμενα ἀναγγελεῖ ὑμῖν.
he may hear he will speak; and the things coming he will announce to you.
14 ἐκεῖνος ἐμὲ δοξάσει, ὅτι ἐκ τοῦ ἐμοῦ [p]λήψεται," καὶ ἀναγ-
He me will glorify, for of mine he will receive, and will an-
γελεῖ ὑμῖν. 15 πάντα ὅσα ἔχει ὁ πατὴρ ἐμά ἐστιν·
nounce to you. All things whatsoever [3]has [1]the [2]Father [5]mine [4]are;
διὰ τοῦτο εἶπον, ὅτι ἐκ τοῦ ἐμοῦ [q]λήψεται," καὶ ἀναγ-
because of this I said, that of mine he will receive, and will an-
γελεῖ ὑμῖν. 16 Μικρὸν καὶ [r]οὐ".θεωρεῖτέ με, καὶ πάλιν
nounce to you. A little [while] and ye do not behold me; and again
μικρὸν καὶ ὄψεσθέ με, [s]ὅτι ἐγὼ ὑπάγω πρὸς τὸν πα-
a little [while] and ye shall see me, because I go away to the Fa-
τέρα." 17 Εἶπον οὖν ἐκ τῶν.μαθητῶν.αὐτοῦ πρὸς
ther. Said therefore [some] of his disciples to
ἀλλήλους, Τί ἐστιν τοῦτο ὃ λέγει ἡμῖν, Μικρὸν καὶ
one another, What is this which he says to us, A little [while] and
οὐ.θεωρεῖτέ με, καὶ πάλιν μικρὸν καὶ ὄψεσθέ με; καὶ
ye do not behold me; and again a little [while] and ye shall see me? and
Ὅτι [t]ἐγὼ" ὑπάγω πρὸς τὸν πατέρα; 18 Ἔλεγον οὖν,
Because I go away to the Father? They said therefore,
[v]Τοῦτο τί ἐστιν" ὃ λέγει, [w]τὸ" μικρόν; οὐκ.οἴδαμεν
[3]This [1]what [2]is which he says, the little [while]? We do not know
τί λαλεῖ. 19 Ἔγνω [x]οὖν" [y]ὁ" Ἰησοῦς ὅτι ἤθελον αὐτὸν
what he speaks. [2]Knew [3]therefore [1]Jesus that they desired [3]him
ἐρωτᾶν, καὶ εἶπεν αὐτοῖς, Περὶ τούτου ζητεῖτε μετ'
[1]to [2]ask, and said to them, Concerning this do ye inquire among
ἀλλήλων, ὅτι εἶπον, Μικρὸν καὶ οὐ.θεωρεῖτέ με, καὶ
one another, that I said, A little [while] and ye do not behold me; and
πάλιν μικρὸν καὶ ὄψεσθέ με; 20 ἀμὴν ἀμὴν λέγω ὑμῖν,
again a little [while] and ye shall see me? Verily verily I say to you,
ὅτι κλαύσετε καὶ θρηνήσετε ὑμεῖς, ὁ.δὲ κόσμος χαρήσεται·
that [2]will [3]weep [4]and [5]will [6]lament [1]ye, but the world will rejoice;
ὑμεῖς.[z]δὲ" λυπηθήσεσθε, [a]ἀλλ'" ἡ.λύπη.ὑμῶν εἰς χαρὰν γενή-
but ye will be grieved, but your grief to joy shall be-
σεται. 21 ἡ γυνὴ ὅταν τίκτῃ, λύπην ἔχει, ὅτι ἦλθεν
come. The woman when she gives birth, grief has, because is come
ἡ.ὥρα.αὐτῆς· ὅταν.δὲ γεννήσῃ τὸ παιδίον, [b]οὐκ ἔτι"
her hour; but when she brings forth the child, no longer
μνημονεύει τῆς θλίψεως, διὰ τὴν χαρὰν ὅτι ἐγεννήθη
she remembers the tribulation, on account of the joy that has been born
ἄνθρωπος εἰς τὸν κόσμον. 22 καὶ ὑμεῖς οὖν [c]λύπην μὲν
a man into the world. And ye therefore grief indeed
νῦν· [d]ἔχετε·" πάλιν.δὲ ὄψομαι ὑμᾶς, καὶ χαρήσεται ὑμῶν
now have; but again I will see you, and [2]shall [3]rejoice [1]your
ἡ καρδία, καὶ τὴν.χαρὰν.ὑμῶν οὐδεὶς [e]αἴρει" ἀφ' ὑμῶν. 23 καὶ
[4]heart, and your joy no one takes from you. And
ἐν ἐκείνῃ τῇ ἡμέρᾳ ἐμὲ οὐκ ἐρωτήσετε οὐδέν. Ἀμὴν ἀμὴν
in that day of me ye shall ask nothing. Verily verily
λέγω ὑμῖν, [f]ὅτι" [g]ὅσα.ἂν" αἰτήσητε τὸν πατέρα [h]ἐν τῷ
I say to you, That whatsoever ye may ask the Father in

that when the time comes, you may remember that I told you of them. But I did not say these things to you from the beginning because I was with you.

5 But now I go to Him who sent Me, and none of you asks Me, Where are You going?

6 But because I have said these things to you, sorrow has filled your heart.

7 But I tell you the truth. It is better for you that I should go away. For if I do not go away the Comforter will not come to you. But if I go, I will send Him to you.

8 And when He comes, He will prove the world wrong about sin and about righteousness and about judgment –

9 about sin, because they do not believe on Me –

10 about righteousness, because I go away to My Father and you no longer see Me –

11 and about judgment, because the prince of this world has been judged.

12 I still have many things to say to you, but you are not able to bear them now.

13 But when He has come, the Spirit of Truth, He will guide you into all the truth. For He will not speak from Himself, but as many things as He hears, He will speak. And He will tell you things of the future.

14 He will glorify Me, for He will take that which is Mine and will tell it to you.

15 All things that the Father has are Mine. This is why I said, He will take of Mine and will tell it to you.

16 A little while and you will not see Me. And again a little while and you will see Me, because I go away to the Father.

17 Then *some* of the disciples said to one another, What is this that He says to us – a little while and you will not see Me, and again a little while and you will see Me? And, Because I go away to the Father?

18 So they said, What is this that He says, A little while? We do not know what He is saying.

19 Jesus knew then that they wanted to ask and He said to them, Do you ask about this among one another, that I said, A little while and you will not see Me, and again, a little while and you will see Me?

20 Indeed, I tell you truly that you will weep and wail, but the world will rejoice. And you will be sorrowful, but your sorrow shall become joy.

21 When she gives birth, a woman has pain because her time has come. But when she brings forth the child, she no longer remembers the pain because of the joy that a man has been born into the world.

22 And so you now truly have sorrow, but I will see you again and your heart will rejoice. And no one will take your joy away from you.

23 And in that day you will ask nothing of Me. Indeed, I tell you truly that as many things as you may ask the Father in My

ὀνόματί.μου δώσει ὑμῖν." 24 ἕως.ἄρτι οὐκ ᾐτήσατε οὐδὲν
my name he will give you. Hitherto ye asked nothing
ἐν τῷ.ὀνόματί.μου· αἰτεῖτε, καὶ [j]λήψεσθε," ἵνα ἡ.χαρὰ.ὑμῶν
in my name: ask, and ye shall receive, that your joy
ᾖ πεπληρωμένη. 25 ταῦτα ἐν παροιμίαις λελάληκα ὑμῖν·
may be full. These things in allegories I have spoken to you;
[k]ἀλλ'[l] ἔρχεται ὥρα ὅτε [l]οὐκ ἔτι" ἐν παροιμίαις λαλήσω
but is coming an hour when no longer in allegories I will speak
ὑμῖν, ἀλλὰ παῤῥησίᾳ περὶ τοῦ πατρὸς [m]ἀναγγελῶ ὑμῖν.
to you, but plainly concerning the Father I will announce to you.
26 ἐν ἐκείνῃ τῇ ἡμέρᾳ ἐν τῷ.ὀνόματί.μου αἰτήσεσθε· καὶ οὐ
In that day in my name ye shall ask; and [3]not
λέγω ὑμῖν ὅτι ἐγὼ ἐρωτήσω τὸν πατέρα περὶ ὑμῶν· 27 αὐ-
[1]I [2]say to you that I will beseech the Father for you, [4]him-
τὸς γὰρ ὁ πατὴρ φιλεῖ ὑμᾶς, ὅτι ὑμεῖς ἐμὲ πεφιλήκατε, καὶ
self [1]for [2]the [3]Father loves you, because ye me have loved, and
πεπιστεύκατε ὅτι ἐγὼ παρὰ [n]τοῦ θεοῦ[l] ἐξῆλθον. 28 ἐξῆλθον
have believed that I from God came out. I came out
[o]παρὰ[l] τοῦ πατρὸς καὶ ἐλήλυθα εἰς τὸν κόσμον· πάλιν ἀφίημι
from the Father and have come into the world; again I leave
τὸν κόσμον καὶ πορεύομαι πρὸς τὸν πατέρα. 29 Λέγουσιν
the world and go to the Father. [3]Say
[p]αὐτῷ[l] οἱ.μαθηταὶ.αὐτοῦ, "Ἴδε, νῦν [q]παῤῥησίᾳ λαλεῖς, καὶ
[4]to [5]him [1]his [2]disciples, Lo, now plainly thou speakest, and
παροιμίαν οὐδεμίαν λέγεις. 30 νῦν οἴδαμεν ὅτι οἶδας
[2]allegory [1]no speakest. Now we know that thou knowest
πάντα, καὶ οὐ χρείαν ἔχεις ἵνα τίς σε ἐρωτᾷ. ἐν τούτῳ
all things, and [2]not [3]need [1]hast that anyone thee should ask. By this
πιστεύομεν ὅτι ἀπὸ θεοῦ ἐξῆλθες. 31 Ἀπεκρίθη αὐτοῖς
we believe that from God thou camest forth. [2]Answered [3]them
[r]ὁ[l] Ἰησοῦς, "Ἄρτι πιστεύετε; 32 ἰδού, ἔρχεται ὥρα καὶ [s]νῦν[l]
[1]Jesus, [6]Now [4]do [5]ye [7]believe? Lo, is coming an hour and now
ἐλήλυθεν, ἵνα σκορπισθῆτε ἕκαστος εἰς τὰ.ἴδια, [t]καὶ ἐμὲ"
has come, that ye will be scattered each to his own, and me
μονον ἀφῆτε· καὶ οὐκ.εἰμὶ μόνος, ὅτι ὁ πατὴρ μετ'
alone ye will leave; and [yet] I am not alone, for the Father with
ἐμοῦ ἐστιν. 33 ταῦτα λελάληκα ὑμῖν ἵνα ἐν ἐμοὶ εἰρήνην
me is. These things I have spoken to you that in me peace
ἔχητε. ἐν τῷ κόσμῳ θλίψιν [v]ἔχετε·" ἀλλὰ θαρσεῖτε,
ye may have. In the world tribulation ye have; but be of good courage,
ἐγὼ νενίκηκα τὸν κόσμον.
I have overcome the world.

17 Ταῦτα ἐλάλησεν [w]ὁ[l] Ἰησοῦς, καὶ [x]ἐπῆρεν" τοὺς ὀφθαλ-
These things spoke Jesus, and lifted up [3]eyes
μοὺς αὐτοῦ εἰς τὸν οὐρανὸν [y]καὶ" εἶπεν, Πάτερ, ἐλήλυθεν ἡ
[2]his to the heaven and said, Father, [3]has [4]come [1]the
ὥρα· δόξασόν σου τὸν υἱόν, ἵνα [z]καὶ" ὁ.υἱός.[a]σου" δοξάσῃ
[2]hour; glorify thy Son, that also thy Son may glorify
σε· 2 καθὼς ἔδωκας αὐτῷ ἐξουσίαν πάσης σαρκός, ἵνα
thee; as thou gavest him authority over all flesh, that [of]
πᾶν ὃ δέδωκας αὐτῷ, [b]δώσῃ" αὐτοῖς ζωὴν αἰώνιον.
all which thou hast given him, he should give to them life eternal.
3 αὕτη.δέ ἐστιν ἡ αἰώνιος ζωή, ἵνα [c]γινώσκωσίν" σε τὸν
And this is the eternal life, that they should know thee the
μόνον ἀληθινὸν θεόν, καὶ ὃν ἀπέστειλας Ἰησοῦν χριστόν.
only true God, and [3]whom [4]thou [5]didst [6]send [1]Jesus [2]Christ.
4 ἐγώ σε ἐδόξασα ἐπὶ τῆς γῆς· τὸ ἔργον [d]ἐτελείωσα" ὃ
I thee glorified on the earth; the work I completed which
δέδωκάς μοι ἵνα ποιήσω· 5 καὶ νῦν δόξασόν με σύ, πά-
thou hast given me that I should do; and now glorify me thou, Fa-
τερ, παρὰ σεαυτῷ, τῇ δόξῃ ᾗ εἶχον πρὸ τοῦ τὸν κόσμον
ther, with thyself, with the glory which I had before the world
εἶναι παρὰ σοί. 6 Ἐφανέρωσά σου τὸ ὄνομα τοῖς ἀνθρώποις
was with thee. I manifested thy name to the men
οὓς [e]δέδωκάς" μοι ἐκ τοῦ κόσμου· σοὶ ἦσαν, [f]καὶ ἐμοὶ"
whom thou hast given me out of the world. Thine they were, and to me
αὐτοὺς [e]δέδωκας·" καὶ τὸν.λόγον.σου [g]τετηρήκασιν." 7 νῦν
them thou hast given, and thy word they have kept. Now
ἔγνωκαν ὅτι πάντα ὅσα [h]δέδωκάς" μοι, παρὰ σοῦ
they have known that all things whatsoever thou hast given me, of thee
[i]ἐστιν·[l] 8 ὅτι τὰ ῥήματα ἃ [k]δέδωκάς" μοι δέδωκα αὐτοῖς·
are; for the words which thou hast given me I have given them,
καὶ αὐτοὶ ἔλαβον, [l]καὶ ἔγνωσαν" ἀληθῶς ὅτι παρὰ σοῦ
and they received [them], and knew truly that from thee
ἐξῆλθον, καὶ ἐπίστευσαν ὅτι σύ με ἀπέστειλας. 9 ἐγὼ περὶ
I came out, and they believed that thou me didst send. I concerning
αὐτῶν ἐρωτῶ· οὐ περὶ τοῦ κόσμου ἐρωτῶ, ἀλλὰ
them make request; not concerning the world make I request, but
περὶ ὧν δέδωκάς μοι, ὅτι σοί εἰσιν. 10 καὶ τὰ
concerning whom thou hast given me, for thine they are: (and [3]things
ἐμὰ πάντα σά ἐστιν, καὶ τὰ.σὰ ἐμά· καὶ δεδόξασμαι
[2]my [1]all [6]thine [5]are, and thine [are] mine:) and I have been glorified

name, He will give you.
24 Up to this time you have not asked anything in My name. Ask and you shall receive,
so that your joy may be full.
25 I have told you these things in parables,
but the hour is coming when I will no longer
speak to you in parables, but I will tell you
plainly about the Father.
26 In that day you will ask in My name –
and I do not say I shall ask the Father for
you,
27 for the Father Himself loves you, because you have loved Me and have believed
that I came out from God.
28 I came out from the Father and have
come into the world. Again, I leave the
world and go to the Father.
29 His disciples said to Him, See, now You
are speaking plainly and not speaking a parable.
30 Now we know that you have known all
things and do not need for anyone to ask
You. By this we believe that you have proceeded from God.
31 Jesus answered them, Do you believe
now?
32 Behold! The time is coming, and now is,
that you will be scattered, each one to his
own home. And you will leave Me alone –
yet I am not alone because the Father is
with Me.
33 I have spoken these things to you so that
you may have peace in Me. You have trouble
in the world, but be of good courage, I have
overcome the world.

CHAPTER 17

1 Jesus said these things and lifted up His
eyes to Heaven and said, Father, the time
has come. Glorify Your Son so that Your
Son may also glorify You –
2 even as You have given Him authority
over all flesh, that He should give everlasting
life to all which You have given to Him.
3 And this is life everlasting, that they
should know You, the only true God, and
Jesus Christ whom You have sent.
4 I have glorified You on the earth. I have
finished the work that You have given Me to
do.
5 And now, O Father, glorify Me beside
Yourself, with the glory which I had beside
You before the world ever was.
6 I made Your name known to the men
whom You have given Me out of the world.
They were Yours and You have given them
to Me, and they have kept Your word.
7 Now they have known that all things
which You have given Me are from You.
8 For the words which You have given Me I
have given them, and they have taken them
to themselves and they know that I truly
proceeded from You. And they believed that
You sent Me.
9 I pray for them. I do not pray for the
world, but for those whom You have given
to Me, because they are Yours,
10 and all My things are Yours, and Yours
are Mine, and I have been glorified in them.

ἐν αὐτοῖς. 11 καὶ [m]οὐκ ἔτι‖ εἰμὶ ἐν τῷ κόσμῳ, καὶ [n]οὗτοι‖ ἐν
in them. And no longer I am in the world, and these in
τῷ κόσμῳ εἰσίν, [o]καὶ ἐγὼ‖ πρός σε ἔρχομαι. πάτερ ἅγιε, τήρη-
the world are, and I to thee come. [2]Father [1]Holy, keep
σον αὐτοὺς ἐν τῷ.ὀνόματί.σου [p]οὓς‖ δέδωκάς μοι, ἵνα
them in thy name whom thou hast given me, that
ὦσιν ἕν, καθὼς [q] ἡμεῖς. 12 ὅτε ἤμην μετ' αὐτῶν [r]ἐν τῷ
they may be one, as we. When I was with them in the
κόσμῳ ἐγὼ ἐτήρουν αὐτοὺς ἐν τῷ.ὀνόματί.σου [s]οὓς‖ δέ-
world I was keeping them in thy name: whom thou
δωκάς μοι [t] ἐφύλαξα, καὶ οὐδεὶς ἐξ αὐτῶν ἀπώλετο, εἰ.μὴ ὁ
hast given me I guarded, and no one of them perished, except the
υἱὸς τῆς ἀπωλείας, ἵνα ἡ γραφὴ πληρωθῇ. 13 νῦν.δὲ
son of perdition, that the scripture might be fulfilled. And now
πρός σε ἔρχομαι, καὶ ταῦτα λαλῶ ἐν τῷ κόσμῳ ἵνα ἔχω-
to thee I come; and these things I speak in the world that they may
σιν τὴν χαρὰν τὴν ἐμὴν πεπληρωμένην ἐν [u]αὐτοῖς.‖ 14 ἐγὼ
have [2]joy [1]my fulfilled in them. I
δέδωκα αὐτοῖς τὸν.λόγον.σου, καὶ ὁ κόσμος ἐμίσησεν αὐτούς,
have given them thy word, and the world hated them,
ὅτι οὐκ.εἰσὶν ἐκ τοῦ κόσμου, καθὼς ἐγὼ οὐκ.εἰμὶ ἐκ τοῦ
because they are not of the world, as I am not of the
κόσμου. 15 οὐκ.ἐρωτῶ ἵνα ἄρῃς αὐτοὺς ἐκ τοῦ
world. I do not make request that thou shouldest take them out of the
κόσμου, ἀλλ' ἵνα τηρήσῃς αὐτοὺς ἐκ τοῦ πονηροῦ.
world, but that thou shouldest keep them out of the evil.
16 ἐκ τοῦ κόσμου οὐκ.εἰσίν, καθὼς ἐγὼ [v]ἐκ τοῦ κόσμου οὐκ
Of the world they are not, as I of the world [2]not
εἰμί.‖ 17 ἁγίασον αὐτοὺς ἐν τῇ.ἀληθείᾳ.[w]σου·‖ ὁ λόγος ὁ σὸς
[1]am. Sanctify them by thy truth; [2]word [1]thy
ἀλήθειά ἐστιν. 18 καθὼς ἐμὲ ἀπέστειλας εἰς τὸν κόσμον,
truth is. As me thou didst send into the world,
κἀγὼ ἀπέστειλα αὐτοὺς εἰς τὸν κόσμον· 19 καὶ ὑπὲρ αὐτῶν
I also sent them into the world; and for them
[x]ἐγὼ‖ ἁγιάζω ἐμαυτόν, ἵνα [y]καὶ αὐτοὶ ὦσιν‖ ἡγιασμένοι ἐν
I sanctify myself, that also they may be sanctified in
ἀληθείᾳ. 20 Οὐ περὶ τούτων δὲ ἐρωτῶ μόνον, ἀλλὰ
truth. [2]Not [3]for [4]these [1]and [7]make [6]I [8]request [5]only, but
καὶ περὶ τῶν [z]πιστευσόντων‖ διὰ τοῦ.λόγου.αὐτῶν εἰς
also for those who shall believe through their word on
ἐμέ· 21 ἵνα πάντες ἓν ὦσιν, καθὼς σύ, [a]πάτερ,‖ ἐν ἐμοί,
me; that all one may be, as thou, Father, [art] in me,
κἀγὼ ἐν σοί, ἵνα καὶ αὐτοὶ ἐν ἡμῖν [b]ἓν‖ ὦσιν· ἵνα ὁ κόσμος
and I in thee, that also they in us one may be, that the world
[c]πιστεύσῃ‖ ὅτι σύ με ἀπέστειλας. 22 [d]καὶ ἐγὼ‖ τὴν δόξαν
may believe that thou me didst send. And I the glory
ἣν [e]δέδωκάς‖ μοι δέδωκα αὐτοῖς, ἵνα ὦσιν ἕν, καθὼς
which thou hast given me have given them, that they may be one, as
ἡμεῖς ἕν [f]ἐσμεν·‖ 23 ἐγὼ ἐν αὐτοῖς, καὶ σὺ ἐν ἐμοί, ἵνα
we one are: I in them, and thou in me, that
ὦσιν τετελειωμένοι εἰς ἕν, [g]καὶ‖ ἵνα γινώσκῃ ὁ κόσμος
they may be perfected into one, and that [3]may [4]know [1]the [2]world
ὅτι σύ με ἀπέστειλας, καὶ ἠγάπησας αὐτοὺς καθὼς ἐμὲ ἠγά-
that thou me didst send, and lovedst them as me thou
πησας. 24 [h]Πάτερ,‖ [i]οὓς‖ [j]δέδωκάς‖ μοι θέλω ἵνα ὅπου εἰμὶ
lovedst. Father, whom thou hast given me I desire that where [2]am
ἐγὼ κἀκεῖνοι ὦσιν μετ' ἐμοῦ, ἵνα θεωρῶσιν τὴν δόξαν τὴν
[1]I they also may be with me, that they may behold [2]glory
ἐμὴν ἣν [k]ἔδωκάς‖ μοι, ὅτι ἠγάπησάς με πρὸ καταβολῆς
[1]my which thou gavest me, for thou lovedst me before [the] foundation
κόσμου 25 [l]Πάτερ‖ δίκαιε, καὶ ὁ κόσμος σε οὐκ.ἔγνω,
of [the] world. [2]Father [1]righteous, and the world thee knew not,
ἐγὼ.δέ σε ἔγνων, καὶ οὗτοι ἔγνωσαν ὅτι σύ με ἀπέστειλας·
but I thee knew, and these knew that thou me didst send.
26 καὶ ἐγνώρισα αὐτοῖς τὸ.ὄνομά.σου, καὶ γνωρίσω·
And I made known to them thy name, and will make [it] known;
ἵνα ἡ ἀγάπη ἣν ἠγάπησάς με ἐν αὐτοῖς ᾖ, κἀγὼ
that the love with which thou lovedst me in them may be; and I
ἐν αὐτοῖς.
in them.

18 Ταῦτα εἰπὼν [m]ὁ‖ Ἰησοῦς ἐξῆλθεν σὺν τοῖς μαθηταῖς
[4]These [5]things [2]having [3]said [1]Jesus went out with [2]disciples
αὐτοῦ πέραν τοῦ χειμάῤῥου [n]τῶν Κέδρων,‖ ὅπου ἦν κῆπος,
[1]his beyond the winter stream of Kedron, where was a garden,
εἰς ὃν εἰσῆλθεν αὐτὸς καὶ οἱ.μαθηταὶ.αὐτοῦ. 2 ᾔδει.δὲ καὶ
into which [2]entered [1]he and his disciples. And [8]knew [2]also
Ἰούδας ὁ παραδιδοὺς αὐτὸν τὸν τόπον· ὅτι πολλάκις
[1]Judas [3]who [4]was [5]delivering [7]up [6]him the place, because [3]often
συνήχθη [o]ὁ‖ Ἰησοῦς ἐκεῖ μετὰ τῶν.μαθητῶν.αὐτοῦ. 3 ὁ οὖν
[2]was [4]gathered [1]Jesus there with his disciples. [2]Therefore
Ἰούδας λαβὼν τὴν σπεῖραν, καὶ ἐκ τῶν ἀρχιερέων καὶ [p]
[1]Judas having received the band, and [2]from [3]the [4]chief [5]priests [6]and

11 And I no longer am in the world, but these are in the world, and I am coming to You. Holy Father, keep them in Your name, all those You have given to Me, so that they may be one, as We are.

12 While I was with them in the world I kept them in Your name. I watched over those You have given to Me and not one of them is lost except the son of perdition, in order that the Scripture might be fulfilled.

13 And now I come to You and I speak these things in the world so that they may have My joy fulfilled in them.

14 I have given them Your word, and the world hated them because they are not of the world, even as I am not of the world.

15 I do not pray for You to take them out of the world, but for You to keep them from evil.

16 They are not of the world, even as I am not of the world.

17 Sanctify them by Your truth. Your word is truth.

18 As You sent Me into the world, I also sent them into the world.

19 And I sanctify Myself for them so that they also may be sanctified in Truth.

20 Neither do I pray for these alone, but for those who shall believe on Me through their word –

21 that they also may be one, as You, Father, are in Me and I am in You, so that they also may be one in Us, so that the world may believe that You sent Me.

22 And the glory which You have given Me, I have given them, so that they may be one even as We are one:

23 I in them, and You in Me, so that they may be made perfect in one and that the world may know that You have sent Me and that You love them as You have loved Me.

24 Father, I desire that those whom You have given Me may be with Me where I am, so that they may see My glory which You gave to Me, because You have loved Me, before the foundation of the world.

25 O righteous Father! The world did not know You, but I knew You, and these have come to know that You have sent Me.

26 And I made Your name known to them and I will make it known, so that the love with which You loved Me may be in them and I in them.

CHAPTER 18

1 When Jesus had spoken these words, He went out with His disciples beyond the brook of Kidron, where there was a garden into which He and His disciples entered.

2 And Judas, who was betraying Him, also knew the place, because Jesus often went there to meet with His disciples.

3 Then taking the band and officers from the chief priests and Pharisees, Judas came

Φαρισαίων ὑπηρέτας, ἔρχεται ἐκεῖ μετὰ φανῶν καὶ λαμπάδων
[7]Pharisees [1]officers, comes there with torches and lamps
καὶ ὅπλων. 4 Ἰησοῦς [q]οὖν εἰδὼς πάντα τὰ ἐρχόμενα
and weapons. Jesus therefore knowing all things that were coming
ἐπ' αὐτόν, [r]ἐξελθὼν εἶπεν αὐτοῖς, Τίνα ζητεῖτε; 5 Ἀπε-
upon him, having gone forth said to them, Whom seek ye? They
κρίθησαν αὐτῷ, Ἰησοῦν τὸν Ναζωραῖον. Λέγει αὐτοῖς [s]ὁ
answered him, Jesus the Nazarean. [2]Says [3]to [4]them
Ἰησοῦς, Ἐγώ εἰμι. Εἱστήκει.δὲ καὶ Ἰούδας ὁ παρα-
[1]Jesus, I am [he]. And [6]was [7]standing [2]also [1]Judas [3]who [4]was [5]de-
διδοὺς αὐτὸν μετ' αὐτῶν. 6 Ὡς οὖν εἶπεν αὐτοῖς, [t]Ὅτι
livering [7]up [6]him with them. When therefore he said to them,
ἐγώ εἰμι, [v]ἀπῆλθον εἰς.τὰ.ὀπίσω καὶ [w]ἔπεσον χαμαί.
I am [he], they went backward and fell to [the] ground.
7 πάλιν οὖν [x]αὐτοὺς ἐπηρώτησεν, Τίνα ζητεῖτε; Οἱ.δὲ
Again therefore [3]them [1]he [2]questioned, Whom seek ye? And they
εἶπον, Ἰησοῦν τὸν Ναζωραῖον. 8 Ἀπεκρίθη [y]ὁ Ἰησοῦς, Εἶπον
said, Jesus the Nazarean. [2]Answered [1]Jesus, I told
ὑμῖν ὅτι ἐγώ εἰμι. εἰ οὖν ἐμὲ ζητεῖτε, ἄφετε τούτους ὑπά-
you that I am [he]. If therefore me ye seek, suffer these to go
γειν· 9 ἵνα πληρωθῇ ὁ λόγος ὃν εἶπεν, Ὅτι οὓς δέ-
away; that might be fulfilled the word which he said, Whom thou
δωκάς μοι οὐκ ἀπώλεσα ἐξ αὐτῶν οὐδένα. 10 Σίμων οὖν
hast given me I lost of them not one. Simon [2]therefore
Πέτρος ἔχων μάχαιραν, εἵλκυσεν αὐτήν, καὶ ἔπαισεν τὸν
[1]Peter having a sword, drew it, and smote the
τοῦ ἀρχιερέως δοῦλον, καὶ ἀπέκοψεν αὐτοῦ τὸ [z]ὠτίον τὸ
[5]of [6]the [4]high [2]priest [1]bondman, and cut off his [2]ear
δεξιόν. ἦν.δὲ ὄνομα τῷ δούλῳ Μάλχος. 11 εἶπεν οὖν
[1]right. And [4]was [1]name [2]the [3]bondman's Malchus. [3]Said [2]therefore
ὁ Ἰησοῦς τῷ Πέτρῳ, Βάλε τὴν.μάχαιράν.[a]σου εἰς τὴν θήκην.
[1]Jesus to Peter, Put thy sword into the sheath;
τὸ ποτήριον ὃ δέδωκέν μοι ὁ πατὴρ οὐ.μὴ.πίω αὐτό;
the cup which [3]has [4]given [5]me [1]the [2]Father should I not drink it?

12 Ἡ οὖν σπεῖρα καὶ ὁ χιλίαρχος καὶ οἱ ὑπηρέται τῶν
The [2]therefore [1]band and the chief captain and the officers of the
Ἰουδαίων συνέλαβον τὸν Ἰησοῦν, καὶ ἔδησαν αὐτόν, 13 καὶ
Jews took hold of Jesus, and bound him; and
[b]ἀπήγαγον αὐτὸν πρὸς Ἄνναν πρῶτον· ἦν.γὰρ πενθερὸς
they led away him to Annas first; for he was father-in-law
τοῦ Καϊάφα, ὃς ἦν ἀρχιερεὺς τοῦ.ἐνιαυτοῦ.ἐκείνου. 14 ἦν.δὲ
of Caiaphas, who was high priest that year. And it was
Καϊάφας ὁ συμβουλεύσας τοῖς Ἰουδαίοις, ὅτι συμφέρει
Caiaphas who gave counsel to the Jews, that it is profitable
ἕνα ἄνθρωπον [c]ἀπολέσθαι ὑπὲρ τοῦ λαοῦ. 15 Ἠκολούθει.δὲ
for one man to perish for the people. Now there followed
τῷ Ἰησοῦ Σίμων Πέτρος καὶ [d]ὁ ἄλλος μαθητής. ὁ.δὲ μαθητὴς
Jesus Simon Peter and the other disciple. And [2]disciple
ἐκεῖνος ἦν γνωστὸς τῷ ἀρχιερεῖ, καὶ συνεισῆλθεν τῷ Ἰησοῦ
[1]that was known to the high priest, and entered with Jesus
εἰς τὴν αὐλὴν τοῦ ἀρχιερέως· 16 ὁ.δὲ.Πέτρος εἱστήκει πρὸς
into the court of the high priest, but Peter stood at
τῇ θύρᾳ ἔξω. ἐξῆλθεν οὖν ὁ μαθητὴς ὁ ἄλλος [e]ὃς ἦν
the door without. Went out therefore the [2]disciple [1]other who was
γνωστὸς [f]τῷ ἀρχιερεῖ, καὶ εἶπεν τῇ θυρωρῷ καὶ εἰσήγα-
known to the high priest, and spoke to the door-keeper and brought
γεν τὸν Πέτρον. 17 λέγει οὖν [g]ἡ παιδίσκη ἡ θυρωρὸς τῷ
in Peter. [6]Says [5]therefore [1]the [2]maid [3]the [4]door-keeper
Πέτρῳ, Μὴ καὶ σὺ ἐκ τῶν μαθητῶν εἶ τοῦ ἀνθρώπου
to Peter, [2]not [4]also [3]thou [5]of [6]the [7]disciples [1]art of [8]man
τούτου; Λέγει ἐκεῖνος, Οὐκ.εἰμί. 18 Εἱστήκεισαν.δὲ οἱ δοῦλοι
[9]this? [4]Says [2]he, I am not. But [6]were [7]standing [1]the [2]bondmen
καὶ οἱ ὑπηρέται ἀνθρακιὰν πεποιηκότες, ὅτι ψῦχος ἦν,
[3]and [4]the [5]officers, a fire of coals having made, for cold it was,
καὶ ἐθερμαίνοντο· ἦν.δὲ [h]μετ' αὐτῶν ὁ Πέτρος ἑστὼς
and were warming themselves; and [2]was [3]with [4]them [1]Peter standing
καὶ θερμαινόμενος. 19 Ὁ.οὖν.ἀρχιερεὺς ἠρώτησεν τὸν Ἰη-
and warming himself. The high priest therefore questioned Je-
σοῦν περὶ τῶν.μαθητῶν.αὐτοῦ, καὶ περὶ τῆς διδαχῆς
sus concerning his disciples, and concerning [2]teaching
αὐτοῦ. 20 ἀπεκρίθη [i]αὐτῷ [k]ὁ Ἰησοῦς, Ἐγὼ παρρησίᾳ
[1]his. [2]Answered [3]him [1]Jesus, I openly
ἐλάλησα τῷ κόσμῳ· ἐγὼ πάντοτε ἐδίδαξα ἐν [m]τῇ συνα-
spoke to the world; I always taught in the syna-
γωγῇ καὶ ἐν τῷ ἱερῷ, ὅπου [n]πάντοτε οἱ Ἰουδαῖοι συνέρχον-
gogue and in the temple, where always the Jews come to-
ται, καὶ ἐν κρυπτῷ ἐλάλησα οὐδέν. 21 τί με [o]ἐπερωτᾷς;
gether, and in secret I spoke nothing. Why me dost thou question?
ἐπερώτησον τοὺς ἀκηκοότας τί ἐλάλησα αὐτοῖς· ἴδε οὗτοι
question those who have heard what I spoke to them; lo, they
οἴδασιν ἃ εἶπον ἐγώ. 22 Ταῦτα.δὲ αὐτοῦ.εἰπόντος εἷς [p]τῶν
know what [2]said [1]I. But [4]these [5]things [1]on [2]his [3]saying one of the

there with torches and lamps and weapons.
4 Then knowing all things that were coming
on Him, Jesus went forward and said to
them, Whom do you seek?
5 They answered Him, Jesus the Naz-a-re-
an. Jesus said to them, I am. And Judas, who
betrayed Him, was standing with them also.
6 Then when He said to them, I am, they
went backward and fell to the ground.
7 Then He asked them again, Whom do you
seek? And they said, Jesus the Naz-a-re-an.
8 Jesus answered, I told you that I am.
Then if it is Me you seek, let these go
9 (so that the Word might be fulfilled, "Of
those whom You have given Me, I did not
lose one").
10 Then Simon Peter drew the sword he
had and struck the servant of the high priest
and cut off his right ear. And the servant's
name was Mal-chus.
11 Then Jesus said to Peter, Put your sword
into the sheath. Should I not drink the cup
which the Father has given Me?

12 Then the band, and the chief captain,
and the officers of the Jews took hold of
Jesus and tied Him up.
13 And they led Him away to Annas first,
for he was father-in-law to Cai-a-phas, who
was high priest that year.
14 And it was Cai-a-phas who advised the
Jews that it is good for one man to die for
the people.
15 And Simon Peter was following Jesus,
and the other disciple *too*. And that disciple
was known to the high priest. And he entered with Jesus into the court of the high
priest
16 – but Peter stood at the door outside.
Then the other disciple who was known to
the high priest went out and spoke to the
doorkeeper and brought Peter inside.
17 Then the girl who kept the door said to
Peter, Are you not of the disciples of this
man too? He said, I am not.
18 And the servants and the officers were
standing and were warming themselves, for
they had made a fire of coals because it was
cold. And Peter was standing with them and
warmed himself.
19 Then the high priest asked Jesus about
His disciples and about His teaching.
20 Jesus answered him, I spoke openly to
the world. I always taught in the synagogue
and in the Temple, where the Jews always
come together. And I said nothing in secret.
21 Why do you ask Me? Ask those who
have heard what I said to them. See! They
know what I said.
22 But as He said these things, one of the
officers standing beside Jesus gave Him a

ὑπηρετῶν παρεστηκὼς" ἔδωκεν ῥάπισμα τῷ
officers standing by gave a blow with the palm of the hand
Ἰησοῦ, εἰπών, Οὕτως ἀποκρίνῃ τῷ ἀρχιερεῖ; 23 Ἀπεκρίθη
to Jesus, saying, Thus answerest thou the high priest? [2]Answered
αὐτῷ [q]ὁ" Ἰησοῦς, Εἰ κακῶς ἐλάλησα, μαρτύρησον περὶ τοῦ
[3]him [1]Jesus, If evil I spoke, bear witness concerning the
κακοῦ· εἰ.δὲ καλῶς, τί με δέρεις; 24 Ἀπέστειλεν [r] αὐτὸν
evil; but if well, why me strikest thou? [2]Sent [3]him
ὁ Ἄννας δεδεμένον πρὸς Καϊάφαν τὸν ἀρχιερέα.
[1]Annas bound to Caiaphas the high priest.
25 Ἦν.δὲ Σίμων Πέτρος ἑστὼς καὶ θερμαινόμενος·
Now [3]was [1]Simon [2]Peter standing and warming himself.
εἶπον οὖν αὐτῷ, Μὴ καὶ σὺ ἐκ τῶν.μαθητῶν.αὐτοῦ
They said therefore to him, [2]Not [4]also [3]thou [5]of [6]his [7]disciples
εἶ; Ἠρνήσατο.ἐκεῖνος, καὶ εἶπεν, Οὐκ.εἰμί. 26 Λέγει εἷς
[1]art? He denied, and said, I am not. Says one
ἐκ τῶν δούλων τοῦ ἀρχιερέως, συγγενὴς ὢν οὗ
of the bondmen of the high priest, kinsman being [of him] of whom
ἀπέκοψεν Πέτρος τὸ ὠτίον, Οὐκ.ἐγώ σε εἶδον ἐν τῷ κήπῳ
[2]cut [3]off [1]Peter the ear, [2]I [3]not [4]thee [1]saw in the garden
μετ' αὐτοῦ; 27 Πάλιν οὖν ἠρνήσατο [s]ὁ" Πέτρος, καὶ εὐθέως
with him? Again therefore [2]denied [1]Peter, and immediately
ἀλέκτωρ ἐφώνησεν.
a cock crew.
28 Ἄγουσιν οὖν τὸν Ἰησοῦν ἀπὸ τοῦ Καϊάφα εἰς τὸ
They lead therefore Jesus from Caiaphas into the
πραιτώριον· ἦν.δὲ [t]πρωΐα·" καὶ αὐτοὶ οὐκ.εἰσῆλθον εἰς τὸ
prætorium, and it was early. And they entered not into the
πραιτώριον, ἵνα μὴ.μιανθῶσιν, [v]ἀλλ' ἵνα" φάγωσιν τὸ
prætorium, that they might not be defiled, but that they might eat the
πάσχα. 29 ἐξῆλθεν οὖν ὁ [w]Πιλάτος" [x] πρὸς αὐτούς, καὶ
passover. [3]Went [4]forth [2]therefore [1]Pilate to them, and
[y]εἶπεν," Τίνα κατηγορίαν φέρετε [z]κατὰ" τοῦ.ἀνθρώπου.τούτου;
said, What accusation bring ye against this man?
30 Ἀπεκρίθησαν καὶ [a]εἶπον" αὐτῷ, Εἰ μὴ.ἦν οὗτος [b]κακο-
They answered and said to him, If [2]were [3]not [1]he an evil
ποιός," οὐκ ἄν σοι παρεδώκαμεν αὐτόν. 31 Εἶπεν
doer, [3]not [4]to [5]thee [1]we [2]would have delivered up him. [3]Said
[c]οὖν" αὐτοῖς [d]ὁ" [w]Πιλάτος," Λάβετε αὐτὸν ὑμεῖς, καὶ
[2]therefore [4]to [5]them [1]Pilate, Take him ye, and
κατὰ τὸν.νόμον.ὑμῶν κρίνατε [e]αὐτόν." Εἶπον [f]οὖν"
according to your law judge him. [4]Said [3]therefore
αὐτῷ οἱ Ἰουδαῖοι, Ἡμῖν οὐκ ἔξεστιν ἀποκτεῖναι οὐδένα·
[5]to [6]him [1]the [2]Jews, To us it is permitted to put [3]to [4]death [1]no [2]one;
32 ἵνα ὁ λόγος τοῦ Ἰησοῦ πληρωθῇ ὃν εἶπεν σημαίνων
that the word of Jesus might be fulfilled which he spoke signifying
ποίῳ θανάτῳ ἤμελλεν ἀποθνήσκειν. 33 Εἰσῆλθεν οὖν
by what death he was about to die. [2]Entered [3]therefore
[g]εἰς τὸ πραιτώριον πάλιν" ὁ [h]Πιλάτος," καὶ ἐφώνησεν τὸν
[4]into [5]the [6]prætorium [7]again [1]Pilate, and called
Ἰησοῦν, καὶ εἶπεν αὐτῷ, Σὺ εἶ ὁ βασιλεὺς τῶν Ἰουδαίων;
Jesus, and said to him, [2]Thou [1]art the king of the Jews?
34 Ἀπεκρίθη [i]αὐτῷ ὁ" Ἰησοῦς, [k]Ἀφ' ἑαυτοῦ" σὺ τοῦτο
[2]Answered [3]him [1]Jesus, From thyself [2]thou [3]this
λέγεις, ἢ ἄλλοι [l]σοι εἶπον" περὶ ἐμοῦ; 35 Ἀπεκρίθη
[1]sayest, [4]or [6]others [7]to [8]thee [5]did say [it] concerning me? [2]Answered
ὁ [h]Πιλάτος," Μήτι ἐγὼ Ἰουδαῖός εἰμι; τὸ ἔθνος τὸ σὸν καὶ
[1]Pilate, [2]I [4]a [5]Jew [3]am? [8]Nation [7]thy and
οἱ ἀρχιερεῖς παρέδωκάν σε ἐμοί· τί ἐποίησας; 36 Ἀπεκρίθη
the chief priests delivered up thee to me: what didst thou? [2]Answered
[m]ὁ" Ἰησοῦς, Ἡ βασιλεία ἡ ἐμὴ οὐκ.ἔστιν ἐκ τοῦ.κόσμου.τούτου·
[1]Jesus, [4]kingdom [3]my is not of this world;
εἰ ἐκ τοῦ.κόσμου.τούτου ἦν ἡ βασιλεία ἡ ἐμή, οἱ ὑπηρέται [n]ἂν
if of this world were [2]kingdom [1]my, [4]attendants
οἱ ἐμοὶ ἠγωνίζοντο" ἵνα μὴ.παραδοθῶ τοῖς Ἰουδαίοις·
[3]my would fight that I might not be delivered up to the Jews;
νῦν.δὲ ἡ βασιλεία ἡ ἐμὴ οὐκ.ἔστιν ἐντεῦθεν. 37 Εἶπεν οὖν
but now [2]kingdom [1]my is not from hence. [3]Said [2]therefore
αὐτῷ ὁ [h]Πιλάτος," Οὐκοῦν βασιλεὺς εἶ σύ; Ἀπεκρίθη [o]ὁ"
[4]to [5]him [1]Pilate, Then a king art thou? [2]Answered
Ἰησοῦς, Σὺ λέγεις, ὅτι βασιλεύς εἰμι [p]ἐγώ.! [q]ἐγὼ! εἰς τοῦτο
[1]Jesus, Thou sayest [it], for a king [2]am [1]I. I for this
γεγέννημαι. καὶ εἰς τοῦτο ἐλήλυθα εἰς τὸν κόσμον, ἵνα
have been born, and for this I have come into the world, that
μαρτυρήσω τῇ ἀληθείᾳ. πᾶς ὁ.ὢν ἐκ τῆς ἀληθείας
I may bear witness to the truth. Everyone that is of the truth
ἀκούει μου τῆς φωνῆς. 38 Λέγει αὐτῷ ὁ [h]Πιλάτος," Τί ἐστιν
hears my voice. [2]Says [3]to [4]him [1]Pilate, What is
ἀλήθεια; Καὶ τοῦτο εἰπών, πάλιν ἐξῆλθεν πρὸς τοὺς
truth? And this having said, again he went out to the
Ἰουδαίους, καὶ λέγει αὐτοῖς, Ἐγὼ οὐδεμίαν [r]αἰτίαν εὑρίσκω ἐν
Jews, and says to them, I not any fault find in

blow with the palm of the hand, saying, Do not answer the high priest that way.

23 Jesus answered him, If I spoke evil, bear witness of the evil; but if well, why do you strike Me?

24 Now Annas had sent Him bound to Cai-a-phas the high priest.

25 And Simon Peter was standing and warming himself. Then they said to him, Are you not of his disciples too? He denied and said, I am not.

26 One of the servants of the high priest (who was a relative of the one whose ear Peter cut off) said, Did I not see you in the garden with him?

27 Again, then, Peter denied it. And immediately a cock crowed.

28 Then they led Jesus from Cai-a-phas to the judgment hall, and it was early. And they did not go into the judgment hall so that they might not be made unclean, and so that they might eat the passover.

29 So Pilate came out to them and said, What charge do you bring against this man?

30 They answered and said to him, If he were not a criminal we would not have delivered him to you.

31 Pilate then said to them, You take him and judge him according to your law. Then the Jews said to him, It is not permitted to us to put anyone to death –

32 (so that the word of Jesus might be fulfilled, which He spoke to show what kind of death He was going to die).

33 Then Pilate went into the judgment hall again and called Jesus and said to Him, Are you the king of the Jews?

34 Jesus answered him, Do you say this of yourself or did others say it to you about Me?

35 Pilate answered, Am I a Jew? Your own nation and the chief priests delivered you up to me. What did you do?

36 Jesus answered, My kingdom is not of this world. If My kingdom were of this world, My servants would fight so that I might not be delivered up to the Jews. But now My kingdom is not from here.

37 Then Pilate said to Him, Then, are you a king? Jesus answered, You say it, because I am a king. For this I have been born, and for this I have come into the world, that I may witness to the truth. Everyone that is of the truth hears My voice.

38 Pilate said to Him, What is truth? And saying this, he went out to the Jews again and said to them, I do not find any fault at all in him.

αὐτῷ." 39 ἔστιν.δὲ συνήθεια ὑμῖν ἵνα ἕνα [s]ὑμῖν ἀπολύσω[h]
him. But it is a custom with you that one to you I should release

ἐν τῷ πάσχα· βούλεσθε οὖν [j]ὑμῖν ἀπολύσω" τὸν βασιλέα
at the passover; will ye therefore to you I should release the king

τῶν Ἰουδαίων; 40 Ἐκραύγασαν οὖν πάλιν [u]πάντες," λέ-
of the Jews? They [3]cried [4]out [2]therefore [5]again [1]all, say-

γοντες, Μὴ τοῦτον, ἀλλὰ τὸν Βαραββᾶν· ἦν.δὲ ὁ Βαραβ-
ing, Not this one, but Barabbas. Now [2]was [1]Barab-

βᾶς λῃστής. 19 Τότε οὖν ἔλαβεν ὁ [h]Πιλάτος" τὸν Ἰησοῦν
bas a robber. Then therefore [2]took [1]Pilate Jesus

καὶ ἐμαστίγωσεν. 2 καὶ οἱ στρατιῶται πλέξαντες στέφανον
and scourged [him]. And the soldiers having platted a crown

ἐξ ἀκανθῶν ἐπέθηκαν αὐτοῦ τῇ κεφαλῇ, καὶ ἱμάτιον πορ-
of thorns put [it] on his head, and a [2]cloak [1]pur-

φυροῦν περιέβαλον αὐτόν, 3 [v]καὶ ἔλεγον, Χαῖρε, ὁ βασιλεὺς
ple cast around him, and said, Hail, king

τῶν Ἰουδαίων· καὶ [w]ἐδίδουν" αὐτῷ ῥαπίσματα.
of the Jews! and they gave him blows with the palm of the hand.

4 [x]Ἐξῆλθεν [y]οὖν[h] πάλιν [z]ἔξω ὁ Πιλάτος," καὶ λέγει αὐτοῖς,
[4]Went [2]therefore [3]again [5]out [1]Pilate, and says to them,

Ἴδε, ἄγω ὑμῖν αὐτὸν ἔξω, ἵνα γνῶτε ὅτι [a]ἐν αὐτῷ
Behold, I bring [3]to [4]you [1]him [2]out, that ye may know that in him

οὐδεμίαν αἰτίαν εὑρίσκω." 5 Ἐξῆλθεν οὖν [b]ὁ Ἰησοῦς ἔξω,
not any fault I find. Went therefore Jesus out,

φορῶν τὸν ἀκάνθινον στέφανον καὶ τὸ πορφυροῦν ἱμάτιον.
wearing the thorny crown and the purple cloak;

καὶ λέγει αὐτοῖς, [c]Ἴδε" ὁ ἄνθρωπος. 6 Ὅτε οὖν [d]εἶδον"
and he says to them, Behold the man! When therefore saw

αὐτὸν οἱ ἀρχιερεῖς καὶ οἱ ὑπηρέται ἐκραύγασαν [e]λέγοντες,"
him the chief priests and the officers they cried out saying,

Σταύρωσον, σταύρωσον[f]. Λέγει αὐτοῖς ὁ [g]Πιλάτος," Λάβετε
Crucify, crucify [him]. [2]Says [3]to [4]them [1]Pilate, Take

αὐτὸν ὑμεῖς καὶ σταυρώσατε· ἐγὼ.γὰρ οὐχ.εὑρίσκω ἐν αὐτῷ
him ye and crucify [him], for I find not in him

αἰτίαν. 7 Ἀπεκρίθησαν [h]αὐτῷ" οἱ Ἰουδαῖοι, Ἡμεῖς νόμον
a fault. [3]Answered [4]him [1]the [2]Jews, We a law

ἔχομεν, καὶ κατὰ τὸν.νόμον.[i]ἡμῶν" ὀφείλει ἀποθανεῖν,
have, and according to our law he ought to die,

ὅτι [k]ἑαυτὸν υἱὸν θεοῦ" ἐποίησεν. 8 Ὅτε οὖν ἤκουσεν
because himself Son of God he made. When therefore [2]heard

ὁ [g]Πιλάτος" τοῦτον τὸν λόγον μᾶλλον ἐφοβήθη, 9 καὶ
[1]Pilate this word [the] more he was afraid, and

εἰσῆλθεν εἰς τὸ πραιτώριον πάλιν, καὶ λέγει τῷ Ἰησοῦ, Πόθεν
went into the prætorium again, and says to Jesus, Whence

εἶ σύ; Ὁ.δὲ.Ἰησοῦς ἀπόκρισιν οὐκ.ἔδωκεν αὐτῷ. 10 λέγει
art thou? But Jesus an answer did not give him. [2]Says

[l]οὖν" αὐτῷ ὁ [g]Πιλάτος," Ἐμοὶ οὐ.λαλεῖς; οὐκ.οἶδας
[3]therefore [4]to [5]him [1]Pilate, To me speakest thou not? Knowest not thou

ὅτι ἐξουσίαν ἔχω [m]σταυρῶσαί σε, καὶ ἐξουσίαν ἔχω ἀπο-
that authority I have to crucify thee, and authority I have to re-

λῦσαί σε"; 11 Ἀπεκρίθη" [o]ὁ" Ἰησοῦς, Οὐκ [p]εἶχες" ἐξουσίαν
lease thee? [2]Answered [1]Jesus, Thou hadst [3]authority

[q]οὐδεμίαν κατ' ἐμοῦ, εἰ μὴ.ἦν [r]σοι δεδομένον" ἄνωθεν·
[1]not [2]any against me if it were not to thee given from above.

διὰ.τοῦτο ὁ [s]παραδιδούς" μέ σοι μείζονα ἁμαρτίαν
On this account he who delivers up me to thee greater sin

ἔχει. 12 Ἐκ τούτου [t]ἐζήτει ὁ Πιλάτος" ἀπολῦσαι αὐτόν.
has. From this sought Pilate to release him;

οἱ.δὲ Ἰουδαῖοι [v]ἔκραζον," λέγοντες, Ἐὰν τοῦτον ἀπο-
but the Jews cried out, saying, If this [man] thou re-

λύσῃς οὐκ.εἶ φίλος τοῦ Καίσαρος. πᾶς ὁ βασιλέα
lease thou art not a friend of Cæsar. Everyone [3]the [4]king

[w]αὑτὸν" ποιῶν ἀντιλέγει τῷ Καίσαρι. 13 Ὁ οὖν.[x]Πιλάτος"
[2]himself [1]making speaks against Cæsar. Pilate therefore

ἀκούσας [y]τοῦτον τὸν λόγον," ἤγαγεν ἔξω τὸν Ἰησοῦν, καὶ
having heard this word, led out Jesus, and

ἐκάθισεν ἐπὶ [z]τοῦ" βήματος, εἰς τόπον λεγόμενον Λιθό-
sat down upon the judgment-seat, at a place called Pave-

στρωτον, Ἑβραϊστὶ.δὲ Γαββαθᾶ· 14 ἦν.δὲ παρασκευὴ
ment, but in Hebrew Gabbatha: (and it was [the] preparation

τοῦ πάσχα, ὥρα [a]δὲ ὡσεὶ" ἕκτη· καὶ λέγει τοῖς Ἰου-
of the passover, [[2]the] [3]hour [1]and about the sixth;) and he says to the Jews,

δαίοις, Ἴδε ὁ.βασιλεὺς.ὑμῶν. 15 [b]Οἱ.δὲ ἐκραύγασαν," [y]Ἆρον
Behold your king! But they cried out, Away,

ἆρον, σταύρωσον αὐτόν. Λέγει αὐτοῖς ὁ [x]Πιλάτος," Τὸν
away, crucify him. [2]Says [3]to [4]them [1]Pilate,

βασιλέα.ὑμῶν σταυρώσω; Ἀπεκρίθησαν οἱ ἀρχιερεῖς, Οὐκ
Your king shall I crucify? [4]Answered [1]the [2]chief [3]priests, [7]Not

ἔχομεν βασιλέα εἰ.μὴ Καίσαρα. 16 Τότε οὖν παρέδωκεν
[5]we [6]have a king except Cæsar. Then therefore he delivered up

αὐτὸν αὐτοῖς ἵνα σταυρωθῇ. Παρέλαβον [c]δὲ τὸν Ἰη-
him to them that he might be crucified. [2]They [3]took [1]and Je-

39 But it is a custom with you that I should release one to you at the Passover. So do you desire that I should release to you the king of the Jews?

40 Then they all cried out again, saying, Not this one, but Bar-ab-bas! Now Bar-ab-bas was a robber.

CHAPTER 19

1 So Pilate then took Jesus and whipped *Him*.

2 And after they had plaited a crown of thorns, the soldiers put it on His head. And they put a purple robe around Him

3 and said, Hail! King of the Jews! And *they* struck Him with the palm of the hand.

4 Pilate then went out again and said to them, See, I bring him out to you so that you may know that I do not find any fault in him.

5 Then Jesus came out wearing the crown of thorns and the purple robe. And he said to them, Behold! The man!

6 When the chief priests and the officers saw Him, then they cried out, Saying, Crucify! Crucify! Pilate said to them, You take and crucify him, for I do not find any fault in him.

7 The Jews answered him, We have a law, and according to our law he ought to die, because he made himself Son of God.

8 Then when Pilate heard this saying, he was more afraid.

9 And he went again into the judgment hall. And he said to Jesus, Where are you from? But Jesus did not answer him.

10 Then Pilate said to Him, Do you refuse to speak to me? Do you not know that I have authority to crucify you and I have authority to let you go?

11 Jesus answered, You would have no authority against Me if it were not given to you from above. Because of this, he who delivers Me up to you has the greater sin.

12 From then on Pilate wanted to let Him go, but the Jews cried out, saying, If you let this one go you are not Caesar's friend. Everyone who makes himself king speaks against Caesar.

13 Then, hearing these words, Pilate led Jesus out. And he sat down on the judgment seat at a place called Pavement (but in Hebrew, Gab-bath-a).

14 And it was the time to prepare the Passover, and about the sixth hour. And he said to the Jews, Behold! Your king!

15 But they cried out, Away! Away! Crucify him! Pilate said to them, Shall I crucify your king? The chief priests answered, We have no king except Caesar.

16 Then he turned Him over to them so that He might be crucified. And they took Jesus and led *Him* away.

σοῦν [d]καὶ ἀπήγαγον·‖ 17 καὶ βαστάζων [e]τὸν.σταυρὸν.αὐτοῦ‖
sus · and led [him] away. And bearing his cross
ἐξῆλθεν εἰς τὸν λεγόμενον κρανίου τόπον, [f]ὃς‖ λέγεται
he went out to the [2]called [3]of [4]a [5]skull [1]place, which is called
Ἑβραϊστὶ Γολγοθᾶ. 18 ὅπου αὐτὸν ἐσταύρωσαν, καὶ μετ᾽
in Hebrew Golgotha: where him they crucified, and with
αὐτοῦ ἄλλους δύο ἐντεῦθεν καὶ ἐντεῦθεν, μέσον.δὲ
him [2]others [1]two on this side and on that side [one], and in the middle
τὸν Ἰησοῦν. 19 [g]Ἔγραψεν.δὲ καὶ τίτλον ὁ [x]Πιλάτος‖ καὶ
Jesus. And [5]wrote [2]also [4]a [3]title [1]Pilate and
ἔθηκεν ἐπὶ τοῦ σταυροῦ· ἦν.δὲ γεγραμμένον. Ἰησοῦς ὁ
put on the cross. And it was written, Jesus the
Ναζωραῖος, ὁ βασιλεὺς τῶν Ἰουδαίων. 20 Τοῦτον οὖν
Nazaræan, the king of the Jews. This [2]therefore
τὸν τίτλον πολλοὶ ἀνέγνωσαν τῶν Ἰουδαίων, ὅτι ἐγγὺς ἦν
[3]title [4]many [5]read of the Jews, for near [3]was
[g]τῆς πόλεως ὁ τόπος,‖ ὅπου ἐσταυρώθη ὁ Ἰησοῦς· καὶ ἦν
[1]the [2]city the place, where was crucified Jesus; and it was
γεγραμμένον Ἑβραϊστί, [h]Ἑλληνιστί, Ῥωμαϊστί.‖ 21 ἔλεγον
written in Hebrew, in Greek, in Latin. [7]Said
οὖν τῷ [i]Πιλάτῳ‖ οἱ ἀρχιερεῖς τῶν Ἰουδαίων, Μὴ.γράφε,
[8]therefore [9]to [10]Pilate [1]the [2]chief [3]priests [4]of [5]the [6]Jews, Write not,
Ὁ βασιλεὺς τῶν Ἰουδαίων· ἀλλ᾽ ὅτι ἐκεῖνος εἶπεν, Βασιλεύς
The king of the Jews, but that he said, King
[k]εἰμι τῶν Ἰουδαίων.‖ 22 Ἀπεκρίθη ὁ [x]Πιλάτος,‖ Ὃ γέ-
I am of the Jews. [2]Answered [1]Pilate, What I have
γραφα γέγραφα. 23 Οἱ οὖν στρατιῶται, ὅτε ἐσταύρωσαν
written I have written. The [2]therefore [1]soldiers, when they crucified
τὸν Ἰησοῦν ἔλαβον τὰ.ἱμάτια.αὐτοῦ, καὶ ἐποίησαν [l]τέσσαρα‖
Jesus took his garments, and made four
μέρη, ἑκάστῳ στρατιώτῃ μέρος, καὶ τὸν χιτῶνα. ἦν.δὲ ὁ
parts, to each soldier a part, and the tunic; but [3]was [1]the
χιτὼν [m]ἄρραφος,‖ ἐκ τῶν ἄνωθεν ὑφαντὸς δι᾽.ὅλου. 24 [n]εἶ-
[2]tunic seamless, from the top woven throughout. They
πον‖ οὖν πρὸς ἀλλήλους, Μὴ.σχίσωμεν αὐτόν, ἀλλὰ
said therefore to one another, Let us not rend it, but
λάχωμεν περὶ αὐτοῦ τίνος ἔσται· ἵνα ἡ γραφὴ πλη-
let us cast lots for it whose it shall be; that the scripture might be
ρωθῇ [o]ἡ λέγουσα,‖ Διεμερίσαντο τὰ.ἱμάτιά.μου ἑαυτοῖς,
fulfilled which says, They divided my garments among them,
καὶ ἐπὶ τὸν.ἱματισμόν.μου ἔβαλον κλῆρον. Οἱ μὲν οὖν
and for my vesture they cast a lot. The [2]therefore
στρατιῶται ταῦτα ἐποίησαν.
[1]soldiers these things did.

25 Εἱστήκεισαν.δὲ παρὰ τῷ σταυρῷ τοῦ Ἰησοῦ ἡ.μήτηρ.αὐ-
And stood by the cross of Jesus his mother,
τοῦ, καὶ ἡ ἀδελφὴ τῆς.μητρὸς.αὐτοῦ, [p]Μαρία‖ ἡ τοῦ
and the sister of his mother, Mary the [wife]
Κλωπᾶ, καὶ [p]Μαρία‖ ἡ Μαγδαληνή. 26 Ἰησοῦς οὖν ἰδὼν
of Clopas, and Mary the Magdalene. Jesus therefore seeing
τὴν μητέρα, καὶ τὸν μαθητὴν παρεστῶτα ὃν ἠγάπα, λέγει
[his] mother, and the disciple standing by whom he loved, says
τῇ.μητρὶ.[q]αὐτοῦ,‖ Γύναι, [r]ἰδοὺ‖ ὁ.υἱός.σου. 27 Εἶτα λέγει τῷ
to his mother, Woman, behold thy son. Then he says to the
μαθητῇ, [r]Ἰδοὺ‖ ἡ.μήτηρ.σου. Καὶ ἀπ᾽ ἐκείνης τῆς ὥρας
disciple, Behold thy mother. And from that hour
ἔλαβεν [s]αὐτὴν ὁ μαθητὴς‖ εἰς τὰ.ἴδια. 28 Μετὰ τοῦτο
[3]took [4]her [1]the [2]disciple to his own [home]. After this,
εἰδὼς ὁ Ἰησοῦς ὅτι [t]πάντα ἤδη‖ τετέλεσται, ἵνα τελειωθῇ
[2]knowing [1]Jesus that all things now have been finished, that might be fulfilled
ἡ γραφὴ λέγει, Διψῶ. 29 Σκεῦος [v]οὖν‖ ἔκειτο ὄξους
the scripture he says, I thirst. A vessel therefore was set [2]of [3]vinegar
μεστόν· [w]οἱ.δὲ πλήσαντες σπόγγον ὄξους, καὶ ὑσσώπῳ‖
[1]full, and they having filled a sponge with vinegar, and [5]hyssop
περιθέντες προσήνεγκαν αὐτοῦ τῷ.στόματι. 30 ὅτε
[1]having [2]put [[3]it] [4]on they brought it to [his] mouth. When
οὖν ἔλαβεν τὸ ὄξος [x]ὁ Ἰησοῦς‖ εἶπεν, Τετέλεσται· καὶ
therefore [2]took [3]the [4]vinegar [1]Jesus he said, It has been finished; and
κλίνας τὴν κεφαλὴν παρέδωκεν τὸ πνεῦμα. 31 Οἱ
having bowed the head he yielded up [his] spirit. The
οὖν Ἰουδαῖοι, [y]ἵνα μὴ.μείνῃ ἐπὶ τοῦ σταυροῦ τὰ
[2]therefore [1]Jews, that might not remain on the cross the
σώματα ἐν τῷ σαββάτῳ, [y]ἐπεὶ παρασκευὴ ἦν,‖ ἦν.γὰρ
bodies on the sabbath, because [the] preparation it was, (for [4]was
μεγάλη ἡ ἡμέρα [z]ἐκείνου‖ τοῦ σαββάτου, ἠρώτησαν τὸν [a]Πι-
[5]great [3]day [1]that [2]sabbath,) requested Pi-
λάτον‖ ἵνα κατεαγῶσιν αὐτῶν τὰ σκέλη, καὶ ἀρθῶσιν.
late that [3]might [4]be [5]broken [1]their [2]legs, and taken away.
32 ἦλθον οὖν οἱ στρατιῶται, καὶ τοῦ μὲν πρώτου κατέαξαν
Came therefore the soldiers, and of the first broke
τὰ σκέλη καὶ τοῦ ἄλλου τοῦ [b]συσταυρωθέντος‖ αὐτῷ· 33 ἐπὶ.δὲ
the legs and of the other who was crucified with him; but to

17 And bearing His cross, He went out to the place called Place of a Skull (which is called in Hebrew, Gol-goth-a).

18 There they crucified Him, and two others with Him, on this side and on that side, and Jesus in the middle.

19 And Pilate also wrote a sign and put it on the cross. And it was inscribed, JESUS THE NAZARENE, THE KING OF THE JEWS.

20 So many of the Jews read this title, for the place where Jesus was crucified was near the city. And it was written in Hebrew, in Greek and in Latin.

21 Then the chief priests of the Jews said to Pilate, Do not write, The king of the Jews, but that he said, I am king of the Jews.

22 Pilate answered, What I have written, I have written.

23 Then when they crucified Jesus, the soldiers took His clothes and made four parts, one part to each soldier – also the coat, but the coat was seamless, woven from the top throughout.

24 So they said to one another, Let us not tear it, but let us throw dice for it *to see* whose it shall be – so that the Scripture might be fulfilled which says, "They divided My clothes among them and they threw lots for My robe." So the soldiers did these things.

25 And His mother stood by the cross of Jesus, also the sister of His mother, Mary the *wife* of Clopas and Mary Magdalene.

26 Then seeing His mother and the disciple whom He loved standing there, Jesus said to His mother, Woman, look! Your son!

27 Then He said to the disciple, Look! Your mother! And from that hour that disciple took her into his own *home.*

28 After this, knowing that all things had been completed, Jesus said, I am thirsty! (so that the Scripture might be fulfilled).

29 Now a vessel full of vinegar was put there. And filling a sponge with vinegar and putting it on hyssop, they brought it to His mouth.

30 Then when Jesus received the vinegar, He said, It has been finished! And bowing His head, He gave up His spirit.

31 Then the Jews asked Pilate that their legs might be broken and that *they be* taken away (so that the bodies might not stay on the cross on the sabbath, because it was the time to prepare the Passover – for that sabbath was an important day).

32 So the soldiers came and broke the legs of the first and of the other who was crucified with Him.

33 But coming to Jesus, when they saw He

τὸν Ἰησοῦν ἐλθόντες, ὡς εἶδον [c]αὐτὸν ἤδη" τεθνηκότα,
Jesus having come, when they saw he already was dead,
οὐ.κατέαξαν αὐτοῦ τὰ σκέλη· 34 ἀλλ' εἷς τῶν στρατιωτῶν
they did not break his legs, but one of the soldiers
λόγχῃ αὐτοῦ τὴν πλευρὰν ἔνυξεν, καὶ [d]εὐθὺς ἐξῆλθεν"
with a spear his side pierced, and immediately came out
αἷμα καὶ ὕδωρ. 35 καὶ ὁ ἑωρακὼς μεμαρτύρηκεν, καὶ
blood and water. And he who has seen has borne witness, and
ἀληθινὴ αὐτοῦ ἐστιν ἡ μαρτυρία, [e]κἀκεῖνος" οἶδεν ὅτι ἀληθῆ
true 2his 1is witness, and he knows that true
λέγει, ἵνα [f] ὑμεῖς [g]πιστεύσητε." 36 ἐγένετο.γὰρ ταῦτα ἵνα
he says, that ye may believe. For 3took 4place 1these 2things that
ἡ γραφὴ πληρωθῇ, Ὀστοῦν.οὐ συντριβήσεται αὐτοῦ.
the scripture might be fulfilled, Not a bone shall be broken of him.
37 καὶ πάλιν ἑτέρα γραφὴ λέγει, Ὄψονται εἰς ὃν
And again another scripture says, They shall look on him whom
ἐξεκέντησαν.
they pierced.

38 Μετὰ.δὲ ταῦτα ἠρώτησεν τὸν [h]Πιλάτον" [i]ὁ" Ἰωσὴφ
And after these things asked Pilate Joseph
[k]ὁ" ἀπὸ Ἀριμαθαίας, ὢν μαθητὴς τοῦ Ἰησοῦ, κεκρυμμένος.δὲ
(from Arimathæa, being a disciple of Jesus, but concealed
διὰ τὸν φόβον τῶν Ἰουδαίων, ἵνα ἄρῃ τὸ σῶμα
through fear of the Jews,) that he might take away the body
τοῦ Ἰησοῦ· καὶ ἐπέτρεψεν ὁ [l]Πιλάτος." [m]ἦλθεν" οὖν καὶ
of Jesus: and 2gave 3leave 1Pilate. He came therefore and
[n]ἦρεν" [o]τὸ σῶμα" [p]τοῦ Ἰησοῦ." 39 ἦλθεν.δὲ καὶ Νικόδημος,
took away the body of Jesus. And came also Nicodemus,
ὁ ἐλθὼν πρὸς [q]τὸν Ἰησοῦν" νυκτὸς τὸ.πρῶτον, φέρων μίγμα
who came to Jesus by night at first, bearing a mixture
σμύρνης καὶ ἀλόης [r]ὡσεὶ" λίτρας ἑκατόν. 40 ἔλαβον οὖν
of myrrh and aloes about 3pounds 1a 2hundred. They took therefore
τὸ σῶμα τοῦ Ἰησοῦ, καὶ ἔδησαν αὐτὸ [s] ὀθονίοις μετὰ τῶν
the body of Jesus, and bound it in linen cloths with the
ἀρωμάτων, καθὼς ἔθος ἐστὶν τοῖς Ἰουδαίοις ἐντα-
aromatics, as a custom is among the Jews to prepare for
φιάζειν. 41 ἦν.δὲ ἐν τῷ τόπῳ ὅπου ἐσταυρώθη κῆπος,
burial. Now there was in the place where he was crucified a garden,
καὶ ἐν τῷ κήπῳ μνημεῖον καινόν, ἐν ᾧ οὐδέπω.οὐδεὶς ἐτέθη.
and in the garden a 2tomb 1new, in which no one ever was laid.
42 ἐκεῖ οὖν διὰ τὴν παρασκευὴν τῶν Ἰουδαίων, ὅτι
There therefore on account of the preparation of the Jews, because
ἐγγὺς ἦν τὸ μνημεῖον, ἔθηκαν τὸν Ἰησοῦν.
near was the tomb, they laid Jesus.

20 Τῇ.δὲ μιᾷ τῶν σαββάτων [t]Μαρία" ἡ Μαγδαληνὴ
But on the first [day] of the week Mary the Magdalene
ἔρχεται πρωΐ σκοτίας ἔτι οὔσης εἰς τὸ μνημεῖον, καὶ βλέπει
comes early 4dark 3still 1it 2being to the tomb, and sees
τὸν λίθον ἠρμένον ἐκ τοῦ μνημείου. 2 τρέχει οὖν καὶ
the stone taken away from the tomb. She runs therefore and
ἔρχεται πρὸς Σίμωνα Πέτρον καὶ πρὸς τὸν ἄλλον μαθητὴν
comes to Simon Peter and to the other disciple
ὃν ἐφίλει ὁ Ἰησοῦς, καὶ λέγει αὐτοῖς, Ἦραν τὸν κύριον
whom 2loved 1Jesus, and says to them, They took away the Lord
ἐκ τοῦ μνημείου, καὶ οὐκ.οἴδαμεν ποῦ ἔθηκαν αὐτόν.
out of the tomb, and we know not where they laid him.
3 Ἐξῆλθεν οὖν ὁ Πέτρος καὶ ὁ ἄλλος μαθητής, καὶ ἤρχοντο
3Went 4forth 2therefore 1Peter and the other disciple, and came
εἰς τὸ μνημεῖον. 4 ἔτρεχον.δὲ οἱ δύο ὁμοῦ· [v]καὶ ὁ" ἄλλος
to the tomb. And 3ran 1the 2two together, and the other
μαθητὴς προέδραμεν τάχιον τοῦ Πέτρου, καὶ ἦλθεν πρῶτος
disciple ran forward faster than Peter, and came first
εἰς τὸ μνημεῖον, 5 καὶ παρακύψας βλέπει [w]κείμενα τὰ ὀθόνια,"
to the tomb, and stooping down he sees lying the linen cloths;
οὐ μέντοι εἰσῆλθεν. 6 ἔρχεται οὖν [x] Σίμων Πέτρος ἀκολου-
3not 4however 1he 2entered. Comes then Simon Peter follow-
θῶν αὐτῷ, καὶ εἰσῆλθεν εἰς τὸ μνημεῖον, καὶ θεωρεῖ τὰ
ing him, and entered into the tomb, and sees the
ὀθόνια κείμενα, 7 καὶ τὸ σουδάριον ὃ ἦν ἐπὶ τῆς κεφαλῆς
linen cloths lying, and the handkerchief which was upon 2head
αὐτοῦ, οὐ μετὰ τῶν ὀθονίων κείμενον, ἀλλὰ χωρὶς ἐν-
1his, not with the linen cloths lying, but 6by 7itself
τετυλιγμένον εἰς ἕνα τόπον. 8 τότε οὖν εἰσῆλθεν καὶ ὁ
1folded 2up 3in 4a 5place. Then therefore entered also the
ἄλλος μαθητὴς ὁ ἐλθὼν πρῶτος εἰς τὸ μνημεῖον, καὶ εἶδεν
other disciple who came first to the tomb, and saw
καὶ ἐπίστευσεν· 9 οὐδέπω.γὰρ ᾔδεισαν τὴν γραφήν, ὅτι
and believed; for not yet knew they the scripture, that
δεῖ αὐτὸν ἐκ νεκρῶν ἀναστῆναι. 10 ἀπῆλθον
it behoves him from among [the] dead to rise. Went away
οὖν πάλιν πρὸς [y]ἑαυτοὺς" οἱ μαθηταί. 11 [z]Μαρία".δὲ
therefore again to their [home] the disciples. But Mary

was already dead, they did not break His
legs.
34 But one of the soldiers pierced His side
with a spear. And immediately there came
out blood and water.
35 And he who has seen this has testified,
and his witness is true. And he knows that
he speaks true things, so that you may believe.
36 For these things were done so that the
Scripture might be fulfilled, "Not a bone of
Him shall be broken."
37 And again another Scripture says, "They
shall look upon Him whom they pierced."
38 And after these things Joseph of Ar-i-
ma-thea (a disciple of Jesus, but secretly
through fear of the Jews) asked Pilate for
permission. So he came and took away the
body of Jesus.
39 And Nic-o-de-mus also came (the one
who at first came to Jesus by night) bearing
a mixture of myrrh and aloes, about a hundred pounds.
40 Then they took Jesus' body and bound
it in linen clothes with the spices, as it was
the custom among the Jews in preparing to
bury.
41 Now there was a garden in the place
where He was crucified, and a new tomb in
the garden, in which no one was ever laid.
42 So, because it was the Jews' time to
make ready, because the tomb was near,
they laid Jesus there.

CHAPTER 20

1 And on the first of the sabbaths, Mary
Magdalene came early to the tomb, while it
was still dark. And *she* saw the stone already
taken away from the tomb.
2 Then she ran and came to Simon Peter
and to the other disciple whom Jesus loved
and said to them, They took away the Lord
out of the tomb. And we do not know
where they laid Him.
3 So Peter and the other disciple hurriedly
left and came to the tomb,
4 and the two were running together. And
the other disciple ran forward faster than
Peter and came first to the tomb.
5 And stooping down he saw the linen
clothes there. Yet he did not go in.
6 Then Simon Peter came following him
and went into the tomb. And *he* saw the
linen clothes lying there,
7 and the handkerchief which was on His
head was not lying with the linen clothes but
folded up in a place by itself.
8 So, then, the other disciple who came to
the tomb first also went in. And he saw and
believed
9 (for they did not yet know the Scripture,
that it was necessary for Him to rise again
from among the dead).
10 Then the disciples returned to their
home.

εἱστήκει πρὸς [a]τὸ μνημεῖον‖ [b]κλαίουσα ἔξω.‖ ὡς οὖν
stood at the tomb [2]weeping [1]outside. As therefore
ἔκλαιεν, παρέκυψεν εἰς τὸ μνημεῖον, 12 καὶ θεωρεῖ δύο ἀγ-
she wept, she stooped down into the tomb, and beholds two an-
γέλους ἐν λευκοῖς καθεζομένους, ἕνα πρὸς τῇ κεφαλῇ καὶ ἕνα
gels in white sitting, one at the head and one
πρὸς τοῖς ποσίν, ὅπου ἔκειτο τὸ σῶμα τοῦ Ἰησοῦ. 13 [c]καὶ‖
at the feet, where was laid the body of Jesus. And
λέγουσιν αὐτῇ ἐκεῖνοι, Γύναι, τί κλαίεις; Λέγει αὐτοῖς,
[2]say [3]to [4]her [1]they, Woman, why weepest thou? She says to them,
Ὅτι ἦραν τὸν.κύριόν.μου, καὶ οὐκ.οἶδα ποῦ ἔθηκαν
Because they took away my Lord, and I know not where they laid
αὐτόν. 14 [d]Καὶ‖ ταῦτα εἰποῦσα ἐστράφη εἰς.τὰ.ὀπίσω, καὶ
him. And these things having said she turned backward, and
θεωρεῖ τὸν Ἰησοῦν ἑστῶτα· καὶ οὐκ.ᾔδει ὅτι [e]ὁ‖ Ἰησοῦς ἐστιν.
beholds Jesus standing, and knew not that Jesus it is.
15 λέγει αὐτῇ *ὁ‖ Ἰησοῦς, Γύναι, τί κλαίεις; τίνα ζητεῖς;
[2]Says [3]to [4]her [1]Jesus, Woman, why weepest thou? Whom seekest thou?
Ἐκείνη δοκοῦσα ὅτι ὁ κηπουρός ἐστιν, λέγει αὐτῷ, Κύριε, εἰ
She thinking that the gardener it is, says to him, Sir, if
σὺ ἐβάστασας αὐτόν, εἰπέ μοι ποῦ [f]αὐτὸν ἔθηκας·‖ κἀγὼ
thou didst carry off him, tell me where him thou didst lay, and I
αὐτὸν ἀρῶ. 16 Λέγει αὐτῇ [g]ὁ‖ Ἰησοῦς, [h]Μαρία.‖ Στρα-
him will take away. [2]Says [3]to [4]her [1]Jesus, Mary. Turn-
φεῖσα ἐκείνη λέγει αὐτῷ[i], Ῥαββουνί· ὃ.λέγεται, διδάσκαλε.
ing round she says to him, Rabboni, that is to say, Teacher.
17 λέγει αὐτῇ [k]ὁ‖ Ἰησοῦς, Μή μου ἅπτου, οὔπω.γὰρ ἀναβέ-
[2]Says [3]to [4]her [1]Jesus, [7]Not [6]me [5]touch, for not yet have I
βηκα πρὸς τὸν.πατέρα.[l]μου·‖ πορεύου.δὲ πρὸς τοὺς ἀδελφούς
ascended to my Father; but go to [2]brethren
μου, καὶ εἰπὲ αὐτοῖς, Ἀναβαίνω πρὸς τὸν.πατέρα.μου καὶ
[1]my, and say to them, I ascend to my Father and
πατέρα.ὑμῶν, καὶ θεόν.μου καὶ θεὸν.ὑμῶν. 18 *Ἔρχεται
your Father, and my God and your God. [4]Comes
[m]Μαρία‖ ἡ Μαγδαληνὴ [n]ἀπαγγέλλουσα‖ τοῖς μαθηταῖς ὅτι
[1]Mary [2]the [3]Magdalene bringing word to the disciples
[o]ἑώρακεν‖ τὸν κύριον, καὶ ταῦτα εἶπεν αὐτῇ. 19 Οὔσης.οὖν
she has seen the Lord, and these things he said to her. It being therefore
ὀψίας τῇ.ἡμέρᾳ.ἐκείνῃ, τῇ μιᾷ [p]τῶν‖.σαββάτων, καὶ τῶν
evening on that day, the first [day] of the week, and the
θυρῶν κεκλεισμένων ὅπου ἦσαν οἱ μαθηταὶ [q]συνηγμένοι,‖ διὰ
doors having been shut where [3]were [1]the [2]disciples assembled, through
τὸν φόβον τῶν Ἰουδαίων, ἦλθεν ὁ Ἰησοῦς καὶ ἔστη εἰς τὸ
fear of the Jews, [2]came [1]Jesus and stood in the
μέσον, καὶ λέγει αὐτοῖς, Εἰρήνη ὑμῖν. 20 Καὶ τοῦτο εἰπὼν
midst, and says to them, Peace to you. And this having said
ἔδειξεν [r]αὐτοῖς τὰς χεῖρας καὶ τὴν πλευρὰν αὐτοῦ.‖ ἐχάρη-
he shewed to them the hands and the side of himself. [3]Rejoiced
σαν οὖν οἱ μαθηταὶ ἰδόντες τὸν κύριον. 21 εἶπεν οὖν
[4]therefore [1]the [2]disciples having seen the Lord. [3]Said [2]therefore
αὐτοῖς [s]ὁ Ἰησοῦς‖ πάλιν, Εἰρήνη ὑμῖν· καθὼς ἀπέσταλκέν
[4]to [5]them [1]Jesus again, Peace to you: as [3]has [4]sent [5]forth
με ὁ πατήρ, κἀγὼ πέμπω ὑμᾶς. 22 Καὶ τοῦτο εἰπὼν
[6]me [1]the [2]Father, I also send you. And this having said
ἐνεφύσησεν, καὶ λέγει αὐτοῖς, Λάβετε πνεῦμα ἅγιον.
he breathed into [them], and says to them, Receive [the] [2]Spirit [1]Holy:
23 [t]ἄν‖.τινων ἀφῆτε τὰς ἁμαρτίας, [v]ἀφίενται‖ αὐτοῖς·
of whomsoever ye may remit the sins, they are remitted to them;
[t]ἄν‖.τινων κρατῆτε, κεκράτηνται. 24 Θωμᾶς.δέ, εἷς ἐκ
of whomsoever ye may retain, they have been retained. But Thomas, one of
τῶν δώδεκα ὁ λεγόμενος Δίδυμος, οὐκ.ἦν μετ' αὐτῶν ὅτε
the twelve called Didymus, was not with them when
ἦλθεν [w]ὁ‖ Ἰησοῦς. 25 ἔλεγον οὖν αὐτῷ οἱ ἄλλοι μαθηταί,
[2]came [1]Jesus. [4]Said [5]therefore [6]to [7]him [1]the [2]other [3]disciples,
Ἑωράκαμεν τὸν κύριον. Ὁ.δὲ εἶπεν αὐτοῖς, Ἐὰν.μὴ ἴδω ἐν
We have seen the Lord. But he said to them, Unless I see in
ταῖς.χερσὶν.αὐτοῦ τὸν τύπον τῶν ἥλων, καὶ βάλω [x]τὸν δάκτυ-
his hands the mark of the nails, and put [2]finger
λόν μου‖ εἰς τὸν [y]τύπον‖ τῶν ἥλων, καὶ βάλω [z]τὴν.χεῖρά.μου‖
[1]my into the mark of the nails, and put my hand
εἰς τὴν.πλευρὰν.αὐτοῦ, οὐ.μὴ πιστεύσω. 26 Καὶ μεθ' ἡμέρας
into his side, not at all will I believe. And after [2]days
ὀκτὼ πάλιν ἦσαν ἔσω οἱ.μαθηταὶ.αὐτοῦ, καὶ Θωμᾶς μετ'
[1]eight again were [3]within [1]his [2]disciples, and Thomas with
αὐτῶν. ἔρχεται ὁ Ἰησοῦς, τῶν θυρῶν κεκλεισμένων, καὶ ἔστη
them. Comes Jesus, the doors having been shut, and stood
εἰς τὸ μέσον καὶ εἶπεν, Εἰρήνη ὑμῖν. 27 Εἶτα λέγει τῷ Θωμᾷ,
in the midst and said, Peace to you. Then he says to Thomas,
Φέρε τὸν.δάκτυλόν.σου ὧδε, καὶ ἴδε τὰς.χεῖράς.μου· καὶ
Bring thy finger here, and see my hands; and
φέρε τὴν.χεῖρά.σου, καὶ βάλε εἰς τὴν.πλευράν.μου· καὶ
bring thy hand, and put [it] into my side; and

[11]But Mary was standing at the tomb, weeping outside. As she was crying, then, she stooped down into the tomb.

[12]And she saw two angels in white, one sitting at the head and one at the feet where the body of Jesus was laid.

[13]And they said to her, Woman, why are you crying? She said to them, Because they took away my Lord and I do not know where they laid Him.

[14]And as she said these things, she turned around and saw Jesus standing there (but she did not know that it was Jesus).

[15]Jesus said to her, Woman, why are you crying? For whom are you searching? Thinking it was the gardener, she said to Him, Sir, if you carried Him away, tell me where you laid Him and I will take Him away.

[16]Jesus said to her, Mary! Turning around, she said to Him, Rab-bo-ni! (that is to say, Master!)

[17]Jesus said to her, Do not touch Me, for I have not yet gone up to My Father. But go to My brothers and say to them, I am going up to My Father and your Father and My God and your God.

[18]Mary Magdalene came bringing word to the disciples that she had seen the Lord, and that He had said these things to her.

[19]Then, it being evening on that day, the first of the sabbaths, and the doors having been shut where the disciples were gathered together (through fear of the Jews), Jesus came and stood in the middle of them. And He said to them, Peace be on you!

[20]And having said this, He showed them His hands and His side. Then the disciples rejoiced when they saw the Lord.

[21]Jesus then said to them again, Peace be on you! As the Father has sent Me, I also send you.

[22]And having said this He breathed on *them* and said to them, Receive the Holy Spirit!

[23]If you forgive the sins of any, they are forgiven to them. If you retain any, they have been retained.

[24]But Thomas, called Did-y-mus, one of the twelve, was not with them when Jesus came.

[25]Then the other disciples said to him, We have seen the Lord. But he said to them, Unless I see the mark of the nails in His hands, and put my finger into the mark of the nails, and put my hand into His side, I will not believe.

[26]And after eight days again His disciples were inside, and Thomas with them. The door was shut, *but* Jesus came in and stood among them, saying, Peace to you!

[27]Then He said to Thomas, Bring your finger here and see My hands. And bring your

μη.γίνου ἄπιστος, ἀλλὰ πιστός. 28 aΚαὶ" ἀπεκρίθη bὁ"
be not unbelieving, but believing. And ²answered
Θωμᾶς καὶ εἶπεν αὐτῷ, Ὁ.κύριός.μου καὶ ὁ.θεός.μου. 29 Λέγει
¹Thomas and said to him, My Lord and my God. ²Says
αὐτῷ cὁ" Ἰησοῦς, "Ὅτι ἑώρακάς 'με, dΘωμᾶ," πεπίστευκας
³to ⁴him ¹Jesus, Because thou hast seen me, Thomas, thou hast believed:
μακάριοι οἱ μὴ.ἰδόντες καὶ πιστεύσαντες.
blessed they who have not seen and have believed.

30 Πολλὰ μὲν οὖν καὶ ἄλλα σημεῖα ἐποίησεν ὁ Ἰη-
Many ³therefore ⁴also ¹other ²signs did Je-
σοῦς ἐνώπιον τῶν.μαθητῶν eαὐτοῦ," ἃ οὐκ.ἔστιν γεγραμ-
sus in presence of his disciples, which are not written
μένα ἐν τῷ.βιβλίῳ.τούτῳ. 31 ταῦτα.δὲ γέγραπται ἵνα
in this book; but these have been written that
fπιστεύσητε" ὅτι gὁ" Ἰησοῦς ἐστιν ὁ χριστὸς ὁ υἱὸς τοῦ
ye may believe that Jesus is the Christ the Son
θεοῦ, καὶ ἵνα πιστεύοντες ζωὴν h ἔχητε ἐν τῷ ὀνόματι
of God, and that believing, life ye may have in ²name
αὐτοῦ.
¹his.

21 Μετὰ ταῦτα ἐφανέρωσεν ἑαυτὸν πάλιν iὁ Ἰησοῦς"
After these things ⁵manifested ⁴himself ²again ¹Jesus
τοῖς μαθηταῖς ἐπὶ τῆς θαλάσσης τῆς Τιβεριάδος· ἐφανέρωσεν.δὲ
to the disciples at the sea of Tiberias. And he manifested
οὕτως· 2 ἦσαν ὁμοῦ Σίμων Πέτρος, καὶ Θωμᾶς ὁ
[himself] thus: There were together Simon Peter, and Thomas
λεγόμενος Δίδυμος, καὶ Ναθαναὴλ ὁ ἀπὸ Κανᾶ τῆς Γαλι-
called Didymus, and Nathanael from Cana of Gali-
λαίας, καὶ οἱ τοῦ Ζεβεδαίου, καὶ ἄλλοι ἐκ τῶν μαθητῶν
lee, and the [sons] of Zebedee, and ²others ³of ⁵disciples
αὐτοῦ δύο. 3 λέγει αὐτοῖς Σίμων Πέτρος, Ὑπάγω ἁλιεύειν.
⁴his ¹two. ⁸Says ⁹to ¹⁰them ⁶Simon ⁷Peter, I go to fish.
Λέγουσιν αὐτῷ, Ἐρχόμεθα καὶ ἡμεῖς σὺν σοί. kἘξῆλθον
They say to him, ³Come ²also ¹we with thee. They went forth
καὶ lἀνέβησαν" εἰς τὸ πλοῖον mεὐθὺς," καὶ ἐν ἐκείνῃ τῇ
and went up into the ship immediately, and during that
νυκτὶ ἐπίασαν οὐδέν. 4 πρωΐας.δὲ ἤδη nγενομένης" ἔστη oὁ"
night they took nothing. And morning already being come ²stood
Ἰησοῦς pεἰς" τὸν αἰγιαλόν· οὐ μέντοι ᾔδεισαν οἱ μαθηταὶ ὅτι
¹Jesus on the shore; ⁵not ³however ⁴knew ¹the ²disciples that
Ἰησοῦς ἐστιν. 5 λέγει οὖν αὐτοῖς qὁ Ἰησοῦς," Παιδία,
Jesus it is. ³Says ²therefore ⁴to ⁵them ¹Jesus, Little children,
μή τι προσφάγιον ἔχετε; Ἀπεκρίθησαν αὐτῷ, Οὔ. 6 rὉ.δὲ
any food have ye? They answered him, No. And he
εἶπεν" αὐτοῖς, Βάλετε εἰς τὰ δεξιὰ μέρη τοῦ πλοίου τὸ δίκτυον,
said to them, Cast to the right side of the ship the net,
καὶ εὑρήσετε. Ἔβαλον οὖν, καὶ sοὐκ ἔτι" αὐτὸ ἑλκῦσαι
and ye shall find. They cast therefore, and no longer it to draw
tἴσχυσαν" ἀπὸ τοῦ πλήθους τῶν ἰχθύων. 7 λέγει οὖν
were they able from the multitude of the fishes. Says therefore
ὁ.μαθητὴς.ἐκεῖνος ὃν ἠγάπα ὁ Ἰησοῦς τῷ Πέτρῳ, Ὁ κύριός
that disciple whom ²loved ¹Jesus to Peter, The Lord
ἐστιν. Σίμων οὖν Πέτρος, ἀκούσας ὅτι ὁ κύριός ἐστιν,
it is. Simon ²therefore ¹Peter, having heard that the Lord it is,
τὸν ἐπενδύτην διεζώσατο· ἦν.γὰρ γυμνός· καὶ ἔβαλεν
[his] upper garment he girded on, for he was naked, and cast
ἑαυτὸν εἰς τὴν θάλασσαν. 8 οἱ.δὲ ἄλλοι μαθηταὶ τῷ
himself into the sea. And the other disciples in the
πλοιαρίῳ ἦλθον· οὐ.γὰρ ἦσαν μακρὰν ἀπὸ τῆς γῆς, vἀλλ'"
small ship came, for not were they far from the land, but
ὡς.ἀπὸ πηχῶν διακοσίων, σύροντες τὸ δίκτυον τῶν
somewhere about ³cubits ¹two ²hundred, dragging the net
ἰχθύων. 9 Ὡς οὖν ἀπέβησαν εἰς τὴν γῆν βλέπουσιν
of fishes. When therefore they went up on the land they see
ἀνθρακιὰν κειμένην καὶ ὀψάριον ἐπικείμενον, καὶ ἄρτον.
a fire of coals lying and fish lying on [it], and bread.
10 λέγει αὐτοῖς wὁ" Ἰησοῦς, Ἐνέγκατε ἀπὸ τῶν ὀψαρίων ὧν
²Says ³to ⁴them ¹Jesus, Bring of the fishes which
ἐπιάσατε νῦν. 11 Ἀνέβη x Σίμων Πέτρος, καὶ εἵλκυσεν τὸ
ye took just now. Went up Simon Peter, and drew the
δίκτυον yἐπὶ τῆς γῆς," μεστὸν zἰχθύων μεγάλων" ἑκατὸν
net to the land, full of ²fishes ¹large a hundred [and]
aπεντηκοντατριῶν·" καὶ τοσούτων ὄντων οὐκ.ἐσχίσθη τὸ
fifty three; and [though] so many there were was not rent the
δίκτυον. 12 Λέγει αὐτοῖς bὁ" Ἰησοῦς, Δεῦτε ἀριστήσατε.
net. ²Says ³to ⁴them ¹Jesus, Come ye, dine.
οὐδεὶς.cδὲ" ἐτόλμα τῶν μαθητῶν ἐξετάσαι αὐτόν, Σὺ τίς
But none ⁴ventured ¹of ²the ³disciples to ask him, ³Thou ¹who
εἶ; εἰδότες ὅτι ὁ κύριός ἐστιν· 13 ἔρχεται dοὖν ὁ" Ἰησοῦς
²art? knowing that the Lord it is. ³Comes ²therefore ¹Jesus
καὶ λαμβάνει τὸν ἄρτον καὶ δίδωσιν αὐτοῖς, καὶ τὸ ὀψάριον
and takes the bread and gives to them, and the fish

hand and put it into My side, and be no longer unbelieving but believing.

28 And Thomas answered and said to Him, My Lord and my God!

29 Jesus said to him, Have you believed because you have seen Me, Thomas? Blessed are the ones who have not seen and have believed.

30 Then Jesus did many other miracles also in the presence of His disciples, which are not written in this book.

31 But these have been written that you may believe that Jesus is the Christ, the Son of God, and that believing you might have life in His name.

CHAPTER 21

1 After these things Jesus showed Himself again to the disciples at the sea of Tiberias. Now He revealed Himself in this way:

2 There were altogether Simon Peter and Thomas called Did-y-mus and Na-than-a-el from Cana of Galilee and the sons of Zeb-e-dee and two others of His disciples.

3 Simon Peter said to them, I am going fishing. They said to him, We will come with you, too. They went out and entered the boat at once. And they caught nothing all that night.

4 But when morning had come, Jesus stood on the shore. However, the disciples did not know that it was Jesus.

5 Jesus then said to them, Little children, do you have any food? They answered Him, No.

6 And He said to them, Throw the net to the right side of the boat and you will find – so they cast, and they were no longer able to draw it because of the abundance of fish.

7 Then that disciple whom Jesus loved said to Peter, It is the Lord. Then, hearing that it was the Lord, Simon Peter put on his outer coat, for he was naked, and threw himself into the sea.

8 And the other disciples came dragging the net of fish in the small ship, for they were not far from the land, only somewhere around three hundred feet off.

9 Then when they went up on the land, they saw a fire of coals lying, and fish lying on it, and bread.

10 Jesus then said to them, Bring some of the fish which you just now caught.

11 Simon Peter went up and drew the net full of large fish to land, a hundred and fifty three – although there were so many, the net was not torn.

12 Jesus said to them, Come and eat. But none of the disciples dared to ask Him, Who are You? For they knew that it was the Lord.

13 Then Jesus came and took the Bread and gave some to them, and some of the fish too.

ὁμοίως. 14 τοῦτο ἤδη τρίτον ἐφανερώθη ᵉὁ‖ Ἰησοῦς
in like manner. This [is] now the third time ⁴was ⁵manifested ¹Jesus
τοῖς.μαθηταῖς.ᶠαὐτοῦ‖ ἐγερθεὶς ἐκ νεκρῶν.
to his disciples having been raised from among [the] dead.
15 "Οτε οὖν ἠρίστησαν, λέγει τῷ Σίμωνι Πέτρῳ ὁ Ἰησοῦς,
When therefore they had dined, ²says ³to ⁴Simon ⁵Peter ¹Jesus,
Σίμων ᵍἸωνᾶ,‖ ἀγαπᾷς με ʰπλεῖον‖ τούτων; Λέγει αὐτῷ,
Simon [son] of Jonas, lovest thou me more than these? He says to him,
Ναί, κύριε· σὺ οἶδας ὅτι φιλῶ σε. Λέγει αὐτῷ,
Yea, Lord; thou knowest that I have affection for thee. He says to him,
Βόσκε τὰ.ἀρνία.μου. 16 Λέγει αὐτῷ πάλιν δεύτερον, Σίμων
Feed my lambs. He says to him again a second time, Simon
ᵍἸωνᾶ,‖ ἀγαπᾷς με; Λέγει αὐτῷ, Ναὶ κύριε· σὺ οἶδας
[son] of Jonas, lovest thou me? He says to him, Yea, Lord; thou knowest
ὅτι φιλῶ σε. Λέγει αὐτῷ, Ποίμαινε τὰ ⁱπρόβατά‖
that I have affection for thee. He says to him, Shepherd ²sheep
μου. 17 Λέγει αὐτῷ τὸ τρίτον, Σίμων ᵏἸωνᾶ,‖ φι-
¹my. He says to him the third time, Simon [son] of Jonas, hast thou
λεῖς με; Ἐλυπήθη ὁ Πέτρος ὅτι εἶπεν αὐτῷ τὸ
affection for me? ²Was ³grieved ¹Peter because he said to him the
τρίτον, Φιλεῖς με; ˡκαὶ‖ ᵐεἶπεν‖ αὐτῷ, Κύριε, ⁿσὺ
third time, Hast thou affection for me? and said to him, Lord, thou
πάντα‖ οἶδας· σὺ γινώσκεις ὅτι φιλῶ σε. Λέγει
all things knowest; thou knowest that I have affection for thee. ²Says
αὐτῷ ᵒὁ Ἰησοῦς,‖ Βόσκε τὰ.ᵖπρόβατά‖.μου. 18 ἀμὴν ἀμὴν
³to ⁴him ¹Jesus, Feed my sheep. Verily verily
λέγω σοι, ὅτε ἦς νεώτερος ἐζώννυες σεαυτόν, καὶ
I say to thee, When thou wast younger thou girdedst thyself, and
περιεπάτεις ὅπου ἤθελες· ὅταν.δὲ γηράσῃς ἐκ-
walkedst where thou didst desire; but when thou shalt be old thou shalt
τενεῖς τὰς.χεῖράς.σου, καὶ ἄλλος ᑫσε ζώσει,‖ καὶ οἴσει ʳ
stretch forth thy hands, and another thee shall gird, and bring [thee]
ὅπου οὐ.θέλεις. 19 Τοῦτο.δὲ εἶπεν σημαίνων ποίῳ
where thou dost not desire. But this he said signifying by what
θανάτῳ δοξάσει τὸν θεόν. καὶ τοῦτο εἰπὼν λέγει αὐτῷ,
death he should glorify God. And this having said he says to him,
Ἀκολούθει μοι. 20 Ἐπιστραφεὶς.ˢδὲ‖ ὁ Πέτρος βλέπει τὸν
Follow me. But having turned Peter sees the
μαθητὴν ὃν ἠγάπα ὁ Ἰησοῦς ἀκολουθοῦντα, ὃς καὶ ἀνέπεσεν
disciple whom ²loved ¹Jesus following, who also reclined
ἐν τῷ δείπνῳ ἐπὶ τὸ.στῆθος.αὐτοῦ καὶ εἶπεν, Κύριε, τίς ἐστιν
at the supper on his breast and said, Lord, who is it
ὁ παραδιδούς σε; 21 Τοῦτον ᵗ ἰδὼν ὁ Πέτρος λέγει τῷ Ἰη-
who is delivering up thee? ³Him ²seeing ¹Peter says to Je-
σοῦ, Κύριε, οὗτος.δὲ τί; 22 Λέγει αὐτῷ ὁ Ἰησοῦς, Ἐὰν
sus, Lord, but of this one what? ²Says ³to ⁴him ¹Jesus, If
αὐτὸν θέλω μένειν ἕως ἔρχομαι, τί πρός σε; σὺ
³him ¹I ²desire to abide till I come, what [is it] to thee? ²Thou
ᵛἀκολούθει μοι.‖ 23 Ἐξῆλθεν οὖν ʷὁ.λόγος.οὗτος‖ εἰς
¹follow me. Went out therefore this word among
τοὺς ἀδελφούς, Ὅτι ὁ.μαθητὴς.ἐκεῖνος οὐκ.ἀποθνήσκει· ˣκαὶ
the brethren, That that disciple does not die. However
οὐκ εἶπεν‖ αὐτῷ ὁ Ἰησοῦς, ὅτι οὐκ ἀποθνήσκει· ἀλλ', Ἐὰν
³not ²said ⁴to ⁵him ¹Jesus, That he does not die; but, If
αὐτὸν θέλω μένειν ἕως ἔρχομαι, ʸτί πρός σε;‖
³him ¹I ²desire to abide till I come, what [is it] to thee?

24 Οὗτός ἐστιν ὁ μαθητὴς ὁ μαρτυρῶν περὶ τούτων,
This is the disciple who bears witness concerning these things,
καὶ ᶻ γράψας ταῦτα· καὶ οἴδαμεν ὅτι ἀληθής ᵃἐστιν ἡ
and [who] wrote these things: and we know that true is
μαρτυρία.αὐτοῦ.‖ 25 ᵇἔστιν.δὲ καὶ ἄλλα πολλὰ ᶜὅσα‖
his witness. And there are also ²other ³things ¹many whatsoever
ἐποίησεν ὁ Ἰησοῦς, ἅτινα ἐὰν γράφηται καθ'.ἕν, ᵈοὐδὲ‖
²did ¹Jesus, which if they should be written one by one, ³not ⁴even
αὐτὸν οἶμαι τὸν κόσμον ᵉχωρῆσαι‖ τὰ γραφόμενα βιβλία.
⁷itself ¹I ²suppose ⁵the ⁶world would contain the ²written ¹books.
ᶠἈμήν.‖ ‖ ᵍ
Amen.

¹⁴This is now the third time Jesus was revealed to His disciples after being raised from among the dead.

¹⁵Then when they had eaten, Jesus said to Simon Peter, Simon, son of Jonas, do you love Me more than these? Peter said to Him, Yes, Lord, You know that I love You. He said to him, Feed My lambs!

¹⁶Again He said to him a second time, Simon, son of Jonas, do you love Me? He said to Him, Yes, Lord, You know that I love You. Jesus said to him, Nurture My sheep!

¹⁷He said to him the third time, Simon, son of Jonas, do you have love for Me? Peter was grieved because He said to Him the third time, Do you love Me? And he said to Him, Lord, You know all things, You know that I love You! Jesus said to him, Feed My sheep.

¹⁸Indeed, I tell you truly, when you were younger you dressed yourself and went where you chose. But when you are old, you shall stretch out your hands and another shall dress you and bring you where you do not choose.

¹⁹And He said this to show by what death he should glorify God. And having said this, He said to him, Follow Me!

²⁰But turning around, Peter saw the disciple whom Jesus loved following (who had rested on His breast at the Supper, saying, Lord, who is it who is betraying You?).

²¹Peter saw him and said to Jesus, Lord, but what about this one?

²²Jesus said to him, If I desire for him to remain until I come, what *is that* to you? You follow Me!

²³Then this saying went out among the brothers that that disciple would not die. But Jesus did not say to him that he would not die, but, if I desire for him to remain until I come, what *is that* to you?

²⁴This is the disciple who bears witness concerning these things and who wrote these things. And we know that his witness is true.

²⁵And there are many other things, as many things as Jesus did, which if they should be written one by one, I suppose not even the world itself would have place for the books written. Amen.

The ACTS of the Holy Apostles

CHAPTER 1

ΤΟΝ μὲν πρῶτον λόγον ἐποιησάμην περὶ πάντων, ὦ
The ³indeed ¹first ²account I made concerning all things, O
Θεόφιλε, ὧν ἤρξατο ʲὁ‖ Ἰησοῦς ποιεῖν.τε καὶ διδάσκειν,
Theophilus, which ²began ¹Jesus both to do and to teach,
2 ἄχρι ἧς.ἡμέρας ἐντειλάμενος τοῖς ἀποστόλοις διὰ
until the day in which, having given command ⁵to ⁶the ⁷apostles ¹by
πνεύματος ἁγίου οὓς ἐξελέξατο, ᵏἀνελήφθη.‖ 3 οἷς
[²the] ⁴Spirit ³Holy whom he chose, he was taken up: to whom

¹Indeed, O Theo-phi-lus, I made the first report as to all the things Jesus set out to do and teach,

²until the day He was taken up (after He had given orders through the Holy Spirit to those apostles He had chosen).

καὶ παρέστησεν ἑαυτὸν ζῶντα μετὰ τὸ.παθεῖν.αὐτόν, ἐν
also he presented himself living after he had suffered, with
πολλοῖς τεκμηρίοις, δι' ἡμερῶν [l]τεσσαράκοντα" ὀπτανόμενος
many proofs, during [2]days [1]forty being seen
αὐτοῖς, καὶ λέγων τὰ περὶ τῆς βασιλείας τοῦ θεοῦ.
by them, and speaking the things concerning the kingdom of God:
4 καὶ συναλιζόμενος [m]παρήγγειλεν αὐτοῖς" ἀπὸ Ἱερο-
and being assembled with [him] he charged them from Jeru-
σολύμων μὴ χωρίζεσθαι, ἀλλὰ περιμένειν τὴν ἐπαγγελίαν
salem not to depart, but to await the promise
τοῦ πατρός, ἣν ἠκούσατέ μου· 5 ὅτι [n]Ἰωάννης" μὲν
of the Father, which [said he] ye heard of me. For John indeed
ἐβάπτισεν ὕδατι, ὑμεῖς.δὲ [o]βαπτισθήσεσθε ἐν πνεύμα-
baptized with water, but ye shall be baptized with [the] [2]Spirit
τι" ἁγίῳ οὐ μετὰ πολλὰς ταύτας ἡμέρας. 6 Οἱ μὲν οὖν
[1]Holy [4]not [3]after many days. They indeed therefore
συνελθόντες [p]ἐπηρώτων" αὐτὸν λέγοντες, Κύριε, εἰ ἐν
having come together asked him, saying, Lord, [3]at
τῷ.χρόνῳ.τούτῳ ἀποκαθιστάνεις τὴν βασιλείαν τῷ Ἰσραήλ;
[4]this [5]time [1]restorest [2]thou the kingdom to Israel?
7 Εἶπεν.[q]δὲ" πρὸς αὐτούς, Οὐχ ὑμῶν ἐστιν γνῶναι χρόνους
And he said to them, [3]Not [4]yours [1]it [2]is to know times
ἢ καιροὺς οὓς ὁ πατὴρ ἔθετο ἐν τῇ.ἰδίᾳ ἐξουσίᾳ· 8 ἀλλὰ
or seasons which the Father placed in his own authority; but
[r]λήψεσθε" δύναμιν, ἐπελθόντος τοῦ ἁγίου πνεύματος ἐφ'
ye will receive power, [4]having [5]come [1]the [2]Holy [3]Spirit upon
ὑμᾶς, καὶ ἔσεσθέ [s]μοι" μάρτυρες ἔν.τε Ἱερουσαλὴμ καὶ [t]ἐν"
you, and ye shall be to me witnesses both in Jerusalem and in
πάσῃ [v]τῇ" Ἰουδαίᾳ καὶ [w]Σαμαρείᾳ" καὶ ἕως ἐσχάτου
all Judæa and Samaria and to [the] uttermost part
τῆς γῆς. 9 Καὶ ταῦτα εἰπών, βλεπόντων αὐτῶν
of the earth. And these things having said, [2]beholding [[3]him] [1]they
ἐπήρθη, καὶ νεφέλη ὑπέλαβεν αὐτὸν ἀπὸ τῶν ὀφθαλμῶν
he was taken up, and a cloud withdrew him from [2]eyes
αὐτῶν.
[1]their.

[3]He also showed Himself alive to them after
His suffering, with many proofs that cannot
be denied, being seen by them for forty days
and speaking the things of God's kingdom.
[4]And gathering *them* together, He commanded them not to leave Jerusalem, but
said, Wait for the promise of the Father
which you heard from Me.
[5]For John indeed baptized with water, but
you shall be baptized in the Holy Spirit not
many days after this.
[6]Then, indeed, when they had come together, they asked Him, saying, Lord, Do You at
this time give the kingdom back to Israel?
[7]And He said to them, It is not yours to
know the times or seasons, which the Father
ordained for His own authority.
[8]But you will receive power when the Holy
Spirit comes upon you. And you shall be
witnesses to Me both in Jerusalem and in all
Judea and Samaria and to the furthest part of
earth
[9]– and when He had said this, they
watched as He was taken up. And a cloud
hid Him from their eyes.

10 Καὶ ὡς ἀτενίζοντες ἦσαν εἰς τὸν οὐρανὸν πορευομένου
And as [3]looking [4]intently [1]they [2]were into the heaven as [2]was [3]going
αὐτοῦ, καὶ ἰδοὺ ἄνδρες δύο παρειστήκεισαν αὐτοῖς ἐν [x]ἐσθῆτι
[1]he, [5]also [6]behold [7]men [8]two stood by them in [2]apparel
λευκῇ," 11 οἳ καὶ [y]εἶπον," Ἄνδρες Γαλιλαῖοι, τί ἑστήκατε [z]ἐμ-
[1]white, who also said, Men Galileans, why do ye stand look-
βλέποντες" εἰς τὸν οὐρανόν; οὗτος ὁ Ἰησοῦς ὁ [a]ἀναληφθεὶς"
ing into the heaven? This Jesus who was taken up
ἀφ' ὑμῶν εἰς τὸν οὐρανὸν οὕτως ἐλεύσεται ὃν.τρόπον
from you into the heaven thus will come in the manner
ἐθεάσασθε αὐτὸν πορευόμενον εἰς τὸν οὐρανόν. 12 Τότε
ye beheld him going into the heaven. Then
ὑπέστρεψαν εἰς Ἱερουσαλὴμ ἀπὸ ὄρους τοῦ καλουμένου
they returned to Jerusalem from [the] mount called
ἐλαιῶνος, ὅ ἐστιν ἐγγὺς Ἱερουσαλήμ, σαββάτου ἔχον
of Olives, which is near Jerusalem, [3]a [4]sabbath's [1]being [2]distant
ὁδόν. 13 Καὶ ὅτε εἰσῆλθον [b]ἀνέβησαν εἰς τὸ ὑπερῷον,"
journey. And when they had entered they went up to the upper chamber,
οὗ ἦσαν καταμένοντες ὅ.τε.Πέτρος καὶ [c]Ἰάκωβος καὶ Ἰωάν-
where were staying both Peter and James and John
νης" καὶ Ἀνδρέας, Φίλιππος καὶ Θωμᾶς, Βαρθολομαῖος καὶ
and Andrew, Philip and Thomas, Bartholomew and
[d]Ματθαῖος," Ἰάκωβος Ἀλφαίου καὶ Σίμων ὁ Ζηλωτής,
Matthew, James [son] of Alphæus and Simon the Zealot,
καὶ Ἰούδας Ἰακώβου. 14 οὗτοι πάντες ἦσαν προσκαρ-
and Jude [brother] of James. These all were [4]steadfastly
τεροῦντες ὁμοθυμαδὸν τῇ προσευχῇ [e]καὶ τῇ δεήσει," σὺν
[5]continuing [1]with [2]one [3]accord in prayer and supplication, with [the]
γυναιξὶν καὶ [f]Μαρίᾳ" τῇ μητρὶ τοῦ Ἰησοῦ, καὶ [g]σὺν" τοῖς
women and Mary the mother of Jesus, and with
ἀδελφοῖς.αὐτοῦ.
his brethren.

[10]And as He was going up, while they
looked up into the heavens, then, behold!
Two men stood beside them in white clothing.
[11]And they said, Men! Galileans! Why do
you stand looking up into the heavens? This
Jesus who was taken up from you into Heaven
will come as you saw Him going up into
Heaven.
[12]Then they returned to Jerusalem from
the Mount of Olives, which is near Jerusalem
– being a sabbath day's journey away.
[13]And when they came in they went up to
the upper room where both Peter and James
and John and Andrew and Philip and
Thomas and Bar-thol-o-mew and Matthew
and James of Alpheus and Simon Zelotes
and Judas, James' *brother,* were staying.
[14]All of these were continuing together in
prayer and looking to God, with the women
and Mary the mother of Jesus, and with His
brothers.

15 Καὶ ἐν ταῖς.ἡμέραις.ταύταις ἀναστὰς Πέτρος ἐν
And in those days [2]having [3]stood [4]up [1]Peter in
μέσῳ τῶν [h]μαθητῶν" εἶπεν· ἦν τε ὄχλος ὀνομάτων
[the] midst of the disciples said, ([2]was [1]and [[3]the] [3]number [4]of [5]names
ἐπὶ.τὸ.αὐτὸ [i]ὡς" ἑκατὸν.[k]εἴκοσιν·" 16 Ἄνδρες ἀδελφοί, ἔδει
[6]together about a hundred and twenty,) Men brethren, it was neces-
πληρωθῆναι τὴν.γραφὴν.[l]ταύτην," ἣν προεῖπεν τὸ
sary [3]to [4]have [5]been [6]fulfilled [1]this [2]scripture, which [5]spoke [6]before [1]the
πνεῦμα τὸ ἅγιον διὰ στόματος [m]Δαβὶδ" περὶ Ἰούδα τοῦ
[3]Spirit [2]the [4]Holy by [the] mouth of David concerning Judas who
γενομένου ὁδηγοῦ τοῖς συλλαβοῦσιν [n]τὸν" Ἰησοῦν· 17 ὅτι
became guide to those who took Jesus; for
κατηριθμημένος ἦν [o]σὺν" ἡμῖν, καὶ ἔλαχεν τὸν κλῆρον τῆς
numbered he was with us, and obtained a part

[15]And in those days, after he stood up in
the midst of the disciples (the group of
people in all were about a hundred and
twenty), Peter said,
[16]Men! Brothers! It was necessary that this
Scripture should be fulfilled, which the Holy
Spirit spoke before by David's mouth, as to
Judas, who guided those who took Jesus.
[17]For he was counted with us and was
given a part in this ministry.

διακονίας.ταύτης. 18 Οὗτος μὲν οὖν ἐκτήσατο χωρίον
in this service. This [man] indeed then got a field
ἐκ [p]τοῦ" μισθοῦ τῆς ἀδικίας, καὶ πρηνὴς γενόμενος
out of the reward of unrighteousness, and [3]headlong [1]having [2]fallen
ἐλάκησεν μέσος, καὶ ἐξεχύθη πάντα τὰ.σπλάγχνα.αὐτοῦ.
burst in [the] midst, and [4]gushed [5]out [1]all [2]his [3]bowels.
19 [q]καὶ γνωστὸν ἐγένετο πᾶσιν τοῖς κατοικοῦσιν Ἱερουσαλήμ,
And known it became to all those dwelling in Jerusalem,
ὥστε κληθῆναι τὸ.χωρίον.ἐκεῖνο τῇ.[r]ἰδίᾳ".διαλέκτῳ.αὐτῶν
so that was called that field in their own language
[s]Ἀκελδαμά," [t]τουτέστιν" χωρίον αἵματος. 20 γέγραπται.γὰρ
Aceldama; that is, field of blood. For it has been written
ἐν βίβλῳ ψαλμῶν, Γενηθήτω ἡ.ἔπαυλις.αὐτοῦ ἔρημος,
in [the] book of Psalms, Let [3]become [1]his [2]homestead desolate,
καὶ μὴ.ἔστω ὁ κατοικῶν ἐν αὐτῇ. καί, Τὴν ἐπισκοπὴν
and let there not be [one] dwelling in it; and, [5]Overseership
αὐτοῦ [v]λάβοι" ἕτερος. 21 Δεῖ οὖν τῶν συνελθόντων
[4]his [1]let [3]take [2]another. It behoves therefore of those [2]consorting
ἡμῖν ἀνδρῶν ἐν παντὶ χρόνῳ [w]ἐν" ᾧ εἰσῆλθεν καὶ
[3]with [4]us [1]men during all [the] time in which came in and
ἐξῆλθεν ἐφ' ἡμᾶς ὁ κύριος Ἰησοῦς, 22 ἀρξάμενος ἀπὸ τοῦ
went out among us the Lord Jesus, beginning from the
βαπτίσματος [x]Ἰωάννου" [y]ἕως" τῆς ἡμέρας ἧς [z]ἀνελήφθη"
baptism of John until the day in which he was taken up
ἀφ' ἡμῶν, μάρτυρα τῆς.ἀναστάσεως.αὐτοῦ [a]γενέσθαι σὺν
from us, [8]a [9]witness [10]of [11]his [12]resurrection [4]to [5]become [6]with
ἡμῖν" ἕνα τούτων. 23 Καὶ ἔστησαν δύο, Ἰωσὴφ τὸν καλού-
[7]us [1]one [2]of [3]these. And they set forth two, Joseph call-
μενον [b]Βαρσαβᾶν," ὃς ἐπεκλήθη Ἰοῦστος, καὶ [c]Ματθίαν."
ed Barsabas, who was surnamed Justus, and Matthias.
24 καὶ προσευξάμενοι [d]εἶπον," Σὺ κύριε, καρδιογνῶστα
And praying they said, Thou Lord, knower of the hearts
πάντων, ἀνάδειξον [e]ἐκ τούτων τῶν δύο ἕνα ὃν ἐξελέξω"
of all, shew of these two [2]one [1]which thou didst choose
25 λαβεῖν τὸν [f]κλῆρον" τῆς.διακονίας ταύτης καὶ ἀποστολῆς,
to receive the part of this service and apostleship,
[g]ἐξ" ἧς παρέβη Ἰούδας, πορευθῆναι εἰς τὸν τόπον
from which [2]transgressing [3]fell [1]Judas, to go to his [2]place
τὸν ἴδιον. 26 Καὶ ἔδωκαν κλήρους [h]αὐτῶν," καὶ ἔπεσεν ὁ
[1]own. And they gave [2]lots [1]their, and [3]fell [1]the
κλῆρος ἐπὶ [c]Ματθίαν," καὶ [i]συγκατεψηφίσθη" μετὰ τῶν ἕνδεκα
[2]lot on Matthias, and he was numbered with the eleven
ἀποστόλων.
apostles.

2 Καὶ ἐν τῷ [k]συμπληροῦσθαι" τὴν ἡμέραν τῆς πεντη-
And during the accomplishing of the day of Pente-
κοστῆς ἦσαν [l]ἅπαντες ὁμοθυμαδὸν" ἐπὶ.τὸ.αὐτό. 2 καὶ
cost they were all with one accord in the same place. And
ἐγένετο ἄφνω ἐκ τοῦ οὐρανοῦ ἦχος ὥσπερ φερομένης
[2]came [1]suddenly out of the heaven a sound as [5]rushing
πνοῆς βιαίας, καὶ ἐπλήρωσεν ὅλον τὸν οἶκον οὗ ἦσαν
[6]of [2]a [4]breath [3]violent, and filled [2]whole [1]the house where they were
[m]καθήμενοι·" 3 καὶ ὤφθησαν αὐτοῖς διαμεριζόμεναι γλῶσσαι
sitting. And there appeared to them divided tongues
ὡσεὶ πυρός, [n]ἐκάθισεν.τε" ἐφ' ἕνα ἕκαστον αὐτῶν· 4 καὶ
as of fire, and sat upon [2]one [1]each of them. And
ἐπλήσθησαν [o]ἅπαντες" πνεύματος ἁγίου, καὶ ἤρξαντο λαλεῖν
they were [2]filled [1]all with [the] [2]Spirit [1]Holy, and began to speak
ἑτέραις γλώσσαις, καθὼς τὸ πνεῦμα ἐδίδου [p]αὐτοῖς ἀποφθέγ-
with other tongues, as the Spirit gave to them to utter
γεσθαι." 5 Ἦσαν.δὲ [q]ἐν" Ἱερουσαλὴμ κατοικοῦντες Ἰουδαῖοι,
forth. Now [3]were [4]in [5]Jerusalem [2]dwelling [1]Jews,
ἄνδρες εὐλαβεῖς ἀπὸ παντὸς ἔθνους τῶν ὑπὸ τὸν οὐρανόν.
[2]men [1]pious from every nation of those under the heaven.
6 γενομένης.δὲ τῆς φωνῆς ταύτης, συνῆλθεν τὸ πλῆθος
But [5]having [6]arisen [1]the [2]rumour [3]of [4]this, [9]came [10]together [7]the [8]multitude
καὶ συνεχύθη· ὅτι ἤκουον εἷς ἕκαστος τῇ.ἰδίᾳ διαλέκτῳ
and were confounded, because [3]heard [2]one [1]each in his own language
λαλούντων αὐτῶν. 7 ἐξίσταντο.δὲ [r]πάντες" καὶ ἐθαύμαζον,
[2]speaking [1]them. And [2]were [3]amazed [1]all and wondered,
λέγοντες [s]πρὸς ἀλλήλους," [t]Οὐκ" ἰδοὺ [v]πάντες" οὗτοι εἰσιν οἱ
saying to one another, [3]Not [1]lo [4]all [5]these [2]are who
λαλοῦντες Γαλιλαῖοι; 8 καὶ πῶς ἡμεῖς ἀκούομεν ἕκαστος
are speaking Galileans? and how [2]we [3]hear each
τῇ.ἰδίᾳ.διαλέκτῳ.ἡμῶν ἐν ᾗ ἐγεννήθημεν, 9 Πάρθοι καὶ
in our own language in which we were born, Parthians and
Μῆδοι καὶ [w]Ἐλαμῖται," καὶ οἱ κατοικοῦντες τὴν Μεσοπο-
Medes and Elamites, and those who inhabit Mesopo-
ταμίαν, Ἰουδαίαν.τε καὶ Καππαδοκίαν, Πόντον καὶ τὴν Ἀσίαν,
tamia, and Judea and Cappadocia, Pontus and Asia,
10 Φρυγίαν.τε καὶ Παμφυλίαν, Αἴγυπτον καὶ τὰ μέρη τῆς
both Phrygia and Pamphylia, Egypt and the parts

18 Now, then, this one bought a field out of the reward of unrighteousness – falling face down. He broke open in the middle and all his bowels gushed out.

19 And it became known to all those living in Jerusalem, so that the field was called in their language, A-kel-da-ma (which means, Field of Blood).

20 For it has been written in the book of Psalms, "Let his home become forsaken and let there be no one living in it," and, "let another take his office."

21 Then it is right that one of those men who have been with us all the time during which the Lord Jesus came and went among us –

22 beginning from the baptism of John, until the day in which He was taken up from us – should become a witness of His resurrection with us.

23 And they chose out two, Joseph called Bar-sa-bas (whose last name was Justus), and Mat-thi-as.

24 And praying they said, Lord, You know all hearts, reveal which one of these two You have chosen

25 to receive a share of this ministry and apostleship, from which Judas fell away by sin, to go to his own place.

26 And they gave their lots, and the lot fell on Mat-thi-as. And he was counted with the eleven apostles.

CHAPTER 2

1 And when the day of Pentecost was being fulfilled, they were all together in one place.

2 And suddenly a sound came out of the sky, like a rushing violent wind! And it filled the whole house where they were sitting.

3 And forked tongues, like fire, appeared to them and sat on each one of them.

4 And they were all filled with the Holy Spirit and began to speak other languages – as the Spirit gave them *ability* to speak.

5 Now there were Jews living in Jerusalem, God-fearing men from every nation under the sky.

6 And when this sound had come, the crowd came together and were bewildered because they were each one hearing them speak in his own language.

7 And they were all amazed and wondered, saying to each other, Listen! Are these not all Galileans who are speaking?

8 And, How do we each hear in our own language in which we were born?

9 Par-thi-ans and Medes and E-lam-ites and those who lived in Mes-o-po-ta-mi-a and Judea and Cap-pa-do-ci-a, Pontus and Asia,

10 Both Phryg-i-a and Pam-phyl-i-a, Egypt and that part of Libya around Cy-re-ne, and strangers from Rome, Jews and proselytes.

Λιβύης τῆς κατὰ Κυρήνην, καὶ οἱ ἐπιδημοῦντες
of Libya which [is] about Cyrene, and the 2sojourning [3here]

Ῥωμαῖοι, Ἰουδαῖοί-τε καὶ προσήλυτοι, 11 Κρῆτες καὶ [w]Ἄραβες,
1Romans, both Jews and proselytes, Cretans and Arabians,

ἀκούομεν λαλούντων αὐτῶν ταῖς-ἡμετέραις γλώσσαις τὰ
we hear 2speaking 1them in our own tongues the

μεγαλεῖα τοῦ θεοῦ; 12 Ἐξίσταντο-δὲ πάντες καὶ [x]διηπόρουν,||
great things of God? And 2were 3amazed 1all and were in perplexity,

ἄλλος-πρὸς-ἄλλον λέγοντες, Τί [y]ἂν-θέλοι|| τοῦτο εἶναι;
one to another saying, What would this be?

13 [v]Ἕτεροι-δὲ [z]χλευάζοντες|| ἔλεγον, "Ὅτι γλεύκους μεμεστω-
But others mocking said, Of new wine 3full

μένοι εἰσίν. 14 Σταθεὶς-δὲ [a]Πέτρος σὺν τοῖς ἕνδεκα ἐπῆρεν
1they 2are. But 2standing 3up 1Peter with the eleven lifted up

τὴν-φωνὴν-αὐτοῦ καὶ ἀπεφθέγξατο αὐτοῖς, "Ἄνδρες Ἰουδαῖοι,
his voice and spoke forth to them, Men Jews,

καὶ οἱ κατοικοῦντες Ἱερουσαλὴμ [o]ἅπαντες,|| τοῦτο ὑμῖν
and 2ye 3who 4inhabit 5Jerusalem 1all, 7this 10to 11you

γνωστὸν ἔστω, καὶ ἐνωτίσασθε τὰ-ῥήματά-μου. 15 οὐ-γὰρ ὡς
9known 6let 8be, and give heed to my words: for not as

ὑμεῖς ὑπολαμβάνετε, οὗτοι μεθύουσιν· ἔστιν-γὰρ ὥρα
ye take it, 2these are drunken, for it is [the] 2hour

τρίτη τῆς ἡμέρας· 16 ἀλλὰ τοῦτό ἐστιν τὸ εἰρημένον
1third of the day; but this is that which has been spoken

διὰ τοῦ προφήτου [b]Ἰωήλ,|| 17 [c]Καὶ|| ἔσται ἐν ταῖς ἐσχάταις
by the prophet Joel, And it shall be in the last

ἡμέραις, λέγει ὁ θεός, ἐκχεῶ ἀπὸ τοῦ-πνεύματός-μου ἐπὶ
days, says God, I will pour out of my Spirit upon

πᾶσαν σάρκα, καὶ προφητεύσουσιν οἱ-υἱοὶ-ὑμῶν καὶ αἱ θυγα-
all flesh; and shall prophesy your sons and 2daugh-

τέρες ὑμῶν· καὶ οἱ-νεανίσκοι-ὑμῶν ὁράσεις ὄψονται, καὶ οἱ
ters 1your; and your young men visions shall see, and

πρεσβύτεροι-ὑμῶν [e]ἐνύπνια|| ἐνυπνιασθήσονται· 18 [f]καί γε||
your elders dreams shall dream; and even

ἐπὶ τοὺς-δούλους-μου καὶ ἐπὶ τὰς-δούλας-μου ἐν ταῖς ἡμέραις
upon my bondmen and upon my bondwomen in 2days

ἐκείναις ἐκχεῶ ἀπὸ τοῦ-πνεύματός-μου, καὶ προφητεύ-
1those will I pour out of my Spirit, and they shall pro-

σουσιν. 19 καὶ δώσω τέρατα ἐν τῷ οὐρανῷ ἄνω καὶ σημεῖα
phesy; and I will give wonders in the heaven above and signs

ἐπὶ τῆς γῆς κάτω, αἷμα καὶ πῦρ καὶ ἀτμίδα καπνοῦ. 20 ὁ
on the earth below, blood and fire and vapour of smoke. The

ἥλιος μεταστραφήσεται εἰς σκότος καὶ ἡ σελήνη εἰς αἷμα,
sun shall be turned into darkness and the moon into blood,

πρὶν [g]ἢ|| ἐλθεῖν [h]τὴν|| ἡμέραν κυρίου τὴν μεγάλην [i]καὶ
before come 5day 6of [7the] 8Lord 1the 2great 3and

ἐπιφανῆ.|| 21 καὶ ἔσται, πᾶς ὃς-[k]ἂν|| ἐπικαλέσηται τὸ
4manifest. And it shall be, everyone whoever shall call upon the

ὄνομα κυρίου σωθήσεται. 22 "Ἄνδρες [l]Ἰσραηλῖται,|| ἀκούσατε
name of [the] Lord shall be saved. Men Israelites, hear

τοὺς-λόγους-τούτους· Ἰησοῦν τὸν Ναζωραῖον, ἄνδρα [m]ἀπὸ
these words: Jesus the Nazaraean, a man by

τοῦ θεοῦ ἀποδεδειγμένον|| εἰς ὑμᾶς δυνάμεσιν καὶ τέρασιν
God set forth to you by works of power and wonders

καὶ σημείοις, οἷς ἐποίησεν δι' αὐτοῦ ὁ θεὸς ἐν μέσῳ ὑμῶν,
and signs, which 2wrought 3by 4him 1God in 2midst 1your,

καθὼς [n]καὶ|| αὐτοὶ οἴδατε, 23 τοῦτον τῇ ὡρισμένῃ βουλῇ
as also yourselves know: him, 3by 4the 5determinate 6counsel

καὶ προγνώσει τοῦ θεοῦ ἔκδοτον [o]λαβόντες|| διὰ [p]χειρῶν||
7and 8foreknowledge 9of 10God 1given 2up, having taken by 2hands

ἀνόμων προσπήξαντες [q]ἀνείλετε·|| 24 ὃν ὁ θεὸς ἀνέστησεν,
1lawless, having crucified ye put to death. Whom God raised up,

λύσας τὰς ὠδῖνας τοῦ θανάτου, καθότι οὐκ-ἦν δυνατὸν
having loosed the throes of death, inasmuch as it was not possible

κρατεῖσθαι αὐτὸν ὑπ' αὐτοῦ. 25 [r]Δαβὶδ-γὰρ λέγει εἰς
[for] 2to 3be 4held 1him by it; for David says as to

αὐτόν, [s]Προωρώμην τὸν κύριον [t]ἐνώπιόν μου [v]διὰ-παντός,||
him, I foresaw the Lord before me continually,

ὅτι ἐκ δεξιῶν-μου ἐστίν, ἵνα μὴ-σαλευθῶ. 26 διὰ-τοῦτο
because at my right hand he is, that I may not be shaken. Therefore

[w]εὐφράνθη|| [x]ἡ-καρδία-μου|| καὶ ἠγαλλιάσατο ἡ-γλῶσσά-μου·
3rejoiced 1my 2heart and 3exulted 1my 2tongue;

ἔτι-δὲ καὶ ἡ-σάρξ-μου κατασκηνώσει [y]ἐπ'|| ἐλπίδι· 27 ὅτι οὐκ
yea more, also my flesh shall rest in hope, for 3not

[z]ἐγκαταλείψεις|| τὴν-ψυχήν-μου εἰς [a]ᾅδου,|| οὐδὲ δώσεις τὸν
1thou 2wilt leave my soul in hades, nor wilt thou give

ὅσιόν σου ἰδεῖν διαφθοράν. 28 ἐγνώρισάς μοι ὁδοὺς
2holy 3one 1thy to see corruption. Thou didst make known to me paths

ζωῆς· πληρώσεις με εὐφροσύνης μετὰ τοῦ-προσώπου-σου.
of life, thou wilt fill me with joy with thy countenance.

29 "Ἄνδρες ἀδελφοί, ἐξὸν εἰπεῖν μετὰ παρρησίας
Men brethren, it is permitted [me] to speak with freedom

11 Cretes and Arabians – we hear them speaking the great things of God in our own languages.

12 And they were all amazed and were in doubt, saying to each other, What does this mean?

13 But others, making fun of them said, They are full of new wine.

14 But standing with the eleven, Peter lifted his voice and spoke to them, Men! Jews! All of you who live in Jerusalem! Let this become known to you and listen to my words.

15 For these men are not drunk, as you suppose, for it is only the third hour of the day.

16 But this is that which the prophet Joel has spoken,

17 "And it shall happen in the last days, God says, I will pour out of My Spirit on all flesh. And your sons and daughters shall prophesy, and your young men shall see visions, and your old men shall dream dreams.

18 And also I will pour out of My Spirit on My slaves and slave-girls in those days, and they shall prophesy.

19 And I will give wonders in the heavens above and miracles on the earth below – blood and fire and vapor of smoke.

20 The sun shall be turned into darkness and the moon into blood, before the coming of the great and glorious day of the Lord.

21 And it shall be that everyone who shall call on the name of the Lord will be saved."

22 Men! Israelites! Hear these words. Jesus the Nazarene *was* a man approved of God among you by mighty works and wonders and miracles, which God worked by Him among you, as you yourselves know.

23 This One who *was* delivered to you by the before-determined counsel and foreknowledge of God, you laid your wicked hands on and killed Him, crucifying Him.

24 God has raised Him up, loosing Him from the pains of death because it was not possible for Him to be held by it.

25 For David said of Him, "I always saw the Lord before Me, because He is at My right hand, that I may not be moved.

26 For this reason My heart rejoiced and My tongue was glad. Yes, more, My flesh shall rest in hope,

27 because You will not leave My soul in Hades, nor will you give Your Holy One to see corruption.

28 You have revealed to Me the ways of life. You will fill Me with joy with Your face."

29 Men! Brothers! I may speak with freedom to you about the patriarch David, that he both died and was buried. And his tomb is among us to this day.

πρὸς ὑμᾶς περὶ τοῦ πατριάρχου [b]Δαβίδ,‖ ὅτι καὶ ἐτελεύτη-
to you concerning the patriarch David, that both he died
σεν καὶ ἐτάφη, καὶ τὸ.μνῆμα.αὐτοῦ ἔστιν ἐν ἡμῖν ἄχρι
and was buried, and his tomb is amongst us unto
τῆς.ἡμέρας.ταύτης. 30 προφήτης οὖν ὑπάρχων, καὶ εἰδὼς
this day. A prophet therefore being, and knowing
ὅτι ὅρκῳ ὤμοσεν αὐτῷ ὁ θεός, ἐκ καρποῦ τῆς ὀσφύος
that with an oath [2]swore [3]to [4]him [1]God, of [the] fruit of [1]loins
αὐτοῦ [c]τὸ.κατὰ σάρκα ἀναστήσειν τὸν χριστόν,‖ καθίσαι ἐπὶ
[2]his as concerning flesh to raise up the Christ, to sit upon
[d]τοῦ.θρόνου‖.αὐτοῦ, 31 προϊδὼν ἐλάλησεν περὶ τῆς ἀνα-
his throne, foreseeing he spoke concerning the resur-
στάσεως τοῦ χριστοῦ, ὅτι [e]οὐ [f]κατελείφθη‖ [g]ἡ.ψυχὴ.αὐτοῦ‖ εἰς
rection of the Christ, that was not left his soul in
[h]ᾅδου,‖ [i]οὐδὲ‖ ἡ.σὰρξ.αὐτοῦ εἶδεν διαφθοράν. 32 τοῦτον τὸν
hades, nor his flesh saw corruption. This
Ἰησοῦν ἀνέστησεν ὁ θεὸς οὗ πάντες ἡμεῖς ἐσμεν μάρτυρες.
Jesus [2]raised [3]up [1]God whereof all we are witnesses.
33 τῇ δεξιᾷ οὖν τοῦ θεοῦ ὑψωθείς, τήν.τε ἐπαγ-
By the right hand therefore of God having been exalted, and the pro-
γελίαν τοῦ [k]ἁγίου πνεύματος‖ λαβὼν παρὰ τοῦ πατρός,
mise of the Holy Spirit having received from the Father,
ἐξέχεεν τοῦτο ὃ [l]νῦν‖ ὑμεῖς [m]βλέπετε καὶ ἀκούετε. 34 οὐ
he poured out this which now ye behold and hear. [4]Not
γὰρ [b]Δαβὶδ‖ ἀνέβη εἰς τοὺς οὐρανούς, λέγει.δὲ αὐτός,
[1]for [2]David [3]ascended into the heavens, but he says himself,
Εἶπεν [n]ὁ‖ κύριος τῷ.κυρίῳ.μου, Κάθου ἐκ δεξιῶν.μου· 35 ἕως
Said the Lord to my Lord, Sit at my right hand, until
ἂν θῶ τοὺς.ἐχθρούς.σου ὑποπόδιον τῶν.ποδῶν.σου. 36 Ἀ-
I place thine enemies a footstool of thy feet. As-
σφαλῶς οὖν γινωσκέτω πᾶς [o]οἶκος Ἰσραήλ, ὅτι [p]καὶ‖
surely therefore let know all [the] house of Israel, that both
κύριον [q]καὶ χριστὸν αὐτὸν‖ [r]ὁ θεὸς ἐποίησεν,‖ τοῦτον τὸν
Lord and Christ him God made, this
Ἰησοῦν ὃν ὑμεῖς ἐσταυρώσατε.
Jesus whom ye crucified.

37 Ἀκούσαντες.δὲ κατενύγησαν [s]τῇ.καρδίᾳ,‖ εἶπόν.τε πρὸς
And having heard they were pricked in heart, and said to
τὸν Πέτρον καὶ τοὺς λοιποὺς ἀποστόλους, Τί [t]ποιήσομεν,‖
Peter and the other apostles, What shall we do,
ἄνδρες ἀδελφοί; 38 Πέτρος.δὲ [v]ἔφη‖ πρὸς αὐτούς, Μετανοή-
men brethren? And Peter said to them, Repent,
σατε[w], καὶ βαπτισθήτω ἕκαστος ὑμῶν [x]ἐπὶ‖ τῷ ὀνόματι Ἰησοῦ
and be baptized each of you in the name of Jesus
χριστοῦ, εἰς ἄφεσιν [y]ἁμαρτιῶν,‖ καὶ [z]λήψεσθε‖ τὴν δωρεὰν
Christ, for remission of sins, and ye will receive the gift
τοῦ ἁγίου πνεύματος. 39 ὑμῖν.γάρ ἐστιν ἡ ἐπαγγελία καὶ
of the Holy Spirit. For to you is the promise and
τοῖς.τέκνοις.ὑμῶν, καὶ πᾶσιν τοῖς εἰς μακράν, [a]ὅσους‖ ἂν
to your children, and to all those at a distance, as many as
προσκαλέσηται κύριος ὁ.θεὸς.ἡμῶν. 40 Ἑτέροις.τε λόγοις
[5]may [6]call [[1]the] [2]Lord [3]our [4]God. And with [1]other [3]words
πλείοσιν [b]διεμαρτύρετο‖ καὶ παρεκάλει [c] λέγων, Σώθητε ἀπὸ
[2]many he earnestly testified and exhorted, saying, Be saved from
τῆς γενεᾶς τῆς.σκολιᾶς.ταύτης. 41 Οἱ.μὲν.οὖν [d]ἀσμένως‖
[3]generation [1]this [2]crooked. Those therefore who gladly
ἀποδεξάμενοι τὸν.λόγον.αὐτοῦ ἐβαπτίσθησαν· καὶ προσετέθη-
had welcomed his word were baptized; and were added
σαν [e] τῇ.ἡμέρᾳ.ἐκείνῃ ψυχαὶ ὡσεὶ τρισχίλιαι. 42 Ἦσαν.δὲ
that day [4]souls [1]about [2]three [3]thousand. And they were
προσκαρτεροῦντες [f] τῇ διδαχῇ τῶν ἀποστόλων καὶ τῇ κοινωνίᾳ
steadfastly continuing in the teaching of the apostles and in fellowship,
[g]καὶ‖ τῇ κλάσει τοῦ ἄρτου καὶ ταῖς προσευχαῖς. 43 [h]ἐγένετο‖
and the breaking of bread and prayers. [2]There [3]came
δὲ πάσῃ ψυχῇ φόβος, πολλά.[i]τε‖ τέρατα καὶ σημεῖα διὰ
[1]and upon every soul fear, and many wonders and signs through
τῶν ἀποστόλων ἐγίνετο.[j] 44 [k]πάντες.δὲ οἱ [l]πιστεύοντες‖ ἦσαν
the apostles took place. And all who believed were
ἐπὶ.τὸ.αὐτὸ καὶ εἶχον ἅπαντα κοινά, 45 καὶ τὰ κτήματα
together and had all things common, and [their] possessions
καὶ τὰς.ὑπάρξεις ἐπίπρασκον, καὶ διεμέριζον αὐτὰ πᾶσιν,
and goods they sold, and divided them to all,
καθότι ἄν τις χρείαν εἶχεν. 46 καθ'.ἡμέραν.τε προσκαρ-
according as anyone [2]need [1]had. And every day steadfastly
τεροῦντες ὁμοθυμαδὸν ἐν τῷ ἱερῷ, κλῶντές.τε κατ'.οἶκον
continuing with one accord in the temple, and breaking [2]in [[3]their] [4]houses
ἄρτον, μετελάμβανον τροφῆς ἐν ἀγαλλιάσει καὶ ἀφελότητι
[1]bread, they partook of food with gladness and simplicity
καρδίας, 47 αἰνοῦντες τὸν θεόν, καὶ ἔχοντες χάριν πρὸς ὅλον
of heart, praising God, and having favour with [2]whole
τὸν λαόν. ὁ.δὲ κύριος προσετίθει τοὺς σωζομένους
[1]the people; and the Lord added [2]those [3]who [4]were [5]being [6]saved

30 *He was* a prophet, and knowing that God had sworn to him with an oath to raise up the Christ out of the fruit of his loins, according to the flesh, to sit on his throne,

31 foreseeing this, then, he spoke about the resurrection of Christ, that His soul was not left in Hades nor His flesh to see corruption.

32 God did raise up this Jesus, of which we are all witnesses.

33 Then, having been exalted by the right hand of God, and having received the promise of the Holy Spirit from the Father, He poured out this which you now see and hear.

34 For David did not go into the heavens, but he himself said, "The Lord said to my Lord, Sit at My right hand

35 until I place Your enemies as a footstool for Your feet."

36 Then let all the house of Israel certainly acknowledge that God made Him both Lord and Christ, this same Jesus that you have crucified.

37 And having heard, they were stabbed in the heart and said to Peter and the other apostles, What shall we do, men and brothers?
38 But Peter said to them, Repent and be baptized, each one of you, in the name of Jesus Christ unto remission of sins, and you will receive the gift of the Holy Spirit.
39 For the promise is to you and to your children and to all those that are afar off, as many as the Lord our God shall call.
40 And with many other words he earnestly testified and pleaded, saying, Be saved from this wicked generation!

41 Then those who gladly welcomed his word were baptized. And there were about three thousand souls added on that day.
42 And they were firmly devoted to the teaching of the apostles, and in fellowship, and in breaking of bread and in prayers.
43 And fear came on every soul, also many wonders and miracles were being done through the apostles.

44 And all who believed were together. And all had things in common.
45 And they sold their valuables and goods and divided them to all as anyone had need.
46 And with one heart they faithfully continued daily in the Temple. And breaking bread in houses, they took their food with gladness and purity of heart,
47 praising God and having favor with all the people. And the Lord added those who were being saved day by day to the church.

καθ᾽.ἡμέραν [m]τῇ ἐκκλησίᾳ.[ll]
[1]daily to the assembly.
3 [n]Ἐπὶ.τὸ.αὐτὸ[ll] [o]δὲ Πέτρος[ll] καὶ [p]Ἰωάννης[ll] ἀνέβαινον
[5]Together [1]and [2]Peter [3]and [4]John went up
εἰς τὸ ἱερὸν ἐπὶ τὴν ὥραν τῆς προσευχῆς τὴν [q]ἐννάτην.[ll]
into the temple at the hour of prayer, the ninth;
2 καί τις ἀνὴρ χωλὸς ἐκ κοιλίας μητρὸς αὐτοῦ ὑπάρχων
and a certain man [2]lame [3]from [6]womb [5]mother's [4]his [1]being
ἐβαστάζετο· ὃν ἐτίθουν καθ᾽.ἡμέραν πρὸς τὴν θύραν τοῦ
was being carried, whom they placed daily at the door of the
ἱεροῦ τὴν λεγομένην Ὡραίαν, τοῦ αἰτεῖν ἐλεημοσύνην παρὰ
temple called Beautiful, to ask alms from
τῶν εἰσπορευομένων εἰς τὸ ἱερόν. 3 ὃς ἰδὼν Πέτρον καὶ
those who were going into the temple; who seeing Peter and
[r]Ἰωάννην[ll] μέλλοντας εἰσιέναι εἰς τὸ ἱερόν, ἠρώτα ἐλεημοσύ-
John being about to enter into the temple, asked [3]alms
νην λαβεῖν. 4 ἀτενίσας.δὲ Πέτρος εἰς αὐτὸν σὺν τῷ [s]Ἰωάν-
[1]to [2]receive. And [2]looking [3]intently [1]Peter upon him with John
νῃ[ll] εἶπεν, Βλέψον εἰς ἡμᾶς. 5 Ὁ.δὲ ἐπεῖχεν αὐτοῖς, προσδοκῶν
said, Look on us. And he gave heed to them, expecting
τι παρ᾽ αὐτῶν λαβεῖν. 6 εἶπεν.δὲ Πέτρος, Ἀργύριον καὶ
something from them to receive. But said Peter, Silver and
χρυσίον οὐχ.ὑπάρχει μοι· ὃ.δὲ ἔχω, τοῦτό σοι δίδωμι.
gold there is not to me, but what I have, this to thee I give:
ἐν τῷ ὀνόματι Ἰησοῦ χριστοῦ τοῦ Ναζωραίου [t]ἔγειραι καὶ[ll]
In the name of Jesus Christ the Nazaræan rise up and
περιπάτει. 7 Καὶ πιάσας αὐτὸν τῆς δεξιᾶς χειρὸς ἤγειρεν[v]·
walk. And having taken him by the right hand he raised up
παραχρῆμα.δὲ ἐστερεώθησαν [w]αὐτοῦ αἱ βάσεις[ll] καὶ τὰ
[him], and immediately were strengthened his feet and
[x]σφυρά·[ll] 8 καὶ ἐξαλλόμενος ἔστη καὶ περιεπάτει, καὶ εἰσῆλ-
ankle bones. And leaping up he stood and walked, and entered
θεν σὺν αὐτοῖς εἰς τὸ ἱερόν, περιπατῶν καὶ ἁλλόμενος [y]καὶ[ll]
with them into the temple, walking and leaping and
αἰνῶν τὸν θεόν. 9 καὶ εἶδεν [z]αὐτὸν πᾶς ὁ λαὸς[ll] περιπα-
praising God. And [4]saw [5]him [1]all [2]the [3]people walk-
τοῦντα καὶ αἰνοῦντα τὸν θεόν· 10 ἐπεγίνωσκόν.[a]τε[ll] αὐτὸν
ing and praising God. And they recognized him
ὅτι [b]οὗτος[ll] ἦν ὁ πρὸς τὴν ἐλεημοσύνην καθήμενος ἐπὶ
that he it was who for alms [was] sitting at
τῇ Ὡραίᾳ πύλῃ τοῦ ἱεροῦ· καὶ ἐπλήσθησαν θάμβους καὶ
the Beautiful gate of the temple, and they were filled with wonder and
ἐκστάσεως ἐπὶ τῷ συμβεβηκότι αὐτῷ. 11 Κρατοῦντος.δὲ
amazement at that which had happened to him. And as [8]held
[c]τοῦ ἰαθέντος χωλοῦ[ll] τὸν Πέτρον καὶ [d] [e]Ἰωάννην,[ll]
[1]the [4]who [5]had [6]been [7]healed [2]lame [[3]man] Peter and John,
συνέδραμεν [f]πρὸς αὐτοὺς πᾶς ὁ λαὸς[ll] ἐπὶ τῇ στοᾷ τῇ
ran together to them all the people in the porch
καλουμένῃ [g]Σολομῶντος,[ll] ἔκθαμβοι. 12 ἰδὼν.δὲ [h] Πέτρος
called Solomon's, greatly amazed. And seeing [it] Peter
ἀπεκρίνατο πρὸς τὸν λαόν, Ἄνδρες [i]Ἰσραηλῖται,[ll] τί θαυ-
answered to the people, Men Israelites, why won-
μάζετε ἐπὶ τούτῳ, ἢ ἡμῖν τί ἀτενίζετε ὡς ἰδίᾳ δυνάμει
der ye at this? or on us why look intently as if by [our] own power
ἢ εὐσεβείᾳ πεποιηκόσιν τοῦ περιπατεῖν αὐτόν; 13 ὁ θεὸς
or piety [we] had made [2]to [3]walk [1]him? The God
Ἀβραὰμ καὶ [k]Ἰσαὰκ καὶ [k]Ἰακώβ, ὁ θεὸς τῶν.πατέρων.ἡμῶν,
of Abraham and Isaac and Jacob, the God of our fathers,
ἐδόξασεν τὸν.παῖδα.αὐτοῦ Ἰησοῦν· ὃν ὑμεῖς [l] παρεδώκατε,
glorified his servant Jesus, whom ye delivered up,
καὶ ἠρνήσασθε [m]αὐτὸν[ll] κατὰ.πρόσωπον [n]Πιλάτου,[ll] κρίναντος
and denied him in the presence of Pilate, [2]having [3]adjudged
ἐκείνου ἀπολύειν. 14 ὑμεῖς.δὲ τὸν ἅγιον καὶ δίκαιον
[1]he to release [him]. But ye the holy and righteous one
ἠρνήσασθε, καὶ ᾐτήσασθε ἄνδρα φονέα χαρισθῆναι ὑμῖν,
denied, and requested a man a murderer to be granted to you,
15 τὸν.δὲ ἀρχηγὸν τῆς ζωῆς ἀπεκτείνατε· ὃν ὁ θεὸς ἤγειρεν
but the Author of life ye killed, whom God raised up
ἐκ νεκρῶν, οὗ ἡμεῖς μάρτυρές ἐσμεν. 16 καὶ ἐπὶ
from among [the] dead, whereof we witnesses are: and by
τῇ πίστει τοῦ.ὀνόματος.αὐτοῦ τοῦτον ὃν θεωρεῖτε καὶ
faith in his name this [man] whom ye behold and
οἴδατε ἐστερέωσεν τὸ.ὄνομα.αὐτοῦ· καὶ ἡ πίστις ἡ δι᾽
know [3]made [4]strong [1]his [2]name; and the faith which [is] by
αὐτοῦ ἔδωκεν αὐτῷ τὴν.ὁλοκληρίαν.ταύτην ἀπέναντι πάντων
him gave to him this complete soundness before all
ὑμῶν. 17 καὶ νῦν, ἀδελφοί, οἶδα ὅτι κατὰ ἄγνοιαν ἐπράξατε,
of you. And now, brethren, I know that in ignorance ye acted,
ὥσπερ καὶ οἱ.ἄρχοντες.ὑμῶν· 18 ὁ.δὲ.θεὸς ἃ προκατήγγειλεν
as also your rulers; but [2]God [1]what before announced
διὰ στόματος πάντων τῶν.προφητῶν.[o]αὐτοῦ[ll] παθεῖν
by [the] mouth of all his prophets [that] [3]should [4]suffer

CHAPTER 3

1 Now about this time Peter and John went up to the Temple at the ninth hour, the hour of prayer.

2 And a certain man who was lame from his mother's womb was being carried, whom they put down daily at the gate of the Temple called Beautiful, so as to beg alms from those who were entering into the Temple.

3 Seeing Peter and John about to go into the Temple, he begged to receive a gift.

4 And Peter and John looked at him and said, Look toward us!

5 And he watched them eagerly, expecting to get something from them.

6 But Peter said, Of silver and gold I have none, but what I have I give to you: In the name of Jesus Christ the Nazarene, get up and walk!

7 And taking him by the right hand, he lifted him up. And instantly his feet and ankle-bones were strengthened.

8 And leaping up, he stood and walked and went into the Temple with them, walking and leaping and praising God.

9 And all the people saw him walking and praising God.

10 And they recognized him, that it was he who was sitting at the Beautiful Gate of the Temple for alms. And they were filled with wonder and amazement at that which had happened to him.

11 And as the lame man who had been healed hugged Peter and John, the people all ran together to them in Solomon's Porch, greatly wondering.

12 And seeing it, Peter answered the people, Men! Israelites! Why do you wonder at this? Or why do you look so intently at us, as if we had made him walk by our own power or goodness?

13 The God of Abraham and Isaac and Jacob, the God of our fathers, glorified His Son, Jesus, whom you betrayed. And *you* denied Him in the presence of Pilate, after he had decided to let Him go.

14 But you denied the holy and righteous One and demanded that a man who was a murderer be given to you *instead.*

15 And you killed the Author of life, whom God raised up from among the dead, of which we are witnesses.

16 And by faith in His name, this one whom you see and know has been made strong by His name. And the faith which is through Him has given him this perfect soundness in the presence of all of you.

17 And now, brothers, I know that you did this without knowing what you did, as is also true of your rulers.

18 But what God had before proclaimed by the mouth of all His prophets, that Christ should suffer, He fulfilled in this way.

τὸν χριστόν[p], ἐπλήρωσεν οὕτως. 19 μετανοήσατε οὖν καὶ
[1]the [2]Christ, he fulfilled thus. Repent therefore and
ἐπιστρέψατε, [q]εἰς" τὸ ἐξαλειφθῆναι ὑμῶν τὰς ἁμαρτίας, ὅπως
be converted, for the blotting out of your sins, so that
ἂν.ἔλθωσιν καιροὶ ἀναψύξεως ἀπὸ προσώπου τοῦ κυρίου,
may come times of refreshing from [the] presence of the Lord,
20 καὶ ἀποστείλῃ τὸν [r]προκεκηρυγμένον" ὑμῖν, [s]Ἰησοῦν
and [that] he may send him who was before proclaimed to you, Jesus
χριστόν," 21 ὃν δεῖ οὐρανὸν μὲν δέξασθαι ἄχρι χρόνων
Christ, whom [2]must [1]heaven indeed receive till times
ἀποκαταστάσεως πάντων, ὧν ἐλάλησεν ὁ θεὸς διὰ
of restoration of all things, of which [2]spoke [1]God by [the]
στόματος [t]πάντων" ἁγίων [v]αὐτοῦ προφητῶν ἀπ' αἰῶνος."
mouth of all [2]holy [1]his prophets from of old.
22 [w]Μωσῆς" μὲν [x]γὰρ" [y]πρὸς τοὺς πατέρας" εἶπεν, "Οτι
[2]Moses [3]indeed [1]for to the fathers said,
προφήτην ὑμῖν ἀναστήσει κύριος ὁ θεὸς [z]ὑμῶν" ἐκ
A prophet to you will [5]raise [6]up [[1]the] [2]Lord [4]God [3]your from among
τῶν.ἀδελφῶν.ὑμῶν, ὡς ἐμέ· αὐτοῦ ἀκούσεσθε κατὰ πάντα
your brethren, like me: him shall ye hear in all things
ὅσα.ἂν λαλήσῃ πρὸς ὑμᾶς. 23 ἔσται.δὲ πᾶσα ψυχὴ
whatsoever he may say to you. And it shall be [that] every soul
ἥτις [a]ἂν".μὴ.ἀκούσῃ τοῦ.προφήτου.ἐκείνου [b]ἐξολοθρευθήσεται"
which may not hear that prophet shall be destroyed
ἐκ τοῦ λαοῦ. 24 Καὶ πάντες.δὲ οἱ προφῆται ἀπὸ
from among the people. And indeed all the prophets from
Σαμουὴλ καὶ τῶν καθεξῆς, ὅσοι ἐλάλησαν καὶ [c]προκατήγ-
Samuel and those subsequent, as many as spoke also before an-
γειλαν" τὰς.ἡμέρας.ταύτας. 25 ὑμεῖς ἐστε [d]υἱοὶ τῶν προφητῶν
nounced these days. Ye are sons of the prophets
καὶ τῆς διαθήκης ἧς [e]διέθετο ὁ θεὸς" πρὸς τοὺς πατέρας
and of the covenant which [2]appointed [1]God to [2]fathers
[f]ἡμῶν," λέγων πρὸς Ἀβραάμ, Καὶ [g]τῷ.σπέρματί.σου ἐνευλο-
[1]our, saying to Abraham, And in thy seed shall be
γηθήσονται πᾶσαι αἱ πατριαὶ τῆς γῆς. 26 ὑμῖν πρῶτον
blessed all the families of the earth. To you first
[h]ὁ θεὸς ἀναστήσας" τὸν.παῖδα.αὐτοῦ [i]Ἰησοῦν," ἀπέστειλεν
God, having raised up his servant Jesus, sent
αὐτὸν εὐλογοῦντα ὑμᾶς ἐν τῷ ἀποστρέφειν ἕκαστον ἀπὸ
him, blessing you in turning each from
τῶν πονηριῶν [k]ὑμῶν."
[2]wickedness [1]your.

4 Λαλούντων.δὲ αὐτῶν πρὸς τὸν λαόν, ἐπέστησαν αὐτοῖς
And as [2]were [3]speaking [1]they to the people, came upon them
οἱ ἱερεῖς καὶ ὁ στρατηγὸς τοῦ ἱεροῦ καὶ οἱ Σαδδουκαῖοι,
the priests and captain of the temple and the Sadducees,
2 διαπονούμενοι διὰ τὸ διδάσκειν αὐτοὺς τὸν λαόν, καὶ
being distressed because [2]teach [1]they the people, and
καταγγέλλειν ἐν τῷ Ἰησοῦ τὴν ἀνάστασιν τὴν ἐκ
announce in Jesus the resurrection which [is] from among
νεκρῶν· 3 καὶ ἐπέβαλον αὐτοῖς τὰς χεῖρας καὶ ἔθεντο
[the] dead; and they laid [2]on [3]them [1]hands and put
εἰς τήρησιν εἰς τὴν αὔριον· ἦν.γὰρ ἑσπέρα ἤδη.
[them] in hold till the morrow; for it was evening already.
4 πολλοὶ.δὲ τῶν ἀκουσάντων τὸν λόγον ἐπίστευσαν,
But many of those who had heard the word believed,
καὶ ἐγενήθη [m]ὁ" ἀριθμὸς τῶν ἀνδρῶν [n]ὡσεὶ" χιλιάδες πέντε.
and [6]became [1]the [2]number [3]of [4]the [5]men about [2]thousand [1]five.
5 Ἐγένετο.δὲ ἐπὶ τὴν αὔριον συναχθῆναι αὐτῶν
And it came to pass on the morrow were gathered together their
τοὺς ἄρχοντας καὶ [o]πρεσβυτέρους καὶ [o]γραμματεῖς [p]εἰς" Ἱε-
rulers and elders and scribes at Je-
ρουσαλήμ, 6 καὶ [q]Ἄνναν τὸν ἀρχιερέα καὶ Καϊάφαν καὶ
rusalem, and Annas the high priest and Caiaphas and
Ἰωάννην καὶ Ἀλέξανδρον," καὶ ὅσοι ἦσαν ἐκ γένους
John and Alexander, and as many as were of [2]family
ἀρχιερατικοῦ. 7 καὶ στήσαντες αὐτοὺς ἐν [r]τῷ" μέσῳ ἐπυν-
[1]high-priestly. And having placed them in the midst they
θάνοντο, Ἐν ποίᾳ δυνάμει ἢ ἐν ποίῳ ὀνόματι [s]ἐποιήσατε
inquired, In what power or in what name did
τοῦτο" ὑμεῖς; 8 Τότε Πέτρος πλησθεὶς πνεύματος ἁγίου
[2]this [1]ye? Then Peter, filled with [the] [2]Spirit [1]Holy,
εἶπεν πρὸς αὐτούς, Ἄρχοντες τοῦ λαοῦ καὶ πρεσβύτεροι
said to them, Rulers of the people and elders
[t]τοῦ Ἰσραήλ," 9 εἰ ἡμεῖς σήμερον ἀνακρινόμεθα ἐπὶ εὐεργεσίᾳ
of Israel, If we this day are examined as to a good work
ἀνθρώπου.ἀσθενοῦς, ἐν τίνι οὗτος [v]σέσωσται," 10 γνωστὸν
[to the] infirm man, by what he has been cured, [3]known
ἔστω πᾶσιν ὑμῖν καὶ παντὶ τῷ λαῷ Ἰσραήλ, ὅτι ἐν τῷ
[1]be [2]it to all you and to all the people of Israel, that in the
ὀνόματι Ἰησοῦ χριστοῦ τοῦ Ναζωραίου, ὃν ὑμεῖς ἐσταυ-
name of Jesus Christ the Nazaræan, whom ye cruci-

19 Then repent and be converted, for the blotting out of your sins, so that the times of refreshing from the presence of the Lord may come,
20 and that He may send Him who was before preached to you, Jesus Christ,
21 whom Heaven must indeed receive until the times when all things shall be restored, of which God spoke by the mouth of all His holy prophets since the world began.

22 For Moses indeed said to the fathers, "The Lord your God will raise up a Prophet to you from among your brothers, *one* like me. You shall hear Him in all things, whatever He may say to you.

23 And it shall be true that every soul who will not listen to that Prophet shall be destroyed from among the people."
24 Yes, and all the prophets from Samuel, and those following, as many as spoke, also told of these things beforehand.

25 You are sons of the prophets and of the covenant which God made with our fathers, saying to Abraham, "And in your Seed shall all the families of the earth be blessed."
26 When He had raised up His Son Jesus, God sent Him to you first, blessing you in turning each one away from your sins.

CHAPTER 4

1 And as they were speaking to the people, the priests and the captain of the Temple and the Sad-du-cees came to them,
2 being much disturbed because they were teaching the people and preaching the resurrection which is from among the dead by Jesus.
3 And they seized them and put them under guard until the next day, for it was evening already.
4 But many of those who had heard the word believed. And the number of the men was about five thousand.
5 And on the next day their rulers and elders and scribes were gathered at Jerusalem.
6 And Annas the high priest, and Cai-a-phas and John and Alexander, and as many as were of the high-priestly family *were there.*
7 And when they had put them in the middle, they asked, By what power or by what name did you do this?
8 Then being filled with the Holy Spirit, Peter said to them, Rulers of the people and elders of Israel,
9 if we are tried today as to the good work *to the* lame man, by what he has been cured,
10 let it be known to you all and to all the people of Israel that in the name of Jesus Christ the Nazarene, whom you crucified, whom God raised from the dead – it is by Him that this one stands before you sound.

ρώσατε, ὃν ὁ θεὸς ἤγειρεν ἐκ νεκρῶν, ἐν τούτῳ
fied, whom God raised from among [the] dead, by him
οὗτος παρέστηκεν ἐνώπιον ὑμῶν ὑγιής. 11 οὗτός ἐστιν ὁ
this [man] stands before you sound. This is the
λίθος ὁ ἐξουθενηθεὶς ὑφ' ὑμῶν τῶν [w]οἰκοδομούντων,"
stone which has been set at nought by you the builders,
ὁ γενόμενος εἰς κεφαλὴν γωνίας. 12 καὶ οὐκ ἔστιν
which is become head of [the] corner. And there is
ἐν ἄλλῳ οὐδενὶ ἡ σωτηρία· [x]οὔτε".γὰρ ὄνομά ἐστιν ἕτερον
in [2]other [1]no one salvation, for neither [4]name [1]is [2]there [3]another
ὑπὸ τὸν οὐρανὸν τὸ δεδομένον ἐν ἀνθρώποις, ἐν ᾧ
under the heaven which has been given among men, by which
δεῖ σωθῆναι ἡμᾶς.
[2]must [3]be [4]saved [1]we.
13 Θεωροῦντες.δὲ τὴν τοῦ Πέτρου παῤῥησίαν καὶ [y]Ἰωάν-
But seeing the [2]of [3]Peter [1]boldness and of John,
νου," καὶ καταλαβόμενοι ὅτι ἄνθρωποι ἀγράμματοί εἰσιν
and having perceived that [3]men [4]unlettered [1]they [2]are
καὶ ἰδιῶται, ἐθαύμαζον, ἐπεγίνωσκόν.τε αὐτοὺς ὅτι σὺν τῷ
and uninstructed, they wondered, and they recognized them that with
Ἰησοῦ ἦσαν. 14 τὸν.[z]δὲ" ἄνθρωπον βλέποντες σὺν αὐτοῖς
Jesus they were. But [2]the [3]man [1]beholding [5]with [6]them
ἑστῶτα τὸν τεθεραπευμένον, οὐδὲν εἶχον ἀντειπεῖν. 15 κελεύ-
[4]standing who had been healed, nothing they had to gainsay. [2]Having
σαντες δὲ αὐτοὺς ἔξω τοῦ συνεδρίου ἀπελθεῖν [a]συνέβαλον"
[3]commanded [1]but them outside the sanhedrim to go they conferred
πρὸς ἀλλήλους, 16 λέγοντες, Τί [b]ποιήσομεν" τοῖς ἀνθρώ-
with one another, saying, What shall we do to [2]men
ποις τούτοις; ὅτι.μὲν.γὰρ γνωστὸν σημεῖον γέγονεν
[1]these? for that indeed a known sign has come to pass
δι' αὐτῶν, πᾶσιν τοῖς κατοικοῦσιν Ἱερουσαλὴμ φανερόν,
through them, [3]to [4]all [5]those [6]inhabiting [7]Jerusalem [[1]is] [2]manifest,
καὶ οὐ.δυνάμεθα [c]ἀρνήσασθαι·" 17 ἀλλ' ἵνα μὴ ἐπὶ.πλεῖον
and we are unable to deny [it]. But that not further
διανεμηθῇ εἰς τὸν λαόν, [d]ἀπειλῇ" ἀπειλησώμεθα αὐτοῖς
it may spread among the people, with a threat let us threaten them
μηκέτι λαλεῖν ἐπὶ τῷ.ὀνόματι.τούτῳ μηδενὶ ἀνθρώπων.
no longer to speak in this name to any man.
(lit. to no)
18 Καὶ καλέσαντες αὐτοὺς παρήγγειλαν [e]αὐτοῖς" [f]τὸ" καθόλου
And having called them they charged them [2]at [3]all
μὴ φθέγγεσθαι μηδὲ διδάσκειν ἐπὶ τῷ ὀνόματι τοῦ Ἰησοῦ.
[1]not to speak nor to teach in the name of Jesus.
19 ὁ.δὲ.Πέτρος καὶ [g]Ἰωάννης" ἀποκριθέντες [h]πρὸς αὐτοὺς
But Peter and John answering to them
εἶπον," Εἰ δίκαιόν ἐστιν ἐνώπιον τοῦ θεοῦ ὑμῶν ἀκούειν
said, Whether right it is before God [3]to [4]you [1]to [2]listen
μᾶλλον ἢ τοῦ θεοῦ κρίνατε. 20 οὐ.δυνάμεθα γὰρ ἡμεῖς ἃ
rather than God, judge ye; [3]cannot [1]for [2]we [6]what
[i]εἴδομεν" καὶ ἠκούσαμεν μὴ.λαλεῖν. 21 Οἱ.δὲ προσαπειλη-
[7]we [8]saw [9]and [10]heard [4]not [5]speak. But they having further
σάμενοι ἀπέλυσαν αὐτούς, μηδὲν εὑρίσκοντες τὸ.πῶς κολά-
threatened let [2]go [1]them, nothing finding as to how they might
σωνται αὐτοὺς διὰ τὸν λαόν, ὅτι πάντες ἐδόξαζον
punish them on account of the people, because all were glorifying
τὸν θεὸν ἐπὶ τῷ γεγονότι. 22 ἐτῶν.γὰρ ἦν
God for that which has taken place; for [6]years [[7]old] [3]was
πλειόνων [k]τεσσαράκοντα" ὁ ἄνθρωπος ἐφ' ὃν [l]ἐγεγόνει"
[4]above [5]forty [1]the [2]man on whom had taken place
τὸ.σημεῖον.τοῦτο τῆς ἰάσεως.
this sign of healing.
23 Ἀπολυθέντες.δὲ ἦλθον πρὸς τοὺς.ἰδίους, καὶ
And having been let go they came to their own [company], and
ἀπήγγειλαν ὅσα πρὸς αὐτοὺς οἱ ἀρχιερεῖς καὶ οἱ πρεσ-
reported whatever to them the chief priests and the el-
βύτεροι [m]εἶπον." 24 οἱ.δὲ ἀκούσαντες, ὁμοθυμαδὸν ἦραν
ders said. And they having heard, with one accord lifted up
φωνὴν πρὸς τὸν θεόν, καὶ [m]εἶπον," Δέσποτα, σὺ [n]ὁ
[their] voice to God, and said, O master, thou [art] the
θεὸς" ὁ ποιήσας τὸν οὐρανὸν καὶ τὴν γῆν καὶ τὴν θάλασσαν
God who made the heaven and the earth and the sea
καὶ πάντα τὰ ἐν αὐτοῖς, 25 [o]ὁ διὰ στόματος" [p]Δαβὶδ"
and all that [are] in them, who by [the] mouth of David
[q]τοῦ".παιδός.σου εἰπών, [r]Ἱνατί" ἐφρύαξαν ἔθνη, καὶ
thy servant didst say, Why did [2]rage [3]haughtily [1]nations, and
λαοὶ ἐμελέτησαν κενά; 26 παρέστησαν οἱ βασιλεῖς τῆς
[2]peoples [1]did meditate vain things? Stood up the kings of the
γῆς, καὶ οἱ ἄρχοντες συνήχθησαν ἐπὶ.τὸ.αὐτὸ κατὰ τοῦ
earth, and the rulers were gathered together against the
κυρίου καὶ κατὰ τοῦ.χριστοῦ.αὐτοῦ. 27 Συνήχθησαν.γὰρ
Lord and against his Christ. For were gathered together
ἐπ'.ἀληθείας [s] ἐπὶ τὸν ἅγιον παῖδά σου Ἰησοῦν, ὃν
of a truth against [2]holy [3]servant [1]thy Jesus, whom

11 This is the Stone which you builders have counted worthless, which has become the Head of the corner.

12 And neither is there salvation in any other, for there is no other name under Heaven given among men by which we must be saved.

13 And seeing the boldness of Peter and of John, and having become aware that they were without learning or education, they wondered. And they took note of them, that they had been with Jesus.

14 And looking at the man who had been healed standing with them, they had nothing to reply.

15 But having ordered them to go outside the san-he-drin, they counseled together,

16 saying, What shall we do to these men? For that a truly notable miracle has taken place through them is plain to all those living in Jerusalem, and we are not able to deny it.

17 But that it spread no further among the people, let us threaten them strictly to speak no more in this name to any man.

18 And having called them, they ordered them not to teach or speak at all in the name of Jesus.

19 But Peter and John answered them and said, Whether it is right before God to listen to you rather than to God, you judge.

20 For we cannot keep from speaking what we saw and heard.

21 But after further threatening, they let them go, finding nothing for which they could punish them (on account of the people) for all the people were glorifying God for that which had been done.

22 For the man on whom this miracle had been performed was over forty years old.

23 And when they had been released, they came to their own friends and told them what the chief priests and the elders said.

24 And having heard, with one accord they lifted up their voice to God and said, O Lord, You are God who made the sky and the earth and the sea, and all that are in them,

25 *the One* who said by the mouth of Your servant David, "Why did the heathen rage and the peoples think foolish things?

26 The kings of the earth stood up and the rulers were gathered together against the Lord and against His Christ."

27 For indeed both Herod and Pontius Pilate, with the heathen and the peoples of Israel, were gathered together against Your holy child Jesus, whom You anointed,

ἔχρισας, [s]Ἡρώδης.τε καὶ Πόντιος [t]Πιλάτος," σὺν ἔθνεσιν
thou didst anoint, both Herod and Pontius Pilate, with nations
καὶ λαοῖς Ἰσραήλ, 28 ποιῆσαι ὅσα ἡ.χείρ.σου καὶ ἡ βουλή
and peoples of Israel, to do whatever thy hand and [2]counsel
[u]σου" προώρισεν γενέσθαι. 29 καὶ τὰ νῦν, κύριε, [v]ἔπιδε"
[1]thy predetermined to come to pass. And now, Lord, look
ἐπὶ τὰς.ἀπειλὰς.αὐτῶν, καὶ δὸς τοῖς.δούλοις.σου μετὰ παρ-
upon their threatenings, and give to thy bondmen with [2]bold-
ῥησίας πάσης λαλεῖν τὸν.λόγον.σου, 30 ἐν τῷ τὴν.χεῖρά.[w]σου"
ness [1]all to speak thy word, in that thy hand
ἐκτείνειν [x]σε" εἰς ἴασιν, καὶ.σημεῖα καὶ τέρατα γίνεσθαι
[2]stretchest [3]out [1]thou for healing, and signs and wonders take place
διὰ τοῦ ὀνόματος τοῦ ἁγίου παιδός σου Ἰησοῦ. 31 Καὶ
through the name [3]holy [4]servant [1]of [2]thy Jesus. And
δεηθέντων αὐτῶν ἐσαλεύθη ὁ τόπος ἐν ᾧ ἦσαν συνηγ-
[2]having [3]prayed [1]they [6]was [7]shaken [4]the [5]place in which they were assem-
μένοι, καὶ ἐπλήσθησαν ἅπαντες [y]πνεύματος ἁγίου," καὶ
bled, and they were [2]filled [1]all with [the] [2]Spirit [1]Holy, and
ἐλάλουν τὸν λόγον τοῦ θεοῦ μετὰ παῤῥησίας.
spoke the word of God with boldness.

32 Τοῦ.δὲ πλήθους τῶν πιστευσάντων ἦν [z]ἡ" καρδία
And of the multitude of those that believed [6]were [1]the [2]heart
καὶ [a]ἡ" ψυχὴ μία· καὶ [b]οὐδὲ" εἷς τι τῶν ὑπαρ-
[3]and [4]the [5]soul one, and not one [2]anything [3]of [4]that [5]which [7]pos-
χόντων αὐτῷ ἔλεγεν ἴδιον εἶναι, ἀλλ' ἦν αὐτοῖς [c]ἅπαντα"
sessed [6]he [1]said [9]his [10]own [8]was, [11]but [14]were [15]to [16]them [12]all [13]things
κοινά. 33 καὶ [d]μεγάλῃ δυνάμει" ἀπεδίδουν τὸ μαρτύριον
common. And with great power [3]gave [4]testimony
οἱ ἀπόστολοι [e]τῆς ἀναστάσεως τοῦ κυρίου Ἰησοῦ," χάρις.τε
[1]the [2]apostles of the resurrection of the Lord Jesus, and [2]grace
μεγάλη ἦν ἐπὶ πάντας αὐτούς. 34 οὐδὲ.γὰρ ἐνδεής τις
[1]great was upon all them. For neither in want [2]anyone
[f]ὑπῆρχεν" ἐν αὐτοῖς· ὅσοι.γὰρ κτήτορες χωρίων ἢ οἰκιῶν
[1]was among them; for as many as owners of estates or houses
ὑπῆρχον, πωλοῦντες ἔφερον τὰς τιμὰς τῶν πιπρα-
were, selling [them] brought the values of those sold,
σκομένων, 35 καὶ ἐτίθουν παρὰ τοὺς πόδας τῶν ἀπο-
and laid [them] at the feet of the apos-
στόλων· [g]διεδίδοτο".δὲ ἑκάστῳ καθότι.ἂν τις χρείαν
tles; and distribution was made to each according as anyone [2]need
εἶχεν.
[1]had.

36 [h]Ἰωσῆς".δὲ ὁ ἐπικληθεὶς Βαρνάβας [i]ὑπὸ" τῶν ἀπο-
And Joses who was surnamed Barnabas by the apos-
στόλων, ὅ ἐστιν μεθερμηνευόμενον, υἱὸς παρακλήσεως,
tles (which is, being interpreted, Son of consolation),
[k]Λευΐτης," Κύπριος τῷ.γένει, 37 ὑπάρχοντος αὐτῷ ἀγροῦ,
a Levite, a Cypriot by birth, having land,
πωλήσας ἤνεγκεν τὸ χρῆμα καὶ ἔθηκεν [l]παρὰ" τοὺς πόδας
having sold [it] brought the money and laid [it] at the feet
τῶν ἀποστόλων 5 Ἀνὴρ.δέ τις [m]Ἀνανίας ὀνόματι,"
of the apostles. But [3]man [1]a [2]certain, Ananias by name,
σὺν [n]Σαπφείρῃ" τῇ.γυναικὶ.αὐτοῦ, ἐπώλησεν κτῆμα, 2 καὶ
with Sapphira his wife, sold a possession, and
ἐνοσφίσατο ἀπὸ τῆς τιμῆς, [o]συνειδυίας" καὶ τῆς γυναικὸς
kept back from the value, being aware of [it] also [2]wife
[p]αὐτοῦ," καὶ ἐνέγκας μέρος.τι παρὰ τοὺς πόδας τῶν
[1]his, and having brought a certain part [3]at [4]the [5]feet [6]of [7]the
ἀποστόλων ἔθηκεν. 3 εἶπεν.δὲ [q] Πέτρος, Ἀνανία, [r]διατί"
[8]apostles [1]laid [[2]it]. But said Peter, Ananias, why
ἐπλήρωσεν ὁ σατανᾶς τὴν.καρδίαν.σου, ψεύσασθαί σε τὸ
did [2]fill [1]Satan thy heart, [3]to [4]lie [5]to [[1]for] [2]thee the
πνεῦμα τὸ ἅγιον, καὶ νοσφίσασθαι [s] ἀπὸ τῆς τιμῆς τοῦ
Spirit the Holy, and to keep back from the value of the
χωρίου; 4 οὐχὶ μένον σοὶ ἔμενεν; καὶ πραθὲν
estate? [6]Not [1]remaining [2]to [3]thee [4]did [5]it remain? and having been sold,
ἐν τῇ.σῇ ἐξουσίᾳ ὑπῆρχεν; τί ὅτι ἔθου ἐν τῇ
in thine own authority was it [not]? why didst thou purpose in
καρδίᾳ.σου τὸ.πρᾶγμα.τοῦτο; οὐκ.ἐψεύσω ἀνθρώποις, ἀλλὰ
thy heart this thing? Thou didst not lie to men, but
τῷ θεῷ. 5 Ἀκούων.δὲ [t] Ἀνανίας τοὺς.λόγους.τούτους, πεσὼν
to God. And [2]hearing [1]Ananias these words, falling down
ἐξέψυξεν· καὶ ἐγένετο φόβος μέγας ἐπὶ πάντας τοὺς
expired. And [3]came [2]fear [1]great upon all who
ἀκούοντας [v]ταῦτα." 6 ἀναστάντες.δὲ οἱ νεώτεροι συνέ-
heard these things. And having risen the younger [men] swathed
στειλαν αὐτόν, καὶ ἐξενέγκαντες ἔθαψαν. 7 Ἐγένετο.δὲ
him, and having carried out buried [him]. And it came to pass
ὡς ὡρῶν τριῶν διάστημα καὶ ἡ.γυνὴ.αὐτοῦ μὴ εἰδυῖα τὸ
about [2]hours [1]three afterwards also his wife, not knowing what
γεγονὸς εἰσῆλθεν. 8 ἀπεκρίθη.δὲ [w]αὐτῇ" [x]ὁ" Πέτρος,
had come to pass, came in. And answered her Peter,

28 to do whatever Your hand and counsel before determined to be done.

29 And now, O Lord, look on their threats, and grant to Your servants to speak Your word with all boldness

30 in the stretching out of Your hand for healing and miracles and wonders to take place through the name of Your holy child Jesus.

31 And when they had prayed, the place in which they had gathered was shaken. And they were filled with the Holy Spirit. And they spoke the word of God with boldness.

32 And of the multitude of those who did believe, their hearts and their souls were one. And no one said that anything which he owned was his own, but all things were common to them.

33 And with great power the apostles told of the resurrection of the Lord Jesus, and great grace was on all of them.

34 For neither was there anyone among them in need, for as many as were owners of land sold them and brought the values of the things sold.

35 And they laid *them* down at the feet of the apostles. And it was given out to each as anyone had need.

36 And Joses, a Levite, who was born in Cyprus, was given the last name of Barnabas by the apostles (which means, Son of consolation).

37 He had land and sold it, bringing the money and laying it at the feet of the apostles.

CHAPTER 5

1 But a certain man named An-a-ni-as and his wife Sap-phi-ra sold a possession

2 and kept back part of the price, his wife also being aware of this. And he brought a certain part and laid it at the feet of the apostles.

3 But Peter said, An-a-ni-as, why did Satan fill your heart for you to lie to the Holy Spirit and to keep part of the land price?

4 While it remained, did it not belong to you? And when it was sold, was it *not* in your own power? Why did you think this thing in your heart? You did not lie to men, but to God!

5 And An-a-ni-as hearing these words fell down and died. And great fear came on all who heard these things.

6 And the younger men got up and wrapped him and carried him out and buried him.

7 And about three hours later his wife came in, not knowing what had happened.

8 And Peter answered her, Tell me if you

Εἰπέ μοι εἰ τοσούτου τὸ χωρίον ἀπέδοσθε; Ἡ.δὲ εἶπεν,
Tell me if for so much the estate ye sold? And she said,
Ναί, τοσούτου. 9 Ὁ.δὲ.Πέτρος [y]εἶπεν‖ πρὸς αὐτήν, Τί
Yes, for so much. And Peter said to her, Why [is it]
ὅτι συνεφωνήθη.ὑμῖν πειράσαι τὸ πνεῦμα κυρίου; ἰδού, οἱ
that ye agreed together to tempt the Spirit of [the] Lord? Lo, the
πόδες τῶν θαψάντων τὸν.ἄνδρα.σου ἐπὶ τῇ θύρᾳ, καὶ
feet of those who buried thy husband [are] at the door, and
ἐξοίσουσίν σε. 10 Ἔπεσεν.δὲ παραχρῆμα [z]παρὰ‖ τοὺς
they shall carry out thee. And she fell down immediately at
πόδας.αὐτοῦ καὶ ἐξέψυξεν· εἰσελθόντες.δὲ οἱ νεανίσκοι
his feet and expired. And having come in the young [men]
[a]εὗρον‖ αὐτὴν νεκράν, καὶ ἐξενέγκαντες ἔθαψαν πρὸς
found her dead; and having carried out they buried [her] by
τὸν.ἄνδρα.αὐτῆς. 11 καὶ ἐγένετο φόβος μέγας ἐφ' ὅλην τὴν
her husband. And 3came 2fear 1great upon 2whole 1the
ἐκκλησίαν, καὶ ἐπὶ πάντας τοὺς ἀκούοντας ταῦτα. 12 Διὰ.δὲ
assembly, and upon all who heard these things. And by
τῶν χειρῶν τῶν ἀποστόλων [b]ἐγένετο‖ σημεῖα καὶ τέρατα
the hands of the apostles came to pass 2signs 3and 4wonders
[c]ἐν τῷ λαῷ πολλά·‖ καὶ ἦσαν ὁμοθυμαδὸν [d]ἅπαντες‖
5among 6the 7people 1many; (and they were 2with 3one 4accord 1all
ἐν τῇ στοᾷ [e]Σολομῶντος·‖ 13 τῶν.δὲ λοιπῶν οὐδεὶς ἐτόλμα
in the porch of Solomon, but of the rest no one durst
κολλᾶσθαι αὐτοῖς, ἀλλ' ἐμεγάλυνεν αὐτοὺς ὁ λαός· 14 μᾶλλον
join them, but 3magnified 4them 1the 2people; 5the 6more
δὲ προσετίθεντο πιστεύοντες τῷ κυρίῳ, πλήθη ἀνδρῶν.τε
8and 7were 10added 9believers to the Lord, multitudes both of men
καὶ γυναικῶν· 15 ὥστε [f]κατὰ‖ τὰς πλατείας ἐκφέρειν τοὺς
and women;) so as in the streets to bring out the
ἀσθενεῖς καὶ τιθέναι ἐπὶ [g]κλινῶν‖ καὶ [h]κραββάτων,‖ ἵνα
sick, and put [them] on beds and couches, that
ἐρχομένου Πέτρου κἂν ἡ σκιὰ [i]ἐπισκιάσῃ‖ τινὶ
7coming 5of 6Peter 1at 2least 3the 4shadow might overshadow some one
αὐτῶν. 16 συνήρχετο.δὲ καὶ τὸ πλῆθος τῶν πέριξ
of them. And came together also the multitude of the 2round 3about
πόλεων [k]εἰς‖ Ἱερουσαλήμ, φέροντες ἀσθενεῖς καὶ ὀχλου-
1cities to Jerusalem, bringing sick ones and those
μένους ὑπὸ πνευμάτων ἀκαθάρτων, οἵτινες ἐθεραπεύοντο
beset by 3spirits 1unclean. who were 2healed
ἅπαντες.
1all.

17 Ἀναστὰς.δὲ ὁ ἀρχιερεὺς καὶ πάντες οἱ σὺν αὐτῷ,
And having risen up the high priest and all those with him,
ἡ οὖσα αἵρεσις τῶν Σαδδουκαίων, ἐπλήσθησαν ζήλου,
which is [the] sect of the Sadducees, were filled with anger,
18 καὶ ἐπέβαλον τὰς χεῖρας [l]αὐτῶν‖ ἐπὶ τοὺς ἀποστόλους καὶ
and laid 2hands 1their on the apostles and
ἔθεντο αὐτοὺς ἐν τηρήσει δημοσίᾳ. 19 ἄγγελος.δὲ κυρίου
put them in [the] 2hold 1public. But an angel of [the] Lord
διὰ [m]τῆς‖ νυκτὸς [n]ἤνοιξεν‖ τὰς θύρας τῆς φυλακῆς,
during the night opened the doors of the prison,
ἐξαγαγών.τε αὐτοὺς εἶπεν, 20 Πορεύεσθε, καὶ σταθέντες
and having brought 2out 1them said, Go ye, and standing
λαλεῖτε ἐν τῷ ἱερῷ τῷ λαῷ πάντα τὰ ῥήματα τῆς ζωῆς
speak in the temple to the people all the words of 2life
ταύτης. 21 Ἀκούσαντες.δὲ εἰσῆλθον ὑπὸ τὸν ὄρθρον εἰς τὸ
1this. And having heard they entered at the dawn into the
ἱερόν, καὶ ἐδίδασκον. παραγενόμενος.δὲ ὁ ἀρχιερεὺς καὶ οἱ
temple, and were teaching. But having come the high priest and those
σὺν αὐτῷ, συνεκάλεσαν τὸ συνέδριον καὶ πᾶσαν τὴν γερου-
with him, they called together the sanhedrim and all the elder-
σίαν τῶν υἱῶν Ἰσραήλ, καὶ ἀπέστειλαν εἰς τὸ δεσμωτήριον
hood of the sons of Israel, and sent to the prison
ἀχθῆναι.αὐτούς. 22 οἱ.δὲ [o]ὑπηρέται παραγενόμενοι‖ οὐχ
to have them brought. But the officers having come 2not
εὗρον αὐτοὺς ἐν τῇ φυλακῇ· ἀναστρέψαντες.δὲ ἀπήγγειλαν,
1did find them in the prison; and having returned they reported,
23 λέγοντες, Ὅτι τὸ [p]μὲν‖ δεσμωτήριον εὕρομεν κεκλεισ-
saying, The 2indeed 1prison we found shut
μένον ἐν πάσῃ ἀσφαλείᾳ, καὶ τοὺς φύλακας [q]ἔξω‖ ἑστῶτας
with all security, and the keepers without standing
[r]πρὸ‖ τῶν θυρῶν· ἀνοίξαντες.δέ, ἔσω οὐδένα εὕρομεν.
before the doors; but having opened, within no one we found.
24 Ὡς.δὲ ἤκουσαν τοὺς.λόγους.τούτους ὅ.τε [s]ἱερεὺς καὶ
And when they heard these words both the priest and
ὁ‖ στρατηγὸς τοῦ ἱεροῦ καὶ οἱ ἀρχιερεῖς διηπόρουν περὶ
the captain of the temple and the chief priests were perplexed concerning
αὐτῶν, τί ἂν.γένοιτο τοῦτο. 25 παραγενόμενος.δέ τις
them, what 2might 3be 1this. But having come a certain one
ἀπήγγειλεν αὐτοῖς [t]λέγων,‖ Ὅτι ἰδοὺ οἱ ἄνδρες οὓς ἔθεσθε
reported to them, saying, Lo, the men whom ye put

sold the land for this much? And she said, Yes, for that much.

9 And Peter said to her, Why did you agree together to tempt the Spirit of the Lord? Behold! The feet of those who buried your husband are at the door, and they will carry you out.

10 And she fell down at his feet and immediately died. And coming in, the younger men found her dead. And they carried *her* out and buried *her* beside her husband.

11 And great fear came on all the church and on all who heard these things.

12 And many miracles and wonders were worked among the people by the hands of the apostles. And they were all together in the porch of Solomon.

13 And of the rest no one dared join them, but the people greatly magnified them.

14 And the more believers were added to the Lord, myriads of both men and women.

15 They brought out the sick into the streets and put *them* on beds and couches so that at least the shadow of Peter might overshadow some one of them.

16 And also the crowds came together from the cities around Jerusalem bringing sick ones and those who were plagued by evil spirits – who were all healed.

17 And becoming aroused, the high priest and all those with him (which is the sect of the Sad-du-cees) were filled with anger.

18 And *they* seized the apostles and put them in the public prison.

19 But an angel of the Lord opened the prison doors during the night and brought them out, saying,

20 Go! Stand in the Temple and preach to the people all the words of this Life!

21 And having heard, they went into the Temple at dawn and were teaching. And the high priest and the ones with him arrived. And they called the san-he-drin together and all the senate of the sons of Israel. And *they* sent to the prison to have them brought.

22 But the officers that came did not find them in the prison. And returning, they reported,

23 saying, Indeed we found the prison shut with all safety, and the keepers standing outside in front of the doors, but when we had opened we did not find anyone inside.

24 And when they heard these words, both the priest and the captain of the Temple and the chief priests were bewildered about them – as to what this might come to.

25 But someone came and told them, saying, Behold! The men whom you put in the prison are in the Temple, standing and teaching the people.

ἐν τῇ φυλακῇ εἰσὶν ἐν τῷ ἱερῷ ἑστῶτες καὶ διδάσκοντες τὸν
in the prison are in the temple standing and teaching the
λαόν. 26 Τότε ἀπελθὼν ὁ στρατηγὸς σὺν τοῖς ὑπηρέταις
people. Then [3]having [4]gone [1]the [2]captain with the officers
[v]ἤγαγεν" αὐτούς, οὐ μετὰ βίας, ἐφοβοῦντο.γὰρ τὸν λαόν,
brought them, not with violence, for they feared the people,
[w]ἵνα" μὴ.λιθασθῶσιν. 27 ἀγαγόντες.δὲ αὐτοὺς ἔστησαν
that they might not be stoned. And having brought them they set
ἐν τῷ συνεδρίῳ· καὶ ἐπηρώτησεν αὐτοὺς ὁ ἀρχιερεύς,
[them] in the sanhedrim. And [4]asked [5]them [1]the [2]high [3]priest,
28 λέγων, [x]Οὐ" παραγγελίᾳ παρηγγείλαμεν ὑμῖν μὴ διδάσ-
saying, [3]Not [4]by [5]a [6]charge [1]did [2]we charge you not to teach
κειν ἐπι τῷ.ὀνόματι.τούτῳ [x];" καὶ ἰδοὺ πεπληρώκατε τὴν Ἰε-
in this name? and lo, ye have filled Je-
ρουσαλὴμ τῆς.διδαχῆς.ὑμῶν, καὶ βούλεσθε ἐπαγαγεῖν ἐφ
rusalem with your teaching, and purpose to bring upon
ἡμᾶς τὸ αἷμα τοῦ.ἀνθρώπου.τούτου. 29 Ἀποκριθεὶς.δὲ [y]ὁ"
us the blood of this man. But [5]answering
Πέτρος καὶ οἱ ἀπόστολοι [z]εἶπον," Πειθαρχεῖν δεῖ
[1]Peter [2]and [3]the [4]apostles said, [4]To [5]obey [1]it [2]is [3]necessary
θεῷ μᾶλλον ἢ ἀνθρώποις. 30 ὁ θεὸς τῶν.πατέρων.ἡμῶν
God rather than men. The God of our fathers
ἤγειρεν Ἰησοῦν, ὃν ὑμεῖς διεχειρίσασθε κρεμάσαντες ἐπὶ
raised up Jesus, whom ye killed, having hanged on
ξύλου· 31 τοῦτον ὁ θεὸς ἀρχηγὸν καὶ σωτῆρα ὕψωσεν τῇ
a tree. Him God a chief and Saviour exalted by the
δεξιᾷ αὐτοῦ, [a]δοῦναι μετάνοιαν τῷ Ἰσραὴλ καὶ ἄφεσιν
right hand of him, to give repentance to Israel and remission
ἁμαρτιῶν. 32 καὶ ἡμεῖς [b]ἐσμεν αὐτοῦ μάρτυρες" τῶν ῥημάτων
of sins. And we are of him witnesses of [2]things
τούτων, καὶ τὸ πνεῦμα [c]δὲ" τὸ ἅγιον, ὃ ἔδωκεν ὁ θεὸς
[1]these, and [2]the [3]Spirit [1]also the Holy, which [2]gave [1]God
τοῖς πειθαρχοῦσιν αὐτῷ. 33 Οἱ.δὲ ἀκούσαντες διεπρίοντο,
to those that obey him. But they having heard were cut
καὶ [d]ἐβουλεύοντο" ἀνελεῖν αὐτούς. 34 ἀναστὰς
[to the heart], and took counsel to put to death them. [7]Having [8]risen [9]up
δέ τις ἐν τῷ συνεδρίῳ Φαρισαῖος, ὀνόματι Γα-
[1]but [2]a [3]certain [[4]man] in the sanhedrim a Pharisee, by name Ga-
μαλιήλ, νομοδιδάσκαλος, τίμιος παντὶ τῷ λαῷ, ἐκέλευσεν
maliel, a teacher of the law, honoured by all the people, commanded
ἔξω βραχύ.[e]τι" [f]τοὺς ἀποστόλους" ποιῆσαι, 35 εἶπέν.τε
[3]out [4]for [5]a [6]short [7]while [8]the [9]apostles [1]to [2]put, and said
πρὸς αὐτούς, Ἄνδρες [g]Ἰσραηλῖται," προσέχετε ἑαυτοῖς
to them, Men Israelites, take heed to yourselves
ἐπὶ τοῖς.ἀνθρώποις.τούτοις τί μέλλετε πράσσειν. 36 πρὸ
as regards these men what ye are about to do; [2]before
γὰρ τούτων τῶν ἡμερῶν ἀνέστη Θευδᾶς, λέγων εἶναί τινα
[1]for these days rose up Theudas, affirming [2]to [3]be [4]somebody
ἑαυτόν, ᾧ [h]προσεκολλήθη ἀριθμὸς ἀνδρῶν, ὡσεὶ" τετρα-
[1]himself, to whom were joined a number of men, about four
κοσίων· ὃς ἀνῃρέθη, καὶ πάντες ὅσοι ἐπείθοντο αὐτῷ
hundred; who was put to death, and all as many as were persuaded by him
διελύθησαν καὶ ἐγένοντο εἰς οὐδέν. 37 μετὰ τοῦτον ἀνέστη
were dispersed and came to nothing. After this one rose up
Ἰούδας ὁ Γαλιλαῖος ἐν ταῖς ἡμέραις τῆς ἀπογραφῆς, καὶ
Judas the Galilean in the days of the registration, and
ἀπέστησεν λαὸν [i]ἱκανὸν" ὀπίσω αὐτοῦ· κἀκεῖνος ἀπώλετο,
drew away [2]people [1]much after him; and he perished,
καὶ πάντες ὅσοι ἐπείθοντο αὐτῷ διεσκορπίσθησαν. 38 καὶ
and all as many as were persuaded by him were scattered abroad. And
τὰ νῦν λέγω ὑμῖν, ἀπόστητε ἀπὸ τῶν.ἀνθρώπων.τούτων, καὶ
now I say to you, Withdraw from these men, and
[k]ἐάσατε" αὐτούς· ὅτι ἐὰν ᾖ ἐξ ἀνθρώπων ἡ.βουλὴ.αὕτη ἢ
let [2]alone [1]them, for if [6]be [7]from [8]men [1]this [2]counsel [3]or
τὸ.ἔργον.τοῦτο, καταλυθήσεται· 39 εἰ.δὲ ἐκ θεοῦ ἐστιν,
[4]this [5]work, it will be overthrown; but if from God it be,
[l]οὐ.δύνασθε" καταλῦσαι [m]αὐτό," μήποτε καὶ θεομάχοι
ye are not able to overthrow it, lest also fighters against God
εὑρεθῆτε. 40 Ἐπείσθησαν.δὲ αὐτῷ· καὶ προσκαλεσάμενοι
ye be found. And they were persuaded by him; and having called to
τοὺς ἀποστόλους, δείραντες παρήγγειλαν μὴ λαλεῖν
[them] the apostles, having beaten they enjoined [them] not to speak
ἐπὶ τῷ ὀνόματι τοῦ Ἰησοῦ, καὶ ἀπέλυσαν [n]αὐτούς." 41 Οἱ
in the name of Jesus, and released them. They
μὲν οὖν ἐπορεύοντο χαίροντες ἀπὸ προσώπου τοῦ
therefore departed rejoicing from [the] presence of the
συνεδρίου ὅτι [o]ὑπὲρ τοῦ ὀνόματος αὐτοῦ κατηξιώθησαν"
sanhedrim that for the name of him they were accounted worthy
ἀτιμασθῆναι· 42 πᾶσάν.τε ἡμέραν ἐν τῷ ἱερῷ καὶ κατ᾽.οἶκον
to be dishonoured. And every day in the temple and in the houses
οὐκ.ἐπαύοντο διδάσκοντες καὶ εὐαγγελιζόμενοι [p]Ἰησοῦν
they ceased not teaching and announcing the glad tidings— Jesus

26 Then the captain, going with the officers brought them without force, for they feared that they might get stoned by the crowd.

27 And bringing them, they set them in the san-he-drin. And the high priest asked them,

28 saying, Did we not strictly command you not to teach in this name? And, look! You have filled Jerusalem with your teaching and intend to bring on us the blood of this man.

29 And Peter and the apostles answering said, It is right to obey God rather than man.

30 The God of our fathers raised up Jesus, whom you killed by crucifixion –

31 a Prince and a Savior *whom* God has exalted by His right hand in order to give repentance to Israel and remission of sins.

32 And we are His witnesses of these things, and the Holy Spirit also, whom God gave to those who obey Him.

33 But having heard, they were cut to the heart and plotted to put them to death.

34 But a certain Pharisee named Ga-mal-i-el, a teacher of the Law, honored by the people, rose up in the san-he-drin and commanded the apostles to be put out for a short while.

35 And *he* said to them, Men! Israelites! Be careful what you are doing as to these men.

36 For before these days Theu-das rose up, boasting himself to be somebody, to whom a number of men (about four hundred) were joined. *He* was killed and all of them were scattered and came to nothing, as many as were following him.

37 After this one, Judas the Galilean rose up in the days of the Census and drew away many people after him. He also was destroyed and all of them were scattered, as many as were following him.

38 And now I say to you, Draw back from these men and let them alone. For if this counsel or this work is of men it will be overthrown.

39 But if it is from God you are not able to overthrow it, for fear that you also may be found to be fighters against God.

40 And they were persuaded by him. And having called the apostles, they beat them and commanded them not to speak in the name of Jesus, then let them go.

41 Then they departed from the presence of the san-he-drin, rejoicing that they were thought worthy to suffer shame for His name.

42 And daily in the Temple and in the houses they did not stop teaching and preaching the gospel of Jesus Christ.

τὸν χριστόν.‖
the Christ.

6 Ἐν.δὲ ταῖς.ἡμέραις.ταύταις πληθυνόντων τῶν μαθητῶν
But in those days [3]multiplying [1]the [2]disciples
ἐγένετο γογγυσμὸς τῶν Ἑλληνιστῶν πρὸς τοὺς Ἑβραίους,
there arose a murmuring of the Hellenists against the Hebrews,
ὅτι παρεθεωροῦντο ἐν τῇ διακονίᾳ τῇ καθημερινῇ αἱ
because were overlooked in the [2]ministration [1]daily
χῆραι.αὐτῶν. 2 προσκαλεσάμενοι.δὲ οἱ δώδεκα τὸ πλῆθος
their widows. And [3]having [4]called [5]to [[6]them] [1]the [2]twelve the multitude
τῶν μαθητῶν, [q]εἶπον,‖ Οὐκ ἀρεστόν ἐστιν ἡμᾶς, καταλείψαν-
of the disciples, said, Not seemly it is [for] us, leaving
τας τὸν λόγον τοῦ θεοῦ, διακονεῖν τραπέζαις. 3 ἐπισκέψασθε
the word of God, to attend tables. Look out
[r]οὖν,‖ [s]ἀδελφοί,‖ ἄνδρας ἐξ ὑμῶν μαρτυρουμένους
therefore, brethren, [2]men [3]from [4]among [5]yourselves, [6]borne [7]witness [8]to
ἑπτά, πλήρεις πνεύματος [t]ἁγίου‖ καὶ σοφίας, οὓς [v]κατα-
[1]seven, full of [the] [2]Spirit [1]Holy and wisdom, whom we will
στήσομεν‖ ἐπὶ τῆς.χρείας.ταύτης· 4 ἡμεῖς.δὲ τῇ προσευχῇ
appoint over this business; but we to prayer
καὶ τῇ διακονίᾳ τοῦ λόγου προσκαρτερήσομεν. 5 Καὶ
and the ministry of the word will steadfastly continue. And
ἤρεσεν ὁ λόγος ἐνώπιον παντὸς τοῦ πλήθους· καὶ
[3]was [4]pleasing [1]the [2]saying before all the multitude; and
ἐξελέξαντο Στέφανον, ἄνδρα [w]πλήρη‖ πίστεως καὶ πνεύ-
they chose Stephen, a man full of faith and [the] [2]Spi-
ματος ἁγίου, καὶ Φίλιππον, καὶ Πρόχορον, καὶ Νικάνορα, καὶ
rit [1]Holy, and Philip, and Prochorus, and Nicanor, and
Τίμωνα, καὶ Παρμενᾶν, καὶ Νικόλαον προσήλυτον Ἀντιοχέα,
Timon, and Parmenas, and Nicolas a proselyte of Antioch,
6 οὓς ἔστησαν ἐνώπιον τῶν ἀποστόλων· καὶ προσευξάμενοι
whom they set before the apostles; and having prayed
ἐπέθηκαν αὐτοῖς τὰς χεῖρας. 7 καὶ ὁ λόγος τοῦ θεοῦ
they laid [2]on [3]them [1]hands. And the word of God
ηὔξανεν, καὶ ἐπληθύνετο ὁ ἀριθμὸς τῶν μαθητῶν ἐν Ἰε-
increased, and [6]was [7]multiplied [1]the [2]number [3]of [4]the [5]disciples in Je-
ρουσαλὴμ σφόδρα, πολύς.τε ὄχλος τῶν ἱερέων ὑπήκουον
rusalem exceedingly, and a great multitude of the priests were obedient
τῇ πίστει.
to the faith.

8 Στέφανος.δὲ πλήρης [x]πίστεως‖ καὶ δυνάμεως ἐποίει
And Stephen, full of faith and power, wrought
τέρατα καὶ σημεῖα μεγάλα ἐν τῷ λαῷ. 9 ἀνέστησαν.δέ
wonders and [2]signs [1]great among the people. And arose
τινες τῶν ἐκ τῆς συναγωγῆς [y]τῆς λεγομένης‖ Λιβερτίνων,
certain of those of the synagogue called Libertines,
καὶ Κυρηναίων, καὶ Ἀλεξανδρέων, καὶ τῶν ἀπὸ Κιλικίας
and of Cyrenians, and of Alexandrians, and of those from Cilicia
[z]καὶ Ἀσίας,‖ [a]συζητοῦντες‖ τῷ Στεφάνῳ· 10 καὶ οὐκ.ἴσχυον
and Asia, disputing with Stephen. And they were not able
ἀντιστῆναι τῇ σοφίᾳ καὶ τῷ πνεύματι ᾧ ἐλάλει. 11 τότε
to resist the wisdom and the spirit by which he spoke. Then
ὑπέβαλον ἄνδρας, λέγοντας, Ὅτι ἀκηκόαμεν αὐτοῦ λαλοῦν-
they suborned men, saying, We have heard him speaking
τος ῥήματα βλάσφημα εἰς [b]Μωσῆν‖ καὶ τὸν θεόν. 12 Συν-
[2]words [1]blasphemous against Moses and God. [2]They
εκίνησάν τε τὸν λαὸν καὶ τοὺς πρεσβυτέρους καὶ τοὺς
[3]stirred [4]up [1]and the people and the elders and the
γραμματεῖς, καὶ ἐπιστάντες συνήρπασαν αὐτόν, καὶ ἤγαγον
scribes, and coming upon they seized him, and brought
εἰς τὸ συνέδριον, 13 ἔστησάν.τε μάρτυρας ψευδεῖς,
[him] to the sanhedrim, And they set [2]witnesses [1]false,
λέγοντας, Ὁ.ἄνθρωπος.οὗτος οὐ.παύεται [c]ῥήματα βλάσφημα
saying, This man does not cease [3]words [2]blasphemous
λαλῶν‖ κατὰ τοῦ τόπου τοῦ ἁγίου [d]τούτου‖ καὶ τοῦ νόμου.
[1]speaking against [3]place [2]holy [1]this and the law;
14 ἀκηκόαμεν.γὰρ αὐτοῦ λέγοντος, Ὅτι Ἰησοῦς ὁ Ναζω-
for we have heard him saying, That [2]Jesus [3]the [4]Naza-
ραῖος οὗτος καταλύσει τὸν.τόπον.τοῦτον, καὶ ἀλλάξει τὰ
rean [1]this will destroy this place, and will change the
ἔθη ἃ παρέδωκεν ἡμῖν Μωϋσῆς. 15 Καὶ ἀτενίσαντες εἰς
customs which [2]delivered [3]to [4]us [1]Moses. And looking intently on
αὐτὸν [e]ἅπαντες‖ οἱ καθεζόμενοι ἐν τῷ συνεδρίῳ [f]εἶδον‖ τὸ
him all who sat in the sanhedrim saw
πρόσωπον.αὐτοῦ ὡσεὶ πρόσωπον ἀγγέλου.
his face as [the] face of an angel.

7 Εἶπεν.δὲ ὁ ἀρχιερεύς, Εἰ [g]ἄρα‖ ταῦτα οὕτως [h]ἔχει‖;
And [4]said [1]the [2]high [3]priest, [6]Then [7]these [8]things [9]so [5]are?
2 Ὁ.δὲ ἔφη, Ἄνδρες ἀδελφοὶ καὶ πατέρες, ἀκούσατε. ὁ θεὸς
And he said, Men brethren and fathers, hearken. The God
τῆς δόξης ὤφθη τῷ.πατρὶ.ἡμῶν Ἀβραὰμ ὄντι ἐν τῇ Μεσο-
of glory appeared to our father Abraham being in Meso-

CHAPTER 6

[1]And in those days the disciples multiplied
and there arose a murmuring of the Grecian
Jews against the Hebrews, because their
widows were overlooked in the daily serving.
[2]And the Twelve, calling the company of the
disciples near, said, It is not right for us to
leave the word of God in order to wait tables
[3]– so, brothers, find seven men from among
yourselves who are of good report, full of
the Holy Spirit and wisdom, whom we can
appoint over this business.
[4]But we will give ourselves continually to
prayer and to the ministry of the word.
[5]And the saying was pleasing before all the
people. And they chose Stephen, a man full of
faith and the Holy Spirit, and Philip and
Proch-o-rus and Ni-ca-nor and Timon and Par-
men-as and Nicolas, a convert from Antioch.
[6]They set these before the apostles. And
when they had prayed, they laid their hands
on them.
[7]And the word of God increased. And the
number of the disciples multiplied greatly in
Jerusalem. And a great multitude of the
priests were obedient to the faith.

[8]And Stephen, full of faith and power,
worked great wonders and miracles among
the people.
[9]And there arose certain ones of those of
the synagogue called Libertines, and of
Cy-ren-i-ans and of Alexandrians and of Ci-
li-ci-ans and Asia, debating with Stephen.
[10]But they were not able to resist the wisdom and the spirit by which he spoke.
[11]Then they secretly urged men on, saying,
We have heard him speaking words that blaspheme Moses and God.
[12]And they stirred up the people and the
elders and the scribes. And coming upon
him, they caught him and brought him to
the san-he-drin.
[13]And they set up false witnesses, saying,
This man does not stop speaking words that
blaspheme this holy place and the Law.
[14]For we have heard him saying that this
Jesus the Nazarene will destroy this place and
will change the customs which Moses gave us.
[15]And all that sat in the san-he-drin, fasten-
ing their eyes on him, saw his face as *if it
were the* face of an angel.

CHAPTER 7

[1]Then the high priest said, Then are these
things so?
[2]And Stephen said, Men! Brothers and
fathers! Listen! The God of glory appeared
to our father Abraham when he was in
Mes-o-po-ta-mi-a before he lived in Haran,

ποταμίᾳ, πρὶν ἢ κατοικῆσαι αὐτὸν ἐν Χαῤῥάν, 3 καὶ εἶπεν
potamia, before [2]dwelt [1]he in Charran, and said
πρὸς αὐτόν, "Ἔξελθε ἐκ τῆς.γῆς.σου καὶ [i]ἐκ[ll] τῆς συγγενείας
to him, Go out from thy land and from [2]kindred
σου, καὶ δεῦρο εἰς[k] γῆν ἣν ἂν σοι δείξω. 4 Τότε ἐξελθὼν
[1]thy and come into land which to thee I will shew. Then going out
ἐκ γῆς Χαλδαίων, κατῴκησεν ἐν Χαῤῥάν, κἀκεῖθεν
from [the] land of Chaldeans, he dwelt in Charran, and thence
μετὰ τὸ ἀποθανεῖν τὸν.πατέρα.αὐτοῦ, μετῴκισεν αὐτὸν εἰς
after [3]died [1]his [2]father, he removed him into
τὴν.γῆν.ταύτην εἰς ἣν ὑμεῖς νῦν κατοικεῖτε· 5 καὶ οὐκ
this land in which ye now dwell. And [3]not
ἔδωκεν αὐτῷ κληρονομίαν ἐν αὐτῇ, οὐδὲ βῆμα.ποδός
[1]he [2]did give to him an inheritance in it, not even a foot's tread;
καὶ ἐπηγγείλατο [l]αὐτῷ δοῦναι[ll] εἰς κατάσχεσιν [m]αὐτήν,[ll] καὶ
and promised to him to give [2]for [3]a [4]possession [1]it, and
τῷ.σπέρματι.αὐτοῦ μετ' αὐτόν, οὐκ.ὄντος αὐτῷ τέκνου.
to his seed after him, there not being to him a child.
6 ἐλάλησεν.δὲ οὕτως ὁ θεός, Ὅτι ἔσται τὸ.σπέρμα.αὐτοῦ
And [2]spoke [3]thus [1]God: That [3]shall [4]be [1]his [2]seed
πάροικον ἐν γῇ ἀλλοτρίᾳ, καὶ δουλώσουσιν αὐτὸ καὶ
a sojourner in a [2]land [1]strange, and they will enslave it and
κακώσουσιν ἔτη τετρακόσια. 7 καὶ τὸ ἔθνος ᾧ [n]ἐὰν[ll]
ill-treat [it] [3]years [1]four [2]hundred; and the nation to which
[o]δουλεύσωσιν,[ll] κρινῶ ἐγώ, [p]εἶπεν ὁ θεός·[ll] καὶ μετὰ
they may be in bondage will [2]judge [1]I, said God; and after
ταῦτα ἐξελεύσονται καὶ λατρεύσουσίν μοι ἐν τῷ τόπῳ
these things they shall come forth and serve me in [2]place
τούτῳ. 8 Καὶ ἔδωκεν αὐτῷ διαθήκην περιτομῆς· καὶ οὕτως
[1]this. And he gave to him a covenant of circumcision; and thus
ἐγέννησεν τὸν Ἰσαάκ, καὶ περιέτεμεν αὐτὸν τῇ ἡμέρᾳ τῇ
he begat Isaac, and circumcised him the [2]day
ὀγδόῃ· καὶ [q]ὁ[ll] Ἰσαὰκ τὸν Ἰακώβ, καὶ [q]ὁ[ll] Ἰακὼβ τοὺς
[1]eighth; and Isaac [begat] Jacob, and Jacob the
δώδεκα πατριάρχας. 9 καὶ οἱ πατριάρχαι ζηλώσαντες τὸν
twelve patriarchs. And the patriarchs, envying
Ἰωσὴφ ἀπέδοντο εἰς Αἴγυπτον· καὶ ἦν ὁ θεὸς μετ'
Joseph, sold [him] into Egypt. And [2]was [1]God with
αὐτοῦ, 10 καὶ [r]ἐξείλετο[ll] αὐτὸν ἐκ πασῶν τῶν.θλίψεων.αὐτοῦ,
him, and delivered him out of all his tribulations,
καὶ ἔδωκεν αὐτῷ χάριν καὶ σοφίαν [s]ἐναντίον[ll] Φαραὼ βασι-
and gave him favour and wisdom before Pharaoh king
λέως Αἰγύπτου, καὶ κατέστησεν αὐτὸν ἡγούμενον ἐπ' Αἴγυπ-
of Egypt, and he appointed him ruler over Egypt
τον καὶ [t]ὅλον τὸν.οἶκον.αὐτοῦ. 11 ἦλθεν.δὲ λιμὸς ἐφ' ὅλην
and [2]whole [1]his house. But [3]came [1]a [2]famine upon [2]whole
τὴν [v]γῆν Αἰγύπτου[ll] καὶ Χαναάν, καὶ θλίψις μεγάλη· καὶ
[1]the land of Egypt and Canaan, and [2]tribulation [1]great, and
οὐχ.[w]εὕρισκον[ll] χορτάσματα οἱ.πατέρες.ἡμῶν. 12 ἀκούσας.δὲ
[3]did [4]not [5]find [6]sustenance [1]our [2]fathers. But [2]having [3]heard
Ἰακὼβ ὄντα [x]σῖτα ἐν Αἰγύπτῳ,[ll] ἐξαπέστειλεν τοὺς πατέρας
[1]Jacob [5]was [4]corn in Egypt, sent forth [2]fathers
ἡμῶν πρῶτον· 13 καὶ ἐν τῷ δευτέρῳ [y]ἀνεγνωρίσθη[ll] Ἰωσὴφ
[1]our first; and at the second time was made known Joseph
τοῖς.ἀδελφοῖς.αὐτοῦ, καὶ φανερὸν ἐγένετο τῷ Φαραὼ τὸ γένος
to his brethren, and [2]known [1]became to Pharaoh the family
[z]τοῦ[ll] [a]Ἰωσήφ.[ll] 14 ἀποστείλας.δὲ Ἰωσὴφ μετεκαλέσατο [b]τὸν
of Joseph. And having sent Joseph he called for
πατέρα.αὐτοῦ Ἰακώβ,[ll] καὶ πᾶσαν τὴν.συγγένειαν.[c]αὐτοῦ,[ll] ἐν
his father Jacob, and all his kindred, in
ψυχαῖς ἑβδομήκοντα πέντε. 15 [d]κατέβη.δὲ[ll] Ἰακὼβ εἰς Αἴγυπ-
[3]souls [1]seventy [2]five. And went down Jacob into Egypt
τον, καὶ ἐτελεύτησεν αὐτὸς καὶ οἱ.πατέρες.ἡμῶν· 16 καὶ
and died, he and our fathers, and
μετετέθησαν εἰς Συχέμ, καὶ ἐτέθησαν ἐν τῷ μνήματι [e]ὃ[ll]
were carried over to Sychem, and were placed in the tomb which
ὠνήσατο Ἀβραὰμ τιμῆς ἀργυρίου παρὰ τῶν υἱῶν [f]Ἐμμὸρ[ll]
[2]bought [1]Abraham for a sum of money from the sons of Emmor
[g]τοῦ[ll] [h]Συχέμ. 17 Καθὼς.δὲ ἤγγιζεν ὁ χρόνος τῆς ἐπαγ-
of Sychem. But as drew near the time of the pro-
γελίας ἧς [i]ὤμοσεν[ll] ὁ θεὸς τῷ Ἀβραάμ, ηὔξησεν ὁ λαὸς καὶ
mise which [2]swore [1]God to Abraham, [3]increased [1]the [2]people and
ἐπληθύνθη ἐν Αἰγύπτῳ, 18 [k]ἄχρις[ll] οὗ ἀνέστη βασιλεὺς
multiplied in Egypt, until arose [2]king
ἕτερος,[l] ὃς οὐκ.ᾔδει τὸν Ἰωσήφ. 19 οὗτος κατασοφισάμενος
[1]another, who knew not Joseph. He having dealt subtilly with
τὸ.γένος.ἡμῶν, ἐκάκωσεν τοὺς.πατέρας.[m]ἡμῶν,[ll] τοῦ ποιεῖν
our race, ill-treated our fathers, making
[n]ἔκθετα τὰ.βρέφη[ll].αὐτῶν εἰς.τὸ μὴ.ζῳογονεῖσθαι. 20 Ἐν ᾧ
[3]exposed [1]their [2]babes that they might not live. In which
καιρῷ ἐγεννήθη [o]Μωσῆς,[ll] καὶ ἦν ἀστεῖος τῷ θεῷ· ὃς ἀνε-
time was born Moses, and was beautiful to God; who was

3 And said to him, "Go away from your country and your relatives and come into the land which I will show to you."
4 Then going out from the land of the Chaldeans, he lived in Haran. And after his father died, He moved him from there into this land in which you now live.
5 And He gave him no inheritance in it, not even a foot-breadth. But *He* promised to give it to him for his own, and to his seed after him (at the time when he had no children).
6 And God spoke in this way: That his seed shall be living in a strange land, and they will bring them into slavery and mistreat them four hundred years.

7 And the nation to whom they shall be in slavery I will judge, said God, and after these things they shall come out and serve Me in this place.
8 And He gave to him a covenant of circumcision. And so he fathered Isaac and circumcised him the eighth day. And Isaac *fathered* Jacob, and Jacob the twelve patriarchs.
9 And moved with envy, the patriarchs sold Joseph into Egypt.
10 But God was with him and delivered him out of all his troubles and gave him favor and wisdom before Pharaoh king of Egypt. And he made him governor over Egypt and all of his house.

11 And there came a famine on all the land of Egypt and Canaan, and great distress, and our fathers found no food.
12 But Jacob heard there was grain in Egypt and sent out our fathers for the first time.
13 And at the second time Joseph was made known to his brothers, and Joseph's kin became known to Pharaoh.
14 And Joseph sent, calling for his father Jacob and all his family, seventy-five souls in all.

15 And Jacob went down into Egypt and died, he and our fathers.
16 And they were carried over to She-chem and were laid in the tomb which Abraham bought for a sum of money from the sons of Emmor of She-chem.
17 But as the time of the promise was drawing near (which God had sworn to Abraham) the people increased and multiplied in Egypt
18 until another king arose, who had not known Joseph.
19 *This king* acted slyly with our race, wickedly abusing our fathers, forcing them to put their babies outside so that they might not live.
20 In this time Moses was born. And he was beautiful to God and was nursed three months in the house of his father.

τράφη μῆνας τρεῖς ἐν τῷ οἴκῳ τοῦ.πατρὸς.ʳαὐτοῦ.ˡ
brought up ²months ¹three in the house of his father.
21 ᑫἐκτεθέντα.δὲ αὐτόν,ˡˡ ʳἀνείλετοˡˡ αὐτὸν ἡ θυγάτηρ Φαραώ,
And ²being ³exposed ¹he, took up him the daughter of Pharaoh,
καὶ ἀνεθρέψατο αὐτὸν ἑαυτῇ εἰς υἱόν. 22 καὶ ἐπαιδεύθη
and brought up him for herself for a son. And ²was ³instructed
ᵒΜωσῆςˡˡ ˢ πάσῃ σοφίᾳ Αἰγυπτίων· ἦν.δὲ δυνατὸς ἐν
¹Moses in all [the] wisdom of [the] Egyptians, and he was mighty in
λόγοις καὶ ᵗἐνˡˡ ἔργοις.ᵛ 23 Ὡς.δὲ ἐπληροῦτο αὐτῷ ʷτεσ-
words and in deeds. And when was fulfilled to him ³of
σαρακονταετὴςˡˡ χρόνος, ἀνέβη ἐπὶ τὴν.καρδίαν.αὐτοῦ ἐπι-
⁴forty ⁵years ¹a ²period, it came into his heart to
σκέψασθαι τοὺς.ἀδελφοὺς.αὐτοῦ τοὺς υἱοὺς Ἰσραήλ. 24 καὶ
look upon his brethren the sons of Israel; and
ἰδών τινα ἀδικούμενον, ἠμύνατο καὶ ἐποίησεν.ἐκδίκησιν
seeing a certain one being wronged, he defended [him] and avenged
τῷ καταπονουμένῳ, πατάξας τὸν Αἰγύπτιον. 25 ἐνόμιζεν.δὲ
him being oppressed, having smitten the Egyptian. For he thought
συνιέναι τοὺς.ἀδελφοὺς.ˣαὐτοῦˡˡ ὅτι ὁ θεὸς διὰ χειρὸς
³would ⁴understand ¹his ²brethren that God by ²hand
αὐτοῦ δίδωσιν ʸαὐτοῖς σωτηρίαν.ˡˡ οἱ.δὲ οὐ.συνῆκαν.
¹his is giving them salvation. But they understood not.
26 τῇ.ᶻτεˡˡ ἐπιούσῃ ἡμέρᾳ ὤφθη αὐτοῖς μαχομένοις, καὶ
And on the following day he appeared to those who were contending, and
ᵃσυνήλασενˡˡ αὐτοὺς εἰς εἰρήνην, εἰπών, Ἄνδρες ἀδελφοί ἐστε
urged them to peace, saying, Men ³brethren ²are
ᵇὑμεῖς·ˡˡ ᶜἱνατίˡˡ ἀδικεῖτε ἀλλήλους; 27 Ὁ.δὲ ἀδικῶν
¹ye, why wrong ye one another? But he who was wronging [his]
τὸν πλησίον ἀπώσατο αὐτόν, εἰπών, Τίς σε κατέστησεν
neighbour thrust away him, saying, Who ²thee ¹appointed
ἄρχοντα καὶ δικαστὴν ἐφ' ᵈἡμᾶςˡˡ; 28 μὴ ἀνελεῖν με
ruler and judge over us? To put to death me
σὺ θέλεις, ὃν.τρόπον ἀνεῖλες ᵉχθὲςˡˡ τὸν Αἰγύπτιον;
²thou ¹wishest, in the way thou puttest to death yesterday the Egyptian?
29 Ἔφυγεν.δὲ ᶠΜωσῆςˡˡ ἐν τῷ.λόγῳ.τούτῳ, καὶ ἐγένετο
And ²fled ¹Moses at this saying, and became
πάροικος ἐν γῇ Μαδιάμ, οὗ ἐγέννησεν υἱοὺς δύο.
a sojourner in [the] land of Madiam, where he begat ²sons ¹two.
30 Καὶ πληρωθέντων ἐτῶν ᵍτεσσαράκονταˡˡ ὤφθη αὐτῷ ἐν
And ³being ⁴fulfilled ²years ¹forty appeared to him in
τῇ ἐρήμῳ τοῦ ὄρους Σινᾶ ἄγγελος ʰκυρίουˡˡ ἐν φλογὶ
the desert of the Mount Sina an angel of [the] Lord in a flame
πυρὸς βάτου. 31 ὁ.δὲ.ᶠΜωσῆςˡˡ ἰδὼν ⁱἐθαύμασενˡˡ τὸ
of fire of a bush. And Moses seeing [it] wondered at the
ὅραμα· προσερχομένου.δὲ αὐτοῦ κατανοῆσαι, ἐγένετο φωνὴ
vision; and ²coming ³near ¹he to consider [it], there was a voice
κυρίου ᵏπρὸς αὐτόν,ˡˡ 32 Ἐγὼ ὁ θεὸς τῶν.πατέρων.σου,
of [the] Lord to him, I [am] the God of thy fathers,
ὁ θεὸς Ἀβραὰμ καὶ ˡὁ θεὸςˡˡ Ἰσαὰκ καὶ ˡὁ θεὸςˡˡ Ἰακώβ.
the God of Abraham and the God of Isaac and the God of Jacob.
Ἔντρομος.δὲ γενόμενος ᶠΜωσῆςˡˡ οὐκ.ἐτόλμα κατανοῆσαι.
And ⁴trembling ²having ³become ¹Moses he durst not consider [it].
33 εἶπεν.δὲ αὐτῷ ὁ κύριος, Λῦσον τὸ ὑπόδημα τῶν ποδῶν
And ³said ⁴to ⁵him ¹the ²Lord, Loose the sandal of ²feet
σου· ὁ.γὰρ τόπος ᵐἐνˡˡ ᾧ ἕστηκας, γῆ ἁγία ἐστίν. 34 ἰδὼν
¹thy, for the place on which thou standest, ³ground ²holy ¹is. Seeing,
εἶδον τὴν κάκωσιν τοῦ.λαοῦ.μου τοῦ ἐν Αἰγύπτῳ, καὶ τοῦ
I saw the ill-treatment of my people in Egypt, and
στεναγμοῦ.ⁿαὐτῶνˡˡ ἤκουσα· καὶ κατέβην ἐξελέσθαι αὐτούς·
their groaning heard, and came down to take ²out ¹them;
καὶ νῦν δεῦρο, ᵒἀποστελῶˡˡ σε εἰς Αἴγυπτον. 35 Τοῦτον τὸν
and now come, I will send thee to Egypt. This
Μωϋσῆν ὃν ἠρνήσαντο εἰπόντες, Τίς σε κατέστησεν ἄρ-
Moses, whom they refused, saying, Who ²thee ¹appointed ru-
χοντα καὶ δικαστήν; τοῦτον ὁ θεὸς ᵖ ἄρχοντα καὶ λυτρωτὴν
ler and judge? him God [²as] ³ruler ⁴and ⁵deliverer
ᑫἀπέστειλεν ἐνˡˡ χειρὶ ἀγγέλου τοῦ ὀφθέντος αὐτῷ ἐν τῇ
¹sent by [the] hand of [the] angel who appeared to him in the
βάτῳ. 36 οὗτος ἐξήγαγεν αὐτούς, ποιήσας τέρατα καὶ
bush. This one led out them, having wrought wonders and
σημεῖα ἐν ʳγῇˡˡ ˢΑἰγύπτουˡˡ καὶ ἐν ἐρυθρᾷ θαλάσσῃ,
signs in [the] land of Egypt and in [the] Red Sea,
καὶ ἐν τῇ ἐρήμῳ ἔτη ᵗτεσσαράκονταˡˡ 37 Οὗτός ἐστιν ὁ
and in the wilderness ²years ¹forty. This is the
Μωϋσῆς ὁ ʷεἰπὼνˡˡ τοῖς υἱοῖς Ἰσραήλ, Προφήτην ὑμῖν
Moses who said to the sons of Israel, A prophet to you
ἀναστήσει ˣκύριοςˡˡ ὁ θεὸς ʸὑμῶνˡˡ ἐκ τῶν ἀδελφῶν
⁵will ⁶raise ⁷up [¹the] ²Lord ⁴God ³your from among ²brethren
ὑμῶν ὡς ἐμέ· ᶻαὐτοῦ ἀκούσεσθε.ˡˡ 38 Οὗτός ἐστιν ὁ γενό-
¹your like me, him ye shall hear. This is he who was
μενος ἐν τῇ ἐκκλησίᾳ ἐν τῇ ἐρήμῳ μετὰ τοῦ ἀγγέλου τοῦ
in the assembly in the wilderness with the angel who

21 And when he was put outside, Pharaoh's daughter took him and brought him up for her own son.
22 And Moses was taught in all the wisdom of the Egyptians. And he was mighty in words and in deeds.
23 And when forty years was fulfilled to him, it came into his heart to see his brothers, the sons of Israel.
24 And seeing a certain one suffering wrong, he defended *him by* striking the Egyptian. And he avenged him who was being abused.
25 For he thought that his brothers would understand that God by his hand was giving them their salvation. But they did not know.
26 And the next day, also, he appeared to them as they fought and urged them to peace, saying, Men, are you brothers. Why do you wrong one another?
27 But he that was doing wrong to his neighbor pushed him away, saying, Who made you a ruler and judge over us?
28 Do you desire to kill me in the way you killed the Egyptian yesterday?
29 And at this saying Moses fled and became a stranger in the land of Midian, where he fathered two sons.
30 And when forty years had passed, an Angel of the Lord appeared to him in the desert of Mount Sinai, in a flame of fire in a bush.
31 And Moses saw and wondered at the sight. And as he was coming near to look, a voice of the Lord came to him:
32 "I am the God of your fathers, the God of Abraham and the God of Isaac and the God of Jacob." And Moses trembled, not daring to look.
33 And the Lord said to him, "Put off the sandals from your feet, for the place where you stand is holy ground."
34 "I have seen the affliction of My people in Egypt, and I have heard their groaning and have come down in order to take them out. And now, come! I will send you into Egypt."
35 This Moses whom they had refused, saying, Who made you a ruler and judge? – this one God sent as ruler and a redeemer, by the hand of the Angel who appeared to him in the Bush.
36 This one led them out, after working wonders and miracles in the land of Egypt and in the Red Sea and in the wilderness forty years.
37 This is the Moses who said to the sons of Israel, "The Lord your God will raise up a Prophet to you from among your brothers, *One* like me. You shall hear Him."
38 This is he who was in the congregation in the wilderness with the Angel who spoke to him in Mount Sinai and with our fathers – who received living words to give to us –

λαλοῦντος αὐτῷ ἐν τῷ ὄρει Σινᾶ, καὶ τῶν.πατέρων.ἡμῶν,
spoke to him in the mount Sina, and with our fathers;
ὃς ἐδέξατο λόγια ζῶντα δοῦναι ἡμῖν· 39 ᾧ οὐκ.ἠθέλησαν
who received [2]oracles [1]living to give to us: to whom [3]would [4]not
ὑπήκοοι γενέσθαι οἱ.πατέρες.ἡμῶν, [a]ἀλλ'‖ ἀπώσαντο, καὶ
[6]subject [5]be [1]our [2]fathers, but thrust [him] away, and
ἐστράφησαν [b]ταῖς.καρδίαις.αὐτῶν εἰς Αἴγυπτον, 40 εἰπόντες
turned back their hearts to Egypt, saying
τῷ Ἀαρών, Ποίησον ἡμῖν θεοὺς οἳ προπορεύσονται ἡμῶν·
to Aaron, Make us gods who shall go before us;
ὁ γὰρ [c]Μωσῆς‖ οὗτος ὃς ἐξήγαγεν ἡμᾶς ἐκ γῆς Αἰγύπ-
for [2]Moses [1]that who brought [2]out [1]us from [the] land of Egypt,
του, οὐκ.οἴδαμεν τί [d]γέγονεν‖ αὐτῷ. 41 Καὶ ἐμοσχοποίησαν
we know not what has happened to him. And they made a calf
ἐν ταῖς.ἡμέραις.ἐκείναις, καὶ ἀνήγαγον θυσίαν τῷ εἰδώλῳ,
in those days, and offered sacrifice to the idol,
καὶ εὐφραίνοντο ἐν τοῖς ἔργοις τῶν.χειρῶν.αὐτῶν. 42 [3]Ἔστρεψεν
and rejoiced in the works of their hands. [3]Turned
δὲ ὁ θεὸς καὶ παρέδωκεν αὐτοὺς λατρεύειν τῇ στρατιᾷ τοῦ
[1]but [2]God and delivered up them to serve the host of the
οὐρανοῦ· καθὼς γέγραπται ἐν βίβλῳ τῶν προφητῶν,
heaven; as it has been written in [the] book of the prophets,
Μὴ σφάγια καὶ θυσίας προσηνέγκατέ μοι ἔτη [e]τεσσαρά-
[4]Slain [5]beasts [6]and [7]sacrifices [1]did [2]ye [3]offer to me [2]years [1]forty
κοντα‖ ἐν τῇ ἐρήμῳ, οἶκος Ἰσραήλ; 43 καὶ ἀνελάβετε τὴν
in the wilderness, O house of Israel? And ye took up the
σκηνὴν τοῦ Μολόχ, καὶ τὸ ἄστρον τοῦ.θεοῦ.[e]ὑμῶν‖ [f]Ῥεμφάν,‖
tabernacle of Moloch, and the star of your god Remphan,
τοὺς τύπους οὓς ἐποιήσατε προσκυνεῖν αὐτοῖς· καὶ μετοικιῶ
the models which ye made to worship them; and I will remove
ὑμᾶς ἐπέκεινα Βαβυλῶνος. 44 Ἡ σκηνὴ τοῦ μαρτυρίου ἦν
you beyond Babylon. The tabernacle of the testimony was
[g]ἐν‖ τοῖς.πατράσιν.ἡμῶν ἐν τῇ ἐρήμῳ, καθὼς διετάξατο
among our fathers in the wilderness, as commanded
ὁ λαλῶν τῷ.[h]Μωσῇ,‖ ποιῆσαι αὐτὴν κατὰ τὸν τύπον
he who spoke to Moses, to make it according to the model
ὃν ἑωράκει· 45 ἣν καὶ εἰσήγαγον διαδεξάμενοι
which he had seen; which also [7]brought [8]in [3]having [4]received [5]by [6]succession
οἱ.πατέρες.ἡμῶν μετὰ Ἰησοῦ ἐν τῇ κατασχέσει τῶν ἐθνῶν,
[1]our [2]fathers with Joshua in the taking possession of the nations,
ὧν [i]ἐξῶσεν‖ ὁ θεὸς ἀπὸ προσώπου τῶν.πατέρων.ἡμῶν,
whom [2]drove [3]out [1]God from [the] face of our fathers,
ἕως τῶν ἡμερῶν [k]Δαβίδ·‖ 46 ὃς εὗρεν χάριν ἐνώπιον τοῦ
until the days of David; who found favour before
θεοῦ, καὶ ᾐτήσατο εὑρεῖν σκήνωμα τῷ [m]θεῷ‖ Ἰακώβ.
God, and asked to find a tabernacle for the God of Jacob;
47 [n]Σολομῶν‖.δὲ [o]ᾠκοδόμησεν‖ αὐτῷ οἶκον. 48 Ἀλλ' οὐχ ὁ
but Solomon built him a house. But [4]not [1]the
ὕψιστος ἐν χειροποιήτοις [p]ναοῖς‖ κατοικεῖ, καθὼς ὁ προ-
[2]Most [3]High in hand-made temples dwells; as the pro-
φήτης λέγει, 49 Ὁ οὐρανός μοι θρόνος ἡ.δὲ γῆ ὑπο-
phet says, The heaven [is] to me a throne and the earth a foot-
πόδιον τῶν.ποδῶν.μου· ποῖον οἶκον οἰκοδομήσετέ μοι; λέγει
stool of my feet: what house will ye build me? says
κύριος· ἢ τίς τόπος τῆς.καταπαύσεώς.μου; 50 οὐχὶ
[the] Lord, or what [the] place of my rest? [2]not
ἡ.χείρ.μου ἐποίησεν ταῦτα πάντα; 51 σκληροτράχηλοι καὶ
[3]my [4]hand [1]made [6]these [7]things [5]all? O stiffnecked and
ἀπερίτμητοι [q]τῇ καρδίᾳ‖ καὶ τοῖς ὠσίν, ὑμεῖς ἀεὶ τῷ πνεύματι
uncircumcised in heart and ears, ye always the Spirit
τῷ ἁγίῳ ἀντιπίπτετε, [r]ὡς‖ οἱ.πατέρες.ὑμῶν, καὶ ὑμεῖς. 52 τίνα
the Holy resist; as your fathers, also ye. Which
τῶν προφητῶν οὐκ.ἐδίωξαν οἱ.πατέρες.ὑμῶν; καὶ ἀπέ-
of the prophets did not [3]persecute [1]your [2]fathers? and they
κτειναν τοὺς προκαταγγείλαντας περὶ τῆς ἐλεύσεως τοῦ
killed those who before announced concerning the coming of the
δικαίου, οὗ νῦν ὑμεῖς προδόται καὶ φονεῖς [s]γεγένησθε·‖
Just One, of whom now ye betrayers and murderers have become!
53 οἵτινες ἐλάβετε τὸν νόμον εἰς διαταγὰς ἀγγέλων, καὶ
who received the law by [the] disposition of angels, and
οὐκ.ἐφυλάξατε.
kept [it] not.

54 Ἀκούοντες.δὲ ταῦτα διεπρίοντο ταῖς.καρδίαις.αὐτῶν,
And hearing these things they were cut to their hearts,
καὶ ἔβρυχον τοὺς ὀδόντας ἐπ' αὐτόν. 55 Ὑπάρχων.δὲ πλήρης
and gnashed the teeth at him. But being full
πνεύματος ἁγίου, ἀτενίσας εἰς τὸν οὐρανόν, εἶδεν
of [the] [2]Spirit [1]Holy, having looked intently into heaven, he saw
δόξαν θεοῦ, καὶ Ἰησοῦν ἑστῶτα ἐκ δεξιῶν τοῦ θεοῦ,
[the] glory of God, and Jesus standing at the right hand of God,
56 καὶ εἶπεν, Ἰδού, θεωρῶ τοὺς οὐρανοὺς [t]ἀνεῳγμένους,‖ καὶ
and said, Lo, I behold the heavens opened, and

39 whom our fathers would not obey. But they pushed him away and turned their hearts back to Egypt,

40 saying to Aaron, Make us gods that will go before us, for we do not know what has happened to this Moses who brought us out of the land of Egypt.

41 And they made a calf in those days and offered sacrifice to the idol and rejoiced in the work of their hands.

42 But God turned and gave them up to worship the bodies of the sky, as it has been written in the book of the Prophets, "Did you offer slain beasts and sacrifices to Me forty years in the wilderness, O house of Israel?

43 And you took up the tent of Moloch and the star of your god Rem-phan – the figures which you made to worship them – and I will remove you beyond Babylon."

44 But the tabernacle of witness was among our fathers in the wilderness, as He who spoke to Moses commanded Him to make it according to the pattern which he had seen,

45 this our fathers received in turn, bringing it in with Joshua when they took possession of the nations which God drove out from before the face of our fathers – until the days of David,

46 who found favor before God. And *he* asked to find a tabernacle for the God of Jacob,

47 but Solomon built Him a house.

48 But the Most High does not live in man-made buildings, as the prophet says,

49 "Heaven is My throne and earth a footstool for My feet. What house will you build Me, says the Lord? Or, Where is the place of My rest?

50 Has not My hand made all these things?"

51 O you stiffnecked and uncircumcised in heart and ears! You always resist the Holy Spirit. As your fathers *were*, so are you!

52 Which one of the prophets did your fathers not persecute? And they killed the ones who prophesied of the coming of the Just One – of whom you now have become betrayers and murderers! –

53 *you* who have received the Law through orders of angels, and did not keep it!

54 And hearing these things they were cut to their hearts and gnashed their teeth at him.

55 But being full of the Holy Spirit, looking into Heaven he saw the glory of God and Jesus standing at the right hand of God.

56 *He* cried out, Look! I see the heavens opened and the Son of man standing at the

τὸν υἱὸν τοῦ ἀνθρώπου ἐκ δεξιῶν ἑστῶτα τοῦ θεοῦ.
the Son of man [2]at [3]the [4]right [[5]hand] [1]standing of God.
57 Κράξαντες.δὲ φωνῇ μεγάλῃ συνέσχον τὰ.ὦτα.αὐτῶν
And crying out with a [2]voice [1]loud they held their ears
καὶ ὥρμησαν ὁμοθυμαδὸν ἐπ' αὐτόν, 58 καὶ ἐκβαλόντες
and rushed with one accord upon him, and having cast [him]
ἔξω τῆς πόλεως ἐλιθοβόλουν. καὶ οἱ μάρτυρες ἀπέθεντο
out of the city they stoned [him]. And the witnesses laid aside
τὰ.ἱμάτια.αὐτῶν παρὰ τοὺς πόδας νεανίου καλουμένου
their garments at the feet of a young man called
Σαύλου. 59 καὶ ἐλιθοβόλουν τὸν Στέφανον, ἐπικαλούμενον
Saul. And they stoned Stephen, invoking
καὶ λέγοντα, Κύριε Ἰησοῦ, δέξαι τὸ.πνεῦμά.μου. 60 θεὶς.δὲ
and saying, Lord Jesus, receive my spirit. And having bowed
τὰ γόνατα ἔκραξεν φωνῇ μεγάλῃ, Κύριε, μὴ.στήσῃς αὐτοῖς
the knees he cried with a [2]voice [1]loud, Lord, lay not to them
[r]τὴν.ἁμαρτίαν.ταύτην.[‖] Καὶ τοῦτο εἰπὼν ἐκοιμήθη.
this sin. And this having said he fell asleep.
8 Σαῦλος.δὲ ἦν συνευδοκῶν τῇ ἀναιρέσει αὐτοῦ.
And Saul was consenting to the killing of him.
Ἐγένετο.δὲ ἐν ἐκείνῃ τῇ ἡμέρᾳ διωγμὸς μέγας ἐπὶ τὴν
And took place on that day a [2]persecution [1]great against the
ἐκκλησίαν τὴν ἐν Ἱεροσολύμοις· πάντες.[w]τε[‖] διεσπάρησαν
assembly which [was] in Jerusalem, and all were scattered
κατὰ τὰς χώρας τῆς Ἰουδαίας καὶ [x]Σαμαρείας[‖]. πλὴν τῶν
throughout the countries of Judæa and Samaria except the
ἀποστόλων. 2 συνεκόμισαν.δὲ τὸν Στέφανον ἄνδρες εὐλαβεῖς,
apostles. And [3]buried [4]Stephen [2]men [1]pious,
καὶ [y]ἐποιήσαντο[‖] κοπετὸν μέγαν ἐπ' αὐτῷ. 3 Σαῦλος.δὲ
and made [2]lamentation [1]great over him. But Saul
ἐλυμαίνετο τὴν ἐκκλησίαν, κατὰ.τοὺς.οἴκους εἰσπορευόμενος,
was ravaging the assembly, [2]house [3]by [4]house [1]entering,
σύρων.τε ἄνδρας καὶ γυναῖκας παρεδίδου εἰς φυλακήν.
and dragging men and women delivered [them] up to prison.
4 Οἱ μὲν οὖν διασπαρέντες διῆλθον, εὐαγγελιζό-
They who therefore had been scattered passed through, announcing the
μενοι τὸν λόγον. 5 Φίλιππος.δὲ κατελθὼν εἰς [z] πόλιν
glad tidings— the word. And Philip, going down to a city
τῆς [x]Σαμαρείας[‖] ἐκήρυσσεν αὐτοῖς τὸν χριστόν. 6 προσεῖχόν
of Samaria, proclaimed to them the Christ; [4]gave [5]heed
[a]τε[‖] οἱ ὄχλοι τοῖς λεγομένοις ὑπὸ τοῦ Φιλίππου ὁμο-
[1]and [2]the [3]crowds to the things spoken by Philip with
θυμαδόν, ἐν.τῷ.ἀκούειν.αὐτοὺς καὶ βλέπειν τὰ σημεῖα ἃ
one accord, when they heard and saw the signs which
ἐποίει. 7 [b]πολλῶν[‖].γὰρ τῶν ἐχόντων πνεύματα ἀκά-
he did. For of many of those who had spirits un-
θαρτα, βοῶντα [c]μεγάλῃ φωνῇ ἐξήρχετο·[‖] πολλοὶ.δὲ
clean, [4]crying [5]with [6]a [7]loud [8]voice [1]they [2]went [3]out; and many
παραλελυμένοι καὶ χωλοὶ ἐθεραπεύθησαν. 8 [d]καὶ ἐγένετο
having been paralysed and lame were healed. And [3]was
χαρὰ μεγάλη[‖] ἐν τῇ.πόλει.ἐκείνῃ.
[2]joy [1]great in that city.

9 Ἀνὴρ.δέ.τις ὀνόματι Σίμων προϋπῆρχεν ἐν τῇ πόλει
But a certain man, by name Simon, was formerly in the city
μαγεύων καὶ [e]ἐξιστῶν[‖] τὸ ἔθνος τῆς [x]Σαμαρείας,[‖] λέγων
using magic arts and amazing the nation of Samaria, saying
εἶναί τινα ἑαυτὸν μέγαν· 10 ᾧ προσεῖχον πάντες
[2]to [3]be [4]some [1]himself great one. To whom [2]were [3]giving [4]heed [1]all
ἀπὸ μικροῦ ἕως μεγάλου, λέγοντες, Οὗτός ἐστιν ἡ δύναμις
from small to great, saying, This one is the power
τοῦ θεοῦ ἡ [f] μεγάλη. 11 Προσεῖχον.δὲ αὐτῷ, διὰ
of God which [is] great. And they were giving heed to him, because
τὸ.ἱκανῷ χρόνῳ ταῖς [g]μαγείαις[‖] ἐξεστακέναι αὐτούς.
that for a long time with the magic arts [he] had amazed them.
12 Ὅτε.δὲ ἐπίστευσαν τῷ Φιλίππῳ εὐαγγελιζομένῳ
But when they believed Philip announcing the glad tidings—
[h]τὰ[‖] περὶ τῆς βασιλείας τοῦ θεοῦ καὶ τοῦ ὀνόματος
the things concerning the kingdom of God and the name
[i]τοῦ[‖] Ἰησοῦ χριστοῦ, ἐβαπτίζοντο ἄνδρες.τε καὶ γυναῖκες.
of Jesus Christ, they were baptized both men and women.
13 ὁ.δὲ.Σίμων καὶ αὐτὸς ἐπίστευσεν, καὶ βαπτισθεὶς ἦν
And Simon also himself believed, and having been baptized was
προσκαρτερῶν τῷ Φιλίππῳ· θεωρῶν τε [k]σημεῖα καὶ δυνά-
steadfastly continuing with Philip; [2]beholding [1]and signs and [2]works [3]of
μεις μεγάλας γινομένας,[‖] ἐξίστατο. 14 Ἀκούσαντες.δὲ οἱ
[4]power [1]great being done, was amazed. And [5]having [6]heard [1]the
ἐν Ἱεροσολύμοις ἀπόστολοι ὅτι δέδεκται ἡ [l]Σαμάρεια[‖] τὸν
[3]in [4]Jerusalem [2]apostles that [2]had [3]received [1]Samaria the
λόγον τοῦ θεοῦ, ἀπέστειλαν πρὸς αὐτοὺς [m]τὸν[‖] Πέτρον καὶ
word of God, they sent to them Peter and
[n]Ἰωάννην·[‖] 15 οἵτινες καταβάντες προσηύξαντο περὶ
John; who having come down prayed for

right hand of God!
57 And crying out with a loud voice, they held their ears and rushed upon him with one mind.
58 And throwing him out of the city, they stoned him. And the witnesses laid their clothes at the feet of a young man named Saul.
59 And they stoned Stephen *as he* prayed, saying Lord Jesus, receive my spirit.
60 And bowing down, he cried with a loud voice, Lord, do not lay this sin to them. And when he had said this, he fell asleep.

CHAPTER 8

1 And Saul was agreeing to his death. And a great persecution against the church which was in Jerusalem came on that day. And they were scattered throughout the countries of Judea and Samaria, except the apostles.
2 And devoted men buried Stephen and there was great weeping over him.
3 But Saul was ravaging the church. Entering house by house and dragging men and women, he delivered them up to prison.

4 Then they who had been scattered went everywhere preaching the gospel, the word.
5 And Philip went down to a city of Samaria and preached Christ to them.
6 And the people with one accord listened to the things Philip said, when they heard and saw the miracles which he did.
7 For evil spirits came out from many of those who were possessed, crying with a loud voice. And many who were paralyzed and lame were healed.
8 And there was great joy in that city.

9 But a certain man named Simon had been using magic arts in the city before. And he had been amazing the nation of Samaria, declaring himself to be someone great.
10 They were all listening to him, both the small and the great, saying, This is the power of God, which is great.
11 And they were giving attention to him because he had amazed them with the magic arts for a long time.
12 But when they believed Philip preaching the gospel, the things about the kingdom of God and the name of Jesus Christ, they were baptized, both men and women.
13 And Simon himself also believed. And when he had been baptized, he continued to follow Philip. And seeing miracles and great works of power being done, he was amazed.
14 And when the apostles in Jerusalem heard that Samaria had received the word of God, they sent Peter and John to them.
15 And when they had come, they prayed for them that they might receive the Holy Spirit

αὐτῶν, ὅπως λάβωσιν πνεῦμα ἅγιον. 16 [o]οὔπω‖·γὰρ
them, that they might receive [the] ²Spirit ¹Holy; for not yet
ἦν ἐπ' οὐδενὶ αὐτῶν ἐπιπεπτωκός, μόνον.δὲ βεβαπ-
was he upon any (lit. no one) of them fallen, but only ³bap-
τισμένοι ὑπῆρχον εἰς τὸ ὄνομα τοῦ κυρίου Ἰησοῦ. 17 τότε
tized ¹they ²were to the name of the Lord Jesus. Then
[p]ἐπετίθουν‖ τὰς χεῖρας ἐπ' αὐτούς, καὶ ἐλάμβανον πνεῦμα
they laid hands upon them, and they received [the] ²Spirit
ἅγιον. 18 [q]Θεασάμενος‖.δὲ ὁ Σίμων ὅτι διὰ τῆς ἐπιθέσεως
¹Holy. But ²having ³seen ¹Simon that by the laying on
τῶν χειρῶν τῶν ἀποστόλων δίδοται τὸ πνεῦμα [r]τὸ ἅγιον,‖
of the hands of the apostles was given the Spirit the Holy,
προσήνεγκεν αὐτοῖς χρήματα, 19 λέγων, Δότε κἀμοὶ τὴν
he offered to them riches, saying, Give also to me
ἐξουσίαν.ταύτην, ἵνα ᾧ.[s]ἂν‖ ἐπιθῶ τὰς χεῖρας, λαμ-
this authority, that on whomsoever I may lay hands, he may re-
βάνῃ πνεῦμα ἅγιον. 20 Πέτρος.δὲ εἶπεν πρὸς αὐτόν,
ceive [the] ²Spirit ¹Holy. But Peter said to him,
Τὸ.ἀργύριόν.σου σὺν σοὶ εἴη εἰς ἀπώλειαν· ὅτι τὴν
Thy money with thee may it be to destruction, because the
δωρεὰν τοῦ θεοῦ ἐνόμισας διὰ χρημάτων κτᾶσθαι. 21 οὐκ
gift of God thou didst think by riches to be obtained. ³Not
ἔστιν σοι μερὶς οὐδὲ κλῆρος ἐν τῷ.λόγῳ.τούτῳ· ἡ.γὰρ
⁴there ²is to thee part nor lot in this matter; for the
καρδία σου οὐκ.ἔστιν εὐθεῖα [t]ἐνώπιον‖ τοῦ θεοῦ. 22 μετανόη-
heart of thee is not right before God. Repent
σον οὖν ἀπὸ τῆς.κακίας.σου ταύτης, καὶ δεήθητι [v]τοῦ θεοῦ,‖
therefore of ²thy ³wickedness ¹this, and supplicate God,
εἰ ἄρα ἀφεθήσεταί σοι ἡ ἐπίνοια τῆς.καρδίας.σου. 23 εἰς
if indeed may be forgiven to thee the thought of thy heart; ²in
γὰρ χολὴν πικρίας καὶ σύνδεσμον ἀδικίας ὁρῶ σε
¹for a gall of bitterness and a bond of unrighteousness I see thee
ὄντα. 24 Ἀποκριθεὶς.δὲ ὁ Σίμων εἶπεν, Δεήθητε ὑμεῖς ὑπὲρ
to be. And ²answering ¹Simon said, Supplicate ye on behalf
ἐμοῦ πρὸς τὸν κύριον, ὅπως μηδὲν ἐπέλθῃ ἐπ' ἐμὲ ὧν
of me to the Lord, so that nothing may come upon me of which
εἰρήκατε. 25 Οἱ μὲν οὖν διαμαρτυράμενοι καὶ λαλή-
ye have spoken. They therefore having earnestly testified and having
σαντες τὸν λόγον τοῦ κυρίου, [w]ὑπέστρεψαν‖ εἰς [x]Ἱερουσαλήμ,‖
spoken the word of the Lord, returned to Jerusalem,
πολλάς.τε κώμας τῶν [y]Σαμαρειτῶν‖ [z]εὐηγγελίσαντο.‖
and [to] many villages of the Samaritans announced the glad tidings.
26 Ἄγγελος.δὲ κυρίου ἐλάλησεν πρὸς Φίλιππον, λέγων,
But an angel of [the] Lord spoke to Philip, saying,
Ἀνάστηθι καὶ [a]πορεύου‖ κατὰ μεσημβρίαν, ἐπὶ τὴν ὁδὸν
Rise up and go towards [the] south, on the way
τὴν καταβαίνουσαν ἀπὸ Ἱερουσαλὴμ εἰς Γάζαν· αὕτη
which goes down from Jerusalem to Gaza: the same
ἐστὶν ἔρημος. 27 καὶ ἀναστὰς ἐπορεύθη· καὶ ἰδού, ἀνὴρ
is desert. And having risen up he went. And lo, a man
Αἰθίοψ εὐνοῦχος δυνάστης Κανδάκης [b]τῆς‖ βασιλίσσης
an Ethiopian, a eunuch, one in power under Candace the queen
Αἰθιόπων, ὃς ἦν ἐπὶ πάσης τῆς.γάζης.αὐτῆς, [c]ὃς‖
of [the] Ethiopians, who was over all her treasure, who
ἐληλύθει προσκυνήσων εἰς Ἱερουσαλήμ, 28 ἦν.τε ὑποστρέφων
had come ³to ⁴worship ¹to ²Jerusalem, and was returning
καὶ καθήμενος ἐπὶ τοῦ.ἅρματος.αὐτοῦ, [d]καὶ‖ ἀνεγίνωσκεν [e]
and sitting in his chariot, and he was reading
τὸν προφήτην Ἡσαΐαν. 29 εἶπεν.δὲ τὸ πνεῦμα τῷ Φιλίππῳ,
the prophet Esaias. And said the Spirit to Philip,
Πρόσελθε καὶ κολλήθητι τῷ.ἅρματι.τούτῳ. 30 Προσδραμὼν.δὲ
Go near and join thyself to this chariot. And running up
ὁ Φίλιππος ἤκουσεν αὐτοῦ ἀναγινώσκοντος [f]τὸν προφήτην
Philip heard him reading the prophet
Ἡσαΐαν,‖ καὶ εἶπεν, [g]Ἆρά.γε‖ γινώσκεις ἃ ἀναγινώσκεις;
Esaias, and said, ³Then ¹dost ²thou know what thou readest?
31 Ὁ.δὲ εἶπεν, Πῶς.γὰρ ἂν.δυναίμην ἐὰν.μή τις [h]ὁδη-
But he said, [No,] for how should I be able unless some one should
γήσῃ‖ με; Παρεκάλεσέν.τε τὸν Φίλιππον ἀναβάντα καθίσαι
guide me? And he besought Philip having come up to sit
σὺν αὐτῷ. 32 ἡ.δὲ περιοχὴ τῆς γραφῆς ἣν ἀνεγίνωσκεν
with him. And the passage of the scripture which he was reading
ἦν αὕτη, Ὡς πρόβατον ἐπὶ σφαγὴν ἤχθη, καὶ ὡς ἀμνὸς
was this, As a sheep to slaughter he was led, and as a lamb
ἐναντίον τοῦ [i]κείροντος‖ αὐτὸν ἄφωνος, οὕτως οὐκ.ἀνοίγει
before him who shears him [is] dumb, thus he opens not
τὸ.στόμα.αὐτοῦ. 33 ἐν τῇ.ταπεινώσει.[k]αὐτοῦ‖ ἡ.κρίσις.αὐτοῦ
his mouth. In his humiliation his judgment
ἤρθη, τὴν.[l]δὲ‖ γενεὰν αὐτοῦ τίς διηγήσεται; ὅτι
was taken away, and the generation of him who shall declare? for
αἴρεται ἀπὸ τῆς γῆς ἡ.ζωὴ.αὐτοῦ. 34 Ἀποκριθεὶς.δὲ ὁ εὐνοῦχος
is taken from the earth his life. And answering the eunuch

16 (for as yet He had fallen on none of them, but they had only been baptized into the name of the Lord Jesus).

17 Then they laid hands on them and they received the Holy Spirit.

18 And when Simon saw that the Holy Spirit was given through the laying on of the hands of the apostles, he offered them money,

19 saying, Give me this power also, that on whomever I may lay hands he may receive the Holy Spirit.

20 But Peter said to him, May your money be destroyed with you, because you thought the gift of God could be gotten by money.

21 You have no part or share in this matter, for your heart is not right in the sight of God.

22 Therefore repent of this wickedness of yours and pray God if indeed the thought of your heart may be forgiven to you.

23 For I see that you are in the gall of bitterness and the chains of unrighteousness.

24 And Simon answered them and said, Pray to the Lord for me, that none of these things which you have said may come on me.

25 Then when they had testified and preached the word of the Lord, they returned to Jerusalem. And they preached the gospel in many villages of the Samaritans.

26 And an angel of the Lord spoke to Philip, saying, Get up and go toward the south, on the highway which goes from Jerusalem to Gaza (which is desert).

27 And he got up and went. And, behold, An Ethiopian man, a eunuch, one in power under Can-da-ce the queen of the Ethiopians, who was her treasurer, who had come to Jerusalem to worship

28 and was returning. And sitting in his chariot, he was reading the prophet Isaiah.

29 And the Spirit said to Philip, Go near and join yourself to this chariot.

30 And running near to him, Philip heard him reading the prophet Isaiah. And *he* said, Do you then know what you are reading?

31 And he said, How could I unless someone should guide me? And he asked Philip to come up to sit with him.

32 And the passage of the Scripture which he was reading was this, "He was led as a sheep to slaughter and as a lamb dumb before his shearer, so He does not open His mouth.

33 In His humiliation His judgment was taken away, and who shall declare His generation? For His life is taken from the earth."

τῷ Φιλίππῳ. εἶπεν, Δέομαί σου, περὶ τίνος ὁ προφήτης
[2]to [3]Philip [1]said, I pray thee, concerning whom [2]the [3]prophet
λέγει . τοῦτο ; περὶ ἑαυτοῦ, ἢ περὶ ἑτέρου.τινός ;
[1]says this? concerning himself, or concerning some other?
35 Ἀνοίξας.δὲ ὁ Φίλιππος τὸ.στόμα.αὐτοῦ, καὶ ἀρξάμενος
And [2]having [3]opened [1]Philip his mouth, and having begun
ἀπὸ τῆς.γραφῆς.ταύτης, εὐηγγελίσατο.αὐτῷ τὸν Ἰη-
from this scripture, announced to him the glad tidings— Je-
σοῦν. 36 ὡς.δὲ ἐπορεύοντο κατὰ τὴν ὁδόν, ἦλθον ἐπί
sus. And as they were going along the way, they came upon
τι ὕδωρ· καί φησιν ὁ εὐνοῦχος, Ἰδοὺ ὕδωρ· τί κωλύει
a certain water, and [3]says [1]the [2]eunuch, Behold water; what hinders
με βαπτισθῆναι; 37 [n]Εἶπεν δὲ ὁ Φίλιππος, Εἰ πιστεύεις ἐξ
me to be baptized? And [2]said [1]Philip, If thou believest from
ὅλης τῆς καρδίας, ἔξεστιν. Ἀποκριθεὶς.δὲ εἶπεν, Πιστεύω
[2]whole [1]the heart, it is lawful. And answering he said, I believe
τὸν υἱὸν τοῦ θεοῦ εἶναι τὸν Ἰησοῦν χριστόν.[‖] 38 Καὶ ἐκέλευ-
[5]the [6]Son [7]of [8]God [3]to [4]be [1]Jesus [2]Christ. And he com-
σεν στῆναι τὸ ἅρμα· καὶ κατέβησαν ἀμφότεροι εἰς
manded [3]to [4]stand [5]still [1]the [2]chariot. And they went down both to
τὸ ὕδωρ, ὅ.τε.Φίλιππος καὶ ὁ εὐνοῦχος· καὶ ἐβάπτισεν αὐτόν.
the water, both Philip and the eunuch, and he baptized him.
39 ὅτε.δὲ ἀνέβησαν ἐκ τοῦ ὕδατος πνεῦμα κυρίου
But when they came up out of the water [the] Spirit of [the] Lord
ἥρπασεν τὸν Φίλιππον· καὶ οὐκ εἶδεν αὐτὸν οὐκέτι ὁ
caught away Philip, and [3]saw [4]him [5]no [6]longer [1]the
εὐνοῦχος, ἐπορεύετο.γὰρ τὴν.ὁδὸν.αὐτοῦ χαίρων. 40 Φίλιππος
[2]eunuch, for he went his way rejoicing. [2]Philip
δὲ εὑρέθη εἰς Ἄζωτον· καὶ διερχόμενος εὐηγ-
[1]but was found at Azotus, and passing through he announced the
γελίζετο τὰς πόλεις πάσας, ἕως τοῦ.ἐλθεῖν.αὐτὸν εἰς
glad tidings [to] [2]the [3]cities [1]all, till he came to
[o]Καισάρειαν.[‖]
Cæsarea.

9 Ὁ.δὲ.Σαῦλος ἔτι [p]ἐμπνέων[‖] ἀπειλῆς καὶ φόνου εἰς
But Saul, still breathing out threatenings and slaughter towards
τοὺς μαθητὰς τοῦ κυρίου, προσελθὼν τῷ ἀρχιερεῖ 2 ᾐτήσατο
the disciples of the Lord, having come to the high priest asked
παρ' αὐτοῦ ἐπιστολὰς εἰς Δαμασκὸν πρὸς τὰς συναγωγάς,
from him letters to Damascus, to the synagogues,
ὅπως [q]ἐάν[‖] τινας εὕρῃ [r]τῆς ὁδοῦ ὄντας[‖] ἄνδρας.τε καὶ
so that if any he found [2]of [3]the [4]way [1]being both men and
γυναῖκας, δεδεμένους ἀγάγῃ εἰς Ἱερουσαλήμ. 3 ἐν.δὲ
women, having bound he might bring [them] to Jerusalem. But in
τῷ πορεύεσθαι ἐγένετο αὐτὸν ἐγγίζειν τῇ Δαμασκῷ, [s]καὶ
proceeding it came to pass he drew near to Damascus, and
ἐξαίφνης[‖] [t]περιήστραψεν αὐτὸν[‖] φῶς [v]ἀπὸ[‖] τοῦ οὐρανοῦ·
suddenly shone round about him a light from the heaven,
4 καὶ πεσὼν ἐπὶ τὴν γῆν ἤκουσεν φωνὴν λέγουσαν αὐτῷ,
and having fallen on the earth he heard a voice saying to him,
Σαούλ, Σαούλ, τί με διώκεις; 5 Εἶπεν.δέ, Τίς εἶ[w],
Saul, Saul, why me dost thou persecute? And he said, Who art thou,
κύριε; Ὁ.δὲ [x]κύριος εἶπεν,[‖] Ἐγώ εἰμι Ἰησοῦς [y] ὃν σὺ
Lord? And the Lord said, I am Jesus whom thou
διώκεις· [z]σκληρόν σοι πρὸς κέντρα λακτίζειν.
persecutest. [It is] hard for thee against [the] goads to kick.
6 Τρέμων.τε καὶ θαμβῶν εἶπεν, Κύριε, τί με θέλεις
And trembling and astonished he said, Lord, What me desirest thou
ποιῆσαι; Καὶ ὁ κύριος πρὸς αὐτόν,[‖] [a]Ἀνάστηθι καὶ
to do? And the Lord [said] to him, Rise up and
εἴσελθε εἰς τὴν πόλιν, καὶ λαληθήσεταί σοι [b]τί[‖] σε δεῖ
enter into the city, and it shall be told thee what thee it behoves
ποιεῖν. 7 Οἱ.δὲ ἄνδρες οἱ συνοδεύοντες αὐτῷ εἱστήκεισαν
to do. But the men who were travelling with him stood
[c]ἐννεοί,[‖] ἀκούοντες μὲν τῆς φωνῆς μηδένα.δὲ θεωροῦντες.
speechless, hearing indeed the voice but no one seeing.
8 ἠγέρθη.δὲ [d]ὁ[‖] Σαῦλος ἀπὸ τῆς γῆς· [e]ἀνεῳγμένων[‖].δὲ τῶν
And rose up Saul from the earth, and having been opened
ὀφθαλμῶν.αὐτοῦ [f]οὐδένα[‖] ἔβλεπεν. χειραγωγοῦντες.δὲ αὐτὸν
his eyes no one he saw. But leading [2]by [3]the [4]hand [1]him
εἰσήγαγον εἰς Δαμασκόν. 9 καὶ ἦν ἡμέρας τρεῖς μὴ βλέ-
they brought [him] to Damascus. And he was [2]days [1]three not see-
πων, καὶ οὐκ.ἔφαγεν οὐδὲ ἔπιεν. 10 Ἦν.δέ τις μαθητὴς
ing, and did not eat nor drink. And there was a certain disciple
ἐν Δαμασκῷ ὀνόματι Ἀνανίας· καὶ εἶπεν πρὸς αὐτὸν [g]ὁ κύριος
in Damascus by name Ananias. And [3]said [4]to [5]him [1]the [2]Lord
ἐν ὁράματι,[‖] Ἀνανία. Ὁ.δὲ εἶπεν, Ἰδοὺ ἐγώ, κύριε.
in a vision, Ananias. And he said, Behold [here am] I, Lord.
11 Ὁ.δὲ κύριος πρὸς αὐτόν, [h]Ἀναστὰς[‖] πορεύθητι ἐπὶ
And the Lord to him [said], Having risen up go into
τὴν ῥύμην τὴν καλουμένην Εὐθεῖαν, καὶ ζήτησον ἐν οἰκίᾳ
the street which is called Straight, and seek in [the] house

34 And the eunuch answering to Philip said,
I beg of you, about whom does the prophet
say this, about himself or about some other?
35 And Philip opened his mouth. And
beginning from this Scripture, *he* preached
to him the gospel of Jesus.
36 And as they were going along the way,
they came to a certain water. And the
eunuch said, Look! Water! What keeps me
from being baptized?
37 And Philip said, If you believe from the
whole heart, it is lawful. And answering he
said, I believe Jesus Christ to be the Son of
God.
38 And he ordered the chariot to stop. And
they both went down into the water, both
Philip and the eunuch. And he baptized him.
39 And when they came up out of the
water, the Spirit of the Lord took Philip
away, so that the eunuch never saw him
again – for he went his way rejoicing.
40 And Philip was found at A-zo-tus. And
going through he preached the gospel to all
the cities until he came to Caesarea.

CHAPTER 9

1 But Saul, still breathing out threatenings
and murders against the Lord's disciples,
went to the high priest,
2 asking for letters from him to the
synagogues at Da-mas-cus, so that if he
found any who were of the Way, whether
men or women, he might bring them bound
to Jerusalem.
3 But in going, he was drawing near to
Da-mas-cus when suddenly a light from
Heaven shone around him.
4 And he fell down on the ground and
heard a voice saying to him, Saul! Saul! Why
do you persecute Me?
5 And he said, Who are you, sir? And
the Lord said, I am Jesus whom you
persecute. *It is* hard for you to kick
against the prods.
6 And trembling and astonished, he said,
Lord, what do you want me to do? And the
Lord said to him, Get up and go into the
city and you will be told what you should
do.
7 But the men who were traveling with him
stood speechless, hearing indeed the voice,
but seeing no one.
8 And Saul got up from the ground. And his
eyes were opened, but he saw no one. But
leading him by the hand, they brought him
to Da-mas-cus.
9 And he was three days without seeing and
did not eat or drink.
10 And there was a certain disciple in
Da-mas-cus named An-a-ni-as. And the Lord
said to him in a vision, An-a-ni-as! And he
said, I am here, Lord.
11 And the Lord said to him, Get up and go
into the street called Straight and ask in the

'Ιούδα Σαῦλον ὀνόματι, Ταρσέα. ἰδοὺ.γὰρ προσεύχεται,
of Judas [one] Saul by name, of Tarsus: for lo he prays,
12 καὶ εἶδεν ἰἐν ὁράματι ἄνδρα" ᵏὀνόματι 'Ανανίαν" εἰσελθόντα
and he saw in a vision a man by name Ananias coming
καὶ ἐπιθέντα αὐτῷ ˡχεῖρα," ὅπως ἀναβλέψῃ. 13 'Απε-
and putting on him a hand, so that he should receive sight. ²An-
κρίθη δὲ ᵐὁ" 'Ανανίας, Κύριε, ⁿἀκήκοα" ἀπὸ πολλῶν περὶ
swered ¹and Ananias, Lord, I have heard from many concerning
τοῦ.ἀνδρὸς.τούτου, ὅσα κακὰ ᵒἐποίησεν τοῖς.ἁγίοις.σου" ἐν
this man, how many evils he did to thy saints in
'Ιερουσαλήμ· 14 καὶ ὧδε ἔχει ἐξουσίαν παρὰ τῶν ἀρχιερέων
Jerusalem; and here he has authority from the chief priests
δῆσαι πάντας τοὺς ἐπικαλουμένους τὸ.ὄνομά.σου. 15 Εἶπεν.δὲ
to bind all who call on thy name. And ³said
πρὸς αὐτὸν ὁ κύριος, Πορεύου, ὅτι σκεῦος ἐκλογῆς ᵖμοι
⁴to ⁵him ¹the ²Lord, Go, for a vessel of election to me
ἐστὶν" οὗτος, τοῦ βαστάσαι τὸ.ὄνομά.μου ἐνώπιον ᵍἐθνῶν ʳ
is this [man], to bear my name before Gentiles
καὶ βασιλέων, υἱῶν.τε 'Ισραήλ. 16 ἐγὼ.γὰρ ὑποδείξω
and kings, and [the] sons of Israel: for I will shew
αὐτῷ ὅσα δεῖ αὐτὸν ὑπὲρ τοῦ.ὀνόματός.μου παθεῖν.
to him how much it behoves him for my name to suffer.
17 'Απῆλθεν.δὲ 'Ανανίας καὶ εἰσῆλθεν εἰς τὴν οἰκίαν, καὶ
And ²went ³away ¹Ananias and entered into the house; and
ἐπιθεὶς ἐπ' αὐτὸν τὰς χεῖρας εἶπεν, Σαοὺλ ἀδελφέ, ὁ
having laid upon him [his] hands he said, ²Saul ¹brother, the
κύριος ἀπέσταλκέν με, 'Ιησοῦς ὁ ὀφθείς σοι ἐν τῇ ὁδῷ
Lord has sent me, Jesus who appeared to thee in the way
ᾗ ἤρχου, ὅπως ἀναβλέψῃς καὶ πλησθῇς πνεύ-
in which thou camest, that thou mightest receive sight and be filled with [the]
ματος ἁγίου. 18 Καὶ εὐθέως ˢἀπέπεσον ἀπὸ τῶν ὀφθαλμῶν
²Spirit ¹Holy. And immediately fell from ²eyes
αὐτοῦ" ᵗὡσεὶ" λεπίδες, ἀνέβλεψέν.τε ᵛπαραχρῆμα," καὶ
¹his as it were scales, and he received sight instantly, and
ἀναστὰς ἐβαπτίσθη, 19 καὶ λαβὼν τροφὴν ἐνίσχυσεν·
having risen up was baptized; and having taken food he was strengthened.
Ἐγένετο.δὲ ʷὁ Σαῦλος" μετὰ τῶν ἐν Δαμασκῷ μαθητῶν ἡμέρας
And ²was ¹Saul with the ²in ³Damascus ¹disciples ⁵days
τινάς· 20 καὶ εὐθέως ἐν ταῖς συναγωγαῖς ἐκήρυσσεν
⁴certain. And immediately in the synagogues he was proclaiming
τὸν ˣχριστόν," ὅτι οὗτός ἐστιν ὁ υἱὸς τοῦ θεοῦ. 21 ἐξίσταντο.δὲ
Christ, that he is the Son of God. And ²were ³amazed
πάντες οἱ ἀκούοντες, καὶ ἔλεγον, Οὐχ οὗτός ἐστιν ὁ πορθήσας
¹all who heard, and said, ²Not ³this ¹is he who destroyed
ʸἐν" 'Ιερουσαλὴμ τοὺς ἐπικαλουμένους τὸ.ὄνομα.τοῦτο, καὶ
in Jerusalem those who called on this name, and
ὧδε εἰς τοῦτο ἐληλύθει ἵνα δεδεμένους αὐτοὺς ἀγάγῃ
here for this had come that ⁵bound ⁴them ¹he ²might ³bring
ἐπὶ τοὺς ἀρχιερεῖς; 22 Σαῦλος.δὲ μᾶλλον ἐνεδυναμοῦτο, καὶ
to the chief priests? But Saul more increased in power, and
ᶻσυνέχυνεν" ᵃτοὺς" 'Ιουδαίους τοὺς κατοικοῦντας ἐν Δαμασκῷ,
confounded the Jews who dwelt in Damascus,
συμβιβάζων ὅτι οὗτός ἐστιν ὁ χριστός. 23 ὡς.δὲ ἐπληροῦντο
proving that this is the Christ. Now when were fulfilled
ἡμέραι ἱκαναί, συνεβουλεύσαντο οἱ 'Ιουδαῖοι ἀνελεῖν αὐ-
²days ¹many, ⁵consulted ⁶together ³the ⁴Jews to put to death him.
τόν· 24 ἐγνώσθη.δὲ τῷ Σαύλῳ ἡ.ἐπιβουλὴ.αὐτῶν. ᵇπαρε-
But became known to Saul their plot. ²They ³were
τήρουν" ᶜτε" τὰς πύλας ἡμέρας.τε καὶ νυκτός, ὅπως αὐτὸν
⁴watching ¹and the gates both day and night, that him
ἀνέλωσιν· 25 λαβόντες.δὲ ᵈαὐτὸν οἱ μαθηταὶ" νυκτὸς
they might put to death; but taking him the disciples by night
ᵉκαθῆκαν διὰ τοῦ τείχους" ᶠ, χαλάσαντες ἐν σπυρίδι.
let down ²through ³the ⁴wall [¹him], lowering [him] in a basket.
26 Παραγενόμενος.δὲ ᵍὁ Σαῦλος" ʰεἰς" 'Ιερουσαλήμ, ⁱἐπει-
And ²having ³arrived ¹Saul at Jerusalem, he at-
ρᾶτο" κολλᾶσθαι τοῖς μαθηταῖς· καὶ πάντες ἐφοβοῦντο
tempted to join himself to the disciples, and all were afraid of
αὐτόν, μὴ πιστεύοντες ὅτι ἐστὶν μαθητής. 27 Βαρνάβας.δὲ
him, not believing that he is a disciple. But Barnabas
ἐπιλαβόμενος αὐτόν, ἤγαγεν πρὸς τοὺς ἀποστόλους, καὶ
having taken him, brought [him] to the apostles, and
διηγήσατο αὐτοῖς πῶς ἐν τῇ ὁδῷ εἶδεν τὸν κύριον, καὶ ὅτι
related to them how in the way he saw the Lord, and that
ἐλάλησεν αὐτῷ, καὶ πῶς ἐν Δαμασκῷ ἐπαῤῥησιάσατο ἐν τῷ
he spoke to him, and how in Damascus he spoke boldly in the
ὀνόματι ᵏτοῦ" 'Ιησοῦ. 28 καὶ ἦν μετ' αὐτῶν εἰσπορευόμενος
name of Jesus. And he was with them coming in
καὶ ἐκπορευόμενος ˡἐν" 'Ιερουσαλήμ, ᵐκαὶ" παῤῥησιαζόμενος
and going out in Jerusalem, and speaking boldly
ἐν τῷ ὀνόματι τοῦ κυρίου ⁿ'Ιησοῦ·" 29 ἐλάλει.τε καὶ συνεζήτει
in the name of the Lord Jesus. And he spoke and discussed

house of Judas for one named Saul of Tarsus
– for, see, he is praying.
12 And he has seen in a vision a man named
An-a-ni-as coming in and putting a hand
upon him so that he might see.
13 And An-a-ni-as answered, Lord, I have
heard from many about this man, how many
evils he has done to Your saints in
Jerusalem.
14 And here he has authority from the chief
priests to chain all who call on Your name.
15 And the Lord said to him, Go! For this
one is a chosen vessel to Me, to bear My
name before nations and kings and the sons
of Israel.
16 For I will show him how much he must
suffer for My name.
17 And An-a-ni-as left and went into the
house. And laying his hands on him, he said,
Brother Saul, the Lord has sent me – Jesus
who appeared to you in the way in which
you came – so that you might receive your
sight and be filled with the Holy Spirit.
18 And immediately something like scales
fell from his eyes, and he received sight
instantly, and *he* rose up and was baptized.
19 And taking food, he was strengthened.
And Saul was with the disciples at Da-mas-
cus certain days.
20 And he at once preached Christ in the
synagogues, that He is the Son of God.
21 And all those who heard were amazed
and said, Is this not he who destroyed
those who call on this Name in Jerusalem,
and who had come here for this, that he
might bring them chained to the chief
priests?
22 But Saul increased the more in strength
and confounded the Jews who lived in
Da-mas-cus, proving that this is the Christ.
23 Now when many days had passed, the
Jews plotted to kill him.
24 But their plan became known to Saul.
They were also watching the gates both day
and night, so that they might kill him.
25 But taking him by night, the disciples let
him down through the wall, lowering him in
a basket.
26 And after Saul had come to Jerusalem,
he tried to join himself to the disciples. But
they were afraid of him, not believing that
he was a disciple.
27 But Barnabas took him and brought him
to the apostles and told them how he had
seen the Lord in the way, and that He spoke
to him, and how he had spoken boldly in
Da-mas-cus in the name of Jesus.
28 And he was with them, coming and
going in Jerusalem, speaking boldly in the
name of the Lord Jesus.
29 And he spoke and reasoned with the
Grecian Jews. But they decided to kill him.

πρὸς τοὺς Ἑλληνιστάς· οἱ.δὲ ἐπεχείρουν [o]αὐτὸν ἀνε-
with the Hellenists; but they took in hand [3]him [1]to [2]put to
λεῖν.‖ 30 ἐπιγνόντες.δὲ οἱ ἀδελφοὶ κατήγαγον αὐτὸν εἰς
death. But having known [it] the brethren brought down him to
[p]Καισάρειαν,‖ καὶ ἐξαπέστειλαν [q]αὐτὸν‖ εἰς Ταρσόν. 31 [r]Αἱ‖
Cæsarea, and sent away him to Tarsus. The
μὲν οὖν [s]ἐκκλησίαι‖ καθ' ὅλης τῆς Ἰουδαίας καὶ Γαλι-
[2]indeed [3]then [1]assemblies throughout [2]whole [1]the of Judæa and Gali-
λαίας καὶ [t]Σαμαρείας‖ [v]εἶχον‖ εἰρήνην, [w]οἰκοδομούμεναι καὶ
lee and Samaria had peace, being built up and
πορευόμεναι‖ τῷ φόβῳ τοῦ κυρίου, καὶ τῇ παρακλήσει τοῦ
going on in the fear of the Lord, and in the comfort of the
ἁγίου πνεύματος [x]ἐπληθύνοντο.‖
Holy Spirit were increased.
32 Ἐγένετο.δὲ Πέτρον διερχόμενον διὰ πάντων,
Now it came to pass [that] Peter, passing through all
κατελθεῖν καὶ πρὸς τοὺς ἁγίους τοὺς κατοικοῦντας
[quarters], went down also to the saints that inhabited
[y]Λύδδαν.‖ 33 εὗρεν.δὲ ἐκεῖ ἄνθρωπόν.τινα [z]Αἰνέαν ὀνόματι,‖
Lydda, And he found there a certain man, Æneas by name,
ἐξ ἐτῶν ὀκτὼ κατακείμενον ἐπὶ [a]κραββάτῳ,‖ ὃς ἦν παρα-
for [2]years [1]eight lying on a couch, who was para-
λελυμένος. 34 καὶ εἶπεν αὐτῷ ὁ Πέτρος, Αἰνέα, ἰᾶταί σε
lysed. And [2]said [3]to [4]him [1]Peter, Æneas, [4]heals [5]thee
Ἰησοῦς [b]ὁ‖ χριστός· ἀνάστηθι καὶ στρῶσον σεαυτῷ.
[1]Jesus [2]the [3]Christ; rise up, and spread [a couch] for thyself.
Καὶ εὐθέως ἀνέστη· 35 καὶ [c]εἶδον‖ αὐτὸν πάντες οἱ
And immediately he rose up. And saw him all those
κατοικοῦντες [y]Λύδδαν‖ καὶ τὸν [d]Σαρωνᾶν,‖ οἵτινες ἐπέστρεψαν
inhabiting Lydda and the Saron, who turned
ἐπὶ τὸν κύριον.
to the Lord.
36 Ἐν.Ἰόππῃ.δέ τις ἦν μαθήτρια ὀνόματι Ταβιθά,
And in Joppa [2]a [3]certain [1]was disciple, by name Tabitha,
ἣ διερμηνευομένη λέγεται Δορκάς· αὕτη ἦν πλήρης [e]ἀγαθῶν
which being interpreted is called Dorcas, She was full of good
ἔργων‖ καὶ ἐλεημοσυνῶν ὧν ἐποίει· 37 ἐγένετο.δὲ ἐν ταῖς
works and of alms which she did. And it came to pass in
ἡμέραις.ἐκείναις ἀσθενήσασαν αὐτὴν ἀποθανεῖν· λούσαν-
those days [that] having sickened she died; [2]having
τες δὲ [f]αὐτὴν ἔθηκαν‖ ἐν [g] ὑπερῴῳ. 38 ἐγγὺς.δὲ
[3]washed [1]and her they put [her] in an upper room. And [3]near
οὔσης [h]Λύδδης‖ τῇ Ἰόππῃ, οἱ μαθηταὶ ἀκούσαντες ὅτι Πέτρος
[2]being [1]Lydda to Joppa, the disciples having heard that Peter
ἐστὶν ἐν αὐτῇ ἀπέστειλαν δύο ἄνδρας πρὸς αὐτόν, παρα-
is in it sent two men to him, beseech-
καλοῦντες [i]μὴ ὀκνῆσαι‖ διελθεῖν ἕως [k]αὐτῶν.‖ 39 ἀναστὰς
ing [him] not to delay to come to them. [2]Having [3]risen [4]up
δὲ Πέτρος συνῆλθεν αὐτοῖς· ὃν παραγενόμενον ἀνήγαγον
[1]and Peter went with them, whom, having arrived they brought
εἰς τὸ ὑπερῷον, καὶ παρέστησαν αὐτῷ πᾶσαι αἱ χῆραι
into the upper room, and stood by him all the widows
κλαίουσαι καὶ ἐπιδεικνύμεναι χιτῶνας καὶ ἱμάτια ὅσα ἐ-
weeping and shewing tunics and garments which [2]was
ποίει μετ' αὐτῶν οὖσα ἡ Δορκάς. 40 ἐκβαλὼν.δὲ ἔξω πάντας
[3]making [5]with [6]them [4]being [1]Dorcas. But [2]having [3]put [5]out [4]all
ὁ Πέτρος, [l] θεὶς τὰ γόνατα προσηύξατο· καὶ ἐπιστρέψας
[1]Peter, having bowed the knees he prayed. And having turned
πρὸς τὸ σῶμα εἶπεν, Ταβιθά, ἀνάστηθι. Ἡ.δὲ ἤνοιξεν
to the body he said, Tabitha, Arise. And she opened
τοὺς.ὀφθαλμοὺς.αὐτῆς· καὶ ἰδοῦσα τὸν Πέτρον ἀνεκάθισεν.
her eyes, and seeing Peter she sat up.
41 δοὺς.δὲ αὐτῇ χεῖρα ἀνέστησεν αὐτήν, φωνήσας.δὲ
And having given her [his] hand he raised up her, and having called
τοὺς ἁγίους καὶ τὰς χήρας παρέστησεν αὐτὴν ζῶσαν. 42 γνω-
the saints and the widows he presented her living. [4]Known
στὸν δὲ ἐγένετο καθ' ὅλης [m]τῆς‖ Ἰόππης, καὶ [n]πολλοὶ
[1]and [2]it [3]became throughout [2]whole [1]the of Joppa, and many
ἐπίστευσαν‖ ἐπὶ τὸν κύριον· 43 ἐγένετο.δὲ [o]ἡμέρας
believed on the Lord. And it came to pass [that] [4]days
ἱκανὰς μεῖναι αὐτὸν‖ ἐν Ἰόππῃ παρά τινι Σίμωνι βυρσεῖ.
[3]many [2]abode [1]he in Joppa with a certain Simon a tanner.
10 Ἀνὴρ.δέ.τις [p]ἦν‖ ἐν [q]Καισαρείᾳ‖ ὀνόματι Κορνήλιος,
But a certain man was in Cæsarea by name Cornelius,
ἑκατοντάρχης ἐκ σπείρης τῆς καλουμένης Ἰταλικῆς, 2 εὐ-
a centurion of a band which is called Italic, pious
σεβὴς καὶ φοβούμενος τὸν θεὸν σὺν παντὶ τῷ.οἴκῳ.αὐτοῦ,
and fearing God with all his house,
ποιῶν.[r]τε‖ ἐλεημοσύνας πολλὰς τῷ λαῷ, καὶ δεόμενος
both doing [2]alms [1]much to the people, and supplicating
τοῦ θεοῦ [s]διαπαντός.‖ 3 εἶδεν ἐν ὁράματι φανερῶς, ὡσεὶ
God continually, He saw in a vision plainly, about

30 But when the brothers knew it, they
brought him down to Caesarea and sent him
away to Tarsus.
31 Then indeed the churches throughout all
of Judea and Galilee and Samaria had peace,
being built up and walking in the fear of the
Lord and in the comfort of the Holy Spirit,
being multiplied.

32 And traveling around, Peter went down
also to the saints that lived at Lydda.
33 And he found there a certain man named
E-ne-as, who had been lying on a bed for
eight years, being paralyzed.
34 And Peter said to him, E-ne-as, Jesus the
Christ heals you! Get up and spread for
yourself. And he immediately got up.
35 And all of those living in Lydda and
Saron saw him and turned to the Lord.

36 And there was a certain disciple at Joppa
named Tab-i-tha (which means she was
called Dorcas). She was full of good works
and of kind-hearted acts which she did.
37 And it happened in those days that she
became ill and died. And after they had
bathed her, they put her in an upper room.
38 And as Lydda was near Joppa, and the
disciples having heard that Peter was there,
they sent two men to him asking him to
come to them without delay.
39 And Peter rose up and went with them.
When he had come, they brought him into
the upper room. And all the widows stood
beside him, weeping and showing coats and
clothes which Dorcas was making with them.
40 But Peter put them all out and kneeled
down and prayed. Then turning to the body,
he said, Tab-i-tha, Get up! And she opened
her eyes. And seeing Peter, she sat up.
41 And he gave her his hand and raised her
up. And when he had called the saints and
the widows, he showed her alive.
42 And it became known throughout all of
Joppa. And many believed on the Lord.
43 And he stayed many days in Joppa with
a tanner named Simon.

CHAPTER 10

1 And there was a certain man in Caesarea
named Cornelius, a captain of the Italian
Band,
2 a pious one who feared God with all his
household, doing also many good deeds to
the people and praying to God continually.
3 About the ninth hour of the day he saw in
a vision plainly an angel of God coming to
him and saying to him, Cornelius!

ὥραν ˇἐννάτην" τῆς ἡμέρας, ἄγγελον τοῦ θεοῦ εἰσελθόντα
[3]hour [1]the [2]ninth of the day, an angel of God coming

πρὸς αὐτόν, καὶ εἰπόντα αὐτῷ, Κορνήλιε. 4 Ὁ.δὲ ἀτε-
to him, and saying to him, Cornelius. But he having looked

νίσας αὐτῷ καὶ ἔμφοβος γενόμενος εἶπεν, Τί ἐστιν, κύριε;
intently on him and [2]afraid [1]becoming said, What is it, Lord?

εἶπεν.δὲ αὐτῷ, Αἱ.προσευχαί.σου καὶ αἱ.ἐλεημοσύναι.σου
And he said to him, Thy prayers and thine alms

ἀνέβησαν εἰς μνημόσυνον [w]ἐνώπιον" τοῦ θεοῦ. 5 καὶ νῦν
are gone up for a memorial before God. And now

πέμψον [x]εἰς Ἰόππην ἄνδρας," καὶ μετάπεμψαι Σίμωνα [y] ὃς
send [2]to [3]Joppa [1]men, and send for Simon who

ἐπικαλεῖται Πέτρος· 6 οὗτος ξενίζεται παρά τινι Σίμωνι
is surnamed Peter. He lodges with a certain Simon

βυρσεῖ, ᾧ ἐστιν οἰκία παρὰ θάλασσαν· [z]οὗτος λαλήσει σοι
a tanner, whose [2]is [1]house by [the] sea; he shall tell thee

τί σε δεῖ ποιεῖν." 7 Ὡς.δὲ ἀπῆλθεν ὁ ἄγγελος ὁ
what [3]thee [1]it [2]behoves to do. And when [3]departed [1]the [2]angel who

λαλῶν [a]τῷ Κορνηλίῳ," φωνήσας δύο τῶν.οἰκετῶν.[b]αὐτοῦ,"
spoke to Cornelius, having called two of his servants,

καὶ στρατιώτην εὐσεβῆ τῶν προσκαρτερούντων αὐτῷ, 8 καὶ
and a [2]soldier [1]pious of those continually waiting on him, and

ἐξηγησάμενος [c]αὐτοῖς ἅπαντα" ἀπέστειλεν αὐτοὺς εἰς τὴν
having related to them all things he sent them to

Ἰόππην. 9 Τῇ.δὲ ἐπαύριον ὁδοιπορούντων [d]ἐκείνων" καὶ
Joppa. And on the morrow, as [2]are [3]journeying [1]these and

τῇ πόλει ἐγγιζόντων, ἀνέβη Πέτρος ἐπὶ τὸ δῶμα προσ-
to the city drawing near, [2]went [3]up [1]Peter on the housetop to

εύξασθαι, περὶ ὥραν ἕκτην. 10 ἐγένετο.δὲ πρόσπεινος,
pray, about [3]hour [1]the [2]sixth. And he became very hungry,

καὶ ἤθελεν γεύσασθαι· παρασκευαζόντων.δὲ [e]ἐκείνων" [f]ἐπέ-
and wished to eat. But as [2]were [3]making [4]ready [1]they [7]fell

πεσεν" ἐπ' αὐτὸν ἔκστασις, 11 καὶ θεωρεῖ τὸν οὐρανὸν ἀνεῳγ-
[8]upon [9]him [5]a [6]trance, and he beholds the heaven opened,

μένον, καὶ καταβαῖνον [g]ἐπ' αὐτὸν" σκεῦός τι ὡς ὀθόνην
and descending upon him a [2]vessel [1]certain, as a [2]sheet

μεγάλην, τέσσαρσιν ἀρχαῖς [h]δεδεμένον, καὶ" καθιέμενον ἐπὶ
[1]great, by four corners bound, and let down upon

τῆς γῆς· 12 ἐν ᾧ ὑπῆρχεν πάντα τὰ τετράποδα [i]τῆς γῆς
the earth; in which were all the quadrupeds of the earth

καὶ τὰ θηρία καὶ τὰ ἑρπετὰ" καὶ [k]τὰ" πετεινὰ τοῦ οὐ-
and the wild beasts and the creeping things and the birds of the hea-

ρανοῦ. 13 καὶ ἐγένετο φωνὴ πρὸς αὐτόν, Ἀναστάς, Πέτρε,
ven. And came a voice to him, Having risen up, Peter,

θῦσον καὶ φάγε. 14 Ὁ.δὲ.Πέτρος εἶπεν, Μηδαμῶς, κύριε· ὅτι
kill and eat. But Peter said, In no wise, Lord; for

οὐδέποτε ἔφαγον πᾶν κοινὸν [l]ἢ" ἀκάθαρτον. 15 Καὶ φωνὴ
never did I eat anything common or unclean. And a voice

πάλιν ἐκ.δευτέρου πρὸς αὐτόν, Ἃ ὁ θεὸς [m]ἐκαθάρισεν,"
[came] again the second time to him, What God cleansed,

σὺ μὴ κοίνου. 16 Τοῦτο.δὲ ἐγένετο ἐπὶ.τρίς· καὶ [n]πάλιν"
[3]thou [2]not [1]make common. And this took place thrice, and again

[o]ἀνελήφθη" τὸ σκεῦος εἰς τὸν οὐρανόν. 17 Ὡς.δὲ ἐν ἑαυτῷ
was taken up the vessel into the heaven. And as [4]in [5]himself

διηπόρει ὁ Πέτρος τί ἂν.εἴη τὸ ὅραμα ὃ εἶδεν, [p]καὶ"
[2]was [3]perplexed [1]Peter what might be the vision which he saw, [2]also

ἰδού, οἱ ἄνδρες οἱ ἀπεσταλμένοι [q]ἀπὸ" τοῦ Κορνηλίου, διε-
[1]behold, the men who were sent from Cornelius, having

ρωτήσαντες τὴν οἰκίαν [r] Σίμωνος, ἐπέστησαν ἐπὶ τὸν πυλῶνα·
inquired for the house of Simon, stood at the porch;

18 καὶ φωνήσαντες ἐπυνθάνοντο εἰ Σίμων ὁ ἐπικαλού-
and having called out they asked if Simon who [is] surnamed

μενος Πέτρος ἐνθάδε ξενίζεται. 19 Τοῦ.δὲ.Πέτρου [s]ἐνθυμου-
Peter [2]here [1]lodges. But as Peter was think-

μένου" περὶ τοῦ ὁράματος, εἶπεν [t]αὐτῷ τὸ πνεῦμα," Ἰδού,
ing over the vision, [3]said [4]to [5]him [1]the [2]Spirit, Behold,

ἄνδρες [v]τρεῖς" [w]ζητοῦσίν" σε· 20 ἀλλὰ ἀναστὰς κατάβηθι,
[2]men [1]three seek thee; but having risen go down,

καὶ πορεύου σὺν αὐτοῖς, μηδὲν διακρινόμενος· [x]διότι" ἐγὼ
and proceed with them, nothing doubting, because I

ἀπέσταλκα αὐτούς. 21 Καταβὰς.δὲ Πέτρος πρὸς τοὺς
have sent them. And [2]having [3]gone [4]down [1]Peter to the

ἄνδρας [y]τοὺς ἀπεσταλμένους ἀπὸ τοῦ Κορνηλίου πρὸς αὐτόν,"
men who were sent from Cornelius to him,

εἶπεν, Ἰδού, ἐγώ εἰμι ὃν ζητεῖτε· τίς ἡ αἰτία δι' ἣν
said, Behold, I am whom ye seek; what [is] the cause for which

πάρεστε; 22 οἱ.δὲ [z]εἶπον," Κορνήλιος ἑκατοντάρχης, ἀνὴρ
ye are come? And they said, Cornelius a centurion, a [2]man

δίκαιος καὶ φοβούμενος τὸν θεόν, μαρτυρούμενός.τε ὑπὸ ὅλου
[1]righteous and fearing God, and borne witness to by [2]whole

τοῦ ἔθνους τῶν Ἰουδαίων, ἐχρηματίσθη ὑπὸ ἀγγέλου
[1]the nation of the Jews, was divinely instructed by [3]angel

4 And when he looked intently at him, he was afraid and said, What is it sir? And he said to him, Your prayers and your charity have come up for a memorial before God.

5 And now send men to Joppa, and send for Simon whose last name is Peter.

6 He is staying with one Simon, a tanner, whose house is by the sea. He will tell you what you ought to do.

7 And when the angel who spoke to Cornelius left, he called two of his servants and a pious soldier from among those who always waited on him.

8 And after he told them all things, he sent them to Joppa.

9 And on the next day, as these were traveling and drawing near to the city, Peter went up on the roof to pray, about the sixth hour.

10 And he became very hungry and wanted to eat. But as they were making ready, a trance fell on him.

11 And he saw the heavens opened up and a certain vessel coming down on him, like a giant sheet tied at the four corners, and being let down on the earth.

12 And in *it* were all kinds of four-footed animals of the earth, and the wild beasts, and creeping things, and the birds of the sky.

13 And a voice came to him, Get up, Peter! Kill and eat!

14 But Peter said, Oh no, Lord, for I never have eaten anything common or unclean.

15 And again the second time a voice *came,* What God has made clean you do not make common!

16 And this took place three times, then the vessel was taken up into Heaven.

17 And even as Peter was bewildered as to what the vision which he saw might mean, then, behold, the men who were sent from Cornelius (having asked for the house of Simon) stood at the gate.

18 And they called out asking if Simon, whose last name was Peter was living there.

19 And even while Peter thought on the vision, the Spirit said to him, See! Three men are looking for you.

20 But get up and go down and go with them, doubting nothing, for I have sent them.

21 And Peter went down to the men who were sent to him from Cornelius. And he said, See! I am the one you seek. Why did you come?

22 And they said, Cornelius, a captain, a righteous and God-fearing man, also one well-spoken of by all the nation of the Jews, was warned by a holy angel to send for you to come to his house and to hear words from you.

ἁγίου, μεταπέμψασθαί σε εἰς τὸν.οἶκον.αὐτοῦ, καὶ ἀκοῦσαι
a holy, to send for thee to his house, and to hear
ῥήματα παρὰ σοῦ. 23 Εἰσκαλεσάμενος οὖν αὐτοὺς ἐξένισεν.
words from thee. Having called in therefore them he lodged
Τῇ.δὲ ἐπαύριον [a]ὁ Πέτρος[‖] ἐξῆλθεν σὺν αὐτοῖς, καί
[them]. And on the morrow Peter went forth with them, and
τινες τῶν ἀδελφῶν τῶν ἀπὸ [b]τῆς[‖] Ἰόππης συνῆλθον αὐτῷ.
certain of the brethren those from Joppa went with him.
24 [c]καὶ τῇ[‖] ἐπαύριον [d]εἰσῆλθον[‖] εἰς τὴν [e]Καισάρειαν·[‖]
And on the morrow they entered into Cæsarea.
ὁ.δὲ.Κορνήλιος ἦν προσδοκῶν αὐτούς, [f]συγκαλεσάμενος[‖] τοὺς
And Cornelius was expecting them, having called together
συγγενεῖς.αὐτοῦ καὶ τοὺς ἀναγκαίους φίλους. 25 Ὡς.δὲ
his kinsmen and intimate friends. And as
ἐγένετο [g] εἰσελθεῖν τὸν Πέτρον, συναντήσας αὐτῷ ὁ Κορνήλιος,
was coming in Peter, having met him Cornelius,
πεσὼν ἐπὶ τοὺς πόδας προσεκύνησεν. 26 ὁ.δὲ.Πέτρος
having fallen at [his] feet did homage. But Peter
[h]αὐτὸν ἤγειρεν,[‖] λέγων, Ἀνάστηθι· [i]κἀγὼ[‖] αὐτὸς ἄνθρωπός
him raised, saying, Rise up: I also myself a man
εἰμι. 27 Καὶ συνομιλῶν αὐτῷ εἰσῆλθεν, καὶ εὑρίσκει συνεληλυθότας
am. And talking with him he went in, and finds gathered together
πολλούς. 28 ἔφη.τε πρὸς αὐτούς, Ὑμεῖς ἐπίστασθε
many. And he said to them, Ye know
ὡς ἀθέμιτόν ἐστιν ἀνδρὶ Ἰουδαίῳ κολλᾶσθαι ἢ προσέρχεσθαι
how unlawful it is for a man a Jew to unite himself or come near
ἀλλοφύλῳ· [k]καὶ ἐμοὶ[‖] [l]ὁ θεὸς ἔδειξεν[‖] μηδένα
to one of another race. And to me God shewed no
κοινὸν ἢ ἀκάθαρτον λέγειν ἄνθρωπον· 29 διὸ καὶ ἀναντιρρήτως
common or unclean to call man. Wherefore also without gainsaying
ἦλθον μεταπεμφθείς. πυνθάνομαι οὖν, τίνι
I came, having been sent for. I inquire therefore, for what
λόγῳ [m]μετεπέμψασθέ[‖] με; 30 Καὶ ὁ Κορνήλιος ἔφη, Ἀπὸ
reason did ye send for me? And Cornelius said, Ago
τετάρτης ἡμέρας μέχρι ταύτης τῆς ὥρας ἤμην [n]νηστεύων, καὶ[‖]
four days until this hour I was fasting, and
τὴν [o]ἐννάτην[‖] [p]ὥραν[‖] προσευχόμενος ἐν τῷ.οἴκῳ.μου· καὶ ἰδού,
the ninth hour praying in my house; and behold,
ἀνὴρ ἔστη ἐνώπιόν μου ἐν ἐσθῆτι λαμπρᾷ, 31 καί φησιν,
a man stood before me in apparel bright, and said,
Κορνήλιε, εἰσηκούσθη σου ἡ προσευχὴ καὶ αἱ.ἐλεημοσύναι.σου
Cornelius, was heard thy prayer and thine alms
ἐμνήσθησαν ἐνώπιον τοῦ θεοῦ. 32 πέμψον οὖν εἰς Ἰόππην,
were remembered before God. Send therefore to Joppa,
καὶ μετακάλεσαι Σίμωνα ὃς ἐπικαλεῖται Πέτρος· οὗτος ξενίζεται
and call for Simon who is surnamed Peter; he lodges
ἐν οἰκίᾳ Σίμωνος βυρσέως παρὰ θάλασσαν· [q]ὃς
in [the] house of Simon a tanner by [the] sea; who
παραγενόμενος λαλήσει σοι.[‖] 33 [r]Ἐξαυτῆς[‖] οὖν ἔπεμψα
having come will speak to thee. At once therefore I sent
πρός σε· σύ.τε καλῶς ἐποίησας παραγενόμενος. νῦν οὖν
to thee; and thou well didst having come. Now therefore
πάντες ἡμεῖς ἐνώπιον τοῦ θεοῦ πάρεσμεν ἀκοῦσαι πάντα τὰ
all we before God are present to hear all things that
προστεταγμένα σοι [s]ὑπὸ[‖] [t]τοῦ θεοῦ.[‖] 34 Ἀνοίξας.δὲ Πέτρος
have been ordered thee by God. And opening Peter
τὸ στόμα εἶπεν, Ἐπ᾽.ἀληθείας καταλαμβάνομαι ὅτι οὐκ
[his] mouth said, Of a truth I perceive that not
ἔστιν [v]προσωπολήπτης[‖] ὁ θεός, 35 ἀλλ᾽ ἐν παντὶ ἔθνει ὁ
is a respecter of persons God, but in every nation he that
φοβούμενος αὐτὸν καὶ ἐργαζόμενος δικαιοσύνην, δεκτὸς αὐτῷ
fears him and works righteousness, acceptable to him
ἐστιν. 36 τὸν λόγον [w]ὃν[‖] ἀπέστειλεν τοῖς υἱοῖς Ἰσραήλ,
is. The word which he sent to the sons of Israel,
εὐαγγελιζόμενος εἰρήνην διὰ Ἰησοῦ χριστοῦ, οὗτός ἐστιν
announcing the glad tidings— peace by Jesus Christ, (he is
πάντων κύριος, 37 ὑμεῖς οἴδατε· τὸ γενόμενον ῥῆμα
of all Lord), ye know; the which came declaration
καθ᾽ ὅλης τῆς Ἰουδαίας, [x]ἀρξάμενον[‖] [y] ἀπὸ τῆς Γαλιλαίας,
through whole the of Judæa, beginning from Galilee,
μετὰ τὸ βάπτισμα ὃ ἐκήρυξεν [z]Ἰωάννης·[‖] 38 Ἰησοῦν τὸν
after the baptism which proclaimed John: Jesus who
ἀπὸ [a]Ναζαρέτ,[‖] ὡς ἔχρισεν αὐτὸν ὁ θεὸς πνεύματι
[was] from Nazareth, how anointed him God with [the] Spirit
ἁγίῳ καὶ δυνάμει, ὃς διῆλθεν εὐεργετῶν καὶ ἰώμενος
Holy and with power, who went through, doing good and healing
πάντας τοὺς καταδυναστευομένους ὑπὸ τοῦ διαβόλου, ὅτι
all that were being oppressed by the devil, because
ὁ θεὸς ἦν μετ᾽ αὐτοῦ· 39 καὶ ἡμεῖς [b]ἐσμεν[‖] μάρτυρες πάντων
God was with him. And we are witnesses of all things
ὧν ἐποίησεν ἔν.τε τῇ χώρᾳ τῶν Ἰουδαίων καὶ [c]ἐν[‖] Ἰε-
which he did both in the country of the Jews and in Je-

23 Then he called them in and housed them. And on the next day Peter went with them. And some of the brothers from Joppa went with him.

24 And on the next day they entered Caesarea. And Cornelius was expecting them, having called together his close friends and his relatives.

25 And as Peter was coming in, Cornelius met him, falling down at his feet, worshiping.

26 But Peter raised him up, saying, Stand up! I myself also am a man.

27 And talking with him, he went in. And he found many gathered together.

28 And he said to them, You know that it is not lawful for a Jewish man to go with or come near to one of another race. But God taught me not to call any man common or unclean.

29 So when I was called, I came without doubt. I therefore ask for what reason did you send for me?

30 And Cornelius said, Four days ago until this hour, I was fasting and praying in my house at the ninth hour. And, behold! A man stood in front of me in bright clothing!

31 And he said, Cornelius, your prayer was heard and your kind deeds were remembered before God.

32 So send to Joppa and call for Simon whose last name is Peter. He is staying in Simon's house, a tanner, by the sea. When he comes he will speak to you.

33 So, I immediately sent to you. And you did well to come. Now, then, we are all here before God to hear all things that God has commanded you.

34 And Peter, opening his mouth, said, Indeed I see that God is not a respecter of persons.

35 But in every nation, he who fears Him and works righteousness is acceptable to Him.

36 The word which He sent to the sons of Israel, preaching the gospel, peace by Jesus Christ (He is Lord of all!) you know.

37 *It is* the message which came throughout all Judea, having begun from Galilee after the baptism which John preached.

38 That God anointed Jesus (who was from Nazareth) with the Holy Spirit and with power. *He* went about doing good and healing all that were pressed down by the devil, because God was with Him.

39 And we are witnesses of all things which He did, both in the country of the Jews, and in Jerusalem (whom they killed by hanging Him on a tree).

ρουσαλήμ· ὃν d ᶜἀνεῖλον‖ κρεμάσαντες ἐπὶ ξύλου.
rusalem; whom they put to death having hanged [him] on a tree.
40 τοῦτον ὁ θεὸς ἤγειρεν f τῇ τρίτῃ ἡμέρᾳ, καὶ ἔδωκεν αὐτὸν
This one God raised up on the third day, and gave him
ἐμφανῆ γενέσθαι, 41 οὐ παντὶ τῷ λαῷ, ἀλλὰ μάρτυσιν τοῖς
[2]manifest [1]to [2]become, not to all the people, but to witnesses who
προκεχειροτονημένοις ὑπὸ τοῦ θεοῦ, ἡμῖν, οἵτινες συνεφάγομεν
had been chosen before by God, to us, who did eat with
καὶ συνεπίομεν αὐτῷ μετὰ τὸ.ἀναστῆναι.αὐτὸν ἐκ
and did drink with him after he had risen from among [the]
νεκρῶν· 42 καὶ παρήγγειλεν ἡμῖν κηρύξαι τῷ λαῷ, καὶ
dead. And he charged us to proclaim to the people, and
διαμαρτύρασθαι ὅτι gαὐτός‖ ἐστιν ὁ ὡρισμένος ὑπὸ τοῦ
to testify fully that he it is who has been appointed by
θεοῦ κριτὴς ζώντων καὶ νεκρῶν. 43 τούτῳ πάντες οἱ προφῆται
God judge of living and dead. To him all the prophets
μαρτυροῦσιν, ἄφεσιν ἁμαρτιῶν λαβεῖν διὰ τοῦ ὀνόματος
bear witness, [that] [8]remission [9]of [10]sins [7]receives [11]through [13]name
αὐτοῦ πάντα τὸν πιστεύοντα εἰς αὐτόν.
[12]his [1]every [2]one [3]that [4]believes [5]on [6]him.

40 This One God raised up on the third day
and caused Him to be seen,
41 not to all the people but to witnesses
chosen before by God, even to us who ate
with Him and drank with Him after He had
risen from the dead.
42 And He commanded us to preach to the
people and to fully testify that He is the One
appointed by God to be the Judge of living
and dead.
43 All the prophets witness to Him, that
through His name everyone that believes on
Him receives remission of sins.

44 Ἔτι λαλοῦντος τοῦ Πέτρου τὰ.ῥήματα.ταῦτα, hἐπέπεσεν‖
[4]Yet [1]as [3]is [5]speaking [2]Peter these words, [6]fell
τὸ πνεῦμα τὸ ἅγιον ἐπὶ πάντας τοὺς ἀκούοντας τὸν λόγον.
[1]the [2]Spirit [3]the [4]Holy upon all those hearing the word.
45 καὶ ἐξέστησαν οἱ ἐκ περιτομῆς πιστοὶ iὅσοι‖ kσυνῆλ-
And were amazed the [2]of [3]the [4]circumcision [1]believers as many as came
θον‖ τῷ Πέτρῳ, ὅτι καὶ ἐπὶ τὰ ἔθνη ἡ δωρεὰ τοῦ lἁγίου
with Peter, that also upon the Gentiles the gift of the Holy
πνεύματος‖ ἐκκέχυται· 46 ἤκουον.γὰρ αὐτῶν λαλούν-
Spirit had been poured out; for they heard them speak-
των γλώσσαις καὶ μεγαλυνόντων τὸν θεόν. τότε ἀπεκρίθη
ing with tongues and magnifying God. Then answered
mὁ‖ Πέτρος, 47 Μήτι τὸ ὕδωρ nκωλῦσαι δύναταί‖ τις
Peter, [5]The [6]water [4]forbid [1]can [2]any [3]one
τοῦ μὴ.βαπτισθῆναι τούτους, οἵτινες τὸ πνεῦμα τὸ ἅγιον
that should not be baptized these, who the Spirit the Holy
ἔλαβον oκαθὼς‖ καὶ ἡμεῖς; 48 προσέταξέν.pτε‖ qαὐτοὺς‖ rβαπ-
received as also we? And he ordered them to be
τισθῆναι ἐν τῷ ὀνόματι τοῦ κυρίου.‖ τότε ἠρώτησαν αὐτὸν
baptized in the name of the Lord. Then they begged him
ἐπιμεῖναι ἡμέρας τινάς.
to remain [2]days [1]some.

44 Even while Peter was speaking these
words, the Holy Spirit fell on all those
hearing the word.
45 And those of the circumcision-believers
(who came with Peter) were amazed that the
gift of the Holy Spirit had also been poured
out on the Gentiles.
46 For they heard them speaking with
languages and magnifying God. Then Peter
said,
47 Can anyone keep back water that these
should not be baptized who have received
the Holy Spirit even as we also did?
48 And he commanded them to be baptized
in the name of the Lord. Then they begged
him to stay certain days.

11 Ἤκουσαν.δὲ οἱ ἀπόστολοι καὶ οἱ ἀδελφοὶ οἱ ὄντες κατὰ
And [3]heard [1]the [2]apostles and the brethren who were in
τὴν Ἰουδαίαν, ὅτι καὶ τὰ ἔθνη ἐδέξαντο τὸν λόγον τοῦ θεοῦ.
Judæa, that also the Gentiles received the word of God;
2 sκαὶ ὅτε‖ ἀνέβη Πέτρος εἰς tἹεροσόλυμα,‖ διεκρίνοντο πρὸς
and when [2]went [3]up [1]Peter to Jerusalem, [5]contended [6]with
αὐτὸν οἱ ἐκ περιτομῆς, 3 λέγοντες, Ὅτι vπρὸς ἄνδρας
[7]him [1]those [2]of [3]the [4]circumcision, saying, To men
ἀκροβυστίαν.ἔχοντας wεἰσῆλθες,‖ καὶ wσυνέφαγες‖ αὐτοῖς.
uncircumcised thou wentest in, and didst eat with them.
4 Ἀρξάμενος.δὲ xὁ‖ Πέτρος ἐξετίθετο αὐτοῖς καθεξῆς λέ-
But [2]having [3]begun [1]Peter he set [it] forth to them in order say-
γων, 5 Ἐγὼ ἤμην ἐν πόλει Ἰόππῃ προσευχόμενος, καὶ
ing, I was in [the] city of Joppa praying, and
εἶδον ἐν ἐκστάσει ὅραμα, καταβαῖνον σκεῦός τι ὡς ὀθόνην
I saw in a trance a vision, [4]descending [1]a [3]vessel [2]certain like a [2]sheet
μεγάλην, τέσσαρσιν ἀρχαῖς καθιεμένην ἐκ τοῦ οὐρανοῦ. καὶ
[1]great, by four corners let down out of the heaven, and
ἦλθεν yἄχρις‖ ἐμοῦ. 6 εἰς ἣν ἀτενίσας κατενόουν,
it came as far as me: on which having looked intently I considered,
καὶ εἶδον τὰ τετράποδα τῆς γῆς καὶ τὰ θηρία καὶ τὰ ἑρ-
and saw the quadrupeds of the earth and the wild beasts and the creeping
πετὰ καὶ τὰ πετεινὰ τοῦ οὐρανοῦ. 7 ἤκουσα.δὲ z φωνῆς λε-
things and the birds of the heaven. And I heard a voice say-
γούσης μοι, Ἀναστάς, Πέτρε, θῦσον καὶ φάγε. 8 εἶπον.δέ,
ing to me, Having risen up, Peter, kill and eat. But I said,
Μηδαμῶς, κύριε· ὅτι aπᾶν‖ κοινὸν ἢ ἀκάθαρτον οὐδέποτε
In no wise, Lord, for anything common or unclean never
εἰσῆλθεν εἰς τὸ.στόμα.μου. 9 ἀπεκρίθη.δέ bμοι‖ φωνὴ ἐκ.δευ-
entered into my mouth. But [3]answered [4]me [1]a [2]voice the second
τέρου ἐκ τοῦ οὐρανοῦ, Ἃ ὁ θεὸς cἐκαθάρισεν,‖ σὺ μὴ
time out of the heaven, What God cleansed, [3]thou [2]not
κοίνου. 10 τοῦτο.δὲ ἐγένετο ἐπὶ.τρίς, καὶ dπάλιν ἀνε-
[1]make common. And this took place thrice, and again was
σπάσθη‖ ἅπαντα εἰς τὸν οὐρανόν. 11 καὶ ἰδού, eἐξαυτῆς‖ τρεῖς
drawn up all into the heaven. And lo, at once three
ἄνδρες ἐπέστησαν ἐπὶ τὴν οἰκίαν ἐν ᾗ fἤμην,‖ ἀπεσταλμένοι
men stood at the house in which I was, sent
ἀπὸ gΚαισαρείας‖ πρός με. 12 εἶπεν.δέ hμοι τὸ πνεῦμα,‖
from Cæsarea to me. And [3]said [4]to [5]me [1]the [2]Spirit,

CHAPTER 11

1 And the apostles and brothers who were
in Judea heard that the Gentiles received the
word of God also.
2 And when Peter went up to Jerusalem,
they of the circumcision argued with him,
3 saying, You went in to men not circumcised and ate with them.
4 But Peter began explaining to them in
order, saying,
5 I was in the city of Joppa praying. And in
a trance I saw a vision: A certain vessel like a
giant sheet came down, lowered by its four
corners out of Heaven. And it came to me.
6 Looking in, I fixed my eyes and saw the
four-footed animals of the earth, and the
wild beasts, and the creeping things, and the
birds of the sky.
7 And I heard a voice saying to me, Get up,
Peter! Kill and eat!
8 But I said, No, Lord, for nothing common
or unclean has entered my mouth.
9 But a voice said to me the second time
out of Heaven, What God made clean, you
do not make common.
10 And this happened three times, and all
was again drawn up into Heaven.
11 And, behold! Immediately three men
stood at the house where I was, having been
sent from Caesarea to me.
12 And the Spirit said for me to go with

συνελθεῖν αὐτοῖς, ¹μηδὲν διακρινόμενον·ᴵᴵ ἦλθον.δὲ σὺν ἐμοὶ
to go with them, nothing doubting. And went with me
καὶ οἱ ἓξ ἀδελφοὶ οὗτοι, καὶ εἰσήλθομεν εἰς τὸν οἶκον τοῦ
also ²six ³brethren ¹these, and we entered into the house of the
ἀνδρός, 13 ἀπήγγειλέν.ᵏτεᴵᴵ ἡμῖν πῶς εἶδεν τὸν ἄγγελον ἐν
man, and he related to us how he saw the angel in
τῷ.οἴκῳ.αὐτοῦ σταθέντα καὶ εἰπόντα ˡαὐτῷ,ᴵᴵ Ἀπόστειλον εἰς
his house standing and saying to him, Send ²to
Ἰόππην ᵐἄνδρας,ᴵᴵ καὶ μετάπεμψαι Σίμωνα τὸν ἐπικαλούμενον
³Joppa ¹men, and send for Simon who is surnamed
Πέτρον, 14 ὃς λαλήσει ῥήματα πρός σε ἐν.οἷς σωθήσῃ
Peter, who shall speak words to thee whereby shalt be saved
σὺ καὶ πᾶς ὁ.οἶκός.σου. 15 ἐν.δὲ τῷ.ἄρξασθαί.με λαλεῖν
thou and all thy house. And in my beginning to speak
ἐπέπεσεν τὸ πνεῦμα τὸ ἅγιον ἐπ' αὐτούς, ὥσπερ καὶ ἐφ'
⁵fell ¹the ²Spirit ³the ⁴Holy upon them, even as also upon
ἡμᾶς ἐν ἀρχῇ 16 ἐμνήσθην.δὲ τοῦ ῥήματος ⁿ κυρίου,
us in [the] beginning. And I remembered the word of [the] Lord,
ὡς ἔλεγεν, ᵒἸωάννηςᴵᴵ μὲν ἐβάπτισεν ὕδατι, ὑμεῖς.δὲ
how he said, John indeed baptized with water, but ye
βαπτισθήσεσθε ἐν πνεύματι ἁγίῳ. 17 Εἰ οὖν τὴν ἴσην
shall be baptized with [the] ²Spirit ¹Holy. If then the like
δωρεὰν ἔδωκεν αὐτοῖς ὁ θεὸς ὡς καὶ ἡμῖν, πιστεύσασιν ἐπὶ
gift ²gave ³to ⁴them ¹God as also to us, having believed on
τὸν κύριον Ἰησοῦν χριστόν, ἐγὼ.ᵖδὲᴵᴵ τίς ἤμην δυνατὸς
the Lord Jesus Christ, and I, who was I, [to be] able
κωλῦσαι τὸν θεόν; 18 Ἀκούσαντες.δὲ ταῦτα ἡσύχασαν,
to forbid God? And having heard these things they were silent,
καὶ ᵠἐδόξαζονᴵᴵ τὸν θεόν, λέγοντες, ʳἌραγεᴵᴵ καὶ τοῖς ἔθνεσιν
and glorified God, saying, Then indeed also to the Gentiles
ὁ θεὸς τὴν μετάνοιαν ˢἔδωκεν εἰς ζωήν.ᴵᴵ
God ²repentance ¹gave unto life.

19 Οἱ μὲν οὖν διασπαρέντες ἀπὸ τῆς θλίψεως τῆς
They indeed therefore who were scattered by the tribulation that
γενομένης ἐπὶ ᵗΣτεφάνῳ,ᴵᴵ διῆλθον ἕως Φοινίκης καὶ Κύπρου
took place upon Stephen, passed through to Phœnicia and Cyprus
καὶ Ἀντιοχείας, μηδενὶ λαλοῦντες τὸν λόγον εἰ.μὴ μόνον
and Antioch, to no one speaking the word except ³only
Ἰουδαίοις. 20 ἦσαν.δέ τινες ἐξ αὐτῶν ἄνδρες Κύπριοι καὶ
¹to ²Jews. But were certain ²of ³them ¹men Cypriots and
Κυρηναῖοι, οἵτινες ᵛεἰσελθόντεςᴵᴵ εἰς Ἀντιόχειαν, ἐλάλουν ʷ
Cyrenians, who having come into Antioch, spoke
πρὸς τοὺς ˣἙλληνιστάςᴵᴵ εὐαγγελιζόμενοι τὸν κύριον
to the Hellenists, announcing the glad tidings— the Lord
Ἰησοῦν. 21 καὶ ἦν χεὶρ κυρίου μετ' αὐτῶν· πολύς.τε
Jesus. And ⁶was [¹the] ²hand ³of [⁴the] ⁵Lord with them, and a great
ἀριθμὸς ʸ πιστεύσας ἐπέστρεψεν ἐπὶ τὸν κύριον. 22 Ἠκούσθη
number having believed turned to the Lord. ⁴Was ⁵heard
δὲ ὁ λόγος εἰς τὰ ὦτα τῆς ἐκκλησίας τῆς ᶻ ἐν ᵃἹερο-
¹and ²the ³report in the ears of the assembly which [was] in Jeru-
σολύμοιςᴵᴵ περὶ αὐτῶν· καὶ ἐξαπέστειλαν Βαρνάβαν ᵇδιελ-
salem concerning them; and they sent forth Barnabas to go
θεῖνᴵᴵ ἕως Ἀντιοχείας. 23 ὃς παραγενόμενος καὶ ἰδὼν
through as far as Antioch: who having come and having seen
τὴν χάριν ᶜ τοῦ θεοῦ ἐχάρη, καὶ παρεκάλει πάντας τῇ.προθέσει
the grace of God rejoiced, and exhorted all with purpose
τῆς καρδίας προσμένειν τῷ κυρίῳ· 24 ὅτι ἦν ἀνὴρ ἀγαθὸς
of heart to abide with the Lord; for he was a ²man ¹good
καὶ πλήρης πνεύματος ἁγίου καὶ πίστεως. καὶ προσετέθη
and full of [the] ²Spirit ¹Holy and of faith. And was added
ὄχλος ἱκανὸς τῷ κυρίῳ. 25 Ἐξῆλθεν.δὲ εἰς Ταρσὸν ᵈὁ Βαρ-
a ²crowd ¹large to the Lord. And ²went ³forth ⁴to ⁵Tarsus ¹Bar-
νάβαςᴵᴵ ἀναζητῆσαι Σαῦλον, 26 καὶ εὑρὼν ᵉαὐτὸνᴵᴵ ἤγαγεν
nabas to seek Saul; and having found him he brought
ᵉαὐτὸνᴵᴵ εἰς Ἀντιόχειαν. ἐγένετο.δὲ ᶠαὐτοὺςᴵᴵ ἐνιαυτὸν
him to Antioch. And it came to pass they a ²year
ὅλον συναχθῆναι ἐν τῇ ἐκκλησίᾳ, καὶ διδάξαι ὄχλον
¹whole were gathered together in the assembly, and taught a ²crowd
ἱκανόν, χρηματίσαι.τε ᵍπρῶτονᴵᴵ ἐν Ἀντιοχείᾳ τοὺς μαθητὰς
¹large: and ³were ⁵called ⁴first ⁷in ⁸Antioch ¹the ²disciples
Χριστιανούς.
⁶Christians.

27 Ἐν.ταύταις.δὲ ταῖς ἡμέραις κατῆλθον ἀπὸ Ἱεροσολύμων
And in these days came down from Jerusalem
προφῆται εἰς Ἀντιόχειαν. 28 ἀναστὰς.δὲ εἷς ἐξ
prophets to Antioch; and ⁷having ⁶risen ⁷up ¹one ²from ³among
αὐτῶν ὀνόματι Ἄγαβος, ʰἐσήμανενᴵᴵ διὰ τοῦ πνεύματος,
⁴them, by name Agabus, he signified by the Spirit,
λιμὸν ⁱμέγανᴵᴵ μέλλειν ἔσεσθαι ἐφ' ὅλην τὴν οἰκουμένην·
A ²famine ¹great is about to be over ²whole ¹the habitable world;
ᵏὅστιςᴵᴵ ˡκαὶᴵᴵ ἐγένετο ἐπὶ Κλαυδίου ᵐΚαίσαρος.ᴵᴵ 29 τῶν.δὲ
which also came to pass under Claudius Cæsar. And the

them, doubting nothing. And six of these
brothers went with me. And we went into
the house of the man.
13 And he told us how he saw the angel
standing in his house and saying to him,
Send men to Joppa and send for Simon,
whose last name is Peter,
14 who shall speak words to you by which
you and all your household shall be saved.
15 And as I began to speak, the Holy Spirit
fell upon them also, even as on us in the
beginning.
16 And I remembered the word of the Lord
saying, John indeed baptized with water, but
you shall be baptized with the Holy Spirit.
17 If then God gave the same gift to them
as also to us, when we had believed on the
Lord Jesus Christ, who was I to be able to
withstand God?
18 And hearing these things, they were
silent and glorified God, saying, Then truly
God gave repentance to life to the Gentiles
also.

19 Then, indeed, they who were scattered
abroad by the persecution that took place
over Stephen, traveled to Phen-ic-i-a and
Cyprus and Antioch, preaching the word to
no one except to Jews only.
20 But certain ones of them were men of
Cyprus and Cy-re-ne who, coming into
Antioch, spoke to the Greek-speaking Jews,
preaching the gospel of the Lord Jesus.
21 And the hand of the Lord was with them
and very many turned to the Lord, believing.
22 And the news about them was heard in
the ears of the church in Jerusalem. And
they sent Barnabas to go to Antioch.
23 *He* rejoiced when he had come and had
seen the grace of God and had encouraged
them to continue in the Lord with purpose
of heart.
24 For he was a good man and full of the
Holy Spirit and of faith. And a great company was added to the Lord.
25 And Barnabas went out to Tarsus to
look for Saul.
26 And having found him, he brought him
to Antioch. For a whole year they gathered
together in the church and taught a huge
crowd. And the disciples were first called
Christians in Antioch.

27 And in these days prophets came down
from Jerusalem to Antioch.
28 And one named Agabus rose up from
among them and showed by the Spirit that a
great famine was going to come over the
whole world (which also happened in the
time of Claudius Caesar).

μαθητῶν καθὼς "ηὐπορεῖτό" τις, ὥρισαν ἕκαστος αὐ-
disciples according as [3]was [4]prospered [1]any [2]one, determined, each of
τῶν εἰς διακονίαν πέμψαι τοῖς κατοικοῦσιν ἐν τῇ Ἰουδαίᾳ
them, for ministration to send to the [2]dwelling [3]in [4]Judæa
ἀδελφοῖς· 30 ὃ καὶ ἐποίησαν, ἀποστείλαντες πρὸς τοὺς
[1]brethren; which also they did, sending [it] to the
πρεσβυτέρους διὰ χειρὸς Βαρνάβα καὶ Σαύλου.
elders by [the] hand of Barnabas and Saul.

12 Κατ'.ἐκεῖνον.δὲ τὸν.καιρὸν ἐπέβαλεν [o]Ἡρώδης ὁ βασι-
And at [1]that time [4]put [5]forth [1]Herod [2]the [3]king
λεὺς" τὰς χεῖρας κακῶσαί τινας τῶν ἀπὸ τῆς ἐκκλησίας.
[his] hands to ill-treat some of those of the assembly;
2 ἀνεῖλεν.δὲ Ἰάκωβον τὸν ἀδελφὸν [p]Ἰωάννου" [q]μαχαίρᾳ."
and he put to death James the brother of John with a sword.
3 [r]καὶ ἰδὼν" ὅτι ἀρεστόν ἐστιν τοῖς Ἰουδαίοις προσέθετο
And having seen that pleasing it is to the Jews he added
συλλαβεῖν καὶ Πέτρον· ἦσαν.δὲ [s] ἡμέραι τῶν.ἀζύμων·
to take also Peter: (and they were days of unleavened bread:)
4 ὃν καὶ πιάσας ἔθετο εἰς φυλακήν, παραδοὺς τέσσαρ-
whom also having seized he put in prison, having delivered to four
σιν τετραδίοις στρατιωτῶν φυλάσσειν αὐτόν, βουλόμενος μετὰ
sets of four soldiers to guard him, purposing after
τὸ πάσχα ἀναγαγεῖν αὐτὸν τῷ λαῷ. 5 ὁ.μὲν.οὖν.Πέτρος
the passover to bring out him to the people. Peter therefore indeed
ἐτηρεῖτο ἐν τῇ φυλακῇ· προσευχὴ.δὲ ἦν [t]ἐκτενὴς" γινομένη
was kept in the prison; but [2]prayer [3]was [1]fervent made
ὑπὸ τῆς ἐκκλησίας πρὸς τὸν θεὸν [v]ὑπὲρ" αὐτοῦ. 6 "Ὅτε.δὲ
by the assembly to God concerning him. But when
[w]ἔμελλεν" [x]αὐτὸν προάγειν" ὁ Ἡρώδης, τῇ.νυκτὶ.ἐκείνῃ ἦν
[2]was [3]about [6]him [4]to [5]bring [7]forth [1]Herod, in that night was
ὁ Πέτρος κοιμώμενος μεταξὺ δύο στρατιωτῶν, δεδεμένος ἁλύ-
Peter sleeping between two soldiers, bound with
σεσιν δυσίν, φύλακές τε πρὸ τῆς θύρας ἐτήρουν τὴν φυλακήν.
[2]chains [1]two, guards also before the door kept the prison.
7 καὶ ἰδού, ἄγγελος κυρίου ἐπέστη, καὶ φῶς ἔλαμψεν ἐν
And behold, an angel of [the] Lord stood by, and a light shone in
τῷ οἰκήματι. πατάξας.δὲ τὴν πλευρὰν τοῦ Πέτρου ἤγειρεν
the building. And having smitten the side of Peter he roused up
αὐτὸν λέγων, Ἀνάστα ἐν τάχει. Καὶ [y]ἐξέπεσον" αὐτοῦ αἱ
him, saying, Rise up in haste. And fell off of him the
ἁλύσεις ἐκ τῶν χειρῶν. 8 εἶπέν.[z]τε" ὁ ἄγγελος πρὸς
chains from [his] hands. And [3]said [1]the [2]angel to
αὐτόν, [a]Περίζωσαι," καὶ ὑπόδησαι τὰ.σανδάλιά.σου. Ἐποίη-
him, Gird thyself about, and bind on thy sandals. [2]He [3]did
σεν δὲ οὕτως. καὶ λέγει αὐτῷ, Περιβαλοῦ τὸ.ἱμάτιόν.σου,
[1]and so. And he says to him, Cast about [thee] thy garment,
καὶ ἀκολούθει μοι. 9 Καὶ ἐξελθὼν ἠκολούθει [b]αὐτῷ·" καὶ
and follow me. And going forth he followed him, and
οὐκ.ᾔδει ὅτι ἀληθές ἐστιν τὸ γινόμενον διὰ τοῦ ἀγ-
did not know that real it is which is happening by means of the an-
γέλου, ἐδόκει.δὲ ὅραμα βλέπειν. 10 διελθόντες.δὲ πρώτην
gel, but thought a vision he saw. And having passed through a first
φυλακὴν καὶ δευτέραν, [c]ἦλθον" ἐπὶ τὴν πύλην τὴν σιδηρᾶν
guard and a second, they came to the [2]gate [1]iron
τὴν φέρουσαν εἰς τὴν πόλιν, ἥτις αὐτομάτη [d]ἠνοίχθη" αὐτοῖς·
that leads into the city, which of itself opened to them;
καὶ ἐξελθόντες προῆλθον ῥύμην μίαν, καὶ εὐθέως
and having gone out they went on through [2]street [1]one, and immediately
ἀπέστη ὁ ἄγγελος ἀπ' αὐτοῦ. 11 καὶ ὁ Πέτρος [e]γενόμενος
departed the angel from him. And Peter having come
ἐν.ἑαυτῷ" εἶπεν, Νῦν οἶδα ἀληθῶς ὅτι ἐξαπέστειλεν
to himself said, Now I know of a truth that [3]sent [4]forth [[1]the]
κύριος τὸν.ἄγγελον.αὐτοῦ, καὶ [f]ἐξείλετό" με ἐκ χειρὸς
[2]Lord his angel, and delivered me out of [the] hand
Ἡρῴδου καὶ πάσης τῆς προσδοκίας τοῦ λαοῦ τῶν Ἰουδαίων.
of Herod and all the expectation of the people of the Jews.
12 συνιδών.τε ἦλθεν ἐπὶ τὴν οἰκίαν [g] Μαρίας τῆς μητρὸς
And considering [it] he came to the house of Mary the mother
[h]Ἰωάννου" τοῦ ἐπικαλουμένου Μάρκου, οὗ ἦσαν ἱκανοὶ
of John who is surnamed Mark, where were many
συνηθροισμένοι καὶ προσευχόμενοι. 13 Κρούσαντος.δὲ [i]τοῦ
gathered together and praying. And [2]having [3]knocked
Πέτρου" τὴν θύραν τοῦ πυλῶνος, προσῆλθεν παιδίσκη ὑπα-
[1]Peter [at] the door of the porch, [3]came [1]a [2]damsel to
κοῦσαι, ὀνόματι Ῥόδη· 14 καὶ ἐπιγνοῦσα τὴν φωνὴν τοῦ
listen, by name Rhoda; and having recognized the voice
Πέτρου, ἀπὸ τῆς χαρᾶς οὐκ.ἤνοιξεν τὸν πυλῶνα, εἰσδρα-
of Peter, from joy she opened not the porch, [2]having
μοῦσα δὲ ἀπήγγειλεν ἑστάναι τὸν Πέτρον πρὸ τοῦ
[3]run [4]in [1]but she reported [2]to [3]be [4]standing [1]Peter before the
πυλῶνος. 15 οἱ.δὲ πρὸς αὐτὴν [k]εἶπον," Μαίνῃ. Ἡ.δὲ
porch. But they to her said, Thou art mad. But she

29 And every one of the disciples decided to send relief to the brothers living in Judea, as much as anyone was able –
30 which they also did, sending it to the elders by the hand of Barnabas and Saul.

CHAPTER 12

1 And at that time Herod the king stretched out his hands to do evil to some of those of the church.
2 And he killed James the brother of John with the sword.
3 And seeing that it was pleasing to the Jews, he went further to seize Peter too. And they were days of unleavened bread.
4 Having caught *Peter* too, he put him in prison, delivering him to four sets of four soldiers each to guard him, thinking to bring him out to the people after the Passover.
5 Then, indeed, Peter was kept in the prison – but the church prayed fervently to God for him.
6 But when Herod was about to bring him out, that night Peter was sleeping between two soldiers, bound with two chains. And there were guards on duty in front of the prison door.

7 And, behold! An angel of the Lord stood by. And a light shone in the building. And hitting Peter on the side, he awakened him, saying, Get up quickly! And the chains fell from his hands. And the angel said to him, Dress yourself and put on your sandals. And he did so.
8 And he said to him, Put your robe around you and follow me.
9 And he followed him, going out but not realizing that this which was happening by means of the angel was really true. But he thought he saw a vision.

10 And going through the first guard and the second, they came to the iron gate that leads into the city, which opened to them of its own accord. And going out, they went on through one street. And suddenly the angel left him.
11 Now coming to himself, Peter said, Now I know that the Lord really sent out His angel and rescued me from Herod's hand and all that the people of the Jews expected.
12 And considering it, he came to the house of Mary the mother of John Mark, where many were gathered together and praying.

13 And when Peter knocked at the door of the gate, a girl named Rhoda came to see who was at the door.
14 And recognizing the voice of Peter, she did not open the gate for pure joy. But running inside she told them of Peter standing in front of the gate.

15 But they said to her, You are insane. But

διϊσχυρίζετο οὕτως ἔχειν. [l]οἱ.δ' ἔλεγον," Ὁ ἄγγελος [m]αὐ-
strongly affirmed thus it was. And they said, The angel of
τοῦ ἐστιν." 16 Ὁ.δὲ.Πέτρος ἐπέμενεν κρούων· ἀνοίξαντες.δὲ
him it is. But Peter continued knocking: and having opened
[n]εἶδον" αὐτόν, καὶ ἐξέστησαν. 17 κατασείσας.δὲ αὐτοῖς
they saw him, and were amazed. And having made a sign to them
τῇ χειρὶ σιγᾷν διηγήσατο [o]αὐτοῖς" πῶς ὁ κύριος αὐτὸν
with the hand to be silent he related to them how the Lord him
ἐξήγαγεν ἐκ τῆς φυλακῆς. εἶπεν.[p]δέ," Ἀπαγγείλατε Ἰακώβῳ
brought out of the prison. And he said, Report to James
καὶ τοῖς ἀδελφοῖς ταῦτα. Καὶ ἐξελθὼν ἐπορεύθη εἰς ἕτερον
and to the brethren these things. And having gone out he went to another
τόπον. 18 γενομένης.δὲ ἡμέρας ἦν τάραχος οὐκ ὀλίγος
place. And [2]having [3]come [1]day there was [3]disturbance [1]no [2]small
ἐν τοῖς στρατιώταις, τί ἄρα ὁ Πέτρος ἐγένετο. 19 Ἡρώδης
among the soldiers, what then [3of] [4]Peter [1]was [2]become. [6]Herod
δὲ ἐπιζητήσας αὐτὸν καὶ μὴ εὑρών, ἀνακρίνας τοὺς
[8]and having sought after [5]him [1]and [2]not [3]having [4]found, having examined the
φύλακας ἐκέλευσεν ἀπαχθῆναι· καὶ κατελθὼν
guards he commanded [them] to be led away [to death]. And having gone down
ἀπὸ τῆς Ἰουδαίας εἰς [q]τὴν" [r]Καισάρειαν" διέτριβεν. 20 [s]Ἦν
from Judæa to Cæsarea he stayed [there]. [3]Was
δὲ [s]ὁ Ἡρώδης" θυμομαχῶν Τυρίοις καὶ Σιδωνίοις·
[1]and [2]Herod in bitter hostility with [the] Tyrians and Sidonians;
ὁμοθυμαδὸν.δὲ παρῆσαν πρὸς αὐτόν, καὶ πείσαντες Βλάστον
but with one accord they came to him, and having gained Blastus
τὸν ἐπὶ τοῦ κοιτῶνος τοῦ βασιλέως, ᾐτοῦντο εἰρήνην,
who [was] over the bedchamber of the king, sought peace,
διὰ τὸ τρέφεσθαι αὐτῶν τὴν χώραν ἀπὸ τῆς βασιλικῆς.
because was nourished their country by the king's.
21 Τακτῇ.δὲ ἡμέρᾳ ὁ Ἡρώδης ἐνδυσάμενος ἐσθῆτα βασιλικήν,
And on a set day Herod having put on [2]apparel [1]royal,
[t]καὶ" καθίσας ἐπὶ τοῦ βήματος, ἐδημηγόρει πρὸς αὐ-
and having sat on the tribunal, was making an oration to them.
τούς. 22 ὁ.δὲ δῆμος ἐπεφώνει, Θεοῦ φωνὴ καὶ οὐκ
And the people were crying out, [3]Of [4]a [5]god [1the] [2]voice and not
ἀνθρώπου. 23 παραχρῆμα.δὲ ἐπάταξεν αὐτὸν ἄγγελος κυ-
of a man! And immediately [6]smote [7]him [1]an [2]angel [3]of [4the]
ρίου, ἀνθ'.ὧν οὐκ ἔδωκεν [v]τὴν" δόξαν τῷ θεῷ· καὶ γενόμενος
[5]Lord, because he gave not the glory to God, and having been
σκωληκόβρωτος ἐξέψυξεν. 24 ὁ.δὲ λόγος τοῦ θεοῦ ηὔξανεν
eaten of worms he expired. But the word of God grew
καὶ ἐπληθύνετο. 25 Βαρνάβας.δὲ καὶ Σαῦλος ὑπέστρεψαν ἐξ
and multiplied. And Barnabas and Saul returned from
Ἰερουσαλήμ, πληρώσαντες τὴν διακονίαν, [w]συμπαραλαβόν-
Jerusalem, having fulfilled the ministration, having taken with
τες" [x]καὶ" [y]Ἰωάννην" τὸν ἐπικληθέντα Μάρκον.
[them] also John who was surnamed Mark.
13 Ἦσαν.δέ [z]τινες" ἐν Ἀντιοχείᾳ κατὰ τὴν οὖσαν
Now there were certain in Antioch in the [2]which [3]was [4there]
ἐκκλησίαν προφῆται καὶ διδάσκαλοι, ὅ.τε.Βαρνάβας καὶ Συμεὼν
[1]assembly prophets and teachers, both Barnabas and Simeon
ὁ καλούμενος Νίγερ, καὶ Λούκιος ὁ Κυρηναῖος, Μαναήν.τε
who was called Niger, and Lucius the Cyrenian, and Manaen,
Ἡρώδου τοῦ [a]τετράρχου" σύντροφος, καὶ Σαῦλος. 2 λειτουρ-
of Herod the tetrarch a foster-brother, and Saul. [3]As [4]were [5]min-
γούντων δὲ αὐτῶν τῷ κυρίῳ καὶ νηστευόντων, εἶπεν τὸ
istering [1]and [2]they to the Lord and fasting, [5]said [1]the
πνεῦμα τὸ ἅγιον, Ἀφορίσατε δή μοι τόν.[b]τε".Βαρνάβαν καὶ
[2]Spirit [3]the [4]Holy, Separate indeed to me both Barnabas and
[c]τὸν" Σαῦλον εἰς τὸ ἔργον ὃ προσκέκλημαι αὐτούς. 3 Τότε
Saul for the work to which I have called them. Then
νηστεύσαντες καὶ προσευξάμενοι, καὶ ἐπιθέντες τὰς χεῖρας
having fasted and prayed, and having laid hands
αὐτοῖς, ἀπέλυσαν. 4 [d]Οὗτοι" μὲν οὖν ἐκπεμφθέντες
on them, they let [them] go. They indeed therefore having been sent forth
ὑπὸ τοῦ [e]πνεύματος τοῦ ἁγίου," κατῆλθον εἰς [f]τὴν" [g]Σελεύ-
by the Spirit the Holy, went down to Seleu-
κειαν," ἐκεῖθέν.τε ἀπέπλευσαν εἰς [f]τὴν" Κύπρον. 5 καὶ γενό-
cia, and thence sailed away to Cyprus. And having
μενοι ἐν Σαλαμῖνι κατήγγελλον τὸν λόγον τοῦ θεοῦ ἐν ταῖς
come into Salamis they announced the word of God in the
συναγωγαῖς τῶν Ἰουδαίων· εἶχον.δὲ καὶ [h]Ἰωάννην"
synagogues of the Jews. And they had also John [as]
ὑπηρέτην. 6 διελθόντες.δὲ [i] τὴν νῆσον ἄχρι Πάφου
an attendant. And having passed through the island as far as Paphos
εὗρόν [j] τινα μάγον ψευδοπροφήτην Ἰουδαῖον, ᾧ ὄνομα
they found a certain magician, a false prophet a Jew, whose name
[k]Βαριησοῦς," 7 ὃς ἦν σὺν τῷ ἀνθυπάτῳ Σεργίῳ Παύλῳ,
[was] Barjesus, who was with the proconsul Sergius Paulus,
ἀνδρὶ συνετῷ. οὗτος προσκαλεσάμενος Βαρνάβαν καὶ
[3]man [1]an [2]intelligent. He having called to [him] Barnabas and

she insisted it was so. And they said, It is his angel.

16 But Peter still kept on knocking. And when they opened up, they saw him and were amazed.

17 But waving to them to be silent, he told them how the Lord brought him out of the prison. And he said, Go tell these things to James and to the brothers. And he left and went into another place.

18 And when day came, there was no small stir among the soldiers. What then had become of Peter?

19 And after searching for him and not finding him, Herod examined the guards, *then* commanded *them* to be led away *to* death. And going down from Judea to Caesarea, he remained.

20 And Herod was bitterly displeased with those from Tyre and Sidon. But having made a friend of Blastus, who was over the king's bedroom, they came all together and begged for peace (because their country was fed by the king's).

21 And on a set day, Herod dressed up in royal clothing and sat on the throne, making a speech to them.

22 And the people were crying out, The voice of a god, and not of a man!

23 But immediately an angel of the Lord struck him, because he did not give the glory to God. And he died, being eaten of worms.

24 But the word of God grew and multiplied.

25 And Barnabas and Saul returned from Jerusalem, having completed their mission, also bringing with them John Mark.

CHAPTER 13

1 Now there were certain prophets and teachers there in the church in Antioch – Barnabas and Simeon (who was called Niger) and Lucius the Cy-ren-i-an and Man-a-en (Herod the tetrarch's foster-brother) and Saul.

2 And as they were serving the Lord and fasting, the Holy Spirit said, Now separate both Barnabas and Saul to Me, for the work to which I have called them.

3 Then when they had fasted and prayed and had laid hands on them, they let them go.

4 Then they went down to Se-leu-ci-a, indeed being sent out by the Holy Spirit. And from there they sailed away to Cyprus.

5 And coming into Sal-a-mis, they preached the word of God in the synagogues of the Jews. And they also had John as a minister.

6 And going through the island as far as Paphos, they found a certain magician, a false prophet, a Jew named Bar-je-sus.

7 *He* was with the proconsul, Ser-gi-us Paulus, an intelligent man, who called Barnabas and Saul, asking to hear the word of

Σαῦλον ἐπεζήτησεν ἀκοῦσαι τὸν λόγον τοῦ θεοῦ· 8 ἀνθίστατο.δὲ
Saul desired to hear the word of God. But there withstood
αὐτοῖς Ἐλύμας ὁ μάγος· οὕτως.γὰρ μεθερμηνεύεται τὸ ὄνομα
them Elymas the magician, (for so is interpreted [2]name
αὐτοῦ· ζητῶν διαστρέψαι τὸν ἀνθύπατον ἀπὸ τῆς πίστεως.
[1]his), seeking to pervert the proconsul from the faith.
9 Σαῦλος.δέ, ὁ καὶ Παῦλος, πλησθεὶς πνεύματος ἁγίου,
But Saul, who also [is] Paul, being filled with [the] [2]Spirit [1]Holy,
[l]καὶ‖ ἀτενίσας εἰς αὐτὸν 10 εἶπεν, Ὦ πλήρης παν-
and having looked steadfastly upon him said, O full of
τὸς δόλου καὶ πάσης ῥᾳδιουργίας, υἱὲ διαβόλου, ἐχθρὲ πάσης
all guile and all craft, son of [the] devil, enemy of all
δικαιοσύνης, οὐ.παύσῃ διαστρέφων τὰς ὁδοὺς κυρίου
righteousness, wilt thou not cease perverting the [2]ways [3]of [4the] [5]Lord
τὰς εὐθείας; 11 καὶ νῦν ἰδού, χεὶρ [m]τοῦ‖ κυρίου ἐπὶ σέ,
[1]straight? And now lo, [the] hand of the Lord [is] upon thee,
καὶ ἔσῃ τυφλός, μὴ βλέπων τὸν ἥλιον ἄχρι καιροῦ.
and thou shalt be blind, not seeing the sun for a season.
Παραχρῆμα.[n]δὲ‖ [o]ἐπέπεσεν‖ ἐπ' αὐτὸν ἀχλὺς καὶ σκότος, καὶ
And immediately fell upon him a mist and darkness, and
περιάγων ἐζήτει χειραγωγούς. 12 τότε ἰδὼν
going about he sought some to lead [him] by the hand. Then [3]having [4]seen
ὁ ἀνθύπατος τὸ γεγονὸς ἐπίστευσεν, [p]ἐκπλησσόμενος‖ ἐπὶ
[1]the [2]proconsul what had happened believed, being astonished at
τῇ διδαχῇ τοῦ κυρίου.
the teaching of the Lord.

13 Ἀναχθέντες.δὲ ἀπὸ τῆς Πάφου οἱ περὶ [q]τὸν‖
And having sailed from Paphos [2with] [3]those [4]about [5him]
Παῦλον ἦλθον εἰς Πέργην τῆς Παμφυλίας. [r]Ἰωάννης‖.δὲ
[1]Paul came to Perga of Pamphylia; and John
ἀποχωρήσας ἀπ' αὐτῶν ὑπέστρεψεν εἰς Ἱεροσόλυμα. 14 αὐ-
having departed from them returned to Jerusalem. [2]They
τοὶ δὲ διελθόντες ἀπὸ τῆς Πέργης παρεγένοντο εἰς Ἀν-
[1]but, having passed through from Perga, came to An-
τιόχειαν [s]τῆς Πισιδίας,‖ καὶ [t]εἰσελθόντες‖ εἰς τὴν συναγωγὴν
tioch of Pisidia, and having gone into the synagogue
τῇ ἡμέρᾳ τῶν σαββάτων ἐκάθισαν. 15 Μετὰ.δὲ τὴν ἀνά-
on the [2]day [1]sabbath they sat down. And after the read-
γνωσιν τοῦ νόμου καὶ τῶν προφητῶν ἀπέστειλαν οἱ ἀρχισυνά-
ing of the law and of the prophets [6]sent [1]the [2]rulers [3]of
γωγοι πρὸς αὐτούς, λέγοντες, [v]Ἄνδρες ἀδελφοί, εἰ [v] ἔστιν
[4]the [5]synagogue to them, saying, Men brethren, if there is
[w]λόγος ἐν ὑμῖν‖ παρακλήσεως πρὸς τὸν λαόν, λέγετε.
a word among you of exhortation to the people, speak.
16 Ἀναστὰς.δὲ Παῦλος, καὶ κατασείσας τῇ χειρί, εἶπεν,
And [2]having [3]risen [4]up [1]Paul, and making a sign with the hand, said,
[w]Ἄνδρες [x]Ἰσραηλῖται,‖ καὶ οἱ φοβούμενοι τὸν θεόν, ἀκούσατε.
Men Israelites, and those fearing God, hearken.
17 ὁ θεὸς τοῦ.λαοῦ.τούτου [y]Ἰσραὴλ‖ ἐξελέξατο τοὺς πατέρας
The God of this people Israel chose [2]fathers
ἡμῶν· καὶ τὸν λαὸν ὕψωσεν ἐν τῇ παροικίᾳ ἐν γῇ
[1]our, and [2]the [3]people [1]exalted in the sojourning in [the] land
[z]Αἰγύπτῳ,‖ καὶ μετὰ βραχίονος ὑψηλοῦ ἐξήγαγεν αὐτοὺς ἐξ
of Egypt, and with [3]arm [1]a [2]high brought them out of
αὐτῆς· 18 καὶ ὡς [a]τεσσαρακονταετῆ‖ χρόνον [b]ἐτροπο-
it, and about [3]forty [4]years [1the] [2]time he bore
φόρησεν αὐτοὺς‖ ἐν τῇ ἐρήμῳ. 19 καὶ καθελὼν ἔθνη ἑπτὰ
[2]manners [1]their in the desert. And having destroyed [2]nations [1]seven
ἐν γῇ Χαναάν, [c]κατεκληροδότησεν‖ [d]αὐτοῖς‖ τὴν.γῆν.αὐ-
in [the] land of Canaan, he gave by lot to them their land.
τῶν. 20 [e]καὶ μετὰ ταῦτα, ὡς ἔτεσιν τετρακοσίοις καὶ
And after these things about [5]years [1]four [2]hundred [3]and
πεντήκοντα‖ ἔδωκεν κριτὰς ἕως Σαμουὴλ [f]τοῦ‖ προφήτου·
[4]fifty he gave judges until Samuel the prophet.
21 κἀκεῖθεν ᾐτήσαντο βασιλέα, καὶ ἔδωκεν αὐτοῖς ὁ θεὸς
And then they asked for a king, and [2]gave [3]to [4]them [1]God
τὸν Σαοὺλ υἱὸν [g]Κίς,‖ ἄνδρα ἐκ φυλῆς [h]Βενιαμίν,‖ ἔτη
Saul son of Cis, a man of [the] tribe of Benjamin, [2]years
[i]τεσσαράκοντα.‖ 22 καὶ μεταστήσας αὐτὸν ἤγειρεν [k]αὐτοῖς
[1]forty. And having removed him he raised up to them
τὸν Δαβὶδ‖ εἰς βασιλέα, ᾧ καὶ εἶπεν μαρτυρήσας,
David for king, to whom also [4]he [5]said [1]having [2]borne [3]witness,
Εὗρον [l]Δαβὶδ‖ τὸν τοῦ Ἰεσσαί, ἄνδρα κατὰ τὴν καρδίαν
I found David the [son] of Jesse, a man according to [2]heart
μου, ὃς ποιήσει πάντα τὰ.θελήματά.μου. 23 Τούτου
[1]my, who will do all my will. [4]Of [5]this [6man,]
ὁ θεὸς ἀπὸ τοῦ σπέρματος κατ' ἐπαγγελίαν [m]ἤγειρεν‖ τῷ
[7]God [1]of [2]the [3]seed according to promise raised up
Ἰσραὴλ σωτῆρα Ἰησοῦν, 24 προκηρύξαντος [n]Ἰωάννου‖
to Israel a Saviour Jesus, [2]having [3]before [4]proclaimed [1]John
πρὸ προσώπου τῆς.εἰσόδου.αὐτοῦ βάπτισμα μετανοίας
before [the] face of his entrance a baptism of repentance

God.

8 But El-y-mus the magician (for that is the meaning of his name) opposed them there, wishing to turn the proconsul from the faith.

9 But Saul (*who is* also Paul), being filled with the Holy Spirit and fixing his eyes on him

10 said, O son of the devil, full of all trickery and cunning, enemy of all righteousness, will you not stop perverting the right ways of the Lord?

11 And now look, the hand of the Lord is on you and you will be blind, not seeing the sun for some time. And immediately a mist and darkness fell on him and he went about asking some to lead him by the hand.

12 Then seeing what had happened, the proconsul believed, being gladly amazed at the teaching of the Lord.

13 Paul and those with him sailed from Paphos and came to Perga of Pam-phyl-i-a. And John left them and returned to Jerusalem.

14 But after going through from Perga, they came to Antioch of Pisidia. And going into the synagogue on the Sabbath day, they sat.

15 And after the reading of the Law and the Prophets, the rulers of the synagogue sent to them, saying, Men, brothers! If there is a word of exhortation with you, say it to the people.

16 And Paul got up and signaled with his hand, saying, Men! Israelites, and those fearing God, listen!

17 The God of this people Israel chose out our fathers and lifted up the people in their stay in the land of Egypt, bringing them out with a high arm.

18 And He endured their ways for about forty years in the desert.

19 And having destroyed seven nations in the land of Canaan, He gave their land to them by lot.

20 And afterwards, about four hundred and fifty years, He gave judges until Samuel the prophet.

21 And then they asked for a king. And God gave them Saul, the son of Kish, a man of the tribe of Benjamin, for forty years.

22 And taking him away, He raised up David for their king, to whom also He witnessed, saying, I found David the son of Jesse a man according to My own heart, who shall do all My will.

23 Of the seed of this one, according to promise, God raised up a Savior to Israel, Jesus,

24 after John had first preached a baptism of repentance to all the people of Israel before His coming.

παντὶ τῷ λαῷ Ἰσραήλ. 25 ὡς.δὲ ἐπλήρου [o]ὁ [p]Ἰωάννης
to all the people of Israel. And as [2]was [3]fulfilling [1]John
τὸν δρόμον, ἔλεγεν, [q]Τίνα με ὑπονοεῖτε εἶναι; οὐκ εἰμὶ
[his] course, he said, Whom me do ye suppose to be? [3]Not [2]am
ἐγώ, ἀλλ' ἰδού, ἔρχεται μετ' ἐμέ, οὗ οὐκ.εἰμὶ ἄξιος τὸ ὑπό-
[1]I [he], but lo, he comes after me, of whom I am not worthy the san-
δημα τῶν ποδῶν λῦσαι. 26 Ἄνδρες ἀδελφοί, υἱοὶ γένους
dal of the feet to loose. Men brethren, sons of [the] race
Ἀβραάμ, καὶ οἱ ἐν ὑμῖν φοβούμενοι τὸν θεόν, [r]ὑμῖν ὁ
of Abraham, and those among you fearing God, to you the
λόγος τῆς.σωτηρίας.ταύτης [s]ἀπεστάλη. 27 οἱ.γὰρ κατοικοῦν-
word of this salvation was sent: for those dwelling
τες ἐν Ἰερουσαλὴμ καὶ οἱ.ἄρχοντες.αὐτῶν, τοῦτον ἀγνοήσαντες
in Jerusalem and their rulers, him not having known
καὶ τὰς φωνὰς τῶν προφητῶν τὰς κατὰ πᾶν σάββατον ἀνα-
and the voices of the prophets who on every sabbath are
γινωσκομένας, κρίναντες ἐπλήρωσαν· 28 καὶ μηδεμίαν
read, [3]having [4]judged [[5]him] [1]they [2]fulfilled. And no one
αἰτίαν θανάτου εὑρόντες ᾐτήσαντο [t]Πιλάτον ἀναιρεθῆναι
cause of death having found they begged Pilate to put [2]to [3]death
αὐτόν. 29 ὡς.δὲ ἐτέλεσαν [v]ἅπαντα τὰ περὶ αὐτοῦ γε-
[1]him. And when they finished all things that concerning him had
γραμμένα, καθελόντες ἀπὸ τοῦ ξύλου, ἔθηκαν εἰς
been written, having taken [him] down from the tree, they put [him] in
μνημεῖον· 30 ὁ.δὲ.θεὸς ἤγειρεν αὐτὸν ἐκ νεκρῶν,
a tomb; but God raised him from among [the] dead,
31 ὃς ὤφθη ἐπὶ ἡμέρας πλείους τοῖς συναναβᾶσιν αὐτῷ
who appeared for [2]days [1]many to those who came up with him
ἀπὸ τῆς Γαλιλαίας εἰς Ἰερουσαλήμ, οἵτινες [w]εἰσιν μάρτυρες
from Galilee to Jerusalem, who are [2]witnesses
αὐτοῦ πρὸς τὸν λαόν. 32 καὶ ἡμεῖς [x]ὑμᾶς εὐαγγελιζόμεθα
[1]his to the people. And we to you announce the glad tidings—
τὴν πρὸς τοὺς πατέρας ἐπαγγελίαν γενομένην, ὅτι ταύτην
the, [3]to [4]the [5]fathers [1]promise [2]made, that this
ὁ θεὸς ἐκπεπλήρωκεν τοῖς τέκνοις [y]αὐτῶν ἡμῖν, ἀναστήσας
God has fulfilled [4]children [3]their [1]to [2]us, having raised up
Ἰησοῦν· 33 ὡς καὶ ἐν [z]τῷ ψαλμῷ τῷ δευτέρῳ γέγραπται,
Jesus; as also in the [2]psalm [1]second it has been written,
Υἱός μου εἶ σύ, ἐγὼ σήμερον γεγέννηκά σε. 34 Ὅτι.δὲ
[4]Son [3]my [1]thou [2]art, I to-day have begotten thee. And that
ἀνέστησεν αὐτὸν ἐκ νεκρῶν, μηκέτι μέλλοντα ὑπο-
he raised him from among [the] dead, no more to be about to
στρέφειν εἰς διαφθοράν, οὕτως εἴρηκεν, Ὅτι δώσω ὑμῖν τὰ
return to corruption, thus he spoke: I will give to you the
ὅσια [a]Δαβὶδ τὰ πιστά. 35 [b]διὸ καὶ ἐν ἑτέρῳ λέγει,
[2]mercies [3]of [4]David [1]faithful. Wherefore also in another he says,
Οὐ.δώσεις τὸν.ὅσιόν.σου ἰδεῖν διαφθοράν. 36 [a]Δαβὶδ
Thou wilt not suffer thy Holy One to see corruption. [2]David
μὲν γὰρ ἰδίᾳ γενεᾷ ὑπηρετήσας τῇ τοῦ θεοῦ βουλῇ
[1]indeed for to his own generation having ministered by the [2]of [3]God [1]counsel
ἐκοιμήθη, καὶ προσετέθη πρὸς τοὺς.πατέρας.αὐτοῦ, καὶ εἶδεν
fell asleep, and was added to his fathers, and saw
διαφθοράν. 37 ὃν.δὲ ὁ θεὸς ἤγειρεν οὐκ.εἶδεν διαφθοράν.
corruption. But he whom God raised up did not see corruption.
38 Γνωστὸν οὖν ἔστω ὑμῖν, ἄνδρες ἀδελφοί, ὅτι διὰ τού-
[4]Known [3]therefore [1]be [2]it to you, men brethren, that through this
του ὑμῖν ἄφεσις ἁμαρτιῶν καταγγέλλεται· 39 [c]καὶ ἀπὸ
one to you remission of sins is announced, and from
πάντων ὧν οὐκ.ἠδυνήθητε ἐν [d]τῷ νόμῳ [e]Μωσέως δι-
all things from which ye could not in the law of Moses be
καιωθῆναι, ἐν τούτῳ πᾶς ὁ πιστεύων δικαιοῦται. 40 βλέ-
justified, in him everyone that believes is justified. Take
πετε οὖν μὴ.ἐπέλθῃ [f]ἐφ' ὑμᾶς τὸ εἰρημένον ἐν
heed therefore that it may not come upon you that which has been said in
τοῖς προφήταις, 41 Ἴδετε, οἱ.καταφρονηταί, καὶ θαυμάσατε
the prophets, Behold, ye despisers, and wonder
καὶ ἀφανίσθητε· ὅτι ἔργον [g]ἐγὼ ἐργάζομαι ἐν ταῖς.ἡμέραις
and perish; for a work I work in [2]days
ὑμῶν, ἔργον [h]ᾧ οὐ.μὴ πιστεύσητε ἐάν τις ἐκδιηγῆται
[1]your, a work which in no wise ye would believe if one should declare it
ὑμῖν. 42 Ἐξιόντων.δὲ [i]ἐκ τῆς συναγωγῆς τῶν Ἰουδαίων,
to you. But [3]having [4]departed [5]from [6]the [7]synagogue [1]the [2]Jews,
παρεκάλουν [k]τὰ ἔθνη εἰς τὸ μεταξὺ σάββατον λαληθῆναι
[10]besought [8]the [9]Gentiles on the next sabbath [3]to [4]be [5]spoken
αὐτοῖς τὰ.ῥήματα.ταῦτα. 43 λυθείσης.δὲ τῆς συναγωγῆς,
[6]to [7]them [1]these [2]words. And [3]having [4]broken [5]up [1]the [2]synagogue,
ἠκολούθησαν πολλοὶ τῶν Ἰουδαίων καὶ τῶν σεβομένων
[15]followed [6]many [7]of [8]the [9]Jews [10]and [11]of [12]the [13]worshipping
προσηλύτων τῷ Παύλῳ καὶ τῷ Βαρνάβᾳ· οἵτινες προσλα-
[14]proselytes Paul and Barnabas, who speak-
λοῦντες αὐτοῖς.ἔπειθον αὐτοὺς [l]ἐπιμένειν τῇ χάριτι τοῦ
ing to them persuaded them to continue in the grace

25 And as John was finishing his course, he
said, Who do you think that I am? I am not
He! But, behold! He is coming after me, of
whom I am not worthy to untie the sandal
of His feet.
26 Men! Brothers! Sons of the race of
Abraham and those among you fearing God!
The word of this salvation was sent to you.
27 For those living in Jerusalem and their
rulers, not knowing Him, nor the voices of
the prophets who are being read on every
Sabbath, they have fulfilled them in judging.
28 And no one being able to find any cause
of death, they begged Pilate to kill Him.
29 And when they finished all things that
had been written of Him, taking Him down
from a tree, they laid Him in a tomb.
30 But God raised Him from among the
dead,
31 *and He* appeared for many days to those
who came up with Him from Galilee to
Jerusalem, who are His witnesses to the
people.
32 And we preach to you the gospel, the
promise made to the fathers,
33 that God has raised up Jesus and has
fulfilled this to us, their children – as it has
been written in the second Psalm also, "You
are My Son. Today I have begotten You."
34 And that He raised Him from among the
dead, never more to return to corruption, He
spoke in this way, "I will give to You the
sure mercies of David."
35 Then He also says in another *Psalm*,
"You will not allow Your Holy One to see
corruption."
36 For when he had served his own generation by the will of God, David died and was
added to his fathers. And he did see corruption.
37 But He whom God raised up did not see
corruption!

38 So, men and brothers, let it be known to
you that through this One remission of sins
is preached.
39 And in Him everyone who believes is
justified from all things from which you
were not able to be justified by the law of
Moses.
40 Then beware that it may not come on
you, that which has been spoken in the
prophets.
41 "You despisers see and wonder and be
ruined! For I work a work in your days, a
work which you in no way would believe if
one should tell you of it."
42 But after the Jews left the synagogue,
the Gentiles asked that these words be
spoken to them on the next Sabbath.
43 And after the synagogue had broken up,
many of the Jews and the devoted converts

θεοῦ.
of God.
44 Τῷ.[m]δὲ‖ [n]ἐρχομένῳ‖ σαββάτῳ σχεδὸν πᾶσα ἡ πόλις
And on the coming sabbath almost all the city
συνήχθη ἀκοῦσαι τὸν λόγον [o]τοῦ θεοῦ.‖ 45 ἰδόντες.δὲ
was gathered together to hear the word of God. But [3]having [4]seen
οἱ Ἰουδαῖοι τοὺς ὄχλους, ἐπλήσθησαν ζήλου, καὶ ἀντέλεγον
[1]the [2]Jews the crowds, were filled with envy, and contradicted
τοῖς ὑπὸ [p]τοῦ‖ Παύλου [q]λεγομένοις,‖ [r]ἀντιλέγοντες καὶ‖
the things [2]by [3]Paul [1]spoken, contradicting and
βλασφημοῦντες. 46 παρρησιασάμενοι.[s]δὲ‖ ὁ Παῦλος καὶ ὁ Βαρ-
blaspheming. But [4]speaking [5]boldly [1]Paul [2]and [3]Bar-
νάβας [t]εἶπον,‖ Ὑμῖν ἦν ἀναγκαῖον πρῶτον λαληθῆναι τὸν
nabas said, To you was necessary first to be spoken the
λόγον τοῦ θεοῦ· ἐπειδὴ.[v]δὲ‖ ἀπωθεῖσθε αὐτόν, καὶ οὐκ ἀξίους
word of God; but since ye thrust away it, and not worthy
κρίνετε ἑαυτοὺς τῆς αἰωνίου ζωῆς, ἰδοὺ στρεφόμεθα εἰς τὰ
ye judge yourselves of eternal life, lo, we turn to the
ἔθνη· 47 οὕτως.γὰρ ἐντέταλται ἡμῖν ὁ κύριος, Τέθεικά σε
Gentiles; for thus has enjoined us the Lord, I have set thee
εἰς φῶς ἐθνῶν, τοῦ.εἶναί.σε εἰς σωτηρίαν ἕως ἐσχά-
for a light of [the] Gentiles, that thou be for salvation to [the] uttermost
του τῆς γῆς. 48 Ἀκούοντα.δὲ τὰ ἔθνη ἔχαιρον, καὶ ἐδόξα-
part of the earth. And hearing [it] the Gentiles rejoiced, and glori-
ζον τὸν λόγον τοῦ κυρίου, καὶ ἐπίστευσαν ὅσοι ἦσαν
fied the word of the Lord, and believed as many as were
τεταγμένοι εἰς ζωὴν αἰώνιον. 49 διεφέρετο.δὲ ὁ λόγος τοῦ
appointed to life eternal. And was carried the word of the
κυρίου [w]δι'‖ ὅλης τῆς χώρας. 50 οἱ.δὲ Ἰουδαῖοι παρώτρυναν
Lord through [2]whole [1]the country. But the Jews excited
τὰς σεβομένας γυναῖκας [x]καὶ‖ τὰς εὐσχήμονας καὶ τοὺς πρώ-
the worshipping [3]women [1]and [2]honourable and the principal
τους τῆς πόλεως, καὶ ἐπήγειραν διωγμὸν ἐπὶ τὸν Παῦλον
men of the city, and stirred up a persecution against Paul
καὶ [y]τὸν‖ Βαρνάβαν, καὶ ἐξέβαλον αὐτοὺς ἀπὸ τῶν.ὁρίων.αὐ-
and Barnabas, and cast out them from their borders.
τῶν. 51 οἱ.δὲ ἐκτιναξάμενοι τὸν κονιορτὸν τῶν.ποδῶν.[z]αὐτῶν‖
But they having shaken off the dust of their feet
ἐπ' αὐτούς, ἦλθον εἰς Ἰκόνιον. 52 οἱ.[a]δὲ‖ μαθηταὶ ἐπλη-
against them, came to Iconium. And the disciples were
ροῦντο χαρᾶς καὶ πνεύματος ἁγίου.
filled with joy and [the] [2]Spirit [1]Holy.

14 Ἐγένετο.δὲ ἐν Ἰκονίῳ κατὰ.τὸ.αὐτὸ εἰσελθεῖν αὐτοὺς
And it came to pass in Iconium [2]together [3]entered [1]they
εἰς τὴν συναγωγὴν τῶν Ἰουδαίων, καὶ λαλῆσαι οὕτως ὥστε
into the synagogue of the Jews, and spoke so that
πιστεῦσαι Ἰουδαίων.τε καὶ Ἑλλήνων πολὺ πλῆθος. 2 οἱ.δὲ
[9]believed [1]both [2]of [3]Jews [4]and [5]Hellenists [6]a [7]great [8]number. But the
[b]ἀπειθοῦντες‖ Ἰουδαῖοι ἐπήγειραν καὶ ἐκάκωσαν τὰς ψυχὰς
disobeying Jews stirred up and made evil-affected the souls
τῶν ἐθνῶν κατὰ τῶν ἀδελφῶν. 3 ἱκανὸν μὲν οὖν χρόνον
of the Gentiles against the brethren. A long [2]therefore [1]time
διέτριψαν παρρησιαζόμενοι ἐπὶ τῷ κυρίῳ, τῷ μαρτυ-
they stayed, speaking boldly, [confiding] in the Lord, who bore wit-
ροῦντι [c]τῷ λόγῳ τῆς.χάριτος.αὐτοῦ, [d]καὶ‖ [e]διδόντι‖ σημεῖα καὶ
ness to the word of his grace, and giving signs and
τέρατα γίνεσθαι διὰ τῶν.χειρῶν.αὐτῶν. 4 ἐσχίσθη.δὲ τὸ
wonders to be done through their hands. And was divided the
πλῆθος τῆς πόλεως· καὶ οἱ.μὲν ἦσαν σὺν τοῖς Ἰουδαίοις
multitude of the city, and some were with the Jews
οἱ.δὲ σὺν τοῖς ἀποστόλοις. 5 Ὡς.δὲ ἐγένετο ὁρμὴ τῶν
and some with the apostles. And when there was a rush [2]of [3]the
ἐθνῶν τε καὶ Ἰουδαίων σὺν τοῖς.ἄρχουσιν.αὐτῶν, ὑβρίσαι
[4]Gentiles [1]both and Jews with their rulers, to insult
καὶ λιθοβολῆσαι αὐτούς, 6 συνιδόντες κατέφυγον εἰς τὰς
and to stone them, being aware they fled to the
πόλεις τῆς Λυκαονίας, [f]Λύστραν, καὶ Δέρβην, καὶ τὴν περί-
cities of Lycaonia, Lystra, and Derbe, and the country
χωρον, 7 κἀκεῖ [g]ἦσαν εὐαγγελιζόμενοι.‖
around, and there they were announcing the glad tidings.
8 Καί τις ἀνὴρ [h]ἐν Λύστροις ἀδύνατος‖ τοῖς ποσὶν ἐκά-
And a certain man in Lystra, impotent in the feet, sat,
θητο, χωλὸς ἐκ κοιλίας μητρὸς.αὐτοῦ [i]ὑπάρχων,‖ ὃς
lame from [the] womb of his mother being, who
οὐδέποτε [k]περιεπεπατήκει.‖ 9 οὗτος [l]ἤκουεν‖ τοῦ Παύλου
never had walked. This [man] heard Paul
λαλοῦντος· ὃς ἀτενίσας αὐτῷ, καὶ ἰδὼν ὅτι [m]πίστιν
speaking, who, having looked intently on him, and seeing that faith
ἔχει‖ τοῦ σωθῆναι, 10 εἶπεν μεγάλῃ [n]τῇ‖ φωνῇ, [o]Ἀνάστηθι
he has to be healed, said with a loud voice, Stand up
ἐπὶ τοὺς.πόδας.σου ὀρθός. Καὶ [p]ἥλλετο‖ καὶ περιεπάτει.
on thy feet upright. And he sprang up and walked.

followed Paul and Barnabas, who spoke to them and persuaded them to continue in the grace of God.

44 And on the coming Sabbath, almost all the city was gathered together to hear the word of God.

45 But seeing the multitudes, the Jews were filled with envy and denied the things spoken by Paul, opposing and blaspheming.

46 But speaking boldly, Paul and Barnabas said, It was right that the word of God should be spoken to you first, but because you thrust it away and do not judge yourselves worthy of everlasting life, behold! We turn to the Gentiles.

47 For so the Lord has commanded us, "I have set You for a light of the Gentiles, for You to be for salvation to the ends of the earth."

48 And the Gentiles heard and rejoiced and glorified the word of the Lord, and as many as were ordained to eternal life believed.

49 And the word of the Lord was spread throughout all that country.

50 But the Jews stirred up the devoted and honorable women, and the chief men of the city, and raised a persecution against Paul and Barnabas. And they expelled them out of their borders.

51 But shaking off the dust of their feet against them, they came to I-co-ni-um.

52 And the disciples were filled with joy and the Holy Spirit.

CHAPTER 14

1 And they entered together into the synagogue of the Jews in I-co-ni-um and spoke so that a great company believed, both of Jews and foreign-born Jews.

2 But the unbelieving Jews stirred up the souls of the Gentiles, making them evil-hearted against the brothers.

3 So they stayed a long time, speaking boldly in the Lord, who bore witness to the word of His grace, giving miracles and wonders to be done through their hands.

4 And the multitude of the city was divided, and some were with the Jews, and some with the apostles.

5 And when there was an attack by both the Gentiles and Jews, with their rulers, in order to abuse and to stone them,

6 they were warned and escaped to the cities of Ly-ca-on-i-a, Lystra and Derbe, and the country around there.

7 And they preached the gospel there.

8 And a certain man who had never walked was sitting in Lystra, having no strength in his feet, being lame from his mother's womb

9 — this one heard Paul speaking, who fixed his eyes on him, seeing that he had faith to be healed.

10 And he said with a loud voice, Stand up on your feet! And he leaped up and walked.

11 Οἱ.[r]δὲ॥ ὄχλοι ἰδόντες ὃ ἐποίησεν [s]ὁ॥ Παῦλος, ἐπῆραν
And the crowds having seen what [2]did [1]Paul, lifted up
τὴν.φωνὴν.αὐτῶν Λυκαονιστὶ λέγοντες, Οἱ θεοὶ ὁμοιωθέντες
their voice in Lycaonian saying, The gods, having become like
ἀνθρώποις κατέβησαν πρὸς ἡμᾶς· 12 ἐκάλουν.τε τὸν [t]μὲν॥
men, are come down to us. And they called
Βαρνάβαν Δία· τὸν.δὲ.Παῦλον Ἑρμῆν, ἐπειδὴ αὐτὸς ἦν ὁ
Barnabas Zeus; and Paul Hermes, because he was the
ἡγούμενος τοῦ λόγου. 13 [v]ὁ.δὲ॥ ἱερεὺς τοῦ Διὸς τοῦ ὄντος
leader in speaking. And the priest of Zeus who was
πρὸ τῆς.πόλεως.[w]αὐτῶν,॥ ταύρους καὶ στέμματα ἐπὶ τοὺς
before their city, oxen and garlands to the
πυλῶνας ἐνέγκας, σὺν τοῖς ὄχλοις ἤθελεν θύειν. 14 Ἀκού-
gates having brought, with the crowds wished to sacrifice. [7]Having
σαντες δὲ οἱ ἀπόστολοι Βαρνάβας καὶ Παῦλος, διαρρήξαντες
[8]heard [1]but [2]the [3]apostles [4]Barnabas [5]and [6]Paul, having rent
τὰ.ἱμάτια.αὐτῶν [x]εἰσεπήδησαν॥ εἰς τὸν ὄχλον, κράζοντες
their garments, rushed in to the crowd, crying
15 καὶ λέγοντες, Ἄνδρες, τί ταῦτα ποιεῖτε; καὶ ἡμεῖς
and saying, Men, why these things do ye? also we
ὁμοιοπαθεῖς ἐσμεν ὑμῖν ἄνθρωποι, εὐαγγελιζόμενοι
[3]of [4]like [5]feelings [1]are [6]with [7]you [2]men, announcing the glad tidings to
ὑμᾶς ἀπὸ τούτων τῶν ματαίων ἐπιστρέφειν ἐπὶ [y]τὸν॥ θεὸν
you from these vanities to turn to God
[y]τὸν॥ ζῶντα, ὃς ἐποίησεν τὸν οὐρανὸν καὶ τὴν γῆν καὶ τὴν
the living, who made the heaven and the earth and the
θάλασσαν καὶ πάντα τὰ ἐν αὐτοῖς· 16 ὃς ἐν ταῖς παρ-
sea and all the things in them; who in the
ῳχημέναις γενεαῖς εἴασεν πάντα τὰ ἔθνη πορεύεσθαι ταῖς
past generations suffered all the nations to go
ὁδοῖς.αὐτῶν· 17 [z]καί.τοι.γε॥ οὐκ ἀμάρτυρον [a]ἑαυτὸν॥ ἀφῆ-
in their [own] ways, though indeed not without witness himself he
κεν [b]ἀγαθοποιῶν,॥ οὐρανόθεν [c]ἡμῖν॥ ὑετοὺς διδοὺς καὶ καιροὺς
left, doing good, from heaven to us [2]rains [1]giving and [3]seasons
καρποφόρους, ἐμπιπλῶν τροφῆς καὶ εὐφροσύνης τὰς καρδίας
fruitful, filling with food and gladness the hearts
[d]ἡμῶν.॥ 18 Καὶ ταῦτα λέγοντες μόλις κατέπαυσαν τοὺς
of us. And these things saying hardly they stopped the
ὄχλους τοῦ.μὴ.θύειν αὐτοῖς. 19 [e]Ἐπῆλθον॥.δὲ ἀπὸ Ἀντιοχείας
crowds from sacrificing to them. But thither came from Antioch
καὶ Ἰκονίου Ἰουδαῖοι, καὶ πείσαντες τοὺς ὄχλους, καὶ λιθά-
and Iconium Jews, and having persuaded the crowds, and having
σαντες τὸν Παῦλον, ἔσυρον ἔξω τῆς πόλεως, [f]νομίσαντες॥
stoned Paul, drew [him] outside the city, supposing
αὐτὸν [g]τεθνάναι.॥ 20 κυκλωσάντων.δὲ [h]αὐτὸν τῶν μαθητῶν,॥
him to have died. But [3]having [4]surrounded [5]him [1]the [2]disciples,
ἀναστὰς εἰσῆλθεν εἰς τὴν πόλιν· καὶ τῇ ἐπαύριον ἐξῆλ-
having risen up he entered into the city. And on the morrow he went
θεν σὺν τῷ Βαρνάβᾳ εἰς Δέρβην. 21 [i]εὐαγγελισάμενοί॥ τε
away with Barnabas to Derbe. And having announced the glad tidings to
τὴν.πόλιν.ἐκείνην, καὶ μαθητεύσαντες ἱκανοὺς ὑπέστρεψαν εἰς
that city, and having discipled many they returned to
τὴν Λύστραν καὶ [k]Ἰκόνιον καὶ [k]Ἀντιόχειαν· 22 ἐπιστηρίζοντες
Lystra and Iconium and Antioch, establishing
τὰς ψυχὰς τῶν μαθητῶν, παρακαλοῦντες ἐμμένειν τῇ
the souls of the disciples, exhorting [them] to continue in the
πίστει, καὶ ὅτι διὰ πολλῶν θλίψεων δεῖ ἡμᾶς εἰσελθεῖν εἰς
faith, and that through many tribulations must we enter into
τὴν βασιλείαν τοῦ θεοῦ. 23 χειροτονήσαντες.δὲ αὐτοῖς [l]πρεσ-
the kingdom of God. And having chosen for them el-
βυτέρους κατ᾽.ἐκκλησίαν,॥ προσευξάμενοι μετὰ νηστειῶν πα-
ders in every assembly, having prayed with fastings they
ρέθεντο αὐτοὺς τῷ κυρίῳ εἰς ὃν πεπιστεύκεισαν. 24 καὶ
committed them to the Lord, on whom they had believed. And
διελθόντες τὴν Πισιδίαν ἦλθον εἰς [m]Παμφυλίαν· 25 καὶ
having passed through Pisidia they came to Pamphylia, and
λαλήσαντες [n]ἐν Πέργῃ॥ τὸν λόγον κατέβησαν εἰς [o]Ἀττάλειαν·॥
having spoken in Perga the word they came down to Attalia;
26 κἀκεῖθεν ἀπέπλευσαν εἰς Ἀντιόχειαν, ὅθεν ἦσαν παρα-
and thence they sailed to Antioch, whence they had been
δεδομένοι τῇ χάριτι τοῦ θεοῦ εἰς τὸ ἔργον ὃ ἐπλήρωσαν.
committed to the grace of God for the work which they fulfilled.
27 παραγενόμενοι.δὲ καὶ συναγαγόντες τὴν ἐκκλησίαν
And having arrived and having gathered together the assembly
[p]ἀνήγγειλαν॥ ὅσα ἐποίησεν ὁ θεὸς μετ᾽ αὐτῶν, καὶ ὅτι ἤνοιξεν
they declared all that [2]did [1]God with them, and that he opened
τοῖς ἔθνεσιν θύραν πίστεως. 28 διέτριβον.δὲ [q]ἐκεῖ॥ χρόνον
to the nations a door of faith. And they stayed there [3]time
οὐκ ὀλίγον σὺν τοῖς μαθηταῖς.
[1]not [2]a little with the disciples.
15 Καί τινες κατελθόντες ἀπὸ τῆς Ἰουδαίας ἐδίδασκον
And certain having come down from Judæa were teaching

11 And when the people saw what Paul did, they cried in the Ly-ca-on-i-an language, saying, The gods have become like men and have come down to us.

12 And they called Barnabas, Zeus; and Paul, Hermes, because he led in the speaking.

13 And the priest of Zeus that is before the city, bringing oxen and garlands to the gates, wanted to sacrifice along with the people.

14 And hearing, the apostles Barnabas and Paul tore their clothes and rushed into the crowd crying out,

15 and saying, Men! Why do you do these things? We also are men with feelings like you – preaching the gospel to you in order to turn you from these worthless things to the living God, who made the heaven and the earth and the sea and all the things in them –

16 who in the ages past allowed all the nations to go on in their own ways,

17 although He really did not leave Himself without witness, doing good by giving rains from Heaven to us and fruitful seasons, and filling our hearts with food and gladness.

18 And saying these things, they barely stopped the people from sacrificing to them.

19 But Jews from Antioch and I-co-ni-um came there. And having persuaded the people, they stoned Paul and dragged him outside the city, supposing him to have died.

20 But the disciples gathered around him, and he got up and went into the city. And on the next day he went away with Barnabas to Derbe.

21 And having preached the gospel to that city, and having taught many, they returned again to Lystra and I-co-ni-um and Antioch –

22 confirming the souls of the disciples, encouraging them to continue in the faith, and that through many afflictions we must enter into the kingdom of God.

23 And after electing elders for them in every church and praying, with fastings, they gave them to the Lord, on whom they had believed.

24 And going through Pi-sid-i-a, they came to Pam-phyl-i-a.

25 And after they had spoken the word in Perga, they came down to At-ta-li-a.

26 And from there they sailed to Antioch, from where they had been delivered up to the grace of God for the work which they had completed.

27 And having come and gathered the church together, they told all that God did with them, and how He opened a door of faith to the Gentiles.

28 And they remained there for some time with the disciples.

CHAPTER 15

1 And certain ones who had come down from Judea were teaching the brothers,

τοὺς ἀδελφούς, "Οτι ἐὰν.μὴ [r]περιτέμνησθε" τῷ ἔθει [s] Μωϋ-
the brethren, Unless ye be circumcised after the custom of Mo-
σέως οὐ.δύνασθε σωθῆναι. 2 Γενομένης [t]οὖν" στάσεως
ses ye cannot be saved. Having taken place therefore a commotion
καὶ [v]συζητήσεως" οὐκ ὀλίγης τῷ Παύλῳ καὶ τῷ Βαρνάβᾳ πρὸς
and discussion not a little by Paul and Barnabas with
αὐτούς, ἔταξαν ἀναβαίνειν Παῦλον καὶ Βαρνάβαν καί
them, they appointed [4]to [5]go [6]up [1]Paul [2]and [3]Barnabas and
τινας ἄλλους ἐξ αὐτῶν πρὸς τοὺς ἀποστόλους καὶ
certain others from amongst them to the apostles and
πρεσβυτέρους εἰς Ἱερουσαλήμ, περὶ τοῦ.ζητήματος.τούτου.
elders to Jerusalem, about this question.

3 οἱ μὲν οὖν προπεμφθέντες ὑπὸ τῆς ἐκκλησίας, διήρ-
They indeed therefore having been sent forward by the assembly passed
χοντο τήν [w] Φοινίκην καὶ [x]Σαμάρειαν," ἐκδιηγούμενοι τὴν
through Phœnicia and Samaria, relating the
ἐπιστροφὴν τῶν ἐθνῶν· καὶ ἐποίουν χαρὰν μεγάλην πᾶσιν
conversion of the nations. And they caused [2]joy [1]great to all
τοῖς ἀδελφοῖς. 4 παραγενόμενοι.δὲ εἰς [y]Ἱερουσαλὴμ" [z]ἀπε-
the brethren. And having come to Jerusalem they were
δέχθησαν" [a]ὑπὸ" τῆς ἐκκλησίας καὶ τῶν ἀποστόλων καὶ τῶν
welcomed by the assembly and the apostles and the
πρεσβυτέρων, ἀνήγγειλάν.τε ὅσα ὁ θεὸς ἐποίησεν μετ' αὐτῶν.
elders, and they declared all that God did with them.

5 ἐξανέστησαν.δέ τινες τῶν ἀπὸ τῆς αἱρέσεως τῶν Φαρισαίων
And rose up certain of those of the sect of the Pharisees
πεπιστευκότες, λέγοντες, "Οτι δεῖ περιτέμνειν αὐτούς,
who believed, saying, It is necessary to circumcise them,
παραγγέλλειν.τε τηρεῖν τὸν νόμον Μωϋσέως. 6 Συνήχ-
and charge [them] to keep the law of Moses. [2]Were [3]gathered
θησαν [b]δὲ" οἱ ἀπόστολοι καὶ οἱ πρεσβύτεροι ἰδεῖν περὶ τοῦ
[4]together [1]and the apostles and the elders to see about
λόγου.τούτου. 7 πολλῆς.δὲ [c]συζητήσεως" γενομένης, ἀνα-
this matter. And much discussion having taken place, [2]having
στὰς Πέτρος εἶπεν πρὸς αὐτούς, "Ανδρες ἀδελφοί, ὑμεῖς
[3]risen [4]up [1]Peter said to them, Men brethren, ye
ἐπίστασθε ὅτι ἀφ' ἡμερῶν ἀρχαίων [d]ὁ θεὸς ἐν ἡμῖν ἐξελέξατο"
know that from [2]days [1]early God among us chose
διὰ τοῦ.στόματός.μου ἀκοῦσαι τὰ ἔθνη τὸν λόγον τοῦ
by my mouth [for] [3]to [4]hear [1]the [2]nations the word of the
εὐαγγελίου, καὶ πιστεῦσαι. 8 καὶ ὁ καρδιογνώστης θεὸς ἐμαρ-
glad tidings, and to believe. And the heart-knowing God bore
τύρησεν αὐτοῖς, δοὺς [e]αὐτοῖς" τὸ πνεῦμα τὸ ἅγιον, καθὼς καὶ
witness to them, giving to them the Spirit the Holy, as also
ἡμῖν· 9 καὶ [f]οὐδὲν".διέκρινεν μεταξὺ ἡμῶν [g]τε" καὶ αὐτῶν,
to us, and put no difference between [2]us [1]both and them,
τῇ πίστει καθαρίσας τὰς.καρδίας.αὐτῶν. 10 νῦν οὖν τί
by the faith having purified their hearts. Now therefore why
πειράζετε τὸν θεόν, ἐπιθεῖναι ζυγὸν ἐπὶ τὸν τράχηλον τῶν
tempt ye God to put a yoke upon the neck of the
μαθητῶν, ὃν οὔτε οἱ.πατέρες.ἡμῶν οὔτε ἡμεῖς ἰσχύσαμεν
disciples, which neither our fathers nor we were able
βαστάσαι; 11 ἀλλὰ διὰ τῆς χάριτος [h] κυρίου Ἰησοῦ [i]χριστοῦ"
to bear? But by the grace of [the] Lord Jesus Christ
πιστεύομεν σωθῆναι, καθ' ὃν.τρόπον κἀκεῖνοι. 12 Ἐσίγησεν
we believe to be saved, in the same manner as they also. [2]Kept [3]silence
δὲ πᾶν τὸ πλῆθος, καὶ ἤκουον Βαρνάβα καὶ Παύλου ἐξη-
[1]and all the multitude, and heard Barnabas and Paul — re-
γουμένων ὅσα ἐποίησεν ὁ θεὸς σημεῖα καὶ τέρατα ἐν τοῖς
lating what [5]did [4]God [1]signs [2]and [3]wonders among the
ἔθνεσιν δι' αὐτῶν. 13 Μετὰ.δὲ τὸ.σιγῆσαι αὐτοὺς ἀπεκρίθη
nations by them. And after [2]were [3]silent [1]they [5]answered
Ἰάκωβος λέγων, "Ανδρες ἀδελφοί, ἀκούσατέ μου. 14 Συμεὼν
[4]James, saying, Men brethren, hear me. Simeon
ἐξηγήσατο καθὼς πρῶτον ὁ θεὸς ἐπεσκέψατο λαβεῖν ἐξ
related how first God visited to take out of
ἐθνῶν λαὸν [k]ἐπὶ" τῷ.ὀνόματι.αὐτοῦ. 15 καὶ τούτῳ συμφω-
nations a people for his name. And with this agree
νοῦσιν οἱ λόγοι τῶν προφητῶν, καθὼς γέγραπται, 16 Μετὰ
the words of the prophets: as it has been written, After
ταῦτα ἀναστρέψω καὶ ἀνοικοδομήσω τὴν σκηνὴν [l]Δαβὶδ"
these things I will return and will build again the tabernacle of David
τὴν πεπτωκυῖαν· καὶ τὰ [m]κατεσκαμμένα" αὐτῆς ἀνοικοδομήσω,
which is fallen; and the ruins of it I will build again,
καὶ ἀνορθώσω αὐτήν, 17 ὅπως ἂν.ἐκζητήσωσιν οἱ κατάλοιποι
and will set up it, so that [5]may [6]seek [7]out [1]the [2]residue
τῶν ἀνθρώπων τὸν κύριον, καὶ πάντα τὰ ἔθνη ἐφ' οὓς ἐπι-
[3]of [4]men the Lord, and all the nations upon whom has
κέκληται τὸ.ὄνομά.μου ἐπ' αὐτούς· λέγει κύριος [n]ὁ" ποιῶν
been called my name upon them, says [the] Lord who does

Unless you are circumcised according to the custom of Moses, you cannot be saved.
[2]So, after an uproar had occurred and Paul and Barnabas had much discussion with them, they appointed Paul and Barnabas and certain others among them to go up to the apostles and elders in Jerusalem as to this question.
[3]Then, indeed, being sent by the church, they went through Phen-ic-i-a and Samaria telling of the conversion of the Gentiles. And they caused great joy to all the brothers.
[4]And coming to Jerusalem, they were welcomed gladly by the church and the apostles and the elders. And they revealed all that God had done with them.

[5]And there were certain believers from the sect of the Pharisees who rose up and said, It is only right to circumcise them and make them keep the law of Moses.
[6]And the apostles and the elders were assembled to see about this matter.
[7]And after there had been much talk, Peter got up and said to them, Men! Brothers! You know that from early days God chose from among us, that the Gentiles were to hear the word of the gospel by my mouth, and to believe.
[8]And the heart-knowing God bore witness to them, giving them the Holy Spirit, even as to us.
[9]And also he put no difference between us and them, for He made their hearts pure by faith.
[10]Now, then, why do you tempt God, to put a yoke on the neck of the disciples, one which neither our fathers nor we were able to bear.
[11]But we believe through the grace of the Lord Jesus Christ, to be saved in the same way as they are, too.
[12]And all the crowd were quiet and listened to Barnabas and Paul telling what miracles and wonders God had done among the Gentiles by them.
[13]And after they were silent, James answered and said, Men! Brothers! Listen to me!
[14]Simon has told how God at first looked out in order to take out of the Gentiles a people for His name.
[15]And the words of the prophets agree with this, as it has been written,
[16]"After these things I will return and will build again the tabernacle of David which has fallen. And I will build the ruins of it again, and I will set it up,
[17]so that the men who are left may seek out the Lord, and all the Gentiles on whom My name has been called, says the Lord, who is doing these things."

ταῦτα [o]πάντα.ǁ 18 [p]Γνωστὰǁ ἀπ' αἰῶνός [q]ἐστιν τῷ θεῷ
[4]these [3]things [1]all. known from eternity are to God
πάντα τὰ.ἔργα.αὐτοῦ.ǁ 19 διὸ ἐγὼ κρίνω μὴ παρενοχλεῖν
all his works. Wherefore I judge not to trouble
τοῖς ἀπὸ τῶν ἐθνῶν ἐπιστρέφουσιν ἐπὶ τὸν θεόν· 20 ἀλλὰ
those who from the nations turn to God; but
ἐπιστεῖλαι αὐτοῖς τοῦ ἀπέχεσθαι [r]ἀπὸǁ τῶν ἀλισγημάτων τῶν
to write to them to abstain from the pollutions of the
εἰδώλων καὶ τῆς πορνείας καὶ [s]τοῦǁ πνικτοῦ καὶ τοῦ αἵματος.
idols and fornication and what is strangled and blood.
21 [t]Μωσῆςǁ.γὰρ ἐκ γενεῶν ἀρχαίων κατὰ.πόλιν τοὺς κη-
For Moses from generations of old in every city [2]those [3]pro-
ρύσσοντας αὐτὸν ἔχει ἐν ταῖς συναγωγαῖς κατὰ.πᾶν σάββατον
claiming [4]him [1]has in the synagogues, every sabbath
ἀναγινωσκόμενος.
being read.

22 Τότε ἔδοξεν τοῖς ἀποστόλοις καὶ τοῖς πρεσβυτέροις
Then it seemed good to the apostles and to the elders
σὺν ὅλῃ τῇ ἐκκλησίᾳ, ἐκλεξαμένους ἄνδρας ἐξ αὐτῶν
with [2]whole [1]the assembly, chosen men from among them
πέμψαι εἰς Ἀντιόχειαν σὺν τῷ Παύλῳ καὶ Βαρνάβᾳ, Ἰούδαν
to send to Antioch with Paul and Barnabas, Judas
τὸν [v]ἐπικαλούμενονǁ [w]Βαρσαβᾶν,ǁ καὶ Σιλᾶν, ἄνδρας ἡγου-
surnamed Barsabas, and Silas, [2]men [1]lead-
μένους ἐν τοῖς ἀδελφοῖς, 23 γράψαντες διὰ χειρὸς.αὐτῶν
ing among the brethren, having written by their hand
[x]τάδε,ǁ Οἱ ἀπόστολοι καὶ οἱ πρεσβύτεροι [y]καὶ οἱǁ ἀδελφοί,
thus: The apostles and the elders and the brethren,
τοῖς κατὰ τὴν Ἀντιόχειαν καὶ Συρίαν καὶ Κιλικίαν ἀδελφοῖς
to those in Antioch and Syria and Cilicia, brethren
τοῖς ἐξ ἐθνῶν, χαίρειν. 24 Ἐπειδὴ ἠκούσαμεν ὅτι
from among [the] nations, greeting. Inasmuch as we have heard that
τινὲς ἐξ ἡμῶν ἐξελθόντες ἐτάραξαν ὑμᾶς λόγοις,
certain from amongst us having gone out troubled you by words,
ἀνασκευάζοντες τὰς.ψυχὰς.ὑμῶν, [z]λέγοντες περιτέμνεσθαι
upsetting your souls, saying [ye must] be circumcised
καὶ τηρεῖν τὸν νόμον,ǁ οἷς οὐ.διεστειλάμεθα· 25 ἔδοξεν
and keep the law; to whom we gave no [such] command; it seemed good
ἡμῖν γενομένοις ὁμοθυμαδόν, [a]ἐκλεξαμένουςǁ ἄνδρας πέμψαι
to us having come with one accord, chosen men to send
πρὸς ὑμᾶς, σὺν τοῖς.ἀγαπητοῖς.ἡμῶν Βαρνάβᾳ καὶ Παύλῳ,
to you, with our beloved Barnabas and Paul,
26 ἀνθρώποις παραδεδωκόσιν τὰς.ψυχὰς.αὐτῶν ὑπὲρ τοῦ
men who have given up their lives for the
ὀνόματος τοῦ.κυρίου.ἡμῶν Ἰησοῦ χριστοῦ. 27 ἀπεστάλκαμεν
name of our Lord Jesus Christ. We have sent
οὖν Ἰούδαν καὶ Σίλαν, καὶ αὐτοὺς διὰ λόγου ἀπαγγέλ-
therefore Judas and Silas, [2]also [1]themselves by word telling
λοντας τὰ αὐτά. 28 ἔδοξεν.γὰρ [b]τῷ ἁγίῳ πνεύματιǁ
[you] the same things. For it seemed good to the Holy Spirit
καὶ ἡμῖν, μηδὲν πλέον ἐπιτίθεσθαι ὑμῖν βάρος πλὴν [c]τῶν
and to us, no further [2]to [3]lay [4]upon [5]you [1]burden than
ἐπάναγκες.τούτων,ǁ 29 ἀπέχεσθαι εἰδωλοθύτων καὶ
these necessary things: to abstain from things sacrificed to idols, and
αἵματος καὶ [d]πνικτοῦǁ καὶ πορνείας· ἐξ ὧν
from blood and from what is strangled, and from fornication; from which
διατηροῦντες ἑαυτούς, εὖ πράξετε. ἔρρωσθε. 30 Οἱ μὲν
keeping yourselves, well ye will do. Farewell. They
οὖν ἀπολυθέντες [e]ἦλθονǁ εἰς Ἀντιόχειαν· καὶ συναγαγόντες
therefore, being let go went to Antioch, and having gathered
τὸ πλῆθος ἐπέδωκαν τὴν ἐπιστολήν. 31 ἀναγνόντες.δὲ ἐχά-
the multitude delivered the epistle. And having read they
ρησαν ἐπὶ τῇ παρακλήσει. 32 Ἰούδας.[f]τεǁ καὶ Σίλας, καὶ αὐ-
rejoiced at the consolation. And Judas and Silas, [2]also [1]them-
τοὶ προφῆται ὄντες, διὰ λόγου πολλοῦ παρεκάλεσαν τοὺς
selves [4]prophets [3]being, by [2]discourse [1]much exhorted the
ἀδελφούς, καὶ ἐπεστήριξαν. 33 Ποιήσαντες.δὲ χρόνον ἀπε-
brethren, and established [them]. And having continued a time they
λύθησαν μετ' εἰρήνης ἀπὸ τῶν ἀδελφῶν πρὸς [g]τοὺς ἀποστό-
were let go in peace from the brethren to the apostles;
λους.ǁ 34 [h]ἔδοξεν.δὲ τῷ Σίλᾳ ἐπιμεῖναι αὐτοῦ.ǁ 35 Παῦλος.δὲ
but it seemed good to Silas to remain there. And Paul
καὶ Βαρνάβας διέτριβον ἐν Ἀντιοχείᾳ, διδάσκοντες καὶ εὐαγ-
and Barnabas stayed in Antioch, teaching and [5]an-
γελιζόμενοι μετὰ καὶ ἑτέρων πολλῶν, τὸν λόγον τοῦ
nouncing [6]the [7]glad [8]tidings [1]with [4]also [3]others [2]many— the word of the
κυρίου.
Lord.

36 Μετὰ.δέ τινας ἡμέρας εἶπεν [i]Παῦλος πρὸς Βαρνάβαν,ǁ
But after certain days said Paul to Barnabas,
Ἐπιστρέψαντες δὴ ἐπισκεψώμεθα τοὺς.ἀδελφοὺς.[k]ἡμῶνǁ κατὰ
Having turned back [2]indeed [1]let [3]us look after our brethren in

18 All His works are known to God from
eternity.
19 Therefore I judge: We are not to trouble
those who turn to God from the Gentiles,
20 but to write to them to keep themselves
from the pollutions of idols, from fornication, and from things strangled, and from
blood.
21 For Moses from ages past has those who
teach him in the synagogues, being read in
the synagogues every Sabbath.

22 Then it seemed good to the apostles and
to the elders, with the whole church, to send
men chosen from among them to Antioch
with Paul and Barnabas – Judas (whose last
name was Barsabas) and Silas, leaders from
among the brothers,
23 writing in this way by their hand: The
apostles and the elders and the brothers
greet those in Antioch and Syria and Cilicia.
Brothers from among the Gentiles:
24 Since we have heard that certain ones
who come from among us have troubled you
with words, unsettling your souls by saying,
Be circumcised and keep the Law – to
whom we gave no command –
25 It seemed good to us, having come together with one purpose, to send chosen men
to you with our beloved Barnabas and Paul,
26 men who have given their lives for the
name of our Lord Jesus Christ.
27 We have therefore sent Judas and Silas,
and they by word will speak the same things

28 – for it seemed good to the Holy Spirit
and to us to lay no further burden on you
than these needful things –
29 to abstain from things sacrificed to idols,
and from blood, and from what is strangled,
and from fornication. If you will keep yourselves from *these*, you will do well. Farewell.
30 Being let go, then, they went to Antioch.
And gathering the company together, *they*
delivered the letter.

31 And having read it, they rejoiced at the
comfort.
32 And Judas and Silas, being prophets
themselves, also encouraged and strengthened the brothers through much discussion.
33 And some time later, they were let go in
peace from the brothers to the apostles.
34 But Silas was pleased to remain there.
35 And Paul and Barnabas remained in Antioch, with many others also, teaching and
preaching the gospel, the word of the Lord.

36 But after some days Paul said to Barnabas, Now let us return and look after our
brothers in every city in which we have
preached the word of the Lord *to see* how
they are.

[1]πᾶσαν πόλιν‖ ἐν αἷς κατηγγείλαμεν τὸν λόγον τοῦ κυρίου,
every city in which we have announced the word of the Lord,
πῶς ἔχουσιν. 37 Βαρνάβας.δὲ [m]ἐβουλεύσατο‖ [n]συμπαρα-
how they are. And Barnabas purposed to take
λαβεῖν‖ [o] [p]τὸν‖ [q]Ἰωάννην‖ τὸν καλούμενον Μάρκον· 38 Παῦ-
with [them] John called Mark; [2]Paul
λος δὲ ἠξίου τὸν ἀποστάντα ἀπ' αὐτῶν ἀπὸ Παμ-
[1]but thought it well him who withdrew from them from Pam-
φυλίας, καὶ μὴ.συνελθόντα αὐτοῖς εἰς τὸ ἔργον, μὴ [r]συμπαρα-
phylia, and went not with them to the work, not to take
λαβεῖν‖ τοῦτον. 39 ἐγένετο [s]οὖν‖ παροξυσμός, ὥστε
[2]with [[3]them] [1]him. Arose therefore a sharp contention so that
ἀποχωρισθῆναι αὐτοὺς ἀπ' ἀλλήλων, τόν.τε.Βαρνάβαν παρα-
[2]departed [1]they from one another, and Barnabas having
λαβόντα τὸν Μάρκον ἐκπλεῦσαι εἰς Κύπρον· 40 Παῦλος.δὲ
taken Mark sailed to Cyprus; but Paul
ἐπιλεξάμενος Σίλαν ἐξῆλθεν, παραδοθεὶς τῇ χάριτι
having chosen Silas went forth, having been committed to the grace
[t]τοῦ θεοῦ‖ ὑπὸ τῶν ἀδελφῶν. 41 διήρχετο.δὲ τὴν Συρίαν
of God by the brethren. And he passed through Syria
καὶ [w] Κιλικίαν, ἐπιστηρίζων τὰς ἐκκλησίας. 16 Κατήντησεν.δὲ [x]
and Cilicia, establishing the assemblies. And he arrived
εἰς Δέρβην καὶ [y] Λύστραν· καὶ ἰδού, μαθητής τις ἦν ἐκεῖ,
at Derbe and Lystra: and behold, a [2]disciple [1]certain was there,
ὀνόματι Τιμόθεος, υἱὸς γυναικός [z]τινος‖ Ἰουδαίας πιστῆς
by name Timotheus, son of a [4]woman [1]certain [2]Jewish [3]believing
πατρὸς.δὲ [a]Ἕλληνος· 2 ὃς ἐμαρτυρεῖτο ὑπὸ τῶν ἐν Λύσ-
but [the] father a Greek, who was borne witness to by the [2]in [3]Lys-
τροις καὶ Ἰκονίῳ ἀδελφῶν. 3 τοῦτον ἠθέλησεν ὁ Παῦλος σὺν
tra [4]and [5]Iconium [1]brethren. This one [2]wished [1]Paul with
αὐτῷ ἐξελθεῖν, καὶ λαβὼν περιέτεμεν αὐτὸν διὰ τοὺς
him to go forth, and having taken he circumcised him on account of the
Ἰουδαίους τοὺς ὄντας ἐν τοῖς.τόποις.ἐκείνοις· ᾔδεισαν.γὰρ
Jews who were in those places, for they [2]knew
[a]ἅπαντες τὸν.πατέρα.αὐτοῦ ὅτι [a]Ἕλλην‖ ὑπῆρχεν. 4 ὡς.δὲ
[1]all his father that a Greek he was. And as
διεπορεύοντο τὰς πόλεις [b]παρεδίδουν‖ αὐτοῖς φυλάσσειν
they passed through the cities they delivered to them to keep
τὰ δόγματα τὰ κεκριμένα ὑπὸ τῶν ἀποστόλων καὶ [c]τῶν‖
the decrees decided on by the apostles and the
πρεσβυτέρων τῶν ἐν [d]Ἱερουσαλήμ.‖ 5 αἱ μὲν οὖν ἐκ-
elders in Jerusalem. The [2]therefore [1]as-
κλησίαι ἐστερεοῦντο τῇ πίστει, καὶ ἐπερίσσευον τῷ ἀριθμῷ
semblies were strengthened in the faith, and abounded in number
καθ'.ἡμέραν.
every day.

6 [e]Διελθόντες‖ δὲ τὴν Φρυγίαν καὶ [f]τὴν‖ Γαλατικὴν
[2]Having [3]passed [4]through [1]and Phrygia and the Galatian
χώραν, κωλυθέντες ὑπὸ τοῦ ἁγίου πνεύματος λαλῆσαι
country, having been forbidden by the Holy Spirit to speak
τὸν λόγον ἐν τῇ Ἀσίᾳ, 7 ἐλθόντες [g] κατὰ τὴν Μυσίαν ἐπείρα-
the word in Asia, having come down to Mysia they at-
ζον [h]κατὰ‖ [i]τὴν‖ Βιθυνίαν [k]πορεύεσθαι·‖ καὶ οὐκ.εἴασεν
tempted to Bithynia to go; and [3]did [4]not [5]suffer
αὐτοὺς τὸ πνεῦμα [l]. 8 παρελθόντες.δὲ τὴν Μυσίαν κατέβη-
[6]them [1]the [2]Spirit; and having passed by Mysia they came
σαν εἰς Τρῳάδα. 9 καὶ ὅραμα διὰ [m]τῆς‖ νυκτὸς [n]ὤφθη τῷ
down to Troas. And a vision during the night appeared
Παύλῳ·‖ Ἀνήρ [o]τις ἦν Μακεδὼν‖ ἑστώς, [p] παρακαλῶν
to Paul: A [2]man [1]certain [5]was [3]of [4]Macedonia standing, beseeching
αὐτὸν καὶ λέγων, Διαβὰς εἰς Μακεδονίαν βοήθησον
him and saying, Having passed over into Macedonia help
ἡμῖν. 10 Ὡς.δὲ τὸ ὅραμα εἶδεν, εὐθέως ἐζητήσαμεν ἐξελθεῖν
us. And when the vision he saw, immediately we sought to go forth
εἰς [q]τὴν‖ Μακεδονίαν, συμβιβάζοντες ὅτι προσκέκληται ἡμᾶς
to Macedonia, concluding that [3]had [4]called [5]us
[r]ὁ κύριος‖ εὐαγγελίσασθαι αὐτούς. 11 Ἀναχθέντες
[1]the [2]Lord to announce the glad tidings to them. Having sailed
[s]οὖν‖ ἀπὸ [t]τῆς‖ Τρῳάδος εὐθυδρομήσαμεν εἰς Σαμο-
therefore from Troas we came with a straight course to Samo-
θρᾴκην, τῇ.[v]τε‖ ἐπιούσῃ εἰς [w]Νεάπολιν,‖ 12 [x]ἐκεῖθέν.τε‖
thracia, and on the following day to Neapolis, and thence
εἰς Φιλίππους, ἥτις ἐστὶν πρώτη τῆς μερίδος [y]τῆς‖
to Philippi, which is [the] first [2]of [[3]that] [4]part
Μακεδονίας πόλις, κολώνια. [z]Ἦμεν.δὲ ἐν ταύτῃ τῇ πόλει δια-
[5]of [6]Macedonia [1]city, a colony. And we were in this city stay-
τρίβοντες ἡμέρας τινάς, 13 τῇ.τε ἡμέρᾳ τῶν σαββάτων
ing [2]days [1]certain. And on the day of the sabbath
ἐξήλθομεν [z]ἔξω‖ τῆς [a]πόλεως‖ παρὰ ποταμόν, οὗ [b]ἐνομίζετο
we went forth outside the city by a river, where was customary
προσευχὴ‖ εἶναι, καὶ καθίσαντες ἐλαλοῦμεν ταῖς συνελ-
prayer to be, and having sat down we spoke to the [2]who [3]came

37 And Barnabas wanted to take John Mark.
38 But Paul did not agree it was good to take the one who had left them *and* the work from Pam-phyl-i-a.
39 So there came about a sharp fit of anger, so that they separated from one another. And Barnabas took Mark and sailed to Cyprus.
40 But Paul chose Silas and left, after being commended to the grace of God by the brothers.
41 And he went through Syria and Cilicia, making the churches strong.

CHAPTER 16

1 And he came to Derbe and Lystra; and, behold! A certain disciple named Timothy was there (the son of a certain woman who was a believing Jewess, but his father was a Greek.)
2 *This one* was recommended by the brothers in Lystra and I-co-ni-um.
3 Paul desired this one to go with him. And he took him and circumcised him because of the Jews who were in those places. For they all knew that his father was a Greek.
4 And as they were going through the cities, they delivered to them the commandments to keep, those decided on by the apostles and elders in Jerusalem.
5 Then the churches were truly strengthened in the faith and increased in number every day.

6 And having gone through Phryg-i-a and the country of Galatia, they were forbidden by the Holy Spirit to speak the word in Asia.
7 After coming down to Mysia, they were trying to go on to Bi-thyn-i-a, but the Spirit did not permit them.
8 And passing by Mysia, they came to Troas.
9 And a vision appeared to Paul during the night: A certain man of Mac-e-do-ni-a was standing and calling to him, saying, Cross over into Mac-e-do-ni-a! Help us!
10 And when he saw the vision, we immediately tried to go into Mac-e-do-ni-a, feeling certain that the Lord had called us to preach the gospel to them.
11 So, after sailing from Troas, we came with a straight course to Sam-o-thrac-i-a. And on the next day *we came* to Ne-a-po-lis,
12 and from there to Phil-ip-pi, which is the chief city of that part of Mac-e-do-ni-a, a colony. And we had been staying in this city for some days.
13 And on the Sabbath day, we went outside the city by a river, where it was the custom for prayer to be made. And sitting down, we spoke to the women who gathered there.

θούσαις γυναιξίν. 14 Καί τις γυνὴ ὀνόματι Λυδία, πορ-
together women. And a certain woman, by name Lydia, a seller
φυρόπωλις πόλεως Θυατείρων, σεβομένη τὸν θεόν, ἤκουεν·
of purple of [the] city of Thyatira, who worshipped God, was hearing;
ἧς ὁ κύριος διήνοιξεν τὴν καρδίαν προσέχειν τοῖς
of whom the Lord opened the heart to attend to the things
λαλουμένοις ὑπὸ τοῦ Παύλου. 15 ὡς.δὲ ἐβαπτίσθη καὶ
spoken by Paul. And when she was baptized and
ὁ.οἶκος.αὐτῆς παρεκάλεσεν λέγουσα, Εἰ κεκρίκατέ με πιστὴν
her house she besought saying, If ye have judged me faithful
τῷ κυρίῳ εἶναι, εἰσελθόντες εἰς τὸν.οἶκόν.μου, μείνατε·
to the Lord to be, having entered into my house, abide.
καὶ παρεβιάσατο ἡμᾶς. 16 Ἐγένετο.δὲ πορευομένων.ἡμῶν
And she constrained us. And it came to pass as we were going
εἰς προσευχήν, παιδίσκην τινὰ ἔχουσαν πνεῦμα Πύθωνος
to prayer, a damsel certain, having a spirit of Python,
ἀπαντῆσαι ἡμῖν, ἥτις ἐργασίαν πολλὴν παρεῖχεν τοῖς
met us, who gain much brought
κυρίοις.αὐτῆς μαντευομένη. 17 αὕτη κατακολουθήσασα τῷ
to her masters by divining. She having followed
Παύλῳ καὶ ἡμῖν ἔκραζεν λέγουσα, Οὗτοι οἱ ἄνθρωποι δοῦλοι
Paul and us cried saying, These men bondmen
τοῦ θεοῦ τοῦ ὑψίστου εἰσίν, οἵτινες καταγγέλλουσιν ἡμῖν
of the God Most High are, who announce to us [the]
ὁδὸν σωτηρίας. 18 Τοῦτο.δὲ ἐποίει ἐπὶ πολλὰς ἡμέρας· δια-
way of salvation. And this she did for many days. Being
πονηθεὶς δὲ ὁ Παῦλος, καὶ ἐπιστρέψας τῷ πνεύματι εἶπεν,
distressed but Paul, and having turned to the spirit said,
Παραγγέλλω σοι ἐν τῷ ὀνόματι Ἰησοῦ χριστοῦ ἐξελθεῖν
I charge thee in the name of Jesus Christ to come out
ἀπ' αὐτῆς. Καὶ ἐξῆλθεν αὐτῇ.τῇ ὥρᾳ. 19 Ἰδόντες.δὲ οἱ κύριοι
from her. And it came out the same hour. And seeing masters
αὐτῆς ὅτι ἐξῆλθεν ἡ ἐλπὶς τῆς.ἐργασίας.αὐτῶν, ἐπιλαβόμενοι
her that was gone the hope of their gain, having taken hold of
τὸν Παῦλον καὶ τὸν Σίλαν εἵλκυσαν εἰς τὴν ἀγορὰν
Paul and Silas they dragged [them] into the market
ἐπὶ τοὺς ἄρχοντας· 20 καὶ προσαγαγόντες αὐτοὺς τοῖς
before the magistrates; and having brought up them to the
στρατηγοῖς εἶπον, Οὗτοι οἱ ἄνθρωποι ἐκταράσσουσιν ἡμῶν
captains said, These men exceedingly trouble our
τὴν πόλιν, Ἰουδαῖοι ὑπάρχοντες· 21 καὶ καταγγέλλουσιν ἔθη
city, Jews being, and announce customs
ἃ οὐκ.ἔξεστιν ἡμῖν παραδέχεσθαι οὐδὲ ποιεῖν, Ῥωμαίοις
which it is not lawful for us to receive nor to do, Romans
οὖσιν. 22 Καὶ συνεπέστη ὁ ὄχλος κατ' αὐτῶν, καὶ οἱ στρα-
being. And rose up together the crowd against them, and the cap-
τηγοὶ περιρρήξαντες αὐτῶν τὰ ἱμάτια ἐκέλευον ῥαβδί-
tains having torn off of them the garments commanded to beat [them]
ζειν· 23 πολλάς.τε ἐπιθέντες αὐτοῖς πληγὰς ἔβαλον
with rods. And many having laid on them stripes they cast [them]
εἰς φυλακήν, παραγγείλαντες τῷ δεσμοφύλακι ἀσφαλῶς τηρεῖν
into prison, charging the jailor safely to keep
αὐτούς· 24 ὃς παραγγελίαν τοιαύτην εἰληφὼς ἔβαλεν αὐτοὺς
them; who a charge such having received thrust them
εἰς τὴν ἐσωτέραν φυλακήν, καὶ τοὺς.πόδας.αὐτῶν ἠσφαλί-
into the inner prison, and their feet secured
σατο εἰς τὸ ξύλον. 25 Κατὰ.δὲ τὸ μεσονύκτιον Παῦλος καὶ
to the stocks. And towards midnight Paul and
Σίλας προσευχόμενοι ὕμνουν τὸν θεόν· ἐπηκροῶντο
Silas praying were singing praises to God, listened to
δὲ αὐτῶν οἱ δέσμιοι. 26 ἄφνω.δὲ σεισμὸς ἐγένετο μέγας,
and them the prisoners. And suddenly earthquake there was a great,
ὥστε σαλευθῆναι τὰ θεμέλια τοῦ δεσμωτηρίου· ἀνεῴχθησάν
so that were shaken the foundations of the prison, were opened
τε παραχρῆμα αἱ θύραι πᾶσαι, καὶ πάντων τὰ δεσμὰ ἀνέθη.
and immediately the doors all, and of all the bonds were loosed.
27 ἔξυπνος.δὲ γενόμενος ὁ δεσμοφύλαξ, καὶ ἰδὼν ἀνεῳγ-
And awoke out of sleep being the jailor, and seeing opened
μένας τὰς θύρας τῆς φυλακῆς, σπασάμενος μάχαιραν ἔμελ-
the doors of the prison, having drawn a sword was
λεν ἑαυτὸν ἀναιρεῖν, νομίζων ἐκπεφευγέναι τοὺς δεσμίους.
about himself to put to death, supposing had escaped the prisoners.
28 ἐφώνησεν.δὲ φωνῇ μεγάλῃ ὁ Παῦλος λέγων, Μηδὲν
But called out with a voice loud Paul saying, No
πράξῃς σεαυτῷ κακόν· ἅπαντες.γάρ ἐσμεν ἐνθάδε. 29 Αἰ-
do to thyself injury; for all we are here. Having
τήσας δὲ φῶτα εἰσεπήδησεν, καὶ ἔντρομος.γενόμενος προσ-
asked for and lights he rushed in, and trembling fell
έπεσεν τῷ Παύλῳ καὶ τῷ Σίλᾳ· 30 καὶ προαγαγὼν αὐτοὺς
down before Paul and Silas. And having brought them
ἔξω ἔφη, Κύριοι, τί με.δεῖ ποιεῖν ἵνα σωθῶ;
out he said, Sirs, what is necessary for me to do that I may be saved?

14 And a certain woman named Lydia, a seller of purple (who was from the city of Thy-a-ti-ra, who worshiped God), was listening – whose heart the Lord opened in order that she might set her mind on the things which Paul preached.

15 And when she and her household had been baptized, she begged us, saying, If you have judged me to be faithful to the Lord, come into my house and stay. And she prevailed upon us.

16 And as we were going to prayer, a certain girl met us, one who had a spirit which could discern things, who brought much profit to her owners by divining.

17 Following Paul and us, she cried, saying, These men are servants of the Most High God, who show to us the way of salvation.

18 And she did this for many days. But being distressed, Paul turned to the spirit and said, I command you in the name of Jesus Christ to come out of her. And it came out that same hour.

19 And seeing that the hope of their profit was gone, her owners caught Paul and Silas and dragged them into the market-place before the rulers.

20 And bringing them up to the judges, they said, These men, who are Jews, trouble our city.

21 And they teach customs which it is not lawful for us as Romans to receive or to do.

22 And the crowd joined together against them. And the judges, after tearing their clothes off them, commanded that they be beaten with rods.

23 And after they laid on them many stripes, they threw them into prison, warning the jailor to keep them safely.

24 After getting such a warning, he showed them into the inner prison and fastened their feet to the wood *stocks*.

25 And towards midnight Paul and Silas were praying and singing hymns to God, and the prisoners listened to them.

26 Then suddenly there was a great earthquake, so that the foundations of the prison were shaken. And immediately all the doors were opened and all of the bonds broken.

27 And the jailor, being awakened out of sleep and seeing the prison doors opened, drew a sword and was about to kill himself – supposing the prisoners had escaped.

28 But Paul called out with a loud voice, saying, Do no harm to yourself! For we are all here.

29 And after he had called for lights, he rushed in and fell trembling in front of Paul and Silas.

30 And after he had called for lights...

31 Οἱ.δὲ εἶπον, Πίστευσον ἐπὶ τὸν κύριον Ἰησοῦν χριστόν,
And they said, Believe on the Lord Jesus Christ,
καὶ σωθήσῃ, σὺ καὶ ὁ.οἶκός.σου. 32 Καὶ ἐλάλησαν αὐτῷ
and thou shalt be saved, thou and thy house. And they spoke to him
τὸν λόγον τοῦ κυρίου, καὶ πᾶσιν τοῖς ἐν τῇ.οἰκίᾳ.αὐτοῦ.
the word of the Lord, and to all those in his house.
33 καὶ παραλαβὼν αὐτοὺς ἐν ἐκείνῃ τῇ ὥρᾳ τῆς νυκτὸς ἔλου-
And having taken them in that hour of the night he wash-
σεν ἀπὸ τῶν πληγῶν, καὶ ἐβαπτίσθη αὐτὸς καὶ οἱ αὐτοῦ
ed [them] from the stripes; and was baptized he and his
πάντες παραχρῆμα. 34 ἀναγαγών.τε αὐτοὺς εἰς τὸν οἶκον
all immediately. And having brought them into house
αὐτοῦ παρέθηκεν τράπεζαν, καὶ ἠγαλλιάσατο πανοικὶ
his he laid a table [for them], and exulted with all [his] house,
πεπιστευκὼς τῷ θεῷ. 35 Ἡμέρας.δὲ γενομένης ἀπέ-
having believed in God. And day having come
στειλαν οἱ στρατηγοὶ τοὺς ῥαβδούχους λέγοντες, Ἀπόλυσον
sent the captains the serjeants, saying, Let go
τοὺς.ἀνθρώπους.ἐκείνους. 36 Ἀπήγγειλεν.δὲ ὁ δεσμοφύλαξ
those men. And reported the jailor
τοὺς.λόγους.τούτους πρὸς τὸν Παῦλον, Ὅτι ἀπεστάλκασιν
these words to Paul, Have sent
οἱ στρατηγοὶ ἵνα ἀπολυθῆτε· νῦν οὖν ἐξελθόντες πο-
the captains that ye may be let go. Now therefore having gone out de-
ρεύεσθε ἐν εἰρήνῃ. 37 Ὁ.δὲ.Παῦλος ἔφη πρὸς αὐτούς, Δείραντες
part in peace. But Paul said to them, Having beaten
ἡμᾶς δημοσίᾳ ἀκατακρίτους, ἀνθρώπους Ῥωμαίους ὑπάρχον-
us publicly uncondemned, men Romans being,
τας, ἔβαλον εἰς φυλακήν, καὶ νῦν λάθρα ἡμᾶς ἐκβάλλου-
they cast [us] into prison, and now secretly us do they thrust
σιν; οὐ γάρ· ἀλλὰ ἐλθόντες αὐτοὶ ἡμᾶς ἐξαγαγέτωσαν.
out? no indeed, but having come themselves us let them bring out.
38 Ἀνήγγειλαν.δὲ τοῖς στρατηγοῖς οἱ ῥαβδοῦχοι τὰ ῥήματα
And reported to the captains the serjeants words
ταῦτα· καὶ ἐφοβήθησαν ἀκούσαντες ὅτι Ῥωμαῖοί εἰσιν.
these. And they were afraid having heard that Romans they are.
39 καὶ ἐλθόντες παρεκάλεσαν αὐτούς, καὶ ἐξαγαγόντες
And having come they besought them, and having brought out
ἠρώτων ἐξελθεῖν τῆς πόλεως. 40 ἐξελθόντες.δὲ ἐκ
they asked [them] to go out of the city. And having gone forth out of
τῆς φυλακῆς εἰσῆλθον εἰς τὴν Λυδίαν· καὶ ἰδόντες τοὺς
the prison they came to Lydia; and having seen the
ἀδελφοὺς παρεκάλεσαν αὐτούς, καὶ ἐξῆλθον.
brethren they exhorted them, and went away.

17 Διοδεύσαντες.δὲ τὴν Ἀμφίπολιν καὶ Ἀπολλωνίαν
And having journeyed through Amphipolis and Apollonia
ἦλθον εἰς Θεσσαλονίκην, ὅπου ἦν ἡ συναγωγὴ τῶν Ἰου-
they came to Thessalonica, where was the synagogue of the Jews.
δαίων. 2 κατὰ.δὲ τὸ εἰωθὸς τῷ Παύλῳ εἰσῆλθεν πρὸς αὐτούς,
And according to the custom with Paul he went in to them,
καὶ ἐπὶ σάββατα τρία διελέγετο αὐτοῖς ἀπὸ τῶν γραφῶν,
and for sabbaths three reasoned with them from the scriptures,
3 διανοίγων καὶ παρατιθέμενος ὅτι τὸν χριστὸν ἔδει πα-
opening and setting forth that the Christ it behoved to have
θεῖν καὶ ἀναστῆναι ἐκ νεκρῶν, καὶ ὅτι οὗτός ἐστιν
suffered and to have risen from among [the] dead, and that this is
ὁ χριστὸς Ἰησοῦς, ὃν ἐγὼ καταγγέλλω ὑμῖν. 4 Καί τινες
the Christ Jesus, whom I announce to you. And some
ἐξ αὐτῶν ἐπείσθησαν, καὶ προσεκληρώθησαν τῷ Παύλῳ καὶ
of them were obedient, and joined themselves to Paul and
τῷ Σίλᾳ, τῶν.τε σεβομένων Ἑλλήνων πολὺ πλῆθος,
to Silas, and of the worshipping Greeks a great multitude,
γυναικῶν.τε τῶν πρώτων οὐκ ὀλίγαι. 5 Ζηλώσαντες.δὲ
and of women the chief not a few. But having become envious
οἱ ἀπειθοῦντες Ἰουδαῖοι, καὶ προσλαβόμενοι τῶν
the disobeying Jews, and having taken to [them] of the
ἀγοραίων τινὰς ἄνδρας πονηρούς, καὶ ὀχλοποιήσαντες
market-loungers certain men evil, and having collected a crowd
ἐθορύβουν τὴν πόλιν· ἐπιστάντες.τε τῇ οἰκίᾳ Ἰάσονος
roused in tumult the city; and having assaulted the house of Jason
ἐζήτουν αὐτοὺς ἀγαγεῖν εἰς τὸν δῆμον· 6 μὴ.εὑρόντες.δὲ
they sought them to bring out to the people; but not having found
αὐτοὺς ἔσυρον τὸν Ἰάσονα καί τινας ἀδελφοὺς ἐπὶ τοὺς
them they dragged Jason and certain brethren before the
πολιτάρχας, βοῶντες, Ὅτι οἱ τὴν οἰκουμένην ἀνα-
city magistrates, crying out, Those who the habitable world have set
στατώσαντες οὗτοι καὶ ἐνθάδε πάρεισιν, 7 οὓς ὑποδέδεκται
in confusion these also here are come, whom has received
Ἰάσων· καὶ οὗτοι πάντες ἀπέναντι τῶν δογμάτων Καίσαρος
Jason; and these all contrary to the decrees of Cæsar
πράττουσιν, βασιλέα λέγοντες ἕτερον εἶναι, Ἰησοῦν.
do, king saying another there is— Jesus.

31 And they said, Believe on the Lord Jesus
Christ and you shall be saved, you and your
household.
32 And they spoke to him the word of the
Lord, and to all those in his household.
33 And taking them in that hour of the
night, he washed their stripes. And he and all
his were baptized at once.
34 And bringing them into his own house,
he laid a table and rejoiced with all his
household, having believed in God.
35 And when day arrived, the judges sent
the floggers, saying, Let those men go.
36 And the jailor spoke these words to Paul,
The judges have sent to say that you may be
set free. Now, then, as you go, go in peace.
37 But Paul said to them, They have had us
publicly beaten, we who are Romans and
not found guilty. And they threw us into
prison. And now they secretly throw us out?
No, indeed! But let them come themselves
and bring us out.
38 And the floggers reported these words to
the judges. And when they heard that they
were Romans, they were full of terror.
39 They came and appealed to them. And
they brought them out and begged them to
go out of the city.
40 And when they had left the prison, they
came to Lydia's. And having seen the brothers, they cheered them and departed.

CHAPTER 17

1 And after they had gone through Am-
phip-o-lis and Ap-ol-lo-ni-a, they came to
Thess-a-lo-ni-ca, where the Jews' synagogue
was.
2 And according to the custom with Paul,
he went in to them. And for three sabbaths
he reasoned with them from the Scriptures,
3 opening and setting out that the Christ
must necessarily have suffered and to have
risen from among the dead, and that this
Jesus whom I preach to you is the Christ.
4 And some of them did believe and joined
themselves to Paul and Silas. And a great
many of the Greeks who worshiped, and
quite a few of the leading women believed.
5 But the unbelieving Jews became jealous
and took some evil men from the market-
loafers and collected a crowd. And they set
the city in a turmoil. And setting themselves
against Jason's house, they tried to bring
them out to the people.
6 But not finding them, they dragged Jason
and some of the brothers before the city
judges, crying out, Those who have turned
the world upside down have come here too,
7 and Jason has received *them.* And all of
these do things contrary to the laws of
Caesar, saying there is another king – Jesus.

8 Ἐτάραξαν.δὲ τὸν ὄχλον καὶ τοὺς πολιτάρχας ἀκούοντας
And they troubled the crowd and the city magistrates hearing
ταῦτα. 9 καὶ λαβόντες τὸ ἱκανὸν παρὰ τοῦ Ἰάσονος καὶ
these things. And having taken security from Jason and
τῶν λοιπῶν ἀπέλυσαν αὐτούς. 10 Οἱ.δὲ ἀδελφοὶ εὐθέως διὰ
the rest they let [2]go [1]them. But the brethren immediately by
[h]τῆς‖ νυκτὸς ἐξέπεμψαν τόν.τε.Παῦλον καὶ τὸν Σιλᾶν εἰς Βέ-
night sent away both Paul and Silas to Be-
ροιαν· οἵτινες παραγενόμενοι, εἰς τὴν συναγωγὴν [i]τῶν Ἰου-
rœa; who, being arrived, into the synagogue of the Jews
δαίων ἀπῄεσαν.‖ 11 οὗτοι.δὲ ἦσαν εὐγενέστεροι τῶν ἐν
went. And these were more noble than those in
Θεσσαλονίκῃ, οἵτινες ἐδέξαντο τὸν λόγον μετὰ πάσης προθυ-
Thessalonica, who received the word with all readi-
μίας, [k]τὸ‖ καθ'.ἡμέραν ἀνακρίνοντες τὰς γραφὰς εἰ ἔχοι
ness, daily examining the scriptures if were
ταῦτα οὕτως. 12 πολλοὶ μὲν οὖν ἐξ αὐτῶν ἐπί-
these things so. Many indeed therefore from among them be-
στευσαν, καὶ τῶν Ἑλληνίδων γυναικῶν τῶν εὐσχημόνων καὶ
lieved, and of the [2]Grecian [3]women [1]honourable and
ἀνδρῶν οὐκ ὀλίγοι. 13 ὡς.δὲ ἔγνωσαν οἱ ἀπὸ τῆς Θεσσαλο-
men not a few. But when [5]knew [1]the [3]from [4]Thessalo-
νίκης Ἰουδαῖοι ὅτι καὶ ἐν τῇ Βεροίᾳ κατηγγέλη ὑπὸ τοῦ
nica [2]Jews that also in Berœa was announced by
Παύλου ὁ λόγος τοῦ θεοῦ, ἦλθον κἀκεῖ σαλεύοντες [l] τοὺς
Paul the word of God, they came also there stirring up the
ὄχλους. 14 εὐθέως.δὲ τότε τὸν Παῦλον ἐξαπέστειλαν οἱ
crowds. And immediately then [5]Paul [3]sent [4]away [1]the
ἀδελφοὶ πορεύεσθαι [m]ὡς‖ ἐπὶ τὴν θάλασσαν· [n]ὑπέμενον.δὲ‖
[2]brethren to go as to the sea; but remained
ὅ.τε.Σίλας καὶ ὁ Τιμόθεος ἐκεῖ. 15 Οἱ.δὲ [o]καθιστῶντες‖ τὸν
both Silas and Timotheus there. But those conducting
Παῦλον ἤγαγον [p]αὐτὸν‖ ἕως Ἀθηνῶν· καὶ λαβόντες ἐντολὴν
Paul brought him unto Athens; and having received a command
πρὸς τὸν Σίλαν καὶ [q] Τιμόθεον, ἵνα ὡς τάχιστα ἔλθω-
to Silas and Timotheus, that as quickly as possible they should
σιν πρὸς αὐτόν, ἐξῄεσαν.
come to him, they departed.

16 Ἐν.δὲ ταῖς Ἀθήναις ἐκδεχομένου αὐτοὺς τοῦ Παύλου,
But in Athens [2]waiting [3]for [4]them [1]Paul,
παρωξύνετο τὸ.πνεῦμα.αὐτοῦ ἐν αὐτῷ [r]θεωροῦντι‖ κατ-
[7]was [8]painfully [9]excited [5]his [6]spirit in him seeing [4]full
είδωλον οὖσαν τὴν πόλιν. 17 διελέγετο μὲν οὖν ἐν τῇ
[5]of [6]idols [3]being [1]the [2]city. He reasoned indeed therefore in the
συναγωγῇ τοῖς Ἰουδαίοις καὶ τοῖς σεβομένοις, καὶ ἐν τῇ
synagogue with the Jews and those who worshipped, and in the
ἀγορᾷ κατὰ.πᾶσαν.ἡμέραν πρὸς τοὺς παρατυγχάνον-
market-place every day with those who met with
τας. 18 τινὲς.δὲ [s] τῶν [t]Ἐπικουρείων‖ καὶ [v]τῶν‖ [w]Στωϊκῶν‖
[him]. But some of the Epicureans and the Stoics,
φιλοσόφων συνέβαλλον αὐτῷ· καί τινες ἔλεγον, Τί ἂν θέλοι
philosophers, encountered him. And some said, What may [3]desire
ὁ.σπερμολόγος.οὗτος λέγειν; Οἱ.δέ, Ξένων δαιμονίων δοκεῖ
[1]this [2]chatterer to say? And some, Of foreign gods he seems
(*lit.* demons)
καταγγελεὺς εἶναι· ὅτι τὸν Ἰησοῦν καὶ τὴν ἀνάστασιν
a proclaimer to be, because [of] Jesus and the resurrection
[x]αὐτοῖς εὐηγγελίζετο.‖ 19 ἐπιλαβόμενοί.τε‖ αὐτοῦ,
to them he announced the glad tidings. And having taken hold of him,
ἐπὶ τὸν [z]Ἄρειον‖ πάγον ἤγαγον λέγοντες, Δυνάμεθα
to the Mars' hill they brought [him], saying, Are we able
γνῶναι τίς ἡ.καινὴ.αὕτη [a]ἡ‖ ὑπὸ σοῦ λαλουμένη διδαχή;
to know what [is] this new [2]which [3]by [4]thee [5]is [6]spoken [1]teaching?

20 ξενίζοντα.γάρ τινα εἰσφέρεις εἰς τὰς.ἀκοὰς.ἡμῶν. βου-
For [2]strange [3]things [1]certain thou bringest to our ears. We
λόμεθα οὖν γνῶναι [b]τί ἂν.θέλοι‖ ταῦτα εἶναι. 21 Ἀθη-
wish therefore to know what [3]may [4]mean [1]these [2]things. [7]Athe-
ναῖοι δὲ πάντες καὶ οἱ ἐπιδημοῦντες ξένοι εἰς οὐδὲν ἕτερον
nians [5]now [6]all and the sojourning strangers in nothing else
[c]εὐκαίρουν‖ ἢ λέγειν τι [d]καὶ‖ ἀκούειν [e] καινότερον.
spent their leisure than to tell [4]something [1]and [2]to [3]hear newer.

22 Σταθεὶς.δὲ [f]ὁ‖ Παῦλος ἐν μέσῳ τοῦ [g]Ἀρείου‖ πάγου
And [2]having [3]stood [1]Paul in [the] midst of Mars' hill
ἔφη, Ἄνδρες Ἀθηναῖοι, κατὰ πάντα ὡς δεισιδαιμονεστέρους
said, Men Athenians, in all things very religious
(*lit.* very reverent to demons)
ὑμᾶς θεωρῶ. 23 διερχόμενος.γὰρ καὶ ἀναθεωρῶν τὰ σεβάσ-
you I behold; for, passing through and beholding [2]objects [3]of
ματα ὑμῶν, εὗρον καὶ βωμὸν ἐν ᾧ ἐπεγέγραπτο,
[4]veneration [1]your, I found also an altar on which had been inscribed,
Ἀγνώστῳ θεῷ. [h]ὃν‖ οὖν ἀγνοοῦντες εὐσεβεῖτε, [i]τοῦτον‖
To an unknown God. Whom therefore not knowing ye reverence, him

8 And they stirred up the people and the city judges who heard these things.

9 But after they had taken bond from Jason and the rest, they let them go.

10 But the brothers immediately sent both Paul and Silas away by night to Berea. When they arrived, *they* went into the synagogue of the Jews.

11 And these were more noble than those in Thess-a-lo-ni-ca, receiving the word with readiness, daily searching the Scriptures as to whether these things were so.

12 Then many of them truly believed, and quite a few of *them were* prominent Greek women and men.

13 But when the Jews from Thess-a-lo-ni-ca found out that the word of God was preached by Paul in Berea also, they came there, too, stirring up the people.

14 And then immediately the brothers sent Paul away to go toward the sea, but both Silas and Timothy remained there.

15 And those bringing Paul brought him to Athens. And after they had received a command that Silas and Timothy should come to him as quickly as possible, they left.

16 But waiting for them in Athens, Paul saw that the city was full of idols. And his spirit was sharply stirred within him.

17 Then truly he disputed in the synagogue with the Jews, and with those who worshiped and with those he met in the market-place every day.

18 But some of the philosophers, the Epi-cu-re-ans and the Stoics, met him. And some said, What would this chatterer desire to say? And others, He seems to be a preacher of strange gods (because he preached the gospel of Jesus and the resurrection to them).

19 And pulling him along, they brought him to Mars Hill, saying, Are we able to know what this new teaching is which is being spoken by you?

20 For you bring strange things to our ears. So we would like to know what these things mean.

21 Now all the A-the-ni-ans and the strangers living there spent their leisure time in nothing else than to tell and to hear some new things.

22 And standing in the middle of Mars Hill, Paul said, Men! A-the-ni-ans! I see you are very fearful of gods in all things.

23 For as I went through and saw the things which you worship, I found also an altar on which had been written, TO THE UNKNOWN GOD. Not knowing then whom you worship, I make Him known to you –

ἐγὼ καταγγέλλω ὑμῖν. 24 ὁ Θεὸς ὁ ποιήσας τὸν κόσμον καὶ
I announce to you. The God who made the world and
πάντα τὰ ἐν αὐτῷ, οὗτος οὐρανοῦ καὶ γῆς [k]κύριος
all things that [are] in it, he of heaven and earth Lord
ὑπάρχων,[l] οὐκ ἐν χειροποιήτοις ναοῖς κατοικεῖ, 25 οὐδὲ ὑπὸ
being, not in hand-made temples dwells, nor by
χειρῶν [l]ἀνθρώπων[l] θεραπεύεται προσδεόμενός τινος, αὐτὸς
hands of men is served as needing anything, himself
διδοὺς πᾶσιν ζωὴν καὶ πνοὴν [m]κατὰ.πάντα·[l] 26 ἐποίησέν.τε
giving to all life and breath in every [respect]; and he made
ἐξ ἑνὸς [n]αἵματος πᾶν ἔθνος ἀνθρώπων, κατοικεῖν ἐπὶ [o]πᾶν
of one blood every nation of men, to dwell upon all
τὸ πρόσωπον[l] τῆς γῆς, ὁρίσας [p]προτεταγμένους[l] και-
the face of the earth, having determined fore-arranged times
ροὺς καὶ τὰς ὁροθεσίας τῆς κατοικίας.αὐτῶν· 27 ζητεῖν [q]τὸν
and the boundaries of their dwelling— to seek the
κύριον, εἰ ἄρα.γε ψηλαφήσειαν αὐτὸν [r]καὶ[l] εὕροιεν,
Lord; if perhaps they might feel after him and might find him,
[s]καιτοιγε[l] οὐ μακρὰν ἀπὸ ἑνὸς ἑκάστου ἡμῶν ὑπάρχοντα.
though indeed [2]not [3]far [4]from [5]one [6]each [7]of [8]us [1]being;
28 ἐν.αὐτῷ.γὰρ ζῶμεν καὶ κινούμεθα καὶ ἐσμέν· ὡς καί τινες
for in him we live and move and are; as also some
τῶν καθ' ὑμᾶς ποιητῶν εἰρήκασιν, Τοῦ.γὰρ καὶ γένος
of the [2]among [3]you [1]poets have said, For of him [2]also [1]offspring
ἐσμέν. 29 Γένος οὖν ὑπάρχοντες τοῦ θεοῦ, οὐκ.ὀφείλομεν
we are. Offspring therefore being of God, we ought not
νομίζειν χρυσῷ ἢ ἀργύρῳ ἢ λίθῳ, χαράγματι τέχνης καὶ
to think to gold or to silver or to stone, a graven thing of art and
ἐνθυμήσεως ἀνθρώπου, τὸ θεῖον εἶναι ὅμοιον. 30 Τοὺς
imagination of man, that which [is] divine to be like. The
μὲν οὖν χρόνους τῆς ἀγνοίας ὑπεριδὼν ὁ θεός, [t]τὰ
[2]indeed [3]therefore times of ignorance [2]having [3]overlooked [1]God,
νῦν[l] [v]παραγγέλλει[l] τοῖς ἀνθρώποις [w]πᾶσιν πανταχοῦ μετα-
now charges men all everywhere to re-
νοεῖν· 31 [x]διότι[l] ἔστησεν ἡμέραν ἐν ᾗ μέλλει κρίνειν τὴν
pent, because he set a day in which he is about to judge the
οἰκουμένην ἐν δικαιοσύνῃ, ἐν ἀνδρὶ ᾧ ὥρισεν, πίστιν
habitable world in righteousness, by a man whom he appointed; [2]proof
παρασχὼν πᾶσιν ἀναστήσας αὐτὸν ἐκ νεκρῶν.
[1]having [2]given to all [in] having raised him from among [the] dead.
32 Ἀκούσαντες.δὲ ἀνάστασιν νεκρῶν, οἱ μὲν ἐχλεύαζον·
And having heard a resurrection of [the] dead, some mocked,
οἱ.δὲ εἶπον,[l] Ἀκουσόμεθά σου [z]πάλιν περὶ τούτου.[l]
and some said, We will hear thee again concerning this.
33 [a]Καὶ[l] οὕτως ὁ Παῦλος ἐξῆλθεν ἐκ μέσου αὐτῶν.
And thus Paul went out from [the] midst of them.
34 τινὲς.δὲ ἄνδρες κολληθέντες αὐτῷ ἐπίστευσαν· ἐν οἷς
But some men joining themselves to him believed; among whom
καὶ Διονύσιος [b]ὁ[l] [c]Ἀρεοπαγίτης,[l] καὶ γυνὴ ὀνόματι Δά-
also [was] Dionysius the Areopagite, and a woman by name Da-
μαρις, καὶ ἕτεροι σὺν αὐτοῖς.
maris, and others with them.
18 Μετὰ.[d]δὲ[l] ταῦτα χωρισθεὶς [e]ὁ Παῦλος[l] ἐκ τῶν
And after these things [2]having [3]departed [1]Paul from
Ἀθηνῶν ἦλθεν εἰς.Κόρινθον· 2 καὶ εὑρών τινα Ἰουδαῖον
Athens, came to Corinth; and having found a certain Jew
ὀνόματι Ἀκύλαν, Ποντικὸν τῷ.γένει, προσφάτως ἐληλυθότα
by name Aquila, of Pontus by race, lately come
ἀπὸ τῆς Ἰταλίας, καὶ Πρίσκιλλαν γυναῖκα.αὐτοῦ, διὰ τὸ
from Italy, and Priscilla his wife, because
[f]διατεταχέναι[l] Κλαύδιον χωρίζεσθαι πάντας τοὺς Ἰουδαίους
[2]had [3]ordered [1]Claudius to depart all the Jews
[g]ἐκ[l] τῆς Ῥώμης, προσῆλθεν αὐτοῖς· 3 καὶ διὰ τὸ ὁμό-
out of Rome, he came to them, and because of [2]the [3]same
τεχνον εἶναι, ἔμενεν παρ' αὐτοῖς καὶ [h]εἰργάζετο·[l] ἦσαν.γὰρ
[4]trade [1]being, he abode with them and worked; for they were
σκηνοποιοὶ [i]τὴν.τέχνην.[l] 4 διελέγετο.δὲ ἐν τῇ συναγωγῇ
tent makers by trade. And he reasoned in the synagogue
κατὰ.πᾶν.σάββατον, ἔπειθέν.τε Ἰουδαίους καὶ Ἕλληνας.
every sabbath, and persuaded Jews and Greeks.
5 Ὡς.δὲ κατῆλθον.ἀπὸ τῆς Μακεδονίας ὅ.τε.Σίλας καὶ ὁ Τι-
And when came down from Macedonia both Silas and Ti-
μόθεος [k]συνείχετο τῷ πνεύματι[l] ὁ Παῦλος διαμαρτυρόμενος
motheus [2]was [3]pressed [4]in [5]spirit [1]Paul earnestly testifying
τοῖς Ἰουδαίοις [l] τὸν χριστὸν Ἰησοῦν. 6 ἀντιτασ-
to the Jews [2to [3be] [4]the [5]Christ [1]Jesus. [7]As [9]set [10]themselves [11]in
σομένων δὲ αὐτῶν καὶ βλασφημούντων, ἐκτιναξάμενος
[12]opposition [6]but [8]they and were blaspheming, having shaken [his]
τὰ ἱμάτια, εἶπεν πρὸς αὐτούς, Τὸ.αἷμα.ὑμῶν ἐπὶ τὴν
garments, he said to them, Your blood [be] upon
κεφαλὴν.ὑμῶν· καθαρὸς ἐγὼ ἀπὸ τοῦ.νῦν εἰς τὰ ἔθνη
your head: [2]pure [3from [4it] [1]I from henceforth to the nations

24 the God who made the world and all the things that are in it. He being Lord of Heaven and earth does not live in temples made with hands.

25 Neither is He served by the hands of men, as if He needed anything, He Himself giving to all life, breath and all things.

26 And He made every nation of men of one blood, to live on all the face of the earth, having ordained the times and boundaries of their living place – which He before determined,

27 so that they might seek the Lord, if perhaps they might feel after Him and might find Him. Though, indeed, He is not far from each one of us,

28 for in Him we live and move and have our being – as also some of your poets have said, For we are also His offspring.

29 Being offspring of God, then, we ought not to think that the Godhead is like gold or silver or stone, engraved by art and the imagination of man.

30 Indeed, then, having before overlooked the times of ignorance, God now commands all men everywhere to repent.

31 Because He has set a Day in which He is going to judge the world in righteousness, by the Man whom He ordained, having given assurance to all *in that* He has raised Him from among the dead.

32 But hearing of a resurrection of the dead, some indeed ridiculed it. But others said, We will hear you again concerning this.

33 And so Paul went out from among them.

34 But some men believed, joining themselves to him, among whom also was Di-o-nys-i-us the Ar-e-op-a-gite and a woman named Dam-a-ris, and others with them.

CHAPTER 18

1 And after these things, Paul left Athens and came to Corinth.

2 And having found a certain Jew named Aquila (born in Pontus) and his wife Priscilla (who had lately come from Italy because Claudius had ordered all the Jews to leave Rome), he came to *live with* them.

3 And because he was of the same trade, he stayed with them and worked. For they were tentmakers by trade.

4 And he reasoned in the synagogue every sabbath and persuaded both Jews and Greeks.

5 And when both Silas and Timothy came down from Mac-e-do-ni-a, Paul was pressed in the spirit, earnestly witnessing to the Jews that Jesus is the Christ.

6 But as they set themselves in opposition and were blaspheming, he shook his robes and said to them, Your blood be on your own head! I am clean. From now on I will go to the Gentiles.

πορεύσομαι. 7 Καὶ μεταβὰς ἐκεῖθεν [m]ἦλθεν[l] εἰς οἰκίαν
will go. And having departed thence he came to [the] house
τινὸς ὀνόματι [n]Ἰούστου, σεβομένου τὸν θεόν, οὗ
of a certain one by name Justus, who worshipped God, of whom
ἡ οἰκία ἦν συνομοροῦσα τῇ συναγωγῇ. 8 Κρίσπος.δὲ ὁ
the house was adjoining the synagogue. But Crispus the
ἀρχισυνάγωγος ἐπίστευσεν τῷ κυρίῳ σὺν ὅλῳ τῷ.οἴκῳ.αὐ-
ruler of the synagogue believed in the [3]Lord with [4]whole [1]his house;
τοῦ· καὶ πολλοὶ τῶν Κορινθίων ἀκούοντες ἐπίστευον καὶ
and many of the Corinthians hearing believed and
ἐβαπτίζοντο. 9 Εἶπεν.δὲ ὁ κύριος [o]δι' ὁράματος ἐν νυκτὶ[ll]
were baptized. And said the Lord by a vision in [the] night
τῷ Παύλῳ, Μὴ.φοβοῦ, ἀλλὰ λάλει καὶ μὴ.σιωπήσῃς· 10 διότι
to Paul, Fear not, but speak and be not silent; because
ἐγώ εἰμι μετὰ σοῦ, καὶ οὐδεὶς ἐπιθήσεταί σοι τοῦ κακῶσαί σε·
I am with thee, and no one shall set on thee to ill-treat thee;
διότι λαός ἐστίν μοι πολὺς ἐν τῇ.πόλει.ταύτῃ. 11 Ἐκάθισέν
because people there is to me much in this city. [2]He [3]remained
[p]τε[ll] ἐνιαυτὸν καὶ μῆνας ἕξ διδάσκων ἐν αὐτοῖς τὸν λόγον
[1]and a year and [2]months [1]six, teaching among them the word
τοῦ θεοῦ.
of God.

12 Γαλλίωνος.δὲ [q]ἀνθυπατεύοντος[ll] τῆς Ἀχαΐας, κατεπ-
But Gallio being proconsul of Achaia, [8]rose
έστησαν ὁμοθυμαδὸν οἱ Ἰουδαῖοι τῷ Παύλῳ, καὶ ἤγαγον
[9]against [3]with [4]one [5]accord [1]the [2]Jews Paul, and led
αὐτὸν ἐπὶ τὸ βῆμα, 13 λέγοντες, Ὅτι παρὰ τὸν νόμον
him to the judgment seat, saying, That contrary to the law
[r]οὗτος ἀναπείθει[ll] τοὺς ἀνθρώπους σέβεσθαι τὸν θεόν.
this [man] persuades men to worship God.
14 Μέλλοντος.δὲ τοῦ Παύλου ἀνοίγειν τὸ στόμα, εἶπεν ὁ
But [2]being [3]about [1]Paul to open [his] mouth, [2]said
Γαλλίων πρὸς τοὺς Ἰουδαίους, Εἰ μὲν [s]οὖν[l] ἦν ἀδί-
[1]Gallio to the Jews, If indeed therefore it was [2]unrighteous-
κημά τι ἢ ῥᾳδιούργημα πονηρόν, ὦ Ἰουδαῖοι, κατὰ λόγον
ness [1]some or [2]criminality [1]wicked, O Jews, according to reason
ἂν [t]ἠνεσχόμην[ll] ὑμῶν, 15 εἰ.δὲ [v]ζήτημά[l] ἐστιν περὶ
I should have borne with you, but if a question it be about
λόγου καὶ ὀνομάτων καὶ νόμου τοῦ καθ' ὑμᾶς, ὄψεσθε
a word and names and a law which [is] among you, ye will see
αὐτοί· κριτὴς.[w]γὰρ[l] ἐγὼ τούτων οὐ.βούλομαι εἶναι.
[to it] yourselves; for a judge I of these things do not wish to be.
16 Καὶ ἀπήλασεν αὐτοὺς ἀπὸ τοῦ βήματος· 17 ἐπιλαβό-
And he drove them from the judgment seat. [5]Having [6]laid
μενοι δὲ πάντες [x]οἱ Ἕλληνες[l] Σωσθένην τὸν ἀρχισυνάγωγον
hold [8]on [1]and [2]all [3]the [4]Greeks Sosthenes the ruler of the synagogue,
ἔτυπτον ἔμπροσθεν τοῦ βήματος· καὶ οὐδὲν τού-
they beat [him] before the judgment seat. And [3]nothing [6]about [7]these
των τῷ Γαλλίωνι ἔμελεν.
[8]things [4]to [5]Gallio [1]it [2]mattered.

18 Ὁ.δὲ.Παῦλος ἔτι προσμείνας ἡμέρας ἱκανάς, τοῖς ἀδελ-
But Paul yet having remained [2]days [1]many, [7]the [8]breth-
φοῖς ἀποταξάμενος, ἐξέπλει εἰς τὴν Συρίαν, καὶ σὺν αὐτῷ
ren [3]having [4]taken [5]leave [6]of sailed away to Syria, and with him
Πρίσκιλλα καὶ Ἀκύλας, κειράμενος [y]τὴν κεφαλὴν ἐν Κεγ-
Priscilla and Aquila, having shorn [his] head in Cen-
χρεαῖς·[l] εἶχεν.γὰρ εὐχήν. 19 [z]κατήντησεν[l].δὲ εἰς Ἔφεσον, κά-
chrea, for he had a vow: and he came to Ephesus, and
κείνους κατέλιπεν [a]αὐτοῦ·[ll] αὐτὸς.δὲ εἰσελθὼν εἰς τὴν
[2]them [1]left there. But he himself having entered into the
συναγωγὴν [b]διελέχθη[ll] τοῖς Ἰουδαίοις. 20 ἐρωτώντων.δὲ
synagogue reasoned with the Jews. And [2]asking [3him]
αὐτῶν ἐπὶ πλείονα χρόνον μεῖναι [c]παρ' αὐτοῖς[l] οὐκ.ἐπένευσεν·
[1]they for a longer time to remain with them he did not accede,
21 [d]ἀλλ' ἀπετάξατο αὐτοῖς,[ll] εἰπών, [e]Δεῖ με πάντως τὴν
but took leave of them, saying, It behoves me by all means the
ἑορτὴν τὴν ἐρχομένην ποιῆσαι εἰς Ἱεροσόλυμα·[ll] πάλιν.δὲ
[3]feast [2]coming to keep at Jerusalem, but again
ἀνακάμψω πρὸς ὑμᾶς, τοῦ θεοῦ θέλοντος. [g]Καὶ[ll] ἀνήχθη ἀπὸ
I will return to you, God willing. And he sailed from
τῆς Ἐφέσου· 22 καὶ κατελθὼν εἰς [h]Καισάρειαν,[ll] ἀναβὰς
Ephesus. And having landed at Cæsarea, having gone up
καὶ ἀσπασάμενος τὴν ἐκκλησίαν κατέβη εἰς Ἀντιόχειαν.
and having saluted the assembly he went down to Antioch.
23 καὶ ποιήσας χρόνον τινὰ ἐξῆλθεν, διερχόμενος καθεξῆς
And having stayed [2]time [1]some he went forth, passing through [8]in [7]order
τὴν Γαλατικὴν χώραν καὶ Φρυγίαν, [i]ἐπιστηρίζων[l] πάντας
[1]the [2]Galatian [5]country [3]and [4]Phrygian, establishing all
τοὺς μαθητάς.
the disciples.
24 Ἰουδαῖος.δέ τις Ἀπολλὼς ὀνόματι, Ἀλεξανδρεὺς τῷ
But a [2]Jew [1]certain, Apollos by name, an Alexandrian

7 And leaving there, he came to the house of a certain one named Justus, who worshiped God, whose house was by the synagogue.
8 And Crispus, the ruler of the synagogue, believed in the Lord with all his household. And many of the Corinthians heard and believed and were baptized.
9 And by a vision in the night, the Lord said to Paul, Do not be afraid, but speak and do not hold back your voice,
10 because I am with you. And no one will attack you, to do evil to you, for I have many people in this city.
11 And he stayed there eighteen months, teaching among them the word of God.

12 And when Gallio was proconsul of Achai-a, the Jews rose up against Paul all together and led him to the judgment seat,
13 saying, This one persuades men to worship God contrary to the law.
14 But as Paul was about to open his mouth, Gallio said to the Jews, Then, indeed, if it was anything unrighteous, or some wicked fraud, O Jews, according to reason I would have borne with you.
15 But if it is a question about words or names and a law which is among you, you will see to it yourselves. For I do not want to be a judge of these things.
16 And he drove them away from the judgment seat.
17 Then all the Greeks took Sos-the-nes the ruler of the synagogue and beat him in front of the judgment seat. But Gallio did not care, not even for these things.

18 But Paul remained many days. And then, taking leave of the brothers, he sailed away to Syria. And Priscilla and Aquila *were* with him. *Paul* had shorn his head in Cen-chre-a because he had a vow.
19 And he came to Eph-e-sus and left them there. But he himself reasoned with the Jews when he had entered into the synagogue.
20 And when they asked him to stay for a longer time with them, he did not agree.
21 But he left them, saying, It is necessary for me by all means to keep the coming feast at Jerusalem, but I will come again to you, God willing. And he sailed from Ephesus.
22 And having landed at Caesarea, he went up and greeted the church before going down to Antioch.
23 And after staying some time, he left, going through the countries of Galatia and Phryg-i-a, in order, strengthening all the disciples.
24 But a certain Jew named Apollos, an Alexandrian by birth, came to Ephesus, a learned man, being mighty in the Scriptures.

γένει, ἀνὴρ λόγιος, κατήντησεν εἰς Ἔφεσον, δυνατὸς ὢν
by birth, [3]man [1]an [2]eloquent, came to Ephesus, [2]mighty [1]being

ἐν ταῖς γραφαῖς. 25 οὗτος ἦν κατηχημένος τὴν ὁδὸν τοῦ
in the scriptures. He was instructed in the way of the

κυρίου, καὶ ζέων τῷ πνεύματι, ἐλάλει καὶ ἐδίδασκεν
Lord, and being fervent in spirit, he spoke and taught

ἀκριβῶς τὰ περὶ [k]τοῦ κυρίου,‖ ἐπιστάμενος μόνον τὸ
accurately the things concerning the Lord, knowing only the

βάπτισμα [l]Ἰωάννου·‖ 26 οὗτός.τε ἤρξατο παῤῥησιάζεσθαι ἐν
baptism of John. And he began to speak boldly in

τῇ συναγωγῇ. ἀκούσαντες.δὲ αὐτοῦ [m]Ἀκύλας καὶ Πρίσκιλλα‖
the synagogue. And [4]having [5]heard [6]him [1]Aquila [2]and [3]Priscilla

προσελάβοντο αὐτόν, καὶ ἀκριβέστερον αὐτῷ ἐξέθεντο τὴν
they took [2]to [3them] [1]him, and more accurately to him expounded the

[n]τοῦ θεοῦ ὁδόν.‖ 27 βουλομένου.δὲ αὐτοῦ διελθεῖν εἰς τὴν
[2]of [3]God [1]way. And [2]being [3]minded [1]he to pass through into

Ἀχαΐαν, προτρεψάμενοι οἱ ἀδελφοὶ ἔγραψαν τοῖς μαθηταῖς
Achaia, [7]exhorting [8them] [1]the [2]brethren [3]wrote [4]to [5]the [6]disciples

ἀποδέξασθαι αὐτόν· ὃς παραγενόμενος συνεβάλετο πολὺ τοῖς
to welcome him, who having arrived helped much those who

πεπιστευκόσιν διὰ τῆς χάριτος· 28 εὐτόνως.γὰρ τοῖς Ἰου-
believed through grace. For powerfully the Jews

δαίοις διακατηλέγχετο δημοσίᾳ, ἐπιδεικνὺς διὰ τῶν γραφῶν,
he confuted publicly, shewing by the scriptures

εἶναι τὸν χριστὸν Ἰησοῦν.
[2]to [3]be [4]the [5]Christ [1]Jesus.

19 Ἐγένετο.δὲ ἐν.τῷ τὸν Ἀπολλὼ εἶναι ἐν Κορίνθῳ, Παῦ-
And it came to pass, while Apollos was in Corinth, Paul,

λον διελθόντα τὰ ἀνωτερικὰ μέρη, [o]ἐλθεῖν‖ εἰς Ἔφεσον·
having passed through the upper parts, came to Ephesus,

καὶ [p]εὑρών‖ τινας μαθητὰς 2 εἶπεν [q]πρὸς αὐτούς, Εἰ
and having found certain disciples he said to them, [The]

πνεῦμα ἅγιον ἐλάβετε πιστεύσαντες; Οἱ.δὲ [r]εἶπον‖ πρὸς
[2]Spirit [1]Holy did ye receive, having believed? And they said to

αὐτόν, Ἀλλ' [s]οὐδὲ‖ εἰ πνεῦμα ἅγιόν ἐστιν, ἠκούσαμεν.
him, Not even if [the] [2]Spirit [1]Holy is, did we hear.

3 [t]Εἶπέν.τε‖ [v]πρὸς αὐτούς,‖ Εἰς τί οὖν ἐβαπτίσθητε; Οἱ.δὲ
And he said to them, To what then were ye baptized? And they

[w]εἶπον,‖ Εἰς τὸ [x]Ἰωάννου‖ βάπτισμα. 4 Εἶπεν.δὲ Παῦλος,
said, To the [2]of [3]John [1]baptism. And [2]said [1]Paul,

[y]Ἰωάννης‖ [z]μὲν‖ ἐβάπτισεν βάπτισμα μετανοίας, τῷ
John indeed baptized [with] a baptism of repentance, to the

λαῷ λέγων, εἰς τὸν ἐρχόμενον μετ' αὐτὸν ἵνα πιστεύσωσιν,
people saying, [2]On [3]him [4]coming [5]after [6]him [1]that they should believe,

[a]τουτέστιν‖ εἰς τὸν [b]χριστὸν‖ Ἰησοῦν. 5 Ἀκούσαντες.δὲ ἐβαπ-
that is, on [2]the [3]Christ [1]Jesus. And having heard they

τίσθησαν εἰς τὸ ὄνομα τοῦ κυρίου Ἰησοῦ. 6 καὶ ἐπιθέντος
were baptized to the name of the Lord Jesus. And [2]having [3]laid

αὐτοῖς τοῦ Παύλου [c]τὰς‖ χεῖρας ἦλθεν τὸ πνεῦμα τὸ ἅγιον
[5]on [6]them [1]Paul [4]hands came the Spirit the Holy

ἐπ' αὐτούς, ἐλάλουν.τε γλώσσαις καὶ [d]προεφήτευον.‖
upon them, and they were speaking with tongues and prophesying

7 ἦσαν.δὲ οἱ πάντες ἄνδρες ὡσεὶ [e]δεκαδύο.‖ 8 Εἰσελθὼν.δὲ
And [4]were [2]the [1]all [3]men about twelve. And having entered

εἰς τὴν συναγωγὴν ἐπαῤῥησιάζετο, ἐπὶ μῆνας τρεῖς διαλεγό-
into the synagogue he spoke boldly, for [2]months [1]three reason-

μενος καὶ πείθων [f]τὰ‖ περὶ τῆς βασιλείας τοῦ θεοῦ.
ing and persuading the things concerning the kingdom of God.

9 Ὡς.δέ τινες ἐσκληρύνοντο καὶ ἠπείθουν, κακολογοῦντες τὴν
But when some were hardened and disobeyed, speaking evil of the

ὁδὸν ἐνώπιον τοῦ πλήθους, ἀποστὰς ἀπ' αὐτῶν ἀφώρισεν
way before the multitude, having departed from them he separated

τοὺς μαθητάς, καθ'.ἡμέραν διαλεγόμενος ἐν τῇ σχολῇ Τυράν-
the disciples, daily reasoning in the school of [3]Tyran-

νου [g]τινός.‖ 10 Τοῦτο.δὲ ἐγένετο ἐπὶ ἔτη δύο, ὥστε πάντας
nus [1]a [2]certain. And this was for [2]years [1]two, so that all

τοὺς κατοικοῦντας τὴν Ἀσίαν ἀκοῦσαι τὸν λόγον τοῦ κυρίου
those who inhabited Asia heard the word of the Lord

[h]Ἰησοῦ,‖ Ἰουδαίους.τε καὶ Ἕλληνας· 11 Δυνάμεις.τε οὐ τὰς
Jesus, both Jews and Greeks. And works of power not

τυχούσας [i]ἐποίει ὁ θεὸς‖ διὰ τῶν χειρῶν Παύλου, 12 ὥστε καὶ
common [2]wrought [1]God by the hands of Paul, so that even

ἐπὶ τοὺς ἀσθενοῦντας [k]ἐπιφέρεσθαι‖ ἀπὸ τοῦ.χρωτὸς.αὐτοῦ
to those being sick were brought from his skin

σουδάρια ἢ σιμικίνθια, καὶ ἀπαλλάσσεσθαι ἀπ' αὐτῶν τὰς
handkerchiefs or aprons, and departed from them the

νόσους, τά.τε πνεύματα τὰ πονηρὰ [l]ἐξέρχεσθαι ἀπ' αὐτῶν.‖
diseases, and the [2]spirits [1]wicked went out from them.

13 Ἐπεχείρησαν δέ τινες [m]ἀπὸ τῶν‖ περιερχομένων Ἰουδαίων
But [7]took [8]in [9]hand [1]certain [2]from [3]the [4]wandering [5]Jews,

ἐξορκιστῶν ὀνομάζειν ἐπὶ τοὺς ἔχοντας τὰ πνεύματα τὰ
[6]exorcists, to name over those who had the [2]spirits

25 He was taught in the way of the Lord. And being fervent in spirit, he spoke and accurately taught the things of the Lord, knowing only the baptism of John.

26 And he began to speak boldly in the synagogue. And when Aquila and Priscilla heard him, they took him and explained the way of God more exactly to him.

27 And when he desired to go through into A-chai-a, the brothers wrote to the disciples encouraging them to welcome him. After arriving, he very much helped those who believed through grace.

28 For he powerfully, publicly proved the Jews to be wrong, showing by the Scriptures that Jesus was the Christ.

CHAPTER 19

1 And while Apollos was in Corinth, Paul came to Ephesus, after he had gone through the upper countries. And finding certain disciples,

2 he said to them, Did you receive the Holy Spirit when you believed? And they said to him, We have never even heard if the Holy Spirit exists.

3 And he said to them, Then to what were you baptized? And they said, To the baptism of John.

4 And Paul said, John indeed baptized *with* the baptism of repentance, saying to the people that they should believe on Him, the One coming after him – that is, on the Christ – Jesus.

5 And hearing this, they were baptized into the name of the Lord Jesus.

6 And after Paul laid his hands on them, the Holy Spirit came on them. And they were speaking in languages and prophesying.

7 And there were about twelve men in all.

8 And entering into the synagogue, he spoke boldly for three months, reasoning and proving the things concerning the kingdom of God.

9 But when some were hardened and did not believe, speaking evil of the Way before the multitude, he left them and separated the disciples – day by day reasoning in the school of a certain Ty-ran-nus.

10 And this was for two years, so that all those who lived in Asia heard the word of the Lord Jesus, both Jews and Greeks.

11 And God worked special miracles by the hands of Paul,

12 so that even handkerchiefs or aprons were brought from his skin to those who were sick, and the diseases left them, and the evil spirits went out from them.

13 But some of the Jews who went around throwing out demons undertook to call the name of the Lord Jesus over those who had

πονηρὰ τὸ ὄνομα τοῦ κυρίου Ἰησοῦ, λέγοντες, [n]Ὁρκίζομεν"
wicked the name of the Lord Jesus, saying, We adjure
ὑμᾶς τὸν Ἰησοῦν ὃν [o]ὁ" Παῦλος κηρύσσει. 14 Ἦσαν.δέ
you [by] Jesus. whom Paul proclaims. And there were
[p]τινες" [q]υἱοὶ" Σκευᾶ Ἰουδαίου ἀρχιερέως ἑπτὰ [q] [r]οἱ" τοῦτο
certain [men] [2]sons [3]of [4]Sceva [5]a [6]Jew, [7]a [8]high [9]priest [1]seven who this
ποιοῦντες. 15 ἀποκριθὲν.δὲ τὸ πνεῦμα τὸ πονηρὸν εἶπεν[s],
were doing. But answering the [2]spirit [1]wicked said,
Τὸν Ἰησοῦν γινώσκω, καὶ τὸν Παῦλον ἐπίσταμαι· ὑμεῖς
Jesus I know, and Paul I am acquainted with; [2]ye
δὲ τίνες ἐστέ; 16 Καὶ [t]ἐφαλλόμενος" [v]ἐπ' αὐτοὺς ὁ ἄνθρω-
[1]but, who are ye? And leaping on them [5]the man
πος" ἐν ᾧ ἦν τὸ πνεῦμα τὸ πονηρόν, [w]καὶ" κατακυριεύσας
in whom was the [2]spirit [1]wicked, and having mastered
[x]αὐτῶν" ἴσχυσεν κατ' αὐτῶν, ὥστε γυμνοὺς καὶ τετραυματισ-
them prevailed against them, so that naked and wounded
μένους ἐκφυγεῖν ἐκ τοῦ.οἴκου.ἐκείνου. 17 τοῦτο.δὲ ἐγένετο
they escaped out of that house. And this became
γνωστὸν πᾶσιν Ἰουδαίοις.τε καὶ Ἕλλησιν τοῖς κατοικοῦσιν τὴν
known to all both Jews and Greeks, those inhabiting
Ἔφεσον, καὶ [y]ἐπέπεσεν" φόβος ἐπὶ πάντας αὐτούς, καὶ ἐμεγα-
Ephesus, and [2]fell [1]fear upon [2]all [1]them, and was mag-
λύνετο τὸ ὄνομα τοῦ κυρίου Ἰησοῦ. 18 Πολλοί.τε τῶν
nified the name of the Lord Jesus. And many of those who
πεπιστευκότων ἤρχοντο ἐξομολογούμενοι καὶ ἀναγγέλλοντες
believed came confessing and declaring
τὰς.πράξεις.αὐτῶν. 19 ἱκανοὶ.δὲ τῶν τὰ περίεργα πρα-
their deeds. And many of those who the curious arts prac-
ξάντων συνενέγκαντες τὰς βίβλους κατέκαιον ἐνώπιον
tised having brought the books burnt [them] before
πάντων· καὶ συνεψήφισαν τὰς τιμὰς αὐτῶν, καὶ εὗρον
all. And they reckoned up the prices of them, and found [it]
ἀργυρίου μυριάδας πέντε. 20 οὕτως κατὰ κράτος [z]ὁ λόγος τοῦ
[3]of [4]silver [2]myriads [1]five. Thus with might the word of the
κυρίου" ηὔξανεν καὶ ἴσχυεν.
Lord increased and prevailed.
21 Ὡς.δὲ ἐπληρώθη ταῦτα ἔθετο ὁ Παῦλος ἐν τῷ πνεύ-
And when were fulfilled these things [2]purposed [1]Paul in the spirit,
ματι, [a]διελθὼν" τὴν Μακεδονίαν καὶ [b]Ἀχαΐαν πορεύε-
having passed through Macedonia and Achaia, to
σθαι εἰς [c]Ἱερουσαλήμ," εἰπών, Ὅτι μετὰ τὸ γενέσθαι με ἐκεῖ
go to Jerusalem, saying, After [2]having [3]been [1]my there
δεῖ με καὶ Ῥώμην ἰδεῖν. 22 Ἀποστείλας.δὲ εἰς [d]τὴν"
it behoves me also Rome to see. And having sent into
Μακεδονίαν δύο τῶν διακονούντων αὐτῷ, Τιμόθεον καὶ
Macedonia two of those who ministered to him, Timotheus and
Ἔραστον, αὐτὸς ἐπέσχεν χρόνον εἰς τὴν Ἀσίαν· 23 Ἐγένετο
Erastus, he remained a time in Asia. [2]Came [3]to [4]pass
δὲ κατὰ τὸν.καιρὸν.ἐκεῖνον τάραχος οὐκ ὀλίγος περὶ τῆς
[1]and at that time [5]disturbance [1]no [2]small about the
ὁδοῦ. 24 Δημήτριος.γάρ τις ὀνόματι, ἀργυροκόπος,
way. For [4]Demetrius [1]a [2]certain [[3]man] by name, a silversmith,
ποιῶν ναοὺς ἀργυροῦς Ἀρτέμιδος, [e]παρείχετο" τοῖς τεχνίταις
making [2]temples [1]silver of Artemis, brought to the artificers
[f]ἐργασίαν οὐκ ὀλίγην·" 25 οὓς συναθροίσας, καὶ τοὺς
[3]gain [1]no [2]little; whom having brought together, and the
περὶ τὰ.τοιαῦτα ἐργάτας, εἶπεν, Ἄνδρες, ἐπίστασθε ὅτι ἐκ
[2]in [3]such [4]things [1]workmen, he said, Men, ye know that from
ταύτης τῆς ἐργασίας ἡ εὐπορία [g]ἡμῶν" ἐστιν· 26 καὶ θεωρεῖτε
this gain the wealth of us is; and ye see
καὶ ἀκούετε ὅτι οὐ μόνον Ἐφέσου ἀλλὰ [h] σχεδὸν πάσης τῆς
and hear that not only of Ephesus but almost of all
Ἀσίας ὁ.Παῦλος.οὗτος πείσας μετέστησεν ἱκανὸν ὄχλον,
Asia this Paul having persuaded turned away a great multitude,
λέγων ὅτι οὐκ.εἰσὶν θεοὶ οἱ διὰ χειρῶν γινόμενοι. 27 οὐ
saying that they are not gods which by hands are made. [2]Not
μόνον δὲ τοῦτο κινδυνεύει ἡμῖν τὸ μέρος εἰς ἀπελεγμὸν
[3]only [1]now [5]this [4]is dangerous to us [lest] the business [2]into [3]disrepute
ἐλθεῖν, ἀλλὰ καὶ τὸ τῆς μεγάλης θεᾶς [i]Ἀρτέμιδος ἱερὸν" εἰς
[1]come, but also the [2]of [3]the [4]great [5]goddess [6]Artemis [1]temple for
[k]οὐδὲν" [l]λογισθῆναι, μέλλειν".[m]δὲ" καὶ καθαιρεῖσθαι [n]τὴν μεγα-
nothing be reckoned, and be about also to be destroyed the ma-
λειότητα" αὐτῆς, ἣν ὅλη [o]ἡ" Ἀσία καὶ ἡ οἰκουμένη σέβεται.
jesty of her, whom all Asia and the habitable world worships.
28 Ἀκούσαντες.δὲ καὶ γενόμενοι πλήρεις θυμοῦ, ἔκρα-
And having heard, and having become full of indignation, they cried
ζον λέγοντες, Μεγάλη ἡ Ἄρτεμις Ἐφεσίων. 29 Καὶ
out saying, Great the Artemis of [the] Ephesians. And
ἐπλήσθη ἡ πόλις [p]ὅλη" [q] συγχύσεως· ὥρμησάν.τε ὁμοθυ-
was [3]filled [1]the [3]city [2]whole with confusion, and they rushed with one
μαδὸν εἰς τὸ θέατρον, συναρπάσαντες Γάϊον καὶ Ἀρί-
accord to the theatre, having seized with [them] Gaius and Ari-

evil spirits, saying, We command you by Jesus, whom Paul preaches!

14 And there were certain ones who were doing this – the seven sons of Sceva, a Jew and a chief priest.

15 But the evil spirit answering said, Jesus I know and Paul I know, but you, who are you?

16 And the man in whom the evil spirit resided leaped on them. And overcoming them, he prevailed against them, so that they fled out of that house naked and wounded.

17 And this became known to all who lived in Ephesus, both Jews and Greeks. And fear fell on all of them. And the name of the Lord Jesus was magnified.

18 And many of those who believed came confessing and declaring their deeds.

19 And many of those who had practiced the magic arts, bringing their books, burned them before all. And they counted up the prices of them and found it fifty thousand pieces of silver.

20 So with power the word of the Lord increased and triumphed.

21 And when these things were ended, going through Mac-e-do-ni-a and A-chai-a, Paul in the Spirit decided to go to Jerusalem, saying, After I have been there, it is necessary for me also to see Rome.

22 And having sent two of those who ministered to him in Mac-e-do-ni-a (Timothy and Erastus), he remained a time in Asia.

23 And there came at that time quite a disturbance about the Way.

24 For a certain one named De-me-tri-us, a silversmith who made silver shrines of Diana, brought much profit to the skilled workers.

25 Bringing these together, and workmen in the same kind of work, he said, Men! You know that our riches come from this work.

26 And you see and hear that not only at Ephesus but almost in all Asia, this Paul has persuaded and turned away a great multitude, saying that they which are made of hands are not gods.

27 Now not only is this dangerous for us, *for fear our* business will become lightly regarded, but also the temple of the great goddess Diana may be despised. And her majesty may also be about to be destroyed, whom all Asia and the world worships.

28 And hearing this, they became full of anger and cried out, saying, Great is Diana of the Ephesians!

29 And the whole city was filled with disorder. And they rushed all together into the theatre, having seized Paul's traveling companions from Mac-e-do-ni-a, Gaius and A-ris-tar-chus.

σταρχον Μακεδόνας, συνεκδήμους [r]τοῦ" Παύλου. 30 [r]τοῦ" [s]δὲ
starchus, Macedonians, fellow-travellers of Paul. But
Παύλου" βουλομένου εἰσελθεῖν εἰς τὸν δῆμον, οὐκ.εἴων αὐτὸν
Paul intending to go in to the people, [3]did [4]not [5]suffer [6]him
οἱ μαθηταί· 31 τινὲς.δὲ καὶ τῶν Ἀσιαρχῶν ὄντες αὐτῷ
[1]the [2]disciples, and some also of the chiefs of Asia being [2]to [3]him
φίλοι, πέμψαντες πρὸς αὐτόν, παρεκάλουν μὴ δοῦναι ἑαυτὸν
[1]friends, having sent to him, urged [him] not to venture himself
εἰς τὸ θέατρον. 32 ἄλλοι.μὲν.οὖν.ἄλλο.τι ἔκραζον.
into the theatre. Some therefore one thing and some another were crying out;
ἦν.γὰρ ἡ ἐκκλησία [t]συγκεχυμένη," καὶ οἱ πλείους οὐκ.ᾔδεισαν
for [3]was [1]the [2]assembly confused, and the most did not know
τίνος [v]ἕνεκεν" συνεληλύθεισαν. 33 ἐκ.δὲ τοῦ ὄχλου
for what cause they had come together. But from among the crowd
[w]προεβίβασαν" Ἀλέξανδρον, [x]προβαλόντων" αὐτὸν τῶν
they put forward Alexander, [3]thrusting [5]forward [4]him [1]the
Ἰουδαίων· ὁ.δὲ.Ἀλέξανδρος κατασείσας τὴν χεῖρα,
[2]Jews: And Alexander, having made a sign with the hand,
ἤθελεν ἀπολογεῖσθαι τῷ δήμῳ. 34 [y]ἐπιγνόντων".δὲ ὅτι
wished to make a defence to the people. But having recognized that
Ἰουδαῖός ἐστιν, φωνὴ ἐγένετο μία ἐκ πάντων, ὡς.ἐπὶ ὥρας
a Jew he is, [4]cry [1]there [2]was [3]one from all, for about [2]hours
δύο [z]κραζόντων," Μεγάλη ἡ Ἄρτεμις Ἐφεσίων. 35 Κατα-
[1]two crying out, Great the Artemis of [the] Ephesians. [4]Having
στείλας δὲ ὁ γραμματεὺς τὸν ὄχλον φησίν, Ἄνδρες Ἐφέσιοι,
[5]calmed [1]and [2]the [3]recorder the crowd says, Men Ephesians,
τίς γάρ ἐστιν [a]ἄνθρωπος" ὃς οὐ.γινώσκει τὴν Ἐφεσίων
[2]what [1]for [4]is [5]there [3]man who knows not the [2]of [[3]the] [4]Ephesians
πόλιν νεωκόρον οὖσαν τῆς μεγάλης [b]θεᾶς" Ἀρτέμιδος καὶ
[1]city [7]temple-keepers [5]as [6]being of the great goddess Artemis, and
τοῦ Διοπετοῦς; 36 ἀναντιῤῥήτων οὖν ὄντων τούτων,
of that fallen from Zeus? Undeniable therefore being these things
δέον ἐστὶν ὑμᾶς κατεσταλμένους ὑπάρχειν, καὶ μηδὲν προ-
necessary it is for you calm to be, and [3]nothing [4]head-
πετὲς [c]πράττειν." 37 ἠγάγετε.γὰρ τοὺς.ἄνδρας.τούτους,
long [1]to [2]do. For ye brought these men, [who are]
οὔτε ἱεροσύλους οὔτε βλασφημοῦντας τὴν [d]θεὰν" [e]ὑμῶν."
neither temple plunderers nor are defaming [2]goddess [1]your.
38 εἰ μὲν οὖν Δημήτριος καὶ οἱ σὺν αὐτῷ τεχνῖται [f]πρός
If indeed therefore Demetrius and the [2]with [3]him [1]artificers against
τινα λόγον ἔχουσιν," ἀγοραῖοι ἄγονται, καὶ ἀνθύπατοί εἰσιν·
anyone a matter have, courts are held, and proconsuls there are:
ἐγκαλείτωσαν ἀλλήλοις. 39 εἰ.δέ τι [g]περὶ ἑτέρων"
let them accuse one another. But if anything concerning other matters
ἐπιζητεῖτε, ἐν τῇ ἐννόμῳ ἐκκλησίᾳ ἐπιλυθήσεται. 40 καὶ.γὰρ
ye inquire, in the lawful assembly it shall be solved. For also
κινδυνεύομεν ἐγκαλεῖσθαι στάσεως περὶ τῆς.σήμερον,
we are in danger to be accused of insurrection in regard to this day,
μηδενὸς αἰτίου ὑπάρχοντος περὶ οὗ [h] δυνησόμεθα ἀπο-
not one cause existing concerning which we shall be able to
δοῦναι λόγον [i] τῆς.συστροφῆς.ταύτης. 41 Καὶ ταῦτα εἰπών,
give a reason for this concourse. And these things having said,
ἀπέλυσεν τὴν ἐκκλησίαν.
he dismissed the assembly.

20 Μετὰ.δὲ τὸ παύσασθαι τὸν θόρυβον, [k]προσκαλεσάμενος[l]
But after [3]ceased [1]the [2]tumult, [5]having [6]called [7]to
ὁ Παῦλος τοὺς μαθητάς, καὶ [l] ἀσπασάμενος, ἐξῆλθεν
[[8]him] [4]Paul the disciples, and saluted [them], went away
[m]πορευθῆναι" εἰς [n]τὴν" Μακεδονίαν. 2 διελθὼν.δὲ τὰ
to go to Macedonia. And having passed through
μέρη.ἐκεῖνα, καὶ παρακαλέσας αὐτοὺς λόγῳ πολλῷ, ἦλ-
those parts, and having exhorted them with [2]discourse [1]much, he
θεν εἰς τὴν Ἑλλάδα· 3 ποιήσας.τε μῆνας τρεῖς, γενο-
came to Greece. And having continued [2]months [1]three, having been
μένης [o]αὐτῷ ἐπιβουλῆς" ὑπὸ τῶν Ἰουδαίων μέλλοντι
made against them a plot by the Jews being about
ἀνάγεσθαι εἰς τὴν Συρίαν, ἐγένετο [p]γνώμη" τοῦ ὑποστρέφειν
to sail into Syria, [3]arose [1]a [2]purpose to return
διὰ Μακεδονίας. 4 συνείπετο.δὲ αὐτῷ [q]ἄχρι τῆς Ἀσίας"
through Macedonia. And accompanied him as far as Asia
Σώπατρος [r] Βεροιαῖος· Θεσσαλονικέων.δὲ Ἀρίσταρχος καὶ
Sopater a Berœan, and of Thessalonians Aristarchus and
Σεκοῦνδος, καὶ Γάϊος Δερβαῖος καὶ Τιμόθεος· Ἀσιανοὶ.δὲ
Secundus, and Gaius of Derbe and Timotheus, and of Asia
Τυχικὸς καὶ Τρόφιμος. 5 οὗτοι [s] [t]προελθόντες" ἔμενον ἡμᾶς
Tychicus and Trophimus. These having gone before waited for us
ἐν [v]Τρωάδι·" 6 ἡμεῖς.δὲ ἐξεπλεύσαμεν μετὰ τὰς ἡμέρας τῶν
in Troas; but we sailed away after the days of the
ἀζύμων ἀπὸ Φιλίππων, καὶ ἤλθομεν πρὸς αὐτοὺς εἰς
unleavened bread from Philippi, and came to them at
τὴν [w]Τρωάδα" [x]ἄχρις" ἡμερῶν πέντε, [y]οὗ" διετρίψαμεν ἡμέρας
Troas in [2]days [1]five, where we stayed [2]days

30 But when Paul wanted to go in to the people, the disciples did not let him go.

31 And some of the chief men of Asia, being his friends, sent to him and urged him not to try to go into the theatre himself.

32 Then some were crying out one thing and some another. For the gathering was excited, and the greater part of them did not know why they had come together.

33 But from among the crowd they put forward Alexander, the Jews pushing him forward. And Alexander, waving with his hand, wanted to give a defense to the people.

34 But when they recognized that he was a Jew, there was one cry from all, crying out for about two hours, Great is Diana of the Ephesians!

35 And after the townclerk calmed the crowd, he said, Men! Ephesians! What is this? Who is the man who does not know that the city of the Ephesians is keeper of the temple of the great goddess Diana, and of that which fell down from Zeus?

36 Then these things being without doubt, you ought to be quiet and to do nothing rashly.

37 For you have brought these men *who are* neither temple-robbers nor blaspheming your goddess.

38 So if De-me-tri-us and those who work with him really have a matter against anyone, court days are held and there are proconsuls – let them accuse one another.

39 But if you ask about other matters, it shall be decided in a lawful meeting.

40 For we are also in danger to be accused of riot in regard to this day, there being not one cause by which we can give a reason for this riotous gathering.

41 And saying these things, he dismissed the assembly.

CHAPTER 20

1 And after the uproar stopped, Paul called and embraced the disciples, and he left to go into Mac-e-do-ni-a.

2 And after he had gone through those parts and had encouraged them with many words, he came to Greece.

3 And after staying three months, as he was about to sail into Syria, he decided to return through Mac-e-do-ni-a, a plot being made against him by the Jews.

4 And Sopater of Berea and A-ris-tar-chus and Se-cun-dus of the Thess-a-lo-ni-ans and Gaius of Derbe and Timothy and Tych-i-cus and Troph-i-mus of Asia went with him as far as Asia.

5 Going before us, these waited in Troas.

6 And after the days of the unleavened bread, we sailed from Philippi. And we came to them at Troas in five days, where we stayed seven days.

ἑπτά. 7 Ἐν.δὲ τῇ μιᾷ τῶν σαββάτων, συνηγμένων
¹seven. And on the first [day] of the week, ³having ⁴been ⁵assembled
ᶻτῶν μαθητῶν τοῦ‖ κλάσαι ἄρτον, ὁ Παῦλος διελέγετο αὐτοῖς,
¹the ²disciples to break bread, Paul discoursed to them,
μέλλων ἐξιέναι τῇ ἐπαύριον, παρέτεινέν.τε τὸν λόγον μέχρι
about to depart on the morrow; and he continued the discourse till
μεσονυκτίου· 8 ἦσαν.δὲ λαμπάδες ἱκαναὶ ἐν τῷ ὑπερῴῳ οὗ
midnight. And ³were ²lamps ¹many in the upper room where
ᵃἦσαν‖ συνηγμένοι. 9 ᵇκαθήμενος‖.δέ τις νεανίας ὀνόματι
they were assembled. And was sitting a certain youth, by name
Εὔτυχος ἐπὶ τῆς θυρίδος, καταφερόμενος ὕπνῳ βαθεῖ, δια-
Eutychus, by the window, overpowered by ²sleep ¹deep, as
λεγομένου τοῦ Παύλου ἐπὶ.πλεῖον, κατενεχθεὶς ἀπὸ
²discoursed ¹Paul for a longer time, having been overpowered by
τοῦ ὕπνου ἔπεσεν ἀπὸ τοῦ τριστέγου κάτω, καὶ ἤρθη
the sleep he fell ²from ³the ⁴third ⁵story ¹down, and was taken up
νεκρός. 10 καταβὰς.δὲ ὁ Παῦλος ἐπέπεσεν αὐτῷ, καὶ ᶜσυμ-
dead. But ²having ³descended ¹Paul fell upon him, and having
περιλαβὼν‖ εἶπεν, Μὴ.θορυβεῖσθε· ἡ.γὰρ ψυχὴ αὐτοῦ ἐν
embraced [him] said, Do not make a tumult, for the life of him in
αὐτῷ ἐστιν. 11 Ἀναβὰς.δὲ καὶ κλάσας ᵈ ἄρτον καὶ γευσά-
him is. And having gone up and having broken bread and having
μενος, ἐφ'.ἱκανόν.τε ὁμιλήσας ᵉἄχρις‖ αὐγῆς, οὕτως ἐξῆλ-
eaten, and for long having conversed until day-break, so he de-
θεν. 12 ἤγαγον.δὲ τὸν παῖδα ζῶντα, καὶ παρεκλήθησαν οὐ
parted. And they brought the boy alive, and were comforted not
μετρίως. 13 Ἡμεῖς.δὲ ᶠπροελθόντες‖ ἐπὶ τὸ πλοῖον ἀνήχθημεν
a little. But we having gone before to the ship sailed
ᵍεἰς‖ τὴν Ἄσσον, ἐκεῖθεν μέλλοντες ἀναλαμβάνειν τὸν Παῦ-
to Assos, ³there ¹being ²about to take in Paul;
λον· οὕτως.γὰρ ʰἦν.διατεταγμένος,‖ μέλλων αὐτὸς πεζεύειν.
for so he had appointed, ²being ³about ¹himself to go on foot.
14 ὡς.δὲ ⁱσυνέβαλεν‖ ἡμῖν εἰς τὴν Ἄσσον, ἀναλαβόντες αὐτὸν
And when he met with us at Assos, having taken ²in ¹him
ἤλθομεν εἰς Μιτυλήνην· 15 κἀκεῖθεν ἀποπλεύσαντες τῇ
we came to Mitylene; and thence having sailed away, on the
ἐπιούσῃ κατηντήσαμεν ᵏἀντικρὺ‖ Χίου· τῇ.δὲ ἑτέρᾳ
following [day] arrived opposite Chios, and the next [day]
παρεβάλομεν εἰς Σάμον· ˡκαὶ μείναντες ἐν Τρωγυλλίῳ,‖ τῇ ᵐ
we arrived at Samos; and having remained at Trogyllium, the
ἐχομένῃ ἤλθομεν εἰς Μίλητον. 16 ⁿἔκρινεν‖.γὰρ ὁ Παῦλος
next [day] we came to Miletus: for ²had ³decided ¹Paul
παραπλεῦσαι τὴν Ἔφεσον, ὅπως μὴ.γένηται αὐτῷ χρονο-
to sail by Ephesus, so that it might not happen to him to spend
τριβῆσαι ἐν τῇ Ἀσίᾳ· ἔσπευδεν.γὰρ εἰ δυνατὸν ᵒἦν‖ αὐτῷ
time in Asia; for he hastened if possible it was for him
τὴν ἡμέραν τῆς πεντηκοστῆς γενέσθαι εἰς ᵖἹεροσόλυμα.‖
the day of Pentecost to be in Jerusalem.
17 Ἀπὸ.δὲ τῆς Μιλήτου πέμψας εἰς Ἔφεσον μετεκαλέσατο
And from Miletus having sent to Ephesus he called for
τοὺς.πρεσβυτέρους τῆς ἐκκλησίας. 18 ὡς.δὲ παρεγένοντο πρὸς
the elders of the assembly. And when they were come to
αὐτὸν ᑫ εἶπεν αὐτοῖς, Ὑμεῖς ἐπίστασθε, ἀπὸ πρώτης ἡμέρας
him he said to them, Ye know, from the first day
ἀφ' ἧς ἐπέβην εἰς τὴν Ἀσίαν, πῶς μεθ' ὑμῶν τὸν.πάντα
on which I arrived in Asia, how with you all the
χρόνον ἐγενόμην, 19 δουλεύων τῷ κυρίῳ μετὰ πάσης ταπεινο-
time I was, serving the Lord with all humi-
φροσύνης καὶ ʳπολλῶν‖ δακρύων καὶ πειρασμῶν, τῶν συμ-
lity and many tears and temptations, which hap-
βάντων μοι ἐν ταῖς ἐπιβουλαῖς τῶν Ἰουδαίων· 20 ὡς
pened to me through the plots of the Jews; how
οὐδὲν ὑπεστειλάμην τῶν συμφερόντων τοῦ.μὴ ἀναγγεῖλαι
nothing I kept back of what is profitable so as not to announce [it]
ὑμῖν, καὶ διδάξαι ὑμᾶς δημοσίᾳ καὶ κατ'.οἴκους, 21 διαμαρ-
to you, and to teach you publicly and from house to house, earnestly
τυρόμενος Ἰουδαίοις.τε καὶ Ἕλλησιν τὴν εἰς ˢτὸν‖ θεὸν
testifying both to Jews and Greeks ²toward ³God
μετάνοιαν καὶ πίστιν ᵗτὴν‖ εἰς τὸν.κύριον.ἡμῶν Ἰησοῦν
¹repentance and faith toward our Lord Jesus
ᵛχριστόν.‖ 22 καὶ νῦν ἰδοὺ ʷἐγὼ δεδεμένος‖ τῷ πνεύματι
Christ. And now, lo, I, bound in the spirit,
πορεύομαι εἰς Ἱερουσαλήμ, τὰ ἐν αὐτῇ συναντήσοντά
go to Jerusalem, the things which in it shall happen
ˣμοι‖ μὴ εἰδώς, 23 πλὴν ὅτι τὸ πνεῦμα τὸ ἅγιον κατὰ.πόλιν
to me not knowing; except that the Spirit the Holy in every city
διαμαρτύρεταιʸ ᶻλέγον‖ ὅτι δεσμά ᵃμε καὶ θλίψεις‖ μένουσιν.
fully testifies, saying that bonds ⁴me ¹and ²tribulations ³await.
24 ἀλλ' οὐδενὸς ᵇλόγον‖ ᶜποιοῦμαι, οὐδὲ ἔχω‖ τὴν ψυχήν
But ⁴of ⁵nothing ³account ¹I ²make, nor hold I ²life
ᵈμου‖ τιμίαν ἐμαυτῷ, ὡς τελειῶσαι τὸν.δρόμον.μου ᵉμετὰ
¹my dear to myself, so as to finish my course with

7 And on the first of the week, when the disciples had been gathered together to break bread, Paul preached to them, being about to leave on the next day. And he continued the sermon until midnight.

8 And there were many lamps in the upper room where they were assembled.

9 And a certain youth named Eu-ty-chus was sitting on the window. Being overpowered by deep sleep as Paul preached for a long time, he sunk down from the sleep and fell from the third story down. And he was taken up dead.

10 But when Paul had come down, he fell on him and embraced him, saying, Do not mourn, for his life is in him.

11 And after he had gone up and had broken and tasted bread, and had talked for a long time, until day-break, he left.

12 And they brought the boy alive and were very much comforted.

13 But going ahead to the ship, we sailed to Assos, intending to take in Paul there – for so he had ordered, intending himself to go on foot.

14 And when he met with us at Assos, we took him in and went to Mit-y-le-ne.

15 And sailing away from there, we arrived the following day across from Chios. And the next day we arrived at Samos. And after remaining in Tro-gyl-li-um, the next day we came to Mi-le-tus.

16 For Paul had decided to sail past Ephesus, so that he might not lose time in Asia. For if it were possible for him, he hurried so as to be at Jerusalem on the day of Pentecost.

17 And sending from Mi-le-tus to Ephesus, he called for the elders of the church.

18 And when they had come to him, he said to them, You know how I was with you at all times from the first day I arrived in Asia,

19 serving the Lord with all lowliness in mind and many tears and trials which happened to me through the plots of the Jews.

20 *You know* how I kept nothing back so as not to tell you of those things that are profitable to you and to teach you publicly, and from house to house –

21 earnestly testifying both to Jews and Greeks repentance toward God and faith toward our Lord Jesus Christ.

22 And now, behold! I go on to Jerusalem bound in the Spirit, not knowing the things which will happen to me in it,

23 except that the Holy Spirit in every city fully testifies, saying that bonds and trials are waiting for me.

24 But I do not think anything of these things, nor do I hold my life dear to myself, so that I may finish my course with joy and the ministry which I received from the Lord Jesus – so as to fully testify the gospel of the grace of God.

χαρᾶς," καὶ τὴν διακονίαν ἣν ἔλαβον παρὰ τοῦ κυρίου Ἰη-
joy, and the ministry which I received from the Lord Je-
σοῦ, διαμαρτύρασθαι τὸ εὐαγγέλιον τῆς χάριτος τοῦ θεοῦ.
sus, to testify fully the glad tidings of the grace of God.
25 καὶ νῦν ἰδοὺ ἐγὼ οἶδα ὅτι οὐκέτι ὄψεσθε τὸ.πρόσωπόν.μου
And now, lo, I know that no more [3]will [4]see [6]my [5]face
ὑμεῖς πάντες, ἐν οἷς διῆλθον κηρύσσων τὴν βασιλείαν
[1]ye [2]all, among whom I have gone about proclaiming the kingdom
[f]τοῦ θεοῦ." 26 [g]διὸ" μαρτύρομαι ὑμῖν ἐν τῇ.σήμερον.ἡμέρᾳ,
of God. Wherefore I testify to you in this day
ὅτι καθαρὸς [h]ἐγὼ" ἀπὸ τοῦ αἵματος πάντων· 27 οὐ.γὰρ
that pure I [am] from the blood of all, for [2]not
ὑπεστειλάμην τοῦ μὴ ἀναγγεῖλαι [i]ὑμῖν" πᾶσαν τὴν βουλὴν
[1]I [3]kept back from announcing to you all the counsel
τοῦ.θεοῦ [j]. 28 προσέχετε [k]οὖν" ἑαυτοῖς καὶ παντὶ τῷ
of God. Take heed therefore to yourselves and to all the
ποιμνίῳ. ἐν.ᾧ ὑμᾶς τὸ πνεῦμα τὸ ἅγιον ἔθετο ἐπισκόπους,
flock, wherein [7]you [1]the [2]Spirit [3]the [4]Holy [5]did [6]set overseers,
ποιμαίνειν τὴν ἐκκλησίαν [l]τοῦ θεοῦ," ἣν περιεποιήσατο διὰ
to shepherd the assembly of God, which he purchased with
τοῦ [m]ἰδίου αἵματος." 29 ἐγὼ.[n]γὰρ" οἶδα [o]τοῦτο," ὅτι εἰσελεύ-
the [2]of [3]his [4]own [1]blood. For I know this, that will
σονται μετὰ τὴν.ἄφιξίν.μου λύκοι βαρεῖς εἰς ὑμᾶς, μὴ
come in after my departure [2]wolves [1]grievous amongst you, not
φειδόμενοι τοῦ ποιμνίου· 30 καὶ ἐξ ὑμῶν.αὐτῶν ἀνα-
sparing the flock; and from amongst your own selves will
στήσονται ἄνδρες λαλοῦντες διεστραμμένα, τοῦ ἀποσπᾶν τοὺς
rise up men speaking perverted things, to draw away the
μαθητὰς ὀπίσω [p]αὐτῶν." 31 διὸ γρηγορεῖτε, μνημονεύοντες
disciples after themselves. Wherefore watch, remembering
ὅτι τριετίαν νύκτα καὶ ἡμέραν οὐκ.ἐπαυσάμην μετὰ δακρύων
that three years night and day I ceased not with tears
νουθετῶν ἕνα ἕκαστον. 32 καὶ [q]τανῦν" παρατίθεμαι ὑμᾶς,
admonishing [2]one [1]each. And now I commit you,
[r]ἀδελφοί," τῷ θεῷ καὶ τῷ λόγῳ τῆς.χάριτος.αὐτοῦ, τῷ δυνα-
brethren, to God and to the word of his grace, which is
μένῳ [s]ἐποικοδομῆσαι" καὶ δοῦναι [t]ὑμῖν" [v] κληρονομίαν ἐν
able to build up and to give you an inheritance among
τοῖς ἡγιασμένοις πᾶσιν. 33 ἀργυρίου ἢ χρυσίου ἢ ἱματισμοῦ
[2]the [3]sanctified [1]all. Silver or gold or clothing
[w]οὐδενὸς" ἐπεθύμησα· 34 αὐτοὶ.[x]δὲ" γινώσκετε ὅτι ταῖς
of no one I desired. But yourselves know that
χρείαις.μου καὶ τοῖς οὖσιν μετ' ἐμοῦ ὑπηρέτησαν αἱ
to my needs and to those who were with me did [3]minister
χεῖρες.αὗται. 35 πάντα ὑπέδειξα ὑμῖν ὅτι οὕτως κοπιῶντας
[1]these [2]hands. All things I shewed you that thus labouring
δεῖ ἀντιλαμβάνεσθαι τῶν ἀσθενούντων, μνημονεύειν.τε
it behoves [us] to aid those being weak, and to remember
τῶν λόγων τοῦ κυρίου Ἰησοῦ ὅτι αὐτὸς εἶπεν, Μακάριόν ἐστιν
the words of the Lord Jesus that himself said, [2]Blessed [3]it [4]is
[y]διδόναι μᾶλλον" ἢ λαμβάνειν. 36 Καὶ ταῦτα εἰπών,
[5]to [6]give [1]more than to receive. And these things having said
θεὶς τὰ.γόνατα.αὐτοῦ σὺν πᾶσιν αὐτοῖς προσηύξατο.
having bowed his knees with [2]all [1]them he prayed.
37 Ἱκανὸς.δὲ [z]ἐγένετο κλαυθμὸς" πάντων· καὶ ἐπιπεσόντες
And [3]much [1]there [2]was weeping of all: and falling
ἐπὶ τὸν τράχηλον τοῦ Παύλου κατεφίλουν αὐτόν· 38 ὀδυνώ-
upon the neck of Paul they ardently kissed him, dis-
μενοι μάλιστα ἐπὶ τῷ λόγῳ ᾧ εἰρήκει, ὅτι οὐκέτι μέλ-
tressed most of all for the word which he had said, that no more they
λουσιν τὸ.πρόσωπον.αὐτοῦ θεωρεῖν. προέπεμπον.δὲ αὐτὸν
are about his face to see. And they accompanied him
εἰς τὸ πλοῖον.
to the ship.

21 Ὡς.δὲ ἐγένετο ἀναχθῆναι ἡμᾶς ἀποσπασθέντας ἀπ'
And when it was [2]sailed [1]we, having drawn away from
αὐτῶν, εὐθυδρομήσαντες ἤλθομεν εἰς τὴν [a]Κῶν," τῇ.δὲ ἑξῆς
them, having run direct we came to Cos, and on the next
εἰς τὴν Ῥόδον, κἀκεῖθεν εἰς Πάταρα. 2 καὶ εὑρόντες
[day] to Rhodes, and thence to Patara. And having found
πλοῖον διαπερῶν εἰς Φοινίκην, ἐπιβάντες ἀνήχθημεν.
a ship passing over into Phœnicia, having gone on board we sailed;
3 [b]ἀναφάναντες".δὲ τὴν Κύπρον, καὶ καταλιπόντες αὐτὴν
and having sighted Cyprus, and having left it
εὐώνυμον ἐπλέομεν εἰς Συρίαν, καὶ [c]κατήχθημεν" εἰς Τύρον·
on the left we sailed to Syria, and brought to at Tyre,
ἐκεῖσε.γὰρ [d]ἦν τὸ πλοῖον" ἀποφορτιζόμενον τὸν γόμον. 4 [e]καὶ
for there was the ship discharging the lading. And
ἀνευρόντες" τοὺς μαθητάς, ἐπεμείναμεν [f]αὐτοῦ" ἡμέρας ἑπτά·
having found out the ^ disciples, we remained there [2]days [1]seven;
οἵτινες τῷ Παύλῳ ἔλεγον διὰ τοῦ πνεύματος, μὴ [g]ἀναβαίνειν"
who to Paul said by the Spirit, not to go up

25 And now, see, I know that you will see my face no more, *you* among whom I have gone about preaching the kingdom of God.

26 Because of this I bear witness to you today that I am pure from the blood of all.

27 For I did not hold back from preaching to you all the counsel of God.

28 Therefore watch yourselves and all the flock in which the Holy Spirit made you overseers, to feed the church of God which He bought with His own blood.

29 For I know this, that after I leave grievous wolves will come in among you, not sparing the flock.

30 And from among your own selves will rise up men speaking evil things, in order to draw away the disciples after them.

31 Watch, therefore, remembering that I did not stop warning each one day and night, with tears, for three years.

32 And now, brethren, I give you up to God and to the word of His grace, which is able to build you up and to give you an inheritance among all those who are sanctified.

33 I have not desired anyone's gold or silver or clothing.

34 But you yourselves know that these hands supplied my needs and to those who were with me.

35 I showed you all things, that working in this way we ought to help those who are weak, and to remember the words of the Lord Jesus, that He Himself said, It is more blessed to give than to receive.

36 And after he had said these things, he kneeled down and prayed with all of them.

37 And there was much weeping by all. And falling on Paul's neck, they kissed him lovingly,

38 sorrowing most of all for that which he had said, that they were to see his face no more. And they went with him to the ship.

CHAPTER 21

1 And after we had torn ourselves away from them, we sailed. After a direct run, we came to Co-os, and on the next day to Rhodes – and from there to Patara.

2 And finding a ship going to Phen-ic-i-a, we went on board and sailed away.

3 And sighting Cyprus, then leaving it behind on the left, we sailed to Syria and landed at Tyre. For the ship was unloading there.

4 And searching out the disciples, we stayed there seven days. *And they* said to Paul, by the Spirit, not to go up to Jerusalem.

εἰς [h]'Ιερουσαλήμ.‖ 5 ὅτε.δὲ ἐγένετο [i]ἡμᾶς ἐξαρτίσαι‖ τὰς ἡμέ-
to Jerusalem. But when it was we completed the days,
ρας, ἐξελθόντες ἐπορευόμεθα, προπεμπόντων ἡμᾶς πάντων
having set out we journeyed, [2]accompanying [3]us [1]all
σὺν γυναιξὶν καὶ τέκνοις ἕως ἔξω τῆς πόλεως· καὶ θέντες
with wives and children as far as outside the city. And having bowed
τὰ γόνατα ἐπὶ τὸν αἰγιαλὸν [k]προσηυξάμεθα. 6 καὶ ἀσπασά-
the knees on the shore we prayed. And having
μενοι‖ ἀλλήλους [l][m]ἐπέβημεν‖ εἰς τὸ πλοῖον, ἐκεῖνοι.δὲ ὑπέ-
saluted one another we went up into the ship, and they re-
στρεψαν εἰς τὰ.ἴδια. 7 'Ἡμεῖς.δὲ τὸν πλοῦν διανύσαντες
turned to their own [homes]. And we, the voyage having completed
ἀπὸ Τύρου κατηντήσαμεν εἰς Πτολεμαΐδα, καὶ ἀσπασάμενοι
from Tyre, arrived at Ptolemais, and having saluted
τοὺς ἀδελφοὺς ἐμείναμεν ἡμέραν μίαν παρ' αὐτοῖς. 8 τῇ.δὲ
the brethren we abode [2]day [1]one with them. And on the
ἐπαύριον ἐξελθόντες [n]οἱ.περὶ.τὸν.Παῦλον‖ [o]ἦλθον‖ εἰς
morrow [6]having [7]gone [8]forth [1]Paul [2]and [3]those [4]with [5]him they came to
[p]Καισάρειαν·‖ καὶ εἰσελθόντες εἰς τὸν οἶκον Φιλίππου τοῦ
Cæsarea; and having entered into the house of Philip the
εὐαγγελιστοῦ, [q]τοῦ‖ ὄντος ἐκ τῶν ἑπτά, ἐμείναμεν παρ' αὐτῷ.
evangelist, being of the seven, we abode with him.
9 τούτῳ.δὲ ἦσαν θυγατέρες [r]παρθένοι τέσσαρες‖ προφη-
Now to this [man] there were [2]daughters [3]virgins [1]four who pro-
τεύουσαι. 10 ἐπιμενόντων.δὲ [s]ἡμῶν‖ ἡμέρας πλείους κατῆλθέν
phesied. And [2]remaining [1]we [4]days [3]many [8]came [9]down
τις ἀπὸ τῆς 'Ιουδαίας προφήτης ὀνόματι Ἄγαβος·
[5]a [6]certain [7]one from Judæa, a prophet, by name Agabus;
11 καὶ ἐλθὼν πρὸς ἡμᾶς, καὶ ἄρας τὴν ζώνην τοῦ
and having come to us, and having taken the girdle
Παύλου, δήσας.[t]τε‖ [v]αὐτοῦ τὰς χεῖρας καὶ τοὺς πόδας‖
of Paul, and having bound of himself the hands and the feet
εἶπεν, Τάδε λέγει τὸ πνεῦμα τὸ ἅγιον, Τὸν ἄνδρα οὗ ἐστιν
said, Thus says the Spirit the Holy, The man of whom is
ἡ.ζώνη.αὕτη οὕτως δήσουσιν ἐν 'Ιερουσαλὴμ οἱ 'Ιουδαῖοι, καὶ
this girdle thus shall [3]bind [4]in [5]Jerusalem [1]the [2]Jews, and
παραδώσουσιν εἰς χεῖρας ἐθνῶν. 12 'Ὡς.δὲ ἠκούσαμεν
deliver up into [the] hands of [the] nations. And when we heard
ταῦτα, παρεκαλοῦμεν ἡμεῖς.τε καὶ οἱ ἐντόπιοι τοῦ
these things, [8]besought [1]both [2]we [3]and [4]those [5]of [6][the] [7]place
μὴ ἀναβαίνειν αὐτὸν εἰς 'Ιερουσαλήμ. 13 [w]ἀπεκρίθη.[x]δὲ‖ ὁ
[10]not [11]to [12]go [13]up [9]him to Jerusalem. But [2]answered
Παῦλος,[y] Τί ποιεῖτε κλαίοντες καὶ συνθρύπτοντές μου τὴν
[1]Paul, What do ye weeping and breaking my
καρδίαν; ἐγὼ.γὰρ οὐ μόνον δεθῆναι ἀλλὰ καὶ ἀποθανεῖν εἰς
heart? for I not only to be bound but also to die at
'Ιερουσαλὴμ ἑτοίμως.ἔχω ὑπὲρ τοῦ ὀνόματος τοῦ κυρίου 'Ιησοῦ.
Jerusalem am ready for the name of the Lord Jesus.
14 Μὴ.πειθομένου.δὲ αὐτοῦ ἡσυχάσαμεν εἰπόντες, [z]Τὸ θέλημα
And [3]not [2]being [4]persuaded [1]he we were silent, saying, The will
τοῦ κυρίου γενέσθω.‖
of the Lord be done.

5But when it came about that we completed those days, we set out and traveled
on. All with their wives and children went
with us as far as the outside of the city. And
kneeling on the shore, we prayed.
6And after embracing one another, we
went up into the ship. And they went back
to their own homes.
7And after we finished the voyage from
Tyre, we arrived at Ptol-e-ma-is, and greeting
the brothers, we stayed one day with them.
8And on the next day, after Paul and those
with him had gone forth, they came to
Caesarea. And entering into the house of
Philip the evangelist (who was of the seven),
we stayed with him.
9Now four virgin daughters who prophesied were born to this one.
10And as we remained many more days, a
certain man came down from Judea, a
prophet named Agabus.
11And when he had come to us and had
taken up Paul's belt, and had tied his hands
and feet, he said, This is what the Holy
Spirit says, This is the way the Jews in Jerusalem will tie up the man who owns this
belt. And they will deliver him into the
hands of the Gentiles.
12And when we heard these things, both
we and those of that place begged him not
to go up to Jerusalem.
13But Paul answered, What are you doing,
weeping and breaking my heart! For I am
not only ready to be bound, but also to die
at Jerusalem for the name of the Lord Jesus.
14And when he was not persuaded, we
became silent, saying, The Lord's will be
done.

15 Μετὰ.δὲ τὰς.ἡμέρας ταύτας [a]ἀποσκευασάμενοι‖ ἀνε-
And after these days, having packed the baggage we
βαίνομεν εἰς [b]'Ιερουσαλήμ.‖ 16 συνῆλθον.δὲ καὶ τῶν
went up to Jerusalem. And went also [some] of the
μαθητῶν ἀπὸ [c]Καισαρείας‖ σὺν ἡμῖν, ἄγοντες παρ' ᾧ
disciples from Cæsarea with us, bringing [one] with whom
ξενισθῶμεν, Μνάσωνί.τινι Κυπρίῳ, ἀρχαίῳ μαθητῇ. 17 Γενο-
we might lodge, a certain Mnason, a Cypriot, an old disciple. [3]Having
μένων δὲ ἡμῶν εἰς 'Ιεροσόλυμα ἀσμένως [d]ἐδέξαντο‖ ἡμᾶς οἱ
[4]arrived [1]and [2]we at Jerusalem [3]gladly [4]received [5]us [1]the
ἀδελφοί. 18 τῇ.[e]δὲ‖ ἐπιούσῃ εἰσῄει ὁ Παῦλος σὺν ἡμῖν
[2]brethren. And on the following [day] [2]went [3]in [1]Paul with us
πρὸς 'Ιάκωβον, πάντες.τε παρεγένοντο οἱ πρεσβύτεροι. 19 καὶ
to James, and all [3]assembled [1]the [2]elders. And
ἀσπασάμενος αὐτοὺς ἐξηγεῖτο καθ'.ἓν.ἕκαστον ὧν ἐποίησεν
having saluted them he related one by one what things [2]wrought
ὁ θεὸς ἐν τοῖς ἔθνεσιν διὰ τῆς.διακονίας.αὐτοῦ. 20 οἱ.δὲ
[1]God among the nations by his ministry. And they
ἀκούσαντες ἐδόξαζον [f]τὸν κύριον·‖ [g]εἶπόν.τε‖ αὐτῷ, Θεωρεῖς,
having heard glorified the Lord. And they said to him, Thou seest,
ἀδελφέ, πόσαι μυριάδες εἰσὶν [h]'Ιουδαίων‖ τῶν πεπι-
brother, how many myriads there are of Jews who have be-
στευκότων, καὶ πάντες ζηλωταὶ τοῦ νόμου ὑπάρχουσιν.
lieved, and all zealous ones of the law are.
21 κατηχήθησαν.δὲ περὶ σοῦ, ὅτι ἀποστασίαν διδάσκεις
And they were informed concerning thee, that [9]apostasy [1]thou [2]teachest
ἀπὸ [i]Μωσέως‖ τοὺς κατὰ τὰ ἔθνη [k]πάντας‖ 'Ιουδαίους,
[10]from [11]Moses [4]the [6]among [7]the [8]nations [3]all [5]Jews,
λέγων μὴ περιτέμνειν αὐτοὺς τὰ τέκνα, μηδὲ τοῖς ἔθεσιν
telling [2]not [3]to [4]circumcise [1]them the children, nor in the customs

15And after these days we packed the
baggage and went up to Jerusalem.
16And some of the disciples from Caesarea
also went up with us, bringing with them a
certain Mnay-son of Cyprus, an old disciple
with whom we might stay.
17After we had arrived in Jerusalem, the
brothers gladly welcomed us.
18And on the next day Paul went in with
us to James. And all the elders were there.
19And greeting them, he told them one by
one what God had worked among the
Gentiles by his ministry.
20And they heard and glorified the Lord.
And they said to him, You see, brothers,
how many myriads of Jews there are who
have believed. And all are zealous of the
Law.
21And as to you, they have been told that
you teach a falling away from Moses, telling
all the Jews among the Gentiles not to
circumcise their children or to walk in *our*
ways.

περιπατεῖν. 22 τί οὖν ἐστιν; πάντως [l]δεῖ πλῆθος
to walk. What then is it? certainly [3]must [1]a [2]multitude
συνελθεῖν·|| ἀκούσονται.[m]γὰρ|| ὅτι ἐλήλυθας. 23 τοῦτο οὖν
come together; for they will hear that thou hast come. This therefore
ποίησον ὅ σοι λέγομεν· εἰσὶν ἡμῖν ἄνδρες τέσσαρες εὐχὴν
do thou what [3]to [4]thee [1]we [2]say: There are with us [2]men [1]four a vow
ἔχοντες ἐφ' ἑαυτῶν· 24 τούτους παραλαβὼν ἁγνίσθητι σὺν
having on themselves; these having taken be purified with
αὐτοῖς, καὶ δαπάνησον ἐπ' αὐτοῖς, ἵνα [n]ξυρήσωνται|| τὴν
them, and be at expense for them, that they may shave the
κεφαλήν, καὶ [o]γνῶσιν|| πάντες ὅτι ὧν κατήχηνται
head; and [2]may [3]know [1]all that of which they have been informed
περὶ σοῦ οὐδέν ἐστιν, ἀλλὰ στοιχεῖς καὶ αὐτὸς
about thee [2]nothing [1]is, but thou [3]walkest [4]orderly [2]also [1]thyself
[p]τὸν νόμον φυλάσσων.|| 25 περὶ.δὲ τῶν πεπιστευκότων
[6]the [7]law [5]keeping. But concerning those who have believed
ἐθνῶν ἡμεῖς [q]ἐπεστείλαμεν.|| κρίναντες [r]μηδὲν.τοιοῦτον
of the nations we wrote, judging [4]no [5]such [6]thing
τηρεῖν αὐτούς, εἰ.μὴ|| φυλάσσεσθαι αὐτοὺς τό τε εἰδωλό-
[2]to [3]observe [1]them, except to keep [2]from [1]themselves things offered
θυτον καὶ [s]τὸ|| αἷμα καὶ πνικτὸν καὶ πορνείαν. 26 Τότε
to idols, and blood, and what is strangled, and fornication. Then
ὁ Παῦλος παραλαβὼν τοὺς ἄνδρας, τῇ ἐχομένῃ ἡμέρᾳ σὺν
Paul having taken the men, on the next day with
αὐτοῖς ἁγνισθεὶς εἰσῄει εἰς τὸ ἱερόν, διαγγέλλων τὴν
them having been purified entered into the temple, declaring the
ἐκπλήρωσιν τῶν ἡμερῶν τοῦ ἁγνισμοῦ, ἕως οὗ προσηνέχθη
fulfilment of the days of the purification, until was offered
ὑπὲρ ἑνὸς ἑκάστου αὐτῶν ἡ προσφορά. 27 ὡς.δὲ. ἔμελλον
for [2]one [1]each of them the offering. But when [4]were [5]about
αἱ ἑπτὰ ἡμέραι συντελεῖσθαι οἱ ἀπὸ τῆς Ἀσίας Ἰουδαῖοι
[1]the [2]seven [3]days to be completed the [2]from [3]Asia [1]Jews
θεασάμενοι αὐτὸν ἐν τῷ ἱερῷ, [t]συνέχεον|| πάντα τὸν ὄχλον,
having seen him in the temple, stirred up all the crowd,
καὶ [v]ἐπέβαλον|| [w]τὰς χεῖρας ἐπ' αὐτόν,|| 28 κράζοντες, Ἄνδρες
and laid hands upon him, crying, Men
[x]Ἰσραηλῖται,|| βοηθεῖτε. οὗτός ἐστιν ὁ ἄνθρωπος ὁ κατὰ
Israelites, help! this is the man who against
τοῦ λαοῦ καὶ τοῦ νόμου καὶ τοῦ.τόπου.τούτου πάντας [y]παν-
the people and the law and this place all every-
ταχοῦ|| διδάσκων· ἔτι.τε καὶ Ἕλληνας εἰσήγαγεν εἰς τὸ ἱερόν,
where teaches, and further also Greeks he brought into the temple,
καὶ κεκοίνωκεν τὸν ἅγιον τόπον τοῦτον. 29 [z]Ἦσαν.γὰρ.προ-
and defiled [2]holy [3]place [1]this. For they had before
εωρακότες Τρόφιμον τὸν Ἐφέσιον ἐν τῇ πόλει σὺν αὐτῷ, ὃν
seen Trophimus the Ephesian in the city with him, whom
ἐνόμιζον ὅτι εἰς τὸ ἱερὸν εἰσήγαγεν ὁ Παῦλος. 30 ἐκινήθη
they supposed that into the temple [2]brought [1]Paul. [4]Was [5]moved
τε ἡ πόλις ὅλη, καὶ ἐγένετο συνδρομὴ τοῦ λαοῦ· καὶ ἐπι-
[3]and [6]the [8]city [7]whole, and there was a concourse of the people; and having
λαβόμενοι τοῦ Παύλου, εἷλκον αὐτὸν ἔξω τοῦ ἱεροῦ· καὶ
laid hold of Paul, they drew him outside the temple, and
εὐθέως ἐκλείσθησαν αἱ θύραι. 31 ζητούντων.[z]δὲ|| αὐτὸν
immediately were shut the doors. But as they were seeking him
ἀποκτεῖναι ἀνέβη φάσις τῷ χιλιάρχῳ τῆς σπείρης,
to kill there came a representation to the chief captain of the band,
ὅτι ὅλη [a]συγκέχυται|| Ἱερουσαλήμ. 32 ὃς [b]ἐξαυτῆς|| [c]παρα-
that all [2]was [3]in [4]a [5]tumult [1]Jerusalem; who at once having
λαβὼν|| στρατιώτας καὶ [d]ἑκατοντάρχους|| κατέδραμεν ἐπ'
taken with [him] soldiers and centurions ran down upon
αὐτούς. οἱ.δὲ ἰδόντες [e]τὸν|| χιλίαρχον καὶ τοὺς στρατιώτας
them. And they having seen the chief captain and the soldiers
ἐπαύσαντο τύπτοντες τὸν Παῦλον. 33 τότε ἐγγίσας
ceased beating Paul. Then [4]having [5]drawn [6]near
ὁ χιλίαρχος ἐπελάβετο αὐτοῦ, καὶ ἐκέλευσεν δεθῆναι
[1]the [2]chief [3]captain laid hold of him, and commanded [him] to be bound
ἁλύσεσιν δυσίν· καὶ ἐπυνθάνετο τίς [f]ἂν||.εἴη, καὶ τί
with [2]chains [1]two, and inquired who he might be, and what
ἐστιν.πεποιηκώς. 34 ἄλλοι.δὲ.ἄλλο.τι [g]ἐβόων||
he had been doing. But some [3]one [4]thing [5]and [6]some [7]another [1]were [2]crying
ἐν τῷ ὄχλῳ· [h]μὴ.δυνάμενος.δὲ|| γνῶναι τὸ ἀσφαλὲς διὰ
in the crowd. And not being able to know the certainty on account of
τὸν θόρυβον, ἐκέλευσεν ἄγεσθαι αὐτὸν εἰς τὴν παρεμ-
the tumult, he commanded [2]to [3]be [4]brought [1]him into the for-
βολήν. 35 ὅτε.δὲ ἐγένετο ἐπὶ τοὺς ἀναβαθμοὺς συνέβη
tress. But when he came on the stairs it happened
βαστάζεσθαι αὐτὸν ὑπὸ τῶν στρατιωτῶν διὰ τὴν βίαν
[2]was [3]borne [1]he by the soldiers because of the violence
τοῦ ὄχλου. 36 ἠκολούθει.γὰρ τὸ πλῆθος τοῦ λαοῦ [i]κράζον,||
of the crowd. For followed the multitude of the people, crying,
Αἶρε αὐτόν. 37 Μέλλων.τε εἰσάγεσθαι εἰς τὴν παρεμβολὴν
Away with him. But being about to be brought into the fortress

22 What, then? A crowd will surely come together, for they will hear that you have come.

23 So, you do what we say to you. There are four men with us who have a vow upon themselves.

24 Taking these, be purified with them. And pay their expenses, so that they may shave their heads – and all may know that the things they have been told about you are not so, but that you yourself also walk in an orderly way, keeping the Law.

25 But as to those of the Gentiles who have believed, we have written – judging that they observe no such thing, only to keep themselves from things offered to idols, and blood and what is strangled and fornication.

26 Then taking the men on the next day, Paul purified himself with them and went into the Temple, so as to declare the fulfilling of the days of purification, until the offering was offered for each one of them.

27 But when the seven days were about to be completed, the Jews from Asia saw him in the Temple and stirred up the people, laying hands on him,

28 crying out, Men! Israelites! Help! This is the man who teaches all everywhere against the people, the Law and this place. And, besides, he has also brought Greeks into the Temple and has defiled this holy place –

29 for they had seen Troph-i-mus the Ephesian with him in the city before, whom they supposed Paul brought into the Temple.

30 And all the city was moved. And there was a running together of the people. And seizing Paul, they dragged him outside the Temple. And the doors were shut at once.

31 But as they were trying to kill him, a report came to the chief captain of the band that all Jerusalem was in a riot.

32 At once taking soldiers and centurions, he ran down on them. And seeing the chief captain and the soldiers, they ceased beating Paul.

33 Then drawing near, the chief captain took him and commanded *him* to be bound with two chains. And he asked who he might be and what he had been doing.

34 But some cried out one thing and some another from the crowd. And not being able to know for certain, because of the tumult, he ordered him brought into the fortress.

35 But when he came on the stairs, it happened he was being carried by the soldiers, because of the violence of the crowd.

36 For the crowd of people followed, crying out, Away with him!

37 But as Paul was about to be brought into the fortress, he asked the chief captain, Is it permitted for me to say something to you?

ὁ Παῦλος λέγει τῷ χιλιάρχῳ, Εἰ ἔξεστίν μοι εἰπεῖν τι
Paul says to the chief captain, Is it permitted to me to say something
πρός σε; Ὁ.δὲ ἔφη, Ἑλληνιστὶ γινώσκεις; 38 οὐκ ἄρα
to thee? And he said, Greek dost thou know? [3]Not [4]then
σὺ εἶ ὁ Αἰγύπτιος ὁ πρὸ τούτων τῶν ἡμερῶν ἀναστα-
[2]thou [1]art the Egyptian who before these days caused a
τώσας καὶ ἐξαγαγὼν εἰς τὴν ἔρημον τοὺς τετρακισχιλίους
confusion and led out into the desert the four thousand
ἄνδρας τῶν σικαρίων; 39 Εἶπεν.δὲ ὁ Παῦλος, Ἐγὼ ἄνθρωπος
men of the assassins? But [2]said [1]Paul, I a man
μέν εἰμι Ἰουδαῖος Ταρσεύς, τῆς Κιλικίας οὐκ ἀσήμου πόλεως
indeed am a Jew of Tarsus, [7]of [8]Cilicia [4]no [3]of [5]insignificant [6]city
πολίτης· δέομαι.δέ σου, ἐπίτρεψόν μοι λαλῆσαι πρὸς τὸν
[1]a [2]citizen, and I beseech thee, allow me to speak to the
λαόν. 40 Ἐπιτρέψαντος.δὲ αὐτοῦ, ὁ Παῦλος ἑστὼς ἐπὶ
people. And [2]having [3]allowed [[4]him] [1]he, Paul standing on
τῶν ἀναβαθμῶν κατέσεισεν τῇ χειρὶ τῷ λαῷ· πολλῆς.δὲ
the stairs made a sign with the hand to the people; and great
σιγῆς γενομένης προσεφώνησεν τῇ Ἑβραΐδι διαλέκτῳ
silence having taken place he spoke to [them] in the Hebrew language
λέγων, 22 Ἄνδρες ἀδελφοὶ καὶ πατέρες, ἀκούσατέ μου τῆς
saying; Men, brethren and fathers, hear my
πρὸς ὑμᾶς [k]νῦν‖ ἀπολογίας. 2 Ἀκούσαντες.δὲ ὅτι τῇ Ἑβραΐδι
[2]to [3]you [4]now [1]defence. And having heard that in the Hebrew
διαλέκτῳ προσεφώνει αὐτοῖς, μᾶλλον παρέσχον ἡσυχίαν. καὶ
language he spoke to them, [3]the [4]more [1]they [2]kept quiet; and
φησιν, 3 Ἐγὼ [l]μέν‖ εἰμι ἀνὴρ Ἰουδαῖος, γεγεννημένος ἐν
he says, I indeed am a man a Jew, born in
Ταρσῷ τῆς Κιλικίας, ἀνατεθραμμένος.δὲ ἐν τῇ.πόλει.ταύτῃ
Tarsus of Cilicia, but brought up in this city
παρὰ τοὺς πόδας Γαμαλιήλ, πεπαιδευμένος κατὰ
at the feet of Gamaliel, having been instructed according to [the]
ἀκρίβειαν τοῦ πατρῴου νόμου, ζηλωτὴς ὑπάρχων τοῦ θεοῦ,
exactness of the ancestral law, [2]a [3]zealous [4]one [1]being for God,
καθὼς πάντες ὑμεῖς ἐστε σήμερον· 4 ὃς ταύτην τὴν ὁδὸν
even as all ye are this day; who this way
ἐδίωξα ἄχρι θανάτου, δεσμεύων καὶ παραδιδοὺς εἰς φυλακὰς
persecuted unto death, binding and delivering up to prisons
ἄνδρας.τε καὶ γυναῖκας, 5 ὡς καὶ ὁ ἀρχιερεὺς μαρτυρεῖ μοι,
both men and women; as also the high priest bears witness to me,
καὶ πᾶν τὸ πρεσβυτέριον· παρ' ὧν καὶ ἐπιστολὰς δεξάμενος
and all the elderhood; from whom also letters having received
πρὸς τοὺς ἀδελφούς, εἰς Δαμασκὸν ἐπορευόμην, ἄξων καὶ τοὺς
to the brethren, to Damascus I went, to bring also those
ἐκεῖσε ὄντας, δεδεμένους εἰς Ἱερουσαλήμ, ἵνα τιμωρη-
there who were, bound to Jerusalem, in order that they might
θῶσιν. 6 ἐγένετο.δέ μοι πορευομένῳ καὶ ἐγγίζοντι τῇ
be punished. And it came to pass to me journeying and drawing near
Δαμασκῷ περὶ μεσημβρίαν ἐξαίφνης ἐκ τοῦ οὐρανοῦ περι-
to Damascus, about mid-day suddenly out of the heaven
αστράψαι φῶς ἱκανὸν περὶ ἐμέ· 7 [m]ἔπεσόν‖.τε εἰς τὸ ἔδαφος,
shone a [2]light [1]great about me. And I fell to the ground,
καὶ ἤκουσα φωνῆς λεγούσης μοι, Σαούλ, Σαούλ, τί με διώ-
and heard a voice saying to me, Saul, Saul, why me perse-
κεις; 8 Ἐγὼ.δὲ ἀπεκρίθην, Τίς εἶ, κύριε; Εἶπέν.τε
cutest thou? And I answered, Who art thou, Lord? And he said
πρός [n]με,‖ Ἐγώ εἰμι Ἰησοῦς ὁ Ναζωραῖος ὃν σὺ διώκεις.
to me, I am Jesus the Nazaræan, whom thou persecutest.
9 Οἱ.δὲ σὺν ἐμοὶ ὄντες τὸ μὲν φῶς ἐθεάσαντο, [o]καὶ ἔμ-
But those [2]with [3]me [1]being the [2]indeed [1]light beheld, and a-
φοβοι ἐγένοντο·‖ τὴν.δὲ φωνὴν οὐκ.ἤκουσαν τοῦ λαλοῦντός
larmed were, but the voice did not hear of him speaking
μοι. 10 εἶπον.δέ, Τί ποιήσω κύριε; Ὁ.δὲ κύριος εἶπεν
to me. And I said, What shall I do, Lord? And the Lord said
πρός με, Ἀναστὰς πορεύου εἰς Δαμασκόν, κἀκεῖ σοι λα-
to me, Having risen up go to Damascus, and there thee it
ληθήσεται περὶ πάντων ὧν τέτακταί σοι ποιῆσαι.
shall be told concerning all things which it has been appointed thee to do.
11 Ὡς.δὲ οὐκ.ἐνέβλεπον ἀπὸ τῆς δόξης τοῦ.φωτὸς.ἐκείνου,
And as I did not see from the glory of that light,
χειραγωγούμενος ὑπὸ τῶν συνόντων μοι, ἦλθον εἰς Δαμασ-
being led by the hand by those being with me, I came to Damas-
κόν. 12 Ἀνανίας.δέ.τις, ἀνὴρ [p]εὐσεβὴς‖ κατὰ τὸν νόμον,
cus. And a certain Ananias, a [2]man [1]pious according to the law,
μαρτυρούμενος ὑπὸ πάντων τῶν κατοικούντων Ἰουδαίων,
borne witness to by all the [2]dwelling [[3]there] [1]Jews,
13 ἐλθὼν πρός [q]με‖ καὶ ἐπιστὰς εἶπέν μοι, Σαοὺλ ἀδελφέ,
coming to me and standing by said to me, [2]Saul [1]brother,
ἀνάβλεψον. Κἀγὼ αὐτῇ.τῇ.ὥρᾳ ἀνέβλεψα εἰς αὐτόν. 14 Ὁ.δὲ
look up. And I in the same hour looked up on him. And he
εἶπεν, Ὁ θεὸς τῶν.πατέρων.ἡμῶν προεχειρίσατό σε γνῶναι
said, The God of our fathers appointed thee to know

And he said, Do you know Greek?
38 Then are you not the Egyptian who before these days caused an uprising and led four thousand men of the assassins into the desert?
39 But Paul said, I really am a Jew, a man of Tarsus in Cilicia, a citizen of no small city – and I beg you, let me speak to the people.
40 And he agreed. Paul stood on the stairs and signaled with his hand to the people. And as a great silence took place, he spoke to them in the Hebrew language, saying,

CHAPTER 22

1 Men! Brothers and Fathers! Hear my defense now to you.
2 And when they heard that he was speaking in the Hebrew language, they were even more silent. And he said,
3 I am really a Jew, a man born in Tarsus of Cilicia, but brought up in this city at the feet of Ga-ma-li-el, being taught according to the strictness of the Law of the fathers, being zealous for God, just as all of you are today.
4 *And I* persecuted this Way to death, arresting and delivering to prisons both men and women –
5 as also the high priest will say of me, and all the elders. From whom I also received letters to the brothers, going to Damascus in order to also bring the ones there to Jerusalem in bonds, so they might be punished.
6 But traveling on and coming near to Damascus about midday, it happened to me! Suddenly out of Heaven a great light shone on me.
7 And I fell to the ground. And I heard a voice saying to me, Saul! Saul! Why do you persecute Me?
8 And I answered, Who are you, sir? And He said to me, I am Jesus the Nazarean whom you persecute.
9 But those who were with me indeed saw the light and were afraid, but did not hear the voice of Him speaking to me.
10 And I said, What shall I do, Lord? And the Lord said to me, Get up! Go to Damascus and there you will be told about all things which have been appointed to you to do.
11 And as I could not see because of that light, I came to Damascus being led by the hand of those who were with me.
12 And a certain An-a-ni-as, a man devoted according to the Law, who was well-spoken of by all the Jews living *there,*
13 came to me. And standing beside me, he said to me, Brother Saul, look up! And in the same hour I looked upon him.
14 And he said, The God of our fathers appointed you to know His will and to see

τὸ.θέλημα.αὐτοῦ, καὶ ἰδεῖν τὸν δίκαιον καὶ ἀκοῦσαι φωνὴν
his will, and to see the Just One, and to hear a voice
ἐκ τοῦ.στόματος.αὐτοῦ· 15 ὅτι ἔσῃ μάρτυς αὐτῷ
out of his mouth; for thou shalt be a witness for him
πρὸς πάντας ἀνθρώπους ὧν ἑώρακας καὶ ἤκουσας. 16 καὶ
to all men of what thou hast seen and heard. And
νῦν τί μέλλεις; ἀναστὰς βάπτισαι καὶ ἀπόλουσαι τὰς
now why delayest thou? Having arisen be baptized and wash away
ἁμαρτίας.σου, ἐπικαλεσάμενος τὸ ὄνομα [r]τοῦ κυρίου.‖ 17 Ἐ-
thy sins, calling on the name of the Lord. [2]It [3]came
γένετο δέ μοι ὑποστρέψαντι εἰς Ἱερουσαλήμ, καὶ προσευ-
[4]to [5]pass [1]and to me having returned to Jerusalem, and on [2]pray-
χομένου μου ἐν τῷ ἱερῷ, γενέσθαι.με ἐν ἐκστάσει, 18 καὶ [s]ἰδεῖν‖
ing [1]my in the temple, I became in a trance, and saw
αὐτὸν λέγοντά μοι, Σπεῦσον καὶ ἔξελθε ἐν τάχει ἐξ Ἱε-
him saying to me, Make haste and go away with speed out of Je-
ρουσαλήμ, διότι οὐ.παραδέξονταί σου [t]τὴν‖ μαρτυρίαν
rusalem, because they will not receive thy testimony
περὶ ἐμοῦ. 19 Κἀγὼ εἶπον, Κύριε, αὐτοὶ ἐπίστανται,
concerning me. And I said, Lord, themselves know
ὅτι ἐγὼ ἤμην φυλακίζων καὶ δέρων κατὰ.τὰς.συναγωγὰς τοὺς
that I was imprisoning and beating in every synagogue those
πιστεύοντας ἐπὶ σέ· 20 καὶ ὅτε [v]ἐξεχεῖτο‖ τὸ αἷμα Στεφάνου
believing on thee; and when was poured out the blood of Stephen
τοῦ.μάρτυρός.σου, καὶ αὐτὸς ἤμην ἐφεστὼς καὶ συνευδοκῶν
thy witness, also myself was standing by and consenting
[w]τῇ ἀναιρέσει αὐτοῦ,‖ καὶ φυλάσσων τὰ ἱμάτια τῶν
to the putting to death of him, and keeping the garments of those who
ἀναιρούντων αὐτόν. 21 Καὶ εἶπεν πρός με, Πορεύου, ὅτι ἐγὼ
killed him. And he said to me, Go, for I
εἰς ἔθνη μακρὰν ἐξαποστελῶ σε. 22 Ἤκουον.δὲ αὐτοῦ ἄχρι
to nations afar off will send forth thee. And they heard him until
τούτου τοῦ λόγου, καὶ ἐπῆραν τὴν.φωνὴν.αὐτῶν λέγοντες,
this word, and lifted up their voice, saying,
Αἶρε ἀπὸ τῆς γῆς τὸν.τοιοῦτον· οὐ.γὰρ [x]καθῆκον‖ αὐτὸν
Away with [4]from [5]the [6]earth [1]such [2]a [3]one, for [3]not [1]it [2]is fit he
ζῆν. 23 Κραυγαζόντων.[y]δὲ‖ αὐτῶν, καὶ ῥιπτούντων
should live. And as [2]were [3]crying [4]out [1]they, and casting off [their]
τὰ ἱμάτια, καὶ κονιορτὸν βαλλόντων εἰς τὸν ἀέρα, 24 ἐκέλευσεν
garments, and [2]dust [1]throwing into the air, [4]commanded
[z]αὐτὸν ὁ χιλίαρχος ἄγεσθαι‖ εἰς τὴν παρεμβολήν, [a]εἰπὼν‖
[5]him [1]the [2]chief [3]captain to be brought into the fortress, bidding
μάστιξιν ἀνετάζεσθαι αὐτόν, ἵνα ἐπιγνῷ δι' ἣν αἰτίαν
[5]by [6]scourges [2]to [3]be [4]examined [1]him, that he might know for what cause
οὕτως ἐπεφώνουν αὐτῷ. 25 ὡς.δὲ [b]προέτεινεν‖ αὐτὸν
thus they cried out against him. But as he stretched forward him
τοῖς ἱμᾶσιν εἶπεν πρὸς τὸν ἑστῶτα ἑκατόνταρχον [c]ὁ
with the thongs [2]said [3]to [4]the [6]who [7]stood [8]by [5]centurion
Παῦλος,‖ Εἰ ἄνθρωπον Ῥωμαῖον καὶ ἀκατάκριτον ἔξεστιν
[1]Paul, A man a Roman and uncondemned is it lawful
ὑμῖν μαστίζειν; 26 Ἀκούσας.δὲ ὁ [d]ἑκατόνταρχος,‖ προσ-
for you to scourge? And [3]having [4]heard [[5]it] [1]the [2]centurion, having
ελθὼν [e]ἀπήγγειλεν τῷ χιλιάρχῳ‖ λέγων, [f]Ὅρα‖ τί μέλ-
gone he reported [it] to the chief captain saying, See what art
λεις ποιεῖν; ὁ.γὰρ.ἄνθρωπος.οὗτος Ῥωμαῖός ἐστιν.
thou about to do? For this man a Roman is.
27 Προσελθὼν.δὲ ὁ χιλίαρχος εἶπεν αὐτῷ, Λέγε μοι, [g]εἶ‖ σὺ
And having come up the chief captain said to him, Tell me, [2]thou
Ῥωμαῖος εἶ; Ὁ.δὲ ἔφη, Ναί. 28 Ἀπεκρίθη.[h]τε‖ ὁ χιλίαρχος,
[3]a [4]Roman [1]art? And he said, Yes. And [4]answered [1]the [2]chief [3]captain,
Ἐγὼ πολλοῦ κεφαλαίου τὴν.πολιτείαν.ταύτην ἐκτησάμην.
I with a great sum this citizenship bought.
Ὁ.δὲ.Παῦλος ἔφη, Ἐγὼ.δὲ καὶ γεγέννημαι. 29 Εὐθέως οὖν
And Paul said, But I also was [free] born. Immediately therefore
ἀπέστησαν ἀπ' αὐτοῦ οἱ μέλλοντες αὐτὸν ἀνετάζειν· καὶ
departed from him those being about [3]him [1]to [2]examine, and
ὁ χιλίαρχος δὲ ἐφοβήθη, ἐπιγνοὺς ὅτι Ῥωμαῖός ἐστιν,
the chief captain also was afraid, having ascertained that a Roman he is,
καὶ ὅτι [i]ἦν.αὐτὸν‖.δεδεκώς. 30 Τῇ.δὲ ἐπαύριον βουλόμενος
and because he had bound him. And on the morrow, desiring
γνῶναι τὸ ἀσφαλὲς τὸ.τί κατηγορεῖται [k]παρὰ‖ τῶν Ἰουδαίων,
to know the certainty wherefore he is accused by the Jews,
ἔλυσεν αὐτὸν [l]ἀπὸ τῶν δεσμῶν,‖ καὶ ἐκέλευσεν [m]ἐλθεῖν‖ τοὺς
he loosed him from the bonds, and commanded to come the
ἀρχιερεῖς καὶ [n]ὅλον‖ τὸ.συνέδριον.[o]αὐτῶν·‖ καὶ καταγαγὼν
chief priests and [2]whole [1]their sanhedrim, and having brought down
τὸν Παῦλον ἔστησεν εἰς αὐτούς.
Paul he set [him] among them.

23 Ἀτενίσας.δὲ [p]ὁ Παῦλος τῷ συνεδρίῳ‖ εἶπεν,
And [2]having [3]looked [4]intently [1]Paul on the sanhedrim said,
Ἄνδρες ἀδελφοί, ἐγὼ πάσῃ συνειδήσει ἀγαθῇ πεπολίτευμαι
Men brethren, I in all [2]conscience [1]good have conducted myself

the Just One and to hear a voice out of His mouth –

15 for you shall be a witness for Him to all men of what you have seen and heard.

16 And now why do you delay? Get up! Be baptized and wash away your sins, calling on the name of the Lord.

17 And when I returned to Jerusalem, and while I was praying in the Temple, I began to be in a trance.

18 And I saw Him saying to me, Hurry and go quickly out of Jerusalem, because they will not receive your testimony about Me.

19 And I said, Lord, they themselves know that I was imprisoning and beating those who believed on You in every synagogue.

20 And when the blood of Stephen, Your witness, was poured out, I also was standing by and agreeing to his death. And I kept the clothes of those who killed him.

21 And He said to me, Go, for I will send you far away to the Gentiles.

22 And they listened to him until he said this, then they lifted up their voice saying, Away from the earth with such a one! For it is not right for him to live.

23 And as they were shouting and throwing off clothes and throwing dust into the air,

24 the chief captains commanded him to be brought into the fortress, ordering him to be examined by lashes, so that he might know why they cried out against him.

25 But as he stretched him out with straps, Paul said to the centurion who stood by, Is it lawful for you to whip a Roman who has not been found guilty?

26 And hearing this, the centurion left and reported to the chief captain, saying, Be careful what you are doing, for this man is a Roman.

27 And the chief captain came up and said to him, Tell me, are you a Roman? And he said, Yes.

28 And the chief captain answered, I bought this citizenship with a great sum. And Paul said, But I was even born *free*.

29 Immediately, then, those who were about to examine him left. And the chief captain was afraid when he found out that he was a Roman and because he had bound him.

30 And on the next day, desiring to know exactly why he was accused by the Jews, he turned him loose from the bonds. And he commanded the chief priests and their entire san-he-drin to come. And he brought Paul down and set him among them.

CHAPTER 23

1 And after looking earnestly on the san-hedrin, Paul said, Men! Brothers! I have behaved myself in all good conscience toward God to this day.

τῷ θεῷ ἄχρι ταύτης τῆς ἡμέρας. 2 Ὁ.δὲ ἀρχιερεὺς Ἀνα-
towards God unto this day. But the high priest Ana-
νίας ἐπέταξεν τοῖς παρεστῶσιν αὐτῷ τύπτειν αὐτοῦ τὸ στόμα
nias ordered those standing by him to smite his mouth.
3 τότε ὁ Παῦλος πρὸς αὐτὸν εἶπεν, Τύπτειν σε μέλλει ὁ
Then Paul to him said, 4To 5smite 6thee 2is 3about
θεός, τοῖχε κεκονιαμένε· καὶ σὺ κάθῃ κρίνων με κατὰ
1God, 8wall 7whited. And thou dost thou sit judging me according to
τὸν νόμον, καὶ παρανομῶν κελεύεις με τύπτεσθαι; 4 Οἱ.δὲ
the law, and contrary to law commandest me to be smitten? And those who
παρεστῶτες [q]εἶπον,‖ Τὸν ἀρχιερέα τοῦ θεοῦ λοιδορεῖς;
stood by said, 4The 5high 6priest 7of 8God 1railest 2thou 3at?
5 Ἔφη.τε ὁ Παῦλος, Οὐκ.ᾔδειν, ἀδελφοί, ὅτι ἐστὶν ἀρχ-
And 2said 1Paul, I was not conscious, brethren, that he is a high
ιερεύς· γέγραπται.γάρ, [r]Ἄρχοντα τοῦ.λαοῦ.σου οὐκ ἐ-
priest; for it has been written, A ruler of thy people 3not 1thou 2shalt
ρεῖς κακῶς. 6 Γνοὺς.δὲ ὁ Παῦλος ὅτι τὸ ἓν μέρος ἐστὶν
speak 2of 1evil. But 2having 3known 1Paul that the one part consists
Σαδδουκαίων τὸ.δὲ ἕτερον Φαρισαίων [s]ἔκραξεν‖ ἐν τῷ συν-
of Sadducees and the other of Pharisees cried out in the sanhe-
εδρίῳ, Ἄνδρες ἀδελφοί, ἐγὼ Φαρισαῖός εἰμι, υἱὸς [t]Φαρισαίου·‖
drim, Men brethren, I a Pharisee am, son of a Pharisee:
περὶ ἐλπίδος καὶ ἀναστάσεως νεκρῶν ἐγὼ κρίνομαι.
concerning a hope and resurrection of [the] dead I am judged.
7 Τοῦτο.δὲ αὐτοῦ [v]λαλήσαντος‖ ἐγένετο στάσις τῶν Φαρι-
And this he having spoken there was a dissension of the Phari-
σαίων καὶ [w]τῶν‖ Σαδδουκαίων, καὶ ἐσχίσθη [x] τὸ πλῆθος·
sees and the Sadducees, and was divided the multitude.
8 Σαδδουκαῖοι [y]μὲν‖ γὰρ λέγουσιν μὴ.εἶναι ἀνάστασιν [z]μηδὲ‖
2Sadducees 3indeed 1for say there is no resurrection nor
ἄγγελον μήτε πνεῦμα· Φαρισαῖοι.δὲ ὁμολογοῦσιν τὰ ἀμφότερα.
angel nor spirit; but Pharisees confess both.
9 ἐγένετο.δὲ κραυγὴ μεγάλη· καὶ ἀναστάντες [a]οἱ‖ [b]γραμ-
And there was a 2clamour 1great, and having risen up the scribes
ματεῖς τοῦ μέρους‖ τῶν Φαρισαίων διεμάχοντο λέγοντες,
of the part of the Pharisees they were contending, saying,
Οὐδὲν κακὸν εὑρίσκομεν ἐν τῷ.ἀνθρώπῳ.τούτῳ· εἰ.δὲ πνεῦμα
Nothing evil we find in this man; and if a spirit
ἐλάλησεν αὐτῷ ἢ ἄγγελος[c], μὴ.θεομαχῶμεν.‖ 10 Πολλῆς.δὲ
spoke to him or an angel, let us not fight against God. And a great
[d]γενομένης στάσεως, εὐλαβηθεὶς‖ ὁ χιλίαρχος μὴ δια-
2arising 1dissension, 6fearing 3the 4chief 5captain lest 2should 3be
σπασθῇ ὁ Παῦλος ὑπ' αὐτῶν, ἐκέλευσεν τὸ στράτευμα
4torn 5in 6pieces 1Paul by them, commanded the troop
καταβὰν ἁρπάσαι αὐτὸν ἐκ μέσου αὐτῶν, ἄγειν.τε
having gone down to take by force him from 2midst 1their, and to bring
εἰς τὴν παρεμβολήν. 11 Τῇ.δὲ ἐπιούσῃ νυκτὶ ἐπιστὰς
[him] into the fortress. But the following night 3standing 4by
αὐτῷ ὁ κύριος εἶπεν, Θάρσει [e]Παῦλε·‖ ὡς.γὰρ διε-
5him 1the 2Lord said, Be of good courage, Paul; for as thou didst
μαρτύρω τὰ περὶ ἐμοῦ εἰς Ἱερουσαλήμ, οὕτως σε.δεῖ
fully testify the things concerning me at Jerusalem, so thou must
καὶ εἰς Ῥώμην μαρτυρῆσαι. 12 Γενομένης.δὲ ἡμέρας, ποιή-
also at Rome bear witness. And it being day, 5having
σαντές [f]τινες τῶν Ἰουδαίων συστροφὴν‖ ἀνεθεμάτισαν
6made 1some 2of 3the 4Jews a combination put 2under 3a 4curse
ἑαυτούς, λέγοντες μήτε φαγεῖν μήτε πιεῖν ἕως.οὗ ἀποκτεί-
1themselves, declaring neither to eat nor to drink till they should
νωσιν τὸν Παῦλον· 13 ἦσαν.δὲ πλείους [g]τεσσαράκοντα‖ οἱ
kill Paul. And they were more than forty who
ταύτην τὴν συνωμοσίαν [h]πεποιηκότες·‖ 14 οἵτινες προσελ-
this conspiracy had made; who having
θόντες τοῖς ἀρχιερεῦσιν καὶ τοῖς πρεσβυτέροις [i]εἶπον,‖ Ἀνα-
come to the chief priests and the elders said, With a
θέματι ἀνεθεματίσαμεν ἑαυτούς, [k]μηδενὸς‖ γεύσασθαι ἕως.οὗ
curse we have cursed ourselves, nothing to taste until
ἀποκτείνωμεν τὸν Παῦλον. 15 νῦν οὖν ὑμεῖς ἐμφανίσατε
we should kill Paul. Now therefore ye make a representation
τῷ χιλιάρχῳ σὺν τῷ συνεδρίῳ, ὅπως [l]αὔριον‖ [m]αὐτὸν
to the chief captain with the sanhedrim, so that to-morrow him
καταγάγῃ πρὸς‖ ὑμᾶς, ὡς μέλλοντας διαγινώσκειν ἀκρι-
he may bring down to you, as being about to examine more
βέστερον τὰ περὶ αὐτοῦ· ἡμεῖς.δέ, πρὸ τοῦ ἐγγίσαι
accurately the things concerning him, and we, before 2drawing 3near
αὐτὸν ἕτοιμοί ἐσμεν τοῦ ἀνελεῖν αὐτόν. 16 Ἀκούσας.δὲ
1his 5ready 4are to put to death him. But 8having 9heard 10of
ὁ υἱὸς τῆς ἀδελφῆς Παύλου [n]τὸ ἔνεδρον,‖ παραγενόμενος
1the 2son 3of 4the 5sister 6of 7Paul the lying in wait, having come near
καὶ εἰσελθὼν εἰς τὴν παρεμβολὴν ἀπήγγειλεν τῷ Παύλῳ.
and entered into the fortress he reported [it] to Paul.
17 προσκαλεσάμενος.δὲ ὁ Παῦλος ἕνα τῶν ἑκατοντάρχων,
And 2having 3called 4to [5him] 1Paul one of the centurions,

2 But the high priest, An-a-ni-as, commanded those standing beside him to hit him on the mouth.

3 Then Paul said to him, God is about to strike you, *you* whitewashed wall! And do you sit judging me according to the Law, yet against Law command me to be struck?

4 And those who stood by said, Do you slander the high priest of God?

5 And Paul said, I did not know, brothers, that he was high priest – for it is written, "You shall not speak evil of the ruler of your people."

6 But knowing that one part were of the Sad-du-cees and the other of the Pharisees, Paul cried out in the san-he-drin, Men! Brothers! I am a Pharisee, son of a Pharisee. I am judged concerning a hope and resurrection of the dead.

7 And when he had said this, there was a striving between the Pharisees and the Sad-du-cees. And the crowd was divided.

8 For indeed, the Sad-du-cees say there is no resurrection or angel or spirit. But the Pharisees believe in both.

9 And there was a great tumult. And the scribes on the side of the Pharisees stood up and contended, saying, We do not find anything evil in this man. And if a spirit spoke to him or an angel, let us not fight against God.

10 And as a great fight began, the chief captain fearing that Paul would be torn in pieces by them, commanded the soldiers to go down to remove him from among them by force and to bring him to the fortress.

11 But the following night, standing by him, the Lord said, Be encouraged, Paul, for as you fully testified the things about Me at Jerusalem, so you must also testify at Rome.

12 And when day came, the Jews made a plot, putting themselves under a curse, saying that they would neither eat or drink until they had killed Paul.

13 And they were more than forty who had made this plot.

14 And coming to the chief priests and elders, *they* said, With a curse we have cursed ourselves, to taste nothing until we have killed Paul.

15 Now, then, you make a statement to the chief captain, with the san-he-drin, so that tomorrow he may bring him down to you – as if you were going to ask more exactly the things about him. And we are ready to put him to death before he comes near.

16 But Paul's nephew heard of the ambush. And coming and entering the fortress, he reported to Paul.

17 And calling one of the centurions, Paul said, Take this young man to the chief cap-

ἔφη, Τὸν.νεανίαν.τοῦτον [o]ἀπάγαγε‖ πρὸς τὸν χιλίαρχον· ἔχει
said, [2]This [3]young [4]man [1]take to the chief captain, [2]he [1]has
γάρ [p]τι ἀπαγγεῖλαι‖ αὐτῷ. 18 Ὁ μὲν οὖν παραλαβὼν
[3]for something to report to him. He indeed therefore having taken
αὐτὸν ἤγαγεν πρὸς τὸν χιλίαρχον, καί φησιν, Ὁ δέσμιος
him brought [him] to the chief captain, and says, The prisoner
Παῦλος προσκαλεσάμενός με ἠρώτησεν τοῦτον τὸν
Paul having called [2]to [[3]him] [1]me asked [me] this
[q]νεανίαν‖ ἀγαγεῖν πρός σε, ἔχοντά τι λαλῆσαί σοι.
young man to lead to thee, having something to say to thee.

19 Ἐπιλαβόμενος.δὲ τῆς.χειρὸς.αὐτοῦ ὁ χιλίαρχος, καὶ
And [4]having [5]taken [6]hold [7]of [8]his [9]hand [1]the [2]chief [3]captain, and
ἀναχωρήσας κατ'.ἰδίαν ἐπυνθάνετο, Τί ἐστιν ὃ ἔχεις
having withdrawn apart inquired, What is it which thou hast
ἀπαγγεῖλαί μοι; 20 Εἶπεν.δέ, Ὅτι οἱ Ἰουδαῖοι συνέθεντο
to report to me? And he said, The Jews agreed
τοῦ ἐρωτῆσαί σε, ὅπως αὔριον [r]εἰς τὸ συνέδριον κατα-
to request thee, that to-morrow into the sanhedrim thou mayest
γάγῃς τὸν Παῦλον, ὡς μέλλοντές‖ τι ἀκριβέστερον
bring down Paul, as being about [3]something [4]more [5]accurately
πυνθάνεσθαι περὶ αὐτοῦ. 21 σὺ οὖν μὴ.πεισθῇς αὐτοῖς·
[1]to [2]inquire concerning him. Thou therefore be not persuaded by them,
ἐνεδρεύουσιν.γὰρ αὐτὸν ἐξ αὐτῶν ἄνδρες πλείους [s]τεσσαρά-
for lie in wait for him, of them [4]men [1]more [2]than [3]forty
κοντα,‖ οἵτινες ἀνεθεμάτισαν ἑαυτοὺς μήτε φαγεῖν μήτε
who put [2]under [3]a [4]curse [1]themselves neither to eat nor
πιεῖν ἕως.οὗ ἀνέλωσιν αὐτόν· καὶ νῦν [t]ἕτοιμοί εἰσιν‖
to drink till they put to death him; and now ready they are
προσδεχόμενοι τὴν ἀπὸ σοῦ ἐπαγγελίαν. 22 Ὁ μὲν οὖν
waiting the [2]from [3]thee [1]promise. The [3]therefore
χιλίαρχος ἀπέλυσεν τὸν [q]νεανίαν,‖ παραγγείλας μηδενὶ
[1]chief [2]captain dismissed the young man, having charged [him] to no one
ἐκλαλῆσαι ὅτι ταῦτα ἐνεφάνισας πρός [v]με.‖ 23 Καὶ
to utter that these things thou didst represent to me. And
προσκαλεσάμενος [w]δύο τινὰς‖ τῶν ἑκατοντάρχων εἶπεν,
having called to [him] [2]two [1]certain of the centurions he said,
Ἑτοιμάσατε στρατιώτας διακοσίους ὅπως πορευθῶσιν ἕως
Prepare soldiers two hundred, that they may go as far as
[x]Καισαρείας,‖ καὶ ἱππεῖς ἑβδομήκοντα, καὶ δεξιολάβους δια-
Cæsarea, and horsemen seventy, and spearmen two
κοσίους, ἀπὸ τρίτης ὥρας τῆς νυκτός· 24 κτήνη.τε παραστῆ-
hundred, for the third hour of the night. And [4]beasts [1]to [2]have [3]pro-
σαι, ἵνα ἐπιβιβάσαντες τὸν Παῦλον διασώσωσιν
vided, that having set [2]on [1]Paul they may carry [him] safe through
πρὸς Φήλικα τὸν ἡγεμόνα· 25 γράψας ἐπιστολὴν [y]περι-
to Felix the governor, having written a letter hav-
έχουσαν‖ τὸν.τύπον.τοῦτον· 26 Κλαύδιος Λυσίας τῷ κρατίστῳ
ing this form: Claudius Lysias to the most excellent
ἡγεμόνι Φήλικι χαίρειν. 27 Τὸν.ἄνδρα.τοῦτον [z]συλληφθέντα‖
governor, Felix, greeting. This man, having been seized
ὑπὸ τῶν Ἰουδαίων, καὶ μέλλοντα ἀναιρεῖσθαι ὑπ' αὐτῶν,
by the Jews, and being about to be put to death by them,
ἐπιστὰς σὺν τῷ στρατεύματι [a]ἐξειλόμην‖ [b]αὐτόν,‖ μαθὼν
having come up with the troop I rescued him, having learnt
ὅτι Ῥωμαῖός ἐστιν. 28 βουλόμενος.[c]δὲ γνῶναι‖ τὴν αἰτίαν
that a Roman he is. And desiring to know the charge
δι' ἣν ἐνεκάλουν αὐτῷ κατήγαγον [d]αὐτὸν‖ εἰς τὸ
on account of which they accused him I brought down him to
συνέδριον.αὐτῶν· 29 ὃν εὗρον ἐγκαλούμενον περὶ ζητη-
their sanhedrim: whom I found to be accused concerning ques-
μάτων τοῦ.νόμου.αὐτῶν, μηδὲν.δὲ ἄξιον θανάτου ἢ δεσμῶν
tions of their law, but [2]no [4]worthy [5]of [6]death [7]or [8]of [9]bonds
[e]ἔγκλημα ἔχοντα.‖ 30 μηνυθείσης.δέ μοι ἐπιβουλῆς εἰς
[3]accusation [1]having. And it having been intimated to me of a plot against
τὸν ἄνδρα [f]μέλλειν‖ ἔσεσθαι [g]ὑπὸ τῶν Ἰουδαίων‖
the man about to be [carried out] by the Jews
[h]ἐξαυτῆς‖ ἔπεμψα πρός σε, παραγγείλας καὶ τοῖς κα-
at once I sent [him] to thee, having charged also the ac-
τηγόροις λέγειν [i]τὰ‖ [k]πρὸς αὐτὸν‖ ἐπὶ σοῦ. [l]Ἔρρωσο.‖
cusers to say the things against him before thee. Farewell.

31 Οἱ μὲν οὖν στρατιῶται, κατὰ τὸ διατεταγμένον
The [2]therefore [1]soldiers, according to the orders given
αὐτοῖς, ἀναλαβόντες τὸν Παῦλον ἤγαγον διὰ [m]τῆς‖ νυκτὸς
to them, having taken Paul brought [him] by night
εἰς τὴν Ἀντιπατρίδα. 32 τῇ.δὲ ἐπαύριον ἐάσαντες τοὺς
to Antipatris, and on the morrow having left the
ἱππεῖς [n]πορεύεσθαι‖ σὺν αὐτῷ, ὑπέστρεψαν εἰς τὴν παρεμ-
horsemen to go with him, they returned to the for-
βολήν· 33 οἵτινες εἰσελθόντες εἰς τὴν [o]Καισάρειαν,‖ καὶ
tress. Who having entered into Cæsarea, and

tain, for he has something to tell him.
18 Indeed, then, taking him he brought him
to the chief captain and said, The prisoner
Paul called me near asking that this young
man be brought to you, for he has something to say to you.
19 And the chief captain took his hand and
drew him off to one side, asking, What is it
that you have to tell me?
20 And he said, The Jews agreed to ask you
to bring Paul down into the san-he-drin
tomorrow, as if they were about to ask
something more exactly about him.

21 So you should not be persuaded by them
– for more than forty men of them lie in
wait for him, putting themselves under a
curse not to eat or drink until they kill him.
And now they are ready, waiting for the promise from you.
22 Then, indeed, the chief captain let the
young man go, after telling him, Tell no one
that you revealed these things to me.
23 And calling a certain two of the
centurions near, he said, Make ready two
hundred soldiers, that they may go as far as
Caesarea, and seventy horsemen and two
hundred spearmen, for the third hour of the
night.
24 And provide animals so that Paul may
ride, that they may carry him safe to Felix
the governor.

25 In this way, he wrote a letter.
26 Claudius Lysias to the most excellent
governor Felix, greeting:
27 This man was caught by the Jews and
was about to be killed by them. Coming up
with the troop, I rescued him.
28 Learning that he was a Roman, and
desiring to know the reason why they were
accusing him, I brought him down to their
council.
29 *But* I found him to be accused concerning questions of their law and having no
charge against him worthy of death or
bonds.

30 But when it was suggested to me that a
plot by the Jews against the man was about
to occur, I sent him at once to you, ordering
the ones who accuse him also to accuse him
before you. Farewell.
31 Then according to the orders given them,
the soldiers took Paul and brought him by
night to An-tip-a-tris.
32 And on the next day, leaving the horsemen to go with him, they went back to the
fortress.

33 And entering into Caesarea, they delivered the letter to the governor, also delivering
Paul to him.

ἀναδόντες τὴν ἐπιστολὴν τῷ ἡγεμόνι, παρέστησαν καὶ τὸν
given up the letter to the governor, presented also
Παῦλον αὐτῷ. 34 ἀναγνοὺς.δὲ [p]ὁ ἡγεμών,‖ καὶ ἐπερω-
Paul to him. And [3]having [4]read [[5]it] [1]the [2]governor, and having
τήσας ἐκ ποίας [q]ἐπαρχίας‖ ἐστίν, καὶ πυθόμενος ὅτι ἀπὸ
asked of what province he is, and having learnt that from
Κιλικίας, 35 Διακούσομαί σου, ἔφη, ὅταν καὶ οἱ κατήγοροί
Cilicia [he is], I will [2]hear [1]fully thee, he said, when also [2]accusers
σου παραγένωνται[r]. Ἐκέλευσέν.τε αὐτὸν‖ ἐν τῷ πραιτωρίῳ
[1]thine may have arrived. And he commanded him in the prætorium
τοῦ Ἡρῴδου φυλάσσεσθαι[s].
of Herod to be kept.

24 Μετὰ.δὲ πέντε ἡμέρας κατέβη ὁ ἀρχιερεὺς Ἀνανίας
And after five days came down the high priest Ananias
μετὰ [t]τῶν πρεσβυτέρων‖ καὶ ῥήτορος Τερτύλλου τινός, οἵτινες
with the elders and an orator [3]Tertullus [1]a [2]certain, who
ἐνεφάνισαν τῷ ἡγεμόνι κατὰ τοῦ Παύλου. 2 κληθέν-
made a representation to the governor against Paul. [3]Having [4]been
τος δὲ αὐτοῦ ἤρξατο κατηγορεῖν ὁ Τέρτυλλος λέγων,
[5]called [1]and [2]he [7]began [8]to [9]accuse [6]Tertullus, saying,
3 Πολλῆς εἰρήνης τυγχάνοντες διὰ σοῦ, καὶ [v]κατορθωμάτων‖
[2]Great [3]peace [1]obtaining through thee, and excellent measures
γινομένων τῷ.ἔθνει.τούτῳ διὰ τῆς.σῆς.προνοίας, πάντῃ.τε
being done for this nation through thy forethought, both in every way
καὶ πανταχοῦ ἀποδεχόμεθα, κράτιστε Φῆλιξ, μετὰ πάσης
and everywhere we gladly accept [it], most excellent Felix, with all
εὐχαριστίας. 4 ἵνα.δὲ μὴ ἐπὶ πλεῖόν σε [w]ἐγκόπτω‖
thankfulness. But that [3]not [7]to [9]longer [8]thee [1]I [2]may [4]be [5]a [6]hindrance
παρακαλῶ ἀκοῦσαί σε ἡμῶν συντόμως τῇ.σῇ.ἐπιεικείᾳ. 5 εὑ-
I beseech [2]to [3]hear [1]thee us briefly in thy clemency. [2]Having
ρόντες γὰρ τὸν.ἄνδρα.τοῦτον λοιμόν, καὶ κινοῦντα [x]στάσιν‖
[3]found [1]for this man a pest, and moving insurrection
πᾶσιν τοῖς Ἰουδαίοις τοῖς κατὰ τὴν οἰκουμένην, πρωτοστάτην
among all the Jews in the habitable world, [2]a [3]leader
τε τῆς τῶν Ναζωραίων αἱρέσεως· 6 ὃς καὶ τὸ ἱερὸν
[1]and of the [2]of [3]the [4]Nazaræans [1]sect; who also the temple
ἐπείρασεν βεβηλῶσαι, ὃν καὶ ἐκρατήσαμεν [y]καὶ κατὰ
attempted to profane, whom also we seized, and according to
τὸν ἡμέτερον νόμον ἠθελήσαμεν [z]κρίνειν. 7 παρελθὼν.δὲ
our law wished to judge; but [5]having [6]come [7]up
Λυσίας ὁ χιλίαρχος μετὰ πολλῆς βίας ἐκ τῶν.χειρῶν.ἡμῶν
[1]Lysias [2]the [3]chief [4]captain with great force out of our hands
ἀπήγαγεν, 8 κελεύσας τοὺς.κατηγόρους.αὐτοῦ ἔρχεσθαι
took away [him], having commanded his accusers to come
[a]ἐπὶ σέ·‖ παρ' οὗ δυνήσῃ αὐτὸς ἀνακρίνας περὶ
to thee, from whom thou wilt be able thyself, having examined concerning
πάντων τούτων ἐπιγνῶναι ὧν ἡμεῖς κατηγοροῦμεν
all these things [6]to [7]know [1]of [2]which [3]we [4]accuse
αὐτοῦ. 9 [b]Συνέθεντο‖.δὲ καὶ οἱ Ἰουδαῖοι, φάσκοντες ταῦτα
[5]him. And [4]agreed [3]also [1]the [2]Jews, declaring these things
οὕτως ἔχειν. 10 Ἀπεκρίθη.[c]δὲ‖ ὁ Παῦλος, νεύσαντος
[3]thus [1]to [2]be. But [2]answered [1]Paul, [5]having [6]made [7]a [8]sign
αὐτῷ τοῦ ἡγεμόνος λέγειν, Ἐκ πολλῶν ἐτῶν ὄντα σε
[9]to [10]him [3]the [4]governor to speak, [5]For [6]many [7]years [3]as [4]being [2]thee
κριτὴν τῷ.ἔθνει.τούτῳ ἐπιστάμενος, [d]εὐθυμότερον‖ τὰ
[8]judge [9]to [10]this [11]nation [1]knowing, more cheerfully [as to] the things
περὶ ἐμαυτοῦ ἀπολογοῦμαι. 11 δυναμένου σου [e]γνῶναι‖
concerning myself I make defence. [2]Being [3]able [1]thou to know
ὅτι οὐ πλείους εἰσίν μοι ἡμέραι [f]ἢ‖ [g]δεκαδύο‖ ἀφ' ἧς
that [3]not [4]more [5]than [1]there [2]are [8]to [9]me [7]days [6]twelve since
ἀνέβην προσκυνήσων [h]ἐν‖ Ἱερουσαλήμ 12 καὶ οὔτε ἐν τῷ
I went up to worship at Jerusalem, and neither in the
ἱερῷ εὗρόν με πρός τινα διαλεγόμενον ἢ [i]ἐπισύστασιν‖
temple did they find me with anyone reasoning, or a tumultuous gathering
ποιοῦντα ὄχλου οὔτε ἐν ταῖς συναγωγαῖς οὔτε κατὰ τὴν
making of a crowd neither in the synagogues nor in the
πόλιν· 13 [k]οὔτε‖ παραστῆσαί [l]με‖ δύνανται [m] περὶ
city; neither [4]to [5]prove [1]are [2]they [3]able [the things] concerning
ὧν [n]νῦν‖ κατηγοροῦσίν μου. 14 ὁμολογῶ.δὲ τοῦτό σοι,
which now they accuse me. But I confess this to thee,
ὅτι κατὰ τὴν ὁδὸν ἣν λέγουσιν αἵρεσιν, οὕτως λατρεύω τῷ
that in the way which they call sect, so I serve the
πατρῴῳ θεῷ, πιστεύων πᾶσιν τοῖς κατὰ τὸν νόμον καὶ [o]
ancestral God, believing all things which throughout the law and
τοῖς προφήταις γεγραμμένοις, 15 ἐλπίδα ἔχων [p]εἰς‖ τὸν θεόν,
the prophets have been written, a hope having in God,
ἣν καὶ αὐτοὶ οὗτοι προσδέχονται, ἀνάστασιν μέλλειν
which also they themselves receive, [that] a resurrection is about
ἔσεσθαι [q]νεκρῶν,‖ δικαίων.τε καὶ ἀδίκων· 16 ἐν.τούτῳ.[r]δὲ‖
to be of [the] dead, both of just and of unjust. And in this
αὐτὸς ἀσκῶ, ἀπρόσκοπον συνείδησιν ἔχειν πρὸς τὸν θεὸν
myself I exercise, [5]without [6]offence [3]a [4]conscience [1]to [2]have towards God

34 And having read it and having asked of what province he was and having learned that *he was* from Cilicia,

35 the governor said, I will hear you fully when your accusers also have come. And he commanded him to be kept in Herod's palace.

CHAPTER 24

1 And after five days An-a-ni-as the high priest came down, with the elders and a certain speaker, Ter-tull-us, who made a statement to the governor against Paul.

2 And when Ter-tull-us was called, he began to accuse, saying,

3 *We are* enjoying great peace through you, and by your forethought very worthy things are being done for this nation. But in every way and everywhere we gladly accept it, most excellent Felix, with all thankfulness.

4 But that I may no longer keep you, I beg you in your mercy to hear us briefly.

5 For we have found this man a pest, and moving rebellion among all the Jews in the world, and a ring-leader of the sect of the Nazareans,

6 also trying to profane the Temple. We also caught him and according to our law wished to judge him.

7 But Lysias, the chief captain, came up with great force and took him out of our hands, commanding his accusers to come to you,

8 from whom you will be able to know that of which we accuse him, after judging for yourself.

9 And the Jews also agreed these things were so.

10 But after the governor signaled him to speak, Paul said, Knowing that for many years you have been a judge to this nation, the more cheerfully I answer about myself.

11 You are able to find out that it is not more than twelve days since I went up to worship at Jerusalem.

12 And neither did they find me arguing with anyone in the Temple, nor making a stir among the people, either in the synagogues or in the city.

13 Nor can they prove the things about which they now accuse me.

14 But I confess this to you, that according to the Way (which they call heresy), so I serve the God of the fathers, believing all things that have been written throughout the Law and the Prophets,

15 having a hope in God which they themselves also hold, that there is going to be a resurrection of the dead, both of the just and the unjust.

16 And in this I exercise myself to have a conscience without offense towards God and men continually.

καὶ τοὺς ἀνθρώπους [s]διαπαντός.‖ 17 δι'.ἐτῶν.δὲ πλειόνων
and men continually. And after [2]years [1]many
[t]παρεγενόμην‖ ἐλεημοσύνας ποιήσων εἰς τὸ.ἔθνος.μου [t].καὶ
I arrived [2]alms [1]bringing to my nation . and
προσφοράς· 18 ἐν [v]οἷς‖ εὗρόν με ἡγνισμένον ἐν τῷ ἱερῷ,
offerings. Amidst which they found me purified in the temple,
οὐ μετὰ ὄχλου οὐδὲ μετὰ θορύβου, τινὲς.[w]δὲ‖ ἀπὸ τῆς
not with crowd nor with tumult. But [it was] certain [2]from
Ἀσίας Ἰουδαῖοι, 19 οὓς [x]δεῖ‖ ἐπὶ σοῦ παρεῖναι καὶ κατηγορεῖν
[3]Asia [1]Jews, who ought before thee to appear and to accuse
εἴ τι ἔχοιεν πρός [y]με·‖ 20 ἢ αὐτοὶ.οὗτοι εἰπάτωσαν,
if anything they may have against me; or these themselves let them say,
[z]εἴ‖ τι εὗρον [a]ἐν ἐμοὶ‖ ἀδίκημα, στάντος.μου ἐπὶ τοῦ
if any [2]they [3]found [4]in [5]me [1]unrighteousness, when I stood before the
συνεδρίου, 21 ἢ περὶ μιᾶς.ταύτης φωνῆς, ἧς [b]ἔκραξα‖
sanhedrim, [other] than concerning this one voice, which I cried out
[c]ἑστὼς ἐν αὐτοῖς,‖ Ὅτι περὶ ἀναστάσεως νεκρῶν ἐγὼ
standing among them: Concerning a resurrection of [the] dead I
κρίνομαι σήμερον [d]ὑφ'‖ ὑμῶν. 22 [e]Ἀκούσας.δὲ ταῦτα ὁ
am judged this day by you. And [2]having [3]heard [4]these [5]things
Φῆλιξ ἀνεβάλετο αὐτούς,‖ ἀκριβέστερον εἰδὼς τὰ περὶ
[1]Felix he put [2]off [1]them, more accurately knowing the things concerning
τῆς ὁδοῦ, [f]εἰπών,‖ Ὅταν Λυσίας ὁ χιλίαρχος καταβῇ,
the way, saying, When Lysias the chief captain may have come down,
διαγνώσομαι τὰ καθ' ὑμᾶς· 23 διαταξάμενός [g]τε‖ τῷ ἑκα-
I will examine the things as to you; having ordered the
τοντάρχῃ τηρεῖσθαι [h]τὸν Παῦλον,‖ ἔχειν.τε ἄνεσιν, καὶ
centurion to keep Paul, and to [let him] have ease, and
μηδένα κωλύειν τῶν.ἰδίων.αὐτοῦ ὑπηρετεῖν [i]ἢ προσέρχεσθαι‖
[3]none [1]to [2]forbid of his own to minister or to come
αὐτῷ. 24 Μετὰ.δὲ [k]ἡμέρας τινὰς‖ παραγενόμενος ὁ Φῆλιξ
to him. And after [2]days [1]certain [4]having [5]arrived [3]Felix
σὺν Δρουσίλλῃ τῇ[l].γυναικὶ.[m]αὐτοῦ‖ οὔσῃ Ἰουδαίᾳ, μετε-
with Drusilla his wife, who was a Jewess, he
πέμψατο τὸν Παῦλον, καὶ ἤκουσεν αὐτοῦ περὶ τῆς εἰς
sent for Paul, and heard him concerning the [2]in
χριστὸν[n] πίστεως. 25 διαλεγομένου.δὲ αὐτοῦ περὶ δικαιο-
[3]Christ [1]faith. And as [2]reasoned [1]he concerning right-
σύνης καὶ ἐγκρατείας καὶ τοῦ κρίματος τοῦ μέλλοντος [o]ἔσεσθαι,‖
eousness and self-control and the judgment about to be,
ἔμφοβος γενόμενος ὁ Φῆλιξ ἀπεκρίθη, Τὸ.νῦν.ἔχον πορεύου·
[2]afraid [1]becoming Felix answered, For the present go,
καιρὸν.δὲ μεταλαβὼν μετακαλέσομαί σε· 26 ἅμα [p]δὲ‖
and an opportunity having found I will call for thee; withal too
καὶ ἐλπίζων ὅτι χρήματα δοθήσεται αὐτῷ ὑπὸ τοῦ Παύλου,
also hoping that riches will be given him by Paul,
[q]ὅπως λύσῃ αὐτόν·‖ διὸ καὶ πυκνότερον αὐτὸν μετα-
that he might loose him: wherefore also oftener him send-
πεμπόμενος ὡμίλει αὐτῷ. 27 Διετίας.δὲ πληρωθείσης
ing for he conversed with him. But two years being completed
ἔλαβεν διάδοχον ὁ Φῆλιξ Πόρκιον Φῆστον· θέλων.τε
[3]received [[2]as] [4]successor [1]Felix Porcius Festus; and wishing
[r]χάριτας‖ καταθέσθαι τοῖς Ἰουδαίοις ὁ Φῆλιξ κατέλιπεν
favours to acquire for himself with the Jews Felix left
τὸν Παῦλον δεδεμένον.
Paul bound.

25 Φῆστος οὖν ἐπιβὰς τῇ [s]ἐπαρχίᾳ,‖ μετὰ τρεῖς
Festus therefore being come into the province, after three
ἡμέρας ἀνέβη εἰς Ἱεροσόλυμα ἀπὸ [t]Καισαρείας.‖ 2 ἐνε-
days went up to Jerusalem from Cæsarea. [2]Made [3]a [4]re-
φάνισαν [v]δὲ‖ αὐτῷ [w]ὁ ἀρχιερεὺς‖ καὶ οἱ πρῶτοι τῶν
presentation [5]before [1]and him the high priest and the chief of the
Ἰουδαίων κατὰ τοῦ Παύλου, καὶ παρεκάλουν αὐτόν, 3 αἰτού-
Jews against Paul, and besought him, ask-
μενοι χάριν κατ' αὐτοῦ, ὅπως μεταπέμψηται αὐτὸν εἰς
ing a favour against him, that he would send for him to
Ἱερουσαλήμ, ἐνέδραν ποιοῦντες ἀνελεῖν αὐτὸν κατὰ τὴν
Jerusalem, an ambush forming to put to death him on the
ὁδόν. 4 ὁ.μὲν.οὖν.Φῆστος ἀπεκρίθη, τηρεῖσθαι τὸν Παῦλον
way. Festus therefore answered, [2]should [3]be [4]kept [1]Paul
[x]ἐν Καισαρείᾳ,‖ ἑαυτὸν.δὲ μέλλειν ἐν.τάχει ἐκπορεύεσθαι.
at Cæsarea, and himself was about shortly to set out.
5 Οἱ οὖν [y]δυνατοὶ ἐν ὑμῖν, φησίν,‖ [z]συγκαταβάντες,‖
Those therefore in-power among you, says he, having gone down too,
εἴ τι ἐστὶν ἐν τῷ ἀνδρὶ [a]τούτῳ,‖ κατηγορείτωσαν αὐτοῦ.
if anything is in [2]man [1]this, let them accuse him.
6 Διατρίψας.δὲ ἐν αὐτοῖς ἡμέρας [b]πλείους ἢ‖ δέκα, κατα-
And having spent among them [4]days [1]more [2]than [3]ten, having
βὰς εἰς [c]Καισάρειαν,‖ τῇ ἐπαύριον καθίσας ἐπὶ τοῦ
gone down to Cæsarea, on the morrow having sat on the
βήματος ἐκέλευσεν τὸν Παῦλον ἀχθῆναι. 7 παραγενομένου
judgment seat he commanded Paul to be brought. [2]Being [1]come

17 And after many years I came bringing alms and offerings to my nation. In which act they found me purified in the Temple – not with a crowd, nor with tumult.
18 But *there were* certain Jews from Asia,
19 who ought to appear before you and to accuse me if they have anything against me.
20 Or let these themselves speak if they found any unrighteousness in me when I stood before the san-he-drin,
21 *except* about this one speech which I cried out as I stood among them: I am judged today by you concerning a resurrection of the dead!
22 And after Felix heard these things, he put them off, knowing more precisely of the things concerning the Way, saying, When Lysias the chief captain comes down, I will know more fully the things about you.
23 *And he* commanded the centurion to keep Paul and to let him have liberty, and to forbid none of his own to minister or come to him.
24 And after certain days, Felix came with his wife Drusilla, who was a Jewess. He sent for Paul and heard him concerning faith in Christ.
25 And as he reasoned about righteousness, and self-control, and the judgment that is coming, Felix became afraid and said, For now go away. And when I have found a convenient time I will call for you.
26 He hoped that Paul would give him money, so that he might let him go. For this reason also he often sent for him and talked with him.
27 But after two years had been completed, Felix welcomed a successor, Porcius Festus. And desiring to obtain favors for himself with the Jews, Felix left Paul in bonds.

CHAPTER 25

1 Then after Festus had come into the province, three days later he went up to Jerusalem from Caesarea.
2 And the high priest and the chief of the Jews made charges to him against Paul;
3 and they begged him, asking a favor against him, that he might send after him so as to *bring him* to Jerusalem (preparing an ambush in order to kill him on the way).
4 Then, indeed, Festus answered that Paul would be kept in Caesarea, and that he himself was shortly to return.
5 He said, Then those in power among you may come down together. Let them accuse him if there is anything *evil* in this man.
6 And after he had stayed among them more than ten days, going down to Caesarea, sitting on the judgment seat, he commanded Paul to be brought.

δὲ αὐτοῦ, περιέστησαν [d] οἱ ἀπὸ Ἱεροσολύμων καταβε-
[1]and [2]he, stood round the [2]from [3]Jerusalem [4]who [5]had [6]come
βηκότες Ἰουδαῖοι, πολλὰ καὶ βαρέα [e]αἰτιάματα‖ [f]φέροντες
[7]down [1]Jews, many and weighty charges bringing
κατὰ τοῦ Παύλου,‖ ἃ οὐκ.ἴσχυον ἀποδεῖξαι, 8 [g]ἀπο-
against Paul, which they were not able to prove: [2]said [3]in
λογουμένου αὐτοῦ,‖ "Οτι οὔτε εἰς τὸν νόμον τῶν Ἰουδαίων
[4]defence [1]he, Neither against the law of the Jews
οὔτε εἰς τὸ ἱερὸν οὔτε εἰς Καίσαρά τι ἥμαρτον.
nor against the temple nor against Cæsar [in] anything sinned I.
9 Ὁ.Φῆστος.δὲ [h]τοῖς Ἰουδαίοις θέλων‖ χάριν κατα-
But Festus, [7]with [8]the [9]Jews [1]wishing [2]favour [3]to [5]acquire [4]for
θέσθαι ἀποκριθεὶς τῷ Παύλῳ εἶπεν, Θέλεις εἰς Ἱεροσόλυμα
[6]himself answering Paul said, Art thou willing to Jerusalem
ἀναβάς, ἐκεῖ περὶ τούτων [i]κρίνεσθαι‖ ἐπ' ἐμοῦ;
having gone up there concerning these things to be judged before me?
10 Εἶπεν.δὲ ὁ Παῦλος, [k] Ἐπὶ τοῦ βήματος Καίσαρος [k]ἑ-
But [2]said [1]Paul, Before the judgment seat of Cæsar stand-
στώς‖ εἰμι, οὗ με.δεῖ κρίνεσθαι. Ἰουδαίους οὐδὲν [l]ἠδί-
ing I am, where it behoves me to be judged. To Jews [3]nothing [1]I [2]did
κησα,‖ ὡς καὶ σὺ κάλλιον ἐπιγινώσκεις. 11 εἰ μὲν [m]γὰρ‖
wrong, as also thou very well knowest. [2]If [3]indeed [1]for
ἀδικῶ καὶ ἄξιον θανάτου πέπραχά τι, οὐ.παραιτοῦμαι
I do wrong and worthy of death have done anything, I do not deprecate
τὸ ἀποθανεῖν· εἰ.δὲ οὐδέν ἐστιν ὧν οὗτοι κατηγοροῦσίν
to die; but if nothing there is of which they accuse
μου, οὐδείς με δύναται αὐτοῖς χαρίσασθαι. Καίσαρα ἐπι-
me, no one me can to them give up. To Cæsar I ap-
καλοῦμαι. 12 Τότε ὁ Φῆστος [n]συλλαλήσας‖ μετὰ τοῦ συμ-
peal. Then Festus, having conferred with the coun-
βουλίου, ἀπεκρίθη, Καίσαρα ἐπικέκλησαι, ἐπὶ Καίσαρα
cil, answered, To Cæsar thou hast appealed, to Cæsar
πορεύσῃ.
thou shalt go.

13 Ἡμερῶν.δὲ διαγενομένων τινῶν, Ἀγρίππας ὁ βασιλεὺς
And [4]days [3]having [2]passed [1]certain, Agrippa the king
καὶ Βερνίκη κατήντησαν εἰς [o]Καισάρειαν,‖ [p]ἀσπασόμενοι‖ τὸν
and Bernice came down to Cæsarea, saluting
Φῆστον. 14 ὡς.δὲ πλείους ἡμέρας διέτριβον ἐκεῖ ὁ Φῆστος
Festus. And when many days they stayed there Festus
τῷ βασιλεῖ ἀνέθετο τὰ κατὰ τὸν Παῦλον λέγων,
[3]the [4]king [1]laid [2]before the things relating to Paul, saying,
Ἀνήρ τις ἐστὶν καταλελειμμένος ὑπὸ Φήλικος δέσμιος,
A [2]man [1]certain there is left by Felix a prisoner,
15 περὶ οὗ, γενομένου μου εἰς Ἱεροσόλυμα, ἐνε-
concerning whom, [3]being [1]on [2]my in Jerusalem, [4]made [5]a [6]re-
φάνισαν οἱ ἀρχιερεῖς καὶ οἱ πρεσβύτεροι τῶν Ἰουδαίων,
presentation [1]the [2]chief [3]priests and the elders of the Jews,
αἰτούμενοι κατ' αὐτοῦ [q]δίκην·‖ 16 πρὸς οὓς ἀπεκρίθην,
asking [3]against [4]him [1]judgment to whom I answered,
ὅτι οὐκ.ἔστιν ἔθος Ῥωμαίοις χαρίζεσθαί τινα ἄνθρωπον
It is not a custom with Romans to give up any man
[r]εἰς ἀπώλειαν,‖ πρὶν ἢ ὁ κατηγορούμενος κατὰ.πρόσωπον
to destruction, before he being accused face to face
ἔχοι τοὺς κατηγόρους, τόπον.τε ἀπολογίας λάβοι
may have the accusers, and opportunity of defence he may get
περὶ τοῦ ἐγκλήματος. 17 συνελθόντων οὖν [s]αὐτῶν‖
concerning the accusation. [2]Having [3]come [4]together [5]therefore [1]they
ἐνθάδε, ἀναβολὴν μηδεμίαν ποιησάμενος, τῇ ἑξῆς καθίσας
here, delay none having made, the next [day] having sat
ἐπὶ τοῦ βήματος ἐκέλευσα ἀχθῆναι τὸν ἄνδρα· 18 περὶ
on the judgment seat I commanded to be brought the man; concerning
οὗ σταθέντες οἱ κατήγοροι οὐδεμίαν αἰτίαν [t]ἐπέφερον‖ ὧν
whom standing up the accusers [2]no [3]charge [1]brought of which
[v]ὑπενόουν ἐγώ‖ [w]· 19 ζητήματα.δέ τινα περὶ τῆς.ἰδίας
[2]supposed [1]I; but [2]questions [1]certain concerning their own
δεισιδαιμονίας εἶχον πρὸς αὐτόν, καὶ περί τινος Ἰησοῦ
system of religion they had against him, and concerning a certain Jesus
(*lit.* demon-worship)
τεθνηκότος, ὃν ἔφασκεν ὁ Παῦλος ζῆν. 20 ἀπορούμενος.δὲ
who is dead, whom [2]affirmed [1]Paul to be alive. And [2]being [3]perplexed
ἐγὼ [x]εἰς‖ τὴν περὶ [y]τούτου‖ ζήτησιν ἔλεγον, εἰ.βούλοιτο
[1]I as to the [2]concerning [3]this [1]inquiry said, Would he be willing
πορεύεσθαι εἰς [z]Ἱερουσαλήμ,‖ κἀκεῖ κρίνεσθαι περὶ
to go to Jerusalem, and there to be judged concerning
τούτων. 21 τοῦ.δὲ.Παύλου ἐπικαλεσαμένου τηρηθῆναι αὐ-
these things. But Paul having appealed for [2]to [3]be [4]kept [1]him-
τὸν εἰς τὴν τοῦ Σεβαστοῦ διάγνωσιν, ἐκέλευσα τηρεῖσθαι
self for the [2]of [3]Augustus [1]cognizance, I commanded [2]to [3]be [4]kept
αὐτὸν ἕως.οὗ [a]πέμψω‖ αὐτὸν πρὸς Καίσαρα. 22 Ἀγρίππας
[1]him till I might send him to Cæsar. [2]Agrippa

7 And when he had come, the Jews who had come down from Jerusalem stood around, bringing many and heavy charges against Paul – which they were not able to prove.

8 He said in defense, Neither against the law of the Jews nor against the Temple nor against Caesar have I committed any sin at all.

9 But Festus, wanting to obtain favor for himself with the Jews, answered Paul, saying, Are you willing to go up to Jerusalem to be judged before me regarding these things?

10 And Paul said, I am standing before the judgment seat of Caesar, where I ought to be judged. I did nothing wrong to the Jews, as you very well know.

11 For if I indeed am unrighteous and have done anything deserving of death, I do not refuse to die. But if there is none of the things of which they accuse me, no one can give me up to them. I appeal to Caesar!

12 Then, after he talked with the council, Festus answered, You have appealed to Caesar. To Caesar you shall go!

13 And after some days passed, Agrippa the king and Bernice came down to Caesarea to greet Festus.

14 And as they stayed there many days, Festus laid the things relating to Paul before the king, saying, There is a certain man left a prisoner by Felix,

15 about whom the chief priests and the elders of the Jews made charges when I was in Jerusalem, asking judgment against him.

16 I answered that it is not a custom of Romans to give up any man to die before he who is accused has his accusers face to face and has an opportunity for defense regarding the crime laid against him.

17 Then when they had come together here making no delay whatever I sat on the judgment seat the next day and commanded the man to be brought.

18 But regarding him, the accusers when they stood up brought no charges such as I expected.

19 But they had certain questions about their own religion with him and about a certain Jesus who is dead, whom Paul claimed to be alive.

20 But being doubtful as to the inquiry about this, I asked if he would be willing to go to Jerusalem and be judged there regarding these things.

21 But when Paul appealed for himself to be kept for the examination of Augustus, I commanded him to be kept until I might send him to Caesar.

22 And Agrippa said to Festus, I would like to hear the man myself. And he said, Tomorrow you shall hear him.

δὲ πρὸς τὸν Φῆστον [b]ἔφη,[ll] Ἐβουλόμην καὶ αὐτὸς τοῦ
[1]and to Festus said, I was desiring also myself the
ἀνθρώπου ἀκοῦσαι. [c]Ὁ.δέ,[ll] Αὔριον, φησίν, ἀκούσῃ αὐτοῦ.
man to hear. And he [2]To-morrow [1]says, thou shalt hear him.
23 Τῇ οὖν ἐπαύριον ἐλθόντος τοῦ Ἀγρίππα καὶ τῆς
On the [2]therefore [1]morrow [4]having [5]come [3]Agrippa and
Βερνίκης μετὰ πολλῆς φαντασίας, καὶ εἰσελθόντων εἰς τὸ
Bernice, with great pomp, and having entered into the
ἀκροατήριον, σύν τε [d]τοῖς[ll] χιλιάρχοις καὶ ἀνδράσιν τοῖς
hall of audience, with both the chief captains and men
κατ᾽.ἐξοχὴν [e]οὖσιν[ll] τῆς πόλεως, καὶ κελεύσαντος τοῦ Φήστου
of eminence being of the city, and [2]having [3]commanded [1]Festus
ἤχθη ὁ Παῦλος. 24 καί φησιν ὁ Φῆστος, Ἀγρίππα βασι-
[5]was [6]brought [4]Paul. And [2]says [1]Festus, [4]Agrippa [3]king
λεῦ, καὶ πάντες οἱ [f]συμπαρόντες[ll] ἡμῖν ἄνδρες, θεωρεῖτε τοῦ-
and all the [2]being [3]present [4]with [5]us [1]men, ye see this
τον περὶ οὗ [g]πᾶν[ll] τὸ πλῆθος τῶν Ἰουδαίων .ἐνέτυχόν
one concerning whom all the multitude of the Jews pleaded
μοι ἔν τε Ἱεροσολύμοις καὶ ἐνθάδε, [h]ἐπιβοῶντες[ll] μὴ
with me in both Jerusalem and here, crying out [that]
δεῖν [i]ζῆν αὐτὸν[ll] μηκέτι 25 ἐγὼ.δὲ [k]καταλαβόμενος[ll] μηδὲν
[2]ought [3]to [4]live [1]he no longer. But I having perceived nothing
ἄξιον [l]θανάτου αὐτὸν[l] πεπραχέναι, [m]καὶ[ll] αὐτοῦ δὲ τούτου
worthy of death he had done, [5]also [4]himself [1]and [2]this [3]one
ἐπικαλεσαμένου τὸν Σεβαστόν, ἔκρινα πέμπειν [n]αὐτόν·[ll]
having appealed to Augustus, I determined to send him,
26 περὶ οὗ ἀσφαλές τι γράψαι τῷ.κυρίῳ οὐκ.ἔχω·
concerning whom [2]certain [1]anything to write to [my] lord I have not.
διὸ προήγαγον αὐτὸν ἐφ᾽ ὑμῶν, καὶ μάλιστα ἐπὶ σοῦ,
Wherefore I brought [2]forth [1]him before you, and specially before thee,
βασιλεῦ Ἀγρίππα, ὅπως τῆς ἀνακρίσεως γενομένης
king Agrippa, so that the examination having taken place
σχῶ τι [o]γράψαι.[ll] 27 ἄλογον.γάρ μοι δοκεῖ πέμ-
I may have something to write; for irrational to me it seems send-
ποντα δέσμιον, μὴ καὶ τὰς κατ᾽ αὐτοῦ αἰτίας σημᾶναι.
ing a prisoner, not also the [2]against [3]him [1]charges to signify.
26 Ἀγρίππας.δὲ πρὸς τὸν Παῦλον ἔφη, Ἐπιτρέπεταί σοι
And Agrippa to Paul said, It is allowed thee
[p]ὑπὲρ[ll] σεαυτοῦ λέγειν. Τότε ὁ Παῦλος [q]ἀπελογεῖτο,[ll] ἐκτείνας
for thyself to speak. Then Paul made a defence, stretching out
τὴν χεῖρα,[q] 2 Περὶ πάντων ὧν ἐγκαλοῦμαι ὑπὸ Ἰου-
the hand: Concerning all of which I am accused by Jews,
δαίων, βασιλεῦ Ἀγρίππα, ἥγημαι ἐμαυτὸν μακάριον [r]μέλλων
king Agrippa, I esteem myself happy being about
ἀπολογεῖσθαι ἐπὶ σοῦ σήμερον·[ll] 3 μάλιστα γνώστην [s]ὄντα
to make defence before thee to-day, especially [3]acquainted [2]being
σε[ll] πάντων τῶν κατὰ Ἰουδαίους ἐθῶν τε καὶ ζητημάτων.
[1]thou of all the [5]among [6]Jews [1]customs [2]and [3]also [4]questions;
διὸ δέομαί [t]σου[t] μακροθύμως ἀκοῦσαί μου. 4 τὴν μὲν οὖν
wherefore I beseech thee patiently to hear me. The [5]then
βίωσίν μου [v]τὴν[v] ἐκ νεότητος, τὴν ἀπ᾽ ἀρχῆς
[1]manner [2]of [4]life [3]my from youth, which from [its] commencement
γενομένην ἐν τῷ.ἔθνει.μου ἐν [w]Ἱεροσολύμοις, ἴσασιν πάντες
was among my nation in Jerusalem, know all
[x]οἱ[ll] Ἰουδαῖοι, 5 προγινώσκοντές με ἄνωθεν, ἐὰν θέλωσιν
the Jews, who before knew me from the first, if they would
μαρτυρεῖν, ὅτι κατὰ τὴν ἀκριβεστάτην αἵρεσιν τῆς
bear witness, that according to the strictest sect
ἡμετέρας [y]θρησκείας[y] ἔζησα Φαρισαῖος. 6 καὶ νῦν ἐπ᾽
of our religion I lived a Pharisee. And now for [the]
ἐλπίδι τῆς [z]πρὸς[z] τοὺς πατέρας [a]ἐπαγγελίας γενομένης ὑπὸ
hope of the [3]to [4]the [5]fathers [1]promise [2]made by
τοῦ θεοῦ ἕστηκα κρινόμενος, 7 εἰς ἣν τὸ.δωδεκάφυλον.ἡμῶν
God, I stand being judged, to which our twelve tribes
ἐν.ἐκτενείᾳ νύκτα καὶ ἡμέραν λατρεῦον ἐλπίζει καταντῆσαι·
intently night and day serving hope to arrive;
περὶ ἧς ἐλπίδος ἐγκαλοῦμαι, [b]βασιλεῦ Ἀγρίππα,[ll] ὑπὸ
concerning which hope I am accused, O king Agrippa, by
[c]τῶν[c] Ἰουδαίων[d]. 8 τί ἄπιστον κρίνεται παρ᾽ ὑμῖν εἰ ὁ θεὸς
the Jews. Why incredible is it judged by you if God
νεκροὺς ἐγείρει; 9 ἐγὼ μὲν οὖν ἔδοξα ἐμαυτῷ πρὸς
[the] dead raises? I indeed therefore thought in myself [8]to
τὸ ὄνομα Ἰησοῦ τοῦ Ναζωραίου δεῖν πολλὰ ἐναντία
[7]the [8]name [9]of [10]Jesus [11]the [12]Nazarean [1]I [2]ought [3]many [4]things [5]contrary
πρᾶξαι· 10 ὃ καὶ ἐποίησα ἐν Ἱεροσολύμοις, καὶ πολλοὺς [e]
to do. Which also I did in Jerusalem, and many
τῶν ἁγίων ἐγὼ [f]φυλακαῖς κατέκλεισα, τὴν παρὰ τῶν ἀρχ-
of the saints I in prisons shut up, the [2]from [3]the [4]chief
ιερέων ἐξουσίαν λαβών· ἀναιρουμένων.τε αὐτῶν
[5]priests [1]authority having received; and [2]being [3]put [4]to [5]death [1]they
κατήνεγκα.ψῆφον. 11 καὶ κατὰ πάσας τὰς συναγωγὰς
I gave [my] vote against [them]. And in all the synagogues

23 So on the next day, Paul was brought out after Agrippa and Bernice had come with a great show, and had entered into the place of hearing with the chief captains and the important men of the city – and after Festus commanded it.
24 And Festus said, King Agrippa, and all the men who are here with us, you see this one about whom all the company of the Jews pleaded with me, both here and in Jerusalem, crying out that he ought not to live any longer.

25 But when I found him to have done nothing deserving of death, and when he also had appealed to Augustus, I decided to send him.
26 I have nothing to write to *my* lord. For this reason I brought him before you, and especially before you, O king Agrippa, so that after the examination has been completed, I may have something to write.
27 For it seems to me unreasonable to send a prisoner and not to state his charges.

CHAPTER 26

1 And Agrippa said to Paul, You may speak for yourself. Then Paul stretched out his hand and spoke for himself:
2 Regarding all of which I am accused by the Jews, king Agrippa, I consider myself happy as I am about to speak for myself before you today.
3 You are especially acquainted with both the customs and questions among Jews. For this reason I ask you to hear me patiently.
4 Truly, then, all the Jews know my way of life from my youth, which from the begging was among my nation in Jerusalem.
5 *They* knew me first, if they would but testify, that I lived a Pharisee according to the strictest sect of our religion.
6 And now I stand, being judged for the hope of the promise made to the fathers by God,
7 to which our twelve tribes hope to attain, serving fervently night and day. *It is* concerning this hope that I am accused by the Jews, O king Agrippa.
8 Why is it thought unbelievable by any of you that God raises the dead?
9 Indeed, I then thought within myself that I ought to do many things contrary to the name of Jesus the Nazarean.
10 Which I also did in Jerusalem, and I shut up in prisons many of the saints, receiving authority from the chief priests. And when they were put to death, I gave my vote against *them*.
11 And often punishing them in all the synagogues, I compelled them to blaspheme.

πολλάκις τιμωρῶν αὐτούς, ἠνάγκαζον βλασφημεῖν· περισ-
often punishing them, I compelled [them] to blaspheme. 4Exceed-
σῶς τε ἐμμαινόμενος αὐτοῖς ἐδίωκον ἕως.καὶ εἰς
ingly 1and 2being 3furious against them I persecuted [them] even as far as to
τὰς ἔξω πόλεις. 12 ἐν οἷς gκαὶ‖ πορευόμενος εἰς τὴν Δα-
foreign cities. During which also journeying to Da-
μασκὸν μετ' ἐξουσίας καὶ ἐπιτροπῆς hτῆς παρὰ‖ τῶν ἀρχ-
mascus, with authority and a commission from the chief
ιερέων, 13 ἡμέρας.μέσης κατὰ τὴν ὁδὸν εἶδον, βασιλεῦ,
priests, at mid-day in the way I saw, O king,
οὐρανόθεν ὑπὲρ τὴν λαμπρότητα τοῦ ἡλίου περιλάμψαν
from heaven above the brightness of the sun 3shining 4round 5about
με φῶς καὶ τοὺς σὺν ἐμοὶ πορευομένους. 14 πάντων.iδὲ‖
6me 1a 2light and those with me journeying. And all
καταπεσόντων ἡμῶν εἰς τὴν γῆν ἤκουσα φωνὴν kλαλοῦσαν‖
3having 4fallen 5down 1of 2us to the ground I heard a voice speaking
πρός με lκαὶ λέγουσαν‖ τῇ Ἑβραΐδι διαλέκτῳ, Σαούλ, Σαούλ,
to me and saying in the Hebrew language, Saul, Saul,
τί με διώκεις; σκληρόν σοι πρὸς κέντρα λακτίζειν.
why me persecutest thou? [it is] hard for thee against goads to kick.
15 Ἐγὼ.δὲ mεἶπον,‖ Τίς εἶ κύριε; Ὁ.δὲ n εἶπεν, Ἐγώ εἰμι
And I said, Who art thou, Lord? And he said, I am
Ἰησοῦς ὃν σὺ διώκεις. 16 ἀλλὰ ἀνάστηθι, καὶ στῆθι ἐπὶ
Jesus whom thou persecutest: but rise up, and stand on
τοὺς.πόδας.σου· εἰς.τοῦτο.γὰρ ὤφθην σοι, προχειρίσασθαί
thy feet; for, for this purpose I appeared to thee, to appoint
σε ὑπηρέτην καὶ μάρτυρα ὧν.τε εἶδες ὧν.τε
thee an attendant and a witness both of what thou didst see and in what
ὀφθήσομαί σοι, 17 ἐξαιρούμενός σε ἐκ τοῦ λαοῦ καὶ o
I shall appear to thee, taking out thee from among the people and
τῶν ἐθνῶν, εἰς οὓς pνῦν σε ἀποστέλλω,‖ 18 ἀνοῖξαι ὀφθαλμοὺς
the nations, to whom now thee I send, to open 2eyes
αὐτῶν, τοῦ.ἐπιστρέψαι ἀπὸ σκότους εἰς φῶς καὶ τῆς ἐξουσίας
1their, that [they] may turn from darkness to light and the authority
τοῦ σατανᾶ ἐπὶ τὸν θεόν, τοῦ.λαβεῖν αὐτοὺς ἄφεσιν ἁμαρ-
of Satan to God, that 2may 3receive 1they remission of sins
τιῶν καὶ κλῆρον ἐν τοῖς ἡγιασμένοις πίστει τῇ
and inheritance among those that have been sanctified by faith that [is]
εἰς ἐμέ. 19 Ὅθεν, βασιλεῦ Ἀγρίππα, οὐκ.ἐγενόμην ἀπειθὴς
in me. Whereupon, O king Agrippa, I was not disobedient
τῇ οὐρανίῳ ὀπτασίᾳ, 20 ἀλλὰ τοῖς ἐν Δαμασκῷ πρῶτον q
to the heavenly vision; but to those in Damascus first
καὶ r Ἱεροσολύμοις, sεἰς‖ πᾶσάν τε τὴν χώραν τῆς Ἰουδαίας
and Jerusalem, 2to 3all 1and the region of Judæa
καὶ τοῖς ἔθνεσιν, tἀπαγγέλλων‖ μετανοεῖν καὶ ἐπιστρέφειν
and to the nations, declaring [to them] to repent and to turn
ἐπὶ τὸν θεόν, ἄξια τῆς μετανοίας ἔργα πράσσοντας. 21 ἕνεκα
to God, 3worthy 4of 5repentance 2works 1doing. On account of
τούτων με vοἱ‖ Ἰουδαῖοι συλλαβόμενοι w ἐν τῷ ἱερῷ, ἐπει-
these things me the Jews having seized in the temple, at-
ρῶντο διαχειρίσασθαι. 22 ἐπικουρίας οὖν τυχὼν τῆς
tempted to kill. Aid therefore having obtained
xπαρὰ‖ τοῦ θεοῦ ἄχρι τῆς.ἡμέρας.ταύτης ἕστηκα, yμαρτυρού-
from God unto this day I have stood, bearing wit-
μενος‖ μικρῷ.τε καὶ μεγάλῳ, οὐδὲν ἐκτὸς λέγων ὧν τε
ness both to small and to great, nothing else saying than what both
οἱ προφῆται ἐλάλησαν μελλόντων γίνεσθαι καὶ zΜωσῆς,‖
the prophets 3said 4was 5about 6to 7happen 1and 2Moses,
23 εἰ παθητὸς ὁ χριστός, εἰ πρῶτος ἐξ ἀναστά-
whether 2should 3suffer 1Christ; whether [he] first through resurrec-
σεως νεκρῶν φῶς μέλλει καταγγέλλειν τῷ a λαῷ καὶ τοῖς
tion of [the] dead 5light 1is 2about 3to 4announce to the people and to the
ἔθνεσιν. 24 Ταῦτα.δὲ αὐτοῦ.ἀπολογουμένου, ὁ Φῆστος με-
nations. And 2these 3things 1uttering in his defence, Festus with
γάλῃ τῇ φωνῇ bἔφη,‖ Μαίνῃ Παῦλε· τὰ πολλά σε γράμ-
loud voice said, Thou art mad, Paul; much 3thee 1learn-
ματα εἰς μανίαν περιτρέπει. 25 Ὁ.δὲ c, Οὐ.μαίνομαι, φησίν,
ing 4to 5madness 2turns. But he, 2I 3am 4not 5mad, 1says,
κράτιστε Φῆστε, dἀλλ'‖ ἀληθείας καὶ σωφροσύνης ῥήματα
most noble Festus, but of truth and discreetness words
ἀποφθέγγομαι· 26 ἐπίσταται.γὰρ περὶ τούτων ὁ βασι-
I utter; for 3is 4informed 5concerning 6these 7things 1the 2king
λεύς, πρὸς ὃν καὶ παῤῥησιαζόμενος λαλῶ· λανθάνειν.γὰρ
to whom also using boldness I speak. For hidden from
αὐτόν τι τούτων οὐ πείθομαι eοὐδέν·‖ οὐ γάρ
him any of these things [are] not I am persuaded; 4not 1for
ἐστιν ἐν γωνίᾳ πεπραγμένον τοῦτο. 27 πιστεύεις βασιλεῦ
7in 8a 9corner 3has 5been 6done 2this. Believest thou, king
Ἀγρίππα τοῖς προφήταις; οἶδα ὅτι πιστεύεις. 28 Ὁ δὲ
Agrippa, the prophets? I know that thou believest. And
Ἀγρίππας πρὸς τὸν Παῦλον fἔφη,‖ Ἐν ὀλίγῳ με gπείθεις‖
Agrippa to Paul said, In a little 3me 1thou 2persuadest

And being extremely maddened against them, I even persecuted them to foreign cities.

12 During which time also *as I was* going to Damascus with authority and a commission from the chief priests,

13 at noon-time, O king, I saw in the road a light from Heaven – brighter than the sun – shining around me and those traveling with me.

14 And as we all were falling down to the ground, I heard a voice speaking to me and saying in the Hebrew language, Saul! Saul! Why do you persecute Me? It is hard for you to kick against the prods.

15 And I said, Who are you, sir? And He said, I am Jesus, whom you persecute.

16 But get up and stand up on your feet, for *it was* for this purpose I appeared to you: to appoint you a servant and a witness, both of what you have seen and in what I shall yet appear to you.

17 I take you out from the people, and the Gentiles to whom I now send you

18 in order to open their eyes so that they may turn from darkness to light and from the authority of Satan to God – so that they may receive forgiveness of sins and inheritance among those that have been sanctified by faith in Me.

19 After this, O king Agrippa, I did not disobey the heavenly vision,

20 but preached to those in Damascus first, and Jerusalem, and in all the region of Judea and to the Gentiles – that they should repent and turn to God, doing works worthy of repentance.

21 Because of these things, catching hold of me in the Temple, the Jews tried to kill me.

22 So then, by the help of God I have stood until this day, bearing witness to both small and great, saying nothing else than what both the prophets and Moses said was going to happen,

23 that Christ should suffer and that through the resurrection of the dead, He was first going to proclaim light to the people and to the Gentiles.

24 And as he was speaking these things in his defense, Festus cried out with a loud voice, You are insane, Paul! Much learning is making you insane.

25 But he said, I am not insane, most noble Festus, but I speak words of truth and sanity

26 – for the king is aware of these things, toward whom I also speak with boldness. For I am persuaded that none of these things are hidden from him, for this has not been done in a corner.

27 King Agrippa, do you believe the prophets? I know that you do believe.

28 And Agrippa said to Paul, Do you *think* to persuade me to become a Christian in but a little while?

χριστιανὸν [h]γενέσθαι.ǁ 29 Ὁ.δὲ.Παῦλος [i]εἶπεν,ǁ [k]Εὐξαίμηνǁ ἂν
a Christian to become. And Paul said, I would wish
τῷ θεῷ, καὶ ἐν ὀλίγῳ καὶ ἐν [l]πολλῷǁ οὐ μόνον σε ἀλλὰ καὶ
to God, both in a little and in much not only thou but also
πάντας τοὺς ἀκούοντάς μου σήμερον γενέσθαι τοιούτους
all those hearing me this day should become such
ὁποῖος κἀγώ εἰμι, παρεκτὸς τῶν.δεσμῶν.τούτων. 30 [m]Καὶ
as I also am, except these bonds. And
ταῦτα εἰπόντος αὐτοῦ,ǁ ἀνέστη ǁ ὁ βασιλεὺς καὶ ὁ ἡγεμὼν
these things ²having ³said ¹he, ⁶rose ⁷up ⁴the ⁵king and the governor
ἥ τε Βερνίκη καὶ οἱ [o]συγκαθήμενοιǁ αὐτοῖς· 31 καὶ ἀνα-
also Bernice and those who sat with them, and having
χωρήσαντες ἐλάλουν πρὸς ἀλλήλους λέγοντες, Ὅτι οὐδὲν
withdrawn they spoke to one another saying, Nothing
θανάτου [p]ἄξιον ἢ δεσμῶνǁ [q] πράσσει ὁ.ἄνθρωπος.οὗτος.
²of ³death ¹worthy or of bonds does this man.
32 Ἀγρίππας.δὲ τῷ Φήστῳ ἔφη, Ἀπολελύσθαι [r]ἐδύνατοǁ ὁ
And Agrippa to Festus said, ⁴Have ⁵been ⁶let ⁷go ³might
ἄνθρωπος.οὗτος εἰ μὴ.[s]ἐπεκέκλητοǁ Καίσαρα.
¹this ²man if he had not appealed to Cæsar.

27 Ὡς.δὲ ἐκρίθη τοῦ.ἀποπλεῖν.ἡμᾶς εἰς τὴν Ἰταλίαν
But when it was decided that ²should ³sail ¹we to Italy
παρεδίδουν τόν.τε.Παῦλον καί τινας ἑτέρους δεσμώτας ἑκα-
they delivered up both Paul and certain other prisoners to a
τοντάρχῃ, ὀνόματι Ἰουλίῳ, σπείρης Σεβαστῆς. 2 ἐπιβάν-
centurion, by name Julius, of the band of Augustus. ²Having ³gone ⁴on
τες δὲ πλοίῳ Ἀδραμυττηνῷ [t]μέλλοντεςǁ πλεῖν [u] τοὺς κατὰ
⁵board ¹and a ship of Adramyttium about to navigate the ²along
τὴν Ἀσίαν [v]τόπους ἀνήχθημεν, ὄντος σὺν ἡμῖν Ἀριστάρχου
³Asia ¹places we set sail, being with us Aristarchus
Μακεδόνος Θεσσαλονικέως. 3 τῇ.τε.ἑτέρᾳ κατήχθημεν εἰς
a Macedonian of Thessalonica. And the next [day] we landed at
Σιδῶνα· φιλανθρώπως.τε ὁ Ἰούλιος τῷ Παύλῳ χρησάμενος
Sidon. And ⁵kindly ¹Julius ⁴Paul ²having ³treated
ἐπέτρεψεν πρὸς [v] φίλους [w]πορευθένταǁ ἐπιμελείας
allowed [him] ²to [³his] ⁴friends ¹going [⁷their] ⁸care
τυχεῖν. 4 κἀκεῖθεν ἀναχθέντες ὑπεπλεύσαμεν τὴν Κύπρον
⁵to ⁶receive. And thence setting sail we sailed under Cyprus
διὰ τὸ τοὺς ἀνέμους εἶναι ἐναντίους. 5 τό.τε.πέλαγος τὸ
because the winds were contrary. And the sea
κατὰ τὴν Κιλικίαν καὶ Παμφυλίαν διαπλεύσαντες [x]κατήλθομεν
along Cilicia and Pamphylia having sailed over we came
εἰς [y]Μύραǁ τῆς Λυκίας. 6 Κἀκεῖ εὑρὼν ὁ [z]ἑκατόνταρχος
to Myra of Lycia. And there ³having ⁴found ¹the ²centurion
πλοῖον Ἀλεξανδρῖνον πλέον εἰς τὴν Ἰταλίαν ἐνεβίβασεν
a ship of Alexandria sailing to Italy he caused ²to ³enter
ἡμᾶς εἰς αὐτό. 7 ἐν.ἱκαναῖς.δὲ ἡμέραις βραδυπλοοῦντες καὶ
¹us into it. And for many days sailing slowly and
μόλις γενόμενοι κατὰ τὴν Κνίδον, μὴ προσεῶντος ἡμᾶς
hardly having come over against Cnidus, ³not ⁴suffering ⁵us
τοῦ ἀνέμου, ὑπεπλεύσαμεν τὴν Κρήτην κατὰ Σαλμώνην·
¹the ²wind, we sailed under Crete over against Salmone;
8 μόλις.τε παραλεγόμενοι αὐτὴν ἤλθομεν εἰς τόπον τινὰ
and hardly coasting along it we came to a ²place ¹certain
καλούμενον Καλοὺς Λιμένας, ᾧ.ἐγγὺς [a]ἦν πόλιςǁ [b]Λασαία.ǁ
called Fair Havens, near which was a city of Lasæa.
9 Ἱκανοῦ δὲ χρόνου διαγενομένου καὶ ὄντος ἤδη ἐπισφαλοῦς
And much time having passed and being already dangerous
τοῦ πλοός, διὰ τὸ καὶ τὴν νηστείαν ἤδη παρεληλυθέναι,
the voyage, because also the fast already had past,
παρῄνει ὁ Παῦλος 10 λέγων αὐτοῖς, Ἄνδρες, θεωρῶ ὅτι μετὰ
²exhorted ¹Paul ⁴saying ³them, Men, I perceive that with
ὕβρεως καὶ πολλῆς ζημίας οὐ μόνον τοῦ [c]φόρτουǁ καὶ τοῦ
disaster and much loss not only of the cargo and of the
πλοίου ἀλλὰ καὶ τῶν.ψυχῶν.ἡμῶν μέλλειν ἔσεσθαι τὸν πλοῦν.
ship but also of our lives is about to be the voyage.
11 Ὁ.δὲ [d]ἑκατόνταρχοςǁ τῷ κυβερνήτῃ καὶ τῷ ναυκλήρῳ
But the centurion by the steersman and the ship-owner
[e]ἐπείθετο μᾶλλονǁ ἢ τοῖς ὑπὸ [f]τοῦǁ Παύλου λεγο-
was persuaded rather than by the things ²by ³Paul ¹spoken.
μένοις. 12 ἀνευθέτου.δὲ τοῦ λιμένος ὑπάρχοντος πρὸς παρα-
And ill-adapted the port being to winter
χειμασίαν, οἱ [g]πλείουςǁ ἔθεντο.βουλὴν ἀναχθῆναι [h]κἀκεῖθεν,ǁ
in, the most counselled to set sail thence also,
[i]εἴπωςǁ δύναιντο καταντήσαντες εἰς Φοίνικα παρα-
if by any means they might be able having arrived at Phœnice to
χειμάσαι, λιμένα τῆς Κρήτης βλέποντα κατὰ λίβα
winter [there], a port of Crete looking towards south-west
καὶ κατὰ χῶρον. 13 ὑποπνεύσαντος.δὲ νότου, δόξαν-
and towards north-west. And ⁴blowing ⁵gently ¹a ²south ³wind, think-
τες τῆς προθέσεως κεκρατηκέναι, ἄραντες ἆσσον
ing the purpose to have gained, having weighed [anchor] ⁴close ⁵by

29 And Paul answered, My prayer to God is that both in a little while and in much measure, you and also all those who are hearing me today should become what I also am, except for these chains.

30 And when he had said these things, the king and the governor and Bernice, and those who sat with them, stood up.

31 And going aside, they spoke to one another saying, This man has done nothing deserving of death or of bonds.

32 And Agrippa said to Festus, This man might have been set free if he had not appealed to Caesar.

CHAPTER 27

1 And when it was decided that we should sail to Italy, they delivered both Paul and certain other prisoners to a centurion of the band of Augustus, whose name was Julius.

2 And after going on board a ship of Ad-ra-myt-ti-um, intending to sail along the coasts of Asia, we set sail. And Ar-is-tar-chus, a Mac-e-do-ni-an from Thess-a-lo-ni-ca was with us.

3 And the next day we landed at Sidon. And Julius, treating Paul kindly, allowed him to go to his friends to receive their care.

4 And setting sail from there we sailed under Cyprus, because the winds were contrary.

5 And after sailing over the sea alongside of Cilicia and Pam-phyl-i-a, we came to Myra, a city of Lycia.

6 And there the centurion found a ship of Alexandria sailing to Italy, and he put us into it.

7 And after sailing slowly for many days and having difficulty coming abreast of Cnidus (the wind not allowing us), we sailed under Crete, opposite Sal-mo-ne.

8 And coasting along it with difficulty, we came to a certain place called Fair Havens, which was near a city of Lasea.

9 And much time being used up and the voyage already dangerous because the Fast was already also past, Paul warned them,

10 saying, Men! I see that the voyage is going to be visited with injury and much loss, not only of the cargo and of the ship, but also of our lives.

11 But the centurion was persuaded more by the pilot and the ship-owner than by the things spoken by Paul.

12 And because the port was not comfortable to winter in, the majority also gave advice to set sail from there to see if they might somehow be able to winter at Phoenix, a port of Crete which looked towards the southwest and towards the northwest.

13 And when a south wind began blowing gently, thinking they had gained their purpose, they lifted anchor and coasted along

παρελέγοντο τὴν Κρήτην. 14 μετ' οὐ πολὺ δὲ ἔβαλεν
[1]they [2]coasted [3]along Crete. [4]After [2]not [3]long [1]but there came
κατ' αὐτῆς ἄνεμος τυφωνικός, ὁ καλούμενος [k]εὐροκλύδων.[‖]
down it a [2]wind [1]tempestuous, called Euroclydon.
15 συναρπασθέντος.δὲ τοῦ πλοίου, καὶ μὴ δυναμένου ἀντ-
And [3]having [4]been [5]caught [1]the [2]ship, and not able to bring
οφθαλμεῖν τῷ ἀνέμῳ, ἐπιδόντες ἐφερόμεθα. 16 νησίον
[her] head to the wind, giving [her] up we were driven along. [8]Small [7]island
δέ τι ὑποδραμόντες καλούμενον [l]Κλαύδην[‖] [m]μόλις
[1]but [4]a [5]certain [2]running [3]under called Clauda [2]hardly
ἰσχύσαμεν[‖] περικρατεῖς γενέσθαι τῆς σκάφης· 17 ἣν ἄραν-
[1]we were able masters to become of the boat; which having taken
τες βοηθείαις ἐχρῶντο, ὑποζωννύντες τὸ πλοῖον· φοβούμενοί
up helps they used, undergirding the ship; [2]fearing
τε μὴ εἰς τὴν σύρτιν ἐκπέσωσιν, χαλάσαντες τὸ σκεῦος
[1]and lest into the quicksand they should fall, having lowered the gear
οὕτως ἐφέροντο. 18 Σφοδρῶς.δὲ χειμαζομένων ἡμῶν
so they were driven. But [3]violently [2]being [4]tempest-tossed [1]we
τῇ ἑξῆς ἐκβολὴν ἐποιοῦντο· 19 καὶ τῇ
on the next [day] [3]a [4]casting [5]out [[6]of [7]cargo] [1]they [2]made, and on the
τρίτῃ αὐτόχειρες τὴν σκευὴν τοῦ πλοίου [n]ἐρρίψαμεν·[‖]
third [day] with [our] own hands the equipment of the ship we cast away.
20 μήτε.δὲ ἡλίου μήτε ἄστρων ἐπιφαινόντων ἐπὶ πλείονας
And neither sun nor stars appearing for many
ἡμέρας, χειμῶνός.τε οὐκ ὀλίγου ἐπικειμένου, λοιπὸν περιῃ-
days, and [3]tempest [1]no [2]small lying on [us], henceforth was taken
ρεῖτο [o]πᾶσα ἐλπὶς[‖] τοῦ.σώζεσθαι.ἡμᾶς. 21 Πολλῆς.[p]δὲ[‖] ἀσιτίας
away all hope of our being saved. And [3]a [4]long [5]abstinence
ὑπαρχούσης, τότε σταθεὶς ὁ Παῦλος ἐν μέσῳ.αὐτῶν εἶπεν,
[1]there [2]being, then [2]standing [3]up [1]Paul in their midst said,
Ἔδει μέν, ὦ ἄνδρες, πειθαρχήσαντάς μοι μὴ ἀνά-
It behoved [you] indeed, O men, having been obedient to me not to have
γεσθαι ἀπὸ τῆς Κρήτης κερδῆσαί.τε τὴν.ὕβριν.ταύτην καὶ
set sail from Crete and to have gained this disaster and
τὴν ζημίαν. 22 καὶ [q]τανῦν[‖] παραινῶ ὑμᾶς εὐθυμεῖν·
loss: and now I exhort you to be of good cheer,
ἀποβολὴ.γὰρ ψυχῆς οὐδεμία ἔσται ἐξ ὑμῶν, πλὴν τοῦ
for [3]loss [4]of [5]life [1]not [2]any shall be from among you, only of the
πλοίου. 23 παρέστη.γάρ μοι [r]τῇ.νυκτὶ.ταύτῃ[‖] [s]ἄγγελος[‖] τοῦ
ship. For stood by me this night an angel
θεοῦ, οὗ εἰμι[t] ᾧ.καὶ λατρεύω,[s] 24 λέγων, Μὴ.φοβοῦ Παῦλε,
of God, whose I am and whom I serve, saying, Fear not, Paul;
Καίσαρί σε δεῖ παραστῆναι· καὶ ἰδοὺ κεχάρισταί σοι ὁ θεὸς
Cæsar thou must stand before; and lo [2]has [3]granted [4]to [5]thee [1]God
πάντας τοὺς πλέοντας μετὰ σοῦ. 25 Διὸ εὐθυμεῖτε ἄνδρες·
all those sailing with thee. Wherefore be of good cheer, men,
πιστεύω.γὰρ τῷ θεῷ ὅτι οὕτως ἔσται καθ' ὃν.τρόπον
for I believe God that thus it shall be according to the way
λελάληταί μοι. 26 εἰς.νῆσον.δέ τινα δεῖ.ἡμᾶς ἐκπεσεῖν.
it has been said to me. But on [3]island [1]a [2]certain we must fall.
27 Ὡς.δὲ τεσσαρεσκαιδεκάτη νὺξ ἐγένετο διαφερομένων
And when the fourteenth night was come [2]being [3]driven [4]about
ἡμῶν ἐν τῷ Ἀδρίᾳ, κατὰ μέσον τῆς νυκτὸς ὑπενόουν
[1]we in the Adriatic, towards [the] middle of the night [3]supposed
οἱ ναῦται προσάγειν τινὰ αὐτοῖς χώραν· 28 καὶ βολίσαντες
[1]the [2]sailors [6]neared [4]some [7]them [5]country, and having sounded
εὗρον ὀργυιὰς εἴκοσι· βραχὺ.δὲ διαστήσαντες καὶ πάλιν
they found [2]fathoms [1]twenty, and [3]a [4]little [1]having [2]gone [5]farther and again
βολίσαντες εὗρον ὀργυιὰς δεκαπέντε· 29 φοβούμενοί.τε
having sounded they found [2]fathoms [1]fifteen; and fearing
[v]μήπως[‖] [w]εἰς[‖] τραχεῖς τόπους [x]ἐκπέσωσιν,[‖] ἐκ πρύμνης
lest on rocky places they should fall, out of [the] stern
ῥίψαντες ἀγκύρας τέσσαρας [y]ηὔχοντο[‖] ἡμέραν γενέσθαι.
having cast [2]anchors [1]four they wished day to come.
30 τῶν.δὲ ναυτῶν ζητούντων φυγεῖν ἐκ τοῦ πλοίου, καὶ
But the sailors seeking to flee out of the ship, and
χαλασάντων τὴν σκάφην εἰς τὴν θάλασσαν, προφάσει ὡς ἐκ
having let down the boat into the sea, with pretext as from
[z]πρώρας[‖] [a]μελλόντων ἀγκύρας[‖] ἐκτείνειν, 31 εἶπεν ὁ Παῦ-
[the] prow being about [4]anchors [1]to [2]cast [3]out, [6]said [5]Paul
λος τῷ ἑκατοντάρχῃ καὶ τοῖς στρατιώταις, Ἐὰν.μὴ οὗτοι
to the centurion and to the soldiers, Unless these
μείνωσιν ἐν τῷ πλοίῳ, ὑμεῖς σωθῆναι οὐ.δύνασθε. 32 Τότε [b]οἱ
abide in the ship ye [2]be [3]saved [1]cannot. Then the
στρατιῶται ἀπέκοψαν[‖] τὰ σχοινία τῆς σκάφης καὶ εἴασαν
soldiers cut away the ropes of the boat and let
αὐτὴν ἐκπεσεῖν. 33 ἄχρι.δὲ.οὗ [c]ἔμελλεν ἡμέρα[‖] γίνεσθαι,
her fall. And until [2]was [3]about [1]day [4]to [5]come,
παρεκάλει ὁ Παῦλος ἅπαντας μεταλαβεῖν τροφῆς, λέγων,
[7]exhorted [6]Paul all to partake of food, saying,
Τεσσαρεσκαιδεκάτην σήμερον ἡμέραν προσδοκῶντες ἄσι-
[4]The [5]fourteenth [1]to-[2]day [[3]is] day watching without

close beside Crete.

14 But not long after this, a stormy wind called Eur-o-cly-don sprang up against it.

15 And the ship was caught and could not bring her head into the wind – giving up, we were driven along.

16 But running under a certain little isle called Clauda, we were hardly able to be masters of the boat.

17 Taking helps, they undergirded the ship. And fearing that they might fall into the quicksand, they let down the mast and were driven along.

18 But as we were being violently tossed by the storm, on the next day they finished throwing out *the cargo*.

19 And on the third day we threw out the tackling of the ship with our own hands.

20 And when neither the sun or the stars appeared for many days, and a great storm lay upon us, all hope of our being saved was taken away from that time.

21 And after a long period of fasting, then Paul stood among them and said, Truly, O men, you ought to have listened to me and should not have set sail from Crete and so have spared yourself this injury and loss.

22 But now I urge you to be of good cheer, for there shall be none of you lose your life, only the ship.

23 For tonight an angel of God stood by me (whose I am and whom I serve)

24 saying, Do not be afraid, Paul, you must stand before Caesar. And, lo, God has given to you all those sailing with you.

25 So be cheerful, men, for I believe God that it shall be so, even as it was said to me.

26 But we must fall on a certain island.

27 And when the fourteenth night came, *as* we were driven about in the Ad-ri-at-ic, towards midnight the sailors supposed that some land was coming near to them.

28 And they sounded and found twenty fathoms. And going on a little, they sounded again and found fifteen fathoms.

29 And being afraid they would fall on rocky places, they threw four anchors out of the stern and wished for day to come.

30 And letting down the boat into the sea, the sailors were trying to escape from the ship, pretending as if *they* were going to throw anchors from the prow.

31 Paul said to the centurion and the soldiers, If these men do not stay in the ship, you cannot be saved.

32 Then the soldiers cut away the ropes of the boat and let her fall.

33 And until day was dawning, Paul called on all to eat, saying, *It is* the fourteenth day today and you have continued watching and fasting, for you have taken nothing.

τοι διατελεῖτε, [d]μηδὲν‖ [e]προσλαβόμενοι.‖ 34 διὸ παρα-
taking food ye continue, nothing having taken. Wherefore I ex-
καλῶ ὑμᾶς [f]προσλαβεῖν‖ τροφῆς· τοῦτο.γὰρ πρὸς τῆς
hort you to take food, for this for
ὑμετέρας.σωτηρίας ὑπάρχει· [g]οὐδενὸς‖.γὰρ ὑμῶν θρὶξ [h]ἐκ‖
your safety is; for of no one of you a hair of
τῆς κεφαλῆς [i]πεσεῖται.‖ 35 [k]Εἰπὼν‖.δὲ ταῦτα καὶ λαβὼν
the head shall fall. And having said these things and having taken
ἄρτον εὐχαρίστησεν τῷ θεῷ ἐνώπιον πάντων, καὶ κλάσας
a loaf he gave thanks to God before all, and having broken [it]
ἤρξατο ἐσθίειν. 36 εὔθυμοι.δὲ γενόμενοι πάντες καὶ αὐ-
began to eat. And [4]of [5]good [6]cheer [2]having [3]become [1]all also them-
τοὶ προσελάβοντο τροφῆς· 37 [l]ἦμεν‖.δὲ [m]ἐν τῷ πλοίῳ αἱ
selves took food. And we were in the ship [2]the
πᾶσαι ψυχαὶ‖ διακόσιαι [n]ἑβδομηκονταέξ.‖ 38 κορεσθέντες.δὲ
[1]all souls two hundred [and] seventy six. And being satisfied
τροφῆς ἐκούφιζον τὸ πλοῖον, ἐκβαλλόμενοι τὸν σῖτον εἰς τὴν
with food they lightened the ship, casting out the wheat into the
θάλασσαν. 39 Ὅτε.δὲ ἡμέρα ἐγένετο τὴν γῆν οὐκ.ἐπεγίνωσκον·
sea. And when [3]day [1]it [2]was the land they did not recognize;
κόλπον.δέ τινα κατενόουν ἔχοντα αἰγιαλόν, εἰς ὃν [o]ἐβου-
but a [2]bay [1]certain they perceived having a shore, on which they
λεύσαντο‖ εἰ δύναιντο ἐξῶσαι τὸ πλοῖον. 40 καὶ τὰς
purposed if they should be able to drive the ship; and [4]the
ἀγκύρας περιελόντες εἴων εἰς τὴν θάλασσαν, ἅμα
[5]anchors [1]having [2]cut [3]away they left in the sea, at the same time
ἀνέντες τὰς ζευκτηρίας τῶν πηδαλίων· καὶ ἐπάραντες τὸν
having loosened the bands of the rudders, and having hoisted the
[p]ἀρτέμονα‖ τῇ πνεούσῃ κατεῖχον εἰς τὸν αἰγιαλόν. 41 περι-
foresail to the wind they made for the shore. [2]Having
πεσόντες δὲ εἰς τόπον διθάλασσον [q]ἐπώκειλαν‖ τὴν ναῦν·
[3]fallen [1]and into a place where two seas met they ran aground the vessel;
καὶ ἡ μὲν πρῷρα ἐρείσασα ἔμεινεν ἀσάλευτος, ἡ.δὲ
and the prow having stuck fast remained immovable, but the
πρύμνα ἐλύετο ὑπὸ τῆς βίας [r]τῶν κυμάτων.‖ 42 τῶν.δὲ
stern was broken by the violence of the waves. And of the
στρατιωτῶν βουλὴ ἐγένετο ἵνα τοὺς δεσμώτας ἀποκτείνωσιν,
soldiers [the] counsel was that the prisoners they should kill,
μήτις ἐκκολυμβήσας [s]διαφύγοι·‖ 43 ὁ.δὲ [t]ἑκατόνταρχος‖
lest anyone having swum out should escape. But the centurion
βουλόμενος διασῶσαι τὸν Παῦλον ἐκώλυσεν αὐτοὺς τοῦ
desiring to save Paul hindered them of [their]
βουλήματος, ἐκέλευσέν.τε τοὺς δυναμένους κολυμβᾶν, [v]ἀπορ-
purpose, and commanded those being able to swim, having
ῥίψαντας‖ πρώτους, ἐπὶ τὴν γῆν ἐξιέναι, 44 καὶ τοὺς
cast [themselves] off first, on the land to go out; and the
λοιπούς, οὓς μὲν ἐπὶ σανίσιν οὓς.δὲ ἐπί τινων.τῶν ἀπὸ τοῦ
rest, some indeed on boards and others on some things from the
πλοίου· καὶ οὕτως ἐγένετο πάντας διασωθῆναι ἐπὶ τὴν γῆν.
ship; and thus it came to pass all were brought safely to the land.

28 Καὶ διασωθέντες τότε [w]ἐπέγνωσαν‖ ὅτι Μελίτη ἡ
And having been saved then they knew that Melita the
νῆσος καλεῖται. 2 Οἱ.[x]δὲ‖ βάρβαροι [y]παρεῖχον‖ οὐ τὴν
island is called. And the barbarians shewed no
τυχοῦσαν φιλανθρωπίαν ἡμῖν· [z]ἀνάψαντες‖.γὰρ πυρὰν προσ-
common philanthropy to us; for having kindled a fire they
ελάβοντο πάντας ἡμᾶς, διὰ τὸν ὑετὸν τὸν ἐφεστῶτα καὶ
received all of us, because of the rain that was present and
διὰ τὸ ψύχος. 3 Συστρέψαντος.δὲ τοῦ Παύλου φρυγάνων [a]
because of the cold. And [2]having [3]gathered [1]Paul [6]of [7]sticks
πλῆθος, καὶ ἐπιθέντος ἐπὶ τὴν πυρὰν ἔχιδνα [b]ἐκ‖ τῆς
[4]a [5]quantity, and having laid [them] on the fire a viper out of the
θέρμης [c]ἐξελθοῦσα‖ καθῆψεν τῆς.χειρὸς.αὐτοῦ. 4 ὡς.δὲ [d]εἶδον‖
heat having come wound about his hand. And when [3]saw
οἱ βάρβαροι κρεμάμενον τὸ θηρίον ἐκ τῆς.χειρὸς.αὐτοῦ
[1]the [2]barbarians [6]hanging [4]the [5]beast from his hand
[e]ἔλεγον πρὸς ἀλλήλους,‖ Πάντως φονεύς ἐστιν ὁ ἄνθρωπος
they said to one another, By all means a murderer is [2]man
οὗτος, ὃν διασωθέντα ἐκ τῆς θαλάσσης ἡ δίκη ζῆν οὐκ
[1]this, whom having been saved from the sea justice [3]to [4]live [2]not
εἴασεν. 5 Ὁ μὲν οὖν [f]ἀποτινάξας‖ τὸ θηρίον εἰς τὸ πῦρ
[1]permitted. He indeed then having shaken off the beast into the fire,
ἔπαθεν οὐδὲν κακόν. 6 οἱ.δὲ προσεδόκων αὐτὸν μέλλειν
suffered no injury. But they were expecting him to be about
[g]πίμπρασθαι‖ ἢ καταπίπτειν ἄφνω νεκρόν· ἐπὶ.πολὺ.δὲ
to become inflamed or to fall down suddenly dead. But for a long time
αὐτῶν προσδοκώντων καὶ θεωρούντων μηδὲν ἄτοπον εἰς αὐτὸν
they expecting and seeing nothing amiss to him
γινόμενον, [h]μεταβαλλόμενοι‖ ἔλεγον [i]θεὸν αὐτὸν εἶναι.‖
happening, changing their opinion said a god he was.
7 Ἐν.δὲ τοῖς περὶ τὸν.τόπον.ἐκεῖνον ὑπῆρχεν χωρία
Now in the [parts] about that place were lands

34 So I beg you to eat, for it is for your safety. For not a hair shall fall from the head of any one of you.

35 And when he had said this, taking bread, he gave thanks to God before all. And he broke it and began to eat.

36 And all became cheerful and themselves also took food.

37 And all the souls in the ship were two hundred and seventy-six.

38 And when they were satisfied with food, they lightened the ship by throwing out the wheat into the sea.

39 And when day dawned, they did not recognize the land. But they saw a certain bay with a beach on which they decided to drive the ship, if they were able to do so.

40 And cutting away the anchors, they left them in the sea. At the same time they loosened the bands of the rudders, and after hoisting the mainsail to the wind, they made for the shore.

41 And falling into a place where two seas met, they ran the ship aground. And indeed the forepart stuck fast and remained fixed, but the stern was broken by the violence of the waves.

42 And the advice of the soldiers was that they should kill the prisoners, lest any one of them should swim out and escape.

43 But desiring to save Paul, the centurion kept them from their purpose and commanded those who could swim to jump off first and go out on the land –

44 and then the rest, some indeed on boards and others on some things from the ship. And so all were brought safely to the land.

CHAPTER 28

1 And having been saved, then they knew that the island was called Mel-i-ta.

2 And the natives showed us unusual kindness. For having kindled a fire, they received all of us (because of the falling rain and because of the cold).

3 And when Paul had gathered a bundle of sticks and had laid them on the fire, a viper came out of the heat and fastened on his hand.

4 And when the natives saw the beast hanging from his hand, they said to one another, No doubt this man is a murderer whom Justice will not allow to live, though he has been saved from the sea.

5 But, indeed, shaking the beast off into the fire, he suffered no harm.

6 But they thought he soon would become inflamed, or would suddenly fall down dead. And after looking for it a long time, and when no evil happened to him, they changed their minds and said that he was a god.

7 Now near that place were lands owned by the island chief, named Pub-li-us, who,

τῷ πρώτῳ τῆς νήσου, ὀνόματι Ποπλίῳ, ὃς ἀνα-
belonging to the chief of the island, by name Publius, who having
δεξάμενος ἡμᾶς [k]τρεῖς ἡμέρας" φιλοφρόνως ἐξένισεν.
received us three days in a friendly way lodged [us].
8 ἐγένετο.δὲ τὸν πατέρα τοῦ Ποπλίου πυρετοῖς καὶ [l]δυσεν-
And it happened the father of Publius 4fevers 5and 6dysen-
τερίᾳ" συνεχόμενον κατακεῖσθαι· πρὸς ὃν ὁ Παῦλος εἰσελ-
tery 2oppressed 3with 1lay, to whom Paul having en-
θὼν καὶ προσευξάμενος, ἐπιθεὶς τὰς χεῖρας αὐτῷ ἰάσατο
tered and having prayed, having laid on [3his] 2hands 1him cured
αὐτόν. 9 τούτου [m]οὖν" γενομένου καὶ οἱ λοιποὶ οἱ [n]ἔχον-
him. This therefore having taken place also the rest who had
τες ἀσθενείας ἐν τῇ νήσῳ" προσήρχοντο καὶ ἐθεραπεύοντο
infirmities in the island came and were healed:
10 οἳ καὶ πολλαῖς τιμαῖς ἐτίμησαν ἡμᾶς, καὶ ἀναγομένοις
who also with many honours honoured us, and on setting sail
ἐπέθεντο τὰ πρὸς [o]τὴν χρείαν."
they laid on [us] the things for [our] need.
11 Μετὰ.δὲ τρεῖς μῆνας ἀνήχθημεν ἐν πλοίῳ παρακεχει-
And after three months we sailed in a ship which had
μακότι ἐν τῇ νήσῳ, Ἀλεξανδρίνῳ, παρασήμῳ Διοσκούροις·
wintered in the island, an Alexandrian, with an ensign [the] Dioscuri.
12 καὶ καταχθέντες εἰς Συρακούσας ἐπεμείναμεν [p]ἡμέρας
And having been brought to at Syracuse we remained 2days
τρεῖς·" 13 ὅθεν περιελθόντες κατηντήσαμεν εἰς Ῥήγιον, καὶ
1three. Whence having gone round we arrived at Rhegium; and
μετὰ μίαν ἡμέραν ἐπιγενομένου νότου δευτεραῖοι
after one day, 4having 5come 6on 1a 2south 3wind, on the second day
ἤλθομεν εἰς Ποτιόλους· 14 οὗ εὑρόντες ἀδελφοὺς παρε-
we came to Puteoli; where having found brethren we were
κλήθημεν [q]ἐπ'" αὐτοῖς ἐπιμεῖναι ἡμέρας ἑπτά· καὶ οὕτως [r]εἰς
entreated 3with 4them 1to 2remain 6days 5seven. And thus to
τὴν Ῥώμην ἤλθομεν." 15 κἀκεῖθεν οἱ ἀδελφοὶ ἀκούσαντες
Rome we came. And thence the brethren having heard
τὰ περὶ ἡμῶν [s]ἐξῆλθον" εἰς ἀπάντησιν ἡμῖν [t]ἄχρις"
the things concerning us came out to meet us as far as
Ἀππίου.Φόρου καὶ Τριῶν Ταβερνῶν· οὓς ἰδὼν ὁ Παῦ-
[the] market-place of Appius and Three Taverns; whom 2seeing 1Paul,
λος, εὐχαριστήσας τῷ θεῷ ἔλαβεν θάρσος.
having given thanks to God he took courage.

16 [u]Ὅτε.δὲ [v]ἤλθομεν" εἰς [w]Ῥώμην [x]ὁ ἑκατόνταρχος παρέ-
And when we came to Rome the centurion de-
δωκεν τοὺς δεσμίους τῷ στρατοπεδάρχῃ·" [y]τῷ.δὲ.Παύλῳ
livered the prisoners to the commander of the camp, but Paul
ἐπετράπη" μένειν καθ'.ἑαυτόν, σὺν τῷ φυλάσσοντι αὐτὸν
was allowed to remain by himself, with the 2who 3kept 4him
στρατιώτῃ. 17 Ἐγένετο.δὲ μετὰ ἡμέρας τρεῖς [z]συγκαλέσασ-
1soldier. And it came to pass after 2days 1three 4called 5to-
θαι" [a]τὸν Παῦλον" τοὺς ὄντας τῶν Ἰουδαίων πρώτους·
gether 3Paul those who were 3of 4the 5Jews 1chief 2ones.
συνελθόντων.δὲ αὐτῶν ἔλεγεν πρὸς αὐτούς, [b]Ἄνδρες
And 2having 3come 4together 1they he said to them, Men
ἀδελφοί, ἐγὼ" οὐδὲν ἐναντίον ποιήσας τῷ λαῷ ἢ τοῖς
brethren, I 3nothing 4against 1having 2done the people or the
ἔθεσιν τοῖς πατρῴοις δέσμιος ἐξ Ἱεροσολύμων παρεδόθην
2customs 1ancestral a prisoner from Jerusalem was delivered
εἰς τὰς χεῖρας τῶν Ῥωμαίων· 18 οἵτινες ἀνακρίναντές με
into the hands of the Romans, who having examined me
ἐβούλοντο ἀπολῦσαι, διὰ τὸ μηδεμίαν αἰτίαν θανάτου
wished to let [me] go, because not one cause of death
ὑπάρχειν ἐν ἐμοί. 19 ἀντιλεγόντων.δὲ τῶν Ἰουδαίων
was there in me. But 3speaking 4against [5it] 1the 2Jews
ἠναγκάσθην ἐπικαλέσασθαι Καίσαρα, οὐχ ὡς τοῦ.ἔθνους.μου
I was compelled to appeal to Cæsar, not as 6my 7nation
ἔχων τι [c]κατηγορῆσαι." 20 διὰ ταύτην οὖν τὴν αἰτίαν
1having 2anything 3to 4lay 5against. For this 2therefore 1cause
παρεκάλεσα ὑμᾶς ἰδεῖν καὶ προσλαλῆσαι· [d]ἕνεκεν".γὰρ
I called for you to see and to speak to [you]; for on account of
τῆς ἐλπίδος τοῦ Ἰσραὴλ τὴν.ἅλυσιν.ταύτην περίκειμαι.
the hope of Israel this chain I have around [me].
21 Οἱ.δὲ πρὸς αὐτὸν [e]εἶπον," Ἡμεῖς οὔτε γράμματα [f]περὶ
And they to him said, We neither letters concerning
σοῦ ἐδεξάμεθα" ἀπὸ τῆς Ἰουδαίας οὔτε παραγενόμενός τις
thee received from Judæa, nor having arrived any one
τῶν ἀδελφῶν ἀπήγγειλεν ἢ ἐλάλησέν τι περὶ σοῦ
of the brethren reported or said anything 2concerning 3thee
πονηρόν. 22 ἀξιοῦμεν.δὲ παρὰ σοῦ ἀκοῦσαι ἃ φρονεῖς·
1evil. But we think well from thee to hear what thou thinkest,
περὶ.μὲν.γὰρ τῆς.αἱρέσεως.ταύτης γνωστόν [g]ἐστιν ἡμῖν"
for indeed as concerning this sect known it is to us
ὅτι πανταχοῦ ἀντιλέγεται. 23 Ταξάμενοι.δὲ αὐτῷ ἡμέραν
that everywhere it is spoken against. And having appointed him a day

having received us kindly kept us for three
days.
8 And it happened that the father of Publius lay overcome with fevers and dysentery
– to whom Paul went in, and having prayed,
he laid his hands on him and healed him.
9 Then this being done, the others in the
island who also had sicknesses came and
were healed.
10 *They* also honored us with many honors,
and when we were sailing, they heaped on us
the things that were needed.
11 And after three months we sailed in a
ship which had wintered in the island, an
Alexandrian ship named The Twin Brothers.
12 And having landed at Syracuse, we
stayed three days.
13 From there, after going around, we came
to Rhe-gi-um. And after one day a south
wind sprang up. The second day we came to
Pu-te-o-li,
14 where we found brothers and were urged
to stay with them seven days. And so we
came toward Rome.
15 And hearing the things about us, the
brothers from there came out to meet us, as
far as the Appian Forum and Three Taverns.
When Paul saw *them,* he gave thanks to God
and was encouraged.

16 And when we came to Rome, the centurion delivered the prisoners to the commander of the camp. But Paul was allowed to
remain by himself, with the soldier who
guarded him.
17 And after three days, Paul called together those who were chief men of the
Jews. And when they had come together, he
said to them, Men! Brothers! I have done
nothing against the people or the customs of
our fathers, *yet* I was given over as a prisoner
from Jerusalem, into the hands of the Romans.
18 When they had examined me, they
wished to let me go, because there was not
one cause of death in me.
19 But the Jews objecting, I was forced to
appeal to Caesar – not as though I had
anything to lay against my nation.
20 For this cause, then, I called for you, to
see and to speak to you. For on account of
the hope of Israel, I am bound with this
chain.
21 And they said to him, We neither received letters from Judea about you, nor did
anyone of the brothers who came report it
or say anything evil about you.
22 But we think it good to hear from you,
what you think, for truly as regarding this
belief, it is known to us that it is spoken
against everywhere.
23 And after setting him a day, many
came to him into his house – to whom he

ʰἧκον" πρὸς αὐτὸν εἰς τὴν ξενίαν πλείονες· οἷς ἐξετίθετο
came to him to the lodging many, to whom he expounded.
διαμαρτυρόμενος τὴν βασιλείαν τοῦ θεοῦ, πείθων.τε αὐτοὺς
fully testifying the kingdom of God, and persuading them
ⁱτὰ" περὶ τοῦ Ἰησοῦ, ἀπό.τε τοῦ νόμου ʰΜωσέως"
the things concerning Jesus, both from the law of Moses
καὶ τῶν προφητῶν, ἀπὸ πρωῒ ἕως ἑσπέρας. 24 καὶ οἱ
and the prophets, from morning to evening. And some
μὲν ἐπείθοντο τοῖς λεγομένοις, οἱ.δὲ ἠπίστουν.
indeed were persuaded of the things spoken, but some disbelieved.
25 ἀσύμφωνοι.δὲ.ὄντες πρὸς ἀλλήλους ἀπελύοντο, εἰπόν-
And disagreeing with one another they departed; ²having
τος τοῦ Παύλου ῥῆμα ἕν, "Ὅτι καλῶς τὸ πνεῦμα τὸ ἅγιον
³spoken ¹Paul ⁵word ⁴one, Well the Spirit the Holy
ἐλάλησεν διὰ Ἡσαΐου τοῦ προφήτου πρὸς τοὺς πατέρας
spoke by Esaias the prophet to ²fathers
ᵐἡμῶν," 26 ⁿλέγον," Πορεύθητι πρὸς τὸν.λαὸν.τοῦτον καὶ
¹our, saying, Go to this people, and
ᵒεἰπέ," Ἀκοῇ ἀκούσετε, καὶ οὐ.μὴ συνῆτε· καὶ βλέποντες
say, In hearing ye shall hear, and in no wise understand, and seeing
βλέψετε, καὶ οὐ.μὴ ἴδητε· 27 ἐπαχύνθη.γὰρ ἡ καρδία
ye shall see, and in no wise perceive. For has grown fat the heart
τοῦ.λαοῦ.τούτου, καὶ τοῖς ὠσὶν βαρέως ἤκουσαν, καὶ
of this people, and with the ears heavily they have heard, and
τοὺς.ὀφθαλμοὺς.αὐτῶν ἐκάμμυσαν· μήποτε ἴδωσιν τοῖς
their eyes they have closed, lest they should see with the
ὀφθαλμοῖς, καὶ τοῖς ὠσὶν ἀκούσωσιν, καὶ τῇ καρδίᾳ
eyes, and with the ears they should hear, and with the heart
συνῶσιν, καὶ ἐπιστρέψωσιν, καὶ ᵖἰάσωμαι" αὐτούς.
they should understand, and should be converted, and I should heal them.
28 Γνωστὸν οὖν ᵠἔστω ὑμῖν," ὅτι τοῖς ἔθνεσιν ἀπεστάλη ʳ
Known therefore be it to you, that to the nations is sent
τὸ σωτήριον τοῦ θεοῦ, αὐτοὶ.καὶ ἀκούσονται. 29 ˢΚαὶ ταῦτα
the salvation of God; and they will hear. And these things
αὐτοῦ εἰπόντος ἀπῆλθον οἱ Ἰουδαῖοι, πολλὴν ἔχοντες ἐν
he having said ³went ⁴away ¹the ²Jews, ⁶much ⁵having ⁸among
ἑαυτοῖς συζήτησιν."
⁹themselves ⁷discussion.
30 ᵗἜμεινεν.δὲ ᵛὁ Παῦλος" διετίαν ὅλην ἐν ἰδίῳ μισ-
And ²abode ¹Paul two ²years ¹whole in his own hired
θώματι, καὶ ἀπεδέχετο πάντας τοὺς εἰσπορευομένους πρὸς
house, and welcomed all who came in to
αὐτόν, 31 κηρύσσων τὴν βασιλείαν τοῦ θεοῦ, καὶ διδάσκων
him, proclaiming the kingdom of God, and teaching
τὰ περὶ τοῦ κυρίου Ἰησοῦ ʷχριστοῦ," μετὰ πάσης
the things concerning the Lord Jesus Christ, with all
παρρησίας ἀκωλύτως. ˣ
freedom unhinderedly.

explained fully witnessing to the kingdom of God and persuaded them of the things about Jesus (both from the law of Moses and from the Prophets), from morning to evening.
24 And some were indeed persuaded of the things spoken, but some did not believe.
25 And without agreeing with one another, they went away, after Paul had spoken one *last* word: Well did the Holy Spirit speak by Isaiah the prophet to our fathers, saying,
26 "Go to this people and say, By hearing you shall hear and in no way understand; and seeing you shall see and in no way perceive.
27 For the heart of this people has grown fat, and they have heard with heavy ears, and they have closed their eyes, for fear that they should see with their eyes and they should hear with their ears and they should understand with their heart and should be converted, and I should heal them."
28 Then let it be known to you that the salvation of God is sent to the Gentiles. And they will hear.
29 And when he had said this, the Jews left, arguing among themselves.
30 And Paul stayed two whole years in his own hired house and welcomed all who came in to him,
31 preaching the kingdom of God and teaching the things about the Lord Jesus Christ, with all freedom, without being hindered.

The Letter to the ROMANS

ΠΑΥΛΟΣ δοῦλος ᵇἸησοῦ χριστοῦ," κλητὸς ἀπόστολος, ἀφω-
Paul, bondman of Jesus Christ, a called apostle, sepa-
ρισμένος εἰς εὐαγγέλιον θεοῦ, 2 ὃ προεπηγγείλατο διὰ
rated to glad tidings of God, which he before promised through
τῶν.προφητῶν.αὐτοῦ ἐν γραφαῖς ἁγίαις, 3 περὶ τοῦ υἱοῦ
his prophets in ²writings ¹holy, concerning ²Son
αὐτοῦ, τοῦ γενομένου ἐκ σπέρματος ᶜΔαβὶδ" κατὰ
¹his, who came of [the] seed of David according to
σάρκα, 4 τοῦ ὁρισθέντος υἱοῦ θεοῦ ἐν δυνάμει, κατὰ
flesh, who was marked out Son of God in power, according to [the]
πνεῦμα ἁγιωσύνης, ἐξ ἀναστάσεως νεκρῶν, Ἰησοῦ χριστοῦ
Spirit of holiness, by resurrection of [the] dead— Jesus Christ
τοῦ.κυρίου.ἡμῶν, 5 δι' οὗ ἐλάβομεν χάριν καὶ ἀποστολὴν
our Lord; by whom we received grace and apostleship
εἰς ὑπακοὴν πίστεως ἐν πᾶσιν τοῖς ἔθνεσιν, ὑπὲρ τοῦ
unto obedience of faith among all the nations, in behalf of
ὀνόματος.αὐτοῦ, 6 ἐν οἷς ἐστε καὶ ὑμεῖς, κλητοὶ Ἰησοῦ
his name, among whom are also ye, called of Jesus
χριστοῦ· 7 πᾶσιν τοῖς οὖσιν ἐν Ῥώμῃ ἀγαπητοῖς θεοῦ,
Christ: to all those who are in Rome beloved of God,
κλητοῖς ἁγίοις· χάρις ὑμῖν καὶ εἰρήνη ἀπὸ θεοῦ πατρὸς.ἡμῶν
called saints: grace to you and peace from God our Father
καὶ κυρίου Ἰησοῦ χριστοῦ.
and Lord Jesus Christ.

CHAPTER 1

1 Paul, a called apostle and bondslave of Jesus Christ, *who was* separated to the Gospel of God
2 (which He promised before through His prophets in the holy Scriptures –
3 *the gospel* about His Son, who came of the seed of David according to the flesh is concerned,
4 who was declared Son of God in power, according to the Spirit of holiness, by resurrection from among the dead
5 Jesus Christ, our Lord, through whom we received grace and apostleship to the obedience of faith among all the nations, for His name's sake,
6 among whom are you also, the called out ones of Jesus Christ) –
7 to all those who are in Rome, beloved, called out saints of God. Grace to you and peace from God our Father and the Lord Jesus Christ.

8 Πρῶτον μὲν εὐχαριστῶ τῷ.θεῷ.μου διὰ Ἰησοῦ χριστοῦ
First, I thank my God through Jesus Christ

[d]ὑπὲρ‖ πάντων ὑμῶν, ὅτι ἡ.πίστις.ὑμῶν καταγγέλλεται ἐν
for [2]all [1]you, that your faith is announced in

ὅλῳ τῷ κόσμῳ· 9 μάρτυς.γάρ μου ἐστὶν ὁ θεός, ᾧ λατρεύω
[2]whole [1]the world; for [4]witness [3]my [2]is [1]God, whom I serve

ἐν τῷ.πνεύματί.μου ἐν τῷ εὐαγγελίῳ τοῦ.υἱοῦ.αὐτοῦ, ὡς
in my spirit in the glad tidings of his Son, how

ἀδιαλείπτως μνείαν ὑμῶν ποιοῦμαι, 10 πάντοτε ἐπὶ τῶν
unceasingly mention of you I make, always at

προσευχῶν.μου δεόμενος, [e]εἴπως‖ ἤδη ποτὲ εὐοδωθήσομαι
my prayers beseeching, if by any means now at length I shall be prospered

ἐν τῷ θελήματι τοῦ θεοῦ ἐλθεῖν πρὸς ὑμᾶς· 11 ἐπιποθῶ.γὰρ
by the will of God to come to you. For I long

ἰδεῖν ὑμᾶς, ἵνα τι μεταδῶ χάρισμα ὑμῖν πνευματικόν,
to see you, that some [3]I [4]may [5]impart [2]gift [6]to [7]you [1]spiritual,

εἰς τὸ στηριχθῆναι ὑμᾶς, 12 τοῦτο.δέ.ἐστιν, [f]συμπαρα-
to the [end] [2]be [3]established [1]ye, that is, to be comforted

κληθῆναι‖ ἐν ὑμῖν διὰ τῆς ἐν ἀλλήλοις πίστεως ὑμῶν.τε
together among you, through the [2]in [3]one [4]another [1]faith, both yours

καὶ ἐμοῦ· 13 οὐ.θέλω.δὲ ὑμᾶς ἀγνοεῖν, ἀδελφοί, ὅτι πολ-
and mine. But I do not wish you to be ignorant, brethren, that many

λάκις προεθέμην ἐλθεῖν πρὸς ὑμᾶς, καὶ ἐκωλύθην ἄχρι τοῦ
times I proposed to come to you, and was hindered until the

δεῦρο, ἵνα [g]καρπόν τινα‖ σχῶ καὶ ἐν ὑμῖν, καθὼς
present, that [2]fruit [1]some I might have also among you, according as

καὶ ἐν τοῖς λοιποῖς ἔθνεσιν. 14 Ἕλλησίν.τε καὶ βαρβάροις,
also among the other nations. Both to Greeks and barbarians,

σοφοῖς.τε καὶ ἀνοήτοις, ὀφειλέτης εἰμί· 15 οὕτως τὸ κατ' ἐμὲ
both to wise and unintelligent, a debtor I am: so as to me

πρόθυμον καὶ ὑμῖν τοῖς ἐν Ῥώμῃ εὐαγ-
[there is] readiness [3]also [4]to [5]you [6]who [[7]are] [8]in [9]Rome [1]to [2]announce

γελίσασθαι. 16 οὐ.γὰρ.ἐπαισχύνομαι τὸ εὐαγγέλιον [h]τοῦ
the glad tidings. For I am not ashamed of the glad tidings of the

χριστοῦ·‖ δύναμις.γὰρ θεοῦ ἐστιν εἰς σωτηρίαν παντὶ τῷ
Christ: for power of God it is unto salvation to every one that

πιστεύοντι, Ἰουδαίῳ.τε [i]πρῶτον‖ καὶ Ἕλληνι. 17 δικαιοσύνη
believes, both to Jew first and to Greek: [2]righteousness

γὰρ θεοῦ ἐν αὐτῷ ἀποκαλύπτεται ἐκ πίστεως εἰς πίστιν,
[1]for of God in it is revealed by faith to faith;

καθὼς γέγραπται, Ὁ.δὲ δίκαιος ἐκ πίστεως ζήσεται.
according as it has been written, But the just by faith shall live.

18 Ἀποκαλύπτεται.γὰρ ὀργὴ θεοῦ ἀπ' οὐρανοῦ ἐπὶ πᾶσαν
For there is revealed wrath of God from heaven upon all

ἀσέβειαν καὶ ἀδικίαν ἀνθρώπων τῶν τὴν ἀλήθειαν ἐν
ungodliness and unrighteousness of men who the truth in

ἀδικίᾳ κατεχόντων. 19 διότι τὸ.γνωστὸν τοῦ θεοῦ
unrighteousness hold. Because that which is known of God

φανερόν ἐστιν ἐν αὐτοῖς, ὁ.[k]γὰρ.θεὸς‖ αὐτοῖς ἐφανέρωσεν·
[2]manifest [1]is among them, for God to them manifested [it];

20 τὰ.γὰρ ἀόρατα αὐτοῦ ἀπὸ κτίσεως κόσμου τοῖς
for the invisible things of him from creation of [the] world by the

ποιήμασιν νοούμενα καθορᾶται, ἥ.τε ἀΐδιος αὐτοῦ δύνα-
things made being understood are perceived, both [2]eternal [1]his power

μις καὶ θειότης, εἰς τὸ εἶναι αὐτοὺς ἀναπολογήτους. 21 διότι
and divinity; for [2]to [3]be [1]them without excuse. Because

γνόντες τὸν θεόν, οὐχ ὡς θεὸν ἐδόξασαν ἢ [l]εὐχαρίσ-
having known God, not as God they glorified [him] or were thank-

τησαν,‖ [m]ἀλλ'‖ ἐματαιώθησαν ἐν τοῖς.διαλογισμοῖς.αὐτῶν, καὶ
ful; but became vain in their reasonings, and

ἐσκοτίσθη ἡ ἀσύνετος αὐτῶν καρδία· 22 φάσκοντες
was darkened the [4]without [5]understanding [2]of [3]them [1]heart: professing

εἶναι σοφοὶ ἐμωράνθησαν, 23 καὶ ἤλλαξαν τὴν δόξαν τοῦ
to be wise they became fools, and changed the glory of the

ἀφθάρτου θεοῦ ἐν ὁμοιώματι εἰκόνος φθαρτοῦ ἀνθρώπου
incorruptible God into a likeness of an image of corruptible man

καὶ πετεινῶν καὶ τετραπόδων καὶ ἑρπετῶν. 24 διὸ [n]καὶ‖
and of birds and quadrupeds and creeping things. Wherefore also

παρέδωκεν αὐτοὺς ὁ θεὸς ἐν ταῖς ἐπιθυμίαις τῶν.καρδιῶν.αὐ-
[2]gave [4]up [3]them [1]God in the desires of their hearts

τῶν εἰς ἀκαθαρσίαν, τοῦ ἀτιμάζεσθαι τὰ.σώματα.αὐτῶν ἐν
to uncleanness, [3]to [4]be [5]dishonoured [1]their [2]bodies between

[o]ἑαυτοῖς·‖ 25 οἵτινες μετήλλαξαν τὴν ἀλήθειαν τοῦ θεοῦ ἐν
themselves: who changed the truth of God into

τῷ ψεύδει, καὶ ἐσεβάσθησαν καὶ ἐλάτρευσαν τῇ κτίσει
falsehood, and reverenced and served the created thing

παρὰ τὸν κτίσαντα, ὅς ἐστιν εὐλογητὸς εἰς τοὺς αἰῶνας.
beyond him who created [it], who is blessed to the ages.

ἀμήν. 26 διὰ.τοῦτο παρέδωκεν αὐτοὺς ὁ θεὸς εἰς πάθη
Amen. For this reason [2]gave [4]up [3]them [1]God to passions

ἀτιμίας· αἵ.τε.γὰρ θήλειαι αὐτῶν μετήλλαξαν τὴν φυσικὴν
of dishonour, [2]both [1]for [4]females [3]their changed the natural

8 First, I thank my God through Jesus
Christ for all of you, that your faith is
spoken of throughout the whole world.
9 For God is my witness (whom I serve in
my spirit in the gospel of His Son) how in my
prayers I mention you without ceasing,
10 always praying, if I by any means now
may be blessed by the will of God to come
to you.
11 For I long to see you so that I may give
to you some spiritual gift, in order that you
may be firmly established.
12 That is, to be comforted together among
you, through faith in one another, both
yours and mine.
13 But I do not want you to be ignorant,
brothers, that I many times purposed to visit
you (so that I might have some fruit among
you too, even as also among the other
Gentiles), but I was kept back until now.
14 I am a debtor both to Greeks and barbarians, both to the wise and the foolish.
15 so that I am ready to preach the gospel
to you who are in Rome also.
16 For I am not ashamed of the gospel of
Christ. For it is the power of God to salvation
to everyone who believes – to the Jew first,
and to the Greek.
17 For in it the righteousness of God is revealed from faith to faith, even as it has been
written, "But the just shall live by faith."

18 For God's wrath is revealed from Heaven
on all ungodliness and unrighteousness of
men, who suppress the truth in unrighteousness.
19 Because that which is known about God
is clearly known within them, for God
plainly showed it to them.
20 For the unseen things of Him from the
creation of the world are clearly seen, being
understood by the things that are made
both His eternal power and Godhead, in
order for them to be without excuse.
21 Because when they knew God, they did
not glorify Him as God, neither were they
thankful. But they became worthless in their
thoughts, and their foolish heart was darkened.
22 Claiming to be wise, they became fools,
23 and they changed the glory of the
immortal God into a likeness of an image of
man that dies, and of birds and four-footed
animals and creeping things.
24 For this reason God also gave them up to
uncleanness in the lusts of their hearts, to
dishonor their bodies between themselves:
25 who changed the truth of God into a lie
and worshiped and served the created thing
more than the Creator, who is blessed
forever. Amen!
26 For this reason God gave them up to vile
passions of dishonor. For even their females
changed the natural use into that which is

χρῆσιν εἰς τὴν παρὰ φύσιν· 27 ὁμοίως.[p]τε" ·καὶ οἱ [q]ἄῤῥενες"
use into that contrary to nature; and in like manner also the males
ἀφέντες τὴν φυσικὴν χρῆσιν τῆς θηλείας, ἐξεκαύθησαν ἐν τῇ
having left the natural use of the female, were inflamed in
ὀρέξει.αὐτῶν εἰς ἀλλήλους, [r]ἄρσενες" ἐν [s]ἄρσεσιν" τὴν
their lust towards one another, males with males
ἀσχημοσύνην κατεργαζόμενοι, καὶ τὴν ἀντιμισθίαν ἣν ἔδει
[3]shame [1]working [2]out, and the recompense which was fit
τῆς.πλάνης.αὐτῶν ἐν ·ἑαυτοῖς ἀπολαμβάνοντες. 28 καὶ
of their error in themselves receiving. And
καθὼς οὐκ.ἐδοκίμασαν τὸν θεὸν ἔχειν ἐν ἐπιγνώσει,
according as they did not approve [3]God [1]to [2]have in [their] knowledge,
παρέδωκεν αὐτοὺς ὁ θεὸς εἰς ἀδόκιμον νοῦν, ποιεῖν τὰ μὴ
[2]gave [4]up [3]them [1]God to an unapproving mind, to do things not
καθήκοντα, 29 πεπληρωμένους πάσῃ ἀδικίᾳ, [t]πορνείᾳ,"
fitting; being filled with all unrighteousness, fornication,
[v]πονηρίᾳ, πλεονεξίᾳ, κακίᾳ·" μεστοὺς φθόνου, φόνου, ἔριδος,
wickedness, covetousness, malice; full of envy, murder, strife,
δόλου, κακοηθείας· ψιθυριστάς, 30 καταλάλους, θεοστυγεῖς,
guile, evil dispositions; whisperers, slanderers, hateful to God,
ὑβριστάς, ὑπερηφάνους, ἀλαζόνας, ἐφευρετὰς κακῶν,
insolent, proud, vaunting, inventors of evil things,
γονεῦσιν ἀπειθεῖς, 31 ἀσυνέτους, ἀσυνθέτους, ἀ-
to parents disobedient, without understanding, perfidious, without
στόργους, [w]ἀσπόνδους," ἀνελεήμονας· 32 οἵτινες τὸ
natural affection, implacable, unmerciful; who the
δικαίωμα τοῦ θεοῦ ἐπιγνόντες, ὅτι οἱ τὰ.τοιαῦτα
righteous judgment of God having known, that those such things
πράσσοντες ἄξιοι θανάτου εἰσίν, οὐ μόνον αὐτὰ ποιοῦσιν,
doing worthy of death are, not only [2]them [1]practise,
ἀλλὰ καὶ συνευδοκοῦσιν τοῖς πράσσουσιν.
but also are consenting to those that do [them].

2 Διὸ ἀναπολόγητος εἶ, ὦ ἄνθρωπε, πᾶς ὁ κρίνων·
Wherefore inexcusable thou art, O man, every one who judgest,
ἐν.ᾧ.γὰρ κρίνεις τὸν ἕτερον, σεαυτὸν κατακρίνεις·
for in that in which thou judgest the other, thyself thou condemnest:
τὰ.γὰρ αὐτὰ πράσσεις ὁ κρίνων. 2 οἴδαμεν [x]δὲ" ὅτι τὸ
for the same things thou doest who judgest. [2]We [3]know [1]but that the
κρῖμα τοῦ θεοῦ ἐστιν κατὰ ἀλήθειαν ἐπὶ τοὺς τὰ τοιαῦτα
judgment of God is according to truth upon those that such things
πράσσοντας. 3 λογίζῃ.δὲ τοῦτο, ὦ ἄνθρωπε, ὁ κρίνων
do. And reckonest thou this, O man, who judgest
τοὺς τὰ.τοιαῦτα πράσσοντας καὶ ποιῶν αὐτά, ὅτι
those that such things do, and practisest them [thyself], that
σὺ ἐκφεύξῃ τὸ κρῖμα τοῦ θεοῦ; 4 ἢ τοῦ πλούτου τῆς χρη-
thou shalt escape the judgment of God? or the riches of the kind-
στότητος αὐτοῦ καὶ τῆς ἀνοχῆς καὶ τῆς μακροθυμίας κατα-
ness of him and the forbearance and the long-suffering despisest
φρονεῖς, ἀγνοῶν ὅτι τὸ χρηστὸν τοῦ θεοῦ εἰς μετάνοιάν σε
thou, not knowing that the kindness of God to repentance thee
ἄγει; 5 κατὰ.δὲ τὴν.σκληρότητά.σου καὶ ἀμετανόητον
leads? but according to thy hardness and impenitent
καρδίαν θησαυρίζεις σεαυτῷ ὀργὴν ἐν ἡμέρᾳ ὀργῆς καὶ ἀπο-
heart treasurest up to thyself wrath in a day of wrath and re-
καλύψεως δικαιοκρισίας τοῦ θεοῦ, 6 ὃς ἀποδώσει ἑκάστῳ
velation of righteous judgment of God, who will render to each
κατὰ τὰ.ἔργα.αὐτοῦ. 7 τοῖς μὲν καθ' ὑπομονὴν ἔργου
according to his works: to those that with endurance in [2]work
ἀγαθοῦ, δόξαν καὶ τιμὴν καὶ ἀφθαρσίαν ζητοῦσιν, ζωὴν
[1]good, glory and honour and incorruptibility are seeking— life
αἰώνιον. 8 τοῖς.δὲ ἐξ ἐριθείας, καὶ ἀπειθοῦσιν [y]μὲν" τῇ
eternal. But to those of contention, and who disobey the
ἀληθείᾳ, πειθομένοις.δὲ τῇ ἀδικίᾳ, [z]θυμὸς καὶ ὀργή,"
truth, but obey unrighteousness— indignation and wrath,
9 θλίψις καὶ στενοχωρία, ἐπὶ πᾶσαν ψυχὴν ἀνθρώπου τοῦ
tribulation and strait, on every soul of man that
κατεργαζομένου τὸ κακόν, Ἰουδαίου.τε πρῶτον καὶ Ἕλληνος·
works out evil, both of Jew first and of Greek;
10 δόξα.δὲ καὶ τιμὴ καὶ εἰρήνη παντὶ τῷ ἐργαζομένῳ τὸ
but glory and honour and peace to everyone that works
ἀγαθόν, Ἰουδαίῳ.τε πρῶτον καὶ Ἕλληνι· 11 οὐ.γάρ.ἐστιν
good, both to Jew first, and to Greek: for there is not
[a]προσωποληψία" παρὰ τῷ θεῷ. 12 ὅσοι.γὰρ ἀνόμως ἥμαρτον,
respect of persons with God. For as many as without law sinned,
ἀνόμως καὶ ἀπολοῦνται· καὶ ὅσοι ἐν νόμῳ ἥμαρτον, διὰ
without law also shall perish; and as many as in law sinned, by
νόμου κριθήσονται, 13 οὐ.γὰρ οἱ ἀκροαταὶ [b]τοῦ" νόμου δίκαιοι
law shall be judged, (for not the hearers of the law [are] just
παρὰ [c]τῷ" θεῷ, ἀλλ' οἱ ποιηταὶ [b]τοῦ" νόμου δικαιωθήσονται.
with God, but the doers of the law shall be justified.
14 Ὅταν.γὰρ ἔθνη τὰ μὴ νόμον ἔχοντα φύσει τὰ
For when nations which [2]not [3]law [1]have by nature the things

contrary to nature –
27 and in the same way also, leaving the
natural use of the woman, the men were
inflamed in their lust towards one another,
men working out shame with men and
receiving within themselves that reward
which was fitting for their deceitful delu-
sion.
28 And just as much as they did not think it
good to have God in *their* knowledge, God
gave them up to a mind that was not fit for
any good, to do those things which were not
right,
29 being filled with all kinds of unrighteousness – fornication, wickedness, covetousness, malice – *being* full of envy, murder,
quarrels, deceit, evil habits. *They became*
whisperers,
30 slanderers, God-haters, insolent, proud,
braggarts, devisers of evil things, disobedient
to parents,
31 without understanding, impossible to
trust, without natural love, unforgiving and
without mercy.
32 *They* knew the righteous judgment of
God, that those doing such things are
worthy of death, *but* not only do *they*
practice them, but they also delight in those
who do so.
2 1 For this reason you are without excuse, O
man, every one who judges, for you condemn yourself in that in which you judge
the other, for you who judge do the same
things.
2 But we know that the judgment of God is
according to truth on those who do such
things.
3 And, O man, who judge those that do such
things, yet keep on practicing them, do you
think this, that you shall escape the
judgment of God?
4 Or do you despise the riches of His goodness and forbearance and long-suffering, not
knowing that the goodness of God leads you
to repentance?
5 But according to your hardness and stub-
born heart, you are storing up wrath for
yourself in the Day of wrath and revelation
of God's righteous Judgment.
6 *For He* will give to each according to his
works:
7 everlasting life indeed to those who with
patience in good work are seeking glory and
honor and incorruptibility.
8 But wrath and anger *shall be given* to the
ones who rebel and who do not obey the
truth, but obey that which is wrong.
9 Trouble and great pain *will come* on every
soul of man who works out evil – both of
the Jew first, and of the Greek.
10 But glory and honor and peace *will come*
to everyone who works out good – both to
the Jew first and to the Greek.
11 For there is no respect of persons with
God.
12 For as many as sinned without Law shall
also be lost without Law. And as many as
sinned within Law shall be judged by Law.
13 (For not the hearers of the Law *are*
righteous with God, but the doers of the
Law will be counted righteous.
14 For when the Gentiles, who do not have
the Law) do by nature the things of the

τοῦ νόμου [d]ποιῇ,[ll] οὗτοι νόμον μὴ ἔχοντες, ἑαυτοῖς εἰσιν
of the law practise, these, law not having, to themselves are
νόμος· 15 οἵτινες ἐνδείκνυνται τὸ ἔργον τοῦ νόμου γραπτὸν
a law; who shew the work of the law written
ἐν ταῖς.καρδίαις.αὐτῶν, [e]συμμαρτυρούσης[ll] αὐτῶν τῆς συνει-
in their hearts, [3]bearing [4]witness [5]with [1]their [2]con-
δήσεως, καὶ μεταξὺ ἀλλήλων τῶν λογισμῶν κατηγορούντων
science, and between one another the reasonings accusing
ἢ καὶ ἀπολογουμένων, 16 ἐν ἡμέρᾳ [f]ὅτε[ll] κρινεῖ ὁ θεὸς
or also defending;) in a day when [2]shall [3]judge [1]God
τὰ κρυπτὰ τῶν ἀνθρώπων, κατὰ τὸ.εὐαγγέλιόν.μου, διὰ
the secrets of men, according to my glad tidings, by
[g]Ἰησοῦ χριστοῦ.[ll]
Jesus Christ.

17 [h]"Ἴδε[ll] σὺ Ἰουδαῖος ἐπονομάζῃ, καὶ ἐπαναπαύῃ [i]τῷ[ll]
Lo, thou a Jew art named, and restest in the
νόμῳ, καὶ καυχᾶσαι ἐν θεῷ, 18 καὶ γινώσκεις τὸ θέλημα, καὶ
law, and boastest in God, and knowest the will, and
δοκιμάζεις τὰ διαφέροντα, κατηχούμενος ἐκ τοῦ
approvest the things that are more excellent, being instructed out of the
νόμου· 19 πέποιθάς.τε σεαυτὸν ὁδηγὸν εἶναι τυφλῶν,
law; and art persuaded [that] thyself a guide art of [the] blind,
φῶς τῶν ἐν σκότει, 20 παιδευτὴν ἀφρόνων, διδάσκαλον
a light of those in darkness, an instructor of [the] foolish, a teacher
νηπίων, ἔχοντα τὴν μόρφωσιν τῆς γνώσεως καὶ τῆς ἀληθείας
of infants, having the form of knowledge and of the truth
ἐν τῷ νόμῳ· 21 ὁ.οὖν διδάσκων ἕτερον, σεαυτὸν οὐ δι-
in the law: thou then that teachest another, thyself [3]not [1]dost
δάσκεις; ὁ κηρύσσων μὴ κλέπτειν, κλέπτεις; 22 ὁ
[2]thou teach? thou that proclaimest not to steal, dost thou steal? thou that
λέγων μὴ μοιχεύειν, μοιχεύεις; ὁ
sayest not to commit adultery, dost thou commit adultery? thou that
βδελυσσόμενος τὰ εἴδωλα, ἱεροσυλεῖς; 23 ὃς ἐν
abhorrest idols, dost thou commit sacrilege? thou who in
νόμῳ καυχᾶσαι, διὰ τῆς παραβάσεως τοῦ νόμου τὸν θεὸν
law boastest, through the transgression of the law [3]God
ἀτιμάζεις; 24 Τὸ.γὰρ ὄνομα τοῦ θεοῦ δι' ὑμᾶς βλασ-
[1]dishonourest [2]thou? For the name of God through you is blas-
φημεῖται ἐν τοῖς ἔθνεσιν, καθὼς γέγραπται. 25 Περι-
phemed among the nations, according as it has been written. [2]Circum-
τομὴ μὲν. γὰρ ὠφελεῖ ἐὰν νόμον πράσσῃς· ἐὰν.δὲ
cision [3]indeed [1]for profits if [the] law thou doest; but if
παραβάτης νόμου ᾖς, ἡ.περιτομή.σου ἀκροβυστία γέγονεν.
a transgressor of law thou art, thy circumcision uncircumcision has become.
26 ἐὰν οὖν ἡ ἀκροβυστία τὰ δικαιώματα τοῦ νόμου φυλάσ-
If therefore the uncircumcision the requirements of the law keep,
σῃ, [k]οὐχὶ[ll] ἡ.ἀκροβυστία.αὐτοῦ εἰς περιτομὴν λογισθήσεται;
[2]not [3]his [4]uncircumcision [5]for [6]circumcision [1]shall be reckoned?
27 καὶ κρινεῖ ἡ ἐκ φύσεως ἀκροβυστία, τὸν νόμον τελοῦσα,
and [8]shall [9]judge [1]the [3]by [4]nature [2]uncircumcision, [6]the [7]law [5]fulfilling,
σὲ τὸν διὰ γράμματος καὶ περιτομῆς παραβάτην νόμου;
thee who with letter and circumcision [art] a transgressor of law?
28 οὐ.γὰρ ὁ ἐν.τῷ.φανερῷ Ἰουδαῖός ἐστιν, οὐδὲ
For not he that [is one] outwardly [2]a [3]Jew, [1]is, neither
ἡ ἐν.τῷ.φανερῷ ἐν σαρκὶ περιτομή· 29 [l]ἀλλ'[ll] ὁ
that outwardly in flesh [is] circumcision: but he that [is]
ἐν.τῷ.κρυπτῷ Ἰουδαῖος, καὶ περιτομὴ καρδίας ἐν πνεύ-
hiddenly a Jew [is one]; and circumcision [is] of heart, in spi-
ματι, οὐ.γράμματι· οὗ ὁ ἔπαινος οὐκ ἐξ ἀνθρώπων,
rit, not in letter; of whom the praise [is] not of men,
[m]ἀλλ'[ll] ἐκ τοῦ θεοῦ.
but of God.

3 Τί οὖν τὸ περισσὸν τοῦ Ἰουδαίου, ἢ τίς ἡ ὠφέλεια
What then [is] the superiority of the Jew? or what the profit
τῆς περιτομῆς; 2 πολὺ κατὰ πάντα τρόπον. πρῶτον μὲν
of the circumcision? Much in every way: [2]first
[n]γὰρ[ll] ὅτι ἐπιστεύθησαν τὰ λόγια τοῦ θεοῦ. 3 τί.γάρ, εἰ
[1]for that they were entrusted with the oracles of God. For what, if
ἠπίστησάν τινες; μὴ ἡ.ἀπιστία.αὐτῶν τὴν πίστιν τοῦ θεοῦ
[3]not [2]believed [1]some? [5]their [6]unbelief [11]the [12]faith [13]of [14]God
καταργήσει; 4 μὴ.γένοιτο· γινέσθω.δὲ ὁ θεὸς ἀληθής,
[4]shall [7]make [8]of [9]no [10]effect? may it not be! but let [2]be [1]God [3]true,
πᾶς.δὲ ἄνθρωπος ψεύστης, [o]καθὼς[ll] γέγραπται, Ὅπως
and every man false, according as it has been written, That
ἂν.δικαιωθῇς ἐν τοῖς.λόγοις.σου, καὶ [p]νικήσῃς[ll] ἐν τῷ
thou shouldest be justified in thy words, and overcome in
κρίνεσθαί.σε. 5 Εἰ.δὲ ἡ.ἀδικία.ἡμῶν θεοῦ δικαιοσύνην συνί-
thy being judged. But if our unrighteousness [2]God's [3]righteousness [1]com-
στησιν, τί ἐροῦμεν; μὴ ἄδικος ὁ θεὸς ὁ ἐπιφέρων τὴν
mend, what shall we say? [is] [2]unrighteous [1]God who inflicts
ὀργήν; κατὰ ἄνθρωπον λέγω. 6 μὴ.γένοιτο· ἐπεὶ πῶς
wrath? According to man I speak. May it not be! since how

Law, not having the Law, they are a law to
themselves,
15 showing the work of the law written in
their hearts, their conscience bearing witness
with them. And the thoughts *which passed*
between one another *will be* accusing or
excusing *them*;
16 on the Day when God shall judge the
hidden things of men according to my
gospel, by Jesus Christ.
17 Behold! You are called a Jew and rest in
the Law and boast in God,
18 and know the will *of God*, and approve
the things that are more excellent, being
instructed out of the Law,
19 and are sure that you yourself are a
guide of the blind, a light of those in
darkness,
20 a teacher of foolish ones, a teacher of
babes, having the pattern of knowledge and
of truth in the Law.
21 You, then, who are teaching another, do
you teach yourself? You who are preaching
not to steal, do you steal?
22 You who are advising not to commit
adultery, do you commit adultery? You who
hate idols, do you rob temples?
23 You who boast in the Law, do you dishon-
or God through the breaking of the Law?
24 For the name of God is blasphemed
among the Gentiles because of you, even as
it has been written.
25 For if you keep the Law, circumcision
indeed profits. But if you are a breaker of
the Law, your circumcision has become no
circumcision.
26 If, then, one not circumcised keeps the
demands of the Law, shall his lack of circumcision not be counted for circumcision?
27 And shall not the one who lacks circumcision by nature *by* fulfilling the Law judge
you, who with letter and circumcision *are* a
breaker of the Law?
28 For he is not a Jew who is *so* outwardly,
neither is circumcision that which is outward
in flesh –
29 but he *is* a Jew who is *so* inwardly. And
circumcision is of the heart, *in* spirit, not in
letter – of whom the praise is not of men,
but of God.
3 1 Then what is the advantage of the Jew?
Or what is the profit of circumcision?
2 Much in every way! For indeed, first, they
were entrusted with the words of God.
3 For what if some did not believe? Will
their not believing make the faith of God of
no use?
4 Let it not be! But let God be true and
every man a liar, just as it has been written,
"that You should be justified in Your words
and may overcome when You are called into
judgment."
5 But if our unrighteousness shows forth
the righteousness of God, what shall we say?
Is God unrighteous, who lays on wrath? (I
speak as a man.)
6 Let it not be *said!* Otherwise how shall

κρινεῖ ὁ θεὸς τὸν κόσμον; 7 εἰ [q]γὰρ" ἡ ἀλήθεια τοῦ θεοῦ
shall [2]judge [1]God the world? [2]If [1]for the truth of God
ἐν τῷ.ἐμῷ.ψεύσματι ἐπερίσσευσεν εἰς τὴν.δόξαν.αὐτοῦ, τί ἔτι
in my lie abounded to his glory, why yet
κἀγὼ ὡς ἁμαρτωλὸς κρίνομαι; 8 καὶ μὴ καθὼς βλασ-
[3]also [2]I [4]as [5]a [6]sinner [1]am judged? and not, according as we are
φημούμεθα, καὶ καθώς φασίν τινες ἡμᾶς λέγειν, "Οτι
injuriously charged and according as [2]affirm [1]some [that] we say,
ποιήσωμεν τὰ.κακὰ ἵνα ἔλθῃ τὰ.ἀγαθά; ὧν τὸ κρῖμα
Let us practise evil things that [3]may [4]come [1]good [2]things? whose judgment
ἔνδικόν ἐστιν.
[2]just [1]is.

9 Τί οὖν; προεχόμεθα; οὐ.πάντως· προῃτιασάμεθα.γὰρ
What then? are we better? not at all: for we before charged
Ἰουδαίους.τε καὶ Ἕλληνας πάντας ὑφ' ἁμαρτίαν εἶναι,
both Jews and Greeks all [3]under [4]sin [[1]with] [2]being:
10 καθὼς γέγραπται, "Οτι οὐκ.ἔστιν δίκαιος οὐδὲ
according as it has been written, There is not a righteous one, not even
εἷς· 11 οὐκ.ἔστιν [r]ὁ" συνιῶν, οὐκ.ἔστιν [s]ὁ" ἐκζητῶν
one: there is not [one] that understands, there is not [one] that seeks after
τὸν θεόν. 12 πάντες ἐξέκλιναν, ἅμα [t]ἠχρειώθη-
God. All did go out of the way, together they became unprofit-
σαν·" οὐκ.ἔστιν [v] ποιῶν χρηστότητα, οὐκ.ἔστιν ἕως
able; there is not [one] practising kindness, there is not so much as
ἑνός. 13 τάφος ἀνεῳγμένος ὁ.λάρυγξ.αὐτῶν, ταῖς γλώσσαις
one; [3]sepulchre [1]an [2]opened [is] their throat, with [2]tongues
αὐτῶν ἐδολιοῦσαν· ἰὸς ἀσπίδων ὑπὸ τὰ.χείλη.αὐτῶν·
[1]their they used deceit: poison of asps [is] under their lips:
14 ὧν τὸ στόμα [w] ἀρᾶς καὶ πικρίας γέμει· 15 ὀξεῖς οἱ
of whom the mouth of cursing and of bitterness is full; swift
πόδες.αὐτῶν ἐκχέαι αἷμα· 16 σύντριμμα καὶ ταλαιπωρία
their feet to shed blood; ruin and misery [are]
ἐν ταῖς.ὁδοῖς.αὐτῶν· 17 καὶ ὁδὸν εἰρήνης οὐκ.ἔγνωσαν.
in their ways; and a way of peace they did not know;
18 οὐκ.ἔστιν φόβος θεοῦ ἀπέναντι τῶν.ὀφθαλμῶν.αὐτῶν.
there is no fear of God before their eyes.
19 Οἴδαμεν.δὲ ὅτι ὅσα ὁ νόμος λέγει, τοῖς ἐν τῷ νόμῳ
Now we know that whatsoever the law says, to those in the law
λαλεῖ· ἵνα πᾶν στόμα φραγῇ, καὶ ὑπόδικος γένηται
it speaks, that every mouth may be stopped, and under judgment be
πᾶς ὁ κόσμος τῷ θεῷ. 20 διότι ἐξ ἔργων νόμου οὐ δικαιω-
all the world to God. Wherefore by works of law [2]not [1]shall be
θήσεται πᾶσα σὰρξ ἐνώπιον αὐτοῦ· διὰ.γὰρ νόμου ἐπί-
justified any (*lit.* all) flesh before him; for through law [is] know-
γνωσις ἁμαρτίας.
ledge of sin.

21 Νυνὶ.δὲ χωρὶς νόμου δικαιοσύνη θεοῦ πεφανέρωται,
But now apart from law righteousness of God has been manifested,
μαρτυρουμένη ὑπὸ τοῦ νόμου καὶ τῶν προφητῶν· 22 δι-
being borne witness to by the law and the prophets: [2]right-
καιοσύνη δὲ θεοῦ διὰ πίστεως Ἰησοῦ χριστοῦ, εἰς πάντας
eousness [1]even of God through faith of Jesus Christ, towards all
[x]καὶ ἐπὶ πάντας" τοὺς πιστεύοντας· οὐ.γάρ.ἐστιν διαστολή·
and upon all those that believe: for there is no difference:
23 πάντες.γὰρ ἥμαρτον καὶ ὑστεροῦνται τῆς δόξης τοῦ θεοῦ,
for all sinned and come short of the glory of God;
24 δικαιούμενοι δωρεὰν τῇ.αὐτοῦ.χάριτι, διὰ τῆς ἀπολυ-
being justified gratuitously by his grace, through the re-
τρώσεως τῆς ἐν χριστῷ Ἰησοῦ, 25 ὃν προέθετο ὁ θεὸς
demption which [is] in Christ Jesus; whom [2]set [3]forth [1]God
ἱλαστήριον διὰ [y]τῆς" πίστεως ἐν τῷ.αὐτοῦ.αἵματι, εἰς ἔν-
a mercy seat through faith in his blood, for a shew-
δειξιν τῆς.δικαιοσύνης.αὐτοῦ, διὰ τὴν πάρεσιν τῶν
ing forth of his righteousness, in respect of the passing by the
προγεγονότων ἁμαρτημάτων 26 ἐν τῇ ἀνοχῇ τοῦ
[2]that [3]had [4]before [5]taken [6]place [1]sins in the forbearance
θεοῦ, πρὸς [z] ἔνδειξιν τῆς.δικαιοσύνης.αὐτοῦ ἐν τῷ νῦν
of God; for [the] shewing forth of his righteousness in the present
καιρῷ, εἰς τὸ εἶναι.αὐτὸν δίκαιον καὶ δικαιοῦντα τὸν ἐκ
time, for his being just and justifying him that [is] of [the]
πίστεως Ἰησοῦ. 27 Ποῦ οὖν ἡ καύχησις; ἐξεκλείσθη.
faith of Jesus. Where then [is] the boasting? It was excluded.
διὰ ποίου νόμου; τῶν ἔργων; οὐχί, ἀλλὰ διὰ νόμου
Through what law? of works? No, but through a law
πίστεως. 28 λογιζόμεθα [a]οὖν" [b]πίστει δικαιοῦσθαι" ἄνθρω-
of faith. [2]We [3]reckon [1]therefore [9]by [10]faith [6]to [7]be [8]justified [4]a [5]man
πον, χωρὶς ἔργων νόμου. 29 ἢ Ἰουδαίων ὁ θεὸς μόνον;
apart from works of law. Of Jews [is he] the God only?
οὐχὶ.[c]δὲ" καὶ ἐθνῶν; ναὶ καὶ ἐθνῶν· 30 [d]ἐπείπερ" εἷς
and not also of Gentiles? Yea, also of Gentiles: since indeed one
ὁ θεὸς ὃς δικαιώσει περιτομὴν ἐκ πίστεως, καὶ
God [it is] who will justify [the] circumcision by faith, and

God judge the world?
7 For if in my lie the truth of God overflowed to His glory, why am I still judged as
a sinner?
8 And why not (as we are wrongly accused,
and as some report that we say), let us
practice evil so that good may come
whose judgment is just.
9 What then? Are we better? Not at all! For
we have before charged both Jews and
Greeks with being all under sin,
10 as it has been written, "There is none
righteous, no, not one!
11 There is none that understands, there is
not one that seeks after God.
12 All have gone out of the way. Together
they have become worthless. There is none
that is doing good, no, not one!
13 Their throat is an opened grave. They
deceived with their tongues. The poison of
asps is under their lips.
14 *Their* mouth is full of cursing and
bitterness.
15 Their feet *are* swift to shed blood.
16 Ruin and misery are in their ways,
17 and they have not known the way of
peace.
18 There is no fear of God before their
eyes."
19 Now we know that whatever the Law
says, it speaks to those within the Law, so
that every mouth may be stopped and all the
world be under judgment to God.
20 For this reason no flesh shall be justified
before Him by works of Law – for *the*
knowledge of sin *comes* by means of Law.
21 But God's righteousness has been
revealed apart from Law, being witnessed by
the Law and the Prophets –
22 even the righteousness of God through
faith of Jesus Christ, towards all and on all
those who believe. For there is no difference,
23 for all have sinned and come short of the
glory of God,
24 being justified as a free gift, by His grace,
through the redemption which is in Christ
Jesus.
25 God has set *Him* out as a mercy seat
through faith in His blood, for the revealing of
His righteousness (through the passing by of
those sins committed beforehand, in the forbearance of God);
26 for the revealing of His righteousness in
the present time, that He might be just and the
justifier of him who is of the faith of Jesus.
27 Where then is the boasting? It was shut
out. By what Law? Of works? No! But by a
law of faith.
28 So we conclude that a man is justified by
faith, without the works of Law.
29 *Is He* the God of the Jews only, and not
of the Gentiles too? Yes, also of Gentiles,
30 since indeed *it is* one God who will
justify the circumcision by faith and those

ἀκροβυστίαν διὰ τῆς πίστεως. 31 νόμον οὖν καταργοῦ-
uncircumcision through faith. [b]Law [3]then [1]do [2]we [4]make of no
μεν διὰ τῆς πίστεως; μὴ.γένοιτο· ἀλλὰ νόμον [c]ἱστῶμεν.‖
effect through faith? May it not be! but [3]law [1]we [2]establish.

4 Τί οὖν ἐροῦμεν [f]Ἀβραὰμ τὸν.πατέρα.ἡμῶν εὑρηκέναι‖
What then shall we say Abraham our father has found
κατὰ σάρκα; 2 εἰ.γὰρ Ἀβραὰμ ἐξ ἔργων ἐδικαιώθη, ἔχει
according to flesh? For if Abraham by works was justified, he has
καύχημα, ἀλλ' οὐ πρὸς [g]τὸν‖ θεόν. 3 τί.γὰρ ἡ γραφὴ
ground of boasting, but not towards God. For what [2]the [3]scripture
λέγει; Ἐπίστευσεν.δὲ Ἀβραὰμ τῷ θεῷ, καὶ ἐλογίσθη αὐτῷ
[1]says? And [2]believed [1]Abraham God, and it was reckoned to him
εἰς δικαιοσύνην. 4 Τῷ.δὲ ἐργαζομένῳ ὁ μισθὸς οὐ.λογίζεται
for righteousness. Now to him that works the reward is not reckoned
κατὰ χάριν, ἀλλὰ κατὰ [i]τὸ‖ ὀφείλημα· 5 τῷ.δὲ
according to grace, but according to debt: but to him that
μὴ.ἐργαζομένῳ, πιστεύοντι.δὲ ἐπὶ τὸν δικαιοῦντα τὸν [k]ἀ-
does not work, but believes on him that justifies the un-
σεβῆ,‖ λογίζεται ἡ.πίστις.αὐτοῦ εἰς δικαιοσύνην. 6 καθάπερ
godly, [3]is [4]reckoned [1]his [2]faith for righteousness. Even as
καὶ [l]Δαβὶδ λέγει τὸν μακαρισμὸν τοῦ ἀνθρώπου ᾧ ὁ θεὸς
also David declares the blessedness of the man to whom God
λογίζεται δικαιοσύνην χωρὶς ἔργων, 7 Μακάριοι ὧν
reckons righteousness apart from works: Blessed [they] of whom
ἀφέθησαν αἱ ἀνομίαι, καὶ ὧν ἐπεκαλύφθησαν αἱ ἁμαρτίαι.
are forgiven the lawlessnesses, and of whom are covered the sins:
8 μακάριος ἀνὴρ [m]ᾧ‖ οὐ.μὴ λογίσηται κύριος ἁμαρτίαν.
blessed [the] man to whom in no wise [3]will [4]reckon [[1]the] [2]Lord sin.
9 Ὁ.μακαρισμὸς.οὖν.οὗτος ἐπὶ τὴν περιτομήν, ἢ καὶ ἐπὶ
[Is] this blessedness then on the circumcision, or also on
τὴν ἀκροβυστίαν; λέγομεν.γὰρ [n]ὅτι‖ ἐλογίσθη τῷ Ἀβραὰμ
the uncircumcision? For we say that was reckoned to Abraham
ἡ πίστις εἰς δικαιοσύνην. 10 πῶς οὖν ἐλογίσθη; ἐν περι-
faith for righteousness. How then was it reckoned? [2]in [3]circum-
τομῇ ὄντι, ἢ ἐν ἀκροβυστίᾳ; οὐκ ἐν περιτομῇ, ἀλλ' ἐν ἀκρο-
cision [1]being, or in uncircumcision? Not in circumcision, but in uncir-
βυστίᾳ· 11 καὶ σημεῖον ἔλαβεν περιτομῆς, σφραγῖδα
cumcision. And [the] sign he received of circumcision, [as] seal
τῆς δικαιοσύνης τῆς πίστεως τῆς ἐν τῇ ἀκροβυστίᾳ,
of the righteousness of the faith which [he had] in the uncircumcision,
εἰς τὸ.εἶναι.αὐτὸν πατέρα πάντων τῶν πιστευόντων [o]δι'‖
for him to be father of all those that believe in
ἀκροβυστίας, εἰς τὸ λογισθῆναι [p]καὶ‖ αὐτοῖς [q]τὴν‖ δικαιο-
uncircumcision, for [4]to [5]be [6]reckoned [3]also [7]to [8]them [1]the [2]righteous-
σύνην· 12 καὶ πατέρα περιτομῆς τοῖς οὐκ ἐκ περιτομῆς
ness; and father of circumcision to those not of circumcision
μόνον, ἀλλὰ καὶ τοῖς στοιχοῦσιν τοῖς ἴχνεσιν τῆς ἐν
only, but also to those that walk in the steps of the [2]during
[r]τῇ ἀκροβυστίᾳ πίστεως τοῦ.πατρὸς ἡμῶν Ἀβραάμ.
[3]uncircumcision [1]faith of our father Abraham.

13 Οὐ.γὰρ διὰ νόμου ἡ ἐπαγγελία τῷ Ἀβραὰμ ἢ τῷ
For not by law the promise [was] to Abraham or
σπέρματι.αὐτοῦ, τὸ κληρονόμον αὐτὸν εἶναι [s]τοῦ‖ κόσμου,
to his seed, that heir he should be of the world,
ἀλλὰ διὰ δικαιοσύνης πίστεως. 14 εἰ.γὰρ οἱ ἐκ νόμου
but by righteousness of faith. For if those of law [be]
κληρονόμοι, κεκένωται ἡ πίστις, καὶ κατήργηται ἡ ἐ-
heirs, [2]has [3]been [4]made [5]void [1]faith, and [3]made [4]of [5]no [6]effect [1]the [2]pro-
παγγελία· 15 ὁ.γὰρ.νόμος ὀργὴν κατεργάζεται· οὗ [t]γὰρ‖ οὐκ
mise. For the law [3]wrath [1]works [2]out; [5]where [6]for [8]not
ἔστιν νόμος, οὐδὲ παράβασις. 16 διὰ.τοῦτο ἐκ πίστεως,
[7]is [9]law, neither [is] transgression. Wherefore of faith
ἵνα κατὰ χάριν, εἰς τὸ εἶναι βεβαίαν τὴν
[it is], that according to grace [it might be], for [3]to [4]be [5]sure [1]the
ἐπαγγελίαν παντὶ τῷ σπέρματι, οὐ τῷ ἐκ τοῦ νόμου μόνον,
[2]promise to all the seed, not to that of the law only,
ἀλλὰ καὶ τῷ ἐκ πίστεως Ἀβραάμ, ὅς ἐστιν πατὴρ
but also to that of [the] faith of Abraham, who is father
πάντων.ἡμῶν, 17 καθὼς γέγραπται, Ὅτι πατέρα πολ-
of us all, (according as it has been written, A father of
λῶν ἐθνῶν τέθεικά σε, κατέναντι οὗ ἐπίστευσεν θεοῦ,
many nations I have made thee,) before [2]whom [3]he [4]believed [1]God,
τοῦ ζωοποιοῦντος τοὺς νεκρούς, καὶ καλοῦντος τὰ μὴ
who quickens the dead, and calls the things not
ὄντα ὡς ὄντα. 18 Ὃς παρ' ἐλπίδα [v]ἐπ'‖ ἐλπίδι ἐπίστευσεν,
being as being; who against hope in hope believed,
εἰς τὸ γενέσθαι αὐτὸν πατέρα πολλῶν ἐθνῶν, κατὰ τὸ
for [2]to [3]become [1]him father of many nations, according to that which
εἰρημένον, Οὕτως ἔσται τὸ.σπέρμα.σου· 19 καὶ μὴ ἀσθενήσας
had been said, So shall be thy seed: and not being weak
τῇ πίστει, [w]οὐ‖ κατενόησεν τὸ.ἑαυτοῦ σῶμα [x]ἤδη‖ νενεκρω-
in the faith, [3]not [1]he [2]considered his own body already become

not circumcised through faith.
31 Do we then do away with Law through
faith? Let it not be! Yes, we establish the Law.

CHAPTER 4

1 What then shall we say our father Abraham, according to the flesh, has found?
2 For if Abraham was justified by works, he
has reason to boast – but not towards God.
3 For what does the Scripture say? "And
Abraham believed God. And it was counted
to him for righteousness."
4 Now to him who works, the reward is not
counted according to grace, but according to
debt.
5 But to him who does not work, but
believes on Him who justifies the ungodly,
his faith is counted for righteousness.
6 Even as David also speaks of the blessedness of the man to whom God credits
righteousness apart from works:
7 "Blessed *are they* whose lawless deeds are
forgiven and whose sins are covered.
8 Blessed *is the* man to whom the Lord will
in no way charge sin."
9 *Is* this blessedness then on the circumcision, or also on those not circumcised? For
we say that faith was credited to Abraham
for righteousness.
10 How then was it credited? Was he in
circumcision, or not in circumcision? Not in
circumcision, but in uncircumcision!
11 And he received the sign of circumcision
as a seal of the righteousness of the faith
which *he had* in uncircumcision – for him to
be father to those who believe, *though still*
in uncircumcision – for righteousness also to
be credited to them.
12 And *that he might be* father of circumcision to those who are not of circumcision
only, but also to those who walk in the steps
of the faith our father Abraham had during
uncircumcision.
13 For the promise that he should be heir
of the world *was* not by law to Abraham, or
to his seed, but by righteousness of faith.
14 For if they who are of the Law *are* heirs,
faith has been made of no value and the
promise is made of no effect.
15 For the Law works out wrath – for
where there is no law *there is* no lawbreak-
ing.
16 Because of this *it is* of faith so that *it
might be* according to grace, so that the
promise might be made sure to all the seed –
not to that which is of the Law only, but
also to that which is of Abraham's faith
(who is father of us all).
17 Even as it has been written, "I have
made you a father of many nations." *This
was* before God, whom he believed, who
gives life to the dead and calls the things
which are not as if they were.
18 *For* in hope *he* believed against hope
that he would become the father of many
nations (according to that which has been
said, "So shall your seed be").
19 And not being weak in the faith, he did
not consider his own body already dead

μένον, ἑκατονταέτης που ὑπάρχων, καὶ τὴν νέκρωσιν
dead, [3]a [4]hundred [5]years [6]old [2]about [1]being, and the deadening
τῆς μήτρας Σάῤῥας· 20 εἰς.δὲ τὴν ἐπαγγελίαν τοῦ θεοῦ οὐ
of the womb of Sarah, and at the promise of God [2]not
διεκρίθη τῇ ἀπιστίᾳ, [y]ἀλλ'‖ ἐνεδυναμώθη τῇ πίστει,
[1]doubted through unbelief; but was strengthened in faith,
δοὺς δόξαν τῷ θεῷ, 21 καὶ πληροφορηθεὶς ὅτι ὃ ἐπήγ-
giving glory to God, and being fully assured that what he has
γελται, δυνατός ἐστιν καὶ ποιῆσαι. 22 διὸ [z]καὶ‖ ἐλογίσθη
promised, able he is also to do; wherefore also it was reckoned
αὐτῷ εἰς δικαιοσύνην. 23 Οὐκ.ἐγράφη δὲ δι' αὐτὸν
to him for righteousness. [2]It [3]was [4]not [5]written [1]but on account of him
μόνον, ὅτι ἐλογίσθη αὐτῷ· 24 ἀλλὰ καὶ δι' ἡμᾶς,
only, that it was reckoned to him, but also on account of us,
οἷς μέλλει λογίζεσθαι, τοῖς πιστεύουσιν ἐπὶ τὸν
to whom it is about to be reckoned, to those that believe on him who
ἐγείραντα Ἰησοῦν τὸν.κύριον.ἡμῶν ἐκ νεκρῶν, 25 ὃς
raised Jesus our Lord from among [the] dead, who
παρεδόθη διὰ τὰ.παραπτώματα.ἡμῶν, καὶ ἠγέρθη διὰ τὴν
was delivered for our offences, and was raised for
δικαίωσιν.ἡμῶν.
our justification.

5 Δικαιωθέντες οὖν ἐκ πίστεως, εἰρήνην [a]ἔχομεν‖
Having been justified therefore by faith, peace we have
πρὸς τὸν θεὸν διὰ τοῦ.κυρίου.ἡμῶν Ἰησοῦ χριστοῦ, 2 δι'
toward God through our Lord Jesus Christ, through
οὗ καὶ τὴν προσαγωγὴν ἐσχήκαμεν [b]τῇ πίστει‖ εἰς τὴν χάριν
whom also access we have by faith into [2]grace
ταύτην ἐν ᾗ ἑστήκαμεν· καὶ καυχώμεθα ἐπ' ἐλπίδι τῆς δόξης
[1]this in which we stand, and we boast in hope of the glory
τοῦ θεοῦ. 3 οὐ.μόνον.δέ, ἀλλὰ καὶ [c]καυχώμεθα‖ ἐν ταῖς
of God. And not only [so], but also we boast in
θλίψεσιν, εἰδότες ὅτι ἡ θλίψις ὑπομονὴν κατεργάζεται,
tribulations, knowing that the tribulation [3]endurance [1]works [2]out;
4 ἡ.δὲ ὑπομονὴ δοκιμήν, ἡ.δὲ δοκιμὴ ἐλπίδα, 5 ἡ.δὲ ἐλπὶς
and the endurance proof; and the proof hope; and the hope
οὐ.καταισχύνει· ὅτι ἡ ἀγάπη τοῦ θεοῦ ἐκκέχυται ἐν
does not make ashamed, because the love of God has been poured out in
ταῖς.καρδίαις.ἡμῶν διὰ πνεύματος ἁγίου τοῦ δοθέντος ἡμῖν.
our hearts by the [2]Spirit [1]Holy which was given to us:
6 [d]Ἔτι.γὰρ‖ χριστὸς ὄντων ἡμῶν ἀσθενῶν [e] κατὰ.καιρὸν
for still [5]Christ [2]being [1]we [3]without [4]strength in due time
ὑπὲρ ἀσεβῶν ἀπέθανεν. 7 μόλις.γὰρ ὑπὲρ δικαίου
for [the] ungodly died. For hardly for a just [man]
τις ἀποθανεῖται· ὑπὲρ.γὰρ τοῦ ἀγαθοῦ τάχα τις
[2]any [3]one [1]will die; for on behalf of the good [man] perhaps some one
καὶ τολμᾷ ἀποθανεῖν· 8 συνίστησιν.δὲ τὴν.ἑαυτοῦ ἀγάπην
even might dare to die; but [2]commends [3]his [4]own [5]love
εἰς ἡμᾶς [f]ὁ θεός,‖ ὅτι ἔτι ἁμαρτωλῶν ὄντων ἡμῶν χριστὸς
[6]to [7]us [1]God, that [2]still [4]sinners [3]being [1]we Christ
ὑπὲρ ἡμῶν ἀπέθανεν. 9 πολλῷ οὖν μᾶλλον, δικαιωθέντες
[2]for [3]us [1]died. Much therefore more, having been justified
νῦν ἐν τῷ.αἵματι.αὐτοῦ, σωθησόμεθα δι' αὐτοῦ ἀπὸ τῆς
now by his blood, we shall be saved by him from
ὀργῆς. 10 εἰ.γὰρ ἐχθροὶ ὄντες κατηλλάγημεν τῷ θεῷ διὰ
wrath. For if, [2]enemies [1]being we were reconciled to God through
τοῦ θανάτου τοῦ.υἱοῦ.αὐτοῦ, πολλῷ μᾶλλον καταλλαγέντες
the death of his Son, much more, having been reconciled
σωθησόμεθα ἐν τῇ.ζωῇ.αὐτοῦ· 11 οὐ.μόνον.δέ, ἀλλὰ καὶ
we shall be saved by his life. And not only [so], but also
καυχώμενοι ἐν τῷ θεῷ διὰ τοῦ.κυρίου.ἡμῶν Ἰησοῦ χριστοῦ,
boasting in God through our Lord Jesus Christ,
δι' οὗ νῦν τὴν καταλλαγὴν ἐλάβομεν.
through whom now the reconciliation we received.
12 Διὰ.τοῦτο ὥσπερ δι' ἑνὸς ἀνθρώπου ἡ ἁμαρτία εἰς τὸν
On this account, as by one man sin into the
κόσμον εἰσῆλθεν, καὶ διὰ τῆς ἁμαρτίας ὁ θάνατος, καὶ οὕτως
world entered, and by sin death, and thus
εἰς πάντας ἀνθρώπους [g]ὁ θάνατος‖ διῆλθεν, ἐφ'.ᾧ πάντες
to all men death passed, for that all
ἥμαρτον. 13 ἄχρι.γὰρ νόμου ἁμαρτία ἦν ἐν κόσμῳ·
sinned: (for until law sin was in [the] world;
ἁμαρτία.δὲ οὐκ.ἐλλογεῖται, μὴ.ὄντος νόμου· 14 [h]ἀλλ'‖
but sin is not put to account, there not being law; but
ἐβασίλευσεν ὁ θάνατος ἀπὸ Ἀδὰμ μέχρι [i]Μωσέως‖ καὶ ἐπὶ
[2]reigned [1]death from Adam until Moses even upon
τοὺς μὴ.ἁμαρτήσαντας ἐπὶ τῷ ὁμοιώματι τῆς παραβάσεως
those who had not sinned in the likeness of the transgression
Ἀδάμ, ὅς ἐστιν τύπος τοῦ μέλλοντος. 15 Ἀλλ' οὐχ
of Adam, who is a figure of the coming [one]. But [shall] not
ὡς τὸ παράπτωμα, οὕτως καὶ τὸ χάρισμα.[k] εἰ.γὰρ τῷ
as the offence, so also [be] the free gift? For if by the

(being a hundred years old) and the deadening of Sarah's womb,

20 and did not stagger at the promise of God through unbelief, but was strengthened in faith, giving glory to God,

21 and was fully persuaded that what *God* has promised, He is also able to do.

22 For this reason also it was counted to him for righteousness.

23 But it was not written that it was credited to him for his sake only,

24 but also for our sake, to whom it is going to be credited – to those that believe on Him who raised our Lord Jesus from the dead,

25 who was delivered for our sins and was raised for our justification.

CHAPTER 5

1 Therefore, having been justified by faith, we have peace toward God through our Lord Jesus Christ.

2 Through *Him*, we also have the entrance of faith into this grace in which we stand. And we fill up with rejoicing in hope of the glory of God.

3 And not only so, but we also rejoice exceedingly in troubles, knowing that trouble works out patience,

4 and patience *works out* proven character, and proven character hope.

5 And this hope does not make us ashamed, because the love of God has been poured out in our hearts by the Holy Spirit, who has been given to us.

6 For while we were still without strength, in due time Christ died for the ungodly.

7 Now one will hardly die for a righteous one – someone might even dare to die for a good one.

8 But God proves His own love to us in that while we were still sinners, Christ died for us!

9 Much more then, having been justified now by His blood, we shall be saved from wrath by Him.

10 For if while we were enemies, we were reconciled to God through the death of His Son, much more we are being reconciled *now* – we shall be saved by His life.

11 And not only so, but we also glory in God through our Lord Jesus Christ, by whom we now have received the reconciliation.

12 Because of this, just as sin entered into the world by one man, and death by sin, so death passed to all men because all sinned.

13 (For until the Law, sin was in the world. But sin is not charged when there is no law.

14 Yet death ruled from Adam until Moses, even on those who had not sinned in the likeness of Adam's transgression, who is a type of Him who is coming.)

15 For the free gift, however, is not like the sin. For if by the sin of the one many died,

τοῦ ἑνὸς παραπτώματι οἱ πολλοὶ ἀπέθανον, πολλῷ μᾶλλον
[2]of [3]the [4]one [1]offence the many died, much more
ἡ χάρις τοῦ θεοῦ καὶ ἡ δωρεὰ ἐν χάριτι τῇ τοῦ ἑνὸς
the grace of God, and the gift in grace, which [is] of the one
ἀνθρώπου Ἰησοῦ χριστοῦ εἰς τοὺς πολλοὺς ἐπερίσσευσεν.
man Jesus Christ, to the many did abound.
16 καὶ οὐχ ὡς δι' ἑνὸς ἁμαρτήσαντος τὸ δώρημα·[k]
And [shall] not as by one having sinned [be] the gift?
τὸ.μὲν.γὰρ κρίμα ἐξ ἑνὸς εἰς κατάκριμα, τὸ.δὲ χάρισμα
For the [2]indeed [1]judgment [was] of one to condemnation, but the free gift
ἐκ πολλῶν παραπτωμάτων εἰς δικαίωμα. 17 εἰ.γὰρ τῷ
[is] of many offences to justification. For if by the
τοῦ ἑνὸς παραπτώματι ὁ θάνατος ἐβασίλευσεν διὰ τοῦ ἑνός,
[2]of [3]the [4]one [1]offence death reigned by the one,
πολλῷ μᾶλλον οἱ τὴν περισσείαν τῆς χάριτος καὶ [m]τῆς
much more those the abundance of grace, and of the
δωρεᾶς‖ τῆς δικαιοσύνης λαμβάνοντες, ἐν ζωῇ βασιλεύσουσιν
gift of righteousness receiving, in life shall reign
διὰ τοῦ ἑνὸς Ἰησοῦ χριστοῦ. 18 Ἄρα οὖν ὡς δι' ἑνὸς παρα-
by the one Jesus Christ:) so then as by one of-
πτώματος εἰς πάντας ἀνθρώπους εἰς κατάκριμα,
fence [it was] towards all men to condemnation,
οὕτως καὶ δι' ἑνὸς δικαιώματος εἰς πάντας ἀνθρώ-
so also by one accomplished righteousness towards all men
πους εἰς δικαίωσιν ζωῆς. 19 ὥσπερ.γὰρ διὰ τῆς παρακοῆς
to justification of life. For as by the disobedience
τοῦ ἑνὸς ἀνθρώπου ἁμαρτωλοὶ κατεστάθησαν οἱ πολλοί,
of the one man [5]sinners [3]were [4]constituted [1]the [2]many,
οὕτως καὶ διὰ τῆς ὑπακοῆς τοῦ ἑνὸς δίκαιοι κατασταθήσονται
so also by the obedience of the one [6]righteous [3]shall [4]be [5]constituted
οἱ πολλοί. 20 Νόμος.δὲ παρεισῆλθεν, ἵνα πλεονάσῃ τὸ
[1]the [2]many. But law came in by the bye, that might abound the
παράπτωμα. οὗ.δὲ ἐπλεόνασεν ἡ ἁμαρτία, ὑπερεπερίσσευσεν
offence; but where abounded sin, overabounded
ἡ χάρις· 21 ἵνα ὥσπερ ἐβασίλευσεν ἡ ἁμαρτία ἐν τῷ θανάτῳ,
grace, that as [2]reigned [1]sin in death,
οὕτως καὶ ἡ χάρις βασιλεύσῃ διὰ δικαιοσύνης εἰς ζωὴν
so also grace might reign through righteousness to life
αἰώνιον, διὰ Ἰησοῦ χριστοῦ τοῦ.κυρίου ἡμῶν.
eternal, through Jesus Christ our Lord.
6 Τί οὖν ἐροῦμεν; [n]ἐπιμενοῦμεν‖ τῇ ἁμαρτίᾳ ἵνα ἡ χάρις
What then shall we say? Shall we continue in sin that grace
πλεονάσῃ; 2 μὴ.γένοιτο. οἵτινες.ἀπεθάνομεν τῇ ἁμαρτίᾳ,
may abound? May it not be! We who died to sin,
πῶς ἔτι ζήσομεν ἐν αὐτῇ; 3 ἢ ἀγνοεῖτε ὅτι ὅσοι
how still shall we live in it? Or are ye ignorant that [2]as [3]many [4]as
ἐβαπτίσθημεν εἰς χριστὸν Ἰησοῦν, εἰς τὸν.θάνατον.αὐτοῦ
[1]we were baptized unto Christ Jesus, unto his death
ἐβαπτίσθημεν; 4 συνετάφημεν οὖν αὐτῷ διὰ τοῦ βαπ-
we were baptized? We were buried therefore with him by bap-
τίσματος εἰς τὸν θάνατον· ἵνα ὥσπερ ἠγέρθη χριστὸς
tism unto death, that as [2]was [3]raised [4]up [1]Christ
ἐκ νεκρῶν διὰ τῆς δόξης τοῦ πατρός, οὕτως καὶ
from among [the] dead by the glory of the Father, so also
ἡμεῖς ἐν καινότητι ζωῆς περιπατήσωμεν. 5 Εἰ.γὰρ σύμφυτοι
we in newness of life should walk. For if conjoined
γεγόναμεν τῷ ὁμοιώματι τοῦ.θανάτου.αὐτοῦ, ἀλλὰ.καὶ
we have become in the likeness of his death, so also
τῆς.ἀναστάσεως ἐσόμεθα· 6 τοῦτο γινώσκοντες, ὅτι ὁ παλαιὸς
of [his] resurrection we shall be; this knowing, that [2]old
ἡμῶν ἄνθρωπος συνεσταυρώθη, ἵνα καταργηθῇ τὸ σῶμα
[1]our man was crucified with [him], that might be annulled the body
τῆς ἁμαρτίας, τοῦ μηκέτι δουλεύειν ἡμᾶς τῇ ἁμαρτίᾳ.
of sin, that [2]no [3]longer [4]be [5]subservient [1]we to sin.
7 ὁ.γὰρ ἀποθανὼν δεδικαίωται ἀπὸ τῆς ἁμαρτίας. 8 Εἰ.δὲ
For he that died has been justified from sin. Now if
ἀπεθάνομεν σὺν χριστῷ, πιστεύομεν ὅτι καὶ [o]συζήσομεν‖
we died with Christ, we believe that also we shall live with
αὐτῷ, 9 εἰδότες ὅτι χριστὸς ἐγερθεὶς ἐκ
him, knowing that Christ having been raised up from among [the]
νεκρῶν, οὐκέτι ἀποθνήσκει· θάνατος αὐτοῦ οὐκέτι κυριεύει.
dead, no more dies: death [5]him [1]no [2]more [3]rules [4]over.
10 [p]ὃ‖.γὰρ ἀπέθανεν, τῇ ἁμαρτίᾳ ἀπέθανεν ἐφάπαξ. [p]ὃ‖.δὲ
For in that he died, to sin he died once for all; but in that
ζῇ, ζῇ τῷ θεῷ. 11 οὕτως καὶ ὑμεῖς λογίζεσθε ἑαυτοὺς[q]
he lives, he lives to God. So also ye reckon yourselves
νεκροὺς μὲν [r]εἶναι‖ τῇ ἁμαρτίᾳ, ζῶντας.δὲ τῷ θεῷ, ἐν χριστῷ
[3]dead [4]indeed [1]to [2]be to sin, but alive to God, in Christ
Ἰησοῦ [s]τῷ.κυρίῳ.ἡμῶν.‖ 12 Μὴ οὖν βασιλευέτω ἡ ἁμαρτία
Jesus our Lord. [2]Not [4]therefore [1]let [5]reign [3]sin
ἐν τῷ.θνητῷ.ὑμῶν σώματι, εἰς τὸ ὑπακούειν [t]αὐτῇ ἐν‖ [v]ταῖς
in your mortal body, for to obey it in

much more the grace of God and the gift in
grace, which is of the one Man, Jesus Christ,
overflowed to the many.
16 And the free gift is not as by one who
sinned (for indeed the judgment is of one to
sentence of death) but the free gift is of
many failings to justification.
17 For if by the fall of one, death ruled
through the one, much more those who are
receiving the abundance of grace and the gift
of righteousness shall rule in life by the One,
Jesus Christ.
18 So, then, as through one fall the *sentence* of death was to all men, so also
through one righteous act *the free gift came*
to all men to justification of life.
19 For as through the one man's failure to
obey the many were placed in the category
of sinners, so also through the obedience of
the One, the many shall be placed in the
category of righteous ones.
20 But the Law came in beside, in order
that the offense might increase. But where
sin abounded,
21 grace abounded much more – so that as
sin ruled in death, so also grace might rule
through righteousness to life everlasting
through Jesus Christ, our Lord.

CHAPTER 6

1 What then, shall we say? Shall we go on in
sin so that grace may abound?
2 Let it not be! We who died to sin, how
shall we still live in it?
3 What? Do you not understand that as
many as were baptized into Christ Jesus, we
were baptized into His death?
4 So we were buried with Him through
baptism into death, so that as Christ was
raised from among the dead by the glory of
the Father, so also we should walk in
newness of life.
5 For if we have been joined together in the
likeness of His death, so we shall also
certainly be in resurrection,
6 knowing this, that our old man was
crucified with *Him* so that the body of sin
might be done away with – so that we no
longer should serve sin.
7 For he that has died has been justified
from sin.
8 Now if we died with Christ, we believe
that we shall also live with Him,
9 knowing that Christ, having been raised
from among the dead, He never dies again.
Death does not rule over Him anymore.
10 For in that He died, He died to sin once
for all. But in that He lives, He lives to God.
11 So also you count yourselves truly dead
to sin, but alive to God in Christ Jesus, our
Lord.
12 Therefore, do not let sin be king in your
mortal body, to obey it in its evil desires.

πιθυμίαις.αὐτοῦ·" 13 μηδὲ παριστάνετε τὰ.μέλη.ὑμῶν ὅπλα
its desires. Neither be yielding your members instruments
ἀδικίας τῇ ἁμαρτίᾳ· ἀλλὰ παραστήσατε ἑαυτοὺς τῷ
of unrighteousness to sin, but yield yourselves
θεῷ ʷὡς" ἐκ νεκρῶν ζῶντας, καὶ τὰ.μέλη.ὑμῶν
to God as ²from ³among [⁴the] ⁵dead ¹alive, and your members
ὅπλα δικαιοσύνης τῷ θεῷ. 14 ἁμαρτία.γὰρ ὑμῶν οὐ
instruments of righteousness to God. For sin ⁵you ²not
κυριεύσει· οὐ.γάρ ἐστε ὑπὸ νόμον, ˣἀλλ'" ὑπὸ χάριν.
shall ³rule ⁴over, for ³not ²are ¹ye under law, but under grace.
15 Τί οὖν; ʸἁμαρτήσομεν" ὅτι οὐκ.ἐσμὲν ὑπὸ νόμον,
What then? shall we sin because we are not under law
ᶻἀλλ'" ὑπὸ χάριν; μὴ.γένοιτο. 16 οὐκ.οἴδατε ὅτι ᾧ
but under grace? May it not be! Know ye not that to whom
παριστάνετε ἑαυτοὺς δούλους εἰς ὑπακοήν, δοῦλοί ἐστε
ye yield yourselves bondmen for obedience, bondmen ye are
ᾧ ὑπακούετε, ἤτοι ἁμαρτίας εἰς θάνατον, ἢ ὑπακοῆς
to him whom ye obey, whether of sin to death, or of obedience
εἰς δικαιοσύνην; 17 χάρις.δὲ τῷ.θεῷ, ὅτι ἦτε δοῦλοι τῆς
to righteousness? But thanks [be] to God, that ye were bondmen
ἁμαρτίας, ὑπηκούσατε.δὲ ἐκ καρδίας εἰς ὃν παρεδόθητε
of sin, but ye obeyed from [the] heart ⁵to ⁶which ⁷ye ⁸were ⁹delivered
τύπον διδαχῆς. 18 ἐλευθερωθέντες.δὲ ἀπὸ τῆς ἁμαρτίας,
¹a ²form ³of ⁴teaching. And having been set free from sin,
ἐδουλώθητε τῇ δικαιοσύνῃ. 19 Ἀνθρώπινον λέγω διὰ
ye became bondmen to righteousness. Humanly I speak on account of
τὴν ἀσθένειαν τῆς.σαρκὸς.ὑμῶν. ὥσπερ.γὰρ παρεστήσατε
the weakness of your flesh. For as ye yielded
τὰ.μέλη.ὑμῶν δοῦλα τῇ ἀκαθαρσίᾳ καὶ τῇ ἀνομίᾳ εἰς τὴν
your members in bondage to uncleanness and to lawlessness unto
ἀνομίαν, οὕτως νῦν παραστήσατε τὰ.μέλη.ὑμῶν δοῦλα τῇ
lawlessness, so now yield your members in bondage
δικαιοσύνῃ εἰς ἁγιασμόν. 20 ὅτε.γὰρ δοῦλοι ἦτε τῆς
to righteousness unto sanctification. For when bondmen ye were
ἁμαρτίας, ἐλεύθεροι ἦτε τῇ δικαιοσύνῃ. 21 τίνα οὖν
of sin, free ye were as to righteousness. What ²therefore
καρπὸν εἴχετε τότε, ᶻ ἐφ'.οἷς νῦν ἐπαισχύνεσθε;
¹fruit had ye then, in the [things] of which now ye are ashamed?
τὸᵃ.γὰρ τέλος ἐκείνων θάνατος. 22 νυνὶ.δὲ ἐλευθερω-
for the end of those things [is] death. But now having been
θέντες ἀπὸ τῆς ἁμαρτίας, δουλωθέντες.δὲ τῷ θεῷ, ἔχετε
set free from sin, and having become bondmen to God, ye have
τὸν.καρπὸν.ὑμῶν εἰς ἁγιασμόν, τὸ.δὲ τέλος ζωὴν αἰώνιον.
your fruit unto sanctification, and the end life eternal.
23 τὰ.γὰρ ὀψώνια τῆς ἁμαρτίας θάνατος· τὸ.δὲ χάρισμα
For the wages of sin [is] death; but the free gift
τοῦ θεοῦ ζωὴ αἰώνιος ἐν χριστῷ Ἰησοῦ τῷ.κυρίῳ.ἡμῶν.
of God life eternal in Christ Jesus our Lord.
7 Ἢ.ἀγνοεῖτε, ἀδελφοί, γινώσκουσιν.γὰρ νόμον λαλῶ, ὅτι
Are ye ignorant, brethren, for to those knowing law I speak, that
ὁ νόμος κυριεύει τοῦ ἀνθρώπου ἐφ' ὅσον χρόνον ζῇ;
the law rules over the man for as long ²as ¹time he may live?
2 ἡ.γὰρ ὕπανδρος γυνὴ τῷ ζῶντι ἀνδρὶ δέδεται νόμῳ·
For the married woman to the living husband is bound by law;
ἐὰν.δὲ ἀποθάνῃ ὁ ἀνὴρ κατήργηται ἀπὸ ᵇτοῦ νόμου" τοῦ
but if should die the husband, she is cleared from the law of the
ἀνδρός. 3 ἄρα.οὖν ζῶντος τοῦ ἀνδρὸς μοιχαλὶς χρηματίσει,
husband: so then, ²living ¹the ²husband, an adulteress she shall be called,
ἐὰν γένηται ἀνδρὶ ἑτέρῳ· ἐὰν.δὲ ἀποθάνῃ ὁ ἀνήρ, ἐλευθέρα
if she be to ²man ¹another; but if should die the husband, free
ἐστὶν ἀπὸ τοῦ νόμου, τοῦ.μὴ.εἶναι.αὐτὴν μοιχαλίδα, γενο-
she is from the law, so as for her not to be an adulteress, having
μένην ἀνδρὶ ἑτέρῳ. 4 ὥστε, ἀδελφοί.μου, καὶ ὑμεῖς ἐθανατώ-
become to ²man ¹another. So that, my brethren, also ye were made
θητε τῷ νόμῳ διὰ τοῦ σώματος τοῦ χριστοῦ, εἰς τὸ γενέσθαι
dead to the law by the body of the Christ, for ²to ³be
ὑμᾶς ἑτέρῳ, τῷ ἐκ νεκρῶν ἐγερθέντι, ἵνα καρπο-
¹you to another, who from among [the] dead was raised, that we should
φορήσωμεν τῷ θεῷ. 5 ὅτε.γὰρ ἦμεν ἐν τῇ σαρκί, τὰ παθή-
bring forth fruit to God. For when we were in the flesh, the pas-
ματα τῶν ἁμαρτιῶν τὰ διὰ τοῦ νόμου ἐνηργεῖτο ἐν
sions of sins, which [were] through the law, wrought in
τοῖς.μέλεσιν.ἡμῶν εἰς τὸ καρποφορῆσαι τῷ θανάτῳ· 6 νυνὶ.δὲ
our members to the bringing forth fruit to death; but now
κατηργήθημεν ἀπὸ τοῦ νόμου, ᶜἀποθανόντες" ἐν ᾧ κατει-
we were cleared from the law, having died [in that] in which we were
χόμεθα, ὥστε δουλεύειν ᵈἡμᾶς" ἐν καινότητι πνεύματος, καὶ
held, so that ²should ³serve ¹we in newness of spirit, and
οὐ παλαιότητι γράμματος.
not in oldness of letter.
7 Τί οὖν ἐροῦμεν; ὁ νόμος ἁμαρτία; μὴ.γένοιτο·
What then shall we say? [Is] the law sin? May it not be!

13 Do not give your members as instruments of unrighteousness to sin, but give yourselves completely to God as *one* alive from the dead, and your members as instruments of righteousness to God.

14 For sin shall not lord it over you, for you are not under Law, but under grace.

15 What then? Shall we sin because we are not under Law, but under grace? Let it not be!

16 Do you not know that to whom you give yourselves as slaves for obedience, you are slaves to him whom you obey – whether of sin to death or of obedience to righteousness.

17 But thanks to God, you were the slaves of sin, but you obeyed from the heart the form of teaching to which you were yielded.

18 And being set free from sin, you became slaves to righteousness.

19 I speak in the manner of men, because of the weakness of your flesh. For as you gave your members up in bondage to uncleanness, and to lawless act after lawless act, so now devote your members in bondage to righteousness to holiness.

20 For when you were the slaves of sin, you were free as to righteousness.

21 What fruit did you have then in the things of which you are now ashamed? For the end of those things is death.

22 But now being set free from sin, and having become bondslaves to God, you have your fruit to holiness, and the end, life everlasting.

23 For the wages of sin is death, but the free gift of God is eternal life through Jesus Christ, our Lord.

CHAPTER 7

1 Do you not understand, brothers (for I speak to those who know law), that the Law rules over a man as long as he lives?

2 For the married woman is bound by law to the living husband. But if the husband dies, she is freed from the law of her husband.

3 So, then, while the husband is alive she will be called an adulteress if she becomes another man's. But if the husband should die, she is free from the law, so as not to be an adulteress if she becomes another man's.

4 So that, my brothers, you also were made dead to the Law through the body of Christ, in order for you to become Another's (who was raised from among the dead so that we could bear fruit to God).

5 For when we were in the flesh, the passions of sin (which *were* through the Law) worked in our members to bear fruit to death.

6 But now we have been set free from the Law, being dead to that in which we were held, so that we should serve in newness of spirit and not in oldness of letter.

7 What then shall we say? *Is* the Law sin?

ἀλλὰ τὴν ἁμαρτίαν οὐκ.ἔγνων εἰ.μὴ διὰ νόμου· τήν.τε.γὰρ
But sin I knew not unless by law: for also
ἐπιθυμίαν οὐκ.ᾔδειν εἰ.μὴ ὁ νόμος ἔλεγεν, Οὐκ
lust I had not been conscious of unless the law said, [3]Not
ἐπιθυμήσεις· 8 ἀφορμὴν.δὲ λαβοῦσα ἡ ἁμαρτία διὰ τῆς
[1]thou [2]shalt lust; but [4]an [5]occasion [2]having [3]taken [1]sin by the
ἐντολῆς [e]κατειργάσατο‖ ἐν ἐμοὶ πᾶσαν ἐπιθυμίαν. χωρὶς.γὰρ
commandment worked out in me every lust; for apart from
νόμου ἁμαρτία νεκρά· 9 ἐγὼ.δὲ ἔζων χωρὶς νόμου
law sin [was] dead. But I was alive apart from law
ποτέ· ἐλθούσης.δὲ τῆς ἐντολῆς, ἡ ἁμαρτία ἀνέζησεν, ἐγὼ.δὲ
once; but having come the commandment, sin revived, but I
ἀπέθανον· 10 καὶ εὑρέθη μοι ἡ ἐντολὴ ἡ
died. And was found to me [that] the commandment which [was]
εἰς ζωήν, [f]αὕτη‖ εἰς θάνατον. 11 ἡ.γὰρ.ἁμαρτία ἀφορμὴν
to life, this [to be] to death: for sin [3]an [4]occasion
λαβοῦσα διὰ τῆς ἐντολῆς ἐξηπάτησέν με, καὶ δι' αὐτῆς
[1]having [2]taken by the commandment, deceived me, and by it
ἀπέκτεινεν. 12 ὥστε ὁ.μὲν.νόμος ἅγιος, καὶ ἡ ἐντολὴ
slew [me]. So that the law indeed [is] holy, and the commandment
ἁγία καὶ δικαία καὶ ἀγαθή. 13 Τὸ οὖν ἀγαθὸν ἐμοὶ
holy and just and good. That which then [is] good, to me
[g]γέγονεν‖ θάνατος; μὴ.γένοιτο· [h]ἀλλὰ‖ ἡ ἁμαρτία, ἵνα
has it become death? May it not be! But sin, that
φανῇ ἁμαρτία, διὰ τοῦ ἀγαθοῦ μοι κατεργαζομένη
it might appear sin, by that which [is] good to me working out
θάνατον, ἵνα γένηται καθ'.ὑπερβολὴν ἁμαρτωλὸς ἡ ἁμαρτία
death; that [2]might [3]become [4]excessively [5]sinful [1]sin
διὰ τῆς ἐντολῆς. 14 Οἴδαμεν.γὰρ ὅτι ὁ νόμος πνευματικός
by the commandment. For we know that the law spiritual
ἐστιν· ἐγὼ.δὲ [i]σαρκικός‖ εἰμι, πεπραμένος ὑπὸ τὴν ἁμαρτίαν.
is; but I [2]fleshly [1]am, having been sold under sin.
15 ὃ.γὰρ κατεργάζομαι, οὐ.γινώσκω· οὐ.γὰρ ὃ θέλω, τοῦτο
For what I work out, I do not own: for not what I will, this
πράσσω· ἀλλ' ὃ μισῶ, τοῦτο ποιῶ. 16 εἰ.δὲ ὃ οὐ.θέλω,
I do; but what I hate, this I practise. But if what I do not will,
τοῦτο ποιῶ, [k]σύμφημι‖ τῷ νόμῳ ὅτι καλός. 17 νυνὶ.δὲ
this I practise, I consent to the law that [it is] right. Now then
οὐκέτι ἐγὼ κατεργάζομαι αὐτό, [l]ἀλλ'‖ ἡ [m]οἰκοῦσα‖ ἐν ἐμοὶ
no longer [2]I [1]am working [3]out [4]it; but the [2]dwelling [3]in [4]me
ἁμαρτία. 18 Οἶδα.γὰρ ὅτι οὐκ.οἰκεῖ ἐν ἐμοί, [n]τουτέστιν‖ ἐν
[1]sin. For I know that there dwells not in me, that is in
τῇ.σαρκί.μου, ἀγαθόν· τὸ.γὰρ.θέλειν παράκειταί μοι, τὸ δὲ
my flesh, good: for to will is present with me, but
κατεργάζεσθαι τὸ καλὸν [o]οὐχ.εὑρίσκω.‖ 19 οὐ.γὰρ ὃ θέλω
to work out the right I find not. For not what [2]I [3]will
ποιῶ ἀγαθόν· [p]ἀλλ'‖ ὃ οὐ.θέλω κακόν, τοῦτο πράσ-
[4]do [5]I [6]practise [1]good; but what [2]I [3]do [4]not [5]will [1]evil, this I do.
σω. 20 εἰ.δὲ ὃ οὐ.θέλω [q]ἐγώ,‖ τοῦτο ποιῶ, οὐκέτι
But if what [2]do [3]not [4]will [1]I, this I practise, [it is] no longer
ἐγὼ κατεργάζομαι αὐτό, [p]ἀλλ'‖ ἡ οἰκοῦσα ἐν ἐμοὶ ἁμαρτία.
I [who] work [2]out [1]it, but the [2]dwelling [3]in [4]me [1]sin.
21 Εὑρίσκω ἄρα τὸν νόμον τῷ θέλοντι ἐμοὶ ποιεῖν τὸ καλόν,
I find then the law [3]who [4]will [1]to [2]me to practise the right,
ὅτι ἐμοὶ τὸ κακὸν παράκειται. 22 συνήδομαι.γὰρ τῷ νόμῳ
that me evil is present with. For I delight in the law
τοῦ θεοῦ κατὰ τὸν ἔσω ἄνθρωπον· 23 βλέπω.δὲ ἕτερον
of God according to the inward man: but I see another
νόμον ἐν τοῖς.μέλεσίν.μου ἀντιστρατευόμενον τῷ νόμῳ τοῦ
law in my members warring against the law
νοός.μου, καὶ αἰχμαλωτίζοντά με [r] τῷ νόμῳ τῆς ἁμαρτίας
of my mind, and leading [2]captive [1]me to the law of sin
τῷ ὄντι ἐν τοῖς.μέλεσίν.μου. 24 ταλαίπωρος ἐγὼ ἄνθρωπος·
which is in my members. O wretched [2]I [1]man!
τίς με ῥύσεται ἐκ τοῦ σώματος τοῦ.θανάτου.τούτου;
who [3]me [1]shall [2]deliver out of the body of this death?
25 [s]εὐχαριστῶ‖ τῷ θεῷ διὰ Ἰησοῦ χριστοῦ τοῦ.κυρίου.ἡμῶν·
I thank God through Jesus Christ our Lord.
ἄρα.οὖν αὐτὸς ἐγὼ τῷ [t]μὲν‖ νοῒ δουλεύω νόμῳ θεοῦ·
So then [2]myself [1]I with the [2]indeed [1]mind serve [2]law [1]God's;
τῇ.δὲ σαρκὶ νόμῳ ἁμαρτίας.
but with the flesh [2]law [1]sin's.

8 Οὐδὲν.ἄρα.νῦν κατάκριμα τοῖς ἐν χριστῷ Ἰησοῦ, [u]μὴ
[There is] then now no condemnation to those in Christ Jesus, [3]not
κατὰ σάρκα περιπατοῦσιν, ἀλλὰ κατὰ πνεῦμα.‖ 2 ὁ.γὰρ
[4]according [5]to [6]flesh [1]who [2]walk, but according to Spirit. For the
νόμος τοῦ πνεύματος τῆς ζωῆς ἐν χριστῷ Ἰησοῦ ἠλευθέρωσέν
law of the Spirit of life in Christ Jesus set [2]free
[v]με‖ ἀπὸ τοῦ νόμου τῆς ἁμαρτίας καὶ τοῦ θανάτου. 3 Τὸ γὰρ
[1]me from the law of sin and of death. For
ἀδύνατον τοῦ νόμου, ἐν.ᾧ ἠσθένει διὰ τῆς σαρκός,
[4]powerless [[3]being] [1]the [2]law, in that it was weak through the flesh,

Let it not be *said*! But I did not know sin except through Law. For I would not have recognized lust unless the Law had said, "You shall not lust."

8 But sin, receiving an opportunity through the commandment, worked out in me every lust. For apart from Law, sin *was* dead.

9 And I was alive apart from Law once, but the commandment came and sin came alive, and I died.

10 And the commandment which *was* to life was found to be death to me.

11 For sin, receiving an opportunity through the commandment, seduced me, and through it killed me.

12 So that the Law truly is holy and the commandment is holy and just and good.

13 That which is good, then, has it become death to me? Let it not be! But sin, that it might be revealed as sin, worked death to me by that which is good – so that sin might become excessively sinful through the commandment.

14 For we know that the Law is spiritual and I am fleshly, being sold under sin.

15 For I do not approve what I do – for I do not do that which I will, but I do this that I hate.

16 But if I do what I do not will, I consent to the Law that *it is* good.

17 Now, then, I am no longer working it out, but the sin living in me *is working it out.*

18 For I know that in me (that is, in my flesh) there dwells no good. For to desire is present with me, but how to work out the good I do not find.

19 For the good that I desire, I do not do. But the evil I do not desire, this I do.

20 But if I do that which I do not desire, *it is* no longer I working it out, but sin living in me.

21 I find, then, a law – that when I desire to do what is right, evil is present with me.

22 For I delight in the law of God according to the inward man.

23 But I see another law in my members warring against the law of my mind and leading me captive to the law of sin which is in my members.

24 O wretched man that I am! Who shall deliver me from the body of this death?

25 I thank God through Jesus Christ, our Lord! So then, I myself with the mind truly serve the law of God, but with the flesh the law of sin.

8 1 *There is* therefore, now no condemnation to those in Christ Jesus, who walk not according to the flesh, but according to the Spirit.

2 For the law of the Spirit of life in Christ Jesus set me free from the law of sin and of death.

3 For what the Law was not able to do, in that it was weak through the flesh, God, *in*

ὁ θεὸς τὸν.ἑαυτοῦ υἱὸν πέμψας ἐν ὁμοιώματι σαρκὸς ἁμαρτίας
God, [3]his [4]own [5]Son [1]having [2]sent, in likeness of flesh of sin,
καὶ περὶ.ἁμαρτίας κατέκρινεν τὴν ἁμαρτίαν ἐν τῇ σαρκί, 4 ἵνα
and for sin, condemned sin in the flesh, that
τὸ δικαίωμα τοῦ νόμου πληρωθῇ ἐν ἡμῖν, τοῖς μὴ κατὰ
the requirement of the law should be fulfilled in us, who not according to
σάρκα περιπατοῦσιν, ἀλλὰ κατὰ πνεῦμα. 5 Οἱ.γὰρ
flesh walk, but according to Spirit. For they that
κατὰ σάρκα ὄντες, τὰ τῆς σαρκὸς φρονοῦσιν· οἱ.δὲ
according to flesh are, the things of the flesh mind; and they
κατὰ πνεῦμα, τὰ τοῦ πνεύματος. 6 τὸ.γὰρ φρόνημα
according to Spirit, the things of the Spirit. For the mind
τῆς σαρκὸς θάνατος· τὸ.δὲ φρόνημα τοῦ πνεύματος, ζωὴ
of the flesh [is] death; but the mind of the Spirit, life
καὶ εἰρήνη. 7 Διότι τὸ φρόνημα τῆς σαρκὸς ἔχθρα εἰς
and peace. Because the mind of the flesh [is] enmity towards
θεόν· τῷ.γὰρ νόμῳ τοῦ θεοῦ οὐχ.ὑποτάσσεται, οὐδὲ.γὰρ δύνα-
God: for to the law of God it is not subject; for neither can
ται· 8 οἱ.δὲ ἐν σαρκὶ ὄντες, θεῷ .ἀρέσαι οὐ.δύνανται.
it [be]; and they that [2]in [3]flesh [1]are, [6]God [5]please [4]cannot.
9 Ὑμεῖς.δὲ οὐκ ἐστὲ ἐν σαρκί, [w]ἀλλ'‖ ἐν πνεύματι, εἴπερ
But ye [2]not [1]are in flesh, but in Spirit, if indeed [the]
πνεῦμα θεοῦ οἰκεῖ ἐν ὑμῖν. εἰ.δέ τις πνεῦμα χριστοῦ
Spirit of God dwells in you; but if anyone [the] Spirit of Christ
οὐκ.ἔχει, οὗτος οὐκ.ἔστιν αὐτοῦ. 10 εἰ.δὲ χριστὸς ἐν ὑμῖν, τὸ
has not, he is not of him: but if Christ [be] in you, the
μὲν σῶμα νεκρὸν [x]δι'‖ ἁμαρτίαν, τὸ.δὲ πνεῦμα ζωὴ
[2]indeed [1]body [is] dead on account of sin, but the Spirit life
διὰ δικαιοσύνην. 11 εἰ.δὲ τὸ πνεῦμα τοῦ ἐγείραντος[y]
on account of righteousness. But if the Spirit of him who raised up
Ἰησοῦν ἐκ νεκρῶν οἰκεῖ ἐν ὑμῖν, ὁ ἐγείρας [z]τὸν‖
Jesus from among [the] dead dwells in you, he who raised up the
[a]χριστὸν ἐκ νεκρῶν‖ ζωοποιήσει καὶ τὰ θνητὰ σώματα
Christ from among [the] dead will quicken also [2]mortal [3]bodies
ὑμῶν διὰ [b]τὸ ἐνοικοῦν αὐτοῦ πνεῦμα‖ ἐν ὑμῖν. 12 Ἄρα
[1]your on account of [3]that [4]dwells [1]his [2]Spirit in you. So
οὖν, ἀδελφοί, ὀφειλέται ἐσμέν οὐ τῇ σαρκί, τοῦ κατὰ σάρκα
then, brethren, debtors we are, not to the flesh, [3]according [4]to [5]flesh
ζῆν· 13 εἰ.γὰρ κατὰ σάρκα ζῆτε, μέλλετε ἀποθνήσκειν·
[1]to [2]live; for if according to flesh ye live, ye are about to die;
εἰ.δὲ πνεύματι τὰς πράξεις τοῦ σώματος θανατοῦτε, ζήσεσθε.
but if by [the] Spirit the deeds of the body ye put to death, ye will live:
14 Ὅσοι.γὰρ πνεύματι θεοῦ ἄγονται, οὗτοί [c]εἰσιν υἱοὶ θεοῦ.‖
for as many as by [the] Spirit of God are led, these are sons of God.
15 οὐ.γὰρ ἐλάβετε πνεῦμα [d]δουλείας‖ πάλιν εἰς φόβον, [e]ἀλλ'‖
For [3]not [1]ye [2]received a spirit of bondage again unto fear, but
ἐλάβετε πνεῦμα υἱοθεσίας, ἐν.ᾧ κράζομεν, Ἀββᾶ, ὁ πατήρ.
ye received a Spirit of adoption, whereby we cry, Abba, Father.
16 Αὐτὸ τὸ πνεῦμα [f]συμμαρτυρεῖ‖ τῷ.πνεύματι.ἡμῶν, ὅτι
[3]Itself [1]the [2]Spirit bears witness with our spirit, that
ἐσμὲν τέκνα θεοῦ. 17 εἰ.δὲ τέκνα, καὶ κληρονόμοι· κληρονόμοι
we are children of God. And if children, also heirs: heirs
μὲν θεοῦ, [f]συγκληρονόμοι.δὲ χριστοῦ· εἴπερ [g]συμπάσχομεν,‖
indeed of God, and joint-heirs of Christ; if indeed we suffer together,
ἵνα καὶ συνδοξασθῶμεν.
that also we may be glorified together.
18 Λογίζομαι.γὰρ ὅτι οὐκ ἄξια τὰ παθήματα τοῦ νῦν
For I reckon that not worthy [are] the sufferings of the present
καιροῦ πρὸς τὴν μέλλουσαν δόξαν ἀποκαλυφθῆναι
time [to be compared] with the [2]about [1]glory to be revealed
εἰς ἡμᾶς. 19 Ἡ.γὰρ ἀποκαραδοκία τῆς κτίσεως τὴν ἀποκά-
to us. For the earnest expectation of the creation [2]the [3]reve-
λυψιν τῶν υἱῶν τοῦ θεοῦ ἀπεκδέχεται. 20 τῇ.γὰρ.ματαιότητι
lation [4]of [5]the [6]sons [7]of [8]God [1]awaits; for to vanity
ἡ κτίσις ὑπετάγη, οὐχ ἑκοῦσα, ἀλλὰ διὰ τὸν ὑπο-
the creation was subjected, not willingly, but by reason of him who sub-
τάξαντα, [h]ἐπ'‖ ἐλπίδι 21 [i]ὅτι‖ καὶ αὐτὴ ἡ κτίσις ἐλευθερω-
jected [it], in hope that also [3]itself [1]the [2]creation shall be
θήσεται ἀπὸ τῆς [j]δουλείας‖ τῆς φθορᾶς εἰς τὴν ἐλευθερίαν
freed from the bondage of corruption into the freedom
τῆς δόξης τῶν τέκνων τοῦ θεοῦ. 22 οἴδαμεν.γὰρ ὅτι πᾶσα ἡ
of the glory of the children of God. For we know that all the
κτίσις [g]συστενάζει‖ καὶ συνωδίνει ἄχρι τοῦ νῦν· 23 οὐ
creation groans together and travails together until now. [2]Not
μόνον δέ, ἀλλὰ καὶ αὐτοὶ τὴν ἀπαρχὴν τοῦ πνεύματος
[3]only [1]and [so], but even ourselves the first-fruit of the Spirit
ἔχοντες, [k]καὶ ἡμεῖς‖ αὐτοὶ ἐν ἑαυτοῖς στενάζομεν, υἱοθεσίαν
having, also we ourselves [2]in [3]ourselves [1]groan, [5]adoption
ἀπεκδεχόμενοι, τὴν ἀπολύτρωσιν τοῦ.σώματος.ἡμῶν. 24 τῇ
[4]awaiting— the redemption of our body.
γὰρ.ἐλπίδι ἐσώθημεν· ἐλπὶς.δὲ βλεπομένη οὐκ.ἔστιν ἐλπίς·
For in hope we were saved; but hope seen is not hope;

sending His own Son in the likeness of sinful flesh, and *to be a sacrifice* for sin, condemned sin in the flesh,

4 in order that the righteous demand of the Law should be fulfilled in us, who walk not according to the flesh but according to the Spirit.

5 For they who are according to the flesh set their mind on the things of the flesh – and they *who are* according to the Spirit on the things of the Spirit.

6 For the mind of the flesh is death, but the mind of the Spirit is life and peace.

7 Because the mind of the flesh is enmity towards God – for it is not subject to the law of God, for neither can it be,

8 and they that are in the flesh are not able to please God.

9 But you are not in the flesh but in the Spirit if the Spirit of God really dwells in you. But if anyone has not the Spirit of Christ, he is not His.

10 But if Christ is in you, the body indeed is dead because of sin, but the Spirit is life because of righteousness.

11 But if the Spirit of Him who raised up Jesus from among the dead dwells in you, He who raised up the Christ from among the dead will also make your death-doomed bodies live because of His Spirit that dwells in you.

12 So, then, brothers, we are not debtors to the flesh, to live according to the flesh.

13 For if you live according to the flesh, you are going to die. But if you by the Spirit put to death the deeds of the body, you will live –

14 for as many as are led by the Spirit of God, these are the sons of God!

15 For you did not receive a spirit of bondage again to fear, but you received a spirit of adoption in which we cry, Abba – Father!

16 The Spirit Himself bears witness with our spirit that we are children of God.

17 And if children, also heirs, truly heirs of God and joint- heirs of Christ, if we indeed suffer together, so that we may also be glorified together.

18 For I calculate that the sufferings of this present time are not worthy *to be compared* with the glory about to revealed to us.

19 For the creation eagerly looks out for the unveiling of the sons of God,

20 for the creation has been made subject to vanity (not of its own will, but because of Him who made it subject) in hope

21 that the creation itself also will be delivered from the bondage of decay into the freedom of the glory of the children of God.

22 For we know that the whole creation groans together and labors together in pain until now.

23 And not only so, but even we ourselves, having the first-fruit of the Spirit, we ourselves groan in ourselves, waiting for adoption – the redemption of our body.

24 For we were saved in hope, but hope

ὃ.γὰρ βλέπει τις τί [m]καὶ‖ ἐλπίζει; 25 εἰ.δὲ ὃ οὐ
for what [3]sees [2]anyone why also does he hope for? But if what [3]not
βλέπομεν ἐλπίζομεν, δι' ὑπομονῆς ἀπεκδεχόμεθα. 26 Ὡσαύτως
[1]we [2]see we hope for, in endurance we await. [2]In [3]like [4]manner
δὲ καὶ τὸ πνεῦμα συναντιλαμβάνεται [n]ταῖς.ἀσθενείαις‖.ἡμῶν·
[1]and also the Spirit jointly helps our weaknesses;
τὸ.γὰρ τί προσευξώμεθα καθὸ δεῖ, οὐκ.οἴδαμεν, [o]ἀλλ'‖
for that which we should pray for according as it behoves, we know not, but
αὐτὸ τὸ πνεῦμα ὑπερεντυγχάνει [p]ὑπὲρ ἡμῶν‖ στεναγμοῖς
[3]itself [1]the [2]Spirit makes intercession for us with groanings
ἀλαλήτοις· 27 ὁ.δὲ [q]ἐρευνῶν‖ τὰς καρδίας οἶδεν τί τὸ
inexpressible But he who searches the hearts knows what [is] the
φρόνημα τοῦ πνεύματος, ὅτι κατὰ θεὸν ἐντυγχάνει ὑπὲρ
mind of the Spirit, because according to God he intercedes for
ἁγίων. 28 Οἴδαμεν.δὲ ὅτι τοῖς ἀγαπῶσιν τὸν θεὸν πάντα
saints. But we know that to those who love God all things
[r]συνεργεῖ‖ εἰς ἀγαθόν, τοῖς κατὰ πρόθεσιν κλητοῖς
work together for good, to those who according to purpose [2]called
οὖσιν. 29 ὅτι οὓς προέγνω, καὶ προώρισεν συμμόρ-
[1]are. Because whom he foreknew, also he predestinated [to be] conformed
φους τῆς εἰκόνος τοῦ.υἱοῦ.αὐτοῦ, εἰς τὸ εἶναι αὐτὸν πρω-
to the image of his Son, for [2]to [3]be [1]him [the] first-
τότοκον ἐν πολλοῖς ἀδελφοῖς· 30 οὓς.δὲ προώρισεν, τούτους
born among many brethren. But whom he predestinated, these
καὶ ἐκάλεσεν· καὶ οὓς ἐκάλεσεν, τούτους καὶ ἐδικαίωσεν· οὓς
also he called; and whom he called, these also he justified; [2]whom
δὲ ἐδικαίωσεν, τούτους καὶ ἐδόξασεν.
[1]but he justified, these also he glorified.

31 Τί οὖν ἐροῦμεν πρὸς ταῦτα; εἰ ὁ θεὸς ὑπὲρ ἡμῶν,
What then shall we say to these things? If God [be] for us,
τίς καθ' ἡμῶν; 32 ὅς γε τοῦ.ἰδίου.υἱοῦ οὐκ.ἐφείσατο, [s]ἀλλ'‖
who against us? Who indeed his own Son spared not, but
ὑπὲρ ἡμῶν πάντων παρέδωκεν αὐτόν, πῶς οὐχὶ καὶ σὺν αὐτῷ
for us all gave up him, how [3]not [4]also [5]with [6]him
τὰ.πάντα ἡμῖν χαρίσεται; 33 τίς ἐγκαλέσει κατὰ
[9]all [10]things [8]us [1]will [2]he [7]grant? Who shall bring an accusation against
ἐκλεκτῶν θεοῦ; θεὸς ὁ δικαιῶν. 34 τίς ὁ κατα-
[the] elect of God? [It is] God who justifies: who he that con-
κρίνων; χριστὸς [t] ὁ ἀποθανών, μᾶλλον.δὲ [v]καὶ‖ ἐγερθείς,
demns? [It is] Christ who died, but rather also is raised up;
ὃς [w]καί‖ ἔστιν ἐν δεξιᾷ τοῦ θεοῦ, ὃς καὶ ἐντυγχάνει ὑπὲρ
who also is at [the] right hand of God; who also intercedes for
ἡμῶν. 35 τίς ἡμᾶς χωρίσει ἀπὸ τῆς ἀγάπης τοῦ χριστοῦ;
us: who us shall separate from the love of Christ?
θλῖψις, ἢ στενοχωρία, ἢ διωγμός, ἢ λιμός, ἢ γυμνότης, ἢ
tribulation, or strait, or persecution, or famine, or nakedness, or
κίνδυνος, ἢ μάχαιρα; 36 καθὼς γέγραπται, Ὅτι [x]ἕνεκά‖.σου
danger, or sword? According as it has been written, For thy sake
θανατούμεθα ὅλην τὴν ἡμέραν· ἐλογίσθημεν ὡς πρόβατα
we are put to death [2]whole [1]the day; we were reckoned as sheep
σφαγῆς. 37 Ἀλλ' ἐν τούτοις πᾶσιν ὑπερνικῶμεν διὰ
of slaughter. But in [2]these [3]things [1]all we more than overcome through
τοῦ ἀγαπήσαντος ἡμᾶς. 38 πέπεισμαι.γὰρ ὅτι οὔτε
him who loved us. For I am persuaded that neither
θάνατος, οὔτε ζωή, οὔτε ἄγγελοι, οὔτε ἀρχαί, [y]οὔτε δυ-
death, nor life, nor angels, nor principalities, nor
νάμεις,‖ οὔτε ἐνεστῶτα, οὔτε μέλλοντα,[y] 39 οὔτε ὕψωμα, οὔτε
powers, nor things present, nor things to be, nor height, nor
βάθος, οὔτε τις κτίσις ἑτέρα δυνήσεται ἡμᾶς χωρίσαι
depth, nor any [2]created [3]thing [1]other will be able us to separate
ἀπὸ τῆς ἀγάπης τοῦ θεοῦ, τῆς ἐν χριστῷ Ἰησοῦ τῷ κυρίῳ
from the love of God, which [is] in Christ Jesus [2]Lord
ἡμῶν.
[1]our.

9 Ἀλήθειαν λέγω ἐν χριστῷ, οὐ.ψεύδομαι, [z]συμμαρτυρούσης‖
Truth I say in Christ, I lie not, bearing witness with
μοι τῆς.συνειδήσεώς.μου ἐν πνεύματι ἁγίῳ, 2 ὅτι λύπη
me my conscience in [the] [2]Spirit [1]Holy, that [2]grief
μοι ἐστὶν μεγάλη, καὶ ἀδιάλειπτος ὀδύνη τῇ.καρδίᾳ.μου·
[3]to [4]me [5]is [1]great, and unceasing sorrow in my heart,
3 ηὐχόμην.γὰρ [a]αὐτὸς ἐγὼ ἀνάθεμα εἶναι‖ ἀπὸ τοῦ χριστοῦ
for I was wishing [2]myself [1]I a curse to be from the Christ
ὑπὲρ τῶν.ἀδελφῶν.μου, τῶν.συγγενῶν.μου κατὰ σάρκα·
for my brethren, my kinsmen according to flesh;
4 οἵτινές εἰσιν [b]Ἰσραηλῖται,‖ ὧν ἡ υἱοθεσία καὶ ἡ δόξα,
who are Israelites, whose [is] the adoption and the glory,
καὶ [c]αἱ διαθῆκαι‖ καὶ ἡ νομοθεσία, καὶ ἡ λατρεία καὶ αἱ
and the covenants and the lawgiving, and the service and the
ἐπαγγελίαι, 5 ὧν οἱ πατέρες, καὶ ἐξ ὧν ὁ χριστὸς τὸ
promises; whose [are] the fathers; and of whom [is] the Christ
κατὰ σάρκα, ὁ ὢν ἐπὶ πάντων θεὸς εὐλογητὸς εἰς τοὺς
according to flesh, who is over all God blessed to the

that is seen is not hope. For what anyone
sees, why does he also hope for it?
25 But if we hope for that which we do not
see, we wait with patience.
26 And in the same way the Spirit also joins
in to help our weaknesses. For we do not
know what we should pray for as we ought,
but the Spirit Himself pleads our case for us
with groanings that cannot be spoken.
27 But He who searches the hearts knows
what is the mind of the Spirit, because He
pleads the case for the saints according to
God.
28 And we know that all things work together for good to those who love God, to
those who are the called according to His
purpose.
29 Because whom He foreknew, He also
predestinated *to be* conformed to the image
of His Son, in order that He might be the
firstborn among many brothers.
30 And whom He predestinated, these He
also called. And whom He called, these He
also justified. And whom He justified, these
He also glorified.
31 What then shall we say to these things?
If God is for us, who *can be* against us?
32 Truly, He who did not withhold His own
Son, but surrendered Him for us all, shall He
not also freely give us all things with Him?
33 Who shall bring any charge against God's
elect? *It is* God who justifies!
34 Who is he that condemns? Christ *is the
One* who died! Yes, rather, He is also raised
up (who also is at the right hand of God,
who also pleads our case for us).
35 Who shall separate us from the love of
Christ? *Shall* trouble or distress or persecution or hunger or nakedness or danger or
sword?
36 As it is written, "For Your sake we are
killed all the day long. We were counted as
sheep for slaughter."
37 But in all these things we more than
conquer through Him who loved us.
38 For I am persuaded that neither death
nor life nor angels nor rulers nor powers nor
things present nor things to come –
39 nor height, nor depth, nor any other
created thing will be able to separate us from
the love of God, which is in Christ Jesus, our
Lord.
9 1 I tell the truth in Christ. I do not lie, my
conscience witnessing with me in the Holy
Spirit,
2 that I have great grief and pain that never
stops in my heart.
3 For I myself was wishing to be a curse
from Christ for my brothers, my kinsmen
according to the flesh –
4 who are Israelites, to whom belong the
sonship and the glory and the convenants
and the Law-giving and the service and the
promises.
5 To whom belong the fathers, and from
whom comes the Christ, according to the
flesh (who is God-blessed over all forever!

αἰῶνας. ἀμήν. 6 Οὐχ οἷον.δὲ ὅτι ἐκπέπτωκεν ὁ λόγος τοῦ
ages. Amen. Not however that has failed the word
θεοῦ. οὐ.γὰρ πάντες οἱ ἐξ Ἰσραήλ, οὗτοι Ἰσραήλ·
of God; for not all [4]which [[5]are] [6]of [7]Israel [1]those [[2]are] [3]Israel:
7 οὐδ' ὅτι εἰσὶν σπέρμα Ἀβραάμ, πάντες τέκνα, ἀλλ'
nor because they are seed of Abraham [are] all children: but,
ἐν Ἰσαὰκ κληθήσεταί σοι σπέρμα. 8 [d]Τουτέστιν,‖ οὐ τὰ
In Isaac shall be called to thee a seed. That is, [2]not [1]the
τέκνα τῆς σαρκός, ταῦτα τέκνα τοῦ θεοῦ· ἀλλὰ τὰ τέκνα
[2]children [3]of [4]the [5]flesh [6]these [[7]are] children of God; but the children
τῆς ἐπαγγελίας λογίζεται εἰς σπέρμα. 9 ἐπαγγελίας.γὰρ
of the promise are reckoned for seed. For of promise
ὁ.λόγος.οὗτος, Κατὰ τὸν.καιρὸν.τοῦτον ἐλεύσομαι, καὶ
this word [is], According to this time I will come, and
ἔσται τῇ Σάρρᾳ υἱός. 10 Οὐ.μόνον.δέ, ἀλλὰ καὶ Ῥε-
there shall be to Sarah a son. And not only [that], but also Re-
βέκκα ἐξ ἑνὸς κοίτην ἔχουσα, Ἰσαὰκ τοῦ.πατρὸς.ἡμῶν·
becca [3]by [4]one [2]conception [1]having, Isaac our father,
11 [e]μήπω‖ γὰρ γεννηθέντων, μηδὲ πραξάντων
[4]not [5]yet [[2]the [3]children] [1]for being born, nor having done
τι ἀγαθὸν ἢ [f]κακόν,‖ ἵνα ἡ κατ' ἐκλογὴν [g]τοῦ θεοῦ
anything good or evil, (that the [4]according [5]to [6]election [2]of [3]God
πρόθεσις‖ μένῃ, οὐκ ἐξ ἔργων, ἀλλ' ἐκ τοῦ καλοῦντος,
[1]purpose might abide, not of works, but of him who calls),
12 [h]ἐρρήθη‖ αὐτῇ, Ὅτι ὁ μείζων δουλεύσει τῷ ἐλάσσονι·
it was said to her, The greater shall serve the lesser:
13 καθὼς γέγραπται, Τὸν Ἰακὼβ ἠγάπησα, τὸν.δὲ Ἠσαῦ
according as it has been written, Jacob I loved, and Esau
ἐμίσησα.
I hated.

14 Τί οὖν ἐροῦμεν; μὴ ἀδικία παρὰ τῷ θεῷ;
What then shall we say? Unrighteousness with God [is there]?
μὴ.γένοιτο· 15 τῷ.[i]γὰρ.Μωσῇ‖ λέγει, Ἐλεήσω ὃν.ἂν
May it not be! For to Moses he says, I will shew mercy to whomsoever
ἐλεῶ, καὶ οἰκτειρήσω ὃν.ἂν οἰκτείρω.
I shew mercy, and I will feel compassion on whomsoever I feel compassion.
16 Ἄρα οὖν οὐ τοῦ θέλοντος, οὐδὲ τοῦ τρέχοντος,
So then [it is] not of him that wills, nor of him that runs,
ἀλλὰ τοῦ [k]ἐλεοῦντος‖ θεοῦ. 17 λέγει.γὰρ ἡ γραφὴ τῷ Φαραώ,
but [3]who [4]shews [5]mercy [1]of [2]God. For says the scripture to Pharaoh,
Ὅτι εἰς αὐτὸ.τοῦτο ἐξήγειρά σε, ὅπως ἐνδείξωμαι ἐν σοὶ
For this same thing I raised out thee, so that I might shew in thee
τὴν.δύναμίν.μου, καὶ ὅπως διαγγελῇ τὸ.ὄνομά.μου ἐν πάσῃ
my power, and so that should be declared my name in all
τῇ γῇ. 18 Ἄρα οὖν ὃν θέλει ἐλεεῖ· ὃν.δὲ θέλει
the earth. So then to whom he will he shews mercy, and whom he will
σκληρύνει.
he hardens.

19 Ἐρεῖς [l]οὖν μοι,‖ Τί[m] ἔτι μέμφεται; τῷ.[n]γὰρ‖ βου-
Thou wilt say then to me, Why yet does he find fault? for [4]the [5]pur-
λήματι αὐτοῦ τίς ἀνθέστηκεν; 20 [o]Μενοῦνγε, ὦ ἄνθρωπε,‖
pose [6]of [7]him [1]who [2]has [3]resisted? Yea, rather, O man,
σὺ τίς εἶ ὁ ἀνταποκρινόμενος τῷ θεῷ; μὴ ἐρεῖ τὸ
[3]thou [1]who [2]art that answerest against God? Shall [4]say [1]the
πλάσμα τῷ πλάσαντι, Τί με ἐποίησας οὕτως;
[2]thing [3]formed to him who formed [it], Why me madest thou thus?
21 Ἢ οὐκ.ἔχει ἐξουσίαν ὁ κεραμεὺς τοῦ πηλοῦ, ἐκ τοῦ
Or has not authority the potter over the clay, out of the
αὐτοῦ φυράματος ποιῆσαι ὃ.μὲν εἰς τιμὴν σκεῦος, ὃ.δὲ
same lump to make one [2]to [3]honour [1]vessel, and another
εἰς ἀτιμίαν; 22 εἰ.δὲ θέλων ὁ θεὸς ἐνδείξασθαι τὴν ὀργήν,
to dishonour? And if [2]willing [1]God to shew wrath,
καὶ γνωρίσαι τὸ.δυνατὸν.αὐτοῦ, ἤνεγκεν ἐν πολλῇ μακρο-
and to make known his power, bore in much long-
θυμίᾳ σκεύη ὀργῆς κατηρτισμένα εἰς ἀπώλειαν· 23 καὶ ἵνα
suffering vessels of wrath fitted for destruction; and that
γνωρίσῃ τὸν πλοῦτον τῆς.δόξης.αὐτοῦ ἐπὶ σκεύη
he might make known the riches of his glory upon vessels
ἐλέους, ἃ προητοίμασεν εἰς δόξαν; 24 οὓς καὶ ἐκάλεσεν
of mercy, which he before prepared for glory, [2]whom [3]also [4]he [5]called
ἡμᾶς οὐ μόνον ἐξ Ἰουδαίων, ἀλλὰ καὶ ἐξ
[1]us not only from among [the] Jews, but also from among [the]
ἐθνῶν· 25 ὡς καὶ ἐν τῷ Ὡσηὲ λέγει, Καλέσω τὸν οὐ
nations? As also in Hosea he says, I will call that which [is] not
λαόν.μου, λαόν.μου· καὶ τὴν οὐκ ἠγαπημένην, ἠγαπημένην.
my people, My People; and that not beloved, Beloved.
26 Καὶ ἔσται, ἐν τῷ τόπῳ οὗ [h]ἐρρήθη‖ [p]αὐτοῖς,‖ Οὐ λαός
And it shall be, in the place where it was said to them, Not [2]people
μου ὑμεῖς, ἐκεῖ κληθήσονται υἱοὶ θεοῦ ζῶντος. 27 Ἠ-
[1]my [are] ye, there they shall be called sons of [3]God [[1]the] [2]living. [2]E-
σαΐας δὲ κράζει· ὑπὲρ τοῦ Ἰσραήλ, Ἐὰν.ᾖ ὁ ἀριθμὸς
saias [1]but cries concerning Israel, If [6]should [7]be [1]the [2]number

Amen!).
6 Not, however, that the word of God has
failed! For those are not all Israel who are
out of Israel.
7 Nor *are* all *of them* children because they
are seed out of Abraham. But, "In Isaac shall
seed be called to you."
8 That is to say, the children of the flesh are
not the ones who are the children of God,
but the children of the promise are counted
as the seed.
9 For this word is of promise, "According
to this time I will come, and there shall be a
son *born* to Sarah."
10 And not only *this,* but also when Rebec-
ca had conceived by one, our father Isaac,
11 (for *the children* had not yet been born,
nor had they done anything good or evil, so
that the purpose of God according to
election might stand, not of works, but of
Him who calls) –
12 It was said to her, "The elder shall serve
the younger" –
13 according as it has been written, "Jacob
have I loved, and Esau have I hated."
14 What then shall we say? *Is there* unrighteousness with God? Let it not be *said*!
15 For He said to Moses, "I will show
mercy to whom I desire to show mercy, and
I will have pity on whom I desire to have
pity."
16 So then *it is* not of him that wills or of
him that runs, but of God who shows mercy.
17 For Scripture says to Pharaoh, "For this
very thing I raised you up, so that I might
show My power in you and so that My name
might be made known in all the earth."
18 So, then, He shows mercy to whom He
desires, and He hardens whom He desires.
19 You will then say to me, Why does He
still find fault, for who has resisted His
purpose?
20 Yes, rather, O man, who are you that
answers against God? Shall the thing formed
say to Him who formed it, Why did you
make me this way?
21 Or, does not the potter have authority
over the clay, out of the same lump to make
one vessel to honor and another to
dishonor?
22 And *what* if God, intending to show
wrath and to make His power known, endured with much long-suffering the vessels
of wrath fitted for destruction.
23 And *also* that He might make known the
riches of His glory on vessels of mercy which
He beforehand prepared for glory –
24 even us whom He also has called, not
only among the Jews, but also from among
the Gentiles.
25 As He says also in Hosea, "I will call that
which is not My people, 'My people!,' and
that which is not loved, 'Beloved!' "
26 And in the place where it was said to
them, "You are not My people, there they
shall be called sons of the living God."
27 But Isaiah cries out in regard to Israel,
"If the number of the sons of Israel are as

τῶν υἱῶν Ἰσραὴλ ὡς ἡ ἄμμος τῆς θαλάσσης, τὸ [r]κατάλειμ-
[3]of [4]the [5]sons [6]of [7]Israel as the sand of the sea, the remnant
μα‖ σωθήσεται· 28 λόγον γὰρ συντελῶν καὶ συντέμνων
shall be saved: for [the] matter [he is] concluding and cutting short
[s]ἐν δικαιοσύνῃ· ὅτι λόγον συντετμημένον‖ ποιήσει
in righteousness: because a matter cut short will [3]do [1]the
κύριος ἐπὶ τῆς γῆς. 29 Καὶ καθὼς προείρηκεν Ἡσαΐας,
[2]Lord upon the earth. And according as said before Esaias,
Εἰ.μὴ κύριος Σαβαὼθ [t]ἐγκατέλιπεν‖ ἡμῖν σπέρμα, ὡς Σόδομα
Unless [the] Lord of Hosts had left us a seed, as Sodom
ἂν.ἐγενήθημεν, καὶ ὡς Γόμορρα ἂν.ὡμοιώθημεν.
we should have become, and as Gomorrha we should have been made like.
30 Τί οὖν ἐροῦμεν; ὅτι ἔθνη τὰ μὴ.διώκοντα δικαιο-
What then shall we say? That Gentiles that follow not after right-
σύνην, κατέλαβεν δικαιοσύνην, δικαιοσύνην.δὲ τὴν ἐκ πίστεως·
eousness, attained righteousness, but righteousness that [is] by faith.
31 Ἰσραὴλ.δὲ διώκων νόμον δικαιοσύνης, εἰς νόμον [v]δι-
But Israel, following after a law of righteousness, to a law of
καιοσύνης‖ οὐκ.ἔφθασεν. 32 [w]διατί;‖ ὅτι οὐκ ἐκ πίσ-
righteousness did not attain. Why? Because [it was] not by faith,
τεως, ἀλλ' ὡς ἐξ ἔργων [x]νόμου·‖ προσέκοψαν.[y]γὰρ‖ τῷ λίθῳ
but as by works of law. For they stumbled at the stone
τοῦ προσκόμματος, 33 καθὼς γέγραπται, Ἰδοὺ τίθημι ἐν
of stumbling, according as it has been written, Behold I place in
Σιὼν λίθον προσκόμματος καὶ πέτραν σκανδάλου· καὶ [z]πᾶς‖
Sion a stone of stumbling and rock of offence: and every one
ὁ πιστεύων ἐπ' αὐτῷ οὐ.καταισχυνθήσεται.
that believes on him shall not be ashamed.

10 Ἀδελφοί, ἡ μὲν εὐδοκία τῆς.ἐμῆς καρδίας, καὶ ἡ
Brethren, the good pleasure of my own heart, and
δέησις [a]ἡ‖ πρὸς τὸν θεὸν ὑπὲρ [b]τοῦ Ἰσραήλ ἐστιν‖ εἰς
supplication to God on behalf of Israel is for
σωτηρίαν. 2 μαρτυρῶ.γὰρ αὐτοῖς ὅτι ζῆλον θεοῦ ἔχουσιν,
salvation. For I bear witness to them that zeal for God they have,
ἀλλ' οὐ κατ' ἐπίγνωσιν. 3 ἀγνοοῦντες.γὰρ τὴν τοῦ θεοῦ
but not according to knowledge. For being ignorant of the [2]of [3]God
δικαιοσύνην, καὶ τὴν.ἰδίαν [c]δικαιοσύνην‖ ζητοῦντες στῆσαι,
[1]righteousness, and their own righteousness seeking to establish,
τῇ δικαιοσύνῃ τοῦ θεοῦ οὐχ.ὑπετάγησαν. 4 τέλος.γὰρ
to the righteousness of God they submitted not. For [3]the [4]end
νόμου χριστὸς εἰς δικαιοσύνην παντὶ τῷ πιστεύοντι.
[5]of [6]law [1]Christ [2]is for righteousness to every one that believes.
5 [d]Μωσῆς‖.γὰρ γράφει [e] τὴν δικαιοσύνην τὴν ἐκ [f]τοῦ‖
For Moses writes [of] the righteousness which [is] of the
νόμου, [g]Ὅτι‖ ὁ ποιήσας [h]αὐτὰ‖ ἄνθρωπος ζήσεται
law, That the [2]having [3]practised [4]those [5]things [1]man shall live
ἐν [i]αὐτοῖς.‖ 6 Ἡ.δὲ ἐκ πίστεως δικαιοσύνη οὕτως λέγει,
by them. But the [2]of [3]faith [1]righteousness thus speaks:
Μὴ.εἴπῃς ἐν [k]τῇ‖.καρδίᾳ.σου, Τίς ἀναβήσεται εἰς τὸν
Thou mayest not say in thy heart, Who shall ascend to the
οὐρανόν; τοῦτ' ἔστιν χριστὸν καταγαγεῖν· 7 ἤ, Τίς κατα-
heaven? that is, Christ to bring down. Or, Who shall
βήσεται εἰς τὴν ἄβυσσον; τοῦτ' ἔστιν χριστὸν ἐκ
descend into the abyss? that is, Christ from among [the]
νεκρῶν ἀναγαγεῖν. 8 ἀλλὰ τί λέγει; Ἐγγύς σου τὸ ῥῆμά
dead to bring up. But what says it? Near thee the word
ἐστιν, ἐν τῷ.στόματί.σου καὶ ἐν τῇ.καρδίᾳ.σου. τοῦτ' ἔστιν τὸ
is, in thy mouth and in thy heart: that is the
ῥῆμα τῆς πίστεως ὃ κηρύσσομεν· 9 ὅτι ἐὰν ὁμολογήσῃς
word of faith which we proclaim, that if thou confess
ἐν τῷ.στόματί.σου κύριον Ἰησοῦν, καὶ πιστεύσῃς ἐν τῇ
with thy mouth [the] Lord Jesus, and believe in
καρδίᾳ.σου ὅτι ὁ θεὸς αὐτὸν ἤγειρεν ἐκ νεκρῶν,
thy heart that God him raised from among [the] dead,
σωθήσῃ· 10 καρδίᾳ.γὰρ πιστεύεται εἰς δικαιοσύνην.
thou shalt be saved. For with [the] heart is belief to righteousness;
στόματι.δὲ ὁμολογεῖται εἰς σωτηρίαν. 11 Λέγει.γὰρ ἡ
and with [the] mouth is confession to salvation. For says the
γραφή, Πᾶς ὁ πιστεύων ἐπ' αὐτῷ οὐ.καταισχυνθήσεται.
scripture, Everyone that believes on him shall not be ashamed.
12 Οὐ.γάρ.ἐστιν διαστολὴ Ἰουδαίου τε καὶ Ἕλληνος· ὁ.γὰρ
For there is not a difference of Jew and Greek; for the
αὐτὸς κύριος πάντων πλουτῶν εἰς πάντας τοὺς ἐπικαλου-
same Lord of all [is] rich toward all that call
μένους αὐτόν. 13 Πᾶς.γὰρ ὃς.ἂν ἐπικαλέσηται τὸ ὄνομα
upon him. For everyone, whoever may call on the name
κυρίου, σωθήσεται. 14 Πῶς οὖν [l]ἐπικαλέσονται‖ εἰς
of [the] Lord, shall be saved. How then shall they call on [him]
ὃν οὐκ.ἐπίστευσαν; πῶς.δὲ [m]πιστεύσουσιν‖ οὗ
whom they believed not? and how shall they believe on [him] of whom
οὐκ.ἤκουσαν; πῶς.δὲ [n]ἀκούσουσιν‖ χωρὶς κηρύσσοντος;
they heard not? and how shall they hear apart from [one] preaching?

the sand of the sea, the remnant shall be saved,
28 for *He is* bringing the matter to an end
and cutting it short in righteousness, because
the Lord will do a short work on the earth."
29 And as Isaiah said before, "Except the
Lord of Hosts had left us a seed, we would have become as Sodom and would have been like Go-mor-rah."
30 What then shall we say? That the
Gentiles that do not follow after righteousness have gotten righteousness, but a righteousness that is by faith.
31 But Israel following after a law of
righteousness did not attain a law of righteousness.
32 Why? Because *it was* not of faith, but as
by works of the Law. For they stumbled at the Stone-of-stumbling
33 even as it has been written, "Behold! I
place in Zion a Stone-of-stumbling and a Rock-of-offense. And everyone who believes on Him shall not be ashamed."

CHAPTER 10

1 Brothers! Indeed, my heart's desire and
prayer to God for Israel's sake is for them to be saved.
2 For I testify to them that they have zeal
for God, but not according to knowledge.
3 For being ignorant of God's righteousness
and trying to set up their own righteousness, they did not put themselves under the righteousness of God.
4 For Christ is the end of the law for right-
eousness to everyone who believes.
5 For Moses tells of the righteousness which
is of the Law, that, "the man who has practiced those things shall live by them."
6 But the righteousness of faith speaks in
this way, "You may not say in your heart, Who shall go up into Heaven?" – that is, in order to bring Christ down.
7 Or, "Who shall go down into the abyss?"
– that is, in order to bring Christ up from among the dead.
8 But what does it say? – "The word is near
you, in your mouth and in your heart" – that is, the word of faith which we preach.
9 So that if you confess the Lord Jesus with
your mouth and believe in your heart that God raised Him from among the dead, you shall be saved.
10 For with the heart man believes to
righteousness, and with the mouth he confesses to salvation.
11 For the Scripture says, "Everyone who
believes on Him shall not be ashamed."
12 For there is no difference between Jew
and Greek. For the same Lord of all is rich toward all that call on Him.
13 For everyone who calls on the name of
the Lord shall be saved.
14 How then shall they call on Him whom
they did not believe? And how shall they believe on Him of whom they have not heard? And how shall they hear without preaching?

15 πῶς.δὲ [o]κηρύξουσιν,ǁ ἐὰν.μὴ ἀποσταλῶσιν; καθὼς
and how shall they preach, unless they be sent? according as
γέγραπται, Ὡς ὡραῖοι οἱ πόδες τῶν [p]εὐαγγελιζο-
it has been written, How beautiful the feet of those announcing the glad
μένων εἰρήνην, τῶνǁ εὐαγγελιζομένων [q]τὰ˩ ἀγαθά.
tidings of peace, of those announcing the glad tidings of good things!
16 Ἀλλ' οὐ πάντες ὑπήκουσαν τῷ εὐαγγελίῳ· Ἡσαΐας.γὰρ
But not all obeyed the glad tidings. For Esaias
λέγει, Κύριε, τίς ἐπίστευσεν τῇ.ἀκοῇ.ἡμῶν; 17 [r]Ἄρα ἡ πίστις
says, Lord, who believed our report? So faith [is]
ἐξ ἀκοῆς, ἡ.δὲ ἀκοὴ διὰ ῥήματος [r]θεοῦ.ǁ 18 ἀλλὰ λέγω,
by report, but the report by [the] word of God. But I say,
Μὴ οὐκ.ἤκουσαν; [s]μενοῦνγεǁ εἰς πᾶσαν τὴν γῆν ἐξῆλθεν
Did they not hear? Yea, rather, Into all the earth went out
ὁ.φθόγγος.αὐτῶν, καὶ εἰς τὰ πέρατα τῆς οἰκουμένης τὰ ῥήματα
their voice, and to the ends of the habitable world [2]words
αὐτῶν. 19 Ἀλλὰ λέγω, Μὴ [t]οὐκ.ἔγνω Ἰσραήλǁ; πρῶτος
[1]their. But I say, Did not [2]know [1]Israel? First,
[u]Μωσῆςǁ λέγει, Ἐγὼ παραζηλώσω ὑμᾶς ἐπ' οὐκ
Moses says, I will provoke to jealousy you through [those] not
ἔθνει, [v]ἐπὶǁ ἔθνει ἀσυνέτῳ παροργιῶ ὑμᾶς. 20 Ἠ-
a nation, through a nation without understanding I will anger you. [2]E-
σαΐας δὲ ἀποτολμᾷ καὶ λέγει, Εὑρέθην [w] τοῖς ἐμὲ μὴ ζη-
saias [1]but is very bold and says, I was found by those [3]me [1]not [2]seek-
τοῦσιν, ἐμφανὴς ἐγενόμην [x] τοῖς ἐμὲ μὴ ἐπερωτῶσιν. 21 πρὸς
ing; manifested I became to those [4]me [1]not [2]enquiring [3]after. [2]To
δὲ τὸν Ἰσραὴλ λέγει, Ὅλην τὴν ἡμέραν ἐξεπέτασα τὰς
[1]but Israel he says, [2]Whole [1]the day I stretched out
χεῖράς.μου πρὸς λαὸν ἀπειθοῦντα καὶ ἀντιλέγοντα.
my hands to a people disobeying and contradicting.

11 Λέγω οὖν, Μὴ ἀπώσατο ὁ θεὸς τὸν.λαὸν.αὐτοῦ[y];
I say then, Did [2]thrust [3]away [1]God his people?
μὴ.γένοιτο· καὶ.γὰρ ἐγὼ [z]Ἰσραηλίτηςǁ εἰμί, ἐκ σπέρματος
May it not be! For also I an Israelite am, of [the] seed
Ἀβραάμ, φυλῆς [a]Βενιαμίν.ǁ 2 οὐκ.ἀπώσατο ὁ θεὸς
of Abraham, of [the] tribe of Benjamin. [2]Did [3]not [4]thrust [5]away [1]God
τὸν.λαὸν.αὐτοῦ, ὃν προέγνω. ἢ οὐκ.οἴδατε ἐν
his people, whom he foreknew. Know ye not in [the history of]
[b]Ἠλίᾳǁ τί λέγει ἡ γραφή; ὡς ἐντυγχάνει τῷ θεῷ κατὰ
Elias what says the scripture? how he pleads with God against
τοῦ Ἰσραήλ, [c]λέγων,ǁ 3 Κύριε, τοὺς.προφήτας.σου ἀπέκτειναν,
Israel, saying, Lord, thy prophets they killed,
[d]καὶǁ τὰ.θυσιαστήριά.σου κατέσκαψαν· κἀγὼ ὑπελείφθην μό-
and thine altars they dug down; and I was left a-
νος, καὶ ζητοῦσιν τὴν.ψυχήν.μου. 4 Ἀλλὰ τί λέγει αὐτῷ ὁ
lone, and they seek my life. But what says to him the
χρηματισμός; Κατέλιπον ἐμαυτῷ ἑπτακισχιλίους ἄνδρας
divine answer? I left to myself seven thousand men
οἵτινες οὐκ.ἔκαμψαν γόνυ τῇ Βάαλ. 5 Οὕτως οὖν καὶ ἐν τῷ
who bowed not a knee to Baal. Thus then also in the
νῦν καιρῷ λεῖμμα κατ' ἐκλογὴν χάριτος γέγονεν.
present time a remnant according to election of grace there has been.
6 εἰ.δὲ χάριτι, οὐκέτι ἐξ ἔργων· ἐπεὶ ἡ χάρις οὐκέτι γίνεται
But if by grace, no longer of works; else grace no longer becomes
χάρις. [e]εἰ.δὲ ἐξ ἔργων, οὐκέτι [f]ἐστὶν˩ χάρις· ἐπεὶ τὸ ἔργον
grace; but if of works, no longer is it grace; else work
οὐκέτι ἐστὶν ἔργον.ǁ
no longer is work.
7 Τί οὖν; ὃ ἐπιζητεῖ Ἰσραήλ, [g]τούτουǁ οὐκ.ἐπέτυχεν,
What then? What [2]seeks [3]for [1]Israel, this it did not obtain;
ἡ.δὲ ἐκλογὴ ἐπέτυχεν· οἱ.δὲ λοιποὶ ἐπωρώθησαν, 8 [h]καθὼςǁ
but the election obtained [it], and the rest were hardened, according as
γέγραπται, Ἔδωκεν αὐτοῖς ὁ θεὸς πνεῦμα κατανύξεως,
it has been written, [2]Gave [3]them [1]God a spirit of slumber,
ὀφθαλμοὺς τοῦ.μὴ βλέπειν, καὶ ὦτα τοῦ.μὴ ἀκούειν, ἕως
eyes so as not to see, and ears so as not to hear, unto
τῆς.σήμερον.ἡμέρας. 9 καὶ [i]Δαβὶδǁ λέγει, Γενηθήτω ἡ τράπεζα
this day. And David says, Let be [2]table
αὐτῶν εἰς παγίδα, καὶ εἰς θήραν, καὶ εἰς σκάνδαλον, καὶ εἰς
[1]their for a snare, and for a trap, and for cause of offence, and for
ἀνταπόδομα αὐτοῖς· 10 σκοτισθήτωσαν οἱ.ὀφθαλμοὶ.αὐτῶν
a recompense to them: let be darkened their eyes
τοῦ.μὴ βλέπειν, καὶ τὸν.νῶτον.αὐτῶν [k]διαπαντὸςǁ [l]σύγ-
so as not to see, and their back continually bow thou
καμψον.ǁ
down.
11 Λέγω οὖν, μὴ ἔπταισαν ἵνα πέσωσιν; μὴ.γένοιτο·
I say then, Did they stumble that they might fall? May it not be!
ἀλλὰ τῷ.αὐτῶν παραπτώματι ἡ σωτηρία τοῖς ἔθνεσιν, εἰς
but by their offence salvation [is] to the nations, for

15 And how shall they preach unless they
are sent? As it has been written, "How
beautiful are the feet of those who are
preaching the gospel of peace, of those
preaching the gospel of good things."
16 But not all obeyed the gospel. For Isaiah
says, "Lord, who believed our report?"
17 So then faith *comes* by hearing and
hearing by the word of God.
18 But I say, Did they not hear? Yes, rather
their voice went out into all the earth, and
their words to the ends of the habitable
world.
19 But I say, Did not Israel know? First,
Moses says, "I will cause you to be jealous
by *those who are* not a nation. I will anger
you by a nation without understanding."
20 And Isaiah is very bold and says, "I was
found by those who were not trying to find
Me. I was revealed to those who were not
seeking after Me."
21 But to Israel He says, "All the day long I
stretched out My hands to an unbelieving
and contradicting people."

CHAPTER 11

1 I say then, Did God cast away His people?
Let it not be *said!* For I also am an Israelite,
of the seed of Abraham, of the tribe of
Benjamin.
2 God did not throw aside His people whom
He foreknew. Do you not know what the
Scripture says *in the history* of Elijah, how
he pleads with God against Israel, saying,
3 "Lord, they killed Your prophets and
they dug down Your altars, and I alone am
left, and they seek my life."
4 But what does the divine answer say to
him – "I left to Myself seven thousand men
who have not bowed a knee to Baal."
5 So then also in the present time there has
come to be a remnant according to the
election of grace.
6 But if by grace, no longer of works –
otherwise grace no longer proves to be grace.
But if of works, it is no longer of grace –
otherwise work no longer proves to be work.
7 What then? Whatever Israel looked for, it
did not obtain. But the chosen have gotten
it, and the rest were blinded –
8 even as it has been written, "God gave
them a spirit of slumber, eyes that do not
see and ears that do not hear," to this day.
9 And David says, "Let their table be for a
snare and for a trap and for a stumbling-
block and for a reward to them.
10 Let their eyes be darkened so as not to
see, and, Bow down their back always."
11 I say, then, Did they stumble so that
they might fall? Let it not be *said*! But by
their falling away, salvation *is granted* to the
Gentiles, so as to cause them to be jealous.

τὸ παραζηλῶσαι αὐτούς. 12 εἰ.δὲ τὸ.παράπτωμα.αὐτῶν
to provoke to jealousy them. But if their offence [be the]
πλοῦτος κόσμου, καὶ τὸ.ἥττημα.αὐτῶν πλοῦτος ἐθνῶν,
wealth of [the] world, and their default [the] wealth of [the] nations,
πόσῳ μᾶλλον τὸ.πλήρωμα.αὐτῶν; 13 Ὑμῖν [m]γὰρ‖ λέγω
how much more their fulness? [2]To [3]you [1]for I speak,
τοῖς ἔθνεσιν· ἐφ'.ὅσον μέν ‖ εἰμι ἐγὼ ἐθνῶν ἀπόστολος,
the nations, inasmuch as [2]am [1]I [4]of [[5]the] [6]nations [3]apostle,
τὴν.διακονίαν.μου δοξάζω, 14 εἴ.πως παραζηλώσω
my service I glorify, if by any means I shall provoke to jealousy
μου τὴν σάρκα, καὶ σώσω τινὰς ἐξ αὐτῶν. 15 εἰ.γὰρ
my flesh, and shall save some from among them. For if
ἡ.ἀποβολὴ.αὐτῶν καταλλαγὴ κόσμου, τίς ἡ [o]πρόσ-
their casting away [be the] reconciliation of [the] world, what the recep-
ληψις,‖ εἰ.μὴ ζωὴ ἐκ νεκρῶν;
tion, except life from among [the] dead?
16 εἰ.δὲ ἡ ἀπαρχὴ ἁγία, καὶ τὸ φύραμα· καὶ εἰ ἡ ῥίζα
Now if the first-fruit [be] holy, also the lump; and if the root
ἁγία, καὶ οἱ κλάδοι. 17 εἰ.δέ τινες τῶν κλάδων ἐξεκλάσθη-
[be] holy, also the branches. But if some of the branches were broken
σαν, σὺ.δὲ ἀγριέλαιος ὢν ἐνεκεντρίσθης ἐν αὐτοῖς, καὶ
off, and thou, a wild olive tree being, wast grafted in amongst them, and
[l]συγκοινωνὸς‖ τῆς ῥίζης [p]καὶ‖ τῆς πιότητος τῆς ἐλαίας
a fellow-partaker of the root and of the fatness of the olive tree
ἐγένου, 18 μὴ.κατακαυχῶ τῶν κλάδων· εἰ.δὲ κατακαυχᾶσαι,
became, boast not against the branches; but if thou boastest against
οὐ σὺ τὴν ῥίζαν βαστάζεις, [q]ἀλλ'‖ ἡ ῥίζα σέ. 19 Ἐ-
[them], [3]not [1]thou [4]the [5]root [2]bearest, but the root thee. Thou
ρεῖς οὖν, Ἐξεκλάσθησαν [r]οἱ‖ κλάδοι, ἵνα ἐγὼ [s]ἐγκεντρισθῶ.‖
wilt say then, Were broken out the branches, that I might be grafted in.
20 Καλῶς· τῇ ἀπιστίᾳ [t]ἐξεκλάσθησαν,‖ σὺ.δὲ τῇ πίστει
Well: by unbelief they were broken out, and thou by faith
ἕστηκας. μὴ.[v]ὑψηλοφρόνει,‖ ἀλλὰ φοβοῦ· 21 εἰ.γὰρ ὁ θεὸς
standest. Be not high-minded, but fear: for if God
τῶν κατὰ φύσιν κλάδων οὐκ.ἐφείσατο, [w]μήπως‖ οὐδέ σου
the [2]according [3]to [4]nature [1]branches spared not— lest neither thee
[x]φείσηται.‖ 22 [y]Ἴδε οὖν χρηστότητα καὶ ἀποτομίαν θεοῦ·
he should spare. Behold then [the] kindness and severity of God:
ἐπὶ μὲν τοὺς πεσόντας, [y]ἀποτομίαν·‖ ἐπὶ.δὲ σε, [z]χρηστό-
upon those that fell, severity; and upon thee, kind-
τητα,‖ ἐὰν [a]ἐπιμείνῃς‖ τῇ χρηστότητι· ἐπεὶ καὶ σὺ ἐκ-
ness, if thou continue in [his] kindness, else also thou wilt
κοπήσῃ. 23 [b]καὶ ἐκεῖνοι‖ δέ, ἐὰν μὴ.[c]ἐπιμείνωσιν‖ τῇ ἀπιστίᾳ,
be cut off. [3]Also [2]they [1]and, if they continue not in unbelief,
[d]ἐγκεντρισθήσονται·‖ δυνατὸς.γὰρ ἐστιν ὁ θεὸς πάλιν [d]ἐγκεν-
shall be grafted in; for able is God again to graft
τρίσαι‖ αὐτούς. 24 εἰ.γὰρ σὺ ἐκ τῆς κατὰ φύσιν ἐξε-
in them. For if thou out of the [4]according [5]to [6]nature [7]wast
κόπης ἀγριελαίου, καὶ παρὰ φύσιν ἐνεκεντρίσθης εἰς
[8]cut [9]off [1]wild [2]olive [3]tree, and, contrary to nature, wast grafted in to
καλλιέλαιον, πόσῳ μᾶλλον οὗτοι οἱ κατὰ φύσιν,
a good olive tree, how much more these who according to nature [are],
[d]ἐγκεντρισθήσονται‖ τῇ.ἰδίᾳ ἐλαίᾳ; 25 Οὐ.γὰρ θέλω ὑμᾶς
shall be grafted into their own olive tree? For [3]not [2]do [1]I wish you
ἀγνοεῖν, ἀδελφοί, τὸ.μυστήριον.τοῦτο, ἵνα μὴ.ἦτε [e]παρ'‖
to be ignorant, brethren, of this mystery, that ye may not be in
ἑαυτοῖς φρόνιμοι, ὅτι πώρωσις ἀπὸ μέρους τῷ Ἰσραὴλ γέ-
yourselves wise, that hardness in part to Israel has
γονεν, ἄχρις.οὗ τὸ πλήρωμα τῶν ἐθνῶν εἰσέλθῃ· 26 καὶ
happened, until the fulness of the nations be come in; and
οὕτως πᾶς Ἰσραὴλ σωθήσεται, καθὼς γέγραπται,
so all Israel shall be saved, according as it has been written,
Ἥξει ἐκ Σιὼν ὁ ῥυόμενος, [f]καὶ‖ ἀποστρέψει ἀσεβείας
Shall come out of Sion the deliverer, and he shall turn away ungodliness
ἀπὸ Ἰακώβ· 27 καὶ αὕτη αὐτοῖς ἡ παρ' ἐμοῦ διαθήκη,
from Jacob. And this [is] [5]to [6]them [1]the [3]from [4]me [2]covenant,
ὅταν ἀφέλωμαι τὰς.ἁμαρτίας.αὐτῶν. 28 Κατὰ μὲν
when I may have taken away their sins. As regards indeed
τὸ εὐαγγέλιον, ἐχθροὶ δι'.ὑμᾶς· κατὰ.δὲ τὴν
the glad tidings, [they are] enemies on your account; but as regards the
ἐκλογήν, ἀγαπητοὶ διὰ τοὺς πατέρας. 29 ἀμεταμέλητα
election, beloved on account of the fathers. [2]Not [3]to [4]be [5]repented [6]of
γὰρ τὰ χαρίσματα καὶ ἡ κλῆσις τοῦ θεοῦ. 30 ὥσπερ.γὰρ
[1]for [are] the gifts and the calling of God. For as
[g]καὶ ὑμεῖς ποτε ἠπειθήσατε τῷ θεῷ, νῦν.δὲ ἠλεήθητε
also ye once were disobedient to God, but now have been shewn mercy
τῇ.τούτων ἀπειθείᾳ· 31 οὕτως καὶ οὗτοι νῦν ἠπείθησαν
through their disobedience; so also these now were disobedient
τῷ.[h]ὑμετέρῳ‖.ἐλέει, ἵνα καὶ αὐτοὶ [i] ἐλεηθῶσιν.
to your mercy, that also they may have mercy shewn [them].
32 συνέκλεισεν.γὰρ ὁ θεὸς τοὺς πάντας εἰς ἀπείθειαν, ἵνα τοὺς
For [2]shut [3]up [4]together [1]God all in disobedience, that

12 But if their falling away is the riches of
the world, and their loss the riches of the
Gentiles, how much more their fullness?
13 For I speak to you, the Gentiles – since
I am the apostle of the Gentiles, I glorify my
ministry –
14 if by any means I shall cause *those who*
are my flesh to be jealous and shall save
some from among them.
15 For if their rejection becomes the reconciliation of the world, what *then* the reception except life from among the dead?
16 Now if the first fruit is holy, the lump is
too. And if the root is holy, the branches are
too.
17 But if some of the branches were broken
off and being a wild olive tree you were
grafted in among them, and came to share
with them the root and of the fatness of the
olive tree,
18 do not boast against the branches. But if
you do boast, *remember* that you do not
bear the root, but the root bears you.
19 You will then say, The branches were
broken off so that I might be grafted in.
20 Well! They were broken off by unbelief.
And you stand by faith. Do not be high-
minded, but fear!
21 For if God did not spare the natural
limbs, perhaps He will not spare you either.
22 Note then the goodness and severity of
God: On those who fell, severity. And on
you, goodness – if you keep on in *His* goodness; otherwise you too will be cut off.
23 And if they do not keep on in unbelief,
they also shall be grafted in. For God is able
to graft them in again.
24 For if you were cut out of the olive tree
which is wild by nature, and, contrary to
nature were grafted into a good olive tree –
how much more shall these who are according to nature be grafted into their own olive
tree?
25 For I do not want you to be ignorant of
this mystery, brothers (so that you may not
be wise in your own selves), that hardness in
part has happened to Israel, until the fullness
of the Gentiles has come in.
26 And so all Israel shall be saved, even as it
has been written, "Out of Zion the Deliverer
shall come. And He shall turn away ungodliness from Jacob.
27 And this is My covenant to them – when
I have taken away their sins."
28 Indeed, as regards the gospel, *they are*
enemies for your sakes. But as regards the
election, beloved for the fathers' sake.
29 For the gifts and the calling of God are
without repentance.
30 For as you also in times past were
unbelieving, but now have been shown
mercy through their unbelief,
31 so also these now have not believed in
regard to your mercy, so that they too may
have mercy shown them.
32 For God shut all up together in unbelief,

πάντας ἐλεήσῃ. 33 ᵀΩ βάθος πλούτου καὶ σοφίας
all he might shew mercy to. O depth of riches both of wisdom
καὶ γνώσεως θεοῦ. ὡς ᵏἀνεξερεύνητα" τὰ.κρίματα.αὐτοῦ, καὶ
and knowledge of God! How unsearchable his judgments, and
ἀνεξιχνίαστοι αἱ.ὁδοὶ.αὐτοῦ. 34 τίς.γὰρ ἔγνω νοῦν
untraceable his ways! For who did know [the] mind
κυρίου; ἢ τίς σύμβουλος.αὐτοῦ ἐγένετο; 35 ἢ τίς προέ-
of [the] Lord, or who his counsellor became? Or who first
δωκεν αὐτῷ, καὶ ἀνταποδοθήσεται αὐτῷ; 36 ὅτι ἐξ αὐτοῦ
gave to him, and it shall be recompensed to him? For of him
καὶ δι' αὐτοῦ καὶ εἰς αὐτὸν τὰ.πάντα· αὐτῷ ἡ δόξα
and through him and unto him [are] all things: to him [be] the glory
εἰς τοὺς αἰῶνας. ἀμήν.
to the ages. Amen.

12 Παρακαλῶ οὖν ὑμᾶς, ἀδελφοί, διὰ τῶν οἰκτιρμῶν τοῦ
I exhort therefore you, brethren, by the compassions
θεοῦ, παραστῆσαι τὰ.σώματα.ὑμῶν θυσίαν ζῶσαν, ἁγίαν,
of God, to present your bodies a 2sacrifice 1living, holy,
ˡεὐάρεστον τῷ θεῷ," τὴν λογικὴν λατρείαν ὑμῶν· 2 καὶ μὴ
well-pleasing to God, 2intelligent 3service 1your. And 2not
ᵐσυσχηματίζεσθε¹ τῷ.αἰῶνι.τούτῳ, ἀλλὰ ⁿμεταμορφοῦσθε" τῇ
1fashion yourselves to this age, but be transformed by the
ἀνακαινώσει τοῦ.νοὸς.ᵒὑμῶν," εἰς τὸ δοκιμάζειν ὑμᾶς τί
renewing of your mind, for to prove by you what [is]
τὸ θέλημα τοῦ θεοῦ τὸ ἀγαθὸν καὶ εὐάρεστον καὶ τέλειον.
7will 8of 9God 1the 2good 3and 4well-pleasing 5and 6perfect.
3 λέγω.γὰρ διὰ τῆς χάριτος τῆς δοθείσης μοι, παντὶ
For I say through the grace which is given to me, to everyone
τῷ.ὄντι ἐν ὑμῖν, μὴ ὑπερφρονεῖν παρ' ὃ δεῖ
that is among you, not to be high-minded above what it behoves [you]
φρονεῖν, ἀλλὰ φρονεῖν εἰς.τὸ σωφρονεῖν, ἑκάστῳ ὡς ὁ
to be minded; but to be minded so as to be sober-minded to each as
θεὸς ἐμέρισεν μέτρον πίστεως. 4 Καθάπερ.γὰρ ἐν ἑνὶ σώματι
God divided a measure of faith. For even as in one body
ᵖμέλη πολλὰ" ἔχομεν, τὰ.δὲ μέλη πάντα οὐ τὴν αὐτὴν
2members 1many we have, but the members all 2not 3the 4same
ἔχει πρᾶξιν· 5 οὕτως οἱ πολλοὶ ἓν σῶμά ἐσμεν ἐν χριστῷ,
1have function; thus 2the 3many 5one 6body 1we 4are in Christ,
ᵠὁ".δὲ.καθ'.εἷς ἀλλήλων μέλη. 6 ἔχοντες.δὲ χαρίσματα
and each one 3of 3each 4other 1members. But having 2gifts
κατὰ τὴν χάριν τὴν δοθεῖσαν ἡμῖν διάφορα· εἴτε
3according 4to 5the 6grace 7which 8is 9given 10to 11us 1different, whether
προφητείαν, κατὰ τὴν ἀναλογίαν τῆς πίστεως· 7 εἴτε δια-
prophecy— according to the proportion of faith; or ser-
κονίαν, ἐν τῇ διακονίᾳ· εἴτε ὁ διδάσκων, ἐν τῇ διδασκαλίᾳ·
vice— in service; or he that teaches— in teaching;
8 εἴτε ὁ παρακαλῶν, ἐν τῇ παρακλήσει· ὁ μεταδιδούς, ἐν
or that exhorts— in exhortation; he that imparts— in
ἁπλότητι· ὁ προϊστάμενος, ἐν σπουδῇ· ὁ ἐλεῶν,
simplicity, he that takes the lead— with diligence; he that shews mercy—
ἐν ἱλαρότητι. 9 Ἡ ἀγάπη ἀνυπόκριτος· ἀποστυγοῦντες τὸ
with cheerfulness. [Let] love [be] unfeigned; abhorring
πονηρόν, κολλώμενοι τῷ ἀγαθῷ· 10 τῇ φιλαδελφίᾳ εἰς ἀλ-
evil, cleaving to good; in brotherly love towards one
λήλους φιλόστοργοι· τῇ τιμῇ ἀλλήλους προηγούμενοι·
another kindly affectioned; in [giving] honour 3one 4another 1going 2before;
11 τῇ σπουδῇ μὴ ὀκνηροί, τῷ πνεύματι ζέοντες, ʳτῷ καιρῷ"
in diligence, not slothful; in spirit, fervent; 2in 3season
δουλεύοντες· 12 τῇ ἐλπίδι χαίροντες, τῇ θλίψει ὑπομένον-
1serving. In hope, rejoicing; in tribulation, endur-
τες, τῇ προσευχῇ προσκαρτεροῦντες· 13 ταῖς χρείαις τῶν
ing; in prayer, stedfastly continuing; to the needs of the
ἁγίων κοινωνοῦντες, τὴν φιλοξενίαν διώκοντες· 14 εὐλογεῖτε
saints communicating; hospitality pursuing. Bless
τοὺς διώκοντας ὑμᾶς· εὐλογεῖτε, καὶ μὴ.καταρᾶσθε. 15 χαί-
those that persecute you; bless, and curse not. Re-
ρειν μετὰ χαιρόντων, ˢκαὶ" κλαίειν μετὰ κλαιόντων. 16 τὸ
joice with rejoicing ones, and weep with weeping ones; the
αὐτὸ εἰς ἀλλήλους φρονοῦντες· μὴ τὰ.ὑψηλὰ φρο-
same thing toward one another minding, not high things mind-
νοῦντες, ἀλλὰ τοῖς ταπεινοῖς συναπαγόμενοι. μὴ.γίνεσθε
ing, but with the lowly going along: be not
φρόνιμοι παρ' ἑαυτοῖς. 17 μηδενὶ κακὸν ἀντὶ κακοῦ ἀποδι-
wise in yourselves: to no one evil for evil ren-
δόντες· προνοούμενοι καλὰ ᵗ ἐνώπιον ᵛπάντων" ἀνθρώπων·
dering: providing right [things] before all men:
18 εἰ δυνατόν, τὸ.ἐξ.ὑμῶν, μετὰ πάντων ἀνθρώπων εἰρη-
if possible, as to yourselves, with all men being
νεύοντες. 19 μὴ ἑαυτοὺς ἐκδικοῦντες, ἀγαπητοί, ἀλλὰ δότε
at peace; not yourselves avenging, beloved, but give
τόπον τῇ ὀργῇ· γέγραπται.γάρ, Ἐμοὶ ἐκδίκησις, ἐγὼ ἀντα-
place to wrath; for it has been written, To me vengeance! I will

so that He might show mercy to all.
33 O the depth of the riches both of the wisdom and knowledge of God! How unsearchable are His judgments! And His ways are past finding out!
34 For who has known the mind of the Lord? Or who became His advisor?
35 Or, who has first given to Him, and it shall be given back to him again?
36 For of Him and through Him and to Him are all things: to Him be glory forever. Amen!

CHAPTER 12

1 Therefore, brothers, I call on you by the mercies of God to present your bodies a living sacrifice, holy, pleasing to God – *which* is your reasonable service.
2 And be not conformed to this world, but be transformed by the renewing of your mind, so that you may prove what is the good and pleasing and perfect will of God.
3 For through the grace which is given to me, I say to everyone that is among you, Do not be high-minded above what you ought to think. But set your mind so as to think wisely, according as God has given to each a measure of faith.
4 For even as one body we have many members, but the members do not have the same use,
5 so we, the many, are one body in Christ, and everyone members of one another.
6 But we have different gifts according to the grace which is given to us. If it is prophecy, *let us prophesy* according to how much faith –
7 or ministry, in serving – or he who teaches, in teaching –
8 or he who comforts, in comforting – he who is giving, with a single heart. And he who is leading, with eagerness – he who shows mercy, in cheerfulness.
9 *Let your* love be without pretending. Hate evil and hold tight to that which is good.
10 *Be* tender-hearted toward one another, in brotherly love, going before one another in giving honor –
11 as to diligence, not careless, but warm in spirit, serving the Lord.
12 *If you are* in hope, rejoicing – in trouble, enduring – in prayer, steadily keeping on,
13 providing for the needs of the saints, following after hospitality.
14 Bless those who persecute you – bless and do not curse.
15 Rejoice with those who rejoice, and weep with those who weep.
16 Be of the same mind toward one another, not minding the high things, but going along with the lowly. Do not be wise in your own selves.
17 Pay no one evil for evil. Think beforehand to provide things honest before all men.
18 If possible, as far as is in you, be at peace with all men.
19 Do not avenge yourselves, beloved, but give place to anger. For it has been written, "Vengeance is Mine, I will repay, says the

ποδώσω, λέγει κύριος. 20 [w]Ἐὰν οὖν[‖] πεινᾷ ὁ ἐχθρός
recompense, says [the] Lord. If therefore should hunger [2]enemy
σου, ψώμιζε αὐτόν· ἐὰν διψᾷ, πότιζε αὐτόν· τοῦτο
[1]thine, feed him; if he should thirst, give [2]drink [1]him; [4]this
γὰρ ποιῶν, ἄνθρακας πυρὸς σωρεύσεις ἐπὶ τὴν κεφαλὴν
[3]for doing, coals of fire thou wilt heap upon [2]head
αὐτοῦ. 21 μὴ.νικῶ ὑπὸ τοῦ κακοῦ, ἀλλὰ νίκα ἐν τῷ
[1]his. Be not overcome by evil, but overcome [2]with
ἀγαθῷ τὸ κακόν.
[3]good [1]evil.

13 Πᾶσα ψυχὴ ἐξουσίαις ὑπερεχούσαις ὑποτασσέσθω.
[2]Every [3]soul [6]to [7]authorities [8]above [[9]him] [1]let [4]be [5]subject.
οὐ.γάρ.ἐστιν ἐξουσία εἰ.μὴ [x]ἀπὸ[‖] θεοῦ· αἱ.δὲ οὖσαι
For there is no authority except from God; and those that are
[y]ἐξουσίαι[‖] ὑπὸ [z]τοῦ[‖] θεοῦ τεταγμέναι.εἰσίν. 2 ὥστε ὁ
authorities, by God have been appointed. So that he that
ἀντιτασσόμενος τῇ ἐξουσίᾳ, τῇ.τοῦ θεοῦ διαταγῇ ἀνθέστηκεν·
sets himself against the authority, the [2]of [3]God [1]ordinance resists;
οἱ.δὲ ἀνθεστηκότες, ἑαυτοῖς κρίμα [a]λήψονται.[‖] 3 οἱ
and they that resist, to themselves judgment shall receive. [2]The
γὰρ ἄρχοντες οὐκ.εἰσὶν φόβος [b]τῶν ἀγαθῶν ἔργων,[‖] ἀλλὰ
[1]for rulers are not a terror to good works, but
[c]τῶν κακῶν.[‖] θέλεις.δὲ μὴ φοβεῖσθαι τὴν ἐξουσίαν; τὸ
to evil [ones]. Dost thou desire not to be afraid of the authority? [2]the
ἀγαθὸν ποίει, καὶ ἕξεις ἔπαινον ἐξ αὐτῆς· 4 θεοῦ.γὰρ
[3]good [1]practise, and thou shalt have praise from it; for of God
διάκονός ἐστίν σοι εἰς τὸ ἀγαθόν. ἐὰν δὲ τὸ κακὸν ποιῇς,
a servant it is to thee for good. But if evil thou practisest,
φοβοῦ· οὐ.γὰρ εἰκῇ τὴν μάχαιραν φορεῖ· θεοῦ.γὰρ διάκονός
fear; for not in vain the sword it wears; for of God a servant
ἐστιν, ἔκδικος εἰς ὀργὴν τῷ τὸ κακὸν πράσσοντι. 5 διὸ
it is, an avenger for wrath to him that [2]evil [1]does. Wherefore
ἀνάγκη ὑποτάσσεσθαι, οὐ μόνον διὰ τὴν ὀργήν,
necessary [it is] to be subject, not only on account of wrath,
ἀλλὰ καὶ διὰ τὴν συνείδησιν. 6 διὰ.τοῦτο.γὰρ καὶ
but also on account of conscience. For on this account also
φόρους τελεῖτε· λειτουργοὶ.γὰρ θεοῦ εἰσιν, εἰς.αὐτὸ.τοῦτο
tribute pay ye; for ministers of God they are, on this same thing
προσκαρτεροῦντες. 7 ἀπόδοτε [d]οὖν[‖] πᾶσιν τὰς ὀφειλάς·
attending continually. Render therefore to all their dues:
τῷ τὸν φόρον, τὸν φόρον· τῷ τὸ τέλος, τὸ τέλος· τῷ
to whom tribute, tribute; to whom custom, custom; to whom
τὸν φόβον, τὸν φόβον· τῷ τὴν τιμήν, τὴν τιμήν. 8 Μηδενὶ
fear, fear; to whom honour, honour. To no one
μηδὲν ὀφείλετε, εἰ.μὴ τὸ [e]ἀγαπᾶν ἀλλήλους·[‖] ὁ.γὰρ
anything (lit. nothing) owe ye, unless to love one another: for he that
ἀγαπῶν τὸν ἕτερον, νόμον πεπλήρωκεν. 9 τὸ γάρ, Οὐ
loves the other, law has fulfilled. For, [3]Not
μοιχεύσεις, οὐ φονεύσεις, οὐ.κλέψεις,
[1]thou [2]shalt commit adultery, Thou shalt not commit murder, Thou shalt not steal,
[f]οὐ.ψευδομαρτυρήσεις,[‖] οὐκ.ἐπιθυμήσεις, καὶ εἴ τις ἑτέρα
Thou shalt not bear false witness, Thou shalt not lust; and if any other com-
ἐντολή, ἐν [g]τούτῳ τῷ λόγῳ[‖] ἀνακεφαλαιοῦται, [h]ἐν τῷ,[‖] Ἀγα-
mandment, in this word it is summed up, in this, Thou
πήσεις τὸν.πλησίον.σου ὡς [i]ἑαυτόν.[‖] 10 Ἡ ἀγάπη τῷ πλη-
shalt love thy neighbour as thyself. Love to the neigh-
σίον κακὸν οὐκ.ἐργάζεται· πλήρωμα οὖν νόμου ἡ ἀγάπη.
bour, evil does not work: [3]fulness [4]therefore [5]of [[6]the] [7]law [1]love [[2]is].
11 Καὶ τοῦτο, εἰδότες τὸν καιρόν, ὅτι ὥρα [k]ἡμᾶς
Also this, knowing the time, that [the] hour [4]we [[1]it [2]is]
ἤδη[‖] ἐξ ὕπνου ἐγερθῆναι· νῦν.γὰρ ἐγγύτερον ἡμῶν ἡ
[3]already out of sleep should be roused; for now nearer [is] of us the
σωτηρία, ἢ ὅτε ἐπιστεύσαμεν. 12 ἡ νὺξ προέκοψεν, ἡ.δὲ
salvation, than when we believed. The night is advanced, and the
ἡμέρα ἤγγικεν. ἀποθώμεθα οὖν τὰ ἔργα τοῦ σκότους,
day has drawn near; we should cast off therefore the works of darkness,
[l]καὶ ἐνδυσώμεθα[‖] τὰ ὅπλα τοῦ φωτός. 13 ὡς ἐν ἡμέρᾳ,
and should put on the armour of light. As in [the] day,
εὐσχημόνως περιπατήσωμεν, μὴ κώμοις καὶ μέθαις, μὴ κοί-
becomingly we should walk; not in revels and drinking, not in cham-
ταις καὶ ἀσελγείαις, μὴ ἔριδι καὶ ζήλῳ· 14 [m]ἀλλ'[‖] ἐνδύσασθε
bering and wantonness, not in strife and emulation. But put on
τὸν κύριον Ἰησοῦν χριστόν, καὶ τῆς σαρκὸς πρόνοιαν μὴ
the Lord Jesus Christ, and [7]of [8]the [9]flesh [4]forethought [2]not
ποιεῖσθε εἰς ἐπιθυμίας.
do take [5]for [6]desire.

14 Τὸν.δὲ ἀσθενοῦντα τῇ πίστει προσλαμβάνεσθε, μὴ εἰς
But him being weak in the faith receive not for
διακρίσεις διαλογισμῶν. 2 [n]Ὃς.μὲν πιστεύει φαγεῖν πάντα,
decisions of reasonings. One believes to eat all things;

Lord."
20 So if your enemy should be hungry, feed
him. If he should be thirsty, give him a drink
– for doing this, you will heap coals of fire
on his head.
21 Do not be overcome by evil, but overcome evil with good.

CHAPTER 13

1 Let every soul put himself under the
higher authorities. For there is no authority
except from God, and the authorities that
exist have been appointed by God.
2 So that he who sets himself against the
authority sets himself against the order of
God. And they who do resist shall receive
judgment to themselves.
3 For the rulers are not frightening to good
works, but to evil. Do you desire not to be
afraid of the authority? Do good and you
shall have praise from it.
4 For it is a servant of God to your good.
But if you do evil, be afraid. For it does not
wear the sword in vain. For it is a servant of
God, a punisher for wrath to him that does
evil.
5 That is why *it is* needful to be under it –
not because of wrath only, but also for the
sake of conscience.
6 For because of this you also pay taxes –
for they are servants of God, always giving
attention to this same thing.
7 Then give to all their dues – taxes to
whom taxes *are due*, custom to whom
custom *is due*, fear to whom fear *is due*, and
honor to whom honor *is due*.
8 Do not owe anything to anyone, except
to love one another – for he who loves the
other has fulfilled the Law.
9 For, "You shall not commit adultery;
You shall not commit murder; You shall not
steal; You shall not bear false witness; You
shall not lust," and if there is any other
commandment it is summed up in this word,
in this, "You shall love your neighbor as
yourself."
10 Love does not work any ill to its
neighbor, so love is the fulfilling of the Law.
11 This also, knowing the time, that *it is*
already the hour that we should be aroused
from sleep – for now our salvation is nearer
than when we believed.
12 The night is far gone and the day is near,
so let us throw off the works of darkness
and put on the armor of light.
13 Let us walk honorably, as in daytime –
not in carousings and drinking, not in
unlawful intercourse and lustful acts, not in
fighting and envy.
14 But put on the Lord Jesus Christ and do
not take thought for the lusts of the flesh.

CHAPTER 14

1 And receive him who is weak in the faith,
not in order to judge his opinions
2 (one believes he may eat all things; an-

ὁ δὲ ἀσθενῶν λάχανα ἐσθίει. 3 ὁ ἐσθίων, τὸν μὴ
another being weak [2]herbs [1]eats. He that eats, [6]him [8]that [9]not
ἐσθίοντα μὴ.ἐξουθενείτω· [n]καὶ ὁ[ll] μὴ.ἐσθίων, τὸν ἐ-
[7]eats [1]let [2]him [3]not [4]despise; and he that eats not, [5]him [6]that
σθίοντα μὴ.κρινέτω· ὁ.θεὸς γὰρ αὐτὸν προσελάβετο. 4 σὺ
[7]eats [1]let [2]him [3]not [4]judge: for God him received. [3]Thou
τίς εἶ ὁ κρίνων ἀλλότριον οἰκέτην; τῷ.ἰδίῳ κυρίῳ στήκει
[1]who [2]art judging another's servant? to his own master he stands
ἢ πίπτει. σταθήσεται.δέ· [o]δυνατὸς.γάρ ἐστιν ὁ θεὸς[ll]
or falls. And he shall be made to stand; for able is God
στῆσαι αὐτόν. 5 [p]Ὃς.μὲν [p]κρίνει ἡμέραν παρ' ἡμέραν,
to make [2]stand [1]him. One judges a day [to be] above a day;
ὃς.δὲ κρίνει πᾶσαν ἡμέραν. ἕκαστος ἐν τῷ.ἰδίῳ νοΐ
another judges every day [to be alike]. [2]Each [3]in [4]his [5]own [6]mind
πληροφορείσθω. 6 ὁ φρονῶν τὴν ἡμέραν, κυρίῳ φρονεῖ·
[1]let be fully assured. He that regards the day, to [the] Lord regards [it];
[q]καὶ ὁ μὴ.φρονῶν τὴν ἡμέραν, κυρίῳ οὐ φρονεῖ.[ll] [r]ὁ
and he that regards not the day, to [the] Lord regards [it] not. He that
ἐσθίων, κυρίῳ ἐσθίει, εὐχαριστεῖ.γὰρ τῷ θεῷ· καὶ ὁ μὴ
eats, to [the] Lord eats, for he gives thanks to God; and he that [2]not
ἐσθίων, κυρίῳ οὐκ.ἐσθίει, καὶ εὐχαριστεῖ τῷ θεῷ. 7 οὐδεὶς
[1]eats, to [the] Lord he eats not, and gives thanks to God. [2]No [3]one
γὰρ ἡμῶν ἑαυτῷ ζῇ, καὶ οὐδεὶς ἑαυτῷ ἀποθνήσκει. 8 ἐάν.τε
[1]for of us to himself lives, and no one to himself dies. [2]Both [3]if
γὰρ ζῶμεν, τῷ κυρίῳ ζῶμεν· ἐάν.τε [s]ἀποθνήσκωμεν,[ll]
[1]for we should live, to the Lord we should live; and if we should die,
τῷ κυρίῳ ἀποθνήσκομεν. ἐάν.τε οὖν ζῶμεν, ἐάν.τε [s]ἀπο-
to the Lord we die: both if then we should live, and if we should
θνήσκωμεν,[ll] τοῦ κυρίου ἐσμέν. 9 εἰς.τοῦτο.γὰρ χριστὸς [t]καὶ[ll]
die, the Lord's we are. For, for this Christ both
ἀπέθανεν καὶ [v]ἀνέστη καὶ ἀνέζησεν,[ll] ἵνα καὶ νεκρῶν καὶ
died and rose and lived again, that both [the] dead and
ζώντων κυριεύσῃ. 10 Σὺ.δὲ τί κρίνεις τὸν ἀδελφόν
living he might rule over. But thou why judgest thou [2]brother
σου; ἢ καὶ σὺ τί ἐξουθενεῖς τὸν.ἀδελφόν.σου; πάντες.γὰρ
[1]thy? or also thou why dost thou despise thy brother? For [2]all
παραστησόμεθα τῷ βήματι [w]τοῦ χριστοῦ.[ll] 11 γέγραπται
[1]we shall stand before the judgment seat of the Christ. [2]It [3]has [4]been [5]written
γάρ, Ζῶ ἐγώ, λέγει κύριος· ὅτι ἐμοὶ κάμψει πᾶν γόνυ,
[1]for, [7]Live [6]I, says [the] Lord, that to me shall bow every knee,
καὶ [x]πᾶσα γλῶσσα ἐξομολογήσεται[ll] τῷ θεῷ. 12 Ἄρα [y]οὖν[ll]
and every tongue shall confess to God. So then
ἕκαστος ἡμῶν περὶ ἑαυτοῦ λόγον [z]δώσει[ll] [a]τῷ θεῷ.[ll] 13 Μη-
each of us concerning himself account shall give to God. No
κέτι οὖν ἀλλήλους κρίνωμεν· ἀλλὰ τοῦτο κρίνατε μᾶλλον,
longer therefore one another should we judge; but this judge ye rather,
τὸ μὴ.τιθέναι πρόσκομμα τῷ ἀδελφῷ ἢ σκάνδαλον.
not to put an occasion of stumbling to the brother or a cause of offence.
14 οἶδα καὶ πέπεισμαι ἐν κυρίῳ Ἰησοῦ, ὅτι οὐδὲν
I know and am persuaded in [the] Lord Jesus, that nothing [is]
κοινὸν δι' [b]ἑαυτοῦ·[ll] εἰ.μὴ τῷ λογιζομένῳ τι κοινὸν
unclean of itself: except to him who reckons anything unclean
εἶναι, ἐκείνῳ κοινόν· 15 εἰ [c]δὲ[ll] διὰ βρῶμα ὁ
to be, to that one unclean [it is]. [2]If [1]but on account of meat
ἀδελφός.σου λυπεῖται, οὐκέτι κατὰ ἀγάπην περιπατεῖς.
thy brother is grieved, no longer according to love thou walkest.
μὴ τῷ.βρώματί.σου ἐκεῖνον ἀπόλλυε ὑπὲρ οὗ χριστὸς ἀπέ-
[2]Not [3]with [4]thy [5]meat [6]him [1]destroy for whom Christ died.
θανεν. 16 Μὴ.βλασφημείσθω οὖν ὑμῶν τὸ ἀγαθόν· 17 οὐ
Let not [4]be [5]evil [6]spoken [7]of [1]therefore [2]your [3]good; [9]not
γάρ ἐστιν ἡ βασιλεία τοῦ θεοῦ βρῶσις καὶ πόσις, ἀλλὰ
[8]for is the kingdom of God eating and drinking; but
δικαιοσύνη καὶ εἰρήνη καὶ χαρὰ ἐν πνεύματι ἁγίῳ· 18 ὁ
righteousness and peace and joy in [the] [2]Spirit [1]Holy. [4]He [5]that
γὰρ ἐν [d]τούτοις[ll] δουλεύων [e]τῷ[ll] χριστῷ εὐάρεστος τῷ θεῷ,
[3]for in these things serves the Christ [is] well-pleasing to God,
καὶ δόκιμος τοῖς ἀνθρώποις. 19 ἄρα οὖν τὰ τῆς εἰρήνης
and approved by men. So then the things of peace
[f]διώκωμεν,[ll] καὶ τὰ τῆς οἰκοδομῆς τῆς.εἰς.ἀλλήλους.
we should pursue, and the things for building up one another.
20 Μὴ ἕνεκεν βρώματος κατάλυε τὸ ἔργον τοῦ θεοῦ.
Not for the sake of meat destroy the work of God.
πάντα μὲν καθαρά, ἀλλὰ κακὸν τῷ ἀνθρώπῳ τῷ
All things indeed [are] pure; but [it is] evil to the man who
διὰ προσκόμματος ἐσθίοντι. 21 καλὸν τὸ μὴ φαγεῖν κρέα,
through stumbling eats. [It is] right not to eat flesh,
μηδὲ πιεῖν οἶνον, μηδὲ ἐν ᾧ ὁ.ἀδελφός.σου προσκόπτει [g]ἢ
nor drink wine, nor in what thy brother stumbles, or
σκανδαλίζεται ἢ ἀσθενεῖ.[ll] 22 Σὺ πίστιν [h]ἔχεις; κατὰ[ll] [i]σαυτὸν[ll]
is offended, or is weak. [2]Thou [3]faith [1]hast? To thyself
ἔχε ἐνώπιον τοῦ θεοῦ· μακάριος ὁ μὴ.κρίνων ἑαυτὸν
have [it] before God. Blessed [is] he that judges not himself

other, being weak, eats vegetables

3 do not let the one who eats despise the one who does not eat and he who does not eat, let him not judge him who eats, for God has adopted him for Himself –

4 he stands or falls to his own master. And he shall be made to stand, for God is able to establish him.

5 One judges one day above another; another judges every day *alike*. Let each be fully assured in his own mind.

6 He who regards the day regards it to the Lord; and he who does not regard the day does not regard it to the Lord. He who eats does so to the Lord, for he gives thanks to God. And he who does not eat, does not eat for the Lord's *sake* and gives thanks to God.

7 For not one of us lives to himself, and not one dies to himself.

8 For both if we should live, we live to the Lord, and if we should die, we die to the Lord. Both, then, if we should live and if we should die, we are the Lord's.

9 For this Christ both died and rose and lived again, so that He might rule over both the living and the dead.

10 But you – why do you judge your brother? Or again, You – why do you belittle your brother? For we shall all stand before the judgment seat of Christ.

11 For it has been written, "I live, says the Lord, so that every knee shall bow to Me and every tongue shall confess to God."

12 So, then, each of us shall give account of himself to God.

13 No longer, then, should we judge one another. But rather judge this – Do not put a stumbling-block or reason to fall before your brother.

14 I know and am persuaded in the Lord Jesus that nothing is unclean of itself – except to him who judges anything to be unclean, to him *it is* unclean.

15 But if your brother is grieved on account of *your* food, you no longer walk according to love. Do not with your food destroy him for whom Christ died.

16 Then do not let your good be slandered.

17 For the kingdom of God is not eating and drinking, but righteousness and peace and joy in the Holy Spirit.

18 For he who serves Christ in these things is pleasing to God and approved by men.

19 So then let us follow the things of peace, and the things that edify one another.

20 Do not throw down the work of God for the sake of food. All things are indeed pure, but *it is* evil to the man who is eating through stumbling.

21 It is not right to eat flesh or drink wine or to *do anything* in which your brother stumbles, or is scandalized, or is weak.

22 Do you have faith? Have it to yourself before God. Happy is he who does not condemn himself by what he approves.

ἐν ᾧ δοκιμάζει. 23 ὁ.δὲ διακρινόμενος, ἐὰν φάγῃ, κατα-
in what he approves. But he that doubts, if he eat, has been
κέκριται, ὅτι οὐκ ἐκ πίστεως· πᾶν.δὲ ὃ οὐκ ἐκ
condemned, because [it is] not of faith; and everything which [is] not of
πίστεως, ἁμαρτία ἐστίν. [k]
faith, [2]sin [1]is.

15 Ὀφείλομεν.δὲ ἡμεῖς οἱ δυνατοὶ τὰ ἀσθενήματα τῶν
But we ought, we who [are] strong, the infirmities of the
ἀδυνάτων βαστάζειν, καὶ μὴ ἑαυτοῖς ἀρέσκειν· 2 ἕκαστος.[l]γὰρ"
weak to bear, and not ourselves to please. For [2]each
ἡμῶν τῷ πλησίον ἀρεσκέτω εἰς τὸ ἀγαθὸν πρὸς οἰκοδομήν.
[3]of [4]us [6]the [7]neighbour [1]let [5]please unto good for building up.
3 καὶ.γὰρ ὁ χριστὸς οὐχ ἑαυτῷ ἤρεσεν, ἀλλά, καθὼς γέ-
For also the Christ [2]not [3]himself [1]pleased; but, according as it has
γραπται, Οἱ ὀνειδισμοὶ τῶν ὀνειδιζόντων σε [m]ἐπέπεσον"
been written, The reproaches of those reproaching thee fell
ἐπ' ἐμέ. 4 Ὅσα.γὰρ προεγράφη, εἰς τὴν ἡμετέραν
on me. For as many things as were written before for our
διδασκαλίαν [n]προεγράφη," ἵνα διὰ τῆς ὑπομονῆς καὶ [o] τῆς
instruction were written before, that through endurance and
παρακλήσεως τῶν γραφῶν τὴν ἐλπίδα ἔχωμεν. 5 ὁ.δὲ
encouragement of the scriptures hope we might have. Now the
θεὸς τῆς ὑπομονῆς καὶ τῆς παρακλήσεως δῴη ὑμῖν τὸ αὐτὸ
God of endurance and encouragement give you [3]the [4]same [5]thing
φρονεῖν ἐν ἀλλήλοις κατὰ [p]χριστὸν Ἰησοῦν·" 6 ἵνα
to [2]mind with one another according to Christ Jesus; that
ὁμοθυμαδὸν ἐν ἑνὶ στόματι δοξάζητε τὸν θεὸν καὶ πατέρα
with one accord with one mouth ye may glorify the God and Father
τοῦ.κυρίου.ἡμῶν Ἰησοῦ χριστοῦ. 7 Διὸ προσλαμβάνεσθε
of our Lord Jesus Christ. Wherefore receive ye
ἀλλήλους, καθὼς καὶ ὁ χριστὸς προσελάβετο [q]ἡμᾶς" εἰς
one another, according as also the Christ received us to
δόξαν [r] θεοῦ.
[the] glory of God.

8 Λέγω [s]δέ," [t]Ἰησοῦν" χριστὸν διάκονον [v]γεγενῆσθαι" περι-
[2]I [3]say [1]but, Jesus Christ a servant has become of cir-
τομῆς ὑπὲρ ἀληθείας θεοῦ, εἰς τὸ βεβαιῶσαι τὰς ἐπαγ-
cumcision for [the] truth of God, for to confirm the pro-
γελίας τῶν πατέρων· 9 τὰ.δὲ ἔθνη ὑπὲρ ἐλέους δοξάσαι τὸν
mises of the fathers; and the nations for mercy to glorify
θεόν, καθὼς γέγραπται, Διὰ τοῦτο ἐξομολογήσομαί
God; according as it has been written, Because of this I will confess
σοι ἐν ἔθνεσιν, καὶ τῷ.ὀνόματί.σου ψαλῶ. 10 Καὶ
to thee among [the] nations, and thy name will I praise. And
πάλιν λέγει, Εὐφράνθητε, ἔθνη, μετὰ τοῦ.λαοῦ.αὐτοῦ. 11 Καὶ
again it says, Rejoice ye, nations, with his people. And
πάλιν[w], Αἰνεῖτε [x]τὸν κύριον πάντα τὰ ἔθνη," καὶ [y]ἐπαινέσατε"
again, Praise the Lord, all the nations, and praise
αὐτὸν πάντες οἱ λαοί. 12 Καὶ πάλιν, Ἡσαΐας λέγει, Ἔ-
him, all the peoples. And again, Esaias says, There
σται ἡ ῥίζα τοῦ Ἰεσσαί, καὶ ὁ ἀνιστάμενος ἄρχειν
shall be the root of Jesse, and he that arises to rule [the]
ἐθνῶν, ἐπ' αὐτῷ ἔθνη ἐλπιοῦσιν. 13 Ὁ.δὲ θεὸς τῆς
nations: in him [the] nations shall hope. Now [2]the [3]God
ἐλπίδος πληρώσαι ὑμᾶς πάσης χαρᾶς καὶ εἰρήνης ἐν τῷ
[4]of [5]hope [1]may fill you with all joy and peace in
πιστεύειν, εἰς τὸ περισσεύειν ὑμᾶς ἐν τῇ ἐλπίδι, ἐν δυνάμει
believing, for [2]to [3]abound [1]you in hope, in power
πνεύματος ἁγίου.
of [the] [2]Spirit [1]Holy.

14 Πέπεισμαι.δέ, ἀδελφοί.μου, καὶ αὐτὸς ἐγὼ περὶ
But [4]am [5]persuaded, [6]my [7]brethren, [2]also [3]myself [1]I concerning
ὑμῶν, ὅτι καὶ αὐτοὶ μεστοί ἐστε ἀγαθωσύνης, πεπληρωμένοι
you that also yourselves full are of goodness, being filled
πάσης [z] γνώσεως, δυνάμενοι καὶ ἀλλήλους νουθετεῖν. 15 [a]τολ-
with all knowledge, being able also one another to admonish. [2]More
μηρότερον" δὲ ἔγραψα ὑμῖν, [b]ἀδελφοί," ἀπὸ μέρους, ὡς
[3]boldly [1]but I did write to you, brethren, in part, as
ἐπαναμιμνήσκων ὑμᾶς, διὰ τὴν χάριν τὴν δοθεῖσάν μοι
reminding you, because of the grace which was given to me
[c]ὑπὸ" τοῦ θεοῦ, 16 εἰς τὸ εἶναί με λειτουργὸν [d]Ἰησοῦ χριστοῦ"
by God, for [2]to [3]be [1]me a minister of Jesus Christ
εἰς τὰ ἔθνη, ἱερουργοῦντα τὸ εὐαγγέλιον τοῦ θεοῦ,
to the nations, administering in sacred service the glad tidings of God,
ἵνα γένηται ἡ προσφορὰ τῶν ἐθνῶν εὐπρόσδεκτος, ἡγιασμένη
that might be the offering up of the nations acceptable, sanctified
ἐν πνεύματι ἁγίῳ. 17 ἔχω οὖν [e] καύχησιν ἐν χριστῷ
by [the] [2]Spirit [1]Holy. I have therefore boasting in Christ
Ἰησοῦ τὰ πρὸς [f]θεόν· 18 οὐ.γὰρ τολμήσω [g]λα-
Jesus [as to] the things pertaining to God. For not will I dare to

23 But he who doubts, if he eats, has been
condemned, because it is not of faith. And
whatever is not of faith is sin.

CHAPTER 15

1 And we who are strong ought to bear the
weaknesses of the weak and not try to please
ourselves.
2 For let everyone of us please his neighbor
for good, to build him up.
3 For even Christ did not please Himself,
but as it has been written, "The curses of
those who were cursing You fell on Me."
4 For whatever things were written in the
past were written before for our learning, so
that through patience and comfort of the
Scriptures we might have hope.
5 Now the God of constancy and comfort
grant you to mind the same thing with one
another according to Christ Jesus.
6 So that with one mind, with one mouth,
you may glorify the God and Father of our
Lord Jesus Christ.
7 Then take one another to your *hearts* just
as Christ also took us to *Himself* to *the* glory
of God.

8 But I say that Jesus Christ has become a
servant of circumcision for the truth of God,
to confirm the promises of the fathers.
9 And for the Gentiles to glorify God for
mercy, as it has been written, "Because of
this I will confess to You among the
Gentiles, and I will praise Your name."
10 And again it says, "Rejoice with His
people, you Gentiles."
11 And again, "Praise the Lord, all the
Gentiles, and praise Him, all the peoples."
12 And again, Isaiah says, "There shall be
the Root of Jesse, and He that arises to reign
over the Gentiles, in Him the Gentiles shall
hope."
13 Now may the God of hope fill you with
all joy and peace in believing, so that you
may abound in hope, in the power of the
Holy Spirit.

14 But, my brothers, I myself am also persuaded about you, that you yourselves are
full of goodness, having been filled with all
knowledge, being able also to warn one
another.
15 But I did more boldly write to you,
brothers, partly to remind you, because of
the grace which was given to me under God.
16 For *it was given* to me to be a minister
of Jesus Christ to the Gentiles, sacredly
ministering the gospel of God, in order that
the offering up of the Gentiles might be
pleasing, sanctified by the Holy Spirit.
17 Therefore I have my glorying in Christ
Jesus in those things having to do with God.
18 For I will not dare speak anything of

λεῖν τι‖ ὧν οὐ κατειργάσατο χριστὸς δι' ἐμοῦ, εἰς
speak anything of what [3]not [2]worked [4]out [1]Christ by me, for [the]
ὑπακοὴν ἐθνῶν, λόγῳ καὶ ἔργῳ, 19 ἐν δυνάμει ση-
obedience of [the] nations, by word and work, in [the] power of
μείων καὶ τεράτων, ἐν δυνάμει πνεύματος [h]θεοῦ·‖ ὥστε.με
signs and wonders, in [the] power of [the] Spirit of God; so as for me
ἀπὸ Ἱερουσαλὴμ καὶ κύκλῳ μέχρι τοῦ Ἰλλυρικοῦ πεπληρω-
from Jerusalem, and in a circuit unto Illyricum, to have fully
κέναι τὸ εὐαγγέλιον τοῦ χριστοῦ· 20 οὕτως.δὲ [i]φιλοτιμού-
preached the glad tidings of the Christ; and so being am-
μενον‖ εὐαγγελίζεσθαι, οὐχ ὅπου ὠνομάσθη χριστός,
bitious to announce the glad tidings, not where [2]was [3]named [1]Christ,
ἵνα μὴ ἐπ' ἀλλότριον θεμέλιον οἰκοδομῶ· 21 ἀλλὰ καθὼς
that not upon another's foundation I might build; but according as
γέγραπται, Οἷς οὐκ.ἀνηγγέλη περὶ αὐτοῦ, ὄψον-
it has been written, To whom it was not announced concerning him, they shall
ται· καὶ οἳ οὐκ.ἀκηκόασιν, συνήσουσιν. 22 Διὸ καὶ ἐνε-
see; and those that have not heard, shall understand. Wherefore also I was
κοπτόμην [k]τὰ.πολλὰ‖ τοῦ.ἐλθεῖν πρὸς ὑμᾶς. 23 νυνὶ.δὲ
hindered many times from coming to you. But now,
μηκέτι τόπον ἔχων ἐν τοῖς.κλίμασιν.τούτοις, ἐπιποθίαν.δὲ
no longer [2]place [1]having in these regions, and [2]a [3]longing
ἔχων [l]τοῦ[l] ἐλθεῖν πρὸς ὑμᾶς ἀπὸ [m]πολλῶν‖ ἐτῶν, 24 ὡς.[n]ἐὰν‖
[1]having to come to you for many years, whenever
πορεύωμαι εἰς τὴν Σπανίαν, [o]ἐλεύσομαι πρὸς ὑμᾶς·‖ ἐλπίζω
I may go to Spain, I will come to you; [2]I [3]hope
γὰρ διαπορευόμενος θεάσασθαι ὑμᾶς, καὶ [p]ὑφ'‖ ὑμῶν προπεμ-
[1]for going through to see you, and by you to be set
φθῆναι ἐκεῖ, ἐὰν ὑμῶν πρῶτον ἀπὸ μέρους ἐμπλησθῶ.
forward thither, if of you first in part I should be filled.
25 Νυνὶ.δὲ πορεύομαι εἰς Ἱερουσαλήμ, διακονῶν τοῖς ἁγίοις.
But now I go to Jerusalem, doing service to the saints;
26 [q]εὐδόκησαν‖.γὰρ Μακεδονία καὶ Ἀχαΐα κοινωνίαν τινὰ
for [4]were [5]pleased [1]Macedonia [2]and [3]Achaia [6]a [8]contribution [7]certain
ποιήσασθαι εἰς τοὺς πτωχοὺς τῶν ἁγίων τῶν ἐν Ἱερουσα-
to make for the poor of the saints who [are] in Jerusa-
λήμ· 27 [q]εὐδόκησαν‖.γὰρ καὶ ὀφειλέται [r]αὐτῶν εἰσιν.‖ εἰ.γὰρ
lem. For they were pleased and [2]debtors [1]their they are; for if
τοῖς.πνευματικοῖς.αὐτῶν ἐκοινώνησαν τὰ ἔθνη, ὀφείλουσιν
in their spiritual things [3]participated [1]the [2]nations, they ought
καὶ ἐν τοῖς σαρκικοῖς λειτουργῆσαι αὐτοῖς. 28 τοῦτο οὖν
also in the fleshly things to minister to them. This therefore
ἐπιτελέσας, καὶ σφραγισάμενος αὐτοῖς τὸν.καρπὸν.τοῦτον,
having finished, and having sealed to them this fruit,
ἀπελεύσομαι δι' ὑμῶν εἰς [s]τὴν‖ Σπανίαν. 29 οἶδα.δὲ ὅτι
I will set off by you into Spain. And I know that
ἐρχόμενος πρὸς ὑμᾶς, ἐν πληρώματι εὐλογίας [t]τοῦ εὐαγγελίου
coming to you, in fulness of blessing of the glad tidings
τοῦ‖ χριστοῦ ἐλεύσομαι. 30 Παρακαλῶ.δὲ ὑμᾶς, [v]ἀδελφοί,‖ διὰ
of Christ I shall come. But I exhort you, brethren, by
τοῦ.κυρίου.ἡμῶν Ἰησοῦ χριστοῦ, καὶ διὰ τῆς ἀγάπης τοῦ
our Lord Jesus Christ, and by the love of the
πνεύματος, συναγωνίσασθαί μοι ἐν ταῖς προσευχαῖς ὑπὲρ
Spirit, to strive together with me in prayers for
ἐμοῦ πρὸς τὸν θεόν· 31 ἵνα ῥυσθῶ ἀπὸ τῶν ἀπει-
me to God, that I may be delivered from those being
θούντων ἐν τῇ Ἰουδαίᾳ, καὶ [w]ἵνα‖ ἡ [x]διακονία‖ μου ἡ
disobedient in Judæa; and that [2]service [1]my which [is]
[y]εἰς‖ Ἱερουσαλὴμ εὐπρόσδεκτος [z]γένηται τοῖς ἁγίοις·‖ 32 ἵνα
for Jerusalem acceptable may be to the saints; that
[a]ἐν χαρᾷ ἔλθω‖ πρὸς ὑμᾶς διὰ θελήματος [b]θεοῦ,‖ [c]καὶ
in joy I may come to you by [the] will of God, and
συναναπαύσωμαι ὑμῖν.‖ 33 ὁ.δὲ θεὸς τῆς εἰρήνης μετὰ
I may be refreshed with you. And the God of peace [be] with
πάντων ὑμῶν. [d]ἀμήν.‖
[2]all [1]you. Amen.

16 Συνίστημι.δὲ ὑμῖν Φοίβην τὴν.ἀδελφὴν.ἡμῶν, οὖσαν
But I commend to you Phœbe, our sister, being
διάκονον τῆς ἐκκλησίας τῆς ἐν [e]Κεγχρεαῖς·‖ 2 ἵνα [f]αὐτὴν προσ-
servant of the assembly in Cenchrea; that her ye may
δέξησθε‖ ἐν κυρίῳ ἀξίως τῶν ἁγίων, καὶ παραστῆτε αὐτῇ
receive in [the] Lord worthily of saints, and ye may assist her
ἐν ᾧ.ἂν ὑμῶν χρῄζῃ πράγματι· καὶ.γὰρ [g]αὕτη‖ προ-
in whatever [2]of [3]you [4]she [5]may [6]need [1]matter; for also she a suc-
στάτις πολλῶν ἐγενήθη, καὶ [h]αὐτοῦ ἐμοῦ.‖ 3 Ἀσπάσασθε
courer of many has been, and [3]myself [1]of [2]me. Salute
[i]Πρίσκιλλαν‖ καὶ Ἀκύλαν τοὺς.συνεργούς.μου ἐν χριστῷ Ἰη-
Priscilla and Aquila my fellow-workers in Christ Je-
σοῦ· 4 οἵτινες ὑπὲρ τῆς.ψυχῆς.μου τὸν.ἑαυτῶν τράχηλον
sus, (who for my life their own neck

what Christ has not done through me, to the
obedience of the Gentiles, by word and deed
19 – of signs and wonders in power, in the
power of God's Spirit, so that I have fully
preached the gospel of Christ from Jerusalem and in a circle as far as Il-lyr-i-cum.
20 And so I was eager to preach the gospel
where Christ had not been named, so that I
might not build on another's foundation,
21 but as it has been written, "They shall
see, to whom nothing was told about Him.
And those that have not heard shall understand."
22 For this reason also I was kept back
many times from coming to you.
23 But now having no more opportunity in
these borders, and having a great longing to
come to you for many years,
24 whenever I go to Spain I will come to
you. For I hope in going through to see you,
and to be sent forward to there by you, if
first I shall share and be satisfied by you.
25 But now I go to Jerusalem, ministering
to the saints.
26 For Mac-e-do-ni-a and A-chai-a were
pleased to make a certain gift to the poor
among the saints who are in Jerusalem.
27 They have been pleased and they have
been their debtors. For if the Gentiles took
part in their spiritual things, they ought also
to minister to them in fleshly things.
28 Then when I have finished this and have
sealed to them this fruit, I will come by you
into Spain.
29 And I am sure that when I come to you,
I shall come in the fullness of blessing of the
gospel of Christ.
30 And I beg you, brothers, by our Lord
Jesus Christ, and by the love of the Spirit, to
strongly help me in prayers to God for me,
31 so that I may be delivered from those in
Judea who are unbelieving, and that my gift
which is for Jerusalem may be pleasing to
the saints,
32 that I may come to you in joy, by the
will of God, and that I may be refreshed by
you.
33 And the God of peace be with you all.
Amen.

CHAPTER 16

1 And I commend to you our sister Phoebe,
who is a servant of the Cen-chre-an church,
2 that you may receive her in the Lord, as
saints should and you may help her in
whatever matter she may need you. For she
also has been a helper of many, and of
myself.
3 Greet Priscilla and Aquila, my fellow-
workers in Christ Jesus,
4 who laid down their own necks for my

ὑπέθηκαν, οἷς οὐκ ἐγὼ μόνος εὐχαριστῶ, ἀλλὰ καὶ πᾶσαι αἱ
laid down: whom not [2]I [1]only thank, but also all the
ἐκκλησίαι τῶν ἐθνῶν· 5 καὶ τὴν κατ' οἶκον αὐτῶν ἐκκλησίαν.
assemblies of the nations,) and the [2]at [4]house [3]their [1]assembly.
ἀσπάσασθε Ἐπαίνετον τὸν.ἀγαπητόν.μου, ὅς ἐστιν ἀπαρχὴ
Salute Epænetus my beloved, who is a first-fruit
τῆς [k]Ἀχαΐας" εἰς χριστόν. 6 ἀσπάσασθε [l]Μαριάμ," ἥτις πολλὰ
of Achaia for Christ. Salute Mary, who [2]much
ἐκοπίασεν εἰς [m]ἡμᾶς." 7 ἀσπάσασθε Ἀνδρόνικον καὶ Ἰουνίαν
[1]laboured for us. Salute Andronicus and Junias
τοὺς.συγγενεῖς.μου καὶ συναιχμαλώτους μου· οἵτινές εἰσιν
my kinsmen and [2]fellow-prisoners [1]my, who are
ἐπίσημοι ἐν τοῖς ἀποστόλοις, οἳ καὶ πρὸ ἐμοῦ [n]γεγόνασιν"
of note among the apostles; who also before me were
ἐν χριστῷ. 8 ἀσπάσασθε [o]Ἀμπλίαν" τὸν.ἀγαπητόν.μου ἐν
in Christ. Salute Amplias my beloved in [the]
κυρίῳ. 9 ἀσπάσασθε Οὐρβανὸν τὸν.συνεργὸν.ἡμῶν ἐν [p]χριστῷ,"
Lord. Salute Urbanus our fellow-worker in Christ,
καὶ Στάχυν τὸν.ἀγαπητόν.μου. 10 ἀσπάσασθε Ἀπελλῆν τὸν
and Stachys my beloved. Salute Apelles the
δόκιμον ἐν χριστῷ. ἀσπάσασθε τοὺς ἐκ τῶν Ἀρι-
approved in Christ. Salute those of the [household] of Ari-
στοβούλου. 11 ἀσπάσασθε [q]Ἡρῳδίωνα" τὸν.[r]συγγενῆ".μου.
stobulus. Salute Herodion my kinsman.
ἀσπάσασθε τοὺς ἐκ τῶν Ναρκίσσου, τοὺς ὄντας ἐν
Salute those of the [household] of Narcissus, who are in [the]
κυρίῳ. 12 ἀσπάσασθε Τρύφαιναν καὶ Τρυφῶσαν τὰς κοπιώσας
Lord. Salute Tryphæna and Tryphosa, who labour
ἐν κυρίῳ. [s]ἀσπάσασθε Περσίδα τὴν ἀγαπητήν, ἥτις πολλὰ
in [the] Lord. Salute Persis the beloved, who much
ἐκοπίασεν ἐν κυρίῳ." 13 ἀσπάσασθε Ῥοῦφον τὸν ἐκλεκτὸν
laboured in [the] Lord. Salute Rufus the chosen
ἐν κυρίῳ, καὶ τὴν.μητέρα.αὐτοῦ καὶ ἐμοῦ. 14 ἀσπάσασθε
in [the] Lord, and his mother and mine. Salute
[t]Ἀσύγκριτον," Φλέγοντα, [v]Ἑρμᾶν," Πατρόβαν, [w]Ἑρμῆν," καὶ
Asyncritus, Phlegon, Hermas, Patrobas, Hermes, and
τοὺς σὺν αὐτοῖς ἀδελφούς. 15 ἀσπάσασθε Φιλόλογον καὶ
the [2]with [3]them [1]brethren, Salute Philologus and
Ἰουλίαν, Νηρέα καὶ τὴν.ἀδελφὴν.αὐτοῦ, καὶ Ὀλυμπᾶν, καὶ
Julias, Nereus and his sister, and Olympas, and
τοὺς σὺν αὐτοῖς πάντας ἁγίους. 16 ἀσπάσασθε ἀλλήλους
[2]the [4]with [5]them [1]all [3]saints. Salute one another
ἐν φιλήματι ἁγίῳ. ἀσπάζονται ὑμᾶς αἱ ἐκκλησίαι [x] τοῦ
with a [2]kiss [1]holy. [7]Salute [8]you [3]the [4]assemblies
χριστοῦ.
[5]of [6]Christ.

17 Παρακαλῶ.δὲ ὑμᾶς, ἀδελφοί, σκοπεῖν τοὺς τὰς διχο-
But I exhort you, brethren to consider those who [2]divi-
στασίας καὶ τὰ σκάνδαλα, παρὰ τὴν διδαχὴν ἣν ὑμεῖς
sions [3]and [4]causes [5]of [6]offence [7]contrary [8]to [9]the [10]teaching [11]which [12]ye
ἐμάθετε, ποιοῦντας· καὶ [y]ἐκκλίνατε" ἀπ' αὐτῶν. 18 οἱ γὰρ
[13]learnt, [1]make, and turn away from them. For
τοιοῦτοι τῷ.κυρίῳ.ἡμῶν [z]Ἰησοῦ" χριστῷ οὐ.δουλεύουσιν, ἀλλὰ
such [3]our [4]Lord [5]Jesus [6]Christ [1]serve [2]not, but
τῇ.ἑαυτῶν κοιλίᾳ· καὶ διὰ τῆς χρηστολογίας καὶ εὐλογίας
their own belly, and by kind speaking and praise
ἐξαπατῶσιν τὰς καρδίας τῶν ἀκάκων. 19 ἡ.γὰρ ὑμῶν ὑπακοὴ
deceive the hearts of the innocent. For the [2]of [3]you [1]obedience
εἰς πάντας ἀφίκετο· [a]χαίρω οὖν τὸ.ἐφ' ὑμῖν." θέλω.δὲ
[5]to [6]all [4]reached. I rejoice therefore concerning you; but I wish
ὑμᾶς σοφοὺς [b]μὲν" εἶναι εἰς τὸ ἀγαθόν, ἀκεραίους.δὲ εἰς τὸ
you wise to be [as] to good, and simple to
κακόν. 20 ὁ.δὲ θεὸς τῆς εἰρήνης συντρίψει τὸν σατανᾶν ὑπὸ
evil. But the God of peace will bruise Satan under
τοὺς.πόδας.ὑμῶν ἐν τάχει. ἡ χάρις τοῦ.κυρίου.ἡμῶν Ἰησοῦ
your feet shortly. The grace of our Lord Jesus
[c]χριστοῦ" μεθ' ὑμῶν. [d]
Christ [be] with you.
21 [e]Ἀσπάζονται" ὑμᾶς Τιμόθεος ὁ.συνεργός.μου καὶ Λούκιος
[12]Salute [13]you [1]Timotheus [2]my [3]fellow-worker [4]and [5]Lucius
καὶ Ἰάσων καὶ Σωσίπατρος οἱ.συγγενεῖς.μου. 22 ἀσπάζομαι
[6]and [7]Jason [8]and [9]Sosipater [10]my [11]kinsmen. [20]Salute
ὑμᾶς ἐγὼ Τέρτιος ὁ γράψας τὴν ἐπιστολὴν ἐν κυρίῳ.
[21]you [14]I [15]Tertius [16]who [17]wrote [18]the [19]epistle in [the] Lord.
23 ἀσπάζεται ὑμᾶς Γάϊος ὁ ξένος μου καὶ [f]τῆς ἐκκλησίας
[2]Salutes [3]you [1]Gaius, the host of me and of the [2]assembly
ὅλης." ἀσπάζεται ὑμᾶς Ἔραστος ὁ οἰκονόμος τῆς πόλεως,
[1]whole. [13]Salutes [14]you [1]Erastus [4]the [5]steward [6]of [7]the [8]city,
καὶ Κούαρτος ὁ ἀδελφός. 24 [g]Ἡ χάρις τοῦ.κυρίου.ἡμῶν
[9]and [10]Quartus [11]the [12]brother. The grace of our Lord
Ἰησοῦ χριστοῦ μετὰ πάντων ὑμῶν. ἀμήν."
Jesus Christ [be] with [2]all [1]you. Amen.

life, whom not only I thank but also all the
churches of the Gentiles.
5 And greet the church at their house, and
my beloved Ep-e-ne-tus, who is a first-fruit
of A-chai-a for Christ.
6 Greet Mary, who did much labor for us.
7 Salute An-dro-ni-cus and Junias, my kinsmen and fellow-prisoners, noted among the
apostles, who also were in Christ before me.
8 Greet Amplias, my beloved in the Lord.
9 Greet Urbanus, our helper in Christ, and
my beloved Stach-ys.
10 Greet Apelles, the approved in Christ *and*
those of the household of A-ris-to-bu-lus.
11 Greet He-ro-di-on, my kinsman. Greet
those of the household of Nar-cis-sus, who
are in the Lord.
12 Greet Try-phe-na and Try-pho-sa, who
labor in the Lord. Greet Persis, the beloved,
who much labored in the Lord.
13 Greet Rufus, the chosen in the Lord, and
his mother and mine.
14 Salute A-syn-cri-tus, Phleg-on, Hermas,
Pat-ro-bas, Hermes and the brothers with
them.
15 Greet Phil-ol-o-gus and Julias, Nereus
and his sister and O-lym-pas, and all the
saints with them.
16 Greet one another with a holy kiss. The
churches of Christ send greetings to you.

17 Now, I beg you, brothers, to consider
those who make the divisions and causes of
stumbling contrary to the teaching which
you have learned. And turn away from
them.
18 For such ones do not serve our Lord
Jesus Christ, but their own belly. And by
smooth words and praise *they* deceive the
hearts of the innocent.
19 For your obedience reached to all. So I
rejoice concerning you. But I would have
you to be wise to good and simple as to evil.
20 And the God of peace will bruise Satan
under your feet shortly. The grace of our
Lord Jesus Christ be with you.

21 Timothy, my fellow-worker, and Lucius
and Jason, and So-sip-a-ter, my kindred greet
you.
22 I, Tertius, who wrote you the epistle in
the Lord greet you.
23 Gaius, the host of the whole church and
me, greets you. Erastus, the steward of the
city, and Quartus the brother, greet you.
24 The grace of our Lord Jesus Christ be
with you all. Amen.

25 [h]Τῷ.δὲ δυναμένῳ ὑμᾶς στηρίξαι κατὰ τὸ εὐαγ-
Now to him who is able you to establish according to [2]glad
γέλιόν μου καὶ τὸ κήρυγμα Ἰησοῦ χριστοῦ, κατὰ ἀπο-
[3]tidings [1]my and the proclamation of Jesus Christ, according to a reve-
κάλυψιν μυστηρίου χρόνοις αἰωνίοις σεσιγημένου,
lation of [the] mystery in times of the ages having been kept secret,
26 φανερωθέντος.δὲ νῦν, διά.τε γραφῶν προφητικῶν, κατ'
but made manifest now, and by [2]scriptures [1]prophetic, according to
ἐπιταγὴν τοῦ αἰωνίου θεοῦ, εἰς ὑπακοὴν πίστεως εἰς πάντα
commandment of the eternal God, for obedience of faith to all
τὰ ἔθνη γνωρισθέντος, 27 μόνῳ σοφῷ θεῷ, διὰ Ἰη-
the nations having been made known—[the] only wise God, through Je-
σοῦ χριστοῦ, ᾧ ἡ δόξα εἰς τοὺς αἰῶνας[i]. ἀμήν.
sus Christ, to whom be glory to the ages. Amen.
[k]Πρὸς Ῥωμαίους ἐγράφη ἀπὸ Κορίνθου, διὰ Φοίβης τῆς
To [the] Romans written from Corinth, by Phœbe
διακόνου τῆς ἐν Κεγχρεαῖς ἐκκλησίας.||
servant of the [2]in [3]Cenchrea [1]assembly.

25 Now to Him that is able to establish you
according to my gospel – and the preaching
of Jesus Christ, according to the revealing of
the mystery (regarding which, silence has
been kept during eternal ages,
26 but now has been made plain), and by
prophetic Scriptures, according to commandment of the everlasting God, made known
for obedience of faith to all the nations,
27 the only wise God, through Jesus Christ,
to whom be the glory forever. Amen.

The FIRST Letter to the CORINTHIANS

CHAPTER 1

ΠΑΥΛΟΣ [b]κλητὸς|| ἀπόστολος [c]Ἰησοῦ χριστοῦ,|| διὰ θελή-
Paul a called apostle of Jesus Christ, by [the] will
ματος θεοῦ, καὶ Σωσθένης ὁ ἀδελφός, 2 τῇ ἐκκλησίᾳ τοῦ
of God, and Sosthenes the brother, to the assembly
θεοῦ [d]τῇ οὔσῃ ἐν Κορίνθῳ,|| ἡγιασμένοις ἐν χριστῷ Ἰη-
of God which is in Corinth, having been sanctified in Christ Je-
σοῦ,[d] κλητοῖς ἁγίοις, σὺν πᾶσιν τοῖς ἐπικαλουμένοις τὸ ὄνομα
sus, called saints, with all those [4]calling [5]on [6]the [7]name
τοῦ.κυρίου.ἡμῶν Ἰησοῦ χριστοῦ ἐν παντὶ τόπῳ, αὐτῶν.[e]τε||
[8]of [9]our [10]Lord [11]Jesus [12]Christ [1]in [2]every [3]place, both theirs
καὶ ἡμῶν· 3 χάρις ὑμῖν καὶ εἰρήνη ἀπὸ θεοῦ πατρὸς.ἡμῶν
and ours: grace to you and peace from God our Father
καὶ κυρίου Ἰησοῦ χριστοῦ.
and [the] Lord Jesus Christ.

4 Εὐχαριστῶ τῷ.θεῷ.μου πάντοτε περὶ ὑμῶν, ἐπὶ τῇ
I thank my God always concerning you, for the
χάριτι τοῦ θεοῦ τῇ δοθείσῃ ὑμῖν ἐν χριστῷ Ἰησοῦ, 5 ὅτι ἐν
grace of God that was given to you in Christ Jesus, that in
παντὶ ἐπλουτίσθητε ἐν αὐτῷ, ἐν παντὶ λόγῳ καὶ πάσῃ
everything ye were enriched in him, in all discourse and all
γνώσει, 6 καθὼς τὸ μαρτύριον τοῦ χριστοῦ ἐβεβαιώθη ἐν
knowledge, according as the testimony of the Christ was confirmed in
ὑμῖν· 7 ὥστε ὑμᾶς μὴ ὑστερεῖσθαι ἐν μηδενὶ χαρίσματι, ἀπεκ-
you, so that ye are behind in not one gift,
δεχομένους τὴν ἀποκάλυψιν τοῦ.κυρίου.ἡμῶν Ἰησοῦ χριστοῦ·
awaiting the revelation of our Lord Jesus Christ;
8 ὃς καὶ βεβαιώσει ὑμᾶς ἕως τέλους, ἀνεγκλήτους ἐν τῇ
who also will confirm you to [the] end, unimpeachable in the
ἡμέρᾳ τοῦ.κυρίου.ἡμῶν Ἰησοῦ χριστοῦ. 9 πιστὸς ὁ θεός, δι'
day of our Lord Jesus Christ. Faithful [is] God, by
οὗ ἐκλήθητε εἰς κοινωνίαν τοῦ.υἱοῦ.αὐτοῦ Ἰησοῦ χριστοῦ
whom ye were called into fellowship of his Son Jesus Christ
τοῦ.κυρίου.ἡμῶν.
our Lord.

1 Paul, called by God's will to be an apostle
of Jesus Christ, and Sos-the-nes the brother,
2 to the church of God which is in Corinth,
who have been sanctified in Christ Jesus,
called-out saints, with all the ones who call
on the name of our Lord Jesus Christ in
every place – both theirs and ours.
3 Grace to you, and peace from God our
Father and the Lord Jesus Christ.
4 I thank my God always because of you,
for the grace of God that was given to you in
Christ Jesus,
5 that you were made rich in Him in everything: in all you say and in all you know
6 – even as the testimony of Christ was
confirmed in you,
7 so that you are not behind in any gift,
waiting for the revealing of our Lord Jesus
Christ,
8 who also will confirm you to the end,
blameless in the day of our Lord Jesus Christ
9 – God is faithful, by whom you were called
into fellowship with His Son, Jesus Christ
our Lord.

10 Παρακαλῶ.δὲ ὑμᾶς, ἀδελφοί, διὰ τοῦ ὀνόματος τοῦ
Now I exhort you, brethren, by the name
κυρίου.ἡμῶν Ἰησοῦ χριστοῦ, ἵνα τὸ αὐτὸ λέγητε πάντες,
of our Lord Jesus Christ, that [4]the [5]same [6]thing [1]ye [3]say [2]all,
καὶ μὴ ᾖ ἐν ὑμῖν σχίσματα, ἦτε.δὲ κατηρτισμένοι
and [3]no [1]there [2]be [5]among [6]you [4]divisions; but ye be knit together
ἐν τῷ αὐτῷ νοῒ καὶ ἐν τῇ αὐτῇ γνώμῃ. 11 ἐδηλώθη.γάρ
in the same mind and in the same judgment. For it was shewn
μοι περὶ ὑμῶν, ἀδελφοί.μου, ὑπὸ τῶν Χλόης,
to me concerning you, my brethren, by those of [the house of] Chloe,
ὅτι ἔριδες ἐν ὑμῖν εἰσιν· 12 λέγω.δὲ τοῦτο, ὅτι ἕκαστος
that strifes among you there are. But I say this, that each
ὑμῶν λέγει, Ἐγὼ μέν εἰμι Παύλου, ἐγὼ.δὲ Ἀπολλώ, ἐγὼ.δὲ
of you says, I am of Paul, and I of Apollos, and I
Κηφᾶ, ἐγὼ.δὲ χριστοῦ. 13 Μεμέρισται ὁ χριστός; μὴ Παῦ-
of Cephas, and I of Christ Has [3]been [4]divided [1]the [2]Christ? [5]Paul
λος ἐσταυρώθη [f]ὑπὲρ|| ὑμῶν; ἢ εἰς τὸ ὄνομα Παύλου ἐβαπ-
[6]was crucified for you? or to the name of Paul were ye
τίσθητε; 14 εὐχαριστῶ [g]τῷ θεῷ|| ὅτι οὐδένα ὑμῶν ἐβάπτισα,
baptized? I thank God that no one of you I baptized,
εἰ.μὴ Κρίσπον καὶ Γάϊον· 15 ἵνα μή τις εἴπῃ ὅτι εἰς τὸ
except Crispus and Gaius, that not anyone should say that unto

10 Now I urge you brothers, by the name of
our Lord Jesus Christ, that you all agree in
what you say and that there be no divisons
among you. But be knit together in the same
mind and in the same judgment.
11 For it was revealed to me about you, my
brothers, by those who are of Chloe, that
there are arguments among you.
12 But I say this, that each of you claims, I
am of Paul, and I of Apollos, and I of Peter,
and I of Christ.
13 Has Christ been divided? Was Paul crucified for you? Or were you baptized into the
name of Paul?
14 I thank God that I did not baptize any
of you, except Crispus and Gaius,
15 so that no one should say that I baptized

ἐμὸν ὄνομα [b]ἐβάπτισα.‖ 16 ἐβάπτισα.δὲ καὶ τὸν Στεφανᾶ
my name I baptized. And I baptized also the [2]of [3]Stephanas
οἶκον· λοιπὸν οὐκ.οἶδα εἴ τινα ἄλλον ἐβάπτισα. 17 Οὐ.γὰρ
[1]house; as to the rest I know not if any other I baptized. For [4]not
ἀπέστειλέν με [i]χριστὸς βαπτίζειν, [k]ἀλλ'‖ εὐαγγελίζεσθαι·
[2]sent [3]me [1]Christ to baptize, but to announce the glad tidings;
οὐκ ἐν σοφίᾳ λόγου, ἵνα μὴ κενωθῇ ὁ σταυρὸς τοῦ χριστοῦ.
not in wisdom of word, that [2]not [1]be made void the cross of the Christ.
18 ὁ.λόγος.γὰρ ὁ τοῦ σταυροῦ τοῖς μὲν ἀπολλυμένοις μωρία
For the word of the cross to those perishing [2]foolishness
ἐστίν, τοῖς.δὲ σωζομένοις ἡμῖν δύναμις θεοῦ ἐστιν. 19 γέ-
[1]is, but [3]who [4]are [5]being [6]saved [1]to [2]us [9]power [10]of [11]God [7]it [8]is. [13]It [14]has
γραπται γάρ, Ἀπολῶ τὴν σοφίαν τῶν σοφῶν, καὶ τὴν
[15]been [16]written [12]for, I will destroy the wisdom of the wise, and the
σύνεσιν τῶν συνετῶν ἀθετήσω. 20 Ποῦ σοφός;
understanding of the understanding ones I will set aside. Where [is the] wise?
ποῦ γραμματεύς; ποῦ [l]συζητητὴς‖ τοῦ.αἰῶνος.τούτου;
where [the] scribe? where [the] disputer of this age?
οὐχὶ.ἐμώρανεν ὁ θεὸς τὴν σοφίαν τοῦ.κόσμου.[m]τούτου‖;
did not [2]make [3]foolish [1]God the wisdom of this world?
21 Ἐπειδὴ.γὰρ ἐν τῇ σοφίᾳ τοῦ θεοῦ οὐκ.ἔγνω ὁ κόσμος διὰ
For since, in the wisdom of God, [5]knew [6]not [1]the [2]world [3]by
τῆς σοφίας τὸν θεόν, εὐδόκησεν ὁ θεὸς διὰ τῆς μωρίας τοῦ
[4]wisdom God, [2]was [3]pleased [1]God by the foolishness of the
κηρύγματος σῶσαι τοὺς πιστεύοντας· 22 ἐπειδὴ καὶ Ἰου-
proclamation to save those that believe. Since both Jews
δαῖοι [n]σημεῖον‖ αἰτοῦσιν, καὶ Ἕλληνες σοφίαν ζητοῦσιν.
[3]a [4]sign [1]ask [2]for, and Greeks [2]wisdom [1]seek;
23 ἡμεῖς.δὲ κηρύσσομεν χριστὸν ἐσταυρωμένον, Ἰουδαίοις
but we proclaim Christ crucified, to Jews
μὲν σκάνδαλον, [o]Ἕλλησιν‖ δὲ μωρίαν· 24 αὐτοῖς.δὲ τοῖς
indeed a cause of offence, [2]to [3]Greeks [1]and foolishness; but to those the
κλητοῖς, Ἰουδαίοις.τε καὶ Ἕλλησιν, χριστὸν θεοῦ δύναμιν καὶ
called, both Jews and Greeks, Christ God's power and
θεοῦ σοφίαν. 25 ὅτι τὸ μωρὸν τοῦ θεοῦ σοφώτερον τῶν
God's wisdom. Because the foolishness of God wiser
ἀνθρώπων ἐστίν· καὶ τὸ ἀσθενὲς τοῦ θεοῦ ἰσχυρότερον τῶν
than men is, and the weakness of God stronger
ἀνθρώπων [p]ἐστίν.‖ 26 Βλέπετε.γὰρ τὴν.κλῆσιν.ὑμῶν, ἀδελφοί,
than men is. For ye see your calling, brethren,
ὅτι οὐ πολλοὶ σοφοὶ κατὰ σάρκα, οὐ πολλοὶ δυνα-
that not many wise according to flesh [there are], not many power-
τοί, οὐ πολλοὶ εὐγενεῖς· 27 ἀλλὰ τὰ μωρὰ τοῦ κόσμου
ful, not many high-born. But the foolish things of the world
ἐξελέξατο ὁ θεός, [q]ἵνα τοὺς σοφοὺς καταισχύνῃ·‖ [r]καὶ τὰ
[2]chose [1]God, that the wise he might put to shame; and the
ἀσθενῆ τοῦ κόσμου ἐξελέξατο ὁ θεός,‖ ἵνα καταισχύνῃ
weak things of the world [2]chose [1]God, that he might put to shame
τὰ ἰσχυρά· 28 καὶ τὰ ἀγενῆ τοῦ κόσμου καὶ τὰ ἐξουθενη-
the strong things; and the low-born of the world, and the de-
μένα ἐξελέξατο ὁ θεός, [s]καὶ‖ τὰ μὴ.ὄντα, ἵνα τὰ
spised [2]chose [1]God, and the things that are not, that the things that
ὄντα καταργήσῃ· 29 ὅπως μὴ [t]καυχήσηται‖ πᾶσα σὰρξ
are he may annul; so that [4]not [3]might [5]boast [1]all [2]flesh
ἐνώπιον [v]αὐτοῦ.‖ 30 ἐξ.αὐτοῦ.δὲ ὑμεῖς ἐστε ἐν χριστῷ Ἰησοῦ,
before him. But of him ye are in Christ Jesus,
ὃς ἐγενήθη [w]ἡμῖν σοφία‖ ἀπὸ θεοῦ δικαιοσύνη.τε καὶ ἁγιασ-
who was made to us wisdom from God and righteousness and sancti-
μὸς καὶ ἀπολύτρωσις· 31 ἵνα, καθὼς γέγραπται,
fication and redemption; that, according as it has been written,
Ὁ καυχώμενος, ἐν κυρίῳ καυχάσθω.
He that boasts, in [the] Lord let him boast.

2 Κἀγὼ ἐλθὼν πρὸς ὑμᾶς, ἀδελφοί, ἦλθον οὐ καθ'
And I having come to you, brethren, came not according to
ὑπεροχὴν λόγου ἢ σοφίας καταγγέλλων ὑμῖν τὸ μαρτύριον
excellency of word or wisdom, announcing to you the testimony
τοῦ θεοῦ. 2 οὐ.γὰρ ἔκρινα [x]τοῦ‖ [y]εἰδέναι τι‖ ἐν ὑμῖν,
of God. For [3]not [1]I [2]decided to know anything among you,
εἰ.μὴ Ἰησοῦν χριστόν, καὶ τοῦτον ἐσταυρωμένον. 3 [z]καὶ ἐγὼ‖
except Jesus Christ, and him crucified. And I
ἐν ἀσθενείᾳ καὶ ἐν φόβῳ καὶ ἐν τρόμῳ πολλῷ ἐγενόμην πρὸς
in weakness and in fear and in [2]trembling [1]much was with
ὑμᾶς· 4 καὶ ὁ.λόγος.μου καὶ τὸ.κήρυγμά.μου οὐκ ἐν πειθοῖς
you; and my word and my preaching [was] not in persuasive
[a]ἀνθρωπίνης‖ σοφίας λόγοις, [b]ἀλλ'‖ ἐν ἀποδείξει πνεύματος
[3]human [2]of [4]wisdom [1]words, but in demonstration of [the] Spirit
καὶ δυνάμεως· 5 ἵνα ἡ.πίστις.ὑμῶν μὴ.ᾖ ἐν σοφίᾳ ἀνθρώ-
and of power; that your faith might not be in wisdom of men,
πων, [b]ἀλλ'‖ ἐν δυνάμει θεοῦ.
but in power of God.
6 Σοφίαν.δὲ λαλοῦμεν ἐν τοῖς τελείοις· σοφίαν.δὲ οὐ τοῦ
But wisdom we speak among the perfect; but wisdom, not

into my name.
16 And I also baptized the household of
Stephanas. As to the rest I do not know any
others I baptized.
17 For Christ did not send me to baptize
but to preach the gospel – not in wisdom of
word, so that the cross of Christ might not
be made of no value.
18 For the word of the Cross is foolishness
to those that are being lost, but to us who are
being saved, it is the power of God.
19 For it has been written, "I will destroy the
wisdom of the wise and I will set aside the
understanding of the intelligent ones."
20 Where is the wise? Where is the scribe?
Where is the lawyer of this age? Did God not
make the wisdom of this world foolish?
21 For since in the wisdom of God the
world did not know God by wisdom, God
was pleased by the foolishness of preaching
to save those that believe.
22 Since both the Jews ask for a sign and
the Greeks look for wisdom,
23 yet we preach Christ crucified – a cause
of stumbling to the Jews and foolishness to
the Greeks,
24 but to those who are the called, both
Jews and Greeks, Christ is God's power and
God's wisdom.
25 Because the foolishness of God is wiser
than men, and the weakness of God is
stronger than men.
26 For you see your calling, brothers, that
there are not many wise according to the
flesh, not many powerful, not many high-
born.
27 But God chose the foolish things of the
world so that He might put the wise to
shame. And God chose the weak things of
the world so that He might put the strong
things to shame.
28 And God chose the low-born of the
world and the things of little value, and the
things that do not exist – so that He might
bring to nothing the things that are –
29 so that no flesh might glory in His
presence.
30 But of Him you are in Christ Jesus, who
was made to us wisdom from God, and righteousness and sanctification and redemption
31 – so that, even as it has been written, "He
that glories, let him glory in the Lord."

CHAPTER 2

1 And when I came to you, brothers, I did
not come with excellency of word or wisdom, declaring to you the testimony of God.
2 For I decided not to know anything
among you except Jesus Christ and Him
crucified.
3 And I was with you in weakness and in
fear and in much trembling.
4 And my word and my preaching *was* not
in moving words of human wisdom, but in
proof of the Spirit and of power –
5 so that your faith might not be in the
wisdom of men, but in the power of God.
6 But we speak wisdom among the perfect.

αἰῶνος.τούτου, οὐδὲ τῶν ἀρχόντων τοῦ.αἰῶνος.τούτου. τῶν
of this age, nor of the rulers of this age, who

καταργουμένων· 7 ἀλλὰ λαλοῦμεν [c]σοφίαν θεοῦ‖ ἐν μυστηρίῳ,
are coming to nought. But we speak wisdom of God in a mystery,

τὴν ἀποκεκρυμμένην ἣν προώρισεν ὁ θεὸς πρὸ τῶν
the hidden [wisdom] which 2predetermined 1God before the

αἰώνων εἰς δόξαν.ἡμῶν, 8 ἣν οὐδεὶς τῶν ἀρχόντων τοῦ
ages for our glory, which no one of the rulers

αἰῶνος.τούτου ἔγνωκεν· εἰ.γὰρ ἔγνωσαν, οὐκ ἂν τὸν κύριον
of this age has known, (for if they had known, 8not 1the 2Lord

τῆς δόξης ἐσταύρωσαν· 9 ἀλλὰ καθὼς γέγραπ-
3of 4the 5glory 6they 7would have crucified,) but according as it has been

ται, "Α ὀφθαλμὸς οὐκ.εἶδεν, καὶ οὖς οὐκ.ἤκουσεν, καὶ
written, Things which eye saw not, and ear heard not, and

ἐπὶ καρδίαν ἀνθρώπου οὐκ.ἀνέβη, [d]ἃ‖ ἡτοίμασεν ὁ θεὸς
into heart of man came not, which 2prepared 1God

τοῖς ἀγαπῶσιν αὐτόν· 10 ἡμῖν.δὲ [e]ὁ θεὸς ἀπεκάλυψεν‖
for those that love him, but to us God revealed [them]

διὰ τοῦ.πνεύματος.[f]αὐτοῦ·‖ τὸ.γὰρ πνεῦμα πάντα [g]ἐρευνᾷ,‖
by his Spirit; for the Spirit all things searches,

καὶ τὰ βάθη τοῦ θεοῦ. 11 τίς.γὰρ οἶδεν ἀνθρώπων τὰ
even the depths of God. For who 3knows 1of 2men the things

τοῦ ἀνθρώπου, εἰ.μὴ τὸ πνεῦμα τοῦ ἀνθρώπου τὸ ἐν
of man, except the spirit of man which [is] in

αὐτῷ; οὕτως καὶ τὰ τοῦ θεοῦ οὐδεὶς [h]οἶδεν,‖ εἰ.μὴ τὸ
him? so also the things of God no one knows, except the

πνεῦμα τοῦ θεοῦ. 12 ἡμεῖς.δὲ οὐ τὸ πνεῦμα τοῦ κόσμου ἐλά-
Spirit of God. But we not the spirit of the world re-

βομεν, ἀλλὰ τὸ πνεῦμα τὸ ἐκ τοῦ θεοῦ, ἵνα εἰδῶμεν
ceived, but the Spirit which [is] from God, that we might know

τὰ ὑπὸ τοῦ θεοῦ χαρισθέντα ἡμῖν. 13 "Α καὶ λαλοῦμεν,
the things by God granted to us: which also we speak,

οὐκ ἐν διδακτοῖς ἀνθρωπίνης σοφίας λόγοις, ἀλλ' ἐν δι-
not in 2taught 3of 4human 5wisdom 1words, but in [those]

δακτοῖς πνεύματος [i]ἁγίου,‖ πνευματικοῖς πνευματικὰ
taught of [the] 2Spirit 1Holy, 6by 7spiritual [8means] 4spiritual 5things

[k]συγκρίνοντες.‖ 14 ψυχικὸς.δὲ ἄνθρωπος οὐ.δέχεται τὰ
3communicating. But [the] natural man receives not the things

τοῦ πνεύματος τοῦ θεοῦ· μωρία.γὰρ αὐτῷ ἐστιν, καὶ
of the Spirit of God, for foolishness to him they are; and

οὐ.δύναται γνῶναι, ὅτι πνευματικῶς ἀνακρίνεται.
he cannot know [them], because spiritually they are discerned;

15 ὁ.δὲ πνευματικὸς ἀνακρίνει [l]μὲν‖ πάντα, αὐτὸς.δὲ ὑπ'
but the spiritual discerns all things, but he by

οὐδενὸς ἀνακρίνεται. 16 τίς.γὰρ ἔγνω νοῦν κυρίου,
no one is discerned. For who did know [the] mind of [the] Lord?

ὃς συμβιβάσει αὐτόν; ἡμεῖς.δὲ νοῦν [m]χριστοῦ‖ ἔχομεν.
who shall instruct him? But we [the] mind of Christ have.

3 [n]Καὶ ἐγώ,‖ ἀδελφοί, οὐκ.ἠδυνήθην λαλῆσαι ὑμῖν ὡς
And I, brethren, was not able to speak to you as

πνευματικοῖς, ἀλλ' ὡς [o]σαρκικοῖς,‖ ὡς νηπίοις ἐν χριστῷ.
to spiritual, but as to fleshly; as to babes in Christ.

2 γάλα ὑμᾶς ἐπότισα, [p]καὶ‖ οὐ βρῶμα· οὔπω.γὰρ [q]ἠδύνασθε,‖
Milk 3you 1I 2gave to drink; and not meat, for not yet were ye able,

ἀλλ' [r]οὔτε‖ [s]ἔτι‖ νῦν δύνασθε· 3 ἔτι.γὰρ σαρκικοί ἐστε.
but neither yet now are ye able; for yet fleshly ye are.

ὅπου.γὰρ ἐν ὑμῖν ζῆλος καὶ ἔρις [t]καὶ διχοστασίαι,‖
For where among you emulation and strife and divisions [there are],

οὐχὶ σαρκικοί ἐστε, καὶ κατὰ ἄνθρωπον περιπατεῖτε;
3not 4fleshly 1are 2ye, and 2according 3to 4man 1walk?

4 ὅταν.γὰρ λέγῃ τις, Ἐγὼ μέν εἰμι Παύλου, ἕτερος.δέ, Ἐγὼ
For when 2may 3say 1one, I am of Paul, and another, I

Ἀπολλώ, [v]οὐχὶ σαρκικοί‖ ἐστε; 5 [w]Τίς‖ οὖν ἐστιν [x]Παῦλος,‖
of Apollos, 3not 4fleshly 1are 2ye? Who then is Paul,

[w]τίς‖ δὲ [y] [x]Ἀπολλώς,‖ [z]ἀλλ' ἢ‖ διάκονοι δι' ὧν ἐπιστεύ-
2who 1and Apollos? but servants through whom ye be-

σατε, καὶ ἑκάστῳ ὡς ὁ κύριος ἔδωκεν; 6 ἐγὼ ἐφύτευσα,
lieved, and to each as the Lord gave? I planted,

Ἀπολλὼς ἐπότισεν, [a]ἀλλ'‖ ὁ θεὸς ηὔξανεν· 7 ὥστε οὔτε
Apollos watered; but God gave growth. So that neither

ὁ φυτεύων ἐστίν τι, οὔτε ὁ ποτίζων, ἀλλ' ὁ αὐξά-
he that plants is anything, nor he that waters; but 2who 3gives

νων θεός. 8 ὁ.φυτεύων.δὲ καὶ ὁ ποτίζων ἕν εἰσιν· ἕκαστος
4growth 1God. But he that plants and he that waters 2one 1are; 4each

δὲ τὸν.ἴδιον μισθὸν [b]λήψεται‖ κατὰ τὸν.ἴδιον κόπον.
3but his own reward shall receive according to his own labour.

9 θεοῦ.γάρ ἐσμεν συνεργοί· θεοῦ γεώργιον, θεοῦ οἰκοδομή
For God's 2we 3are 1fellow-workers; God's husbandry, God's building

ἐστε. 10 Κατὰ τὴν χάριν τοῦ θεοῦ τὴν δοθεῖσάν μοι, ὡς
ye are. According to the grace of God which was given to me, as

σοφὸς ἀρχιτέκτων θεμέλιον [c]τέθεικα,‖ ἄλλος.δὲ ἐποικοδομεῖ·
a wise architect [the] foundation I have laid, and another builds up.

But not the wisdom of this age or of the rulers of this age, who are coming to nothing,

7 but we speak the wisdom of God in a mystery, that which God has hidden and ordained for our glory before the world–

8 which not one of the rulers of this world has known (for if they had known, they would not have crucified the Lord of Glory).

9 But even as it has been written, "Eye has not seen and ear has not heard," nor has it entered into the heart of man, "the things which God has prepared for those that love Him."

10 But God has revealed *them* to us by His Spirit. For the Spirit searches all things, even the deep things of God.

11 For who among men knows the things of man, except the spirit of man which is in him? So also no one knows the things of God except the Spirit of God.

12 But we have not received the spirit of the world, but the Spirit which is from God, so that we might know the things given to us by God –

13 which we also speak, not in the words which man's wisdom teaches, but in *the words* the Holy Spirit teaches, explaining spiritual things by spiritual *means.*

14 But the natural man does not receive the things of the Spirit of God, for they are foolishness to him – neither can he know *them,* because they are spiritually understood.

15 But the spiritual one understands all things and he is judged by no one.

16 For who has known the mind of the Lord? Who shall teach Him? And we have the mind of Christ.

CHAPTER 3

1 And, brothers, I could not speak to you as to spiritual ones, but as to fleshly ones, as to babes in Christ.

2 I gave you milk to drink and not solid food, for you were not yet able to bear it. But even now you are not yet able,

3 for you are still fleshly. For since divisions and jealousy and fighting are among you, are you not fleshly and walking as men?

4 For when one says, I am of Paul, and another, I am of Apollos, are you not fleshly?

5 Who then is Paul, and who is Apollos, but ministers through whom you believed, and as the Lord gave to each.

6 I planted. Apollos watered. But God gave growth.

7 So that he who plants is not anything, nor is he who waters, but God who gives growth!

8 But he who plants and he who waters are one. But each one shall receive his own reward according to his own labor.

9 For we are fellow-workers of God. You are God's field, God's building.

10 I have laid the foundation as a wise architect, according to the grace of God which was given to me. And another builds.

ἕκαστος.δὲ βλεπέτω πῶς ἐποικοδομεῖ· 11 θεμέλιον.γὰρ ἄλλον
But [2]each [1]let take heed how he builds up. For [2]foundation [1]other
οὐδεὶς δύναται θεῖναι παρὰ τὸν κείμενον, ὅς ἐστιν [d]Ἰη-
no one is able to lay besides that which is laid, which is Je-
σοῦς ὁ χριστός.[‖] 12 εἰ.δέ τις ἐποικοδομεῖ ἐπὶ τὸν θεμέλιον
sus the Christ. Now if anyone build up on [2]foundation
[e]τοῦτον[‖] [f]χρυσόν, ἄργυρον,[‖] λίθους τιμίους, ξύλα, χόρτον,
[1]this gold, silver, [2]stones [1]precious, wood, grass,
καλάμην, 13 ἑκάστου τὸ ἔργον φανερὸν γενήσεται· ἡ.γὰρ
straw, of each the work manifest will become; for the
ἡμέρα δηλώσει· ὅτι ἐν πυρὶ ἀποκαλύπτεται· καὶ ἑκάστου
day will declare [it], because in fire it is revealed; and of each
τὸ ἔργον ὁποῖόν ἐστιν, τὸ πῦρ [g] δοκιμάσει. 14 εἴ τινος τὸ
the work what sort it is, the fire will prove. If of anyone the
ἔργον [h]μένει[‖] ὃ [i]ἐπῳκοδόμησεν,[‖] μισθὸν [k]λήψεται·[‖] 15 εἴ
work abides which he built up, a reward he shall receive. If
τινος τὸ ἔργον κατακαήσεται, ζημιωθήσεται· αὐτὸς.δὲ
of anyone the work shall be consumed, he shall suffer loss, but himself
σωθήσεται, οὕτως.δὲ ὡς διὰ πυρός. 16 Οὐκ.οἴδατε ὅτι ναὸς
shall be saved, but so as through fire. Know ye not that [2]temple
θεοῦ ἐστε, καὶ τὸ πνεῦμα τοῦ θεοῦ οἰκεῖ ἐν ὑμῖν; 17 εἴ τις
[3]God's ye are, and the Spirit of God dwells in you? If anyone
τὸν ναὸν τοῦ θεοῦ φθείρει, φθερεῖ [l]τοῦτον[l] ὁ
the temple of God corrupt, [3]shall [4]bring [6]to [6]corruption [5]him
θεός· ὁ.γὰρ ναὸς τοῦ θεοῦ ἅγιός ἐστιν, οἵτινές ἐστε ὑμεῖς.
[2]God; for the temple of God [2]holy [1]is, which [2]are [1]ye.
18 μηδεὶς ἑαυτὸν ἐξαπατάτω· εἴ τις δοκεῖ σοφὸς
[4]No [5]one [7]himself [3]let [6]deceive: if anyone [3]thinks [[4]himself] [7]wise
εἶναι ἐν ὑμῖν ἐν τῷ.αἰῶνι.τούτῳ, μωρὸς γενέσθω, ἵνα
[5]to [6]be. [1]among [2]you in this age, foolish let him become, that
γένηται σοφός. 19 ἡ.γὰρ σοφία τοῦ.κόσμου.τούτου μωρία
he may be wise. For the wisdom of this world foolishness
παρὰ [m]τῷ θεῷ ἐστιν· γέγραπται.γάρ, Ὁ δρασσόμενος τοὺς
with God is; for it has been written, He takes the
σοφοὺς ἐν τῇ.πανουργίᾳ.αὐτῶν. 20 καὶ πάλιν, Κύριος
wise in their craftiness. And again, [The] Lord
γινώσκει τοὺς διαλογισμοὺς τῶν σοφῶν, ὅτι εἰσὶν μάταιοι.
knows the reasonings of the wise, that they are vain.
21 Ὥστε μηδεὶς καυχάσθω ἐν ἀνθρώποις· πάντα.γὰρ ὑμῶν
So that [2]no [3]one [1]let boast in men; for all things [2]yours
ἐστιν, 22 εἴτε Παῦλος, εἴτε Ἀπολλώς, εἴτε Κηφᾶς, εἴτε
[1]are. Whether Paul, or Apollos, or Cephas. or [the]
κόσμος, εἴτε ζωή, εἴτε θάνατος, εἴτε ἐνεστῶτα, εἴτε μέλλοντα·
world, or life, or death, or present things, or coming things,
πάντα ὑμῶν [n]ἐστιν·[‖] 23 ὑμεῖς.δὲ χριστοῦ· χριστὸς.δὲ θεοῦ.
all [2]yours [1]are; and ye Christ's, and Christ God's.

4 Οὕτως ἡμᾶς λογιζέσθω ἄνθρωπος ὡς ὑπηρέτας χριστοῦ
So [5]of [6]us [1]let [4]reckon [2]a [3]man as attendants of Christ
καὶ οἰκονόμους μυστηρίων θεοῦ. 2 [o]ὃ δὲ[‖] λοιπόν, ζητεῖται
and stewards [3]mysteries [1]of [2]God's. But as to the rest, it is required
ἐν τοῖς οἰκονόμοις ἵνα πιστός τις εὑρεθῇ. 3 ἐμοὶ.δὲ εἰς ἐλά-
in stewards that faithful one be found. But to me the small-
χιστόν ἐστιν ἵνα ὑφ' ὑμῶν ἀνακριθῶ, ἢ ὑπὸ ἀνθρωπίνης
est matter it is that by you I be examined, or by man's
ἡμέρας· ἀλλ' οὐδὲ ἐμαυτὸν ἀνακρίνω. 4 οὐδὲν.γὰρ ἐμαυτῷ
day. But neither myself do I examine. For of nothing in myself
σύνοιδα· ἀλλ' οὐκ ἐν τούτῳ δεδικαίωμαι· ὁ.δὲ ἀνα-
I am conscious; but not by this have I been justified: but he who ex-
κρίνων με κύριός ἐστιν. 5 ὥστε μὴ πρὸ καιροῦ τι
amines me [the] Lord is. So that not before [the] time anything
κρίνετε, ἕως ἂν ἔλθῃ ὁ κύριος, ὃς καὶ φωτίσει τὰ
judge, until may have come the Lord, who both will bring to light the
κρυπτὰ τοῦ σκότους, καὶ φανερώσει τὰς βουλὰς τῶν
hidden things of darkness, and will make manifest the counsels
καρδιῶν· καὶ τότε ὁ ἔπαινος γενήσεται ἑκάστῳ ἀπὸ τοῦ θεοῦ.
of hearts; and then praise shall be to each from God.
6 Ταῦτα.δέ, ἀδελφοί, μετεσχημάτισα εἰς ἐμαυτὸν καὶ [p]Ἀ-
Now these things, brethren, I transferred to myself and A-
πολλὼ[‖] δι' ὑμᾶς, ἵνα ἐν ἡμῖν μάθητε τὸ μὴ ὑπὲρ
pollos on account of you, that in us ye may learn not [3]above
[q]ὃ[‖] γέγραπται [r]φρονεῖν,[‖] ἵνα μὴ εἷς ὑπὲρ τοῦ ἑνὸς
[4]what [5]has [6]been [7]written [1]to [2]think, that not one for one
φυσιοῦσθε κατὰ τοῦ ἑτέρου. 7 τίς.γάρ σε διακρίνει;
ye be puffed up against the other. For who thee makes to differ?
τί.δὲ ἔχεις ὃ οὐκ.ἔλαβες; εἰ.δὲ καὶ ἔλαβες,
And what hast thou which thou didst not receive? but if also thou didst receive,
τί καυχᾶσαι ὡς μὴ λαβών; 8 ἤδη κεκορεσμένοι ἐστέ,
why boastest thou as not having received? Already satiated ye are;
ἤδη ἐπλουτήσατε, χωρὶς ἡμῶν ἐβασιλεύσατε· καὶ ὄφελόν
already ye were enriched; apart from us ye reigned; and I would

But let each one be careful how he builds.
11 For no one can lay any other foundation
than that which is laid, which is Jesus Christ.
12 Now if anyone build on this foundation
gold, silver, precious stones, wood, grass or
straw,
13 the work of each one will be revealed. For
the Day will make it known, because it is
revealed in fire. And the fire will test the
work of each one, what kind it is.
14 If the work of any man which he built
endures, he shall receive a reward.
15 If the work of anyone is burned, he shall
suffer loss. But he himself shall be saved, but
so as by fire.
16 Do you not know you are the sanctuary
of God, and the Spirit of God dwells in you?
17 If anyone defiles the sanctuary of God,
God will destroy him, for the sanctuary of
God is holy, since you are of such.
18 Let no one deceive himself! If anyone of
you imagines he is wise in this age, let him
become foolish so that he may be wise.
19 For the wisdom of this world is foolishness with God. For it has been written, "He
takes the wise in their own wickedness."
20 And again, "The Lord knows the thoughts
of the wise, that they are worthless."
21 So let no man glory in men. For all
things are yours,
22 whether Paul or Apollos or Peter or the
world or life or death or things present or
things to come – all are yours,
23 and you are Christ's, and Christ is God's.

CHAPTER 4

1 Let man think of us as ministers of Christ
and keepers of the mysteries of God.
2 But as to the rest, it is necessary in
managers one must be found faithful.
3 But to me it is a very small thing that I
should be judged by you, or by man's day.
But neither do I judge myself.
4 For I am aware of nothing of myself. But
I have not been justified by this, but He who
judges me is the Lord.
5 Then do not judge anything before the
time, until the Lord has come, who will both
bring to light the hidden things of darkness
and reveal the thoughts of all hearts. And
then shall each one have praise from God.
6 And these things, brothers, I have changed
to fit Apollos and myself for your sakes, so
that you may learn in us not to think above
what has been written, in order that none of
you may be puffed up against one another.
7 For who makes you to differ? And what
do you have which you did not receive? But
now if you did receive, why do you boast as
one who did not receive?
8 You are already satisfied! You are already
rich! You ruled as kings without us! And I

γε ἐβασιλεύσατε, ἵνα καὶ ἡμεῖς ὑμῖν [s]συμβασιλεύσωμεν.‖
surely ye did reign, that also we [4]you [1]might [2]reign [3]with.
9 δοκῶ.γὰρ [t]ὅτι‖ ὁ θεὸς ἡμᾶς τοὺς ἀποστόλους ἐσχάτους ἀπέ-
For I think that God us the apostles last set
δειξεν ὡς ἐπιθανατίους· ὅτι θέατρον ἐγενήθημεν τῷ κόσμῳ,
forth as appointed to death. For a spectacle we became to the world,
καὶ ἀγγέλοις καὶ ἀνθρώποις. 10 ἡμεῖς μωροὶ διὰ
both to angels and to men. We [are] fools on account of
χριστόν, ὑμεῖς.δὲ φρόνιμοι ἐν χριστῷ· ἡμεῖς ἀσθενεῖς, ὑμεῖς.δὲ
Christ, but ye prudent in Christ; we weak, but ye
ἰσχυροί· ὑμεῖς ἔνδοξοι, ἡμεῖς.δὲ ἄτιμοι. 11 ἄχρι τῆς ἄρτι
strong; ye glorious, but we without honour. To the present
ὥρας καὶ πεινῶμεν καὶ διψῶμεν, καὶ [v]γυμνητεύομεν,‖ καὶ
hour both we hunger and thirst, and are naked, and
κολαφιζόμεθα, καὶ ἀστατοῦμεν, 12 καὶ κοπιῶμεν, ἐργα-
are buffeted, and wander without a home, and labour, work-
ζόμενοι ταῖς.ἰδίαις χερσίν· λοιδορούμενοι, εὐλογοῦμεν· διω-
ing with our own hands. Railed at, we bless; per-
κόμενοι, ἀνεχόμεθα· 13 [w]βλασφημούμενοι,‖ παρακαλοῦμεν·
secuted, we bear; evilly spoken to, we beseech:
ὡς περικαθάρματα τοῦ κόσμου ἐγενήθημεν, πάντων
as [the] refuse of the world we are become, of all [the]
περίψημα ἕως ἄρτι. 14 Οὐκ ἐντρέπων ὑμᾶς γράφω ταῦτα,
off-scouring until now. Not shaming you do I write these things,
[x]ἀλλ'‖ ὡς τέκνα μου ἀγαπητὰ [y]νουθετῶ.‖ 15 ἐὰν.γὰρ
but as [3]children [1]my [2]beloved I admonish [you]. For if
μυρίους παιδαγωγοὺς ἔχητε ἐν χριστῷ, ἀλλ' οὐ πολ-
ten thousand tutors ye should have in Christ, yet not [1]many
λοὺς πατέρας· ἐν.γὰρ χριστῷ Ἰησοῦ διὰ τοῦ εὐαγγελίου
fathers; for in Christ Jesus through the glad tidings
ἐγὼ ὑμᾶς ἐγέννησα. 16 παρακαλῶ οὖν ὑμᾶς, μιμηταί μου
I you did beget. I exhort therefore you, [2]imitators [3]of [4]me
γίνεσθε.
[1]become.

17 Διὰ τοῦτο [z]ἔπεμψα ὑμῖν Τιμόθεον, ὅς ἐστιν [a]τέκνον
On account of this I sent to you Timotheus, who is [3]child
μου‖ ἀγαπητὸν καὶ πιστὸν ἐν κυρίῳ, ὃς ὑμᾶς ἀναμνήσει
[1]my [2]beloved and faithful in [the] Lord, who [3]you [1]will [2]remind of
τὰς.ὁδούς.μου τὰς ἐν χριστῷ,[b] καθὼς πανταχοῦ ἐν πάσῃ
my ways that [are] in Christ, according as everywhere in every
ἐκκλησίᾳ διδάσκω. 18 ὡς μὴ.ἐρχομένου δέ μου πρὸς ὑμᾶς
assembly I teach. [2]As [5]to [5]not [6]coming [1]now [4]my to you
ἐφυσιώθησάν τινες· 19 ἐλεύσομαι.δὲ ταχέως πρὸς ὑμᾶς, ἐὰν
[2]were [3]puffed [4]up [1]some; but I shall come shortly to you, if
ὁ κύριος θελήσῃ, καὶ γνώσομαι, οὐ τὸν λόγον τῶν
the Lord will, and I will know, not the word of those who
πεφυσιωμένων, ἀλλὰ τὴν δύναμιν. 20 οὐ.γὰρ ἐν λόγῳ ἡ
are puffed up, but the power. For not in word the
βασιλεία τοῦ θεοῦ, ἀλλ' ἐν δυνάμει. 21 τί θέλετε; ἐν
kingdom of God [is], but in power. What will ye? with
ῥάβδῳ ἔλθω πρὸς ὑμᾶς, ἢ ἐν ἀγάπῃ πνεύματί.τε [c]πρᾳό-
a rod I should come to you, or in love and a spirit of meek-
τητος‖;
ness?

5 Ὅλως ἀκούεται ἐν ὑμῖν πορνεία, καὶ τοιαύτη πορνεία
Commonly [2]is [3]reported [4]among [5]you [1]fornication, and such fornication
ἥτις οὐδὲ ἐν τοῖς ἔθνεσιν [d]ὀνομάζεται,‖ ὥστε γυναῖκά
which not even among the nations is named, so as [6]wife
τινα τοῦ πατρὸς ἔχειν. 2 καὶ ὑμεῖς πεφυσιωμένοι ἐστέ,
[1]one [4his] [5]father's [2]to [3]have. And ye [2]puffed [3]up [1]are,
καὶ οὐχὶ μᾶλλον ἐπενθήσατε, ἵνα [e]ἐξαρθῇ‖ ἐκ μέσου.ὑμῶν
and not rather did mourn, that might be taken out of your midst
ὁ τὸ.ἔργον.τοῦτο [f]ποιήσας;‖ 3 ἐγὼ μὲν.γὰρ [g]ὡς‖ ἀπὼν τῷ
he who this deed did! [2]I [1]for as being absent
σώματι, παρὼν.δὲ τῷ πνεύματι, ἤδη κέκρικα ὡς παρών,
in body, but being present in spirit, already have judged as being present,
τὸν οὕτως τοῦτο κατεργασάμενον, 4 ἐν τῷ ὀνόματι τοῦ
him who so [3]this [1]worked [2]out, in the name
κυρίου.[h]ἡμῶν‖ Ἰησοῦ [i]χριστοῦ,‖ συναχθέντων ὑμῶν καὶ
of our Lord Jesus Christ, being gathered together ye and
τοῦ ἐμοῦ πνεύματος, σὺν τῇ δυνάμει τοῦ.κυρίου.[k]ἡμῶν‖ Ἰησοῦ
my spirit, with the power of our Lord Jesus
[l]χριστοῦ,‖ 5 παραδοῦναι τὸν.τοιοῦτον τῷ σατανᾷ εἰς ὄλεθρον
Christ— to deliver such a one to Satan for destruction
τῆς σαρκός, ἵνα τὸ πνεῦμα σωθῇ ἐν τῇ ἡμέρᾳ τοῦ κυρίου
of the flesh, that the spirit may be saved in the day of the Lord
[l]Ἰησοῦ.‖ 6 Οὐ καλὸν τὸ.καύχημα.ὑμῶν· οὐκ.οἴδατε ὅτι μικρὰ
Jesus. Not good [is] your boasting. Know ye not that a little
ζύμη ὅλον τὸ φύραμα ζυμοῖ; 7 ἐκκαθάρατε [m]οὖν‖ τὴν πα-
leaven [3]whole [2]the [4]lump [1]leavens? Purge out therefore the

wish you surely did rule, so that we also
might rule with you.
9 For I believe that God has set us, the
apostles, out last, as it were appointed to
death. For we became a spectacle to the
world, both to angels and to men.
10 We are fools for Christ's sake, but you are
wise in Christ. We are weak, but you are
strong. You are glorious, but we have no
honor.
11 Even until now we both hunger and
thirst, and are naked and are beaten and
wander about without a home.
12 And *we* labor, working with our own
hands – being cursed, we bless – being
persecuted, we bear it –
13 being defamed, we beg. We are made as
filth of the world, dirt wiped off by all to
this day.
14 I do not write these things to shame you,
but I warn you as my beloved children.
15 For if you have ten thousand teachers in
Christ, yet not many fathers – for I fathered
you in Christ Jesus through the gospel.
16 So I urge you, be imitators of me.

17 For this reason I sent Timothy to you,
who is my beloved child and one faithful in
the Lord, who will remind you of my ways
that are in Christ – just as I teach everywhere in every church.
18 Now as to my not coming to you, some
were puffed up.
19 But I will come to you shortly, if the
Lord will. And I will not mark the word of
those who are proud, but the power.
20 For the kingdom of God is not in word,
but in power!
21 What do you want, that I should come
to you with a rod, or in love and in a spirit
of meekness?

CHAPTER 5

1 It is commonly said *there is* fornication among you – and such fornication
as is not even named among the Gentiles,
that one should have his father's wife.
2 And you are proud and have not rather
mourned, so that he who did this deed might
be taken away from among you.
3 For indeed, I (as being absent in body but
present in spirit) have already judged him who
has done this thing, as though I were present,
4 in the name of our Lord Jesus Christ (you
being gathered together with my spirit, with
the power of our Lord Jesus Christ)
5 to deliver such a one to Satan in order to
destroy the flesh, so that the spirit may be
saved in the day of the Lord Jesus.
6 Your boasting is not good. Do you not
know that a little leaven will leaven a whole
lump?
7 So purge out the old leaven so that you

λαιὰν ζύμην, ἵνα ἦτε νέον φύραμα, καθώς ἐστε ἄζυμοι·
old leaven, that ye may be a new lump, according as ye are unleavened.
καὶ.γὰρ τὸ.πάσχα.ἡμῶν [n]ὑπὲρ ἡμῶν‖ [o]ἐτύθη‖ χριστός.
For also [2]our [3]passover [6]for [7]us [4]was [5]sacrificed [1]Christ.
8 ὥστε ἑορτάζωμεν, μὴ ἐν ζύμῃ παλαιᾷ, μηδὲ ἐν
So that we should celebrate the feast, not with [2]leaven [1]old, nor with
ζύμῃ κακίας καὶ πονηρίας, ἀλλ' ἐν ἀζύμοις [p]εἰλι-
leaven of malice and wickedness, but with unleavened [bread] of
κρινείας‖ καὶ ἀληθείας.
sincerity and of truth.
9 Ἔγραψα ὑμῖν ἐν τῇ ἐπιστολῇ, μὴ συναναμίγνυσθαι
I wrote to you in the epistle, not to associate with
πόρνοις· 10 [q]καὶ‖ οὐ πάντως τοῖς πόρνοις τοῦ.κόσμου.τού-
fornicators; and not altogether with the fornicators of this world,
του, ἢ τοῖς πλεονέκταις, [r]ἢ‖ ἅρπαξιν, ἢ εἰδωλολάτραις· ἐπεὶ
or with the covetous, or rapacious, or idolaters, since
[s]ὀφείλετε‖ ἄρα ἐκ τοῦ κόσμου ἐξελθεῖν. 11 [t]νυνὶ‖.δὲ ἔγραψα
ye ought then out of the world to go. But now, I wrote
ὑμῖν μὴ συναναμίγνυσθαι, ἐάν τις ἀδελφὸς ὀνομαζόμενος
to you not to associate with [him], if anyone [2]brother [1]designated
[v]ᾖ‖ πόρνος, ἢ πλεονέκτης, ἢ εἰδωλολάτρης, ἢ λοίδορος,
[be] either a fornicator, or covetous, or idolater, or railer,
ἢ μέθυσος, ἢ ἅρπαξ· τῷ.τοιούτῳ· μηδὲ συνεσθίειν. 12 τί
or a drunkard, or rapacious; with such a one not even to eat. [2]What
γάρ μοι [w]καὶ‖ τοὺς ἔξω κρίνειν; οὐχὶ τοὺς ἔσω ὑμεῖς
[1]for [is it] to me also those outside to judge, [4]not [6]those [7]within [1]ye
κρίνετε; 13 τοὺς.δὲ ἔξω ὁ θεὸς [x]κρίνει.‖ [y]καὶ ἐξαρεῖτε‖
[2]do [3]ye [5]judge? But those outside God judges. And ye shall put out
τὸν πονηρὸν ἐξ ὑμῶν.αὐτῶν.
the wicked person from among yourselves.

6 Τολμᾷ τις ὑμῶν, πρᾶγμα ἔχων πρὸς τὸν ἕτερον,
Dare anyone of you, a matter having against the other,
κρίνεσθαι ἐπὶ τῶν ἀδίκων, καὶ οὐχὶ ἐπὶ τῶν ἁγίων; 2 [z]οὐκ
go to law before the unrighteous, and not before the saints? [3]Not
οἴδατε ὅτι οἱ ἅγιοι τὸν κόσμον κρινοῦσιν; καὶ εἰ ἐν ὑμῖν
[1]know [2]ye that the saints [3]the [4]world [1]will [2]judge? and if by you
κρίνεται ὁ κόσμος, ἀνάξιοί ἐστε κριτηρίων ἐλαχίστων; 3 οὐκ
is judged the world, [3]unworthy [1]are [2]ye of judgments the smallest? [3]Not
οἴδατε ὅτι ἀγγέλους κρινοῦμεν; [a]μήτι.γε‖ βιωτικά;
[1]know [2]ye that angels we shall judge? much more then things of this life?
4 βιωτικὰ μὲν οὖν κριτήρια ἐὰν ἔχητε, τοὺς
[8]Things [9]of [10]this [11]life [4]then [5]judgment [[6]as [7]to] [1]if [2]ye [3]have, who
ἐξουθενημένους ἐν τῇ ἐκκλησίᾳ, τούτους [b]καθίζετε.‖ 5 πρὸς
are least esteemed in the assembly, [4]those [1]set [2]ye [3]up. For
ἐντροπὴν ὑμῖν [c]λέγω.‖ οὕτως οὐκ.[d]ἔστιν‖ ἐν ὑμῖν [e]σοφὸς
shame to you I speak. Thus is there not among you a wise [man]
οὐδὲ εἷς,‖ ὃς δυνήσεται διακρῖναι ἀνὰ.μέσον τοῦ ἀδελφοῦ
not even one, who shall be able to decide between [2]brother
αὐτοῦ; 6 ἀλλὰ ἀδελφὸς μετὰ ἀδελφοῦ κρίνεται, καὶ
[1]his [and brother]? But brother with brother goes to law, and
τοῦτο ἐπὶ ἀπίστων; 7 ἤδη μὲν [f]οὖν‖ ὅλως ἥττημα
this before unbelievers! Already indeed therefore altogether a default
[g]ἐν‖ ὑμῖν ἐστιν, ὅτι κρίματα ἔχετε μεθ' ἑαυτῶν. [h]διατί‖ οὐχὶ
among you is, that law-suits ye have among yourselves. Why not
μᾶλλον ἀδικεῖσθε; [h]διατί‖ οὐχὶ μᾶλλον ἀποστερεῖσθε; 8 ἀλλὰ
rather suffer wrong? why not rather be defrauded? But
ὑμεῖς ἀδικεῖτε καὶ ἀποστερεῖτε, καὶ [i]ταῦτα‖ ἀδελφούς.
ye do wrong and defraud, and these things [to your] brethren.
9 ἢ οὐκ.οἴδατε ὅτι ἄδικοι [k]βασιλείαν θεοῦ‖ οὐ κληρονο-
Or know ye not that unjust ones [the] kingdom of God [2]not [1]shall in-
μήσουσιν; Μὴ.πλανᾶσθε· οὔτε πόρνοι, οὔτε εἰδωλολάτραι,
herit? Be not misled; neither fornicators, nor idolaters,
οὔτε μοιχοί, οὔτε μαλακοί, οὔτε ἀρσενο-
nor adulterers, nor abusers of themselves as women, nor abusers of them-
κοῖται, 10 οὔτε κλέπται, οὔτε πλεονέκται, [l]οὔτε‖ μέθυσοι,
selves with men, nor thieves, nor covetous, nor drunkards,
οὐ λοίδοροι, οὐχ ἅρπαγες, βασιλείαν θεοῦ [m]οὐ‖ κληρονο-
nor railers, nor rapacious, [the] kingdom of God shall
μήσουσιν. 11 καὶ ταῦτά τινες.ἦτε· [n]ἀλλὰ‖ ἀπελού-
inherit. And these things some of you were; but ye were
σασθε, ἀλλὰ ἡγιάσθητε, [o]ἀλλ'‖ ἐδικαιώθητε, ἐν τῷ ὀνόματι
washed, but ye were sanctified, but ye were justified, in the name
τοῦ κυρίου [p] Ἰησοῦ, [q] καὶ ἐν τῷ πνεύματι τοῦ.θεοῦ ἡμῶν.
of the Lord Jesus, and by the Spirit of our God.
12 Πάντα μοι ἔξεστιν, ἀλλ' οὐ πάντα συμφέρει· πάντα
All things to me are lawful, but not all things do profit; all things
μοι ἔξεστιν, ἀλλ' οὐκ ἐγὼ ἐξουσιασθήσομαι ὑπό τινος.
to me are lawful, but [3]not [1]I [2]will be brought under the power of any.
13 Τὰ βρώματα τῇ κοιλίᾳ, καὶ ἡ κοιλία τοῖς βρώμασιν·
Meats for the belly, and the belly for meats;

may be a new lump, according as you are
unleavened. For even Christ our Passover is
sacrificed for us.
8 Then let us keep the feast, not with old
leaven, nor with leaven of malice and wickedness, but with sincerity and truth, *which is*
not leavened.
9 I wrote to you in a letter not to keep
company with fornicators,
10 and not altogether with the fornicators
of this world, or with the covetous, or robbers or worshipers of idols – for then you
would have to go out of the world.
11 But now I wrote to you not to keep
company with *him*, if anyone called a
brother is either a fornicator or covetous or
an idolator or a reviler or a drunkard or a
robber. Do not even eat with such a one.
12 For what *is it* to me to judge those who
are outside too? Do you not judge those
who are inside?
13 But God judges those who are outside.
And you shall put that wicked person out
from among yourselves!

CHAPTER 6

1 If anyone of you has a matter against
another, do you dare go to law before the
unjust and not before the saints?
2 Do you not know that the saints will
judge the world? And if the world is judged
by you, are you unworthy to judge the
smallest matters?
3 Do you not know that we shall judge
angels? How much more then the things of
this life?
4 If then you have judgment *as to* things of
this life, set those up who are least esteemed
in the church.
5 I speak to your shame. So! Is there not a
wise one among you, not even one who is
able to decide between his brother *and
another brother?*
6 But brother goes to law with brother. And
this before unbelievers!
7 Already, then, there is a failure among
you, that you have lawsuits among yourselves. Why do not you instead suffer injustice. Why not rather be cheated?
8 But you do wrong and cheat, and these
things to brothers!
9 Do you not know that the unjust shall not
inherit the kingdom of God? Do not be
deceived, neither fornicators, nor idolaters,
nor adulterers, nor abusers of themselves as
women, nor abusers of themselves with men,
10 nor thieves, nor covetous ones, nor
drunkards, nor name-callers, nor robbers
shall inherit the kingdom of God.
11 And some of you were these things. But
you were washed, but you were sanctified,
but you were justified in the name of the
Lord Jesus and by the Spirit of our God.
12 All things are lawful to me, but not all
things do good. All things are lawful to me,
but I will not be brought under the power of
any.
13 Food is for the belly, and the belly is for

ὁ.δὲ.θεὸς καὶ ταύτην καὶ ταῦτα ʹ καταργήσει. τὸ.δὲ σῶμα
but God both this and these will bring to nought: but the body [is]
οὐ τῇ πορνείᾳ, ἀλλὰ τῷ κυρίῳ, καὶ ὁ κύριος τῷ σώματι·
not for fornication, but for the Lord, and the Lord for the body.
14 ὁ.δὲ.θεὸς καὶ τὸν κύριον ἤγειρεν, καὶ [r]ἡμᾶς[l] [s]ἐξεγερεῖ‖ διὰ
And God both the Lord raised up, and us will raise out by
τῆς.δυνάμεως.αὐτοῦ. 15 οὐκ.οἴδατε ὅτι τὰ.σώματα.ὑμῶν μέλη
his power, Know ye not that your bodies members
χριστοῦ ἐστιν; ἄρας οὖν τὰ μέλη τοῦ χριστοῦ, ποιήσω
of Christ are? Having taken then the members of the Christ, shall I make
πόρνης μέλη; μὴ.γένοιτο. 16 ἢ οὐκ.οἴδατε ὅτι ὁ
[them] [2]of [3]a [4]harlot [1]members? May it not be! Or know ye not that he that
κολλώμενος τῇ πόρνῃ, ἓν σῶμά ἐστιν; Ἔσονται.γάρ, [t]φησίν,‖
is joined to the harlot, [2]one [3]body [1]is? For shall be, he says,
οἱ δύο εἰς σάρκα μίαν· 17 ὁ.δὲ κολλώμενος τῷ κυρίῳ, ἓν
the two for [2]flesh [1]one. But he that is joined to the Lord, [2]one
πνεῦμά ἐστιν. 18 Φεύγετε τὴν πορνείαν. πᾶν ἁμάρτημα ὃ
[3]spirit [1]is. Flee fornication. Every sin which
ἐὰν ποιήσῃ ἄνθρωπος, ἐκτὸς τοῦ σώματός ἐστιν· ὁ.δὲ
[3]may [4]practise [1]a [2]man, without the body is, but he that
πορνεύων, εἰς τὸ.ἴδιον σῶμα ἁμαρτάνει. 19 ἢ οὐκ
commits fornication, against his own body sins. Or [3]not
οἴδατε ὅτι τὸ.σῶμα.ὑμῶν ναὸς τοῦ ἐν ὑμῖν ἁγίου πνεύματός
[1]know [2]ye that your body a temple of the [3]in [4]you [1]Holy [2]Spirit
ἐστιν, οὗ ἔχετε ἀπὸ θεοῦ, καὶ οὐκ ἐστὲ ἑαυτῶν; 20 ἠγορά-
is, which ye have from God; and [3]not [2]are [1]ye your own? [2]ye [3]were
σθητε γὰρ τιμῆς· δοξάσατε δὴ τὸν θεὸν ἐν τῷ σώματι
[4]bought [1]for with a price; glorify [2]indeed [1]God in [2]body
ὑμῶν, [v]καὶ ἐν τῷ.πνεύματι.ὑμῶν, ἅτινά ἐστιν τοῦ θεοῦ.‖
[1]your, and in your spirit, which are God's.

7 Περὶ.δὲ ὧν ἐγράψατέ [w]μοι,‖ καλὸν ἀνθρώπῳ
But concerning what things ye wrote to me: [It is] good for a man
γυναικὸς μὴ ἅπτεσθαι· 2 διὰ.δὲ τὰς πορνείας ἕκαστος
[4]a [5]woman [1]not [2]to [3]touch; but on account of fornication [2]each
τὴν.ἑαυτοῦ.γυναῖκα ἐχέτω, καὶ ἑκάστη τὸν.ἴδιον ἄνδρα ἐχέτω.
[4]his [5]own [6]wife [1]let [3]have, and [2]each [4]her [5]own [6]husband [1]let [3]have.
3 τῇ γυναικὶ ὁ ἀνὴρ τὴν [x]ὀφειλομένην εὔνοιαν‖ ἀπο-
To the wife [2]the [3]husband [5]due [6]benevolence [1]let
διδότω· ὁμοίως.[y]δὲ‖ καὶ ἡ γυνὴ τῷ ἀνδρί. 4 ἡ γυνὴ τοῦ.ἰδίου
[4]render, and likewise also the wife to the husband. The wife her own
σώματος οὐκ.ἐξουσιάζει, [z]ἀλλ'‖ ὁ ἀνήρ· ὁμοίως.δὲ καὶ ὁ
body has not authority over, but the husband; and likewise also the
ἀνὴρ τοῦ.ἰδίου σώματος οὐκ.ἐξουσιάζει, [z]ἀλλ'‖ ἡ γυνή. 5 μὴ
husband his own body has not authority over, but the wife. [2]Not
ἀποστερεῖτε ἀλλήλους, εἰ.μή τι ἂν ἐκ συμφώνου πρὸς καιρόν,
[1]defraud one another, unless by consent for a season,
ἵνα [a]σχολάζητε‖ [b]τῇ νηστείᾳ καὶ‖ τῇ προσευχῇ, καὶ πάλιν
that ye may be at leisure for fasting and for prayer, and again
[c]ἐπὶ.τὸ.αὐτὸ ,συνέρχησθε,‖ ἵνα μὴ πειράζῃ ὑμᾶς ὁ σατανᾶς
into one place come together, that [3]not [2]may [4]tempt [5]you [1]Satan
διὰ τὴν.ἀκρασίαν.ὑμῶν. 6 τοῦτο.δὲ λέγω κατὰ [d]συγ-
because of your incontinence. But this I say by way of per-
γνώμην,‖ οὐ κατ' ἐπιταγήν. 7 θέλω [e]γὰρ‖ πάντας ἀνθρώ-
mission, not by way of command. [2]I [3]wish [1]but all men
πους εἶναι ὡς.καὶ ἐμαυτόν· [z]ἀλλ'‖ ἕκαστος ἴδιον [f]χάρισμα
to be even as myself: but each his own gift
ἔχει‖ ἐκ θεοῦ, [g]ὃς‖ μὲν οὕτως, [g]ὃς‖.δὲ οὕτως. 8 Λέγω.δὲ
has from God; one so, and another so. But I say
τοῖς ἀγάμοις καὶ ταῖς χήραις, καλὸν αὐτοῖς [h]ἐστιν‖ ἐὰν [i]
to the unmarried and to the widows, good for them it is if
μείνωσιν ὡς κἀγώ. 9 εἰ.δὲ οὐκ.ἐγκρατεύονται, γαμησά-
they should remain as even I. But if they have not self-control, let them
τωσαν· [k]κρεῖσσον[l].γάρ [l]ἐστιν‖ [m]γαμῆσαι‖ ἢ πυροῦσθαι.
marry; for better it is to marry than to burn.
10 Τοῖς.δὲ γεγαμηκόσιν παραγγέλλω, οὐκ ἐγώ, [z]ἀλλ'‖ ὁ
But to the married I charge, not I, but the
κύριος, γυναῖκα ἀπὸ ἀνδρὸς μὴ [n]χωρισθῆναι·‖ 11 ἐὰν.δὲ καὶ
Lord, wife from husband not to be separated; (but if also
χωρισθῇ, μενέτω ἄγαμος, ἢ τῷ ἀνδρὶ καταλλαγήτω·
she be separated, let her remain unmarried, or to the husband be reconciled;)
καὶ ἄνδρα γυναῖκα μὴ ἀφιέναι. 12 Τοῖς.δὲ λοιποῖς [o]ἐγὼ λέγω,‖
and husband [4]wife [1]not [2]to [3]leave. But to the rest I say,
οὐχ ὁ κύριος, εἴ τις ἀδελφὸς γυναῖκα ἔχει ἄπιστον, καὶ
not the Lord, If any brother [4]wife [1]has [2]an [3]unbelieving, and
[p]αὐτὴ‖ συνευδοκεῖ οἰκεῖν μετ' αὐτοῦ, μὴ.ἀφιέτω αὐτήν·
she consents to dwell with him, let him not leave her.
13 καὶ γυνὴ [q]ἥτις‖ ἔχει ἄνδρα ἄπιστον, καὶ [r]αὐτὸς‖
And a woman who has [3]husband [1]an [2]unbelieving, and he
συνευδοκεῖ οἰκεῖν μετ' αὐτῆς, μὴ.ἀφιέτω [s]αὐτόν.‖ 14 ἡγίασται
consents to dwell with her, let her not leave him. [2]Is [3]sanctified

food, but God will bring both this and these to nothing. But the body is not for fornication, but for the Lord. And the Lord is for the body.

14 And God has both raised up the Lord and will raise us up by His power.

15 Do you know that your bodies are members of Christ? Shall I then take the members of Christ and share *His* members with a harlot? Let it not be!

16 Or do you not know that he who is joined to a harlot is one body? For He says, "The two shall be one flesh."

17 But he who is joined to the Lord is one spirit.

18 Flee fornication! Every sin that a man does is outside the body. But he who commits fornication sins against his own body.

19 Or do you not know that your body is the temple of the Holy Spirit in you, which you have from God?And you are not your own.

20 You were bought with a price. Then glorify God in your body and in your spirit, which are God's.

7 1 But as to the things you wrote me: *It is* good for a man not to touch a woman.

2 But because of fornication, let each one have his own wife. And let each one have her own husband.

3 Let the husband give what is due to the wife, and in the same way also the wife to the husband.

4 The wife does not have authority over her own body, but the husband *does.* And in the same way the husband does not have authority over his own body, but the wife.

5 Do not deprive one another, except by agreement for a time, so that you may be free for fasting and prayer. But come together again into one place so that Satan may not tempt you because of your inability to contain yourselves.

6 But I say this by way of permission, not by way of command.

7 For I wish that all men were even as myself. But each one has his own gift from God, one in this way and another in that.

8 But I say to the unmarried and the widows, it is good for them if they should remain as I am.

9 However, if they do not have control of themselves, let them marry. For it is better to marry than to burn.

10 But to the married I command (not I, but the Lord), The wife should not be separated from her husband.

11 But if she is separated, let her remain unmarried or be reconciled to her husband. And the husband *ought* not to leave his wife.

12 But to the rest I say (not the Lord), If any brother has an unbelieving wife and she agrees to live with him, let him not leave her.

13 And the woman who has an unbelieving husband and he agrees to live with her, let her not leave him

γὰρ ὁ ἀνὴρ ὁ ἄπιστος ἐν τῇ γυναικί, καὶ ἡγίασται ἡ γυνὴ
for the [2]husband [1]unbelieving in the wife, and is sanctified the [2]wife
ἡ ἄπιστος ἐν τῷ [t]ἀνδρί·ǁ ἐπεὶ ἄρα τὰ.τέκνα.ὑμῶν ἀκάθαρτά
[1]unbelieving in the husband; else then your children unclean
ἐστιν, νῦν.δὲ ἅγιά ἐστιν. 15 εἰ.δὲ ὁ ἄπιστος χωρίζεται,
are, but now [2]holy [1]are. But if the unbeliever separates himself,
χωριζέσθω. οὐ.δεδούλωται ὁ ἀδελφὸς ἢ ἡ ἀδελφὴ ἐν
let him separate himself; is not under bondage the brother or the sister in
τοῖς τοιούτοις· ἐν.δὲ εἰρήνῃ κέκληκεν [v]ἡμᾶςǁ ὁ θεός. 16 τί
such [cases], but in peace [2]has [3]called [4]us [1]God. [6]What
γὰρ οἶδας, γύναι, εἰ τὸν ἄνδρα σώσεις; ἢ τί οἶδας,
[7]for knowest thou, O wife, if the husband thou shalt save? or what knowest thou,
ἄνερ, εἰ τὴν γυναῖκα σώσεις; 17 εἰ.μὴ. ἑκάστῳ ὡς
O husband, if the wife thou shalt save? Only to each as
[w]ἐμέρισενǁ [x]ὁ θεός,ǁ ἕκαστον ὡς κέκληκεν [x]ὁ κύριος,ǁ οὕτως
[2]divided [1]God, each as [3]has [4]called [1]the [2]Lord, so
περιπατείτω· καὶ οὕτως ἐν ταῖς ἐκκλησίαις πάσαις διατάσ-
let him walk; and thus in [2]the [3]assemblies [1]all I order.
σομαι. 18 Περιτετμημένος τις ἐκλήθη; μὴ.ἐπι-
Having been circumcised [2]any [3]one [1]was called? let him not be
σπάσθω. ἐν ἀκροβυστίᾳ [y]τις ἐκλήθη;ǁ μὴ.περι-
uncircumcised: in uncircumcision [2]any [3]one [1]was called? let him not be
τεμνέσθω. 19 ἡ περιτομὴ οὐδέν ἐστιν, καὶ ἡ ἀκροβυστία οὐδέν
circumcised. Circumcision [2]nothing [1]is, and uncircumcision [2]nothing
ἐστιν, ἀλλὰ τήρησις ἐντολῶν θεοῦ. 20 ἕκαστος ἐν τῇ κλήσει
[1]is, but keeping [2]commandments [1]God's. Each in the calling
ᾗ ἐκλήθη, ἐν ταύτῃ μενέτω. 21 δοῦλος ἐκλή-
in which he was called, in this let him abide. Bondman [being] wast
θης; μή σοι μελέτω· ἀλλ' εἰ.καὶ δύνασαι ἐλεύθερος
thou called, not to thee let it be a care; but and if thou art able [3]free
γενέσθαι, μᾶλλον χρῆσαι. 22 ὁ.γὰρ ἐν κυρίῳ κληθεὶς
[1]to [2]become, [5]rather [6]use [it]. For he [3]in [4the] [5]Lord [1]being [2]called
δοῦλος, ἀπελεύθερος κυρίου ἐστίν· ὁμοίως [z]καὶǁ ὁ
[being] a bondman, a freedman of [the] Lord is; likewise also he
ἐλεύθερος κληθείς, δοῦλός ἐστιν χριστοῦ. 23 τιμῆς ἠγορά-
free being called, a bondman is of Christ. With a price ye were
σθητε· μὴ.γίνεσθε δοῦλοι ἀνθρώπων. 24 ἕκαστος ἐν.ᾧ ἐκλή-
bought; become not bondmen of men. Each wherein he was
θη, ἀδελφοί, ἐν τούτῳ μενέτω παρὰ [a]τῷǁ θεῷ.
called, brethren, in that let him abide with God.

25 Περὶ.δὲ τῶν παρθένων ἐπιταγὴν κυρίου οὐκ.ἔχω·
But concerning virgins, commandment of [the] Lord I have not;
γνώμην.δὲ δίδωμι, ὡς ἠλεημένος ὑπὸ κυρίου πιστὸς
but judgment I give, as having received mercy from [the] Lord [3]faithful
εἶναι. 26 νομίζω οὖν τοῦτο καλὸν ὑπάρχειν διὰ τὴν ἐν-
[1]to [2]be. I think then this [2]good [1]is because of the pre-
εστῶσαν ἀνάγκην, ὅτι καλὸν ἀνθρώπῳ τὸ οὕτως εἶναι.
sent necessity, that [it is] good for a man so to be.
27 δέδεσαι γυναικί; μὴ.ζήτει λύσιν. λέλυσαι ἀπὸ
Hast thou been bound to a wife? seek not to be loosed. Hast thou been loosed from
γυναικός; μὴ.ζήτει γυναῖκα. 28 ἐὰν.δὲ καὶ [b]γήμῃς,ǁ
a wife? seek not a wife. But if also thou mayest have married,
οὐχ.ἥμαρτες· καὶ ἐὰν γήμῃ [c]ἡǁ παρθένος, οὐχ
thou didst not sin; and if [3]may [4]have [5]married [1]the [2]virgin, [6]not
ἥμαρτεν· θλίψιν.δὲ τῇ σαρκὶ ἕξουσιν οἱ τοιοῦτοι· ἐγὼ.δὲ
[6]she [7]did sin: but tribulation in the flesh [2]shall [3]have [1]such; but I
ὑμῶν φείδομαι. 29 Τοῦτο.δέ φημι, ἀδελφοί, [d] ὁ καιρὸς συν-
[2]you [1]spare. But this I say, brethren, the season strait-
εσταλμένος· [e]τὸ.λοιπόν ἐστιν,ǁ ἵνα καὶ [f]οἱǁ ἔχοντες γυναῖκας,
ened [is]. For the rest is, that even those having wives,
ὡς μὴ ἔχοντες ὦσιν· 30 καὶ οἱ κλαίοντες, ὡς μὴ κλαίοντες· καὶ
[2]as [3]not [4]having [1]be; and those weeping, as not weeping; and
οἱ χαίροντες, ὡς μη χαίροντες· καὶ οἱ ἀγοράζοντες, ὡς μὴ
those rejoicing, as not rejoicing; and those buying, as not
κατέχοντες 31 καὶ οἱ χρώμενοι [g]τῷ.κόσμῳ.τούτῳ,ǁ ὡς μὴ
possessing; and those using this world, as not
καταχρώμενοι. παράγει.γὰρ τὸ σχῆμα τοῦ.κόσμου.τούτου.
using [it] as their own; for passes away the fashion of this world.
32 θέλω.δὲ ὑμᾶς ἀμερίμνους εἶναι. ὁ ἄγαμος μεριμνᾷ τὰ
But I wish you without care to be. The unmarried cares for the things
τοῦ κυρίου, πῶς [h]ἀρέσειǁ τῷ κυρίῳ· 33 ὁ.δὲ γαμήσας
of the Lord, how he shall please the Lord; but he that is married
μεριμνᾷ τὰ τοῦ κόσμου, πῶς [h]ἀρέσειǁ τῇ γυναικί.
cares for the things of the world, how he shall please the wife.

34 [i]μεμέρισταιǁ ἡ [k]γυνὴǁ καὶ ἡ παρθένος. [l]ἡ ἄγαμοςǁ μεριμνᾷ
Divided are the wife and the virgin. The unmarried cares for
τὰ τοῦ κυρίου, ἵνα ᾖ ἁγία [m]καὶǁ [n] σώματι καὶ [n]
the things of the Lord, that she may be holy both in body and
πνεύματι· ἡ.δὲ γαμήσασα μεριμνᾷ τὰ τοῦ κόσμου,
spirit; but she that is married cares for the things of the world,

14 For the unbelieving husband is sanctified
in the wife. And the unbelieving wife is sanctified in the husband. For otherwise your
children are unclean, but now are holy.
15 But if the unbeliever separates himself,
let him separate himself. The brother or the
sister is not under bondage in such cases, But
God has called us in peace.
16 For what do you know, O wife, whether
you shall save your husband? Or what do
you know, O husband, whether you shall
save your wife?
17 But to each one as God has given, as the
Lord has called each, so let him walk. And
so I order in all the churches.
18 Was anyone called who had been
circumcised? Let him not be uncircumcised.
Was anyone called not being circumcised?
Let him not be circumcised.
19 Circumcision is nothing. And not being
circumcised is nothing. But keeping God's
commandments *is everything.*
20 Each one in the calling in which he was
called, let him remain in this.
21 Were you called a slave? Do not let it be
a care to you. Bit if you are able to become
free, make your life useful.
22 For he who is called a slave in the Lord
is a free man of the Lord. And so is he who
is called free, *he* is a slave of Christ.
23 You were bought with a price. Do not
become the slaves of men.
24 Brothers, in whichever way he was called, let each one live with God in that way.
25 Now as to virgins, I do not have any
commandment of the Lord. Yet I give judgment as one who has received mercy from
the Lord to be faithful.
26 This then is *what* I think is good
(because of the present distress): that *it is*
good for a man to be this way.
27 Have you been bound to a wife? Do not
try to be free. Have you been freed from a
wife? Do not look for a wife.
28 But if you also should get married, you
have not sinned. And if a virgin has gotten
married, she has not sinned, but shall have
much trouble in the flesh. But I spare you.
29 But this I say, my brothers, the time is
short. The rest is: That even those who have
wives should be as not having *them* –
30 and those weeping as not weeping – and
the ones rejoicing as not rejoicing - and the
ones buying as not owning anything –
31 and the ones using this world as not
using it as their very own – for the ways of
this world are passing away.
32 But I desire for you to be free from care.
The unmarried one cares for the things of
the Lord, how he shall please the Lord.
33 But he that is married cares for the
things of the world, how he shall please his
wife.
34 The wife and the virgin are different.
The unmarried one cares for the things of
the Lord, that she may be holy both in body
and spirit. But she that is married cares for
the things of the world, how she shall please

πῶς [o]ἀρέσει‖ τῷ ἀνδρί. 35 τοῦτο.δὲ πρὸς τὸ.ὑμῶν.αὐτῶν
how she shall please the husband. But this for your own
[p]συμφέρον‖ λέγω· οὐχ ἵνα βρόχον ὑμῖν ἐπιβάλω, ἀλλὰ
profit I say; not that a noose [5]you [1]I [2]may [3]cast [4]before. but
πρὸς τὸ εὔσχημον καὶ [q]εὐπρόσεδρον‖ τῷ κυρίῳ ἀπερι-
for what [is] seemly, and waiting on the Lord without
σπάστως. 36 εἰ.δέ τις ἀσχημονεῖν ἐπὶ τὴν παρθένον
distraction. But if anyone [[2]he] [3]behaves [4]unseemly [5]to [7]virginity
αὐτοῦ νομίζει, ἐὰν ᾖ ὑπέρακμος, καὶ οὕτως ὀφείλει γίνε-
[6]his [1]thinks, if he be beyond [his] prime, and so it ought to
σθαι, ὃ θέλει ποιείτω, οὐχ.ἁμαρτάνει· γαμείτωσαν. 37 ὃς.δὲ
be, what he wills let him do, he does not sin: let them marry. But he who
ἕστηκεν [r]ἑδραῖος ἐν τῇ καρδίᾳ,‖ μὴ ἔχων ἀνάγκην, ἐξουσίαν.δὲ
stands firm in heart, not having necessity, but authority
ἔχει περὶ τοῦ.ἰδίου θελήματος, καὶ τοῦτο κέκρικεν ἐν τῇ [s]
has over his own will, and this has judged in
καρδίᾳ.[t]αὐτοῦ‖ [v]τοῦ‖ τηρεῖν τὴν.ἑαυτοῦ παρθένον, καλῶς
his heart to keep his own virginity, well
[w]ποιεῖ.‖ 38 ὥστε καὶ ὁ [x]ἐκγαμίζων καλῶς ποιεῖ· [y]ὁ.δὲ‖
he does. So that also he that gives in marriage [2]well [1]does; and he that
μὴ [z]ἐκγαμίζων‖ κρεῖσσον [w]ποιεῖ.‖ 39 Γυνὴ δέδεται [a]νόμῳ‖
[2]not [1]gives in marriage [2]better [1]does. A wife is bound by law
ἐφ' ὅσον χρόνον ζῇ ὁ.ἀνὴρ.αὐτῆς· ἐὰν.δὲ κοι-
for as long [2]as [1]time [5]may [6]live [3]her [4]husband; but if may have fallen
μηθῇ ὁ ἀνὴρ [b]αὐτῆς,‖ ἐλευθέρα ἐστὶν ᾧ θέλει γαμη-
asleep the husband of her, free she is to whom she wills to be
θῆναι, μόνον ἐν κυρίῳ. 40 μακαριωτέρα.δέ ἐστιν ἐὰν οὕτως
married, only in [the] Lord. But happier she is if so
μείνῃ, κατὰ τὴν ἐμὴν γνώμην· δοκῶ.δὲ κἀγὼ
she should remain, according to my judgment; and I think I also
πνεῦμα θεοῦ ἔχειν.
[3]Spirit [2]God's [1]have.

8 Περὶ.δὲ τῶν.εἰδωλοθύτων, οἴδαμεν, ὅτι πάντες γνῶσιν
But concerning things sacrificed to idols, we know, (for [2]all [4]knowledge
ἔχομεν. ἡ γνῶσις φυσιοῖ, ἡ δὲ ἀγάπη οἰκοδομεῖ. 2 εἰ.[c]δέ‖
[1]we [3]have: knowledge puffs up, but love builds up. But if
τις δοκεῖ [d]εἰδέναι‖ τι, [e]οὐδέπω.οὐδὲν ἔγνωκεν‖
anyone thinks to have known anything, nothing yet he has known
καθὼς δεῖ γνῶναι. 3 εἰ.δέ τις ἀγαπᾷ τὸν θεόν,
according as it is necessary to know. But if anyone love God,
οὗτος ἔγνωσται ὑπ' αὐτοῦ. 4 περὶ τῆς βρώσεως οὖν τῶν
he is known by him:) concerning the eating then
εἰδωλοθύτων, οἴδαμεν ὅτι οὐδὲν εἴδωλον ἐν κόσμῳ,
of things sacrificed to idols, we know that nothing an idol [is] in [the] world,
καὶ ὅτι οὐδεὶς θεὸς [f]ἕτερος‖ εἰ.μὴ εἷς. 5 καὶ.γὰρ εἴπερ
and that [there is] no [2]God [1]other except one. For even if indeed
εἰσὶν λεγόμενοι θεοί, εἴτε ἐν οὐρανῷ εἴτε ἐπὶ [g]τῆς‖
there are [those] called gods, whether in heaven or on the
γῆς· ὥσπερ εἰσὶν θεοὶ πολλοὶ καὶ κύριοι πολλοί· 6 [h]ἀλλ'‖
earth, as there are gods many and lords many, but
ἡμῖν εἷς θεὸς ὁ πατήρ, ἐξ οὗ τὰ.πάντα, καὶ ἡμεῖς
to us [there is] one God the Father, of whom [are] all things, and we
εἰς αὐτόν· καὶ εἷς κύριος Ἰησοῦς χριστός, δι' οὗ τὰ.πάντα,
for him; and one Lord Jesus Christ, by whom [are] all things,
καὶ ἡμεῖς δι' αὐτοῦ. 7 ἀλλ' οὐκ ἐν πᾶσιν ἡ γνῶσις· τινὲς
and we by him. But not in all [is] the knowledge: [2]some
δὲ τῇ [i]συνειδήσει‖ [k]τοῦ εἰδώλου ἕως ἄρτι‖ ὡς εἰδωλό-
[1]but with conscience of the idol, until now [2]as [3]of [4]a [5]thing [6]sacrificed
θυτον ἐσθίουσιν, καὶ ἡ.συνείδησις.αὐτῶν ἀσθενὴς οὖσα
[7]to [8]an [9]idol [1]eat, and their conscience, [2]weak [1]being,
μολύνεται. 8 βρῶμα.δὲ ἡμᾶς οὐ.[l]παρίστησιν‖ τῷ θεῷ· οὔτε
is defiled. But meat us does not commend to God; [2]neither
[m]γὰρ‖ ἐὰν [n]φάγωμεν περισσεύομεν· οὔτε ἐὰν μὴ.φάγωμεν
[1]for if we eat have we an advantage; neither if we eat not
ὑστερούμεθα.‖ 9 βλέπετε.δὲ μήπως ἡ ἐξουσία ὑμῶν αὕτη
do we come short. But take heed lest [3]power [2]your [1]this
πρόσκομμα γένηται [o]τοῖς ἀσθενοῦσιν.‖ 10 ἐὰν.γάρ
an occasion of stumbling become to those being weak. For if
τίς ἴδῃ [p]σε,‖ τὸν ἔχοντα γνῶσιν, ἐν [q]εἰδωλείῳ‖ κατακείμενον,
anyone see thee, who hast knowledge, in an idol-temple reclining
οὐχὶ ἡ συνείδησις αὐτοῦ ἀσθενοῦς ὄντος οἰκοδο-
[at table], [2]not [3]the [4]conscience [5]of [6]him [8]weak [7]being [1]will be
μηθήσεται εἰς.τὸ τὰ.εἰδωλόθυτα ἐσθίειν; 11 [r]καὶ ἀπο-
built up so as [3]things [4]sacrificed [5]to [6]idols [1]to [2]eat? and will
λεῖται‖ ὁ ἀσθενῶν [s]ἀδελφὸς ἐπὶ τῇ.σῇ.γνώσει,‖ δι' ὃν χριστὸς
perish the weak brother on thy knowledge, for whom Christ
ἀπέθανεν. [t] 12 οὕτως.δὲ ἁμαρτάνοντες εἰς τοὺς ἀδελφούς,
died. Now thus sinning against the brethren,
καὶ τύπτοντες αὐτῶν τὴν συνείδησιν ἀσθενοῦσαν, εἰς χριστὸν
and wounding their [2]conscience [1]weak, against Christ

her husband.
35 And I say this for your own good, not
that I may place a snare in front of you, but
for that which is right and that you may
serve the Lord without being distracted.
36 But if anyone considers it is behaving
indecently towards his virginity (if he be
beyond *his* prime, and so it ought to be), let
him do what he chooses – he does not sin –
let them marry.
37 But he who stands firm in his heart, not
having any need, but who has authority over
his own will (and he has judged this thing in
his heart, to keep his own virginity), he does
well.
38 So that he that gives in marriage does well,
and he that does not give in marriage does
better.
39 A wife is bound by law for as long as her
husband is living. But if her husband is dead,
she is free to be married to whom she pleases
– only in the Lord.
40 But according to my judgment, she is
happier if she could stay unmarried. And I
believe I have the Spirit of God.

CHAPTER 8

1 Now about things sacrificed to idols, we
know that we all have knowledge. Knowledge puffs up, but love builds up.
2 But if anyone thinks he knows anything,
he has not known anything as he ought to
know it.
3 But if anyone loves God, he is known by
Him.
4 Then, as to eating things sacrificed to
idols, we know that an idol is nothing in the
world. And *there is* no other God except
one.
5 For even though there are *those* called
gods, whether in the heavens or on the earth,
as there are many gods and many lords,
6 yet to us *there is* one God the Father, of
whom are all things, and we for Him – and
one Lord Jesus Christ by whom are all things
– and we by Him.
7 But this knowledge is not in all. But some
being fully aware of the idol eat as of a thing
sacrificed to an idol even until now. And
their conscience being weak are defiled
8 But food does not commend us to God.
For neither if we eat are we the better, nor if
we do not eat are we the worse.
9 But be careful for fear this strength of
yours may become a cause of stumbling to
those who are weak.
10 For if anyone sees you who have knowledge dining in an idol-temple, will not the
weak one's conscience be lifted up so as to
eat things sacrificed to idols?
11 And through your knowledge the weak
brother, for whom Christ died, will fall.
12 But sinning in this way against the
brothers and wounding their weak conscience, you are sinning against Christ.

ἁμαρτάνετε. 13 ʸδιόπερ‖ εἰ βρῶμα σκανδαλίζει τὸν ἀδελφόν
ye sin. Wherefore if meat cause ³to ⁴offend ²brother
μου, οὐ.μὴ φάγω κρέα εἰς.τὸν.αἰῶνα, ἵνα μὴ τὸν ἀδελφόν
¹my, not at all should I eat flesh for ever, that ¹not ⁶brother
μου σκανδαλίσω.
⁵my ¹I ²may ⁴cause to offend.

9 Οὐκ.εἰμὶ ˣἀπόστολος‖; οὐκ.εἰμὶ ˣἐλεύθερος‖; οὐχὶ Ἰησοῦν
Am I not an apostle? am I not free? ³not ⁵Jesus
ʸχριστὸν‖ τὸν.κύριον.ἡμῶν ᶻἑώρακα‖; οὐ τὸ.ἔργον.μου ὑμεῖς
⁶Christ ⁷our ⁸Lord ¹have ²I ⁴seen? ¹⁰not ¹²my ¹³work ¹¹ye
ἐστε ἐν κυρίῳ; 2 εἰ ἄλλοις οὐκ.εἰμὶ ἀπόστολος, ἀλλά
⁹are in [the] Lord? If to others I am not an apostle, yet
γε ὑμῖν εἰμι· ἡ.γὰρ σφραγὶς ᵃτῆς.ἐμῆς.ἀποστολῆς‖ ὑμεῖς
at any rate to you I am; for the seal of my apostleship ye
ἐστε ἐν κυρίῳ. 3 ἡ.ἐμὴ.ἀπολογία τοῖς ἐμὲ ἀνακρίνουσιν
are in [the] Lord. My defence to those ³me ¹who ²examine
ᵇαὕτη ἐστίν,‖ 4 Μὴ οὐκ.ἔχομεν ἐξουσίαν φαγεῖν καὶ ᶜπιεῖν‖;
⁵this ⁴is: Have we not authority to eat and to drink?
5 μὴ οὐκ.ἔχομεν ἐξουσίαν ἀδελφὴν γυναῖκα περιάγειν, ὡς καὶ
have we not authority a sister, a wife, to take about, as also
οἱ λοιποὶ ἀπόστολοι, καὶ οἱ ἀδελφοὶ τοῦ κυρίου, καὶ Κηφᾶς;
the other apostles, and the brethren of the Lord, and Cephas?
6 ἢ μόνος ἐγὼ καὶ Βαρνάβας οὐκ.ἔχομεν ἐξουσίαν ᵈτοῦ‖ μὴ
Or only I and Barnabas have we not authority not
ἐργάζεσθαι; 7 Τίς στρατεύεται ἰδίοις ὀψωνίοις ποτέ;
to work? Who serves as a soldier at his own charges at any time?
τίς φυτεύει ἀμπελῶνα, καὶ ᵉἐκ τοῦ καρποῦ‖ αὐτοῦ οὐκ.ἐσθίει;
who plants a vineyard, and of the fruit of it does not eat?
ᶠἢ‖ τίς ποιμαίνει ποίμνην, καὶ ἐκ τοῦ γάλακτος τῆς ποίμνης
or who shepherds a flock, and of the milk of the flock
οὐκ.ἐσθίει; 8 μὴ κατὰ ἄνθρωπον ταῦτα λαλῶ; ἢ ᵍοὐχὶ
does not eat? according to a man these things do I speak, or ²not
καὶ ὁ νόμος ταῦτα‖ λέγει; 9 ἐν.γὰρ τῷ ʰΜωσέως‖ νόμῳ
³also ⁴the ⁵law ⁶these ⁷things ¹says? For in the ²of ³Moses ¹law
γέγραπται, Οὐ.ⁱφιμώσεις‖ βοῦν ἀλοῶντα. μὴ τῶν
it has been written, Thou shalt not muzzle an ox treading out corn. ⁴For ⁵the
βοῶν μέλει τῷ θεῷ; 10 ἢ δι' ἡμᾶς πάντως λέγει;
⁶oxen ¹is ²there ³care with God? or because of us altogether says he [it]?
δι'.ἡμᾶς.γὰρ ἐγράφη, ὅτι ʲἐπ' ἐλπίδι ὀφείλει‖ ὁ ἀροτριῶν
For because of us it was written, that in hope ought he that ploughs
ἀροτριᾶν, καὶ ὁ ἀλοῶν ᵏτῆς.ἐλπίδος.αὐτοῦ μετέχειν
to plough, and he that treads out corn, ⁵of ⁶his ⁷hope ³to ⁴partake
ἐπ' ἐλπίδι.‖ 11 Εἰ ἡμεῖς ὑμῖν τὰ πνευματικὰ ἐσπείραμεν,
¹in ²hope. If we to you spiritual things did sow, [is it]
μέγα εἰ ἡμεῖς ὑμῶν τὰ σαρκικὰ θερίσομεν; 12 εἰ ἄλλοι
a great thing if we your fleshly things shall reap? If others
τῆς ˡἐξουσίας ὑμῶν‖ μετέχουσιν, οὐ μᾶλλον ἡμεῖς;
²of ³the ⁴authority ⁵over ⁶you ¹partake, [should] not rather we?
ἀλλ' οὐκ.ἐχρησάμεθα τῇ.ἐξουσίᾳ.ταύτῃ· ἀλλὰ πάντα στέ-
But we did not use this authority; but all things we
γομεν, ἵνα μὴ ᵐἐγκοπήν τινα‖ δῶμεν τῷ εὐαγγελίῳ τοῦ
bear, that not ²hindrance ¹any we should give to the glad tidings of the
χριστοῦ. 13 οὐκ.οἴδατε ὅτι οἱ τὰ.ἱερὰ ἐργαζόμενοι, ⁿ
Christ. Know ye not that those [²at] ³sacred ⁴things ¹labouring, [the
ἐκ τοῦ ἱεροῦ ἐσθίουσιν· οἱ τῷ θυσιαστηρίῳ ᵒπροσεδ-
things] of the temple eat; those ²at ³the ⁴altar ¹attend-
ρεύοντες,‖ τῷ θυσιαστηρίῳ συμμερίζονται; 14 οὕτως καὶ ὁ
ing, with the altar partake? So also the
κύριος διέταξεν τοῖς τὸ εὐαγγέλιον καταγγέλλουσιν, ἐκ τοῦ
Lord did order to those the glad tidings announcing, of the
εὐαγγελίου ζῆν. 15 ἐγὼ.δὲ ᵖοὐδενὶ ἐχρησάμην‖ τούτων·
glad tidings to live. But I ²none ¹used of these things.
οὐκ.ἔγραψα.δὲ ταῦτα ἵνα οὕτως γένηται ἐν ἐμοί·
Now I did not write these things that thus it should be with me; [²it ³were]
καλὸν γάρ μοι μᾶλλον ἀποθανεῖν, ἢ τὸ.καύχημά.μου ᵠἵνα
⁴good ¹for for me rather to die, than ³my ⁴boasting ¹that
τις‖ ʳκενώσῃ.‖ 16 ἐὰν.γὰρ εὐαγγελίζωμαι, οὐκ.ἔστιν
²anyone should make void. For if I announce the glad tidings, there is not
μοι καύχημα· ἀνάγκη.γάρ μοι ἐπίκειται· οὐαὶ.ˢδέ‖ μοι
²to ³me ¹boasting; for necessity ⁴me ¹is ²laid ³upon; ⁶woe ⁵but to me
ἐστὶν ἐὰν μὴ.ᵗεὐαγγελίζωμαι.‖ 17 εἰ.γὰρ ἑκὼν τοῦτο
it is if I should not announce the glad tidings. For if willingly this
πράσσω, μισθὸν ἔχω· εἰ.δὲ ἄκων οἰκονομίαν πεπί-
I do, a reward I have; but if unwillingly an administration I am en-
στευμαι. 18 τίς οὖν ᵛμοί‖ ἐστιν ὁ μισθός; ἵνα εὐαγ-
trusted with. What then ²my ¹is reward? That in announcing
γελιζόμενος ἀδάπανον θήσω τὸ εὐαγγέλιον ʷτοῦ
the glad tidings ⁴without ⁵expense ⁶I ⁷should ⁸make ⁹the ¹⁰glad ¹¹tidings ¹of ²the
χριστοῦ,‖ εἰς.τὸ μὴ καταχρήσασθαι τῇ.ἐξουσίᾳ.μου ἐν τῷ
³Christ, so as not using as my own my authority in the

13 So if food causes my brother to stumble, I would never eat flesh forever, in order that I may not cause my brother to stumble.

CHAPTER 9

1 Am I not an apostle? Am I not free? Have I not seen Jesus Christ our Lord? Are you not my work in the Lord?
2 If I am not an apostle to others, yet without doubt I am to you. For you are the seal of my apostleship in the Lord.
3 My answer to those who judge me is this:
4 Do we not have authority to eat and to drink?
5 Do we not have authority to lead around a sister, a wife, as the other apostles, and Peter, and the brothers of the Lord also *do*.
6 Or *is it* only Barnabas and I who have no right to quit working?
7 Who at any time serves as a soldier at his own expense? Who plants a vineyard and does not eat of the fruit at any time? Or who shepherds a flock and does not partake of the milk of the flock?
8 Do I speak these things according to the ways of men? Or does not the Law also say these things?
9 For it has been written in the Law of Moses, "You shall not muzzle an ox treading out corn." Is it *because* God cares for the oxen?
10 Or *does* He say it only because of us? It was written for us, because he who plows ought to plow in hope. And he who treads out grain in hope *ought* to share in hope.
11 If we have sown spiritual things to you, *it is* a great thing if we shall reap your fleshly things?
12 If others share in the authority over you, *should* not rather we? But we did not use this authority. But we endure all things for fear that we should hinder the gospel of Christ.
13 Do you not know that those who labor *about* holy things eat of the temple? Those attending the altar share with the altar.
14 Even so the Lord has commanded to those who preach the gospel, to live of the gospel.
15 But I did not use any of these things. And I did not write these things that it should be so with me. For *it would be* better for me to die than that anyone should make my glorying without effect.
16 For if I preach the gospel, there is no glory to me, for great necessity is laid on me and it is a calamity to me if I do not preach the gospel.
17 For if I do this willingly, I have a reward. But if against my will, I am entrusted with stewardship.
18 What then is my reward? – that in preaching the gospel I should make the gospel of Christ free – so that I may not misuse my authority in the gospel.

εὐαγγελίῳ. 19 Ἐλεύθερος.γὰρ ὢν ἐκ πάντων, πᾶσιν ἐμαυτὸν
glad tidings. For free being from all, to all myself
ἐδούλωσα, ἵνα τοὺς πλείονας κερδήσω· 20 καὶ ἐγενόμην
I became bondman, that the more I might gain. And I became
τοῖς Ἰουδαίοις ὡς Ἰουδαῖος, ἵνα Ἰουδαίους κερδήσω· τοῖς
to the Jews as a Jew, that Jews I might gain: to those
ὑπὸ νόμον ὡς ὑπὸ νόμον, [x] ἵνα τοὺς ὑπὸ νόμον κερδήσω·
under law as under law, that those under law I might gain:
21 τοῖς ἀνόμοις ὡς ἄνομος, μὴ ὢν ἄνομος [y]θεῷ,[ll] ἀλλ'
to those without law as without law, (not being without law to God, but
ἔννομος [z]χριστῷ,[ll] ἵνα [a]κερδήσω[ll] ἀνόμους. 22 ἐγενόμην
within law to Christ,) that I might gain those without law. I became
τοῖς ἀσθενέσιν [b]ὡς[ll] ἀσθενής, ἵνα τοὺς ἀσθενεῖς κερδήσω.
to the weak as weak, that the weak I might gain.
τοῖς.πᾶσιν γέγονα [c]τὰ[ll].πάντα, ἵνα πάντως τινὰς σώσω.
To all these I have become all things, that by all means some I might save.
23 [d]τοῦτο[ll] δὲ ποιῶ διὰ τὸ εὐαγγέλιον, ἵνα [e]συγκοινωνὸς[ll]
[2]This [1]and I do on account of the glad tidings, that a fellow-partaker
αὐτοῦ γένωμαι.
with it I might be.

24 Οὐκ.οἴδατε ὅτι οἱ ἐν σταδίῳ τρέχοντες πάντες μὲν
Know ye not that those who in a race-course run all
τρέχουσιν, εἷς.δὲ λαμβάνει τὸ βραβεῖον; οὕτως τρέχετε, ἵνα
run, but one receives the prize? Thus run, that
καταλάβητε. 25 πᾶς.δὲ ὁ ἀγωνιζόμενος, πάντα ἐγκρα-
ye may obtain. But everyone that strives, in all things controls
τεύεται· ἐκεῖνοι μὲν οὖν ἵνα φθαρτὸν στέφανον λάβωσιν,
himself: they indeed then that a corruptible crown they may receive,
ἡμεῖς.δὲ ἄφθαρτον. 26 ἐγὼ τοίνυν οὕτως τρέχω, ὡς οὐκ
but we an incorruptible. I therefore so run, as not
ἀδήλως· οὕτως πυκτεύω, ὡς οὐκ ἀέρα δέρων· 27 [g]ἀλλ'[ll]
uncertainly; so I combat, as not [the] air beating. But
ὑπωπιάζω μου τὸ σῶμα, καὶ δουλαγωγῶ, μήπως ἄλλοις
I buffet my body, and bring [it] into servitude, lest to others
κηρύξας αὐτὸς ἀδόκιμος γένωμαι.
having preached [2]myself [5]rejected [1]I [3]might [4]be.

10 Οὐ.θέλω [h]δὲ[ll] ὑμᾶς ἀγνοεῖν, ἀδελφοί, ὅτι οἱ πατέρες
[2]I [3]wish [4]not [1]now you to be ignorant, brethren, that [2]fathers
ἡμῶν πάντες ὑπὸ τὴν νεφέλην ἦσαν, καὶ πάντες διὰ τῆς
[1]our all under the cloud were, and all through the
θαλάσσης διῆλθον, 2 καὶ πάντες εἰς τὸν [i]Μωσῆν[ll] [k]ἐβαπτίσαντο[ll]
sea passed, and all to Moses were baptized
ἐν τῇ νεφέλῃ καὶ ἐν τῇ θαλάσσῃ, 3 καὶ πάντες τὸ αὐτὸ [l]βρῶμα
in the cloud and in the sea, and all the same [2]meat
πνευματικὸν ἔφαγον,[ll] 4 καὶ πάντες τὸ αὐτὸ [m]πόμα πνευ-
[1]spiritual ate, and all the same [2]drink [1]spi-
ματικὸν ἔπιον·[ll] ἔπινον.γὰρ ἐκ πνευματικῆς ἀκολουθούσης
ritual drank; for they drank of a spiritual [2]following
πέτρας· ἡ.[n]δὲ πέτρα[ll] ἦν ὁ χριστός. 5 ἀλλ' οὐκ ἐν τοῖς
[1]rock, and the rock was the Christ: yet not with the
πλείοσιν αὐτῶν [o]εὐδόκησεν[ll] ὁ θεός· κατεστρώθησαν.γὰρ ἐν
most of them was [2]well [3]pleased [1]God; for they were strewed in
τῇ ἐρήμῳ. 6 ταῦτα.δὲ τύποι ἡμῶν ἐγενήθησαν, εἰς τὸ μὴ
the desert. But these things types for us became, for [2]not
εἶναι ἡμᾶς ἐπιθυμητὰς κακῶν, καθὼς κἀκεῖνοι ἐπεθύμη-
[3]to [4]be [1]us desirers of evil things, according as they also desired,
σαν. 7 μηδὲ εἰδωλολάτραι γίνεσθε, καθώς τινες αὐτῶν· [p]ὡς[ll]
Neither idolaters be ye, according as some of them; as
γέγραπται, Ἐκάθισεν ὁ λαὸς φαγεῖν καὶ [q]πιεῖν,[ll] καὶ ἀν-
it has been written, [3]Sat [4]down [1]the [2]people to eat and to drink, and rose
έστησαν παίζειν. 8 μηδὲ πορνεύωμεν, καθώς τινες
up to play. Neither should we commit fornication, according as some
αὐτῶν ἐπόρνευσαν, καὶ [r]ἔπεσον[ll] [s]ἐν[ll] μιᾷ ἡμέρᾳ εἰκοσιτρεῖς
of them committed fornication, and fell in one day twenty-three
χιλιάδες. 9 μηδὲ ἐκπειράζωμεν τὸν [t]χριστόν,[ll] καθὼς [v]καί[ll]
thousand. Neither should we tempt the Christ, according as also
τινες αὐτῶν [w]ἐπείρασαν,[ll] καὶ ὑπὸ τῶν ὄφεων [x]ἀπώλοντο.[ll]
some of them tempted, and by the serpents perished.
10 μηδὲ γογγύζετε, [y]καθὼς[ll] [v]καί[ll] τινες αὐτῶν ἐγόγγυσαν,
Neither murmur ye, according as also some of them murmured,
καὶ ἀπώλοντο ὑπὸ τοῦ ὀλοθρευτοῦ. 11 ταῦτα.δὲ [z]πάντα[ll]
and perished by the destroyer. Now these things all [as]
[a]τύποι[ll] [b]συνέβαινον[ll] ἐκείνοις· ἐγράφη.δὲ πρὸς νουθεσίαν
types happened to them, and were written for [2]admonition
ἡμῶν εἰς οὓς τὰ τέλη τῶν αἰώνων [c]κατήντησεν.[ll] 12 ὥστε
[1]our on whom the ends of the ages are arrived. So that
ὁ δοκῶν ἑστάναι, βλεπέτω μὴ πέσῃ. 13 Πειρασμὸς
he that thinks to stand, let him take heed lest he fall. Temptation
ὑμᾶς οὐκ.εἴληφεν εἰ.μὴ ἀνθρώπινος· πιστὸς.δὲ ὁ θεός, ὃς
you has not taken except what belongs to man; and faithful [is] God, who

19 For being free from all, I myself became
a slave to all, so that I might gain the most.
20 And I became as a under Law, so that I
might gain those under Law –
21 and to those outside Law as outside Law
(not being outside law to God, but under
law to Christ), that I might gain those
outside Law.
22 To the weak, I became as weak, so that I
might gain the weak. To all these I have
become all things so that by all means I
might save some.
23 And I do this for the sake of the gospel,
so that I might be one who shares in it.
24 Do you not know that the ones who run
in a race really all run, but only one receives
the prize? So run that you may win.
25 But everyone who tries to win in all
things controls himself. Then they really *do*
it so that they may win a crown that
vanishes away, but we *one* that lasts forever.
26 So then I do not run uncertainly, nor
fight as one beating the air.
27 But I keep my body under discipline and
bring it into captivity lest I may by some
means be rejected myself, after having
preached to others.

CHAPTER 10

1 Now I do not want you to be ignorant,
brothers, that our fathers were all under the
cloud. And all passed through the sea.
2 And all were baptized into Moses in the
cloud and in the sea.
3 And all ate the same spiritual food.
4 And all drank the same spiritual drink –
for they drank of the spiritual rock following *them*, and that Rock was Christ.
5 Yet God was not pleased with most of
them, for they were slain in the desert.
6 But these things became examples for us,
so that we may not be persons who lust after
evil things, even as they also lusted.
7 Neither be worshipers of idols, even as
some of them, for it has been written, "The
people sat down to eat and to drink and got up
to play."
8 Neither should we commit fornication,
even as some of them committed fornication
(and twenty-three thousand fell in one day.)
9 Nor would we try Christ, as some also of
them tested Him and were slain by serpents.
10 Nor should you murmur, as some of
them murmured and were killed by the
destroyer.
11 Now all these things happened as examples to them and were written down for
warning to us, on whom the ends of the ages
have come –
12 so let him that thinks that he stands be
careful lest he fall.
13 No temptation has taken you except
what is common to man. But God is faithful,

οὐκ.ἐάσει ὑμᾶς πειρασθῆναι ὑπὲρ ὃ δύνασθε, ἀλλὰ ποιήσει
will not suffer you to be tempted above what ye are able, but will make
σὺν τῷ πειρασμῷ καὶ τὴν ἔκβασιν, τοῦ.δύνασθαι [e]ὑμᾶς‖
with the temptation also the issue, for [2]to [3]be [4]able [1]you
ὑπενεγκεῖν. 14 Διόπερ, ἀγαπητοί.μου, φεύγετε ἀπὸ τῆς
to bear [it]. Wherefore, my beloved, flee from
εἰδωλολατρείας. 15 ὡς φρονίμοις λέγω· κρίνατε ὑμεῖς ὅ
idolatry. As to intelligent ones I speak: judge ye what
φημι. 16 τὸ ποτήριον τῆς εὐλογίας ὃ εὐλογοῦμεν, οὐχὶ
I say. The cup of blessing which we bless, [3]not
κοινωνία [f]τοῦ αἵματος τοῦ χριστοῦ ἐστιν;‖ τὸν ἄρτον ὃν
[4]fellowship [5]of [6]the [7]blood [8]of [9]the [10]Christ [1]is [2]it? The bread which
κλῶμεν, οὐχὶ κοινωνία τοῦ σώματος τοῦ χριστοῦ ἐστιν;
we break, [3]not [4]fellowship [5]of [6]the [7]body [8]of [9]the [10]Christ [1]is [2]it?
17 ὅτι εἷς ἄρτος, ἓν σῶμα οἱ πολλοί ἐσμεν· οἱ γὰρ πάντες
Because [5]one [6]loaf, [7]one [8]body [2]the [3]many [1]we [4]are; for [2]all
ἐκ τοῦ ἑνὸς ἄρτου μετέχομεν. 18 βλέπετε τὸν Ἰσραὴλ κατὰ
[3]of [4]the [5]one [6]loaf [1]we partake. See Israel according to
σάρκα· [g]οὐχὶ‖ οἱ ἐσθίοντες τὰς θυσίας, κοινωνοὶ
flesh: [2]not [3]those [4]eating [5]the [6]sacrifices, [7]fellow-partakers
τοῦ θυσιαστηρίου εἰσίν; 19 τί οὖν φημι; ὅτι [h]εἴδωλον‖ τί
[8]with [9]the [10]altar [1]are? What then say I? that an idol anything
ἐστιν; ἢ ὅτι [h]εἰδωλόθυτον‖ τί ἐστιν; 20 ἀλλ' ὅτι
is, or that what is sacrificed to an idol anything is? but that
ἃ [i]θύει‖ [k]τὰ ἔθνη,‖ δαιμονίοις [l]θύει,‖ καὶ οὐ θεῷ[m]·
what [3]sacrifice [1]the [2]nations, to demons they sacrifice, and not to God.
οὐ.θέλω.δὲ ὑμᾶς κοινωνοὺς τῶν δαιμονίων γίνεσθαι.
But I do not wish you fellow-partakers with demons to be.
21 οὐ.δύνασθε ποτήριον κυρίου πίνειν, καὶ ποτήριον
Ye cannot [the] cup of [the] Lord drink, and [the] cup
δαιμονίων· οὐ.δύνασθε τραπέζης κυρίου μετέχειν καὶ
of demons: ye cannot of [the] table of [the] Lord partake and
τραπέζης δαιμονίων. 22 ἢ παραζηλοῦμεν τὸν κύριον;
of [the] table of demons. Or, do we provoke to jealousy the Lord?
μὴ ἰσχυρότεροι αὐτοῦ ἐσμεν;
stronger than he are we?
23 Πάντα [n]μοι‖ ἔξεστιν, ἀλλ' οὐ πάντα συμφέρει·
All things for me are lawful, but [4]not [1]all [2]things [3]are profitable;
πάντα [n]μοι‖ ἔξεστιν, ἀλλ' οὐ πάντα οἰκοδομεῖ. 24 μηδεὶς
all things for me are lawful, but [3]not [1]all [2]do build up. [1]No [2]one
τὸ ἑαυτοῦ ζητείτω, ἀλλὰ τὸ τοῦ ἑτέρου [o]ἕκαστος.‖
[5]that [6]of [7]himself [1]let [4]seek, but [3]that [4]of [5]the [6]other [1]each [2]one.
25 Πᾶν τὸ ἐν μακέλλῳ πωλούμενον ἐσθίετε, μηδὲν ἀνα-
Everything that in a market is sold eat, nothing in-
κρίνοντες διὰ τὴν συνείδησιν· 26 τοῦ.[p]γὰρ. κυρίου‖
quiring on account of conscience. For [4]the [5]Lord's [[3]is]
ἡ γῆ καὶ τὸ πλήρωμα αὐτῆς. 27 εἰ.[q]δέ‖ τις καλεῖ ὑμᾶς
[1]the [2]earth and the fulness of it. But if anyone [4]invite [5]you
τῶν ἀπίστων, καὶ θέλετε πορεύεσθαι, πᾶν τὸ παρατιθέμενον
[1]of [2]the [3]unbelieving, and ye wish to go, all that is set before
ὑμῖν ἐσθίετε, μηδὲν ἀνακρίνοντες διὰ τὴν συνείδησιν.
you eat, nothing inquiring on account of conscience.
28 ἐὰν.δέ τις ὑμῖν εἴπῃ, Τοῦτο [r]εἰδωλόθυτόν‖ ἐστιν· μὴ
But if anyone to you say, This [2]offered [3]to [4]an [5]idol [1]is, [7]not
ἐσθίετε, δι' ἐκεῖνον τὸν μηνύσαντα καὶ τὴν συνείδησιν·
[6]do eat, on account of him that shewed [it], and the conscience;
[s]τοῦ.γὰρ κυρίου ἡ γῆ καὶ τὸ πλήρωμα αὐτῆς.‖ 29 συνεί-
for [4]the [5]Lord's [[3]is] [1]the [2]earth and the fulness of it. [2]Con-
δησιν δὲ λέγω, οὐχὶ τὴν ἑαυτοῦ, ἀλλὰ τὴν τοῦ ἑτέρου.
science [1]but, I say, not that of thyself, but that of the other;
ἵνα.τί.γὰρ ἡ.ἐλευθερία.μου κρίνεται ὑπὸ ἄλλης συνειδήσεως;
for why [2]my [3]freedom [1]is judged by another's conscience?
30 εἰ.[t]δὲ‖ ἐγὼ χάριτι μετέχω, τί βλασφημοῦμαι ὑπὲρ οὗ
But if I with thanks partake, why am I evil spoken of for what
ἐγὼ εὐχαριστῶ; 31 Εἴτε οὖν ἐσθίετε, εἴτε πίνετε, εἴτε
I give thanks? Whether therefore ye eat, or ye drink, or
τι ποιεῖτε, πάντα εἰς δόξαν θεοῦ ποιεῖτε. 32 ἀπρόσκοποι
anything ye do, all things to [2]glory [1]God's do. Without offence
[v]γίνεσθε καὶ Ἰουδαίοις‖ καὶ Ἕλλησιν καὶ τῇ ἐκκλησίᾳ τοῦ
be ye both to Jews and Greeks and to the assembly
θεοῦ· 33 καθὼς κἀγὼ πάντα πᾶσιν ἀρέσκω, μὴ ζητῶν
of God. According as I also all in all things please; not seeking
τὸ ἐμαυτοῦ [w]συμφέρον,‖ ἀλλὰ τὸ τῶν πολλῶν, ἵνα σωθῶ-
the [2]of [3]myself [1]profit, but that of the many, that they may
σιν. 11 μιμηταί μου γίνεσθε, καθὼς κἀγὼ χριστοῦ.
be saved. Imitators of me be, according as I also [am] of Christ.
2 Ἐπαινῶ.δὲ ὑμᾶς, [x]ἀδελφοί,‖ ὅτι πάντα μου μέ-
Now I praise you, brethren, that in all things me ye have
μνησθε, καὶ καθὼς παρέδωκα ὑμῖν, τὰς παραδόσεις κατ-
remembered; and according as I delivered to you, the traditions ye
έχετε. 3 θέλω.δὲ ὑμᾶς εἰδέναι, ὅτι παντὸς ἀνδρὸς ἡ κεφαλὴ
keep. But I wish you to know, that of every man [4]the [5]head

who will not allow you to be tempted above what you are able. But with the temptation, He will make a way of escape, so that you may be able to bear it.
14 Therefore, my dear loved ones, flee from idol-worshiping.
15 I speak as to wise men. You judge what I say.
16 The cup of blessing which we bless, is it not the partaking of the blood of Christ? The bread which we break, is it not the partaking of the body of Christ?
17 Because we, the many, are one loaf, one body, for we all partake of the one loaf.
18 Look at Israel according to the flesh. Are not the ones eating the sacrifices those who share with the altar?
19 What do I say then, that the idol is anything or that which is offered in sacrifice is anything?
20 *No!* But the things the Gentiles sacrifice, they sacrifice to demons and not to God. But I do not want you to share with demons
21 – you cannot drink the Lord's cup and the cup of demons! You cannot eat of the Lord's table and the table of demons!
22 Or do we provoke the Lord to jealousy? Are we stronger than He is?
23 All things are lawful for me, but not all things are profitable. All things are lawful for me, but not all things edify.
24 Let no one pursue his own *welfare*, but each one the other's.
25 Eat everything that is sold in a market, in no way inquiring because of conscience.
26 "For the earth is the Lord's, and the fullness of it."
27 But if anyone of the unbelievers invites you and you desire to go, eat all that is set before you, in no way inquiring because of conscience.
28 But if anyone says to you, This is a thing sacrificed to an idol, do not eat for his sake who showed it, and the conscience: "For the earth is the Lord's, and the fullness of it."
29 But conscience, I say, not that of yourself, but that of the other man. For why is my freedom judged by another's conscience?
30 But if I partake by grace, why am I slandered for that for which I give thanks?
31 Therefore, whether you eat or drink or whatever you do, do all to the glory of God.
32 Do not give any occasion of stumbling, either to the Jews or the Greeks or to the church of God
33 Even as I also please in all things, not pursuing my own profit, but that of the many, so that they may be saved.

CHAPTER 11

1 Be imitators of me, even as I also *am* of Christ.
2 Now, brothers, I praise you that you have remembered me in all things, holding fast the teachings just as I taught them to you.
3 But I want you to know that Christ is the

ὁ χριστός ἐστιν· κεφαλὴ.δὲ γυναικὸς ὁ ἀνήρ· κεφαλὴ.δὲ
¹the ²Christ ³is, but head of [the] woman [is] the man, and head
ʸχριστοῦ, ὁ θεός. 4 πᾶς ἀνὴρ προσευχόμενος ἢ προφητεύων,
of Christ, God. Every man praying or prophesying,
κατὰ κεφαλῆς ἔχων, καταισχύνει τὴν.κεφαλὴν.αὐτοῦ.
[anything] on [his] head having, puts to shame his head.
5 πᾶσα.δὲ γυνὴ προσευχομένη ἢ προφητεύουσα ἀκατακαλύπτῳ
But every woman praying or prophesying ⁴uncovered
τῇ κεφαλῇ, καταισχύνει τὴν.κεφαλὴν.ᶻἑαυτῆς·‖ ἕν.γάρ
¹with ²the ³head, puts to shame her head; for one
ἐστιν καὶ τὸ αὐτὸ τῇ.ἐξυρημένῃ. 6 εἰ.γὰρ οὐ.κατακαλύπτεται γυνή, καὶ κειράσθω· εἰ.δὲ αἰσχρὸν γυναικὶ τὸ
it is and the same with having been shaven. For if be not covered a woman, also let her be shorn. But if [it be] shameful to a woman
κείρασθαι ἢ ξυρᾶσθαι, κατακαλυπτέσθω. 7 ἀνὴρ.μὲν.γὰρ οὐκ
to be shorn or to be shaven, let her be covered. For man indeed ²not
ὀφείλει κατακαλύπτεσθαι τὴν κεφαλήν, εἰκὼν καὶ δόξα θεοῦ
¹ought to have ³covered ¹the ²head, image and glory of God
ὑπάρχων· ᵃγυνὴ.δὲ δόξα ἀνδρός ἐστιν· 8 οὐ.γάρ ἐστιν ἀνὴρ
being; but woman glory of man is. For not is man
ἐκ γυναικός, ἀλλὰ γυνὴ ἐξ ἀνδρός· 9 καὶ.γὰρ οὐκ ἐκτίσθη
of woman, but woman of man. For also not was created
ἀνὴρ διὰ τὴν γυναῖκα, ἀλλὰ γυνὴ διὰ τὸν ἄνδρα·
man on account of the woman, but woman on account of the man.
10 διὰ τοῦτο ὀφείλει ἡ γυνὴ ἐξουσίαν ἔχειν ἐπὶ τῆς κεφαλῆς, διὰ τοὺς ἀγγέλους. 11 πλὴν οὔτε ᵇἀνὴρ
Because of this ought the woman authority to have on the head, on account of the angels. However neither [is] man
χωρὶς γυναικός, οὔτε γυνὴ χωρὶς ἀνδρός,‖ ἐν κυρίῳ·
apart from woman, nor woman apart from man, in [the] Lord.
12 ὥσπερ.γὰρ ἡ γυνὴ ἐκ τοῦ ἀνδρός, οὕτως καὶ ὁ ἀνὴρ
For as the woman of the man [is], so also the man
διὰ τῆς γυναικός, τὰ.δὲ.πάντα ἐκ τοῦ θεοῦ. 13 ἐν ὑμῖν.αὐτοῖς
by the woman [is]; but all things of God. In yourselves
κρίνατε· πρέπον ἐστὶν γυναῖκα ἀκατακάλυπτον τῷ θεῷ
judge: becoming is it for a woman uncovered to God
προσεύχεσθαι; 14 ᶜἢ‖ οὐδὲ ᵈαὐτὴ ἡ φύσις‖ διδάσκει ὑμᾶς,
to pray? Or ²not ³even ⁵itself ⁴nature ¹does teach you,
ὅτι ἀνὴρ μὲν ἐὰν κομᾷ, ἀτιμία αὐτῷ ἐστιν· 15 γυνὴ
that ²a ³man ¹if have long hair a dishonour to him it is? ³A ⁴woman
δὲ ἐὰν κομᾷ, δόξα αὐτῇ ἐστιν; ὅτι ἡ κόμη ἀντὶ
¹but ²if have long hair, glory to her it is; for the long hair instead
περιβολαίου δέδοται ᵉαὐτῇ·‖ 16 εἰ.δέ τις δοκεῖ φιλόνεικος
of a covering is given to her. But if anyone thinks ³contentious
εἶναι, ἡμεῖς τοιαύτην συνήθειαν οὐκ.ἔχομεν, οὐδὲ αἱ ἐκκλησίαι
¹to ²be, we ³such ⁴custom ¹have ²not, nor the assemblies
τοῦ θεοῦ.
of God.
17 Τοῦτο.δὲ ᶠπαραγγέλλων οὐκ.ἐπαινῶ,‖ ὅτι οὐκ
But [²as ⁴to] ³this ¹charging [³you] I do not praise [you], that not
εἰς τὸ ᵍκρεῖττον,‖ ʰἀλλ'‖ εἰς τὸ ⁱἧττον‖ συνέρχεσθε. 18 πρῶτον
for the better, but for the worse ye come together. ²First
μὲν γὰρ συνερχομένων ὑμῶν ἐν ᵏτῇ‖ ἐκκλησίᾳ, ἀκούω σχίσματα ἐν ὑμῖν ὑπάρχειν, καὶ μέρος.τι πιστεύω· 19 δεῖ.γὰρ
¹indeed for coming together ye in the assembly, I hear divisions among you to be, and partly I believe [it]. For there must
καὶ αἱρέσεις ἐν ὑμῖν εἶναι, ἵνα ˡ οἱ δόκιμοι φανεροὶ γένωνται
also sects among you be, that the approved manifest may become
ἐν ὑμῖν. 20 συνερχομένων οὖν ὑμῶν ἐπὶ.τὸ.αὐτό, οὐκ
among you. Coming together therefore ye into one place, ³not
ἔστιν κυριακὸν δεῖπνον φαγεῖν· 21 ἕκαστος.γὰρ τὸ.ἴδιον
¹it ²is [the] Lord's supper to eat. For each one his own
δεῖπνον προλαμβάνει ἐν τῷ φαγεῖν, καὶ ὃς.μὲν πεινᾷ ὃς.δὲ
supper takes first in eating, and one is hungry and another
μεθύει. 22 μὴ γὰρ οἰκίας οὐκ.ἔχετε εἰς τὸ ἐσθίειν καὶ πίνειν;
is drunken. For houses have ye not for eating and drinking?
ἢ τῆς ἐκκλησίας τοῦ θεοῦ καταφρονεῖτε, καὶ καταισχύνετε
or the assembly of God do ye despise, and put to shame
τοὺς μὴ.ἔχοντας; τί ᵐὑμῖν εἴπω‖; ⁿἐπαινέσω‖ ὑμᾶς ᵒἐν
them that have not? What to you should I say? shall I praise you in
τούτῳ; οὐκ‖.ἐπαινῶ. 23 Ἐγὼ.γὰρ παρέλαβον ἀπὸ τοῦ κυρίου,
this? I do not praise. For I received from the Lord
ὃ καὶ παρέδωκα ὑμῖν, ὅτι ὁ κύριος Ἰησοῦς ἐν τῇ νυκτὶ
that which also I delivered to you, that the Lord Jesus in the night
ᾗ ᵖπαρεδίδοτο,‖ ἔλαβεν ἄρτον, 24 καὶ εὐχαριστήσας
in which he was delivered up took bread, and having given thanks
ἔκλασεν, καὶ εἶπεν, ᑫΛάβετε, φάγετε·‖ τοῦτό μου ἐστὶν τὸ
he broke [it], and said, Take, eat, this of me is the
σῶμα τὸ ὑπὲρ ὑμῶν ʳκλώμενον·‖. τοῦτο ποιεῖτε εἰς τὴν
body which for you [is] being broken: this do in
ἐμὴν ἀνάμνησιν. 25 Ὡσαύτως καὶ τὸ ποτήριον, μετὰ τὸ
remembrance of me. In like manner also the cup, after

Head of every man, but the head of the woman is the man, and the Head of Christ is God.
4 Every man who prays or prophesies *with anything* on his head puts his head to shame
5 – and every woman who prays or prophesies with her head uncovered puts her head to shame. For it is one and the same as if her head had been shaved.
6 For if a woman is not covered, let her also have her hair cut off. But if it is shameful for a woman to have her hair cut off or to be shaven, let her be covered.
7 For, indeed, being the image and glory of God, man ought not to have his head covered. But woman is the glory of man.
8 For man is not of the woman, but woman of the man.
9 For also man was not created for the sake of the woman, but woman for man's sake.
10 For this reason the woman ought to have authority on the head, for the sake of the angels.
11 And man is not apart from the woman, or woman apart from the man, in the Lord. the Lord.
12 For as woman is of the man, so the man also by the woman – but all things are of God.
13 Judge within yourselves: Is it becoming for a woman to pray to God uncovered?
14 Or does not even nature itself teach you it is a dishonor to him if a man has long hair.
15 But if a woman has long hair, it is to her glory, for the long hair is given to her in the place of a covering.
16 But if anyone thinks to be full of argument, we have no such custom, nor the churches of God.
17 But commanding you as to this, I do not praise *you*, because you come together not for the better but for the worse.
18 For first of all I hear that you have divisions among you when you come together in the churches. And I partly believe it.
19 For there must also be heresies among you in order that the approved may be made known among you.
20 So when you come together into one place, it is not to eat the Lord's supper.
21 For each one takes his own supper first in eating, and one is hungry and another is drunken.
22 What! Do you not have houses for eating and drinking? Or do you despise the church of God, and put those who have nothing to shame? What should I say to you? Shall I praise you in this? I do not praise you!
23 For I received from the Lord that which I also delivered to you, that the Lord Jesus took bread (in the night in which He was betrayed),
24 and after giving thanks, He broke *it* and said, Take, eat! This is My body, which is being broken for you. Do this in remembrance of Me.
25 In the same way also, having dined, *He*

δειπνῆσαι, λέγων, Τοῦτο τὸ ποτήριον ἡ καινὴ διαθήκη ἐστὶν
having supped, saying, This cup the new covenant is
ἐν τῷ.ἐμῷ.αἵματι· τοῦτο ποιεῖτε, ὁσάκις ˢἂν‖ πίνητε,
in my blood: this do, as often as ye may drink [it],
εἰς τὴν.ἐμὴν.ἀνάμνησιν. 26 Ὁσάκις.γὰρ ˢἂν‖ ἐσθίητε τὸν
in remembrance of me. For as often as ye may eat
ἄρτον.τοῦτον, καὶ τὸ.ποτήριον.ᵗτοῦτο‖ πίνητε, τὸν θάνατον
this bread, and this cup may drink, the death
τοῦ κυρίου καταγγέλλετε, ᵛἄχρις‖ οὗ ʷἂν‖ ἔλθῃ. 27 Ὥστε
of the Lord ye announce, until he may come. So that
ὃς.ἂν ἐσθίῃ τὸν.ἄρτον.ˣτοῦτον‖ ἢ πίνῃ τὸ ποτήριον
whosoever should eat this bread or should drink the cup
τοῦ κυρίου ἀναξίως, ἔνοχος ἔσται τοῦ σώματος καὶ ʸ αἵματος
of the Lord unworthily, guilty shall be of the body and blood
τοῦ κυρίου. 28 δοκιμαζέτω.δὲ ᶻἄνθρωπος ἑαυτόν,‖ καὶ οὕτως
of the Lord. But let ³prove ¹a ²man himself, and thus
ἐκ τοῦ ἄρτου ἐσθιέτω, καὶ ἐκ τοῦ ποτηρίου πινέτω· 29 ὁ.γὰρ
of the bread let him eat, and of the cup let him drink. For he that
ἐσθίων καὶ πίνων ᵃἀναξίως,‖ κρίμα ἑαυτῷ ἐσθίει καὶ πίνει,
eats and drinks unworthily, judgment to himself eats and drinks,
μὴ διακρίνων τὸ σῶμα ᵇτοῦ κυρίου.‖ 30 διὰ τοῦτο ἐν ὑμῖν
not discerning the body of the Lord. Because of this among you
πολλοὶ ἀσθενεῖς καὶ ἄρρωστοι, καὶ κοιμῶνται ἱκανοί.
many [are] weak and infirm, and are fallen asleep many.
31 εἰ ᶜγὰρ‖ ἑαυτοὺς διεκρίνομεν, οὐκ.ἂν.ἐκρινόμεθα· 32 κρινό-
²If ¹for ourselves. we scrutinized, we should not be judged. ⁴Being
μενοι δέ, ὑπὸ ᵈ κυρίου παιδευόμεθα, ἵνα μὴ σὺν τῷ
³judged ¹but, by [the] Lord we are disciplined, that not with the
κόσμῳ κατακριθῶμεν. 33 Ὥστε, ἀδελφοί.μου, συνερχόμενοι
world we should be condemned. So that, my brethren, coming together
εἰς τὸ φαγεῖν, ἀλλήλους ἐκδέχεσθε· 34 εἰ.ᵉδέ‖ τις πεινᾷ,
for to eat, one another wait for. But if anyone be hungry,
ἐν.οἴκῳ ἐσθιέτω· ἵνα μὴ εἰς κρίμα συνέρχησθε. τὰ.δὲ
at home let him eat, that not for judgment ye may come together; and the
λοιπά, ὡς.ἂν ἔλθω, διατάξομαι.
other things whenever I may come, I will set in order.

12 Περὶ.δὲ τῶν πνευματικῶν, ἀδελφοί, οὐ.θέλω ὑμᾶς
But concerning spirituals, brethren, I do not wish you
ἀγνοεῖν. 2 οἴδατε ὅτι ᶠ ἔθνη ἦτε, πρὸς τὰ εἴδωλα τὰ ἄφωνα
to be ignorant. Ye know that Gentiles ye were, ³to ⁵idols ⁴dumb
ὡς ἂν.ἤγεσθε, ἀπαγόμενοι· 3 διὸ γνωρίζω ὑμῖν, ὅτι
⁶as ⁷ye ⁸might ⁹be ¹⁰led, ¹led ²away. Therefore I give ²to ³know ¹you, that
οὐδεὶς ἐν πνεύματι θεοῦ λαλῶν λέγει ἀνάθεμα ʰἸησοῦν·‖
no one in [the] Spirit of God speaking says accursed [is] Jesus;
καὶ οὐδεὶς δύναται εἰπεῖν ⁱΚύριον Ἰησοῦν,‖ εἰ.μὴ ἐν πνεύ-
and no one can say Lord Jesus, except in [the] ²Spirit
ματι ἁγίῳ. 4 διαιρέσεις.δὲ χαρισμάτων εἰσίν, τὸ.δὲ αὐτὸ
¹Holy. But diversities of gifts there are, but the same
πνεῦμα· 5 καὶ διαιρέσεις διακονιῶν εἰσίν, καὶ ὁ αὐτὸς κύριος·
Spirit; and diversities of services there are, and the same Lord;
6 καὶ διαιρέσεις ἐνεργημάτων εἰσίν, ᵏὁ.δὲ‖ αὐτός ˡἐστιν‖ θεός,
and diversities of operations there are, but the same ²it ³is ¹God,
ὁ ἐνεργῶν τὰ.πάντα ἐν πᾶσιν. 7 ἑκάστῳ.δὲ δίδοται ἡ φανέ-
who operates all things in all. But to each is given the mani-
ρωσις τοῦ πνεύματος πρὸς τὸ συμφέρον. 8 ᾧ.μὲν.γὰρ διὰ
festation of the Spirit for profit. For to one by
τοῦ πνεύματος δίδοται λόγος σοφίας, ἄλλῳ.δὲ λόγος
the Spirit is given a word of wisdom; and to another a word
γνώσεως, κατὰ τὸ αὐτὸ πνεῦμα· 9 ἑτέρῳ.ᵐδὲ‖ πίστις,
of knowledge, according to the same Spirit; and to a different one faith,
ἐν τῷ αὐτῷ πνεύματι· ἄλλῳ.δὲ χαρίσματα ἰαμάτων, ἐν τῷ
in the same Spirit; and to another gifts of healing, in the
ⁿαὐτῷ‖ πνεύματι· 10 ἄλλῳ.δὲ ἐνεργήματα δυνάμεων,
same Spirit; and to another operations of works of power;
ἄλλῳ.ᵒδὲ‖ προφητεία, ἄλλῳ.ᵖδὲ‖ ᵠδιακρίσεις‖ πνευμάτων,
and to another prophecy; and to another discerning of spirits;
ἑτέρῳ.ʳδὲ‖ γένη γλωσσῶν, ἄλλῳ.δὲ ˢἑρμηνεία‖ γλωσ-
and to a different one kinds of tongues; and to another interpretation of
σῶν· 11 πάντα.δὲ ταῦτα ἐνεργεῖ τὸ ἓν καὶ τὸ αὐτὸ πνεῦ-
tongues. But all these things ⁷operates ¹the ²one ³and ⁴the ⁵same ⁶Spirit,
μα, διαιροῦν ἰδίᾳ ἑκάστῳ καθὼς βούλεται. 12 Καθάπερ
dividing separately to each according as he wills. ²Even ³as
γὰρ τὸ σῶμα ἕν ἐστιν καὶ μέλη ᵗἔχει πολλά,‖ πάντα.δὲ τὰ
¹for the body ²one ¹is and ³members ¹has ²many, but all the
μέλη τοῦ σώματος ᵛτοῦ ἑνός,‖ πολλὰ ὄντα, ἕν ἐστιν σῶμα·
members of the ²body ¹one, ⁴many ³being, ⁶one ⁵are body:
οὕτως καὶ ὁ χριστός. 13 καὶ.γὰρ ἐν ἑνὶ πνεύματι ἡμεῖς
so also [is] the Christ. For also by one Spirit we
πάντες εἰς ἓν σῶμα ἐβαπτίσθημεν, εἴτε Ἰουδαῖοι εἴτε Ἕλ-
all into one body were baptized, whether Jews or
ληνες, εἴτε δοῦλοι εἴτε ἐλεύθεροι· καὶ πάντες ʷεἰς‖ ἓν πνεῦμα
Greeks, whether bondmen or free and all into one Spirit

took the cup, saying, This cup is the new
covenant in My blood. Do this, as often as
you drink it, in remembrance of Me.
26 For as often as you eat this bread and
drink this cup, you solemnly proclaim the
death of the Lord until He comes.
27 So that whoever shall eat this bread or
shall drink the cup of the Lord in an
unworthy way shall be guilty of the body
and the blood of the Lord.
28 But let a man closely examine himself,
then let him eat of the bread and let him
drink of the cup in this way.
29 For he who eats and drinks unworthy,
eats and drinks judgment to himself, not
seeing through to the body of the Lord.
30 For this reason, many among you are
weak and sickly. And many are dead.
31 For if we examine ourselves closely, we
would not be judged.
32 But when we are judged, we are corrected by the Lord, so that we might not be
condemned with the world.
33 So then, brothers, when you come together in order to eat, wait for one another.
34 But if anyone is hungry, let him eat at
home – so that you may not come together
for judgment. And the other things I will set
in order when I come.

12 1 But as to spiritual gifts, brothers, I do not
want you to be ignorant.
2 You know that you were Gentiles carried
away to dumb idols, even as you were led.
3 For this reason I impart to you the
knowledge that no one who is speaking by
the Spirit of God says that Jesus is accursed.
And no one can say that Jesus is Lord
except by the Holy Spirit.
4 But there are different kinds of gifts, yet
the same Spirit.
5 And there are different kind of ministries,
yet the same Lord.
6 And there are different kinds of workings,
yet it is the same God who works all things in
all.
7 But to each one of us the showing forth
of the Spirit is given for profit.
8 For to one a word of wisdom is given by
the Spirit. And to another a word of knowledge according to the same Spirit.
9 And to a different one faith *is given*, in
the same Spirit – and to another gifts of
healing, in the same Spirit;
10 and to another the working of mighty
works, and to another prophecy, and to
another discerning of spirits, and to a different one is *given many* kinds of languages,
and to another the interpretation of
languages.
11 But the one and the same Spirit works all
these things, giving separately to each one as
He desires.
12 For as the body is one and has many
parts, but all the parts of the body, though
many, are one body – so also is Christ.
13 For by one Spirit also we were baptized
into one body, whether Jews or Greeks,
whether slaves or free men. And all were

ἐποτίσθημεν. 14 Καὶ.γὰρ τὸ σῶμα οὐκ.ἔστιν ἓν μέλος, ἀλλὰ
were made to drink. For also the body is not one member, but
πολλά. 15 ἐὰν εἴπῃ ὁ πούς, Ὅτι οὐκ.εἰμὶ χείρ, οὐκ.εἰμὶ
many. If should say the foot, Because I am not a hand, I am not
ἐκ τοῦ σώματος· οὐ παρὰ τοῦτο οὐκ.ἔστιν ἐκ τοῦ σώματος[x];
of the body: on account of this is it not of the body?
16 καὶ ἐὰν εἴπῃ τὸ οὖς, Ὅτι οὐκ.εἰμὶ ὀφθαλμὸς οὐκ.εἰμὶ ἐκ
And if should say the ear, Because I am not an eye I am not of
τοῦ σώματος· οὐ παρὰ τοῦτο οὐκ.ἔστιν ἐκ τοῦ σώματος[x];
the body: on account of this is it not of the body?
17 εἰ ὅλον τὸ σῶμα ὀφθαλμός, ποῦ ἡ ἀκοή; εἰ ὅλον
If [2]whole [1]the body [were] an eye, where the hearing? if [the] whole
ἀκοή, ποῦ ἡ ὄσφρησις; 18 [y]νυνὶ ǁ.δὲ ὁ θεὸς ἔθετο τὰ μέλη,
hearing, where the smelling? But now God set the members,
ἓν ἕκαστον αὐτῶν ἐν τῷ σώματι, καθὼς ἠθέλησεν. 19 εἰ.δὲ
[2]one [1]each of them in the body, according as he would. But if
ἦν [z]τὰ ǁ πάντα ἓν μέλος, ποῦ τὸ σῶμα; 20 νῦν.δὲ πολλὰ
[3]were [1]all one member, where the body? But now many
[a]μὲν ǁ μέλη, ἓν.δὲ σῶμα. 21 οὐ.δύναται.[b]δὲ ǁ [c]ὀφ-
[are the] members, but one body. And is not able [the]
θαλμὸς εἰπεῖν τῇ χειρί, Χρείαν σου οὐκ.ἔχω· ἢ πάλιν ἡ
eye to say to the hand, Need of thee I have not; or again the
κεφαλὴ τοῖς ποσίν, Χρείαν ὑμῶν οὐκ.ἔχω. 22 ἀλλὰ πολλῷ
head to the feet, Need of you I have not. But much
μᾶλλον τὰ δοκοῦντα μέλη τοῦ σώματος ἀσθενέστερα ὑπάρ-
rather the [5]which [6]seem [1]members [2]of [3]the [4]body [9]weaker [7]to
χειν, ἀναγκαῖά ἐστιν· 23 καὶ ἃ δοκοῦμεν [d]ἀτιμότερα ǁ
[8]be, necessary are; and those which we think more void of honour
εἶναι τοῦ σώματος, τούτοις τιμὴν περισσοτέραν περιτίθεμεν·
to be of the body, [4]these [7]honour [5]more [6]abundant [1]we [2]put [3]about;
καὶ τὰ ἀσχήμονα ἡμῶν εὐσχημοσύνην περισσοτέραν ἔχει·
and the uncomely [parts] of us comeliness more abundant have;
24 τὰ.δὲ εὐσχήμονα ἡμῶν οὐ χρείαν ἔχει. [e]ἀλλ' ǁ ὁ θεὸς
but the comely [parts] of us [2]no [3]need [1]have. But God
συνεκέρασεν τὸ σῶμα, τῷ [f]ὑστεροῦντι ǁ περισσοτέραν
tempered together the body, to that being deficient more abundant
δοὺς τιμήν, 25 ἵνα μὴ.ᾖ [g]σχίσμα ǁ ἐν τῷ
[3]having [2]given [1]honour, that there might not be division in the
σώματι, ἀλλὰ τὸ αὐτὸ ὑπὲρ ἀλλήλων μεριμνῶσιν τὰ
body, but [5]the [6]same [8]for [9]one [10]another [3]might [4]have [7]concern [1]the
μέλη· 26 καὶ [h]εἴτε ǁ πάσχει ἓν μέλος, [i]συμπάσχει ǁ πάντα
[2]members. And if suffers one member, suffers with [it] all
τὰ μέλη· εἴτε δοξάζεται [k]ἓν ǁ μέλος, [l]συγχαίρει ǁ πάντα τὰ
the members; if be glorified one member, rejoice with [it] all the
μέλη. 27 ὑμεῖς.δέ ἐστε σῶμα χριστοῦ, καὶ μέλη ἐκ
members. Now ye are [the] body of Christ, and members in
μέρους. 28 Καὶ οὓς μὲν ἔθετο ὁ θεὸς ἐν τῇ ἐκκλησίᾳ πρῶ-
particular. And [4]certain [2]did [3]set [1]God in the assembly: first,
τον ἀποστόλους, δεύτερον προφήτας, τρίτον διδασκάλους,
apostles; secondly, prophets; thirdly, teachers;
ἔπειτα δυνάμεις, [m]εἶτα ǁ χαρίσματα ἰαμάτων, [n]ἀντιλήψεις, ǁ
then works of power; then gifts of healings; helps;
κυβερνήσεις, γένη γλωσσῶν. 29 μὴ πάντες ἀπόστολοι; μὴ
governments; kinds of tongues. [Are] all apostles?
πάντες προφῆται; μὴ πάντες διδάσκαλοι; μὴ πάντες δυνά-
all prophets? all teachers? [have] all works of
μεις; 30 μὴ πάντες χαρίσματα ἔχουσιν ἰαμάτων; μὴ πάντες
power? [2]all [3]gifts [1]have of healings? [2]all
γλώσσαις λαλοῦσιν; μὴ πάντες διερμηνεύουσιν; 31 Ζηλοῦτε
[1]do speak with tongues? [2]all [1]do interpret? [2]Be [3]emulous [4]of
δὲ τὰ χαρίσματα τὰ [o]κρείττονα· ǁ καὶ ἔτι καθ'.ὑπερβολὴν
[1]but the [6]gifts [5]better, and yet [2]more [3]surpassing
ὁδὸν .ὑμῖν δείκνυμι.
[1]a [4]way to you I shew.

13 Ἐὰν ταῖς γλώσσαις τῶν ἀνθρώπων λαλῶ καὶ τῶν
If with the tongues of men I speak and
ἀγγέλων, ἀγάπην.δὲ μὴ.ἔχω, γέγονα χαλκὸς ἠχῶν ἢ
of angels, but love have not, I have become [2]brass [1]sounding or
κύμβαλον ἀλαλάζον. 2 [p]καὶ ἐὰν ǁ ἔχω προφητείαν, καὶ εἰδῶ
a [2]cymbal [1]clanging. And if I have prophecy, and know
τὰ μυστήρια πάντα καὶ πᾶσαν τὴν γνῶσιν, [q]καὶ ἐὰν ǁ ἔχω
[2]mysteries [1]all and all knowledge, and if I have
πᾶσαν τὴν πίστιν, ὥστε ὄρη [r]μεθιστάνειν, ǁ ἀγάπην.δὲ
all faith, so as mountains to remove, but love
μὴ.ἔχω, [s]οὐθέν ǁ εἰμι. 3 [t]καὶ ἐὰν ǁ [v]ψωμίσω ǁ πάντα τὰ
have not, nothing I am. And if I give away in food all
ὑπάρχοντά.μου, [w]καὶ ἐὰν ǁ παραδῶ τὸ.σῶμά.μου ἵνα [x]καυθή-
my goods, and if I deliver up my body that I may be
σωμαι, ǁ ἀγάπην.δὲ μὴ.ἔχω, [y]οὐδὲν ǁ ὠφελοῦμαι. 4 Ἡ ἀγάπη
burned, but love have not, nothing I am profited. Love
μακροθυμεῖ, χρηστεύεται· ἡ ἀγάπη οὐ.ζηλοῖ· [z]ἡ ἀγάπη ǁ οὐ
has patience, is kind; love is not envious; love [2]not

made to drink into one Spirit.
14 For also the body is not one member,
but many.
15 If the foot should say, Because I am not
a hand, I am not of the body, is it then not
of the body?
16 And if the ear should say, Because I am
not an eye, I am not of the body, is it then
not of the body?
17 If the whole body *were* an eye, where
would the hearing be? If all hearing, where
would the smelling be?
18 But now God set each one of the parts in
the body, just as He pleased.
19 But if all were one part, where *would* the
body be?
20 But now, indeed, many are the members,
but one body.
21 And the eye cannot say to the hand, I do
not need you. Nor again the head to the
feet, I do not need you.
22 But much rather the parts of the body
which seem to be weaker are necessary –
23 and those of the body which we consider
less honorable, to these we give the more
honor. And our unpresentable *members* have
the greater propriety.
24 But our presentable *members* have no
need. But God tempered the body together,
giving more honor to that which has need,
25 so that there should not be any division
within the body, but that the members
might have the same care for one another.
26 And if one part suffers, all the parts
suffer with it – if one part is glorified, all
the parts rejoice together.
27 Now you are the body of Christ, and
members in particular.
28 And God has set certain ones in the
church – first, apostles – secondly, prophets
– thirdly, teachers – then works of power –
then gifts of healings, helps, governments,
different kinds of languages.
29 Are all apostles, all prophets, all teachers? *Do* all do works of power?
30 Do all have gifts of healing? Do all
speak in foreign tongues? Do all interpret?
31 But zealously strive for the better gifts,
and yet I show you a more excellent way.

CHAPTER 13

1 If I speak in the tongues of men and
angels, but have not love, I have become as
sounding brass or a clanging cymbal.
2 And if I have prophecy and know all
mysteries and all knowledge, and if I have all
faith (so that *I could* remove mountains),
but do not have love, I am nothing.
3 And if I give all my goods in order to feed
the poor, and I give my body to be burned,
but *have not* love, I have gained nothing.
4 Love has patience, is kind – love is not
jealous – love is not vain, is not puffed up.

περπερεύεται, οὐ.φυσιοῦται, 5 οὐκ.ἀσχημονεῖ, οὐ.ζητεῖ τὰ
is vain-glorious, is not puffed up, acts not unseemly, seeks not the things
ἑαυτῆς, οὐ.παροξύνεται, οὐ.λογίζεται τὸ κακόν, 6 οὐ.χαίρει
of its own, is not quickly provoked, reckons not evil, rejoices not
ἐπὶ τῇ ἀδικίᾳ, [a]συγχαίρει".δὲ τῇ ἀληθείᾳ, 7 πάντα στέγει,
at unrighteousness, but rejoices with the truth; all things covers,
πάντα πιστεύει, πάντα ἐλπίζει, πάντα ὑπομένει. 8 Ἡ ἀγάπη
all things believes, all things hopes, all things endures. Love
οὐδέποτε [b]ἐκπίπτει." εἴτε.[c]δὲ" προφητεῖαι, καταργηθήσονται·
never fails; but whether prophecies, they shall be done away;
εἴτε γλῶσσαι, παύσονται· εἴτε γνῶσις, καταργηθήσεται.
whether tongues, they shall cease; whether knowledge it shall be done away.
9 ἐκ.μέρους.γὰρ γινώσκομεν, καὶ ἐκ μέρους προφητεύομεν·
For in part we know, and in part we prophesy;
10 ὅταν.δὲ ἔλθῃ τὸ τέλειον, [d]τότε" τὸ ἐκ μέρους καταργηθήσεται.
but when may come that which is perfect, then that in part shall be done away.
11 ὅτε ἤμην νήπιος, [e]ὡς νήπιος ἐλάλουν, [f]ὡς
When I was an infant, as an infant I spoke, as
νήπιος ἐφρόνουν, ὡς νήπιος ἐλογιζόμην· ὅτε.[g]δὲ" γέγονα
an infant I thought, as an infant I reasoned; but when I became
ἀνήρ, κατήργηκα τὰ τοῦ νηπίου. 12 βλέπομεν.γὰρ
a man, I did away with the things of the infant. For we see
ἄρτι δι' ἐσόπτρου ἐν αἰνίγματι, τότε.δὲ πρόσωπον πρὸς
now through a glass obscurely, but then face to
πρόσωπον· ἄρτι γινώσκω ἐκ μέρους, τότε.δὲ ἐπιγνώσομαι
face; now I know in part, but then I shall know
καθὼς καὶ ἐπεγνώσθην. 13 νυνὶ.δὲ μένει πίστις, ἐλπίς,
according as also I have been known. And now abides faith, hope,
ἀγάπη, τὰ.τρία.ταῦτα· μείζων.δὲ τούτων ἡ ἀγάπη.
love; these three things; but the greater of these [is] love.

14 Διώκετε τὴν ἀγάπην· ζηλοῦτε.δὲ τὰ πνευματικά,
Pursue love, and be emulous of spirituals,
μᾶλλον.δὲ ἵνα προφητεύητε. 2 ὁ.γὰρ λαλῶν γλώσσῃ, οὐκ
but rather that ye may prophesy. For he that speaks with a tongue, not
ἀνθρώποις λαλεῖ, ἀλλὰ [h]τῷ" θεῷ· οὐδεὶς.γὰρ ἀκούει, πνεύματι
to men speaks, but to God: for no one hears; [2]in [3]spirit
δὲ λαλεῖ μυστήρια· 3 ὁ.δὲ προφητεύων, ἀνθρώποις λαλεῖ
[1]but he speaks mysteries. But he that prophesies, to men speaks
οἰκοδομὴν καὶ παράκλησιν καὶ παραμυθίαν. 4 ὁ λαλῶν
[for] building up and encouragement and consolation. He that speaks
γλώσσῃ, ἑαυτὸν οἰκοδομεῖ· ὁ.δὲ προφητεύων, ἐκκλησίαν
with a tongue, himself builds up; but he that prophesies, [the] assembly
οἰκοδομεῖ. 5 θέλω.δὲ πάντας ὑμᾶς λαλεῖν γλώσσαις, μᾶλλον
builds up. Now I desire all you to speak with tongues, [2]rather
δὲ ἵνα προφητεύητε· μείζων [i]γὰρ" ὁ προφητεύων ἢ
[1]but that ye should prophesy: [2]greater [1]for [is] he that prophesies than
ὁ λαλῶν γλώσσαις, ἐκτὸς εἰ.μὴ διερμηνεύῃ, ἵνα ἡ ἐκ-
he that speaks with tongues, unless he should interpret, that the as-
κλησία οἰκοδομὴν λάβῃ. 6 [k]Νυνὶ".δέ, ἀδελφοί, ἐὰν ἔλθω
sembly building up may receive. And now, brethren, if I come
πρὸς ὑμᾶς γλώσσαις λαλῶν, τί ὑμᾶς ὠφελήσω, ἐὰν μὴ
to you with tongues speaking, what you shall I profit, unless
ὑμῖν λαλήσω ἢ ἐν ἀποκαλύψει, ἢ ἐν γνώσει, ἢ ἐν προ-
to you I shall speak either in revelation, or in knowledge, or in pro-
φητείᾳ, ἢ [l]ἐν" διδαχῇ; 7 ὅμως τὰ ἄψυχα φωνὴν διδόντα,
phecy, or in teaching? Even lifeless things a sound giving,
εἴτε αὐλὸς εἴτε κιθάρα, ἐὰν διαστολὴν [m]τοῖς φθόγγοις"
whether pipe or harp, if distinction to the sounds
μὴ.δῷ, πῶς γνωσθήσεται τὸ αὐλούμενον ἢ τὸ κιθαρι-
they give not, how shall be known that being piped or being
ζόμενον; 8 καὶ.γὰρ ἐὰν ἄδηλον [n]φωνὴν σάλπιγξ" δῷ, τίς
harped? For also if an uncertain sound a trumpet give, who
παρασκευάσεται εἰς πόλεμον; 9 οὕτως καὶ ὑμεῖς διὰ τῆς
shall prepare himself for war? So also ye, by means of the
γλώσσης ἐὰν.μὴ εὔσημον λόγον δῶτε, πῶς γνωσθήσεται τὸ
tongue unless an intelligible speech ye give, how shall be known that
λαλούμενον; ἔσεσθε.γὰρ εἰς ἀέρα λαλοῦντες. 10 Τοσαῦτα,
being spoken? for ye will be [2]into [3the] [4]air [1]speaking. So many,
εἰ τύχοι, γένη φωνῶν [o]ἐστιν" ἐν κόσμῳ, καὶ οὐδὲν [p]αὐ-
it may be, kinds of sounds there are in [the] world, and none of
τῶν" ἄφωνον· 11 ἐὰν οὖν μὴ.εἰδῶ τὴν δύναμιν
them without [distinct] sound. If therefore I know not the power
τῆς φωνῆς, ἔσομαι τῷ λαλοῦντι βάρβαρος· καὶ ὁ
of the sound, I shall be to him that speaks a barbarian; and he that
λαλῶν, ἐν ἐμοὶ βάρβαρος. 12 οὕτως καὶ ὑμεῖς, ἐπεὶ ζηλωταί
speaks, [3]for [4]me [1]a [2]barbarian. So also ye, since emulous
ἐστε πνευμάτων, πρὸς τὴν οἰκοδομὴν τῆς ἐκκλησίας ζητεῖτε
ye are of spirits, for the building up of the assembly seek
ἵνα περισσεύητε. 13 [q]Διόπερ" ὁ λαλῶν γλώσσῃ, προσευ-
that ye may abound. Wherefore he that speaks with a tongue, let him
χέσθω ἵνα διερμηνεύῃ. 14 ἐὰν.[r]γὰρ" προσεύχωμαι γλώσσῃ,
pray that he may interpret. For if I pray with a tongue,

5 *Love* does not behave indecently, does
not pursue its own things, is not easily provoked. *Love* thinks no evil,
6 does not rejoice in unrighteousness, but
rejoices in the truth.
7 *Love* silently bears all things, believes all
things, hopes all things, endures all things.
8 Love never fails. But if there are prophecies, they shall be abolished – if languages,
they shall stop – if knowledge, it shall cease.
9 For we know in part and we prophesy in
part,
10 but when that which is perfect comes,
then that which is in part shall cease to be.
11 When I was a child, I spoke as a child, I
thought as a child, I reasoned as a child –
but when I became a man, I did away with
childish things.
12 For now we see in a mirror dimly, but
then face to face. Now I know in part, but
then I shall know even as I also have been
known.
13 And now faith, hope and love remain,
these three things, but the greatest of these
is love.
14 1 Run after love and desire spiritual gifts, but
rather that you may prophesy the word.
2 For he who speaks in tongues does not
speak to men, but to God – for no one
hears, but he in spirit speaks mysteries.
3 But he who prophesies to men speaks for
building up and to encourage and to comfort
them in the faith.
4 He who speaks in tongues builds himself
up, but he who prophesies builds up the
church.
5 Now I wish you all to speak in languages,
but even more that you might prophesy. For
he who prophesies is greater than he who
speaks with languages (unless he should interpret so that the church may receive
benefit).
6 But now, brothers, if I come to you
speaking with foreign languages, what good
shall I do you, unless I speak to you either in
way of revelation, or of knowledge or
teaching, or of prophecy.
7 Even when things without life give a
sound (whether pipe or harp), if they do not
give a difference in the sounds, how shall it
be known what is being piped or harped?
8 And, too, if a trumpet gives an uncertain
sound, who shall get ready for war?
9 You, too, unless you give an understand-
able speech by means of the language, how
shall it be known what you are saying? For
you will be speaking into the air.
10 It may be that there are so many kinds
of sounds in the world, and none of them
without distinction in sound.
11 Then if I do not know the meaning of
the sound, I will be a barbarian to him who
speaks – and he who speaks *will be* a barbarian to me.
12 So you also, since you are zealous of
spiritual gifts, look for ways you may excel
for the building up of the church.
13 Then he who speaks in a tongue, let him
pray that he can interpret.

τὸ.πνεῦμά.μου προσεύχεται, ὁ.δὲ.νοῦς.μου ἄκαρπός ἐστιν.
my spirit prays, but my understanding unfruitful is.

15 τί οὖν ἐστιν; προσεύξομαι τῷ πνεύματι, προσεύξομαι
What then is it? I will pray with the Spirit, [2]I [3]will [4]pray

δὲ καὶ τῷ νοΐ· ψαλῶ τῷ πνεύματι, ψαλῶ
[1]but also with the understanding. I will praise with the Spirit, [2]I [3]will [4]praise

[s]δὲ‖ καὶ [t]τῷ‖ νοΐ. 16 ἐπεὶ ἐὰν [v]εὐλογήσῃς‖ [w]τῷ‖
[1]but also with the understanding. Else if thou bless with the

πνεύματι, ὁ ἀναπληρῶν τὸν τόπον τοῦ ἰδιώτου πῶς
spirit, he that fills the place of the uninstructed how

ἐρεῖ τὸ ἀμὴν ἐπὶ τῇ.σῇ.εὐχαριστίᾳ, ἐπειδὴ τί λέγεις
shall he say the Amen at thy giving of thanks, since what thou sayest

οὐκ.οἶδεν; 17 σὺ.μὲν.γὰρ καλῶς εὐχαριστεῖς, [x]ἀλλ'‖ ὁ ἕτερος
he knows not? For thou indeed well givest thanks, but the other

οὐκ.οἰκοδομεῖται. 18 εὐχαριστῶ τῷ θεῷ [y]μου,‖ πάντων ὑμῶν
is not built up. I thank [2]God [1]my, [7]than [8]all [9]of [10]you

μᾶλλον [z]γλώσσαις λαλῶν·‖ 19 [a]ἀλλ'‖ ἐν ἐκκλησίᾳ θέλω πέντε
[6]more [4]with [5]tongues [3]speaking; but in [the] assembly I desire five

λόγους [b]διὰ τοῦ νοός‖ μου λαλῆσαι, ἵνα καὶ ἄλλους
words with [2]understanding [1]my to speak, that also others

κατηχήσω, ἢ μυρίους λόγους ἐν γλώσσῃ. 20 Ἀδελφοί, μὴ
I may instruct, than ten thousand words in a tongue. Brethren, [2]not

παιδία γίνεσθε ταῖς.φρεσίν· ἀλλὰ τῇ κακίᾳ νηπιάζετε,
[3]children [1]be in [your] minds, but in malice be babes;

ταῖς.δὲ φρεσὶν τέλειοι γίνεσθε. 21 ἐν τῷ νόμῳ γέγρα-
but in [your] minds [2]full [3]grown [1]be. In the law it has been

πται, Ὅτι ἐν ἑτερογλώσσοις, καὶ ἐν χείλεσιν [c]ἑτέροις,‖ λα-
written, By other tongues, and by [2]lips [1]other I will

λήσω τῷ.λαῷ.τούτῳ, καὶ οὐδ' οὕτως εἰσακούσονταί μου,
speak to this people, and not even thus will they hear me,

λέγει κύριος. 22 Ὥστε αἱ γλῶσσαι εἰς σημεῖόν εἰσιν, οὐ
saith [the] Lord. So that the tongues for a sign are, not

τοῖς πιστεύουσιν, ἀλλὰ τοῖς ἀπίστοις· ἡ.δὲ.προφητεία,
to those that believe, but to the unbelievers; but prophecy,

οὐ τοῖς ἀπίστοις, ἀλλὰ τοῖς πιστεύουσιν. 23 ἐὰν οὖν
not to the unbelievers, but to those that believe. If therefore

[d]συνέλθῃ‖ ἡ ἐκκλησία ὅλη ἐπὶ.τὸ.αὐτό, καὶ πάντες [e]γλώσ-
[4]come [5]together [1]the [3]assembly [2]whole in one place, and all with

σαις λαλῶσιν,‖ εἰσέλθωσιν.δὲ ἰδιῶται ἢ ἄπιστοι,
tongues should speak, and come in uninstructed ones or unbelievers,

οὐκ.ἐροῦσιν ὅτι μαίνεσθε; 24 ἐὰν.δὲ πάντες προφητεύωσιν,
will they not say that ye are mad? But if all prophesy,

εἰσέλθῃ.δέ τις ἄπιστος ἢ ἰδιώτης, ἐλέγχεται ὑπὸ πάν-
and should come in some unbeliever or uninstructed, he is convicted by all,

των, ἀνακρίνεται ὑπὸ πάντων, 25 [f]καὶ οὕτως‖ τὰ κρυπτὰ
he is examined by all; and thus the secrets

τῆς.καρδίας.αὐτοῦ φανερὰ γίνεται· καὶ οὕτως πεσὼν ἐπὶ
of his heart manifest become; and thus, falling upon

πρόσωπον, προσκυνήσει τῷ θεῷ, ἀπαγγέλλων ὅτι [g]ὁ θεὸς
[his] face, he will do homage to God, declaring that God

ὄντως‖ ἐν ὑμῖν ἐστιν.
indeed amongst you is.

26 Τί οὖν ἐστιν, ἀδελφοί; ὅταν συνέρχησθε, ἕκαστος
What then is it, brethren? when ye may come together, each

[h]ὑμῶν‖ ψαλμὸν ἔχει, διδαχὴν ἔχει, [i]γλῶσσαν ἔχει, ἀποκά-
of you a psalm has, a teaching has, a tongue has, a reve-

λυψιν ἔχει,‖ ἑρμηνείαν ἔχει· πάντα πρὸς οἰκοδομὴν [k]γε-
lation has, an interpretation has. All things for building up let be

νέσθω.‖ 27 εἴτε γλώσσῃ τις λαλεῖ, κατὰ δύο ἢ τὸ
done. If with a tongue anyone speak, [let it be] by two or the

πλεῖστον τρεῖς, καὶ ἀνὰ.μέρος, καὶ εἷς διερμηνευέτω. 28 ἐὰν.δὲ
most three, and in succession, and [2]one [1]let interpret; and if

μὴ.ᾖ [l]διερμηνευτής,‖ σιγάτω ἐν ἐκκλησίᾳ· ἑαυτῷ.δὲ
there be not an interpreter, let him be silent in an assembly; and to himself

λαλείτω καὶ τῷ θεῷ. 29 προφῆται.δὲ δύο ἢ τρεῖς λαλεί-
let him speak and to God. And prophets [2]two [3]or [4]three [1]let

τωσαν, καὶ οἱ ἄλλοι διακρινέτωσαν· 30 ἐὰν.δὲ ἄλλῳ
speak, and [2]the [3]others [1]let discern. But if to another

ἀποκαλυφθῇ καθημένῳ, ὁ πρῶτος σιγάτω. 31 δύ-
[5]should [4]be [3]a [6]revelation [1]sitting [2]by, [8]the [9]first [7]let be silent. [2]Ye

νασθε γὰρ καθ'.ἕνα πάντες προφητεύειν, ἵνα πάντες μαν-
[3]can [1]for one by one all prophesy, that all may

θάνωσιν, καὶ πάντες παρακαλῶνται· 32 καὶ πνεύματα
learn, and all may be exhorted. And spirits

προφητῶν προφήταις ὑποτάσσεται· 33 οὐ.γάρ ἐστιν ἀκατα-
of prophets to prophets are subject. For [3]not [1]he [2]is [6]of [7]dis-

στασίας ὁ θεός, [m]ἀλλ'‖ εἰρήνης, ὡς ἐν πάσαις ταῖς ἐκκλησίαις
order [4]the [5]God, but of peace, as in all the assemblies

τῶν [n]ἁγίων.
of the saints.

34 Αἱ‖ γυναῖκες [o]ὑμῶν‖ ἐν ταῖς ἐκκλησίαις σιγάτωσαν.
[2]Women [1]your in the assemblies let them be silent

14 For if I pray in a tongue, my spirit prays, but my understanding is without fruit.

15 What, then? I will pray with the spirit, but I will pray also with the understanding. I will praise with the spirit, but I will also praise with the understanding.

16 Otherwise if you bless with the spirit, he who occupies the place of the unlearned, how shall he say the amen at your giving of thanks, since he does not know what you say?

17 For you, indeed, give thanks well, but the other is not being edified.

18 I thank my God that I speak more with languages than all of you,

19 but in the church I had rather speak five words with my understanding, so that I also may teach others, than ten thousand words in a foreign tongue.

20 Brothers, do not be children in your minds, but be infants in malice and be full-grown in your minds.

21 It has been written in the Law, "By other tongues and by other lips I will speak to this people, and even so they will not hear Me, says the Lord."

22 So that the tongues are not for a sign to those who believe, but to the ones who do not believe. But prophecy is not to the ones who do not believe, but to those who believe –

23 if then the whole church comes together in one place, and all should speak with foreign tongues, and unlearned ones or unbelievers come in, will they not say that you are insane?

24 But if all proclaim the word, and some unbeliever or unlearned one should come in, he is convicted by all, he is tried by all –

25 and so the secrets of his heart may become known. And so, falling on his face, he will worship God, saying that God is indeed among you.

26 What, then, brothers? When you come together, each of you has a psalm, has a teaching, has a tongue, has a revelation, has an interpretation. Let all things be done for building up.

27 If anyone speak with a foreign tongue, *let it be* by two, or at the most three, and one after another, and let one interpret.

28 And if there is no interpreter, let him be silent in the church and let him speak to himself and to God.

29 And let two or three prophets speak, and let others judge.

30 But if there should be a revelation to another sitting by, let the first be silent.

31 For one by one you can all proclaim the word, so that all may learn and all may be encouraged.

32 And the spirits of prophets are subject to prophets.

33 For He is not the God of confusion, but of peace, as in all the churches of the saints.

34 Let your women be silent in the churches,

οὐ.γὰρ.[p]ἐπιτέτραπται[ll] αὐταῖς λαλεῖν, [m]ἀλλ'[ll] [q]ὑποτάσσεσθαι,[ll]
for it is not allowed to them to speak; but to be in subjection,
καθὼς καὶ ὁ νόμος λέγει. 35 εἰ.δέ τι μαθεῖν θέλουσιν,
according as also the law says. But if anything to learn they wish,
ἐν.οἴκῳ τοὺς.ἰδίους ἄνδρας ἐπερωτάτωσαν· αἰσχρὸν.γάρ ἐστιν
at home their own husbands let them ask; for a shame it is
[r]γυναιξὶν ἐν ἐκκλησίᾳ λαλεῖν.[ll]
for women in assembly to speak.
36 [s]Ἢ ἀφ' ὑμῶν ὁ λόγος τοῦ θεοῦ ἐξῆλθεν; ἢ εἰς ὑμᾶς
Or [3]from [4]you [5]the [6]word [7]of [8]God [1]went [2]out, or to you
μόνους κατήντησεν; 37 εἴ τις δοκεῖ προφήτης εἶναι ἢ
only did it arrive? If anyone thinks a prophet to be or
πνευματικός, ἐπιγινωσκέτω ἃ γράφω ὑμῖν, ὅτι [s]τοῦ[ll]
spiritual, let him recognize the things I write to you, that of the
κυρίου [t]εἰσὶν[ll] [v]ἐντολαί·[ll] 38 εἰ.δέ τις ἀγνοεῖ, [w]ἀγνοείτω.[ll]
Lord they are commands. But if any be ignorant, let him be ignorant.
39 Ὥστε, ἀδελφοί[x], ζηλοῦτε τὸ προφητεύειν, καὶ τὸ λαλεῖν
So that, brethren, be emulous to prophesy, and to speak
[y]γλώσσαις μὴ.κωλύετε.[ll] 40 πάντα [z] εὐσχημόνως καὶ κατὰ
with tongues do not forbid. All things becomingly and with
τάξιν γινέσθω.
order let be done.
15 Γνωρίζω.δὲ ὑμῖν, ἀδελφοί, τὸ εὐαγγέλιον ὃ εὐηγ-
But I make known to you, brethren, the glad tidings which I an-
γελισάμην ὑμῖν, ὃ καὶ παρελάβετε, ἐν ᾧ καὶ ἑστήκατε,
nounced to you, which also ye received, in which also ye stand,
2 δι' οὗ καὶ σώζεσθε. τίνι λόγῳ [b]εὐηγγελισάμην[ll] ὑμῖν
by which also ye are being saved, [5]what [6]word [7]I [8]announced [9]to [10]you
εἰ κατέχετε, ἐκτὸς εἰ.μὴ εἰκῇ ἐπιστεύσατε. 3 Παρέδωκα.γὰρ
[1]if [2]ye [3]hold [4]fast, unless in vain ye believed. For I delivered
ὑμῖν ἐν πρώτοις, ὃ καὶ παρέλαβον, ὅτι χριστὸς ἀπέθανεν
to you in the first place, what also I received, that Christ died
ὑπὲρ τῶν.ἁμαρτιῶν.ἡμῶν, κατὰ τὰς γραφάς· 4 καὶ ὅτι
for our sins, according to the scriptures; and that
ἐτάφη, καὶ ὅτι ἐγήγερται τῇ [c]τρίτῃ ἡμέρᾳ,[ll] κατὰ τὰς
he was buried; and that he was raised the third day, according to the
γραφάς· 5 καὶ ὅτι ὤφθη Κηφᾷ, [d]εἶτα[ll] τοῖς δώδεκα. 6 ἔπειτα
scriptures; and that he appeared to Cephas, then to the twelve. Then
ὤφθη ἐπάνω πεντακοσίοις ἀδελφοῖς ἐφάπαξ, ἐξ ὧν οἱ
he appeared to above five hundred brethren at once, of whom the
[e]πλείους[ll] μένουσιν ἕως ἄρτι, τινὲς.δὲ [f]καὶ[ll] ἐκοιμήθησαν.
greater part remain until now, but some also are fallen asleep.
7 ἔπειτα ὤφθη Ἰακώβῳ, *εἶτα[ll] τοῖς ἀποστόλοις πᾶσιν.
Then he appeared to James; then to [2]the [3]apostles [1]all;
8 ἔσχατον.δὲ πάντων, ὡσπερεὶ τῷ.ἐκτρώματι ὤφθη κἀμοί.
and last of all, as to an abortion, he appeared also to me.
9 ἐγὼ.γάρ εἰμι ὁ ἐλάχιστος τῶν ἀποστόλων, ὃς οὐκ.εἰμὶ
For I am the least of the apostles, who am not
ἱκανὸς καλεῖσθαι ἀπόστολος, διότι ἐδίωξα τὴν ἐκκλησίαν
fit to be called apostle, because I persecuted the assembly
τοῦ θεοῦ. 10 χάριτι.δὲ θεοῦ εἰμι ὅ εἰμι, καὶ ἡ.χάρις.αὐτοῦ
of God. But by grace of God I am what I am, and his grace
ἡ εἰς ἐμὲ οὐ κενὴ ἐγενήθη, ἀλλὰ περισσότερον αὐ-
which [was] towards me not void has been, but more abundantly than
τῶν πάντων ἐκοπίασα· οὐκ.ἐγὼ.δέ, [g]ἀλλ'[ll] ἡ χάρις τοῦ θεοῦ
them all I laboured, but not I, but the grace of God
[h]ἡ σὺν ἐμοί. 11 εἴτε οὖν ἐγὼ εἴτε ἐκεῖνοι, οὕτως κηρύσ-
with me. Whether therefore I or they, so we
σομεν, καὶ οὕτως ἐπιστεύσατε. 12 Εἰ.δὲ χριστὸς κηρύσσεται,
preach, and so ye believed. Now if Christ is preached,
[i]ὅτι ἐκ νεκρῶν[ll] ἐγήγερται, πῶς λέγουσίν [k]τινες
that from among [the] dead he has been raised, how say some
ἐν ὑμῖν[ll] ὅτι ἀνάστασις νεκρῶν οὐκ.ἔστιν; 13 εἰ.δὲ ἀνά-
among you that a resurrection of [the] dead there is not? But if a resur-
στασις νεκρῶν οὐκ.ἔστιν, οὐδὲ χριστὸς ἐγήγερται· 14 εἰ.δὲ
rection of [the] dead there is not, neither Christ has been raised: but if
χριστὸς οὐκ.ἐγήγερται, κενὸν.ἄρα [l] τὸ.κήρυγμα.ἡμῶν, κενὴ
Christ has not been raised, then void [is] our proclamation, [2]void
[m]δὲ[ll] καὶ ἡ.πίστις.ὑμῶν. 15 εὑρισκόμεθα.δὲ καὶ ψευδομάρτυρες
[1]and also your faith. And we are found also false witnesses
τοῦ θεοῦ, ὅτι ἐμαρτυρήσαμεν κατὰ τοῦ θεοῦ ὅτι ἤγειρεν
of God; for we witnessed concerning God that he raised up
τὸν χριστόν, ὃν οὐκ.ἤγειρεν εἴπερ ἄρα νεκροὶ οὐκ
the Christ, whom he raised not if then [the] dead [2]not
ἐγείρονται· 16 εἰ.γὰρ νεκροὶ οὐκ.ἐγείρονται, οὐδὲ χριστὸς
[1]are raised. For if [the] dead are not raised, neither Christ
ἐγήγερται· 17 εἰ.δὲ χριστὸς οὐκ.ἐγήγερται, ματαία ἡ πίστις
has been raised: but if Christ has not been raised, vain [2]faith
ὑμῶν[o]· ἔτι ἐστὲ ἐν ταῖς.ἁμαρτίαις.ὑμῶν· 18 ἄρα.καὶ οἱ
[1]your [is]; still ye are in your sins. And then those that
κοιμηθέντες ἐν χριστῷ ἀπώλοντο. 19 εἰ ἐν τῇ.ζωῇ.ταύτῃ
fell asleep in Christ perished. If in this life

for it is not permitted to them to speak, but to
be in subjection, even as the Law also says.
35 But if they desire to learn anything, let
them ask their husbands at home – for it is a
shame for women to speak in church.
36 For did the word of God come out from
you? Or did it come only to you?
37 If anyone thinks to be a prophet, or to be
spiritual, let him recognize these things I write
to you, that they are commands of the Lord.
38 But if anyone is ignorant, let him be
ignorant.
39 So, then, my brothers, be zealous to
prophesy, and do not forbid to speak in
other languages.
40 Let all things be done decently and in
order.
15 1 And, brothers, I reveal to you the gospel
which I preached to you, which you also
received, in which you also stand,
2 by which you also are being saved, if you
hold fast the word which I preached to you,
(unless you believed in vain).
3 For I transferred to you first of all what I
also received, that Christ died for our sins,
according to the Scriptures,
4 and that He was buried, and that He was
raised the third day, according to the Scriptures,
5 and that He appeared to Peter, then to the
twelve.
6 Then He appeared to over five hundred
brothers at once, of whom most remain until
now (but some also are dead).
7 After that He appeared to James, then to
all the apostles.
8 And last of all, as if to one born out of
due time, He appeared also to me.
9 For I am the least of the apostles, who am
not fit to be called Apostle, because I persecuted the church of God.
10 But by the grace of God, I am what I
am, and His grace which was towards me has
not been without fruit – but I labored more
abundantly than all of them (yet not I, but
the grace of God with me).
11 Whether, then, they or I, so we preach,
and so you believed.
12 Now if Christ is preached, that He has
been raised from among the dead, how do
some of you say that there is no resurrection
of the dead?
13 But if there is no resurrection of the
dead, neither has Christ been raised.
14 But if Christ has not been raised, then
our preaching is worthless and your faith is
also worthless.
15 And, too, we are found to be false witnesses of God. For we witnessed of God that
He raised up the Christ, *but* He did not raise
Him if it be so that the dead are not raised.
16 For if the dead are not raised, neither
has Christ been raised.
17 But if Christ has not been raised, your
faith is foolish – you are still in your sins.
18 And when those that have fallen asleep
in Christ have been lost.
19 If we have hope in Christ in this life

[p]ἠλπικότες.ἐσμὲν ἐν χριστῷ" μόνον, ἐλεεινότεροι πάντων ἀν-
[2]we [3]have [4]hope [5]in [6]Christ [1]only, more miserable than all
θρώπων ἐσμέν.
men we are.
20 Νυνὶ.δὲ χριστὸς ἐγήγερται ἐκ νεκρῶν, ἀπαρχὴ
But now Christ has been raised from among [the] dead, first-fruit
τῶν κεκοιμημένων [q]ἐγένετο." 21 ἐπειδὴ.γὰρ δι' ἀνθρώπου
of those fallen asleep he became. For since by man [is]
[r]ὁ" θάνατος, καὶ δι' ἀνθρώπου ἀνάστασις νεκρῶν. 22 ὥσπερ
death, also by man resurrection of [the] dead. [2]As
γὰρ ἐν τῷ Ἀδὰμ πάντες ἀποθνήσκουσιν, οὕτως καὶ ἐν τῷ
[1]for in Adam all die, so also in the
χριστῷ πάντες ζωοποιηθήσονται. 23 ἕκαστος.δὲ ἐν τῷ.ἰδίῳ
Christ all shall be made alive. But each in his own
τάγματι· ἀπαρχὴ χριστός, ἔπειτα οἱ [s] χριστοῦ ἐν τῇ
rank: [[2]the] [3]first-fruit [1]Christ, then those of Christ at
παρουσίᾳ αὐτοῦ· 24 εἶτα τὸ τέλος, ὅταν [t]παραδῷ" τὴν
his coming. Then the end, when he shall have given up the
βασιλείαν τῷ θεῷ καὶ πατρί, ὅταν καταργήσῃ
kingdom to him who [is] God and Father; when he shall have annulled
πᾶσαν ἀρχὴν καὶ πᾶσαν ἐξουσίαν καὶ δύναμιν· 25 δεῖ.γὰρ
all rule and all authority and power. For it behoves
αὐτὸν βασιλεύειν, [v]ἄχρις" οὗ [w]ἂν" θῇ πάντας τοὺς
him to reign, until he shall have put all
ἐχθροὺς [x] ὑπὸ τοὺς.πόδας.αὐτοῦ. 26 ἔσχατος ἐχθρὸς καταρ-
enemies under his feet. [The] last enemy an-
γεῖται ὁ θάνατος. 27 Πάντα.γὰρ ὑπέταξεν ὑπὸ τοὺς
nulled [is] death. For all things he put in subjection under
πόδας.αὐτοῦ· ὅταν.δὲ εἴπῃ [y]ὅτι" πάντα ὑποτέτακται,
his feet. But when it be said that all things have been put in subjection,
δῆλον ὅτι ἐκτὸς τοῦ ὑποτάξαντος αὐτῷ τὰ.πάντα·
[it is] manifest that [it is] except him who put in subjection to him all things.
28 ὅταν.δὲ ὑποταγῇ αὐτῷ τὰ.πάντα, τότε
But when shall have been put in subjection to him all things, then
[z]καὶ" αὐτὸς ὁ υἱὸς ὑποταγήσεται τῷ ὑποτάξαντι
also [3]himself [1]the [2]Son will be put in subjection to him who put in subjection
αὐτῷ τὰ.πάντα, ἵνα ᾖ ὁ θεὸς [a]τὰ" πάντα ἐν πᾶσιν.
to him all things, that [2]may [3]be [1]God all in all.
29 Ἐπεὶ τί ποιήσουσιν οἱ βαπτιζόμενοι ὑπὲρ τῶν νεκρῶν
Since what shall they do who are baptized for the dead
εἰ ὅλως νεκροὶ οὐκ ἐγείρονται; τί καὶ βαπτίζονται ὑπὲρ
if [4]at [5]all [[1]the] [2]dead [3]not are raised? why also are they baptized for
[b]τῶν νεκρῶν"; 30 τί καὶ ἡμεῖς κινδυνεύομεν πᾶσαν ὥραν;
the dead? Why also [2]we [1]are in danger every hour?
31 καθ'.ἡμέραν ἀποθνήσκω, νὴ τὴν [c]ἡμετέραν" καύχησιν, [d]
Daily I die, by our boasting,
ἣν ἔχω ἐν χριστῷ Ἰησοῦ τῷ.κυρίῳ.ἡμῶν. 32 εἰ κατὰ
which I have in Christ Jesus our Lord. If according to
ἄνθρωπον ἐθηριομάχησα ἐν Ἐφέσῳ, τί μοι τὸ [e]ὄφελος,
man I fought with beasts in Ephesus, what to me the profit,
εἰ νεκροὶ οὐκ.ἐγείρονται;" φάγωμεν καὶ πίωμεν,
if [the] dead are not raised? We may eat and we may drink;
αὔριον.γὰρ ἀποθνήσκομεν. 33 μὴ.πλανᾶσθε· φθείρουσιν ἤθη
for to-morrow we die. Be not misled: [3]corrupt [5]manners
[f]χρήσθ'" ὁμιλίαι κακαί. 34 ἐκνήψατε δικαίως, καὶ μὴ
[4]good [2]companionships [1]evil. Awake up righteously, and [2]not
ἁμαρτάνετε· ἀγνωσίαν.γὰρ θεοῦ τινες ἔχουσιν· πρὸς ἐντροπὴν
[1]sin; for ignorance of God some have: to [2]shame
ὑμῖν [g]λέγω."
[1]your I speak.

35 [h]Ἀλλ'" ἐρεῖ τις, Πῶς ἐγείρονται οἱ νεκροί; ποίῳ
But will say some one, How are raised the dead? [2]with [3]what
δὲ σώματι ἔρχονται; 36 [i]ἄφρον," σὺ ὃ σπείρεις, οὐ
[1]and body do they come? Fool; [2]thou [1]what sowest, [3]not
ζωοποιεῖται ἐὰν.μὴ ἀποθάνῃ· 37 καὶ ὃ σπείρεις, οὐ τὸ σῶμα
[4]is quickened unless it die. And what thou sowest, not the body
τὸ γενησόμενον σπείρεις, ἀλλὰ γυμνὸν κόκκον, εἰ τύχοι,
that shall be thou sowest, but a bare grain, it may be
σίτου ἤ τινος τῶν λοιπῶν· 38 ὁ.δὲ.θεὸς [j]αὐτῷ δίδωσιν"
of wheat or of some one of the rest; and God to it gives
σῶμα καθὼς ἠθέλησεν, καὶ ἑκάστῳ τῶν σπερμάτων [k]τὸ".ἴδιον
a body according as he willed, and to each of the seeds its own
σῶμα. 39 οὐ πᾶσα σὰρξ ἡ αὐτὴ σάρξ· ἀλλὰ ἄλλη μὲν
body. Not every flesh [is] the same flesh, but one
[l]σὰρξ" ἀνθρώπων, ἄλλη.δὲ σὰρξ κτηνῶν, ἄλλη.δὲ [m] [n]ἰχθύων,
flesh of men, and another flesh of beasts, and another of fishes,
ἄλλη.δὲ πτηνῶν." 40 καὶ σώματα ἐπουράνια, καὶ
and another of birds. And bodies [there are] heavenly, and
σώματα ἐπίγεια· [o]ἀλλ'" ἑτέρα μὲν ἡ τῶν ἐπουρανίων
bodies earthly: but different [is] the [2]of [3]the [4]heavenly
δόξα, ἑτέρα.δὲ ἡ τῶν ἐπιγείων. 41 ἄλλη δόξα ἡλίου,
[1]glory, and different that of the earthly: one glory of [the] sun,

only, we are more miserable than all men.
20 But now Christ has been raised from
among the dead. He has become the first-
fruit of those who are dead.
21 For since death *came* through man, resurrection of the dead also *came* through man,
22 – for as all die in Adam, so also all shall
be made alive in Christ.
23 But each in his own order: Christ the
first-fruit, then they who are of Christ in His
coming,
24 then comes the end – whenever He delivers up the kingdom to Him who is God
and Father – whenever He shall have put
down all rule and all authority and power.
25 For He must reign until He has put all
enemies under His feet –
26 the last enemy put down is death.
27 For He put all things in subjection under
His feet. But when it is said that all things are
put in subjection, plainly that excepts Him
who put all things in subjection to Him.
28 And when all things shall have been put
in subjection to Him, then the Son Himself
also will be subject to Him who put all
things under Him – so that God may be all
in all.
29 Otherwise, what shall they do who are
being baptized for the dead, if the dead are
not raised at all? And why are they also
being baptized for the dead?
30 Why also are we in danger every hour?
31 Day by day I die, by our glorying which
I have in Christ Jesus our Lord.
32 If after the manner of a man I have
fought with wild beasts in Ephesus, what is
the gain to me if the dead are not raised? –
"Let us eat and drink, for tomorrow we
die."
33 Do not be led astray, evil compan-
ionships ruin good habits.
34 Be awake, as is right, and do not sin. For
some do not have the knowledge of God – I
speak this to your shame.

35 But someone will say, How are the dead
raised, and with what body do they come?
36 Fool! What you sow is not made alive
unless it dies.
37 And what you sow, you do not sow the
body which shall come to be, but the bare
grain – it may be of wheat or of some other.
38 And God gives a body to it as He
pleased, and to each of the seeds its own
body.
39 Not all flesh is the same flesh, but one
flesh of men and another flesh of beasts, and
another of fish and another of birds.
40 And heavenly bodies and earthly bodies
exist, but the glory of the heavenly is different, and that of the earthly different –
41 one glory of the sun and another glory

καὶ ἄλλη δόξα σελήνης, καὶ ἄλλη δόξα ἀστέρων ἀστὴρ
and another glory of [the] moon, and another glory of [the] stars; ²star
γὰρ ἀστέρος διαφέρει ἐν δόξῃ. 42 οὕτως καὶ ἡ ἀνάστασις
¹for ⁴from ⁵star ³differs in glory. So also [is] the resurrection
τῶν νεκρῶν. σπείρεται ἐν φθορᾷ, ἐγείρεται ἐν ἀφθαρσίᾳ·
of the dead. It is sown in corruption, it is raised in incorruptibility.
43 σπείρεται ἐν ἀτιμίᾳ, ἐγείρεται ἐν δόξῃ· σπείρεται ἐν ἀ-
It is sown in dishonour, it is raised in glory. It is sown in weak-
σθενείᾳ, ἐγείρεται ἐν δυνάμει· 44 σπείρεται σῶμα ψυχικόν,
ness, it is raised in power. It is sown a ²body ¹natural,
ἐγείρεται σῶμα πνευματικόν. ᵖἔστιν σῶμα ψυχικόν, ᵍκαὶ
it is raised a ²body ¹spiritual: there is a ²body ¹natural, and
ἔστιν" ʳσῶμα" πνευματικόν. 45 οὕτως καὶ γέγραπται,
there is a ²body ¹spiritual. So also it has been written,
Ἐγένετο ὁ πρῶτος ˢἄνθρωπος" Ἀδὰμ εἰς ψυχὴν ζῶσαν· ὁ
⁵Became ¹the ²first ³man ⁴Adam a ²soul ¹living; the
ἔσχατος Ἀδὰμ εἰς πνεῦμα ζωοποιοῦν. 46 ἀλλ' οὐ πρῶτον
last Adam a ²spirit ¹quickening. But not first [was]
τὸ πνευματικόν, ἀλλὰ τὸ ψυχικόν, ἔπειτα τὸ πνευματικόν.
the spiritual, but the natural, then the spiritual:
47 ὁ πρῶτος ἄνθρωπος ἐκ γῆς, χοϊκός· ὁ δεύτερος ἄν-
the first man out of earth, made of dust; the second
θρωπος, ᵗὁ κύριος" ἐξ οὐρανοῦ. 48 οἷος ὁ χοϊκός, τοιοῦτοι
man, the Lord out of heaven. Such as he made of dust, such
καὶ οἱ χοϊκοί· καὶ οἷος ὁ ἐπουράνιος, τοιοῦτοι καὶ οἱ
also [are] those made of dust; and such as the heavenly [one], such also the
ἐπουράνιοι· 49 καὶ καθὼς ἐφορέσαμεν τὴν εἰκόνα τοῦ
heavenly [ones]. And according as we bore the image of the [one]
χοϊκοῦ, ᵛφορέσομεν" καὶ τὴν εἰκόνα τοῦ ἐπουρανίου.
made of dust, we shall bear also the image of the [²one] ¹heavenly.
50 Τοῦτο.δέ φημι, ἀδελφοί, ὅτι σὰρξ καὶ αἷμα βασιλείαν
But this I say, brethren, that flesh and blood [the] kingdom
θεοῦ κληρονομῆσαι οὐ.ʷδύνανται," οὐδὲ ἡ φθορὰ τὴν ἀ-
of God ²inherit ¹cannot, nor ³corruption ⁴incor-
φθαρσίαν ˣκληρονομεῖ."
ruptibility ¹does ²inherit.
51 Ἰδοὺ μυστήριον ὑμῖν λέγω· Πάντες ʸμὲν" ᶻοὐ κοιμηθη-
Lo a mystery to you I tell: All ³not ¹we ²shall
σόμεθα·" πάντες.δὲ ἀλλαγησόμεθα, 52 ἐν ἀτόμῳ, ἐν
fall asleep, but all we shall be changed, in an instant, in [the]
ῥιπῇ ὀφθαλμοῦ, ἐν τῇ ἐσχάτῃ σάλπιγγι· σαλπίσει.γάρ,
twinkling of an eye, at the last trumpet; for a trumpet shall sound,
καὶ οἱ νεκροὶ ᵃἐγερθήσονται" ἄφθαρτοι, καὶ ἡμεῖς ἀλλαγησό-
and the dead shall be raised incorruptible, and we shall be
μεθα. 53 δεῖ.γὰρ τὸ.φθαρτὸν.τοῦτο ἐνδύσασθαι ἀφθαρσίαν,
changed. For it behoves this corruption to put on incorruptibility,
καὶ τὸ.θνητὸν.τοῦτο ἐνδύσασθαι ἀθανασίαν. 54 ὅταν.δὲ τὸ
and this mortal to put on immortality. But when
φθαρτὸν.τοῦτο ἐνδύσηται ἀφθαρσίαν, καὶ τὸ.θνητὸν.τοῦτο
this corruptible shall have put on incorruptibility, and this mortal
ἐνδύσηται ἀθανασίαν, τότε γενήσεται ὁ λόγος ὁ γε-
shall have put on immortality, then shall come to pass the word that has
γραμμένος, Κατεπόθη ὁ θάνατος εἰς νῖκος. 55 Ποῦ σου,
been written: ²Was ³swallowed ⁴up ¹death in victory. Where of thee,
θάνατε, τὸ ᵇκέντρον"; ποῦ σου, ᶜᾅδη," τὸ ᵇνῖκος"; 56 Τὸ.δὲ
O death, the sting? where of thee, O hades, the victory? Now the
κέντρον τοῦ θανάτου ἡ ἁμαρτία· ἡ.δὲ δύναμις τῆς ἁμαρ-
sting of death [is] sin, and the power of sin
τίας ὁ νόμος· 57 τῷ.δὲ.θεῷ χάρις τῷ διδόντι ἡμῖν τὸ νῖκος
the law; but to God [be] thanks, who gives us the victory
διὰ τοῦ.κυρίου.ἡμῶν Ἰησοῦ χριστοῦ. 58 Ὥστε, ἀδελφοί.μου
by our Lord Jesus Christ. So that, my brethren
ἀγαπητοί, ἑδραῖοι γίνεσθε, ἀμετακίνητοι, περισσεύοντες ἐν τῷ
beloved, ²firm ¹be, immovable, abounding in the
ἔργῳ τοῦ κυρίου πάντοτε, εἰδότες ὅτι ὁ.κόπος.ὑμῶν οὐκ.ἔστιν
work of the Lord always, knowing that your toil is not
κενὸς ἐν κυρίῳ.
void in [the] Lord.

16 Περὶ.δὲ τῆς λογίας τῆς εἰς τοὺς ἁγίους, ὥσπερ
Now concerning the collection which [is] for the saints, as
διέταξα ταῖς ἐκκλησίαις τῆς Γαλατίας, οὕτως καὶ ὑμεῖς
I directed the assemblies of Galatia, so also ye
ποιήσατε. 2 κατὰ.μίαν ᵈσαββάτων" ἕκαστος ὑμῶν παρ'
do. Every first [day] of the week ²each ³of ⁴you ⁶by
ἑαυτῷ τιθέτω, θησαυρίζων ὅ.τι ᵉἂν" εὐοδῶται, ἵνα μὴ
⁷him ¹let ⁵put, treasuring up whatever he may be prospered in, that not
ὅταν ἔλθω τότε λογίαι γίνωνται. 3 ὅταν.δὲ παραγένω-
when I may come then collections there should be. And when I shall have
μαι, οὓς.ᶠἐὰν" δοκιμάσητε δι' ἐπιστολῶν τούτους πέμψω
arrived, whomsoever ye may approve by epistles these I will send
ἀπενεγκεῖν τὴν.χάριν.ὑμῶν εἰς Ἰερουσαλήμ· 4 ἐὰν.δὲ ᵍᾖ
to carry your bounty to Jerusalem: and if it be

of the moon and another glory of the stars –
for a star differs from a star in glory.
42 So also is the resurrection of the dead.
The body is sown in decay, it is raised in *a*
state that cannot decay.
43 It is sown in dishonor, it is raised in glory.
It is sown in weakness, it is raised in power.
44 It is sown a natural body, it is raised a
spiritual body. There is a natural body and
there is a spiritual body.
45 So also it is written, "The first man,
Adam, became a living soul," the last Adam
became a life-giving Spirit.
46 But that which is spiritual is not first,
but the natural, then the spiritual.
47 The first man is of the earth, earthy. The
second man is the Lord out of Heaven.
48 Just as he who is made of dust is, so also
are those made of dust. And just like the
Heavenly One is, so also *will be* the heavenly
ones.
49 And as we bore the image of him made
of dust, so we shall also bear the image of
the Heavenly One.
50 But I say this, brothers, that flesh and
blood cannot inherit the kingdom of God,
nor does rottenness inherit purity.

51 See, I tell you a heavenly secret! We shall
not all die, but we shall all be changed –
52 in an instant, in the twinkling of an
eye, at the last trumpet – for a trumpet will
sound and the dead will be raised forever
pure, and we shall be changed.
53 For rottenness must put on purity, and
this mortal must put on immortality.
54 But when this decaying one shall have
put on purity, and this mortal has put on
immortality, then is fulfilled the word that is
written, "Death was swallowed up in victory.
55 O death, where is your sting? O grave,
where is your victory?"
56 Now the sting of death is sin, and the
power of sin is the Law.
57 But thanks to God, who gives us the
victory through our Lord Jesus Christ!
58 So, then, my beloved brothers, be firm
and unmovable, multiplying in the work of
the Lord always, knowing that your labor is
not without fruit in the Lord.

CHAPTER 16

1 Now about the collection which is for the
saints, as I gave order to the churches of
Galatia, you also do the same.
2 On the first of the week, let each of you
store up whatever he has prospered so that
when I come there will be no collections.
3 And when I arrive, whomever you shall
approve by letters, I will send these to carry
your gifts of charity to Jerusalem.

ἄξιον[ll] τοῦ.κἀμὲ πορεύεσθαι, σὺν ἐμοὶ πορεύσονται. 5 Ἐλεύ-
suitable for me also to go, with me they shall go. ²I ³will
σομαι δὲ πρὸς ὑμᾶς ὅταν Μακεδονίαν διέλθω·
⁴come ¹but to you when Macedonia I shall have gone through;
Μακεδονίαν.γὰρ διέρχομαι. 6 πρὸς.ὑμᾶς.δὲ τυχὸν παραμενῶ,
for Macedonia I do go through. And with you it may be I shall stay,
ἢ καὶ παραχειμάσω, ἵνα ὑμεῖς με προπέμψητε οὗ.ἐὰν
or even I shall winter, that ye me may set forward wheresoever
πορεύωμαι. 7 οὐ.θέλω.γὰρ ὑμᾶς ἄρτι ἐν παρόδῳ ἰδεῖν· ἐλπίζω
I may go. For I will not ³you ⁴now ⁵in ⁶passing ¹to ²see, ⁸I ⁹hope
[h]δὲ[ll] χρόνον τινὰ ἐπιμεῖναι πρὸς ὑμᾶς, ἐὰν ὁ κύριος [i]ἐπι-
⁷but a ²time ¹certain to remain with you, if the Lord per-
τρέπῃ.[ll] 8 ἐπιμενῶ.δὲ ἐν Ἐφέσῳ ἕως τῆς πεντηκοστῆς·
mit. But I shall remain in Ephesus till Pentecost.
9 θύρα.γάρ μοι ἀνέῳγεν μεγάλη καὶ ἐνεργής, καὶ ἀντι-
For a door to me has been opened great and efficient, and op-
κείμενοι πολλοί.
posers [are] many.

10 Ἐὰν.δὲ ἔλθῃ Τιμόθεος, βλέπετε ἵνα ἀφόβως γένηται
Now if ²come ¹Timotheus, see that without fear he may be
πρὸς ὑμᾶς· τὸ.γὰρ ἔργον κυρίου ἐργάζεται, ὡς [k]καὶ ἐγώ.[ll]
with you; for the work of [the] Lord he works, as even I.
11 μή τις οὖν αὐτὸν ἐξουθενήσῃ· προπέμψατε.δὲ αὐτὸν
²Not ³anyone ¹therefore him should despise; but set forward him
ἐν εἰρήνῃ, ἵνα ἔλθῃ πρός [l]με[ll] ἐκδέχομαι.γὰρ αὐτὸν μετὰ
in peace, that he may come to me; for I await him with
τῶν ἀδελφῶν. 12 Περὶ.δὲ Ἀπολλὼ τοῦ ἀδελφοῦ, πολλὰ
the brethren. And concerning Apollos the brother, much
παρεκάλεσα αὐτὸν ἵνα ἔλθῃ πρὸς ὑμᾶς μετὰ τῶν
I exhorted him that he should go to you with the
ἀδελφῶν· καὶ πάντως.οὐκ ἦν θέλημα ἵνα νῦν ἔλθῃ,
brethren; and not at all was [his] will that now he should come;
ἐλεύσεται δὲ ὅταν εὐκαιρήσῃ. 13 Γρηγορεῖτε, στήκετε
but he will come when he shall have opportunity. Watch ye; stand fast
ἐν τῇ πίστει, ἀνδρίζεσθε, [m]κραταιοῦσθε. 14 πάντα
in the faith, quit yourselves like men, be strong. ²All ⁴things
ὑμῶν ἐν ἀγάπῃ γινέσθω.
³your ⁵in ⁶love ¹let be done.

15 Παρακαλῶ.δὲ ὑμᾶς, ἀδελφοί· οἴδατε τὴν οἰκίαν Στεφανᾶ,
But I exhort you, brethren, (ye know the house of Stephanas,
ὅτι ἐστὶν ἀπαρχὴ τῆς Ἀχαΐας, καὶ εἰς διακονίαν τοῖς ἁγίοις
that it is ²first-fruit ¹Achaia's, and ⁷for ⁸service ⁴to ⁵the ⁶saints
ἔταξαν ἑαυτούς· 16 ἵνα καὶ ὑμεῖς ὑποτάσσησθε τοῖς
¹they ²appointed ³themselves,) that also ye be subject
τοιούτοις, καὶ παντὶ τῷ συνεργοῦντι καὶ κοπιῶντι. 17 Χαίρω
to such, and to everyone working with [us] and labouring. ²I ³rejoice
δὲ ἐπὶ τῇ παρουσίᾳ Στεφανᾶ καὶ [n]Φουρτουνάτου[ll] καὶ Ἀχαϊκοῦ,
¹but at the coming of Stephanas and Fortunatus and Achaicus;
ὅτι τὸ [o]ὑμῶν[ll] ὑστέρημα [p]οὗτοι[ll] ἀνεπλήρωσαν· 18 ἀνέπαυ-
because your deficiency these filled up. ²They ³re-
σαν γὰρ τὸ ἐμὸν πνεῦμα καὶ τὸ ὑμῶν. ἐπιγινώσκετε οὖν
freshed ¹for my spirit and yours; recognize therefore
τοὺς τοιούτους. 19 Ἀσπάζονται ὑμᾶς αἱ ἐκκλησίαι τῆς Ἀσίας·
such. ⁵Salute ⁶you ¹the ²assemblies ³of ⁴Asia.
[q]ἀσπάζονται[ll] ὑμᾶς ἐν κυρίῳ πολλὰ Ἀκύλας καὶ [r]Πρίσ-
¹⁰Salute ¹¹you ¹³in [¹⁴the] ¹⁵Lord ¹²much ⁷Aquila ⁸and ⁹Pris-
κιλλα,[ll] σὺν τῇ κατ' οἶκον.αὐτῶν ἐκκλησίᾳ· 20 ἀσπάζονται
cilla, with the ²in ³their ⁴house ¹assembly. ⁴Salute
ὑμᾶς οἱ ἀδελφοὶ πάντες. ἀσπάσασθε ἀλλήλους ἐν φιλήματι
⁵you ²the ³brethren ¹all. Salute ye one another with a ²kiss
ἁγίῳ.
¹holy.

21 Ὁ ἀσπασμὸς τῇ.ἐμῇ χειρὶ Παύλου· 22 εἴ τις οὐ.φιλεῖ
The salutation ³by ⁴my [⁵own] ⁶hand ¹of ²Paul. If anyone love not
τὸν κύριον [s]Ἰησοῦν χριστόν,[ll] ἤτω ἀνάθεμα· μαρὰν ἀθά.
the Lord Jesus Christ, let him be accursed: Maran atha.
23 ἡ χάρις τοῦ κυρίου Ἰησοῦ [t]χριστοῦ[ll] μεθ' ὑμῶν. 24 ἡ
The grace of the Lord Jesus Christ [be] with you.
ἀγάπη.μου μετὰ πάντων ὑμῶν ἐν χριστῷ Ἰησοῦ. [v]ἀμήν.[ll]
My love [be] with ²all ¹you in Christ Jesus. Amen.
[w]Πρὸς Κορινθίους πρώτη ἐγράφη ἀπὸ Φιλίππων, διὰ
²To [³the] ⁴Corinthians ¹first written from Philippi, by
Στεφανᾶ καὶ Φουρτουνάτου καὶ Ἀχαϊκοῦ καὶ Τιμοθέου.[ll]
Stephanas and Fortunatus and Achaicus and Timotheus.

4 And if it is suitable for me to go also, they
shall go with me.
5 But I will come to you when I have gone
through Mac-e-do-ni-a, for I do go through
Mac-e-do-ni-a.
6 And it may be that I will stay with you,
or I may even winter *there*, so that you may
send me wherever I may go.
7 For I do not want to see you now in
passing, but I hope to stay a while with you,
if the Lord permit.
8 But I shall stay in Ephesus until Pentecost
9 – for a door has been opened to me, wonderful and mighty, but many oppose us.
10 Now if Timothy comes, see that he is
without fear among you. For he works the
work of the Lord, even as I do.
11 Let no one then despise him, but send
him on in peace so that he may come to me,
for I look for him with the brothers.
12 And as to Apollos the brother, I urged
him to come to you with the brothers. But it
was not his will to come now, but he will come
when he has an opportunity.
13 Watch! Stand fast in the faith! Be men!
Be strong!
14 Let all your things be done in love.

15 But I beg you, brothers, you know the
house of Stephenas, that it is the first-fruit
of Achaia and they have devoted themselves
to minister to the saints –
16 that you be subject to such and to everyone working and laboring with us.
17 And I rejoice at the coming of Stephenas
and Fortunatus and Achaicus, for they filled
up what was lacking on your part.
18 For they refreshed my spirit and yours.
Then recognize such men.
19 The churches of Asia greet you. Aquila
and Priscilla greet you in the Lord, with the
church in their house.
20 All the brothers greet you. Greet one
another with a holy kiss.

21 The greeting of Paul, by my own hand.
22 If anyone does not love the Lord Jesus
Christ, let him be accursed. The Lord comes.
23 The grace of the Lord Jesus Christ be with
you.
24 My love be with you all in Christ Jesus.
Amen.

ΠΑΥΛΟΣ ἀπόστολος [b]Ἰησοῦ χριστοῦ|| διὰ θελήματος θεοῦ,
Paul, apostle of Jesus Christ by will of God,

καὶ Τιμόθεος ὁ ἀδελφός, τῇ ἐκκλησίᾳ τοῦ θεοῦ τῇ οὔσῃ ἐν
and Timotheus the brother, to the assembly of God which is in

Κορίνθῳ, σὺν τοῖς ἁγίοις πᾶσιν τοῖς οὖσιν ἐν ὅλῃ τῇ Ἀ-
Corinth, with [2]the [3]saints [1]all who are in [2]whole [1]the [of] A-

χαΐᾳ· 2 χάρις ὑμῖν καὶ εἰρήνη ἀπὸ [c]θεοῦ|| πατρὸς ἡμῶν καὶ
chaia. Grace to you and peace from God our Father and

κυρίου Ἰησοῦ χριστοῦ.
[the] Lord Jesus Christ.

3 Εὐλογητὸς ὁ θεὸς καὶ πατὴρ τοῦ κυρίου ἡμῶν Ἰησοῦ
Blessed [be] the God and Father of our Lord Jesus

χριστοῦ, ὁ πατὴρ τῶν οἰκτιρμῶν καὶ θεὸς πάσης παρακλή-
Christ, the Father of compassions, and God of all encourage-

σεως, 4 ὁ παρακαλῶν ἡμᾶς ἐπὶ πάσῃ τῇ θλίψει ἡμῶν, εἰς
ment; who encourages us in all our tribulation, for

τὸ δύνασθαι ἡμᾶς παρακαλεῖν τοὺς ἐν πάσῃ θλίψει, διὰ
[2]to [3]be [4]able [1]us to encourage those in every tribulation, through

τῆς παρακλήσεως ἧς παρακαλούμεθα αὐτοὶ ὑπὸ τοῦ
the encouragement with which we are encouraged ourselves by

θεοῦ· 5 ὅτι καθὼς περισσεύει τὰ παθήματα τοῦ χριστοῦ
God. Because according as abound the sufferings of the Christ

εἰς ἡμᾶς, οὕτως διὰ [d] χριστοῦ περισσεύει καὶ ἡ παράκλησις
toward us, so through Christ abounds also [2]encouragement

ἡμῶν. 6 εἴτε δὲ θλιβόμεθα, ὑπὲρ τῆς ὑμῶν παρακλήσεως
[1]our. But whether we are troubled, [it is] for your encouragement

καὶ σωτηρίας, [e]τῆς ἐνεργουμένης ἐν ὑπομονῇ τῶν αὐτῶν
and salvation, being wrought in [the] endurance of the same

παθημάτων ὧν καὶ ἡμεῖς πάσχομεν·|| [f]εἴτε παρακαλούμεθα,
sufferings which [2]also [1]we suffer, whether we are encouraged,

ὑπὲρ τῆς ὑμῶν παρακλήσεως[e] [g]καὶ σωτηρίας·||| καὶ ἡ ἐλπὶς
[it is] for your encouragement and salvation; (and [2]hope

ἡμῶν βεβαία ὑπὲρ ὑμῶν[f]· 7 εἰδότες ὅτι [h]ὥσπερ|| κοινωνοί
[1]our [is] sure for you;) knowing that as partners

ἐστε τῶν παθημάτων, οὕτως καὶ τῆς παρακλήσεως. 8 Οὐ γὰρ
ye are of the sufferings, so also of the encouragement. For [3]not

θέλομεν ὑμᾶς ἀγνοεῖν, ἀδελφοί, [i]ὑπὲρ|| τῆς θλίψεως ἡμῶν
[2]do [1]we wish you to be ignorant, brethren, as to our tribulation

τῆς γενομένης [k]ἡμῖν|| ἐν τῇ Ἀσίᾳ, ὅτι καθ' ὑπερβολὴν [l]ἐβαρή-
which happened to us in Asia, that excessively we were

θημεν ὑπὲρ δύναμιν,|| ὥστε ἐξαπορηθῆναι ἡμᾶς καὶ τοῦ ζῆν·
burdened beyond [our] power, so as for us to despair even of living.

9 [m]ἀλλ'|| αὐτοὶ ἐν ἑαυτοῖς τὸ ἀπόκριμα τοῦ θανάτου ἐσχή-
But ourselves in ourselves the sentence of death we have

καμεν, ἵνα μὴ πεποιθότες ὦμεν ἐφ' ἑαυτοῖς, ἀλλ' ἐπὶ τῷ
had, that we should not have trust in ourselves, but in

θεῷ τῷ ἐγείροντι τοὺς νεκρούς· 10 ὃς ἐκ τηλικούτου θανάτου
God who raises the dead; who from so great a death

[n]ἐρρύσατο|| ἡμᾶς [o]καὶ ῥύεται,|| εἰς ὃν ἠλπίκαμεν [p]ὅτι|| καὶ
delivered us and does deliver; in whom we have hope that also

ἔτι ῥύσεται, 11 συνυπουργούντων καὶ ὑμῶν ὑπὲρ ἡμῶν
still he will deliver; labouring together [2]also [1]ye for us

τῇ δεήσει, ἵνα ἐκ πολλῶν προσώπων τὸ εἰς ἡμᾶς χάρισμα
by supplication, that by many persons the [2]towards [3]us [1]gift

διὰ πολλῶν εὐχαριστηθῇ ὑπὲρ ἡμῶν. 12 Ἡ
[9]through [10]many [4]might [5]be [6]subject [7]of [8]thanksgiving for us.

γὰρ καύχησις ἡμῶν αὕτη ἐστίν, τὸ μαρτύριον τῆς συνειδήσεως
For our boasting this is, the testimony of [2]conscience

ἡμῶν, ὅτι ἐν [q]ἁπλότητι|| καὶ [r]εἰλικρινείᾳ|| [s] θεοῦ, οὐκ ἐν σοφίᾳ
[1]our, that in simplicity and sincerity of God, (not in [2]wisdom

σαρκικῇ, ἀλλ' ἐν χάριτι θεοῦ, ἀνεστράφημεν ἐν τῷ κόσμῳ,
[1]fleshly, but in grace of God,) we had our conduct in the world,

περισσοτέρως δὲ πρὸς ὑμᾶς. 13 οὐ γὰρ ἄλλα γράφομεν
and more abundantly towards you. For not other things do we write

ὑμῖν [t]ἀλλ'|| ἢ ἃ ἀναγινώσκετε, ἢ καὶ ἐπιγινώσκετε, ἐλπίζω δὲ
to you but what ye read, or even recognize; and I hope

ὅτι [v]καὶ|| ἕως τέλους ἐπιγνώσεσθε, 14 καθὼς καὶ ἐπέ-
that even to [the] end ye will recognize, according as also ye did

γνωτε ἡμᾶς ἀπὸ μέρους, ὅτι καύχημα ὑμῶν ἐσμεν, καθάπερ
recognize us in part, that [3]your [4]boasting [1]we [2]are, even as

καὶ ὑμεῖς ἡμῶν ἐν τῇ ἡμέρᾳ τοῦ κυρίου [w] Ἰησοῦ. 15 Καὶ
also ye [are] ours in the day of the Lord Jesus. And

ταύτῃ τῇ πεποιθήσει ἐβουλόμην [x]πρὸς ὑμᾶς ἐλθεῖν πρότερον,||
with this confidence I purposed [3]to [4]you [1]to [2]come previously,

ἵνα δευτέραν χάριν [y]ἔχητε·|| 16 καὶ δι' ὑμῶν [z]διελθεῖν||
that a second favour ye might have; and by you to pass through

εἰς Μακεδονίαν, καὶ πάλιν ἀπὸ Μακεδονίας ἐλθεῖν πρὸς ὑμᾶς,
to Macedonia, and again from Macedonia to come to you,

καὶ ὑφ' ὑμῶν προπεμφθῆναι εἰς τὴν Ἰουδαίαν. 17 τοῦτο οὖν
and by you to be set forward to Judæa. This therefore

CHAPTER 1

1 Paul, an apostle of Jesus Christ by God's
will, and Timothy the brother, to the church
of God which is in Corinth, with all the
saints who are in all Achaia.
2 Grace to you and peace from God our
Father and the Lord Jesus Christ.

3 Blessed be the God and Father of our
Lord Jesus Christ, the Father of mercies and
God of all comfort,
4 who comforts us in all our trouble, en-
abling us to comfort those in every tribulation, through that comfort with which we
ourselves are comforted by God.
5 For as the sufferings of Christ abound to
us, so also our comfort increases by Christ.
6 But if we are troubled, *it is* for your comfort and salvation, being worked out in the
endurance of the same sufferings we suffer.
If we are encouraged, it is for your comfort
and salvation –
7 and our hope for you is certain, knowing
that even as you share the sufferings, so you
share also the comfort.
8 For, brothers, we do not want you to be
ignorant as to our trouble which happened
to us in Asia, that we were heavily pressed
down beyond strength, so as for us to even
lose hope of living.
9 But we ourselves have had the sentence of
death within us, so that we might not trust in
ourselves, but in God who raises the dead.
10 *For He* rescued us from so great a death
and is delivering us, in whom we have hope
that He also will still deliver us
11 with you also laboring together by
prayer for us, so that the gracious gift to us
by many may be the cause of thanksgiving
by many for our benefit.
12 For our rejoicing is this, the testimony of
our conscience, that we have conducted ourselves in the world in honest and godly sincerity – not in fleshly wisdom, but in the
grace of God – especially so toward you.
13 For we do not write any other things to
you but what you read, or even recognize.
And I hope that you will know to the end –
14 even as you also in part recognized us,
that we are your joy, even as you are ours in
the day of the Lord Jesus.
15 And being sure of this, I intended to
come to you before now, so that you might
have a second benefit,
16 and to go by you through to Mac-e-do-
ni-a, and again to come to you from Mac-e-
do-ni-a, and to be brought to Judea by you.
17 This then being my purpose, did I indeed

[a]βουλευόμενος,‖ μή τι ἄρα τῇ ἐλαφρίᾳ ἐχρησάμην; ἢ ἃ
purposing, [3]indeed [4]lightness [1]did [2]I [4]use? or what
βουλεύομαι, κατὰ σάρκα βουλεύομαι, ἵνα ᾖ παρ'
I purpose, according to flesh do I purpose, that there should be with
ἐμοὶ τὸ ναὶ ναί, καὶ τὸ οὒ οὔ; 18 πιστὸς.δὲ ὁ θεός, ὅτι ὁ
me yea yea, and nay nay? Now faithful God [is], that
λόγος.ἡμῶν ὁ πρὸς ὑμᾶς οὐκ [b]ἐγένετο‖ ναὶ καὶ οὔ. 19 ὁ.[c]γὰρ
our word to you [2]not [1]was yea and nay. For the
τοῦ θεοῦ‖ υἱὸς [d]Ἰησοῦς χριστὸς‖ ὁ ἐν ὑμῖν δι' ἡμῶν κη-
[2]of [3]God [1]Son, Jesus Christ, who among you by us was
ρυχθείς, δι' ἐμοῦ καὶ Σιλουανοῦ καὶ Τιμοθέου, οὐκ.ἐγένετο ναὶ
proclaimed, (by me and Silvanus and Timotheus,) was not yea
καὶ οὔ, ἀλλὰ ναὶ ἐν αὐτῷ γέγονεν. 20 ὅσαι.γὰρ ἐπαγγελίαι
and nay, but yea in him has been. For whatever promises
θεοῦ, ἐν αὐτῷ τὸ ναί, [e]καὶ ἐν αὐτῷ‖ τὸ ἀμήν,
of God [there are], in him [is] the yea, and in him the Amen,
τῷ θεῷ πρὸς δόξαν δι' ἡμῶν. 21 ὁ.δὲ βεβαιῶν ἡμᾶς σὺν
[3]to [4]God [1]for [2]glory by us. Now he who confirms us with
ὑμῖν εἰς χριστόν, καὶ χρίσας ἡμᾶς, θεός· 22 ὁ καὶ σφραγι-
you unto Christ, and anointed us, [is] God, who also sealed
σάμενος ἡμᾶς, καὶ δοὺς τὸν [f]ἀρραβῶνα‖ τοῦ πνεύματος ἐν
us, and gave the earnest of the Spirit in
ταῖς.καρδίαις.ἡμῶν.
our hearts.

23 Ἐγὼ.δὲ μάρτυρα τὸν θεὸν ἐπικαλοῦμαι ἐπὶ τὴν ἐμὴν
But I [3]as [4]witness [2]God [1]call upon my
ψυχήν, ὅτι φειδόμενος ὑμῶν οὐκέτι ἦλθον εἰς Κόρινθον.
soul, that sparing you not yet did I come to Corinth.
24 οὐχ ὅτι κυριεύομεν ὑμῶν τῆς πίστεως, ἀλλὰ συνεργοί
Not that we rule over your faith, but fellow-workers
ἐσμεν τῆς.χαρᾶς.ὑμῶν, τῇ.γὰρ.πίστει ἑστήκατε. 2 Ἔκρινα.δὲ
are of your joy: for by faith ye stand. But I judged
ἐμαυτῷ τοῦτο, τὸ μὴ πάλιν [g]ἐλθεῖν ἐν λύπῃ πρὸς ὑμᾶς.‖
with myself this, not again to come in grief to you.
2 εἰ.γὰρ ἐγὼ λυπῶ ὑμᾶς, καὶ τίς [h]ἐστιν‖ ὁ εὐφραίνων με, εἰ.μὴ
For if I grieve you, [2]also [1]who is it that gladdens me, except
ὁ λυπούμενος ἐξ ἐμοῦ; 3 καὶ ἔγραψα [i]ὑμῖν‖ τοῦτο αὐτό,
he who is grieved by me? And I wrote to you this same,
ἵνα.μὴ ἐλθὼν λύπην [k]ἔχω‖ ἀφ' ὧν ἔδει με
lest having come grief I might have from [those] of whom it behoves me
χαίρειν· πεποιθὼς ἐπὶ πάντας ὑμᾶς, ὅτι ἡ.ἐμὴ.χαρὰ
to rejoice; trusting in [2]all [1]you, that my joy [[2]that]
πάντων ὑμῶν ἐστιν. 4 ἐκ.γὰρ πολλῆς θλίψεως καὶ συνοχῆς
[3]of [5]all [4]you [1]is. For out of much tribulation and distress
καρδίας ἔγραψα ὑμῖν διὰ πολλῶν δακρύων, οὐχ ἵνα λυπη-
of heart I wrote to you through many tears; not that ye might
θῆτε, ἀλλὰ τὴν ἀγάπην ἵνα γνῶτε ἣν ἔχω περισ-
be grieved, but [2]the [3]love [1]that ye might know which I have more
σοτέρως εἰς ὑμᾶς. 5 Εἰ.δέ τις λελύπηκεν, οὐκ ἐμὲ
abundantly towards you. But if anyone has grieved, [3]not [5]me
λελύπηκεν, [l]ἀλλ'‖ ἀπὸ.μέρους, ἵνα μὴ.ἐπιβαρῶ, πάντας
[1]he [2]has [4]grieved, but in part (that I may not overcharge) [2]all
ὑμᾶς. 6 ἱκανὸν τῷ.τοιούτῳ ἡ.ἐπιτιμία.αὕτη ἡ ὑπὸ τῶν
[1]you. Sufficient to such a one [is] this rebuke which [is] by the
πλειόνων· 7 ὥστε τοὐναντίον [m]μᾶλλον‖ ὑμᾶς χαρίσασθαι
greater part; so that on the contrary rather ye should forgive
καὶ παρακαλέσαι, μήπως τῇ.περισσοτέρᾳ λύπῃ κατα-
and encourage, lest with more abundant grief should be swal-
ποθῇ ὁ.τοιοῦτος. 8 διὸ παρακαλῶ ὑμᾶς κυρῶσαι εἰς
lowed up such a one. Wherefore I exhort you to confirm [2]towards
αὐτὸν ἀγάπην. 9 εἰς.τοῦτο.γὰρ καὶ ἔγραψα, ἵνα γνῶ
[3]him [1]love. For, for this also did I write, that I might know
τὴν δοκιμὴν ὑμῶν, εἰ εἰς πάντα ὑπήκοοί ἐστε. 10 ᾧ.δέ
the proof of you, if to everything obedient ye are. But to whom
τι χαρίζεσθε, [n]καὶ ἐγώ·‖ καὶ.γὰρ ἐγὼ [o]εἴ τι κεχάρισ-
anything ye forgive, also I; for also I if anything I have for-
μαι, ᾧ κεχάρισμαι,‖ δι' ὑμᾶς, ἐν προσώπῳ χριστοῦ,
given, of whom I have forgiven, [is] for sake of you, in [the] person of Christ;
11 ἵνα μὴ.πλεονεκτηθῶμεν ὑπὸ τοῦ σατανᾶ· οὐ.γὰρ αὐτοῦ
that we should not be overreached by Satan, for not of his
τὰ νοήματα ἀγνοοῦμεν.
thoughts are we ignorant.

12 Ἐλθὼν.δὲ εἰς τὴν [p]Τρῳάδα‖ εἰς τὸ εὐαγγέλιον τοῦ
Now having come to Troas for the glad tidings of the
χριστοῦ, καὶ θύρας μοι ἀνεῳγμένης ἐν κυρίῳ, 13 οὐκ
Christ, also a door to me having been opened in [the] Lord, [3]not
ἔσχηκα ἄνεσιν τῷ.πνεύματί.μου τῷ.μὴ.εὑρεῖν.με Τίτον τὸν
[1]I [2]had ease in my spirit at my not finding Titus
ἀδελφόν.μου· ἀλλὰ ἀποταξάμενος αὐτοῖς, ἐξῆλθον εἰς Μακε-
my brother; but having taken leave of them, I went out to Mace-
δονίαν. 14 Τῷ.δὲ.θεῷ χάρις τῷ πάντοτε θριαμβεύοντι
donia. But to God [be] thanks, who always leads in triumph

use lightness? Or the things that I plan, do I purpose according to the flesh, so that there should be yes, yes – and, no, no – with me?

18 But God is faithful, that our word to you was not yes and no.

19 For the Son of God, Jesus Christ (who was preached among you by us – Silvanus, Timothy and me) was not yes and no, but in Him it was, Yes!

20 For however many promises of God *there are*, in Him is the Yes and in Him is the Amen, for glory to God by us.

21 Now He who establishes us with you in Christ and anoints us in God,

22 who also has sealed us and has given the earnest of the Spirit in our hearts.

23 But I call on God as witness on my soul that I have not yet come to Corinth so as to spare you.

24 Not that we rule over your faith, but are fellow-workers of your joy. For you stand by faith.

CHAPTER 2

1 But I decided with myself, not to come to you again in sorrow.

2 For I make you sorry, who is it that will make me glad, but he who is made sorry by me?

3 And I wrote this very thing for fear that when I come I might have sorrow from *those* concerning whom I ought to rejoice,

4 trusting in you all, that my joy is *the joy* of all of you. For through many tears I wrote you out of much trouble and agony of heart, not that you might be saddened, but that you might know the overflowing love which I have towards you.

5 But if anyone has caused sorrow, he has not caused me sorrow, but in part all of you (*I say* this that I may not bear down too heavily).

6 This punishment which was *put on him* by most of you is enough for such a person.

7 So that on the contrary you should *now* forgive and encourage this one for fear he should be overcome with floods of sorrow.

8 So I urge you to make him sure of love.

9 For to this end also I wrote, that I might know the proof of you, if you are obedient in everything.

10 But to whom you forgive anything, I also. For also if I have forgiven anything, I have forgiven it for you, in Christ's person.

11 So that we should not be overreached by Satan, for we are not ignorant of his devices.

12 But when I had come to Troas for the gospel of Christ, and a door had been opened to me by the Lord,

13 I did not have any rest in my spirit because I did not find my brother Titus. But I left them and went out to Mac-e-do-ni-a.

14 But thanks be to God, who always leads us in triumph in Christ, and who reveals by

ἡμᾶς ἐν τῷ χριστῷ, καὶ τὴν ὀσμὴν τῆς γνώσεως αὐτοῦ
us in the Christ, and the odour of the knowledge of him
φανεροῦντι δι' ἡμῶν ἐν παντὶ τόπῳ. 15 ὅτι χριστοῦ
makes manifest through us in every place. For of Christ
εὐωδία ἐσμὲν τῷ θεῷ ἐν τοῖς σῳζομένοις καὶ ἐν τοῖς ἀπολ-
a sweet perfume we are to God in those being saved and in those perish-
λυμένοις· 16 οἷς.μὲν ὀσμὴ [q] θανάτου εἰς θάνατον· οἷς.δέ,
ing; to the ones, an odour of death to death, but to the others,
ὀσμὴ [q] ζωῆς εἰς ζωήν. καὶ πρὸς ταῦτα τίς ἱκανός;
an odour of life to life; and for these things who [is] competent?
17 οὐ.γάρ ἐσμεν ὡς οἱ πολλοί, καπηλεύοντες τὸν λόγον
For 3not 1we 2are as the many, making gain by corrupting the word
τοῦ θεοῦ, [r]ἀλλ'‖ ὡς ἐξ [s]εἰλικρινείας,‖ ἀλλ' ὡς ἐκ θεοῦ, [t]κατ-
of God, but as of sincerity, but as of God. be-
ενώπιον‖ [u]τοῦ‖ θεοῦ, ἐν χριστῷ λαλοῦμεν.
fore God, in Christ we speak.
3 Ἀρχόμεθα πάλιν ἑαυτοὺς [v]συνιστάνειν‖; [w]εἰ‖.μὴ χρῄ-
Do we begin again ourselves to commend? unless we
ζομεν, ὥς [x] τινες, [y]συστατικῶν‖ ἐπιστολῶν πρὸς ὑμᾶς, ἢ ἐξ
need, as some, commendatory epistles to you, or 3from
ὑμῶν [z]συστατικῶν‖; 2 ἡ.ἐπιστολὴ.ἡμῶν ὑμεῖς ἐστε, [a]ἐγγεγραμ-
4you 1commendatory [2ones]? Our epistle ye are, having been
μένη‖ ἐν ταῖς.καρδίαις.ἡμῶν, γινωσκομένη καὶ ἀναγινω-
inscribed in our hearts, being known and being
σκομένη ὑπὸ πάντων ἀνθρώπων· 3 φανερούμενοι ὅτι ἐστὲ
read by all men, being manifested that ye are
ἐπιστολὴ χριστοῦ διακονηθεῖσα ὑφ' ἡμῶν, [a]ἐγγεγραμμένη‖
2epistle 1Christ's, ministered by us; having been inscribed,
οὐ μέλανι, ἀλλὰ πνεύματι θεοῦ ζῶντος, οὐκ ἐν πλαξὶν
not with ink, but with [the] Spirit of 3God [1the] 2living; not on tablets
λιθίναις, [b]ἀλλ'‖ ἐν πλαξὶν [c]καρδίας‖ σαρκίναις. 4 Πεποί-
of stone, but on 2tablets 3of [4the] 5heart 1fleshy. 7Confi-
θησιν δὲ τοιαύτην ἔχομεν διὰ τοῦ χριστοῦ πρὸς τὸν θεόν·
dence 6and such have we through the Christ towards God:
5 οὐχ ὅτι [d]ἱκανοί ἐσμεν ἀφ' ἑαυτῶν λογίσασθαί τι‖ ὡς ἐξ
not that competent we are from ourselves to reckon anything as of
[e]ἑαυτῶν,‖ ἀλλ' ἡ.ἱκανότης.ἡμῶν ἐκ τοῦ θεοῦ· 6 ὃς καὶ
ourselves, but our competency [is] of God; who also
ἱκάνωσεν ἡμᾶς διακόνους καινῆς διαθήκης, οὐ γράμ-
made 2competent 1us [as] servants of a new covenant; not of let-
ματος, ἀλλὰ πνεύματος· τὸ.γὰρ γράμμα [f]ἀποκτείνει,‖ τὸ.δὲ
ter, but of Spirit; for the letter kills, but the
πνεῦμα ζωοποιεῖ. 7 Εἰ.δὲ ἡ διακονία τοῦ θανάτου ἐν [g]γράμ-
Spirit quickens. But if the service of death in let-
μασιν,‖ ἐντετυπωμένη [h]ἐν‖ λίθοις, ἐγενήθη ἐν δόξῃ, ὥστε
ters, having been engraven in stones, was produced with glory, so as
μὴ.δύνασθαι ἀτενίσαι τοὺς υἱοὺς Ἰσραὴλ εἰς τὸ πρόσω-
5not 6to 7be 8able 9to 10look 11intently 1the 2children 3of 4Israel into the face
πον [i]Μωσέως,‖ διὰ τὴν δόξαν τοῦ.προσώπου.αὐτοῦ, τὴν
of Moses, on account of the glory of his face, which
καταργουμένην· 8 πῶς οὐχὶ μᾶλλον ἡ διακονία τοῦ πνεύμα-
is being annulled; how not rather the service of the Spirit
τος ἔσται ἐν δόξῃ; 9 εἰ.γὰρ [k]ἡ διακονία‖ τῆς κατακρίσεως
shall be in glory? For if the service of condemnation [be]
δόξα, πολλῷ μᾶλλον περισσεύει ἡ διακονία τῆς δικαιοσύνης
glory, much rather abounds the service of righteousness
[l]ἐν‖ δόξῃ. 10 καὶ.γὰρ [m]οὐδὲ‖ δεδόξασται τὸ
in glory. For even neither 8has 9been 9made 10glorious 1that 2which
δεδοξασμένον ἐν τούτῳ τῷ μέρει, [n]ἕνεκεν‖ τῆς ὑπερ-
4has 5been 6made 7glorious in this respect, on account of the sur-
βαλλούσης δόξης. 11 εἰ.γὰρ τὸ καταργούμενον διὰ
passing glory. For if that which is being annulled [was] through
δόξης, πολλῷ μᾶλλον τὸ μένον ἐν δόξῃ. 12 Ἔχοντες
glory, much rather that which remains [is] in glory. Having
οὖν τοιαύτην ἐλπίδα, πολλῇ παρρησίᾳ χρώμεθα· 13 καὶ
therefore such hope, much boldness we use: and
οὐ καθάπερ [o]Μωσῆς‖ ἐτίθει κάλυμμα ἐπὶ τὸ πρόσωπον [p]ἑαυ-
not according as Moses put a veil on the face of him-
τοῦ,‖ πρὸς τὸ μὴ ἀτενίσαι τοὺς υἱοὺς Ἰσραὴλ εἰς τὸ τέλος
self, for 5not 6to 7look 8intently 1the 2sons 3of 4Israel to the end
τοῦ καταργουμένου· 14 [q]ἀλλ'‖ ἐπωρώθη τὰ.νοήματα.αὐτῶν.
of that being annulled. But were hardened their thoughts,
ἄχρι.γὰρ τῆς σήμερον [r] τὸ αὐτὸ κάλυμμα ἐπὶ τῇ ἀναγνώσει
for unto the present the same veil at the reading
τῆς παλαιᾶς διαθήκης μένει, μὴ ἀνακαλυπτόμενον, [s]ὅ τι‖
of the old covenant remains, not uncovered, which
ἐν χριστῷ καταργεῖται· 15 ἀλλ' ἕως σήμερον, ἡνίκα [t]ἀνα-
in Christ is being annulled. But unto this day, when is
γινώσκεται‖ [o]Μωσῆς,‖ κάλυμμα ἐπὶ τὴν.καρδίαν.αὐτῶν κεῖται·
read Moses, a veil upon their heart lies.
16 ἡνίκα.[v]δ' ἂν‖ ἐπιστρέψῃ πρὸς κύριον, περιαιρεῖται τὸ
But when it shall have turned to [the] Lord, is taken away the

us in every place the sweet odor of the knowledge of Him.

15 For we are to God a sweet perfume in Christ, in those who are being saved, and in those who are being lost.

16 To the ones *we are* a savor of death unto death, and to the others a savor of life to life – and who is good enough for these things?

17 For we are not as the many, profiting by corrupting the word of God, but as of truthfulness, but as of God. In the sight of God, we speak in Christ.

CHAPTER 3

1 Do we begin again to recommend ourselves? Or do we, like some, need letters to recommend us to you – or from you to recommend us?

2 You are our letter, having been inscribed in our hearts, being known and read by all men,

3 showing that you are Christ's letter, served by us, not being written with ink, but with the Spirit of the living God – not on tablets of stone, but on fleshly tablets of the heart.

4 And we have such trust through Christ towards God.

5 Not that we are able of ourselves to judge anything as of ourselves, but our ability to judge is of God

6 who has also made us able ministers of the new covenant, not of the letter, but of the Spirit – for the letter kills, but the Spirit gives life.

7 But if the ministry of death, in letters cut into stones, was brought into being with glory (so that the children of Israel were not able to look into the face of Moses, because of the shining glory of his face), which was to cease –

8 now much rather shall the ministry of the Spirit be with glory!

9 For if the ministry of condemnation was glory, much more does the ministry of righteousness exceed in glory.

10 For even that which has been made glorious has not been made glorious in this respect – because of the glory which is far greater.

11 For if that which is to cease *was* through glory, much more that which remains is with glory.

12 Having such hope, then, we use great plainness of speech.

13 And not like Moses, who put a veil over his face so that the children of Israel could not look to the end of that being annulled.

14 But their minds were blinded. For until this very day, the same veil remains on the reading of the Old Testament, not removed because it is to be done away in Christ.

15 But until today, when Moses is read, a veil lies on their heart.

16 But when it shall have turned to the Lord, the veil is taken away.

κάλυμμα. 17 Ὁ.δὲ κύριος τὸ πνεῦμά ἐστιν· οὗ.δὲ τὸ πνεῦμα
veil. Now the Lord the Spirit is; and where the Spirit
κυρίου, [w]ἐκεῖ[‖] ἐλευθερία. 18 ἡμεῖς.δὲ πάντες ἀνακεκα-
of [the] Lord [is], there [is] freedom. But we all with un-
λυμμένῳ προσώπῳ τὴν δόξαν κυρίου κατοπτριζόμενοι,
covered face the glory of [the] Lord beholding as in a mirror, [to]
τὴν αὐτὴν εἰκόνα μεταμορφούμεθα ἀπὸ δόξης εἰς δόξαν,
the same image are being transformed from glory to glory,
καθάπερ ἀπὸ κυρίου πνεύματος.
even as from [the] Lord [the] Spirit.

4 Διὰ.τοῦτο ἔχοντες τὴν.διακονίαν.ταύτην, καθὼς ἠλεή-
Therefore, having this service, according as we re-
θημεν, οὐκ.[x]ἐκκακοῦμεν·[‖] 2 [y]ἀλλ'[‖] ἀπειπάμεθα τὰ κρυπτὰ
ceived mercy, we faint not. But we renounced the hidden things
τῆς αἰσχύνης, μὴ περιπατοῦντες ἐν πανουργίᾳ μηδὲ δολοῦν-
of shame, not walking in craftiness, nor falsify-
τες τὸν λόγον τοῦ θεοῦ, ἀλλὰ τῇ φανερώσει τῆς ἀληθείας
ing the word of God, but by manifestation of the truth
[z]συνιστῶντες[‖] ἑαυτοὺς πρὸς πᾶσαν συνείδησιν ἀνθρώπων
commending ourselves to every conscience of men
ἐνώπιον τοῦ θεοῦ. 3 Εἰ.δὲ καὶ ἔστιν κεκαλυμμένον τὸ εὐαγ-
before God. But if also is covered [2]glad
γέλιον ἡμῶν, ἐν τοῖς ἀπολλυμένοις ἐστὶν κεκαλυμμένον· 4 ἐν
tidings [1]our, in those perishing it is covered; in
οἷς ὁ θεὸς τοῦ.αἰῶνος.τούτου ἐτύφλωσεν τὰ νοήματα τῶν
whom the god of this age blinded the thoughts of the
ἀπίστων, εἰς.τὸ μὴ αὐγάσαι [a]αὐτοῖς[‖] τὸν φωτισμὸν τοῦ
unbelieving, so as not to beam forth to them the radiancy of the
εὐαγγελίου [c]τῆς[‖] δόξης τοῦ χριστοῦ, ὅς ἐστιν εἰκὼν τοῦ
glad tidings of the glory of the Christ, who is [the] image
θεοῦ. 5 οὐ.γὰρ ἑαυτοὺς κηρύσσομεν, ἀλλὰ [d]χριστὸν Ἰη-
of God. For not ourselves do we proclaim, but Christ Je-
σοῦν[‖] κύριον· ἑαυτοὺς.δὲ δούλους.ὑμῶν διὰ Ἰησοῦν.
sus Lord, and ourselves your bondmen for the sake of Jesus.
6 ὅτι ὁ θεὸς ὁ εἰπὼν ἐκ σκότους φῶς [e]λάμψαι,[‖] ὃς
Because [it is] God who spoke out of darkness light to shine, who
ἔλαμψεν ἐν ταῖς.καρδίαις.ἡμῶν, πρὸς φωτισμὸν τῆς γνώ-
shone in our hearts, for [the] radiancy of the know-
σεως τῆς δόξης [f]τοῦ θεοῦ[‖] ἐν προσώπῳ [g]Ἰησοῦ[‖] χριστοῦ.
ledge of the glory of God in [the] face of Jesus Christ.
7 [h]Ἔχομεν.δὲ τὸν.θησαυρὸν.τοῦτον ἐν ὀστρακίνοις σκεύεσιν,
But we have this treasure in earthen vessels,
ἵνα ἡ ὑπερβολὴ τῆς δυνάμεως ᾖ τοῦ θεοῦ, καὶ μὴ ἐξ
that the surpassingness of the power may be of God, and not from
ἡμῶν· 8 ἐν παντὶ θλιβόμενοι, ἀλλ' οὐ στενοχωρούμενοι·
us: in every [way] oppressed, but not straitened;
ἀπορούμενοι, ἀλλ' οὐκ ἐξαπορούμενοι· 9 διωκόμενοι, ἀλλ' οὐκ
perplexed, but not utterly at a loss; persecuted, but not
ἐγκαταλειπόμενοι· καταβαλλόμενοι, ἀλλ' οὐκ ἀπολλύμενοι·
forsaken; cast down, but not destroyed;
10 πάντοτε τὴν νέκρωσιν τοῦ [h]κυρίου[‖] Ἰησοῦ ἐν τῷ σώματι
always the dying of the Lord Jesus in the body
περιφέροντες, ἵνα καὶ ἡ ζωὴ τοῦ Ἰησοῦ ἐν [i]τῷ σώματι[‖] ἡμῶν
bearing about, that also the life of Jesus in [2]body [1]our
φανερωθῇ. 11 ἀεὶ.γὰρ ἡμεῖς οἱ ζῶντες εἰς θάνατον παρα-
may be manifested; for always we who live to death are de-
διδόμεθα διὰ Ἰησοῦν, ἵνα καὶ ἡ ζωὴ τοῦ Ἰησοῦ φανε-
livered on account of Jesus, that also the life of Jesus may be
ρωθῇ ἐν τῇ θνητῇ σαρκὶ ἡμῶν. 12 Ὥστε ὁ [k]μὲν[‖] θάνατος
manifested in [2]mortal [3]flesh [1]our; so that death
ἐν ἡμῖν ἐνεργεῖται, ἡ.δὲ.ζωὴ ἐν ὑμῖν· 13 ἔχοντες.δὲ τὸ αὐτὸ
in us works, and life in you. And having the same
πνεῦμα τῆς πίστεως, κατὰ τὸ γεγραμμένον, Ἐπίστευσα,
spirit of faith, according to what has been written, I believed,
διὸ [l]ἐλάλησα, καὶ ἡμεῖς πιστεύομεν, διὸ καὶ λαλοῦμεν·
therefore I spoke; [2]also [1]we believe, therefore also we speak;
14 εἰδότες ὅτι ὁ ἐγείρας τὸν [m]κύριον[‖] Ἰησοῦν, καὶ ἡμᾶς
knowing that he who raised up the Lord Jesus, also us
[n]διὰ[‖] Ἰησοῦ ἐγερεῖ, καὶ παραστήσει σὺν ὑμῖν. 15 τὰ
through Jesus will raise up, and will present with you.
γὰρ πάντα δι' ὑμᾶς, ἵνα ἡ χάρις πλεονάσασα
For all things [are] for the sake of you, that the grace, abounding
διὰ τῶν πλειόνων τὴν εὐχαριστίαν περισσεύσῃ εἰς τὴν
through the most, [3]thanksgiving [1]may [2]cause to exceed to the
δόξαν τοῦ θεοῦ.
glory of God.

16 Διὸ οὐκ.[o]ἐκκακοῦμεν·[‖] ἀλλ' εἰ καὶ ὁ ἔξω ἡμῶν ἄν-
Wherefore we faint not; but if indeed [2]outward [1]our
θρωπος διαφθείρεται, ἀλλ' ὁ [p]ἔσωθεν[‖] ἀνακαινοῦται
man is being brought to decay, yet the inward is being renewed
ἡμέρᾳ.καὶ.ἡμέρᾳ. 17 τὸ.γὰρ παραυτίκα ἐλαφρὸν τῆς θλίψεως
day by day. For the momentary lightness of [2]tribulation

17 Now the Lord is the Spirit. And where
the Spirit of the Lord is, there is freedom!
18 But we all with unveiled face beholding
the glory of the Lord, as in a mirror, are
being changed into the same image from
glory to glory as from the Spirit of the Lord.

CHAPTER 4

1 Then, since we have this ministry, even as
we have received mercy, we do not faint.
2 But we have forsaken the hidden things of
shame, not walking in sly ways or falsely
using the word of God. But by revealing the
truth, we are approving ourselves to every
conscience of men in the sight of God.
3 But if our gospel is hidden, it is hidden in
those who are being lost –
4 in whom the god of this world has blinded
the minds of the ones who do not believe, so
that the brightness of the gospel of the glory
of Christ (who is the image of God) should
not dawn on them.
5 For we do not preach ourselves, but
Christ Jesus the Lord, and ourselves your
servants for the sake of Jesus.
6 Because the God who commanded light to
shine out of darkness *is He* who has shone in
our hearts *to give* the brightness of the
knowledge of the glory of God in the face of
Jesus Christ.
7 But we have this treasure in earthen vessels, so that the surpassing greatness of the
power may be of God and not from ourselves.
8 In every *way we are* pressed down, but not
hemmed in – in doubt, but not without hope
9 persecuted, but not forsaken – thrown
down, but not destroyed.
10 *We are* always bearing about in our body
the dying of the Lord Jesus, so that the life
of the Lord Jesus may be revealed in our
body, too.
11 For we who live are always being delivered
to death for Jesus' sake, so that the life of
Jesus may be revealed in our dying flesh, too.
12 So death indeed works in us, and life in
you.
13 But we have the same spirit of faith, as it
has been written, "I believed, so I spoke."
We also believe, so we also speak,
14 knowing that He who raised up the
Lord Jesus will raise us up through Jesus also
and will present us with you.
15 For all things are for your sake, in order
that the abounding grace may excel through
the thanksgiving of the greatest number, to
the glory of God.

16 For this reason we do not faint. But even
if our outward man is decaying, yet the
inward man is being renewed day by day.
17 For the lightness of our affliction (which

ἡμῶν καθ᾽.ὑπερβολὴν.εἰς.ὑπερβολὴν αἰώνιον βάρος δόξης
[1]our [4]excessively [5]surpassing [3]an eternal weight of glory
κατεργάζεται ἡμῖν, 18 μὴ σκοπούντων ἡμῶν τὰ βλεπό-
works out for us; [2]not [3]considering [1]we the things seen,
μενα, ἀλλὰ τὰ μὴ βλεπόμενα· τὰ.γὰρ βλεπόμενα
but the things not seen; for the things seen [are]
πρόσκαιρα· τὰ.δὲ μὴ βλεπόμενα αἰώνια. 5 οἴδαμεν.γὰρ
temporary, but the things not seen eternal. For we know
ὅτι ἐὰν ἡ ἐπίγειος ἡμῶν οἰκία τοῦ σκήνους καταλυθῇ, οἰκο-
that if [2]earthly [1]our house of the tabernacle be destroyed, a build-
δομὴν ἐκ θεοῦ ἔχομεν, οἰκίαν ἀχειροποίητον, αἰώνιον ἐν τοῖς
ing from God we have, a house not made with hands, eternal in the
οὐρανοῖς. 2 καὶ.γὰρ ἐν τούτῳ στενάζομεν, τὸ.οἰκητήριον.ἡμῶν
heavens. For indeed in this we groan, our dwelling
τὸ ἐξ οὐρανοῦ ἐπενδύσασθαι ἐπιποθοῦντες· 3 [q]εἴγε"
which [is] from heaven [2]to [3]be [4]clothed [5]with [1]longing; if indeed
καὶ ἐνδυσάμενοι, οὐ γυμνοὶ εὑρεθησόμεθα. 4 καὶ.γὰρ οἱ
also being clothed, not naked we shall be found. For indeed [2]who
ὄντες ἐν τῷ σκήνει στενάζομεν βαρούμενοι· [r]ἐπειδὴ" οὐ
[3]are [4]in [5]the [6]tabernacle [1]we groan being burdened; since [3]not
θέλομεν ἐκδύσασθαι, [s]ἀλλ᾽" ἐπενδύσασθαι, ἵνα καταποθῇ
[1]we [2]do wish to be unclothed, but to be clothed upon, that may be swallowed up
τὸ θνητὸν ὑπὸ τῆς ζωῆς. 5 ὁ.δὲ κατεργασάμενος ἡμᾶς εἰς
the mortal by life. Now he who wrought out us for
αὐτὸ.τοῦτο θεός, ὁ [t]καὶ" δοὺς ἡμῖν τὸν [v]ἀρραβῶνα" τοῦ
this same thing [is] God, who also gave to us the earnest of the
πνεύματος. 6 Θαῤῥοῦντες οὖν πάντοτε, καὶ εἰδότες ὅτι
Spirit. Being [2]confident [3]therefore [1]always, and knowing that
ἐνδημοῦντες ἐν τῷ σώματι ἐκδημοῦμεν ἀπὸ τοῦ κυρίου·
being at home in the body we are from home away from the Lord,
7 διὰ.πίστεως.γὰρ περιπατοῦμεν, οὐ διὰ εἴδους· 8 θαῤῥοῦμεν δέ,
(for by faith we walk, not by sight;) we are confident,
καὶ εὐδοκοῦμεν μᾶλλον ἐκδημῆσαι ἐκ τοῦ σώματος καὶ
and are pleased rather to be from home out of the body and
ἐνδημῆσαι πρὸς τὸν κύριον. 9 Διὸ καὶ φιλοτιμούμεθα,
to be at home with the Lord. Wherefore also we are ambitious,
εἴτε ἐνδημοῦντες εἴτε ἐκδημοῦντες, εὐάρεστοι αὐτῷ εἶναι.
whether being at home or being from home, well-pleasing to him to be.
10 τοὺς.γὰρ.πάντας ἡμᾶς φανερωθῆναι δεῖ ἔμπροσθεν τοῦ
For [2]all [1]we [4]be [5]manifested [3]must before the
βήματος τοῦ χριστοῦ, ἵνα κομίσηται ἕκαστος τὰ
judgment seat of the Christ, that [2]may [3]receive [1]each the things [done]
διὰ τοῦ σώματος, πρὸς ἃ ἔπραξεν, εἴτε ἀγαθὸν εἴτε
in the body, according to what he did, whether good or
[w]κακόν." 11 Εἰδότες οὖν τὸν φόβον τοῦ κυρίου, ἀνθρώπους
evil. Knowing therefore the terror of the Lord, [3]men
πείθομεν, θεῷ.δὲ πεφανερώμεθα· ἐλπίζω.δὲ καὶ ἐν ταῖς
[1]we [2]persuade, but to God we have been manifested, and I hope also in
συνειδήσεσιν.ὑμῶν πεφανερῶσθαι. 12 οὐ.[x]γὰρ" πάλιν ἑαυτοὺς
your consciences to have been manifested. For not again ourselves
συνιστάνομεν ὑμῖν, ἀλλὰ ἀφορμὴν διδόντες ὑμῖν καυχήματος
do we commend to you, but occasion are giving to you of boasting
ὑπὲρ ἡμῶν, ἵνα ἔχητε πρὸς τοὺς ἐν προσώπῳ
in behalf of us, that ye may have [such] towards those [2]in [3]appearance
καυχωμένους καὶ [y]οὐ" καρδίᾳ. 13 εἴτε.γὰρ ἐξέστημεν,
[1]boasting and not in heart. For whether we were beside ourselves,
θεῷ· εἴτε σωφρονοῦμεν, ὑμῖν. 14 ἡ.γὰρ ἀγάπη
[it was] to God; or are sober-minded [it is] for you. For the love
τοῦ χριστοῦ συνέχει ἡμᾶς, κρίναντας τοῦτο, ὅτι [z]εἰ" εἷς ὑπὲρ
of the Christ constrains us, having judged this, that if one [2]for
πάντων ἀπέθανεν, ἄρα οἱ πάντες ἀπέθανον· 15 καὶ ὑπὲρ
[3]all [1]died, then all died; and for
πάντων ἀπέθανεν, ἵνα οἱ ζῶντες μηκέτι ἑαυτοῖς ζῶ-
all he died, that they who live no longer to themselves should
σιν, ἀλλὰ τῷ ὑπὲρ αὐτῶν ἀποθανόντι καὶ ἐγερθέντι.
live, but to him who for them died and was raised again.
16 ὥστε ἡμεῖς ἀπὸ τοῦ.νῦν οὐδένα οἴδαμεν κατὰ σάρκα·
So that we from now no one know according to flesh;
εἰ.[a]δὲ" καὶ ἐγνώκαμεν κατὰ σάρκα χριστόν, ἀλλὰ νῦν
but if even we have known according to flesh Christ, yet now
οὐκέτι γινώσκομεν 17 ὥστε εἴ τις ἐν χριστῷ,
no longer we know [him]. So that if anyone [be] in Christ [there is]
καινὴ κτίσις· τὰ ἀρχαῖα παρῆλθεν, ἰδοὺ γέγονεν καινὰ
a new creation: the old things passed away; lo, have become new
[b]τὰ.πάντα." 18 τὰ.δὲ.πάντα ἐκ τοῦ θεοῦ, τοῦ καταλλάξαν-
all things: and all things [are] of God, who reconciled
τος ἡμᾶς ἑαυτῷ διὰ [c]Ἰησοῦ" χριστοῦ, καὶ δόντος ἡμῖν τὴν
us to himself by Jesus Christ, and gave to us the
διακονίαν τῆς καταλλαγῆς· 19 ὡς ὅτι θεὸς ἦν ἐν χριστῷ
service of reconciliation: how that God was in Christ [the]
κόσμον καταλλάσσων ἑαυτῷ, μὴ λογιζόμενος αὐτοῖς τὰ
world reconciling to himself, not reckoning to them

is but for a moment) is working out for us a
far more excellent eternal weight of glory.
18 We do not look at the things which are
seen, but at the things which are not seen –
for the things which are seen are not lasting,
but the things which are not seen are
everlasting.

CHAPTER 5

1 For we know that if our earthly house of
this tabernacle is taken down, we have a
building from God, a house not made with
hands, eternal in Heaven.
2 For indeed in this we groan, for we long
to be clothed with our house which is from
Heaven.
3 For if indeed we shall be found clothed,
we shall not be naked.
4 For indeed we who are in the tabernacle
groan, being burdened – since we do not
wish to be unclothed, but to be clothed – so
that the mortal may be swallowed up by life.
5 Now He who has made us fit for this same
thing is God, who also has given to us the
first-fruit of the Spirit.
6 So, being always fully assured, knowing
that while we are at home in the body, we
are absent from the Lord,
7 (for we walk by faith, not by sight),
8 we are fully assured and are pleased rather
to be away from home, out of the body, and
to be at home with the Lord.
9 Because of this, too, we are striving to be
pleasing to Him, whether we are at home or
away from home.
10 For we all must appear before the judgment seat of Christ – so that each may
receive the things done in the body, according to what he did, whether good or evil.
11 Knowing therefore the terror of the
Lord, we persuade men. But to God we have
been known, and I hope we have been
known in your conscience also
12 For we do not again recommend ourselves to you, but we are giving you an
occasion to glory for our sake – so that you
may have something *to answer* to those *who*
glory in appearance and not in heart.
13 For if we were beside ourselves, *it was* to
God – or are of sound mind, *it is* for you.
14 For the love of Christ presses us on every
side. For we have judged this, that if one
died for all, then all died.
15 And He died for all, so that they who
live should no longer live to themselves, but
to Him who died for them and was raised.
16 So that from now on, we know no one
according to the flesh, but even if we have
known Christ according to the flesh, yet
now we no longer know *Him.*
17 So that if anyone is in Christ, *he is* a new
creation – the old things have passed away.
Behold! All things have become new!
18 And all things are of God, who reconciled us to Himself by Jesus Christ. And He
gave us the ministry of reconciliation –
19 that is, that God was in Christ
reconciling the world to Himself, not count-

παραπτώματα.αὐτῶν, καὶ θέμενος ἐν ἡμῖν τὸν λόγον τῆς
their offences, and having put in us the word
καταλλαγῆς. 20 ὑπὲρ χριστοῦ οὖν πρεσβεύομεν, ὡς
of reconciliation. For Christ therefore we are ambassadors, as it were
τοῦ θεοῦ παρακαλοῦντος δι' ἡμῶν· δεόμεθα ὑπὲρ χριστοῦ,
God exhorting by us, we beseech for Christ,
καταλλάγητε τῷ θεῷ· 21 τὸν.dγὰρ" μὴ.γνόντα ἁμαρτίαν
Be reconciled to God. For him who knew not sin
ὑπὲρ ἡμῶν ἁμαρτίαν ἐποίησεν, ἵνα ἡμεῖς eγινώμεθα" δι-
4for 5us 3sin 1he 2made, that we might become right-
καιοσύνη θεοῦ ἐν αὐτῷ.
eousness of God in him.

6 Συνεργοῦντες.δὲ καὶ παρακαλοῦμεν μὴ εἰς κενὸν τὴν
But working together 2also 1we exhort 3not 4in 5vain 6the
χάριν τοῦ θεοῦ δέξασθαι ὑμᾶς· 2 λέγει.γάρ, Καιρῷ δεκτῷ
8grace 7of 9God 9to 10receive 1you: (for he says, In a time accepted
ἐπήκουσά σου, καὶ ἐν ἡμέρᾳ σωτηρίας ἐβοήθησά σοι· ἰδοὺ νῦν
I listened to thee, and in a day of salvation I helped thee: lo, now
καιρὸς εὐπρόσδεκτος, ἰδοὺ νῦν ἡμέρα σωτηρίας· 3 μηδεμίαν
[the] time well-accepted; behold, now [the] day of salvation:) not one
ἐν μηδενὶ διδόντες προσκοπήν, ἵνα μὴ.μωμηθῇ ἡ διακονία·
3in 4anything 2giving 1offence, that be not blamed the service;
(lit nothing)
4 ἀλλ' ἐν παντὶ fσυνιστῶντες" ἑαυτοὺς ὡς θεοῦ διάκονοι,
but in everything commending ourselves as God's servants,
ἐν ὑπομονῇ πολλῇ, ἐν θλίψεσιν, ἐν ἀνάγκαις, ἐν στενο-
in 2endurance 1much, in tribulations, in necessities, in straits,
χωρίαις, 5 ἐν πληγαῖς, ἐν φυλακαῖς, ἐν ἀκαταστασίαις, ἐν
in stripes, in imprisonments, in commotions, in
κόποις, ἐν ἀγρυπνίαις, ἐν νηστείαις, 6 ἐν ἁγνότητι, ἐν γνώσει,
labours, in watchings, in fastings, in pureness, in knowledge,
ἐν μακροθυμίᾳ, ἐν χρηστότητι, ἐν πνεύματι ἁγίῳ, ἐν ἀγάπῃ
in long-suffering, in kindness, in [the] 2Spirit 1Holy, in love
ἀνυποκρίτῳ, 7 ἐν λόγῳ ἀληθείας, ἐν δυνάμει θεοῦ,
unfeigned, in [the] word of truth, in [the] power of God;
διὰ τῶν ὅπλων τῆς δικαιοσύνης τῶν δεξιῶν καὶ ἀριστερῶν,
through the arms of righteousness on the right hand and left,
8 διὰ δόξης καὶ ἀτιμίας, διὰ δυσφημίας καὶ εὐφημίας· ὡς
through glory and dishonour, through evil report and good report: as
πλάνοι, καὶ ἀληθεῖς· 9 ὡς ἀγνοούμενοι, καὶ ἐπιγινωσκόμενοι·
deceivers, and true; as being unknown, and well-known;
ὡς ἀποθνήσκοντες, καὶ ἰδοὺ ζῶμεν· ὡς παιδευόμενοι, καὶ
as dying, and lo we live; as disciplined, and
μὴ θανατούμενοι· 10 ὡς λυπούμενοι, ἀεὶ.δὲ χαίροντες· ὡς
not put to death; as sorrowful, but always rejoicing; as
πτωχοί, πολλοὺς.δὲ πλουτίζοντες· ὡς μηδὲν ἔχοντες, καὶ
poor, but many enriching; as nothing having, and
πάντα κατέχοντες.
all things possessing.

11 Τὸ.στόμα.ἡμῶν ἀνέῳγεν πρὸς ὑμᾶς, Κορίνθιοι, ἡ
Our mouth has been opened to you, Corinthians,
καρδία.ἡμῶν πεπλάτυνται· 12 οὐ.στενοχωρεῖσθε ἐν ἡμῖν,
our heart has been expanded. Ye are not straitened in us,
στενοχωρεῖσθε.δὲ ἐν τοῖς.σπλάγχνοις.ὑμῶν. 13 τὴν.δὲ αὐτὴν
but ye are straitened in your bowels; but the same
ἀντιμισθίαν, ὡς τέκνοις λέγω, πλατύνθητε καὶ ὑμεῖς.
[as] recompense, (as to children I speak,) be expanded also ye.

14 Μὴ.γίνεσθε ἑτεροζυγοῦντες ἀπίστοις· τίς.γὰρ με-
Be not diversely yoked with unbelievers; for what par-
τοχὴ δικαιοσύνῃ καὶ ἀνομίᾳ; hτίς.δὲ" κοινωνία φωτὶ
ticipation [has] righteousness and lawlessness? and what fellowship light
πρὸς σκότος; 15 τίς.δὲ συμφώνησις iχριστῷ" πρὸς kΒελίαρ";
with darkness? and what concord Christ with Beliar,
ἢ τίς μερὶς πιστῷ μετὰ ἀπίστου; 16 τίς.δὲ lσυγκατά-
or what part to a believer with an unbeliever? and what agree-
θεσις" ναῷ θεοῦ μετὰ εἰδώλων; mὑμεῖς" γὰρ ναὸς θεοῦ
ment a temple of God with idols? 2ye 1for a temple of 3God
nἐστε" ζῶντος, καθὼς εἶπεν ὁ θεός, "Οτι ἐνοικήσω ἐν
4are [the] 2living, according as 2said 1God, I will dwell among
αὐτοῖς, καὶ oἐμπεριπατήσω" καὶ ἔσομαι αὐτῶν θεός, καὶ
them, and walk among [them]; and I will be their God, and
αὐτοὶ ἔσονταί pμοι" λαός. 17 διὸ qἐξέλθετε" ἐκ μέσου
they shall be to me a people. Wherefore come out from the midst
αὐτῶν καὶ ἀφορίσθητε, λέγει κύριος, καὶ ἀκαθάρτου
of them and be separated, says [the] Lord, and [the] unclean
μὴ.ἅπτεσθε· κἀγὼ εἰσδέξομαι ὑμᾶς, 18 καὶ ἔσομαι ὑμῖν εἰς
touch not. and I will receive you; and I will be to you for
πατέρα, καὶ ὑμεῖς ἔσεσθέ μοι εἰς υἱοὺς καὶ θυγατέρας, λέγει
a father, and ye shall be to me for sons and daughters, says
κύριος παντοκράτωρ. 7 Ταύτας οὖν ἔχοντες τὰς
[the] Lord Almighty. 3These 2therefore 1having
ἐπαγγελίας, ἀγαπητοί, καθαρίσωμεν ἑαυτοὺς ἀπὸ παντὸς
promises, beloved, we should cleanse ourselves from every

ing their trespasses against them. And *He* has
put in us the word of reconciliation.
20 So we are ambassadors for Christ, as
though God were calling through us – we
beseech for Christ's sake, be reconciled to
God.
21 For He made Him who knew no sin *to*
be sin for us, so that we might become the
righteousness of God in Him.

6 1 But working together, we also call on you
not to receive the grace of God in vain.
2 (For He says, "In an accepted time I have
heard you, and in a day of salvation I have
helped you." – Behold! Now is the accepted
time. Behold! Now is the day of salvation).
3 Not giving any occasion of stumbling in
anything, so that the ministry may not be
blamed.
4 but in everything *we are* setting ourselves
out as God's servants – in much patience, in
troubles, in emergencies, in difficulties,
5 in stripes, in imprisonments, in riots, in
labors, in watchings, in fastings,
6 in pureness, in knowledge, in long-suffering, in kindness, in the Holy Spirit, in true
love,
7 in the word of truth, in the power of God,
through the weapons of righteousness on the
right hand and the left,
8 through glory and dishonor, through evil
report and good report – as deceivers, and
yet true –
9 as unknown, and yet well-known – as
dying, and yet, look, we live! – as flogged,
and yet not put to death –
10 as sorrowful, but yet always rejoicing –
as poor, but yet enriching many – as having
nothing, and yet possessing all things.
11 Our mouth is opened to you, O Corinthians, our heart has been made larger.
12 You are not made narrow in us, but you
are cramped in your own bowels.
13 But for the same reward (I speak as to
children) be also made larger.
14 Do not be unequally yoked with unbelievers. For what partnership *does* righteousness *have* with lawlessness? And what
fellowship *does* light *have* with darkness?
15 And what agreement *does* Christ have
with Be-li-al? Or what part *does* a believer
have with an unbeliever?
16 And what agreement *does* a sanctuary of
God *have* with idols? For you are a sanctuary of the living God, even as God said, "I
will live in them and walk with them. And I
will be their God and they shall be My
people."
17 So come out from among them and be
separate, says the Lord. Do not touch the
unclean and I will receive you.
18 And I will be a Father to you, and you
shall be sons and daughters to Me, says the
Lord Almighty.

7 1 Then, loved ones, having these promises,
let us make ourselves clean from every

μολυσμοῦ σαρκὸς καὶ πνεύματος, ἐπιτελοῦντες ἁγιωσύνην ἐν
defilement of flesh and spirit, perfecting holiness in
φόβῳ θεοῦ.
fear of God.
2 Χωρήσατε ἡμᾶς· οὐδένα ἠδικήσαμεν, οὐδένα ἐφθείραμεν,
Receive us: no one did we wrong, no one did we corrupt,
οὐδένα ἐπλεονεκτήσαμεν. 3 [r]οὐ πρὸς κατάκρισιν‖ λέγω·
no one did we overreach. Not for condemnation I speak,
προείρηκα.γὰρ ὅτι ἐν ταῖς.καρδίαις.ἡμῶν ἐστε εἰς τὸ συν-
for I have before said that in our hearts ye are, for to die
αποθανεῖν καὶ [s]συζῆν.‖ 4 πολλή μοι παῤῥησία πρὸς
together and to live together. Great [is] to me boldness towards
ὑμᾶς, πολλή μοι καύχησις ὑπὲρ ὑμῶν· πεπλήρωμαι
you, great to me boasting in respect of you; I have been filled
τῇ παρακλήσει, ὑπερπερισσεύομαι τῇ χαρᾷ ἐπὶ πάσῃ τῇ
with encouragement; I overabound with joy at all
θλίψει.ἡμῶν. 5 Καὶ.γὰρ ἐλθόντων ἡμῶν εἰς Μακεδονίαν,
our tribulation. For indeed, [2]having [3]come [1]we into Macedonia,
οὐδεμίαν [t]ἔσχηκεν‖ ἄνεσιν ἡ.σὰρξ.ἡμῶν, ἀλλ' ἐν παντὶ
[4]not [5]any [3]had [6]ease [1]our [2]flesh, but in every [way]
θλιβόμενοι· ἔξωθεν μάχαι, ἔσωθεν φόβοι. 6 ἀλλ' ὁ
being oppressed; without contentions, within fears. But he who
παρακαλῶν τοὺς ταπεινοὺς παρεκάλεσεν ἡμᾶς ὁ θεὸς ἐν τῇ
encourages those brought low encouraged us— God—by the
παρουσίᾳ Τίτου· 7 οὐ.μόνον.δὲ ἐν τῇ παρουσίᾳ.αὐτοῦ, ἀλλὰ
coming of Titus; and not only by his coming, but
καὶ ἐν τῇ παρακλήσει ᾗ παρεκλήθη ἐφ' ὑμῖν,
also by the encouragement with which he was encouraged as to you;
ἀναγγέλλων ἡμῖν τὴν.ὑμῶν.ἐπιπόθησιν, τὸν.ὑμῶν.ὀδυρμόν,
relating to us your longing, your mourning,
τὸν.ὑμῶν.ζῆλον ὑπὲρ ἐμοῦ, ὥστε.με μᾶλλον χαρῆναι. 8 Ὅτι
your zeal for me; so as for me the more to be rejoiced. For
εἰ καὶ ἐλύπησα ὑμᾶς ἐν τῇ ἐπιστολῇ, οὐ.μεταμέλομαι, εἰ καὶ
if also I grieved you in the epistle, I do not regret [it], if even
μετεμελόμην· βλέπω.[v]γὰρ‖ ὅτι ἡ.ἐπιστολὴ ἐκείνη εἰ καὶ πρὸς
I did regret; for I see that that epistle, if even for
ὥραν ἐλύπησεν ὑμᾶς. 9 νῦν χαίρω, οὐχ ὅτι ἐλυπήθητε, ἀλλ'
an hour, grieved you. Now I rejoice, not that ye were grieved, but
ὅτι ἐλυπήθητε εἰς μετάνοιαν· ἐλυπήθητε.γὰρ κατὰ θεόν,
that ye were grieved to repentance; for ye were grieved according to God,
ἵνα ἐν μηδενὶ ζημιωθῆτε ἐξ ἡμῶν. 10 ἡ.γὰρ κατὰ
that in nothing ye might suffer loss by us. For the [2]according [3]to
θεὸν λύπη μετάνοιαν εἰς σωτηρίαν ἀμεταμέλητον [w]κατερ-
[4]God [1]grief repentance to salvation not to be regretted works
γάζεται‖ ἡ.δὲ τοῦ κόσμου λύπη θάνατον κατεργάζεται.
out; but the [2]of [3]the [4]world [1]grief death works out.
11 ἰδοὺ.γὰρ αὐτὸ.τοῦτο τὸ κατὰ θεὸν λυπηθῆναι [x]ὑμᾶς,‖
For lo, this same thing, according to God [2]to [3]have [4]been [5]grieved [1]you,
πόσην [y]κατειργάσατο‖ [z]ὑμῖν σπουδήν, ἀλλὰ ἀπολογίαν,
how much [2]it [3]worked [4]out [5]in [6]you [1]diligence, but [what] defence,
ἀλλὰ ἀγανάκτησιν, ἀλλὰ φόβον, ἀλλὰ ἐπιπόθησιν, ἀλλὰ
but indignation, but fear, but longing, but
ζῆλον, [a]ἀλλ'‖ ἐκδίκησιν; ἐν παντὶ συνεστήσατε ἑαυτοὺς
zeal, but vengeance! in every [way] ye proved yourselves
ἁγνοὺς εἶναι [b]ἐν‖ τῷ πράγματι. 12 ἄρα εἰ καὶ ἔγραψα ὑμῖν,
[3]pure [1]to [2]be in the matter. Then if also I wrote to you,
οὐχ [c]εἵνεκεν‖ τοῦ ἀδικήσαντος, οὐδὲ [c]εἵνεκεν‖ τοῦ
not for the sake of him who did wrong, nor for the sake of him who
ἀδικηθέντος· [d]ἀλλ'‖ [c]εἵνεκεν‖ τοῦ φανερωθῆναι τὴν σπουδὴν
suffered wrong, but for the sake of [7]being [8]manifested [2]diligence
[e]ὑμῶν‖ τὴν ὑπὲρ [f]ἡμῶν‖ πρὸς ὑμᾶς ἐνώπιον τοῦ θεοῦ.
[1]your [3]which [[4]is] [5]for [6]us to you before God.
13 Διὰ τοῦτο παρακεκλήμεθα ἐπὶ [g]τῇ παρακλήσει
On account of this we have been encouraged in [2]encouragement
[h]ὑμῶν·‖ περισσοτέρως.δὲ‖ μᾶλλον ἐχάρημεν ἐπὶ τῇ χαρᾷ
[1]your, and the more abundantly rather we rejoiced at the joy
Τίτου, ὅτι ἀναπέπαυται τὸ.πνεῦμα.αὐτοῦ ἀπὸ πάντων
of Titus, because has been refreshed his spirit by all
ὑμῶν· 14 ὅτι εἴ τι αὐτῷ ὑπὲρ ὑμῶν κεκαύχημαι, οὐ
of you. Because if anything to him about you I have boasted, [2]not
κατῃσχύνθην· ἀλλ' ὡς πάντα ἐν ἀληθείᾳ ἐλαλήσαμεν
[1]I [3]was put to shame; but as all things in truth we spoke
ὑμῖν, οὕτως καὶ ἡ καύχησις [k]ἡμῶν‖ [l]ἡ‖ ἐπὶ Τίτου
to you, so also the boasting of us which [was] to Titus
ἀλήθεια ἐγενήθη· 15 καὶ τὰ.σπλάγχνα.αὐτοῦ περισσοτέρως
truth became; and his bowels more abundantly
εἰς ὑμᾶς ἐστιν, ἀναμιμνησκομένου τὴν πάντων ὑμῶν
towards you are, remembering the [2]of [3]all [4]of [5]you
ὑπακοήν, ὡς μετὰ φόβου καὶ τρόμου ἐδέξασθε αὐτόν.
[1]obedience, how with fear and trembling ye received him.
16 χαίρω [m]ὅτι ἐν παντὶ θαῤῥῶ ἐν ὑμῖν.
I rejoice that in everything I am confident in you.

defilement of flesh and spirit, perfecting holiness in the fear of God.
2 Make room for us – we have done you no wrong. We have not corrupted anyone. We have not taken advantage of anyone.
3 I do not speak to condemn you, for I have said before that you are in our hearts, for us to live together and to die together.
4 Great is my freedom of speech to you. Great is my glorying on your behalf. I am filled with comfort. I am overflowing with joy at our tribulation.
5 For, indeed, when we had come into Mac-e-do-ni-a, our flesh had no rest. But we were troubled on every side, with fightings on the outside and fears on the inside.
6 But the God who comforts those who are brought low, comforted us by the coming of Titus.
7 And not only by his coming, but also by the comfort with which he was comforted in regard to you. *For he* told us of your longing, your mourning and your eagerness for me, so that I rejoiced all the more.
8 Because even if I made you sorry in the letter, I do not repent (if even I did repent, for I see that the letter did make you sorry, even if for only an hour).
9 Now I rejoice, not that you were made sorry, but that you were made sorry to the point of repentance. For you were made sorry in God's way, so that you might not suffer loss by us.
10 For godly sorrow works repentance to salvation, not to be regretted. But the sorrow of the world works death.
11 For, look at this same thing (your being made sorry in God's way): What carefulness it worked out in you! *What* clearing of yourselves! *What* anger! *What* fear! *What* desire! *What eagerness!* Yes, what punishment! In every way you have proved yourselves to be clear in the matter.
12 So then even if I wrote to you, it was not for the sake of him who did wrong (nor for the sake of him who suffered wrong), but so that our care for you in the sight of God might appear to you.
13 For this reason we have been much comforted in your comfort. And much more fully have we rejoiced over the joy of Titus, because his spirit has been refreshed by all of you.
14 For if I have boasted anything to him about you, I was not put to shame. But as we spoke all things in truth to you, so also our boasting before Titus turned out to be truth.
15 And his tender feelings towards you are far greater, remembering the obedience of you – how you received him with fear and trembling.
16 So I am joyful that in everything I am fully assured in you.

8 Γνωρίζομεν.δὲ ὑμῖν, ἀδελφοί, τὴν χάριν τοῦ θεοῦ τὴν
But we make known to you, brethren, the grace of God which
δεδομένην ἐν ταῖς ἐκκλησίαις τῆς Μακεδονίας· 2 ὅτι ἐν πολλῇ
has been given in the assemblies of Macedonia; that in much
δοκιμῇ θλίψεως ἡ περισσεία τῆς.χαρᾶς.αὐτῶν καὶ ἡ κατὰ
proof of tribulation the abundance of their joy and
βάθους πτωχεία αὐτῶν ἐπερίσσευσεν εἰς [n]τὸν πλοῦτον‖ τῆς
[2]deep [3]poverty [1]their abounded to the riches
ἁπλότητος.αὐτῶν· 3 ὅτι κατὰ δύναμιν, μαρτυρῶ,
of their liberality. For according to [their] power, I bear witness,
καὶ [o]ὑπὲρ‖ δύναμιν αὐθαίρετοι, 4 μετὰ πολ-
and beyond [their] power [they were] willing of themselves, with much
λῆς παρακλήσεως δεόμενοι ἡμῶν τὴν χάριν καὶ τὴν κοινωνίαν
entreaty beseeching of us, [5]the [6]grace [7]and [8]the [9]fellowship
τῆς διακονίας τῆς εἰς τοὺς ἁγίους [p]δέξασθαι.ἡμᾶς·‖
[10]of [11]the [12]service [13]which [14]was [15]for [16]the [17]saints [1]for [2]us [3]to [4]receive.
5 καὶ οὐ καθὼς ἠλπίσαμεν, [q]ἀλλ'‖ ἑαυτοὺς ἔδωκαν πρῶ-
And not [only] according as we hoped, but themselves they gave first
τον τῷ κυρίῳ, καὶ ἡμῖν διὰ θελήματος θεοῦ 6 εἰς.τὸ παρα-
to the Lord, and to us by [the] will of God. So that [2]ex-
καλέσαι ἡμᾶς Τίτον, ἵνα καθὼς προενήρξατο, οὕτως καὶ
horted [1]we Titus, that according as he before began, so also
ἐπιτελέσῃ εἰς ὑμᾶς καὶ τὴν.χάριν.ταύτην. 7 Ἀλλ' ὥσπερ
he might complete with you also this grace. But even as
ἐν παντὶ περισσεύετε, πίστει, καὶ λόγῳ, καὶ γνώσει, καὶ
in every [way] ye abound, in faith, and word, and knowledge, and
πάσῃ σπουδῇ, καὶ τῇ ἐξ ὑμῶν ἐν ἡμῖν ἀγάπῃ, ἵνα καὶ ἐν
all diligence, and in the [2]from [3]you [4]to [5]us [1]love, that also in
ταύτῃ τῇ χάριτι περισσεύητε· 8 οὐ κατ' ἐπιταγὴν λέγω,
this grace ye should abound. Not according to a command do I speak,
ἀλλὰ διὰ τῆς ἑτέρων σπουδῆς καὶ τὸ τῆς [r]ὑμετέρας‖ ἀγάπης
but through the [2]of [3]others [1]diligence and the [2]of [3]your [4]love
γνήσιον δοκιμάζων· 9 γινώσκετε.γὰρ τὴν χάριν τοῦ κυρίου
[1]genuineness proving. For ye know the grace of [2]Lord
ἡμῶν Ἰησοῦ χριστοῦ, ὅτι δι' ὑμᾶς ἐπτώχευσεν
[1]our Jesus Christ, that [3]for [4]the [5]sake [6]of [7]you [8]he [9]became [10]poor
πλούσιος ὤν, ἵνα ὑμεῖς τῇ.ἐκείνου.πτωχείᾳ πλουτήσητε.
[2]rich [1]being; that ye by his poverty might be enriched.
10 καὶ γνώμην ἐν τούτῳ δίδωμι· τοῦτο.γὰρ ὑμῖν συμφέρει,
And a judgment in this I give, for this for you is profitable,
οἵτινες οὐ μόνον τὸ ποιῆσαι, ἀλλὰ καὶ τὸ θέλειν προενήρ-
who not only the doing, but also the being willing began
ξασθε ἀπὸ.πέρυσι· 11 νυνὶ.δὲ καὶ τὸ ποιῆσαι ἐπιτελέσατε,
before a year ago. But now also [2]the [3]doing [1]complete;
ὅπως καθάπερ ἡ προθυμία τοῦ θέλειν, οὕτως καὶ
so that even as [there was] the readiness of the being willing, so also
τὸ ἐπιτελέσαι ἐκ τοῦ ἔχειν. 12 Εἰ.γὰρ ἡ προθυμία πρό-
the completing out of that [ye] have. For if the readiness is pre-
κειται, καθὸ [s]ἐὰν‖ ἔχῃ [t]τις‖ εὐπρόσδεκτος, οὐ καθὸ
sent, according as [2]may [3]have [1]anyone [he is] accepted, not according as
οὐκ.ἔχει. 13 οὐ.γὰρ ἵνα ἄλλοις ἄνεσις, ὑμῖν.[v]δὲ‖
he has not. For [it is] not that to others [there may be] ease, but for you
θλίψις· ἀλλ' ἐξ ἰσότητος, ἐν τῷ νῦν καιρῷ τὸ ὑμῶν περίσ-
pressure, but of equality, in the present time your abun-
σευμα εἰς τὸ.ἐκείνων.ὑστέρημα, 14 ἵνα καὶ τὸ ἐκείνων περίσ-
dance for their deficiency, that also their abun-
σευμα γένηται εἰς τὸ.ὑμῶν.ὑστέρημα· ὅπως γένηται
dance may be for your deficiency, so that there should be
ἰσότης· 15 καθὼς γέγραπται, Ὁ τὸ πολὺ οὐκ
equality. According as it has been written, He that [gathered] much [2]not
ἐπλεόνασεν· καὶ ὁ τὸ ὀλίγον οὐκ.ἠλαττόνησεν.
[1]had over, and he that [gathered] little did not lack.
16 Χάρις.δὲ τῷ θεῷ, τῷ [w]διδόντι‖ τὴν αὐτὴν σπουδὴν ὑπὲρ
But thanks to God, who gives the same diligence for
ὑμῶν ἐν τῇ καρδίᾳ Τίτου· 17 ὅτι τὴν μὲν παράκλησιν ἐ-
you in the heart of Titus. For the [2]indeed [1]exhortation he
δέξατο, σπουδαιότερος.δὲ ὑπάρχων, αὐθαίρετος ἐξῆλθεν
received, but more diligent being, of his own accord he went out
πρὸς ὑμᾶς. 18 συνεπέμψαμεν.δὲ [x]μετ' αὐτοῦ τὸν ἀδελφὸν‖
to you. But we sent with him the brother
οὗ ὁ ἔπαινος ἐν τῷ εὐαγγελίῳ διὰ πασῶν τῶν ἐκ-
of whom the praise [is] in the glad tidings through all the as-
κλησιῶν· 19 οὐ.μόνον.δέ, ἀλλὰ καὶ χειροτονηθεὶς ὑπὸ τῶν
semblies; and not only [so], but also having been chosen by the
ἐκκλησιῶν συνέκδημος.ἡμῶν [y]σὺν‖ τῇ.χάριτι.ταύτῃ τῇ
assemblies [is] our fellow-traveller with this grace, which [is]
διακονουμένῃ ὑφ' ἡμῶν πρὸς τὴν [z]αὐτοῦ‖ τοῦ κυρίου δόξαν
served by us to the [5]himself [2]of [3]the [4]Lord [1]glory
καὶ προθυμίαν [a]ὑμῶν·‖ 20 στελλόμενοι τοῦτο, μή
and [a witness of] [2]readiness [1]your; avoiding this, lest
τις ἡμᾶς μωμήσηται ἐν τῇ.ἁδρότητι.ταύτῃ τῇ διακονου-
anyone us should blame in this abundance which [is] served

CHAPTER 8

1 But we make known to you, brothers, the
grace of God which has been given in the
churches of Mac-e-do-ni-a –
2 that in a great testing-time of trouble, the
overflowing of their joy and their deep
poverty multiplied to the riches of their
generous giving.
3 For I testify that as they were able, and
beyond their ability, *they were* willing –
4 with great desire begging us, for us to
receive the grace and the fellowship of the
ministry which was for the saints.
5 And not as we hoped, but they gave themselves first to the Lord and to us, by the will
of God.
6 So we called on Titus, that even as he
began before, so also he should complete
this grace to you too.
7 But even as you excel in everything – in
faith and speech and knowledge and all
eagerness and in your love to us – in this
grace you should excel also.
8 I do not speak according to a command,
but through the eagerness of others, and
testing of the trueness of your love.
9 For you know the grace of our Lord Jesus
Christ, that being rich, He became poor for
your sake, so that you might be made rich
by His being poor.
10 And I give my judgment in this matter,
for this is good for you, who began before
not only to do, but also to be willing a year
before.
11 But now finish the doing of it so that as
there was a readiness to be willing, so, too, a
finishing *now giving* out if all you own.
12 For if there is a willing mind, *it is*
accepted according to what a man may have
– not according to what he does not have.
13 For *it is* not that *I intend* for others to
be eased and for you *to be* burdened,
14 but of equalness – now your surplus for
their need – also, *then,* their surplus may be
for your need, so that there should be an
equalness.
15 Even as it has been written, "He that
gathered much had nothing left over, and he
that gathered little did not lack anything."
16 But thanks to God, who gives the same
care for you in the heart of Titus.
17 For, indeed, he accepted the exhortation, but being more eager, of his own
accord, he went out to you.
18 And we sent with him the brother whose
praise in the gospel is in all the churches.
19 And not only so, but also he had been
chosen by the churches as our traveling companion with this gift, which is managed by
us to the glory of the Lord Himself, and
your willing mind.
20 *We are* arranging this for fear that
anyone should blame us in this rich collection which is managed by us,

μένῃ ὑφ' ἡμῶν· 21 [b]προνοούμενοι" καλὰ οὐ μόνον ἐνώπιον
by us; providing things right not only before
κυρίου, ἀλλὰ καὶ ἐνώπιον ἀνθρώπων. 22 Συνεπέμψαμεν.δὲ
[the] Lord, but also before men. And we sent with
αὐτοῖς τὸν.ἀδελφὸν.ἡμῶν ὃν ἐδοκιμάσαμεν ἐν πολλοῖς πολ-
them our brother whom we proved in many things often
λάκις σπουδαῖον ὄντα, νυνὶ.δὲ πολὺ σπουδαιότερον πεποι-
diligent to be, and now much more diligent by the [2]con-
θήσει πολλῇ τῇ εἰς ὑμᾶς. 23 εἴτε ὑπὲρ Τίτου,
fidence [1]great which [is] towards you. Whether as regards Titus,
κοινωνὸς ἐμὸς καὶ εἰς ὑμᾶς συνεργός· εἴτε ἀδελφοὶ
[he is] [2]partner [1]my and for you a fellow-worker; or [2]brethren
ἡμῶν, ἀπόστολοι ἐκκλησιῶν, δόξα. χριστοῦ. 24 Τὴν
[1]our, [they are] messengers of assemblies, [2]glory [1]Christ's. The
οὖν ἔνδειξιν τῆς.ἀγάπης.ὑμῶν, καὶ ἡμῶν καυχήσεως ὑπὲρ
[4]therefore [1]proof of your love, and of our boasting about
ὑμῶν, εἰς αὐτοὺς [c]ἐνδείξασθε" [d]καὶ" εἰς πρόσωπον τῶν ἐκκλησιῶν.
you, [3]to [4]them [1]shew [2]ye and in face of the assemblies.

9 Περὶ.μὲν.γὰρ τῆς διακονίας τῆς εἰς τοὺς ἁγίους
For concerning the service which [is] for the saints
περισσόν μοι ἐστὶν τὸ γράφειν ὑμῖν. 2 οἶδα.γὰρ τὴν προθυ-
superfluous for me it is writing to you. For I know [2]readi-
μίαν ὑμῶν ἣν ὑπὲρ ὑμῶν καυχῶμαι Μακεδόσιν, ὅτι
ness [1]your which concerning you I boast of to Macedonians; that
Ἀχαΐα παρεσκεύασται ἀπὸ.πέρυσι· καὶ [e]ὁ" [f]ἐξ" ὑμῶν ζῆλος
Achaia has been prepared a year ago, and the [2]of [3]you [1]zeal
ἠρέθισεν τοὺς πλείονας. 3 ἔπεμψα.δὲ τοὺς ἀδελφούς, ἵνα.μὴ
provoke the greater number. But I sent the brethren, lest
τὸ.καύχημα.ἡμῶν τὸ ὑπὲρ ὑμῶν κενωθῇ ἐν τῷ
our boasting which [is] about you should be made void in
μέρει.τούτῳ· ἵνα καθὼς ἔλεγον, παρεσκευασμένοι ἦτε,
this respect, that according as I said, prepared ye may be;
4 μήπως ἐὰν ἔλθωσιν σὺν ἐμοὶ Μακεδόνες, καὶ εὕρωσιν ὑμᾶς
lest perhaps if should come with me Macedonians, and find you
ἀπαρασκευάστους, καταισχυνθῶμεν ἡμεῖς, ἵνα μὴ.λέγωμεν
unprepared, [2]should [3]be [4]put [5]to [6]shame [1]we, (that we may not say
ὑμεῖς, ἐν τῇ.ὑποστάσει.ταύτῃ [g]τῆς καυχήσεως." 5 ἀναγκαῖον
ye,) in this confidence of boasting. Necessary
οὖν ἡγησάμην παρακαλέσαι τοὺς ἀδελφοὺς ἵνα προέλ-
therefore I esteemed [it] to exhort the brethren that they should
θωσιν [h]εἰς" ὑμᾶς, καὶ προκαταρτίσωσιν τὴν [i]προκατηγ-
go before to you, and should complete beforehand [3]fore-
γελμένην" εὐλογίαν ὑμῶν ταύτην ἑτοίμην εἶναι οὕτως ὡς
announced [4]blessing [2]your [1]this [7]ready [5]to [6]be thus as
εὐλογίαν, [k]καὶ" μὴ [l]ὥσπερ" πλεονεξίαν. 6 Τοῦτο.δέ, ὁ
a blessing, and not as [of] covetousness. But this [I say], he that
σπείρων φειδομένως, φειδομένως καὶ θερίσει· καὶ ὁ σπείρων
sows sparingly, sparingly also shall reap; and he that sows
ἐπ' εὐλογίαις, ἐπ' εὐλογίαις καὶ θερίσει. 7 ἕκαστος καθὼς
on blessings, on blessings also shall reap: each according as
[m]προαιρεῖται" τῇ καρδίᾳ· μὴ ἐκ.λύπης ἢ ἐξ ἀνάγκης· ἱλαρὸν
he purposes in the heart; not grievingly, or of necessity; [2]a [3]cheerful
γὰρ δότην ἀγαπᾷ ὁ θεός. 8 [n]δυνατὸς.δὲ" ὁ θεὸς πᾶσαν χάριν
[1]for giver [2]loves [1]God. For able [is] God every grace
περισσεῦσαι εἰς ὑμᾶς, ἵνα ἐν παντὶ πάντοτε πᾶσαν
to make abound towards you, that in every [way] always all
αὐτάρκειαν ἔχοντες, περισσεύητε εἰς πᾶν ἔργον ἀγαθόν·
sufficiency having, ye may abound to every [2]work [1]good:
9 καθὼς γέγραπται, Ἐσκόρπισεν, ἔδωκεν τοῖς πένησιν·
according as it has been written, He scattered abroad, he gave to the poor,
ἡ.δικαιοσύνη.αὐτοῦ μένει εἰς.τὸν.αἰῶνα. 10 Ὁ.δὲ ἐπιχορηγῶν
his righteousness abides for ever. Now he that supplies
[o]σπέρμα" τῷ σπείροντι καὶ ἄρτον εἰς βρῶσιν [p]χορηγήσαι"
seed to him that sows and bread for eating may he supply
καὶ [q]πληθύναι" τὸν.σπόρον.ὑμῶν, καὶ [r]αὐξήσαι" τὰ [s]γεννή-
and may he multiply your sowing, and may he increase the fruits
ματα" τῆς.δικαιοσύνης.ὑμῶν. 11 ἐν παντὶ πλουτιζόμενοι
of your righteousness: in every [way] being enriched
εἰς πᾶσαν ἁπλότητα, ἥτις κατεργάζεται δι' ἡμῶν εὐχαρισ-
to all liberality, which works out through us thanks-
τίαν [t]τῷ" θεῷ· 12 ὅτι ἡ διακονία τῆς.λειτουργίας.ταύτης
giving to God. Because the service of this ministration
οὐ μόνον ἐστὶν προσαναπληροῦσα τὰ ὑστερήματα τῶν ἁγίων,
not only is completely filling up the deficiencies of the saints,
ἀλλὰ καὶ περισσεύουσα διὰ πολλῶν εὐχαριστιῶν τῷ θεῷ·
but also abounding through many thanksgivings to God;
13 διὰ τῆς δοκιμῆς τῆς.διακονίας.ταύτης δοξάζοντες τὸν
through the proof of this service [they] glorifying
θεὸν ἐπὶ τῇ ὑποταγῇ τῆς.ὁμολογίας.ὑμῶν εἰς τὸ εὐαγγέλιον
God at the subjection, by your confession, to the glad tidings
τοῦ χριστοῦ, καὶ ἁπλότητι τῆς κοινωνίας εἰς αὐτοὺς καὶ
of the Christ, and liberality of the communication towards them and

21 providing all things honest, not only in the sight of the Lord, but also in the sight of men.

22 And we sent our brother with them, whom we often proved to be earnest in many things, and now much more earnest by the great assurance which *I have* toward you.

23 *If anyone* asks about Titus, *he is* my partner and fellow-helper for you – or our brothers, *they are* messengers of the churches, the glory of Christ.

24 So demonstrate to them and before the churches, the proof of your love and of our boasting about you.

CHAPTER 9

1 For as to the ministry which is for the saints, it is not necessary for me to write you
2 – for I know your readiness of mind, of which I boast to the Mac-e-do-ni-ans concerning you, that A-chai-a was ready a year ago. And your eagerness aroused very many.
3 Yet I sent the brothers for fear that our boasting (which is about you) should be in vain in this respect, so that as I said, you may be ready –

4 fearing that perhaps the Mac-e-do-ni-ans should come with me and find you not ready. We (not to say you) would be put to shame in this confident boldness.

5 So I judged it needful to call on the brothers, that they should go in advance to you and collect beforehand your promised gift. The same is to be ready as a blessing, and not as of selfishness.

6 But this *is true*, he that sows very little shall also reap very little. And he who sows with blessings shall also reap with blessings.

7 Each one *give* as he purposes in his heart, not out of sorrow or out of need, for God loves a cheerful giver.

8 For God is able to make every grace increase abundantly to you, so that in every way you *will* always have enough of every kind and may increase in every good work.

9 Even as it has been written, "He has scattered abroad, he has given to the poor, his righteousness remains forever."

10 Now He that supplies seed to the sower and bread for eating, may He supply you and may He multiply your sowing, and may He increase the fruits of your righteousness

11 *so that* in every way *you may* be enriched to every kind of generous giving, which truly works out through us thanksgiving to God.

12 Because the ministry of this service is not only fully supplying the needs of the saints, but also multiplying over and over through many thanksgivings to God.

13 So through the proof of this service, *they are* glorifying God for your freely expressed obedience to the gospel of Christ, and generous giving of the fellowship towards them and towards all.

εἰς πάντας, 14 καὶ αὐτῶν.δεήσει ὑπὲρ ὑμῶν, ἐπιποθούν-
towards all; and in their supplication for you, a longing
των ὑμᾶς διὰ τὴν ὑπερβάλλουσαν χάριν τοῦ θεοῦ ἐφ'
for you, on account of the surpassing grace of God upon
ὑμῖν. 15 χάρις.[v]δὲ‖ τῷ θεῷ ἐπὶ τῇ ἀνεκδιηγήτῳ αὐτοῦ δωρεᾷ.
you. Now thanks [be] to God for [2]indescribable [1]his free gift.
10 Αὐτὸς.δὲ ἐγὼ Παῦλος παρακαλῶ ὑμᾶς διὰ.τῆς [w]πρᾳό-
Now [2]myself [1]I Paul exhort you by the meek-
τητος‖ καὶ ἐπιεικείας τοῦ χριστοῦ, ὃς κατὰ πρόσωπον μὲν
ness and gentleness of the Christ, who as to appearance [am]
ταπεινὸς ἐν ὑμῖν, ἀπὼν.δὲ θαῤῥῶ εἰς ὑμᾶς· 2 δέομαι.δὲ
mean among you, but absent am bold towards you; but I beseech
τὸ μὴ παρὼν θαῤῥῆσαι τῇ πεποιθήσει ᾗ
that [5]not [1]being [2]present [3]I [4]should be bold with the confidence with which
λογίζομαι τολμῆσαι ἐπί τινας τοὺς λογιζομένους ἡμᾶς ὡς
I reckon to be daring towards some who reckon of us as
κατὰ σάρκα περιπατοῦντας. 3 ἐν.σαρκὶ.γὰρ περιπατοῦντες,
[2]according [3]to [4]flesh [1]walking. For in flesh walking,
οὐ κατὰ σάρκα στρατευόμεθα· 4 τὰ.γὰρ ὅπλα τῆς [x]στρα-
not according to flesh do we war. For the arms of [2]war-
τείας‖.ἡμῶν οὐ σαρκικά, ἀλλὰ δυνατὰ τῷ θεῷ πρὸς
fare [1]our [are] not fleshly, but powerful through God to [the]
καθαίρεσιν ὀχυρωμάτων· 5 λογισμοὺς καθαιροῦντες καὶ πᾶν
overthrow of strong-holds; [2]reasonings [1]overthrowing and every
ὕψωμα ἐπαιρόμενον κατὰ τῆς γνώσεως τοῦ θεοῦ, καὶ αἰχμα-
high thing lifting itself up against the knowledge of God, and leading
λωτίζοντες πᾶν νόημα εἰς τὴν ὑπακοὴν τοῦ χριστοῦ, 6 καὶ
captive every thought into the obedience of the Christ; and
ἐν ἑτοίμῳ ἔχοντες ἐκδικῆσαι πᾶσαν παρακοήν, ὅταν πλη-
[2]in [3]readiness [1]having to avenge all disobedience, when may have
ρωθῇ ὑμῶν ἡ ὑπακοή. 7 Τὰ κατὰ πρόσωπον
been fulfilled your obedience. The things according to appearance
βλέπετε; εἴ τις πέποιθεν ἑαυτῷ χριστοῦ εἶναι, τοῦτο
do ye look at? If anyone is persuaded in himself of Christ to be, this
λογιζέσθω πάλιν [y]ἀφ'‖.ἑαυτοῦ, ὅτι καθὼς αὐτὸς χριστοῦ,
let him reckon again of himself, that according as he [is] of Christ,
οὕτως καὶ ἡμεῖς [z]χριστοῦ.‖ 8 ἐάν.[a]τε‖.γὰρ [b]καὶ‖ περισ-
so also [are] we of Christ. For and if even more a-
σότερόν τι [c]καυχήσωμαι‖ περὶ τῆς.ἐξουσίας.ἡμῶν, ἧς
bundantly somewhat I should boast concerning our authority, which
ἔδωκεν ὁ κύριος [d]ἡμῖν‖ εἰς οἰκοδομὴν καὶ οὐκ εἰς καθαίρεσιν
[3]gave [1]the [2]Lord to us for building up and not for overthrowing
ὑμῶν, οὐκ.αἰσχυνθήσομαι 9 ἵνα μὴ.δόξω ὡς ἂν ἐκφοβεῖν
you, I shall not be put to shame; that I may not seem as if frightening
ὑμᾶς διὰ τῶν ἐπιστολῶν. 10 ὅτι αἱ [e]μὲν ἐπιστολαί,
you by means of epistles: because the epistles,
φησίν,‖ βαρεῖαι καὶ ἰσχυραί· ἡ.δὲ παρουσία τοῦ σώματος
says he, [are] weighty and strong, but the presence of the body
ἀσθενής, καὶ ὁ λόγος [f]ἐξουθενημένος.‖ 11 τοῦτο λογιζέσθω
weak, and the speech naught. This let [4]reckon
ὁ τοιοῦτος, ὅτι οἷοί ἐσμεν τῷ λόγῳ δι' ἐπιστολῶν ἀπόντες,
[1]such [2]a [3]one, that such as we are in word by epistles being absent,
τοιοῦτοι καὶ παρόντες τῷ ἔργῳ. 12 Οὐ.γὰρ τολμῶμεν
such [we are] also being present in deed. For [3]not [2]dare [1]we
[g]ἐγκρῖναι‖ ἢ [h]συγκρῖναι‖ ἑαυτούς τισιν τῶν ἑαυτοὺς συν-
rank among or compare [2]with [1]ourselves some who themselves com-
ιστανόντων, ἀλλὰ αὐτοὶ ἐν ἑαυτοῖς ἑαυτοὺς μετροῦντες, καὶ
mend; but these by themselves themselves measuring, and
[h]συγκρίνοντες‖ ἑαυτοὺς ἑαυτοῖς, οὐ.[i]συνιοῦσιν.‖ 13 ἡμεῖς
comparing themselves with themselves, do not understand. [2]We
δὲ [k]οὐχὶ‖ εἰς τὰ ἄμετρα καυχησόμεθα, ἀλλὰ κατὰ
[1]now not to the things beyond measure will boast, but according to
τὸ μέτρον τοῦ κανόνος οὗ ἐμέρισεν ἡμῖν ὁ θεὸς μέτρου
the measure of the rule which [5]divided [6]to [7]us [1]the [2]God [3]of [4]measure
ἐφικέσθαι ἄχρι καὶ ὑμῶν. 14 [l]οὐ γὰρ ὡς‖ μὴ ἐφικνούμενοι εἰς
to reach [2]to [1]also you. [2]Not [1]for as not reaching to
ὑμᾶς ὑπερεκτείνομεν ἑαυτούς· ἄχρι.γὰρ καὶ ὑμῶν ἐφθάσαμεν
you do we overstretch ourselves, (for to [2]also [1]you we came
ἐν τῷ εὐαγγελίῳ τοῦ χριστοῦ· 15 οὐκ εἰς τὰ ἄμετρα
in the glad tidings of the Christ;) not [2]to [3]the [4]things [5]beyond [6]measure
καυχώμενοι ἐν ἀλλοτρίοις κόποις, ἐλπίδα.δὲ ἔχοντες, αὐξανο-
[1]boasting in others' labours, but hope having, [3]increas-
μένης τῆς.πίστεως.ὑμῶν, ἐν ὑμῖν μεγαλυνθῆναι κατὰ
ing [1]your [2]faith, among you to be enlarged according to
τὸν.κανόνα.ἡμῶν εἰς περισσείαν, 16 εἰς τὰ ὑπερέκεινα ὑμῶν
our rule to abundance, to that beyond you
εὐαγγελίσασθαι, οὐκ ἐν ἀλλοτρίῳ κανόνι εἰς τὰ
to announce the glad tidings, not [3]in [4]another's [5]rule [6]as [7]to [8]things
ἕτοιμα καυχήσασθαι. 17 Ὁ.δὲ καυχώμενος, ἐν κυρίῳ
[9]ready [1]to [2]boast. But he that boasts, in [the] Lord
καυχάσθω· 18 οὐ.γὰρ ὁ ἑαυτὸν [n]συνιστῶν,‖ ἐκεῖνός ἐστιν
let him boast, For not he that himself commends, this [one] is

14 And in their prayer for you is a longing for you, because of the overflowing grace of God on you.

15 Now thanks to God for His unspeakable free gift.

CHAPTER 10

1 Now I myself, Paul, call on you by the meekness and gentleness of Christ – I, who indeed to look on, am lowly among you, but absent, I am bold toward you.

2 I ask, however, that when *I am* present, I may not be bold with the confidence with which I think to be daring against some, who judge us as walking according to the flesh.

3 For *even if we are* walking in the flesh, we do not war to the flesh.

4 For the weapons of our warfare are not fleshly, but mighty through God to the pulling down of strongholds,

5 overthrowing imaginations and every high thing lifting itself up against the knowledge of God – and bringing into captivity every thought to the obedience of Christ –

6 and having a readiness to avenge all who refuse to obey, as soon as you have fulfilled your obedience.

7 Do you look at things according to the outward appearance? If anyone is certain within himself that he is Christ's, let him think this again within himself – that even as he is Christ's, so also are we Christ's.

8 Yes, even if I should boast somewhat more fully about our authority (which the Lord gave us for building up and not for pulling you down), I will not be put to shame

9 so that I may not seem to be frightening you by letters:

10 Because (he says), truly *Paul's* letters are weighty and strong, but the presence of his body is weak and his speech is contemptible.

11 Let such a one think this, that such as we are in word through letters when absent, so also in action when present.

12 For we dare not rank ourselves among or compare ourselves with some who commend themselves (but measuring themselves by themselves, and comparing themselves with themselves, they are not perceptive).

13 Now we will not boast as to the things beyond measure, but according to the measure of the rule, which the God of measure gave to us, one reaching even to you.

14 For we do not outstretch ourselves, as though we did not reach to you. For we have come to you before also in the gospel of Christ –

15 not boasting in other men's labors, as to the things beyond measure, but we had hope – your faith increasing among you – to be increased more and more, according to our rule to overflowing abundance.

16 *And this* so as to preach the gospel to that *region* beyond you, not to boast in another's rule in regard to the things ready to hand.

17 But he that boasts, let him glory in the Lord.

18 For not he that commends himself is the

δόκιμος, [o]ἀλλ'‖ ὃν ὁ κύριος συνίστησιν.
approved, but whom the Lord commends.

11 [n]Ὄφελον [p]ἀνείχεσθέ‖ μου μικρὸν [q] [r]τῇ ἀφροσύνῃ·‖
I would ye were bearing with me a little in folly;
ἀλλὰ καὶ ἀνέχεσθέ μου. 2 ζηλῶ.γὰρ ὑμᾶς θεοῦ ζή-
but indeed bear with me. For I am jealous as to you [4]of [5]God [1]with [[2]the]
λῳ· ἡρμοσάμην.γὰρ ὑμᾶς ἑνὶ ἀνδρὶ παρθένον ἁγνὴν
[3]jealousy, for I have espoused you to one man [4]a [6]virgin [5]chaste
παραστῆσαι τῷ χριστῷ· 3 φοβοῦμαι.δὲ μήπως ὡς ὁ
[1]to [2]present [[3]you] to the Christ. But I fear lest by any means as the
ὄφις [s]Εὔαν ἐξηπάτησεν‖ ἐν τῇ.πανουργίᾳ.αὐτοῦ, [t]οὕτως‖
serpent [2]Eve [1]deceived in his craftiness, so
φθαρῇ τὰ.νοήματα.ὑμῶν ἀπὸ τῆς ἁπλότητος [v] τῆς
should be corrupted your thoughts from simplicity which [is]
εἰς [w]τὸν‖ χριστόν. 4 εἰ.μὲν.γὰρ ὁ ἐρχόμενος ἄλλον Ἰησοῦν
as to the Christ. For if indeed he that comes another Jesus
κηρύσσει ὃν οὐκ.ἐκηρύξαμεν, ἢ πνεῦμα ἕτερον λαμβάνετε
proclaims whom we did not proclaim, or a [2]spirit [1]different ye receive
ὃ οὐκ.ἐλάβετε, ἢ εὐαγγέλιον ἕτερον ὃ οὐκ.ἐδέξασθε,
which ye did not receive, or [2]glad [3]tidings [1]different which ye did not accept,
καλῶς [x]ἠνείχεσθε.‖ 5 Λογίζομαι [y]γὰρ‖ μηδὲν ὑστερη-
well were ye bearing with [it]. [2]I [3]reckon [1]for in nothing to have been
κέναι τῶν [z]ὑπὲρ.λίαν‖ ἀποστόλων. 6 εἰ.δὲ καὶ ἰδιώτης
behind those in a surpassing degree apostles. But if even unpolished
τῷ λόγῳ, ἀλλ' οὐ τῇ γνώσει· ἀλλ' ἐν παντὶ [a]φανε-
in speech [I am], yet not in knowledge; but in every [way] made
ρωθέντες‖ ἐν πᾶσιν εἰς ὑμᾶς. 7 ἢ ἁμαρτίαν.ἐποίησα, ἐμαυτὸν
manifest in all things to you. Or did I commit sin, [2]myself
ταπεινῶν ἵνα ὑμεῖς ὑψωθῆτε, ὅτι δωρεὰν τὸ τοῦ θεοῦ
[1]humbling that ye might be exalted, because gratuitously the [3]of [4]God
εὐαγγέλιον εὐηγγελισάμην ὑμῖν; 8 ἄλλας ἐκκλησίας ἐσύλησα,
[1]glad [2]tidings I announced to you? Other assemblies I despoiled,
λαβὼν ὀψώνιον πρὸς τὴν ὑμῶν διακονίαν· 9 καὶ
having received wages for [2]towards [3]you [1]service. And
παρὼν πρὸς ὑμᾶς καὶ ὑστερηθείς, οὐ κατενάρκησα
being present with you and having been deficient, I did lazily burden
[b]οὐδενός·‖ τὸ.γὰρ ὑστέρημά μου προσανεπλήρωσαν οἱ ἀδελ-
no one, (for the deficiency of me [3]completely [4]filled [5]up [1]the [2]breth-
φοὶ ἐλθόντες ἀπὸ Μακεδονίας· καὶ ἐν παντὶ ἀβαρῆ
ren who came from Macedonia,) and in everything not burdensome
[c]ὑμῖν ἐμαυτὸν‖ ἐτήρησα καὶ τηρήσω. 10 ἔστιν ἀλήθεια
to you myself I kept and will keep. [5]Is [[1]the] [2]truth
χριστοῦ ἐν ἐμοὶ ὅτι ἡ.καύχησις.αὕτη [d]οὐ.σφραγίσεται‖ εἰς ἐμὲ
[3]of [4]Christ in me that this boasting shall not be sealed up as to me
ἐν τοῖς κλίμασιν τῆς Ἀχαΐας. 11 [e]διατί‖; ὅτι οὐκ.ἀγαπῶ
in the regions of Achaia. Why? because I do not love
ὑμᾶς; ὁ θεὸς οἶδεν· 12 ὃ.δὲ ποιῶ, καὶ ποιήσω, ἵνα ἐκ-
you? God knows. But what I do, also I will do, that I may
κόψω τὴν ἀφορμὴν τῶν θελόντων ἀφορμήν, ἵνα ἐν.ᾧ καυ-
cut off the occasion of those wishing an occasion, that wherein they
χῶνται εὑρεθῶσιν καθὼς καὶ ἡμεῖς. 13 οἱ.γὰρ.τοιοῦτοι
boast they may be found according as also we. For such [are]
ψευδαπόστολοι, ἐργάται δόλιοι, μετασχηματιζόμενοι εἰς ἀπο-
false apostles, [2]workers [1]deceitful, transforming themselves into apo-
στόλους χριστοῦ· 14 καὶ [f]οὐ θαυμαστόν·‖ αὐτὸς.γὰρ ὁ
stles of Christ. And not wonderful [is it], for [2]himself
σατανᾶς μετασχηματίζεται εἰς ἄγγελον φωτός· 15 οὐ
[1]Satan transforms himself into an angel of light. [It is] not
μέγα οὖν εἰ καὶ οἱ.διάκονοι.αὐτοῦ μετασχηματίζον-
a great thing therefore if also his servants transform themselves
ται ὡς διάκονοι δικαιοσύνης, ὧν τὸ τέλος ἔσται κατὰ
as servants of righteousness; of whom the end shall be according to
τὰ.ἔργα.αὐτῶν.
their works.

16 Πάλιν λέγω, μή τίς με δόξῃ ἄφρονα εἶναι· εἰ.δὲ
Again I say, Not anyone [3]me [1]should [2]think a fool to be; but if
μήγε, κἂν ὡς ἄφρονα δέξασθέ με, ἵνα [g]μικρόν τι κἀγὼ‖
otherwise, even as a fool receive me, that [2]little [1]some I also
καυχήσωμαι. 17 ὃ λαλῶ, οὐ [h]λαλῶ κατὰ κύριον,‖
may boast. What I speak, [3]not [2]do [1]I speak according to [the] Lord,
ἀλλ' ὡς ἐν ἀφροσύνῃ, ἐν ταύτῃ τῇ ὑποστάσει τῆς καυχήσεως.
but as in folly, in this confidence of boasting.
18 ἐπεὶ πολλοὶ καυχῶνται κατὰ [i]τὴν‖ σάρκα, κἀγὼ καυ-
Since many boast according to flesh, I also will
χήσομαι. 19 ἡδέως.γὰρ ἀνέχεσθε τῶν ἀφρόνων, φρόνιμοι
boast. For [4]gladly [1]ye [5]bear [6]with [7]fools [3]intelligent
ὄντες· 20 ἀνέχεσθε.γὰρ εἴ τις ὑμᾶς καταδουλοῖ, εἴ τις
[2]being. For ye bear [it] if anyone [2]you [1]bring into bondage, if anyone
κατεσθίει, εἴ τις λαμβάνει, εἴ τις ἐπαίρεται,
devour [you], if anyone take [from you], if anyone exalt himself,
εἴ τις [k]ὑμᾶς εἰς πρόσωπον‖ δέρει. 21 κατὰ ἀτιμίαν λέγω,
if anyone [2]you [3]on [4]the [5]face [1]beat. As to dishonour I speak

one approved, but the one whom the Lord
commends.

CHAPTER 11

1 I wish that you would bear with me a
little in my foolishness. No, rather, do bear
with me.
2 For I am jealous over you with the jealousy of God. For I have promised you to
one Man, so as to present you a pure virgin
to Christ.
3 But I fear that by some means, as the
serpent deceived Eve in his cunning, so your
thoughts might be spoiled from the pureness
which is due to Christ.
4 For if indeed, he that comes preaches
another Jesus, whom we have not preached,
or you receive another spirit which you have
not received – or another gospel which you
never welcomed, you might well bear with
it.
5 For I suppose myself to have been behind
the highest apostles in no way.
6 But even if I am not polished in speech,
yet it is not so in knowledge. But in every
way, I have made *the truth* clear to you in
all things.
7 Or did I commit a sin, humbling myself so
that you might be exalted, because I
preached the gospel of God to you without
charge?
8 I stripped other churches, receiving wages
in order to minister to you.
9 And when I was present with you and had
need, I did not lazily burden anyone, but my
need was completely supplied by the
brothers who came from Mac-e-do-ni-a. And
in everything I kept myself from being a
burden to you – and will keep myself.
10 The truth of Christ is in me, so that this
boasting of mine shall not be stopped in the
regions of A-chai-a.
11 Why? Because I do not love you? God
knows!
12 But what I am doing I still will do, so
that I may cut off the opportunity of those
desiring an opportunity – so that in that
which they boast, they may be found
according as we are.
13 For such ones are false apostles, misleading workers, changing themselves over
into apostles of Christ.
14 And *it is* no wonder, for Satan himself
transforms himself into an angel of light.
15 *It is* not a great thing, then, if his servants also transform themselves as ministers
of righteousness, whose end shall be
according to their works.
16 Again I say, No one should think me to
be a fool! But if not, receive me even as a
fool so that I may boast a little.
17 What I say, I do not say according to the
Lord, but as in foolishness, in this boldness
of boasting.
18 Since many boast according to the flesh,
I also will boast.
19 For you gladly bear with the foolish,
being wise.
20 For you allow it if anyone brings you
into bondage, if anyone devours you, if
anyone takes *from you,* if anyone prides
himself, if anyone strikes you on the face.
21 I speak as to dishonor, as though we

ὡς ὅτι ἡμεῖς [l]ἠσθενήσαμεν·‖ ἐν.ᾧ.δ' ἂν τις τολμᾷ, ἐν
as that we were weak; but wherein anyone may be daring, (in
ἀφροσύνῃ λέγω, τολμῶ κἀγώ. 22 Ἑβραῖοί εἰσιν; κἀγώ·
folly I speak,) [2]am [3]daring [1]I also. Hebrews are they? I also.
[m]Ἰσραηλῖταί‖ εἰσιν; κἀγώ· σπέρμα Ἀβραάμ εἰσιν; κἀγώ·
Israelites are they? I also. Seed of Abraham are they? I also.
23 διάκονοι χριστοῦ εἰσιν; παραφρονῶν λαλῶ, [n]ὑπὲρ
Servants of Christ are they? (as being beside myself I speak,) above
ἐγώ·‖ ἐν κόποις περισσοτέρως, [o]ἐν πληγαῖς ὑπερ-
[measure] I [too]; in labours more abundantly, in stripes above
βαλλόντως, ἐν φυλακαῖς περισσοτέρως,‖ ἐν θανάτοις πολ-
measure, in imprisonments more abundantly, in deaths often.
λάκις. 24 ὑπὸ Ἰουδαίων πεντάκις [p]τεσσαράκοντα‖
From Jews five times forty [stripes]
παρὰ μίαν ἔλαβον, 25 τρὶς [q]ἐῤῥαβδίσθην,‖ ἅπαξ ἐλιθάσθην,
except one I received. Thrice I was beaten with rods, once I was stoned,
τρὶς ἐναυάγησα, νυχθήμερον ἐν τῷ βυθῷ πεποίηκα·
three times I was shipwrecked, a night and a day in the deep I have passed:
26 ὁδοιπορίαις πολλάκις· κινδύνοις ποταμῶν, κινδύνοις
in journeyings often, in perils of rivers, in perils
λῃστῶν, κινδύνοις ἐκ γένους, κινδύνοις ἐξ ἐθνῶν,
of robbers, in perils from [my own] race, in perils from [the] nations,
κινδύνοις ἐν πόλει, κινδύνοις ἐν ἐρημίᾳ, κινδύνοις ἐν
in perils in [the] city, in perils in [the] desert, in perils on
θαλάσσῃ, κινδύνοις ἐν ψευδαδέλφοις· 27 [r]ἐν‖ κόπῳ καὶ
[the] sea, in perils among false brethren; in labour and
μόχθῳ, ἐν ἀγρυπνίαις πολλάκις, ἐν λιμῷ καὶ δίψει, ἐν νη-
toil, in watchings often, in hunger and thirst, in fast-
στείαις πολλάκις, ἐν ψύχει καὶ γυμνότητι· 28 χωρὶς τῶν
ings often, in cold and nakedness. Besides the things
παρεκτός, [s]ἡ ἐπισύστασίς μου‖ ἡ καθ'.ἡμέραν, ἡ μέριμνα
without, the crowding on me daily, the care
πασῶν τῶν ἐκκλησιῶν. 29 τίς ἀσθενεῖ, καὶ οὐκ.ἀσθενῶ; τίς
concerning all the assemblies. Who is weak, and I am not weak? who
σκανδαλίζεται, καὶ οὐκ ἐγὼ πυροῦμαι; 30 εἰ καυχᾶσθαι
is offended, and [3]not [1]I [2]do burn? If [3]to [4]boast
δεῖ, τὰ τῆς.ἀσθενείας.μου καυχήσομαι. 31 Ὁ
[1]it [2]behoves, [in] the things concerning my infirmity I will boast. The
θεὸς καὶ πατὴρ τοῦ.κυρίου.[t]ἡμῶν‖ Ἰησοῦ [v]χριστοῦ‖ οἶδεν, ὁ
God and Father of our Lord Jesus Christ knows, he who
ὢν εὐλογητὸς εἰς τοὺς αἰῶνας, ὅτι οὐ.ψεύδομαι. 32 ἐν Δα-
is blessed to the ages, that I do not lie. In Da-
μασκῷ ὁ ἐθνάρχης Ἀρέτα τοῦ βασιλέως ἐφρούρει τὴν
mascus the ethnarch of Aretas the king was guarding the
[w]Δαμασκηνῶν πόλιν,‖ πιάσαι με [x]θέλων·‖ 33 καὶ διὰ
[2]of [3]the [4]Damascenes [1]city, [6]to [7]take [8]me [5]wishing. And through
θυρίδος ἐν σαργάνῃ ἐχαλάσθην διὰ τοῦ τείχους, καὶ
a window in a basket I was let down through the wall, and
ἐξέφυγον τὰς.χεῖρας.αὐτοῦ.
escaped his hands.

12 Καυχᾶσθαι [y]δὴ οὐ.συμφέρει μοι· ἐλεύσομαι.γὰρ‖ [z] εἰς
To boast indeed is not profitable to me; for I will come to
ὀπτασίας καὶ ἀποκαλύψεις κυρίου· 2 οἶδα ἄνθρωπον ἐν
visions and revelations of [the] Lord. I know a man in
χριστῷ πρὸ.ἐτῶν δεκατεσσάρων, εἴτε ἐν σώματι οὐκ.οἶδα,
Christ [2]years [3]ago [1]fourteen, (whether in [the] body I know not,
εἴτε ἐκτὸς [a]τοῦ‖ σώματος οὐκ.οἶδα· ὁ θεὸς οἶδεν· ἁρπαγέντα
or out of the body I know not, God knows,) [4]caught [5]away
τὸν.τοιοῦτον ἕως τρίτου οὐρανοῦ. 3 καὶ οἶδα τὸν τοιοῦτον
[1]such [2]a [3]one to [the] third heaven. And I know such
ἄνθρωπον, εἴτε ἐν σώματι εἴτε [b]ἐκτὸς‖ τοῦ σώματος [c]οὐκ
a man, (whether in [the] body or out of the body [3]not
οἶδα·‖ ὁ θεὸς οἶδεν· 4 ὅτι ἡρπάγη εἰς τὸν παράδεισον,
[1]I [2]know, God knows:) that he was caught away to Paradise,
καὶ ἤκουσεν ἄῤῥητα ῥήματα, ἃ οὐκ.ἐξὸν ἀνθρώπῳ
and heard unutterable sayings, which it is not permitted to man
λαλῆσαι. 5 ὑπὲρ τοῦ.τοιούτου καυχήσομαι· ὑπὲρ.δὲ ἐμαυτοῦ
to speak. Concerning such a one I will boast, but concerning myself
οὐ.καυχήσομαι, εἰ.μὴ ἐν ταῖς.ἀσθενείαις.[d]μου·‖ 6 ἐὰν.γὰρ
I will not boast, unless in my weaknesses. For if
θελήσω καυχήσασθαι, οὐκ.ἔσομαι ἄφρων· ἀλήθειαν.γὰρ
I should desire to boast, I shall not be a fool; for truth
ἐρῶ· φείδομαι.δέ, μή τις· εἰς ἐμὲ λογίσηται ὑπὲρ ὃ
I will say; but I forbear, lest anyone as to me should reckon above what
βλέπει με, ἢ ἀκούει [e]τι‖ ἐξ ἐμοῦ. 7 Καὶ τῇ ὑπερβολῇ
he sees me, or hears anything of me. And by the surpassingness
τῶν ἀποκαλύψεων [f]ἵνα μὴ.ὑπεραίρωμαι, ἐδόθη μοι σκόλοψ
of the revelations that I might not be exalted, was given to me a thorn
τῇ σαρκί, ἄγγελος [g]σατᾶν‖ ἵνα με κολαφίζῃ, [h]ἵνα μὴ
for the flesh, a messenger of Satan, that me he might buffet, that [3]not
ὑπεραίρωμαι.‖ 8 [i] ὑπὲρ τούτου τρὶς τὸν κύριον παρεκάλεσα,
[1]I [2]might be exalted. For this thrice the Lord I besought

were weak. But in whatever anyone may be
daring (I speak in foolishness), I too am
daring.
22 Are they Hebrews? So am I! Are they
Israelites? So am I! Are they the seed of
Abraham? So am I!
23 Are they ministers of Christ? (I am
speaking as one myself): I am more! I excel
them in labors much more richly, and in
stripes beyond measure – I have been many
more times in prison and often in deaths.
24 Five times I received from the Jews forty
stripes minus one.
25 I was beaten with rods three times, I was
stoned, I was shipwrecked three times. I
have passed a night and a day in the deep.
26 *I have been* in travels often, in dangers of
rivers, in dangers of robbers, in dangers from
my countrymen, in dangers from the
heathen, in dangers in the city, in dangers in
the desert, in dangers on the sea, in dangers
among false brothers.
27 *I have been* in toil and hardship, often in
sleeplessness, in hunger and thirst, often in
fastings, in cold and nakedness.
28 Besides the things on the outside, the
care of all the churches is crowding in on me
daily.
29 Who is weak, and I am not weak? Who is
caused to stumble, and I do not burn?
30 If it is right for me to boast in the things
regarding my weakness, I will boast.
31 The God and Father of our Lord Jesus
Christ, He who is blessed forever, knows that
I do not lie.
32 In Damascus the governor under Ar-e-tas
the king was guarding the city of the Dam-a-
scenes desiring to arrest me.
33 But I was lowered through a window in a
basket through the wall and escaped his
grasp.
12 1 Indeed, *it is* not profitable for me to
boast. For I will come to visions and revelations of the Lord.
2 I know a man in Christ (fourteen years
ago – whether in the body I do not know,
or out of the body I do not know; God
knows) – such a one was caught away into
the third Heaven.
3 And I know such a man (whether in the
body or out of the body I do not know; God
knows) –
4 that he was caught up into Paradise. And
he heard unspeakable words, which it is not
allowed to man to speak.
5 About such a one I will boast, but about
myself I will not boast, except in my
weaknesses.
6 For if I should desire to boast, I shall not
be a fool. For I will tell the truth. But I will
restrain myself for fear that anyone should
think of me above what he sees me to be, or
what he hears of me.
7 And so that I might not be made proud
by the magnificence of the heavenly visions,
a thorn in the flesh was given to me, a
messenger of Satan, that he might beat
against me, so that I might not be proud.
8 For this thing I begged the Lord three

ἵνα ἀποστῇ ἀπ᾽ ἐμοῦ· 9 καὶ εἴρηκέν μοι, Ἀρκεῖ σοι ἡ
that it might depart from me, And he said to me, Suffices thee
χάρις.μου· ἡ.γὰρ δύναμίς [k]μου‖ ἐν ἀσθενείᾳ [l]τελειοῦται.‖
my grace; for the power of me in weakness is perfected.
ἥδιστα οὖν μᾶλλον καυχήσομαι ἐν ταῖς.ἀσθενείαις.[m]μου‖
Most gladly therefore rather will I boast in my weaknesses
ἵνα ἐπισκηνώσῃ ἐπ᾽ ἐμὲ ἡ δύναμις τοῦ χριστοῦ. 10 διὸ
that may dwell upon me the power of the Christ. Wherefore
εὐδοκῶ ἐν ἀσθενείαις, ἐν ὕβρεσιν, ἐν ἀνάγκαις, ἐν διωγ-
I take pleasure in weaknesses, in insults, in necessities, in perse-
μοῖς, [n]ἐν‖ στενοχωρίαις, ὑπὲρ χριστοῦ· ὅταν.γὰρ ἀσθενῶ,
cutions, in straits, for Christ: for when I may be weak,
τότε δυνατός εἰμι.
then powerful I am.
11 Γέγονα ἄφρων [o]καυχώμενος·‖ ὑμεῖς με ἠναγκάσατε.
I have become a fool boasting; ye me compelled:
ἐγὼ.γὰρ ὤφειλον ὑφ᾽ ὑμῶν συνίστασθαι· οὐδὲν.γὰρ
for I ought by you to have been commended; for nothing
ὑστέρησα τῶν [p]ὑπὲρ.λίαν‖ ἀποστόλων, εἰ καὶ οὐδέν εἰμι.
I was behind those in a surpassing degree apostles, if also nothing I am.
12 Τὰ μὲν σημεῖα τοῦ ἀποστόλου [q]κατειργάσθη‖ ἐν ὑμῖν
The [2]indeed [1]signs of the apostle were worked out among you
ἐν πάσῃ ὑπομονῇ, [r]ἐν‖ σημείοις [s]καὶ‖ τέρασιν καὶ δυνάμεσιν.
in all endurance, in signs and wonders and works of power.
13 τί.γάρ ἐστιν ὃ [t]ἡττήθητε‖ ὑπὲρ τὰς λοιπὰς ἐκ-
For in what is it that ye were inferior beyond the rest [of the] as-
κλησίας, εἰ.μὴ ὅτι αὐτὸς ἐγὼ οὐ.κατενάρκησα ὑμῶν; χαρί-
semblies, unless that [2]myself [1]I did not lazily burden you? For-
σασθέ μοι τὴν.ἀδικίαν.ταύτην. 14 ἰδοὺ τρίτον [u] ἑτοίμως ἔχω
give me this injustice. Lo, a third time ready I am
ἐλθεῖν πρὸς ὑμᾶς, καὶ οὐ καταναρκήσω [v]ὑμῶν·‖ οὐ.γὰρ.ζητῶ
to come to you, and I will not lazily burden you; for I do not seek
τὰ ὑμῶν, [w]ἀλλ᾽‖ ὑμᾶς. οὐ.γὰρ ὀφείλει τὰ τέκνα τοῖς
the things of you, but you; for [4]not [3]ought [1]the [2]children for the
γονεῦσιν θησαυρίζειν, [x]ἀλλ᾽‖ οἱ γονεῖς τοῖς τέκνοις. 15 ἐγὼ.δὲ
parents to treasure up, but the parents for the children. Now I
ἥδιστα δαπανήσω καὶ ἐκδαπανηθήσομαι ὑπὲρ τῶν ψυχῶν
most gladly will spend and will be utterly spent for [2]souls
ὑμῶν· εἰ [y]καὶ‖ περισσοτέρως ὑμᾶς [z]ἀγαπῶν,‖ [a]ἧττον‖ [b]ἀγαπῶ-
[1]your, if even more abundantly [2]you [1]loving, less I am loved.
μαι.‖ 16 Ἔστω.δέ, ἐγὼ οὐ.κατεβάρησα ὑμᾶς· [w]ἀλλ᾽‖ ὑπάρχων
But be it so, I did not burden you; but being
πανοῦργος δόλῳ ὑμᾶς ἔλαβον. 17 μή τινα ὧν ἀπέσταλκα
crafty with guile you I took. Any of whom I have sent
πρὸς ὑμᾶς, δι᾽ αὐτοῦ ἐπλεονέκτησα ὑμᾶς; 18 παρεκάλεσα
to you, by him did I overreach you? I besought
Τίτον, καὶ συναπέστειλα τὸν ἀδελφόν· μή τι ἐπλεονέκτησεν
Titus, and sent with [him] the brother: Did [2]overreach
ὑμᾶς Τίτος; οὐ τῷ αὐτῷ πνεύματι περιεπατήσαμεν; οὐ
[3]you [1]Titus? Not by the same spirit walked we? Not
τοῖς αὐτοῖς ἴχνεσιν;
in the same steps?
19 [c]Πάλιν‖ δοκεῖτε ὅτι ὑμῖν ἀπολογούμεθα;[c] [d]κατενώ-
Again do ye think that to you we are making a defence? be-
πιον‖ [e]τοῦ‖ θεοῦ ἐν χριστῷ λαλοῦμεν· τὰ.δὲ.πάντα, ἀγαπητοί,
fore God in Christ we speak; and all things, beloved,
ὑπὲρ τῆς.ὑμῶν.οἰκοδομῆς. 20 φοβοῦμαι.γάρ, μήπως ἐλθὼν
for your building up. For I fear, lest perhaps having come
οὐχ οἵους θέλω εὕρω ὑμᾶς, κἀγὼ εὑρεθῶ ὑμῖν οἷον
not such as I wish I should find you, and I be found by you such as
οὐ.θέλετε· μήπως [f]ἔρεις,‖ [g]ζῆλοι,‖ θυμοί, ἐριθεῖαι,
ye do not wish: lest perhaps [there be] strifes, jealousies, indignations, contentions,
καταλαλιαί, ψιθυρισμοί, φυσιώσεις, ἀκαταστασίαι· 21 μὴ
evil speakings, whisperings, puffings up, commotions; lest
πάλιν [h]ἐλθόντα με‖ [i]ταπεινώσῃ‖ [k] ὁ θεός μου πρὸς ὑμᾶς,
again having come [5]me [3]should [4]humble [2]God [1]my as to you,
καὶ πενθήσω πολλοὺς τῶν προημαρτηκότων, καὶ
and I should mourn over many of those who have before sinned, and
μὴ.μετανοησάντων ἐπὶ τῇ ἀκαθαρσίᾳ καὶ πορνείᾳ καὶ ἀσελ-
have not repented upon the uncleanness and fornication and licen-
γείᾳ ᾗ ἔπραξαν.
tiousness which they practised.
13 Τρίτον.τοῦτο ἔρχομαι πρὸς ὑμᾶς. ἐπὶ στόματος
This third time I am coming to you. In [the] mouth
δύο μαρτύρων καὶ τριῶν σταθήσεται πᾶν ῥῆμα. 2 προεί-
of two witnesses or of three shall be established every matter. I have be-
ρηκα καὶ προλέγω, ὡς παρὼν τὸ δεύτερον, καὶ
fore declared and I say beforehand, as being present the second time, and
ἀπὼν [l]νῦν [l]γράφω‖ τοῖς προημαρτηκόσιν, καὶ τοῖς
being absent now I write to those who have before sinned, and to [2]the
λοιποῖς πᾶσιν, ὅτι ἐὰν ἔλθω εἰς τὸ πάλιν οὐ.φείσομαι. 3 ἐπεὶ
[3]rest [1]all, that if I come again I will not spare. Since

times, that it might be taken away from me.
9 And He said to me, My grace is sufficient
for you, for My strength is made perfect in
weakness. Most gladly, then, will I rather
glory in my weaknesses, so that the power of
Christ may rest on me.
10 So I take pleasure in weaknesses, in
insults, in dire needs, in persecutions, in
tight circumstances for Christ – for when I
am weak, then I am strong.
11 *In this* boasting I have become a fool.
You made me do it. For I ought to have
been praised by you, for I was in no way
behind the highest apostles, though I am
nothing.
12 Truly the signs of an apostle were
worked out among you in all patience, in
miracles, and in wonders and works of
power.
13 For in what is it that you were worse
than the other churches, except that I myself did not lazily burden you? Forgive me
this injustice.
14 Behold! I am ready to come to you a third
time. And I will not lazily burden you, for I do
not seek your things, but you. For the children ought not to lay up treasure for the
parents, but the parents for the children.
15 Now I most gladly will spend and be
fully spent for your souls (even if loving you
more and more, I am loved the less).
16 But even so, I did not burden you. But
being crafty, I caught you with bait.
17 Did I take advantage of you by any of
the ones I have sent to you?
18 I begged Titus and sent the brother
along. Did Titus take advantage of you? Did
we not walk by the same spirit? Did *we* not
walk in the same steps?
19 Again, do you think that we are defending
ourselves? We speak before God in Christ
but in all things, my loved ones, for your
gain.
20 For I fear that by some means when I
come I may not find you as I wish, and that
I may be found by you such as you do not
wish – fearing there may be fightings, envyings, outbursts of anger, party arguments,
salders, whisperings, proud thoughts and
tumults.
21 *I fear* that when I come again, my God
will humble me in regard to you, and I
should have to weep over many of those
who have sinned already and have not
repented of the uncleanness and
fornication and lustfulness which they
have practiced.

13 1 I am coming to you this third time. In the
mouth of two or three witnesses, every
matter shall be settled.
2 I have told you before and I now tell you
beforehand (as being present the second
time, and being absent now, I write to those
who have sinned before, and to all the rest)
that if I come again I will not spare.
3 Since you look for a proof of Christ

δοκιμὴν ζητεῖτε τοῦ ἐν ἐμοὶ λαλοῦντος χριστοῦ, ὃς εἰς
a proof ye seek ⁴in ⁵me ³speaking ¹of ²Christ, (who towards
ὑμᾶς οὐκ.ἀσθενεῖ, ἀλλὰ δυνατεῖ ἐν ὑμῖν· 4 καὶ.γὰρ [m]εἰ
you is not weak, but is powerful in you, for indeed if
ἐσταυρώθη ἐξ ἀσθενείας, ἀλλὰ ζῇ ἐκ δυνάμεως θεοῦ·
he was crucified in weakness, yet he lives by ²power ¹God's;
καὶ.γὰρ [n] ἡμεῖς ἀσθενοῦμεν ἐν αὐτῷ, ἀλλὰ [o]ζησόμεθα σὺν
for indeed we are weak in him, but we shall live with
αὐτῷ ἐκ δυνάμεως θεοῦ [p]εἰς ὑμᾶς· 5 ἑαυτοὺς πειράζετε
him by ²power ¹God's towards you,) yourselves try ye
εἰ ἐστὲ ἐν τῇ πίστει, ἑαυτοὺς δοκιμάζετε. ἢ οὐκ.ἐπιγινώσκετε
if ye are in the faith; yourselves prove: or do ye not recognize
ἑαυτούς, ὅτι [q]Ἰησοῦς χριστὸς ἐν ὑμῖν [r]ἐστιν; εἰ.μή τι ἀδό-
yourselves, that Jesus Christ in you is, unless re-
κιμοί ἐστε. 6 ἐλπίζω.δὲ ὅτι γνώσεσθε ὅτι ἡμεῖς οὐκ.ἐσμὲν
jected ye are? Now I hope that ye will know that we are not
ἀδόκιμοι. 7 [s]εὔχομαι.δὲ πρὸς τὸν θεὸν μὴ ποιῆσαι ὑμᾶς
rejected. But I pray to God [that] ²may ³do ¹ye
κακὸν μηδέν, οὐχ ἵνα ἡμεῖς δόκιμοι φανῶμεν, ἀλλ' ἵνα ὑμεῖς
⁵evil ⁴nothing; not that we approved may appear, but that ye
τὸ καλὸν ποιῆτε, ἡμεῖς.δὲ ὡς ἀδόκιμοι ὦμεν. 8 οὐ.γὰρ
what [is] right may do, and we as rejected be. For not
δυνάμεθά τι κατὰ τῆς ἀληθείας, [t]ἀλλ' ὑπὲρ τῆς ἀληθείας.
have we ²power ¹any against the truth, but for the truth.
9 χαίρομεν.γὰρ ὅταν ἡμεῖς ἀσθενῶμεν, ὑμεῖς.δὲ δυνατοὶ ἦτε·
For we rejoice when we may be weak, and ye powerful may be.
τοῦτο.[v]δὲ καὶ εὐχόμεθα, τὴν.ὑμῶν.κατάρτισιν. 10 διὰ.τοῦτο
But this also we pray for, your perfecting. On this account
ταῦτα ἀπὼν γράφω, ἵνα παρὼν μὴ ἀποτόμως χρή-
these things being absent I write, that being present not with severity I may
σωμαι, κατὰ τὴν ἐξουσίαν ἣν [w]ἔδωκέν μοι ὁ κύριος εἰς
treat [you], according to the authority which ³gave ⁴me ¹the ²Lord for
οἰκοδομὴν καὶ οὐκ εἰς καθαίρεσιν.
building up and not for overthrowing.

11 Λοιπόν, ἀδελφοί, χαίρετε, καταρτίζεσθε, παρακαλεῖσθε,
For the rest, brethren, rejoice; be perfected; be encouraged;
τὸ.αὐτὸ φρονεῖτε, εἰρηνεύετε· καὶ ὁ θεὸς τῆς ἀγάπης καὶ
⁴the ²same ³thing ¹mind; be at peace; and the God of love and
εἰρήνης ἔσται μεθ' ὑμῶν. 12 Ἀσπάσασθε ἀλλήλους ἐν ἁγίῳ
peace shall be with you. Salute one another with a holy
φιλήματι. ἀσπάζονται ὑμᾶς οἱ ἅγιοι πάντες. 13 Ἡ χάρις
kiss. ⁴Salute ⁵you ²the ³saints ¹all. The grace
τοῦ κυρίου Ἰησοῦ χριστοῦ, καὶ ἡ ἀγάπη τοῦ θεοῦ, καὶ ἡ
of the Lord Jesus Christ, and the love of God, and the
κοινωνία τοῦ ἁγίου πνεύματος μετὰ πάντων ὑμῶν. [x]ἀμήν.
fellowship of the Holy Spirit [be] with ²all ¹you. Amen.
[y]Πρὸς Κορινθίους δευτέρα ἐγράφη ἀπὸ Φιλίππων τῆς
²To [³the] ⁴Corinthians ¹second written from Philippi
Μακεδονίας, διὰ Τίτου καὶ Λουκᾶ.
of Macedonia, by Titus and Lucas.

speaking in me (who is not weak towards
you, but is powerful in you –
4 for indeed, if He was crucified because of
weakness, yet He lives by God's power – for
indeed, we are weak in Him, but we shall live
with Him by God's power towards you),
5 examine yourselves, whether you are in
the faith. Test your own selves. Or do you
not recognize yourselves that Jesus Christ is
in you, unless you are rejected ones.
6 Now I hope that you will know that we
are not rejected.
7 But I pray to God that you may do
nothing evil, not that we may appear to be
approved, but that you may do what is right,
even though we are rejected.
8 For we have no power against the truth,
but for the truth.
9 For we rejoice when we are weak and you
are strong. But this also, we pray for your
being made perfect.
10 Because of this, I write these things
while absent, so that when I am present I
may not treat you with sharpness –
according to the authority which the Lord
gave me for building you up and not for
pulling you down.
11 Finally, brothers, be joyful, be made
perfect, be comforted, be of one mind, be at
peace.
12 Greet one another with a holy kiss.
13 All saints greet you.
14 The grace of the Lord Jesus Christ, and
the love of God, and the fellowship of the
Holy Spirit be with you, Amen.

The Letter to the GALATIANS

ΠΑΥΛΟΣ ἀπόστολος, οὐκ ἀπ' ἀνθρώπων οὐδὲ δι' ἀν-
Paul apostle, not from men nor through
θρώπου, ἀλλὰ διὰ Ἰησοῦ χριστοῦ, καὶ θεοῦ πατρὸς τοῦ
man, but through Jesus Christ, and God [the] Father, who
ἐγείραντος αὐτὸν ἐκ νεκρῶν, 2 καὶ οἱ σὺν ἐμοὶ
raised him from among [the] dead, and ²the ⁴with ⁵me
πάντες ἀδελφοί, ταῖς ἐκκλησίαις τῆς Γαλατίας· 3 χάρις ὑμῖν
¹all ³brethren, to the assemblies of Galatia. Grace to you
καὶ εἰρήνη ἀπὸ θεοῦ πατρὸς καὶ κυρίου ἡμῶν Ἰησοῦ χρισ-
and peace from God [the] Father and ²Lord ¹our Jesus Christ,
τοῦ, 4 τοῦ δόντος ἑαυτὸν [b]ὑπὲρ τῶν.ἁμαρτιῶν.ἡμῶν, ὅπως
who gave himself for our sins, so that
ἐξέληται ἡμᾶς ἐκ τοῦ [c]ἐνεστῶτος αἰῶνος πονηροῦ,
he might deliver us out of the present ²age ¹evil,
κατὰ τὸ θέλημα τοῦ θεοῦ καὶ πατρὸς ἡμῶν, 5 ᾧ
according to the will of ²God ³and ⁴Father ¹our; to whom [be]
ἡ δόξα εἰς τοὺς αἰῶνας τῶν αἰώνων. ἀμήν.
the glory to the ages of the ages. Amen.
6 Θαυμάζω ὅτι οὕτως ταχέως μετατίθεσθε ἀπὸ τοῦ
I wonder that thus quickly ye are being changed from him who
καλέσαντος ὑμᾶς ἐν χάριτι χριστοῦ, εἰς ἕτερον εὐαγ-
called you in ²grace ¹Christ's, to a different glad
γέλιον· 7 ὃ οὐκ.ἔστιν ἄλλο, εἰ.μή τινές εἰσιν οἱ ταράσ-
tidings, which is not another; but ³some ¹there ²are who trou

CHAPTER 1

1 Paul, an apostle (not from men, nor by
man, but through Jesus Christ and God the
Father, who raised Him from the dead),
2 and all the brothers with me to the
churches of Galatia.
3 Grace and peace to you from God the
Father and our Lord Jesus Christ,
4 who gave Himself for our sins so that He
might deliver us out of the present evil age,
according to the will of our God and Father,
5 to *Him* be the glory forever and ever.
Amen.
6 I marvel that you are so quickly moving
away from Him who called you into the
grace of Christ, to another gospel –
7 which is not another, but there are some
who trouble you and desire to twist the

σοντες ὑμᾶς, καὶ θέλοντες μεταστρέψαι τὸ εὐαγγέλιον τοῦ
ble you, and desire to pervert the glad tidings of the
χριστοῦ. 8 ἀλλὰ καὶ ἐὰν ἡμεῖς ἢ ἄγγελος ἐξ οὐρανοῦ [d]εὐαγ-
Christ: but even if we or an angel out of heaven should an-
γελίζηται" [e]ὑμῖν" παρ' ὃ εὐηγγελισάμεθα ὑμῖν, ἀνάθεμα
nounce glad tidings to you contrary to what we announced to you, accursed
ἔστω. 9 ὡς προειρήκαμεν, καὶ ἄρτι πάλιν λέγω, εἴ τις
let him be. As we have said before, 2also 1now again I say, If anyone
ὑμᾶς εὐαγγελίζεται παρ' ὃ παρελάβετε, ἀνάθεμα
[to] you announces glad tidings contrary to what ye received, accursed
ἔστω. 10 ἄρτι.γὰρ ἀνθρώπους πείθω ἢ τὸν θεόν; ἢ
let him be. For now men do I persuade or God? or
ζητῶ ἀνθρώποις ἀρέσκειν; εἰ.[f]γὰρ" ἔτι ἀνθρώποις ἤρεσκον,
do I seek men to please? For if yet men I were pleasing,
χριστοῦ δοῦλος οὐκ.ἂν.ἤμην.
Christ's bondman I should not be.
11 Γνωρίζω [g]δὲ" ὑμῖν, ἀδελφοί, τὸ εὐαγγέλιον τὸ εὐαγ-
2I 3make 4known 1but to you, brethren, the glad tidings which was
γελισθὲν ὑπ' ἐμοῦ, ὅτι οὐκ.ἔστιν κατὰ ἄνθρωπον· 12 οὐδὲ
announced by me, that it is not according to man. 2Neither
γὰρ ἐγὼ παρὰ ἀνθρώπου παρέλαβον αὐτό, [h]οὔτε" ἐδιδάχθην,
1for I from man received it, nor was I taught [it],
ἀλλὰ δι' ἀποκαλύψεως Ἰησοῦ χριστοῦ. 13 Ἠκούσατε.γὰρ τὴν
but by a revelation of Jesus Christ. For ye heard of
ἐμὴν.ἀναστροφήν ποτε ἐν τῷ Ἰουδαϊσμῷ, ὅτι καθ'.ὑπερβολὴν
my conduct once in Judaism, that excessively
ἐδίωκον τὴν ἐκκλησίαν τοῦ θεοῦ καὶ ἐπόρθουν αὐτήν·
I was persecuting the assembly of God and was ravaging it;
14 καὶ προέκοπτον ἐν τῷ Ἰουδαϊσμῷ ὑπὲρ πολλοὺς συνηλικιώτας
and was advancing in Judaism beyond many contemporaries
ἐν τῷ.γένει.μου, περισσοτέρως ζηλωτὴς ὑπάρχων τῶν πατρι-
in my [own] race, more abundantly zealous being 4of 6fathers
κῶν μου παραδόσεων. 15 ὅτε.δὲ εὐδόκησεν [i]ὁ θεὸς" ὁ
5my 1for [2the] 3traditions. But when 2was 3pleased 1God, who
ἀφορίσας με ἐκ κοιλίας μητρός.μου, καὶ καλέσας διὰ τῆς
selected me from 3womb 1my 2mother's, and called [me] by
χάριτος.αὐτοῦ, 16 ἀποκαλύψαι τὸν.υἱὸν.αὐτοῦ ἐν ἐμοί, ἵνα
his grace, to reveal his Son in me, that
εὐαγγελίζωμαι.αὐτὸν ἐν τοῖς ἔθνεσιν· εὐθέως
I should announce him as the glad tidings among the nations, immediately
οὐ.προσανεθέμην σαρκὶ καὶ αἵματι, 17 οὐδὲ [k]ἀνῆλθον" εἰς
I conferred not with flesh and blood, nor went I up to
Ἱεροσόλυμα πρὸς τοὺς πρὸ ἐμοῦ ἀποστόλους, [l]ἀλλ'"
Jerusalem to those [who were] 2before 3me 1apostles, but
ἀπῆλθον εἰς Ἀραβίαν, καὶ πάλιν ὑπέστρεψα εἰς Δαμασκόν.
I went away into Arabia, and again returned to Damascus.
18 Ἔπειτα μετὰ [m]ἔτη τρία" ἀνῆλθον εἰς Ἱεροσόλυμα ἱσ-
Then after 2years 1three I went up to Jerusalem to make
τορῆσαι "Πέτρον," καὶ ἐπέμεινα πρὸς αὐτὸν ἡμέρας
acquaintance with Peter, and I remained with him 2days
δεκαπέντε· 19 ἕτερον.δὲ τῶν ἀποστόλων οὐκ.εἶδον, εἰ.μὴ
1fifteen; but other of the apostles I saw not, except
Ἰάκωβον τὸν ἀδελφὸν τοῦ κυρίου. 20 ἃ.δὲ γράφω ὑμῖν,
James the brother of the Lord. Now what [things] I write to you,
ἰδοὺ ἐνώπιον τοῦ θεοῦ, ὅτι οὐ.ψεύδομαι. 21 Ἔπειτα ἦλθον εἰς
lo, before God, I lie not. Then I came into
τὰ κλίματα τῆς Συρίας καὶ τῆς Κιλικίας· 22 ἤμην.δὲ ἀ-
the regions of Syria and Cilicia; but I was un-
γνοούμενος τῷ.προσώπῳ ταῖς ἐκκλησίαις τῆς Ἰουδαίας ταῖς
known by face to the assemblies of Judæa which
ἐν χριστῷ· 23 μόνον.δὲ ἀκούοντες ἦσαν, Ὅτι ὁ
[are] in Christ, only 3hearing 1they 2were, That he who
διώκων ἡμᾶς ποτε, νῦν εὐαγγελίζεται τὴν πίστιν
2persecuted 3us 1once, now announces the glad tidings— the faith,
ἥν ποτε ἐπόρθει. 24 καὶ ἐδόξαζον ἐν ἐμοὶ τὸν θεόν.
which once he ravaged: and they were glorifying 2in 3me 1God.

2 Ἔπειτα διὰ δεκατεσσάρων ἐτῶν πάλιν ἀνέβην εἰς Ἱε-
Then after fourteen years again I went up to Je-
ροσόλυμα μετὰ Βαρνάβα, [o]συμπαραλαβὼν" καὶ Τίτον·
rusalem with Barnabas, taking with [me] also Titus;
2 ἀνέβην.δὲ κατὰ ἀποκάλυψιν, καὶ ἀνεθέμην αὐτοῖς τὸ
but I went up according to revelation, and laid before them the
εὐαγγέλιον· ὃ κηρύσσω ἐν τοῖς ἔθνεσιν, κατ'.ἰδίαν.δὲ τοῖς
glad tidings which I proclaim among the nations, but privately to those
δοκοῦσιν, μήπως εἰς κενὸν τρέχω ἢ ἔδραμον· 3 ἀλλ'
of repute, lest somehow in vain I should be running or had run; (but
οὐδὲ Τίτος ὁ σὺν ἐμοί, Ἕλλην· ὤν, ἠναγκάσθη περι-
not even Titus who [was] with me, 2a 3Greek 1being, was compelled to be
τμηθῆναι. 4 διὰ.δὲ τοὺς παρεισάκτους ψευδ-
circumcised;) and [this] on account of the 3brought 4in 5stealthily 1false
αδέλφους, οἵτινες παρεισῆλθον κατασκοπῆσαι τὴν ἐλευθερίαν
2brethren, who came in by stealth to spy out 2freedom

gospel of Christ.
8 But even if we or an angel from Heaven
should preach any other gospel to you than
that which we have preached to you, let him
be anathema.
9 As we have said before, I also now say
again, If anyone preaches any other gospel
to you contrary to what you received, let
him be anathema.
10 For now do I persuade men or God? Or do
I seek to please men? For if I were yet pleasing
men, I would not be the servant of Christ.
11 But I assure you, brothers, the gospel
that I preached is not according to men.
12 For I did not receive it from man, nor
was I taught it, except by a heavenly
revelation of Jesus Christ.
13 For you have heard of my way of life at
one time in the Jewish religion, how I was
beyond measure in persecution of the
church of God and was destroying it.
14 And I was progressing in the Jewish
religion beyond many others of my age in
my own race, for *I was* zealous for the
traditions of my fathers.
15 But when it pleased God, who separated
me from my mother's womb, and called me
by His grace,
16 to reveal His Son in me, that I might
preach the gospel about Him in the nations,
I did not immediately talk it over with flesh
and blood.
17 Nor did I go up to Jerusalem to those
apostles before me, but I went away into
Arabia, and I returned again to Damascus.
18 Then after three years, I went up to
Jerusalem to make friends with Peter. And I
remained with him fifteen days.
19 But I did not see any other of the
apostles, except James, the Lord's brother.
20 Now what I write to you, behold, before
God I do not lie.
21 Then I came into the regions of Syria
and Cilicia.
22 But I was not known by face to the
churches of Judea which were in Christ.
23 Only they heard that he who persecuted
them in times past was now preaching the
gospel, the faith that he once destroyed.
24 And they were glorifying God in me.

CHAPTER 2

1 Then after fourteen years I again went up
to Jerusalem with Barnabas, taking Titus
with me also.
2 But I went up according to revelation and
laid before them the gospel which I preach
among the Gentiles but privately to those
thought to be important, for fear that somehow I might be running, or had run, in vain.
3 (But not even Titus, who was with me,
being a Greek, was forced to be circumcised).
4 But *this was* on account of the false
brothers brought in secretly, who stole in to

ἡμῶν ἣν ἔχομεν ἐν χριστῷ Ἰησοῦ, ἵνα ἡμᾶς [p]καταδουλώ-
[1]our which we have in Christ Jesus, that us they might bring
σωνται·‖ 5 οἷς οὐδὲ πρὸς ὥραν εἴξαμεν τῇ ὑποταγῇ,
into bondage; to whom not even for an hour did we yield in subjection,
ἵνα ἡ ἀλήθεια τοῦ εὐαγγελίου διαμείνῃ πρὸς ὑμᾶς. 6 Ἀπὸ
that the truth of the glad tidings might continue with you. [2]From
δὲ τῶν δοκούντων εἶναί τι, ὁποῖοί ποτε ἦσαν οὐδέν
[1]but those reputed to be something, whatsoever they were [2]no
μοι διαφέρει· πρόσωπον [q]θεὸς ἀνθρώπου οὐ λαμ-
[4]to [5]me [1]makes [3]difference: [the] person [3]God [1]of [2]man [5]not [4]does
βάνει· ἐμοὶ γὰρ οἱ δοκοῦντες οὐδὲν προσανέθεντο, 7 ἀλλὰ
accept; for to me those of repute nothing conferred; but
τοὐναντίον, ἰδόντες ὅτι πεπίστευμαι τὸ εὐαγγέλιον
on the contrary, having seen that I have been entrusted with the glad tidings
τῆς ἀκροβυστίας, καθὼς Πέτρος τῆς περιτομῆς· 8 ὁ
of the uncircumcision, according as Peter [that] of the circumcision, ([2]he [3]who
γὰρ ἐνεργήσας Πέτρῳ εἰς ἀποστολὴν τῆς περιτομῆς, ἐνήργη-
[1]for wrought in Peter for apostleship of the circumcision, wrought
σεν [r]καὶ ἐμοὶ‖ εἰς τὰ ἔθνη· 9 καὶ γνόντες τὴν χάριν τὴν
also in me towards the nations,) and having known the grace which
δοθεῖσάν μοι, Ἰάκωβος καὶ Κηφᾶς καὶ [s]Ἰωάννης,‖ οἱ δο-
was given to me, James and Cephas and John, those re-
κοῦντες στῦλοι εἶναι, δεξιὰς ἔδωκαν ἐμοὶ καὶ Βαρνάβᾳ
puted [3]pillars [1]to [2]be, [the] right hands [3]they [4]gave [5]to [6]me [7]and [8]Barnabas
κοινωνίας, ἵνα ἡμεῖς [t] εἰς τὰ ἔθνη, αὐτοὶ δὲ εἰς τὴν
[1]of [2]fellowship, that we [should go] to the nations, and they to the
περιτομήν· 10 μόνον τῶν πτωχῶν ἵνα μνημονεύωμεν, ὃ
circumcision: only the poor that we should remember, which
καὶ ἐσπούδασα αὐτὸ τοῦτο ποιῆσαι.
[3]also [4]I [5]was [6]diligent [1]very [2]thing to do.
11 Ὅτε δὲ ἦλθεν [v]Πέτρος‖ εἰς Ἀντιόχειαν, κατὰ πρόσωπον
But when [2]came [1]Peter to Antioch, to [the] face
αὐτῷ ἀντέστην, ὅτι κατεγνωσμένος ἦν. 12 πρὸ τοῦ γὰρ
him I withstood, because to be condemned he was: for before that
ἐλθεῖν τινας ἀπὸ Ἰακώβου, μετὰ τῶν ἐθνῶν συνήσθιεν· ὅτε δὲ
[2]came [1]some from James, with the nations he was eating; but when
[w]ἦλθον,‖ ὑπέστελλεν καὶ ἀφώριζεν ἑαυτόν, φοβούμενος
they came, he was drawing back and was separating himself, being afraid of
τοὺς ἐκ περιτομῆς· 13 καὶ συνυπεκρίθησαν αὐτῷ καὶ οἱ
those of [the] circumcision; and conjointly dissembled with him also the
λοιποὶ Ἰουδαῖοι, ὥστε καὶ Βαρνάβας συναπήχθη αὐτῶν
rest of [the] Jews, so that even Barnabas was carried away [2]their
τῇ ὑποκρίσει. 14 Ἀλλ᾽ ὅτε εἶδον ὅτι οὐκ ὀρθοποδοῦσιν
[1]by dissimulation. But when I saw that they walk not uprightly
πρὸς τὴν ἀλήθειαν τοῦ εὐαγγελίου, εἶπον τῷ [x]Πέτρῳ‖
according to the truth of the glad tidings, I said to Peter
ἔμπροσθεν πάντων, Εἰ σύ, Ἰουδαῖος ὑπάρχων, ἐθνικῶς
before all, If thou, [2]a [3]Jew [1]being, nation-like
[y]ζῇς καὶ οὐκ Ἰουδαϊκῶς,‖ [z]τί‖ τὰ ἔθνη ἀναγκάζεις Ἰου-
livest and not Jewishly, why the nations dost thou compel to ju-
δαΐζειν; 15 Ἡμεῖς φύσει Ἰουδαῖοι, καὶ οὐκ ἐξ ἐθνῶν
daize? We, [2]by [3]nature [1]Jews, and not [2]of [[3]the] [4]nations
ἁμαρτωλοί, 16 εἰδότες [a] ὅτι οὐ δικαιοῦται ἄνθρωπος ἐξ ἔργων
[1]sinners, knowing that [3]is [4]not [5]justified [1]a [2]man by works
νόμου, ἐὰν μὴ διὰ πίστεως [b]Ἰησοῦ χριστοῦ,‖ καὶ ἡμεῖς εἰς
of law, but through faith of Jesus Christ, also we on
χριστὸν Ἰησοῦν ἐπιστεύσαμεν, ἵνα δικαιωθῶμεν ἐκ πίστεως
Christ Jesus believed, that we might be justified by faith
χριστοῦ, καὶ οὐκ ἐξ ἔργων νόμου· [c]διότι‖ [d]οὐ δικαιωθήσεται
of Christ, and not by works of law; because shall not be justified
ἐξ ἔργων νόμου‖ πᾶσα σάρξ. 17 εἰ δὲ ζητοῦντες δικαιωθῆναι
by works of law any flesh. Now if seeking to be justified
(lit. all)
ἐν χριστῷ εὑρέθημεν καὶ αὐτοὶ ἁμαρτωλοί, [e]ἆρα‖ χριστὸς
in Christ we [3]were [4]found [2]also [1]ourselves sinners, [is] then Christ
ἁμαρτίας διάκονος; [f] μὴ γένοιτο. 18 εἰ γὰρ ἃ κατέλυσα
[2]of [3]sin [1]minister? May it not be! For if what I threw down
ταῦτα πάλιν οἰκοδομῶ, παραβάτην ἐμαυτὸν [g]συνίστημι.‖
these things again I build, a transgressor myself I constitute.
19 Ἐγὼ γὰρ διὰ νόμου νόμῳ ἀπέθανον, ἵνα θεῷ ζήσω.
For I through law to law died, that to God I may live.
20 χριστῷ συνεσταύρωμαι· ζῶ δέ, οὐκέτι ἐγώ, ζῇ δὲ
[6]Christ [1]I [2]have [3]been [4]crucified [5]with, yet I live, no longer I, but [2]lives
ἐν ἐμοὶ χριστός· ὃ δὲ νῦν ζῶ ἐν σαρκί, ἐν πίστει
[3]in [4]me [1]Christ; but that which now I live in flesh, in faith
ζῶ τῇ [h]τοῦ υἱοῦ τοῦ θεοῦ,‖ τοῦ ἀγαπήσαντός με καὶ παρα-
I live, that of the Son of God, who loved me and gave
δόντος ἑαυτὸν ὑπὲρ ἐμοῦ. 21 οὐκ ἀθετῶ τὴν χάριν τοῦ θεοῦ·
up himself for me. I do not set aside the grace of God;
εἰ γὰρ διὰ νόμου δικαιοσύνη, ἄρα χριστὸς δωρεὰν
for if through law righteousness [is], then Christ [2]for [3]nought
ἀπέθανεν.
[1]died.

spy out our freedom which we have in Christ Jesus, so that they might enslave us –
5 to whom we did not give in, not even for an hour, so that the truth of the gospel might continue with you.
6 But from those who were thought to be something (whatever they were makes no difference to me – God does not accept the person of man), for those who were thought to be important did not add anything to me.
7 But on the contrary, seeing that I had been charged with the gospel to the uncircumcised (even as Peter to the circumcision
8 – for He who worked in Peter towards the apostleship of the circumcision also worked in me towards the Gentiles),
9 and when they saw the grace which was given to me, James and Peter and John (those esteemed as pillars) gave the right hand of fellowship to Barnabas and me that we *should go* to the Gentiles and they to the circumcision.
10 Only *asking* that we should remember the poor, which very thing I was also trying to do.
11 But when Peter came to Antioch, I set my face against him, because he was to be blamed.
12 For before some came from James, he was eating with the Gentiles; but when they came, he was afraid of the circumcision party, drawing back and keeping himself apart.
13 And the rest of the Jews also acted the hypocrite with him, so that even Barnabas was carried away by their dissimulation.
14 But when I saw that they did not walk uprightly, according to the truth of the gospel, I said to Peter in the presence of all, If you, being a Jew, live like the Gentiles and not like the Jews, why do you force the Gentiles to live like the Jews?
15 We Jews by nature, and not sinners of the Gentiles
16 know that a man is not justified by works of the Law, but through faith in Jesus Christ. We too have believed on Jesus Christ that we might be justified by faith in Christ and not by works of the Law – for by the works of the Law shall no flesh be justified.
17 But if, while we seek to be justified in Christ, we were found to be sinners, is Christ then the minister of sin? Let it not be *said*!
18 For if I build again these things which I pulled down, I make myself a sinner.
19 For I through the Law died to the Law, so that I may live to God.
20 I have been crucified with Christ. Nevertheless I live, yet not I, but Christ lives in me. And the *life* which I now live in the flesh, I live by the faith of the Son of God, who loved me and gave Himself for me.
21 I do not set aside the grace of God. For if righteousness *is* through the Law, then Christ died without obtaining anything.

3 Ὦ ἀνόητοι Γαλάται, τίς ὑμᾶς ἐβάσκανεν [l]τῇ ἀληθείᾳ
O senseless Galatians, who you bewitched, [4]the [5]truth
μὴ πείθεσθαι;[ll] οἷς κατ' ὀφθαλμοὺς Ἰησοῦς χριστὸς προε-
not [2]to [3]obey? [7]whose [8]before eyes Jesus Christ was openly
γράφη [l]ἐν ὑμῖν[ll] ἐσταυρωμένος; 2 τοῦτο μόνον θέλω μαθεῖν
set forth among you— crucified? This only I wish to learn
ἀφ' ὑμῶν, ἐξ ἔργων νόμου τὸ πνεῦμα ἐλάβετε, ἢ ἐξ ἀκοῆς
from you, by works of law the Spirit receive ye, or by report
πίστεως; 3 οὕτως ἀνόητοί ἐστε; ἐναρξάμενοι πνεύματι, νῦν
of faith? So senseless are ye? Having begun in Spirit, now
σαρκὶ ἐπιτελεῖσθε; 4 τοσαῦτα ἐπάθετε εἰκῇ; εἴγε
in flesh are ye being perfected? So many things did ye suffer in vain? if indeed
καὶ εἰκῇ. 5 ὁ οὖν ἐπιχορηγῶν ὑμῖν τὸ πνεῦμα, καὶ
also in vain. He who therefore supplies to you the Spirit, and
ἐνεργῶν δυνάμεις ἐν ὑμῖν, ἐξ ἔργων νόμου ἢ ἐξ ἀκοῆς
works works of power among you, [is it] by works of law or by report
πίστεως; 6 καθὼς Ἀβραὰμ ἐπίστευσεν τῷ θεῷ, καὶ ἐλογίσθη
of faith? Even as Abraham believed God, and it was reckoned
αὐτῷ εἰς δικαιοσύνην. 7 γινώσκετε ἄρα ὅτι οἱ ἐκ πίστεως,
to him for righteousness. Know then that they that of faith
οὗτοί [k]εἰσιν υἱοὶ[ll] Ἀβραάμ. 8 προϊδοῦσα.δὲ ἡ γραφὴ
[are], these are sons of Abraham; and [3]foreseeing [1]the [2]scripture
ὅτι ἐκ πίστεως δικαιοῖ τὰ ἔθνη ὁ θεός, προευηγγελί-
that by faith [2]justifies [3]the [4]nations [1]God, before announced glad
σατο τῷ Ἀβραάμ, [ll]Ὅτι [l]ἐνευλογηθήσονται[ll] ἐν σοὶ πάντα τὰ
tidings to Abraham: Shall be blessed in thee all the
ἔθνη. 9 ὥστε οἱ ἐκ πίστεως εὐλογοῦνται σὺν τῷ πιστῷ
nations. So that those of faith are being blessed with the believing
Ἀβραάμ. 10 ὅσοι.γὰρ ἐξ ἔργων νόμου εἰσίν, ὑπὸ κατάραν
Abraham. For as many as of works of law are, under a curse
εἰσίν· γέγραπται.γάρ, [m]Ἐπικατάρατος πᾶς ὃς οὐκ ἐμ-
are. For it has been written, Cursed [is] everyone who [2]not [1]does
μένει [n]ἐν[ll] πᾶσιν τοῖς γεγραμμένοις ἐν τῷ βιβλίῳ τοῦ νόμου,
continue in all things which have been written in the book of the law
τοῦ ποιῆσαι αὐτά. 11 [ll]Ὅτι.δὲ ἐν νόμῳ οὐδεὶς δικαιοῦται
to do them. But that in virtue of law no one is being justified
παρὰ τῷ θεῷ δῆλον· ὅτι ὁ δίκαιος ἐκ πίστεως ζήσεται·
with God [is] manifest; because the just by faith shall live;
12 ὁ.δὲ νόμος οὐκ.ἔστιν ἐκ πίστεως, [o]ἀλλ'[ll] ὁ ποιήσας
but the law is not of faith; but, the [2]who [3]did
αὐτὰ [p]ἄνθρωπος[ll] ζήσεται ἐν αὐτοῖς. 13 χριστὸς ἡμᾶς
[4]these [5]things [1]man shall live in virtue of them. Christ us
ἐξηγόρασεν ἐκ τῆς κατάρας τοῦ νόμου, γενόμενος ὑπὲρ ἡμῶν
ransomed from the curse of the law, having become for us
κατάρα· [q]γέγραπται.γάρ,[ll] Ἐπικατάρατος πᾶς ὁ κρεμά-
a curse, (for it has been written, Cursed [is] everyone who hangs
μενος ἐπὶ ξύλου· 14 ἵνα εἰς τὰ ἔθνη ἡ εὐλογία τοῦ Ἀβραὰμ
on a tree,) that to the nations the blessing of Abraham
γένηται ἐν [r]χριστῷ Ἰησοῦ,[ll] ἵνα τὴν ἐπαγγελίαν τοῦ πνεύμα-
might come in Christ Jesus, that the promise of the Spirit
τος λάβωμεν διὰ τῆς πίστεως.
we might receive through faith.

15 Ἀδελφοί, κατὰ ἄνθρωπον λέγω, ὅμως ἀνθρώπου
Brethren, (according to man I am speaking,) even of man
κεκυρωμένην διαθήκην οὐδεὶς ἀθετεῖ ἢ ἐπιδιατάσσεται.
a confirmed covenant no one sets aside, or adds thereto.
16 τῷ.δὲ.Ἀβραὰμ [s]ἐρρήθησαν[ll] αἱ ἐπαγγελίαι, καὶ τῷ σπέρματι
But to Abraham were spoken the promises, and to [2]seed
αὐτοῦ· οὐ.λέγει, Καὶ τοῖς σπέρμασιν, ὡς ἐπὶ πολλῶν, [t]ἀλλ'[ll]
[1]his: he does not say, And to seeds, as of many; but
ὡς ἐφ' ἑνός, Καὶ τῷ.σπέρματί.σου, ὅς ἐστιν χριστός. 17 τοῦτο
as of one, And to thy seed; which is Christ. [2]This
δὲ λέγω, διαθήκην προκεκυρωμένην ὑπὸ τοῦ θεοῦ [v]εἰς χριστ-
[1]now I say, [the] covenant confirmed beforehand by God to Christ,
τὸν[ll] ὁ μετὰ [w]ἔτη τετρακόσια καὶ τριάκοντα[ll] γεγονὼς
the [5]after [10]years [6]four [7]hundred [8]and [9]thirty [2]which [3]took [4]place
νόμος οὐκ.ἀκυροῖ, εἰς.τὸ καταργῆσαι τὴν ἐπαγγελίαν. 18 εἰ
[1]law does not annul so as to make of no effect the promise. [2]If
γὰρ ἐκ νόμου ἡ κληρονομία, οὐκέτι ἐξ ἐπαγγελίας·
[1]for by law [be] the inheritance, [it is] no longer by promise;
τῷ.δὲ.Ἀβραὰμ δι' ἐπαγγελίας κεχάρισται ὁ θεός. 19 Τί
but to Abraham through promise [2]granted [[3]it] [1]God. Why
οὖν ὁ νόμος; τῶν παραβάσεων χάριν [x]προσετέθη,[ll]
then the law? [5]transgressions [1]for [2]the [3]sake [4]of it was added,
ἄχρις οὗ ἔλθῃ τὸ σπέρμα ᾧ ἐπήγγελται,
until should have come the seed to whom promise has been made,
διαταγεὶς δι' ἀγγέλων ἐν χειρὶ μεσίτου. 20 ὁ.δὲ
having been ordained through angels in [3]hand [1]a [2]mediator's. But the
μεσίτης ἑνὸς οὐκ.ἔστιν, ὁ.δὲ.θεὸς εἷς ἐστιν.
mediator [3]of [4]one [1]is [2]not, but God [2]one [1]is.
21 Ὁ.οὖν.νόμος κατὰ τῶν ἐπαγγελιῶν [y]τοῦ θεοῦ[ll];
The law then [is it] against the promises of God?

CHAPTER 3

1 O foolish Galatians, who has bewitched you that you should not obey the truth – before whose eyes Jesus Christ crucified was openly set out among you?

2 This only I desire to learn from you: Did you receive the Spirit by works of the Law? or by the hearing of faith?

3 Are you so foolish? Having begun in the Spirit, are you now made perfect by flesh?

4 Did you suffer so many things without cause? If indeed *it was* also without cause.

5 He then who supplies the Spirit to you and works miracles among you, *is it* by works of the Law, or by the hearing of faith?

6 *It is* even as Abraham believed God and it was counted to him for righteousness.

7 Know then that they that are of faith, these are the sons of Abraham.

8 And the Scripture, foreseeing that God justifies the Gentiles by faith, preached before the gospel to Abraham *saying,* "All the nations shall be blessed in you."

9 So that those who are of faith are being blessed with the believing Abraham.

10 For as many as are of the works of the Law are under a curse – for it is written, "Cursed is everyone who does not continue in all things which have been written in the book of the Law to do them."

11 But that no one is being justified by Law in the sight of God is plainly seen, because, "The just shall live by faith."

12 But the Law is not of faith, but, "The man who has done these shall live by them."

13 Christ redeemed us from the Law's curse – being made a curse for us, for it is written, "Cursed is everyone who hangs on a tree" –

14 that Abraham's blessing might come to the Gentiles in Christ Jesus, so that we might gain the promise of the Spirit through faith.

15 Brothers! I speak in the way of man – no one sets aside even a confirmed covenant of man, or adds to it.

16 But to Abraham and to his seed the promises were spoken. He does not say, And to seeds, as of many, but as of one – "And to your Seed," which is Christ.

17 I say this now, the covenant settled first by God to Christ, the Law (which came four hundred and thirty years after) cannot set aside, so as to do away with the promise.

18 For if the inheritance is by Law, *it is* no longer by promise – but God gave it to Abraham by promise.

19 Why then the Law? It was added because of transgressions, until the Seed should come to the promised ones (having been ordained through angels in a mediator's hand).

20 But a mediator is not *a mediator* of one, but God is one.

21 *Is* the Law then against the promises of

μὴ.γένοιτο· εἰ.γὰρ ἐδόθη νόμος ὁ δυνάμενος ζωοποιῆσαι,
May it not be! For if was given a law which was able to quicken,
ὄντως [a]ἂν ἐκ νόμου ἦν[‖] ἡ δικαιοσύνη· 22 ἀλλὰ συνέ-
indeed by law would have been righteousness; but [3]shut
κλεισεν ἡ γραφὴ τὰ.πάντα [a]ὑπὸ[‖] ἁμαρτίαν, ἵνα ἡ ἐπαγγελία
[4]up [1]the [2]scripture all things under sin, that the promise
ἐκ πίστεως Ἰησοῦ χριστοῦ δοθῇ τοῖς πιστεύουσιν.
by faith of Jesus Christ might be given to those that believe.
23 Πρὸ.τοῦ.δὲ ἐλθεῖν τὴν πίστιν, ὑπὸ νόμον ἐφρουρούμεθα,
But before [2]came [1]faith, under law we were guarded,
[b]συγκεκλεισμένοι[‖] εἰς τὴν μέλλουσαν πίστιν ἀποκαλυφθῆναι·
having been shut up to the [2]being [3]about [1]faith to be revealed.
24 ὥστε ὁ νόμος παιδαγωγὸς ἡμῶν γέγονεν εἰς χριστόν, ἵνα
So that the law [2]tutor [1]our has been [up] to Christ, that
ἐκ πίστεως δικαιωθῶμεν· 25 ἐλθούσης.δὲ τῆς πίστεως,
by faith we might be justified. But [2]having [3]come [1]faith,
οὐκέτι ὑπὸ παιδαγωγόν ἐσμεν. 26 πάντες.γὰρ υἱοὶ θεοῦ
no longer under a tutor we are; for all sons of God
ἐστε διὰ τῆς πίστεως ἐν χριστῷ Ἰησοῦ· 27 ὅσοι.γὰρ εἰς
ye are through faith in Christ Jesus. For as many as to
χριστὸν ἐβαπτίσθητε, χριστὸν ἐνεδύσασθε. 28 οὐκ.ἔνι Ἰου-
Christ were baptized, [5]Christ [1]ye [2]did [3]put [4]on. There is not Jew
δαῖος οὐδὲ Ἕλλην· οὐκ.ἔνι δοῦλος οὐδὲ ἐλεύθερος· οὐκ.ἔνι
nor Greek; there is not bondman nor free; there is not
ἄρσεν καὶ θῆλυ· [c]πάντες[‖].γὰρ ὑμεῖς εἷς ἐστε ἐν.χριστῷ Ἰησοῦ·
male and female; for all ye one are in Christ Jesus:
29 εἰ.δὲ ὑμεῖς χριστοῦ, ἄρα τοῦ Ἀβραὰμ σπέρμα ἐστέ,
but if ye [are] Christ's, then Abraham's seed ye are,
[d]καὶ[‖] [e]κατ'[‖] ἐπαγγελίαν κληρονόμοι.
and according to promise heirs.

4 Λέγω.δέ, ἐφ' ὅσον χρόνον ὁ κληρονόμος νήπιός ἐστιν,
Now I say, for as long [2]as [1]time the heir an infant is,
οὐδὲν διαφέρει δούλου, κύριος πάντων ὤν· 2 ἀλλὰ
nothing he differs from a bondman, [though] [2]lord [3]of [4]all [1]being; but
ὑπὸ ἐπιτρόπους ἐστὶν καὶ οἰκονόμους ἄχρι τῆς προθεσμίας
under guardians he is and stewards until the time before appointed
τοῦ πατρός. 3 οὕτως καὶ ἡμεῖς, ὅτε ἦμεν νήπιοι, ὑπὸ τὰ
of the father. So also we, when we were infants, under the
στοιχεῖα τοῦ κόσμου [f]ἦμεν[‖] δεδουλωμένοι· 4 ὅτε.δὲ ἦλθεν τὸ
elements of the world were held in bondage; but when came the
πλήρωμα τοῦ χρόνου, ἐξαπέστειλεν ὁ θεὸς τὸν.υἱὸν.αὐτοῦ,
fulness of the time, [2]sent [3]forth [1]God his Son,
γενόμενον ἐκ γυναικός, γενόμενον ὑπὸ νόμον, 5 ἵνα τοὺς
come of woman, come under law, that those
ὑπὸ νόμον ἐξαγοράσῃ, ἵνα τὴν υἱοθεσίαν ἀπολάβωμεν.
under law he might ransom, that adoption we might receive.
6 ὅτι.δέ ἐστε υἱοί, ἐξαπέστειλεν ὁ θεὸς τὸ πνεῦμα τοῦ
But because ye are sons, [2]sent [3]forth [1]God the Spirit
υἱοῦ.αὐτοῦ εἰς τὰς καρδίας [g]ὑμῶν,[‖] κρᾶζον, Ἀββᾶ ὁ πατήρ.
of his Son into [2]hearts [1]your, crying, Abba, Father.
7 ὥστε οὐκέτι εἶ δοῦλος, [h]ἀλλ'[‖] υἱός· εἰ.δὲ υἱός, καὶ
So no longer thou art bondman, but son; and if son, also
κληρονόμος [i]θεοῦ διὰ χριστοῦ.[‖] 8 Ἀλλὰ τότε μὲν οὐκ
heir of God through Christ. But then indeed not
εἰδότες θεόν, ἐδουλεύσατε τοῖς [k]μὴ φύσει[‖] οὖσιν
knowing God, ye were in bondage to those who not by nature are
θεοῖς· 9 νῦν.δέ, γνόντες θεόν, μᾶλλον.δὲ γνωσθέντες
gods; but now, having known God, but rather having been known
ὑπὸ θεοῦ, πῶς ἐπιστρέφετε πάλιν ἐπὶ τὰ ἀσθενῆ καὶ πτωχὰ
by God, how do ye turn again to the weak and beggarly
στοιχεῖα οἷς πάλιν ἄνωθεν [l]δουλεύειν[‖] θέλετε; 10 ἡμέρας
elements to which again anew to be in bondage ye desire? Days
παρατηρεῖσθε, καὶ μῆνας, καὶ καιρούς, καὶ ἐνιαυτούς.[m] 11 φο-
ye observe, and months, and times, and years. I am
βοῦμαι ὑμᾶς, μήπως εἰκῇ κεκοπίακα εἰς ὑμᾶς.
afraid of you, lest somehow in vain I have laboured as to you.
12 Γίνεσθε ὡς ἐγώ, ὅτι.κἀγὼ ὡς ὑμεῖς, ἀδελφοί, δέο-
Be as I [am], for I also [am] as ye, brethren, I be-
μαι ὑμῶν· οὐδέν με ἠδικήσατε. 13 οἴδατε.δὲ ὅτι δι'
seech you: in nothing me ye wronged. But ye know that in
ἀσθένειαν τῆς σαρκὸς εὐηγγελισάμην ὑμῖν τὸ.πρότερον,
weakness of the flesh I announced the glad tidings to you at the first;
14 καὶ τὸν πειρασμόν [n]μου τὸν[‖] ἐν τῇ.σαρκί.μου οὐκ ἐξου-
and [2]temptation [1]my in my flesh [3]not [1]ye [2]de-
θενήσατε οὐδὲ ἐξεπτύσατε, [h]ἀλλ'[‖] ὡς ἄγγελον θεοῦ ἐ-
spised nor rejected with contempt; but as an angel of God ye
δέξασθέ με, ὡς χριστὸν Ἰησοῦν. 15 [o]τίς[‖] οὖν [p]ἦν[‖] ὁ μακαρισμὸς
received me, as Christ Jesus. What then was [2]blessedness
ὑμῶν; μαρτυρῶ.γὰρ ὑμῖν ὅτι, εἰ δυνατόν, τοὺς ὀφθαλμοὺς
[1]your? for I bear [2]witness [1]you that, if possible, [2]eyes
ὑμῶν ἐξορύξαντες [q]ἂν[‖] ἐδώκατέ μοι. 16 ὥστε ἐχθρὸς
[1]your having plucked out ye would have given [them] to me. So [2]enemy

God? Let it not be! For if a law had been given which was able to give life, indeed righteousness would have been by Law.

22 But the Scripture shut up all things under sin so that the promise by faith of Jesus Christ might be given to those that believe.

23 But before faith came, we were kept under Law, being shut up to the faith which was going to be revealed.

24 So that the Law has been our schoolmaster until Christ, so that we might be justified by faith.

25 But faith coming on, we are no longer under a schoolmaster –

26 for you are all sons of God through faith in Christ Jesus.

27 For as many as were baptized into Christ have put on Christ.

28 There is not Jew or Greek, nor is there slave or freeman, nor is there male or female, for you all are one in Christ Jesus.

29 But if you are Christ's, then you are Abraham's seed and heirs as to the promise.

4 1 But I say, for as long a time as the heir is an infant, he does not differ any from a slave – though he is lord of all.

2 But he is under guardians and managers until the time set before by the father.

3 So we, too, when in infancy, were held in slavery under the principles of the world.

4 But when the fullness of time came, God sent out His Son, coming from a woman, coming under Law,

5 so that He might redeem the ones under Law, so that we might receive sonship.

6 But because you are sons, God sent the Spirit of His Son into your hearts, crying Abba – Father!

7 So that you are no longer a slave, but a son – and if a son, also an heir of God through Christ.

8 But then indeed not knowing God, you were a slave to those who by nature are not gods.

9 But now *that you* have known God (or, rather, that you have been known by God), how can you turn again to the weak and poor principles to which you again desire to be in slavery?

10 You carefully keep days and months and times and years.

11 I am afraid of you for fear that somehow I have labored to no avail regarding you.

12 Brothers! I beg of you, be as *I am*, for I also *am* as you are. You did not wrong me in anything.

13 But you know that through weakness of the flesh, I preached the gospel to you at first

14 – and you despised not my temptation in the flesh, nor spit on *me*. But you received me as an angel of God, even as Jesus Christ.

15 What then was your happiness? For I tell you that if possible you would have plucked out your eyes and have given them to me.

ὑμῶν γέγονα ἀληθεύων ὑμῖν; 17 Ζηλοῦσιν ὑμᾶς
'your have I become speaking truth to you? They are zealous after you
οὐ καλῶς, ἀλλὰ ἐκκλεῖσαι [r]ὑμᾶς" θέλουσιν, ἵνα αὐτοὺς
not rightly, but to exclude you [from us] they desire, that them
ζηλοῦτε. 18 καλὸν.δὲ [s]τὸ" ζηλοῦσθαι ἐν καλῷ
ye may be zealous after. But right [it is] to be zealous in a right [thing]
πάντοτε, καὶ μὴ μόνον ἐν τῷ.παρεῖναί.με πρὸς ὑμᾶς, 19 [t]τεκ-
at all times, and not only in my being present with -you— [2]little
νία" μου, οὓς πάλιν ὠδίνω [v]ἄχρις" οὗ μορφωθῇ
[3]children [1]my, of whom again I travail until shall have been formed
χριστὸς ἐν ὑμῖν· 20 ἤθελον.δὲ παρεῖναι πρὸς ὑμᾶς ἄρτι, καὶ
Christ in you: and I was wishing to be present with you now, and
ἀλλάξαι τὴν.φωνήν.μου, ὅτι ἀποροῦμαι ἐν ὑμῖν.
to change my voice, for I am perplexed as to you.

21 Λέγετέ μοι, οἱ ὑπὸ νόμον θέλοντες εἶναι, τὸν νόμον
Tell me, ye who under law wish to be, the law
οὐκ.ἀκούετε; 22 γέγραπται.γάρ, ὅτι Ἀβραὰμ δύο υἱοὺς
do ye not hear? For it has been written, that Abraham two sons
ἔσχεν· ἕνα ἐκ τῆς παιδίσκης, καὶ ἕνα ἐκ τῆς ἐλευθέρας·
had; one of the maid-servant, and one of the free [woman].
23 [w]ἀλλ'" ὁ [x]μὲν" ἐκ τῆς παιδίσκης, κατὰ σάρκα [y]γε-
But he of the maid-servant, according to flesh has
γέννηται·" ὁ.δὲ ἐκ τῆς ἐλευθέρας, [z]διὰ τῆς" ἐπαγγελίας.
been born, and he of the free [woman], through the promise.
24 ἅτινά ἐστιν ἀλληγορούμενα· αὗται.γάρ εἰσιν [a]αἱ" δύο
Which things are allegorized; for these are the two
διαθῆκαι· μία μὲν ἀπὸ ὄρους Σινᾶ, εἰς [b]δουλείαν" γεννῶσα,
covenants; one from mount Sina, to bondage bringing forth,
ἥτις ἐστὶν Ἄγαρ. 25 τὸ γὰρ [c]Ἄγαρ" Σινᾶ ὄρος ἐστὶν ἐν τῇ
which is Agar. For Agar [3]Sina mount [1]is in
Ἀραβίᾳ, [d]συστοιχεῖ".δὲ τῇ νῦν Ἰερουσαλήμ, δουλεύει
Arabia, and corresponds to the now Jerusalem, [2]she [3]is [4]in [5]bondage
[e]δὲ" μετὰ τῶν.τέκνων.αὐτῆς. 26 ἡ.δὲ ἄνω Ἰερουσαλήμ, ἐλευ-
[1]and with her children; but the [2]above [1]Jerusalem, [4]free
θέρα ἐστίν, ἥτις ἐστὶν μήτηρ [f]πάντων" ἡμῶν· 27 γέγραπται
[3]is, which is mother of all of us. [2]It [3]has [4]been [5]written
γάρ, Εὐφράνθητι στεῖρα ἡ οὐ.τίκτουσα· ῥῆξον καὶ βόησον
[1]for, Rejoice, O barren that bearest not; break forth and cry,
ἡ οὐκ.ὠδίνουσα· ὅτι πολλὰ τὰ τέκνα τῆς ἐρήμου μᾶλλον ἢ
that travailest not; because many the children of the desolate more than
τῆς ἐχούσης τὸν ἄνδρα. 28 [g]Ἡμεῖς".δέ, ἀδελφοί, κατὰ Ἰσαάκ,
of her that has the husband. But we, brethren, like Isaac,
ἐπαγγελίας τέκνα [h]ἐσμέν·" 29 ἀλλ' ὥσπερ τότε ὁ κατὰ
[3]of [4]promise [2]children [1]are. But as then he who according to
σάρκα γεννηθεὶς ἐδίωκεν τὸν κατὰ πνεῦμα, οὕτως καὶ
flesh was born persecuted him [born] according to Spirit, so also
νῦν. 30 ἀλλὰ τί λέγει ἡ γραφή; Ἔκβαλε τὴν παιδίσκην
now. But what says the scripture? Cast out the maid-servant
καὶ τὸν.υἱὸν.αὐτῆς, οὐ.γὰρ.μὴ [i]κληρονομήσῃ" ὁ υἱὸς τῆς
and her son, for in no wise may [6]inherit [1]the [2]son [3]of [4]the
παιδίσκης μετὰ τοῦ υἱοῦ τῆς ἐλευθέρας. 31 [k]Ἄρα," ἀδελ-
[5]maid-servant with the son of the free [woman]. So then, breth-
φοί, οὐκ.ἐσμὲν παιδίσκης τέκνα, ἀλλὰ τῆς ἐλευθέρας.
ren, we are not [2]of [3]a [4]maid-servant [1]children, but of the free [woman].

5 Τῇ ἐλευθερίᾳ [l]οὖν" [m]ᾗ" [n]χριστὸς ἡμᾶς" ἠλευθέρω-
In the freedom therefore wherewith Christ us made free,
σεν, [o]στήκετε," [p]καὶ μὴ πάλιν ζυγῷ [q]δουλείας" ἐνέχεσθε. 2 Ἴδε
stand fast, and not again in a yoke of bondage be held. Lo,
ἐγὼ Παῦλος λέγω ὑμῖν, ὅτι ἐὰν περιτέμνησθε, χριστὸς ὑμᾶς
I Paul say to you, that if ye be circumcised, Christ [3]you
οὐδὲν ὠφελήσει· 3 μαρτύρομαι.δὲ πάλιν παντὶ ἀνθρώπῳ
[2]nothing [1]shall [2]profit. And I testify again to every man
περιτεμνομένῳ, ὅτι ὀφειλέτης ἐστὶν ὅλον τὸν νόμον ποιῆσαι.
being circumcised, that a debtor he is [2]whole [1]the law to do.
4 κατηργήθητε ἀπὸ [r]τοῦ" χριστοῦ, οἵτινες ἐν νόμῳ δι-
Ye are deprived of all effect from the Christ, whosoever in law are
καιοῦσθε, τῆς χάριτος ἐξεπέσατε· 5 ἡμεῖς.γὰρ πνεύματι
being justified; grace ye fell from. For we, by [the] Spirit
ἐκ πίστεως ἐλπίδα δικαιοσύνης ἀπεκδεχόμεθα. 6 ἐν.γὰρ
by faith [the] hope of righteousness await. For in
χριστῷ Ἰησοῦ οὔτε περιτομή τι ἰσχύει, οὔτε ἀκροβυστία,
Christ Jesus neither circumcision [3]any [1]is [2]of force, nor uncircumcision;
ἀλλὰ πίστις δι' ἀγάπης ἐνεργουμένη. 7 Ἐτρέχετε καλῶς·
but faith [2]by [3]love [1]working. Ye were running well:
τίς ὑμᾶς [s]ἀνέκοψεν" [t]τῇ" ἀληθείᾳ μὴ πείθεσθαι; 8 ἡ πεισ-
who [2]you [1]hindered [6]the [7]truth [3]not [4]to [5]obey? The persua-
μονὴ οὐκ ἐκ τοῦ καλοῦντος ὑμᾶς. 9 Μικρὰ ζύμη ὅλον
sion [is] not of him who calls you. A little leaven [3]whole
τὸ φύραμα ζυμοῖ. 10 ἐγὼ [v] πέποιθα εἰς ὑμᾶς ἐν κυρίῳ,
[2]the [4]lump [1]leavens. I am persuaded as to you in [the] Lord,
ὅτι οὐδὲν.ἄλλο.φρονήσετε, ὁ.δὲ ταράσσων ὑμᾶς βαστάσει τὸ
that ye will have no other mind, and he troubling you shall bear the

16 Have I then become your enemy by
telling you the truth?
17 They are eagerly after you, *but* not with
honor. But they desire to keep you so that
you may *run* eagerly after them.
18 But it is right to be zealous in a right
thing at all times, and not only when I am
present with you.
19 *You* are my little children, for whom I
labor in pain again until Christ shall have
been formed in you –
20 and I desire to be there with you now
and to change my voice, for I am doubtful
about you.
21 Tell me, you who desire to be under Law
– do you not hear the Law?
22 For it has been written that Abraham
had two sons, one out of the slave-woman
and one out of the free woman.
23 But he that was out of the slave-woman
had been born after the flesh, and he that was
out of the free woman through the promise.
24 Which things are an allegory, for these are
the two covenants – one from Mount Sinai,
bringing into slavery, which is Hagar.
25 For Hagar is Mount Sinai in Arabia and
answers to the present Jerusalem. And she is
in slavery with her children.
26 But the Jerusalem which is above is free,
which is the mother of us all.
27 For it has been written, "Rejoice, O unfruitful one that does not bear. Break forth
and cry, you who have no birth-pains. Because
more are the children of the deserted one
than of her who has the husband."
28 But, brothers, we like Isaac are children
of the promise.
29 But as then he who was born according
to the flesh persecuted him *who was born*
according to the Spirit, so it is now.
30 But what does the Scripture say?
"Throw out the slave-woman and her son, for
the son of the slave-woman shall not in any
way inherit with the son of the free woman."
31 So, then, brothers, we are not children of
the slave-woman, but of the free woman.

CHAPTER 5

1 Then stand firm in the freedom with
which Christ has made us free. And do not
be held again in the yoke of slavery.
2 Behold! I, Paul, say to you that if you are
circumcised, Christ will be no profit to you.
3 And I again testify to every man being
circumcised that he is a debtor to do the
whole Law.
4 You are set aside from Christ, you who are
being justified in Law. You fell from grace.
5 For we through the Spirit wait for the hope
of righteousness by faith.
6 For in Christ Jesus neither circumcision
nor the lack of circumcision is worth
anything, but faith working by love.
7 You were running well. Who kept you
back that you did not obey the truth?
8 This false belief is not of Him who calls.
9 A little leaven leavens the whole lump.
10 I am persuaded as to you that you will
have no other mind in the Lord. But he who
is troubling you shall bear the judgment,

κρίμα, ὅστις [w]ἂν" ᾖ.
judgment, whosoever he may be.
11 Ἐγὼ.δέ, ἀδελφοί, εἰ περιτομὴν ἔτι κηρύσσω, τί ἔτι διώ-
But I, brethren, if circumcision yet I proclaim, why yet am I
κομαι; ἄρα κατήργηται τὸ σκάνδαλον τοῦ σταυροῦ.
persecuted? Then has been done away the offence of the cross.
12 ὄφελον καὶ ἀποκόψονται οἱ ἀναστατοῦντες
I would 3even 1they 2would cut themselves off who throw 2into 3confusion
ὑμᾶς. 13 Ὑμεῖς.γὰρ ἐπ' ἐλευθερίᾳ ἐκλήθητε, ἀδελφοί· μόνον
1you. For ye for freedom were called, brethren; only
μὴ τὴν ἐλευθερίαν εἰς ἀφορμὴν τῇ σαρκί, ἀλλὰ διὰ τῆς
[use] not the freedom for an occasion to the flesh, but by
ἀγάπης δουλεύετε ἀλλήλοις. 14 ὁ.γὰρ.πᾶς νόμος ἐν ἑνὶ
love serve ye one another. For the whole law in one
λόγῳ [x]πληροῦται," ἐν τῷ, Ἀγαπήσεις τὸν.πλησίον.σου ὡς
word is fulfilled, in Thou shalt love thy neighbour as
[y]ἑαυτόν." 15 εἰ.δὲ ἀλλήλους δάκνετε καὶ κατεσθίετε, βλέπετε
thyself; but if one another ye bite and devour, take heed
μὴ [z]ὑπὸ" ἀλλήλων ἀναλωθῆτε.
3not 5by 6one 7another 1ye 2be 4consumed.

16 Λέγω.δέ, Πνεύματι περιπατεῖτε, καὶ ἐπιθυμίαν σαρκὸς
But I say, By [the] Spirit walk ye, and 2desire 1flesh's
οὐ.μὴ τελέσητε. 17 ἡ.γὰρ.σὰρξ ἐπιθυμεῖ κατὰ τοῦ πνεύ-
in no wise should ye fulfil. For the flesh desires against the Spirit,
ματος, τὸ.δὲ πνεῦμα κατὰ τῆς σαρκός· ταῦτα [a]δὲ" [b]ἀντί-
and the Spirit against the flesh; 2these 3things 1and are op-
κειται ἀλλήλοις," ἵνα μὴ ἃ.[c]ἂν" θέλητε ταῦτα ποιῆτε.
posed to one another, that not whatsoever ye may wish those things ye should do;
18 εἰ.δὲ πνεύματι ἄγεσθε, οὐκ.ἐστὲ ὑπὸ νόμον. 19 φανερὰ
but if by [the] Spirit ye are led, ye are 2no 1under law. 2Manifest
δέ ἐστιν τὰ ἔργα τῆς σαρκός, ἅτινά ἐστιν [d]μοιχεία," πορνεία,
1now are the works of the flesh, which are adultery, fornication,
ἀκαθαρσία, ἀσέλγεια, 20 εἰδωλολατρεία, φαρμακεία, ἔχθραι,
uncleanness, licentiousness, idolatry, sorcery, enmities,
[e]ἔρεις, ζῆλοι," θυμοί, ἐριθεῖαι, διχοστασίαι, αἱρέσεις,
strifes, jealousies, indignations, contentious, divisions, sects,
21 φθόνοι, [f]φόνοι," μέθαι, κῶμοι, καὶ τὰ ὅμοια τούτοις·
envyings, murders, drunkennesses, revels, and things like these;
ἃ προλέγω ὑμῖν, καθὼς [g]καὶ" προεῖπον, ὅτι οἱ
as to which I tell 2beforehand 1you, even as also I said before, that they who
τὰ.τοιαῦτα πράσσοντες βασιλείαν θεοῦ οὐ.κληρονομήσουσιν.
such things do 2kingdom 1God's shall not inherit.
22 ὁ.δὲ καρπὸς τοῦ πνεύματός ἐστιν ἀγάπη, χαρά, εἰρήνη,
But the fruit of the Spirit is love, joy, peace,
μακροθυμία, χρηστότης, ἀγαθωσύνη, πίστις, 23 [h]πρᾳότης,"
long-suffering, kindness, goodness, faith, meekness,
ἐγκράτεια· κατὰ τῶν.τοιούτων οὐκ.ἔστιν νόμος. 24 οἱ.δὲ
self-control: against such things there is no law. But they that [are]
τοῦ χριστοῦ [i] τὴν σάρκα ἐσταύρωσαν σὺν τοῖς παθήμασιν καὶ
of the Christ 2the 3flesh 1crucified with the passions and
ταῖς ἐπιθυμίαις. 25 εἰ ζῶμεν πνεύματι, πνεύματι καὶ
the desires. If we live by [the] Spirit, by [the] Spirit also
στοιχῶμεν. 26 μὴ.γινώμεθα κενόδοξοι, ἀλλήλους προκα-
we should walk. We should not become vain-glorious, one another provok-
λούμενοι, [k]ἀλλήλοις" φθονοῦντες.
ing, one another envying.

6 Ἀδελφοί, ἐὰν καὶ [l]προληφθῇ" ἄνθρωπος ἔν τινι παρα-
Brethren, if even be taken a man in some of-
πτώματι, ὑμεῖς οἱ πνευματικοὶ καταρτίζετε τὸν.τοιοῦτον ἐν
fence, ye, the spiritual [ones], restore such a one in
πνεύματι [m]πρᾳότητος," σκοπῶν σεαυτὸν μὴ καὶ σὺ πει-
a spirit of meekness, considering thyself lest also thou be
ρασθῇς. 2 ἀλλήλων τὰ βάρη βαστάζετε, καὶ οὕτως [n]ἀνα-
tempted. One another's burdens bear ye, and thus ful-
πληρώσατε" τὸν νόμον τοῦ χριστοῦ. 3 εἰ.γὰρ δοκεῖ τις
fil the law of the Christ. For if 2thinks 1anyone
εἶναί τι, μηδὲν ὤν, [o]ἑαυτὸν φρεναπατᾷ." 4 τὸ.δὲ ἔργον
to be something, 2nothing 1being, himself he deceives: but the work
ἑαυτοῦ δοκιμαζέτω ἕκαστος, καὶ τότε εἰς ἑαυτὸν μόνον τὸ
of himself let 2prove 1each, and then as to himself alone the
καύχημα ἕξει, καὶ οὐκ εἰς τὸν.ἕτερον· 5 ἕκαστος.γὰρ τὸ
boasting he will have, and not as to another. For each
ἴδιον φορτίον βαστάσει.
his own load shall bear.
6 Κοινωνείτω.δὲ ὁ κατηχούμενος τὸν λόγον τῷ
Let 7share 1him 2being 3taught 4in 5the 6word with him that
κατηχοῦντι ἐν πᾶσιν ἀγαθοῖς. 7 μὴ.πλανᾶσθε, θεὸς οὐ μυκ-
teaches in all good things. Be not misled; God 2not 1is
τηρίζεται· ὃ.γὰρ.[p]ἐὰν" σπείρῃ ἄνθρωπος, τοῦτο καὶ θερί-
mocked; for whatsoever 3may 4sow 1a 2man, that also he shall
σει· 8 ὅτι ὁ σπείρων εἰς τὴν.σάρκα.ἑαυτοῦ, ἐκ τῆς σαρκὸς
reap. For he that sows to his own flesh, from the flesh

whoever he may be.
11 But I, brothers, if I still preach circumcision, why am I yet persecuted? Then the
stumbling-block of the cross has ceased.
12 I wish that they who are causing you to
doubt would even cut themselves off.
13 For you were called to freedom,
brothers. Only do not use the freedom for
an opportunity to the flesh, but serve one
another by love.
14 For all the Law is fulfilled in one word,
"You shall love your neighbor as yourself."
15 But if you bite and devour one another,
be careful that you are not destroyed by one
another.
16 But I say, Walk in the Spirit and you will
not fulfill the lust of the flesh.
17 For the flesh lusts against the Spirit, and
the Spirit against the flesh. And these are
contrary to one another: so that you cannot
do the things that you want to do.
18 But if you are led by the Spirit, you are
not under Law.
19 Now the works of the flesh are clearly
revealed – adultery, fornication, uncleanness
and lustfulness,
20 idolatry, practicing of evil magic, hatreds
– fightings, jealousies, outbursts of anger,
party arguments, differences, false teachings,
21 envyings, murders, drunkenness, wild
parties and things like these. As to *these* I
tell you now, as I also said before, that they
who do such things shall not inherit the
kingdom of God.
22 But the fruit of the Spirit is love, joy,
peace, long-suffering, kindness, goodness,
faith,
23 meekness, self-control – against such
things there is no law.
24 But they that are Christ's, crucified the
flesh with its passions and lusts.
25 If we live by the Spirit, we should also
walk by the Spirit.
26 We should not seek after self-glory, provoking one another, envying one another.

CHAPTER 6

1 Brothers, if a man is taken in some fault,
you, who are spiritual restore him in a spirit
of meekness, considering yourself for fear
that you also may be tempted.
2 Bear one another's burdens, and so fulfill
the law of Christ.
3 For if anyone thinks himself to be something, being nothing, he is fooling himself.
4 But let each prove his own work and then
he alone will have rejoicing, not in another.
5 For each shall carry his own load.
6 Let him who is taught in the word share
with him who teaches in all good things.
7 Be not deceived, God is not mocked – for
whatever a man sows, that he shall also reap.
8 For he that sows to his own flesh shall
reap from the flesh everlasting misery, but

θερίσει φθοράν· ὁ.δὲ σπείρων εἰς τὸ πνεῦμα, ἐκ τοῦ
shall reap corruption; but he that sows to the Spirit, from the
πνεύματος θερίσει ζωὴν αἰώνιον. 9 τὸ δὲ καλὸν ποιοῦντες
Spirit shall reap life eternal: but [in] well doing
μὴ.[q]ἐκκακῶμεν·‖ καιρῷ.γὰρ ἰδίῳ θερίσομεν, μὴ ἐκλυόμενοι.
we should not lose heart; for in [2]time [1]due [5]we [6]shall [7]reap [4]not [3]fainting.
10 ἄρα οὖν ὡς καιρὸν [r]ἔχομεν‖ ἐργαζώμεθα τὸ ἀγαθὸν πρὸς
So then as occasion we have we should work good towards
πάντας, μάλιστα.δὲ πρὸς τοὺς οἰκείους τῆς πίστεως.
all, and specially towards those of the household of faith.
11 [s]Ἴδετε πηλίκοις ὑμῖν γράμμασιν ἔγραψα τῇ.ἐμῇ.χειρί.
See in how large [4]to [5]you [1]letters [2]I [3]wrote with my [own] hand.
12 ὅσοι θέλουσιν εὐπροσωπῆσαι ἐν σαρκί, οὗτοι
As many as wish to have a fair appearance in [the] flesh, these
ἀναγκάζουσιν ὑμᾶς περιτέμνεσθαι, μόνον ἵνα [s]μὴ‖ τῷ
compel you to be circumcised, only that not for the
σταυρῷ τοῦ χριστοῦ [s] [t]διώκωνται.‖ 13 οὐδὲ.γὰρ οἱ
cross of the Christ they may be persecuted. For neither they who
[u]περιτεμνόμενοι‖ αὐτοὶ νόμον φυλάσσουσιν· ἀλλὰ θέ-
are being circumcised themselves [the] law keep; but they
λουσιν ὑμᾶς περιτέμνεσθαι, ἵνα ἐν τῇ.ὑμετέρᾳ.σαρκὶ καυ-
wish you to be circumcised, that in your flesh they
χήσωνται. 14 ἐμοὶ.δὲ μὴ.γένοιτο καυχᾶσθαι εἰ.μὴ ἐν τῷ
might boast. But for me may it not be to boast except in the
σταυρῷ τοῦ κυρίου.ἡμῶν Ἰησοῦ χριστοῦ· δι' οὗ ἐμοὶ
cross of our Lord Jesus Christ; through whom to me [the]
κόσμος ἐσταύρωται, κἀγὼ [v]τῷ‖ κόσμῳ. 15 [w]ἐν γὰρ χριστῷ
world has been crucified, and I to the world. [2]In [1]for Christ
Ἰησοῦ οὔτε‖ περιτομή [x]τι ἰσχύει,‖ οὔτε ἀκροβυστία,
Jesus neither circumcision [3]any [1]is [2]of force, nor uncircumcision;
ἀλλὰ καινὴ κτίσις. 16 καὶ ὅσοι τῷ.κανόνι.τούτῳ στοι-
but a new creation. And as many as by this rule shall
χήσουσιν, εἰρήνη ἐπ' αὐτοὺς καὶ ἔλεος, καὶ ἐπὶ τὸν Ἰσραὴλ
walk, peace [be] upon them and mercy, and upon the Israel
τοῦ θεοῦ.
of God.
17 Τοῦ.λοιποῦ, κόπους μοι μηδεὶς παρεχέτω· ἐγὼ.γὰρ τὰ
For the rest, [5]troubles [6]to [7]me [2]no [3]one [1]let [4]give, for I the
στίγματα τοῦ [y]κυρίου‖ Ἰησοῦ ἐν τῷ.σώματί.μου βαστάζω.
brands of the Lord Jesus in my body bear.
18 Ἡ χάρις τοῦ.κυρίου.ἡμῶν Ἰησοῦ χριστοῦ μετὰ τοῦ πνεύ-
The grace of our Lord Jesus Christ [be] with [2]spi-
ματος ὑμῶν, ἀδελφοί. ἀμήν.
rit [1]your, brethren. Amen.
[z]Πρὸς Γαλάτας ἐγράφη ἀπὸ Ῥώμης.‖
To [the] Galatians written from Rome.

he that sows to the Spirit shall reap everlasting life from the Spirit.
[9]But let us not lose heart in doing well, for in due time we shall reap, if we do not faint.
[10]So then as we are able, we should do good to all, and especially towards those of the household of faith.
[11]See, in what large letters I have written you with my own hand?
[12]As many as desire to have a show in the flesh, these force you to be circumcised – only that they may not be persecuted for the cross of Christ.
[13]For they themselves who are being circumcised do not keep the Law, but they desire you to be circumcised so they might boast in your flesh.
[14]But may it never be for me to boast, except in the cross of our Lord Jesus Christ, through whom the world has been crucified to me, and I to the world.
[15]For in Christ Jesus neither circumcision is worth anything, or the lack of circumcision, but a new creation.
[16]And as many as shall walk by this rule, peace and mercy be on them and on the Israel of God.
[17]For the rest, let no one cause me troubles, for I bear in my body the brands of the Lord Jesus.
[18]The grace of our Lord Jesus Christ be with your spirit, brothers. Amen.

The Letter to the EPHESIANS

ΠΑΥΛΟΣ ἀπόστολος [b]Ἰησοῦ χριστοῦ‖ διὰ θελήματος θεοῦ,
Paul, apostle of Jesus Christ by will of God,
τοῖς ἁγίοις τοῖς οὖσιν [c]ἐν Ἐφέσῳ‖ καὶ πιστοῖς ἐν χριστῷ
to the saints who are at Ephesus and faithful in Christ
Ἰησοῦ· 2 χάρις ὑμῖν καὶ εἰρήνη ἀπὸ θεοῦ πατρὸς.ἡμῶν καὶ
Jesus. Grace to you and peace from God our Father and
κυρίου Ἰησοῦ χριστοῦ.
[the] Lord Jesus Christ.
3 Εὐλογητὸς ὁ θεὸς καὶ πατὴρ τοῦ.κυρίου.ἡμῶν Ἰησοῦ
Blessed [be] the God and Father of our Lord Jesus
χριστοῦ, ὁ εὐλογήσας ἡμᾶς ἐν πάσῃ εὐλογίᾳ πνευματικῇ ἐν
Christ, who blessed us with every [2]blessing [1]spiritual in
τοῖς ἐπουρανίοις [d] χριστῷ, 4 καθὼς ἐξελέξατο ἡμᾶς ἐν αὐτῷ
the heavenlies with Christ; according as he chose us in him
πρὸ καταβολῆς κόσμου, εἶναι.ἡμᾶς ἁγίους καὶ ἀμώ-
before [the] foundation of [the] world, for us to be holy and blame-
μους κατενώπιον αὐτοῦ [e]ἐν ἀγάπῃ,‖ 5 προορίσας ἡμᾶς εἰς
less before him in love; having predestinated us for
υἱοθεσίαν διὰ Ἰησοῦ χριστοῦ εἰς αὐτόν, κατὰ τὴν εὐδο-
adoption through Jesus Christ to himself, according to the good
κίαν τοῦ.θελήματος.αὐτοῦ, 6 εἰς ἔπαινον δόξης τῆς χάρι-
pleasure of his will, to [the] praise of [the] glory of [2]grace
τος αὐτοῦ, [f]ἐν.ᾗ‖ ἐχαρίτωσεν ἡμᾶς ἐν τῷ ἠγαπημένῳ·
[1]his, wherein he made [2]objects [3]of [4]grace [1]us in the Beloved:
7 ἐν ᾧ ἔχομεν τὴν ἀπολύτρωσιν διὰ τοῦ.αἵματος.αὐτοῦ,
in whom we have redemption through his blood,
τὴν ἄφεσιν τῶν παραπτωμάτων, κατὰ [g]τὸν πλοῦτον‖ τῆς
the remission of offences, according to the riches

CHAPTER 1

[1]Paul, an apostle of Jesus Christ, by the will of God, to the saints who are at Ephesus and the faithful in Christ Jesus:
[2]Grace to you and peace, from God our Father and the Lord Jesus Christ.
[3]Blessed is the God and Father of our Lord Jesus Christ, who has blessed us with every spiritual blessing in the heavenlies in Christ
[4]according as He has chosen us in Him before the foundation of the world, for us to be holy and blameless before Him in love.
[5]*For He* had marked us out beforehand for adoption through Jesus Christ to Himself, according to the good pleasure of His will –
[6]to the praise of the glory of His grace, in which He made us the receivers of grace in the Beloved.
[7]In whom we have redemption through His blood, the forgiveness of sins, according to the riches of His grace –

χάριτος.αὐτοῦ· 8 ἧς ἐπερίσσευσεν εἰς ἡμᾶς ἐν πάσῃ
of his grace; which he caused to abound toward us in all
σοφίᾳ καὶ φρονήσει, 9 γνωρίσας ἡμῖν τὸ μυστήριον τοῦ
wisdom and intelligence, having made known to us the mystery
θελήματος.αὐτοῦ, κατὰ τὴν.εὐδοκίαν.αὐτοῦ, ἣν προέθετο
of his will, according to his good pleasure, which he purposed
ἐν αὐτῷ 10 εἰς οἰκονομίαν τοῦ πληρώματος τῶν καιρῶν,
in himself for [the] administration of the fulness of times;
ἀνακεφαλαιώσασθαι τὰ.πάντα ἐν τῷ χριστῷ, τά.[h]τε‖ [i]ἐν‖
to head up all things in the Christ, both the things in
τοῖς οὐρανοῖς καὶ τὰ ἐπὶ τῆς γῆς· 11 ἐν αὐτῷ, ἐν ᾧ
the heavens and the things upon the earth; in him, in whom
καὶ [k]ἐκληρώθημεν,‖ προορισθέντες κατὰ πρό-
also we obtained an inheritance, being predestinated according to [the] pur-
θεσιν τοῦ τὰ.πάντα ἐνεργοῦντος κατὰ τὴν βουλὴν
pose of him who [2]all [3]things [1]works according to the counsel
τοῦ.θελήματος.αὐτοῦ, 12 εἰς τὸ εἶναι ἡμᾶς εἰς ἔπαινον
of his will, for [2]to [3]be [1]us to [the] praise
τῆς‖.δόξης.αὐτοῦ, τοὺς προηλπικότας ἐν τῷ χριστῷ· 13 ἐν
of his glory; who have fore-trusted in the Christ: in
ᾧ καὶ ὑμεῖς, ἀκούσαντες τὸν λόγον τῆς ἀληθείας, τὸ εὐαγ-
whom also ye, having heard the word of the truth, the glad
γέλιον τῆς.σωτηρίας.ὑμῶν, ἐν ᾧ καὶ πιστεύσαντες ἐσφρα-
tidings of your salvation— in whom also, having believed, ye were
γίσθητε τῷ πνεύματι τῆς ἐπαγγελίας τῷ ἁγίῳ, 14 [m]ὅς‖ ἐστιν
sealed with the Spirit of promise the Holy, who is
ἀῤῥαβὼν τῆς.κληρονομίας.ἡμῶν, εἰς ἀπολύτρωσιν τῆς
[the] earnest of our inheritance, to [the] redemption of the
περιποιήσεως, εἰς ἔπαινον τῆς.δόξης.αὐτοῦ.
acquired possession, to praise of his glory.

15 Διὰ τοῦτο κἀγὼ ἀκούσας [1] τὴν καθ' ὑμᾶς πίστιν ἐν
Because of this I also having heard of the [2]among [3]you [1]faith in
τῷ κυρίῳ Ἰησοῦ, καὶ [n]τὴν ἀγάπην‖ τὴν εἰς πάντας τοὺς
the Lord Jesus, and the love which [is] toward all the
ἁγίους, 16 οὐ.παύομαι εὐχαριστῶν ὑπὲρ ὑμῶν, μνείαν [o]ὑμῶν‖
saints, do not cease giving thanks for you, mention of you
ποιούμενος ἐπὶ τῶν.προσευχῶν.μου· 17 ἵνα ὁ θεὸς τοῦ κυρίου
making in my prayers, that the God of [2]Lord
ἡμῶν Ἰησοῦ χριστοῦ, ὁ πατὴρ τῆς δόξης, δῴη ὑμῖν πνεῦμα
[1]our Jesus Christ, the Father of glory, may give to you [the] spirit
σοφίας καὶ ἀποκαλύψεως ἐν ἐπιγνώσει αὐτοῦ, 18 πεφω-
of wisdom and revelation in [the] knowledge of him, [6]being
τισμένους τοὺς ὀφθαλμοὺς τῆς [p]διανοίας‖ ὑμῶν, εἰς τὸ εἰδέναι
[7]enlightened [1]the [2]eyes [5]mind [3]of [4]your, for [2]to [3]know
ὑμᾶς τίς ἐστιν ἡ ἐλπὶς τῆς.κλήσεως.αὐτοῦ, [q]καὶ‖ τίς ὁ πλοῦ-
[1]you what is the hope of his calling, and what the riches
τος τῆς δόξης τῆς.κληρονομίας.αὐτοῦ ἐν τοῖς ἁγίοις, 19 καὶ
of the glory of his inheritance in the saints, and
τί τὸ ὑπερβάλλον μέγεθος τῆς.δυνάμεως.αὐτοῦ εἰς ἡμᾶς
what the surpassing greatness of his power towards us
τοὺς πιστεύοντας κατὰ τὴν ἐνέργειαν τοῦ κράτους τῆς
who believe according to the working of the might
ἰσχύος.αὐτοῦ, 20 ἣν [r]ἐνήργησεν‖ ἐν τῷ χριστῷ ἐγείρας
of his strength, which he wrought in the Christ, having raised
αὐτὸν ἐκ [s] νεκρῶν, καὶ [t]ἐκάθισεν‖ [v] ἐν δεξιᾷ
him from among [the] dead, and he set [him] at [2]right [3]hand
αὐτοῦ ἐν τοῖς [w]ἐπουρανίοις,‖ 21 ὑπεράνω πάσης ἀρχῆς
[1]his in the heavenlies, above every principality
καὶ ἐξουσίας καὶ δυνάμεως καὶ κυριότητος, καὶ παντὸς ὀνό-
and authority and power and lordship, and every name
ματος ὀνομαζομένου οὐ μόνον ἐν τῷ.αἰῶνι.τούτῳ, ἀλλὰ καὶ
named, not only in this age, but also
ἐν τῷ μέλλοντι· 22 καὶ [x] πάντα ὑπέταξεν ὑπὸ τοὺς πόδας
in the coming [one]; and all things he put under [2]feet
αὐτοῦ· καὶ αὐτὸν ἔδωκεν κεφαλὴν ὑπὲρ πάντα τῇ ἐκ-
[1]his, and [2]him [1]gave [to be] head over all things to the as-
κλησίᾳ, 23 ἥτις ἐστὶν τὸ.σῶμα.αὐτοῦ, τὸ πλήρωμα τοῦ
sembly, which is his body, the fulness of him who
[y]πάντα ἐν πᾶσιν πληρουμένου **2** καὶ ὑμᾶς ὄντας νεκροὺς
all things in all fills— and you being dead
τοῖς παραπτώμασιν καὶ ταῖς ἁμαρτίαις[z], 2 ἐν αἷς ποτε
in offences and sins, in which once
περιεπατήσατε κατὰ τὸν αἰῶνα τοῦ.κόσμου.τούτου, κατὰ
ye walked according to the age of this world, according to
τὸν ἄρχοντα τῆς ἐξουσίας τοῦ ἀέρος, τοῦ πνεύματος τοῦ νῦν
the ruler of the authority of the air, the spirit that now
ἐνεργοῦντος ἐν τοῖς υἱοῖς τῆς ἀπειθείας· 3 ἐν οἷς καὶ ἡμεῖς
works in the sons of disobedience: among whom also we
πάντες ἀνεστράφημέν ποτε ἐν ταῖς ἐπιθυμίαις τῆς σαρκὸς
all had our conduct once in the desires of [2]flesh
ἡμῶν, ποιοῦντες τὰ θελήματα τῆς σαρκὸς καὶ τῶν διανοιῶν,
[1]our, doing the things willed of the flesh and of the thoughts,

8 which He caused to abound toward us in all wisdom and understanding.

9 *For He* had made known to us the mystery of His will, according to His good pleasure which He purposed in Himself –

10 for in the dispensation of the fullness of time *He purposed* to head up all things in Christ, the things in Heaven and the things on earth, in Him,

11 in whom we also have been chosen to an inheritance, being predestinated according to the purpose of Him who works all things according to the counsel of His own will –

12 for us to be to the praise of His glory, who have first trusted in Christ.

13 And in Him, you having heard the word of truth, the gospel of your salvation, also having believed in Him, you were sealed with the Holy Spirit of promise,

14 who is the first-fruit of our inheritance, to the redemption of the purchased possession, to the praise of His glory.

15 Because of this, I also (hearing of your faith in the Lord Jesus and *your* love toward all the saints),

16 do not stop giving thanks for you, making mention of you in my prayers,

17 that the God of our Lord Jesus Christ, the Father of glory, may give to you the spirit of wisdom and revelation in the knowledge of Him –

18 *that* the eyes of your understanding may be enlightened, so that you may know what is the hope of His calling and what are the riches of the glory of His inheritance in the saints,

19 and what is the exceeding greatness of His power towards us, who believe according to the working of His mighty strength

20 which He worked in Christ when He raised Him from among the dead. And He set Him at His right hand in the heavenlies,

21 above all rule, authority, power, lordship and every name that is named – not only in this age, but also in the coming one.

22 And He put all things under His feet and gave Him to be Head over all things to the church,

23 which is His body, the fullness of Him who fills all things in all.

CHAPTER 2

1 And *He made* you *live* who were once dead in trespasses and sins –

2 in which you once walked according to the course of this world, according to the prince of the power of the air, the spirit that now works in the sons of disobedience,

3 among whom also we conducted ourselves in times past in the lusts of our flesh (doing the things willed by the flesh and the mind), and were by nature the children of wrath, just like the rest of them.

καὶ [a]ἦμεν‖ [b]τέκνα φύσει‖ ὀργῆς, ὡς καὶ οἱ λοιποί· 4 ὁ.δὲ.θεός,
and were children, by nature, of wrath, as even the rest: but God,
πλούσιος ὢν ἐν ἐλέει, διὰ τὴν πολλὴν ἀγάπην αὐτοῦ
[2]rich [1]being in mercy, because of [2]great [3]love [1]his
ἣν ἠγάπησεν ἡμᾶς, 5 καὶ ὄντας ἡμᾶς νεκροὺς τοῖς
wherewith he loved us, [2]also [3]being [1]we dead
παραπτώμασιν, συνεζωοποίησεν [c] τῷ χριστῷ· χάριτί ἐστε
in offences, quickened [us] with the Christ, (by grace ye are
σεσωσμένοι· 6 καὶ συνήγειρεν, καὶ συνεκάθισεν ἐν τοῖς
saved,) and raised [us] up together, and seated [us] together in the
ἐπουρανίοις ἐν χριστῷ Ἰησοῦ· 7 ἵνα ἐνδείξηται ἐν τοῖς
heavenlies in Christ Jesus, that he might shew in the
αἰῶσιν τοῖς ἐπερχομένοις [d]τὸν· ὑπερβάλλοντα πλοῦτον‖
ages that [are] coming the surpassing riches
τῆς.χάριτος.αὐτοῦ ἐν χρηστότητι ἐφ' ἡμᾶς ἐν χριστῷ Ἰησοῦ·
of his grace in kindness toward us in Christ Jesus.
8 τῇ γὰρ χάριτί ἐστε σεσωσμένοι διὰ [e]τῆς‖ πίστεως· καὶ
For by grace ye are saved through faith; and
τοῦτο οὐκ ἐξ ὑμῶν, θεοῦ τὸ δῶρον· 9 οὐκ ἐξ ἔργων, ἵνα
this not of yourselves; [it is] God's gift: not of works, that
μή τις καυχήσηται. 10 αὐτοῦ.γάρ ἐσμεν ποίημα, κτισθέν-
not anyone might boast. For his [2]we [3]are [1]workmanship, created
τες ἐν χριστῷ Ἰησοῦ ἐπὶ ἔργοις ἀγαθοῖς, οἷς προητοίμασεν ὁ
in Christ Jesus for [2]works [1]good, which [2]before [3]prepared
θεὸς ἵνα ἐν αὐτοῖς περιπατήσωμεν.
[1]God that in them we should walk.
11 Διὸ μνημονεύετε ὅτι [f]ὑμεῖς ποτε‖ τὰ ἔθνη ἐν
Wherefore remember that ye once the nations in [the]
σαρκί, οἱ λεγόμενοι ἀκροβυστία ὑπὸ τῆς λεγομένης περιτο-
flesh, who are called uncircumcision by that called circum-
μῆς ἐν σαρκὶ χειροποιήτου, 12 ὅτι ἦτε [g]ἐν‖ τῷ.καιρῷ.ἐκείνῳ
cision in [the] flesh made by hand— that ye were at that time
χωρὶς χριστοῦ, ἀπηλλοτριωμένοι τῆς πολιτείας τοῦ Ἰσραήλ,
apart from Christ, alienated from the commonwealth of Israel,
καὶ ξένοι τῶν διαθηκῶν τῆς ἐπαγγελίας, ἐλπίδα μὴ ἔχον-
and strangers from the covenants of promise, hope not hav-
τες, καὶ ἄθεοι ἐν τῷ κόσμῳ· 13 νυνὶ.δὲ ἐν χριστῷ Ἰησοῦ,
ing, and without God in the world: but now in Christ Jesus,
ὑμεῖς οἱ ποτὲ ὄντες μακρὰν [h]ἐγγὺς ἐγενήθητε‖ ἐν τῷ αἵματι
ye who once were afar off near are become by the blood
τοῦ χριστοῦ. 14 αὐτὸς.γάρ ἐστιν ἡ.εἰρήνη.ἡμῶν, ὁ ποιήσας
of the Christ. For he is our peace, who made
τὰ ἀμφότερα ἕν, καὶ τὸ μεσότοιχον τοῦ φραγμοῦ λύσας·
both one, and the middle wall of the fence broke down,
15 τὴν ἔχθραν ἐν τῇ.σαρκὶ.αὐτοῦ, τὸν νόμον τῶν ἐντολῶν
[6]the [7]enmity [3]in [4]his [5]flesh, [8]the [9]law [10]of [11]commandments
ἐν δόγμασιν καταργήσας· ἵνα τοὺς δύο κτίσῃ ἐν [i]ἑαυ-
[12]in [13]decrees [1]having [2]annulled, that the two he might create in him-
τῷ‖ εἰς ἕνα καινὸν ἄνθρωπον, ποιῶν εἰρήνην· 16 καὶ ἀπο-
self into one new man, making peace; and might
καταλλάξῃ τοὺς ἀμφοτέρους ἐν ἑνὶ σώματι τῷ θεῷ διὰ τοῦ
reconcile both in one body to God through the
σταυροῦ, ἀποκτείνας τὴν ἔχθραν ἐν αὐτῷ· 17 καὶ ἐλθὼν
cross, having slain the enmity by it; and having come
εὐηγγελίσατο εἰρήνην ὑμῖν τοῖς μακρὰν καὶ[k]
he announced the glad tidings— peace to you who [were] afar off and
τοῖς ἐγγύς, 18 ὅτι.δι' αὐτοῦ ἔχομεν τὴν προσαγωγὴν οἱ
to those near. For through him we have access
ἀμφότεροι ἐν ἑνὶ πνεύματι πρὸς τὸν πατέρα. 19 ἄρα οὖν
both by one Spirit to the Father. So then
οὐκέτι ἐστὲ ξένοι καὶ πάροικοι, [l]ἀλλὰ‖ [m] [n]συμπολῖται‖ τῶν
no longer are ye strangers and sojourners, but fellow-citizens of the
ἁγίων καὶ οἰκεῖοι τοῦ θεοῦ, 20 ἐποικοδομηθέντες ἐπὶ τῷ
saints and of the household of God, being built up on the
θεμελίῳ τῶν ἀποστόλων καὶ προφητῶν, ὄντος ἀκρο-
foundation of the apostles and prophets, [4]being [[5]the] [6]corner-
γωνιαίου αὐτοῦ [o]Ἰησοῦ χριστοῦ,‖ 21 ἐν ᾧ πᾶσα [p]ἡ‖ οἰκοδομὴ
stone [3]himself [1]Jesus [2]Christ, in whom all the building
συναρμολογουμένη αὔξει εἰς ναὸν ἅγιον ἐν κυρίῳ, 22 ἐν
fitted together increases to a [2]temple [1]holy in [the] Lord; in
ᾧ καὶ ὑμεῖς συνοικοδομεῖσθε εἰς κατοικητήριον τοῦ θεοῦ
whom also ye are being built together for a habitation of God
ἐν πνεύματι.
in [the] Spirit.

3 Τούτου.χάριν ἐγὼ Παῦλος ὁ δέσμιος τοῦ χριστοῦ [q]Ἰη-
For this cause I Paul prisoner of the Christ Je-
σοῦ‖ ὑπὲρ ὑμῶν τῶν ἐθνῶν· 2 εἴγε ἠκούσατε τὴν οἰκονομίαν
sus for you nations, if indeed ye heard of the administration
τῆς χάριτος τοῦ θεοῦ τῆς δοθείσης μοι εἰς ὑμᾶς, 3 [r]ὅτι‖
of the grace of God which was given to me towards you, that
κατὰ ἀποκάλυψιν [s]ἐγνώρισέν‖ μοι τὸ μυστήριον, καθὼς
by revelation he made known to me the mystery, (according as

4 But God, being rich in mercy, because of
His great love with which He loved us
5 (even when we were dead in sins), He
made us alive together with Christ (by grace
you are saved),
6 and raised us up together and seated us
together in the heavenlies in Christ Jesus –
7 so that in the ages to come He might show
the exceeding riches of His grace in kindness
toward us in Christ Jesus.
8 For by grace you are saved, through faith,
not of works, that not anyone could boast.
9 not of works, that not anyone could
boast.
10 For we are His workmanship, created in
Christ Jesus to good works that God prepared before that we should walk in them.
11 For this reason remember that you were
Gentiles in the flesh (who are called,
Uncircumcision by those called Circumcision
in the flesh made by hand),
12 that at that time you were without
Christ, being separated from the commonwealth of Israel and strangers from the
covenants of promise – having no hope and
without God in the world.
13 But now in Christ Jesus, you who were
at one time far off are made near by the
blood of Christ.
14 For He is our peace, who has made us
both one and who has broken down the
middle wall of the partition *between us*
15 (having in His flesh done away with the
ill-will, the Law of commandments contained in ordinances), so that He might in
Himself make the two into one new man,
making peace *between them*,
16 and might reconcile both to God in one
body through the cross, slaying the ill-will
by it.
17 And having come, He preached the
gospel of peace to you who *were* far off and
to those near.
18 For through Him we both have a way to
come to the Father by one Spirit.
19 So, then, you are no longer strangers and
foreigners, but fellow-citizens of the saints
and of the household of God.
20 *For you* have been built on the foundation of the apostles and prophets, Jesus
Christ Himself being the chief cornerstone –
21 in whom all the building fitted together
grows into a holy temple in the Lord.
22 In whom also you are being built together into a dwelling-place of God in the Spirit.

CHAPTER 3

1 For this reason, I, Paul, *am* prisoner of
Jesus Christ for you Gentiles.
2 If indeed you have heard of the ministry
of the grace of God which has been given to
me towards you
3 that by revelation He revealed to me the
mystery (as I wrote before in a few words,

προέγραψα ἐν.ὀλίγῳ, 4 πρὸς ὃ δύνασθε ἀναγινώσκοντες
I wrote before briefly, by which ye are able, reading [it],

νοῆσαι τὴν.σύνεσίν.μου ἐν τῷ μυστηρίῳ τοῦ.χριστοῦ· 5 ὃ
to perceive my understanding in the mystery of the Christ,) which

[t]ἐν" ἑτέραις γενεαῖς οὐκ.ἐγνωρίσθη τοῖς υἱοῖς τῶν ἀνθρώ-
in other generations was not made known to the sons of men,

πων, ὡς νῦν ἀπεκαλύφθη τοῖς ἁγίοις ἀποστόλοις αὐτοῦ καὶ
as now it was revealed to [2]holy [3]apostles [1]his and

προφήταις ἐν πνεύματι· 6 εἶναι τὰ ἔθνη [v]συγκληρονόμα"
prophets in [the] Spirit, [3]to [4]be [1]the [2]nations joint-heirs

καὶ [w]σύσσωμα" καὶ [v]συμμέτοχα" τῆς.ἐπαγγελίας.[x]αὐτοῦ" ἐν
and a joint-body and joint-partakers of his promise in

[y]τῷ" χριστῷ[z], διὰ τοῦ εὐαγγελίου, 7 οὗ [a]ἐγενόμην" διάκονος
the Christ through the glad tidings; of which I became servant

κατὰ τὴν δωρεὰν τῆς χάριτος τοῦ θεοῦ [b]τὴν δοθεῖσάν"
according to the gift of the grace of God given

μοι κατὰ τὴν ἐνέργειαν τῆς.δυνάμεως.αὐτοῦ· 8 ἐμοὶ
to me, according to the working of his power. To me,

τῷ ἐλαχιστοτέρῳ πάντων [c]τῶν" ἁγίων ἐδόθη ἡ.χάρις.αὕτη,
the less than the least of all the saints, was given this grace,

[d]ἐν" τοῖς ἔθνεσιν εὐαγγελίσασθαι [e]τὸν" ἀνεξιχνίαστον
among the nations to announce the glad tidings— the unsearchable

[f]πλοῦτον" τοῦ χριστοῦ, 9 καὶ φωτίσαι [g]πάντας" τίς
riches of the Christ, and to enlighten all [as to] what [is]

ἡ [h]κοινωνία" τοῦ μυστηρίου τοῦ ἀποκεκρυμμένου ἀπὸ τῶν
the fellowship of the mystery which has been hidden from the

αἰώνων ἐν τῷ θεῷ, τῷ τὰ.πάντα κτίσαντι [i]διὰ Ἰησοῦ χριστοῦ,"
ages in God, who all things created by Jesus Christ,

10 ἵνα γνωρισθῇ νῦν ταῖς ἀρχαῖς καὶ ταῖς ἐξουσίαις ἐν
that might be known now to the principalities and the authorities in

τοῖς ἐπουρανίοις διὰ τῆς ἐκκλησίας ἡ πολυποίκιλος σοφία
the heavenlies through the assembly the multifarious wisdom

τοῦ θεοῦ, 11 κατὰ πρόθεσιν τῶν αἰώνων, ἣν ἐποίησεν
of God, according to [the] purpose of the ages, which he made

ἐν [k]χριστῷ Ἰησοῦ τῷ.κυρίῳ.ἡμῶν, 12 ἐν ᾧ ἔχομεν τὴν παρ-
in Christ Jesus our Lord, in whom we have bold-

ῥησίαν καὶ [l]τὴν" προσαγωγὴν ἐν πεποιθήσει διὰ τῆς πίστεως
ness and access in confidence by the faith

αὐτοῦ. 13 διὸ αἰτοῦμαι μὴ [m]ἐκκακεῖν" ἐν ταῖς θλίψεσίν
of him. Wherefore I beseech [you] not to faint at [2]tribulations

μου ὑπὲρ ὑμῶν, ἥτις ἐστὶν δόξα.ὑμῶν. 14 τούτου.χάριν
[1]my for you, which is your glory. For this cause

κάμπτω τὰ.γόνατά.μου πρὸς τὸν πατέρα [n]τοῦ.κυρίου.ἡμῶν
I bow my knees to the Father of our Lord

Ἰησοῦ χριστοῦ," 15 ἐξ οὗ πᾶσα πατριὰ ἐν οὐρανοῖς καὶ
Jesus Christ, of whom every family in [the] heavens and

ἐπὶ γῆς ὀνομάζεται, 16 ἵνα [o]δῴη" ὑμῖν κατὰ [p]τὸν
on earth is named, that he may give you according to the

πλοῦτον" τῆς.δόξης.αὐτοῦ, δυνάμει κραταιωθῆναι διὰ τοῦ
riches of his glory, with power to be strengthened by

πνεύματος.αὐτοῦ εἰς τὸν ἔσω ἄνθρωπον, 17 κατοικῆσαι τὸν
his Spirit in the inner man; [for] [3]to [4]dwell [1]the

χριστὸν διὰ τῆς πίστεως ἐν ταῖς.καρδίαις.ὑμῶν· 18 ἐν ἀγάπῃ
[2]Christ, through faith, in your hearts, in love

ἐρριζωμένοι καὶ τεθεμελιωμένοι ἵνα ἐξισχύσητε κατα-
being rooted and founded, that ye may be fully able to ap-

λαβέσθαι σὺν πᾶσιν τοῖς ἁγίοις τί τὸ πλάτος καὶ μῆκος
prehend with all the saints what [is] the breadth and length

καὶ [q]βάθος καὶ ὕψος," 19 γνῶναί.τε τὴν ὑπερβάλλουσαν
and depth and height; and to know the surpassing

τῆς γνώσεως ἀγάπην τοῦ χριστοῦ, ἵνα πληρωθῆτε εἰς πᾶν
knowledge love of the Christ; that ye may be filled unto all

τὸ πλήρωμα τοῦ θεοῦ. 20 τῷ.δὲ δυναμένῳ ὑπὲρ πάντα
the fulness of God. But to him who is able above all things

ποιῆσαι [r]ὑπὲρ.ἐκ.περισσοῦ" ὧν αἰτούμεθα ἢ νοοῦμεν, κατὰ
to do exceedingly above what we ask or think, according to

τὴν δύναμιν τὴν ἐνεργουμένην ἐν ἡμῖν, 21 αὐτῷ ἡ δόξα
the power which works in us, to him [be] glory

ἐν τῇ ἐκκλησίᾳ [s]ἐν χριστῷ Ἰησοῦ, εἰς πάσας τὰς γενεὰς τοῦ
in the assembly in Christ Jesus, to all the generations of the

αἰῶνος τῶν αἰώνων. ἀμήν. 4 Παρακαλῶ οὖν ὑμᾶς ἐγὼ
age of the ages. Amen. I exhort therefore you, I

ὁ δέσμιος ἐν κυρίῳ, ἀξίως περιπατῆσαι τῆς κλήσεως
the prisoner in [the] Lord, [3]worthily [1]to [2]walk of the calling

ἧς ἐκλήθητε, 2 μετὰ πάσης ταπεινοφροσύνης καὶ [t]πρᾳό-
wherewith ye were called, with all humility and meek-

τητος," μετὰ μακροθυμίας, ἀνεχόμενοι ἀλλήλων ἐν ἀγάπῃ,
ness, with longsuffering, bearing with one another in love;

3 σπουδάζοντες τηρεῖν τὴν ἑνότητα τοῦ πνεύματος ἐν τῷ
being diligent to keep the unity of the Spirit in the

συνδέσμῳ τῆς εἰρήνης. 4 [u]Ἓν σῶμα καὶ ἓν πνεῦμα, καθὼς καὶ
bond of peace. One body and one Spirit, even as also

4 by the reading of which you are able to understand my knowledge in the mystery of Christ),

5 which was not made known to the sons of men in other generations, as it now has been revealed to His holy apostles and prophets in the Spirit –

6 that the Gentiles were to be heirs together and of the same body and sharers of His promise in Christ, through the gospel.

7 Of which *gospel* I was made a minister, according to the gift of the grace of God given to me, according to the working of His divine power.

8 This grace was given to me (*who am* less than the least of all the saints), to preach the gospel of the unsearchable riches of Christ among the Gentiles,

9 and to make all see what is the fellowship of the mystery which has been hidden from eternity in God, who created all things by Jesus Christ –

10 so that now to the rulers and the authorities in the heavenlies might be known by the church the manifold wisdom of God

11 (according to the eternal purpose which He purposed in Christ Jesus our Lord,

12 in whom we have boldness and a way of approach, in confidence, through His faith).

13 So I desire that you do not faint at my trials for you, which is your glory.

14 For this cause I bow my knees to the Father of our Lord Jesus Christ,

15 of whom the whole family in Heaven and earth is named,

16 *asking* that He may give you according to the riches of His glory to be strengthened with power in the inner man, through His Spirit

17 that through faith Christ may dwell in your hearts, that you, being rooted and grounded in love,

18 may be fully able to grasp firmly with your mind (along with all the saints) what is the breadth and length and depth and height;

19 and to know the love of Christ which goes beyond our knowledge, so that you may be filled to all the fullness of God.

20 Now to Him who is able to do exceedingly above all that we ask or think, according to the power that works in us,

21 to Him be glory in the church by Christ Jesus throughout all ages, world without end, Amen.

CHAPTER 4

1 Then I, the prisoner in the Lord, urge you to walk worthy of the calling with which you were called,

2 with all humility, meekness and long-suffering, bearing with one another in love,

3 being careful to keep the unity of the Spirit in the bond of peace.

ἐκλήθητε ἐν μιᾷ ἐλπίδι τῆς.κλήσεως.ὑμῶν· 5 εἷς κύριος, μία
ye were called in one hope of your calling; one Lord, one
πίστις, ἓν βάπτισμα· 6 εἷς θεὸς καὶ πατὴρ πάντων, ὁ
faith, one baptism; one God and Father of all, who [is]
ἐπὶ πάντων, καὶ διὰ πάντων, καὶ ἐν πᾶσιν [v]ὑμῖν.‖
over all, and through all, and in [2]all [1]you.
7 ἑνὶ.δὲ.ἑκάστῳ ἡμῶν ἐδόθη [w]ἡ‖ χάρις κατὰ τὸ μέτρον
But to each one of us was given grace according to the measure
τῆς δωρεᾶς τοῦ χριστοῦ. 8 διὸ λέγει, Ἀναβὰς εἰς
of the gift of the Christ. Wherefore he says, Having ascended up on
ὕψος ᾐχμαλώτευσεν αἰχμαλωσίαν, [x]καὶ‖ ἔδωκεν δόματα τοῖς
high he led [2]captive [1]captivity, and gave gifts
ἀνθρώποις. 9 Τὸ.δὲ ἀνέβη, τί ἐστιν εἰ.μὴ ὅτι καὶ κατέβη
to men. But that he ascended, what is it but that also he descended
[y]πρῶτον‖ εἰς τὰ κατώτερα [z]μέρη‖ τῆς γῆς; 10 ὁ καταβὰς
first into the lower parts of the earth? He that descended
αὐτός ἐστιν καὶ ὁ ἀναβὰς ὑπεράνω πάντων τῶν οὐρανῶν,
[2]the [3]same [1]is also who ascended above all the heavens,
ἵνα πληρώσῃ τὰ.πάντα. 11 καὶ αὐτὸς ἔδωκεν τοὺς.μὲν ἀπο-
that he might fill all things; and he gave some apo-
στόλους, τοὺς.δὲ προφήτας, τοὺς.δὲ εὐαγγελιστάς, τοὺς.δὲ
stles, and some prophets, and some evangelists, and some
ποιμένας καὶ διδασκάλους, 12 πρὸς τὸν καταρτισμὸν τῶν
shepherds and teachers, with a view to the perfecting of the
ἁγίων, εἰς ἔργον διακονίας, εἰς οἰκοδομὴν τοῦ σώματος τοῦ
saints; for work of [the] service, for building up of the body of the
χριστοῦ· 13 μέχρι καταντήσωμεν οἱ πάντες εἰς τὴν ἑνότητα
Christ; until we [2]may [3]arrive [1]all at the unity
τῆς πίστεως καὶ τῆς ἐπιγνώσεως τοῦ υἱοῦ τοῦ θεοῦ, εἰς ἄνδρα
of the faith and of the knowledge of the Son of God, at a [2]man
τέλειον, εἰς μέτρον ἡλικίας τοῦ πληρώματος τοῦ
[1]full-grown, at [the] measure of [the] stature of the fulness of the
χριστοῦ· 14 ἵνα μηκέτι ὦμεν νήπιοι, κλυδωνιζόμενοι καὶ
Christ; that no longer we may be infants, being tossed and
περιφερόμενοι παντὶ ἀνέμῳ τῆς διδασκαλίας ἐν τῇ [a]κυβείᾳ‖
carried about by every wind of the teaching in the sleight
τῶν ἀνθρώπων, ἐν πανουργίᾳ πρὸς τὴν [b]μεθοδείαν‖ τῆς
of men, in craftiness with a view to the systematizing
πλάνης· 15 ἀληθεύοντες.δὲ ἐν ἀγάπῃ αὐξήσωμεν εἰς αὐτὸν
of error; but holding the truth in love we may grow up into him
τὰ.πάντα, ὅς ἐστιν ἡ κεφαλή, [c]ὁ‖ χριστός, 16 ἐξ οὗ πᾶν
in all things, who is the head, the Christ: from whom all
τὸ σῶμα συναρμολογούμενον καὶ [d]συμβιβαζόμενον‖ διὰ πάσης
the body, fitted together and compacted by every
ἁφῆς τῆς ἐπιχορηγίας κατ' ἐνέργειαν ἐν μέτρῳ
joint of supply according to [the] working in [its] measure
ἑνὸς.ἑκάστου μέρους, τὴν αὔξησιν τοῦ σώματος ποιεῖται εἰς
of each one part, the increase of the body makes for itself to
οἰκοδομὴν [e]ἑαυτοῦ‖ ἐν ἀγάπῃ.
[the] building up of itself in love.
17 Τοῦτο οὖν λέγω καὶ μαρτύρομαι ἐν κυρίῳ, μηκέτι
This therefore I say, and testify in [the] Lord, [3]no [4]longer
ὑμᾶς.περιπατεῖν, καθὼς καὶ τὰ [f]λοιπὰ‖ ἔθνη περιπατεῖ ἐν
[1]that [2]ye walk even as also the rest, [the] nations, are walking in
ματαιότητι τοῦ.νοὸς.αὐτῶν, 18 [g]ἐσκοτισμένοι‖ τῇ δια-
[the] vanity of their mind, being darkened in the under-
νοίᾳ, ὄντες ἀπηλλοτριωμένοι τῆς ζωῆς τοῦ θεοῦ, διὰ
standing, being alienated from the life of God, on account of
τὴν ἄγνοιαν τὴν οὖσαν ἐν αὐτοῖς, διὰ τὴν πώρωσιν
the ignorance which is in them, on account of the hardness
τῆς.καρδίας.αὐτῶν· 19 οἵτινες ἀπηλγηκότες ἑαυτοὺς
of their heart, who having cast off all feeling, themselves
παρέδωκαν τῇ ἀσελγείᾳ εἰς ἐργασίαν ἀκαθαρσίας πάσης
gave up to licentiousness, for [the] working of [2]uncleanness [1]all
ἐν πλεονεξίᾳ· 20 ὑμεῖς.δὲ οὐχ οὕτως ἐμάθετε τὸν χριστόν,
with craving. But ye [2]not [3]thus [1]learned the Christ,
21 εἴγε αὐτὸν ἠκούσατε καὶ ἐν αὐτῷ ἐδιδάχθητε, καθώς
if indeed him ye heard and in him were taught, according as
ἐστιν ἀλήθεια ἐν τῷ Ἰησοῦ· 22 ἀποθέσθαι.ὑμᾶς κατὰ
is [the] truth in Jesus; for you to have put off according to
τὴν προτέραν ἀναστροφὴν τὸν παλαιὸν ἄνθρωπον, τὸν
the former conduct the old man, which
φθειρόμενον κατὰ τὰς ἐπιθυμίας τῆς ἀπάτης· 23 ἀνα-
is corrupt according to the desires of deceit; [2]to [3]be [4]re-
νεοῦσθαι [h]δὲ‖ τῷ πνεύματι τοῦ.νοὸς.ὑμῶν· 24 καὶ ἐνδύσασθαι
newed [1]and in the spirit of your mind; and to have put on
τὸν καινὸν ἄνθρωπον, τὸν κατὰ θεὸν κτισθέντα ἐν δι-
the new man, which according to God was created in right-
καιοσύνῃ καὶ ὁσιότητι τῆς ἀληθείας. 25 Διὸ ἀποθέμενοι τὸ
eousness and holiness of truth. Wherefore having put off
ψεῦδος, λαλεῖτε ἀλήθειαν ἕκαστος μετὰ τοῦ.πλησίον.αὐτοῦ·
falsehood, speak truth each with his neighbour,

4 *There is* one body and one Spirit, as you
also were called in one hope of your calling –
5 one Lord, one faith, one baptism –
6 one God and Father of all, who is above
all and through all and in you all.
7 But to each one of us grace was given according to the measure of the gift of Christ.
8 So He says, "Having ascended on high, He
led captivity captive and gave gifts to men."
9 Now if He ascended, what is it but *proof*
that He also first came down into the lower
parts of the earth?
10 He that came down is the same also who
went up far above all the heavens, so that He
might fill all things.
11 And He indeed gave some to be apostles,
and some prophets, and some evangelists,
and some pastors and teachers,
12 so as to perfect the saints for the work
of the ministry, for edifying the body of
Christ,
13 until we all come to the unity of the
faith and of the knowledge of the Son of
God, to a full-grown man, to the measure of
the stature of the fullness of Christ –
14 so that we may no longer be infants,
being tossed to and fro and carried about by
every wind of doctrine, in the underhanded-
ness of men, in skillful trickery, with a view
to the establishing of error.
15 But speaking the truth in love, we may
grow up into Him in all things, who is the
Head – Christ.
16 From whom all the body, fitted and
brought together by every assisting joint,
according to the working of each part in its
own measure, producing the growth of the
body to the building up of itself in love.
17 This I say, then, and testify in the Lord
that you no longer walk even as also the rest
of the Gentiles are walking, in the vanity of
their mind,
18 being darkened in the understanding,
being made strangers to the life of God
because of the ignorance which is in them,
because of the hardness of their heart.
19 *For* having thrown off all feeling, *they*
gave themselves up to lust, for the working
of all uncleanness with greediness.
20 But you have not so learned Christ –
21 if indeed you heard Him and were taught
in Him, as the truth is in Jesus.
22 For you *ought* to have put off the old
man (according to your way of living before)
which is corrupt according to deceitful lusts,
23 and to be renewed in the spirit of your
mind,
24 and to have put on the new man (who in
God's image was created in righteousness
and true holiness).
25 Because of this, stop lying, let each
speak truth with his neighbor, because we
are members of one another.

ὅτι ἐσμὲν ἀλλήλων μέλη. 26 Ὀργίζεσθε καὶ μὴ ἁμαρ-
because we are of one another members. Be angry, and 2not 1sin;

τάνετε· ὁ ἥλιος μὴ ἐπιδυέτω ἐπὶ ἱτῷ παροργισμῷ ὑμῶν,
5the 6sun 3let 4not set upon your provocation,

27 kμήτε‖ δίδοτε τόπον τῷ διαβόλῳ. 28 ὁ κλέπτων μηκέτι
neither give place to the devil. He that steals 4no 5more

κλεπτέτω, μᾶλλον δὲ κοπιάτω, ἐργαζόμενος lτὸ ἀγαθὸν
1let 2him 3steal, but rather let him labour, working what [is] good

ταῖς χερσίν,‖ ἵνα ἔχῃ μεταδιδόναι τῷ χρείαν ἔχοντι.
with [his] hands, that he may have to impart to him that 2need 1has.

29 πᾶς λόγος σαπρὸς ἐκ τοῦ στόματος ὑμῶν μὴ ἐκ-
5Any 7word 6corrupt 10out 11of 12your 13mouth 4not 3let
(lit. every)

πορευέσθω, mἀλλ'‖ εἴ τις ἀγαθὸς πρὸς οἰκοδομὴν τῆς χρείας,
8go 9forth, but if any good for building up in respect of need,

ἵνα δῷ χάριν τοῖς ἀκούουσιν. 30 καὶ μὴ λυπεῖτε τὸ
that it may give grace to them that hear. And grieve not the

πνεῦμα τὸ ἅγιον τοῦ θεοῦ, ἐν ᾧ ἐσφραγίσθητε εἰς ἡμέραν
Spirit the Holy of God, by which ye were sealed for [the] day

ἀπολυτρώσεως. 31 πᾶσα πικρία καὶ θυμὸς καὶ ὀργὴ καὶ
of redemption. All bitterness, and indignation, and wrath, and

κραυγὴ καὶ βλασφημία ἀρθήτω ἀφ' ὑμῶν, σὺν πάσῃ
clamour, and evil speaking let be removed from you, with all

κακίᾳ· 32 γίνεσθε nδὲ‖ εἰς ἀλλήλους χρηστοί, εὔσπλαγχνοι,
malice; and be to one another kind, tender-hearted,

χαριζόμενοι ἑαυτοῖς, καθὼς καὶ ὁ θεὸς ἐν χριστῷ ἐχαρί-
forgiving each other, according as also God in Christ for-

σατο oὑμῖν.‖ 5 Γίνεσθε οὖν μιμηταὶ τοῦ θεοῦ, ὡς τέκνα
gave you. Be ye therefore imitators of God, as children

ἀγαπητά· 2 καὶ περιπατεῖτε ἐν ἀγάπῃ, καθὼς καὶ ὁ χριστὸς
beloved, and walk in love, even as also the Christ

ἠγάπησεν pἡμᾶς,‖ καὶ παρέδωκεν ἑαυτὸν ὑπὲρ qἡμῶν‖ προσ-
loved us, and gave up himself for us, an of-

φορὰν καὶ θυσίαν τῷ θεῷ εἰς ὀσμὴν εὐωδίας.
fering and a sacrifice to God for an odour of a sweet smell.

3 Πορνεία δὲ καὶ rπᾶσα ἀκαθαρσία‖ ἢ πλεονεξία μηδὲ
But fornication and all uncleanness or covetousness not even

ὀνομαζέσθω ἐν ὑμῖν, καθὼς πρέπει ἁγίοις· 4 sκαὶ‖ αἰσχρό-
let it be named among you, even as is becoming to saints; and filthi-

της tκαὶ‖ μωρολογία ἢ εὐτραπελία, vτὰ οὐκ ἀνήκοντα,‖ ἀλλὰ
ness and foolish talking or jesting, which are not becoming; but

μᾶλλον εὐχαριστία. 5 τοῦτο γὰρ wἔστε γινώσκοντες‖ ὅτι πᾶς
rather thanksgiving. For this ye know that any
(lit. every)

πόρνος, ἢ ἀκάθαρτος, ἢ πλεονέκτης, xὅς‖ ἐστιν εἰδωλολά-
fornicator, or unclean person, or covetous, who is an idolater,

τρης, οὐκ ἔχει κληρονομίαν ἐν τῇ βασιλείᾳ τοῦ χριστοῦ καὶ
has not inheritance in the kingdom of the Christ and

θεοῦ. 6 μηδεὶς ὑμᾶς ἀπατάτω κενοῖς λόγοις· διὰ
of God. 2No 3one 5you 1let 4deceive with empty words; 2on 3account 4of

ταῦτα γὰρ ἔρχεται ἡ ὀργὴ τοῦ θεοῦ ἐπὶ τοὺς υἱοὺς τῆς
5these 6things 1for comes the wrath of God upon the sons

ἀπειθείας. 7 μὴ οὖν γίνεσθε yσυμμέτοχοι‖ αὐτῶν. 8 ἦτε
of disobedience. 2Not 3therefore 1be joint-partakers with them; 2ye 3were

γάρ ποτε σκότος, νῦν δὲ φῶς ἐν κυρίῳ· ὡς τέκνα φωτὸς
1for once darkness, but now light in [the] Lord; as children of light

περιπατεῖτε· 9 ὁ γὰρ καρπὸς τοῦ zπνεύματος‖ ἐν πάσῃ
walk, (for the fruit of the Spirit [is] in all

ἀγαθωσύνῃ καὶ δικαιοσύνῃ καὶ ἀληθείᾳ· 10 δοκιμάζοντες τί
goodness and righteousness and truth,) proving what

ἐστιν εὐάρεστον τῷ κυρίῳ. 11 καὶ μὴ aσυγκοινωνεῖτε‖ τοῖς
is well-pleasing to the Lord; and have no fellowship with the

ἔργοις τοῖς ἀκάρποις τοῦ σκότους, μᾶλλον δὲ καὶ ἐλέγχετε·
2works 1unfruitful of darkness, but rather also reprove;

12 τὰ γὰρ bκρυφῆ‖ γινόμενα ὑπ' αὐτῶν αἰσχρόν ἐστιν καὶ
for the things in secret being done by them shameful it is even

λέγειν. 13 τὰ δὲ πάντα ἐλεγχόμενα ὑπὸ τοῦ φωτὸς φανεροῦ-
to say. But all of them being reproved by the light are made mani-

ται· πᾶν γὰρ τὸ φανερούμενον φῶς ἐστιν. 14 διὸ
fest; for 4everything 1that 2which 3makes 5manifest 7light 6is. Wherefore

λέγει, c"Εγειραι‖ ὁ καθεύδων, καὶ ἀνάστα ἐκ τῶν
he says, Arouse, [thou] that sleepest, and rise up from among the

νεκρῶν, καὶ ἐπιφαύσει σοι ὁ χριστός. 15 Βλέπετε οὖν
dead, and shall shine upon thee the Christ. Take heed therefore

dπῶς ἀκριβῶς‖ περιπατεῖτε, μὴ ὡς ἄσοφοι, ἀλλ' ὡς σοφοί,
how accurately ye walk, not as unwise, but as wise,

16 ἐξαγοραζόμενοι τὸν καιρόν, ὅτι αἱ ἡμέραι πονηραί εἰσιν.
ransoming the time, because the days 2evil 1are.

17 διὰ τοῦτο μὴ γίνεσθε ἄφρονες, ἀλλὰ eσυνιέντες‖ τί τὸ
On this account be not foolish, but understanding what the

θέλημα τοῦ κυρίου. 18 καὶ μὴ μεθύσκεσθε οἴνῳ, ἐν ᾧ
will of the Lord [is]. And be not drunk with wine, in which

26 Be angry, but do not sin, do not let the sun go down on your wrath,
27 nor give place to the devil.
28 Let the thieving one steal no more, but rather let him labor, working what is good with his hands, so that he may have *something* to give to him that has need.
29 Let no filthy word go out of your mouth – but if anything *is said*, for good, use in building up one's needs, that it may give grace to those who hear.
30 And do not grieve the Holy Spirit of God, by whom you were sealed to the day of redemption.
31 Let all bitterness and wrath and anger and tumult and evil-speaking be put away from you, along with all evil-hearted feelings
32 – and be kind to one another, tender-hearted, forgiving each other, even as also God forgave you in Christ.

CHAPTER 5

1 Then be imitators of God, as loved children,
2 and walk in love, even as also Christ loved us and gave Himself for us an offering and a sacrifice to God for an odor of a sweet smell.
3 But as to fornication and all uncleanness or greediness, let it not be even named among you, as is becoming to saints –
4 *let there be* no filthiness or foolish talking or joking, which are not becoming, but rather thanksgiving.
5 For you know this, that no fornicator or unclean person or covetous one (who is an idolater) has any inheritance in the kingdom of Christ and of God.
6 Let no one deceive you with empty words – for the wrath of God comes on the sons of disobedience because of these things.
7 So do not be partners with them,
8 for you were once darkness, but now light in the Lord – walk as children of light.
9 For the fruit of the Spirit is in all goodness and righteousness and truth.
10 *Be always* proving what is the Lord's will,
11 and have no fellowship with the unfruitful works of darkness, but rather warn them.
12 For it is shameful even to speak the things which are being done by them in secret.
13 But all of them, being exposed by the light, are clearly revealed – for that which clearly reveals everything is light.
14 So He says, "Wake up, sleeper, and rise up from the dead! And Christ will shine on you."
15 Then be careful how you walk, not as unwise but as wise ones,
16 redeeming the time because the days are evil.
17 So do not be foolish, but understanding what the will of the Lord is.

ἐστιν ἀσωτία· ἀλλὰ πληροῦσθε ἐν πνεύματι, 19 λα-
is dissoluteness; but be filled with [the] Spirit, speak-
λοῦντες ἑαυτοῖς [f] ψαλμοῖς καὶ ὕμνοις καὶ ᾠδαῖς [g]πνευματι-
ing to each other in psalms and hymns and [2]songs [1]spiritual,
καῖς," ᾄδοντες καὶ ψάλλοντες [h]ἐν" [i]τῇ καρδίᾳ" ὑμῶν τῷ κυρίῳ,
singing and praising with [2]heart [1]your to the Lord;
20 εὐχαριστοῦντες πάντοτε ὑπὲρ πάντων ἐν ὀνόματι τοῦ
giving thanks at all times for all things in [the] name
κυρίου.ἡμῶν Ἰησοῦ χριστοῦ τῷ θεῷ καὶ πατρί· 21 ὑπο-
of our Lord Jesus Christ to him who [is] God and Father, submit-
τασσόμενοι ἀλλήλοις ἐν φόβῳ [k]θεοῦ."
ting yourselves to one another in [the] fear of God.

22 Αἱ γυναῖκες, τοῖς.ἰδίοις ἀνδράσιν [l]ὑποτάσσεσθε," ὡς τῷ
Wives, to your own husbands submit yourselves, as to the
κυρίῳ· 23 ὅτι [m]ὁ" ἀνήρ ἐστιν κεφαλὴ τῆς γυναικός, ὡς καὶ
Lord, for the husband is head of the wife, as also
ὁ χριστὸς κεφαλὴ τῆς ἐκκλησίας, [n]καὶ" αὐτός [o]ἐστιν" σωτὴρ
the Christ [is] head of the assembly, and he is Saviour
τοῦ σώματος· 24 [p]ἀλλ'" [q]ὥσπερ" ἡ ἐκκλησία ὑποτάσσεται τῷ
of the body. But even as the assembly is subjected to the
χριστῷ, οὕτως καὶ αἱ γυναῖκες τοῖς.[r]ἰδίοις" ἀνδράσιν ἐν παντί.
Christ, so also wives to their own husbands in everything.
25 Οἱ ἄνδρες, ἀγαπᾶτε τὰς.γυναῖκας.[s]ἑαυτῶν," καθὼς καὶ ὁ
Husbands, love your own wives, even as also the
χριστὸς ἠγάπησεν τὴν ἐκκλησίαν, καὶ ἑαυτὸν παρέδωκεν ὑπὲρ
Christ loved the assembly, and himself gave up for
αὐτῆς· 26 ἵνα αὐτὴν ἁγιάσῃ, καθαρίσας τῷ λουτρῷ
it, that it he might sanctify, having cleansed [it] by the washing
τοῦ ὕδατος ἐν ῥήματι, 27 ἵνα παραστήσῃ [t]αὐτὴν" ἑαυτῷ
of water by [the] word, that he might present it to himself
ἔνδοξον τὴν ἐκκλησίαν μὴ ἔχουσαν σπίλον ἢ ῥυτίδα ἤ τι
[3]glorious [1]the [2]assembly, not having spot, or wrinkle, or any
τῶν.τοιούτων, ἀλλ' ἵνα ᾖ ἁγία καὶ ἄμωμος. 28 οὕτως
of such things; but that it might be holy and blameless. So
[v]ὀφείλουσιν [w] οἱ ἄνδρες" ἀγαπᾷν τὰς.ἑαυτῶν.γυναῖκας ὡς
ought husbands to love their own wives as
τὰ.ἑαυτῶν σώματα· ὁ ἀγαπῶν τὴν ἑαυτοῦ γυναῖκα ἑαυτὸν
their own bodies: he that loves his own wife [2]himself
ἀγαπᾷ· 29 οὐδεὶς.γάρ ποτε τὴν.ἑαυτοῦ σάρκα ἐμίσησεν,
[1]loves. For no one at any time his own flesh hated,
[x]ἀλλ'" ἐκτρέφει καὶ θάλπει αὐτήν, καθὼς καὶ ὁ [y]κύριος" τὴν
but nourishes and cherishes it, even as also the Lord the
ἐκκλησίαν. 30 ὅτι μέλη ἐσμὲν τοῦ.σώματος.αὐτοῦ, [z]ἐκ τῆς
assembly: for members we are of his body, of
σαρκὸς.αὐτοῦ, καὶ ἐκ τῶν.ὀστέων.αὐτοῦ." 31 Ἀντὶ τούτου
his flesh, and of his bones. Because of this
καταλείψει ἄνθρωπος [a]τὸν" πατέρα [b]αὐτοῦ" καὶ [c]τὴν" μητέρα,
[3]shall [4]leave [1]a [2]man [6]father [5]his and mother,
καὶ προσκολληθήσεται [d]πρὸς τὴν γυναῖκα" [e]αὐτοῦ," καὶ ἔσον-
and shall be joined to [2]wife [1]his, and [3]shall
ται οἱ δύο εἰς σάρκα μίαν. 32 Τὸ.μυστήριον.τοῦτο μέγα ἐστίν·
[4]be [1]the [2]two for [5]flesh [6]one. This mystery [2]great [1]is,
ἐγὼ.δὲ λέγω εἰς χριστὸν καὶ [f]εἰς" τὴν ἐκκλησίαν. 33 πλὴν
but I speak as to Christ and as to the assembly. However
καὶ ὑμεῖς οἱ.καθ'.ἕνα, ἕκαστος τὴν.ἑαυτοῦ γυναῖκα οὕτως ἀγα-
also ye everyone, [2]each [4]his [5]own [6]wife [7]so [1]let
πάτω ὡς ἑαυτόν· ἡ.δὲ γυνὴ ἵνα φοβῆται τὸν ἄνδρα.
[3]love as himself; and the wife that she may fear the husband.

6 Τὰ τέκνα, ὑπακούετε τοῖς.γονεῦσιν.ὑμῶν [g]ἐν κυρίῳ·"
Children, obey your parents in [the] Lord,
τοῦτο.γάρ ἐστιν δίκαιον. 2 Τίμα τὸν.πατέρα.σου καὶ τὴν
for this is just. Honour thy father and
μητέρα· ἥτις ἐστὶν ἐντολὴ πρώτη ἐν ἐπαγγελίᾳ· 3 ἵνα
mother, which is [3]commandment [1]the [2]first with a promise, that
εὖ σοι γένηται, καὶ ἔσῃ μακροχρόνιος ἐπὶ τῆς γῆς.
well with thee it may be, and thou mayest be long-lived on the earth.
4 Καὶ οἱ πατέρες, μὴ.παροργίζετε τὰ.τέκνα.ὑμῶν, [x]ἀλλ'" ἐκ-
And fathers, do not provoke your children, but bring
τρέφετε αὐτὰ ἐν παιδείᾳ καὶ νουθεσίᾳ κυρίου.
up them in [the] discipline and admonition of [the] Lord.

5 Οἱ δοῦλοι, ὑπακούετε τοῖς [h]κυρίοις κατὰ σάρκα"
Bondmen, obey [your] masters according to flesh
μετὰ φόβου καὶ τρόμου, ἐν ἁπλότητι [i]τῆς".καρδίας.ὑμῶν, ὡς
with fear and trembling, in simplicity of your heart, as
τῷ χριστῷ· 6 μὴ κατ' [k]ὀφθαλμοδουλείαν" ὡς ἀνθρωπάρεσκοι,
to the Christ; not with eye-service as men-pleasers;
ἀλλ' ὡς δοῦλοι [l]τοῦ' χριστοῦ, ποιοῦντες τὸ θέλημα τοῦ θεοῦ
but as bondmen of the Christ, doing the will of God
ἐκ ψυχῆς, 7 μετ' εὐνοίας δουλεύοντες [m] τῷ κυρίῳ καὶ
from [the] soul, with good will doing service to the Lord and
οὐκ ἀνθρώποις· 8 εἰδότες ὅτι [n]ὃ.ἐάν.τι ἕκαστος" ποιήσῃ
not to men; knowing that whatsoever [2]each [3]may [4]have [5]done

18 And do not be drunk with wine, in which is debauchery, but be filled with the Spirit,

19 speaking to each other in psalms and hymns and spiritual songs, singing and making melody in your heart to the Lord,

20 giving thanks at all times for all things to Him who is God and Father, in the name of our Lord Jesus Christ,

21 submitting yourselves to one another in the fear of God.

22 Wives, submit yourselves to your own husbands as to the Lord.

23 For the husband is head of the wife, as Christ is Head of the church, and He is Savior of the body.

24 But as the church is subject to Christ, so also wives to their own husbands in everything.

25 Husbands, love your own wives, as Christ also loved the church and gave Himself for it

26 that He might set it apart, having cleansed it by the washing of water by the word –

27 so that He might present it to Himself a glorious church, not having spot or wrinkle or any such thing, but that it might be holy and blameless.

28 So husbands ought to love their own wives as their own bodies. He that loves his own wife loves himself.

29 For no one ever yet hated his own flesh, but nourishes and warmly cares for it, even as the Lord does the church.

30 For we are members of His body, of His flesh and of His bones.

31 For this cause a man shall leave his father and mother and shall be joined to his wife – and the two shall be one flesh.

32 This is a great mystery, but I speak as to Christ and as to the church.

33 However, you also, every one of you, let each love his own wife as himself, and the wife that she fear her husband.

CHAPTER 6

1 Children, obey your parents in the Lord, for that is right.

2 Honor your father and mother, which is the first commandment with promise,

3 so that it may be well with you and you may live long on the earth.

4 And fathers, anger not your children, but rear them in the mind and fear of the Lord.

5 Slaves, obey the masters according to the flesh, with fear and trembling, in purity of your heart, even as to Christ.

6 Do not *serve* with eye-service, as men-pleasers, but as servants of Christ, doing the will of God from the heart.

7 With good will do service to the Lord and not to men,

8 knowing that whatever good each may have done, he shall receive this from the

ἀγαθόν, τοῦτο [o]κομιεῖται‖ παρὰ [p]τοῦ‖ κυρίου, εἴτε δοῦλος
good, this he shall receive from the Lord, whether bondman
εἴτε ἐλεύθερος. 9 Καὶ οἱ κύριοι, τὰ.αὐτὰ ποιεῖτε πρὸς
or free. And masters, the same things do towards
αὐτούς, ἀνιέντες τὴν ἀπειλήν· εἰδότες ὅτι καὶ [q]ὑμῶν.αὐτῶν
them, giving up threatening, knowing that also your own
ὁ‖ κύριός ἐστιν ἐν οὐρανοῖς, καὶ [r]προσωποληψία‖ οὐκ.ἔστιν
master is in [the] heavens, and respect of persons there is.not
παρ' αὐτῷ.
with him.

10 [s]Τὸ.λοιπόν,‖ [t]ἀδελφοί.μου,‖ ἐνδυναμοῦσθε ἐν κυρίῳ,
For the rest, my brethren, be empowered in [the] Lord,
καὶ ἐν τῷ κράτει τῆς.ἰσχύος.αὐτοῦ. 11 ἐνδύσασθε τὴν παν-
and in the might of his strength. Put on the pan-
οπλίαν τοῦ θεοῦ, πρὸς τὸ δύνασθαι ὑμᾶς στῆναι πρὸς τὰς
oply of God, for [2]to [3]be [4]able [1]you to stand against the
[w]μεθοδείας‖ τοῦ διαβόλου· 12 ὅτι οὐκ.ἔστιν [x]ἡμῖν‖ ἡ πάλη
artifices of the devil: because [3]is [4]not [5]to [6]us [1]the [2]wrestling
πρὸς αἷμα καὶ σάρκα, ἀλλὰ πρὸς τὰς ἀρχάς, πρὸς τὰς
against blood and flesh, but against principalities, against
ἐξουσίας, πρὸς τοὺς κοσμοκράτορας τοῦ σκότους [y]τοῦ αἰῶνος‖
authorities, against the world-rulers of the darkness of [2]age
[z]τούτου,‖ πρὸς τὰ πνευματικὰ τῆς πονηρίας ἐν τοῖς ἐπου-
[1]this, against the spiritual [powers] of wickedness in the hea-
ρανίοις. 13 διὰ τοῦτο ἀναλάβετε τὴν πανοπλίαν τοῦ θεοῦ,
venlies. Because of this take up the panoply of God,
ἵνα δυνηθῆτε ἀντιστῆναι ἐν τῇ ἡμέρᾳ τῇ πονηρᾷ, καὶ ἅπαντα
that ye may be able to withstand in the [2]day [1]evil, and all things
κατεργασάμενοι στῆναι. 14 στῆτε οὖν περιζωσάμενοι τὴν
having worked out to stand. Stand therefore, having girt about
ὀσφὺν.ὑμῶν ἐν ἀληθείᾳ, καὶ ἐνδυσάμενοι τὸν θώρακα τῆς
your loins with truth, and having put on the breastplate
δικαιοσύνης, 15 καὶ ὑποδησάμενοι τοὺς πόδας ἐν ἑτοι-
of righteousness, and having shod the feet with [the] pre-
μασίᾳ τοῦ εὐαγγελίου τῆς εἰρήνης· 16 [a]ἐπὶ‖ πᾶσιν ἀναλα-
paration of the glad tidings of peace: besides all having
βόντες τὸν θυρεὸν τῆς πίστεως, ἐν ᾧ δυνήσεσθε πάντα
taken up the shield of faith, with which ye will be able all
τὰ βέλη τοῦ πονηροῦ [b]τὰ‖ πεπυρωμένα σβέσαι· 17 καὶ
the [2]darts [3]of [4]the [5]wicked [6]one [1]burning to quench. Also
τὴν περικεφαλαίαν τοῦ σωτηρίου δέξασθε, καὶ τὴν μάχαιραν
the helmet of salvation receive, and the sword
τοῦ πνεύματος, ὅ ἐστιν ῥῆμα θεοῦ· 18 διὰ πάσης προσευχῆς
of the Spirit, which is [2]word [1]God's; by all prayer
καὶ δεήσεως προσευχόμενοι ἐν παντὶ καιρῷ ἐν πνεύματι,
and supplication praying in every season in [the] Spirit,
καὶ εἰς αὐτὸ [c]τοῦτο‖ ἀγρυπνοῦντες ἐν πάσῃ προσκαρτερήσει
and unto this very thing watching with all perseverance
καὶ δεήσει περὶ πάντων τῶν ἁγίων, 19 καὶ ὑπὲρ ἐμοῦ, ἵνα
and supplication for all saints; and for me that
μοι [d]δοθείη‖ λόγος ἐν ἀνοίξει τοῦ.στόματός.μου ἐν
to me may be given utterance in [the] opening of my mouth with
παῤῥησίᾳ, γνωρίσαι τὸ μυστήριον [e]τοῦ εὐαγγελίου,‖ 20 ὑπὲρ
boldness to make known the mystery of the glad tidings, for
οὗ πρεσβεύω ἐν ἁλύσει, ἵνα ἐν αὐτῷ παῤῥησιάσωμαι
which I am an ambassador in a chain, that in it I may be bold
ὡς δεῖ με λαλῆσαι.
as it behoves me to speak.

21 Ἵνα.δὲ [f]εἰδῆτε καὶ ὑμεῖς‖ τὰ κατ' ἐμέ, τί
But that [3]may [4]know [2]also [1]ye the things concerning me, what
πράσσω, πάντα [g]ὑμῖν γνωρίσει‖ Τυχικὸς ὁ ἀγαπητὸς
I am doing, all things to you will make known Tychicus the beloved
ἀδελφὸς καὶ πιστὸς διάκονος ἐν κυρίῳ· 22 ὃν ἔπεμψα
brother and faithful servant in [the] Lord; whom I sent
πρὸς ὑμᾶς εἰς αὐτὸ.τοῦτο, ἵνα γνῶτε τὰ περὶ
to you for this very thing, that ye might know the things concerning
ἡμῶν καὶ παρακαλέσῃ τὰς.καρδίας.ὑμῶν.
us and he might encourage your hearts.

23 Εἰρήνη τοῖς ἀδελφοῖς καὶ ἀγάπη μετὰ πίστεως ἀπὸ
Peace to the brethren, and love with faith from
θεοῦ πατρὸς καὶ κυρίου Ἰησοῦ χριστοῦ. 24 Ἡ χάρις μετὰ
God [the] Father and Lord Jesus Christ. Grace with
πάντων τῶν ἀγαπώντων τὸν.κύριον.ἡμῶν Ἰησοῦν χριστὸν
all those that love our Lord Jesus Christ
ἐν ἀφθαρσίᾳ. [h]ἀμήν.‖
in incorruption. Amen.

[i]Πρὸς Ἐφεσίους ἐγράφη ἀπὸ Ῥώμης, διὰ Τυχικοῦ.‖
To [the] Ephesians written from Rome, by Tychicus.

Lord, whether a slave or a freeman.
9 And masters, do the same towards them, giving up threatening, knowing that also your own Master is in Heaven, and there is no respect of persons with Him.

10 For the rest, my brothers, be powerful in the Lord, and in the might of His strength.
11 Put on all God's armor so you may be able to withstand the wiles of the devil.
12 For we wrestle not against flesh and blood, but against rulers and authorities and the rulers of this world's darkness, against spiritual powers of wickedness in the air.
13 Then take up all God's armor so that you may be able to stand in the evil day – and when you have done all, to stand.
14 Then stand firm, with the girdle of truth circling your waist, putting on the breastplate of righteousness,
15 and shoeing your feet with the readiness of the gospel of peace –
16 above all, taking up the shield of faith, with which you will be able to put out all the burning darts of the wicked one.
17 Also the helmet of salvation, and the Spirit's sword, which is God's word.
18 *Be* always praying with all prayer and humble looking to the Spirit, and watching to this very thing, with all steadfastness and humble seeking for all saints,
19 and *pray* for me that skill in speaking may be given me, in the opening of my mouth with boldness to make known the mystery of the gospel,
20 for which I am an ambassador in a chain, that I may be bold in it, as I ought to speak.

21 But that you also may know my affairs, what I am doing, Tych-i-cus the beloved brother and faithful servant in the Lord will reveal all to you,
22 whom I sent to you for this very thing, that you might know our affairs, and that he might comfort your hearts.

23 Peace to the brothers and love with faith from God the Father and the Lord Jesus Christ.
24 Grace be with all those that love our Lord Jesus Christ in purity. Amen.

The Letter to the PHILIPPIANS

ΠΑΥΛΟΣ καὶ Τιμόθεος δοῦλοι [l]Ἰησοῦ χριστοῦ, πᾶσιν τοῖς
Paul and Timotheus, bondmen of Jesus Christ, to all the
ἁγίοις ἐν χριστῷ Ἰησοῦ τοῖς οὖσιν ἐν Φιλίπποις, σὺν
saints in Christ Jesus who are in Philippi, with [the]
ἐπισκόποις καὶ διακόνοις· 2 χάρις ὑμῖν καὶ εἰρήνη ἀπὸ θεοῦ
overseers and those who serve. Grace to you and peace from God
πατρὸς ἡμῶν καὶ κυρίου [m]Ἰησοῦ χριστοῦ.
our Father and [the] Lord Jesus Christ.
3 Εὐχαριστῶ τῷ θεῷ μου ἐπὶ πάσῃ τῇ μνείᾳ ὑμῶν,
I thank my God on the whole remembrance of you,
4 πάντοτε ἐν πάσῃ δεήσει μου ὑπὲρ πάντων ὑμῶν μετὰ
always in 2every 3supplication 1my for 2all 1you with
χαρᾶς τὴν δέησιν ποιούμενος, 5 ἐπὶ τῇ κοινωνίᾳ ὑμῶν εἰς
joy 2supplication 1making, for your fellowship in
τὸ εὐαγγέλιον, ἀπὸ [n] πρώτης ἡμέρας ἄχρι τοῦ νῦν· 6 πε-
the glad tidings, from [the] first day until now; being
ποιθὼς αὐτὸ τοῦτο, ὅτι ὁ ἐναρξάμενος ἐν ὑμῖν ἔργον
persuaded of this very thing, that he who began in you a 2work
ἀγαθὸν ἐπιτελέσει [o]ἄχρις ἡμέρας [l]Ἰησοῦ χριστοῦ·
1good will complete [it] until [the] day of Jesus Christ:
7 καθώς ἐστιν δίκαιον ἐμοὶ τοῦτο φρονεῖν ὑπὲρ πάντων ὑμῶν,
as it is righteous for me this to think as to 2all 1you,
διὰ τὸ ἔχειν με ἐν τῇ καρδίᾳ ὑμᾶς, ἔν τε τοῖς δεσμοῖς μου
because 2have 3me 4in 5the 6heart 1ye, both in my bonds
καὶ [p] τῇ ἀπολογίᾳ καὶ βεβαιώσει τοῦ εὐαγγελίου, [q]συγ-
and in the defence and confirmation of the glad tidings, fellow-
κοινωνούς μου τῆς χάριτος πάντας ὑμᾶς ὄντας. 8 μάρτυς γάρ
partakers of my grace all ye are. For 4witness
μου [r]ἐστιν ὁ θεός, ὡς ἐπιποθῶ πάντας ὑμᾶς ἐν σπλάγ-
3my 2is 1God, how I long after 2all 1you in [the] bowels
χνοις [s]Ἰησοῦ χριστοῦ. 9 καὶ τοῦτο προσεύχομαι, ἵνα ἡ ἀγάπη
of Jesus Christ. And this I pray, that 2love
ὑμῶν ἔτι μᾶλλον καὶ μᾶλλον [t]περισσεύῃ ἐν ἐπιγνώσει καὶ
1your yet more and more may abound in knowledge and
πάσῃ αἰσθήσει, 10 εἰς τὸ δοκιμάζειν ὑμᾶς τὰ δια-
all intelligence, for 2to 3approve 1you the things that are
φέροντα, ἵνα ἦτε εἰλικρινεῖς καὶ ἀπρόσκοποι εἰς ἡμέραν
excellent, that ye may be pure and without offence for [the] day
χριστοῦ, 11 πεπληρωμένοι [v]καρπῶν δικαιοσύνης [w]τῶν
of Christ, being filled with fruits of righteousness which [are]
διὰ Ἰησοῦ χριστοῦ, εἰς δόξαν καὶ ἔπαινον θεοῦ.
by Jesus Christ, to 2glory 3and 4praise 1God's.
12 Γινώσκειν δὲ ὑμᾶς βούλομαι, ἀδελφοί, ὅτι τὰ κατ'
But 4to 5know 3you 1I 2wish, brethren, that the things concerning
ἐμὲ μᾶλλον εἰς προκοπὴν τοῦ εὐαγγελίου ἐλήλυθεν·
me rather to [the] advancement of the glad tidings have turned out,
13 ὥστε τοὺς δεσμούς μου φανεροὺς ἐν χριστῷ γενέσθαι
so as my bonds 4manifest 5in 6Christ 1to 2have 3become
ἐν ὅλῳ τῷ πραιτωρίῳ καὶ τοῖς λοιποῖς πᾶσιν· 14 καὶ τοὺς
in 2whole 1the prætorium and to 2the 3rest 1all; and the
πλείονας τῶν ἀδελφῶν ἐν κυρίῳ πεποιθότας τοῖς δεσμοῖς
most of the brethren 2in [3the] 4Lord 1trusting by 2bonds
μου περισσοτέρως τολμᾶν ἀφόβως τὸν λόγον [x]λαλεῖν. 15 Τινὲς
1my 4more 5abundantly 3dare 10fearlessly 8the 9word 6to 7speak. Some
μὲν καὶ διὰ φθόνον καὶ ἔριν, τινὲς δὲ καὶ δι' εὐδοκίαν τὸν
indeed even from envy and strife, but some also from good-will the
χριστὸν κηρύσσουσιν. 16 οἱ μὲν [y]ἐξ ἐριθείας [z]τὸν χριστὸν
Christ are proclaiming. Those indeed out of contention the Christ
καταγγέλλουσιν οὐχ ἁγνῶς, οἰόμενοι θλῖψιν [a]ἐπιφέρειν
are announcing, not purely, supposing tribulation to add
τοῖς δεσμοῖς μου· 17 οἱ δὲ [y]ἐξ ἀγάπης, εἰδότες ὅτι εἰς ἀπο-
to my bonds, but these out of love, knowing that for de-
λογίαν τοῦ εὐαγγελίου κεῖμαι. 18 τί γάρ; πλὴν [b] παντὶ
fence of the glad tidings I am set. What then? nevertheless in every
τρόπῳ, εἴτε προφάσει εἴτε ἀληθείᾳ, χριστὸς καταγγέλλεται·
way, whether in pretext or in truth, Christ is announced;
καὶ ἐν τούτῳ χαίρω, ἀλλὰ καὶ χαρήσομαι. 19 οἶδα γὰρ ὅτι
and in this I rejoice, yea, also I will rejoice: for I know that
τοῦτό μοι ἀποβήσεται εἰς σωτηρίαν διὰ τῆς ὑμῶν δεήσεως,
this for me shall turn out to salvation through your supplication,
καὶ ἐπιχορηγίας τοῦ πνεύματος Ἰησοῦ χριστοῦ, 20 κατὰ
and [the] supply of the Spirit of Jesus Christ: according to
τὴν ἀποκαραδοκίαν καὶ ἐλπίδα μου, ὅτι ἐν οὐδενὶ αἰσχυνθή-
2earnest 3expectation 4and 5hope 1my, that in nothing I shall be
σομαι, ἀλλ' ἐν πάσῃ παρρησίᾳ, ὡς πάντοτε, καὶ νῦν μεγα-
ashamed, but in all boldness, as always, also now shall be
λυνθήσεται χριστὸς ἐν τῷ σώματί μου εἴτε διὰ ζωῆς εἴτε διὰ
magnified Christ in my body whether by life or by
θανάτου. 21 Ἐμοὶ γὰρ τὸ ζῆν χριστός, καὶ τὸ ἀποθανεῖν
death. For to me to live [is] Christ, and to die
κέρδος. 22 εἰ δὲ τὸ ζῆν ἐν σαρκί, τοῦτό μοι καρπὸς ἔργου·
gain; but if to live in flesh, this for me [is] fruit of labour:

CHAPTER 1

1 Paul and Timothy, servants of Jesus
Christ, to all the saints in Christ Jesus who
are in Philippi, with the overseers and
deacons.
2 Grace to you and peace from God our
Father and the Lord Jesus Christ.
3 I thank my God for all my remembrance
of you.
4 Always in my every prayer for all of you,
I make request with joy
5 for your fellowship in the gospel, from
the first day until now,
6 being persuaded of this very thing, that
He who began a good work in you will finish
it unto the day of Jesus Christ.
7 Even as it is right for me to think this of
you all, because you have me in your heart,
both in my bonds and in the defense and
confirmation of the gospel, you are all
sharers of my grace.
8 For God is my witness how I long for you
all in the tender affections of Jesus Christ.
9 And this I pray, that your love may
increase more and more in knowledge and all
judgment,
10 so that you may discern the things that
differ, that you may be pure and without
blame to the day of Christ,
11 being filled with the fruits of righteousness, which are by Jesus Christ, to the glory
and praise of God.
12 But I want you to know, brothers, that
the things concerning me have turned out to
the progress of the gospel,
13 so that inside the palace, and to all the
rest, my bonds have become known to be in
Christ.
14 And the most of the brothers in the
Lord, being assured by my bonds, dare much
more boldly to speak the word without fear
15 Some indeed are preaching Christ even
from envy and strife, but some also from
good will.
16 The ones who are indeed preaching
Christ in order to stir up trouble, not sin-
cerely, but, thinking to add troubles to my
bonds.
17 But the ones *who do so* out of love
know that I am set for the defense of the
gospel.
18 What then? Nevertheless, in every way,
whether pretending or in truth, Christ is
preached. And I rejoice in this. Yes, I will
rejoice
19 because I know that this will turn out to
be salvation for me, through your prayer and
the supply of the Spirit of Jesus Christ.
20 Even according to my hope and eager
belief that I shall not be ashamed in anything, but in all boldness, as always, so now
Christ shall be magnified in my body,
whether by life or by death.
21 For *to* me to live is Christ! And to die is
gain!

καὶ τί αἱρήσομαι οὐ.γνωρίζω· 23 συνέχομαι [c]γὰρ" ἐκ τῶν
and what I shall choose I know not. [2]I [3]am [4]pressed [1]for by the
δύο, τὴν ἐπιθυμίαν ἔχων εἰς τὸ ἀναλῦσαι, καὶ σὺν χριστῷ
two, [2]the [3]desire [1]having for to depart, and with Christ
εἶναι, πολλῷ[d].μᾶλλον κρεῖσσον· 24 τὸ.δὲ.ἐπιμένειν [e]ἐν"
to be, [for it is] very much better; but to remain in
τῇ σαρκὶ ἀναγκαιότερον δι' ὑμᾶς· 25 καὶ τοῦτο
the flesh [is] more necessary for the sake of you; and this
πεποιθὼς οἶδα ὅτι μενῶ καὶ [f]συμπαραμενῶ" πᾶσιν
being persuaded of, I know that I shall abide and continue with [2]all
ὑμῖν εἰς τὴν.ὑμῶν.προκοπὴν καὶ χαρὰν τῆς πίστεως, 26 ἵνα
[1]you; for your advancement and joy of faith; that
τὸ.καύχημα.ὑμῶν περισσεύῃ ἐν χριστῷ Ἰησοῦ ἐν ἐμοὶ διὰ
your boasting may abound in Christ Jesus in me through
τῆς.ἐμῆς.παρουσίας πάλιν πρὸς ὑμᾶς. 27 Μόνον ἀξίως τοῦ
my presence again with you. Only worthily of the
εὐαγγελίου τοῦ χριστοῦ πολιτεύεσθε, ἵνα εἴτε ἐλθὼν καὶ
glad tidings of the Christ conduct yourselves, that whether having come and
ἰδὼν ὑμᾶς, εἴτε ἀπὼν [g]ἀκούσω" τὰ περὶ ὑμῶν,
having seen you, or being absent I might hear the things concerning you,
ὅτι στήκετε ἐν ἑνὶ πνεύματι, μιᾷ ψυχῇ συναθλοῦντες
that ye stand fast in one spirit, with one soul striving together
τῇ πίστει τοῦ εὐαγγελίου, 28 καὶ μὴ πτυρόμενοι ἐν μη-
with the faith of the glad tidings; and being frightened in no-
δενὶ ὑπὸ τῶν ἀντικειμένων· ἥτις [h]αὐτοῖς μέν ἐστιν" ἔν-
thing by those who oppose; which to them is a demon-
δειξις ἀπωλείας, [i]ὑμῖν" δὲ σωτηρίας, καὶ τοῦτο ἀπὸ θεοῦ·
stration of destruction, [2]to [3]you [1]but of salvation, and this from God;
29 ὅτι ὑμῖν ἐχαρίσθη τὸ ὑπὲρ χριστοῦ, οὐ μόνον τὸ
because to you it was granted concerning Christ, not only
εἰς αὐτὸν πιστεύειν, ἀλλὰ καὶ τὸ ὑπὲρ αὐτοῦ πάσχειν·
[3]on [4]him [1]to [2]believe, but also concerning him to suffer,
30 τὸν αὐτὸν ἀγῶνα ἔχοντες οἷον [k]ἴδετε" ἐν ἐμοί, καὶ νῦν
the same conflict having such as ye saw in me, and now
ἀκούετε ἐν ἐμοί.
hear of in me.

2 Εἴ τις οὖν παράκλησις ἐν χριστῷ, εἴ τι παρα-
If [2]any [1]then encouragement [there be] in Christ, if any conso-
μύθιον ἀγάπης, εἴ τις κοινωνία πνεύματος, εἴ [l]τινα" σπλάγ-
lation of love, if any fellowship of [the] Spirit, if any bowels
χνα καὶ οἰκτιρμοί, 2 πληρώσατέ μου τὴν χαράν, ἵνα
and compassions, fulfil my joy, that
τὸ.αὐτὸ.φρονῆτε, τὴν αὐτὴν ἀγάπην ἔχοντες, [m]σύμψυχοι,"
ye may be of the same mind, the same love having, joined in soul,
τὸ ἓν φρονοῦντες· 3 μηδὲν [n]κατὰ" ἐριθείαν [o]ἢ" κενο-
the one thing minding— nothing according to contention or vain-
δοξίαν, ἀλλὰ τῇ ταπεινοφροσύνῃ ἀλλήλους ἡγούμενοι ὑπερ-
glory, but in humility one another esteeming a-
έχοντας ἑαυτῶν. 4 μὴ τὰ ἑαυτῶν [p]ἕκαστος"
bove themselves, [2]not [4]the [5]things [6]of [7]themselves [3]each
[q]σκοπεῖτε," ἀλλὰ καὶ τὰ ἑτέρων [r]ἕκαστος." 5 Τοῦτο
[1]consider, but [2]also [3]the [4]things [5]of [6]others [1]each. [2]This
[s]γὰρ φρονείσθω" ἐν ὑμῖν ὃ καὶ ἐν χριστῷ Ἰησοῦ, 6 ὃς
[1]for [3]let mind be in you which also in Christ Jesus [was]; who,
ἐν μορφῇ θεοῦ ὑπάρχων, οὐχ ἁρπαγμὸν ἡγήσατο τὸ εἶναι
in [the] form of God subsisting, [3]not [4]rapine [1]esteemed [2]it to be
[t]ἴσα[t] θεῷ, 7 [v]ἀλλ'" ἑαυτὸν ἐκένωσεν, μορφὴν δούλου
equal with God; but [2]himself [1]emptied, [7]form [8]a [9]bondman's
λαβών, ἐν ὁμοιώματι ἀνθρώπων γενόμενος· 8 καὶ σχή-
[5]having [6]taken, in [the] likeness of men having become; and in
ματι εὑρεθεὶς ὡς ἄνθρωπος, ἐταπείνωσεν ἑαυτόν, γενό-
figure having been found as a man, he humbled himself, having
μενος ὑπήκοος μέχρι θανάτου, θανάτου.δὲ σταυροῦ. 9 διὸ
become obedient unto death, even death of [the] cross. Wherefore
καὶ ὁ θεὸς αὐτὸν ὑπερύψωσεν καὶ ἐχαρίσατο αὐτῷ [w]ὄνομα
also God him highly exalted and granted to him a name
τὸ ὑπὲρ πᾶν ὄνομα· 10 ἵνα ἐν τῷ ὀνόματι Ἰησοῦ πᾶν
which [is] above every name, that at the name of Jesus every
γόνυ κάμψῃ ἐπουρανίων καὶ ἐπιγείων καὶ καταχθονίων·
knee should bow of [beings] in heaven and on earth and under the earth,
11 καὶ πᾶσα γλῶσσα [x]ἐξομολογήσηται" ὅτι κύριος Ἰησοῦς
and every tongue should confess that [[3]is] [4]Lord [1]Jesus
χριστὸς εἰς δόξαν θεοῦ πατρός.
[2]Christ to [the] glory of God [the] Father.
12 Ὥστε, ἀγαπητοί.μου, καθὼς πάντοτε ὑπηκούσατε, μὴ
So that, my beloved, even as always ye obeyed, not
ὡς ἐν τῇ.παρουσίᾳ.μου μόνον, ἀλλὰ νῦν πολλῷ μᾶλλον ἐν
as in my presence only, but now much rather in
τῇ.ἀπουσίᾳ.μου, μετὰ φόβου καὶ τρόμου τὴν.ἑαυτῶν σωτηρίαν
my absence, with fear and trembling your own salvation
κατεργάζεσθε· 13 [y]ὁ".θεὸς.γάρ ἐστιν ὁ ἐνεργῶν ἐν ὑμῖν καὶ τὸ
work out, for God it is who works in you both

22 But if I live in the flesh, this is the fruit of my labor, yet what I shall choose I do not know.

23 For I am pressed down by the two – having a desire to depart and to be with Christ (very much better) –

24 but to stay here in the flesh is more needful for your sake.

25 And being certain of this, I know that I shall stay and continue with you all, to your progress and joy in faith –

26 so that your rejoicing may abound in Christ Jesus in me, through my being again with you.

27 Only keep yourselves doing the things worthy of the gospel of Christ, so that whether I come and see you or am absent, I might hear about you, that you stand firm in one spirit, with one soul, working together for the faith of the gospel.

28 And do not be frightened in anything by those who are against you, which is indeed a proof of loss to them, but of salvation to you – and this from God.

29 Because it was given to you as a favor for Christ's sake, not only to believe on Him, but also to suffer for His sake,

30 having the same struggle which you saw in me, and now hear to be in me.

2 1 Then if *there is* any consolation in Christ, if any comfort of love, if any fellowship of the Spirit, if any tenderness and mercies,

2 fill my joy, so that you may be of the same mind, having the same love, one in soul and minding this one thing.

3 *Let* nothing be done according to a desire to quarrel or to glory in self. But in lowliness of mind let each think one another to be better than himself.

4 Do not let each one consider his own things, but each one the things of others too.

5 For let this mind be in you which was also in Christ Jesus,

6 who, being in the form of God, thought it not robbery to be equal with God,

7 but emptied Himself and took on Him the form of a servant and was made in the likeness of men.

8 And being found in fashion as a man, He humbled Himself and became obedient to death, even the death of *a* cross.

9 For this reason God also highly exalted Him and gave Him a name which is above every other name –

10 so that at the name of Jesus every knee should bow (of those in Heaven and on earth and under the earth),

11 and every tongue should confess that Jesus Christ is Lord, to the glory of God the Father.

12 So, then, my beloved, even as you always obeyed, not in my presence only, but now much rather in my absence, work out your own salvation with fear and trembling.

θέλειν καὶ τὸ ἐνεργεῖν ὑπὲρ τῆς εὐδοκίας. 14 πάντα
to will and to work according to [his] good pleasure. [2]All [3]things
ποιεῖτε χωρὶς γογγυσμῶν καὶ διαλογισμῶν, 15 ἵνα [z]γένησθε"
[1]do apart from murmurings and reasonings, that ye may be
ἄμεμπτοι καὶ ἀκέραιοι, τέκνα θεοῦ [a]ἀμώμητα" [b]ἐν μέσῳ"
faultless and simple, children of God unblamable in [the] midst
γενεᾶς σκολιᾶς καὶ διεστραμμένης, ἐν οἷς φαίνεσθε ὡς
of a generation crooked and perverted; among whom ye appear as
φωστῆρες ἐν κόσμῳ, 16 λόγον ζωῆς ἐπέχοντες, εἰς καύχημα
luminaries in [the] world, [the] word of life holding forth, for a boast
ἐμοὶ εἰς ἡμέραν χριστοῦ, ὅτι οὐκ εἰς κενὸν ἔδραμον οὐδὲ εἰς
to me in [2]day [1]Christ's, that not in vain I ran, nor in
κενὸν ἐκοπίασα. 17 [c]ἀλλ'" εἰ καὶ σπένδομαι ἐπὶ τῇ θυσίᾳ καὶ
vain laboured. But if also I am poured out on the sacrifice and
λειτουργίᾳ τῆς.πίστεως.ὑμῶν, χαίρω καὶ [d]συγχαίρω" πᾶσιν
ministration of your faith, I rejoice, and rejoice with all
ὑμῖν· 18 τὸ.[e]δ'".αὐτὸ καὶ ὑμεῖς χαίρετε καὶ [d]συγχαίρετέ" μοι.
you. And in the same also [2]ye [1]rejoice and rejoice with me.
19 Ἐλπίζω.δὲ ἐν [f]κυρίῳ" Ἰησοῦ Τιμόθεον ταχέως πέμψαι
But I hope in [the] Lord Jesus [3]Timotheus [4]soon [1]to [2]send
ὑμῖν, ἵνα κἀγὼ εὐψυχῶ, γνοὺς τὰ περὶ
to you, that I also may be of good courage, having known the things concerning
ὑμῶν· 20 οὐδένα.γὰρ ἔχω ἰσόψυχον, ὅστις γνησίως τὰ
you. For no one have I like-minded, who genuinely the things
περὶ ὑμῶν μεριμνήσει· 21 οἱ.πάντες.γὰρ τὰ ἑαυτῶν
relative to you will care for. For all the things of themselves
ζητοῦσιν, οὐ τὰ [h]τοῦ" [i]χριστοῦ Ἰησοῦ." 22 τὴν.δὲ δοκιμὴν
are seeking, not the things of Christ Jesus. But the proof
αὐτοῦ γινώσκετε, ὅτι ὡς πατρὶ τέκνον, σὺν ἐμοὶ ἐδούλευσεν
of him ye know, that, as [3]to [4]a [5]father [1]a [2]child, with me he served
εἰς τὸ εὐαγγέλιον. 23 τοῦτον μὲν οὖν ἐλπίζω πέμψαι ὡς
for the glad tidings. Him therefore I hope to send [3]when
ἂν [k]ἀπίδω" τὰ περὶ ἐμέ, ἐξαυτῆς· 24 πέ-
[4]I [5]shall [6]have [7]seen [8]the [9]things [10]concerning [11]me [1]at [2]once: [13]I [14]am
ποιθα δὲ ἐν κυρίῳ ὅτι καὶ αὐτὸς ταχέως ἐλεύσομαι.
[15]persuaded [12]but in [the] Lord that also [2]myself [4]soon [1]I [3]shall come:
25 Ἀναγκαῖον.δὲ ἡγησάμην Ἐπαφρόδιτον τὸν ἀδελφὸν καὶ
but necessary I esteemed [it] [5]Epaphroditus, [7]brother [8]and
συνεργὸν καὶ [l]συστρατιώτην" μου, ὑμῶν.δὲ ἀπόστολον καὶ
[9]fellow-worker [10]and [11]fellow-soldier [6]my, [12]but [13]your [14]messenger [15]and
λειτουργὸν τῆς.χρείας.μου, πέμψαι πρὸς ὑμᾶς· 26 ἐπειδὴ
[16]minister [17]of [18]my [19]need, [1]to [2]send [3]to [4]you, since
ἐπιποθῶν ἦν πάντας ὑμᾶς[m], καὶ ἀδημονῶν διότι
[3]longing [4]after [1]he [2]was [6]all [5]you, and [was] deeply depressed because
ἠκούσατε ὅτι ἠσθένησεν· 27 καὶ.γὰρ ἠσθένησεν παραπλήσιον
ye heard that he was sick; for indeed he was sick like
θανάτῳ· [n]ἀλλ'" ὁ θεὸς [o]αὐτὸν ἠλέησεν," οὐκ.αὐτὸν.δὲ μόνον,
to death, but God him had mercy on, and not him alone,
ἀλλὰ καὶ ἐμέ, ἵνα μὴ λύπην ἐπὶ [p]λύπῃ" σχῶ. 28 σπου-
but also me, that not sorrow upon sorrow I might have. The more
δαιοτέρως οὖν ἔπεμψα αὐτόν, ἵνα ἰδόντες αὐτὸν πάλιν
diligently therefore I sent him, that seeing him again
χαρῆτε, κἀγὼ ἀλυπότερος ὦ. 29 προσδέχεσθε οὖν
ye might rejoice, and I the less sorrowful might be. Receive therefore
αὐτὸν ἐν κυρίῳ μετὰ πάσης χαρᾶς, καὶ τοὺς τοιούτους
him in [the] Lord with all joy, and such
ἐντίμους ἔχετε· 30 ὅτι διὰ τὸ ἔργον [q]τοῦ" [r]χριστοῦ"
in honour hold; because for the sake of the work of the Christ
μέχρι θανάτου ἤγγισεν, [s]παραβουλευσάμενος" τῇ ψυχῇ,
unto death he went near, having disregarded [his] life,
ἵνα ἀναπληρώσῃ τὸ.ὑμῶν.ὑστέρημα τῆς πρός με λειτουργίας.
that he might fill up your deficiency [4]of the [2]towards [3]me [1]ministration.

3 Τὸ.λοιπόν, ἀδελφοί.μου, χαίρετε ἐν κυρίῳ· τὰ αὐτὰ
For the rest, my brethren, rejoice in [the] Lord: the same things
γράφειν ὑμῖν, ἐμοὶ μὲν οὐκ ὀκνηρόν, ὑμῖν.δὲ ἀσφαλές.
to write to you, to me [is] not irksome, and for you safe.
2 βλέπετε τοὺς κύνας, βλέπετε τοὺς κακοὺς ἐργάτας, βλέπετε
See to dogs, see to evil workers, see to
τὴν κατατομήν· 3 ἡμεῖς.γάρ ἐσμεν ἡ περιτομή, οἱ πνεύματι
the concision. For we are the circumcision, who [3]in [4]spirit
[t]θεῷ" λατρεύοντες, καὶ καυχώμενοι ἐν χριστῷ Ἰησοῦ, καὶ οὐκ
[2]God [1]serve, and boast in Christ Jesus, and not
ἐν σαρκὶ πεποιθότες,[v] 4 καίπερ ἐγὼ ἔχων πεποίθησιν καὶ ἐν
in flesh trust. Though I have trust even in
σαρκί· [v]εἴ τις δοκεῖ ἄλλος πεποιθέναι ἐν σαρκί, ἐγὼ μᾶλλον·
flesh; if any [2]thinks [1]other to trust in flesh, I rather:
5 [w]περιτομῇ ὀκταήμερος, ἐκ γένους Ἰσραήλ, φυλῆς
[as to] circumcision, on [the] eighth day; of [the] race of Israel, of [the] tribe
[x]Βενιαμίν," Ἑβραῖος ἐξ Ἑβραίων, κατὰ νόμον Φαρισαῖος,
of Benjamin, Hebrew of Hebrews; according to [the] law a Pharisee;
6 κατὰ [y]ζῆλον" διώκων τὴν ἐκκλησίαν, κατὰ δικαιοσύ-
according to zeal, persecuting the assembly; according to righteous-

13For it is God who works in you both to
will and to do of His good pleasure.
14Do all things without complaints and
questionings,
15so that you may be blameless and harmless, children of God, without spot in the
midst of a generation which is crooked and
perverted – among whom you shine as lights
in the world,
16holding out the word of life, to my joy
in the day of Christ, that I did not run without gain, nor labor in vain.
17But if I also am offered on the sacrifice
and service of your faith, I rejoice. And I
rejoice together with you all.
18And you also take joy in the same and
rejoice with me.
19But I trust in the Lord Jesus to send
Timothy to you soon, so that I also may be
encouraged when I know your affairs.
20For I have no one of the same mind who
will genuinely care for your affairs.
21For all are seeking their own things, not
the things of Christ Jesus.
22But you know the proof of him, that, as
a child to a father, he served with me for the
gospel.
23So I hope to send him at once whenever
I have seen how things go with me.
24But I trust in the Lord that I also myself
shall come shortly.
25Yet I thought it needful to send you
E-paph-ro-di-tus, my brother and fellow-
soldier and fellow-worker, but your messenger and minister to my need.
26He has been longing for you all and was
full of heaviness because you had heard that
he was sick.
27For indeed he was sick, even as near to
death, but God had mercy on him – and not
on him only, but also on me, so that I might
not have sorrow on top of sorrow.
28I sent him, then, the more carefully, that
seeing him again you might rejoice and that I
might be the less sorrowful.
29Then receive him in the Lord with all
gladness and hold him in honor,
30because he went near death for the sake
of the work of Christ, disregarding life so
that he might fill up your failure toward me.

1Finally, my brothers, rejoice in the Lord.
To be writing the same things to you is not
truly tiresome to me, but *it is* safe for you.
2Look out for dogs. Look out for evil
workers. Look out for the concision *party*.
3For we are the circumcision who serve
God in spirit and rejoice in Christ Jesus and
do not trust in the flesh.
4Though I too might trust in the flesh, *for*
if any other thinks to trust in the flesh, I
more,
5being circumcised the eighth day, of the
race of Israel, of the tribe of Benjamin – a
Hebrew of the Hebrews. According to the
Law, a Pharisee,

νην τὴν ἐν νόμῳ γενόμενος ἄμεμπτος. 7 [z]ἀλλ'‖ ἅτινα
ness which [is] in [the] law, having become blameless; but what things
[a]ἦν μοι‖ κέρδη, ταῦτα ἥγημαι διὰ τὸν χριστὸν
were to me gain, these I have esteemed, on account of Christ,
ζημίαν· 8 ἀλλὰ [b]μενοῦνγε‖ καὶ ἡγοῦμαι πάντα ζημίαν
loss. But yea rather, also I am esteeming all things loss
εἶναι διὰ τὸ ὑπερέχον τῆς γνώσεως [c] χριστοῦ Ἰησοῦ
to be on account of the excellency of the knowledge of Christ Jesus
τοῦ.κυρίου.μου, δι' ὃν τὰ.πάντα ἐζημιώθην, καὶ ἡγοῦ-
my Lord, on account of whom all things I suffered loss of, and esteem
μαι σκύβαλα [d]εἶναι,‖ ἵνα χριστὸν κερδήσω, 9 καὶ εὑρεθῶ
[them] refuse to be, that Christ I may gain; and be found
ἐν αὐτῷ, μὴ ἔχων ἐμὴν.δικαιοσύνην τὴν ἐκ νόμου, ἀλλὰ
in him, not having my righteousness which [is] of law, but
τὴν διὰ πίστεως χριστοῦ, τὴν ἐκ θεοῦ δικαιοσύνην ἐπὶ
that which by faith of Christ [is], the [2]of [3]God [1]righteousness on
τῇ πίστει, 10 τοῦ γνῶναι αὐτὸν καὶ τὴν δύναμιν τῆς ἀνα-
faith, to know him and the power of [2]resur-
στάσεως αὐτοῦ, καὶ [e]τὴν‖ κοινωνίαν [f]τῶν‖.παθημάτων.αὐτοῦ,
rection [1]his, and the fellowship of his sufferings,
[g]συμμορφούμενος‖ τῷ.θανάτῳ.αὐτοῦ, 11 εἴ.πως καταντήσω
being conformed to his death, if by any means I may arrive
εἰς τὴν ἐξανάστασιν [h]τῶν‖ νεκρῶν. 12 οὐχ ὅτι ἤδη ἔλαβον,
at the resurrection of the dead. Not that [2]already [1]I received,
ἢ ἤδη τετελείωμαι· διώκω.δὲ εἰ [i]καὶ‖ καταλάβω
or already have been perfected; but I am pursuing, if also I may lay hold,
ἐφ'.ᾧ καὶ [k]κατελήφθην‖ ὑπὸ [l]τοῦ χριστοῦ [m]Ἰησοῦ.‖ 13 ἀδελ-
for that also I was laid hold of by the Christ Jesus. Bre-
φοί, ἐγὼ ἐμαυτὸν [n]οὐ‖ λογίζομαι κατειληφέναι· ἓν.δέ,
thren, I myself [2]not [1]do reckon to have laid hold; but one thing—
τὰ μὲν ὀπίσω ἐπιλανθανόμενος, τοῖς.δὲ ἔμπροσθεν
the things behind forgetting, and to the things before
ἐπεκτεινόμενος, 14 κατὰ σκοπὸν διώκω [o]ἐπὶ‖ τὸ βραβεῖον
stretching out, towards [the] goal I pursue for the prize
τῆς ἄνω κλήσεως τοῦ θεοῦ ἐν χριστῷ Ἰησοῦ. 15 Ὅσοι
of the [2]on [3]high [1]calling of God in Christ Jesus. As many as
οὖν τέλειοι τοῦτο.φρονῶμεν· καὶ εἴ τι ἑτέρως
therefore [are] perfect should be of this mind; and if [in] anything differently
φρονεῖτε, καὶ τοῦτο ὁ θεὸς ὑμῖν ἀποκαλύψει. 16 πλὴν εἰς.ὃ
ye are minded, [2]also [1]this God to you will reveal. But whereto
ἐφθάσαμεν, τῷ αὐτῷ στοιχεῖν [p]κανόνι, τὸ.αὐτὸ.φρονεῖν.‖
we attained, by the same [2]to [3]walk [1]rule, to be of the same mind.
17 [q]Συμμιμηταί‖ μου γίνεσθε, ἀδελφοί, καὶ σκοπεῖτε τοὺς
[2]Imitators [3]together [4]of [5]me [1]be, brethren, and consider those
οὕτως περιπατοῦντας καθὼς ἔχετε τύπον ἡμᾶς. 18 πολ-
thus walking as ye have [[2]for] [3]a [4]pattern [1]us; [2]many
λοὶ γὰρ περιπατοῦσιν οὓς πολλάκις ἔλεγον ὑμῖν, νῦν.δὲ
[1]for are walking [of] whom often I told you, and now
καὶ κλαίων λέγω, τοὺς ἐχθροὺς τοῦ σταυροῦ τοῦ
even weeping I tell [you, they are] the enemies of the cross
χριστοῦ· 19 ὧν τὸ τέλος ἀπώλεια, ὧν ὁ θεὸς ἡ κοιλία,
of Christ: whose end [is] destruction, whose God [is] the belly,
καὶ ἡ δόξα ἐν τῇ.αἰσχύνῃ.αὐτῶν, οἱ τὰ.ἐπίγεια φρονοῦντες.
and the glory in their shame, who earthly things mind:
20 ἡμῶν.γὰρ τὸ πολίτευμα ἐν οὐρανοῖς ὑπάρχει, ἐξ οὗ
for of us the commonwealth in [the] heavens exists, from which
καὶ σωτῆρα ἀπεκδεχόμεθα κύριον Ἰησοῦν χριστόν, 21 ὃς
also [as] Saviour we are awaiting [the] Lord Jesus Christ, who
μετασχηματίσει τὸ σῶμα τῆς ταπεινώσεως ἡμῶν, [r]εἰς τὸ γε-
will transform [2]body [3]of [4]humiliation [1]our, for [2]to
νέσθαι αὐτὸ‖ [s]σύμμορφον‖ τῷ σώματι τῆς.δόξης.αὐτοῦ, κατὰ
[3]become [1]it conformed to [2]body [3]of [1]his [4]glory, according to
τὴν ἐνέργειαν τοῦ.δύνασθαι.αὐτὸν καὶ ὑποτάξαι [t]ἑαυτῷ‖
the working of his power even to subdue to himself
τὰ.πάντα.
all things.

4 Ὥστε, ἀδελφοί.μου ἀγαπητοὶ καὶ ἐπιπόθητοι, χαρὰ καὶ
So that, my brethren beloved and longed for, [2]joy [3]and
στέφανός μου, οὕτως στήκετε ἐν κυρίῳ, ἀγαπητοί. 2 [u]Εὐω-
[4]crown [1]my, thus stand fast in [the] Lord, beloved. Euo-
δίαν‖ παρακαλῶ, καὶ Συντύχην παρακαλῶ, τὸ.αὐτὸ.φρονεῖν
dia I exhort, and Syntyche I exhort, to be of the same mind
ἐν κυρίῳ· 3 [v]καὶ‖ ἐρωτῶ καὶ σε, [w]σύζυγε γνήσιε,‖ [x]συλ-
in [the] Lord. And I ask also thee, [2]yoke-fellow [1]true, as-
λαμβάνου‖ αὐταῖς, αἵτινες ἐν τῷ εὐαγγελίῳ συνήθλησάν
sist these [women], who in the glad tidings strove together
μοι, μετὰ καὶ Κλήμεντος, καὶ τῶν λοιπῶν συνεργῶν.μου,
with me; with also Clement, and the rest of my fellow-workers,
ὧν τὰ ὀνόματα ἐν βίβλῳ ζωῆς.
whose names [are] in [the] book of life.

4 Χαίρετε ἐν κυρίῳ πάντοτε· πάλιν ἐρῶ, χαίρετε.
Rejoice in [the] Lord always: again I will say, rejoice.

6 according to zeal, persecuting the church. According to righteousness which is in the Law, I had become blameless.

7 But all things which were gain to me, these I have counted loss for Christ.

8 But no, rather, I also count all things to be but loss because of the excellency of the knowledge of Christ Jesus my Lord – for whose sake I have suffered the loss of all things and count *them but* refuse in order that I might gain Christ,

9 and to be found in Him, not having my own righteousness (which is of the Law), but that which is through the faith of Christ – the righteousness of God which is by faith,

10 that I may know Him and the power of His resurrection, and the fellowship of His sufferings, being conformed to His death:

11 If by any means I may attain to the resurrection of the dead.

12 Not as though I had already received or already have been perfected, but I am pressing on if perhaps I may also obtain that for which I also was taken hold of by Christ Jesus.

13 Brothers, I do not count myself to have taken possession, but one thing I do, forgetting those things which are behind and reaching out to those things which are before,

14 I press toward the mark for the prize of the high calling of God in Christ Jesus.

15 So, let us, as many as are perfect, be of this mind. And if you think differently in anything, God will reveal this to you also.

16 But as to that we have attained, let us walk by the same rule, to be of the same mind.

17 Be imitators of me, brothers, and consider those walking this way, for you have us for a pattern.

18 For many are walking (of whom I often told you and now even weeping, I tell you) as enemies of the cross of Christ –

19 whose end is destruction, whose god is the belly, whose glory is in their shame, who mind earthly things.

20 For our citizenship is in Heaven, from which we also are looking for the Lord Jesus Christ as Savior,

21 who will completely transform our body of humiliation, for it to be made like His glorious body – according to the almighty working of His power, even to put all things under Himself.

4 1 So, then, my brothers, ones loved and longed for, my crown and joy, stand firm in this way in the Lord, dearly beloved.

2 I call on Eu-od-i-a and on Syn-ty-che to be of one mind in the Lord.

3 And I ask you also, true friend, help these who labored with me in the gospel, and with Clement and the rest of my fellow-workers, whose names are in the Book of Life.

4 Rejoice in the Lord always. Again I say,

5 τὸ.ἐπιεικὲς.ὑμῶν γνωσθήτω πᾶσιν ἀνθρώποις. ὁ κύριος
[2]Your [3]gentleness [1]let be known to all men. The Lord [is]
ἐγγύς. 6 Μηδὲν μεριμνᾶτε, ἀλλ' ἐν παντὶ τῇ.προσευχῇ
near. Nothing be careful about, but in everything by prayer
καὶ τῇ.δεήσει μετὰ εὐχαριστίας τὰ.αἰτήματα.ὑμῶν γνωρι-
and by supplication with thanksgiving [2]your [3]requests [1]let be made
ζέσθω πρὸς τὸν θεόν· 7 καὶ ἡ εἰρήνη τοῦ θεοῦ ἡ ὑπερέχουσα
known to God; and the peace of God which surpasses
πάντα νοῦν φρουρήσει τὰς.καρδίας.ὑμῶν καὶ τὰ νοήματα
every understanding shall guard your hearts and [2]thoughts
ὑμῶν ἐν χριστῷ Ἰησοῦ. 8 Τὸ.λοιπόν, ἀδελφοί, ὅσα
[1]your in Christ Jesus. For the rest, brethren, whatsoever [things]
ἐστὶν ἀληθῆ, ὅσα σεμνά, ὅσα δίκαια, ὅσα ἁγνά,
are true, whatsoever venerable, whatsoever just, whatsoever pure,
ὅσα προσφιλῆ, ὅσα εὔφημα, εἴ τις ἀρετὴ καὶ εἴ τις
whatsoever lovely, whatsoever of good report; if any virtue and if any
ἔπαινος, ταῦτα λογίζεσθε· 9 ἃ καὶ ἐμάθετε καὶ παρελάβετε
praise, these things consider. What also ye learned and received
καὶ ἠκούσατε καὶ εἴδετε ἐν ἐμοί, ταῦτα πράσσετε· καὶ ὁ θεὸς
and heard and saw in me, these things do; and the God
τῆς εἰρήνης ἔσται μεθ' ὑμῶν. 10 Ἐχάρην.δὲ ἐν κυρίῳ
of peace shall be with you. But I rejoiced in [the] Lord
μεγάλως, ὅτι ἤδη.ποτὲ ἀνεθάλετε τὸ ὑπὲρ ἐμοῦ φρονεῖν·
greatly, that now at length ye revived [your] [2]of [3]me [1]thinking;
ἐφ'.ᾧ καὶ ἐφρονεῖτε, ἠκαιρεῖσθε.δέ. 11 οὐχ ὅτι
although also ye were thinking, but ye were lacking opportunity. Not that
καθ' ὑστέρησιν λέγω· ἐγὼ.γὰρ ἔμαθον ἐν οἷς εἰμι,
as to destitution I speak; for I learned in what [circumstances] I am,
αὐτάρκης εἶναι. 12 οἶδα.[y]δὲ" ταπεινοῦσθαι, οἶδα.καὶ
content to be. And I know [how] to be brought low, and I know [how]
περισσεύειν· ἐν παντὶ καὶ ἐν πᾶσιν μεμύημαι καὶ χορτά-
to abound. In everything and in all things I am initiated both to be
ζεσθαι καὶ πεινᾶν, καὶ περισσεύειν καὶ ὑστερεῖσθαι· 13 πάντα
full and to hunger, both to abound and to be deficient. [5]All [6]things
ἰσχύω ἐν τῷ ἐνδυναμοῦντί με [z]χριστῷ." 14 πλὴν
[1]I [2]am [3]strong [4]for in the [2]who [3]empowers [4]me [1]Christ. But
καλῶς ἐποιήσατε, [a]συγκοινωνήσαντές" μου τῇ θλίψει. 15 οἴδατε
well ye did, having fellowship in my tribulation. [2]Know
δὲ καὶ ὑμεῖς, Φιλιππήσιοι, ὅτι ἐν ἀρχῇ τοῦ εὐαγγελίου,
[1]and also ye, O Philippians, that in [the] beginning of the glad tidings,
ὅτε ἐξῆλθον ἀπὸ Μακεδονίας, οὐδεμία μοι ἐκκλησία ἐκοι-
when I came out from Macedonia, not any [4]with [5]me [1]assembly [2]had
νώνησεν εἰς λόγον δόσεως καὶ [b]λήψεως," εἰ.μὴ ὑμεῖς
[3]fellowship with regard to an account of giving and receiving, except ye
μόνοι· 16 ὅτι καὶ ἐν Θεσσαλονίκῃ καὶ ἅπαξ καὶ δὶς [c]εἰς" τὴν
alone; because also in Thessalonica both once and twice for
χρείαν.μοι ἐπέμψατε. 17 οὐχ ὅτι ἐπιζητῶ τὸ δόμα, [d]ἀλλ'"
my need ye sent. Not that I seek after gift, but
ἐπιζητῶ τὸν καρπὸν τὸν πλεονάζοντα εἰς λόγον.ὑμῶν·
I seek after fruit that abounds to your account.
18 ἀπέχω.δὲ πάντα καὶ περισσεύω· πεπλήρωμαι, δεξάμενος
But I have all things and abound; I am full, having received
παρὰ Ἐπαφροδίτου τὰ παρ' ὑμῶν, ὀσμὴν εὐωδίας,
from Epaphroditus the things from you, an odour of a sweet smell,
θυσίαν δεκτήν, εὐάρεστον τῷ θεῷ. 19 ὁ δὲ θεός.μου πληρώσει
a sacrifice acceptable, well-pleasing to God. But my God will fill up
πᾶσαν χρείαν.ὑμῶν κατὰ [e]τὸν.πλοῦτον".αὐτοῦ ἐν δόξῃ ἐν
all your need according to his riches in glory in
χριστῷ Ἰησοῦ. 20 τῷ.δὲ θεῷ καὶ πατρὶ ἡμῶν ἡ δόξα εἰς
Christ Jesus. But to the God and Father of us [be] glory to
τοὺς αἰῶνας τῶν αἰώνων. ἀμήν.
the ages of the ages. Amen.

21 Ἀσπάσασθε πάντα ἅγιον ἐν χριστῷ Ἰησοῦ. ἀσπάζον-
Salute every saint in Christ Jesus. [8]Sa-
ται ὑμᾶς οἱ σὺν ἐμοὶ ἀδελφοί. 22 ἀσπάζονται ὑμᾶς πάν-
lute [9]you [1]the [3]with [4]me [2]brethren. [10]Salute [11]you [7]all
τες οἱ ἅγιοι, μάλιστα.δὲ οἱ ἐκ τῆς Καίσαρος οἰκίας. 23 Ἡ
[8]the [9]saints, and especially those of the [2]of [3]Cæsar [1]household. The
χάρις τοῦ.κυρίου [f]ἡμῶν" Ἰησοῦ χριστοῦ μετὰ [g]πάντων
grace of our Lord Jesus Christ [be] with [2]all
ὑμῶν." [h]ἀμήν.[h]
[1]you. Amen.

[i]Πρὸς Φιλιππησίους ἐγράφη ἀπὸ Ῥώμης, δι' Ἐπα-
To [the] Philippians written from Rome, by Epa-
φροδίτου."
phroditus.

Rejoice!
5 Let your sweet reasonableness be known
to all men. The Lord is near.
6 Do not be anxious about anything, but in
everything, by prayer and by request, with
gratitude, let your desires be known to God.
7 And the peace of God which passes all
understanding shall keep your hearts and
minds through Christ Jesus.
8 Finally, brothers, whatever *things* are true
whatever is honorable whatever is right
whatever is pure whatever is lovely
whatever is of good report if *there is* any
virtue and if there is any praise, think on
these things.
9 Do those things which you also learned,
received and heard and saw in me. And the
God of peace shall be with you.
10 But I rejoiced in the Lord greatly, that
now at last your care of me has come alive
again. Although you also cared, but you did
not have opportunity.
11 Not that I speak as to need, for I have
learned to be content in whatever state I am.
12 I know both how to be humbled and I
know how to abound. In everything and in
all things, I have been taught how to be both
full and hungry – both to have plenty and
to have less than enough.
13 I can do all things through Christ who
strengthens me.
14 But you did well, having fellowship with
me in my troubles.
15 And you know, too, O Philippians, that
in the beginning of the gospel (when I came
out of Mac-e-do-ni-a) no church shared with
me as to giving and receiving, but you
only.
16 Because even in Thess-a-lo-ni-ca you sent
both once and again for my need.
17 Not that I look for a gift, but I look for
fruit that multiplies to your account.
18 But I have all things, and more than
enough. I am full, receiving from E-paph-
ro-di-tus the things from you, an odor of
sweet smell, an acceptable sacrifice, well-
pleasing to God.
19 But my God will fill up all your need
according to His riches in glory in Christ
Jesus.
20 Now may glory be to God and our
Father forever and ever. Amen.
21 Greet every saint in Christ Jesus. The
brothers with me greet you.
22 All the saints greet you, and especially
those of the household of Caesar.
23 The grace of our Lord Jesus Christ be
with you all. Amen.

ΠΑΥΛΟΣ ἀπόστολος [l]Ἰησοῦ χριστοῦ διὰ θελήματος θεοῦ, καὶ
Paul apostle of Jesus Christ by [2]will [1]God's, and
Τιμόθεος ὁ ἀδελφός, 2 τοῖς ἐν [m]Κολασσαῖς ἁγίοις καὶ πισ-
Timotheus the brother, to the [7]in [8]Colosse [1]saints [2]and [3]faith-
τοῖς ἀδελφοῖς ἐν χριστῷ·[n] χάρις ὑμῖν καὶ εἰρήνη ἀπὸ θεοῦ
ful [4]brethren [5]in [6]Christ. Grace to you and peace from God
πατρὸς ἡμῶν [o]καὶ κυρίου Ἰησοῦ χριστοῦ.
our Father and [the] Lord Jesus Christ.
3 Εὐχαριστοῦμεν τῷ θεῷ [p]καὶ πατρὶ τοῦ κυρίου ἡμῶν Ἰη-
We give thanks to the God and Father of our Lord Je-
σοῦ χριστοῦ, πάντοτε [q]περὶ ὑμῶν προσευχόμενοι· 4 ἀκού-
sus Christ, continually [2]for [3]you [1]praying, having
σαντες τὴν πίστιν ὑμῶν ἐν χριστῷ Ἰησοῦ, καὶ τὴν ἀγάπην
heard of your faith in Christ Jesus, and the love
[r]τὴν εἰς πάντας τοὺς ἁγίους, 5 διὰ τὴν ἐλπίδα
which [ye have] towards all the saints, on account of the hope
τὴν ἀποκειμένην ὑμῖν ἐν τοῖς οὐρανοῖς, ἣν προηκούσατε
which [is] laid up for you in the heavens; which ye heard of before
ἐν τῷ λόγῳ τῆς ἀληθείας τοῦ εὐαγγελίου, 6 τοῦ παρόντος εἰς
in the word of the truth of the glad tidings, which are come to
ὑμᾶς, καθὼς καὶ ἐν παντὶ τῷ κόσμῳ, [s]καὶ ἔστιν καρποφορού-
you, even as also in all the world, and are bringing forth
μενον[t], καθὼς καὶ ἐν ὑμῖν, ἀφ' ἧς ἡμέρας ἠκούσατε καὶ
fruit, even as also among you, from the day in which ye heard and
ἐπέγνωτε τὴν χάριν τοῦ θεοῦ ἐν ἀληθείᾳ· 7 καθὼς [u]καὶ
knew the grace of God in truth: even as also
ἐμάθετε ἀπὸ Ἐπαφρᾶ τοῦ ἀγαπητοῦ συνδούλου ἡμῶν, ὅς
ye learned from Epaphras [2]beloved [3]fellow-bondman [1]our, who
ἐστιν πιστὸς ὑπὲρ [v]ὑμῶν διάκονος τοῦ χριστοῦ, 8 ὁ καὶ
is [2]faithful [6]for [7]you [1]a [3]servant [4]of [5]Christ, who also
δηλώσας ἡμῖν τὴν ὑμῶν ἀγάπην ἐν πνεύματι.
signified to us your love in [the] Spirit.
9 Διὰ τοῦτο καὶ ἡμεῖς ἀφ' ἧς ἡμέρας ἠκούσαμεν,
On account of this also we from the day in which we heard [of it],
οὐ παυόμεθα ὑπὲρ ὑμῶν προσευχόμενοι καὶ αἰτούμενοι ἵνα
do not cease [2]for [3]you [1]praying and asking that
πληρωθῆτε τὴν ἐπίγνωσιν τοῦ θελήματος αὐτοῦ ἐν πάσῃ
ye may be filled with the knowledge of his will in all
σοφίᾳ καὶ συνέσει πνευματικῇ, 10 περιπατῆσαι [w]ὑμᾶς
wisdom and [2]understanding [1]spiritual, [5]to [6]walk [[3]for] [4]you
ἀξίως τοῦ κυρίου εἰς πᾶσαν [x]ἀρέσκειαν· ἐν παντὶ ἔργῳ ἀγαθῷ
worthily of the Lord to all pleasing, in every [2]work [1]good
καρποφοροῦντες καὶ αὐξανόμενοι [y]εἰς τὴν ἐπίγνωσιν τοῦ
bringing forth fruit and growing into the knowledge
θεοῦ· 11 ἐν πάσῃ δυνάμει δυναμούμενοι κατὰ τὸ κράτος
of God; with all power being strengthened according to the might
τῆς δόξης αὐτοῦ εἰς πᾶσαν ὑπομονὴν καὶ μακροθυμίαν μετὰ
of his glory to all endurance and longsuffering with
χαρᾶς· 12 εὐχαριστοῦντες τῷ πατρί, τῷ [z]ἱκανώσαντι [a]ἡμᾶς
joy; giving thanks to the Father, who made [2]competent [1]us
εἰς τὴν μερίδα τοῦ κλήρου τῶν ἁγίων ἐν τῷ φωτί, 13 ὃς
for the share of the inheritance of the saints in the light, who
[b]ἐρρύσατο ἡμᾶς ἐκ τῆς ἐξουσίας τοῦ σκότους, καὶ μετέστη-
delivered us from the authority of darkness, and trans-
σεν εἰς τὴν βασιλείαν τοῦ υἱοῦ τῆς ἀγάπης αὐτοῦ, 14 ἐν
lated [us] into the kingdom of the Son of his love: in
ᾧ ἔχομεν τὴν ἀπολύτρωσιν [c]διὰ τοῦ αἵματος αὐτοῦ, τὴν
whom we have redemption through his blood, the
ἄφεσιν τῶν ἁμαρτιῶν· 15 ὅς ἐστιν εἰκὼν τοῦ θεοῦ τοῦ
remission of sins; who is [the] image of God the
ἀοράτου, πρωτότοκος πάσης κτίσεως· 16 ὅτι ἐν αὐτῷ ἐ-
invisible, firstborn of all creation; because by him were
κτίσθη τὰ πάντα, [d]τὰ ἐν τοῖς οὐρανοῖς καὶ [e]τὰ ἐπὶ τῆς
created all things, the things in the heavens and the things upon the
γῆς, τὰ ὁρατὰ καὶ τὰ ἀόρατα, εἴτε θρόνοι εἴτε κυριότητες
earth, the visible and the invisible, whether thrones, or lordships,
εἴτε ἀρχαὶ εἴτε ἐξουσίαι· τὰ πάντα δι' αὐτοῦ καὶ εἰς αὐτὸν
or principalities, or authorities: all things by him and for him
ἔκτισται· 17 καὶ αὐτός ἐστιν πρὸ πάντων, καὶ τὰ πάντα
have been created. And he is before all, and all things
ἐν αὐτῷ συνέστηκεν· 18 καὶ αὐτός ἐστιν ἡ κεφαλὴ τοῦ σώμα-
in him subsist. And he is the head of the body,
τος τῆς ἐκκλησίας· ὅς ἐστιν ἀρχή, πρωτότοκος ἐκ
the assembly; who is [the] beginning, firstborn from among
τῶν νεκρῶν, ἵνα γένηται ἐν πᾶσιν αὐτὸς πρωτεύων·
the dead, that [2]might [3]be [4]in [5]all [6]things [1]he holding the first place;
19 ὅτι ἐν αὐτῷ εὐδόκησεν πᾶν τὸ πλήρωμα κατοικῆσαι,
because in him [4]was [5]pleased [1]all [2]the [3]fulness to dwell,
20 καὶ δι' αὐτοῦ ἀποκαταλλάξαι τὰ πάντα εἰς αὐτόν, εἰρη-
and by him to reconcile all things to itself, having
νοποιήσας διὰ τοῦ αἵματος τοῦ σταυροῦ αὐτοῦ, [f]δι' αὐτοῦ,
made peace by the blood of his cross, by him,

CHAPTER 1

1 Paul, an apostle of Jesus Christ by the will
of God, and Timothy our brother,
2 to the saints and faithful brothers in
Christ in Co-loss-e. Grace and peace to you
from God the Father and the Lord Jesus
Christ.
3 We give thanks to the God and Father of
our Lord Jesus Christ, praying always for
you,
4 hearing of your faith in Christ Jesus and
the love which you have toward all the
saints,
5 through the hope which is laid up for you
in Heaven, which you heard of before in the
word of the truth of the gospel
6 which has come to you, even as also into
all the world, and has been bringing forth
fruit, even as among you also, from the day
in which you heard and knew the grace of
God in truth.
7 Even as you learned from Ep-a-phras our
beloved fellow-servant, who is a faithful
minister of Christ for you,
8 who also declared to us your love in the
Spirit.
9 For this cause, too, since the day we
heard, we do not stop praying for you and
asking that you may be filled with the
knowledge of His will in all wisdom and
spiritual understanding,
10 *and for* you to walk worthily of the
Lord to all pleasing, bearing fruit in every
good work and growing into the knowledge
of God –
11 *that you may be* strengthened with all
power, according to the might of His glory,
to all patience and long-suffering with joy –
12 giving thanks to the Father, who has
made us fit for a share in the inheritance of
the saints in light,
13 who has delivered us from the power of
darkness and has translated us into the kingdom of His dearly beloved Son.
14 *In Him*, we have redemption through His
blood, the forgiveness of sins,
15 *He* who is the image of the God who
cannot be seen, the first-born of all creation.
16 Because all things were created by Him,
the things in Heaven and the things on the
earth – that which can be seen and that which
cannot be seen, whether thrones or lordships
or chief rulers or authorities – all things
have been created by Him and for Him.
17 And He is before all things, and all things
are held together in Him.
18 And He is the Head of the body, the
church, who is the beginning, the first-born
from among the dead, that He might have
the pre-eminence in all things,
19 because all the fullness *was* pleased to
dwell in Him,
20 and through Him, making peace by the
blood of His cross, to reconcile all things to

εἴτε τὰ ἐπὶ τῆς γῆς, εἴτε τὰ ἐν τοῖς οὐρανοῖς. 21 καὶ
whether the things on the earth, or the things in the heavens. And
ὑμᾶς ποτε ὄντας ἀπηλλοτριωμένους καὶ ἐχθροὺς τῇ διανοίᾳ
you once being alienated and enemies in mind
ἐν τοῖς ἔργοις τοῖς πονηροῖς. νυνὶ.δὲ [g]ἀποκατήλλαξεν· 22 ἐν
by [2]works [1]wicked, yet now he reconciled in
τῷ σώματι τῆς.σαρκὸς.αὐτοῦ διὰ τοῦ θανάτου[h], παρα-
the body of his flesh through death, to pre-
στῆσαι ὑμᾶς ἁγίους καὶ ἀμώμους καὶ ἀνεγκλήτους κατενώ-
sent you holy and unblamable and unimpeachable before
πιον αὐτοῦ· 23 εἴγε ἐπιμένετε τῇ πίστει τεθεμελιωμένοι
him, if indeed ye continue in the faith founded
καὶ ἑδραῖοι, καὶ μὴ μετακινούμενοι ἀπὸ τῆς ἐλπίδος τοῦ
and firm, and not being moved away from the hope of the
εὐαγγελίου οὗ ἠκούσατε, τοῦ κηρυχθέντος ἐν πάσῃ [i]τῇ‖
glad tidings, which ye heard, which were proclaimed in all the
κτίσει τῇ ὑπὸ τὸν οὐρανόν, οὗ ἐγενόμην ἐγὼ Παῦλος
creation which [is] under heaven, of which [3]became [1]I [2]Paul
διάκονος.
servant.

24 Νῦν χαίρω ἐν τοῖς.παθήμασίν.[k]μου‖ ὑπὲρ ὑμῶν, καὶ
Now, I am rejoicing in my sufferings for you, and
ἀνταναπληρῶ τὰ ὑστερήματα τῶν θλίψεων τοῦ χριστοῦ
I am filling up that which is behind of the tribulations of the Christ
ἐν τῇ.σαρκί.μου ὑπὲρ τοῦ.σώματος.αὐτοῦ, ὅ ἐστιν ἡ ἐκ-
in my flesh for his body, which is the as-
κλησία· 25 ἧς ἐγενόμην ἐγὼ διάκονος κατὰ τὴν οἰκονο-
sembly; of which [2]became [1]I servant, according to the adminis-
μίαν τοῦ θεοῦ τὴν δοθεῖσάν μοι εἰς ὑμᾶς πληρῶσαι τὸν
tration of God which [is] given me towards you to complete the
λόγον τοῦ θεοῦ, 26 τὸ μυστήριον τὸ ἀποκεκρυμμένον ἀπὸ
word of God, the mystery which has been hidden from
τῶν αἰώνων καὶ ἀπὸ τῶν γενεῶν, [l]νυνὶ‖.δὲ ἐφανερώθη
ages and from generations, but now was made manifest
τοῖς.ἁγίοις.αὐτοῦ· 27 οἷς ἠθέλησεν ὁ θεὸς γνωρίσαι [m]τίς
to his saints; to whom [2]did [3]will [1]God to make known what
ὁ‖ πλοῦτος τῆς δόξης τοῦ.μυστηρίου.τούτου ἐν τοῖς ἔ-
the riches of the glory of this mystery [are] among the na-
θνεσιν, [n]ὅς‖ ἐστιν χριστὸς ἐν ὑμῖν ἡ ἐλπὶς τῆς δόξης· 28 ὃν
tions, which is Christ in you the hope of glory: whom
ἡμεῖς καταγγέλλομεν, νουθετοῦντες πάντα ἄνθρωπον, καὶ
we announce, admonishing every man, and
διδάσκοντες πάντα ἄνθρωπον ἐν πάσῃ σοφίᾳ, ἵνα παρα-
teaching every man in all wisdom, that we may
στήσωμεν πάντα ἄνθρωπον τέλειον ἐν χριστῷ [o]Ἰησοῦ.‖
present every man perfect in Christ Jesus.
29 εἰς.ὃ καὶ κοπιῶ, ἀγωνιζόμενος κατὰ τὴν ἐνέργειαν
Whereunto also I labour, striving according to [2]working
αὐτοῦ τὴν ἐνεργουμένην ἐν ἐμοὶ ἐν δυνάμει.
[1]his which works in me in power.

2 Θέλω.γὰρ ὑμᾶς εἰδέναι ἡλίκον ἀγῶνα ἔχω [p]περὶ‖ ὑμῶν
For I wish you to know how great conflict I have for you,
καὶ τῶν ἐν [q]Λαοδικείᾳ,‖ καὶ ὅσοι οὐχ.[r]ἑωράκασιν‖ τὸ πρόσω-
and those in Laodicea, and as many as have not seen [2]face
πόν μου ἐν σαρκί, 2 ἵνα παρακληθῶσιν αἱ.καρδίαι.αὐτῶν,
[1]my in flesh; that may be encouraged their hearts,
[s]συμβιβασθέντων‖ ἐν ἀγάπῃ, καὶ εἰς [t]πάντα πλοῦτον‖ τῆς
being knit together in love, and to all riches of the
πληροφορίας τῆς συνέσεως, εἰς ἐπίγνωσιν τοῦ μυστηρίου
full assurance of understanding; to [the] knowledge of the mystery
τοῦ θεοῦ [v]καὶ πατρὸς καὶ τοῦ‖ [w]χριστοῦ,‖ 3 ἐν ᾧ εἰσιν
of God and of [the] Father and of the Christ; in which are
πάντες οἱ θησαυροὶ τῆς σοφίας καὶ [x]τῆς‖ γνώσεως ἀπόκρυ-
all the treasures of wisdom and of knowledge hid.
φοι. 4 τοῦτο.[y]δὲ‖ λέγω, ἵνα [z]μή τις‖ ὑμᾶς παραλογίζηται ἐν
And this I say, that not anyone you may beguile by
πιθανολογίᾳ· 5 εἰ.γὰρ καὶ τῇ σαρκὶ ἄπειμι, ἀλλὰ τῷ
persuasive speech. For if indeed in the flesh I am absent, yet
πνεύματι σὺν ὑμῖν εἰμί, χαίρων καὶ βλέπων ὑμῶν τὴν τάξιν,
in spirit with you I am, rejoicing and seeing your order,
καὶ τὸ στερέωμα τῆς εἰς χριστὸν πίστεως.ὑμῶν. 6 ὡς οὖν
and the firmness [4]in [5]Christ [1]of [2]your [3]faith. As therefore
παρελάβετε τὸν χριστὸν Ἰησοῦν τὸν κύριον, ἐν αὐτῷ περιπα-
ye received the Christ, Jesus the Lord, in him walk,
τεῖτε, 7 ἐρριζωμένοι καὶ ἐποικοδομούμενοι ἐν αὐτῷ, καὶ
having been rooted and being built up in him, and
βεβαιούμενοι [a]ἐν‖ τῇ πίστει, καθὼς ἐδιδάχθητε, περισσεύοντες
being confirmed in the faith, even as ye were taught, abounding
[b]ἐν αὐτῇ‖ ἐν εὐχαριστίᾳ.
in it with thanksgiving.

8 Βλέπετε μή τις [c]ὑμᾶς ἔσται‖ ὁ συλαγωγῶν
Take heed lest [4]anyone [10]you [1]there [2]shall [3]be [5]who [6]makes [7]a [8]prey [9]of

Himself – through Him, whether the things on earth or the things in Heaven.

21 And you, who were once alienated and enemies in your mind by wicked works, yet now He has reconciled

22 in the body of His flesh, through death, to present you holy and without blame and without charge before Him,

23 if you continue in the faith grounded and settled and are not moved away from the hope of the gospel which you heard, which was preached in all the creation that is under the heavens, of which I, Paul, became a minister.

24 Now I am rejoicing in my sufferings for you. And I am filling up that which is behind of the afflictions of Christ in my flesh, for His body, which is the church.

25 Of which I became a minister, according to the administration of God, which is given to me for you, to fulfill the word of God –

26 the mystery which has been hidden from the ages, and from generations, but now has been revealed to His saints.

27 *To them* God desired to reveal what are the riches of the glory of this mystery in the nations – which is Christ in you, the hope of glory.

28 We preach, warning every man and teaching every man in all wisdom so that we may present every man perfect in Christ Jesus.

29 For which I also labor, working according to the working of Him who works in me in power.

CHAPTER 2

1 For I want you to know how great a struggle I am having for your sake, and for those in La-od-i-ce-a, and as many as have not seen my face in the flesh,

2 so that their hearts may be comforted, being knit together in love, and to all riches of the full assurance of understanding, to the knowledge of the mystery of God and of the Father and of Christ,

3 in whom are all the treasures of wisdom and of knowledge hidden.

4 And I say this so that no one may bewitch you by winning words.

5 For though I am indeed absent in the flesh, yet I am with you in spirit, rejoicing and beholding your order and the firmness of your faith in Christ.

6 Then, as you received Christ Jesus the Lord, walk in Him –

7 being rooted and built up in Him, and being established in the faith, even as you were taught, increasing in it with gratitude.

8 Be careful that there may not be anyone who captures you by means of philosophy

διὰ τῆς φιλοσοφίας καὶ κενῆς ἀπάτης, κατὰ τὴν παρά-
through philosophy and empty deceit, according to the tra-
δοσιν τῶν ἀνθρώπων, κατὰ τὰ στοιχεῖα τοῦ κόσμου, καὶ
dition of men, according to the elements of the world, and
οὐ κατὰ χριστόν· 9 ὅτι ἐν αὐτῷ κατοικεῖ πᾶν τὸ πλήρωμα
not according to Christ. For in him dwells all the fulness
τῆς θεότητος σωματικῶς,· 10 καί ἐστε ἐν αὐτῷ πεπληρωμένοι·
of the Godhead bodily; and ye are [2]in [3]him [1]complete,
[d]ὅς" ἐστιν ἡ κεφαλὴ πάσης ἀρχῆς καὶ ἐξουσίας· 11 ἐν ᾧ
who is the head of all principality and authority, in whom
καὶ περιετμήθητε περιτομῇ ἀχειροποιήτῳ, ἐν τῇ ἀπ-
also ye were circumcised with circumcision not made by hand, in the put-
εκδύσει τοῦ σώματος [e]τῶν ἁμαρτιῶν" τῆς σαρκός, ἐν τῇ περι-
ting off of the body of the sins of the flesh, in the circum-
τομῇ τοῦ χριστοῦ, 12 συνταφέντες αὐτῷ ἐν τῷ [f]βαπτίσματι·"
cision of the Christ; having been buried with him in baptism,
ἐν ᾧ καὶ συνηγέρθητε διὰ τῆς πίστεως τῆς ἐνερ-
in which also ye were raised with [him] through the faith of the work-
γείας τοῦ θεοῦ τοῦ ἐγείραντος αὐτὸν ἐκ [g]τῶν" νεκρῶν.
ing of God who raised him from among the dead.
13 καὶ ὑμᾶς νεκροὺς ὄντας [h]ἐν" τοῖς παραπτώμασιν καὶ τῇ
And you, [2]dead [1]being in offences and in the
ἀκροβυστίᾳ τῆς.σαρκὸς.ὑμῶν, [i]συνεζωποίησεν" [k]σὺν αὐτῷ,
uncircumcision of your flesh, he quickened together with him,
χαρισάμενος [l]ἡμῖν" πάντα τὰ παραπτώματα· 14 ἐξαλείψας
having forgiven us all the offences; having blotted out
τὸ καθ' ἡμῶν χειρόγραφον τοῖς δόγμασιν, ὃ ἦν ὑπεναν-
the [5]against [6]us [1]handwriting [2]in [3]the [4]decrees, which was adverse
τίον ἡμῖν, καὶ αὐτὸ ἦρκεν ἐκ τοῦ μέσου, προσηλώσας
to us, also it he has taken out of the midst, having nailed
αὐτὸ τῷ σταυρῷ, 15 ἀπεκδυσάμενος τὰς ἀρχὰς καὶ τὰς
it to the cross; having stripped the principalities and the
ἐξουσίας ἐδειγμάτισεν ἐν.παρρησίᾳ, θριαμβεύσας
authorities, he made a show [of them] publicly, leading in triumph
αὐτοὺς ἐν αὐτῷ.
them in it.
16 Μὴ οὖν τις ὑμᾶς κρινέτω ἐν βρώσει [m]ἢ" ἐν πόσει,
[2]Not [3]therefore [4]anyone [6]you [1]let [5]judge in meat or in drink,
ἢ ἐν μέρει ἑορτῆς ἢ [n]νουμηνίας" ἢ σαββάτων· 17 [o]ἅ" ἐστιν
or in respect of feast, or new moon, or sabbaths, which are
σκιὰ τῶν.μελλόντων, τὸ.δὲ σῶμα [p]τοῦ" χριστοῦ. 18 μη-
a shadow of things to come; but the body [is] of the Christ. [2]No
δεὶς ὑμᾶς καταβραβευέτω θέλων ἐν ταπεινοφροσύνῃ καὶ
[3]one [5]you [1]let [4]defraud of the prize, doing [his] will in humility and
[q]θρησκείᾳ" τῶν ἀγγέλων, ἃ [r]μὴ" [s]ἑώρακεν" ἐμβατεύων,
worship of the angels, [3]things [4]which [7]not [5]he [6]has [8]seen [1]intruding [2]into,
εἰκῇ φυσιούμενος ὑπὸ τοῦ νοὸς τῆς.σαρκὸς.αὐτοῦ, 19 καὶ οὐ
vainly puffed up by the mind of his flesh, and not
κρατῶν τὴν κεφαλήν, ἐξ οὗ πᾶν τὸ σῶμα διὰ τῶν ἁφῶν
holding fast the head, from whom all the body, by the joints
καὶ συνδέσμων ἐπιχορηγούμενον καὶ [t]συμβιβαζόμενον," αὔξει
and bands being supplied and knit together, increases
τὴν αὔξησιν τοῦ θεοῦ.
[with] the increase of God.
20 Εἰ [v]οὖν" ἀπεθάνετε σὺν [w]τῷ" χριστῷ ἀπὸ τῶν στοιχείων
If then ye died with the Christ from the elements
τοῦ κόσμου, τί ὡς ζῶντες ἐν κόσμῳ δογματί-
of the world, why as if alive in [the] world do ye subject yourselves
ζεσθε;[x] 21 Μὴ.ἅψῃ, μηδὲ.γεύσῃ, μηδὲ.θίγῃς·
to decrees? Thou mayest not handle, Thou mayest not taste, Thou mayest not touch,
22 ἅ ἐστιν πάντα εἰς φθορὰν τῇ ἀποχρήσει· κατὰ
(which things are all unto corruption in the using,) according to
τὰ ἐντάλματα καὶ διδασκαλίας τῶν ἀνθρώπων·[x] 23 ἅτινά
the injunctions and teachings of men, which
ἐστιν λόγον μὲν ἔχοντα σοφίας ἐν [y]ἐθελοθρησκείᾳ"
are [2]an [3]appearance [4]indeed [1]having of wisdom in voluntary worship
καὶ ταπεινοφροσύνῃ [z]καὶ" [a]ἀφειδίᾳ" σώματος, οὐκ ἐν
and humility and unsparing treatment of [the] body, not in
τιμῇ τινι πρὸς πλησμονὴν τῆς σαρκός.[x]
[3]honour [1]a [2]certain for satisfaction of the flesh.
3 Εἰ οὖν συνηγέρθητε τῷ χριστῷ, τὰ ἄνω ζητεῖτε,
If therefore ye were raised with Christ, [2]the [3]things [4]above [1]seek,
οὗ ὁ χριστός ἐστιν ἐν δεξιᾷ τοῦ θεοῦ καθήμενος·
where the Christ is [2]at [3the] [4]right [5]hand [6]of [7]God [1]sitting:
2 τὰ ἄνω φρονεῖτε, μὴ τὰ ἐπὶ τῆς γῆς. 3 ἀπεθάνετε
[9]the [10]things [11]above [8]mind, not the things on the earth; [2]ye [3]died
γάρ, καὶ ἡ.ζωὴ.ὑμῶν κέκρυπται σὺν τῷ χριστῷ ἐν τῷ θεῷ·
[1]for, and your life has been hid with the Christ in God.
4 ὅταν ὁ χριστὸς φανερωθῇ ἡ.ζωὴ.[b]ἡμῶν," τότε καὶ
When the Christ [3]may [4]be [5]manifested [1]our [2]life, then also
ὑμεῖς σὺν αὐτῷ φανερωθήσεσθε ἐν δόξῃ.
ye with him shall be manifested in glory.

and empty deceit, according to the teaching
of men, according to the rules of the world
and not according to Christ.
9 For in Him dwells all the fullness of the
Godhead bodily.
10 And you are complete in Him, who is
the Head of all rule and authority.
11 And you were circumcised in Him with
circumcision not done by hand, in the
putting off of the body of the sins of the
flesh, in the circumcision of Christ,
12 being buried with Him in baptism, in
which you were also raised with Him
through the faith of the almighty working of
God, who raised Him from among the dead.
13 And you, being dead in your sins and the
uncircumcision of your flesh, He has made
alive together with Him, forgiving you all
your sins,
14 blotting out the handwriting in the
decrees against us, which stood out against
us, and He has taken it out of the way,
nailing it to the cross.
15 Stripping the rulers and the authorities,
He made a show of them publicly,
triumphing over them in it.
16 So, do not let anyone judge you in meat
or in drink or in respect of a feast or the new
moon or sabbaths –
17 which are a shadow of things to come,
but the body is of Christ.
18 Let no one cheat you of your reward,
doing his own will in lowliness and worship
of angels, pushing into things which he has
not seen, without a cause puffed up by his
fleshly mind.
19 And not holding fast the Head, from
whom all the body, by the joints and bands
which are given and knit together, increases
with the increase of God.
20 If, then, you died with Christ from the
principles of the world, why do you put
yourself under its ordinances, as if you were
living in the world?
21 You may not handle – you may not
taste – you may not touch –
22 which things are all to vanish away in the
using – *these are* according to the commandments and teachings of men
23 which indeed have an appearance of
wisdom in will worship and lowliness and
harsh treatment of the body – not in any
honor for the satisfying of the flesh.

CHAPTER 3

1 If, then, you were raised with Christ,
pursue those things which are above, where
Christ is sitting at the right hand of God.
2 Set your mind on the things above, not on
the things on the earth.
3 For you died and your life has been hidden with Christ in God.
4 When Christ, our life, shall appear, then
you also shall appear with Him in glory.

5 Νεκρώσατε οὖν τὰ μέλη [c]ὑμῶν" τὰ ἐπὶ τῆς γῆς,
Put to death therefore [2]members [1]your which [are] on the earth,
πορνείαν, ἀκαθαρσίαν, πάθος, ἐπιθυμίαν κακήν, καὶ τὴν
fornication, uncleanness, passion, [2]desire [1]evil, and
πλεονεξίαν, ἥτις ἐστὶν εἰδωλολατρεία, 6 δι' [d]ἃ"
covetousness, which is idolatry. On account of which things
ἔρχεται [e]ἡ" ὀργὴ τοῦ θεοῦ [f]ἐπὶ τοὺς υἱοὺς τῆς ἀπειθείας·"
comes the wrath of God upon the sons of disobedience.
7 ἐν οἷς καὶ ὑμεῖς περιεπατήσατέ ποτε ὅτε ἐζῆτε ἐν
Among whom also ye walked once when ye were living in
[g]αὐτοῖς·" 8 νυνὶ.δὲ ἀπόθεσθε καὶ ὑμεῖς τὰ.πάντα, ὀργήν,
these things. But now, put off also ye, all [these] things, wrath,
θυμόν, κακίαν, βλασφημίαν, αἰσχρολογίαν ἐκ τοῦ στόμα-
indignation, malice, blasphemy, foul language out of [2]mouth
τος ὑμῶν. 9 Μὴ.ψεύδεσθε εἰς ἀλλήλους, ἀπεκδυσάμενοι τὸν
[1]your. Do not lie to one another, having put off the
παλαιὸν ἄνθρωπον σὺν ταῖς.πράξεσιν.αὐτοῦ, 10 καὶ ἐνδυσά-
old man with his deeds, and having
μενοι τὸν νέον τὸν ἀνακαινούμενον εἰς ἐπίγνωσιν κατ'
put on the new that [is] being renewed into knowledge according to
εἰκόνα τοῦ κτίσαντος αὐτόν· 11 ὅπου οὐκ.ἔνι
[the] image of him who created him; where there is not
Ἕλλην καὶ Ἰουδαῖος, περιτομὴ καὶ ἀκροβυστία, βάρβαρος,
Greek and Jew, circumcision and uncircumcision, barbarian,
Σκύθης, δοῦλος, [h]ἐλεύθερος· ἀλλὰ [i]τὰ".πάντα καὶ ἐν πᾶσιν
Scythian, bondman, free; but [3]all [4]things [5]and [6]in [7]all
χριστός.
[[2]is] [1]Christ.

12 Ἐνδύσασθε οὖν, ὡς ἐκλεκτοὶ [k]τοῦ" θεοῦ, ἅγιοι καὶ
Put on therefore, as elect of God, holy and
ἠγαπημένοι, σπλάγχνα [l]οἰκτιρμῶν," χρηστότητα, ταπεινο-
beloved, bowels of compassions, kindness, humi-
φροσύνην, [m]πρᾳότητα," μακροθυμίαν· 13 ἀνεχόμενοι ἀλ-
lity, meekness, long-suffering; bearing with one
λήλων, καὶ χαριζόμενοι ἑαυτοῖς, ἐάν τις πρός τινα ἔχῃ
another, and forgiving each other, if any against any should have
μομφήν· καθὼς καὶ ὁ "χριστὸς" ἐχαρίσατο ὑμῖν, οὕτως καὶ
a complaint; even as also the Christ forgave you, so also [do]
ὑμεῖς· 14 ἐπὶ.πᾶσιν.δὲ τούτοις τὴν ἀγάπην, [o]ἥτις" ἐστὶν
ye. And to all these [add] love, which is [the]
σύνδεσμος τῆς τελειότητος· 15 καὶ ἡ εἰρήνη [p]τοῦ θεοῦ" βρα-
bond of perfectness. And the peace of God let
βευέτω ἐν ταῖς.καρδίαις.ὑμῶν, εἰς ἣν καὶ ἐκλήθητε ἐν ἑνὶ σώ-
preside in your hearts, to which also ye were called in one
ματι· καὶ εὐχάριστοι γίνεσθε. 16 ὁ λόγος τοῦ χριστοῦ ἐνοικείτω
body, and thankful be. The word of the Christ let dwell
ἐν ὑμῖν πλουσίως, ἐν πάσῃ σοφίᾳ· διδάσκοντες καὶ νουθε-
in you richly, in all wisdom; teaching and admon-
τοῦντες ἑαυτοὺς ψαλμοῖς [q]καὶ" ὕμνοις [r]καὶ" ᾠδαῖς πνευματι-
ishing each other in psalms and hymns and [2]songs [1]spiritual
καῖς ἐν [s]χάριτι ᾄδοντες ἐν [t]τῇ καρδίᾳ" ὑμῶν [v]τῷ κυρίῳ."
with grace singing in [2]heart [1]your to the Lord.
17 καὶ πᾶν ὅ.τι.[w]ἂν" ποιῆτε ἐν λόγῳ ἢ ἐν ἔργῳ, πάντα
And everything, whatsoever ye may do in word or in work, [do] all
ἐν ὀνόματι [x]κυρίου Ἰησοῦ," εὐχαριστοῦντες τῷ θεῷ [y]καὶ"
in [the] name of [the] Lord Jesus, giving thanks to God and
πατρὶ δι' αὐτοῦ.
[the] Father by him.

18 Αἱ γυναῖκες, ὑποτάσσεσθε τοῖς.[z]ἰδίοις" ἀνδράσιν, ὡς
Wives, subject yourselves to your own husbands, as
ἀνῆκεν ἐν κυρίῳ. 19 Οἱ ἄνδρες, ἀγαπᾶτε τὰς γυναῖκας[a]
is becoming in [the] Lord. Husbands, love the wives,
καὶ μὴ.πικραίνεσθε πρὸς αὐτάς. 20 Τὰ τέκνα, ὑπακούετε
and be not bitter against them. Children, obey
τοῖς γονεῦσιν κατὰ.πάντα· τοῦτο.γάρ [b]ἐστιν εὐάρεστον" [c]τῷ"
the parents in all things; for this is well-pleasing to the
κυρίῳ. 21 Οἱ πατέρες, μὴ.[d]ἐρεθίζετε" τὰ.τέκνα.ὑμῶν, ἵνα μὴ
Lord. Fathers, do not provoke your children, that [2]not
ἀθυμῶσιν. 22 Οἱ δοῦλοι, ὑπακούετε κατὰ.πάντα τοῖς
[1]they [3]be disheartened. Bondmen, obey in all things the
κατὰ σάρκα κυρίοις, μὴ ἐν [e]ὀφθαλμοδουλείαις" ὡς ἀν-
[2]according [3]to [4]flesh [1]masters, not with eye-services, as
θρωπάρεσκοι, [f]ἀλλ'" ἐν ἁπλότητι καρδίας, φοβούμενοι [g]τὸν
men-pleasers, but in simplicity of heart, fearing
θεόν." 23 [h]καὶ πᾶν.ὅ.τι" ἐὰν ποιῆτε, ἐκ.ψυχῆς ἐργάζεσθε, ὡς
God. And whatsoever ye may do, [2]heartily [1]work, as
τῷ κυρίῳ καὶ οὐκ ἀνθρώποις· 24 εἰδότες ὅτι ἀπὸ κυρίου
to the Lord and not to men; knowing that from [the] Lord
[i]ἀπολήψεσθε" τὴν ἀνταπόδοσιν τῆς κληρονομίας· τῷ.[k]γὰρ"
ye shall receive the recompense of the inheritance, for the
κυρίῳ χριστῷ δουλεύετε. 25 ὁ.[l]δὲ" ἀδικῶν [m]κομιεῖται.
Lord Christ ye serve. But he that does wrong shall receive [for]

[5]So put to death your members which are
on the earth: fornication, uncleanness,
passion, evil lust and covetousness (which is
idolatry).
[6]Which things are the reason the wrath of
God comes on the sons of disobedience,
[7]among whom you also walked at one
time, when you were living in these things.
[8]But now, you must also put off these
things – wrath, anger, evil-hearted feelings,
blasphemy, filthy language out of your
mouth.
[9]Do not lie to one another, *for you* have
put off the old man with his works
[10]and have put on the new *man* that is
being renewed in knowledge according to
the image of Him who created him,
[11]where there is neither Greek nor Jew,
circumcision nor uncircumcision, barbarian,
Scyth-i-an, slave or freeman – but Christ is
all things and in all.

[12]Then put on as the elect of God, holy
and beloved, tender feelings of mercy,
kindness, humility, meekness, long-suffering
[13]bearing with one another and forgiving
each other, if anyone should have a complaint against any. Even as Christ forgave
you, you also do the same.
[14]And to all these things, *add on* love,
which is the bond of perfectness.
[15]And let the peace of God rule in your
hearts, to which you also were called in one
body and be thankful.
[16]Let the word of Christ live in you richly,
in all wisdom, teaching and urging one
another in psalms, hymns and spiritual
songs, singing with grace in your heart to the
Lord.
[17]And whatever you do in word or in
deed, do all in the name of the Lord Jesus,
giving thanks to God and the Father by Him.

[18]Wives, be subject to your own husbands,
as is becoming in the Lord.
[19]Husbands, love your wives and do not be
bitter against them.
[20]Children, obey your parents in all things,
for this is well- pleasing to the Lord.
[21]Fathers, do not anger your children so
that they may not be discouraged.
[22]Slaves, obey your masters in all things as
to the flesh – not with eye-service, as
men-pleasers, but in pureness of heart, fearing God.
[23]And whatever you do, work heartily, as
to the Lord and not to men,
[24]knowing that you shall receive the reward of the inheritance from the Lord, for
you serve the Lord Christ.
[25]But he that does wrong shall receive for
what he did wrong. And there is no respect

ὃ ἠδίκησεν, καὶ οὐκ.ἔστιν [n]προσωποληψία.‖ 4 Οἱ κύριοι,
what he did wrong, and there is no respect of persons. Masters,
τὸ δίκαιον καὶ τὴν ἰσότητα τοῖς δούλοις
that which [is] just and that which [is] equal to bondmen
παρέχεσθε, εἰδότες ὅτι καὶ ὑμεῖς ἔχετε κύριον ἐν [o]οὐρανοῖς.‖
give, knowing that also ye have a Master in [the] heavens.
2 Τῇ προσευχῇ προσκαρτερεῖτε, γρηγοροῦντες ἐν αὐτῇ ἐν
In prayer stedfastly continue, watching in it with
εὐχαριστίᾳ· 3 προσευχόμενοι ἅμα καὶ περὶ ἡμῶν, ἵνα ὁ θεὸς
thanksgiving; praying withal also for us, that God
ἀνοίξῃ ἡμῖν θύραν τοῦ λόγου λαλῆσαι τὸ μυστήριον τοῦ
may open to us a door of the word to speak the mystery of the
χριστοῦ, δι' [p]ὃ‖ καὶ δέδεμαι, 4 ἵνα φανε-
Christ, on account of which also I have been bound, that I may make
ρώσω αὐτὸ ὡς δεῖ με λαλῆσαι. 5 Ἐν σοφίᾳ περιπατεῖτε
manifest it as it behoves me to speak. In wisdom walk
πρὸς τοὺς ἔξω, τὸν καιρὸν ἐξαγοραζόμενοι. 6 ὁ λόγος
towards those without, [2]the [3]time [1]ransoming. [Let] [2]word
ὑμῶν πάντοτε ἐν χάριτι, ἅλατι ἠρτυμένος, εἰδέναι πῶς
[1]your [be] always with grace, [2]with [3]salt [1]seasoned, to know how
δεῖ ὑμᾶς ἑνὶ.ἑκάστῳ ἀποκρίνεσθαι.
it behoves you [3]each [4]one [1]to [2]answer.
7 Τὰ κατ' ἐμὲ πάντα γνωρίσει ὑμῖν Τυχικὸς
[2]The [3]things [4]concerning [5]me [1]all [7]will [8]make [9]known [10]to [11]you [6]Tychicus
ὁ ἀγαπητὸς ἀδελφὸς καὶ πιστὸς διάκονος καὶ σύνδουλος
the beloved brother and faithful servant and fellow-bondman
ἐν κυρίῳ, 8 ὃν ἔπεμψα πρὸς ὑμᾶς εἰς αὐτὸ.τοῦτο, ἵνα
in [the] Lord; whom I sent to you for this very thing, that
[q]γνῷ‖ τὰ περὶ [r]ὑμῶν‖ καὶ παρακαλέσῃ τὰς
he might know the things concerning you, and might encourage
καρδίας.ὑμῶν, 9 σὺν Ὀνησίμῳ, τῷ πιστῷ καὶ ἀγαπητῷ
your hearts; with Onesimus, the faithful and beloved
ἀδελφῷ, ὅς ἐστιν ἐξ ὑμῶν· πάντα ὑμῖν [s]γνωριοῦσιν‖
brother, who is of you. All things [2]to [3]you [4]they [5]will [6]make [7]known
τὰ ὧδε.
[1]here.
10 Ἀσπάζεται ὑμᾶς Ἀρίσταρχος ὁ.συναιχμάλωτός.μου, καὶ
[4]Salutes [5]you [1]Aristarchus [2]my [3]fellow-prisoner, and
Μάρκος ὁ ἀνεψιὸς Βαρνάβα, περὶ οὗ ἐλάβετε ἐντολάς·
Mark, the cousin of Barnabas, concerning whom ye received orders,
ἐὰν ἔλθῃ πρὸς ὑμᾶς, δέξασθε αὐτόν· 11 καὶ Ἰησοῦς ὁ λεγό-
(if he come to you, receive him,) and Jesus called
μενος Ἰοῦστος, οἱ ὄντες ἐκ περιτομῆς· [t] οὗτοι μόνοι
Justus, who are of [the] circumcision. These [are the] only
συνεργοὶ εἰς τὴν βασιλείαν τοῦ θεοῦ, οἵτινες ἐγενήθησάν
fellow-workers for the kingdom of God, who were
μοι παρηγορία. 12 ἀσπάζεται ὑμᾶς Ἐπαφρᾶς ὁ ἐξ ὑμῶν
to me a consolation. [2]Salutes [3]you [1]Epaphras who [is] of you,
δοῦλος χριστοῦ[u], πάντοτε ἀγωνιζόμενος ὑπὲρ ὑμῶν ἐν ταῖς
a bondman of Christ, always striving for you in
προσευχαῖς, ἵνα [v]στῆτε‖ τέλειοι καὶ [w]πεπληρωμένοι‖ ἐν
prayers, that ye may stand perfect and complete in
παντὶ θελήματι τοῦ θεοῦ. 13 μαρτυρῶ.γὰρ αὐτῷ ὅτι ἔχει
every will of God. For I bear witness to him that he has
[x]ζῆλον πολὺν‖ ὑπὲρ ὑμῶν καὶ τῶν ἐν [y]Λαοδικείᾳ‖ καὶ τῶν
[2]zeal [1]much for you and them in Laodicea and them
ἐν Ἱεραπόλει. 14 ἀσπάζεται ὑμᾶς Λουκᾶς ὁ ἰατρὸς ὁ ἀγα-
in Hierapolis. [5]Salutes [6]you [1]Luke [2]the [4]physician [3]be-
πητός, καὶ Δημᾶς. 15 ἀσπάσασθε τοὺς ἐν [y]Λαοδικείᾳ‖ ἀδελ-
loved, and Demas. Salute the [2]in [3]Laodicea [1]breth-
φούς, καὶ [z]Νυμφᾶν‖ καὶ τὴν κατ'.οἶκον.[a]αὐτοῦ‖ ἐκκλησίαν·
ren, and Nymphas, and the [2]in [3]his [4]house [1]assembly.
16 καὶ ὅταν ἀναγνωσθῇ παρ' ὑμῖν ἡ ἐπιστολή, ποιήσατε
And when may be read among you, the epistle, cause
ἵνα καὶ ἐν τῇ Λαοδικέων ἐκκλησίᾳ ἀναγνωσθῇ, καὶ
that also in the [2]of [[3]the] [4]Laodiceans [1]assembly it may be read, and
τὴν ἐκ [b]Λαοδικείας‖ ἵνα καὶ ὑμεῖς ἀναγνῶτε· 17 καὶ εἴπατε
that from Laodicea that also ye may read. And say
Ἀρχίππῳ, Βλέπε τὴν διακονίαν ἣν παρέλαβες ἐν
to Archippus, Take heed to the service which thou didst receive in [the]
κυρίῳ, ἵνα αὐτὴν πληροῖς. 18 Ὁ ἀσπασμὸς τῇ.ἐμῇ.χειρὶ
Lord, that it thou fulfil. The salutation [3]by [4]my [[5]own] [6]hand
Παύλου. μνημονεύετέ μου τῶν δεσμῶν. ἡ χάρις μεθ'
[1]of [2]Paul. Remember my bonds. Grace [be] with
ὑμῶν. [c]ἀμήν.‖
you. Amen.
[d]Πρὸς Κολασσαεῖς ἐγράφη ἀπὸ Ῥώμης, διὰ Τυχικοῦ καὶ
To [the] Colossians written from Rome, by Tychicus and
Ὀνησίμου.‖
Onesimus.

of persons.

CHAPTER 4

1 Masters, give that which is right and that
which is equal to slaves, knowing that you
have a Master in Heaven.
2 Continue in prayer, watching in it with
thanksgiving,
3 praying at the same time for us also, that
God may open to us a door of the word,
that we may speak the mystery of Christ
(for which reason I also have been imprison-
ed),
4 so that I may make it clear, as I ought to
speak.
5 Walk in wisdom toward those who are on
the outside, redeeming the time.
6 *Let* your speech be always with grace,
seasoned with salt, to know how you ought
to answer each one.
7 Tych-i-cus, the beloved brother and faithful minister and fellow-servant in the Lord,
will make known to you all the things about
me.
8 I sent him to you for this very thing, so
that he might know the things concerning
you and might comfort your hearts,
9 along with O-nes-i-mus, a faithful and
much loved brother, who is one of you.
They will make known to you all things
here.
10 Ar-is-tar-chus my fellow-prisoner greets
you, and Mark the cousin of Barnabas, about
whom you received orders (if he comes to
you, receive him),
11 and Jesus who is called Justus, who are
of the circumcision. These are the only
fellow-workers for the kingdom of God who
were a comfort to me.
12 Ep-a-phras greets you, who is one of
you, a servant of Christ, always laboring for
you in prayers, that you may stand perfect
and complete in all the will of God.
13 For I bear witness to him that he has
much feeling for you and for those in
La-od-i-ce-a and for those in Hi-er-a-po-lis.
14 Luke the beloved physician greets you,
and Demas.
15 Greet the brothers in La-od-i-ce-a and
Nym-phas and the church in his house.
16 And when this letter is read among you,
cause that it be read also in the church of
the La-od-i-ce-ans – and that you may also
read *the one* from La-od-i-ce-a.
17 And say to Ar-chip-pus, Take heed to
the ministry which you received in the Lord,
that you fulfill it.
18 The signature of Paul, by my own hand.
Remember my bonds. Grace be with you.
Amen.

ΠΑΥΛΟΣ καὶ Σιλουανὸς καὶ Τιμόθεος, τῇ ἐκκλησίᾳ Θεσ-
Paul and Silvanus and Timotheus, to the assembly of Thes-
σαλονικέων ἐν θεῷ πατρὶ καὶ κυρίῳ Ἰησοῦ χριστῷ·
salonians in God [the] Father and [the] Lord Jesus Christ.
χάρις ὑμῖν καὶ εἰρήνη [f]ἀπὸ θεοῦ πατρὸς.ἡμῶν καὶ κυρίου
Grace to you and peace from God our Father and [the] Lord
Ἰησοῦ χριστοῦ.‖
Jesus Christ.
2 Εὐχαριστοῦμεν τῷ θεῷ πάντοτε περὶ πάντων ὑμῶν,
We give thanks to God always concerning all you,
μνείαν [g]ὑμῶν‖ ποιούμενοι ἐπὶ τῶν.προσευχῶν.ἡμῶν, 3 ἀδια-
[2]mention [3]of [4]you [1]making at our prayers, un-
λείπτως μνημονεύοντες ὑμῶν τοῦ ἔργου τῆς πίστεως καὶ τοῦ
ceasingly remembering your work of faith and
κόπου τῆς ἀγάπης καὶ τῆς ὑπομονῆς τῆς ἐλπίδος τοῦ κυρίου
labour of love and endurance of hope of [2]Lord
ἡμῶν Ἰησοῦ χριστοῦ, ἔμπροσθεν τοῦ θεοῦ καὶ πατρὸς ἡμῶν·
[1]our Jesus Christ, before [2]God [3]and [4]Father [1]our;
4 εἰδότες, ἀδελφοὶ ἠγαπημένοι ὑπὸ [h]θεοῦ, τὴν.ἐκλογὴν.ὑμῶν·
knowing, brethren beloved by God, your election.
5 ὅτι τὸ.εὐαγγέλιον.ἡμῶν οὐκ.ἐγενήθη [i]εἰς‖ ὑμᾶς ἐν λόγῳ
Because our glad tidings came not to you in word
μόνον, ἀλλὰ καὶ ἐν δυνάμει καὶ ἐν πνεύματι ἁγίῳ, καὶ [k]ἐν‖
only, but also in power and in [the] [2]Spirit [1]Holy, and in
πληροφορίᾳ πολλῇ, καθὼς οἴδατε οἷοι ἐγενήθημεν [l]ἐν‖
[2]full [3]assurance [1]much, even as ye know what we were among
ὑμῖν δι' ὑμᾶς. 6 καὶ ὑμεῖς μιμηταὶ ἡμῶν ἐγενήθητε
you for the sake of you: and ye imitators of us became
καὶ τοῦ κυρίου, δεξάμενοι τὸν λόγον ἐν θλίψει πολλῇ
and of the Lord, having accepted the word in [2]tribulation [1]much
μετὰ χαρᾶς πνεύματος ἁγίου, 7 ὥστε γενέσθαι ὑμᾶς [m]τύπους‖
with joy of [the] [2]Spirit [1]Holy, so that [2]became [1]ye patterns
πᾶσιν τοῖς πιστεύουσιν ἐν τῇ Μακεδονίᾳ καὶ [n] τῇ Ἀχαΐᾳ.
to all those believing in Macedonia and Achaia:
8 ἀφ'.ὑμῶν.γὰρ ἐξήχηται ὁ λόγος τοῦ κυρίου οὐ μόνον ἐν
for from you has sounded out the word of the Lord not only in
τῇ Μακεδονίᾳ καὶ [o]Ἀχαΐᾳ, [p]ἀλλ'‖ [q]καὶ‖ ἐν παντὶ τόπῳ ἡ
Macedonia and Achaia, but also in every place
πίστις.ὑμῶν ἡ πρὸς τὸν θεὸν ἐξελήλυθεν, ὥστε μὴ
your faith which [is] towards God has gone abroad, so as [5]no
χρείαν [r]ἡμᾶς.ἔχειν‖ λαλεῖν τι· 9 αὐτοὶ.γὰρ περὶ
[6]need [1]for [2]us [3]to [4]have to say anything; for themselves concerning
ἡμῶν ἀπαγγέλλουσιν ὁποίαν εἴσοδον [s]ἔχομεν‖ πρὸς ὑμᾶς,
us relate what entrance in we have to you,
καὶ πῶς ἐπεστρέψατε πρὸς τὸν θεὸν ἀπὸ τῶν εἰδώλων, δου-
and how ye turned to God from idols, to
λεύειν θεῷ ζῶντι καὶ ἀληθινῷ, 10 καὶ ἀναμένειν τὸν υἱὸν
serve a [4]God [1]living [2]and [3]true, and to await [2]Son
αὐτοῦ ἐκ τῶν οὐρανῶν, ὃν ἤγειρεν ἐκ [t] νεκρῶν, Ἰη-
[1]his from the heavens, whom he raised from among [the] dead— Je-
σοῦν τὸν ῥυόμενον ἡμᾶς [v]ἀπὸ‖ τῆς ὀργῆς τῆς ἐρχομένης.
sus, who delivers us from the [2]wrath [1]coming.
2 Αὐτοὶ.γὰρ οἴδατε, ἀδελφοί, τὴν.εἴσοδον.ἡμῶν τὴν
For [2]yourselves [1]ye know, brethren, our entrance in which [we had]
πρὸς ὑμᾶς, ὅτι οὐ κενὴ γέγονεν. 2 ἀλλὰ [w]καὶ‖ προπαθόν-
to you, that not void it has been; but also having before suf-
τες καὶ ὑβρισθέντες, καθὼς οἴδατε, ἐν Φιλίπποις, ἐπαρ-
fered and having been insulted, even as ye know, at Philippi, we
ῥησιασάμεθα ἐν τῷ.θεῷ.ἡμῶν λαλῆσαι πρὸς ὑμᾶς τὸ εὐαγγέλιον
were bold in our God to speak to you the glad tidings
τοῦ θεοῦ ἐν πολλῷ ἀγῶνι. 3 Ἡ γὰρ παράκλησις ἡμῶν οὐκ
of God in much conflict. For [2]exhortation [1]our [was] not
ἐκ πλάνης, οὐδὲ ἐξ ἀκαθαρσίας, [x]οὔτε‖ ἐν δόλῳ, 4 ἀλλὰ καθὼς
of error, nor of uncleanness, nor in guile; but even as
δεδοκιμάσμεθα ὑπὸ τοῦ θεοῦ πιστευθῆναι τὸ εὐαγγέλιον,
we have been approved by God to be entrusted with the glad tidings,
οὕτως λαλοῦμεν, οὐχ ὡς ἀνθρώποις ἀρέσκοντες, ἀλλὰ [y]τῷ‖
so we speak; not as [2]men [1]pleasing, but
θεῷ, τῷ δοκιμάζοντι τὰς καρδίας [z]ἡμῶν.‖ 5 Οὔτε.γάρ ποτε
God, who proves the hearts of us. For neither at any time
ἐν λόγῳ [a]κολακείας‖ ἐγενήθημεν, καθὼς οἴδατε, οὔτε
with word of flattery were we [with you], even as ye know, nor
ἐν προφάσει πλεονεξίας, θεὸς μάρτυς, 6 οὔτε ζητοῦντες
with a pretext of covetousness, God [is] witness; nor seeking
ἐξ ἀνθρώπων δόξαν, οὔτε ἀφ'.ὑμῶν οὔτε ἀπ' ἄλλων,
from men glory, neither from you nor from others, [though]
δυνάμενοι ἐν.βάρει εἶναι ὡς χριστοῦ ἀπόστολοι; 7 [b]ἀλλ'‖
having power [3]burdensome [1]to [2]be as Christ's apostles; but
ἐγενήθημεν [c]ἤπιοι‖ ἐν μέσῳ.ὑμῶν, ὡς [d]ἂν‖ τροφὸς θάλπῃ
we were gentle in your midst, as a nurse would cherish
τὰ.ἑαυτῆς τέκνα. 8 οὕτως [e]ἱμειρόμενοι‖ ὑμῶν, εὐδοκοῦμεν
her own children. Thus yearning over you, we were pleased

CHAPTER 1

1 Paul and Silvanius and Timothy to the church of the Thess-a-lo-ni-ans, in God the Father and the Lord Jesus Christ. Grace to you and peace from God our Father and the Lord Jesus Christ.

2 We give thanks to God always for you all, making mention of you in our prayers.

3 We never stop remembering your work of faith and labor of love and patience of hope – which is of our Lord Jesus Christ, in the sight of our God and Father –

4 knowing, beloved brothers, your election by our God.

5 For our gospel did not come to you in word only, but also in power and in the Holy Spirit and in much assurance – you know what kind of men we were among you, for your sake.

6 And you became imitators of us and of the Lord, after you had graciously embraced the word, in much affliction and with much joy in the Holy Spirit.

7 *So much so* that you became examples to all those who believe in Mac-e-do-ni-a and A-chai-a.

8 For the word of the Lord sounded out from you, not only in Mac-e-do-ni-a and A-chai-a, but also in every place your faith (which is towards God) has gone abroad, so that there is no need for us to say anything.

9 For *they* themselves witness what kind of entrance we had to you, even how you turned from idols to God in order to serve the living and true God –

10 and to wait for His Son from Heaven (whom He raised from the dead – Jesus) who delivers us from the wrath to come.

CHAPTER 2

1 For, brothers, you yourselves know our coming to you, that it was not fruitless.

2 But even after we had been shamefully treated and had suffered before (even as you know, at Philippi), we were bold in our God to preach the gospel of God to you in much agony.

3 For our call to you was not misleading, nor of uncleanness, nor of trickery.

4 But even as we have been approved by God to be trusted with the gospel, so we speak – not so as to please men, but God, who tests our hearts.

5 For at no time were we flattering in words – as you know, nor with an excuse for covetousness – God is our witness.

6 Nor *were we* seeking glory from men (not from you nor from others) – as the apostles of Christ we had power to be burdensome,

7 but we were gentle in your midst, even as a nurse warmly loves her own children.

8 Longing over you in this way, we were pleased to have given you not only the gos-

μεταδοῦναι ὑμῖν οὐ μόνον τὸ εὐαγγέλιον τοῦ θεοῦ, ἀλλὰ
to have imparted to you not only the glad tidings of God, but
καὶ τὰς ἑαυτῶν ψυχάς, διότι ἀγαπητοὶ ἡμῖν [f]γεγένησθε.‖
also our own lives, because beloved to us ye have become.
9 μνημονεύετε.γάρ, ἀδελφοί, τὸν.κόπον.ἡμῶν καὶ τὸν μόχθον·
For ye remember, brethren, our labour and the toil,
νυκτὸς.[g]γὰρ‖ καὶ ἡμέρας ἐργαζόμενοι, πρὸς τὸ μὴ ἐπιβαρῆσαί
for night and day working, for not to burden
τινα ὑμῶν, ἐκηρύξαμεν εἰς ὑμᾶς τὸ εὐαγγέλιον τοῦ θεοῦ.
anyone of you, we proclaimed to you the glad tidings of God.
10 ὑμεῖς μάρτυρες καὶ ὁ θεός, ὡς ὁσίως καὶ δικαίως καὶ
Ye [are] witnesses, and God, how holily and righteously and
ἀμέμπτως ὑμῖν τοῖς πιστεύουσιν ἐγενήθημεν, 11 καθάπερ
blamelessly with you that believe we were: even as
οἴδατε, ὡς ἕνα.ἕκαστον ὑμῶν, ὡς πατὴρ τέκνα ἑαυτοῦ, παρα-
ye know, how each one of you, as a father [3]children [1]his [2]own, ex-
καλοῦντες ὑμᾶς καὶ παραμυθούμενοι 12 καὶ [h]μαρτυρούμενοι,‖
horting you and consoling and testifying,
εἰς τὸ [i]περιπατῆσαι‖ ὑμᾶς ἀξίως τοῦ θεοῦ τοῦ καλοῦντος
for [2]to [3]have [4]walked [1]you worthily of God, who calls
ὑμᾶς εἰς τὴν.ἑαυτοῦ βασιλείαν καὶ δόξαν. 13 [k]Διὰ τοῦτο
you to his own kingdom and glory. Because of this
καὶ ἡμεῖς εὐχαριστοῦμεν τῷ θεῷ ἀδιαλείπτως, ὅτι παραλα-
also we give thanks to God unceasingly, that, having re-
βόντες λόγον ἀκοῆς παρ' ἡμῶν τοῦ θεοῦ ἐδέξασθε οὐ
ceived [the] word of [the] report [3]by [4]us [1]of [2]God, ye accepted not
λόγον ἀνθρώπων, ἀλλὰ καθώς ἐστιν ἀληθῶς, λόγον θεοῦ, ὃς
[2]word [1]men's, but even as it is truly, [2]word [1]God's, which
καὶ ἐνεργεῖται ἐν ὑμῖν τοῖς πιστεύουσιν. 14 ὑμεῖς.γὰρ μιμηταὶ
also works in you who believe. For ye imitators
ἐγενήθητε, ἀδελφοί, τῶν ἐκκλησιῶν τοῦ θεοῦ τῶν οὐσῶν ἐν τῇ
became, brethren, of the assemblies of God which are in
Ἰουδαίᾳ ἐν χριστῷ Ἰησοῦ, ὅτι [l]ταὐτὰ‖ ἐπάθετε καὶ ὑμεῖς
Judæa in Christ Jesus; because the same things [3]suffered [2]also [1]ye
ὑπὸ τῶν.ἰδίων συμφυλετῶν καθὼς καὶ αὐτοὶ ὑπὸ τῶν Ἰου-
from your own countrymen as also they from the Jews,
δαίων, 15 τῶν καὶ τὸν κύριον ἀποκτεινάντων Ἰησοῦν καὶ
who [2]both [3]the [4]Lord [1]killed Jesus and
τοὺς.[m]ἰδίους‖ προφήτας, καὶ [n]ὑμᾶς‖ ἐκδιωξάντων, καὶ θεῷ
their own prophets, and [2]you [1]drove out, and [4]God
μὴ.ἀρεσκόντων, καὶ πᾶσιν ἀνθρώποις ἐναντίων, 16 κω-
[1]do [2]not [3]please, and [4]all [3]to [5]men [[1]are] [2]contrary, for-
λυόντων ἡμᾶς τοῖς ἔθνεσιν λαλῆσαι ἵνα σωθῶσιν, εἰς
bidding us to the nations to speak that they may be saved, for
τὸ ἀναπληρῶσαι αὐτῶν τὰς ἁμαρτίας πάντοτε· [o]ἔφθασεν‖.δὲ
to fill up their sins always: but is come
ἐπ' αὐτοὺς ἡ ὀργὴ εἰς.τέλος.
upon them the wrath to the uttermost.
17 Ἡμεῖς.δέ, ἀδελφοί, ἀπορφανισθέντες ἀφ' ὑμῶν πρὸς
But we, brethren, having been bereaved of you for
καιρὸν ὥρας προσώπῳ οὐ καρδίᾳ, περισσοτέρως ἐσπου-
time of an hour in face, not in heart, more abundantly were
δάσαμεν τὸ.πρόσωπον.ὑμῶν ἰδεῖν ἐν πολλῇ ἐπιθυμίᾳ· 18 [q]διό‖
diligent your face to see with much desire; wherefore
ἠθελήσαμεν ἐλθεῖν πρὸς ὑμᾶς, ἐγὼ μὲν Παῦλος καὶ ἅπαξ
we wished to come to you, I indeed Paul, both once
καὶ δίς, καὶ ἐνέκοψεν ἡμᾶς ὁ σατανᾶς. 19 τίς.γὰρ ἡμῶν
and twice, and [2]hindered [3]us [1]Satan; for what [is] our
ἐλπὶς ἢ χαρὰ ἢ στέφανος καυχήσεως; ἢ οὐχὶ καὶ ὑμεῖς
hope or joy or crown of boasting? or [are] not even ye
ἔμπροσθεν τοῦ.κυρίου.ἡμῶν Ἰησοῦ [r]χριστοῦ‖ ἐν τῇ αὐτοῦ
before our Lord Jesus Christ at his
παρουσίᾳ; 20 ὑμεῖς.γάρ ἐστε ἡ.δόξα.ἡμῶν καὶ ἡ χαρά.
coming? for ye are our glory and joy.
3 Διὸ μηκέτι στέγοντες, [s]εὐδοκήσαμεν‖ καταλειφθῆναι
Wherefore no longer enduring, we thought good to be left
ἐν Ἀθήναις μόνοι, 2 καὶ ἐπέμψαμεν Τιμόθεον τὸν ἀδελφὸν
in Athens alone, and sent Timotheus [2]brother
ἡμῶν καὶ [t]διάκονον‖ τοῦ θεοῦ [v]καὶ συνεργὸν ἡμῶν‖ ἐν τῷ
[1]our and servant of God and [2]fellow-worker [1]our in the
εὐαγγελίῳ τοῦ χριστοῦ, εἰς τὸ στηρίξαι ὑμᾶς καὶ παρακαλέσαι
glad tidings of the Christ, for to establish you and to encourage
[w]ὑμᾶς‖ [x]περὶ‖ τῆς.πίστεως.ὑμῶν 3 [y]τῷ‖ [z]μηδένα σαίνεσθαι‖
you concerning your faith that no one be moved
ἐν ταῖς.θλίψεσιν ταύταις· αὐτοὶ.γὰρ οἴδατε ὅτι εἰς τοῦτο
by these tribulations. (For yourselves know that for this
κείμεθα· 4 καὶ.γὰρ ὅτε πρὸς ὑμᾶς ἦμεν, προελέγομεν ὑμῖν
we are set; for also, when with you we were, we told [2]beforehand [1]you
ὅτι μέλλομεν θλίβεσθαι, καθὼς καὶ ἐγένετο καὶ οἴ-
we are about to suffer tribulation, even as also it came to pass and ye
δατε· 5 διὰ τοῦτο κἀγὼ μηκέτι στέγων, ἔπεμψα εἰς τὸ
know.) Because of this I also no longer enduring, sent for

pel of God, but our own souls also, because
you have become dear to us.
9 For, brothers, you remember our labor
and hard work. For working day and night,
so as not to weigh any one of you down, we
preached the gospel of God to you.
10 You and God are witnesses how holily
and righteously and blamelessly we behaved
ourselves among you that believe.
11 Even as you know how *we were* as a
father to his own children to each of you,
appealing and encouraging and urging,
12 and testifying for you to walk worthily
of God, who calls you to His own kingdom
and glory.
13 For this reason also we give thanks to
God without stopping, that when you had
received the word of God, hearing it by us,
you did not take it as the word of men, but
as the word of God, as it truly is – which
also works in you who believe.
14 For, brothers, you became imitators of
the churches of God in Judea, which are in
Christ Jesus, because you also suffered the
same things from your own countrymen,
even as they from the Jews,
15 who both killed the Lord Jesus and their
own prophets, and have persecuted us, and
do not please God and are contrary to all
men.
16 *They are* telling us not to preach to the
Gentiles so that they may be saved in order
to fill up their sins always. But the wrath of
God has come on them to the uttermost.
17 But, brothers, when we were taken away
from you for an hour's time (in presence,
not in heart), we were more eagerly trying to
see your face with much longing.
18 So again and again we wished to come to
you (even I, Paul), but Satan held us back.
19 For what is our hope or joy or crown of
rejoicing – or are you not also to be in the
presence of our Lord Jesus Christ at His
coming.
20 For you are our glory and joy.

CHAPTER 3

1 So when we could no longer bear it, we
decided to be left alone in Athens
2 and sent Timothy our brother and minister of God, and our fellow-worker in the
gospel of Christ, in order to establish you
and encourage you as to your faith –
3 so that no one should be troubled by
these afflictions. For you know that we are
appointed for this.
4 For even when we were with you, we told
you beforehand that we were going to suffer
affliction (as it also happened, and you
know).
5 Because of this also, I could not bear it
any longer and sent to know your faith, for

γνῶναι τὴν.πίστιν.ὑμῶν, μήπως ἐπείρασεν ὑμᾶς ὁ
to know your faith, lest perhaps [4]did [5]tempt [6]you [1]he [2]who
πειράζων, καὶ εἰς κενὸν γένηται ὁ.κόπος.ἡμῶν. 6 Ἄρτι.δὲ
[3]tempts, and void should become our labour. But now
ἐλθόντος Τιμοθέου πρὸς ἡμᾶς ἀφ' ὑμῶν, καὶ εὐαγγελισα-
[2]having [3]come [1]Timotheus to us from you, and having announced
μένου ἡμῖν τὴν πίστιν καὶ τὴν ἀγάπην ὑμῶν, καὶ ὅτι
glad tidings to us [of] [2]faith [3]and [4]love [1]your, and that
ἔχετε μνείαν ἡμῶν ἀγαθὴν πάντοτε, ἐπιποθοῦντες ἡμᾶς
ye have [3]remembrance [4]of [5]us [2]good [1]always, longing [3]us
ἰδεῖν, καθάπερ καὶ ἡμεῖς ὑμᾶς, 7 διὰ τοῦτο παρεκλή-
[1]to [2]see, even as also we you: because of this we were encou-
θημεν, ἀδελφοί, ἐφ' ὑμῖν, ἐπὶ πάσῃ τῇ [a]θλίψει καὶ ἀνάγκῃ‖
raged, brethren, as to you, in all [2]tribulation [3]and [4]necessity
ἡμῶν, διὰ τῆς.ὑμῶν.πίστεως· 8 ὅτι νῦν ζῶμεν ἐὰν ὑμεῖς
[1]our, through your faith, because now we live if ye
[b]στήκετε‖ ἐν κυρίῳ. 9 τίνα.γὰρ εὐχαριστίαν δυνάμεθα
should stand fast in [the] Lord. For what thanksgiving are we able
τῷ θεῷ ἀνταποδοῦναι περὶ ὑμῶν, ἐπὶ πάσῃ τῇ χαρᾷ
[3]to [4]God [1]to [2]render concerning you, for all the joy
ᾗ χαίρομεν δι' ὑμᾶς ἔμπροσθεν τοῦ.θεοῦ.ἡμῶν,[c]
wherewith we rejoice on account of you before our God,
10 νυκτὸς καὶ ἡμέρας [d]ὑπὲρ.ἐκπερισσοῦ‖ δεόμενοι εἰς τὸ ἰδεῖν
night and day exceedingly beseeching for to see
ὑμῶν τὸ πρόσωπον, καὶ καταρτίσαι τὰ.ὑστερήματα τῆς πίστεως
your face, and to perfect the things lacking in [2]faith
ὑμῶν; 11 Αὐτὸς.δὲ ὁ θεὸς καὶ πατὴρ.ἡμῶν καὶ ὁ.κύριος.ἡμῶν
[1]your? But [6]himself [3]God [4]and [2]our [5]Father [7]and [8]our [9]Lord
Ἰησοῦς [e]χριστὸς‖ κατευθύναι τὴν.ὁδὸν.ἡμῶν πρὸς ὑμᾶς.
[10]Jesus [11]Christ [1]may direct our way to you.
12 ὑμᾶς.δὲ ὁ κύριος πλεονάσαι καὶ περισσεύσαι τῇ
But [5]you [2]the [3]Lord [1]may [4]make to exceed and to abound
ἀγάπῃ εἰς ἀλλήλους καὶ εἰς πάντας, καθάπερ καὶ ἡμεῖς
in love toward one another and toward all, even as also we
εἰς ὑμᾶς, 13 εἰς τὸ στηρίξαι ὑμῶν τὰς καρδίας ἀμέμπτους
toward you, for to establish your hearts blameless
ἐν ἁγιωσύνῃ ἔμπροσθεν τοῦ θεοῦ καὶ πατρὸς ἡμῶν, ἐν τῇ
in holiness before [2]God [3]and [4]Father [1]our, at the
παρουσίᾳ τοῦ.κυρίου.ἡμῶν Ἰησοῦ [f]χριστοῦ‖ μετὰ πάντων τῶν
coming of our Lord Jesus Christ with all
ἁγίων.αὐτοῦ.[g]
his saints.

4 [h]Τὸ‖.λοιπὸν οὖν, ἀδελφοί, ἐρωτῶμεν ὑμᾶς καὶ παρα-
For the rest then, brethren, we beseech you and we
καλοῦμεν ἐν κυρίῳ Ἰησοῦ, [i]καθὼς παρελάβετε παρ' ἡμῶν
exhort in [the] Lord Jesus, even as ye received from us
τὸ πῶς δεῖ ὑμᾶς περιπατεῖν καὶ ἀρέσκειν θεῷ, [k]ἵνα περισ-
how it behoves you to walk and please God, that ye should
σεύητε μᾶλλον. 2 οἴδατε.γὰρ τίνας παραγγελίας ἐδώκαμεν
abound more. For ye know what injunctions we gave
ὑμῖν διὰ τοῦ κυρίου Ἰησοῦ. 3 τοῦτο.γάρ ἐστιν [l] θέλημα τοῦ
you through the Lord Jesus. For this is [2]will
θεοῦ, ὁ.ἁγιασμὸς.ὑμῶν, ἀπέχεσθαι ὑμᾶς ἀπὸ τῆς πορνείας,
[1]God's, your sanctification, [3]to [4]abstain [[1]for] [2]you from fornication,
4 εἰδέναι ἕκαστον ὑμῶν τὸ.ἑαυτοῦ σκεῦος κτᾶσθαι ἐν
[4]to [5]know [1]each [2]of [3]you [how] [3]his [4]own [5]vessel [1]to [2]possess in
ἁγιασμῷ καὶ τιμῇ, 5 μὴ ἐν πάθει ἐπιθυμίας καθάπερ καὶ
sanctification and honour, (not in passion of lust even as also
τὰ ἔθνη τὰ μὴ.εἰδότα τὸν θεόν· 6 τὸ μὴ ὑπερβαίνειν καὶ
the nations who know not God,) not to go beyond and
πλεονεκτεῖν ἐν τῷ πράγματι τὸν.ἀδελφὸν.αὐτοῦ, διότι ἔκ-
to overreach in the matter his brother; because [the] a-
δικος [m]ὁ‖ κύριος περὶ πάντων τούτων, καθὼς καὶ
venger [is] the Lord concerning all these things, even as also
[n]προείπαμεν‖ ὑμῖν καὶ διεμαρτυράμεθα. 7 οὐ.γὰρ ἐκάλεσεν
we told [2]before [1]you and fully testified. For [4]not [2]called
ἡμᾶς ὁ θεὸς ἐπὶ ἀκαθαρσίᾳ, [o]ἀλλ'‖ ἐν ἁγιασμῷ. 8 τοιγαροῦν
[3]us [1]God to uncleanness, but in sanctification. So then
ὁ ἀθετῶν, οὐκ ἄνθρωπον ἀθετεῖ, ἀλλὰ τὸν θεόν, τὸν
he that sets aside, [2]not [3]man [1]sets aside, but God, who
[p]καὶ‖ [q]δόντα‖ [r]τὸ.πνεῦμα.αὐτοῦ‖ τὸ ἅγιον εἰς [s]ἡμᾶς.‖
also gave his [2]Spirit [1]Holy to us.
9 Περὶ.δὲ τῆς φιλαδελφίας οὐ χρείαν [t]ἔχετε‖ γρά-
Now concerning brotherly love [3]no [4]need [1]ye [2]have [for me] to
φειν ὑμῖν, αὐτοὶ.γὰρ ὑμεῖς θεοδίδακτοί ἐστε εἰς τὸ ἀγαπᾷν
write to you, for [2]yourselves [1]ye [4]taught [5]of [6]God [3]are for to love
ἀλλήλους· 10 καὶ.γὰρ ποιεῖτε αὐτὸ εἰς πάντας τοὺς ἀδελ-
one another. For also ye do this towards all the bre-
φοὺς [v]τοὺς‖ ἐν ὅλῃ.τῇ.Μακεδονίᾳ. παρακαλοῦμεν.δὲ ὑμᾶς,
thren who [are] in the whole of Macedonia; but we exhort you,
ἀδελφοί, περισσεύειν μᾶλλον, 11 καὶ φιλοτιμεῖσθαι ἡσυχάζειν
brethren, to abound more, and endeavour earnestly to be quiet

fear that perhaps the tempter should tempt
you and make our labor to no avail.
6 But now Timothy has come to us from
you and has told us good news as to your
faith and love (and that you always have a
good remembrance of us, longing to see us,
even as we also you).
7 So we were comforted over you, through
your faith, brothers, in all our affliction and
need –
8 because now we live, if you stand firm in
the Lord.
9 For what thanks can we return to God as
to you, for all the joy which we rejoice before our God on account of you –
10 night and day, praying to see your face
and perfect the things lacking in your faith?
11 But may our God and Father Himself
and our Lord Jesus Christ direct our way to
you.
12 And may the Lord make you increase
and multiply in love toward one another and
toward all, as we also do toward you,
13 so that your hearts may be established
blameless in holiness before our God and
Father at the coming of our Lord Jesus
Christ with all His saints.

CHAPTER 4

1 For the rest, then, brothers, we beg you
and encourage you in the Lord Jesus that as
you received from us how you ought to walk
and please God, that you should do far more
2 – for you know what commandments we
gave you through the Lord Jesus.
3 For this is God's will, your sanctification,
for you to keep away from fornication,
4 so that each of you may know how to
possess his own vessel in purity and honor
5 (not in passions of lust, even as the Gentiles also, who do not know God)
6 not overreaching and cheating his brother
in the matter, because the Lord is the
avenger in these things, even as we also told
you before and fully declared *to you.*
7 For God did not call us to uncleanness,
but to holiness.
8 So then he that despises does not despise
man but God, who also gave His Holy Spirit
to us.
9 Now as to brotherly love, you have no
need for me to write to you, for you yourselves are taught by God to love each other.
10 For you also do this toward all the brothers who are in all Mac-e-do-ni-a. But, brothers, we call on you to grow more and
more.
11 And try earnestly to be quiet and to
mind your own business, and to work with

καὶ πράσσειν τὰ.ἴδια, καὶ ἐργάζεσθαι ταῖς.[w]ἰδίαις‖.χερσὶν
and to do your own things, and to work with [2]own [3]hands
ὑμῶν, καθὼς ὑμῖν παρηγγείλαμεν, 12 ἵνα περιπατῆτε εὐ-
[1]your, even as on you we enjoined, that ye may walk be-
σχημόνως πρὸς τοὺς ἔξω, καὶ μηδενὸς χρείαν ἔχητε.
comingly towards those without, and of no one [3]need [1]may [2]have.
13 Οὐ [x]θέλω‖ δὲ ὑμᾶς ἀγνοεῖν, ἀδελφοί, περὶ
[4]Not [2]I [3]do [5]wish [1]but you to be ignorant, brethren, concerning
τῶν [y]κεκοιμημένων,‖ ἵνα μὴ.λυπῆσθε, καθὼς καὶ οἱ λοιποὶ
those who have fallen asleep, that ye be not grieved, even as also the rest
οἱ μὴ.ἔχοντες ἐλπίδα. 14 εἰ.γὰρ πιστεύομεν ὅτι Ἰησοῦς ἀπέ-
who have no hope. For if we believe that Jesus died
θανεν καὶ ἀνέστη, οὕτως καὶ ὁ θεὸς τοὺς κοιμηθέντας
and rose again, so also God those who are fallen asleep
διὰ τοῦ Ἰησοῦ ἄξει σὺν αὐτῷ. 15 τοῦτο.γὰρ ὑμῖν λέ-
through Jesus will bring with him. For this to you we
γομεν ἐν λόγῳ κυρίου, ὅτι ἡμεῖς οἱ ζῶντες, οἱ περι-
say in [the] word of [the] Lord, that we the living who re-
λειπόμενοι εἰς τὴν παρουσίαν τοῦ κυρίου, οὐ.μὴ φθάσωμεν
main to the coming of the Lord, in no wise may anticipate
τοὺς κοιμηθέντας· 16 ὅτι αὐτὸς ὁ κύριος ἐν κελεύσ-
those who are fallen asleep; because [3]himself [1]the [2]Lord with a shout of com-
ματι, ἐν φωνῇ ἀρχαγγέλου καὶ ἐν σάλπιγγι θεοῦ κατα-
mand, with [2]voice [1]archangel's and with trumpet of God shall
βήσεται ἀπ' οὐρανοῦ, καὶ οἱ νεκροὶ ἐν χριστῷ ἀναστήσονται
descend from heaven, and the dead in Christ shall rise
πρῶτον· 17 ἔπειτα ἡμεῖς οἱ ζῶντες οἱ περιλειπόμενοι, ἅμα
first; then we the living who remain, together
σὺν αὐτοῖς ἁρπαγησόμεθα ἐν νεφέλαις εἰς ἀπάντησιν
with them shall be caught away in [the] clouds for [the] meeting
τοῦ κυρίου εἰς ἀέρα, καὶ οὕτως πάντοτε σὺν κυρίῳ ἐσό-
of the Lord in [the] air; and thus always with [the] Lord we shall
μεθα. 18 ὥστε παρακαλεῖτε ἀλλήλους ἐν τοῖς.λόγοις.τούτοις.
be. So encourage one another with these words.
5 Περὶ.δὲ τῶν χρόνων καὶ τῶν καιρῶν, ἀδελφοί, οὐ χρείαν
But concerning the times and the seasons, brethren, [3]no [4]need
ἔχετε ὑμῖν γράφεσθαι· 2 αὐτοὶ.γὰρ ἀκριβῶς οἴδατε ὅτι
[1]ye [2]have for you to be written [to], for [2]yourselves [4]accurately [1]ye [3]know that
[z]ἡ‖ ἡμέρα κυρίου ὡς κλέπτης ἐν νυκτὶ οὕτως ἔρχεται·
the day of [the] Lord as a thief by night so comes.
3 ὅταν.[a]γὰρ‖ λέγωσιν, Εἰρήνη καὶ ἀσφάλεια, τότε αἰφνί-
For when they may say, Peace and security, then sud-
διος αὐτοῖς [b]ἐφίσταται‖ ὄλεθρος, ὥσπερ ἡ.ὠδὶν τῇ
den [3]upon [4]them [2]comes [1]destruction, as travail to her
ἐν.γαστρὶ.ἐχούσῃ, καὶ οὐ.μὴ ἐκφύγωσιν. 4 ὑμεῖς.δέ, ἀδελ-
that is with child; and in no wise shall they escape. But ye, bre-
φοί, οὐκ.ἐστὲ ἐν σκότει, ἵνα [c]ἡ ἡμέρα ὑμᾶς‖ ὡς [d]κλέπτης‖
thren, are not in darkness, that the day you as a thief
καταλάβῃ· 5 πάντες [e]ὑμεῖς υἱοὶ φωτός ἐστε καὶ υἱοὶ ἡμέρας·
should overtake: all ye sons of light are and sons of day;
οὐκ.ἐσμὲν νυκτὸς οὐδὲ σκότους. 6 ἄρα οὖν μὴ.καθεύδωμεν
we are not of night nor of darkness. So then we should not sleep
ὡς [f]καὶ‖ οἱ λοιποί, ἀλλὰ γρηγορῶμεν καὶ νήφωμεν.
as also the rest, but we should watch and we should be sober;
7 οἱ.γὰρ καθεύδοντες νυκτὸς καθεύδουσιν, καὶ οἱ μεθυ-
for they that sleep [2]by [3]night [1]sleep, and they that are
σκόμενοι νυκτὸς μεθύουσιν· 8 ἡμεῖς.δὲ ἡμέρας ὄντες νήφω-
drunken [3]by [4]night [1]get [2]drunk; but we [2]of [3]day [1]being should be
μεν, ἐνδυσάμενοι θώρακα πίστεως καὶ ἀγάπης, καὶ
sober, having put on [the] breastplate of faith and love, and [as]
περικεφαλαίαν ἐλπίδα σωτηρίας· 9 ὅτι οὐκ ἔθετο ἡμᾶς
helmet [2]hope [1]salvation's; because [3]not [2]has [4]set [5]us
ὁ θεὸς εἰς ὀργήν, [g]ἀλλ'‖ εἰς περιποίησιν σωτηρίας διὰ τοῦ
[1]God for wrath, but for obtaining salvation through
κυρίου.ἡμῶν Ἰησοῦ χριστοῦ, 10 τοῦ ἀποθανόντος [h]ὑπὲρ‖ ἡμῶν,
our Lord Jesus Christ, who died for us,
ἵνα εἴτε γρηγορῶμεν εἴτε καθεύδωμεν, ἅμα σὺν αὐτῷ
that whether we may watch or we may sleep, together with him
ζήσωμεν. 11 διὸ παρακαλεῖτε ἀλλήλους, καὶ οἰκοδομεῖτε εἷς
we may live. Wherefore encourage one another, and build up one
τὸν ἕνα, καθὼς καὶ ποιεῖτε.
the other, even as also ye are doing.
12 Ἐρωτῶμεν.δὲ ὑμᾶς, ἀδελφοί, εἰδέναι τοὺς κοπιῶντας
But we beseech you, brethren, to know those who labour
ἐν ὑμῖν, καὶ προϊσταμένους ὑμῶν ἐν κυρίῳ, καὶ νουθε-
among you, and take the lead of you in [the] Lord, and admo-
τοῦντας ὑμᾶς, 13 καὶ ἡγεῖσθαι αὐτοὺς [i]ὑπὲρ.ἐκπερισσοῦ‖ ἐν
nish you, and to esteem them exceedingly in
ἀγάπῃ διὰ τὸ.ἔργον.αὐτῶν. εἰρηνεύετε ἐν [k]ἑαυτοῖς.‖
love on account of their work. Be at peace among yourselves.
14 παρακαλοῦμεν.δὲ ὑμᾶς, ἀδελφοί, νουθετεῖτε τοὺς ἀτάκτους,
But we exhort you, brethren, admonish the disorderly,

your own hands, as we commanded you,
12 that you may walk decently towards the
ones on the outside and that you may have
need of no one.
13 But I do not want you to be ignorant,
brothers, about those who have died (so that
you may not be sorrowful, even as also the
rest who have no hope).
14 For if we believe that Jesus died and rose
again, even so God will also bring with Him
all those who have died in Jesus.
15 For we say this to you in the Lord's
word that we who are alive and left to the
coming of the Lord may not in any way go
before those who are dead.
16 Because the Lord Himself will come
down from Heaven with a shout, with the
voice of the archangel and with the trumpet
of God. And the dead in Christ shall rise
first,
17 then those who are left alive shall be
caught up together with those in the clouds
to meet the Lord in the air. And so we shall
always be with the Lord.
18 So comfort each other with these words.

CHAPTER 5

1 But as to the times and the seasons,
brothers, you do not need me to write to
you.
2 For you yourselves know perfectly well
that the day of the Lord comes as a thief in
the night.
3 For when they say, Peace and safety! –
then sudden destruction comes on them as
labor pains on her that is with child. And
they shall in no way escape.
4 But you, brothers, are not in darkness,
that the Day should overtake you as a thief.
5 You are all sons of light and sons of day.
We are not sons of night nor of darkness.
6 So then we should not sleep as the rest do
– but we should watch and be sober.
7 For the sleepers sleep by night, and the
drunken get drunk by night,
8 but we who are of the day should be full
of self-control and put on the breastplate of
faith and love, and the hope of salvation as a
helmet.
9 For God has not appointed us to wrath,
but to the getting of salvation through our
Lord Jesus Christ,
10 who died for us so that if we watch or
sleep, we may live together with Him.
11 Then encourage one another and build
up one another, even as you also are doing.
12 But, brothers, we beg you to recognize
those who labor among you and who are
taking the lead of you and warning you.
13 And esteem them very highly in love
because of their work. Be at peace among
yourselves also.
14 But, brothers, we call on you to warn

παραμυθεῖσθε τοὺς ὀλιγοψύχους, ἀντέχεσθε τῶν ἀσθενῶν, μα-
console [1]the faint-hearted, sustain the weak, be
κροθυμεῖτε πρὸς πάντας. 15 ὁρᾶτε μή τις κακὸν ἀντὶ κακοῦ
patient towards all. See that not anyone evil for evil
τινὶ [l]ἀποδῷ·[ll] ἀλλὰ πάντοτε τὸ ἀγαθὸν διώκετε [m]καὶ[ll] εἰς
to anyone render, but always the good pursue both towards
ἀλλήλους καὶ εἰς πάντας. 16 πάντοτε χαίρετε. 17 ἀδια-
one another and towards all; always rejoice; unceas-
λείπτως προσεύχεσθε. 18 ἐν παντὶ εὐχαριστεῖτε· τοῦτο γὰρ [n]
ingly pray; in everything give thanks, for this
θέλημα θεοῦ ἐν χριστῷ Ἰησοῦ εἰς ὑμᾶς. 19 τὸ πνεῦμα
[is the] will of God in Christ Jesus towards you; the Spirit
μὴ [o]σβέννυτε.[ll] 20 προφητείας μὴ ἐξουθενεῖτε. 21 πάντα [p]
do not quench; prophecies do not set at naught; all things
δοκιμάζετε· τὸ καλὸν κατέχετε. 22 ἀπὸ παντὸς εἴδους πονη-
prove, the right hold fast; from every form of wicked-
ροῦ ἀπέχεσθε. 23 Αὐτὸς δὲ ὁ θεὸς τῆς εἰρήνης ἁγιάσαι
ness abstain. Now [6]himself [2]the [3]God [4]of [5]peace [1]may sanctify
ὑμᾶς ὁλοτελεῖς· καὶ ὁλόκληρον ὑμῶν τὸ πνεῦμα καὶ ἡ ψυχὴ
you wholly; and [3]entire [2]your [4]spirit [5]and [6]soul
καὶ τὸ σῶμα ἀμέμπτως ἐν τῇ παρουσίᾳ τοῦ κυρίου ἡμῶν
[7]and [8]body [11]blameless [12]at [13]the [14]coming [15]of [16]our [17]Lord
Ἰησοῦ χριστοῦ τηρηθείη. 24 πιστὸς ὁ καλῶν ὑμᾶς,
[18]Jesus [19]Christ [1]may [9]be [10]preserved. [He is] faithful who calls you,
ὃς καὶ ποιήσει. 25 Ἀδελφοί, προσεύχεσθε [q] περὶ ἡμῶν.
who also will perform [it]. Brethren, pray for us.
26 ἀσπάσασθε τοὺς ἀδελφοὺς πάντας ἐν φιλήματι ἁγίῳ.
Salute [2]the [3]brethren [1]all with a [2]kiss [1]holy.
27 [r]ὁρκίζω[ll] ὑμᾶς τὸν κύριον ἀναγνωσθῆναι τὴν ἐπιστο-
I adjure you [by] the Lord [that] be read the epistle
λὴν πᾶσιν τοῖς [s]ἁγίοις[ll] ἀδελφοῖς. 28 ἡ χάρις τοῦ κυρίου ἡμῶν
to all the holy brethren. The grace of our Lord
Ἰησοῦ χριστοῦ μεθ' ὑμῶν. [t]ἀμήν.[ll]
Jesus Christ [be] with you. Amen.
[v]Πρὸς Θεσσαλονικεῖς πρώτη ἐγράφη ἀπὸ Ἀθηνῶν.[ll]
[2]To [3the] [4]Thessalonians [1]first written from Athens.

the unruly ones, comfort the faint-hearted,
hold up the weak and be patient towards all.
15 See that no one gives evil for evil to anyone, but always follow that which is good,
both towards one another and towards all.
16 Rejoice evermore.
17 Pray without ceasing.
18 In everything give thanks, for this is
the will of God in Christ Jesus towards
you.
19 Do not quench the Spirit.
20 Do not despise prophecies.
21 Test all things, hold to what is excellent.
22 Keep back from every form of evil.
23 And may the God of Peace Himself fully
sanctify you, and may your whole spirit and
soul and body be kept blameless at the
coming of our Lord Jesus Christ –
24 *He* who calls you is faithful, who also
will do it.
25 Brothers, pray for us.
26 Greet all the brothers with a holy kiss.
27 I charge you by the Lord that this letter
be read to all the holy brothers.
28 The grace of our Lord Jesus Christ be
with you. Amen.

The SECOND Letter to the THESSALONIANS

CHAPTER 1

ΠΑΥΛΟΣ καὶ Σιλουανὸς καὶ Τιμόθεος, τῇ ἐκκλησίᾳ Θεσ-
Paul and Silvanus and Timotheus, to the assembly of Thes-
σαλονικέων ἐν θεῷ πατρὶ ἡμῶν καὶ κυρίῳ Ἰησοῦ χριστῷ·
salonians in God [2]Father [1]our and Lord Jesus Christ.
2 χάρις ὑμῖν καὶ εἰρήνη ἀπὸ θεοῦ πατρὸς [b]ἡμῶν[ll] καὶ κυρίου
Grace to you and peace from God [2]Father [1]our and Lord
Ἰησοῦ χριστοῦ.
Jesus Christ.
3 Εὐχαριστεῖν ὀφείλομεν τῷ θεῷ πάντοτε περὶ ὑμῶν,
[3]To [4]thank [1]we [2]ought God always concerning you,
ἀδελφοί, καθὼς ἄξιόν ἐστιν, ὅτι ὑπεραυξάνει ἡ πίστις
brethren, even as meet it is, because increases exceedingly [2]faith
ὑμῶν, καὶ πλεονάζει ἡ ἀγάπη ἑνὸς ἑκάστου πάντων ὑμῶν
[1]your, and abounds the love of [2]one [1]each of [2]all [1]you
εἰς ἀλλήλους· 4 ὥστε [c]ἡμᾶς αὐτοὺς[ll] ἐν ὑμῖν [d]καυχᾶσθαι[ll] ἐν
to one another; so as for us ourselves [3]in [4]you [1]to [2]boast in
ταῖς ἐκκλησίαις τοῦ θεοῦ ὑπὲρ τῆς ὑπομονῆς ὑμῶν καὶ πίστεως
the assemblies of God for your endurance and faith
ἐν πᾶσιν τοῖς διωγμοῖς ὑμῶν καὶ ταῖς θλίψεσιν αἷς ἀνέ-
in all your persecutions and the tribulations which ye are
χεσθε, 5 ἔνδειγμα τῆς δικαίας κρίσεως τοῦ θεοῦ, εἰς τὸ
bearing; a manifest token of the righteous judgment of God, for
καταξιωθῆναι ὑμᾶς τῆς βασιλείας τοῦ θεοῦ, ὑπὲρ ἧς
[2]to [3]be [4]accounted [5]worthy [1]you of the kingdom of God, for which
καὶ πάσχετε· 6 εἴπερ δίκαιον παρὰ θεῷ ἀνταποδοῦναι
also ye suffer, if at least righteous [it is] with God to recompense
τοῖς θλίβουσιν ὑμᾶς θλίψιν, 7 καὶ ὑμῖν τοῖς θλιβο-
to those who oppress you tribulation, and to you that are op-
μένοις ἄνεσιν μεθ' ἡμῶν, ἐν τῇ ἀποκαλύψει τοῦ κυρίου Ἰησοῦ
pressed repose with us, at the revelation of the Lord Jesus
ἀπ' οὐρανοῦ μετ' ἀγγέλων δυνάμεως αὐτοῦ, 8 ἐν [e]πυρὶ φλογός,[ll]
from heaven with [the] angels of his power, in a fire of flame,
διδόντος ἐκδίκησιν τοῖς μὴ εἰδόσιν θεόν, καὶ τοῖς μὴ
awarding vengeance on those that [2]not [1]know God, and those that [2]not
ὑπακούουσιν τῷ εὐαγγελίῳ τοῦ κυρίου ἡμῶν Ἰησοῦ [f]χριστοῦ·[ll]
[1]obey the glad tidings of our Lord Jesus Christ,
9 οἵτινες δίκην τίσουσιν, [g]ὄλεθρον[ll] αἰώνιον, ἀπὸ
who [the] penalty shall suffer, [2]destruction [1]eternal, from [the]

1 Paul and Silvanus and Timothy to the
church of the Thess-a-lo-ni-ans in God our
Father and the Lord Jesus Christ.
2 Grace and peace to you from God our
Father and the Lord Jesus Christ.
3 We are bound to always thank God as to
you, brothers, even as it is right to do so,
because your faith grows more and more and
the love of each and every one of you is
overflowing toward one another.
4 *It is so evident* that we boast in you in the
churches of God, for your patience and faith
in all your persecutions and the troubles,
which you are bearing –
5 *this being* clear proof of the righteous
judgment of God, for you to be counted
worthy of the kingdom of God, for which
you also suffer.
6 *This I say* because it is a righteous thing
with God to repay trouble to those who give
you trouble,
7 and to give rest with us to you who are
troubled, at the revealing of the Lord Jesus
from Heaven with the angels of His power.
8 In flaming fire *He will be* taking vengeance on those that do not know God and
on those who do not obey the gospel of our
Lord Jesus Christ,
9 who shall suffer the penalty: everlasting

προσώπου τοῦ κυρίου, καὶ ἀπὸ τῆς δόξης τῆς.ἰσχύος.αὐτοῦ,
presence of the Lord, and from the glory of his strength,
10 ὅταν ἔλθῃ ἐνδοξασθῆναι ἐν τοῖς.ἁγίοις.αὐτοῦ καὶ
when he shall have come to be glorified in his saints and
θαυμασθῆναι ἐν πᾶσιν τοῖς [b]πιστεύουσιν,‖ ὅτι ἐπιστεύθη
to be wondered at in all them that believe, (because [5]was [6]believed
τὸ.μαρτύριον.ἡμῶν ἐφ' ὑμᾶς, ἐν τῇ.ἡμέρᾳ.ἐκείνῃ. 11 εἰς ὃ
[1]our [2]testimony [3]to [4]you,) in that day. For which
καὶ προσευχόμεθα πάντοτε περὶ ὑμῶν, ἵνα ὑμᾶς ἀξιώσῃ
also we pray always for you, that [5]you [3]may [4]count [6]worthy
τῆς κλήσεως ὁ.θεὸς.ἡμῶν, καὶ πληρώσῃ πᾶσαν εὐδοκίαν
[7]of [8]the [9]calling [1]our [2]God, and may fulfil every good pleasure
ἀγαθωσύνης καὶ ἔργον πίστεως ἐν δυνάμει· 12 ὅπως ἐν-
of goodness and work of faith with power, so that may
δοξασθῇ τὸ ὄνομα τοῦ.κυρίου.ἡμῶν Ἰησοῦ [i]χριστοῦ‖ ἐν ὑμῖν,
be glorified the name of our Lord Jesus Christ in you,
καὶ ὑμεῖς ἐν αὐτῷ, κατὰ τὴν χάριν τοῦ.θεοῦ.ἡμῶν καὶ
and ye in him, according to the grace of our God and
κυρίου Ἰησοῦ χριστοῦ.
of [the] Lord Jesus Christ.

2 Ἐρωτῶμεν.δὲ ὑμᾶς, ἀδελφοί, ὑπὲρ τῆς παρουσίας τοῦ
Now we beseech you, brethren, by the coming
κυρίου.ἡμῶν Ἰησοῦ χριστοῦ καὶ ἡμῶν ἐπισυναγωγῆς ἐπ'
of our Lord Jesus Christ and our gathering together to
αὐτόν, 2 εἰς τὸ μὴ ταχέως σαλευθῆναι ὑμᾶς ἀπὸ τοῦ νοός,
him, for [2]not [5]quickly [3]to [4]be [6]shaken [1]you in mind,
[k]μήτε‖ θροεῖσθαι, μήτε διὰ πνεύματος, μήτε διὰ λόγου, μήτε
nor to be troubled, neither by spirit, nor by word, nor
δι' ἐπιστολῆς ὡς δι' ἡμῶν, ὡς ὅτι ἐνέστηκεν ἡ ἡμέρα τοῦ
by epistle, as if by us, as that is present the day of the
[l]χριστοῦ.‖ 3 Μή τις ὑμᾶς ἐξαπατήσῃ κατὰ μηδένα τρόπον·
Christ. Not anyone [3]you [1]should [2]deceive in any way,
(*lit.* no)
ὅτι ἐὰν.μὴ ἔλθῃ ἡ ἀποστασία πρῶτον
because [it will not be] unless shall have come the apostasy first,
καὶ ἀποκαλυφθῇ ὁ ἄνθρωπος τῆς [m]ἁμαρτίας,‖ ὁ υἱὸς
and shall have been revealed the man of sin, the son
τῆς ἀπωλείας, 4 ὁ ἀντικείμενος καὶ ὑπεραιρόμενος ἐπὶ πάντα
of perdition, he who opposes and exalts himself above all
λεγόμενον θεὸν ἢ σέβασμα, ὥστε.αὐτὸν εἰς τὸν ναὸν
called God or object of veneration: so as for him in the temple
τοῦ θεοῦ [n]ὡς θεὸν‖ καθίσαι, ἀποδεικνύντα ἑαυτὸν ὅτι ἐστὶν
of God as God to sit down, setting forth himself that he is
θεός. 5 οὐ.μνημονεύετε ὅτι ἔτι ὢν πρὸς ὑμᾶς, ταῦτα
God. Do ye not remember that, yet being with you, these things
ἔλεγον ὑμῖν; 6 καὶ νῦν τὸ κατέχον οἴδατε, εἰς τὸ ἀπο-
I said to you? And now that which restrains ye know, for [2]to [3]be
καλυφθῆναι αὐτὸν ἐν τῷ.[o]ἑαυτοῦ‖ καιρῷ. 7 τὸ.γὰρ μυστήριον
[4]revealed [1]him in his own time. For the mystery
ἤδη ἐνεργεῖται τῆς ἀνομίας, μόνον ὁ κατέχων
[1]already [4]is [5]working [3]of [2]lawlessness; only [there is] he who restrains
ἄρτι ἕως ἐκ μέσου γένηται· 8 καὶ τότε ἀποκαλυ-
at present until out of [the] midst he be [gone], and then will be re-
φθήσεται ὁ ἄνομος, ὃν ὁ κύριος [p] [q]ἀναλώσει‖ τῷ
vealed the lawless [one], whom the Lord will consume with the
πνεύματι τοῦ.στόματος.αὐτοῦ, καὶ καταργήσει τῇ ἐπιφανείᾳ
breath of his mouth, and annul by the appearing
τῆς.παρουσίας.αὐτοῦ· 9 οὗ ἐστιν ἡ παρουσία κατ'
of his coming; whose [2]is [1]coming according to [the]
ἐνέργειαν τοῦ σατανᾶ ἐν πάσῃ δυνάμει καὶ σημείοις καὶ τέρασιν
working of Satan in every power and signs and wonders
ψεύδους, 10 καὶ ἐν πάσῃ ἀπάτῃ [r]τῆς‖ ἀδικίας [s]ἐν‖ τοῖς
of falsehood, and in every deceit of unrighteousness in them that
ἀπολλυμένοις, ἀνθ'.ὧν τὴν ἀγάπην τῆς ἀληθείας οὐκ.ἐδέξαντο
perish, because the love of the truth they received not
εἰς τὸ σωθῆναι αὐτούς· 11 καὶ διὰ τοῦτο [t]πέμψει‖
for [2]to [3]be [4]saved [1]them. And on account of this [2]will [3]send
αὐτοῖς ὁ θεὸς ἐνέργειαν πλάνης, εἰς τὸ πιστεῦσαι αὐτοὺς
[4]to [5]them [1]God a working of error, for [2]to [3]believe [1]them
τῷ ψεύδει· 12 ἵνα κριθῶσιν [v]πάντες‖ οἱ μὴ.πιστεύσαντες
what [is] false, that may be judged all who believed not
τῇ ἀληθείᾳ, [w]ἀλλ'‖ εὐδοκήσαντες [x]ἐν‖ τῇ ἀδικίᾳ.
the truth, but delighted in unrighteousness.
13 Ἡμεῖς.δὲ ὀφείλομεν εὐχαριστεῖν τῷ θεῷ πάντοτε περὶ
But we ought to give thanks to God always concerning
ὑμῶν, ἀδελφοὶ ἠγαπημένοι ὑπὸ κυρίου, ὅτι [y]εἵλετο‖ ὑμᾶς
you, brethren beloved by [the] Lord, that [2]chose [3]you
ὁ θεὸς [z]ἀπ' ἀρχῆς‖ εἰς σωτηρίαν ἐν ἁγιασμῷ πνεύματος
[1]God from [the] beginning to salvation in sanctification of [the] Spirit
καὶ πίστει ἀληθείας, 14 εἰς.ὃ [a]ἐκάλεσεν [b]ὑμᾶς‖ διὰ τοῦ
and belief of [the] truth; whereto he called you by
εὐαγγελίου.ἡμῶν, εἰς περιποίησιν δόξης τοῦ κυρίου
our glad tidings, to [the] obtaining of [the] glory of [2]Lord

death from the presence of the Lord and from the glory of His strength –

10 when He shall come to be glorified in His saints and to be admired in all those who believe in that Day – because our report to you was believed.

11 To this end also we always pray for you, that our God may count you worthy of *this* calling and may complete all the good pleasure of His goodness and the work of faith with power,

12 so that the name of our Lord Jesus Christ may be glorified in you, and you in Him, according to the grace of our God and the Lord Jesus Christ.

CHAPTER 2

1 Now we beg you, brothers, by the coming of our Lord Jesus Christ and our gathering together to Him,

2 that you may not be quickly shaken in mind or be troubled, either by spirit or by word or by letter, as if by us, as if the day of Christ is at hand.

3 Let no one deceive you in any way, because that Day *will not come* unless the falling away has come first, and unless the man of sin has been revealed, the son of perdition

4 who sets himself against and lifts himself above all that is called God, or any object of worship – so as for him to sit down as God in the Temple of God, setting himself out to be God.

5 Do you not remember that while I was with you I told you these things?

6 And now you know that which holds back, to the end that he might be revealed in his own time.

7 For the mystery of lawlessness is already working, until he who is now holding back is taken out of the way.

8 And then the Lawless One will be revealed, whom the Lord will destroy with the breath of His mouth and will bring to nothing by the brightness of His coming.

9 *This one's* coming is according to the working Satan with all power and signs and lying wonders,

10 and with all the false acting of unrighteousness in those that are lost – because they did not receive the love of the truth to the end that they might be saved.

11 And for this cause God will send a working of error to them, so that they should believe the lie,

12 so that all those who did not believe the truth, but delighted in unrighteousness, may be judged.

13 But we are bound to give thanks to God always regarding you, brothers, beloved by the Lord, because God has from the beginning chosen you to salvation through sanctification of the Spirit and belief of the truth

14 – to which He called you by our gospel,

ἡμῶν Ἰησοῦ χριστοῦ. 15 ἄρα οὖν, ἀδελφοί, στήκετε, καὶ
[1]our Jesus Christ. So then, brethren, stand firm, and
κρατεῖτε τὰς παραδόσεις ἃς ἐδιδάχθητε, εἴτε διὰ λόγου
hold fast the traditions which ye were taught, whether by word
εἴτε δι' ἐπιστολῆς.ἡμῶν. 16 αὐτὸς.δὲ ὁ κύριος ἡμῶν Ἰησοῦς
or by our epistle. But [5]himself [2]Lord [1]our [3]Jesus
[c] χριστός, καὶ [d]ὁ‖ θεὸς [e]καὶ‖ πατὴρ ἡμῶν, ὁ ἀγαπήσας ἡμᾶς
[4]Christ, and [2]God [3]and [4]Father [1]our, who loved us,
καὶ δοὺς παράκλησιν αἰωνίαν καὶ.ἐλπίδα ἀγαθὴν ἐν χάριτι,
and gave [us] [2]encouragement [1]eternal and [2]hope [1]good by grace,
17 παρακαλέσαι ὑμῶν τὰς καρδίας, καὶ στηρίξαι [f]ὑμᾶς‖
may he encourage your hearts, and may he establish you
ἐν παντὶ [g]λόγῳ καὶ ἔργῳ‖ ἀγαθῷ.
in every [2]word [3]and [4]work [1]good.

3 Τὸ.λοιπόν, προσεύχεσθε, ἀδελφοί, περὶ ἡμῶν, ἵνα ὁ
For the rest, pray, brethren, for us, that the
λόγος τοῦ κυρίου τρέχῃ καὶ δοξάζηται, καθὼς καὶ πρὸς
word of the Lord may run and may be glorified, even as also with
ὑμᾶς, 2 καὶ ἵνα ῥυσθῶμεν ἀπὸ τῶν ἀτόπων καὶ πονηρῶν
you; and that we may be delivered from perverse and wicked
ἀνθρώπων· οὐ.γὰρ πάντων ἡ πίστις. 3 πιστὸς
men, for [3]not [6]of [7]all [[2]is] [1]faith [[4]the [5]portion]. [2]Faithful
δέ ἐστιν [h]ὁ κύριος,‖ ὃς στηρίξει ὑμᾶς καὶ φυλάξει
[1]but is the Lord, who will establish you and will keep [you]
ἀπὸ τοῦ πονηροῦ. 4 πεποίθαμεν.δὲ ἐν κυρίῳ ἐφ' ὑμᾶς,
from evil. But we trust in [the] Lord as to you,
ὅτι ἃ παραγγέλλομεν [i]ὑμῖν,‖ [k] [l]καὶ‖ ποιεῖτε καὶ
that the things which we charge you, both ye are doing and
ποιήσετε. 5 ὁ.δὲ κύριος κατευθύναι ὑμῶν τὰς καρδίας εἰς
will do. But [2]the [3]Lord [1]may direct your hearts into
τὴν ἀγάπην τοῦ θεοῦ, καὶ εἰς [m] ὑπομονὴν τοῦ χριστοῦ.
the love of God, and into [the] endurance of the Christ.
6 Παραγγέλλομεν.δὲ ὑμῖν, ἀδελφοί, ἐν ὀνόματι τοῦ
Now we charge you, brethren, in [the] name
κυρίου.[n]ἡμῶν‖ Ἰησοῦ χριστοῦ, στέλλεσθαι ὑμᾶς ἀπὸ παν-
of our Lord Jesus Christ, [that] [2]withdraw [1]ye from every
τὸς ἀδελφοῦ ἀτάκτως περιπατοῦντος, καὶ μὴ κατὰ τὴν
brother [2]disorderly [1]walking, and not according to the
παράδοσιν ἣν [o]παρέλαβεν‖ παρ' ἡμῶν. 7 αὐτοὶ.γὰρ οἴδατε
tradition which he received from us. For [2]yourselves [1]ye know
πῶς δεῖ μιμεῖσθαι ἡμᾶς· ὅτι οὐκ.ἠτακτήσαμεν
how it behoves [you] to imitate us, because we behaved not disorderly
ἐν ὑμῖν, 8 οὐδὲ δωρεὰν ἄρτον ἐφάγομεν παρά τινος, [p]ἀλλ'‖
among you; nor for nought bread did we eat from anyone; but
ἐν κόπῳ καὶ μόχθῳ, [q]νύκτα καὶ ἡμέραν‖ ἐργαζόμενοι, πρὸς τὸ
in labour and toil, night and day working, for
μὴ ἐπιβαρῆσαί τινα ὑμῶν· 9 οὐχ ὅτι οὐκ.ἔχομεν ἐξουσίαν,
not to be burdensome to anyone of you. Not that we have not authority,
ἀλλ' ἵνα ἑαυτοὺς τύπον δῶμεν ὑμῖν εἰς τὸ μιμεῖσθαι ἡμᾶς.
but that ourselves a pattern we might give to you for to imitate us.
10 καὶ.γὰρ ὅτε ἦμεν πρὸς ὑμᾶς τοῦτο παρηγγέλλομεν ὑμῖν,
For also when we were with you this we charged you,
ὅτι εἴ τις οὐ.θέλει ἐργάζεσθαι, μηδὲ ἐσθιέτω. 11 ἀκούομεν
that if anyone does not wish to work, neither let him eat. [2]We [3]hear
γάρ τινας περιπατοῦντας ἐν ὑμῖν ἀτάκτως, μηδὲν ἐργαζο-
[1]for some are walking among you disorderly, not at all work-
μένους, ἀλλὰ περιεργαζομένους. 12 τοῖς.δὲ.τοιούτοις παραγ-
ing, but being busy bodies. Now such we
γέλλομεν καὶ παρακαλοῦμεν [r]διὰ τοῦ.κυρίου.ἡμῶν Ἰησοῦ
charge and exhort by our Lord Jesus
χριστοῦ,‖ ἵνα μετὰ ἡσυχίας ἐργαζόμενοι, τὸν.ἑαυτῶν ἄρτον
Christ, that with quietness working, their own bread
ἐσθίωσιν. 13 ὑμεῖς.δέ, ἀδελφοι, μὴ.[s]ἐκκακήσητε‖ καλοποιοῦν-
they may eat. But ye, brethren, do not lose heart [in] well-doing.
τες. 14 εἰ.δέ τις οὐχ.ὑπακούει τῷ.λόγῳ.ἡμῶν διὰ τῆς ἐπι-
But if anyone obey not our word by the epis-
στολῆς, τοῦτον σημειοῦσθε [t]καὶ‖ [v]μὴ.συναναμίγνυσθε‖ αὐτῷ,
tle, [2]that [[3]man] [1]mark and associate not with him,
ἵνα ἐντραπῇ· 15 καὶ μὴ ὡς ἐχθρὸν ἡγεῖσθε, ἀλλὰ
that he may be ashamed; and not as an enemy esteem [him], but
νουθετεῖτε ὡς ἀδελφόν. 16 αὐτὸς.δὲ ὁ κύριος τῆς εἰρήνης
admonish [him] as a brother. But [6]himself [2]the [3]Lord [4]of [5]peace
δῴη ὑμῖν τὴν εἰρήνην διὰ.παντὸς ἐν παντὶ [w]τρόπῳ.‖ ὁ
[1]may give you peace continually in every way. The
κύριος μετὰ πάντων ὑμῶν.
Lord [be] with all you.
17 Ὁ ἀσπασμὸς τῇ.ἐμῇ.χειρὶ Παύλου, ὅ ἐστιν σημεῖον
The salutation [3]by [4]my [[5]own] [6]hand [1]of [2]Paul, which is [the] sign
ἐν πάσῃ ἐπιστολῇ· οὕτως γράφω. 18 ἡ χάρις τοῦ.κυρίου.ἡμῶν
in every epistle; so I write. The grace of our Lord
Ἰησοῦ χριστοῦ μετὰ πάντων ὑμῶν. [x]ἀμήν.‖
Jesus Christ [be] with [2]all [1]you. Amen.

to gain the glory of our Lord Jesus Christ.
15 So then, brothers, stand firm and
strongly hold to the teachings which you
were taught, whether by word or by our
letter.
16 But may our Lord Jesus Christ Himself
and our God and Father, who loved us and
has given us everlasting encouragement and
good hope by grace,
17 encourage your hearts. And may He
establish you in every good word and work.

CHAPTER 3

1 For the rest, brothers, pray for us, that
the word of the Lord may run freely and
may be glorified even as it also has with you,
2 and that we may be delivered from perverse and wicked men, for faith is not of all.
3 But the Lord is faithful, who will establish
you and keep you from evil.
4 And we trust in the Lord as to you, that
you are both doing and will do the things
which we command you.
5 And may the Lord direct your hearts into
the love of God, and into the patience of
Christ.
6 Now we command you, brothers, in the
name of our Lord Jesus Christ: Withdraw
from every brother who is walking in an
unruly way, and not according to the
teaching which he received from us.
7 For you yourselves know how it is right
to act like us, because we did not behave in
an unruly way among you.
8 Nor did we eat bread from anyone without charge, but in labor and hardship, night
and day, *we were* working so as not to be a
burden to any one of you.
9 Not that we do not have authority, but so
that we might give ourselves as a pattern to
you in order *for you* to act like us.
10 For even when we were with you we
commanded you this, that if anyone does
not want to work, neither let him eat.
11 For we hear that some are walking in an
unruly way among you, not working at all,
but being busybodies.
12 Now by the Lord Jesus Christ we command and urge these that they *ought to be*
working with quietness, that they may eat
their own bread.
13 But you, brothers, do not lose heart in
doing good.
14 But if anyone does not obey our word
by this letter, note him and do not associate
with him, so that he may be ashamed.
15 But do not count him as an enemy, but
warn him as a brother.
16 And may the Lord of peace give you
peace continually in every way. The Lord be
with you all.
17 The greeting of Paul, by my own hand,
which is the sign in every letter, so I write.
18 The grace of our Lord Jesus Christ be
with all of you. Amen.

[y]Πρὸς Θεσσαλονικεῖς δευτέρα ἐγράφη ἀπὸ Ἀθηνῶν.[ǁ]
[2]To [3the] [4]Thessalonians [1]second written from Athens.

The FIRST Letter to TIMOTHY

ΠΑΥΛΟΣ ἀπόστολος [b]Ἰησοῦ χριστοῦ[ǁ] κατ' ἐπιταγὴν
Paul, apostle of Jesus Christ according to [the] command
θεοῦ σωτῆρος.ἡμῶν, καὶ [c]κυρίου[ǁ] [d]Ἰησοῦ χριστοῦ[ǁ] τῆς
of God our Saviour, and of [the] Lord Jesus Christ
ἐλπίδος.ἡμῶν, 2 Τιμοθέῳ γνησίῳ τέκνῳ ἐν πίστει· χάρις,
our hope, to Timotheus, [my] true child in faith; grace,
ἔλεος, εἰρήνη ἀπὸ θεοῦ πατρὸς.[e]ἡμῶν[ǁ] καὶ χριστοῦ Ἰησοῦ
mercy, peace, from God our Father and Christ Jesus
τοῦ.κυρίου.ἡμῶν.
our Lord.

3 Καθὼς παρεκάλεσά σε προσμεῖναι ἐν Ἐφέσῳ,
Even as I besought thee to remain in Ephesus, [when I was]
πορευόμενος εἰς Μακεδονίαν, ἵνα παραγγείλῃς τισὶν μὴ
going to Macedonia, that thou mightest charge some not
ἑτεροδιδασκαλεῖν, 4 μηδὲ προσέχειν μύθοις καὶ γενεαλογίαις
to teach other doctrines, nor to give heed to fables and [2]genealogies
ἀπεράντοις, αἵτινες [f]ζητήσεις[ǁ] παρέχουσιν μᾶλλον ἢ [g]οἰκονο-
[1]interminable, which [2]questionings [1]bring rather than [2]adminis-
μίαν[ǁ] θεοῦ τὴν ἐν πίστει· 5 τὸ.δὲ τέλος τῆς παραγγελίας
tration [1]God's which [is] in faith. But the end of the charge
ἐστὶν ἀγάπη ἐκ καθαρᾶς καρδίας καὶ συνειδήσεως ἀγαθῆς
is love out of [2]pure [1]a heart and a [2]conscience [1]good
καὶ πίστεως ἀνυποκρίτου· 6 ὧν τινες ἀστοχήσαντες,
and faith unfeigned; from which some, having missed the mark,
ἐξετράπησαν εἰς ματαιολογίαν, 7 θέλοντες εἶναι νομοδιδάσ-
turned aside to vain talking, wishing to be law-teachers,
καλοι, μὴ νοοῦντες μήτε ἃ λέγουσιν, μήτε περὶ τίνων
understanding neither what they say, nor concerning what
διαβεβαιοῦνται. 8 οἴδαμεν.δὲ ὅτι καλὸς ὁ νόμος, ἐάν τις
they strongly affirm. Now we know that good [is] the law, if anyone
αὐτῷ νομίμως [h]χρῆται,[ǁ] 9 εἰδὼς τοῦτο, ὅτι δικαίῳ
[2]it [3]lawfully [1]use, knowing this, that for a righteous [one]
νόμος οὐ.κεῖται, ἀνόμοις.δὲ καὶ ἀνυποτάκτοις, ἀσεβέσιν
law is not enacted, but for lawless and insubordinate [ones], for [the] ungodly
καὶ ἁμαρτωλοῖς, ἀνοσίοις καὶ βεβήλοις, [i]πατραλῴαις[ǁ]
and sinful, for [the] unholy and profane, for smiters of fathers
καὶ [k]μητραλῴαις,[ǁ] ἀνδροφόνοις, 10 πόρνοις, ἀρσενο-
and smiters of mothers; for slayers of man, fornicators, abusers of them-
κοίταις, ἀνδραποδισταῖς, ψεύσταις, ἐπιόρκοις, καὶ εἴ
selves with men, men-stealers, liars, perjurers, and if
τι ἕτερον τῇ ὑγιαινούσῃ διδασκαλίᾳ ἀντίκειται, 11 κατὰ
any [2]thing [1]other to sound teaching is opposed, according to
τὸ εὐαγγέλιον τῆς δόξης τοῦ μακαρίου θεοῦ, ὃ ἐπιστεύ-
the glad tidings of the glory of the blessed God, which [2]was [3]entrusted
θην ἐγώ. 12 [l]καὶ[ǁ] χάριν.ἔχω τῷ ἐνδυναμώσαντί με χριστῷ
[4]with [1]I. And I thank him who strengthened me, Christ
Ἰησοῦ τῷ.κυρίῳ.ἡμῶν, ὅτι πιστόν με ἡγήσατο, θέμενος εἰς
Jesus our Lord, that faithful me he esteemed, appointing [me] to
διακονίαν, 13 [m]τὸν[ǁ] πρότερον ὄντα [n] βλάσφημον καὶ διώκτην
service, [2]previously [1]being a blasphemer and persecutor
καὶ ὑβριστήν· [o]ἀλλ'[ǁ] ἠλεήθην, ὅτι ἀγνοῶν ἐποίησα
and insolent; but I was shewn mercy, because being ignorant I did
ἐν ἀπιστίᾳ· 14 ὑπερεπλεόνασεν.δὲ ἡ χάρις τοῦ.κυρίου.ἡμῶν
[it] in unbelief. But superabounded the grace of our Lord
μετὰ πίστεως καὶ ἀγάπης τῆς ἐν χριστῷ Ἰησοῦ. 15 πιστὸς
with faith and love which [is] in Christ Jesus. Faithful
ὁ λόγος καὶ πάσης ἀποδοχῆς ἄξιος, ὅτι χριστὸς Ἰησοῦς
[is] the word, and of all acceptation worthy, that Christ Jesus
ἦλθεν εἰς τὸν κόσμον ἁμαρτωλοὺς σῶσαι, ὧν πρῶτός
came into the world sinners to save, of whom [the] first
εἰμι ἐγώ. 16 ἀλλὰ διὰ.τοῦτο ἠλεήθην, ἵνα ἐν ἐμοὶ
[2]am [1]I. But for this reason I was shewn mercy, that in me, [the]
πρώτῳ ἐνδείξηται [p]Ἰησοῦς χριστὸς[ǁ] τὴν [q]πᾶσαν[ǁ] μακρο-
first, [3]might [4]shew [5]forth [1]Jesus [2]Christ the whole long-
θυμίαν, πρὸς ὑποτύπωσιν τῶν μελλόντων πιστεύειν ἐπ'
suffering, for a delineation of those being about to believe on
αὐτῷ εἰς ζωὴν αἰώνιον. 17 τῷ.δὲ βασιλεῖ τῶν αἰώνων,
him to life eternal. Now to the King of the ages, [the]
ἀφθάρτῳ, ἀοράτῳ, μόνῳ [r]σοφῷ[ǁ] θεῷ, τιμὴ καὶ δόξα εἰς τοὺς
incorruptible, invisible, only wise God, honour and glory to the
αἰῶνας τῶν αἰώνων. ἀμήν. 18 ταύτην τὴν παραγγελίαν
ages of the ages. Amen. This charge

CHAPTER 1

1 Paul, an apostle of Jesus Christ, according
to the command of God our Savior and of
the Lord Jesus Christ, our Hope,
2 to Timothy, *my* true child in the faith.
Grace, mercy and peace from God our
Father and Christ Jesus our Lord.
3 Even as I asked you to remain in Ephesus
when I was going into Mac-e-do-ni-a, so that
you might charge some to teach no other
doctrines,
4 nor to listen to fables and endless genealogies (which bring doubts rather than God's
administration, which is in faith).
5 Now the end of the commandment is love
out of a pure heart and a good conscience
and an unpretended faith.
6 From which some having missed the mark
have turned aside to empty talking,
7 desiring to be teachers of the Law, understanding neither what they say nor about *the
things* they strongly affirm.
8 Now we know that the Law is good if a
man use it lawfully,
9 knowing this that the law is not made for
a righteous man, but for the lawless and
unruly – for the ungodly and sinful – for
the unholy and profane – for those who
strike fathers and mothers – for murderers,
10 prostitutes, abusers of themselves with
men, men-stealers, liars, perjurers, and anything else which is against sound doctrine,
11 according to the gospel of the glory of
the blessed God, with which I was entrusted.
12 And I thank Christ Jesus our Lord, who
strengthened me, because He counted me
faithful, putting me into the ministry,
13 who before was a blasphemer and a
persecutor and proud, but I was shown
mercy, because being ignorant I did it in
unbelief.
14 But the grace of our Lord abounded
exceedingly with faith and love, which is in
Christ Jesus.
15 This is a faithful saying and worthy of all
acceptance, that Christ Jesus came into the
world to save sinners, of whom I am chief.
16 But for this reason I was shown mercy,
that in me, the chief *of sinners,* Jesus Christ
might show forth His entire long-suffering,
as an example to those who are going to
believe on Him to life everlasting.
17 Now to the King eternal, invisible,
immortal, the only wise God, be honor and
glory forever and ever. Amen.
18 This charge I commit to you, my son

παρατίθεμαί σοι, τέκνον Τιμόθεε, κατὰ τὰς προ-
I commit to thee, [my] child Timotheus, according to the [2]going
αγούσας ἐπὶ σε προφητείας, ἵνα [s]στρατεύῃ ἐν αὐταῖς τὴν
[3]before [2]as [3]to [4]thee [1]prophecies, that thou mightest war by them the
καλὴν στρατείαν, 19 ἔχων πίστιν καὶ ἀγαθὴν συνείδησιν,
good warfare, holding faith and [2]good [1]a conscience;
ἥν τινες ἀπωσάμενοι, περὶ τὴν πίστιν ἐναυάγησαν·
which [conscience] some, having cast away, as to faith made shipwreck;
20 ὧν ἐστιν Ὑμέναιος καὶ Ἀλέξανδρος, οὓς παρέδωκα τῷ
of whom are Hymenæus and Alexander, whom I delivered up
σατανᾷ, ἵνα παιδευθῶσιν μὴ βλασφημεῖν.
to Satan, that they may be disciplined not to blaspheme.

2 Παρακαλῶ οὖν πρῶτον πάντων ποιεῖσθαι δεήσεις,
I exhort therefore, first of all, to be made supplications,
προσευχάς, ἐντεύξεις, εὐχαριστίας, ὑπὲρ πάντων ἀνθρώ-
prayers, intercessions, thanksgivings, for all men;
πων, 2 ὑπὲρ βασιλέων καὶ πάντων τῶν ἐν ὑπεροχῇ ὄντων,
for kings and all that in dignity are,
ἵνα ἤρεμον καὶ ἡσύχιον βίον διάγωμεν ἐν πάσῃ εὐσεβείᾳ καὶ
that a tranquil and quiet life we may lead in all piety and
σεμνότητι· 3 τοῦτο γὰρ καλὸν καὶ ἀποδεκτὸν ἐνώπιον τοῦ
gravity; for this [is] good and acceptable before
σωτῆρος ἡμῶν θεοῦ, 4 ὃς πάντας ἀνθρώπους θέλει σωθῆναι
our Saviour God, who [2]all [3]men [1]wishes to be saved
καὶ εἰς ἐπίγνωσιν ἀληθείας ἐλθεῖν. 5 εἷς γὰρ θεός, εἷς καὶ
and to [4]knowledge [5]of [[6]the] [7]truth [1]to [2]come. For [3]one God [[2]is], and one
μεσίτης θεοῦ καὶ ἀνθρώπων, ἄνθρωπος χριστὸς Ἰη-
[the] mediator of God and men, [the] man Christ Je-
σοῦς, 6 ὁ δοὺς ἑαυτὸν ἀντίλυτρον ὑπὲρ πάντων, [v]τὸ μαρ-
sus, who gave himself a ransom for all, the tes-
τύριον καιροῖς ἰδίοις, 7 εἰς ὃ ἐτέθην ἐγὼ
timony [to be rendered] in [3]times [1]its [2]own, to which [2]was [3]appointed [1]I
κῆρυξ καὶ ἀπόστολος· ἀλήθειαν λέγω [w]ἐν χριστῷ, οὐ
a herald and apostle, ([the] truth I speak in Christ, [3]not
ψεύδομαι· διδάσκαλος ἐθνῶν, ἐν πίστει καὶ ἀληθείᾳ.
[1]I [2]do lie,) a teacher of [the] nations, in faith and truth.
8 Βούλομαι οὖν προσεύχεσθαι τοὺς ἄνδρας ἐν παντὶ τόπῳ,
I will therefore [3]to [4]pray [1]the [2]men in every place,
ἐπαίροντας ὁσίους χεῖρας χωρὶς ὀργῆς καὶ διαλογισμοῦ·
lifting up holy hands apart from wrath and reasoning.
9 ὡσαύτως [x]καὶ [y]τὰς γυναῖκας ἐν καταστολῇ κοσμίῳ μετὰ
In like manner also the women in [2]guise [1]seemly with
αἰδοῦς καὶ σωφροσύνης κοσμεῖν ἑαυτάς, μὴ ἐν πλέγμασιν,
modesty and discreetness to adorn themselves, not with plaitings,
[z]ἢ [a]χρυσῷ, ἢ μαργαρίταις, ἢ ἱματισμῷ πολυτελεῖ, 10 [b]ἀλλ'
or gold, or pearls, or [2]clothing [1]costly, but
ὃ πρέπει γυναιξὶν ἐπαγγελλομέναις θεοσέβειαν, δι'
what is becoming to women professing [the] fear of God, by
ἔργων ἀγαθῶν. 11 Γυνὴ ἐν ἡσυχίᾳ μανθανέτω ἐν πάσῃ
[2]works [1]good. [4]A [5]woman [7]in [8]quietness [1]let [6]learn in all
ὑποταγῇ· 12 [c]γυναικὶ δὲ διδάσκειν οὐκ ἐπιτρέπω, οὐδὲ αὐ-
subjection; but a woman to teach I do not allow, nor to exercise
θεντεῖν ἀνδρός, [d]ἀλλ' εἶναι ἐν ἡσυχίᾳ. 13 Ἀδὰμ γὰρ
authority over man, but to be in quietness; for Adam
πρῶτος ἐπλάσθη, εἶτα Εὕα. 14 καὶ Ἀδὰμ οὐκ ἠπατήθη· ἡ δὲ
first was formed, then Eve: and Adam was not deceived; but the
γυνὴ [e]ἀπατηθεῖσα ἐν παραβάσει γέγονεν· 15 σωθήσεται δὲ
woman, having been deceived, in transgression has become. But she shall be saved
διὰ τῆς τεκνογονίας, ἐὰν μείνωσιν ἐν πίστει καὶ ἀγάπῃ
through the childbearing, if they abide in faith and love
καὶ ἁγιασμῷ μετὰ σωφροσύνης.
and sanctification with discreetness.

3 Πιστὸς ὁ λόγος· εἴ τις ἐπισκοπῆς ὀρέγεται,
Faithful [is] the word: if any [4]overseership [1]stretches [2]forward [3]to
καλοῦ ἔργου ἐπιθυμεῖ. 2 δεῖ οὖν τὸν ἐπίσκοπον [f]ἀνεπί-
of [2]good [1]a work he is desirous. It behoves then the overseer irreproach-
ληπτον εἶναι, μιᾶς γυναικὸς ἄνδρα, [g]νηφάλεον, σώφρονα,
able to be, [2]of [3]one [4]wife [1]husband, sober, discreet,
κόσμιον, φιλόξενον, διδακτικόν· 3 μὴ πάροινον, μὴ πλήκτην,
decorous, hospitable, apt to teach; not given to wine, not a striker,
[h]μὴ αἰσχροκερδῆ, [i]ἀλλ' ἐπιεικῆ, ἄμαχον, ἀφιλάργυρον·
not greedy of base gain, but gentle, not contentious, not loving money;
4 τοῦ ἰδίου οἴκου καλῶς προϊστάμενον, τέκνα ἔχοντα ἐν
his own house well ruling, [his] children having in
ὑποταγῇ μετὰ πάσης σεμνότητος· 5 εἰ δέ τις τοῦ ἰδίου οἴκου
subjection with all gravity; (but if one his own house
προστῆναι οὐκ οἶδεν, πῶς ἐκκλησίας θεοῦ ἐπιμελήσεται;
[how] to rule knows not, how [the] assembly of God shall he take care of?)
6 μὴ νεόφυτον, ἵνα μὴ τυφωθεὶς εἰς κρίμα ἐμπέσῃ
not a novice, lest being puffed up, into [the] crime [4]he [5]may [6]fall
τοῦ διαβόλου. 7 δεῖ δὲ [k]αὐτὸν καὶ μαρτυρίαν καλὴν
[1]of [2]the [3]devil. But it behoves [1]him also a [2]testimony [1]good

Timothy, according to the prophecies going
before as to you, in order that you might
war a good warfare by them,
19 holding faith and a good conscience,
which some have put away, making shipwreck as to faith,
20 of whom are Hy-me-ne-us and Alexander
– whom I have delivered to Satan, that they
may learn not to blaspheme.

2 1 First of all, then, I advise you that
petitions, prayers, holy requests and thanksgivings be made for all men,
2 for kings and all that are in high places –
that we may lead a peaceable and quiet life
in all godliness and honor.
3 For this is good and pleasing in the sight
of God our Savior,
4 who will have all men saved and to come
to the knowledge of the truth.
5 For *there is* one God and one Mediator
between God and men, the man Christ Jesus,
6 who gave Himself a ransom for all, the
witness *to be given* in due time –
7 to which I was ordained a herald and
apostle (I speak the truth in Christ and do
not lie), a teacher of the Gentiles, in faith
and truth.
8 Then I desire that the men pray in every
place, lifting up holy hands, without anger
and doubting.
9 In the same way, also, that the women
dress themselves in decent clothes, with
modesty and sensibleness – not with braided
hair, nor gold, nor pearls, nor expensive
clothing.
10 But as is becoming to women who
profess godliness, *let them beautify themselves* by good works.
11 Let a woman learn in silence, in all
subjection.
12 But I do not allow a woman to teach, or
to exercise authority over man – but to be
in silence.
13 For Adam was formed first, then Eve.
14 And Adam was not deceived, but the
woman, being fully deceived, has come to be
in transgression.
15 But she shall be saved through the
bearing of children, if they continue in faith
and love and holiness, with being sensible.

3 1 This is a true saying: If anyone wants to
be a bishop, he desires a good work.
2 A bishop, then, must be blameless, the
husband of one wife, temperate, discreet,
modest, hospitable, skilled in teaching,
3 not given to wine, not quarrelsome, not
greedy of ill profit, but considerate, not full
of strife, not loving money.
4 *He must* rule his own house well, having
his children in obedience, with all honor.
5 (Now if a man does not know how to rule
his own house, how shall he take care of the
church of God)?
6 *He must* not be a new convert, for fear

ἔχειν ἀπὸ τῶν ἔξωθεν, ἵνα.μὴ εἰς ὀνειδισμὸν ἐμπέσῃ καὶ
to have from those without, lest into reproach he may fall and [the]
παγίδα τοῦ διαβόλου. 8 Διακόνους ὡσαύτως σεμνούς, μὴ
snare of the devil. Those who serve, in like manner, grave, not
διλόγους, μὴ οἴνῳ πολλῷ προσέχοντας, μὴ αἰσχροκερδεῖς,
double-tongued, not to [2]wine [1]much given, not greedy of base gain,
9 ἔχοντας τὸ μυστήριον τῆς πίστεως ἐν καθαρᾷ συνειδήσει.
holding the mystery of the faith in [2]pure [1]a conscience.
10 καὶ.οὗτοι.δὲ δοκιμαζέσθωσαν πρῶτον, εἶτα διακονείτωσαν,
And these also let them be proved first, then let them serve,
ἀνέγκλητοι ὄντες. 11 γυναῖκας ὡσαύτως σεμνάς, μὴ δια-
[2]unimpeachable [1]being. Women in like manner grave, not slan-
βόλους, [l]νηφαλέους,‖ πιστὰς ἐν πᾶσιν. 12 διάκονοι ἔστω-
derers, sober, faithful in all things. [2]Those [3]who [4]serve [1]let
σαν μιᾶς γυναικὸς ἄνδρες, τέκνων καλῶς προϊστάμενοι
[5]be [7]of [8]one [9]wife [6]husbands, [[12]their] [13]children [11]well [10]ruling
καὶ τῶν.ἰδίων οἴκων. 13 οἱ.γὰρ καλῶς διακονήσαντες, βαθμὸν
and their own houses. For those well having served, a [2]degree
ἑαυτοῖς καλὸν περιποιοῦνται, καὶ πολλὴν παρρησίαν ἐν
[3]for [4]themselves [1]good acquire, and much boldness in
πίστει τῇ ἐν χριστῷ Ἰησοῦ.
faith which [is] in Christ Jesus.
14 Ταῦτά σοι γράφω, ἐλπίζων ἐλθεῖν πρός σε [m]τάχιον·‖
These things to thee I write, hoping to come to thee more quickly;
15 ἐὰν.δὲ βραδύνω, ἵνα εἰδῇς πῶς δεῖ ἐν
but if I should delay, that thou mayest know how it behoves [one] in [the]
οἴκῳ θεοῦ ἀναστρέφεσθαι, ἥτις ἐστὶν ἐκκλησία θεοῦ
house of God to conduct oneself, which is [the] assembly of [3]God [[1]the]
ζῶντος, στῦλος καὶ ἑδραίωμα τῆς ἀληθείας. 16 καὶ ὁμολο-
[2]living, pillar and base of the truth. And confes-
γουμένως μέγα ἐστὶν τὸ τῆς εὐσεβείας μυστήριον· [n]θεὸς‖
sedly great is the [2]of [3]piety [1]mystery: God
ἐφανερώθη ἐν σαρκί, ἐδικαιώθη ἐν πνεύματι, ὤφθη ἀγ-
was manifested in flesh, was justified in [the] Spirit, was seen by
γέλοις, ἐκηρύχθη ἐν ἔθνεσιν, ἐπιστεύθη ἐν κόσμῳ,
angels, was proclaimed among [the] nations, was believed on in [the] world,
[o]ἀνελήφθη‖ ἐν δόξῃ.
was received up in glory.

4 Τὸ.δὲ πνεῦμα ῥητῶς λέγει, ὅτι ἐν ὑστέροις καιροῖς ἀπο-
But the Spirit expressly speaks, that in latter times [3]shall
στήσονταί τινες τῆς πίστεως, προσέχοντες πνεύμασιν πλάνοις
[2]depart [4]from [1]some the faith, giving heed to [2]spirits [1]deceiving
καὶ διδασκαλίαις δαιμονίων 2 ἐν ὑποκρίσει ψευδολόγων,
and teachings of demons in hypocrisy of speakers of lies,
[p]κεκαυτηριασμένων‖ τὴν.ἰδίαν συνείδησιν, 3 κωλυόντων
being cauterized [as to] their own conscience, forbidding
γαμεῖν, ἀπέχεσθαι βρωμάτων, ἃ ὁ θεὸς ἔκτισεν εἰς
to marry, [bidding] to abstain from meats, which God created for
[q]μετάληψιν‖ μετὰ εὐχαριστίας τοῖς πιστοῖς καὶ ἐπεγνωκόσιν
reception with thanksgiving for the faithful and who know
τὴν ἀλήθειαν. 4 ὅτι πᾶν κτίσμα θεοῦ καλόν, καὶ οὐδὲν
the truth. Because every creature of God [is] good, and nothing
ἀπόβλητον, μετὰ εὐχαριστίας λαμβανόμενον· 5 ἁγιάζεται
to be rejected, with thanksgiving being received; [2]it [3]is [4]sanctified
γὰρ διὰ λόγου θεοῦ καὶ ἐντεύξεως. 6 Ταῦτα ὑποτι-
[1]for by [2]word [1]God's and intercourse [with him]. These things laying
θέμενος τοῖς ἀδελφοῖς, καλὸς ἔσῃ διάκονος [r]Ἰησοῦ
before the brethren, [2]good [4]thou [5]wilt [6]be [1]a [3]servant of Jesus
χριστοῦ,‖ ἐντρεφόμενος τοῖς λόγοις τῆς πίστεως, καὶ τῆς
Christ, being nourished with the words of the faith, and of the
καλῆς διδασκαλίας ᾗ παρηκολούθηκας. 7 Τοὺς.δὲ βεβήλους
good teaching which thou hast closely followed. But the profane
καὶ .γραώδεις μύθους παραιτοῦ· γύμναζε.δὲ σεαυτὸν πρὸς
and old wives' fables refuse, but exercise thyself to
εὐσέβειαν· 8 ἡ.γὰρ.σωματικὴ γυμνασία πρὸς ὀλίγον ἐστὶν
piety; for bodily exercise for a little is
ὠφέλιμος· ἡ.δὲ.εὐσέβεια πρὸς πάντα ὠφέλιμός ἐστιν, ἐπαγγε-
profitable, but piety for everything [2]profitable [1]is, pro-
λίαν ἔχουσα ζωῆς τῆς .νῦν καὶ τῆς μελλούσης.
mise having of life, of that which [is] now and of that which [is] coming.
9 πιστὸς ὁ λόγος καὶ πάσης ἀποδοχῆς ἄξιος. 10 εἰς.τοῦτο.γὰρ
Faithful [is] the word and of all acceptation worthy; for, for this
[s]καὶ‖ κοπιῶμεν καὶ [t]ὀνειδιζόμεθα,‖ ὅτι ἠλπίκαμεν ἐπὶ θεῷ
both we labour and are reproached, because we have hope in a [2]God
ζῶντι, ὅς ἐστιν σωτὴρ πάντων ἀνθρώπων, μάλιστα πιστῶν.
[1]living, who is Preserver of all men, specially of believers.
11 Παράγγελλε ταῦτα καὶ δίδασκε. 12 μηδείς σου τῆς
Charge these things and teach. [2]No [3]one [5]thy
νεότητος καταφρονείτω, ἀλλὰ τύπος γίνου τῶν πιστῶν ἐν
[6]youth [1]let [4]despise, but a pattern be of the believers in
λόγῳ, ἐν ἀναστροφῇ, ἐν ἀγάπῃ, [v]ἐν πνεύματι,‖ ἐν πίστει,
word, in conduct, in love, in [the] Spirit, in faith,

that being puffed up with pride he may fall into the crime of the devil.

7 And he ought to have a good report from those on the outside, so that he may not fall into shame and the snare of the devil.

8 In the same way the deacons *must be* honorable, not double-tongued, not given to much wine, not greedy of ill profit,

9 holding the mystery of the faith in a pure conscience.

10 And let these also be tested first, then let them serve, being blameless.

11 In the same way let *their* women be honorable, not given to slander, temperate, faithful in all things.

12 Let the deacons be husband of one wife, ruling their children and their own houses well.

13 For the ones who have served well get for themselves a good portion and great boldness in the faith which is in Christ Jesus.

14 I write these things to you, hoping to come to you more quickly.

15 But if I should delay long, *I write to you* so that you know how you ought to behave yourself in the house of God, which is the church of the living God, the support and foundation of the truth.

16 And without doubt, great is the mystery of godliness – God was manifest in flesh, was justified in the Spirit, was seen by angels, was preached among the Gentiles, was believed on in the world and was received up in glory.

4 1 The Spirit plainly says that in the latter times some shall depart from the faith, turning to spirits that lead astray and teachings of demons,

2 and of men who speak lies in hypocrisy, their conscience being seared,

3 forbidding men to marry, not to eat meats which God created to be received with gratitude by those who believe and know the truth.

4 For everything created by God is good. And nothing is to be refused, but to be received with thanksgiving.

5 For it is made holy by the word of God and by prayer.

6 By laying these things before the brothers, you will be a good servant of Jesus Christ, being fed with the words of the faith and of the good teaching which you have followed.

7 But refuse the profane and the old wives' tales. And exercise yourself to godliness.

8 For exercise of the body is of a little profit, but godliness is of profit for everything, having a promise of life – that which is now and that which is to come.

9 This is a faithful saying and worthy of all belief.

10 For it is for this that we both labor and suffer shame, because we have hope in the living God, who is the Preserver of all men, especially of believers.

ἐν ἁγνείᾳ. 13 ἕως ἔρχομαι, πρόσεχε τῇ ἀναγνώσει, τῇ παρα-
in purity. Till I come, give heed to reading, to exhor-
κλήσει, τῇ διδασκαλίᾳ. 14 μὴ.ἀμέλει τοῦ ἐν σοὶ χαρίσματος,
tation, to teaching. Be not negligent of the [2]in [3]thee [1]gift,
ὃ ἐδόθη σοι διὰ προφητείας μετὰ ἐπιθέσεως τῶν χει-
which was given to thee through prophecy with laying on of the hands
ρῶν τοῦ πρεσβυτερίου. 15 ταῦτα μελέτα, ἐν τούτοις ἴσθι·
of the elderhood. These things meditate on, in them be,
ἵνα σου ἡ.προκοπὴ φανερὰ ᾖ [w]ἐν[‖] πᾶσιν. 16 ἔπεχε
that thy advancement manifest may be among all. Give heed
σεαυτῷ καὶ τῇ διδασκαλίᾳ· ἐπίμενε αὐτοῖς· τοῦτο.γὰρ
to thyself and to the teaching; continue in them; for this
ποιῶν, καὶ σεαυτὸν σώσεις καὶ τοὺς ἀκούοντάς σου.
doing, both thyself thou shalt save and those that hear thee.

5 Πρεσβυτέρῳ μὴ.ἐπιπλήξῃς, ἀλλὰ παρακάλει ὡς
An elder do not sharply rebuke, but exhort [him] as
πατέρα· νεωτέρους ὡς ἀδελφούς· 2 πρεσβυτέρας ὡς
a father; younger [men] as brethren; elder [women] as
μητέρας· νεωτέρας ὡς ἀδελφάς, ἐν πάσῃ ἁγνείᾳ. 3 χήρας
mothers; younger as sisters, with all purity. [2]Widows
τίμα τὰς ὄντως χήρας. 4 εἰ.δέ τις χήρα τέκνα ἢ ἔκγονα
[1]honour that [are] [2]indeed [1]widows; but if any widow [2]children [3]or [4]descendants
ἔχει, μανθανέτωσαν πρῶτον τὸν.ἴδιον οἶκον εὐσεβεῖν, καὶ
[1]have, let them learn first [as to] their own house to be pious, and
ἀμοιβὰς ἀποδιδόναι τοῖς.προγόνοις· τοῦτο.γάρ ἐστιν [x]καλὸν
[3]recompense [1]to [2]render to [their] parents; for this is good
καὶ[‖] ἀπόδεκτον ἐνώπιον τοῦ θεοῦ. 5 ἡ.δὲ ὄντως χήρα
and acceptable before God. Now she who [is] [3]indeed [1]a [2]widow,
καὶ μεμονωμένη ἤλπικεν ἐπὶ [y]τὸν[‖] θεόν, καὶ προσμένει ταῖς
and left alone, has [her] hope in God, and continues
δεήσεσιν καὶ ταῖς προσευχαῖς νυκτὸς καὶ ἡμέρας· 6 ἡ.δὲ
in supplications and prayers night and day. But she that
σπαταλῶσα, ζῶσα τέθνηκεν. 7 καὶ ταῦτα παράγγελλε,
lives in self-gratification, living is dead. And these things charge,
ἵνα [z]ἀνεπίληπτοι[‖] ὦσιν. 8 εἰ.δέ τις τῶν.ἰδίων καὶ μάλιστα
that irreproachable they may be. But if anyone his own and specially
[a]τῶν[‖] οἰκείων οὐ.[b]προνοεῖ,[‖] τὴν πίστιν ἤρνηται, καὶ
[his] household does not provide for, the faith he has denied, and
ἔστιν ἀπίστου χείρων. 9 Χήρα καταλεγέσθω μὴ
is [2]than [3]an [4]unbeliever [1]worse. [6]A [7]widow [5]let be put on the list [2]not
ἔλαττον ἐτῶν ἑξήκοντα γεγονυῖα, ἑνὸς ἀνδρὸς γυνή, 10 ἐν
[3]less [4]than [6]years [5]sixty [1]being, of one man wife, in
ἔργοις καλοῖς μαρτυρουμένη, εἰ ἐτεκνοτρόφησεν, εἰ ἐξενο-
[2]works [1]good being borne witness to, if she brought up children, if she enter-
δόχησεν, εἰ ἁγίων πόδας ἔνιψεν, εἰ θλιβομένοις ἐπήρ-
tained strangers, if saints' feet she washed, if to the oppressed she impart-
κεσεν, εἰ παντὶ ἔργῳ ἀγαθῷ ἐπηκολούθησεν. 11 Νεωτέρας.δὲ
ed relief, if every [2]work [1]good she followed after. But younger
χήρας παραιτοῦ· ὅταν.γὰρ [c]καταστρηνιάσωσιν[‖] τοῦ
widows refuse; for when they may have grown wanton against
χριστοῦ, γαμεῖν θέλουσιν, 12 ἔχουσαι κρίμα ὅτι τὴν
Christ, to marry they wish, having judgment because [their]
πρώτην πίστιν ἠθέτησαν. 13 ἅμα.δὲ καὶ ἀργαὶ μανθά-
first faith they cast off. And withal also [to be] idle they
νουσιν, περιερχόμεναι τὰς οἰκίας· οὐ.μόνον.δὲ ἀργαί, ἀλλὰ
learn, going about to the houses; and not only idle, but
καὶ φλύαροι καὶ περίεργοι, λαλοῦσαι τὰ μὴ.δέοντα. 14 βού-
also tattlers and busy-bodies, speaking things [they] ought not. I
λομαι οὖν νεωτέρας γαμεῖν, τεκνογονεῖν, οἰκοδεσποτεῖν,
will therefore younger [ones] to marry, to bear children, to rule the house,
μηδεμίαν ἀφορμὴν διδόναι τῷ ἀντικειμένῳ λοιδορίας χάριν.
[3]no [4]occasion [1]to [2]give to the adversary [3]of [4]reproach [1]on [2]account.
15 ἤδη.γάρ τινες ἐξετράπησαν ὀπίσω τοῦ σατανᾶ. 16 Εἴ τις
For already some are turned aside after Satan. If any
[d]πιστὸς ἢ[‖] πιστὴ ἔχει χήρας, [e]ἐπαρκείτω[‖] αὐ-
believing [man] or believing [woman] have widows, let him impart relief to
ταῖς, καὶ μὴ βαρείσθω ἡ ἐκκλησία, ἵνα ταῖς ὄντως χήραις
them, and not let be burdened the assembly, that to the [2]indeed [1]widows
ἐπαρκέσῃ.
it may impart relief.

17 Οἱ καλῶς προεστῶτες πρεσβύτεροι διπλῆς τιμῆς
The [6]well [2]who [3]take [4]the [5]lead [1]elders of double honour
ἀξιούσθωσαν, μάλιστα οἱ κοπιῶντες ἐν λόγῳ καὶ διδασ-
let be counted worthy, specially those labouring in word and teach-
καλίᾳ. 18 λέγει.γὰρ ἡ γραφή, [f]Βοῦν ἀλοῶντα οὐ φι-
ing; for says the scripture, An ox treading out corn [3]not [1]thou
μώσεις·[‖] καί, Ἄξιος ὁ ἐργάτης τοῦ.μισθοῦ.αὐτοῦ. 19 Κατὰ
[2]shalt muzzle, and, Worthy [is] the workman of his hire. Against
πρεσβυτέρου κατηγορίαν μὴ.παραδέχου, ἐκτὸς εἰ.μὴ ἐπὶ
an elder an accusation receive not, unless on [the testi-
δύο ἢ τριῶν μαρτύρων. 20 Τοὺς [g]ἁμαρτάνοντας ἐνώπιον
mony of] two or three witnesses. Those that sin [2]before

11 Command and teach these things.
12 Let no one despise your youth, but be
an example of the believers in word, in
conduct, in love, in spirit, in faith and in
purity.
13 Until I come, pay attention to reading,
to comforting and to teaching.
14 Do not neglect the gift in you, which
was given to you through prophecy, with the
laying on of the hands of the body of elders.
15 Think on these things. Be wholly in
them that your progress may be plain to all.
16 Pay close attention to yourself and to
the teaching. Continue in them, for in doing
this you shall both save yourself and those
who hear you.
5 1 Do not sharply rebuke an elder. But call
on him as a father and the younger *men* as
brothers;
2 the elder *women* as mothers and the
younger *women* as sisters, in all purity.
3 Honor widows who are widows indeed.
4 But if any widow has children or grand-
children, let them learn first to be godly as
to their own house and to give a return to
their parents, for this is good and pleasing in
the sight of God.
5 Now she who is a widow indeed and left
alone trusts in God. And *she* continues in
petitions and prayers night and day.
6 But she who lives in the pleasing of herself
is dead, *though* living.
7 And command these things so that they
may be without blame.
8 But if anyone does not provide for his
own, especially for *his own* household, he
has denied the faith and is worse than an
unbeliever.
9 Let a widow be put on the list at not less
than sixty years of age, the wife of one man,
10 well reported of for good works – if she
has brought up children, if she has treated
strangers hospitably, if she has washed the
feet of the saints, if she has given relief to
those in trouble, if she has followed after
every good work.
11 But refuse younger widows. For when
they have grown lustful against Christ, they
desire to marry,
12 being guilty, because they threw off
their first faith.
13 And with it all they also learn *to be* idle,
going about to the houses. And not only
idle, but also tattlers and busybodies, saying
things they ought not to say.
14 Then, I want the younger ones to marry,
to bear children, to guide the house, but to
give no occasion to the adversary because of
evil-speaking.
15 For some have already turned aside after
Satan.
16 If any believing man or believing woman
may have widows, let him give relief to them
– and do not let the church be burdened, so
that it may give relief to those who are

πάντων ἔλεγχε, ἵνα καὶ οἱ λοιποὶ φόβον ἔχωσιν. 21 Διαμαρ-
³all ¹convict, that also the rest ²fear ¹may ²have. I earnestly
τύρομαι ἐνώπιον τοῦ θεοῦ καὶ [h]κυρίου Ἰησοῦ χριστοῦ[i] καὶ
testify before God and [the] Lord Jesus Christ and
τῶν ἐκλεκτῶν ἀγγέλων, ἵνα ταῦτα φυλάξῃς χωρὶς
the elect angels, that these things thou shouldest keep, apart from
προκρίματος, μηδὲν ποιῶν κατὰ [i]πρόσκλισιν.[i]
prejudice, nothing doing by partiality.

22 Χεῖρας ταχέως μηδενὶ ἐπιτίθει, μηδὲ κοινώνει ἁμαρτίαις
Hands quickly on no one lay, nor share in sins
ἀλλοτρίαις· σεαυτὸν ἁγνὸν τήρει. 23 μηκέτι ὑδροπότει, [k]ἀλλ'[j]
of others. Thyself pure keep. No longer drink water, but
οἴνῳ ὀλίγῳ χρῶ διὰ τὸν.στόμαχόν.[l]σου καὶ τὰς πυκνάς
⁴wine ²a ³little ¹use on account of thy stomach and ²frequent
σου ἀσθενείας. 24 Τινῶν ἀνθρώπων αἱ ἁμαρτίαι πρόδηλοί
¹thy infirmities. Of some men the sins manifest
εἰσιν, προάγουσαι εἰς κρίσιν· τισὶν.δὲ καὶ ἐπακολουθοῦσιν.
are, going before to judgment; and some also they follow after.
25 ὡσαύτως [m]καὶ τὰ [n]καλὰ ἔργα[l] πρόδηλά [o]ἐστιν·[ll] καὶ τὰ
In like manner also good works manifest are, and those that
ἄλλως ἔχοντα, κρυβῆναι οὐ.[p]δύναται.[ll]
otherwise are, ²be ³hid ¹cannot.

6 Ὅσοι εἰσὶν ὑπὸ ζυγὸν δοῦλοι, τοὺς ἰδίους δεσπότας
As many ²as ³are ⁴under ⁵yoke ¹bondmen, their own masters
πάσης τιμῆς ἀξίους ἡγείσθωσαν, ἵνα μὴ τὸ ὄνομα τοῦ θεοῦ
of all honour worthy let them esteem, that not the name of God
καὶ ἡ διδασκαλία βλασφημῆται. 2 οἱ.δὲ πιστοὺς ἔχοντες
and the teaching be blasphemed. And they that ²believing ¹have
δεσπότας, μὴ.καταφρονείτωσαν, ὅτι ἀδελφοί εἰσιν· ἀλλὰ
masters, let them not despise [them], because brethren they are; but
μᾶλλον δουλευέτωσαν, ὅτι πιστοί εἰσιν καὶ ἀγα-
rather let them serve [them], because believing [ones] they are and be-
πητοὶ οἱ τῆς εὐεργεσίας ἀντιλαμβανόμενοι. ταῦτα δίδασκε
loved who ⁵the ⁶good ⁷service ¹are ²being ³helped ⁴by. These things teach
καὶ παρακάλει. 3 Εἴ τις ἑτεροδιδασκαλεῖ, καὶ [q]μὴ.προσέρχεται[ll]
and exhort. If anyone teaches other doctrine, and draws not near
ὑγιαίνουσιν λόγοις τοῖς τοῦ.κυρίου.ἡμῶν Ἰησοῦ χριστοῦ, καὶ
²sound ¹to words those of our Lord Jesus Christ, and
τῇ κατ' εὐσέβειαν διδασκαλίᾳ, 4 τετύφωται, μηδὲν
the ²according ³to ⁴piety ¹teaching, he is puffed up, nothing
ἐπιστάμενος, ἀλλὰ νοσῶν περὶ ζητήσεις καὶ λογομαχίας,
knowing, but sick about questions and disputes of words,
ἐξ ὧν γίνεται φθόνος, ἔρις, βλασφημίαι, ὑπόνοιαι πονηραί,
out of which come envy, strife, evil speakings, ²suspicions ¹wicked,
5 [r]παραδιατριβαὶ[ll] διεφθαρμένων ἀνθρώπων τὸν νοῦν, καὶ
vain argumentations ³corrupted ¹of ²men in mind, and
ἀπεστερημένων τῆς ἀληθείας, νομιζόντων πορισμὸν εἶναι τὴν
destitute of the truth, holding ⁴gain ²to ³be
εὐσέβειαν· [s]ἀφίστασο ἀπὸ τῶν τοιούτων.[l] 6 Ἔστιν.δὲ πορισμὸς
¹piety; withdraw from such. But ⁴is ⁶gain
μέγας ἡ εὐσέβεια μετὰ αὐταρκείας. 7 οὐδὲν.γὰρ εἰσηνέγκαμεν
⁵great ¹piety ²with ³contentment. For nothing we brought
εἰς τὸν κόσμον, [t]δῆλον[l] ὅτι οὐδὲ ἐξενεγκεῖν τι δυνά-
into the world, [it is] manifest that neither to carry out anything are we
μεθα· 8 ἔχοντες.δὲ διατροφὰς καὶ σκεπάσματα, τούτοις ἀρ-
able. But having sustenance and coverings, with these we shall
κεσθησόμεθα. 9 Οἱ.δὲ βουλόμενοι πλουτεῖν, ἐμπίπτουσιν εἰς
be satisfied. But those desiring to be rich, fall into
πειρασμὸν καὶ παγίδα καὶ ἐπιθυμίας πολλὰς ἀνοήτους καὶ
temptation and a snare and ⁶desires ¹many ²unwise ³and
βλαβεράς, αἵτινες βυθίζουσιν τοὺς ἀνθρώπους εἰς ὄλεθρον
⁴hurtful, which sink men into destruction
καὶ ἀπώλειαν. 10 ῥίζα.γὰρ πάντων τῶν κακῶν ἐστιν ἡ φιλ-
and perdition. For a root of all evils is the love
αργυρία· ἧς τινες ὀρεγόμενοι ἀπεπλανήθησαν ἀπὸ τῆς
of money; which some stretching after were seduced from the
πίστεως, καὶ ἑαυτοὺς περιέπειραν ὀδύναις πολλαῖς. 11 Σὺ
faith, and themselves pierced with ²sorrows ¹many. ⁴Thou
δέ, ὦ ἄνθρωπε [u]τοῦ[l] θεοῦ, ταῦτα φεῦγε· δίωκε.δὲ δικαιο-
³but, O man of God, these things flee, and pursue right-
σύνην, εὐσέβειαν, πίστιν, ἀγάπην, ὑπομονήν, [v]πραότητα·[ll]
eousness, piety, faith, love, endurance, meekness.
12 ἀγωνίζου τὸν καλὸν ἀγῶνα τῆς πίστεως· ἐπιλαβοῦ τῆς
Combat the good combat of the faith. Lay hold
αἰωνίου ζωῆς, εἰς ἣν [w]καὶ[l] ἐκλήθης, καὶ ὡμολόγησας
of eternal life, to which also thou wast called, and didst confess
τὴν καλὴν ὁμολογίαν ἐνώπιον πολλῶν μαρτύρων. 13 Παραγ-
the good confession before many witnesses. I
γέλλω [x]σοι[ll] ἐνώπιον [y]τοῦ[ll] θεοῦ τοῦ [z]ζωοποιοῦντος[ll] τὰ.πάντα,
charge thee before God who quickens all things,

widows indeed.
17 Let the elders who are good in leading be
counted worthy of double honor, especially
those laboring in word and teaching.
18 For the Scripture says, "You shall not
muzzle an ox that is treading out corn," and,
"The laborer is worthy of his reward."
19 Do not receive an accusation against an
elder except on *the testimony of* two or
three witnesses.
20 Convict those that sin before all so that
the rest may have fear.
21 I earnestly witness before God and the
Lord Jesus Christ and the elect angels that
you should keep these things, without pre-
ferring one before another, doing nothing by
being partial.
22 Do not lay hands suddenly on anyone,
nor take part in the sins of others. Keep
yourself pure.
23 Do not drink water any longer, but use a
little wine on account of your stomach and
your many infirmities.
24 The sins of some men are plain, going
before to judgment and some also they
follow after.
25 In the same way also the good works *of
some* are plain, and those that are not so
cannot be hidden.
6 1 Let as many slaves as are under the yoke
count their own masters worthy of all honor
so that the name and the teaching of God
may not be blasphemed.
2 And the ones who have believing masters,
let them not despise them because they are
brothers. But rather let them serve because
they are faithful and beloved, who are being
helped by good workmanship. Teach and
urge on *them* these things.
3 If anyone teaches otherwise and does not
approve of sound words (even those of our
Lord Jesus Christ) and of the teaching which
is according to godliness,
4 he is puffed up, knowing nothing – sick
about questions and arguments, out of
which come envy, quarrels, evil-speaking,
filthy suspicions,
5 empty arguments of men ruined in mind
and totally without the truth – supposing
godliness to be profit. Withdraw from these.
6 But godliness with contentment is great
gain.
7 For we did not bring anything into this
world, *and it is* clear that we are not able to
carry anything out of it.
8 But having food and clothing, we shall be
satisfied with these.
9 But those who want to be rich fall into
temptation and a snare. And *they fall* into
many foolish and hurtful lusts which plunge
men into death and everlasting ruin.
10 For the love of money is a root of all
kinds of evil. Some who have reached out
after *money* have wandered from the faith
and have pierced themselves through with
many sorrows.

καὶ χριστοῦ Ἰησοῦ τοῦ μαρτυρήσαντος ἐπὶ Ποντίου [a]Πι-
and Christ Jesus who witnessed before Pontius Pi-
λάτου" τὴν καλὴν ὁμολογίαν, 14 τηρῆσαί.σε τὴν ἐντολὴν
late the good confession, that thou keep the commandment
ἄσπιλον, [b]ἀνεπίληπτον," μέχρι τῆς ἐπιφανείας τοῦ κυρίου
spotless, irreproachable, until the appearing of [2]Lord
ἡμῶν Ἰησοῦ χριστοῦ, 15 ἣν καιροῖς.ἰδίοις δείξει ὁ
[1]our Jesus Christ; which in its own times [6]shall [7]shew [1]the
μακάριος καὶ μόνος δυνάστης, ὁ βασιλεὺς τῶν βασιλευόν-
[2]blessed [3]and [4]only [5]Ruler, the King of those being kings
των καὶ κύριος τῶν κυριευόντων, 16 ὁ μόνος ἔχων ἀθα-
and Lord of those being lords; who alone has im-
νασίαν, φῶς οἰκῶν ἀπρόσιτον, ὃν εἶδεν οὐδεὶς
mortality, [2]in [4]light [1]dwelling [3]unapproachable, whom [5]did [6]see [1]no [2]one
ἀνθρώπων οὐδὲ ἰδεῖν δύναται, ᾧ τιμὴ καὶ κράτος
[3]of [4]men nor to see is able; to whom honour, and might
αἰώνιον. ἀμήν.
eternal. Amen.

17 Τοῖς πλουσίοις ἐν τῷ νῦν αἰῶνι παράγγελλε, μὴ
To the rich in the present age charge, not
[c]ὑψηλοφρονεῖν," μηδὲ ἠλπικέναι ἐπὶ πλούτου ἀδηλότητι,
to be high-minded, nor to have hope in [3]of [4]riches [1]the] [2]uncertainty;
ἀλλ' [d]ἐν" [e]τῷ" θεῷ [f]τῷ ζῶντι," τῷ παρέχοντι ἡμῖν [g] [h]πλου-
but in [3]God [1]the [2]living, who gives us richly
σίως πάντα" εἰς ἀπόλαυσιν· 18 ἀγαθοεργεῖν, πλουτεῖν ἐν
all things for enjoyment; to do good, to be rich in
ἔργοις καλοῖς, εὐμεταδότους εἶναι, κοινωνικούς, 19 ἀπο-
[2]works [1]good, liberal in distributing to be, ready to communicate, trea-
θησαυρίζοντας ἑαυτοῖς θεμέλιον καλὸν εἰς τὸ μέλλον, ἵνα
suring up for themselves a [2]foundation [1]good for the future, that
ἐπιλάβωνται τῆς [i]αἰωνίου" ζωῆς.
they may lay hold of eternal life.

20 Ὦ Τιμόθεε, τὴν [k]παρακαταθήκην" φύλαξον,
O Timotheus, the deposit committed [to thee] keep,
ἐκτρεπόμενος τὰς βεβήλους κενοφωνίας, καὶ ἀντιθέσεις τῆς
avoiding profane empty babblings, and oppositions
ψευδωνύμου.γνώσεως· 21 ἥν τινες ἐπαγγελλόμενοι, περὶ
of falsely-named knowledge, which some professing, in reference to
τὴν πίστιν ἠστόχησαν. Ἡ χάρις [l]μετὰ σοῦ." [m]ἀμήν."
the faith missed the mark. Grace [be] with thee. Amen.

[n]Πρὸς Τιμόθεον πρώτη ἐγράφη ἀπὸ Λαοδικείας, ἥτις
[2]To [3]Timothy [1]first written from Laodicæa, which
ἐστὶν μητρόπολις Φρυγίας τῆς Πακατιανῆς."
is the chief city of Phrygia Pacatiana.

The SECOND Letter to TIMOTHY

ΠΑΥΛΟΣ ἀπόστολος [b]Ἰησοῦ χριστοῦ" διὰ θελήματος θεοῦ
Paul, apostle of Jesus Christ by [the] will of God
κατ' ἐπαγγελίαν ζωῆς τῆς ἐν χριστῷ Ἰησοῦ, 2 Τι-
according to promise of life which [is] in Christ Jesus, to Ti-
μοθέῳ ἀγαπητῷ τέκνῳ· χάρις, ἔλεος, εἰρήνη ἀπὸ θεοῦ
motheus [my] beloved child: Grace, mercy, peace from God [the]
πατρὸς καὶ χριστοῦ Ἰησοῦ τοῦ.κυρίου ἡμῶν.
Father and Christ Jesus our Lord.

3 Χάριν.ἔχω τῷ θεῷ, ᾧ λατρεύω ἀπὸ προγόνων ἐν
I am thankful to God, whom I serve from [my] forefathers with
καθαρᾷ συνειδήσει, ὡς ἀδιάλειπτον ἔχω τὴν περὶ σοῦ μνείαν
pure conscience, how unceasingly I have the [2]of [3]thee [1]remembrance
ἐν ταῖς.δεήσεσίν.μου [c]νυκτὸς καὶ ἡμέρας," 4 ἐπιποθῶν σε
in my supplications night and day, longing [3]thee
ἰδεῖν, μεμνημένος σου τῶν δακρύων, ἵνα χαρᾶς πληρωθῶ·
[1]to [2]see, remembering thy tears, that with joy I may be filled;
5 ὑπόμνησιν [d]λαμβάνων" τῆς ἐν σοὶ ἀνυποκρίτου πίστεως,
[2]remembrance [1]taking of the [3]in [4]thee [1]unfeigned [2]faith,
ἥτις ἐνῴκησεν πρῶτον ἐν τῇ.μάμμῃ.σου Λωΐδι καὶ τῇ μητρί
which dwelt first in thy grandmother Lois and in [2]mother
σου [e]Εὐνείκῃ," πέπεισμαι.δὲ ὅτι καὶ ἐν σοί. 6 Δι' ἣν αἰτίαν
[1]thy Eunice, and I am persuaded that also in thee. For which cause
ἀναμιμνήσκω σε ἀναζωπυρεῖν τὸ χάρισμα τοῦ θεοῦ, ὅ ἐστιν
I remind thee to kindle up the gift of God which is
ἐν σοὶ διὰ τῆς ἐπιθέσεως τῶν.χειρῶν.μου· 7 οὐ.γὰρ ἔδωκεν
in thee by the laying on of my hands. For [4]not [5]gave
ἡμῖν ὁ θεὸς πνεῦμα δειλίας, ἀλλὰ δυνάμεως καὶ ἀγάπης
[3]us [1]God a spirit of cowardice, but of power, and of love,
καὶ σωφρονισμοῦ. 8 μὴ οὖν ἐπαισχυνθῇς τὸ
and of wise discretion. [4]Not [1]therefore [2]thou [3]shouldest be ashamed of the
μαρτύριον τοῦ.κυρίου.ἡμῶν, μηδὲ ἐμὲ τὸν.δέσμιον.αὐτοῦ· ἀλλὰ
testimony of our Lord, nor me his prisoner; but

11 But you, O man of God, flee these
things. And follow after righteousness, godliness, faith, love, patience and meekness.
12 Fight the good fight of faith. Lay hold
on eternal life, to which you were also called
and have confessed a good confession before
many witnesses.
13 I charge you in the sight of God (who
makes all things live), and of Christ Jesus
(who witnessed a good confession before
Pontius Pilate),
14 that you keep the commandment without spot and without blame until the appearing of our Lord Jesus Christ.
15 *For He* in His own times will show who
is the blessed and only Ruler, the King of
kings and Lord of lords –
16 who alone has the power not to die,
living in light which is unapproachable,
whom no one has seen or is able to see – to
whom be honor and power everlasting.
Amen.
17 To the rich in this world, warn against
high-mindedness or hope in the uncertainty
of riches, but *let them hope* in the living
God who gives us richly all things to enjoy.
18 *Urge them* to do good, to be rich in good
works, to be ready to give, ready to share in
fellowship,
19 treasuring up for themselves a good
foundation for the time to come, so that
they may lay hold on everlasting life.
20 O Timothy, keep that which is deposited
with you, keeping away from unholy, empty
babblings and the contrary teachings of
falsely named science –
21 which some have professed having
missed the mark as to the faith. Grace be
with you. Amen.

1 1 Paul, an apostle of Jesus Christ by the will
of God, according to the promise of life
which is in Christ Jesus,
2 to Timothy, *my* beloved child: Grace,
mercy and peace from God the Father and
Christ Jesus our Lord.
3 I am thankful to God (whom I serve with
pure conscience from my forefathers) that
without ceasing, I remember you in my
prayers night and day,
4 greatly longing to see you, remembering
your tears, that I may be filled with joy,
5 calling to mind your genuine faith, which
first was in your grandmother Lois, and in
your mother Eunice. And I am persuaded
that it is in you also.
6 For which cause I remind you to stir up
the gift of God, which is in you by the
laying on of my hands.
7 For God has not given us a spirit of
fearfulness, but of power and of love and of
a sound mind.
8 So you should not be ashamed of the
testimony of our Lord or of me, His

[f]συγκακοπάθησον‖ τῷ εὐαγγελίῳ κατὰ δύναμιν θεοῦ, 9 τοῦ
suffer evils along with the glad tidings according to [2]power [1]God's; who
σώσαντος ἡμᾶς καὶ καλέσαντος κλήσει ἁγίᾳ, οὐ κατὰ
saved us and called [us] with a [2]calling [1]holy, not according to
τὰ.ἔργα.ἡμῶν, ἀλλὰ [g]κατ'‖ ἰδίαν πρόθεσιν καὶ χάριν· τὴν
our works, but according to his own purpose and grace, which
δοθεῖσαν ἡμῖν ἐν χριστῷ Ἰησοῦ πρὸ χρόνων.αἰωνίων,
[was] given us in Christ Jesus before the ages of time,
10 φανερωθεῖσαν.δὲ νῦν διὰ τῆς ἐπιφανείας τοῦ.σωτῆρος.ἡμῶν
but made manifest now by the appearing of our Saviour
[h]Ἰησοῦ χριστοῦ,‖ καταργήσαντος μὲν τὸν θάνατον, φωτίσαν-
Jesus Christ, who annulled death, [2]brought [3]to
τος δὲ ζωὴν καὶ ἀφθαρσίαν διὰ τοῦ εὐαγγελίου, 11 εἰς ὃ
[4]light [1]and life and incorruptibility by the glad tidings; to which
ἐτέθην ἐγὼ κῆρυξ καὶ ἀπόστολος καὶ διδάσκαλος
[2]was [3]appointed [1]I a herald and apostle and teacher
[i]ἐθνῶν.‖ 12 δι' .ἣν αἰτίαν καὶ ταῦτα πάσχω· ἀλλ' οὐκ
of [the] nations. For which cause also these things I suffer; but [3]not
ἐπαισχύνομαι, οἶδα.γὰρ ᾧ πεπίστευκα, καὶ πέπεισμαι ὅτι
[1]I [2]am ashamed; for I know whom I have believed, and am persuaded that
δυνατός ἐστιν τὴν παραθήκην μου φυλάξαι εἰς ἐκείνην
able he is the deposit committed [to him] of me to keep for that
τὴν ἡμέραν. 13 ὑποτύπωσιν ἔχε ὑγιαινόντων λόγων, ὧν
day. [2]A [3]delineation [1]have of sound words, which [words]
παρ' ἐμοῦ ἤκουσας, ἐν πίστει καὶ ἀγάπῃ τῇ ἐν χριστῷ
from me thou didst hear, in faith and love which [are] in Christ
Ἰησοῦ. 14 τὴν καλὴν [j]παρακαταθήκην‖ φύλαξον διὰ
Jesus. The good deposit committed [to thee] keep by [the]
πνεύματος ἁγίου τοῦ ἐνοικοῦντος ἐν ἡμῖν. 15 Οἶδας τοῦτο,
[2]Spirit [1]Holy which dwells in us. Thou knowest this,
ὅτι ἀπεστράφησάν με πάντες οἱ ἐν τῇ Ἀσίᾳ, ὧν ἐστιν
that turned away from me all who [are] in Asia, of whom is
[k]Φύγελλος‖ καὶ [l]Ἑρμογένης.‖ 16 Δῴη ἔλεος ὁ κύριος τῷ
Phygellus and Hermogenes. May [3]grant [4]mercy [1]the [2]Lord to the
Ὀνησιφόρου οἴκῳ· ὅτι πολλάκις με ἀνέψυξεν, καὶ τὴν
[2]of [3]Onesiphorus [1]house, because oft me he refreshed, and
ἅλυσίν.μου οὐκ.[m]ἐπῃσχύνθη,‖ 17 ἀλλὰ γενόμενος ἐν Ῥώμῃ,
my chain was not ashamed of; but having been in Rome,
[n]σπουδαιότερον‖ ἐζήτησέν με καὶ εὗρεν· 18 δῴη αὐτῷ
more diligently he sought out me and found [me]— may [3]grant [4]to [5]him
ὁ κύριος εὑρεῖν ἔλεος παρὰ κυρίου ἐν ἐκείνῃ τῇ ἡμέρᾳ· καὶ
[1]the [2]Lord to find mercy from [the] Lord in that day— and
ὅσα ἐν Ἐφέσῳ διηκόνησεν βέλτιον σὺ γινώσκεις.
how much in Ephesus he served [3]better [[4]than [5]I [6]need [7]say] [1]thou [2]knowest.
2 Σὺ οὖν, τέκνον.μου, ἐνδυναμοῦ ἐν τῇ χάριτι τῇ
Thou therefore, my child, be strong in the grace which [is]
ἐν χριστῷ Ἰησοῦ· 2 καὶ ἃ ἤκουσας παρ' ἐμοῦ
in Christ Jesus. And the things which thou didst hear of me
διὰ πολλῶν μαρτύρων, ταῦτα παράθου πιστοῖς ἀνθρώποις,
with many witnesses, these commit to faithful men,
οἵτινες ἱκανοὶ ἔσονται καὶ ἑτέρους διδάξαι. 3 [o]σὺ οὖν
such as competent shall be also others to teach. Thou therefore
κακοπάθησον‖ ὡς καλὸς στρατιώτης [p]Ἰησοῦ χριστοῦ.‖ 4 οὐδεὶς
suffer hardship as [2]good [1]a soldier of Jesus Christ. No one
στρατευόμενος ἐμπλέκεται ταῖς τοῦ βίου [q]πραγματείαις,‖
serving as a soldier entangles himself with the [2]of [3]life [1]affairs,
ἵνα τῷ στρατολογήσαντι ἀρέσῃ. 5 ἐὰν.δὲ καὶ ἀθλῇ
that him who enrolled him as a soldier he may please. And if also [2]contend
τις, οὐ.στεφανοῦται ἐὰν.μὴ νομίμως ἀ-
[[3]in [4]the [5]games] [1]anyone, he is not crowned unless lawfully he shall
θλήσῃ. 6 τὸν κοπιῶντα γεωργὸν δεῖ πρῶτον τῶν
have contended. The [3]labour [1]husbandman [2]must before of the
καρπῶν μεταλαμβάνειν.
fruits partaking.
7 Νόει [r]ἃ‖ λέγω· [s]δῴη‖ γάρ σοι ὁ κύριος σύνεσιν
Consider the things I say, [2]may [6]give [1]for [5]thee [3]the [4]Lord understanding
ἐν πᾶσιν. 8 Μνημόνευε Ἰησοῦν χριστὸν ἐγηγερμένον ἐκ
in all things. Remember Jesus Christ raised from among
νεκρῶν, ἐκ σπέρματος [t]Δαβίδ,‖ κατὰ τὸ εὐαγγέλιόν
[the] dead, of [the] seed of David, according to [2]glad [3]tidings
μου· 9 ἐν ᾧ κακοπαθῶ μέχρι δεσμῶν ὡς κακοῦργος· [v]ἀλλ'‖
[1]my, in which I suffer hardship unto bonds as an evil doer: but
ὁ λόγος τοῦ θεοῦ οὐ.δέδεται. 10 διὰ τοῦτο πάντα ὑπο-
the word of God is not bound. Because of this all things I en-
μένω διὰ τοὺς ἐκλεκτούς, ἵνα καὶ αὐτοὶ σωτηρίας τύ-
dure for sake of the elect, that also they [the] salvation may
χωσιν τῆς ἐν χριστῷ Ἰησοῦ μετὰ δόξης αἰωνίου. 11 πιστὸς
obtain which [is] in Christ Jesus with [2]glory [1]eternal. Faithful
ὁ λόγος· εἰ.γὰρ συναπεθάνομεν, καὶ [w]συζήσομεν·‖
[is] the word; for if we died together with [him], also we shall live together;
12 εἰ ὑπομένομεν, καὶ [x]συμβασιλεύσομεν·‖ εἰ [y]ἀρνούμεθα,‖
if we endure, also we shall reign together; if we deny

prisoner. But suffer hardship along with the
gospel according to the power of God,
9 who saved us and called us with a holy
calling, not according to our works, but
according to His own purpose and grace,
which was given to us in Christ Jesus before
the world began,
10 but now revealed by the appearing of
our Savior Jesus Christ, who truly made
death of no effect and who brought life and
immortality to light by the gospel,
11 to which I was appointed a preacher and
an apostle and a teacher of the Gentiles.
12 For which cause I also suffer these
things. But I am not ashamed, for I know
whom I have believed and am persuaded that
He is able to keep that which I have
committed *to Him* against that Day.
13 Hold the pattern of sound words which
you have heard from me, in faith and love
which are in Christ Jesus.
14 That good trust given to you, keep by
the Holy Spirit who dwells in us.
15 This you know, that all those who are in
Asia have turned away from me – of which
kind is Phy-gel-lus and Her-mog-e-nes.
16 May the Lord grant mercy to the house
of O-nes-i-phor-us, because he often refreshed me and because he was not ashamed of
my chain.
17 But when he was in Rome, he earnestly
looked for me and found me.
18 May the Lord grant to him to find mercy
from the Lord in that Day. And how much
he helped in Ephesus you know best.
2 1 Therefore, my son, you must be strong in
the grace which is in Christ Jesus.
2 And the things which you heard from me,
with many witnesses, entrust these things to
faithful men, ones that will be able to teach
others too.
3 Then, suffer hardship as a good soldier of
Jesus Christ.
4 No one who is serving as a soldier tangles
himself up with the affairs of this life, that
he may please him who made him a soldier.
5 And even if one contests *in the games,* he
is not crowned unless he has contested
according to the rules.
6 The farmer must work before sharing in
the fruits.
7 Consider what I say, for the Lord may
give you understanding in all things.
8 Remember Jesus Christ, *who was* raised
from among the dead, of the seed of David,
according to my gospel,
9 in which I suffer hardship like an evildoer,
even to chains. But the word of God is not
chained.
10 Because of this I endure all things for the
sake of the elect, so that they may also
obtain the salvation which is in Christ Jesus,
with everlasting glory.
11 This is a faithful saying, for if we died
together with *Him,* we also shall live with
Him.

κἀκεῖνος ἀρνήσεται ἡμᾶς· 13 εἰ ἀπιστοῦμεν, ἐκεῖνος
[him], he also will deny us; if we are unfaithful, he
πιστὸς μένει· ἀρνήσασθαι[z] ἑαυτὸν οὐ.δύναται.
faithful abides; to deny himself he is not able.
14 Ταῦτα ὑπομίμνησκε, διαμαρτυρόμενος ἐνώπιον
[2]These [3]things [4]put [5]in [6]remembrance [1]of, testifying earnestly before
[a]τοῦ κυρίου[‖] [b]μὴ λογομαχεῖν[‖] [c]εἰς[‖] οὐδὲν χρήσιμον, ἐπὶ
the Lord not to dispute about words [2]for [3]nothing [1]profitable, to
καταστροφῇ τῶν ἀκουόντων. 15 σπούδασον σεαυτὸν
subversion of those who hear. Be diligent [3]thyself
δόκιμον παραστῆσαι τῷ θεῷ, ἐργάτην ἀνεπαίσχυντον, ὀρθο-
[4]approved [1]to [2]present to God, a workman not ashamed, straight-
τομοῦντα τὸν λόγον τῆς ἀληθείας· 16 τὰς.δὲ.βεβήλους κενο-
ly cutting the word of truth; but profane empty
φωνίας περιΐστασο· ἐπὶ πλεῖον γὰρ προκόψουσιν ἀσεβείας
babblings stand aloof from, [2]to [3]more [1]for they will advance of ungodliness,
17 καὶ ὁ.λόγος.αὐτῶν ὡς γάγγραινα νομὴν ἕξει· ὧν ἐστιν
and their word as a gangrene pasture will have; of whom is
Ὑμέναιος καὶ Φιλητός, 18 οἵτινες περὶ τὴν ἀλήθειαν
Hymenæus and Philetus; who concerning the truth
ἠστόχησαν, λέγοντες [d]τὴν[‖] ἀνάστασιν ἤδη γεγονέναι.
missed the mark, asserting the resurrection already to have taken place;
καὶ ἀνατρέπουσιν τήν τινων πίστιν. 19 ὁ [e]μέντοι[‖] στερεὸς
and are overthrowing the [2]of [3]some [1]faith. Nevertheless [2]firm
θεμέλιος τοῦ θεοῦ ἕστηκεν, ἔχων τὴν.σφραγῖδα.ταύτην, Ἔγνω
[3]foundation [1]God's stands, having this seal, [3]Knows
κύριος τοὺς ὄντας αὐτοῦ, καὶ Ἀποστήτω ἀπὸ ἀδι-
[[1]the] [2]Lord those that are his, and Let depart from unright-
κίας πᾶς ὁ ὀνομάζων τὸ ὄνομα [f]χριστοῦ.[‖] 20 ἐν μεγάλῃ
eousness everyone who names the name of Christ. [2]In [4]great
δὲ οἰκίᾳ οὐκ.ἔστιν μόνον σκεύη χρυσᾶ καὶ ἀργυρᾶ, ἀλλὰ
[1]but [3]a house there are not only vessels golden and silver, but
καὶ ξύλινα καὶ ὀστράκινα, καὶ ἃ μὲν εἰς τιμήν, ἃ.δὲ εἰς
also wooden and earthen, and some to honour, others to
ἀτιμίαν. 21 ἐὰν οὖν τις ἐκκαθάρῃ ἑαυτὸν ἀπὸ τούτων,
dishonour. If therefore one shall have purged himself from these,
ἔσται σκεῦος εἰς τιμήν, ἡγιασμένον, [g]καὶ[‖] εὔχρηστον
he shall be a vessel to honour, having been sanctified, and serviceable
τῷ δεσπότῃ, εἰς πᾶν ἔργον ἀγαθὸν ἡτοιμασμένον.
to the master, for every [2]work [1]good having been prepared.
22 τὰς.δὲ.νεωτερικὰς ἐπιθυμίας φεῦγε· δίωκε.δὲ δικαιοσύνην,
But youthful lusts flee, and pursue righteousness,
πίστιν, ἀγάπην, εἰρήνην μετὰ [h] τῶν ἐπικαλουμένων τὸν
faith, love, peace with those that call on the
κύριον ἐκ καθαρᾶς καρδίας. 23 τὰς.δὲ.μωρὰς καὶ ἀπαι-
Lord out of [2]pure [1]a heart. But foolish and undis-
δεύτους ζητήσεις παραιτοῦ, εἰδὼς ὅτι γεννῶσιν μάχας·
ciplined questionings refuse, knowing that they beget contentions.
24 δοῦλον.δὲ κυρίου οὐ.δεῖ μάχεσθαι, [i]ἀλλ'[‖] ἤπιον
And [3]a [4]bondman [5]of [[6]the] [7]Lord [1]it [2]behoves not to contend, but gentle
εἶναι πρὸς πάντας, διδακτικόν, ἀνεξίκακον, 25 ἐν [k]πρᾳότητι[‖]
to be towards all; apt to teach; forbearing; in meekness
παιδεύοντα τοὺς ἀντιδιατιθεμένους, μήποτε [l]δῷ[‖] αὐτοῖς
disciplining those that oppose, if perhaps [2]may [3]give [4]them
ὁ θεὸς μετάνοιαν εἰς ἐπίγνωσιν ἀληθείας, 26 καὶ ἀνα-
[1]God repentance to acknowledgment of [the] truth, and they may
νήψωσιν ἐκ τῆς τοῦ διαβόλου παγίδος, ἐζωγρημένοι ὑπ'
awake up out of the [2]of [3]the [4]devil [1]snare, having been taken by
αὐτοῦ εἰς τὸ ἐκείνου θέλημα.
him for his will.

3 Τοῦτο.δὲ [m]γίνωσκε,[‖] ὅτι ἐν ἐσχάταις ἡμέραις ἐνστή-
But this know thou, that in [the] last days [3]will [4]be
σονται καιροὶ χαλεποί. 2 ἔσονται.γὰρ οἱ ἄνθρωποι φίλαυτοι,
[5]present [2]times [1]difficult; for [2]will [3]be [1]men lovers of self,
φιλάργυροι, ἀλαζόνες, ὑπερήφανοι, βλάσφημοι, γονεῦσιν
lovers of money, vaunting, proud, evil speakers, to parents
ἀπειθεῖς, ἀχάριστοι, ἀνόσιοι, 3 ἄστοργοι, ἄσπονδοι,
disobedient, unthankful, unholy, without natural affection, implacable,
διάβολοι, ἀκρατεῖς, ἀνήμεροι, ἀφιλάγαθοι, 4 προδόται,
slanderers, incontinent, savage, not lovers of good, betrayers,
προπετεῖς, τετυφωμένοι, φιλήδονοι μᾶλλον ἢ φιλόθεοι,
headlong, puffed up, lovers of pleasure rather than lovers of God;
5 ἔχοντες μόρφωσιν εὐσεβείας, τὴν.δὲ δύναμιν αὐτῆς ἠρνη-
having a form of piety, but the power of it deny-
μένοι. καὶ τούτους ἀποτρέπου. 6 ἐκ.τούτων.γάρ εἰσιν οἱ
ing: and these turn away from. For of these are those who
ἐνδύνοντες εἰς τὰς οἰκίας καὶ [n]αἰχμαλωτεύοντες τὰ[‖] γυναικάρια
[are] entering into houses and leading captive silly women
σεσωρευμένα ἁμαρτίαις, ἀγόμενα ἐπιθυμίαις ποικίλαις, 7 πάν-
laden with sins, led away by [2]lusts [1]various, al-
τοτε μανθάνοντα καὶ μηδέποτε εἰς ἐπίγνωσιν ἀληθείας
ways learning and never to [the] knowledge of [the] truth

12 If we endure, we shall also reign with
Him. If we deny Him, He will also deny us.
13 If we are unfaithful, He remains faithful,
for He cannot deny Himself.
14 Remind them of these things, testifying
strongly before the Lord: Do not argue
about words to no profit, to the subversion
of the ones who hear,
15 study to show yourself approved to God,
a workman that does not need to be
ashamed, rightly dividing the word of truth.
16 But keep away from unholy, empty
babblings, for they will go forward to more
ungodliness,
17 and their word will feed *on them* like
stinking, rotting flesh – of whom is Hy-me-
ne-us and Phi-le-tus,
18 who missed the mark as to the truth,
saying that the resurrection has already
taken place (and are overthrowing the faith
of some).
19 But the foundation of God stands sure,
having this seal: "The Lord knows those that
are His," and, "Let everyone who names the
name of Christ depart from unrighteousness."
20 But in a great house there are not only
vessels of gold and silver, but wooden and
earthen vessels too. And some are to honor,
others to dishonor.
21 So if one has purged himself from these,
he shall be a vessel to honor, being set apart
and made useful to the Master, being prepared for every good work.
22 But flee youthful lusts and pursue after
righteousness, faith, love and peace with the
ones who call on the Lord with a pure heart.
23 But stay away from foolish and ignorant
arguments, knowing that they cause quarrels
24 – and it is not right for a servant of the
Lord to quarrel, but to be gentile towards
all, quick to teach, patient –
25 in meekness teaching those who set
themselves against themselves – perhaps
God may give them repentance so as to have
a full knowledge of the truth,
26 and *then* they may wake up out of the
snare of the devil, those who have been
taken captive by him, to do his will.
3 1 But you know this, that in the last days
dangerous times will come.
2 For men will be lovers of themselves,
lovers of money, braggarts, proud, blasphe-
mers, not obeying parents, unthankful,
unholy,
3 without natural feeling, refusing to yield,
false accusers, without self-control, savage,
not lovers of good,
4 traitors, reckless, puffed up – lovers of
pleasure rather than lovers of God,
5 having a form of godliness but denying
the power of it – but turn away from these!
6 For of these are the ones who creep into
houses and lead away silly women loaded
with sins, led on by different kinds of lusts
7 always learning and never able to come to

ἐλθεῖν δυνάμενα. 8 ὃν.τρόπον.δὲ Ἰαννῆς καὶ Ἰαμβρῆς ἀντέ-
[2]to [3]come [1]able. Now in the way Jannes and Jambres with-
στησαν Μωϋσεῖ, οὕτως καὶ οὗτοι ἀνθίστανται τῇ ἀληθείᾳ,
stood Moses, thus also these withstand the truth,
ἄνθρωποι κατεφθαρμένοι τὸν.νοῦν, ἀδόκιμοι περὶ
men utterly corrupted in mind, found worthless as regards
τὴν πίστιν. 9 ἀλλ' οὐ.προκόψουσιν ἐπὶ.πλεῖον· ἡ γὰρ ἄνοια
the faith. But they shall not advance farther, for [2]folly
αὐτῶν ἔκδηλος ἔσται πᾶσιν, ὡς καὶ ἡ ἐκείνων ἐγένετο.
[1]their fully manifest shall be to all, as also that of those became.
10 σὺ.δὲ [o]παρηκολούθηκάς" μου τῇ διδασκαλίᾳ, τῇ ἀγωγῇ,
But thou hast closely followed my teaching, conduct,
τῇ προθέσει, τῇ πίστει, τῇ μακροθυμίᾳ, τῇ ἀγάπῃ, τῇ ὑπομονῇ,
purpose, faith, patience, love, endurance,
11 τοῖς διωγμοῖς, τοῖς παθήμασιν, οἷά μοι ἐγένετο ἐν Ἀν-
persecutions, sufferings: such as to me happened in An-
τιοχείᾳ, ἐν Ἰκονίῳ, ἐν Λύστροις· οἵους διωγμοὺς ὑπ-
tioch, in Iconium, in Lystra; what manner of persecutions I en-
ήνεγκα, καὶ ἐκ πάντων με [p]ἐῤῥύσατο" ὁ κύριος. 12 καὶ
dured; and out of all [4]me [3]delivered [1]the [2]Lord. And
πάντες δὲ οἱ θέλοντες [q]εὐσεβῶς ζῆν" ἐν χριστῷ Ἰησοῦ
all indeed who wish piously to live in Christ Jesus
διωχθήσονται· 13 πονηροὶ.δὲ ἄνθρωποι καὶ γόητες προ-
will be persecuted. But wicked men and impostors shall
κόψουσιν ἐπὶ τὸ χεῖρον, πλανῶντες καὶ πλανώμενοι. 14 σὺ.δὲ
advance to worse, misleading and being misled. But thou
μένε ἐν οἷς ἔμαθες καὶ ἐπιστώθης, εἰδὼς παρὰ
abide in the things thou didst learn, and wast assured of, having known from
[r]τίνος" ἔμαθες, 15 καὶ ὅτι ἀπὸ βρέφους [s]τὰ" ἱερὰ
whom thou didst learn [them]; and that from a babe the sacred
γράμματα οἶδας, τὰ δυνάμενά σε σοφίσαι εἰς
letters thou hast known, which [are] able [3]thee [1]to [2]make wise to
σωτηρίαν, διὰ πίστεως τῆς ἐν χριστῷ Ἰησοῦ. 16 πᾶσα
salvation, through faith which [is] in Christ Jesus. Every
γραφὴ θεόπνευστος καὶ ὠφέλιμος πρὸς διδασκαλίαν, πρὸς
scripture [is] God-inspired and profitable for teaching, for
[t]ἔλεγχον," πρὸς ἐπανόρθωσιν, πρὸς [v]παιδείαν" τὴν ἐν
conviction, for correction, for discipline which [is] in
δικαιοσύνῃ· 17 ἵνα ἄρτιος ᾖ ὁ τοῦ θεοῦ ἄνθρωπος, πρὸς
righteousness; that complete may be the [2]of [3]God [1]man, to
πᾶν ἔργον ἀγαθὸν ἐξηρτισμένος.
every [2]work [1]good fully fitted.

4 Διαμαρτύρομαι [w]οὖν ἐγὼ" ἐνώπιον τοῦ θεοῦ καὶ [x]τοῦ
[2]Earnestly [3]testify [4]therefore [1]I before God and the
κυρίου" [y]Ἰησοῦ χριστοῦ," τοῦ μέλλοντος κρίνειν ζῶντας καὶ
Lord Jesus Christ, who is about to judge living and
νεκροὺς [z]κατὰ" τὴν.ἐπιφάνειαν.αὐτοῦ καὶ τὴν βασιλείαν
dead according to his appearing and [2]kingdom
αὐτοῦ, 2 κήρυξον τὸν λόγον, ἐπίστηθι εὐκαίρως ἀκαίρως,
[1]his, proclaim the word; be urgent in season, out of season,
ἔλεγξον, [a]ἐπιτίμησον, παρακάλεσον," ἐν πάσῃ μακροθυμίᾳ
convict, rebuke, encourage, with all patience
καὶ διδαχῇ. 3 ἔσται.γὰρ καιρὸς ὅτε τῆς ὑγιαινούσης δι-
and teaching. For there will be a time when sound teach-
δασκαλίας οὐκ.ἀνέξονται, ἀλλὰ κατὰ τὰς [b]ἐπιθυμίας
ing they will not bear; but according to [3]desires
τὰς.ἰδίας" ἑαυτοῖς ἐπισωρεύσουσιν διδασκάλους, κνηθό-
[1]their [2]own to themselves will heap up teachers,
μενοι.τὴν.ἀκοήν· 4 καὶ ἀπὸ μὲν τῆς ἀληθείας τὴν ἀκοὴν ἀπο-
having an itching ear; and from the truth the ear they will
στρέψουσιν, ἐπὶ.δὲ τοὺς μύθους ἐκτραπήσονται. 5 σὺ.δὲ
turn away, and to fables will be turned aside. But thou,
νῆφε ἐν πᾶσιν, κακοπάθησον, ἔργον ποίησον εὐαγ-
be sober in all things, suffer hardships, [the] work do of an
γελιστοῦ, τὴν.διακονίαν.σου πληροφόρησον. 6 Ἐγὼ.γὰρ ἤδη
evangelist, thy service fully carry out. For I already
σπένδομαι, καὶ ὁ καιρὸς τῆς.[c]ἐμῆς.ἀναλύσεως" ἐφ-
am being poured out, and the time of my release is
έστηκεν. 7 τὸν [d]ἀγῶνα τὸν καλὸν" ἠγώνισμαι, τὸν .δρόμον
come. The [3]combat [2]good I have combated, the course
τετέλεκα, τὴν πίστιν τετήρηκα· 8 λοιπὸν ἀπόκειταί μοι
I have finished, the faith I have kept. Henceforth is laid up for me
ὁ τῆς δικαιοσύνης στέφανος, ὃν ἀποδώσει μοι ὁ κύριος
the [2]of [3]righteousness [1]crown, which [6]will [7]render [8]to [9]me [1]the [2]Lord
ἐν ἐκείνῃ τῇ ἡμέρᾳ, ὁ δίκαιος κριτής· οὐ.μόνον.δὲ ἐμοί,
[10]in [11]that [12]day [3]the [4]righteous [5]judge; and not only to me,
ἀλλὰ καὶ πᾶσιν τοῖς ἠγαπηκόσιν τὴν.ἐπιφάνειαν.αὐτοῦ.
but also to all who love his appearing.
9 Σπούδασον ἐλθεῖν πρός με ταχέως. 10 Δημᾶς.γάρ με
Be diligent to come to me quickly; for Demas [2]me
ἐγκατέλιπεν, ἀγαπήσας τὸν νῦν αἰῶνα, καὶ ἐπορεύθη εἰς
[1]forsook, having loved the present age, and is gone to

the knowledge of the truth.
8 Now as Jan-nes and Jam-bres opposed
Moses, so also these resist the truth, being
men completely rotten in mind, worthless as
to the faith.
9 But they shall not go any further, for
their foolishness shall be very clear to all,
just as theirs also was.
10 But you have closely studied my teaching, way of life, purpose, faith, long-suffering, love, patience,
11 persecutions and sufferings – which happened to me in Antioch, in I-co-ni-um, in
Lystra. *And you know* what kind of persecutions I endured, and that the Lord delivered
me out of them all.
12 And indeed all who desire to live godly
in Christ Jesus will be persecuted.
13 But evil men and pretenders shall go on
to worse, leading astray and being led astray.
14 But you keep on in the things you have
learned and of which you have been made
sure, knowing from whom you have learned.
15 And also that from a babe you have
known the Holy Scriptures, which is able to
make you wise to salvation, through faith
which is in Christ Jesus.
16 All Scripture is God-breathed and profitable for teaching, for reproof, for correction,
for instruction in righteousness,
17 so that the man of God may be perfect,
fully fitted to all good works.

CHAPTER 4

1 I then call on you in the sight of God and
the Lord Jesus Christ (who shall judge the
living and the dead at His appearing and His
kingdom)
2 to preach the word – be urgent in season
and out of season – convict, correct, and
encourage with all patience and teaching.
3 For the time will come when they will not
endure sound doctrine, but they will heap
up to themselves teachers who tickle the ear
according to their own lusts.
4 And they will turn away their ear from
the truth and will be turned aside to fairy
tales.
5 But be clear-minded in all things, suffer
hardships, do the work of an evangelist and
fully carry out your ministry.
6 For I already am being poured out, and
the time of my release is here.
7 I have fought a good fight. I have finished
the course. I have kept the faith.
8 Now the crown of righteousness is laid up
for me, which the Lord, the righteous Judge,
will give me in that Day – and not only to
me, but also to all who love His appearing.
9 Try to come to me quickly.
10 For Demas has deserted me, having loved
this present world. And he has gone back
to Thess-a-lo-ni-ca. Crescens *has gone* to
Galatia and Titus to Dalmatia.

Θεσσαλονίκην· Κρήσκης εἰς [e]Γαλατίαν,‖ Τίτος εἰς [f]Δαλματίαν·‖
Thessalonica; Crescens to Galatia, Titus to Dalmatia.
11 Λουκᾶς ἐστιν μόνος μετ' ἐμοῦ. Μάρκον ἀναλαβὼν ἄγε
Luke [2]is [1]alone with me. Mark having taken bring
μετὰ σεαυτοῦ· ἔστιν.γάρ μοι εὔχρηστος εἰς διακονίαν. 12 Τυ-
with thyself, for he is [2]to [3]me [1]useful for service. [2]Ty-
χικὸν δὲ ἀπέστειλα εἰς Ἔφεσον. 13 Τὸν [g]φαιλόνην‖ ὃν
chicus [1]but I sent to Ephesus. The cloak which
ἀπέλιπον ἐν [h]Τρωάδι‖ παρὰ Κάρπῳ, ἐρχόμενος φέρε, καὶ τὰ
I left in Troas with Carpus, [when] coming bring, and the
βιβλία, μάλιστα τὰς μεμβράνας. 14 Ἀλέξανδρος ὁ χαλκεὺς
books, especially the parchments. Alexander the smith
πολλά μοι κακὰ ἐνεδείξατο· [i]ἀποδῴη‖ αὐτῷ ὁ
[2]many [5]against [6]me [3]evil [4]things [1]did. May [3]render [4]to [5]him [1]the
κύριος κατὰ τὰ.ἔργα.αὐτοῦ· 15 ὃν καὶ σὺ φυλάσσου,
[2]Lord according to his works. Whom also thou be ware of,
λίαν.γὰρ [k]ἀνθέστηκεν‖ τοῖς ἡμετέροις λόγοις. 16 Ἐν τῇ
for exceedingly he has withstood our words. In
πρώτῃ.μου ἀπολογίᾳ οὐδείς μοι [l]συμπαρεγένετο,‖ ἀλλὰ πάντες
my first defence no one [3]me [2]stood [4]with, but all
με ἐγκατέλιπον· μὴ αὐτοῖς λογισθείη· 17 ὁ.δὲ κύριός
me forsook. Not to them may it be reckoned. But the Lord
μοι παρέστη, καὶ ἐνεδυνάμωσέν με, ἵνα δι' ἐμοῦ τὸ κή-
[3]me [1]stood [2]by, and strengthened me, that through me the pro-
ρυγμα πληροφορηθῇ, καὶ [m]ἀκούσῃ‖ πάντα τὰ ἔθνη· καὶ
clamation might be fully made, and [4]should [5]hear [1]all [2]the [3]nations; and
[n]ἐρρύσθην‖ ἐκ στόματος λέοντος. 18 [o]καὶ‖ ῥύσεταί με
I was delivered out of [the] [2]mouth [1]lion's. And [3]will [4]deliver [5]me
ὁ κύριος ἀπὸ παντὸς ἔργου πονηροῦ, καὶ σώσει εἰς τὴν
[1]the [2]Lord from every [2]work [1]wicked, and will preserve [me] for
βασιλείαν.αὐτοῦ τὴν ἐπουράνιον· ᾧ ἡ δόξα εἰς τοὺς
his kingdom the heavenly; to whom [be] glory unto the
αἰῶνας τῶν αἰώνων. ἀμήν.
ages of the ages. Amen.
19 Ἄσπασαι Πρίσκαν καὶ Ἀκύλαν, καὶ τὸν Ὀνησιφόρου
Salute Prisca and Aquila, and the [2]of [3]Onesiphorus
οἶκον. 20 Ἔραστος ἔμεινεν ἐν Κορίνθῳ· Τρόφιμον.δὲ ἀπέλιπον
[1]house. Erastus remained in Corinth, but Trophimus I left
ἐν Μιλήτῳ ἀσθενοῦντα. 21 Σπούδασον πρὸ χειμῶνος ἐλθεῖν.
in Miletus sick. Be diligent before winter to come.
Ἀσπάζεταί σε Εὔβουλος, καὶ Πούδης, καὶ [q]Λῖνος,‖ καὶ
[2]Salutes [3]thee [1]Eubulus, and Pudens, and Linus, and
Κλαυδία, καὶ οἱ ἀδελφοὶ πάντες. 22 Ὁ κύριος [r]Ἰησοῦς‖
Claudia, and [2]the [3]brethren [1]all. The Lord Jesus
[s]χριστὸς‖ μετὰ τοῦ.πνεύματός.σου. ἡ χάρις μεθ' ὑμῶν.
Christ [be] with thy spirit. Grace [be] with you.
[t]ἀμήν.‖
Amen.
[v]Πρὸς Τιμόθεον δευτέρα, τῆς Ἐφεσίων ἐκκλη-
[2]To [3]Timotheus [1]second, [8]of [9]the [11]of [[12]the] [13]Ephesians [10]assem-
σίας πρῶτον ἐπίσκοπον χειροτονηθέντα, ἐγράφη ἀπὸ
bly [[5]the] [6]first [7]overseer [4]chosen, written from
Ῥώμης, ὅτε ἐκ.δευτέρου παρέστη Παῦλος τῷ Καίσαρι
Rome, when a second time [2]was [3]placed [4]before [1]Paul Cæsar
Νέρωνι.‖
Nero.

11 Only Luke is with me. Take Mark and
bring him with you, for he is useful to me
for the ministry.
12 But I sent Tych-i-cus to Ephesus.
13 When you come, bring the cloak I left in
Troas with Carpus, and the books, especially
the parchments.
14 Alexander the coppersmith did many
evil things against me. May the Lord give to
him according to his works.
15 You also beware, for he has greatly
resisted our words.
16 In my first defense no one stood with
me, but everyone left me. May it not be
charged to them.
17 But the Lord stood by me and strengthened me, so that through me the preaching
might be fully known, and so that all the
Gentiles should hear – and I was
delivered out of the mouth of the lion.
18 And the Lord will deliver me from
every evil work, and will keep me for His
heavenly kingdom – to whom be glory
forever and ever. Amen.
19 Greet Priscilla and Aquila and the house
of O-nes-i-phor-us.
20 Erastus stayed in Corinth, but I left
Troph-i-mus sick in Miletus.
21 Try to come before winter. Eu-bu-lus
greets you, and Pudens, and Linus, and
Claudia and all the brothers.
22 The Lord Jesus Christ be with your
spirit. Grace be with you. Amen.

The Letter to TITUS

ΠΑΥΛΟΣ δοῦλος θεοῦ, ἀπόστολος.δὲ Ἰησοῦ χριστοῦ κατὰ
Paul bondman of God, and apostle of Jesus Christ according to
πίστιν ἐκλεκτῶν θεοῦ καὶ ἐπίγνωσιν ἀληθείας τῆς
[the] faith [3]elect [1]of [2]God's and knowledge of [the] truth which [is]
κατ' εὐσέβειαν, 2 ἐπ' ἐλπίδι ζωῆς αἰωνίου, ἣν ἐπηγ-
according to piety; in [the] hope of life eternal, which [6]pro-
γείλατο ὁ ἀψευδὴς θεὸς πρὸ χρόνων.αἰωνίων, 3 ἐ-
mised [1]the [3]who [4]cannot [5]lie [2]God before the ages of time,
φανέρωσεν.δὲ καιροῖς.ἰδίοις τὸν.λόγον.αὐτοῦ, ἐν κηρύγματι
but manifested in its own seasons his word in [the] proclamation
ὃ ἐπιστεύθην ἐγὼ κατ' ἐπιταγὴν τοῦ σωτῆρος
which [2]was [3]entrusted [4]with [1]I according to [the] commandment of [2]Saviour
ἡμῶν θεοῦ, 4 Τίτῳ γνησίῳ τέκνῳ κατὰ κοινὴν
[1]our God; to Titus [my] true child according to [our] common
πίστιν, χάρις, [b]ἔλεος,‖ εἰρήνη ἀπὸ θεοῦ πατρός, καὶ
faith: Grace, mercy peace from God [the] Father, and [the]
[c]κυρίου Ἰησοῦ χριστοῦ‖ τοῦ.σωτῆρος.ἡμῶν
Lord Jesus Christ our Saviour.
5 Τούτου.χάριν [d]κατέλιπόν σε ἐν Κρήτῃ, ἵνα τὰ.λείποντα
For this cause I left thee in Crete, that the things lacking

1 1 Paul, a servant of God and an apostle of
Jesus Christ, according to the faith of God's
elect and the full knowledge of the truth
which is according to godliness –
2 in the hope of eternal life, which the God
who cannot lie promised before the world
began,
3 (but it is revealed in its own time in the
preaching of His word, with which I was
entrusted according to the commandment of
our Savior God),
4 to Titus, *my* true child according to our
common faith: Grace, mercy and peace from
God our Father and the Lord Jesus Christ,
our Savior.
5 For this cause I left you in Crete, so that

[e]ἐπιδιορθώσῃ," καὶ καταστήσῃς κατὰ.πόλιν πρεσ-
thou mightest go on to set right, and mightest appoint in every city
βυτέρους, ὡς ἐγώ σοι διεταξάμην· 6 εἴ τις ἐστιν ἀνέγ-
elders, as I [2]thee [1]ordered: if anyone is unim-
κλητος, μιᾶς γυναικὸς ἀνήρ, τέκνα ἔχων πιστά, μὴ ἐν
peachable, [2]of [3]one [4]wife [1]husband, [7]children [5]having [6]believing, not under
κατηγορίᾳ ἀσωτίας ἢ ἀνυπότακτα. 7 δεῖ.γὰρ τὸν ἐπί-
accusation of dissoluteness or insubordinate. For it behoves the over-
σκοπον ἀνέγκλητον εἶναι, ὡς θεοῦ οἰκονόμον· μὴ αὐθάδη,
seer unimpeachable to be, as God's steward; not selfwilled,
μὴ ὀργίλον, μὴ πάροινον, μὴ πλήκτην, μὴ αἰσχροκερδῆ,
not passionate, not given to wine, not a striker, not greedy of base gain,
8 ἀλλὰ φιλόξενον, φιλάγαθον, σώφρονα, δίκαιον, ὅσιον, ἐγ-
but hospitable, a lover of good, discreet, just, holy, tem-
κρατῆ, 9 ἀντεχόμενον τοῦ κατὰ τὴν διδαχὴν πιστοῦ
perate, holding to the [3]according [4]to [5]the [6]teaching [1]faithful
λόγου, ἵνα δυνατὸς ᾖ καὶ παρακαλεῖν ἐν τῇ διδασκαλίᾳ
[2]word, that able he may be both to encourage with [2]teaching
τῇ ὑγιαινούσῃ, καὶ τοὺς ἀντιλέγοντας ἐλέγχειν. 10 εἰσὶν.γὰρ
[1]sound, and those who gainsay to convict. For there are
πολλοὶ [f]καὶ" ἀνυπότακτοι ματαιολόγοι καὶ φρεναπάται, μά-
many and insubordinate vain talkers and mind-deceivers, espe-
λιστα [g] οἱ ἐκ [h] περιτομῆς, 11 οὓς δεῖ ἐπιστο-
cially those of [the] circumcision, whom it is necessary to stop the
μίζειν· οἵτινες ὅλους οἴκους ἀνατρέπουσιν, διδάσκοντες
mouths of, who whole houses overthrow, teaching
ἃ μὴ.δεῖ, αἰσχροῦ κέρδους χάριν· 12 εἶπέν
things which [they] ought not, [4]base [5]gain [1]for [2]sake [3]of. [14]Said
τις ἐξ αὐτῶν ἴδιος.αὐτῶν προφήτης, Κρῆτες ἀεὶ
[6]one [7]of [8]themselves [11]of [12]their [13]own [9]a [10]prophet, Cretans always [are]
ψεῦσται, κακὰ θηρία, γαστέρες ἀργαί. 13 ἡ.μαρτυρία.αὕτη
liars, evil wild beasts, [2]gluttons [1]lazy. This testimony
ἐστὶν ἀληθής· δι' ἣν αἰτίαν ἔλεγχε αὐτοὺς ἀποτόμως, ἵνα
is true; for which cause convict them with severity, that
ὑγιαίνωσιν ἐν τῇ πίστει, 14 μὴ προσέχοντες Ἰουδαϊκοῖς
they may be sound in the faith, not giving heed to Jewish
μύθοις καὶ ἐντολαῖς ἀνθρώπων ἀποστρεφομένων τὴν ἀλή-
fables and commandments of men, turning away from the truth.
θειαν. 15 πάντα [i]μὲν" καθαρὰ τοῖς καθαροῖς· τοῖς.δὲ
All things [are] pure to the pure; but to those who
[k]μεμιασμένοις" καὶ ἀπίστοις οὐδὲν καθαρόν, ἀλλὰ μεμίαν-
are defiled and unbelieving nothing [is] pure; but are de-
ται αὐτῶν καὶ ὁ νοῦς καὶ ἡ.συνείδησις. 16 θεὸν ὁμολογοῦσιν
filed [2]their [1]both mind and [their] conscience. God they profess
εἰδέναι, τοῖς.δὲ.ἔργοις ἀρνοῦνται, βδελυκτοὶ ὄντες καὶ
to know, but in works deny [him], [2]abominable [1]being and
ἀπειθεῖς, καὶ πρὸς πᾶν ἔργον ἀγαθὸν ἀδόκιμοι.
disobedient, and as to every [2]work [1]good found worthless.
2 Σὺ.δὲ λάλει ἃ πρέπει τῇ ὑγιαινούσῃ διδασ-
But [2]thou [1]speak the things that become sound teach-
καλίᾳ· 2 πρεσβύτας νηφαλίους εἶναι, σεμνούς, σώ-
ing: [the] aged [men] [3]sober [1]to [2]be, grave, dis-
φρονας, ὑγιαίνοντας τῇ πίστει, τῇ ἀγάπῃ, τῇ ὑπομονῇ·
creet, sound in faith, in love, in endurance;
3 πρεσβύτιδας ὡσαύτως ἐν καταστήματι ἱερο-
[the] aged [women] in like manner in deportment as becomes
πρεπεῖς, μὴ διαβόλους, [l]μὴ" οἴνῳ πολλῷ δεδουλωμένας,
sacred ones, not slanderers, not [3]to [4]wine [2]much [1]enslaved,
καλοδιδασκάλους, 4 ἵνα [m]σωφρονίζωσιν" τὰς νέας
teachers of what is right; that they may school the young [women]
φιλάνδρους εἶναι, φιλοτέκνους, 5 σώφρονας,
lovers of [their] husbands to be, lovers of [their] children, discreet,
ἁγνάς, [n]οἰκουρούς," ἀγαθάς, ὑποτασσομένας τοῖς.ἰδίοις ἀν-
chaste, keepers at home, good, subject to their own hus-
δράσιν, ἵνα μὴ ὁ λόγος τοῦ θεοῦ βλασφημῆται. 6 Τοὺς
bands, that not the word of God may be evil spoken of. The
νεωτέρους ὡσαύτως παρακάλει σωφρονεῖν, [o] 7 περὶ
younger [men] in like manner exhort to be discreet; in
πάντα σεαυτὸν παρεχόμενος τύπον καλῶν ἔργων, ἐν τῇ
all things thyself holding forth a pattern of good works; in
διδασκαλίᾳ [p]ἀδιαφθορίαν," σεμνότητα, [q]ἀφθαρσίαν," 8 λόγον
teaching uncorruptness, gravity, incorruption, [2]speech
ὑγιῆ, ἀκατάγνωστον, ἵνα ὁ.ἐξ.ἐναντίας ἐντραπῇ, μηδὲν
[1]sound, not to be condemned; that he who is opposed may be ashamed, [2]nothing
ἔχων [r]περὶ ὑμῶν λέγειν" φαῦλον. 9 Δούλους [s]ἰδίοις
[1]having [6]concerning [7]you [4]to [5]say [3]evil. Bondmen to their own
δεσπόταις" ὑποτάσσεσθαι, ἐν πᾶσιν εὐαρέστους εἶναι, μὴ
masters to be subject, in everything well-pleasing to be, not
ἀντιλέγοντας, 10 μὴ νοσφιζομένους, ἀλλὰ [t]πίστιν πᾶσαν"
contradicting; not purloining, but [4]fidelity [2]all
ἐνδεικνυμένους ἀγαθήν· ἵνα τὴν διδασκαλίαν [v] τοῦ σωτῆρος
[1]shewing [3]good, that the teaching [3]Saviour

you might set in order the things that were
lacking, and that you might ordain elders in
every city, even as I had ordered you to do:
6 If any man is blameless, the husband of
one wife, having faithful children, not
accused of behaving loosely or being unruly
7 (for a bishop ought to be blameless, as
God's minister, not self-willed, nor full of
passion, nor given to wine, nor quarrelsome,
nor greedy of ill profit –
8 but hospitable, a lover of all that is good,
of a sound mind, just, holy, temperate,
9 clinging to the faithful word according to
the doctrine, so that he may be able both to
encourage with sound teaching and to convict the ones who speak against the truth).
10 For there are many unruly and empty
talkers and those who lead the mind astray
– especially those of the circumcision,
11 whose mouth must be stopped, who
overthrow whole houses, teaching things
which they ought not, for the sake of ill
profit.
12 One of themselves, a prophet of their
own said, The people of Crete are always
liars, evil beasts, lazy gluttons.
13 This statement is true, for which cause
convict them sharply so that they may be
sound in the faith,
14 not listening to Jewish tales and
commandments of men, turning away from
the truth.
15 Unto the pure, all things are pure. But to
the defiled and unbelieving, nothing is pure,
but both their mind and conscience are
defiled.
16 They claim to know God, but in works
deny Him, being hateful and disobedient.
And as to every good work, they are useless.
2 1 But speak the things that become sound
doctrine –
2 the aged men to be controlled, sensible, of
a sound mind, sound in faith, in love, in
patience –
3 the aged women also to behave as is right
for holy ones – not false accusers, not slaves
to wine, teachers of what is right –
4 so that they may teach the young women
to be lovers of their husbands and lovers of
their children,
5 right-minded, chaste, keepers at home,
good, obedient to their husbands – so that
the word of God may not be blasphemed.
6 In the same way encourage the younger
men to be right-minded –
7 in all things holding yourself out as a
pattern of good works: in doctrine, in
purity, being sensible, sincere,
8 of sound speech which cannot be condemned, so that he who is against you, may
be ashamed, having nothing evil to say of
you.
9 *Tell* slaves to be obedient to their masters,
to be pleasing in everything, not complaining,
10 not stealing, but showing all good faith

ʷὑμῶν‖ θεοῦ κοσμῶσιν ἐν πᾶσιν. 11 Ἐπεφάνη.γὰρ ἡ
¹of ²your God they may adorn in all things. For ¹¹appeared ¹the
χάρις τοῦ θεοῦ ˣἡ‖ σωτήριος πᾶσιν ἀνθρώποις,
²grace ³of ⁴God ⁵which ⁶brings ⁷salvation ⁸for ⁹all ¹⁰men,
12 παιδεύουσα ἡμᾶς ἵνα ἀρνησάμενοι τὴν ἀσέβειαν καὶ τὰς
instructing us that, having denied ungodliness and
κοσμικὰς.ἐπιθυμίας, σωφρόνως καὶ δικαίως καὶ εὐσεβῶς ζή-
worldly desires, discreetly and righteously and piously we
σωμεν ἐν τῷ νῦν αἰῶνι, 13 προσδεχόμενοι τὴν μακαρίαν
should live in the present age, awaiting the blessed
ἐλπίδα καὶ ἐπιφάνειαν τῆς δόξης τοῦ μεγάλου θεοῦ καὶ σωτῆ-
hope and appearing of the glory ³great ⁴God ⁵and ⁶Sa-
ρος ἡμῶν ʸἸησοῦ χριστοῦ,‖ 14 ὃς ἔδωκεν ἑαυτὸν ὑπὲρ ἡμῶν,
viour ¹of ²our Jesus Christ; who gave himself for us,
ἵνα λυτρώσηται ἡμᾶς ἀπὸ πάσης ἀνομίας, καὶ καθαρίσῃ
that he might redeem us from all lawlessness, and might purify
ἑαυτῷ λαὸν περιούσιον, ζηλωτὴν καλῶν ἔργων. 15 Ταῦτα
to himself a people peculiar, zealous of good works. These things
λάλει, καὶ παρακάλει, καὶ ἔλεγχε μετὰ πάσης ἐπιταγῆς.
speak, and exhort, and convict with all command.
μηδείς σου περιφρονείτω.
²No ³one ⁵thee ¹let ⁴despise.

3 Ὑπομίμνησκε αὐτοὺς ἀρχαῖς ᶻκαὶ‖ ἐξουσίαις ὑποτάσ-
Put ²in ³remembrance ¹them to rulers and to authorities to be
σεσθαι, πειθαρχεῖν, πρὸς πᾶν ἔργον ἀγαθὸν ἑτοίμους εἶναι,
subject, to be obedient, ⁴to ⁵every ⁷work ⁶good ³ready ¹to ²be,
2 μηδένα βλασφημεῖν, ἀμάχους εἶναι, ἐπιεικεῖς,
no one to speak evil of, not ³contentious ¹to ²be, [to be] gentle,
πᾶσαν ἐνδεικνυμένους ᵃπρᾳότητα‖ πρὸς πάντας ἀνθρώπους.
²all ¹shewing meekness towards all men.
3 ἦμεν.γάρ ποτε καὶ ἡμεῖς ἀνόητοι, ἀπειθεῖς, πλανώ-
For ²were ³once ⁴also ¹we without intelligence, disobedient, led
μενοι, δουλεύοντες ἐπιθυμίαις καὶ ἡδοναῖς ποικίλαις, ἐν κακίᾳ
astray, serving ²lusts ³and ⁴pleasures ¹various, in malice
καὶ φθόνῳ διάγοντες, στυγητοί, μισοῦντες ἀλλήλους· 4 ὅτε.δὲ
and envy living, hateful, hating one another. But when
ἡ χρηστότης καὶ ἡ φιλανθρωπία ἐπεφάνη τοῦ.σωτῆρος.ἡμῶν
the kindness and the love to man ⁵appeared ¹of ²our ³Saviour
θεοῦ, 5 οὐκ ἐξ ἔργων τῶν ἐν δικαιοσύνῃ ᵇὧν‖ ἐποιήσαμεν
⁴God, not by works which [were] in righteousness which ²practised
ἡμεῖς, ἀλλὰ κατὰ ᶜτὸν.αὐτοῦ.ἔλεον‖ ἔσωσεν ἡμᾶς, διὰ
¹we, but according to his mercy he saved us, through [the]
λουτροῦ ᵈπαλιγγενεσίας‖ καὶ ἀνακαινώσεως πνεύματος ἁγίου,
washing of regeneration and renewing of [the] ²Spirit ¹Holy,
6 οὗ ἐξέχεεν ἐφ' ἡμᾶς πλουσίως διὰ Ἰησοῦ χριστοῦ τοῦ
which he poured out on us richly through Jesus Christ
σωτῆρος.ἡμῶν· 7 ἵνα δικαιωθέντες τῇ.ἐκείνου.χάριτι, κληρο-
our Saviour; that having been justified by his grace, heirs
νόμοι ᵉγενώμεθα‖ κατ' ἐλπίδα ζωῆς αἰωνίου.
we should become according to [the] hope of life eternal.
8 Πιστὸς ὁ λόγος, καὶ περὶ τούτων βούλομαί σε δια-
Faithful [is] the word, and concerning these things I desire thee to
βεβαιοῦσθαι, ἵνα φροντίζωσιν καλῶν ἔργων προΐστασθαι
affirm strongly, that ⁸may ⁷take ⁹care ¹³good ¹⁴works ⁹to ¹⁰be ¹¹forward ¹²in
οἱ πεπιστευκότες ᶠτῷ‖ θεῷ. ταῦτά ἐστιν ᵍτὰ‖ καλὰ καὶ
¹they ²who ³have ⁴believed ⁵God. These things are good and
ὠφέλιμα τοῖς ἀνθρώποις· 9 μωρὰς.δὲ ζητήσεις καὶ γενεαλο-
profitable to men; but foolish questions and genealo-
γίας καὶ ʰἔρεις‖ καὶ μάχας νομικὰς περιΐστασο· εἰσὶν
gies and strifes and contentions about [the] law stand aloof from; ²they ³are
γὰρ ἀνωφελεῖς καὶ μάταιοι. 10 Αἱρετικὸν ἄνθρωπον μετὰ
¹for unprofitable and vain. A sectarian man after
μίαν καὶ δευτέραν νουθεσίαν παραιτοῦ, 11 εἰδὼς ὅτι ἐξέ-
one and a second admonition reject, knowing that is
στραπται ὁ τοιοῦτος, καὶ ἁμαρτάνει, ὢν αὐτοκατάκριτος.
perverted such a one, and sins, being self-condemned.
12 Ὅταν πέμψω Ἀρτεμᾶν πρός σε ἢ Τυχικόν, σπούδα-
When I shall send Artemas to thee, or Tychicus, be dili-
σον ἐλθεῖν πρός με εἰς Νικόπολιν· ἐκεῖ.γὰρ κέκρικα
gent to come to me to Nicopolis; for there I have decided
παραχειμάσαι. 13 Ζηνᾶν τὸν νομικὸν καὶ ⁱἈπολλὼ‖ σπου-
to winter. Zenas the lawyer and Apollos dili-
δαίως πρόπεμψον, ἵνα μηδὲν αὐτοῖς ᵏλείπῃ.‖ 14 μαν-
gently set forward, that nothing to them may be lacking; ²let
θανέτωσαν δὲ καὶ οἱ ἡμέτεροι καλῶν ἔργων προΐστασθαι
⁴learn ¹and ⁴also ³ours ¹⁰good ¹¹works ⁶to ⁷be ⁸forward ⁹in
εἰς τὰς ἀναγκαίας χρείας, ἵνα μὴ.ὦσιν ἄκαρποι. 15 Ἀσ-
for necessary wants, that they may not be unfruitful. ⁵Sa-
πάζονταί σε οἱ μετ' ἐμοῦ πάντες. ἄσπασαι τοὺς φι-
lute ⁶thee ²those ³with ⁴me ¹all. Salute those who
λοῦντας ἡμᾶς ἐν πίστει. ἡ χάρις μετὰ πάντων ὑμῶν.
love us in [the] faith. Grace [be] with ²all ¹you.

– so that they may adorn the teaching of your Savior God in all things.
11 For the grace of God, *that grace* which brings salvation, has become clearly known to all men,
12 teaching us that, denying ungodliness and worldly lusts, we should live wisely and righteously and godly in this present world,
13 looking for that blessed hope, and the glorious appearing of our great God and Savior Jesus Christ,
14 who gave Himself for us so that He might redeem us from all iniquity, and purify to Himself a peculiar people, zealous of good works.
15 These things speak, and exhort and rebuke with all authority. Let no one despise you.

CHAPTER 3

1 Remind them to be subject to rulers and to authorities, to be obedient, to be ready to every good work,
2 to speak evil of no one, to be peaceful, gentle, showing all meekness toward all men.
3 For we also were once foolish, disobedient, led astray, serving various lusts and pleasures – living in malice and envy, hateful and hating one another.
4 But when the kindness and love of God our Savior toward man appeared –
5 not by works of righteousness which we have done, but according to His mercy He saved us, by the washing of regeneration and renewing of the Holy Spirit,
6 which He poured out on us richly through Jesus Christ our Savior,
7 so that being justified by His grace, we should become heirs according to the hope of eternal life.
8 This saying is a faithful saying, and I desire you to strongly insist on these things, so that they who have believed God may be careful to maintain good works. These things are good and profitable to men.
9 But keep back from foolish questions and genealogies, and arguments and quarrels about the Law – for they are unprofitable and vain.
10 After the first and second warning, avoid a man who is a heretic,
11 knowing that such a one is turned out of the way and sins, being judged so by himself.
12 When I shall send Ar-te-mas to you, or Tych-i-cus, try to come to me to Ni-cop-o-lis. For I have decided to winter there.
13 Try to send Zenas the lawyer and Apollos, so that nothing may be lacking to them.
14 And let ours also learn to maintain good works for necessary uses, so that they may not be without fruit.
15 All those with me greet you. Greet those who love us in the faith. Grace be with you all. Amen.

[l]ἀμήν.‖
Amen.
[m]Πρὸς Τίτον, τῆς Κρητῶν ἐκκλησίας πρῶτον ἐπί-
To Titus [4]of [5]the [7]of [the] [8]Cretans [6]assembly [2]first [3]over-
σκοπον χειροτονηθέντα, ἐγράφη ἀπὸ Νικοπόλεως τῆς Μακε-
seer [1]chosen, written from Nicopolis of Mace-
δονίας.‖
donia.

The Letter to PHILEMON

ΠΑΥΛΟΣ δέσμιος χριστοῦ Ἰησοῦ, καὶ Τιμόθεος ὁ ἀδελφός,
Paul, prisoner of Christ Jesus, and Timotheus the brother,
Φιλήμονι τῷ ἀγαπητῷ καὶ συνεργῷ.ἡμῶν, 2 καὶ Ἀπφίᾳ τῇ
to Philemon the beloved and our fellow-worker, and to Apphia the
[b]ἀγαπητῇ,[r] καὶ Ἀρχίππῳ τῷ.[c]συστρατιώτῃ‖.ἡμῶν, καὶ τῇ
beloved, and to Archippus our fellow-soldier, and to the
κατ' οἶκόν.σου ἐκκλησίᾳ· 3 χάρις ὑμῖν καὶ εἰρήνη ἀπὸ θεοῦ
[2]in [3]thy [4]house [1]assembly: Grace to you and peace from God
πατρὸς.ἡμῶν καὶ κυρίου Ἰησοῦ χριστοῦ.
our Father and [the] Lord Jesus Christ.
4 Εὐχαριστῶ τῷ.θεῷ.μου, πάντοτε μνείαν σου ποιούμενος
I thank my God, always mention of thee making
ἐπὶ τῶν.προσευχῶν.μου, 5 ἀκούων σου τὴν ἀγάπην καὶ τὴν
at my prayers, hearing of thy love and
πίστιν ἣν ἔχεις [d]πρὸς‖ τὸν κύριον Ἰησοῦν καὶ εἰς πάν-
faith which thou hast towards the Lord Jesus, and towards all
τας τοὺς ἁγίους, 6 ὅπως ἡ κοινωνία τῆς.πίστεώς.σου ἐνεργὴς
the saints, so that the fellowship of thy faith efficient
γένηται ἐν ἐπιγνώσει παντὸς ἀγαθοῦ [e]τοῦ‖ ἐν
may become in [the] acknowledgment of every good [thing] which [is] in
[f]ὑμῖν‖ εἰς χριστὸν [g]Ἰησοῦν.‖ 7 [h]χάριν‖ γὰρ [i]ἔχομεν πολλὴν‖
you towards Christ Jesus. [5]Thankfulness [1]for [2]we [3]have [4]great
καὶ παράκλησιν ἐπὶ τῇ.ἀγάπῃ.σου, ὅτι τὰ σπλάγχνα
and encouragement by occasion of thy love, because the bowels
τῶν ἁγίων ἀναπέπαυται διὰ σοῦ, ἀδελφέ.
of the saints have been refreshed by thee, brother.
8 Διὸ πολλὴν ἐν χριστῷ παρρησίαν ἔχων ἐπιτάσσειν σοι
Wherefore much [2]in [3]Christ [1]boldness having to order thee
τὸ ἀνῆκον, 9 διὰ τὴν ἀγάπην μᾶλλον παρακαλῶ·
what [is] becoming, for the sake of love rather I exhort,
τοιοῦτος ὢν ὡς Παῦλος πρεσβύτης, νυνὶ.δὲ καὶ δέσμιος
such a one being as Paul [the] aged, and now also prisoner
[k]Ἰησοῦ χριστοῦ·‖ 10 παρακαλῶ σε περὶ τοῦ ἐμοῦ τέκνου, ὃν
of Jesus Christ. I exhort thee for my child, whom
ἐγέννησα ἐν τοῖς δεσμοῖς [l]μου,‖ Ὀνήσιμον, 11 τόν ποτέ σοι
I begot in [2]bonds [1]my, Onesimus, once to thee
ἄχρηστον, νυνὶ.δὲ [m] σοι καὶ ἐμοὶ εὔχρηστον, ὃν ἀνέπεμ-
unserviceable, but now to thee and to me serviceable: whom I sent
ψα[n]· 12 [o]σὺ.δὲ‖ αὐτόν, [p]τουτέστιν‖ τὰ ἐμὰ σπλάγχνα,
back [to thee]: but thou him, (that is, my bowels,)
[q]προσλαβοῦ·‖ 13 ὃν ἐγὼ ἐβουλόμην πρὸς ἐμαυτὸν κατέχειν,
receive: whom I was desiring with myself to keep,
ἵνα ὑπὲρ σοῦ [r]διακονῇ μοι‖ ἐν τοῖς δεσμοῖς τοῦ εὐαγγελίου·
that for thee he might serve me in the bonds of the glad tidings;
14 χωρὶς.δὲ τῆς.σῆς.γνώμης οὐδὲν ἠθέλησα ποιῆσαι, ἵνα μὴ
but apart from thy mind nothing I wished to do, that not
ὡς κατὰ.ἀνάγκην τὸ.ἀγαθόν.σου ᾖ, ἀλλὰ κατὰ.ἑκούσιον.
as of necessity thy good might be, but of willingness:
15 τάχα.γὰρ διὰ τοῦτο ἐχωρίσθη πρὸς ὥραν,
for perhaps because of this he was separated [from thee] for a time,
ἵνα αἰώνιον αὐτὸν ἀπέχῃς· 16 οὐκέτι ὡς δοῦλον,
that eternally him thou mightest possess; no longer as a bondman,
[s]ἀλλ'‖ ὑπὲρ δοῦλον, ἀδελφὸν ἀγαπητόν, μάλιστα ἐμοί,
but above a bondman, a brother beloved, specially to me,
πόσῳ.δὲ μᾶλλόν σοι καὶ ἐν σαρκὶ καὶ ἐν κυρίῳ;
and how much rather to thee both in [the] flesh and in [the] Lord?
17 εἰ οὖν [t]ἐμὲ‖ ἔχεις κοινωνόν, προσλαβοῦ αὐτὸν ὡς
If therefore me thou holdest a partner, receive him as
ἐμέ· 18 εἰ.δέ τι ἠδίκησέν σε ἢ ὀφείλει, τοῦτο ἐμοὶ [v]ἐλλόγει.‖
me; but if anything he wronged thee, or owes, this put to my account.
19 ἐγὼ Παῦλος ἔγραψα τῇ.ἐμῇ χειρί, ἐγὼ ἀποτίσω· ἵνα
I Paul wrote [it] with my [own] hand; I will repay; that
μὴ.λέγω σοι ὅτι καὶ σεαυτόν μοι προσοφείλεις. 20 Ναί,
I may not say to thee that even thyself to me thou owest also. Yea,
ἀδελφέ, ἐγώ σου ὀναίμην ἐν κυρίῳ· ἀνάπαυσόν μου
brother, [2]I [3]of [4]thee [1]may have profit in [the] Lord: refresh my
τὰ σπλάγχνα ἐν [w]κυρίῳ.‖ 21 πεποιθὼς τῇ.ὑπακοῇ.σου
bowels in [the] Lord. Being persuaded of thy obedience

1 Paul, a prisoner of Christ Jesus, and
Timothy our brother, to Phi-le-mon, our
dearly beloved friend and fellow-worker,
2 and to Ap-phi-a the beloved, and to
Ar-chip-pus our fellow-soldier, and to the
church in your house:
3 Grace to you and peace from God our
Father and the Lord Jesus Christ.
4 I thank my God, making mention of you
always in my prayers,
5 hearing of your love and faith which you
have towards the Lord Jesus and towards all
the saints,
6 so that the fellowship of your faith may
be efficient in the acknowledgment of every
good thing which is among you toward
Christ Jesus.
7 For we have great joy and encouragement
on account of your love, because the hearts
of the saints have been refreshed by you,
brother.
8 For this reason, I *might* have much boldness in Christ to command you to do what
is right.
9 But for love's sake, I beg you, being such
a one as Paul the aged, and now also a
prisoner of Jesus Christ.
10 I beg you for my child O-nes-i-mus,
whom I have begotten in my bonds.
11 At one time he was not profitable to you,
but now profitable to both you and me.
12 I have sent *him* back to you. And do
receive him, that is, my own heart.
13 For I desired to keep him with me so
that he might minister to me for you, in the
bonds of the gospel.
14 But I did not want to do anything apart
from your mind, so that your good might
not be as by force, but of willingness.
15 For perhaps because of this he was
separated for a time, so that you might
possess him forever –
16 no longer a slave, but above a slave, a
beloved brother, especially to me, but now
much more to you, both in the flesh and in
the Lord.
17 If, then, you count me as a partner,
receive him as if it were me.
18 And if he has wronged you or owes anything, put this to my account.
19 I, Paul, wrote it with my own hand – I
will repay it (that I may not say to you that
you owe even yourself to me too).
20 Yes, brother, may I have joy of you
in the Lord? Refresh my heart in the

ἔγραψά σοι, εἰδὼς ὅτι καὶ ὑπὲρ [x]ὃ" λέγω ποιήσεις.
I wrote to thee, knowing that even above what I may say thou wilt do.
22 "Ἅμα.δὲ καὶ ἑτοίμαζέ μοι ξενίαν· ἐλπίζω.γὰρ ὅτι διὰ
But withal also prepare me a lodging; for I hope that through
τῶν.προσευχῶν.ὑμῶν χαρισθήσομαι ὑμῖν. 23 [y]Ἀσπάζονταί[1]
your prayers I shall be granted to you. [13]Salute
σε Ἐπαφρᾶς ὁ συναιχμάλωτός μου ἐν χριστῷ Ἰησοῦ,
[14]thee [1]Epaphras [3]fellow-prisoner [2]my [4]in [5]Christ [6]Jesus;
24 Μάρκος, Ἀρίσταρχος, Δημᾶς, Λουκᾶς, οἱ.συνεργοί.μου.
[7]Mark, [8]Aristarchus, [9]Demas, [10]Luke, [11]my [12]fellow-workers.
25 ἡ χάρις τοῦ.κυρίου.[z]ἡμῶν[a] Ἰησοῦ χριστοῦ μετὰ τοῦ
The grace of our Lord Jesus Christ [be] with
πνεύματος.ὑμῶν. [a]ἀμήν."
your spirit. Amen.
[b]Πρὸς Φιλήμονα ἐγράφη ἀπὸ Ῥώμης, διὰ Ὀνησίμου
To Philemon written from Rome, by Onesimus
οἰκέτου."
a servant.

Lord.
21 Being persuaded of your obedience, I
wrote to you, knowing that you will do even
more than what I say.
22 And at the same time, prepare me a
place to stay, too, for I hope that through
your prayers I shall be given to you.
23 Ep-a-phras, my fellow-prisoner in Christ
Jesus,
24 Mark, Ar-is-tar-chus, Demas and Luke,
my fellow-workers, greet you.
25 The grace of the Lord Jesus Christ be
with your spirit. Amen.

The Letter to the HEBREWS

CHAPTER 1

ΠΟΛΥΜΕΡΩΣ καὶ πολυτρόπως πάλαι ὁ θεὸς λαλήσας
In many parts and in many ways of old God having spoken
τοῖς πατράσιν ἐν τοῖς προφήταις, ἐπ' [b]ἐσχάτων" τῶν ἡμερῶν
to the fathers in the prophets, in [2]last [3]days
τούτων, ἐλάλησεν ἡμῖν ἐν.υἱῷ, 2 ὃν ἔθηκεν κληρονό-
[1]these spoke to us in Son, whom he appointed heir
μον πάντων, δι' οὗ καὶ [c]τοὺς αἰῶνας ἐποίησεν," 3 ὃς ὢν
of all things, by whom also the worlds he made: who being
ἀπαύγασμα τῆς.δόξης καὶ χαρακτὴρ τῆς ὑποστάσεως
[the] effulgence of [his] glory and [the] exact expression of [2]substance
αὐτοῦ, φέρων.τε τὰ.πάντα τῷ ῥήματι τῆς.δυνάμεως.αὐτοῦ,
[1]his, and upholding all things by the word of his power,
[d]δι' ἑαυτοῦ" καθαρισμὸν [e]ποιησάμενος τῶν ἁμαρτιῶν"
by himself [the] purification having made of [2]sins
[f]ἡμῶν," ἐκάθισεν ἐν δεξιᾷ τῆς μεγαλωσύνης ἐν ὑψηλοῖς,
[1]our, sat down on [the] right hand of the greatness on high,
4 τοσούτῳ κρείττων γενόμενος τῶν ἀγγέλων, ὅσῳ
by so much better having become than the angels, as much as
διαφορώτερον παρ' αὐτοὺς κεκληρονόμηκεν ὄνομα. 5 Τίνι.γὰρ
[3]more [4]excellent [5]beyond [6]them [1]he [2]has [8]inherited [7]a [8]name. For to which
εἶπέν ποτε τῶν ἀγγέλων, Υἱός μου εἶ σύ, ἐγὼ σήμερον
[4]said [5]he [6]ever [1]of [2]the [3]angels, [8]Son [7]my art thou: I to-day
γεγέννηκά σε; καὶ πάλιν, Ἐγὼ ἔσομαι αὐτῷ εἰς πατέρα,
have begotten thee? and again, I will be to him for Father,
καὶ αὐτὸς ἔσται μοι εἰς υἱόν; 6 ὅταν.δὲ πάλιν εἰσαγάγῃ
and he shall be to me for Son? and [2]when [1]again he brings in
τὸν πρωτότοκον εἰς τὴν οἰκουμένην, λέγει, Καὶ προσκυνη-
the first-born into the habitable world, he says, And let wor-
σάτωσαν αὐτῷ πάντες ἄγγελοι θεοῦ. 7 Καὶ πρὸς μὲν
ship him all [the] angels of God. And as to
τοὺς ἀγγέλους λέγει, Ὁ ποιῶν τοὺς.ἀγγέλους.αὐτοῦ πνεύ-
the angels he says, Who makes his angels spi-
ματα, καὶ τοὺς.λειτουργοὺς.αὐτοῦ πυρὸς φλόγα· 8 πρὸς.δὲ
rits, and his ministers [3]of [4]fire [1]a [2]flame; but as to
τὸν υἱόν, Ὁ.θρόνος.σου, ὁ θεός, εἰς τὸν αἰῶνα τοῦ αἰῶνος·
the Son, Thy throne, O God, [is] to the age of the age.
[g]ῥάβδος [h] εὐθύτητος [i]ἡ" ῥάβδος τῆς.βασιλείας.σου. 9 ἠγά-
a sceptre of uprightness [is] the sceptre of thy kingdom. Thou
πησας δικαιοσύνην καὶ ἐμίσησας [k]ἀνομίαν." διὰ τοῦτο
didst love righteousness and didst hate lawlessness; because of this
ἔχρισέν σε ὁ θεὸς ὁ.θεός.σου ἔλαιον ἀγαλλιάσεως παρὰ τοὺς
[4]anointed [5]thee [1]God [2]thy [3]God with [the] oil of exultation above
μετόχους.σου. 10 Καί, Σὺ κατ'.ἀρχάς, κύριε, τὴν γῆν ἐθε-
thy companions. And, Thou in the beginning, Lord, the earth didst
μελίωσας, καὶ ἔργα τῶν.χειρῶν.σου εἰσιν οἱ οὐρανοί· 11 αὐτοὶ
found, and works of thy hands are the heavens. They
ἀπολοῦνται, σὺ.δὲ διαμένεις· καὶ πάντες ὡς ἱμάτιον παλαιω-
shall perish, but thou continuest; and [they] all as a garment shall grow
θήσονται, 12 καὶ ὡσεὶ περιβόλαιον [l]ἑλίξεις" αὐτούς[m], καὶ
old, and as a covering thou shalt roll up them, and
ἀλλαγήσονται· σὺ.δὲ ὁ αὐτὸς εἶ, καὶ τὰ.ἔτη.σου οὐκ ἐκλεί-
they shall be changed; but thou the same art, and thy years [2]not [1]shall
ψουσιν. 13 Πρὸς.τίνα.δὲ τῶν ἀγγέλων εἴρηκέν ποτε, Κάθου ἐκ
fail. But as to which of the angels said he ever, Sit at
δεξιῶν.μου, ἕως.ἂν.θῶ τοὺς.ἐχθρούς.σου ὑποπόδιον τῶν
my right hand until I place thine enemies [as] a footstool [1]for
ποδῶν.σου; 14 οὐχὶ πάντες εἰσὶν λειτουργικὰ πνεύματα, εἰς
[3]feet [2]thy? [6]Not [7]all [4]are [5]they ministering spirits, for

1 At many places and in many ways God
has spoken in times past to the fathers in the
prophets –
2 in these last days He has spoken to us in
the Son, whom He has appointed heir of all
things – by whom also He made the worlds.
3 *And He* who is the shining splendor of His
glory and the express image of His Person,
(and who is upholding all things by the word
of His power), when He had purged our sins
by Himself, He sat down on the right hand
of the Majesty on high,
4 having become so much better than the
angels, He has inherited a far more excellent
name than they.
5 For to which of the angels has He at any
time said, "You are My Son. Today I have
begotten You?" And again, "I will be a
Father to Him and He shall be a Son to
Me?"
6 And again, when He brought the First-
born into the world, He said, "And let all
the angels of God worship Him."
7 And of the angels He said, "Who makes
His angels spirits and His ministers a flame of
fire."
8 But as to the Son, "Your throne, O God,
is forever and ever. A sceptre of righteousness is the sceptre of Your kingdom.
9 You have loved righteousness and hated
lawlessness. Because of this, God, Your God,
has anointed You with the oil of gladness
above Your companions."
10 And, "You, O Lord, in the beginning
laid the foundations of the earth. And the
heavens are the works of Your hands.
11 They shall vanish away, but You shall
continue. And they shall all grow old like a
garment –
12 and as a covering You shall fold them
up, and they shall be changed. But You are
the same, and Your years shall not fail."
13 But to which of the angels did He ever
say, "Sit on My right hand until I place Your
enemies as a footstool at Your feet?"
14 Are they not all ministering spirits sent

διακονίαν ἀποστελλόμενα διὰ τοὺς μέλλοντας κληρονο-
service being sent forth on account of those being about to inherit
μεῖν σωτηρίαν;
salvation?

2 Διὰ τοῦτο δεῖ περισσοτέρως [n]ἡμᾶς προσέχειν‖
On account of this it behoves more abundantly us to give heed
τοῖς ἀκουσθεῖσιν, μήποτε [o]παραῤῥυῶμεν.‖ 2 εἰ.γὰρ
to the things heard, lest at any time we should slip away. For if
ὁ δι' ἀγγέλων λαληθεὶς λόγος ἐγένετο βέβαιος, καὶ πᾶσα
the 3by 4angels 2spoken 1word was confirmed, and every
παράβασις καὶ παρακοὴ ἔλαβεν ἔνδικον μισθαποδοσίαν, 3 πῶς
transgression and disobedience received just recompense, how
ἡμεῖς ἐκφευξόμεθα τηλικαύτης ἀμελήσαντες σωτηρίας; ἥτις
2we 1shall escape 5so 6great [1if 2we] 3have 4neglected a salvation? which
ἀρχὴν λαβοῦσα λαλεῖσθαι διὰ τοῦ κυρίου, ὑπὸ
3a 4commencement 1having 2received to be spoken [of] by the Lord, 5by
τῶν ἀκουσάντων εἰς ἡμᾶς ἐβεβαιώθη, 4 συνεπιμαρτυ-
6those 7that 8heard 3to 4us 1was 2confirmed; 10bearing 11witness
ροῦντος τοῦ θεοῦ σημείοις τε καὶ τέρασιν, καὶ ποικίλαις
12with [13them] 9God 15by 16signs 14both and wonders, and various
δυνάμεσιν, καὶ πνεύματος ἁγίου μερισμοῖς, κατὰ τὴν
acts of power, and 2of [3the] 5Spirit 4Holy 1distributions, according to
αὐτοῦ θέλησιν.
his will.

5 Οὐ.γὰρ ἀγγέλοις ὑπέταξεν τὴν οἰκουμένην τὴν μέλ-
For not to angels did he subject the habitable world which is to
λουσαν, περὶ ἧς λαλοῦμεν· 6 διεμαρτύρατο.δέ που τὶς
come, of which we speak; but 2fully 3testified 4somewhere 1one
λέγων, Τί ἐστιν ἄνθρωπος, ὅτι μιμνήσκῃ αὐτοῦ; ἢ υἱὸς
saying, What is man, that thou art mindful of him, or son
ἀνθρώπου, ὅτι ἐπισκέπτῃ [p]αὐτόν;‖ 7 ἠλάττωσας αὐτὸν
of man, that thou visitest him? Thou didst make 2lower 1him
βραχύ τι παρ' ἀγγέλους· δόξῃ καὶ τιμῇ ἐστεφάνωσας
3little 2some than [the] angels; with glory and honour thou didst crown
(or for a little)
αὐτόν, [q]καὶ κατέστησας αὐτὸν ἐπὶ τὰ ἔργα τῶν.χειρῶν.σου·‖
him, and didst set him over the works of thy hands;
8 πάντα ὑπέταξας ὑποκάτω τῶν.ποδῶν.αὐτοῦ. Ἐν.[r]γὰρ
all things thou didst subject under his feet. For in
τῷ‖ ὑποτάξαι [s]αὐτῷ‖ τὰ.πάντα, οὐδὲν ἀφῆκεν αὐτῷ ἀνυπότακ-
subjecting to him all things, nothing he left to him unsubject.
τον· νῦν.δὲ οὔπω ὁρῶμεν αὐτῷ τὰ.πάντα ὑποτεταγμένα·
But now not yet do we see to him all things subjected;
9 τὸν.δὲ βραχύ τι παρ' ἀγγέλους ἠλαττωμένον βλέπομεν
but 4who 8little 7some 10than [11the] 12angels [5was] 6made 9lower 1we 2see
(or for a little)
Ἰησοῦν διὰ τὸ πάθημα τοῦ θανάτου δόξῃ καὶ τιμῇ
3Jesus on account of the suffering of death with glory and with honour
ἐστεφανωμένον, ὅπως χάριτι θεοῦ ὑπὲρ παντὸς γεύσηται
crowned; so that by [the] grace of God for every one he might taste
(or every thing)
θανάτου. 10 Ἔπρεπεν.γὰρ αὐτῷ, δι' ὃν τὰ.πάντα καὶ δι'
death. For it was becoming to him, for whom [are] all things and by
οὗ τὰ.πάντα, πολλοὺς υἱοὺς εἰς δόξαν ἀγαγόντα, τὸν
whom [are] all things, many sons to glory bringing, the
ἀρχηγὸν τῆς.σωτηρίας.αὐτῶν διὰ παθημάτων τελειῶσαι.
leader of their salvation through sufferings to make perfect.
11 ὅ.τε.γὰρ ἁγιάζων καὶ οἱ ἁγιαζόμενοι, ἐξ ἑνὸς πάντες·
For both he who sanctifies and those sanctified of one [are] all;
δι' ἣν αἰτίαν οὐκ.ἐπαισχύνεται ἀδελφοὺς αὐτοὺς καλεῖν, 12 λέ-
for which cause he is not ashamed 4brethren 3them 1to 2call, say-
γων, Ἀπαγγελῶ τὸ.ὄνομά.σου τοῖς.ἀδελφοῖς.μου, ἐν μέσῳ
ing, I will declare thy name to my brethren; in [the] midst
ἐκκλησίας ὑμνήσω.σε. 13 Καὶ πάλιν, Ἐγὼ ἔσομαι
of [the] assembly I will sing praise to thee. And again, I will be
πεποιθὼς ἐπ' αὐτῷ. Καὶ πάλιν, Ἰδοὺ ἐγὼ καὶ τὰ παιδία ἅ
trusting in him. And again, Behold I and the children which
μοι ἔδωκεν ὁ θεός. 14 Ἐπεὶ οὖν τὰ παιδία κεκοινώνηκεν
3me 2gave 1God. Since therefore the children have partaken
[t]σαρκὸς καὶ αἵματος,‖ καὶ αὐτὸς παραπλησίως μετέσχεν
of flesh and blood, also he in like manner took part in
τῶν.αὐτῶν, ἵνα διὰ τοῦ θανάτου καταργήσῃ τὸν τὸ κράτος
the same, that through death he might annul him who 2the 3might
ἔχοντα τοῦ θανάτου, [w]τουτέστιν‖ τὸν διάβολον, 15 καὶ ἀπαλ-
1has of death, that is, the devil; and might set
λάξῃ τούτους ὅσοι φόβῳ θανάτου διὰ παντὸς τοῦ.ζῇν
free those whosoever by fear of death through all their lifetime
ἔνοχοι ἦσαν [x]δουλείας.‖ 16 οὐ.γὰρ δήπου ἀγγέλων ἐπιλαμ-
2subject 1were to bondage. For not indeed of angels takes he
βάνεται, ἀλλὰ σπέρματος Ἀβραὰμ ἐπιλαμβάνεται. 17 ὅθεν
hold, but of [the] seed of Abraham he takes hold. Wherefore
ὤφειλεν κατὰ πάντα τοῖς.ἀδελφοῖς ὁμοιωθῆναι, ἵνα ἐλεή-
it behoved [him] in all things to [his] brethren to be made like, that a merci-

out in order to serve those who are going to be heirs of salvation?

2 1 Because of this, we ought to give the more earnest attention to the things which we have heard, for fear that at any time we might slip away.

2 For if the word spoken by angels was confirmed, and every disobedience and breaking of the Law received a just repayment,

3 how shall we escape if we neglect so great a salvation? Which *salvation* was spoken of by the Lord in the beginning, being confirmed to us by those that heard –

4 God bearing witness both with signs and wonders and with different kinds of mighty works, and with gifts of the Holy Spirit, according to His own will.

5 For He did not put the world which is to come under angels of which we speak.

6 But one fully testified in a certain place, saying, "What is man that You care to remember him, or the son of man that You visit him?

7 For a little while You made him lower than the angels. You crowned him with glory and honor and set him over the works of Your hands.

8 You have put all things under his feet." For in putting all things under him, He did not leave anything that is not under him. But now we do not yet see all things under him –

9 but we do see Jesus crowned with glory and honor, who, on account of the suffering of death was for a little while made lower than the angels, so that by the grace of God He might taste death for every *son.*

10 For it was proper to Him (for whom are all things and by whom are all things), in bringing many sons to glory, to make the Author of their salvation perfect through sufferings.

11 For both He that makes holy and those who are being made holy are all of One – for which cause He is not ashamed to call them brothers,

12 saying, "I will declare Your name to My brothers. I will sing praise to You in the midst of the congregation."

13 And again, "I will put My trust in Him." And again, "See! I and the children which God has given Me."

14 Since, then, the children have partaken of flesh and blood, He also in the same way took part of the same – so that through death He might defeat him who has the power of death, that is, the devil –

15 and that He might deliver all those who through fear of death were subject to life-long slavery.

16 For without doubt He does not take hold of angels, but He takes hold of the seed of Abraham.

17 So He needed in every way to be made

μων γένηται καὶ πιστὸς ἀρχιερεὺς τὰ πρὸς τὸν θεόν,
ful 5he 6might 7be 1and 2faithful 3high 4priest [in] things relating to God,
εἰς τὸ ἱλάσκεσθαι τὰς ἁμαρτίας τοῦ λαοῦ. 18 ἐν.ᾧ.γὰρ
for to make propitiation for the sins of the people; for in that
πέπονθεν αὐτὸς πειρασθείς, δύναται τοῖς πειραζομένοις
he 2has 3suffered 1himself having been tempted, he is able those being tempted
βοηθῆσαι.
to help.

3 Ὅθεν, ἀδελφοὶ ἅγιοι, κλήσεως ἐπουρανίου μέτοχοι,
Wherefore, 2brethren 1holy, of [the] 2calling 1heavenly partakers,
κατανοήσατε τὸν ἀπόστολον καὶ ἀρχιερέα τῆς.ὁμολογίας.ἡμῶν
consider the apostle and high priest of our confession,
χριστὸν Ἰησοῦν· 2 πιστὸν ὄντα τῷ ποιήσαντι αὐτόν, ὡς
Christ Jesus, 2faithful 1being to him who appointed him, as
καὶ Μωσῆς ἐν ὅλῳ τῷ.οἴκῳ.αὐτοῦ. 3 πλείονος.γὰρ δόξης
also Moses in all his house. For 2of 3more 4glory
οὗτος παρὰ Μωσῆν ἠξίωται, καθ᾽.ὅσον πλείονα τιμὴν
1he than Moses has been counted worthy, by how much more honour
ἔχει τοῦ οἴκου ὁ κατασκευάσας αὐτόν· 4 πᾶς.γὰρ οἶκος
has 5than 6the 7house 1he 2who 3built 4it. For every house
κατασκευάζεται ὑπό τινος· ὁ.δὲ τὰ.πάντα κατασκευάσας
is built by some one; but he who all things built [is]
θεός. 5 καὶ Μωσῆς μὲν πιστὸς ἐν ὅλῳ τῷ.οἴκῳ.αὐτοῦ ὡς
God. And Moses indeed [was] faithful in all his house as
θεράπων, εἰς μαρτύριον τῶν λαληθησομένων·
a ministering servant, for a testimony of the things going to be spoken;
6 χριστὸς.δὲ ὡς υἱὸς ἐπὶ τὸν.οἶκον.αὐτοῦ, οὗ οἶκός ἐσμεν
but Christ as Son over his house, whose house are
ἡμεῖς, ἐάνπερ τὴν παῤῥησίαν καὶ τὸ καύχημα τῆς ἐλπίδος
we, if indeed the boldness and the boasting of the hope
μέχρι τέλους βεβαίαν κατάσχωμεν.
unto [the] end firm we should hold.

7 Διό, καθὼς λέγει τὸ πνεῦμα τὸ ἅγιον, Σήμερον ἐὰν τῆς
Wherefore, even as says the Spirit the Holy, To-day if
φωνῆς.αὐτοῦ ἀκούσητε, 8 μὴ.σκληρύνητε τὰς.καρδίας.ὑμῶν,
his voice ye will hear, harden not your hearts,
ὡς ἐν τῷ παραπικρασμῷ, κατὰ τὴν ἡμέραν τοῦ πειρασμοῦ ἐν
as in the provocation, in the day of temptation, in
τῇ ἐρήμῳ, 9 οὗ ἐπείρασάν με οἱ.πατέρες.ὑμῶν, ἐδοκίμασάν
the wilderness, where 3tempted 4me 1your 2fathers, proved
με, καὶ εἶδον τὰ.ἔργα.μου τεσσαράκοντα ἔτη· 10 διὸ προσ-
me, and saw my works forty years. Wherefore I was
ώχθισα τῇ γενεᾷ ἐκείνῃ, καὶ εἶπον, Ἀεὶ πλανῶνται τῇ
indignant with 2generation 1that, and said, Always they err
καρδίᾳ· αὐτοὶ.δὲ οὐκ.ἔγνωσαν τὰς.ὁδούς.μου· 11 ὡς ὤμοσα ἐν
in heart; and they did not know my ways; so I swore in
τῇ.ὀργῇ.μου, Εἰ εἰσελεύσονται εἰς τὴν.κατάπαυσίν.μου. 12 Βλέ-
my wrath, If they shall enter into my rest. Take
πετε, ἀδελφοί, μήποτε ἔσται ἔν τινι ὑμῶν καρδία πονηρὰ
heed, brethren, lest perhaps shall be in anyone of you a 2heart 1wicked
ἀπιστίας ἐν τῷ ἀποστῆναι ἀπὸ θεοῦ ζῶντος· 13 ἀλλὰ
of unbelief in departing from 3God [1the] 2living. But
παρακαλεῖτε ἑαυτοὺς καθ᾽.ἑκάστην.ἡμέραν, ἄχρις.οὗ τὸ σήμερον
encourage yourselves every day as long as 1to-day
καλεῖται, ἵνα μὴ σκληρυνθῇ τις ἐξ ὑμῶν ἀπάτῃ τῆς
2it is 3called, that not may be hardened any of you by [the] deceitfulness
ἁμαρτίας· 14 μέτοχοι.γὰρ γεγόναμεν τοῦ χριστοῦ, ἐάνπερ
of sin. For companions we have become of the Christ, if indeed
τὴν ἀρχὴν τῆς ὑποστάσεως μέχρι τέλους βεβαίαν κατά-
the beginning of the assurance unto [the] end firm we
σχωμεν· 15 ἐν τῷ.λέγεσθαι, Σήμερον ἐὰν τῆς.φωνῆς.αὐτοῦ
should hold; in its being said, To-day if his voice
ἀκούσητε, μὴ.σκληρύνητε τὰς.καρδίας.ὑμῶν, ὡς ἐν τῷ παραπι-
ye will hear, harden not your hearts, as in the provoca-
κρασμῷ. 16 τινὲς.γὰρ ἀκούσαντες παρεπίκραναν, ἀλλ᾽ οὐ
tion. For some having heard provoked, but not
πάντες οἱ ἐξελθόντες ἐξ Αἰγύπτου διὰ Μωσέως. 17 τίσιν.δὲ
all who came out from Egypt by Moses. And with whom
προσώχθισεν τεσσαράκοντα ἔτη; οὐχὶ τοῖς ἁμαρ-
was he indignant forty years? [Was it] not with those who
τήσασιν, ὧν τὰ κῶλα ἔπεσεν ἐν τῇ ἐρήμῳ; 18 τίσιν.δὲ
sinned, of whom the carcases fell in the wilderness? And to whom
ὤμοσεν μὴ.εἰσελεύσεσθαι εἰς τὴν.κατάπαυσιν.αὐτοῦ, εἰ.μὴ
swore he [that they] shall not enter into his rest, except
τοῖς ἀπειθήσασιν; 19 καὶ βλέπομεν ὅτι οὐκ.ἠδυνήθησαν
to those who disobeyed? And we see that they were not able
εἰσελθεῖν δι᾽ ἀπιστίαν. 4 Φοβηθῶμεν οὖν μήποτε
to enter in on account of unbelief. We should fear therefore lest perhaps
καταλειπομένης ἐπαγγελίας εἰσελθεῖν εἰς τὴν.κατάπαυσιν.αὐ-
3being 4left 1a 2promise to enter into his rest,
τοῦ, δοκῇ τις ἐξ ὑμῶν ὑστερηκέναι. 2 καὶ.γὰρ ἐσμεν.εὐηγ-
4might 5seem 1any 2of 3you to come short. For indeed we have had

like His brothers, so that He might be a merciful and faithful High Priest in things relating to God, to make atonement for the sins of the people.

18 For in that He Himself has suffered, having been tempted, He is able to help those who are tempted.

CHAPTER 3

1 Then, holy brothers, who share in the heavenly calling, consider the Apostle and High Priest whom we confess – Christ Jesus,

2 who was faithful to Him who appointed Him, even as Moses also in all his house.

3 For He was counted worthy of more glory than Moses, just as He who has built *the house* has more honor than the house.

4 For every house is built by someone, but He that built all things is God.

5 And Moses truly was faithful in all his house, as a servant, for a witness of those things which were going to be spoken later.

6 But Christ *was faithful* as a Son over His own house (whose house we are, if we hold fast the boldness and rejoicing of the hope firm to the end).

7 For this reason, as the Holy Spirit says, "Today, if you will hear His voice,

8 do not harden your hearts, as in the *day they* provoked Me, in the day of temptation in the wilderness,

9 where your fathers tempted Me, proved Me and saw My works forty years."

10 For this reason, "I was not pleased with that generation and said, They always go astray in their hearts and they have not known My ways.

11 So I swore in My wrath, They shall not enter into My rest."

12 Be careful, brothers, for fear that there may be in any of you an evil heart of unbelief in falling away from the living God.

13 But encourage one another day by day, while it is called Today – so that none of you may be hardened through the deceitfulness of sin.

14 For we have become companions of Christ, if we truly hold the beginning of our trust firm to the end –

15 so long as it is said, "Today, if you will hear His voice, do not harden your hearts, as in the *day they* provoked Me."

16 For some provoked God when they heard, but not all who came out from Egypt by Moses.

17 But with whom was He displeased forty years – if not with those who sinned, whose bodies fell in the wilderness?

18 And to whom did He swear that they should not enter into His rest, but to those that did not believe?

19 So we see that they could not enter in because of unbelief.

4 1 Let us fear, then, lest a promise being left to enter into His rest, any of you should seem to come short.

γελισμένοι, καθάπερ κἀκεῖνοι· ἀλλ' οὐκ ὠφέλησεν ὁ
glad tidings announced [to us] even as also they; but not did profit [2]the
λόγος τῆς ἀκοῆς ἐκείνους, μὴ [t]συγκεκραμένος‖ τῇ πίστει
[3]word [4]of [5]the [6]report [1]them, not having been mixed with faith
τοῖς ἀκούσασιν. 3 εἰσερχόμεθα.γὰρ εἰς [v]τὴν‖ κατάπαυσιν
in those who heard. For we enter into the rest,
οἱ πιστεύσαντες, καθὼς εἴρηκεν, Ὡς ὤμοσα ἐν τῇ.ὀργῇ.μου,
who believed; as he has said, So I swore in my wrath,
Εἰ εἰσελεύσονται εἰς τὴν.κατάπαυσίν.μου· καίτοι τῶν ἔργων
If they shall enter into my rest; though verily the works
ἀπὸ καταβολῆς κόσμου γενηθέντων. 4 Εἴρηκεν.γάρ που
from [the] foundation of [the] world were done. For he has said somewhere
περὶ τῆς ἑβδόμης οὕτως, Καὶ κατέπαυσεν ὁ θεὸς ἐν τῇ
concerning the seventh [day] thus, And [2]rested [1]God on the
ἡμέρᾳ τῇ ἑβδόμῃ ἀπὸ πάντων τῶν.ἔργων.αὐτοῦ· 5 καὶ ἐν τού-
[2]day [1]seventh from all his works: and in this
τῳ πάλιν, Εἰ εἰσελεύσονται εἰς τὴν.κατάπαυσίν.μου. 6 Ἐπεὶ
[place] again, If they shall enter into my rest. Since
οὖν ἀπολείπεταί τινας εἰσελθεῖν εἰς αὐτήν, καὶ οἱ πρό-
therefore it remains [for] some to enter into it, and those who
τερον εὐαγγελισθέντες οὐκ.εἰσῆλθον [w]δι'‖ ἀπείθειαν, 7 πά-
formerly heard glad tidings did not enter in on account of disobedience, again
λιν τινὰ ὁρίζει ἡμέραν, Σήμερον, ἐν [x]Δαβὶδ‖ λέγων, μετὰ
a certain [2]he [3]determines [1]day, To-day, in David saying, after
τοσοῦτον χρόνον, καθὼς [y]εἴρηται,‖ Σήμερον ἐὰν τῆς φωνῆς
so long a time, (according as it has been said,) To-day, if [2]voice
αὐτοῦ ἀκούσητε, μὴ.σκληρύνητε τὰς.καρδίας.ὑμῶν. 8 Εἰ.γὰρ
[1]his ye will hear, harden not your hearts. For if
αὐτοὺς Ἰησοῦς κατέπαυσεν, οὐκ ἂν περὶ ἄλλης ἐλά-
[3]them [1]Jesus [2]gave [4]rest, not concerning another [2]would [3]he [4]have
(i.e. Joshua)
λει μετὰ.ταῦτα ἡμέρας· 9 ἄρα ἀπολείπεται σαββατισμὸς τῷ
[5]spoken [6]afterwards [1]day. Then remains a sabbatism to the
λαῷ τοῦ.θεοῦ. 10 ὁ.γὰρ εἰσελθὼν εἰς τὴν.κατάπαυσιν.αὐτοῦ,
people of God. For he that entered into his rest,
καὶ αὐτὸς κατέπαυσεν ἀπὸ τῶν.ἔργων.αὐτοῦ, ὥσπερ ἀπὸ
also he rested from his works, as [3]from
τῶν ἰδίων ὁ θεός. 11 Σπουδάσωμεν οὖν εἰσελθεῖν εἰς
[4]his [5]own [1]God [[2]did]. We should be diligent therefore to enter into
ἐκείνην τὴν κατάπαυσιν, ἵνα.μὴ ἐν τῷ αὐτῷ τις ὑποδείγ-
that rest, lest [4]after [5]the [6]same [1]anyone [7]example
ματι πέσῃ τῆς ἀπειθείας. 12 Ζῶν.γὰρ ὁ λόγος τοῦ θεοῦ καὶ
[2]may [3]fall of disobedience. For living [is] the word of God and
ἐνεργής, καὶ τομώτερος ὑπὲρ πᾶσαν μάχαιραν δίστομον, καὶ
efficient, and sharper than every [2]sword [1]two-edged, even
διϊκνούμενος ἄχρι μερισμοῦ ψυχῆς.[z]τε‖ καὶ πνεύματος, ἁρ-
penetrating to [the] division both of soul and spirit, [2]of
μῶν τε καὶ μυελῶν, καὶ κριτικὸς ἐνθυμήσεων καὶ ἐννοιῶν
[3]joints [1]both and marrows, and [is] a discerner of [the] thoughts and intents
καρδίας· 13 καὶ οὐκ.ἔστιν κτίσις ἀφανὴς ἐνώπιον αὐτοῦ·
of [the] heart. And there is not a created thing unapparent before him;
πάντα.δὲ γυμνὰ καὶ τετραχηλισμένα τοῖς ὀφθαλμοῖς αὐτοῦ,
but all things [are] naked and laid bare to the eyes of him,
πρὸς ὃν ἡμῖν ὁ λόγος.
with whom [is] our account.

14 [a]Ἔχοντες.οὖν ἀρχιερέα μέγαν διεληλυθότα τοὺς
Having therefore a [2]high [3]priest [1]great [who] has passed through the
οὐρανούς, Ἰησοῦν τὸν υἱὸν τοῦ θεοῦ, κρατῶμεν τῆς ὁμο-
heavens, Jesus the Son of God, we should hold fast the con-
λογίας. 15 οὐ.γὰρ ἔχομεν ἀρχιερέα μὴ δυνάμενον [a]συμπα-
fession. For not have we a high priest not able to sym-
θῆσαι‖ ταῖς.ἀσθενείαις.ἡμῶν, [b]πεπειραμένον‖.δὲ κατὰ πάντα
pathise with our infirmities, but [who] has been tempted in all things
καθ'.ὁμοιότητα χωρὶς ἁμαρτίας. 16 προσερχώμεθα οὖν
according to [our] likeness, apart from sin. We should come therefore
μετὰ παῤῥησίας τῷ θρόνῳ τῆς χάριτος, ἵνα λάβωμεν [c]ἔλεον,‖
with boldness to the throne of grace, that we may receive mercy,
καὶ χάριν εὕρωμεν εἰς εὔκαιρον βοήθειαν.
and [3]grace [1]may [2]find for opportune help.

5 Πᾶς.γὰρ ἀρχιερεὺς ἐξ ἀνθρώπων λαμβανόμενος, ὑπὲρ
For every high priest from among men being taken for
ἀνθρώπων καθίσταται τὰ πρὸς τὸν θεόν, ἵνα προσφέρῃ
men is constituted in things relating to God, that he may offer
δῶρά.[d]τε‖ καὶ θυσίας ὑπὲρ ἁμαρτιῶν, 2 μετριοπαθεῖν δυνά-
both gifts, and sacrifices for sins; [3]to [4]exercise [5]forbearance [1]being
μενος τοῖς ἀγνοοῦσιν καὶ πλανωμένοις, ἐπεὶ καὶ αὐτὸς
[2]able with those being ignorant and erring, since also himself
περίκειται ἀσθένειαν· 3 καὶ [e]διὰ ταύτην‖ ὀφείλει,
is encompassed with infirmity; and on account of this [infirmity] he ought,
καθὼς περὶ τοῦ λαοῦ, οὕτως καὶ περὶ [f]ἑαυτοῦ‖ προσφέρειν
even as for the people, so also for himself to offer
[g]ὑπὲρ‖ ἁμαρτιῶν. 4 Καὶ οὐχ ἑαυτῷ τις λαμβάνει τὴν τιμήν,
for sins. And not to himself anyone takes the honour,

2 For the gospel has been preached to us, as well as to them. But the word of the message did not do them any good, not being mixed with faith in the ones who heard.

3 For we who have believed do enter into rest, as He said, "As I have sworn in My wrath, they shall not enter into My rest." Though truly the works were finished from the foundation of the world –

4 for He has spoken in a certain place of the seventh day in this way, "And God rested on the seventh day from all His works."

5 And in this place again, "They shall not enter into My rest."

6 Since, then, it remains for some to enter into it – and those to whom it was first announced did not enter in because of unbelief –

7 He again marks out a certain day, saying in David, "Today" (after so long a time). Even as it is said, "Today, if you will hear His voice, do not harden your hearts."

8 For if Joshua had given them rest, then He would not have afterwards spoken about another day.

9 So then, there is still a rest to the people of God.

10 For He that entered into His rest, He also rested from His works, as God did from His.

11 Let us, then, labor to enter into the rest for fear that anyone should fall according to the same example of unbelief.

12 For the word of God is living and powerful and sharper than any two-edged sword, piercing even to the dividing apart of both soul and spirit, and of both the joints and marrow – and a heart of the thoughts and intentions of the heart.

13 And there is not any creature that is not clearly revealed before Him. But all things are naked and opened to the eyes of Him to whom we must give account.

14 Therefore, having a great High Priest who has passed through the heavens, Jesus the Son of God, let us hold firmly to what we confess.

15 For we do not have a High Priest who cannot be touched with the feeling of our weaknesses, but One who has been tempted in all things like *us, but* without sin.

16 So let us draw near to the throne of grace with boldness, so that we may receive mercy and find grace to help in time of need.

CHAPTER 5

1 For every high priest taken from among men is appointed for men in things relating to God – so that he may offer both gifts and sacrifices for sins,

2 being able to have pity on the ignorant and those that wander out of the way, since he himself also is hemmed in with weakness.

3 And because of this he ought, even as for the people, so also for himself to offer for sins.

ἀλλὰ [h]ὁ" καλούμενος ὑπὸ τοῦ θεοῦ, [i]καθάπερ" καὶ [h]ὁ" Ἀαρών.
but [h]he being called by God, even as also Aaron.
5 οὕτως καὶ ὁ χριστὸς οὐχ ἑαυτὸν ἐδόξασεν γενηθῆναι ἀρχ-
Thus also the Christ not himself did glorify to become a high
ιερέα, ἀλλ' ὁ λαλήσας πρὸς αὐτόν, Υἱός μου εἶ σύ, ἐγὼ σή-
priest; but he who said to him, [2]Son [1]my art thou, I to-
μερον γεγέννηκά σε. 6 καθὼς καὶ ἐν ἑτέρῳ λέγει, Σὺ
day have begotten thee. Even as also in another [place] he says, Thou [art]
ἱερεὺς εἰς.τὸν.αἰῶνα κατὰ τὴν τάξιν Μελχισεδέκ. 7 "Ος ἐν
a priest for ever according to the order of Melchisedec. Who in
ταῖς ἡμέραις τῆς.σαρκὸς.αὐτοῦ δεήσεις.τε καὶ ἱκετηρίας πρὸς
the days of his flesh both supplications and entreaties [3]to
τὸν δυνάμενον σώζειν αὐτὸν ἐκ θανάτου, μετὰ κραυ-
[4]him [5]who [[6]was] [7]able [8]to [9]save [10]him [11]from [12]death, [13]with [15]cry-
γῆς ἰσχυρᾶς καὶ δακρύων προσενέγκας, καὶ εἰσακουσθεὶς ἀπὸ
ing [14]strong [16]and [17]tears [1]having [2]offered, and having been heard in
τῆς.εὐλαβείας, 8 καίπερ ὢν υἱός, ἔμαθεν ἀφ' ὧν
that [he] feared; though being a son, he learned, from the things which
ἔπαθεν τὴν ὑπακοήν, 9 καὶ τελειωθεὶς ἐγένετο [k]τοῖς
he suffered, obedience; and having been perfected became to [2]those [3]that
ὑπακούουσιν αὐτῷ πᾶσιν" αἴτιος σωτηρίας αἰωνίου· 10 προσ-
[4]obey [5]him [1]all, author of [2]salvation [1]eternal; having
αγορευθεὶς ὑπὸ τοῦ θεοῦ ἀρχιερεὺς κατὰ τὴν τάξιν Μελ-
been saluted by God [as] high priest according to the order of Mel-
χισεδέκ. 11 Περὶ οὗ πολὺς ἡμῖν.ὁ.λόγος καὶ δυσερμή-
chisedec. Concerning whom [[3]is] [4]much [1]our [2]discourse and difficult in inter-
νευτος λέγειν, ἐπεὶ νωθροὶ γεγόνατε ταῖς.ἀκοαῖς. 12 καὶ.γὰρ
pretation to speak, since sluggish ye have become in hearing. For truly
ὀφείλοντες εἶναι διδάσκαλοι διὰ τὸν χρόνον, πάλιν
[when ye] ought to be teachers because of the time, again
χρείαν ἔχετε τοῦ.διδάσκειν ὑμᾶς τίνα τὰ στοιχεῖα τῆς
need ye have of [one] to teach you what [are] the elements of the
ἀρχῆς τῶν λογίων τοῦ θεοῦ· καὶ γεγόνατε χρείαν ἔχοντες
beginning of the oracles of God, and have become [2]need [1]having
γάλακτος, [l]καὶ" οὐ στερεᾶς τροφῆς. 13 πᾶς.γὰρ ὁ μετέχων
of milk, and not of solid food; for everyone that partakes
γάλακτος ἄπειρος λόγου δικαιοσύνης· νήπιος.γάρ ἐστιν·
of milk [is] unskilled in [the] word of righteousness, for an infant he is;
14 τελείων.δέ ἐστιν ἡ στερεὰ τροφή, τῶν διὰ τὴν
but [4]for [[5]the] [6]fully [7]grown [3]is [1]solid [2]food, who on account of
ἕξιν τὰ αἰσθητήρια γεγυμνασμένα ἐχόντων πρὸς διάκρισιν
habit [2]the [3]senses [4]exercised [1]have for distinguishing
καλοῦ τε καὶ κακοῦ.
[2]good [1]both and evil.

6 Διὸ ἀφέντες τὸν τῆς ἀρχῆς τοῦ χριστοῦ λόγον, ἐπὶ
Wherefore, having left the [2]of [3]the [4]beginning [5]of [6]the [7]Christ [1]discourse, to
τὴν τελειότητα φερώμεθα· μὴ πάλιν θεμέλιον καταβαλλόμενοι
the full growth we should go on; not again a foundation laying
μετανοίας ἀπὸ νεκρῶν ἔργων, καὶ πίστεως ἐπὶ θεόν, 2 βαπ-
of repentance from dead works, and faith in God, [4]of [5]wash-
τισμῶν [m]διδαχῆς," ἐπιθέσεώς.τε χειρῶν, ἀναστάσεώς.[n]τε" νε-
ings [1]of [[2]the] [3]doctrine, and of laying on of hands, and of resurrection of [the]
κρῶν, καὶ κρίματος αἰωνίου. 3 καὶ τοῦτο ποιήσομεν, [o]ἐάνπερ"
dead, and of [2]judgment [1]eternal; and this will we do, if indeed
ἐπιτρέπῃ ὁ θεός. 4 ἀδύνατον.γὰρ τοὺς ἅπαξ φωτισθέντας,
[2]permit [1]God. For [it is] impossible, those once enlightened,
γευσαμένους.τε τῆς δωρεᾶς τῆς ἐπουρανίου, καὶ μετόχους
and [who] tasted of the [2]gift [1]heavenly, and partakers
γενηθέντας πνεύματος ἁγίου, 5 καὶ καλὸν γευσαμένους
became of [the] [2]Spirit [1]Holy, and [[2]the] [3]good [1]tasted
θεοῦ ῥῆμα δυνάμεις.τε μέλλοντος αἰῶνος, 6 καὶ
[5]of [6]God [4]word and [the] works of power of [the] [2]to [3]come [1]age, and
παραπεσόντας, πάλιν ἀνακαινίζειν εἰς μετάνοιαν, ἀνασταυ-
[who] fell away, again to renew to repentance, crucify-
ροῦντας ἑαυτοῖς τὸν υἱὸν τοῦ θεοῦ καὶ παραδειγ-
ing for themselves [as they do] the Son of God, and exposing
ματίζοντας. 7 γῆ.γὰρ ἡ πιοῦσα τὸν ἐπ' αὐτῆς [p]πολλάκις
[him] publicly. For ground which drank the [4]upon [5]it [3]often
ἐρχόμενον" ὑετόν, καὶ τίκτουσα βοτάνην εὔθετον ἐκείνοις
[2]coming [1]rain, and produces [2]herbage [1]fit for those
δι' οὓς καὶ γεωργεῖται, μεταλαμβάνει εὐλογίας ἀπὸ τοῦ
for sake of whom also it is tilled, partakes of blessing from
θεοῦ· 8 ἐκφέρουσα.δὲ ἀκάνθας καὶ τριβόλους, ἀδόκιμος καὶ
God; but [that] bringing forth thorns and thistles [is] rejected and
κατάρας ἐγγύς, ἧς τὸ τέλος εἰς καῦσιν. 9 Πεπείσμεθα.δὲ
[3]a [4]curse [1]near [2]to, of which the end [is] for burning. But we are persuaded
περὶ ὑμῶν, ἀγαπητοί, τὰ.[q]κρείττονα" καὶ ἐχόμενα
concerning you, beloved, better things, and [things] connected with
σωτηρίας, εἰ καὶ οὕτως λαλοῦμεν. 10 οὐ.γὰρ ἄδικος ὁ θεὸς
salvation, [2]if [1]even thus we speak. For not unrighteous [is] God
ἐπιλαθέσθαι τοῦ.ἔργου.ὑμῶν καὶ [r]τοῦ κόπου" τῆς ἀγάπης ἧς
to forget your work and the labour of love which

4 And no one takes this honor to himself,
but he is called by God, even as Aaron also.
5 So also Christ did not glorify Himself to
become a High Priest, but He who said to
Him, "You are My Son, Today I have begotten You."
6 As He said in another *Psalm* also, "You
are a priest forever, after the order of
Mel-chiz-e-dek."
7 *For He*, in the days of His flesh, after
offering up both requests and prayers to
Him who was able to save Him from death,
(with strong crying and tears, and having
been heard in that He feared God,
8 even though He was a Son), He learned
obedience from the things which He suffered.
9 And being made perfect, He became the
Author of eternal salvation to all those who
obey Him,
10 being called by God to be High Priest
after the order of Mel-chiz-e-dek,
11 about whom we have many things to
say and not easy to be explained since you
have become dull of hearing.
12 For, indeed, because of the time, you
ought to be teachers, yet you need one to
teach you again the first principles of the
words of God, having become *ones who* have
need of milk and not of solid food.
13 For every one that uses milk is not
skilled in the word of righteousness, for he is
an infant.
14 But solid food belongs to the ones who
are of full age, those who through habit have
their senses exercised to judge both good
and evil.
6 1 Then, leaving the principles of the teaching of Christ, let us go on to full growth –
not laying again the foundation of repentance from dead works and of faith toward
God –
2 of the teaching of baptisms and of laying
on of hands and of the raising of the dead
and of everlasting judgment.
3 And this we will do if God permits.
4 For those who were once enlightened and
who have tasted of the heavenly gift, and
who became partakers of the Holy Spirit,
5 and who have tasted the good word of
God and the works of power of the age to
come,
6 and who have fallen away, *it is* not possible to renew them again to repentance. *For
they are* crucifying to themselves the Son of
God and putting Him to an open shame.
7 (For the earth, which drinks in the rain
that often comes on it and produces plants
fit for those for whom it is worked, shares
God's blessing.
8 But *that ground* which brings forth thorns
and thistles is rejected, and is near to being
cursed – the end of which is to be burned).
9 But, loved ones, even though we speak
this way, we are persuaded better things of
you, and *things* that go along with salvation.
10 For God is not unrighteous to forget

ἐνεδείξασθε εἰς τὸ.ὄνομα.αὐτοῦ, διακονήσαντες τοῖς ἁγίοις καὶ
ye did shew to his name, having served to the saints and
διακονοῦντες. 11 ἐπιθυμοῦμεν.δὲ ἕκαστον ὑμῶν τὴν αὐτὴν
[still] serving. But we desire each of you the same
ἐνδείκνυσθαι σπουδὴν πρὸς τὴν πληροφορίαν τῆς ἐλπίδος ἄχρι
[2]to [3]shew [1]diligence to the full assurance of the hope unto
τέλους· 12 ἵνα μὴ νωθροὶ γένησθε, μιμηταὶ.δὲ τῶν διὰ
[the] end; that [3]not [4]sluggish [1]ye [2]be, but imitators of those who through
πίστεως καὶ μακροθυμίας κληρονομούντων τὰς ἐπαγγελίας.
faith and long patience inherit the promises.
13 Τῷ.γὰρ.Ἀβραὰμ ἐπαγγειλάμενος ὁ θεός, ἐπεὶ κατ' οὐδενὸς
For [4]to [5]Abraham [2]having [3]promised [1]God, since by no one
εἶχεν μείζονος ὀμόσαι, ὤμοσεν καθ' ἑαυτοῦ, 14 λέγων, [s]Ἦ‖.μὴν
he had greater to swear, swore by himself, saying, Surely
εὐλογῶν εὐλογήσω σε, καὶ πληθύνων πληθυνῶ σε· 15 καὶ
blessing I will bless thee, and multiplying I will multiply thee; and
οὕτως μακροθυμήσας ἐπέτυχεν τῆς ἐπαγγελίας. 16 ἄνθρω-
thus having had long patience he obtained the promise. [2]Men
ποι [t]μὲν‖ γὰρ κατὰ τοῦ μείζονος ὀμνύουσιν, καὶ πάσης αὐτοῖς
[3]indeed [1]for [5]by [6]the [7]greater [4]swear, and of all [2]to [3]them
ἀντιλογίας πέρας εἰς βεβαίωσιν ὁ ὅρκος· 17 ἐν.ᾧ περισσό-
[1]gainsaying an end for confirmation [is] the oath. Wherein [3]more [4]a-
τερον βουλόμενος ὁ θεὸς ἐπιδεῖξαι τοῖς κληρονόμοις τῆς ἐπαγ-
bundantly [2]desiring [1]God to shew to the heirs of pro-
γελίας τὸ ἀμετάθετον τῆς.βουλῆς.αὐτοῦ, ἐμεσίτευσεν ὅρκῳ,
mise the unchangeableness of his counsel, interposed by an oath,
18 ἵνα διὰ δύο πραγμάτων ἀμεταθέτων, ἐν οἷς ἀδύνατον
that by two [2]things [1]unchangeable, in which [it was] impossible
ψεύσασθαι [v]θεόν, ἰσχυρὰν παράκλησιν ἔχωμεν οἱ κατα-
[3]to [4]lie [[1]for] [2]God, strong encouragement we might have who fled
φυγόντες κρατῆσαι τῆς προκειμένης ἐλπίδος· 19 ἣν ὡς
for refuge to lay hold on the [2]set [3]before [[4]us] [1]hope, which as
ἄγκυραν ἔχομεν τῆς ψυχῆς [w]ἀσφαλῆ‖.τε καὶ βεβαίαν, καὶ εἰσ-
an anchor we have of the soul both certain and firm, and en-
ερχομένην εἰς τὸ ἐσώτερον τοῦ καταπετάσματος, 20 ὅπου
tering into that within the veil; where
πρόδρομος ὑπὲρ ἡμῶν εἰσῆλθεν Ἰησοῦς, κατὰ τὴν τάξιν
[as] forerunner for us [2]entered [1]Jesus, according to the order
Μελχισεδὲκ ἀρχιερεὺς γενόμενος εἰς.τὸν.αἰῶνα.
of Melchisedec a high priest having become for ever.
7 Οὗτος.γὰρ ὁ Μελχισεδέκ, βασιλεὺς Σαλήμ, ἱερεὺς τοῦ θεοῦ
For this Melchisedec, king of Salem, priest of God
[x]τοῦ‖ ὑψίστου, [y]ὁ‖ συναντήσας Ἀβραὰμ ὑποστρέφοντι ἀπὸ τῆς
the most high, who met Abraham returning from the
κοπῆς τῶν βασιλέων, καὶ εὐλογήσας αὐτόν· 2 ᾧ καὶ δεκάτην
smiting of the kings, and having blessed him; to whom also [3]a [4]tenth
ἀπὸ πάντων ἐμέρισεν Ἀβραάμ· πρῶτον μὲν ἑρμηνευόμενος
[5]of [6]all [2]divided [1]Abraham; first being interpreted
βασιλεὺς δικαιοσύνης, ἔπειτα.δὲ καὶ βασιλεὺς Σαλήμ, ὅ ἐστιν
king of righteousness, and then also king of Salem, which is
βασιλεὺς εἰρήνης· 3 ἀπάτωρ, ἀμήτωρ, ἀγενεαλόγητος·
king of peace; without father, without mother, without genealogy;
μήτε ἀρχὴν ἡμερῶν, μήτε ζωῆς τέλος ἔχων· ἀφωμοιωμένος.δὲ
neither beginning of days nor [2]of [3]life [1]end having, but assimilated
τῷ υἱῷ τοῦ θεοῦ, μένει ἱερεὺς εἰς.τὸ.διηνεκές. 4 Θεωρεῖτε.δὲ
to the Son of God, abides a priest in perpetuity. Now consider
πηλίκος οὗτος, ᾧ [z]καὶ‖ δεκάτην Ἀβραὰμ ἔδωκεν ἐκ
how great this [one was], to whom [5]even [6]a [7]tenth [1]Abraham [4]gave [8]out [9]of
τῶν ἀκροθινίων ὁ πατριάρχης. 5 καὶ οἱ μὲν ἐκ τῶν
[10]the [11]spoils [2]the [3]patriarch. And they indeed from among the
[a]υἱῶν‖ [b]Λευΐ‖ τὴν ἱερατείαν λαμβάνοντες, ἐντολὴν ἔχουσιν
sons of Levi, [3]the [4]priesthood [[1]who] [2]receive, commandment have
[c]ἀποδεκατοῦν‖ τὸν λαὸν κατὰ τὸν νόμον, [d]τουτέστιν,‖
to take tithes from the people according to the law, that is [from]
τοὺς.ἀδελφοὺς.αὐτῶν, καίπερ ἐξεληλυθότας ἐκ τῆς ὀσφύος
their brethren though having come out of the loins
Ἀβραάμ· 6 ὁ.δὲ μὴ.γενεαλογούμενος ἐξ αὐτῶν δεδεκάτω-
of Abraham; but he [who] reckons no genealogy from them has tithed
κεν [e]τὸν‖ Ἀβραάμ, καὶ τὸν ἔχοντα τὰς ἐπαγγελίας [f]εὐλό-
Abraham, and [3]him [4]who [5]had [6]the [7]promises, [1]has
γηκεν·‖ 7 χωρὶς.δὲ πάσης ἀντιλογίας τὸ ἔλαττον ὑπὸ τοῦ
[2]blessed. But apart from all gainsaying the inferior by the
κρείττονος εὐλογεῖται. 8 καὶ ὧδε μὲν δεκάτας ἀποθνήσκοντες
superior is blessed. And here [4]tithes [[2]that] [3]die
ἄνθρωποι λαμβάνουσιν· ἐκεῖ.δέ, μαρτυρούμενος ὅτι ζῇ.
[1]men [5]receive; but there [one] witnessed of that he lives;
9 καί, ὡς.ἔπος.εἰπεῖν, [g]διὰ‖ Ἀβραὰμ καὶ [h]Λευΐ‖ ὁ δεκάτας
and, so to speak, through Abraham, also Levi, who [2]tithes
λαμβάνων δεδεκάτωται· 10 ἔτι.γὰρ ἐν τῇ ὀσφύϊ τοῦ.πατρὸς
[1]receives, has been tithed. For yet in the loins of [his] father
ἦν, ὅτε συνήντησεν αὐτῷ [i]ὁ‖ Μελχισεδέκ. 11 Εἰ μὲν οὖν
he was when [2]met [3]him [1]Melchisedec. If indeed then

your work and labor of love, which you have shown toward His name, in that you have ministered to the saints and do minister.

11 And we earnestly desire that each of you will show the same eagerness, to the full assurance of the hope to the end –

12 so that you will not be dull, but imitators of those who inherit the promises through patience and faith.

13 For when God was promising to Abraham, He swore by Himself, because He could not swear by any greater One,

14 saying, "Surely blessing I will bless you, and multiplying I will multiply you."

15 And so, having had patience, he received the promise.

16 For men indeed swear by the greater. And an oath to make things sure is the end of all argument to them.

17 In which way, desiring to more fully declare to the heirs of promise, that His purpose does not change, God came in with an oath –

18 so that by two things that cannot change (in which it was not possible for God to lie), we might have strong comfort – we who have fled for refuge in order to lay hold upon the hope set before us –

19 which we have as an anchor of the soul, both certain and sure, and entering into that inside the veil,

20 where Jesus *as our* Forerunner has entered for our sake, having become a High Priest forever according to the order of Mel-chiz-e-dek.

7 1 For this Mel-chiz-e-dek, (who was king of Salem and priest of the most high God), met Abraham returning from the slaughter of the kings and blessed him.

2 Abraham also gave a tenth of all to him. First of all, his name being translated is king of righteousness. And then also king of Salem, which is, king of peace –

3 without father, without mother, without genealogy, having neither beginning of days nor end of life – but being made similar to the Son of God, he remains a priest forever.

4 Now consider how great this man was, to whom even the patriarch Abraham gave a tenth of the spoils.

5 And indeed they that are of the sons of Levi, receiving the office of the priesthood, have a commandment to take tithes of the people according to the Law – that is, from their brothers, even though they come out of the loins of Abraham.

6 But he, whose line is not counted from them, received tithes from Abraham and blessed him who had the promises.

7 And without contradiction, the lesser is blessed by the greater.

8 And here dying men receive tithes, but there *one of whom it is* witnessed that he lives.

9 And as I may so say, Levi also, who re-

τελείωσις διὰ τῆς [k]Λευϊτικῆς'' ἱερωσύνης ἦν, ὁ.λαὸς.γὰρ
perfection by the Levitical priesthood were, for the people [[8]based]
ἐπ' [l]αὐτῇ'' [m]νενομοθέτητο,'' τίς ἔτι χρεία κατὰ
[6]upon [7]it [1]had [2]received [[3]the] [4]law, what still need [was there] according to
τὴν τάξιν Μελχισεδὲκ ἕτερον ἀνίστασθαι ἱερέα, καὶ οὐ
the order of Melchisedec [for] another [2]to [3]arise [1]priest; and not
κατὰ τὴν τάξιν Ἀαρὼν λέγεσθαι; 12 μετατιθεμένης.γὰρ
according to the order of Aaron to be named? For [3]being [4]changed
τῆς ἱερωσύνης, ἐξ ἀνάγκης καὶ νόμου μετάθεσις γίνεται.
[1]the [2]priesthood, from necessity also of law a change takes place.
13 ἐφ'.ὃν.γὰρ λέγεται ταῦτα, φυλῆς ἑτέρας μετέσχηκεν, ἀφ'.ἧς
For he of whom are said these things, a [2]tribe [1]different has part in, of which
οὐδεὶς προσέσχηκεν τῷ θυσιαστηρίῳ· 14 πρόδηλον.γὰρ ὅτι
no one has given attendance at the altar. For [it is] manifest that
ἐξ Ἰούδα ἀνατέταλκεν ὁ.κύριος.ἡμῶν, εἰς ἣν φυλὴν [n]οὐδὲν
out of Juda has sprung our Lord, as to which tribe [3]nothing
περὶ ἱερωσύνης'' [o]Μωσῆς'' ἐλάλησεν. 15 Καὶ περισσότερον
[4]concerning [5]priesthood [1]Moses [2]spoke. And more abundantly
ἔτι κατάδηλόν ἐστιν, εἰ κατὰ τὴν ὁμοιότητα Μελχισεδὲκ
yet quite manifest it is, since according to the similitude of Melchisedec
ἀνίσταται ἱερεὺς ἕτερος, 16 ὃς οὐ κατὰ νόμον ἐντο-
arises a [2]priest [1]different, who not according to law of [2]command-
λῆς [p]σαρκικῆς'' γέγονεν, ἀλλὰ κατὰ δύναμιν ζωῆς
ment [1]fleshly has been constituted, but according to power of [2]life
ἀκαταλύτου· 17 [q]μαρτυρεῖ'.γάρ, Ὅτι σὺ ἱερεὺς εἰς τὸν
[1]indissoluble. For he testifies, Thou [art] a priest for
αἰῶνα κατὰ τὴν τάξιν Μελχισεδέκ. 18 Ἀθέτησις μὲν.γὰρ
ever after the order of Melchisedec. [2]A [3]putting [4]away [1]for
γίνεται προαγούσης ἐντολῆς, διὰ τὸ.αὐτῆς.ἀσθενὲς
there is of the [2]going before [1]commandment, because of its weakness
καὶ ἀνωφελές, 19 οὐδὲν.γὰρ ἐτελείωσεν ὁ νόμος, ἐπεισ-
and unprofitableness, (for [4]nothing [3]perfected [1]the [2]law,) [[6]the] [7]intro-
αγωγὴ δὲ κρείττονος ἐλπίδος, δι' ἧς ἐγγίζομεν τῷ θεῷ. 20 Καὶ
duction [5]and of a better hope by which we draw near to God. And
καθ'.ὅσον οὐ χωρὶς ὁρκωμοσίας· οἱ μὲν γάρ,
by how much [it was] not apart from [the] swearing of an oath, ([2]they [1]for
χωρὶς ὁρκωμοσιας εἰσὶν ἱερεῖς γεγονότες, 21 ὁ.δέ,
without [the] swearing of an oath are [2]priests [1]become, but he
[r]μετὰ' ὁρκωμοσίας, διὰ τοῦ λέγοντος πρὸς αὐτόν,
with [the] swearing of an oath, by him who says, as to him,
Ὤμοσεν κύριος καὶ οὐ.μεταμεληθήσεται, Σὺ ἱερεὺς εἰς τὸν
[3]swore [[1]the] [2]Lord, and will not repent, Thou [art] a priest for
αἰῶνα [s]κατὰ τὴν τάξιν Μελχισεδέκ·'' 22 κατὰ.[t]τοσοῦτον''[u]
ever according to the order of Melchisedec,) by so much
κρείττονος διαθήκης γέγονεν ἔγγυος Ἰησοῦς. 23 Καὶ οἱ
of a better covenant [2]has become [4]surety [1]Jesus. And they
μὲν πλείονές εἰσιν.[v]γεγονότες ἱερεῖς'' διὰ τὸ θανάτῳ κω-
[2]many [1]are priests on account of by death being
λύεσθαι παραμένειν· 24 ὁ.δέ, διὰ τὸ.μένειν.αὐτὸν εἰς
hindered from continuing; but he, because of his abiding for
τὸν αἰῶνα, ἀπαράβατον ἔχει τὴν ἱερωσύνην· 25 ὅθεν καὶ
ever, [4]intransmissible [1]has [2]the [3]priesthood. Whence also
σώζειν εἰς.τὸ.παντελὲς δύναται τοὺς προσερχομένους δι'
to save completely he is able those who approach by
αὐτοῦ τῷ θεῷ, πάντοτε ζῶν εἰς.τὸ.ἐντυγχάνειν ὑπὲρ αὐτῶν.
him to God, always living to intercede for them.
26 τοιοῦτος.γὰρ ἡμῖν [w]ἔπρεπεν ἀρχιερεύς, ὅσιος, ἄκακος,
For such [5]us [4]became [1]a [2]high [3]priest, holy, harmless,
ἀμίαντος, κεχωρισμένος ἀπὸ τῶν.ἁμαρτωλῶν, καὶ ὑψηλότερος
undefiled, separated from sinners, and [2]higher
τῶν οὐρανῶν γενόμενος· 27 ὃς οὐκ.ἔχει καθ'.ἡμέραν ἀνάγ-
than [3]the [4]heavens [1]become: who has not day by day neces-
ην, ὥσπερ οἱ ἀρχιερεῖς, πρότερον ὑπὲρ τῶν.ἰδίων ἁμαρτιῶν
ty, as the high priests, first for his own sins
υσίας ἀναφέρειν, ἔπειτα τῶν τοῦ λαοῦ· τοῦτο.γὰρ
crifices [1]to [2]offer [3]up, then for those of the people; for this
οίησεν [x]ἐφάπαξ,'' ἑαυτὸν [y]ἀνενέγκας.'' 28 ὁ.νόμος.γὰρ ἀν-
ne did once for all, [4]himself [1]having [2]offered [3]up. For the law
ώπους καθίστησιν ἀρχιερεῖς, ἔχοντας ἀσθένειαν· ὁ.λόγος.δὲ
en [1]constitutes high priests, [who] have infirmity; but the word
ῆς ὁρκωμοσίας τῆς μετὰ τὸν νόμον, υἱὸν εἰς τὸν
the swearing of the oath, which [is] after the law, a Son for
ῶνα τετελειωμένον.
er has perfected.
8 Κεφάλαιον.δὲ ἐπὶ τοῖς λεγομένοις, τοιοῦτον
Now a summary of the things being spoken of [is], [3]such
ομεν ἀρχιερέα, ὃς ἐκάθισεν ἐν δεξιᾷ τοῦ θρόνου τῆς
[2]have a high priest, who sat down on [the] right hand of the throne of the
αλωσύνης ἐν τοῖς οὐρανοῖς, 2 τῶν ἁγίων λειτουργός, καὶ
greatness in the heavens; [2]of [3]the [4]holies [1]minister, and
ς σκηνῆς τῆς ἀληθινῆς, ἣν ἔπηξεν ὁ κύριος, [z]καὶ'' οὐκ
ne [2]tabernacle [1]true which [3]pitched [1]the [2]Lord and not

ceives tithes, has paid tithes through
Abraham.
10 For he was yet in the loins of his father
when Mel-chiz-e-dek met him.
11 Truly, then, if perfection were by the
priesthood of Levi, (for under it the people
received the Law), what further need *was*
there that another priest should rise after the
order of Mel-chiz-e-dek – and not named
under the order of Aaron?
12 For the priesthood being changed, a
change of law must also come about.
13 For He of whom these things are spoken
belongs to another tribe, of which no one
has given attendance at the altar.
14 For plainly our Lord has sprung out of
Judah, of which tribe Moses said nothing as
to priesthood.
15 And it is still more plain, since a different priest arises,
16 who is made according to the likeness of
Mel-chiz-e-dek – not according to the law of
a fleshly commandment, but according to
the power of an endless life.
17 For He testifies, "You are a Priest forever, after the order of Mel-chiz-e-dek."
18 For indeed there is a putting away of the
foregoing commandment because of its
weakness and lack of gain –
19 for the Law did not make anything perfect, but *there is* an introduction of a better
Hope by which we draw near to God.
20 And since *He was* not *made priest* without an oath,
21 for they are made priests without the
swearing of an oath, but He was made priest
with the swearing of an oath by Him who
said to Him, "The Lord swore and will not
repent, You are a Priest forever after the
order of Mel-chiz-e-dek" –
22 by so much Jesus was made a surety of a
better covenant.
23 And they truly were many priests,
because they were hindered from continuing
by death.
24 But He, because He lives forever, has a
priesthood that cannot be changed.
25 Therefore He is able also to save to the
uttermost those that come to God by Him,
since He ever lives to make intercession for
them.
26 For such a High Priest was fitting for us
– holy, harmless, undefiled and separated
from sinners and made higher than the
heavens.
27 One who does not, as those high priests,
need to offer sacrifices daily, first for His
own sins and then for the people's – for this
He did once for all when He offered up
Himself.
28 For the Law makes men high priests who
have infirmity. But the word of the oath,
which came after the Law, has perfected the
Son forever.
8 1 Now the sum of the things which we have
spoken *is this:* We have such a High Priest,

ἄνθρωπος.
man.
3 Πᾶς.γὰρ ἀρχιερεὺς εἰς τὸ προσφέρειν δῶρά.τε καὶ θυσίας
For every high priest for to offer both gifts and sacrifices
καθίσταται· ὅθεν ἀναγκαῖον ἔχειν τι καὶ τοῦ-
is constituted; whence [it is] necessary [4]to [5]have [6]something [7]also [[1]for] [2]this
τον ὃ προσενέγκῃ. 4 εἰ.μὲν [a]γὰρ‖ ἦν ἐπὶ γῆς, οὐδ᾽
[3]one which he may offer. [2]If [3]indeed [1]for he were on earth, not even
ἂν.ἦν ἱερεύς, ὄντων [b]τῶν ἱερέων‖ τῶν προσφερόντων
would he be a priest, there being the priests who offer
κατὰ [c]τὸν‖ νόμον τὰ δῶρα, 5 οἵτινες ὑποδείγματι καὶ
according to the law the gifts, who [the] representation and
σκιᾷ λατρεύουσιν τῶν ἐπουρανίων, καθὼς κεχρημάτισ-
shadow serve of the heavenlies, according as [2]was [3]divinely [4]in-
ται [d]Μωσῆς‖ μέλλων ἐπιτελεῖν τὴν σκηνήν, Ὅρα,.γάρ
structed [1]Moses being about to construct the tabernacle; for, see,
φησιν, [e]ποιήσῃς‖ πάντα κατὰ τὸν τύπον τὸν δειχθέντα
says he, thou make all things according to the pattern which was shewn
σοι ἐν τῷ ὄρει. 6 [f]νυνὶ.δὲ διαφορωτέρας [g]τέτευχεν‖
thee in the mountain. But now a more excellent [2]he [3]has [4]obtained
λειτουργίας, ὅσῳ καὶ κρείττονός ἐστιν διαθήκης μεσίτης,
[1]ministry by so much as also of a better [2]he [3]is [1]covenant mediator,
ἥτις ἐπὶ κρείττοσιν ἐπαγγελίαις νενομοθέτηται. 7 Εἰ.γὰρ
which upon better promises has been established. For if
ἡ.πρώτη.ἐκείνη ἦν ἄμεμπτος, οὐκ ἂν δευτέρας ἐζητεῖτο
that first [one] were faultless, not for a second would [2]be [3]sought
τόπος. 8 μεμφόμενος.γὰρ [h]αὐτοῖς‖ λέγει, Ἰδού, ἡμέραι ἔρ-
[1]place. For finding fault, [3]to [4]them [1]he [2]says, Lo, days are
χονται, λέγει κύριος, καὶ συντελέσω ἐπὶ τὸν οἶκον
coming, saith [the] Lord, and I will ratify as regards the house
Ἰσραὴλ καὶ ἐπὶ τὸν οἶκον Ἰούδα διαθήκην καινήν· 9 οὐ
of Israel and as regards the house of Juda a [2]covenant [1]new; not
κατὰ τὴν.διαθήκην ἣν ἐποίησα τοῖς.πατράσιν.αὐτῶν,
according to the covenant which I made with their fathers,
ἐν ἡμέρᾳ ἐπιλαβομένου.μου τῆς.χειρὸς.αὐτῶν ἐξαγαγεῖν
in [the] day of my taking hold of their hand to lead
αὐτοὺς ἐκ γῆς Αἰγύπτου· ὅτι αὐτοὶ οὐκ.ἐνέμειναν ἐν
them out of [the] land of Egypt; because they did not continue in
τῇ.διαθήκῃ.μου, κἀγὼ ἠμέλησα αὐτῶν, λέγει κύριος. 10 ὅτι
my covenant, and I disregarded them, saith [the] Lord. Because
αὕτη ἡ διαθήκη[k] ἣν διαθήσομαι τῷ οἴκῳ Ἰσραὴλ μετὰ
this [is] the covenant which I will covenant with the house of Israel after
τὰς.ἡμέρας.ἐκείνας, λέγει κύριος, διδοὺς νόμους.μου εἰς
those days, says [the] Lord, giving my laws into
τὴν.διάνοιαν αὐτῶν καὶ ἐπὶ [l]καρδίας‖ αὐτῶν ἐπιγράψω αὐτούς·
their mind, also upon [2]hearts [1]their I will inscribe them;
καὶ ἔσομαι αὐτοῖς εἰς θεόν, καὶ αὐτοὶ ἔσονταί μοι εἰς λαόν.
and I will be to them for God, and they shall be to me for people.
11 καὶ οὐ.μὴ διδάξωσιν ἕκαστος τὸν [m]πλησίον‖ αὐτοῦ, καὶ
And not at all shall they teach each [2]neighbour [1]his, and
ἕκαστος τὸν.ἀδελφὸν.αὐτοῦ, λέγων, Γνῶθι τὸν κύριον· ὅτι
each his brother, saying, Know the Lord; because
πάντες εἰδήσουσίν με, ἀπὸ μικροῦ [n]αὐτῶν‖ ἕως
all shall know me, from [the] little [one] of them to [the]
μεγάλου αὐτῶν· 12 ὅτι ἵλεως ἔσομαι ταῖς.ἀδικίαις.αὐτῶν,
great [one] of them. Because merciful I will be to their unrighteousnesses,
καὶ τῶν.ἁμαρτιῶν.αὐτῶν [o]καὶ τῶν.ἀνομιῶν.αὐτῶν‖ οὐ.μὴ
and their sins and their lawlessnesses in no wise
μνησθῶ ἔτι. 13 Ἐν τῷ λέγειν καινήν, πεπαλαίωκεν
will I remember more. In the saying New, he has made old
τὴν πρώτην· τὸ.δὲ παλαιούμενον καὶ γηράσκον ἐγγὺς
the first; but that which grows old and aged [is] near
ἀφανισμοῦ.
disappearing.
9 [p]Εἶχεν‖ μὲν οὖν [q]καὶ‖ ἡ πρώτη [r]σκηνὴ‖ δικαιώματα
[4]Had [7]indeed [5]therefore [6]also [1]the [2]first [3]tabernacle ordinances
λατρείας, τό.τε ἅγιον κοσμικόν. 2 σκηνὴ.γὰρ κατε-
of service, and the sanctuary, a worldly [one]. For a tabernacle was
σκευάσθη ἡ πρώτη, ἐν ᾗ ἥ.τε λυχνία καὶ ἡ τρά-
prepared, the first, in which [were] both the lampstand and the ta-
πεζα καὶ ἡ πρόθεσις τῶν ἄρτων, ἥτις λέγεται [s]ἅγια.‖ 3 μετὰ
ble and the presentation of the loaves, which is called holy; [2]after
δὲ τὸ δεύτερον καταπέτασμα σκηνὴ ἡ λεγομένη [t]ἅγια‖
[1]but the second veil a tabernacle which [is] called holy
ἁγίων, 4 χρυσοῦν ἔχουσα θυμιατήριον, καὶ τὴν κιβωτὸν τῆς
of holies, [2]a [3]golden [1]having censer, and the ark of the
διαθήκης περικεκαλυμμένην πάντοθεν χρυσίῳ, ἐν ᾗ
covenant, having been covered round [3]in [4]every [5]part [1]with [2]gold, in which
στάμνος χρυσῆ ἔχουσα τὸ μάννα, καὶ ἡ ῥάβδος Ἀαρὼν
[was the] [2]pot [1]golden having the manna, and the rod of Aaron
ἡ βλαστήσασα, καὶ αἱ πλάκες τῆς διαθήκης· 5 ὑπεράνω.δὲ
that sprouted, and the tablets of the covenant; and above

who has sat down on the right hand of the throne of the Majesty in Heaven,

2 a Minister of the holy places and of the true tabernacle which the Lord pitched, and not man.

3 For every high priest is appointed to offer gifts and sacrifices. So this One must have something which He may offer.

4 For indeed if He were on earth, He would not be a priest – there are the priests who offer gifts according to the Law,

5 who serve the pattern and shadow of heavenly things, even as Moses was divinely instructed when he was about to make the tabernacle, for He says, "See that you make all things according to the pattern which was shown to you in the mountain."

6 But now He has gotten a more excellent ministry, by so much He is also the Mediator of a better covenant, which was built on better promises.

7 For if that first covenant had been without fault, then no place would have been sought for the second.

8 For finding fault He said to them, "See! The days come, says the Lord, when I shall make a new covenant with the house of Israel and with the house of Judah –

9 not according to the covenant which I made with their fathers in the day when I took them by the hand to lead them out of the land of Egypt" – because they did not keep on in My covenant and I stopped taking care of them, says the Lord.

10 "For this is the covenant which I will make with the house of Israel: After those days, says the Lord, I will put My laws in their mind and write them in their hearts – and I will be their God and they shall be My people.

11 And they shall no more teach each one his neighbor, and each one his brother, saying, Know the Lord – for all shall know Me, from the least of them to the greatest of them.

12 For I will be merciful to their wrongdoings, and I will not remember their sins and their lawless deeds any more."

13 By saying, "New," He has made the first *covenant* old. Now that which decays and grows old is ready to disappear.

9 1 Truly, then, the first tabernacle also had holy orders of worship and an earthly Holy Place.

2 For there was a tabernacle prepared, the first one – in which were the lampstand and the table and the showbread – which is called the Holy Place.

3 And after the second veil, the tabernacle which is called the Holy of Holies –

4 which had the golden censer, and the ark of the covenant which was covered with gold in every part, in which was the golden pot with the manna, and Aaron's rod that budded, and the tables of the covenant –

αὐτῆς [t]χερουβὶμ" δόξης κατασκιάζοντα τὸ ἱλαστήριον·
it [the] cherubim of glory overshadowing the mercy seat;
περὶ ὧν οὐκ.ἔστιν νῦν λέγειν κατὰ.μέρος.
concerning which it is not now [the time] to speak in detail.
6 Τούτων.δὲ οὕτως κατεσκευασμένων, εἰς μὲν τὴν πρώτην
Now these things thus having been prepared, into the first
σκηνὴν [v]διαπαντὸς" εἰσίασιν οἱ ἱερεῖς τὰς λατρείας ἐπιτελοῦν-
tabernacle at all times enter the priests, the services accomplish-
τες· 7 εἰς.δὲ τὴν δευτέραν ἅπαξ τοῦ.ἐνιαυτοῦ μόνος ὁ ἀρχιε-
ing; but into the second once in the year alone the high
ρεύς, οὐ χωρὶς αἵματος, ὃ προσφέρει ὑπὲρ ἑαυτοῦ καὶ
priest, not apart from blood, which he offers for himself and
τῶν τοῦ λαοῦ ἀγνοημάτων· 8 τοῦτο δηλοῦντος τοῦ πνεύ-
the [4]of [5]the [6]people [1]sins [2]of [3]ignorance: [11]this [12]signifying [7]the [8]Spirit
ματος τοῦ ἁγίου, μήπω πεφανερῶσθαι τὴν τῶν ἁγίων
[9]the [10]Holy, [that] not yet has been made manifest the [2]of [3]the [4]holies
ὁδὸν ἔτι τῆς πρώτης σκηνῆς ἐχούσης στάσιν· 9 ἥτις
[1]way, [9]still [5]the [6]first [7]tabernacle [8]having a standing; which [is]
παραβολὴ εἰς τὸν καιρὸν τὸν ἐνεστηκότα, καθʼ [w]ὃν' δῶρά.τε
a simile for the [2]time [1]present, in which both gifts
καὶ θυσίαι προσφέρονται, μὴ δυνάμεναι κατὰ συνείδησιν τε-
and sacrifices are offered, not being able as to conscience to
λειῶσαι τὸν λατρεύοντα, 10 μόνον ἐπὶ βρώμασιν καὶ
perfect him who serves, [consisting] only in meats and
πόμασιν καὶ διαφόροις βαπτισμοῖς, [x]καὶ [y]δικαιώμασιν' σαρκός,
drinks and divers washings, and ordinances of flesh,
μέχρι καιροῦ διορθώσεως ἐπικείμενα. 11 Χριστὸς.δὲ
[2]until [[3]the] [4]time [5]of [6]setting [7]things [8]right [1]imposed. But Christ
παραγενόμενος ἀρχιερεὺς τῶν [z]μελλόντων' ἀγαθῶν, διὰ τῆς
being come high priest of the coming good things, by the
μείζονος καὶ τελειοτέρας σκηνῆς, οὐ χειροποιήτου, [a]τουτέστιν"
greater and more perfect tabernacle, not made by hand, (that is,
οὐ ταύτης τῆς κτίσεως, 12 οὐδὲ διʼ αἵματος τράγων καὶ
not of this creation,) nor by blood of goats and
μόσχων, διὰ.δὲ τοῦ.ἰδίου.αἵματος εἰσῆλθεν [b]ἐφάπαξ' εἰς
calves, but by his own blood, entered once for all into
τὰ ἅγια, αἰωνίαν λύτρωσιν [c]εὑράμενος." 13 εἰ.γὰρ τὸ αἷμα
the holies, eternal redemption having found. For if the blood
[d]ταύρων καὶ τράγων', καὶ σποδὸς δαμάλεως ῥαντίζουσα τοὺς
of bulls and of goats, and ashes of a heifer sprinkling the
κεκοινωμένους, ἁγιάζει πρὸς τὴν τῆς σαρκὸς καθαρότητα,
defiled, sanctifies for the [2]of [3]the [4]flesh [1]purity,
14 πόσῳ μᾶλλον τὸ αἷμα τοῦ χριστοῦ, ὃς διὰ πνεύματος
how much rather the blood of the Christ who through [the] [2]Spirit
αἰωνίου ἑαυτὸν προσήνεγκεν ἄμωμον τῷ θεῷ, καθαριεῖ τὴν
[1]eternal [4]himself [3]offered spotless to God, shall purify
συνείδησιν [e]ὑμῶν" ἀπὸ νεκρῶν ἔργων, εἰς τὸ λατρεύειν θεῷ
[2]conscience [1]your from dead works for to serve [3]God [[1]the]
ζῶντι[f]; 15 Καὶ διὰ.τοῦτο διαθήκης καινῆς μεσίτης ἐστίν,
[2]living! And for this reason of a [2]covenant [1]new [5]mediator [3]he [4]is,
ὅπως θανάτου γενομένου, εἰς ἀπολύτρωσιν τῶν ἐπὶ τῇ
so that, death having taken place for redemption of the [2]under [3]the
πρώτῃ διαθήκῃ παραβάσεων, τὴν ἐπαγγελίαν λάβωσιν
[4]first [5]covenant [1]transgressions, the promise [10]might [11]receive
οἱ κεκλημένοι τῆς αἰωνίου κληρονομίας. 16 ὅπου.γὰρ
[5]they [6]who [7]have [8]been [9]called [1]of [2]the [3]eternal [4]inheritance. (For where
διαθήκη, θάνατον ἀνάγκη φέρεσθαι τοῦ
[there is] a testament, [[4]for [5]the] [6]death [[1]it [2]is] [3]necessary [10]to [11]come [12]in [7]of [8]the
διαθεμένου· 17 διαθήκη.γὰρ ἐπὶ.νεκροῖς βεβαία, ἐπεὶ
[9]testator. For a testament in the case of [the] dead [is] affirmed, since
μήποτε ἰσχύει ὅτε ζῇ ὁ διαθέμενος.[g] 18 ὅθεν [h]οὐδʼ"
in no way it is of force when [3]is [4]living [1]the [2]testator.) Whence neither
ἡ πρώτη χωρὶς αἵματος [i]ἐγκεκαίνισται." 19 λαληθείσης
the first apart from blood has been inaugurated. [4]Having [5]been [6]spoken
γὰρ πάσης ἐντολῆς κατὰ [k]νόμον ὑπὸ Μωϋσέως παντὶ
for [2]every [3]commandment according to law by Moses to all
τῷ λαῷ, λαβὼν τὸ αἷμα τῶν μόσχων καὶ [l]τράγων, μετὰ
the people, having taken the blood of calves and of goats, with
ὕδατος καὶ ἐρίου κοκκίνου καὶ ὑσσώπου, αὐτό.τε τὸ βιβλίον
water and [2]wool [1]scarlet and hyssop, both [3]itself [1]the [2]book
καὶ πάντα τὸν λαὸν [m]ἐρράντισεν," 20 λέγων, Τοῦτο τὸ
and all the people he sprinkled, saying, This [is] the
αἷμα τῆς διαθήκης ἧς ἐνετείλατο πρὸς ὑμᾶς ὁ θεός. 21 καὶ
blood of the covenant which [2]enjoined [3]to [4]you [1]God. And
τὴν σκηνὴν δὲ καὶ πάντα τὰ σκεύη τῆς λειτουργίας τῷ
the tabernacle too and all the vessels of the ministration with
αἵματι ὁμοίως [m]ἐρράντισεν.' 22 καὶ σχεδὸν ἐν αἵματι
blood in like manner he sprinkled; and almost [3]with [4]blood
πάντα καθαρίζεται κατὰ τὸν νόμον, καὶ χωρὶς αἱματ-
[1]all [2]things are purified according to the law, and apart from blood-
εκχυσίας οὐ.γίνεται ἄφεσις. 23 Ἀνάγκη οὖν τὰ μὲν
shedding there is no remission. [it was] necessary then [for] the

5 and above it the cherubim of glory overshadowing the mercy-seat (of which we
cannot now speak part by part).

6 Now when these things had been prepared
in this way, the priests went at all times into
the first tabernacle, doing the duties *of God.*
7 But into the second the high priest *went*
alone once a year, not without blood, which
he offered for himself and for the errors of
the people.
8 The Holy Spirit was illustrating by this
that the way into the *Holy* of Holies was not
yet revealed, the first tabernacle still having
a standing.
9 Which was a parable for the present time,
in which were offered both gifts and sacrifices that, as regards the conscience, could
not make him who served perfect –
10 only in meats and drinks and different
kinds of washings, and fleshly rules put on
them until the time of setting things right.
11 But when Christ had come as a High
Priest of good things to come, by a greater
and more perfect tabernacle, not made with
hands (that is, not of this creation,)
12 not by the blood of goats and calves, but
by His own blood He entered in once for all
into the Holy of *Holies,* having obtained
everlasting redemption.
13 For if the blood of bulls and of goats
and the ashes of a heifer sprinkling the
unclean, sanctifies for the purity of the
flesh,
14 how much more shall the blood of Christ
(who through the eternal Spirit offered
Himself without spot to God) purge your
conscience from dead works to serve the
living God!
15 And for this reason, He is the Mediator
of the new covenant, so that, by means of
death for the redemption of the sins under
the first covenant, they who have been
called might receive the promise of the everlasting inheritance.
16 For where *there is* a testament, the death
of the one who made it must be brought in.
17 For a testament is affirmed after men are
dead – otherwise it is of no force at all while
the one who made it is living.
18 From which *we see* that neither was the
first *covenant* put into effect without blood.
19 For when Moses had spoken every commandment to all the people according to the
Law, he took the blood of calves and goats,
along with water and scarlet wool and
hyssop and sprinkled both the book and all
the people,
20 saying, "This is the blood of the covenant which God has commanded to you."
21 And he sprinkled with blood both the
tabernacle and all the vessels of the ministry.
22 And almost all things are purified with

ὑποδείγματα τῶν ἐν τοῖς οὐρανοῖς τούτοις καθαρίζεσθαι,
representations of the things in the heavens with these to be purified,
αὐτὰ.δὲ τὰ ἐπουράνια κρείττοσιν θυσίαις παρὰ ταύτας.
but 3themselves 1the 2heavenlies with better sacrifices than these.
24 οὐ.γὰρ εἰς χειροποίητα [n]ἅγια εἰσῆλθεν" [o]ὁ" χριστός, ἀντί-
For not into 2made 3by 4hands 1holies entered the Christ, fi-
τυπα τῶν ἀληθινῶν, ἀλλ' εἰς αὐτὸν τὸν οὐρανόν, νῦν ἐμφα-
gures of the true [ones], but into 2itself 1heaven, now to
νισθῆναι τῷ.προσώπῳ τοῦ θεοῦ ὑπὲρ ἡμῶν· 25 οὐδ' ἵνα
appear before the face of God for us: nor that
πολλάκις προσφέρῃ ἑαυτόν, ὥσπερ ὁ ἀρχιερεὺς εἰσέρχεται εἰς
often he should offer himself, even as the high priest enters into
τὰ ἅγια κατ'.ἐνιαυτὸν ἐν αἵματι ἀλλοτρίῳ· 26 ἐπεὶ ἔ-
the holies year by year with 2blood 1another's; since it was neces-
δει αὐτὸν πολλάκις παθεῖν ἀπὸ καταβολῆς κόσμου·
sary for him often to have suffered from [the] foundation of [the] world.
[p]νῦν.δὲ ἅπαξ ἐπὶ συντελείᾳ τῶν αἰώνων, εἰς ἀθέτη-
But now once in [the] consummation of the ages, for [the] putting
σιν[q] ἁμαρτίας, διὰ τῆς.θυσίας.αὐτοῦ πεφανέρωται. 27 καὶ
away of sin by his sacrifice he has been manifested. And
καθ'.ὅσον ἀπόκειται τοῖς ἀνθρώποις ἅπαξ ἀποθανεῖν, μετὰ
for as much as it is apportioned to men once to die, 2after
δὲ τοῦτο κρίσις· 28 οὕτως [r] ὁ χριστὸς ἅπαξ προσενεχθεὶς
1and this, judgment; thus the Christ, once having been offered
εἰς τὸ πολλῶν ἀνενεγκεῖν ἁμαρτίας, ἐκ.δευτέρου χωρὶς
for 5of 6many 1to 2bear [3the] 4sins, a second time 8apart 9from
ἁμαρτίας ὀφθήσεται τοῖς αὐτὸν ἀπεκδεχομένοις εἰς
10sin 1shall 2appear 3to 4those 5that 7him 6await for
σωτηρίαν.
salvation.

10 Σκιὰν.γὰρ ἔχων ὁ νόμος τῶν μελλόντων ἀγαθῶν, οὐκ
For 4a 5shadow 3having 1the 2law of the coming good things, not
αὐτὴν τὴν εἰκόνα τῶν πραγμάτων, κατ'.ἐνιαυτὸν ταῖς.αὐταῖς
3itself 1the 2image of the things, year by year with the same
θυσίαις [s]ἃς' προσφέρουσιν εἰς.τὸ.διηνεκὲς οὐδέποτε [t]δύναται"
sacrifices which they offer in perpetuity never is able
τοὺς προσερχομένους τελειῶσαι. 2 ἐπεὶ [v]οὐκ'.ἂν.ἐπαύσαντο
3those 4who 5approach 1to 2perfect. Since would they not have ceased
προσφερόμεναι, διὰ τὸ μηδεμίαν ἔχειν ἔτι συνείδησιν
to be offered, on account of 7no 9any 6having 8longer 10conscience
ἁμαρτιῶν τοὺς λατρεύοντας, ἅπαξ [w]κεκαθαρμένους"; 3 ἀλλ'
11of 12sins 1those 2who 3serve 4once 5purged? But
ἐν αὐταῖς ἀνάμνησις ἁμαρτιῶν κατ'.ἐνιαυτόν. 4 ἀδύ-
in these a remembrance of sins year by year [there is]. 4Impos-
νατον γὰρ αἷμα ταύρων καὶ τράγων ἀφαιρεῖν ἁμαρ-
sible [2it 3is] 1for [for the] blood of bulls and of goats to take away sins.
τίας. 5 Διὸ εἰσερχόμενος εἰς τὸν κόσμον λέγει, [x]Θυσίαν καὶ
Wherefore coming into the world he says, Sacrifice and
προσφορὰν' οὐκ.ἠθέλησας, σῶμα.δὲ κατηρτίσω μοι· 6 ὁλο-
offering thou willedst not, but a body thou didst prepare me. Burnt
καυτώματα καὶ περὶ ἁμαρτίας οὐκ.[y]εὐδόκησας."
offerings and [sacrifices] for sin thou delightedst not in.
7 τότε εἶπον, Ἰδοὺ ἥκω, ἐν κεφαλίδι βιβλίου γέγραπται
Then I said, Lo, I come, (in [the] roll of [the] book it is written
περὶ ἐμοῦ, τοῦ ποιῆσαι, ὁ θεός, τὸ.θέλημά.σου. 8 Ἀνώτερον
of me,) to do, O God, thy will. Above
λέγων, "Ὅτι [z]θυσίαν" καὶ [a]προσφορὰν' καὶ ὁλοκαυτώματα
saying, Sacrifice and offering and burnt offerings
καὶ περὶ ἁμαρτίας οὐκ.ἠθέλησας, οὐδὲ [b]εὐδόκησας,"
and [sacrifices] for sin thou willedst not, nor delightedst in,
αἵτινες κατὰ [c]τὸν' νόμον προσφέρονται, 9 τότε εἴρηκεν,
(which according to the law are offered); then he said,
Ἰδοὺ ἥκω τοῦ ποιῆσαι, [d]ὁ θεός." τὸ.θέλημά.σου. ἀναιρεῖ τὸ
Lo, I come, to do, O God, thy will. He takes away the
πρῶτον, ἵνα τὸ δεύτερον στήσῃ· 10 ἐν ᾧ θελήματι
first, that the second he may establish; by which will
ἡγιασμένοι ἐσμὲν [e]οἱ' διὰ τῆς προσφορᾶς τοῦ σώματος [f]τοῦ"
3sanctified 1we 2are through the offering of the body
Ἰησοῦ χριστοῦ [g]ἐφάπαξ." 11 Καὶ πᾶς μὲν [h]ἱερεὺς' ἕστηκεν
of Jesus Christ once for all. And every priest stands
καθ'.ἡμέραν λειτουργῶν, καὶ τὰς αὐτὰς πολλάκις προσφέρων
day by day ministering, and the same 2often 1offering
θυσίας, αἵτινες οὐδέποτε δύνανται περιελεῖν ἁμαρτίας·
3sacrifices, which never are able to take away sins.
12 [i]αὐτὸς".δὲ μίαν ὑπὲρ ἁμαρτιῶν προσενέγκας θυσίαν, εἰς
But he, 3one 4for 5sins 1having 2offered 6sacrifice, in
τὸ διηνεκὲς ἐκάθισεν ἐν δεξιᾷ τοῦ θεοῦ, 13 τὸ.λοιπὸν
perpetuity sat down at [the] right hand of God, henceforth
ἐκδεχόμενος ἕως τεθῶσιν οἱ.ἐχθροὶ.αὐτοῦ ὑποπόδιον τῶν
awaiting until be placed his enemies [as] a footstool
ποδῶν αὐτοῦ. 14 μιᾷ.γὰρ προσφορᾷ τετελείωκεν εἰς.τὸ.διη-
for 2feet 1his. For by one offering he has perfected in perpe-

blood according to the Law. And without
shedding of blood is no remission.
23 Necessarily, then, the patterns of the
things in the heavens should be purified with
these. But the heavenly things themselves
were purified with better sacrifices than
these.
24 For Christ has not entered into the Holy
of *Holies* made with hands, (the figures of
the true), but into Heaven itself – now to
appear in the presence of God for us.
25 Nor yet *is it necessary* that He should
offer Himself often – as the high priest
enters into the Holy Place every year with
another's blood –
26 for then He would have had to suffer
often from the foundation of the world. But
now, once, in the end of ages, He has
appeared to put away sin by the sacrifice of
Himself.
27 And in view of the fact that it is
appointed to men once to die, and after this
the Judgment –
28 so Christ, having been once offered to
bear the sins of many, shall appear a second
time without sin to those that look for Him,
to salvation.
10:1 For the Law had a shadow of the good
things to come, not the image itself of those
things. So it can never make those who come
near perfect with the same sacrifices which
they offer over and over year after year.
2 Otherwise, would they not have ceased
being offered? Because the worshipers, when
they had been once for all purged, would
have had no more conscience of sins!
3 But in those *sacrifices there is* a remembering of sins year by year.
4 For it is not possible that the blood of
bulls and of goats should take away sins.
5 For this reason, coming into the world,
He says, "Sacrifice and offering You did not
desire. You prepared a body for Me.
6 In burnt offerings and *sacrifices* for sin,
You did not delight.
7 Then I said, Lo, in the roll of the Book it
is written of Me. I come to do Your will, O
God."
8 Above when He said, "Sacrifice and offering, and burnt offerings and *sacrifices* for sin
You did not desire, nor delight in them,"
(which are offered according to the Law),
9 then He said, "Lo, I come to do Your
will, O God," He takes away the first so that
He may set up the second –
10 by which will we are sanctified through
the offering of the body of Jesus Christ once
for all.
11 And every priest stands day by day
ministering, and often offering the same
sacrifices, which can never take away sins.
12 But this Man, after He had offered one
sacrifice for sins forever, sat down on the
right hand of God,
13 from then on expecting until His
enemies should be placed as a footstool for

νεκὲς τοὺς ἁγιαζομένους. 15 Μαρτυρεῖ.δὲ ἡμῖν καὶ τὸ πνεῦμα
tuity the sanctified. And bears witness to us also the Spirit
τὸ ἅγιον· μετὰ.γὰρ τὸ [k]προειρηκέναι, 16 Αὕτη ἡ δια-
the Holy; for after the having said before, This [is] the cove-
θήκη ἣν διαθήσομαι πρὸς αὐτοὺς μετὰ τὰς.ἡμέρας.ἐκείνας,
nant which I will covenant towards them after those days,
λέγει κύριος, διδοὺς νόμους.μου ἐπὶ καρδίας.αὐτῶν, καὶ ἐπὶ
says [the] Lord: giving my laws into their hearts, also into
τῶν διανοιῶν αὐτῶν ἐπιγράψω αὐτούς· 17 καὶ τῶν ἁμαρτιῶν
2minds 1their I will inscribe them; and 2sins
αὐτῶν καὶ τῶν.ἀνομιῶν.αὐτῶν οὐ.μὴ [m]μνησθῶ ἔτι.
1their and their lawlessnesses in no wise will I remember any more.
18 ὅπου.δὲ ἄφεσις τούτων, οὐκέτι προσφορὰ περὶ
But where remission of these [is], no longer [is there] an offering for
ἁμαρτίας.
sin.

19 Ἔχοντες οὖν, ἀδελφοί, παῤῥησίαν εἰς τὴν.εἴσοδον
Having therefore, brethren, boldness for entrance into
τῶν ἁγίων ἐν τῷ αἵματι Ἰησοῦ, 20 ἣν ἐνεκαίνισεν ἡμῖν
the holies by the blood of Jesus, 7which 8he 9dedicated 10for 11us
ὁδὸν πρόσφατον καὶ ζῶσαν διὰ τοῦ καταπετάσματος, [n]τουτ-
1a 4way 2newly 3made 5and 6living through the veil, that
έστιν τῆς.σαρκὸς.αὐτοῦ, 21 καὶ ἱερέα μέγαν ἐπὶ τὸν οἶκον
is, his flesh; and a 2priest 1great over the house
τοῦ θεοῦ, 22 προσερχώμεθα μετὰ ἀληθινῆς καρδίας ἐν
of God [having], we should approach with a true heart, in
πληροφορίᾳ πίστεως, [o]ἐῤῥαντισμένοι τὰς καρδίας ἀπὸ συν-
full assurance of faith, having been sprinkled [as to] the hearts from a 2con-
ειδήσεως πονηρᾶς, καὶ [p]λελουμένοι τὸ σῶμα ὕδατι
science 1wicked, and having been washed [as to] the body with 2water
καθαρῷ·[q] 23 κατέχωμεν τὴν ὁμολογίαν τῆς ἐλπίδος ἀκλινῆ,
1pure. We should hold fast the confession of the hope unwavering,
πιστὸς.γὰρ ὁ ἐπαγγειλάμενος· 24 καὶ κατανοῶμεν ἀλ-
for [is] faithful he who promised; and we should consider one
λήλους εἰς παροξυσμὸν ἀγάπης καὶ καλῶν ἔργων, 25 μὴ
another for provoking to love and to good works; not
ἐγκαταλείποντες τὴν ἐπισυναγωγὴν ἑαυτῶν, καθὼς
forsaking the assembling together of ourselves, even as [the]
ἔθος τισίν, ἀλλὰ παρακαλοῦντες· καὶ τοσούτῳ
custom [is] with some; but encouraging [one another], and by so much
μᾶλλον ὅσῳ βλέπετε ἐγγίζουσαν τὴν ἡμέραν. 26 ἑκου-
[the] more as ye see drawing near the day. [2Where] 1will-
σίως γὰρ ἁμαρτανόντων ἡμῶν μετὰ.τὸ.λαβεῖν τὴν ἐπίγνωσιν
ingly 3for 5sin 4we after receiving the knowledge
τῆς ἀληθείας, οὐκέτι περὶ ἁμαρτιῶν ἀπολείπεται θυσία·
of the truth, no longer 3for 4sins 5remains 1a 2sacrifice,
27 φοβερὰ.δέ τις ἐκδοχὴ κρίσεως, καὶ πυρὸς ζῆλος ἐσ-
but a 2fearful 1certain expectation of judgment, and 2of 3fire 1fervour 5to
θίειν μέλλοντος τοὺς ὑπεναντίους. 28 ἀθετήσας τις
6devour 4about the adversaries. 3Having 4set 5aside 1any 2one
νόμον [r]Μωσέως χωρὶς οἰκτιρμῶν ἐπὶ δυσὶν
[the] law of Moses, 2without 3compassions 4on [5the 6testimony 7of] 8two
ἢ τρισὶν μάρτυσιν ἀποθνήσκει· 29 πόσῳ δοκεῖτε χείρονος
9or 10three 11witnesses 1dies: how much 3think 4ye 1worse
ἀξιωθήσεται τιμωρίας ὁ τὸν υἱὸν τοῦ θεοῦ
5shall 6he 7be 8counted 9worthy 10of 2punishment who the Son of God
καταπατήσας, καὶ τὸ αἷμα τῆς διαθήκης κοινὸν ἡγησά-
trampled upon, and 3the 4blood 5of 6the 7covenant 2common 1esteem-
μενος ἐν.ᾧ ἡγιάσθη, καὶ τὸ πνεῦμα τῆς χάριτος
ed wherewith he was sanctified, and the Spirit of grace
ἐνυβρίσας; 30 οἴδαμεν.γὰρ τὸν εἰπόντα, Ἐμοὶ ἐκδίκησις,
insulted! For we know him who said, To me 2vengeance
ἐγὼ ἀνταποδώσω, [s]λέγει κύριος· καὶ πάλιν,
[1belongs]; I will recompense, says [the] Lord: and again, [The]
[t]Κύριος κρινεῖ τὸν.λαὸν.αὐτοῦ. 31 Φοβερὸν τὸ ἐμπεσεῖν
Lord will judge his people. [It is] a fearful thing to fall
εἰς χεῖρας θεοῦ ζῶντος.
into [the] hands of 3God [1the] 2living.

32 Ἀναμιμνήσκεσθε.δὲ τὰς πρότερον ἡμέρας, ἐν αἷς φωτισ-
But call to remembrance the former days in which, having
θέντες πολλὴν ἄθλησιν ὑπεμείνατε παθημάτων· 33 τοῦτο
been enlightened, 2much 3conflict 1ye 2endured of sufferings; partly,
μέν, ὀνειδισμοῖς.τε καὶ θλίψεσιν θεατριζόμενοι· τοῦτο.δέ,
both in reproaches and tribulations being made a spectacle; and partly,
κοινωνοὶ τῶν οὕτως ἀναστρεφομένων γενηθέντες·
3partners 4of 5those 6thus 7passing 8through [9them] 1having 2become.
34 καὶ.γὰρ τοῖς.[v]δεσμοῖς.μου συνεπαθήσατε, καὶ τὴν ἁρπαγὴν
For both with my bonds ye sympathized, and the plunder
τῶν.ὑπαρχόντων.ὑμῶν μετὰ χαρᾶς προσεδέξασθε, γινώσκοντες
of your possessions with joy ye received, knowing
ἔχειν [w]ἐν [x]ἑαυτοῖς κρείττονα ὕπαρξιν [y]ἐν οὐρανοῖς καὶ
to have in yourselves a better 3possession 4in [5the] 6heavens 1and

His feet.
14 For by one offering He has perfected
forever those who are sanctified.
15 And the Holy Spirit also is a witness to
us: for after *He said* before,
16 "This is the covenant that I will make
with them after those days, says the Lord, I
will put My laws into their hearts and I will
write them in their minds," also,
17 "their sins and lawlessnesses I will
remember no more."
18 Now where remission of these *is, there is*
no longer an offering for sin.
19 Brothers, since then we have boldness to
enter into the Holiest by the blood of Jesus,
20 by a new and living way which He has
consecrated for us through the veil, that is to
say, His flesh –
21 and *since we have* a High Priest over the
house of God,
22 let us draw near with a true heart in full
assurance of faith, having our hearts sprinkled from an evil conscience, and our bodies
having been washed with pure water.
23 Let us hold fast the confession of our
hope without wavering – for He who promised is faithful.
24 And we should consider one another,
encouraging to love and good works,
25 not forsaking the assembling of ourselves
together, as the manner of some is, but
encouraging *one another* – and so much the
more as you see the Day approaching.
26 For if we sin willingly after we have
received the knowledge of the truth, there
remains no more sacrifice for sins,
27 but a certain fearful looking forward to
judgment and burning jealousy, *which is*
going to devour those who are against *God.*
28 He who set aside the law of Moses died
without mercy, under two or three witnesses.
29 How much worse punishment do you
think he shall be thought worthy *to receive*
who has trampled underfoot the Son of
God, and has counted the blood of the
covenant with which he was sanctified an
unholy thing, and who has insulted the
Spirit of grace?
30 For we know Him who said, "Vengeance
is Mine! I will repay, says the Lord!" And
again, "The Lord will judge His people."
31 It is a fearful thing to fall into the hands
of the living God.
32 But call to memory the days before, in
which (after you had been given light) you
endured a great fight of afflictions.
33 Partly you were made a public spectacle,
both in ugly charges and in trials. And partly
you had become companions of those
enduring *these things.*
34 For you both sympathized with me in
my bonds and took joyfully the plundering
of your goods – knowing in yourselves that
you have better and more enduring riches in

μένουσαν. 35 μὴ.ἀποβάλητε οὖν τὴν.παῤῥησίαν.ὑμῶν,
[2]abiding. Cast not away therefore your boldness
ἥτις ἔχει [2]μισθαποδοσίαν μεγάλην.‖ 36 ὑπομονῆς.γὰρ ἔχετε
which has [2]recompense [1]great. For of endurance ye have
χρείαν, ἵνα τὸ θέλημα τοῦ θεοῦ ποιήσαντες κομίσησθε τὴν
need, that the will of God having done ye may receive the
ἐπαγγελίαν. 37 ἔτι.γὰρ [2]μικρὸν.ὅσον.ὅσον, ὁ ἐρχόμενος
promise. For yet a very little while, he who comes
ἥξει, καὶ οὐ.[a]χρονιεῖ.‖ 38 ὁ.δὲ [b]δίκαιος‖ ἐκ πίστεως ζήσε-
will come, and will not delay. But the just by faith shall
ται· καὶ ἐὰν ὑποστείληται, οὐκ.εὐδοκεῖ ἡ.ψυχή.μου ἐν αὐτῷ.
live; and if he draw back, [3]delights [4]not [1]my [2]soul in him.
39 ἡμεῖς.δὲ οὐκ.ἐσμὲν ὑποστολῆς εἰς ἀπώλειαν, ἀλλὰ
But we are not of [those] drawing back to destruction, but
πίστεως εἰς περιποίησιν ψυχῆς.
of faith to saving [the] soul.
11 [c]Ἔστιν.δὲ πίστις ἐλπιζομένων ὑπόστασις, πραγμά-
Now [2]is [1]faith of [things] hoped for [the] assurance, of things
των ἔλεγχος οὐ βλεπομένων. 2 ἐν.ταύτῃ.γὰρ ἐμαρτυ-
[[3]the] [4]conviction [1]not [2]seen. For by this [3]were [4]borne
ρήθησαν οἱ πρεσβύτεροι. 3 Πίστει νοοῦμεν κατηρτίσθαι
[5]witness [6]to [1]the [2]elders. By faith we apprehend to have been framed
τοὺς αἰῶνας ῥήματι θεοῦ, εἰς.τὸ μὴ ἐκ φαινομένων
the worlds by [the] word of God, so that [6]not [7]from [[8]things] [9]appearing
[c]τὰ βλεπόμενα‖ γεγονέναι. 4 Πίστει πλείονα θυσίαν
[1]the [2]things [3]seen [4]have [5]being. By faith [2]a [3]more [4]excellent [5]sacrifice
Ἄβελ παρὰ Κάϊν προσήνεγκεν τῷ θεῷ, δι' ἧς ἐμαρτυ-
[1]Abel than Cain offered to God, by which he was borne wit-
ρήθη εἶναι δίκαιος, μαρτυροῦντος ἐπὶ τοῖς.δώροις.αὐτοῦ [d]τοῦ
ness to as being righteous, [2]bearing [3]witness [4]to [5]his [6]gifts
θεοῦ‖ καὶ δι' αὐτῆς ἀποθανὼν ἔτι [e]λαλεῖται.‖ 5 Πίστει Ἐνὼχ
[1]God, and through it, having died, yet speaks. By faith Enoch
μετετέθη τοῦ μὴ ἰδεῖν θάνατον, καὶ οὐχ.[f]εὑρίσκετο,‖ διότι
was translated not to see death, and was not found, because
μετέθηκεν αὐτὸν ὁ θεός· πρὸ.γὰρ τῆς.μεταθέσεως.[g]αὐτοῦ‖ με-
[2]translated [3]him [1]God; for before his translation he has
μαρτύρηται [h]εὐηρεστηκέναι‖ τῷ θεῷ. 6 χωρὶς.δὲ πίστεως
been borne witness to to have well pleased God. But apart from faith
ἀδύνατον εὐαρεστῆσαι· πιστεῦσαι.γὰρ δεῖ τὸν
[it is] impossible to well please [him]. For [8]to [9]believe [1]it [2]behoves [3]him [4]who
προσερχόμενον [i]τῷ‖ θεῷ. ὅτι ἐστίν, καὶ τοῖς ἐκζητοῦσιν
[5]approaches [6]to [7]God, that he is, and [that] for those who seek [2]out
αὐτὸν μισθαποδότης γίνεται. 7 Πίστει χρηματισ-
[1]him a rewarder he becomes. By faith [2]having [3]been [4]divinely [5]in-
θεὶς Νῶε περὶ τῶν μηδέπω βλεπομένων, εὐλαβη-
structed [1]Noah concerning the things not yet seen, having been moved
θεὶς κατεσκεύασεν κιβωτὸν εἰς σωτηρίαν τοῦ οἴκου
with fear, prepared an ark for [the] salvation of [2]house
αὐτοῦ· δι' ἧς κατέκρινεν τὸν κόσμον, καὶ τῆς κατὰ πίστιν
[1]his; by which he condemned the world, and of the [2]according [3]to [4]faith
δικαιοσύνης ἐγένετο κληρονόμος. 8 Πίστει [k]καλούμενος Ἀ-
[1]righteousness became heir. By faith being called A-
βραὰμ ὑπήκουσεν ἐξελθεῖν εἰς [l]τὸν‖ τόπον ὃν [m]ἤμελλεν‖
braham obeyed to go out into the place which he was about
λαμβάνειν εἰς κληρονομίαν, καὶ ἐξῆλθεν, μὴ ἐπιστάμενος ποῦ
to receive for an inheritance, and went out, not knowing where
ἔρχεται. 9 Πίστει παρῴκησεν εἰς [n]τὴν‖ γῆν τῆς ἐπαγγελίας,
he is going. By faith he sojourned in the land of the promise,
ὡς ἀλλοτρίαν, ἐν σκηναῖς κατοικήσας μετὰ Ἰσαὰκ καὶ
as [in] a strange [country], in tents having dwelt with Isaac and
Ἰακὼβ τῶν [o]συγκληρονόμων‖ τῆς ἐπαγγελίας τῆς αὐτῆς·
Jacob, the joint-heirs of the [2]promise [1]same;
10 ἐξεδέχετο.γὰρ τὴν τοὺς θεμελίους ἔχουσαν πόλιν, ἧς
for he was waiting for the [3]foundations [2]having [1]city, of which [the]
τεχνίτης καὶ δημιουργὸς ὁ θεός. 11 Πίστει καὶ αὐτὴ Σάῤῥα
artificer and constructor [is] God. By faith also [2]herself [1]Sarah
δύναμιν εἰς καταβολὴν σπέρματος ἔλαβεν, καὶ παρὰ καιρὸν
power for [the] conception of seed received, and beyond [2]age
ἡλικίας [p]ἔτεκεν,‖ ἐπεὶ πιστὸν ἡγήσατο τὸν ἐπαγγειλάμενον.
[1]seasonable gave birth; since faithful she esteemed him who promised.
12 διὸ καὶ ἀφ' ἑνὸς [q]ἐγεννήθησαν,‖ καὶ.ταῦτα νενεκρω-
Wherefore also from one were born, and that too of [one] having
μένου, καθὼς τὰ ἄστρα τοῦ οὐρανοῦ τῷ πλήθει, καὶ [r]ὡσεὶ‖
become dead, even as the stars of the heaven in multitude, and as
ἄμμος ἡ παρὰ τὸ χεῖλος τῆς θαλάσσης ἡ ἀναρίθμητος.
[3]sand [4]which [[5]is] [6]by [7]the [8]shore [9]of [10]the [11]sea [1]the [2]countless.
13 Κατὰ πίστιν ἀπέθανον οὗτοι πάντες, μὴ [s]λαβόντες‖ τὰς
In faith [3]died [2]these [1]all, not having received the
ἐπαγγελίας, ἀλλὰ πόῤῥωθεν αὐτὰς ἰδόντες, [t]καὶ πεισθέν-
promises, but from afar them having seen, and having been per-
τες,‖ καὶ ἀσπασάμενοι, καὶ ὁμολογήσαντες ὅτι ξένοι καὶ
suaded, and having embraced [them], and having confessed that strangers and

Heaven.
35 Then do not throw away your confidence, which has great reward.
36 For you have need of patience so that
after you have done the will of God you
may receive the promise.
37 For yet a little while, and He that shall
come will come and will not delay.
38 "Now the just shall live by faith. But if
any draw back, My soul shall have no
pleasure in him."
39 But we are not of the ones who draw
back to perdition, but of those who believe
to the saving of the soul.
11 1 Now faith is the substance of things
hoped for, the evidence of things not seen.
2 For by this the elders were given a good
report.
3 By faith we understand that the worlds
were framed by the word of God, that the
things which are seen were not made of
things which appear.
4 By faith Abel offered to God a more
excellent sacrifice than Cain, by which he
received witness that he was righteous, God
testifying of his gifts – and by it, though he
has died, he still speaks.
5 By faith Enoch was translated so that he
should not see death. And *he* was not found
because God had translated him, for before
he was translated he had this witness, that he
pleased God.
6 But without faith it is impossible to please
God. For he who comes to God must believe
that He is, and that He is a rewarder of the
ones who carefully seek Him out.
7 By faith Noah, (being warned by God of
things not yet seen and moved with fear),
prepared an ark for the saving of his house.
By this he judged the world guilty and
became heir of the righteousness which is by
faith.
8 By faith Abraham obeyed when he was
called to go out into a place which he was
going to receive for an inheritance. And he
went out without knowing where he was
going.
9 By faith he stayed in the land of the
promise, as in a strange country, living in
tents with Isaac and Jacob, the heirs with
him of the same promise.
10 For he looked for a city which has foundations, whose builder and maker is God.
11 Through faith also Sarah herself got the
strength to conceive seed and was delivered
of a child when she was beyond a seasonable
age – because she judged Him faithful who
had promised.
12 By reason of this also, there sprang up
from one (and that too of one who had
become dead) *as many* as the stars of the sky
in multitude and as countless as the sand by
the seashore.
13 These all died in faith, not having
received the promises. But they had seen

παρεπίδημοί εἰσιν ἐπὶ τῆς γῆς. 14 οἱ.γὰρ τοιαῦτα λέ-
sojourners they are on the earth. For they who such things
γοντες, ἐμφανίζουσιν ὅτι πατρίδα ἐπιζητοῦσιν. 15 καὶ.εἰ
say, make manifest that [their] own country they are seeking. And if
μὲν ἐκείνης [v]ἐμνημόνευον" ἀφ' ἧς [w]ἐξῆλθον," εἶ-
indeed [4]that [1]they [2]were [3]remembering from whence they came out, they might
χον.ἂν καιρὸν ἀνακάμψαι· 16 [x]νυνὶ".δὲ κρείττονος ὀρέ-
have had opportunity to have returned; but now a better they stretch
γονται, [y]τουτέστιν," ἐπουρανίου· διὸ οὐκ.ἐπαισχύνεται
forward to, that is, a heavenly; wherefore [2]is [3]not [4]ashamed [5]of
αὐτοὺς ὁ θεός, θεὸς ἐπικαλεῖσθαι αὐτῶν· ἡτοίμασεν.γὰρ αὐτοῖς
[6]them [1]God. [11]God [7]to [8]be [9]called [10]their; for he prepared for them
πόλιν.
a city.

17 Πίστει προσενήνοχεν Ἀβραὰμ τὸν Ἰσαὰκ πειραζόμενος,
By faith [4]has [5]offered [6]up [1]Abraham [7]Isaac [2]being [3]tried,
καὶ τὸν.μονογενῆ προσέφερεν ὁ τὰς ἐπαγγελίας ἀνα-
and [?his] [10]only-begotten [8]was [7]offering [9]up [1]he [2]who [4]the [5]promises [3]ac-
δεξάμενος, 18 πρὸς ὃν ἐλαλήθη, "Ὅτι ἐν Ἰσαὰκ κληθήσεταί
cepted, as to whom it was said, In Isaac shall be called
σοι σπέρμα· 19 λογισάμενος ὅτι καὶ ἐκ νεκρῶν
thy seed; reckoning that even from among [the] dead
[z]ἐγείρειν δυνατὸς" ὁ θεός, ὅθεν αὐτὸν καὶ ἐν παραβολῇ
[4]to [5]raise [3]able [[2]was] [1]God, whence him also in a simile
ἐκομίσατο. 20 Πίστει [a] περὶ μελλόντων [b]εὐλόγησεν" Ἰσαὰκ
he received. By faith concerning things coming [2]blessed [1]Isaac
τὸν Ἰακὼβ καὶ τὸν Ἠσαῦ. 21 Πίστει Ἰακὼβ ἀποθνήσκων
Jacob and Esau. By faith Jacob dying
ἕκαστον τῶν υἱῶν Ἰωσὴφ [b]εὐλόγησεν" καὶ προσεκύνησεν
[2]each [3]of [4]the [5]sons [6]of [7]Joseph [1]blessed and worshipped
ἐπὶ τὸ ἄκρον τῆς.ῥάβδου.αὐτοῦ. 22 Πίστει Ἰωσὴφ τελευτῶν
on the top of his staff. By faith Joseph, dying,
περὶ τῆς ἐξόδου τῶν υἱῶν Ἰσραὴλ ἐμνημόνευσεν, καὶ
concerning the going forth of the sons of Israel made mention, and
περὶ τῶν.ὀστέων.αὐτοῦ ἐνετείλατο.
concerning his bones gave command.

23 Πίστει [c]Μωσῆς" γεννηθεὶς ἐκρύβη τρίμηνον ὑπὸ
By faith Moses, having been born, was hid three months by
τῶν.πατέρων.αὐτοῦ διότι εἶδον ἀστεῖον τὸ παιδίον· καὶ
his parents because they saw [4]beautiful [1]the [2]little [3]child; and
οὐκ.ἐφοβήθησαν τὸ [d]διάταγμα" τοῦ βασιλέως. 24 Πίστει
did not fear the injunction of the king. By faith
[e]Μωσῆς" μέγας γενόμενος ἠρνήσατο λέγεσθαι υἱὸς θυγατρὸς
Moses, great having become, refused to be called son of [2]daughter
Φαραώ, 25 μᾶλλον ἑλόμενος [f]συγκακουχεῖσθαι" τῷ λαῷ
[1]Pharaoh's; [2]rather [1]having [3]chosen to suffer affliction with the people
τοῦ θεοῦ, ἢ πρόσκαιρον ἔχειν ἁμαρτίας ἀπόλαυσιν·
of God, than [[3]the] [4]temporary [1]to [2]have [6]of [7]sin [5]enjoyment;
26 μείζονα πλοῦτον ἡγησάμενος τῶν [g]ἐν" [h]Αἰγύπτῳ" θη-
greater riches having esteemed [6]than [7]the [9]in [10]Egypt [8]trea-
σαυρῶν τὸν ὀνειδισμὸν τοῦ χριστοῦ· ἀπέβλεπεν.γὰρ εἰς τὴν
sures [1]the [2]reproach [3]of [4]the [5]Christ; for he had respect to the
μισθαποδοσίαν. 27 Πίστει κατέλιπεν Αἴγυπτον, μὴ φοβηθεὶς
recompense. By faith he left Egypt, not having feared
τὸν θυμὸν τοῦ βασιλέως· τὸν.γὰρ ἀόρατον ὡς ὁρῶν
the indignation of the king; for [3]the [4]invisible [[5]one] [1]as [2]seeing
ἐκαρτέρησεν. 28 Πίστει πεποίηκεν τὸ πάσχα καὶ τὴν πρόσ-
he persevered. By faith he has kept the passover and the affu-
χυσιν τοῦ αἵματος, ἵνα μὴ ὁ.[i]ὀλοθρεύων" τὰ πρωτότοκα θί-
sion of the blood, lest the destroyer of the firstborn [ones] might
γῃ αὐτῶν. 29 Πίστει διέβησαν τὴν ἐρυθρὰν θάλασσαν
touch them. By faith they passed through the Red Sea
ὡς διὰ ξηρᾶς[k] ἧς πεῖραν.λαβόντες οἱ Αἰγύπτιοι
as through dry [land]; of which [3]having [4]made [5]trial [1]the [2]Egyptians
κατεπόθησαν. 30 Πίστει τὰ τείχη [l]Ἱεριχὼ" [m]ἔπεσεν", κυ-
were swallowed up. By faith the walls of Jericho fell, having
κλωθέντα ἐπὶ ἑπτὰ ἡμέρας. 31 Πίστει Ῥαὰβ ἡ πόρνη οὐ
been encircled for seven days. By faith Rahab the harlot [2]not
συναπώλετο τοῖς ἀπειθήσασιν, δεξαμένη τοὺς κατασκό-
[1]did [3]perish [4]with those who disobeyed, having received the spies
πους μετ' εἰρήνης.
with peace.

32 Καὶ τί ἔτι λέγω; ἐπιλείψει.[n]γάρ με" διηγούμενον ὁ
And what more do I say? For [4]will [5]fail [6]me [3]relating [1]the
χρόνος περὶ Γεδεών, [o]Βαράκ [p]τε καὶ" Σαμψὼν [q]καὶ" Ἰεφθάε,
[2]time of Gedeon, Barak also and Sampson and Jephthae,
[r]Δαβίδ" τε καὶ Σαμουὴλ καὶ τῶν προφητῶν· 33 οἳ διὰ πίστεως
David also and Samuel and of the prophets: who by faith
κατηγωνίσαντο βασιλείας, [s]εἰργάσαντο" δικαιοσύνην, ἐπέτυχον
overcame kingdoms, wrought righteousness, obtained
ἐπαγγελιῶν, ἔφραξαν στόματα λεόντων, 34 ἔσβεσαν δύναμιν
promises, stopped mouths of lions, quenched [the] power

them at a distance and were persuaded of
them and embraced *them.* And they confessed that they were strangers and pilgrims
on the earth.
14 For they who say such things make it
clear that they are looking for their own
country.
15 And truly, if they had been thinking of
that from which they came, they might have
had opportunity to have returned.
16 But now they stretch forward to a better
country, that is, a heavenly country. For this
reason God is not ashamed to be called their
God, for He has prepared a city for them.
17 By faith Abraham, when he was tested,
offered up Isaac. And he that had received
the promises was offering up his only-
begotten,
18 of whom it was said, "In Isaac shall your
seed be called."
19 *For he was supposing* that God was able
to raise him up, even from the dead – from
which he did get him back too, in a way of
speaking.
20 By faith Isaac blessed Jacob and Esau in
regard to things to come.
21 By faith Jacob, when he was dying,
blessed each of the sons of Joseph, and he
worshiped, *leaning* on the top of his staff.
22 By faith Joseph, when he died, talked
about the departing of the children of Israel
and gave commandment about his bones.
23 By faith Moses, when he was born, was
hidden three months by his parents -
because they saw the little child was very
beautiful and they were not afraid of the
king's commandment.
24 By faith Moses, when he had become a
man, refused to be called the son of
Phar-a-oh's daughter,
25 choosing rather to suffer affliction with
the people of God than to have the temporary enjoyment of sin.
26 *For he* had counted the reproach of
Christ greater riches than the treasures of
Egypt, for he looked forward to a reward.
27 By faith he left Egypt, not fearing the
anger of the king. For he kept on, as seeing
Him who is invisible.
28 By faith he kept the Passover and the
sprinkling of blood, for fear that He who
killed the first-born should touch them.
29 By faith they passed through the Red
Sea as by dry land. But the Egyptians, trying
to do *the same*, were swallowed up.
30 By faith the walls of Jericho fell down,
after they had been circled for seven days.
31 By faith Rahab the harlot did not die
with the ones who did not believe, when she
had received the spies with peace.
32 And what more shall I say? For the time
would fail me to tell of Gideon and Barak
and Samson and Jeph-thah and David and
Samuel and of the prophets
33 who through faith put down kingdoms,
worked righteousness, received the promises,

πυρός, ἔφυγον στόματα [t]μαχαίρας,‖ [v]ἐνεδυναμώθησαν‖ ἀπὸ
of fire, escaped [the] mouths of [the] sword, acquired strength out of
ἀσθενείας, ἐγενήθησαν ἰσχυροὶ ἐν πολέμῳ, παρεμβολὰς
weakness, became mighty in war, [2the] 3armies
ἔκλιναν ἀλλοτρίων· 35 ἔλαβον [w]γυναῖκες‖ ἐξ ἀνα-
1made 4to 2give 3way 4of 5strangers. 10Received 9women by resur-
στάσεως τοὺς.νεκροὺς.αὐτῶν· ἄλλοι.δὲ ἐτυμπανίσθησαν, οὐ
rection their dead; and others were tortured, not
προσδεξάμενοι τὴν ἀπολύτρωσιν, ἵνα κρείττονος ἀναστάσεως
having accepted redemption, that a better resurrection
τύχωσιν· 36 ἕτεροι.δὲ ἐμπαιγμῶν καὶ μαστίγων πεῖραν
they might obtain; and others 2of 3mockings 4and 5of 6scourgings 1trial
ἔλαβον, ἔτι.δὲ δεσμῶν καὶ φυλακῆς· 37 ἐλιθάσθησαν,
received, yea, moreover, of bonds and of imprisonment. They were stoned,
[x]ἐπρίσθησαν, ἐπειράσθησαν,‖ ἐν φόνῳ [y]μαχαίρας‖ ἀπέθα-
were sawn asunder, were tempted, by slaughter of [the] sword they
νον· περιῆλθον ἐν μηλωταῖς, ἐν αἰγείοις δέρμασιν, ὑστερού-
died; they wandered in sheep-skins, in goats' skins, being des-
μενοι, θλιβόμενοι, κακουχούμενοι, 38 ὧν οὐκ.ἦν ἄξιος ὁ
titute, being oppressed, being evil treated, (of whom 3was 4not 5worthy 1the
κόσμος· [z]ἐν‖ ἐρημίαις πλανώμενοι καὶ ὄρεσιν καὶ σπηλαίοις
2world,) in deserts wandering and in mountains and in caves
καὶ ταῖς ὀπαῖς τῆς γῆς. 39 Καὶ οὗτοι πάντες μαρτυρη-
and in the holes of the earth. And these all, having been borne
θέντες διὰ τῆς πίστεως, οὐκ.ἐκομίσαντο [a]τὴν ἐπαγγελίαν,‖
witness to through faith, did not receive the promise,
40 τοῦ θεοῦ περὶ ἡμῶν κρεῖττόν τι προβλεψαμένου, ἵνα.μὴ
God for us 2better 1something having foreseen, that not
χωρὶς ἡμῶν τελειωθῶσιν.
apart from us they should be made perfect.

12 Τοιγαροῦν καὶ ἡμεῖς τοσοῦτον ἔχοντες περικείμενον
Therefore also we 2so 3great 1having 4encompassing
ἡμῖν νέφος μαρτύρων, ὄγκον ἀποθέμενοι πάντα καὶ
5us 4a 5cloud 6of 7witnesses, 14weight 10having 11laid 12aside 13every and
τὴν εὐπερίστατον ἁμαρτίαν, δι' ὑπομονῆς τρέχωμεν τὸν
the easily-surrounding sin, with endurance we should run the
προκείμενον ἡμῖν ἀγῶνα, 2 ἀφορῶντες εἰς τὸν τῆς πίστεως
2lying 3before 4us 1race, looking away to 2the 6of 7faith
ἀρχηγὸν καὶ τελειωτὴν Ἰησοῦν, ὃς ἀντὶ τῆς προκει-
3leader 4and 5completer 1Jesus: who in view of the 2ly-
μένης αὐτῷ χαρᾶς ὑπέμεινεν σταυρόν, αἰσχύνης
ing 3before 4him 1joy endured [the] cross, [the] shame
καταφρονήσας, ἐν.δεξιᾷ.τε τοῦ θρόνου τοῦ θεοῦ [b]ἐκάθι-
having despised, and at [the] right hand of the throne of God sat
σεν.‖ 3 ἀναλογίσασθε.γὰρ τὸν τοιαύτην ὑπομεμενηκότα
down. For consider well him who 2so 3great 1has 4endured
ὑπὸ τῶν ἁμαρτωλῶν εἰς [c]αὐτὸν‖ ἀντιλογίαν, ἵνα μὴ κά-
6from 7sinners 8against 9himself 5gainsaying, that 2not 1ye 3be
μητε, ταῖς.ψυχαῖς.ὑμῶν ἐκλυόμενοι. 4 Οὔπω μέχρις αἵματος
4wearied, 6in 7your 8souls 5fainting. Not yet unto blood
ἀντικατέστητε πρὸς τὴν ἁμαρτίαν ἀνταγωνιζόμενοι, 5 καὶ
resisted ye 2against 3sin 1wrestling, and
ἐκλέλησθε τῆς παρακλήσεως, ἥτις ὑμῖν ὡς υἱοῖς διαλέ-
ye have quite forgotten the exhortation, which to you, as to sons, he ad-
γεται·[d] Υἱέ.μου, μὴ.ὀλιγώρει [e]παιδείας‖ κυρίου, μηδὲ ἐκ-
dresses: My son, despise not [the] discipline of [the] Lord, nor
λύου ὑπ' αὐτοῦ ἐλεγχόμενος. 6 ὃν.γὰρ ἀγαπᾷ κύριος
faint, by him being reproved; for whom 3loves [1the] 2Lord
παιδεύει· μαστιγοῖ.δὲ πάντα υἱὸν ὃν παραδέχεται. 7 [f]Εἰ‖
he disciplines, and scourges every son whom he receives. If
[g]παιδείαν‖ ὑπομένετε, ὡς υἱοῖς ὑμῖν προσφέρεται
discipline ye endure, 6as 7with 8sons 4with 5you 2is 3dealing
ὁ θεός· τίς.γάρ [h]ἐστιν‖ υἱὸς ὃν οὐ.παιδεύει πατήρ;
1God; for who is [the] son whom 3disciplines 4not [1the] 2Father?
8 εἰ.δὲ χωρίς ἐστε [i]παιδείας,‖ ἧς μέτοχοι γεγόνασιν πάν-
But if 3without 1ye 2are discipline, of which 4partakers 2have 3become 1all,
τες, ἄρα νόθοι [j]ἐστὲ καὶ οὐχ υἱοί.‖ 9 εἶτα τοὺς μὲν τῆς σαρκὸς
then bastards ye are and not sons. Moreover the 4flesh
ἡμῶν πατέρας εἴχομεν παιδευτάς, καὶ [k]ἐνετρε-
2of 3our 1fathers we have had [as] those who discipline [us], and we respected
πόμεθα·‖ οὐ [l]πολλῷ‖ μᾶλλον ὑποταγησόμεθα τῷ πατρὶ
[them]; 2not 4much 5rather 1shall 3we be in subjection to the Father
τῶν πνευμάτων, καὶ ζήσομεν; 10 οἱ.μὲν.γὰρ πρὸς ὀλίγας
of spirits, and shall live? For they indeed for a few
ἡμέρας κατὰ τὸ δοκοῦν αὐτοῖς ἐπαίδευον· ὁ.δὲ ἐπὶ
days according to that which seemed good to them disciplined; but he for
τὸ συμφέρον, εἰς τὸ μεταλαβεῖν τῆς.ἁγιότητος.αὐτοῦ. 11 πᾶσα
profit, for [us] to partake of his holiness. 2Any (lit. every)
[m]δὲ παιδεία‖ πρὸς μὲν τὸ.παρὸν οὐ.δοκεῖ χαρᾶς εἶναι,
1but discipline for the present seems not [3matter] 4of 5joy 1to 2be,
ἀλλὰ λύπης· ὕστερον.δὲ καρπὸν εἰρηνικὸν τοῖς δι' αὐτῆς
but of grief; but afterwards 3fruit 2peaceable 4to 5those 11by 12it

stopped the mouths of lions,

34 put out the power of fire, escaped the edges of the sword. Out of weakness they were made strong. Becoming mighty in war, they turned the armies of strangers to flight.

35 Women received their dead by resurrection. And others were tortured, refusing to accept deliverance so that they might obtain a better resurrection.

36 And others underwent mockings and whippings – and even more, of chains and of being in prison –

37 they were stoned, they were cut apart with saws, they were tempted and were slain with the sword. They wandered about in sheepskins and goatskins, being in want, afflicted, tormented,

38 (of whom the world was not worthy); they wandered in deserts and in mountains and in dens and caves of the earth.

39 And all of these, when they had gotten a good report through faith, did not receive the promise.

40 God had provided some better thing for us, so that they should not be made perfect apart from us.

12 1 Then, since we are also circled about with so great a cloud of witnesses, let us lay aside every weight, and the sin which so easily encircles us. And let us run with patience the race that is set before us,

2 looking to Jesus, the Author and Finisher of our faith, who for the joy that was set before Him endured the cross, despising the shame, and sat down at the right hand of the throne of God.

3 For carefully consider Him who endured such great slander of sinners against Himself, for fear that you may become wearied and faint in your minds,

4 you have not yet resisted to blood, wrestling against sin.

5 And you have forgotten the comforting call which He speaks to you as to sons, "My son, do not despise the chastening of the Lord, nor faint when being corrected by Him.

6 For whom the Lord loves, He corrects, and He whips every son whom He receives."

7 If you endure correction, God is dealing with you as sons for who is the son whom the father does not correct?

8 But if you are without discipline, of which all have become partakers, then you are bastards and not sons.

9 Furthermore, we have had fathers of our flesh who corrected us, and we respected them. Shall we not much rather be put under the Father of spirits and live?

10 For they indeed corrected for a few days according to that which seemed good to them but He for good, so that we might share His holiness.

11 Now chastening for the present does not seem to be joyous, but grievous. But after-

γεγυμνασμένοις ἀποδίδωσιν δικαιοσύνης.
2having 3been 4exercised 1renders 4of 5righteousness.

12 Διὸ τὰς παρειμένας χεῖρας καὶ τὰ παραλελυμένα γόνατα
Wherefore the 2hanging 3down 1hands and the enfeebled knees

ἀνορθώσατε· 13 καὶ τροχιὰς ὀρθὰς ⁿποιήσατε‖ τοῖς.ποσὶν.ὑμῶν,
lift up; and 2paths 1straight make for your feet,

ἵνα.μὴ τὸ χωλὸν ἐκτραπῇ, ἰαθῇ.δὲ
lest that which [is] lame be turned aside; but that 2it 3may 4be 5healed

μᾶλλον. 14 εἰρήνην διώκετε μετὰ πάντων, καὶ τὸν ἁγιασμόν,
1rather. Peace pursue with all, and sanctification,

οὗ χωρὶς οὐδεὶς ὄψεται τὸν κύριον· 15 ἐπισκοποῦντες μή
3which 1apart 2from no one shall see the Lord; looking diligently lest

τις.ὑστερῶν ἀπὸ τῆς χάριτος τοῦ θεοῦ· μή τις ῥίζα πικρίας
any lack the grace of God; lest any root of bitterness

ἄνω φύουσα ἐνοχλῇ, καὶ ᵒδιὰ ταύτης‖ μιανθῶσιν ᵖ
2up 1springing should trouble [you], and by this be defiled

πολλοί· 16 μή τις πόρνος ἢ βέβηλος, ὡς Ἠσαῦ, ὃς
many; lest [there be] any fornicator or profane person, as Esau, who

ἀντὶ βρώσεως μιᾶς ᵠἀπέδοτο‖ τὰ πρωτοτόκια ʳαὐτοῦ.‖ 17 ἴστε
for 2meal 1one sold 2birthright 1his; 4ye 5know

γὰρ ὅτι καὶ μετέπειτα θέλων κληρονομῆσαι τὴν εὐλογίαν ἀπε-
3for that also afterwards, wishing to inherit the blessing, he was

δοκιμάσθη· μετανοίας.γὰρ τόπον οὐχ.εὗρεν, καίπερ μετὰ δακ-
rejected, for 2of 3repentance 1place he found not, although with

ρύων ἐκζητήσας αὐτήν.
tears having earnestly sought it.

18 Οὐ.γὰρ προσεληλύθατε ψηλαφωμένῳ ˢὄρει,‖ καὶ
For 3not 1ye 2have come to 3being 4touched [1the] 2mount and

κεκαυμένῳ πυρί, καὶ γνόφῳ, καὶ ᵗσκότῳ,‖ καὶ θυέλλῃ,
having been kindled with fire, and to obscurity, and to darkness, and to tempest,

19 καὶ σάλπιγγος ἤχῳ, καὶ φωνῇ ῥημάτων, ἧς οἱ
and 2trumpet's 1to sound, and to voice of words; which [voice] they that

ἀκούσαντες παρῃτήσαντο μὴ προστεθῆναι αὐτοῖς
heard excused themselves [asking] 3not 4to 5be 6addressed 7to 8them [1the]

λόγον· 20 οὐκ.ἔφερον.γὰρ τὸ διαστελλόμενον, Κἂν θηρίον
2word; (for they could not bear that [which] was commanded: And if a beast

θίγῃ τοῦ ὄρους λιθοβοληθήσεται, ᵘἢ βολίδι κατατοξευ-
should touch the mountain, it shall be stoned, or with a dart shot

θήσεται·‖ 21 καί, οὕτως φοβερὸν ἦν τὸ φανταζόμενον,
through; and, so fearful was the spectacle [that]

ᵛΜωσῆς‖ εἶπεν, Ἔκφοβός εἰμι καὶ ἔντρομος· 22 ἀλλὰ προσ-
Moses said, 3greatly 4afraid 1I 2am and trembling:) but ye have

εληλύθατε Σιὼν ὄρει, καὶ πόλει θεοῦ ζῶντος, Ἱερου-
come to 2Sion 1mount; and [the] city of 3God [1the] 2living, 5Jeru-

σαλὴμ ἐπουρανίῳ, καὶ μυριάσιν ʷἀγγέλων 23 πανηγύρει,
salem 4heavenly; and to myriads of angels, [the] universal gathering;

καὶ ἐκκλησίᾳ πρωτοτόκων ˣἐν οὐρανοῖς ἀπογεγραμ-
and to [the] assembly of [the] firstborn [ones] in [the] heavens regis-

μένων,‖ καὶ κριτῇ θεῷ πάντων, καὶ πνεύμασιν δικαίων
tered; and to [2the] 3judge 1God of all; and to [the] spirits of [the] just

τετελειωμένων, 24 καὶ διαθήκης νέας μεσίτῃ Ἰησοῦ, καὶ
[who] have been perfected; and 4of 5a 7covenant 6fresh 3mediator 1to 2Jesus; and

αἵματι ῥαντισμοῦ ʸκρείττονα‖ λαλοῦντι παρὰ τὸν ᶻἌβελ
to [the] blood of sprinkling, 2better 3things 1speaking than Abel.

25 Βλέπετε μὴ.παραιτήσησθε τὸν λαλοῦντα. εἰ.γὰρ ἐκεῖνοι
Take heed ye refuse not him who speaks. For if they

οὐκ.ᶻἔφυγον,‖ ᵃτὸν‖ ἐπὶ ᵇτῆς‖ γῆς παραιτησάμενοιᵃ χρη-
escaped not, 3him 4that 5on 6the 7earth [1who] 2refused divine-

ματίζοντα, ᶜπολλῷ‖.μᾶλλον ἡμεῖς οἱ τὸν ἀπ' οὐρανῶν
ly instructed [them], much more we who 4him 5from [6the] 7heavens

ἀποστρεφόμενοι, 26 οὗ ἡ φωνὴ τὴν γῆν ἐσάλευσεν τότε,
1turn 2away 3from! whose voice 2the 3earth 1shook then;

νῦν.δὲ ἐπήγγελται, λέγων, Ἔτι ἅπαξ ἐγὼ ᵈσείω‖ οὐ μόνον
but now he has promised, saying, Yet once I shake not only

τὴν γῆν, ἀλλὰ καὶ τὸν οὐρανόν. 27 Τὸ.δὲ Ἔτι.ἅπαξ, δηλοῖ
the earth, but also the heaven. But the Yet once, signifies

ᵉτῶν σαλευομένων τὴν‖ μετάθεσιν, ὡς πεποιημένων,
3of 4the [5things] 6shaken 1the 2removing, as having been made,

ἵνα μείνῃ τὰ μὴ.σαλευόμενα. 28 διὸ βασιλείαν
that 5may 6remain 1the [2things] 3not 4shaken. Wherefore a kingdom

ἀσάλευτον παραλαμβάνοντες, ἔχωμεν χάριν, δι' ἧς
not to be shaken receiving, may we have grace, by which

λατρεύωμεν εὐαρέστως τῷ θεῷ μετὰ ᶠαἰδοῦς καὶ εὐλαβείας.‖
we may serve 2well 3pleasingly 1God with reverence and fear.

29 καὶ.γὰρ ὁ.θεὸς.ἡμῶν πῦρ καταναλίσκον.
For also our God [is] a 2fire 1consuming.

13 Ἡ φιλαδελφία μενέτω. 2 τῆς φιλοξενίας μὴ ἐπιλαν-
2Brotherly 3love 1let abide; of hospitality 2not 1be for-

θάνεσθε· διὰ.ταύτης.γὰρ ἔλαθόν τινες ξενίσαντες ἀγγέλους.
getful; for by this unawares some entertained angels.

3 μιμνήσκεσθε τῶν δεσμίων, ὡς συνδεδεμένοι· τῶν κακου-
Be mindful of prisoners, as bound with [them]; those being

wards it yields up the peaceable fruit of righteousness to those who have been exercised by it.

12 For this reason lift up the hands which hang down and the feeble knees.

13 And make straight paths for your feet for fear that the lame will be turned out of the way – but rather that it may be healed.

14 Eagerly pursue peace with all men, and holiness, without which no one shall see the Lord.

15 Look carefully for fear that there should be anyone lacking of the grace of God, lest any root of bitterness should spring up and trouble you (and by this many are made unclean) –

16 for fear any fornicator or ungodly person (as Esau, who for one meal sold his birthright.

17 For you know that afterward he was rejected when he desired to inherit the blessing, though he sought it carefully, with tears – for he did not find any place of repentance).

18 For you have not come to the mountain that could be touched and which had been kindled with fire, and to blackness, and to darkness, and to storm,

19 and to a sound of a trumpet, and the sound of words – on which they that had heard the voice earnestly begged that the word not be addressed to them.

20 For they could not bear that which was commanded, "And if a beast should touch the mountain, it shall be stoned or thrust through with a dart."

21 And so terrible was the sight that Moses said, I am greatly afraid and trembling.

22 But you have come up to Mount Zion and to the City of the living God, the heavenly Jerusalem, and to a countless company of angels,

23 to the general gathering and church of the first-born, who are written in Heaven – and to God the judge of all, and to the spirits of just men made perfect,

24 and to Jesus, the Mediator of the new covenant – and to the blood of sprinkling, speaking better things than that of Abel.

25 See that you do not refuse Him who speaks. For if they did not escape who refused Him that divinely warned them on earth, much more we *shall not escape* who turn away from Him who is from Heaven –

26 whose voice then shook the earth, but now He has promised, saying, "Yet once I will shake not only the earth, but the heaven too."

27 And the, "Yet once," clearly shows the removing of those things that are shaken, as of things that have been made – so that the things which cannot be shaken may remain.

28 Then, since we are receiving a kingdom that cannot be shaken, let us have grace by which we may serve God in a pleasing way, with reverence and godly fear.

χουμένων, ὡς καὶ αὐτοὶ ὄντες ἐν σώματι. 4 τίμιος
evil-treated, as also yourselves being in [the] body. Honourable [let]
ὁ γάμος ἐν πᾶσιν, καὶ ἡ κοίτη ἀμίαντος· πόρ-
marriage [be held] in every [way], and the bed [be] undefiled; ²for-
νους ᵍδὲ¹ καὶ μοιχοὺς κρινεῖ ὁ θεός. 5 ἀφιλάργυρος
nicators ¹but and adulterers ²will ³judge ¹God. Without love of money [let
ὁ τρόπος· ἀρκούμενοι τοῖς.παροῦσιν· αὐτὸς
your] manner of life [be], satisfied with present [circumstances]; ²he
γὰρ εἴρηκεν, Οὐ.μή σε ἀνῶ, οὐδ'.οὐ.μή σε ʰἐγκαταλίπω.ᴵ
¹for has said, In no wise thee will I leave, nor in any wise thee will I forsake.
6 ὥστε θαῤῥοῦντας.ἡμᾶς.λέγειν, Κύριος ἐμοὶ βοηθός,
So that we may boldly say, [The] Lord [is] to me a helper,
ⁱκαὶᴵ οὐ.φοβηθήσομαι·ᵏ τί ποιήσει μοι ἄνθρωπος;
and I will not be afraid: what shall ²do ³to ⁴me ¹man?
7 Μνημονεύετε τῶν.ἡγουμένων.ὑμῶν, οἵτινες ἐλάλησαν
Remember your leaders, who spoke
ὑμῖν τὸν λόγον τοῦ θεοῦ· ὧν ἀναθεωροῦντες τὴν ἔκβασιν
to you the word of God; of whom, considering the issue
τῆς.ἀναστροφῆς, μιμεῖσθε τὴν.πίστιν. 8 Ἰησοῦς χριστὸς
of [their] conduct, imitate [their] faith. Jesus Christ
ˡχθὲςᴵ καὶ σήμερον ὁ αὐτός, καὶ εἰς τοὺς αἰῶνας. 9 διδα-
yesterday and to-day [is] the same, and to the ages. With
χαῖς ποικίλαις καὶ ξέναις μὴ.ᵐπεριφέρεσθε·ᴵ καλὸν.γὰρ
⁴teachings ¹various ²and ³strange be not carried about; for [it is] good [for]
χάριτι βεβαιοῦσθαι τὴν καρδίαν, οὐ βρώμασιν, ἐν οἷς οὐκ
⁶with ⁷grace ³to ⁴be ⁵confirmed ¹the ²heart. not meats; in which ²not
ὠφελήθησαν οἱ ⁿπεριπατήσαντες.ᴵ 10 Ἔχομεν θυσια-
¹were ³profited those who walked [therein]. We have an al-
στήριον ἐξ οὗ φαγεῖν οὐκ.ἔχουσιν ἐξουσίαν οἱ τῇ σκηνῇ
tar of which to eat they have not authority who the tabernacle
λατρεύοντες. 11 ὧν.γὰρ εἰσφέρεται ζώων τὸ αἷμα
serve; for of those ²whose ⁴is ⁵brought ¹animals ³blood [as sacri-
ᵒπερὶ ἁμαρτίαςᴵ εἰς τὰ ἅγια ᵖ διὰ τοῦ ἀρχιερέως, τούτων
fices] for sin into the holies by the high priest, of these
τὰ σώματα κατακαίεται ἔξω τῆς παρεμβολῆς· 12 διὸ καὶ
the bodies are burned outside the camp. Wherefore also
Ἰησοῦς, ἵνα ἁγιάσῃ διὰ τοῦ.ἰδίου αἵματος τὸν λαόν,
Jesus, that he might sanctify by his own blood the people,
ἔξω τῆς πύλης ἔπαθεν. 13 τοίνυν ἐξερχώμεθα πρὸς αὐτὸν
outside the gate suffered: therefore we should go forth to him
ἔξω τῆς παρεμβολῆς, τὸν.ὀνειδισμὸν.αὐτοῦ φέροντες· 14 οὐ
outside the camp, his reproach bearing; ⁴not
γὰρ ἔχομεν ὧδε μένουσαν πόλιν, ἀλλὰ τὴν μέλλουσαν ἐπι-
¹for ²we ³have here an abiding city, but the coming one we are
ζητοῦμεν. 15 Δι' αὐτοῦ ᵍοὖνᴵ ἀναφέρωμεν θυσίαν αἰνέσεως
seeking for. By him therefore we should offer [the] sacrifice of praise
ʳδιαπαντὸςᴵ τῷ θεῷ, ˢτουτέστιν,ᴵ καρπὸν χειλέων ὁμολογούν-
continually to God, that is, fruit of [the] lips confess-
των τῷ.ὀνόματι.αὐτοῦ. 16 τῆς.δὲ.εὐποιΐας καὶ κοινωνίας
ing to his name. But of doing good and of communicating
μὴ.ἐπιλανθάνεσθε· τοιαύταις.γὰρ θυσίαις εὐαρεστεῖται ὁ θεός.
be not forgetful, for with such sacrifices is ²well ³pleased ¹God.
17 Πείθεσθε τοῖς.ἡγουμένοις.ὑμῶν, καὶ ὑπείκετε· αὐτοὶ.γὰρ
Obey your leaders, and be submissive: for they
ἀγρυπνοῦσιν ὑπὲρ τῶν.ψυχῶν.ὑμῶν, ὡς λόγον ἀποδώσον-
watch for your souls, as ⁴account ¹about ²to ³ren-
τες· ἵνα μετὰ χαρᾶς τοῦτο ποιῶσιν, καὶ μὴ στενάζοντες·
der; that with joy this they may do, and not groaning,
ἀλυσιτελὲς.γὰρ ὑμῖν τοῦτο. 18 Προσεύχεσθε περὶ
for unprofitable for you [would [be], this. Pray for
ἡμῶν· ᵗπεποίθαμενᴵ.γάρ, ὅτι καλὴν συνείδησιν ἔχομεν, ἐν
us: for we are persuaded, that, a good conscience we have, in
πᾶσιν καλῶς θέλοντες ἀναστρέφεσθαι· 19 περισσοτέρως.δὲ
all things ⁵well ¹wishing ²to ³conduct ⁴ourselves. But more abundantly
παρακαλῶ τοῦτο ποιῆσαι, ἵνα τάχιον ἀποκατασταθῶ
I exhort [you] this to do, that more quickly I may be restored
ὑμῖν. 20 Ὁ.δὲ θεὸς τῆς εἰρήνης, ὁ ἀναγαγὼν ἐκ
to you. And the God of peace, who brought again from among [the]
νεκρῶν τὸν ποιμένα τῶν προβάτων τὸν μέγαν ἐν
dead the Shepherd of the sheep the great [one] in [the power of
αἵματι διαθήκης αἰωνίου, τὸν.κύριον.ἡμῶν Ἰησοῦν,
the] blood of [the] ²covenant ¹eternal, our Lord Jesus,
21 καταρτίσαι ὑμᾶς ἐν παντὶ ᵛἔργῳᴵ ἀγαθῷ, εἰς τὸ ποιῆσαι
perfect you in every ²work ¹good, for to do
τὸ.θέλημα.αὐτοῦ, ʷποιῶν ἐν ˣὑμῖνᴵ τὸ εὐάρεστον ἐνώ-
his will, doing in you that which [is] well pleasing be-
πιον αὐτοῦ, διὰ Ἰησοῦ χριστοῦ· ᾧ ἡ δόξα εἰς τοὺς
fore him, through Jesus Christ; to whom [be] glory to the
αἰῶνας τῶν αἰώνων. ἀμήν. 22 Παρακαλῶ.δὲ ὑμᾶς, ἀδελ-
ages of the ages. Amen. But I exhort you, breth-
φοί, ʸἀνέχεσθεᴵ τοῦ λόγου τῆς παρακλήσεως· καὶ.γὰρ διὰ
ren, bear the word of exhortation, for also in

29 For also, "Our God is a consuming fire."

CHAPTER 13

1 Let brotherly love continue.
2 Do not forget to welcome strangers for
in this way some have entertained angels
without knowing it.
3 Remember the ones who are prisoners, as
if bound with them and the ones being
ill-treated, as if you were also *ill-treated* in
body.
4 Marriage is honorable in every way, and
the marriage bed is clean but fornicators
and adulterers God will judge.
5 *Let your* way of life be free from the love
of money. *Be* satisfied with *what you have*
now. For He has said, "I will never leave you
nor ever forsake you."
6 So that we may boldly say, "The Lord is
my Helper, and I will not fear. What shall
man do to me?"
7 Remember your leaders, who have spoken
the word of God to you. Consider carefully
what has come out of their conduct. Imitate
their faith:
8 Jesus Christ, the same yesterday and
today and forever.
9 Do not be carried about with different
and strange doctrines – for it is good for the
heart to be established with grace, not with
foods, in which those who walked *in them*
were not helped.
10 We have an altar of which they who
serve the tabernacle do not have a right to
eat.
11 For the bodies of those animals whose
blood is brought into the Holy Place by the
high priest, for sin, are burned outside the
camp.
12 For this reason also Jesus suffered outside the camp, so that He might purify the
people with His own blood.
13 Then, let us go out to Him outside the
camp, bearing His reproach.
14 For we do not have any lasting city, but
we are seeking the one to come.
15 By Him, then, let us offer the sacrifice of
praise to God continually – that is, the fruit
of our lips, giving thanks to His name.
16 But do not forget to do good and to
share what you have, for God is well-pleased
with such sacrifices.
17 Obey your leaders and submit, for they
watch for your souls as ones that are about
to give account, so that they may do it with
joy and not with sadness – for this *would*
not *be* good for you.
18 Pray for us – for we trust we have a
good conscience, in all things willing to live
honestly.
19 But I rather urge you to do this so that I
may be more quickly given back to you.
20 Now the God of peace (who brought
again from the dead our Lord Jesus, that
great Shepherd of the sheep, through the

βραχέων ἐπέστειλα ὑμῖν.
few words I wrote to you.
23 Γινώσκετε τὸν ἀδελφὸν [z] Τιμόθεον ἀπολελυμένον, μεθ'
Know ye the brother Timotheus has been released; with
οὗ, ἐὰν τάχιον ἔρχηται, ὄψομαι ὑμᾶς. 24 Ἀσπάσασθε
whom, if sooner he should come, I will see you. Salute
πάντας τοὺς.ἡγουμένους.ὑμῶν, καὶ πάντας τοὺς ἁγίους.
all your leaders, and all the saints.
ἀσπάζονται ὑμᾶς οἱ ἀπὸ τῆς Ἰταλίας. 25 ἡ χάρις μετὰ
[4]Salute [5]you [1]they [2]from [3]Italy. Grace [be] with
πάντων ὑμῶν. [a]ἀμήν.[a]
[2]all [1]you. Amen.
[b]Πρὸς Ἑβραίους ἐγράφη ἀπὸ τῆς Ἰταλίας, διὰ Τιμοθέου.[b]
To [the] Hebrews written from Italy, by Timotheus.

blood of the everlasting covenant),
21 make you perfect in every good work to
do His will, working in you that which is
pleasing in His sight, through Jesus Christ –
to whom be glory forever and ever. Amen.
22 Now I call on you, brothers, bear with
the word of exhortation, for I have written
to you in few words.
23 Know that our brother Timothy has
been set free, with whom, if he should come
shortly, I will see you.
24 Greet all your leaders and all the saints.
Those from Italy greet you.
25 Grace be with you all. Amen.

The Letter of JAMES

ΙΑΚΩΒΟΣ θεοῦ καὶ κυρίου Ἰησοῦ χριστοῦ δοῦλος, ταῖς
James [2]of [3]God [4]and [5]of [[6]the] [7]Lord [8]Jesus [9]Christ [1]bondman, to the
δώδεκα φυλαῖς ταῖς ἐν τῇ διασπορᾷ χαίρειν.
twelve tribes which [are] in the dispersion, greeting.
2 Πᾶσαν χαρὰν ἡγήσασθε, ἀδελφοί.μου, ὅταν πειρασμοῖς
All joy esteem [it], my brethren, when [6]temptations
περιπέσητε ποικίλοις, 3 γινώσκοντες ὅτι τὸ δοκίμιον ὑμῶν
[1]ye [2]may [3]fall [4]into [5]various, knowing that the proving of your
τῆς πίστεως κατεργάζεται ὑπομονήν· 4 ἡ.δὲ.ὑπομονὴ ἔργον
faith works out endurance. But [2]endurance [[4]its] [6]work
τέλειον ἐχέτω, ἵνα ἦτε τέλειοι καὶ ὁλόκληροι, ἐν μηδενὶ λει-
[5]perfect [1]let [3]have, that ye may be perfect and complete, in nothing lack-
πόμενοι. 5 εἰ.δέ τις ὑμῶν λείπεται σοφίας, αἰτείτω παρὰ τοῦ
ing. But if anyone of you lack wisdom, let him ask from [2]who
διδόντος θεοῦ πᾶσιν ἁπλῶς, καὶ μὴ.ὀνειδίζοντος, καὶ δοθήσε-
[3]gives [1]God to all freely, and reproaches not, and it shall be
ται αὐτῷ. 6 αἰτείτω.δὲ ἐν πίστει, μηδὲν διακρινόμενος· ὁ.γὰρ
given to him: but let him ask in faith, nothing doubting. For he that
διακρινόμενος ἔοικεν κλύδωνι θαλάσσης ἀνεμιζομένῳ καὶ
doubts is like a wave of [the] sea being driven by the wind and
ῥιπιζομένῳ. 7 μὴ.γὰρ οἰέσθω ὁ.ἄνθρωπος.ἐκεῖνος, ὅτι [d]λή-
being tossed; for [2]not [1]let [5]suppose [3]that [4]man that he
ψεταί[d] τι παρὰ τοῦ κυρίου· 8 ἀνὴρ δίψυχος,
shall receive anything from the Lord; [he is] a [2]man [1]double-minded,
ἀκατάστατος ἐν πάσαις ταῖς.ὁδοῖς.αὐτοῦ. 9 Καυχάσθω.δὲ
unstable in all his ways. But let [6]boast
ὁ ἀδελφὸς ὁ ταπεινὸς ἐν τῷ.ὕψει.αὐτοῦ· 10 ὁ.δὲ πλούσιος
[1]the [2]brother [3]of [4]low [5]degree in his elevation, and the rich
ἐν τῇ.ταπεινώσει.αὐτοῦ, ὅτι ὡς ἄνθος χόρτου παρελεύ-
in his humiliation, because as [1]flower [[3]the] [2]grass's he will pass
σεται. 11 ἀνέτειλεν.γὰρ ὁ ἥλιος σὺν τῷ.καύσωνι, καὶ ἐξή-
away. For [3]rose [1]the [2]sun with [its] burning heat, and dried
ρανεν τὸν χόρτον, καὶ τὸ ἄνθος αὐτοῦ ἐξέπεσεν, καὶ ἡ εὐ-
up the grass, and the flower of it fell, and the
πρέπεια τοῦ.προσώπου.αὐτοῦ ἀπώλετο· οὕτως καὶ ὁ πλούσιος
comeliness of its appearance perished: thus also the rich
ἐν ταῖς.πορείαις.αὐτοῦ μαρανθήσεται. 12 Μακάριος ἀνὴρ
in his goings shall wither. Blessed [is the] man
ὃς ὑπομένει πειρασμόν· ὅτι δόκιμος γενόμενος [e]λήψεται[e]
who endures temptation; because [2]proved [1]having [2]been he shall receive
τὸν στέφανον τῆς ζωῆς, ὃν ἐπηγγείλατο [f]ὁ κύριος[f] τοῖς
the crown of life, which [3]promised [1]the [2]Lord to those that
ἀγαπῶσιν αὐτόν.
love him.
13 Μηδεὶς πειραζόμενος λεγέτω, Ὅτι ἀπὸ [g]τοῦ[g] θεοῦ πειρά-
[2]No [3]one [4]being [5]tempted [1]let say, From God I am
ζομαι· ὁ.γὰρ.θεὸς ἀπείραστός ἐστιν κακῶν, πειράζει.δὲ αὐτὸς
tempted. For God [2]not [3]to [4]be [5]tempted [1]is by evils, and [2]tempts [1]himself
οὐδένα. 14 ἕκαστος.δὲ πειράζεται, [h]ὑπὸ[h] τῆς.ἰδίας ἐπιθυμίας
no one. But each one is tempted, by his own lust
ἐξελκόμενος καὶ δελεαζόμενος· 15 εἶτα ἡ ἐπιθυμία συλλαβοῦσα
being drawn away and being allured; then lust having conceived
τίκτει ἁμαρτίαν· ἡ.δὲ.ἁμαρτία ἀποτελεσθεῖσα ἀποκύει
gives birth to sin; but sin having been completed brings forth
θάνατον. 16 Μὴ.πλανᾶσθε, ἀδελφοί μου ἀγαπητοί· 17 πᾶσα
death. Be not misled, [3]brethren [1]my [2]beloved. Every
δόσις ἀγαθὴ καὶ πᾶν δώρημα τέλειον ἄνωθέν ἐστιν
[2]act [3]of [4]giving [1]good and every [2]gift [1]perfect [6]from [7]above [3]is
καταβαῖνον ἀπὸ τοῦ πατρὸς τῶν φώτων, παρ' ᾧ οὐκ.ἔνι
[4]coming [5]down from the Father of lights, with whom there is not
παραλλαγή, ἢ τροπῆς ἀποσκίασμα. 18 βουληθεὶς ἀπε-
variation, or [2]of [3]turning [1]shadow. Having willed [it] he be-

1 1 James, a servant of God and of the Lord
Jesus Christ, to the twelve tribes which are
in the Dispersion, greeting:
2 My brothers, count it all joy when you
fall into different kinds of temptations,
3 knowing that the proving of your faith
works patience.
4 But let patience have its perfect work, so
that you may be perfect and complete,
lacking nothing.
5 But if any of you lack wisdom let him ask
it from God, who freely gives to all and does
not reproach. And it shall be given to him.
6 But let him ask in faith, doubting nothing.
For he who doubts is like a wave of the sea
which is being driven and tossed by the wind
7 – for do not let that man think that he
shall receive anything from the Lord –
8 a double-minded man who is not depen-
dable in any of his ways.
9 But let the brother who is low rejoice in
being lifted up.
10 *And let the* rich *brother rejoice* in being
made humble, because he will pass away like
the flower of the grass.
11 For the sun rose with burning heat and
dried up the grass – so also the rich shall dry
up in his ways.
12 Blessed is the man who endures temptations, for when he is tried he shall receive
the crown of life which the Lord has
promised to those who love Him.
13 Let no one say when he is tempted, It is
because I am tempted of God. For God cannot be tempted by evils, and He himself
tempts no one.
14 But each one is tempted when he is
drawn away and seduced by his own lust.
15 Then when lust has conceived, it gives
birth to sin. And when it is fully finished, sin
brings forth death.
16 Do not be led astray, my beloved
brothers.
17 Every good and perfect gift is from
above, coming down from the Father of
lights, with whom there is no change nor
shadow of turning.
18 After He had willed it, He brought us
forth by the word of truth, in order for us to

κύησεν ἡμᾶς λόγῳ ἀληθείας, εἰς τὸ εἶναι ἡμᾶς ἀπαρχήν
gat us by [the] word of truth, for 2to 3be 1us 7first-fruits
τινα τῶν.αὐτοῦ.κτισμάτων.
4a 5sort 6of of his creatures.
19 i"Ὥστε," ἀδελφοί μου ἀγαπητοί, ἔστω k πᾶς ἄνθρωπος
So that, 3brethren 1my 2beloved, let 3be 1every 2man
ταχὺς εἰς τὸ ἀκοῦσαι, βραδὺς εἰς τὸ λαλῆσαι, βραδὺς εἰς ὀργήν.
swift to hear, slow to speak, slow to wrath;
20 ὀργὴ.γὰρ ἀνδρὸς δικαιοσύνην θεοῦ lοὐ.κατεργάζεται."
for 2wrath 1man's 7righteousness 6God's 3works 4not 5out.
21 Διὸ ἀποθέμενοι πᾶσαν ῥυπαρίαν καὶ περισσείαν κα-
Wherefore, having laid aside all filthiness and abounding of wick-
κίας, ἐν πραΰτητι δέξασθε τὸν ἔμφυτον λόγον, τὸν δυνά-
edness, in meekness accept the implanted word, which [is]
μενον σῶσαι τὰς.ψυχὰς.ὑμῶν. 22 γίνεσθε.δὲ ποιηταὶ λόγου,
able to save your souls. But be ye doers of [the] word,
καὶ μὴ mμόνον ἀκροαταί," παραλογιζόμενοι ἑαυτούς. 23 ὅτι
and not only hearers, beguiling yourselves. Because
εἴ τις ἀκροατὴς λόγου ἐστὶν καὶ οὐ ποιητής, οὗτος
if any man a hearer of [the] word is and not a doer, this one
ἔοικεν ἀνδρὶ κατανοοῦντι τὸ πρόσωπον τῆς γενέσεως αὐτοῦ
is like to a man considering 3face 2natural 1his
ἐν ἐσόπτρῳ· 24 κατενόησεν.γὰρ ἑαυτὸν καὶ ἀπελήλυθεν, καὶ
in a mirror: for he considered himself and has gone away, and
εὐθέως ἐπελάθετο ὁποῖος ἦν. 25 ὁ.δὲ παρακύψας εἰς
immediately forgot what 3like 1he 2was. But he that looked into
νόμον τέλειον τὸν τῆς ἐλευθερίας, καὶ παραμείνας,
[the] 2law 1perfect, that of freedom, and continued in [it],
n"οὗτος" οὐκ ἀκροατὴς ἐπιλησμονῆς γενόμενος, ἀλλὰ ποιητὴς
this one not a 2hearer 1forgetful having been, but a doer
ἔργου, οὗτος μακάριος ἐν τῇ.ποιήσει.αὐτοῦ ἔσται. 26 Εἴ
of [the] work, this one blessed in his doing shall be. If
οτις δοκεῖ θρῆσκος εἶναι pἐν ὑμῖν," μὴ χαλιναγωγῶν
anyone 3seems 6religious 4to 5be 1among 2you, not bridling
γλῶσσαν.αὐτοῦ, qἀλλ'" ἀπατῶν καρδίαν.rαὐτοῦ," τούτου
his tongue, but deceiving his heart, of this one
μάταιος ἡ sθρησκεία." 27 sθρησκεία" καθαρὰ καὶ ἀμίαντος
vain [is] the religion. Religion pure and undefiled
παρὰ tτῷ" θεῷ καὶ πατρὶ αὕτη ἐστίν, ἐπισκέπτεσθαι ὀρ-
before God and [the] Father 2this 1is: to visit or-
φανοὺς καὶ χήρας ἐν τῇ.θλίψει.αὐτῶν, ἄσπιλον ἑαυτὸν τηρεῖν
phans and widows in their tribulation, unspotted 3oneself 1to 2keep
ἀπὸ τοῦ κόσμου.
from the world.
2 Ἀδελφοί.μου, μὴ ἐν vπροσωποληψίαις" ἔχετε τὴν πίστιν
My brethren, 2not 4with 5respect 6of 7persons 1do 3have the faith
τοῦ.κυρίου.ἡμῶν Ἰησοῦ χριστοῦ τῆς δόξης· 2 ἐὰν.γὰρ
of our Lord Jesus Christ, [Lord] of glory; for if
εἰσέλθῃ εἰς wτὴν".συναγωγὴν.ὑμῶν ἀνὴρ χρυσοδακτύλιος
may have come into your synagogue a man with gold rings
ἐν ἐσθῆτι λαμπρᾷ, εἰσέλθῃ.δὲ καὶ πτωχὸς ἐν ῥυπαρᾷ
in 2apparel 1splendid, and may have come in also a poor [man] in vile
ἐσθῆτι, 3 xκαὶ ἐπιβλέψητε ἐπὶ τὸν φοροῦντα τὴν ἐσθῆτα
apparel, and ye may have looked upon him who wears the 2apparel
τὴν λαμπράν, καὶ εἴπητε yαὐτῷ," Σὺ κάθου ὧδε καλῶς, καὶ
1splendid, and may have said to him, Thou sit thou here well, and
τῷ πτωχῷ εἴπητε, Σὺ στῆθι ἐκεῖ, ἢ κάθου zὧδε" ὑπὸ
to the poor may have said, Thou stand thou there, or sit thou here under
τὸ.ὑποπόδιόν.μου· 4 aκαὶ' οὐ διεκρίθητε ἐν ἑαυτοῖς,
my footstool: 4also 3not 1did 2ye make a difference among yourselves,
καὶ ἐγένεσθε κριταὶ διαλογισμῶν πονηρῶν; 5 Ἀκούσατε,
and became judges [having] 2reasonings 1evil? Hear,
ἀδελφοί μου ἀγαπητοί, οὐχ ὁ θεὸς ἐξελέξατο τοὺς πτωχοὺς
3brethren 1my 2beloved: 5not 6God 4did choose the poor
bτοῦ κόσμου" cτούτου," πλουσίους ἐν πίστει, καὶ κληρονόμους
3world 1of 2this, rich in faith, and heirs
τῆς βασιλείας ἧς ἐπηγγείλατο τοῖς ἀγαπῶσιν αὐτόν;
of the kingdom which he promised to those that love him?
6 ὑμεῖς.δὲ ἠτιμάσατε τὸν πτωχόν. dοὐχ" οἱ πλούσιοι
But ye dishonoured the poor [man]. 2Not 3the 4rich
καταδυναστεύουσιν eὑμῶν," καὶ αὐτοὶ ἕλκουσιν ὑμᾶς
1do oppress you, and [2not] 1they 1do drag you
εἰς κριτήρια; 7 οὐκ αὐτοὶ βλασφημοῦσιν τὸ καλὸν
before [the] tribunals? 2not 3they 1do blaspheme the good
ὄνομα τὸ ἐπικληθὲν ἐφ' ὑμᾶς; 8 Εἰ μέντοι νόμον τελεῖτε
name which was called upon you? If indeed [the] 2law 3ye 4keep
βασιλικόν, κατὰ τὴν γραφήν, Ἀγαπήσεις τὸν.πλησίον.σου
1royal according to the scripture, Thou shalt love thy neighbour
ὡς σεαυτόν, καλῶς ποιεῖτε· 9 εἰ δὲ fπροσωποληπτεῖτε," ἁμαρ-
as thyself, 3well 1ye 2do. But if ye have respect of persons, 3sin
τίαν ἐργάζεσθε, ἐλεγχόμενοι ὑπὸ τοῦ νόμου ὡς παραβάται.
1ye 2work, being convicted by the law as transgressors.

be a kind of first-fruits of His creatures.

[19]Then, my beloved brothers, let every man be swift to hear, slow to speak, slow to anger.

[20]For the anger of man does not work out the righteousness of God.

[21]For this reason, when you have laid aside all filthiness and overflowing of wickedness, receive in meekness the implanted word, which is able to save your souls.

[22]But be doers of the word and not hearers only, deceiving yourselves.

[23]Because if anyone is a hearer of the word and not a doer, this one is like a man studying his natural face in a mirror.

[24]For he studied himself and went away. And immediately he forgot what he was like.

[25]But he that looked into the perfect law of liberty and continued in it, this one has not been a forgetful hearer, but a doer of the work. This one shall be blessed in his doing.

[26]If anyone among you thinks himself to be religious – but not bridling his tongue, but is deceiving his heart – this one's religion is worthless.

[27]Pure and undefiled religion before God and the Father is this: to visit the fatherless and widows in their afflictions – to keep oneself unspotted from the world.

CHAPTER 2

[1]My brothers, do not have the faith of our Lord Jesus Christ, *the Lord* of glory, with partiality to persons.

[2]For if a man with gold rings and fancy clothing comes into your gathering – and if a poor man in dirty clothes also comes in –

[3]and if you have looked on him who wears fancy clothing and have said to him, You sit here in a good place – and if you have said to the poor man, You stand there, or, You sit here under my footstool –

[4]did you not make a difference among yourselves? And did you not become judges with evil judgments?

[5]My beloved brothers, hear this! Did not God choose the poor of this world rich in faith and heirs of the kingdom which He promised to those that love Him?

[6]But you despised the poor man. Do not the rich oppress you? And do they not drag you before the judgment seats?

[7]Do they not blaspheme the good name by which you were called?

[8]If you truly keep the royal law according to the Scripture, "You shall love your neighbor as yourself," you do well.

[9]But if you have partiality toward persons, you work sin, being found guilty by the Law as law-breakers.

10 ὅστις.γὰρ ὅλον τὸν νόμον [g]τηρήσει, πταίσει[‖] δὲ ἐν ἑνί,
For whosoever [2]whole [1]the law shall keep, [2]shall [3]stumble [1]but in one
γέγονεν πάντων ἔνοχος. 11 ὁ.γὰρ εἰπών, Μὴ μοι-
[point], he has become [2]of [3]all [1]guilty. For he who said, [3]not [1]Thou
χεύσῃς, εἶπεν καί, Μὴ.φονεύσῃς· εἰ δὲ
[2]mayest commit adultery, said also, Thou mayest not commit murder. Now if
οὐ.[h]μοιχεύσεις, φονεύσεις[‖] δέ, γέγονας
[4]thou shalt not commit adultery, [2]shalt [3]commit [4]murder [1]but, thou hast become
παραβάτης νόμου. 12 Οὕτως λαλεῖτε καὶ οὕτως ποιεῖτε, ὡς
a transgressor of [the] law. So speak ye and so do, as
διὰ νόμου ἐλευθερίας μέλλοντες κρίνεσθαι· 13 ἡ.γὰρ.κρίσις
by [the] law of freedom being about to be judged; for judgment
[i]ἀνίλεως[‖] τῷ μὴ.ποιήσαντι ἔλεος· [k]καὶ[‖] κατα-
[will be] without mercy to him that wrought not mercy. And [2]boasts
καυχᾶται ἔλεος κρίσεως.
[3]over [1]mercy judgment.

14 Τί [l]τὸ[‖] ὄφελος, ἀδελφοί.μου, ἐὰν πίστιν [m]λέγῃ τις[‖]
What [is] the profit, my brethren, if [5]faith [2]say [1]anyone
ἔχειν, ἔργα.δὲ μὴ.ἔχῃ; μὴ δύναται ἡ πίστις σῶσαι αὐτόν;
[[3]he] [4]has, but works have not? is [2]able [1]faith to save him?
15 ἐὰν.[n]δὲ[‖] ἀδελφὸς ἢ ἀδελφὴ γυμνοὶ ὑπάρχωσιν, καὶ λειπό-
Now if a brother or a sister [2]naked [1]be, and desti-
μενοι [o]ὦσιν[‖] τῆς ἐφημέρου τροφῆς, 16 εἴπῃ.δέ τις αὐτοῖς
tute may be of daily food, and [5]say [1]anyone [6]to [7]them
ἐξ ὑμῶν, Ὑπάγετε ἐν εἰρήνῃ, θερμαίνεσθε καὶ χορτά-
[2]from [3]amongst [4]you, Go in peace; be warmed and be fill-
ζεσθε, μὴ.δῶτε.δὲ αὐτοῖς τὰ ἐπιτήδεια τοῦ σώματος, τί
ed; but give not to them the needful things for the body, what [is]
[p]τὸ[‖] ὄφελος; 17 οὕτως καὶ ἡ πίστις ἐὰν μὴ [q]ἔργα ἔχῃ[‖] νεκρά
the profit? So also faith, if [3]not [4]works [1]it [2]have, [6]dead
ἐστιν καθ' ἑαυτήν. 18 ἀλλ' ἐρεῖ τις Σὺ πίστιν ἔχεις,
[5]is by itself. But [3]will [4]say [1]some[2]one, Thou [2]faith [1]hast
κἀγὼ ἔργα ἔχω· δεῖξόν μοι τὴν.πίστιν.σου [r]ἐκ[‖] τῶν ἔργων
and I [2]works [1]have. Shew me thy faith from [2]works
[s]σου,[‖] κἀγὼ [t]δείξω σοι[‖] ἐκ τῶν.ἔργων.μου τὴν πίστιν [u]μου.[‖]
[1]thy, and I will shew thee from my works [2]faith [1]my.
19 σὺ πιστεύεις ὅτι [v]ὁ θεὸς εἷς ἐστιν.[‖] καλῶς ποιεῖς· καὶ τὰ
Thou believest that God [2]one [1]is. [5]Well [3]thou [4]doest; even the
δαιμόνια πιστεύουσιν, καὶ φρίσσουσιν. 20 θέλεις.δὲ γνῶναι,
demons believe, and shudder. But wilt thou know,
ὦ ἄνθρωπε κενέ, ὅτι ἡ πίστις χωρὶς τῶν ἔργων [w]νεκρά[‖] ἐστιν;
O [2]man [1]empty, that faith apart from works dead is?
21 Ἀβραὰμ ὁ.πατὴρ.ἡμῶν οὐκ ἐξ ἔργων ἐδικαιώθη, ἀνε-
[3]Abraham [4]our [5]father [2]not [7]by [8]works [1]was [6]justified, having
νέγκας Ἰσαὰκ τὸν.υἱὸν.αὐτοῦ ἐπὶ τὸ θυσιαστήριον; 22 βλέ-
offered Isaac his son upon the altar? Thou
πεις ὅτι ἡ πίστις [x]συνήργει[‖] τοῖς.ἔργοις.αὐτοῦ, καὶ ἐκ τῶν
seest that faith was working with his works, and by
ἔργων ἡ πίστις ἐτελειώθη;[y] 23 καὶ ἐπληρώθη ἡ γραφὴ ἡ
works faith was perfected. And was fulfilled the scripture which
λέγουσα, Ἐπίστευσεν.δὲ Ἀβραὰμ τῷ θεῷ, καὶ ἐλογίσθη
says, Now [2]believed [1]Abraham God, and it was reckoned
αὐτῷ εἰς δικαιοσύνην, καὶ φίλος θεοῦ ἐκλήθη. 24 Ὁρᾶτε
to him for righteousness, and friend of God he was called. Ye see
[z]τοίνυν[‖] ὅτι ἐξ ἔργων δικαιοῦται ἄνθρωπος, καὶ οὐκ ἐκ πίστεως
then that by works is justified a man, and not by faith
μόνον.[a] 25 ὁμοίως.δὲ καὶ Ῥαὰβ ἡ πόρνη οὐκ ἐξ ἔργων
only. But in like manner also [3]Rahab [4]the [5]harlot [2]not [7]by [8]works
ἐδικαιώθη, ὑποδεξαμένη τοὺς ἀγγέλους, καὶ ἑτέρᾳ ὁδῷ
[1]was [6]justified, having received the messengers, and by another way
ἐκβαλοῦσα; 26 ὥσπερ.γὰρ τὸ σῶμα χωρὶς πνεύματος
having put [them] forth? For as the body apart from spirit
νεκρόν ἐστιν, οὕτως καὶ ἡ πίστις χωρὶς [b]τῶν[‖] ἔργων νεκρά
[2]dead [1]is, so also faith apart from works [2]dead
ἐστιν.
[1]is.

3 Μὴ πολλοὶ διδάσκαλοι γίνεσθε, ἀδελφοί.μου, εἰδότες ὅτι
[2]Not [3]many [4]teachers [1]be, my brethren, knowing that
μεῖζον κρίμα [c]ληψόμεθα·[‖] 2 πολλὰ.γὰρ πταίομεν ἅπαντες.
greater judgment we shall receive. For [3]often [1]we [4]stumble [2]all.
εἴ τις ἐν λόγῳ οὐ.πταίει, οὗτος τέλειος ἀνήρ, δυνατὸς
If anyone in word stumble not, this one [is] a perfect man, able
χαλιναγωγῆσαι καὶ ὅλον τὸ σῶμα. 3 [d]Ἰδοὺ[‖] τῶν ἵππων
to bridle also [2]whole [1]the body. Lo, [6]of [7]the [8]horses
τοὺς χαλινοὺς εἰς τὰ στόματα βάλλομεν [e]πρὸς[‖] τὸ πείθεσθαι
[1]the [2]bits [3]in [4]the [5]mouths we put, for [2]to [3]obey
αὐτοὺς ἡμῖν,[‖] καὶ ὅλον τὸ.σῶμα.αὐτῶν μετάγομεν. 4 Ἰδοὺ
[1]them us, and [2]whole [1]their body we turn about. Lo,
καὶ τὰ πλοῖα τηλικαῦτα ὄντα, καὶ ὑπὸ [g]σκληρῶν ἀνέμων[‖]
also the ships, [2]so [3]great [1]being, and by violent winds
ἐλαυνόμενα, μετάγεται ὑπὸ ἐλαχίστου πηδαλίου, ὅπου
being driven, are turned about by a very small rudder, wherever

10 For whoever shall keep the whole Law,
but shall stumble in one *point,* he has
become guilty of all.
11 For He who said, "You shall not commit
adultery," also said, "You shall not kill."
But if you do not commit adultery, but
commit murder, you have become a
lawbreaker.
12 Speak and do in such a way as if you are
about to be judged by the law of liberty.
13 For judgment *will be* without mercy to
him who did not do mercy. And mercy
rejoices over judgment.
14 My brothers, What good is it if someone
says he has faith, but does not have works?
Can faith save him?
15 Now if a brother or a sister is naked and
is in need of daily food,
16 and if any of you say to them, Go in
peace, be warmed and filled, but does not
give to them the things needed for the body,
what good is it?
17 Even so, faith, if it does not have works,
is dead by itself.
18 But someone will say, You have faith,
and I have works. Show me your faith apart
from your works, and I will show you my
faith from my works.
19 You believe that God is one? You do
well. The demons also believe and tremble.
20 But will you know, O empty-headed
man, that faith apart from works is dead!
21 Was not our father Abraham declared
just by works when he had offered his son
Isaac on the altar?
22 You see that faith was working with his
works, and faith was made complete by
works.
23 And the Scripture was fulfilled which
says, "And Abraham believed God, and it
was counted to him for righteousness. And
he was called, Friend of God."
24 You see, then, that a man is declared just
by works, and not by faith only.
25 And in the same way, was not Rahab the
harlot declared just by works, when she
had taken in the messengers and had sent
them out another way?
26 For just as the body apart from the
spirit is dead, so faith apart from works is
also dead.

CHAPTER 3

1 My brothers, be not many teachers,
knowing that we shall receive greater
judgment.
2 For we all often stumble. If anyone does
not stumble in word, he is a mature man
who is able to bridle the whole body too.
3 Behold! We put bits into the mouths of
horses for them to obey us. And we turn
about their whole body.
4 See! The ships also are very great and
are driven by violent winds, *yet* they are
turned about by a very small rudder,

[h]ἂν" ἡ ὁρμὴ τοῦ εὐθύνοντος [i]βούληται." 5 οὕτως καὶ
the impulse of him who steers may will. Thus also
ἡ γλῶσσα μικρὸν μέλος ἐστίν, καὶ [k]μεγαλαυχεῖ." Ἰδού,
the tongue a little member is, and boasts great things. Lo,
[l]ὀλίγον· πῦρ ἡλίκην ὕλην ἀνάπτει· 6 [m]καὶ" ἡ γλῶσσα
a little fire how large a wood it kindles; and the tongue [is]
πῦρ, ὁ κόσμος τῆς ἀδικίας. [n]οὕτως" ἡ γλῶσσα καθίσταται
fire, the world of unrighteousness. Thus the tongue is set
ἐν τοῖς.μέλεσιν.ἡμῶν, [o]ἡ" σπιλοῦσα ὅλον τὸ σῶμα, καὶ φλο-
in our members, the defiler [of] [2]whole [1]the body, and setting
γίζουσα τὸν τροχὸν τῆς γενέσεως, καὶ φλογιζομένη ὑπὸ τῆς
on fire the course of nature, and being set on fire by
γεέννης· 7 πᾶσα.γὰρ φύσις θηρίων.τε καὶ πετεινῶν, ἑρπε-
gehenna. For every species both of beasts and of birds, [2]of [3]creeping
τῶν τε καὶ ἐναλίων, δαμάζεται καὶ δεδάμασται τῇ
[4]things [1]both and things of the sea, is subdued and has been subdued by
φύσει τῇ ἀνθρωπίνῃ· 8 τὴν.δὲ γλῶσσαν οὐδεὶς [p]δύναται
[3]species [1]the [2]human; but the tongue no one [3]is [4]able
ἀνθρώπων δαμάσαι·" [q]ἀκατάσχετον' κακόν, μεστὴ ἰοῦ
[1]of [2]men to subdue; [it is] an unrestrainable evil, full of [2]poison
θανατηφόρου. 9 ἐν.αὐτῇ εὐλογοῦμεν [r]τὸν θεὸν" καὶ πατέρα,
[1]death-bringing. Therewith we bless God and [the] Father,
καὶ ἐν.αὐτῇ καταρώμεθα τοὺς ἀνθρώπους τοὺς καθ'
and therewith we curse men who according to [the]
ὁμοίωσιν θεοῦ γεγονότας· 10 ἐκ τοῦ αὐτοῦ στόματος ἐξέρ-
likeness of God are made. Out of the same mouth goes
χεται εὐλογία καὶ κατάρα. οὐ χρή, ἀδελφοί.μου, ταῦτα
forth blessing and cursing. [6]Not [5]ought, [1]my [2]brethren, [3]these [4]things
οὕτως γίνεσθαι. 11 μήτι ἡ.πηγὴ ἐκ τῆς αὐτῆς ὀπῆς
thus to be. [3]The [4]fountain [5]out [6]of [7]the [8]same [9]opening
βρύει τὸ γλυκὺ καὶ τὸ πικρόν; 12 μὴ δύναται, ἀδελφοί
[1]pours [2]forth sweet and bitter? Is able, [2]brethren
μου, συκῆ ἐλαίας ποιῆσαι, ἢ ἄμπελος σῦκα; [s]οὕτως" [t]οὐδεμία
[1]my, a fig-tree olives to produce, or a vine figs? Thus no
πηγὴ ἁλυκὸν καὶ" γλυκὺ ποιῆσαι ὕδωρ.
fountain [is able] salt and sweet [2]to [3]produce [1]water.
13 Τίς σοφὸς καὶ ἐπιστήμων ἐν ὑμῖν; δειξάτω ἐκ τῆς
Who [is] wise and understanding among you; let him shew out of
καλῆς ἀναστροφῆς τὰ.ἔργα αὐτοῦ ἐν πραΰτητι σοφίας. 14 εἰ.δὲ
good conduct his works in meekness of wisdom; but if
ζῆλον πικρὸν ἔχετε καὶ ἐριθείαν ἐν τῇ καρδίᾳ.ὑμῶν, μὴ κατα-
[2]emulation [1]bitter ye have and contention in your heart, [2]not [1]do
καυχᾶσθε [u]καὶ ψεύδεσθε κατὰ τῆς ἀληθείας." 15 Οὐκ ἔστιν
boast against and lie against the truth. [3]Not [2]is
αὕτη ἡ σοφία ἄνωθεν κατερχομένη, [v]ἀλλ'" ἐπίγειος, ψυ-
[1]this the wisdom from above coming down, but earthly, na-
χική, δαιμονιώδης. 16 ὅπου γὰρ ζῆλος καὶ ἐριθεία, ἐκεῖ
tural, devilish. For where emulation and contention [are], there
ἀκαταστασία καὶ πᾶν φαῦλον πρᾶγμα. 17 ἡ.δὲ ἄνωθεν
[is] commotion and every evil thing. But the [2]from [3]above
σοφία πρῶτον μὲν ἁγνή ἐστιν, ἔπειτα εἰρηνική, ἐπιεικής,
[1]wisdom [5]first [6]pure [4]is, then peaceful, gentle,
εὐπειθής, μεστὴ ἐλέους καὶ καρπῶν ἀγαθῶν, ἀδιάκριτος [w]καὶ"
yielding, full of mercy and of [2]fruits [1]good, impartial and
ἀνυπόκριτος. 18 καρπὸς.δὲ [x]τῆς" δικαιοσύνης ἐν εἰρήνῃ σπεί-
unfeigned. But [the] fruit of righteousness in peace is
ρεται τοῖς ποιοῦσιν εἰρήνην. 4 Πόθεν πόλεμοι καὶ [y]
sown for those that make peace. Whence [come] wars and
μάχαι ἐν ὑμῖν; οὐκ ἐντεῦθεν, ἐκ τῶν.ἡδονῶν.ὑμῶν
fightings among you? [Is it] not thence, from your pleasures,
τῶν στρατευομένων ἐν τοῖς.μέλεσιν.ὑμῶν; 2 ἐπιθυμεῖτε, καὶ
which war in your members? Ye desire, and
οὐκ.ἔχετε· φονεύετε καὶ ζηλοῦτε, καὶ οὐ.δύνασθε ἐπιτυχεῖν.
have not; ye kill and are emulous, and are not able to obtain;
μάχεσθε καὶ πολεμεῖτε, [z]οὐκ.ἔχετε [a]δέ," διὰ τὸ μὴ αἰτεῖσθαι
ye fight and war, [2]ye [3]have [4]not [1]but because [2]not [1]ask
ὑμᾶς· 3 αἰτεῖτε, καὶ οὐ.λαμβάνετε, διότι κακῶς αἰτεῖσθε ἵνα
[3]you. Ye ask, and receive not, because evilly ye ask, that
ἐν ταῖς.ἡδοναῖς.ὑμῶν δαπανήσητε. 4 [b]Μοιχοὶ καὶ" μοιχα-
in your pleasures ye may spend [it]. Adulterers and adulte-
λίδες, οὐκ.οἴδατε ὅτι ἡ φιλία τοῦ κόσμου, ἔχθρα [c]τοῦ
resses, know ye not that the friendship of the world enmity [with]
θεοῦ ἐστιν;" ὃς.[d]ἂν' οὖν βουληθῇ φίλος εἶναι τοῦ κόσμου,
God is? Whosoever therefore be minded a friend to be of the world,
ἐχθρὸς τοῦ θεοῦ καθίσταται. 5 ἢ δοκεῖτε ὅτι κενῶς ἡ γρα-
an enemy of God is constituted. Or think ye that in vain the scrip-
φὴ λέγει;[e] πρὸς φθόνον ἐπιποθεῖ τὸ πνεῦμα ὃ [f]κατῴκησεν'
ture speaks? with envy does [3]long [1]the [2]Spirit which took up [his] abode
ἐν ἡμῖν;[g] 6 μείζονα.δὲ δίδωσιν χάριν· διὸ λέγει, Ὁ θεὸς
in us? But [3]greater [1]he [2]gives grace. Wherefore he says, God
ὑπερηφάνοις ἀντιτάσσεται, ταπεινοῖς.δὲ δίδωσιν χάριν.
[4]the] [5]proud [1]sets [2]himself [3]against, but to [the] lowly he gives grace.

wherever the pleasure of the helmsman
may desire.
5 So also the tongue is a little member,
and it boasts great things. Behold, a little
fire! How large a forest it will set on fire!
6 And the tongue is a fire, a world of
unrighteousness. So the tongue is set in our
members, the defiler of the whole body –
both setting on fire the course of nature,
and being set on fire by hell.
7 For every species, both of animals and
of birds, both of creeping things and things
of the sea, is tamed and has been tamed by
mankind.
8 But no one among men is able to tame
the tongue. It is an evil that cannot be controlled, full of deadly poison.
9 We bless our God and Father with it,
and with it we curse men who are made
according to the image of God.
10 Out of the same mouth issues blessing
and cursing. My brothers, these things
ought not to be so.
11 Does the fountain out of the same
opening pour forth sweet and bitter?
12 My brothers, is a fig-tree able to bring
forth olives, or a vine, figs? So no fountain
is *able* to bring forth salt and sweet water.
13 Who is wise and understanding among
you? Out of good behavior let him show
his works, in meekness of wisdom.
14 But if you have bitter jealousy and
fighting in your heart, do not boast and lie
against the truth.
15 This is not that wisdom which comes
down from above, but it is earthly, beastly,
devilish.
16 For where jealousy and fighting are,
there is confusion and every evil thing.
17 But the wisdom that is from above is
first pure, then peaceful, gentle, yielding,
full of mercy and of good fruits, not
partial and not pretended.
18 And the fruit of righteousness is sown
in peace for those that make peace.
4 1 Where do wars and fightings among you
originate? Do *they* not *come from* this,
from your lusts which war in your
members?
2 You desire and do not have. You kill
and are jealous and are not able to obtain.
You fight and war, but you do not have
what you want because you do not ask.
3 You ask and do not receive, because you
ask in the wrong way, that you may waste
it on your lusts.
4 You adulterers and adulteresses! Do you
not know that the friendship of the world
is enmity with God?
5 Or do you think the Scripture says in
vain, The spirit which dwells in us yearns
to envy?
6 But He gives more grace. For this reason
He says, "God set Himself against the
proud, but He gives grace to those who are

7 Ὑποτάγητε οὖν τῷ θεῷ. ἀντίστητε [h] τῷ διαβόλῳ, καὶ
Subject yourselves therefore to God. Resist the devil, and
φεύξεται ἀφ' ὑμῶν· 8 ἐγγίσατε τῷ θεῷ, καὶ ἐγγιεῖ ὑμῖν.
he will flee from you. Draw near to God, and he will draw near to you.
καθαρίσατε χεῖρας, ἁμαρτωλοί, καὶ ἁγνίσατε καρδίας,
Have cleansed [your] hands, sinners, and have purified [your] hearts,
δίψυχοι. 9 ταλαιπωρήσατε καὶ πενθήσατε [i]καὶ" κλαύσατε.
ye double minded. Be wretched, and mourn, and weep.
ὁ.γέλως.ὑμῶν εἰς πένθος μεταστραφήτω, καὶ ἡ.χαρὰ εἰς
[2]Your [3]laughter [4]to [5]mourning [1]let be turned, and [your] joy to
κατήφειαν. 10 ταπεινώθητε ἐνώπιον [k]τοῦ" κυρίου, καὶ ὑψώ-
heaviness. Humble yourselves before the Lord, and he will
σει ὑμᾶς.
exalt you.

11 Μὴ.καταλαλεῖτε ἀλλήλων, ἀδελφοί· ὁ καταλαλῶν
Speak not against one another, brethren. He that speaks against
ἀδελφοῦ, [l]καὶ" κρίνων τὸν.ἀδελφὸν.αὐτοῦ, καταλαλεῖ
[his] brother, and judges his brother, speaks against [the]
νόμου, καὶ κρίνει νόμον· εἰ.δὲ νόμον κρίνεις, οὐκ
law, and judges [the] law. But if [the] law thou judgest, [3]not
εἶ ποιητὴς νόμου, ἀλλὰ κριτής. 12 εἷς ἐστιν ὁ νομο-
[1]thou [2]art a doer of [the] law, but a judge. One is the law-
θέτης[m], ὁ δυνάμενος σῶσαι καὶ ἀπολέσαι· σὺ [n] τίς εἶ [o]ὃς
giver, who is able to save and to destroy: [3]thou [1]who [2]art that
κρίνεις" τὸν [p]ἕτερον";
judgest the other?

13 Ἄγε νῦν οἱ λέγοντες, Σήμερον [q]καὶ" αὔριον [r]πορευ-
Go to now, ye who say, To-day and to-morrow we may
σώμεθα" εἰς τήνδε.τὴν.πόλιν, καὶ [s]ποιήσωμεν" ἐκεῖ ἐνιαυτὸν
go into such a city and may spend there [2]year
[t]ἕνα" καὶ [v]ἐμπορευσώμεθα," καὶ [w]κερδήσωμεν·" 14 οἵτινες οὐκ
[1]one and may traffic, and may make gain, ye who [2]not
ἐπίστασθε [x]τὸ" τῆς αὔριον· ποία.[y]γὰρ" ἡ.ζωὴ.ὑμῶν;
[1]know what on the morrow [will be], (for what [is] your life?
ἀτμὶς [z]γάρ" [a]ἐστιν" ἡ πρὸς ὀλίγον φαινομένη, ἔπειτα
A vapour even it is, which for a little [while] appears, [2]then
[b]δὲ" ἀφανιζομένη· 15 ἀντὶ τοῦ λέγειν.ὑμᾶς, Ἐὰν ὁ κύριος
[1]and disappears,) instead of your saying, If the Lord
θελήσῃ, καὶ [c]ζήσωμεν," καὶ [d]ποιήσωμεν" τοῦτο ἢ ἐκεῖνο.
should will and we should live, also we may do this or that.
16 νῦν.δὲ καυχᾶσθε ἐν ταῖς.[e]ἀλαζονείαις".ὑμῶν· πᾶσα καύχη-
But now ye boast in your vauntings: all [2]boasting
σις τοιαύτη πονηρά ἐστιν. 17 εἰδότι οὖν καλὸν ποιεῖν,
[1]such evil is. To [him] knowing therefore good to do,
καὶ μὴ ποιοῦντι, ἁμαρτία αὐτῷ ἐστιν.
and not doing [it], sin to him it is.

5 Ἄγε νῦν οἱ.πλούσιοι, κλαύσατε ὀλολύζοντες ἐπὶ ταῖς
Go to now, [ye] rich, weep, howling over
ταλαιπωρίαις ὑμῶν ταῖς ἐπερχομέναις. 2 ὁ πλοῦτος
[2]miseries [1]your that [are] coming upon [you]. [2]Riches
ὑμῶν σέσηπεν, καὶ τὰ.ἱμάτια.ὑμῶν σητόβρωτα γέγονεν·
[1]your have rotted, and your garments moth-eaten have become.
3 ὁ.χρυσὸς.ὑμῶν καὶ ὁ ἄργυρος κατίωται, καὶ ὁ.ἰὸς.αὐτῶν
Your gold and silver has been eaten away, and their canker
εἰς μαρτύριον ὑμῖν ἔσται, καὶ φάγεται τὰς.σάρκας.ὑμῶν ὡς
for a testimony against you shall be, and shall eat your flesh as
πῦρ· ἐθησαυρίσατε ἐν ἐσχάταις ἡμέραις. 4 ἰδού, ὁ μισθὸς
fire. Ye treasured up in [the] last days. Lo, the hire
τῶν ἐργατῶν τῶν ἀμησάντων τὰς.χώρας.ὑμῶν, ὁ [f]ἀπεστερη-
of the workmen who harvested your fields, which has been
μένος" ἀφ' ὑμῶν κράζει, καὶ αἱ βοαὶ τῶν θερισάντων εἰς
kept back by you, cries out, and the cries of those who reaped, into
τὰ ὦτα κυρίου Σαβαὼθ [g]εἰσεληλύθασιν." 5 ἐτρυφήσατε
the ears of [the] Lord of Hosts have entered. Ye lived in indulgence
ἐπὶ τῆς γῆς, καὶ ἐσπαταλήσατε. ἐθρέψατε τὰς.καρδίας.ὑμῶν
upon the earth, and lived in self-gratification; ye nourished your hearts
[h]ὡς" ἐν ἡμέρᾳ σφαγῆς. 6 κατεδικάσατε, ἐφονεύσατε τὸν δί-
as in a day of slaughter; ye condemned, ye killed, the
καιον· οὐκ.ἀντιτάσσεται ὑμῖν.
just; he does not resist you.

7 Μακροθυμήσατε οὖν, ἀδελφοί, ἕως τῆς παρουσίας τοῦ
Be patient therefore, brethren, till the coming of the
κυρίου. ἰδού, ὁ γεωργὸς ἐκδέχεται τὸν τίμιον καρπὸν τῆς
Lord. Lo, the husbandman awaits the precious fruit of the
γῆς, μακροθυμῶν ἐπ' αὐτῷ ἕως [i]ἂν" λάβῃ [j]ὑετὸν" [k]πρώ-
earth, being patient for it until it receive [the] [4]rain [1]ear-
ιμον" καὶ ὄψιμον· 8 μακροθυμήσατε καὶ ὑμεῖς, στηρίξατε
ly [2]and [3]latter. Be patient also ye: establish
τὰς.καρδίας.ὑμῶν, ὅτι ἡ παρουσία τοῦ κυρίου ἤγγικεν.
your hearts, because the coming of the Lord has drawn near.
9 Μὴ.στενάζετε [l]κατ' ἀλλήλων, ἀδελφοί," ἵνα μὴ [m]κατακρι-
Groan not against one another, brethren, that [3]not [1]ye [2]be con-

humble."

7 Then put yourself under God. Resist the devil and he will run from you.

8 Come near to God and He will come near to you. Clean your hands, sinners! And purify your hearts, you double-minded ones!

9 Be sorrowful and mourn and weep. Let your laughter be turned to mourning and your joy to shame.

10 Humble yourselves before the Lord, and He will exalt you.

11 Do not speak evil against one another, brothers. He who speaks against his brother and who judges his brother speaks against the Law and judges the Law. But if you judge the Law, you are not a doer of the Law, but a judge.

12 One is the Lawgiver, who is able to save and destroy. Who are you that judges another?

13 Come now, you who say, Today and tomorrow we will go into such a city and will spend a year there, and we will buy and sell, and we will make a profit –

14 you who do not know what *will be* tomorrow. For what is your life? For it is a mist that appears for a little while and then vanishes.

15 Instead, you say, If the Lord is willing and we should live, we also may do this or that.

16 But now you rejoice in your boastings. All such rejoicing is evil.

17 Then to him who knows to do good and does not do it, it is sin to him.

5 1 Come, rich men, weep, howling over your miseries which are coming on you.

2 Your riches have rotted and your clothes have become moth-eaten.

3 Your gold and silver has been eaten away, and their rust shall be for a witness against you and shall eat your flesh like fire. You have heaped up treasure in the last days.

4 Look! The wages of the workers who harvested your fields cry out, (which you have kept back,) and the cries of the ones who reaped have entered into the ears of the Lord of Hosts.

5 You lived in pleasure on the earth and satisfied yourself. You have nourished your hearts, as in a day of slaughter.

6 You have condemned and killed the just – he does not resist you.

7 Then, brothers, be patient until the coming of the Lord. See, the farmer waits for the precious fruit of the earth, having patience for it until it gets the early and late rain.

8 You also be patient. Make your hearts strong, because the coming of the Lord has approached.

9 Do not grumble against one another,

ῆτε·" ἰδού, [n] κριτὴς πρὸ τῶν θυρῶν ἕστηκεν. 10 Ὑπό-
lemned. Lo, [the] judge before the door stands. [As] an ex-
δειγμα λάβετε [o]τῆς κακοπαθείας, ἀδελφοί.μου," καὶ τῆς
ample 9take 1of 2suffering 3evils, 7my 8brethren, 4and
μακροθυμίας, τοὺς προφήτας οἳ ἐλάλησαν [p] τῷ ὀνόματι κυ-
5of 6patience, the prophets who spoke in the name of [the]
ρίου. 11 ἰδού, μακαρίζομεν τοὺς [q]ὑπομένοντας." τὴν ὑπο-
Lord. Lo, we call blessed those who endure. The en-
μονὴν Ἰὼβ ἠκούσατε, καὶ τὸ τέλος κυρίου [r]εἴδετε," ὅτι
durance of Job ye have heard of, and the end of [the] Lord ye saw; that
πολύσπλαγχνός ἐστιν ὁ κύριος καὶ οἰκτίρμων. 12 Πρὸ
full of tender pity is the Lord and compassionate. 2Before
πάντων δέ, ἀδελφοί.μου, μὴ.ὀμνύετε, μήτε τὸν οὐρανόν,
all 4things 1but my brethren, swear not, neither [by] heaven,
μήτε τὴν γῆν, μήτε ἄλλον.τινὰ ὅρκον· ἤτω.δὲ ὑμῶν τὸ ναί,
nor the earth; nor any other oath; but let be of you the yea,
ναί, καὶ τὸ οὔ, οὔ· ἵνα μὴ [s]εἰς ὑπόκρισιν" πέσητε. 13 κακο-
yea, and the nay, nay, that not into hypocrisy ye may fall. Does 4suf-
παθεῖ τις ἐν ὑμῖν; προσευχέσθω· εὐθυμεῖ τις;
fer 5hardships 1anyone 2among 3you? let him pray: is 2cheerful 1anyone?
ψαλλέτω. 14 ἀσθενεῖ τις ἐν ὑμῖν; προσκαλεσάσθω
let him praise; is 2sick 1anyone among you? let him call to [him]
τοὺς πρεσβυτέρους τῆς ἐκκλησίας, καὶ προσευξάσθωσαν ἐπ'
the elders of the assembly, and let them pray over
αὐτόν, ἀλείψαντες [t]αὐτὸν" ἐλαίῳ ἐν τῷ ὀνόματι [v]τοῦ" κυρίου·
him, having anointed him with oil in the name of the Lord;
15 καὶ ἡ εὐχὴ τῆς πίστεως σώσει τὸν κάμνοντα, καὶ ἐγε-
and the prayer of faith shall save the exhausted one, and 3will
ρεῖ αὐτὸν ὁ κύριος· κἂν ἁμαρτίας ᾖ.πεποιηκώς,
raise 5up 6him 1the 2Lord; and if 7sins 1he 2be [3one 4who] 5has 6committed,
ἀφεθήσεται αὐτῷ. 16 ἐξομολογεῖσθε [w] ἀλλήλοις
shall be forgiven him. Confess to one another [your]
τὰ παραπτώματα," καὶ [y]εὔχεσθε" ὑπὲρ ἀλλήλων, ὅπως ἰαθῆ-
offences, and pray for one another, that ye may be
τε. πολὺ ἰσχύει δέησις δικαίου ἐνεργουμένη.
healed. 9Much 8prevails [1the] 3supplication 4of 5a 6righteous [7man] 2operative.
17 [z]Ἠλίας" ἄνθρωπος ἦν ὁμοιοπαθὴς ἡμῖν, καὶ προσευχῇ
Elias 2a 3man 1was of like feelings to us, and with prayer
προσηύξατο τοῦ μὴ βρέξαι· καὶ οὐκ.ἔβρεξεν ἐπὶ τῆς γῆς
he prayed [for it] not to rain; and it did not rain upon the earth
ἐνιαυτοὺς τρεῖς καὶ μῆνας ἕξ. 18 καὶ πάλιν προσηύξατο, καὶ
2years 1three and 2months 1six; and again he prayed, and
ὁ οὐρανὸς [a]ὑετὸν ἔδωκεν," καὶ ἡ γῆ ἐβλάστησεν τὸν
the heaven 2rain 1gave, and the earth caused 3to 4sprout
καρπὸν αὐτῆς.
2fruit 1its.

19 Ἀδελφοί, [b] ἐάν τις ἐν ὑμῖν πλανηθῇ ἀπὸ τῆς ἀλη-
Brethren, if anyone among you err from the truth,
θείας, καὶ ἐπιστρέψῃ τις αὐτόν, 20 [c]γινωσκέτω" ὅτι ὁ
and 2bring 3back 1anyone him, let him know that he who
ἐπιστρέψας ἁμαρτωλὸν ἐκ πλάνης ὁδοῦ.αὐτοῦ, σώσει
brings back a sinner from [the] error of his way, shall save
ψυχὴν [d] ἐκ θανάτου, καὶ καλύψει πλῆθος ἁμαρτιῶν. [e]
a soul from death, and shall cover a multitude of sins.

[e]Ἰακώβου ἐπιστολή."
2Of 3James 1epistle.

brothers, so that you may not be judged.
Look! The Judge stands before the door.
10 My brothers, as an example of suffering
evils, and of patience, take the prophets
who spoke in the name of the Lord.
11 See, the ones who hold out to the end
we call happy. You have heard of the
patience of Job. And you saw the end of
the Lord, that the Lord is full of pity and
tender mercy.
12 But above all, my brothers, do not
swear – not by Heaven, nor the earth, nor
any other oath. But let your yes be yes and
your no be no – that you may not fall into
hypocrisy.
13 Does anyone among you suffer hardships
– let him pray. Is anyone cheerful – let him
sing the praise of God.
14 Is anyone sick among you – let him call
the elders of the church and let them pray
over him, anointing him with oil in the name
of the Lord.
15 And the prayer of faith shall save the
one who is sick, and the Lord will raise him
up. And if he is one who has committed sins,
it shall be forgiven him.
16 Confess your faults to one another and
pray for one another, so that you may be
healed. The fervent, working prayer of a
righteous man has much power.
17 Elijah was a man who had the same kind
of feelings we have, and he prayed in prayer
for it not to rain. And it did not rain on the
earth three years and six months.
18 And he prayed again, and the sky gave
rain, and the earth bore its fruit.
19 Brothers, if anyone of you goes astray
from the truth and if any one brings him
back,
20 let him know that he who converts a
sinner from the error of his way shall save a
soul from death and shall cover a multitude
of sins.

The FIRST Letter of PETER

CHAPTER 1

ΠΕΤΡΟΣ ἀπόστολος Ἰησοῦ χριστοῦ, ἐκλεκτοῖς παρεπιδήμοις
Peter, apostle of Jesus Christ, to [the] elect sojourners
διασπορᾶς Πόντου, Γαλατίας, Καππαδοκίας, Ἀσίας, καὶ
of [the] dispersion of Pontus, of Galatia, of Cappadocia, of Asia, and
Βιθυνίας, 2 κατὰ πρόγνωσιν θεοῦ πατρός, ἐν ἁγιασ-
Bithynia, according to [the] foreknowledge of God [the] Father, by sanctifi-
μῷ πνεύματος, εἰς ὑπακοὴν καὶ ῥαντισμὸν αἵματος
cation of [the] Spirit, unto [the] obedience and sprinkling of [the] blood
Ἰησοῦ χριστοῦ· χάρις ὑμῖν καὶ εἰρήνη πληθυνθείη.
of Jesus Christ: Grace to you and peace be multiplied.
3 Εὐλογητὸς ὁ θεὸς καὶ πατὴρ τοῦ.κυρίου.ἡμῶν Ἰησοῦ
Blessed [be] the God and Father of our Lord Jesus
χριστοῦ, ὁ κατὰ τὸ.πολὺ.αὐτοῦ ἔλεος ἀναγεννήσας [g]ἡμᾶς"
Christ, who according to his great mercy begat 2again 1us
εἰς ἐλπίδα ζῶσαν δι' ἀναστάσεως Ἰησοῦ χριστοῦ ἐκ
to a 2hope 1living through [the] resurrection of Jesus Christ from among
νεκρῶν, 4 εἰς κληρονομίαν ἄφθαρτον καὶ ἀμίαντον καὶ
[the] dead, to an inheritance incorruptible and undefiled and

1 Peter, an apostle of Jesus Christ, to the
elect strangers of the Dispersion of Pontus of
Galatia, of Cap-pa-do-ci-a, of Asia and of
Bi-thyn-i-a –
2 *elected* according to *the* foreknowledge of
God the Father, in a setting apart by the
Spirit, to obedience and sprinkling of the
blood of Jesus Christ: Grace and peace be
multiplied to you.
3 Blessed be the God and Father of our
Lord Jesus Christ, who, according to His
great mercy, brought us forth again to a
living hope, through the resurrection of
Jesus Christ from among the dead,
4 to an inheritance which cannot rot away

ἀμάραντον, τετηρημένην ἐν οὐρανοῖς εἰς [h]ἡμᾶς," 5 τοὺς ἐν
unfading, reserved in [the] heavens for us, who by
δυνάμει θεοῦ φρουρουμένους διὰ πίστεως, εἰς σωτηρίαν
[the] power of God [are] being guarded through faith, for salvation
ἑτοίμην ἀποκαλυφθῆναι ἐν καιρῷ ἐσχάτῳ· 6 ἐν.ᾧ ἀγαλ-
ready to be revealed in [the] [2]time [1]last. Wherein ye ex-
λιᾶσθε, ὀλίγον ἄρτι, εἰ δέον [i]ἐστίν," λυπηθέντες
ult, for a little while at present, if necessary it is, having been put to grief
ἐν ποικίλοις πειρασμοῖς, 7 ἵνα τὸ δοκίμιον ὑμῶν τῆς πίστεως
in various trials, that the proving of your faith,
[k]πολὺ τιμιώτερον" χρυσίου τοῦ ἀπολλυμένου, διὰ πυρὸς δὲ
(much more precious than gold that perishes,) [2]by [3]fire [1]though
δοκιμαζομένου, εὑρεθῇ εἰς ἔπαινον καὶ [l]τιμὴν καὶ δόξαν," ἐν
being proved, be found to praise and honour and glory, in
ἀποκαλύψει Ἰησοῦ χριστοῦ· 8 ὃν οὐκ [m]εἰδότες" ἀγαπᾶτε,
[the] revelation of Jesus Christ, whom not having seen ye love;
εἰς ὃν ἄρτι μὴ ὁρῶντες, πιστεύοντες.δέ, ἀγαλλιᾶσθε
on whom now [though] not looking, but believing, ye exult
χαρᾷ ἀνεκλαλήτῳ καὶ δεδοξασμένῃ, 9 κομιζόμενοι τὸ τέλος
with joy unspeakable and glorified, receiving the end
τῆς.πίστεως.ὑμῶν, σωτηρίαν ψυχῶν· 10 περὶ ἧς
of your faith, [the] salvation of [your] souls; concerning which
σωτηρίας ἐξεζήτησαν καὶ [n]ἐξηρεύνησαν" προφῆται οἱ περὶ
salvation [9]sought [10]out [11]and [12]searched [13]out [1]prophets, [2]who [4]of
τῆς εἰς ὑμᾶς χάριτος προφητεύσαντες, 11 [o]ἐρευνῶντες" εἰς
[5]the [7]towards [8]you [6]grace [3]prophesied; searching to
τίνα ἢ ποῖον καιρὸν ἐδήλου τὸ ἐν αὐτοῖς πνεῦμα
what or what manner of time [7]was [8]signifying [1]the [5]in [6]them [2]Spirit
χριστοῦ, προμαρτυρόμενον τὰ εἰς.χριστὸν παθήματα, καὶ
[3]of [4]Christ, testifying beforehand of the [[2]belonging] [3]to [4]Christ [1]sufferings, and
τὰς μετὰ ταῦτα δόξας· 12 οἷς ἀπεκαλύφθη ὅτι οὐχ ἑαυτοῖς,
the [2]after [3]these [1]glories; to whom it was revealed, that not to themselves
[p]ἡμῖν" δὲ διηκόνουν αὐτά, ἃ νῦν ἀνηγγέλη ὑμῖν διὰ
[2]to [3]us [1]but were serving those things, which now were announced to you by
τῶν εὐαγγελισαμένων ὑμᾶς [q]ἐν" πνεύματι ἁγίῳ ἀπο-
those who announced the glad tidings to you in [the] [2]Spirit [1]Holy
σταλέντι ἀπ' οὐρανοῦ, εἰς ἃ ἐπιθυμοῦσιν ἄγγελοι παρακύψαι.
sent from heaven, into which [2]desire [1]angels to look.
13 Διὸ ἀναζωσάμενοι τὰς ὀσφύας τῆς.διανοίας.ὑμῶν, νή-
Wherefore having girded up the loins of your mind, be-
φοντες, τελείως ἐλπίσατε ἐπὶ τὴν φερομένην ὑμῖν χάριν ἐν
ing sober, perfectly hope in the [2]being [3]brought [4]to [5]you [1]grace at
ἀποκαλύψει Ἰησοῦ χριστοῦ. 14 ὡς τέκνα ὑπακοῆς, μὴ
[the] revelation of Jesus Christ; as children of obedience, not
[r]συσχηματιζόμενοι" ταῖς πρότερον ἐν τῇ.ἀγνοίᾳ.ὑμῶν ἐπιθυ-
fashioning yourselves to the former [2]in [3]your [4]ignorance [1]de-
μίαις, 15 ἀλλὰ κατὰ τὸν καλέσαντα ὑμᾶς ἅγιον καὶ
sires; but according as he who called you [is] holy, also
αὐτοὶ ἅγιοι ἐν πάσῃ ἀναστροφῇ γενήθητε· 16 διότι
[3]yourselves [4]holy [5]in [6]all [[7]your] [8]conduct [1]be [2]ye; because
[s]γέγραπται, Ἅγιοι [t]γένεσθε," [u]ὅτι" ἐγὼ ἅγιός [v]εἰμι." 17 Καὶ
it has been written, [3]Holy [1]be [2]ye, because I [2]holy [1]am. And
εἰ πατέρα ἐπικαλεῖσθε τὸν [w]ἀπροσωπολήπτως" κρίνοντα
if [as] Father ye call on him who without regard of persons judges
κατὰ τὸ ἑκάστου ἔργον, ἐν φόβῳ τὸν τῆς.παροικίας.ὑμῶν
according to the [2]of [3]each [1]work, in fear the [2]of [3]your [4]sojourn
χρόνον ἀναστράφητε· 18 εἰδότες ὅτι οὐ φθαρτοῖς, ἀρ-
[1]time pass ye, knowing that not by corruptible things, by
γυρίῳ ἢ χρυσίῳ, ἐλυτρώθητε ἐκ τῆς.ματαίας.ὑμῶν ἀναστροφῆς
silver or by gold, ye were redeemed from your vain manner of life
πατροπαραδότου, 19 ἀλλὰ τιμίῳ αἵματι ὡς ἀμνοῦ
handed down from [your] fathers, but by precious blood as of a lamb
ἀμώμου καὶ ἀσπίλου χριστοῦ· 20 προεγνωσ-
without blemish and without spot [the blood] of Christ: having been fore-
μένου μὲν πρὸ καταβολῆς κόσμου, φανερωθέντος.δὲ ἐπ'
known indeed before [the] foundation of [the] world, but manifested at
[x]ἐσχάτων" τῶν χρόνων δι' ὑμᾶς, 21 τοὺς δι' αὐτοῦ
[the] last times for the sake of you, who by him
[y]πιστεύοντας" εἰς θεόν, τὸν ἐγείραντα αὐτὸν ἐκ νεκρῶν,
believe in God, who raised up him from among [the] dead,
καὶ δόξαν αὐτῷ δόντα, ὥστε τὴν.πίστιν.ὑμῶν καὶ ἐλπίδα εἶναι
and glory to him gave, so as for your faith and hope to be
εἰς θεόν. 22 Τὰς.ψυχὰς.ὑμῶν ἡγνικότες ἐν τῇ ὑπακοῇ τῆς
in God. Your souls having purified by obedience to the
ἀληθείας [z]διὰ πνεύματος" εἰς φιλαδελφίαν ἀνυπόκριτον, ἐκ
truth through [the] Spirit to brotherly love unfeigned, out of
[a]καθαρᾶς" καρδίας ἀλλήλους ἀγαπήσατε ἐκτενῶς· 23 ἀναγε-
[2]pure [3]a heart one another love ye fervently. Having been
γεννημένοι οὐκ ἐκ σπορᾶς φθαρτῆς, ἀλλὰ ἀφθάρτου, διὰ
begotten again, not of [2]seed [1]corruptible, but of incorruptible, by
λόγου ζῶντος θεοῦ καὶ μένοντος [b]εἰς.τὸν.αἰῶνα." 24 διότι
[the] word [3]living [1]of [2]God and abiding for ever. Because

one which is undefiled and never fades away, reserved in Heaven for us,

5 who are being kept by the power of God through faith to salvation, ready to be revealed in the last time –

6 in which you greatly rejoice. *But* now, for a little while, since it is necessary, you are being put to grief in many different trials –

7 so that the proving of your faith, being much more precious than of gold, (which perishes even though proved by fire,) may be found to praise and honor and glory in the revealing of Jesus Christ.

8 You have not seen *Him, but* you love *Him* – in whom you rejoice with unspeakable joy and full of glory, without now seeing *Him*, but believing –

9 receiving the completion of your faith, the salvation of your souls.

10 Of which salvation the prophets, (who told beforehand of the grace of God towards you), looked for and carefully searched out –

11 searching what, or what manner of time, the Spirit of Christ within them was declaring. *For He* testified beforehand of the sufferings of Christ and the glories proceeding from them.

12 To whom it was revealed that they were not ministering those things to themselves, but to us – which things now have been revealed to you by those who preached the gospel to you in the Holy Spirit sent from Heaven – into which things the angels desire to look.

13 For this reason tighten up the waist of your mind. Be watchful. Hope to the end in the grace which is being brought to you in the revealing of Jesus Christ

14 as obedient children, not following the pattern of your old lusts in your ignorance,

15 but as He who has called you is holy, you yourselves also be holy in all you do,

16 because it has been written, "Be holy, because I am holy."

17 And since you call on Him as Father, who without any respect to persons judges according to everyone's work, pass the time of your stay here in fear.

18 *For* you know that you were not redeemed by things that rot away, by silver or by gold, from your worthless way of life that was handed down from your fathers,

19 but *you were redeemed* by the precious blood of Christ, as a lamb without blemish and without spot.

20 *For* truly He had been foreknown before the foundation of the world, but was revealed at the last times for your sake,

21 who through Him believe in God, who raised Him up from among the dead and gave glory to Him – so that your faith and hope might be in God.

22 Since you have purified your souls in obedience to the truth through the Spirit to

πᾶσα σὰρξ [c]ὡς" χόρτος, καὶ πᾶσα δόξα [d]ἀνθρώπου" ὡς
all flesh [is] as grass, and all [the] glory of man as [the]
ἄνθος [e]χόρτου. ἐξηράνθη ὁ χόρτος, καὶ τὸ ἄνθος [e]αὐτοῦ[l]
flower of grass. [3]Withered [1]the [2]grass, and the flower of it
ἐξέπεσεν· 25 τὸ.δὲ ῥῆμα κυρίου μένει εἰς.τὸν.αἰῶνα. Τοῦτο.δέ
fell away; but the word of [the] Lord abides for ever. But this
ἐστιν τὸ ῥῆμα τὸ εὐαγγελισθὲν εἰς ὑμᾶς.
is the word which was announced to you.
2 Ἀποθέμενοι οὖν πᾶσαν κακίαν καὶ πάντα δόλον καὶ
Having laid aside therefore all malice and all guile and
ὑποκρίσεις καὶ φθόνους καὶ πάσας καταλαλιάς, 2 ὡς ἀρτιγέν-
hypocrisies and envyings and all evil speakings, as new-
νητα βρέφη, τὸ λογικὸν ἄδολον γάλα ἐπιποθήσατε, ἵνα ἐν
born babes, the [2]mental [1]genuine milk long ye after, that by
αὐτῷ αὐξηθῆτε,[f] 3 [g]εἴπερ[l] ἐγεύσασθε ὅτι χρηστὸς ὁ κύριος.
it ye may grow, if indeed ye did taste that [3is] [4]good [1]the [2]Lord.
4 πρὸς ὃν προσερχόμενοι, λίθον ζῶντα, ὑπὸ ἀνθρώπων μὲν
To whom coming, a [2]stone [1]living, by men indeed
ἀποδεδοκιμασμένον, παρὰ.δὲ θεῷ ἐκλεκτόν, ἔντιμον, 5 καὶ αὐ-
rejected, but with God chosen, precious, also your-
τοὶ ὡς λίθοι ζῶντες [i]οἰκοδομεῖσθε," οἶκος πνευματικός,[k]
selves, as [2]stones [1]living, are being built up, a [2]house [1]spiritual,
ἱεράτευμα ἅγιον, ἀνενέγκαι πνευματικὰς θυσίας εὐπροσδέκτους
a [2]priesthood [1]holy to offer spiritual sacrifices acceptable
[l]τῷ θεῷ διὰ Ἰησοῦ χριστοῦ. 6 [m]Διὸ καὶ[l] περιέχει [n]ἐν τῇ
to God by Jesus Christ. Wherefore also it is contained in the
γραφῇ," Ἰδοὺ τίθημι ἐν Σιὼν λίθον ἀκρογωνιαῖον, ἐκλεκτόν,
scripture: Behold, I place in Sion a [2]stone [1]corner, chosen,
ἔντιμον· καὶ ὁ πιστεύων ἐπ' αὐτῷ οὐ.μὴ καταισχυνθῇ.
precious: and he that believes on him in no wise should be put to shame.
7 Ὑμῖν οὖν ἡ τιμὴ τοῖς πιστεύουσιν· [o]ἀπει-
To you therefore [3is] [4]the [5]preciousness [1]who [2]believe; [7]to [8those] [9]dis-
θοῦσιν[l] δέ, [p]λίθον" ὃν ἀπεδοκίμασαν οἱ οἰκοδομοῦντες,
obeying [6]but, [the] stone which [3]rejected [1]those [2]building,
οὗτος ἐγενήθη εἰς κεφαλὴν γωνίας, 8 καὶ λίθος προσκόμ-
this became head of [the] corner, and a stone of stum-
ματος καὶ πέτρα σκανδάλου· οἳ προσκόπτουσιν τῷ λόγῳ
bling and a rock of offence; who stumble at the word,
ἀπειθοῦντες, εἰς ὃ καὶ ἐτέθησαν· 9 ὑμεῖς.δὲ γένος ἐκ-
being disobedient, to which also they were appointed. But ye [are] a [2]race
λεκτόν, βασίλειον ἱεράτευμα, ἔθνος ἅγιον, λαὸς εἰς περι-
[1]chosen, a kingly priesthood, a [2]nation [1]holy, a people for a pos-
ποίησιν, ὅπως τὰς ἀρετὰς ἐξαγγείλητε τοῦ ἐκ σκότους
session, that the virtues ye might set forth of him who out of darkness
ὑμᾶς καλέσαντος εἰς τὸ.θαυμαστὸν.αὐτοῦ φῶς· 10 οἵ ποτε
[2]you [1]called to his wonderful light; who once
οὐ λαός, νῦν.δὲ λαὸς θεοῦ· οἱ οὐκ.ἠλεημένοι,
[were] not a people, but now [are] [2]people [1]God's; who had not received mercy,
νῦν.δὲ ἐλεηθέντες.
but now received mercy
11 Ἀγαπητοί, παρακαλῶ ὡς παροίκους καὶ παρεπιδή-
Beloved, I exhort [you] as strangers and sojourners,
μους, ἀπέχεσθαι[q] τῶν σαρκικῶν ἐπιθυμιῶν, αἵτινες στρατεύον-
to abstain from fleshly desires, which war
ται κατὰ τῆς ψυχῆς· 12 τὴν.ἀναστροφὴν.ὑμῶν ἐν τοῖς
against the soul; [2]your [3]manner [4]of [5]life [7]among [8]the
ἔθνεσιν ἔχοντες καλήν, ἵνα ἐν.ᾧ καταλαλοῦσιν ὑμῶν ὡς
[9]nations [1]having [6]right that wherein they speak against you as
κακοποιῶν, ἐκ τῶν καλῶν ἔργων [r]ἐποπτεύσαντες" δοξά-
evil doers, through [your] good works having witnessed they
σωσιν τὸν θεὸν ἐν ἡμέρᾳ ἐπισκοπῆς.
may glorify God in [the] day of visitation.
13 Ὑποτάγητε [s]οὖν" πάσῃ ἀνθρωπίνῃ κτίσει, διὰ
Be in subjection therefore to every human institution for the sake of
τὸν κύριον· εἴτε βασιλεῖ, ὡς ὑπερέχοντι· 14 εἴτε ἡγεμόσιν,
the Lord; whether to [the] king as supreme, or to governors
ὡς δι' αὐτοῦ πεμπομένοις εἰς ἐκδίκησιν [t]μὲν" κακοποιῶν,
as by him sent, for vengeance [on] evil doers,
ἔπαινον.δὲ ἀγαθοποιῶν· 15 ὅτι οὕτως ἐστὶν τὸ θέλημα
and praise [to] well doers; (because so is the will
τοῦ θεοῦ, ἀγαθοποιοῦντας φιμοῦν τὴν τῶν ἀφρόνων
of God, [by] well doing to put to silence the [2]of [3]senseless
ἀνθρώπων ἀγνωσίαν· 16 ὡς ἐλεύθεροι, καὶ μὴ ὡς ἐπικά-
[4]men [1]ignorance;) as free, and not [3]as [4]a
λυμμα ἔχοντες τῆς κακίας τὴν ἐλευθερίαν, ἀλλ' ὡς [v]δοῦλοι
[5]cloak [1]having [6]of [7]malice [2]freedom, but as bondmen
θεοῦ." 17 πάντας τιμήσατε, τὴν ἀδελφότητα ἀγαπᾶτε, τὸν
of God. [1]All [4]shew [2]honour [3]to, [6]the [7]brotherhood [5]love,
θεὸν φοβεῖσθε, τὸν βασιλέα τιμᾶτε.
[9]God [8]fear, [11]the [12]king [10]honour.
18 Οἱ οἰκέται, ὑποτασσόμενοι ἐν παντὶ φόβῳ τοῖς.δεσ-
Servants, being subject with all fear to [your]

brotherly love which is not pretended, love
one another fervently out of a pure heart.
23 *For* you have been born again, not of
seed which can rot away, but of seed that
can never corrupt, by the word of God living
and remaining forever.
24 Because all flesh is as grass, and all the
glory of man is like the flower of grass the
grass withered and the flower of it fell away.
25 But the word of the Lord goes on
forever. And this is the gospel which was
preached to you.
2 1 So, laying aside all malice and all guile and
hypocrisies and jealousies and all evil words,
2 like newborn babies, long for the pure milk
of the word, so that you may grow by it –
3 if indeed you have tasted that the Lord is
good.
4 Coming to Him, the Living Stone (indeed
refused by men, but elect, precious with
God.)
5 you also as living stones are being built up
into a spiritual house, a holy priesthood, to
offer up spiritual sacrifices pleasing to God
through Jesus Christ.
6 For this reason also it is contained in the
Scriptures, "Behold! I place in Zion an elect,
precious Cornerstone – and he that believes
on Him in no way shall be put to shame."
7 *He is* precious therefore to you who
believe, but to the unbelieving *He is* the
Stone which the builders rejected, which
became the Head-of-the-corner,
8 and a Stone-of-stumbling and a Rock-of-
offense – to the unbelieving ones who
stumble at the Word, not believing, to which
they also were appointed.
9 But you are a chosen generation, a royal
priesthood, a holy nation, a people who
belong to God, so that you might show forth
the praise of Him who called you out of
darkness into His wonderful light –
10 you who once *were* not a people, but
now *are the* people of God: you who had
not received mercy, but now have received
mercy.
11 Beloved, I urge you as strangers and
pilgrims to keep yourselves away from
fleshly lusts, which war against the soul.
12 Make your behavior wholesome among
the Gentiles, so that (with regard to that
which they speak against you as evil-doers)
through witnessing your good works, they
may glorify God in the day of His visitation.
13 Then be obedient to every law of man
for the Lord's sake, whether to a king as
supreme,
14 or to governors as sent by Him to punish
evil-doers and to praise those who do well.
15 Because so is the will of God, that the
ignorance of foolish men may be put to
silence by the doing of good.
16 As free men (yet not using freedom as a
cover of evil feeling, but as servants of God),
17 honor all men, love the brotherhood,

πόταις, οὐ μόνον τοῖς ἀγαθοῖς καὶ ἐπιεικέσιν, ἀλλὰ καὶ
masters, not only to the good and gentle, but also
τοῖς σκολιοῖς. 19 τοῦτο.γὰρ χάρις, εἰ διὰ συνείδησιν
to the crooked. For this [is] acceptable if for sake of conscience
θεοῦ ὑποφέρει τις λύπας, πάσχων ἀδίκως. 20 ποῖον.γὰρ
towards God [2]endures [1]anyone griefs, suffering unjustly. For what
κλέος, εἰ ἁμαρτάνοντες καὶ κολαφιζόμενοι ὑπομενεῖτε;
glory [is it], if sinning and being buffeted ye endure it?
ἀλλ' εἰ ἀγαθοποιοῦντες καὶ πάσχοντες ὑπομενεῖτε, τοῦτο
but if doing good and suffering ye endure [it], this [is]
χάρις παρὰ θεῷ. 21 εἰς.τοῦτο.γὰρ ἐκλήθητε, ὅτι καὶ
acceptable with God. For to this ye were called; because also
χριστὸς ἔπαθεν ὑπὲρ [x]ἡμῶν,‖ [y]ἡμῖν‖ ὑπολιμπάνων ὑπογραμ-
Christ, suffered for us, [2]us [1]leaving a model
μόν, ἵνα ἐπακολουθήσητε τοῖς.ἴχνεσιν.αὐτοῦ· 22 ὃς ἁμαρτίαν
that ye should follow after in his steps; who [3]sin
οὐκ.ἐποίησεν, οὐδὲ εὑρέθη δόλος ἐν τῷ.στόματι.αὐτοῦ· 23 ὃς
[1]did [2]no, neither was [2]found [1]guile in his mouth; who,
λοιδορούμενος οὐκ.ἀντελοιδόρει, πάσχων οὐκ.ἠπείλει,
being railed at, railed not in return; [when] suffering threatened not;
παρεδίδου.δὲ τῷ κρίνοντι δικαίως· 24 ὃς τὰς
but gave [himself] over to him who judges righteously; who
ἁμαρτίας.ἡμῶν αὐτὸς ἀνήνεγκεν ἐν τῷ.σώματι.αὐτοῦ ἐπὶ τὸ
our sins himself bore in his body on the
ξύλον, ἵνα ταῖς.ἁμαρτίαις ἀπογενόμενοι, τῇ δικαιοσύνῃ ζή-
tree, that, to sins [we] being dead, to righteousness we
σωμεν· οὗ.τῷ.μώλωπι.[z]αὐτοῦ‖ ἰάθητε. 25 ἦτε.γὰρ ὡς πρό-
may live; by whose bruise ye were healed. For ye were as
βατα [a]πλανώμενα·‖ ἀλλ' ἐπεστράφητε νῦν ἐπὶ τὸν ποιμένα
sheep going astray, but are returned now to the shepherd
καὶ ἐπίσκοπον τῶν.ψυχῶν.ὑμῶν.
and overseer of your souls.

3 Ὁμοίως, [b]αἱ‖ γυναῖκες, ὑποτασσόμεναι τοῖς.ἰδίοις ἀν-
Likewise, wives, being subject to your own hus-
δράσιν, ἵνα καὶ εἴ τινες ἀπειθοῦσιν τῷ λόγῳ, διὰ τῆς τῶν
bands, that, even if any are disobedient to the word, by the [2]of [3]the
γυναικῶν ἀναστροφῆς ἄνευ λόγου [c]κερδηθήσωνται,‖ 2 ἐπο-
[4]wives [1]conduct without [the] word they may be gained, hav-
πτεύσαντες τὴν ἐν φόβῳ ἁγνὴν ἀναστροφὴν ὑμῶν·
ing witnessed [[4]carried [5]out] [6]in [7]fear [2]chaste [3]conduct [1]your;
3 ὧν ἔστω.οὐχ ὁ ἔξωθεν ἐμπλοκῆς [d]τριχῶν,‖ [e]καὶ‖
whose [2]let [3]it [4]not [5]be [6]the [7]outward [[8]one] [9]of [10]braiding [11]of [12]hair, [13]and
περιθέσεως χρυσίων, ἢ ἐνδύσεως ἱματίων κόσμος·
[14]putting [15]around [16]of [17]gold, [18]or [19]putting [20]on [21]of [22]garments [1]adorning;
4 ἀλλ' ὁ κρυπτὸς τῆς καρδίας ἄνθρωπος, ἐν τῷ ἀφθάρτῳ
but the hidden [2]of [3]the [4]heart [1]man, in the incorruptible
τοῦ [f]πρᾳέος καὶ ἡσυχίου‖ πνεύματος, ὅ ἐστιν ἐνώπιον
[ornament] of the meek and quiet spirit, which is before
τοῦ θεοῦ πολυτελές. 5 οὕτως.γάρ ποτε καὶ αἱ ἅγιαι γυναῖκες
God of great price. For thus formerly also the holy women
αἱ ἐλπίζουσαι [g]ἐπὶ τὸν‖ θεὸν ἐκόσμουν ἑαυτάς, ὑποτασσό-
those hoping in God adorned themselves, being sub-
μεναι τοῖς.ἰδίοις ἀνδράσιν· 6 ὡς Σάρρα [h]ὑπήκουσεν‖ τῷ
ject to their own husbands; as Sarah obeyed
Ἀβραάμ, κύριον αὐτὸν καλοῦσα, ἧς ἐγενήθητε τέκνα· ἀγα-
Abraham, [2]lord [3]him [1]calling; of whom ye became children, do-
θοποιοῦσαι καὶ μὴ.φοβούμεναι μηδεμίαν πτόησιν. 7 Οἱ
ing good and not fearing [with] any consternation.
(lit. no)
ἄνδρες ὁμοίως, συνοικοῦντες κατὰ γνῶσιν, ὡς ἀσθε-
Husbands likewise, dwelling with [them] according to knowledge, as with a
νεστέρῳ σκεύει τῷ γυναικείῳ ἀπονέμοντες τιμήν, ὡς
weaker [even] [4]vessel [1]with [2]the [3]female, rendering [them] honour, as
καὶ [i]συγκληρονόμοι‖ χάριτος ζωῆς, εἰς τὸ μὴ [k]ἐκκόπτεσ-
also [being] joint-heirs of [the] grace of life, so as [3]not [4]to [5]be [6]cut
θαι τὰς.προσευχὰς.ὑμῶν.
[7]off [1]your [2]prayers.

8 Τὸ.δὲ.τέλος, πάντες ὁμόφρονες, συμπαθεῖς, φιλ-
Finally, all [being] of one mind, sympathizing, loving
άδελφοι, εὔσπλαγχνοι, [l]φιλόφρονες·‖ 9 μὴ ἀποδιδόντες
the brethren, tender hearted, friendly, not rendering
κακὸν ἀντὶ κακοῦ, ἢ λοιδορίαν ἀντὶ λοιδορίας· τοὐναντίον.δὲ
evil for evil, or railing for railing; but on the contrary,
εὐλογοῦντες, [m]εἰδότες‖ ὅτι εἰς τοῦτο ἐκλήθητε, ἵνα εὐλογίαν
blessing, knowing that to this ye were called, that blessing
κληρονομήσητε. 10 ὁ.γὰρ θέλων ζωὴν ἀγαπᾷν, καὶ ἰδεῖν
ye should inherit. For he that wills [3]life [1]to [2]love, and to see
ἡμέρας ἀγαθάς, παυσάτω τὴν.γλῶσσαν.[n]αὐτοῦ‖ ἀπὸ
[2]days [1]good, let him cause to cease his tongue from
κακοῦ, καὶ χείλη [n]αὐτοῦ‖ τοῦ μὴ λαλῆσαι δόλον. 11 ἐκκλι-
evil, and [2]lips [1]his not to speak guile. Let him turn
νάτω[o] ἀπὸ κακοῦ, καὶ ποιησάτω ἀγαθόν· ζητησάτω εἰρήνην,
aside from evil, and let him do good. Let him seek peace

fear God, honor him who rules.
18 Servants, be obedient to your masters
with all fear – not only to the good and
gentle ones, but also to the wicked ones.
19 For this is pleasing, if for the sake of
conscience towards God anyone patiently
endures sorrows, suffering unjustly.
20 For what glory *is it* if you patiently
endure *when you are* sinning and are being
punished. But if you patiently endure, doing
good and suffering *for it,* this is pleasing to
God.
21 For you are called to this, because Christ
also suffered for us, leaving us an example so
that you should follow His steps –
22 who did not sin, nor was guile found in
His mouth,
23 who did not speak evil in return when
evil was being spoken to Him. He did not
threaten when He was suffering, but He gave
Himself over to Him who judges righteously.
24 *He* Himself bore our sins in His own
body on the tree, so that we, being dead to
sins, might live to righteousness – by whose
stripes you were healed.
25 For you were as sheep going astray, but
you are now returned to the Shepherd and
Bishop of your souls.
3 1 In the same way, wives be subject to your
husbands, so that even if any do not believe
the word, they may without a word be won
by the behavior of the wives –
2 watching your pure behavior in fear.
3 *When you* beautify yourself, let it not be
by the outward braiding of the hair and
putting on of gold, or by putting on of
clothes,
4 but *let it be* the hidden man of the heart,
in the *beauty* of a meek and quiet spirit
which can never be corrupted – which is of
great value in the sight of God.
5 For in this way in the old days too, the
holy women (the ones who were trusting in
God) made themselves beautiful, being
subject to their own husbands –
6 as Sarah obeyed Abraham, calling him
lord – whose children you became, doing
good and not fearing any terror.
7 In the same way, you husbands live with
your wives according to knowledge, giving
honor as to a weaker vessel, as also being
heirs together of the grace of life, so that
your prayers may not be cut off.
8 Finally, all of you be of one mind. Have
pity, loving the brothers, tenderhearted and
friendly.
9 Never give evil for evil, nor evil-speaking
for evil-speaking. But on the contrary, give
blessing, knowing that you were called to
this, that you should inherit blessing.
10 For he that wants to love life and see
good days, let him stop his tongue from evil
and his lips from speaking deceit.
11 Let him turn aside from evil and let him

καὶ διωξάτω αὐτήν. 12 ὅτι [p]οἱ[ǁ] ὀφθαλμοὶ κυρίου ἐπὶ
and let him pursue it: because the eyes of [the] Lord [are] on
δικαίους, καὶ ὦτα.αὐτοῦ εἰς δέησιν.αὐτῶν· πρόσωπον.δὲ
[the] righteous, and his ears towards their supplication. But [the] face
κυρίου ἐπὶ ποιοῦντας κακά. 13 καὶ τίς ὁ κακώ-
of [the] Lord [is] against those doing evil. And who [is] he that shall in-
σων ὑμᾶς, ἐὰν τοῦ ἀγαθοῦ [q]μιμηταὶ[ǁ] γένησθε;
jure you, if [2]of [3]that [4]which [5is] [6]good [1]imitators ye should be?
14 ἀλλ' εἰ καὶ πάσχοιτε διὰ δικαιοσύνην, μακάριοι.
But if also ye should suffer on account of righteousness, blessed [are ye];
τὸν.δὲ.φόβον.αὐτῶν μὴ.φοβηθῆτε, μηδὲ ταραχθῆτε·
but their fear ye should not be afraid of, neither should ye be troubled;
15 κύριον.δὲ τὸν [r]θεὸν[ǁ] ἁγιάσατε ἐν ταῖς.καρδίαις.ὑμῶν·
but [3]Lord [2]the [4]God [1]sanctify in your hearts,
ἕτοιμοι.[s]δὲ[ǁ] ἀεὶ πρὸς ἀπολογίαν παντὶ τῷ αἰτοῦντι ὑμᾶς
and ready [be] always for a defence to everyone that asks you
λόγον περὶ τῆς ἐν ὑμῖν ἐλπίδος, [t]μετὰ πρᾳΰτητος καὶ
an account concerning the [2]in [3]you [1]hope, with meekness and
φόβου· 16 συνείδησιν ἔχοντες ἀγαθήν, ἵνα ἐν.ᾧ [v]καταλαλῶ-
fear; [2]a [4]conscience [1]having [3]good, that whereas they may speak
σιν[ǁ] [w]ὑμῶν ὡς κακοποιῶν,[ǁ] καταισχυνθῶσιν οἱ ἐπηρεάζοντες
against you as evil doers, they may be ashamed who calumniate
ὑμῶν τὴν ἀγαθὴν ἐν χριστῷ ἀναστροφήν. 17 κρεῖττον.γὰρ
your good [4]in [5]Christ [1]manner [2]of [3]life. For [it is] better,
ἀγαθοποιοῦντας, εἰ [x]θέλει[ǁ] τὸ θέλημα τοῦ θεοῦ, πάσχειν,
[8for [9]you] [10]doing [11]good, [1]if [6]wills [7it] [2]the [3]will [4]of [5]God, to suffer,
ἢ κακοποιοῦντας· 18 ὅτι καὶ χριστὸς ἅπαξ περὶ ἁμαρ-
than doing evil; because [2]indeed [1]Christ once for sins
τιῶν [y]ἔπαθεν[ǁ] δίκαιος ὑπὲρ ἀδίκων, ἵνα ἡμᾶς προσαγάγῃ
suffered, [the] just for [the] unjust, that us he might bring
[z]τῷ[ǁ] θεῷ, θανατωθεὶς μὲν σαρκί, ζωοποιηθεὶς.δὲ [a]τῷ[ǁ]
to God; having been put to death in flesh, but made alive by the
πνεύματι, 19 ἐν ᾧ καὶ τοῖς ἐν φυλακῇ πνεύμασιν πορευθεὶς
Spirit, in which also to the [2]in [3]prison [1]spirits having gone
ἐκήρυξεν, 20 ἀπειθήσασίν ποτε, ὅτε [b]ἅπαξ ἐξεδέχετο[ǁ] ἡ
he preached, [who] disobeyed sometime, when once was waiting the
τοῦ θεοῦ μακροθυμία ἐν ἡμέραις Νῶε, κατασκευα-
[2]of [3]God [1]longsuffering in [the] days of Noe, [while was] being pre-
ζομένης κιβωτοῦ, εἰς ἣν [c]ὀλίγαι,[ǁ] [d]τουτέστιν[ǁ] ὀκτώ, ψυχαὶ
pared [the] ark, into which few, that is eight souls,
διεσώθησαν δι' ὕδατος, 21 [e]ὃ[ǁ] καὶ [f]ἡμᾶς[ǁ] ἀντίτυπον νῦν
were saved through water, which [2]also [5]us [1]figure [4]now
σώζει βάπτισμα, οὐ σαρκὸς ἀπόθεσις ῥύπου, ἀλλὰ
[3]saves [even] baptism, not of flesh a putting away of [the] filth, but
συνειδήσεως ἀγαθῆς ἐπερώτημα εἰς θεόν, δι' ἀνα-
[5]of [6]a [8]conscience [7]good [1the] [2]demand [3]towards [4]God, by [the] re-
στάσεως Ἰησοῦ χριστοῦ, 22 ὅς ἐστιν ἐν δεξιᾷ [g]τοῦ[ǁ] θεοῦ,
surrection of Jesus Christ, who is at [the] right hand of God,
πορευθεὶς εἰς οὐρανόν, ὑποταγέντων αὐτῷ ἀγγέλων καὶ
gone into heaven, [6]having [7]been [8]subjected [9]to [10]him [1]angels [2]and
ἐξουσιῶν καὶ δυνάμεων.
[3]authorities [4]and [5]powers.
4 Χριστοῦ οὖν παθόντος [h]ὑπὲρ ἡμῶν[ǁ] σαρκί, καὶ ὑμεῖς τὴν
Christ then having suffered for us in [the] flesh, also ye [4]the
αὐτὴν ἔννοιαν ὁπλίσασθε· ὅτι ὁ παθὼν [i]ἐν[ǁ] σαρκί,
[5]same [6]mind [1]arm [2]yourselves [3]with; for he that suffered in [the] flesh
πέπαυται ἁμαρτίας· 2 εἰς τὸ μηκέτι ἀνθρώπων ἐπιθυμίαις,
has done with sin; no longer [10]men's [9]to [11]lusts,
ἀλλὰ θελήματι θεοῦ τὸν ἐπίλοιπον ἐν σαρκὶ βιῶσαι χρόνον.
[12]but [13]to [15]will [14]God's [3]the [4]remaining [6]in [7the] [8]flesh [1]to [2]live [5]time.
3 ἀρκετὸς.γὰρ [k]ἡμῖν[ǁ] ὁ παρεληλυθὼς χρόνος [l]τοῦ βίου,[ǁ] τὸ
For [is] sufficient for us the past time of life the
[m]θέλημα[ǁ] τῶν ἐθνῶν [n]κατεργάσασθαι,[ǁ] πεπορευμένους ἐν
will of the nations to have worked out, having walked in
ἀσελγείαις, ἐπιθυμίαις, οἰνοφλυγίαις, κώμοις, πότοις, καὶ
licentiousness, lusts, wine-drinking, revels, drinkings, and
ἀθεμίτοις εἰδωλολατρείαις· 4 ἐν.ᾧ ξενίζονται, μὴ συν-
unhallowed idolatries. Wherein they think it strange [2]not [3]run-
τρεχόντων ὑμῶν εἰς τὴν αὐτὴν τῆς ἀσωτίας ἀνάχυσιν,
ning [4]with [5them] [1]your to the same [2]of [3]dissoluteness [1]overflow,
βλασφημοῦντες· 5 οἳ ἀποδώσουσιν λόγον τῷ ἑτοίμως
speaking evil [of you]; who shall render account to him [3]ready
ἔχοντι κρῖναι ζῶντας καὶ νεκρούς. 6 εἰς.τοῦτο.γὰρ καὶ
[1]who [2]is to judge [the] living and [the] dead. For to this [end] also
νεκροῖς εὐηγγελίσθη, ἵνα κριθῶσιν μὲν
to [the] dead were the glad tidings announced, that they might be judged indeed
κατὰ ἀνθρώπους σαρκί, ζῶσιν.δὲ κατὰ θεὸν πνεύματι.
as regards men in [the] flesh; but might live as regards God in [the] Spirit.
7 Πάντων.δὲ τὸ τέλος ἤγγικεν· σωφρονήσατε οὖν
But of all things the end has drawn near: be sober-minded therefore,
καὶ νήψατε εἰς [o]τὰς[ǁ] προσευχάς· 8 πρὸ πάντων [p]δὲ[ǁ] τὴν
and be watchful unto prayers; [2]before [3]all [4]things [1]but

do good. Let him seek peace, and let him
run after it,
12 because the eyes of the Lord are on the
righteous, and His ears *are open* to their
prayers. But the face of the Lord is against
the ones who are doing evil.
13 And who is he that shall hurt you if you
are imitators of that which is good?
14 But if you also should suffer on account
of righteousness, *you are* blessed. But you
should not be afraid of their fear, nor should
you be troubled.
15 But sanctify the Lord God in your hearts
and be ready always to give an answer to
everyone that asks you a reason for the hope
that is in you, with meekness and fear –
16 having a good conscience, so that in the
thing regarding which they speak against you
as evil-doers, they who lie against your good
behavior in Christ may be ashamed.
17 For it is better, if the will of God desires
it so, to suffer while doing good than while
doing evil.
18 Because even Christ once for all suffered
for sins, the Just for the unjust, so that He
might bring us to God, being put to death in
the flesh but made alive by the Spirit.
19 In which also, going to the spirits in
prison, He preached
20 to those who did not believe in times
past, when at one time the long-suffering of
God was waiting – in the days of Noah,
while the ark was being prepared – in which
a few, that is, eight souls were saved through
water:
21 which antitype now also saves us, *even*
baptism – not a putting away of the filth of
the flesh, but the answer of a good conscience towards God through the resurrection of Jesus Christ,
22 who is at the right hand of God. For He
has gone into Heaven – angels and leaders
and powers being subjected to Him.
4 1 Since, then, Christ has suffered for us in
the flesh, you also arm yourselves with the
same mind. For he that has suffered in the
flesh has been set free from sin,
2 to the end that he no longer will live the
rest of the time in the flesh to the lusts of
men, but to the will of God.
3 For the time of life already past is enough
for us to have worked out the will of the
heathen, when we walked in wantonness,
lusts, drunkenness, parties, carousings, and
unholy idol-worshiping.
4 In which *matter* they think it strange that
you do not run with them into the same
overflow of shamelessness, speaking evil.
5 They shall give account to Him who is
ready to judge the living and the dead.
6 For to this end also the gospel was
preached to the dead, so that they might be
truly judged according to men in the flesh,
but might live according to God in the
Spirit.

εἰς ἑαυτοὺς ἀγάπην ἐκτενῆ ἔχοντες, ὅτι [q] ἀγάπη [r]καλύψει‖
among yourselves [3]love [2]fervent [1]having, because love will cover

πλῆθος ἁμαρτιῶν. 9 φιλόξενοι εἰς ἀλλήλους ἄνευ [s]γογγυσ-
a multitude of sins; hospitable to one another, without murmur-

μῶν·‖ 10 ἕκαστος καθὼς ἔλαβεν χάρισμα, εἰς ἑαυτοὺς
ings; each according as he received a gift, to each other

αὐτὸ διακονοῦντες, ὡς καλοὶ οἰκονόμοι ποικίλης χάριτος
[2]it [1]serving, as good stewards of [the] various grace

θεοῦ· 11 εἴ τις λαλεῖ, ὡς λόγια θεοῦ· εἴ τις διακονεῖ, ὡς
of God. If anyone speaks— as oracles of God; if anyone serves— as

ἐξ ἰσχύος ἧς χορηγεῖ ὁ θεός· ἵνα ἐν πᾶσιν δοξάζηται ὁ
of strength which [2]supplies [1]God; that in all things may be glorified

θεὸς διὰ Ἰησοῦ χριστοῦ, ᾧ ἐστιν ἡ δόξα καὶ τὸ κράτος
God through Jesus Christ, to whom is the glory and the might

εἰς τοὺς αἰῶνας τῶν αἰώνων. ἀμήν.
to the ages of the ages. Amen.

12 Ἀγαπητοί, μὴ ξενίζεσθε τῇ ἐν ὑμῖν πυρώσει
[4] Beloved, take not as strange the [4]amongst [5]you [1]fire [[2]of [3]persecution]

πρὸς πειρασμὸν ὑμῖν γινομένῃ, ὡς ξένου ὑμῖν
for trial to you [which is] taking place, as if a strange thing to you

συμβαίνοντος· 13 ἀλλὰ [t]καθὸ‖ κοινωνεῖτε τοῖς τοῦ χρισ-
[is] happening; but according as ye have share in the [2]of

τοῦ παθήμασιν, χαίρετε, ἵνα καὶ ἐν τῇ ἀποκαλύψει τῆς δόξης
[3]Christ [1]sufferings, rejoice, that also in the revelation of [2]glory

αὐτοῦ χαρῆτε ἀγαλλιώμενοι. 14 εἰ ὀνειδίζεσθε ἐν
[1]his ye may rejoice exulting. If ye are reproached in [the]

ὀνόματι χριστοῦ, μακάριοι· ὅτι τὸ τῆς δόξης[v] καὶ
name of Christ, blessed [are ye]; because the [spirit] of glory and

τὸ τοῦ θεοῦ πνεῦμα ἐφ' ὑμᾶς ἀναπαύεται· [w]κατὰ μὲν αὐτοὺς
the [2]of [3]God [1]Spirit upon you rests; on their part

βλασφημεῖται, κατὰ δὲ ὑμᾶς δοξάζεται.‖ 15 μὴ γὰρ τις
he is blasphemed, but on your part he is glorified. Assuredly [2]not [3]anyone

ὑμῶν πασχέτω ὡς φονεύς, ἢ κλέπτης, ἢ κακοποιός, ἢ ὡς
[4]of [5]you [1]let suffer as a murderer, or thief, or evil doer, or as

[x]ἀλλοτριοεπίσκοπος.[1] 16 εἰ δὲ ὡς χριστιανός, μὴ αἰσχυ-
overlooker of other people's matters; but if as a christian, [2]not [1]let [3]him

νέσθω, δοξαζέτω δὲ τὸν θεὸν ἐν τῷ [y]μέρει‖ τούτῳ. 17 ὅτι
be ashamed, but let him glorify God in [2]respect [1]this. Because

ὁ καιρὸς τοῦ ἄρξασθαι τὸ κρίμα ἀπὸ τοῦ οἴκου τοῦ θεοῦ·
the time [for] [3]to [4]have [5]begun [1]the [2]judgment from the house of God

εἰ δὲ πρῶτον ἀφ' ἡμῶν, τί τὸ τέλος τῶν ἀπειθούντων
[is come]; but if first from us, what the end of those disobeying

τῷ τοῦ θεοῦ εὐαγγελίῳ; 18 καὶ εἰ ὁ δίκαιος μόλις σώζεται,
the [3]of [4]God [1]glad [2]tidings? And if the righteous with difficulty is saved,

ὁ ἀσεβὴς καὶ [z] ἁμαρτωλὸς ποῦ φανεῖται; 19 ὥστε καὶ
[3]the [4]ungodly [5]and [6]sinner [1]where [2]shall appear? Wherefore also

οἱ πάσχοντες κατὰ τὸ θέλημα τοῦ θεοῦ, [a]ὡς‖ πιστῷ
they who suffer according to the will of God as to a faithful

κτίστῃ παρατιθέσθωσαν τὰς ψυχὰς [b]ἑαυτῶν‖ ἐν [c]ἀγαθοποιΐᾳ.‖
Creator let them commit their souls in well doing.

5 Πρεσβυτέρους [d] [e]τοὺς‖ ἐν ὑμῖν παρακαλῶ ὁ [f]συμ-
Elders who [are] among you I exhort who [am] a

πρεσβύτερος καὶ μάρτυς τῶν τοῦ χριστοῦ παθημάτων, ὁ
fellow elder and witness of the [2]of [3]the [4]Christ [1]sufferings, who

καὶ τῆς μελλούσης ἀποκαλύπτεσθαι δόξης κοινωνός, 2 ποι-
also of the [2]about [3]to [4]be [5]revealed [1]glory [am] partaker: shep-

μάνατε τὸ ἐν ὑμῖν ποίμνιον τοῦ θεοῦ, [g]ἐπισκοποῦντες‖ μὴ
herd the [4]among [5]you [1]flock [2]of [3]God, exercising oversight not

ἀναγκαστῶς, [h]ἀλλ'‖ ἑκουσίως[i]· μηδὲ αἰσχροκερδῶς, ἀλλὰ προ-
by constraint, but willingly; not for base gain, but readi-

θύμως· 3 μηδ' ὡς κατακυριεύοντες τῶν κλήρων, ἀλλὰ
ly; not as exercising lordship over [your] possessions, but

τύποι γινόμενοι τοῦ ποιμνίου. 4 καὶ φανερωθέντος
patterns being of the flock. And [4]having [5]been [6]manifested

τοῦ ἀρχιποίμενος, κομιεῖσθε τὸν ἀμαράντινον τῆς δόξης
[1]the [2]chief [3]shepherd, ye shall receive the unfading [2]of [3]glory

στέφανον.
[1]crown.

5 Ὁμοίως, νεώτεροι, ὑποτάγητε πρεσβυτέροις· πάντες
Likewise, [ye] younger [ones], be subject to [the] elder [ones], [2]all

δὲ ἀλλήλοις [k]ὑποτασσόμενοι‖ τὴν ταπεινοφροσύνην ἐγκομβώ-
[1]and one to another being subject [3]humility [1]bind

σασθε· ὅτι ὁ θεὸς ὑπερηφάνοις ἀντιτάσσεται, ταπεινοῖς
[2]on; because God [the] proud sets himself against, [2]to [[3]the] [4]humble

δὲ δίδωσιν χάριν. 6 ταπεινώθητε οὖν ὑπὸ τὴν κραταιὰν
[1]but gives grace. Be humbled therefore under the mighty

[l]χεῖρα‖ τοῦ θεοῦ, ἵνα ὑμᾶς ὑψώσῃ ἐν καιρῷ[m]. 7 πᾶσαν
hand of God, that you he may exalt in [due] time; all

τὴν μέριμναν ὑμῶν [n]ἐπιρρίψαντες‖ ἐπ' αὐτόν, ὅτι αὐτῷ
your care having cast upon him, because with him

μέλει περὶ ὑμῶν. 8 νήψατε, γρηγορήσατε, [o]ὅτι‖ ὁ ἀντίδικος
there is care about you. Be sober, watch, because [2]adversary

7 But the end of all things has come near. So be right-minded and be watchful as to prayers.

8 And above all things, have earnest love among yourselves, for love will cover a multitude of sins.

9 Be hospitable to one another, without grumblings.

10 According as each has received a gift, minister it to each other, as good managers of the manifold grace of God.

11 If anyone speaks, *let him speak* as the very words of God – if anyone ministers, as of the strength which God supplies – so that in all things God may be glorified through Jesus Christ, to whom is the glory and the power forever and ever. Amen.

12 Beloved, do not be surprised at the fire *of persecution which is* taking place among you for your trial, as if a strange thing is happening to you.

13 But even as you share in the sufferings of Christ, rejoice that also in the revealing of His glory, you may be beside yourself with joy.

14 If you are slandered for the name of Christ, *you are* blessed, because the Spirit of God and of glory rests on you. On their part He is blasphemed, but on your part He is glorified.

15 For let none of you suffer as a murderer or thief or evil-doer or as a meddler.

16 But if *one suffers* as a Christian, let him not be ashamed, but let him glorify God because of this.

17 For the time *has come* for the judgment to begin at the house of God. But if it first *begins* from us, what shall be the end of the ones who do not believe the gospel of God?

18 And if the righteous is saved with difficulty, where shall the ungodly and the sinner appear?

19 Then also those who suffer according to the will of God, as to a faithful Creator, let them commit their souls to Him in doing well.

5 1 I, (who am a fellow-elder and witness of the sufferings of Christ, who also am a partaker of the glory about to be revealed), urge the elders who are among you

2 to shepherd the flock of God which is among you. Watch carefully over them, not by force, but willingly – not for evil gain, but with a ready mind –

3 not as lording it over the things you have been given, but being examples to the flock.

4 And when the chief Shepherd has been revealed, you shall receive the crown of glory that never fades away.

5 In the same way, *let the* younger be subject to the elders. And all of you be subject to one another. Be clothed with an humble mind – because God sets Himself against the proud, but gives grace to the humble.

ὑμῶν διάβολος, ὡς λέων ὠρυόμενος, περιπατεῖ, ζητῶν [p]τίνα"
[1]your [the] [*] devil, as a [2]lion [1]roaring, goes about, seeking whom
[q]καταπίῃ·" 9 ᾧ ἀντίστητε στερεοὶ τῇ πίστει, εἰδότες τὰ
he may swallow up. Whom resist, firm in faith, knowing the
αὐτὰ τῶν παθημάτων τῇ ἐν [r] κόσμῳ ὑμῶν.ἀδελφότητι
same sufferings [7]which [[8]is] [9]in [[10]the] [11]world [4]in [5]your [6]brotherhood
ἐπιτελεῖσθαι. 10 ὁ.δὲ θεὸς πάσης χάριτος, ὁ καλέσας
[1]are [2]being accomplished. But the God of all grace, who called
[s]ἡμᾶς εἰς τὴν αἰώνιον αὐτοῦ δόξαν ἐν χριστῷ [t]Ἰησοῦ,' ὀλίγον
us to [3]eternal [1]his glory in Christ Jesus, a little while
παθόντας, αὐτὸς [v]καταρτίσαι ὑμᾶς," [w]στηρίξαι, σθενώ-
[ye] having suffered, [2]himself [1]may perfect you, may he establish, may he
σαι,[\] [x]θεμελιώσαι· 11 αὐτῷ [y]ἡ δόξα καὶ τὸ κράτος εἰς
strengthen, may he found [you]: to him [be] the glory and the might, to
τοὺς αἰῶνας τῶν αἰώνων. ἀμήν.
the ages of the ages. Amen.

12 Διὰ Σιλουανοῦ ὑμῖν [z]τοῦ" πιστοῦ ἀδελφοῦ, ὡς λογίζο-
By Silvanus, [4]to [5]you [1]the [2]faithful [3]brother, as I reckon,
μαι, δι'.ὀλίγων ἔγραψα, παρακαλῶν καὶ ἐπιμαρτυρῶν ταύτην
briefly I wrote, exhorting and testifying this
εἶναι ἀληθῆ χάριν τοῦ θεοῦ, εἰς ἣν [a]ἑστήκατε." 13 Ἀσπά-
to be [the] true grace of God, in which ye stand. [7]Sa-
ζεται ὑμᾶς ἡ ἐν Βαβυλῶνι συνεκλεκτή, καὶ Μάρκος
lutes [8]you [1]she [3]in [4]Babylon [2]elected [5]with [[6]you], and Mark
ὁ.υἱός.μου. 14 ἀσπάσασθε ἀλλήλους ἐν φιλήματι ἀγάπης
my son. Salute one another with a kiss of love.
εἰρήνη ὑμῖν πᾶσιν τοῖς ἐν χριστῷ [b]Ἰησοῦ.[a] [c]ἀμήν."
Peace [be] with you all who [are] in Christ Jesus. Amen.

[d]Πέτρου ἐπιστολὴ καθολικὴ πρώτη."
[4]Of [5]Peter [3]Epistle [2]General [1]First.

[6]Humble yourselves, then, under the
mighty hand of God, so that He may lift you
up in due time:
[7]throwing all your care on Him, because
He cares about you.
[8]Be careful! Watch! Because your enemy,
the devil, walks around like a roaring lion
looking for any he may devour.
[9]Resist firm in the faith, knowing that the
same kind of sufferings are being sent on
your brothers who are in the world.
[10]But may the God of all grace Himself
(who has called us to His everlasting glory in
Christ Jesus) make you perfect after you
have suffered a little while. May He make
you stand firm. May He strengthen you. May
He settle you.
[11]To Him be the glory and the power
forever and ever. Amen.
[12]By Sil-va-nus, a faithful brother to you,
as I think, I have written briefly, urging and
testifying this to be the true grace of God, in
which you stand.
[13]The *church that is* in Babylon, elected
with you, greets you, and Mark, my son.
[14]Greet one another with a kiss of love.
Peace be with you all who are in Christ
Jesus. Amen.

The SECOND Letter of PETER

[f]ΣΥΜΕΩΝ" Πέτρος δοῦλος καὶ ἀπόστολος Ἰησοῦ χριστοῦ,
Simeon Peter, bondman and apostle of Jesus Christ,
τοῖς ἰσότιμον ἡμῖν λαχοῦσιν πίστιν ἐν δικαιο-
to those who [2]like [3]precious [5]with [6]us [1]obtained [4]faith through [the] right-
σύνῃ τοῦ.θεοῦ.ἡμῶν καὶ σωτῆρος [g] Ἰησοῦ χριστοῦ· 2 χάρις
eousness of our God and Saviour Jesus Christ: Grace
ὑμῖν καὶ εἰρήνη πληθυνθείη ἐν ἐπιγνώσει τοῦ θεοῦ, καὶ
to you and peace be multiplied in [the] knowledge of God, and
Ἰησοῦ τοῦ.κυρίου.ἡμῶν.
of Jesus our Lord.

3 Ὡς[h] πάντα ἡμῖν τῆς θείας.δυνάμεως αὐτοῦ τὰ
As [8]all [9]things [6]to [7]us [2]divine [3]power [1]his [10]which [[11]pertain]
πρὸς ζωὴν καὶ εὐσέβειαν δεδωρημένης, διὰ τῆς ἐπιγνώσεως
[12]to [13]life [14]and [15]piety [4]has [5]given, through the knowledge
τοῦ καλέσαντος ἡμᾶς [i]διὰ δόξης καὶ ἀρετῆς," 4 δι' ὧν
of him who called us by glory and virtue, through which
τὰ [k]μέγιστα ἡμῖν καὶ τίμια" ἐπαγγέλματα δεδώρηται, ἵνα
[6]the [7]greatest [4]to [5]us [8]and [9]precious [10]promises [1]he [2]has [3]given, that
διὰ τούτων γένησθε θείας κοινωνοὶ φύσεως, ἀπο-
through these ye may become [2]of [[3]the] [4]divine [1]partakers nature, hav-
φυγόντες τῆς ἐν [l]κόσμῳ ἐν ἐπιθυμίᾳ φθορᾶς. 5 καὶ
ing escaped the [2]in [[3]the] [4]world [5]through [6]lust [1]corruption. [12]also
[m]αὐτὸ.τοῦτο' δέ, σπουδὴν πᾶσαν παρεισενέγκαν-
[8]for [9]this [10]very [11]reason [7]but, [18]diligence, [17]all [14]having [15]brought [13]in [16]be-
τες, ἐπιχορηγήσατε ἐν τῇ.πίστει.ὑμῶν τὴν ἀρετήν, ἐν.δὲ τῇ ἀρετῇ
sides, supply ye in your faith virtue, and in virtue
τὴν γνῶσιν, 6 ἐν.δὲ τῇ γνώσει τὴν ἐγκράτειαν, ἐν.δὲ τῇ ἐγκρα-
knowledge, and in knowledge self-control, and in self-con-
τείᾳ τὴν ὑπομονήν, ἐν.δὲ τῇ ὑπομονῇ τὴν εὐσέβειαν, 7 ἐν.δὲ
trol endurance, and in endurance piety, and in
τῇ εὐσεβείᾳ τὴν φιλαδελφίαν, ἐν.δὲ τῇ φιλαδελφίᾳ τὴν ἀγάπην.
piety brotherly love, and in brotherly love love:
8 ταῦτα.γὰρ ὑμῖν [n]ὑπάρχοντα' καὶ πλεονάζοντα, οὐκ
for these things [1]in [2]you [1]being and abounding [[3]to [4]be] [5]neither
ἀργοὺς οὐδὲ ἀκάρπους καθίστησιν εἰς τὴν τοῦ.κυρίου.ἡμῶν
[6]idle [7]nor [8]unfruitful [1]make [[2]you] as to the [2]of [3]our [4]Lord
Ἰησοῦ χριστοῦ ἐπίγνωσιν· 9 ᾧ.γὰρ μὴ.πάρεστιν ταῦτα
[5]Jesus [6]Christ [1]knowledge; for with whom are not present these things
τυφλός ἐστιν, μυωπάζων, λήθην.λαβὼν τοῦ καθαρισμοῦ τῶν
blind he is, short sighted, having forgotten the purification
πάλαι αὐτοῦ [o]ἁμαρτιῶν." 10 Διὸ μᾶλλον, ἀδελφοί, σπου-
[4]of [5]old [1]of [2]his [3]sins. Wherefore rather, brethren, be dili-
δάσατε [p] βεβαίαν ὑμῶν τὴν κλῆσιν καὶ ἐκλογὴν [q]ποιεῖσθαι·[a]
gent [7]sure [3]your [4]calling [5]and [6]election [1]to [2]make,

CHAPTER 1

[1]Simon Peter, a servant and apostle of
Jesus Christ, to those who have received the
same precious faith with us through the
righteousness of our God and Savior Jesus
Christ.
[2]Grace and peace be multiplied to you in
the knowledge of God and of Jesus our Lord
[3]– Even as His godly power has given to us
all things which have to do with life and
godliness, through the knowledge of Him
who called us by *His* glory and power –
[4]through which He has given to us very
great and precious promises, so that through
these you may become partakers of the
divine nature – having escaped the rottenness that is in the world through lust.
[5]And for this very reason also, after you
have added diligence, fill out your faith with
goodness – and your goodness with knowledge –
[6]and your knowledge with self-control –
and your self-control with patience – and
your patience with godliness –
[7]and your godliness with brotherly love –
and your brotherly love with love.
[8]For if these things are in you and are
plentiful, they do not make you either idle
or unfruitful as to the knowledge of our
Lord Jesus Christ.
[9]For he who does not have these things is
blind, not seeing very far, having forgotten
that *he was* made pure from his old sins.
[10]For this reason, brothers, give all the

ταῦτα.γὰρ ποιοῦντες οὐ.μὴ πταίσητέ ποτε. 11 οὕτως
for these things doing in no wise shall ye stumble at any time. 2Thus
γὰρ πλουσίως ἐπιχορηγηθήσεται ὑμῖν ἡ εἴσοδος εἰς τὴν αἰώ-
1for 5richly 3shall 4be supplied to you the entrance into the eter-
νιον βασιλείαν τοῦ.κυρίου.ἡμῶν καὶ σωτῆρος Ἰησοῦ χριστοῦ.
nal kingdom of our Lord and Saviour Jesus Christ.
12 Διὸ [r]οὐκ.ἀμελήσω‖ [s]ὑμᾶς ἀεὶ‖ ὑπομιμνήσκειν
Wherefore I will not neglect 3you 4always 1to 2put in remembrance
περὶ τούτων, καίπερ εἰδότας, καὶ ἐστηριγμένους ἐν
concerning these things, although knowing [them] and having been established in
τῇ παρούσῃ ἀληθείᾳ. 13 δίκαιον.δὲ ἡγοῦμαι, ἐφ'.ὅσον εἰμὶ ἐν
the present truth. But right I esteem it, as long as I am in
τούτῳ τῷ σκηνώματι, διεγείρειν ὑμᾶς ἐν ὑπομνήσει·
this tabernacle, to stir up you by putting [you] in remembrance,
14 εἰδὼς ὅτι ταχινή ἐστιν ἡ ἀπόθεσις τοῦ.σκηνώματός.μου,
knowing that speedily is the putting off of my tabernacle
καθὼς καὶ ὁ.κύριος.ἡμῶν Ἰησοῦς χριστὸς ἐδήλωσέν μοι.
[to be], as also our Lord Jesus Christ signified to me;
15 σπουδάσω.δὲ καὶ ἑκάστοτε ἔχειν.ὑμᾶς μετὰ
but I will be diligent also at every time for you to have [it in your power] after
τὴν.ἐμὴν ἔξοδον τὴν τούτων μνήμην.ποιεῖσθαι. 16 οὐ.γὰρ
my departure 5these 6things 1to 2have 3in 4remembrance. For not
σεσοφισμένοις μύθοις ἐξακολουθήσαντες ἐγνωρίσαμεν ὑμῖν τὴν
4cleverly-imagined 5fables 1having 2followed 3out we made known to you the
τοῦ.κυρίου.ἡμῶν Ἰησοῦ χριστοῦ δύναμιν καὶ παρουσίαν, ἀλλ'
4of 5our 6Lord 7Jesus 8Christ 1power 2and 3coming, but
ἐπόπται γενηθέντες τῆς.ἐκείνου μεγαλειότητος. 17 λαβὼν
eye-witnesses having been of his majesty. 2Having 3received
γὰρ παρὰ θεοῦ πατρὸς τιμὴν καὶ δόξαν, φωνῆς ἐνεχθεί-
1for from God [the] Father honour and glory, 2a 3voice 4having 5been
σης αὐτῷ τοιᾶσδε ὑπὸ τῆς μεγαλοπρεποῦς δόξης, [t]Οὗτός
6brought 7to 8him 1such by the very excellent glory: This
ἐστιν ὁ.υἱός.μου ὁ ἀγαπητός,‖ εἰς ὃν ἐγὼ εὐδόκησα. 18 καὶ
is my Son the beloved, in whom I have found delight. And
ταύτην τὴν φωνὴν ἡμεῖς ἠκούσαμεν ἐξ οὐρανοῦ ἐνεχθεῖσαν,
this voice we heard 2from 3heaven 1brought,
σὺν αὐτῷ ὄντες ἐν τῷ [v]ὄρει τῷ ἁγίῳ.‖ 19 καὶ ἔχομεν βεβαι-
5with 6him 4being on the 2mount 1holy. and we have more
ότερον τὸν προφητικὸν λόγον, ᾧ καλῶς ποιεῖτε προσέχοντες,
sure the prophetic word, to which 3well 1ye 2do taking heed,
ὡς λύχνῳ φαίνοντι ἐν αὐχμηρῷ τόπῳ, ἕως.οὗ ἡμέρα διαυγάσῃ,
as to a lamp shining in an obscure place, until day should dawn,
καὶ φωσφόρος ἀνατείλῃ ἐν ταῖς.καρδίαις.ὑμῶν· 20 τοῦτο
and [the] morning star should arise in your hearts; this
πρῶτον γινώσκοντες, ὅτι πᾶσα προφητεία γραφῆς ἰδίας
first knowing, that 2any 3prophecy 4of 5scripture 7of 8its 9own
(*lit.* every)
ἐπιλύσεως οὐ.γίνεται. 21 οὐ.γὰρ θελήματι ἀνθρώπου ἠνέχθη
10interpretation 6is 1not, for not by [the] will of man was 2brought
[w]ποτὲ προφητεία,‖ [x]ἀλλ'‖ ὑπὸ πνεύματος ἁγίου φερό-
3at 4any 5time 1prophecy, but, 3by [4the] 6Spirit 5Holy 1being
μενοι ἐλάλησαν [y]οἱ‖ [z]ἅγιοι‖ [a]θεοῦ ἄνθρωποι.
2borne, 12spoke 7the 8holy 10of 11God 9men.
2 Ἐγένοντο.δὲ καὶ ψευδοπροφῆται ἐν τῷ λαῷ, ὡς καὶ
But there were also false prophets among the people, as also
ἐν ὑμῖν ἔσονται ψευδοδιδάσκαλοι, οἵτινες παρεισάξουσιν
among you will be false teachers, who will bring in stealthily
αἱρέσεις ἀπωλείας, καὶ τὸν ἀγοράσαντα αὐτοὺς δεσπότην ἀρ-
2sects 1destructive, and 2the 4who 5bought 6them 3Master 1de-
νούμενοι, ἐπάγοντες ἑαυτοῖς ταχινὴν ἀπώλειαν· 2 καὶ πολλοὶ
nying, bringing upon themselves swift destruction; and many
ἐξακολουθήσουσιν αὐτῶν ταῖς [b]ἀπωλείαις,‖ δι' οὓς ἡ ὁδὸς
will follow out their destructive ways, through whom the way
τῆς ἀληθείας βλασφημηθήσεται· 3 καὶ ἐν πλεονεξίᾳ πλασ-
of the truth will be evil spoken of. And through covetousness with
τοῖς λόγοις ὑμᾶς ἐμπορεύσονται· οἷς τὸ κρίμα ἔκπαλαι
well-turned words you they will make gain of: for whom judgment of old
οὐκ.ἀργεῖ, καὶ ἡ.ἀπώλεια.αὐτῶν οὐ.νυστάζει. 4 Εἰ.γὰρ ὁ θεὸς
is not idle, and their destruction slumbers not. For if God
ἀγγέλων ἁμαρτησάντων οὐκ.ἐφείσατο, ἀλλὰ [c]σειραῖς‖
[the] angels who sinned spared not, but 8to 9chains
ζόφου ταρταρώσας παρέδωκεν
10of 11darkness 1having 2cast [3them] 4to 5the 6deepest 7abyss delivered [them]
εἰς κρίσιν [d]τετηρημένους·‖ 5 καὶ ἀρχαίου κόσμου οὐκ
for judgment having been kept; and [the] ancient world 2not
ἐφείσατο, [e]ἀλλ'‖ ὄγδοον Νῶε δικαιοσύνης κήρυκα ἐφύ-
1spared, but [3the] 4eighth 2Noe 7of 8righteousness 5a 6herald 1pre-
λαξεν, κατακλυσμὸν κόσμῳ ἀσεβῶν ἐπάξας· 6 καὶ
served, [the] flood upon [the] world of [the] ungodly having brought in; and
πόλεις Σοδόμων καὶ Γομόρρας τεφρώσας κατα-
[the] cities of Sodom and Gomorrha having reduced to ashes with an
στροφῇ κατέκρινεν, ὑπόδειγμα μελλόντων ἀσε-
1overthrow condemned [them], 3an 4example [5to 6those] 7being 8about 9to 10live

more carefulness to make your calling and
election sure. For doing these things, you
will never stumble at any time.
11For so shall the entrance into the everlasting kingdom of our Lord and Savior
Jesus Christ be richly furnished to you.
12For this reason I will not fail to cause
you to remember these things, even though
you know and have been firmly settled in
the present truth.
13But I think that as long as I am in this
earthly tabernacle, it is good to stir you up
to remember.
14*For I* know that the putting off of my
earthly tabernacle is going to be soon, even
as our Lord Jesus Christ showed to me.
15But I will also do my best always to see
that you have these things in your memory
after I am gone.
16For we have not followed cleverly in-
vented fables when we make known to you
the power and coming of our Lord Jesus
Christ, but we were eye-witnesses of His
Majesty.
17For when He had received honor and
glory from God the Father, such a voice
came to Him from the magnificent glory,
"This is My Son, the Beloved, in whom I am
well-pleased."
18And we heard this voice which came
down from Heaven, when we were with Him
on the holy mountain.
19And we have the word of the prophets
confirmed – to which you do well to pay
attention, as you would to a lamp shining in
a dark place, until the day should dawn and
the Morning-Star should rise in your hearts
20knowing this first, that not any prophecy of the Scripture is of its own
interpretation.
21For prophecy was never at any time
brought by the will of man, but the holy
men of God spoke, being borne along by the
Holy Spirit.
2 1But there were also false prophets among
the people, just as there will also be false
teachers among you, who secretly will bring
in false teachings which destroy. And they
will deny the Master who bought them,
bringing on themselves quick destruction.
2And many shall follow their destroying
ways. Because *of them* the way of truth shall
be evil spoken of.
3And through greediness they will make
gain of you through well-turned words – for
whom judgment from of old is not idle, and
their destruction does not sleep.
4For God did not spare the angels who
sinned, but when He had thrown them into
the deepest hell, He gave them up into
chains of darkness to be kept to Judgment.
5And He did not spare the old world, but
saved Noah the eighth *person*, a preacher of
righteousness, bringing in the flood on the
world of the ungodly.
6And turning the cities of Sodom and

ρ́εῖν τεθεικώς· 7 καὶ δίκαιον Λώτ, καταπονούμενον ὑπὸ τῆς
[11]ungodly [1]having [2]set; and righteous Lot, oppressed by the
τῶν ἀθέσμων ἐν ἀσελγείᾳ ἀναστροφῆς, [f]ἐρρύσατο·[‖] 8 βλέμ-
[4]of [5]the [6]lawless [2]in [3]licentiousness [1]conduct he delivered, ([4]through
ματι γὰρ καὶ ἀκοῇ [g]ὁ[‖] δίκαιος, [h]ἐγκατοικῶν[‖] ἐν αὐτοῖς,
[5]seeing [1]for and hearing, the righteous [man], dwelling among them,
ἡμέραν ἐξ ἡμέρας ψυχὴν δικαίαν ἀνόμοις ἔργοις
day by day [[2]his] [4]soul [3]righteous [5]with [[6]their] [7]lawless [8]works
ἐβασάνιζεν· 9 οἶδεν κύριος εὐσεβεῖς ἐκ [i]πειρασμοῦ[‖]
[1]tormented,) [11]knows [[9]the] [10]Lord [how the] pious out of temptation
ῥύεσθαι. ἀδίκους.δὲ εἰς ἡμέραν κρίσεως κολαζομένους
to deliver, and [the] unrighteous to a day of judgment [3]to [4]be [5]punished
τηρεῖν· 10 μάλιστα.δὲ τοὺς ὀπίσω σαρκὸς ἐν ἐπιθυμίᾳ
[1]to [2]keep; and specially those who after [the] flesh in [the] lust
μιασμοῦ πορευομένους, καὶ κυριότητος καταφρονοῦντας.
of pollution walk, and lordship despise. [They
Τολμηταί, αὐθάδεις, δόξας οὐ.τρέμουσιν βλασφημοῦντες·
are] daring, self-willed; [7]glories [1]they [2]tremble [3]not [4]speaking [5]evil [6]of;
11 ὅπου ἄγγελοι ἰσχύϊ καὶ δυνάμει μείζονες ὄντες, οὐ φέ-
where angels [3]in [4]strength [5]and [6]power [2]greater [1]being, [8]not [7]do
ρουσιν κατ' αὐτῶν [k]παρὰ κυρίῳ[‖] βλάσφημον κρίσιν.
bring against them, before [the] Lord, a railing charge.
12 οὗτοι.δέ, ὡς ἄλογα ζῶα [l]φυσικὰ γεγενημένα[‖] εἰς ἅλω-
But these, as [2]irrational [3]animals [1]natural born for cap-
σιν καὶ φθοράν, ἐν οἷς ἀγνοοῦσιν βλασφημοῦντες, ἐν
ture and corruption, [3]in [4]what [5]they [6]are [7]ignorant [8]of [1]speaking [2]evil, in
τῇ.φθορᾷ.αὐτῶν [m]καταφθαρήσονται,[‖] 13 κομιούμενοι
their corruption shall utterly perish, being about to receive [the]
μισθὸν ἀδικίας, ἡδονὴν ἡγούμενοι τὴν ἐν.ἡμέρᾳ τρυφήν,
reward of unrighteousness; [4]pleasure [1]esteeming [2]ephemeral [3]indulgence;
σπῖλοι καὶ μῶμοι, ἐντρυφῶντες ἐν ταῖς [n]ἀπάταις[‖] αὐτῶν, συν-
spots and blemishes, luxuriating in [2]deceits [1]their, feast-
ευωχούμενοι ὑμῖν, 14 ὀφθαλμοὺς ἔχοντες μεστοὺς μοιχαλίδος
ing with you; eyes having full of an adulteress,
καὶ [o]ἀκαταπαύστους[‖] ἁμαρτίας, δελεάζοντες ψυχὰς ἀστηρίκ-
and that cease not from sin, alluring souls unestablish-
τους, καρδίαν γεγυμνασμένην [p]πλεονεξίαις[‖] ἔχοντες, κατάρας
ed; [2]a [3]heart [4]exercised [5]in [6]craving [1]having, [8]of [9]curse
τέκνα, 15 [q]καταλιπόντες[‖] [r]τὴν[‖] εὐθεῖαν ὁδόν, ἐπλανήθησαν,
[8]children; having left the straight way, they went astray,
ἐξακολουθήσαντες τῇ ὁδῷ τοῦ Βαλαὰμ τοῦ Βοσόρ, ὃς
having followed in the way of Balaam, [son] of Bosor, who [the]
μισθὸν ἀδικίας ἠγάπησεν, 16 ἔλεγξιν.δὲ ἔσχεν ἰδίας
reward of unrighteousness loved; but reproof had of his own
παρανομίας· ὑποζύγιον ἄφωνον, ἐν ἀνθρώπου φωνῇ
wickedness, [the] [2]beast [3]of [4]burden [1]dumb, in man's voice
φθεγξάμενον, ἐκώλυσεν τὴν τοῦ προφήτου παραφρονίαν.
speaking, forbade the [2]of [3]the [4]prophet [1]madness.
17 οὗτοί εἰσιν πηγαὶ ἄνυδροι, [s]νεφέλαι[‖] ὑπὸ λαίλαπος ἐλαυ-
These are fountains without water, clouds by storm being
νόμεναι, οἷς ὁ ζόφος τοῦ σκότους [t]εἰς.αἰῶνα[‖] τετήρηται.
driven, to whom the gloom of darkness for ever is kept.
18 ὑπέρογκα.γὰρ ματαιότητος φθεγγόμενοι, δελεάζουσιν
For great swelling [words] of vanity speaking, they allure
ἐν ἐπιθυμίαις σαρκός, [v]ἀσελγείαις, τοὺς [w]ὄντως[‖]
with [the] desires of [the] flesh, by licentiousnesses, those who indeed
[x]ἀποφυγόντας[‖] τοὺς ἐν πλάνῃ ἀναστρεφομένους, 19 ἐλευ-
escaped from those who [2]in [3]error [1]walk, [6]free-
θερίαν αὐτοῖς ἐπαγγελλόμενοι, αὐτοὶ δοῦλοι ὑπάρχοντες
dom [5]them [4]promising, themselves [2]bondmen [1]being
τῆς φθορᾶς· ᾧ.γάρ τις ἥττηται, τούτῳ [y]καὶ[‖] δε-
of corruption; for by whom anyone has been subdued, by him also he is
δούλωται. 20 εἰ.γὰρ ἀποφυγόντες τὰ μιάσματα τοῦ κόσμου
held in bondage. For if having escaped the pollutions of the world
ἐν ἐπιγνώσει τοῦ κυρίου [z] καὶ σωτῆρος Ἰησοῦ χριστοῦ,
through [the] knowledge of the Lord and Saviour Jesus Christ,
τούτοις.δὲ πάλιν ἐμπλακέντες ἡττῶνται, γέγονεν
but [8]by [9]these [1]again [2]having [3]been [4]entangled [5]they [6]are [7]subdued, has become
αὐτοῖς τὰ ἔσχατα χείρονα τῶν πρώτων. 21 [a]κρεῖττον[‖]
to them the last [state] worse than the first. [2]Better
γὰρ ἦν αὐτοῖς μὴ ἐπεγνωκέναι τὴν ὁδὸν τῆς δικαιοσύνης,
[1]for it were for them not to have known the way of righteousness,
ἢ ἐπιγνοῦσιν [b] [c]ἐπιστρέψαι[‖] [d]ἐκ[‖] τῆς παραδοθείσης αὐ-
than having known [it] to have turned from the [3]delivered [4]to
τοῖς ἁγίας ἐντολῆς. 22 συμβέβηκεν.[e]δὲ[‖] αὐτοῖς τὸ τῆς
[5]them [1]holy [2]commandment. But has happened to them the [word] of the
ἀληθοῦς παροιμίας, Κύων ἐπιστρέψας ἐπὶ τὸ.ἴδιον ἐξέραμα·
true proverb: [The] dog having returned to his own vomit;
καί, Ὗς λουσαμένη, εἰς [f]κύλισμα[‖] βορβόρου.
and, [The] [2]sow [1]washed, to [her] rolling place in [the] mire.

3 Ταύτην ἤδη, ἀγαπητοί, δευτέραν ὑμῖν γράφω ἐπιστολήν,
This now, beloved, a second [2]to [3]you [4]I [5]write [1]epistle,

Go-mor-rah into ashes, He condemned them with an overthrow – setting an example to those who were going to live ungodly.
7 And he delivered righteous Lot, tormented by the filthy behavior of the lawless
8 for day by day that just man's righteous soul was tormented with their lawless works, as he lived among them, seeing and hearing.
9 The Lord knows how to deliver the godly out of temptation and to keep the unjust to a day of judgment to be punished,
10 and especially those who walk after the flesh in the lust of uncleanness and who hate government, being bold and self-willed. They do not fear to speak evil of rulers,
11 when *even* angels, who are greater in strength and power, do not bring a shaming charge against them before the Lord.
12 But like the natural animals who have no reason, who have been born to be caught and destroyed, speaking hurtfully in things they know nothing of, they shall utterly be destroyed in their own rottenness,
13 being about to receive the reward of lawlessness. *For they* count it pleasure to riot in the daytime, being spotty and disgraceful ones, taking great joy in their lies as they feast with you,
14 having eyes full of an adulteress and that cannot cease from sin, alluring to themselves souls that are not settled. *They* have a heart full of the desire to have more and more – cursed children –
15 leaving the right way, they went astray, following in the way of Balaam the son of Beor, who loved the reward of unrighteousness
16 (but he was reproved of his own wickedness when the dumb beast of burden spoke in the voice of man, forbidding the madness of the prophet).
17 These are springs without water, clouds being driven by storm, for whom the blackness of darkness is kept forever.
18 For in speaking great swelling *words* of vanity, by the lusts of the flesh and by wicked looseness, they draw those who indeed had escaped from the ones who walk in error,
19 promising them freedom while they themselves are the slaves of corruption – for by whom anyone has been overcome, by the same he also is held in slavery.
20 For if through the knowledge of the Lord and Savior Jesus Christ they have escaped the filthy vices of the world, but when they have become tangled up in these again, they are overcome – their last *state* is worse than their first.
21 For it would have been better for them not to have known the way of righteousness than to know and to have turned away from the holy commandment delivered to them.
22 But the *word* of the true proverb has happened to them: The dog has returned to

ἐν αἷς διεγείρω ὑμῶν ἐν ὑπομνήσει τὴν εἰλικρι-
in [both] which I stir up your 3in 4putting [5you] 6in 7remembrance 1pure
νῆ διάνοιαν, 2 μνησθῆναι τῶν προειρημένων ῥημάτων ὑπὸ τῶν
2mind, to be mindful of the 2spoken 3before 1words by the
ἁγίων προφητῶν, καὶ τῆς τῶν ἀποστόλων gἡμῶν‖ ἐντολῆς,
holy prophets, and of the 9the 10apostles 7by 8us 1commandment
τοῦ κυρίου καὶ σωτῆρος· 3 τοῦτο πρῶτον γινώσκοντες, ὅτι
2of 3the 4Lord 5and 6Saviour; this first knowing, that
ἐλεύσονται ἐπ᾽ hἐσχάτου‖ τῶν ἡμερῶν i ἐμπαῖκται, κατὰ
will come at the close of the days mockers, according to
τὰς.ἰδίας.kαὐτῶν ἐπιθυμίας‖ πορευόμενοι, 4 καὶ λέγοντες, Ποῦ
their own lusts walking, and saying, Where
ἐστιν ἡ ἐπαγγελία τῆς.παρουσίας.αὐτοῦ; ἀφ᾽.ἧς.γὰρ οἱ πατέ-
is the promise of his coming? for since the fa-
ρες ἐκοιμήθησαν, πάντα οὕτως διαμένει ἀπ᾽ ἀρχῆς κτί-
thers fell asleep, all things thus continue from [the] beginning of [the]
σεως. 5 λανθάνει.γὰρ αὐτοὺς τοῦτο θέλοντας, ὅτι
creation. For 2is 3hidden 4from 5them 1this, [they] willing [it], that
οὐρανοὶ ἦσαν ἔκπαλαι, καὶ γῆ ἐξ ὕδατος καὶ δι᾽ ὕδατος
heavens were of old, and an earth out of water and in water
συνεστῶσα, τῷ τοῦ θεοῦ λόγῳ, 6 δι᾽ ὧν ὁ τότε
subsisting, by the 2of 3God 1word, through which [waters] the then
κόσμος ὕδατι κατακλυσθεὶς ἀπώλετο· 7 οἱ.δὲ νῦν οὐρανοὶ
world with water having been deluged perished. But the now heavens
καὶ ἡ γῆ lαὐτοῦ‖ λόγῳ τεθησαυρισμένοι εἰσίν, πυρὶ τηρού-
and the earth by his word 2treasured 3up 1are, for fire being
μενοι εἰς ἡμέραν κρίσεως καὶ ἀπωλείας τῶν ἀσεβῶν ἀνθρώπων.
kept to a day of judgment and destruction of ungodly men.
8 ἓν.δὲ.τοῦτο μὴ.λανθανέτω ὑμᾶς, ἀγαπητοί, ὅτι μία ἡμέρα
But this one thing let not be hidden from you, beloved, that one day
παρὰ κυρίῳ ὡς χίλια ἔτη, καὶ χίλια ἔτη ὡς ἡμέρα
with [the] Lord [is] as a thousand years, and a thousand years as 2day
μία. 9 οὐ.βραδύνει mὁ‖ κύριος τῆς ἐπαγγελίας, ὥς τινες βρα-
1one. 5Does 6not 7delay 3the 4Lord the promise, as some 2de-
δυτῆτα ἡγοῦνται· ἀλλὰ μακροθυμεῖ nεἰς‖ oἡμᾶς,‖ μὴ βουλό-
3lay 1esteem, but is longsuffering towards us, not will-
μενός τινας ἀπολέσθαι, ἀλλὰ πάντας εἰς μετάνοιαν χωρῆ-
ing [for] any to perish, but all to repentance to
σαι. 10 ἥξει.δὲ pἡ‖ ἡμέρα κυρίου ὡς κλέπτης qἐν νυκτί,‖
come. But shall come the day of [the] Lord as a thief in [the] night,
ἐν ᾗ rοἱ‖ οὐρανοὶ ῥοιζηδὸν παρελεύσονται, στοιχεῖα.δὲ
in which the heavens with rushing noise shall pass away, and [the] elements
καυσούμενα sλυθήσονται,‖ καὶ γῆ καὶ τὰ ἐν αὐτῇ ἔργα
burning with heat shall be dissolved, and [the] earth and the 2in 3it 1works
tκατακαήσεται.‖
shall be burnt up.

11 Τούτων vοὖν‖ πάντων λυομένων, ποταποὺς
These things then all being to be dissolved, what kind of [persons]
δεῖ ὑπάρχειν ὑμᾶς ἐν ἁγίαις ἀναστροφαῖς καὶ εὐσεβείαις,
ought 2to 3be 1ye in holy conduct and piety,
12 προσδοκῶντας καὶ σπεύδοντας τὴν παρουσίαν τῆς τοῦ
expecting and hastening the coming of the
θεοῦ ἡμέρας δι᾽ ἣν οὐρανοὶ πυρούμενοι λυθή-
2of 3God 1day by reason of which [the] heavens, being on fire, shall be dis-
σονται, καὶ στοιχεῖα καυσούμενα wτήκεται;‖ 13 καινοὺς
solved, and [the] elements burning with heat shall melt? 2New
δὲ οὐρανοὺς καὶ xγῆν καινὴν‖ yκατὰ‖ zτὸ ἐπάγγελμα‖ αὐτοῦ
1but heavens and 3earth 1a 2new according to 2promise 1his,
προσδοκῶμεν, ἐν οἷς δικαιοσύνη κατοικεῖ. 14 διό, ἀγαπη-
we expect, in which righteousness dwells. Wherefore, belov-
τοί, ταῦτα προσδοκῶντες, σπουδάσατε ἄσπιλοι καὶ ἀμώ-
ed, these things expecting be diligent without spot and unblam-
μητοι αὐτῷ εὑρεθῆναι ἐν εἰρήνῃ, 15 καὶ τὴν τοῦ.κυρίου.ἡμῶν
able by him to be found in peace; and the 2of 3our 4Lord
μακροθυμίαν, σωτηρίαν ἡγεῖσθε· καθὼς καὶ ὁ ἀγαπητὸς
1longsuffering, 7salvation 5esteem 6ye; according as also 2beloved
ἡμῶν ἀδελφὸς Παῦλος κατὰ τὴν aαὐτῷ δοθεῖσαν‖ σοφίαν
1our brother Paul according to the 3to 4him 2given 1wisdom
ἔγραψεν ὑμῖν, 16 ὡς καὶ ἐν πάσαις bταῖς‖ ἐπιστολαῖς, λαλῶν
wrote to you, as also in all [his] epistles, speaking
ἐν αὐταῖς περὶ τούτων· ἐν cοἷς‖ ἐστιν δυσνόητά
in them concerning these things, among which are 3hard 4to 5be 6understood
τινα, ἃ οἱ ἀμαθεῖς καὶ ἀστήρικτοι στρεβλοῦσιν, ὡς
1some 2things, which the untaught and unestablished wrest, as
καὶ τὰς λοιπὰς γραφάς, πρὸς τὴν.ἰδίαν.αὐτῶν ἀπώλειαν.
also the other scriptures, to their own destruction.
17 Ὑμεῖς οὖν, ἀγαπητοί, προγινώσκοντες φυλάσσεσθε,
Ye therefore, beloved, knowing beforehand, beware,
ἵνα.μὴ τῇ τῶν ἀθέσμων πλάνῃ συναπαχθέντες, ἐκπέ-
lest with the 2of 3the 4lawless [5ones] 1error having been led away, ye should
σητε τοῦ.ἰδίου στηριγμοῦ· 18 αὐξάνετε.δὲ ἐν χάριτι καὶ
fall from your own steadfastness: but grow in grace, and

his own vomit – and, the sow who was
washed to her rolling place in the mud.
3 1This second letter, loved ones, I now write
to you, in which I stir up your pure mind to
remember to
2pay attention to the words spoken before
by the holy prophets and of the commandment of the Lord and Savior by us, the
apostles.
3First, know this, that scoffers will come in
the last days, walking according to their own
lusts,
4and saying, Where is the promise of His
coming? For since the fathers fell asleep, all
things continue this way from the beginning
of creation.
5For by their own will this is hidden from
them, that by the word of God the heavens
were of old, and the earth *was made* to stand
out of the water, and in the water
6(through which *waters* the old world was
destroyed when it had been flooded with
water).
7But the heavens and the earth which now
exist are kept by the same word, being kept
for fire to the day of judgment and destruction of ungodly men.
8But do not let this one thing be hidden
from you, beloved, that one day is with the
Lord as a thousand years, and a thousand
years as one day.
9The Lord is not slow as to the promise, as
some think of slowness, but *He* is long-
suffering towards us, not willing for any to
be lost, but all to come to repentance.
10But the day of the Lord shall come as a
thief in the night – in which the heavens
shall disappear with a great noise and the
elements shall melt away with burning heat
– and the earth and the works in it shall be
burned up.
11Since, then, all these things are to be
melted away, what kind of *persons* ought
you to be in holy behavior and godliness –
12looking for and rushing the coming of
the Day of God, on account of which the
heavens (being on fire) will melt away, and
the elements shall melt, burning with heat!
13But according to His promise, we look
for new heavens and a new earth, in which
righteousness dwells.
14For this reason, loved ones, since you are
looking for these things, be careful to be
found by Him in peace, without spot and
without blame.
15And think of the long-suffering of our
Lord as salvation even as our beloved
brother Paul wrote to you, according to
the wisdom given to him
16(as also he speaks about these things
in all his letters, among which things
there are some things hard to understand,
which the ignorant and unsettled ones
pervert, as *they* also *do* the other
Scriptures, to their own destruction)
17So you, beloved, knowing beforehand,

γνώσει τοῦ.κυρίου.ἡμῶν καὶ σωτῆρος Ἰησοῦ χριστοῦ.
in [the] knowledge of our Lord and Saviour Jesus Christ.
αὐτῷ ἡ δόξα καὶ νῦν καὶ εἰς ἡμέραν αἰῶνος. ἀμήν.
To him [be] glory both now and to [the] day of eternity. Amen.

The FIRST Letter of JOHN

Ὃ ἦν ἀπ' ἀρχῆς, ὃ ἀκηκόαμεν, ὃ ἑω-
That which was from [the] beginning, that which we have heard, that which we
ράκαμεν τοῖς.ὀφθαλμοῖς.ἡμῶν, ὃ ἐθεασάμεθα καὶ αἱ χεῖρες
have seen with our eyes, that which we gazed upon and 2hands
ἡμῶν ἐψηλάφησαν περὶ τοῦ λόγου τῆς ζωῆς· 2 καὶ ἡ ζωὴ
1our handled concerning the Word of life; (and the life
ἐφανερώθη, καὶ ἑωράκαμεν, καὶ μαρτυροῦμεν, καὶ ἀπαγγέλ-
was manifested, and we have seen, and bear witness, and re-
λομεν ὑμῖν τὴν ζωὴν τὴν αἰώνιον, ἥτις ἦν πρὸς τὸν πατέρα,
port to you the 2life 1eternal, which was with the Father,
καὶ ἐφανερώθη ἡμῖν· 3 ὃ ἑωράκαμεν καὶ ἀκηκόαμεν,
and was manifested to us:) that which we have seen and have heard
ἀπαγγέλλομεν ὑμῖν, ἵνα καὶ ὑμεῖς κοινωνίαν ἔχητε μεθ'
we report to you, that also ye fellowship may have with
ἡμῶν· καὶ ἡ κοινωνία δὲ ἡ ἡμετέρα μετὰ τοῦ πατρὸς καὶ
us; and 2fellowship 3indeed 1our [is] with the Father, and
μετὰ τοῦ.υἱοῦ.αὐτοῦ Ἰησοῦ χριστοῦ· 4 καὶ ταῦτα γράφο-
with his Son Jesus Christ. And these things we
μεν ὑμῖν, ἵνα ἡ χαρὰ ἡμῶν ᾖ πεπληρωμένη.
write to you that 2joy 1our may be full.

5 Καὶ αὕτη ἐστὶν ἡ ἐπαγγελία ἣν ἀκηκόαμεν ἀπ'
And this is the message which we have heard from
αὐτοῦ, καὶ ἀναγγέλλομεν ὑμῖν, ὅτι ὁ θεὸς φῶς ἐστιν, καὶ
him, and announce to you, that God 2light 1is, and
σκοτία ἐν αὐτῷ οὐκ.ἔστιν οὐδεμία. 6 ἐὰν εἴπωμεν ὅτι
darkness in him is not any at all. If we should say that
κοινωνίαν ἔχομεν μετ' αὐτοῦ, καὶ ἐν τῷ σκότει περιπατῶμεν,
fellowship we have with him, and in darkness should walk,
ψευδόμεθα, καὶ οὐ.ποιοῦμεν τὴν ἀλήθειαν· 7 ἐὰν.δὲ ἐν τῷ
we lie, and do not practise the truth. But if in the
φωτὶ περιπατῶμεν, ὡς αὐτός ἐστιν ἐν τῷ φωτί, κοινωνίαν
light we should walk, as he is in the light, fellowship
ἔχομεν μετ' ἀλλήλων, καὶ τὸ αἷμα Ἰησοῦ χριστοῦ τοῦ υἱοῦ
we have with one another, and the blood of Jesus Christ 2Son
αὐτοῦ καθαρίζει ἡμᾶς ἀπὸ πάσης ἁμαρτίας. 8 ἐὰν εἴπωμεν
1his cleanses us from every sin. If we should say
ὅτι ἁμαρτίαν οὐκ.ἔχομεν, ἑαυτοὺς πλανῶμεν καὶ ἡ ἀλήθεια
that sin we have not, ourselves we deceive, and the truth
οὐκ.ἔστιν ἐν ἡμῖν. 9 ἐὰν ὁμολογῶμεν τὰς.ἁμαρτίας.ἡμῶν,
is not in us. If we should confess our sins,
πιστός ἐστιν καὶ δίκαιος, ἵνα ἀφῇ ἡμῖν τὰς ἁμαρτίας,
faithful he is and righteous, that he may forgive us the sins,
καὶ καθαρίσῃ ἡμᾶς ἀπὸ πάσης ἀδικίας. 10 ἐὰν εἴπωμεν
and may cleanse us from all unrighteousness. If we should say
ὅτι οὐχ.ἡμαρτήκαμεν, ψεύστην ποιοῦμεν αὐτόν, καὶ ὁ λόγος
that we have not sinned, a liar we make him, and 2word
αὐτοῦ οὐκ.ἔστιν ἐν ἡμῖν.
1his is not in us.

2 Τεκνία μου, ταῦτα γράφω ὑμῖν, ἵνα μὴ.ἁμάρτητε·
2Little children 1my, these things I write to you, that ye may not sin;
καὶ ἐάν τις ἁμάρτῃ, παράκλητον ἔχομεν πρὸς τὸν πατέρα,
and if anyone should sin, a Paraclete we have with the Father,
Ἰησοῦν χριστὸν δίκαιον· 2 καὶ αὐτὸς ἱλασμός ἐστιν
Jesus Christ [the] righteous; and he [the] propitiation is
περὶ τῶν.ἁμαρτιῶν.ἡμῶν· οὐ περὶ τῶν.ἡμετέρων δὲ μόνον,
for our sins; 2not 3for 4ours 1but only,
ἀλλὰ καὶ περὶ ὅλου τοῦ κόσμου.
but also for 2whole 1the world.

3 Καὶ ἐν τούτῳ γινώσκομεν ὅτι ἐγνώκαμεν αὐτόν, ἐὰν
And by this we know that we have known him, if
τὰς.ἐντολὰς.αὐτοῦ τηρῶμεν. 4 ὁ λέγων, Ἔγνωκα αὐτόν,
his commandments we keep. He that says, I have known him,
καὶ τὰς.ἐντολὰς.αὐτοῦ μὴ.τηρῶν, ψεύστης ἐστίν, καὶ ἐν τούτῳ
and his commandments is not keeping, a liar is, and in him
ἡ ἀλήθεια οὐκ.ἔστιν· 5 ὃς.δ'.ἂν τηρῇ αὐτοῦ τὸν λόγον,
the truth is not; but whoever may keep his word,
ἀληθῶς ἐν τούτῳ ἡ ἀγάπη τοῦ θεοῦ τετελείωται. ἐν τούτῳ
truly in him the love of God has been perfected. By this
γινώσκομεν ὅτι ἐν αὐτῷ ἐσμεν. 6 ὁ λέγων ἐν αὐτῷ
we know that in him we are. He that says in him [he]
μένειν, ὀφείλει, καθὼς ἐκεῖνος περιεπάτησεν, καὶ αὐτὸς οὕτως
abides, ought, even as he walked, also himself so

be careful for fear that you may be led away with the error of the lawless and may fall from your own firm stand.
18 But grow in grace and in the knowledge of our Lord and Savior Jesus Christ. To Him be glory both now and to the day of eternity.
Amen.

CHAPTER 1

1 *We report to you* that which was heard from the beginning, that which we have heard, that which we have seen with our eyes, that which we looked on and handled with our hands, as regards the Word of life.
2 And the Life was revealed. And we have seen and bear witness and report to you that everlasting Life which was with the Father, and *which was* revealed to us.
3 We report to you what we have seen and what we have heard, so that you also may have fellowship with us. And truly our fellowship is with the Father, and with His Son, Jesus Christ.
4 And we write these things to you so that your joy may be full.
5 And this is the message which we have heard from Him and pass on to you, that God is light, and there is no darkness in Him at all.
6 If we say that we have fellowship with Him and walk in darkness, we lie and we do not practice the truth.
7 But if we walk in the light as He is in the light, we have fellowship with one another – and the blood of Jesus Christ His son cleanses us from all sin.
8 If we say that we have no sin, we are deceiving ourselves, and the truth is not in us.
9 If we confess our sins, He is faithful and just to forgive us our sins, and to cleanse us from all unrighteousness.
10 If we say that we have not sinned, we make Him a liar, – and His word is not in us.

CHAPTER 2

1 My little children, I write these things to you so that you may not sin. And if anyone should sin, we have an Advocate with the Father, Jesus Christ the righteous;
2 and He is the propitiation for our sins, but not for ours only, but also for all the world.
3 And by this we know that we have known Him, if we keep His commandments.
4 He that says, I have known Him, but is not keeping His commandments, is a liar, and the truth is not in him.
5 But whoever keeps His word, truly the love of God has been perfected in him. By this we know that we are in Him.
6 He that says he lives in Him ought also to walk in the same way as He walked.

περιπατεῖν. 7 [t]ἀδελφοί,ǁ οὐκ ἐντολὴν καινὴν γράφω ὑμῖν,
to walk. Brethren, not a [2]commandment [1]new I write to you,
ἀλλ' ἐντολὴν παλαιάν, ἣν εἴχετε ἀπ' ἀρχῆς· ἡ
but [3]commandment [1]an [2]old, which ye had from [the] beginning: the
ἐντολὴ ἡ παλαιά ἐστιν ὁ λόγος ὃν ἠκούσατε [v]ἀπ'
[2]commandment [1]old is the word which ye heard from [the]
ἀρχῆς.ǁ 8 πάλιν ἐντολὴν καινὴν γράφω ὑμῖν, ὅ ἐστιν
beginning. Again a [2]commandment [1]new I write to you, which is
ἀληθὲς ἐν αὐτῷ καὶ ἐν ὑμῖν, ὅτι ἡ σκοτία παράγεται,
true in him and in you, because the darkness is passing away,
καὶ τὸ φῶς τὸ ἀληθινὸν ἤδη φαίνει. 9 ὁ λέγων ἐν τῷ
and the [2]light [1]true already shines. He that says in the
φωτὶ εἶναι, καὶ τὸν.ἀδελφὸν.αὐτοῦ μισῶν, ἐν τῇ σκοτίᾳ ἐστὶν
light [he] is, and [2]his [3]brother [1]hates, in the darkness is
ἕως ἄρτι. 10 ὁ ἀγαπῶν τὸν.ἀδελφὸν αὐτοῦ, ἐν τῷ φωτὶ
until now. He that loves his brother, in the light
μένει, καὶ σκάνδαλον [w]ἐν αὐτῷ οὐκ.ἔστιν.ǁ 11 ὁ.δὲ
abides, and [4]cause [5]of [6]offence [7]in [8]him [1]there [2]is [3]not. But he that
μισῶν τὸν.ἀδελφὸν.αὐτοῦ, ἐν τῇ σκοτίᾳ ἐστίν, καὶ ἐν τῇ σκοτίᾳ
hates his brother, in the darkness is, and in the darkness
περιπατεῖ, καὶ οὐκ.οἶδεν ποῦ ὑπάγει, ὅτι ἡ σκοτία ἐτύφ-
walks, and knows not where he goes, because the darkness blind-
λωσεν τοὺς.ὀφθαλμοὺς.αὐτοῦ.
ed his eyes.

12 Γράφω ὑμῖν, τεκνία, ὅτι ἀφέωνται ὑμῖν
I write to you, little children, because have been forgiven you [your]
αἱ ἁμαρτίαι διὰ τὸ.ὄνομα.αὐτοῦ.
sins for the sake of his name.

13 Γράφω ὑμῖν, πατέρες, ὅτι ἐγνώκατε τὸν ἀπ'
I write to you, fathers, because ye have known him who [is] from
ἀρχῆς. Γράφω ὑμῖν, νεανίσκοι, ὅτι νενικήκατε τὸν
[the] beginning. I write to you, young men, because ye have overcome the
πονηρόν. [x]Γράφωǁ ὑμῖν, παιδία, ὅτι ἐγνώκατε τὸν
wicked [one]. I write to you, little children, because ye have known the
πατέρα.
Father.

14 Ἔγραψα ὑμῖν, πατέρες, ὅτι ἐγνώκατε τὸν
I wrote to you, fathers, because ye have known him who [is]
ἀπ' ἀρχῆς. Ἔγραψα ὑμῖν, νεανίσκοι, ὅτι ἰσχυροί ἐστε,
from [the] beginning. I wrote to you, young men, because strong ye are
καὶ ὁ λόγος τοῦ θεοῦ ἐν ὑμῖν μένει, καὶ νενικήκατε τὸν
and the word of God in you abides, and ye have overcome the
πονηρόν. 15 μὴ.ἀγαπᾶτε τὸν κόσμον, μηδὲ τὰ ἐν τῷ
wicked [one]. Love not the world, nor the things in the
κόσμῳ· ἐάν τις ἀγαπᾷ τὸν κόσμον, οὐκ ἔστιν ἡ ἀγάπη
world. If anyone should love the world, [7]not [8]is [1]the [2]love
τοῦ πατρὸς ἐν αὐτῷ· 16 ὅτι πᾶν τὸ ἐν τῷ κόσμῳ,
[3]of [4]the [5]Father in him; because all that which [is] in the world,
ἡ ἐπιθυμία τῆς σαρκός, καὶ ἡ ἐπιθυμία τῶν ὀφθαλμῶν, καὶ
the desire of the flesh, and the desire of the eyes, and
ἡ [y]ἀλαζονείαǁ τοῦ βίου, οὐκ.ἔστιν ἐκ τοῦ πατρός, [z]ἀλλ'ǁ ἐκ
the vaunting of life, is not of the Father, but of
τοῦ κόσμου ἐστίν. 17 καὶ ὁ κόσμος παράγεται, καὶ ἡ ἐπι-
the world is; and the world is passing away, and the
θυμία αὐτοῦ· ὁ.δὲ ποιῶν τὸ θέλημα τοῦ θεοῦ μένει εἰς τὸν
lust of it, but he that does the will of God abides for
αἰῶνα. 18 Παιδία, ἐσχάτη ὥρα ἐστίν· καὶ καθὼς
ever. Little children, [the] last hour it is, and according as
ἠκούσατε ὅτι [a]ὁǁ ἀντίχριστος ἔρχεται, καὶ νῦν ἀντίχριστοι
ye heard that the antichrist is coming, even now [2]antichrists
πολλοὶ γεγόνασιν· ὅθεν γινώσκομεν ὅτι ἐσχάτη ὥρα ἐστίν.
[1]many have arisen, whence we know that [the] last hour it is.
19 ἐξ ἡμῶν [b]ἐξῆλθον,ǁ ἀλλ' οὐκ.ἦσαν ἐξ ἡμῶν· εἰ.γὰρ
From among us they went out, but they were not of us; for if
[c]ἦσαν ἐξ ἡμῶν,ǁ μεμενήκεισαν.ἂν μεθ' ἡμῶν· ἀλλ' ἵνα φανε-
they were of us, they would have remained with us, but that they
ρωθῶσιν ὅτι οὐκ.εἰσὶν πάντες ἐξ ἡμῶν. 20 καὶ ὑμεῖς
might be made manifest that [2]are [3]not [1]all of us. And ye
χρίσμα ἔχετε ἀπὸ τοῦ ἁγίου, καὶ οἴδατε [d]πάντα.ǁ
[the] anointing have from the holy [one], and ye know all things.
21 οὐκ.ἔγραψα ὑμῖν ὅτι οὐκ.οἴδατε τὴν ἀλήθειαν, ἀλλ' ὅτι
I wrote not to you because ye know not the truth, but because
οἴδατε αὐτήν, καὶ ὅτι πᾶν ψεῦδος ἐκ τῆς ἀληθείας οὐκ ἔστιν.
ye know it, and that [2]any [3]lie [5]of [6]the [7]truth [1]not [4]is.
(lit. every)
22 Τίς ἐστιν ὁ ψεύστης εἰ.μὴ ὁ ἀρνούμενος ὅτι Ἰησοῦς οὐκ
Who is the liar but he that denies that Jesus
ἔστιν ὁ χριστός; οὗτός ἐστιν ὁ ἀντίχριστος ὁ ἀρνούμενος
is the Christ? He is the antichrist who denies
τὸν πατέρα καὶ τὸν υἱόν. 23 πᾶς ὁ ἀρνούμενος τὸν υἱόν,
the Father and the Son. Everyone that denies the Son,
οὐδὲ τὸν πατέρα ἔχει. [e] 24 Ὑμεῖς [f]οὖνǁ ὃ ἠκούσατε ἀπ'
neither [3]the [4]Father [1]has [2]he. Ye therefore what ye heard from

7 Brothers, I do not write a new commandment to you, but an old commandment which you had from the beginning. The old commandment is the word which you heard from the beginning.

8 Again I write to you a new commandment, which is true in Him and in you – because the darkness is passing away and the true Light already shines.

9 He that says he is in the light and hates his brother is in the darkness even until now.

10 He that loves his brother rests in the light and there is no cause of stumbling in him.

11 But he that hates his brother is in the darkness and walks in the darkness, and he does not know where he goes, because the darkness blinds his eyes.

12 I write to you, little children, because your sins have been forgiven you for His name's sake.

13 I write to you, fathers, because you have known Him who *is* from *the* beginning. I write to you, young men, because you have overcome the wicked *one*. I write to you, little children, because you have known the Father.

14 I wrote to you, fathers, because you have known Him who is from the beginning. I wrote to you, young men, because you are strong and the word of God lives in you, and you have overcome the wicked one.

15 Do not love the world nor the things in the world! If anyone loves the world, the love of the Father is not in him,

16 because all that which is in the world – the lust of the flesh, and the lust of the eyes, and the pride of life, is not of the Father, but is of the world.

17 And the world is passing away, and the lust of it. But he that does the will of God remains forever.

18 Little children, it is the last hour. And as you heard that the antichrist is coming, even now many antichrists have arisen, from which we know that it is the last hour.

19 They went out from among us, but they were not of us – for if they were of us, they would have remained with us. But *it was so* that they might become known that they all are not of us.

20 But you have an anointing from the Holy One and you know all things.

21 I did not write to you because you do not know the truth, but because you know it – and that no lie is ever of the truth.

22 Who is a liar but he who denies that Jesus is the Christ? He is the antichrist who denies the Father and the Son.

23 Everyone that denies the Son does not have the Father either.

24 You, then, let that dwell in you which

ἀρχῆς, ἐν ὑμῖν μενέτω. ἐὰν ἐν ὑμῖν μείνῃ ὃ ἀπ'
[the] beginning, in you let it abide: if in you should abide what from
ἀρχῆς ἠκούσατε, καὶ ὑμεῖς ἐν τῷ υἱῷ καὶ [g]ἐν[l] τῷ πατρὶ
[the] beginning ye heard, also ye in the Son and in the Father
μενεῖτε. 25 καὶ αὕτη ἐστὶν ἡ ἐπαγγελία, ἣν αὐτὸς ἐπηγ-
shall abide. And this is the promise which he pro-
γείλατο ἡμῖν, τὴν ζωὴν τὴν αἰώνιον. 26 ταῦτα ἔγραψα ὑμῖν
mised us, life eternal. These things I wrote to you
περὶ τῶν πλανώντων ὑμᾶς. 27 καὶ ὑμεῖς τὸ χρῖσμα
concerning those who lead [2]astray [1]you: and you the anointing
ὃ ἐλάβετε ἀπ' αὐτοῦ, [h]ἐν ὑμῖν μένει,[h] καὶ οὐ χρείαν ἔχετε
which ye received from him, in you abides, and not need ye have
ἵνα τις διδάσκῃ ὑμᾶς· ἀλλ' ὡς τὸ [i]αὐτὸ[l] χρῖσμα διδάσκει
that anyone should teach you; but as the same anointing teaches
ὑμᾶς περὶ πάντων, καὶ ἀληθές ἐστιν, καὶ οὐκ.ἔστιν ψεῦ-
you concerning all things, and true is, and is not a
δος· καὶ καθὼς ἐδίδαξεν ὑμᾶς, [j]μενεῖτε[j] ἐν αὐτῷ.
lie; and even as it taught you, ye shall abide in him.

28 Καὶ νῦν, τεκνία, μένετε ἐν αὐτῷ· ἵνα [k]ὅταν[l] φανερω-
And now, little children, abide in him, that when he be mani-
θῇ, [l]ἔχωμεν[l] παῤῥησίαν, καὶ μὴ αἰσχυνθῶμεν ἀπ'.αὐτοῦ,
fested we may have boldness, and not be put to shame from before him
ἐν τῇ.παρουσίᾳ.αὐτοῦ.
at his coming.

29 Ἐὰν εἰδῆτε ὅτι δίκαιός ἐστιν, γινώσκετε ὅτι [m] πᾶς ὁ
If ye know that righteous he is, ye know that everyone who
ποιῶν τὴν δικαιοσύνην, ἐξ αὐτοῦ, [n]γεγέννηται.[n] 3 Ἴδετε πο-
practises righteousness of him has been begotten. See
ταπὴν ἀγάπην δέδωκεν ἡμῖν ὁ πατήρ, ἵνα τέκνα θεοῦ
what love [3]has [4]given [5]to [6]us [1]the [2]Father, that children of God
κληθῶμεν[o]· διὰ τοῦτο ὁ κόσμος οὐ.γινώσκει ἡμᾶς,
we should be called. On account of this the world knows not us,
ὅτι οὐκ.ἔγνω αὐτόν. 2 ἀγαπητοί, νῦν τέκνα θεοῦ ἐσμεν,
because it knew not him. Beloved, now children of God are we,
καὶ οὔπω ἐφανερώθη τί ἐσόμεθα· οἴδαμεν.[p]δὲ[l] ὅτι ἐὰν
and not yet was it manifested what we shall be; but we know that if
φανερωθῇ, ὅμοιοι αὐτῷ ἐσόμεθα, ὅτι ὀψόμεθα αὐτὸν καθώς
he be manifested, like him we shall be, for we shall see him as
ἐστιν. 3 καὶ πᾶς ὁ ἔχων τὴν.ἐλπίδα.ταύτην ἐπ' αὐτῷ,
he is. And everyone that has this hope in him,
ἁγνίζει ἑαυτόν, καθὼς ἐκεῖνος ἁγνός ἐστιν.
purifies himself, even as he [2]pure [1]is.

4 Πᾶς ὁ ποιῶν τὴν ἁμαρτίαν, καὶ τὴν ἀνομίαν ποιεῖ·
Everyone that practises sin, also lawlessness practises;
καὶ [q]ἡ ἁμαρτία ἐστὶν ἡ ἀνομία. 5 καὶ οἴδατε ὅτι ἐκεῖνος
and sin is lawlessness. And ye know that he
ἐφανερώθη, ἵνα τὰς ἁμαρτίας [r]ἡμῶν[l] ἄρῃ· καὶ
was manifested, that [2]sins [1]our he might take away; and
ἁμαρτία ἐν αὐτῷ οὐκ.ἔστιν. 6 πᾶς ὁ ἐν αὐτῷ μένων οὐχ
sin in him is not. [2]Anyone [3]that [5]in [6]him [4]abides [1]not (lit. everyone)
ἁμαρτάνει· πᾶς ὁ ἁμαρτάνων οὐχ ἑώρακεν αὐτόν, οὐδὲ
sins: [2]anyone [3]that [4]sins [1]not has seen him, nor (lit. everyone)
ἔγνωκεν αὐτόν.
has known him.

7 Τεκνία, μηδεὶς πλανάτω ὑμᾶς· ὁ ποιῶν τὴν
Little children, [2]no [3]one [1]let [4]lead [6]astray [5]you; he that practises
δικαιοσύνην, δίκαιός ἐστιν, καθὼς ἐκεῖνος δίκαιός ἐστιν. 8 ὁ
righteousness, righteous is, even as he righteous is. He that
ποιῶν τὴν ἁμαρτίαν, ἐκ τοῦ διαβόλου ἐστίν· ὅτι ἀπ'
practises sin, of the devil is; because from [the]
ἀρχῆς ὁ διάβολος ἁμαρτάνει. εἰς τοῦτο ἐφανερώθη ὁ υἱὸς
beginning the devil sins. For this was manifested the Son
τοῦ θεοῦ, ἵνα λύσῃ τὰ ἔργα τοῦ διαβόλου. 9 πᾶς ὁ
of God, that he might undo the works of the devil. [2]Anyone [3]that (lit. everyone)
γεγεννημένος ἐκ τοῦ θεοῦ ἁμαρτίαν οὐ ποιεῖ, ὅτι σπέρμα
[4]has [5]been [6]begotten [7]of [8]God, [10]sin [1]not [9]practises, because [2]seed
αὐτοῦ ἐν αὐτῷ μένει· καὶ οὐ.δύναται ἁμαρτάνειν, ὅτι ἐκ τοῦ
[1]his in him abides, and he is not able to sin, because of
θεοῦ γεγέννηται. 10 ἐν τούτῳ φανερά ἐστιν τὰ τέκνα τοῦ
God he has been begotten. In this manifest are the children
θεοῦ καὶ τὰ τέκνα τοῦ διαβόλου. πᾶς ὁ μὴ [s]ποιῶν
of God and the children of the devil. [2]Anyone [3]that [5]not [4]practises (lit. everyone)
δικαιοσύνην[s] οὐκ ἔστιν ἐκ τοῦ θεοῦ, καὶ ὁ μὴ.ἀγαπῶν τὸν
[6]righteousness [1]not is of God, and he that loves not
ἀδελφὸν αὐτοῦ. 11 ὅτι αὕτη ἐστὶν ἡ ἀγγελία ἣν ἠκούσατε
[2]brother [1]his. Because this is the message which ye heard
ἀπ' ἀρχῆς, ἵνα ἀγαπῶμεν ἀλλήλους· 12 οὐ καθὼς
from [the] beginning; that we should love one another: not as
Κάϊν ἐκ τοῦ πονηροῦ ἦν, καὶ ἔσφαξεν τὸν ἀδελφὸν
Cain [who] of the wicked [one] was, and slew [2]brother

you heard from the beginning. If what you
heard from the beginning dwells in you,
you also will dwell in the Son and in the
Father.
25 And this is the promise He promised us
– life everlasting.
26 I wrote these things to you concerning
those who lead you astray.
27 And the anointing which you received
from Him remains in you, and you have no
need that anyone should teach you. But
even as the same anointing teaches you
about all things, and is true, and is not a
lie – and even as it taught you – you shall
live in Him.
28 And now, little children, remain in Him
so that when He is revealed we may have
boldness and may not be put to shame before Him at His coming.
29 If you know that He is righteous, you
know that everyone who practices righteousness has been born of Him.

CHAPTER 3

1 See what love the Father has given to us,
that we should be called the children of
God! For this reason, the world does not
know us, because it did not know Him.
2 Beloved, now we are children of God, and
it does not yet appear what we shall be. But
we know that when He shall appear, we shall
be like Him – for we shall see Him as He is.
3 And everyone that has this hope in him
purifies himself, even as He is pure.
4 Everyone that practices sin also practices
lawlessness – and sin is lawlessness.
5 And you know that He was revealed so
that He might take away our sins – and in
Him there is no sin.
6 Everyone who remains in Him does not
sin. Everyone that sins has not seen Him and
has not known Him.
7 Little children, do not let anyone lead
you astray. He that practices righteousness is
righteous, even as He is righteous.
8 He that practices sin is of the devil,
because the devil sins from the beginning.
For this the Son of God was revealed, that
He might undo the works of the devil.
9 Anyone that has been born of God does
not practice sin, because His seed remains in
Him, and he is not able to sin because he has
been born of God.
10 In this the children of God and the children of the devil are revealed – anyone that
does not practice righteousness is not of
God, and *also* he that does not love his
brother.
11 Because this is the message which you
have heard from the beginning, that we
should love one another
12 not like Cain, who was of the wicked
one and killed his brother. And why did he
kill him? Because his works were wicked and

αὐτοῦ· καὶ χάριν τίνος ἔσφαξεν αὐτόν; ὅτι τὰ.ἔργα.αὐτοῦ
[1]his; and on account of what slew he him? because his works
πονηρὰ ἦν, τὰ.δὲ τοῦ.ἀδελφοῦ.αὐτοῦ δίκαια.
[2]wicked [1]were, and those of his brother righteous.
13 [t]Μὴ.θαυμάζετε, ἀδελφοί [v]μου," εἰ μισεῖ ὑμᾶς ὁ κόσμος.
Wonder not, [2]brethren [1]my, if [3]hates [4]you [1]the [2]world.
14 ἡμεῖς οἴδαμεν ὅτι μεταβεβήκαμεν ἐκ τοῦ θανάτου εἰς τὴν
We know that we have passed from death to
ζωήν, ὅτι ἀγαπῶμεν τοὺς ἀδελφούς· ὁ μὴ.ἀγαπῶν
life, because we love the brethren. He that loves not [his]
[w]τὸν ἀδελφόν," μένει ἐν τῷ θανάτῳ. 15 πᾶς ὁ μισῶν τὸν
brother, abides in death. Everyone that hates
ἀδελφὸν αὐτοῦ, ἀνθρωποκτόνος ἐστίν, καὶ οἴδατε ὅτι πᾶς
[2]brother [1]his a murderer is, and ye know that [2]any (lit. every)
ἀνθρωποκτόνος οὐκ ἔχει ζωὴν αἰώνιον ἐν [x]αὐτῷ" μένουσαν.
[3]murderer [1]not has life eternal [2]in [3]him [1]abiding.
16 Ἐν τούτῳ ἐγνώκαμεν τὴν ἀγάπην, ὅτι ἐκεῖνος ὑπὲρ
By this we have known love, because he for
ἡμῶν τὴν.ψυχὴν.αὐτοῦ ἔθηκεν· καὶ ἡμεῖς ὀφείλομεν ὑπὲρ τῶν
us his life laid down; and we ought for the
ἀδελφῶν τὰς ψυχὰς [y]τιθέναι." 17 ὃς.δ'.ἂν ἔχῃ τὸν
brethren [our] lives to lay down. But whoever may have
βίον τοῦ κόσμου, καὶ θεωρῇ τὸν.ἀδελφὸν.αὐτοῦ χρείαν
[3]means [4]of [5]life [1]the [2]world's, and may see his brother [2]need
ἔχοντα, καὶ κλείσῃ τὰ.σπλάγχνα.αὐτοῦ ἀπ' αὐτοῦ, πῶς ἡ
[1]having, and may shut up his bowels from him, how [2]the
ἀγάπη τοῦ θεοῦ μένει ἐν αὐτῷ;
[3]love [4]of [5]God [1]abides in him?
18 Τεκνία [z]μου," μὴ.ἀγαπῶμεν λόγῳ μηδὲ [a] γλώσσῃ,
[2]Little [3]children [1]my, we should not love in word, nor with tongue,
[b]ἀλλ'" [c]ἔργῳ καὶ ἀληθείᾳ. 19 [d]καὶ" ἐν τούτῳ [e]γινώσκομεν"
but in work and in truth. And by this we know
ὅτι ἐκ τῆς ἀληθείας ἐσμέν, καὶ ἔμπροσθεν αὐτοῦ πείσομεν
that of the truth we are, and before him shall persuade
τὰς.καρδίας.ἡμῶν· 20 [f]ὅτι" ἐὰν καταγινώσκῃ ἡμῶν ἡ καρδία,
our hearts, that if [3]should [4]condemn [1]our [2]heart,
ὅτι μείζων ἐστὶν ὁ θεὸς τῆς.καρδίας.ἡμῶν καὶ γινώσκει πάντα.
that greater is God than our heart and knows all things.
21 ἀγαπητοί, ἐὰν ἡ καρδία [g]ἡμῶν" μὴ.καταγινώσκῃ ἡμῶν,
Beloved, if [2]heart [1]our should not condemn us,
παῤῥησίαν ἔχομεν πρὸς τὸν θεόν, 22 καὶ ὃ.ἐὰν αἰτῶμεν,
boldness we have towards God, and whatsoever we may ask,
λαμβάνομεν [h]παρ'" αὐτοῦ, ὅτι τὰς.ἐντολὰς.αὐτοῦ τηροῦμεν,
we receive from him, because his commandments we keep,
καὶ τὰ ἀρεστὰ ἐνώπιον αὐτοῦ ποιοῦμεν. 23 καὶ αὕτη
and the things pleasing before him we practise. And this
ἐστὶν ἡ.ἐντολὴ.αὐτοῦ, ἵνα [i]πιστεύσωμεν" τῷ ὀνόματι τοῦ
is his commandment, that we should believe on the name
υἱοῦ.αὐτοῦ Ἰησοῦ χριστοῦ, καὶ ἀγαπῶμεν ἀλλήλους, καθὼς
of his Son Jesus Christ, and should love one another, even as
ἔδωκεν ἐντολὴν ἡμῖν. 24 καὶ ὁ τηρῶν τὰς.ἐντολὰς.αὐτοῦ,
he gave commandment to us. And he that keeps his commandments,
ἐν αὐτῷ μένει, καὶ αὐτὸς ἐν αὐτῷ· καὶ ἐν τούτῳ γινώσκομεν
in him abides, and he in him: and by this we know
ὅτι μένει ἐν ἡμῖν, ἐκ τοῦ πνεύματος οὗ ἡμῖν ἔδωκεν.
that he abides in us, by the Spirit which to us he gave.

those of his brother were righteous.
13 Do not wonder, my brothers, if the
world hates you.
14 We know that we have passed out of
death into life because we love the brothers.
He that does not love his brother continues
in death.
15 Anyone who hates his brother is a murderer – and you know that no murderer has
everlasting life abiding in him.
16 By this we know love, because He laid
down His life for us – and we ought to lay
down our lives for our brothers.
17 But whoever has the means of life of the
world and sees that his brother has need, and
shuts up his tender feelings from him, how
does the love of God live in him?
18 My little children, we should not love in
word nor with tongue, but in work and in
truth.
19 And by this we know that we are of the
truth and shall assure our hearts before Him.
20 For if our heart condemns us, God is
greater than our heart and knows all things.
21 Beloved, if our heart does not condemn
us, we have confidence towards God.
22 And whatever we may ask, we receive
from Him, because we keep His commandments and we practice the things which are
pleasing in His sight.
23 And this is His commandment, that we
should believe on the name of His Son, Jesus
Christ. And we should love one another,
even as He commanded us.
24 And he that keeps His commandments
lives in Him, and He in him – and by this we
know that He lives in us, by the Spirit which
He gave to us.

4 Ἀγαπητοί, μὴ παντὶ πνεύματι πιστεύετε, ἀλλὰ δοκιμά-
Beloved, [2]not [3]every [4]spirit [1]believe, but prove
ζετε τὰ πνεύματα, εἰ ἐκ τοῦ θεοῦ ἐστιν· ὅτι πολλοὶ ψευδο-
the spirits, if of God they are; because many false
προφῆται ἐξεληλύθασιν εἰς τὸν κόσμον. 2 ἐν τούτῳ γινώσκετε
prophets have gone out into the world. By this ye know
τὸ πνεῦμα τοῦ θεοῦ· πᾶν πνεῦμα ὃ ὁμολογεῖ Ἰησοῦν χριστὸν
the Spirit of God: every spirit which confesses Jesus Christ
ἐν σαρκὶ ἐληλυθότα, ἐκ τοῦ θεοῦ ἐστιν. 3 καὶ πᾶν πνεῦμα
[2]in [3]flesh [1]come, of God is; and [2]any (lit. every) [3]spirit
ὃ μὴ.ὁμολογεῖ τὸν Ἰησοῦν [k]χριστὸν ἐν σαρκὶ ἐληλυθότα," ἐκ
[4]which [5]confesses [6]not [7]Jesus [8]Christ [10]in [11]flesh [9]come, [13]of
τοῦ θεοῦ οὐκ ἔστιν· καὶ τοῦτό ἐστιν τὸ τοῦ ἀντιχρίστου,
[14]God [1]not [12]is: and this is that [power] of the antichrist,
ὃ ἀκηκόατε ὅτι ἔρχεται, καὶ νῦν ἐν τῷ κόσμῳ ἐστὶν ἤδη.
[of] which ye heard that it comes, and now in the world is it already.
4 Ὑμεῖς ἐκ τοῦ θεοῦ ἐστε, τεκνία, καὶ νενικήκατε αὐτούς·
Ye of God are, little children, and have overcome them,
ὅτι μείζων ἐστὶν ὁ ἐν ὑμῖν ἢ ὁ ἐν τῷ κόσμῳ.
because greater is he who [is] in you than he who [is] in the world.
5 αὐτοὶ ἐκ τοῦ κόσμου εἰσίν, διὰ τοῦτο ἐκ τοῦ κόσμου λα-
They of the world are; because of this of the world they
λοῦσιν, καὶ ὁ κόσμος αὐτῶν ἀκούει. 6 ἡμεῖς ἐκ τοῦ θεοῦ
talk, and the world [2]them [1]hears. We of God

CHAPTER 4

1 Beloved, do not believe every spirit, but
test the spirits, if they are of God. For many
false prophets have gone out into the world.
2 By this you know the Spirit of God: every
spirit which confesses that Jesus Christ has
come in the flesh is of God.
3 And any spirit which does not confess
that Jesus Christ has come in the flesh is not
of God. And this is that *spirit* of the antichrist of which you have heard that it
comes. And now it is already in the world.
4 Little children, you are of God and have
overcome them because He who is in you is
greater than he who is in the world.
5 They are of the world. This is why they
talk of the world, and the world hears
them.
6 We are of God. He that knows God

ἐσμεν· ὁ γινώσκων τὸν θεόν, ἀκούει ἡμῶν· ὃς οὐκ.ἔστιν
are; he that knows God, hears us; he that is not
ἐκ τοῦ θεοῦ, οὐκ.ἀκούει ἡμῶν. ἐκ τούτου γινώσκομεν τὸ πνεῦμα
of God, hears not us. By this we know the spirit
τῆς ἀληθείας καὶ τὸ πνεῦμα τῆς πλάνης.
of truth and the spirit of error.
7 Ἀγαπητοί, ἀγαπῶμεν ἀλλήλους· ὅτι ἡ ἀγάπη ἐκ τοῦ
Beloved, we should love one another; because love [2]of
θεοῦ ἐστιν, καὶ πᾶς ὁ ἀγαπῶν, ἐκ τοῦ θεοῦ γεγέννηται,
[3]God [1]is, and everyone that loves, of God has been begotten,
καὶ γινώσκει τὸν θεόν. 8 ὁ μὴ.ἀγαπῶν, οὐκ.ἔγνω τὸν θεόν·
and knows God. He that loves not, knew not God;
ὅτι ὁ θεὸς ἀγάπη ἐστίν. 9 ἐν τούτῳ ἐφανερώθη ἡ ἀγάπη
because God [2]love [1]is. In this was manifested the love
τοῦ θεοῦ ἐν ἡμῖν, ὅτι τὸν.υἱὸν.αὐτοῦ τὸν μονογενῆ ἀπέ-
of God as to us, that his Son the only-begotten [2]has
σταλκεν ὁ θεὸς εἰς τὸν κόσμον, ἵνα ζήσωμεν δι' αὐτοῦ.
[3]sent [1]God into the world, that we might live through him.
10 ἐν τούτῳ ἐστὶν ἡ ἀγάπη, οὐχ ὅτι ἡμεῖς ἠγαπήσαμεν τὸν
In this is love, not that we loved
θεόν, ἀλλ' ὅτι αὐτὸς ἠγάπησεν ἡμᾶς, καὶ ἀπέστειλεν τὸν υἱὸν
God, but that he loved us, and sent [2]Son
αὐτοῦ ἱλασμὸν περὶ τῶν.ἁμαρτιῶν.ἡμῶν. 11 ἀγαπητοί, εἰ
[1]his a propitiation for our sins. Beloved, if
οὕτως ὁ θεὸς ἠγάπησεν ἡμᾶς, καὶ ἡμεῖς ὀφείλομεν ἀλλήλους
[2]so [1]God loved us, also we ought one another
ἀγαπᾷν. 12 θεὸν οὐδεὶς πώποτε τεθέαται· ἐὰν ἀγαπῶμεν
to love. [6]God [1]no [2]one [6]at [7]any [8]time [3]has [4]seen; if we should love
ἀλλήλους, ὁ θεὸς ἐν ἡμῖν μένει, καὶ ἡ.ἀγάπη.αὐτοῦ [1]τετελειω-
one another, God in us abides, and his love [2]perfect-
μένη ἐστὶν ἐν ἡμῖν.[ll] 13 ἐν τούτῳ γινώσκομεν ὅτι ἐν αὐτῷ
ed [1]is in us. By this we know that in him
μένομεν, καὶ αὐτὸς ἐν ἡμῖν, ὅτι ἐκ τοῦ.πνεύματος.αὐτοῦ
we abide, and he in us, because of his Spirit
δέδωκεν ἡμῖν. 14 καὶ ἡμεῖς τεθεάμεθα καὶ μαρτυροῦμεν ὅτι
he has given to us. And we have seen and bear witness that
ὁ πατὴρ ἀπέσταλκεν τὸν υἱὸν σωτῆρα τοῦ κόσμου.
the Father has sent the Son [as] Saviour of the world.
15 [m]Ὃς.ἂν ὁμολογήσῃ ὅτι Ἰησοῦς ἐστιν ὁ υἱὸς τοῦ θεοῦ, ὁ
Whosoever may confess that Jesus is the Son of God,
θεὸς ἐν αὐτῷ μένει, καὶ αὐτὸς ἐν τῷ θεῷ. 16 καὶ ἡμεῖς ἐγνώ-
God in him abides, and he in God. And we have
καμεν καὶ πεπιστεύκαμεν τὴν ἀγάπην ἣν ἔχει ὁ θεὸς ἐν ἡμῖν.
known and have believed the love which [2]has [1]God as to us.
ὁ θεὸς ἀγάπη ἐστίν, καὶ ὁ μένων ἐν τῇ ἀγάπῃ, ἐν τῷ θεῷ
God [2]love [1]is, and he that abides in love, in God
μένει, καὶ ὁ θεὸς ἐν αὐτῷ[m]. 17 ἐν τούτῳ τετελείωται ἡ ἀγάπη
abides, and God in him. In this has been perfected love
μεθ' ἡμῶν, ἵνα παρρησίαν ἔχωμεν ἐν τῇ ἡμέρᾳ τῆς κρίσεως,
with us, that boldness we may have in the day of judgment,
ὅτι καθὼς ἐκεῖνός ἐστιν, καὶ ἡμεῖς ἐσμεν ἐν τῷ.κόσμῳ.τούτῳ.
that even as he is, also we are in this world.
18 φόβος οὐκ.ἔστιν ἐν τῇ ἀγάπῃ, [n]ἀλλ'[ll] ἡ τελεία ἀγάπη ἔξω
[4]Fear [1]there [2]is [3]not in love, but perfect love [2]out
βάλλει τὸν φόβον, ὅτι ὁ φόβος κόλασιν ἔχει· ὁ.δὲ φοβού-
[1]casts fear; because fear [2]torment [1]has, and he that fears
μενος οὐ.τετελείωται ἐν τῇ ἀγάπῃ. 19 ἡμεῖς [o] ἀγαπῶμεν
has not been made perfect in love. We love
[p]αὐτὸν[l] ὅτι [q]αὐτὸς[l] πρῶτος ἠγάπησεν ἡμᾶς.
him because he first loved us.
20 Ἐάν τις εἴπῃ, Ὅτι ἀγαπῶ τὸν θεόν, καὶ τὸν ἀδελ-
If anyone should say, I love God, and [4]bro-
φὸν αὐτοῦ μισῇ, ψεύστης ἐστίν· ὁ.γὰρ μὴ.ἀγαπῶν τὸν
ther [3]his [1]should [2]hate, a liar he is. For he that loves not
ἀδελφὸν.αὐτοῦ ὃν ἑώρακεν, τὸν θεὸν ὃν οὐχ.ἑώρακεν,
his brother whom he has seen, [7]God [8]whom [9]he [10]has [11]not [12]seen,
[r]πῶς[ll] δύναται ἀγαπᾷν; 21 καὶ ταύτην τὴν ἐντολὴν ἔχο-
[1]how [2]is [3]he [4]able [5]to [6]love? And this commandment we
μεν ἀπ' αὐτοῦ, ἵνα ὁ ἀγαπῶν τὸν θεὸν ἀγαπᾷ καὶ τὸν
have from him, that he that loves God should love also
ἀδελφὸν αὐτοῦ. 5 Πᾶς ὁ πιστεύων ὅτι Ἰησοῦς ἐστιν ὁ
[2]brother [1]his. Everyone that believes that Jesus is the
χριστὸς ἐκ τοῦ θεοῦ γεγέννηται· καὶ πᾶς ὁ ἀγαπῶν τὸν
Christ, of God has been begotten; and everyone that loves him that
γεννήσαντα ἀγαπᾷ [s]καὶ[l] τὸν γεγεννημένον ἐξ αὐτοῦ. 2 ἐν
begat, loves also him that has been begotten of him. By
τούτῳ γινώσκομεν ὅτι ἀγαπῶμεν τὰ τέκνα τοῦ θεοῦ, ὅταν τὸν
this we know that we love the children of God, when
θεὸν ἀγαπῶμεν καὶ τὰς.ἐντολὰς.αὐτοῦ [t]τηρῶμεν.[l] 3 αὕτη.γάρ
God we love and his commandments keep. For this
ἐστιν ἡ ἀγάπη τοῦ θεοῦ, ἵνα τὰς.ἐντολὰς.αὐτοῦ τηρῶμεν·
is the love of God, that his commandments we should keep;

hears us. He that is not of God does not hear us. By this we know the spirit of truth and the spirit of error.

7 Beloved, we should love one another, because love is of God, and everyone that loves has been born of God and knows God.

8 He that does not love never knew God, because God is love.

9 In this the love of God was revealed in us, that God has sent His son, the Only-begotten, into the world so that we might live through Him.

10 In this is love, not that we loved God, but that He loved us and sent His Son to be the propitiation for our sins.

11 Beloved, if God so loved us, we ought also to love one another.

12 No one has seen God at any time. If we love one another, God lives in us and His love is perfected in us.

13 By this we know we live in Him and He in us, that He has given to us from His Spirit.

14 And we have seen and testify that the Father has sent the Son as Savior of the world.

15 Whoever may confess that Jesus is the Son of God, God lives in him and he in God.

16 And we have known and have believed the love which God has in us. God is love, and he that continues in love continues in God, and God in him.

17 In this has love been perfected with us, that we may have boldness in the Day of Judgment, that as He is, so are we in this world.

18 There is no fear in love, but perfect love thrusts out fear, for fear has torment, and he that fears has not been made perfect in love.

19 We love Him because He first loved us.

20 If anyone says, I love God – and hates his brother – he is a liar. For he that does not love his brother whom he has seen, how is he able to love God whom he has not seen?

21 And we have this commandment from Him, that he that loves God should also love his brother.

CHAPTER 5

1 Whoever believes that Jesus is the Christ has been born of God. And whoever loves Him who brought to birth also loves him that has been born of Him.

2 By this we know that we love the children of God, when we love God and keep His commandments.

3 For this is the love of God that we should keep His commandments, and His com-

καὶ αἱ.ἐντολαὶ.αὐτοῦ βαρεῖαι οὐκ.εἰσιν. 4 ὅτι πᾶν τὸ γε-
and his commandments burdensome are not. Because all that has
γεννημένον ἐκ τοῦ θεοῦ νικᾷ τὸν κόσμον· καὶ αὕτη ἐστὶν
been begotten of God overcomes the world; and this is
ἡ νίκη ἡ νικήσασα τὸν κόσμον, ἡ.πίστις.ἡμῶν. 5 τίς[v]
the victory which overcame the world, our faith. Who
ἐστιν ὁ νικῶν τὸν κόσμον, εἰ.μὴ ὁ πιστεύων ὅτι Ἰησοῦς
is he that overcomes the world, but he that believes that Jesus
ἐστιν ὁ υἱὸς τοῦ θεοῦ;
is the Son of God?
6 Οὗτός ἐστιν ὁ ἐλθὼν δι' ὕδατος καὶ αἵματος, Ἰησοῦς
This is he who came by water and blood, Jesus
[w]ὁ[1] χριστός· οὐκ ἐν τῷ ὕδατι μόνον, [x]ἀλλ'[1] ἐν τῷ ὕδατι καὶ[y]
the Christ; not by water only, but by water and
τῷ αἵματι· καὶ τὸ πνεῦμά ἐστιν τὸ μαρτυροῦν ὅτι τὸ πνεῦμά
blood. And the Spirit it is that bears witness, because the Spirit
ἐστιν ἡ ἀλήθεια. 7 ὅτι τρεῖς εἰσιν οἱ μαρτυροῦντες [z]ἐν τῷ
is the truth. Because three there are who bear witness in
οὐρανῷ, ὁ πατήρ, ὁ λόγος, καὶ τὸ ἅγιον πνεῦμα· καὶ οὗτοι
heaven, the Father, the Word, and the Holy Ghost; and these
οἱ τρεῖς ἕν εἰσιν. 8 καὶ τρεῖς εἰσιν οἱ μαρτυροῦντες ἐν τῇ
three one are. And three there are who bear witness on
γῇ,[1] τὸ πνεῦμα, καὶ τὸ ὕδωρ, καὶ τὸ αἷμα, καὶ οἱ τρεῖς εἰς τὸ
earth, the Spirit, and the water, and the blood; and the three to the
ἕν εἰσιν. 9 εἰ τὴν μαρτυρίαν τῶν ἀνθρώπων λαμβάνο-
one [point] are. If the witness of men we re-
μεν, ἡ μαρτυρία τοῦ θεοῦ μείζων ἐστίν· ὅτι αὕτη ἐστὶν
ceive, the witness of God [2]greater [1]is. Because this is
ἡ μαρτυρία τοῦ θεοῦ, [a]ἣν[1] μεμαρτύρηκεν περὶ τοῦ.υἱοῦ.αὐτοῦ.
the witness of God which he has witnessed concerning his Son.
10 ὁ πιστεύων εἰς τὸν υἱὸν τοῦ θεοῦ ἔχει τὴν μαρτυρίαν [b] ἐν
He that believes on the Son of God has the witness in
[c]ἑαυτῷ·[1] ὁ μὴ.πιστεύων [d]τῷ θεῷ[1] ψεύστην πεποίηκεν αὐτόν,
himself; he that believes not God [4]a [5]liar [1]has [2]made [3]him.
ὅτι οὐ.πεπίστευκεν εἰς τὴν μαρτυρίαν, ἣν μεμαρτύρηκεν ὁ
because he has not believed in the witness which [2]has [3]witnessed
θεὸς περὶ τοῦ.υἱοῦ.αὐτοῦ. 11 καὶ αὕτη ἐστὶν ἡ μαρτυρία
[1]God concerning his Son. And this is the witness,
ὅτι ζωὴν αἰώνιον ἔδωκεν ἡμῖν ὁ θεός· καὶ αὕτη ἡ ζωὴ ἐν τῷ
that life eternal [2]gave [3]to [4]us [1]God; and this life [2]in
υἱῷ αὐτοῦ ἐστιν. 12 ὁ ἔχων τὸν υἱόν, ἔχει τὴν ζωήν· ὁ
[4]Son [3]his [1]is: he that has the Son, has life: he that
μὴ.ἔχων τὸν υἱὸν τοῦ θεοῦ, τὴν ζωὴν οὐκ.ἔχει.
has not the Son of God, life has not.
13 Ταῦτα ἔγραψα ὑμῖν [e]τοῖς πιστεύουσιν εἰς τὸ ὄνομα
These things I wrote to you who believe on the name
τοῦ υἱοῦ τοῦ θεοῦ,[1] ἵνα εἰδῆτε ὅτι ζωὴν [f]ἔχετε αἰώνιον,[1] [g]καὶ
of the Son of God, that ye may know that [4]life [1]ye [2]have [3]eternal, and
ἵνα πιστεύητε[1] εἰς τὸ ὄνομα τοῦ υἱοῦ τοῦ θεοῦ. 14 καὶ αὕτη
that ye may believe on the name of the Son of God. And this
ἐστὶν ἡ παῤῥησία ἣν ἔχομεν πρὸς αὐτόν, [h]ὅτι ἐάν τι[1]
is the boldness which we have towards him, that if anything
αἰτώμεθα κατὰ τὸ.θέλημα.αὐτοῦ, ἀκούει ἡμῶν· 15 καὶ
we may ask according to his will, he hears us. And
[i]ἐάν[1] οἴδαμεν ὅτι ἀκούει ἡμῶν, ὃ.[k]ἂν[1] αἰτώμεθα, οἴδαμεν ὅτι
if we know that he hears us, whatsoever we may ask, we know that
ἔχομεν τὰ αἰτήματα ἃ ᾐτήκαμεν [l]παρ'[1] αὐτοῦ.
we have the requests which we have asked from him.
16 Ἐάν τις [m]ἴδῃ[1] τὸν.ἀδελφὸν.αὐτοῦ ἁμαρτάνοντα
If anyone should see his brother sinning
ἁμαρτίαν μὴ πρὸς θάνατον, αἰτήσει, καὶ δώσει αὐτῷ ζωήν,
a sin not to death, he shall ask, and he shall give him life
τοῖς ἁμαρτάνουσιν μὴ πρὸς θάνατον. ἔστιν ἁμαρτία
for those that sin not to death. There is a sin
πρὸς θάνατον· οὐ περὶ ἐκείνης λέγω ἵνα ἐρωτήσῃ.
to death; not concerning that do I say that he should beseech.
17 πᾶσα ἀδικία ἁμαρτία ἐστίν, καὶ ἔστιν ἁμαρτία οὐ πρὸς
Every unrighteousness [2]sin [1]is; and there is a sin not to
θάνατον. 18 οἴδαμεν ὅτι πᾶς ὁ γεγεννημένος ἐκ τοῦ θεοῦ
death. We know that [2]anyone [3]that [4]has [5]been [6]begotten [7]of [8]God
(*lit.* everyone)
οὐχ ἁμαρτάνει· [n]ἀλλ'[1] ὁ γεννηθεὶς ἐκ τοῦ θεοῦ τηρεῖ [o]ἑαυ-
[1]not sins, but he that was begotten of God keeps him-
τόν,[1] καὶ ὁ πονηρὸς οὐχ.ἅπτεται αὐτοῦ. 19 οἴδαμεν ὅτι
self, and the wicked [one] does not touch him. We know that
ἐκ τοῦ θεοῦ ἐσμεν, καὶ ὁ κόσμος ὅλος ἐν τῷ πονηρῷ κεῖται.
of God we are, and the [2]world [1]whole in the wicked [one] lies.
20 [p]οἴδαμεν δὲ ὅτι ὁ υἱὸς τοῦ θεοῦ ἥκει, καὶ δέδωκεν ἡμῖν
And we know that the Son of God is come, and has given us
διάνοιαν ἵνα [q]γινώσκωμεν[1] τὸν ἀληθινόν· καὶ ἐσμεν
an understanding that we might know him that [is] true; and we are
ἐν τῷ ἀληθινῷ, ἐν τῷ.υἱῷ.αὐτοῦ Ἰησοῦ χριστῷ. οὗτός
in him that [is] true, in his Son Jesus Christ. He

mandments are not too heavy.
4 Because all that has been born of God
overcomes the world. And this is the victory that has overcome the world, *even*
our faith.
5 Who is he that overcomes the world but
he that believes that Jesus is the Son of
God?
6 This is He that came by means of water
and blood, Jesus the Christ not by water
only, but by water and blood. And it is the
Spirit that bears witness, because the Spirit
is the truth.
7 *For there are three who bear witness in*
Heaven, the Father, the Word, and the Holy
Spirit, and these three are one.
8 There are three who bear witness on the
earth, the Spirit and the water and the blood
and the three are *witnesses* to the one.
9 If we receive the witness of men, the
witness of God is greater. Because this is the
witness of God which He has witnessed
concerning His Son.
10 He that believes on the Son of God has
the witness in himself. He that does not
believe God has made Him a liar because
he has not believed in the witness which God
has testified concerning His Son.
11 And this is the witness that God gave to
us, everlasting life and this life is in His
Son.
12 He that has the Son has life. He that
does not have the Son of God does not have
life.
13 I wrote these things to you who believe
on the name of the Son of God, so that you
may know you have eternal life, and so that
you may believe on the name of the Son of
God.
14 And this is the confidence which we
have towards Him, that if we ask anything
according to His will, He hears us
15 and if we know that He hears us, whatever we may ask, we know that we have the
prayers which we have asked from Him.
16 If anyone should see a brother sinning a
sin not unto death, he shall ask, and He shall
give him life for those that do not sin unto
death. There is a sin unto death I do not
say that he should ask in regard to that.
17 All unrighteousness is sin and there is
a sin not to death.
18 We know that everyone who has been
born of God does not sin, but he who was
born of God guards himself, and the wicked
one does not touch him.
19 We know that we are of God, and the
whole world lies in the wicked *one.*
20 And we know that the Son of God has
come, and He has given us an understanding
so that we can know Him that is true. And
we are in Him that is true, in His Son Jesus
Christ. He is the true God and everlasting
life.

ἐστιν ὁ ἀληθινὸς θεός, καὶ ʳἡ' ζωὴ αἰώνιος.
is the true God, and life eternal.
21 Τεκνία, φυλάξατε ˢἑαυτούς' ἀπὸ τῶν εἰδώλων. ᵗἀμήν.‖
Little children, keep yourselves from idols. Amen.
ᵛ'Ιωάννου ἐπιστολὴ καθολικὴ πρώτη.‖
⁴Of ⁵John ³epistle ²general ¹first.

21 Little children, keep yourselves from idols. Amen.

The SECOND Letter of JOHN

'Ο πρεσβύτερος ᵇἐκλεκτῇ' ᶜκυρίᾳ' καὶ τοις.τέκνοις.αὐτῆς,
The elder to [the] elect lady and her children,
οὓς ἐγὼ ἀγαπῶ ἐν ἀληθείᾳ, καὶ οὐκ ἐγὼ μόνος, ἀλλὰ καὶ
whom I love in truth, and not I only, but also
πάντες οἱ ἐγνωκότες τὴν ἀλήθειαν, 2 διὰ τὴν ἀλή-
all those who have known the truth, for sake of the
θειαν τὴν μένουσαν ἐν ἡμῖν, καὶ μεθ' ἡμῶν ἔσται εἰς.τὸν.αἰῶνα·
truth which abides in us, and with us shall be for ever.
3 ἔσται μεθ' ᵈἡμῶν' χάρις, ἔλεος, εἰρήνη παρὰ θεοῦ πατρὸς
²Shall ¹be ⁴with ⁵us ¹grace, mercy, peace, from God [the] Father,
καὶ παρὰ ᵉκυρίου‖ 'Ιησοῦ χριστοῦ τοῦ υἱοῦ τοῦ πατρός, ἐν
and from [the] Lord Jesus Christ, the Son of the Father, in
ἀληθείᾳ καὶ ἀγάπῃ.
truth and love.
4 'Εχάρην λίαν ὅτι εὕρηκα ἐκ τῶν.τέκνων.σου περιπα-
I rejoiced exceedingly that I have found of thy children walk-
τοῦντας ἐν ἀληθείᾳ, καθὼς ἐντολὴν ἐλάβομεν παρὰ τοῦ
ing in truth, as commandment we received from the
πατρός. 5 καὶ νῦν ἐρωτῶ σε, ᶠκυρία,‖ οὐχ ὡς ἐντολὴν
Father And now I beseech thee, lady, not as a ²commandment
ᵍγράφω σοι καινήν,' ἀλλὰ ἣν ʰεἴχομεν' ἀπ' ἀρ-
³I ⁴write ⁵to ⁶thee ¹new, but that which we were having from [the] begin-
χῆς, ἵνα ἀγαπῶμεν ἀλλήλους. 6 καὶ αὕτη ἐστὶν ἡ ἀγάπη,
ning, that we should love one another. And this is love,
ἵνα περιπατῶμεν κατὰ τὰς.ἐντολὰς.αὐτοῦ. αὕτη ⁱἐστὶν ἡ
that we should walk according to his commandments. This is the
ἐντολή,' ᵏκαθὼς ἠκούσατε ἀπ' ἀρχῆς, ἵνα ἐν αὐτῇ
commandment, even as ye heard from [the] beginning, that in it
περιπατῆτε· 7 ὅτι πολλοὶ πλάνοι ˡεἰσῆλθον' εἰς τὸν
ye might walk. Because many deceivers entered into the
κόσμον, οἱ μὴ.ὁμολογοῦντες 'Ιησοῦν χριστὸν ἐρχόμενον ἐν
world, those who do not confess Jesus Christ coming in
σαρκί· οὗτός ἐστιν ὁ πλάνος καὶ ὁ ἀντίχριστος. 8 βλέπετε
flesh— this is the deceiver and the antichrist. See to
ἑαυτούς, ἵνα μὴ ᵐἀπολέσωμεν' ἃ ⁿεἰργασάμεθα,' ἀλλὰ
yourselves, that ²not ¹we ³may lose what things we wrought, but
μισθὸν πλήρη ᵒἀπολάβωμεν.‖ 9 πᾶς ὁ ᵖπαραβαίνων,' καὶ
a ²reward ¹full we may receive. ²Anyone ³who ⁴transgresses, ⁵and
(lit. everyone)
μὴ.μένων ἐν τῇ διδαχῇ τοῦ χριστοῦ, θεὸν οὐκ ἔχει· ὁ
⁶abides ⁷not ⁸in ⁹the ¹⁰teaching ¹¹of ¹²the ¹³Christ, ¹⁵God ¹not ¹⁴has. He that
μένων ἐν τῇ διδαχῇ ᵠτοῦ χριστοῦ,' οὗτος καὶ τὸν πατέρα
abides in the teaching of the Christ, this [one] both the Father
καὶ τὸν υἱὸν ἔχει. 10 εἴ τις ἔρχεται πρὸς ὑμᾶς, καὶ ταύτην
and the Son has. If anyone comes to you, and this
τὴν διδαχὴν οὐ.φέρει, μὴ.λαμβάνετε αὐτὸν εἰς οἰκίαν,
teaching does not bring, do not receive him into [the] house,
καὶ χαίρειν αὐτῷ μὴ.λέγετε· 11 ὁ.ʳγὰρ λέγων' αὐτῷ χαίρειν,
and ³Hail ! ⁴to ⁵him ¹say ²not ; for he who says to him Hail !
κοινωνεῖ τοῖς ἔργοις αὐτοῦ τοῖς πονηροῖς.
partakes in ³works ¹his ²evil.
12 Πολλὰ ἔχων ὑμῖν γράφειν, οὐκ.ˢἠβουλήθην' διὰ χάρ-
Many things having ³to ⁴you ¹to ²write, I would not with pa-
του καὶ μέλανος· ᵗἀλλὰ ἐλπίζω' ᵘἐλθεῖν' πρὸς ὑμᾶς, καὶ στόμα
per and ink; but I hope to come to you, and mouth
πρὸς στόμα λαλῆσαι, ἵνα ἡ χαρὰ ʷἡμῶν' ˣῇ.πεπληρωμένη.‖
to mouth to speak, that ²joy ¹our may be full.
13 ἀσπάζεταί σε τὰ τέκνα τῆς ἀδελφῆς σου τῆς ʸἐκλεκ-
⁷Salute ⁸thee ¹the ²children ⁶sister ³of ⁴thine ⁵elect.
τῆς.‖ ᶻἀμήν.‖
Amen.

ᵃ'Ιωάννου ἐπιστολὴ δευτέρα.‖
³Of ⁴John ²epistle ¹second.

1 The elder to the elect lady and her children, whom I love in truth. And not only I, but also all those who have known the truth.

2 for the sake of the truth which lives in us and shall be with us forever.

3 Grace, mercy and peace shall be with us, from God the Father and from the Lord Jesus Christ, the Son of the Father, in truth and love.

4 I was so very happy that I have found some of your children walking in truth, just as we received commandment from the Father.

5 And now I beg of you, lady, not as though I were writing a new commandment to you, but that which we had from the beginning, that we should love one another.

6 And this is love, that we walk according to His commandment. This is the commandment, even as you heard from the beginning, that you might walk in it.

7 Because many deceivers have gone out into the world, those who do not confess that Jesus Christ is coming in the flesh – this is the deceiver and the antichrist.

8 Watch yourselves so that you may not lose what things we have worked out, but that we may receive a full reward.

9 Whoever oversteps and does not continue in the teaching of Christ does not have God. He that continues in the teaching of Christ is the one who has both the Father and the Son.

10 If anyone comes to you and does not bring this teaching, do not receive him into your house, and do not speak to him a cheerful greeting.

11 For he who speaks to him a cheerful greeting takes part in his evil works.

12 Since I have many things to write to you, I do not want to *write* with paper and ink, but I hope to come to you and to speak mouth to mouth so that our joy may be full.

13 The children of your elect sister greet you. Amen.

Ὁ πρεσβύτερος Γαΐῳ τῷ ἀγαπητῷ, ὃν ἐγὼ ἀγαπῶ ἐν
The elder to Gaius the beloved, whom I love in
ἀληθείᾳ.
truth.
2 Ἀγαπητέ, περὶ πάντων εὔχομαί σε εὐοδοῦσθαι καὶ
Beloved, concerning all things I wish thee to prosper and
ὑγιαίνειν, καθὼς εὐοδοῦταί σου ἡ ψυχή. 3 ἐχάρην γὰρ
be in health, even as prospers thy soul. For I rejoiced
λίαν ἐρχομένων ἀδελφῶν καὶ μαρτυρούντων σου τῇ
exceedingly, coming [the] brethren and bearing witness of thy
ἀληθείᾳ, καθὼς σὺ ἐν ἀληθείᾳ περιπατεῖς. 4 μειζοτέραν τού-
truth, even as thou in truth walkest. Greater than
των οὐκ ἔχω χαράν, ἵνα ἀκούω τὰ ἐμὰ τέκνα ἐν
these things I have not joy, that I should hear of my children in
ἀληθείᾳ περιπατοῦντα. 5 Ἀγαπητέ, πιστὸν ποιεῖς ὃ ἐὰν
truth walking. Beloved, faithfully thou doest whatever
ἐργάσῃ εἰς τοὺς ἀδελφοὺς καὶ εἰς τοὺς
thou mayest have wrought towards the brethren and towards
ξένους, 6 οἳ ἐμαρτύρησάν σου τῇ ἀγάπῃ ἐνώπιον ἐκ-
strangers, (who witnessed of thy love before [the] as-
κλησίας· οὓς καλῶς ποιήσεις προπέμψας ἀξίως τοῦ θεοῦ·
sembly) whom well thou wilt do setting forward worthily of God;
7 ὑπὲρ γὰρ τοῦ ὀνόματος ἐξῆλθον μηδὲν λαμβάνοντες
for for the name they went forth, nothing taking
ἀπὸ τῶν ἐθνῶν. 8 ἡμεῖς οὖν ὀφείλομεν ἀπολαμβάνειν
from the nations. We therefore ought to receive
τοὺς τοιούτους, ἵνα συνεργοὶ γινώμεθα τῇ ἀληθείᾳ. 9 Ἔ-
such, that fellow-workers we may be with the truth. I
γραψα τῇ ἐκκλησίᾳ· ἀλλ' ὁ φιλοπρωτεύων αὐτῶν
wrote to the assembly; but who loves to be first among them
Διοτρεφὴς οὐκ ἐπιδέχεται ἡμᾶς. 10 διὰ τοῦτο, ἐὰν ἔλθω,
Diotrephes, receives not us. On account of this, if I come,
ὑπομνήσω αὐτοῦ τὰ ἔργα ἃ ποιεῖ, λόγοις
I will bring to remembrance of him the works which he does, with words
πονηροῖς φλυαρῶν ἡμᾶς· καὶ μὴ ἀρκούμενος ἐπὶ τούτοις,
evil prating against us; and not satisfied with these,
οὔτε αὐτὸς ἐπιδέχεται τοὺς ἀδελφούς, καὶ τοὺς βουλομέ-
neither himself receives the brethren, and those who would
νους κωλύει, καὶ ἐκ τῆς ἐκκλησίας ἐκβάλλει. 11 Ἀγα-
he forbids, and from the assembly casts [them] out. Be-
πητέ, μὴ μιμοῦ τὸ κακόν, ἀλλὰ τὸ ἀγαθόν. ὁ
loved, do not imitate that which [is] evil, but what [is] good. He that
ἀγαθοποιῶν, ἐκ τοῦ θεοῦ ἐστιν· ὁ δὲ κακοποιῶν οὐχ ἑώ-
does good, of God is; but he that does evil not has
ρακεν τὸν θεόν. 12 Δημητρίῳ μεμαρτύρηται ὑπὸ πάντων, καὶ
seen God. To Demetrius witness is borne by all, and
ὑπ' αὐτῆς τῆς ἀληθείας· καὶ ἡμεῖς δὲ μαρτυροῦμεν, καὶ
by itself the truth; and we also bear witness, and
οἴδατε ὅτι ἡ μαρτυρία ἡμῶν ἀληθής ἐστιν.
ye know that our witness true is.
13 Πολλὰ εἶχον γράφειν, ἀλλ' οὐ θέλω διὰ μέλανος καὶ
Many things I had to write, but I will not with ink and
καλάμου σοι γράψαι· 14 ἐλπίζω δὲ εὐθέως ἰδεῖν σε,
pen to thee to write; but I hope immediately to see thee
καὶ στόμα πρὸς στόμα λαλήσομεν. 15 Εἰρήνη σοι. ἀσπά-
and mouth to mouth we shall speak. Peace to thee. Sa-
ζονταί σε οἱ φίλοι. ἀσπάζου τοὺς φίλους κατ' ὄνομα.
lute thee the friends. Salute the friends by name.
Ἰωάννου ἐπιστολὴ καθολικὴ τρίτη.
Of John epistle general third.

[1]The elder to Gaius the beloved, whom I love in truth.

[2]Beloved, in regard to all things I wish you to do well and to be in good health, even as your soul is doing well.

[3]For I was very happy when the brothers came and testified of your truth, even as you walk in truth.

[4]I have no joy greater than this, that I should hear of my children walking in truth.

[5]Beloved, faithfully you do whatever you do for the brothers and for strangers

[6](who witnessed of your love before the church), whom you will do well to set forward in a way worthy of God.

[7]For they went out for the Name, taking nothing from the nations.

[8]We then ought to receive such, that we may be fellow-helpers with the truth.

[9]I wrote to the church, but Di-ot-re-phes, who loves to be chief among them, did not receive us.

[10]For this reason, if I come, I will bring the works which he does to his memory, speaking against us with evil words. And not satisfied with these, he himself does not receive the brothers. And he forbids those who would do so, throwing them out of the church.

[11]Beloved, do not follow that which is evil, but what is good. He that does good is of God, but he that does evil has not seen God.

[12]De-me-tri-us has a good report by all, and by the truth itself. And we also bear witness, and you know that our witness is true.

[13]I had many things to write, but I do not want to write to you with pen and ink.

[14]But I hope to see you shortly, and we shall speak mouth to mouth. Peace be to you. The friends greet you. Greet the friends by name.

The Letter of JUDE

ΙΟΥΔΑΣ Ἰησοῦ χριστοῦ δοῦλος, ἀδελφὸς δὲ Ἰακώβου, τοῖς
Jude, of Jesus Christ bondman, and brother of James, to the
ἐν θεῷ πατρὶ ἡγιασμένοις καὶ Ἰησοῦ χριστῷ τετηρη-
in God [the] Father sanctified and in Jesus Christ kept
μένοις κλητοῖς· 2 ἔλεος ὑμῖν καὶ εἰρήνη καὶ ἀγάπη
called [ones]. Mercy to you and peace, and love
πληθυνθείη.
be multiplied.
3 Ἀγαπητοί, πᾶσαν σπουδὴν ποιούμενος γράφειν ὑμῖν
Beloved, all diligence using to write to you
περὶ τῆς κοινῆς σωτηρίας, ἀνάγκην ἔσχον γράψαι ὑμῖν,
concerning the common salvation, necessity I had to write to you,
παρακαλῶν ἐπαγωνίζεσθαι τῇ ἅπαξ παραδοθείσῃ τοῖς
exhorting [you] to contend earnestly for the once delivered to the
ἁγίοις πίστει. 4 παρεισέδυσαν γάρ τινες ἄνθρωποι, οἱ
saints faith. For came in stealthily certain men, they who

[1]Jude, a servant of Jesus Christ and brother of James, to the ones who are set apart in God the Father and kept in Jesus Christ the called ones.

[2]Mercy and peace and love be multiplied to you.

[3]Beloved, using all carefulness to write to you regarding the common salvation, I had need to write to you urging you to earnestly contend for the faith once for all delivered to the saints.

[4]For certain men came secretly creeping in,

πάλαι προγεγραμμένοι εἰς τοῦτο τὸ κρίμα, ἀσεβεῖς
of old have been before marked out to this sentence, ungodly [persons]
τὴν τοῦ θεοῦ.ἡμῶν [d]χάριν[‖] μετατιθέντες εἰς ἀσέλγειαν καὶ τὸν
[2]the [4]of [5]our [6]God [3]grace [1]changing into licentiousness and [3]the
μόνον δεσπότην [e]θεὸν[‖] καὶ κύριον.ἡμῶν Ἰησοῦν χριστὸν
[2]only [4]master— [5]God [6]and [7]our [8]Lord [9]Jesus [10]Christ
ἀρνούμενοι.
[1]denying.

5 Ὑπομνῆσαι.δὲ ὑμᾶς βούλομαι, εἰδότας [f]ὑμᾶς[‖] ἅπαξ
But [3]put [4]in [6]remembrance [5]you [1]I [2]would, [8]knowing [7]you once
[g]τοῦτο,[‖] ὅτι [h]ὁ[‖] [i]κύριος[‖] λαὸν ἐκ γῆς Αἰγύπτου σώ-
this, that the Lord a people out of [the] land of Egypt having
σας, τὸ.δεύτερον τοὺς μὴ.πιστεύσαντας ἀπώλεσεν. 6 ἀγ-
saved, in the second place those who believed not he destroyed.
γέλους τε τοὺς μὴ.τηρήσαντας τὴν.ἑαυτῶν ἀρχήν, ἀλλὰ
[2]Angels [1]and who kept not their own first-state, but
ἀπολιπόντας τὸ.ἴδιον οἰκητήριον, εἰς κρίσιν μεγάλης
left their own dwelling, unto [the] judgment of [the] great
ἡμέρας δεσμοῖς ἀϊδίοις ὑπὸ ζόφον τετήρηκεν· 7 ὡς Σόδομα
day in [2]bonds [1]eternal under darkness he keeps; as Sodom
καὶ Γόμοῤῥα, καὶ αἱ περὶ αὐτὰς πόλεις, τὸν ὅμοιον [l]τού-
and Gomorrha, and the [2]around [3]them [1]cities, in like [2]with
τοις τρόπον[‖] ἐκπορνεύσασαι, καὶ ἀπελθοῦσαι
[3]them [1]manner having given themselves to fornication and having gone
ὀπίσω σαρκὸς ἑτέρας, πρόκεινται δεῖγμα, πυρὸς αἰωνίου
after [2]flesh [1]other, are set forth as an example, [4]of [6]fire [5]eternal
δίκην ὑπέχουσαι. 8 ὁμοίως.μέντοι καὶ οὗτοι ἐνυπνια-
[[3]the] [3]penalty [1]undergoing. Yet in like manner also these dream-
ζόμενοι, σάρκα μὲν μιαίνουσιν, κυριότητα.δὲ ἀθετοῦσιν,
ers [[2]the] [3]flesh [1]defile, and [3]lordship [1]set [2]aside,
δόξας.δὲ βλασφημοῦσιν. 9 [m]ὁ.δὲ[‖] Μιχαὴλ ὁ ἀρχάγγελος,
and [4]glories [1]speak [2]evil [3]of. But Michael the archangel,
[n]ὅτε[‖] τῷ διαβόλῳ διακρινόμενος διελέγετο περὶ τοῦ [o]Μω-
when with the devil disputing he reasoned about the [2]of
σέως[‖] σώματος, οὐκ.ἐτόλμησεν κρίσιν ἐπενεγκεῖν βλασ-
[3]Moses [1]body, did not dare [6]a [7]charge [1]to [2]bring [3]against [[4]him] [6]rail-
φημίας, [p]ἀλλ'[‖] εἶπεν, Ἐπιτιμήσαι σοι κύριος. 10 οὗτοι.δὲ
ing, but said, [3]Rebuke [4]thee [[1]the] [2]Lord. But these,
ὅσα μὲν οὐκ.οἴδασιν βλασφημοῦσιν· ὅσα.δὲ
whatever things they know not they speak evil of; but whatever things
φυσικῶς, ὡς τὰ ἄλογα ζῶα, ἐπίστανται, ἐν τούτοις
naturally, as the irrational animals, they understand, in these things
φθείρονται. 11 οὐαὶ αὐτοῖς· ὅτι τῇ ὁδῷ τοῦ Κάϊν
they corrupt themselves. Woe to them! because in the way of Cain
ἐπορεύθησαν, καὶ τῇ πλάνῃ τοῦ Βαλαὰμ μισθοῦ ἐξεχύθησαν,
they went, and to the error of Balaam for reward rushed,
καὶ τῇ ἀντιλογίᾳ τοῦ Κορὲ ἀπώλοντο. 12 οὗτοί εἰσιν [q] ἐν
and in the gainsaying of Korah perished. These are in
ταῖς.ἀγάπαις.ὑμῶν σπιλάδες, συνευωχούμενοι [r] ἀφόβως,[r]
your love feasts sunken rocks, feasting together [with you] fearlessly,
ἑαυτοὺς ποιμαίνοντες· νεφέλαι ἄνυδροι, ὑπὸ ἀνέμων
[2]themselves [1]pasturing; clouds without water, by winds
[s]περιφερόμεναι·[‖] δένδρα φθινοπωρινὰ ἄκαρπα δὶς ἀποθα-
being carried about, [2]trees [1]autumnal, without fruit, twice dead,
νόντα ἐκριζωθέντα· 13 κύματα ἄγρια θαλάσσης ἐπαφρίζοντα
rooted up; [2]waves [1]wild of [the] sea, foaming out
τὰς.ἑαυτῶν αἰσχύνας· ἀστέρες πλανῆται, οἷς ὁ ζόφος τοῦ
their own shames; [2]stars [1]wandering, to whom the gloom
σκότους εἰς.[t]τὸν[‖].αἰῶνα τετήρηται. 14 [v]προεφήτευσεν[‖].δὲ καὶ
of darkness for ever has been kept. And [8]prophesied [7]also
τούτοις ἕβδομος ἀπὸ Ἀδὰμ Ἐνώχ, λέγων, Ἰδού,
[8]as [9]to [10]these [[2]the] [3]seventh [4]from [5]Adam, [1]Enoch, saying, Behold,
ἦλθεν κύριος ἐν [w]μυριάσιν ἁγίαις[‖] αὐτοῦ, 15 ποιῆσαι
[6]came [[1]the] [2]Lord amidst [3]myriads [2]holy [1]his, to execute
κρίσιν κατὰ πάντων, καὶ [x]ἐξελέγξαι[‖] πάντας τοὺς ἀσεβεῖς
judgment against all, and to convict all the ungodly
[y]αὐτῶν[‖] περὶ πάντων τῶν ἔργων [z]ἀσεβείας[‖] αὐτῶν ὧν
of them concerning all [2]works [3]of [4]ungodliness [1]their which
ἠσέβησαν, καὶ περὶ πάντων τῶν σκληρῶν [a] ὧν
they did ungodlily, and concerning all the hard [things] which
ἐλάλησαν κατ' αὐτοῦ ἁμαρτωλοὶ ἀσεβεῖς. 16 οὗτοί εἰσιν
[3]spoke [4]against [5]him [2]sinners [1]ungodly. These are
γογγυσταί, μεμψίμοιροι, κατὰ τὰς.ἐπιθυμίας.αὐτῶν πορευό-
murmurers, complainers, [2]after [3]their [4]lusts [1]walk-
μενοι· καὶ τὸ.στόμα.αὐτῶν λαλεῖ ὑπέρογκα, θαυμάζοντες
ing; and their mouth speaks great swelling [words], admiring
πρόσωπα ὠφελείας χάριν. 17 ὑμεῖς.δέ, ἀγαπητοί, μνή-
persons [5]profit [1]for [2]the [3]sake [4]of. But ye, beloved, re-
σθητε τῶν [b]ῥημάτων τῶν προειρημένων[‖] ὑπὸ τῶν ἀπο-
member the words which have been spoken before by the apo-
στόλων τοῦ.κυρίου.ἡμῶν Ἰησοῦ χριστοῦ· 18 ὅτι ἔλεγον ὑμῖν,
stles of our Lord Jesus Christ, that they said to you,

they who were before of old marked out to this condemnation, ungodly ones who are changing the grace of our God into evil-doing and denying the only Master our God and Lord, Jesus Christ.

5 But I would have you remember, though you once knew this, that when the Lord had saved a people out of the land of Egypt, in the second place He destroyed those who did not believe.

6 And angels who did not keep their own original state, but left their own dwelling-place, He keeps in everlasting chains under darkness to the judgment of the great Day.

7 Just as Sodom and Go-mor-rah (and the cities around them in the same manner with them) had given themselves to fornication and had gone after other flesh, they are set forth as an example, undergoing punishment of everlasting fire.

8 Yet in the same way these dreamers also defile the flesh, despise government and speak evil of leaders.

9 But Michael the archangel, when he was setting himself against the devil, arguing about the body of Moses, did not dare to bring an evil charge against him. But *he* said, The Lord rebuke you!

10 But these – whatever things they do not know, they speak evil of – but what they know by nature, like the animals without reason, they corrupt themselves in these things.

11 Woe to them! Because they have gone in the way of Cain and have run greedily into the error of Balaam for reward, and have been lost in the contradiction of Korah.

12 These are hidden rocks in your love feasts, feasting together *with you*, without fear setting themselves out to pasture. *They are* clouds without water, being carried about by winds. *They are* autumn trees without fruit, twice dead, plucked up by the roots.

13 *They are* wild waves of the sea foaming out their own shame – wandering stars to whom the blackness of darkness has been kept forever.

14 And Enoch, the seventh from Adam, also foretold of these, saying, "Behold, the Lord comes with myriads of His holy ones

15 to execute judgment against all, and to convict all the ones who were ungodly among them regarding all their works of ungodliness which they did in an ungodly way – and regarding all the hard things which ungodly sinners spoke against Him."

16 These are murmurers, complainers, walking after their own lusts. And their mouth speaks great swelling *words*, admiring persons for the sake of gain.

17 But you, beloved, remember the words which have been spoken before by the apostles of our Lord Jesus Christ

[c]ὅτι' [v]ἐν ἐσχάτῳ χρόνῳ" ἔσονται ἐμπαῖκται, κατὰ τὰς
that in [the] last time there will be mockers, [2]after
ἑαυτῶν ἐπιθυμίας πορευόμενοι τῶν ἀσεβειῶν. 19 οὗτοί εἰσιν
[3]their [4]own [5]desires [1]walking of ungodlinesses. These are
οἱ ἀποδιορίζοντες[e], ψυχικοί, πνεῦμα μὴ
they who set apart [themselves], natural [men], [3]the] [4]Spirit [1]not
ἔχοντες. 20 ὑμεῖς.δέ, ἀγαπητοί, [f]τῇ.ἁγιωτάτῃ.ὑμῶν πίστει
[2]having. But ye, beloved, on your most holy faith
ἐποικοδομοῦντες ἑαυτούς," ἐν πνεύματι ἁγίῳ προσευχό-
building up yourselves, in [the] [2]Spirit [1]Holy pray-
μενοι, 21 ἑαυτοὺς ἐν ἀγάπῃ θεοῦ τηρήσατε, προσδεχό-
ing, [2]yourselves [3]in [[4]the] [5]love [6]of [7]God [1]keep, await-
μενοι τὸ ἔλεος τοῦ.κυρίου.ἡμῶν Ἰησοῦ χριστοῦ, εἰς ζωὴν
ing the mercy of our Lord Jesus Christ unto life
αἰώνιον. 22 καὶ οὓς μὲν [g]ἐλεεῖτε διακρινόμενοι·" 23 [h]οὓς.δὲ
eternal. And [2]some [1]pity, making a difference but others
ἐν φόβῳ σώζετε, ἐκ τοῦ πυρὸς ἁρπάζοντες," μισοῦντες
with fear save, out of the fire snatching [them]; hating
καὶ τὸν ἀπὸ τῆς σαρκὸς ἐσπιλωμένον χιτῶνα.
even the [3]by [4]the [5]flesh [2]spotted [1]garment.
24 Τῷ.δὲ δυναμένῳ φυλάξαι [i]αὐτοὺς" ἀπταίστους, καὶ
But to him who is able to keep them without stumbling, and
στῆσαι κατενώπιον τῆς.δόξης.αὐτοῦ ἀμώμους ἐν ἀγαλ-
to set [them] before his glory blameless with exul-
λιάσει, 25 μόνῳ [k]σοφῷ" θεῷ σωτῆρι.ἡμῶν, [l] δόξα [m]καὶ"
tation, to [the] only wise God our Saviour, [be] glory and
μεγαλωσύνη, κράτος καὶ ἐξουσία, [n] καὶ νῦν καὶ εἰς πάντας
greatness, might and authority, both now, and to all
τοὺς αἰῶνας. ἀμήν.
the ages. Amen.
[o]Ἐπιστολὴ Ἰούδα καθολική."
[2]Epistle [3]of [4]Jude [1]general.

[18]that they told you that there will be
mockers in the last time, walking after their
own ungodly lusts.
[19]These are they who set *themselves* apart,
animal-like ones who do not have the Spirit.
[20]But you, beloved, building yourselves up
in your most holy faith, praying in the Holy
Spirit,
[21]keep yourselves in the love of God,
looking for the mercy of our Lord Jesus
Christ to everlasting life.
[22]And have pity on some, making a difference.
[23]But save others with fear, snatching
them out of the fire, hating even the
clothing spotted by the flesh.
[24]And to Him who is able to keep you
from falling, and to present you without
blame before the presence of His glory, with
unspeakable joy
[25]to the only wise God, our Savior, be
glory and majesty, authority and power,
both now and forever. Amen.

The REVELATION of John

ΑΠΟΚΑΛΥΨΙΣ Ἰησοῦ χριστοῦ, ἣν ἔδωκεν αὐτῷ ὁ θεός,
Revelation of Jesus Christ, which [2]gave [3]to [4]him [1]God,
δεῖξαι τοῖς.δούλοις.αὐτοῦ ἃ δεῖ γενέσθαι ἐν.τάχει, καὶ
to shew to his bondmen what things must take place shortly: and
ἐσήμανεν ἀποστείλας διὰ τοῦ.ἀγγέλου.αὐτοῦ τῷ.δούλῳ.αὐτοῦ
he signified [it], having sent by his angel to his bondman
[b]Ἰωάννῃ," 2 ὃς ἐμαρτύρησεν τὸν λόγον τοῦ θεοῦ καὶ τὴν
John, who testified the word of God and the
μαρτυρίαν Ἰησοῦ χριστοῦ, ὅσα [c]τε' [d]εἶδεν." 3 μακά-
testimony of Jesus Christ, [2]whatsoever [3]things [1]and he saw. Bless-
ριος ὁ ἀναγινώσκων, καὶ οἱ ἀκούοντες [e]τοὺς λόγους"
ed [is] he that reads, and they that hear the words
τῆς προφητείας, καὶ τηροῦντες τὰ ἐν αὐτῇ γεγραμμένα·
of the prophecy, and keep the things [2]in [3]it [1]written;
ὁ.γὰρ καιρὸς ἐγγύς.
for the time [is] near.
4 [f]Ἰωάννης" ταῖς ἑπτὰ ἐκκλησίαις ταῖς ἐν τῇ Ἀσίᾳ·
John to the seven assemblies which [are] in Asia:
χάρις ὑμῖν καὶ εἰρήνη ἀπὸ [g]τοῦ' ὁ ὢν καὶ ὁ ἦν καὶ ὁ
Grace to you and peace from him who is and who was and who[is]
ἐρχόμενος· καὶ ἀπὸ τῶν ἑπτὰ πνευμάτων [h]ἃ' [i]ἐστιν' ἐνώπιον
to come; and from the seven Spirits which are before
τοῦ.θρόνου.αὐτοῦ· 5 καὶ ἀπὸ Ἰησοῦ χριστοῦ, ὁ μάρτυς ὁ
his throne; and from Jesus Christ, the [2]witness
πιστός, ὁ πρωτότοκος [k]ἐκ' τῶν νεκρῶν, καὶ ὁ ἄρχων τῶν
[1]faithful, the firstborn from among the dead, and the ruler of the
βασιλέων τῆς γῆς· τῷ [l]ἀγαπήσαντι" ἡμᾶς, καὶ [m]λού-
kings of the earth. To him who loved us, and wash-
σαντι' ἡμᾶς [n]ἀπὸ' τῶν.ἁμαρτιῶν.[o]ἡμῶν" ἐν τῷ.αἵματι.αὐτοῦ·
ed us from our sins in his blood,
6 καὶ ἐποίησεν [p]ἡμᾶς" [q]βασιλεῖς καὶ' ἱερεῖς τῷ θεῷ καὶ πατρὶ
and made us kings and priests to [2]God [3]and [4]Father
αὐτοῦ· αὐτῷ ἡ δόξα καὶ τὸ κράτος εἰς τοὺς αἰῶνας [r]τῶν
[1]his: to him [be] the glory and the might to the ages of the
αἰώνων." ἀμήν.
ages. Amen.
7 Ἰδού, ἔρχεται μετὰ τῶν νεφελῶν, καὶ ὄψεται αὐτὸν πᾶς
Behold, he comes with the clouds, and shall see him every
ὀφθαλμός, καὶ οἵτινες αὐτὸν ἐξεκέντησαν· καὶ κόψονται
eye, and they which [2]him [1]pierced, and [7]shall [8]wail
ἐπ' αὐτὸν πᾶσαι αἱ φυλαὶ τῆς γῆς. ναί, ἀμήν.
[9]on [10]account [11]of [12]him [1]all [2]the [3]tribes [4]of [5]the [6]earth. Yea, amen.
8 Ἐγώ εἰμι τὸ [s]Α" καὶ τὸ [t]Ω,' [v]ἀρχὴ καὶ τέλος·" λέγει
I am the A and the Ω, beginning and ending, says

CHAPTER 1

[1]The revelation of Jesus Christ, which God
gave to Him to show to His servants those
things which must take place shortly. And
He made it known by sending His angel to
His servant John,
[2]who bore record of the word of God and
the witness of Jesus Christ, and whatever
things he saw.
[3]Blessed is he that reads and those that
hear the words of this prophecy, and keep
the things written in it, for the time is near.
[4]John, to the seven churches which are in
Asia: Grace to you and peace from Him who
is and who was and who is to come – and
from the seven Spirits which are before His
throne
[5]and from Jesus Christ, the faithful Witness, the First-born from among the dead
and the Ruler of the kings of the earth. To
Him who loved us and washed us from our
sins in His blood
[6]and made us kings and priests to His God
and Father – to Him be the glory and the
might forever and ever. Amen.
[7]Behold! He comes with the clouds! And
every eye shall see Him and those who
pierced Him *shall see Him* – and all the
tribes of the earth shall wail on account of
Him. Even so, Amen.
[8]I am the A and the Z, the Beginning and
the Ending, says the Lord, who is and who

[w]ὁ κύριος," ὁ ὢν καὶ ὁ ἦν καὶ ὁ ἐρχόμενος, ὁ παντο-
the Lord, who is and who was and who [is] to come, the Al-
κράτωρ.
mighty.

9 Ἐγὼ [x]Ἰωάννης," ὁ [y]καὶ" ἀδελφὸς ὑμῶν καὶ [z]συγκοινωνὸς[z]
I John, also [2]brother [1]your and fellow-partaker
ἐν τῇ θλίψει καὶ [a]ἐν τῇ[1] βασιλείᾳ καὶ ὑπομονῇ [b c]Ἰησοῦ χριστοῦ," ἐγενόμην ἐν τῇ νήσῳ τῇ καλουμένῃ Πάτμῳ, διὰ
in the tribulation and in the kingdom and endurance of Jesus Christ, was in the island which [is] called Patmos, because of
τὸν λόγον τοῦ θεοῦ καὶ [d]διὰ" τὴν μαρτυρίαν Ἰησοῦ [e]χριστοῦ."
the word of God and because of the testimony of Jesus Christ.

10 ἐγενόμην ἐν πνεύματι ἐν τῇ κυριακῇ ἡμέρᾳ· καὶ
I became in [the] Spirit on the Lord's day, and
ἤκουσα ὀπίσω μου φωνὴν μεγάλην ὡς σάλπιγγος,
I heard behind me a [2]voice [1]loud as of a trumpet,

11 λεγούσης, [f]Ἐγώ εἰμι τὸ Α καὶ τὸ Ω, ὁ πρῶτος καὶ ὁ ἔσχατος· καί," Ὃ βλέπεις γράψον εἰς βιβλίον, καὶ πέμψον ταῖς [g]ἐκκλησίαις [h]ταῖς ἐν Ἀσίᾳ," εἰς Ἔφεσον, καὶ εἰς [i]Σμύρναν," καὶ εἰς Πέργαμον, καὶ εἰς [k]Θυάτειρα," καὶ εἰς Σάρδεις, καὶ εἰς [l]Φιλαδέλφειαν," καὶ εἰς [m]Λαοδίκειαν."
saying, I am the A and the Ω, the first and the last; and, What thou seest write in a book, and send to the assemblies which [are] in Asia: to Ephesus, and to Smyrna, and to Pergamos, and to Thyatira, and to Sardis, and to Philadelphia, and to Laodicea.

12 καὶ ἐπέστρεψα βλέπειν τὴν φωνὴν ἥτις [n]ἐλάλησεν" μετ' ἐμοῦ· καὶ ἐπιστρέψας εἶδον ἑπτὰ λυχνίας χρυσᾶς,
And I turned to see the voice which spoke with me, and having turned I saw seven [2]lampstands [1]golden,

13 καὶ ἐν μέσῳ τῶν [o]ἑπτὰ" λυχνιῶν ὅμοιον [p]υἱῷ" ἀνθρώπου, ἐνδεδυμένον ποδήρη, καὶ περιεζωσμένον πρὸς τοῖς [q]μαστοῖς" ζώνην [r]χρυσῆν."
and in [the] midst of the seven lampstands [one] like [the] Son of man, clothed in [a garment] reaching to the feet, and [4]girt [5]about [6]with [1]at [2]the [3]breasts [7]a [9]girdle [8]golden:

14 ἡ.δὲ.κεφαλὴ.αὐτοῦ καὶ αἱ τρίχες λευκαὶ [s]ὡσεὶ[s] ἔριον λευκόν, ὡς χιών· καὶ οἱ.ὀφθαλμοὶ.αὐτοῦ ὡς φλὸξ πυρός·
and his head and hair white as if [2]wool [1]white, as snow; and his eyes as a flame of fire;

15 καὶ οἱ.πόδες.αὐτοῦ ὅμοιοι χαλκολιβάνῳ ὡς ἐν καμίνῳ [t]πεπυρωμένοι·" καὶ ἡ.φωνὴ.αὐτοῦ ὡς φωνὴ ὑδάτων πολλῶν·
and his feet like fine brass, as if [3]in [4]a [5]furnace [1they] [2]glowed; and his voice as [the] voice of [2]waters [1]many,

16 καὶ ἔχων ἐν τῇ δεξιᾷ [v]αὐτοῦ χειρὶ" ἀστέρας ἑπτά· καὶ ἐκ τοῦ.στόματος.αὐτοῦ ῥομφαία δίστομος ὀξεῖα ἐκπορευομένη· καὶ ἡ.ὄψις.αὐτοῦ ὡς ὁ ἥλιος φαίνει ἐν τῇ.δυνάμει.αὐτοῦ.
and having in [2]right [1]his hand [2]stars [1]seven, and out of his mouth a [3]sword [2]two-edged [1]sharp going forth, and his countenance as the sun shines in its power.

17 καὶ ὅτε εἶδον αὐτόν, ἔπεσα πρὸς τοὺς.πόδας.αὐτοῦ ὡς νεκρός· καὶ [w]ἐπέθηκεν" τὴν.δεξιὰν.αὐτοῦ [x]χεῖρα" ἐπ' ἐμέ, λέγων [y]μοι," Μὴ.φοβοῦ· ἐγώ εἰμι ὁ πρῶτος καὶ ὁ ἔσχατος,
And when I saw him, I fell at his feet as dead: and he laid his right hand upon me, saying to me, Fear not; I am the first and the last,

18 καὶ ὁ ζῶν, καὶ ἐγενόμην νεκρός, καὶ ἰδοὺ ζῶν εἰμι εἰς τοὺς αἰῶνας τῶν αἰώνων· [z]ἀμήν·" καὶ ἔχω τὰς κλεῖς τοῦ [a]ᾅδου καὶ τοῦ θανάτου."
and the living [one]: and I became dead, and behold [3]alive [1]I [2]am to the ages of the ages, Amen; and have the keys of hades and of death.

19 γράψον [b] ἃ εἶδες, καὶ ἅ εἰσιν, καὶ ἃ μέλλει [c]γίνεσθαι[1] μετὰ ταῦτα·
Write the things which thou sawest and the things which are, and the things which are about to take place after these.

20 τὸ μυστήριον τῶν ἑπτὰ ἀστέρων [d]ὧν" εἶδες [e]ἐπὶ τῆς δεξιᾶς" μου, καὶ τὰς ἑπτὰ λυχνίας τὰς χρυσᾶς. οἱ ἑπτὰ ἀστέρες ἄγγελοι τῶν ἑπτὰ ἐκκλησιῶν εἰσιν· καὶ [f]αἱ[1] [g]ἑπτὰ λυχνίαι" [h]ἃς εἶδες" ἑπτὰ ἐκκλησίαι εἰσίν.
The mystery of the seven stars which thou sawest on [2]right [3]hand [1]my, and the seven [2]lampstands [1]golden. The seven stars [2]angels [3]of [4]the [5]seven [6]assemblies [1]are; and the seven lampstands which thou sawest [2]seven [3]assemblies [1]are.

2 Τῷ ἀγγέλῳ [i]τῆς" [k]Ἐφεσίνης" ἐκκλησίας γράψον, Τάδε λέγει ὁ κρατῶν τοὺς ἑπτὰ ἀστέρας ἐν τῇ.δεξιᾷ.αὐτοῦ, ὁ περιπατῶν ἐν μέσῳ τῶν ἑπτὰ λυχνιῶν τῶν [l]χρυσῶν·"
To the angel of the Ephesian assembly write: These things says he who holds the seven stars in his right hand, who walks in [the] midst of the seven [2]lampstands [1]golden.

2 Οἶδα τὰ.ἔργα.σου, καὶ τὸν κόπον [m]σου," καὶ τὴν ὑπομονήν σου, καὶ ὅτι οὐ.δύνῃ βαστάσαι κακούς, καὶ [n]ἐπειράσω" τοὺς [o]φάσκοντας εἶναι ἀποστόλους[1] καὶ οὐκ.εἰσίν,
I know thy works, and [2]labour [1]thy, and [2]endurance [1]thy, and that thou canst not bear evil [ones]; and thou didst try those who declare [themselves] to be apostles and are not,

was and who is to come – the Almighty.
9 I, John, even your brother and companion
in the trials and in the kingdom and patience
of Jesus Christ, was in the island which is
called Patmos, because of the word of God,
and because of the testimony of Jesus
Christ.
10 I came to be in the Spirit on the Lord's
day, and I heard behind me a loud voice, as
of a trumpet,
11 saying, I am the A and the Z, the First
and the Last. And, What you see write in a
book and send it to the churches in Asia: to
Ephesus and to Smyrna and to Per-ga-mos
and to Thy-a-ti-ra and to Sardis and to
Phil-a-del-phi-a and to La-od-i-ce-a.
12 And I turned to see the voice which
spoke with me. And turning I saw seven
golden lampstands.
13 And in the middle of the seven lampstands, *I saw One* like the Son of man,
clothed in a garment reaching to the feet,
and tied at the breasts with a golden band.
14 And His head and hair were white like
wool, like snow. And His eyes were like a
flame of fire.
15 And His feet were like fine brass, as if
made to glow in a furnace. And His voice
was like the voice of many waters.
16 And He had seven stars in His right hand
and a sharp two-edged sword going forth out
of His mouth. And His face was as the sun
shines in its power.
17 And when I saw Him, I fell at His feet as
dead. And He laid His right hand on me,
saying to me, Do not fear. I am the First and
the Last
18 and the Living One. And I became dead,
and, Look! I am alive forever and ever.
Amen. And I have the keys of hell and of
death.
19 Write the things which you saw, and the
things which are, and the things which are
going to take place after these things.
20 The mystery of the seven stars which
you saw on My right hand, and the seven
golden lampstands. The seven stars are the
angels of the seven churches, and the seven
lampstands which you saw are the seven
churches.

CHAPTER 2

1 To the angel of the church of Ephesus
write: He who holds the seven stars in His
right hand, He that is walking in the midst of
the seven golden lampstands, says these
things,
2 I know your works and your labor and
your patience, and that you cannot bear evil
men, and that you tried the ones pretending
to be apostles and are not, and that you
found them to be liars.

καὶ εὗρες αὐτοὺς ψευδεῖς, 3 καὶ [p]ἐβάστασας καὶ ὑπομονὴν
and didst find them liars; and didst bear and [2]endurance
ἔχεις, καὶ" διὰ τὸ.ὄνομά.μου [q]κεκοπίακας καὶ οὐ.κέκμηκας."
[1]hast, and for the sake of my name hast laboured and hast not wearied:
4 [r]ἀλλ'" ἔχω κατὰ σοῦ, ὅτι τὴν.ἀγάπην.σου τὴν πρώτην
but I have against thee, that thy [2]love [1]first
[s]ἀφῆκας." 5 μνημόνευε οὖν πόθεν [t]ἐκπέπτωκας," καὶ
thou didst leave. Remember therefore whence thou hast fallen from, and
μετανόησον, καὶ τὰ πρῶτα ἔργα ποίησον· εἰ.δὲ μή, ἔρχομαι
repent, and the first works do: but if not, I am coming
σοι [v]τάχει," καὶ κινήσω τὴν.λυχνίαν.σου ἐκ τοῦ τόπου
to thee quickly, and I will remove thy lampstand out of [2]place
αὐτῆς, ἐὰν.μὴ μετανοήσῃς. 6 ἀλλὰ τοῦτο ἔχεις, ὅτι
[1]its, except thou shouldest repent. But this thou hast, that
μισεῖς τὰ ἔργα τῶν Νικολαϊτῶν, ἃ κἀγὼ μισῶ. 7 ὁ
thou hatest the works of the Nicolaitanes, which I also hate. He that
ἔχων οὖς ἀκουσάτω τί τὸ πνεῦμα λέγει ταῖς[w] ἐκκλησίαις·
has an ear, let him hear what the Spirit says to the assemblies.
τῷ [x]νικῶντι' δώσω αὐτῷ φαγεῖν ἐκ τοῦ ξύλου τῆς ζωῆς
To him that overcomes, I will give to him to eat of the tree of life
ὅ ἐστιν ἐν [y]μέσῳ τοῦ παραδείσου" τοῦ θεοῦ[z].
which is in [the] midst of the paradise of God.

8 Καὶ τῷ ἀγγέλῳ [a]τῆς" [b]ἐκκλησίας Σμυρναίων" γράψον,
And to the angel of the assembly of Smyrneans write:
Τάδε λέγει ὁ πρῶτος καὶ ὁ ἔσχατος, ὃς ἐγένετο νεκρὸς
These things says the first and the last, who became dead
καὶ ἔζησεν· 9 Οἶδά σου [c]τὰ ἔργα καὶ" τὴν θλίψιν καὶ τὴν
and lived. I know thy works and tribulation and
πτωχείαν· [d]πλούσιος.δὲ" εἶ· καὶ τὴν βλασφημίαν [e] τῶν
poverty; but rich thou art; and the calumny of those who
λεγόντων Ἰουδαίους εἶναι ἑαυτούς, καὶ οὐκ.εἰσίν, ἀλλὰ συν-
declare [4]Jews [2]to [3]be [1]themselves, and are not, but a syn-
αγωγὴ τοῦ σατανᾶ. 10 [f]μηδὲν" φοβοῦ ἃ μέλλεις
agogue of Satan. [2]Not [3]at [4]all [1]fear the things which thou art about
πάσχειν. ἰδού,[g] μέλλει [h]βαλεῖν' [i]ἐξ ὑμῶν ὁ διάβολος'
to suffer. Lo, [3]is [4]about [5]to [6]cast [7some] [8]of [9]you [1]the [2]devil
εἰς φυλακήν, ἵνα πειρασθῆτε· καὶ [k]ἕξετε" θλίψιν ἡμερῶν
into prison, that ye may be tried; and ye shall have tribulation [2]days
δέκα. γίνου πιστὸς ἄχρι θανάτου, καὶ δώσω σοι τὸν στέ-
[1]ten. Be thou faithful unto death, and I will give to thee the
φανον τῆς ζωῆς. 11 ὁ ἔχων οὖς ἀκουσάτω τί τὸ πνεῦμα
crown of life. He that has an ear, let him hear what the Spirit
λέγει ταῖς ἐκκλησίαις· ὁ νικῶν οὐ.μὴ ἀδικηθῇ ἐκ
says to the assemblies. He that overcomes in no wise shall be injured of
τοῦ θανάτου τοῦ δευτέρου.
the [2]death [1]second.

12 Καὶ τῷ ἀγγέλῳ τῆς ἐν Περγάμῳ ἐκκλησίας γράψον,
And to the angel of the [2]in [3]Pergamos [1]assembly write:
Τάδε λέγει ὁ ἔχων τὴν ῥομφαίαν τὴν δίστομον τὴν
These things says he who has the [3]sword [2]two-edged
ὀξεῖαν· 13 Οἶδα [l]τὰ.ἔργα.σου καὶ" ποῦ κατοικεῖς, ὅπου ὁ
[1]sharp, I know thy works and where thou dwellest, where the
θρόνος τοῦ σατανᾶ, καὶ κρατεῖς τὸ.ὄνομά.μου, καὶ οὐκ
throne of Satan [is]; and thou holdest fast my name, and [2]not
ἠρνήσω τὴν πίστιν μου [m]καὶ' ἐν ταῖς ἡμέραις [n]ἐν" [o]αἷς' [p]Ἀν-
[1]didst [3]deny my faith even in the days in which An-
τίπας" ὁ.μάρτυς.μου ὁ πιστός[q], ὃς ἀπεκτάνθη παρ' ὑμῖν,
tipas my [2]witness [1]faithful [was], who was killed among you,
ὅπου [r]κατοικεῖ ὁ σατανᾶς." 14 [s]ἀλλ'' ἔχω κατὰ σοῦ ὀλίγα,
where [2]dwells [1]Satan. But I have against thee a few things;
[t]ὅτι" ἔχεις ἐκεῖ κρατοῦντας τὴν διδαχὴν Βαλαάμ, ὃς
because thou hast there [those] holding the teaching of Balaam, who
ἐδίδασκεν [v]ἐν" [w]τῷ' Βαλὰκ βαλεῖν σκάνδαλον ἐνώπιον τῶν
taught Balak to cast a snare before the
υἱῶν Ἰσραήλ, φαγεῖν εἰδωλόθυτα καὶ πορνεῦσαι.
sons of Israel, to eat things sacrificed to idols and to commit fornication.
15 οὕτως ἔχεις καὶ σὺ κρατοῦντας τὴν διδαχὴν [x]τῶν"
So hast also thou [those] holding the teaching of the
Νικολαϊτῶν [y]ὃ μισῶ." 16 μετανόησον[z]· εἰ.δὲ μή, ἔρχομαί
Nicolaitanes, which thing I hate. Repent! but if not, I am coming
σοι ταχύ, καὶ πολεμήσω μετ' αὐτῶν ἐν τῇ ῥομφαίᾳ τοῦ
to thee quickly, and will make war with them with the sword
στόματός.μου. 17 ὁ ἔχων οὖς ἀκουσάτω τί τὸ πνεῦμα
of my mouth. He that has an ear, let him hear what the Spirit
λέγει ταῖς ἐκκλησίαις· τῷ [a]νικῶντι' δώσω αὐτῷ [b]φαγεῖν
says to the assemblies. To him that overcomes, I will give to him to eat
ἀπὸ" τοῦ μάννα τοῦ κεκρυμμένου, καὶ δώσω αὐτῷ ψῆφον
of the [2]manna [1]hidden; and I will give to him a [2]pebble
λευκήν, καὶ ἐπὶ τὴν ψῆφον ὄνομα καινὸν γεγραμμένον, ὃ
[1]white, and on the pebble a [2]name [1]new written, which
οὐδεὶς [c]ἔγνω' εἰ.μὴ ὁ λαμβάνων.
no one knew except he who receives [it].

3 And *I know* that you did bear up, and
that you have patience, and that for My
name's sake you have labored and have not
become weary.
4 But I have this against you, that you left
your first love.
5 Remember then where you have fallen
from, and repent, and do the first works –
and if not, I will come to you quickly and
will move your lampstand out of its place –
unless you repent.
6 But this you have, that you hate the
works of the Nic-o-la-i-tans, which I also
hate.
7 He that has an ear, let him hear what the
Spirit says to the churches. To the one who
overcomes I will give him to eat of the tree
of life, which is in the middle of the paradise
of God.
8 And to the angel of the church of Smyrna
write: The First and the Last, who became
dead and lived, says these things
9 I know your works and trouble and
poverty, but you are rich. And *I know* the
evil speaking of those who claim themselves
to be Jews and are not, but are a synagogue
of Satan.
10 Do not at all fear the things which you
are about to suffer. Behold! The devil is
about to throw some of you into prison so
that you may be tested. And you shall have
ten days of trials. Be faithful to death, and I
will give you the crown of life.
11 He that has an ear, let him hear what the
Spirit says to the churches. He that overcomes shall never in any way be hurt by the
second death.
12 And to the angel of the church in
Per-gam-os write: He who has the sharp
two-edged sword says these things:
13 I know your works and where you live,
where the throne of Satan is and you hold
My name fast and did not deny My faith
even in the days in which An-ti-pas was My
faithful witness who was killed among
you, where Satan lives.
14 But I have a few things against you,
because you have there those who are
holding to the teaching of Balaam, who
taught Balak to throw a stumbling-block before the sons of Israel, to eat things sacrificed to idols and to commit fornication.
15 So do you also have those who are
holding to the teaching of the Nic-o-la-i-tans,
which thing I hate.
16 Repent! But if not, I will come to you
quickly and I will make war with them with
the sword in My mouth.
17 He that has an ear, let him hear what the
Spirit says to the churches. To him that
overcomes, I will give to him to eat of the
hidden manna. And I will give to him a
white stone, and on the stone a new name
has been written which no one knew except he who received it.

18 Καὶ τῷ ἀγγέλῳ [d]τῆς" ἐν Θυατείροις ἐκκλησίας γράψον,
And to the angel of the [2]in [3]Thyatira [1]assembly write:
Τάδε λέγει ὁ υἱὸς τοῦ θεοῦ, ὁ ἔχων τοὺς ὀφθαλμοὺς
These things says the Son of God, he who has [2]eyes
[e]αὐτοῦ" ὡς [f]φλόγα" πυρός, καὶ οἱ.πόδες.αὐτοῦ ὅμοιοι χαλκολι-
[1]his as a flame of fire, and his feet like fine
βάνῳ· 19 Οἶδά σου τὰ ἔργα καὶ τὴν [g]ἀγάπην, καὶ τὴν δια-
brass. I know thy works, and love, and ser-
κονίαν, καὶ τὴν πίστιν" καὶ [h]τὴν" ὑπομονήν [i]σου," καὶ τὰ ἔργα
vice, and faith, and [2]endurance [1]thy, and [2]works
σου, [k]καὶ" τὰ ἔσχατα πλείονα τῶν πρώτων. 20 [l]ἀλλ'"
[1]thy, and the last [to be] more than the first. But
ἔχω κατὰ σοῦ [m]ὀλίγα," ὅτι [n]ἐᾷς" τὴν γυναῖκα[o] [p]Ἰεζα-
I have against thee a few things that thou sufferest the woman Jeze-
βήλ," [q]τὴν λέγουσαν" [r]ἑαυτὴν" προφῆτιν, [s]διδάσκειν καὶ πλα-
bel, her who calls herself a prophetess, to teach and to
νᾶσθαι" ἐμοὺς δούλους, πορνεῦσαι καὶ [t]εἰδωλό-
mislead my bondmen to commit fornication and [3]things [4]sacrificed [5]to
θυτα φαγεῖν." 21 καὶ ἔδωκα αὐτῇ χρόνον ἵνα μετανοήσῃ [v]ἐκ
[6]idols [1]to [2]eat. And I gave her time that she might repent of
τῆς.πορνείας.αὐτῆς, καὶ οὐ.μετενόησεν." 22 ἰδού, [w]ἐγὼ" βάλλω
her fornication; and she repented not. Lo, I cast
αὐτὴν εἰς κλίνην, καὶ τοὺς μοιχεύοντας μετ' αὐτῆς εἰς
her into a bed, and those who commit adultery with her into
θλίψιν μεγάλην, ἐὰν.μὴ [xa]μετανοήσωσιν" ἐκ τῶν ἔργων
[2]tribulation [1]great, except they should repent of [2]works
[ya]αὐτῶν." 23 καὶ τὰ.τέκνα.αὐτῆς ἀποκτενῶ ἐν θανάτῳ· καὶ
[1]their. And her children I will kill with death; and
γνώσονται πᾶσαι αἱ ἐκκλησίαι ὅτι ἐγώ εἰμι ὁ [za]ἐρευνῶν"
[4]shall [5]know [1]all [2]the [3]assemblies that I am he who searches
νεφροὺς καὶ καρδίας· καὶ δώσω ὑμῖν ἑκάστῳ κατὰ τὰ
reins and hearts; and I will give to you each according to
ἔργα ὑμῶν. 24 ὑμῖν.δὲ λέγω [a]καὶ" λοιποῖς τοῖς ἐν
[2]works [1]your. But to you I say, and to [the] rest who [are] in
Θυατείροις, ὅσοι οὐκ.ἔχουσιν τὴν διδαχὴν.ταύτην, [b]καὶ"
Thyatira, as many as have not this teaching, and
οἵτινες οὐκ.ἔγνωσαν τὰ [c]βάθη" τοῦ σατανᾶ, ὡς λέγουσιν, Οὐ
who knew not the depths of Satan, as they say; [3]not
[d]βαλῶ" ἐφ' ὑμᾶς ἄλλο βάρος· 25 πλὴν ὃ ἔχετε κρατή-
[1]I [2]will [4]cast upon you any other burden; but what ye have hold
σατε, [e]ἄχρις" οὗ.ἂν.ἥξω. 26 καὶ ὁ νικῶν καὶ ὁ
fast till I shall come. And he that overcomes, and he that
τηρῶν ἄχρι τέλους τὰ.ἔργα.μου, δώσω αὐτῷ ἐξουσίαν
keeps until [the] end my works, I will give to him authority
ἐπὶ τῶν ἐθνῶν· 27 καὶ ποιμανεῖ αὐτοὺς ἐν ῥάβδῳ σι-
over the nations, and he shall shepherd them with [3]rod [1]an
δηρᾷ· ὡς τὰ σκεύη τὰ.κεραμικὰ συντρίβεται, ὡς κἀγὼ
[2]iron, as vessels of pottery are broken in pieces; as I also
εἴληφα παρὰ τοῦ.πατρός.μου· 28 καὶ δώσω αὐτῷ τὸν
have received from my Father; and I will give to him the
ἀστέρα τὸν πρωϊνόν. 29 ὁ ἔχων οὖς ἀκουσάτω τί τὸ
[2]star [1]morning. He that has an ear, let him hear what the
πνεῦμα λέγει ταῖς ἐκκλησίαις.
Spirit says to the assemblies.

3 Καὶ τῷ ἀγγέλῳ τῆς ἐν Σάρδεσιν ἐκκλησίας γράψον,
And to the angel of the [2]in [3]Sardis [1]assembly write:
Τάδε λέγει ὁ ἔχων τὰ [f] πνεύματα τοῦ θεοῦ καὶ τοὺς
These things says he who has the Spirits of God and the
ἑπτὰ ἀστέρας· Οἶδά σου τὰ ἔργα, ὅτι [g]τὸ" ὄνομα ἔχεις ὅτι
seven stars. I know thy works, that [3]the [4]name [1]thou [2]hast that
ζῇς, καὶ νεκρὸς εἶ. 2 γίνου γρηγορῶν, καὶ [h]στήριξον"
thou livest, and [2]dead [1]art. Be watchful, and strengthen
τὰ.λοιπὰ ἃ [i]μέλλει" ἀποθανεῖν· οὐ.γὰρ.εὕρηκά
the things that remain, which are about to die, for I have not found
σου [j]τὰ" ἔργα πεπληρωμένα ἐνώπιον τοῦ θεοῦ[k]. 3 μνημόνευε
thy works complete before God. Remember
[l]οὖν" πῶς εἴληφας καὶ ἤκουσας, καὶ τήρει, καὶ
therefore how thou hast received and heard, and keep [it] and
μετανόησον· ἐὰν οὖν μὴ.γρηγορήσῃς, ἥξω [m]ἐπὶ σὲ"
repent. If therefore thou shalt not watch I will come upon thee
ὡς κλέπτης, καὶ οὐ.μὴ [n]γνῷς" ποίαν ὥραν ἥξω
as a thief, and in no wise shalt thou know what hour I shall come
ἐπὶ σέ. 4 [o] [p]ἔχεις ὀλίγα" ὀνόματα [q]καὶ" ἐν Σάρδεσιν, ἃ οὐκ
upon thee. Thou hast a few names also in Sardis which [2]not
ἐμόλυναν τὰ.ἱμάτια.αὐτῶν· καὶ περιπατήσουσιν μετ' ἐμοῦ ἐν
[1]defiled their garments, and they shall walk with me in
λευκοῖς, ὅτι ἄξιοί εἰσιν. 5 ὁ νικῶν, [r]οὗτος" περι-
white, because worthy they are. He that overcomes, he shall
βαλεῖται ἐν ἱματίοις λευκοῖς· καὶ οὐ.μὴ ἐξαλείψω τὸ ὄνομα
be clothed in [2]garments [1]white; and in no wise will I blot out [2]name
αὐτοῦ ἐκ τῆς βίβλου τῆς ζωῆς, καὶ [s]ἐξομολογήσομαι" τὸ ὄνομα
[1]his from the book of life, and will confess [2]name

18 And to the angel of the church in Thy-a-
ti-ra write: The Son of God, He who has His
eyes like a flame of fire and His feet like fine
brass, says these things –
19 I know your works and love and service
and faith and your patience and your works
– even the last more than the first.
20 But I have a few things against you, that
you allow that woman Jez-e-bel (the one
who calls herself a prophetess), to teach and
to lead My servants astray to commit fornication and to eat things sacrificed to idols.
21 And I gave her time so that she might
repent of her fornication, and she did not
repent.
22 Behold! I will throw her into a bed
and those who commit adultery with her
into great trouble, unless they should repent
of their works.
23 And I will kill her children with death.
And all the churches shall know that I am
He who searches the inner parts and hearts.
And I will give to each of you according to
your works.
24 But to you I say, and to the rest who are
in Thy-a-ti-ra (as many as do not have this
teaching, and who did not know the deep
things of Satan, as they say), I will not put
on you any other load.
25 But what you have, hold fast until I
come.
26 And he that overcomes, and he that
keeps My works until the end, I will give him
authority over the nations.
27 And he shall shepherd them with a rod
of iron, even as vessels of pottery are broken
in pieces, even as I also have received from
My Father –
28 and I will give to him the Morning Star.
29 He that has an ear, let him hear what
the Spirit says to the churches.

CHAPTER 3

1 And to the angel of the church in Sardis
write: He who has the Spirits of God and the
seven stars says these things. I know your
works, that you have the name that you live,
and are dead.
2 Be watchful and make strong the things
that remain, which are about to die. For I
have not found your works perfect before
God.
3 Remember then how you have received
and heard, and keep them, and repent. If
then you will not watch, I will come on you
as a thief, and you shall not know in what
hour I shall come on you.
4 You have a few names also in Sardis
which have not made their robes unclean.
And they shall walk with Me in white,
because they are worthy.
5 He that overcomes, this one shall be
clothed in white robes, and I will never in
any way blot out his name from the Book of
Life, but I will confess his name before My

αὐτοῦ ἐνώπιον τοῦ.πατρός.μου καὶ ἐνώπιον τῶν ἀγγέλων
[1]his before my Father and before [2]angels
αὐτοῦ. 6 ὁ ἔχων οὖς ἀκουσάτω τί τὸ πνεῦμα λέγει
[1]his. He that has an ear, let him hear what the Spirit says
ταῖς ἐκκλησίαις.
to the assemblies.

7 Καὶ τῷ ἀγγέλῳ τῆς ἐν [t]Φιλαδελφείᾳ[ll] ἐκκλησίας γράψον,
And to the angel of the [2]in [3]Philadelphia [1]assembly write:
Τάδε λέγει [v]ὁ ἅγιος, ὁ ἀληθινός,[ll] ὁ ἔχων τὴν [w]κλεῖδα[ll]
These things says the Holy, the True; he who has the key
[x]τοῦ[ll] [y]Δαβίδ,[ll] ὁ ἀνοίγων καὶ οὐδεὶς [z]κλείει,[ll] [a]καὶ[1] [b]κλείει[ll] καὶ
of David, who opens and no one shuts, and shuts and
οὐδεὶς [c]ἀνοίγει·[ll] 8 Οἶδά σου τὰ ἔργα· ἰδού, δέδωκα ἐνώπιόν
no one opens. I know thy works. Lo, I have set before
σου θύραν [d]ἀνεῳγμένην,[1] [e]καὶ[ll] οὐδεὶς δύναται κλεῖσαι αὐτήν·
thee [3]door [1]an [2]opened, and no one is able to shut it,
ὅτι μικρὰν ἔχεις δύναμιν, καὶ ἐτήρησάς μου τὸν λόγον,
because [3]a [4]little [1]thou [2]hast power, and didst keep my word,
καὶ οὐκ.ἠρνήσω τὸ.ὄνομά.μου. 9 ἰδού, [f]δίδωμι[ll] ἐκ τῆς συνα-
and didst not deny my name. Lo, I give of the syna-
γωγῆς τοῦ σατανᾶ τῶν λεγόντων ἑαυτοὺς Ἰουδαίους εἶναι,
gogue of Satan those that declare themselves [3]Jews [1]to [2]be,
καὶ οὐκ.εἰσίν, ἀλλὰ ψεύδονται· ἰδού, ποιήσω αὐτοὺς ἵνα
and are not, but do lie; lo, I will cause them that
[g]ἥξωσιν[ll] καὶ [h]προσκυνήσωσιν[ll] ἐνώπιον τῶν.ποδῶν.σου,
they should come and should do homage before thy feet,
καὶ γνῶσιν ὅτι ἐγὼ ἠγάπησά σε. 10 ὅτι ἐτήρησας τὸν
and should know that I loved thee. Because thou didst keep the
λόγον τῆς.ὑπομονῆς.μου, κἀγώ σε τηρήσω ἐκ τῆς ὥρας τοῦ
word of my endurance, I also thee will keep out of the hour
πειρασμοῦ τῆς μελλούσης ἔρχεσθαι ἐπὶ τῆς οἰκουμένης
of trial which [is] about to come upon the [2]habitable [3]world
ὅλης, πειράσαι τοὺς κατοικοῦντας ἐπὶ τῆς γῆς. 11 [i]Ἰδού,[ll]
[1]whole, to try them that dwell upon the earth. Behold,
ἔρχομαι ταχύ· κράτει ὃ ἔχεις, ἵνα μηδεὶς λάβῃ τὸν
I come quickly: hold fast what thou hast, that no one take
στέφανόν σου. 12 ὁ νικῶν, ποιήσω αὐτὸν στύλον ἐν τῷ
[2]crown [1]thy. He that overcomes, I will make him a pillar in the
ναῷ τοῦ.θεοῦ.μου, καὶ ἔξω οὐ.μὴ ἐξέλθῃ ἔτι, καὶ γράψω
temple of my God, and out not at all shall he go more; and I will write
ἐπ' αὐτὸν τὸ ὄνομα τοῦ.θεοῦ.μου, καὶ τὸ ὄνομα τῆς πόλεως
upon him the name of my God, and the name of the city
τοῦ.θεοῦ.μου, τῆς καινῆς Ἱερουσαλήμ, [k]ἡ καταβαίνουσα[ll]
of my God, the new Jerusalem, which comes down
ἐκ τοῦ οὐρανοῦ ἀπὸ τοῦ.θεοῦ.μου, καὶ τὸ.ὄνομά.μου τὸ
out of heaven from my God, and my [2]name
καινόν. 13 ὁ ἔχων οὖς ἀκουσάτω τί τὸ πνεῦμα λέγει
[1]new. He that has an ear, let him hear what the Spirit says
ταῖς ἐκκλησίαις.
to the assemblies.

14 Καὶ τῷ ἀγγέλῳ τῆς [l]ἐκκλησίας Λαοδικέων[1] γράψον,
And to the angel of the assembly of [the] Laodiceans write:
Τάδε λέγει ὁ ἀμήν, ὁ μάρτυς ὁ πιστὸς καὶ ἀληθινός, ἡ
These things says the Amen, the witness faithful and true, the
ἀρχὴ τῆς κτίσεως τοῦ θεοῦ· 15 Οἶδά σου τὰ ἔργα, ὅτι οὔτε
beginning of the creation of God. I know thy works, that neither
ψυχρὸς εἶ, οὔτε ζεστός· ὄφελον ψυχρὸς [m]εἴης,[1] ἢ ζεστός·
cold thou art, nor hot; I would cold thou wert or hot.
16 οὕτως ὅτι χλιαρὸς εἶ, καὶ οὔτε [n]ψυχρὸς οὔτε ζεστός,[ll]
Thus because lukewarm thou art, and neither cold nor hot,
μέλλω σε ἐμέσαι ἐκ τοῦ.στόματός.μου. 17 ὅτι λέγεις,
I am about [3]thee [1]to [2]spue out of my mouth. Because thou sayest,
[o]Ὅτι πλούσιός εἰμι καὶ πεπλούτηκα καὶ [p]οὐδενὸς[1] χρείαν ἔχω,
Rich I am, and have grown rich and [3]of [4]nothing [2]need [1]have,
καὶ οὐκ.οἶδας ὅτι σὺ εἶ ὁ ταλαίπωρος καὶ [q] [r]ἐλεεινός,[1] καὶ
and knowest not that thou art the wretched, and miserable, and
πτωχὸς καὶ τυφλὸς καὶ γυμνός· 18 συμβουλεύω σοι ἀγοράσαι
poor, and blind, and naked; I counsel thee to buy
παρ' ἐμοῦ χρυσίον πεπυρωμένον ἐκ πυρός, ἵνα πλουτήσῃς,
from me gold purified by fire, that thou mayest be rich;
καὶ ἱμάτια λευκά, ἵνα περιβάλῃ καὶ μὴ.φανερωθῇ
and [2]garments [1]white, that thou mayest be clothed, and may not be made manifest
ἡ αἰσχύνη τῆς.γυμνότητός.σου· καὶ [s]κολλούριον[1] [t]ἔγχρισον·
the shame of thy nakedness; and [4]eye-salve [1]anoint [2]thou [3]with
τοὺς.ὀφθαλμούς.σου, ἵνα βλέπῃς. 19 ἐγὼ ὅσους ἐὰν φιλῶ,
thine eyes, that thou mayest see. I as many as I love
ἐλέγχω καὶ παιδεύω· [v]ζήλωσον[1] οὖν καὶ μετανόησον.
I rebuke and discipline; be thou zealous therefore and repent.
20 ἰδού, ἕστηκα ἐπὶ τὴν θύραν καὶ κρούω· ἐάν τις ἀκούσῃ
Behold, I stand at the door and knock; if anyone hear
τῆς.φωνῆς.μου, καὶ ἀνοίξῃ τὴν θύραν, [w] εἰσελεύσομαι πρὸς
my voice and open the door, I will come in to

Father and before His angels.

6 He that has an ear, let him hear what the Spirit says to the churches.

7 And to the angel of the church in Phil-a-del-phi-a write: The Holy, the True, He that has the key of David, He that opens and no one shuts, and shuts and no one opens, says these things

8 I know your works. Behold! I have set an open door before you, and no one is able to shut it, because you have a little power and did keep My word and did not deny My name.

9 See! I give *you those* of the synagogue of Satan, the ones claiming themselves to be Jews and are not, but lie. Behold! I will make them come and bow down before your feet, and to know that I loved you.

10 Because you kept the word of My patience, I also will keep you out of the hour of trial which is about to come on the whole world to try those who live on the earth.

11 Behold! I come quickly! Hold fast that which you have so that no one may take your crown.

12 He that overcomes I will make him a pillar in the temple of My God. And he shall never go out any more. And I will write the name of My God on him, and the name of the city of My God – the new Jerusalem which comes down out of Heaven from My God – and My new name.

13 He that has an ear, let him hear what the Spirit says to the churches.

14 And to the angel of the church of the La-od-i-ce-ans write: The Amen, the faithful and true Witness, the Beginning of the creation of God, says these things –

15 I know your works, that you are neither cold nor hot. I wish that you were cold or hot.

16 So, because you are lukewarm and neither cold nor hot, I am about to spit you out of My mouth.

17 Because you say, I am rich and have need of nothing – and do not know that you are wretched and miserable and poor and blind and naked –

18 I advise you to buy from Me gold made pure by fire, so that you may be rich, and white robes so that you may be clothed, and the shame of your nakedness may not be revealed – and to anoint your eyes with eye salve so that you may see.

19 As many as I love, I rebuke and discipline. So be fervent and repent.

20 Behold! I stand at the door and knock. If anyone hears My voice and opens the door, I will come in to him and will dine

αὐτόν, καὶ δειπνήσω μετ' αὐτοῦ, καὶ αὐτὸς μετ' ἐμοῦ. 21 ὁ
him, and will sup with him, and he with me. He that
νικῶν, δώσω αὐτῷ καθίσαι μετ' ἐμοῦ ἐν τῷ.θρόνῳ.μου, ὡς
overcomes, I will give to him to sit with me in my throne, as
κἀγὼ ἐνίκησα, καὶ ἐκάθισα μετὰ τοῦ.πατρός.μου ἐν τῷ θρόνῳ
I also overcame, and sat down with my Father in [2]throne
αὐτοῦ. 22 ὁ ἔχων οὖς ἀκουσάτω τί τὸ πνεῦμα λέγει
[1]his. He that has an ear, let him hear what the Spirit says
ταῖς ἐκκλησίαις.
to the assemblies.

4 Μετὰ ταῦτα [x]εἶδον,‖ καὶ ἰδοὺ θύρα [y]ἠνεῳγμένη‖ ἐν τῷ
After these things I saw, and behold a door opened in
οὐρανῷ, καὶ ἡ φωνὴ ἡ πρώτη ἣν ἤκουσα ὡς σάλπιγγος
heaven, and the [2]voice [1]first which I heard [was] as of a trumpet
λαλούσης μετ' ἐμοῦ, [z]λέγουσα,‖ [a]Ἀνάβα‖ ὧδε, καὶ δείξω
speaking with me, saying, Come up hither, and I will shew
σοι [b]ἃ‖ δεῖ γενέσθαι μετὰ ταῦτα.[c] 2 [d]καὶ‖ εὐθέως
to thee what things must take place after these things. And immediately
ἐγενόμην ἐν πνεύματι· καὶ ἰδού, θρόνος ἔκειτο ἐν τῷ
I became in [the] Spirit; and behold, a throne was set in the
οὐρανῷ, καὶ ἐπὶ [e]τοῦ θρόνου‖ καθήμενος· 3 καὶ ὁ καθή-
heaven, and upon the throne [one] sitting, and he who [was] sit-
μενος [f]ἦν· ὅμοιος ὁράσει λίθῳ ἰάσπιδι καὶ [g]σαρδίνῳ·‖ καὶ
ting was like in appearance to a [2]stone [1]jasper and a sardius; and
ἶρις κυκλόθεν τοῦ θρόνου [h]ὅμοιος‖ ὁράσει σμαραγ-
a rainbow [was] around the throne like in appearance to an eme-
δίνῳ. 4 καὶ κυκλόθεν τοῦ θρόνου [i]θρόνοι‖ εἴκοσι [k]καὶ· [l]τέσ-
rald. And around the throne [4]thrones [1]twenty [2]and
σαρες,‖ καὶ ἐπὶ τοὺς [m]θρόνους εἶδον τοὺς εἴκοσι καὶ τέσσαρας‖
[3]four, and on the thrones I saw twenty and four
πρεσβυτέρους καθημένους, περιβεβλημένους [n]ἐν‖ ἱματίοις
elders sitting, clothed in [2]garments
λευκοῖς· καὶ [o]ἔσχον‖ ἐπὶ τὰς.κεφαλὰς.αὐτῶν στεφάνους [p]χρυσ-
[1]white; and they had on their heads [2]crowns [1]gold-
οῦς.‖ 5 καὶ ἐκ τοῦ θρόνου ἐκπορεύονται ἀστραπαὶ καὶ
en. And out of the throne go forth lightnings and
[q]βρονταὶ καὶ φωναί·‖ καὶ ἑπτὰ λαμπάδες πυρὸς καιόμεναι
thunders and voices; and seven lamps of fire burning
ἐνώπιον τοῦ θρόνου[r], [s]αἵ‖ [t]εἰσιν‖ [v]τὰ‖ ἑπτὰ πνεύματα τοῦ
before the throne, which are the seven Spirits
θεοῦ· 6 καὶ ἐνώπιον τοῦ θρόνου [w] θάλασσα ὑαλίνη, ὁμοία
of God; and before the throne a [2]sea [1]glass, like
κρυστάλλῳ. καὶ ἐν μέσῳ τοῦ θρόνου καὶ κύκλῳ τοῦ θρόνου
crystal. And in [the] midst of the throne and around the throne
[x]τέσσαρα‖ ζῶα γέμοντα ὀφθαλμῶν [y]ἔμπροσθεν‖ καὶ
four living creatures, full of eyes before and
ὄπισθεν. 7 καὶ τὸ ζῶον τὸ πρῶτον ὅμοιον λέοντι,
behind; and the [2]living [3]creature [1]first [was] like a lion,
καὶ τὸ δεύτερον ζῶον ὅμοιον μόσχῳ, καὶ τὸ τρίτον ζῶ-
and the second living creature like a calf, and the third living
ον [z]ἔχον‖ τὸ πρόσωπον [a]ὡς‖ [b]ἄνθρωπος,‖ καὶ τὸ τέταρτον
creature having the face as a man, and the fourth
ζῶον ὅμοιον ἀετῷ [c]πετωμένῳ.‖ 8 καὶ [d] [e]τέσσαρα‖
living creature like [3]eagle [1]a [2]flying. And [the] four
ζῶα, ἓν.[f]καθ'.ἑαυτό,‖ [g]εἶχον‖ ἀνὰ πτέρυγας ἕξ,
living creatures, each for itself had respectively [2]wings [1]six;
κυκλόθεν καὶ ἔσωθεν [h]γέμοντα‖ ὀφθαλμῶν, καὶ ἀνάπαυσιν οὐκ
around and within full of eyes; and [4]cessation [3]not
ἔχουσιν ἡμέρας καὶ νυκτός, [i]λέγοντα,‖ Ἅγιος, ἅγιος, ἅγιος
[1]they [2]have day and night, saying, Holy, holy, holy,
κύριος ὁ θεὸς ὁ παντοκράτωρ, ὁ ἦν καὶ ὁ ὢν καὶ ὁ
Lord God Almighty, who was, and who is, and who [is]
ἐρχόμενος. 9 καὶ ὅταν δώσουσιν τὰ ζῶα δόξαν καὶ
to come. And when [4]shall [5]give [1]the [2]living [3]creatures glory and
τιμὴν καὶ εὐχαριστίαν τῷ καθημένῳ ἐπὶ [k]τοῦ θρόνου,‖ τῷ
honour and thanksgiving to him who sits upon the throne, who
ζῶντι εἰς τοὺς αἰῶνας τῶν αἰώνων, 10 πεσοῦνται οἱ εἴκοσι [l]καὶ‖
lives to the ages of the ages, shall fall the twenty and
τέσσαρες πρεσβύτεροι ἐνώπιον τοῦ καθημένου ἐπὶ τοῦ
four elders before him who sits upon the
θρόνου, καὶ [m]προσκυνοῦσιν‖ τῷ ζῶντι εἰς τοὺς αἰῶνας τῶν
throne, and they worship him who lives to the ages of the
αἰώνων, καὶ [n]βάλλουσιν‖ τοὺς.στεφάνους.αὐτῶν ἐνώπιον τοῦ
ages; and cast their crowns before the
θρόνου, λέγοντες, 11 Ἄξιος εἶ, [o]κύριε,‖ λαβεῖν τὴν δόξαν
throne, saying, Worthy art thou, O Lord, to receive glory
καὶ τὴν τιμὴν καὶ [p]τὴν‖ δύναμιν· ὅτι σὺ ἔκτισας τὰ
and honour and power: because thou didst create
πάντα, καὶ διὰ τὸ.θέλημά.σου [q]εἰσίν‖ καὶ ἐκτίσθησαν.
all things, and for thy will they are, and were created.

5 Καὶ εἶδον ἐπὶ τὴν δεξιὰν τοῦ καθημένου ἐπὶ τοῦ
And I saw on the right hand of him who sits upon the

with him, and he with Me.

21 He that overcomes, I will give to him to sit with Me on My throne, even as I also overcame and sat down with My Father on His throne.

22 He that has an ear, let him hear what the Spirit says to the churches.

CHAPTER 4

1 After these things I looked, and behold! A door opened in Heaven! And the first voice I heard was like that of a trumpet speaking with me, saying, Come up here and I will show you what things must happen after these things.

2 And instantly I came to be in the Spirit. And, behold! A throne was set in Heaven, and One was sitting on the throne.

3 And He who was sitting there looked like a jasper stone and a sardius. And a rainbow was around the throne, looking like an emerald.

4 And twenty-four thrones were around the throne. And I saw twenty-four elders sitting on the thrones, clothed in white robes. And they had golden crowns on their heads.

5 And out of the throne lightnings and thunders and voices went forth. And seven lamps of fire were burning in front of the throne, which are the seven Spirits of God.

6 And a sea of glass was in front of the throne, like crystal. And in the midst of the throne, and around the throne, were four living creatures, full of eyes in front and behind.

7 And the first living creature was like a lion. And the second living creature was like a calf. And the third living creature had the face of a man. And the fourth living creature was like a flying eagle.

8 And each one of the four living creatures has six wings about him, and within *they were* full of eyes. And they never stop day and night, saying, Holy, holy, holy, Lord God Almighty, who was and who is and who is to come.

9 And when the living creatures give glory and honor and thanksgiving to Him who sits on the throne, who lives forever and ever,

10 the twenty-four elders fall down before Him who sits on the throne. And they worship Him who lives forever and ever, and throw their crowns before the throne, saying,

11 O Lord, You are worthy to receive glory and honor and power, because You created all things, and they are and were created for Your pleasure.

CHAPTER 5

1 And I saw a book on the right hand of

θρόνου βιβλίον γεγραμμένον ἔσωθεν καὶ ὄπισθεν, κατεσφρα-
throne a book, written within and on [the] back, having been
γισμένον σφραγῖσιν ἑπτά. 2 καὶ εἶδον ἄγγελον ἰσχυρὸν κη-
sealed with ²seals ¹seven. And I saw ³angel ¹a ²strong pro-
ρύσσοντα[r] φωνῇ μεγάλῃ, Τίς [s]ἐστιν[‖] ἄξιος ἀνοῖξαι τὸ
claiming with a ²voice ¹loud, Who is worthy to open the
βιβλίον, καὶ λῦσαι τὰς σφραγῖδας αὐτοῦ; 3 καὶ οὐδεὶς [t]ἠδύ-
book, and to loose the seals of it? And no one was
νατο[‖] ἐν τῷ οὐρανῷ, [v]οὐδὲ[‖] ἐπὶ τῆς γῆς, [v]οὐδὲ[‖] ὑποκάτω τῆς
able in the heaven, nor upon the earth, nor under the
γῆς, ἀνοῖξαι τὸ βιβλίον, [w]οὐδὲ[‖] βλέπειν αὐτό. 4 καὶ [x]ἐγὼ[‖]
earth, to open the book, nor to look at it. And I
ἔκλαιον [y]πολλά,[‖] ὅτι οὐδεὶς ἄξιος εὑρέθη ἀνοῖξαι [z]καὶ ἀνα-
was weeping much because no one worthy was found to open and to
γνῶναι[‖] τὸ βιβλίον, οὔτε βλέπειν αὐτό. 5 καὶ εἷς ἐκ τῶν
read the book, nor to look at it. And one of the
πρεσβυτέρων λέγει μοι, Μὴ.κλαῖε· ἰδού, ἐνίκησεν ὁ λέων
elders says to me, Do not weep. Behold, ³overcame ¹the ²Lion
ὁ [a]ὢν[‖] ἐκ τῆς φυλῆς Ἰούδα, ἡ ῥίζα [b]Δαβίδ,[‖] ἀνοῖξαι
which is of the tribe of Juda, the root of David, [so as] to open
τὸ βιβλίον, καὶ [c]λῦσαι[‖] τὰς ἑπτὰ σφραγῖδας αὐτοῦ. 6 καὶ
the book, and to loose the seven seals of it. And
εἶδον [d]καὶ[‖] [e]ἰδού,[‖] ἐν μέσῳ τοῦ θρόνου καὶ τῶν τεσσάρων
I saw, and behold, in [the] midst of the throne and of the four
ζώων, καὶ ἐν μέσῳ τῶν πρεσβυτέρων, ἀρνίον [f]ἑστη-
living creatures, and in [the] midst of the elders, a Lamb stand-
κὸς[‖] ὡς ἐσφαγμένον, [g]ἔχον[‖] κέρατα ἑπτὰ καὶ ὀφθαλμοὺς
ing as having been slain, having ²horns ¹seven and ²eyes
ἑπτά, [h]οἵ[‖] εἰσιν τὰ [i]ἑπτὰ[‖] [k]τοῦ θεοῦ πνεύματα[‖] [la]τὰ[‖] [ma]ἀπε-
¹seven, which are the seven ²of ³God ¹Spirits which have
σταλμένα[‖] εἰς πᾶσαν τὴν γῆν. 7 καὶ ἦλθεν, καὶ εἴληφεν [na]τὸ
been sent into all the earth: and he came and took the
βιβλίον[‖] ἐκ τῆς δεξιᾶς τοῦ καθημένου ἐπὶ τοῦ θρόνου.
book out of the right hand of him who sits on the throne.
8 καὶ ὅτε ἔλαβεν τὸ βιβλίον τὰ [o]τέσσαρα[‖] ζῶα καὶ οἱ
And when he took the book the four living creatures and the
[p]εἰκοσιτέσσαρες[‖] πρεσβύτεροι [q]ἔπεσον[‖] ἐνώπιον τοῦ ἀρνίου,
four-and-twenty elders fell before the Lamb,
ἔχοντες ἕκαστος [r]κιθάρας[‖] καὶ φιάλας [s]χρυσᾶς[‖] γεμούσας θυ-
having each harps and ²bowls ¹golden full of
μιαμάτων, αἵ εἰσιν αἱ προσευχαὶ τῶν ἁγίων· 9 καὶ ᾄδουσιν
incenses, which are the prayers of the saints. And they sing
ᾠδὴν καινήν, λέγοντες, Ἄξιος εἶ λαβεῖν τὸ βιβλίον, καὶ
a ²song ¹new, saying, Worthy art thou to take the book, and
ἀνοῖξαι τὰς.σφραγῖδας.αὐτοῦ· ὅτι ἐσφάγης καὶ ἠγόρασας
to open its seals; because thou wast slain, and didst purchase
τῷ θεῷ [t]ἡμᾶς[‖] ἐν τῷ.αἵματί.σου, ἐκ πάσης φυλῆς καὶ γλώσ-
²to ³God ¹us by thy blood, out of every tribe and tongue
σης καὶ λαοῦ καὶ ἔθνους, 10 καὶ ἐποίησας [v]ἡμᾶς[‖] [w]τῷ.θεῷ.ἡμῶν[‖]
and people and nation, and didst make us to our God
[x]βασιλεῖς[‖] καὶ ἱερεῖς· καὶ [y]βασιλεύσομεν[‖] ἐπὶ τῆς γῆς 11 Καὶ
kings and priests; and we shall reign over the earth. And
εἶδον, καὶ ἤκουσα[z] φωνὴν ἀγγέλων πολλῶν [a]κυκλόθεν[‖] τοῦ
I saw, and I heard [the] voice of ²angels ¹many around the
θρόνου καὶ τῶν ζώων καὶ τῶν πρεσβυτέρων·[b] καὶ χιλι-
throne and of the living creatures and of the elders; and thou-
άδες χιλιάδων, 12 λέγοντες φωνῇ μεγάλῃ, [c]Ἄξιόν[‖] ἐστιν
sands of thousands; saying with a ²voice ¹loud, Worthy is
τὸ ἀρνίον τὸ ἐσφαγμένον λαβεῖν τὴν δύναμιν καὶ [d] πλοῦτον
the Lamb that has been slain to receive power, and riches,
καὶ σοφίαν καὶ ἰσχὺν καὶ τιμὴν καὶ δόξαν καὶ εὐλογίαν.
and wisdom, and strength, and honour, and glory, and blessing.
13 Καὶ πᾶν κτίσμα ὃ [e]ἐστιν[‖] ἐν τῷ οὐρανῷ, καὶ [f]ἐν τῇ γῇ,[‖]
And every creature which is in the heaven and in the earth
καὶ ὑποκάτω τῆς γῆς, καὶ ἐπὶ τῆς θαλάσσης [g]ἅ[‖] [h]ἐστιν,[‖]
and under the earth, and ⁴on ⁵the ⁶sea ¹those ²that ³are,
καὶ τὰ ἐν αὐτοῖς [i]πάντα,[‖] [k]ἤκουσα [l]λέγοντας,[‖] Τῷ
and ²the ³things ⁴in ⁵them ¹all, heard I saying, To him who
καθημένῳ ἐπὶ [m]τοῦ θρόνου[‖] καὶ τῷ ἀρνίῳ ἡ εὐλογία καὶ ἡ
sits on the throne, and to the Lamb, Blessing, and
τιμὴ καὶ ἡ δόξα καὶ τὸ κράτος εἰς τοὺς αἰῶνας τῶν αἰώνων.
honour, and glory, and might, to the ages of the ages.
14 Καὶ τὰ [n]τέσσαρα[‖] ζῶα ἔλεγον, [oa]Ἀμήν· καὶ οἱ [pa]εἰκοσι-
And the four living creatures said, Amen; and the four-and-
τέσσαρες[‖] πρεσβύτεροι ἔπεσαν, καὶ προσεκύνησαν
twenty elders fell down and worshipped [him who]
[qa]ζῶντι εἰς τοὺς αἰῶνας τῶν αἰώνων.[‖]
lives to the ages of the ages.

6 Καὶ [ra]εἶδον[‖] ὅτε ἤνοιξεν τὸ ἀρνίον μίαν ἐκ τῶν [sa] σφρα-
And I saw when ³opened ¹the ²Lamb one of the seals,
γίδων. καὶ ἤκουσα ἑνὸς ἐκ τῶν τεσσάρων ζώων λεγον-
and I heard ⁵one ⁷of ⁸the ⁹four ¹⁰living ¹¹creatures ¹²say-

Him written on the inside and on the back,
having been sealed with seven seals.
2 And I saw a strong angel shouting with a
loud voice, Who is worthy to open the book
and to loose the seals of it?
3 And no one in Heaven or on the earth or
under the earth was able to open the book,
or to look at it.
4 And I was crying very much because no
one was found who was worthy to open and
to read the book, or to look at it.
5 And one of the elders said to me, Do not
cry. Look! The Lion which is of the tribe of
Judah, the Root of David, has overcome *so
as* to open the book and to loose the seven
seals of it.
6 And I saw, and behold! In the midst of
the throne and of the four living creatures,
and in the midst of the elders, a Lamb was
standing, just as if it had been slain, having
seven horns and seven eyes (which are the
seven Spirits of God which have been sent
into all the earth).
7 And He came and took the book out of the
right hand of Him who sits on the throne.
8 And when He took the book, the four living
creatures and the twenty-four elders fell
down before the Lamb. *And* each had harps
and golden bowls full of incenses, which are
the prayers of the saints.
9 And they sang a new song, saying, You are
worthy to take the book and to open its seals,
because You were slain and have purchased us
to God by Your blood, out of every tribe and
tongue and people and nation.
10 And You have made us kings and priests
to our God. And we shall rule over the earth.
11 And I saw, and I heard the voice of many
angels around the throne, and of the living
creatures, and of the elders – and the
number of them was myriads of myriads and
thousands of thousands,
12 saying, with a loud voice, Worthy is the
Lamb that has been slain to receive power
and riches and wisdom and strength and
honor and glory and blessing.
13 And I heard every creature which is in
Heaven, and in the earth, and under the
earth, the ones that are on the sea, and all
the things in them, saying, To Him who sits
on the throne, and to the Lamb, blessing and
honor and glory and might forever and ever.
14 And the four living creatures said, Amen.
And the twenty-four elders fell down and
worshiped *Him who* lives forever and ever.

CHAPTER 6

1 And I saw when the Lamb opened one of
the seals. And I heard one of the four living

τος, ὡς φωνῆς βροντῆς, Ἔρχου καὶ βλέπε. 2 Καὶ εἶδον,
ing, as a voice of thunder, Come and see. And I saw,
καὶ ἰδού, ἵππος λευκός, καὶ ὁ καθήμενος ἐπ' αὐτῷ ἔχων
and behold, a horse white, and he sitting on it having
τόξον· καὶ ἐδόθη αὐτῷ στέφανος, καὶ ἐξῆλθεν νικῶν, καὶ
a bow; and was given to him a crown, and he went forth overcoming and
ἵνα νικήσῃ.
that he might overcome.

3 Καὶ ὅτε ἤνοιξεν τὴν δευτέραν σφραγῖδα ἤκουσα τοῦ
And when he opened the second seal I heard the
δευτέρου ζώου λέγοντος, Ἔρχου καὶ βλέπε. 4 Καὶ
second living creature saying, Come and see. And
ἐξῆλθεν ἄλλος ἵππος πυῤῥός· καὶ τῷ καθημένῳ ἐπ' αὐτῷ
went forth another horse red; and to him sitting on it
ἐδόθη αὐτῷ λαβεῖν τὴν εἰρήνην ἀπὸ τῆς γῆς, καὶ ἵνα
was given to him to take peace from the earth, and that
ἀλλήλους σφάξωσιν· καὶ ἐδόθη αὐτῷ μάχαιρα μεγάλη.
one another they should slay; and was given to him a sword great.

5 Καὶ ὅτε ἤνοιξεν τὴν τρίτην σφραγῖδα ἤκουσα τοῦ τρίτου
And when he opened the third seal I heard the third
ζώου λέγοντος, Ἔρχου καὶ βλέπε. Καὶ εἶδον, καὶ
living creature saying, Come and see. And I saw, and
ἰδού, ἵππος μέλας, καὶ ὁ καθήμενος ἐπ' αὐτῷ ἔχων ζυγὸν
behold, a horse black, and he sitting on it having a balance
ἐν τῇ χειρὶ αὐτοῦ. 6 καὶ ἤκουσα φωνὴν ἐν μέσῳ τῶν
in his hand. And I heard a voice in [the] midst of the
τεσσάρων ζώων λέγουσαν, Χοῖνιξ σίτου δηναρίου,
four living creatures, saying, A chœnix of wheat for a denarius,
καὶ τρεῖς χοίνικες κριθῆς δηναρίου· καὶ τὸ ἔλαιον καὶ τὸν
and three chœnixes of barley for a denarius: and the oil and the
οἶνον μὴ ἀδικήσῃς.
wine thou mayest not injure.

7 Καὶ ὅτε ἤνοιξεν τὴν σφραγῖδα τὴν τετάρτην, ἤκουσα
And when he opened the seal fourth, I heard [the]
φωνὴν τοῦ τετάρτου ζώου λέγουσαν, Ἔρχου καὶ
voice of the fourth living creature saying, Come and
βλέπε. 8 Καὶ εἶδον, καὶ ἰδού, ἵππος χλωρός, καὶ ὁ καθήμενος
see. And I saw, and behold, a horse pale, and he sitting
ἐπάνω αὐτοῦ, ὄνομα αὐτῷ ὁ Θάνατος, καὶ ὁ ᾅδης ἀκο-
on it, name his [was] Death, and hades fol-
λουθεῖ μετ' αὐτοῦ· καὶ ἐδόθη αὐτοῖς ἐξουσία ἀποκτεῖναι
lows with him; and was given to them authority to kill
ἐπὶ τὸ τέταρτον τῆς γῆς ἐν ῥομφαίᾳ καὶ ἐν λιμῷ καὶ ἐν
over the fourth of the earth with sword and with famine and with
θανάτῳ, καὶ ὑπὸ τῶν θηρίων τῆς γῆς.
death, and by the beasts of the earth.

9 Καὶ ὅτε ἤνοιξεν τὴν πέμπτην σφραγῖδα εἶδον ὑποκάτω
And when he opened the fifth seal I saw under
τοῦ θυσιαστηρίου τὰς ψυχὰς τῶν ἐσφαγμένων διὰ τὸν
the altar the souls of those having been slain because of the
λόγον τοῦ θεοῦ, καὶ διὰ τὴν μαρτυρίαν ἣν εἶχον, 10 καὶ
word of God, and because of the testimony which they held; and
ἔκραζον φωνῇ μεγάλῃ, λέγοντες, Ἕως πότε, ὁ δεσ-
they were crying with a voice loud, saying, Until when, O Mas-
πότης ὁ ἅγιος καὶ ὁ ἀληθινός, οὐ κρίνεις καὶ ἐκδικεῖς
ter, the holy and the true, dost thou not judge and avenge
τὸ αἷμα ἡμῶν ἀπὸ τῶν κατοικούντων ἐπὶ τῆς γῆς; 11 Καὶ
our blood on those who dwell on the earth? And
ἐδόθησαν ἑκάστοις στολαὶ λευκαί, καὶ ἐῤῥέθη αὐτοῖς ἵνα
were given to each robes white; and it was said to them that
ἀναπαύσωνται ἔτι χρόνον μικρόν, ἕως οὗ πληρώσονται
they should rest yet a time little, until shall be fulfilled
καὶ οἱ σύνδουλοι αὐτῶν καὶ οἱ ἀδελφοὶ αὐτῶν, οἱ μέλλοντες
both their fellow-bondmen and their brethren, those being about
ἀποκτείνεσθαι ὡς καὶ αὐτοί.
to be killed as also they.

12 Καὶ εἶδον ὅτε ἤνοιξεν τὴν σφραγῖδα τὴν ἕκτην· καὶ
And I saw when he opened the seal sixth, and
ἰδού, σεισμὸς μέγας ἐγένετο, καὶ ὁ ἥλιος ἐγένετο μέλας
behold, earthquake a great there was, and the sun became black
ὡς σάκκος τρίχινος, καὶ ἡ σελήνη ἐγένετο ὡς αἷμα, 13 καὶ
as sackcloth hair, and the moon became as blood, and
οἱ ἀστέρες τοῦ οὐρανοῦ ἔπεσαν εἰς τὴν γῆν, ὡς συκῆ βάλλει
the stars of the heaven fell unto the earth, as a fig-tree casts
τοὺς ὀλύνθους αὐτῆς, ὑπὸ μεγάλου ἀνέμου σειομένη· 14 καὶ
its untimely figs, by a great wind being shaken. And
οὐρανὸς ἀπεχωρίσθη ὡς βιβλίον εἱλισσόμενον, καὶ πᾶν
heaven departed as a book being rolled up, and every
ὄρος καὶ νῆσος ἐκ τῶν τόπων αὐτῶν ἐκινήθησαν· 15 καὶ
mountain and island out of their places were moved. And
οἱ βασιλεῖς τῆς γῆς, καὶ οἱ μεγιστᾶνες, καὶ οἱ πλούσιοι, καὶ
the kings of the earth, and the great, and the rich, and

creatures saying, as with a voice of thunder, Come and see.

2 And I saw. And behold, a white horse! And He that was sitting on it had a bow. And a crown was given to Him. And He went out overcoming, and so that He might overcome.

3 And when He opened the second seal, I heard the second living creature saying, Come and see.

4 And another, a red horse went out. And to him that was sitting on it was given *power* to take peace from the earth – and so that they should kill one another. And a great sword was given to him.

5 And when He opened the third seal, I heard the third living creature saying, Come and see. And I saw. And behold, a black horse! And he that was sitting on it had a pair of scales in his hand.

6 And I heard a voice from within the four living creatures, saying, A quart of wheat for a piece of money, and three quarts of barley for a piece of money. And you may not hurt the oil and the wine.

7 And when He opened the fourth seal, I heard the voice of the fourth living creature saying, Come and see.

8 And I looked. And, behold, a pale horse! And he who was sitting on it was named Death. And hell accompanied him. And they were given the right to kill with a sword over the fourth part of the earth – even with famine and with death, and by the beasts of the earth.

9 And when He opened the fifth seal, I saw under the altar the souls of those who had been killed because of the word of God, and because of the witness which they held.

10 And they were crying with a loud voice, saying, O Master, the Holy and the True, how long will You not judge and avenge our blood on those who live on the earth?

11 And to each were given white robes. And it was said to them that they should rest yet a little time, until both their fellow-servants and their brothers (the ones about to be killed as they were) should have their number complete.

12 And I saw when He opened the sixth seal, and behold, there was a great earthquake! And the sun became black as sackcloth made of hair. And the moon became as blood.

13 And the stars of the sky fell on the earth, like a fig-tree casts its figs out of season when shaken by a mighty wind.

14 And the heaven departed as a scroll when it is rolled together; and every mountain and island were moved out of their places.

15 And the kings of the earth, and the great ones, and the rich, and the chief captains, and the powerful ones, and every slave, and every freeman hid themselves in the caves

οἱ χιλίαρχοι,' καὶ οἱ [m]δυνατοί," καὶ πᾶς δοῦλος καὶ [n]πᾶς"
the chief captains, and the powerful, and every bondman, and every
ἐλεύθερος ἔκρυψαν ἑαυτοὺς εἰς τὰ σπήλαια καὶ εἰς τὰς
free [man] hid themselves in the caves and in the
πέτρας τῶν ὀρέων, 16 καὶ λέγουσιν τοῖς ὄρεσιν καὶ ταῖς
rocks of the mountains; and they say to the mountains and to the
πέτραις, [o]Πέσετε ἐφ' ἡμᾶς, καὶ κρύψατε ἡμᾶς ἀπὸ προσ-
rocks, Fall on us, and hide us from [the] face
ώπου τοῦ καθημένου ἐπὶ [p]τοῦ θρόνου," καὶ ἀπὸ τῆς ὀργῆς
of him who sits on the throne, and from the wrath
τοῦ ἀρνίου· 17 ὅτι ἦλθεν ἡ ἡμέρα ἡ μεγάλη τῆς ὀργῆς
of the Lamb; because is come the [2]day [1]great [4]wrath
[q]αὐτοῦ,' καὶ τίς δύναται σταθῆναι;
[3]of [5]his, and who is able to stand?

7 [r]Καὶ" μετὰ [s]ταῦτα" [t]εἶδον" τέσσαρας ἀγγέλους ἑστῶτας
And after these things I saw four angels standing
ἐπὶ τὰς τέσσαρας γωνίας τῆς γῆς, κρατοῦντας τοὺς τέσσαρας
upon the four corners of the earth, holding the four
ἀνέμους τῆς γῆς, ἵνα μὴ πνέῃ ἄνεμος ἐπὶ τῆς γῆς, μήτε
winds of the earth, that no [2]might [3]blow [1]wind on the earth, nor
ἐπὶ τῆς θαλάσσης, μήτε ἐπὶ [v]πᾶν' δένδρον. 2 Καὶ [t]εἶδον" ἄλ-
on the sea, nor upon any (lit. every) tree. And I saw an-
λον ἄγγελον [w]ἀναβάντα' ἀπὸ [x]ἀνατολῆς" ἡλίου, ἔχοντα
other angel having ascended from [the] rising of [the] sun, having
σφραγῖδα θεοῦ ζῶντος· καὶ ἔκραξεν φωνῇ μεγάλῃ
[the] seal of [3]God [[1]the] [2]living; and he cried with a [2]voice [1]loud
τοῖς τέσσαρσιν ἀγγέλοις, οἷς ἐδόθη αὐτοῖς ἀδικῆσαι τὴν
to the four angels to whom it was given to them to injure the
γῆν καὶ τὴν θάλασσαν, 3 λέγων, Μὴ ἀδικήσητε τὴν γῆν,
earth and the sea, saying, Injure not the earth,
μήτε τὴν θάλασσαν, μήτε τὰ δένδρα, [y]ἄχρις" [z]οὗ" [a]σφραγίζω-
nor the sea, nor the trees, until we
μεν" τοὺς δούλους τοῦ θεοῦ ἡμῶν ἐπὶ τῶν μετώπων αὐτῶν.
seal the bondmen of our God on their foreheads.
4 Καὶ ἤκουσα τὸν ἀριθμὸν τῶν ἐσφραγισμένων· [b]ρμδ'' χιλιάδες,
And I heard the number of the sealed, 144 thousand,
ἐσφραγισμένοι ἐκ πάσης φυλῆς υἱῶν Ἰσραήλ· 5 ἐκ
sealed out of every tribe of [the] sons of Israel; out of [the]
φυλῆς Ἰούδα, [c]ιβ'' χιλιάδες ἐσφραγισμένοι· ἐκ φυλῆς
tribe of Judah, 12 thousand sealed; out of [the] tribe
Ῥουβήν, [c]ιβ'' χιλιάδες [d]ἐσφραγισμένοι·' ἐκ φυλῆς Γάδ,
of Reuben, 12 thousand sealed; out of [the] tribe of Gad,
[c]ιβ'' χιλιάδες [d]ἐσφραγισμένοι·' 6 ἐκ φυλῆς Ἀσήρ, [c]ιβ''
12 thousand sealed; out of [the] tribe of Aser, 12
χιλιάδες [d]ἐσφραγισμένοι·" ἐκ φυλῆς [e]Νεφθαλείμ,' [c]ιβ''
thousand sealed; out of [the] tribe of Nepthalim, 12
χιλιάδες [d]ἐσφραγισμένοι·" ἐκ φυλῆς [f]Μανασσῆ," [c]ιβ''
thousand sealed; out of [the] tribe of Manasses, 12
χιλιάδες [d]ἐσφραγισμένοι" 7 ἐκ φυλῆς Συμεών, [c]ιβ'' χιλι-
thousand sealed; out of [the] tribe of Simeon, 12 thou-
άδες [d]ἐσφραγισμένοι·" ἐκ φυλῆς [g]Λευΐ,' [c]ιβ'' χιλιάδες
sand sealed; out of [the] tribe of Levi, 12 thousand
[d]ἐσφραγισμένοι·" ἐκ φυλῆς [h]Ἰσαχάρ," [c]ιβ'' χιλιάδες [d]ἐσφρα-
sealed; out of [the] tribe of Issachar, 12 thousand seal-
γισμένοι·" 8 ἐκ φυλῆς Ζαβουλών, [c]ιβ'' χιλιάδες [d]ἐσφρα-
ed; out of [the] tribe of Zabulon, 12 thousand seal-
γισμένοι·" ἐκ φυλῆς Ἰωσήφ, [c]ιβ'' χιλιάδες [d]ἐσφραγισμένοι·"
ed; out of [the] tribe of Joseph, 12 thousand sealed;
ἐκ φυλῆς [i]Βενιαμίν,' [c]ιβ'' χιλιάδες ἐσφραγισμένοι.
out of [the] tribe of Benjamin, 12 thousand sealed.
9 Μετὰ ταῦτα [t]εἶδον,' [k]καὶ' [l]ἰδού,' [m]ὄχλος πολύς," ὃν
After these things I saw, and behold, a [2]crowd [1]great, which
ἀριθμῆσαι αὐτὸν οὐδεὶς [n]ἠδύνατο,' ἐκ παντὸς ἔθνους καὶ
[5]to [6]number [7]it [1]no [2]one [3]was [4]able, out of every nation and
φυλῶν καὶ λαῶν καὶ γλωσσῶν, [o]ἑστῶτες ἐνώπιον τοῦ θρόνου
tribes, and peoples, and tongues, standing before the throne
καὶ ἐνώπιον τοῦ ἀρνίου, [p]περιβεβλημένοι" στολὰς λευκάς, καὶ
and before the Lamb, clothed with [2]robes [1]white, and
[q]φοίνικες ἐν ταῖς χερσὶν αὐτῶν· 10 καὶ [r]κράζοντες' φωνῇ
palms in their hands; and crying with a [2]voice
μεγάλῃ, λέγοντες, Ἡ σωτηρία [s]τῷ καθημένῳ ἐπὶ τοῦ
[1]loud, saying, Salvation to him who sits on the
θρόνου τοῦ θεοῦ ἡμῶν," καὶ τῷ ἀρνίῳ. 11 Καὶ πάντες οἱ ἄγ-
throne of our God, and to the Lamb. And all the an-
γελοι [t]ἑστήκεσαν" κύκλῳ τοῦ θρόνου καὶ τῶν πρεσβυτέρων καὶ
gels stood around the throne and the elders and
τῶν τεσσάρων ζώων, καὶ [v]ἔπεσον' ἐνώπιον τοῦ θρόνου
the four living creatures, and fell before the throne
ἐπὶ [w]πρόσωπον" αὐτῶν, καὶ προσεκύνησαν τῷ θεῷ, 12 λέγον-
on [2]face [1]their, and worshipped God, say-
τες, Ἀμήν· ἡ εὐλογία καὶ ἡ δόξα καὶ ἡ σοφία καὶ ἡ εὐχαριστία
ing, Amen Blessing, and glory, and wisdom, and thanksgiving,

and in the rocks of the mountains.
16 And they said to the mountains and to the rocks, Fall on us and hide us from the face of Him who sits on the throne, and from the wrath of the Lamb
17 because the great day of His wrath has come, and who is able to stand?

CHAPTER 7

1 And after these things I saw four angels standing on the four corners of the earth, holding the four winds of the earth, so that no wind might blow on the earth, or on the sea or on any tree.
2 And I saw another angel, who had come up from the rising of the sun, and who had the seal of the living God. And he cried with a loud voice to the four angels to whom it was given to them to hurt the earth and the sea,
saying,
3 Do not hurt the earth or the sea or the trees until we seal the servants of our God on their foreheads.
4 And I heard the number of the sealed ones – one hundred and forty-four thousand, sealed out of every tribe of the sons of Israel.
5 Out of the tribe of Judah, twelve thousand were sealed. Out of the tribe of Reuben, twelve thousand were sealed. Out of the tribe of Gad, twelve thousand were sealed.
6 Out of the tribe of Asher, twelve thousand were sealed. Out of the tribe of Naphtali, twelve thousand were sealed. Out of the tribe of Manasseh, twelve thousand were sealed.
7 Out of the tribe of Simeon, twelve thousand were sealed. Out of the tribe of Levi, twelve thousand were sealed. Out of the tribe of Issachar, twelve thousand were sealed.
8 Out of the tribe of Zebulun, twelve thousand were sealed. Out of the tribe of Joseph, twelve thousand were sealed. Out of the tribe of Benjamin, twelve thousand were sealed.

9 After these things I looked, and behold, a great crowd! And no one was able to count it – out of every nation and *of all* tribes and peoples and tongues – standing in front of the throne and in front of the Lamb, clothed with white robes, and having palm branches in their hands.
10 And crying with a loud voice, they said, Salvation to our God who sits on the throne, and to the Lamb.
11 And all the angels and the elders and the four living creatures stood around the throne. And they fell on their faces before the throne and worshiped God,
12 saying, Amen – Blessing and glory and wisdom and thanksgiving and honor and

καὶ ἡ τιμὴ καὶ ἡ δύναμις καὶ ἡ ἰσχὺς τῷ.θεῷ.ἡμῶν εἰς τοὺς
and honour, and power, and strength, to our God to the
αἰῶνας τῶν αἰώνων. ˣἀμήν.‖
ages of the ages. Amen.
13 Καὶ ἀπεκρίθη εἷς ἐκ τῶν πρεσβυτέρων, λέγων μοι, Οὗτοι
And ⁵answered ¹one ²of ³the ⁴elders, saying to me, These
οἱ περιβεβλημένοι τὰς στολὰς τὰς λευκάς, τίνες εἰσίν, καὶ
who are clothed with the ²robes ¹white, who are they, and
πόθεν ἦλθον; 14 Καὶ εἴρηκα αὐτῷ, Κύριεʸ, σὺ οἶδας. Καὶ
whence came they? And I said to him, [My] lord, thou knowest. And
εἶπέν μοι, Οὗτοί εἰσιν οἱ ἐρχόμενοι ᶻἐκ τῆς θλίψεως τῆς‖
he said to me, These are they who come out of the ²tribulation
μεγάλης, καὶ ἔπλυναν τὰς.στολὰς.αὐτῶν, καὶ ἐλεύκαναν
¹great, and they washed their robes, and made white
ᵃστολὰς‖ ᵇαὐτῶν‖ ἐν τῷ αἵματι τοῦ ἀρνίου. 15 διὰ τοῦτό
²robes ¹their in the blood of the Lamb. Because of this
εἰσιν ἐνώπιον τοῦ θρόνου τοῦ θεοῦ, καὶ λατρεύουσιν αὐτῷ
are they before the throne of God, and serve him
ἡμέρας καὶ νυκτὸς ἐν τῷ.ναῷ.αὐτοῦ· καὶ ὁ καθήμενος ἐπὶ
day and night in his temple; and he who sits on
ᶜτοῦ θρόνου‖ σκηνώσει ἐπ' αὐτούς. 16 οὐ.πεινάσουσιν
the throne shall tabernacle over them. They shall not hunger
ἔτι, οὐδὲ ᵈ διψήσουσιν ἔτι, ᵉοὐδὲ‖ μὴ πέσῃ ἐπ' αὐ-
any more, neither shall they thirst any more, nor at all shall fall upon
τοὺς ὁ ἥλιος, οὐδὲ πᾶν καῦμα· 17 ὅτι τὸ ἀρνίον τὸ
them the sun, nor any heat; because the Lamb which [is]
ᶠἀνάμεσον‖ τοῦ θρόνου ποιμανεῖ αὐτούς, καὶ ὁδηγήσει αὐτοὺς
in [the] midst of the throne will shepherd them, and will lead them
ἐπὶ ᵍζώσας‖ πηγὰς ὑδάτων, καὶ ἐξαλείψει ὁ θεὸς πᾶν
to living fountains of waters, and ²will ³wipe ⁴away ¹God every
δάκρυον ʰἀπὸ‖ τῶν.ὀφθαλμῶν.αὐτῶν.
tear from their eyes.

8 Καὶ ⁱὅτε‖ ἤνοιξεν τὴν σφραγῖδα τὴν ἑβδόμην, ἐγένετο
And when he opened the ²seal ¹seventh, ⁴was
σιγὴ ἐν τῷ οὐρανῷ ὡς ᵏἡμιώριον.‖ 2 Καὶ ˡεἶδον‖ τοὺς ἑπτὰ
³silence in the heaven about half-an-hour. And I saw the seven
ἀγγέλους, οἳ ἐνώπιον τοῦ θεοῦ ἑστήκασιν, καὶ ἐδόθησαν
angels, who ²before ³God ¹stand, and were given
αὐτοῖς ἑπτὰ σάλπιγγες. 3 καὶ ἄλλος ἄγγελος ἦλθεν, καὶ
to them seven trumpets. And another angel came and
ἐστάθη ἐπὶ ᵐτὸ θυσιαστήριον,‖ ἔχων λιβανωτὸν χρυσοῦν· καὶ
stood at the altar, having a ²censer ¹golden; and
ἐδόθη αὐτῷ θυμιάματα πολλά, ἵνα ⁿδώσῃ‖ ταῖς
³was ¹given ⁵to ⁶him ²incense ¹much, that he might give [it] to the
προσευχαῖς τῶν ἁγίων πάντων ἐπὶ τὸ θυσιαστήριον τὸ
prayers of ²the ³saints ¹all upon the ²altar
χρυσοῦν τὸ ἐνώπιον τοῦ θρόνου. 4 καὶ ἀνέβη ὁ καπνὸς
¹golden which [was] before the throne. And went up the smoke
τῶν θυμιαμάτων ταῖς προσευχαῖς τῶν ἁγίων, ἐκ χειρὸς
of the incense with the prayers of the saints, out of [the] hand
τοῦ ἀγγέλου, ἐνώπιον τοῦ θεοῦ. 5 καὶ εἴληφεν ὁ ἄγγελος ᵒτὸ‖
of the angel, before God. And ³took ¹the ²angel the
λιβανωτόν, καὶ ἐγέμισεν ᵖαὐτὸ‖ ἐκ τοῦ πυρὸς τοῦ θυσιαστη-
censer, and filled it from the fire of the altar,
ρίου, καὶ ἔβαλεν εἰς τὴν γῆν· καὶ ἐγένοντο ᑫφωναὶ καὶ
and cast [it] into the earth: and there were voices, and
βρονταὶ καὶ ἀστραπαὶ καὶ σεισμός.
thunders, and lightnings, and an earthquake.
6 Καὶ οἱ ἑπτὰ ἄγγελοι ʳ ἔχοντες τὰς ἑπτὰ σάλπιγγας ἡτοί-
And the seven angels having the seven trumpets pre-
μασαν ˢἑαυτοὺς‖ ἵνα σαλπίσωσιν.
pared themselves that they might sound [their] trumpets.
7 Καὶ ὁ πρῶτος ᵗἄγγελος‖ ἐσάλπισεν, καὶ ἐγένετο
And the first angel sounded [his] trumpet; and there was
χάλαζα καὶ πῦρ ᵛμεμιγμένα‖ ʷ αἵματι, καὶ ἐβλήθη εἰς τὴν
hail and fire mingled with blood, and it was cast upon the
γῆν· ˣ καὶ τὸ τρίτον τῶν δένδρων κατεκάη, καὶ πᾶς χόρτος
earth: and the third of the trees was burnt up, and all ²grass
χλωρὸς κατεκάη.
¹green was burnt up.
8 Καὶ ὁ δεύτερος ἄγγελος ἐσάλπισεν, καὶ ὡς
And the second angel sounded [his] trumpet; and as [it were]
ὄρος μέγα πυρὶ καιόμενον ἐβλήθη εἰς τὴν θάλασσαν· καὶ
a ²mountain ¹great ⁴with ⁵fire ³burning was cast into the sea, and
ἐγένετο τὸ τρίτον τῆς θαλάσσης αἷμα. 9 καὶ ἀπέθανεν τὸ
⁶became ¹the ²third ³of ⁴the ⁵sea blood; and ¹⁴died ¹the
τρίτον τῶν κτισμάτων τῶν ἐν τῇ θαλάσσῃ τὰ ἔχοντα
²third ³of ⁴the ⁵creatures ⁶which [⁷were] ⁸in ⁹the ¹⁰sea ¹¹which ¹²have
ψυχάς, καὶ τὸ τρίτον τῶν πλοίων ʸδιεφθάρη.‖
¹³life; and the third of the ships was destroyed.
10 Καὶ ὁ τρίτος ἄγγελος ἐσάλπισεν, καὶ ἔπεσεν ἐκ
And the third angel sounded [his] trumpet; and ⁴fell ⁵out ⁶of

power and strength to our God forever and
ever. Amen.
13 And one of the elders answered, saying
to me, These who are clothed with the white
robes, who are they? And where do they
come from?
14 And I said to him, Sir, you know. And
he said to me, These are the ones who come
out of the great tribulation. And they have
washed their robes and have made their
robes white in the blood of the Lamb.
15 This is why they are before the throne of
God, and they serve Him day and night in
His Temple. And He who sits on the throne
shall spread His tent over them.
16 They shall not hunger any more, nor
shall they thirst any more – nor shall the
sun ever fall on them, or any heat,
17 because the Lamb which is in the midst
of the throne will shepherd them. And He
will lead them to living fountains of water.
And God will wipe away every tear from
their eyes.

CHAPTER 8

1 And when He opened the seventh seal,
there was silence in Heaven about half-an-hour.
2 And I saw the seven angels who stand before God. And seven trumpets were given to
them.
3 And another angel came and stood at the
altar. And he had a golden censer, and much
incense was given to him so that he might give
it with the prayers of all the saints on the
golden altar which was before the throne.
4 And the smoke of the incense went up with
the prayers of the saints out of the hand of
the angel before God.
5 And the angel took the censer and filled it
from the fire of the altar and threw it onto
the earth. And there were voices and
thunders and lightnings and an earthquake.
6 And the seven angels who had the seven
trumpets got themselves ready, so that they
could sound trumpets.
7 And the first angel sounded his trumpet.
And there came hail and fire mixed with
blood, and it was thrown upon the earth.
And the third part of the trees was burned
up, and all the green grass was burned up.
8 And the second angel sounded his trumpet – and as *it were* a great mountain burning
with fire was thrown into the sea, and the
third part of the sea also became blood.
9 And the third part of the creatures which
was in the sea died – those which have life.
And the third part of the ships were destroyed.
10 And the third angel sounded his trumpet.
And a great star fell out of the sky, burning

τοῦ οὐρανοῦ ἀστὴρ μέγας καιόμενος ὡς λαμπάς, καὶ ἔπεσεν
[7]the [8]heaven [1]a [3]star [2]great, burning as a lamp, and it fell
ἐπὶ τὸ τρίτον τῶν ποταμῶν, καὶ ἐπὶ τὰς πηγὰς[z] ὑδάτων.
upon the third of the rivers, and upon the fountains of waters.
11 καὶ τὸ ὄνομα τοῦ ἀστέρος λέγεται[a] Ἄψινθος· καὶ [b]γίνεται
And the name of the star is called Wormwood; and [3]becomes
τὸ τρίτον[c] εἰς ἄψινθον, καὶ πολλοὶ [d] ἀνθρώπων ἀπέθανον
[1]the [2]third into wormwood, and [3]many [1]of [2]men died
ἐκ τῶν ὑδάτων, ὅτι ἐπικράνθησαν.
of the waters, because they were made bitter.
12 Καὶ ὁ τέταρτος ἄγγελος ἐσάλπισεν, καὶ ἐπλήγη
And the fourth angel sounded [his] trumpet; and was smitten
τὸ τρίτον τοῦ ἡλίου καὶ τὸ τρίτον τῆς σελήνης καὶ τὸ τρίτον
the third of the sun, and the third of the moon, and the third
τῶν ἀστέρων, ἵνα σκοτισθῇ τὸ τρίτον αὐτῶν, καὶ ἡ
of the stars; that should be darkened the third of them, and the
ἡμέρα μὴ [e]φαίνῃ τὸ τρίτον αὐτῆς, καὶ ἡ νὺξ ὁμοίως.
day [2]not [1]should appear [for] the third of it, and the night likewise.
13 Καὶ [f]εἶδον, καὶ ἤκουσα ἑνὸς [g]ἀγγέλου πετωμένου ἐν
And I saw, and heard one angel flying in
μεσουρανήματι, λέγοντος φωνῇ μεγάλῃ, Οὐαί, οὐαί, οὐαί,
mid-heaven, saying with a [2]voice [1]loud, Woe, woe, woe,
[h]τοῖς κατοικοῦσιν ἐπὶ τῆς γῆς, ἐκ τῶν λοιπῶν φωνῶν
to those who dwell on the earth, from the remaining voices
τῆς σάλπιγγος τῶν τριῶν ἀγγέλων τῶν μελλόντων σαλ-
of the trumpet of the three angels who [are] about to sound
πίζειν.
[their] trumpets.

like a lamp. And it fell on the third part of the rivers, and on the fountain of waters.

11 And the name of the star is called Wormwood. And a third *of the waters* became wormwood. And many men died of the waters because they were made bitter.

12 And the fourth angel sounded his trumpet. And the third part of the sun was struck, and the third part of the moon, and the third part of the stars – so that the third part of them might be made dark and the day should not shine for a third of it, and the night also.

13 And I saw and heard one angel flying in the middle of Heaven, saying with a loud voice, Woe! Woe! Woe to those who live on the earth, from the rest of the voices of the trumpet of the three angels who are going to sound their trumpets!

9 Καὶ ὁ πέμπτος ἄγγελος ἐσάλπισεν, καὶ [i]εἶδον
And the fifth angel sounded [his] trumpet; and I saw
ἀστέρα ἐκ τοῦ οὐρανοῦ πεπτωκότα εἰς τὴν γῆν, καὶ ἐδό-
a star out of the heaven fallen to the earth, and there was
θη αὐτῷ ἡ κλεὶς τοῦ φρέατος τῆς ἀβύσσου. 2 καὶ ἤνοιξεν
given to it the key of the pit of the abyss. And it opened
τὸ φρέαρ τῆς ἀβύσσου. καὶ ἀνέβη καπνὸς ἐκ τοῦ φρέατος
the pit of the abyss; and there went up smoke out of the pit
ὡς καπνὸς καμίνου μεγάλης, καὶ [k]ἐσκοτίσθη ὁ ἥλιος
as [the] smoke of a [2]furnace [1]great; and [3]was [4]darkened [1]the [2]sun
καὶ ὁ ἀὴρ ἐκ τοῦ καπνοῦ τοῦ φρέατος. 3 καὶ ἐκ τοῦ καπνοῦ
and the air by the smoke of the pit. And out of the smoke
ἐξῆλθον ἀκρίδες εἰς τὴν γῆν, καὶ ἐδόθη [l]αὐταῖς ἐξουσία,
came forth locusts unto the earth, and was given to them power,
ὡς ἔχουσιν ἐξουσίαν οἱ σκορπίοι τῆς γῆς· 4 καὶ ἐῤῥέθη
as [6]have [7]power [1]the [2]scorpions [3]of [4]the [5]earth; and it was said
[l]αὐταῖς ἵνα μὴ [m]ἀδικήσωσιν τὸν χόρτον τῆς γῆς, οὐδὲ πᾶν
to them, that [3]not [1]they [2]should injure the grass of the earth, nor any
χλωρόν, οὐδὲ πᾶν δένδρον, εἰ.μὴ τοὺς ἀνθρώπους [n]μόνους
green thing, nor any tree, but the men only
οἵτινες οὐκ.ἔχουσιν τὴν σφραγῖδα τοῦ θεοῦ ἐπὶ τῶν μετώπων
who have not the seal of God on [2]foreheads
[o]αὐτῶν. 5 καὶ ἐδόθη [p]αὐταῖς ἵνα μὴ.ἀποκτείνωσιν αὐτούς,
[1]their. And it was given to them that they should not kill them,
ἀλλ' ἵνα [q]βασανισθῶσιν μῆνας πέντε· καὶ ὁ βασανισμὸς
but that they should be tormented [2]months [1]five; and [2]torment
αὐτῶν ὡς βασανισμὸς σκορπίου, ὅταν παίσῃ ἄν-
[1]their [was] as [the] torment of a scorpion, when it may strike a
θρωπον· 6 καὶ ἐν ταῖς.ἡμέραις.ἐκείναις ζητήσουσιν οἱ ἄνθρω-
man. And in those days [2]shall [3]seek [1]men
ποι τὸν θάνατον, καὶ [r]οὐχ [s]εὑρήσουσιν αὐτόν· καὶ ἐπιθυμή-
death, and [2]not [1]shall find it; and shall
σουσιν ἀποθανεῖν, καὶ [t]φεύξεται [v]ὁ θάνατος ἀπ' αὐτῶν.
desire to die, and [2]shall [3]flee [1]death from them.
7 καὶ τὰ ὁμοιώματα τῶν ἀκρίδων [w]ὅμοια ἵπποις ἡτοι-
And the likenesses of the locusts [were] like to horses pre-
μασμένοις εἰς πόλεμον, καὶ ἐπὶ τὰς.κεφαλὰς.αὐτῶν ὡς στέφανοι
pared for war, and upon their heads as crowns
ὅμοιοι [x]χρυσῷ, καὶ τὰ.πρόσωπα.αὐτῶν ὡς πρόσωπα ἀνθρώ-
like gold; and their faces as faces of
πων· 8 καὶ [y]εἶχον τρίχας ὡς τρίχας γυναικῶν· καὶ οἱ ὀδόντες
men; and they had hair as [2]hair [1]women's; and [2]teeth
αὐτῶν ὡς λεόντων ἦσαν· 9 καὶ εἶχον θώρακας ὡς θώρακας
[1]their [4]as [5]of [6]lions [3]were; and they had breastplates as [2]breastplates
σιδηροῦς· καὶ ἡ φωνὴ τῶν.πτερύγων.αὐτῶν ὡς φωνὴ
[1]iron; and the sound of their wings [was] as [the] sound
ἁρμάτων ἵππων πολλῶν τρεχόντων εἰς πόλεμον. 10 καὶ
of chariots of [2]horses [1]many running to war; and
ἔχουσιν οὐρὰς [z]ὁμοίας σκορπίοις, καὶ κέντρα·[a] [b]ἦν ἐν ταῖς
they have tails like scorpions, and stings; [4]was [5]in
οὐραῖς αὐτῶν [c]καὶ ἡ.ἐξουσία.αὐτῶν ἀδικῆσαι τοὺς ἀνθρώπους
[7]tails [6]their [1]and [2]their [3]power to injure men
μῆνας πέντε. 11 [d]καὶ ἔχουσιν [e]ἐφ' αὐτῶν βασιλέα [f]τὸν
[2]months [1]five. And they have over them a king, the

CHAPTER 9

1 And the fifth angel sounded his trumpet. And I saw a star which had fallen to the earth out of the sky. And there was given to it the key of the bottomless pit.

2 And it opened the bottomless pit. And smoke went up out of the pit, pike the smoke of a great furnace. And the sun and the air were made dark by the smoke of pit.

3 And out of the smoke came forth locusts onto the earth. And power was given to them as the scorpions of the earth have power.

4 And it was commanded them, that they should not hurt the grass of the earth or any green thing or any tree, but only the men who do not have the seal of God on their foreheads.

5 And it was given to them that they should not kill them, but that they should be tormented five months. And their torment is like the torment of a scorpion when it strikes a man.

6 And in those days men shall seek death and will not find it. And they shall desire to die, and death shall flee from them.

7 And the shapes of the locusts were like horses ready for war. And on their heads, crowns like gold, and their faces like the faces of men.

8 And they had hair like the hair of women. And their teeth were like the teeth of lions.

9 And they had breastplates of iron. And the sound of their wings was like the sound of chariots, of many horses running to war.

10 And they have tails like scorpions, and stings. And their power to hurt men five months was in their tails.

11 And they have a king over them, the

ἄγγελον τῆς ἀβύσσου· [k] ὄνομα αὐτῷ Ἑβραϊστὶ Ἀβαδδών, καὶ
angel of the abyss: his name in Hebrew Abaddon, and
ἐν τῇ Ἑλληνικῇ ὄνομα ἔχει Ἀπολλύων.
in the Greek [for] name he has Apollyon.
12 Ἡ οὐαὶ ἡ μία ἀπῆλθεν· ἰδού, [l]ἔρχονται'' ἔτι δύο οὐαὶ
[3]Woe [1]the [2]first is past. Lo, [4]come [1]yet [2]two [3]woes
μετὰ ταῦτα.
after these things.
13 Καὶ ὁ ἕκτος ἄγγελος ἐσάλπισεν, καὶ ἤκουσα φωνὴν
And the sixth angel sounded [his] trumpet; and I heard [2]voice
μίαν ἐκ τῶν [i]τεσσάρων' κεράτων τοῦ θυσιαστηρίου τοῦ χρυσοῦ
[1]one from the four horns of the [3]altar [2]golden
τοῦ ἐνώπιον τοῦ θεοῦ, 14 [h]λέγουσαν'' τῷ ἕκτῳ ἀγγέλῳ
which [is] before God, saying to the sixth angel
[l]ὃς εἶχε'' τὴν σάλπιγγα, Λῦσον τοὺς τέσσαρας ἀγγέλους τοὺς
who had the trumpet, Loose the four angels who
δεδεμένους ἐπὶ τῷ ποταμῷ τῷ μεγάλῳ Εὐφράτῃ. 15 Καὶ ἐλύ-
are bound at the [2]river [1]great Euphrates. And were
θησαν οἱ τέσσαρες ἄγγελοι οἱ ἡτοιμασμένοι εἰς τὴν ὥραν καὶ
loosed the four angels who had been prepared for the hour and
ἡμέραν καὶ μῆνα καὶ ἐνιαυτόν, ἵνα ἀποκτείνωσιν τὸ τρίτον
day and month and year, that they might kill the third
τῶν ἀνθρώπων. 16 καὶ ὁ ἀριθμὸς [n] στρατευμάτων τοῦ ἱππι-
of men; and the number of [the] armies of the caval-
κοῦ [o]δύο μυριάδες'' μυριάδων· [p]καὶ'' ἤκουσα τὸν ἀριθμὸν
ry [was] two myriads of myriads, and I heard the number
αὐτῶν. 17 καὶ οὕτως [q]εἶδον'' τοὺς ἵππους ἐν τῇ ὁράσει, καὶ
of them. And thus I saw the horses in the vision, and
τοὺς καθημένους ἐπ' αὐτῶν, ἔχοντας θώρακας πυρίνους καὶ
those sitting on them, having breastplates fiery, and
ὑακινθίνους καὶ θειώδεις· καὶ αἱ κεφαλαὶ τῶν ἵππων
hyacinthine, and brimstone-like; and the heads of the horses [were]
ὡς κεφαλαὶ λεόντων, καὶ ἐκ τῶν.στομάτων.αὐτῶν ἐκπορεύε-
as heads of lions, and out of their mouths goes
ται πῦρ καὶ καπνὸς καὶ θεῖον. 18 [r]ὑπὸ'' τῶν τριῶν [s] τούτων
out fire and smoke and brimstone. By [2]three [1]these
ἀπεκτάνθησαν τὸ τρίτον τῶν ἀνθρώπων, ἐκ τοῦ πυρὸς καὶ
were killed the third of the men, by the fire and
[t]ἐκ'' τοῦ καπνοῦ καὶ [t]ἐκ'' τοῦ θείου, τοῦ ἐκπορευομένου ἐκ
by the smoke and by the brimstone, which goes forth out of
τῶν.στομάτων.αὐτῶν. 19 [v]αἱ.γὰρ ἐξουσίαι αὐτῶν ἐν τῷ
their mouths. For the powers of them [2]in
στόματι αὐτῶν εἰσιν·'' αἱ.γὰρ.οὐραὶ.αὐτῶν ὅμοιαι ὄφεσιν,
[4]mouth [3]their [1]are; for their tails [are] like serpents,
ἔχουσαι κεφαλάς, καὶ ἐν αὐταῖς ἀδικοῦσιν. 20 καὶ οἱ λοιποὶ
having heads, and with them they injure. And the rest
τῶν ἀνθρώπων οἳ οὐκ.ἀπεκτάνθησαν ἐν ταῖς.πληγαῖς.ταύταις,
of the men who were not killed by these plagues,
[w]οὔτε'' μετενόησαν ἐκ τῶν ἔργων τῶν.χειρῶν.αὐτῶν, ἵνα μὴ
[1]not [2]even [1]repented of the works of their hands, that [3]not
[x]προσκυνήσωσιν'' τὰ δαιμόνια, καὶ [y] εἴδωλα τὰ χρυσᾶ καὶ
[1]they [2]should do homage to the demons, and [2]idols [1]the golden and
τὰ ἀργυρᾶ καὶ τὰ χαλκᾶ καὶ τὰ λίθινα καὶ τὰ ξύλινα,
silver and brazen and stone and wooden,
ἃ οὔτε βλέπειν [z]δύναται,'' οὔτε ἀκούειν, οὔτε περιπατεῖν·
which neither [3]to [4]see [1]are [2]able, nor to hear, nor to walk.
21 καὶ οὐ.μετενόησαν ἐκ τῶν.φόνων.αὐτῶν, οὔτε ἐκ τῶν
And they repented not of their murders, nor of
[a]φαρμακειῶν'' αὐτῶν, οὔτε ἐκ τῆς.πορνείας.αὐτῶν, οὔτε ἐκ
[2]sorceries [1]their, nor of their fornications, nor of
τῶν.κλεμμάτων.αὐτῶν.
their thefts.

10 Καὶ εἶδον ἄλλον ἄγγελον ἰσχυρὸν καταβαίνοντα ἐκ τοῦ
And I saw another [2]angel [1]strong coming down out of the
οὐρανοῦ, περιβεβλημένον νεφέλην, καὶ [b] ἶρις ἐπὶ [c]τῆς κεφ-
heaven, clothed with a cloud, and a rainbow on the
αλῆς''[d], καὶ τὸ.πρόσωπον.αὐτοῦ ὡς ὁ ἥλιος, καὶ οἱ.πόδες.αὐτοῦ
head, and his face as the sun, and his feet
ὡς στῦλοι πυρός· 2 καὶ [e]εἶχεν'' ἐν τῇ.χειρὶ.αὐτοῦ βιβλαρίδιον
as pillars of fire, and he had in his hand a little book
[f]ἀνεῳγμένον·'' καὶ ἔθηκεν τὸν.πόδα.αὐτοῦ τὸν δεξιὸν ἐπὶ [g]τὴν
open. And he placed his [2]foot [1]right upon the
θάλασσαν,'' τὸν.δὲ εὐώνυμον ἐπὶ [h]τὴν γῆν,'' 3 καὶ ἔκραξεν
sea, and the left upon the earth, and cried
φωνῇ μεγάλῃ ὥσπερ λέων μυκᾶται· καὶ ὅτε ἔκραξεν,
with a [2]voice [1]loud as a lion roars. And when he cried,
ἐλάλησαν αἱ ἑπτὰ βρονταὶ τὰς.ἑαυτῶν.φωνάς· 4 καὶ ὅτε
[4]spoke [1]the [2]seven [3]thunders their voices. And when
ἐλάλησαν αἱ ἑπτὰ βρονταὶ [i]τὰς.φωνὰς.ἑαυτῶν,'' [k]ἔμελλον'
[4]spoke [1]the [2]seven [3]thunders their voices, I was about
γράφειν· καὶ ἤκουσα φωνὴν ἐκ τοῦ οὐρανοῦ, λέγουσάν [l]μοι,''
to write: And I heard a voice out of the heaven, saying to me,

angel of the bottomless pit. His name in Hebrew is A-bad-don. And in the Greek language, he has A-poll-yon for his name.
12 The first woe is past. Behold! There are still two woes to come after these things.
13 And the sixth angel sounded his trumpet. And I heard one voice from the four horns of the golden altar which is before God,
14 saying to the sixth angel who had the trumpet, Release the four angels who are bound at the great river Euphrates.
15 And the four angels were released who had been made ready for the hour and day and month and year – that they might kill the third part of men.
16 And the number of the armies of the horsemen was two myriads of myriads. And I heard the number of them.
17 And so I saw the horses in the vision, and the ones who were sitting on them. They had fire-colored breastplates, even dusky red and brimstone-like. And the heads of the horses were as the heads of lions. And out of their mouths came out fire and smoke and brimstone.
18 The third part of men were killed by these three, by the fire and by the smoke and by the brimstone which came out of their mouths.
19 For their powers are in their mouths – for their tails are like snakes with heads, and with them they hurt.
20 And the rest of men, who were not killed by these plagues, did not even repent of the works of their hands, that they should not worship the demons, and the golden and the silver and the brass and the stone and the wooden idols – which can neither see nor hear nor walk.
21 And they did not repent of their murders, nor of their magic arts, nor of their fornications, nor of their thefts.

CHAPTER 10

1 And I saw another mighty angel coming down out of Heaven, clothed with a cloud, and a rainbow on his head, and his face like the sun, and his feet like pillars of fire.
2 And he had a little book open in his hand. And he placed his right foot on the sea and his left on the earth.
3 And he cried with a loud voice, just as a lion roars. And when he cried, the seven thunders spoke their sounds.
4 And when the seven thunders spoke their sounds, I was about to write. And I heard a voice out of Heaven saying to me, Seal up

Σφράγισον ἃ ἐλάλησαν αἱ ἑπτὰ βρονταί, καὶ μὴ ᵐταῦτα¹
Seal what [things] ⁴spoke ¹the ²seven ³thunders, and ²not ³them
γράψῃς. 5 Καὶ ὁ ἄγγελος, ὃν εἶδον ἑστῶτα ἐπὶ τῆς θαλάσσης
¹write. And the angel whom I saw standing on the sea
καὶ ἐπὶ τῆς γῆς, ἦρεν τὴν.χεῖρα.αὐτοῦ ⁿ εἰς τὸν οὐρανόν,
and on the earth, lifted up his hand to the heaven,
6 καὶ ὤμοσεν ἐν τῷ ζῶντι εἰς τοὺς αἰῶνας τῶν αἰώνων, ὃς
and sware by him who lives to the ages of the ages, who
ἔκτισεν τὸν οὐρανὸν καὶ τὰ ἐν αὐτῷ, καὶ τὴν γῆν καὶ
created the heaven and the things in it, and the earth and
τὰ ἐν αὐτῇ, ᵒκαὶ τὴν θάλασσαν καὶ τὰ ἐν αὐτῇ,¹
the things in it, and the sea and the things in it,
Ὅτι χρόνος ᵖοὐκ ἔσται ἔτι·ᴵᴵ 7 ᵍἀλλ᾽¹ ἐν ταῖς ἡμέραις τῆς
Delay ¹no ³shall ²be longer; but in the days of the
φωνῆς τοῦ ἑβδόμου ἀγγέλου, ὅταν μέλλῃ σαλπίζειν,
voice of the seventh angel, when he is about to sound [the] trumpet,
καὶ ʳτελεσθῇ¹ τὸ μυστήριον τοῦ θεοῦ, ὡς εὐηγ-
also should be completed the mystery of God, as he did announce
γέλισεν ˢτοῖς.ἑαυτοῦ.δούλοις τοῖς προφήταις.ᴵᴵ
the glad tidings to his bondmen the prophets.
8 Καὶ ἡ φωνὴ ἣν ἤκουσα ἐκ τοῦ οὐρανοῦ, πάλιν
And the voice which I heard out of the heaven [was] again
ᵗλαλοῦσα¹ μετ᾽ ἐμοῦ, καὶ ᵛλέγουσα,¹ Ὕπαγε λάβε τὸ ʷβιβλα-
speaking with me, and saying, Go, take the little
ρίδιον¹ τὸ ἠνεῳγμένον ἐν τῇ χειρὶ ˣ ἀγγέλου τοῦ ἑστῶτος
book which is open in the hand of [the] angel who is standing
ἐπὶ τῆς θαλάσσης καὶ ἐπὶ τῆς γῆς. 9 Καὶ ʸἀπῆλθονᴵᴵ πρὸς τὸν
on the sea and on the earth. And I went to the
ἄγγελον, λέγων αὐτῷ, ᶻΔός¹ μοι τὸ βιβλαρίδιον. Καὶ λέγει
angel, saying to him, Give me the little book. And he says
μοι, Λάβε καὶ κατάφαγε αὐτό· καὶ πικρανεῖ σου τὴν
to me, Take and eat ²up ¹it: and it shall make bitter thy
κοιλίαν, ἀλλ᾽ ἐν τῷ.στόματι.σου ἔσται γλυκὺ ὡς μέλι. 10 Καὶ
belly, but in thy mouth it shall be sweet as honey. And
ἔλαβον τὸ βιβλαρίδιον ἐκ τῆς χειρὸς τοῦ ἀγγέλου, καὶ κατέ-
I took the little book out of the hand of the angel, and ate
φαγον αὐτό· καὶ ἦν ἐν τῷ.στόματί.μου ὡς μέλι γλυκύ· καὶ
²up ¹it; and it was in my mouth ²as ³honey ¹sweet; and
ὅτε ἔφαγον αὐτό, ἐπικράνθη ἡ.κοιλία.μου. 11 καὶ ᶜλέγειᴵᴵ
when I did eat it, ³was ⁴made ⁵bitter ¹my ²belly. And he says
μοι, Δεῖ.σε πάλιν προφητεῦσαι ἐπὶ λαοῖς καὶ ᵈ ἔθνεσιν καὶ
to me, Thou must again prophesy as to peoples, and nations, and
γλώσσαις καὶ βασιλεῦσιν πολλοῖς.
tongues, and ²kings ¹many.

11 Καὶ ἐδόθη μοι κάλαμος ὅμοιος ῥάβδῳ, ᵉ λέγων, ᶠἜγει-
And was given to me a reed like a staff, saying, Rise,
ραι,¹ καὶ μέτρησον τὸν ναὸν τοῦ θεοῦ, καὶ τὸ θυσιαστήριον,
and measure the temple of God, and the altar,
καὶ τοὺς προσκυνοῦντας ἐν αὐτῷ· 2 καὶ.τὴν αὐλὴν τὴν
and those who worship in it. And the court which
ᵍἔσωθενᴵ τοῦ ναοῦ ἔκβαλε ʰἔξω,ᴵᴵ καὶ μὴ αὐτὴν μετρήσῃς,
[is] within the temple cast out, and ²not ³it ¹measure;
ὅτι ἐδόθη τοῖς ἔθνεσιν· καὶ τὴν πόλιν τὴν ἁγίαν
because it was given [up] to the nations, and the ²city ¹holy
πατήσουσιν μῆνας ⁱτεσσαράκοντα · ᵏ δύο. 3 καὶ δώσω
shall they trample upon ³months ¹forty ²two. And I will give
τοῖς.δυσὶν.μάρτυσίν.μου, καὶ προφητεύσουσιν ἡμέρας
[power] to my two witnesses, and they shall prophesy ⁷days
χιλίας διακοσίας ἑξήκοντα, ˡπεριβεβλημένοιᴵᴵ σάκ-
¹a ²thousand ³two ⁴hundred [⁵and] ⁶sixty, clothed in sack-
κους. 4 οὗτοί εἰσιν αἱ δύο ἐλαῖαι, καὶ ᵐ δύο λυχνίαι
cloth. These are the two olive trees, and [the] two lampstands
αἱ ἐνώπιον ⁿτοῦ¹ ᵒθεοῦ¹ τῆς γῆς ᵖἑστῶσαι.¹ 5 καὶ εἴ τις
which ²before ³the ⁴God ⁵of ⁶the ⁷earth ¹stand. And if anyone
αὐτοὺς ᵍθέλῃᴵᴵ ἀδικῆσαι, πῦρ ἐκπορεύεται ἐκ τοῦ στόματος
⁵them ¹should ²will ³to ⁴injure, fire goes out of ²mouth
αὐτῶν, καὶ κατεσθίει τοὺς.ἐχθροὺς.αὐτῶν· καὶ εἴ τις ʳαὐτοὺς
¹their, and devours their enemies. And if anyone ⁵them
θέλῃ¹ ἀδικῆσαι, οὕτως δεῖ.αὐτὸν ἀποκτανθῆναι. 6 οὗτοι
¹should ²will ³to ⁴injure, thus must he be killed. These
ἔχουσιν ˢ ᵗἐξουσίαν κλεῖσαι τὸν οὐρανόν,¹ ἵνα μὴ ᵛβρέχῃ
have authority to shut the heaven, that no ²may ³fall
ὑετὸς ἐν ἡμέραις αὐτῶν τῆς προφητείας·¹ καὶ ἐξουσίαν
¹rain in [the] days of their prophecy; and authority
ἔχουσιν ἐπὶ τῶν ὑδάτων, στρέφειν αὐτὰ εἰς αἷμα, καὶ πατά-
they have over the waters, to turn them into blood, and to
ξαι τὴν γῆν ʷ ˣπάσῃ πληγῇ, ὁσάκις ἐὰν θελήσωσιν.ᴵᴵ 7 καὶ
smite the earth with every plague, as often as they may will. And
ὅταν τελέσωσιν τὴν.μαρτυρίαν.αὐτῶν, τὸ θηρίον τὸ
when they shall have completed their testimony, the beast who
ἀναβαῖνον ἐκ τῆς ἀβύσσου ποιήσει ʸπόλεμον μετ᾽ αὐτῶν,ᴵᴵ
comes up out of the abyss will make war with them,

the things which the seven thunders spoke and do not write them.

5 And the angel whom I saw standing on the sea and on the earth lifted up his hand to Heaven.

6 And he swore by Him who lives forever and ever, who created the sky and the things in it, and the earth and the things in it, and the sea and the things in it that there should no longer be any time.

7 But in the days of the voice of the seventh angel, when he is going to sound the trumpet, the mystery of God should also be completed, even as He preached to His servants the prophets.

8 And the voice which I heard out of Heaven was again speaking with me and saying, Go! Take the little book which is open in the hand of the angel who is standing on the sea and on the earth.

9 And I went to the angel, saying to him, Give me the little book. And he said to me, Take and eat it up. And it shall make your belly bitter, but it shall be sweet as honey in your mouth.

10 And I took the little book out of the hand of the angel and ate it up. And it was like sweet honey in my mouth, and when I had eaten it, my belly was made bitter.

11 And he said to me, You must again prophesy in regard to many peoples and nations and tongues and kings.

CHAPTER 11

1 And a reed like a staff was given to me, saying, Get up and measure the Temple of God, and the altar, and the ones who worship in it.

2 And leave out the court which is outside the Temple, and do not measure it – because it was given to the Gentiles and they shall trample the holy city underfoot for forty-two months.

3 And I will give *power* to my two witnesses. And they shall prophesy one thousand two hundred and sixty days, dressed in sackcloth.

4 These are the two olive trees and the two lampstands which stand before the God of the earth.

5 And if anyone should desire to hurt them, fire comes out of their mouth and eats their enemies. And if anyone should desire to hurt them, he must be killed in the same way.

6 These have authority to shut up the sky, so that no rain may fall in their days of prophecy – and they have authority over the waters to turn them into blood, and to strike the earth with every plague, as often as they desire.

7 And when they shall have finished their witnessing, the beast who comes up out of the bottomless pit will make war with them. And he will overcome them and will kill them.

καὶ νικήσει αὐτούς, καὶ ἀποκτενεῖ αὐτούς. 8 καὶ ᶻτὰ
and will overcome them, and will kill them: and
πτώματα αὐτῶν ἐπὶ τῆς πλατείας ᵃᵃπόλεως τῆς με-
²bodies ¹their [will be] on the street of ²city ¹the
γάλης, ἥτις καλεῖται πνευματικῶς Σόδομα καὶ Αἴγυπτος,
³great, which is called spiritually Sodom and Egypt,
ὅπου καὶ ὁ κύριος ᵇἡμῶν ἐσταυρώθη. 9 καὶ ᶜβλέψουσιν
where also ²Lord ¹our was crucified. And ¹¹shall ¹²see [¹some]
ἐκ τῶν λαῶν καὶ φυλῶν καὶ γλωσσῶν καὶ ἐθνῶν ᵈτὰ πτώ-
²of ³the ⁴peoples ⁵and ⁶tribes ⁷and ⁸tongues ⁹and ¹⁰nations ¹⁴bodies
ματα αὐτῶν ἡμέρας τρεῖς ᵉκαὶ ἥμισυ, καὶ τὰ πτώματα αὐτῶν
¹³their ¹⁶days ¹⁵three and a half, and their bodies
οὐκ ᶠἀφήσουσιν τεθῆναι εἰς ᵍμνήματα. 10 καὶ οἱ κατ-
³not ¹they ²will suffer to be put into tombs. And they that
οικοῦντες ἐπὶ τῆς γῆς ʰχαροῦσιν ἐπ' αὐτοῖς, καὶ ⁱεὐφρανθή-
dwell on the earth will rejoice over them, and will make
σονται καὶ δῶρα ᵏπέμψουσιν ἀλλήλοις, ὅτι οὗτοι οἱ δύο
merry, and gifts will send to one another, because these, the two
προφῆται ἐβασάνισαν τοὺς κατοικοῦντας ἐπὶ τῆς γῆς.
prophets, tormented them that dwell upon the earth.
11 καὶ μετὰ τὰς τρεῖς ἡμέρας καὶ ἥμισυ, πνεῦμα ζωῆς
And after the three days and a half, [the] spirit of life
ἐκ τοῦ θεοῦ εἰσῆλθεν ˡἐπ' αὐτούς, καὶ ἔστησαν ἐπὶ τοὺς
from God did enter into them, and they stood upon
πόδας αὐτῶν, καὶ φόβος μέγας ᵐἔπεσεν ἐπὶ τοὺς θεωροῦντας
²feet ¹their; and ²fear ¹great fell upon those beholding
αὐτούς. 12 καὶ ἤκουσαν ⁿφωνὴν μεγάλην ἐκ τοῦ οὐρανοῦ,
them: and they heard a ²voice ¹great out of the heaven,
ᵒλέγουσαν αὐτοῖς, ᵖἈνάβητε ὧδε. Καὶ ἀνέβησαν εἰς τὸν
saying to them, Come up hither. And they went up to the
οὐρανὸν ἐν τῇ νεφέλῃ, καὶ ἐθεώρησαν αὐτοὺς οἱ ἐχθροὶ αὐτῶν.
heaven in the cloud; and ³beheld ⁴them ¹their ²enemies.
13 Καὶ ἐν ἐκείνῃ τῇ ὥρᾳ ἐγένετο σεισμὸς μέγας, καὶ τὸ
And in that hour there was ³earthquake ¹a ²great, and the
δέκατον τῆς πόλεως ἔπεσεν, καὶ ἀπεκτάνθησαν ἐν τῷ σεισμῷ
tenth of the city fell, and there were killed in the earthquake
ὀνόματα ἀνθρώπων χιλιάδες ἑπτά· καὶ οἱ λοιποὶ ἔμφοβοι
³names ⁴of ⁵men ²thousand ¹seven. And the rest ²afraid
ἐγένοντο, καὶ ἔδωκαν δόξαν τῷ θεῷ τοῦ οὐρανοῦ.
¹became, and gave glory to the God of the heaven.
14 Ἡ οὐαὶ ᑫἡ δευτέρα ἀπῆλθεν· ἰδού, ἡ οὐαὶ ἡ τρίτη
³Woe ¹the ²second is past: lo, the ²woe ¹third
ἔρχεται ταχύ.
comes quickly.
15 Καὶ ὁ ἕβδομος ἄγγελος ἐσάλπισεν, καὶ ἐγένοντο
And the seventh angel sounded [his] trumpet; and ³were
φωναὶ μεγάλαι ἐν τῷ οὐρανῷ, ʳλέγουσαι, ˢἘγένοντο αἱ
²voices ¹great in the heaven, saying, ⁶Are ⁷become ¹the
βασιλεῖαι τοῦ κόσμου τοῦ κυρίου ἡμῶν, καὶ τοῦ χριστοῦ αὐτοῦ,
²kingdoms ³of ⁴the ⁵world our Lord's, and his Christ's,
καὶ βασιλεύσει εἰς τοὺς αἰῶνας τῶν αἰώνων. 16 Καὶ ᵗοἱ
and he shall reign to the ages of the ages. And the
εἴκοσι ᵛκαὶ τέσσαρες πρεσβύτεροι ʷοἱ ἐνώπιον τοῦ θεοῦ ˣκαθή-
twenty and four elders, who before God sit
μενοι ἐπὶ τοὺς θρόνους αὐτῶν, ἔπεσαν ἐπὶ τὰ πρόσωπα αὐτῶν,
on their thrones, fell upon their faces,
καὶ προσεκύνησαν τῷ θεῷ, 17 λέγοντες, Εὐχαριστοῦμέν σοι,
and worshipped God, saying, We give thanks to thee,
κύριε ὁ θεὸς ὁ παντοκράτωρ, ὁ ὢν καὶ ὁ ἦν ʸκαὶ ὁ
Lord God Almighty, [He] who is, and who was, and who [is]
ἐρχόμενος, ᶻὅτι εἴληφας τὴν δύναμίν σου τὴν μεγάλην,
coming, that thou hast taken ³power ¹thy ²great,
καὶ ἐβασίλευσας. 18 καὶ τὰ ἔθνη ὠργίσθησαν, καὶ ἦλθεν ἡ
and reigned. And the nations were angry, and is come
ὀργή σου, καὶ ὁ καιρὸς τῶν νεκρῶν, κριθῆναι, καὶ δοῦναι τὸν
²wrath ¹thy, and the time of the dead to be judged, and to give the
μισθὸν τοῖς δούλοις σου τοῖς προφήταις, καὶ τοῖς ἁγίοις καὶ
reward to thy bondmen the prophets, and to the saints, and
τοῖς φοβουμένοις τὸ ὄνομά σου, ᵃτοῖς μικροῖς καὶ τοῖς
to those who fear thy name, the small and the
μεγάλοις, καὶ διαφθεῖραι τοὺς ᵇδιαφθείροντας τὴν γῆν.
great; and to bring to corruption those who corrupt the earth.
19 Καὶ ἠνοίγη ὁ ναὸς τοῦ θεοῦ ᶜἐν τῷ οὐρανῷ, καὶ ὤφ-
And was opened the temple of God in the heaven, and was
θη ἡ κιβωτὸς τῆς διαθήκης ᵈαὐτοῦ ἐν τῷ ναῷ αὐτοῦ· καὶ
seen the ark of his covenant in his temple: and
ἐγένοντο ἀστραπαὶ καὶ φωναὶ καὶ βρονταὶ καὶ σεισμὸς καὶ
there were lightnings and voices and thunders and an earthquake and
χάλαζα μεγάλη.
²hail ¹great.
12 Καὶ σημεῖον μέγα ὤφθη ἐν τῷ οὐρανῷ, γυνὴ περι-
And a ²sign ¹great was seen in the heaven; a woman cloth-

8 And their bodies shall be on the great city's street, which is called spiritually Sodom, and Egypt – where our Lord was crucified.

9 And *some* of the peoples and tribes and tongues and nations shall see their bodies three days and a half. And they will not allow their bodies to be put into graves.

10 And they that live on the earth will rejoice over them, and they will make merry and will send gifts to one another, because these two prophets tormented those who live on the earth.

11 And after three days and a half, the Spirit of life from God entered into them, and they stood on their feet. And great fear fell on those seeing them.

12 And they heard a great voice out of Heaven saying to them, Come up here! And they went up to Heaven in the cloud. And their enemies saw them.

13 And in that hour there was a great earthquake. And the tenth part of the city fell, and seven thousand persons of men were killed in the earthquake. And the rest became afraid and gave glory to the God of Heaven.

14 The second woe is past. Behold, the third woe comes quickly!

15 And the seventh angel sounded his trumpet. And there were great voices in Heaven, saying, The kingdoms of the world have become our Lord's and His Christ's – and He shall reign forever and ever.

16 And the twenty-four elders who sat before God on their thrones fell on their faces and worshiped God,

17 saying, We give thanks to You, O Lord God Almighty, who is and who was and who is to come. For You have taken Your great power and have ruled.

18 And the nations were angry, and Your wrath has come. And the time *has come* for the dead to be judged and to give the reward to Your servants the prophets, and to the saints, and to the ones who fear Your name, the small and the great – and to bring to ruin those who have corrupted the earth.

19 And the Temple of God in Heaven was opened. And the ark of His covenant was seen in His Temple. And there were lightnings and voices and thunders and an earthquake and great hail.

CHAPTER 12

1 And a great wonder appeared in Heaven – a woman clothed with the sun, and the

βεβλημένη τὸν ἥλιον, καὶ ἡ σελήνη ὑποκάτω τῶν.ποδῶν.αὐτῆς,
ed with the sun, and the moon under her feet,
καὶ ἐπὶ τῆς.κεφαλῆς.αὐτῆς στέφανος ἀστέρων δώδεκα· 2 καὶ
and on her head a crown of [2]stars [1]twelve; and
ἐν.γαστρὶ.ἔχουσα, [e] [f]κράζει‖ ὠδίνουσα καὶ βασανιζομένη
being with child she cries being in travail, and being in pain
τεκεῖν.
to bring forth.
3 Καὶ ὤφθη ἄλλο σημεῖον ἐν τῷ οὐρανῷ, καὶ ἰδού, δρά-
And was seen another sign in the heaven, and behold, a [3]dra-
κων [g]μέγας πυῤῥός,‖ ἔχων κεφαλὰς ἑπτὰ καὶ κέρατα δέκα· καὶ
gon [1]great [2]red, having [2]heads [1]seven and [2]horns [1]ten, and
ἐπὶ τὰς.κεφαλὰς.αὐτοῦ [h]διαδήματα ἑπτά·‖ 4 καὶ ἡ.οὐρὰ.αὐτοῦ
upon his heads [2]diadems [1]seven; and his tail
σύρει τὸ τρίτον τῶν ἀστέρων τοῦ οὐρανοῦ, καὶ ἔβαλεν αὐτοὺς
drags the third of the stars of the heaven, and he cast them
εἰς τὴν γῆν. καὶ ὁ δράκων ἕστηκεν ἐνώπιον τῆς γυναικὸς τῆς
to the earth. And the dragon stands before the woman who
μελλούσης τεκεῖν, ἵνα ὅταν τέκῃ, τὸ.τέκνον.αὐτῆς
is about to bring forth, that when she should bring forth, her child
καταφάγῃ. 5 καὶ ἔτεκεν υἱὸν [i]ἄῤῥενα,‖ ὃς μέλλει ποι-
he might devour. And she brought forth a [2]son [1]male, who is about to
μαίνειν πάντα τὰ ἔθνη ἐν ῥάβδῳ σιδηρᾷ· καὶ ἡρπάσθη
shepherd all the nations with [3]rod [1]an [2]iron: and was caught away
τὸ.τέκνον.αὐτῆς πρὸς τὸν θεὸν καὶ [k] τὸν.θρόνον.αὐτοῦ. 6 καὶ
her child to God and his throne. And
ἡ γυνὴ ἔφυγεν εἰς τὴν ἔρημον, ὅπου ἔχει [l] τόπον ἡτοιμασ-
the woman fled into the wilderness, where she has a place pre-
μένον ἀπὸ τοῦ θεοῦ, ἵνα ἐκεῖ [m]τρέφωσιν‖ αὐτὴν ἡμέρας
pared of God, that there they should nourish her [7]days
χιλίας διακοσίας ἑξήκοντα.
[1]a [2]thousand [3]two [4]hundred [[5]and] [6]sixty.
7 Καὶ ἐγένετο πόλεμος ἐν τῷ οὐρανῷ· [n]ὁ‖ Μιχαὴλ καὶ
And there was war in the heaven: Michael and
οἱ.ἄγγελοι.αὐτοῦ [o]ἐπολέμησαν κατὰ‖ τοῦ δράκοντος, καὶ ὁ
his angels warred against the dragon, and the
δράκων ἐπολέμησεν, καὶ οἱ.ἄγγελοι.αὐτοῦ· 8 καὶ οὐκ [p]ἴσχυ-
dragon warred, and his angels; and [3]not [1]they [2]pre-
σαν,‖ [q]οὔτε‖ τόπος εὑρέθη αὐτῶν ἔτι ἐν τῷ οὐρανῷ. 9 καὶ
vailed, nor [3]place [1]was [4]found [2]their any more in the heaven. And
ἐβλήθη ὁ δράκων ὁ μέγας, ὁ ὄφις ὁ ἀρχαῖος, ὁ καλού-
was cast [out] the [2]dragon [1]great, the [2]serpent [1]ancient, who is
μενος διάβολος, καὶ ὁ σατανᾶς, ὁ πλανῶν τὴν οἰκουμένην
called Devil, and the Satan, who misleads the [2]habitable
ὅλην, ἐβλήθη εἰς τὴν γῆν, καὶ οἱ.ἄγγελοι.αὐτοῦ
[[3]world] [1]whole, he was cast into the earth, and his angels
μετ᾽ αὐτοῦ ἐβλήθησαν. 10 Καὶ ἤκουσα φωνὴν μεγάλην [r]λέ-
[3]with [4]him [1]were [2]cast. And I heard a [2]voice [1]great
γουσαν ἐν τῷ οὐρανῷ,‖ Ἄρτι ἐγένετο ἡ σωτηρία καὶ ἡ δύνα-
saying in the heaven, Now is come the salvation and the power
μις καὶ ἡ βασιλεία τοῦ.θεοῦ.ἡμῶν, καὶ ἡ ἐξουσία τοῦ χριστοῦ
and the kingdom of our God, and the authority [3]Christ
αὐτοῦ· ὅτι [s]κατεβλήθη‖ ὁ [t]κατήγορος‖ τῶν.ἀδελφῶν.ἡμῶν,
[1]of [2]his; because is cast down the accuser of our brethren,
ὁ κατηγορῶν [v]αὐτῶν‖ ἐνώπιον τοῦ.θεοῦ.ἡμῶν ἡμέρας καὶ
who accuses them before our God day and
νυκτός. 11 καὶ αὐτοὶ ἐνίκησαν αὐτὸν διὰ τὸ αἷμα τοῦ
night. And they overcame him by reason of the blood of the
ἀρνίου, καὶ διὰ τὸν λόγον τῆς.μαρτυρίας.αὐτῶν, καὶ
Lamb, and by reason of the word of their testimony, and
[w]οὐκ‖ ἠγάπησαν τὴν.ψυχὴν.αὐτῶν ἄχρι θανάτου. 12 διὰ
[2]not [1]loved their life unto death. Because of
τοῦτο εὐφραίνεσθε [x]οἱ‖ οὐρανοὶ καὶ οἱ ἐν αὐτοῖς σκηνοῦντες.
this rejoice ye heavens and [ye] who in them tabernacle.
οὐαὶ [y]τοῖς κατοικοῦσιν‖ [z]τὴν γῆν καὶ τὴν θάλασσαν,‖ ὅτι
Woe to those who inhabit the earth and the sea, because
κατέβη ὁ διάβολος πρὸς ὑμᾶς ἔχων θυμὸν μέγαν, εἰ-
is come down the devil to you having [2]fury [1]great, know-
δὼς ὅτι ὀλίγον καιρὸν ἔχει.
ing that a short time he has.
13 Καὶ ὅτε εἶδεν ὁ δράκων ὅτι ἐβλήθη εἰς τὴν γῆν,
And when [3]saw [1]the [2]dragon that he was cast into the earth,
ἐδίωξεν τὴν γυναῖκα ἥτις ἔτεκεν τὸν [a]ἄῤῥενα.‖ 14 καὶ
he persecuted the woman which brought forth the male [child]. And
ἐδόθησαν τῇ γυναικὶ [b] δύο πτέρυγες τοῦ ἀετοῦ τοῦ μεγάλου,
were given to the woman two wings of the [2]eagle [1]great,
ἵνα πέτηται εἰς τὴν ἔρημον εἰς τὸν.τόπον.αὐτῆς, ὅπου τρέ-
that she might fly into the wilderness into her place, where she is
φεται ἐκεῖ καιρόν, καὶ καιρούς, καὶ ἥμισυ καιροῦ, ἀπὸ
nourished there a time, and times, and half a time, from [the]
προσώπου τοῦ ὄφεως. 15 καὶ ἔβαλεν ὁ ὄφις [c]ὀπίσω τῆς
face of the serpent. And [3]cast [1]the [2]serpent [8]after [9]the

moon under her feet. And on her head was a crown of twelve stars.

2 And she was with child, and she cried, being in labor and in pain to bring forth.

3 And another wonder appeared in Heaven – and behold! A great red dragon which had seven heads and ten horns and seven crowns on his heads!

4 And his tail drags the third part of the stars of the sky. And he threw them onto the earth. And the dragon stands in front of the woman who is about to bear, so that when she should bear her child, he might eat it.

5 And she brought forth a male, a son who is going to shepherd all the nations with a rod of iron. And her child was caught away to God and His throne.

6 And the woman fled into the wilderness, where she has a place made ready by God, so that there they should take care of her a thousand two hundred and sixty days.

7 And there was war in Heaven: Michael and his angels made war against the dragon. And the dragon and his angels made war.

8 And they did not prevail, nor was their place found in Heaven any more.

9 And the great dragon was thrown out, the old serpent who is called the devil, and Satan – who leads the whole world astray. He was thrown onto the earth, and his angels were thrown out with him.

10 And I heard a great voice saying in Heaven, Now the salvation and the power and the kingdom of our God, and the authority of His Christ, has been accomplished – because the accuser of our brothers is throw down, who accuses them before our G day and night.

11 And they overcame him because of the blood of the Lamb, and because of the word of their testimony. And they did not love their life *even* unto death.

12 Because of this, rejoice O heavens, and you who live in them. Woe to those who live on the earth and in the sea, because the devil has come down to you. And he has great anger, knowing that he has only a short time.

13 And when the dragon saw that he was thrown onto the earth, he persecuted the woman who brought forth the manchild.

14 And two wings of the great eagle were given to the woman, so that she might fly into the wilderness into her place – where she is taken care of for a time, and times and half a time, from the face of the serpent.

15 And the serpent put out water from his

γυναικὸς ἐκ τοῦ.στόματος.αὐτοῦ[1] ὕδωρ ὡς ποταμόν, ἵνα
[10]woman [4]out [5]of [6]his [7]mouth water as a river, that
[d]ταύτην[ll] . ποταμοφόρητον ποιήσῃ. 16 καὶ
[4]her [[8]as [9]one] [7]carried [8]away [9]by [10]a [11]river [1]he [2]might [3]make. And
ἐβοήθησεν ἡ γῆ τῇ γυναικί, καὶ ἤνοιξεν ἡ γῆ τὸ στόμα
[3]helped [1]the [2]earth the woman, and [3]opened [1]the [2]earth [5]mouth
αὐτῆς, καὶ κατέπιεν τὸν ποταμὸν ὃν ἔβαλεν ὁ δράκων
[4]its, and swallowed up the river which [3]cast [1]the [2]dragon
ἐκ τοῦ.στόματος.αὐτοῦ. 17 καὶ ὠργίσθη ὁ δράκων [e]ἐπὶ[l]
out of his mouth. And [3]was [4]angry [1]the [2]dragon with
τῇ γυναικί, καὶ ἀπῆλθεν ποιῆσαι πόλεμον μετὰ τῶν λοιπῶν
the woman, and went to make war with the rest
τοῦ.σπέρματος.αὐτῆς, τῶν τηρούντων τὰς ἐντολὰς τοῦ
of her seed, who keep the commandments
θεοῦ, καὶ ἐχόντων τὴν μαρτυρίαν [f]τοῦ[l] Ἰησοῦ [g]χριστοῦ.[ll]
of God, and have the testimony of Jesus Christ.
18 Καὶ [h]ἐστάθην[ll] ἐπὶ τὴν ἄμμον τῆς θαλάσσης· 13 καὶ
And I stood upon the sand of the sea; and
εἶδον ἐκ τῆς θαλάσσης θηρίον ἀναβαῖνον, ἔχον [i]κεφαλὰς
I saw out of the sea a beast rising, having [2]heads
ἑπτὰ καὶ κέρατα δέκα·[ll] καὶ ἐπὶ τῶν.κεράτων.αὐτοῦ δέκα δια-
[1]seven and [2]horns [1]ten, and on its horns ten dia-
δήματα, καὶ ἐπὶ τὰς.κεφαλὰς.αὐτοῦ [k]ὄνομα[ll] βλασφημίας.
dems, and upon its heads [the] name of blasphemy.
2 καὶ τὸ θηρίον ὃ εἶδον ἦν ὅμοιον παρδάλει, καὶ οἱ πόδες
And the beast which I saw was like to a leopard, and [2]feet
αὐτοῦ ὡς [l]ἄρκτου,[l] καὶ τὸ.στόμα.αὐτοῦ ὡς στόμα [m]λέοντος.[ll]
[1]its as of a bear, and its mouth as [the] mouth of a lion;
καὶ ἔδωκεν αὐτῷ ὁ δράκων τὴν.δύναμιν.αὐτοῦ, καὶ τὸν θρόνον
and [3]gave [4]to [5]it [1]the [2]dragon his power, and [2]throne
αὐτοῦ, καὶ ἐξουσίαν μεγάλην. 3 καὶ [n]εἶδον[ll] μίαν [o] τῶν κεφα-
[1]his, and [2]authority [1]great. And I saw one [3]heads
λῶν αὐτοῦ ὡς ἐσφαγμένην εἰς θάνατον· καὶ ἡ πληγὴ τοῦ
[1]of [2]its as slain to death; and the wound
θανάτου αὐτοῦ ἐθεραπεύθη, καὶ [p]ἐθαυμάσθη[ll] [q]ἐν[ll] [r]ὅλῃ τῇ
[3]death [1]of [2]its was healed: and there was wonder in [2]whole [1]the
γῇ[l] ὀπίσω τοῦ θηρίου. 4 καὶ προσεκύνησαν [s]τὸν δράκοντα[ll]
earth after the beast. And they did homage to the dragon,
[t]ὃς[ll] ἔδωκεν [v]ἐξουσίαν τῷ θηρίῳ, καὶ προσεκύνησαν [w]τὸ
who gave authority to the beast; and they did homage to the
θηρίον,[ll] λέγοντες, Τίς ὅμοιος τῷ θηρίῳ; [x]τίς δύναται
beast, saying, Who [is] like to the beast? who is able
πολεμῆσαι μετ' αὐτοῦ; 5 καὶ ἐδόθη αὐτῷ στόμα λαλοῦν
to make war with it? And was given to it a mouth speaking
μεγάλα καὶ [y]βλασφημίας·[ll] καὶ ἐδόθη αὐτῷ ἐξουσία [z] ποιῆ-
great things and blasphemy; and was given to it authority to
σαι μῆνας [a]τεσσαράκοντα [b]δύο·[ll] 6 καὶ ἤνοιξεν τὸ.στόμα.αὐτοῦ
act [3]months [1]forty [2]two. And it opened its mouth
εἰς [c]βλασφημίαν[ll] πρὸς τὸν θεόν, βλασφημῆσαι τὸ ὄνομα
for blasphemy against God, to blaspheme [2]name
αὐτοῦ, καὶ τὴν.σκηνὴν.αὐτοῦ, [d]καὶ[l] τοὺς ἐν τῷ οὐρανῷ
[1]his, and his tabernacle, and those who [2]in [3]the [4]heaven
σκηνοῦντας. 7 [e]καὶ ἐδόθη αὐτῷ [f]πόλεμον ποιῆσαι[l] μετὰ τῶν
[1]tabernacle. And was given to it [3]war [1]to [2]make with the
ἁγίων, καὶ νικῆσαι αὐτούς·[ll] καὶ ἐδόθη αὐτῷ ἐξουσία ἐπὶ
saints, and to overcome them; and was given to it authority over
πᾶσαν φυλὴν [g] καὶ γλῶσσαν καὶ ἔθνος. 8 καὶ προσκυνήσου-
every tribe, and tongue, and nation; and shall do homage
σιν [h]αὐτῷ[l] πάντες οἱ κατοικοῦντες ἐπὶ τῆς γῆς [i]ὧν[l] οὐ
to it all who dwell on the earth of whom [2]not
γέγραπται [k]τὰ ὀνόματα[l] ἐν [l]τῇ βίβλῳ[ll] τῆς ζωῆς τοῦ
[1]have been written the names [7]in [8]the [9]book [10]of [11]life [12]of [13]the
ἀρνίου [m] ἐσφαγμένου ἀπὸ καταβολῆς κόσμου. 9 Εἴ
[15]Lamb [14]slain [1]from [[2]the] [3]founding [4]of [[5]the] [6]world. If
τις ἔχει οὖς, ἀκουσάτω. 10 Εἴ τις [n] [o]αἰχμαλωσίαν[ll]
anyone has an ear, let him hear. If anyone [[2]into] [3]captivity
[p]συνάγει,[ll] εἰς αἰχμαλωσίαν ὑπάγει· εἴ τις ἐν [q]μαχαίρᾳ[ll]
[1]gathers, into captivity he goes. If anyone with [the] sword
[r]ἀποκτενεῖ,[l] [s]δεῖ[ll] αὐτὸν ἐν [q]μαχαίρᾳ[l] ἀποκτανθῆναι· ὧδέ
will kill, [2]must [1]he with [the] sword be killed. Here
ἐστιν ἡ ὑπομονὴ καὶ ἡ πίστις τῶν ἁγίων.
is the endurance and the faith of the saints.
11 Καὶ εἶδον ἄλλο θηρίον ἀναβαῖνον ἐκ τῆς γῆς, καὶ
And I saw another beast rising out of the earth, and
εἶχεν κέρατα δύο ὅμοια ἀρνίῳ, καὶ ἐλάλει ὡς δράκων. 12 καὶ
it had [2]horns [1]two like to a lamb, and spoke as a dragon; and
τὴν ἐξουσίαν τοῦ πρώτου θηρίου πᾶσαν ποιεῖ ἐνώπιον
[2]the [3]authority [4]of [5]the [6]first [7]beast [1]all it exercises before
αὐτοῦ· καὶ ποιεῖ τὴν γῆν καὶ τοὺς [t]κατοικοῦντας ἐν αὐτῇ[l]
it, and causes the earth and those who dwell in it
ἵνα [v]προσκυνήσωσιν[l] τὸ θηρίον τὸ πρῶτον, οὗ ἐθερα-
that they should do homage to the [2]beast [1]first, of whom was

mouth like a river *to go* after the woman, so that he might cause her to be carried away with the river.

16 And the earth helped the woman, and the earth opened its mouth and swallowed up the river which the dragon put forth out of his mouth.

17 And the dragon was angry with the woman and went to war with the rest of her children who keep the commandments of God, and who have the testimony of Jesus Christ.

CHAPTER 13

1 And I stood on the sea-sand. And rising out of the sea I saw a beast with seven heads and ten horns. And on its horns were ten crowns. And on its heads was the name of blasphemy.

2 And the beast I saw was like a leopard, and its *feet* like a bear's feet, and its mouth like a lion's mouth. And the dragon gave his power to it, and his throne and his great authority.

3 And I saw one of its heads as dead. And its deadly wound was healed. And the whole earth wondered after the beast.

4 And they worshiped the dragon who gave authority to the beast. And they worshiped the beast, saying, Who is like the beast? Who is able to make war with it?

5 And to it was given a mouth to speak great things, and blasphemy. And authority was given to it to act forty-two months.

6 And it opened its mouth for blasphemy against God, to blaspheme His name and His tabernacle and those who dwell in Heaven.

7 And it was given to it to make war with the saints and to subdue them. And it was given power over every tribe and tongue and nation.

8 And all earth's inhabitants shall worship it – *that is, all those* whose names have not been written in the Book of Life of the Lamb, slain from the foundation of the world.

9 If anyone has an ear, let him hear.

10 If anyone brings into captivity, into captivity he goes. If anyone will kill by a sword, with a sword he must be killed. Here is the patience and the faith of the saints.

11 And I saw another beast rising out of the earth. And it had two horns like a lamb, and it spoke like a dragon.

12 And it uses all the authority of the first beast before it. And it causes the earth and the ones who live in it to worship the first

πεύθη ἡ πληγὴ τοῦ.θανάτου.αὐτοῦ· 13 καὶ ποιεῖ σημεῖα
healed the wound of its death. And it works [2]signs

μεγάλα, [w]ἵνα καὶ πῦρ ποιῇ' [x]καταβαίνειν ἐκ τοῦ οὐ-
[1]great, that even fire it should cause to come down out of the hea-

ρανοῦ' εἰς τὴν γῆν ἐνώπιον τῶν ἀνθρώπων. 14 καὶ πλανᾷ
ven to the earth before men. And it misleads

τοὺς κατοικοῦντας ἐπὶ τῆς γῆς, διὰ τὰ σημεῖα ἃ
those who dwell on the earth, by reason of the signs which

ἐδόθη αὐτῷ ποιῆσαι ἐνώπιον τοῦ θηρίου, λέγων τοῖς
it was given to it to work before the beast, saying to those who

κατοικοῦσιν ἐπὶ τῆς γῆς, ποιῆσαι [z]εἰκόνα' τῷ θηρίῳ [a]ὃ'
dwell on the earth, to make an image to the beast, which

ἔχει τὴν πληγὴν τῆς [b]μαχαίρας' καὶ ἔζησεν. 15 καὶ ἐδόθη
has the wound of the sword, and lived. And it was given

[c]αὐτῷ' [d]δοῦναι πνεῦμα' τῇ εἰκόνι τοῦ θηρίου, ἵνα καὶ λα-
to it to give breath to the image of the beast, that [7]also [8]should

λήσῃ ἡ εἰκὼν τοῦ θηρίου, καὶ ποιήσῃ, [e] ὅσοι [f]ἂν' μὴ
[9]speak [1]the [2]image [3]of [4]the [5]beast, and should cause as many as [2]not

[g]προσκυνήσωσιν' [h]τὴν εἰκόνα' τοῦ θηρίου [i]ἵνα' ἀποκτανθῶσιν.
[1]would do homage to the image of the beast that they should be killed.

16 καὶ ποιεῖ πάντας, τοὺς μικροὺς καὶ τοὺς μεγάλους, καὶ
And it causes all, the small and the great, and

τοὺς πλουσίους καὶ τοὺς πτωχούς, καὶ τοὺς ἐλευθέρους καὶ
the rich and the poor, and the free and

τοὺς δούλους, ἵνα [k]δώσῃ' αὐτοῖς χάραγμα ἐπὶ τῆς χειρὸς
the bondmen, that it should give them a mark on [2]hand

αὐτῶν τῆς δεξιᾶς, ἢ ἐπὶ [l]τῶν μετώπων' αὐτῶν, 17 [m]καὶ' ἵνα
[1]their [2]right, or on [2]foreheads [1]their; and that

μή.τις δύνηται ἀγοράσαι ἢ πωλῆσαι, εἰ.μὴ ὁ ἔχων τὸ
no one should be able to buy or to sell, except he who has the

χάραγμα [n]ἢ' [o]τὸ ὄνομα' τοῦ θηρίου, ἢ τὸν ἀριθμὸν τοῦ
mark or the name of the beast, or the number

ὀνόματος αὐτοῦ. 18 Ὧδε ἡ σοφία ἐστίν. ὁ ἔχων [p]τὸν'
[2]name [3]of [1]its. Here [2]wisdom [1]is. He who has

νοῦν, ψηφισάτω τὸν ἀριθμὸν τοῦ θηρίου· ἀριθμὸς.γὰρ
understanding let him count the number of the beast: for [2]number

ἀνθρώπου ἐστίν, καὶ ὁ.ἀριθμὸς.αὐτοῦ [q] [r]χξς'.'
[3]a [4]man's it is; and its number [is] 666.

14 Καὶ [s]εἶδον,' καὶ ἰδού, [t] ἀρνίον [v]ἑστηκὸς' ἐπὶ τὸ ὄρος
And I saw, and behold, [the] Lamb standing upon mount

Σιών, καὶ μετ' αὐτοῦ ἑκατὸν [w]τεσσαράκοντα τέσσαρες'
Sion, and with him a hundred [and] forty four

χιλιάδες, ἔχουσαι τὸ ὄνομα [x] τοῦ.πατρὸς.αὐτοῦ γεγραμμένον
thousand, having the name of his Father written

ἐπὶ τῶν.μετώπων.αὐτῶν. 2 καὶ ἤκουσα φωνὴν ἐκ τοῦ οὐ-
on their foreheads. And I heard a voice out of the hea-

ρανοῦ ὡς φωνὴν ὑδάτων πολλῶν, καὶ ὡς φωνὴν βροντῆς
ven as a voice of [2]waters [1]many, and as a voice of [2]thunder

μεγάλης· καὶ [y]φωνὴν ἤκουσα' [za]κιθαρῳδῶν κιθαριζόντων ἐν
[1]great: and a voice I heard of harpers harping with

ταῖς.κιθάραις.αὐτῶν. 3 καὶ ᾄδουσιν [aa]ὡς' ᾠδὴν καινὴν ἐνώ-
their harps. And they sing as a [2]song [1]new be-

πιον τοῦ θρόνου, καὶ ἐνώπιον τῶν τεσσάρων ζώων καὶ
fore the throne, and before the four living creatures and

τῶν πρεσβυτέρων· καὶ οὐδεὶς [ba]ἠδύνατο' μαθεῖν τὴν ᾠδήν,
the elders. And no one was able to learn the song

εἰ.μὴ αἱ ἑκατὸν [c]τεσσαράκοντα τέσσαρες'. χιλιάδες, οἱ
except the hundred [and] forty four thousand, who

ἠγορασμένοι ἀπὸ τῆς γῆς. 4 οὗτοί εἰσιν οἳ μετὰ
have been purchased from the earth. These are they who with

γυναικῶν οὐκ.ἐμολύνθησαν· παρθένοι.γάρ εἰσιν· οὗτοί [d]εἰσιν'
women were not defiled, for virgins they are: these are

οἱ ἀκολουθοῦντες τῷ ἀρνίῳ ὅπου ἂν [e]ὑπάγῃ.' οὗτοι
they who follow the Lamb wheresoever he may go. These

ἠγοράσθησαν ἀπὸ τῶν ἀνθρώπων, ἀπαρχὴ τῷ θεῷ καὶ
were purchased from among men [as] firstfruits to God and

τῷ ἀρνίῳ. 5 καὶ ἐν τῷ.στόματι.αὐτῶν οὐχ.εὑρέθη [f]δόλος·'
to the Lamb: and in their mouth was not found guile;

ἄμωμοι.[g]γάρ' εἰσιν [h]ἐνώπιον τοῦ θρόνου τοῦ θεοῦ.'
for blameless they are before the throne of God.

6 Καὶ εἶδον [i]ἄλλον' ἄγγελον [j]πετώμενον' ἐν μεσου-
And I saw another angel flying in mid-

ρανήματι, ἔχοντα εὐαγγέλιον αἰώνιον εὐαγγελίσαι [k]
heaven, having [the] [2]glad [3]tidings [1]everlasting to announce [to]

τοὺς [l]κατοικοῦντας' ἐπὶ τῆς γῆς, καὶ [m] πᾶν ἔθνος καὶ φυλὴν
those who dwell on the earth, and every nation and tribe

καὶ γλῶσσαν καὶ λαόν, 7 [n]λέγοντα' [o]ἐν' φωνῇ μεγάλῃ,
and tongue and people, saying with a [2]voice [1]loud,

Φοβήθητε τὸν θεόν, καὶ δότε αὐτῷ δόξαν, ὅτι ἦλθεν ἡ ὥρα
Fear God, and give to him glory, because is come the hour

τῆς.κρίσεως.αὐτοῦ· καὶ προσκυνήσατε τῷ ποιήσαντι τὸν
of his judgment; and do homage to him who made the

beast – whose deadly wound was healed.

13 And it works great miracles, that even fire should be made to come down out of the sky to the earth in the sight of men.

14 And it leads astray those who live on the earth, because of the miracles which were given to it to work in the sight of the beast, commanding those who live on the earth to make an image to the beast – which has the wound of the sword, and lived.

15 And it was given to it to give breath to the image of the beast, so that the image of the beast could even speak. And it would cause as many as would not worship the image of the beast to be killed.

16 And all the small and the great and the rich and the poor and the free and the slave, it will force to receive a mark on their right hand, or on their foreheads –

17 and that no one will be able to buy or sell unless he has the mark, or the name of the beast, or the number of its name.

18 Here is wisdom: Let him who has understanding count the number of the beast – for it is a man's number, and its number is six hundred and sixty-six.

CHAPTER 14

1 And I saw, and behold! A Lamb standing on Mount Zion! And with Him were a hundred and forty-four thousand who had the name of His Father written on their foreheads.

2 And I heard a sound out of Heaven like the sound of many waters, and like a sound of great thunder. And I heard a sound of harpers playing on their harps

3 And they sing as it were a new song before the throne, and before the four living creatures and the elders. And no one was able to learn the song except the hundred and forty-four thousand who had been redeemed from the earth.

4 These are they who were not made unclean with women – for they are virgins. These are they who follow the Lamb wherever He goes. These were redeemed from among men as first-fruits to God and to the Lamb.

5 And in their mouth was found no guile, for they are blameless before the throne of God.

6 And I saw another angel flying in Heaven's midst, who had the everlasting gospel to preach to earth's inhabitants, even to every nation and tribe and tongue and people,

7 saying with a loud voice, Fear God and give glory to Him, because the hour of His judgment has come. And worship Him who made the sky and the earth and the sea

οὐρανὸν καὶ τὴν γῆν καὶ θάλασσαν καὶ πηγὰς ὑδάτων.
heaven and the earth and sea and fountains of waters.
8 Καὶ ἄλλος ἄγγελος ἠκολούθησεν, λέγων, Ἔπεσεν ἔπε-
And another angel followed, saying, Is fallen, is
σεν Βαβυλὼν ἡ πόλις ἡ μεγάλη· ὅτι ἐκ τοῦ οἴνου τοῦ
fallen Babylon city the great, because of the wine of the
θυμοῦ τῆς πορνείας αὐτῆς πεπότικεν πάντα ἔθνη.
fury of her fornication she has given to drink all nations.
9 Καὶ τρίτος ἄγγελος ἠκολούθησεν αὐτοῖς, λέγων ἐν
And a third angel followed them, saying, with
φωνῇ μεγάλῃ, Εἴ τις τὸ θηρίον προσκυνεῖ καὶ τὴν
a voice loud, If anyone the beast does homage to and
εἰκόνα αὐτοῦ, καὶ λαμβάνει χάραγμα ἐπὶ τοῦ μετώπου αὐτοῦ,
image its, and receives a mark on his forehead
ἢ ἐπὶ τὴν χεῖρα αὐτοῦ, 10 καὶ αὐτὸς πίεται ἐκ τοῦ οἴνου
or upon his hand, also he shall drink of the wine
τοῦ θυμοῦ τοῦ θεοῦ, τοῦ κεκερασμένου ἀκράτου ἐν τῷ
of the fury of God which is mixed undiluted in the
ποτηρίῳ τῆς ὀργῆς αὐτοῦ, καὶ βασανισθήσεται ἐν πυρὶ καὶ
cup of his wrath, and he shall be tormented in fire and
θείῳ ἐνώπιον τῶν ἁγίων ἀγγέλων, καὶ ἐνώπιον τοῦ
brimstone, before the holy angels, and before the
ἀρνίου· 11 καὶ ὁ καπνὸς τοῦ βασανισμοῦ αὐτῶν ἀναβαίνει
Lamb. And the smoke of their torment goes up
εἰς αἰῶνας αἰώνων· καὶ οὐκ ἔχουσιν ἀνάπαυσιν ἡμέρας καὶ
to ages of ages, and they have no respite day and
νυκτὸς οἱ προσκυνοῦντες τὸ θηρίον καὶ τὴν εἰκόνα αὐτοῦ, καὶ
night who do homage to the beast and its image, and
εἴ τις λαμβάνει τὸ χάραγμα τοῦ ὀνόματος αὐτοῦ. 12 Ὧδε
if anyone receives the mark of its name. Here [the]
ὑπομονὴ τῶν ἁγίων ἐστιν· ὧδε οἱ τηροῦντες τὰς ἐν-
endurance of the saints is, here they who keep the command-
τολὰς τοῦ θεοῦ καὶ τὴν πίστιν Ἰησοῦ.
ments of God and the faith of Jesus.
13 Καὶ ἤκουσα φωνῆς ἐκ τοῦ οὐρανοῦ, λεγούσης μοι,
And I heard a voice out of the heaven, saying to me,
Γράψον, Μακάριοι οἱ νεκροὶ οἱ ἐν κυρίῳ ἀποθνήσκοντες
Write, Blessed the dead who in [the] Lord die
ἀπάρτι. Ναί, λέγει τὸ πνεῦμα, ἵνα ἀναπαύσωνται ἐκ
from henceforth. Yea, saith the Spirit, that they may rest from
τῶν κόπων αὐτῶν· τὰ δὲ ἔργα αὐτῶν ἀκολουθεῖ μετ' αὐτῶν.
their labours; and works their follow with them.
14 Καὶ εἶδον, καὶ ἰδού, νεφέλη λευκή, καὶ ἐπὶ τὴν νεφέλην
And I saw, and behold, a cloud white, and upon the cloud
καθήμενος ὅμοιος υἱῷ ἀνθρώπου, ἔχων ἐπὶ τῆς
[one] sitting like [the] Son of man, having on
κεφαλῆς αὐτοῦ στέφανον χρυσοῦν, καὶ ἐν τῇ χειρὶ αὐτοῦ δρέ-
head his a crown golden, and in his hand a
πανον ὀξύ. 15 καὶ ἄλλος ἄγγελος ἐξῆλθεν ἐκ τοῦ ναοῦ,
sickle sharp. And another angel came out of the temple,
κράζων ἐν μεγάλῃ φωνῇ τῷ καθημένῳ ἐπὶ τῆς νεφέλης,
crying with loud voice to him sitting on the cloud,
Πέμψον τὸ δρέπανόν σου, καὶ θέρισον, ὅτι ἦλθέν σοι ἡ
Send thy sickle and reap; because is come to thee the
ὥρα τοῦ θερίσαι, ὅτι ἐξηράνθη ὁ θερισμὸς τῆς γῆς. 16 Καὶ
hour to reap, because is dried the harvest of the earth. And
ἔβαλεν ὁ καθήμενος ἐπὶ τὴν νεφέλην τὸ δρέπανον αὐτοῦ
put forth he sitting upon the cloud his sickle
ἐπὶ τὴν γῆν, καὶ ἐθερίσθη ἡ γῆ.
upon the earth, and was reaped the earth.
17 Καὶ ἄλλος ἄγγελος ἐξῆλθεν ἐκ τοῦ ναοῦ τοῦ ἐν τῷ
And another angel came out of the temple which [is] in the
οὐρανῷ, ἔχων καὶ αὐτὸς δρέπανον ὀξύ. 18 καὶ ἄλλος ἄγ-
heaven, having also he a sickle sharp. And another an-
γελος ἐξῆλθεν ἐκ τοῦ θυσιαστηρίου, ἔχων ἐξουσίαν ἐπὶ τοῦ
gel came out of the altar, having authority over
πυρός, καὶ ἐφώνησεν κραυγῇ μεγάλῃ τῷ ἔχοντι τὸ δρέπανον
fire, and he called with a cry loud to him having sickle
τὸ ὀξύ, λέγων, Πέμψον σου τὸ δρέπανον τὸ ὀξύ, καὶ τρύγη-
the sharp, saying, Send thy sickle sharp, and gather
σον τοὺς βότρυας τῆς γῆς, ὅτι ἤκμασαν αἱ σταφυλαὶ
the bunches of the earth; because are fully ripe grapes
αὐτῆς. 19 Καὶ ἔβαλεν ὁ ἄγγελος τὸ δρέπανον αὐτοῦ εἰς
her. And put forth the angel his sickle to
τὴν γῆν, καὶ ἐτρύγησεν τὴν ἄμπελον τῆς γῆς, καὶ ἔβαλεν
the earth, and gathered the vine of the earth, and cast [the fruit]
εἰς τὴν ληνὸν τοῦ θυμοῦ τοῦ θεοῦ τὴν μεγάλην. 20 καὶ
into winepress of the fury of God the great. And
ἐπατήθη ἡ ληνὸς ἔξω τῆς πόλεως, καὶ ἐξῆλθεν αἷμα
was trodden the winepress outside the city, and came forth blood
ἐκ τῆς ληνοῦ ἄχρι τῶν χαλινῶν τῶν ἵππων, ἀπὸ
out of the winepress as far as the bits of the horses, to the distance of

and the fountains of water.

8 And another angel followed, saying, The great city, Babylon, is fallen, is fallen because she has given to all nations to drink of the wine of the fury of her fornication.

9 And a third angel followed them, saying with a loud voice, If anyone worships the beast and its image and receives a mark on his forehead or on his hand,

10 he also shall drink of the wine of the wrath of God which is poured full strength into the cup of His anger. And he shall be tormented in fire and brimstone before the holy angels, and in the sight of the Lamb.

11 And the smoke of their torment rises forever and ever. And they have no rest day and night, those who worship the beast and its image, and if anyone takes the mark of its name.

12 Here is the patience of the saints. Here are they who keep the commandments of God and the faith of Jesus.

13 And I heard a voice out of Heaven saying to me, Write, Blessed are the dead who die in the Lord from now on. Yes, says the Spirit, that they may rest from their labors. And their works follow with them.

14 And I saw, and behold, a white cloud! And on the cloud One like the Son of man was sitting. And He had a golden crown on His head. And in His hand was a sharp sickle.

15 And another angel came out of the Temple crying with a loud voice to Him who sat on the cloud, Send forth Your sickle and reap, because the hour has come for You to reap, because the harvest of the earth is ripe.

16 And He who sat on the cloud put forth His sickle on the earth and reaped the earth.

17 And another angel came from the Temple which is in Heaven; he also had a sharp sickle.

18 And another angel came out of the altar, who had authority over fire. And he called with a loud cry to him who had the sharp sickle, saying, Send your sharp sickle and gather the clusters of the vine of the earth, for her grapes are fully ripe.

19 And the angel put forth his sickle into the earth and gathered the vine of the earth, and he threw *the fruit* into the great winepress of the wrath of God.

20 And the winepress was trodden outside the city, and blood came forth out of the winepress even to the bits of the horses, to the distance of two hundred miles.

σταδίων χιλίων ἑξακοσίων.
[4]furlongs [1]a [2]thousand [3]six [4]hundred.

15 Καὶ [a]εἶδον‖ ἄλλο σημεῖον ἐν τῷ οὐρανῷ μέγα καὶ θαυ-
And I saw another sign in the heaven, great and won-
μαστόν, ἀγγέλους ἑπτά, ἔχοντας πληγὰς ἑπτὰ τὰς ἐσχάτας,
derful: [2]angels [1]seven, having [2]plagues [1]seven, the last;
ὅτι ἐν αὐταῖς ἐτελέσθη ὁ θυμὸς τοῦ θεοῦ.
because in them was completed the fury of God.
2 Καὶ [a]εἶδον‖ ὡς θάλασσαν ὑαλίνην μεμιγμένην πυρί,
And I saw as a [2]sea [1]glass mingled with fire,
καὶ τοὺς νικῶντας ἐκ τοῦ θηρίου καὶ ἐκ τῆς.εἰκόνος.αὐτοῦ
and the overcomers of the beast, and of its image,
καὶ [b]ἐκ τοῦ.χαράγματος.αὐτοῦ,‖ ἐκ τοῦ ἀριθμοῦ τοῦ ὀνόματος
and of its mark, of the number [2]name
αὐτοῦ, ἑστῶτας ἐπὶ τὴν θάλασσαν τὴν ὑαλίνην, ἔχοντας
[1]of [3]its, standing upon the [2]sea [1]glass, having
κιθάρας τοῦ θεοῦ. 3 καὶ ᾄδουσιν τὴν ᾠδὴν [c]Μωσέως‖ [d]δού-
harps of God. And they sing the song of Moses, bond-
λου τοῦ θεοῦ, καὶ τὴν ᾠδὴν τοῦ ἀρνίου, λέγοντες, Μεγάλα καὶ
man of God, and the song of the Lamb, saying, Great and
θαυμαστὰ τὰ.ἔργα.σου, κύριε ὁ θεὸς ὁ παντοκράτωρ· δί-
wonderful [are] thy works, Lord God Almighty; right-
καιαι καὶ ἀληθιναὶ αἱ.ὁδοί.σου, ὁ βασιλεὺς τῶν [e]ἁγίων.‖
eous and true [are] thy ways, [thou] King of saints.
4 τίς οὐ μὴ φοβηθῇ [f]σε,‖ κύριε, καὶ [g]δοξάσῃ‖ τὸ.ὄνομά.σου;
Who [2]not [1]should fear thee, O Lord, and glorify thy name?
ὅτι μόνος ὅσιος· ὅτι πάντα τὰ ἔθνη ἥξουσιν καὶ
for [thou] only [art] holy; for all the nations shall come and
προσκυνήσουσιν ἐνώπιόν σου· ὅτι τὰ.δικαιώματά.σου
do homage before thee; for thy righteous [acts] (*lit.* righteousnesses)
ἐφανερώθησαν.
were manifested.
5 Καὶ μετὰ ταῦτα [a]εἶδον,‖ καὶ [h]ἰδού,‖ ἠνοίγη ὁ ναὸς
And after these things I saw, and behold, was opened the temple
τῆς σκηνῆς τοῦ μαρτυρίου ἐν τῷ οὐρανῷ· 6 καὶ ἐξῆλθον οἱ
of the tabernacle of the testimony in the heaven; and came forth the
ἑπτὰ ἄγγελοι [i] ἔχοντες τὰς ἑπτὰ πληγάς, ἐκ τοῦ ναοῦ,
seven angels [5]having [6]the [7]seven [8]plagues [1]out [2]of [3]the [4]temple,
ἐνδεδυμένοι [k]λίνον‖ καθαρὸν [l]καὶ‖ λαμπρόν, καὶ περιεζωσμένοι
clothed in linen pure and bright, and girt with
περὶ τὰ στήθη ζώνας χρυσᾶς. 7 καὶ ἓν ἐκ τῶν τεσσάρων
[3]about [4]the [5]breasts [2]girdles [1]golden. And one of the four
ζώων ἔδωκεν τοῖς ἑπτὰ ἀγγέλοις ἑπτὰ φιάλας χρυσᾶς,
living creatures gave to the seven angels seven [2]bowls [1]golden,
γεμούσας τοῦ θυμοῦ τοῦ θεοῦ τοῦ ζῶντος εἰς τοὺς αἰῶνας
full of the fury of God, who lives to the ages
τῶν αἰώνων. 8 καὶ ἐγεμίσθη ὁ ναὸς καπνοῦ ἐκ τῆς δόξης
of the ages. And [3]was [4]filled [1]the [2]temple with smoke from the glory
τοῦ θεοῦ, καὶ ἐκ τῆς.δυνάμεως.αὐτοῦ· καὶ οὐδεὶς [m]ἠδύνατο‖
of God, and from his power: and no one was able
εἰσελθεῖν εἰς τὸν ναόν, ἄχρι τελεσθῶσιν αἱ ἑπτὰ πληγαὶ τῶν
to enter into the temple until were completed the seven plagues of the
ἑπτὰ ἀγγέλων.
seven angels.

16 Καὶ ἤκουσα [n]φωνῆς μεγάλης‖ ἐκ τοῦ ναοῦ, λεγούσης
And I heard a [2]voice [1]loud out of the temple, saying
τοῖς ἑπτὰ ἀγγέλοις, Ὑπάγετε, καὶ [o]ἐκχέατε‖ τὰς [p] φιάλας τοῦ
to the seven angels, Go, and pour out the bowls of the
θυμοῦ τοῦ θεοῦ εἰς τὴν γῆν.
fury of God into the earth.
2 Καὶ ἀπῆλθεν ὁ πρῶτος, καὶ ἐξέχεεν τὴν.φιάλην.αὐτοῦ
And [3]departed [1]the [2]first, and poured out his bowl
[q]ἐπὶ‖ τὴν γῆν· καὶ ἐγένετο ἕλκος κακὸν καὶ πονηρὸν [r]εἰς‖ τοὺς
on to the earth; and came a sore, evil and grievous, upon the
ἀνθρώπους τοὺς ἔχοντας τὸ χάραγμα τοῦ θηρίου, καὶ τοὺς
men who had the mark of the beast, and those
[s]τῇ.εἰκόνι.αὐτοῦ προσκυνοῦντας.‖
[3]to [4]his [5]image [1]doing [2]homage.
3 Καὶ ὁ δεύτερος [t]ἄγγελος‖ ἐξέχεεν τὴν.φιάλην.αὐτοῦ εἰς
And the second angel poured out his bowl into
τὴν θάλασσαν· καὶ ἐγένετο αἷμα ὡς νεκροῦ, καὶ πᾶσα ψυχὴ
the sea; and it became blood, as of [one] dead; and every [2]soul
[v]ζῶσα‖ ἀπέθανεν [w] ἐν τῇ θαλάσσῃ.
[1]living died in the sea.
4 Καὶ ὁ τρίτος [x]ἄγγελος‖ ἐξέχεεν τὴν.φιάλην.αὐτοῦ εἰς
And the third angel poured out his bowl into
τοὺς ποταμοὺς καὶ [y]εἰς‖ τὰς πηγὰς τῶν ὑδάτων· καὶ [z]ἐγένετο‖
the rivers, and into the fountains of waters; and they became
αἷμα. 5 καὶ ἤκουσα τοῦ ἀγγέλου τῶν ὑδάτων λέγοντος,
blood. And I heard the angel of the waters saying,
Δίκαιος, [a]κύριε,‖ εἶ, ὁ ὢν καὶ ὁ ἦν [b]καὶ ὁ‖ ὅσιος, ὅτι
Righteous, O Lord, art thou, who art and who wast and the holy one, that

CHAPTER 15

1 And I saw another wonder in Heaven, great and wonderful – seven angels who had the seven last plagues. For the wrath of God was completed in them.
2 And I saw as it were a sea of glass mixed with fire. And the ones who had overcome the beast, and its image, and its mark, and the number of its name, were standing on the sea of glass, having God's harps.
3 And they sang the song of Moses, a servant of God, and the song of the Lamb, saying, Great and wonderful are Your works, Lord God Almighty. Righteous and true are Your ways, O King of the saints.
4 Who shall not fear You and glorify Your name, O Lord? For You only are holy. For all the nations shall come and worship before You – for Your righteous deeds have been revealed.
5 And after these things I saw, and behold – the Temple of the tabernacle of the testimony in Heaven was opened.
6 And the seven angels came out of the Temple. They had the seven plagues. They were clothed in pure and bright linen and were tied at the breasts with golden bands.
7 And one of the four living creatures gave to the seven angels seven golden bowls full of the wrath of God, who lives forever.
8 And the Temple was filled with smoke from the glory of God, and from His power. And no one was able to enter into the Temple until the seven plagues of the seven angels were finished.

CHAPTER 16

1 And I heard a loud voice out of the Temple saying to the seven angels, Go and pour out bowls of God's wrath onto the earth.
2 And the first went. And he poured out his bowl onto the earth. And an evil and vicious sore came on the men who had the mark of the beast and those worshiping his image.
3 And the second angel poured out his bowl onto the sea. And it looked like a dead man's blood. And every living soul in the sea died.
4 And the third angel poured out his bowl onto the rivers and onto the fountains of waters. And they became blood.
5 And I heard the angel of the waters saying, O Lord, You are righteous, He who

ταῦτα ἔκρινας· 6 ὅτι [c]αἷμα" ἁγίων καὶ προ-
these things thou didst judge; because [the] blood of saints and of pro-
φητῶν ἐξέχεαν, καὶ αἷμα αὐτοῖς [d]ἔδωκας" [e]πιεῖν·" ἄξιοι
phets they poured out, and blood to them thou didst give to drink; [2]worthy
[f]γάρ" εἰσιν. 7 Καὶ ἤκουσα [g]ἄλλου ἐκ" τοῦ θυσιαστηρίου λέ-
[1]for they are. And I heard another out of the altar say-
γοντος, Ναί, κύριε ὁ θεὸς ὁ παντοκράτωρ, ἀληθιναὶ καὶ δίκαιαι
ing, Yea, Lord God Almighty, true and righteous
αἱ.κρίσεις.σου.
[are] thy judgments.

8 Καὶ ὁ τέταρτος [x]ἄγγελος" ἐξέχεεν τὴν.φιάλην.αὐτοῦ ἐπὶ
And the fourth angel poured out his bowl upon
τὸν ἥλιον· καὶ ἐδόθη αὐτῷ καυματίσαι τοὺς ἀνθρώπους ἐν
the sun; and it was given to it to scorch men with
πυρί· 9 καὶ ἐκαυματίσθησαν οἱ ἄνθρωποι καῦμα μέγα, κα
fire. And [2]were [3]scorched [1]men with [2]heat [1]great, an
ἐβλασφήμησαν τὸ ὄνομα τοῦ θεοῦ τοῦ.ἔχοντος [h] ἐξουσίαν ἐπ
they blasphemed the name of God, who has authority over
τὰς.πληγὰς.ταύτας, καὶ οὐ.μετενόησαν δοῦναι αὐτῷ δόξαν.
these plagues, and did not repent to give him glory.

10 Καὶ ὁ πέμπτος [i]ἄγγελος" ἐξέχεεν τὴν.φιάλην.αὐτοῦ ἐπὶ
And the fifth angel poured out his bowl upon
τὸν θρόνον τοῦ θηρίου· καὶ ἐγένετο ἡ.βασιλεία.αὐτοῦ ἐσκοτω-
the throne of the beast; and [3]became [1]its [2]kingdom dark-
μένη· καὶ [k]ἐμασσῶντο" τὰς.γλώσσας.αὐτῶν ἐκ τοῦ πόνου,
ened; and they were gnawing their tongues for the distress,
11 καὶ ἐβλασφήμησαν τὸν θεὸν τοῦ οὐρανοῦ ἐκ τῶν πόνων
and blasphemed the God of the heaven for [2]distresses
αὐτῶν καὶ ἐκ τῶν.ἑλκῶν.αὐτῶν, καὶ οὐ.μετενόησαν ἐκ τῶν
[1]their and for their sores, and did not repent of
ἔργων αὐτῶν.
[2]works [1]their.

12 Καὶ ὁ ἕκτος [l]ἄγγελος" ἐξέχεεν τὴν.φιάλην.αὐτοῦ ἐπὶ τὸν
And the sixth angel poured out his bowl upon the
ποταμὸν τὸν μέγαν [l]τὸν" Εὐφράτην· καὶ ἐξηράνθη τὸ ὕδωρ
[2]river [1]great, the Euphrates; and was dried up [2]water
αὐτοῦ, ἵνα ἑτοιμασθῇ ἡ ὁδὸς τῶν βασιλέων τῶν ἀπὸ
[1]its, that might be prepared the way of the kings [2]the [1]from
[m]ἀνατολῶν" ἡλίου. 13 Καὶ [n]εἶδον" ἐκ τοῦ στόματος τοῦ
rising of [the] sun. And I saw out of the mouth of the
δράκοντος, καὶ ἐκ τοῦ στόματος τοῦ θηρίου, καὶ ἐκ τοῦ
dragon, and out of the mouth of the beast, and out of the
στόματος τοῦ ψευδοπροφήτου, πνεύματα τρία ἀκάθαρτα
mouth of the false prophet, [3]spirits [1]three [2]unclean
[o]ὅμοια βατράχοις" 14 εἰσὶν.γὰρ πνεύματα [p]δαιμόνων" ποι-
like frogs; for they are spirits of demons do-
οῦντα [q]σημεῖα ἐκπορεύεσθαι" ἐπὶ τοὺς βασιλεῖς [r]τῆς γῆς καὶ
ing signs, to go forth to the kings of the earth and
τῆς οἰκουμένης ὅλης, συναγαγεῖν αὐτοὺς εἰς [s] πόλεμον
of the [2]habitable [[3]world] [1]whole to gather together them unto battle
τῆς [t]ἡμέρας ἐκείνης τῆς μεγάλης" τοῦ θεοῦ τοῦ παντοκράτορος.
of [3]day [1]that [2]great of God the Almighty.
15 Ἰδού, ἔρχομαι ὡς κλέπτης. μακάριος ὁ γρηγορῶν,
Behold, I come as a thief. Blessed [is] he that watches,
καὶ τηρῶν τὰ.ἱμάτια.αὐτοῦ, ἵνα μὴ γυμνὸς περιπατῇ, καὶ
and keeps his garments, that not naked he may walk, and
βλέπωσιν τὴν.ἀσχημοσύνην.αὐτοῦ. 16 καὶ συνήγαγεν
they see his shame. And he gathered together
αὐτοὺς εἰς τὸν τόπον τὸν καλούμενον Ἑβραϊστὶ [v]Ἀρμα-
them to the place which is called in Hebrew Arma-
γεδδών."
geddon.

17 Καὶ ὁ ἕβδομος [w]ἄγγελος" ἐξέχεεν τὴν.φιάλην.αὐτοῦ
And the seventh angel poured out his bowl
[x]εἰς" τὸν ἀέρα· καὶ ἐξῆλθεν φωνὴ [y]μεγάλη" [z]ἀπὸ" τοῦ ναοῦ
into the air; and came out a [2]voice [1]loud from the temple
[a]τοῦ οὐρανοῦ," ἀπὸ τοῦ θρόνου, λέγουσα, Γέγονεν. 18 Καὶ
of the heaven, from the throne, saying, It is done. And
ἐγένοντο [b]φωναὶ καὶ βρονταὶ καὶ ἀστραπαί," καὶ σεισμὸς
there were voices and thunders and lightnings; and [4]earthquake
ἐγένετο μέγας, οἷος οὐκ.ἐγένετο ἀφ' οὗ [c]οἱ ἄνθρωποι ἐγέ-
[1]there [2]was [3]a [4]great, such as was not since men
νοντο" ἐπὶ τῆς γῆς, τηλικοῦτος σεισμὸς οὕτως μέγας. 19 καὶ
were on the earth so mighty an earthquake, so great. And
ἐγένετο ἡ πόλις ἡ μεγάλη εἰς τρία μέρη, καὶ αἱ πόλεις τῶν
[4]became [1]the [3]city [2]great into three parts; and the cities of the
ἐθνῶν [d]ἔπεσον·" καὶ Βαβυλὼν ἡ μεγάλη ἐμνήσθη ἐνώπιον
nations fell; and Babylon the great was remembered before
τοῦ θεοῦ, δοῦναι αὐτῇ τὸ ποτήριον τοῦ οἴνου τοῦ θυμοῦ τῆς
God, to give her the cup of the wine of the fury
ὀργῆς αὐτοῦ. 20 καὶ πᾶσα νῆσος ἔφυγεν, καὶ ὄρη οὐχ
[3]wrath [1]of [2]his. And every island fled; and [2]mountains [1]no

is and who was, and the Holy One, that You have judged these things.

6 For they poured out the blood of the saints and of the prophets, and You gave them blood to drink, for they deserve it.

7 And I heard another out of the altar saying, Yes, Lord God Almighty, true and righteous are Your judgments.

8 And the fourth angel poured out his bowl upon the sun. And it was given to him to scorch men with fire.

9 And men were scorched with great heat, so that they blasphemed the name of God – who has authority over these plagues. And they did not repent to give Him glory.

10 And the fifth angel poured out his bowl on the throne of the beast. And its kingdom became darkened. And they were biting their tongues from the pain.

11 And they blasphemed the God of Heaven for their pains and for their sores. And they did not repent of their works.

12 And the sixth angel poured out his bowl on the great river Eu-phra-tes. And its water was dried up, so that the ways of the kings from the east might be made ready.

13 And I saw coming out of the mouth of the dragon, and out of the mouth of the beast, and out of the mouth of the false prophet, three unclean spirits, like frogs.

14 For they are the spirits of demons, working miracles, to go out to the kings of the earth and of the whole world to gather them together to the battle of that great day of God, the Almighty.

15 Behold! I come as a thief. Blessed is he that is alert and keeps his clothes on, that he may not walk naked and they see his shame.

16 And he gathered them together into the place which is called in Hebrew, Armageddon.

17 And the seventh angel poured out his bowl into the air. And a loud voice came out from the Temple of Heaven, from the throne, saying, It is done!

18 And there were voices and thunders and lightnings. And there was a great earthquake, such as has not occurred since men were on the earth – so mighty and so great an earthquake *was it.*

19 And the great city fell into three parts; and the cities of the nations fell. And the great Babylon was remembered by God, to give her the cup of the wine of the fury of His wrath.

20 And every island fled away. And no mountains were found.

εὑρέθησαν. 21 καὶ χάλαζα μεγάλη ὡς.ταλαντιαία καταβαίνει
were found; and a [2]hail [1]great as of a talent weight comes down
ἐκ τοῦ οὐρανοῦ ἐπὶ τοὺς ἀνθρώπους· καὶ ἐβλασφήμησαν οἱ
out of the heaven upon men; and [2]blasphemed
ἄνθρωποι τὸν θεόν, ἐκ τῆς πληγῆς τῆς χαλάζης· ὅτι με-
[1]men God, because of the plague of the hail, for
γάλη ἐστὶν ἡ.πληγὴ.αὐτῆς σφόδρα.
great [3]is [4]its [5]plague [1]exceeding.

17 Καὶ ἦλθεν εἷς ἐκ τῶν ἑπτὰ ἀγγέλων τῶν ἐχόντων τὰς
And came one of the seven angels of those having the
ἑπτὰ φιάλας, καὶ ἐλάλησεν μετ' ἐμοῦ, λέγων [e]μοι,' Δεῦρο,
seven bowls, and spoke with me, saying to me, Come here,
δείξω σοι τὸ κρίμα τῆς πόρνης τῆς μεγάλης, τῆς καθη-
I will shew thee the sentence of the [2]harlot [1]great, who sits
μένης ἐπὶ [f]τῶν' ὑδάτων [f]τῶν' πολλῶν· 2 μεθ' ἧς ἐπόρνευ-
upon the [2]waters [1]many; with whom [6]committed [7]for-
σαν οἱ βασιλεῖς τῆς γῆς, καὶ ἐμεθύσθησαν [g]ἐκ τοῦ οἴνου
nication [1]the [2]kings [3]of [4]the [5]earth; and were made drunk with the wine
τῆς.πορνείας.αὐτῆς οἱ κατοικοῦντες τὴν γῆν.' 3 Καὶ
of her fornication those that dwell on the earth. And
ἀπήνεγκέν με εἰς ἔρημον ἐν πνεύματι· καὶ [h]εἶδον' γυναῖκα
he carried away me [4]to [5]a [6]wilderness [1]in [[2]the] [3]Spirit; and I saw a woman
καθημένην ἐπὶ θηρίον κόκκινον, [i]γέμον ὀνομάτων' βλασφημίας,
sitting upon a [2]beast [1]scarlet, full of names of blasphemy,
[k]ἔχον' κεφαλὰς ἑπτὰ καὶ κέρατα δέκα. 4 καὶ ἡ γυνὴ [l]ἡ'
having [2]heads [1]seven and [2]horns [1]ten. And the woman
περιβεβλημένη [m]πορφύρᾳ' καὶ [n]κοκκίνῳ,' [o]καὶ' κεχρυσωμένη
clothed in purple and scarlet, and decked (*lit.* gilded)
[p]χρυσῷ' καὶ λίθῳ τιμίῳ καὶ μαργαρίταις, ἔχουσα [q]χρυσοῦν
with gold and [2]stone [1]precious and pearls, having a golden
ποτήριον' ἐν τῇ.χειρὶ.αὐτῆς, [r]γέμον' βδελυγμάτων καὶ [s]ἀκαθ-
cup in her hand, full of abominations and of unclean-
άρτητος' πορνείας.αὐτῆς, 5 καὶ ἐπὶ τὸ.μέτωπον.αὐτῆς
ness of her fornication; and upon her forehead
ὄνομα γεγραμμένον, Μυστήριον, Βαβυλὼν ἡ μεγάλη, ἡ
a name written, Mystery, Babylon the Great, the
μήτηρ τῶν πορνῶν καὶ τῶν βδελυγμάτων τῆς γῆς. 6 Καὶ
mother of the harlots and of the abominations of the earth. And
[t]εἶδον' τὴν γυναῖκα μεθύουσαν ἐκ τοῦ αἵματος τῶν ἁγίων, καὶ
I saw the woman drunk with the blood of the saints, and
ἐκ τοῦ αἵματος τῶν μαρτύρων Ἰησοῦ· καὶ ἐθαύμασα, ἰδὼν
with the blood of the witnesses of Jesus. And I wondered, having seen
αὐτήν, θαῦμα μέγα. 7 Καὶ εἶπέν μοι ὁ ἄγγελος, [v]Διατί'
her, with [2]wonder [1]great. And [3]said [4]to [5]me [1]the [2]angel, Why
ἐθαύμασας; ἐγώ [w]σοὶ ἐρῶ' τὸ μυστήριον τῆς γυναικός,
didst thou wonder? I thee will tell the mystery of the woman,
καὶ τοῦ θηρίου τοῦ βαστάζοντος αὐτήν, τοῦ ἔχοντος τὰς
and of the beast which carries her, which has the
ἑπτὰ κεφαλὰς καὶ τὰ δέκα κέρατα. 8 [x] Θηρίον ὃ εἶδες,
seven heads and the ten horns. [The] beast which thou sawest
ἦν, καὶ οὐκ.ἔστιν, καὶ μέλλει ἀναβαίνειν ἐκ τῆς ἀβύσσου,
was, and is not, and is about to come up out of the abyss,
καὶ εἰς ἀπώλειαν [y]ὑπάγειν' καὶ [z]θαυμάσονται' οἱ κατοι-
and into destruction to go; and shall wonder they who dwell
κοῦντες ἐπὶ τῆς γῆς, ὧν [a]οὐ.γέγραπται' [b]τὰ ὀνόματα' ἐπὶ
on the earth, of whom are not written the names in
τὸ βιβλίον τῆς ζωῆς ἀπὸ καταβολῆς κόσμου, [c]βλέ-
the book of life from [the] foundation of [the] world, see-
ποντες' τὸ θηρίον [d]ὅ τι' ἦν, καὶ οὐκ ἔστιν, [e]καίπερ ἐστίν.[f]
ing the beast which was and [2]not [1]is, and yet is.
9 ὧδε ὁ νοῦς ὁ ἔχων σοφίαν. αἱ ἑπτὰ κεφαλαί, [f]ὄρη
Here [is] the mind which has wisdom: The seven heads [3]mountains
εἰσὶν ἑπτά,' ὅπου ἡ γυνὴ κάθηται ἐπ' αὐτῶν. 10 καὶ βα-
[1]are [2]seven, where the woman sits on them. And
σιλεῖς ἑπτά εἰσιν· οἱ πέντε ἔπεσαν, [g]καὶ' ὁ εἷς ἔστιν, ὁ
[4]kings [3]seven [1]there [2]are: the five are fallen, and the one is, the
ἄλλος οὔπω ἦλθεν· καὶ ὅταν ἔλθῃ, ὀλίγον αὐτὸν.δεῖ
other [2]not [3]yet [1]is come: and when he shall have come, a little while he must
μεῖναι. 11 καὶ τὸ θηρίον ὃ ἦν, καὶ οὐκ ἔστιν, καὶ [h]αὐτὸς'
remain. And the beast which was, and [2]not [1]is, [4]also [3]he
ὄγδοός ἐστιν, καὶ ἐκ τῶν ἑπτά ἐστιν, καὶ εἰς ἀπώλειαν
[6]an [7]eighth [5]is, and of the seven is, and into destruction
ὑπάγει. 12 καὶ τὰ δέκα κέρατα ἃ εἶδες, δέκα βασιλεῖς
goes. And the ten horns which thou sawest ten kings
εἰσιν, οἵτινες βασιλείαν [i]οὔπω' ἔλαβον, [k]ἀλλ'' ἐξουσίαν ὡς
are, which [4]a [5]kingdom [2]not [3]yet [1]received, but authority as
βασιλεῖς μίαν ὥραν λαμβάνουσιν μετὰ τοῦ θηρίου. 13 οὗτοι
kings one hour receive with the beast. These
μίαν [l]γνώμην ἔχουσιν,' καὶ τὴν δύναμιν καὶ [m]τὴν' ἐξουσίαν
one mind have, and the power and the authority

21 And a great hail, like the weight of a
talent, came down out of the sky on men.
And men blasphemed God because of the
plague of the hail. For its plague was very
great.

CHAPTER 17

1 And one of the seven angels (of those
who had the seven bowls) came and spoke
with me, saying to me, Come here. I will
show you the judgment of the great harlot
who sits on the many waters
2 with whom the kings of the earth fornicated. And those that live on the earth
were made drunk with the wine of her
fornication.
3 And he carried me away in the Spirit
into a wilderness. And I saw a woman sitting on a scarlet beast, full of names of
blasphemy and having seven heads and ten
horns.
4 And the woman was dressed in purple
and scarlet and was gilded with gold and
precious stones and pearls. And she had a
golden cup in her hand which was full of
hateful things, and of the uncleanness of
her fornication.
5 And a name was written on her
forehead, MYSTERY, BABYLON THE
GREAT, the mother of the harlots and of
the hateful things of the earth.
6 And I saw the woman drunk with
the blood of the saints, and with the
blood of the witnesses of Jesus. And I
wondered with great wonder when I saw
her.
7 And the angel said to me, Why did you
wonder? I will tell you the mystery of the
woman and of the beast which carries her
– which has the seven heads and the ten
horns.
8 The beast which you saw was, and is
not, and is about to come up out of the
bottomless pit, and to go into perdition.
And they who live on the earth, whose
names are not written in the Book of Life
from the foundation of the world, will wonder when they see the beast which was, and
is not, and yet is.
9 Here is the mind which has wisdom: The
seven heads are seven mountains, where the
woman sits on them.
10 And there are seven kings – the five have
fallen, and the one is, and the other has not
yet come. And when he comes, he must
remain a little while.
11 And the beast which was, and is not, he
also is an eighth, and is of the seven, and
goes into perdition.
12 And the ten horns which you saw are ten
kings, which have not yet received a kingdom, but will receive authority as kings one
hour with the beast.
13 These have one mind. And they shall

[n]ἑαυτῶν" τῷ θηρίῳ [o]διαδιδώσουσιν." 14 οὗτοι μετὰ τοῦ
of themselves to the beast they shall give up. These with the
ἀρνίου πολεμήσουσιν, καὶ τὸ ἀρνίον νικήσει αὐτούς, ὅτι
Lamb war will make, and the Lamb will overcome them; because
κύριος κυρίων ἐστὶν καὶ βασιλεὺς βασιλέων· καὶ οἱ
Lord of lords he is and King of kings: and those that [are]
μετ' αὐτοῦ, κλητοὶ καὶ ἐκλεκτοὶ καὶ πιστοί. 15 Καὶ [p]λέγει"
with him, called, and chosen, and faithful. And he says
μοι, Τὰ ὕδατα ἃ εἶδες, οὗ ἡ πόρνη κάθηται, λαοὶ καὶ
to me, The waters which thou sawest, where the harlot sits, [2]peoples [3]and
ὄχλοι εἰσίν, καὶ ἔθνη καὶ γλῶσσαι. 16 καὶ τὰ δέκα κέρατα
[4]multitudes [1]are, and nations and tongues. And the ten horns
ἃ εἶδες [q]ἐπὶ' τὸ θηρίον, οὗτοι μισήσουσιν τὴν πόρνην,
which thou sawest upon the beast, these shall hate the harlot,
καὶ ἠρημωμένην ποιήσουσιν αὐτὴν καὶ γυμνήν, καὶ τὰς
and desolate shall make her and naked, and
σάρκας αὐτῆς φάγονται, καὶ αὐτὴν κατακαύσουσιν [r]ἐν' πυρί.
[4]flesh [3]her [1]shall [2]eat, and [3]her [1]shall [2]burn with fire;
17 ὁ.γὰρ.θεὸς ἔδωκεν εἰς τὰς.καρδίας.αὐτῶν ποιῆσαι τὴν
for God gave to their hearts to do
γνώμην αὐτοῦ, [s]καὶ ποιῆσαι μίαν γνώμην," καὶ δοῦναι τὴν
[2]mind [1]his, and to do one mind, and to give
βασιλείαν αὐτῶν τῷ θηρίῳ, ἄχρι [t]τελεσθῇ τὰ ῥήματα"
[2]kingdom [1]their to the beast, until should be fulfilled the sayings
τοῦ θεοῦ. 18 καὶ ἡ γυνὴ ἣν εἶδες, ἔστιν ἡ πόλις ἡ
of God. And the woman whom thou sawest is the [2]city
μεγάλη, ἡ ἔχουσα βασιλείαν ἐπὶ τῶν βασιλέων τῆς γῆς.
[1]great, which has kingship over the kings of the earth.

18 [v]Καὶ" μετὰ ταῦτα εἶδον [w] ἄγγελον καταβαίνοντα ἐκ
And after these things I saw an angel descending out of
τοῦ οὐρανοῦ, ἔχοντα ἐξουσίαν μεγάλην· καὶ ἡ γῆ ἐφω-
the heaven, having [2]authority [1]great: and the earth was enlight-
τίσθη ἐκ τῆς.δόξης.αὐτοῦ. 2 καὶ ἔκραξεν [x]ἐν.ἰσχύϊ, φωνῇ
ened with his glory. And he cried mightily with a [2]voice
μεγάλῃ," λέγων, [y]Ἔπεσεν [z]ἔπεσεν" Βαβυλὼν ἡ μεγάλη, καὶ
[1]loud, saying, Is fallen, is fallen Babylon the great, and
ἐγένετο κατοικητήριον [z]δαιμόνων," καὶ φυλακὴ παντὸς πνεύ-
is become a habitation of demons, and a hold of every [3]spi-
ματος ἀκαθάρτου[a], καὶ φυλακὴ παντὸς ὀρνέου ἀκαθάρτου καὶ
rit [1]unclean, and a hold of every [4]bird [1]unclean [2]and
μεμισημένου· 3 ὅτι ἐκ [b]τοῦ οἴνου" τοῦ θυμοῦ τῆς πορ-
[3]hated: because of the wine of the fury [3]forni-
νείας αὐτῆς [c]πέπωκεν" πάντα τὰ ἔθνη, καὶ οἱ βασιλεῖς
cation [1]of [2]her [7]have [8]drunk [4]all [5]the [6]nations; and the kings
τῆς γῆς μετ' αὐτῆς ἐπόρνευσαν, καὶ οἱ ἔμποροι τῆς
of the earth with her did commit fornication, and the merchants of the
γῆς ἐκ τῆς δυνάμεως τοῦ.στρήνους.αὐτῆς ἐπλούτησαν.
earth through the power of her luxury were enriched.
4 Καὶ ἤκουσα ἄλλην φωνὴν ἐκ τοῦ οὐρανοῦ, λέγουσαν,
And I heard another voice out of the heaven, saying,
[d]Ἐξέλθετε" [e]ἐξ αὐτῆς ὁ.λαός.μου," ἵνα μὴ.[f]συγκοινωνήσητε"
Come ye out of her, my people, that ye may not have fellowship
ταῖς.ἁμαρτίαις.αὐτῆς, καὶ [g]ἵνα μὴ.λάβητε ἐκ τῶν πληγῶν
in her sins, and that ye may not receive of [2]plagues
αὐτῆς·" 5 ὅτι [h]ἠκολούθησαν" αὐτῆς αἱ ἁμαρτίαι ἄχρι τοῦ
[1]her: for [3]followed [1]her [2]sins as far as the
οὐρανοῦ, καὶ ἐμνημόνευσεν ὁ θεὸς τὰ.ἀδικήματα.αὐτῆς. 6 ἀπό-
heaven, and [2]remembered [1]God her unrighteousnesses. Ren-
δοτε αὐτῇ ὡς καὶ αὐτὴ ἀπέδωκεν [i]ὑμῖν," καὶ διπλώσατε [k]αὐτῇ'
der to her as also she rendered to you; and double ye to her
[l]διπλᾶ κατὰ τὰ.ἔργα.αὐτῆς· ἐν τῷ ποτηρίῳ ᾧ ἐκέρασεν,
double, according to her works. In the cup which she mixed,
κεράσατε αὐτῇ διπλοῦν. 7 ὅσα ἐδόξασεν [m]ἑαυτὴν' καὶ
mix ye to her double. So much as she glorified herself and
ἐστρηνίασεν, τοσοῦτον δότε αὐτῇ βασανισμὸν καὶ πένθος·
lived luxuriously, so much give to her torment and mourning.
ὅτι ἐν τῇ.καρδίᾳ.αὐτῆς λέγει, [n]Κάθημαι βασίλισσα, καὶ
Because in her heart she says, I sit a queen, and
χήρα οὐκ.εἰμί, καὶ πένθος οὐ.μὴ ἴδω. 8 Διὰ τοῦτο
a widow I am not: and mourning in no wise may I see. On account of this
ἐν μιᾷ ἡμέρᾳ ἥξουσιν αἱ.πληγαὶ.αὐτῆς, θάνατος καὶ πένθος
in one day shall come her plagues, death and mourning
καὶ λιμός· καὶ ἐν πυρὶ κατακαυθήσεται· ὅτι ἰσχυρὸς [o]κύριος"
and famine, and with fire she shall be burnt; for strong [is the] Lord
ὁ θεὸς ὁ [p]κρίνων" αὐτήν. 9 καὶ [q]κλαύσονται' [r]αὐτήν," καὶ
God who judges her. And shall weep for her, and
κόψονται ἐπ' [s]αὐτῇ" οἱ βασιλεῖς τῆς γῆς, οἱ μετ' αὐτῆς πορ-
shall bewail for her, the kings of the earth, who with her commit-
νεύσαντες καὶ στρηνιάσαντες, ὅταν βλέπωσιν τὸν καπνὸν
ted fornication and lived luxuriously, when they see the smoke
τῆς.πυρώσεως.αὐτῆς, 10 ἀπὸ μακρόθεν ἑστηκότες διὰ
of her burning, [2]from [3]afar [1]standing on account of

give up their power and authority to the beast.

14 These will make war with the Lamb. And the Lamb will overcome them, because He is Lord of lords and King of kings. And those that are with Him are the called and chosen and faithful ones.

15 And he says to me, The waters which you saw, where the harlot sits, are people and multitudes and nations and tongues.

16 And the ten horns which you saw on the beast, these shall hate the harlot. And they shall make her poor and naked. And they shall eat her flesh and shall burn her with fire.

17 For God has put into their hearts to do His will and to act in one mind, and to give the kingdom to the beast, until the words of God shall be fulfilled.

18 And the woman you saw is the great city, which has kingship over the kings of the earth.

CHAPTER 18

1 And after these things, I saw an angel coming down out of Heaven. And he had great authority, and the earth was lighted up by his glory.

2 And he cried mightily with a loud voice, saying, Babylon the great s fallen, is fallen! And it has become a home of demons, and a prison of every unclean spirit, and a hold of every unclean and hated bird –

3 because all the nations have drunk of the wine of the fury of her fornication. And the kings of the earth fornicated with her. And the merchants of the earth were made rich through the power of her luxury.

4 And I heard another voice out of Heaven, saying, Come out of her, My people, so that you do not have any part in her sins, and so that you may not receive of her plagues,

5 for her sins followed as far as Heaven, and God remembered her wicked deeds.

6 Give to her even as she also gave to you, and double to her double, according to her works. In the cup which she mixed, mix to her twice as much.

7 As much as she glorified herself and lived in luxury, so much torment and sadness give to her. Because she says in her heart, I sit as a queen, and I am not a widow and, I will in no way see sorrow

8 because of this her plagues shall come in one day death and sorrow and hungering and she shall be burned with fire. For the Lord God who judges her is strong.

9 And the kings of the earth shall weep for her and shall wail for her, those who committed fornication with her and lived in luxury when they see the smoke of her burning,

10 standing at a distance because of the fear of her torment, saying, Woe! Woe! The great

τὸν φόβον τοῦ.βασανισμοῦ.αὐτῆς, λέγοντες, Οὐαί, οὐαί, ἡ
the fear of her torment, saying, Woe, woe, the
πόλις ἡ μεγάλη Βαβυλών, ἡ πόλις ἡ ἰσχυρά, ὅτι [t]ἐν" μιᾷ ὥρᾳ
[2]city [1]great, Babylon, the [2]city [1]strong! for in one hour
ἦλθεν ἡ.κρίσις.σου. 11 Καὶ οἱ ἔμποροι τῆς γῆς κλαίουσιν καὶ
is come thy judgment. And the merchants of the earth weep and
πενθοῦσιν ἐπ' [v]αὐτῇ," ὅτι τὸν.γόμον.αὐτῶν οὐδεὶς ἀγοράζει
mourn for her, because their lading no one buys
οὐκέτι· 12 γόμον χρυσοῦ, καὶ ἀργύρου, καὶ λίθου τιμίου,
any more; (*lit.* no more) lading of gold, and of silver, and of [2]stone [1]precious,
καὶ [w]μαργαρίτου," καὶ [x]βύσσου," καὶ πορφύρας, καὶ [y]σηρικοῦ,"
and of pearl, and of fine linen, and of purple, and of silk,
καὶ κοκκίνου· καὶ πᾶν ξύλον θύϊνον, καὶ πᾶν σκεῦος ἐλεφάν-
and of scarlet, and all [2]wood [1]thyine, and every article of
τινον, καὶ πᾶν σκεῦος ἐκ ξύλου τιμιωτάτου, καὶ χαλκοῦ, καὶ
ivory, and every article of [3]wood [1]most [2]precious, and of brass, and
σιδήρου, καὶ μαρμάρου, 13 καὶ [z]κινάμωμον," [a]καὶ θυμιάματα
of iron, and of marble, and cinnamon, and incense,
καὶ μύρον, καὶ λίβανον, καὶ οἶνον, καὶ ἔλαιον, καὶ σεμίδαλιν,
and ointment, and frankincense, and wine, and oil, and finest flour,
καὶ σῖτον, καὶ κτηνη, καὶ πρόβατα, καὶ ἵππων, καὶ ῥεδῶν,
and wheat, and cattle, and sheep, and of horses, and of chariots,
καὶ σωμάτων, καὶ ψυχὰς ἀνθρώπων. 14 καὶ ἡ ὀπώρα [c]τῆς
and of slaves, (*lit.* of bodies) and souls of men. And the ripe fruits of the
ἐπιθυμίας τῆς ψυχῆς.σου" [d]ἀπῆλθεν" ἀπὸ σοῦ, καὶ πάντα τὰ
desire of thy soul are departed from thee, and all the
λιπαρὰ καὶ [e]τὰ" λαμπρὰ [f]ἀπῆλθεν" ἀπὸ σοῦ, καὶ [g]οὐκέτι"
fat things and the bright things are departed from thee, and [4]any [5]more (*lit.* no more)
[h]οὐ.μὴ εὑρήσῃς αὐτά." 15 οἱ ἔμποροι τούτων οἱ
[1]in [2]no [3]wise shouldst thou find them. The merchants of these things, who
πλουτήσαντες ἀπ' αὐτῆς, ἀπὸ μακρόθεν στήσονται διὰ
were enriched from her, from afar shall stand because of
τὸν φόβον τοῦ.βασανισμοῦ.αὐτῆς, κλαίοντες καὶ πενθοῦντες,
the fear of her torment, weeping and mourning,

16 [i]καὶ' λέγοντες, Οὐαί, οὐαί, ἡ πόλις ἡ μεγάλη, ἡ περι-
and saying, Woe, woe, the [2]city [1]great, which [was] cloth-
βεβλημένη [k]βύσσινον" καὶ πορφυροῦν καὶ [k]κόκκινον," καὶ
ed with fine linen and purple and scarlet, and
κεχρυσωμένη [l]ἐν" [m]χρυσῷ" καὶ λίθῳ τιμίῳ καὶ [n]μαργαρί-
decked (*lit.* gilded) with gold and [2]stone [1]precious and pearls!
ταις·" 17 ὅτι μιᾷ ὥρᾳ ἠρημώθη ὁ τοσοῦτος πλοῦτος. Καὶ
for in one hour was made desolate so great wealth. And
πᾶς κυβερνήτης, καὶ [o]πᾶς ἐπὶ τῶν πλοίων ὁ ὅμιλος," καὶ
every steersman, and all [3]in [4]ships [1]the [2]company, and
ναῦται, καὶ ὅσοι τὴν.θάλασσαν.ἐργάζονται, ἀπὸ.μακρόθεν
sailors, and as many as trade by sea, afar off
ἔστησαν, 18 καὶ [p]ἔκραζον," [q]ὁρῶντες" τὸν καπνὸν τῆς πυρώ-
stood, and cried, seeing the smoke [3]burn-
σεως αὐτῆς, λέγοντες, Τίς ὁμοία τῇ πόλει [r]τῇ μεγάλῃ;
ing [1]of [2]her, saying, What [city is] like to the [2]city [1]great?
19 Καὶ [s]ἔβαλον' χοῦν ἐπὶ τὰς κεφαλὰς.αὐτῶν, καὶ [t]ἔκραζον"
And they cast dust upon their heads, and cried,
κλαίοντες καὶ πενθοῦντες, λέγοντες, Οὐαί, οὐαί, ἡ πόλις ἡ
weeping and mourning, saying, Woe, woe, the [2]city
μεγάλη, ἐν ᾗ ἐπλούτησαν πάντες οἱ ἔχοντες [v] πλοῖα ἐν τῇ
[1]great, in which were enriched all who had ships in the
θαλάσσῃ ἐκ τῆς.τιμιότητος.αὐτῆς, ὅτι μιᾷ ὥρᾳ ἠρημώ-
sea through her costliness! for in one hour she was made
θη. 20 Εὐφραίνου ἐπ' [w]αὐτήν," οὐρανέ, καὶ οἱ ἅγιοι [x] ἀπό-
desolate. Rejoice over her, O heaven, and [ye] holy apo-
στολοι καὶ οἱ προφῆται, ὅτι ἔκρινεν ὁ θεὸς τὸ.κρίμα.ὑμῶν ἐξ
stles and [ye] prophets; for [2]did [3]judge [1]God your judgment upon
αὐτῆς. 21 Καὶ ἦρεν εἷς ἄγγελος ἰσχυρὸς λίθον ὡς [y]μύλον"
her. And [4]took [5]up [1]one [3]angel [2]strong a stone, as a [2]millstone
μέγαν, καὶ ἔβαλεν εἰς τὴν θάλασσαν, λέγων, Οὕτως ὁρμή-
[1]great, and cast [it] into the sea, saying, Thus with
ματι βληθήσεται Βαβυλὼν ἡ μεγάλη πόλις, καὶ οὐ.μὴ
violence shall be cast down Babylon the great city, and not at all
εὑρεθῇ ἔτι. 22 καὶ φωνὴ κιθαρῳδῶν καὶ μουσικῶν καὶ
may be found longer: and voice of harpers and musicians and
αὐλητῶν καὶ σαλπιστῶν οὐ.μὴ ἀκουσθῇ ἐν σοὶ ἔτι, καὶ
flute-players and trumpeters not at all may be heard in thee longer, and
πᾶς τεχνίτης πάσης τέχνης οὐ.μὴ εὑρεθῇ ἐν σοὶ ἔτι, καὶ
any (*lit.* every) artificer of any (*lit.* of every) art not at all may be found in thee longer, and
φωνὴ μύλου οὐ.μὴ ἀκουσθῇ ἐν σοὶ ἔτι, 23 καὶ φῶς
sound of millstone not at all may be heard in thee longer, and light
λύχνου οὐ.μὴ [z]φανῇ' [a]ἐν" σοὶ ἔτι, καὶ φωνὴ νυμφίου καὶ
of lamp not at all may shine in thee longer, and voice of bridegroom and

city, Babylon, the strong city! For in one
hour your judgment has come.
11 And the merchants of the earth weep
and grieve for her, because no one buys their
goods any more,
12 goods of gold and of silver and of
precious stone and of pearl and of fine linen
and of purple and of silk and of scarlet and
all thyine wood, and every article of ivory,
and every article of most precious wood, and
of brass and of iron and of marble,
13 and cinnamon, and incense, and
ointment, and frankincense, and wine, and
oil, and finest flour, and wheat, and cattle,
and sheep, and of horses, and of chariots,
and of the bodies of souls of men.
14 And the ripe fruit of the lust of your
soul has gone away from you. And all the
fat things and all the bright things have left
you – and you shall never find them any
more.
15 The merchants of these things, who
were made rich from her, shall stand at a
distance because of the fear of her torment,
crying and grieving,

16 and saying, Woe! Woe! to the great city
which was clothed in fine linen and purple
and scarlet and which was made golden with
gold and precious stones and pearls.
17 For in one hour so much wealth was
made nothing. And every ship-pilot, and all
the company in ships, and sailors, and as
many as trade by sea, stood far away,
18 and cried when they saw the smoke of
her burning, saying, What *city is* like this
great city?
19 And they threw dust on their heads and
cried, weeping and wailing, saying, Woe!
Woe! to the great city, in which all who had
ships in the sea were made rich from her
riches. For in one hour she was made
nothing.
20 Rejoice over her, O Heaven, and holy
apostles and prophets. For God has judged
your judgment on her.
21 And one mighty angel took up a stone,
like a great millstone, and threw it into the
sea, saying, In this way Babylon the great
city shall be thrown down with great power,
and it will never be found any more,
22 – and the sound of harpers and musicians and flute-players and trumpet-players
shall never be heard in you any more. And
no skillful workers of any trade shall be
found in you any longer. And the sound of
the millstone shall never be heard in you any
longer.
23 And the light of a lamp shall never shine
in you any longer. And the voice of the
bridegroom and of the bride shall never be

νύμφης οὐ.μὴ ἀκουσθῇ ἐν σοὶ ἔτι· ὅτι [b]οἱ‖.ἔμποροί.σου
of bride not at all may be heard in thee longer; for thy merchants
ἦσαν οἱ μεγιστᾶνες τῆς γῆς, ὅτι ἐν τῇ.[c]φαρμακείᾳ'.σου ἐπλα-
were the great ones of the earth, for by thy sorcery were
νήθησαν πάντα τὰ ἔθνη. 24 καὶ ἐν αὐτῇ [d]αἷμα‖ προφη-
misled all the nations. And in her [the] blood of pro-
τῶν καὶ ἁγίων εὑρέθη, καὶ πάντων τῶν ἐσφαγμένων ἐπὶ τῆς
phets and saints was found, and of all the slain on the
γῆς.
earth.

19 [e]Καὶ‖ μετὰ ταῦτα ἤκουσα [f] φωνὴν [g]ὄχλου
And after these things I heard a [2]voice [3]of [4]a [6]multitude
πολλοῦ μεγάλην‖ ἐν τῷ οὐρανῷ, [h]λέγοντος,‖ Ἀλληλούϊα· ἡ
[5]great [1]loud in the heaven, saying, Hallelujah: the
σωτηρία καὶ ἡ δόξα [i]καὶ ἡ τιμὴ‖ καὶ ἡ δύναμις [k]κυρίῳ
salvation and the glory and the honour and the power to the Lord
τῷ.θεῷ.ἡμῶν·‖ 2. ὅτι ἀληθιναὶ καὶ δίκαιαι αἱ.κρίσεις.αὐτοῦ·
our God: for true and righteous [are] his judgments;
ὅτι ἔκρινεν τὴν πόρνην τὴν μεγάλην, ἥτις ἔφθειρεν τὴν γῆν
for he judged the [2]harlot [1]great, who corrupted the earth
ἐν τῇ.πορνείᾳ.αὐτῆς, καὶ ἐξεδίκησεν τὸ αἷμα τῶν δούλων
with her fornication, and he did avenge the blood [3]bondmen
αὐτοῦ ἐκ [l]τῆς‖.χειρὸς.αὐτῆς. 3 Καὶ δεύτερον εἴρηκαν, Ἀλλη-
[1]of [2]his at her hand. And a second time they said, Halle-
λούϊα· Καὶ ὁ.καπνὸς.αὐτῆς ἀναβαίνει εἰς τοὺς αἰῶνας τῶν
lujah. And her smoke goes up to the ages of the
αἰώνων. 4 Καὶ [m]ἔπεσαν‖ οἱ [n]πρεσβύτεροι οἱ εἴκοσι καὶ τέσ-
ages. And fell down the [4]elders [1]twenty [2]and
σαρες,‖ καὶ τὰ [o]τέσσαρα‖ ζῶα, καὶ προσεκύνησαν τῷ
[3]four, and the four living creatures and worshipped
θεῷ τῷ καθημένῳ ἐπὶ [p]τοῦ θρόνου,‖ λέγοντες, Ἀμήν· Ἀλλη-
God who sits on the throne, saying, Amen, Halle-
λούϊα. 5 Καὶ φωνὴ [q]ἐκ‖ τοῦ θρόνου ἐξῆλθεν λέγουσα, Αἰνεῖτε
lujah. And a voice out of the throne came forth, saying, Praise
[r]τὸν.θεὸν‖.ἡμῶν πάντες οἱ.δοῦλοι.αὐτοῦ, [s]καὶ‖ οἱ.φοβούμενοι
our God all [ye] his bondmen, and [ye] who fear
αὐτὸν [t]καὶ‖ οἱ μικροὶ καὶ οἱ μεγάλοι. 6 Καὶ ἤκουσα ὡς φωνὴν
him, both the small and the great. And I heard as a voice
ὄχλου πολλοῦ, καὶ [v]ὡς‖ φωνὴν ὑδάτων πολλῶν, καὶ ὡς
of a [2]multitude [1]great, and as a voice of [2]waters [1]many, and as
φωνὴν βροντῶν ἰσχυρῶν, [w]λέγοντας,‖ Ἀλληλούϊα· ὅτι ἐβασί-
a voice of [2]thunders [1]strong, saying, Hallelujah, for has
λευσεν κύριος ὁ θεὸς [x] ὁ παντοκράτωρ. 7 χαίρωμεν καὶ
reigned [the] Lord God the Almighty. We should rejoice and
[y]ἀγαλλιώμεθα,‖ καὶ [z]δῶμεν‖ τὴν δόξαν αὐτῷ· ὅτι ἦλθεν ὁ
should exult; and should give glory to him; for is come the
γάμος τοῦ ἀρνίου, καὶ ἡ.γυνὴ.αὐτοῦ ἡτοίμασεν ἑαυτήν. 8 Καὶ
marriage of the Lamb, and his wife did make [2]ready [1]herself. And
ἐδόθη αὐτῇ ἵνα περιβάληται βύσσινον [a]καθαρὸν καὶ
it was given to her that she should be clothed in fine linen, pure and
λαμπρόν·‖ τὸ.γὰρ βύσσινον τὰ δικαιώματά [b]ἐστιν τῶν
bright; for the fine linen [2]the [3]righteousnesses [1]is of the
ἁγίων.‖ 9 Καὶ λέγει μοι, Γράψον, Μακάριοι οἱ εἰς τὸ
saints. And he says to me, Write, Blessed [are] they who to the
δεῖπνον τοῦ γάμου τοῦ ἀρνίου κεκλημένοι. Καὶ λέγει μοι,
supper of the marriage of the Lamb are called. And he says to me,
Οὗτοι οἱ λόγοι [c] ἀληθινοί [d]εἰσιν τοῦ θεοῦ.‖ 10 Καὶ [e]ἔπεσον‖
These [2]the [4]words [3]true [1]are of God. And I fell
ἔμπροσθεν τῶν.ποδῶν.αὐτοῦ προσκυνῆσαι αὐτῷ· καὶ λέγει
before his feet to do homage to him. And he says
μοι, Ὅρα μή· σύνδουλός σου εἰμὶ καὶ τῶν ἀδελ-
to me, See [thou do it] not. Fellow-bondman of thee I am and [1]breth-
φῶν σου τῶν ἐχόντων τὴν μαρτυρίαν [f]τοῦ‖ Ἰησοῦ· τῷ θεῷ
ren [1]of [2]thy who have the testimony of Jesus. To God
προσκύνησον· ἡ.γὰρ μαρτυρία [f]τοῦ‖ Ἰησοῦ ἐστιν τὸ πνεῦμα
do homage. For [6]the [7]testimony [8]of [9]Jesus [5]is [1]the [2]spirit
τῆς προφητείας.
[3]of [4]prophecy.

11 Καὶ εἶδον τὸν οὐρανὸν [g]ἀνεῳγμένον,‖ καὶ ἰδού, ἵππος
And I saw the heaven opened, and behold, a [2]horse
λευκός, καὶ ὁ καθήμενος ἐπ' αὐτόν, [h]καλούμενος πιστὸς‖
[1]white, and he who sits upon it, called Faithful
καὶ ἀληθινός, καὶ ἐν δικαιοσύνῃ κρίνει καὶ πολεμεῖ· 12 οἱ
and True, and in righteousness he judges and makes war.
δὲ ὀφθαλμοὶ αὐτοῦ [i]ὡς‖ φλὸξ πυρός, καὶ ἐπὶ τὴν κεφαλὴν
And [2]eyes [1]his [were] as a flame of fire, and upon [2]head
αὐτοῦ διαδήματα πολλά, ἔχων [k] ὄνομα γεγραμμένον ὃ οὐδεὶς
[1]his [4]diadems [3]many, having a name written which no one
οἶδεν εἰ.μὴ αὐτός· 13 καὶ περιβεβλημένος ἱμάτιον [l]βεβαμ-
knows but himself, and clothed with a garment dip-

heard in you any more. For your merchants were the great ones of the earth, for by your magic arts all the nations were led astray.

24 And in her the blood of prophets and saints was found, and of all those who were killed on the earth.

CHAPTER 19

1 And after these things I heard a loud voice of a great multitude in Heaven, saying, Hallelujah! Salvation and glory and honor and power to the Lord our God!

2 For His judgments are true and righteous. For He judged the great harlot, who made the earth rotten with her fornication. And He has avenged the blood of His servants at her hand.

3 And a second time they cried, Hallelujah! And her smoke goes up forever and ever.

4 And the twenty-four elders and the four living creatures fell down and worshiped God who sits on the throne, saying, Amen – Hallelujah!

5 And a voice out of the throne came, saying, Praise our God, all His servants, and you who fear Him, both the small and the great.

6 And I heard as it were a voice of a great multitude, and as a sound of many waters, and as a sound of strong thunders, saying, Hallelujah! For the Lord God Almighty has been in control.

7 Let us rejoice and glory. And let us give to Him glory. For the marriage of the Lamb has come, and His wife has made herself ready.

8 And fine linen was given to her for clothing, pure and bright – for the fine linen was the righteousness of the saints.

9 And he says to me, Write: Blessed are they who are called to the supper of the marriage of the Lamb. And he says to me, These are the true words of God.

10 And I fell at his feet to worship him. And he says to me, See that you do not do it. For I am a fellow-servant of you and of your brothers who hold the testimony of Jesus. Worship God. For the testimony of Jesus is the spirit of prophecy.

11 And I saw Heaven opened. And behold, a white horse! And He who was sitting on it is called Faithful and True. And He judges and makes war in righteousness.

12 And His eyes *were* as a flame of fire, and on His head were many crowns. He had a name written which no one knows but Himself.

13 And He was clothed in a robe dipped in

μένον" αἵματι· καὶ ᵐκαλεῖται" τὸ.ὄνομα.αὐτοῦ, Ὁ λόγος τοῦ
ped in blood; and ³is ⁴called ¹his ²name, The Word
θεοῦ. 14 Καὶ τὰ στρατεύματα ⁿ ἐν τῷ οὐρανῷ ἠκολούθει αὐτῷ
of God. And the armies in the heaven were following him
ἐφ' ἵπποις λευκοῖς, ἐνδεδυμένοι βύσσινον λευκὸν ᵒκαὶ' καθαρόν.
upon ²horses ¹white, clothed in fine linen, white and pure.
15 καὶ ἐκ τοῦ.στόματος.αὐτοῦ ἐκπορεύεται ῥομφαία ὀξεῖα,
And out of his mouth goes forth a ²sword ¹sharp,
ἵνα ἐν αὐτῇ ᵖπατάσσῃ' τὰ ἔθνη· καὶ αὐτὸς ποιμανεῖ
that with it he might smite the nations; and he shall shepherd
αὐτοὺς ἐν ῥάβδῳ σιδηρᾷ· καὶ αὐτὸς πατεῖ τὴν ληνὸν τοῦ
them with ²rod ¹an ²iron; and he treads the press of the
οἴνου τοῦ θυμοῦ ᵠκαὶ' τῆς ὀργῆς τοῦ θεοῦ τοῦ παντοκρά-
wine of the fury and of the wrath of God the Almighty.
τορος. 16 καὶ ἔχει ἐπὶ τὸ ἱμάτιον καὶ ἐπὶ τὸν.μηρὸν.αὐτοῦ
And he has upon [his] garment and upon his thigh
ʳτὸ" ὄνομα γεγραμμένον, Βασιλεὺς βασιλέων καὶ κύριος
the name written, King of kings and Lord
κυρίων.
of lords.

17 Καὶ εἶδον ἕνα ἄγγελον ἑστῶτα ἐν τῷ ἡλίῳ· καὶ
And I saw one angel standing in the sun; and
ἔκραξεν ˢ φωνῇ μεγάλῃ λέγων πᾶσιν τοῖς ὀρνέοις τοῖς
he cried with a ²voice ¹loud, saying to all the birds which
ᵗπετωμένοις' ἐν μεσουρανήματι, Δεῦτε ᵛκαὶ συνάγεσθε' εἰς
fly in mid-heaven, Come and gather yourselves to
τὸ δεῖπνον ʷτοῦ μεγάλου" θεοῦ, 18 ἵνα φάγητε σάρκας βα-
the supper of the great God, that ye may eat flesh of
σιλέων, καὶ σάρκας χιλιάρχων, καὶ σάρκας ἰσχυρῶν,
kings, and flesh of chief captains, and flesh of strong [men],
καὶ σάρκας ἵππων καὶ τῶν καθημένων ἐπ' ˣαὐτῶν," καὶ
and flesh of horses and of those who sit on them, and
σάρκας πάντων, ἐλευθέρων ʸ καὶ δούλων, καὶ μικρῶν ᶻ καὶ
flesh of all, free and bond, and small and
μεγάλων.
great.

19 Καὶ ᵃεἶδον" τὸ θηρίον, καὶ τοὺς βασιλεῖς τῆς γῆς,
And I saw the beast, and the kings of the earth,
καὶ τὰ στρατεύματα ᵇαὐτῶν" συνηγμένα ποιῆσαι ᶜ πόλε-
and ²armies ¹their gathered together to make
μον μετὰ τοῦ καθημένου ἐπὶ τοῦ ἵππου, καὶ μετὰ τοῦ
war with him who sits on the horse, and with
στρατεύματος αὐτοῦ. 20 καὶ ἐπιάσθη τὸ θηρίον, καὶ ᵈ ᵉμετὰ
²army ¹his. And was taken the beast, and with
τούτου ὁ" ψευδοπροφήτης ὁ ποιήσας τὰ σημεῖα ἐνώπιον
him the false prophet who wrought the signs before
αὐτοῦ, ἐν οἷς ἐπλάνησεν τοὺς λαβόντας τὸ χάραγμα τοῦ
him, by which he misled those who received the mark of the
θηρίου, καὶ τοὺς προσκυνοῦντας τῇ.εἰκόνι.αὐτοῦ· ζῶντες
beast, and those who do homage to his image. Alive
ἐβλήθησαν οἱ δύο εἰς τὴν λίμνην τοῦ πυρὸς ᶠτὴν καιομένην"
were cast the two into the lake of fire which burns
ἐν ᵍτῷ" θείῳ. 21 καὶ οἱ λοιποὶ ἀπεκτάνθησαν ἐν τῇ
with brimstone; and the rest were killed with the
ῥομφαίᾳ τοῦ καθημένου ἐπὶ τοῦ ἵππου, τῇ ʰἐκπο-
sword of him who sits on the horse, [the sword] which goes
ρευομένῃ' ἐκ τοῦ.στόματος.αὐτοῦ· καὶ πάντα τὰ ὄρνεα ἐχορ-
forth out of his mouth; and all the birds were
τάσθησαν ἐκ τῶν.σαρκῶν.αὐτῶν.
filled with their flesh.

20 Καὶ ⁱεἶδον" ἄγγελον καταβαίνοντα ἐκ τοῦ οὐρανοῦ,
And I saw an angel descending out of the heaven,
ἔχοντα τὴν ʲκλεῖδα' τῆς ἀβύσσου, καὶ ἅλυσιν μεγάλην ἐπὶ
having the key of the abyss, and a ²chain ¹great in
τὴν.χεῖρα.αὐτοῦ. 2 καὶ ἐκράτησεν τὸν δράκοντα, ᵏτὸν ὄφιν
his hand. And he laid hold of the dragon, the ²serpent
τὸν ἀρχαῖον," ˡὅς ἐστιν' διάβολος καὶ ᵐ σατανᾶς, καὶ ἔδησεν
¹ancient, who is [the] devil and Satan, and bound
αὐτὸν χίλια ἔτη, 3 καὶ ἔβαλεν αὐτὸν εἰς τὴν ἄβυσσον, καὶ
him a thousand years, and cast him into the abyss, and
ἔκλεισεν ⁿαὐτόν," καὶ ἐσφράγισεν ἐπάνω αὐτοῦ, ἵνα μὴ
shut him [up], and sealed over him, that ³not
ᵒπλανήσῃ" ᵖτὰ ἔθνη ἔτι," ἄχρι τελεσθῇ τὰ χίλια
¹he ²should mislead the nations longer, until were completed the thousand
ἔτη· ᵠκαὶ" μετὰ ταῦτα δεῖ.ʳαὐτὸν λυθῆναι" μικρὸν
years; and after these things he must be loosed a little
χρόνον.
time.

4 Καὶ ⁱεἶδον" θρόνους, καὶ ἐκάθισαν ἐπ' αὐτούς, καὶ κρίμα
And I saw thrones; and they sat upon them, and judgment
ἐδόθη αὐτοῖς· καὶ τὰς ψυχὰς τῶν πεπελεκισμένων διὰ
was given to them; and the souls of those beheaded on account of

blood. And His name is called, The Word of
God.
14 And the armies in Heaven were following
Him on white horses, clothed with fine
linen, white and pure.
15 And out of His mouth a sharp sword
goes forth, in order that He might strike the
nations with it. And He shall shepherd them
with a rod of iron. And He treads the press
of the wine of the fury and wrath of God
Almighty.
16 And He has on His robe and on His thigh
the name written, KING OF KINGS AND
LORD OF LORDS.
17 And I saw one angel standing in the sun.
And he cried with a loud voice, saying to all
the birds which fly in the sky, Come and
gather yourselves to the supper of the great
God,
18 so that you may eat the flesh of kings,
and the flesh of chief captains, and the flesh
of strong men, and the flesh of horses, and
those who sit on them, and the flesh of all –
free and slaves, small and great.
19 And I saw a beast, and the kings of the
earth, and their armies gathered together to
make war with Him who sits on the horse
and with His army.
20 And the beast was taken, and the false
prophet with him (who worked the miracles
before him, by which he led astray those
who received the mark of the beast, and
those who worshiped the image). These two
were thrown alive into the Lake of Fire,
which burns with brimstone.
21 And the rest were killed with the sword
of Him who sits on the horse, which goes
forth out of His mouth. And all the birds
were filled with their flesh.

CHAPTER 20

1 And I saw an angel coming down out of
Heaven. And he had the key of the bottomless pit and a great chain in his hand.
2 And he laid hold of the dragon, the old
serpent, who is the devil and Satan, and
bound him for a thousand years.
3 And he threw him into the bottomless pit
and shut him up and set a seal over him so
that he should not lead the nations astray
any longer – until the thousand years were
fulfilled. And after these things he must be
set free a little time.
4 And I saw thrones. And they sat on them.
And judgment was given to them. And *I saw*
the souls of those who were beheaded because of their testimony to Jesus and

τὴν μαρτυρίαν Ἰησοῦ, καὶ διὰ τὸν λόγον τοῦ θεοῦ, καὶ
the testimony of Jesus, and on account of the word of God, and
οἵτινες οὐ.προσεκύνησαν [s]τῷ θηρίῳ,[ll] [t]οὔτε[ll] [v]τὴν.εἰκόνα[ll].αὐτοῦ,
those who did not do homage to the beast, nor his image,
καὶ οὐκ.ἔλαβον τὸ χάραγμα ἐπὶ τὸ.μέτωπον.[w]αὐτῶν,[ll] καὶ ἐπὶ
and did not receive the mark upon their forehead, and upon
τὴν.χεῖρα.αὐτῶν· καὶ ἔζησαν, καὶ ἐβασίλευσαν μετὰ [x] χριστοῦ
their hand; and they lived and reigned with Christ
[y]τὰ[ll] χίλια ἔτη· 5 [z] οἱ.[a]δὲ[ll] λοιποὶ τῶν νεκρῶν οὐκ [b]ἀνέζησαν
the thousand years: but the rest of the dead [2]not [1]lived again
ἕως[ll] τελεσθῇ τὰ χίλια ἔτη. αὕτη ἡ ἀνάστασις
till may have been completed the thousand years. This [is] the [2]resurrection
ἡ πρώτη. 6 μακάριος καὶ ἅγιος ὁ ἔχων μέρος ἐν τῇ ἀνα-
[1]first. Blessed and holy he who has part in the [2]resur-
στάσει τῇ πρώτῃ· ἐπὶ τούτων ὁ [c]θάνατος ὁ δεύτερος[ll] οὐκ.ἔχει
rection [1]first: over these the [2]death [1]second has no
ἐξουσίαν, [d]ἀλλ'[ll] ἔσονται ἱερεῖς τοῦ θεοῦ καὶ τοῦ χριστοῦ,
authority; but they shall be priests of God and of the Christ,
καὶ [e]βασιλεύσουσιν[ll] μετ' αὐτοῦ [f] χίλια ἔτη. 7 Καὶ ὅταν τε-
and shall reign with him a thousand years. And when may
λεσθῇ τὰ χίλια ἔτη, λυθήσεται ὁ σατανᾶς ἐκ τῆς
have been completed the thousand years, will be loosed Satan out of
φυλακῆς αὐτοῦ, 8 καὶ ἐξελεύσεται πλανῆσαι τὰ ἔθνη τὰ
[2]prison [1]his, and will go out to mislead the nations which [are]
ἐν ταῖς τέσσαρσιν γωνίαις τῆς γῆς, τὸν Γὼγ καὶ [g]τὸν[ll] Μαγώγ,
in the four corners of the earth, Gog and Magog,
συναγαγεῖν αὐτοὺς εἰς [h] πόλεμον, ὧν ὁ ἀριθμὸς [i] ὡς
to gather together them unto war, of whom the number [is] as
ἡ ἄμμος τῆς θαλάσσης. 9 καὶ ἀνέβησαν ἐπὶ τὸ πλάτος τῆς
the sand of the sea. And they went up upon the breadth of the
γῆς, καὶ [k]ἐκύκλωσαν[ll] τὴν παρεμβολὴν τῶν ἁγίων, καὶ τὴν
earth, and encircled the camp of the saints, and the
πόλιν τὴν ἠγαπημένην· καὶ κατέβη πῦρ [l]ἀπὸ τοῦ θεοῦ ἐκ
[2]city [1]beloved: and [2]came [3]down [1]fire from God out of
τοῦ οὐρανοῦ,[ll] καὶ κατέφαγεν αὐτούς· 10 καὶ ὁ διάβολος ὁ
the heaven and devoured them: and the devil who
πλανῶν αὐτοὺς ἐβλήθη εἰς τὴν λίμνην τοῦ πυρὸς καὶ [m]
misleads them was cast into the lake of fire and
θείου, ὅπου [n] τὸ θηρίον καὶ ὁ ψευδοπροφήτης· καὶ
of brimstone, where [are] the beast and the false prophet; and
βασανισθήσονται ἡμέρας καὶ νυκτὸς εἰς τοὺς αἰῶνας τῶν
they shall be tormented day and night for the ages of the
αἰώνων.
ages.

11 Καὶ εἶδον θρόνον [o]λευκὸν μέγαν,[ll] καὶ τὸν καθήμενον
And I saw a [3]throne [2]white [1]great and him who sits
[p]ἐπ'[ll] [q]αὐτοῦ,[ll] οὗ ἀπὸ [r] προσώπου ἔφυγεν ἡ γῆ καὶ ὁ οὐ-
on it, [2]whose [1]from face fled the earth and the hea-
ρανός, καὶ τόπος οὐχ.εὑρέθη αὐτοῖς. 12 καὶ εἶδον τοὺς
ven, and place was not found for them. And I saw the
νεκρούς, [s]μικροὺς καὶ μεγάλους.[ll] ἑστῶτας ἐνώπιον [t]τοῦ θεοῦ,[ll]
dead, small and great, standing before God,
καὶ βιβλία [v]ἠνεῴχθησαν·[ll] καὶ [w]βιβλίον ἄλλο[ll] [x]ἠνεῴχθη,[ll]
and books were opened; and [2]book [1]another was opened,
ὅ ἐστιν τῆς ζωῆς· καὶ ἐκρίθησαν οἱ νεκροὶ ἐκ τῶν
which is [that] of life. And were judged the dead out of the things
γεγραμμένων ἐν τοῖς βιβλίοις, κατὰ τὰ.ἔργα.αὐτῶν.
written in the books according to their works.
13 καὶ ἔδωκεν ἡ θάλασσα τοὺς [y]ἐν αὐτῇ νεκρούς,[ll] καὶ ὁ
And [5]gave [6]up [1]the [2]sea the [3]in [4]it [1]dead, and
θάνατος καὶ ὁ ᾅδης [z]ἔδωκαν[ll] τοὺς [a]ἐν αὐτοῖς νεκρούς·[ll] καὶ ἐ-
death and hades gave up the [2]in [3]them [1]dead; and they
κρίθησαν ἕκαστος κατὰ τὰ.ἔργα.αὐτῶν. 14 καὶ ὁ θάνατος
were judged each according to their works: and death
καὶ ὁ ᾅδης ἐβλήθησαν εἰς τὴν λίμνην τοῦ πυρός· οὗτός [b]ἐστιν
and hades were cast into the lake of fire. This is
ὁ δεύτερος θάνατος.[ll] [c] 15 καὶ εἴ τις οὐχ.εὑρέθη ἐν τῇ
the second death. And if anyone was not found in the
βίβλῳ τῆς ζωῆς γεγραμμένος, ἐβλήθη εἰς τὴν λίμνην τοῦ
book of life written, he was cast into the lake
πυρός.
of fire.

21 Καὶ εἶδον οὐρανὸν καινὸν καὶ γῆν καινήν· ὁ.γὰρ
And I saw a [2]heaven [1]new and [3]earth [1]a [2]new; for the
πρῶτος οὐρανὸς καὶ ἡ πρώτη γῆ [d]παρῆλθεν,[ll] καὶ ἡ θά-
first heaven and the first earth were passed away, and the
λασσα οὐκ ἔστιν ἔτι.
sea [2]no [1]is longer.
2 Καὶ [e]ἐγὼ Ἰωάννης[ll] [f]εἶδον[ll] τὴν πόλιν τὴν ἁγίαν[f], [4]Ἰερ-
And I John saw the [2]city [1]holy, [4]Jer-
ουσαλὴμ καινήν[f], καταβαίνουσαν [g]ἀπὸ τοῦ θεοῦ ἐκ τοῦ οὐ-
usalem [3]new, coming down from God out of hea-

because of the word of God, and those who did not receive the mark on their forehead and on their hand. And they lived and ruled with Christ the thousand years.

5 But the rest of the dead did not live again until the thousand years had been fulfilled. This is the first resurrection.

6 Blessed and holy is he who has part in the first resurrection – over these the second death has no power, but they shall be priests of God and of Christ and shall rule with Him a thousand years.

7 And when the thousand years have been fulfilled, Satan will be set free from his prison.

8 And he will go out to lead the nations astray which are in the four corners of the earth – Gog and Magog – and to gather them together to war, whose number is as the sand of the sea.

9 And they went the breadth of the earth and circled around the camp of the saints and the beloved city. And fire came down from God out of Heaven and consumed them.

10 And the devil who led them astray was thrown into the Lake of Fire and of Brimstone, where the beast and the false prophet were. And they shall be tormented day and night forever and ever.

11 And I saw a great white throne, and Him who sits on it – from whose face the earth and the sky fled away, and no place was found for them.

12 And I saw the dead, small and great, standing before God. And the books were opened. And another book was opened, which is the Book of Life. And the dead were judged out of the things written in the books, according to their works.

13 And the sea gave up its dead. And death and hell gave up the dead in them. And they were judged each according to their works.

14 And death and hell were cast into the Lake of Fire. This is the second death.

15 And if anyone was not found written in the Book of Life, he was thrown into the Lake of Fire.

CHAPTER 21

1 And I saw a new heaven and a new earth – for the first heaven and the first earth were gone, and the sea no longer existed.

2 And I, John, saw the holy city, New Jerusalem, coming down from God out of Heaven, prepared as a bride made ready for

ρανοῦ," ἡτοιμασμένην ὡς νύμφην κεκοσμημένην τῷ ἀνδρὶ
ven, prepared as a bride adorned for [2]husband
αὐτῆς. 3 καὶ ἤκουσα φωνῆς μεγάλης ἐκ τοῦ [h]οὐρανοῦ,"
[1]her. And I heard a [2]voice [1]great out of the heaven,
λεγούσης, Ἰδού, ἡ σκηνὴ τοῦ θεοῦ μετὰ τῶν ἀνθρώπων,
saying, Behold, the tabernacle of God [is] with men,
καὶ σκηνώσει μετ' αὐτῶν· καὶ αὐτοὶ [i]λαοὶ" αὐτοῦ ἔσονται,
and he shall tabernacle with them, and they [4]peoples [3]his [1]shall [2]be,
καὶ αὐτὸς ὁ θεὸς [k]ἔσται μετ' αὐτῶν" [l]θεὸς.αὐτῶν." 4 καὶ ἐξα-
and [2]himself [1]God shall be with them their God. And [2]shall
λείψει [m]ὁ θεὸς" πᾶν δάκρυον [n]ἀπὸ" τῶν.ὀφθαλμῶν.αὐτῶν,
[3]wipe [4]away [1]God every tear from their eyes;
καὶ [o]ὁ" θάνατος οὐκ.ἔσται ἔτι· οὔτε πένθος, οὔτε κραυγή,
and death shall be no longer, nor mourning, nor crying,
οὔτε πόνος οὐκ ἔσται ἔτι· [p]ὅτι" τὰ πρῶτα [q]ἀπῆλθον."
nor distress [3]any [1]shall [2]be longer, because the former things are passed away.
5 Καὶ εἶπεν ὁ καθήμενος ἐπὶ [r]τοῦ θρόνου," Ἰδού, καινὰ
And said he who sits on the throne, Lo, new
[s]πάντα ποιῶ." Καὶ λέγει [t]μοι," Γράψον· ὅτι οὗτοι οἱ λόγοι
all things I make. And he says to me, Write, because these words
[v]ἀληθινοὶ καὶ πιστοί" εἰσιν. 6 Καὶ εἶπέν μοι, [w]Γέγονεν." ἐγώ
true and faithful are. And he said to me, It is done. I
[x]εἰμι" τὸ [y]Α" καὶ τὸ [z]Ω," ἡ ἀρχὴ καὶ τὸ τέλος. ἐγὼ τῷ
am the A and the Ω, the beginning and the end. I to him that
διψῶντι δώσω [a] ἐκ τῆς πηγῆς τοῦ ὕδατος τῆς ζωῆς δωρεάν.
thirsts will give of the fountain of the water of life gratuitously.
7 ὁ νικῶν κληρονομήσει [b]πάντα," καὶ ἔσομαι αὐτῷ θεός,
He that overcomes shall inherit all things, and I will be to him God,
καὶ αὐτὸς ἔσται μοι [c]ὁ" υἱός. 8 [da]δειλοῖς.δὲ" καὶ ἀπίστοις [ea]
and he shall be to me son: but to [the] fearful, and unbelieving,
καὶ ἐβδελυγμένοις καὶ φονεῦσιν καὶ πόρνοις καὶ [fa]φαρμακεῦσιν"
and abominable, and murderers, and fornicators, and sorcerers,
καὶ εἰδωλολάτραις, καὶ πᾶσιν τοῖς [ga]ψευδέσιν," τὸ.μέρος.αὐτῶν
and idolaters, and all liars, their part
ἐν τῇ λίμνῃ τῇ καιομένῃ πυρὶ καὶ θείῳ, ὅ ἐστιν
[is] in the lake which burns with fire and brimstone; which is [the]
[ha]δεύτερος θάνατος."
second death.

9 Καὶ ἦλθεν [i]πρός με" εἷς [k] τῶν ἑπτὰ ἀγγέλων τῶν ἐχόν-
And came to me one of the seven angels which had
των τὰς ἑπτὰ φιάλας [l]τὰς γεμούσας" τῶν ἑπτὰ πληγῶν τῶν
the seven bowls full of the seven [2]plagues
ἐσχάτων, καὶ ἐλάλησεν μετ' ἐμοῦ, λέγων, Δεῦρο, δείξω
[1]last, and spoke with me, saying, Come hither, I will shew
σοι τὴν νύμφην [m]τοῦ ἀρνίου τὴν γυναῖκα." 10 Καὶ ἀπήνεγκέν
thee the bride [2]Lamb's [1]the wife. And he carried away
με ἐν πνεύματι [n]ἐπ'" ὄρος μέγα καὶ ὑψηλόν, καὶ ἔδειξέν
me in [the] Spirit to a mountain great and high, and shewed
μοι τὴν πόλιν [o]τὴν μεγάλην," τὴν ἁγίαν Ἱερουσαλήμ, κατα-
me the [2]city [1]great, the holy Jerusalem, de-
βαίνουσαν ἐκ τοῦ οὐρανοῦ ἀπὸ τοῦ θεοῦ, 11 ἔχουσαν τὴν
scending out of the heaven from God, having the
δόξαν τοῦ θεοῦ· [p]καὶ" ὁ.φωστὴρ.αὐτῆς ὅμοιος λίθῳ τιμιω-
glory of God, and her radiance [was] like a stone most pre-
(lit. her luminary)
τάτῳ, ὡς λίθῳ ἰάσπιδι κρυσταλλίζοντι· 12 [q]ἔχουσάν τε"
cious, as a [3]stone [2]jasper [1]crystal-like; having also
τεῖχος μέγα καὶ ὑψηλόν, [r]ἔχουσαν" πυλῶνας δώδεκα, [s]καὶ ἐπὶ
a wall great and high; having [2]gates [1]twelve, and at
[t]τοῖς πυλῶσιν" ἀγγέλους δώδεκα," καὶ ὀνόματα ἐπιγεγραμ-
the gates [2]angels [1]twelve, and names inscrib-
μένα, ἅ ἐστιν [v] τῶν δώδεκα φυλῶν [w]τῶν" υἱῶν Ἰσραήλ·
ed, which are [those] of the twelve tribes of the sons of Israel.
13 [x]ἀπ'" [y]ἀνατολῆς" πυλῶνες τρεῖς· [z] ἀπὸ βοῤῥᾶ
On [the] east [2]gates [1]three; on [the] north
πυλῶνες τρεῖς· [z] ἀπὸ νότου πυλῶνες τρεῖς· [z] ἀπὸ
[2]gates [1]three; on [the] south [2]gates [1]three, on [the]
δυσμῶν πυλῶνες τρεῖς. 14 καὶ τὸ τεῖχος τῆς πόλεως [a]ἔχον"
west [2]gates [1]three. And the wall of the city having
θεμελίους δώδεκα, καὶ [b]ἐν αὐτοῖς" ὀνόματα τῶν δώδεκα
[2]foundations [1]twelve, and in them names of the twelve
ἀποστόλων τοῦ ἀρνίου. 15 καὶ ὁ λαλῶν μετ' ἐμοῦ εἶχεν [c]
apostles of the Lamb. And he speaking with me had
κάλαμον χρυσοῦν, ἵνα μετρήσῃ τὴν πόλιν, καὶ τοὺς πυ-
a [2]reed [1]golden, that he might measure the city, and
λῶνας αὐτῆς, καὶ τὸ.τεῖχος.αὐτῆς. 16 καὶ ἡ πόλις τετράγωνος
[2]gates [1]its, and its wall. And the city [2]four-square
κεῖται, καὶ τὸ.μῆκος.αὐτῆς [d]τοσοῦτόν ἐστιν" ὅσον [e]καὶ" τὸ
[1]lies, and its length so much is as also the
πλάτος. καὶ ἐμέτρησεν τὴν πόλιν τῷ καλάμῳ ἐπὶ [f]σταδίων"
breadth. And he measured the city with the reed— [3]furlongs
δώδεκα χιλιάδων· τὸ μῆκος καὶ τὸ πλάτος καὶ τὸ ὕψος αὐτῆς
[1]twelve [2]thousand; the length and the breadth and the height of it

her Husband.
3 And I heard a great voice out of Heaven,
saying, Behold! The tabernacle of God is
with men. And He shall dwell with them,
and they shall be His people, and God Himself shall be with them as their God.
4 And God shall wipe away every tear from
their eyes. And there shall be no more death
or sorrow or crying, nor shall there any
longer be pain – for the former things are
gone.
5 And He who sits on the throne said, See! I
make all things new. And He says to me,
Write – because these words are true and
faithful.
6 And He said to me, It is done. I am the A
and the Z, the Beginning and the End. To
him that thirsts I will give of the fountain of
the water of life freely.
7 He that overcomes shall inherit all things,
and I will be God to him, and he shall be a
son to Me.
8 But to fearful and unbelieving and hateful
ones and murderers and fornicators and
users of magic arts and worshipers of idols
and all liars, their part is in the Lake which
burns with fire and brimstone – which is the
second death.

9 And one of the seven angels which had
the seven bowls full of the seven last plagues
came to me and spoke with me, saying,
Come here, I will show you the bride, the
Lamb's wife.
10 And he carried me away in the Spirit to
a great and high mountain. And he showed
me the great city, the holy Jerusalem,
coming down out of Heaven from God.
11 And it has the glory of God, and her
shining was like a most precious stone, even
as a crystal-like jasper stone –
12 it also has a great and high wall, having
twelve gates. And at the gates were twelve
angels. And the names were written on
them, which are of the twelve tribes of the
sons of Israel.
13 On the east were three gates, on the
north three gates, on the south three gates
and on the west three gates.
14 And the wall of the city was twelve
foundations. And on them the names of the
twelve apostles of the Lamb *were written.*
15 And he that was speaking with me had a
golden reed, in order that he might measure
the city and its gates and its wall.
16 And the city is laid out as a square. And
its length is as much as the width also. And
he measured the city with the reed – twelve
thousand furlongs – the length and the
width and the height of it are equal.

ἴσα ἐστίν. 17 καὶ ἐμέτρησεν τὸ.τεῖχος.αὐτῆς ἑκατὸν
[a]equal [1]are. And he measured its wall, a hundred [and]

[g]τεσσαράκοντα τεσσάρων‖ πηχῶν μέτρον ἀνθρώπου, ὅ ἐστιν
forty four cubits, [3]measure [1]a [2]man's, which is,

ἀγγέλου. 18 καὶ [i]ἦν‖ ἡ [k]ἐνδόμησις‖ τοῦ.τείχους.αὐτῆς
[the] angel's. And [6]was [1]the [2]structure [3]of [4]its [5]wall

ἴασπις· καὶ ἡ πόλις χρυσίον καθαρόν, [l]ὁμοία‖ ὑάλῳ καθαρῷ.
jasper; and the city [2]gold [1]pure, like [2]glass [1]pure:

19 [m]καὶ‖ οἱ θεμέλιοι τοῦ τείχους τῆς πόλεως παντὶ λίθῳ
and the foundations of the wall of the city with every [2]stone

τιμίῳ κεκοσμημένοι. ὁ θεμέλιος ὁ πρῶτος ἴασπις· ὁ
[1]precious [were] adorned: the [2]foundation [1]first, jasper; the

δεύτερος σάπφειρος· ὁ τρίτος [n]χαλκηδών·‖ ὁ τέταρτος σμά-
second, sapphire; the third, chalcedony; the fourth, eme-

ραγδος· 20 ὁ πέμπτος [o]σαρδόνυξ·‖ ὁ ἕκτος [p]σάρδιος·‖ ὁ
rald; the fifth, sardonyx; the sixth, sardius; the

ἕβδομος χρυσόλιθος· ὁ ὄγδοος βήρυλλος· ὁ [q]ἔνατος‖ τοπά-
seventh, chrysolite; the eighth, beryl; the ninth, to-

ζιον· ὁ δέκατος [r]χρυσόπρασος·‖ ὁ ἑνδέκατος ὑάκινθος· ὁ
paz; the tenth, chrysoprasus; the eleventh, jacinth; the

δωδέκατος ἀμέθυστος. 21 καὶ οἱ δώδεκα πυλῶνες, δώδεκα
twelfth, amethyst. And the twelve gates, twelve

μαργαρῖται· ἀνὰ εἷς ἕκαστος τῶν πυλώνων ἦν ἐξ ἑνὸς
pearls; [3]respectively [2]one [1]each of the gates was of one

μαργαρίτου· καὶ ἡ πλατεῖα τῆς πόλεως, χρυσίον καθαρόν, ὡς
pearl; and the street of the city [2]gold [1]pure, as

ὕαλος [s]διαφανής.‖ 22 Καὶ ναὸν οὐκ εἶδον ἐν αὐτῇ· ὁ.γὰρ
[2]glass [1]transparent. And [4]temple [3]no [1]I [2]saw in it; for the

κύριος ὁ θεὸς ὁ παντοκράτωρ [t] ναὸς.αὐτῆς ἐστιν, καὶ τὸ
Lord God Almighty its temple is, and the

ἀρνίον. 23 καὶ ἡ πόλις οὐ χρείαν ἔχει τοῦ ἡλίου, οὐδὲ τῆς
Lamb. And the city [2]no [3]need [1]has of the sun, nor of the

σελήνης, ἵνα φαίνωσιν [v]ἐν‖ αὐτῇ· ἡ.γὰρ δόξα τοῦ θεοῦ ἐφώ-
moon, that they should shine in it; for the glory of God en-

τισεν αὐτήν, καὶ ὁ λύχνος αὐτῆς τὸ ἀρνίον. 24 καὶ [w]τὰ
lightened it, and the lamp of it [is] the Lamb. And the

ἔθνη τῶν σωζομένων ἐν τῷ.φωτὶ.αὐτῆς περιπατήσουσιν·‖ καὶ
nations of the saved in its light shall walk; and

οἱ βασιλεῖς τῆς γῆς φέρουσιν τὴν δόξαν [x]καὶ τὴν τιμὴν‖ αὐτῶν
the kings of the earth bring [2]glory [3]and [4]honour [1]their

εἰς αὐτήν. 25 καὶ οἱ.πυλῶνες.αὐτῆς οὐ.μὴ κλεισθῶσιν ἡμέρας·
unto it. And its gates not at all shall be shut by day;

νὺξ γὰρ οὐκ ἔσται ἐκεῖ. 26 καὶ οἴσουσιν τὴν δόξαν καὶ
[3]night [1]for [2]no shall be there. And they shall bring the glory and

τὴν τιμὴν τῶν ἐθνῶν εἰς αὐτήν. 27 καὶ οὐ.μὴ εἰσέλθῃ εἰς
the honour of the nations unto it. And in no wise may enter into

αὐτὴν πᾶν [y]κοινοῦν,‖ καὶ [z]ποιοῦν‖ βδέλυγμα καὶ ψεῦ-
it anything defiling, and practising abomination and a
(*lit.* everything)

δος· εἰ.μὴ οἱ γεγραμμένοι ἐν τῷ βιβλίῳ τῆς ζωῆς τοῦ
lie; but those who are written in the book of life of the

ἀρνίου.
Lamb.

22 Καὶ ἔδειξέν μοι [a]καθαρὸν‖ ποταμὸν ὕδατος ζωῆς,
And he shewed me [2]pure [1]a river of water of life,

λαμπρὸν ὡς κρύσταλλον, ἐκπορευόμενον ἐκ τοῦ θρόνου τοῦ
bright as crystal, going forth out of the throne

θεοῦ καὶ τοῦ ἀρνίου. 2 ἐν μέσῳ τῆς.πλατείας.αὐτῆς, καὶ τοῦ
of God and of the Lamb. In the midst of its street, and of the

ποταμοῦ, ἐντεῦθεν καὶ [b]ἐντεῦθεν,‖ ξύλον ζωῆς, [c]ποιοῦν‖
river, on this side and on that side, [the] tree of life, producing

καρποὺς δώδεκα, κατὰ [d]μῆνα‖ [e]ἕνα‖ ἕκαστον [f]ἀποδιδοῦν‖ τὸν
[2]fruits [1]twelve, [4]month [3]each yielding

καρπὸν αὐτοῦ· καὶ τὰ φύλλα τοῦ ξύλου εἰς θεραπείαν τῶν
[2]fruit [1]its; and the leaves of the tree for healing of the

ἐθνῶν. 3 Καὶ πᾶν [g]κατανάθεμα‖ οὐκ ἔσται ἔτι· καὶ ὁ θρόνος
nations. And [2]any [3]curse [1]not shall be longer; and the throne
(*lit.* every)

τοῦ θεοῦ καὶ τοῦ ἀρνίου ἐν αὐτῇ ἔσται· καὶ οἱ.δοῦλοι.αὐτοῦ
of God and of the Lamb in it shall be; and his bondmen

λατρεύσουσιν αὐτῷ· 4 καὶ ὄψονται τὸ.πρόσωπον.αὐτοῦ, καὶ
shall serve him, and they shall see his face; and

τὸ.ὄνομα.αὐτοῦ ἐπὶ τῶν.μετώπων.αὐτῶν. 5 καὶ νὺξ οὐκ ἔσται
his name on their foreheads [is]. And [2]night [1]no shall be

[h]ἐκεῖ‖ καὶ [i]χρείαν οὐκ ἔχουσιν‖ [k]λύχνου καὶ φωτὸς [l]ἡλίου,‖
there, and [4]need [3]no [1]they [2]have of a lamp and of light of [the] sun,

ὅτι κύριος ὁ θεὸς [m]φωτίζει‖ αὐτούς· καὶ βασιλεύσουσιν
because [the] Lord God enlightens them, and they shall reign

εἰς τοὺς αἰῶνας τῶν αἰώνων.
to the ages of the ages.

6 Καὶ εἶπέν μοι, Οὗτοι οἱ λόγοι πιστοὶ καὶ ἀληθινοί·
And he said to me, These words [are] faithful and true;

17 And he measured its wall, a hundred and forty-four cubits, a measure of a man, that is, the angel's.

18 And the wall was made of jasper. And the city was pure gold, like pure glass.

19 And the foundations of the wall of the city were decorated with every precious stone. The first foundation was jasper. The second was sapphire – the third, chalcedony – the fourth, emerald.

20 The fifth was sardonyx – the sixth, sardius – the seventh, chrysolite – the eighth, beryl – the ninth, topaz – the tenth, chrysoprasus – the eleventh, hyacinth – the twelfth, amethyst.

21 And the twelve gates were twelve pearls, each one of the gates in turn was one pearl. And the street of the city was pure gold, like glass one can see through.

22 And I saw no temple in it – for the Lord God Almighty is its Temple, and the Lamb.

23 And the city has no need of the sun or of the moon, that they should shine in it – for the glory of God gave it light, and its lamp is the Lamb.

24 And the nations of the ones who are saved shall walk in its light. And the kings of the earth bring their glory and honor into it.

25 And its gates shall never be shut by day, for no night shall be there.

26 And they shall bring the glory and the honor of the nations into it.

27 And in no way may anything that is unclean and which practices abomination and a lie enter into it, only those who are written in the Book of Life of the Lamb!

CHAPTER 22

1 And he showed me a pure river of water of life, clear as crystal, going forth out of the throne of God and the Lamb.

2 In the middle of its street, and of the river, on this side and on that side, a tree of life was producing twelve fruits – yielding its fruit each month. And the leaves of the tree were for the healing of the nations.

3 And there shall be no curse any more. And the throne of God and of the Lamb shall be in it. And His servants shall serve Him.

4 And they shall see His face. And His name is on their foreheads.

5 And no night shall be there. And they have no need of a lamp and of sunlight, because the Lord God gives them light! And they shall rule forever and ever.

6 And he said to me, These words are faithful and true. And the Lord God of the

καὶ [n] κύριος ὁ θεὸς τῶν [o]ἁγίων‖ προφητῶν ἀπέστειλεν τὸν
and [the] Lord God of the holy prophets sent
ἄγγελον αὐτοῦ δεῖξαι τοῖς.δούλοις.αὐτοῦ ἃ δεῖ γε-
[2]angel [1]his to shew his bondmen the things which must come
νέσθαι ἐν.τάχει. 7 [p]Ἰδού, ἔρχομαι ταχύ. μακάριος ὁ
to pass soon. Behold, I am coming quickly. Blessed [is] he who
τηρῶν τοὺς λόγους τῆς προφητείας τοῦ.βιβλίου.τούτου. 8 [q]Καὶ
keeps the words of the prophecy of this book. And
ἐγὼ‖ Ἰωάννης ὁ [r]βλέπων ταῦτα καὶ ἀκούων·‖
I John [was] he who [was] seeing [3]these [4]things [1]and [2]hearing.
καὶ ὅτε ἤκουσα καὶ [s]ἔβλεψα‖ [t]ἔπεσα‖ προσκυνῆσαι ἔμπροσθεν
And when I heard and saw I fell down to do homage before
τῶν ποδῶν τοῦ ἀγγέλου τοῦ [u]δεικνύοντός‖ μοι ταῦτα. 9 καὶ
the feet of the angel who [was] shewing me these things. And
λέγει μοι, Ὅρα μή· σύνδουλός σου [v]γάρ‖ εἰμι, καὶ
he says to me, See [thou do it] not: [4]fellowbondman [5]of [6]thee [1]for [2]I [3]am, and
τῶν.ἀδελφῶν.σου τῶν προφητῶν, καὶ τῶν τηρούντων τοὺς
of thy brethren the prophets, and of those who keep the
λόγους τοῦ.βιβλίου.τούτου· τῷ θεῷ προσκύνησον. 10 Καὶ
words of this book: to God do homage. And
λέγει μοι, Μὴ.σφραγίσῃς τοὺς λόγους τῆς προφητείας τοῦ
he says to me, Seal not the words of the prophecy
βιβλίου τούτου· [w]ὅτι‖ ὁ καιρὸς [x]ἐγγύς ἐστιν. 11 ὁ ἀδι-
[3]book [1]of [2]this; because the time [2]near [1]is. He that is un-
κῶν ἀδικησάτω ἔτι· καὶ [y]ὁ ῥυπῶν‖ [z]ῥυπωσάτω‖
righteous let him be unrighteous still; and he that is filthy let him be filthy
ἔτι· καὶ ὁ δίκαιος [a]δικαιωθήτω‖ ἔτι· καὶ ὁ ἅγιος
still; and he that [is] righteous let him be righteous still; and he that [is] holy
ἁγιασθήτω ἔτι. 12 [b]Καὶ‖ ἰδού, ἔρχομαι ταχύ, καὶ ὁ
let him be sanctified still. And, behold, I am coming quickly, and
μισθός μου μετ' ἐμοῦ, ἀποδοῦναι ἑκάστῳ ὡς τὸ ἔργον [c]αὐτοῦ
[2]reward [1]my with me, to render to each as [2]work [1]his
ἔσται.‖ 13 ἐγώ [d]εἰμι‖ τὸ [e]Α‖ καὶ τὸ [f]Ω,‖ [g]ἀρχὴ καὶ τέλος,
shall be. I am the A and the Ω, [the] beginning and end,
ὁ πρῶτος καὶ ὁ ἔσχατος.‖ 14 Μακάριοι οἱ [h]ποιοῦν-
the first and the last. Blessed [are] they that do
τες τὰς.ἐντολὰς.αὐτοῦ,‖ ἵνα ἔσται ἡ.ἐξουσία.αὐτῶν ἐπὶ τὸ
his commandments, that [3]shall [4]be [1]their [2]authority to the
ξύλον τῆς ζωῆς, καὶ τοῖς πυλῶσιν εἰσέλθωσιν εἰς τὴν πόλιν.
tree of life, and by the gates they should go in to the city.
15 ἔξω.[i]δὲ‖ οἱ κύνες καὶ οἱ φαρμακοὶ καὶ οἱ πόρνοι καὶ
But without [are] the dogs, and the sorcerers, and the fornicators, and
οἱ φονεῖς καὶ οἱ εἰδωλολάτραι, καὶ πᾶς [k]ὁ‖ [l]φιλῶν καὶ
the murderers, and the idolaters, and everyone that loves and
ποιῶν‖ ψεῦδος.
practises a lie.
16 Ἐγὼ Ἰησοῦς ἔπεμψα τὸν.ἄγγελόν.μου μαρτυρῆσαι
I Jesus sent mine angel to testify
ὑμῖν ταῦτα [m]ἐπὶ‖ ταῖς ἐκκλησίαις· ἐγώ εἰμι ἡ ῥίζα καὶ
to you these things in the assemblies. I am the root and
τὸ γένος [n]τοῦ‖ [o]Δαβίδ,‖ ὁ ἀστὴρ ὁ λαμπρὸς [p]καὶ‖ [q]ὀρθρι-
the offspring of David, the [4]star [1]bright [2]and [3]morn-
νός.‖ 17 Καὶ τὸ πνεῦμα καὶ ἡ νύμφη λέγουσιν, [r]Ἐλθέ.‖
ing. And the Spirit and the bride say, Come.
καὶ ὁ ἀκούων εἰπάτω, [r]Ἐλθέ.‖ καὶ ὁ διψῶν [s]ἐλθέτω,‖
And he that hears let him say, Come. And he that thirsts let him come;
[t]καὶ‖ ὁ θέλων [v]λαμβανέτω τὸ‖ ὕδωρ ζωῆς δωρεάν.
and he that wills, let him take the water of life gratuitously.
18 [w]Συμμαρτυροῦμαι.γὰρ‖ παντὶ [x] ἀκούοντι τοὺς λόγους
For I jointly testify to everyone hearing the words
τῆς προφητείας τοῦ.βιβλίου.τούτου· ἐάν τις [ya]ἐπιτιθῇ πρὸς
of the prophecy of this book, If anyone should add to
ταῦτα,‖ ἐπιθήσει [za]ὁ θεὸς ἐπ' αὐτὸν‖ τὰς πληγὰς τὰς γε-
these things, [2]shall [3]add [1]God unto him the plagues which are
γραμμένας ἐν [aa] βιβλίῳ.τούτῳ· 19 καὶ ἐάν τις [ba]ἀφαιρῇ‖
written in this book. And if anyone should take
ἀπὸ τῶν λόγων [ca]βίβλου‖ τῆς.προφητείας.ταύτης, [da]ἀφαιρή-
from the words of [the] book of this prophecy, [2]shall [3]take
σει‖ ὁ θεὸς τὸ.μέρος.αὐτοῦ ἀπὸ [ea]βίβλου‖ τῆς ζωῆς, καὶ
[4]away [1]God his part from [the] book of life, and
[f]ἐκ‖ τῆς πόλεως τῆς ἁγίας, [g]καὶ‖ τῶν γεγραμμένων
out of the [2]city [1]holy, and of those who are written
ἐν [h] βιβλίῳ τούτῳ.
in [2]book [1]this.
20 Λέγει ὁ μαρτυρῶν ταῦτα, Ναί ἔρχομαι ταχύ.
[4]Says [1]he [2]who [3]testifies [4]these [5]things, Yea, I am coming quickly.
Ἀμήν. [i]Ναί,‖ ἔρχου, κύριε Ἰησοῦ.
Amen; yea, come, Lord Jesus.
21 Ἡ χάρις τοῦ.κυρίου.[k]ἡμῶν‖ Ἰησοῦ [l]χριστοῦ‖ μετὰ
The grace of our Lord Jesus Christ [be] with
[m]πάντων‖ [n]ὑμῶν.‖ [o] [p]Ἀμήν.‖ [q]
[2]all [1]you. Amen.

holy prophets sent His angel to show His servants the things which must soon happen.

7 Behold! I come quickly. Blessed is he who keeps the words of the prophecy of this book.

8 And I, John, was he who was seeing and hearing these things. And when I heard and saw, I bowed to worship before the feet of the angel who was showing me these things.

9 And he says to me, Behold! Do not do it! For I am a fellow- servant of you and of your brothers, the prophets, and of those who keep the words of this book. Worship God.

10 And he says to me, Do not seal the words of the prophecy of this book – the time is near.

11 He that is unrighteous, let him continue to be unrighteous; and he that is filthy, let him continue to be filthy; and he that is righteous, let him continue to be righteous; and he that is holy, let him continue to be holy.

12 And behold, I come quickly! And My reward is with Me – to give to each according as his work shall be.

13 I am the A and the Z, the Beginning and the End, the First and the Last.

14 Blessed are they that do His commandments, that they may have a right to the tree of life, and that they should go into the city by the gates.

15 But on the outside are the dogs, and the workers of magic arts, and the fornicators, and the murderers, and the worshippers of idols and everyone who loves and practices a lie.

16 I, Jesus, sent My angel to testify these things to you for the churches. I am the Root and Offspring of David, the bright and Morning Star.

17 And the Spirit and the bride say, Come. And he that hears, let him say, Come. And he that thirsts, let him come. And whoever will, let him take the water of life freely.

18 For I testify to everyone hearing the words of the prophecy of this book, If anyone should add to these things, God shall add to him the plagues which are written in this book.

19 And if anyone should take from the words of this book of this prophecy, God shall take away his part from the Book of Life, and out of the holy city, and out of the things which are written in this book.

20 He who testifies these things says, Yes, I come quickly! Amen. Yes, come, Lord Jesus!

21 The grace of our Lord Jesus Christ be with all of you. Amen